D1095827

# THE NEW GROVE
# DICTIONARY OF MUSIC AND MUSICIANS

*Volume Twelve*

# The New
# GROVE
# Dictionary
# of Music and
# Musicians

EDITED BY

## Stanley Sadie

## 12

*Meares – Mutis*

MACMILLAN PUBLISHERS LIMITED, LONDON
GROVE'S DICTIONARIES OF MUSIC INC., WASHINGTON, DC
PENINSULA PUBLISHERS LIMITED, HONG KONG

First Edition of *A Dictionary of Music and Musicians*, planned and edited by SIR GEORGE GROVE, DCL, in
four volumes, with an Appendix edited by J. A. Fuller Maitland, and an Index by Mrs Edmond
Wodehouse, 1878, 1880, 1883, 1890.
Reprinted 1890, 1900

Second Edition, edited by J. A. FULLER MAITLAND, in five volumes, 1904–10

Third Edition, edited by H. C. COLLES, in five volumes, 1927

Fourth Edition, edited by H. C. COLLES, in five volumes, with Supplementary Volume, 1940

Fifth Edition, edited by ERIC BLOM, in nine volumes, 1954: with Supplementary Volume, 1961
Reprinted 1961, 1973, 1975

American Supplement, edited by WALDO SELDEN PRATT, in one volume, 1920
Reprinted, with new material, 1920, 1928, 1935, 1952

*The New Grove Dictionary of Music and Musicians*,
edited by STANLEY SADIE, in twenty volumes, 1980

Published by Macmillan Publishers Limited, London. This edition is distributed outside the United
Kingdom and Europe by Peninsula Publishers Limited, Hong Kong, a member of the Macmillan
Publishers Group, and by its appointed agents. In the United States of America and Canada, Peninsula
Publishers have appointed Grove's Dictionaries of Music Inc., Washington, DC, as sole distributor.

Text keyboarded, corrected, page-made-up and filmset by
Richard Clay (The Chaucer Press) Ltd, Bungay, Suffolk, England

Illustrations originated by Fletcher & Son Ltd, Norwich, England

Music examples processed by Halstan & Co. Ltd, Amersham, England

Printed and bound by Bright Sun Printing Press Co., Ltd, Hong Kong

**British Library Cataloguing in Publication Data**

The New Grove dictionary of music and
musicians.
  1. Music – Dictionaries
 I. Sadie, Stanley
 780′.3     ML100

ISBN 0–333–23111–2

**Library of Congress Cataloging in Publication Data**
Main entry under title:

The New Grove dictionary of music and musicians.
  Includes bibliographies.
  1. Music – Dictionaries.
  2. Music – Bio-bibliography.
 I. Grove, George, Sir, 1820–1900.
 II. Sadie, Stanley.
 ML100.N48    780′.3    79–26207

ISBN 0–333–23111–2

# Contents

# General Abbreviations

| | | | |
|---|---|---|---|
| A | alto, contralto [voice] | Bte | Benedicite |
| a | alto [instrument] | Bucks. | Buckinghamshire (GB) |
| AB | see BA | Bulg. | Bulgarian |
| ABC | American Broadcasting Company; Australian Broadcasting Commission | BVM | Blessed Virgin Mary |
| | | BWV | Bach-Werke-Verzeichnis [Schmieder, catalogue of J. S. Bach's works] |
| Abt. | Abteilung [section] | | |
| acc. | accompaniment, accompanied by | | |
| AD | anno Domini | | |
| add, addl | additional | | |
| add, addn | addition | *c* | circa [about] |
| ad lib | ad libitum | Calif. | California (USA) |
| Ag | Agnus Dei | CanD | Cantate Domino |
| all | alleluia | carn. | Carnival |
| AM | see MA | CBC | Canadian Broadcasting Corporation |
| a.m. | ante meridiem [before noon] | CBE | Commander of the Order of the British Empire |
| amp | amplified | | |
| AMS | American Musicological Society | CBS | Columbia Broadcasting System (USA) |
| Anh. | Anhang [appendix] | CBSO | City of Birmingham Symphony Orchestra |
| anon. | anonymous(ly) | CeBeDeM | Centre Belge de Documentation Musicale |
| ant | antiphon | cel | celesta |
| appx | appendix | CEMA | Council for the Encouragement of Music and the Arts [now the Arts Council of Great Britain] |
| arr. | arrangement, arranged by/for | | |
| ASCAP | American Society of Composers, Authors and Publishers | | |
| | | cf | confer [compare] |
| attrib. | attribution, attributed to | c.f. | cantus firmus |
| Aug | August | CH | Companion of Honour |
| aut. | autumn | chap. | chapter |
| | | Chin. | Chinese |
| | | chit | chitarrone |
| | | Cie | Compagnie |
| B | bass [voice] | cimb | cimbalom |
| B | Brainard catalogue [Tartini] | cl | clarinet |
| b | bass [instrument] | clvd | clavichord |
| *b* | born | cm | centimetre(s) |
| BA | Bachelor of Arts | CNRS | Centre National de la Recherche Scientifique (F) |
| Bar | baritone [voice] | | |
| bar | baritone [instrument] | Co. | Company; County |
| BBC | British Broadcasting Corporation | Cod. | Codex |
| BC | British Columbia (Canada) | col. | column |
| BC | before Christ | coll. | collected by |
| bc | basso continuo | collab. | in collaboration with |
| Bd. | Band [volume] | comm | communion |
| Berks. | Berkshire (GB) | conc. | concerto |
| Berwicks. | Berwickshire (GB) | cond. | conductor, conducted by |
| bk | book | Conn. | Connecticut (USA) |
| BLitt | Bachelor of Letters/Literature | cont | continuo |
| BM | British Museum | Corp. | Corporation |
| BMI | Broadcast Music Inc. (USA) | c.p.s. | cycles per second |
| BMus | Bachelor of Music | Cr | Credo, Creed |
| bn | bassoon | CSc | Candidate of Historical Sciences |
| Bros. | Brothers | Ct | countertenor |
| Bs | Benedictus | Cz. | Czech |

| | | | |
|---|---|---|---|
| D | Deutsch catalogue [Schubert]; Dounias catalogue [Tartini] | GmbH | Gesellschaft mit beschränkter Haftung [limited-liability company] |
| d. | denarius, denarii [penny, pence] | govt. | government [district in USSR] |
| *d* | died | grad | gradual |
| Dan. | Danish | GSM | Guildhall School of Music and Drama, London |
| db | double bass | | |
| DBE | Dame Commander of the Order of the British Empire | gui | guitar |
| dbn | double bassoon | H | Hoboken catalogue [Haydn]; Helm catalogue [C. P. E. Bach] |
| DC | District of Columbia (USA) | | |
| Dec | December | Hants. | Hampshire (GB) |
| ded. | dedication, dedicated to | Heb. | Hebrew |
| DeM | Deus misereatur | Herts. | Hertfordshire (GB) |
| Dept | Department | HMS | His/Her Majesty's Ship |
| Derbys. | Derbyshire (GB) | HMV | His Master's Voice |
| dir. | director, directed by | hn | horn |
| diss. | dissertation | Hon. | Honorary; Honourable |
| DLitt | Doctor of Letters/Literature | hpd | harpsichord |
| DMus | Doctor of Music | HRH | His/Her Royal Highness |
| DPhil | Doctor of Philosophy | Hung. | Hungarian |
| DSc | Doctor of Science/Historical Sciences | Hunts. | Huntingdonshire (GB) |
| | | Hz | Hertz [c.p.s.] |
| ed. | editor, edited (by) | | |
| edn. | edition | IAML | International Association of Music Libraries |
| e.g. | exempli gratia [for example] | | |
| elec | electric, electronic | ibid | ibidem [in the same place] |
| EMI | Electrical and Musical Industries | i.e. | id est [that is] |
| Eng. | English | IFMC | International Folk Music Council |
| eng hn | english horn | Ill. | Illinois (USA) |
| ens | ensemble | IMS | International Musicological Society |
| esp. | especially | Inc. | Incorporated |
| etc | et cetera [and so on] | inc. | incomplete |
| ex., exx. | example, examples | incl. | includes, including |
| | | Ind. | Indiana (USA) |
| f, ff | following page, following pages | inst | instrument, instrumental |
| f., ff. | folio, folios | int | introit |
| *f* | forte | IPEM | Institute for Psycho-acoustics and Electronic Music, Brussels |
| facs. | facsimile | | |
| fasc. | fascicle | ISCM | International Society for Contemporary Music |
| Feb | February | | |
| *ff* | fortissimo | ISM | Incorporated Society of Musicians (GB) |
| *fff* | fortississimo | ISME | International Society of Music Educators |
| fig. | figure [illustration] | It. | Italian |
| fl | flute | | |
| *fl* | floruit [he/she flourished] | Jan | January |
| *fp* | fortepiano | Jap. | Japanese |
| Fr. | French | *Jb* | Jahrbuch [yearbook] |
| frag. | fragment | Jg. | Jahrgang [year of publication/volume] |
| FRAM | Fellow of the Royal Academy of Music, London | jr | junior |
| | | Jub | Jubilate |
| FRCM | Fellow of the Royal College of Music, London | | |
| FRCO | Fellow of the Royal College of Organists, London | K | Kirkpatrick catalogue [D. Scarlatti]; Köchel catalogue [Mozart; no. after / is from 6th edn.] |
| FRS | Fellow of the Royal Society, London | | |
| | | kbd | keyboard |
| Gael. | Gaelic | KBE | Knight Commander of the Order of the British Empire |
| Ger. | German | | |
| Gk. | Greek | KCVO | Knight Commander of the Royal Victorian Order |
| Gl | Gloria | | |
| Glam. | Glamorgan (GB) | kHz | kilohertz |
| glock | glockenspiel | km | kilometre(s) |
| Glos., Gloucs. | Gloucestershire (GB) | Ky | Kyrie |
| | | Ky. | Kentucky (USA) |

| | | | |
|---|---|---|---|
| £ | libra, librae [pound, pounds sterling] | Oct | October |
| L | Longo catalogue [D. Scarlatti] | off | offertory |
| Lancs. | Lancashire (GB) | OM | Order of Merit |
| Lat. | Latin | Ont. | Ontario (Canada) |
| Leics. | Leicestershire (GB) | op., opp. | opus, opera |
| lib | libretto | op cit | opere citato [in the work cited] |
| Lincs. | Lincolnshire (GB) | opt. | optional |
| lit | litany | orch | orchestra, orchestral |
| LittD | Doctor of Letters/Literature | orchd | orchestrated (by) |
| LlB | Bachelor of Laws | org | organ |
| LlD | Doctor of Laws | orig. | original(ly) |
| LP | long-playing record | ORTF | Office de Radiodiffusion-Télévision Fran-çaise |
| LPO | London Philharmonic Orchestra | | |
| LSO | London Symphony Orchestra | OUP | Oxford University Press |
| Ltd | Limited | ov. | overture |
| | | | |
| M. | Monsieur | P | Pincherle catalogue [Vivaldi] |
| MA | Master of Arts | p. | pars (1p. = *prima pars*, etc) |
| Mag | Magnificat | p., pp. | page, pages |
| mand | mandolin | *p* | piano |
| mar | marimba | p.a. | per annum |
| Mass. | Massachusetts (USA) | PC | number of chanson in A. Pillet and H. Carstens: *Bibliographie der Troubadours* (Halle, 1933) |
| MBE | Member of the Order of the British Empire | | |
| Mez | mezzo-soprano | Penn. | Pennsylvania (USA) |
| *mf* | mezzo-forte | perc | percussion |
| mic | microphone | perf. | performance, performed (by) |
| Mich. | Michigan (USA) | pf | piano |
| Minn. | Minnesota (USA) | PhD | Doctor of Philosophy |
| Mlle | Mademoiselle | pic | piccolo |
| mm | millimetre(s) | pl. | plate; plural |
| Mme | Madame | p.m. | post meridiem [after noon] |
| MMus | Master of Music | PO | Philharmonic Orchestra |
| mod | modulator | Pol. | Polish |
| Mon. | Monmouthshire (GB) | Port. | Portuguese |
| movt | movement | posth. | posthumous(ly) |
| MP | Member of Parliament (GB) | POW | prisoner of war |
| *mp* | mezzo-piano | *pp* | pianissimo |
| MS | manuscript | *ppp* | pianississimo |
| MSc | Master of Science(s) | pr. | printed |
| Mt | Mount | PRO | Public Record Office, London |
| MusB, | Bachelor of Music | prol | prologue |
|   MusBac | | PRS | Performing Right Society (GB) |
| MusD, | Doctor of Music | Ps | Psalm |
|   MusDoc | | ps | psalm |
| MusM | Master of Music | pseud. | pseudonym |
| | | pt. | part |
| | | ptbk | partbook |
| NBC | National Broadcasting Company (USA) | pubd | published |
| n.d. | no date of publication | pubn | publication |
| NJ | New Jersey (USA) | | |
| no. | number | | |
| Nor. | Norwegian | qnt | quintet |
| Northants. | Northamptonshire (GB) | qt | quartet |
| Notts. | Nottinghamshire (GB) | | |
| Nov | November | | |
| n.p. | no place of publication | R | [in signature] editorial revision |
| nr. | near | R. | number of chanson in G. Raynaud: *Biblio-graphie des chansonniers français des XIIIe et XIVe siècles* (Paris, 1884) and H. Spanke: *G. Raynauds Bibliographie des altfranzösischen Liedes* (Leiden, 1955) |
| NSW | New South Wales (Australia) | | |
| Nunc | Nunc dimittis | | |
| NY | New York State (USA) | | |
| | | R | response |
| ob | oboe | R | Ryom catalogue [Vivaldi] |
| obbl | obbligato | *R* | photographic reprint |
| OBE | Officer of the Order of the British Empire | *r* | recto |

| | | | | |
|---|---|---|---|---|
| RAF | Royal Air Force | | T | tenor [voice] |
| RAI | Radio Audizioni Italiane | | t | tenor [instrument] |
| RAM | Royal Academy of Music, London | | TeD | Te Deum |
| RCA | Radio Corporation of America | | Tenn. | Tennessee (USA) |
| RCM | Royal College of Music, London | | timp | timpani |
| re | response | | tpt | trumpet |
| rec | recorder | | Tr | treble [voice] |
| recit | recitative | | tr | tract; treble [instrument] |
| red. | reduction, reduced for | | trans. | translation, translated by |
| repr. | reprinted | | transcr. | transcription, transcribed by/for |
| Rev. | Reverend | | trbn | trombone |
| rev. | revision, revised (by/for) | | | |
| RIdIM | Répertoire International d'Iconographie Musicale | | U. | University |
| RILM | Répertoire International de Littérature Musicale | | UHF | ultra-high frequency |
| | | | UK | United Kingdom of Great Britain and Northern Ireland |
| RISM | Répertoire International des Sources Musicales | | unacc. | unaccompanied |
| | | | unattrib. | unattributed |
| RMCM | Royal Manchester College of Music | | UNESCO | United Nations Educational, Scientific and Cultural Organization |
| RNCM | Royal Northern College of Music, Manchester | | | |
| | | | unperf. | unperformed |
| RO | Radio Orchestra | | unpubd | unpublished |
| Rom. | Romanian | | US | United States [adjective] |
| RPO | Royal Philharmonic Orchestra (GB) | | USA | United States of America |
| RSFSR | Russian Soviet Federated Socialist Republic | | USSR | Union of Soviet Socialist Republics |
| RSO | Radio Symphony Orchestra | | | |
| Rt Hon. | Right Honourable | | V | versicle |
| RTE | Radio Telefís Eireann (Ireland) | | v, vv | voice, voices |
| Russ. | Russian | | v., vv. | verse, verses |
| RV | Ryom catalogue [Vivaldi] | | *v* | verso |
| | | | va | viola |
| | | | vc | cello |
| S | San, Santa, Santo, São [Saint]; soprano [voice] | | vcle | versicle |
| | | | VEB | Volkseigener Betrieb [people's own industry] |
| S. | south, southern | | | |
| $ | dollars | | Ven | Venite |
| s | soprano [instrument] | | VHF | very high frequency |
| s. | solidus, solidi [shilling, shillings] | | vib | vibraphone |
| SACEM | Société d'Auteurs, Compositeurs et Editeurs de Musique (F) | | viz | videlicet [namely] |
| | | | vle | violone |
| San | Sanctus | | vn | violin |
| Sask. | Saskatchewan (Canada) | | vol. | volume |
| sax | saxophone | | | |
| Sept | September | | | |
| seq | sequence | | W. | west, western |
| ser. | series | | Warwicks. | Warwickshire (GB) |
| *sf, sfz* | sforzando, sforzato | | Wilts. | Wiltshire (GB) |
| sing. | singular | | wint. | winter |
| SJ | Societas Jesu (Society of Jesus) | | Wisc. | Wisconsin (USA) |
| SO | Symphony Orchestra | | WoO, woo | Werke ohne Opuszahl [works without opus number] |
| SPNM | Society for the Promotion of New Music (GB) | | | |
| spr. | spring | | Worcs. | Worcestershire (GB) |
| SS | Saints | | WQ | Wotquenne catalogue [C. P. E. Bach] |
| Ss | Santissima, Santissimo | | ww | woodwind |
| SSR | Soviet Socialist Republic | | | |
| St | Saint, Sint, Szent | | | |
| Staffs. | Staffordshire (GB) | | xyl | xylophone |
| Ste | Sainte | | | |
| str | string(s) | | | |
| sum. | summer | | Yorks. | Yorkshire (GB) |
| Sup | superius | | | |
| suppl. | supplement, supplementary | | | |
| Swed. | Swedish | | | |
| sym. | symphony, symphonic | | | |
| synth | synthesizer | | z | Zimmerman catalogue [Purcell] |

# Bibliographical Abbreviations

All bibliographical abbreviations used in this dictionary are listed below, following the typography used in the text of the dictionary. Broadly, *italic* type is used for periodicals and for reference works; roman type is used for anthologies, series etc (titles of individual volumes are italicized).

Full bibliographical information is not normally supplied in the list below if it is available elsewhere in the dictionary. Its availability is indicated as follows: D – in the article 'Dictionaries and encyclopedias of music'; E – in the article 'Editions, historical'; and P – in the list forming §III of the article 'Periodicals' (in this case the number in that list of the periodical concerned is added, in brackets). For other items, in particular national (non-musical) biographical dictionaries, basic bibliographical information is given here; and in some cases extra information is supplied to clarify the abbreviation used.

Festschriften and congress reports are not, in general, covered in this list. Although Festschrift titles are usually shortened in the dictionary, sufficient information is always given for unambiguous identification (dedicatee; occasion, if the same person is dedicatee of more than one Festschrift; place and date of publication; and where the dedicatee has an entry the editor's name may be found); for fuller information on musical Festschriften up to 1967 see W. Gerboth: *An Index to Musical Festschriften and Similar Publications* (New York, 1969). The only congress report series listed below are those of the international and the German musicological associations; for others cited in the dictionary, sufficient information is always given for identification (society or topic; place; date of occurrence); full information may be found in J. Tyrrell and R. Wise: *A Guide to International Congress Reports in Music, 1900–1975* (London, 1979).

| | |
|---|---|
| *AcM* | *Acta musicologica*  P [Intl 5] |
| *ADB* | *Allgemeine deutsche Biographie* (Leipzig, 1875–1912) |
| AM | Antiphonale monasticum pro diurnis horis (Paris, Tournai and Rome, 1934) |
| *AMe* (*AMeS*) | *Algemene muziekencyclopedie* (and suppl.)  D |
| *AMf* | *Archiv für Musikforschung*  P [D776] |
| AMI | L'arte musicale in Italia  E |
| AMP | Antiquitates musicae in Polonia  E |
| *AMw* | *Archiv für Musikwissenschaft*  P [D552] |
| *AMZ* | *Allgemeine musikalische Zeitung*  P [D32, 154, 170] |
| *AMz* | *Allgemeine Musik-Zeitung*  P [D203] |
| *AnM* | *Anuario musical*  P [E91] |
| *AnMc* | *Analecta musicologica* (some vols. in series Studien zur italienisch-deutschen Musikgeschichte), Veröffentlichungen der Musikabteilung des Deutschen historischen Instituts in Rom (Cologne, 1963–) |
| *AnnM* | *Annales musicologiques*  P [F638] |
| AntMI | Antiquae musicae italicae  E |
| AR | Antiphonale sacrosanctae romanae ecclesiae pro diurnis horis (Paris, Tournai and Rome, 1949) |
| AS | Antiphonale sarisburiense, ed. W. H. Frere (London, 1901–25/R1967) |
| | |
| *Baker 5, 6* | *Baker's Biographical Dictionary of Musicians* (5/1958 and 1971 suppl., 6/1978)  D |
| *BAMS* | *Bulletin of the American Musicological Society*  P [US540] |
| *BeJb* | *Beethoven-Jahrbuch* [1953–]  P [D925] |
| *BJb* | *Bach-Jahrbuch*  P [D434] |
| BMB | Biblioteca musica bononiensis  E |
| *BMw* | *Beiträge zur Musikwissenschaft*  P [D1013] |
| BNB | Biographie nationale [belge] (Brussels, 1866–) |
| *BordasD* | *Dictionnaire de la musique* (Paris: Bordas, 1970–76)  D |
| *Bouwsteenen:* ·*JVNM* | *Bouwsteenen: jaarboek der Vereeniging voor Nederlandsche muziekgeschiedenis*  P [NL20] |
| *BrownI* | H. M. Brown: *Instrumental Music Printed before 1600: a Bibliography* (Cambridge, Mass., 2/1967) |
| *BSIM* | *Bulletin français de la S[ociété] I[nternationale de] M[usique]* [previously *Le Mercure musical*; also other titles]  P [F364] |

| | |
|---|---|
| *BUCEM* | *British Union-catalogue of Early Music*, ed. E. Schnapper (London, 1957) |
| *BurneyH* | C. Burney: *A General History of Music from the Earliest Ages to the Present* (London, 1776–89) [p. nos. refer to edn. of 1935/R1957] |
| *BWQ* | *Brass and Woodwind Quarterly*  P [US756] |
| | |
| CaM | Catalogus musicus  E |
| CEKM | Corpus of Early Keyboard Music  E |
| CEMF | Corpus of Early Music in Facsimile  E |
| *CHM* | *Collectanea historiae musicae* (in series Biblioteca historiae musicae cultores) (Florence, 1953–) |
| CM | Le choeur des muses  E |
| *CMc* | *Current Musicology*  P [US747] |
| CMI | I classici musicali italiani  E |
| CMM | Corpus mensurabilis musicae  E |
| *CMz* | *Cercetări de muzicologie*  P [R29] |
| CS | E. de Coussemaker: *Scriptorum de musica medii aevi nova series* (Paris, 1864–76/R1963) |
| *ČSHS* | *Československý hudební slovník*  D |
| CSM | Corpus scriptorum de musica  E |
| *CSPD* | *Calendar of State Papers (Domestic)* (London, 1856–1972) |
| Cw | Das Chorwerk  E |
| | |
| *DAB* | *Dictionary of American Biography* (New York, 1928–) |
| *DAM* | *Dansk aarbog for musikforskning*  P [DK88] |
| *DBF* | *Dictionnaire de biographie française* (Paris, 1933–) |
| *DBI* | *Dizionario biografico degli italiani* (Rome, 1960–) |
| *DBL* | *Dansk biografisk leksikon* (Copenhagen, 1887–1905, 2/1933–) |
| *DBP* | *Dicionário biográfico de musicos portuguezes*  D |
| DČHP | Dějiny české hudby v příkladech  E |
| DDT | Denkmäler deutscher Tonkunst  E |
| DHM | Documenta historicae musicae  E |
| *DJbM* | *Deutsches Jahrbuch der Musikwissenschaft*  P [D980] |
| DM | Documenta musicologica  E |
| *DNB* | *Dictionary of National Biography* (London, 1885–1901, suppls.) |
| DTB | Denkmäler der Tonkunst in Bayern  E |
| DTÖ | Denkmäler der Tonkunst in Österreich  E |

EDM   Das Erbe deutscher Musik   E
EECM   Early English Church Music   E
*EIT*   *Ezhegodnik imperatorskikh teatrov*   P [USSR17]
*EitnerQ*   R. Eitner: *Biographisch-bibliographisches Quellen-Lexikon*   D
*EitnerS*   R. Eitner: *Bibliographie der Musik-Sammelwerke des XVI. und XVII. Jahrhunderts* (Berlin, 1877)
EKM   English (later Early) Keyboard Music   E
EL   The English Lute-songs
EM   The English Madrigalists   E
*EM*   *Ethnomusicology*   P [US664]
*EMDC*   *Encyclopédie de la musique et dictionnaire du Conservatoire*   D
EMN   Exempla musica neerlandica   E
EMS   The English Madrigal School   E
*ES*   *Enciclopedia dello spettacolo*   D
ESLS   The English School of Lutenist-songwriters   E

*FAM*   *Fontes artis musicae*   P [Intl 16]
*FasquelleE*   *Encyclopédie de la musique* (Paris: Fasquelle, 1958–61)   D
FCVR   Florilège du concert vocal de la renaissance   E
*FétisB* (*FétisBS*)   F.-J. Fétis: *Biographie universelle des musiciens* (2/1860–65) (and suppl.)   D

*GerberL*   R. Gerber: *Historisch-biographisches Lexikon der Tonkünstler*   D
*GerberNL*   R. Gerber: *Neues historisch-biographisches Lexikon der Tonkünstler*   D
*GfMKB*   *Gesellschaft für Musikforschung Kongressbericht* [1950–]
GMB   *Geschichte der Musik in Beispielen*, ed. A. Schering (Leipzig, 1931)   E
GR   *Graduale sacrosanctae romanae ecclesiae* (Tournai, 1938)
*Grove 1(–5)*   G. Grove, ed.: *A Dictionary of Music and Musicians*, 2nd–5th edns. as *Grove's Dictionary of Music and Musicians*   D
*Grove 6*   *The New Grove Dictionary of Music and Musicians*   D
GS   *Graduale sarisburiense*, ed. W. H. Frere (London, 1894/R1967)
GS   M. Gerbert: *Scriptores ecclesiastici de musica sacra* (St Blasien, 1784/R1963)
*GSJ*   *The Galpin Society Journal*   P [GB415]

HAM   *Historical Anthology of Music*, ed. A. T. Davison and W. Apel, i (Cambridge, Mass., 1946, rev. 2/1949); ii (Cambridge, Mass., 1950)   E
*HawkinsH*   J. Hawkins: *A General History of the Science and Practice of Music* (London, 1776) [p. nos. refer to edn. of 1853/R1963]
*HJb*   *Händel-Jahrbuch*   P [D712, 968]
HM   Hortus musicus   E
*HMT*   *Handwörterbuch der musikalischen Terminologie*   D
*HMw*   Handbuch der Musikwissenschaft, ed. E. Bücken (Potsdam, 1927–) [monograph series]
*HMYB*   *Hinrichsen's Musical Year Book*   P [GB381]
HPM   Harvard Publications in Music   E
*HR*   *Hudebni revue*   P [CS80]
*HRo*   *Hudebni rozhledy*   P [CS176]
*HV*   *Hudebni věda*   P [CS204]

*IIM*   *Izvestiya na Instituta za muzika*   P [BG14]
IMa   Instituta et monumenta   E
IMi   Istituzioni e monumenti dell'arte musicale italiana   E
*IMSCR*   *International Musicological Society Congress Report* [1930–]
*IMusSCR*   *International Musical Society Congress Report* [1906–11]
*IRASM*   *International Review of the Aesthetics and Sociology of Music*   P [Intl 32]
*IRMO*   S. L. Ginzburg: *Istoriya russkoy muziki v notnïkh obraztsakh*   D
*IRMAS*   *The International Review of Music Aesthetics and Sociology*   P [Intl 32]
*IZ*   *Instrumentenbau-Zeitschrift*   P [D806]

*JAMS*   *Journal of the American Musicological Society*   P [US613]

*JbMP*   *Jahrbuch der Musikbibliothek Peters*   P [D336]
*JEFDSS*   *The Journal of the English Folk Dance and Song Society*   P [GB341]
*JFSS*   *Journal of the Folk-song Society*   P [GB183]
*JIFMC*   *Journal of the International Folk Music Council*   P [Intl 10]
*JMT*   *Journal of Music Theory*   P [US683]
*JRBM*   *Journal of Renaissance and Baroque Music*   P [US590]
*JRME*   *Journal of Research in Music Education*   P [US665]
*JVNM*   see *Bouwsteenen: JVNM*   P [NL20]

*KJb*   *Kirchenmusikalisches Jahrbuch*   P [D284]
*KM*   *Kwartalnik muzyczny*   P [PL35, 64]

*LaborD*   *Diccionario de la música Labor*   D
*LaMusicaD*   *La musica: dizionario*   D
*LaMusicaE*   *La musica: enciclopedia storica*   D
*LM*   *Lucrări de muzicologie*   P [R27]
*LSJ*   *The Lute Society Journal*   P [GB487]
*LU*   *Liber usualis missae et officii pro dominicis et festis duplicibus cum cantu gregoriano* (Solesmes, 1896; many later edns., incl. Tournai, 1963)

*MA*   *The Musical Antiquary*   P [GB240]
MAB   Musica antiqua bohemica   E
MAM   Musik alter Meister   E
MAP   Musica antiqua polonica   E
MAS   [publications of the British] Musical Antiquarian Society   E
MB   Musica britannica   E
MC   Musica da camera   E
*MD*   *Musica disciplina*   P [US590]
*ME*   *Muzïkal'naya entsiklopediya*   D
MEM   Mestres de l'escolania de Montserrat   E
*Mf*   *Die Musikforschung*   P [D839]
*MGG*   *Die Musik in Geschichte und Gegenwart*   D
MH   Musica hispana   E
*MJb*   *Mozart-Jahrbuch des Zentralinstituts für Mozartforschung* [1950–]   P [A254]
*ML*   *Music and Letters*   P [GB280]
MLMI   Monumenta lyrica medii aevi italica   E
*MM*   *Modern Music*   P [US488]
*MMA*   *Miscellanea musicologica* [Australia]   P [AUS19]
MMB   Monumenta musicae byzantinae   E
MMBel   Monumenta musicae belgicae   E
*MMC*   *Miscellanea musicologica* [Czechoslovakia]   P [CS191]
MME   Monumentos de la música española   E
MMFTR   Monuments de la musique française au temps de la renaissance   E
*MMg*   *Monatshefte für Musikgeschichte*   P [D188]
MMI   Monumenti di musica italiana   E
MMN   Monumenta musicae neerlandicae   E
MMP   Monumenta musicae in Polonia   E
*MMR*   *The Monthly Musical Record*   P [GB75]
MMRF   Les maîtres musiciens de la renaissance française   E
MMS   Monumenta musicae svecicae   E
*MO*   *Musical Opinion*   P [GB90]
*MQ*   *The Musical Quarterly*   P [US447]
*MR*   *The Music Review*   P [GB376]
MRM   Monuments of Renaissance Music   E
MRS   Musiche rinascimentali siciliane   E
*MS*   *Muzïkal'nïy sovremennik*   P [USSR37]
MSD   Musicological Studies and Documents, ed. A. Carapetyan (Rome, 1951–)
*MT*   *The Musical Times*   P [GB33]
MVH   Musica viva historica   E
MVSSP   Musiche vocali strumentali sacre e profane   E
Mw   Das Musikwerk   E
*MZ*   *Muzikološki zbornik*   P [YU37]

*NA*   *Note d'archivio per la storia musicale*   P [I186]
*NBJb*   *Neues Beethoven-Jahrbuch*   P [D636]
*NBL*   *Norsk biografisk leksikon* (Oslo, 1921–)
*NDB*   *Neue deutsche Biographie* (Berlin, 1953–)
NM   Nagels Musikarchiv   E
*NNBW*   *Nieuw Nederlandsch biografisch woordenboek* (Leiden, 1911–37)
*NÖB*   *Neue österreichische Biographie* (Vienna, 1923)

| | |
|---|---|
| NOHM | *The New Oxford History of Music*, ed. E. Wellesz, J. A. Westrup and G. Abraham (London, 1954–) |
| NRMI | *Nuova rivista musicale italiana*  P [I 282] |
| NZM | *Neue Zeitschrift für Musik*  P [D75, 1088] |
| | |
| OHM | *The Oxford History of Music*, ed. W. H. Hadow (Oxford, 1901–5, enlarged 2/1929–38) |
| OM | *Opus musicum*  P [CS222] |
| ÖMz | *Österreichische Musikzeitschrift*  P [A233] |
| | |
| PalMus | Paléographie musicale (Solesmes, 1889–) [see entry SOLESMES] |
| PAMS | *Papers of the American Musicological Society*  P [US543] |
| PÄMw | Publikationen älterer praktischer und theoretischer Musikwerke  E |
| PBC | Publicaciones del departamento de música de la Biblioteca de Catalunya  E |
| PG | *Patrologiae cursus completus*, ii: Series graeca, ed. J.-P. Migne (Paris, 1857–1912) |
| PGfM | Publikationen der Gesellschaft für Musikforschung  E |
| PIISM | Pubblicazioni dell'Istituto italiano per la storia della musica  E |
| PL | *Patrologiae cursus completus*, i: Series latina, ed. J.-P. Migne (Paris, 1844–64) |
| PM | Portugaliae musica  E |
| PMA | *Proceedings of the Musical Association*  P [GB80] |
| PMFC | Polyphonic Music of the Fourteenth Century  E |
| PNM | *Perspectives of New Music*  P [US724] |
| PRM | *Polski rocznik muzykologiczny*  P [PL85] |
| PRMA | *Proceedings of the Royal Musical Association*  P [GB80] |
| PSB | *Polskich słownik biograficzny* (Kraków, 1935) |
| PSFM | Publications de la Société française de musicologie  E |
| | |
| *Quaderni della RaM* | *Quaderni della Rassegna musicale*  P [I 272] |
| | |
| *Rad JAZU* | *Rad Jugoslavenske akademije znanosti i umjetnosti* (Zagreb, 1867–) |
| RaM | *La rassegna musicale*  P [I 197] |
| RBM | *Revue belge de musicologie*  P [B126] |
| RdM | *Revue de musicologie*  P [F462] |
| ReM | *La revue musicale* [1920–]  P [F475] |
| RHCM | *Revue d'histoire et de critique musicales* [1901]; *La revue musicale* [1902–10]  P [F320] |
| RicordiE | *Enciclopedia della musica* (Milan: Ricordi, 1963–4)  D |
| RiemannL 12 | *Riemann Musik Lexicon* (12/1959–75)  D |
| RIM | *Rivista italiana di musicologia*  P [I 280] |
| RISM | *Répertoire international des sources musicales* [see entry under this title] |
| RMARC | R[oyal] M[usical] A[ssociation] *Research Chronicle*  P [GB496] |
| RMFC | *Recherches sur la musique française classique*  P [F677] |
| RMG | *Russkaya muzikal'naya gazeta*  P [USSR19] |
| RMI | *Rivista musicale italiana*  P [I 84] |
| RMS | Renaissance Manuscript Studies  E |
| RN | *Renaissance News*  P [see US590] |
| RRMBE | Recent Researches in the Music of the Baroque Era  E |
| RRMR | Recent Researches in the Music of the Renaissance  E |

| | |
|---|---|
| SartoriB | C. Sartori: *Bibliografia della musica strumentale italiana stampata in Italia fino al 1700* (Florence, 1952–68) |
| SBL | *Svenska biografiskt lexikon* (Stockholm, 1918–) |
| SchmidlD (SchmidlDS) | C. Schmidl: *Dizionario dei musicisti* (and suppl.)  D |
| SCMA | Smith College Music Archives  E |
| SeegerL | H. Seeger: *Musiklexikon*  D |
| SEM | [University of California] Series of Early Music  E |
| SH | *Slovenská hudba*  P [CS192] |
| SIMG | *Sammelbände der Internationalen Musik-Gesellschaft*  P [Intl 2] |
| SM | *Studia musicologica Academiae scientiarum hungaricae*  P [H49] |
| SMA | *Studies in Music* [Australia]  P [AUS20] |
| SMd | Schweizerische Musikdenkmäler  E |
| SML | *Schweizer Musiker Lexikon*  D |
| SMM | Summa musicae medii aevi  E |
| SMN | *Studia musicologica norvegica*  P [N45] |
| SMP | *Słownik muzyków polskich*  D |
| SMw | *Studien zur Musikwissenschaft*  P [D536] |
| SMz | *Schweizerische Musikzeitung/Revue musicale suisse*  P [CH4] |
| SOB | Süddeutsche Orgelmeister des Barock  E |
| SovM | *Sovetskaya muzika*  P [USSR66] |
| STMf | *Svensk tidskrift för musikforskning*  P [S46] |
| | |
| TCM | Tudor Church Music  E |
| TM | Thesauri musici  E |
| TVNM | *Tijdschrift van de Vereniging voor Nederlandse muziekgeschiedenis*  P [NL26] |
| | |
| UVNM | Uitgaven der Vereniging voor Nederlandse muziekgeschiedenis  E |
| | |
| VMPH | Veröffentlichungen der Musik-Bibliothek Paul Hirsch  E |
| VMw | *Vierteljahrsschrift für Musikwissenschaft*  P [D282] |
| VogelB | E. Vogel: *Bibliothek der gedruckten weltlichen Vocalmusik Italiens, aus den Jahren 1500 bis 1700* (Berlin, 1892); rev., enlarged, by A. Einstein (Hildesheim, 1962); further addns in *AnMc*, nos.4, 5, 9 and 12; further rev. by F. Lesure and C. Sartori as *Bibliografia della musica italiana vocale profana pubblicata dal 1500 al 1700* (Geneva, 1977) |
| | |
| WaltherML | J. G. Walther: *Musicalisches Lexicon oder Musicalische Bibliothec*  D |
| WDMP | Wydawnictwo dawnej muzyki polskiej  E |
| WE | Wellesley Edition  E |
| WECIS | Wellesley Edition Cantata Index Series  E |
| | |
| YIFMC | *Yearbook of the International Folk Music Council*  P [Intl 31] |
| | |
| ZfM | *Zeitschrift für Musik*  P [D75] |
| ZHMP | Zrodła do historii muzyki polskiej  E |
| ZI | *Zeitschrift für Instrumentenbau*  P [D249] |
| ZIMG | *Zeitschrift der Internationalen Musik-Gesellschaft*  P [Intl 3] |
| ZL | *Zenei lexikon*  D |
| ZMw | *Zeitschrift für Musikwissenschaft*  P [D556] |

# Library Sigla

The system of library sigla in this dictionary follows that used in its publications (Series A) by Répertoire International des Sources Musicales, Kassel, by permission. Below are listed the sigla to be found; a few of them are additional to those in the published RISM lists, but have been established in consultation with the RISM organization. Some original RISM sigla that have now been changed are retained here.

In the dictionary, sigla are always printed in *italic*. In any listing of sources a national sigillum applies without repetition until it is contradicted. For German sigla, the intermediate *brd* and *ddr* are excluded; the list below shows in which part of Germany or Berlin each library is located.

Within each national list, entries are alphabetized by sigillum, first by capital letters (showing the city or town) and then by lower-case ones (showing the institution or collection).

## *A*: AUSTRIA

| | |
|---|---|
| *Ee* | Eisenstadt, Esterházy-Archiv |
| *Eh* | ——, Haydn Museum |
| *Ek* | ——, Stadtpfarrkirche |
| *F* | Fiecht, Benediktinerordensstift St Georgenberg |
| *Gd* | Graz, Diözesan Archiv |
| *Gk* | ——, Hochschule für Musik und Darstellende Kunst |
| *Gl* | ——, Steiermärkische Landesbibliothek am Joanneum |
| *Gmi* | ——, Musikwissenschaftliches Institut der Universität |
| *Gu* | ——, Universitätsbibliothek |
| *GÖ* | Furth bei Göttweig, Benediktinerstift |
| *GÜ* | Güssing, Franziskaner Kloster |
| *H* | Herzogenburg, Chorherrenstift |
| *HE* | Heiligenkreuz, Zisterzienserstift |
| *Ik* | Innsbruck, Konservatorium |
| *Imf* | ——, Museum Ferdinandeum |
| *Imi* | ——, Musikwissenschaftliches Institut der Universität |
| *Iu* | ——, Universitätsbibliothek |
| *Iw* | ——, Prämonstratenser-Chorherrenstift Wilten |
| *KN* | Klosterneuburg, Augustiner-Chorherrenstift |
| *KR* | Kremsmünster, Benediktinerstift |
| *L* | Lilienfeld, Zisterzienser-Stift |
| *LA* | Lambach, Benediktinerstift |
| *LEx* | Leoben, Pfarrbibliothek St Xaver |
| *LIm* | Linz, Oberösterreichisches Landesarchiv |
| *LIs* | ——, Bundesstaatliche Studienbibliothek |
| *M* | Melk an der Donau, Benediktinerstift |
| *MB* | Michaelbeuern, Benediktinerabtei |
| *MÖ* | Mödling, Pfarrkirche St Othmar |
| *MZ* | Mariazell, Benediktiner-Priorat |
| *N* | Neuburg, Pfarrarchiv |
| *NS* | Neustift, Pfarrarchiv |
| *R* | Rein, Zisterzienserstift |
| *Sca* | Salzburg, Museum Carolino Augusteum |
| *Sd* | ——, Dom-Musikarchiv |
| *Sk* | ——, Kapitelbibliothek |
| *Sm* | ——, Internationale Stiftung Mozarteum |
| *Smi* | ——, Musikwissenschaftliches Institut der Universität |
| *Sn* | ——, Nonnberg, Benediktiner-Frauenstift |
| *Ssp* | ——, St Peter Benediktiner-Erzabtei |
| *SB* | Schlierbach, Stift |
| *SCH* | Schlägl, Prämonstratenser-Stift |
| *SE* | Seckau, Benediktinerabtei |
| *SEI* | Seitenstetten, Benediktinerstift |
| *SF* | St Florian, Augustiner-Chorherrenstift |
| *SH* | Solbad Hall, Franziskaner-Kloster |
| *SL* | St Lambrecht, Benediktiner-Abtei |
| *SP* | St Pölten, Diözesanarchiv |
| *SPL* | St Paul, Stift |
| *ST* | Stams, Zisterzienserstift |
| *STE* | Steyr, Stadtpfarrarchiv |
| *TU* | Tulln, Pfarrkirche St Stephan |
| *Wd* | Vienna, Stephansdom |
| *Wdo* | ——, Zentralarchiv des Deutschen Ordens |
| *Wdtö* | ——, Gesellschaft zur Herausgabe von Denkmälern der Tonkunst in Österreich |
| *Wgm* | ——, Gesellschaft der Musikfreunde |
| *Wh* | ——, Pfarrarchiv Hernals |
| *Whb* | ——, Hauptverband des Österreichischen Buchhandels |
| *Wk* | ——, Pfarrkirche St Karl Borromäus |
| *Wkann* | ——, Hans Kann, private collection |
| *Wkh* | ——, Kirche am Hof |
| *Wkm* | ——, Kunsthistorisches Museum |
| *Wl* | ——, Archiv für Niederösterreich (Landesarchiv) |
| *Wm* | ——, Minoritenkonvent |
| *Wmg* | ——, Pfarre, Maria am Gestade |
| *Wmi* | ——, Musikwissenschaftliches Institut der Universität |
| *Wmk* | ——, Akademie für Musik und Darstellende Kunst |
| *Wn* | ——, Österreichische Nationalbibliothek, Musiksammlung |
| *Wögm* | ——, Österreichische Gesellschaft für Musik |
| *Wp* | ——, Musikarchiv, Piaristenkirche Maria Treu |
| *Wph* | ——, Wiener Philharmoniker, Archiv und Bibliothek |
| *Wps* | ——, Priesterseminar |
| *Ws* | ——, Schottenstift |
| *Wsa* | ——, Stadtarchiv |
| *Wsp* | ——, St Peter, Musikarchiv |
| *Wst* | ——, Stadtbibliothek, Musiksammlung |
| *Wu* | ——, Universitätsbibliothek |
| *Ww* | ——, Pfarrarchiv Währing |
| *Wweinmann* | ——, Alexander Weinmann, private collection |
| *Wwessely* | ——, Othmar Wessely, private collection |
| *WAY* | Waydhofen an der Ybbs, Pfarre |
| *WE* | Wels, Stift |
| *WIL* | Wilhering, Zisterzienserstift |
| *Z* | Zwettl, Zisterzienserstift |

## *B*: BELGIUM

| | |
|---|---|
| *Aa* | Antwerp, Stadsarchief |
| *Aac* | ——, Archief en Museum voor het Vlaamse Culturleven |
| *Ac* | ——, Koninklijk Vlaams Muziekconservatorium |
| *Ak* | ——, Onze-Lieve-Vrouwkathedraal |
| *Amp* | ——, Museum Plantijn–Moretus |
| *Apersoons* | ——, Guido Persoons, private collection |
| *As* | ——, Stadsbibliotheek |
| *Asa* | ——, Kerkebestuur St-Andries |
| *Asj* | ——, Collegiale en Parochiale Kerk St-Jacob |
| *Averwilt* | ——, F. Verwilt, private collection |
| *AN* | ——, Anderlecht, St-Guiden Kerk |
| *Ba* | Brussels, Archives de la Ville |
| *Bc* | ——, Conservatoire Royal de Musique |
| *Bcdm* | ——, Centre Belge de Documentation Musicale [CeBeDeM] |
| *Bg* | ——, Eglise de Ste Gudule |
| *Bi* | ——, Institut de Psycho-acoustique et de Musique Electronique |

xiv

| | |
|---|---|
| *Br* | ——, Bibliothèque Royale Albert 1er/Koninklijke Bibliotheek Albert I |
| *Brtb* | ——, Radiodiffusion-Télévision Belge |
| *Bsp* | ——, Société Philharmonique |
| *BRc* | Bruges, Stedelijk Muziekconservatorium |
| *D* | Diest, St Sulpitiuskerk |
| *Gar* | Ghent [Gent, Gand], Stadsarchief |
| *Gc* | ——, Koninklijk Muziekconservatorium |
| *Gcd* | ——, Culturele Dienst Province Ost Vlaanderen |
| *Geb* | ——, St Baafsarchief med Bibliotheek Van Damme |
| *Gu* | ——, Rijksuniversiteit, Centrale Bibliotheek |
| *K* | Kortrijk, St Martinskerk |
| *Lc* | Liège, Conservatoire Royal de Musique |
| *Lu* | ——, Université de Liège |
| *Llc* | Lier, Conservatoire |
| *Llg* | ——, St Gummaruskerk |
| *LV* | Louvain, Dominikanenklooster |
| *LVu* | ——, Université de Louvain |
| *M* | Mons, Conservatoire Royal de Musique |
| *MA* | Morlanwelz-Mariemont, Musée de Mariemont |
| *MEa* | Mechelen, Archief en Stadsbibliotheek |
| *MEs* | ——, Stedelijke Openbare Bibliotheek |
| *OU* | Oudenaarde, Parochiale Kerk |
| *Tc* | Tournai, Chapitre de la Cathédrale |
| *Tv* | ——, Bibliothèque de la Ville |
| *TI* | Tienen, St Germanuskerk |
| *Z* | Zoutleeuw, St Leonarduskerk |

### BR: BRAZIL

| | |
|---|---|
| *Rem* | Rio de Janeiro, Escola de Música, Universidade Federal do Rio de Janeiro |
| *Rn* | ——, Biblioteca Nacional |

### C: CANADA

| | |
|---|---|
| *E* | Edmonton, University of Alberta |
| *Fc* | Fredericton, Christ Church Cathedral |
| *Ku* | Kingston, Queens University, Douglas Library |
| *Lu* | London, University of Western Ontario, Lawson Memorial Library |
| *Mc* | Montreal, Conservatoire de Musique et d'Art Dramatique |
| *Mfisher* | ——, Sidney T. Fisher, private collection [in *Tu*] |
| *Mm* | ——, McGill University, Faculty and Conservatorium of Music and Redpath Libraries |
| *On* | Ottawa, National Library of Canada |
| *Qc* | Quebec, Cathédrale de la Sainte-Trinité |
| *Qul* | ——, Université Laval |
| *SAu* | Sackville, Mt Allison University |
| *SJm* | St John, New Brunswick Museum |
| *Tb* | Toronto, Canadian Broadcasting Corporation |
| *Tm* | ——, Royal Ontario Museum |
| *Tolnick* | ——, Harvey J. Olnick, private collection |
| *Tp* | ——, Toronto Public Library, Music Branch |
| *Tu* | ——, University of Toronto, Faculty of Music |
| *Vu* | Vancouver, University of British Columbia Library, Fine Arts Division |
| *W* | Winnipeg, University of Manitoba |

### CH: SWITZERLAND

| | |
|---|---|
| *A* | Aarau, Aargauische Kantonsbibliothek |
| *AShoboken* | Ascona, Anthony van Hoboken, private collection |
| *Bchristen* | Basle, Werner Christen, private collection |
| *Bm* | ——, Musikakademie der Stadt |
| *Bmi* | ——, Musikwissenschaftliches Institut der Universität |
| *Bu* | ——, Öffentliche Bibliothek der Universität, Musiksammlung |
| *BA* | Baden, Historisches Museum (Landvogtei-Schloss) |
| *BEk* | Berne, Konservatorium |
| *BEl* | ——, Schweizerische Landesbibliothek |
| *BEms* | ——, Musikwissenschaftliches Seminar der Universität |
| *BEsu* | ——, Stadt- und Universitätsbibliothek; Bürgerbibliothek |
| *BI* | Biel, Stadtbibliothek |
| *C* | Chur, Kantonsbibliothek Graubünden |
| *D* | Disentis, Stift |
| *E* | Einsiedeln, Benediktinerkloster |
| *EN* | Engelberg, Stift |
| *Fcu* | Fribourg, Bibliothèque Cantonale et Universitaire |
| *Ff* | ——, Franziskaner-Kloster |
| *Fk* | ——, Kapuziner-Kloster |
| *Fsn* | ——, Kapitel St Nikolaus |
| *FF* | Frauenfeld, Thurgauische Kantonsbibliothek |
| *Gamoudruz* | Geneva, Emile Amoudruz, private collection |
| *Gc* | ——, Conservatoire de Musique |
| *Gpu* | ——, Bibliothèque Publique et Universitaire |

| | |
|---|---|
| *GLtschudi* | Glarus, A. Tschudi, private collection |
| *Lmg* | Lucerne, Allgemeine Musikalische Gesellschaft |
| *Ls* | ——, Stiftsarchiv St Leodegar |
| *Lz* | ——, Zentralbibliothek |
| *LAc* | Lausanne, Conservatoire de Musique |
| *LAcu* | ——, Bibliothèque Cantonale et Universitaire |
| *LU* | Lugano, Biblioteca Cantonale |
| *Mbernegg* | Maienfeld, Sprecher von Bernegg, private collection |
| *MO* | Morges, Bibliothèque de la Ville |
| *MÜ* | Müstair, Frauenkloster |
| *N* | Neuchâtel, Bibliothèque Publique |
| *R* | Rheinfelden, Christkatholisches Pfarramt |
| *S* | Sion, Bibliothèque Cantonale du Valais |
| *Sa* | ——, Staatsarchiv |
| *Sk* | ——, Kathedrale |
| *SA* | Sarnen, Bibliothek des Kollegiums |
| *SAf* | ——, Frauenkloster |
| *SCH* | Schwyz, Kantonsbibliothek |
| *SGs* | St Gall, Stiftsbibliothek |
| *SGv* | ——, Stadtbibliothek |
| *SH* | Schaffhausen, Stadtbibliothek |
| *SM* | St Maurice, Bibliothèque de l'Abbaye |
| *SO* | Solothurn, Zentralbibliothek, Musiksammlung |
| *TH* | Thun, Stadtbibliothek |
| *W* | Winterthur, Stadtbibliothek |
| *Wpeer* | ——, Peer private collection |
| *Zi* | Zurich, Israelitische Kulturgemeinde |
| *Zjacobi* | ——, Erwin R. Jacobi, private collection |
| *Zk* | ——, Konservatorium und Musikhochschule |
| *Zma* | ——, Schweizerisches Musik-Archiv |
| *Zms* | ——, Musikwissenschaftliches Seminar der Universität |
| *Zp* | ——, Pestalozzianum |
| *Zz* | ——, Zentralbibliothek |
| *ZG* | Zug, Stadtbibliothek |
| *ZO* | Zofingen, Stadtbibliothek |
| *ZU* | Zuoz, Gemeindearchiv |

### CO: COLOMBIA

| | |
|---|---|
| *B* | Bogotá, Catedral |

### CS: CZECHOSLOVAKIA

| | |
|---|---|
| *Bb* | Brno, Klášter Milosrdných Bratří [in *Bm*] |
| *Bm* | ——, Ústav Dějin Hudby Moravského Musea, Hudebněhistorické Oddělení |
| *Bu* | ——, Státní Vědecká Knihovna, Universitní Knihovna |
| *BA* | Bakov nad Jizerou, pobočka Státní Archívu v Mladé Boleslavi |
| *BEL* | Bělá pod Bezdězem, Městské Muzeum |
| *BER* | Beroun, Okresní Archív |
| *BRa* | Bratislava, Okresní Archív |
| *BRe* | ——, Evanjelícka a. v. Cirkevná Knižnica |
| *BRhs* | ——, Knižnica Hudobného Seminara Filosofickej Fakulty University Komenského |
| *BRnm* | ——, Slovenské Národné Muzeum, Hudobné Oddělenie |
| *BRsa* | ——, Štátny Ústredný Archív Slovenskej Socialistickej Republiky |
| *BRsav* | ——, Slovenská Akadémia Vied |
| *BRu* | ——, Univerzitná Knižnica |
| *BREsi* | Březnice, Děkanský Kostel Sv Ignáce |
| *BSk* | Banská Štiavnica, Farský Rímsko-Katolícky Kostol, Archív Chóru |
| *CH* | Cheb, Okresní Archív |
| *CHOd* | Choceň, Děkanský Úřad |
| *CHOm* | ——, Městské Muzeum |
| *H* | Hronov, Muzeum Aloise Jiráska |
| *HK* | Hradec Králové, Muzeum |
| *HOm* | Hořice, Vlastivědné Muzeum |
| *J* | Jur pri Bratislave, Okresní Archív, Bratislava-Vidick |
| *JIa* | Jindřichův Hradec, Státní Archív |
| *JIm* | ——, Vlastivědné Muzeum |
| *K* | Český Krumlov, Pracoviště Státního Archívu Třeboň, Hudební Sbírka |
| *KL* | Klatovy, Okresní Archív |
| *KO* | Košice, Městsky Archív |
| *KOL* | Kolín, Děkanský Chrám |
| *KRa* | Kroměříž, Státní Zámek a Zahrady, Historicko-Umělecké Fondy, Hudební Archív |
| *KRA* | Králíky, Děkanský Úřad |
| *KRE* | Kremnica, Městsky Archív |
| *KU* | Kutná Hora, Oblastní Muzeum |
| *KVd* | Karlovy Vary, Děkanský Úřad |
| *KVso* | ——, Karlovarský Symfonický Orchestr |
| *L* | Levoča, Rímsko-Katolícky Farský Kostol |
| *LIa* | Česká Lípa, Okresní Archív |

| | |
|---|---|
| *LIT* | Litoměřice, Státní Archív |
| *LO* | Loukov, Farní Úřad |
| *Mms* | Martin, Matica Slovenská, Oddělenie Hudobných Pamiatok |
| *Mnm* | ——, Slovenské Národné Muzeum, Archív |
| *MB* | Mladá Boleslav, Okresní Archív |
| *ME* | Mělník, Okresní Archív |
| *MH* | Mnichovo Hradiště, Vlastivědné Muzeum |
| *N* | Nítra, Státní Archív |
| *ND* | Nové Dvory, Farní Úřad |
| *NM* | Nové Mesto nad Váhom, Rímsko-Katolický Farský Kostol |
| *OLa* | Olomouc, Státní Oblastní Archív v Opava |
| *OLu* | ——, Státní Vědecká Knihovna, Universitní Knihovna |
| *OP* | Opava, Slezské Muzeum |
| *OS* | Ostrava, Československý Rozhlas, Hudební Archív |
| *OSE* | Osek, Klášter |
| *Pa* | ——, Státní Ústřední Archív |
| *Pak* | Prague, Archív Metropolitní Kapituly |
| *Pdobrovského* | ——, Knihovna Josefa Dobrovského |
| *Ph* | ——, Československá Církev Holešovice |
| *Pis* | ——, Československo Hudební Informační Středisko |
| *Pk* | ——, Archív Státní Konservatoře v Praze |
| *Pnm* | ——, Národní Muzeum, Hudební Oddělení |
| *Pp* | ——, Archív Pražského Hradu |
| *Ppp* | ——, Památník Národního Pisemnictví na Strahově |
| *Pr* | ——, Československý Rozhlas, Hudební Archív Různá Provenience |
| *Pra* | ——, Rodinní Archív Karla Kovařovice |
| *Ps* | ——, Strahovská Knihovna [in *Ppp*] |
| *Psf* | ——, Kostel Sv Franciscus |
| *Psj* | ——, Kostel Sv Jakuba |
| *Pu* | ——, Státní Knihovna ČSSR, Universitní Knihovna |
| *PLa* | Plzeň, Městsky Archív |
| *PLm* | ——, Západočeské Muzeum |
| *PLA* | Plasy, Okresní Archív |
| *POa* | Poděbrady, pobočka Státní Archívu Nymburk |
| *POm* | ——, Helichovo Muzeum |
| *PR* | Příbram, Okresný Muzeum |
| *PRE* | Prešov, Rímsko-Katolický Farský Kostol |
| *RA* | Rakovník, Státní Archív |
| *RAJ* | Rajhrad, Klášter [in *Bm*] |
| *RO* | Rokycany, Okresný Muzeum |
| *ROZ* | Rožnava, Biskupský Archív |
| *RY* | Rychnov, Muzeum Orlicka |
| *Sk* | Spišská Kapitula, Katedrálny Rímsko-Katolický Kostol, Knižnica Spišskej Kapituly |
| *SNV* | Spišská Nová Ves, Rímsko-Katolický Farský Kostol |
| *SO* | Sokolov, Státní Archív |
| *TC* | Třebíč, Městsky Archív |
| *TN* | Trenčín, Okresní Archív |
| *TR* | Trnava, Dóm Sv Mikuláša |
| *TRB* | Třebenice, Klášter |
| *TRE* | Třebőn, Státní Archív |
| *TU* | Turnov, Okresný Muzeum |
| *VE* | Velenice, Farní Úřad |
| *VM* | Vysoké Mýto, Okresný Muzeum |
| *ZA* | Zámrsk, Státní Archív |

### CU: CUBA

| | |
|---|---|
| *Hn* | Havana, Biblioteca Nacional |
| *Hse* | ——, Biblioteca de la Sociedad Económica de Amigos del País |

### D: GERMANY

| | |
|---|---|
| *Aa* | Augsburg, BRD, Kantoreiarchiv St Annen |
| *Af* | ——, Bibliothek der Fuggerschen Domänenkanzlei |
| *Ahk* | ——, Dominikanerkloster Heilig-Kreuz |
| *As* | ——, Staats- und Stadtbibliothek |
| *Asa* | ——, Stadtarchiv |
| *AAd* | Aachen, BRD, Bischöfliche Diözesanbibliothek |
| *AAg* | ——, Kaiser Karl-Gymnasium, Lehrerbibliothek |
| *AAm* | ——, Domarchiv |
| *AAst* | ——, Stadtbibliothek |
| *AB* | Amorbach, BRD, Fürstlich Leiningische Bibliothek, private collection |
| *ABG* | Annaberg-Buchholz, DDR, Pfarramt, Kirchenbibliothek |
| *ABGa* | ——, Kantoreiarchiv St Annen |
| *AD* | Adolfseck bei Fulda, BRD, Schloss Fasanerie, Bibliothek der Kurhessischen Hausstiftung |
| *ALa* | Altenburg, DDR, Landesarchiv (Historisches Staatsarchiv) |
| *ALs* | ——, Stadtarchiv |
| *ALt* | ——, Bibliothek des Landestheaters |
| *AM* | Amberg, BRD, Staatliche Provinzialbibliothek |
| *AN* | Ansbach, BRD, Regierungsbibliothek |
| *AÖ* | Altötting, BRD, Kapuziner-Kloster St Konrad |
| *ARk* | Arnstadt, DDR, Kirchenbibliothek |
| *ARsk* | ——, Stadt- und Kreisbibliothek |
| *ARsm* | ——, Schlossmuseum |
| *ASh* | Aschaffenburg, BRD, Hofbibliothek |
| *ASm* | ——, Stadtbücherei |
| *ASsb* | ——, Stiftsbibliothek |
| *B* | Berlin, Staatsbibliothek Preussischer Kulturbesitz [W] |
| *Ba* | ——, Amerika-Gedenkbibliothek (Berliner Zentralbibliothek) [W]; Deutsche Akademie der Künste [E] |
| *Bch* | ——, Musikbücherei Charlottenburg [W] |
| *Bdhm* | ——, Deutsche Hochschule für Musik Hanns Eisler [E] |
| *Bds* | ——, Deutsche Staatsbibliothek (formerly Königliche Bibliothek; Preussische Staatsbibliothek; Öffentliche Wissenschaftliche Bibliothek), Musikabteilung [E] |
| *Bdso* | ——, Deutsche Staatsoper [E] |
| *Be* | ——, Institut für Musikerziehung der Humboldt-Universität [E] |
| *Bgk* | ——, Streit'sche Stiftung [in *Bs*] [E] |
| *Bhbk* | ——, Staatliche Hochschule für Bildende Kunst [W] |
| *Bhesse* | ——, A. Hesse, private collection [E] |
| *Bhm* | ——, Staatliche Hochschule für Musik und Darstellende Kunst [W] |
| *Bim* | ——, Staatliches Institut für Musikforschung Preussischer Kulturbesitz [W] |
| *Bk* | ——, Staatliche Museen Preussischer Kulturbesitz [W] |
| *Bko* | ——, Komische Oper [E] |
| *Blk* | ——, Bezirks-Lehrerbibliothek Kreuzberg [W] |
| *Bm* | ——, Marienkirche [E] |
| *Bmb* | ——, Internationale Musikbibliothek, Verband Deutscher Komponisten und Musikwissenschaftler [E] |
| *Bmi* | ——, Musikwissenschaftliches Institut der Freien Universität [W]; Musikwissenschaftliches Institut der Humboldt-Universität [E] |
| *Bmm* | ——, Märkisches Museum [E] |
| *Bn* | ——, Nikolaikirche [E] |
| *Bp* | ——, Pädagogisches Zentrum [W] |
| *Br* | ——, Deutscher Demokratischer Rundfunk, Notenarchiv [E] |
| *Bs* | ——, Berliner Stadtbibliothek [E] |
| *Bst* | ——, Stadtbücherei, Hauptstelle Berlin-Wilmersdorf [W] |
| *Btu* | ——, Universitätsbibliothek der Technischen Universität [W] |
| *Btum* | ——, Lehrstuhl für Musikgeschichte der Technischen Universität [W] |
| *Bu* | ——, Universitätsbibliothek der Freien Universität [W] |
| *Buh* | ——, Universitätsbibliothek der Humboldt-Universität [E] |
| *BAa* | Bamberg, BRD, Staatsarchiv |
| *BAf* | ——, Franziskaner-Kloster |
| *BAs* | ——, Staatsbibliothek |
| *BAL* | Ballenstedt, DDR, Stadtbibliothek |
| *BAR* | Bartenstein, BRD, Fürst zu Hohenlohe-Bartensteinsches Archiv, private collection |
| *BAUd* | Bautzen, DDR, Domstift und Bischöfliches Ordinariat |
| *BAUk* | ——, Stadt- und Kreisbibliothek |
| *BB* | Benediktbeuren, BRD, Pfarrkirche |
| *BD* | Brandenburg an der Havel, DDR, Domstift |
| *BDH* | Bad Homburg von der Höhe, BRD, Stadtbibliothek |
| *BE* | Berleburg, BRD, Fürstlich Sayn-Wittgenstein-Berleburgsche Bibliothek, private collection |
| *BEU* | Beuron, BRD, Benediktiner-Erzabtei |
| *BEV* | Bevensen, BRD, Superintendantur, Ephoratsbibliothek und Bibliothek Sursen |
| *BFa* | Burgsteinfurt, BRD, Gymnasium Arnoldinum |
| *BFb* | ——, Fürstlich Bentheimsche Bibliothek [in *MÜu*] |
| *BG* | Beuerberg über Wolfratshausen, BRD, Pfarramt, Stiftskirche |
| *BGD* | Berchtesgaden, BRD, Katholisches Pfarramt |
| *BH* | Bayreuth, BRD, Stadtbücherei |
| *BI* | Bielefeld, BRD, Städtisches Ratsgymnasium |
| *BIB* | Bibra, DDR, Pfarrarchiv |
| *BIR* | Birstein über Wächtersbach, BRD, Fürst von Ysenburgisches Archiv und Schlossbibliothek, private collection |

| | |
|---|---|
| *BIT* | Bitterfeld, DDR, Kreismuseum |
| *BK* | Bernkastel-Kues, BRD, Cusanusstift |
| *BKÖ* | Bad Köstritz, DDR, Pfarrarchiv |
| *BMek* | Bremen, BRD, Bücherei der Bremer Evangelischen Kirche |
| *BMs* | ——, Staats- und Universitätsbibliothek |
| *BNba* | Bonn, BRD, Beethoven-Haus und Beethoven-Archiv |
| *BNek* | ——, Gemeindeverband der Evangelischen Kirche |
| *BNms* | ——, Musikwissenschaftliches Seminar der Universität |
| *BNu* | ——, Universitätsbibliothek |
| *BO* | ——, Bollstedt, Pfarramt |
| *BOCHb* | Bochum, BRD, Bergbaumuseum |
| *BOCHmi* | ——, Musikwissenschaftliches Institut der Ruhr-Universität |
| *BOCHs* | ——, Stadtbibliothek, Musikbücherei |
| *BORp* | Borna, DDR, Pfarrkirche |
| *BS* | Brunswick, BRD, Stadtarchiv und Stadtbibliothek |
| *BTH* | Barth, DDR, Kirchenbibliothek |
| *BÜ* | Büdingen, BRD, Fürstlich Ysenburg- und Büdingisches Archiv und Schlossbibliothek |
| *BW* | Burgwindheim über Bamberg, BRD, Katholisches Pfarramt |
| *Cl* | Coburg, BRD, Landesbibliothek |
| *Cm* | ——, Moritzkirche |
| *Cv* | ——, Kunstsammlung der Veste Coburg |
| *CA* | Castell, BRD, Fürstlich Castell'sche Bibliothek |
| *CD* | Crottendorf, DDR, Kantoreiarchiv |
| *CR* | Crimmitschau, DDR, Stadtkirche St Laurentius |
| *CZ* | Clausthal-Zellerfeld, BRD, Kirchenbibliothek |
| *CZu* | ——, Universitätsbibliothek |
| *Dhm* | Dresden, DDR, Hochschule für Musik Carl Maria von Weber |
| *Dkh* | ——, Katholische Hofkirche |
| *Dl* | ——, Bibliothek und Museum Löbau [in *Dlb*] |
| *Dla* | ——, Staatsarchiv |
| *Dlb* | ——, Sächsische Landesbibliothek |
| *Dmb* | ——, Musikbibliothek |
| *Ds* | ——, Staatstheater |
| *DB* | Dettelbach über Kitzingen, BRD, Franziskanerkloster |
| *DEl* | Dessau, DDR, Universitäts- und Landesbibliothek |
| *DEs* | ——, Stadtarchiv, Rathaus |
| *DI* | Dillingen an der Donau, BRD, Kreis- und Studienbibliothek |
| *DIp* | ——, Bischöfliches Priesterseminar |
| *DIN* | Dinkelsbühl, BRD, Katholisches Pfarramt St Georg |
| *DIP* | Dippoldiswalde, DDR, Evangelisch-Lutherisches Pfarramt |
| *DL* | Delitzsch, DDR, Museum und Bibliothek |
| *DM* | Dortmund, BRD, Stadt- und Landesbibliothek |
| *DO* | Donaueschingen, BRD, Fürstlich Fürstenbergische Hofbibliothek, private collection |
| *DÖ* | Döbeln, DDR, Pfarrbibliothek St Nikolai |
| *DÖF* | Döffingen über Bölingen, BRD, Pfarrbibliothek |
| *DS* | Darmstadt, BRD, Hessische Landes- und Hochschulbibliothek |
| *DSim* | ——, Internationales Musikinstitut |
| *DSk* | ——, Kirchenleitung der Evangelischen Kirche in Hessen und Nassau |
| *DT* | Detmold, BRD, Lippische Landesbibliothek |
| *DÜgg* | Düsseldorf, BRD, Staatliches Görres-Gymnasium |
| *DÜha* | ——, Hauptstaatsarchiv |
| *DÜk* | ——, Goethe-Museum |
| *DÜl* | ——, Landes- und Stadtbibliothek |
| *DÜmb* | ——, Stadtbüchereien, Musikbücherei |
| *DÜR* | Düren, BRD, Stadtbücherei, Leopold-Hoesch-Museum |
| *Ek* | Eichstätt, BRD, Kapuzinerkloster |
| *Es* | ——, Staats- und Seminarbibliothek |
| *Ew* | ——, Benediktinerinnen-Abtei St Walburg |
| *EB* | Ebrach, BRD, Katholisches Pfarramt |
| *EBS* | Ebstorf, BRD, Kloster |
| *EF* | Erfurt, DDR, Wissenschaftliche Bibliothek der Stadt |
| *EFd* | ——, Dombibliothek |
| *EFs* | ——, Stadt- und Bezirksbibliothek |
| *EIa* | Eisenach, DDR, Stadtarchiv |
| *EIb* | ——, Bachhaus und Bachmuseum |
| *EIl* | ——, Landeskirchenrat |
| *EIHp* | Eichtersheim, BRD, Pfarrbibliothek |
| *EL* | Eisleben, DDR, Andreas-Bibliothek |
| *EM* | Emden, BRD, Grosse Kirche |
| *EMM* | Emmerich, BRD, Staatliches Gymnasium |
| *EN* | Engelberg, BRD, Franziskanerkloster |
| *ERms* | Erlangen, BRD, Musikwissenschaftliches Seminar der Universität |
| *ERu* | ——, Universitätsbibliothek |
| *ES* | Essen, BRD, Musikbücherei der Stadtbücherei |
| *EU* | Eutin, BRD, Kreisbibliothek |
| *F* | Frankfurt am Main, BRD, Stadt- und Universitätsbibliothek |
| *Fkm* | ——, Museum für Kunsthandwerk |
| *Fmi* | ——, Musikwissenschaftliches Institut der Johann Wolfgang von Goethe-Universität |
| *Fsg* | ——, Philosophisch-Theologische Hochschule St Georgen |
| *Fsm* | ——, Bibliothek für Neuere Sprachen und Musik |
| *FBa* | Freiberg, DDR, Stadtarchiv |
| *FBb* | ——, Bergakademie, Bücherei |
| *FBo* | ——, Geschwister-Scholl-Oberschule, Historische Bibliothek |
| *FBsk* | ——, Stadt- und Kreisbibliothek |
| *FF* | Frankfurt an der Oder, DDR, Stadt- und Bezirksbibliothek |
| *FG* | Freyburg, DDR, Pfarrarchiv |
| *FLa* | Flensburg, BRD, Stadtarchiv |
| *FLs* | ——, Staatliches Gymnasium |
| *FRcb* | Freiburg im Breisgau, BRD, Collegium Borromaeum |
| *FRms* | ——, Musikwissenschaftliches Seminar der Universität |
| *FRu* | ——, Universitätsbibliothek |
| *FRls* | Friedberg, BRD, Stadtbibliothek |
| *FRlts* | ——, Theologisches Seminar der Evangelischen Kirche in Hessen und Nassau |
| *FS* | Freising, BRD, Dombibliothek |
| *FUf* | Fulda, BRD, Kloster Frauenberg |
| *FUl* | ——, Hessische Landesbibliothek |
| *FUp* | ——, Bischöfliches Priesterseminar, Bibliothek der Philosophisch-Theologischen Hochschule |
| *Ga* | Göttingen, BRD, Staatliches Archivlager |
| *Gb* | ——, Johann Sebastian Bach-Institut |
| *Gms* | ——, Musikwissenschaftliches Seminar der Universität |
| *Gs* | ——, Niedersächsische Staats- und Universitätsbibliothek |
| *GA* | Gaussig bei Bautzen, DDR, Schlossbibliothek |
| *GAH* | Gandersheim, BRD, Stiftsbibliothek |
| *GAM* | Gau-Algesheim, BRD, Stadtarchiv |
| *GAR* | Gars am Inn, BRD, Philosophisch-Theologische Ordenhochschule der Redemptoristen |
| *GBB* | Grossbrembach, DDR, Pfarrarchiv |
| *GBR* | Grossbreitenbach bei Arnstadt, DDR, Pfarrbibliothek |
| *GD* | Gaesdonck über Goch, BRD, Collegium Augustinianum |
| *GE* | Gelenau, DDR, Pfarrarchiv |
| *GERk* | Gera, DDR, Kirchenarchiv |
| *GERs* | ——, Stadtmuseum |
| *GERsb* | ——, Stadt- und Bezirksbibliothek |
| *GEY* | Geyer, DDR, Kirchenbibliothek |
| *GF* | Grossfahrer, DDR, Pfarrarchiv Starcklof-Eschenberger |
| *GHk* | Geithain, DDR, Evangelisch-Lutherisches Pfarramt |
| *GHNa* | Grossenhain, DDR, Archiv |
| *GHNk* | ——, Kirche |
| *GI* | Giessen, BRD, Justus Liebig-Universität |
| *GL* | Goslar, BRD, Marktkirchenbibliothek |
| *GLA* | Glashütte, DDR, Pfarrarchiv |
| *GM* | Grimma, DDR, Göschenhaus, Johannes Sturm, private collection |
| *GMl* | ——, Landesschule |
| *GO* | Gotha, DDR, Evangelisch-Lutherische Stadtkirchengemeinde |
| *GOa* | ——, Augustinerkirche |
| *GOg* | ——, Gymnasium |
| *GOl* | ——, Forschungsbibliothek [former Landesbibliothek] |
| *GOs* | ——, Stadtarchiv |
| *GOsk* | ——, Stadt- und Kreisbibliothek |
| *GÖp* | Görlitz, DDR, Evangelischer Parochialverband |
| *GÖs* | ——, Stadtbibliothek |
| *GÖsp* | ——, Pfarramt St Peter |
| *GOL* | Goldbach bei Gotha, DDR, Pfarrarchiv |
| *GRim* | Greifswald, DDR, Institut für Musikwissenschaft |
| *GRk* | ——, Konsistorialbibliothek |
| *GRu* | ——, Ernst-Moritz-Arndt-Universität |
| *GRÜ* | Grünhain, DDR, Pfarramt |
| *GÜ* | Güstrow, DDR, Heimatmuseum |
| *GZ* | Greiz, DDR, Stadt- und Kreisbibliothek |
| *GZbk* | ——, Staatliche Bücher- und Kupferstichsammlung |

| | |
|---|---|
| *GZmb* | ——, Städtische Musikbibliothek |
| *GZsa* | ——, Historisches Staatsarchiv |
| *Ha* | Hamburg, BRD, Staatsarchiv |
| *Hch* | ——, Gymnasium Christianeum |
| *Hhm* | ——, Harburg, Helmsmuseum |
| *Hj* | ——, Gelehrtenschule des Johanneum |
| *Hkm* | ——. Kunstgewerbemuseum |
| *Hmb* | ——, Musikbücherei der Hamburger Öffentlichen Bücherhallen |
| *Hmg* | ——, Museum für Hamburgische Geschichte |
| *Hmi* | ——, Musikwissenschaftliches Institut der Universität |
| *Hs* | ——, Staats- und Universitätsbibliothek |
| *Hsa* | ——, Senatsarchiv |
| *Hth* | ——, Universität, Theatersammlung |
| *HAf* | Halle an der Saale, DDR, Hauptbibliothek und Archiv der Franckeschen Stiftungen [in *HAu*] |
| *HAh* | ——, Händel-Haus |
| *HAmi* | ——, Institut für Musikwissenschaft der Martin-Luther-Universität |
| *HAmk* | ——, Marienbibliothek |
| *HAs* | ——, Stadt- und Bezirksbibliothek |
| *HAu* | ——. Universitäts- und Landesbibliothek Sachsen-Anhalt |
| *HAI* | Hainichen, DDR, Heimatmuseum |
| *HB* | Heilbronn, BRD, Stadtarchiv |
| *HCHs* | Hechingen, BRD, Stiftskirche |
| *HD* | Hermsdorf, DDR, Pfarrarchiv |
| *HEk* | Heidelberg, BRD, Evangelisches Kirchenmusikalisches Institut |
| *HEms* | ——, Musikwissenschaftliches Seminar der Universität |
| *HEu* | ——, Universitätsbibliothek |
| *HER* | Herrnhut, DDR, Archiv der Brüder-Unität |
| *HEY* | Heynitz, DDR, Pfarrbibliothek |
| *HG* | Havelberg, DDR, Museum |
| *HHa* | Hildburghausen, DDR, Stadtarchiv |
| *HIb* | Hildesheim, BRD, Beverin'sche Bibliothek |
| *HIm* | ——, St Michaelskirche |
| *HIp* | ——, Bischöfliches Priesterseminar |
| *HL* | Haltenbergstetten, BRD, Schloss über Niederstetten, Fürst zu Hohenlohe-Jagstberg'sche Bibliothek, private collection |
| *HLN* | Hameln, BRD, Stadtbücherei des Schiller-Gymnasiums |
| *HN* | Herborn, BRD, Evangelisches Theologisches Seminar |
| *HO* | Hof an der Saale, BRD, Jean Paul-Gymnasium |
| *HOr* | ——, Stadtarchiv, Ratsbibliothek |
| *HOE* | Hohenstein-Ernstthal, DDR, Kantoreiarchiv der Christophorikirche |
| *HOG* | Hofgeismar, BRD, Predigerseminar |
| *HOR* | Horst, BRD, Evangelisch-Lutherisches Pfarramt |
| *HR* | Harburg über Donauwörth, BRD, Fürstlich Oettingen-Wallerstein'sche Bibliothek, private collection |
| *HSj* | Helmstedt, BRD, Juleum |
| *HSk* | ——, Kantorat zu St Stephani [in *W*] |
| *HSm* | ——, Kloster Marienberg |
| *HSwandersleb* | ——, Bibliothek Pastor Wandersleb |
| *HTa* | Halberstadt, DDR, Stadtarchiv |
| *HTd* | ——, Dombibliothek |
| *HTg* | ——, Gleimhaus |
| *HVh* | Hanover, BRD, Staatliche Hochschule für Musik und Theater |
| *HVk* | ——, Arbeitsstelle für Gottesdienst und Kirchenmusik der Evangelisch-Lutherischen Landeskirche |
| *HVl* | ——, Niedersächsische Landesbibliothek |
| *HVs* | ——, Stadtbibliothek |
| *HVsa* | ——, Staatsarchiv |
| *HVth* | ——, Technische Hochschule |
| *HX* | Höxter, BRD, Kirchenbibliothek St Nikolaus |
| *Iek* | Isny, BRD, Evangelische Kirche St Nikolai |
| *Iq* | ——, Fürstlich Quadt'sche Bibliothek, private collection |
| *ILk* | Ilmenau, DDR, Kirchenbibliothek |
| *ILs* | ——, Stadtarchiv |
| *IN* | Indersdorf über Dachau, BRD, Katholisches Pfarramt |
| *Jmb* | Jena, DDR, Ernst Abbe-Bücherei, Musikbücherei |
| *Jmi* | ——, Musikwissenschaftliches Institut der Friedrich-Schiller-Universität |
| *Ju* | ——, Universitätsbibliothek der Friedrich-Schiller-Universität |
| *JA* | Jahnsdorf bei Stollberg, DDR, Pfarrarchiv |
| *JE* | Jever, BRD, Marien-Gymnasium |
| *Kdma* | Kassel, BRD, Deutsches Musikgeschichtliches Archiv |
| *Kl* | ——, Murhardsche Bibliothek der Stadt und Landesbibliothek |
| *Km* | ——, Musikakademie |
| *Ksp* | ——, Louis-Spohr-Gedenk- und Forschungsstätte |
| *KA* | Karlsruhe, BRD, Badische Landesbibliothek |
| *KAsp* | ——, Pfarramt St Peter |
| *KAu* | ——, Universitätsbibliothek |
| *KAL* | Kaldenkirchen, BRD, Pfarrbibliothek |
| *KARj* | Karl-Marx-Stadt, DDR, Jacobi-Kirche |
| *KARr* | ——, Ratsarchiv |
| *KARs* | ——, Stadt- und Bezirksbibliothek |
| *KBs* | Koblenz, BRD, Stadtbibliothek |
| *KBEk* | Koblenz-Ehrenbreitstein, BRD, Provinzialat der Kapuziner |
| *KFm* | Kaufbeuren, BRD, Stadtpfarrkirche St Martin |
| *KFs* | ——, Stadtbücherei |
| *Kll* | Kiel, BRD, Schleswig-Holsteinische Landesbibliothek |
| *KImi* | ——, Musikwissenschaftliches Institut der Christian-Albrecht Universität |
| *KIu* | ——, Universitätsbibliothek |
| *KIN* | Kindelbrück, DDR, Pfarrarchiv, Evangelisches Pfarramt |
| *KMk* | Kamenz, DDR, Evangelisch-Lutherische Hauptkirche |
| *KMl* | ——, Lessingmuseum |
| *KMs* | ——, Stadtarchiv |
| *KNd* | Cologne, BRD, Erzbischöfliche Diözesan- und Dombibliothek |
| *KNh* | ——, Staatliche Hochschule für Musik |
| *KNhi* | ——, Joseph Haydn-Institut |
| *KNmi* | ——, Musikwissenschaftliches Institut der Universität |
| *KNu* | ——, Universitäts- und Stadtbibliothek |
| *KÖ* | Köthen, DDR, Heimatmuseum |
| *KPk* | Kempten, BRD, Kirchenbibliothek, Evangelisch-Lutherisches Pfarramt St Mang |
| *KPs* | ——, Stadtbücherei |
| *KPsl* | ——, Stadtpfarrkirche St Lorenz |
| *KR* | Kleinröhrsdorf über Bischofswerda, DDR, Pfarrkirchenbibliothek |
| *KT* | Klingenthal, DDR, Kirchenbibliothek |
| *KU* | Kulmbach, BRD, Stadtarchiv |
| *KZa* | Konstanz, BRD, Stadtarchiv |
| *KZr* | ——, Rosgarten-Museum |
| *KZs* | ——, Städtische Wessenberg-Bibliothek |
| *Lm* | Lüneburg, BRD, Michaelisschule |
| *Lr* | ——, Ratsbücherei |
| *LA* | Landshut, BRD, Historischer Verein für Niederbayern |
| *LAU* | Laubach, BRD, Gräflich Solms-Laubach'sche Bibliothek |
| *LB* | Langenburg, BRD, Fürstlich Hohenlohe-Langenburg'sche Schlossbibliothek, private collection |
| *LCH* | Lich, BRD, Fürstlich Solms-Lich'sche Bibliothek, private collection |
| *LEb* | Leipzig, DDR, Bach-Archiv |
| *LEbh* | ——, Breitkopf & Härtel, Verlagsarchiv |
| *LEdb* | ——, Deutsche Bücherei, Musikaliensammlung |
| *LEm* | ——, Musikbibliothek der Stadt |
| *LEmh* | ——, Hochschule für Musik |
| *LEmi* | ——, Musikwissenschaftliches Institut der Karl-Marx-Universität |
| *LEsm* | ——, Museum für Geschichte der Stadt |
| *LEt* | ——, Thomasschule |
| *LEu* | ——, Universitätsbibliothek der Karl-Marx-Universität |
| *LFN* | Laufen an der Salzach, BRD, Stiftsarchiv |
| *LHD* | Langhennersdorf über Freiberg, DDR, Pfarramt |
| *LI* | Lindau, BRD, Stadtbibliothek |
| *LIM* | Limbach am Main, BRD, Pfarramt |
| *LL* | Langula über Mühlhausen, DDR, Pfarramt |
| *LM* | Leitheim über Donauwörth, BRD, Schlossbibliothek Freiherr von Tucher |
| *LO* | Loccum über Wunstorf, BRD, Klosterbibliothek |
| *LÖ* | Lössnitz, DDR, Pfarrarchiv |
| *LR* | Lahr, BRD, Lehrerbibliothek des Scheffel-Gymnasiums |
| *LST* | Lichtenstein, DDR, Kantoreiarchiv von St Laurentius |
| *LÜd* | Lübeck, BRD, Distler Archiv |
| *LÜh* | ——, Bibliothek der Hansestadt |
| *LUC* | Luckau, DDR, Nikolaikirche |
| *Ma* | Munich, BRD, Franziskanerkloster St Anna |
| *Mb* | ——, Benediktinerabtei St Bonifaz |
| *Mbm* | ——, Metropolitankapitel |
| *Mbn* | ——, Bayerisches Nationalmuseum |
| *Mbs* | ——, Bayerische Staatsbibliothek |

| | |
|---|---|
| *SAAu* | ——, Universitätsbibliothek |
| *SBg* | Straubing, BRD, Johannes Turmair-Gymnasium |
| *SBj* | ——, Kirchenbibliothek St Jakob |
| *SBk* | ——, Karmeliter-Kloster |
| *SCHhv* | Schwäbisch Hall, BRD, Historischer Verein für Württembergisch-Franken |
| *SCHm* | ——, Archiv der St Michaelskirche |
| *SCHr* | ——, Ratsbibliothek im Stadtarchiv |
| *SCHEY* | Scheyern über Pfaffenhofen, BRD, Benediktiner-abtei |
| *SCHM* | Schmölln, DDR, Archiv der Stadtkirche |
| *SCHMI* | Schmiedeberg bei Dresden, DDR, Pfarramt |
| *SCHWherold* | Schwabach, BRD, Herold collection |
| *SCHWk* | ——, Kirchenbibliothek |
| *SDF* | Schlehdorf, BRD, Katholische Pfarrkirche |
| *SF* | Schweinfurt-Oberndorf, BRD, Kirchen- und Pfarr-bibliothek des Evangelisch-Lutherischen Pfarramts |
| *SFsj* | ——, Pfarramt St Johannis, Sakristei-Bibliothek |
| *SGh* | Schleusingen, DDR, Heimatmuseum |
| *SHk* | Sondershausen, DDR, Stadtkirche |
| *SHs* | ——, Stadt- und Kreisbibliothek |
| *SHsk* | ——, Schlosskirche |
| *SI* | Sigmaringen, BRD, Fürstlich Hohenzollernsche Hofbibliothek, private collection |
| *SLk* | Salzwedel, DDR, Katharinenkirche |
| *SLm* | ——, J. F. Danneil-Museum |
| *SLmk* | ——, Marienkirche |
| *SNed* | Schmalkalden, DDR, Evangelisches Dekanat |
| *SNh* | ——, Heimatmuseum Schloss Wilhelmsburg |
| *SO* | Soest, BRD, Stadtbibliothek im Stadtarchiv |
| *SÖNp* | Schönau bei Heidelberg, BRD, Pfarrbibliothek |
| *SPlb* | Speyer, BRD, Pfälzische Landesbibliothek, Musik-abteilung |
| *SPlk* | ——, Bibliothek des Protestantischen Landes-kirchenrats der Pfalz |
| *SPF* | Schulpforta, DDR, Heimoberschule |
| *SSa* | Stralsund, DDR, Bibliothek des Stadtarchivs |
| *ST* | Stade, BRD, Predigerbibliothek [in *ROT*] |
| *STO* | Stolberg, DDR, Bibliothek |
| *SUa* | Sulzenbrücken, DDR, Pfarrarchiv |
| *SUH* | Suhl, DDR, Stadt- und Bezirksbibliothek Martin Andersen Nexö |
| *SWl* | Schwerin, DDR, Wissenschaftliche Allgemein-bibliothek [former Mecklenburgische Landes-bibliothek] |
| *SWs* | ——, Stadt- und Bezirksbibliothek, Musikabteilung |
| *SWsk* | ——, Schlosskirchenchor |
| *SWth* | ——, Mecklenburgisches Staatstheater |
| *SZ* | Schleiz, DDR, Stadtkirche |
| *Tes* | Tübingen, BRD, Evangelisches Stift |
| *Tl* | ——, Schwäbisches Landesmusikarchiv [in *Tmi*] |
| *Tmi* | ——, Musikwissenschaftliches Institut der Eberhard-Karls-Universität |
| *Tu* | ——, Universitätsbibliothek |
| *Tw* | ——, Bibliothek des Wilhelmstiftes |
| *TAB* | Tabarz, DDR, Pfarrarchiv, Evangelisch-Lutheri-sches Pfarramt |
| *TEG* | Tegernsee, BRD, Pfarrkirche, Katholisches Pfarr-amt |
| *TEI* | Teisendorf, BRD, Katholisches Pfarramt |
| *TH* | Themar, DDR, Pfarramt |
| *TIT* | Tittmoning, BRD, Kollegiatstift |
| *TO* | Torgau, DDR, Johann-Walter-Kantorei |
| *TOek* | ——, Evangelische Kirchengemeinde |
| *TOs* | ——, Stadtarchiv |
| *TRb* | Trier, BRD, Bistumarchiv und Dombibliothek |
| *TRp* | ——, Priesterseminar |
| *TRs* | ——, Stadtbibliothek |
| *Us* | Ulm, BRD, Stadtbibliothek |
| *Usch* | ——, Von Schermar'sche Familienstiftung |
| *UDa* | Udestedt über Erfurt, DDR, Pfarrarchiv, Evangelisch-Lutherisches Pfarramt |
| *V* | Villingen, BRD, Städtische Sammlung |
| *VI* | Viernau, DDR, Pfarramt |
| *W* | Wolfenbüttel, BRD, Herzog August Bibliothek |
| *Wa* | ——, Niedersächsisches Staatsarchiv |
| *WA* | Waldheim, DDR, Stadtkirche St Nikolai |
| *WAB* | Waldenburg, DDR, Kirchenmusikalische Bibliothek von St Bartholomäus |
| *WB* | Weissenburg, BRD, Stadtbibliothek |
| *WBB* | Walberg, BRD, Albertus-Magnus-Akademie, Biblio-thek St Albert |
| *WD* | Wiesentheid, BRD, Musiksammlung des Grafen von Schönborn-Wiesentheid, private collection |
| *WE* | Weiden, BRD, Pfannenstiel'sche Bibliothek, Evan-gelisch-Lutherisches Pfarramt |

| | |
|---|---|
| *WEH* | Weierhof, BRD, Mennonitische Forschungsstelle |
| *WEL* | Weltenburg, BRD, Benediktinerkloster |
| *WER* | Wernigerode, DDR, Heimatmuseum, Harzbücherei |
| *WERk* | Wertheim am Main, BRD, Evangelisches Pfarramt |
| *WERl* | ——, Fürstlich Löwenstein'sche Bibliothek, private collection |
| *WEY* | Weyarn, BRD, Pfarrkirche [in *FS*] |
| *WF* | Weissenfels, DDR, Heimatmuseum |
| *WFg* | ——, Heinrich-Schütz-Gedenkstätte |
| *WGk* | Wittenberg, DDR, Stadtkirche |
| *WGl* | ——, Reformationsgeschichtliches Museum, Luther-halle |
| *WGp* | ——, Evangelisches Predigerseminar |
| *WH* | Windsheim, BRD, Stadtbibliothek |
| *WIl* | Wiesbaden, BRD, Hessische Landesbibliothek |
| *WILd* | Wilster, BRD, Stadtarchiv (Doos'sche Bibliothek) |
| *WL* | Wuppertal, BRD, Wissenschaftliche Stadtbibliothek |
| *WM* | Wismar, DDR, Stadtarchiv |
| *WO* | Worms, BRD, Stadtbibliothek |
| *WRdn* | Weimar, DDR, Deutsches Nationaltheater |
| *WRgm* | ——, Goethe-National-Museum |
| *WRgs* | ——, Goethe–Schiller-Archiv und Franz-Liszt-Museum |
| *WRh* | ——, Franz-Liszt-Hochschule |
| *WRhk* | ——, Herderkirche |
| *WRiv* | ——, Institut für Volksmusikforschung |
| *WRl* | ——, Landeshauptarchiv |
| *WRs* | ——, Stadtbücherei, Musikbücherei |
| *WRtl* | ——, Thüringische Landesbibliothek, Musiksamm-lung |
| *WRz* | ——, Zentralbibliothek der Deutschen Klassik |
| *WS* | Wasserburg am Inn, BRD, Chorarchiv St Jakob, Pfarramt |
| *WÜms* | Würzburg, BRD, Musikwissenschaftliches Seminar der Universität |
| *WÜsa* | ——, Stadtarchiv |
| *WÜu* | ——, Universitätsbibliothek |
| *X* | Xanten, BRD, Stifts- und Pfarrbibliothek |
| *Z* | Zwickau, DDR, Ratsschulbibliothek |
| *Zmk* | ——, Domkantorei der Marienkirche |
| *Zsch* | ——, Robert-Schumann-Haus |
| *ZE* | Zerbst, DDR, Stadtarchiv |
| *ZEo* | ——, Bücherei der Erweiterten Oberschule |
| *ZGh* | Zörbig, DDR, Heimatmuseum |
| *ZGsj* | ——, Pfarramt St Jacobi |
| *ZI* | Zittau, DDR, Stadt- und Kreisbibliothek |
| *ZIa* | ——, Stadtarchiv |
| *ZL* | Zeil, BRD, Fürstlich Waldburg-Zeil'sches Archiv, private collection |
| *ZW* | Zweibrücken, BRD, Bibliotheca Bipontina, Wissen-schaftliche Bibliothek am Herzog-Wolfgang-Gymnasium |
| *ZZ* | Zeitz, DDR, Heimatmuseum |
| *ZZs* | ——, Stiftsbibliothek |

## *DK*: DENMARK

| | |
|---|---|
| *A* | Århus, Statsbiblioteket |
| *Dschoenbaum* | Dragør, Camillo Schoenbaum, private collection |
| *Hfog* | Hellerup, Dan Fog, private collection |
| *Kc* | Copenhagen, Carl Claudius Musikhistoriske Sam-ling |
| *Kh* | ——, Københavns Kommunes Hovedbiblioteket |
| *Kk* | ——, Det Kongelige Bibliotek |
| *Kmk* | ——, Det Kongelige Danske Musikkonservatorium |
| *Km(m)* | ——, Musikhistorisk Museum |
| *Ks* | ——, Samfundet til Udgivelse af Dansk Musik |
| *Kt* | ——, Teaterhistorisk Museum |
| *Ku* | ——, Universitetsbiblioteket 1. Afdeling |
| *Kv* | ——, Københavns Universitet, Musikvidenskabeligt Institut |
| *Ol* | Odense, Landsarkivet for Fyen, Karen Brahes Bib-liotek |
| *Ou* | ——, Universitetsbibliotek |
| *Rk* | Ribe, Stifts- og Katedralskoles Bibliotek |
| *Sa* | Sorø, Sorø Akademis Bibliotek |

## *E*: SPAIN

| | |
|---|---|
| *Ac* | Ávila, Catedral |
| *Asa* | ——, Monasterio de S Ana (Real Monasterio de Encarnació) |
| *Ast* | ——, Monasterio del S Tomás, Archivo de la Iglesia |
| *AL* | Alquezar, Colegiata |
| *ALB* | Albarracín, Colegiata |
| *AS* | Astorga, Catedral |
| *Ba* | Barcelona, Real Academia de Ciencias y Artes |
| *Bac* | ——, Corona de Aragón |

| | |
|---|---|
| *Bc* | ——, Biblioteca de Cataluña |
| *Bca* | ——, Catedral |
| *Bcapdevila* | ——, Felipe Capdevila Rovira, private collection |
| *Bcm* | ——, Conservatorio Superior Municipal de Música |
| *Bih* | ——, Instituto Municipal de Historia (formerly Archivo Histórico de la Ciudad) |
| *Bim* | ——, Instituto Español de Musicología |
| *Bit* | ——, Instituto del Teatro (formerly Museo del Arte Escénico) |
| *Boc* | ——, Biblioteca Orfeó Catalá |
| *Bsm* | ——, S María del Mar |
| *Bu* | ——, Biblioteca del Universidad |
| *BA* | Badajoz, Catedral |
| *BUa* | Burgos, Catedral |
| *BUlh* | ——, Monasterio de Las Huelgas |
| *BUm* | ——, Museo Arqueológico |
| *BUp* | ——, Biblioteca Provincial |
| *BUse* | ——, Parroquia de S Esteban |
| *C* | Córdoba, Catedral |
| *CA* | Calahorra, Catedral |
| *CAL* | Calatayud, Colegiata de S María |
| *CAR* | Cardona, Archivo Comunal |
| *CU* | Cuenca, Catedral |
| *CUi* | ——, Instituto de Música Religiosa |
| *CZ* | Cádiz, Archivo Capitular |
| *E* | El Escorial, Real Monasterio de S Lorenzo |
| *G* | Gerona, Biblioteca Catedralicia |
| *Gm* | ——, Museo Diocesano |
| *Gp* | ——, Biblioteca Pública |
| *Gs* | ——, Seminario Gerundense |
| *GRc* | Granada, Catedral |
| *GRcr* | ——, Capilla Real |
| *GU* | Guadalupe, Real Monasterio de S María |
| *H* | Huesca, Catedral |
| *J* | Jaca, Catedral |
| *JA* | Jaén, Catedral |
| *LPA* | Las Palmas, Catedral de Canarias |
| *La* | León, Catedral |
| *Lc* | ——, Colegiata de S Isidoro |
| *Lp* | ——, Biblioteca Pública Provincial |
| *LEc* | Lérida, Catedral |
| *LEm* | ——, Museo Diocesano |
| *Ma* | Madrid, Real Academia de Bellas Artes de S Fernando |
| *Mah* | ——, Archivo Histórico Nacional (Real Academia de la Historia) |
| *Mam* | ——, Biblioteca Musical Circulante |
| *Mat* | ——, Museo-Archivo Teatral |
| *Mc* | ——, Conservatorio Superior de Música |
| *Mca* | ——, Casa de Alba, private collection |
| *Mcns* | ——, Congregación de Nuestra Señora |
| *Mic* | ——, Instituto de Cultura Hispánica, Sección de Música |
| *Mit* | ——, Ministerio de Información y Turismo |
| *Mlg* | ——, Fundación Lazaro Galdiano |
| *Mm* | ——, Biblioteca Municipal |
| *Mmc* | ——, Casa Ducal de Medinaceli, Bartolomé March Servera, private collection |
| *Mn* | ——, Biblioteca Nacional |
| *Mp* | ——, Palacio Real |
| *Mpm* | ——, Patronato Marcelino Menéndez y Pelayo del Consejo Superior de Investigaciones Científicas |
| *Mrt* | ——, Radio Nacional de España-Televisión |
| *Msa* | ——, Sociedad General de Autores de España |
| *Msi* | ——, Ciudad Universitaria, Facultad de Filosofía y Letras, Biblioteca de S Isidoro |
| *MA* | Málaga, Catedral |
| *MO* | Montserrat, Monasterio de S María |
| *MON* | Mondoñedo, Catedral |
| *OL* | Olot, Biblioteca Popular |
| *OR* | Orense, Catedral |
| *ORI* | Orihuela, Catedral |
| *OS* | Osma, Catedral |
| *OV* | Oviedo, Catedral Metropolitana |
| *P* | Plasencia, Catedral |
| *PAc* | Palma de Mallorca, Catedral |
| *PAp* | ——, Biblioteca Provincial |
| *PAMc* | Pamplona, Catedral |
| *PAMm* | ——, Museo Sarasate |
| *PAS* | Pastrana, Iglesia Parroquial |
| *RO* | Roncesvalles, Monasterio de S María |
| *Sc* | Seville, Catedral |
| *Sco* | ——, Biblioteca Capitular Colombina [in *Sc*] |
| *SA* | Salamanca, Catedral |
| *SAcalo* | ——, José López-Calo, private collection |
| *SAu* | ——, Universidad Pontificia, Biblioteca Universitaria |

| | |
|---|---|
| *SAuf* | ——, Universidad Pontificia, Facultad de Filosofía y Letras |
| *SAN* | Santander, Biblioteca de Menéndez y Pelayo |
| *SC* | Santiago de Compostela, Catedral |
| *SCu* | ——, Biblioteca Universitaria |
| *SD* | Santo Domingo de la Calzada, Archivo |
| *SE* | Segovia, Catedral |
| *SEG* | Segorbe, Catedral |
| *SI* | Silos, Monasterio Benedictino (Abadía) de S Domingo |
| *SIG* | Sigüenza, Catedral |
| *SIM* | Simancas, Archivo General |
| *SO* | Soria, Biblioteca Pública |
| *Tc* | Toledo, Archivo Capitular |
| *Tp* | ——, Biblioteca Pública Provincial y Museo de la Santa Cruz |
| *TAc* | Tarragona, Catedral |
| *TAp* | ——, Biblioteca Pública |
| *TO* | Tortosa, Catedral |
| *TU* | Tudela, Colegiata (formerly Catedral) de S María |
| *TZ* | Tarazona, Catedral |
| *U* (also *SU*) | Seo de Urgel, Catedral |
| *V* | Valladolid, Catedral |
| *Vp* | ——, Parroquia de Santiago |
| *VAa* | Valencia, Archivo, Biblioteca y Museos Municipales |
| *VAc* | ——, Catedral |
| *VAcm* | ——, Conservatorio Superior de Música |
| *VAcp* | ——, Colegio y Seminario del Corpus Christi del Patriarca |
| *VAim* | ——, Instituto Valenciano de Musicología |
| *VAu* | ——, Biblioteca Universitaria |
| *VI* | Vich, Museo Episcopal |
| *VIT* | Vitoria, Catedral |
| *Zac* | Saragossa, Archivo de Música del Cabildo |
| *Zcc* | ——, Colegio Calasanci |
| *Zfm* | ——, Facultad de Medicina |
| *Zp* | ——, Biblioteca Pública |
| *Zs* | ——, Biblioteca Capitular de la Seo |
| *Zsc* | ——, Seminario de S Carlos |
| *Zu* | ——, Biblioteca Universitaria |
| *Zvp* | ——, Iglesia Metropolitana [in *Zac*] |
| *ZA* | Zamora, Catedral |

*EIRE*: IRELAND

| | |
|---|---|
| *C* | Cork, University College |
| *Da* | Dublin, Royal Irish Academy |
| *Dam* | ——, Royal Irish Academy of Music |
| *Dcb* | ——, Chester Beatty Library |
| *Dcc* | ——, Christ Church Cathedral |
| *Dm* | ——, Marsh's Library |
| *Dmh* | ——, Mercer's Hospital |
| *Dn* | ——, National Library and Museum of Ireland |
| *Dpc* | ——, St Patrick's Cathedral |
| *Dtc* | ——, Trinity College |
| *Duc* | ——, University College |

*ET*: EGYPT

| | |
|---|---|
| *S* | Mt Sinai |

*F*: FRANCE

| | |
|---|---|
| *A* | Avignon, Bibliothèque Municipale, Musée Calvet |
| *Aa* | ——, Archives Départementales de Vaucluse |
| *AB* | Abbeville, Bibliothèque Municipale |
| *AG* | Agen, Archives Départementales de Lot-et-Garonne |
| *AI* | Albi, Bibliothèque Municipale |
| *AIXc* | Aix-en-Provence, Conservatoire |
| *AIXm* | ——, Bibliothèque Municipale, Bibliothèque Méjanes |
| *AIXmc* | ——, Maîtrise de la Cathédrale |
| *AL* | Alençon, Bibliothèque Municipale |
| *AM* | Amiens, Bibliothèque Municipale |
| *AN* | Angers, Bibliothèque Municipale |
| *ANG* | Angoulême, Bibliothèque Municipale |
| *ANN* | Annecy, Bibliothèque Municipale |
| *APT* | Apt, Cathédrale Ste Anne |
| *AR* | Arles, Bibliothèque Municipale |
| *AS* | Arras, Bibliothèque Municipale |
| *ASO* | Asnières-sur-Oise, François Lang, private collection |
| *AU* | Auxerre, Bibliothèque Municipale |
| *AUT* | Autun, Bibliothèque Municipale |
| *AV* | Avallon, Société d'Etudes d'Avallon |
| *AVR* | Avranches, Bibliothèque Municipale |
| *B* | Besançon, Bibliothèque Municipale |
| *Ba* | ——, Bibliothèque de l'Archevêché |
| *Be* | ——, Ecole Nationale de Musique |
| *BD* | Bar-le-Duc, Bibliothèque Municipale |
| *BE* | Beauvais, Bibliothèque Municipale |
| *BER* | Bernay, Bibliothèque Municipale |

| | |
|---|---|
| *BG* | Bourg-en-Bresse, Bibliothèque Municipale et Musée de l'Ain |
| *BL* | Blois, Bibliothèque Municipale |
| *BO* | Bordeaux, Bibliothèque Municipale |
| *BOI* | Boisguillaume, Musée Boieldieu |
| *BOU* | Bourbourg, Bibliothèque Municipale |
| *BR* | Brest, Bibliothèque Municipale |
| *BS* | Bourges, Bibliothèque Municipale |
| *BSM* | Boulogne-sur-Mer, Bibliothèque Municipale |
| *C* | Carpentras, Bibliothèque Inguimbertine et Musée de Carpentras |
| *CA* | Cambrai, Bibliothèque Municipale |
| *CAc* | ——, Cathédrale |
| *CAD* | Cadouin, Bibliothèque de l'Abbaye |
| *CAH* | Cahors, Bibliothèque Municipale |
| *CAL* | Calais, Bibliothèque Municipale |
| *CC* | Carcassonne, Bibliothèque Municipale |
| *CF* | Clermont-Ferrand, Bibliothèque Municipale et Universitaire, Section Centrale et Section Lettres |
| *CH* | Chantilly, Musée Condé |
| *CHA* | Châteauroux, Bibliothèque Municipale |
| *CHE* | Cherbourg, Bibliothèque et Archives Municipales |
| *CHM* | Chambéry, Bibliothèque Municipale |
| *CHR* | Chartres, Bibliothèque Municipale |
| *CN* | Caen, Bibliothèque Municipale |
| *CNc* | ——, Conservatoire National de Musique |
| *CO* | Colmar, Bibliothèque Municipale |
| *COs* | ——, Consistoire de l'Eglise de la Confession d'Augsbourg à Colmar |
| *COUm* | Coutances, Bibliothèque Municipale |
| *COUs* | ——, Grand Séminaire |
| *CSM* | Châlons-sur-Marne, Bibliothèque Municipale |
| *CV* | Charleville, Bibliothèque Municipale |
| *Dc* | Dijon, Bibliothèque du Conservatoire |
| *Dm* | ——, Bibliothèque Municipale (Bibliothèque Publique) |
| *DI* | Dieppe, Bibliothèque Municipale |
| *DO* | Dôle, Bibliothèque Municipale |
| *DOU* | Douai, Bibliothèque Municipale |
| *E* | Epinal, Bibliothèque Municipale |
| *EP* | Epernay, Bibliothèque Municipale |
| *EV* | Evreux, Bibliothèque Municipale |
| *F* | Foix, Bibliothèque Municipale |
| *G* | Grenoble, Bibliothèque Municipale |
| *Ge* | ——, Ecole Régionale de Musique, de Danse et d'Art Dramatique |
| *GAP* | Gap, Archives Départementales des Hautes-Alpes |
| *H* | Hyères, Bibliothèque Municipale |
| *Lc* | Lille, Conservatoire |
| *Lfc* | ——, Facultés Catholiques |
| *Lm* | ——, Bibliothèque Municipale |
| *LA* | Laon, Bibliothèque Municipale |
| *LB* | Libourne, Bibliothèque Municipale |
| *LG* | Limoges, Bibliothèque Municipale |
| *LH* | Le Havre, Bibliothèque Municipale |
| *LM* | Le Mans, Bibliothèque Municipale |
| *LO* | Louviers, Bibliothèque Municipale |
| *LP* | Le Puy-en-Velay, Bibliothèque Municipale |
| *LR* | La Rochelle, Bibliothèque Municipale |
| *LV* | Laval, Bibliothèque Municipale |
| *LYc* | Lyons, Conservatoire National de Musique |
| *LYm* | ——, Bibliothèque Municipale |
| *Mc* | Marseilles, Conservatoire de Musique et de Déclamation |
| *Mm* | ——, Bibliothèque Municipale |
| *MAC* | Mâcon, Bibliothèque Municipale |
| *MD* | Montbéliard, Bibliothèque Municipale |
| *MEL* | Melun, Bibliothèque Municipale |
| *MH* | Mulhouse, Bibliothèque Municipale |
| *MIL* | Millau, Bibliothèque Municipale |
| *MIR* | Mirecourt, Bibliothèque Municipale |
| *ML* | Moulins, Bibliothèque Municipale |
| *MLN* | Montluçon, Bibliothèque Municipale |
| *MO* | Montpellier, Faculté de Médecine de l'Université |
| *MOv* | ——, Bibliothèque de la Ville et du Musée Fabre |
| *MON* | Montauban, Bibliothèque Municipale |
| *MZ* | Metz, Bibliothèque Municipale |
| *Nd* | Nantes, Bibliothèque du Musée Dobrée |
| *Ne* | ——, Ecole Nationale de Musique, d'Art Dramatique et de Danse |
| *Nm* | ——, Bibliothèque Municipale |
| *NAc* | Nancy, Conservatoire |
| *NAm* | ——, Bibliothèque Municipale |
| *NAR* | Narbonne, Bibliothèque Municipale |
| *NI* | Nice, Bibliothèque Municipale |
| *NIc* | ——, Conservatoire de Musique |
| *NO* | Noyon, Bibliothèque Municipale |
| *NS* | Nîmes, Bibliothèque Municipale |
| *NT* | Niort, Bibliothèque Municipale |
| *O* | Orleans, Bibliothèque Municipale |
| *Pa* | Paris, Bibliothèque de l'Arsenal |
| *Pal* | ——, American Library in Paris |
| *Pbf* | ——, Centre de Documentation Benjamin Franklin |
| *Pc* | ——, Conservatoire National de Musique [in *Pn*] |
| *Pcf* | ——, Comédie-Française, Bibliothèque |
| *Pcrs* | ——, Centre National de la Recherche Scientifique |
| *Pe* | ——, Schola Cantorum (Ecole Supérieure de Musique, Danse et Art Dramatique) |
| *Pgérard* | ——, Yves Gérard, private collection |
| *Pi* | ——, Bibliothèque de l'Institut |
| *Pim* | ——, Institut de Musicologie de l'Université, Bibliothèque Pierre Aubry |
| *Pis* | ——, Institut Supérieur de Musique Liturgique |
| *Pm* | ——, Bibliothèque Mazarine |
| *Pma* | ——, Musée National des Arts et Traditions Populaires |
| *Pmeyer* | ——, André Meyer, private collection |
| *Pmg* | ——, Musée Guimet |
| *Pmh* | ——, Musée de l'Homme |
| *Pn* | ——, Bibliothèque Nationale |
| *Po* | ——, Bibliothèque–Musée de l'Opéra |
| *Pphon* | ——, Phonothèque Nationale, Bibliothèque et Musée |
| *Ppincherle* | ——, Marc Pincherle, private collection [dispersed 1975] |
| *Ppo* | ——, Bibliothèque Polonaise de Paris |
| *Prothschild* | ——, Germaine, Baronne Edouard de Rothschild, private collection |
| *Prt* | ——, Office de Radiodiffusion-Télévision Française |
| *Psc* | ——, Société des Auteurs et Compositeurs Dramatiques |
| *Pse* | ——, Société des Auteurs, Compositeurs et Editeurs de Musique |
| *Psg* | ——, Bibliothèque Ste Geneviève |
| *Pshp* | ——, Bibliothèque de la Société d'Histoire du Protestantisme |
| *Psi* | ——, Séminaire Israélite de France |
| *Pthibault* | ——, Geneviève Thibault, private collection |
| *PAU* | Pau, Bibliothèque Municipale |
| *PE* | Périgueux, Bibliothèque Municipale |
| *PO* | Poitiers, Bibliothèque Municipale |
| *POu* | ——, Faculté des Lettres de l'Université de Poitiers, Section de Musicologie |
| *Rc* | Rouen, Conservatoire |
| *R(m)* | ——, Bibliothèque Municipale |
| *RE* | Rennes, Bibliothèque Municipale |
| *RO* | Roanne, Bibliothèque Municipale |
| *RSc* | Rheims, Bibliothèque de la Cathédrale |
| *Sc* | Strasbourg, Conservatoire |
| *Sg(sc)* | ——, Grand Séminaire (Séminaire Catholique) |
| *Sim* | ——, Institut de Musicologie de l'Université |
| *Sm* | ——, Archives et Bibliothèque Municipale |
| *Sn* | ——, Bibliothèque Nationale et Universitaire |
| *Ssa* | ——, Société des Amis des Arts de Strasbourg |
| *Ssp* | ——, Séminaire Protestant |
| *SA* | Salins, Bibliothèque Municipale |
| *SAU* | Saumur, Bibliothèque Municipale |
| *SCL* | St-Claude, Bibliothèque Municipale |
| *SDE* | St-Denis, Bibliothèque Municipale |
| *SDI* | St-Dié, Bibliothèque Municipale |
| *SE* | Sens, Bibliothèque Municipale |
| *SEL* | Sélestat, Bibliothèque Municipale |
| *SERRANT* | Serrant, Château |
| *SO* | Solesmes, Abbaye St-Pierre |
| *SOI* | Soissons, Bibliothèque Municipale |
| *SQ* | St-Quentin, Bibliothèque Municipale |
| *T* | Troyes, Bibliothèque Municipale |
| *TH* | Thiers, Bibliothèque Municipale |
| *TLc* | Toulouse, Conservatoire |
| *TLd* | ——, Musée Dupuy |
| *TLm* | ——, Bibliothèque Municipale |
| *TO* | Tours, Bibliothèque Municipale |
| *TOgs* | ——, Grand Séminaire |
| *TOul* | ——, Bibliothèque Universitaire, Section Lettres |
| *TOur* | ——, Centre d'Etudes Supérieures de la Renaissance |
| *TOU* | Toulon, Ecole Nationale de Musique |
| *TOUm* | ——, Bibliothèque Municipale |
| *TOUs* | ——, Société des Amis du Vieux Toulon |
| *TU* | Tulle, Bibliothèque Municipale |
| *V* | Versailles, Bibliothèque Municipale |
| *VA* | Vannes, Bibliothèque Municipale |
| *VAL* | Valenciennes, Bibliothèque Municipale |
| *VE* | Vesoul, Bibliothèque Municipale |
| *VN* | Verdun, Bibliothèque Municipale |

| | |
|---|---|
| | ***GB*: GREAT BRITAIN** |
| *A* | Aberdeen, University Library, King's College |
| *AB* | Aberystwyth, National Library of Wales |
| *AM* | Ampleforth, Abbey and College Library, St Lawrence Abbey |
| *Bp* | Birmingham, Public Libraries |
| *Bu* | ——, University of Birmingham, Barber Institute of Fine Arts |
| *BA* | Bath, Municipal Library |
| *BEas* | Bedford, Bedfordshire Archaeological Society |
| *BEcr* | ——, Bedfordshire County Record Office |
| *BEp* | ——, Public Library Music Department |
| *BENcoke* | Bentley (Hants.), Gerald Coke, private collection |
| *BEV* | Beverley, East Yorkshire County Record Office |
| *BO* | Bournemouth, Central Library |
| *BRb* | Bristol, Baptist College Library |
| *BRp* | ——, Public Libraries, Central Library |
| *BRu* | ——, University of Bristol Library |
| *Ccc* | Cambridge, Corpus Christi College |
| *Cchc* | ——, Christ's College |
| *Cclc* | ——, Clare College |
| *Cfm* | ——, Fitzwilliam Museum |
| *Cgc* | ——, Gonville and Caius College |
| *Cjc* | ——, St John's College |
| *Cjec* | ——, Jesus College |
| *Ckc* | ——, Rowe Music Library, King's College |
| *Cmc* | ——, Magdalene College |
| *Cp* | ——, Peterhouse |
| *Cpc* | ——, Pembroke College |
| *Cpl* | ——, Pendlebury Library of Music |
| *Ctc* | ——, Trinity College |
| *Cu* | ——, University Library |
| *Cumc* | ——, University Music Club |
| *Cus* | ——, Cambridge Union Society |
| *CA* | Canterbury, Cathedral |
| *CAR* | Carlisle, Cathedral |
| *CDp* | Cardiff, Public Libraries, Central Library |
| *CDu* | ——, University College of South Wales and Monmouthshire |
| *CF* | Chelmsford, Essex County Record Office |
| *CH* | Chichester, Diocesan Record Office |
| *CHc* | ——, Cathedral |
| *DRc* | Durham, Cathedral |
| *DRu* | ——, University Library |
| *DU* | Dundee, Public Libraries |
| *En* | Edinburgh, National Library of Scotland |
| *Enc* | ——, New College Library |
| *Ep* | ——, Public Library, Central Public Library |
| *Er* | ——, Reid Music Library of the University of Edinburgh |
| *Es* | ——, Signet Library |
| *Eu* | ——, University Library |
| *EL* | Ely, Cathedral |
| *EXc* | Exeter, Cathedral |
| *EXcl* | ——, Central Library |
| *EXed* | ——, East Devon Area Record Office |
| *EXu* | ——, University Library |
| *Ge* | Glasgow, Euing Music Library |
| *Gm* | ——, Mitchell Library |
| *Gsma* | ——, Scottish Music Archive |
| *Gtc* | ——, Trinity College |
| *Gu* | ——, University Library |
| *GL* | Gloucester, Cathedral |
| *H* | Hereford, Cathedral |
| *HAdolmetsch* | Haslemere, Carl Dolmetsch, private collection |
| *Lam* | London, Royal Academy of Music |
| *Lbbc* | ——, British Broadcasting Corporation |
| *Lbc* | ——, British Council |
| *Lbm* | ——, British Library, Reference Division (formerly British Museum) (= *Lbl*) |
| *Lcm* | ——, Royal College of Music |
| *Lco* | ——, Royal College of Organists |
| *Lcs* | ——, Vaughan Williams Memorial Library (Cecil Sharp Library) |
| *Ldc* | ——, Dulwich College |
| *Lgc* | ——, Gresham College (Guildhall Library) |
| *Lkc* | ——, University of London, King's College |
| *Llp* | ——, Lambeth Palace |
| *Lmic* | ——, British Music Information Centre |
| *Lmp* | ——, Marylebone Public Library |
| *Lpro* | ——, Public Record Office |
| *Lsc* | ——, Sion College |
| *Lsm* | ——, Royal Society of Musicians of Great Britain |
| *Lsp* | ——, St Paul's Cathedral |
| *Ltc* | ——, Trinity College of Music |
| *Lu* | ——, University of London, Music Library |

| | |
|---|---|
| *Lva* | ——, Victoria and Albert Museum |
| *Lwa* | ——, Westminster Abbey |
| *Lwcm* | ——, Westminster Central Music Library |
| *LA* | Lancaster, District Central Library |
| *LAu* | ——, University Library |
| *LEbc* | Leeds, University of Leeds, Brotherton Collection |
| *LEc* | ——, Leeds Public Libraries, Music Department, Central Library |
| *LF* | Lichfield, Cathedral |
| *LI* | Lincoln, Cathedral |
| *LVp* | Liverpool, Public Libraries, Central Library |
| *LVu* | ——, University Music Department |
| *Mch* | Manchester, Chetham's Library |
| *Mcm* | ——, Royal Northern College of Music |
| *Mp* | ——, Central Public Library, Henry Watson Music Library |
| *Mr* | ——, John Rylands University Library, Deansgate Branch |
| *Mrothwell* | ——, Evelyn Rothwell, private collection |
| *Mu* | ——, John Rylands University Library |
| *NO* | Nottingham, University Library |
| *NW* | Norwich, Central Library |
| *NWr* | ——, Norfolk and Norwich Record Office |
| *Ob* | Oxford, Bodleian Library |
| *Obc* | ——, Brasenose College |
| *Och* | ——, Christ Church |
| *Ojc* | ——, St John's College |
| *Olc* | ——, Lincoln College |
| *Omc* | ——, Magdalen College |
| *Onc* | ——, New College |
| *Ooc* | ——, Oriel College |
| *Oqc* | ——, Queen's College |
| *Ouf* | ——, University, Faculty of Music |
| *Oumc* | ——, University Music Club and Union |
| *P* | Perth, Sandeman Music Library |
| *R* | Reading, University, Music Library |
| *RI* | Ripon, Cathedral |
| *RO* | Rochester, Cathedral |
| *SA* | St Andrews, University Library |
| *SB* | Salisbury, Cathedral |
| *SH* | Sherborne, Sherborne School Library |
| *SHR* | Shrewsbury, Shropshire County Record Office |
| *SOp* | Southampton, Public Library |
| *SR* | Studley Royal, Fountains Abbey MS 23 [in *LEc*] |
| *STb* | Stratford-on-Avon, Shakespeare's Birthplace Trust |
| *STm* | ——, Shakespeare Memorial Library |
| *T* | Tenbury, St Michael's College [Toulouse–Philidor collection now largely in *F-Pn*, *V*] |
| *W* | Wells, Cathedral |
| *WB* | Wimborne, Minster |
| *WC* | Winchester, Chapter Library |
| *WCc* | ——, Winchester College |
| *WI* | Wigan, Public Library |
| *WO* | Worcester, Cathedral |
| *WRch* | Windsor, St George's Chapter Library |
| *WRec* | ——, Eton College |
| *Y* | York, Minster |
| *Yi* | ——, Borthwick Institute of Historical Research |
| | |
| | ***GR*: GREECE** |
| *Ae* | Athens, Ethnike Biblioteke tes Hellados |
| *AT* | Mt Athos, Koutloumousi Monastery |
| *ATSch* | ——, Chilandari Monastery |
| *ATSdionision* | ——, Dionision Monastery |
| *ATSgreat lavra* | ——, Monastery of the Great Lavra |
| *ATSiviron* | ——, Iviron Monastery |
| *ATSserbian* | ——, Serbian Monastery |
| *ATSvatopedi* | ——, Vatopedi Monastery |
| *LA* | Lavra |
| *P* | Patmos |
| | |
| | ***H*: HUNGARY** |
| *Ba* | Budapest, Magyar Tudományos Akadémia Régi Könyvek Tára és Kézirattár |
| *Ba(mi)* | ——, Magyar Tudományos Akadémia Zenetudományi Intézet Könyvtára |
| *Bb* | ——, Bartók Béla Zeneművészeti Szakközépiskola Könyvtára |
| *Bev* | ——, Evangélikus Országos Könyvtár |
| *Bf* | ——, Belvárosi Főplébániatemplom Kottatára |
| *Bj* | ——, Józsefvárosi Evangélikus Egyházközseg Kottatára |
| *Bl* | ——, Liszt Ferenc Zeneművészeti Főiskola Könyvtára |
| *Bm* | ——, Budavári Nagyboldogasszony Templom Kottatára |

| | | | |
|---|---|---|---|
| *Bn* | ——, Országos Széchényi Könyvtára | *AT* | Atri, Museo della Basilica Cattedrale, Biblioteca Capitolare |
| *Bo* | ——, Állami Operaház | | |
| *Bp* | ——, Piarista Gimnázium Könyvtára | *Baf* | Bologna, Accademia Filarmonica |
| *Br* | ——, Ráday Gyűjtemény, Könyvtár és Levéltár | *Bam* | ——, Biblioteca della Casa di Risparmio (Biblioteca Ambrosini) |
| *Bs* | ——, Központi Szemináriumi Könyvtár | | |
| *Bst* | ——, Szent István Bazilika Kottatára | *Bas* | ——, Archivio di Stato |
| *Bu* | ——, Egyetemi Könyvtár | *Bc* | ——, Civico Museo Bibliografico Musicale |
| *BA* | Bártfa, church of St Aegidius [in *Bn*] | *Bca* | ——, Biblioteca Comunale dell'Arciginnasio |
| *CSg* | Csurgó, Csokonai Vitéz Mihály Gimnázium Könyvtára | *Bl* | ——, Conservatorio di Musica G. B. Martini |
| | | *Bof* | ——, Oratorio dei Filippini |
| *DR* | Debrecen, Tiszántúli Református Egyházkerület Nagykönyvtára | *Bpm* | ——, Facoltà di Magistero dell'Università degli Studi, Scuola di Perfezionamento in Musicologia |
| *DRm* | ——, Déri Múzeum | *Bsd* | ——, Convento di S Domenico |
| *DRu* | ——, Kossuth Lajos Tudományegyetem Könyvtára | *Bsf* | ——, Convento di S Francesco |
| *Ea* | Esztergom, Komárom Megyei Levéltár | *Bsm* | ——, Biblioteca Conventuale S Maria dei Servi |
| *Efko* | ——, Főszékesegyházi Kottatár | *Bsp* | ——, Basilica di S Petronio |
| *Efkö* | ——, Főszékesegyházi Könyvtár | *Bu* | ——, Biblioteca Universitaria |
| *Em* | ——, Keresztény Múzeum Könyvtára | *BAca* | Bari, Biblioteca Capitolare |
| *EG* | Eger, Főegyházmegyei Könyvtár | *BAcp* | ——, Conservatorio di Musica Nicola Piccinni |
| *EGb* | ——, Bazilika Kottatára | *BAgiovine* | ——, Alfredo Giovine, private collection |
| *Gc* | Győr, Püspöki Papnevelő Intézet Könyvtára | *BAn* | ——, Biblioteca Nazionale Sagarriga Visconti-Volpi |
| *Gk* | ——, Székesegyházi Kottatár | *BAR* | Barletta, Biblioteca Comunale Sabino Loffredo |
| *Gm* | ——, Xántus János Múzeum | *BDG* | Bassano del Grappa, Biblioteca Civica |
| *Gz* | ——, Zeneművészeti Szakközépiskola Könyvtára | *BE* | Belluno, Biblioteca del Seminario |
| *GGn* | Gyöngyös, Országos Széchényi Könyvtár, Bajza József Műemlékkönyvtár | *BEc* | ——, Biblioteca Civica |
| | | *BGc* | Bergamo, Biblioteca Civica Angelo Mai |
| *GYm* | Gyula, Múzeum | *BGi* | ——, Civico Istituto Musicale Gaetano Donizetti |
| *KE* | Keszthely, Országos Széchényi Könyvtár Helikon Könyvtára | *BI* | Bitonto, Biblioteca Comunale Vitale Giordano |
| | | *BRa* | Brescia, Ateneo di Scienze, Lettere ed Arti |
| *KI* | Kiskunhalas, Református Egyházközség Könyvtára | *BRd* | ——, Duomo |
| *KŐ* | Kőszeg, Plébániatemplom Kottatára | *BRi* | ——, Istituto Musicale A. Venturi |
| *KŐm* | ——, Jurisich Múzeum | *BRp* | ——, Archivio di S Maria della Pace |
| *MOp* | Mosonmagyaróvár, 1. sz Plébániatemplom Kottatára | *BRq* | ——, Biblioteca Civica Queriniana |
| | | *BRs* | ——, Seminario Vescovile |
| *NY* | Nyiregyháza, Református Városi Egyházközség Könyvtára | *BRsg* | ——, S Giovanni Evangelista (Cappella del Ss Sacramento) |
| *P* | Pécs, Székesegyházi Kottatár | *BRsmg* | ——, Madonna delle Grazie |
| *PA* | Pápa, Dunántúli Református Egyházkerület Könyvtára | *BRss* | ——, S Salvatore |
| | | *BRE* | Bressanone, Seminario Vescovile Vicentinum |
| *PH* | Pannonhalma, Szent Benedekrend Központi Főkönyvtára | *BRI* | Brindisi, Biblioteca Pubblica Arcivescovile Annibale de Leo |
| *Se* | Sopron, Evangélikus Egyházközség Könyvtára | *BV* | Benevento, Archivio Capitolare |
| *Sg* | ——, Berzsenyi Dániel Gimnázium Könyvtára | *BVa* | ——, Archivio di Stato |
| *Sl* | ——. Liszt Ferenc Múzeum | *BVam* | ——, Biblioteca e Archivio Storico Provinciale Antonio Mellusi |
| *Sp* | ——, Szentlélekről és Szent Mihályról Nevezett Városplébánia Kottatára | *BVT* | Borgo Val di Toro, Biblioteca Comunale Manara |
| *Sst* | ——, Storno Gyűjtemény | *BZa* | Bolzano, Archivio di Stato |
| *SA* | Sárospatak, Tiszáninneni Református Egyházkerület Nagykönyvtára | *BZc* | ——, Conservatorio di Musica Claudio Monteverdi |
| | | *BZd* | ——, Duomo |
| *SD* | Szekszárd, Balogh Ádám Megyei Múzeum | *BZf* | ——, Biblioteca dei Minori Francescani |
| *SFk* | Székesfehérvár, Püspöki Könyvtár | *BZtoggenburg* | ——, Count Toggenburg, private collection |
| *SFm* | ——, István Király Múzeum | *CAc* | Cagliari, Biblioteca Comunale |
| *SFs* | ——, Székesegyházi Kottatár | *CAcon* | ——, Conservatorio di Musica Giovanni Pierluigi da Palestrina |
| *SG* | Szeged, Somogyi Könyvtár | | |
| *SGm* | ——, Móra Ferenc Múzeum | *CAsm* | ——, Cattedrale S Maria |
| *SGu* | ——, Szegedi Orvostudományi Egyetem Könyvtára | *CAu* | ——, Biblioteca Universitaria |
| *SY* | Szombathely, Püspöki Könyvtár | *CAP* | Capua, Museo Provinciale Campano |
| *SYb* | ——, Berzsenyi Dániel Megyei Könyvtár | *CARcc* | Castell'Arquato, Chiesa Collegiata |
| *SYm* | ——, Smidt Múzeum | *CARc(p)* | ——, Archivio Capitolare (Archivio Parrochiale) |
| *T* | Tata, Plébániatemplom Kottatára | *CATa* | Catania, Archivio di Stato |
| *V* | Vác, Székesegyházi Kottatár | *CATc* | ——, Biblioteche Riunite Civica e Antonio Ursino Recupero |
| *VE* | Veszprém, Püspöki Könyvtár | | |
| *VEs* | ——, Székesegyházi Kottatár | *CATm* | ——, Museo Belliniano |
| | | *CATss* | ——, Società di Storia Patria per la Sicilia Orientale |

## *I*: ITALY

| | | | |
|---|---|---|---|
| | | *CC* | Città di Castello, Duomo |
| *Ac* | Assisi, Biblioteca Comunale | *CCc* | ——, Biblioteca Comunale |
| *Ad* | ——, Cattedrale S Rufino | *CDA* | Codogna, Biblioteca Civica Popolare L. Ricca |
| *Af* | ——, S Francesco | *CEb(sm)* | Cesena, Badia S Maria del Monte |
| *AC* | Acicatena, Biblioteca Comunale | *CEc* | ——, Biblioteca Comunale Malatestiana |
| *AG* | Agrigento, Biblioteca Lucchesiana | *CEN* | Cento, S Biagio |
| *AGI* | Agira, Biblioteca Comunale | *CF* | Cividale del Friuli, Archivio Capitolare |
| *AGN* | Agnone, Biblioteca Emidiana | *CFm* | ——, Museo Archeologico Nazionale |
| *AL* | Albenga, Cattedrale | *CHR* | Chieri, Facoltà Teologica dei Gesuiti |
| *ALEa* | Alessandria, Archivio di Stato | *CHT* | Chieta, Biblioteca Provinciale Angelo Camillo de Meis |
| *ALEi* | ——, Istituto Musicale Antonio Vivaldi | | |
| *AN* | Ancona, Biblioteca Comunale | *CHV* | Chiavenna, Biblioteca Capitolare Laurenziana |
| *ANcap* | ——, Biblioteca Capitolare | *CLE* | Corleone, Biblioteca Comunale Francesco Bentivegna |
| *ANd* | ——, Archivio della Cappella del Duomo | | |
| *AO* | Aosta, Seminario Maggiore | *CLO* | Corlono, Chiesa della Reggia Ducale |
| *AP* | Ascoli Picena, Biblioteca Comunale | *CMac* | Casale Monferrato, Archivio Capitolare |
| *AQ* | Aquileia, Archivio della Basilica | *CMbc* | ——, Biblioteca Civica |
| *ARc* | Arezzo, Biblioteca Consorziale | *CMs* | ——, Seminario Vescovile |
| *ARd* | ——, Duomo | *CMI* | Camogli, Biblioteca Comunale Nicolo Cueno |
| *ASc(d)* | Asti, Archivio Capitolare (Duomo) | *CMO* | Camerino, Biblioteca Valentiniana e Comunale |
| *ASi* | ——, Istituto Musicale Giuseppe Verdi | *COc* | Como, Biblioteca Comunale |
| *ASs* | ——, Seminario Vescovile | *COd* | ——, Duomo |

| | |
|---|---|
| *CORc* | Correggio, Biblioteca Comunale |
| *COS* | Cosenza, Biblioteca Civica |
| *CPa* | Carpi, Archivio Paolo Guaitoli della Commissione di Storia Patria de Carpi |
| *CPc* | ——, Biblioteca Comunale |
| *CR* | Cremona, Biblioteca Statale |
| *CRd* | ——, Duomo |
| *CRE* | Crema, Biblioteca Comunale |
| *CREi* | ——, Istituto Musicale L. Folcioni |
| *CT* | Cortona, Biblioteca Comunale e dell'Accademia Etrusca |
| *CZorizio* | Cazzago S Martino, Orizio private collection |
| *DO* | Domodossola, Biblioteca e Archivio dei Rosminiani di Monte Calvaro |
| *E* | Enna, Biblioteca Comunale |
| *Fa* | Florence, Ss Annunziata |
| *Faq* | ——, Pius XII Institute, Graduate School of Fine Arts, Aquinas Library |
| *Fas* | ——, Archivio di Stato |
| *Fc* | ——, Conservatorio di Musica Luigi Cherubini |
| *Fd* | ——, Duomo |
| *Ffabbri* | ——, M. Fabbri, private collection |
| *Fl* | ——, Biblioteca Medicea-Laurenziana |
| *Fm* | ——, Biblioteca Marucelliana |
| *Fn* | ——, Biblioteca Nazionale Centrale |
| *Folschki* | ——, Olschki private collection |
| *Fr* | ——, Biblioteca Riccardiana e Moreniana |
| *Fs* | ——, Seminario Arcivescovile Maggiore |
| *Fsa* | ——, Biblioteca Domenicana, Chiesa S Maria Novella |
| *Fsm* | ——, Convento S Marco |
| *Fu* | ——, Università degli Studi, Facoltà di Lettere e Filosofia |
| *FA* | Fabriano, Biblioteca Comunale |
| *FAd* | ——, Duomo |
| *FAN* | Fano, Biblioteca Comunale Federiciana |
| *FBR* | Fossombrone, Biblioteca Civica Passionei |
| *FEbonfigliuoli* | Ferrara, Bonfigliuoli private collection |
| *FEc* | ——, Biblioteca Comunale Ariostea |
| *FEd* | ——, Duomo |
| *FEmichelini* | ——, Bruto Michelini, private collection |
| *FELc* | Feltre, Biblioteca Comunale |
| *FELd* | ——, Duomo |
| *FELm* | ——, Museo Civico |
| *FEM* | Finale Emilia, Biblioteca Comunale |
| *FERc* | Fermo, Biblioteca Comunale |
| *FERd* | ——, Duomo |
| *FERl* | ——, Liceo Musicale Girolamo Frescobaldi |
| *FERmichelini* | ——, Bruno Michelini, private collection |
| *FOc* | Forlì, Biblioteca Comunale Aurelio Saffi |
| *FOd* | ——, Duomo |
| *FOG* | Foggia, Biblioteca Provinciale |
| *FOLc* | Foligno, Biblioteca Comunale |
| *FOLd* | ——, Duomo |
| *FOSc* | Fossano, Biblioteca Civica |
| *FZac(d)* | Faenza, Archivio Capitolare (Duomo) |
| *FZc* | ——, Biblioteca Comunale |
| *FZsavini* | ——, Ino Savini, private collection |
| *Gc* | Genoa, Biblioteca Civica Berio |
| *Gf* | ——, Biblioteca Franzoniana |
| *Ggrasso* | ——, Lorenzina Grasso, private collection |
| *Gi(l)* | ——, Conservatorio di Musica Nicolò Paganini |
| *Gim* | ——, Istituto Mazziniano |
| *Gsc* | ——, S Caterina |
| *Gsmb* | ——, S Maria della Castagna |
| *Gsmd* | ——, S Maria di Castello, Biblioteca dei Domenicani |
| *Gu* | ——, Biblioteca Universitaria |
| *GA* | Ganna, Badia Benedittina |
| *GE* | Gemona, Duomo |
| *GN* | Giulianova, Biblioteca Comunale Vincenzo Bindi |
| *GO* | Gorizia, Seminario Teologico Centrale |
| *GR* | Grottaferrata, Badia Greca |
| *GUA* | Guastalla, Biblioteca Municipale Maldotti |
| *GUBsp* | Gubbio, Biblioteca Comunale Sperelliana |
| *I* | Imola, Biblioteca Comunale |
| *IE* | Iesi, Archivio Comunale |
| *IV* | Ivrea, Biblioteca Capitolare |
| *La* | Lucca, Archivio di Stato |
| *Lc* | ——, Biblioteca Capitolare Feliniana |
| *Li* | ——, Istituto Musicale Luigi Boccherini |
| *Ls* | ——, Seminario Vescovile |
| *LA* | L'Aquila, Biblioteca Provinciale Salvatore Tommasi |
| *LE* | Lecce, Biblioteca Provinciale Nicola Bernardini |
| *LI* | Livorno, Biblioteca Comunale Labronica Francesco Domenico Guerrazzi |
| *LOc* | Lodi, Biblioteca Capitolare |
| *LOcl* | ——, Biblioteca Comunale Laudense |
| *LT* | Loreto, Archivio Storico della Cappella Lauretana |
| *LU* | Lugo, Biblioteca Comunale Fabrizio Trisi |
| *Ma* | Milan, Biblioteca Ambrosiana |
| *Malfieri* | ——, Trecani degli Alfieri, private collection |
| *Mb* | ——, Biblioteca Nazionale Braidense |
| *Mc* | ——, Conservatorio di Musica Giuseppe Verdi |
| *Mca* | ——, Archivio della Curia Arcivescovile |
| *Mcap(d)* | ——, Cappella Musicale del Duomo |
| *Mcom* | ——, Biblioteca Comunale |
| *Md* | ——, Archivio della Cappella Musicale del Duomo |
| *Mdonà* | ——, Mariangelo Donà, private collection |
| *Mr* | ——, Archivio Storico Ricordi (Casa Editrice) |
| *Ms* | ——, Biblioteca Teatrale Livia Simoni |
| *Msartori* | ——, Claudio Sartori, private collection |
| *Mt* | ——, Biblioteca Trivulziana |
| *Mvidusso* | ——, Carlo Vidusso, private collection |
| *MAa* | Mantua, Archivio di Stato |
| *MAad* | ——, Archivio Storico Diocesano |
| *MAav* | ——, Accademia Virgiliana di Scienze, Lettere ed Arti |
| *MAc* | ——, Biblioteca Comunale |
| *MAi* | ——, Istituto Musicale Lucio Campiani |
| *MAp* | ——, Duomo S Pietro |
| *MAs* | ——, Seminario Vescovile |
| *MAC* | Macerata, Biblioteca Comunale Mozzi-Borgetti |
| *MACa* | ——, Archivio di Stato |
| *MC* | Monte Cassino, Biblioteca dell'Abbazia |
| *ME* | Messina, Biblioteca Universitaria |
| *MEmeli* | ——, Alfonso Meli, private collection |
| *MEnicotra* | ——, Arturo Nicotra, private collection |
| *MEs* | ——, Biblioteca Painiana del Seminario Arcivescovile |
| *MFc* | Molfetta, Biblioteca Comunale Giovanni Panunzio |
| *MFsr* | ——, Pontificio Seminario Regionale Pio XI |
| *MFsv* | ——, Seminario Vescovile |
| *MOa* | Modena, Accademia Nazionale di Scienze, Lettere ed Arti |
| *MOd* | ——, Duomo |
| *MOdep* | ——, Deputazione di Storia Patria per le Antiche Province Modenesi |
| *MOe* | ——, Biblioteca Estense |
| *MOf* | ——, Archivio Ferni |
| *MOl* | ——, Liceo Musicale Orazio Vecchi |
| *MOs* | ——, Archivio di Stato |
| *MTventuri* | Montecatini-Terme, Antonio Venturi, private collection |
| *MV* | Montevergine, Biblioteca del Santuario |
| *MZ* | Monza, Insigne Basilica di S Giovanni Battista |
| *MZc* | ——, Biblioteca Civica |
| *Na* | Naples, Archivio di Stato |
| *Nc* | ——, Conservatorio di Musica S Pietro a Majella |
| *Nf* | ——, Biblioteca Oratoriana dei Filippini |
| *Nlp* | ——, Biblioteca Lucchesi-Palli [in *Nn*] |
| *Nn* | ——, Biblioteca Nazionale Vittorio Emanuele III |
| *Ns* | ——, Seminario Arcivescovile |
| *Nsn* | ——, Società Napoletana di Storia Patria |
| *Nu* | ——, Biblioteca Universitaria |
| *NO* | Novacello, Biblioteca dell'Abbazia |
| *NON* | Nonantola, Seminario Abbaziale |
| *NOVc* | Novara, Biblioteca Civica |
| *NOVd* | ——, Archivio Musicale Classico del Duomo |
| *NOVg* | ——, Archivio e Biblioteca di S Gaudenzio |
| *NOVi* | ——, Civico Istituto Musicale Brera |
| *NOVsg* | ——, Archivio Musicale di S Gaudenzio |
| *NT* | Noto, Biblioteca Comunale |
| *Oc* | Orvieto, Biblioteca Comunale Luigi Fumi |
| *Od* | ——, Biblioteca dell'Opera del Duomo |
| *OR* | Oristano, Seminario Arcivescovile |
| *ORT* | Ortona, Biblioteca Comunale |
| *OS* | Ostiglia, Biblioteca Musicale Greggiati |
| *OSI* | Osimo, Biblioteca Comunale |
| *Pbonelli* | Padua, E. Bonelli, private collection |
| *Pc* | ——, Biblioteca Capitolare |
| *Pca* | ——, Biblioteca Antoniana, Basilica del Santo |
| *Pci* | ——, Museo Civico, Biblioteca Civica e Archivio Comunale |
| *Pi(l)* | ——, Istituto Musicale Cesare Pollini |
| *Ppapafava* | ——, Novello Papafava dei Carreresi, private collection |
| *Ps* | ——, Seminario Vescovile |
| *Pu* | ——, Biblioteca Universitaria |
| *PAac* | Parma, Archivio Capitolare |
| *PAas* | ——, Archivio di Stato |
| *PAc* | ——, Conservatorio di Musica Arrigo Boito |
| *PAi* | ——, Istituto di Studi Verdiani |
| *PAsg* | ——, S Giovanni Evangelista |
| *PAst* | ——, Madonna della Steccata |

| | |
|---|---|
| *PAt* | ——, Teatro Regio |
| *PAL* | Palestrina, Biblioteca Comunale Fantoniana |
| *PAVc* | Pavia, S Maria del Carmine |
| *PAVi* | ——, Civico Istituto Musicale Franco Vittadini |
| *PAVs* | ——, Seminario Vescovile |
| *PAVsm* | ——, S Michele |
| *PAVsp* | ——, S Pietro in Ciel d'Oro |
| *PAVu* | ——, Biblioteca Universitaria |
| *PCa* | Piacenza, Collegio Alberoni |
| *PCc* | ——, Biblioteca Comunale Passerini Landi |
| *PCcon* | ——, Conservatorio di Musica G. Nicolini |
| *PCd* | ——, Duomo |
| *PCsa* | ——, Biblioteca e Archivio Capitolare di S Antonino |
| *PCsm* | ——, S Maria di Campagna |
| *PEc* | Perugia, Biblioteca Comunale Augusta |
| *PEd* | ——, Cattedrale |
| *PEl* | ——, Conservatorio di Musica Francesco Morlacchi |
| *PEsp* | ——, S Pietro |
| *PEA* | Pescia, Biblioteca Comunale Carlo Magnani |
| *PESc* | Pesaro, Conservatorio di Musica Gioacchino Rossini |
| *PEScerasa* | ——, Amadeo Cerasa, private collection [now *VTcerasa*] |
| *PESd* | ——, Duomo |
| *PESo* | ——, Biblioteca Oliveriana |
| *PIa* | Pisa, Archivio di Stato |
| *PIarc* | ——, Biblioteca Arcivescovile Cardinale Pietro Maffi |
| *PIc* | ——, Museo Nazionale di S Matteo |
| *PIca* | ——, Biblioteca Cateriniana |
| *PIcc* | ——, Archivio e Biblioteca Certosa di Calci |
| *PIp* | ——, Archivio Musicale dell'Opera della Primaziale |
| *PIr* | ——, Biblioteca Raffaelli |
| *PIraffaelli* | ——, Raffaelli private collection |
| *PIs* | ——, Fondo Simoneschi |
| *PIst* | ——, Chiesa dei Cavalieri di S Stefano |
| *PIN* | Pinerolo, Biblioteca Comunale Camillo Allinudi |
| *PLa* | Palermo, Archivio di Stato |
| *PLcom* | ——, Biblioteca Comunale |
| *PLcon* | ——, Conservatorio Vincenzo Bellini |
| *PLd* | ——, Duomo |
| *PLi* | ——, Istituto di Storia della Musica, Facoltà di Lettere, Università degli Studi |
| *PLm* | ——, Teatro Massimo |
| *PLn* | ——, Biblioteca Nazionale |
| *PLpagano* | ——, Roberto Pagano, private collection |
| *PLs* | ——, Baron Pietro Emanuele Sgadari di Lo Monaco, private collection [in Casa di Lavoro e Preghiera Padre Massini] |
| *PLsd* | ——, Archivio Storico Diocesano |
| *PO* | Potenza, Biblioteca Provinciale |
| *POa* | ——, Archivio di Stato |
| *POd* | ——, Duomo |
| *PR* | Prato, Duomo |
| *PS* | Pistoia, Cattedrale |
| *PSc* | ——, Biblioteca Comunale Forteguerriana |
| *Ra* | Rome, Biblioteca Angelica |
| *Rac* | ——, Accademia di Francia |
| *Raf* | ——, Accademia Filarmonica Romana |
| *Ras* | ——, Archivio di Stato |
| *Rc* | ——, Biblioteca Casanatense |
| *Rcg* | ——, Curia Generalizia dei Padri Gesuiti; Pontificio Collegio Germano-Ungarico |
| *Rchristoff* | ——, Boris Christoff, private collection |
| *Rcns* | ——, Archivio della Chiesa Nazionale Spagnuola |
| *Rco* | ——, Congregazione dell'Oratorio |
| *Rcsg* | ——, Oratorio di S Girolamo della Cantà |
| *Rdi* | ——, Discoteca di Stato |
| *Rdp* | ——, Archivio Doria-Pamphili, private collection |
| *Rf* | ——, Archivio dei Filippini |
| *Rgiazotto* | ——, Remo Giazotto, private collection |
| *Ria* | ——, Istituto Nazionale di Archeologia e Storia dell'Arte |
| *Rif* | ——, Istituto di Fisiologia dell'Università |
| *Rig* | ——, Istituto Storico Germanico |
| *Rims* | ——, Pontificio Istituto di Musica Sacra |
| *Rla* | ——, Biblioteca Lancisiana |
| *Rli* | ——, Accademia Nazionale dei Lincei e Corsiniana |
| *Rlib* | ——, Basilica Liberiana |
| *Rn* | ——, Biblioteca Nazionale Centrale Vittorio Emanuele III |
| *Rp* | ——, Biblioteca Pasqualini [in *Rsc*] |
| *Rps* | ——, Pio Sodalizio de Piceni |
| *Rsc* | ——, Conservatorio di Musica S Cecilia |
| *Rsg* | ——, S Giovanni in Laterano |
| *Rsgf* | ——, Arciconfraternita di S Giovanni dei Fiorentini |
| *Rslf* | ——, S Luigi de' Francesi |
| *Rsm* | ——, Archivio Capitolare di S Maria Maggiore [in *Rvat*] |
| *Rsmm* | ——, S Maria di Monserrato |
| *Rsmt* | ——, S Maria in Trastevere |
| *Rsp* | ——, Santo Spirito in Sassia |
| *Rss* | ——, S Sabina (Venerabile Convento) |
| *Rv* | ——, Biblioteca Vallicelliana |
| *Rvat* | ——, Biblioteca Apostolica Vaticana |
| *RA* | Ravenna, Duomo |
| *RAc* | ——, Biblioteca Comunale Classense |
| *RAs* | ——, Seminario Arcivescovile dei Ss Angeli Custodi |
| *REas* | Reggio Emilia, Archivio di Stato |
| *REc* | ——, Archivio e Biblioteca Capitolare del Duomo |
| *REd* | ——, Archivio Capitolare del Duomo |
| *REm* | ——, Biblioteca Municipale |
| *REsp* | ——, Archivio Capitolare di S Prospero |
| *RIM* | Rimini, Biblioteca Civica Gambalunga |
| *RO* | Rosate, S Stefano |
| *RVE* | Rovereto, Biblioteca Civica Girolamo Tartarotti |
| *RVI* | Rovigo, Accademia dei Concordi |
| *Sac* | Siena, Accademia Musicale Chigiana |
| *Sas* | ——, Archivio di Stato |
| *Sc* | ——, Biblioteca Comunale degli Intronati |
| *Sd* | ——, Archivio Musicale dell'Opera del Duomo |
| *Smo* | ——, Biblioteca annessa al Monumento Nazionale di Monte Oliveti Maggiore |
| *SA* | Savona, Biblioteca Civica Anton Giulio Barrili |
| *SAL* | Saluzzo, Archivio del Duomo |
| *SAS* | Sassari, Biblioteca Universitaria |
| *SDF* | San Daniele del Friuli, Biblioteca Civica Guarneriana |
| *SE* | Senigallia, Biblioteca Comunale Antonelliana |
| *SI* | Siracusa, Biblioteca Comunale |
| *SML* | Santa Margherita Ligure, Biblioteca Comunale Francesco Domenico Costa |
| *SO* | Sant'Oreste, Collegiata di S Lorenzo |
| *SON* | Sondrio, Biblioteca Civica Pio Rajna |
| *SPc* | Spoleto, Biblioteca Comunale |
| *SPd* | ——, Duomo |
| *SPE* | Spello, Collegiata S Maria Maggiore |
| *ST* | Stresa, Biblioteca Rosminiana |
| *SUsb* | Subiaco, Biblioteca S Benedetto |
| *SUss* | ——, Monumenta Nazionale dell'Abbazia di S Scolastica |
| *Ta* | Turin, Archivio di Stato |
| *Tb* | ——, Convento di Benevagienna |
| *Tci* | ——, Biblioteca Civica Musicale Andrea della Corte |
| *Tco* | ——, Conservatorio Statale di Musica Giuseppe Verdi |
| *Td* | ——, Duomo |
| *Tf* | ——, Accademia Filarmonica |
| *Ti* | ——, Istituto Salesiano Valsalice |
| *Tmc* | ——, Museo Civico |
| *Tn* | ——, Biblioteca Nazionale Universitaria |
| *Tr* | ——, Biblioteca Reale |
| *Trt* | ——, Archivio Musicale Radiotelevisione Italiana |
| *TE* | Terni, Istituto Musicale G. Briccialdi |
| *TEc* | ——, Biblioteca Comunale |
| *TI* | Termini-Imerese, Biblioteca Liciniana |
| *TLP* | Torre del Lago Puccini, Museo di Casa Puccini |
| *TOD* | Todi, Biblioteca Comunale Lorenzo Feoni |
| *TOL* | Tolentino, Biblioteca Comunale Filelfica |
| *TRa* | Trent, Archivio di Stato |
| *TRc* | ——, Biblioteca Comunale |
| *TRmd* | ——, Museo Diocesano |
| *TRmn* | ——, Museo Nazionale |
| *TRmr* | ——, Museo del Risorgimento |
| *TRE* | Tremezzo, Count Gian Ludovico Sola-Cabiati, private collection |
| *TRN* | Trani, Biblioteca Comunale G. Bovio |
| *TRP* | Trapani, Biblioteca Fardelliana |
| *TSci(com)* | Trieste, Biblioteca Civica |
| *TScm* | ——, Civici Musei di Storia ed Arte |
| *TScon* | ——, Conservatorio di Musica G. Tartini |
| *TSmt* | ——, Civico Museo Teatrale di Fondazione Carlo Schmidl |
| *TSsc* | ——, Fondazione Giovanni Scaramangà de Altomonte |
| *TSsg* | ——, Archivio della Cappella della Cattedrale S Giusto |
| *TVca(d)* | Treviso, Biblioteca Capitolare (Duomo) |
| *TVco* | ——, Biblioteca Comunale |
| *Us* | Urbino, Cappella del Sacramento (Duomo) |
| *Usf* | ——, S Francesco [in *Uu*] |
| *Uu* | ——, Biblioteca Universitaria |
| *UD* | Udine, Duomo |
| *UDa* | ——, Archivio di Stato |

| | |
|---|---|
| *UDc* | ——, Biblioteca Comunale Vincenzo Joppi |
| *UDi* | ——, Istituto Musicale Jacopo Tomadini |
| *URBc* | Urbania, Biblioteca Comunale |
| *URBcap* | ——, Biblioteca Capitolare (Duomo) |
| *Vas* | Venice, Archivio di Stato |
| *Vc* | ——, Conservatorio di Musica Benedetto Marcello |
| *Vcg* | ——, Biblioteca Casa di Goldoni |
| *Vlevi* | ——, Fondazione Ugo Levi |
| *Vmarcello* | ——, Andrighetti Marcello, private collection |
| *Vmc* | ——, Museo Civico Correr |
| *Vnm* | ——, Biblioteca Nazionale Marciana |
| *Vqs* | ——, Accademia Querini-Stampalia |
| *Vs* | ——, Seminario Patriarcale |
| *Vsf* | ——, Conventuale di S Francesco |
| *Vsm* | ——, Procuratoria di S Marco |
| *Vsmc* | ——, S Maria della Consolazione detta Della Fava |
| *Vt* | ——, Teatro la Fenice |
| *VAa* | Varese, Archivio Prepositurale di S Vittore |
| *VAc* | ——, Biblioteca Civica |
| *VCc* | Vercelli, Biblioteca Civica |
| *VCd* | ——, Duomo (Biblioteca Capitolare) |
| *VCs* | ——, Seminario Vescovile |
| *VD* | Viadana, Biblioteca Civica |
| *VEaf* | Verona, Società Accademia Filarmonica |
| *VEas* | ——, Archivio di Stato |
| *VEc* | ——, Biblioteca Civica |
| *VEcap* | ——, Biblioteca Capitolare (Cattedrale) |
| *VEs* | ——, Seminario Vescovile |
| *VEsg* | ——, S Giorgio in Braida |
| *VG* | Voghera, Collegiata di S Lorenzo |
| *VIb* | Vicenza, Biblioteca Civica Bertoliana |
| *VId* | ——, Duomo |
| *VImc* | ——, Museo Civico |
| *VImr* | ——, Museo del Risorgimento |
| *VIs* | ——, Seminario Vescovile |
| *VIGsa* | Vigévano, Duomo S Ambrogio |
| *VIGsi* | ——, S Ignazio |
| *VIM* | Vimercate, S Stefano |
| *VO* | Volterra, Biblioteca Guarnacci |
| *VTc* | Viterbo, Biblioteca Comunale degli Ardenti |
| *VTcarosi* | ——, Attilio Carosi, private collection |
| *VTcerasa* | ——, Amadeo Cerasa, private collection |
| *VTp* | ——, Biblioteca Pio XII, Pontificio Seminario Regionale |
| *VTs* | ——, Seminario Diocesano |
| *VTM* | Ventimiglia, Civica Biblioteca Aprosiana |

### IL: ISRAEL

| | |
|---|---|
| *J* | Jerusalem, Jewish National and University Library |
| *Jp* | ——, Patriarchal Library |
| *S* | Mt Sinai |
| *SS* | St Sabas, Monastery |

### IS: ICELAND

| | |
|---|---|
| *Rn* | Reykjavik, National Library |

### J: JAPAN

| | |
|---|---|
| *Tm* | Tokyo, Musashino Ongaku Daigaku |
| *Tma(Tmc)* | ——, Bibliotheca Musashino Academia Musicae |
| *Tn* | ——, Nanki Music Library, Ohki private collection |

### N: NORWAY

| | |
|---|---|
| *Bo* | Bergen, Offentlige Bibliotek |
| *Bu* | ——, Universitetsbiblioteket |
| *Oic* | Oslo, Norwegian Music Information Centre |
| *Oim* | ——, Institutt for Musikkvitenskap, Universitet |
| *Ok* | ——, Musik-Konservatoriet |
| *Onk* | ——, Norsk Komponistforening |
| *Or* | ——, Norsk Rikskringkastings |
| *Ou* | ——, Universitetsbiblioteket |
| *Oum* | ——, Universitetsbiblioteket, Norsk Musikksamling |
| *T* | Trondheim, Kongelige Norske Videnskabers Selskab |
| *Tmi* | ——, Musikkvitenskapelig Institutt |

### NL: THE NETHERLANDS

| | |
|---|---|
| *Ad* | Amsterdam, Stichting Donemus |
| *At* | ——, Toonkunst-Bibliotheek |
| *Au* | ——, Universiteitsbibliotheek |
| *Avnm* | ——, Bibliotheek der Vereniging voor Nederlandse Muziekgeschiedenis [in *At*] |
| *AN* | Amerongen, Archief van het Kasteel der Graven Bentinck, private collection |

| | |
|---|---|
| *Bl* | Bilthoven, Stichting Gaudeamus |
| *D* | Deventer, Stads- of Athenaeumbibliotheek |
| *DHa* | The Hague, Koninklijk Huisarchief |
| *DHgm* | ——, Gemeentemuseum |
| *DHk* | ——, Koninklijke Bibliotheek |
| *DHmw* | ——, Rijksmuseum |
| *G* | Groningen, Universiteitsbibliotheek |
| *Hs* | Haarlem, Stadsbibliotheek |
| *HIr* | Hilversum, Radio Nederland |
| *L* | Leiden, Gemeentearchief |
| *Lml* | ——, Museum Lakenhal |
| *Lt* | ——, Bibliotheca Thysiana [in *Lu*] |
| *Lu* | ——, Bibliotheek der Rijksuniversiteit |
| *Lw* | ——, Bibliothèque Wallonne |
| *LE* | Leeuwarden, Provinciale Bibliotheek van Friesland |
| *R* | Rotterdam, Gemeentebibliotheek |
| *'sH* | 's-Hertogenbosch, Archief van de Illustre Lieve Vrouwe Broederschap |
| *Uim* | Utrecht, Instituut voor Muziekwetenschap der Rijksuniversiteit |
| *Usg* | ——, St Gregorius Vereniging, Bibliotheek [in *Uim*] |
| *Uu* | ——, Bibliotheek der Rijksuniversiteit |

### NZ: NEW ZEALAND

| | |
|---|---|
| *Ap* | Auckland, Public Library |
| *Au* | ——, University Library |
| *Dp* | Dunedin, Public Library |
| *Wt* | Wellington, Alexander Turnbull Library |

### P: PORTUGAL

| | |
|---|---|
| *AN* | Angra do Heroismo, Biblioteca Pública e Arquivo Distrital |
| *AR* | Arouca, Museu Regional de Arte Sacra do Mosteiro de Arouca |
| *AV* | Aveiro, Museu de Aveiro, Mosteiro de Jesus |
| *BA* | Barreiro, Biblioteca Municipal |
| *BRp* | Braga, Biblioteca Pública e Arquivo Distrital |
| *BRs* | ——, Sé de Braga |
| *C* | Coimbra, Biblioteca Geral da Universidade |
| *Cm* | ——, Biblioteca Municipal |
| *Cmn* | ——, Museu Nacional de Machado de Castro |
| *Cs* | ——, Sé Nova |
| *Cug* | ——, Biblioteca Geral da Universidade |
| *Cul* | ——, Faculdade de Letras da Universidade |
| *CA* | Cascais, Museu-Biblioteca Condes de Castro Guimarães |
| *Em* | Elvas, Biblioteca Públia Hortênsia |
| *EVc* | Évora, Arquivo da Sé |
| *EVp* | ——, Biblioteca Pública e Arquivo Distrital |
| *F* | Figuera da Foz, Biblioteca Pública Municipal Pedro Fernandes Tomás |
| *G* | Guimarães, Arquivo Municipal Alfredo Pimenta |
| *La* | Lisbon, Palácio Nacional da Ajuda |
| *Laa* | ——, Academia de Amadores de Musica (Conservatorio Municipal) |
| *Lac* | ——, Academia das Cieńcias |
| *Lan* | ——, Arquivo Nacional de Torre do Tombo |
| *Lc* | ——, Conservatorio Nacional |
| *Lcg* | ——, Fundação Calouste Gulbenkian |
| *Lf* | ——, Fábrica da Sé Patriarcal |
| *Lif* | ——, Instituto de Franca |
| *Ln* | ——, Biblioteca Nacional |
| *Lr* | ——, Emissora Nacional de Radiodifusão |
| *Ls* | ——, Sociedade de Escritores e Compositores Portugueses |
| *Lt* | ——, Teatro Nacional de S Carlos |
| *LA* | Lamego, Biblioteca da Sé |
| *LE* | Leiria, Biblioteca Erudita e Arquivo Distrital (Biblioteca Pública) |
| *Mp* | Mafra, Palácio Nacional |
| *Pa* | Oporto, Ateneu Comercial |
| *Pc* | ——, Conservatorio de Musica |
| *Pcom* | ——, Biblioteca Comunale |
| *Peh* | ——, Museu de Etnografia e Historia |
| *Pf* | ——, Clube Fenianos Portuenses |
| *Pm* | ——, Biblioteca Pública Municipal |
| *PD* | Ponta Delgada, Biblioteca Pública e Arquivo Distrital |
| *PL* | Ponte de Lima, Arquivo da Misericórdia |
| *PO* | Portalegre, Arquivo da Sé |
| *Va* | Viseu, Arquivo Distrital |
| *Vm* | ——, Museu Grão Vasco |
| *Vs* | ——, Arquivo da Sé |
| *VV* | Vila Viçosa, Casa da Bragança, Museu-Biblioteca |

### *PL*: POLAND

| | |
|---|---|
| B | Bydgoszcz, Biblioteka Miejska |
| BA | Barczew, Archiwum Kościoła Parafialnego |
| Cb | Cieszyn, Biblioteka Śląska, Oddział Cieszyn |
| Cp | ——, Biblioteka Tschammera w Kościele Ewangelickim |
| CZp | Częstochowa, Klasztor OO. Paulinów na Jasnej Górze |
| GD | Gdańsk, Biblioteka Polskiej Akademii Nauk |
| GNd | Gniezno, Archiwum Archidiecezjalne |
| GR | Grodzisk, Klasztor OO. Cystersów |
| Kc | Kraków, Biblioteka Czartoryskich |
| Kcz | ——, Biblioteka Czapskich |
| Kd | ——, Klasztor OO. Dominikanów |
| Kj | ——, Biblioteka Jagiellońska |
| Kk | ——, Kapituła Metropolitalna |
| Kp | ——, Biblioteka Polskiej Akademii Nauk |
| Kpa | ——, Archiwum Państwowe |
| Kz | ——, Biblioteka Czartoryskich |
| KA | Katowice, Biblioteka Śląska |
| KO | Kórnik, Polska Akademia Nauk, Biblioteka Kórnicka |
| Lk | Lublin, Biblioteka Katolickiego Uniwersytetu |
| Lw | ——, Biblioteka Wojewódzka i Miejska im. H. Łopacińskiego |
| ŁA | Łancut, Muzeum |
| ŁO | Łowicz, Biblioteka Seminarium |
| MO | Mogiła, Klasztor OO. Cystersów |
| OB | Obra, Klasztor OO. Cystersów |
| Pa | Poznań, Biblioteka Archidiecezjalna |
| Pr | ——, Miejska Biblioteka Publiczna im. Edwarda Raczyńskiego |
| Pu. | ——, Biblioteka Uniwersytecka |
| PE | Pelplin, Biblioteka Seminarium Duchownego |
| PŁp | Płock, Biblioteka Towarzystwa Naukowego |
| R | Raków, Archiwum Kościelne |
| SA | Sandomierz, Seminarium Duchownego |
| SZ | Szalowa, Archiwum Parafialne |
| Tu | Toruń, Biblioteka Uniwersytecka |
| TA | Tarnów, Archiwum Archidiecezjalne |
| Wm | Warsaw, Biblioteka Muzeum Narodowego |
| Wn | ——, Biblioteka Narodowa |
| Wp | ——, Biblioteka Publiczna |
| Ws | ——, Biblioteka Synodalna Ewangelicka |
| Wtm | ——, Biblioteka Warszawskiego Towarzystwa Muzycznego |
| Wu | ——, Biblioteka Uniwersytecka |
| WL | Wilanów, Biblioteka, Oddział Muzeum Narodowego Warszawy |
| WRol | Wrocław, Biblioteka Ossolineum Leopoldiensis |
| WRu | ——, Biblioteka Uniwersytecka |

### *R*: ROMANIA

| | |
|---|---|
| Ab | Aiud, Biblioteca Documentară Bethlen |
| Ba | Bucharest, Biblioteca Academiei Republicii Socialiste România |
| Bc | ——, Biblioteca Centrală de Stat |
| BRm | Braşov, Biblioteca Municipală |
| Sb | Sibiu, Muzeul Brukenthal |
| TMt | Tîrgu Mureş, Biblioteca Documentară Teleki |

### *S*: SWEDEN

| | |
|---|---|
| A | Arvika, Folkliga Musikskolan |
| E | Enköping, Samrealskolans Arkiv |
| ES | Eskilstuna, Stadsbiblioteket |
| Gem | Göteborg, Etnografiska Museet |
| Ghl | ——, Hvitfeldtska Högre Allmänna Läroverket |
| Gu | ——, Universitetsbiblioteket (formerly Stadsbiblioteket) |
| GÄ | Gävle, Vasaskolans Bibliotek |
| Hfryklund | Hälsingborg, D. Daniel Fryklund, private collection [in *Skma*] |
| Hs | ——, Stadsbiblioteket |
| J | Jönköping, Per Brahegymnasiet |
| K | Kalmar, Stifts- och Gymnasiebiblioteket |
| KA | Karlstad, Stadsbiblioteket |
| KAT | Katrineholm, Stadsbiblioteket |
| KH | Karlshamn, Museums Biblioteket |
| L | Lund, Universitetsbiblioteket |
| Lbarnekow | ——, Barnekow private collection |
| LB | Leufsta Bruk, De Geer private collection |
| LI | Linköping, Stifts- och Landsbiblioteket |
| M | Malmö, Stadsbiblioteket |
| N | Norrköping, Stadsbiblioteket |
| Ö | Örebro, Karolinska Skolans Bibliotek |
| ÖS | Östersund, Jämtlands Läns Bibliotek |
| Sdt | Stockholm, Drottningholms Teatermuseum |

| | |
|---|---|
| Sic | ——, Stims Informationscentral för Svensk Musik |
| Sk | ——, Kungliga Biblioteket |
| Skma | ——, Kungliga Musikaliska Akademiens Bibliotek |
| Sm | ——, Musikmuseet |
| Smf | ——, Stiftelsen Musikkulturens Främjande |
| Sn | ——, Nordiska Museet |
| Ssr | ——, Sveriges Radio |
| St | ——, Kungliga Teaterns Bibliotek |
| SK | Skara, Stifts- och Landsbiblioteket |
| STd | Strängnäs, Domkyrkobiblioteket |
| STr | ——, Roggebiblioteket |
| Uifm | Uppsala, Institutionen för Musikforskning vid Uppsala Universitetet |
| Uu | ——, Universitetsbiblioteket |
| V | Västerås, Stadsbiblioteket |
| Vll | Visby, Landsarkivet |
| Vls | ——, Stadsbiblioteket |
| VX | Växjö, Landsbiblioteket |

### *SF*: FINLAND

| | |
|---|---|
| A | Turku [Åbo], Sibelius Museum Musikvetenskapliga Institutionen vid Åbo Akademi, Bibliotek & Arkiv |
| Aa | ——, Åbo Akademis, Bibliotek |
| Hko | Helsinki, Helsingin Kaupunginorkester |
| Hmt | ——, Musiikin Tiedotuskeskus |
| Hr | ——, Oy Yleisradio AB, Nuotisto |
| Hs | ——, Sibelius-Akatemian Kirjasto |
| Hy | ——, Helsingin Yliopiston Kirjasto |
| Hyf | ——, Helsingin Yliopiston Kirjasto, Department of Finnish Music |
| TA | Tampere, Tampereen Yliopiston Kansanperinteen Laitos |

### *US*: UNITED STATES OF AMERICA

| | |
|---|---|
| AA | Ann Arbor, University of Michigan Music Library |
| AB | Albany, New York State Library |
| AL | Allentown (Penn.), Muhlenberg College, John A. W. Haas Library |
| AM | Amherst (Mass.), Amherst College, Robert Frost Building |
| ATu | Atlanta (Georgia), Emory University Library |
| AU | Aurora (NY), Wells College Library |
| AUS | Austin, University of Texas |
| Ba | Boston, Athenaeum Library |
| Bbs | ——, Bostonian Society |
| Bc | ——, New England Conservatory of Music |
| Bco | ——, American Congregational Society, Congregational Library |
| Bfa | ——, Fine Arts Museum |
| Bge | ——, School of Fine Arts, General Education Library |
| Bh | ——, Harvard Musical Association |
| Bhh | ——, Handel and Haydn Society |
| Bhs | ——, Massachusetts Historical Society |
| Bl | ——, Grand Lodge of Masons in Massachusetts, A. F. and A. M. Library |
| Bm | ——, University, Mugar Memorial Library |
| Bp | ——, Public Library, Music Department |
| Bth | ——, University, School of Theology |
| BAep | Baltimore, Enoch Pratt Free Library, Fine Arts and Music Department |
| BAhs | ——, Maryland Historical Society |
| BApi | ——, City Library, Peabody Institute |
| BAu | ——, Johns Hopkins University Libraries |
| BAw | ——, Walters Art Gallery |
| BAT | Baton Rouge, Louisiana State University Library |
| BE | Berkeley, University of California, Music Library |
| BER | Berea (Ohio), Baldwin-Wallace College, Ritter Library of the Conservatory |
| BETm | Bethlehem (Penn.), Archives of the Moravian Church in Bethlehem |
| BETu | ——, Lehigh University, Lucy Packer Lindeman Memorial Library |
| BG | Bangor (Maine), Public Library |
| BK | Brunswick (Maine), Bowdoin College, Department of Music |
| BLl | Bloomington, Indiana University, Lilly Library |
| BLu | ——, Indiana University, School of Music Library |
| BO | Boulder, University of Colorado Music Library |
| BRc | Brooklyn, Brooklyn College Music Library |
| BRp | ——, Public Library |
| BU | Buffalo, Buffalo and Erie County Public Library |
| Charding | Chicago, W. N. H. Harding, private collection [in *GB-Ob*] |
| Chs | ——, Chicago Historical Society Library |
| Cn | ——, Newberry Library |

| | | | |
|---|---|---|---|
| Cu | ——, University Music Library | LU | Lincoln University (Penn.), Vail Memorial Library |
| CA | Cambridge, Harvard University Music Libraries | M | Milwaukee, Public Library, Art and Music Department |
| CAR | Carlisle (Penn.), Dickinson College | | |
| CDhs | Concord, New Hampshire Historical Society | MI | Middletown (Conn.), Wesleyan University, Olin Memorial Library |
| CDs | ——, New Hampshire State Library | | |
| CG | Coral Gables (Florida), University of Miami Music Library | MORduncan | Morgantown, Richard E. Duncan, private collection |
| CHua | Charlottesville, University of Virginia, Alderman Library | MSp | Minneapolis, Public Library |
| | | MSu | ——, University of Minnesota Music Library |
| CHum | ——, University of Virginia Music Library | MV | Mt Vernon (Virginia), Mt Vernon Ladies Association of the Union Collection |
| CHH | Chapel Hill, University of North Carolina Music Library | Nf | Northampton (Mass.), Forbes Library |
| CIhc | Cincinnati, Hebrew Union College | Nsc | ——, Smith College, Werner Josten Music Library |
| CIu | ——, University of Cincinnati College-Conservatory of Music | NAZ | Nazareth (Penn.), Moravian Historical Society |
| | | NBs | New Brunswick, Theological Seminary, Gardner A. Sage Library |
| CLm | Cleveland, Museum of Art, Cantatorium | | |
| CLp | ——, Public Library, Fine Arts Department | NBu | ——, Rutgers University Library |
| CLwr | ——, Western Reserve University, Freiberger Library and Music House Library | NEm | Newark (NJ), Newark Museum |
| | | NEp | ——, Public Library |
| COu | Columbus, Ohio State University Music Library | NH | New Haven, Yale University, School of Music Library |
| CR | Cedar Rapids, Iowa Masonic Library | | |
| Dp | Detroit, Public Library, Music and Performing Arts Department | NORts | New Orleans, Theological Seminary |
| | | NORtu | ——, Tulane University, Howard Tilton Memorial Library |
| DB | Dearborn (Mich.), Henry Ford Museum and Greenfield Village | | |
| | | NP | Newburyport (Mass.), Public Library |
| DE | Denver (Colorado), Public Library, Art and Music Division | NYcc | New York, City College Library, Music Library |
| | | NYcu | ——, Columbia University Music Library |
| DM | Durham (North Carolina), Duke University Libraries | NYfo | ——, Fordham University Library |
| | | NYfuld | ——, James J. Fuld, private collection |
| DN | Denton, North Texas State University Music Library | NYgo | ——, University, Gould Memorial Library |
| | | NYgr | ——, Grolier Club |
| DO | Dover (New Hampshire), Public Library | NYhc | ——, Hunter College Library |
| Eg | Evanston (Ill.), Garrett Theological Seminary | NYhs | ——, New York Historical Society |
| Eu | ——, Northwestern University, Music Library | NYhsa | ——, Hispanic Society of America |
| ECstarr | Eastchester (NY), Saul Starr, private collection | NYj | ——, Juilliard School of Music |
| EXd | Exeter (New Hampshire), Phillips Exeter Academy, Davis Library | NYlateiner | ——, Jacob Lateiner, private collection |
| | | NYma | ——, Mannes College of Music, Clara Damrosch Mannes Memorial Library |
| EXp | ——, Public Library | | |
| FW | Fort Worth, Southwest Baptist Theological Seminary | NYmc | ——, City Museum, Theatre and Music Department |
| | | NYmm | ——, Metropolitan Museum of Art, Thomas J. Watson Library |
| G | Gainesville, University of Florida Library, Rare Book Collection | | |
| | | NYp | ——, Public Library at Lincoln Center, Library and Museum of the Performing Arts |
| GA | Gambier (Ohio), Kenyon College Divinity School, Colburn Library | | |
| | | NYpm | ——, Pierpont Morgan Library |
| GB | Gettysburg, Lutheran Theological Seminary | NYq | ——, Queens College of the City University, Paul Klapper Library, Music Library |
| GR | Granville (Ohio), Denison University Library | | |
| GRE | Greenville (Delaware), Eleutherian Mills Historical Library | NYts | ——, Union Theological Seminary |
| | | OA | Oakland (Calif.), Public Library |
| Hhs | Hartford, Connecticut Historical Society Library | OAm | ——, Mills College, Margaret Prall Music Library |
| Hm | ——, Case Memorial Library, Hartford Seminary Foundation | OB | Oberlin, Oberlin College Conservatory of Music |
| | | Pc | Pittsburgh, Carnegie Library |
| Hp | ——, Public Library, Art and Music Department | Pfinney | ——, Theodore M. Finney, private collection [in Pu] |
| Hs | ——, Connecticut State Library | Ps | ——, Theological Seminary, Clifford E. Barbour Library |
| Hw | ——, Trinity College, Watkinson Library | | |
| HA | Hanover (New Hampshire), Dartmouth College, Baker Library | Pu | ——, University of Pittsburgh, Theodore Finney Music Library |
| | | PD | Portland, Maine Historical Society |
| HB | Harrisonburg (Virginia), Eastern Mennonite College, Menno Simons Historical Library and Archives | PER | Perryville (Missouri), St Mary's Seminary |
| | | PHbo | Philadelphia, St Charles Borromeo Theological Seminary |
| HG | Harrisburg, Pennsylvania State Library | | |
| HO | Hopkinton, New Hampshire Antiquarian Society | PHbs | ——, William Bacon Stevens Library |
| HU | Huntingdon (Penn.), Juniata College, L. A. Beechly Library | PHchs | ——, American Catholic Historical Society of Philadelphia |
| I | Ithaca (NY), Cornell University Music Library | PHci | ——, Curtis Institute of Music |
| IO | Iowa, University of Iowa Music Library | PHem | ——, Eric Mandell Collection of Jewish Music |
| K | Kent (Ohio), Kent State University Library | PHf | ——, Free Library of Philadelphia |
| Lu | Lawrence, University of Kansas Libraries | PHhs | ——, Historical Society of Pennsylvania |
| LAu | Los Angeles, University of California, Walter H. Rubsamen Music Library | PHkm | ——, Lutheran Theological Seminary |
| | | PHlc | ——, Library Company of Philadelphia |
| LAuc | ——, University of California, William Andrews Clark Memorial Library | PHma | ——, Musical Academy |
| | | PHphs | ——, Presbyterian Historical Society |
| LAusc | ——, University of Southern California School of Music | PHps | ——, American Philosophical Society |
| | | PHr | ——, Philip H. and A. S. W. Rosenbach Foundation |
| LB | Lewisburg (Penn.), Bucknell University, Ellen Clark Bertrand Library | PHtr | ——, Trinity Lutheran Church of Germantown |
| | | PHts | ——, Westminster Theological Seminary |
| LChs | Lancaster (Penn.), Lancaster County Historical Society | PHu | ——, University of Pennsylvania, Otto E. Albrecht Music Library |
| LCm | ——, Lancaster Mennonite Historical Library and Archives | Pllevy | ——, Pikesville (Maryland), Lester S. Levy, private collection |
| LCts | ——, Theological Seminary of the United Church of Christ | PL | Portland (Oregon), Library Association of Portland, Music Department |
| LEX | Lexington, University of Kentucky, Margaret I. King Library | PO | Poughkeepsie, Vassar College, George Sherman Dickinson Music Library |
| LOs | Louisville (Ky.), Southern Baptist Theological Seminary, James P. Boyce Centennial Library | PRs | Princeton, Theological Seminary |
| | | PRu | ——, University, Harvey S. Firestone Memorial Library |
| LOu | ——, University, School of Music Library | | |

| | |
|---|---|
| *PROhs* | Providence, Rhode Island Historical Society |
| *PROu* | ——, Brown University Libraries |
| *R* | ——, Rochester, University, Eastman School of Music, Sibley Music Library |
| *RI* | Richmond, Virginia State Library |
| *Sp* | Seattle, Public Library |
| *Su* | ——, University of Washington Music Library |
| *SA* | Salem (Mass.), Essex Institute, James Duncan Phillips Library |
| *SB* | Santa Barbara, University of California, Library |
| *SFp* | San Francisco, Public Library, Fine Arts Department, Music Division |
| *SFs* | ——, Sutro Library |
| *SFsc* | ——, San Francisco State College Library, Frank V. de Bellis Collection |
| *SHE* | Sherman (Texas), Austin College, Arthur Hopkins Library |
| *SLc* | St Louis, Concordia Seminary |
| *SLf* | ——, Fontbonne College |
| *SLkrohn* | ——, Ernst C. Krohn, private collection |
| *SLug* | ——, Washington University, Gaylord Music Library |
| *SLC* | Salt Lake City, University of Utah Library |
| *SM* | San Marino (Calif.), Henry E. Huntington Library and Art Gallery |
| *SPmoldenhauer* | Spokane (Washington), Hans Moldenhauer, private collection |
| *STu* | Stanford, University, Division of Humanities and Social Sciences, Music Library |
| *SW* | Swarthmore (Penn.), Swarthmore College Library |
| *SY* | Syracuse, University Music Library and George Arents Research Library |
| *Tm* | Toledo, Toledo Museum of Art |
| *TA* | Tallahassee, Florida State University, Robert Manning Strozier Library |
| *U* | Urbana, University of Illinois Music Library |
| *Ufraenkel* | ——, Fraenkel collection |
| *UP* | University Park, Pennsylvania State University Library |
| *Wc* | Washington, DC, Library of Congress, Music Division |
| *Wca* | ——, Cathedral |
| *Wcu* | ——, Catholic University of America Music Library |
| *Wgu* | ——, Georgetown University Libraries |
| *Ws* | ——, Folger Shakespeare Libraries |
| *Wsc* | ——, Scottish Rite Masons, Supreme Council |
| *Wsi* | ——, Smithsonian Institution, Music Library |
| *WA* | Watertown (Mass.), Perkins School for the Blind |
| *WC* | Waco (Texas), Baylor University Music Library |
| *WE* | Wellesley (Mass.), Wellesley College Library |
| *WELhartzler* | Wellman (Iowa), J. D. Hartzler, private collection |
| *WGc* | Williamsburg (Virginia), College of William and Mary |
| *WGw* | ——, Colonial Williamsburg Research Department, historical collection |
| *WI* | Williamstown (Mass.), Williams College, Chapin Library |
| *WM* | Waltham (Mass.), Brandeis University Library, Music Library, Goldfarb Library |
| *WOa* | Worcester (Mass.), American Antiquarian Society |
| *WS* | Winston-Salem (North Carolina), Moravian Music Foundation |

#### *USSR*: UNION OF SOVIET SOCIALIST REPUBLICS

| | |
|---|---|
| *J* | Jelgava, Muzei |
| *Kan* | Kiev, Tsentral'naya Naukova Biblioteka, Akademiya Nauk URSR |
| *Kk* | ——, Biblioteka Gosudarstvennoy Konservatoriy imeni P. I. Chaykovskovo |
| *KA* | Kaliningrad, Oblastnaya Biblioteka |
| *KAg* | ——, Gosudarstvennaya Biblioteka |
| *KAu* | ——, Universitetskaya Biblioteka |
| *KI* | Kishinev, Biblioteka Gosudarstvennoy Konservatoriy imeni G. Muzichesku |
| *Lan* | Leningrad, Biblioteka Akademii Nauk SSSR |
| *Lia* | ——, Gosudarstvennïy Tsentral'nïy Istoricheskïy Arkhiv |
| *Lil* | ——, Institut Russkoy Literaturï |
| *Lit* | ——, Leningradsky Gosudarstvennïy Institut Teatra, Muzïki i Kinematografii |
| *Lk* | ——, Biblioteka Leningradskoy Gosudarstvennoy Konservatoriy imeni N. A. Rimskovo-Korsakova |
| *Lph* | ——, Muzïkal'naya Biblioteka Leningradskoy Gosudarstvennoy Filarmonii |
| *Lsc* | ——, Gosudarstvennaya Ordena Trudovovo Krasnovo Znameni Publichnaya Biblioteka imeni M. E. Saltïkova-Shchedrina |
| *Lt* | ——, Leningradskiy Gosudarstvennïy Teatral'nïy Muzey |
| *Ltob* | ——, Tsentral'naya Muzïkal'naya Biblioteka Gosudarstvennovo Akademicheskovo Teatra Operï i Baleta imeni S. M. Kirova |
| *LV* | L'vov, Biblioteka Gosudarstvennoy Konservatoriy imeni N. V. Lysenko |
| *Mcl* | Moscow, Gosudarstvennïy Tsentral'nïy Literaturnïy Arkhiv |
| *Mcm* | ——, Gosudarstvennïy Tsentral'nïy Muzey Muzïkal'noy Kul'turï imeni M. I. Glinki |
| *Mk* | ——, Gosudarstvennaya Konservatoriya imeni P. I. Chaykovskovo, Nauchnaya Muzïkal'naya Biblioteka imeni S. I. Taneyeva |
| *Ml* | ——, Gosudarstvennaya Ordena Lenina Biblioteka SSSR imeni V. I. Lenina |
| *Mm* | ——, Gosudarstvennïyi Istoricheskïyi Muzei |
| *Mt* | ——, Gosudarstvennïyi Teatral'nïyi Muzei imeni A. Bakhrushina |
| *MI* | Minsk, Biblioteka Belorusskoy Gosudarstvennoy Konservatoriy |
| *O* | Odessa, Biblioteka Gosudarstvennoy Konservatoriy imeni A. V. Nezhdanovoy |
| *R* | Riga, Biblioteka Gosudarstvennoy Konservatoriy Latviyskoy imeni J. Vitola |
| *TAu* | Tartu, Universitetskaya Biblioteka |
| *TAL* | Tallinn, Biblioteka Gosudarstvennoy Konservatoriy |
| *TB* | Tbilisi, Biblioteka Gosudarstvennoy Konservatoriy imeni V. Saradzhisvili |
| *V* | Vilnius, Biblioteka Gosudarstvennoy Konservatoriy Litovskoy SSR |

#### *YU*: YUGOSLAVIA

| | |
|---|---|
| *Bn* | Belgrade, Narodna Biblioteka N. R. Srbije |
| *Dsd* | Dubrovnik, Knjižnica Samostana Dominikanaca |
| *Dsmb* | ——, Franjevački Samostan Mala Braća |
| *La* | Ljubljana, Knjižnica Akademije za Glasbo |
| *Lf* | ——, Knjižnica Franciškanškega Samostana |
| *Ls* | ——, Škofijski Arhiv in Biblioteka |
| *Lsa* | ——, Slovenska Akademija Znanosti in Umjetnosti |
| *Lsk* | ——, Arhiv Stolnega Kora |
| *Lu* | ——, Narodna in Univerzitetna Knjižnica |
| *MAk* | Maribor, Glazbeni Arhiv Katedrale |
| *MAs* | ——, Knjižnica Škofijskega Arhiv |
| *NM* | Novo Mesto, Knjižnica Franciškanškega Samostana |
| *NMc* | ——, Glazbeni Arhiv Katedrale |
| *O* | Ohrid, Narodno Museum |
| *Sk* | Split, Glazbeni Arhiv Katedrale |
| *Ssf* | ——, Knjižnica Samostana Sv Frane |
| *Za* | Zagreb, Jugoslavenska Akademija Znanosti i Umjetnosti |
| *Zda* | ——, Državni Arhiv |
| *Zha* | ——, Hrvatski Glazbeni Zavod |
| *Zk* | ——, Glazbeni Arhiv Katedrale |
| *Zs* | ——, Glazbeni Arhiv Bogoslovnog Sjemeništa |
| *Zu* | ——, Nacionalna i Sveučilišna Biblioteka |

*Volume Twelve*

# Meares–Mutis

# A Note on the Use of the Dictionary

This note is intended as a short guide to the basic procedures and organization of the dictionary. A fuller account will be found in the Introduction, vol.1, pp.xi–xx.

**Abbreviations** in general use in the dictionary are listed on pp.vii–x; bibliographical ones (periodicals, reference works, editions etc) are listed on pp.xi–xiii.

**Alphabetization** of headings is based on the principle that words are read continuously, ignoring spaces, hyphens, accents, bracketed matter etc, up to the first comma; the same principle applies thereafter. 'Mc' and 'M'' are listed as 'Mac', 'St' as 'Saint'.

**Bibliographies** are arranged chronologically (within section, where divided), in order of year of first publication, and alphabetically by author within years.

**Cross-references** are shown in small capitals, with a large capital at the beginning of the first word of the entry referred to. Thus 'The instrument is related to the BASS TUBA' would mean that the entry referred to is not '**Bass tuba**' but '**Tuba, bass**'.

**Work-lists** are normally arranged chronologically (within section, where divided). Italic symbols used in them (like *D-Dlb* or *GB-Lbm*) refer to the libraries holding sources, and are explained on pp. xiv–xxx; each national sigillum stands until contradicted.

# M

## CONTINUED

**Meares** [Mears, Meers]. Two English instrument makers, music printers and publishers, father and son, who were active in London in the late 17th and early 18th centuries. Richard Meares the elder is traceable in London by his instrument labels as early as 1669. He was a skilled maker of viols, lutes and other instruments, which were distinguished by their tasteful purfling and woodwork. By 1713 he had engaged in printing and publishing music. His son Richard Meares the younger, who made a few instruments but later turned his attention entirely to publishing, appears to have been

*Opening of Act 2 of Handel's 'Radamisto' published by Meares in 1720*

involved in the printing side of the business from 1717 or earlier, though the evidence is confused. In 1722 both the father's and the son's names are found on imprints, but Meares the elder seems to have died or retired about this time, and thereafter only the son's name appears. According to Hawkins, Meares the younger continued the business until his death about 1743. The Meares firm became one of Walsh's chief rivals, and each frequently pirated the other's publications. The firm's best publications and printed work rank among the finest of the period, and include Croft's *Musicus apparatus academicus* (1720), Handel's *Radamisto* (1720; see illustration) and *Suites de pieces* (1720), John Church's *An Introduction to Psalmody* (1723), and sonatas by Castrucci, Corelli, Geminiani and others. THOMAS CROSS often engraved the plates of the firm's publications.

The two Richard Meares should not be confused with a typographical music printer named H. Meere, who printed one or two works for Walsh in 1716–19, or with W. Mears, a bookseller active about 1713 to 1734, who published the text and music of several ballad operas and some editions of the Psalms with music.

### BIBLIOGRAPHY

*HawkinsH*
F. Kidson: *British Music Publishers, Printers and Engravers* (London, 1900/*R*1974)
C. Humphries and W. C. Smith: *Music Publishing in the British Isles* (London, 1954, 2/1970)
W. Henley: *Universal Dictionary of Violin and Bow Makers* (Brighton, 1959–60)

PETER WARD JONES

**Mears & Stainbank.** Firm of bell founders, since 1968 called the WHITECHAPEL BELL FOUNDRY.

**Measure (i).** An English dance term, current from about 1550 to about 1650, which denotes a choreographed sequence of dance steps in slow or moderate duple time, roughly corresponding to one strain of music. It probably derives from the French *mesure* (It. *misura*), a technical dance term which had a similar meaning in the literatures of the basse danse and bassadanza in the 15th century and the early 16th. The slow ceremonial character of this dance is described by Sir John Davies in his *Orchestra, or a Poem of Dancing* (1596):

> Yet all the feet whereon these Measures goe,
> Are onely Spondees, solemnpe, grave and slow.

The measures are distinguished from ordinary dance steps in that they are a varied series of choreographed units set to one or more dances, usually pavans and almans, and performed by a rehearsed group of dancers, for others as well as for their own gratification. Examples are the figured dances of the masquers in the English court masques, and the elaborate measured dance sequences performed by the barristers at the Inns of Court during this period. Because measures are so often set to pavans, the two are often considered synonymous, but this is not the case: neither pavans nor almans are measures unless choreographed for performance. The term 'measures' is hardly ever found as a musical title (it is not used in Adson's *Courtly Masquing Ayres*, 1621, or John Playford's volumes, 1655 and 1662), but it appears frequently in literary sources in lieu of 'pavan' or 'alman' when referring to those dances (Knowlton). Gombosi's attempt to identify the measures only with the passamezzo pavans cannot be accepted in the light of recent findings, but many pavans of the passamezzo variety were used for dancing the measures. This may account for the anglicized 'passing-measures' pavans and galliards of Byrd, Bull and Philips among others. The terms 'old measures' and 'new measures' are also encountered. The interpretation offered by Gombosi, that these refer to the *passamezzo antico* and *moderno* respectively, likewise cannot be credited, since the references are obviously to either old or newly choreographed dances (see Cunningham, appx.vii, where the first dance of the 'Oulde Measures' is entitled 'Quadrian Pavin', the English equivalent of *passamezzo moderno*). The term 'measures' is also used in literary sources to refer to dances and dancing in general.

BIBLIOGRAPHY

O. Gombosi: 'Some Musical Aspects of the English Court Masque', *JAMS*, i (1948), 3

J. P. Cunningham: *Dancing in the Inns of Court* (London, 1965)

J. E. Knowlton: *Some Dances of the Stuart Masque Identified and Analyzed* (diss., Indiana U., 1966)

MURRAY LEFKOWITZ

**Measure (ii).** A term in American usage equivalent to 'bar' in English usage when referring to a metrical unit rather than 'bar-line'; for 'bar-line' the American term is 'bar'. *See* BAR.

**Meccanica** (It.). ACTION.

**Mechanical Copyright Protection Society** (MCPS). *See* COPYRIGHT COLLECTING SOCIETIES, §II(iii).

**Mechanical instrument.** A musical instrument in which the sound is produced automatically or mechanically, usually without a performer, although some instruments involve a degree of human participation.

1. Types of musical movement.  2. History.

1. TYPES OF MUSICAL MOVEMENT. The most important part of a mechanical instrument or automatophone is the device for regulating the musical sounds, that is, a cylinder, punched cardboard strip, metal disc, or whatever. Of these, the cylinder is by far the oldest. Various sorts of cylinders are illustrated in figs.1, 2, 7, 9.

The cylinder functions as follows: as it revolves slowly, the pegs on its circumference, placed at right angles to its axis, perform certain mechanical actions which can be transmitted over a considerable distance by means of simple levers. When the levers are brought into contact with the valves of the pipes, the pipes sound for as long as the pegs touch the levers. The length of the notes depends on the width of the pegs; the wider the pegs, the longer the valves remain open and the longer the pipe

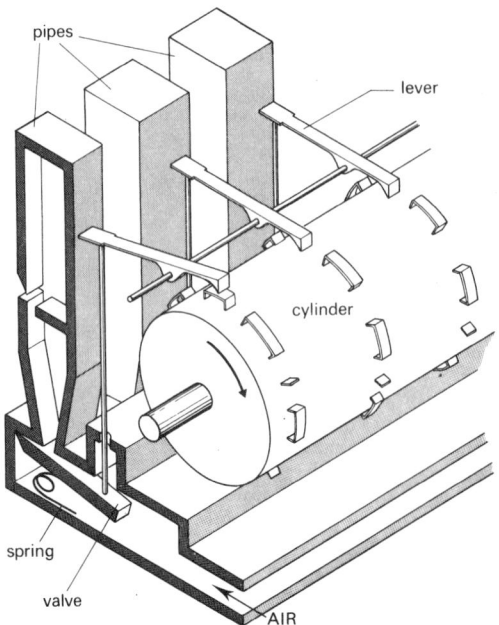

*1. Cylinder mechanism used in mechanical organs*

sounds; the narrower the pegs the shorter the notes. This sort of mechanism is illustrated in fig.1.

To sound pipes of varying pitch, the pegs are placed diagonally on the cylinder. Several pegs sound at once if the pegs are placed in a line along the cylinder axis. The placing of a number of pegs of varying width on the cylinder in order to produce a certain melody or harmony forms the chief principle of automatophonic

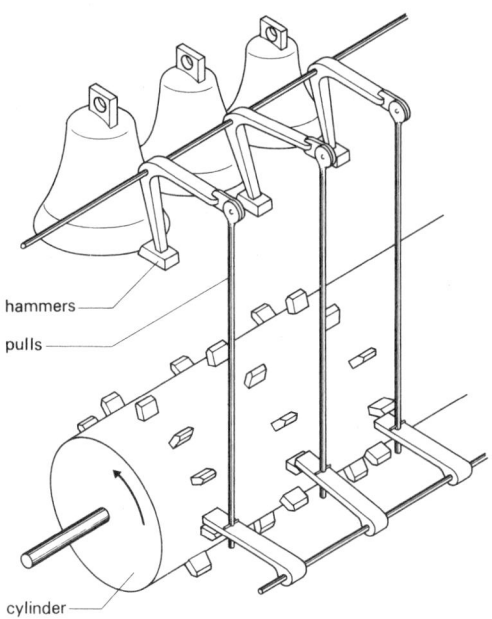

*2. Cylinder mechanism used in carillons and chiming clocks*

instruments. It then remains to ensure that the cylinder revolves regularly, to maintain an even tempo. The faithful reproduction of the music thus depends primarily on the correct placing of the pegs on the circumference of the cylinder, that is on the correct transferring of the melody to the cylinder circumference with the aid of the pegs: the correct placing of the pegs is the greatest problem in the construction of these instruments.

The cylinder is made of pieces of well-seasoned wood, usually oak, glued firmly together to prevent distortion. The shape of the pegs, at first of hard wood and later invariably of metal, has varied at different periods. From the 18th century wire bridges were used to produce long notes in place of the simple nails employed earlier. The cylinders used in carillons and chiming clocks (fig.2) were constructed to play only one melody and had a large number of holes into which the relevant pegs were fitted (for instance, the cylinder of the Delft carillon in Belgium had 7240 holes, that in Salzburg 7964, and that in Malmédy as many as 8979). The large number of holes permits the later repinning of the cylinder and thus the changing of the tune. In practice this is not done for carillons more frequently than once a month, since the repinning of the cylinder is difficult and requires much skill and patience. Apart from this, the carillon cylinder's diameter is fairly large, often over a metre, so it can play quite a long tune in one revolution (*see also* CARILLON).

The technique of transferring musical compositions to the cylinder was described in detail by M. D. J. Engramelle. He too considered the greatest problem in constructing automatophonic instruments to be the determination of the exact place where the pegs were to be hammered in (or pressed in with pliers), so as to open the pipe valves correctly and at the proper moment, and suggested various methods for the drawing up of what he called 'situation plans' which were to be traced on the cylinder to facilitate this work. The operation was then called 'annotating' the cylinder. Not only did Engramelle describe how this was done, but he invented a special set of symbols for the purpose and drew up plans for various compositions. The plans were then used to make so-called workshop charts in the form of a flattened-out cylinder, i.e. a rectangle, the width of the cylinder and the length of its circumference. Horizontal lines were to be drawn on this paper, corresponding to the bars of the composition, and vertical lines representing the notes (for illustration, *see* ENGRAMELLE, MARIE DOMINIQUE JOSEPH). The positions of the pegs were then marked in by means of dots and strokes. The finished plan was to be traced on to the cylinder and the pegs driven in. The pegs set out on the surface of the cylinder often made it possible to read an otherwise unknown composition. Experts have reconstructed many historically valuable pieces from cylinders now no longer capable of playing, or from cylinders of instruments no longer available.

The disadvantage of cylinders, in spite of the improvements made on them, was that they could record at the most eight compositions, and only a few instruments with interchangeable cylinders were produced.

The French instrument maker Alexandre François Debain invented an ingenious mechanism described in 1846 in his treatise *Antiphonel-harmonium suppléant de l'organiste*. The antiphonel was to replace the organist, and not just any organist, but – to quote the inventor – 'a faultless player who never plays a false note or a false chord'. According to many experts, including Auber, Berlioz, Halévy and Thomas, the antiphonel was remarkable for the ease with which it could be used with any keyboard instrument, for the precision of its performance and for the simplicity of its mechanism. It was an oblong box with a metal lid through which keys resembling those on a keyboard passed. These keys, however, acted in the opposite direction and were operated by jacks with tempered steel hooks at the end; the hooks passed through a comb about 3 cm wide. The five octaves of the keyboard were thus squeezed into the relatively narrow space occupied by the comb.

The composition was not transferred to the cylinder, but to a wooden desk called the planchette, with special iron pegs which replaced the player's fingers. As the planchette moved across the lid of the box, by means of a lever or crank, the iron pegs engaged with the jacks, which acted on the keyboard of the instrument. When used with the harmonium, this mechanism produced dynamic shades by means of different peg heights.

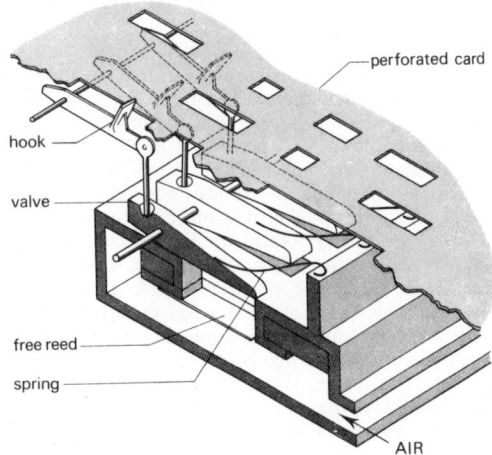

*3. Mechanism with free reeds activated by a perforated card*

The ideal of Engramelle, who envisaged automatophonic instruments that would permit faithful reproduction of the music, was brought closer to realization by the invention of Martin Corteuile, who in 1852 took out a patent for a perforated cardboard strip, on which the holes engaged with the jacks of the antiphonel; the holes represented the musical score.

Then came the perforated card invented by the Nantes instrument maker J. A. Testé (fig.3). In this there were levers to control the valves which vibrated the free metal reeds. At the other end of the levers jacks were placed in a row as long as the box and protruding slightly above the lid. In this position the valves were open, and when the pedals were pressed all the reeds vibrated simultaneously. Above the jacks was a round metal ledge whose edge almost touched the lid of the instrument. This piece of metal contained the same number of grooves as jacks, and the latter rose through the holes to open the valves. If a cardboard strip was passed between the metal ledge and the lid, all the jacks went down, closed the valves, and rose only when a hole in the cardboard allowed them to do so. Testé called his instrument the cartonium. When played, the cardboard

*4. Manopan with perforated card after Testé's model (Národní Muzeum, Prague)*

strip on which the holes were arranged according to the music moved regularly across the jacks. Smooth movement was ensured by means of rubber rollers, turned by a crank, which kept the cardboard in position.

Testé's cartonium system was used in practically all the automatophonic instruments with free metal reeds: intonas, aristonas, manopans (fig.4) etc. The metal jacks which engaged with the valves of the individual reeds were pressed down by a perforated disc or strip. The mechanism was so simple and so easy to handle that this type of automatophonic instrument was still in use after pneumatic devices were used in other instruments.

A way to use a perforated tin disc with music boxes was devised in the 1880s (fig.5). Paul Lochmann's mechanism made use of little wheels with hooks, arranged in the shape of a star, which engaged with the teeth of a steel comb. The hooks plucked the teeth of the comb when they came into contact as the disc revolved. Most instruments had two combs, some had as many as four, one above the other. This 'tandem' arrangement required two sets of wheels to pluck the combs. Paul

*5. Double-disc musical box (the 'Symphonium'), German, late 19th century (private collection)*

Riessner and Gustav Brachhausen further improved this system by having only one set of wheels pluck the two combs. Since they placed the combs tooth against tooth, one of them had to be plucked in a downward direction, which required special mufflers for the bottom comb.

New patents were continually being granted for the construction of the disc mechanism. In 1882 Miguel Boom invented a universal disc, on which the projections could be changed freely, thus varying the music. Ellis Parr constructed an apparatus for reperforating used discs. Ferdinand Schaub perfected the disc projections. Only one thing was now lacking: a means of changing the discs easily, preferably without human assistance. This was finally achieved by the Regina Company of Rahway, NJ, which made polyphons with an automatic device for changing the discs.

The equally ingenious pneumatic system was invented about the same time. It represented an important turning-point in the efforts to achieve a more faithful reproduction of music. In 1842 a Lyons mechanic named Charles Félix Seytre patented an instrument called the autophon which – as stated in the patent – played 'all kinds of melodies with the aid of perforated cards, similar to the jacquart, with square or oblong holes according to the length of the notes to be played'. The holes were linked with pipes which conducted compressed air from the pedal bellows to the small cylinders attached to each of the keys of the instrument. In each of the cylinders there was a small air-driven piston which moved a jack, which in turn made the hammer strike the string from below. A similar instrument, worked by sucked-in air, was described by the French organ maker Napoléon Fourneaux. A pneumatic piano was made in New York by Merritt Gally, who patented his invention in 1881. Patents for pneumatic pianos were granted to Bishop & Down four years later.

The last improvement in this field was the invention of the pianola by the American engineer E. S. Votey; it was patented in 1897. Seven years later the firm of M. Welte & Söhne was founded in Freiburg for the manufacture of fonolas. These were in fact the same kind of instrument under two names. The name 'pianola' was used as a trademark by the Anglo-American Aeolian Company and later came to denote any automatophonic piano with a pneumatic system (*see* PLAYER PIANO).

Perforated strips for the pianola were made in two ways. In the metronome method every bar of the composition was of the same duration, as if timed by a metronome. In practice this was achieved by means of a prepared scheme showing the distance between the holes on the perforated ledge and the same distance for the note lengths. Each note of the composition was marked at the appropriate place; the duration was indicated by a stroke at the point where the perforation was to be made. When the whole piece had been recorded in this fashion, perforation was carried out mechanically at the places indicated. The finished strip was tested on the pianola and any mistakes corrected. This produced a master-roll from which cardboard matrices could be made, thus permitting the simultaneous perforation of a large number of rolls. The second, and better, method was entirely mechanical. The perforated strips were produced by means of an electrical recording made during the musician's performance. As he played the piano, every key he touched switched on the current, which activated the requisite electromagnet; this, in turn, activated a mechanism recording the strength of each stroke. Slight errors in the pianist's performance could be corrected, and the recording thus obtained was used to produce perforated strips for reproduction.

As there were perforated strips for the pianola, so perforated cards were made for other automatophonic instruments, in particular for orchestrions. The manufacture of these cards called for considerable skill and precision. The 'orchestrator' (the person who transferred the music to the strip) had first to study the composition in question, particularly if it happened to be an orchestral piece. The prepared pattern was printed on strips of cardboard glued together in the shape of a book. After the card had been perforated it was tested on the instrument for which it was intended, so that any errors made during the transfer of the composition or during the perforation could be corrected. This mastercard served mass reproduction in the same way as the master-roll did for the pianola. Additional perforated cards were frequently used with organs and harmoniums to control the registers.

The slightest error on the cylinder or in the perforated strip resulted in faulty reproduction, easily discernible by the ear, so great care was required in constructing the instruments; every detail had to be calculated with an accuracy of at least a fiftieth of a second. This meant that some of the pegs on the cylinder or the perforations in the strips had to be placed with a precision of up to half a millimetre. Atmospheric conditions or wear could lead to changes in the mechanism which were slight, but sufficient to cause audible faults in the reproduction, especially in the rhythm. There was no way to correct these changes, and when heard repeatedly they became offensive. However, as long as such variations remained within certain limits, they combined with the agogic variations due to the irregular movement of the cylinder or the perforated strip to create a substantial part of the specific charm of mechanical musical reproduction.

2. HISTORY. The endeavour to create sound by mechanical means, without the assistance and intervention of man, can be traced to the remote past. At first, these efforts had practical reasons (signalling) as well as being for cult purposes (to create voices as of the dead). On the Indonesian paddy fields water currents in the irrigation channels still set in motion tuned bamboo tubes, which strike rhythmically against stones and produce repeating musical phrases.

The effects of air currents on string instruments are known from ancient times. An Indian legend mentions a musical instrument called the vīṇā, whose strings sounded in the wind; and in ancient China there existed several kinds of AEOLIAN HARP. The Malay people thrust into the earth a long bamboo tube with holes into which air is driven; the pitch of the resulting notes changes according to the velocity and direction of the air current.

However, all these sound-producing devices lack the most important part of automatophons – the mechanical 'brain'. This was invented only when technology and music were combined. The first attempts in this field were made by the ancient peoples of Asia and Egypt; their automatic statues inspired Hero of Alexandria to devise a mechanically struck instrument (see HYDRAULIS). The Alexandrian tradition was kept alive in Byzantium after the fall of the Roman Empire, and science

and technology later reached the Arabs and Persians. From 813 to 833 three brothers, Muhammad, Ahamad and Hasan, called Banū Mūsā, then outstanding organizers of Arab science in Baghdad, constructed the first historically documented automatophon, whose 'brain' was a revolving cylinder with pegs.

In Europe, Leo the Philosopher devised automata with artificial trees and singing birds in the first half of the 9th century for Theophilus Ikonomachus, Emperor of Byzantium. Konrad von Würzburg (c1250) mentioned an artificial tree with birds perched on it, moving their wings and singing. Mechanical instruments – a spinet and two drums with a cylinder – were also constructed by Leonardo da Vinci in the late 15th century.

The creation and performance of music by mechanical means reached a sophisticated stage of development when watchmaking replaced sand-glasses with complicated and artistically executed clockwork mechanism. Clock towers were often equipped with carillons which played a melody by means of a cylinder with pins (see fig.2 above). Fétis said that the first manufacturer of carillons was a 15th-century Dutchman named Koecke. In the course of the 16th and 17th centuries carillons were made in Holland and Belgium, the greatest being in Amsterdam, Breda, Goes, Middelburg and Delft. They were played by the so-called 'carilloneurs' by means of a keyboard.

In the late Renaissance, artistic cabinets also contained organ automatophons, or mechanical organs. The most famous one, the so-called Pomeranian art cabinet, had a mechanical organ made by A. Langenbucher and M. Genser; it was destroyed in World War II. Mechanical spinets were made, especially in Augsburg (Samuel Bidermann, Eisenburger), but the Nuremberg artists Werner, Bullman, Hell, Farfler, Hautsch and others, who built various mechanical instruments, are also mentioned. With the end of the Renaissance came the end of interest in art cabinets, and automatophons found less elegant homes. They became larger, and interchangeable cylinders allowed a larger repertory. Smaller organs were incorporated in clocks (flute-playing clocks), while larger mechanisms were placed in secretaires, mirrors and other furniture.

From the second half of the 18th century and during the whole Biedermeier period, flute-playing clocks with beautifully executed cases were extremely popular. A number of composers, including Mozart, Haydn and C. P. E. Bach, wrote music for these instruments. In the second half of the 18th century their centres of manufacture included London (C. Higginson, J. Cox, E. Norton, W. Carpenter, Marriott) and Berlin (C. Möllinger, C. E. Kleemeyer, K. Ehrbar, J. Elfroth), and later Vienna (Gurck, J. A. Hoyer, Maelzel brothers) and Prague (J. H. D. Sander, P. Heinrich, V. Vencl, B. Biswanger). Mechanical clocks were sometimes combined with stringed automatophons (harp clocks) or carillons. Cheap clocks with glass carillons were manufactured by farmers in the Black Forest.

The first barrel organs appeared in the 18th century. The smallest, the so-called 'bird organs', were intended to teach birds to sing. The mechanism was simple: a horizontal wooden barrel fitted with pegs was turned by a crank handle in a wooden case; the pegs engaged with valves on several small pipes, and the air chamber was supplied by bellows worked by the same crank handle (see BIRD INSTRUMENTS). Larger barrel organs were used by beggars, but also found their way to some smaller and poorer churches, where they replaced the organ. The English firm of Flight & Robson manufactured a large number of barrel organs for the church; they played psalms, preludes and hymns, as well as church songs. There are still some in churches in Shelland (Suffolk) and Barnston (Essex). Gavioli, an Italian who lived in Paris at the beginning of the 19th century, was an outstanding maker of barrel organs. Factory manufacture of the instruments was later concentrated in France, Germany and the Austro-Hungarian monarchy. In larger barrel organs the case was divided into two parts: in the upper part were the barrel, the tracture and the bellows, and in the lower part three registers of pipes were placed transversely. The bass pipes were covered, while the other registers, always an octave higher, had double labial pipes. The accommodation of so many pipes in so small a space called for much ingenuity and led to the development at the beginning of the 1860s of barrel organs with upright pipes, using labial as well as reed pipes. This type of

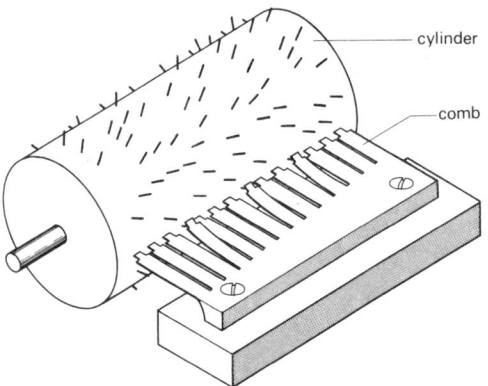

7. *Metal comb and cylinder of a musical box*

barrel organ was known as the 'Wiener Werkl', as Vienna was then the only place manufacturing them.

The construction of barrel organs was considerably influenced by the introduction of free reeds and at the close of the 19th century barrel organs with pipes gave place to cheaper and smaller ones with free reeds. The reeds were often sounded by an interchangeable piece of perforated cardboard (fig.3), or by a folded strip of cardboard instead of by the barrel. This was the basic principle of many automatophons manufactured under different names, such as intona, ariston, manopan, mignon etc. Three fundamental types of automatophons with free reeds were manufactured: the first was based on the barrel or cylinder (barrel organs), the second on the perforated cardboard, and the third on the pneumatic system. All three types survived until the 1920s.

Attempts to imitate the sound of the orchestra resulted in the invention of orchestrions, or mechanical organs (see fig.6), which were often combined with percussion instruments, such as drums, cymbals or triangles, or with a piano. Cherubini and Beethoven composed for J. N. Maelzel's panharmonicon. The most ingenious and interesting orchestrion was constructed in 1821 by the Dutchman Dietrich Nicolaus Winkel, who named his new instrument the 'componium' (now in the Museum of Musical Instruments in Brussels). The componium consists of an orchestrion proper and a special mechanism which plays variations on a given composition of 80 bars. The bars are interchanged by a lengthwise gearing of two cylinders, thus creating endless variations.

Remarkable for the size and volume of sound are the apollonicon, built in 1817 by the English barrel organ maker Flight, and the orchestrions of the Kaufmann family, whose automatophons (symphonicon, salpingion, aulodion, 'trumpeter') were displayed for a number of years in their own 'acoustic cabinet' in Dresden. Very good orchestrions were manufactured by J. H. Heller in Berne, J. Deutschmann in Vienna, Mamert Hock in Saarlouis, James and John Blessing in the Black Forest, and by the Riemer brothers in Chrastava in Bohemia. Most of these musical instruments were used in amusement enterprises, in circuses and with merry-go-rounds (*see* FAIRGROUND ORGAN). It was impossible to separate the individual strands of the composition, and the mechanical playing of the violin part did not help to create the impression of an orchestra. Strength of tone was the most important aspect of orchestrions and much less attention was paid to the quality of the music. Because of this orchestrions never rose above the level of the barrel organ.

Good tone, small size and reasonable price contributed to the development and wide distribution of musical boxes in the 19th century. These instruments are based on a metal comb with teeth of different lengths. The first musical boxes were called *carillons à musique* and were sounded by a disc with steel pins. Their manufacture was particularly concentrated in Switzerland, where miniature mechanisms with 15 to 25 teeth were built into various luxury articles, such as watches, seals, walking-sticks, small boxes, candy boxes, jewel caskets and tobacco boxes. At the close of the 18th century David Lecoultre replaced the disc by a pinned cylinder parallel to the comb (fig.7). The teeth of the comb were no longer mounted separately, but in groups of three, four or five, and each group set in a metal plate. In about 1820 the teeth were cut from sheet steel, and several years later dampers were added.

Other improvements of musical boxes included the introduction of resonators, or small lead weights, which were fixed to the underside of the steel bass teeth. The most important of the Geneva manufacturers were the Nicole brothers, who constructed in about 1840 the first musical box of the fortepiano type, containing two combs of different lengths. Increasing interest and demand on the foreign markets were satisfied by newly-established factories. One of the most important manufacturers was E. Paillard, who founded his factory in St Croix in 1875. The interchangeability of standardized cylinders was a major innovation. But despite these improvements musical boxes could not play more compositions than could cylinder-based mechanisms, and instruments with interchangeable cylinders were extremely expensive. This problem was solved by the German Paul Lochmann, who used a steel disc with protrusions in place of the cylinder (see fig.5 above). In combination with a special mechanism the disc plucked the teeth of the comb the moment the protrusions touched them. These so-called polyphons were characterized by clear, strong tone, and at the beginning

6. *Mechanical organ by Gavioli & Cie, Waldkirch and Paris*

8. *Musical box mounted in a photograph album, late 19th century (private collection)*

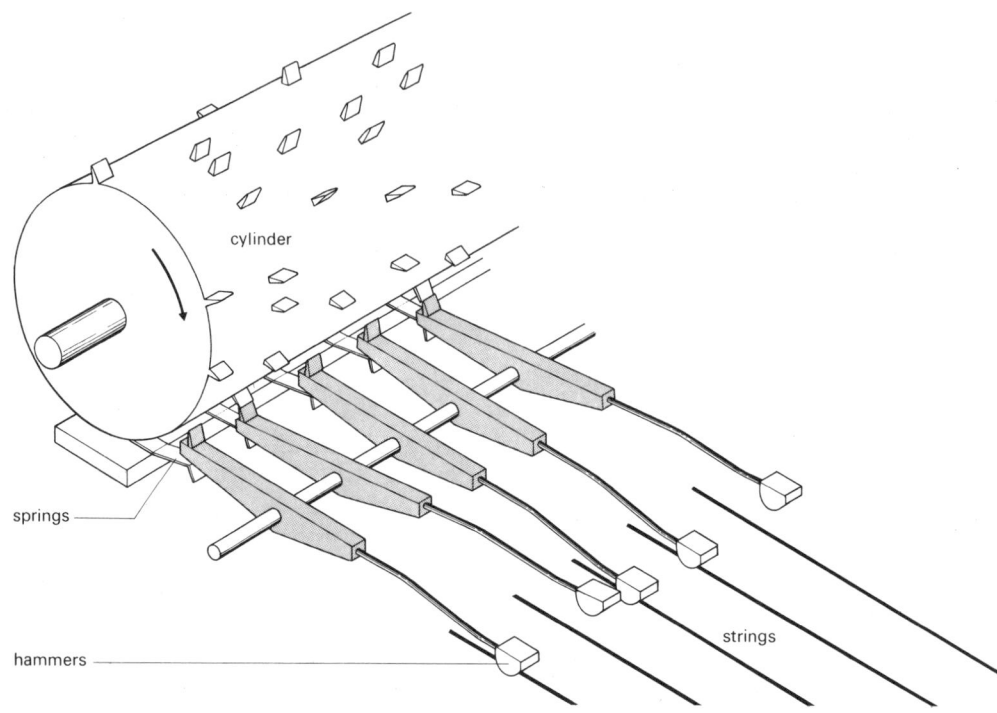

9. *Mechanism of a mechanical piano*

of the 20th century an automatic disc-changing device was also introduced.

Their quiet sound and the difficulty of keeping them constantly tuned are the main reasons why more intensive mechanization of stringed musical instruments did not take place until the 19th century. In addition to barrel organs, 'crank-handle pianos', also known as 'piano organs', appeared at that time in Italy and England. In south Italy these musical instruments still provide music for puppet plays. They are more sturdily built than ordinary pianos, in order to withstand frequent use and the effects of the weather. Their felt hammers are covered with leather and the strings are quadrupled. This gives them a sharp sound rather like a xylophone. The mechanism is very simple: the pins on the cylinder press a lever which engages with the hammer (fig.9). There are no dampers, except on some lower notes, and the pins on the cylinder are not adapted to achieve dynamic effects. A similar construction was used for the so-called 'piano orchestrions', which were equipped with additional instruments including the xylophone, drums, cymbal and triangle.

An important change came with the introduction of the pneumatic mechanism, an impulse to which was given by the perforated strip. Patent rights for the use of a pneumatic mechanism for the piano were issued in the USA as early as 1860, but in practice it was only used 20 years later, when Jean Carpentier constructed his 'mélographe' for the registration of compositions, and the 'mélotrope' for re-playing these compositions with the aid of a perforated strip of paper.

At first the pneumatic mechanism was separate from the piano proper, but later it was built in the piano in such a manner that the piano could also be played without it. These 'pianolas' or 'phonolas' were operated by pedals. Electrically operated instruments were introduced later. To replace the performer's ten fingers the pianola was equipped with 88 mechanical 'fingers', which could be used freely with the perforated strip. It was possible, for example, to play bass tunes without the sustaining pedal, or to play arpeggios and accurate trills without fear that the mechanical 'fingers' would be cramped. The pianola made possible rhythmical extravagance and harmonizations never previously attempted by composers, regardless of the requirements of the fingering. In addition, it was possible to control the tempo and muting of the composition, thus giving the 'musician' handling the instrument an illusion that the performance was his own. A prerequisite for perfect operation of the pianola was the ability to handle the pedals rhythmically for the phrasing of the composition. Thus, the technique of operating the pianola had to be as instinctive as that of singing or speaking. (For illustrations, *see* PLAYER PIANO.)

Four types of pneumatic pianos reached a high degree of perfection in the last phase of their development. These were pianolas of the Duo-Art type made by Aeolian; the Welte-Mignon type made by Welte & Söhne; the phonola made by Hupfeld; and the pianola constructed by the Ampico Corporation. Music from the Ampico piano rolls, when issued on LP records in 1966, surprised the public by its technical perfection. The phonola required someone to regulate the tempo, phrasing and volume during the performance, while the Duo-Art, Welte-Mignon and Ampico pianolas could not deviate from an exact and authentic reproduction of the original performance with all its fine distinctions of attack, use of pedal, and choice of tempo and volume.

The pianola was for a long time considered a mere mechanical piano, to play only compositions written for the piano proper. Not until other musical machines (e.g. the gramophone and the radio) were overtaking it in popularity did the pianola enjoy a reputation as an instrument in its own right, requiring special music and even new compositions (Hindemith and Stravinsky, among others, composed for the pianola). The Aeolian Company in East Rochester, USA, made an attempt to resume the manufacture of pianolas after World War II, but production was stopped again in 1951, apparently for lack of interest.

The complicated system by which bowed instruments are played prevented any attempts at their mechanization for a long time. Frequent attempts had previously been made to replace the bow with some other mechanism, but always without success. It was evident that the usual bow was of no use, and that an endless rotating bow must be introduced. This problem was not solved until 1908, when the first mechanical violin, the 'virtuosa', was constructed in the USA. This was an ordinary violin placed in an instrument containing a number of levers and mechanical 'fingers'; a disc replaced the bow. In 1911 the 'violina' was constructed in Vienna; it consisted of three violins grouped around a common axis and pressed at a given moment against a rotating bow (see fig.10); the pressure was automatically regulated. The 'violiniste', made in 1920, was a violin pendant to the pianola. An ordinary violin was placed in a mobile cradle and the individual strings of the instrument were played by rotating it. The bow moved at the required speed according to the desired performance. It was also possible to change the pressure of the bow on the strings at any moment, thus allowing the use of various techniques, such as martelé, spiccato and staccato.

This was the last stage in the development of automatophons; the advance of musical machines eliminated them so quickly that in the 1930s they virtually ceased to exist. Their extinction, however, has not meant the end of attempts to replace the musical performer with a machine; modern electronic and cybernetic music-making machines are evidence of these efforts. Automatophons are the only musical instruments that have kept past musical practice alive for our generation. Their cylinders and perforated strips fulfil the same function as modern sound recordings; they provide valuable information about the tuning of musical instruments, performing practice and the tempo of compositions in the past.

BIBLIOGRAPHY

S. de Caus: Les raisons des forces mouvantes (Frankfurt am Main, 1615, rev. 2/1624)
R. de Fluctibus: De naturae simia (Oppenheim, 1618)
A. Kircher: Musurgia universalis (Rome, 1650/R1970)
C. Schott: Technica curiosa (Nuremberg, 1664)
A. Kircher: Phonurgia nova (Kempten, 1673/R1966)
C. Schott: Magia universalis naturae et artis (Bamberg, 1674)
J. Vaucanson: Le mécanisme du fluteur automate (Paris, 1738)
M. D. J. Engramelle: La tonotechnie ou l'art de noter les cylindres (Paris, 1775)
E. T. A. Hoffmann: Die Automate (Berlin, 1819)
J. H. M. Pope: Geschichte aller Erfindungen und Entdeckungen (Stuttgart, 1837)
L. Hupfeld: Dea-Violina (Leipzig, 1909)
Welte & Söhne: List of Music for the Welte-Mignon Autographpiano (New York, 1912)
H. L. Atta: The Piano-player (New York, 1914)
W. B. White: The Player-piano Up to Date (New York, 1914)
F. M. Feldhaus: Die Technik der Vorzeit (Leipzig, 1914)
E. Newman: The Piano-player and its music (London, 1920)
S. Grew: The Art of the Player-piano (London, 1922)
A. Chapuis and E. Gelis: Le monde des automates (Paris, 1928)
A. Chapuis: Automates, machines automatiques et méchanisme (Lausanne, 1928)
A. Protz: Mechanische Musikinstrumente (Kassel, 1939)
A. Chapuis: Les automates dans les oeuvres d'imagination (Neuchâtel, 1950)
A. Chapuis and E. Droz: Les automates (Neuchâtel, 1950)
A. Chapuis: Histoire de la boîte à musique et de la musique mécanique (Lausanne, 1955)
A. Buchner: Hudební automaty (Prague, 1959; Eng. trans., 1959)
F. K. Frieberg: Musica ex machina (Berlin, 1960)
E. Simon: Mechanische Musikinstrumente früherer Zeiten und ihre Musik (Wiesbaden, 1966)
L. G. Langwill and N. Boston: Church and Chamber Barrel-organs, their Origin, Makers, Music and Location: a Chapter in English Church Music (Edinburgh, 1967, rev. and enlarged 2/1970)
Q. D. Bowers: A Guidebook of Automatic Musical Instruments (New York, 1967–8)
A. W. J. G. Ord-Hume: Player Piano (London, 1970)
——: Clockwork Music: an Illustrated Musical History of Mechanical Musical Instruments (London, 1973)
The History of Music Machines (New York, 1975) [exhibition catalogue]
                                    ALEXANDR BUCHNER

**Mechanik** [Mechanismus] (Ger; Fr. *méchanique*). ACTION.

10. Mechanical violin: Hupfeld's 'Phonoliszt-Violina', Leipzig, c1912 (British Piano Museum, Brentford, London)

**Mechetti.** Austrian firm of music publishers. Carlo Mechetti (*b* Lucca, 1748; *d* Vienna, 30 Jan 1811) was for many years a steward in the service of Count Karl Colloredo. His associations with members of the higher aristocracy benefited his business transactions to such an extent that he soon acquired a considerable fortune, and on 3 November 1798 he took out an art dealer's licence. He appointed as his assistant his nephew Pietro Mechetti (*b* Lucca, 20 April 1777; *d* Vienna, 25 July 1850), whom he subsequently adopted. The deed of partnership (28 February 1807) made Pietro a public partner in the firm of Carlo Mechetti e Nipote, which was by then publishing music. Pietro Mechetti was granted a new art dealer's licence on 10 July 1810. His uncle made him sole inheritor and, after Carlo's death, Pietro showed his gratitude by always signing the name of the firm (registered on 18 February 1811) as Pietro Mechetti qdm. Carlo. The publishing of music gained impetus only after the Napoleonic Wars. Through reliable business management the firm of Mechetti was always able to hold its own against its larger competitors, Haslinger and Diabelli. Pietro's son Karl (1811–47) became a manager of the firm but died at the age of 37; Pietro survived him by three years. After his death his widow Therese continued the firm under the name Pietro Mechetti sel. Witwe until her death (28 June 1855). The publishing rights then passed to C. A. Spina.

The publication programme was generally above average and included the first edition of Beethoven's *Polonaise* op.89, new editions of opp.10 and 13 and some of his arrangements; the firm also issued first editions of Mendelssohn, Moscheles, Nicolai, Schubert (D356), Schumann and Spohr, and numerous works by Czerny, Donizetti, Fahrbach, Fesca, von Krufft, Leidesdorf, Payer, Pixis, Pohl, Rossini, Vanhal and Voříšek. Like Haslinger and Diabelli, Mechetti was obliged to publish light music in order to finance the less commercial publications, and thus became the principal publisher of Josef Lanner and the younger Johann Strauss. The firm ran several important series, including the *Aurora d'Italia e di Germania* (352 numbers), containing separate pieces from the most popular Italian and German operas, the *Anthologie musicale* (over 100 numbers), *Der musikalische Sammler* (95 numbers) and three series of *Terpsichore*, which included dance and ballet music. Among the firm's catalogues are the *Verlags-Katalog* (1846, 1st suppl. 1847) and two publishers' reports issued by Therese (1853–4), all in the Gesellschaft der Musikfreunde, Vienna.

BIBLIOGRAPHY
O. E. Deutsch: *Music Publishers' Numbers* (London, 1946; Ger. trans., rev. 1961)
C. Junker: *Festschrift zur Feier des hundertjährigen Bestehens der Korporation . . . 1807–1907* (Vienna, 1907)
M. Kratochwil: *Monographie über Carlo Mechetti* (Vienna, 1958)
A. Weinmann: *Verlags-Verzeichnis Pietro Mechetti qdm. Carlo* (Vienna, 1966)

ALEXANDER WEINMANN

**Měchura** [Miechura], **Leopold Eugen** (*b* Prague, 2 Feb 1804; *d* Votín, nr. Klatovy, 11 Feb 1870). Bohemian composer. He studied philosophy and law at the University of Prague and composition with Tomášek and B. D. Weber. He retired to the family estate at Votín in southern Bohemia to devote himself to composition, directing his musical energies in a nationalistic vein in the last decade of his life (the famous Czech nationalist Palacký was his brother-in-law). After a concert of his works in Prague on 22 March 1868 he was recognized as an important national composer. His most significant works are the cantatas *Pohřeb na Kaňku* ('The burial on Kaňk Hill') to a text by A. V. Šmilovský (1866), *Štědrý den* ('Christmas eve') to a text by K. J. Erben (1867) and the three-act opera *Marie Potocká* to a libretto by Josef Kolář after a play by Pushkin (1869), which was produced posthumously at the Prague National Theatre on 13 Jan 1871. His instrumental music, most of which exists in manuscript (in *CS-Pnm*), includes 16 string quartets and six symphonies.

BIBLIOGRAPHY
M. Očadlík: 'Opery L. E. Měchury', *Sborník praci k padesátým narozeninám Profesora Dra Zdeňka Nejedlého* (Prague, 1928), 129

GRACIAN ČERNUŠÁK/R

**Meck, Joseph** [Giuseppe] (*b* probably at Knöringen, nr. Günzburg, 1690; *d* Eichstätt, 2 Dec 1758). German composer. He probably attended a Jesuit Gymnasium in south Germany and studied music in Italy. From about 1711 until his death he was in the service of the Eichstätt court, at first as a violinist, from February 1714 as a chamber musician and valet, from 1715 (while continuing as a valet) as vice-Hofkapellmeister and from 1721 as Hofkapellmeister. With the modest forces at his disposal, he was responsible for all aspects of music at the court. Concertos form the most important element in his surviving output. All of them – 18 for violin, one for oboe – are solo concertos of the Vivaldian type. Along with such men as Heinichen, Pisendel and Stölzel he was thus one of the earliest composers to disseminate Vivaldi's style in Germany; indeed his op.1 is the first published collection of solo concertos by a German composer. The wide cultivation of his concertos testifies to his contemporaries' high opinion of them. His vocal music, on the other hand, is of little interest; neither his cantata-like works, which aspire to virtuosity, nor his hymns, which are simple pieces for everyday use, rise above a pedestrian level. Though his music was known to Corrette (*Art de se perfectionner dans le violon*, 1782), he was generally forgotten after his death.

WORKS
*(catalogue in Beckmann, 1975)*
12 concerti, 3, 4 vn, va, vc, bc, op.1 (Amsterdam, 1720–21)
Conc., 3 vn, va, bc, anon. in 6 concerti . . . del sig. F. M. Veracini, A. Vivaldi, G. M. Alberti, Salvini e G. Torelli (Amsterdam, *c*1717) [wrongly attrib. Vivaldi = P217]
4 vn concs., G, A, *D-B*, *S-Uu*, g, *D-F*, *SWs*, B♭, *A-Wgm* (inc.); ob conc., F, *S-L*; conc., C, probably vn, lost, transcr. org by J. G. Walther, *D-B*, ed. in DDT, xxvi–xxvii (1906/*R*), ed. H. Lohmann in *J. G. Walther: Ausgewählte Orgelwerke*, iii (Wiesbaden, 1966)
2 partitas, a, lute, vn, b, Universitätsbibliothek, Salzburg

Offertory, 4vv, vn, bc, 1742; Miserere, 5vv, 2 vn, org (inc.): Diözesanarchiv, Eichstätt; Pater mi, 4vv, 2 vn, bc, 1743; Vesperae breves, 4vv, 2 vn, bc, 1754; 42 hymns, mostly 4vv, org: St Walburg Abbey, Eichstätt
2 occasional works, 30 pieces for Jesuit school dramas, music lost

BIBLIOGRAPHY
*EitnerQ; WaltherML*
G. Bereths: *Die Musikpflege am kurtrierischen Hofe zu Koblenz-Ehrenbreitstein* (Mainz, 1964), 141f
K. Beckmann: 'A. Vivaldi oder J. Meck?: zum Echtheitsproblem des Concerto P 217', *IMSCR, xi Copenhagen 1972*, 253
——: 'Zur Echtheitsfrage des Concerto RV 275', *Vivaldi Informations*, ii (1973), 7; abridged version, *Musik und Kirche*, xliv (1974), 176
——: *Joseph Meck (1690–1758): Leben und Werk des Eichstätter Hofkapellmeisters* (Bochum, 1975)
based on *MGG* (xvi, 1231–2) by permission of Bärenreiter
KLAUS BECKMANN

**Meckenheuser, Johann Georg** (*b* Goslar, 1666). German organist and theoretician. He was educated at the monastery at Hamersleben, where he was later organist. In 1727 he is known to have been the organist at the church of St Wisbert in Quedlinburg.

Meckenheuser's one known work, *Die sogenannte: Allerneuste, musicalische Temperatur* (Quedlinburg, 1727) expounds a temperament based on an arithmetical division of the ditonic (Pythagorean) comma. Although seven of the 12 notes of the octave are slightly sharp, the division produces an adequate equal temperament. Meckenheuser, however, encountered difficulties in the practical application of his temperament. Adlung (p.311) recounted a disastrous episode experienced by Meckenheuser when he tried to tune the organ at Goslar to his monochord: a fault not of the temperament, but of technique. The treatise was directed with considerable bitterness at Mattheson, who Meckenheuser claimed knew nothing of calculation and even less of musical temperament.

BIBLIOGRAPHY
J. Adlung: *Anleitung zu der musikalischen Gelahrtheit* (Erfurt, 1758/R1953, 2/1783)
J. N. Forkel: *Allgemeine Litteratur der Musik* (Leipzig, 1792/R1962)
CECIL ADKINS

**Meco, Richard.** *See* MICO, RICHARD.

**Medek, Tilo** (*b* Jena, 22 Jan 1940). German composer. He studied musicology at Berlin University (1959–64), also taking composition lessons with Wagner-Régeny until 1967. From 1964 he worked as a freelance composer. He was awarded the 1967 Gaudeamus prize for *Todesfuge*, an impressive piece using dense, blurred choral textures to symbolize the unthinking masses of Nazi Germany; against these textures is set the lyrical purity of the soprano solo. Medek has professed to have lost interest in such techniques and has ranged freely in his subsequent music, from *Die betrunkene Sonne*, a children's story which unfortunately lacks a memorable tune, to *Lesarten*, in which music by Mozart, Beethoven, Schumann and others is cleverly transformed in a way that quickly outstays its welcome.

WORKS
(*selective list*)
Dramatic: Einzug (short opera, after I. Babel), 1969; David und Goliath, ballet, 1972; many scores for the theatre, cinema and television
Vocal: Johann Wallbergens natürliche Zauberkünste, S, speaker, Viennese salon orch, 1965; Todesfuge (Celan), S, 4 SATB choruses, 1966; Dekret (Lenin), speaker, 4 perc, 1967; Die betrunkene Sonne, speaker, orch, 1968; many song cycles
Inst: Verschüttete Bauernflöte, org, 1969; Kaminstücke, pf, 1968–70; Lesarten, 2 pf, 1967–71; Fl Conc., 1973; Sym., 1973

Principal publishers: Deutscher Verlag, Peters, VEB
DAVID BLAKE

**Meder, Johann Gabriel** (*b* Erfurt; *fl* c1755–1800). German composer. His relationship, if any, to Johann Valentin Meder has not been established. He is known to have been a music teacher and leader of the winter concerts in Amsterdam about 1755, and may have written some of his works for them. His *Principes de musique pour le chant* appeared in 1800. Meder's works, all printed by Hummel in Amsterdam and Berlin, include six *Sinfonies à 8* op.1 (1764), three *Sinfonies à 12* op.3 (1783), a *Sinfonie périodique* op.4 (1786), six marches for harpsichord (*c*1795), six marches for wind quintet (*c*1795), a *Recueils d'air* for

wind quintet (1797) and the harpsichord trios *L'illusion du printemps* op.6 (1797).

BIBLIOGRAPHY
*EitnerQ*; *GerberL*
C. F. Cramer, ed.: *Magazin der Musik*, i (Hamburg, 1783/R1970), 767
C. Johansson: *J. J. & B. Hummel Music-publishing and Thematic Catalogues* (diss., U. of Stockholm, 1972)
ERIK KJELLBERG

**Meder, Johann Valentin** (*b* Wasungen, nr. Meiningen, baptized 3 May 1649; *d* Riga, end of July 1719). German composer, organist and singer. He came from a musical family, his father and four brothers all being organists or Kantors. He studied theology at Leipzig in 1669 and then at Jena but soon became a professional singer. He was employed as court singer at Gotha in 1671, Bremen in 1672–3, Hamburg in 1673 and Copenhagen and Lübeck (where he met Buxtehude) in 1674. From 1674 to 1680 he was Kantor at the Gymnasium at Reval (now Tallinn). After a sojourn in Riga in 1685–6 he succeeded Balthasar Erben as Kapellmeister at St Marien, Danzig, in 1687. In 1698 Danzig city council refused to allow a performance of his opera *Die wiederverehligte Coelia*. He had it performed instead in the nearby town of Schottland, which led to his being dismissed from his post. After briefly being employed as Kantor at the cathedral at Königsberg, he went in 1700 to Riga, where he held a similar position until his death.

According to Mattheson, Meder was a singer of repute, an excellent organist and a notable composer. He knew Italian in his youth and was familiar with the music of Italian composers such as Carissimi and Cesti. But for the wars in which the Swedish king was involved for so many years, Meder, as Mattheson pointed out, would probably have become director of music at the Swedish court in Stockholm.

Of four stage works that Meder is known to have written only *Die beständige Argenia* survives, performed in Reval in 1680 by the students of the gymnasium. Dedicated to the newly married Swedish king, Carl XI, and his queen, it reveals his skilful handling of recitative and arioso and of strophic songs which predominate over larger forms such as the through-composed aria. His *Nero* was the first German opera to be performed in Danzig, in November 1695; it was indebted to N. A. Strungk's opera of the same name (1693), for he used not only the same text but a few of Strungk's arias too.

As a composer of sacred music Meder shows to some extent the influence of Buxtehude. Much of his output in this field is lost. Of the surviving works one of the most notable is his oratorio Passion of 1700. It includes a number of interpolated chorales, set as solos, duets and choruses; and, anticipating Bach's treatment, the words of Jesus are normally set as arioso. The work includes a good deal of expressive writing.

WORKS
MOTETS ETC
Ach, Herr mich armen Sünder, 4vv, vn discordato, 2 va, vle, *PL-GD*
Ach Herr, straffe mich nicht, 1v, 2 vn, vle, bc, Reval, 1679, *S-Uu* (holograph)
Die höllische Schlange, dialogue cantata, 4vv, 2 vn, 2 va da braccio, vle, bc, *Uu* (listed in *EitnerQ* as Begrüsset seystu holdseelige)
Gott, du bist derselbst mein König, 3vv, 2 vn, va, vc, 2 clarinos, bc, timp ad lib, *Uu*
Gott hilf mir, 1v, 4 vn, bc, *Uu*
Gott, mein Hertz ist bereit, 3vv, 2 vn, va, b va, bc; 2 ob, bn, ad lib; *Uu*
Herzlich tut mich verlangen (Himmlische Valet Music), 4vv, vn dulcisono, 2 va, vc, vle, 2 recorders, 2 ob, bn, bc (org), *PL-GD*

In principio erat verbum, 3vv, 2 vn, *S-Uu*
Jubilate Deo omnis terra, 1v, clarino, vn, vle, bc, *Uu*
Leben wir, so leben wir dem Herrn, 4vv, 2 vn, va da gamba, vc, bc, *Uu*
Meine Seel säuffzt und stöhnet (Andächtige Communion Musique), 4vv, 5 viols, 2 ob, bn, Riga, 1714, *PL-GD*
Preise, Jerusalem, 12vv, 3 orch, 1687, *GD*
Quid est hoc, quod sentio, 3vv, 2 vn, va da gamba, bc, *S-Uu*
Singet, lobsinget mit Herzen und Zungen, 4 solo vv, chorus, 2 vn, va, vc, 2 ob, bn, *PL-GD*
Sufficit nunc Domine, 1v, vn, 4 va da gamba, bc, *S-Uu*
Vox mitte clamorem, 3vv, 3 vn, bc, *Uu*
Wie murren denn die Leute, dialogue cantata, 2vv, 2 vn, 2 va, bn, bc, Riga, 1684, *Uu* (holograph)
Wünschet Jerusalem Gluck, 12vv, 3 orch, 1686, *PL-GD*

OTHER SACRED

Passions oratorium (according to St Matthew), solo vv, chorus, small orch., 1700, *D-Bds*
In tribulatione invocavimus, 5 solo vv, 4 vn, bn, bc, *Bds*, *Wa* (as solo cantata)

SECULAR

Vor-Jahrs-Erstlinge . . . Ariette und . . . Braut-Tanz (Riga, 1685)
Die beständige Argenia, opera, Reval, 1680, *S-Sk*; ed. in EDM, 1st ser., lxviii (1973)
Die befreyete Andromeda, opera-ballet, Weissenfels, 1688, lost
Der polnische Pracher . . . musicalischen Concentum, 5 insts, 1689, *PL-GD*
Nero (opera, G. C. Corradi, after C. Pallavicino), Danzig, 1695, lost
Die wiederverehligte Coelia, opera, Schottland, 1698, lost

LOST WORKS

Capricci, 2 vn, bc (org) (Danzig, 1698), according to Mattheson; trio and chaconne, 2 vn, bc (hpd), possibly from this collection, *S-Uu*
Musicalischer Dialogus auf bevorstehendes Hl. Weynachtsfest, 1686
Kürmusik zur Ratswahl, 1698
Gott, der du wehlst die Regenten auf Erden, 3 choruses
Languet cor meum, 1v, bc, according to *EitnerQ*
2 sacred songs, 1698; 6 sacred songs, undated

About 130 sacred works in MSS presented to Riga council after Meder's death, incl. 14 masses, 5 Magnificat, and Passions, known only from inventory, see Bolte (1891)

BIBLIOGRAPHY

J. Mattheson: *Grundlage einer Ehren-Pforte* (Hamburg, 1740); ed. M. Schneider (Berlin, 1910/*R*1969)
J. Bolte: 'Johann Valentin Meder', *VMw*, vii (1891), 43
———: *Das Danziger Theater im 16. und 17. Jahrhundert* (Hamburg, 1895)
———: 'J. V. Meders Stammbuch', *SIMG*, i (1899–1900), 530
W. Lott: 'Zur Geschichte der Passionskomposition von 1650–1800', *AMw*, iii (1921), 285
———: 'Zur Geschichte der Passionsmusiken auf Danziger Boden mit Bevorzugung der oratorischen Passion', *AMw*, vii (1925), 297–328
L. Schiedermair: *Die deutsche Oper* (Leipzig, 1930, rev. 2/1940, 3/1943)
H. Rauschning: *Geschichte der Musik und Musikpflege in Danzig* (Danzig, 1931)
Å. Vretblad: 'J. V. Meder och hans opera "Die beständige Argenia" ', *STMf*, xix (1937), 65
N. Busch: 'Alt-Rigas Musikkultur', *Baltische Monatshefte* (1937), 642
Å. Davidsson: *Musikbibliographische Beiträge* (Uppsala and Wiesbaden, 1954)
C.-A. Moberg: 'Drag i Östersjöområdets musikliv på Buxtehudes tid' [Sketch of musical life in the Östersjö area in Buxtehude's day], *STMf*, xxxix (1957), 15–88
B. Smallman: *The Background of Passion Music* (London, 1957, rev., enlarged 2/1970)
F. Krummacher: *Die Überlieferung der Choralbearbeitungen in der frühen evangelischen Kantate* (Berlin, 1965)
B. Smallman: 'A Forgotten Oratorio Passion', *MT*, cxv (1974), 118
ERIK KJELLBERG

**Mederitsch(-Gallus), Johann (Georg Anton)** (*b* Vienna, baptized 27 Dec 1752; *d* Lemberg [now L'vov], 18 Dec 1835). Austrian composer, teacher and Kapellmeister. After study with Wagenseil he became Kapellmeister of the Olmütz (Olomouc) theatre (1781–2), then returned to Vienna, where he was a double bass player in the German Theatre Orchestra as late as 1792. His years in Vienna saw the successful production of a number of Singspiels, and in about 1800 he was piano teacher to the poet Grillparzer, then nine years old. He was Kapellmeister at Ofen (Buda) in 1793, possibly until 1796, and in 1798, and from 1817 he lived at Lemberg. The poverty and sadness of Mederitsch's old age were touchingly described in a letter to Moscheles from the younger Mozart, written on 25 October 1827; his summary of Mederitsch ('perhaps the greatest contrapuntist of our age') may be set against his father's frivolous comments (letter of 5 February 1783). Mederitsch's gratitude to Mozart's son is attested by his bequeathing to him the autograph scores of his works, some 80 in all, which after Mozart's death passed to the Mozarteum, Salzburg. Mederitsch was well known and respected in his day; according to the above letter of the younger Mozart, his incidental music to *Macbeth* was known even in London. However, he is now remembered mainly as the composer of Act 1 (Act 2 was by Winter) of *Babylons Pyramiden*, one of the works in which Schikaneder tried in vain to repeat the success of *Die Zauberflöte*.

WORKS

All stage works first performed in Vienna, unless otherwise stated; most works MS in *A-Sm*, complete list in Aigner.

Der redliche Verwalter (J. F. Schmidt), Bauernfeindscher Saal, 26 Aug 1779
Arkatastor und Illiane, melodrama (F. Zawitzer), Bauernfeindscher Saal, 14 Oct 1779
Der Schlosser, Olomouc, 1781
Die Seefahrer/Der grossmüthige Seefahrer (after Ilein), Leopoldstadt Theatre, 14 Oct 1782
Die Rekruten, wobei Kasperl einen lustigen Bauernjungen und Rekruten spielt, Leopoldstadt Theatre, 6 Dec 1782; attrib. doubtful
Rose, oder Pflicht und Liebe im Streit (G. Stephanie the Younger), Burgtheater, 9 Feb 1783
Der letzte Rausch, 1795; probably written in 1788
Babylons Pyramiden, Act 1 (E. Schikaneder), Freihaus-Theater auf der Wieden, 25 Oct 1797
Incidental music for The Tempest, Hamlet, Macbeth and other plays
Symphonies, concertos, much piano and chamber music; masses, motets

BIBLIOGRAPHY

G. Gugitz: 'Der seltsame Herr Gallus-Mederitsch', *ÖMz*, vii/1 (1952), 15
W. Hummel: *W. A. Mozarts Söhne* (Kassel, 1956), 151ff, 332
F. Grillparzer: *Selbstbiographie*, Sämtliche Werke, iv (Munich, 1965), 15, 25, 30, 52f
T. Aigner: *Johann Gallus Mederitsch (1752–1835): Leben und thematisches Verzeichnis der Werke* (diss., U. of Salzburg, 1973; thematic index, Wilhelming, 1974)
PETER BRANSCOMBE

**Medesimo tempo** (It.: 'the same pace'). A direction to maintain a tempo in spite of apparent disturbances, particularly changes of time signature or note value; *l'istesso tempo* was also used. By the later 19th century these directions were increasingly replaced by equivalence equations.

**Medial cadence** [inverted cadence]. A CADENCE whose penultimate chord is in inversion, as opposed to a 'radical cadence', whose chords are in root position. In some American writings the medial cadence is referred to as a type of imperfect cadence. The term is also sometimes applied to endings in plainsong and modal polyphony that are not on the final of the mode.

**Mediant.** (1) The third step or DEGREE of the major or minor scale, so called because of its intermediate position between the key note, or tonic, and the 5th degree, or dominant. It is the note 'that determines the mode' of a scale (Rousseau, *Dictionnaire de musique*, 1768), since the interval it makes with the tonic major or minor 3rd determines whether the scale is major or minor.

(2) In any of the four authentic church modes, the scale step that lies a 3rd below the tenor (sometimes

called the dominant), namely *f* in the Dorian mode, *a* in the Phrygian and Lydian, and *b* in the Mixolydian.

**Mediation** (Lat. *mediatio*). The mediant cadence, or inflection (*see* INFLECTION, §I) which occurs halfway through a psalm tone. Various types of mediation exist; for example, mediations of one or of two accents, with or without syllables of preparation. *See also* PSALM, §II, 2.

**Médiator** (Fr.). PLECTRUM.

**Medici.** Italian family of music patrons. They were renowned for their patronage of learning, literature, the arts and science.

1. Introduction. 2. Beginnings to 1537. 3. 1537–1737.

1. INTRODUCTION. The Medici ruled over Florence with few interruptions for more than 300 years. Their political genius as well as their proverbial wealth, played no small part in their rise from principal citizens (1434–1532) to absolute rulers of Florence and her Tuscan dominion (1532–1737). The international influence achieved by several members of this family of merchant princes (among them Lorenzo the Magnificent, Popes Leo X and Clement VII and Queens Catherine and Marie of France) and a series of astute dynastic marriages also help explain the Medici's prominent position in the social and cultural history of Italy and the rest of Europe.

The two main branches of the family were founded by Cosimo (1389–1464) and Lorenzo (1395–1440), both of them the sons of the banker Giovanni di Bicci de' Medici (1360–1429), whose ancestors had settled in Florence as early as 1201. Cosimo's line, which included all of the famous Medici of the earlier Renaissance, died out in the seventh generation, and the succession then passed to Lorenzo's line, which carried on the family through six more generations. At the time of the succession (1537) Lorenzo's line was represented by yet another Cosimo (1519–74), who reigned first as Duke of Florence (1537–69) and then as Grand Duke of Tuscany (1569–74). On his mother's side this Cosimo was a direct descendant of the first Cosimo, and thus both branches of the family were united in his person.

2. BEGINNINGS TO 1537. The humanistic, artistic and literary interests of the first Cosimo and his line have long been celebrated, though information about their patronage of music and musicians has only recently been brought to light. Under Cosimo's aegis the first musical chapels, emulating those of northern Europe, were instituted in 1438 at the cathedral and baptistry at Florence. He was also apparently responsible for selecting the musicians engaged at the time, among whom was the Avignon composer Beltrame Feragut. An active policy of recruiting northern musicians for the new chapels was carried out by Cosimo's sons Piero (1416–69) and Giovanni (1421–63). Both were friends of Dufay, who in a well-known letter to them of 22 February 1456 promised to send them some chansons and four Lamentations for Constantinople that he had recently composed. Giovanni, who was a lutenist, was a close friend and early patron of the great Florentine organist Antonio Squarcialupi. Piero is important in music history because of his acquisition, some time before 1456, of the famous collection of Notre Dame

polyphony housed to this day in the Biblioteca Mediceo-Laurenziana, Florence.

Florentine musical life flourished with unprecedented vigour during the reign of Piero's son Lorenzo the Magnificent (1449–92). His unceasing endeavours succeeded in attracting to the city's chapels as well as to his own private service some of the most famous singers and composers of the time, including Isaac, Alexander Agricola and Johannes Ghiselin. Lorenzo himself was a singer of no mean achievement. He is said to have performed often for the delectation of his friends, among them the poet–improviser Baccio Ugolini, who created the title role in Poliziano's *Orfeo*. As a youth Lorenzo had sought to have one of his poems set by Dufay, of whose music he was an ardent admirer. Later in life he had several of his *canti carnascialeschi* set by his favourite musician, Isaac. Isaac subsequently composed the music for Poliziano's lament on Lorenzo's death, *Quis dabit capiti meo aquam*, as well as a motet, *Optime pastor*, honouring the accession in 1513 of Lorenzo's second son Giovanni (1475–1521) to the papal throne as Leo X.

Medici patronage of music and musicians reached its apogee during Leo's reign. He was a thoroughly trained musician, as is shown by a few of his extant compositions, and his knowledge of music theory reputedly was exceeded only by his love of musical performance. It has been estimated that under him the papal chapel employed the unprecedented number of 32 musicians, notably composers such as Gaspar van Weerbeke, Antoine Bruhier, Andreas de Silva, Carpentras, Jean Conseil, Marbrianus de Orto, Francisco de Peñalosa, Bernardo Pisano and Costanzo Festa. Several works by these men are found in the famous Medici Codex of 1518, a sumptuously decorated manuscript commissioned for the wedding of Leo's nephew Lorenzo, Duke of Urbino, and Madeleine de la Tour d'Auvergne. Leo was also fond of instrumental music and patronized many of the famous players of his day, among them the lutenist–composer Francesco Canova da Milano.

Leo's cousin Giulio (1478–1534) succeeded to the papacy as Clement VII in 1523. As a cardinal, Clement had taken a great interest in Florentine musical matters and seems to have been responsible for the appointments of Verdelot, Charles d'Argentille, Mattio Rampollini and several other outstanding musicians to the city's chapels. Despite the many political vicissitudes of his pontificate he remained an avid patron of music and sought to maintain the standard of excellence in the papal chapel that had been established by Leo some years earlier. Among the musicians employed by him were Conseil, Festa, Pisano, Pierre Fontaine, Pernot Vermont, d'Argentille and Ivo Barry. Instrumentalists such as Francesco Canova da Milano and Laurentius da Gaeta were also given favours by this last Medici pope.

3. 1537–1737. With the accession of Duke Cosimo I in 1537 official Medicean patronage of music in Florence was resumed on a broad scale. At his instance the chapels at the cathedral and baptistry were reorganized and enlarged, and his favourite musician, Francesco Corteccia, appointed to direct them. Cosimo and his immediate successors – Francesco I (ruled 1574–87), Ferdinando I (ruled 1587–1609) and Cosimo II (ruled 1609–21) – maintained an active interest in the chapels as well as the prerogative of nominating their choirmasters, the most famous of whom after Corteccia were

*Prince Ferdinando de' Medici (2nd from right) surrounded by his musicians; Pietro Salvetti (seated left, with cello), Giovanni Battista Gigli, called 'il Tedeschino' (centre, with theorbo), Vincenzo Olivicciani, the singer (4th from right), and probably Antonio Rivani, the harpsichordist (extreme right): painting by Anton Domenico Gabbiani (1652–1726) in the Palazzo Pitti, Florence*

Cristofano Malvezzi, Luca Bati and Marco da Gagliano. At court, Cosimo I began the practice of retaining singers, instrumentalists and dancers, and it was continued on an even more lavish scale by his sons and grandson: in the first decades of the 17th century in particular innumerable ballets were performed. Musicians associated with the court in this period include Alessandro Striggio (i), Marenzio, Caccini, Peri, Antonio and Vittoria Archilei, Cavalieri, Francesco Rasi, Lorenzo Allegri, Antonio Brunelli and Vincenzo Calestani; the last two worked at Pisa. Several of these composers were among the earliest and most persuasive monodists.

Cosimo I also initiated the policy of associating important family and state occasions with extraordinary musical festivities. For his own wedding to Eleonora of Toledo in 1539 he commissioned several occasional pieces from Corteccia, Festa and others and also had Corteccia compose music for the *intermedi* of Antonio Landi's comedy *Il commodo*. Other events during his reign, such as the baptisms and weddings of his children or the arrivals of distinguished visitors, were observed in a similar manner. The most elaborate of the Florentine *intermedi*, those for Girolamo Bargagli's *La pellegrina*, were presented in 1589 as part of the festivities attending the marriage of Ferdinando I and Christine of Lorraine. Much of the music for these *intermedi* was composed by Malvezzi and Marenzio. In 1600 the union of Maria de' Medici and Henri IV of France was celebrated with performances of Caccini's *Il rapimento di Cefalo* and Peri's *Euridice*, the first complete extant opera. Notable works presented later in the 17th century include Marco da Gagliano's *La Flora*, on

the occasion of Margherita de' Medici's marriage to Duke Odoardo Farnese of Parma in 1628, and Jacopo Melani's *Ercole in Tebe*, for the wedding of the future Grand Duke Cosimo III and Marguérite Louise of Orleans in 1661.

Medici patronage of music and musicians followed a somewhat erratic course during the reigns of the last three grand dukes. Under Ferdinando II (ruled 1621–70) the chapels at the cathedral and baptistry, comprising 32 singers and directed by G. B. da Gagliano until 1651, continued to flourish, as did the ensembles of voices and instruments maintained by the court. Invitations to visit Florence were extended to prominent composers such as Luigi Rossi and Frescobaldi, and magnificent court productions were arranged of operas, mascheratas, equestrian ballets and aquatic spectacles with music. The Medici, including Ferdinando himself and his brothers Prince Mattias (1613–67) and Cardinal Gian Carlo (1611–63), also lent their support to the establishment of academies which produced new operas by Tuscan musicians and librettists, among them, the Melani brothers, Domenico Anglesi and G. A. Moniglia.

During the reign of Cosimo III (1670–1723) court-sponsored musical events declined steadily, since he cared little for music. Court indifference notwithstanding, some members of the ducal family, notably Cosimo's brother Cardinal Francesco Maria (1660–1711) and his son, the heir apparent Prince Ferdinando (1663–1713), indulged their love of music by supporting both private and public performances of operas, ballets and oratorios. As a youth, Ferdinando had studied counterpoint with G. M. Pagliardi and acquired a passion for music that remained with him until his premature death. Among the musicians he patronized were Bartolomeo Cristofori, Handel, Pasquini, Veracini, G. M. Casini, Pietro Sanmartini, and Alessandro and Domenico Scarlatti. Alessandro Scarlatti composed several operas and sacred works expressly for him. Medici rule petered out with Gian Gastone (ruled 1723–37), whose notorious indolence, allied to the troubled political conditions of the time, precluded notable musical activity at his court.

*See also* FLORENCE, §§1–2.

BIBLIOGRAPHY

R. Galluzzi: *Storia del granducato di Toscana* (Livorno, 1781, rev. 2/1822)
F. X. Haberl: 'Die römische "Schola Cantorum" und die päpstlichen Kapellsänger bis zur Mitte des 16. Jahrhunderts', *VMw*, iii (1887), 251
A. Solerti: *Le origini del melodramma* (Turin, 1903/*R*1969)
——: *Gli albori del melodramma* (Milan, 1904/*R*1969)
——: *Musica, ballo e drammatica alla corte medicea dal 1600 al 1637* (Florence, 1905/*R*1968, 1969)
R. Gandolfi: 'La cappella musicale della corte di Toscana (1539–1859)', *RMI*, xvi (1909), 506
G. F. Young: *The Medici* (London, 1909, repr. 1930)
F. Ghisi: *Feste musicali della Firenze medicea (1480–1589)* (Florence, 1939/*R*1969)
B. Becherini: 'Relazioni di musici fiamminghi con la corte dei Medici: nuovi documenti', *La rinascita*, iv (1941), 87
E. Barfucci: *Lorenzo de' Medici e la società artistica del suo tempo* (Florence, 1945)
F. Schevill: *The Medici* (New York, 1949/*R*1960)
L. Parigi: *Laurentiana: Lorenzo dei Medici cultore della musica* (Florence, 1954)
H.-W. Frey: 'Regesten zur päpstlichen Kapelle unter Leo X und zu seiner privat Kapelle', *Mf*, viii (1955), 58, 178, 412; ix (1956), 139
L. Schrade: 'Les fêtes du mariage de Francesco dei Medici et de Bianca Cappello', *Les fêtes de la Renaissance I: CNRS Abbaye de Royaumont 1955*, 107
H. Engel: *Luca Marenzio* (Florence, 1956)
A.-M. Bragard: 'Détails nouveaux sur les musiciens de la cour du Pape Clément VII', *RBM*, xii (1958), 5
R. L. Weaver: *Florentine Comic Operas of the Seventeenth Century* (diss., U. of North Carolina, 1958)
F. A. D'Accone: 'The Singers of San Giovanni in Florence during the 15th Century', *JAMS*, xiv (1961), 307
M. Fabbri: *Alessandro Scarlatti e il Principe Ferdinando dei Medici* (Florence, 1961)
F. A. D'Accone: 'Heinrich Isaac in Florence: New and Unpublished Documents', *MQ*, xlix (1963), 471
D. P. Walker, ed.: *Musique des intermèdes de 'La pellegrina'* (Paris, 1963)
A. M. Nagler: *Theatre Festivals of the Medici, 1539–1637* (New Haven, Conn., 1964/*R*1976)
C. V. Palisca: 'The First Performance of *Euridice*', *Queens College Twenty-fifth Anniversary Festschrift (1937–1962)* (Flushing, NY, 1964), 1
J. Haar: 'A Gift of Madrigals to Cosimo I: the Ms. Florence, Bibl. Naz. Centrale, Magl. XIX, 130', *RIM*, i (1966), 167
E. E. Lowinsky: *The Medici Codex of 1518: a Choirbook of Motets dedicated to Lorenzo de' Medici, Duke of Urbino* (Chicago, 1968)
A. Minor and B. Mitchell, eds.: *A Renaissance Entertainment: Festivities for the Marriage of Cosimo I, Duke of Florence, in 1539* (Columbia, Missouri, 1968)
W. H. Rubsamen: 'The Music for "Quant'è bella giovinezza" and other Carnival Songs by Lorenzo de' Medici', *Art, Science, and History in the Renaissance*, ed. C. Singleton (Baltimore, 1968), 163
G. Bertelà and A. Tofani, eds.: *Feste e apparati medicei da Cosimo I a Cosimo II* (Florence, 1969)
W. Osthoff: *Theatergesang und darstellende Musik in der italienischen Renaissance* (Tutzing, 1969)
N. Pirrotta and E. Povoledo: *Li due Orfei: da Poliziano a Monteverdi* (Turin, 1969, rev. 2/1975)
D. Kämper: 'Studien zur instrumentalen Ensemblemusik des 16. Jahrhunderts', *AnMc*, no.10 (1970) [whole vol.]
F. A. D'Accone: 'The Musical Chapels at the Florentine Cathedral and Baptistry during the First Half of the 16th Century', *JAMS*, xxiv (1971), 1
H. M. Brown: 'Psyche's Lament: some Music for the Medici Wedding in 1565', *Words and Music: the Scholar's View . . . in Honor of A. Tillman Merritt* (Cambridge, Mass., 1972), 1
H. W. Kaufmann: 'Music for a Noble Florentine Wedding (1539)', *Words and Music: the Scholar's View . . . in Honor of A. Tillman Merritt* (Cambridge, Mass., 1972), 161
H. C. Slim: *A Gift of Madrigals and Motets* (Chicago, 1972)
H. M. Brown: *Sixteenth-century Instrumentation: the Music for the Florentine Intermedii*, MSD, xxx (1973)
F. Hammond: 'Musicians at the Medici Court in the Mid-seventeenth Century', *AnMc*, no.14 (1974), 151
——: 'Musical Instruments at the Medici Court in the Mid-seventeenth Century', *AnMc*, no.15 (1975), 202

FRANK A. D'ACCONE

**Medici, Mario** (*b* Modena, 19 June 1913). Italian music critic, administrator and composer. He took a diploma in composition at the Bologna Liceo (1935), and after doing war service was librarian at Bologna Conservatory (1947–54) and Parma Conservatory (1954–63). As a music critic he has written for *Giornale dell'Emilia* and *Il resto del Carlino* (1947–54); he was co-editor of *Melodramma* (1953–4). In 1968 he was appointed artistic director of the Verona Arena. He founded and became director of the Istituto di Studi Verdiani at Parma in 1959, editing its journal *Verdi* and the reports of its conferences. Most of his compositions were written in the 1930s and include works for piano, a violin sonatina, *Introduzione a commedia* for strings and timpani, *Procedimento amoroso* for soprano and 13 instruments, and a piano concerto.

WRITINGS

ed.: *Parma e Toscanini* (Parma, 1958)
*La musica del 'Corsaro' di Verdi* (Venice, 1963)
*Osservazioni sulla Biblioteca musicale di Parma* (Parma, 1964)
ed.: *1° congresso internazionale di studi verdiani: Venezia 1966*
ed.: *2° congresso internazionale di studi verdiani: Verona 1969*
ed.: *3° congresso internazionale di studi verdiani: Milano 1972*

CAROLYN M. GIANTURCO

**Medieval.** The Middle Ages (Fr. *moyen âge*; Ger. *Mittelalter*; It. *medioevo*) were initially marked by a violent disruption of most political and social structures of the Western world, and by utterly depressed conditions of life, followed by a very long, slow recovery. Nevertheless, the period has an impressive record of artistic and cultural accomplishments. Nor is its musical legacy of lesser importance; although many of its mental processes and habits of perception have since become strange, there are other fundamental aspects of today's music that are heavily indebted to the music of the Middle Ages.

1. Origin of the term and chronology. 2. The central experience of plainsong. 3. Music of the clergy and music of the laity. 4. Rhythm and the music of scholasticism. 5. The transition to the Renaissance.

1. ORIGIN OF THE TERM AND CHRONOLOGY. Both the adjective 'medieval' and the English term for the period, like their equivalents in other languages, derive from the Latin expressions (such as *medium aevum, media aetas, media tempestas*) in which Renaissance humanists voiced their contention that a whole millennium between the end of the ancient civilization and the 15th-century 'rebirth' of culture, literature and art had been but a despicable parenthesis of 'Gothic' obscurity. Historians have long since rejected their bias (though some of it still lingers in the expression 'the Dark Ages') and yet retained the habit of considering such an enormous lapse of time as a single period. Most often the years 476 (end of the Roman empire in the West) and 1453 (fall of Constantinople to the Turks) are given as limits, admittedly conventional, of the period. But other events have also been considered as landmarks to an era; accordingly the initial date has been set at such widely diverging times as the year 250 (beginning of the barbarian invasions) or about 675 (cessation of all sea-

borne Mediterranean trade due to the Arab conquests, and emergence of the Carolingian dynasty). Similarly, the final date has been either anticipated to the beginning of the 14th century and of Italian humanism, or postponed to the spreading of Lutheran reform in the 1520s, not to mention Trevelyan's interesting contention that the Middle Ages lasted to the end of the 18th century.

Music historians have generally avoided a precise definition and seemingly adhered to generally accepted views when referring in the titles of their works to the music 'of' or 'in' the Middle Ages. What follows such titles, however, goes back as far as the very beginning of the Christian era, to speculate which musical elements the new faith may have derived from the synagogue, innovated to meet new conditions, or absorbed from the heterogeneous milieu in which it was spreading. All this, it must be said, forms at best a prehistory of medieval music, for not until the 9th century is there a definite body of music to discuss, or theoretical treatises that are more than mere echoes of classical writing on music. Both are the result of the establishment during the 8th century of a highly unified liturgy for the Western church, a process that is in turn to be related to the historical trend by which the bishops of Rome, having loosened their dependence on the distant Eastern emperors, sought the support of the Carolingian kings. Accordingly, the latest date suggested by general historians, about 675, would seem most suitable for the beginning of what may be called the Latin Middle Ages in music – to be integrated, for the consideration of the Byzantine and related liturgies, by the concept of roughly parallel Greek Middle Ages.

While the border between classical times and the Middle Ages can be seen as an extended no-man's-land, the problem at the other end is an abundance and variety of musical documents, in which new features are not easily separated from old. It would be easier to set the line at the beginning of the 14th century and of the Ars Nova (as suggested, for instance, by Riemann and Abbiati), were not even that novelty too dependent on medieval ideas. No special event in music can assume the symbolic function of a landmark; yet most of the 15th century saw changes which gradually modified the concept and practice of music.

2. THE CENTRAL EXPERIENCE OF PLAINSONG. The history of early medieval music practically coincides with that of plainsong, not because medieval people were so deeply absorbed by religious concerns as to lose all interest in mundane activities, but because the church, with its spiritual hold on society and virtual monopoly of culture, inevitably attracted, and most often produced, the best in every art. Music was part of church life and culture; all clerics had to partake in the practical experience of singing; many added to it the theoretical knowledge of the *ars musica*, inherited from the ancients as one of the disciplines propaedeutic to a liberal education. Even church music, however, comes into the focus of history only from the moment (8th–9th centuries) when a drive for liturgical uniformity prompted the codification of the liturgical repertory. Two procedures were then developed to ensure the transmission and performance of the melodies in their established form and both were to affect deeply the whole history of Western music: namely, the classification of the melodies according to the system of the eight modes (in use until the 18th century) and the gradual

refinement of the early neumes from a purely mnemonic aid into a precise pitch notation whose basic principles have not yet been supplanted. More important than the suppression of two major 'dialects' of plainsong (the Gallican and Mozarabic chants) was the transition from the flexibility and relative freedom of an oral transmission to the dependence on a written text to be (at least in principle) faithfully reproduced at each performance.

The restoration of plainsong by the Benedictines of Solesmes has made this oldest body of medieval music familiar. Its purely melodic essence, its bland ways of stressing the poles of tonal attraction, the flexibility of its rhythm (no matter how much scholars disagree on the details of its interpretation) are all easily perceived. But it takes an insider's knowledge to appreciate fully the ways in which the melodies are shaped, related to their texts, and incorporated in the symbolic meaning of the individual celebration and of the whole cycle of the liturgical year. To some extent this re-creates the typical relationship of most medieval music to its listeners: monastic rites, as well as those of episcopal churches, were acts of devotion to be performed independently of any attendance; and from this came a basic attitude according to which music addressed itself to its own performers and to all participants in the liturgical action rather than to an outside audience.

On such premises it was natural that most musical activities should centre on plainsong. As befitted the aura of sanctity surrounding the chant, musical creativity followed lines suggested by the ecclesiastical trend towards comment on and amplification of sacred texts. Tropes (among which the older forms of sequence must be included) increased the festive solemnity of a given melody by ingeniously interweaving and integrating into its traditional context either new words or new words and music. Similarly, note-against-note parallel ORGANUM (actually a special mode of performance of a liturgical melody, not an improvisation on it) enriched the chant, giving it a fuller resonance.

Polyphonic singing *supra librum* (that is, from the books of plainsong, the *voces organales* being somewhat mechanically added at sight even when contrary and oblique motions were admitted) lasted long after the evolution of more artful kinds of polyphony, in which the musical glossing and the increasing melodic and rhythmic autonomy of the added voices required their being written down and actually gave rise to new compositions. Gradually the flow of the new voice parts slowed down the momentum of the liturgical melody, so that it could no longer be considered to be the *vox principalis*, at least from the musical point of view; and yet the name of 'tenor', now given to the sustained notes of the chant in the gigantic organa of the Notre Dame period, still denotes a spiritual as well as a phonic support to the whole polyphonic structure.

The *concors discordia* of the polyphonic additions to the traditional liturgical melody can be considered as a simultaneous musical troping, an analogy strengthened by its festive destination and by the fact that polyphony, usually applied only to the soloistic sections of a responsorial melody, alternated in performance with the singing of the monophonic choral responds. A further step in this direction, the addition of verbal tropes to certain sections of an organum (the so-called clausulas), led to the creation of the medieval motet with a different text in each voice, resulting in a simultaneous troping and a *concors discordia* in both musical and textual terms.

*Gregory the Great dictating the antiphonary, assisted by the Holy Spirit: miniature from a 9th-century MS fragment from Metz (F-Pn lat.1141, f.3r)*

3. MUSIC OF THE CLERGY AND MUSIC OF THE LAITY. The historical importance of the church's commitment to the preservation of its music seems even more impressive when it is contrasted with the precarious conditions under which all non-liturgical music has survived. A whole class of Latin songs comes first – settings of classical verse, historical laments, spiritual and love-songs, goliardic songs, monophonic conductus – surviving with increasing frequency from the 9th century to the 13th. Their classification depends on subject matter and on the type of source in which the pieces are found, but should not obscure the trait they all have in common of a high literacy. This can only point to the single cultural élite then in existence: the clergy, secular and regular, or even irregular (although it is unrealistic to see the extremes of ostentatious ribaldry and pious contrition as accurately mirroring the status of wandering versus non-wandering clerks). This being the very milieu which was the depositary of musical theory and notation, one is surprised to see how casual was the attention paid to non-liturgical music. The melodies, if at all present in the sources, are mostly notated with highly imprecise neumes, providing no more than a mnemonic aid to long-vanished memories (the main source of the so-called *Carmina burana*, D-Mbs clm 4660, is a typical instance). In addition, instances of the double use of certain melodies with different texts, or of the use of pre-existing (?popular) tunes suggest that the association of text and music was mostly one of mere convenience with no expressive congruity, music serv-

ing as a vehicle easily dropped or replaced. An exception must possibly be made for the monophonic conductus; but then this term is applied only to late pieces, which survive with the polyphonic conductus and organa of the Notre Dame period in manuscripts of a specifically musical nature, already alerted to the importance of the composer and his work.

The later repertory of Latin songs overlaps with the rise of a musical poetry in various vernacular tongues, heralded by the Provençal troubadours at the beginning of the 12th century and introducing the peculiar themes of feudal life and chivalric love above all. Provençal art also spread to Spain and Italy and was soon echoed by the trouvères of northern France and the Minnesinger of Germany. Undoubtedly, this was an art addressed to lay audiences and most often produced by laymen, ranging from the highest nobility (including Guilhem, Count of Poitiers, or Thibaut, King of Navarre) to men of humble birth who had gained admission to court life by virtue of their talents. Connected with its courtly nature is the proud assertion of authorship and the occasional presence of *razos* explaining the circumstances in which a given poem had been conceived; less clear however is the degree to which the authorship of the poetry extended to the music. Here too there is evidence that the same melody could be used for more than one poem: in certain cases it was part of the game to answer a poem by another that could be sung to the tune of the former; this is one of the implications of the term 'sirventes', but the practice was by no means restricted to that single type of song. *Joglars* or *jougleörs*, entrusted with the performance of the songs of troubadours or trouvères, perhaps occasionally supplied or adapted melodies for masters who were musically less gifted.

There has been and still is little agreement as to the possible antecedents of this novel art. Popular, ecclesiastical and Arabic sources have been mentioned, or else a combination of various elements (*see* TROUBADOURS, TROUVÈRES). From the musical point of view, the extant melodies perhaps bear some analogy with liturgical music in their form; but they do not really fit the pattern of any of the ecclesiastical modes. In a few cases there is evidence of melodies being derived from popular tunes or related to the practice of soloists and chorus singing in alternation to accompany a dance (the melodies of *Kalenda maya* and *A l'entrada del tens clar* are well-known instances); yet it would be far-fetched to draw general conclusions from a few special cases. Even more so since popular music obviously had no use for notation (a prevailing condition for all kinds of music until at least the 8th century) and nothing can be known about its nature.

Related as it is to the origins of various modern literatures, the music of the troubadour type has experienced a revival whose fervour tends to make light of many unsolved, and possibly insoluble, philological problems. It is an open question whether the authors themselves always wrote down the texts of their poems; but such doubt is even stronger with regard to the music, for it would seem that the idea of writing down a melody was quite foreign to most 12th-century men. The fact is that no music is provided in the sources of secular song until about 1250, and even then it is done irregularly in only a small minority of the extant manuscripts. This would lend credence to the idea that the melodies were mostly committed to oral tradition, but also that they were thought less essential than the poetic texts and to some extent expendable (the same doubt obtains for the collections of *laude*, cantigas and *Geisslerlieder*, religious songs of lay communities of Italy, Spain and Germany, which are collected in manuscripts of the late 13th and early 14th centuries). Even the second-hand nature of the extant versions has historical value; yet a major obstacle to their revival in performance lies in their notation, which is precise in regard to the melodic contours of the songs, but gives no hint about rhythm, whose reconstruction remains highly controversial. This is all the more regrettable since many of the simpler, mainly syllabic melodies show a clear attraction in spite of their rhythmic ambiguity; but one is at a loss with the clusters of melismatic groups of many others.

4. RHYTHM AND THE MUSIC OF SCHOLASTICISM. It is hard to tell cause from effect in the historical process by which a regular rhythmic pulse asserted itself in the polyphony of the Notre Dame period, to become a basic feature (be it called mode, measure or beat) in the later development of Western music. Undoubtedly a precise temporal relation between the upper parts of an organum had become an essential requirement to hold together these florid, fast-spinning lines against the long sustained notes of the tenor; and the solution given to the problem, based mainly on the insistent repetition of a few rhythmic formulae (*modi* or *maneriae*), was well suited to the limitations of a system of notation that had been created for plainsong and could not signify rhythmic variety. Yet it is impossible to deny the artistic achievements that transcended the technical strictures – the elation of the compelling rhythmic drive that assumed the role of a shaping factor in place of the tenor, now a mere ritual presence, deprived of melodic momentum by the exuberant expansion of the other parts. It is significant that the first surviving document of the new trend, Léonin's cycle of two-voice organa for the liturgy of Notre Dame in Paris (the *Magnus liber organi*), dates from about the time when the building of the cathedral was started in 1163; for the artistic conquest of rhythm in the works of Léonin and in the three- and four-voice organa of his successor Pérotin parallels the conquest of gravity and space in contemporary Gothic architecture. The names of Léonin and Pérotin, appearing from the anonymity of medieval polyphony, also assert a leadership which Paris was to exert in art music until about the beginning of the 15th century.

Following generations indulged mainly in a kind of decorative remodelling of the established repertory of organa, providing them with new, interchangeable clausulas (whereby they showed a persisting concern with rhythm, a clausula being the section of an organum where the tenor, temporarily engaged in a melisma, took part in the rhythmic interplay with the other parts), or else enriching the clausulas with verbal tropes which opened the way to the medieval motet.

Troped clausulas are already motets, but still tentative in two respects: they sometimes have the same text in all the upper parts, and sometimes have a different trope for each part, thereby providing the verbal *concordia discors* that was to prevail in the motet; and the tropes are sometimes religious Latin texts, sometimes secular texts in French. The same clausula music may have been performed both within and without the liturgy, as a troped section of an organum or as an independent piece (a solution that may also have previously applied to the instrumental performance of an untroped clausula). Thus the shift of interest from the liturgical organa and quasi-liturgical conductus to the new genre, typical of the so-called Ars Antiqua period, must be seen as a shift in the purpose of polyphony from the service of God to the entertainment of men, or to art for art's sake.

An entertainment not for everybody. Newly composed motets (with no clausula derivation) show a marked preference for secular themes; but the naivety of some apparently popular texts is quite disingenuous, for the pieces to which they belong have different texts in the various voices, subtly interrelated among themselves and with the tenor. Nor do the motets give up using a fragment of plainsong as a tenor: since this is no longer a liturgical requirement it is meant only to provide hints to the texts of the upper parts (a reversal of the traditional process of polyphony). All the indications point to a milieu of insiders, acquainted with the techniques of liturgical polyphony. Such a milieu is mainly that of the University of Paris, appearing in the first decades of the 13th century as an institution no longer subject to a direct ecclesiastical control, but still having strong ties with ecclesiastical culture and aiming to provide a curriculum orientated towards an ecclesiastical career. Motet texts actually contain references to Paris and to student life, as well as, occasionally, to the composition of a new *triplum* or *quadruplum* (upper parts of a motet); Latin texts, mostly devotional, sometimes touch on points of religious life and mores.

The 13th-century motet actually set polyphony on a course of increasing sophistication – not surprising in the century and place of the most important manifestations of scholastic thought. The very way in which a motet was composed, giving first the chosen tenor a rhythmic *ordo* (i.e. superimposing a rhythmic formula or, later, a preconceived isorhythmic symmetry on its natural rhythm) and then adding the other parts one by one, lent itself to an interaction of musical and intellectual elements; and it prized ingenuity over spontaneity. Then came the notational problems posed by the syllabic setting of the upper parts, which were no longer helped, as in the troped clausula, by the performers' previous knowledge of the music and its rhythm. They were solved by means of different shapes given to the notes and ligatures according to their different rhythmic values. Such *figurae* also made it possible to break the uniformity of modal rhythms; but their adoption gave rise to considerable theoretical argument that appears in a series of writings on *musica figurata*, most of them from Paris. It is unfortunately typical of the period that innovations were supported or opposed by the theorists through captious reasoning more often based on symbolism and analogy than on practicality; thus ternary rhythm, whose preference is ultimately a question of tradition and taste, was justified by reference to a series of conceptual triads, above all the 'perfection' of the Holy Trinity.

Introducing binary rhythm in the practice of art polyphony was but one of the novelties characterizing 14th-century Ars Nova, a period named after the title of a famous tract by Philippe de Vitry (1291–1361). Musical novelty is aggressively displayed in Vitry's motets by the rhythmic animation of the upper voices pitched against slow instrumental tenors, by the occasional introduction of instrumental contratenors and by a general increase of harmonic tensions. A strong intellectual component, less easily perceived by listeners, is the isorhythmic structure underlying the tenors and eventually extended to the contratenors, that is, the sharpening of the previous *ordo* into a complex overlapping of melodic and rhythmic repetitions. It is tempting to describe the hidden rigorous scaffolding as an image of the natural world, its empirical variety ruled by underlying mathematical laws, as it appeared to contemporary thinkers dismayed by the failures of metaphysical speculation; this would give to the assumed naturalness of the Ars Nova a strong scholastic flavour. Actually, it is known that Vitry's rejection of the bias against binary rhythm found strong theoretical support in the musical writings of Jehan des Murs, a mathematician and astronomer who was teaching at the Sorbonne in the 1320s; later Vitry also associated with other modernistic masters such as Leo Hebraeus and Nicholas d'Oresme.

With Vitry, a royal officer, later a bishop, and Guillaume de Machaut (c1300–1377), an almoner for John of Luxembourg and then a canon at Rheims, polyphony, though still produced by ecclesiastics, entered court life. This new development, already evident in the involvement of Vitry's motets in political events, and in his part in the musical insertions of the ROMAN DE FAUVEL (c1316), suggested to Machaut, a most fertile poet and composer, what has been aptly described as a romantic restoration of old chivalric ideals. Most of his motets and his large production of ballades, rondeaux and other lyrical pieces (polyphonic settings of forms belonging to a monophonic tradition of troubadour–trouvère descent) deal with themes of chivalric love. More important, however, are the musical aspects of his art; for, while his motets go further than Vitry's in the development of complex isorhythmic structures, partly extending them to the upper parts, his works in 'ballade style' reverse the long-established tradition of selecting an existing melody as a tenor to be the generating kernel of polyphony; they call instead for a free, newly composed instrumental tenor (often doubled by a contratenor) to support the songlike predominance of the upper vocal part.

There is a humanistic ring in Machaut's obvious intent to evade the introverted narrowness of a polyphony for insiders and to reach out for at least a small audience; and there is often a sensuous expressive appeal in the rich flow of his melodic invention which might seem to anticipate the future. Such qualities, however, are motivated by a nostalgia typical of the most conservative 'waning of the Middle Ages' attitude; nor did Machaut, a highly artificial poet, refrain from the most sophisticated artistry in many of his ballades, rondeaux and lais as well as in his motets. As a result, Machaut's remarkable personal success (made evident by the number and beauty of the manuscripts collecting his works) prompted the following generation to develop the 'ballade style' once more in the direction of a style for connoisseurs, as suitable as the somewhat reduced production of motets for the celebration of historical figures and events (more particularly those connected with Gaston Fébus, Count of Foix, or with the papal court in Avignon). The new specialistic involution went mainly in the direction of a further refinement of rhythm, whose expressive aims, however, appear soon to have given way to a pronounced interest in the aspects of notation, practically resulting in a kind of musical nominalism. The century thus ended on a phase of 'mannered' style and notation, of late labelled ARS SUBTILIOR because of the way in which it exaggerated the already subtle rules of *musica figurata* as described by Jehan des Murs and Philippe de Vitry.

This was also the point of arrival of a parallel line of Italian secular polyphony, which had suddenly appeared in the 1330s from a little-known background of liturgical polyphony whose extent scholars are only beginning to realize. The Italian Ars Nova (as it is often called, although there is a tendency to restyle it trecento music) owed its short-lived brilliance to the lukewarm and discontinuous patronage of some lordly courts of northern Italy and to the slightly more persistent interest of some Florentine circles of intellectuals. Its main charm lies in what would have been called its *dulcedo*, that is, its direct appeal to the listener; but the ecclesiastics who almost exclusively produced it (and had probably derived it from their own practices in private musical entertainment) gradually came under the spell of *subtilitas*, identifying it with the more complex style and notational procedures of French music. The process of assimilation was intensified by the frequent influx of foreign prelates and their musicians during the Great Schism and finally led during the first decade of the 15th century to a complete abandonment of the peculiar forms and techniques of the Italian tradition and to a complete identification with the introverted refinement of the French Ars Subtilior.

5. THE TRANSITION TO THE RENAISSANCE. The strong medieval motivation of the French Ars Nova and the frailty of the Italian equivalent should discourage all attempts to see them as the start of the Renaissance. Doubts have also been cogently raised as to the propriety of a dividing line set at the beginning of the 15th century; even writers who have adopted such a solution (possibly under the spell of a belief that all arts should be aligned chronologically) have felt the need for a distinction between early and late (or high) Renaissance (Reese, Blume), or else for a geographical discrimination according to which a progressive Italian taste would gradually have modified the Gothic elements still haunting the polyphony of the northern countries (Sachs; but a 'Gothic hangover' was mentioned also by Blume). A later date was favoured by Besseler, for whom true Renaissance ideals in music were those stated by Castiglione in his *Il cortegiano*, and by Van den Borren, who identified the musical Renaissance with 'the triumph of pervasive imitation' (c1520). Both writers spoke of 15th-century music as still medieval and largely dominated by the 'late Gothic' ideals and tastes of the Burgundian court. It might be more appropriate to see it as belonging to a transitional phase, during which the widening of the social background supporting art music and the formation of an international style, incorporating elements of the 'peripheral' polyphonic schools into the essentially French 'central' tradition, were the main symptoms of change.

The merging of the two *artes novae* in the sophisticated involution of the Ars Subtilior shows how thin a support even secular polyphony had been able to muster outside its original ecclesiastical milieu. During most of the 15th century men of all stations, in France or elsewhere, continued to find a major source of pleasure in the not necessarily unrefined practices of unwritten music. Even the dukes of Burgundy, famous patrons to famous polyphonists, employed large numbers of minstrels and instrumentalists and sent them periodically to the leading centres of minstrelsy to learn the latest of the trade. As regards Italy, progressive humanists either ignored or despised the 'scholastic' intricacies of polyphony, praising instead the directness of popular (unwritten) music, the only one, according to them, that could lead to a revival of the glories of ancient music. The picture was completely changed, however, by the end of the century, and Renaissance 'society' (that is, upper and upper-middle classes) had come, if not to reject entirely all practices of unwritten music (which long survived more particularly in dance music), at least to see polyphony as the flower of musical artistry.

An important role in the transition was played by the music of the chapels. Neither a new kind of institution (they go back to Carolingian times), nor the purely musical institutions one might assume, chapels at this time were still small groups of ecclesiastics attached to a high prelate or to a secular prince (as Machaut had been attached to John of Luxembourg) and adding to the task of providing private religious services for his household that of aiding in administrative and political affairs. As singing was part of the former, it gradually became a matter of prestige, favoured by the model of the Burgundian court, to have some distinguished musicians among the members of one's chapel, many of whom (Dufay, for instance) held university degrees and were eager to be granted ecclesiastical benefits in reward for their many-sided services. That many such musicians were born and trained in the Low Countries must be related to the prosperity, unaffected by the woes of a chronic war, enjoyed by that region, whose cathedrals were thus allowed to inherit many of the elaborate ways of music-making of the Parisian churches. This also contributed to the stylistic unification that had already been started during the Great Schism and received a new impetus from the following series of councils, as well as from the opportunities they gave to musicians of different countries to meet and know each other. Features of the Italian polyphonic style had already entered the international language of polyphony through the works of foreign composers who had absorbed them while sojourning in Italy: the harmonious sound of the English polyphony (Martin le Franc's *contenance angloise*) made a strong impression at the Council of Konstanz (1414–18) and soon exerted a powerful influence on the formation of the so-called Netherlands or (better) Franco-Flemish style.

It is difficult to determine how long it may have taken for the works of musically gifted chaplains to gain full appreciation from the average court gentleman or lady-in-waiting. During the first half of the century chapel music generally favoured simple settings of parts of the Ordinary for the Mass and of hymns and the *Magnificat* for Vespers, a kind of *Gebrauchsmusik*, most often written in the so-called 'ballade style' (one vocal part supported by instrumental tenor and contratenor). The same style, applied to parts of the Proper, started a new, simpler type of motet, while the medieval isorhythmic motet was not completely abandoned but was reserved for very special celebrations. Court composers, however, appear to have been even more successful with their secular pieces, for the second half of the century is marked by a considerable increase in the production of polyphonic chansons (here, too, English composers and the *contenance angloise* had a considerable influence). Some pieces were such hits that it became fashionable for gentlemen or ladies to adopt their incipits as per-

sonal mottoes and have them embroidered or engraved on possessions. The progress may have been somewhat slower in Italy; yet the courts of Naples, Ferrara and Milan set the pace for an acceptance of the international repertory in spite of all humanistic misgivings; finally, the last decades of the century saw the creation of an Italian secular production, the frottola repertory, setting polyphonically types of texts that had previously belonged to the popular–humanistic tradition.

The tendency of some historians to speak of 'Gothic' elements lingering in the music of the 15th century and to relate them to the influence of the Burgundian court has already been mentioned. While one cannot deny either the weight of that influence or the fact that the dukes of Burgundy nostalgically sought some revival of medieval ideals, it is also evident that their pattern of life, embellished with all the ornaments that art could provide, was soon to set the model for the typical Renaissance man. Similarly, the adjective 'Gothic' might also need reconsideration. The stylistic phenomena to which it is applied appear to have had their starting-point in the need felt by composers, shortly before the middle of the century, to set the Ordinary of the Mass as a cycle, unified by the use in all five sections of similar head-motifs and the same tenor (often of secular origin). There were no liturgical or practical reasons for such procedures, but only an artistic motivation and a feeling for a coherent order and balance of parts, neither of which have Gothic connotations. That the lesser composers (but occasionally also the greatest) may often have paid great attention to the technical side of the innovation and engaged in ambitious exhibitions of contrapuntal and notational ingenuity (including canonic writing) should be seen as deriving from a persisting habit among polyphonists (encouraged in the major chapels by the competition arising from their larger numbers of musical chaplains) of writing for their colleagues even more than for an external audience – a trait more likely to be related to a scholastic than to a Gothic turn of mind. Disregarding the most exceptional tours de force, it is worth noticing that the new developments were of great importance for the future of music, marking for the first time the awareness of a distinction to be made between a religious and a secular style, or, at later times, between serious and lighter genres. That technical complexity was required to reach an intensity and depth of expression has always been a persistent feeling through the centuries and is not the least momentous element in the legacy of the Middle Ages.

BIBLIOGRAPHY

F. Ludwig: 'Die geistliche nichtliturgische, weltliche einstimmige und die mehrstimmige Musik des Mittelalters', *Handbuch der Musikgeschichte*, ed. G. Adler (Frankfurt am Main, 1924, rev. 2/1930/R1961)

H. Besseler: *Die Musik des Mittelalters und der Renaissance* (Potsdam, 1931)

T. Gérold: *Histoire de la musique des origines à la fin du XIV<sup>e</sup> siècle* (Paris, 1936)

A. Pirro: *Histoire de la musique de la fin du XIV<sup>e</sup> siècle à la fin du XVI<sup>e</sup>* (Paris, 1940)

G. Reese: *Music in the Middle Ages* (New York, 1940)

A. Hughes, ed.: *Early Medieval Music up to 1300*, NOHM, ii (1954, rev. 2/1955)

S. Corbin: *L'église à la conquête de sa musique* (Paris, 1960)

A. Hughes and G. Abraham, eds.: *Ars Nova and the Renaissance: 1300–1540*, NOHM, iii (1960)

N. Bridgman: *La vie musicale au quattrocento* (Paris, 1964)

A. Seay: *Music in the Medieval World* (Englewood Cliffs, NJ, 1965)

J. Caldwell: *Medieval Music* (London, 1978)

R. Hoppin: *An Introduction to Medieval Music* (New York, 1978)

NINO PIRROTTA

**Medieval drama.**

I. Introduction. II. Liturgical drama. III. Vernacular drama. IV. Medieval drama in Eastern Europe. V. The end of the Middle Ages.

### *I. Introduction*

1. Definitions, genres and scholarship. 2. Elements and traditions of medieval music drama.

1. DEFINITIONS, GENRES AND SCHOLARSHIP. The many Latin terms used by medieval writers to refer to dramatic representations include *ordo*, *officium*, *ludus*, *festum*, *miraculum* (rare), *misterium* and, most frequently, *representatio*. Each vernacular has an equivalent variety. None of these terms is used consistently, nor is any used exclusively (cf English 'play') to denote a drama. The terms 'tragedy' and 'comedy' are very rare and are not applicable in their traditional meanings. Of the above terms, *ordo* and *officium* are commonly used to describe liturgical ceremonies as well as plays; this draws attention to a fundamentally important but elusive distinction between ritual and drama. When describing vernacular plays, medieval writers used the terms 'miracle' and 'mystery' without distinction; in this article, 'miracle' denotes a play based on the life of a saint, 'mystery' a play on a biblical or apocryphal subject.

The corpus of medieval drama in Latin and the major European vernaculars is huge. It comprises, essentially, two types of religious drama. In the first, traditionally called the 'liturgical drama', music is integral: the whole text of the play is sung monophonically and the language is Latin. In the second, vernacular drama, the music may still be important, but only as an adjunct: the main action is conducted in the spoken vernacular, with songs and instrumental music, plainchant and polyphony, introduced as appropriate. The principal vernaculars to be considered are English, French, German, Italian and Spanish, in all of which a substantial repertory of plays has survived; and there is a smaller corpus from eastern Europe. In addition to these religious plays there are isolated secular plays of various types from the 13th century onwards. It is not until the end of the Middle Ages that coherent traditions of secular drama can be traced (English interludes, French farces and *sotties*, etc). In all medieval secular plays the music is incidental.

An older generation of scholars (Chambers, Young etc) assumed that the liturgical drama was not only earlier in time but seminal in effect – that medieval drama evolved as a continuous single species from the amoeba of simple, formal beginnings (in the famous QUEM QUERITIS dialogue) to the *homo sapiens* of ever more realistic forms in the mystery cycles of the later Middle Ages. Such metaphors of organic growth, together with the patterns they imposed on the material, have been increasingly questioned over the years (see Hardison, 1965). Unfortunately a consideration of the nature and function of music in medieval drama has not played much part either in the formation or in the critique of the traditional interpretation.

The first substantial collection of the musical texts of liturgical plays, Coussemaker's *Drames liturgiques du moyen-âge* (1860), still holds the field, despite its inaccuracies; but numerous single plays are available in scholarly periodicals and separate editions (see for example Lipphardt, 1963, Krieg, 1956, Vecchi, 1954) and in performing editions with English translation (see

Smoldon, 1960 etc, and Greenberg, 1959). The ten plays of the important Fleury Playbook have been published in an edition by Tintori and Monterosso (1958). The musical insertions into vernacular plays are rarely notated. There is no collected edition of such pieces (but see Brown, 1963, for a late French secular repertory).

Musical study of the drama still lags behind the literary; but the studies and articles of Lipphardt (especially his 'Liturgische Dramen' in *MGG*), of Corbin (in *LaMusicaE*, on the Song of the Sibyl (1952), and on the planctus, in *La déposition*, 1960) and of Smoldon (*NOHM*, ii, and *Grove 5*) are the necessary starting-point for serious study. On the literary side the works of fundamental importance in English are E. K. Chambers's *The Medieval Stage* (1903), still unsurpassed as a general survey, and Karl Young's *The Drama of the Medieval Church* (1933), which gives the literary texts of almost the entire corpus of Latin religious drama. Young's work must now be supplemented from Walther Lipphardt (1975). Grace Frank's *The Medieval French Drama* (1954) and N. D. Shergold's *A History of the Spanish Stage* (1967) are the only scholarly books in English covering their subjects; there are no equivalents for German or Italian plays.

In this article plays from the 10th century up to the Reformation are surveyed. The ecclesiastical upheavals of the 16th century brought about the suppression of medieval traditions of religious drama in Protestant countries and modified them severely in countries which remained Catholic.

Controversy has gone on for years as to what constitutes drama. For some inquirers dialogue has been essential; for others, impersonation (pretending to be someone in the story). Thus, for Young (1933), the moving ecclesiastical ceremonies of Holy Week are only in the loosest sense dramatic, since the element of impersonation is almost lacking. For present purposes, and indeed for the medieval period in principle, the concept of impersonation cannot be regarded as crucial – except in monologue. In this article the widest definition is used, admitting as drama any action in which the speeches, or songs, of two or more personages (realistic or symbolic) are opposed or juxtaposed.

2. ELEMENTS AND TRADITIONS OF MEDIEVAL MUSIC DRAMA. No-one now believes either that European drama perished utterly with the destruction of the Roman theatres in the 6th century, or that it had to be invented again in the 10th. All the evidence, fragmentary as it is, testifies to a wealth of dramatic activity of various kinds in the early Middle Ages, much of it involving music. Travelling minstrels, variously designated as *mimi*, *histriones*, *joculatores*, *menestrelli*, *lusatores* etc, combined music and acting with other sorts of entertainment – tumbling, bear-leading, juggling, puppetry (*see* MINSTREL). These were professionals, playing (in many senses) for hire. Their repertory may have included simple pieces of the *fabliau* type (a comic tale, often grotesque or obscene), such as the *Interludium de clerico et puella* (13th century) and *Le garçon et l'aveugle* (13th century; see Axton, 1974); mimed monologues, such as Rutebeuf's *Dit de l'herberie* (13th century; cf the sales talk of the spice merchant in the Resurrection plays); scolding matches, 'flytings', *estrifs*, or demonstrations of clever repartee, such as *Le roi d'Angleterre et le jongleur d'Ely* (13th century); courtly narratives with interpolated song, such as the *chante-*

*fable* AUCASSIN ET NICOLETTE (13th century); and semi-dramatic lyrics, like *Mei amic*, an 11th-century Provençal song dialogue for the Annunciation. To have some cognizance of this professional and of other traditions is essential if the musical elements of the drama are to be seen in their proper nature.

One important tradition is that of the dance-song, both courtly and popular. The dancing by courtiers and their ladies of 'rondets de carole' was described by Jehan Bretel in the *Tournoi de Chauvenci* (13th century); and scraps of (apparently) courtly dance-song are preserved in *Guillaume de Dole* by Jean Renart and in other courtly poems (refrains; *see* REFRAIN). Knowledge of popular dance-song is gained chiefly from courtly adaptations or imitations – though in this early period the distinction between two 'cultures', courtly and popular, is far less sharp than later. Such miniature song-dramas include versions of *Bele Aelis* (e.g. that by the trouvère Baude de la Kakerie); the Provençal song of the April queen, *Al'entrada del tens clar*; perhaps *Tempus est jocundum* from the CARMINA BURANA (*c*1230); and the English *Maiden in the mor lay* (Dronke, 1968). In German drama especially (from the later Passion play of the *Carmina burana* onwards), Mary Magdalen's sinful life is depicted as a dance with her in the centre; she buys cosmetics, sings and dances to entice her lovers. A different type of courtly activity produced the Teutonic warrior-play; its existence and the presence of musical effects in it were mentioned by the German chronicler Gerhoh of Reichersberg (*c*1160), and its influence can be traced in the sung liturgical–political play *Antichristus* (*c*1160) from Tegernsee (Axton, 1974). A later courtly milieu delighted in the dramatic spectacle of the chivalric tournament, a species of mimed heroic drama at which ladies were present and music and dancing added to the social delights (Wickham, 1959).

Other types of lyric besides dance-song may have sprouted into drama. These include the *aube* or ALBA (lovers' dawn-song), the CHANSON DE TOILE ('weaving-song'; usually a woman's dramatic monologue), the *bergerie* (shepherds' games) and the pastourelle (knight encounters maiden). The two last, for instance, with associated music, form the basis of Adam de La Halle's *Robin et Marion* (see §III, 2(iii) below). Another lyric type, the debate (Provençal *joc partit*; Fr. JEU-PARTI) is self-evidently a dramatic form and has a long musical as well as poetic history (*see* TROUBADOURS, TROUVÈRES). Sung dramatic debates range from the sublime (Hildegard of Bingen's *Ordo virtutum*, *c*1155, in the morality tradition) to the near-ridiculous (some of the courtly riddles of Adam de La Halle and his contemporaries in 13th-century Arras). However, of all European song forms, that which most specifically contributed to the drama is the Italian LAUDA SPIRITUALE; the earliest Italian vernacular plays are *laude* in dialogue (see §III, 3(iv) below). But the tradition of the Latin PLANCTUS or lament was even more widespread, and some historians have seen the whole of medieval drama embryonically in the scene where Mary sorrows at the foot of the cross. In German drama the *Marienklage* is of central importance (see §III, 2(i) below). The planctus naturally developed as sung dialogue between the lamenter and the bystanders (Mary and the apostle St John; Rachel and her consolers).

Another element of importance particularly for the formation of the religious drama was the Song of the Sibyl, a prophecy of Christ's birth, of great antiquity. It found its way into the Christmas liturgy in the 8th century and in the drama belongs with the *Ordo prophetarum*, the Procession of the Prophets. Its music is well as its words are traditional (Corbin, *RdM*, 1952). The Procession of the Prophets originated from a famous sermon *Contra judeos*, attributed to St Augustine, which was read at Christmas Matins and incorporated the Song of the Sibyl and many other prophecies. Other sermons, such as the Spanish *Castissimum Marie virginis*, may also have been dramatized (Donovan, 1958).

However, the most imaginative and impressive form of drama in the early Middle Ages remains the liturgy itself. Honorius of Autun, in *Gemma anime* (*c*1100), described the Mass as a drama analogous to ancient tragedy (trans. Hardison, 1965; Latin text in Young, 1933, i, 82):

> our tragic author [i.e. the celebrant] represents by his gestures in the theatre of the Church before the Christian people the struggle of Christ ... By the extension of his hands he represents the extension of Christ on the Cross. By the chant of the Preface he expresses the cry of Christ on the Cross.

More strikingly dramatic than the Mass in their imaginative impact are, in particular, the ceremonies of Holy Week. The blessing of palms, for instance, on Palm Sunday was followed by a procession to a place symbolizing the Mount of Olives, to the singing of *Gloria laus*. Sometimes, especially in Germany, a figure representing Christ riding on an ass (the *Palmesel*) was brought into the church. (A procession is part of the action in many liturgical plays; the Corpus Christi procession, instituted in 1264 (confirmed 1311), contributed to the growth of vernacular drama.)

Two ceremonies are particularly dramatic: the *Depositio crucis*, commemorating the burial of Christ; and the *Elevatio crucis*, celebrating the Resurrection (Young, 1933, i, 112ff; Corbin, *La déposition*, 1960). A striking liturgical action, which was to have a long history both in the liturgical drama and in the mystery cycles and Passion plays, was sometimes combined with these two ceremonies and sometimes with the return of the Palm Sunday procession to the church; this was the HARROWING OF HELL, in which Christ descends to Hell, calls on Satan to open the gates ('Tollite portas'; cf Psalm xxiv) and releases the imprisoned souls of the patriarchs. At the abbey of Barking, Essex, in the 14th century these souls were represented by the members of the convent who were 'imprisoned' in the chapel of St Mary Magdalen. The existence of such a wide variety of dramatic and semi-dramatic ceremonies within the authorized liturgy of Mass and Office should be some safeguard against placing too high an importance on the single dialogue-trope, the *Quem queritis*, as the source of everything that can truly be called drama inside and outside the medieval church.

## II. Liturgical drama

1. Chronology and distribution. 2. The repertory: dramatic and musical material. 3. The repertory: dramatic presentation. 4. Sources. 5. Notations and problems of transcription. 6. Musical style and musical structure. 7. Interpretation and performance: (i) The Padua 'Annunciation' (ii) Mézières' 'Presentation' (iii) 'Play of Daniel' (iv) Fleury 'Play of the Innocents'.

1. CHRONOLOGY AND DISTRIBUTION. Scholars have continued to use the traditional term 'liturgical drama' to describe the corpus of sung religious dialogues, ceremonies and plays in Latin since it was first coined (Clément, 1848–51). Despite its drawbacks – many of

the plays are para-liturgical rather than strictly a part of the liturgy – the term has more than one appropriateness: the plays are found for the most part in liturgical books, and they are animated by the spirit of the liturgy and not by that of the theatre, a totally anachronistic term and concept. Their liturgical spirit, a spirit of ceremonial reverence and joy, adds to the difficulty already discussed of distinguishing between liturgical drama and the drama of the liturgy, between play and ceremony. On the evidence of text and music alone the distinction is often impossible. Helmut de Boor (1967) defined ceremony (*ordo, officium*) as 'everything that was created for presentation within the limits of ecclesiastical ritual'; play, as everything outside the realm of liturgy, whether in Latin or in the vernacular, whether performed in church or out. But a distinction that is so hard to draw in practice perhaps does not matter greatly. What matters is to regard each piece as an entity, combining in itself the elements of text, music and drama. Unless special circumstances are involved, all types of text are here referred to as 'plays'.

The complexity of the repertory can be gauged by considering as a starting-point some manuscripts associated with one of the main dramatic centres, the abbey of St Martial at Limoges. They were formerly in the abbey library and reflect the intense musical activities of an 'école aquitaine' (Chailley, 1960). Out of a group of nearly 20 manuscripts, three are of special interest. *F-Pn* lat.1154 (9th–10th century) contains (among other items, liturgical and non-liturgical) planctus (laments) on the death of Charlemagne and others, pieces on the Last Judgment, hymns, a prose to St Martial and the Song of the Sibyl (*see* EARLY LATIN SECULAR SONG). *F-Pn* lat.1240 (10th century) contains the earliest surviving version of the *Quem queritis* (facs. in Young, 1933, i, pl.6; conjectural transcr. in Smoldon, 1968). *F-Pn* lat.1139 (1096–9) contains an isolated version of the *Quem queritis* (i.e. without liturgical context), with rubric 'Hoc est de mulieribus'; the play *Sponsus*, followed by a prophet play; and an *Ordo Rachelis*, a short liturgical play of the Holy Innocents containing Rachel's dramatic lament. (For this repertory as a whole *see* SAINT MARTIAL and SOURCES, MS, §§II–III.)

These three manuscripts alone provide an ensemble of items, all of them written down by the end of the 11th century and some much earlier. They show how diverse elements can be found in the same milieu (allowing for a range of date) and, in the case of the third manuscript, how at an early date the same compiler would collect plays both 'rudimentary' (*Quem queritis*) and 'advanced' (*Sponsus*, which contains vernacular stanzas and refrains) with a liturgical ceremony (*Ordo Rachelis*) which is in effect no more than a simple dramatic trope of two speeches to the responsory *Sub altare Dei*. It cannot be too often emphasized that there is no orderly chronological development to be discerned in the liturgical drama. The fact that the well-known description of a quite elaborate *Visitatio sepulchri* play at Winchester (see Young, 1933, i, 249) dates from the 10th century is a further reminder. A useful chronological index of liturgical plays, based on Young, was compiled by Hardison (1965, appx II).

The complexity of time is matched by a complexity of place: the liturgical drama was not diffused in equal richness all over Europe. In addition to the 'school' of St Martial already mentioned, St Gall (Switzerland) and

Winchester were important early centres. The latter may have derived ceremonies from Ghent and Fleury (St Benoît-sur-Loire); and Fleury was sufficiently active in the 12th century to have produced the playbook which now bears its name (this attribution is questioned; Corbin, 1953, proposed nearby Blois). In France 'the greatest number of texts and the longest plays come from the northern provinces of Rheims and Sens' (Wright, 1936). Here, as elsewhere, both monasteries and cathedrals contributed. An expanded Easter dialogue is associated with the region of Passau (southeast Germany), the Mary Magdalen scene (with introductory laments) with Normandy and Norman Sicily (Lipphardt, *MGG*). In Italy, Padua and Cividale were especially productive; and in Spain, the cities of Catalonia and the island of Mallorca (Donovan, 1958). The liturgical drama, despite its early start in 10th-century Winchester, is not widely represented in the records of medieval England; but Lichfield, Barking, Lincoln, Malmesbury and York are known to have had plays. It should further be remembered that England was a hub of Norman culture in the two centuries following the Norman Conquest; and the widespread appointment of Norman abbots and bishops is likely to have stimulated the introduction of liturgical ceremonies and plays from one of the liveliest dramatic regions in Europe. However, no single extended dramatic representation survives.

2. THE REPERTORY: DRAMATIC AND MUSICAL MATERIAL. The analysis of the repertory by type and subject has the authority of Young (1933). His analysis has been followed by most later scholars of the drama and by musicologists and is still a convenient frame of understanding. Its neat and helpful divisions and the orderliness with which simple examples precede complex ones must not, however, mislead the inquirer into false assumptions, already referred to, about orderly chronological development. As liturgical drama is in the strictest sense music drama, to describe the repertory of some 600 texts assembled by Young (1933) and Donovan (1958, from north-east Spain) is in fact to describe the scope of the musical repertory.

The simplest forms of dramatic ceremony or play are dialogue tropes of the introit of the Mass (see fig.1). By far the most important and common are the *Quem queritis* dialogues of Easter (quoted in TROPE (i), §3 and ex.2) and Christmas. At Easter the dialogue is between 'Christicole' (worshippers of Christ) and 'celicole' (dwellers in Heaven); in many texts the former are precisely identified with the three Marys visiting the tomb of Christ and the latter with angels at the tomb. At Christmas the dialogue is between the shepherds seeking the crib and the midwives (non-scriptural). Other dialogue tropes exist: for example, a 14th-century Spanish one for the Assumption of the BVM (Donovan).

Particularly in its enlarged forms the Easter dialogue is frequently found, from the 10th century to the 16th, in a different liturgical position. Instead of being attached to the introit of the Mass, it is placed after the third responsory of Matins of Easter, *Dum transisset sabbatum*; it is also amplified by prefatory and concluding sentences, mostly well-known antiphons. The enlarged dialogues are known generically as the *Visitatio sepulchri*; they account for over 400 surviving texts, about two-thirds of the total repertory. Three degrees of dramatic elaboration are normally distin-

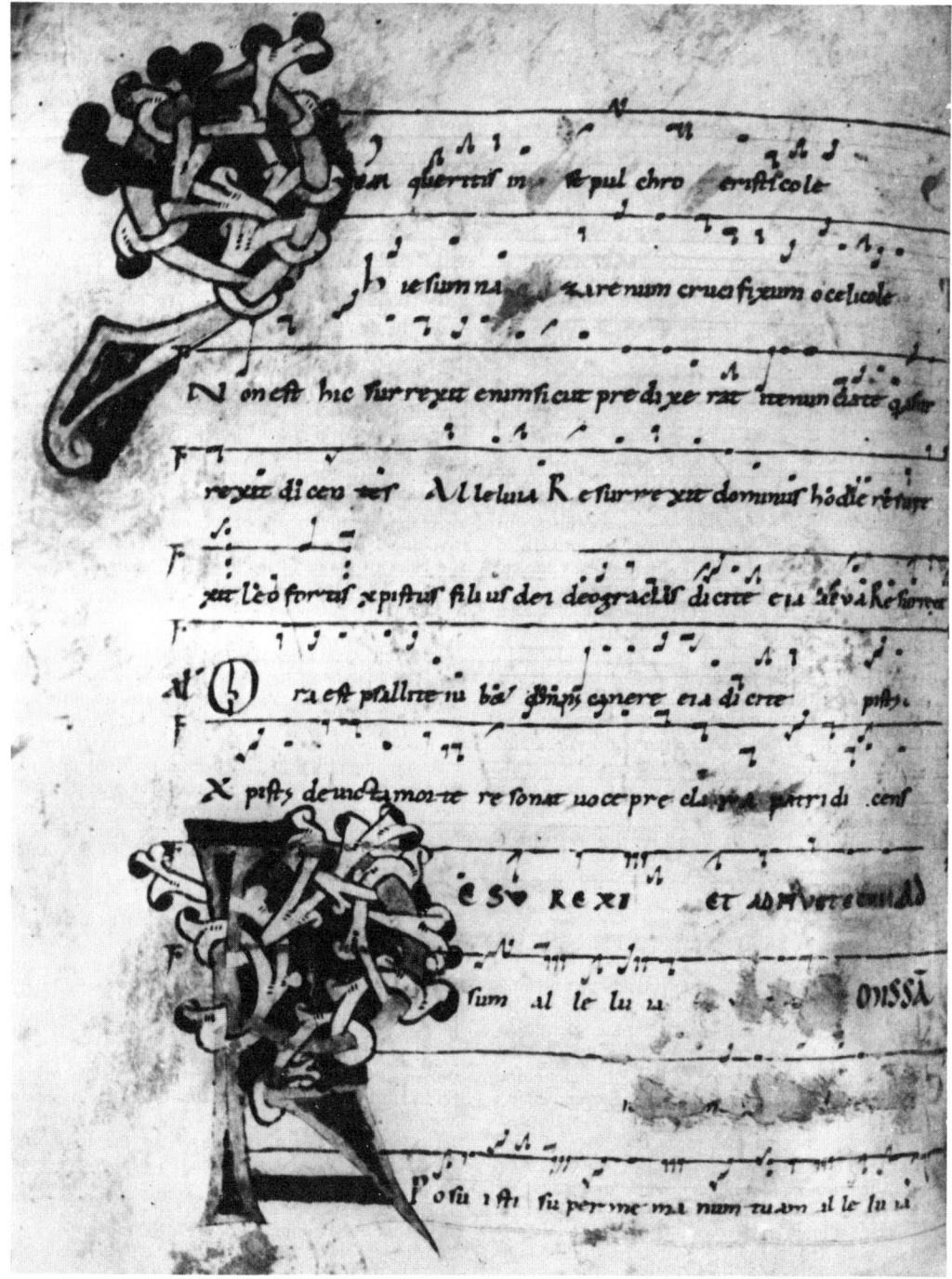

1. A version of the 'Quem queritis' dialogue from a Ravenna troper, 11th–12th century (I-MOd O.1.17, f.104v); the dialogue leads via the trope 'Alleluia resurrexit' into the introit 'Resurrexi' and the Mass; the neumes are heighted around a single line

guished: 'one in which the dialogue is conducted by the Marys and the angel, a second in which are added the apostles, Peter and John, and a third which provides a role for the risen Christ' (Young, 1933, i, p.239). The Visitatio sepulchri, it is essential to realize, is never

extended backwards to include scenes from the Passion and Crucifixion; it exists solely to celebrate the joy of the Resurrection.

Musically, these elaborations call for additions of various kinds. Traditional antiphons, already mentioned, are added, such as *Alleluia, Surrexit Dominus de sepulchro* (found in such early books as Hartker's Antiphonary, *CH-SGs* 390–91; PalMus, 2nd ser., i); *Venite et videte locum* (Hartker, and Winchester Troper); *Currebant duo simul* (Hartker); and, by way of preface, [*Et dicebant ad invicem:*] *Quis revolvet nobis lapidem ab ostio monumenti?* (Hartker). The Easter sequence *Victime paschali* (11th century, attributed to Wipo, an imperial chaplain) is sung in various dramatic arrangements but always to the traditional melody (*Liber usualis*, 780). Hymns, for example *Jesu nostra redempcio*, are sung by the Marys or by the apostles, and *Christ ist erstanden* by the congregation near the end (before the final *Te Deum*). Laments (planctus) are sung by the three Marys as they approach the tomb, the most common set of three being the 15-syllable *Heu, nobis internas mentes, Jam percusso ceu pastore* and *Sed eamus et ad eius*; the music of these is thought to be non-Gregorian (see §II, 6). Exx.1–3 (pp.26–7) give transcriptions of (1) the introit trope in its simplest form to the traditional melody (*F-Pn* lat.8898; 12th-century rituale from Soissons); (2) an expanded dialogue with dramatization of the *Victime paschali* (*Pn* lat.10482; 14th-century breviary from Paris or Melun); (3) the opening of a *Visitatio sepulchri* with the laments of the Marys, in which the traditional words are modified and a new melody provided (*CH-EN* 314, from Engelberg).

Four liturgical plays celebrating the Resurrection in even more elaborate forms were assembled by Young under the title *Ludus paschalis* (the nearest manuscript title is *Ordo paschalis*); they are from Klosterneuburg, Tours, ?Origny-Ste-Benoîte (near St Quentin) and ?Fleury. The longest of these, from Tours, unfortunately incomplete, includes scenes between Pilate and the Roman soldiers, between the Marys and two merchants, the appearance of Christ to the disciples, and the incident of doubting Thomas. The play in the Origny manuscript has rubrics in French and some portions of the dialogue. Seven further plays of the Easter season celebrate the journey to Emmaus (the PEREGRINUS plays). The feasts of the Ascension and of Whitsuntide were celebrated with dramatic liturgical ceremonies and, often, ingenious machines; they do not, however, seem to have developed as drama, except perhaps in Catalonia (see Donovan).

The most complex of all liturgical plays related to Easter are Passion plays (two in the *Carmina burana* manuscript, one from Sulmona and one from Monte Cassino; see Sticca, 1970). The most interesting is the longer of the two Passion plays in the *Carmina burana*. Although normally classed as liturgical drama, this and the other lesser Passions are borderline cases. Their inclusion is warranted by the fact that they are almost entirely in Latin and set to music throughout. (There is no such thing as a spoken religious drama in Latin at this period, except for the moral, pseudo-Terentian plays of the 10th-century nun HROTSWITHA of Gandersheim.) The reasons for excluding them would be that they have no demonstrable connection with the liturgy, and that they treat a subject, Christ's Passion, which is outside the sphere of joyous celebration that characterizes the liturgical drama. The theme of the human, suffering Christ is the proper province of vernacular drama. Musically there is a difference too: 'The number of liturgical pieces incorporated [in the major *Carmina burana* Passion] is relatively small, and ... these are used chiefly as choral introductions to separate

scenes' (Young, 1933, i, 533). Unfortunately the neumes of this play are unheighted in the manuscript; most of the music is therefore locked up in a code that cannot be broken. There are, however, a number of identifiable melodies (see Lipphardt, *MGG*), including those of the laments *Planctus ante nescia* and *Flete, fideles anime*. These well-known compositions in sequence form had an independent existence which is well attested (ex.4 gives the opening of the melody of

Ex.4 *I-Pc* C. 56 ff.32-32v

*Here begins the lament of the Blessed Virgin Mary*: Lament, O faithful in heart; lament, O best sisters: that lamentation and tears, these tokens of grief, may be multiplied. Let the womb of the mother lament; I suffer the pangs of Mary the mother, I who used to be counted happy in the child I bore.

*Flete, fideles* from *I-Pc* C.56). The planctus is a non-liturgical genre. Its performance in a liturgical context was invariably on Good Friday (Corbin, *LaMusicaE*), a day on which liturgical plays like those so far described were never presented. Its use here, and frequent occurrence in vernacular Passion plays (see §III, 2(i) below), show the introduction of an important new musical element. It has also led to the question, fascinating but insoluble, as to which came first, Passion play or planctus. (If an origin for the Passion play is to be sought, the most obvious – the traditional liturgical recitation of the Gospel accounts during Holy Week – must apparently be discounted, since until the 15th century the recitation was performed by a single deacon (Young, 1910).)

The other great season of liturgical rejoicing, Christmas, also produced its plays. The dramatic centre of these is again the moment of celebration – the adoration of the shepherds (*Officium pastorum*) and the adoration of the Magi (*Officium stelle*). In comparison with those of Easter, few introit tropes survive for the Mass of Christmas. Once again, the documents do not support any theory of gradual evolution or of regular imitation by 'Christmas playwrights' of Easter successes. Some 20 Christmas plays can be dated as early as the 11th century: about half are fairly simple dialogues (shep-

Ex.1 *F-Pn* lat. 8898 f. 97

Quem que – ri – tis in se – pul – chro o chri – sti – co – le? Ihe – sum na – za – re – num cru – ci – fi – xum o ce – li – co – le. Non est hic; sur – re – xit sic – ut pre – di – xe – rat. I – te nun – ci – a – te qui – a sur – re – xit. Al – le – lu – ya, re – sur – re – xit do – mi – nus. Ho – di – e, re – sur – re – xit le – o for – tis, Chri – ste fi – li – us de – i, de – o gra – ti – as. Di – ci – te: e – y – a!

Whom do you seek in the tomb, O followers of Christ? Jesus of Nazareth who was crucified, O celestial ones. He is not here; he has risen as he foretold. Go and tell that he is risen. Alleluya, the Lord is risen. Today a strong lion is risen, Christ the Son of God, thanks be to God. Sing: eya!

Ex.2 *F-Pn* lat.10482 ff.176v–177

*Angeli ad mulieres:* Quem que – ri – tis in se – pul – chro o chri – sti – co – le?

*Mulieres ad angelum:* Je – sum na – za – re – num cru – ci – fi – xum o ce – li – co – le.

*Angeli:* Non est hic; sur – rex – it si – cut pre – di – xe – rat. I – te nun – ci – a – te qui – a sur – rex – it.

*Tunc vertant se mulieres ad chorum et veniant cantando prosam:* Vic – ti – mae [pas – cha – li] lau – des im – mo – lant, chri – sti – a – ni.

Ag – nus re – de – mit o – ves, Chri – stus in – no – cens pa – tri re – con – ci – li – a – vit pec – ca – to – res.

Mors et vi – ta du – el – lo con – fli – xe – re mi – ran – do; dux vi – te mor – tu – us reg – nat vi – vus.

*Tunc cantor stet in medio chori et dicat mulieribus:* Dic no – bis, Ma – ri – a, quid vi – dis – ti in vi – a?

*Prima mulier:* Se – pul – chrum Chri – sti vi – ven – tis et glo – ri – am vi – di re – sur – gen – tis,

*Secunda mulier:* An – ge – li – cos tes – tes su – da – ri – um et ves – tes.

*Tercia mulier:* Sur – rex – it Chri – stus spes nos – tra, pre – ce – det su – os in Ga – ly – le – am.

*Cantor:* Cre-den-dum est ma-gis so-li Ma-ri-e ve-ra-ci quam Ju-de-o-rum tur-be fal-la-ci.

*Chorus:* Sci-mus Chri-stum sur-rex-is-se a___ mor-tu-is ve-re; tu no-bis vic-tor rex mi-se-re-re.

*The angels sing to the women*: Whom do you seek in the tomb, O followers of Christ? *The women sing to the angels*: Jesus of Nazareth who was crucified, O celestial ones. *The angels sing*: He is not here; he has risen as he foretold. Go and tell that he is risen. *Then the women turn to the choir and come singing the prose*: Christians offer a sacrifice of praise to the paschal victim. A lamb has redeemed the sheep, sinless Christ has reconciled sinners to the Father. Death and life contended in that stupendous combat; the Lord of life, who died, reigns immortal. *Then the cantor stands in mid-choir and sings to the women*: Tell us, Mary, what did you see in the way? *The first woman*: The tomb of the living Christ and the glory of the resurrection. *The second woman*: The angels as witness, the shroud and the napkin. *The third woman*: Christ our hope is risen, and will go before his own to Galilee. *The cantor*: Truthful Mary alone is more to be believed than the crowd of deceitful Jews. *Choir*: We know Christ is indeed risen from the dead; have mercy upon us, victor, King.

Ex.3 *CH-EN* 314 ff.74*v*–75*v*

*Antiphona. Sola:* He-u! no-bis in-ter-nas men-tes quan-ti pul-sant ge-mi-tus pro nos-tro con-so-la-to-re,___ quo pri-va-mur___ mi-se-re, quem cru-del-is Iu-de-o-rum___ mor-ti de-dit___ po-pu-lus.

*Antiphona. Sola:* Iam___ per-cus-so ceu___ pas-to-re, o-ves___ er-rant mi-se-re; sic ma-gis-tro dis-ce-den-te,___ tur-ban-tur dis-ci-pu-li, at-que nos, ab-sen-te e-o,___ do-lor te-net___ ni-mi-us.

*Antiphona. Sola scilicet Maria Magdalena:* Sed___ e-a-mus et___ ad e-ius pro-pe-re-mus, tum-u-lum; si di-le-xi-mus vi-ven-tem___ di-li-ga-mus___ mor-tu-um.

*Omnes tres:* Quis re-vol-vet___ no-bis ab hos-ti-o la-pi-dem quem te-ge-re san-ctum cer-ni-mus se-pul-chrum?

*Angeli:* Quem que-ri-tis o tre-mu-lae mu-li-e-res in hoc tu-mu-lo ge-men-tes?

*Antiphona. Omnes tres:* Je-sum Na-za-re-num___ cru-ci-fi-xum, o ce-li-co-le.

*Antiphon. One woman*: Alas! what deep sighs rack our inmost souls on account of our Comforter, of whom we unfortunates are deprived, whom the cruel race of Jews gave to be slain. *Antiphon. [Another] woman*: As, when their shepherd is struck down, the sheep wander in distress: so now the disciples are troubled when their master goes away, and in his absence no-one's grief is greater than ours. *Antiphona. [Another] woman, that is Mary Magdalene*: But let us go and hurry to his tomb; if we rejoiced in him when he was alive, let us also care for him now he is dead. *All three*: Who for us will roll away from the entrance the stone which conceals the holy tomb from our eyes? *Angels*: Whom do you seek, O fearful women, weeping by this tomb? *Antiphon. All three*: Jesus of Nazareth who was crucified, O celestial ones.

herds and midwives, the latter not usually identified by name); the others are elaborately developed plays about the Magi and Herod (*Ordo ad representandum Herodem* is the Fleury title), sometimes including a meeting with the shepherds as well, and presented at the end of Matins. Following the *Officium stelle* of Laon (*F-LA* 263) in unbroken sequence is the scene of the Slaughter of the Innocents (no music in the manuscript); in other sources the scene is a separate play-unit, as required by its liturgical affiliation – Holy Innocents Day (28 December), nine days before the Magi feast, Epiphany (6 January).

Musically as well as textually the elements of the Christmas plays are analogous to those of Easter: an introit trope using an 'original' melody (the Christmas melody usually differs from the Easter one); traditional antiphons (e.g. *Venite, adoremus eum*, of Epiphany); melodies of apparently secular character and/or origin (see the exchange *Salve, pater inclite* between Herod and his son in the Fleury play); sequences (e.g. Notker's *Quid tu, virgo* – Fleury and Freising); hymns (e.g. *Hostis Herodes impie, Salvete, flores martyrum*); a formal planctus, Rachel's lament, the centrepiece of liturgical plays on the Slaughter of the Innocents, in the Freising text entitled *Ordo Rachelis*. Exx.5 and 6 give a Christmas dialogue headed 'Quod fit in nocte natalis Domini', from Padua (*I-Pc* C.56, a processional); and the dramatic exchange between Herod and Archelaus, from the Fleury Playbook.

Ex.5 *I-Pc* C. 56 f.1

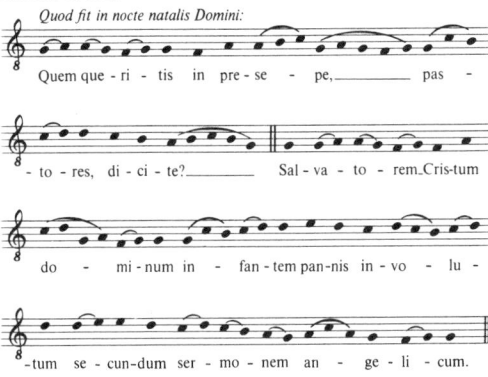

Quod fit in nocte natalis Domini:

Quem que-ri-tis in pre-se - pe,_____ pas - -to - res, di-ci - te?_____ Sal-va - to - rem_Cris-tum do - mi-num in - fan-tem pan-nis in-vo - lu - -tum se - cun-dum ser - mo - nem an - ge - li - cum.

*What is done on Christmas Eve:* Whom do you seek in the manger, O shepherds, say? Our Saviour, Christ the Lord, a child wrapped in swaddling clothes, as the angels told.

The only fully comprehensive Christmas play is that in the *Carmina burana*; the greater part is notated, but in unheighted neumes without indication of pitch or rhythm. The play contains all the episodes discussed above and opens in addition with an *Ordo prophetarum*: Augustine sits enthroned with Isaiah, Daniel, the Sibyl and Aaron on his right, and their opponents, the leader of the Synagogue with a group of Jews, on his left. The Procession of the Prophets has already been mentioned (§I, 3); it was dramatized many times as a separate Christmas play (see also §III, 2(ii)).

The plays of Easter and Christmas account numerically for nearly the whole repertory of liturgical drama. The few other plays, however, include some of the most remarkable as individual compositions: on an Old Testament subject, the *Play of Daniel* from Beauvais; from the New Testament, the Fleury *Raising of Lazarus*

and *Conversion of St Paul*; of plays dealing with the end of all things, the Provençal *Sponsus* and the Tegernsee *Antichristus*; and a group of saints' plays (miracles), all honouring St Nicholas (Fleury Playbook and elsewhere).

With the plays of the saints should perhaps be classed those which honour the greatest saint of all, the Blessed Virgin, at her four major feasts – the Presentation in the Temple, the Annunciation (then celebrated in December), the Purification (presentation of Jesus in the Temple) and the Assumption. Of these, two Annunciation plays from northern Italy (Padua and Cividale) have musical notation, while Philippe de Mézières' play for the feast of the Presentation gives elaborate musical directions (§II, 7(ii) below).

3. THE REPERTORY: DRAMATIC PRESENTATION. The presentation of these dramatic ceremonies and plays was essentially all of a piece with their nature and purpose – liturgical. The concept of 'theatre' is, it must be repeated, totally anachronistic. This means that all the subsidiary terms normally used to describe dramatic events are to some extent misleading – 'stage', 'properties', 'scenery', 'costumes', even 'actors' and 'audience'; they imply a type of dramatic experience which may be quite alien to the liturgical or near-liturgical occasion. At the same time one must beware of thinking that all liturgical plays were the same and that the kind of dramatic mimesis involved was consistent and unchangeable. The more elaborate plays, for example, often 'seem to have been composed in their extant forms in a spirit of literary and dramatic independence, and to have been attached to the liturgy as appendages rather than as intimate accompaniments of central acts of worship' (Young, 1933, ii, 399). It is only in these more ambitious presentations, like the Fleury *Conversion of St Paul*, that the staging plan is implied which was to become standard for the medieval vernacular dramas in their larger forms: the plan of *sedes* and *platea* (see fig.6 below). The *sedes* ('seats') or *loci* ('houses', 'mansions') were structures or raised platforms identifiable with specific localities – Jerusalem, Saul's house, etc; the *platea* ('place') was an unlocalized acting area between and in front of the *sedes*. In §II, 7 below, some remarkable, and remarkably varied, individual plays are discussed; the present section describes general principles based on simpler plays.

The 'stage' is the church itself, which is also the 'auditorium'. The two are not always clearly distinguished from a spatial point of view; a procession moving from station to station creates its own 'stage' locality as required. For the *Visitatio sepulchri* no 'houses' are required, unless the sepulchre to which the Marys go to find Jesus can be so called. It should be noted that the Easter sepulchre was not a piece of scenery for a play but a normal part of the Holy Week and Easter ceremonies (see fig.2). It could be a temporary wood or canvas structure, or (especially in England) a permanent erection in stone (Brooks, 1921). The sepulchre proper might be a chest or coffer placed within the larger structure (the *monumentum*). But even this degree of representation was not strictly necessary; the altar could, and often did, represent the sepulchre. In Christmas ceremonies and plays the dramatic object of comparable importance to the Easter sepulchre was the crib, *presepe*. As a focus for popular devotion the crib owes much to St Francis of Assisi, who in 1223 obtained papal per-

Ex.6 *F-O* 201 p. 211

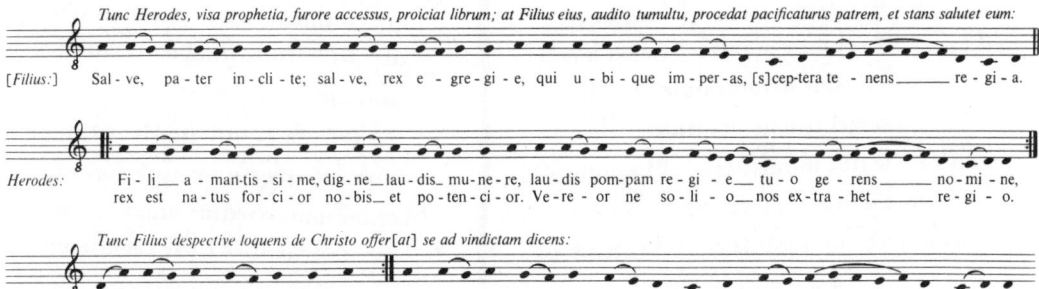

*Tunc Herodes, visa prophetia, furore accessus, proiciat librum; at Filius eius, audito tumultu, procedat pacificaturus patrem, et stans salutet eum:*

[*Filius:*] Sal - ve, pa - ter in - cli - te; sal - ve, rex e - gre - gi - e, qui u - bi - que im - per - as, [s]cep - tera te - nens_____ re - gi - a.

*Herodes:* Fi - li__ a - man - tis - si - me, dig - ne__ lau - dis_ mu - ne - re, lau - dis pom - pam re - gi - e_ tu - o ge - rens_____ no - mi - ne, rex est na - tus for - ci - or no - bis_ et po - ten - ci - or. Ve - re - or ne so - li - o__ nos ex - tra - het_____ re - gi - o.

*Tunc Filius despective loquens de Christo offer[at] se ad vindictam dicens:*

[*Filius:*] Con - tra il - lum re - gu - lum, iu - be,__ pa - ter,__ fi - li - um hoc in - i - re_____ pre - li - um! con - tra na - tum par - vu - lum

Then Herod, having seen the prophecy, is overcome with fury, and flings the book from him; whereupon his son, having heard the tumult, comes forward to pacify his father, and stands and greets him: Hail, great father; hail, excellent king, who reign throughout all the world, wielding the sceptre of the kingdom. Herod: Most beloved son, worthy to be offered praise, whose name bears with it the glory of the realm, a king is born that is stronger and more powerful than we. I fear lest he will banish us from our royal throne. Then the son, speaking contemptuously of Christ offers himself for vengeance, singing: Father, on that prince, on the new-born infant, command your son to declare present war.

mission to erect a crib (with live ox and ass) at Greccio; but it had been in use before this for centuries. Once again, it is not in the narrow sense a stage property; if no crib had been erected, the altar would serve.

A 14th-century *Visitatio* from Essen (in the Münsterarchiv) with remarkably full rubrics ('stage directions' only anachronistically) brings other features to notice, of which one is very unusual: the collegiate church at Essen was for both canons and canonesses, so in their *Visitatio* the parts of the Marys were taken by women, those of the angels by men. Normally all the roles, male or female, were taken by persons of one sex. Another characteristic follows traditional practice – the

2. The Three Marys approaching the sepulchre: illustration from the Hartker Antiphonary (c980–1011) (CH-SGs 391, f.33r); it may show the kind of erection which was used in churches for the play/ceremony 'Visitatio sepulchri'; the Three Marys in the picture are clearly not realistic figures

'costuming'; the angels wear ecclesiastical vestments and do not 'pretend' to be other than clerics (this, however, varies from play to play). A third feature, confirming the absence of full dramatic illusion, is that they are allowed a book to sing from 'if they do not have it by heart' and there is light to read it by (Young, 1933, i, p.333). The degree of 'let's pretend' varies, and phrases such as 'in the likeness of those who are searching', 'in imitation of an angel', 'in a high [or loud] voice as if rejoicing', occur in early and late texts and do indicate some move towards dramatic illusion.

The general style of 'acting' must also have varied somewhat from place to place, and from century to century. But it is a safe conjecture that it was generally restrained and formal even in the larger plays. One remarkable and fully rubricated text, with music, throws some light on this (Young, i, pl.12): a 14th-century *Planctus Marie* from Cividale del Friuli (*I-CFm* CI). Over each phrase of text and music is written a direction to the singer such as: 'Here shall she turn to the men with arms outstretched', 'Here shall she wring her hands', 'Here shall she point to Christ with open palms', 'Here with head bowed she shall throw herself at the feet of Christ'. The verbal text is highly patterned and elaborately rhetorical; the gestures and movements must surely have been in keeping – not subtle, shaded, infinitely expressive, but immediately recognizable, demonstrative and impressive.

The style of singing, the use (or not) of instruments and other matters of musical presentation are considered in §II, 7 below.

4. SOURCES. The liturgical plays are found in a variety of sources, mostly liturgical service-books (see fig.3), but also playbooks, poetical anthologies and miscellanies. The huge majority of *Quem queritis* dialogues is found in tropers: a St Martial troper (*F-Pn* lat.1240), mentioned in §II, 1 above, and the Winchester Troper (*GB-Ob* 775). The extended dialogue *Visitatio sepulchri* occurs in a wider variety of service-books. The so-called Dublin play, for example, is found in two manuscripts, both processionals (*EIRE-Dm* Z.4.2.20; *GB-Ob* Rawl.liturg.d.4); another version, headed 'In Resurrectione Domini', comes from a *Liber responsalis* in the monastery of Einsiedeln, Switzerland (*CH-E* 300),

*3. Opening from a 'Liber responsalis' from Strasbourg, c1200 (GB-Lbm Add.23922, ff.8v-9r), showing the way most liturgical 'plays' (here a play of 'The Three Kings') are embedded in liturgical service books; at the Octave of Epiphany at Vespers, after the 'Magnificat', the play begins (left-hand page) with one Magus singing 'Stella fulgore mimio'; the music is written in unmeasured, unheighted neumes*

where however it is not liturgically placed. The tendency to detach the more elaborate dialogues and plays from their liturgical context is most marked in the case of three highly individual manuscripts. The first and most famous is the *Carmina burana* manuscript from the monastery of Benediktbeuern (*D-Mbs* 4660), which contains among many remarkable items a fragmentary play, *De rege Egipti*, a *Ludus paschalis*, two Passion plays, a *Peregrinus* and an elaborate Christmas play. The second manuscript, also well known, can be claimed as the most truly 'dramatic' of all the sources: the Fleury Playbook (*F-O* 201). The manuscript itself is a large 13th-century religious miscellany; but in the midst of it are inserted four gatherings containing ten plays – the first playbook of its kind. The third manuscript is that rare thing in medieval times, a book to which an author's name can be attached: that of Hilarius, a wandering scholar and pupil of Abelard. His book (*F-Pn* lat.11331, 12th century) contains poems, verse letters and three plays, but without musical notation. Sometimes even a quite elaborate play is substantially the same in several sources. Such is the case with the *Officium stelle* of Rouen (*F-Pn* 904, with music, *Pn* 1213, *R* 222, *R* 382, *R* 384). But generally the more elaborate the play, the less likely this is to occur.

The entire, or partial, absence of musical notation from sources of liturgical plays does not mean that they were not sung. Nor does the use of the Latin verb *dicere* in rubrics, instead of *cantare*, imply the spoken word,

since both verbs are used, apparently interchangeably, in the texts of plays with music throughout and in liturgical books. (The sources of the liturgical drama are listed comprehensively by Lipphardt in 'Liturgische Dramen', *MGG*, where a distinguishing asterisk is given to those which contain music. The sources are listed there by provenance or present location but without shelf-marks, for which Young must be consulted; see also Lipphardt, 1975.)

5. NOTATIONS AND PROBLEMS OF TRANSCRIPTION. Medieval church plays are written in a great variety of notations corresponding to the notations of other melodic music of the period *c*900–*c*1500. In the case of plays closely attached to the liturgy of Christmas or Easter (i.e. the huge majority of surviving musical texts), the notation of the play is identical to that of the liturgical context and presents the same difficulties. Thus the 10th-century St Gall version of the *Quem queritis* is in Franco-German unheighted neumes; the St Martial (*see* TROPE (i), ex.2) in Aquitanian with some indication of comparative pitch by heightening. The clarification of pitch is carried one stage further in, for example, a troper from Ravenna (*I-MOd* O.1.17, 11th–12th century), in which the north Italian neumes are almost precisely heighted by the use of a single line (with faint subsidiaries), with F clef (see fig.1 above). Two lines, usually F and one other, are given to help the singer in a gradual-troper from Piacenza (*I-PCd* 65, 11th–12th

century). Finally (though the sequence is not neatly chronological), most of the longer plays, except those in the *Carmina burana* manuscript, are written in a notation which clearly indicates pitches on a four-line staff; the Fleury Playbook is written in the neumes characteristic of northern France in the 12th century (see fig.5, p.38); they, like the neumes of Gregorian chant in the same period, are beginning to approximate to the now familiar square shapes. These are more evident still in the *Ludus paschalis* of Origny-Ste-Benoîte (*F-SQ* 86). A style of notation slightly less liturgical in its associations is found in the early 13th-century manuscript *GB-Lbm* Eg.2615 (containing the *Play of Daniel*; see fig.4, p.36); but even there the notation is nearer to that of the liturgical monophonic than to that of the polyphonic pieces in the same manuscript (the characteristic canted *punctum*, a rhomboid form, is much used in both sections).

The satisfactory transcription of the liturgical drama is bedevilled not only by the problem of pitch but also by the other problem that besets the study of early monody in general – that of rhythm. It presents itself in two forms: briefly, how should the liturgical chants and melodic passages modelled freely on them be interpreted, and how should melodies of a more secular character be interpreted? In answer to the first question, there is no reason to think that in their somewhat enlarged and freer context the liturgical chants in any way changed their style. If the chant was normally sung rhythmically in a modified equal-note style, then certainly it was so sung in a dramatic setting. On the other hand, melodies such as *Astra tenenti, cunctipotenti* or *Jubilemus regi nostro, magno ac potenti* (from the *Play of Daniel*) with their strongly accentual Latin verse texts seem to invite the metrical interpretation that most editors give them – triple in the first case (ex.7) and duple or triple in the second (ex.8). More complicated melodies, such as the planctus of Rachel in the Fleury *Play of the Innocents*, need, as do other melismatic songs (e.g. of the troubadours and trouvères), more flexible treatment. There is no agreed style for the transcription and editing of liturgical plays. Weakland (1961) proposed, and in his edition of the *Play of Daniel* exemplified, the above distinction between unmeasured liturgical and metricalized 'secular' melody. Monterosso (1958) rendered the whole text of the Fleury Playbook according to the principles of pre-Franconian, modal notation. Krieg (1956) adopted a more flexible but continuously modal interpretation for the whole of the Tours Easter play, prose and verse passages alike. The solution adopted by Coussemaker (1860) of transcribing the music of the plays into traditional Gregorian square notation is non-committal but practical, as is the modern equivalent of unmeasured note heads. Each play

presents its individual problems; but it seems both unhistorical and unmusical not to recognize in many plays the co-existence of different melodic styles, whose proper interpretation is bound up with that of Gregorian chant in the Middle Ages and of other monophonic music (in Latin and in the vernaculars).

Ex.8 *GB-Lbm* Egerton 2615 f. 94*v*

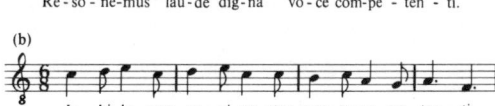
(a)
Ju - bi - le - mus  re - gi no-stro  mag-no ac po - ten - ti.

Re - so - ne-mus  lau-de dig-na    vo - ce com-pe - ten - ti.

(b)
Ju - bi - le - mus  re - gi no-stro  mag- no ac  po - ten - ti.

Re - so - ne - mus  lau - de dig - na    vo - ce com-pe - ten - ti.

Let us rejoice in our great and powerful king. Let us sing fit praises with tuneful voices.

6. MUSICAL STYLE AND MUSICAL STRUCTURE. The way in which both the simplest and the more complex liturgical plays incorporate material direct from the seasonal liturgy has already been briefly described (§II, 2). A common extension, for instance, to the basic *Quem queritis* dialogue consists of the antiphon *Alleluia, Resurrexit Dominus, hodie resurrexit leo fortis, Christus, filius Dei* (e.g. in *F-APT* 4). As this antiphon shows, the melody is not necessarily constant: the version in the two later Easter plays (Fleury and Rouen) differs from that in the Worcester monastic antiphonary (13th century; PalMus, 1st ser., xii). The problem of the precise sources of the melodies used in the plays needs much research.

The analysis of their musical style and structure is also not far advanced. The assimilation round the newly composed basic dialogues of Easter and Christmas of known liturgical or para-liturgical material (e.g. sequences) from varied contexts posed problems of dramatic and of musical unity. The musical problem resolves itself into various related questions. How was the deviser or arranger (the words 'composer' and 'playwright' are best avoided) to achieve a consistent musical style? What devices of melodic repetition (sequence, 'rhyme', motif) were admissible? How could modal congruity, tonal unity, be achieved? What dramatic criteria did the musician have to satisfy?

A consistent musical style was achieved, no doubt almost unconsciously, by the use of the idiom of Gregorian chant. In the case of the simplest dramatic ceremonies, mere dialogue tropes, the whole intention of the arranger was in any case liturgical. The fact that the musical phraseology of the *Quem queritis* itself is analogous to that of other liturgical melodies should cause no surprise. From Brandel (1966) it appears that the closest analogy is that of the Whitsuntide antiphon *Paraclitus autem* (*Liber usualis*, 900); the fact that liturgically the two are not at all closely connected makes it likely that the borrowing was unconscious.

Ex.7 *GB-Lbm* Egerton 2615 f. 94

As-tra te - nen - ti,  Cunc-ti-po- ten - ti,  Tur-ba vi-
- ri - lis  Et pu - e - ri - lis  Con-ti - o  plau - dit.

To the ruler of the stars, to the all-powerful one, this host of men and assembly of youths give honour.

Brandel further noted that the chant of the Marys as they approach the sepulchre, 'Ad monumentum venimus gementes' (see ex.3), has a close parallel in Gloria XIII (*Liber usualis*, 51, 'Et in terra') and that its main melodic marking (rising 3rd superimposed on rising 5th) occurs appropriately in the Easter Tuesday Alleluia verse *Surrexit dominus de sepulchro* (*Liber usualis*, 790; see exx.9 and 10). In his thorough study of the

Ex.9 *LU* 51

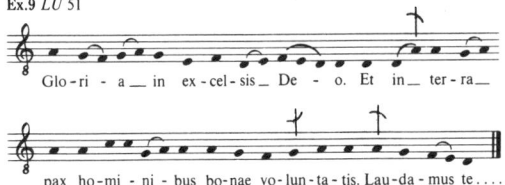

Glo-ri – a __ in ex-cel-sis _ De – o. Et in_ ter-ra_

pax ho-mi – ni - bus bo-nae vo-lun-ta-tis. Lau-da-mus te ....

Glory be to God on high. And on earth peace, goodwill toward men. We praise Thee ...

Ex.10 *LU* 790

Sur – re - xit _____

_____ Do – mi -

- nus de se – - - - pul – - - - -chro ...

The Lord is risen from the tomb ...

13th-century Tours *Ludus paschalis* Krieg (1956) showed the extent of the melodic debt in unidentified chants, by approaching the problem from the opposite angle. The parts of the liturgy most familiar to the medieval singer were the Ordinary of the Mass and the Requiem Mass. Musical thoughts were naturally taken from these as well as from the chants of the most important season of the Christian year – Passiontide and Easter. One of the haunting cadences of the Easter sequence *Victime paschali* mentioned above, 'quid vidisti in via?' (C–F–E–D–E–C–D), recurs over 15 times in the Tours play; the descending phrase 'Christus innocens patris' (A–G–A–G–F–E–C) ten or 11 times; 'gloriam vidi resurgentis' (G–F–G–A–G–F–G–F–E–D) again more than 15. Phrases from the Lamentations of Jeremiah, the Gloria, Sanctus and Benedictus of Mass I (*in tempore paschali*) and the *Popule meus* are also taken from the Lent and Easter liturgies; and the sequence *Dies irae*, the responsory *Libera me, Domine*, and *Fac eas, Domine* (from the offertory *Domine Jesu Christe*) from the Requiem Mass (Krieg, 1956). The arranger-composer of a play such as this from Tours must have been a cleric who lived this music throughout the year in a singing community. He put it together ('com-posed' it) with intellectual control certainly, but out of a teeming hoard of deeply known and only half-consciously transmuted material.

However, the presence in a play of a large number of known liturgical melodies and the widespread use of innumerable known motifs to form 'new' melodies does not in itself bring about musical unity in a continuous composition. The problem of tonal, or more specifically

modal, unity has to be solved. The subtle adjustments, for example, demanded by the shift of the Christmas dialogue from the beginning of Mass to the end of Matins were analysed by Lipphardt (*MGG*, col.1022). In a play as long as the Tours *Ludus paschalis* the problem is on a bigger scale. In this play the predominant mode is the D mode; but the quite long scene in which the Marys buy spices from the merchant is entirely in the F mode (or, more exactly, as it requires B♭'s, in the transposed C mode). There may be a deliberate choice here, since the musical content of the scene is a single melody

Ex.11 *F-TO* 927 f.1v

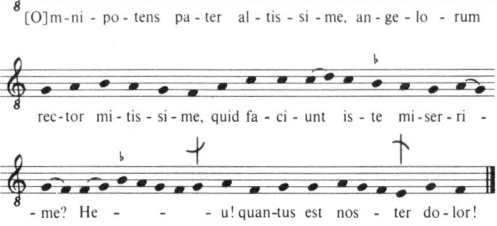

[O]m-ni – po - tens pa-ter al-tis-si-me, an-ge-lo – rum

rec-tor mi-tis-si-me, quid fa – ci-unt is-te mi-ser-ri -

- me? He – - - - u! quan-tus est nos – ter do-lor!

All powerful, most high father, most gentle ruler of the angels, what can we do in this dreadful plight? Alas, what grief is ours!

repeated some ten times (ex.11). The D mode predominates also in the Fleury *Visitatio sepulchri*; but here a big shift occurs in the middle of the play for the scene in the garden, starting with the angel's question 'Mulier quid ploras?'. This is in the E mode and opens a series of 'speeches' all in this mode. At the end of the series, when the linen cloths are placed on the altar, there is a brief interlude of six phrases oscillating between finals on F and G (as the Marys celebrate the Resurrection) and two familiar antiphons [*Nolite timere vos;*] *ite nunciate*, on E, and the final triumphant *Resurrexit hodie Dominus, leo fortis Christus filius Dei*, on D. More needs to be known about the emotional effects associated with different modes before the precise intention behind these changes can be defined. Their nature at least is clear. Lipphardt (1963), from a modal analysis of the Le Mans *Versus ad faciendum Herodem*, concluded that 'the musical technique which can here be characterized as adaptation is one that has been many times described – it is that of the psalm "differences" [the variant endings which ensure smooth transitions between psalm and antiphon] and it is in keeping with the liturgical character of the play' (*see* PSALM, §II).

Analysis of the musical structure of the plays has to take two other aspects into account: the frequent use of what may be called 'narrative melody', and the presence of contrasting material (melodies not modelled on plainchant). The first feature is most evident in such a play as the Fleury *Tres filie*, a 'miracle' of St Nicholas. The story is not lacking in dramatic possibilities: it tells how the saint 'by timely gifts of gold to an indigent father, rescues the three daughters from careers of prostitution' (Young, 1933, ii, 311). Yet it is sung throughout almost entirely to the same melody. This could be thought a special technique for a special purpose, were it not that, as already seen, episodes in fully dramatic and musically developed liturgical plays, such as those from Tours, Origny-Ste-Benoîte and Fleury, could be presented in a similarly stylized way – for example the lively merchant scene in the Origny *Ludus paschalis*,

Ex.12 *F-SQ* 86 p. 611

We have lost our solace, Jesus Christ, all full of sweetness: he was fair and full of kind love. Alas! the true one loved us well.

which uses one tune 16 times (ex.12). Possibly this was the sort of melody to which narrative poems (*chansons de geste* and saints' lives) were sung. There are certain obvious similarities between it and the melody of the Tours merchant scene (ex.11). Each tune hovers around the major 3rd or 4th above the final, making only brief flights above this, and has an impersonal, yet malleable, character analogous to, though musically distinct from, psalm tones.

The presence of contrasting (i.e. non-liturgical) material has been most convincingly demonstrated in the case of the planctus. 'In the melodies of [the developed Easter plays] the different music worlds of the Middle Ages are ... harmoniously juxtaposed. In the figure of Mary they are indeed knit together into the unity of a dramatic action' (Lipphardt, 1948). One mark of 'secular' influence in the planctus is the characteristic fall of a 5th as at the phrase 'Sed eamus' in ex.3. Such a fall is also found, however, in the very same D mode, in the liturgical antiphon *Ad monumentum venimus* (see above). Its secular nature is more apparent when it occurs in the C or G modes, as in Rachel's lament from the Fleury *Slaughter of the Innocents* (ex.13, pp.34–5: 'Heu! teneri partus'). This progression has something in common with, for instance, melodies in one of the most popular planctus of the period, the *Planctus ante nescia*; see, for example, the phrase 'Reddite mestissime' (ex.14). The tradition of the planctus was one that came ready-made, or ready at least for adaptation, to the arrangers of the more complex liturgical plays and provided a corpus of melody different from, but assimilable to, Gregorian chant.

Ex.14 *F-EV* 39 f. 2

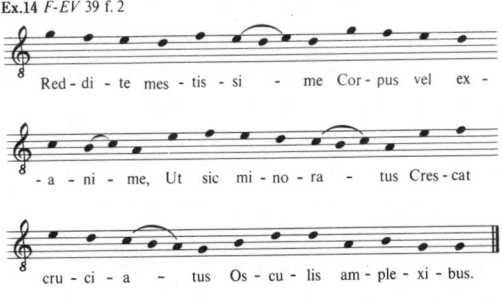

Restore the body to this most sad and fainting woman, so that the crucified one in his humiliation may be enriched with kisses and embraces.

7. INTERPRETATION AND PERFORMANCE. These linked aspects will be discussed with special reference to a few plays of marked individuality which have received less

than their due above. The problem of musical interpretation cannot be considered in isolation from other aspects, though attempts to do so have been common enough. The whole style and meaning of the liturgical drama depends on non-realistic conventions of staging, properties and costumes, on a relationship unfamiliar in the 20th century between actors and 'audience' (?congregation, ?bystanders – *populus* is the neutral term most frequent in the texts), on a style of acting (movement and gesture) and doubtless of singing far removed from 20th-century styles. Music is not only an inseparable part of this complex but a major one – principally in the form of song, but also as the music of instruments. The questions which need to be considered concern music and character, music and 'atmosphere', music as expression and music as symbol, an iconography in sound.

(i) *The Padua 'Annunciation'*. This play (in *I-Pc* CI, 13th century) is a tellingly simple dramatic ceremony which, although of a rare genre, is thoroughly typical in its general style (see Vecchi, 1954). It took place on the day of the feast 'after dinner', as an addition to the authorized liturgy, not as a dramatization of part of it. It opens with a procession of the main characters from sacristy to church. It uses expected liturgical material – the epistle for the day (called the 'prophecy'), the gospel (*Missus est angelus Gabriel*), antiphons (*Ave Maria, gratia plena, Ecce ancilla domini, Benedicta tu in mulieribus*, etc). It ends with an *alternatim* performance of the *Magnificat* for choir and organ.

The central action of the play is symbolic: the dove, immemorial symbol of the Holy Spirit, plunges from the roof of the church and is received by Mary under her cloak. This symbolic use of 'properties' is paralleled by a symbolic use of space (Gabriel comes from the choir, the 'heavenly' part of the church, to visit Mary in the nave, the 'earthly' region), a symbolic time (Mary's journey to Elizabeth's house takes only a few seconds), and symbolic gesture (Mary is to stand and welcome the dove with, literally, 'open arms'). This dramatic style may be summed up not as realism but as realization. The deviser of such a ceremony aimed not to reconstruct a dimly grasped historical event but to honour the Virgin by realizing, making real, a truth about her in the most vivid terms available. His most vivid terms were not, even in drama, naturalistic and causal, a copy of everyday life, but typological and symbolic.

The most important points to be made about the function of the music are negative. First, the music has nothing to do with the presentation of character in the sense of individual personality. Gabriel, the Virgin Mary and Elizabeth all sing in the same style – the style of singing plainchant in 13th-century Padua, whatever that may have been. Moreover, the two principal women's parts were sung, as nearly always, by grown men. Their musical utterances are no more personal than their formal gestures. Working powerfully against any concept of musical 'personality' for the singers is the very fact that the music for the play is a potpourri of familiar chants, associated for the congregation with a liturgical solemnity and communal rejoicing, not with the expression of individual feeling. A second negative point is that the music is not concerned with creating or reinforcing 'atmosphere' – not in the sense that, for instance, Debussy could create through music the sunless atmosphere of underground caves in Act 3 of *Pelléas et Mélisande*. There is, of course, a legitimate

Ex.13 *F-O* 201 pp. 216—19

*Postea, iacentibus infantibus, angelus ab excelso admoneat eos, dicens:* Vos qui in pul-ve-re es-tis, ex-per-gis-ci-mi-ni et cla-ma-te!

*Infantes iacentes:* Qua-re non de-fen - - - dis san-gui-nem nos - tram, de-us nos-ter?

*Angelus:* Ad - huc sus-ti-ne-te mo-di-cum tem - - pus, do-nec im-ple-a - - - tur nu-me-rus fra - - trum ves-tro - - - rum.

*Tunc inducatur Rachel, et due consolatrices; et stans super pueros plangat, cadens aliquando, dicens:*

He - u! te-ne - ri par-tus, la-ce - ros quos cer-ni-mus ar-tus! He-u! dul-ces na - ti, so-la ra-bi-e iu-gu-la-ti! He-u! quem nec pi-e-tas nec ves - tra co-er-cu-it e-tas! He-u! ma-tres mi-se-re, que co-gi-mur is-ta vi-de-re! He-u! quid nunc a-gi-mus cur non hec fac-ta sub-i-mus! He-u! qui-a me-mo-res nos-tros-que le-va-re do-lo-res Gau-di-a non pos-sunt nam dul-ci-a pig-no-ra de-sunt!

*Consolatrices excipientes eam cadentem dicentes:* No-li vir-go Ra - - chel, no-li dul-cis-si-ma ma-ter; pro ne-ce par-vo-rum fle-tus re-ti-ne-re do-lo-rum. Si que tris-tar-is ex-ul-ta que la-cri-ma-ris. nam-que tu-i na-ti vi-vunt su-per as-tra be-a-ti.

*Item Rachel dolens:* Heu! heu! heu! quo-mo-do gau-de-bo, dum mor-tu-a mem-bra vi-de-bo; dum sic com-mo-ta fu-e-ro per vis-ce-ra to-ta? Me fa-ci-ent ve-re pu-e-ri si-ne fi-ne do-le-re. O do-lor! O pa-trum mu-ta-ta-que gau-di-a ma-trum ad lu-gu-bres luc-tus! La-cri-ma-rum

fun - di - te fle - tus, Iu - de - e flo - rem pa - tri - e la - cri - man - do do - lo - rem!

*Item consolatrices:* Quid tu__ vir - go ma - ter__ Ra - chel plo - ras for - mo - sa, cu - ius__

vul - tus Ia - cob__ de - lec - tat? Ce - u so - ro - ris an - ni - cu - le lip - pi - tu - do e - um_____

iu - vat! Ter - ge__ ma - ter flen - tes_____ o - cu - los. Quam te__ de - cent ge - na - rum ri - vu - li?

*Item Rachel:* Heu!__ heu!__ heu!__ quid me in - cu - sas - tis fle - tus in - cas - sum fu - dis - se;

cum sim or - ba - ta na - to, pau - per - ta - tem me - am cu - ra - ret, Qui non__ hos - ti - bus

ce - de - ret an - gus - tos ter - mi - nos, quos mi - chi Ia - cob ad - qui - si - vit, quí - que sto - li - dis

fra - tri - bus, quos mul - tos, pro[h] do - lor, ex - tu - li, es - set pro - fu - tu - rus?

*Afterwards, when the children have been slain, an angel counsels them from on high, singing:* You who lie in the dust, rouse yourselves and cry out! *The slain children:* O our God, why did you not defend our blood? *Angel:* Wait a little while, and the number of your brethren shall increase. *Then Rachel is led in, and two women consoling her; and standing over the children she weeps, sometimes falling down, singing:* Alas! tender children, whose torn limbs we see! Alas, sweet sons, your throats cut in a single fit of rage! Alas, neither pity nor your age could protect you! Alas, wretched mothers, that we should be compelled to see this thing! Alas, what can we do now, why should not we too undergo the same! Alas, for our bitter memories cannot be relieved by joy now that our pledges of sweetness are no more! *The consoling women raise her when she has fallen, singing:* Young wife Rachel, sweetest mother, stop; restrain the tears of your grief at the slaying of the little ones. As you have sorrowed, rejoice as you have wept: for your children live in bliss above the stars. *Then Rachel sings, lamenting:* Alas! alas! alas! how shall I rejoice when I see the dead limbs; when I am thus stricken to the heart? The children will cause me to lament for evermore. O grief! O, the joy of fathers and mothers changed into sorrow! Pour forth floods of tears, weeping in grief for the flower of the land of Judah! *Then the consoling women:* Why do you weep, O fair young mother Rachel, whose countenance delighted Jacob? As if the reddened eyes of an old woman please him! Dry your weeping eyes, O mother. How can these streaming cheeks become you? *Then Rachel:* Alas! alas! alas! how can you reproach me for pouring forth vain tears, when I am bereft of my child, who would have cared for me in poverty, guarded from foes the little plot which Jacob bestowed on me, who would have helped the strong brothers whom, alas, I have borne?

sense in which the music of the Padua play 'creates an atmosphere' – one of restraint and dignity, a liturgical atmosphere, helping to give the play a significance beyond the merely temporal and occasional. What is certain, however, is that in this and other small-scale plays the atmosphere is not peculiar to the play – it is an intensification of the liturgical experience proper to the feast.

(ii) *Mézières' 'Presentation'.* One noticeable feature of the Padua play and of the great majority of liturgical plays is the complete absence of any reference to the playing of instruments. Since the method of staging the plays is described very fully in some instances, this negative evidence must be given weight. A remarkable *ordo*, however, written by the French nobleman Philippe de Mézières (*F-Pn* lat.17330), prescribing in the fullest detail for his *Festum Presentationis Beate Marie Virginis*, is one of the few which do mention instrumental music. It helps to clarify the problem.

This ambitiously conceived liturgical ceremony, which has impersonation, action, dialogue, and all the usual features of a play, was composed for the introduc-tion into the Western church of the feast of the Presentation (Avignon, 1372); it had the approval of the pope and the ecclesiastical hierarchy at Avignon, a fact which gives the *ordo* unusual authority. The ceremony is based on an apocryphal story; its climax comes when Mary, impersonated by a 'very beautiful little girl' three or four years old, climbs the temple steps to the altar and is presented by her parents, Joachim and Anna, to the bishop, who receives her 'in the person of God the Father'. Structurally the play is in three parts (Procession, Praises [*Laudes Marie*] and Presentation); it is followed without a break by the Mass (during which Mary sits on a special platform), by a short civic procession and by a banquet. There is a great deal of singing (the *ordo* does not provide notated melodies) of the usual kind. And in addition 'two young men who shall play sweet [?soft] instruments' are named in the cast and frequently referred to in the rubrics as *pulsatores*. Their instruments are never specified; the verb 'pulsare' was used in medieval Latin for the playing of drums, trumpets, plucked instruments and, with great frequency, bells. Perhaps the young men played more than one kind of instrument; this seems likely, since

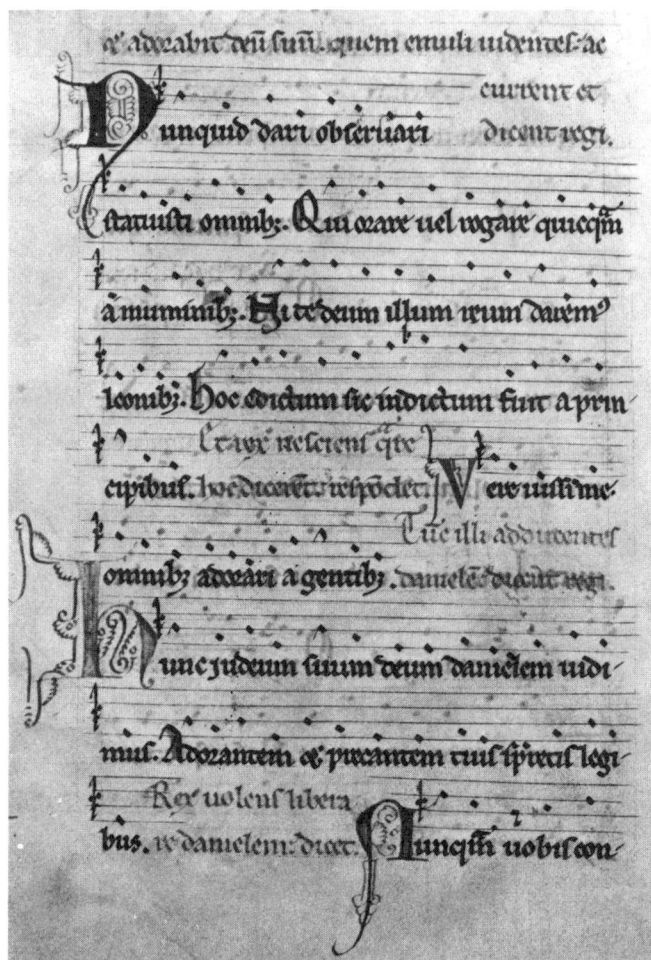

*4. Page from the 'Play of Daniel', from Beauvais, early 13th century (GB-Lbm Eg.2615, f.105v), in which the king's counsellors are accusing Daniel, in his absence, of persisting in forbidden worship; the notation is characterized by rhomboid puncta (not to be confused with mensural semibreves) written on a four-line staff*

their main function was the usual function of instrumental musicians – to accompany movement. They played processional, 'escort' music, as the characters went from place to place. For this loud instruments must have been required. But when they played for an angel singing 'some song in the style of a *rondellus* ... in the vernacular', string music would have been more appropriate. The musicians were also required to quieten the populace down after the expulsion of the character Synagogue from the church, which was expected to cause noisy laughter.

There are one or two points of particular interest. The instrumental music was not, except in the unusual case of the devotional vernacular song, used to support singing; the liturgical items were apparently unaccompanied. Only two instrumentalists were employed for a dramatic ceremony of great magnificence, although all the resources of the papal court were presumably available. The musicians are specifically required to be silent during the Presentation scene itself, the liturgical climax; and they retire altogether, escorting the main actors, before the introit of the Mass is sung. From the limited use of musical instruments on such a grand occasion, it can perhaps be inferred that the liturgical drama as a whole did not often have occasion to employ

them. The only frequent known exceptions are organs and bells.

(*iii*) '*Play of Daniel*'. There is however another play, of equal though different magnificence, the celebrated early 13th-century Beauvais *Play of Daniel* (*GB-Lbm* Eg.2615; see fig.4) which must be taken into consideration; this play, the opening lines state, was devised by the young people (*juventus*: ?students of the cathedral school) of Beauvais 'in honour of Christ'. In fact, it celebrates Christmas; at the end an angel 'shall suddenly cry out "Natus est Christus" '. Daniel was chosen as the subject not out of a historical whim but because he was a prophet of Christ's coming. The play tells the familiar Bible story (*Daniel* v.1ff).

There are at least 50 distinct melodies in the play, unrepeated and untraced in other sources. These are largely syllabic and seem to fit naturally into the patterns created by the accentual Latin verses. One or two pieces are in a florid plainchant style, but only the last item, the Christmas hymn *Nuntium vobis fero*, can be identified liturgically. These facts alone make it unique.

Relevant to the problem of instrumental music is the large number of processional items, all with text: 'conductus regine'; 'conductus Danielis venientis ad regem';

'conductus referentium vasa ante Danielem', etc. But only one rubric in the whole play specifically mentions instrumental music; it announces the coming of Darius who will kill Belshazzar and seize his throne – 'At once King Darius shall appear with his princes, and the *cythariste* and princes shall proceed before him singing [*psallentes*] these words'. The term 'cythariste' suggests that an element of scriptural stylization, based on Old Testament writings, can creep even into stage directions. The reference in the poetic text itself is even more stylized: 'let drums resound; let the harp players pluck their strings; let the musicians' instruments sound his praises'. Nevertheless, there is no reason to believe that the students of Beauvais were more restrained than Philippe de Mézières; the nature of the play, depicting the glory and the fall of kings, indeed calls for fanfares and the like. But neither text nor liturgical tradition supports the idea of lavish and continuous musical accompaniment. The only other play of comparable magnitude on a comparable subject, the 12th-century Tegernsee *Antichristus* (*D-Mbs* lat.19411), is full of regal characters, but instrumental effects are nowhere specified. It is easy to be misled by the appeal of colourful modern productions of such plays.

Among the numerous rubrics of the *Play of Daniel* are two which raise a further large problem of interpretation – that of the actor's proper singing style. The rubrics are 'stupefactus clamabit' and 'dicens lacrimabiliter'. Were Belshazzar's astonishment and Darius's grief to appear in their voices? It certainly seems so. But these are the only stylistic suggestions in 392 lines of text. Some plays, however, are more explicit. The common rubrics 'alta voce', 'mediocri voce' and 'humili voce' are found also in the liturgy proper, referring rather to loudness or pitch than to style. But other rubrics seem to require a distinct emotional colouring to be given to the chant in performance. Examples taken from texts of the *Visitatio sepulchri* alone are: 'mediocri voce dulcisone' ('in a medium voice, sweetly'); 'submissa voce quasi in aurem dicentes' ('in a low voice as if speaking into [his] ear'); 'voce sonora' ('in a resonant voice'); 'cantantes multum suppressa voce' (? 'in a very hushed voice'); 'alte vociferantes' ('shouting out loud'); 'devote . . . aliquantulum remisse' ('with devotion and rather gently'). Other adjectives and adverbs applied to singing are *simplex, blande, lenis, auctorabilis, alacris, querulus, lentus, flebilis* and *moderatus et admodum gravis*. This aspect of the plays is insufficiently studied; but there appears to be an unexpected dimension of psychological realism here. The problem is how the implications of these rubrics can be squared with other indications in the plays of formality, impersonality and emotional restraint.

*(iv) Fleury 'Play of the Innocents'*. Problems of interpretation and performance must be solved separately for each individual play. But to formulate true generalizations about the function of music in liturgical drama, plays more typical than the *Play of Daniel* and *Antichristus* must be chosen for analysis. A play which sums up the central traditions of liturgical drama is *The Slaughter of the Innocents* from the Fleury Playbook (see fig.5). It opens with the Innocents (the choristers of the choir) processing through the church singing *O quam gloriosum est regnum* (antiphon of Vespers, Vigil of All Saints). Then 'a lamb, suddenly appearing, bearing a cross, shall go before them . . . and they following sing,

"Emitte agnum, Domine" ' (antiphon of Lauds, second Sunday before Christmas). This procession continues during the angel's warning to Joseph, Herod's attempted suicide on hearing the news of the escape of the Magi and his command for the slaying of the children. As the slayers approach, the Innocents salute the lamb once more, 'Salve, Agnus Dei'. The distraught mothers are allowed a prayer of five words for mercy. Immediately an angel appears and exhorts the slain children to rise and cry out. Dead on the ground, they sing a sentence from a responsory of Matins of Innocents' Day, 'Quare non defendis sanguinem nostrum, Deus noster?' ('Why dost thou not defend our blood, O our Lord?'). They continue to lie prostrate during the long fourfold lament of Rachel, but rise to their feet when the angel sings the antiphon 'Sinite parvulos' ('Suffer the little children', antiphon of Lauds of Innocents' Day) and process to the choir, praising Christ in the words of the sequence *Festa Christi*. Archelaus succeeds Herod as king (in dumbshow), the angel summons the holy family back to Galilee, Joseph sings *Gaude, gaude* (antiphon of the Assumption of the BVM), and the play ends with the *Te Deum*.

This brief summary cannot do justice to the skill with which the deviser has blended three planes of reality – a traditional historical story (entirely scriptural), a liturgical celebration (for the feast of the Holy Innocents) and a planctus of typological significance (Rachel is the Old Testament type of the mourning mother; *Jeremiah* xxxi.15). But it demonstrates the typically non-realistic character of the play. The slaughtered children are not little Jewish two-year-olds but the Innocents of *Revelation* xiv.1ff, the 144,000 virgins who follow the lamb, singing in procession in the heavenly city. When they are swiftly and decorously slaughtered, they are not so dead that they cannot continue to sing.

The music of the play, like the text, is a mosaic of passages from the service-books: at least ten separate liturgical chants are quoted from half a dozen different services; they are mostly traditional antiphons. Rachel's lament excepted, the music was borrowed or adapted from, or composed in imitation of, liturgical plainsong. The measure and restraint of the liturgical utterances are exemplified in the angel's exhortation to the slain children to be patient until the time appointed, 'Adhuc sustinete modicum tempus' (ex.13); there is nothing more violent in this G mode melody than one rising triad, and almost all movement is by step. Rachel's lament, on the other hand, belongs to the musical tradition of the planctus, with roots in secular ceremonial and affinities to courtly song; its words are highly emotional and rhetorical: 'Alas, delicate children, whose torn limbs we see! Alas, sweet sons, your throats cut in a single fit of rage'. The melody is correspondingly less restrained and more patterned than plainchant. Various features are notable: the melismatic exclamations of grief, the sequential setting of 'Heu, heu, heu', the recurrence of musical 'rhyme' at the end of each hexameter, and the occasional bold melodic jumps. The transition from this comparatively extroverted, emotional style back to authentic liturgical chant at the end of the play is beautifully accomplished by the antiphon which Rachel sings as she falls on the bodies of the children, *Anxiatus est in me spiritus meus* (antiphon of Lauds of Good Friday).

The contribution of music to the dramatic experience can be summed up as follows (Stevens, 1968). First, the composition is singularly unified in tone. There is variety in the music, not only between the planctus and plainchant (traditional or newly composed) but also, within both of these, between a melismatic and a syllabic style (exx.17, 19). The final impression, however, is of unity. Second, the use of known chant has what might be called an 'iconographic' power. Through the psalm-antiphon *Anxiatus est* the grief of Rachel, already generalized through the symbolism of her character, is identified with the sorrows of the psalmist and (by recalling the liturgy of Good Friday) with the sufferings of Christ himself. Melodies sung at memorable moments of the church year bring a wealth of reference and meaning to the drama. Finally, the liturgical music proper has a direct emotional effect in contrast to the human suffering conveyed in the central scene of Rachel. Negatively, in its grave restraint and complete lack of flamboyant emotion, it prevents the listener becoming too involved in the human situation for itself. Positively, it lifts him

with its serene movement above temporal anxieties into that other world, beyond time, the truths of which the liturgical drama was created to celebrate.

### III. Vernacular drama

1. Introduction and presentation. 2. Early and miscellaneous plays: (i) Complaints of the BVM: 'Marienklagen' (ii) 'Sponsus', the 'Play of Adam', 'St Agnes' and the Shrewsbury fragments (iii) Early secular drama. 3. The main traditions: (i) English (ii) French (iii) German (iv) Italian (v) The Spanish peninsula.

1. INTRODUCTION AND PRESENTATION. A broad division between vernacular, spoken plays and Latin, sung plays is obvious and necessary (see §I above); and to postulate two traditions of medieval religious drama is a necessary corrective to the old one-line evolutionary theory. But it would be wrong to suggest that these roughly parallel lines could never meet. There are a number of plays, especially in German (the *Marienklagen*; see §III, 2(i)), the Innsbruck *Osterspiel*, etc (see §III, 3(iii)), but also in other vernaculars (e.g. the 'Bodleian' *Burial and*

5. *Page from the Fleury Playbook, 12th century (F-O 201, p.217), showing Rachel's lament (beginning 'Heu! teneri partus' on the 3rd staff) from 'The Slaughter of the Innocents'; it is preceded by the rubric 'Tunc inducatur Rachel et due consolatrices, et stans super pueros plangat cadens aliquando dicens'; the neumes, approximating to square shapes, are written on a four-line staff*

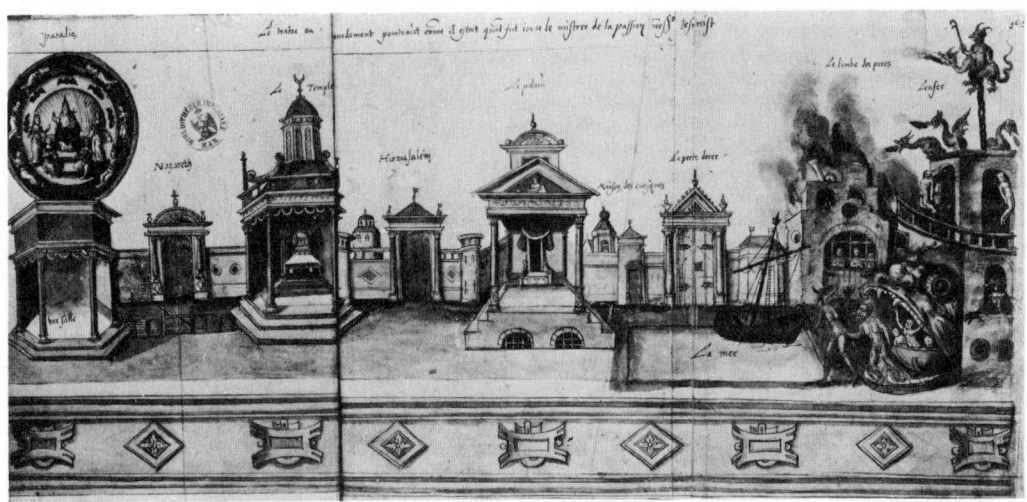

6. *Painting by Hubert Cailleau of the theatre for the 'Mystère de la Passion à Valenciennes' (1547) showing medieval 'simultaneous' staging where each 'mansion' represents a different locality (F-Pn fr.12536)*

*Resurrection*; see §III, 3(i)), for which the term 'vernacular liturgical drama' is appropriate. The *Marienklagen*, at least, and the English *Burial and Resurrection* seem uncontaminated by the cruder, more farcical secular elements; they are in fact less contaminated than certain Latin 'liturgical' dramas themselves. Above all, one must bear in mind the extraordinary variety of vernacular drama in every European country (even though the surviving sources may not do justice to it), compared with which the Latin ecclesiastical drama is almost monolithic. Moreover, it was not entirely a religious drama (see §III, 2(iii)) even if most of the plays that survive are religious.

Despite this variety, certain general propositions about the staging of medieval vernacular plays hold true: the presentation of time and place was non-naturalistic; 'scenery' was a matter of a few 'houses' (*sedes, lieux* etc) and properties of an emblematic kind (an arch to represent a temple, a tree to represent a garden, etc); costume was generally more naturalistic and 'in character' than in the liturgical plays, but contemporary and not historical (Annas and Caiaphas were dressed as medieval bishops, not as Jewish priests of the pre-Christian era); the great majority of performances took place out of doors by daylight, and the audience was far less insulated from the actors than it is in a modern theatre with footlights and spotlights. In short, the medieval vernacular drama was part-formal, part-naturalistic, but always contemporary.

Most medieval plays are rather sparsely provided with directions for their performance. For instance, it is not known where and when, let alone how, the *Sponsus* (§III, 2(ii)) was performed. The picture has to be built up from one or two well-documented plays, like the *Play of Adam* (§III, 2(ii)) and from the voluminous but disconnected information which can be pieced together from texts and archives about the major forms of religious drama.

As in liturgical drama the basic means of presentation for all forms is an unlocalized acting area, or 'place' (Lat. *platea*; Fr. *place*), around which, or behind, or in which, are a number of localized 'houses', 'scaffolds' or 'page-

ants' (Lat. *sedes*; Fr. *lieux, estages, sièges*: see fig.6). The 'houses' sometimes completely surrounded the 'place' (diagrams survive for the Cornish *Ordinalia* and for the morality *The Castle of Perseverance*, fig.7); on other occasions a half-circle was perhaps set up (the Anglo-Norman *La seinte resureccion*, on the basis of a detailed prologue; the miniature by Jean Fouquet of a play on the martyrdom of St Apollonia; *see* ICONOGRAPHY OF MUSIC, fig.4, and Southern, 1957). Insofar as there was a special 'house' for musicians, it was likely to be God's 'house' (i.e. Heaven).

The presentation of the English mystery cycles has been a matter of debate. The idea has long been current that they were always mounted on pageant-wagons and drawn through the streets of the city, each playlet or scene being acted in turn at a large number of stopping-places. This can never have been true of all the cycles (the 'N-Town', for instance, has elaborate stage directions suggesting a stationary presentation 'in the round'), but may in a modified form have been true of some. 'Coventry adopted the technique of true-processional production but the number of stations was limited to two or three' (Nelson, 1974). Even this processional production involved no radical departure from the principles described above; the plays required not only a main pageant cart but also subsidiary 'scaffolds' which were wheeled along with it, and the players also made use of the street itself as the 'place'.

General types of medieval dramatic activity and their presentation were described at length by Wickham (1959); the English mystery plays, and their relationship to Corpus Christi and its procession, by Nelson (1974); the staging of the Wakefield, or Towneley, plays by Rose (1961); *The Castle of Perseverance* by Southern (1957); the staging of several individual French plays by Axton (Axton and Stevens, 1971); the French *mystères* by Cohen (1926, 3/1951); the German plays by Michael (1963); and a huge amount of information about dramatic representations in Spain was collected by Shergold (1967). The thesis that the visual arts (ivories, carvings, stone-bosses) depict properties, costumes and décor was most persuasively

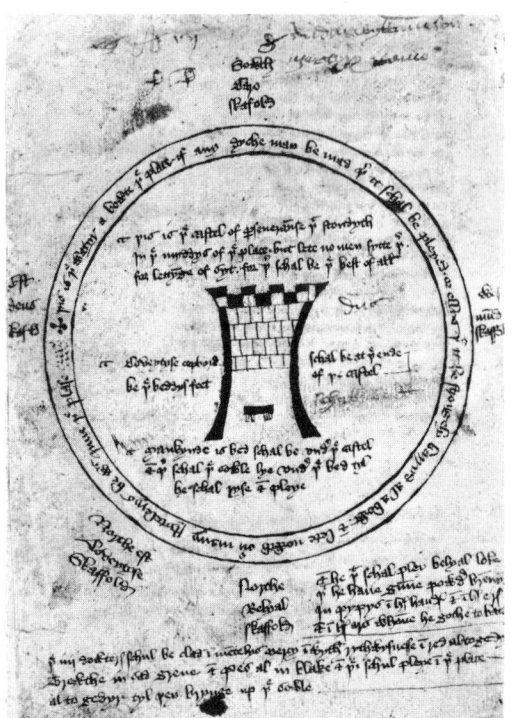

7. *Diagram of the staging of 'The Castle of Perseverance' showing medieval dramatic presentation 'in the round' (Washington, Folger Shakespeare Library V.a.354, f.191v)*

argued and illustrated by Hildburgh (1949) and Anderson (1963).

## 2. EARLY AND MISCELLANEOUS PLAYS.

*(i) Complaints of the BVM: 'Marienklagen'.* The complaint of Mary is a unique form of the Passion play and one in which music plays a prominent part. The planctus of the Blessed Virgin was sung beneath the crucifix of many German and north Italian churches on Good Friday. The event was extra-liturgical and had therefore no fixed time, but often nevertheless took place during the Office itself (Corbin, 1960). Some 50 *Marienklagen* survive in German manuscripts; they differ in extent and in detail but are essentially identical, even in their musical substance. There is no full-length musical study of the *Marienklagen*. Essential information is found in basic articles by Lipphardt (1932–4, 1948), in editions (especially Kühl, 1898), and in the studies of Schönbach (1874), Wechssler on Romance vernacular 'complaints' (1893) and Corbin (1960).

Two *Marienklagen*, one from Munich and one from Bordesholm, Lower Saxony, are of special interest. The Munich text (*D-Mbs* cgm 716) shows the vernacular 'lament' emerging, as it were, from the Latin planctus, in this case from the best known of all, the *Planctus ante nescia*; here it occurs in its simplest form, a monologue chanted by the Virgin. The Bordesholm text, on the other hand, is almost 900 lines long, but still almost entirely sung, and has elaborate directions for performance. Again, no orderly chronological development can be inferred; the 'simple' Munich text dates from the

15th century. The remaining sources range between these extremes of dramatic monologue and extended Passion play. The Munich text starts with the words and melody of the *Planctus ante nescia* and later quotes from another famous sequence, *Flete, fideles*; the rest of the text is in German, with very few rubrics (e.g. 'Quum vadit ad crucem': 'he advances towards the cross'). Towards the end the melody departs entirely from its model and from any liturgical pattern, becoming extremely animated and florid, with extended melodic exclamations. 'The supposition that here we have to do with common courtly formulae of the chivalric *Totenklage* [death lament] is confirmed by the introduction of the Nibelung strophe as the highest expression of lamentation in the Trier *Marienklage*' (Lipphardt, *MGG*; Geering, 1949). Such a melody as that shown in ex.15 would be in the sharpest contrast to its Good Friday liturgical context. Lipphardt and Corbin have both emphasized the non-liturgical spirit of the planctus tradition; it is most clearly evinced in these vernacular 'complaints'.

The Bordesholm *Marienklage* shows how wide the range of musical material could be. There are liturgical chants, especially from Holy Week (the hymn *Crux fidelis*; the responsory *Tenebrae factae sunt*, at the end; the antiphon *Anxiatus est*, occurring in seven other *Marienklagen*, at the beginning). There are also known melodies from the repertory of Minnesang, for example Neidhart von Reuental's *May hat wunniglich entsprossen* and Walther von der Vogelweide's *Kreuzfahrerweise* (Abert, 1948). And there may be additional echoes of the chivalric *Totenklage*.

There is a further interest in the Bordesholm manuscript, not in the text itself but in a most unusual preface:

Here begins the most devout complaint of the most Blessed Virgin Mary with the most pitiful and most devout music [*cum misericordissima et devotissima nota*]: the Blessed Virgin delivers this complaint most devoutly, with the assistance of four devout persons. It takes place on Good Friday before dinner, in the church in front of the choir on a slightly raised platform – or outside the church if the weather is good. This complaint is not a stage play [*ludus*] nor a sport [*ludibrium*] but

Ex.15 *D-Mbs* cgm 716 ff. 151v–152

indeed a complaint and a lamentation; it depicts the deep shared sorrow [*compassio*] of Mary, glorious Virgin. When it is done by good and sincere men ... it truly arouses the bystanders to genuine tears and compassion ... This complaint can easily be performed in two and a half hours. Everything that these five persons have to do shall be done without haste and without undue delay, in good modest fashion. The man who takes the part of Christ is a devout priest [*devotus sacerdos*]; Mary is a young man [*juvenis*]; John the Evangelist, a priest; Mary Magdalen and the mother of John, young men.

The preface speaks for itself, but two points are particularly worth noting: the insistence that the play is neither *ludus* nor *ludibrium*, that it transcends the categories of fiction and of entertainment and that it is true; and the evident paradox of presenting a highly emotional and deliberately emotive situation in a restrained and measured manner. This clearly raises problems of musical interpretation relating not only to the *Marienklagen* but also to the religious drama as a whole.

(*ii*) '*Sponsus*', *the* '*Play of Adam*', '*St Agnes*' *and the Shrewsbury fragments.* A number of isolated religious plays survive from the Middle Ages which do not belong either to the liturgical drama or to the main traditions of vernacular drama. Like the *Marienklagen* and, indeed, many German Passion plays, they mingle Latin and vernacular and give music an important place. They differ widely in date and in general style.

The first, *Sponsus* (see §II, 1 above), comes from a well-known late 11th-century manuscript of St Martial (*F-Pn* lat.1139); it is just under 100 lines long. The play dramatizes in a mixture of Latin and Provençal the parable of the wise and foolish virgins (*Matthew* xxv.1–13) and ends with the coming of the bridegroom (*sponsus*). The play differs from the parable in putting more emphasis on the distress of the foolish and less on the joy of the wise; in introducing new characters – the angel Gabriel, *demones* (the earliest devils of medieval drama), and merchants, who refuse to sell oil to the foolish; and in being more radically an allegory of advent and judgment (Christ is bridegroom and judge; Heaven is the marriage feast).

Although *Sponsus* is often classed as a liturgical play, the text 'bears no evidence of attachment to the liturgy, or having developed from liturgical pieces', or of having been performed in church (Young, 1933, ii, 361). Chailley (1960), on palaeographical, metrical, musical, thematic (literary) and other grounds, believed it to belong with the prophet play which follows it in the manuscript. Advent seems to be its proper season (see, further, Thomas, 1951). The standard scholarly editions (with music) are by Thomas (1951) and D'Avalle (1965); there is also a practical edition, by Smoldon (?1965), with comments on the musical notation.

Musically, also, *Sponsus* has nothing in common with other Latin church plays: it uses no liturgical chants but relies entirely on four melodies of a non-Gregorian character, which may or may not be metrical in keeping with the accentual Latin verse texts. Ex.16 gives the opening melody of the play in the alternative transcriptions adopted by Smoldon and D'Avalle. The unfortunate ambiguity of pitch further clouds the issues of interpretation. However, the fact that a melody may have to serve the purposes of more than one character (e.g. melody 3, for merchants as well as the foolish virgins) means that theories of leitmotifs must be regarded as strained as well as anachronistic (cf St Nicholas plays, §II, 6 above). The music helps the listener to stand away from the characters, not to identify with them.

Ex.16 *F-Pn* lat. 1139 f. 53

The Bridegroom that is Christ is here: be watchful, O virgins! men rejoice and will rejoice in his coming.

The second isolated drama, the *Play of Adam*, is in fact three plays in sequence: Creation and Fall of Man, Cain and Abel, and prophet play. The sole surviving manuscript (*F-TO* 927, 12th century) is in Anglo-Norman and the play is generally thought to have been written in England. It differs from *Sponsus* in that the action is conducted entirely in the spoken vernacular; there is no musical notation in the text, but the singularly detailed Latin stage directions require the singing of two Latin lessons and seven responsories. The only English edition of the play, by Studer (1918), has been superseded by those of Aebischer (1963), Sletsjoe (1968) and Noomen (1971). The basic musical study is by Chailley (in Cohen, 1936). Chailley supplied contemporary responsories from an antiphoner of St Maur-des-Fossés (*F-Pn* lat.12044); Doyle (1948) supplied them from an antiphoner in Worcester Cathedral Library (see PalMus, 1st ser., xii). Muir's monograph (1973) is the only full-length study, but somewhat neglects the music.

The *Play of Adam* is remarkable in several ways: for a depth of psychological penetration almost unrivalled in medieval European drama; for the fullness of its stage directions; and for its unique combination of musical and spoken dramatic effects. The power and subtlety with which the myth is re-created as a human drama is in the strongest imaginative contrast to the effect of the liturgical chants. In ancient use all these responsories belonged to the nocturns of Matins of Septuagesima (formerly of Sexagesima) and it is to this liturgical season, though not precisely (it is thought) to this liturgical Office, that the play pertains. There is another reason for not overestimating, with older scholars, the new 'freedom' and 'emancipation' of the play: like *Sponsus* and the *Play of Daniel*, the *Play of Adam* leads to the prophecies of Christ's coming, and like almost all medieval religious drama on Old Testament themes is a play about Christ. Adam's formal lament after the Fall is directed partly against his wife's treachery, but above all it proclaims Man's redemption.

The dramatic method of the play of the Fall (which contains six of the responsories) is generally to announce themes in the chanted responsories and then to work them out in the form of dramatic 'tropes'. Thus the responsory *Formavit igitur Dominus* ('And the Lord God formed man of the dust of the ground . . .') precedes God's speech describing the creation of Adam (ex.17).

Ex.17 *GB-WO* F.160 p. 72 (Pal Mus xii)

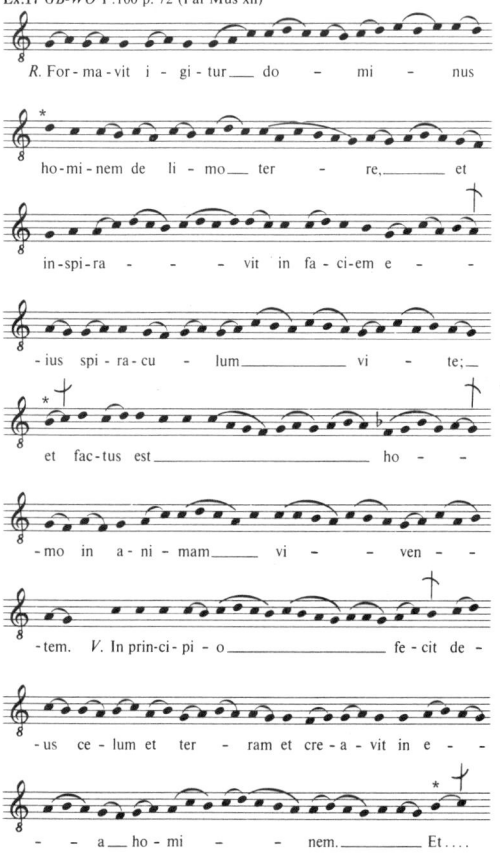

R. And the Lord God formed man of the dust of the ground, and breathed into his nostrils the breath of life; and man became a living soul.
V. In the beginning God created the heaven and the earth, and in them he created man.

In a reading of the play it is easy to overlook the 'primary, framing power of liturgical music in and around the play' (Stevens, 1968): these majestic responsories, unfolding at length, need to be heard. The singers are named as the *chorus*, probably the choir of the church. They take no part in the dramatic action themselves but clearly in some sense represent the heavenly host. Their plainchant singing is always associated with God's own appearances and actions (this is why there is only one responsory in the Cain and Abel play) – a fact which relates the musical dramatic technique of the *Play of Adam* to the technique of the later mysteries (§III, 2(i) above).

The Provençal saints' play *St Agnes* contrasts with both *Sponsus* and the *Play of Adam*. It was copied in the 14th century (*I-Rvat* Chigi C.V.151) and probably writ-

ten not much earlier. The most convenient modern edition is by Jeanroy (1931) with musical appendix by Gérold (see also Hoepffner, 1950, and Monaci, 1880, with facsimiles). The unoriginal story, full of the sensational clichés of medieval hagiography, tells of Agnes's refusal to marry the son of the Roman prefect, Simpronius, and of the consequence: she is brought to trial and sentenced to be put in a brothel. Her hair grows miraculously to cover her nakedness, an angelic light repels all advances, and the brothel becomes a house of prayer. In the end, having survived burning at the stake, she dies calmly and is escorted to Paradise by angels.

There are 19 or 20 musical (i.e. sung) passages in the play, of which almost all are called planctus, irrespective of whether they are so or not. 15 of the melodies are notated, in square (unmeasured) notation on a four-line staff (i.e. in the style of the troubadour chansonniers); of these three are incomplete, and for another the staff has not been filled in. In addition two liturgical antiphons are given, both from Vespers of the Common of Virgins. A typical Latin stage direction (the text is liberally supplied with them) reads: 'Mater facit planctum in sonu albe Reis glorios, verai lums et clardat' ('The mother makes her complaint to the tune of the dawn-song *Reis glorios*'). This celebrated *alba* by Giraut de Borneilh (c1165–1200) survives; most of the other named tunes do not. Ex.18 gives the two versions. The freedom with which the known melody has been modified does not encourage belief that (for instance) the other versions

Ex.18

are necessarily very close to those current two centuries earlier. The dramatic function of the music in the play is unusually varied. There are the expected associations with divine action ('Angelus facit planctum in sonu Veni creator spiritus') and with lamentation (the mother's planctus and others); but music is also a vehicle for prayer (e.g. of the prostitutes after their conversion and baptism). The instrumental music of *tibicinatores* is also required for an angelic *silete* (see §III, 3(ii) below).

The so-called Shrewsbury fragments (Shrewsbury School Library, MS VI; discovered in 1890) present unsolved problems, especially musical ones. The text provides a single actor's part (with cues) for three plays: an *Officium pastorum*, a *Visitatio sepulchri* (the manuscript has the title *Officium Resurrectionis in die Pasche*) and a *Peregrinus*. The English passages are in a north-west Midlands dialect and were spoken; the Latin passages were evidently sung and nine of them are notated in black mensural notation on a five-line staff. The manuscript was written in the early 15th century almost entirely by one scribe (see Davis, 1970). The first thorough edition of the text was made by Young (1933, ii, appx B); that by Davis has musical transcriptions by Harrison. The other contents of the manuscript are mostly processional pieces (listed by Young) but ff.8–14 contain the part of the Jews from the Passions of Palm Sunday and Holy Week.

The rubrics of the manuscript and the nature of the Latin texts suggest that the plays were presented in a church; one processional indicates a church in which St Chad was especially honoured, such as Lichfield Cathedral where, it is known, liturgical plays on precisely these three subjects were performed.

It is puzzling that a single actor's disconnected parts should have been so dignified by their context and presentation. But the precise nature of the music for him is even more puzzling. Of the nine notated items, six are known texts from liturgical plays or from the liturgy. 'Mane nobiscum', for example, in the *Peregrinus* play is an ancient antiphon (Hartker, etc) which was used in plays at Saintes, Fleury, Benediktbeuern, Frankfurt etc (Schuler, 1951); the problem is to know whether the melodies notated are measured monophony for solo or unison singing, upper or middle parts of polyphonic compositions, faburden parts, or something else. The actor–singer of this manuscript was the Third Shepherd, the Third Mary and, probably, the disciple Cleophas. It is likely then that the polyphony, if such there was, was for three voices.

The Shrewsbury fragments have commonly been regarded as an essential link in the 'evolutionary' theory of medieval drama showing the emergence of vernacular plays from liturgical (some parallel between the English speeches of this *Officium pastorum* and York play no.15 is unquestioned). But in the hundreds of surviving English liturgical or para-liturgical manuscripts no parallel can be found.

*(iii) Early secular drama.* There is only one surviving secular play with a significant amount of music, Adam de La Halle's *Robin et Marion*; its quality makes the loss of others regrettable. It appears to have been written about 1283, when Adam was in the service of Robert II, Count of Artois. At that time the count was in southern Italy, but the play is thoroughly 'Artesian', not Italian in any sense; it was written to amuse expatriate northern French soldiers as part of the Christmas

festivities. It is a sophisticated piece of light entertainment consisting of a dramatized pastourelle (a lyric depicting an amorous encounter between a shepherdess and a roving knight) with a dramatized *bergerie* (a lyric describing the songs, dances and games of a group of shepherds). The materials are traditional, but their combination into this musical comedy is Adam's own achievement. The play survives in three manuscripts, the earliest and most authoritative being *F-Pn* fr.25566 (the 'complete works' of Adam de La Halle, *c*1300); *F-AIXm* 572 also contains the music, but *F-Pn* fr.1569 has only empty staves. There have been numerous editions of the play from 1822 onwards, none in English. Varty's (1960) lists previous editions and prints the music, which is also available in a modern English translation of the play (Axton and Stevens, 1971). Essential information from the musical point of view is provided by Gennrich's edition (1962) and Chailley's article (1950).

The music consists of 16 melodies dispersed throughout the play. (Adam's other play, *Le jeu de la feuillée*, contains only one, but of the same type, sung by three fairies.) They are short, rhythmical and syllabic; the notation, in complete contrast to that of Adam's courtly chansons (*F-Pn* fr.25566) is clearly metrical though not totally unambiguous. It is rather unlikely that Adam wrote any of them himself; they belong to the category of courtly popular melodies known as *refrains* (*see* REFRAIN) and several of them are found elsewhere. The melody of *Robins m'aime*, for instance, is also used as the motetus of a three-voice motet; that of *Avoec tele compaignie* occurs in the narrative poem *Renart le nouvel* and elsewhere (Gennrich, 1962). The melodies in fact belong with the words, and the author–composer has imported both together into the play. In this he followed the courtly fashion of the times. 'The melodies of the play of *Robin et Marion* possess practically all the characteristics of the "refrain-centos" of the *romances* and chansons of the period – especially of the pastourelles and *bergeries*' (Chailley, 1950) (in particular they are metrically independent from their context). The instruments introduced – a *chievrete* (a species of bagpipe) and two *cornes* (horns) – are also entirely in keeping with the lighthearted aristocratic stylization of country life.

One must not make heavy weather of the musical side of this delightful and essentially traditional entertainment; *Robin et Marion* is indeed a *jeu*, a playing. The element of dramatic illusion is very lightly handled, and the play has something of the nature of a revue (though without the overt topical references of *Le jeu de la feuillée*).

3. THE MAIN TRADITIONS.
*(i) English.* Fewer plays survive from medieval England than from France or Germany, but they are probably representative of dramatic activity at least in the Midlands and the north. Complete mystery cycles survive from Wakefield (the 'Towneley' plays), York, Chester and (probably) the Norfolk region (the 'Hegge' or 'N-Town' plays, published under the misleading title *Ludus Coventriae*). A cycle in medieval Cornish also survives in three sections: an *Origo mundi*, a Passion and a Resurrection (no events after the Ascension are represented). No texts survive of the Passion plays known to have been performed in London and southern England, nor of the 'Creed' and 'Pater noster' plays.

Isolated mystery plays survive from Norwich, Newcastle, Northampton, Brome (Suffolk) and elsewhere; the most interesting fragments of a supposed cycle are the two 'Corpus Christi plays' from Coventry ('true-Coventry' plays). Performances of saints' plays are recorded but very few survive; however, the manuscript (*GB-Ob* Digby 133; ed. Furnivall) contains a long play of St Mary Magdalen derived largely from *The Golden Legend* (a collection of saints' legends). The tradition of folk drama rests almost entirely on 19th- and 20th-century evidence, apart from the remarkable discovery of an early 16th-century Scottish Plough Play in a musical version (ed. in MB, xv, 1957). The four main cycles each contain plays covering the history of the world from the Creation to the Last Judgment. The contents of the cycles and the location of their manuscripts are listed in Chambers (1903, ii, appx X); his appendix Y (pp.329–406) lists representations of medieval plays from all over Britain (see also Stratman, 1972, i, pp.345ff).

Little actual music is given in the English manuscripts: there are two English songs in the Coventry Plays, some two-voice Latin polyphony in the York cycle, a short monophonic Gloria in the Chester cycle. The number and usefulness of musical stage directions varies from cycle to cycle, but the Chester and Hegge cycles each contain over 30. Beuscher (1930) listed and analysed the musical repertory; Moore (1923), Stevens (1957–8), Carpenter (1968) and Dutka (1973) described the dramatic function of the music.

Most of the musical directions require the singing of liturgical Latin texts, presumably to plainsong (canticles, antiphons, hymns, sequences, communions, offertories and *versus alleluiatici*). These liturgical pieces are not normally those connected with the liturgical drama itself, which in any case covers only a small fraction of the huge subject matter of the mystery cycles; but they are often liturgically appropriate. Thus the Digby *Candlemass Day Play* (Slaughter of the Innocents combined with Purification) contains the stage direction: 'here shal Symeon bere Iesu in his armys, goyng a procession rounde aboute the tempill; and al this wyle the virgynis synge nunc dimittis'. The *Nunc dimittis*, besides being the canticle of Compline, was special to the feast of the Purification, when it was sung with its antiphon *Lumen ad revelationem* at the blessing of the candles (Sarum Processional). In the Hegge play on the same subject, the Latin line (?gloss, ? musical direction, ? spoken text) 'Suscepimus Deus misericordiam tuam' may refer to the introit and gradual for the feast (Sarum Gradual). The hymns include: *Veni, Creator* (Chester *Play of the Holy Ghost*; York plays of the Baptism, the Temptation and Pentecost); *Jhesu, corona virginum* (Hegge, *Presentation BVM*); *Stella celi extirpavit* (Hegge, *Shepherds' Play*); *Gloria laus* (Hegge, *Entry into Jerusalem*); *Salvator mundi* (Wakefield, *Harrowing of Hell*; Chester, *Last Judgment*). (In the last case the processional antiphon, not the hymn, may have been meant, since the angels sing it 'coming and going'.) There is one striking exception to the general observation that the liturgical songs are unconnected with the liturgical drama. The isolated *Christ's Burial and Resurrection* (*GB-Ob* E. museo 160; ed. Furnivall with Digby plays but not now thought to have any connection with them) makes extensive use of the Easter sequence *Victime paschali* (see above). The play is in effect an English *Marienklage*, with a *Visitatio sepulchri*

added to it as second part ('This is a play to be playede, on[e] part on Gud-friday afternone, & the other part opon Esterday after the Resurrectione, in the morowe'). The Latin sequence is sung in dramatic dialogue by the three Marys, Peter, Andrew and John. The rubric is of unusual interest: 'These three [Marys] shall sing it right through to "Dic nobis" in polyphony [*cantifracto*] or at least antiphonally [*in pallinodio*]'.

Indications of Latin polyphony are rare and seldom unambiguous. But such directions as 'the hefne syngynge', 'they shal synge in hefne this hympne: "Jhesu corona" ' may well refer to professional polyphonic singing (by the 'angels' on the scaffold of 'Heaven'). The elaborate vocal style of the angelic musicians (perhaps the clerks of the local cathedral) is invariably the subject of comment by the shepherds ('I dar say that he broght/ foure and twenty to a long': Wakefield, *Second Shepherds' Play*). The simple measured monophonic *Gloria in excelsis Deo* of the Chester plays (ex.19, from *GB-Lbm* Harl.2124) does not seem adequate to the occasion.

Ex.19 *GB-Lbm* Harley 2124 f. 42

Glo-ri-a___ [glo-ri-a] in ex-cel-sis de-
-o, de-o,___ de-o, de-o.

Ex.20 *GB-Lbm* 35290 f. 235v

Sur———ge [pro-pe-ra me-
Sur———ge pro-pe-ra me-
[MS:-xima]

———a, co-lum-ba me-
———a, co-lum-ba me-

-a, ta-ber-na-cu-lum___glo—ri—
-a, ta-ber-na-cu-lum___glo—ri—

-e, vas-cu-lum vi——te, tem-plum-
-e, vas-cu-lum vi——te, tem-plum___

ce—les———te.]
ce—les———te.

Play 46 of the York cycle (*GB-Lbm* 35290; text ed. L. T. Smith) is uniquely valuable as containing the only fully notated Latin polyphonic music in an English dramatic source (see fig.8): it is *The Appearance of Our Lady to St Thomas*, staged by the Weavers' Guild. Three songs are sung by angels in the course of a vision of the Blessed Virgin vouchsafed to doubting Thomas to restore his faith: *Surge, propera mea, columba mea, Veni de Libano sponsa* and *Veni, electa mea*. The texts are strongly reminiscent of passages in the *Song of Songs*. For an unexplained reason each text is set twice, once in the course of the play (notated in score), once at the end of the play (each part written separately at length and not aligned with its fellow). It is not clear whether or not the settings are alternatives for performance. The music (see ex.20) is in a characteristic 15th-century style, reminiscent of some of the carols, for two equal voices of limited range, with long melodies, a strong metrical pulse, marked cross-rhythms, and a non-expressive relationship between the words and the music. The settings in the second group are rather more ornate. All the settings are in triple time (see Wall, 1971, with transcriptions by Steiner).

Part-singing to simple vernacular texts certainly took place as well. The *Second Shepherds' Play* (Wakefield) contains a three-voice song, the first shepherd taking 'the tenory', the second 'the tryble so hye' and the third 'the meyne'. In the Towneley *First Shepherds' Play* the further remark 'Syng we in syght' suggests a style of improvised singing such as English discant (Carpenter, 1951; *see* DISCANT, §II). The Cornish plays require part-singing in Hell from Beelzebub, Satan and other devils. But vernacular singing is not synonymous with part-singing even in late manuscripts. In the Chester *Deluge* the psalm Noah and his family sing in the ark is *Save mee, O God* (probably Psalm xlix, in the metrical version of Sternhold and Hopkins) probably to be sung in unison; and it is even less likely that the drinking-song of Noah's wife and her 'good gossops' was a contrapuntal artefact.

Once again a single unique survival helps to fill the gap. The 'true-Coventry' *Shepherds' Play* is the only dramatic source of vernacular partsong with music. Unfortunately, the original manuscript (completed ?1534) was burnt in 1879; the songs have to be reconstructed from Sharp (1825) who gave an unsatisfactory literal transcript of the original notation. Part-music is sung on three separate occasions, but there are only two musical settings: *As I outrode this enderes night* with the second verse 'Doune from heaven' (a refrain-song in an early 16th-century chordal style with a few simple imitative entries), and *Lully, lulla ... O sisters too* (a carol, in simple chordal style).

Concerning instrumental music the English sources are disappointingly silent. The very late Chester manuscripts (five of the complete cycle, all *c*1600; see Craig, 1955) give some idea, especially in the *Creation and Fall of Man*, how frequently the minstrels may have been called on. They are to play music (unspecified) when God creates the world, when God takes Adam to Paradise, when God re-enters after the Fall, twice when Adam and Eve are expelled, and when God appears to Cain. But this evidence may be valid only for Elizabethan performances. No English 'director's copy' survives comparable to (for example) the documents of Frankfurt and Mons (ed. Cohen, 1925). Information about instrumental music has to be pieced together from

8. *One of the two-part songs given in the text of the play 'The Appearance of Our Lady to St Thomas' from the York cycle, 15th century (GB-Lbm Add.35290, f.236r); this is the only surviving example of notated polyphonic music in an English medieval play-text*

the texts, from the rare stage direction and from account books (the records of Chester and Coventry are especially helpful). Hegge stage directions refer to trumpets ('hic dum buccinant'), harps or lutes (*citharis*) and ?organs (*organa*). The colourful mid-16th-century Coventry accounts list payments: to 'the trumpeter', for regals, for 'dromming', to 'six musicissions', to 'two clarks for singing', 'to Thomas Nycles for settyng a songe' (Craig, 1902). This does not amount to anything very lavish. Directions such as 'fluryshe' and 'pipe ... that we may dance' (especially at the end of Cornish plays) indicate what the musicians were principally required for – fanfares and dance music. The long Digby *Candlemass Day Play* begins and ends with the minstrels playing and the 'virgynes' dancing to 'solace' the people.

Religious plays in the vernacular raise problems about the dramatic function of music which do not exist in liturgical drama. No set of vernacular plays, and in particular no English cycle, is sufficiently well rubricated to show exactly the occasions on which music was required, the precise nature of the pieces, or the effects they were intended to produce. Certain broad uses of music emerge, however, as well-established principles. Music has a threefold function: it assists the stage-business, imitates the effects of real life and provides dramatic symbolism. The stage-business principally required music to cover the exits and entrances (i.e. the movements of main characters to and from their 'scaffolds', 'pageants', 'houses', 'stages' etc). After the Prologue of the Croxton *Play of the Sacrament* (by two *vexillatores*, banner-bearers), the minstrel is exhorted to 'blow up with a mery stevyn' (a cheerful sound), probably to announce the entry of the first player, Aristorius Mercator. This 'fanfare' could, however, also be a call for silence (cf the *silete* of the French and German plays). Such music was not necessarily instrumental: the Digby *Play of Mary Magdalene* contains the curious direction 'here shall entyr a shyp with a mery song' (however, 'song' could mean simply 'music' in this period). In the Hegge Magi play Herod tells his minstrel to 'blowe up a good blast' while he goes to his chamber to change his clothes. This is evidently a short musical interlude marking the end of a scene. Examples could be multiplied.

The music of stage-business merges naturally with the music of dramatic naturalism. That King Herod has a minstrel (the trumpeter?) in attendance at court imitates the conditions of actual medieval life (no medieval dramatist attempted to portray the historical realities of the Christian story). Religious ceremonies, Christian, pagan or Jewish (e.g. in the Hegge plays, the blessing of Mary's parents Joachim and Anna in the Temple) are enriched with appropriate liturgical chants and actions ('There they shal synge this sequens. "Benedicta sit beata Trinitas", And in that tyme Ysakar with his ministerys ensensyth the Autere'). At the entry into Jerusalem 'myghtfull songes' are sung 'here on a rawe' (cf the 'royal entries', 'joyeuses entrées', of medieval city life). Music is also used to depict misery. The tradition of the *planctus* does not appear to have taken root in England, and there are no surviving settings of laments that can be connected with plays; formal laments do however appear in play texts and are sometimes directed to be sung (e.g. Norwich, *Fall*; Cornish, *Resurrection*).

The boundary between naturalistic imitation and dramatic symbolism is equally hard to draw precisely (this applies to the whole dramatic technique, not simply the music). The trumpeters 'blow up' while Herod changes his clothes, play as the 'servyse' of the feast comes in, and entertain Herod and his knights by celebrating the imagined death of the Christ-child; they also symbolize the pretensions of earthly kingship, the lust of the eyes and pride of life. The startling irruption of Death into this scene makes it, in effect, a Dance of Death in which music (especially that of trumpets) is a principal symbol of illusory power (as the dance is of youth and vitality): 'At this point whilst the minstrels are trumpeting [*buccinant*], let Death kill Herod and two of his knights, suddenly; and let the Devil take them' (Hegge, *Death of Herod*). The most important and perpetually recurrent symbolism, however, is that of music as an image of the divine. 'When God appears on a "scaffold" between two angels, or more, playing musical instruments, we know that God is in his heaven . . . a place of order and harmony'. He would be literally in 'Heaven', too – the usual term for his 'scaffold' (see York, *Creation*; Chester, *Fall of Lucifer*, etc). 'Music is never employed in the English drama "for atmosphere"; it is never there for an emotive effect. It is there, like God's beard of gold, or the horned animal heads of the devils, because it signifies something' (Stevens, 1957–8). By a natural extension of the symbol, music is used to signify the divine authority of God's messengers, the

angels (Hegge, *Annunciation*; and passim in all cycles and most individual plays). A further extension enables music to represent human gladness and gratitude in response to God's acts of power and love: that of Adam and the prophets released from limbo (Harrowing of Hell plays); Mary's humble acceptance of Gabriel's message (Annunciation plays); and above all the shepherds', whose glad songs have been discussed above (there is no shepherds' play without music).

(*ii*) *French.* The earliest religious plays, after those discussed (§III, 2(ii–iii)), are miracles, plays based on miraculous incidents in saints' lives. Two of the earliest are *Le jeu de Saint Nicolas* of JEHAN BODEL and Rutebeuf's *Le miracle de Théophile*; neither text contains music or directions for music. However a collection survives from the 14th century, *Les miracles de Notre Dame* (20 dramatized miracles in *F-Pn* fr.819–20, the 'Cangé MSS'); in each play the Virgin works a miracle of salvation for a miserable sinner (a pregnant abbess, a child handed over to the Devil, a bribed pope, etc). As in other European countries, the 14th and 15th centuries saw the growth of massive religious play cycles in France. Unlike the surviving English cycles French ones do not usually cover all history from the Creation to the Last Judgment; their distinguishing feature is often a framework of the Trial of Man. The earliest is *La passion du Palatinus* (14th century; ed. Frank, 1922), which opens with the entry into Jerusalem; *Le jour du jugement* (14th century; ed. Roy, 1903–4) deals only with Antichrist and the Last Judgment but has 94 characters, imposing theatrical effects and music. The 15th-century plays of most interest to the music historian are *La passion de Semur* (Creation to Ascension, 9582 lines, performed in two days; ed. Roy, 1903–4); *La nativité, la passion et la résurrection de nostre Saulveur Jhesu-Crist* of ARNOUL GREBAN (including also Creation, over 30,000 lines, four days; ed. Jodogne, 1965); the Rouen *L'incarnation et la nativité* (1474; 12,800 lines, two days; ed. Verdier, 1886); and the *Vie* (or *Mystère*) *de Saint Louis* (before 1472; 224 characters, three days; ed. Michel, 1871). Each play in the large repertory of *mystères* and miracles is analysed in detail in Petit de Julleville's *Les mystères* (1880, ii). Only *Le jour du jugement* (*F-B* 579) and *La passion de Semur* (*F-Pn* fr.904) contain musical notation; the Rouen *Incarnation* has room for part-music to be filled in (by hand – the text is printed). For accounts of music on the medieval French stage, see especially Pirro (1940) and Brown (1963). Editions of French vernacular plays are listed in Stratman (2/1972, ii, items 7050–7661).

As in other vernacular dramas the principal music is plainsong. In the *Mystère de Saint Louis* a litany is sung by a bishop, an abbot and a dean. Hymns are frequent: *Vexilla regis* (*Saint Louis*), *Veni Redemptor gentium* (*Mystère de Saint Vincent*, 1476), *Gloria tibi Domine* (*Martyre de Saint Denis*), *Aurora lucis* (*Resurrection de Jesus-Christ* by Eloy du Mont). Liturgical chants include the *Stabat mater* (Jean Michel's *Passion*, based on Greban's), *Regina celi*, antiphon of the BVM (Du Mont) and, expectedly, the concluding *Te Deum*. The fact that choirs of angels are the most frequent singers does not mean that such music was sung polyphonically. Some hymns, however, may have been sung in fauxbourdon (Reese, 1954), and elsewhere there is incontrovertible evidence for polyphonic singing. In Arnoul

Greban's *Passion* a 'motet d'onneur' is sung in Hell: Lucifer assigns the tenor to Satan, the 'contre' to himself, 'le dessus' to Beelzebub, the 'haulte double' to Berich, and 'un trouble' to Cerberus. Eventually they sing the rondeau: 'La dure mort eternelle/c'est la chançon des dampnés'. Further infernal counterpoint occurs in Arnoul Greban's brother Simon's *Actes des apôtres* (see Lebègue, 1929), where however Cerberus 'mon gros garcon' is assigned to the 'bazitonans' with 'two really thunderous devils'. The learned compiler of the Rouen *Incarnation* required three-voice performance of angelsong (tenor, contratenor and concordans); and, with trinitarian symbolism, the utterances of God in the Greban and Michel *Passion* plays are also for three voices (in Michel's, 'haut dessus, une haute contre, et une basse contre bien accordés').

One important distinguishing feature of French religious drama, in marked contrast to the English, is its association from at least the 14th century with a tradition of musical and literary competitions, the PUY. The most informative early document is *Les miracles de Notre Dame*, written between about 1339 and 1382 by members of the Guild of Goldsmiths in Paris. As Frank (1954) stated:

The 23 lyrical serventoys [sirventes; *see* TROUBADOURS, TROUVÈRES] in praise of the Virgin which appear between certain plays point to a kind of poetical contest fostered by the religious and literary members of the puy that sponsored the Miracles: these pieces refer to the prince du puy at times and once to a serventoys couronné au dit puy.

At Amiens 'ung jeu de mistère' was performed at the annual Candlemas banquet; this suggests how the Parisian miracles may have been done. The interspersed serventoys are in a favourite troubadour–trouvère form (five stanzas of ten lines with envoi) and were presumably set to music. The songs within the plays give the same impression of literary sophistication and were certainly sung. In accordance with a recurrent pattern, when miraculous intervention is necessary, the Virgin summons the archangels Gabriel and Michael to escort her to earth: they do this singing a rondeau, and the Virgin's return to the skies is often similarly accompanied. The rondeaux, then, function as a sort of conductus. The tradition (as it seems to be) of interpolated art song continues in the big Passion plays of Greban and Michel. In the shepherd scene (Greban, day 1), four shepherds, apparently singing (perhaps only reciting) in dialogue, perform a string of rondeaux. Even the farcical *Le garçon et l'aveugle* (13th century; ed. Roques, 2/1921) incorporates a song in honour of the Virgin. In the Rouen *Incarnation* spoken rondeaux in dialogue introduce the composed songs at important moments; and in one shepherd scene a 'champ [?chant] royal' is performed with an envoi apparently addressed to the 'princes' of a *puy*.

A last type of vernacular song is the planctus (*complainte*). The Autun *Passion* twice signifies 'La complainte Nostre Dame', and the early *Passion du Palatinus* has laments as do the liturgical plays for Mary Magdalen repentant, for the Virgin at the cross, and for the three Marys visiting Christ's tomb. No music survives, and the tradition never acquired the importance that it did in German-speaking countries with the *Marienklage* (§III, 2(i)).

Instrumental music enlivened the plays from the earliest onwards. One of the *Miracles de Notre Dame* (play no.3) contains parts for three minstrels, and in the same play the wicked bishop sends for 'les jugleurs' for a celebration. Practically every *mystère* or miracle demands some kind of instrumental support, provided by the local waits or town band, or hired from outside. The Montferrand *Passion* in 1477 evidently had a total performing ensemble of 'two organists, seven trumpeters, and four unspecified ménétriers, to which should be added two more "tronpetes de la tour" ' (Brown, 1963). The composition, if not the size, of the group seems to have been standard. The unspecified musicians would probably play *haut* wind instruments – shawms and sackbuts – combining to provide the usual dance band. The dance of Salome was an expected feature of the St John the Baptist scenes; sometimes a tambourin (drum) accompanied her, or pipe and tabor (Mons, *Passion*). Elsewhere dances are indicated: the *morisque* (Michel's *Passion*; Semur etc), the *orliennaise* (the basse danse, ?Orleans) and a 'sauterelle' (*Mystère de Saint Louis*). The stage directions of the Rouen *Incarnation* require instrumentalists to join the singers in the chansons which decorate the play, but in each case they alternate with the singers; they do not accompany them.

The dramatic function of music in the plays conforms to international patterns. The function is threefold: to imitate naturalistic effects in stage terms, to further the stage-business and to act as symbol. These categories inevitably overlap. The naturalistic effects include music for feasts (*Miracles de Notre Dame*), for a coronation (*Mystère de Saint Louis*: all the instruments available played for the Sultan's), for a royal entry (e.g. *La vengeance nostre Seigneur*: trumpets and clarions) and for royal proclamations (*Mystère des trois doms*). The feigned naturalism of the angel musicians in the Rouen *Incarnation* is especially interesting. These particular musicians could evidently only sing, but when the 'joueurs d'instrumens' played behind and out of sight, the angels were to 'act as if they were playing'. The stage-business includes the entrances and exits of important characters, for which fanfares were commonly used. But perhaps the most common signals for a musical event of some kind are the directions 'pause' (or 'pose') and 'silete'. The latter originated as a call for order – 'Keep silence, keep silence' (see §III, 3(iii)), and was sung by angels, the principal musicians available. Thence it became the generic term (with 'pause') for a musical interlude, often marking the end of one scene and the beginning of another. In the Greban *Passion* (to choose one out of scores of examples) the creation of Eve ends with God saying: 'Arise my angels, legion by legion, ... and sing a joyous *silete*' – God the Father retires to his 'siège' and the angels sing. Such interludes covered the movement of actors about the 'place' (the main acting area) and in and out of their 'houses' (*sièges, lieux, mansions, estages* etc). The director's book for the Mons *Passion* of 1501 (*Le livre de conduite du régisseur*; see Cohen, 1925) says 'If God takes too long [i.e. in getting from one position to another], *silete*'. The same book requires a *silete* during the mimed building of Noah's ark. On this occasion the alternative to a *silete* is a 'poze d'orghues', or minstrel music 'de quelque instrument'. Elsewhere a 'poze de menestraux' is specified. The French documents, unlike the German, never specify, let alone notate, the precise music to be performed. Minstrels presumably played pieces from their regular repertory on these occasions (Brown, 1963).

The symbolic effects of music in the French plays correspond to those described for the English cycles. Music symbolizes first and foremost the joy and order of Heaven and heavenly truth; it therefore accompanies the appearances and acts of God and his messengers the angels. So frequent and expected is this function of dramatic music that in the plays from the Bibliothèque Ste Geneviève (ed. Jubinal, 1837) the angels are sometimes told to come and go 'sans chanter'. Only the best music is good enough for Heaven; hence, perhaps, the requirement (Mons, 1501) that the angels in Paradise should sing 'en chose faicte' (i.e. *res facta*, thus 'counterpoint'). The divine significance of music can be transferred to a pagan temple ('pose d'orgues': Mons, 1501). The obverse of heavenly music is hellish din. Hell is the place for thunders and tempests: after the Fall of Lucifer, 'here they must make a great storm' (Greban). Polyphonic singing in Hell has already been noted, from the same Passion. Infernal singing could evidently take on a deliberately discordant aspect: in the *Liber beate Barbare* (Petit de Julleville, 1880, ii) Lucifer orders a chanson 'with unmelodious music'.

Once again however the difficulty and danger of establishing hard and fast categories to describe dramatic function are evident. They can be illustrated from the shepherds' plays. Of these one of the most extended and sophisticated representations is in the Rouen *Incarnation*, 1474. The shepherd scenes occur on the second day. At their first entrance four individually named shepherds sing rondeaux in dialogue (see above); a little later they sing 'Requiescant in pace'. Their next scene is, most unusually, a music lesson. Anathot, a young shepherd, asks his elder, Ludin, what the art of singing is called. Ludin replies 'Music'. Anothat exclaims 'Music, what a frightful word!'. At this Ludin instructs him in music with frequent reference to the theory of Jehan des Murs. They finish with a two-part song. At the crib five shepherds sing *En paissant nos brebis* (printed staff left void). Further episodes contain a 'praise' of great shepherds of the past and the long three-voice chanson which Ludin and Anathot compose to conclude the whole play (no music).

In these scenes music is presented as part of the natural (naturalistic, in dramatic terms) presentation of shepherd life – pipes and tabors, and dancing and singing, inevitably go with them; as an extension of the shepherds' poetic creativity (the shepherd David is a type of the poet–musician and often appears as a minstrel with harp in vernacular drama); and as a symptom and symbol of their simple integrity and devotion (pastoral idealization of religious experience).

*(iii) German.* The surviving repertory of plays in the German vernacular is larger, more varied and musically more interesting than that of any other language. The five main types of play are: Easter plays in which the central scene is the visit of the three Marys to the sepulchre; Easter plays in which the complaint of Mary (the *planctus Marie*) is extensively developed – the *Marienklagen*; Passion plays (*Passionen*) treating the events of Holy Week more comprehensively; Corpus Christi plays (*Fronleichnamspiele*) somewhat similar to the English mystery cycles in their scope; and Christmas plays. There also existed in parts of Germany, as elsewhere, a tradition of folk plays. These were associated principally with the celebrations (revels) of Shrove Tuesday (*Fastnachtspiele*). Music and dance certainly played some part in them, but their study belongs rather to folklore and anthropology.

The vernacular religious drama of Germany (i.e. of the German-speaking countries) is generally said to begin with the *Osterspiel* of Muri (13th century). The drama was still flourishing in the early 17th century (e.g. in Lucerne) and is demonstrably the same in essentials, though influenced by the events and the theological upheavals of the Reformation. As in England, the plays reached their peak of popularity and creativity in the 15th and early 16th centuries. From the 14th century onwards certain districts were particularly active in play production: the mid-western districts around Frankfurt and, later, the Tyrol; but the religious drama was widespread and plays survive from many towns, including Breslau, Regensburg, Augsburg and Konstanz.

There is no complete collected edition of German medieval plays. The most substantial collections are by Mone (1841, 1846), Froning (1891–2) and Hartl (1936–42); the latest edition does not always provide the best text. None of these contains music. A useful up-to-date account of the drama from a literary and dramatic standpoint is W. F. Michael's *Das deutsche Drama des Mittelalters* (1971), with bibliography, descriptions of the contents of the plays and full details about editions. The sources of all liturgical and vernacular Easter plays are described, and their contents listed (by song incipit) and cross-referred in Schuler's *Die Musik der Osterfeiern, Osterspiele und Passionen des Mittelalters* (1951). His 50-page introduction is the longest single account of the music of the Easter plays (Christmas and other plays do not figure in his book). More comprehensive and up to date, though inevitably compressed, is the appropriate section of Lipphardt's fundamental article in *MGG*. Editions are listed in Stratman (2/1972, ii, items 7992–8184).

The five principal sources of information about music in the plays are: accounts of payments to performers (e.g. Lucerne, 1571); documents relating to their production (e.g. the 'Frankfurter Dirigierrolle', early 14th century, ed. Froning); stage directions, normally in Latin; references in stage directions or in the text to the required music; and actual notated music. Music was evidently required for all productions, but unfortunately only a few play manuscripts fall into the fifth category. In the comprehensive list of sources given by Lipphardt (*MGG*) those which contain written music are asterisked; of these the most important, *Marienklagen* excepted, are the Alsfeld *Passion* (see Dreimüller, 1936), the Vienna *Passion* (see Orel, 1926) and the Erlau Plays (see Osthoff, 1942). The music is generally monophonic, whether its origin is ecclesiastical or secular, and even in quite late sources is written in *Hufnagel* neumes, the characteristic unmeasured German notation. Some sources contain some mensural notation (e.g. Erlau) and a few have part-music in the form of rounds or canons (Osnabruck, Lucerne). In the late plays (or rather, late versions of plays) more elaborate part-music was certainly called for. A simple two-voice *Silete, silete* from the Trier play *Theophilus* (ed. Bohn, 1877) and a vernacular *Nu hört, wo sik Theophil gaf* in the same style survive. In the Lucerne plays the Kantorei (choir of professional singers) sang 'figuraliter' (usually interpreted as polyphonic music) and 'devota cantio ad organum' (elsewhere a 'Positif' is named) and 'brevis moteta' (Evans, 1943; Schuler, 1951). Such musical requirements belong, however, to the very end of the medieval dramatic tradition. In general the play music belongs to the history of monophonic music, but the surviving evidence does not allow of any dogmatic assertion to this effect, and earlier fashions of polyphony may have served earlier generations.

The different musical traditions which come together in the vernacular drama cannot be understood without reference to the curious dramatic amalgam that occurs in many plays. A fair sample of the potpourri is provided by the late 14th-century 'Innsbruck' *Osterspiel* (*A-Iu*, ed. Meir, 1963; the manuscript is of mid-German provenance). In this the often grotesque comedy is quite naively juxtaposed with liturgical, or quasi-liturgical, action and music. It has the interest of being the earliest surviving *Osterspiel*, apart from the *Osterspiel* of Muri, the unique early vernacular play (13th century). Unlike the Muri play, the 'Innsbruck' play set a pattern: the Vienna and Erlau plays are closely related to it. It may therefore fairly be taken as displaying the essential features and raising the essential problems of the vernacular music drama. These features can be summarized as the alternation or juxtaposition of song and speech, the wide range of musical material, and the equally wide range of musical function.

The bizarre contrasts of mood and treatment which occur in most German vernacular plays (except the *Marienklagen*) are mirrored not only linguistically in the use of various kinds of Latin (liturgical prose, rhymed hymns and sequences, goliardic verse) and of German (from doggerel narrative to laments in a high style), but also musically in the combination of very different musical traditions. They are, briefly: the old liturgical plainsong, together with newer pieces from the repertory of tropes and sequences; 'quasi-plainsong' from the repertory of the liturgical drama itself; the planctus; courtly and 'clerical' song (i.e. epic song, Minnesang and goliard song); and popular song, religious and secular. To these should be added a category of professional instrumental music about which regrettably little is or ever can be known.

The variety of Latin song and plainsong is exemplified by the Wölfenbüttel *Osterspiel* (ed. Schönemann, 1855). Among the various items are familiar antiphons (e.g. *Quis revolvet*), hymns (e.g. *Jesu, nostra redemptio*), laments of the Marys (*Heu, nobis internas* etc; cf Origny *Ludus paschalis*), the Trisagion ('Sancte Deus . . . sancte fortis . . . sancte et immortalis') and the Easter sequence *Victime paschali*. As this brief list shows, a vernacular *Osterspiel* is inevitably closely linked both to other *Osterspiele* and to the larger plays within the Latin liturgical tradition – in particular the *Ludi paschales* of Origny, Klosterneuburg and Tours. Basically there is only one *Osterspiel*, in a number of variant forms. This comment applies equally (perhaps more) to their music. Every single piece of liturgical or quasi-liturgical chant from the Wölfenbüttel play can be paralleled elsewhere, commonly in ten or 12 sources (Schuler, 1951, listed 31 occurrences of the antiphon *Mulier quid ploras*); antiphons and hymns (or hymn-like strophic songs) are especially frequent, and the Trisagion formula from the Good Friday liturgy occurs in no fewer than 19 vernacular plays (like a number of other Latin chants it does not seem to appear in liturgical drama). Until all these plays are available in sound scholarly texts with their music, it will be impossible to say how wide the musical variations are and what their significance is.

Not all the music in the Wölfenbüttel *Osterspiel* is of liturgical origin or shows liturgical affinities. Lipphardt (1948) argued that the three strophes *Heu nobis internas*, *Jam percusso* and *Sed eamus* have no relation to hymn, sequence or any other form. Melodies of this type belong to the planctus tradition whose development in German drama has already been sketched (§III, 2(i) above, *Marienklagen*).

One recurrent scene in vernacular drama especially encouraged the introduction of worldly song (far more worldly than the serious melodies just discussed) – the sinful early career of Mary Magdalen. In the Erlauer *Mary Magdalen Play* (Erlau IV; see Osthoff, 1942) there are 713 German lines and ten Latin; 90 lines are musically notated; 26 have void staves. The text is full of remarks such as 'Ich will preisen meinen leib mit tanzen und mit raien', and 'wir schullen singen, springen, raien den maien auf der Strasse'. The melodies have a 'popular' lilt and the rich individual character of late medieval song. The Alsfeld *Passion* (c1500) also has some notated songs, one being strongly reminiscent, verbally at least, of the songs of the goliards; Rubin, the merchant's man, sings it to advertise his master: 'Hic est magister Ypocras/de gracia bovina'. A slightly less blasphemous version is sung by the same character in the 'Innsbruck' *Osterspiel* and in other plays.

To draw sharp distinctions between the different sources of songs in the vernacular drama is unrealistic; but the range of non-liturgical song is wide. The 'Hessische' *Weihnachtsspiel* (? from Friedberg; see Lipphardt, 1958) is of particular interest, for it contains Christmas songs, some of them still sung today, of a kind different from and more artless than any previously mentioned. One stage direction runs: 'And so the serving-man and Joseph dance around the crib singing: *In dulce jubilo*. And then the angels begin *Sunt impleta*'. Other popular religious songs include *Eya, eya, virgo Deum genuit*, *Puer nobis nascitur* and *Eyn Kint geborn zu Bethleem*.

It is one thing to identify the different musical traditions – liturgical and para-liturgical, courtly and popular – which contribute to the vernacular drama; it is another to describe the dramatic function of the music in all its variety. It is clear that, in the first place, music had some strictly practical uses. The most striking, and perhaps comic to present-day ways of thinking, is the use of angel song, as in the French plays, to keep the audience quiet, or rather to bring them to order. The song *Silete, silete, silentium habete* appears from the early 14th century onwards and is associated with the larger plays. A change from one acting-place to another causes disturbance and noise, the *silete* quells it. In the St Gall Passion almost every 'entrance' is heralded by the *silete* (Schuler, 1951). They were doubtless usually monophonic. Ex.21 gives a setting from the Vienna *Osterspiel* (1472) edited by Osthoff.

These angels are scarcely part of the dramatic action at all, though it is interesting that angels are in fact chosen. (It is also puzzling how 'duo pueri', for example, could by their singing have quelled the noise of a holiday crowd.) Music employed to create an illusion – of social pomp, good cheer, conviviality – is more clearly part of the action. The marriage feast at Cana called for music; so, in the Lucerne Passions, did the entourage of Goliath and the travels of Joseph and his brothers. There are comparatively few German Christmas plays, and of these none has music-making by shepherds 'in the fields abiding', unlike the English plays.

As a dramatic symbol (rather than as a mimetic aid in the simpler sense) music has several functions: first and

Ex.21 *D-TRs 75*

foremost, to represent divine order (as in the French and English plays); second, and paradoxically, as an image of sin (the Jews frequently sing and dance in their idolatry; Mary Magdalen finds 'mundi delectatio' in the same; Herodias dances); third, as an image – as well as a direct expression – of human happiness (the 'Hessische' Christmas play); and last, as part of the representation of human sorrow and pain (the planctus of the three Marys and of the Virgin Mary).

(*iv*) *Italian.* The medieval Italian drama can be distinguished from the drama of England, France and Germany by two characteristics: an early tendency towards spectacular visual effects, and the strong influence of a tradition of popular religious song. The combination of spectacle with music was described by a Russian visitor to the 1439 Council at Florence who saw a representation of the Annunciation at the Chiesa dell'-Annunziata: 'God the Father was surrounded by an angel choir and by children with various kinds of musical instruments ... Gabriel hovered on a cable from God's throne to the Blessed Virgin, waving his wings and uttering a song of joy' (Lipphardt, *MGG*). This spectacular element developed later in the large-scale *rappresentazioni sacre*.

More austere, to judge from the texts, was the tradition of popular *laude*. The LAUDA SPIRITUALE received powerful impetus from the hysterical religious revivalism of 1260 in Perugia. When the hysteria died down and the processions of flagellants ceased, the *laude* fostered by the Franciscans were taken up by fraternities, such as the Disciplinati di Santa Croce in Urbino. The earliest 'dramatic' *laude* come from a songbook of this guild – *De compassione Filii ad matrem tempore Passionis sue* and *De compassione matris ad Filium.* These are strictly monologues; but dialogues followed: *De mutua compassione* and *De planctu Virginis* (Bartholomaeis, 1943, i). A famous early *lauda* in dramatic form is the *Donna del Paradiso,* attributed to JACOPONE DA TODI. It opens with John telling 'the Lady of Paradise' that her son has been taken prisoner and Mary asking how this could be. John tells her of Judas's betrayal, and Mary asks Mary Magdalen to help her. The scene changes (no explicit directions for dramatic performance are given in this or any other manuscripts);

Mary begs Pilate not to allow Christ to be tormented, the Jews cry out 'Crucifige! Crucifige!' and so on, in formal couplets and quatrains, through a brief narrative of the Crucifixion. The only other speaker is Christ himself who urges his mother to serve his disciples and to take John as her son:

> Mamma, col core aflitto
> entro a le man te metto
> de Joanne mio diletto.

No music survives for this or any other *laude drammatiche.* But it is certain that they were sung, and reasonable to suppose that, being in similar metres, they were sung to the same type of melody as survives in the two musical *laudari* at Cortona (*I-CT* 91) and at Florence (*Fn* Magl.II.1.122). The simpler syllabic melodies of the Cortona manuscript seem more appropriate than the more melismatic later ones. The function of the music in such strophically composed verse dialogues would be little more than narrative; the music would be a passionless vehicle for the story (as in a folk ballad), not an amplification of or comment on its meaning.

For the fraternities of laymen such as the Disciplinati di Giustizia, di S Fiorenzo and di S Francesco at Perugia, the *laudari* were the equivalent of missal, antiphoner, troper etc for clerics (Bartholomaeis, 1943); they covered the whole liturgical year. Some days were set aside for the singing of *laude liriche,* others for *laude drammatiche* (also called *devozioni*) which were performed on such feasts as Sundays in Advent, Christmas eve, Christmas Day, Epiphany, Purification, Annunciation, etc. Bartholomaeis printed a cycle of *laude* from Perugia starting *In Dominica de Adventu* (an Antichrist 'play') and ending with *Ufficio dei defunti;* 46 *laude* (*Laudes evangeliorum*) cover Lent and Holy Week. Lipphardt saw in the *laude* of the lamenting Virgin the genesis of the German *Marienklage.* The production of *laude* spread beyond Perugia, Orvieto and other smaller Umbrian cities to Aquila, Rome, Siena and Florence.

The larger form of Italian medieval drama, the *rappresentazione sacra,* flourished in Tuscany in the 15th and 16th centuries. Florence, where elaborate processions and pageants were mounted in honour of St John the Baptist, was the principal centre. With one exception, *La Passione di Gesù Cristo* from Revello (Piedmont), Italian sacred drama did not take the comprehensive, cyclic form of English mystery plays and French *mystères.* Characteristic hagiographical titles are *Rappresentazione di Santa Margherita, ... di San Giovanni e Paolo* (by Lorenzo de' Medici, performed 1489 in Florence), *... di Rosanna* (a secular story dressed up as a saint's legend) and *... di Santa Uliva* (the same). Subjects of biblical plays include the Magi (Siena), the Annunciation (Aquila), the Resurrection (Pordenone) and Abraham and Isaac (Florence).

The *rappresentazioni sacre* were magnificent productions organized by the confraternities. The *Rappresentazione di Santa Uliva* (? 16th century), for example, was performed over two days with gorgeous scenery, musical intermezzos and appearances of mythological beings somewhat loosely connected to the main plot (Bartholomaeis, 1943, iii, pp.3ff). It is rich in musical stage directions: the sung items of the play include a *lauda,* hunting-songs, psalms and the *Te Deum;* the instruments prescribed include *corno, tromba* and *tamburi.* The play also demanded elaborate choreography (Bartholomaeis, iii, pp.40, 61 etc), described fully in the stage directions.

The music of these plays included, then, both secular and sacred songs, both monophony and polyphony (in the *Rappresentazione di Santa Margherita* (? early 16th century) a caccia is sung, *Iamo alla caccia*). The functions of music are the expected ones (symbolic, ceremonial etc) common to other vernacular repertories, with perhaps more emphasis on the spectacle and dance. Even in this late repertory dance-songs are specified: for instance, at the end of the Florence *Abraham and Isaac* 'Sarah and all the rest of the household, except Abraham, and the two angels ... all together perform a dance [ballo] singing this *lauda*'. A more theological dance is specified in the preliminary rubric to a Christmas play from Siena: the angels leave their 'capanna' (? scaffold-stage) and 'faccino coro' (? make a dance); 'with great reverence they adore the Lord, and while the shepherds are on their way, they dance'. The shepherds themselves, after offering their gifts to the Christ-child, go to their station (*luogo*) 'ballando e saltando e facendo gran festa'. A last feature of the plays worth consideration is the unusual use of music during scenes of the Passion and Crucifixion. In *La Passione e Resurrezione del Colosseo* (Rome, ?1489) a 'chorus of shepherds', and a 'second chorus of kings' (? the Magi) sing songs of lament and dire prophecy as Christ is brought by the Pharisees to Herod. They sing again while Christ is put on the cross. At the death of Christ, and the rending of the veil of the Temple, 'the angels come to the cross' and sing (presumably, rather than declaim) sentences from the Easter Preface and from the *Via crucis*. The music of the *rappresentazioni sacre* was discussed by Becherini (1951) and Reese (1954, pp.171ff); literary texts were provided by Ancona (1872).

(*v*) *The Spanish peninsula.* Different categories again are required to describe the drama of the Spanish peninsula, which does not obviously follow either the Italian or the French pattern. Such evidence as there is suggests that in liturgical drama French influence predominated. Ripoll and other Catalonian centres had close liturgical links with French centres such as Limoges and Fleury. Donovan's study of Spanish liturgical drama (1958) is the only major contribution to source material since Young (1933). The distribution of surviving sources seems to indicate that the Latin church drama 'penetrated Castile and non-Catalonian Spain sporadically, and on a very limited scale, rather than as a vast uniform movement'. It is almost totally absent from Portuguese sources (Corbin, 1952). However, many plays may simply have been lost. López-Morales (1968) held that there was no dramatic tradition, either liturgical or vernacular, in Spain before Encina. Apart from a few brief religious texts in Latin which are arguably dramatic and the *Auto de los Reyes Magos* (see below), which is probably the work of a Gascon priest who settled in Toledo, there is little evidence of dramatic activity in Spain until the second half of the 15th century. But from the 1490s onwards Madrid, Seville, Salamanca, Valencia, Toledo and many other towns are known to have had plays. The whole Spanish scene is surveyed with a wealth of detail, particularly relating to dramatic presentation, by Shergold (1967). A great deal of music and varied musical effects were involved; neither has been comprehensively studied (see, however,

Salazar, 1938, and Chase, 1939).

The most striking features of the Spanish scene are: the survival of a fair number of ecclesiastical vernacular plays (many, it seems, by foreign hands), associated with church and liturgy; a rich, well-documented tradition of dramatic pageantry (as distinct from plays proper) associated with the processions of Corpus Christi; the absence of anything resembling the French and English mystery cycles; and a developing tradition of religious moralities, culminating in the *autos sacramentales* of the late 16th and 17th centuries, celebrating the mystery of the Eucharist and performed on Corpus Christi day.

The earliest surviving play in the vernacular is the incomplete *Auto de los Reyes Magos* of the late 12th century. It is different in form and spirit from liturgical plays on the same subject: the lively realistic spoken dialogues of the three astronomers break off in a scene where the traditional gifts of gold, frankincense and myrrh are used to test, not to celebrate, the divinity of the infant Christ (Sturdevant, 1927). The fragment has no music.

After this play there is a long gap in the evidence, conceivably a break in tradition, the only exceptions being one or two isolated plays, such as the St Mary Magdalen play of 14th-century Mallorca. The earliest plays about which we have musical information are *autos*, one-act plays of the late 15th century. Unusually, by comparison with other countries, they are mostly by named authors. Gómez Manrique's *Representacion del nacimiento de Nuestro Senor* was written between 1467 and 1481 for the convent of Calabazanos. At the end the nuns sing a cradle song in chorus to what may possibly be a popular tune. At the turn of the century plays were written by several individuals of distinguished musical talent, of whom the first and best was Juan del Encina. Half a dozen of his plays were first published in 1496, having been already performed in the courtly chapel of his patrons, the Duke and Duchess of Alba. Later works were performed at the court of the Catholic monarchs and perhaps elsewhere. The first six are little more than dialogues between mock-realistic shepherds speaking an anti-literary peasant brogue. The two earliest are Nativity *eglogas*, followed by two Easter ones and then two that are carnivalesque. These Nativity and Easter playlets combine motifs from liturgical plays (*Visitatio sepulchri* and *Peregrinus*) with autobiographical and/or secular material – the three Marys are replaced by two hermits and at the sepulchre they meet not only an angel but also St Veronica, who shows them her miraculous handkerchief. The rumbustious behaviour, crude jokes, yet naively reverent attitude of some of these personages, recall aspects of the English mystery cycles. The next half-dozen introduce other figures such as a squire who falls in love with a peasant girl, peasants who are corrupted by the courtly life, a hermit who is seduced by a nymph, students who 'rag' two peasants, and finally, courtly lovers set against comic peasants, bawds, gobetweens and Venus herself. All but two of Encina's *eglogas*, to judge from the printed texts, ended with the singing of a villancico, no doubt composed by Encina himself. Four such villancicos have survived (*Cancionero musical de Palacio*, ed. H. Anglès, nos.165, 167 and 174; *Cancionero musical de Segovia*, f.207v: *Gran gasajo siento yo* – ex.22, transcribed by J. A. Sage). These are typical villancicos of the period: four-part refrain songs of virelai pattern, three being more popular in type and no.167 more courtly. The villancicos for *eglogas* VIII and XIV, and perhaps others, were accompanied by dancing. As Encina's technique developed, the villancico was integrated more closely into the structure of the play.

Encina's contemporary Lucas Fernandez was also a playwright, as well as *maestro de capilla* of Salamanca Cathedral from 1498. In 1514 he published *Farsas y églogas*, plays after Encina's manner, and with them a pastoral dialogue sung perhaps throughout to the same tune. His *Auto de la Pasión* (1514) contains a planctus of the Blessed Virgin as well as the final villancico. The Portuguese dramatist Gil Vicente, highly talented in his own right, may have followed Encina in some of his plays: he too wrote courtly-popular pieces for royalty, and versions of his plays printed later in the 16th century suggest that several were performed in chapel at Christmas matins. But the courtliness of these playwrights must not be exaggerated. The so-called *Mystery of Elche*, in Catalan, on the Assumption of the Virgin, a 'semi-popular' religious drama still performed each August at Elche, is provided with music throughout. The music, formerly thought to be by Encina and his contemporaries (*NOHM*, iv, p.803), is of the 16th and 17th centuries.

The connection between the vernacular and the liturgical drama seems closer in Spain than elsewhere. In addition to the *Auto de la Pasión* by Fernandez, the following plays display evident knowledge of actions and motifs from the liturgical drama and some of them were performed within the liturgy itself: a 'three-act' Passion play by Alonso de Melgar, printed at Burgos, 1520, with a Resurrection 'eclogue' derived from the *Ordo prophetarum* (among the prophets, who sing plainchant, was David, with a vihuela, and the Erythrean Sibyl, settings of whose song are found in contemporary cancioneros); Gil Vicente's *Auto da Sibila Cassandra*, with Christmas crib; Jorge de Montemayor's Nativity plays 'presented in church . . . each given after one of the nocturns of Matins' (Shergold); a Good Friday *auto* (Burgos, 1552) containing a planctus of the Virgin, *Ay dolo, dueñas, dolo*; such planctus are reminiscent of German *Marienklagen* and Italian *laude* discussed above (§§III, 2(i) and III, 3(iv)). This tradition of vernacular religious plays is perhaps better called ecclesiastical than liturgical; but in its breadth and variety it shows an unusual tolerance of vernacular song in church and is closely associated with the liturgy. This tolerance declined after 1568 with the reform of the breviary.

An interesting, and perhaps independent, dramatic tradition in Majorca is revealed by a manuscript (*E-Bc* 1139) discovered in 1889 and not yet published in entirety. It contains the *Consueta del Rey Asuero* (*Esther* i–vii): the dialogue is sung almost entirely to well-known plainsong hymns: Ahasuerus uses the melody of *Eterne rerum*; Vashti and Esther, *Vexilla regis*; and so on. A planctus melody is also called for; and the wise men can sing 'to the tune that they wish' (Shergold, 1967, p.61, from Plaja, 1953). A sung drama constitutes yet another link with the liturgical.

Many of the plays so far mentioned can be definitely associated, like the liturgical plays, with the ecclesiastical events of Christmas and Easter. The dramatic activities of the feast of Corpus Christi slightly more resemble those that took place in the north of Europe. The mystery plays of Valencia, for example (16th–19th century), consist, in a manuscript copy of 1672, of three

Ex.22 Juan del Encina: Egloga II, final *villancico*

Eng. trans.:

'I feel a great joy.
Hey! Ho!'
'So do I, by my faith!
Ho! Ha!
For He who gave us life
has been born to save us.
Ho! Ha! Hey! Ho!
This night he was born.'

plays: one of Adam and Eve, one of St Christopher and one of 'Rey Herodes' – hardly a cycle, but not obviously seasonal. The manuscript (*E-VAa*) gives the music for most of the passages which are to be sung (Alcahalí, 1903). The dramatic use of music follows the familiar pattern: for God's creation of Adam and Eve the sky opens 'ab molta musica'; and God ascends 'en musica'. In addition Adam and Eve sing, to express their penitence, both in Latin and in Spanish, 'a duo'.

In many instances it is very hard to tell whether references to *misteris* are to plays properly so called or simply to pageants (involving tableaux, mime, dance, music, but not spoken dialogue). The Valencian accounts for 1517 contain payments for a float called 'the *Te Deum*': the Virgin was on it, and musicians were paid £1 4s. (Shergold, 1967). And the *representació* of St Vincent required payments to musicians and dancers. Much research remains to be done; but it is certain that early 16th-century Spain was eminently rich in dramatic pageantry and that music was prominent in it, both for itself and as an accompaniment to procession and dance.

Finally, mention may be made of a perhaps peculiarly Spanish thing – a danced religious play. The *Danza del Santísimo Nacimiento* (*c*1560) has eight angels and eight shepherds; both groups sang villancicos and the shepherds danced, both to the singing and to instrumental music. It was performed in church, probably after Matins.

### IV. Medieval drama in eastern Europe.
Although only a start has been made in bringing to light the riches of east European collections of liturgical manuscripts, enough is known to suggest that the main forms of Western liturgical drama were adopted in the East. Bartkowski (1973) discussed 29 witnesses to the *Visitatio sepulchri* found in Polish manuscripts from the 13th century onwards. Both his and Lewański's surveys are copiously illustrated. Not only the expected German traditions appear to be represented in Eastern books. Bužga ('Liturgische Dramen', *MGG*) referred to Norman plays in 12th-century Prague. Young had already drawn attention to several individual features in the *Visitationes* of Prague books.

Apart from the *Visitatio* may be mentioned a Czech play (in fragments in Zlomek; see Černý) concerning the spice merchant, and the remains of a large-scale cycle of plays of Lucifer, Mary Magdalen, the spice merchant, the Harrowing of Hell, and the Roman soldiers at the tomb, now in Schlägl monastery (see Máchal, 1908).

### V. The end of the Middle Ages.
There was no neat end to the Middle Ages or to its drama. Some traditions persisted, others were suppressed, others died a natural death. In Protestant countries such as England the traditional mystery cycles were discouraged and eventually eradicated by the reformers (Gardiner, 1946); in Spain, on the other hand, not only vernacular religious plays but some liturgical plays (e.g. the SONG OF THE SIBYL)

continued strongly for centuries – in some cases right through to the 20th century (Shergold, 1967).

The bewildering variety of drama, old and new, in the late 15th and 16th centuries defies adequate classification; but it is possible perhaps to distinguish three main milieux: the court; schools and colleges; and towns and cities ('popular' drama). Even this broad classification is unsatisfactory, because, although each milieu had certain distinct and unique features, the types of dramatic activity practised in the others inevitably infiltrated it.

The 'drama' of courts (ceremonies, entertainments and plays) was often sumptuous, and sumptuously provided with music. The dramatic events that could be supported and embellished with music included (to give them their English names) mummings, masks and disguisings, royal entries, tournaments and interludes. The mumming (Fr. *momerie*; Sp. *momo*, etc) consisted simply of a visit by masked, and perhaps originally silent, dice players to someone's house (e.g. Henry VIII, with a band of courtiers pretending to be shepherds, visited Wolsey in 1536); drum and fife were the usual accompaniment. The mask (masque; It. *mascherata*, etc), clearly indigenous in northern Europe but influenced by Italian custom, had as its centrepiece a dance of courtly persons with music played by professionals on loud (*haut*) instruments. In the more complex masks, in early Tudor England often called disguisings, the courtly dancers were wheeled into the hall on an elaborate pageant-car, on which instrumentalists and singers might be stationed (Stevens, 1961, chap.11). Representative pageants were a feature, too, of elaborate court banquets in other parts of Europe (Shergold, chap.5): in Paris (1389) the city of Troy, on wheels, was attacked by a tentful of Greeks, also on wheels (Loomis, 1958). The function of music on such gaudy royal occasions was essentially to draw attention to the spectacle, and to be in itself something worth seeing (musicians were appropriately disguised). The celebrated Feast of the Pheasant (Lille, 1454) had elaborate musical–culinary effects – 28 musicians in a pie, etc (see Reese, 1954). The long and detailed descriptions of festivities for Cosimo I de' Medici's marriage (Florence, 1539) show that the musical offerings could be worthwhile in themselves as well as spectacular: as the bride entered the city 'a madrigal by Francesco Corteccia was sung in eight parts by a chorus of 24 voices accompanied by 4 cornettos and 4 trombones, all placed on the top of the gate' (Dent, 1968). Royal entries such as this were a familiar part of the European scene (see Kernodle, 1944); music there had the same functions, part-visual and part-aural, as in indoor festivities. The English interlude (similar to, if not derived from, the Spanish *entremés* and the French *entremet*) probably derived its name and nature from being a 'playing' (*ludus*) between (*inter*) other things, such as the courses of a banquet. In Italy the acts of spoken drama were separated by *intermedi*, 'mainly *tableaux vivants* and dumb-shows, with or without dances' (Dent). Not only the terminology but the events themselves were variable and multiform. The invisible, hidden musicians of the *intermedi* are more reminiscent of the English mask or disguising than of the interlude.

'Interlude', in effect, like its continental equivalents, tends to mean simply a play. In England interludes were generally didactic and often allegorical. They were acted at court, but were not necessarily of the court. This brings us to the large, indefinable area of 'popular' drama

– drama, that is, intended for popular consumption, usually by named authors and performed professionally or semi-professionally. (It is not to be confused with folk drama.) The moral interlude, or morality play (if it is presented allegorically), tends to use music in a predictable way – to make a moral point. 'Music and dancing are . . . associated with the sinful part of man' (Stevens, 1961); the characters who sing have such names as Sensual Appetite, Pride, Riot, Abominable Living, and their music is taken from the popular repertory – *Jack boy, is thy bow ibroke?*, *Wassayle wassayle out of the mylke payle* – with dances to match. Not all moralities are continuously moral; *Mankind*, for instance, has many bawdy moments and a bawdy Christmas song, sung by the wicked characters (the music, as is normal, does not survive). Rastell's *A New Interlude and a Mery of the Nature of the iiij Elements* (?1525–30) contains the only song with music for a printed English play; it is in three parts.

In France, besides *moralités*, there was a more clearly defined comic dramatic tradition, in the *farses* and *sotties*. Secular drama in France was comprehensively surveyed in detail by Brown (1963), who listed over 400 known theatrical chansons and printed from various sources the music of 60. He distinguished two main types of chanson used in plays – the *chanson musicale* (in the main literary and musical tradition) and the *chanson rustique* (originating as a single line of melody). Music is, again, associated with low life, the pleasures of the tavern and a lack of moral firmness – that is, when it is not introduced purely for entertainment's sake or to oil the dramatic action. Other forms of 'popular' or muncipal dramatic activity (they cannot properly be called plays) included: in England, civic mummings (e.g. at Kennington, 1377, 'for the disport of the yong Prince Richard' – 130 citizens, disguised, accompanied by minstrels; see Wickham, 1959); in Italy, the Carnivals of the seasons before Lent and after 1 May (Calendimaggio), involving the singing and dancing of *canti carnascialeschi* and torchlight processions with decorated pageants (*carri*) of maskers (Reese, 1954, pp.167ff); and in France, the festivities of the *societés joyeuses* – 'play-acting societies' (Brown) such as the Enfants-sans-Souci of Paris, the Bazochiens (law clerks of Paris) and the Infanterie of Dijon (see Brown for a detailed description of the 'mardi gras' festival, i.e. carnival fête, put on by the Abbaye des Conards of Rouen).

Finally, there developed at the end of the Middle Ages, particularly in Germany, an 'educational' drama, the *Schuldrama*. Under the influence of humanism, with its renewed emphasis on classical rhetoric (the mastery of the art of communication through words), a practical dramatic training in the power of language was grafted on to an already strong medieval tradition of debate, as a mode of education, as well as of business and entertainment. 'The subjects treated, both by Protestants and Catholics, were designed for moral edification and derived from the Old Testament and from classical history' (Dent). The plays commonly ended with a Latin chorus, in appropriate metre, which might be danced as well as sung. The straightforward melodies, in the style of chorales, were later harmonized in an equally straightforward style (see Liliencron, 1890, with musical examples). The composer Johann Walter (i), associate of Luther, and Kantor of the town of Torgau from 1526, wrote music for such plays.

A similar tradition, though less centrally important, left traces in other European countries (Sternfeld, 1948). In England there were plays, mostly in Latin to begin with, at universities and in schools (e.g. at Magdalen College, Oxford, from 1486). The song schools, such as St Paul's, were active from early in the 16th century and it is likely that one of the impulses behind the early Elizabethan consort song, for voice and viols, was the need to complement the rhetorical exercises of the set speeches with fittingly 'rhetorical' music (Brett, 1961–2). The music in school drama has to be educational as well as dramatically correct.

## BIBLIOGRAPHY

### GENERAL

R. Froning: *Das Drama des Mittelalters* (Stuttgart, 1891–2)
W. Creizenach: *Geschichte des neueren Dramas* (Halle, 1893–1916)
E. K. Chambers: *The Medieval Stage* (Oxford, 1903)
W. Stammler: 'Drama, Mittelalter', *Reallexicon der deutschen Literatur-Geschichte*, i, ed. P. Merker and W. Stammler (Berlin, 1925), 218
A. Nicoll: *Masks, Mimes and Miracles: Studies in the Popular Theatre* (New York, 1931)
J. Gregor: *Weltgeschichte des Theaters* (Zurich, 1933)
E. Hartl: *Das Drama des Mittelalters* (Leipzig, 1936–42)
J. Smits van Waesberghe: *Musiek en drama in de Middelleeuwen* (Amsterdam, 1942)
*Enciclopedia dello spettacolo* (Rome, 1954–62)
G. Reese: *Music in the Renaissance* (New York, 1954, rev. 2/1959)
C. J. Stratman: *Bibliography of Medieval Drama* (Berkeley, 1954, rev., enlarged 2/1972)
H. Kindermann: *Theatergeschichte Europas* (Salzburg, 1957–62)
E. A. Bowles: 'The Role of Musical Instruments in Medieval Sacred Drama', *MQ*, xlv (1959), 67
W. Salmen: *Der fahrende Musiker im europäischen Mittelalter* (Kassel, 1960)
E. Wolff: 'Die Terminologie des mittelalterlichen Dramas in bedeutungsgeschichtlichen Sicht', *Anglia*, lxxviii (1960), 1
J. D. A. Ogilvy: 'Mimi, Scurrae, Histriones, Entertainers of the Early Middle Ages', *Speculum*, xxxviii (1963), 603
H. M. Gamer: 'Mimes, Musicians, and the Origin of the Medieval Religious Play', *Deutsche Beiträge zur geistigen Überlieferung*, v (1965), 9
L. Schmidt: *Le théâtre populaire européen* (Paris, 1965)
S. Schoenbaum: 'Medieval Supplement', *Research Opportunities in Renaissance Drama*, x– (1967–)
P. Dronke: *The Medieval Lyric* (London, 1968, rev. 2/1978)
*The Medieval Drama: 3rd Annual Conference of the Center for Medieval Studies: Binghamton 1969*
R. Axton: *European Drama of the Early Middle Ages* (London, 1974)
C. J. Thaiss: 'An Index to vols I–XVI of *Research Opportunities in Renaissance Drama*', *Research Opportunities in Renaissance Drama*, xvii (1974), 35
G. Wickham: *The Medieval Theatre* (London, 1974)
D. Bevington, ed.: *Medieval Drama* (Boston, 1975) [incl. 27 liturgical plays, bilingual texts]

### LITURGICAL DRAMA: GENERAL STUDIES

K. Young: *The Drama of the Medieval Church* (Oxford, 1933/R1951) [standard and comprehensive; prints texts of all ceremonies and plays; no music]
E. A. Schuler: *Die Musik der Osterfeiern, Osterspiele und Passionen des Mittelalters* (Kassel, 1951)
S. Corbin: *Essai sur la musique portugaise au Moyen-Age, 1100–1385* (Paris, 1952)
W. L. Smoldon: 'Liturgical Drama', *NOHM*, ii (1954), 175–219
——: 'Liturgical Music Drama', *Grove 5*
G. Frank: 'Liturgico, Dramma', *ES*
R. B. Donovan: *The Liturgical Drama in Medieval Spain* (Toronto, 1958)
W. Lipphardt: 'Liturgische Dramen', *MGG*
S. Corbin: 'Teatro religioso', *LaMusicaE*
O. B. Hardison: *Christian Rite and Christian Drama in the Middle Ages* (Baltimore, 1965)
C. C. Flanigan: 'The Liturgical Drama and its Tradition: a Review of Scholarship 1965–75', *Research Opportunities in Renaissance Drama*, xviii (1975), 81
W. Lipphardt, ed.: *Lateinische Osterfeiern und Osterspiele*, i (Berlin, 1975)
B. Stäblein: *Schriftbild der einstimmigen Musik*, Musikgeschichte in Bildern, iii/4 (Leipzig, 1975)
F. Collins: *Medieval Church Dramas: a Repertory of Complete Plays* (Charlottesville, 1976)

### LITURGICAL DRAMA AND LATIN PLAYS: SPECIAL STUDIES AND EDITIONS

F. Clément: 'Le drame liturgique au Moyen-Age', *Annales*

*archéologiques*, vii (1847), 307; viii (1848), 36, 77, 304; ix (1849), 27, 162; x (1850), 154; xi (1851), 6

A. de La Fons-Mélicoq: 'Cérémonies dramatiques et anciens usages dans les églises du nord de la France', *Annales archéologiques*, x (1850), 92

W. Luzarche: *Office de Pâques ou de la Résurrection* (Tours, 1856)

E. de Coussemaker: *Drames liturgiques du moyen-âge* (Rennes, 1860/*R*1964)

A. Schubiger: *Musikalische Spicilegien*, PÄMw, v (1876)

W. Meyer: 'Der *Ludus de Antichristo* und Bemerkungen über die lateinischen Rhythmen des 12 Jh.', *Sitzungsberichte der Kgl. Bayerischen Akademie der Wissenschaften zu München: Philosophisch-philologische und historische Klasse* (1882), 1–192; repr. in W. Meyer: *Gesammelte Abhandlungen zur mittellateinischen Rhythmik*, i (Berlin, 1905), 136–339

K. Lange: *Die lateinischen Osterfeiern* (Munich, 1887)

B. Venzmer: *Die Chöre im geistlichen Drama des deutschen Mittelalters* (Ludwigslust, 1897)

W. Meyer: 'Fragmenta Burana', *Festschrift zur Feier des hundertfünfzigjährigen Bestehens der Königlichen Gesellschaft der Wissenschaften zu Göttingen* (Berlin, 1901)

P. Wagner: 'Das Dreikönigspiel zu Freiburg in der Schweiz', *Freiburger Geschichtsblatt*, x (1903), 77

H. Anz: *Die lateinischen Magierspiele* (Leipzig, 1905)

A. Gastoué: *Documents pour servir à l'histoire des origines du théâtre musicale: le drame liturgique: le Mystère des vierges folles* (Paris, 1906)

H. Loriquet, A. Colette and J. Pothier: *Le graduel de l'église cathédrale de Rouen au XIIIᵉ siècle* (Rouen, 1907) [facs. of *F-Pn* lat.904]

H. Pfeiffer: 'Klosterneuburger Osterfeier und Osterspiel', *Jb des Stiftes Klosterneuburg*, i (1908), 1–56 [with 5 facs. from *A-KN* 574]

K. Young: 'Observations on the Origin of the Medieval Passion Play', *Proceedings of the Modern Language Association of America*, xxv (1910), 309

H. Omont: 'Le Mystère d'Emmaüs', *Bibliothèque de l'Ecole des Chartes*, lxxiv (1913), 257 [*F-Pn* n.a.lat.1064, from Beauvais]

P. Wagner: 'Ein rheinisches Osterspiel in einer Hs. des 17 Jh.', *Zeitschrift für deutsches Altertum und deutsche Litteratur*, lvi (1918), 100

N. Brooks: *The Sepulchre of Christ in Art and Liturgy* (Urbana, 1921)

H. J. W. Tillyard, trans.: *Plays of Roswitha* (London, 1923)

H. Rueff: 'Das rheinische Osterspiel der Berliner Hs, ms. germ. fol. 1219', *Abhandlungen der Gesellschaft der Wissenschaften zu Göttingen: Philosophisch-historische Klasse*, new ser., xviii (1925), 1–224

Abtei Sankt Hildegard, ed.: *Hildegard of Bingen: Ordo Virtutum, ein Singspiel* (Berlin, 1927)

K. Meyer: 'Über die Melodiebildung in den geistlichen Spielen des früheren Mittelalters', *Beethoven-Zentenarfeier: Wien 1927*, 145

J. B. Fuller, ed.: *Hilarii versus et ludi* (New York, 1929)

F. Liuzzi: 'L'espressione musicale nel dramma liturgico', *Studi medievali*, new ser., i (1929), 74–109

O. E. Albrecht: *Four Latin Plays of St. Nicholas from the 12th Century Fleury Playbook* (Philadelphia, 1935)

T. Gérold: 'Les drames liturgiques médiévaux en Catalogne', *Revue d'histoire et de philosophie religieuses*, xvi (1936), 429

H. Sievers: *Die lateinischen Osterspiele der Stiftskirche St Blasius zu Braunschweig* (Wolfenbüttel, 1936)

E. Wright: *The Dissemination of the Liturgical Drama in France* (Bryn Mawr, 1936)

M. S. de Vito: *L'origine del dramma liturgico* (Milan, 1938)

M. H. Marshall: 'The Dramatic Traditions Established by the Liturgical Plays', *Proceedings of the Modern Language Association of America*, lvi (1941), 962

J. Woerdeman: 'The Source of the Easter Play', *Orate fratres*, xx (1945–6), 262

W. L. Smoldon: 'The Easter Sepulchre Music Drama', *ML*, xxvii (1946), 1

A. A. Abert: 'Das Nachleben des Minnesangs im liturgischen Spiel', *Mf*, i (1948), 95

W. Lipphardt: *Die Weisen der lateinischen Osterspiele des 12. und 13. Jahrhunderts* (Kassel, 1948)

P. Aebischer: 'Un ultime écho de la *Procession des prophètes*: le *Cant de la Sibilla* de la nuit de noël à Majorque', *Mélanges ... offerts à Gustave Cohen* (Paris, 1950), 261

R. Marichal: 'Les drames liturgiques du "Livre de la Trésorerie" d'Origny-Ste-Benoîte', *Mélanges ... offerts à Gustave Cohen* (Paris, 1950), 37

M. H. Marshall: 'Aesthetic Values of the Liturgical Drama', *English Institute Essays 1950*, 89

J. Poll: 'Ein Osterspiel enthalten im Processionale der alten Kapelle von Regensburg', *KJb*, xxxiv (1950), 35

S. Corbin: 'Le Cantus Sibyllae: origines et premiers textes', *RdM*, xxxi (1952), 1

T. Schmid: 'Das Osterspiel in Schweden', *Kyrkohistorisk arsskrift* (1952), 1 [incl. 6 *Visitatio* texts]

J. Smits van Waesberghe: 'Das niederländische Osterspiel', *IMSCR*, v Utrecht 1952, 371

S. Corbin: 'Le ms 201 d'Orléans: drames liturgiques dits de Fleury', *Romania*, lxxiv (1953), 1–43

J. Smits van Waesberghe: 'A Dutch Easter Play', *MD*, vii (1953), 15

G. Vecchi: 'Innodia e dramma sacro', *Studi mediolatini e volgare*, i (1953), 226

———: *Uffici drammatichi padovani* (Florence, 1954)

J. Chailley: 'Le drame liturgique médiéval à St. Martial', *Revue de l'histoire du théâtre*, vii (1955), 127

E. Krieg: *Das lateinische Osterspiel von Tours* (Würzburg, 1956)

J. Smits van Waesberghe: 'Das Nürnberger Osterspiel', *Festschrift Joseph Schmidt-Görg zum 60. Geburtstag* (Bonn, 1957), 303

P. Damilano: 'Il dramma liturgico in Italia', *Musica sacra*, lxxxii (1958), 130

G. Tintori and R. Monterosso: *Sacre rappresentazioni nel manoscritto 201 della Biblioteca Municipale di Orléans* (Cremona, 1958) [with facs.]

N. Greenberg, ed.: *The Play of Daniel* (Oxford, 1959) [transcr. R. Weakland, 'narration' W. H. Auden]

J. Chailley: *L'école musicale de St. Martial de Limoges jusqu'à la fin du XIᵉ siècle* (Paris, 1960)

S. Corbin: *La déposition liturgique du Christ au Vendredi Saint: sa place dans l'histoire des rites et du théâtre religieux* (Lisbon and Paris, 1960)

———: 'Le Jeu de Daniel à l'abbaye de Royaumont', *Cahiers de civilisation médiévale*, iii (1960), 373

W. L. Smoldon, ed.: *The Play of Daniel* (London, 1960) [performing edn.]

———: *Herod: a Medieval Nativity Play* (London, 1960) [performing edn.]

H. Wagenaar-Nolthenius: 'Sur la construction musicale du drame liturgique', *Cahiers de civilisation médiévale*, iii (1960), 449

R. Weakland: 'The Rhythmic Modes and Medieval Latin Drama', *JAMS*, xiv (1961), 131

W. L. Smoldon: 'The Music of the Medieval Church Drama', *MQ*, xlviii (1962), 476

C. C. Sterne, ed.: *The Son of Getron* (Pittsburgh, 1962) [performing edn.]

C. W. Jones: *The St. Nicholas Liturgy and its Literary Relationships* (Berkeley, 1963) [with essay on music by G. Reaney]

W. Lipphardt: 'Das Herodesspiel von Le Mans nach den HSS Madrid, Bibl. Nac. 288 u. 289', *Organicae voces: Festschrift Joseph Smits van Waesberghe* (Amsterdam, 1963), 107

E. A. Bowles: 'Musical Instruments in the Medieval Corpus Christi Procession', *JAMS*, xvii (1964), 251

W. Elders: 'Gregorianisches in liturgischen Dramen der Hs. Orléans 201', *AcM*, xxxvi (1964), 169

W. L. Smoldon, ed.: *Visitatio sepulchri* (Oxford, 1964) [performing edn.]

M. Bernard: 'L'Officium Stellae nivernais', *RdM*, li (1965), 52

W. L. Smoldon: 'Medieval Lyrical Melody and the Latin Church Dramas', *MQ*, li (1965), 507

W. L. Smoldon and N. Greenberg, eds.: *The Play of Herod* (Oxford, 1965) [performing edn.]

R. Brandel: 'Some Unifying Devices in the Religious Music Drama of the Middle Ages', *Aspects of Medieval and Renaissance Music: a Birthday Offering to Gustave Reese* (New York, 1966), 40

J. Chailley: 'Du drame liturgique aux prophètes de Notre-Dame-la-Grande', *Mélanges offerts à René Crozet* (Poitiers, 1966), 835

B. Stäblein: 'Zur Musik des Ludus de Antichristo', *Zum 70. Geburtstag von Joseph Müller-Blattau* (Kassel, 1966), 312

W. L. Smoldon, ed.: *Planctus Mariae* (Oxford, 1966) [performing edn.]

H. Wagenaar-Nolthenius: 'Der "Planctus Judei" und der Gesang jüdischer Märtyrer in Blois anno 1171', *Mélanges offerts à René Crozet* (Poitiers, 1966), 881

H. A. W. de Boor: *Die Textgeschichte der lateinischen Osterfeiern* (Tübingen, 1967)

'Liturgical and Secular Elements in Medieval Liturgical Drama', *IMSCR*, x Ljubljana 1967, 271

W. L. Smoldon, ed.: *Officium pastorum* (Oxford, 1967) [performing edn.]

———: 'The Melodies of the Medieval Church-drama and their Significance', *Comparative Drama*, ii (1968), 185

J. E. Stevens: 'Music in some Early Medieval Plays', *Studies in the Arts*, ed. F. Warner (Oxford, 1968), 21

W. L. Smoldon: 'The Origins of the Quem queritis and the Easter Sepulchre Music-drama, as demonstrated by their Musical Settings', *The Medieval Drama: 3rd Annual Conference of the Center for Medieval Studies: Binghamton 1969*, 121

W. Arlt: *Ein Festoffizium des Mittelalters aus Beauvais in seiner liturgischen und musikalischen Bedeutung* (Cologne, 1970) [edn. of *GB-Lbm* Eg.2615]

R. B. Donovan: 'Two Celebrated Centers of Medieval Liturgical Drama: Fleury and Ripoll', *The Medieval Drama and its Claudelian Revival*, ed. E. C. Dunn and others (Washington, 1970)

P. Dronke: *Poetic Individuality in the Middle Ages* (Oxford, 1970) [with edn. of Hildegard of Bingen: *Ordo Virtutum*, and edn. by I. D. Bent of planctus of Abelard and songs of Hildegard]

P. Evans, ed.: *The Early Trope Repertory of St Martial de Limoges* (Princeton, 1970)

O. B. Hardison: 'Gregorian Easter Vespers and Early Liturgical Drama', *The Medieval Drama and its Claudelian Revival*, ed. E. C. Dunn and others (Washington, 1970), 27

H. Homeyer, ed.: *Hrotsvitha: Opera* (Paderborn, 1970)

M. D. Moore: *The Visitatio Sepulchri of the Medieval Church* (diss., U. of Rochester, NY, 1970)

T. Stemmler: *Liturgische Feiern und geistliche Spiele* (Tübingen, 1970)

S. Sticca: *The Latin Passion Play: its Origins and Development* (New York, 1970)

C. E. Elder: 'Eine noch unbekannte Osterfeier aus St. Nikola in Passau', *Festschrift Bernhard Bischoff* (Stuttgart, 1971), 449

W. Lipphardt: 'Die Mainzer *Visitatio Sepulchri*', *Medievalia litteraria: Festschrift für Helmut de Boor* (Munich, 1971), 171

W. G. Stryker, ed.: 'An Easter Play in Finland', *Studies in Medieval, Renaissance and American Literature: a Festschrift honoring Troy C. Crenshaw, Lorraine Sherley, Ruth Speer Angell* (Fort Worth, 1971), 45, 197

F. Collins: *The Production of Medieval Church Music-drama* (Charlottesville, 1972)

D. N. Dumville: 'Liturgical Drama and Panegyric Responsory from the Eighth Century', *Journal of Theological Studies*, new ser., xxiii (1972), 374–406

W. Lipphardt: 'Die *Visitatio Sepulchri* (III. Stufe) von Gernrode', *Daphnis*, i (1972), 1

C. C. Flanigan: 'The Liturgical Context of the Quem queritis Trope', *Comparative Drama*, viii (1974), 45

——: 'The Roman Rite and the Origins of the Liturgical Drama', *University of Toronto Quarterly*, xliii (1974), 263

D. H. Ogden: 'The Use of Architectural Space in Medieval Music-drama', *Comparative Drama*, viii (1974), 63

D. Dolan: *Le drame liturgique de Pâques en Normandie et en Angleterre au moyen âge* (Paris, 1975)

D. G. Hughes: 'The First Magdalene Lament of the Tours Easter Play', *JAMS*, xxix (1976), 276

T. McGee: 'The Liturgical Placements of the *Quem quaeritis* Dialogue', *JAMS*, xxix (1976), 1

MARIENKLAGEN

O. Schönemann: *Der Sündenfall und Marienklage* (Hanover, 1855)

A. Schönbach: *Über die Marienklagen* (Graz, 1874)

P. Bohn: 'Marienklage: Handschrift der Trierischen Stadtsbibliothek aus dem 15. Jahrhd.', *MMg*, ix (1877), 1, 17

E. Wechssler: *Die romanischen Marienklagen* (Halle, 1893)

G. Kühl: 'Die Bordesholmer Marienklage', *Jb des Vereins für niederdeutsche Sprachforschung*, xxiv (1898), 1–75, i–xiv

F. Ermini: *Lo Stabat mater e i pianti della Vergine nella lirica del medio evo* (Città di Castello, 1916)

F. J. Tanquerey: *Plaintes de la Vierge en anglo-français* (Paris, 1921)

W. Lipphardt: 'Marienklage und Liturgie', *Jb für Liturgiewissenschaft*, xiv (1932), 198

——: 'Altdeutsche Marienklagen', *Singgemeinde*, ix (1933), 65

——: 'Studien zu den Marienklagen', *Beiträge zur Geschichte der deutschen Sprache und Literatur*, lviii (1934), 390–444

A. Geering: 'Die Nibelungenmelodie in der Trierer Marienklage', *IMSCR*, iv Basle 1949, 118

W. Irtenkauf: 'Die "Donaueschinger Marienklage": eine neue wohl aus Österreich stammende Quelle für die Marienklagen und Magdalenszenen des 15 Jh.', *Carinthia*, cxlviii (1958), 359

PLAYS OF SPONSUS, AGNES, THE FALL OF ADAM; ADAM DE LA HALLE

E. Monaci: *Il misterio provenzale di S. Agnese dal ms. Chigiano C.V.151* (Rome, 1880) [with facs.]

——: *Facsimili di documenti per la storia delle lingue e delle letterature romanze* (Rome, 1910) [*Sponsus*]

P. Studer, ed.: *Le mystère d'Adam* (Manchester, 1918)

F. Liuzzi: 'Drammi musicali dei secoli XI–XIV, i: Le vergine savie e le vergine folli', *Studi medievali*, new ser., iii (1930), 82

A. Jeanroy, ed.: *Le jeu de Sainte Agnes* (Paris, 1931) [music ed. T. Gérold]

F. Liuzzi: 'Il dramma delle vergini savie e delle vergine folli e l'uffizio liturgico orientale di S. Agata', *IV° congresso nazionale di studi romani: Roma 1935*, i, 587

G. Cohen: *Le Jeu d'Adam et d'Eve: mystère du XII° siècle* (Paris, 1936, 10/1948) [music ed. J. Chailley]

O. Ursprung: 'Das Sponsus-spiel', *AMf*, iii (1938), 80

J. W. Doyle, trans.: *Adam, a Play* (Sydney, 1948)

J. Chailley: 'La nature musicale du Jeu "Robinet Marion" ', *Mélanges... offerts à Gustave Cohen* (Paris, 1950), 111

E. Hoepffner: 'Les intermèdes musicaux dans le jeu provençal de sainte Agnès', *Mélanges... offerts à Gustave Cohen* (Paris, 1950), 97

L. P. Thomas, ed.: *Le 'Sponsus' (mystère des vierges sages et des vierges folles)* (Paris, 1951) [see also review by J. Chailley, *RBM*, vi (1952), 153]

K. Varty, ed.: *Le Jeu de Robin et de Marion* (London, 1960)

F. Gennrich, ed.: *Adam de la Halle: Le Jeu de Robin et de Marion – Li Rondel Adam* (Langen bei Frankfurt am Main, 1962)

P. Aebischer, ed.: *Le mystère d'Adam: Ordo representacionis Ade* (Geneva and Paris, 1963)

d'A. S. Avalle and R. Monterosso, eds.: *Sponsus: Dramma delle vergini prudenti e delle vergini stolte* (Milan and Naples, 1965) [with 6 facs.]

W. L. Smoldon, ed.: *Sponsus: an 11th Century Mystère* (London, n.d.) [performing edn.]

W. Noomen: 'Le *Jeu d'Adam*: étude descriptive et analytique', *Romania*, lxxxix (1968), 145–93

L. Sletsjoe, ed.: *Le Mystère d'Adam: édition diplomatique accompagnée d'une reproduction photographique du ms. de Tours* (Paris, 1968)

W. Noomen, ed.: *Le Jeu d'Adam* (Paris, 1971)

L. R. Muir: *Liturgy and Drama in the Anglo-Norman Adam* (Oxford, 1973)

ENGLISH PLAYS

T. Sharp: *Dissertation on the Pageants or Dramatic Mysteries Anciently Performed at Coventry* (Coventry, 1825)

F. J. Furnivall, ed.: *The Digby Plays* (London, 1882, 2/1896 in Early English Text Society, extra ser.)

L. T. Smith, ed.: *York Plays* (Oxford, 1885)

H. Craig, ed.: *Two Coventry Corpus Christi Plays*, Early English Text Society, extra ser., lxxxvii (London, 1902, 2/1957)

J. K. Moore: 'The Tradition of Angelic Singing in the English Drama', *Journal of English and Germanic Philology*, xxii (1923), 89

E. Beuscher: *Die Gesangseinlagen in den englischen Mysterien* (Münster, 1930)

F. Collins: 'Music in the Craft Cycles', *Proceedings of the Modern Language Association of America*, xlvii (1932), 613

J. R. Moore: 'Miracle Plays, Minstrels and Jigs', *Proceedings of the Modern Language Association of America*, xlviii (1933), 942

V. Shull: 'Clerical Drama in Lincoln Cathedral, 1318–1561', *Proceedings of the Modern Language Association of America*, lii (1937), 946

H. C. Gardiner: *Mysteries' End: an Investigation into the Last Days of the Medieval Religious Stage* (New Haven, 1946)

W. L. Hildburgh: 'English Alabaster Carvings as Records of the Medieval Religious Drama', *Archaeologia*, xciii (1949), 51–101

C. F. Hoffmann: 'The Source of the Words of the Music in York LVI', *Modern Language Notes*, lxv (1950), 236

N. C. Carpenter: 'Music in the Secunda Pastorum', *Speculum*, xxvi (1951), 696

H. Craig: *English Religious Drama of the Middle Ages* (Oxford, 1955)

J. B. Cutts: 'The Second Coventry Carol', *RN*, x (1957), 3

R. Southern: *The Medieval Theatre in the Round: a Study of the Staging of Castle of Perseverance and Related Matters* (London, 1957)

J. Stevens: 'Music in Medieval English Drama', *PRMA*, lxxxiv (1957–8), 81

G. Wickham: *Early English Stages: 1300 to 1600* (London, 1959)

M. Rose, ed. and trans.: *The Wakefield Mystery Plays* (London, 1961)

M. D. Anderson: *Drama and Imagery in English Medieval Churches* (Cambridge, 1963)

J. Gassner, ed.: *Medieval and Tudor Drama* (New York, 1963)

N. C. Carpenter: 'Music in the Chester Plays', *Papers on English Language and Literature*, i (1965), 195

V. A. Kolve: *The Play called Corpus Christi* (London, 1966)

R. Longsworth: *The Cornish Ordinalia: Religion and Dramaturgy* (Cambridge, Mass., and London, 1967)

N. C. Carpenter: 'Music in the English Mystery Plays', *Music in English Renaissance Drama*, ed. T. H. Long (Lexington, 1968), 1–31

N. Davis, ed.: *Non-cycle Plays and Fragments*, Early English Text Society, suppl. text i (London, 1970) [music of Shrewsbury frags. ed. F. Ll. Harrison]

C. Wall: 'York Pageant XLVI and its Music', *Speculum*, xlvi (1971), 689 [music ed. R. Steiner]

J. Dutka: 'Music and the English Mystery Plays', *Comparative Drama*, vii (1973), 135

——: 'Mysteries, Minstrels and Music', *Comparative Drama*, viii (1974), 112

S. J. Kahrl: *Traditions of Medieval English Drama* (London, 1974)

A. H. Nelson: *The Medieval English Stage: Corpus Christi Pageants and Plays* (Chicago, 1974)

S. K. Rankin: 'Shrewsbury School MS VI: a Medieval Part-book?', *PRMA*, cii (1975–6), 129

FRENCH PLAYS

A. Jubinal: *Mystères inédits du quinzième siècle* (Paris, 1837) [from MSS in *F-Psg*]

A. J. V. Leroux de Lincy and F. Michel, eds.: *Recueil de farces, moralités et sermons joyeux* (Paris, 1837)

F. Michel, ed.: *Le mystère de Saint Louis roi de France*, Roxburghe Club (London, 1871)

G. Paris and U. Robert, eds.: *Les Miracles de Notre Dame* (Paris, 1876–93)

L. Petit de Julleville: *Histoire du théâtre en France: les mystères* (Paris, 1880)

P. le Verdier, ed.: *Mystère de l'Incarnation et Nativité de Notre Sauveur*

*et Rédempteur Jésus-Christ* (Rouen, 1884–6)
L. Petit de Julleville: *Répertoire du théâtre comique en France au moyen âge* (Paris, 1886)
F. W. Bourdillon, ed.: *Cest daucasī & de nicolete* (Oxford, 1896) [with facs.]
E. Roy: *Le Mystère de la Passion en France du XIV<sup>e</sup> au XVI<sup>e</sup> siècle* (Paris, 1903–4)
E. Faral, ed.: *Mimes français du XIII<sup>e</sup> siècle* (Paris, 1910)
M. Roques, ed.: *Le garçon et l'aveugle* (Paris, 2/1921/R)
G. Frank, ed.: *La Passion du Palatinus, mystère du XIV<sup>e</sup> siècle* (Paris, 1922)
G. Cohen, ed.: *Le livre de conduite du régisseur et le compte des dépenses pour le Mystère de la Passion, joué à Mons en 1501* (Paris and Oxford, 1925)
——: *Histoire de la mise-en-scène dans le théâtre religieux français du moyen-âge* (Paris, 1926, 3/1951)
W. P. Shepard, ed.: *La Passion provençale du MS Didot* (Paris, 1928)
R. Lebègue: *Le mystère des Actes des apôtres* (Paris, 1929)
G. Cohen: *Le théâtre en France au moyen âge* (Paris, 1931)
D. Penn: *The Staging of the Miracles of Notre Dame par personnages of the MS Cangé* (New York, 1933)
G. Frank, ed.: *La Passion d'Autun* (Paris, 1934)
J. Handschin: 'Das Weihnachts-Mysterium von Rouen als musik-geschichtliche Quelle', *AcM*, vii (1935), 98
A. Pirro: *Histoire de la musique de la fin du XIVe siècle à la fin du XVIe siècle* (Paris, 1940)
J. Rolland: *Essai paléographique et bibliographique sur le théâtre profane en France avant le XV<sup>e</sup> siècle* (Paris, 1945)
G. Frank: *The Medieval French Drama* (Oxford, 1954)
M. Roques, ed.: *Aucassin et Nicolette*, Les classiques français du moyen âge (Paris, 2/1954)
A. and R. Bossuat: *Deux moralités inédites* (Paris, 1955)
H. M. Brown: *Music in the French Secular Theater, 1400–1550* (Cambridge, Mass., 1963) [music exx. in vol.ii]
O. Jodogne: 'Recherches sur les débuts du théâtre religieux en France', *Cahiers de civilisation médiévale*, xxix (1965), 1
——, ed.: *Le mystère de la Passion d'Arnoul Gréban* (Brussels, 1965)
E. Konigson: *La représentation d'un mystère de la Passion à Valenciennes en 1547* (Paris, 1969)
A. Pulega: *Ludi e spettacoli nel medioevo: I tornei di dame* (Milan, 1970)
R. Axton and J. Stevens, trans.: *Medieval French Plays* (Oxford, 1971) [with music]
M. Lazar: *Le jugement dernier: Lo jutgamen general: drame provençal du XV<sup>e</sup> siècle* (Paris, 1971)
P. Matarasso, trans.: *Aucassin and Nicolette and Other Tales* (Harmondsworth, 1971)
N. Wilkins: 'Music in the 14th-century Miracles de Nostre Dame', *MD*, xxviii (1974), 39–75

GERMAN PLAYS

F. J. Mone: *Altdeutsche Schauspiele* (Leipzig, 1841)
——: *Schauspiele des Mittelalters* (Karlsruhe, 1846)
O. Schönemann: *Der Sünderfall und Marienklage: zwei niederdeutsche Schauspiele* (Hanover, 1855)
K. Weinhold: *Weihnachtsspiele und Lieder aus Süddeutschland und Schlesien* (Graz, 1870)
P. Bohn: 'Theophilus: niederdeutsches Schauspiel aus einer Handschrift des 15. Jahrhunderts der Trierischen Stadtbibliothek', *MMg*, ix (1877), 3, 24
G. Milchsack: *Heidelberger Passionspiel* (Stuttgart, 1880)
——: *Egerer Fronleichnamsspiel* (Stuttgart, 1881)
K. F. Kummer: *Sechs altdeutsche Mysterien* (Vienna, 1882)
R. Froning: *Frankfurter Chroniken und annalistische Aufzeichnungen*, i (Frankfurt am Main, 1884) [contains Frankfurter Dirigier-rolle]
R. Brandstetter: 'Musik und Gesang in den Luzerner Osterspielen', *Der Geschichtsfreund*, xl (1885), 145
J. E. Wackernell: *Altdeutsche Passionsspiele aus Tirol* (Graz, 1897)
E. Refardt: 'Die Musik der Basler Volksschauspiele des 16. Jahrhunderts', *AMw*, iii (1921), 199
M. J. Rudwin: *A Historical and Bibliographical Survey of the German Religious Drama* (Pittsburgh, 1925)
A. Orel: 'Die Weisen im "Wiener Passionsspiel" aus dem 13. Jahrhundert', *Mitteilungen des Vereins für Geschichte der Stadt Wien*, vi (1926), 72 [with transcrs.]
O. Sengpiel: *Die Bedeutung der Prozession für das geistliche Spiel des Mittelalters in Deutschland* (Breslau, 1932)
K. Dreimüller: *Die Musik des Alsfelder Passionsspiels* (Vienna, 1936)
J. Müller-Blattau: *Germanische Erbe in deutscher Tonkunst* (Berlin, 1938)
H. H. Breuer: *Das mittelniederdeutsche Osnabrücker Osterspiel: der Ursprung des Osterspiels und die Prozession* (Osnabrück, 1939)
H. Osthoff: 'Deutsche Liedweisen und Wechselgesänge im mittelalterlichen Drama', *AMf*, vii (1942), 65
M. B. Evans: *The Passion Play of Lucerne: an Historical and Critical Introduction* (New York, 1943)
H. Osthoff: *Die Musik im Drama des deutschen Mittelalters: Quellen und Forschungsziele* (Kassel, 1943)

G. O. Arlt: 'The Vocal Music of the Lucerne Passion Play', *BAMS*, viii (1945), 24
W. F. Michael: *Die geistliche Prozessionsspiele in Deutschland* (Baltimore and Göttingen, 1947)
K. Dreimüller: 'Die Musik im geistlichen Spiel des späten Mittelalters', *KJb*, xxxiv (1950), 27
K. Fellerer: 'Die Nottulner Osterfeier', *Westfalia sacra*, ii (1950)
H. Kettering: 'Die Essener Osterfeier', *KJb*, xxxvi (1952), 7
L. Kaff: *Mittelalterlicher Oster- und Passionsspiele aus Oberösterreich* (Linz, 1956)
W. Lipphardt: 'Das hessische Weihnachtspiel', *Convivium symbolicum*, ii (1958), 23, 66
R. Steinbach: *Die deutschen Oster- und Passionsspiele des Mittelalters* (Cologne and Vienna, 1960)
R. Meir, ed.: *Das Innsbrucker Osterspiel and das Osterspiel von Muri* (Stuttgart, 1963)
W. F. Michael: *Frühformen der deutschen Bühne* (Berlin, 1963)
W. L. Boletta: *The Role of Music in Medieval German Drama: Easter Plays and Passion Plays* (diss., Vanderbilt U., 1967)
W. F. Michael: *Das deutsche Drama des Mittelalters* (Berlin and New York, 1971)

ITALIAN PLAYS

A. d'Ancona: *Sacre rappresentazioni dei secoli, XIV, XV e XVI* (Florence, 1872)
——: *Origini del teatro italiano* (Florence, 1877, 2/1891)
V. de Bartholomaeis: *Origini della poesia drammatica italiana* (Turin, 1924, rev. 2/1952)
J. S. Kennard: *Italian Theatre: a History of the Italian Theatre from its Beginnings to the Present Day* (New York, 1932)
D. M. Inguanez: 'Un dramma della Passione del secolo XII', *Miscellanea cassinese*, xii (1936), 7–38; repr. in *Latomus*, xx (1961), 568
V. de Bartholomaeis, ed.: *Laude drammatiche e rappresentazioni sacre* (Florence, 1943/R1967)
F. Ghisi: 'Le musiche di Isaac per il *San Giovanni e Paolo* di Lorenzo il Magnifico', *RaM*, xvi (1943), 264
B. Becherini: 'La musica nelle sacre rappresentazioni', *RMI*, liii (1951), 193–241
A. Cioni: *Bibliografia delle sacre rappresentazioni* (Florence, 1961)

SPANISH PLAYS

J. del Encina: *Teatro completo*, ed. M. Cañete and F. A. Barbieri (Madrid, 1893)
R. Menéndez Pidal, ed.: 'Auto de los Reyes Magos', *Revista de archivos, bibliotecas y museos*, 3rd ser., iv (1900), 453 [with facs.]
F. Pedrell: 'La Festa d'Elche', *SIMG*, ii (1900–01), 203
J. Ruiz de Lihory, Barón de Alcahali: *Música en Valencia* (Valencia, 1903)
J. P. W. Crawford: *Spanish Drama before Lope de Vega* (Philadelphia, 1922)
L. Fernandez: *Farsas y églogas*, ed. E. Cotarelo y Mori (Madrid, 1926)
J. B. Trend: *The Music of Spanish History to 1600* (Oxford, 1926)
W. Sturdevant: *The Misterio de los Reyes Magos: its Position in the Development of the Medieval Legend of the Three Kings* (Baltimore, 1927)
J. E. Gillet, ed.: '*Danza del Santísimo Nacimento*, a Sixteenth-century Play by Pedro Suárez de Robles', *Proceedings of the Modern Language Association of America*, xliii (1928), 614
H. Corbató: *Los misterios del Corpus de Valencia* (Berkeley, 1932)
H. Anglés: *La música a Catalunya fins al segle XIII* (Barcelona, 1935)
R. B. Williams: *The Staging of Plays in the Spanish Peninsula prior to 1555* (Iowa City, 1935)
A. Salazar: 'Music in the Primitive Spanish Theatre before Lope de Vega', *PAMS 1938*, 94
A. Chase: 'Origins of the Lyric Theatre in Spain', *MQ*, xxv (1939), 292
J. Gillet: 'The *Memorias* of Felipe Fernández Vallejo and the History of the Early Spanish Drama', *Essays and Studies in Honor of Carleton Brown* (New York, 1940), 264
A. Livermore: 'The Spanish Dramatists and their Use of Music', *ML*, xxv (1944), 140
G. Diaz Plaja: 'La Consueta del Rey Asuero', *Boletin de la Real Academia de buenas letras de Barcelona*, xxv (1953), 227
F. L. Carreter: *Teatro medieval: textos integros* (Valencia, 1958)
S. Pestana, ed.: *Auto de los Reyes Magos: texto castellano anónimo de século XII* (Lisbon, 1965)
N. D. Shergold: *A History of the Spanish Stage from Medieval Times until the End of the 17th Century* (Oxford, 1967)
H. López-Morales, ed.: *Églogas completas de Juan del Enzina* (Madrid, 1968)

EAST EUROPEAN PLAYS

G. Milchsack: *Egerer Fronleichnamsspiel* (Stuttgart, 1881)
J. Truhlář: 'O staročeských dramatech velikonočních' [On old Czech Easter plays], *Časopis národního musea*, lvi (1891), 3–43
Z. Nejedlý: 'Magister Záviše und seine Schule', *SIMG*, vii (1905–6), 41
J. Máchal: *Staročeské skladby dramatické původu liturgického* [Old Czech dramatic compositions of liturgical origin] (Prague, 1908)
Z. Nejedlý: *Dějiny husitského zpěvu za válek husitských*, ii [History of

Hussite song during the Hussite wars] (Prague, 1913/R1954)
F. Oberpfalcer and J. Plavec: *Nejstarší české hry divadelní* [The oldest Czech play] (Prague, 1941)
J. Vilikovský: *Písemnictví českého středověku* [Czech medieval literature] (Prague, 1948)
Z. Jachimecki: *Muzyka polska w rozwoju historycznym* [Polish music in its historical development] (Kraków, 1948–51)
V. Černý: 'Staročeský Mastičkář' [The old Czech vendor of ointments], *Rozpravy Československé akademie věd*, lxv (1955), 7
A. Škarka: 'Roudnický plankt' [Marienklage from Raudnitz], *Listy filologické*, lxxix (1956), 187
J. Lewański: 'Dramat i dramatyznacje liturgiczne w średniowieczu Polskim' [Medieval Polish liturgical drama], *Musica medii aevi*, i (1965), 96–174
*Dějiny českeho divadla*, i: *Od počátků do sklonku 18. stoleti* [History of the Czech theatre, i: From its beginnings to the close of the 18th century] (Prague, 1968)
A. and E. Mrygoń: *Bibliografia polskiego piśmiennictwa muzykologicznego* [A bibliography of Polish musicological literature] (Warsaw, 1972)
B. Bartkowski: '*Visitatio sepulchri* w Polskich przekazach średniowiecznych' [*Visitatio sepulchri* in Polish medieval MSS], *Musica medii aevi*, iv (1973), 129–63
P. Rado and L. Mezey: *Libri liturgici manuscripti bibliothecarum Hungariae et limitropharum regionum* (Budapest, 1973)

NEW DRAMATIC TYPES

M. de Montifaud, ed.: *Les triomphes de l'abbaye des Conards avec une notice sur la fête des fous* (Paris, 1874, 2/1877)
R. von Liliencron: 'Die Chorgesänge des lateinisch-deutschen Schuldramas im XVI. Jahrhundert', *VMw*, vi (1890), 309
J. Jelinek: *The Music of the Morality Plays* (diss., U. of Chicago, 1920)
K. M. Lea: *Italian Popular Comedy* (Oxford, 1934/R1962)
E. B. Jules: *Song in the Tudor Interlude* (diss., Yale U., 1936)
O. Michaelis: *Johann Walter, 1496–1570, der Musiker-Dichter in Luthers Gefolgschaft* (Leipzig and Hamburg, 1939)
H. G. Harvey: *The Theatre of the Basoche* (Cambridge, Mass., 1941)
G. Kernodle: *From Art to Theatre* (Chicago, 1944) [incl. extensive bibliography]
F. W. Sternfeld: 'Music in the Schools of the Reformation', *MD*, ii (1948), 99
G. Cohen, ed.: *Recueil de farces françaises inédites du XVᵉ siècle* (Cambridge, Mass., 1949)
*Les fêtes de la Renaissance I: CNRS Abbaye de Royaumont 1955*
T. W. Craik: *The Tudor Interlude: Stage, Costume and Acting* (Leicester, 1958)
L. H. Loomis: 'Secular Dramatics in the Royal Palace, Paris, 1378, 1389, and Chaucer's "Tregetoures"', *Speculum*, xxxiii (1958), 242
J. E. Stevens: *Music and Poetry in the Early Tudor Court* (London, 1961)
P. Brett: 'The English Consort Song: 1570–1625', *PRMA*, lxxxviii (1961–2), 73
H. M. Brown: *Music in the French Secular Theater, 1400–1550* (Cambridge, Mass., 1963)
E. J. Dent, rev. F. W. Sternfeld: 'Music and Drama', *NOHM*, iv (1968), 784–820
J. H. Long, ed.: *Music in English Renaissance Drama* (Lexington, 1968)
P. J. Houle: *The English Morality and Related Drama: a Bibliographical Survey* (Hamden, Conn., 1972)
R. A. Potter: *The English Morality Play: Origins, History, and Influence of a Dramatic Tradition* (London and Boston, 1975)
                    JOHN STEVENS (with JACK SAGE, III, 3(v))

**Medina, Fernand Pérez de** (*fl* 1479). Spanish composer. He entered Isabella's chapel as a singer on 7 November 1477. The queen evidently favoured him, for on 28 July 1479 she ordered that he be exempted from taxation in Seville where he lived. She also raised his annual salary by 3800 to 20,000 maravedís. Two secular pieces by him appear in the Cancionero Musical de Palacio. A moralizing villancico, *No ay plazer en esta vida* (ed. in MME, v, 1947, no.56) for four voices has a 'si placet' first contra. The three-voice canción, *Es por vos si tengo vida* (MME, v, 1947, no.70), is florid in style. One sacred work survives, a setting of the *Salve regina* (*E-Sco* 5–5–20), an antiphon text particularly popular in Spain. Plainsong verses alternate with those in polyphony; the verse, 'Et Jesum' is perhaps the earliest example of five-part writing by a Spanish composer.

BIBLIOGRAPHY
R. Stevenson: *Spanish Music in the Age of Columbus* (The Hague, 1960), 180ff
                                        ISABEL POPE

**Mediņš.** Latvian family of musicians.

**(1) Jāzeps Mediņš** (*b* Kaunas, 13 Feb 1877; *d* Riga, 12 June 1947). Composer and conductor, brother of (2) Jēkabs Mediņš and (3) Jānis Mediņš. He graduated from the First Riga Musical Institute in 1896 (violin, cello and piano) and then became a teacher and director of the same institute. Subsequently he worked as a conductor at the Riga Latvian theatre (1906–11) and the Baku town opera theatre (1916–22), and as répétiteur and conductor at the Latvian National Opera in Riga (1922–5). Ill-health compelled him to give up his work, but he taught the piano at the Riga Conservatory from 1945 to 1947, as professor from 1946. He was awarded the title Honoured Art Worker of the Latvian SSR in 1945. As a composer he showed talents for lyrical drama and colourful orchestration. His greatest work was the opera *Vaidelote* ('The priestess'), but he was also one of the first notable Latvian symphonists.

WORKS
*(selective list)*
Operas: Vaidelote [The priestess] (after Aspāzija), 1922–4, Riga, 1927; Zemdegi [The Zemdegs family], 1947, completed by M. Zariņš
Orch: Vn Conc., 1911; Armeņu melodija, 1932; Latvju zeme [The Latvian land], sym. sketch, 1935; Sym. no.2 'Ziedonī' [In springtime], 1937; Sym. no.3, E♭, 1941
Other works: Str Qt, F, 1941; vn and vc pieces, many choral and solo songs

Principal publisher: Latvijas valsts izdevniecība

BIBLIOGRAPHY
M. Zālīte: *Jāzeps Mediņš* (Riga, 1951)

**(2) Jēkabs Mediņš** (*b* Riga, 22 March 1885; *d* Riga, 27 Nov 1971). Composer, conductor and teacher, brother of (1) Jāzeps Mediņš and (3) Jānis Mediņš. He graduated from the First Riga Musical Institute (violin, organ and piano) in 1905 and studied further at the Berlin Hochschule für Musik summer courses (1910–14). Subsequently he taught in Valmiera, Sizraņa, and in the teachers' institute at Jelgava (1921–44), directed the Jelgava People's Conservatory (1921–41) and taught the choral conducting class at the Riga Conservatory (1944–71, professor from 1945, rector 1949–51). He was chairman of the Soviet Latvian Composers' Union (1948–50) and one of the chief conductors of the Soviet Latvian song festivals. In 1960 he was awarded the title People's Artist of the Latvian SSR.

WORKS
*(selective list)*
Orch: Leġenda, 1909; Cl Conc., 1948; Hn Conc. no.1, 1949; Kokle Conc., 1952; Org Conc., 1954; Hn Conc. no.2, 1962; 6 other concs.
Vocal: cantatas, many choral songs, solo songs, folksong arrs.
Chamber and inst: 3 str qts, inst pieces

Principal publishers: Latvijas valsts izdevniecība, Muzgiz, Sovetskij kompozitor

WRITINGS
*Kora zinātņu pamati* [The foundations of choral science] (Riga, 1956)
*Silueti* [Silhouettes] (Riga, 1968) [autobiography]

**(3) Jānis Mediņš** (*b* Riga, 9 Oct 1890; *d* Stockholm, 4 March 1966). Composer and conductor, brother of (1) Jāzeps Mediņš and (2) Jēkabs Mediņš. He graduated from the First Riga Musical Institute (piano, violin and cello) in 1909. From 1913 to 1915 he was a violist and conductor at the Latvian opera in Riga, later becoming opera conductor of the Latvian National Opera (1920–28) and, from 1928 to 1944, chief conductor of the Latvian Radio SO and artistic director of Latvian radio.

He taught in the special instrumentation class at the Riga Conservatory, where he was appointed professor in 1929. From 1944 to 1948 he lived in Germany, and from 1948 in Stockholm.

A composer of characteristically national neo-Romantic tendency, Mediņš achieved particular success in the genres of opera and ballet, symphonic music and solo song. Alongside Alfrēds Kalniņš, he was one of the founders of Latvian opera, being involved with progressive Latvian dramatic composition. His opera *Uguns un nakts* ('Fire and night') concerns the people's struggle for freedom; its dramatically and powerfully drawn heroes are characterized both chorally and symphonically. Struggle against the idea of despotism is expressed in the opera *Dievi un cilvēki* ('Gods and men'), which includes some original experiments in Egyptian colouring. *Sprīdītis* ('Tom Thumb') is based on characters from folktales, and Mediņš's last opera, *Luteklīte* ('The little darling'), is for children. His *Mīlas uzvara* ('Love's victory', 1935) was the first Latvian ballet. After his death his manuscripts were donated to 14 libraries in Europe and North America (see Dunkele).

### WORKS
*(selective list)*

Operas: Uguns un nakts [Fire and night] (2 operas, J. Rainis), 1913–19, Riga, 1921, rev. as single opera, Riga, 1924; Dievi un cilvēki [Gods and men] (after L. Paegle), Riga, 1922; Sprīdītis [Tom Thumb] (A. Brigadere), Riga, 1927; Luteklīte [The little darling] (children's opera), Riga, 1939

Ballet: Mīlas uzvara [Love's victory], 1935

Orch: Suite no.1, 1922; Imanta, sym. sketch, 1923; Zilais kalns [The blue mountain], sym. sketch, 1924; Vc Conc., 1928; Suite no.3 'Dzimtene' [The fatherland], 1933; Pf Conc., 1934; Nakts Getzemanes dārzā [The night in the garden of Gethsemane], sym. poem; Pie baznīcas [By the church], str; 2 other suites, pieces for band

Chamber and inst: Balāde, pf, 1922; 2 pf trios, 1930, 1958; Vc Sonata, 1945; Str Qt, c, 1946; 2 sonatas, vn, pf, 1946, 1954; Sonatina, vc, pf, 1947; Suite, vc, pf, 1951; Rhapsody, 2 pf, 1954; Sonata, accordion, 1955; 23 dainas, pf

Vocal: 8 cantatas, choral songs, *c*130 solo songs

Principal publishers: Latvijas skaņražu kopa, Liesma, Rode, Universal

### WRITINGS

*Toņi un pustoņi* [Tones and semitones] (Stockholm, 1964) [autobiography]

### BIBLIOGRAPHY

I. Dunkele: 'Ārzemju bibliotekām nosūtītie Jāna Mediņa skaņdarbī' [Mediņš's works sent to foreign libraries], *Latvju mūzika*, ii (1969), 170

—— : 'Jāņa Mediņa nepublicētie skaņdarbi' [Mediņš's unpublished works], *Latvju mūzika*, ii (1969), 172

JĒKABS VĪTOLIŅŠ

**Mediolano** (*fl* late 14th century). Composer, probably northern Italian, from Milan. Only one work is known by him, a four-voice Sanctus, conspicuously Dorian in mode, in the Paduan fragment *GB-Ob* 229 (no.4).

### BIBLIOGRAPHY

B. J. Layton: *Italian Music for the Ordinary of the Mass 1350–1450* (diss., Harvard U., 1960), 135ff

K. von Fischer and F. A. Gallo, eds.: *Italian Sacred Music*, PMFC, xii (1974)

KURT VON FISCHER

**Meditatio** (Lat.). MEDIATION.

**Medium** (Lat.). Synonym for AMBITUS in the treatise *Speculum musice* and in the work of Tinctoris.

**Medius** (Lat.: 'middle'). (1) In 16th- and 17th-century English music, a term sometimes used synonymously with MEANE.

(2) The name sometimes given to the highest partbook of a set, particularly in liturgical sources; the alternative terms 'cantus', 'discantus' and 'superius' are also found. See PARTBOOKS.

**Medley.** English term for a succession of well-known tunes strung together, generally without any formal construction (though examples in the Fitzwilliam Virginal Book regularly repeat each tune in a varied form, and one of the vocal medleys surviving from the 16th century is built on an ostinato bass; see QUODLIBET). A medley is similar to a potpourri, though generally of a smoother construction. The constituent tunes are very often from a similar source, as for example 'a medley of tunes from X' or 'a medley of songs by Y'.

The 'medley overture', which might contain scraps of concerto, opera airs, folktunes and popular dance-tunes, was invented by Richard Charke; such a work by him, with others by Arne and Lampe, was published in *Six Medley or Comic Overtures in Seven Parts* (1763). The form was revived in Victorian times, but the later medley overture generally consisted of a string of tunes from the work it precedes. The term applies to opera overtures by Boieldieu, Auber and Hérold as well as to those to many operettas, including some of Sullivan's.

**Medtner, Nikolay Karlovich.** See METNER, NIKOLAY KARLOVICH.

**Meer, John Henry van der** (*b* The Hague, 9 Feb 1920). Dutch musicologist, resident in Germany. He studied musicology at the University of Utrecht with Albert Smijers and Eduard Reeser and took the doctorate in 1961 with a thesis on Fux as an opera composer. He taught music theory and history at the Conservatory of Utrecht (1946–54) and music history at the Royal Conservatory at The Hague (1948–55). In 1954 Van der Meer became curator of the music department of the Gemeentemuseum at The Hague. He held this post until 1963, when he was appointed curator of the collection of musical instruments of the Germanisches Nationalmuseum at Nuremberg. He is an authority on organology and most of his more recent publications deal with musical instruments.

### WRITINGS

'De muziekhistorische bibliotheek van het Haagse Gemeentemuseum', *'s-Gravenhage*, xiv (1959), 25 [with Eng. summary]

*Johann Josef Fux als Opernkomponist* (diss., U. of Utrecht; Bilthoven, 1961)

'Sweelinck und Nürnberg?', *TVNM*, xx/1–2 (1964), 37

with A. Berner and G. Thibault: *Preservation and Restoration of Musical Instruments* (London, 1967)

'Die Verwendung der Blasinstrumente im Orchester bei Haydn und seinen Zeitgenossen', *Der junge Haydn: Internationale Arbeitstagung des Instituts für Aufführungspraxis: Graz 1970*, 202

*The Carel van Leeuwen Boomkamp Collection of Musical Instruments* (Amsterdam, 1971)

'Einige Probleme bei der Besetzung der Kammermusik für Streicher des Barock', *Musica cameralis: Brno VI 1971*, 49

*Germanisches Nationalmuseum Nürnberg: Wegweiser durch die Sammlung historischer Musikinstrumente* (Nuremberg, 1971)

'Musikinstrumentenbau in Bayern bis 1800', *Musik in Bayern*, ed. R. Münster and H. Schmidt (Tutzing, 1972), ii, 17

'Studien zum Cembalobau in Italien', *Festschrift to Ernst Emsheimer* (Stockholm, 1974), 131, 275

'Das Arpicordo-Problem nochmals erörtert', *AcM*, xlix (1977), 275

ELLINOR BIJVOET

**Me'erāf.** Liturgical book of the Ethiopian Church containing the Common of the Office; see ETHIOPIAN RITE, MUSIC OF THE.

**Meers.** See MEARES.

**Meerti, Elisa.** See BLAES, ELISA.

**Mees, Joseph-Henri(-Ignace)** (*b* Brussels, 28 May 1777; *d* Paris, 18 Dec 1858). South Netherlands composer, conductor, publisher, theorist and teacher. He was the son of Henri Mees (*b* Brussels, 1757; *d* Warsaw, 31 Jan 1820), principal baritone of the Brussels Grand Théâtre, and of Anne-Marie Vitzthumb, a singer. He showed precocious musical talent: at the age of five he sang in a church choir, at seven he began to study the violin and at ten he played in the orchestra of the Grand Théâtre. He had further violin studies with J.-E. Pauwels and lessons in harmony and counterpoint with his grandfather Ignaz Vitzthumb. In 1794, during the second French occupation, the family emigrated to Hamburg, where Henri Mees and other Brussels artists established a theatre for the Comédie-Française; Joseph-Henri occasionally sang secondary roles and conducted the orchestra there. He also opened a music shop, from which he published works from the Parisian repertory.

In 1798 he founded a weekly musical periodical, the *Journal d'Apollon pour le forte-piano*; publication continued until 1804, even though Mees went to Brunswick in 1800 to direct the French theatre at the ducal court. There he married Mlle de Saint-Romain, a former singer at the Paris Opéra. Later he travelled to Germany, Sweden and France (residing briefly in Bordeaux and Rouen, where he became honorary president of the Philharmonic Society), and finally to England; he was one of the first exponents of the *méloplaste* method (a simplified method of reading music using numbers instead of notes) in London. In 1816 he returned to Brussels and founded a music academy, which he directed with J. F. Snel until 1830. In 1824 he established a similar school in Antwerp; both institutions used the *méloplaste* method. He was also engaged in Brussels as court composer (1819–22) and honorary violinist (1827–9) for the private music of Prince William of Orange-Nassau. During the Revolution of 1830 he emigrated, travelling to Paris, Italy, England and finally Kiev, where he directed a music academy and taught music at the imperial boarding-school. He conducted at the St Petersburg Opera from 1838 and in 1855 moved to Paris.

Mees's compositions include an opera, a sacred oratorio and other vocal works. He edited two musical journals in addition to the *Journal d'Apollon*: the *Journal de chant* (Brussels, ?1817–19) and the *Maître à chanter, ou Le troubadour cosmopolite* (?Brussels, 1827). He also prepared new editions of Castil-Blaze's *Dictionnaire de musique moderne* (Brussels, 1828) and Grétry's *Mémoires, ou Essais sur la musique* (Brussels, 1829), adding to the former an *Abrégé historique sur la musique moderne*.

### WORKS
*(printed works published in Brussels unless otherwise stated)*

Le fermier belge (opéra comique, 1, P. Lesbroussart), Brussels, Théâtre du Parc, 9 Nov 1816
Esther, sacred oratorio, frags. perf. Brussels, 1823
Secular vocal: Cantate à grand orchestre, S, T, chorus, orch, 1818, vocal score (?1818); Le civisme, ou Le belge ami zélé de la patrie (J. B. J. Caroli), patriotic cantata, S/T, harp/(pf, gui) (n.d.); Chant national, 2 T, B, wind band (n.d.); Hymne aux arts et à l'amitié (J.-H. Mees), S, T, B, gui, pf (n.d.); Hymne à la paix: strophe à la Sainte-Alliance, T, chorus (n.d.); A l'oranger, hymn, 2 S/2 T, B, pf (Brussels and London, n.d.); Les troubadours, serenade, 2 T, Bar, gui, pf (n.d.); Les mirlitons, trio comique; other works, incl. many romances
Pedagogical: Tableaux synoptique du méloplaste (1827); Explication de la basse chiffrée (1827); Etrennes lyriques: méthode raisonnée pour exercer la voix (1828); Théorie de la musique mise en canons, 4vv (1828)

### BIBLIOGRAPHY
*EitnerQ; FétisB*
A. Choron and F. Fayolle: *Dictionnaire historique des musiciens* (Paris, 1810–11/*R*1971)
*Almanach royal de la cour, des provinces méridionales et de la ville de Bruxelles* (1816–30)
E. Gregoir: *Galerie biographique des artistes-musiciens belges* (Brussels, 1862)
——: *Les artistes-musiciens belges au XVIIIme et au XIXme siècle* (Brussels, 1885)
P. Bergmans: 'Mees (Joseph-Henri)', *BNB*
——: 'Le séjour à Hambourg du musicien bruxellois Joseph-Henri Mees', *Académie royale de Belgique: bulletin de la classe des beaux-arts*, x (1928), 67
R. Vannes: *Dictionnaire des musiciens (compositeurs)* (Brussels, 1947)

PAUL RASPÉ

**Meester, Louis de** (*b* Roeselare, West Flanders, 28 Oct 1904). Belgian composer. He began his career playing in bars and nightclubs and working with touring operetta companies; as a composer he is self-taught. From 1933 to 1937 he was director of the Meknes Conservatory, Morocco, and in 1945 he became a sound engineer with the Flemish section of Belgian radio. He used his technical knowledge of electronics in a major work for the first time in his radio opera *De grote verzoeking van St Antonius*, which won the 1957 Italia Prize. In 1962 Belgian radio appointed him artistic director of the Institute for Electronic Music and Psychoacoustics (IPEM) attached to Ghent University. Co-founder and leader of the composers' group Spectra, he has been tireless in his electronic research, compiling a collection of sounds recorded on about 100 hours of tape. De Meester is an outgoing composer, using novel techniques to express his feelings; much of his work has been in incidental music.

### WORKS
*(selective list)*

Dramatic: De grote verzoeking van St Antonius [The great temptation of St Anthony], radio opera, 1957; Twee is te weinig, drie is te veel [Two is not enough, three is too many] (television opera, T. Brulin), 1965; De paradijsgeuzen [The birds of paradise] (opera, G. Martens), 1967; De tijd der waanzin, music for son et lumière, wind, elec, Ronse, 1972; incidental music for radio, television, theatre and cinema
Elec: Incantations, 1958; Spectrum 64, 1964, collab Spectra; Patent 2003, 1964, collab. Spectra; Nocturne malgache, 1965; Spielerei, 1969; Mimodrama, 1975
Orch: Capriccio, 1946; Magreb, va, orch, 1946; Sinfonietta buffa, 1949; 2 pf concs., 1952, 1956; Musica per archi, 1955; Amalgames, 1956; Marine, 1958; Serenade, str, hpd, 1959; Concertino, double chamber orch, 1965; Scherzettino, fl, ob, str, 1971
Vocal: Betje trompet, reciter, orch, 1950; La voix du silence (Carème), Bar, female chorus, speaking chorus, 1952; Ballade van de gebarsten trommel (M. Coole), speaker, orch, 1973
Chamber: Sonatina, vc, pf, 1946; Divertimento, wind qnt, 1946; 3 str qts, 1947, 1954, 1959; Tafelmuziek, 2 wind, 3 str, 1953; Divertimento a 4, pf qt, 1970

Principal publishers: CeBeDeM, Metropolis
MSS in IPEM

CORNEEL MERTENS

**Méfano, Paul** (*b* Bassorah, Iraq, 6 March 1937). French composer. He studied at the Ecole Normale de Musique, at the Paris Conservatoire (1960–64) with Dandelot, Messiaen and Milhaud, and at the Basle Academy of Music with Boulez, Stockhausen and Pousseur. His very attractive Boulezian early works (up to and including *Paraboles*) established his reputation, and he soon found a much more individual style, marked by a clear feeling for drama and lyricism and a predilection for setting large sound blocks in conflict. *La cérémonie* reveals these qualities in their most perfect balance. After that work Méfano undertook experiments in electronics; *La messe des vouleurs* was a successful essay in the combination of live and electronic resources. Working as a music teacher and adviser in the municipalities of Chatillon and Champigny, he has produced several notable series of broadcasts. In 1971 he received the Enesco Prize of the SACEM.

### WORKS

Incidences, orch, pf, 1960; Madrigal (Eluard), 3 female vv, ens, 1962; Mélodies (Khayyam, Ittomaro, Apollinaire, Bonnefoy), S, ens, 1962; Paraboles (Bonnefoy), dramatic S, ens, 1964; Interférences, hn, pf, ens, 1966; Lignes (Méfano), B, brass, perc, amp bn, amp dbn, 1968; La cérémonie (Méfano), S, Ct, Bar, 3 orch and choral groups, 1970 Old Oedib (Bible), speaker, inst, tape, ring mods, 1970; Intersection, 6-track tape, 1970; Bi-function, 2 musicians, tape, elec, 1971; La messe des voleurs . . . [les voleurs de messe] (Méfano), 4 solo vv, 3 ww, 3 brass, 3 perc, 3 str, Hammond org, 6-track tape, elec, 1972; Signes/oubli, 6 ww, 4 brass, 2 perc, 8 str, Hammond org, elec gui, 1972; 'N', fl, elec, 1972; Would you like it?, ww, brass, str, 1973; L'ombre de mon âme, fl, 1975; Ondes, 15 insts, 1975; Eventail, elec fl, 1976

Principal publishers: Heugel, Salabert

DOMINIQUE JAMEUX

**Megalynarion.** A TROPARION that accompanies the ninth ode of a Byzantine KANŌN for certain feasts; its opening phrase is taken from the *Magnificat*.

**Meged.** An alternative spelling of *meghedi*, a type of hymn of the Armenian Church; *see* ARMENIAN RITE, MUSIC OF THE.

**Megerle, Abraham** (*b* Wasserburg am Inn, 9 Feb 1607; *d* Altötting, 29 May 1680). Austrian composer and organist. In 1617 he became a chorister in Archduchess Anna Katharina's court chapel at Innsbruck and also a pupil of Johann Stadlmayr. He was later appointed organist. In 1633 or shortly before, he left for Konstanz, where he was ordained in 1634 and became cathedral Kapellmeister. His activities during the next few years included the reorganization of the music at the prince-bishop's court in order to meet contemporary liturgical and musical needs. He also went on long journeys in the diocese. From 1640 to 1651 he was Kapellmeister to the Prince-Bishop of Salzburg, and he organized church music there in his capacity as a music inspector in and around Salzburg. In 1651 he entered the collegiate foundation at Altötting, where he remained until his death and where he taught the preacher Abraham a Sancta Clara, who dedicated a eulogy to him. The rapid and successful progress of his professional career brought him to the notice of the Emperor Ferdinand III, whose goodwill he gained by dedicating musical works to him (including an 'enigmatic little piece') and who raised him to the nobility in 1652. In 1662 he was appointed apostolic prothonotary and *notarius juratus*. His autobiography, *Speculum musico-mortuale* (1672), is of interest as a typical example of the Baroque way of thinking. Megerle was a very prolific composer: according to his own testimony he wrote some 2000 sacred works, most of which, however, are lost (see Albert, 1927; see also Pass for a further source of information). Johann Kaspar Kerll thought highly of him, and he himself boasted that he was a 'world-renowned man'. Albert considered him equally adept as a composer of polyphonic and polychoral works as of monody, and drew attention to his occasional 'bold syntheses of the various practices'. His *Ars musica* (1647) comprises three volumes of antiphonal pieces, for the church's year, for two to 24 voices.

### WORKS

Ars musica solemni concertu, 2–24vv, insts, op.1 (Salzburg, 1647)
Psalmodia Jesus et Mariae sacra . . . liber primus, 2–10vv, insts, op.2 (Munich, 1657)
Francisce diligis me, canon, 4vv (n.p., n.d.)

c120 works, 4, 5vv: masses, hymns, motets, antiphonal works, *A-Wn*, *D-Mbs*, *Rp*

LOST WORKS

Konstanzer Weynachtsgesänger
Antiphonalium mit newem Chorall
Litanies, masses, 4 funeral works, occasional works

### WRITINGS

*Electuarium*, 2 vols., 1660, lost
*Scala musica caelestis*, before 1670, lost
*Speculum musico-mortuale, das ist Musicalischer Todtenspiegel* (n.p., 1672) [autobiography]

### BIBLIOGRAPHY

H. Albert: *Abraham Megerle* (Munich, 1927) [incl. full list of works and bibliography]
——: 'Megerle, Abraham', *MGG*
W. Pass: 'Das Musikalieninventar der Pfarrkirche St. Nikolaus in Feldkirch aus dem Jahre 1699', *Montfort*, xx (Dornbirn, 1968), 187, 190

WALTER PASS

**Meghedi.** A type of hymn of the Armenian Church; *see* ARMENIAN RITE, MUSIC OF THE.

**Megli, Domenico Maria.** *See* MELLI, DOMENICO MARIA.

**Mehrstimmigkeit** (Ger.). POLYPHONY.

**Mehta, Zubin** (*b* Bombay, 29 April 1936). Indian conductor. Son of Mehli Mehta, a violinist and the founder-conductor of the Bombay SO, he learnt the piano and the violin as a child and formed an ambition to conduct. He was persuaded to study medicine, which he abandoned at 18 to enter the Vienna Academy, where he studied with Hans Swarowsky and played the double bass in the orchestra. After forming student orchestras to conduct, he entered the first international conductors' competition organized by the Royal Liverpool PO in 1958 and won the major prize (for British and Commonwealth entrants) of a year as musical assistant in Liverpool.

When this expired Mehta was offered no further employment in Britain, but he quickly made a favourable impression as a guest conductor with the Vienna PO, and in Montreal and Los Angeles deputizing for other conductors. His spectacular success led to his appointment to the Montreal SO (1960–67), and to the Los Angeles SO, as associate conductor in 1960, and musical director in 1962. He was then the youngest to hold such an appointment with a leading orchestra in the USA, and the first in North America to share a joint appointment with two major orchestras. At Los Angeles he transformed an undistinguished orchestra into a superior ensemble within a few years, spreading his own and the orchestra's reputation by some outstanding gramophone records.

Mehta made his début at the Metropolitan Opera in 1965 (*Aida*). He first conducted in London at an RPO concert in 1961, and later formed close links with the Israel PO, conducting it on a European tour in 1968 and becoming its chief musical adviser in 1970. In 1976 his appointment as director of the New York PO was announced. He made his London opera début with *Otello* at Covent Garden in 1977. His performances generally favour romantic warmth of expression and voluptuous sonority, combined with bold attack and rhythmic vigour and reinforced by boundless self-confidence. An awareness of his audience is often reflected in platform gestures indicative not so much of the musical content as of the desired response of the audience to it.

BIBLIOGRAPHY
Anon: 'Gypsy Boy', *Time* (19 Jan 1968), 50

NOËL GOODWIN

**Méhul, Etienne-Nicolas** (*b* Givet, 22 June 1763; *d* Paris, 18 Oct 1817). French composer. He was the greatest French symphonist between Gossec and Berlioz and the composer of many important *opéras comiques*.

1. LIFE. Méhul was the second child of four; apart from him only his sister Marie-Catherine (*b* 1764), the mother of the composer Daussoigne-Méhul, survived infancy. His father was *maître d'hôtel* to the Count of Montmorency and later (by 1782) a wine merchant. He first apprenticed his son to the old blind organist of the Franciscan convent at Givet. This teacher died when Méhul was about ten; many sources state that Méhul himself acted as organist at the convent, possibly on his teacher's death. Between 1773 and 1775 the wealthy abbey of Lavaldieu at Monthermé, 50 km from Givet, appointed the German organist Wilhelm Hanser as musical director. Hanser began a music school and, in about 1775, Méhul was accepted as a pupil. Tradition has it that he was supported financially by the Givet community, so that he could live as a pensioner at Lavaldieu. Surpassing his contemporaries, Méhul became Hanser's assistant organist.

In 1778 or 1779 Méhul was taken to Paris; reputedly his chronically precarious health prevented his acceptance into a novitiate at Lavaldieu. No record has been found of an organist's post supposedly acquired for Méhul during these early Paris years. Neither is there any proven evidence of a meeting with Gluck, who finally left Paris in autumn 1779.

Méhul's new teacher was the composer Jean-Frédéric Edelmann, distinguished for his keyboard sonatas of dramatic, even orchestral design. Edelmann's opera *Ariane dans l'isle de Naxos* (1782) was a success that was to influence Méhul's treatment of musical drama. Meanwhile, under the patronage of Mme de Silly (in whose dwelling he lived) Méhul published in 1783 his first book of keyboard sonatas. An ode given the previous year at the Concert Spirituel was well received, and it is possible that Méhul thereafter began work on setting opera librettos for practice. The second set of sonatas, almost the only surviving music from these years of growing maturity, is assured and musically individual. During this period Méhul taught keyboard instruments, but as soon as he was able he gave this up to devote himself to composition.

As the result of a competition set by the Paris Opéra, the theatre accepted Valadier's libretto *Cora* in 1785. By 1789 Méhul had written the music, which remained unperformed for two years. It was, however, in *opéra comique* that Méhul's chief work was to be done, and in developing the tradition of Grétry and Dalayrac he had the invaluable collaboration of the librettist François-Benoît Hoffman. Their first venture – Méhul's first performed opera – was *Euphrosine* (1790). In its modified three-act form this held the stage for over 40 years and was given in many other cities. Méhul's name became famous overnight, particularly on account of the duet, 'Gardez-vous de la jalousie'. The next venture, with Hoffman, was a large-scale opera, *Adrien*. Although it was in rehearsal before the end of 1791, its production was postponed (until 1799) owing to the political difficulties entailed in portraying emperors and monarchs on stage. *Stratonice* (1792), a domestic drama in

*1. Etienne-Nicolas Méhul: portrait (1795) by Joseph Ducreux in the Musée de Versailles*

antique setting, had most recently been treated by Rameau (Act 2 of *Les fêtes de Polymnie*) and Langlé (*Antiochus et Stratonice*, 1786). Méhul chose a style of 'antique simplicity', as Framery noted, and the air 'Versez tous vos chagrins dans le sein paternel' became known throughout France. Méhul himself, as letters show, was perfectly conscious of his reputation and artistic responsibilities. He anticipated the criticism he knew would follow each unexpected move. Like Berlioz after him, he was labelled a noisy composer by those too much aware of his imitators. Méhul's next librettist, Arnault, testified: 'Out of the world, or even in the middle of it, he was entirely absorbed in his art. Lodged with friends who saw to his needs, he left his seclusion . . . only to direct his rehearsals'.

*Le jeune sage et le vieux fou* (1793), a comedy with an adept and witty libretto and music, was the last major work for some years to remain unaffected by the political crisis. So far, Méhul had not participated in the Revolutionary festivals, which had occurred with increasing frequency since 1790. Indeed, like most musicians, he had benefited from aristocratic friends. But Robespierre was now in the ascendant, intensifying France's secularization.

On 8 November 1793 the National Convention decreed the formation of an Institut National de Musique, with Gossec as musical director. A number of composers immediately joined the salaried staff, among them Le Sueur and Méhul on 21 November. On 30 November Méhul's first republican hymn was sung (the *Hymne à la raison*) in the converted church of St Roch. This was followed (10 December) by the Overture in F, his only full-scale piece for wind ensemble and probably the best of the many that were produced during the period, and by further civic pieces in 1794 and after. By far the most popular was the *Chant du départ* (words by

M. J. Chénier), first publicly heard on 4 July 1794 and performed thereafter on innumerable public occasions. Though it was not used in the First Empire, the song was revived periodically in the 19th century, particularly in 1830, 1848 and 1870.

Méhul's opera *Horatius Coclès* (1794) was one of many French works to use a classical setting to convey a republican message. Like many neo-classical paintings, it was a state commission. Music from the as yet unperformed *Adrien* was incorporated for convenience. The other important *opéras comiques* of the 1790s are *Mélidore et Phrosine* (1794) and *Ariodant* (1799). Only the overture to *Le jeune Henri* (1797), 'La chasse du jeune Henri', was successful.

In March or April 1794 the Comédie-Italienne granted Méhul an annual pension of 1000 francs, a great privilege for a young composer. When the Paris Conservatoire was founded he was made one of its five inspectors (7 August 1795). In the following December he was the only musician appointed by the government to sit as a member of the French Institute (Gossec was elected shortly afterwards), and in 1804 he was made one of the first members of the Légion d'honneur.

*La prise du pont de Lodi*, a dramatization of the Austrian defeat of 10 May 1796, may have been ordered by Napoleon himself. The new leader had already shown active interest in music and in spring 1797 asked Méhul to join the artists accompanying the Egyptian campaign. Although he declined to go (the post went to Villoteau) he continued to meet Napoleon and dedicated the comedy *L'irato* to him in 1801. After the victory of Marengo (June 1800) Napoleon commissioned a work from Méhul to celebrate both this and the fall of the Bastille. The resulting *Chant national du 14 juillet 1800*, given in the Invalides, was composed for two full-sized choirs and orchestras and a third group of high voices accompanied by two harps and solo horn. In its use of spatially conceived effects, this cantata is a notable ancestor of Berlioz's Requiem, written for performance in the same building.

After 1800 Méhul staunchly maintained an independence of style in the face of growing appreciation of Mozart and the Italian opera composers. (The interests of the latter were fostered by Napoleon and his circle.) *Bion* (1800) was the first of a series of small-scale comedies, uneven in quality, in which a new lightness of touch is manifest. The failure rate of his operas increased but their overtures were successful (thus indicating Méhul's path towards symphonic works) and many single numbers became popular. *Joseph* (1807), his most famous *opéra comique*, was his last important operatic work. The only female solo part is a breeches part (Benjamin). There is no sub-plot, and the music effectively conveys an idealized atmosphere of antiquity and religion. Disenchanted with stage composition, Méhul turned to purely symphonic writing, and the two published symphonies (1808–9) are, with *Joseph*, the climax of his achievement. The G minor symphony was performed by Mendelssohn and praised by Schumann.

Ill-health gradually caused Méhul to withdraw from musical life but he continued to compose and to teach at the Conservatoire. He produced a spate of Napoleonic cantatas (1810–11), but his chief stage work after 1807, *Les amazones* (1811), failed. The fall of the First Empire increased his sense of decline, and was followed by the vindictive closure of the Conservatoire by the Bourbon restoration, and its subsequent reduction to a

'school of music'. But *La journée aux aventures* (1816) was a success; after this, a few months in the south of France could only delay the final progress of tuberculosis.

Méhul's dedication to composition was rigorous; he was not primarily a performing musician (he wrote no concertos). He was – as he freely admitted – fond of success; yet even stronger was his honesty and utter dislike of flattery. This made him enemies, particularly within the Paris Opéra, and it had a permanent effect on his career. His marriage (1800) was not successful, and his wife moved to Lyons, surviving him by 40 years. However, his love of intelligent company brought many friendships with artists, actors and writers. He enjoyed the company of women; to Cherubini his gaiety seemed, however, 'more calculated than frank', and his Romantically melancholic imagination was the aspect of his character that was widely recognized by his contemporaries.

2. WORKS. Méhul was the most original composer of his time in France to be concerned with the art of orchestration. Numerous effects that he developed were taken up generally. In particular he expanded the role of the cello (both solo and tutti) in the tenor register, made extensive use of stopped horn notes (see ex.1) and used subdivided strings. In almost all his operas he found innumerable ways of building orchestral tone into the whole musical and dramatic fabric of his scores.

Méhul's use of harmony, like his approach to form, could be striking and original over small areas, but was less controlled and effective on a large scale. In exploring new types of modulation (ex.1) he could sound as headstrong as Beethoven; like Beethoven too, he sometimes had recourse to loud dissonances of great power. Structurally, his harmony was always deter-

*2. Beginning of the overture to Act 1 of Méhul's 'Uthal', from the first edition of the score (c1806)*

Ex.1 Elegiac Cantata, 'Brillant Céphale', *F-Pn* MS 2295 f.14*v*

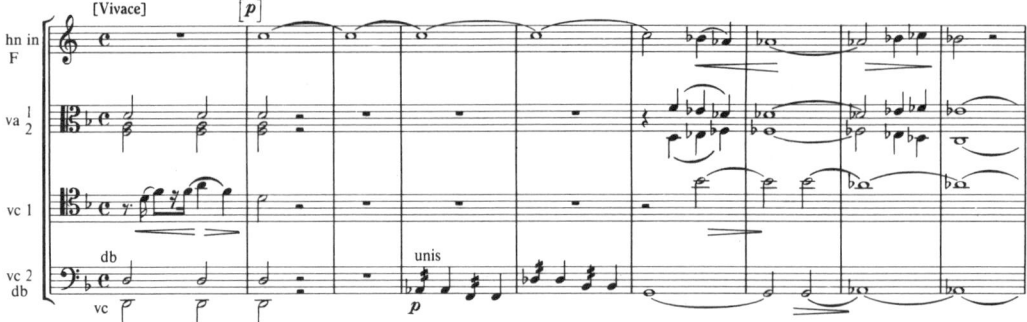

mined by Classical principles, and in fact a proportion of his pieces stay perilously close to tonic and dominant throughout.

Méhul's operatic style was formed in the 1780s. Gluck's example was developed at the Opéra by younger French composers, including Lemoyne, whose assertive rhythms, syncopations and sometimes heavy orchestration were in turn developed by Méhul, Cherubini and others in *opéras comiques* from 1790. Méhul's vocal style centred on a compromise between accurate declamation of the French language and the demands of Classical phrase structure. His melody is often contained within a fairly narrow tessitura; this perhaps typically French feature is seen at its best in his *romances*. However, his large ambitions brought important results in the dramatic use of the orchestra in both physical and psychological description. He also composed some apt operatic ensembles, certain of which enjoyed a long existence in the concert hall.

Above all, Méhul sought to give each opera the musical atmosphere proper to its setting, whether biblical, Nordic, Roman, chivalric or simply comic. In this, and particularly in the means by which he realized musical atmosphere, he may be seen as a Romantic. His use of technical devices such as the reminiscence-motif, his experiments with orchestration, his demand for large forces and his ability to modify his idiom over a whole work all indicate the forward-looking nature of his art.

Méhul's first surviving opera score, *Cora*, was written for the Opéra; the incomplete manuscripts show in particular an impressive storm scene in Act 3, with soloists and chorus. It was in developing the genre of *opéra comique*, however, that he played a crucial part; after *Cora* he wrote only three more recitative operas. For a time in France many *opéras comiques* dispensed with comic elements altogether (Dalayrac's *Nina* in 1786 was probably the first), but Méhul's *Euphrosine* is a mixture of the comic and the serious. The duet in Act 2, 'Gardez-vous de la jalousie', remained one of his outstanding conceptions. It is an unprecedented combination of psychological description (derived from Gluck's example) and motivic development as found in Haydn's symphonies and quartets. Moreover, the chromatic harmony that delays the frenzied final cadence was a shock that left few who heard it unaffected. Grétry and Berlioz both recorded their admiration for it. As a further innovation, Méhul brought back the musical motif of jealousy at two later points in the opera.

This duet immediately sealed Méhul's reputation, and for a time he avoided similar subjects. *Stratonice* (1792)

in fact depicts the magnanimous rejection of jealousy by the Asian king of ancient times, Seleucus. The music of the two commissions, *Horatius Coclès* and *La prise du pont de Lodi*, is dry if aggressively appropriate; Méhul called it his 'iron style'.

In *Mélidore et Phrosine* Méhul developed the turbulent vein of *Euphrosine* on a broad scale. The story tells of the tragic consequences of a love affair thwarted by blind jealousy. Musically it is rich – a storm rages through most of the last act – but the drama is ineptly treated at the end. A 'motto theme' is used ('Love be our guide') and occurs in all three acts at significant moments. Other music is also recalled in Act 3. The composer later wished to revise the work for the Opéra with recitatives, but the scheme came to nothing.

*Doria*, *La caverne* and *Le jeune Henri* were withheld from publication; judging from what remains, *La caverne* contains the best music. When *Adrien* finally reached the stage in 1799 it stood little chance of success; spectacular elements had been emphasized to satisfy the Opéra management, and even without the Revolution the magnanimous emperor or general would have been too *passé* a figure to hold interest for long.

The climax of Méhul's work before 1800 was *Ariodant* (1799), his most polished *opéra comique*. In this careful reworking of Ariosto, 'good' and 'evil' couples placed in opposition, jealous love and a courtly setting in the Middle Ages all make comparison with *Euryanthe* and *Lohengrin* inevitable. Musico-dramatic unity is assisted by recurring material, and the first two acts have dramatic finale structures. The last act is the weakest: the lack of music at the dénouement detracts from the success of the whole, as was also the case in *Héléna* (1803). In the sequence of comic works which began with *Bion*, Méhul's writing became very economical in texture; one consequence was the total rejection of violin tone (violinists play violas) in the Ossianic opera *Uthal* (1806), derived from the poem *Berrathon*. Regrettably, the musician could do little to redeem the inexpert libretto; the overture, which is of great value, far outweighs much of the remainder.

In *Joseph* Méhul was luckier. The familiar Bible story (treated extremely simply), the trappings of antique scenery and costumes, the sentimentality of the tale and the genre of *opéra comique* mingled well. The music is varied, with examples of anguished music (for Simeon), dramatic ensembles and evocative antique hymns. Méhul also admitted a directly tuneful idiom, without sounding definitely German or Italian.

The opera overtures deserve separate mention because many are remarkably inspired examples of form and tone-painting. *Le jeune sage et le vieux fou* first gives musical caricatures of the main characters: the serious youth (two unaccompanied flutes) and the jovial old man (cellos and double basses alone). Then follows a set of studies in orchestral, rather than thematic, variation. The overture 'La chasse du jeune Henri' is a famous study in description, incorporating hunting-calls. Answering horn-calls in a hunting-overture were anticipated in J. P. A. Martini's *Annette et Lubin* (1789), but Méhul's music is far better and has never completely disappeared from the repertory. *Ariodant* has a prelude beginning with a long statement for three solo cellos, accompanied by the rest of the section and by double basses. The Adagio opening to the overture to *Joanna* is a kind of orchestral passacaglia. *Héléna*'s overture is 'interrupted' by trumpet-calls taken from music to Act 1; this idea was adapted by Beethoven in *Fidelio*.

Méhul's opera overtures after 1800 point the way stylistically to the symphonies, only three of which survive complete. In these the challenge of Mozart and early Beethoven was taken up with (for France) unparalleled individuality. Only an artist who had pursued his work with uncompromising honesty could have responded in such a way to the German examples, and Méhul's lead was hardly followed by Frenchmen before Berlioz. The works outwardly resemble Haydn's; the traditional forms clothe an intensity of rhythmic drive and unity comparable with Beethoven's Fifth Symphony. When this is allied to the Mozartian pathos of G minor (in Méhul's First Symphony) the results are very impressive. The slow movements are the weakest. In the finale of the Symphony in D the solo timpani part contains (as in Beethoven's Violin Concerto) important and unifying thematic material.

Of the first set of keyboard sonatas, no.2 in C minor is the least conventional, being forceful and at times dissonant and using a range of true piano figuration. The recapitulation of the first movement is severely curtailed, yet a satisfactory degree of thematic unity

prevails. The second set is a considerable advance on the first, with more control of form, greater abundance of themes and a more extensive use of idiomatic piano writing. The first movement of the second sonata (A minor) is particularly impressive as the first real indication of Méhul's predilection for intensive monothematic development. In France Méhul's obvious musical integrity and loyalty to the concept of French musical art influenced virtually all his colleagues, in particular Boieldieu, Berton and Hérold, his pupil. (It is important to note that Méhul did not reject the music of Italy any more than did Berlioz after him; and German music was a vital influence in Paris well before the Revolution.) There is evidence that Beethoven acquainted himself with Méhul's music from the early years to the last period, and that the trumpet-calls in *Fidelio* were only one of several cases of borrowing. Ringer (1951), pointing to Mendelssohn's performance of Méhul's G minor symphony, also suggested creative influences. In Weber's music the debts are more palpable: technical features like the use of operatic reminiscence-motifs, the chromatic delay of cadences and dramatic scoring of *romances*. Weber also learnt from Méhul's orchestration, both from its various dramatic colours and from its dynamic function in the drama. Méhul's melodic invention sometimes influenced Weber too (exx.2 and 3).

The large number of surviving printed scores indicates the spread of Méhul's music on a European scale. In particular the later comedies (some of whose overtures are still in the repertory) found audiences both in the theatre and the concert hall. *Joseph* has had an almost unbroken performing history. Its easily assimilable melodies and sentiments have always pleased audiences; Wagner admiringly performed it in 1838 in Riga, and his stepfather Geyer sang in Weber's Dresden production of 1817. It may indeed have been an ancestor of *Parsifal*, for the operas share a mood of ritual and the figures of a 'good' man, an 'evil', guilty outsider and a patriarch.

Méhul's writings include prefaces to *Ariodant* and *L'irato*, minor reports and *Funérailles* for Grétry published by the Institut (Paris, 1813). In addition to the works listed below there are many autographs of alternative and deleted pieces from operas, unpublished *romances* and fragments of cantatas in the Bibliothèque Nationale and the Opéra library.

Ex.2
(a) Méhul: *Mélidore et Phrosine*, overture

(b) Weber: *Der Freischütz*, overture

Ex.3
(a) Méhul: *Ariodant*, 'Mais pourquoi'

(b) Weber: *Oberon*, march

### WORKS

(*all printed works published in Paris unless otherwise stated*)

OPERAS

All opéras comiques, first performed in Paris, unless otherwise stated.

TF – *Théâtre Favart*    OC – *Opéra-Comique*

Euphrosine, ou Le tyran corrigé (5, F.-B. Hoffman), TF, 4 Sept 1790 (1791), rev. with 4, later 3 acts as Euphrosine et Coradin
Cora (opera, 4, Valadier), Opéra, 15 Feb 1791, autograph frags., *F-Pn*, inc. parts, *Po*; orig. entitled Alonso et Cora
Stratonice (1, Hoffman), TF, 3 May 1792 (c1792), perf. with recits by L. J. Daussoigne-Méhul, Opéra, 30 March 1821, *Po*
Le jeune sage et le vieux fou (1, Hoffman), TF, 28 March 1793 (c1793)
Horatius Coclès (opera, 1, A. V. Arnault), Opéra, 18 Feb 1794 (c1794)
Le congrès des rois (3, Desmaillot [A. F. Eve]), TF, 26 Feb 1794, ?lost, collab. H.-M. Berton, Blasius, Cherubini, Dalayrac, Devienne, Deshayes, Grétry, L. Jadin, R. Kreutzer, Solié, A. E. Trial
Mélidore et Phrosine (3, Arnault), TF, 6 May 1794 (c1794)
Doria, ou La tyrannie détruite (3, G. M. J. B. Legouvé, C. J. L. d'Avrigny), TF, 12 March 1795, autograph of 6 pieces, *Pn*, *Po*
La caverne (3, N. J. Forgeot), TF, 5 Dec 1795, autograph of 6 pieces, *Pn*
Le jeune Henri (2, J. N. Bouilly), TF, 1 May 1797, nearly complete autograph, *Pn*; orig. entitled La jeunesse d'Henri IV

La prise du pont de Lodi (1, E. J. B. Delrieu), Feydeau, 15 Dec 1797, nearly complete MS, *Pn*
Adrien (opera, 3, Hoffman), Opéra, 4 June 1799, autograph frags., *Pn*, MSS, *B-Bc, F-Po, Pn, US-COu*; orig. entitled Adrien, empéreur de Rome
Ariodant (3, Hoffman), TF, 11 Oct 1799 (*c*1800)
Epicure (3, C. A. Demoustier), TF, 14 March 1800, collab. Cherubini; rev. in 2 acts; Cherubini's autograph, *D-Bds*, autograph of 3 pieces, *F-Pn*
Bion (1, Hoffman), TF, 27 Dec 1800 (*c*1800)
L'irato, ou L'emporté (1, B. J. Marsollier), OC, 17 Feb 1801 (*c*1805)
Une folie (2, J. N. Bouilly), OC, 5 April 1802 (*c*1802)
Le trésor supposé, ou Le danger d'écouter aux portes (1, Hoffman), OC, 29 July 1802 (*c*1802)
Joanna (2, Marsollier), OC, 23 Nov 1802, autograph, *Pn*; excerpts arr. Méhul pubd separately (*c*1803)
Héléna (3, Bouilly), OC, 1 March 1803 (*c*1805)
Le baiser et la quittance, ou Une aventure de garnison (3, L. B. Picard, C. de Longchamps and J. M. A. M. Dieulafoi), OC, 18 June 1803, *B-Ba, Bc, F-Pn, R(m)*; collab. Boieldieu, R. Kreutzer, Nicolo
L'heureux malgré lui (2, C. G. d'A. de Saint-Just), OC, 29 Dec 1803, autograph, *Pn*
Les deux aveugles de Tolède (1, Marsollier), OC, 28 Jan 1806 (*c*1806)
Uthal (1, J. M. B. B. de Saint-Victor), OC, 17 May 1806 (*c*1806)
Gabrielle d'Estrées, ou Les amours d'Henri IV (3, Saint-Just), OC, 25 June 1806 (*c*1806)
Joseph (3, A. Duval), OC, 17 Feb 1807 (*c*1807)
Les amazones, ou La fondation de Thèbes (opera, 3, V. J. E. de Jouy), Opéra, 17 Dec 1811, frags., *Pn*, MS and autograph, *Po*; orig. entitled Amphion, ou Les amazones
Le prince troubadour (1, Duval), OC, 24 May 1813 (*c*1813)
L'oriflamme (1, C. G. Etienne, L. P. Baour-Lormian), Opéra, 1 Feb 1814, Méhul's ov., *Po*; the remainder (?1814) collab. H.-M. Berton, R. Kreutzer, Paer
La journée aux aventures (3, P. D. A. Chapelle, L. Mézières-Miot), OC, 16 Nov 1816 (1817)
Valentine de Milan (3, Bouilly), OC, 28 Nov 1822 (Paris and Berlin, 1823); completed by Daussoigne-Méhul
Many excerpts and arrs. of the above works published separately
Unperf. operas: Psyché (C. H. F. de Moline), lost; Anacréon (P. J. J. Bernard), lost; Lausus et Lydie (Valadier), lost; La taupe et les papillons (1), ?1797, autograph of 6 pieces, *Pn*; Sésostris (3, Arnault, Jouy), *c*1810, inc., autograph of Act 3, *Po*
Doubtful: Lausus (3), collab. J. Lenoble, mentioned by Fétis; L'Amour et Psyché (opera-ballet, Voisenon), collab. Lenoble, mentioned by Fétis
4 operas (Euphrosine, Ariodant, Uthal, Joseph) pubd in facs., Early Romantic Opera, xxxviii–lxi (New York, 1977)

### OTHER STAGE

*(all first performed in Paris)*

Le jugement de Paris (ballet, 3, P. G. Gardel), Opéra, 5 March 1793, *Po* [incl. music by Gluck, Haydn, R. Kreutzer, 'Michel', Nicolo, I. Pleyel], rev. in 1 act
Timoléon (incidental music, 3, M. J. Chénier), Théâtre de la République, 11 Sept 1794, *Pn, US-Bp*, ov. pubd
La dansomanie (ballet, 2, Gardel), Opéra, 14 June 1800, *F-Po*, arr. pf, vn (*c*1800), incl. music by Mozart and others
Daphnis et Pandrose (ballet, 2, Gardel), Opéra, 14 Jan 1803, *Po*, incl. music by Dalvimare, Devienne, Duvernoy, Gluck, Haydn, Himmel, R. Kreutzer, Martini, Miller, Winter
Les Hussites, ou Le siège de Naumbourg (incidental music, 3, Duval), Théâtre de la Porte St Martin, 14 June 1804, lost
Persée et Andromède (ballet, 3, Gardel), Opéra, 8 June 1810, *Po*, incl. music by Haydn, Paer, Steibelt, Méhul (from Ariodant)
? Ov., choruses and entr'actes for Oedipe roi (tragedy, Chénier), 1804, unperf.

### CHORAL

wb – *acc. wind band*

Mass, A♭, with solo vv, orch, ?1804, probably for Napoleon's coronation but not perf. there; vocal score (*c*1879), MSS, *A-KN, Wgm, CS-BRm, US-NYp*
Hymne à la raison [later, Hymne patriotique] (Chénier), with 3 solo vv, orch, 1793 (1794); Le chant des victoires (Chénier), wb (1794); Le chant du départ (Chénier), wb (1794); Hymne chanté par le peuple à la fête de Bara et Viala (C. J. L. d'Avrigny), kbd acc. (1794); Hymne des vingt-deux (Chénier), with 1v, wb (1795); Le chant du retour (Chénier), wb (1797); Hymne pour la fête des époux (J. F. Ducis), with solo vv, wb (1798); La naissance d'Oscar Leclerc (L. M. Revellière Lepeaux), with 2 solo vv, str
Chant national du 14 juillet 1800 (L. J. P. Fontanes), solo vv, 3 choirs, 3 inst ensembles (1800); Hymne à la paix, perf. 1801, lost; Jetez des fleurs, kbd acc., pubd in P. J. B. Chaussard: Fêtes et courtisanes de la Grèce, i, 2nd edn. only (1803), 187, and in Masson (1934); Chant lyrique pour l'inauguration de la statue votée à Sa Majesté l'Empereur et Roi (Arnault), acc. orch, 1807 (n.d.); Chant du retour pour la

Grande-Armée (Arnault), acc. 4 hn (1808); O doux printemps (Arnault), cantata for the marriage of Napoleon and the Archduchess Marie-Louise, acc. orch, April 1810, *F-Po*; Comblé de bonheur (Chant triomphal), cantata, acc. orch, ?1810, *Po*
Du trône où jusqu'à Toi (Arnault), cantata for their Imperial Majesties, acc. orch, June 1810, *Pn*; Le chant d'Ossian (Arnault), acc. orch, June 1811 [on the birth of the King of Rome], lost; Pourquoi sous un ciel aussi beau (Arnault), cantata, acc. orch, July 1811 [on the birth of the King of Rome], lost, collab. Catel, Cherubini; O France! à tes destins prospères (Arnault), chorus, acc. orch, 1811 [on the birth of the King of Rome], *Po*
Elegiac cantata ('Brillant Céphale'), male solo vv, male chorus, insts, autograph, *Pn*
Doubtful: Domine salvum, 2 choirs, 2 orch, 1802–4, *Pn*; Quel tumulte, scène, trio et choeur, with solo vv, orch, *Pn*

### SONGS, REVOLUTIONARY WORKS FOR ONE VOICE

*(all acc. pf or harp unless otherwise indicated)*

Qu'ils sont charmans, for J. B. Radet: Le faucon, gui acc. (1793); Le petit Nantais (L. F. Jauffret) (1794), pubd in Gougelot (1937–43); Hymne à l'éternel ('Quelle solennité') (Hue) (1794); L'ordre du jour (Lille) (1794); Chant funèbre à la mémoire du représentant du peuple Féraud (Baour-Lormian), acc. wind band, unison vv ad lib (1795); Réponse du vieux pasteur (A. F. Coupigny), sung in L. Jadin: Le cabaleur, 1795
Hymne du IX thermidor ('Salut neuf thermidor') (Chénier) (1795); L'infortunée Lyonnaise (Jauffret) (1795), pubd in Gougelot (1937–43); Le chien victime de sa fidélité (Jauffret) (1795), pubd in Gougelot (1937–43); Oscar et Dermide (Arnault, after Ossian), pubd in Six romances anacréontiques, ii (1796), also in Gougelot (1937–43); Hymne sur la paix ('O jour de gloire') (C. Pipelet de Leury) (1797); Le 18 fructidor ('Un vaste deuil') (Lebrun-Tossa) (1798)
Ode XXXIX: Les plaisirs d'un buveur (Anacreon, trans. J.-B. Gail), pubd in 9 odes d'Anacréon, collab. Cherubini, Gossec, Le Sueur (1798–9); Ode XIX: Tout boit dans la nature [set to Greek words with roughly trans. underlay] (Anacreon), pubd in 9 odes d'Anacréon (1798–9); Chant d'amour et de douleur (Chaussard), pubd in Chaussard: Fêtes et courtisanes de la Grèce (1801); La chanson de l'hirondelle (Chaussard), pubd in Chaussard: Fêtes et courtisanes de la Grèce
Le bain (Chaussard), pubd in Chaussard: Fêtes et courtisanes de la Grèce; Chanson de Roland (sung in Act 3 of Duval: Guillaume le conquérant, 1803), with chorus (?1803–4); Le baiser (Saint-Amand) (1808); Le bouquet d'une amie (Saint-Amand) (1808); Bayard mourant (C. Brifaut) (1814); Le retour de l'éxilé (Brifaut) (1815); Eginhard et Emma (Brifaut) (1816)
Chant montagnard, *Pn*; Adieux du pélerin, pubd posth. with new words by Deschamps in *Ternaire*; Retour au foyer, pubd posth. with new words by Deschamps in *Ternaire*; Le vieux pâtre, pubd posth. with new words by Deschamps in *Ternaire*
Doubtful: Des premiers amours, gui acc., *Pn*; De l'amitié j'entends la voix, *Pn*; Canons, pf acc., pubd jointly with Berton and Cherubini as Nouveau recueil de 22 canons (Brussels, n.d.)
Other songs listed in Gougelot (1937–43), lost

### OTHER VOCAL

Ode sacrée (J. B. Rousseau), perf. 1782, lost; Philoctète à Lemnos (A. Renou), scène, lost; Scène française, perf. 1789, lost
Contributions to *Principes élémentaires de musique arrêtés par les membres du Conservatoire* (Paris, 1799–1800) and *Solfèges pour servir à l'étude dans le Conservatoire . . . seconde partie* (Paris, 1801–2)

### INSTRUMENTAL

Orch: Sym., perf. 1797, ?lost; Sym., C, perf. 1802, ?inc.; (the remainder with Méhul's own numbering) no.1, g (1809); no.2, D (1809); no.3, C, perf. 1809; no.4, E, perf. 1810; no.5, A, *c*1810, inc., unperf.: *A-Wn, F-Pn* (some autograph)
Wind ensemble: Ov., F, 1793 (1794), score, ed. W. S. Dudley (1968); March, F, autograph, *Pn*
Chamber: Ouverture burlesque, pf, vn, 3 mirlitons, tpt, perc (n.d.)
Kbd: 3 sonates, hpd/pf, op.1 (1783); 3 sonates, hpd/pf, vn ad lib, bk 2 (1788)
Kbd arrs.: ov. and dances from Edelmann: Le feu (n.d.); dances from Gossec: Thésée, and Gluck: Orphée et Euridice, in Journal de clavecin, i (1782); music from J.-B. Lemoyne: Phèdre (1787); music from many of his own operas

### BIBLIOGRAPHY

#### GENERAL

A. Choron and F. Fayolle: *Dictionnaire historique des musiciens* (Paris, 1810–11/R1971)
H. Berlioz: *Les soirées de l'orchestre* (Paris, 1852; Eng. trans., 1956/R1973)
C. Pierre: *B. Sarrette et les origines du Conservatoire national* (Paris, 1895)
——: *Le Magasin de musique à l'usage des fêtes nationales et du*

*Conservatoire* (Paris, 1895/*R*1954)

——: *Musique des fêtes et cérémonies de la Révolution française* (Paris, 1899)

——: *Le Conservatoire national de musique et de déclamation: documents historiques et administratifs* (Paris, 1900)

——: *Les hymnes et chansons de la Révolution* (Paris, 1904)

C. Bellaigue: *Etudes musicales, troisième série* (Paris, 1907), 380

G. Pierné and H. Woollett: 'Histoire de l'orchestration: les successeurs de Gluck et l'aube de l'opéra-comique', *EMDC*, II/iv (1929), 2282

H. Gougelot: *La romance française sous la Révolution et l'Empire* (Melun, 1937–43) [incl. many songs by Méhul]

B. Schwartz: *French Instrumental Music between the Revolutions (1789 to 1830)* (diss., Columbia U., 1950)

G. Favre: *La musique française de piano avant 1830* (Paris, 1953)

A. L. Ringer: 'The Chasse as a Musical Topic of the 18th Century', *JAMS*, vi (1953), 148

G. Knepler: 'Die Technik der sinfonischen Durchführung in der französischen Revolutionsoper', *BMw*, i (1959), 4

R. M. Longyear: 'Notes on the Rescue Opera', *MQ*, xlv (1959), 49

G. Knepler: *Musikgeschichte des 19. Jahrhunderts* (Berlin, 1961)

W. S. Newman: *The Sonata in the Classic Era* (Chapel Hill, 1963, rev. 2/1972)

A.-P. de Mirimonde: 'Musiciens isolés et portraits de l'école française du XVIIIᵉ siècle dans les collections nationales: III. – Révolution et Empire', *Revue du Louvre*, xvii (1967), 81

W. Dean: 'Opera under the French Revolution', *PRMA*, xciv (1967–8), 77

W. S. Dudley: *Orchestration in the Musique d'harmonie of the French Revolution* (diss., U. of California, Berkeley, 1968)

W. Dean: 'Beethoven and Opera', *The Beethoven Companion*, ed. D. Arnold and N. Fortune (London, 1971), 374

P. Citron, ed.: *H. Berlioz: Correspondance générale*, i (Paris, 1972)

C. Godfrey: 'Gros and Méhul', *Burlington Magazine*, cxiv (1972), 769

B. Deane: 'The French Operatic Overture from Grétry to Berlioz', *PRMA*, xcix (1972–3), 67

D. Charlton: *Orchestration and Orchestral Practice in Paris, 1789–1810* (diss., U. of Cambridge, 1974)

C. Pierre: *Histoire du Concert spirituel 1725–1790* (Paris, 1975)

E. J. Dent: *The Rise of Romantic Opera*, ed. W. Dean (Cambridge, 1976)

#### BIOGRAPHICAL

A. C. Quatremère de Quincy: *Funérailles de M. Méhul, Institut royal de France* (Paris, 1817)

——: 'Notice historique sur la vie et les oeuvres de M. Méhul', *Institut royal de France: Séance publique de l'Académie royale des beaux-arts du 2 octobre 1819* (Paris, 1819); also pubd in Quatremère de Quincy: *Recueil de notices historiques* (Paris, 1834)

F.-J. Fétis: 'Biographie: Méhul (Etienne Henri)', *Revue musicale*, vii (1830) [2nd ser., i], 193 [see also 'Correspondance', ibid, 237, anon. letter on *Stratonice*]

A. V. Arnault: *Souvenirs d'un sexagénaire*, ii (Paris, 1833), 16ff, 66ff

'Méhul et Boïeldieu', *Gazette musicale de Paris*, ii (1835), 293

J. N. Bouilly: *Mes récapitulations* (Paris, 1836–7), ii, 3ff, 319ff, 337ff

P. A. Vieillard: *Méhul, sa vie et ses oeuvres* (Paris, 1859)

La Mara [I. M. Lipsius]: *Musikerbriefe aus fünf Jahrhunderten*, i (Leipzig, 1886), 338

A. Pougin: *Méhul: sa vie, son génie, son caractère* (Paris, 1889, 2/1893)

H. Parent de Curzon: 'Méhul, sa vie et son oeuvre', *Musiciens du temps passé* (Paris, 1893), 117–72

A. Pougin: 'Méhul et Pleyel', *Le ménestrel*, lx (1894), 266

——: 'Notice sur Méhul par Cherubini', *RMI*, xvi (1909), 750

R. Brancour: *Méhul* (Paris, 1912)

H. Radiguer: 'E.-N. Méhul', *EMDC*, I/iii (1921), 1630

J. Tiersot: *Lettres de musiciens écrites en français du XVᵉ au XXᵉ siècle*, i (Turin, 1924), 266ff

C. Barzel: 'Notes et documents de musique: la jeunesse et le roman de Méhul', *Mercure de France* (15 Sept 1932), 730

M. Pincherle: *Musiciens peints par eux-mêmes* (Paris, 1939)

#### WORKS

'Recension', *AMZ*, x (1807–8), col.11 [review of pf sonatas]

'Nachrichten: Siebentes Concert', *AMZ*, xii (1809–10), col.1040 [review of syms.]

E. T. A. Hoffmann: review of La chasse du jeune Henri, *AMZ*, xiv (1812), col.743; repr. in Hoffmann: *Schriften zur Musik*, ed. F. Schnapp (Munich, 1963), 115

——: review of Ariodant, *Dramaturgisches Wochenblatt*, ii/25 (22 June 1816), 195; repr. in Hoffmann: *Schriften zur Musik*, ed. F. Schnapp (Munich, 1963), 308

J.-B. Weckerlin: 'Les quatre versions de la romance de Joseph, opéra de Méhul', *Revue et gazette musicale de Paris*, xlii (1875), 252

E. Gigout: 'La messe du couronnement, de Méhul', *Revue et gazette musicale de Paris*, xlvii (1880), 5

E. Hanslick: *Die Moderne Oper*, v: *Musikalisches und Literarisches* (Berlin, 1889), 241–65

C. Jourday: 'A propos du Chant national du 14 juillet', *RHCM*, i (1901), 278

H. Quittard: 'L'*Uthal* de Méhul', *La revue musicale … dir. J. Combarieu*, viii (1908), 295

H. Strobel: 'Die Opern von E. N. Méhul', *ZMw*, vi (1923–4), 362–402

G. de Saint-Foix: 'Les premiers pianistes parisiens: les six sonates de Méhul', *ReM*, vii/1 (1925), 43

P.-M. Masson: 'Les "Chants anacréontiques" de Méhul', *RdM*, xv (1934), no.51, p.129; no.52, p.197

——: 'L'oeuvre dramatique de Méhul', *Annales de l'Université de Paris*, xii (1937), 523

A. L. Ringer: 'A French Symphonist at the Time of Beethoven: Etienne Nicolas Méhul', *MQ*, xxxvii (1951), 543

D. Charlton: 'Motive and Motif: Méhul before 1791', *ML*, lvii (1976), 362

DAVID CHARLTON

**Mei, Girolamo** [Peretola, Decimo Corinella da] (*b* Florence, 27 May 1519; *d* Rome, July 1594). Italian humanist, editor of Greek texts and historian of Greek music. His pioneering research into Greek music was of fundamental importance and a decisive influence on the emergence of monody and music drama.

1. LIFE. Mei studied with the philosopher and humanist Piero Vettori, whom he assisted in editing and annotating the tragedies of Aeschylus and Euripides and works by Aristotle, Cicero, Thucydides, Ptolemy and other classical authors. In 1540, the year of its founding, he was admitted into the Accademia Fiorentina, then called Accademia de'Umidi. He was also a member of the Accademia dei Pianigiani, for which he wrote several treatises in its private jargon under the pseudonym Decimo Corinella da Peretola, and in 1585 he was honoured with non-resident membership of the Accademia degli Alterati. A journey to Rome in 1546 led to a position with the Bishop of Agen in France, but he was back in Florence in August 1547, then in Rome again in 1548. He departed for France a second time to serve the Bishop of Fréjus, but the job fell through, and he became a companion and tutor to Guglielmo Guadagni at Lyons. In a letter to Vettori of 3 July 1551 he announced that he had begun the study of Greek music theory because his patron loved music, but his progress was slow, as they travelled almost continuously. In 1554 Mei moved to Padua where he attended lectures at the university. In 1559 he went to Rome to seek a position and finally found one in July 1561 as one of the secretaries of Cardinal Giovanni Ricci da Montepulciano. In the same year he resumed his research into Greek music and between 1566 and 1573 wrote his major musical treatise, *De modis musicis antiquorum*, which he dedicated to Vettori. After the cardinal's death in 1574, he moved to the palace of the wealthy nobleman Giovanni Francesco Ridolfi. Between 1572 and 1581 he exchanged more than 30 letters with Vincenzo Galilei, a correspondence from which Galilei learnt most of what he knew about Greek music.

2. WORKS. *De modis* is the first conscientious study of the most difficult problem in Greek music, the history and theory of the *tonoi*. It was based on a thorough reading of all the writings on music that have survived. Book 1 (completed in 1567) describes the 15-string system, the tetrachords, the three genera and the various tunings. The second book (completed in 1568) discusses the species of consonances, particularly of the octave, and the *tonoi* according to Aristoxenus, Ptolemy, Aristides, Martianus Capella and Boethius. Book 3 (completed in 1571) deals with the modern theory of the modes from Boethius to Glarean. Book 4 (completed in

1573) considers the practice of the *tonoi* and *harmoniae* and their place in education, moral conduct and therapeutics, as well as their use in tragedy, comedy, satire and dithyramb. It was here that Mei announced his theory that the ancient tragedies and comedies were sung in their entirety, accompanied in unison by the aulos, a theory that had wide repercussions in Florentine and Ferrarese literary and musical circles.

Mei clearly distinguished the ancient *tonoi* from the church modes. He showed that the Greek *tonoi* served to transpose the 15-note system downwards and upwards from its central 'Dorian' position. His interpretation of Ptolemy's rather special system results, however, in a different set of keys from that assumed by modern scholars. For Mei the Ptolemaic *tonoi* from Hypodorian to Mixolydian are analogous to the keys of D, F, A♭, C, E, G and B♭ because he built the characteristic octave species of each *tonos* around the dynamic *mese* instead of within the central Dorian octave, assigning, as normal, the 'lowest' octave species to the highest *tonos*. The essential feature of the Greek system for Mei was the possibility it afforded composers to vary the range of their melodies according to the 'ethos' or emotional and moral effect that they wished to arouse, using the low *tonoi* for abject and humble subjects, the intermediate for quiet and moderate affections and the high for excited feelings. He reasoned from the evidence in the sources that the Greeks did not know polyphony; rather their music consisted always of a single line, even if several sang and played together or many sang in a chorus. As a result they recognized only the octave, 5th and 4th as consonances, the so-called imperfect consonances being a modern concept deriving from the practice of 'singing several airs together'.

In his later writings – the unfinished Italian treatise that begins 'Come potesse tanto la musica appresso gli antichi', a letter to Agostino del Nero that greatly stimulated G. B. Doni to pursue research in Greek music, and letters to Galilei and Bardi – Mei drew some lessons for modern music from his findings. He concluded that the modern modes, unlike the ancient, lacked diversity of pitch and therefore of affection. Polyphony, with its many parts, 'conveys to the soul of the listener at the same time diverse and contrary affections as it mixes indistinctly together melodies and modes that are completely dissimilar and of natures contrary to each other' (Palisca, 1960, 73). Similarly contrary rhythms and tempos are also juxtaposed. Most of all Mei deplored 'the disordered perturbation, mix-up, and entanglement of the words' (Palisca, 1960, 74). Counterpoint, he maintained, had developed out of a desire of musicians to show off their prowess and was useless for anything else, particularly for the expression of the feelings and meanings of a text.

Although Mei, residing permanently in Rome, could not participate in the conversations in Bardi's Camerata, his letters stirred the group's concern with the reform of modern music and led to its experiments with monody. Galilei's *Dialogo* was directly inspired by Mei's letters: its challenge to Zarlino's tuning theories, the critique of polyphonic music and the information on Greek music that it contains are all based on Mei's letters. The Greek hymns and the tables of notation published there were also sent to Galilei by Mei, who found the hymns in a MS in the library of Ranuccio Farnese in about 1564 (now *I-Nn* III C 4). At a time of transition in musical aesthetics he provided the impetus and the humanistic justification for explorations that led to the first music dramas, to the new recitative style and to expressive monody in general.

WRITINGS

*Discorso sopra la musica antica e moderna* (Venice, 1602/*R*1968 ed. G. Massera)

*De modis musicis antiquorum libri IV* (MS, *I-Rvat*, autograph; *F-Pn, I-Bc, Fr*)

*De nomi delle corde del monochordo* (MS, *I-Ma, US-R*)

*Trattato di musica: come potesse tanto la musica appresso gli antichi* (MS, *F-Pn, I-Rvat*)

Essays on Tuscan prose, poetry and history and academic discourses, letters, several ed. in Palisca (1960)

BIBLIOGRAPHY

*Relatione della vita del Sig. Girolamo Mei fatta dal Sig. Zenobio Mei* (MS, *I-Rvat*)

C. V. Palisca, ed.: *Girolamo Mei (1519–1594): Letters on Ancient and Modern Music to Vincenzo Galilei and Giovanni Bardi*, MSD, iii (1960, 2/1977) [incl. full list of works, letters and sources]

B. R. Hanning: *The Influence of Humanistic Thought and Italian Renaissance Poetry on the Formation of Opera* (diss., Yale U., 1968)

C. V. Palisca: 'The "Camerata Fiorentina": a Reappraisal', *Studi musicali*, i (1972), 203–36

CLAUDE V. PALISCA

**Mei, Orazio** (*b* Pisa, 26 May 1731; *d* Livorno, 1 March 1788). Italian composer and organist. The son of Francesco Saverio Mei, violinist at the church of the Cavalieri di S Stefano in Pisa, he had his first music lessons from his father and from his uncle Nicola Mei, organist at the cathedral, and then studied composition under G. C. M. Clari. He was organist at the church of the Cavalieri di S Stefano in 1748, when he unsuccessfully requested leave. From 1759 to 1763 he was organist at the cathedral, succeeding his uncle, and from 1763 until his death *maestro di cappella* at Livorno Cathedral. He was also a good harpsichordist.

Gervasoni described Mei as 'a serious man, of somewhat retiring and melancholy temperament, amiable, honest, modest and highly religious'. He was best known for his church music in the severe style and for his fugues. His *Stabat mater*, singled out by Fétis, incorporates both Baroque and Classical elements with some success and attains a great intensity of emotional expression, largely the result of his skilful use of both melodic and harmonic chromaticism.

WORKS

Sacred: Stabat mater, c, SATB, str, bc, Brompton Oratory, London; Laetatus sum, 4vv, insts, *I-PIp*; numerous works mentioned by Gervasoni, incl. masses, 2 requiems, Te Deum, hymns, introits, graduals, litanies, motets, Lamentations, sacred arias; La circoncisione, oratorio, 4vv, insts

Other works: 3 hpd sonatas, *Gi(l)*; 3 concs., hpd/pf, orch; 6 sonatas, hpd, vn; fugues, org/hpd; La musica a Fille, cantata; all mentioned by Gervasoni

BIBLIOGRAPHY

*FétisB*

C. Gervasoni: *Nuova teoria di musica* (Parma, 1812)

E. Roche: 'Orazio Mei', *MT*, cxvi (1975), 273

FRANCO BAGGIANI, ELIZABETH ROCHE

**Meibom** [Meiboom, Meibomius], **Marcus** (*b* Tönning, Schleswig-Holstein, 1620–21; *d* Utrecht, 15 Feb 1711). Danish polyhistor. He is first heard of at Königsberg, where he enrolled at the university on 20 June 1644 to study law. On 29 September 1645, however, he matriculated as a student of medicine at Leiden. Here his age is given as 24 (indicating that his traditionally accepted date of birth, 1626, is wrong) and his birthplace as Tönning, which at that time was under the Danish crown. It was, however, neither in law nor medicine but as a philologist and mathematician that he was to make his mark. He dedicated his *Antiquae musicae auctores septem* (Amsterdam, 1652) to Queen Christina of Sweden, and in May of that year he arrived at her court at Stockholm. He was named as assistant royal librarian, but his stay in Sweden was cut short because of a violent altercation with Bourdelot, the queen's personal physician and favourite. According to an old tradition (see Hawkins) the queen had invited him to have some reconstructions of ancient instruments made and to perform the music that had been the subject of his scholarship. He was unfortunately – or maliciously – encouraged to sing; meeting with general ridicule, apparently led by Bourdelot, he boxed the latter's ears, for which he was dismissed from the court.

In 1653 Meibom went to Copenhagen, where he was taken under the protection of King Frederik III. Despite the common assumption that he was installed there as librarian of the royal library, it seems that in the first instance at least he was simply granted a pension as a deserving scholar. On the title-page of his book *Dialogus de proportionibus* (Copenhagen, 1655) he is described as 'consiliarus regius', though it is not known whether any civil service duties were attached to the title. A number of archival references after 1660 show the king was using Meibom's great learning to order and catalogue the expanding royal library, though apparently he was still not given the coveted official appointment of librarian. In 1661 he declined an approach made to him on behalf of Queen Christina to become her librarian in Rome on the grounds that her frequent changes of residence would make it impossible for him to find the peace and quiet that his studies and the state of his health required. At the same time he made it clear that he was not satisfied with his position, but it is not known whether or not he actually applied for the rather surprising position of director of customs at Elsinore in which he was next found, in 1664. He resigned from this post in 1668 and emigrated with his family to Holland, where, apart from three years (1674–7) in England, he spent the rest of his life. Except for a teaching appointment which he held for a year after arriving in Amsterdam, he seems to have occupied no official position, and he refused an invitation to become professor of Hebrew at Leiden. In 1691 it was reported that he was living in poverty, supporting himself by reading proofs. In 1705 he was obliged to sell part of his library by auction; he himself prepared the auction catalogue, in which no fewer than 5848 items are carefully classified. It is interesting to observe that on the title-page he described himself, after nearly 40 years, as 'sometime councillor to Frederik III, King of Denmark'. The rest of his library was sold in May 1711, after his death.

*Antiquae musicae auctores septem*, his first big work, is also his most important contribution to musical scholarship. In its two quarto volumes he provided an edition of the Greek texts of Aristoxenus, Cleonides (under an attribution to Euclid), Nicomachus, Alypius, Gaudentius, Bacchius, Aristides Quintilianus and Martianus Capella (*Satyricon*, bk 9), with a Latin translation and commentary. *Dialogus de proportionibus*, the only other work in which he discussed music, is in the form of a dialogue between a number of Greek mathematicians in which they discuss not only mathematical proportions but the musical proportions as well.

BIBLIOGRAPHY

*HawkinsH*
J. Moller: *Cimbria literata*, iii (Copenhagen, 1744), 443ff
A. Hammerich: *Dansk musikhistorie indtil ca.1700* (Copenhagen, 1921)
H. F. Rørdam: 'Meibom, Marcus', *DBL*
C. S. Petersen: 'Marcus Meibom og Villem Lange', *Fund og forskning*, i (1954), 1–39

JOHN BERGSAGEL

**Meier, Bernhard** (*b* Freiburg, 15 Dec 1923). German musicologist. He studied musicology with Zenck and Gurlitt, history with G. Ritter, and philology with W. Rehm at Freiburg University. He took the doctorate at Freiburg in 1952 with a dissertation on Obrecht's settings of the Mass. From 1955 he was an assistant lecturer in the musicology institute of Tübingen University, where in 1963 he was awarded his *Habilitation* in musicology on the basis of all his published writings. He was then appointed lecturer and in 1969 *ausserplanmässiger Professor* in musicology at Tübingen University. His research is chiefly concerned with Renaissance music and theory. His studies on Obrecht, Lassus, Cipriano de Rore, *musica reservata* and tonal theory and practice in the 15th and 16th centuries are supported by close familiarity with the sources.

WRITINGS

'Die Harmonik im cantus firmus-haltigen Satz des 15. Jahrhunderts', *AMw*, ix (1952), 27
*Studien zur Messkomposition Jacob Obrechts* (diss., U. of Freiburg, 1952)
'Die Handschrift Porta 714 als Quelle zur Tonartenlehre des 15. Jahrhunderts', *MD*, vii (1953), 175
'Zyklische Gesamtstruktur und Tonalität in den Messen Jacob Obrechts', *AMw*, x (1953), 289
'Caput: Bemerkungen zur Messe Dufays und Ockeghems', *Mf*, vii (1954), 268
'The Musica Reservata of Adrianus Petit Coclico and its Relationship to Josquin', *MD*, x (1956), 67–105
'Bemerkungen zu Lechners "Motectae Sacrae" von 1575', *AMw*, xiv (1957), 83
'Alter und neuer Stil in lateinisch textierten Werken von Orlando di Lasso', *AMw*, xv (1958), 151
'Reservata-Probleme: ein Bericht', *AcM*, xxx (1958), 77
'Heinrich Loriti Glareanus als Musiktheoretiker', *Beiträge zur Freiburger Wissenschafts- und Universitätsgeschichte*, xxii (1960), 65–112
'Wortausdeutung und Tonalität bei Orlando di Lasso', *KJb*, xlvii (1963), 75–104
'Modale Korrektur und Wortausdeutung im Choral der Editio Medicaea', *KJb*, liii (1969), 101–32
'Zur Musikhistoriographie des 19. Jahrhunderts', *Die Ausbreitung des Historismus über die Musik*, ed. W. Wiora (Regensburg, 1969), 169–206
'Staatskompositionen von Cyprian de Rore', *TVNM*, xxi/2 (1969), 81–118
*Die Tonarten der klassischen Vokalpolyphonie* (Utrecht, 1974)

EDITIONS

J. Barbireau: *Opera omnia*, CMM, vii (1954–7)
J. Arcadelt und andere Meister: *Sechs italienische Madrigale*, Cw, lviii (1956)
J. Clemens non Papa: *Drei Motetten*, Cw, lxxii (1958)
C. de Rore: *Opera omnia*, CMM, xiv (1959–)
G. Nasco, S. Rosetti, P. Taglia: *Fünf Madrigale auf Texte von Francesco Petrarca*, Cw, lxxxviii (1961)

HANS HEINRICH EGGEBRECHT

**Meier, Gustav** (*b* Wettingen, 13 Aug 1929). American conductor of Swiss birth. He attended the Zurich Conservatory, 1944–8 and 1951–3, studying under Paul Müller. In 1952 and 1953 he was also a student at the Accademia Chigiana in Siena. After spending two years as conductor of the Imperial Court Orchestra in Addis Ababa, Ethiopia, he was appointed assistant conductor of the Zurich Opera, where he worked from 1956 to 1958. Meanwhile, in 1957, he had spent the first of two summers at the Berkshire Music Center,

Tanglewood, studying under Eleazar de Carvalho, and in 1958 he moved permanently to the USA. In addition to guest engagements with a number of American and European orchestras and opera companies, Meier was conductor of the New Haven Chorale, 1960–73, and professor of conducting at Yale University, 1961–73. In 1973 he was appointed to a similar post at the Eastman School of Music in Rochester, New York, and he has served as musical director and conductor of the Greater Bridgeport SO in Connecticut. Some of his most distinguished work has been with contemporary music, in which his ability to render lucidly the textures of such music as Elliott Carter's later works has been especially valuable.

BERNARD JACOBSON

**Meier, Johann David.** See MAYER, JOHANN DAVID.

**Meier, Peter** (*fl* 1633–70). German composer. A city musician in Hamburg, he was one of the most prolific members of the north German school of songwriters in the mid-17th century. He composed most of the songs in Johann Rist's *Des edlen Daphnis aus Cimbrien besungene Florabella* (Hamburg, 1651) and also contributed to other collections, including Rist's *Neue himlische Lieder* (Lüneburg, 1651) and Philipp von Zesen's *Dichterische Jugendflammen* (Hamburg, 1651) and *Dichterische Rosen- und Liljentahl* (Hamburg, 1670). In 1633 he wrote a *Braut-Lied*, probably for the wedding of Johann Kruss. His more serious songs include poignant intervals and rhythms, and in his lighter pieces he successfully captured the simplicity of street songs.

BIBLIOGRAPHY

H. Kretzschmar: *Geschichte des neuen deutschen Liedes* (Leipzig, 1911/*R*1966)
W. Vetter: *Das frühdeutsche Lied* (Münster, 1928)
R. H. Thomas: *Poetry and Song in the German Baroque* (Oxford, 1963)
JOHN H. BARON

**Mei-Figner, Medea.** See FIGNER, MEDEA.

**Meifred, Pierre-Joseph Emile** (*b* Colmar, 13 Nov 1791; *d* Paris, 28 Aug 1867). French horn player and designer. As a child he learnt music merely as a polite accomplishment, and after schooling entered the Ecole des Arts et Métiers at Chalons. He was attached for a time to the secretarial staff of the Empress Josephine, but in 1815 turned professionally to music and entered Dauprat's horn class at the Paris Conservatoire. In 1818 he gained the *premier prix* in horn playing and the following year joined the orchestra of the Théâtre-Italien. He also played in the Opéra orchestra from 1822 until 1850. About 1830, criticism of the inefficiency of French military bands led Meifred to propose the founding of a school for army musicians. The Gymnase Militaire came into being as a result in 1836, but Meifred was passed over twice for the directorship, in favour first of the clarinettist Berr and later of Carafa. Though awarded the cross of the Légion d'honneur in 1848, Meifred's military status remained that of bandmaster in the National Guard. He was a founder-member, and for some years secretary, of the Société des Concerts du Conservatoire, which owed much of its success to his organizing talent.

Mechanically and progressively minded, Meifred devoted himself to the development of the valve horn, then recently introduced from Germany, and at the first Conservatoire concert (9 March 1828) he played a solo of his own composition on this instrument – its first public appearance in France. Together with the Paris instrument maker Labbaye, he greatly improved the German model, adding tuning-slides to the valves and thus making it possible to use crooks in different pitches. In 1834, with Deshays, Meifred patented a valve with movable shutters within the actual windway (French patent no.4002), though this proved too expensive to market commercially; no specimens are known to have survived. (A somewhat similar arrangement of shutters in the windway is found on a trumpet of 1825 made by Nathan Adams of Lowell, Massachusetts.) It is almost certain that the instrument maker Halary, while designing a system of horn valves in which the third valve raised the pitch of the instrument instead of lowering it, called Meifred into consultation. The latter adopted this arrangement for his own use, an example still followed by many horn players in France. In 1832 a valve horn class was inaugurated at the Conservatoire, with Meifred as professor, but this was discontinued after his retirement in 1864 and not resumed until 1903 under Brémond.

WRITINGS

*De l'étendue, de l'emploi et des ressources du cor* (Paris, 1829)
*Méthode de cor chromatique ou à pistons* (Paris, 1840, rev. 2/1849)
'Notice sur la fabrication des instruments de musique en cuivre', *Annuaire de la Société des anciens élèves des écoles nationales des arts-et-métiers, année 1851* (Paris, 1851)

BIBLIOGRAPHY

R. Morley-Pegge: *The French Horn* (London, 1960, rev. 2/1973)
R. Eliason: 'Early American Valves for Brass Instruments', *GSJ*, xxiii (1970), 86
REGINALD MORLEY-PEGGE/PHILIP BATE

**Meigret [Maigret], Robert** (*b* Le Mans, 1508; *d* Le Mans, 1568). French composer. Between 1543 and 1557 30 chansons by him were published in Paris by Attaingnant and Du Chemin. Guillaume Morlaye's *Premier livre de tablature de leut* (Paris, 1552³⁴) attributes to 'Megret' a piece entitled *Auparavant*; in fact it is an arrangement of the four-voice chanson *Auparavant que j'eusse congnoissance* published five years earlier by Attaingnant (*RISM* 1547¹¹) and ascribed to 'Olivier'. The composer may be identical with the Maigret who, according to the contemporary bibliographer La Croix du Maine, was regarded as one of the most learned musicians of his day. Fétis mentioned three four-voice chansons by Maigret printed in Le Roy & Ballard's third *Recueil des chansons*, which is now lost. A five-voice motet printed by Girolamo Scotto (*RISM* 1567³) is ascribed to 'Giacomo Migret'.

All 30 of Meigret's chanson texts are courtly amorous *épigrammes*; most are set in the suave, generally homophonic manner typical of the Parisian chansons of the 1540s illustrated in the works of Sandrin, Janequin and Certon.

WORKS

*(all for 4vv)*

A mon depart, 1547⁸; Amour m'oyant souvant gémir, 1543¹¹; Amour voyant m'amye, 1547¹¹; Ce bon parler, 1545⁸; Celle que j'ay pour maistresse choisie, 1548⁴; Comme au malade, 1557¹²; Descens du ciel, o royne Calliope, 1549¹⁹; D'ung nouveau cas, 1545⁸⁻⁹; En vous voyant, 1547⁸; Ha petit chien, 1547¹¹; J'ay bonne grace, 1546¹⁰; J'ay veu que j'estoys cher tenu, 1547⁸; La grant douceur de vostre cler visaige, 1549²⁰; La nuict passée, 1543¹¹⁻¹²; La vraye amour, 1545⁸; Le fruict sans goust, 1548⁴; L'oeil messager, 1548⁴

Malheur me suit, 1545⁸; N'en parlez plus de l'amour, 1548⁴; Par le seul traict de voz yeulx, 1544⁷; Si la beaulté et doulce contenance, 1546¹⁴; Si la faveur a costumée, 1546¹⁴; S'il est ainsy qu'on estaint la challeur, 1549¹⁹; Si l'endurer segret sans espérance, 1547⁸; Triste est mon cueur, 1547⁸; Tu pers amour, 1549²⁰; Ung doulx regard, 1545⁸;

Venez regretz, 1544[7]; Venus ung jour en veneur se déguise, 1546[14]; Vostre gent corps, 1543[11]

BIBLIOGRAPHY

*FétisB*
R. de Juvigny, ed.: *Les bibliothèques françoises de La Croix du Maine et de du Verdier*, ii (Paris, 1772), 391

FRANK DOBBINS

**Meiland** [Meyland, Mayland], **Jacob** [Jakob] (*b* Senftenberg, Lower Lusatia, 1542; *d* Hechingen, Württemberg, 31 Dec 1577). German composer. About 1550 he became a choirboy at the Dresden Hofkapelle, where he would thus have been a pupil up to 1554 of Johann Walter (i) and then of Matthaeus le Maistre. In 1558 he entered Leipzig University. He later went to Flanders to improve his musical knowledge, and he may also have visited Italy, but there is no documentary evidence of this. He then lived briefly at Nuremberg, whence in 1563 he joined the newly formed Kantorei of the Protestant Margrave Georg Friedrich of Brandenburg-Ansbach. Towards the end of 1564 he became its director. Early in 1565 it was decided to establish a Hofkapelle too, and he was also appointed its first director. During his years at Ansbach he travelled widely – for example to Saxony, Württemberg and Bavaria – no doubt in search of singers for his own Kapelle or for the Dresden Hofkapelle but also perhaps to further his own acquaintance with a variety of noted personalities. In 1572 he left Ansbach, probably because of poor health, and moved to Frankfurt am Main, but because of persistent illness he remained without a permanent post and lived in straitened circumstances there until 1576. He then moved to the court at Celle, but it is not certain whether he held an appointment there. On 17 July 1577 he took up his final post, as Kapellmeister to Count Eitel Friedrich von Hohenzollern at Hechingen, but he died within six months.

In spite of a short career hampered by ill-health, Meiland was a relatively prolific and much respected composer, who could obviously also boast a good classical education. His music was widely known, both in his lifetime and after his death, in both printed and manuscript sources. Influenced mainly by Clemens non Papa and to some extent by Lassus too, he mainly cultivated the Latin motet, but he is also of interest in two other spheres, Passion music and secular songs. His three German responsorial Passions, which are in the tradition of Walter, are historically important because he was the first to break with the customary use in the turbae of fauxbourdon deriving from the liturgical Passion tone, and in so doing he increased the dramatic potential of the form. His two collections of German secular songs for four and five voices (1569–75) are among the most important such volumes before H. L. Hassler's *Lustgarten* (1601).

WORKS

SACRED VOCAL

Cantiones sacrae cum harmonicis numeris, 5, 6vv (Nuremberg, 1564; enlarged 2/1569, 3/1572, 4/1573)
Selectae cantiones, 5, 6vv (Nuremberg, 1572)
Cantiones aliquot novae . . . quibus adiuncta sunt officia due, 5vv (Frankfurt, 1575)
Sacrae aliquot cantiones latinae et germanicae . . . sequentes duas cantiones in honorem domini Sigismundi Feyerabend et Hieronymi eius filii, 4, 5vv (Frankfurt am Main, 1575); 2 ed. C. von Winterfeld: *Der evangelische Kirchengesang*, i (Leipzig, 1843/R1966); 1 ed. in Schmid
Harmoniae sacrae selectae ac compositiones divinae, 5vv (Erfurt, 1588)
Cygneae cantiones latinae et germanicae, 4, 5vv, ed. E. Schelius (Wittenberg, 1590)

Mass; 5 Lat. motets, 4, 6vv; 2 Ger. hymns, 4vv: 1564[3], 1564[5], 1610[12], H. Praetorius: Liber missarum (Hamburg, 1622)
3 Passions: St Mark, 1567; St John, 1568; St Matthew, 1570: *D-AN, As, SGh*; St Mark Passion ed. in *Handbuch der deutschen evangelischen Kirchenmusik*, i/3–4 (Göttingen, 1939)
10 motets, 5, 6vv, *AN, LÜh* [probably copies of works in Cantiones sacrae, 2/1569]

SECULAR VOCAL

Newe ausserlesene teutsche Liedlein, 4, 5vv (Nuremberg, 1569)
Newe ausserlesene teutsche Gesäng, 4, 5vv (Frankfurt, 1575)
5 Ger. songs, 1622[15]
For lost works see Schmidt (1956)

BIBLIOGRAPHY
O. Kade: *Die ältere Passionskomposition bis zum Jahre 1631* (Gütersloh, 1893)
C. Valentin: *Geschichte der Musik in Frankfurt am Main vom Anfange des XIV. bis zum Anfange des XVIII. Jahrhunderts* (Frankfurt am Main, 1906/R1972)
R. Oppel: *Jacob Meiland (1542–1577)* (Pfungstadt, 1911)
H. J. Moser: *Die mehrstimmige Vertonung des Evangeliums*, i (Leipzig, 1931/R1968)
G. Schmidt: *Die Musik am Hofe der Markgrafen von Brandenburg-Ansbach* (Kassel, 1956)
——: 'Zur Quellenlage der Passionen Jakob Meilands', *Jb für Liturgik und Hymnologie*, iii (1957), 124
E. F. Schmid: *Musik an den schwäbischen Zollernhöfen der Renaissance* (Kassel, 1962)
M. Ruhnke: *Beiträge zu einer Geschichte der Hofmusikkollegien im 16. Jahrhundert* (Berlin, 1963)
K. W. Niemöller: *Untersuchungen zu Musikpflege und Musikunterricht an den deutschen Lateinschulen vom ausgehenden Mittelalter bis um 1600* (Regensburg, 1969)
E.-L. Berz: *Die Notendrucker und ihre Verleger in Frankfurt am Main von den Anfängen bis etwa 1630* (Kassel, 1970)

WALTER BLANKENBURG

**Mei Lan-fang** (*b* Peking, 22 Oct 1894; *d* Peking, 8 Aug 1961). Chinese opera actor. He came from a well-known theatrical family and was trained at Fu-lien-ch'eng, the most important school for actors in Peking. His fame began in 1913 when he visited Shanghai. From then on he was in great demand both inside and outside China; he went to Japan in 1919, 1924 and 1956, to the USA in 1930 and to Europe in 1935. A versatile actor, he mastered *k'un-ch'ü* as well as Peking opera. He was most famous as a *ch'ing-i*, but could perform any of the *tan* roles and was an excellent acrobat. After the Communists came to power he helped them in their drama reform and took part in numerous conferences and committees; he joined the Chinese Communist Party in 1959. He made several films and gramophone records and is regarded as the most famous 20th-century Peking opera actor (*see* CHINA, §III, 2(i)).

BIBLIOGRAPHY
Mei Lan-fang, ed.: *Hsü chi-ch'uan: Wu-t'ai sheng-huo ssu-shih nien* [40 years on the stage] (Shanghai, 1952–4)
A. C. Scott: *Mei Lan-fang: Leader of the Pear Garden* (Hong Kong, 1959)

COLIN MACKERRAS

**Meili, Max** (*b* Winterthur, 11 Dec 1899; *d* Zurich, 17 March 1970). Swiss tenor. He studied in Winterthur with P. Deutsch and in Munich with F. von Kraus, then appeared as a concert singer all over Europe. He quickly became known as a distinguished specialist in early music, particularly Monteverdi and Schütz. In 1933 he was among the co-founders of the Schola Cantorum Basiliensis, at whose concerts he frequently sang medieval and Renaissance music; in 1955 he founded the Collegium Cantorum Turicense, which under his direction sang Schütz's Passions and Monteverdi's *Orfeo*, among other works. Recordings of music by these composers and by Buxtehude and Bach bear witness to his stylish and vital singing.

KURT VON FISCHER/JÜRG STENZL

**Meinardus, Ludwig Siegfried** (*b* Hooksiel, Oldenburg, 17 Sept 1827; *d* Bielefeld, 10 July 1896). German conductor, writer on music and composer. After initial education at the Jever Gymnasium, he was advised by Schumann to concentrate on composition. He entered the Leipzig Conservatory in 1846 but soon left, preferring private instruction from Riccius. He then conducted small theatre companies in Erfurt and Nordhausen, and in 1850 went to Berlin to study with A. B. Marx and later with Liszt at Weimar. He was conductor of the Glogau Singakademie (1853–65) and was then appointed to the Dresden Conservatory. In 1874 he settled at Hamburg, where he was critic of the *Hamburger Korrespondent*, and in 1887 he moved to Bielefeld as organist.

Meinardus's most successful work was the oratorio *Luther in Worms* op.36 (Leipzig, 1876); he wrote five further oratorios, two operas (neither performed), two symphonies (*c*1875, 1879) and much choral and chamber music. He is more important, however, for his writings, notably a memoir of Mattheson (Leipzig, 1879), an autobiographical sketch (Gotha, 1874) and his collected criticisms.

J. A. FULLER MAITLAND/R

**Meiningen.** Thuringian town in the German Democratic Republic. Founded around 1000, it became the seat of the Henneberg counts; from 1680 to 1918 it was the residence of the dukes of Saxe-Meiningen, whose palace, the Schloss Elisabethenburg, was the centre of the town's musical life. In 1490 the famous scholar Andreas Ornithoparcus was born in the town. The ducal Kapelle flourished in the 16th century under such Kantors as Samuel and Christoph Fischer; the composer Johann Steuerlein, secretary to the court and official poet from 1589 to 1613, made a German version of the Passion attributed to Obrecht for use in Meiningen. After 1680 the town, as an independent duchy, was able to import fine artists from the court of Brunswick-Wolfenbüttel through the family connections of Duke Bernhard I. Thus G. C. Schürmann, after working in Brunswick, was transferred to Meiningen on his return from a trip to Italy in 1703, with the intention that he should establish an opera tradition; to this end he performed a number of his own works there. On his departure in 1706 Johann Ludwig Bach, the so-called 'Meiningen Bach' and a cousin of Johann Sebastian, became Hofkapellmeister, having assisted Schürmann for a time; he worked there until his death in 1731. J. S. Bach used Johann Ludwig's cantatas in Leipzig, where he was host to the latter's son Samuel Anton; Samuel Anton subsequently returned to Meiningen and became a court official, as did his brother Gottlob Friedrich. A number of the Meiningen Bachs were also gifted painters; their work survives in the Schloss Elisabethenburg (see Young). Many operas, Singspiels and ballets were given at the court in the early 18th century, including J. L. Bach's *Jubel-Freude* (1717).

A period of relative unimportance, musically speaking, followed; in the early 19th century the Hofkapelle was small, comprising no more than 20 players, augmented for special occasions. However, in 1831 a new Hoftheater was built, inaugurated with a performance of Auber's *Fra Diavolo*, and later in the 19th century Duke Georg II considerably enlarged the Hofkapelle and, by inviting many leading musicians to conduct it, raised it to become one of the finest orchestras in Germany. Under Georg II the theatre's productions also became

renowned, and significantly influenced modern stage techniques. Among the musicians associated with the orchestra were Bülow (Kapellmeister 1880–85), Brahms, Wagner, Richard Strauss (Kapellmeister 1885–6) and Reger (Kapellmeister 1911–14); the best-known orchestra member was the clarinettist and assistant conductor Richard Mühlfeld, for whom Brahms wrote his clarinet sonatas and the quintet. In 1885 the orchestra gave the premières of Brahms's Fourth Symphony and Strauss's Horn Concerto no.1, while Brahms's setting of Goethe's *Gesang der Parzen* was dedicated to the duke (1882). In 1895 a festival was held under the direction of Fritz Steinbach; it consisted entirely of works by Bach, Beethoven and Brahms. In 1901, the year before a successful visit to London, the orchestra introduced Elgar's *Enigma Variations* to Germany, playing the work in Leipzig, Berlin and Eisenach as well as Meiningen. This period of intense activity was brought to a close by World War I. The theatre is now maintained by the municipality and chamber concerts are given in the palace, now a museum with a music collection including letters of Bülow, Brahms, Wagner, Reger and others.

BIBLIOGRAPHY
C. Mühlfeld: *Die herzogliche Hofkapelle in Meiningen* (Meiningen, 1910)
A. Humann: *Analekten zur Sachsen-Meiningenschen Kirchen- und Schulgeschichte* (Hildburghausen, 1918)
E. von Hase-Koehler, ed.: *M. Reger: Briefe eines deutschen Meisters: ein Lebensbild* (Leipzig, 1928)
G. Kraft: *Die thüringische Musikkultur um 1600*, i (Würzburg, 1941)
P. Bach: 'Die Meininger Bache', *Johann Sebastian Bach in Thüringen* (Weimar, 1950), 217
G. Kraft: *Musikgeschichte der Stadt Meiningen* (Weimar, 1958)
E. Engel: *Musik in Thüringen* (Cologne, 1966)
T. Hahm: *Die Gastspiele des Meininger Hoftheaters im Urteil der Zeitgenossen unter besonderer Berücksichtigung der Gastspiele in Berlin und Wien* (diss., U. of Cologne, 1970)
P. M. Young: *The Bachs* (London, 1970)
F. Landgraf: *Die Lehrer des Kreises Meiningen* (MS, *D-MEIl*)
PERCY M. YOUNG

**Meinl & Lauber.** German brass instrument makers. The firm's three partners are Franz Meinl (*b* Graslitz, 20 May 1910), his son Ewald (*b* Schönlind, Czechoslovakia, 10 Oct 1937), and Johann Lauber (*b* Plauen, Czechoslovakia, 10 Nov 1919). Franz Meinl was trained by Ignaz Hamm in Rothau, and worked for Gebrüder Stowasser and Bohland & Fuchs (Graslitz). After 1947 he worked on his own in Lenggries and from 1951 in Geretsried (both in Bavaria) making brass instrument bells for other firms. Johann Lauber was trained with Gebrüder Stowasser (1934–7); from 1950 to 1957 he was employed by Böhm & [Andreas] Meinl (Geretsried). Ewald Meinl trained from 1951 to 1955 with his great-uncle, Wenzel Meinl. In 1955 Franz and Ewald founded their own bell-making shop; the firm took on its present name with the entrance of Johann Lauber the following year.

Besides being bell makers, they have gained an international reputation for reproductions of historical brass instruments (from 1967 Baroque trumpets, developed with Edward Tarr, from 1968 trombones with Thomas Cramer, from 1970 horns with Horace Fitzpatrick). They copy the instruments of leading makers, mainly from Nuremberg, using thin hand-rolled tubing. In 1972 they produced a piccolo B♭/A trumpet with two detachable bells, with Rolf Quinque (of Munich).

EDWARD H. TARR

**Meise, Heinrich zur.** *See* FRAUENLOB.

**Meissner** [Meisner], **(Adolf) Philipp (Ernst)** (*b* Burgpreppach, nr. Hofheim, Lower Franconia, 24 Sept 1748; *d* Würzburg, 6 July 1816). German clarinettist, teacher and composer. He showed musical talent at an early age, and took clarinet lessons with the court clarinettist Martin Hessler. When he was barely 16 he played before Prince-Bishop Adam Friedrich of Würzburg; he left school in 1766 and, on the prince-bishop's advice, left Würzburg to further his studies by travelling. At Strasbourg he was taken into the service of Cardinal Prince Constantin of Rohan, with whom he went to Paris. Within three years he was a chamber musician in the employ of the Count of Branca and afterwards was first clarinet in the royal guards' band and in the Opéra orchestra. He often played with great success at the Concert Spirituel and at the Concert des Amateurs, and won no less approval when he appeared at the court at Versailles.

Now a recognized virtuoso, Meissner returned to Würzburg and in 1776 was appointed court and chamber musician in the prince-bishop's Kapelle, a position he held for some 30 years; he later also directed the so-called Turkish Music. He travelled widely in Germany and Switzerland. He founded a clarinet school at Würzburg where his pupils included such notable figures as F. J. Beer, C. A. Göpfert and the Würzburg clarinettist Kleinheuss. Siebold praised his 'full, ringing tone' and 'beautiful, tender execution' on the clarinet.

WORKS
*(published in Mainz unless otherwise stated)*
Harmoniestücke für Blasinstrumente (Leipzig, n.d.) (2 vols.); 2 qts, cl, vn, va, vc (1813) (1814; repr. attrib. 'Kinzi', 1819, 1882); duos, 2 cl, op.3 (n.d.), 2 as op.4 (n.d.), 3 without op. no. (n.d.)
MS concs., variations, cl, lost

BIBLIOGRAPHY
L. Bechstein: *Clarinette: Seitenstück zu den Fahrten eines Musikanten* (Leipzig, 1840) [incl. Meissner's autobiography]
U. Rau: *Die Kammermusik für Klarinette und Streichinstrumente im Zeitalter der Wiener Klassik* (diss., U. of Saarbrücken, 1975)

based on *MGG* (xvi, 1253–4) by permission of Bärenreiter
ULRICH RAU

**Meissonnier, Jean Antoine.** French publisher, partner of Jacques Léopold HEUGEL.

**Meister** [Maistre], **Johann Friedrich** (*b* Peine, nr. Brunswick, before 1638; *d* Flensburg, 28 Oct 1697). German composer and organist. In 1677, with the help of N. A. Strungk, Kapellmeister at Hanover, he was appointed director of music in the Hofkapelle of Duke Ferdinand Albrecht I of Brunswick-Lüneburg at the castle of Bevern. At the beginning of October 1678 he was imprisoned, escaped with the help of friends and, although a warrant was issued for his arrest, entered the service of Bishop August Friedrich of Lübeck at Eutin. From 18 April 1683 until his death, he was organist of St Marien, Flensburg. His relationship with the ducal family at the castle at nearby Glücksburg was almost one of friendship: he performed there, and members of the duke's family were godparents to two of his children. He appears to have led an adventurous life and to have been at odds with authority not only in his earlier days but later in life too; he must have owed it to his aristocratic patrons that this had no serious consequences for him during his time at Flensburg. As court musician he no doubt wrote a good deal of secular music, but only 14 church cantatas by him survive. They are similar to works by Buxtehude in their choice of texts and musical forms; they are technically competent but tend to be virtuoso rather than expressive works.

WORKS
Fürstliche Holstein-Glücksburgische musikalische Gemüths-Belustigung (Hamburg, 1693), 12 vols.; lost, cited in Moller
Il giardino del piacere, overo raccolta di diversi fiori musicali, come sonate, fughe, imitationi, ciacone, 2 vn/vle, bc (hpd) (Hamburg, 1695)
14 cantatas, 1–5vv, 2–6 insts, bc, *D-B*

BIBLIOGRAPHY
J. Moller: *Cimbria literata*, ii (Copenhagen, 1744)
P. Zimmermann: 'Herzog Ferdinand Albrechts I. zu Braunschweig und Lüneburg theatralische Aufführungen im Schlosse zu Bevern', *Jb des Geschichtsvereins für das Herzogtum Braunschweig*, iii (1904)
H. Schilling: *Tobias Eniccelius, Friedrich Meister, Nicolaus Hanff: ein Beitrag zur Geschichte der evangelischen Frühkantate in Schleswig-Holstein* (diss., U. of Kiel, 1934)
H. P. Detlefsen: *Musikgeschichte der Stadt Flensburg bis zum Jahre 1850* (Kassel, 1959)
H. Kümmerling: *Katalog der Sammlung Bokemeyer* (Kassel, 1970)
MICHAEL SPAETH

**Meistergesang.** A German tradition of songwriting and performance among the rising bourgeois classes that flourished particularly in the 16th century. It provided the lower and middle classes in the cities with a religious and secular education: whether as active members or as audience at the concerts, they could become aware of matters which would otherwise have been unavailable or difficult for them to learn. It thereby contributed to the increasing literacy of the bourgeoisie that characterizes the transition from the Middle Ages to the modern era. Wagner's opera *Die Meistersinger von Nürnberg* (1868) has given many people at least some idea of German Meistergesang; but of course the romantic–poetic picture Wagner presented bears only partial resemblance to the information collected from research by literary scholars and musicologists. The following brief, general description is an attempt to give an account of the present state of research.

1. Definition. 2. Sources. 3. Origins, locations, personalities. 4. The themes of the poetry. 5. The music. 6. Organization of the guilds and performance of lieder at the concerts. 7. Spruchgedichte and stage plays.

1. DEFINITION. Meistergesang is the composition and performance of Meisterlieder by the Meistersinger. Meistersinger were those citizens of German cities, usually south German imperial cities, who from the 14th century to the 17th (with isolated examples still in the 18th and 19th centuries) formed themselves into guilds (*Gesellschaften*) for the composition and performance of Meisterlieder. (Current usage refers to the Meistersinger guilds as *Singschulen* (singing schools), although the Meistersinger themselves applied this term only to the events in which they performed their lieder publicly, in the sense of a concert.) As a rule the Meistersinger were artisans belonging to a town's middle and lower classes, although clergymen, lawyers and teachers were also found among them. They participated in the guilds in addition to their normal occupation. They all composed their lieder in German, basing them on more or less similar subjects, which altered in the course of time, and according to generally accepted artistic rules codified in the *Tabulaturen* of the 16th century and which changed only slightly over the centuries. At both the public *Singschulen* and the private *Zechsingen*, lieder were always performed strictly in accordance with the *Schulordnungen* (regulations). Throughout the country guilds were organized along the same or similar lines (the organizational regulations appeared in the *Schulordnung*); and there was much active exchange among the guilds, doubtless encouraged by the tradition of *Wanderjahre*. Finally, all the guilds were under the strict control of the city authorities who superintended

*1. Guild of the Meistersinger of Memmingen: miniature from the 'Stammund Meisterbuch der Memminger Meistersinger' (1626) (Stadtarchiv, Memmingen)*

the observance of the *Schulordnung* as well as general moral, religious and political laws. The Meistersinger, moreover, shared a distinct consciousness of their art and its significance. They are organically and typologically related, although not identical, to the German 12th–15th century *Sangspruchdichter*.

2. SOURCES. Numerous sources are available for Meistergesang research, and they are still far from fully investigated. The most important are the approximately 120 manuscripts containing the Meistersinger lieder, whose number is estimated at about 16,000. The earliest of these manuscripts comes from the beginning of the 15th century, the latest from the 18th century. Generally they contain only the texts and not the melodies. Some contain the lieder of one particular Meistersinger, but the majority contain collections by different poets, often from diverse origins and times. There are no general principles governing either the choice or the order of the collections. The manuscripts are dispersed among numerous libraries, the most extensive and significant collections being in West Berlin, Dresden, Munich, Nuremberg, Weimar and Zwickau. In 1969 the Nuremberg Stadtbibliothek began to establish a central collection of copies of all Meistersinger manuscripts.

The melodies, which were part of an almost exclusively oral tradition, are found in only a few sources. The most important and comprehensive of these are the Colmarer Liederhandschrift, *D-Mbs* Cgm4997 (*c*1470, presumably from Mainz); the Valentin Voigt manuscript *Ju* E1.f.100 (1558, Magdeburg); Adam Puschman's *Singebuch*, formerly in Breslau Stadtbibliothek 356, lost since 1945 (1584–8, Breslau); manuscripts of the Nuremberg Meistersinger Benedict von Watt in *D-B* germ.f.25 (*c*1603) and f.24 (*c*1615), and in *D-Nst* Will III.784 (*c*1616); and *D-Nst* Will III.792–6 (*c*1670 and after). Relatively few printed Meisterlieder were circulated in the 15th and 16th centuries, since after

1540 it was expressly forbidden to perform printed lieder at the *Singschulen*.

Further important sources of information are the extant *Tabulaturen* and *Schulordnungen*, the earliest of which is the *Schulzettel* (1540) of the Nuremberg Meistersinger. The *Gründlicher Bericht des deutschen Meistergesanges* of ADAM PUSCHMAN (1571, 2/1596) disseminated the *Tabulatur* and *Schulordnung* in print. Testimony which reveals the Meistersinger's own awareness of their art and tradition is especially significant. To this category belong numerous songs whose subject is the Meistergesang itself, chronicles, and prefaces to manuscripts. One extensive musical and literary history from the viewpoint of the Meistersinger is *Von der edlen und hochberühmbten Kunst der Musica*, written in 1598 by the Strasbourg theologian and Meistersinger Cyriac Spangenberg (1528–1604). Information about the public face of the Meistersinger can be gathered particularly from the records of their meetings, which in Nuremberg and Augsburg were preserved for a long time, as well as from other archive material, especially correspondence with city authorities. Other sources include posters announcing Meistersinger's events, paintings and other art objects. Finally there are informative reports about Meistergesang from contemporaries who were not themselves Meistersinger. The most important of these is the treatise on the Meistersinger of Nuremberg by the scholar Johann Christoph Wagenseil in his book *De civitate noribergensi commentatio* (1697). This account was Wagner's most important source. (For further description of Meistergesang sources *see* SOURCES, MS, §III, 5, and figs.27–8.)

3. ORIGINS, LOCATIONS, PERSONALITIES. Nothing is known as to why, when or where the first Meistersinger guild was founded. The Meistersinger of the 16th and 17th centuries assumed that it had begun in Mainz. It probably began some time in the 14th century. The

Meistersinger themselves honoured a number of famous poets of the 13th and 14th centuries as the founders of their art. The best-known of the so-called *alte Meister* were Walther von der Vogelweide (*fl c*1198–*c*1230), Reinmar von Zweter (*c*1227–50), der Marner (*c*1230–70), Konrad von Würzburg (*d* 1287), Frauenlob (*d* 1318), Regenbogen (*d* after 1318) and Heinrich von Mügeln (*d* after 1371) (*see* MINNESANG). None of them was a municipal Meistersinger for whom composing and singing was an avocation: they were professional travelling poets, who sang for aristocratic audiences; their verses dealt primarily with religious, moral, chivalric and political topics. Present-day research refers to these poets as 'Sangspruchdichter'. They may be considered the 'founders' of Meistergesang only insofar as the Meistersinger of the 14th and 15th centuries frequently imitated their poems and until the 18th century used a number of their *Töne* (*see* TON) for their own lieder. There are however significant differences between the Meistersinger and the *Sangspruchdichter*.

In the 15th and early 16th centuries there appear to have been Meistersinger guilds in Mainz, Nuremberg, Augsburg and Strasbourg, among other places; but specific information survives only about the Nuremberg Meistersinger. The best-known Nuremberg singers in this period were Fritz Kettner (documented 1392–1430), the baker Konrad Nachtigall (*c*1410–1484/5), the nailmaker Fritz Zorn (documented 1442–7) and the weaver Lienhard Nunnenbeck (documented 1514–15), the teacher of Hans Sachs. The most important Nuremberg Meistersinger at this time was the barber and surgeon Hans Folz (*c*1435 or 1440–1513) from Worms, who in addition to many Meisterlieder also wrote carnival plays (*Fastnachtspiele*) and many other poems. After 1520 the guild received new stimulus through the activities of the shoemaker HANS SACHS (1494–1576), who provided an impetus far beyond Nuremberg for both the founding and renewal of Meistersinger guilds. His best-known contemporaries in Nuremberg were Hans Vogel (*d* between 1549 and 1554), Kunz Füllsack (traceable after 1517) and Wolf Buchner (traceable after 1521). Between 1556 and 1560 the Silesian Adam Puschman (1532–1600) also lived in Nuremberg. Between 1590 and 1630 Nuremberg Meistergesang experienced its last flowering. The most significant singers of this period were GEORG HAGER (1552–1634), Wolf Bauttner (1573–1634), Benedict von Watt (1569–1616), Hans Winter (1591–1627) and Ambrosius Metzger (1573–1632). The Nuremberg guild continued its existence after this time, finally disbanding only in 1774.

The most important Meistersinger guilds of the 16th and 17th centuries, besides that in Nuremberg, were in Augsburg (re-established 1534; the most famous poets of the 16th century being Raphael Duller, Onoferus Schwarzenbach, Sebastian Wild and Johann Spreng), Colmar (founded by Jörg Wickram in 1546), Breslau (founded in 1571; Wolfgang Herold and Adam Puschman), Strasbourg (re-established 1597; Peter Pfort, Cyriac and Wolfhart Spangenberg [Lycosthenes Psellionoros Andropediacus]), Mainz, Freiburg, Nördlingen, Ulm and Memmingen (see fig.1). In addition there were guilds in Austria (Schwaz, Wels, Steyr, Eferding) and Moravia (Iglau). That in Ulm existed until 1839, and the last Meistersinger of Memmingen died in 1922.

4. THE THEMES OF THE POETRY. The majority of lieder surviving from before the Reformation deal with religious subjects, primarily the Virgin Mary, the Trinity, Christmas, the Passion, the Resurrection and the Creation. In addition there are songs in praise of Meistergesang, invitations to song, riddles, poems on the seven liberal arts, and a few narrative poems. Political subjects, so common in the verses of the *Sangspruchdichter*, are absent from Meistergesang, most probably because they were forbidden from the beginning by the censorship which customarily operated in the cities.

Meistergesang came into the service of the Reformation, becoming predominantly Lutheran, through Hans Sachs, who with his contemporaries and followers aimed to incorporate Luther's translation of the Bible into verse, keeping it unchanged in language and content wherever possible. At the same time, secular Meistergesang began to become more important (fables, farces, historical material, narratives of medieval and humanistic origin, and songs about Meistergesang itself). During the late flowering of Nuremberg Meistergesang, around 1600, the development of larger song cycles seems to have been characteristic, above all with Benedict von Watt and Ambrosius Metzger.

5. THE MUSIC. Meisterlieder always consist of an odd number of stanzas, the minimum being three. The Meistersinger actually referred to their lieder as *Bare* (singular *Bar*; *see also* BAR FORM). The most important formal musical feature of the Meisterlieder is that they are not composed and sung in an individual verse form, each with its own melody. The composers almost always made use of existing *Töne* (singular *Ton*, synonymous with *Weise*), many of which had not been written by the Meistersinger themselves. By 1600 the number of different, traditionally accumulated *Töne* stood at about 600. Some stemmed from the *Sangspruchdichter* of the 13th to 15th centuries; others were in the course of time attributed to the *alte Meister*, although the true originators of the *unechte* (not genuine) *Töne* were obscure Meistersinger. Thus from the 15th century to the 17th, for example, over 30 *Töne* were ascribed to Frauenlob, although only seven of them can actually be traced back to him. Finally, from the 15th century onwards, numerous *Töne* were composed by the Meistersinger whose name they bore.

The Meistersinger's *Töne* normally consist of at least seven, but usually 12 or more, verse lines with an end rhyme. Most *Töne* have about 20 lines, but in the 16th and 17th centuries there were also occasional huge *Töne* with more than 100 lines. The shortest line consisted of one syllable, while the longest must contain no more than 13 syllables, as each line should be sung in one breath, according to a 16th-century rule. (But some *Töne* have longer lines.) The rhyme scheme is both free and varied.

The verse and melody of the *Töne* are always constructed as follows: after the first part (first *Stollen*) follows the second part (second *Stollen*), which corresponds exactly both metrically and musically. The first and second *Stollen* together form the *Aufgesang*. Then follows the third part, the *Abgesang*, which is metrically and musically different. In principle, the length of individual parts is left open. Among the *Sangspruchdichter* in the 13th century this *AAB* structure was strictly adhered to and later taken over by the Meistersinger. In present-day German this verse form is called *Kanzonenform*; musicologists speak of BAR FORM. Compare the ten-line *Veilchenweise* (ex.1) by Hans Folz to which is added the first stanza of a farce composed by Hans Sachs on 20 April 1546. The melody of the last lines of its *Abgesang* is identical with the last two lines of the *Stollen*. Reference at the end of the *Abgesang* to the melody of the *Aufgesang* is characteristic of many *Meistertöne*, and it was not unusual for the whole of the *Stollen* melody to be repeated at the end of the *Abgesang* (a repetition referred to as the third *Stollen*).

Ex.1
*Ton:* Hans Folz: *Veilchenweise, D-B germ.f.25, p.170*
Text: Hans Sachs: *Der narr mit dem wintmachen* (after Goetze and Drescher)

Ein car - di - nal
Die sün schin hais,

Rait auf ein mal
Im rûn der schwais

In walt nach waid - mons sa - chen.
Ue - ber sein fai - sten pa - chen.

Als er kam haim vnd sas zw disch,

Da zaigt er auf den fle - der - wisch,

Man solt im frisch

Ein küe - len win - de ma - chen.

The Meistersinger melodies are all monophonic, even in the 16th century and after. They were always performed unaccompanied, normally by a solo voice, but occasionally by a chorus. In their musical work the Meistersinger carry through to the 18th century the German monophonic song tradition which can be traced back to the late 12th century, in particular the tradition of the *Sangspruchdichter*. Their historical orientation becomes more and more of an anachronism and explains why Meistergesang was a peripheral phenomenon in music history, at least from the second half of the 16th century: the general development of music bypassed the Meistergesang tradition, for the Meistersinger firmly rejected all its innovations.

Only a few of the more essential characteristics of Meistergesang melody can be described here. The manuscripts normally transmit the music without any indication of rhythm: the occasional suggestions of mensural notation in certain 16th-century sources are often contradictory and have little authority. One may assume that the normal rule was 'declamatory' rhythm determined by the text. Modal rhythm, whose application Gennrich extended to include Meistergesang, should be dismissed: the sources give not the slightest indication of it.

In their tonality the melodies are extremely varied and scarcely open to any meaningful generalization, apart from the observation that Meistersinger melodies cannot be explained in terms of church modes (see

Schumann, 1972). The stylistic development is more easily discussed because several melodies come from the *Sangspruchdichter* of the 13th and 14th centuries and survive in 14th-century sources as well as in Meistersinger manuscripts of the 15th to 17th centuries (see the example of Klingsor's *Schwarzer Ton* in the articles TON (i) and SOURCES, MS, §III). Comparing the versions of a single melody from manuscripts of different centuries can provide important clues to the characteristics of the melodic style. Variants in the melismas stand out (ex.2). Apparently melismas were frequent in the 14th century, extremely rare in the 15th and far more common again in the 16th and 17th. But in their use of these melismas the 16th- and 17th-century manuscripts are closer to the 15th century than to the 14th: they use them primarily to mark the ends of the melodic lines whereas in the 14th century the melismas are much more evenly distributed across the whole line. Particularly long melismas really began to appear only in the 16th century and were used increasingly afterwards.

Ex.2 Heinrich von Meissen: *Würgendrüssel* (opening)

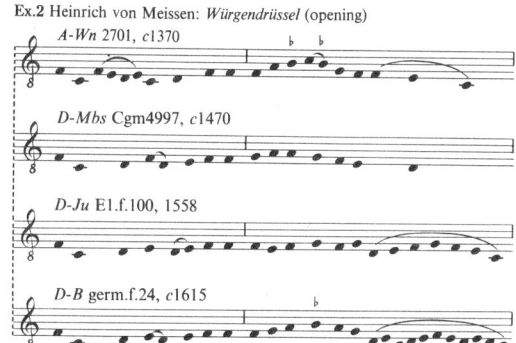

A-Wn 2701, c1370

D-Mbs Cgm4997, c1470

D-Ju El.f.100, 1558

D-B germ.f.24, c1615

The vocal range often seems much smaller in the later centuries than in the 14th. Further, there are more large leaps (of a 4th and more) from the 15th century on. This is evidently symptomatic of a changed stylistic ideal: elegance of melody was preferred in the 14th century, as the use of melisma shows, but later the emphasis was more towards clarity of movement from one note to the next.

The transmission of the melodies has both written and oral characteristics. Many Meistersinger were not musically literate: they were advised to learn the melodies by heart and remember them. This led to many unconsciously introduced variants of the original melodic conception. On the other hand the melodies were doubtless also worked over, improved and adapted when they were written down, as is particularly clear from melodies whose written history stretches back to the 14th century. It is difficult to generalize about the agreements and differences in the melodic lines in versions from different centuries. Some melodies remain substantially the same in spite of the changes in melodic preference already described, but for others the original melodic version is scarcely perceptible in later versions. In some cases it is as though the old melodies have been forgotten and new ones have been written to the metrical scheme. Over the centuries the melodies were adapted, consciously as well as unconsciously, to bring them into the most rational and easily perceptible forms with regular repetition of the individual melodic sections. Often structures which had originally been extremely complicated were simplified enormously: for performer and listener alike, simplicity of form was an ideal.

There is still much work to be done on the degree of contact between the style of Meistergesang and of other musical forms in the 14th, 15th and 16th centuries, in particular the German Gesellschaftslied and folksong. Some melodic similarities have been established between Meisterlieder melodies and Protestant hymns; but the the connection has yet to be defined precisely. Some particularly popular *Meistertöne* were actually used as hymns in the 16th century but in other cases of similarity the connection more probably rests merely on common usage of existing melodic models and has nothing to do with any direct interchange. It also remains to be shown whether the melodies of any of the Meistersinger have particular melodic characteristics or personal styles. There are several indications that this may be so.

6. ORGANIZATION OF THE GUILDS AND PERFORMANCE OF LIEDER AT THE CONCERTS. The extant *Schulordnungen* (school regulations) from the 16th and 17th centuries offer an insight into the organization of the Meistersinger guilds (*Gesellschaften*) as well as into the customary practices of the concerts (*Singschulen*). The following sketch comes from the Nuremberg *Schulordnung* in the 16th and 17th centuries; the other guilds were basically similar. It is not known whether the Nuremberg guild was organized in this way in the 15th century.

The 12 oldest singers formed the nucleus of the Nuremberg guild. The directors were the three chosen *Merker* (markers), of whom the youngest functioned as clerk. Next came the two elected *Büchsenmeister* (treasurers), who presented annual accounts to the guild each year on the Sunday before St Thomas's Day (21 December). On the same day membership fees were paid, elections took place, and new members were received.

A public concert was normally held once a month on a Sunday after the midday service. From the 16th century in Nuremberg the singing took place in various disused churches. (St Katherine's, which appears in Wagner's *Meistersinger*, was not available to the Nuremberg Meistersinger until after 1620.) The concerts were advertised by posters in the town (see fig.2). The focal point of the concert was the *Hauptsingen* (main performance), at which were allowed only lieder based on the scriptures and whose *Ton* was at least 20 lines long. The performance was always solo. During it the markers sat in a cubicle (*Gemerk*), which was draped in black material. Their task was to judge whether the song being performed conformed both in content and language to the Lutheran Bible. In addition, they noted whether both text and performance conformed to the strict rules of the *Tabulatur* and whether the melody was correctly performed. They listed every error, and the singer with the fewest errors was the winner. If several had the same number of mistakes or if there were none at all, the singers had to compete until there was an obvious winner. As a prize he received a silver chain hung with coins, the largest of which depicted King David, the patron of the Meistersinger. The winner was allowed to keep the chain until the next concert. In addition, he was allowed to be one of the *Merker* at the next concert. Besides the public *Hauptsingen*, the

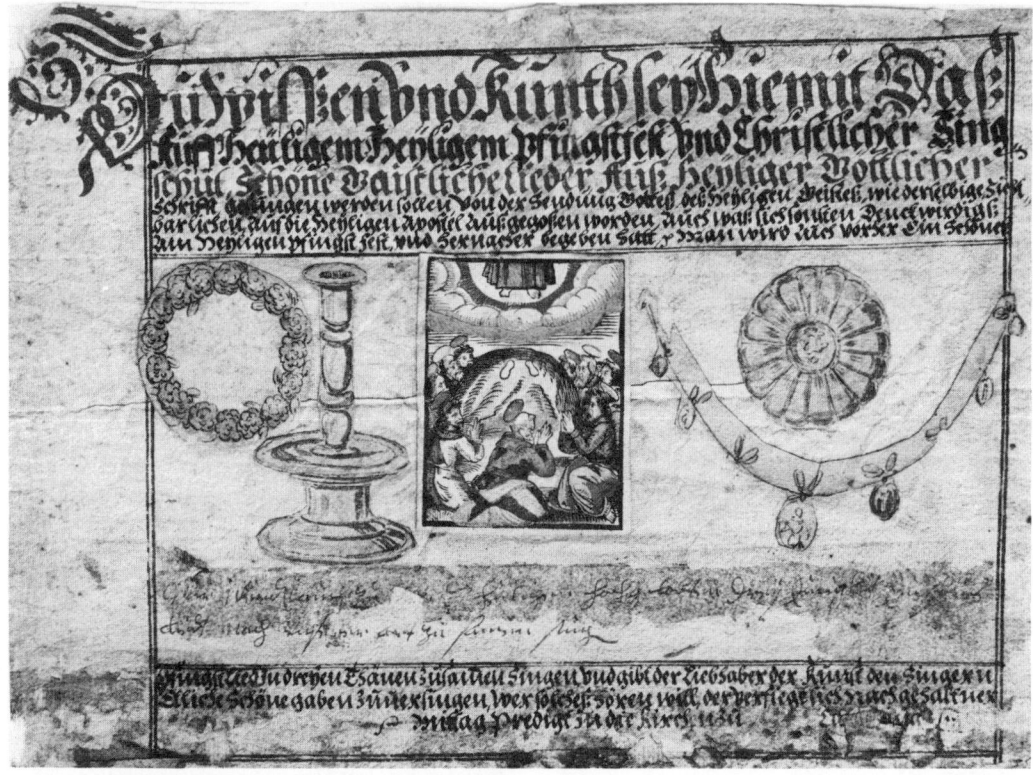

2. *Poster advertising a concert of the Meistersinger of Nuremberg* (D-Nst)

Meistersinger usually held their own private *Zechsingen* at an inn, at which secular Meisterlieder were sung. This concert also retained the character of a competition.

Whoever wished to become a member of the guild first of all studied (was a *Schüler*) with one of its members; his main task was to learn a number of *Töne* and the most important rules of the *Tabulatur*. The widely held opinion that one could become a Meistersinger only by composing a *Ton* is not correct: many highly respected Meistersinger never composed a *Ton*. Even the writing of song texts was apparently not mandatory: many Meistersinger seem not to have been poets; they could perfectly well limit themselves to the performance of other people's songs.

7. SPRUCHGEDICHTE AND STAGE PLAYS. The literary activity of the Meistersinger was not solely confined to the composition and performance of Meisterlieder. In addition, some Meistersinger wrote *Spruchgedichte* (poems in rhymed couplets) and theatrical works. The *Spruchgedichte* were intended for spoken performance and were often printed. They dealt with a wide range of subjects, religious problems as well as political events, historical narratives and farcical or sentimental occurrences, advice for leading a good life, poems in honour of a city, etc. In many places the Meistersinger guilds publicly performed dramatic works. Hans Folz in the 15th century and Hans Sachs in the 16th were by far the most productive artists in these areas, which strictly speaking had nothing to do with Meistergesang itself. From the 15th century until the 17th there were numerous writers of *Spruchgedichte* and plays who were not Meistersinger.

### BIBLIOGRAPHY

#### BIBLIOGRAPHICAL

A. Taylor and F. H. Ellis: *A Bibliography of Meistergesang*, Indiana University Studies, cxiii (Bloomington, Ind., 1936)

A. Taylor: *The Literary History of Meistergesang* (New York, 1937/R1966)

J. Janota: 'Neue Forschungen zur deutschen Dichtung des Spätmittelalters (1230–1500), 1957–1968', *Deutsche Vierteljahrsschrift für Literaturwissenschaft und Geistesgeschichte*, xlv (1971), Sonderheft

B. Könneker: *Hans Sachs* (Stuttgart, 1971)

B. Nagel: *Meistersang* (Stuttgart, 2/1971)

N. Holzberg: *Hans-Sachs-Bibliographie* (Nuremberg, 1976)

#### EDITIONS

A. von Keller, ed.: *C. Spangenberg: Von der Musica und den Meistersängern* (Stuttgart, 1861)

K. Bartsch, ed.: *Meisterlieder der Kolmarer Handschrift* (Stuttgart, 1862/R1962)

R. Jonas, ed.: *A. Puschman: Gründlicher Bericht des deutschen Meistergesangs* (Halle, 1888)

E. Goetze and C. Drescher, eds.: *H. Sachs: Sämtliche Fabeln und Schwänke* (Halle, 1893–1913)

P. Runge, ed.: *Die Sangesweisen der Colmarer Handschrift* (Leipzig, 1896/R1965)

K. Drescher, ed.: *Nürnberger Meistersinger Protokolle von 1575 bis 1689* (Stuttgart, 1897/R1963)

——: *Das Gemerkbüchlein des Hans Sachs (1555–1561) nebst einem Anhange: die Nürnberger Meistersinger-Protokolle von 1595–1605* (Halle, 1898)

G. Münzer, ed.: *Das Singebuch des Adam Puschman* (Leipzig, 1906/R1970)

A. L. Mayer, ed.: *Die Meisterlieder des Hans Folz* (Berlin, 1908)

F. Frauchiger: *Dresden M 13: a Fifteenth-century Collection of Religious Meisterlieder* (diss., U. of Chicago, 1938)

C. Grönlund: *Studien zu Peter Probst, dem Nürnberger Dramatiker und Meistersinger, mit einer Neuausgabe des Textes der Lieder und Sprüche* (Lund, 1945)

C. H. Bell: *Georg Hager: a Meistersinger of Nürnberg (1552–1634)* (Berkeley, 1947)

——: *The Meistersingerschule at Memmingen and its 'Kurtze Entwerffung'* (Berkeley, 1952)

B. Nagel, ed.: *Meistersang: Meisterlieder und Singschulzeugnisse* (Stuttgart, 1965)

A. Vizkelety, ed.: *W. Spangenberg: Sämtliche Werke*, i (Berlin, 1971)

E. and H. Kiepe, eds.: *Epochen der deutschen Lyrik*, ii: *Gedichte, 1300–1500* (Munich, 1972)

H. Brunner, ed.: *J. C. Wagenseil: Buch von der Meister-Singer holdseligen Kunst* (Göppingen, 1975)

H. Brunner, U. Müller and F. V. Spechtler, eds.: *Die Kolmarer Liederhandschrift* (Göppingen, 1976)

H. Brunner and J. Rettelbach, eds.: *Die Töne der Meistersinger: die Handschriften Will III.792, 793, 794, 795, 796 der Stadtbibliothek Nürnberg* (Göppingen, 1978)

#### LITERATURE

J. C. Wagenseil: 'Buch von der Meister-Singer holdseligen Kunst', *De civitate noribergensi commentatio* (Altdorf, 1697/R1975)

J. Grimm: *Über den altdeutschen Meistergesang* (Göttingen, 1811)

F. Schnorr von Carolsfeld: *Zur Geschichte des deutschen Meistersanges* (1872)

——: 'Zwei neue Meistersängerhandschriften', *Archiv für Litteraturgeschichte*, iii (1874), 49

K. J. Schröer: 'Meistersinger in Österreich', *Germanistische Studien: Supplement zur Germania*, ii (Vienna, 1875), 197–239

E. Goetze: 'Monographie über den Meistersänger Adam Puschman von Gorlitz, nebst Beiträgen zur Geschichte des deutschen Meistergesanges', *Neues lausitzisches Magazin*, liii (1877), 59–157

H. Widmann: *Zur Geschichte und Literatur des Meistergesanges in Oberösterreich* (Vienna, 1885)

C. Mey: *Der Meistersinger in Geschichte und Kunst* (Leipzig, 1892, 2/1901)

T. Hampe: 'Spruchsprecher, Meistersinger und Hochzeitslader, vornehmlich in Nürnberg', *Mitteilungen aus dem Germanischen Nationalmuseum* (Nuremberg, 1894), 25, 60

*Hans Sachs-Forschungen: Festschrift zur vierhundertsten Geburtsfeier des Dichters* (Nuremberg, 1894)

A. Hartmann: *Deutsche Meisterlieder-Handschriften in Ungarn* (Munich, 1894)

F. W. E. Roth: 'Zur Geschichte der Meistersänger zu Mainz und Nürnberg', *Zeitschrift für Kulturgeschichte*, iii (1896), 261

A. Dreyer: 'Hans Sachs in München und die gleichzeitigen Münchener Meistersänger', *Analecta germanica: Herman Paul . . . dargebracht* (Amberg, 1906), 323–90

W. Nagel: *Studien zur Geschichte der Meistersänger* (Langensalza, 1909)

J. Bolte: 'Der Nürnberger Meistersinger Hans Vogel', *Archiv für das Studium der neueren Sprachen und Literaturen*, cxxvii (1911), 273

R. Staiger: *Benedict von Watt* (Leipzig, 1913)

W. Brandl: *Sebastian Wild: ein Augsburger Meistersinger* (Weimar, 1914)

R. Pfeiffer: *Die Meistersingerschule zu Augsburg und der Homerübersetzer Johannes Spreng* (Munich, 1919)

F. Eberth: *Die Liedweisen der Kolmarer Handschrift und ihre Einordnung und Stellung in der Entwicklungsgeschichte der deutschen Liedweise im 14.–16. Jahrhundert* (diss., U. of Göttingen, 1933)

H. O. Burger: *Die Kunstauffassung der frühen Meistersinger* (Berlin, 1936)

M. J. Schroeder: *Mary-Verse in Meistergesang* (Washington, DC, 1942/R1970)

F. H. Ellis: 'Analysis of the Berlin MS Germ.Quart 414', *Publications of the Modern Language Association of America*, lxi (1946), 947–96

M. J. Schroeder: 'Topical Outline of Subject-matter in the Berlin MS Germ.Quart 414', *Publications of the Modern Language Association of America*, lxi (1946), 997

B. Nagel: *Der deutsche Meistersang* (Heidelberg, 1952)

H. Rosenfeld: 'Der historische Meistersinger Sixt Bechmesser und der Meistergesang', *Euphorion*, xlvii (1953), 271

G. Trathnigg: 'Die Welser Meistersinger-Handschriften', *Jb des Musealvereins Wels* (1954), 127–80

E. Geiger: *Der Meistergesang des Hans Sachs* (Berne, 1956)

F. Schnell: *Zur Geschichte der Meistersingerschule zu Augsburg* (Augsburg, 1958)

F. Streinz: *Die Singschule in Iglau und ihre Beziehungen zum allgemeinen deutschen Meistergesang* (Munich, 1958)

I. Urban: 'Antike Dichtung in den weltlichen Liedern des Meistersingers J. Spreng', *Euphorion*, lv (1961), 146

H. Müller: 'Zur Blütezeit des Strassburger Meistergesangs 1591 bis zum Dreissigjährigen Krieg', *Zeitschrift für die Geschichte des Oberrheins*, cx (1962), 151

C. Petzsch: 'Studien zum Meistergesang des Hans Folz', *Deutsche Vierteljahrsschrift für Literaturwissenschaft und Geistesgeschichte*, xxxvi (1962), 190–247

——: 'Zu Albrecht Lesch, Jörg Schechner und zur Frage der Münchener Meistersingerschule', *Zeitschrift für deutsches Altertum*, xcvi (1965), 121

——: 'Zur sogenannten, Hans Folz zugeschriebenen Meistergesangsreform', *Beiträge zur Geschichte der deutschen Sprache und Literatur*, lxxxviii (Tübingen, 1966), 110–142

H. Fischer: 'Hans Folz: Altes und Neues zur Geschichte seines Lebens und seiner Schriften', *Zeitschrift für deutsches Altertum*, xcv (1966), 212

G. Freistadt: *Zur Abhängigkeit der Liederhandschriften Kolmar und Donaueschingen* (diss., U. of Göttingen, 1966)

B. Nagel, ed.: *Der deutsche Meistersang* (Darmstadt, 1967)

H. Brunner: 'Epenmelodien', *Formen mittelalterlicher Literatur: Siegfried Beyschlag zu seinem 65. Geburtstag* (Göppingen, 1970), 149

C. Petzsch: 'Parat-(Barant-)Weise, Bar und Barform', *AMw*, xxviii (1971), 33

G. Pfeiffer, ed.: *Nürnberg: Geschichte einer europäischen Stadt* (Munich, 1971)

E. Schumann: *Stilwandel und Gestaltveränderung im Meistersang: vergleichende Untersuchungen zur Musik der Meistersinger* (Kassel, 1972)

R. Münster and H. Schmid: *Musik in Bayern*, i: *Bayerische Musikgeschichte* (Tutzing, 1972)

B. Wachinger: *Sängerkrieg: Untersuchungen zur Spruchdichtung des 13. Jahrhunderts* (Munich, 1973)

G. Mayer: *Probleme der Sangspruchüberlieferung* (diss., U. of Munich, 1974)

H. Brunner: *Die alten Meister: Studien zu Überlieferung und Rezeption der mittelhochdeutschen Sangspruchdichter im Spätmittelalter und in der frühen Neuzeit* (Munich, 1975)

B. Stäblein: *Schriftbild der einstimmigen Musik*, Musikgeschichte in Bildern, iii/4 (Leipzig, 1975)

C. Petzsch: 'Jörg Wickrams Singergesellschaft und ihre grosse Liederhandschrift', *Annuaire de Colmar*, xxv (1975–6), 91

——: 'Singschule: ein Beitrag zur Geschichte des Begriffes', *Zeitschrift für deutsche Philologie*, xcv (1976), 400

B. A. Taylor: 'Der Beitrag des Hans Sachs und seiner Nürnberger Vorgänger zu der Entwicklung der Meistersinger-Tabulatur', *Hans Sachs und Nürnberg: Festschrift zum 400. Todestages* (Nuremberg, 1976)

——: 'Emendation and Misinterpretation: an Examination of Lied XXXIII of the Kolmarer Handschrift', *Seminar: a Journal of Germanic Studies*, xii (1976), 129

H. Kugler: *Handwerk und Meistergesang* (Göttingen, 1977)

HORST BRUNNER

**Meistre, Matthaeus le.** *See* LE MAISTRE, MATTHAEUS.

**Mejer, Johann David.** *See* MAYER, JOHANN DAVID.

**Mejorana.** A Panamanian dance genre. It consists of a quatrain rhymed *abba* (the *redondilla*) which sets forth a basic textual theme developed subsequently in four *décimas*, each using one line of the quatrain. The characteristically descending melodies are often performed with falsetto and melisma. A collective dance like the *cuadrilla*, the *mejorana* is accompanied by the *mejoranera* (a small five-string guitar) and the larger *bocona*, which create hemiola rhythms in combination with the melodies of the violin and the male voice. The *mejoranera* guitar is also called *mejorana*.

WILLIAM GRADANTE

**Mejoranera** [*mejorana*]. A small, short-necked five-string guitar. It is normally made of cedar, with nylon strings. It is tuned either 'by 6' or 'by 25' as in ex.1. In the 1970s it was replacing the similarly shaped four-string *socavón* (or *bocona*), and it typically provides a strummed accompaniment for rural Panamanian dances including *punto*, *cumbia* and *mejorana* (dance and song).

Ex.1 *Mejoranera*: alternative tunings.

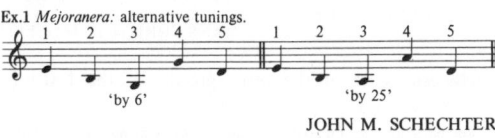

JOHN M. SCHECHTER

**Mel.** A subjective unit of pitch based on judgments of melodic sequences of notes. The relationship between the mel scale for an average listener and the physical frequency scale is given in SOUND, §4.

**Mel, Gaudio.** Possibly an alternative name for CLAUDE GOUDIMEL.

**Mel** [Melle], **Rinaldo del** [Raynaldus, Renatus, René, Renerus] (*b* Mechlin [now Mechelen], *c*1554; *d c*1598). Flemish composer, mainly active in Italy. He was of a landed family whose fortunes were closely linked to the Duchy of Lorraine. In 1547 his parents were living in Mechlin, where his father was chamberlain to the Duchess of Lorraine with responsibility for the management of nearby ducal holdings. After the conquests of Henri II of France, Christine of Denmark, mother of the ten-year-old Renée of Lorraine, and the Duchess of D'Arschot were in Mechlin in 1554; in the dedication of his *Sacrae cantiones* (1588), Mel mentioned that he was named after Renée. He was probably born in 1554 and was thus eight (the average age of admittance) when in 1562 he entered the choir school of St Rombaud Cathedral, where he studied under Séverin Cornet. After completing his schooling, probably in 1572, he went to Lisbon, where, according to Baini, he was employed as *maestro di cappella* at court. It is not known whether he actually functioned as such, or, as Doorslaer suggested, was sent there to mature in the protected environment that the Lisbon court (related by marriage to the Lorraine court) would have provided for the young son of a favoured family.

After Spain annexed Portugal in 1580 Mel went to Rome, where his name appears in that year on a subscription list for two new bells for the Flemish church, S Maria in Campo Santo. Whether or not he studied composition with Palestrina as Baini claimed, his first published works indicate that he was well acquainted with Palestrina's style. The title-pages and dedications of his printed books show that in addition to his continued allegiance to Lorraine (and, by Renée's marriage, to the Bavarian court), he enjoyed the friendship and patronage of the Valignani, the Henrici and Cardinal Gabriel Paleotto. He was in Chieti in 1583–4 and travelled north to Venice in January. On 6 July 1584 he accepted the appointment of *maestro di cappella* at Rieti Cathedral, but his absences on personal affairs angered the church authorities and he remained in the post for less than a year.

During the next six years Mel travelled a good deal, spending parts of 1585 in Rome and Aquila, 1586 in Magliano Capo di Sabina, 1587–8 in Liège (stopping in Venice in January 1587, and arriving in Liège in July to assume the post of *maestro di cappella* to Duke Ernst of Bavaria) and 1588–9 in Antwerp. By 1591 he had returned to Italy and entered the service of Paleotto at Magliano. Paleotto had recently been placed in charge of the diocese of Sabina; he was responsible for many improvements in Magliano during his six-year governorship and appointed Mel music director of the cathedral and the newly founded seminary. Mel remained in the area, apart from short trips to Rome and nearby Calvi, until the end of August 1596, when, according to the dedication of his *Madrigaletti spirituali a tre voci*, he intended to depart for Tortona in order to take title to lands granted him that year by Dorothy of Lorraine. The fact that eight new chansons by him were published in an Antwerp collection (*RISM* 1597[10]) suggests that he may by that time have returned to the Netherlands.

Mel was well educated and a prolific composer whose aristocratic lineage and connections seem to have ensured him at least a modest fame. His sacred pieces show him to have been a craftsman, well trained in Netherlands counterpoint and a diligent imitator of the Palestrinian style. His secular works illustrate a growing tendency to concentrate melodic interest in the treble part (a contemporary statement that he was responsible for the invention of a new kind of polyphony in which the musical structure was borne by the soprano part while the other voices were directed 'cantare e sostenere la mula', is somewhat obtuse). Like many Roman composers, he was fond of cyclic madrigals, and set in their entirety such famous canzoni as Petrarch's *Standomi un giorno*. His eight four- and five-stanza cycles included in his books of three-part *Madrigaletti* are perhaps of greater historical note – semi-popular material destined for local amateurs and quasi-religious fraternities. They are characterized by textural contrasts of chordal declamation alternating with imitative passages, the latter usually consisting of two voices moving in parallel 3rds or 6ths with the third voice entering in imitation a breve or two later. In *Tre gratiosi amanti*, a typical cycle, sectional repetition plays an important role. His three-part writing is diatonic and uses many progressions based on chords with roots a 5th apart.

WORKS

*(published in Venice unless otherwise stated)*

SECULAR VOCAL

Madrigali, 4–6vv (1583)
Il primo libro de madrigali, 6vv (1584)
Il primo libro de madrigali, 5vv (1584)
Il primo libro de madrigali, 5, 6vv (1585²⁶)
Il primo libro de madrigaletti, 3vv (1585)
Il secondo libro delli madrigaletti, 3vv (1586)
Il terzo libro de madrigali, 5vv (1587)
Madrigali, 6vv (Antwerp, 1588)
Il secondo libro de madrigali, 6vv (1593) [incl. works from 1588 edn.]
Il quinto libro de madrigali, 5vv (1594)
Il terzo libro delli madrigaletti, 3vv (1594)
Il terzo libro delli madrigali, 6vv (1595) [incl. works from 1588 edn.]
Madrigaletti spirituali . . . libro quarto, 3vv (1596)

Madrigali . . . libro quarto, 4, 5vv, lost, cited in Giunta catalogue (see Kast)

6 chansons, 4 madrigals, 2 canzonets, 3 other works: 1586¹⁰, 1595⁶, 1595¹⁴, 1597¹⁰, 1597¹⁵, 1600¹⁰, 1601⁵, 1605²¹, 1607¹⁴

SACRED VOCAL

Liber primus motettorum, 4–8vv (1581)
Liber tertius . . . motectorum, 5, 6vv (1585⁴)
Sacrae cantiones . . . cum litania de Beatae Virginis Mariae, 5–8, 12vv (Antwerp, 1588)
Liber quintus motectorum, 6, 8, 12vv (1595)

16 spiritual canzonets, 12 motets, 4–6vv, litany, 5vv, 2 other works, 6vv: 1586², 1586³, 1588², 1590⁵, 1591¹³, 1591²⁶, 1592⁵, 1596², 1598², 1599⁶, 1610²; litany ed. F. Commer, Musica sacra, xxvi (Regensburg, 1885), and R. von Maldeghem, Trésor musical, xii (Brussels, 1876)

Works in *A-Wn, D-As, Bds, Dlb, Mbs, MÜp, Nla, GB-Lbm, Lcm, I-Rvat, PL-WRu, USSR-KA*, Turchini Library, Naples

BIBLIOGRAPHY

G. Baini: *Memorie storico-critiche della vita e delle opere di Giovanni Pierluigi da Palestrina* (Rome, 1828/R1966), i, 23; ii, 126f
R. Eitner: 'Mitteilungen', *MMg*, xx (1888), 190
G. van Doorslaer: 'René del Mel, compositeur du XVIme siècle', *Annales de l'Académie royale d'archéologie de Belgique*, 6th ser., ix (1921), 221–88
P. Magnette: 'Essai sur la musique et les musiciens au Pays de Liège', *RMI*, xxviii (1921), 217
A. Sacchetti-Sassetti: 'La cappella musicale del Duomo di Rieti', *NA*, xvii (1940), 141; xviii (1941), 49, 71
G. Reese: 'Maldeghem and his Buried Treasure: a Bibliographical Study', *Notes*, vi (1948–9), 109
P. Kast: 'Die Musikdrucke des Cataloges Giunta von 1604', *AnMc*, no.2 (1965), 41
P. A. Myers: *An Analytical Study of the Italian Cyclic Madrigals published by Composers working in Rome, ca. 1540–1614* (diss., U. of Illinois, 1971), 226ff, 322f

PATRICIA ANN MYERS

**Melachrino, George (Miltiades)** (*b* London, 1 May 1909; *d* London, 18 June 1965). English orchestra leader, composer and arranger. After studies at Trinity College of Music, London, where he formed a dance orchestra (1939), he formed the Melachrino Strings in 1945. This 50-piece ensemble became noted in Europe and the USA for its radio broadcasts and recordings of light music, including *Music for Relaxation*, *Music for Two People Alone* and *Rêverie*; it was famous for its sweet, sentimental style, which was widely imitated.

**Melanchthon [Schwarzerd], Philipp** (*b* Bretten, 16 Feb 1497; *d* Wittenberg, 19 April 1560). German evangelical theologian. He was a great-nephew of the humanist Reuchlin. He became a student at Heidelberg University in 1509, transferring in 1512 to Tübingen, where he took the Master's degree in 1514. In 1518 he took up a post teaching Greek at Wittenberg, where, influenced by Luther, he took the degree of Bachelor of Theology in 1520. In the same year he was appointed professor there, remaining for the rest of his life. His regulations for education in Saxony, which came into effect in 1528 and which became standard in other areas of Germany, influenced decisively the curriculum of German evangelical universities and Lateinschulen. These regulations set aside an hour each day for music. He was also involved in drawing up the educational regulations for other regions and eventually earned the sobriquet 'Praeceptor Germaniae'. He expounded his views on music in various introductions to published musical works: Rhau's *Selectae harmoniae* (*RISM* 1538¹) and *Officia de Nativitate* (*RISM* 1545⁵), *Zehn deutsche Psalmen Davids* (Wittenberg, 1552) by Johann Reuschlin and Lossius's Cantional of 1553. Melanchthon considered music to be the 'worthy practice of piety', an aid 'to the strengthening of faith', and even a means to the understanding of God. He influenced Protestant hymn writing only indirectly, with such Latin hymns as *Vespera iam venit*, which were also translated into German. His books on rhetoric doubtless encouraged the application of the rules of rhetoric to Protestant church music. Among his students at Wittenberg University were Adrianus Petit Coclico, Sixt Dietrich, Georg Forster and Lucas Lossius. He had a close association with the Wittenberg printer Georg Rhau and the Saxon Kapellmeister Johann Walter.

BIBLIOGRAPHY

F. Blume: *Die evangelische Kirchenmusik*, HMw, x (1931, rev. 2/1965 as *Geschichte der evangelischen Kirchenmusik*)
W. Gurlitt: 'Johannes Walter und die Musik der Reformationszeit', *Luther-Jb*, xv (1933), 1–112
——: 'Musik und Rhetorik', *Helicon: revue internationale des problèmes généraux de la littérature*, v (1943), 67
W. Lueken: *Lebensbilder der Liederdichter und Melodisten* (Göttingen, 1957)
F. Krautwurst: 'Philipp Melanchthon und die Musik', *Gottesdienst und Kirchenmusik* (1960), 109
K. W. Niemöller: *Untersuchungen zu Musikpflege und Musikunterricht an den deutschen Lateinschulen vom ausgehenden Mittelalter bis um 1600* (Regensburg, 1969)

HANS-CHRISTIAN MÜLLER

**Melanesia.** One of the three groups of the PACIFIC ISLANDS.

1. Introduction. 2. Fiji: (i) Instruments (ii) Forms and functions (iii) Composition (iv) Musical structure. 3. New Caledonia. 4. New Hebrides: (i) Genres and musical structure (ii) Instruments (iii) Acculturated music. 5. Papua New Guinea: (i) General (ii) The sing-sing (iii) Wailing (iv) Instruments. 6. Solomon Islands: (i) Bougainville (Papuan-speaking peoples) (ii) Malaita (Melanesian-speaking peoples) (iii) Ontong Java (Polynesian-speaking peoples).

1. INTRODUCTION. Melanesia (Gk. *melas*: 'black', *nēsos*: 'island') lies south of the equator and north-east of Australia, between Indonesia to the west and Polynesia to the east (for map, *see* PACIFIC ISLANDS, fig.1). Geographically the major island aggregates are New Guinea; the Bismarck Archipelago (including the Admiralty group, New Britain and New Ireland); the Solomon Islands; the New Hebrides; New Caledonia (and Loyalty Islands); and the Fiji Islands. There are also many small island groups. Not all boundaries of governmental units of the mid-1970s coincide with these geographic designations.

The people and languages in Melanesia are now quite diverse, although they first originated in south-east Asia. This diversity reflects both the great length of time between the initial human settlement of New Guinea (estimated at 30,000 years ago) and the much later settlements of most of the other islands (within the past 5000 years) and long periods of isolation. Scattered post-settlement contacts with Malay and Chinese sailors preceded European discovery of Melanesia by several centuries. European contacts were themselves diverse in national origin, purpose and extent of influence. Some anthropologists stress diversity above all other characteristics of Melanesia and eschew generalizations about aspects of culture within the area. Furthermore, only a small number of the many music cultures have been studied. Political developments towards self rule, an important element of change in the 1970s, will affect not only the style and repertory but also the role of music in these societies.

Papua New Guinea, an independent nation in the British Commonwealth since 1975, includes the island of New Guinea east of 141° E (the western portion being part of the Republic of Indonesia), the Bismarck Archipelago, Bougainville (geographically one of the Solomon Islands), and small islands near these. The population includes both Papuans and Melanesians, and a small percentage of others. Papua New Guinea presents the greatest cultural variety within one government in all the Pacific Islands countries (*see* PACIFIC ISLANDS, §3). Some peoples in the mountain interior (like a few mountain tribes in the Philippines and South America) have been totally isolated from contact with European culture until the 1960s or 1970s – even their contact with peoples of the New Guinea coast was infrequent until after World War II. In contrast, the people of the Trobriand Islands (about 880 km from the island of New Guinea) and other islands in the Massim area at the southern end of New Guinea have traditionally engaged in a far-flung inter-island ceremonial trade (the 'Kula ring'). In much of Papua New Guinea, traditional music and dance is performed in traditional contexts; where Christian influence (both Catholic and Protestant) is strong, hymn tunes are sung; and soon after World War II in cosmopolitan Port Moresby and some coastal towns the 'cup-tea sing-sing' (an urban substitute for the social functions of the traditional village sing-sing) and, later, the beer halls became the centre for performances of pan-Pacific pop that were influenced by the Philippines and Australia as well as Hawaii.

The Solomon Islands (formerly the British Solomon Islands Protectorate) achieved independence in 1978. Most inhabitants are Melanesians (the Papuans of the north-western Solomons being citizens of Papua New Guinea), but there are also some islands, called Polynesian outliers, settled by Polynesians at a later period than the Papuan and Melanesian settlements, and there is a post-World War II settlement of Micronesians from the Gilbert Islands. Traditional music and dance is still performed in traditional contexts in some villages and in modified contexts in others. Hymn tunes and some other musical styles have been introduced by Christian missionaries (Catholic and Protestant). Popular secular music, much of it with pidgin English text and the style of pan-Pacific pop, predominates in the larger centres.

A distinctive innovation is the bamboo band, which first appeared in the 1920s and 1930s, and in the 1970s is becoming increasingly popular. The bamboo band incorporates some principles of traditional bamboo instruments such as stamping tubes and panpipes. It is composed of several multiple rafts of large tuned bamboo pipes lashed to frames which are stacked horizontally on the ground, the open end of the pipes being struck with the sole of a rubber-thong sandal held in one hand. The highest pitched set is assigned the melody, the lowest a part comparable to that of a plucked string bass, and other sets are given parts filling in the harmony. Guitar and voice are often added to the ensemble. The repertory consists mainly of love songs and 'folk songs' and the performance style is characterized by a vigorous beating of rhythmic patterns borrowed from Western popular dance music.

The New Hebrides, a double chain of about 80 islands, has a land area of about 14,700 sq km. In the 1970s the islands were governed by a condominium of Britain and France, but Christian missions have had the greatest interest in and impact on the native peoples, who speak many languages and dialects. In some islands at a considerable distance from the capital, traditional music and dance are performed in their traditional contexts (*see* PACIFIC ISLANDS, §2); in others hymn tunes and simple Western-style popular music prevail.

New Caledonia, an overseas territory of France, embraces the island of New Caledonia, the Isle of Pines, the Loyalty Islands, and the Huon Islands. In Noumea, the capital, the majority of citizens are of French ancestry and most music is urban French in style, although song texts reflect the local environment. Cultural variety is provided by the many workers who have been imported for the nickel mines from all parts of the Territory, from Wallis and Futuna (islands with Polynesian cultures near Samoa, administered by France), from Indonesia, Vietnam and other places. Although some indigenous Melanesian traditional dances and chants are performed, complete performances of ceremonies are no longer given in traditional social context; elements from them, however, are being used in the development of modern dance-drama.

Fiji is considered Melanesian in geography and in the ethnic origin of its people although its music and dance relate more closely to those of western Polynesia than to those of other Melanesian cultures. However, stylistic features such as intensity of tone production, close simultaneous dissonant intervals, and muscular vitality and precision in dance set Fiji's traditions apart from those of the neighbouring, comparatively relaxed, western Polynesian cultures. In the 1970s, in the two largest urban centres, Nadi and Suva, pan-Pacific pop was extremely popular both with local citizens and tourists. Traditional *meke*, performances combining dance, songs, instrumental and body-percussion accompaniment, are valued for representing Fijian culture to international audiences both at home and abroad. Police and military bands are well-known in the Pacific area for their popularity with local citizens, the precision of their playing, and for their incorporation of choral singing and the playing of traditional Fijian instruments into the brass band repertory. Since Fiji became an independent Dominion within the British Commonwealth in 1970, its people's pride in its traditional heritage has been more visible. But people also respect the cultural traditions of the large Indian and Chinese sections of the population, and those of Europe; school music teachers are attempting to embrace as many of these traditions as possible in their classes.

2. FIJI. The Fiji group, since 1970 an independent nation, comprises about 320 islands, the largest of which is Viti Levu, covering 10,388 sq km. The music of Fiji represents the indigenous traditions and those of India, China, Europe (Fiji is a Dominion of the British Commonwealth) and other Pacific islands. Rotuma Island, for example, which is politically though not culturally linked with Fiji, is a Polynesian society, and the Banabans, who came to Fiji from Ocean Island, have a Micronesian culture. The indigenous Fijians are classified as Melanesian, although they have a considerable admixture of Polynesian blood. Fijian musical styles and structures include and combine elements of Polynesian and Melanesian music.

Fiji's 14 provinces mostly represent social and cultural as well as political divisions. They include the two largest islands, Viti Levu and Vanua Levu (which have several different styles), the Lau group on the eastern boundary, Lomaiviti ('in the centre of Fiji'), Kandavu to the south of the main group, and the Yasawa group to the west. The musical styles vary from area to area and so any generalizations about Fijian music are bound to be inaccurate. This article is based mainly on the styles found in Viti Levu.

(i) *Instruments.* Fijians play both indigenous instruments, which include several kinds of *lali*, as well as the *derua*, *dulali*, *bitu sanisani* and *davui*, and introduced instruments such as the guitar, ukelele and mandolin. The *lali* (slit-drum) was formerly a means of communication, announcing all events of social significance; wars, victories, births and deaths were each announced by a distinctive rhythmic pattern. The large *lali* are now used for calling people to church or for calling them together. The *lali* is made of hardwood, shaped and hollowed out to produce a deep resonance which can be heard at a distance of 8 km. Usually a pair is used, one being larger than the other (fig.1), by one or two players (depending on the function of the *lali* beat) using wooden beaters. A smaller type of *lali*, the *lali ni meke* (fig.2), accompanies chanting and dances. It has a slender shape and is between 75 and 100 cm long, made of hardwood and tapered at either end with a rectangular block hollowed out of the central portion. The best sound is thought to be produced by one person cradling the *lali* in his arms at chest level while the other person beats it, the chest thus providing a further resonator.

*Derua* are bamboo stamping tubes of varying lengths (fig.2), beaten on the ground or on mats. Sometimes a large section of bamboo with a rectangle cut out of it is used as a *lali. Lali ni meke, cobo* (clapping with cupped hands) and sometimes the *derua* provide the rhythmic basis of Fijian music.

*Bitu sanisani* and *dulali* are types of flute. *Bitu sanisani* refers both to the instrument and to the small type of bamboo from which it is made. The origin of the *dulali* (nose flute; fig.3) is ascribed to one of the gods of Fijian mythology; it is rarely played now. It consists of a section of bamboo approximately 60 cm long and 5 cm in diameter, with five holes evenly spaced along the length and three additional holes evenly spaced around the midpoint. There is a theory that Fijian melodic and harmonic structure is based on the notes of the *dulali*.

The *davui* (conch-shell trumpet made from a Triton shell; fig.4) was formerly used in times of war and is now blown (for instance) to announce fresh fish for sale. As a ceremonial instrument it is blown continuously on the death of a very high chief until his burial.

(ii) *Forms and functions.* The many different genres in Fijian music are all part of the social fabric of the society and are predominantly native; introduced forms include hymns and songs. Fijians have names for different voice parts: the first is called *laga* ('to sing'); the second, higher than the first, is called *tagica* ('to cry' or 'to chime in'); the *druku* ('bass'), sung at several different pitch levels, is in effect the chorus; *vaqiqivatu* is a bass that sings intermittently; and *vakasalavoavoa* is the descant voice.

Lullabies, sung by grandmothers, are rhythmic and have a limited vocal range. Singing games are sung or chanted to young children by the older children. Young men and very occasionally young women sing songs in Fijian, sometimes to an original tune (*sere ni cumu*) but more often to the tune of a currently popular Western song. The *sere ni cumu* has been popular since the early 1920s and many songs with original music were composed during World War II. *Taralala*, a side-by-side dance introduced by missionaries as a kindergarten entertainment, is now a form of social dance with vocal and instrumental accompaniment.

*Taro* ('catechism') and *same* (from 'psalm') are unaccompanied forms sung in church by mature women of all ages, usually led by older women. In the *taro* an older woman generally reads the question (*taro*) and the others chant the answer. *Same* are *vucu* ('narratives') with texts suitable for church use, such as Bible stories; the *laga, tagica* and *druku* voices are used. Hymns are sung by the whole congregation and unaccompanied choirs sing anthems.

*Vakalutuivoce* ('the dropping of the oar') are sung by two people while rowing a boat or going down the river by bamboo raft. The two voices form a vocal counterpoint.

*Vucu* are narratives accompanied by *lali ni meke*, hand-clapping and *derua* and sung by the *laga, tagica* and *druku* voices. Perhaps the most complex form of Fijian music is the *meke*, in which voices, *lali*, *cobo* and dance are combined; the one exception is the *meke ni yaqona* which is the highest form of the kava-drinking ceremony. Different types of *meke* include the *meke ni valu* (war dance), a general term incorporating *meke i wau* (men's club dance) and *meke wesi* or *meke moto* (men's spear dance); *ruasa*, a men's standing dance with distinctive hand gestures; the *meke iri* (men's or women's fan dance); *seasea* (women's standing dance); and *vakamalolo* (a sitting dance performed by men or women). All these *meke* are group dances, and although

1. *A pair of lali (slit-drums) at Ban Tailevu, Fiji, 1959*

2. *Lali ni meke (slit-drum) and derua (stamping tubes) at Rewa, Fiji, 1958*

there are certain positions in the line which indicate elevated status, the overall appearance and group co-ordination of the dancers is important. Men's dance movements are vigorous and virile while women's are graceful but controlled. Since the society has a communal structure, the interest is in group excellence rather than individual achievement or skill.

(*iii*) *Composition.* Methods of composition in Fiji vary greatly. Some music is composed in much the same way as Western music, either the words first or the tune, according to individual composers. Composition in the traditional manner, however, follows a ritual pattern. Only certain people are entitled to compose; these are the *dau ni vucu*, who follow a priest-like ritual before producing a composition. The most important figure in any *meke* is the *dau ni vucu*, whose inspiration brings forth not only music, but also a narrative in the form of

3. *Dulali* (*nose flute*) at Nananu, Tailevu, Fiji, 1957

a poem, often with specialized language and idioms that heighten the beauty of the narrative (often 12 or more verses). The *dau ni vucu* is responsible for all aspects of the *meke* – music, poetry, dance, accompanying instrumentation and costumes – and for teaching all aspects of the *meke*.

There are several traditional ways in which a *meke* may come to be composed. Sometimes it is requested by the people of the village and inspired by the god representing the composer's origins. Sometimes the inspiration comes from the *veli*, elf-like creatures whose unpredictability, brisk movement and light-footedness is reflected in the resulting *meke*. All spear dances are inspired by *veli*, as are some *vakamalolo*. Spear dances are noted for their quick movement and abrupt changes of direction; *vakamalolo* inspired by *veli* tend to be faster than most sitting dances and include both sudden changes of direction and unconventional body positions.

Other *meke* not of a warlike nature, such as the *seasea* or some *vakamalolo* and some songs, are inspired by the spirits of stillborn children. These *meke* and songs are held to be particularly original, in that they are the melodies of children who never had a chance to utter a cry on earth; the belief is that these melodies can be found and taken from their burial places. In this form

of composition the lines of the *meke* are not 'remembered' by the *dau ni vucu* who blurts them out, but by the friends who come with him. If they are not able to remember all the lines assigned to them, the forgotten lines must be omitted and not replaced with others. As a result these *meke* frequently have an unequal number of lines in each verse and the narrative is disjointed.

(*iv*) *Musical structure.* In the older style of *meke*, *same* and *vucu* there is a close relationship between the notes that can be produced on the Fijian nose flute and the melodic range of the *laga* and *tagica*. The melody of the *meke* style of the 1920s and earlier was based on five pitches with a range of a 5th or less, the central and lowest having the greatest importance. In the *same* melody of ex.1 the notes are diatonic in the range of a 5th, with a raised fourth degree ($c'$, $d'$, $e'$, $f\sharp'$ and $g'$); the melodic line centres round $e'$, and $c'$, the lowest note, is frequently repeated. In the *meke* melody of ex.2 the notes ($f'$, $g'$, $a'$, $b\flat'$ and $c''$) are also diatonic, but the fourth degree is not raised as it is in the first example. Again, however, the melody moves around the third degree and the lowest note, $f'$, is repeated. Harmony of this period was in clusters rather than spread out in chords. A typical harmonic structure consisted of a 2nd doubled at the 5th and the octave and possibly again at the upper 5th. The 2nd ranged in size from a major 2nd to an interval slightly larger than a minor 2nd.

The type of *meke* taught in schools and gaining widespread currency varies from the traditional harmonic structure; it resembles a major triad in second inversion, the 5th being used as a drone in the bass and the upper two voices singing the root and 3rd, rising to the 2nd and 4th and returning to the root and 3rd. One voice combines the functions of the *laga* and *tagica*. The traditional style of *meke* begins with the *laga* which is joined, after several beats, by the *tagica*, beginning a 2nd above, and a few bars later by the chorus or *druku*. At the end of the verse all the voices slow down and resolve to a unison, the upper voices resolving downwards. Sometimes the *vaqiqivatu* enters after the singing is well under way, in which case the *tagica* sings in the *vakasalavoavoa* ('descant') style. The entry of the *lali* and cupped hand-clapping (*cobo*) coincide with that of the chorus. The *lali* is beaten in a rhythmic pattern, repeated until just before the end of the verse when it changes to signal the end of the verse. *Cobo* marks the pulse and also changes near the end of the verse. A false beat on the *lali* or clap of the hands is considered a shameful mistake.

*Vucu* differs from *meke* only in that there is no dancing. *Same* is like *vucu* except that there is no accompaniment, and the subject matter is taken from Bible

Ex.1 *Same* melody (Thompson, 1966)

Ji - su___ sa___ le - qa na lo - ma - na

Ex.2 *Meke* melody; transcr. C. Saumaiwai

'u la' ki ta - ta - ga    ki Nu-ku-a - lo - fi

e la - u - ti   A - di...etc

stories. In *taro*, the question is usually spoken and the response chanted; the pitch of the chant rises slightly at the beginning and then remains fixed around one note until the end of the response. The final notes are greatly slowed and increase in intensity until the last, which is lower in pitch and short, and has little intensity.

*Vakalutuivoce* is sung by two people. Although the melodic line often has a range of a 4th or more, the two voices are usually a 2nd or 3rd apart. One voice begins and is joined towards the end of the first phrase by the second voice which sings in counterpoint to it. Lullabies and singing games are chanted or sung to simple tunes; lullabies are often improvised, or adapted from well-known versions. *Taralala*, *sere ni cumu* and other songs are often composed informally and deal with various subjects, mainly romantic. Fijian men frequently use a strong falsetto in these forms.

Most forms of Fijian vocal music are divided into verses. The rhyme scheme usually follows a set pattern of vowel sounds for each line-ending, the pattern sometimes being changed for another at the beginning of a new verse. Generally the musical pattern is either fairly consistent throughout the composition or takes the form of alternating slow and fast passages, as is frequently the case in spear dances, where a slow section of little activity is followed by a fast section of intense activity.

3. NEW CALEDONIA. One of the largest islands of Melanesia, New Caledonia is the capital of an overseas territory of the French Republic by the same name which includes the Loyalty Islands and others (see §1). The indigenous culture is Melanesian; however, even before European discovery (by Captain Cook in 1774), there had been some admixture of Polynesian elements (from Tonga), especially in the Loyalty Islands. Since the arrival of Christian missionaries in 1840, and the establishment of control by France in 1853, European influence has been extensive. Even so, by the mid-1970s, no ethnomusicological research had yet been conducted, the principal sources of information being only reports by travellers, missionaries and ethnographers, and a few recordings.

The Melanesian *pilu* was formerly an important ceremony. As described by Leenhardt, its preparation required several years and the events lasted several weeks, involving people from other villages and tribes and following a prescribed order of activities which included many dances and chants. The *pilu* was essential to the functioning of traditional New Caledonian society, but it was slow to accommodate introduced European elements, and so disappeared as a result of colonial domination. In the mid-1970s some *pilu* themes were beginning to be used in modern dance-dramas. The designation *pilu-pilu* is now applied to many genres and styles of traditional dance and music (including some with European influence) in the territory of New Caledonia. In presentations for international audiences, traditions from the Loyalty Islands, quite Polynesian in style, predominate. The most important event in the territory now is the July 14 Fête (from the French Bastille Day).

A distinctive characteristic of the Melanesian dance music performed in New Caledonia in the 1970s was the extensive use of whistling – with sharp percussive blasts, trill effects etc. Both whistling (between the teeth) and hissing were part of the tradition before European

*4. Davui (conch-shell trumpets) at a mourning ceremony, Rairaiwaqa, Suva, Fiji, 1958*

influence; now a policeman's whistle is sometimes substituted. Body percussion (stamping and clapping), mostly in regular alternations of strong and weak pulses, extends throughout an entire dance section and is resumed for the following section. Vigorous grunts by men and the beating of pads made from leaves, both in rhythmic patterns, as well as arhythmic shouts from the men, are also characteristic of the musical style; in some dances these make up the entire sound texture. In other dances, accompaniment can include chant or song, bamboo stamping tubes and a box struck with the hands.

*5. Curved bamboo nose flute from New Caledonia*

An ancient traditional percussion instrument still used by most of the 36 tribes on the island of New Caledonia is a pair of beaters made from triangular pieces of hibiscus or other bark. A long, curved nose flute made of short pieces of bamboo stuck together with vegetable glue was formerly used (fig.5). Slit-drums, though important elsewhere in Melanesia (e.g. the New Hebrides), were not part of the traditional inventory of instruments on New Caledonia. In the Loyalty Islands aerophones reported include a straight bamboo flute, the conch trumpet and pieces of cane partly filled with water to obtain the desired pitch when blown; reports also mentioned a beaten gourd.

Certain traditional chants and songs in the territory (some of which incorporate musical elements introduced by Christian missionaries) are sung by groups of women in two or more parts with some contrapuntal movement; these songs are sung in low tessitura with smooth vocal blend, and favour simultaneous 3rds, the intentional use of dissonance and unison cadences. Other types of song are sung by mixed groups, with a more penetrating vocal production and with some of the women's parts in high tessitura. Characteristically the melodies have narrow ranges (between a 3rd and a 5th) and short phrases which are repeated many times. Certain melodies may be sung to more than one text. Some texts are successions of vowels only, while others recount some celebrated event, such as a past victory in war.

4. NEW HEBRIDES. The New Hebrides group, of which the main islands are Espíritu Santo, Malekula, Pentecost, Aoba, Maewo, Ambrim, Tana and Efate, lies about 800 km west of Fiji and 400 km north-east of New Caledonia, between 167–70° E and 13–20° S.

(i) *Genres and musical structure*. In the New Hebrides traditional music is performed at public and ceremonial occasions and also in private. Ritual ceremonies such as incision, marriage and grade-taking in the pig-killing cultures, and the unique *gol* of south Pentecost Island, which involves jumping from a specially constructed tower with vines tied to the legs, always include music; it accompanies dancing and the climaxes of certain ceremonies, for example the presentation of pigs at grade-taking ceremonies, which is heralded by certain slit-drum rhythms. In many areas traditional dances are now performed at church festivals and for government events such as the opening of a new council building, in fact for any public event which requires celebration. There is no public music except in such contexts.

Of the many types of solo music, most are performed privately. Some islands have solo songs specially composed for a particular ceremony, in honour of the person involved, or even, as in the case of the grade-taking in Ambrim, 'insult' songs. Magic songs intended to procure personal benefits such as a good yam harvest or the attendance of pig-owners with their pigs at the singer's grade-taking ceremony, are still in use in some areas, and naturally are performed in great secrecy. Songs often occur in the narration of traditional stories, and are sung by the story-teller. At Lombaha on the island of Aoba songs of the important solo genre *tanumwe* have complex texts, dealing with the subject in highly allusive language. The songs associated with certain dances (e.g. *savagoro* and *bolo* in the northern islands) are also performed as 'private' solo songs. Other songs include lullabies, songs sung in children's games, counting songs etc.

Dances are to a certain extent borrowed by one island from another, which involves singing in other islands' languages and sometimes in an archaic language no longer understood. In the Banks Islands each island has in addition to its own language its own corresponding song language, distinct from the ordinary language of the other islands. Many dances begin with a preliminary vocalization on vowels or meaningless syllables which serve to identify the type of song or dance to be performed.

While most of the traditional music performed is now of unknown authorship, there are still composers (men and women) in the islands where traditional music survives who are commissioned to compose new songs for particular occasions or in honour of particular persons. The song is taught orally to the performers; in Banks Islands languages the composer is said to 'measure' the song and the performer to 'sew' it, the singer as it were drawing out his song stitch by stitch.

The form of most dance-songs is responsorial and repetitive, as in the *lenga*, for example, a dance common to the northern and central islands of the group. The chorus of dancers is arranged in lines and a leader carrying a bamboo slit-drum acts as soloist. Usually the soloist sings a short rhythmic phrase which is answered by the chorus; and this exchange is repeated several times while the dance movement continues; at the end of a particular section of the dance the soloist introduces a new phrase which receives a new answer from the chorus. The whole section (i.e. old phrases plus new phrases) is at once repeated and this repetition continues until the dance is completed. As the soloist takes up his phrase at the end of the chorus's response the two parts often overlap, introducing a rudimentary element of polyphony. The *savagoro*, another dance which is extremely popular in all the northern islands and the Banks Islands, is often performed in an impromptu fashion on a festive occasion. It is danced on the spot in a close circle by as many as wish to join in. The song, which is responsorial, is accompanied either by hand-clapping on the off-beats, or (in the Banks Islands) by pounding sticks on a board laid above a hole in the ground. A dance found on Aoba called *ahi bue* ('bamboo song') takes its name from *bue*, the bundle of dried bamboos placed on forked sticks which acts as the percussion instrument. At the repetition of the final section of each movement, when the players of the bamboos break into a 6/8 metre, onlookers may run in anticlockwise circles around the line of dancers. Similar points for public participation occur in many dance forms.

Most songs have a duple rhythmic organization, although in some places slit-drums are beaten in triple time. Sometimes hemiola appears between the voices and the various slit-drums. At certain points in some dances there are pauses, a tightening of the rhythm or momentary changes of rhythm. The songs of the *savagoro*, which when performed as a dance fit into a strict rhythm of clapping or stick-pounding, appear when sung by themselves as 'private' music to be rhythmically very unpredictable and acquire a melancholy character which is absent from the dance performance. Some dances are introduced by an unaccompanied solo song, the dancers remaining motionless; its rhythm may follow irregular speech stresses.

Except in one area the vocal part of traditional music is monophonic, though sometimes a variety of rhythms played on the slit-drums forms a kind of counterpoint. But in north Malekula the voices are frequently in polyphony of a kind which seems to be based on a drone, even when the drone itself is not continuous. It is not known why this area alone has polyphonic songs; polyphony is extremely common in songs of the Solomon Islands, the Loyalty Islands and Fiji.

Ex.3 Magic song used to 'pull' pigs, east Aoba; rec. and transcr. P. Crowe

Ex.4 from weeping song, *talang lang ana* genre similar to *tanumwe*, north Pentecost; rec. and transcr. P. Crowe

The Gairoro tree is sounding
The Gairoro tree is sounding,
  is bending, searching up,
  is bending, searching me
The Gairoro tree is sounding
The Gairoro tree is sounding,
  tempting me
Eh! Mwae will not allow me,
  place getting dark,
  let us two go.....

The commonest mode found in the melodies is anhemitonic pentatonic represented by C–D–E–G–A (ex.3), but many songs are either 'fanfares' (i.e. a major triad in various inversions) or are made up of three or four alternate major and minor 3rds (ex.4). Sometimes the highest of the series appears an octave lower, producing the series G–A–C–E instead of the normal A–C–E–G. Passages of such 3rds sometimes occur in otherwise pentatonic songs. Occasionally a passing note is added to the series of 3rds on an intermediate degree within one of the 3rds: when this involves a whole tone it produces the common pentatonic mode and so shows

the relationship between this mode and the series of 3rds; sometimes however the added note involves a semitone.

(*ii*) *Instruments*. By far the most important instrument is the slit-drum, made of logs or of lengths of bamboo. Those made from logs occur everywhere: in the islands north of Malekula and Ambrim they are placed horizontally on the ground and are undecorated, while in these two islands and in islands to the south they are buried upright in the ground and normally carved on the upper part with representations of the human face (see fig.6). In areas with upright slit-drums, however, portable horizontal ones also occur. In south Pentecost and possibly elsewhere slit-drums are sometimes placed at an angle of 45°, resting on a forked stick. Both vertical and horizontal slit-drums vary in size, from the length of a single node of bamboo to up to 7m for wooden drums. In some places they are used singly and in others in groups of varying sizes. In groups they are normally used to play rhythms in counterpoint. Used singly, as in the Small Nambas mortuary rite on Malekula, they play a complicated series of rhythms accompanying the chants. Slit-drums are normally struck with short sticks or with the butt end of the coconut frond, but formerly in the Banks Islands the middle performer of the three playing the same large slit-drum beat it with his hands while his neighbours used sticks. Slit-drums are used mainly during ceremonies and dances, to accompany the singing or announce a significant event in the ceremony. In some places they are still used to send messages: for example on Aoba there is now a particular rhythm played on a small slit-drum to call people to church. Bamboo slit-drums are used for certain kinds of dances. They are held in one hand and beaten with a stick held in the other hand (as by the soloist in the *lenga*), or held by one performer and beaten by another (as in some Banks Islands dances), or laid on the ground in groups (as in the Torres Islands), in which case all the performers play the same rhythm.

Other idiophones include the *bue* (bamboo bundles) of Aoba, described in §4(i) above as accompaniment to the dance *ahi bue*; the ground-resonated percussion beam, still used in the Banks Islands, Maewo, Paama and Espíritu Santo and formerly used on Ambrim, which is made from the buttress root of a tree and beaten with sticks; and shell rattles attached to the dancers' legs, widely used in certain dances. Bullroarers and certain leaves are now rarely used as instruments but were formerly used to simulate the voices of spirits. On Motalava in the Banks Islands the singing in a certain dance is accompanied by the scraping of the butt of a leaf-stalk against a stone, which produces a surprisingly loud rasping sound; although this is now recognized not to be the voice of a spirit, the performers remain inside a leaf enclosure and only men are allowed to see the instrument. It is called *natmat woywoy*, the name of the spirit concerned. On Ambrim formerly another type of leaf was held between the palms and blown on to simulate the voice of spirits.

The most commonly used aerophone is the conch-shell trumpet. It is used as a signalling instrument, both for calling people together and to mark significant moments in ceremonies. The pitch can be slightly varied by putting the fist into the shell's opening. Bamboo end-blown flutes are commonly made, but largely for the tourist trade, since they are played rarely and never in a

6. *Upright and horizontal slit-drums at Iapktas, south-central Malekula, New Hebrides, 1974*

public context. The distances between the holes are calculated by finger sizes: an ineffective notch may be cut off and another begun, which upsets the pitch relationship but does not seem to disturb the maker. Panpipes were once common: in remote parts of Espíritu Santo instruments with 10 pipes (*bue balabala hangavulu*) are still used in polyphonic ensembles.

A remarkable instrument reputedly still current in south-west Malekula and on Ambrim, *temes naainggol* (Malekula) or *tematne are* (Ambrim), consists of a wooden vessel rather like a deep mortar into which the performer blows through a reed tube (see fig.7), producing a booming note. The performer uses several of these vessels, each of a different pitch, and dexterously withdraws his reed pipe from one and inserts it into another as he accompanies the singing.

A musical bow was formerly made, and in the 1970s there was still at least one player in north Ambrim. One end of the bow is held in the teeth and the string is plucked with a piece of coconut-leaf rib (fig.8).

(*iii*) *Acculturated music.* Types of Western music which New Hebrideans have borrowed and which are extremely popular include songs of the cowboy type accompanied by a ukelele or guitar, and gospel hymn tunes, especially of the Moody and Sankey variety (*see* GOSPEL MUSIC, §I). New music is being composed in these styles and authentic Western music of these types is often adapted in performance, either by changes of melodic intervals (semitones becoming whole tones and vice versa, especially where the semitone is used for modulation in the Western tune), or by changes of harmony, or even by the insertion of extra beats and the shortening of long notes, seemingly without any aware-

ness that the rhythm has been made irregular. In certain islands traditional music has almost completely disappeared and only these borrowed Western styles are commonly known. This has occurred mainly where people were taught that the traditional music had 'heathen' associations and was unfit for Christians; where this has happened the islanders have been amazed to learn that Christian people in other islands still perform their traditional songs and dances without any sense of impropriety. The disappearance of certain customary music and rites from Hiw which survive in the other Torres islands is attributed to the fact that those who knew them died without passing them on to their children. The learning of music and rites is often connected with initiation into grades of society and where this initiation is neglected, the traditions associated with it may disappear. However, there are large enough areas in the New Hebrides where traditional music is still composed and performed to ensure that it will survive as a cultural expression of the people.

Recordings of New Hebridean traditional music are held in the archive of Maori and Pacific Music (Crowe Collection) at the Department of Anthropology, University of Auckland, New Zealand; the library (Crowe Collection) at the University of New South Wales, Sydney, and the music department (MacIntyre Collection) of Monash University, Melbourne, Australia; and at the Pitt Rivers Museum (Layard Collection), Oxford. The New Hebrides Cultural Centre, Port Vila, began a systematic collection of oral traditions, including music and dance, in 1976.

5. PAPUA NEW GUINEA.

(*i*) *General.* Papua New Guinea, which achieved

independence in 1975, includes the eastern half of the large island of New Guinea, some small islands of the Torres Straits, the Bismarcks and the northern Solomon Islands, i.e. Buka and Bougainville. (The Solomon Islands as a whole are discussed in §6.)

A nation of unusual cultural diversity, Papua New Guinea has a population of about 2·5 million, with from 500 to 750 languages. A general discussion of the music of Papua New Guinea can only highlight kinds of musical activities rather than outline the many music systems. Most examples will be drawn from the highland peoples who were relatively uninfluenced by other cultures until World War II. Though styles differ from place to place, responsorial group singing is characteristic of Papua New Guinea. The focus of activities is on kin groups or whole communities rather than on individuals. Songs are an integral part of community life, and since the musical tradition is wholly oral, responsorial styles with a leader and chorus serve as a mnemonic scheme, aiding in the recall and retention of repertory. The song leader merely starts the song, and does not lead it in the sense of directing or teaching it. Because music-making normally requires group participation, the occasions for music are specific. They may include male initiation ceremonies, female puberty celebrations, courting, activities related to warfare, virility rites and other male cult rituals, garden fertility rites, social feasts and mourning.

(*ii*) *The sing-sing.* Some occasions require elaborate preparations. Costumes with feather head-dresses and painted emblems mounted on poles are displayed at the most spectacular feasts, called in pidgin English 'sing-sings'. These include dancing as well as singing and are nearly always held at night, either inside a large house belonging to the men of the village or out of doors, on a ground in the centre of the village. Some sing-sings used to be associated with tribal warfare, and their purpose was to lead up to an attack or to celebrate killings. This type of sing-sing and much of the music associated with initiation ceremonies have been discontinued. (During the trusteeship of the Australian government (1919–73) inter-tribal fighting and cruel practices of mutilation, performed as part of initiation and mourning rites, were made punishable by law.) In the highlands, a girl's first menstruation is still marked by a five-day celebration, during which time she feasts, sings and dances with her female age-mates. Sing-sings for courting have disappeared from the Eastern Highlands Province but are still performed in the Western Highlands Province. Some virility rites of the male cult are still observed; a repertory of songs developed from these rituals because during their seclusion from women the men devoted themselves to singing and to such crafts as making arrows, bows, arm- and leg-bands. Garden fertility rites and male purification rites, with accompanying songs, are still practised by some. Sing-sings are held in conjunction with pig feasts and involve social or trading obligations; songs sung on these occasions include a wide range of topics. At very large gatherings, several groups may perform at the same time.

(*iii*) *Wailing.* Mourning the dead takes many forms in Papua New Guinea. All vocal mourning is called by the one general term, 'wailing', which is not necessarily restricted to songs with texts expressing lamentation for the dead, even though such texts do occur, in the Northern Province, for example. In the Southern Highlands Province, the Duna people were heard wailing on one pitch (*a'*) as they approached a local funeral. This single pitch was sustained for several minutes at a time, with only slight variation in volume as singers drew a new breath. In the Eastern Highlands Province, wailing refers to the simultaneous acts of weeping and singing. The songs sung at mourning do not necessarily speak of death, but their style contrasts with that of dance-songs.

(*iv*) *Instruments.* All instruments are made from natural materials such as wood, various canes and bamboo, tree-fruits, gourds, seeds, shells and animal skins.

Flutes, pipes and horns, both end-blown and side-blown, are distributed throughout the mainland and outlying islands, and can be classified according to their construction (whether of bamboo, wood, clay or shell). Bamboo aerophones have the widest distribution. Transverse flutes are usually ceremonial and are common in the northern half of Papua New Guinea, extending into the Northern Province. In the Eastern Highlands, young men learn to play large transverse flutes, approximately 12 cm in diameter and 90 cm long, with the embouchure in the centre. The men later progress to a smaller, stopped flute, side-blown at the stopped end, which is

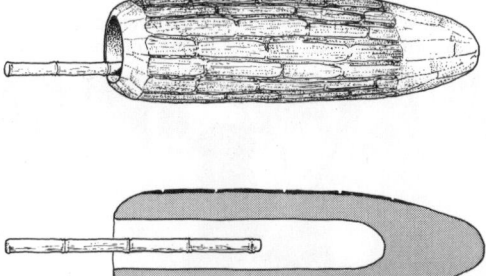

7. *Temes naainggol (wooden vessel with reed tube); general view and section*

8. *Musical bow from north Ambrim, New Hebrides, 1949*

9. *Transverse ('sacred') flutes of the Siane, Eastern Highlands Province, Papua New Guinea*

which seek the source of female strength, believed to be superior to that of the male. In general, 'sacred flutes' and other aerophones in the Sepik Province are longer than their counterparts in the highlands.

End-blown flutes are made of cane, about 2 cm in diameter, with two to seven finger-holes. Tunings vary, as do playing techniques. The end of the flute may be put directly into the mouth, or the sound may be produced by blowing across the end. End-blown flutes are usually mouth-blown, but nose flutes are found in some areas (e.g. Morobe Province). Together with the clustered panpipes (see below), end-blown flutes are perhaps the most personal instruments in Papua New Guinea, because they are played individually, which gives scope for improvisation and an intimacy of expression not possible on instruments played only in ensemble. The end-blown flute is not a ceremonial instrument.

Stopped pipes with only one pitch are found in various dimensions and arrangements. In the past, Usarufas of the Eastern Highlands played cane pipes in sets, each man sounding one pipe. These pipes were played in procession as part of the preliminaries to important pig feasts, and were sounded antiphonally by two groups, each group having pipes of three contrasting lengths and sounding them in unison. Stopped pipes, lashed together in a single or double row (the latter is not indigenous to the mainland) or in a circular cluster, are commonly termed panpipes. A small set of four panpipes, ranging from 10 to 12 cm long, is typical of the Eastern Highlands Province. They are played only by young boys.

harder to play; the famous 'sacred flutes' or 'spirit flutes' belong to this category (fig.9). Traditionally played in pairs by two men initiated at the same time, the term 'sacred' is applied because these flutes are not to be seen by uninitiated males, and are forbidden to women under any circumstances. There is a widespread belief that women originally possessed these flutes and that men then stole them, forbidding women ever to see them again. This parallels other accounts of male rituals

10. *Garamut (slit-drums) of the Iatmul people, Aibom, Sepik Province, Papua New Guinea, 1956*

However, the clustered or bundled panpipes typical of the Southern Highlands and Western Highlands Provinces are played by adults and are considered capable of expressing personal feelings. Players of the clustered panpipes breathe lightly into them, producing a faintly audible sound not unlike wind in the trees, whereas Eastern Highlands players produce a piercing sound by blowing the pipes vigorously.

Wooden horns (or trumpets) are played in the Sepik regions. They may be end-blown or side-blown. End-blown horns are played like a bugle or sung through like a megaphone. The side-blown horn is an elongated cone decorated with carvings and ochre. A figure is often carved at the stopped end near the embouchure and the presence of carved figures such as a crocodile, bird or human shape usually identifies an instrument of the mainland as Sepik-made. An interesting horn made on the island of Bougainville is a hollow wooden cylinder about 1·2 metres long, with one end rounded off by a coconut shell with a centred embouchure. Horn playing with compressed lips is a style closely identified with the lowlands and coastal peoples. Horns of bamboo and shell are sparsely distributed around the mainland. Bamboo horns range from decorated types with wooden mouthpieces inserted in the end to unadorned lengths of bamboo with a small hole pierced through the node. Conch-shell trumpets, prevalent along the coasts, have been introduced into the highlands. Small ocarinas made of clay or tree-fruit come from Maprik, Chimbu and Eastern Highlands regions.

The bullroarer exists in all districts of Papua New Guinea, but its importance is declining. It was formerly much used in male cults and initiations, and like the 'sacred flutes' was believed to have special power, being forbidden to women and children.

The most outstanding idiophone is the *garamut* (pidgin English), a wooden slit-drum, which is struck with one or two wooden beaters (fig.10). Although not found in the highlands, it is known to all Sepik peoples and off-shore islanders. It exists in various shapes and sizes and is played and used in many ways. A small *garamut* measures about 38 cm long; large ones photographed in the Maprik and Sepik regions are 1·2 metres in diameter and 3·5 to 4·5 metres long. An average *garamut* is approximately 45 by 180 cm. They are nearly always painted with ochre, with the two ends carved in the shape of crocodile heads, human figures, birds or a combination of these. Some ceremonial *garamuts* are very ornate. The beaters may also be ornately carved, ranging in length from about 38 cm to 1·5 metres. Players usually strike the *garamut* to one side of the slit, using the end of the beater rather than its side. The slit-drum may be played suspended or stood on end, but generally it rests on the ground. In addition to being used to accompany certain songs, the slit-drum is used to transmit messages to another village or to individuals beyond calling distance. Its uses are thus a combination of the ceremonial, the social and the practical. (Some peoples of the Central Province accompany singing and dancing with an unslit hollow-log drum.)

On the island of New Britain, two slats of thoroughly dried wood are held across the lap and struck with sticks. Tolai men on the island play them to attract young women. A similar idiophone is played in the Maprik Province of the mainland. Other struck idiophones include arrows struck against bows (Chimbu

Province) and gourd lime-pots tapped with spatulas to accompany singing (Goodenough Island), but these uses are secondary.

Various other bamboo idiophones are popular east of the mainland. On the mainland itself (Northern Province) there are bamboo stamping tubes, which are struck on the ground during a sing-sing, and short lengths of open bamboo tubes (approximately 30 cm) which men and women play in unison while seated and singing. A hand is cupped over the end of the tube, and the other end is struck against the bare thigh to mark the beat of the song. The bamboo jew's harp, played throughout the mainland, is made from a 17- or 20-cm piece of bamboo, approximately 2·5 cm in diameter, one side of which is cut away from the node at one end (fig.11). The remaining side is tapered, and a narrow tongue is cut into it which the player taps with the back of his thumb. Jew's harps are played generally by adolescent boys who 'talk' through the rhythm. Sometimes, when using them

11. *Bamboo jew's harp of the Siane people, Eastern Highlands Province, Papua New Guinea*

for courting, the boys speak a girl's name as they play; at other times, they imitate bird calls, bubbling water etc.

The best-known rattle in Papua New Guinea is made of bunches of tree-fruit (*Panguin edule*), which are slit, hollowed and dried. Coastal and island peoples tie them below the knee when they dance. In the highlands (where they are imported) drummers wear them on the wrist of their drumming-hand or tie them to the drum itself. In the Morobe Province, men tie them around the necks of their hunting dogs. Clusters of longer, bean-like seed pods, sometimes combined with pieces of bone and shell, are used for rattles in the Southern Highlands and Northern Provinces. Rattles were originally used to accompany dancing in the highlands. Eastern Highlands men shook bamboo rattles, and women shook gourd ones filled with seeds, or sometimes dancers rolled a piece of split cane between their palms. Few highlands people have retained these rattles as sing-sing instruments; rattles and stamping tubes have been replaced by the drum, copied from that of coastal peoples. A rubbed idiophone traditionally played at important funerals on New Ireland consists of a block of wood, with three deep cavities cut into it, which emits three tones when rubbed vigorously across these open-

*12. Friction block from New Ireland (Conservatoire Royal de Musique, Brussels)*

ings (fig.12). Scraped idiophones are rare. Lime gourds, used in conjunction with betel-nut chewing, often have notched sticks or spatulas which, when scraped along the mouth of the gourd container, act as a rasp; these are heard occasionally as song accompaniment in regions where the betel-nut is grown, or where it has been introduced.

The basic membranophone of Papua New Guinea is the *kundu* (pidgin English), shaped like an elongated hourglass (fig.13). A squat version of this drum is made in the Upper Sepik region, and cone-shaped ones occur in the Southern Highlands Province, the latter tapered to two points like an open 'fish-mouth', or ending in the shape of an overturned dish. Other drums are variations of these shapes. Drumheads are made of possum-, snake- or lizard-skin. The size of the drum depends upon the size of the available animal skin, but 17 cm is

*13. Kundu (hourglass drums) at Goroka, Eastern Highlands Province, Papua New Guinea*

an average diameter. Sometimes a handle spanning the narrowest girth is carved into the drum. Drums with handles or decoration are rarely found in the Eastern Highlands, but lowlands peoples often have intricately carved drums which may be painted as well. Because the drum is used at sing-sings, the players are always in motion, and the shape of the *kundu* is thus functional, in that the player can easily grasp it at the 'neck' or handle, and strike it with the free hand. In the Eastern Highlands, drums are tuned by soaking the drumhead in water, spitting a mucilage, made by chewing a particular leaf, around the rim of the drum (some peoples use blood instead), and finally stretching the skin over the rim and tying it in place. After the drumhead has dried for a day in the sun, three or four pellets of resin are heated and pressed on to the centre of it to reinforce the tension. These are removed, heated and reapplied if the tension slackens during performance. The ceremonial significance of making or playing drums differs from one region to the next. In the Eastern Highlands the drum was only introduced in the mid-20th century and has little or no ritual significance, but drum making is ceremonial in parts of the Southern Highlands Province.

A chordophone popular with island and lowlands peoples consists of a length of bamboo with a narrow strand cut away from its surface; the ends are left attached, and a small wedge of wood placed under the strand serves as a bridge. The instrument is played by tapping the raised strand with a stick. Sago cultures make a one-string chordophone based on the same principle, by separating a strand from a sago frond and placing a bridge at either end. The musical bow, used in the Southern Highlands and Western Highlands Provinces, is played solo and for the player's own enjoyment. The bow is about 30 cm long when strung; its string is cut from the fibrous roots of the plant *Frecinetiea kanehirae*, and is tied to both ends of the bow, or is doubled back on itself, making a two-string chordophone. Players pluck the string with a short stick. The pitch is lowered by bending the bow slightly to lessen the tension.

Instruments played only by children include whistling tops, whizzers, reed whistles and panpipes. The jew's harp could also be classified as a toy, because, although there is no stigma attached to playing it, adults seldom do.

Instruments are commonly designated 'male' or 'female', especially if played in pairs. The terms may simply refer to the larger ('male') or smaller ('female') of two instruments, or may relate their shape to human anatomy. Musical instruments in Papua New Guinea are, generally speaking, the men's domain. Men are the instrument makers, and women use instruments only in group efforts, such as singing while striking a bamboo cylinder on the thigh, or shaking a rattle in the sing-sing. On islands off the mainland, women are known to play slit-drums, but on the mainland women instrumentalists are rare.

6. SOLOMON ISLANDS. The archipelago of the Solomon Islands, total population about 300,000, is politically divided in two parts. To the north-west, Bougainville and Buka (with some small neighbouring islands) form the Province of North Solomons of Papua New Guinea. The Solomon Islands to the south-east were long under British protection. The largest urban area is Honiara, on Guadalcanal, with a population of about 15,000. There

are three indigenous ethnic groups scattered throughout the islands: Papuans, Melanesians and Polynesians, distinguished primarily by linguistic classification. In race and culture the divisions between the three groups are more blurred. Papuan or non-Austronesian languages are spoken on more than half of the island of Bougainville and on some other smaller islands. The great majority of Solomon Islanders speak Melanesian languages. Smaller groups speaking a Polynesian language live on Polynesian outlier islands (see §1).

(*i*)  *Bougainville*  (*Papuan-speaking peoples*).  In Bougainville songs are often composed for an important feast at the request of a political leader, and may later be transposed as music for the panpipes. Among the Siuai, the composer makes new panpipes to fit the melody he wishes to play, and the other musicians make their instruments after that model. Among the Terei, the final tuning of the panpipes takes place in the course of a dance: the pitches of the leader's panpipes are used as a reference for the new instruments. Among the Siuai and elsewhere, the panpipes are discarded after the feast. There are panpipes of one raft and also of two rafts, the second raft consisting of tubes open at the lower end. Panpipes ensembles, composed of instruments of different sizes, sometimes also include trumpets made of bamboo or carved wood. It was particularly on the scales of panpipes from the north-west Solomons (Bougainville and Choiseul), but also on panpipes from Brazil, that Erich von Hornbostel based and elaborated his well-known theory of 'blown 5ths'. Among the Siuai, the important leaders have ensembles of slit-drums at their meeting house which are struck in unison to signify the number of pigs brought to the feast. Such ceremonial feasts, in the course of which pigs are killed in large numbers, may be commemorative funeral feasts, 'social-climbing' feasts for raising one's social rank, or initiation rituals for adolescent boys. Panpipes and slit-drums, regarded as 'prestige' instruments, are an inseparable part of them. Other instrumental pieces may reproduce, through their rhythm, verbal phrases, though with no intention of conveying a message.

(*ii*) *Malaita* (*Melanesian-speaking peoples*). The inhabitants of Malaita (about 60,000 people) speak some 11 languages, some of which, particularly in the north, are closely related. Malaita's music may be divided geographically into that of the north and that of the south (the centre shares characteristics of both). Musical terminology is similar in the different languages: the generic term for vocal music is *nguu* (there are also specific terms for each kind of song); instrumental music is called *'au* ('bamboo'), as all instrumental music except that for slit-drums is played on bamboo instruments.

Solo songs, such as lullabies, are known throughout the island. Songs performed by choruses of men sitting in two rows facing each other and singing in two parts are characteristic of the northern half of the island. The words of their songs, which recount historical traditions, are sometimes sung by the entire choir, sometimes by a song-leader. Certain kinds of song are accompanied by sticks struck against each other, others by jingles (nut-seeds tied to sticks). Other songs accompany activities, the cracking of canarium nuts or the pounding of taro for feasts, or paddling in the large plank canoes. Unlike the men, women sing in unison. No choruses are known in the southern half of Malaita, where usually two people sing together, in two parts. This style is characteristic of the women's songs (funeral laments, enumerative songs and even lullabies) as well as the men's (performed during paddling or the pounding of taro). Another type of song is sung by men to the accompaniment of large bamboo tubes, stamped on the ground or struck against the palm of the hand.

In their instrumental music Malaitans distinguish between 'blown bamboos' and 'struck bamboos'. Some instruments are played unaccompanied, others in ensembles. Instruments played solo in the 'blown bamboo'

14. *Bundle panpipes* (*with seven pipes*) *of the 'Are'are people, Malaita, Solomon Islands*

category include three types of flute made from single bamboo tubes: the transverse flute, the end-blown flute, held obliquely, and the notched flute. The transverse flute is stopped at both ends by the nodes in the bamboo; single holes cut on the reed-wall near each end serve as mouthpiece and finger-hole. The oblique flute may be stopped or open at the lower end: if stopped, the instrument requires a finger-hole; if open, the musician stops or reopens the bottom opening of the tube with his index finger. The notched flute exists only in the south, in Small Malaita. Open at the lower end, it requires two finger-holes or none. In all three types of flute supplementary pitches are obtained by overblowing. The three instruments are played primarily by women for their own amusement. In the southern half of Malaita there is a type of panpipes consisting of a single raft, in which the pipes are not arranged in decreasing sequence. This irregular order is explained by the manner of playing: the musician always blows simultaneously into two adjacent tubes, thus obtaining a two-part melody.

15. *Obliquely held bundle panpipes of the Kwaio people, Malaita, Solomon Islands*

This instrument has five to 13 tubes depending on the region and the type. It is played during the gathering of canarium nuts or to call a woman to a forest tryst. There are in addition two types of bundle panpipes. One type, held vertically, consists of seven to nine open bamboo pipes (fig.14). The musician holds the instrument 1 or 2 cm from his mouth. Keeping his hand nearly motionless, the musician moves his head to direct the breath into the different tubes. In one variant known among the Kwaio, the bottom ends of the tubes are closed by nodes. The other type of bundle panpipes, held obliquely like the oblique flute, is composed of three or four thin open-ended bamboo tubes (fig.15). A small circular hole at the node forms the mouthpiece of each tube. The musician places the tube he wishes to sound obliquely against his mouth; part of the air current also enters the opposite tube. His head remains still, and his hand moves the instrument. Besides the fundamental tones, harmonics are used, their sonority being very weak and delicate. These panpipes are found in the southern part

16. *Stamping tubes of the 'Are'are people, Malaita, Solomon Islands*

of Malaita and seem unknown elsewhere in the world. Both types of bundle panpipes are played for the personal enjoyment of the musician, except among the Fataleka in the northern part of Malaita, where the first type is used in a cycle of funeral feasts.

The category of 'struck bamboos' includes two instruments, the musical bow and stamping tubes, which are played unaccompanied. The musical bow consists of a bamboo tube open at both ends, to which are attached two strings (tuned to the same pitch) made from a single plant fibre. If the bamboo is too rigid and does not bend sufficiently the strings must be raised by bridges, and the instrument then nears the zither family. The bamboo is placed between the lips, thus adding harmonics formed in the mouth to the basic sound obtained by plucking the two strings. The stamping tubes consist of ten bamboo rods, between 13 and 50 cm long, each stopped at the bottom end by a node. The musician, sitting, holds four tubes in each hand and one with each foot (between two toes), and beats them on stones placed on the ground (fig.16). Stamping tubes are known elsewhere in the Pacific, but generally each person plays one or at most two tubes. It seems that only in the southern half of Malaita and nowhere else in the world are the rhythmical, melodic and polyphonic resources of this instrument exploited to such an extent.

Stamping tubes can also be played as an ensemble instrument, in which case the stamping tubes are distributed among two or three players playing ten or twelve tubes in all. As in solo performance, this music is played for amusement, by both men and women. But the most important instrumental ensembles are groups of slit-drums and panpipes played at the great ceremonial feasts held in connection with the ancestor cult or to enhance the prestige of chiefs. The solo slit-drum is known to all peoples in Malaita and is used to send messages, but slit-drum ensembles are found only in southern Malaita and have an essentially musical function. Depending on the region, the ensemble consists of three to twelve slit-drums of different sizes. The instruments are placed horizontally on stands constructed of plant materials, the slit pointed towards the player, who drums on its upper edge with two sticks. Among the 'Are'are the instruments are played in unison; in Small Malaita the three slit-drums are each struck in a different rhythm. Many prohibitions, dietary and sexual, must be observed during the making of new slit-drums, ending with the inaugural ritual when the ensemble is played in public for the first time.

In Malaita there are seven types of panpipes ensembles, with many variants, each type with its own name. The panpipes played in ensembles all consist of one row of tubes stopped at the lower end and arranged in decreasing order of size. The basic scale used is one in which the octave is divided into seven approximately equal intervals (also found in Cambodia, Thailand and Guinea). This scale appears in two forms, one where all the instruments of an ensemble have the complete scale (as in the northern *'au sisile* and the southern *'au tahana*), and one where two instruments share the scale, complementing each other: thus pitches 1, 3, 5, 7 etc belong to one instrument and pitches 2, 4, 6, 8 etc to the other (as in the northern *'au 'ero* and the southern *'au keto* and *'au taka'iori*). Another ensemble in southern Malaita, the *'au paina*, consists of instruments whose tuning is pentatonic. The number of instruments and of the tubes on each instrument, the tessitura of the ensemble as a whole, the number of polyphonic parts, the playing in parallel octaves and the repertory vary according to the type of ensemble. Thus, the *'au tahana* is composed of four instruments of two sizes, each instrument with a tessitura of nearly two octaves. The musicians play in two-part polyphony, each part being doubled at the octave. The *'au paina* has eight instruments played in two-part polyphony, each part quadrupled at the octave. The largest instrument may reach 160 cm in length (fig.17), the others then being 80, 40 and 20 cm long. The tessitura of the ensemble as a whole is five octaves. The *'au sisile* in the north consists of a variable number of instruments (eight to twenty) of the same size, with a tessitura of approximately two octaves. The musicians play in four-part polyphony and there are no doublings at the octave. Among the Kwaio, at the island's centre, the *'au sisile* always consists of eight instruments: four of one size with a tessitura of two octaves, and four instruments of three tubes each, tuned in 3rds. Some pieces are played in four parts (some parts doubled or trebled at the octave), other pieces in six, seven and even eight parts. Some ensembles have no rhythmic accompaniment (e.g. the *'au tahana, 'au keto* and *'au paina*), in others the musicians wear rattles around the ankles (*'au sisile, 'au 'ero*); in still others (e.g. the *'au taka'iori*) the dancers beat on leaf bundles. In the *'au sisile* of the Kwaio, the seated musicians strike their right thighs violently with one hand. New panpipes are made using older instruments as models. The expert craftsman measures the interior length of the tube with a thin rod used as a plummet. To obtain the correct tube length of an instrument to be tuned to the upper octave, the measurements are halved. Conversely, to make an instrument tuned to the lower octave the measuring rod is bent in half before being inserted in the model instrument; the unbent rod then gives the desired length.

Instrumental music in Malaita mostly consists of 'programme music', in the broad sense (or 'descriptive music' in a more restricted sense). Each piece, composed according to rigorous rules, has a title indicating the theme of the composition, for example the songs of birds, the croaking of frogs, the whirring of insects, cries of animals, the patter of drops of water on a leaf, the murmur of streams, the roar of the sea, the crackling of tree branches, or other natural sounds. Human sounds also can be the theme of a piece, such as the crying of an infant, the moaning of the sick or wounded, sleepers' snoring, spoken words, and sounds made at work. Some compositions are based on songs or melodies played on other instruments. A piece may translate a visual movement, such as the swaying of a spider or the comings and goings of people. The history of the composition and the name of the composer are passed on to young musicians, but non-musicians are usually ignorant of these aspects, and often do not even know the name of a composition. The title and composer of some pieces believed to be very old are no longer known even among musicians. These pieces are now known as part of the repertory of a celebrated musician or of a village.

(*iii*) *Ontong Java* (*Polynesian-speaking peoples*). The traditional music of the Ontong Java atoll, like that of all Polynesia, is essentially vocal. In Ontong Java

instruments are used exclusively for the rhythmical accompaniment of song: small slit-drums, sometimes replaced or complemented by pieces of wood or bamboo struck with two sticks; bamboo stamping tubes (each singer plays only one tube); fans struck on the palm of the hand. Some types of song are danced: the musical beach games of young girls consist for the most part of sitting dances. Most standing dances have a slow first part in which the dancers, men or women, stay in place; then there is a great acceleration of tempo, at which point the dancers advance with rapid motions towards

17. *Large panpipes of the 'au paina ensemble, 'Are'are people, Malaita, Solomon Islands*

the choir sitting on the ground. Formerly many types of song were performed only once a year, in the course of an important ritual dedicated to the ancestral gods. Other songs were associated with the birth of the first child, with funerals, or were sung for amusement. The songs are performed by male, female or mixed choirs, with the exception of prayers which are chanted by the ritual leader. Two archaic vocal styles are characteristic of Ontong Java (as of all Polynesia): one-note recitative and speech-song. Passages of both styles also appear in songs which otherwise use several pitches. Songs in two- or three-part polyphony have a drone.

## BIBLIOGRAPHY

FIJI

A. C. Capell, ed.: *A New Fijian Dictionary* (Glasgow and Sydney, 1941, rev.2/1957)
C. Thompson: 'Fijian Music and Dance', *Transactions and Proceedings of the Fiji Society*, xi (Suva, 1966), 14
J. Rabukawaqa: *Early Fijian Music* (Suva, 1973)

NEW CALEDONIA

S. H. Ray: 'The People and Language of Lifu, Loyalty Islands', *Journal of the Royal Anthropological Institute*, xlvii (1917), 273

F. Saracin and J. Roux: *Nova Caledonia* (Munich, 1929), 218ff

M. Leenhardt: *Documents néo-calédoniens* (Paris, 1932), 509f

——: *Gens de la Grande Terre* (Paris, 1937), 159ff

——: *Notes d'ethnologie néo-calédonienne* (Paris, 1939), 143–78

NEW HEBRIDES

F. Speiser: *Ethnographische Materialien aus den Neuen Hebriden und den Banks-Inseln* (Berlin, 1923)

A. B. Deacon: *Malekula: a Vanishing People in the New Hebrides* (London, 1934/R1970)

J. W. Layard: *Stone Men of Malekula* (London, 1942)

R. Clausen: *A Musicological Study of the Layard Collection of Recorded Malekulan Music in its Sociological and Ritual Setting* (diss., U. of Oxford, 1958)

H. Fischer: *Schallgeräte in Ozeanien: Bau und Spieltechnik, Verbreitung und Funktion* (Strasbourg and Baden-Baden, 1958)

P. O'Reilly: *Bibliographie méthodique, analytique et critique des Nouvelles-Hébrides* (Paris, 1958)

A. MacIntyre: *Music of the Small Islands off Malekula* (diss., Monash U., Melbourne, 1970)

M. Bitter: 'Les Nouvelles-Hébrides: chants, danses et documents', Musidisc 30 CV1273 [disc notes]

P. Crowe: 'Music and Grade-taking on East Aoba', *Musicology*, iv (Sydney, 1974), 64

PAPUA NEW GUINEA

R. M. Berndt: *Excess and Restraint: Social Control among a New Guinea Mountain People* (Chicago and London, 1962)

V. Chenoweth: 'Song Structure of a New Guinea Highlands Tribe', *EM*, x (1966), 285

J. Kunst: *Music in New Guinea* (The Hague, 1967)

V. Chenoweth: 'Managalasi Mourning Songs', *EM*, xii (1968), 415

——: 'An Investigation of the Singing Styles of the Dunas', *Oceania*, xxxix (1969), 218

V. Chenoweth and D. Bee: 'Comparative-generative Models of a New Guinea Melodic Structure', *American Anthropologist*, lxxiii (1971), 773

A. Moyle: 'Music', *Encyclopaedia of Papua and New Guinea*, ed. P. Ryan, ii (Carlton, Victoria, 1972)

V. Chenoweth: *Usarufa Music* (diss., U. of Auckland, 1974)

G. D. Spearritt: 'Music of the Middle Sepik River (New Guinea) – a Preliminary Survey', *SMA*, viii (1974)

V. Chenoweth, ed.: *Musical Instruments of Papua New Guinea* (Ukarumpa, Papua New Guinea, 1976)

SOLOMON ISLANDS

E. M. von Hornbostel: 'Die Musik auf den nord-westlichen Salomo-Inseln', *Forschungen auf den Salomo-Inseln und dem Bismarck-Archipel*, ed. R. Thurnwald, i (Berlin, 1912), 462–504

D. L. Oliver: *A Solomon Island Society: Kinship and Leadership among the Siuai of Bougainville* (Cambridge, Mass., 1955)

H. Fischer: *Schallgeräte in Ozeanien: Bau und Spieltechnik, Verbreitung und Funktion* (Strasbourg and Baden-Baden, 1958)

H. Zemp: 'Flûtes de Pan mélanésiennes, 'Are'are, i–ii', 'Musique mélanésienne, 'Are'are, iii', Vogue LDM 30104/5/6 (1969–71) [disc notes]

——: 'Musique de Guadalcanal: Solomon Islands', Ocora OCR 74 (1970) [disc notes]

——: 'Instruments de musique de Malaita', *Journal de la Société des Océanistes*, xxvii/30 (1971), 31; xxviii/34 (1972), 7–48

——: 'Polynesian Traditional Music of Ontong Java (Solomon Islands)', Vogue LD 786 (1971) and LDM 30109 (1972) [disc notes]

——: 'Fabrication de flûtes de Pan aux Iles Salomon', *Objets et mondes*, xii/3 (1972), 247

——: 'Fataleka and Baegu Music: Malaita, Solomon Islands', UNESCO Collection–Musical Sources 6018 (1973) [disc notes]

H. Zemp and J. Schwarz: 'Echelles équiheptaphoniques des flûtes de Pan chez les 'Are'are (Malaita, Iles Salomon)', *YIFMC*, v (1973), 85–121

C. Duvelle: 'Papua New Guinea: Manus, Bougainville', Ocora OCR 86 (1975) [disc notes]

J. Rossen: 'Polynesian Songs and Games from Bellona (Mungiki), Solomon Islands', Ethnic Folkways FE 4273 [disc notes]

——: 'The *Suahongi* of Bellona: Polynesian Ritual Music', *EM*, xxii (1978), 397–439

H. Zemp: ''Are'are Classification of Musical Types and Instruments', *EM*, xxii (1978), 37–67

——: 'Aspects of 'Are'are Musical Theory', *EM*, xxiii (1979), 5–48

R. Sheridan: 'Music of New Guinea', Wattle Records D2 [disc notes] [7 items from the Province of North Solomons of Papua New Guinea]

BARBARA B. SMITH (1, 3)
CHRIS THOMPSON SAUMAIWAI (2)
PETER CROWE, DEREK A. RAWCLIFFE (4)
VIDA CHENOWETH (5), HUGO ZEMP (6)

**Melani.** Italian family of musicians. At least three related families of this name from Pistoia produced musicians during the 17th century. The most prominent were the seven sons of Domenico di Sante Melani, bellringer of Pistoia Cathedral from 1624 to 1650. Of these the most important were the two oldest, Jacopo and Atto, and the youngest, Alessandro, who are discussed separately below. The others were: Francesco Maria (Padre Filippo) (*b* Pistoia, 3 Dec 1628; *d* ?Florence, c1703), a Servite monk allowed to leave the order while remaining a priest, who was a soprano in the service of Archduke Sigismund of Austria in 1657–63, sang a leading role in Cavalli's *Serse* in Paris in 1660 and served the Grand Duke of Tuscany as a singer from 1672 to 1700; Jacinto (*b* Pistoia, 1631; *d* Pistoia, 1705), bellringer in succession to his father; Bartolomeo (*b* Pistoia, 6 March 1634; *d* Pistoia, 1703), an alto at Pistoia Cathedral from 1654 to 1656, in the chapel of the Duke of Bavaria in Munich from 1657 to 1660 (though he sang at the Pergola and Cocomero theatres, Florence, in 1661), *maestro di cappella* of Pistoia Cathedral from 1668 to 1677 and from then on organist there until his death; and Vincentio Paolo (*b* Pistoia, 15 Jan 1637; *d* before 1667), known to have been a soprano at Pistoia Cathedral between 1650 and 1659 and to have sung at the Teatro della Pergola, Florence, in 1661. Three further musicians belonging to other branches of the Melani deserve mention: Antonio (*b* Pistoia, *d* ?Austria), Kapellmeister to Archduke Ferdinand Karl of Austria at Innsbruck in 1659 and composer of *Scherzi musicali, ossia capricci, e balletti* for one or two violins and optional viola (Innsbruck, 1659); Domenico (*b* Pistoia, 7 March 1629; *d* Florence, 12 July 1693), a soprano in the service of Queen Christina of Sweden from 1652 to 1654 and in Dresden from then until 1680, when he retired to Florence; and Nicola (*b* Pistoia, before 1632), a soprano who accompanied Domenico to Dresden.

**(1) Jacopo Melani** (*b* Pistoia, 6 July 1623; *d* Pistoia, 19 Aug 1676). Composer and organist. In 1644 he accompanied his brother (2) Atto Melani to Paris. He was elected organist of Pistoia Cathedral on 24 November 1645 and in 1657 became *maestro di cappella*. He also served Prince Mattias de' Medici by composing music (none of which has survived) for his birthday and for Easter celebrations. He moved to Rome in 1667. On 7 October 1673 his name reappears in records as organist of Pistoia Cathedral and continues to do so until his death, although as payments were to someone else he may not actually have assumed the office.

Jacopo Melani was the leading 17th-century composer of comic operas. Only two of them survive. He may have begun to compose opera as early as 1652, for he was engaged at that date in some capacity by Grimani in Venice; during that season an anonymous opera, *Helena rapita da Theseo* (erroneously attributed to Cavalli), was performed at Grimani's theatre, SS Giovanni e Paolo. Melani was a member (with the duty of composing) of the Florentine Accademia dei Sorgenti, for which he composed *intermedi* to *La donna più costante* in 1655 and probably also to *Scipione in Cartagine*, an opera with a text probably by G. A. Moniglia, in 1657. He composed the music for five of the seven operas mounted by the Immobili, a Florentine dramaturgical academy, in their theatre, the Pergola: *Il potestà di Colognole* (1657), better, though incorrectly, known as *La Tancia*; *Il pazzo per forza* (1658); *Il vecchio balordo* (1659); *Ercole in Tebe* (1661); and *La vedova* (composed in 1662 but not performed until 1680, under the sub-title *Amor vuol inganno*). All the librettos are by G. A. Moniglia. *Ercole*, a *festa teatrale* composed for the wedding of Cosimo de' Medici and Marguerite of Orleans, set the style for the operas composed for the coronations of Louis XIV (Cavalli's *Ercole amante*, 1662) and Leopold I of Austria ( Cesti's *Il pomo d'oro*, 1668).

For Rome he is known to have composed only one opera, *Il Girello* (Palazzo Colonna, 1668), with libretto by Filippo Acciaiuoli and a prologue composed by Stradella. *Il Girello*, a satirical work containing pointed criticism of absolutism, inaugurated a second period of Roman comic opera, which affords a direct link between 17th- and 18th-century comic opera. One of the most frequently performed operas of the century, it was staged throughout Italy between 1669 and 1676 by a touring troupe of *comici*, with whom Melani may have been associated. His remaining three operas were again to librettos by Moniglia. He composed *Il ritorno d'Ulisse* (1669) and *Enea in Italia* (1670) for performance in Pisa during the annual winter sojourn of the Medici court, and. *Tacere et amare* for an academy of Florentine gentlemen in 1674.

The four scores that survive are *Il potestà di Colognole*, *Ercole in Tebe*, *Il Girello* and *Enea in Italia* in various MSS (in *D-Bs*; *F-Pn*; *GB-Lbm*; *I-Fc*, *Fn*, *MOe*, *Nc*, Rospigliosi collection, Pistoia, *Rvat*).

(2) **Atto Melani** (*b* Pistoia, 31 March 1626; *d* Paris, 1714). Alto and composer. He was sent by his patron, Mattias de' Medici, to study in Rome with Luigi Rossi and Marc'Antonio Pasqualini and was then sent in 1644 to Paris, where he quickly won the favour of Mazarin and Queen Anne. During further visits to Paris he performed in such operas as Rossi's *Orfeo* (1647) and Cavalli's *Serse* (1660). Mazarin and Mattias also used Atto, ostensibly only a singer, as a secret diplomatic courier. Thus he travelled continually from one court to another, gathering favours for himself as he did so from an astonishing number of European princes; he was rewarded by being made a gentleman of the chamber to Louis XIV and a naturalized French citizen. But the death of Mazarin in 1661 undermined his secure position. Francesco Buti, librettist and impresario for Louis' coronation opera, *Ercole amante* (1662) by Cavalli, pointedly omitted a suitable role for him, and after becoming indiscreetly involved in the scandal surrounding the fall from favour of Fouquet, the superintendent of finances, he was exiled from France.

He attached himself to Cardinal Giulio Rospigliosi in Rome; his last recorded appearance as a singer took place at the Casa Rospigliosi in 1668. Otherwise his occupation was ecclesiastical politics. He even claimed to be chiefly responsible for the election of Rospigliosi to the papacy as Clement IX in 1667. His connections with Rospigliosi doubtless led to the move to Rome in 1667 of his brothers Jacopo and Alessandro, the latter's appointments to S Maria Maggiore and S Luigi dei Francesi and Atto's own restoration to the good graces of Louis XIV. He returned to France in 1679 and remained there, involved in politics and diplomacy, for the rest of his life. Since he was awarded certain benefices he is sometimes referred to as 'Abbate Melani'.

His extant compositions include 15 solo cantatas and one duet. One cantata, *Io voglio esser infelice*, was published in M. Silvani's *Canzonette per camera* (Bologna, 1670), and several must have become very popular

judging by the number of MSS (in *A-Wn*; *D-MÜs*, *Kl*; *F-Pc*, *Pn*, *Pthibault*; *GB-Cfm*, *Ckc*, *Lbm*; *I-Bc*, *Fc*, *Fn*, *MOe*, *Nc*, *Rc*, *Rvat*; *US-LAuc*) in which they appear. However, his importance lies primarily in the historical record of musical events between 1644 and 1661 found in his numerous letters to various patrons.

(3) **Alessandro Melani** (*b* Pistoia, 4 Feb 1639; *d* Rome, Oct 1703). Composer. He sang at Pistoia Cathedral between 1650 and 1660. He then became *maestro di cappella* in Orvieto and Ferrara. He returned to Pistoia in December 1666 and became *maestro di cappella* of the cathedral in June 1667, replacing his brother Jacopo. Four months later he was elected *maestro di cappella* of S Maria Maggiore, Rome; he assumed a similar position at S Luigi dei Francesi no later than July 1672 and remained there until his death. In Rome he enjoyed the patronage of Ferdinando de' Medici, his name appearing among 'celebrated professors of music protected by the Prince of Tuscany' in 1695, and of Francesco II d'Este, who in 1690 commissioned an oratorio from him, probably *Lo scisma nel sacerdozio* (which is lost). The justification for the admission of Alessandro's nephews to the minor nobility of Tuscany speaks of unspecified services to the King of Poland; the fact that he composed an oratorio, *Golia abbatuto*, in 1685 (to celebrate the Holy League against the Turks negotiated by Pope Innocent XI and including the King of Poland) strongly suggests that these services combined politics and music.

As a composer of liturgical music for Rome, Melani was an important precursor of Alessandro Scarlatti. In addition to his three published collections and isolated motets in other published volumes many other works survive in MS; the majority are for eight, nine or ten voices and they constitute a surprisingly large corpus of polychoral music which has yet to be studied. Of eight oratorios ascribed to him the most frequently performed was one variously titled *Il fratricidio di Caino*, *Il sacrificio di Abele* and *Abele*. *S Dimna* (Rome, 1683) is a pasticcio that brought together the three dominant composers in Rome in the second half of the century: Melani, Pasquini and Scarlatti. Alessandro, his brother Jacopo and later Pasquini, Stradella, Antonio Olivieri, Cosimo Bani and above all Alessandro Scarlatti constitute a second school of Roman opera. As noted above under (1), the revival of opera in Rome began with Jacopo Melani's *Il Girello* in 1668. In the following year at the Teatro Colonna, also with Filippo Acciaiuoli as the impresario, Alessandro's first datable opera, *L'empio punito*, was performed; it is chiefly interesting as the first opera on the subject of Don Juan. These two operas together established a bridge between the lyrical, comic style of mid-century Tuscan opera and the second flowering of Roman opera. But it should be noted that neither composer ever wrote another opera for Rome. Nor are any revivals of their operas recorded in Rome, though Alessandro continued to be a leading composer of oratorio and liturgical music there. Instead his operas were more in demand in Florence and Bologna.

### WORKS

#### OPERAS

L'empio punito (F. Acciaiuoli), Colonna, Rome, 1669, *I-Rvat*

Il trionfo della continenza considerato in Scipione Africano (G. Montevecchi), Fano, 1677, *D-MÜs*

Le reciproche gelosie (F. Nencini), Siena, 1677, *I-Rvat* (with title, Scherzo musicale); Florence, 1691, as Il sospetto senza fondamento

Roberto ovvero Il carceriere di se medesimo (L. Adimari), Florence,

Accademia degli Infuocati, 1681, *F-Pn, I-Bc, MOe*; copies of *F-Pn* in *B-Bc, US-Wc*; also Modena, 1684, as La calma fra le tempeste
Ama chi t'ama (Nencini), Siena, 1682, *I-Bc* (with title Chi geloso non è amar non sa), *MOe*; also Bologna, 1688, with title Gli amori di Lidia e Clori
S Dinna, with B. Pasquini and A. Scarlatti, Rome, 1687, lost
Idaspe, *Rvat*
Capriccio a 3, bacchettone, soldato e giocatore, intermedio, *A-Wn*
L'Europa, introduzione, *Wn*
Rinaldo, intermedio a cinque, *GB-Lbm, I-MOe*

ORATORIOS
La morte di Oloferne [La Giuditta] (Nencini), Rome, S Giovanni de' Fiorentini, 1675, lost
Il fratricidio di Caino [Abele; Il sacrificio di Abele] (B. Pamphili), Rome, Palazzo Pamphili, 1677, lost
S Francesca Romana, Palermo, 1682, lost
Golia abbatuto, Rome, 1685, *GB-Cfm*
Il giudizio di Salomone, Bologna, 1686, lost
Lo scisma del sacerdozio, ?Modena, 1691, lost
Giuditta, Florence, 1693, lost
S Rosa di Viterbo, Florence, 1693, *F-Pc*
S Eugenia (G. Bussi), 1686, *F-LYm*
S Filippo Neri, lost, lib pubd (Lucca, 1715)

SACRED
Mottetti sacri, 2–5vv, op.1 (Rome, 1670)
Delectus sacrorum concentum, 2–5vv, bc, op.2 (Rome, 1673)
Concerti spirituali, 2, 3, 5vv, op.3 (Rome, 1682)
?Motetti, 1–3, 5vv, bc, op.4 (Rome, 1698), lost
6 masses, mass sections, 3 requiems, over 100 litanies, canticles, hymns and motets in MSS: *A-Wn; D-Bs, MÜs; F-Pc, Pn; GB-Lbm, Och; I-Bc, Nc, Nf, PS, Rsc, Rvat; S-Uu*

CHAMBER
28 cantatas, notably A bella gloria in seno, cantate in onore di Luigi XIV, ?Rome, 1678, *I-Vqs*; Oratio Coclite, *Fc*; Dialogo di Lilla e Lidio, *D-MÜs*; All'armi pensieri, *GB-Lbm, I-Rc*
74 arias in *A-Wn; B-Bc, Lc; D-Bs, Kl, MÜs, Mbs; F-Pc, Pn, Pthibault; GB-Cfm, Ckc, DRc, Lbm, Ob; I-Bc, Fc, Fl, Fn, MOe, Nc, Rc, Rvat, Vqs*, Gatti Kraus's private collection, Fiesole; *US-LAuc*
2 canzonettas, *F-Pn, I-Rc*
Sonata a 5 for 2 vn, va, 2 tpt/ob, bc, *S-Uu*; sinfonia a 5, *GB-Ob*

BIBLIOGRAPHY
A. Ademollo: 'Un campanajo e la sua famiglia', *Fanfulla della domenica* (1883), no.52
——: *I primi fasti della musica italiana a Parigi* (Milan, 1884)
——: *La storia del 'Girello'* (Milan, 1890)
H. Prunières: *L'opéra italien en France* (Paris, 1913)
A. Damerini: 'La partitura dell'*Ercole in Tebe* di Jacopo Melani con appendice sui musicisti fratelli di Jacopo', *Bollettino storico pistoiese*, xix (1917), 45
L. Feininger: 'La scuola policorale del sei e settecento', *CHM*, ii (1956), 193
R. L. Weaver: *Florentine Comic Operas of the Seventeenth Century* (diss., U. of North Carolina, 1958)
M. Borrelli: *Una interessante raccolta di libretti a stampa di oratori della fine del Seicento presso la Biblioteca dell'Oratorio di Londra* (Naples, 1962)
P. M. Caponi: 'Melani', *ES*
R. L. Weaver: '*Il Girello*, a 17th-century Burlesque Opera', *Quadrivium*, xii/2 (1971), 141
——: *Alessandro and Atto Melani*, WECIS, viii–ix (1972)
U. Pineschi: 'Jacopo Melani e Lodovico Giustini organisti nella chiesa della Congregazione dello Spirito Santo di Pistoia', *Bollettino storico pistoiese*, lxxv (1973), 89
L. Bianconi and T. Walker: 'Dalla *Finta pazza* alla *Veremonda*: storie di Febiarmonici', *RIM*, x (1975), 379–454
C. Gianturco: 'Evidence for a Late Roman School of Opera', *ML*, lvi (1975), 4
J. W. Hill: 'Le relazioni di Antonio Cesti con la corte e i teatri di Firenze', *RIM*, xi (1976), 27
R. L. Weaver: 'Materiali per le biografie dei fratelli Melani', *RIM*, xii (1977), 252
R. L. Weaver and N. W. Weaver: *A Chronology of Florentine Theater 1590–1750* (Detroit, 1978)

ROBERT LAMAR WEAVER

**Melanippides** (*fl* 5th century BC). Greek dithyrambic poet and composer. Born on Melos, he died at the court of King Perdiccas II of Macedon (*c*450–413 BC), whom he had served as a musician. Xenophon and Plutarch ranked him with the greatest artists of earlier times, among them Homer, Simonides and Euripides (Xenophon, *Memorabilia*, i, chap.4, §3; Plutarch, *Non*

*posse suaviter*, chap.13, §1095*d*). In the *Suda* lexicon he is credited with extensive innovations in dithyrambic composition. The critical tone of this reference probably reflects the estimate given in a fragment from the *Chiron*, a comedy doubtfully ascribed to Pherecrates. Music herself – *Mousikē* in the older sense, which included poetry – appeared on the stage, dishevelled and badly knocked about. Melanippides, she declared, had been the first to 'undo' her and make her 'looser' (*chalarōteran*, 'more slack') with an array of *chordai*. As a musical term, *chordē* may mean either 'note' or 'string'. The latter sense is necessary for the *double entendre* which characterizes the whole of Music's lament. Nevertheless, the passage is not reliable evidence for any increase in the number of lyre strings. *Chalaros* does not appear to have any serious ethical meaning here, nor is its meaning even within a musical context clearly established.

The factual basis may be discernible in Aristotle's explanation (*Rhetoric*, iii, chap.9, §1409*b*25ff) of an attack by a minor poet on Melanippides' use of the extended *anabolē*: he stated that it had been substituted for metrical correspondence in the antistrophic portions of the dithyramb. From the time of Homer onwards, the *anabolē* had been an instrumental prelude; Melanippides pressed it into service as an interlude of some sort. The author of the Pseudo-Plutarchian *De musica* associated him with the new importance accorded to the aulos and an increase in the number of *chordai*; in rapid succession he is categorized as a *melopoios*, i.e. a lyric poet, and again as a dithyrambic poet (chap.30, §1141*c*–*d*; chap.15, §1136*c*; for the lament of *Mousikē* see chap.30, §§1141*d*–1142*a*). The first of these descriptions does not imply a lack of poetic content, as has been supposed. Although the second may be an interpolation, the fact remains that from a very early period Melanippides was regarded as a librettist-composer, one who made the text secondary to displays of virtuosity on the aulos. The term *anabolē*, which properly described instrumental music, could therefore be applied to his interludes. Translations such as 'lyric solo' reflect a modern preoccupation with the text.

Melanippides was thought to have been the forerunner of such controversial dithyrambic poets as Philoxenus and Timotheus; the *Chiron* passage strongly supports this conclusion. Surviving fragments of his works, not clearly identifiable as dithyrambs, have stilted diction and a mild degree of metrical slackness. They include lines from a *Marsyas* (frag.2, ed. Edmonds) which portray Athena casting the double aulos from her: she calls the twin pipes 'defilers of the body', sources of self-inflicted *kakotēs*. This term regularly denoted moral rather than physical shortcomings. Here it stands in curious conjunction with the tradition (*see* MARSYAS) that Athena's disgust was provoked by an awareness of the facial distortion resulting from playing upon the pipes. Athenaeus (bk xiv, p.616*e*, the source of the *Marsyas* fragment) suggested that Melanippides meant to attack aulos playing when he made Athena speak thus. The evidence indicates instead that he championed the aulos and the astrophic metrics which were a necessary consequence of its growing predominance in the dithyramb.

BIBLIOGRAPHY
H. W. Smyth: *Greek Melic Poets* (London and New York, 1900/*R*1963), 132f, 453ff
J. M. Edmonds, ed. and trans.: *Lyra graeca* (London and New York,

1922–7, 2/1928–40), iii, 230–39
A. W. Pickard-Cambridge: *Dithyramb Tragedy and Comedy* (Oxford, 1927, rev. 2/1962 by T. B. L. Webster), 39ff
D. L. Page, ed.: *Poetae melici graeci* (Oxford, 1962), 392ff
U. Knoche: 'Melanippides', *Lexikon der alten Welt* (Zurich and Stuttgart, 1965), 1163
W. D. Anderson: *Ethos and Education in Greek Music* (Cambridge, Mass., 1966), 55, 231f
L. Richter: 'Die neue Musik der griechischen Antike', *AMw*, xxv (1968), 8, 12

WARREN ANDERSON

**Melartin, Erkki** [Erik] **(Gustav)** (*b* Käkisalmi, 7 Feb 1875; *d* Pukinmäki, 14 Feb 1937). Finnish composer. He studied at the Helsinki Music Institute (1892–9) and in Vienna with Fuchs (1899–1901); in addition, he read art history at Basle University and travelled throughout Europe to study. He taught at the Helsinki Music Institute (1898, 1901–7), where he was director from 1911 to 1936, and he conducted the orchestra of the Viipuri Friends of Music (1908–11). As a nationalist symphonist Melartin remained in the shadow of Sibelius; he is best remembered for his shorter lyric pieces, including the salon music which brought him greatest popularity. He was also a mystic; his ideas, somewhat influenced by eastern religions, were presented in the opera *Aino*, though the lame and derivative music of this work hampers the comprehensibility of his philosophy.

WORKS
(*selective list*)

Stage: Aino, opera, 1907; Sininen helmi [The blue pearl], ballet, 1930
8 syms.: c, 1902; e, 1904; F, 1907; E, 1913; (Sinfonia brevis), a, 1916; 1924; 2 syms. inc.
Other orch works: 3 sym. poems; 3 lyric suites; 3 festival preludes; Serenade, str; Karjalaisia kuvia [Karelian pictures]; Vn Conc.; Sursum corda; incidental music
Chamber: 4 str qts; Qt, 2 tpt, trbn, hn; Qt, 4 hn; Trio, fl, cl, bn; 2 vn sonatas; Sonata, fl, harp; vn and vc pieces
Vocal: over 300 solo songs; Legend Marjatta with orch; *c*40 choruses
Pf: over 350 pieces incl. Sonata, Fantasia apocaliptica, Intermezzi, Lyrische Stücke, Der traurige Garten, Stimmungen, Feuillets d'album; Marionettes, suite for 4 hands
Principal publishers: Finnish Broadcasting Company, Fazer

HANNU ILARI LAMPILA

**Melba,** Dame **Nellie** [Mitchell, Helen Porter] (*b* Richmond, Melbourne, 19 May 1861; *d* Sydney, 23 Feb 1931). Australian soprano of Scottish descent. She had already made some concert appearances in Melbourne (the source of her adopted stage name) before going to Europe in 1886. A year's study in Paris with the famous and formidable Mathilde Marchesi transformed her from a gifted beginner into a brilliant vocalist, soon to be regarded as the most accomplished and most famous soprano of her time.

Melba made her début on 13 October 1887 at the Théâtre de la Monnaie, Brussels, as Gilda, and during that season went on to sing Violetta, Lucia di Lammermoor, Lakmé and Ophelia. In 1888 she appeared at Covent Garden as Lucia, and in the same year at the Paris Opéra as Ophelia. Her rare beauty of tone and perfection of technique created an immediate stir, but these virtues were not at first matched by equivalent qualities of taste and musicianship. Her great achievements really began with her Juliet and Marguerite in Paris (1889 and 1890 respectively) and soon afterwards in London; she had studied both parts with Gounod, and often sang them with Jean de Reszke, who became a decisive influence on her musical development. Bernard Shaw, who had formerly complained of her artistic

*Nellie Melba as Ophelia in Ambroise Thomas' 'Hamlet'*

inadequacies, wrote of her in 1892 as 'transfigured, awakened, no longer to be identified by the old descriptions'.

Within a few years the world was at her feet. Between 1892 and 1894 she made some highly successful Italian appearances which included both Gilda and Lucia at La Scala; in 1893 (again as Lucia) she began an association with the Metropolitan that lasted, with intermissions, until 1910; she also sang for Hammerstein's Manhattan Opera, and with the Chicago company. Besides numerous international concert tours, she organized operatic seasons in Australia in 1911, and again in 1924. But Covent Garden always remained, as she said, her 'artistic home'. Except for two seasons (1909 and 1912) she sang there every year until World War I, and made occasional reappearances thereafter; her farewell to the house took place on 8 June 1926, when she was heard in the Balcony Scene from *Roméo et Juliette*, the first part of Act 4 of *Otello*, and the last two acts of *La bohème*. Extensive recordings, by the then novel electrical process, were made of this emotional occasion, which was followed by an Albert Hall concert farewell, some isolated charity appearances, and closely similar *Otello–Bohème* operatic farewells in Sydney and Melbourne at the end of a third Australian season in 1928, in which she did not otherwise appear. In 1918 she had been made a DBE.

During the earlier part of her career, Melba concentrated on the more brilliant French and Italian roles mentioned above, but from 1899 until her retirement Mimì became the most famous of all her parts. Her repertory was not large, and contained no Mozart; but at various times it included also Rosina and Semiramis, Micaëla and Manon, the Queen in *Les Huguenots*, the title roles in Bemberg's *Elaine* and Saint-Saëns' *Hélène* (both written for her, and both negligible), Aida and Nedda, and (in Italian) Elisabeth and Elsa. She once attempted the heavier part of Brünnhilde in *Siegfried* (Metropolitan, 1896, in German with Jean de Reszke), but immediately withdrew from so rash an enterprise. With that exception, she invariably employed her tone well within its natural limits, and it was thanks to this admirable restraint and to her perfect method that she retained her powers largely unimpaired throughout a long career.

Her timbre has often been called silvery, but there is ample evidence that her voice had also a 'clarion quality'. The phrase is that of the American critic, W. J. Henderson, who added: 'It had splendour. The tones glowed with a starlike brilliance'. Her trill, staccato singing, and scales, both diatonic and chromatic, were as precise as if played on a keyboard; and in smoothness and steadiness of tone, in spontaneity of emission and virtually flawless intonation, perhaps no singer of this century has equalled her. 'From B flat below the clef to the high F', wrote Henderson, '... the scale was beautifully equalized throughout and there was not the smallest change in the quality from bottom to top.'

Between 1904 and 1926 Melba made some 150 records. The earliest series, made in London, show the voice in a generally fresher and more brilliant state than some of the later American issues, but among the latter there are also some notable achievements, such as the solos from *Otello* and the *La bohème*, and the duet with Caruso from the first act of the latter, with its softly floated concluding high C, which is the sole (though worthy) souvenir of a famous partnership. In 1926, after her Covent Garden farewell, she made a few electric recordings, which capture a roundness and depth in the tone that were previously wanting. One might obtain some notion of her powers in her prime by superimposing, in imagination, the full tones of her 1926 'Dite alla giovine' (*La traviata*) upon the fabulous agility of her florid records of 1904.

BIBLIOGRAPHY

A. Murphy: *Melba* (London, 1909)
N. Melba: *Melodies and Memories* (London, 1925)
P. Colson: *Melba* (London, 1931)
H. H. Harvey and G. Whelan: 'Nellie Melba', *Record Collector*, iv (1949), 203 [with discography]
J. Hetherington: *Melba* (London, 1967)

DESMOND SHAWE-TAYLOR

**Melbourne.** Australian city, capital of Victoria. Founded in 1834, 46 years later than Sydney, Melbourne quickly became the largest and most active city in Australia when gold was discovered in Victoria in the 1850s. Musical growth paralleled the growth of the city, and only 30 years after settlement music had already achieved a sophistication unequalled elsewhere in Australia. The Melbourne Philharmonic Society, established in 1852, was the first choral society formed in Australia, and was the best-known of the many local groups which formed the large 19th-century festival choirs. Opera seasons occupied at least four months of each year from 1860 onwards (much more than at present); composition was encouraged, as were performances of choral, orchestral and chamber music.

Melbourne has produced at least as much opera as many leading European centres. Under William Saurin Lyster (1827–80) there were as many as 100 opera performances a year in Melbourne; he also toured New Zealand and the eastern Australian states with his company. He was active between 1861 and 1880, but his influence lasted for the next 50 years. Touring companies – the Melba–Williamson Company, the Quinlan Opera Company (which in 1912 produced the *Ring*), the Gonsalez Company and others – were attracted to Australia, and during this time many fine singers emerged such as Ada Crossley, Amy Castles, John Brownlee and Florence Austral; the most famous was Nellie Mitchell who changed her name to Melba (derived from Melbourne) when she became internationally famous.

During the Depression and after, large-scale performances of grand opera were rare, but interest in singing was maintained by means of the *Sun* Aria Competition, the Mobil Quest and Australian Broadcasting Commission vocal competitions. After the Williamson–Sutherland season in 1965 opera began to regain the popularity it had in the 19th century. The Australian Opera, the company created by the Elizabethan Trust in 1956, gives an annual two-month season in Melbourne's Princess Theatre. Melbourne singers who have achieved international reputations include Marjorie Lawrence, William Herbert, Ronald Dowd, John Lanigan, Margreta Elkins, Lauris Elms, John Shaw and Marie Collier.

Orchestral music began in the gold-rush era when Charles Winterbottom presented the Popular Promenade Concerts. In the 1860s orchestral music became firmly established through the composer, conductor and pianist Charles Horsley. The high standard of orchestral music by the 1880s was evident in the appearance of efficient festival orchestras. The large 1882 festival employed a choir of 1107 and an orchestra of 121, and the 1888–9 Centennial International Exhibition had an orchestra of 80 players and a large choir which gave 244 concerts during the six-month festival. This led to the desire to found a permanent orchestra, which was attempted by Marshall Hall in the 1890s. Alberto Zelman conducted the Melbourne SO from 1906 to 1927, when Fritz Hart succeeded him. In 1932, with the advent of the Australian Broadcasting Company, the orchestra was re-formed on a different basis; it was enlarged in 1934 and again in 1936, when it came under the control of the Australian Broadcasting Commission (ABC). At this time it had 40–45 members, augmented to 70–75 for symphony concerts. In the period 1949–64 it was known as the Victorian SO. Resident conductors have included Kurt Wöss, Georges Tzipine, Willem van Otterloo and Fritz Rieger. Bernard Heinze, the conductor for many years and one of the most significant figures in the country's recent musical history, introduced concerts for schoolchildren and ABC Youth Concerts; these series have been copied in all other states. The orchestra has a basic strength of 85 players and 13,000 regular subscribers as well as thousands of additional listeners attracted by open-air concerts at the Myer Music Bowl (see illustration) and the Summer Promenade concerts conducted by John Hopkins.

The Musical Society of Victoria, founded in 1861 by Charles Horsley, has continuously promoted chamber and solo music. Musica Viva (formed 1945) has an

*Concert at the Myer Music Bowl, Melbourne*

active following of 1500 subscribers to its chamber music concerts (*see also* AUSTRALIA). The Melbourne branch of the International Society for Contemporary Music, promoted by the composers Keith Humble and George Dreyfus, presents new music by Australian and foreign composers, as does the Astra Chamber Orchestra and Choir, conducted by George Logie Smith.

In 1891 a chair of music was endowed at Melbourne University by Sir Francis Ormond, with Marshall Hall as first professor, and three years later the conservatorium was formed in conjunction with the university. A second chair of music was established in 1975, with Peter Dennison its first incumbent, alongside the existing chair, then occupied by George Frederick Loughlin. In addition there is the Melba Memorial Conservatorium, established in 1895, and the new chair of music at Monash University, inaugurated in 1965 by the appointment of Trevor Jones. Monash University specializes in ethnomusicological studies.

Australia's oldest music-publishing house, Allan & Co., is in Melbourne. It was established in 1850 as a 'Music and Pianoforte Saloon' and was associated extensively with selling music and instruments, concert promotion and later with music publishing.

For bibliography *see* AUSTRALIA.

ANN CARR-BOYD

**Melbourne String Quartet.** Australian string quartet formed in 1972 by LEONARD DOMMETT.

**Melcelius** [Meltzelius, Mältzel, Möltzel, Melcl], **Jiří** (*b* Horšovský Týn, 1624; *d* Prague, 31 March 1693). Bohemian composer. Melcelius was a member of the Premonstratensian order. His life was passed in a succession of ecclesiastical musical appointments, the most notable of which was at the Prague church of St Benedict between 1663 and 1669. There he was organist and choirmaster and was apparently responsible for modernizing the repertory and building up an archive. In his old age he retired to the Strahov monastery in Prague.

The surviving music of Melcelius is all sacred (MSS in *CS-KRa* and *CS-K* and in *CS-Pnm*). A ten-part instrumental sonata is listed in the inventory of Tovačov Castle, but has not been found. Like most of his Czech contemporaries Melcelius was strongly influenced by the musical style of Michna and showed a similar skill in manipulating large choral forces with solid string accompaniments and frequent use of obbligato trombones and clarinos. He wrote seven masses, two vesper settings, two motets, one requiem and one *Te Deum*.

BIBLIOGRAPHY

*ČSHS*
E. Trolda: 'Jiří Melzel', *Cyril*, lix (1933), 9
J. Racek: 'Inventář hudebnin tovačovského zámku z konce 17. století', *Musikologie*, i (1938), 45

ADRIENNE SIMPSON

**Melcer-Szczawiński, Henryk** (*b* Kalisz, 21 Sept 1869; *d* Warsaw, 18 April 1928). Polish pianist, composer, teacher and conductor. After lessons with his violinist father, he performed from the age of eight in provincial towns. He studied mathematics at Warsaw University, and music at the Warsaw Music Institute under Rudolf Strobl (piano) and Zygmunt Noskowski (composition). After gaining his diploma in 1890 he made a long tour of Russia as an accompanist. He then resumed his studies under Leschetizky in Vienna, and subsequently gave concerts in many European cities, including Paris, Berlin, St Petersburg, Vienna, Dresden, Leipzig and Kiev. In 1895 he won prizes at the Anton Rubinstein competition in Berlin for performances of his own Piano Concerto in E minor and Piano Trio in G minor, and in the same year took charge of the piano class at the Helsinki Conservatory. From 1896 or 1897 until 1899 he was professor at the Lwów Conservatory, winning in 1898 a prize for his C minor Piano Concerto in the Paderewski competition in Leipzig. He was director of the music society in Łódź (1899–1902), conductor and director of the Lwów Philharmonia from 1902, and for a few years from 1903 was responsible for the piano class at the Vienna Conservatory. At this time he also played in many concerts, including annual engagements in Warsaw, Kraków, Lwów, Leipzig, Berlin and St Petersburg. He returned to Poland in 1908 to take up the conductorship of the Warsaw Philharmonic (1910–12) and the Warsaw Opera (1915–16). From 1919 he was on the staff of the Warsaw Conservatory, where he was in charge of the piano class (1919–28), the orchestra (1925–6) and, after the death of Roman Statkowski, the composition class; he was also director of the conservatory (1922–7). A highly cultured man as well as a gifted teacher and organizer, Melcer-Szczawiński raised the educational and artistic standards of the conservatory, preparing a new constitution, drafting a new system of examinations, and founding a viola class (1923) and a class in the methods of piano teaching (1925); he also reorganized the ensemble classes and extended the conservatory's concert activities. A conflict with the ministry of education caused his resignation from the directorship.

Melcer-Szczawiński's playing was characterized by an immaculate technique, an objective sense of interpretation and an extensive repertory which included all Bach's preludes and fugues as well as Chopin's études and Beethoven's sonatas. The 'sonata evenings' at which he played with the violinist Wacław Kochański won particular fame in Warsaw. His main achievement, however, was as a teacher and concert promoter. As a composer he represented late Romanticism. His style was in the tradition of Chopin and Schumann, but in his instrumentation, harmony and forms he assimilated into his music some of the advances made by Liszt and Tchaikovsky (particularly in his concertos and transcriptions of Moniuszko's songs), by Wagner (*Protesilas i Laodamia*) and by Wolf and Reger (five songs to words by Dehmel). In his piano writing he emphasized virtuosity and colour.

### WORKS

Maria (opera, 3, S. Szczawiński, after A. Malczewski), 1903–4, Warsaw, 1904
Protesilas i Laodamia (opera, S. Wyspiański), 1902, Paris, 1925, fragments
Pani Twardowska, ballad, T, chorus, orch (A. Mickiewicz), 1898 (Kraków, 1956)
Symphony, c, 1900, lost
Pf concerto no.1, e, 1895 (arr. pf, Vienna, 1904)
Pf concerto no.2, c, 1898 (arr. 2 pf, Kiev, 1913)
Pf trio, g, op.2, 1895 (Berlin, c1900)
Sonata, G, vn, pf, c1896 (Kraków, c1910)
Trois morceaux caracteristiques, op.5, pf, 1895 (Leipzig, before 1910)
Morceau fantastique, pf (Kraków, 1908)
Trois pensées musicales, pf (Warsaw, after 1910)
5 pieśni [5 songs] (R. Dehmel) (Kraków, c1909)
3 pieśni [3 songs] (M. Konopnicka, J. Jedlicz-Kapuściński, K. Tetmajer) (Kraków, c1910)
Pf transcrs. of songs by Moniuszko (Warsaw, 1901)

### BIBLIOGRAPHY

*SMP*
A. Chybiński: 'Henryk Melcer', *Młoda muzyka* (1908), no.6, p.1; (1909), no.1, p.1
J. W. Reiss: *Henryk Melcer* (Warsaw, 1949)
S. Śledziński, ed.: *150 lat Państwowej Wyższej Szkoły Muzycznej w Warszawie* (Kraków, 1960), 134ff
T. L. Błaszczyk: *Dyrygenci polscy i obcy w Polsce działający w XIX i XX wieku* [Polish and foreign conductors active in the 19th and 20th centuries] (Kraków, 1964)

BARBARA CHMARA-ŻACZKIEWICZ

**Melchior, Lauritz** [Hommel, Lebrecht] (*b* Copenhagen, 20 March 1890; *d* Santa Monica, 18 March 1973). Danish tenor, later naturalized American. Having sung as a treble, he trained with Paul Bang at the Royal Opera School, Copenhagen, and made his début at the Royal Opera on 2 April 1913 as Silvio in *Pagliacci*, going on to sing various other baritone roles. Subsequent studies with the Danish tenor Vilhelm Herold revealed the true nature of Melchior's voice, and he made a second début at the same theatre on 8 October 1918 in the title role of

*Lauritz Melchior as Siegfried*

*Tannhäuser*. With the help of the English novelist Hugh Walpole, who heard him sing at a London concert in 1919, Melchior was enabled to study the Wagner repertory intensively with Anna Bahr-Mildenburg and other eminent teachers, and made what might be termed a third, or 'international', début at Covent Garden on 14 May 1924 as Siegmund. Later that year he sang Siegmund and Parsifal at Bayreuth, and returned there regularly until 1931. From 1926 to 1939 he appeared every year at Covent Garden, where he quickly became a mainstay of the Wagner repertory, especially as Siegmund, Siegfried and Tristan; Othello, sung either in German or in a very Teutonic-sounding Italian, was his only non-Wagnerian London role.

Melchior's Metropolitan début on 20 February 1926, as Tannhäuser, was not outstandingly successful; his great New York period began only with his return, after a year's absence and further study, to sing Siegfried and Tristan in 1929. Thenceforward his activities centred on this house, where he remained a pillar of the Wagnerian wing for more than two decades until disagreements with the Bing regime caused him to take his leave, as Lohengrin, on 2 February 1950. During those years he made frequent guest appearances in Europe and at the Colón in Buenos Aires. Latterly he scored some success in Broadway shows and films, but continued also to make occasional concert and radio appearances in his old repertory, even singing Siegmund with the Danish Radio Orchestra in March 1960 to celebrate his 70th birthday.

In his later years Melchior sang little but Wagner, and concentrated on the heaviest roles, in each of which he appeared over 100 times – as Tristan over 200 times. These figures suggest something of the stamina and endurance that made of this huge Dane – huge in every dimension, as in voice – the only Wagner tenor of recent times who could still sound fresh in the last acts of *Tristan* and *Götterdämmerung*. A certain baritonal warmth remained a welcome feature of his singing, but there was no corresponding constriction in his top notes, and Siegfried's lusty high C in the scene with the Rhinemaidens always rang thrillingly through the house. These virtues, coupled with a vivid and expressive enunciation of the text, induced his admirers to overlook his dramatic limitations and even some musical defects – vagueness in the matter of rhythm and note values – which caused him to avoid the more lyrical and musically complex role of Walther von Stolzing. The heroic scale of his singing, whether in recollection, or as experienced again through the gramophone, has made it increasingly clear that he was the outstanding *Heldentenor* of the century.

From 1913 (in his baritone days) Melchior recorded extensively for numerous companies. His best pre-war years are fully documented by his recording as Siegmund (with Lotte Lehmann and Bruno Walter) and by a composite but almost complete account of the young Siegfried's music, supplemented by substantial extracts from *Götterdämmerung*, *Tristan und Isolde*, *Lohengrin* and *Parsifal* either with Frida Leider or with Kirsten Flagstad (1939–40). There are also many privately issued off-the-air recordings of complete Wagner performances, mainly from Metropolitan broadcasts.

BIBLIOGRAPHY
E. B. Mortensen and J. Zachs: 'A Lauritz Melchior Discography', *Record News*, iii (1959), 433; iv (1959), 12, 49
H. Hansen: *Lauritz Melchior: a Discography* (Copenhagen, 1965, 2/1972)
DESMOND SHAWE-TAYLOR

**Melchior de Brissia.** *See* PREPOSITUS BRIXIENSIS.

**Melchite rite, music of the.** *See* SYRIAN CHURCH MUSIC.

**Melcl, Jiří.** *See* MELCELIUS, JIŘÍ.

**Mele, Giovanni Battista** (*b* Naples, 1701; *d* ?Naples, after 1752). Italian composer. On 25 November 1710 he entered the Neapolitan conservatory Poveri di Gesù Cristo, where he studied for about 12 years with Gaetano Greco. He then went to Spain, where in 1736 he became known to the public through his opera *Por amor y por lealtad* at the Teatro de la Cruz in Madrid. He became associated with the court of Philip V, and composed several Italian serenatas for court events. After the death of Philip V in 1746, Mele was retained by Ferdinand VI, and served with his compatriots Francesco Corselli and Francesco Corradini as a composer of Italian operas and conductor of the orchestra at the Nuovo Real Teatro in the palace of Buen Retiro. His first work for Buen Retiro was *Angelica e Medoro*, a *festa teatrale* composed for the birthday celebrations of the music-loving Queen Maria Barbara in 1747. His last known work, *Armida placata*, an *opera seria*, was performed at Buen Retiro in 1750 and revived there the next year. In 1752 Mele requested permission to return to Naples; his fate thereafter is unknown.

WORKS
*(all stage works performed in Madrid)*

Por amor y por lealtad recobrar la majestad (opera seria, D. V. de Camacho, after Metastasio: Demetrio in Siria), de la Cruz, 31 Jan 1736
Amor constancia y mujer (opera seria, de Camacho, after Metastasio), de los Canos, Feb 1737
Serenata per la ricupperata salute di Sua Maesta, 5vv, insts, Casa del Monsignor L. G. di Vaureal, 1744, *F-Pc*
Serenata in occasione di festeggiarse i solenni sponsali della Real Infanta di Spagna, Donna Maria Teresa, con il Delfino di Francia, 5vv, insts, Casa del Monsignor L. G. di Vaureal, 1744, Pc
Angelica e Medoro (festa teatrale, Metastasio), Buen Retiro, 1747, *I-Nc*
La clemencia de Tito (seria, I. de Luzán y Suelves, after Metastasio), Buen Retiro, carn. 1747, Act 3 [Act 1, F. Corselli; Act 2, F. Corradini]
El Vellon de oro conquistado (opera seria, Pico della Mirandola), Buen Retiro, 23 Sept 1747, lib. only, *GB-Lbm*
El Polifemo (seria, P. Rolli), Buen Retiro, carn. 1748, Act 3 [Act 1, Corselli; Act 2, Corradini]
Endimion y Diana (serenata), spr. 1749
El Artajerjes (opera seria, after Metastasio), Buen Retiro, carn. 1749, recits and some arias
Armida placata (opera seria, G. A. Migliavacca, after Metastasio), Buen Retiro, 12 April 1750, lib. only (1751 perf.), *Lbm*
Concerto, fl, vns, violetta, b, *I-Nc*

BIBLIOGRAPHY
L. Carmen y Milan: *Cronica de la ópera italiana en Madrid desde el año 1748 hasta nuestros dias* (Madrid, 1878)
E. Cotarelo y Mori: *Orígenes y establecimiento de la ópera en España hasta 1800* (Madrid, 1917)
R. Kirkpatrick: *Domenico Scarlatti* (New York, 1953)
A. Mondolfi: 'G. B. Mele, musicista felice', *Gazzetta musicale di Napoli* (1956), June, 94
HANNS-BERTOLD DIETZ

**Meleket.** Interlinear signs of Ethiopic notation; *see* ETHIOPIAN RITE, MUSIC OF THE.

**Melfiche, Cola.** *See* FALCO, MICHELE.

**Melfio, Bastiano** (*b* Tosi [now Tursi]; *fl* 1564–87). Italian composer. According to the title-page of his earliest known publication, *Il primo libro de madrigali a quatro voci* (Rome, 1564), he was at that time the holder of a canonry at Torsi, near Pistica, in the Basilicata. The book contains a number of extended cycles including a three-section setting of Petrarch's *Di persona era*, a text often set as wedding music and which had previously been used by Lassus, Lupacchino, Martoretta and Nicolo Dorati. More than 20 years later he published another collection, *Il primo libro de madrigali a cinque voci* (Venice, 1587).

IAIN FENLON

**Melfio, Gioan Battista** (*b* Bisignano, Calabria; *fl* 1555–6). Italian composer. He was a priest. His only recorded publication, *Il primo libro de gli madrigali a quattro voci* (Venice, 1556), is, according to its dedication, also his first. It is dated 30 September 1555 from Naples and contains settings of Petrarch's verse including *Padre del ciel*, a text which continued to be popular until the end of the century, and of *Dunque baciar* from Ariosto's *Orlando furioso*.

IAIN FENLON

**Melgaz [Melgás], Diogo Dias** (*b* Cuba, Portugal, 11 April 1638; *d* Évora, 10 March 1700). Portuguese composer and teacher. On 11 May 1647 he was admitted as a choirboy at Évora Cathedral, where his teacher was Bento Nunes Pegado. He was elected master of the boys on 14 March 1662, *mestre da crasta* in 1663 and *mestre de capela* in about 1678. In 1697 his former pupil Pedro Vaz Rêgo began to substitute for him because he had become blind. Melgaz died in such poverty that his brother had to borrow 4000 réis to pay his funeral expenses. He was the first Évora composer to write functional harmony, to use bar-lines in his works and to write an instrumental accompaniment (in *P-EVc* 7, ff.59*v*–62) that does not duplicate any other part.

WORKS

2 masses, 16 motets, 3 Passion settings, *P-EVc*; 3 motets ed. J. E. dos Santos, *A polifonia clássica portuguesa* (Lisbon, 1937); 1 ed. in Alegria: *História*

Salve regina, 4vv, *Lf*

BIBLIOGRAPHY

*DBP*

A. F. Barata: 'Diogo Dias de Melgás', *Arquivo transtagano*, ii (1934), 135

J. Mazza: 'Dicionário biográfico de músicos portugueses', *Ocidente*, xxiii (1943), 256, 361; xxiv (1944), 358

M. de Sampayo Ribeiro: *Nossa Senhora na música de Portugal* (Braga, 1948), 30

M. de Sampayo Ribeiro, ed.: *Cadernos do repertório coral polyphonia, Série azul*, v (Lisbon, 1959) [9 Lenten motets]

J. A. Alegria: *História da escola de música da Sé de Évora* (Lisbon, 1973), 75ff, 168ff

——: *Arquivo das músicas da Sé de Évora* (Lisbon, 1973), 15ff, 53, 64

ROBERT STEVENSON

**Meli [Melij], Pietro Paolo.** See MELLI, PIETRO PAOLO.

**Melikov, Arif (Jangirovich)** (*b* Baku, 13 Sept 1933). Soviet composer. He studied the *tar* at the Baku Music College (1946–54) and composition under Karayev at the Azerbaijan State Conservatory (1955–8). While at the conservatory he composed his first serious works, including his graduation piece, the First Symphony. In 1958 he was appointed to teach at the conservatory, where in 1971 he was made assistant professor. He became a board member of the Azerbaijani Composers' Union in 1959, and in 1965 he received the title Honoured Artist of the Azerbaijani SSR.

Melikov completed his finest work, the ballet *Legenda o lyubvi* ('Legend of love'), in 1961. It is a work concerned with one of the eternal subjects of eastern poetry: pure and tragic love. The ballet's number form does not impede a continuous intensive development, for Melikov's inclination towards contrast, an inherent feature of his style, is conditioned by the drama of Nazïm Khikmet. Moments of extreme action alternate with portrait scenes of a psychological character. In many ways *Legend of Love* continues the tradition of Karayev's ballets, but at the same time it contains many original features, among them a novel interpretation of *mugam* methods of development. The work's direct melody and skilful stagecraft have won it lasting popularity. Melikov's next major composition was the symphonic poem *Metamorfozï*, which is built on a logical transformation of three themes. This piece and, more particularly, the Second Symphony mark important stages in the composer's creative evolution, his

expressive means becoming more complex and his link with folk music more distant.

WORKS

*(selective list)*

Stage: Legenda o lyubvi [Legend of love] (ballet, N. Khikmet), 1961, Leningrad, Kirov, 1961; Volnï [Waves] (operetta), Baku, 1967; Dvse [Two] (ballet), 1969, Leningrad, Kirov, 1969; Alibaba i sorok razboynikov [Alibaba and the 40 thieves] (ballet), 1973

Cantatas: Rodina [Homeland]; Golos zemli [Voice of the earth] (Vagif), 1972

Orch: Fl Concertino, 1955; Skazka [Tale], sym. poem, 1957; Sym. no.1, 1958; Pamyati Fizuli [To the memory of Fizuli], sym. poem, 1959; Metamorfozï, sym. poem, 1964; Sym. no.2, 1970; Sym. no.3, 1973; 3 other sym. poems, 6 suites, 3 suites for folk orch

Other works: 2 song cycles (Khikmet), other vocal music, inst pieces, incidental music, 10 film scores etc

BIBLIOGRAPHY

B. L'vov-Anokhin: 'Dva novïkh baleta', *Muzïkal'naya zhizn'* (1961), no.12, p.6

I. Kuznetsova: 'Prekrasnoye dolzhno bït' velichavo' [The beautiful must be majestic], *SovM* (1965), no.7, p.82

I. Kagan: 'Kompozitor A. Melikov', *Literaturnïy Azerbaydzhan* (1967), no.12, p.113

S. Kasimova: 'Muzïkal'naya zhizn' Baku [The musical life of Baku], *Iskusstvo Azerbaydzhana* (1968), no.12, p.135

F. Farkhadova: *Muzïkal'no-stsenicheskiye proizvedeniya molodïkh kompozitorov Azerbaydzhana* [The musico-scenic works of young Azerbaijani composers] (Baku, 1971)

G. Shokhman: 'Simfonicheskiye novinki', *SovM* (1972), no.9, p.27 [on Sym. no.2]

YURIY GABAY

**Melik-Pashayev, Alexander Shamil'yevich** (*b* Tbilisi, 23 Oct 1905; *d* Moscow, 18 June 1964). Georgian conductor and composer. He studied with Nikolay Tcherepnin at the Tbilisi Conservatory and then became pianist and leader of the orchestra at the Tbilisi Opera from 1921, and conductor from 1924. He studied conducting with Alexander Gauk at Leningrad Conservatory (1928–30) and returned to Tbilisi in 1930 as chief conductor. From 1931 he was conductor, and from 1953 chief conductor at the Bol'shoy Theatre in Moscow, where he remained until 1962. An outstanding operatic conductor, he was much admired for his control and shaping of large-scale Romantic works with careful attention to detail and balance of musical and dramatic character. As well as conducting memorable productions of operas by Verdi, Meyerbeer, Tchaikovsky and Rimsky-Korsakov, he introduced new operas by Chishko, Dzerzhinsky, Kabalevsky, Shaporin and others to the Bol'shoy Theatre repertory. He also conducted concerts and occasionally appeared abroad, making his British début in a revival of Tchaikovsky's *The Queen of Spades* at Covent Garden in 1961. He composed a number of works, including a symphony, and was made People's Artist of the USSR in 1951.

WRITINGS

'Put' dirizhora' [The path of a conductor], *Sovetskoye iskusstvo* (12 Oct 1938)

'Mïsli opernovo dirizhora' [Thoughts of an operatic conductor], *SovM* (1951), no.12

'Pikovaya dama v Kovent-Gardene' [*The Queen of Spades* at Covent Garden], *SovM* (1962), no.4

BIBLIOGRAPHY

R. Glezer: 'Master opernovo teatra' [The master of opera theatre], *SovM* (1961), no.9

M. Chulaki: 'Pamyati bol'shovo khudozhnika' [Memories of a great artist], *Muzïkal'naya zhizn'* (1964), no.7

R. Glezer: 'Pamyati Aleksandra Shamil'yevicha Melik-Pashayeva', [Memories of Melik-Pashayev] *SovM* (1964), no.9

G. B. Bernandt and I. M. Yampol'sky: *Kto pisal o muzïke* [Writers on music], ii (Moscow, 1974) [incl. list of writings]

I. M. YAMPOL'SKY

**Melik'yan, Romanos Hovakimi** (*b* Kiziyar, northern Caucasus, 1 Dec 1883; *d* Erevan, 30 March 1935).

Armenian composer and teacher. He graduated from the Rostov music college in 1905, and then studied in Moscow with Ippolitov-Ivanov, Taneyev and Yavorsky (1905–7) and at the St Petersburg Conservatory with Kalafati and Shteynberg (1910–14). In 1908 he organized in Tbilisi the Music League, an Armenian society which did important work in education. Melik'yan was appointed director of music at the House of Armenian Culture in Moscow (1918), and in 1921 he founded a music workshop (from 1923 the conservatory) in Erevan. He was founder-director of the Erevan Theatre of Opera and Ballet (1933); he also established a choral association there. As a composer he made a brilliant contribution to Armenian song, both in original pieces and folksong arrangements. The national quality in his music, established through modal harmony, had an influence on later Armenian composers, such as Step'anyan. In the cycle *Ashnan togher* ('Autumn lines') the delicate use of tone-colour reveals a link with impressionism; *Zmrukhti* ('Emeralds') are decorative pieces, subtle in their treatment of the texts and varied in their piano textures. These features are developed in *Zar-var* ('Sparklets'), a cycle addressed to school-children.

### WORKS
*(selective list)*

Song cycles: Ashnan togher [Autumn lines], 1907–10; Eskizï, folksong arrs., 1912; Zmrukhti [Emeralds] (T'umanyan, D. Demirdjyan, A. Isahakyan, A. Khnkoyan, trad.), 1918; Zar-var [Sparklets], 1922; Pesni novovo bïta [Songs of the new life], n.d.; Krasnoarmeyskiye pesni [Red Armenian songs], n.d.; Shkol'nïye pesni [School songs], n.d.; Pionerskiye pesni [Pioneer songs], n.d.

### BIBLIOGRAPHY
XX dari hay noraguyn kompozitorner, i (Venice, 1926), 27ff
G. Geodakyan: *Romanos Melik'yan: kyank'n ev steghdsagordsut'yun* (Erevan, 1960)
Kh. Tordjyan: *Romanos Melik'yan* (Erevan, 1960)

SVETLANA SARKISIAN

**Meliš** [Zminský], **Emanuel (Antonín)** (*b* Zminný, nr. Pardubice, 15 Oct 1831; *d* Vršovice, Prague, 27 June 1916). Czech writer on music. Abandoning his law studies in Prague, he turned to journalism and soon to music journalism with his essay 'Stav nynější hudby u nás' ('The present state of music in Bohemia') in *Lumír* (1857). He founded and edited the first regular Czech music journal, *Dalibor* (1858–64; 1869), to which he contributed valuable historical articles and the first biographies of Smetana (1863) and the Slovak Ján Levoslav Bella (1869). Through his bibliographical research he became the first Czech musical lexicographer and contributed entries on Czech musicians to contemporary encyclopedias. He was also involved with numerous committees concerned with church music, military music, opera and choirs. In the 1870s he turned his attention to economic questions: he established an experimental farm and an agricultural journal and ran an inn.

### WRITINGS
'Stav hudby v Čechách v XVIII. století' [The state of music in Bohemia in the 18th century], *Dalibor*, iv (1861), 12
'Bedřich Smetana', *Dalibor*, v (1863), 185
'Vývin českých písní' [The evolution of Czech songs], *Dalibor*, vi (1863), 57
'Ženské skladatelky' [Women composers], *Dalibor*, vi (1863), 34
with J. Bergman: *Průvodce v oboru českých tištěných písní: od roku 1800–1862* [A guide to Czech printed songs, 1800–62] (Prague, 1863)
*Průvodce hudební a divadelní* [A musical and theatrical guide] (Prague, 1868, 2/1869)
'H. Berlioz', *Dalibor*, viii (1869), 67
*Průvodce hudební* [A musical guide] (Prague, 1869)
'Taneční hudba na začátku XIX. století' [Dance music at the beginning of the 19th century], *Dalibor*, viii (1869), 9
*Stručné dějiny ruské hudby* [A short history of Russian music] (Prague, 1870)
Articles in *Riegrův Slovník naučný* [Rieger's encyclopedia] and Mendel's *Musikalisches Conversations-Lexikon*

JOHN TYRRELL

**Melis, György** (*b* Szarvas, 2 July 1923). Hungarian baritone. He studied under Olga Rélévhegyi at the Budapest Academy of Music, making his début at the Budapest Opera House in 1959 as Morales (*Carmen*). He has taken both lyric baritone and heroic baritone roles, notably in Mozart and Verdi operas, to which he brings subtle technique, colourful acting ability and a confident sense of style. As Don Giovanni he has appeared internationally – Glyndebourne (1961), Brussels (1961, 1963), Vienna, Berlin, South America and Moscow. He is also a fine lieder singer and frequently performs in oratorio. His recordings include Bluebeard (in Bartók's opera) under Ferencsik and Rigoletto.

PÉTER P. VÁRNAI

**Melisma** (Gk.: 'song'). A group of more than five or six notes sung to a single syllable. The term may be applied universally, but has been most used in reference to medieval western music, particularly chant. 'Melismatic' indicates one end of a spectrum; the other is 'syllabic', or one note to each syllable. An intermediate category, with several notes to a syllable, is termed 'neumatic'.

Some scholars have regarded the melisma, on account of its great antiquity, as a mysterious stylistic phenomenon signifying a Near Eastern provenance, a magical and incantational function, or a combination of both. A broader view of musical history, however, and a more judicious study of specific documents may show the melisma in a different light; the contributions of the Byzantinists (who have dispelled many of the superstitions about Byzantine chant) are also of importance in this respect. Melismas are found in song ranging from the time of antiquity to the present day; in fact, they may be indigenous to any music, and not necessarily mere manifestations of extra-musical factors.

St Augustine in a famous passage written about 400 commented on the expressive essence of the melisma (*jubilus* or *jubilatio* in his terminology): he felt that singing without words expressed a joy too deep for words. It is thus the suspension of the normal relationship between words and music (i.e. syllabic) that is the basis of the melisma's extraordinary power.

In western chant all phases of the spectrum (syllabic–neumatic–melismatic) are represented. Melismas of a melismatic chant are usually spectacular and readily apparent; they often contain 20 to 30 notes in a florid pattern. Generally only a few syllables of a chant are treated in this manner, the rest being set in syllabic or neumatic style.

In the older repertories, melismas could occur in a variety of positions within the chant; later they tended to acquire set positions or functions. Melismas distinguished by their sophistication and sense of rhapsody are more commonly found in graduals, tracts and responsories in the Gregorian repertory, presumably dating from the 7th and 8th centuries; they are closely related to the formulaic process of composition that is a characteristic of such chants (*see* CENTONIZATION). Comparable melismas occur in other western repertories – Milanese, north Italian, Mozarabic, Old Roman – but caution must be exercised in determining the original state of these repertories, for their earliest sources are usually as late as the 11th or 12th centuries: the research of the Byzantinists seems to suggest that a vast increase in melismatic activity can occur in the later sources of a chant repertory.

Melismas also appear, perhaps most characteristically, in the Gregorian Mass ALLELUIA: a melisma occuring on the last syllable, '-ia', came to be called the JUBILUS (absent from the Byzantine alleluia); another (different) melisma is often present within the verse. The jubilus melisma usually reappears on the last syllable of the verse and is further repeated if the alleluia is included after the verse.

From a hypothetical chronology of 7th- and 8th-century Gregorian alleluias, jubili may be seen to become longer rather than shorter. This is true also of the melismas within the verse, which are even more spectacular in later alleluias (compare the verses of *Alleluia, Dies sanctificatus* for Christmas and *Alleluia, Christus resurgens* for the 4th Sunday after Easter).

Some sources provide very extended melismas, sometimes called *melodiae secundae*, as optional replacements for the jubilus in the repetition of the alleluia after the verse. These may date from the 11th or 12th century, although those in the Mozarabic León antiphoner may be 10th-century or even earlier. In the Frankish repertory these extended replacements for the repetition of the jubilus were called *sequentiae*, and were one of the ingredients of the prosa.

In early medieval chant melismas were often detachable entities and could be inserted into or removed from a chant, or transferred to another chant. In consequence they tended to acquire stereotyped melodic characteristics. The most famous instance is provided by Amalar of Metz (*c*830) who referred to a melisma sung at Rome in the responsory *In medio* but transferred by Frankish singers to the Christmas responsory *Descendit*. This melisma has a melodic shape popular at that period: a dramatic rise by leap immediately repeated and followed by a longer stepwise descent often in three-note sequences (e.g. *c–b–a, b–a–g* etc). The later (8th-century) Gregorian alleluia also shows these melodic characteristics. A special set of melismas accompanied the enēchēmata (*see* ENĒCHĒMA). (Huglo has shown that the corresponding Byzantine models again lacked the melismas.) These and other melismas were often called '(p)neumae' in the Middle Ages.

The *Descendit* melisma and other similar ones were sometimes provided with texts set in syllabic style. Some scholars have concluded that such a rationalization of the melisma is a basic aspect of the development of western music. However, examples exist to show that within post-Gregorian and medieval chant, melismas were cultivated even more intensely than before.

Particularly difficult questions are raised by the 'double notation' employed for certain categories, especially sequences and Kyries. From the 10th century, these melodies were written in two forms, one melismatic, with only the text 'alleluia' (for sequences) or 'Kyrie eleison', the other in syllabic style with the complete text of the chant in question (in Kyries, this text has been called inappropriately a trope). The question is whether the melismatic notation implies melismatic performance. In the case of the Kyrie this seems likely; in the case of the sequence, not. If the sequence melodies were to be performed as melismas,

they would far exceed in length and degree of organization any other melismas in western chant.

Newer forms of medieval chant, such as the Aquitanian *versus*, also contain melismas which often appear in well-defined functions at the beginning or end of sections in otherwise basically syllabic or neumatic settings. A remarkable and characteristic melisma occurs at the beginning of the famous *Alma Redemptoris mater* (dating apparently from the 12th century).

The use of the melisma in chant is closely related to its use in polyphony: on the one hand, chant melismas of various kinds served as tenors for organa, motets and derived forms ranging from the settings in the 12th-century *Magnus liber* to the 15th-century masses built on the CAPUT melisma; on the other hand, the upper parts of organa were often melismatic, owing to their great extension, even when the tenor was syllabic. The caudae of the polyphonic conductus are, in polyphony, analogous to melismas in the 11th-century *versus*. Melismatic style has been employed regularly in polyphonic vocal music from Machaut's song forms to the present day. (*See also* NEUMA.)

BIBLIOGRAPHY

P. Wagner: *Einführung in die gregorianischen Melodien*, i (Leipzig, 1895, 3/1911/R1970)

K. Wachsmann: *Untersuchungen zum vorgregorianischen Gesang* (Regensburg, 1935)

E. Wellesz: *A History of Byzantine Music and Hymnography* (Oxford, 1949, 2/1960)

L. Brou: 'Séquences et tropes dans la liturgie mozarabe', *Hispania sacra*, iv (1951), 27

J. Handschin: 'Trope, Sequence and Conductus', *NOHM*, ii (1954), 128–74

E. Werner: *The Sacred Bridge* (New York, 1959)

C. Thodberg: *Der byzantinische Alleluiarionzyklus*, MMB, Subsidia, viii (1966)

M. Huglo: *Les tonaires* (Paris, 1971)

RICHARD L. CROCKER

**Melismatic style.** In plainsong, the setting of text characterized by florid groups of notes called melismas, each of which is sung to one syllable, as for example in most Kyries and alleluias. It is contrasted with neumatic or group style (mainly two to four notes per syllable) and syllabic style (mainly one note per syllable).

**Melk.** Lower Austrian town, with a Benedictine Abbey. The strategic location of the fortress Medelica (Melk) on a slope overlooking the Danube led the Babenbergs, Austria's medieval rulers, to establish their court there in 976. Benedictine monks were invited to join the court in 1089, and shortly after 1110, when the Babenbergs moved to Klosterneuburg, the Benedictines became the owners of Melk and a large area of land. This link with the Austrian monarchal line made the wealthy abbey one of the Empire's most powerful institutions and created ideal conditions for cultural development in later centuries.

Soon after their arrival in Melk the Benedictines founded a boys' choir; *pueri* are mentioned as early as 1140 and a cloister school, training boys for singing in processions and daily church services, is described in a manuscript dating from 1160. A great fire (1297) destroyed the library and most records of this formative musical period, but the *Melker Marienlied* (*c*1125) survives, bearing added marginal neumes notating the 14th-century polyphonic ballade 'Fujez de moi'. In the 15th century the abbey was the centre of a monastic reform movement, which influenced liturgical music throughout Austria and southern Germany. The ideal of the 'Melk

Reform' was the 'total renunciation of polyphony, organ playing and the participation of choirboys and lay vocalists in the divine service' (Angerer), although some of these practices were already well-established in Melk.

During the late Renaissance a group of musicians of many nationalities was active at the abbey, including the Slav Jacob Handl, the Netherlander Lambert de Sainne and perhaps also the Venetian Giovanni Valentini. The first organist was recorded in 1565, and a cornettist is found among the salaried musicians after 1598. Melk choirboys were in demand and were sent to join choirs in Prague and Vienna at the request of the Habsburg emperors. Valentini, Imperial Court Kapellmeister from 1629 to 1649, may have been the earliest of a number of musicians trained in Melk who obtained important musical posts in Vienna; others were Augustin Kürzinger (Kapellmeister at St Stephen's Cathedral, 1667–78) and Albrechtsberger (court organist and Kapellmeister at St Stephen's, 1772–1809).

The elimination of the Turkish threat to Austria in 1683 and the election of Berthold Dietmayr as Abbot of Melk (1700–39) initiated another era of fruitful creative activity. Dietmayr commissioned Jakob Prandtauer to rebuild the abbey in Baroque style, and a costly organ was installed by the Viennese builder Gottfried Sonnholz in 1731. Dramatic productions, recorded as early as 1690, were given in temporary quarters until the completion of a theatre around 1736. The repertory consisted of Latin dramas with incidental music (*ludi caesarei*), secular choral cantatas (*applausi musici*) and Singspiels, mostly occasional works by local composers. Under the direction of a *regens chori*, usually a monk, a sizeable body of performers was maintained by the abbey: 15 choirboys and up to 12 professional musicians, supplemented by a number of monks and servants. A calendar rich with musical events and feast days, in addition to extravagant entertainments for visiting nobility, kept the musicians busy. Music in the second half of the 18th century was provided by the 'Melk Circle' of composers: Kimmerling (a pupil of Haydn in 1760–61), Albrechtsberger, Franz Schneider, Paradeiser and Maximilian Stadler. This productive period came to an abrupt end in the 1780s as a result of the monastic reforms of Emperor Joseph II, when virtually the entire musical apparatus, including the boys' choir, was dissolved.

With the support of abbots Anton Reyberger and Marian Zwinger (1810–37), music was revived in the post-Napoleonic period. Musical forces were available for the performances of oratorios and masses by Haydn, Beethoven, Winter, Naumann and others. A valuable thematic catalogue of the abbey's entire music collection was begun in 1821 by Adam Krieg, *regens chori* from 1812 to 1825, and was continued into the 20th century by a succession of lay and clerical music directors.

The task of revitalizing the abbey's musical institutions after World War II fell to Adolf Trittinger (d 1971), a pupil of Guido Adler. The boys' choir entered its 9th century of existence, the Melk Summer Festivals were initiated, and interest in the abbey's musical past was promoted. These activities reached a peak in 1970 with the installation of a new organ designed by Hans Haselböck and built by Gregor Hradetsky in Krems. With 3280 pipes and 45 stops the instrument is the largest tracker-action organ in Austria. Despite considerable loss sustained during and between the world wars, the abbey's music archive contains one of the richest collections in Lower Austria, with some 14,000 manuscripts and printed editions representing over 800 composers, primarily of the 18th and 19th centuries (including many unica and rare copies). A catalogue of the collection is in Vienna (*A-Wn*).

BIBLIOGRAPHY
'Bericht über den Musikzustand des löbl: Stiftes Mölk in alter und neuer Zeit', *Wiener allgemeine musikalische Zeitung*, ii (1818), cols.349–52, 357–60, 365–7
I. F. Keiblinger: *Geschichte des Benediktinerstiftes Melk in Niederösterreich, seiner Besitzungen und Umgebungen* (Vienna, 1851)
F. Dworschak: 'Joseph Haydn und Karl Joseph Weber von Fürnberg . . . und der Melker Kreis', *Unsere Heimat*, new ser., v (1932), 187
L. Nowak: 'Das Melker Marienlied: die Geschichte eines niederösterreichischen Liedes', *Unsere Heimat*, new ser., vii (1934), 184
A. Trittinger: 'Die Sonnholz-Orgel der Stiftskirche in Melk', *Jahresbericht des öffentlichen Stiftsgymnasiums der Benediktiner zu Melk a.d.D.*, xc (1948), 1
E. Kummer: 'Die alte Melker Klosterschule bis 1418', *Jahresbericht des öffentlichen Stiftsgymnasiums der Benediktiner zu Melk a.d.D.*, c (1957–8), 6
A. Trittinger: 'Die musikhistorische Bedeutung des Stiftes Melk im österreichischen Musikschaffen', *Jahresbericht des öffentlichen Stiftsgymnasiums der Benediktiner zu Melk a.d.D.*, cv (1962–3), 5
F. W. Riedel: 'Abt Berthold Dietmayr von Melk und der kaiserliche Hofkapellmeister Johann Joseph Fux: zur Musikkultur Niederösterreichs im Barockzeitalter', *Unsere Heimat*, xxxvi (1965), 58
R. N. Freeman: 'Zwei Melker Musikkataloge aus der zweiten Hälfte des 18. Jahrhunderts', *Mf*, xxiii (1970), 176
—: *The Practice of Music at Melk Monastery in the Eighteenth Century* (diss., U. of California, Los Angeles, 1971)
J. F. Angerer: 'Die liturgisch-musikalische Erneuerung der Melker Reform: Studien zur Erforschung der Musikpraxis in den Benediktinerklöstern des 15. Jahrhunderts', *Österreichische Akademie der Wissenschaften: philosophisch-historische Klasse: Sitzungsberichte*, cclxxxvii (Vienna, 1974)
ROBERT N. FREEMAN

**Melkite rite, music of the.** See SYRIAN CHURCH MUSIC.

**Melkus, Eduard** (*b* Baden, nr. Vienna, 1 Sept 1928). Austrian violinist. He was educated in Vienna, studying the violin under Ernst Moravec (1943–53) and musicology at Vienna University under Erich Schenk (1951–3); he continued his violin studies under Firmin Touche, Peter Rybar and Alexander Schaichet. In 1958 he was appointed professor of violin and viola at the Vienna Hochschule für Musik, and he has given many lectures, master classes and interpretation courses elsewhere, including several German universities, Amsterdam and Cambridge as well as Chicago and elsewhere in the USA. Melkus specializes in music of the Baroque and Classical periods and has done much to encourage the revival of both original performing styles and neglected early repertory. In 1965 he founded the Vienna Capella Academica, an ensemble that aims to use instruments in original 18th-century condition, though that objective is not rigorously pursued. His gramophone records include sonatas by Biber, Corelli and Handel, dance music of the 17th, 18th and early 19th centuries, and concertos by Bach; they are distinguished by his sweet tone, his fluent and gentle phrasing, his lively rhythms, and the effervescent brilliance of his ornamentation.

BIBLIOGRAPHY
J. Creighton: *Discopaedia of the Violin, 1889–1971* (Toronto, 1974)
STANLEY SADIE

**Mell, Davis** [David, Davie] (*b* Wilton, nr. Salisbury, 15 Nov 1604; *d* London, 4 April 1662). English violinist and composer. He was apprenticed to a clockmaker but had joined the court band by the time of the funeral of

James I and is frequently mentioned in the accounts of the Lord Chamberlain between 1629 and 1641. He played an important part in the production of Shirley's masque *The Triumph of Peace* (1633–4), receiving £20 for composing music for the ante-masques and accompanying the Grandmasquers' dances. Mell was listed in Playford's *Musicall Banquet* (London, 1651) as a music teacher and one of London's 'excellent and able masters'.

He also achieved some prominence as a violinist in the Commonwealth period; he is mentioned in the diaries of Pepys and Evelyn, and in a poem written in 1653 by Nicholas Hookes of Trinity College, Cambridge. Mell became a member of Cromwell's private band of musicians in the following year. Also in the band was John Hingeston, who together with Mell and four others petitioned a parliamentary committee 'for the Advancement of Music' on 19 February 1657 for the alleviation of musicians in hardship and the establishment of a 'Corporation of College of Musitians in London'. Mell visited Oxford in March 1658, an event remembered by Anthony Wood, who, like Evelyn two years earlier, was moved to write that 'after Baltzar came into England and showed his most wonderful parts on that instrument, [Davis] Mell was not so admired, yet he played sweeter, was a well-bred gentleman and not given to excessive drinking as Baltzar was'.

At the Restoration Mell was appointed Master of the King's Band together with George Hudson at a yearly salary of £110, and in the following year he was described as a member of the King's 'Broken consort'. He and Hudson were criticized on 31 May 1661 and instructed to 'give orders to prevent former neglects'. Baltzar became orchestral leader on 30 November 1661 and John Banister (i) took over nine months later.

Mell's surviving music is confined to instrumental dance forms and comprises 54 dance pieces for treble (violin) and basso continuo grouped into 12 suites in Playford's *Courtly Masquing Ayres* (London, 1662). He contributed a set of variations for violin and basso continuo on the tune *John come kiss me now* to the several editions of Playford's *Division Violin* (1685–1706). The extent of his violin technique is greater than has formerly been supposed, as is illustrated by the 64 dance pieces grouped into 12 'suites' for violin in *GB-Och* 433. Many pieces in this MS (probably autograph) incorporate difficult double stopping (see particularly the 'suites' in A minor and C minor). This feature also appears in the second D minor 'suite' (ff. 35–6) together with scordatura strongly reminiscent of the music of contemporary German violinist-composers, such as Biber, Schmelzer and J. J. Walther. The basses only of five instrumental dance pieces are in *Ob* Mus.Sch.D 220 (dated 1654), another five in *Lbm* Add.15118, and *Mell's Battell* is in the Thomas Britton Partbooks (in *US-NYp*).

BIBLIOGRAPHY

*HawkinsH*

H. C. de Lafontaine: *The King's Musick* (London, 1909/*R*1973)
P. Scholes: *The Puritans and Music* (London, 1934)
D. Boyden: *The History of Violin Playing from its Origins to 1761* (London, 1965)
M. Lefkowitz: 'The Longleat Papers of Bulstrode Whitlock', *JAMS*, xviii (1965), 42

NORMAN JOSEPHS

**Mell, Gaudio.** Possibly an alternative name for CLAUDE GOUDIMEL.

**Melle, Rinaldo del** [Raynaldus, Renatus, René, Renerus]. *See* MEL, RINALDO DEL.

**Mellers, Wilfrid (Howard)** (*b* Leamington, 26 April 1914). English composer and musicologist. He was educated at Leamington College and Cambridge University, where he read English and music (1933–8), but studied composition at the same time with Wellesz and Rubbra in Oxford. He held appointments at Dartington Hall (1938–40) and Downing College, Cambridge (1945–8), where he was supervisor in English and music, before becoming staff tutor in music to the extra-mural department of Birmingham University (1948–59). From 1960 to 1963 he was Andrew Mellon Professor of Music in the University of Pittsburgh, and in 1964 was appointed professor of music at the University of York. Birmingham University awarded him the DMus in 1963.

Initially, Mellers was more highly regarded for his writings than his compositions. From the late 1930s he wrote a vast number of articles for leading periodicals on a great variety of subjects but with particular emphasis on English and French music of the 20th century. Some of these were published collectively in 1948 as *Studies in Contemporary Music*. His first published book was *Music and Society* (1946), which reflected Mellers's keen interest in the social background of music, an interest that continued and grew with important consequences for his own compositions. This same interest underlies the point of view that Mellers pursues in his major musicological works: a definitive study of François Couperin; the post-1700 volumes of *Man and his Music*; and an important history of American music, *Music in a New Found Land*, perhaps Mellers's most significant publication to date. These and subsequent studies also reveal Mellers's concern for an understanding of the nature of artistic creation, in particular how it is affected by the interrelationship of music, poetry and drama (examined in *Harmonious Meeting*), how it can be illuminated by an examination of intuitive, 'untutored' creators such as pop and folk musicians (explored especially in his study of the Beatles' music) and how, in the 20th century, it has involved the striking of a more delicate and acute balance and reconciliation between tradition and revolution (the fundamental issue in *Caliban Reborn*). Mellers's training as a literary scholar obviously served him well in developing these investigations and has made a mark on his prose style which, though dangerously overladen with metaphor and other devices and often bordering on the glib, does have the merit of illuminating his ideas in a vivid and frequently provocative fashion.

Mellers's fundamental concerns as a scholar have also influenced his attitude to education. Given the opportunity in 1964 to inaugurate a degree course in music at York, he seized the chance to re-think the basic tenets of an academic musical education and developed a course that approached 'music as human experience', that aimed to make students aware 'of what being a musician means and has meant' by a process of self-discovery. Instead of a comprehensive course in music history with compartmentalized practical skills taught separately, students were given a number of varied topics or works to investigate in depth, applying every possible technique at their command – socio-historical investigation, performing practice, analysis, stylistic imitation, vocal and instrumental skills, individual and group composition – and thus deciding for themselves the relevance of each subject to their own interests and abilities. Mellers believed that the exploration of music in depth in this way, by making and doing, was also a process of self-exploration from which education would spring. His compositions for children to perform start from the same premise.

As a composer Mellers has never achieved the recognition that his writings brought him as a scholar, but his compositions have always followed an intensely individual path, providing the necessary creative outlet for original ideas nurtured by his musicological studies and educational concerns. As one might expect, the majority of his output is vocal and his choice of texts eclectic. However, this has as much to do with the nature of the commissions he has received as with his natural inclination towards literary inspiration. Indeed many of the commissions Mellers has fulfilled have required unusual instrumental forces, and his sensitive deployment of diverse colour combinations is one of the striking features of his work; but after the 1950s he rarely had the opportunity to exploit this gift in purely instrumental terms. Nevertheless, many works of the early 1970s exploit the exploration of selective instrumental palettes almost as a constructional technique in itself; this is especially true of *The Gates of the Dream* (1973), written for students of Mellers's own department at York.

For Mellers, like many composers of his generation, the English Baroque proved to be a significant creative stimulus. His early musical language, heard to best effect in the Viola Sonata and String Trio, is essentially diatonic but with an individual melodic character created by a delicate use of chromaticism and dissonance. The variation forms of the Baroque are in evidence throughout his output and, as the titles and forces of his works suggest, the spirit of the era has had a lasting, continuous influence on his own creativity.

From the time of his American sojourn several other important influences began to appear in Mellers's compositions. The curious cultural mélange he experienced in the USA stimulated his own explorations into the interrelationship of 'concert' music, jazz, folk and pop music, carried furthest in *Yeibichai* (written for the 1969 Proms). As an adjunct to this he has incorporated the musical and literary manifestations of primitive cultures in works like *Life Cycle* and *Natalis invicti solis*, in which he attempted to convey the spirit of fundamental human experiences through the medium of 'concert' music. Inevitably, this has led Mellers to consider the part theatrical projection plays in a concert piece, the way an audience can be involved in a human situation when all the performers are, in a sense, actors with whom it is possible to identify oneself. This conception lies behind *The Listening Light* and is logically extended in the monodrama *The Ancient Wound* and in *Venery for Six Plus*.

As a matter of course Mellers's musical language has expanded to accommodate the new sound worlds he has tried to evoke. For example, in *Cloud Canticle* (1969) the diatonicism of his earliest style is still present but now takes its place in a more flexible sound spectrum that incorporates glissandos, clusters, indeterminately pitched and non-pitched sounds as well as controlled improvisation, all to some extent influenced by Mellers's interest in the recreation of natural, animal and primitive human sounds in a ritualized musical context.

## WORKS

### STAGE

Prometheus (incidental music, Aeschylus), S, T, Bar, chorus, chamber orch, 1947; Lysistrata (play in music, Aristophanes), S, Bar, speaking chorus, fl, ob, cl, bn, tpt, perc, db, 1948; The Tragicall History of Christopher Marlowe (opera, 4, 2 interludes, R. J. White), 1950–52; The Ancient Wound (monodrama, P. Garvie), singing actress, 2 speakers, 9 insts, tape, 1970

### ACCOMPANIED CHORAL

2 Motets in diem pacis (Isaiah), vv, brass, 1945; 4 Carols, boys' vv, cel, 1946; The Song of Ruth (R. J. White, after Bible), S, Mez, Bar, female vv, orch, 1948; News from Greece (R. F. Willetts), Mez, vv, 3 tpt, 2 pf, perc, 1949; The White Island (Herrick), S, female vv, str, 1951; The Hedge of Flowers (D. J. Holbrook), masque, girls' vv, small orch, 1960; 3 Resurrection Hymns of Emily Dickinson, vv, org, 1960; Chants and Litanies of Carl Sandberg, male vv, pf, perc, 1960

Missa brevis, vv, org, 1962; Rootabaga Story (Sandberg), narrator, girls' vv, boys' vv, pf, perc, 1962; A Ballad of Anyone (Cummings), vv, pf, perc, 1964; The Happy Meadow (Y. Winters), cantata, children's vv, recs, perc, 1964; Te Deum, vv, org, 1966; Runes and Carolunes (Pigmy and Eskimo dance-songs, C. Mellers), children's vv, insts, 1967; Life Cycle (Eskimo and African bushmen trad., trans. Bowra), cantata, 3 choruses, 2 orchs, 1967

Yeibichai (G. Snyder), coloratura S, scat singer, vv, jazz trio, orch, tapes, 1968; The Word Unborn (R. Duncan), double chorus, fl, cl, trbn, 2 perc, vc, 1970; Sun-flower: the Divine Tetrad of William Blake, solo vv, vv, orch, 1972–3

### UNACCOMPANIED CHORAL

4 Shakespeare Songs, SSA, 1944; 2 Motets in diem lamentationis (Apocrypha), 1950; Primavera, 6 canzonets, SSA, 1954; Canticum incarnationis (Raine), SSATTB, 1960; Ex nihilo and Lauds (Raine, Auden), 1960; To Mistress Isabel Pennell (Skelton), SATB, 1961; Early Light (Holbrook), 2 partsongs, SATB, 1966; Christmas Eve, SATB, 1966; Resurrection Canticle (Hopkins), 16vv, 1969; Cloud Canticle (R. Johnson), double chorus, 1969

### SOLO VOCAL

The Forgotten Garden (H. Vaughan), cantata, T, str qt, 1945; Conversion in the Garden (St Augustine), cantata, Bar, str, 1947; 3 Latin Canticles, S, org, 1948; 5 Songs of Night (after Gk.), A, eng hn, str qt, 1947, rev. 1949; Aristophanic Extravaganza (Willetts, after Aristophanes), cantata, Ct, pf, hpd, cel, gui, perc, 1949; 3 16th-century Poems, Ct, fl, gui, 1949; Yggdrasil (C. Hassall), cantata, S, A, T, B, chamber orch, 1950; Nausicaa's Welcome (Willetts), cantata, S, Bar, str qt, 1951

Some of Gravity, Some of Mirth (medieval and Elizabethan), S, pf, 1951; 3 Invocations (after Gk.), A, pf, 1951; Carmina felium, S, cl, bn, pf qt, 1952; Merry Margaret (Skelton), T, 1952; Spells (Raine), S, fl, ob, perc, va, 1960; Journey to Love (W. C. Williams), song cycle, S, pf, 1960; Threnodies from the Waters (Beddoes), S, pf, 1961; Songs of Sleep, T, va, pf, 1962; Voices and Creatures (Roethke), speaker, fl, perc, 1962, rev. 1969; Lacrimae amoris (anon., Raleigh), Ct, 3 male vv, 1963

Rose of May: a Threnody for Ophelia (Shakespeare), speaker, S, fl, cl, str qt, 1964; A May Magnificat (Hopkins), Mez, chamber orch, 1966; The Ship of Death (Lawrence), cantata, S, T, cl, b cl, str qt, 1966; Love Story, S, Ct, vc, hpd, 1967, rev. as The Listening Light (Roethke), S, Bar, Baroque ob, Baroque tpt, hpd, str qt, 1974; De vegetabilibus et animalibus (R. Johnson), S, cl, harp, vn, vc, 1971; Venery for 6 Plus, 1v, fl, cl, tpt, perc, db, tape, 1972

The Gates of the Dream (Blake), 6 inst/vocal trios, 1973; The Key and the Kingdom, dancing S, improvising fls and harp/pf, 1974; White Bird Blues (P. Holden), (dancing S, accordion)/(S, fl, cl, harp, va, db), 1974; The Echoing Green (Blake), S, cl, 1974

### INSTRUMENTAL

Orch: Festival Galliard, 1951; Sym., 1953; Alba in 9 Metamorphoses, fl, orch, 1961; Noctambule and Sun-dance, wind band, 1962

Chamber: Str Trio, 1945; Sonata, va, pf, 1946; Serenade, ob, cl, bn, 1946; Galliard, trbn, pf, 1952; Sonatina, tr rec, pf, 1956; Eclogue, tr rec, hpd, perc, vn, vc, 1960; Trio, fl, vc, pf, 1962; Laus amoris, 5 movts, str, 1964; Threnody, 11 str, 1975

Solo inst: Sonata, vc, 1961; Cantilena e ciacona, vn, 1962; Cat Charms, 9 pieces, pf, 1965; Natalis invicti solis, pf, 1968; Opus alchymicum, org, 1969; A Blue Epiphany for J. B. Smith, gui, 1973

Principal publishers: Galliard, Mills, Novello

## WRITINGS

### BOOKS

*Music and Society* (London, 1946)
*Studies in Contemporary Music* (London, 1948)
*François Couperin and the French Classical Tradition* (London, 1950)
*Music in the Making* (London, 1950)
*Man and his Music*, iii–iv (London, 1957–8)
*Music in a New Found Land* (London, 1964/R1975)

*Harmonious Meeting: a Study of the Relationship between English Music, Poetry and Theatre, c.1600–1900* (London, 1965)
*Caliban Reborn: Renewal in Twentieth-century Music* (New York, 1967)
*The Resources of Music* (Cambridge, 1968) [school project incl. composition *Life Cycle*]
*Twilight of the Gods: the Beatles in Retrospect* (London, 1973)
*The Dance of God: a Study of J. S. Bach* (in preparation)
*The Invisible Church: a Study of Beethoven* (in preparation)

ARTICLES
'Bernard van Dieren (1884 [*recte* 1887]–1936): Musical Intelligence and "The New Language" ', *Scrutiny*, v (1936–7), 263
'Delius and Peter Warlock', *Scrutiny*, v (1936–7), 384
'The Problem of Busoni', *ML*, xviii (1937), 240
'Problemas formales de la música cinematografica', *Nuestra musica*, vi (1951), 254
'Recent Trends in British Music', *MQ*, xxxviii (1952), 185
'Erik Satie et la musique "fonctionnelle" ', *ReM* (1952), no.214, p.33
'Opera buffa and the Common Man', *Opera*, x (1959), 141
'An American Aboriginal', *Tempo* (1963), no.64, p.2
'The Avant-garde in America', *PRMA*, xc (1963–4), 1
'Music for 20th-century Children', *MT*, cv (1964), 342, 421, 500
'John Joubert and the "Blessed City" ', *MT*, cv (1964), 814
'Egon Wellesz: an 80th-birthday Tribute', *MT*, cvi (1965), 766
'The New Troubadours: Reflections on Pop and Modern Folk Music', *Musicology*, ii (1965–7), 3
'Edgar Varèse – a Great Central Figure', *Composer* (1966), no.18, p.10
'Stravinsky and Jazz', *Tempo* (1967), no.81, p.29
'The Scope of School Music: Notes on a University Course', *Music in Education*, xxxii (1968), 130
'Couperin and his Church Music', *MT*, cix (1968), 522
'Couperin on the Harpsichord', *MT*, cix (1968), 1010
'1930: "Symphony of Psalms" ', *Tempo* (1971), no.97, p.19
'The Key and the Kingdom; Reflections on Music, Childhood and Education', *Australian Journal of Music Education* (1971), no.9, p.13; (1972), no.10, p.7
'Music in a Modern University: a Question of Priorities', *SMA*, vi (1972), 1; abridged in *MT*, cxiv (1973), 245
'Music's Bestiary', *Guildhall School of Music and Drama Review* (1974), 14

BIBLIOGRAPHY
A. Hutchings: 'Wilfrid Mellers', *Music Survey*, ii (1949), 72
R. Nettel: 'Wilfrid Mellers and his Music', *MMR*, lxxx (1950), 91
E. Blom: 'Zwischen vierzig und fünfzig', *Musica*, xii (1958), 408
R. Henderson: 'The Music of Wilfrid Mellers', *MT*, civ (1963), 178
R. Kostelanetz: 'Modern Music Criticism and the Literate Layman', *PNM*, vi (1967), 119
F. Mulhern: *The Moment of 'Scrutiny'* (London, 1979)
LESLIE EAST

**Melli [Megli], Domenico Maria** (*b* Reggio Emilia; *fl* early 17th century). Italian composer and lawyer. He was a relative, possibly a cousin, of Pietro Paolo Melli, who in his third *Intavolatura* (1616) calls him his 'parente carissimo'. In 1600 he was a singer at Reggio Emilia Cathedral. On the title-page of his first publication he is called a doctor of law, and in the same year he signed the dedication of his second book from Padua, where he was presumably living at the time. As a composer he possibly regarded himself as an amateur; if he was it is probably no accident that all his known music survives in books devoted primarily to monodies, which were specially popular with amateur composers in early 17th-century Italy. He was indeed the only composer besides Caccini (whose *Le nuove musiche* is generally held to have inaugurated the tremendous fashion for monody) to publish monodies during the first years of the century: since its dedication is dated 26 March 1602 it is even possible that his first volume of *Musiche* antedates *Le nuove musiche*, for which the printing licence was granted on 30 June 1602. Melli is a lesser composer than Caccini, though there are similarities between them, especially in the predominantly bland diatonic harmony and in the relationship of vocal line and bass (which with Melli is almost entirely unfigured): in the music of both composers the polarization of voice and bass presents one of the essential features of monody,

especially in madrigals. As in the books of other early monodists, madrigals predominate in Melli's output of 59 solo songs and seven duets and dialogues: the first book consists wholly of them (*pace* the title-page of the reprints), and in the other two books there are more of them than of strophic pieces. Like other amateur composers, but unlike Caccini, Melli occasionally wrote striking chromatic progressions to underline appropriate words: examples occur in *Rapii bacio gradito* in the first book and at the opening of *Languisco e moro* in the second. His melodic invention is rarely very noteworthy, though the tunes and rhythms of some of his light strophic songs are lively. A disadvantage of some of his madrigals is the frequency of perfect cadences, which can generally not be concealed by polyphony in the monodic medium. Compared with Caccini's his madrigals are also remarkably free of ornamentation, perhaps because he was writing with amateur singers in mind. The later third book shows little development of form or style over the earlier ones, and it is perhaps not surprising that he appears to have published no more music after it.

WORKS
Musiche composte sopra alcuni madrigali di diversi, 1v, bc (Venice, 1602, 2/1603 and 3/1609 as Le prime musiche . . . madrigali et arie a una e due voci [there are no arias, or music for 2vv]); 1 ed. in Fortune (1954), appx iv, 4
Le seconde musiche . . . madrigali, canzonette, arie, & dialoghi, 1–2vv, bc (Venice, 1602, 2/1609; 1 of these in 1610²⁰, ed. P. Stroud, London, 1968); 1 ed. in Ambros, 788f
Le terze musiche . . . madrigali, arie, scherzi, sonetti, dialoghi, & altre, 1–2vv, bc (Venice, 1609)

BIBLIOGRAPHY
A. W. Ambros: *Geschichte der Musik*, iv (Leipzig, rev. 3/1909 by H. Leichtentritt), 787ff, 857, 860
N. Fortune: 'Italian Secular Monody from 1600 to 1635: an Introductory Survey', *MQ*, xxxix (1953), 171
——: *Italian Secular Song from 1600 to 1635: the Origins and Development of Accompanied Monody* (diss., U. of Cambridge, 1954)
J. Racek: *Stilprobleme der italienischen Monodie* (Prague, 1965)
N. Fortune: 'Solo Song and Cantata', *NOHM*, iv (1968), 160, 212
G. Casali: 'La cappella musicale della cattedrale di Reggio Emilia all'epoca di Aurelio Signoretti (1567–1631)', *RIM*, viii (1973), 197
NIGEL FORTUNE

**Melli [Meli, Melij, Mely], Pietro Paolo** (*b* Reggio Emilia; *fl* 1612–20). Italian composer and lutenist; he was related to Domenico Maria Melli, whom in his third *Intavolatura* (1616) he called his 'parente carissimo'. He became a member of the imperial court orchestra in Vienna in 1612 on the accession of the Emperor Matthias, whom he had possibly also served previously. In 1619 he was among the few musicians retained by the new emperor, Ferdinand II, from Matthias's orchestra; this and his high salary of 300 florins (the third highest after those of Giovanni Priuli and Giovanni Valentini), with an additional payment of 60 florins, show that he enjoyed great esteem. In his fourth *Intavolatura* (1616) he described himself as lutenist and chamber musician to the emperor, and gentleman of the court. Vander Straeten stated that he was in Ferrara in 1620 as a musician and lutenist of Ferdinand II. Boetticher's reference to Melli's music as close in style to Monteverdi's is supported by Melli's placing first in his second *Intavolatura* (1614) a galliard dedicated to Monteverdi.

WORKS
Intavolatura di liuto attiorbato, libro secondo, nel quale si contiene corrente, volte, gagliarde, preludi et l tastata, 1 capriccio, 1 corrente, et 1 volta cromatiche, 1 aria di Firenze passeggiata dall'autore [etc] (Venice, 1614)
Intavolatura di liuto attiorbato, libro terzo, nel quale si contiene varie sonate in 1 cordatura . . . differente ancora da quella che già 4 anni io mandai alle stampe nel fine del mio primo libro [etc] (Venice, 1616)

Intavolatura di liuto attiorbato, libro IV (Venice, 1616)
Intavolatura di liuto attiorbato e di tiorba, libro V (Venice, 1620)
1 galliard, lute, in 1617[26]

BIBLIOGRAPHY
L. von Köchel: *Die kaiserliche Hof-Musikkapelle in Wien von 1543 bis 1867* (Vienna, 1869)
E. vander Straeten: *La musique aux Pays-bas avant le XIXᵉ siècle*, vi (Brussels, 1882/R1969), 109
W. Boetticher: *Studien zur solistischen Lautenpraxis des 16. und 17. Jahrhunderts* (Berlin, 1943), xxxv, 177, 333f
E. F. Schmid: *Musik an den schwäbischen Zollernhöfen der Renaissance* (Kassel, 1962)
H. Federhofer: *Musikpflege und Musiker am Grazer Habsburgerhof der Erzherzöge Karl und Ferdinand von Innerösterreich (1564–1619)* (Mainz, 1967)
W. Kirkendale: *L'Aria di Fiorenza, id est Il Ballo del Gran Duca* (Florence, 1972), 29, 49, 66, 68
THEOPHIL ANTONICEK

**Mellnäs, Arne** (*b* Stockholm, 30 Aug 1933). Swedish composer and teacher. He studied at the Stockholm Musikhögskolan (1953–63), where Larsson and Blomdahl were among his composition teachers. In 1959 he took lessons with Blacher at the Berlin Hochschule für Musik and privately with Deutsch in Paris and with Ligeti in Vienna; he studied electronic music with Koenig at the Gaudeamus Foundation in 1962–3. Mellnäs returned to the Stockholm Musikhögskolan to teach theory (1963–72) and then orchestration. He first became internationally known as a composer in 1963, when the Ligeti-influenced orchestral piece *Collage* won first prize in the Gaudeamus competition. In subsequent works he has used the newest compositional developments, which he has studied during the course of frequent travels. He was one of the first Swedes to introduce aleatory and deliberately theatrical elements into instrumental music: in *Tombola*, for example, the choice of alternative courses is determined by throwing dice on to the piano strings. *Aura*, originally composed as a text score, was a *succès de scandale* at the 1967 ISCM Festival, partly as a result of its incorporation of exploding balloons. Mellnäs has also composed pieces that are popular with schools and amateurs.

WORKS
*(selective list)*

Opera: Minibuff, 1967; Erik den helige (church opera, B. V. Wall), 1975
Orch: Music for Orch, 1958; Chiasmos, 1961; Collage, 1962; Aura, 1964; Transparence, 1972; Blow, wind insts, 1974
Choral: Succsim (Mellnäs), 1965; Aglepta, children's vv, 1969; Dream (Cummings), 1970; Vae . . ., chorus, org ad lib, 1972; Noel, 2 S, children's vv, chamber orch, 1972; Mara Mara minne, chorus, elec ad lib, 1973; Bossa buffa, 1973; Forsan (Virgil), 1973; Seeker of Truth (Cummings), 1973; A Wind has Blown (Cummings), 1973; Höst (W. Aspenström), 1973; 3 körsatser (T. Danielsson), 1973
Chamber: Tombola, ens, 1963; Gestes sonores, variable ens, 1964; Fixations, org, 1967; Quasi niente, 1–4 str trios, 1968; Capricorn Flakes, pf, hpd, vib + glock, 1970; Cabrillo, cl, trbn, vc, perc, 1970; Agréments, hpd, 1970; Schizofoni, pf, 1971; Ceremus [incl. Display, 3rd movt], fl, cl, tpt, trbn, db, perc, 1973; Fragments for Family Flute, 1–4 fl, 1973; Fragile, variable ens, 1973; The Mummy and the Hummingbird, rec, hpd, 1974; Soliloquium IV, bn, elec, 1976
Solo org: Omnia tempus habent, S, 1972; Sub luna (Chin., trans. Wahlund), S, fl/ob, vn, harp, 1973
Tape: Intensity 6·5, 1966; Conglomérat, 1968; Kaleidovision, 1969; Eufoni, 1969; Far out, 1970

Principal publishers: Hansen, Peters

WRITINGS
'Arbetsbok', *Nutida musik*, vi/8 (1963), 4
'Ur en kluddbok' [From a sketchbook], *Nutida musik*, ix/1–2 (1965), 43 [on *Gestes sonores*]
'Fixerade idéer', *Nutida musik*, xi/1–2 (1967), 59
with L. Edlund: *Det musikaliska hantverket* [The music trade] (Stockholm, 1968)
'Usch: en imaginär dialog', *Nutida musik*, xii/1 (1968), 59
'Anteckningar från ett höghus' [Notes from a skyscraper], *Tonfallet* (1969), no.10, p.1

with F. Rabe and L. J. Werle: 'Kann ein Komponist vom Komponieren leben?', *Melos*, xxxvi (1969), 162
'Den svenske tonsättarens situation', *Nutida musik*, xiv/2 (1970), 32
'Lidelsefulla skärvor' [Passionate fragments], *Nutida musik*, xiv/3 (1971), 8

BIBLIOGRAPHY
B.-E. Johnson: 'Fixations', *Nutida musik*, xi/1–2 (1967), 58
R. Moran: 'Om Arne Mellnäs Eufoni och Monotrem', *Nutida musik*, xiii/3 (1969), 30
B.-E.Johnson:'Kurzbiographien und Werkkommentare',*Elektronische Durchreise* (1971), 10
ROLF HAGLUND

**Mellon Chansonnier** (*US-NHu* 91). See SOURCES, MS, §IX, 8.

**Mellophone.** A valved brass instrument of circular form in E♭, or F (below the cornet), common in the USA, corresponding to the English TENOR COR and similarly intended to replace the horn in boys' marching bands etc. In the 1950s C. G. Conn Inc. brought out a new model, the mellophonium, with a bell of full orchestral horn width but projecting forwards to suit stage performances by bands. See CORNOPHONE.
ANTHONY C. BAINES

**Melngailis, Emīlis** (*b* Igate, 15 Feb 1874; *d* Riga, 20 Dec 1954). Latvian ethnomusicologist and composer. He studied at the Dresden Conservatory (1896–7) and under Rimsky-Korsakov at the St Petersburg Conservatory (1898–1901). After ten years spent as a teacher in Tashkent he returned to Latvia in 1920 and became active as a folk music collector, choral conductor and composer. From 1944 until his death he was a professor at the Latvian Conservatory. His principal achievement was his collection of folk music, amounting to more than 5000 items of mainly Latvian material but including some Lithuanian, Kirghiz and Jewish music. He published *Latviešu dancis* (Riga, 1949) and *Latviešu mūzikas folkloras materiāli* (Riga, 1951–3). Folksong transcriptions for chorus form the most notable part of his compositional output, but he also produced a ballet and some small instrumental pieces. His work as a music critic was affected by his brusque and temperamental nature.

BIBLIOGRAPHY
S. Stumbre: *Emīlis Melngailis* (Riga, 1959)
V. Bērzkalns: 'Emīļa Melngaiļa dziesma' [The Song of Emīlis Melngailis], *Latvju mūzika*, viii (Kalamazoo, Mich., 1975), 687
JOACHIM BRAUN

**Mel'nikov, Ivan Alexandrovich** (*b* St Petersburg, 4 March 1832; *d* St Petersburg, 8 July 1906). Russian baritone. He received his early musical training as a choirboy. After working for some years in trade and as an inspector of Volga boats, he joined (in 1862) the Free Music School choir, conducted by Lomakin with whom he also took private lessons. He made such good progress that he was persuaded to go to Italy to study with Repetto, a master of bel canto. In 1867 Mel'nikov made his St Petersburg début in *I puritani*, and was immediately acclaimed as an artist of the highest order. He appeared regularly at the Mariinsky Theatre, where he achieved particular success in Russian opera. Among his best-known roles were the Miller in Dargomïzhsky's *Rusalka*, the title role in Borodin's *Prince Igor*, Ruslan in Glinka's *Ruslan and Lyudmila* (in 1871 Stasov described him as the greatest of the Ruslans) and Boris Godunov in Musorgsky's opera (a part he created). With the exception of *Iolanta*, he sang in every opera by Tchaikovsky, who greatly admired his talents and dedicated a song to him. Mel'nikov was, however, unsuccessful as Eugene Onegin, a part he sang when his voice was past its best: the *Sanktpeterburgskiye vedomosti* commented that he sang 'not with his voice but with his reputation'. But he remained a great favourite with St Petersburg audiences until he retired after a farewell performance in *Prince Igor* in 1890. Mel'nikov went to the Russian stage at a time when standards were generally low. Modest Tchaikovsky remarked that he excelled in declamatory passages and was superb in cantilena, and his artistry encouraged both composers and audiences to take a greater interest in opera. After his retirement he became a producer at the Mariinsky Theatre (1890–92) and also founded a choir, which was noted for its fine performances. He published a collection of choral pieces, *Sbornik russkikh khorov* (Moscow, 1894), and in 1905 his reminiscences of Adelina Patti and Nápravník ('Adelina Patti i E. F. Nápravník: otrïvki iz vospominaniy') were published in the *Peterburgskiy dnevnik teatrala* (nos.2 and 3–4).

BIBLIOGRAPHY
A. E. Molchanov: 'Perechen' roley I. A. Mel'nikova, ispolnennïkh im v techeniye 25 let evo stsenicheskoy deyatel'nosti' [A list of the roles performed by Mel'nikov during his 25 years on stage], *EIT 1892–3*, 363
I. A. Mel'nikov: 'Avtobiografiya', *RMG* (1906)
N. Findeyzen: 'Vmesto nekrologa pevtsa' [Instead of an obituary of a singer], *RMG* (1906)
M. Montagu-Nathan: 'Shaliapin's Precursors', *ML*, xxxiii (1959), 232
M. MONTAGU-NATHAN/JENNIFER SPENCER

**Melodeon.** An early name for the American organ, a HARMONIUM with suction bellows. Later a popular name for the button ACCORDION, as distinct from the piano accordion.

ANTHONY C. BAINES

**Melodia.** An ORGAN STOP.

**Mélodie** (Fr.: 'melody'). The accompanied French song of the 19th and 20th centuries, usually a setting for voice and piano of a serious lyric poem.

1. 19th century. 2. 20th century.

1. 19TH CENTURY. The complex origins of the *mélodie* can be traced to two song types, the 18th-century French *romance* and the lieder of Schubert. An exclusively strophic song of a rather naive nature (*see* ROMANCE, §3(i)), the *romance* appeared in *opéra comique* during the 18th century and later flourished in the salons of the Empire and Restoration, when it attained a modest artistic level. By the 1820s the composition of *romances* took on commercial aspects that brought about a sharp decline in quality; partly as a result of this, a new type of song arose in the fourth decade of the 19th century. The genesis of the *mélodie* was also prompted by other developments, particularly the influence of Romantic poetry, which supplied composers with literary texts requiring the abandonment of earlier compositional styles and techniques, like rigidly strophic forms and the domination of the voice over the accompaniment. Another important stimulus was provided by Schubert's lieder, hundreds of which appeared in French translations or adaptations. The earliest use of the word *mélodie* for a type of song probably occurred in the 1820s; its eventual adoption was related to the popularity in France of Thomas Moore's *Irish Melodies* and the subsequent setting of their texts by various French composers. Although Moore's tunes remained mostly unknown in France, the continental

vogue for his *Melodies* stimulated the introduction of folk and exotic elements into French song. The most decisive factor leading to the adoption of the name *mélodie* for a vocal piece, however, was its application to French translations of Schubert's lieder to distinguish them from current *romances*.

Berlioz was the first major composer to be associated with the *mélodie*. His early songs were still *romances*, showing, along with 18th-century harmonies and regularity of melodic phrase, abortive attempts to break the strophic mould. The *Neuf mélodies imitées de l'anglais* (1829), generally known as the *Mélodies irlandaises*, contain harmonic and rhythmic audacities and some examples of musical word painting. *Elégie*, the last song of the group, is a 'declaimed' poem depicting the last farewells of Robert Emmet, the condemned Irish hero; although technically deficient in some ways, it is notable for its through-composed structure and its use of a sort of Sprechgesang. Berlioz's *La captive* (1832), which enjoyed a certain popularity, was originally a simple strophic song, to which the composer added a cello part two years later; in 1848 he arranged it for contralto and orchestra, virtually creating a new work. Many of Berlioz's songs were remodelled for expanded resources and some were inserted into large compositions (for example the *Symphonie fantastique* and *Benvenuto Cellini*). His most important *mélodies* are the six of *Les nuits d'été* (1840 or 1841), based on poems from Gautier's *La comédie de la mort* and displaying daring phrase structure and often a declamatory style; the vocal part is welded to the accompaniment by the use of shared germinal motifs, and deep emotion is evoked by original harmonic combinations and strong dissonances. Of Berlioz's later songs, only *La mort d'Ophélie* (1847) is noteworthy, although its harmony is simple. The melodic line is divided between the right hand of the piano part and the voice; the strongly lyrical vocal line is quite moving.

Giacomo Meyerbeer wrote *mélodies* to French texts, and many of his German and Italian songs also appeared in French versions. His songs were well liked by both public and critics, even Berlioz seeing him as an ally in the struggle against the insipid *romance*. Meyerbeer's songs show the influence of Italian bel canto in their vocal parts and of German music in the rich harmonies of the accompaniments. He took few structural liberties, generally using strophic or schematic forms. The declamation of text is handled more skilfully than in his operas, voice and accompaniment are well integrated, and there is some word painting. Although the technical adroitness of his songs is admirable, Meyerbeer's complete lack of true lyricism and his occasionally exaggerated pathos have caused their not unjustified abandonment. Their chief value lies in their influence on Gounod and others.

The dozen or so *mélodies* of Liszt, all but one published between 1840 and 1850, remained virtually ignored until the end of the century, probably because of the demands they make upon performer and public. Liszt's best examples show the influence of the German lied. *Oh! Quand je dors*, one of his best French songs, has a profound unity, matching the rich imagery of Hugo's poem and penetrating its subtlety of thought. Liszt's last *mélodie*, *Tristesse*, composed in 1872 to Alfred de Musset's poem, is more a declamatory lied, almost a recitative, following the delicate nuances of the words and with some passages left unaccompanied.

Wagner wrote six French songs in Paris in winter 1839–40, to poems by Hugo, Ronsard, Béranger and Heine. Except for *Dors, mon enfant*, which is essentially German, the songs show a French flavour and lean towards the traditional *romance* style; this is especially true of *Mignonne*. But in general their interest is more biographical than artistic. Félicien David left about 60 *mélodies*, similar to *romances* but exhibiting a natural simplicity rather than the pretentious dullness characteristic of so many *romances*. Schubert's influence may occasionally be seen in the use of double pedal points and slow waltz rhythms. David's *mélodies* written to poems called *orientales* show more daring and inspiration, especially those in *Les perles d'Orient* (1845); some of these too are much influenced by Schubert.

Ravel credited Gounod with the establishment of the independently French character of the *mélodie*. Gounod's best songs have a typically Gallic grace, displaying perfect craftsmanship and stylistic elegance while retaining freshness and simplicity. He was the first to render consistently and faithfully the difficult rhythms of the French language in song. Unfortunately only a few of his approximately 200 *mélodies* achieve this high level (e.g. *Au rossignol, L'absent, Chanson du printemps, Ô ma belle rebelle, Medjé, Venise*). In most of his vocal works Gounod lapsed into a kind of routine that wasted his craftsmanship in shallow sentimentality.

He set a standard, however, for several younger composers, each of whom added his personal characteristics to Gounod's model. The 48 *mélodies* of Bizet are uneven, and as a group do not rank with his best works. They are notable, nevertheless, for their drama, original harmonies, brilliant vocal writing and expression of local colour. For this last he used harmonic and melodic means as well as the rhythmic patterns favoured by Berlioz, David, Monpou, Massé and Reber in their *boléros, orientales* and *chansons*; his resources for the depiction of exotic atmosphere included melismatic vocal lines, and, to simulate primitivism, parallel harmony (as in *Guitare* and *Adieux de l'hôtesse arabe*). Sometimes the result is excessively theatrical. Gounod's influence is most apparent in Bizet's accompaniments, where, however, such devices as pedal points and dissonance are more daringly structured. Délibes' serious *mélodies* seem the most French of those already mentioned, perhaps deriving their piquant tone and charm from the style of his youthful *chansonnettes*. He depicted the exotic settings of his songs by the same means as did Gounod and Bizet, using folk elements in the rhythm, melody and harmony; he extended their innovations, particularly in his use of harmony. Délibes' melodic lines are simple and graceful, with a limited range, and the structures of his *mélodies* are generally confined to clear and schematic designs (such as rondo or ternary form). Although the prosody shows imperfections, the clarity, grace and balance (as in *Avril*, to a text by Rémy Belleau) emphasize the Gallic character. He lacked, however, the ability to express passion or profound emotion.

Jules Massenet may be called Gounod's true successor as a *mélodie* composer. The essence of his style is not exoticism but the highly refined expression of a delicate sentimentality. His 260 songs outnumber those of any other major French composer and more nearly approximate the number written by Schumann or Wolf. Massenet must be credited with freeing the *mélodie* from the square phrase, introducing a sort of musical prose that is analogous to the free verse written by contemporary poets. He created a unity in which the voice and piano parts are both needed for presentation of the musical thought: one often completes a phrase begun by the other, the piano sometimes connects two unaccompanied vocal phrases, or the principal melody appears in the piano while the voice 'declaims'. Massenet's drive toward synthesis is apparent in another innovation: he was the first in France to write true song cycles. In these works, which he called *poèmes* (e.g. *Poème d'avril* and *Poème du souvenir*, both to texts by Armand Silvestre), the set of *mélodies* grows out of a particular subject, preceded by a prelude whose motifs reappear at the end. The influence of Schumann (especially of *Frauenliebe und Leben*) may be seen in the attitude to the form of the cycle, in the important role given to the piano, in the interdependence of voice and instrument and in the quasi-improvised passages. Massenet's idiom is at its best in the cyclic works. His separate songs include some of real merit, but too many whose technical competence does not compensate for their saccharine sentimentality and lack of real inspiration. Despite the astounding popularity of his songs in the fashionable salons of the time, his too-frequent use of melancholy moods decreased their appeal as the years passed. Nevertheless Massenet was an important influence on the songwriting of younger composers, among whom Fauré and Debussy expressed admiration for him.

Other *mélodie* composers of the period remembered principally for their instrumental music include Saint-Saëns, Lalo and Franck. Saint-Saëns began writing songs at the age of six and in all wrote about 150. The works dating from his adolescence show a poetic sensitivity not generally credited to him. The influence of Schubert and Schumann is seen in the wide intervals of the melodic line and in the lyrical atmosphere pervaded with feelings of intimate warmth, nostalgia and deep emotion (as in *Rêverie*). His talent for the humorous and picturesque is displayed in such works as *Le pas d'armes du Roi Jean* (1852). In the collection of *Mélodies persanes* (1870) he succumbed to the vogue for orientalism, but the technical devices by which he conveyed it were unoriginal: archaic modal harmonies, persisting and monotonous rhythms and extended melismas. Among the varied songs written after 1885 the contemplative *mélodies*, free of exoticism or archaicism, are the strongest, but lack the sensitivity of his youthful works. Lalo was the first to have his *mélodies* performed in Germany, a circumstance that was perhaps due to their elaborate piano accompaniments as well as to the particularly German kind of lyricism they display. They are influenced by Schubert and Schumann, and even foreshadow Brahms and Wolf. Lalo was unusually successful at conveying the atmosphere of a lyrical text; his sensitivity in this respect brought to French song an element lacking until then. His 35 *mélodies* are eclectic in nature and cover a wide panorama of human feelings; but he obviously rejected the opportunity offered by certain texts to exploit local colour. His technical procedures include ingenious rhythmic and harmonic inventions, and declamatory melodic writing close to arioso or recitative. In his introduction of humour and cheerfulness into the *mélodie* Lalo was a precursor of Chabrier.

The 22 *mélodies* of Franck are uneven, many of them being marked by defects in the rhythmic setting of the text but showing interesting or even daring harmonies.

Among the better songs are *Le mariage des roses* (1871; text by E. David), which has a simple and natural gracefulness, and *La procession* (1888; text by Brizeux), a dramatic *mélodie* for voice and orchestra on a religious theme. Franck's importance to the history of the *mélodie* lies not in his own compositions but in his pedagogical role, for his first important pupil was Henri Duparc, through whose works the *mélodie* became one of the most important musical genres cultivated in France.

Duparc's *Cinq mélodies* op.2 (1868) show the influences of Gounod in the arpeggios and subtle syncopations, of Liszt in the juxtaposition of distant chords, and of the young Wagner in the appoggiaturas and chromaticism – all features that reappear in Duparc's later works where they are more deeply imprinted with his personal stamp. *L'invitation au voyage* (1870) renders Baudelaire's visionary nostalgia with an expressiveness that enhances the poetic thought and already marks the composer's full maturity. With this *mélodie* French song entered a new era. Duparc's subsequent works, written to texts by Gautier, Leconte de Lisle, Sully-Prudhomme and others, maintained the same level. Almost all express profound melancholy, although realized in diverse moods and atmospheres (compare the transparency of *Sérénade florentine*, the sombre luxuriance of *Lamento*, the passion of *La fuite*, the drama of *La vague et la cloche* and *Le manoir de Rosemonde* and the quiet turbulence of *Phidylé*). Duparc's vocal lines are extremely expressive, and often use augmented intervals. The essence of his style, however, lies in the piano part, which is replete with dissonant non-harmonic notes and rhythmic complications. Harmonically Duparc went far beyond the lucid triadic arpeggios of his predecessors; the use of sequences of unrelated chords is carried to an extreme in his last *mélodie*, *La vie antérieure* (1884), set for voice and orchestra to a text of Baudelaire, where, for example, a dominant chord in the key of F resolves on to an F♯ triad. Never before in this modest musical genre had such personal expressiveness been dared.

Although Fauré started to compose songs in the manner of Gounod, many of his early *mélodies* already show a distinctive musical personality. Occasional expressions of exuberance or pathos (as in *Chanson du pêcheur*, *Après un rêve* and *Fleur jetée*) disappeared in his later works where, by contrast, his strong attraction to poetry of formal classicism (by Leconte de Lisle and Armand Silvestre) may be seen. The first of these 'Parnassian' songs, *Lydia*, was written before 1871; later examples include *Le secret* (1882), *Les roses d'Ispahan* (1884), *La rose* (c1889), *Le parfum impérissable* (1897) and *La fleur qui va sur l'eau* (1903). Another aspect of his art is revealed in the settings of verse by Paul Verlaine, who became Fauré's favourite poet in the 1890s. Despite his choice of the most diverse texts (the cycles *Cinq mélodies de Venise*, 1890, and *La bonne chanson*, 1891–2), Fauré, unlike Lalo or Saint-Saëns, maintained the homogeneity of his style; its characteristics are a balanced melodic line, correct though not pedantic declamation, a preference for the middle voices (mezzo-soprano and baritone), moderate harmonic tension involving mediant relationships, and flexible structure. During his last 20 years Fauré wrote four song cycles – *La chanson d'Eve* and *Le jardin clos*, (Charles van Lerberghe), *Mirages* (Baroness de Brimont) and *L'horizon chimérique* (Jean de La Ville de Mirmont) – in which his restrained lyricism is expressed with extreme refinement. Both the vocal line, with its limited range and small intervals, and the harmonic subtleties of the piano part sustain the intimacy of these late works. The approximately 100 songs Fauré contributed to the repertory may be the most quintessentially French ever written; the often-asserted relationship with the styles of Schumann and the Wagner-orientated school of Franck does not hold. Fauré's influence on the younger generation, including Ravel, was considerable.

Several of Franck's younger pupils who wrote songs of high quality include Charles Bordes, Guy Ropartz and especially Ernest Chausson, who may be considered a historical link between Duparc and Debussy. Chausson's *Sept mélodies* op.2 (1882) follow the Gounod–Massenet pattern to some extent, but in the *Quatre mélodies* op.8 (1882–8) there are hints of impressionist harmony alongside Franckian chord relationships. The cycle *Serres chaudes* (1893–6) is a setting of a symbolist text by Maeterlinck. Chausson's last song, *Chanson perpetuelle* (1898) for voice and orchestra or piano quintet, is a masterpiece expressing, as do many of his other works, the *fin de siècle* spirit.

In contrast with the *mélodies* of Chausson, the few of Chabrier breathe a spirit of gaiety, sometimes mixed with a note of good-natured irony (*Chanson pour Jeanne*, to a text of Catulle Mendès, 1886, and *Toutes les fleurs*, Rostand, 1889). Four pieces written on animal texts, including Rostand's *Ballade des gros dindons* (1889) and *Pastorale des cochons roses* (1889), foreshadowed a genre to be cultivated by Ravel and Poulenc. Another composer who flourished at the end of the century was Reynaldo Hahn. Although like Fauré he preferred to set Parnassian poetry, Hahn's charm remains rather superficial.

2. 20TH CENTURY. In the 19th century the term 'mélodie' signified a composition which recognizably combined and unified poetic and musical form. By the time of Debussy's Baudelaire settings and *Proses lyriques*, however, the process had become free and personal. Moreover, *mélodie* normally implied a basic lyrical and reflective quality rather than dramatic expression or narrative; it is difficult to think of Debussy's scena-like *Colloque sentimental* as a *mélodie*. Nevertheless the term, used very loosely, has persisted, implying a type of song distinct from the German lied.

French poets, well aware of the supple, musical quality of French poetry – springing from the nature of the language, in which etymological word-stress is eliminated so that the word is subordinate to the phrase, and in which tonic stress is subtly variable but generally falls on the final voiced syllable of a word – sometimes resisted musical setting and sometimes welcomed it. Alfred de Musset even wrote some *Chansons à mettre en musique*. In particular, the poetry of Verlaine has been important in the development of French song. Verlaine avoided high-flown rhetoric, followed no tradition, and showed himself to be a master of classical forms and a daring innovator, a symbolist poet who (with Baudelaire and Mallarmé) explored the relation between appearance and reality, with suggestive overtones and associations, creating an elusive dream-world of nostalgia and secret ecstatic delight.

The particular character of this poetry is strongly reflected in Debussy's songs. In the artistic world that he inhabited, poetry, painting and music were combining and strongly influencing each other. In Verlaine,

Debussy seemed to find a kindred spirit, sensitive, highly sensual and ruthless. With the *Ariettes oubliées* and the two sets of *Fêtes galantes*, to poems of Verlaine, Debussy's individuality found complete expression. With his sympathy and understanding of the literary movements of his time, he was able to penetrate to the heart of a poem, realizing every shade of meaning, and beyond to a feeling that only music could express. While Fauré, the sensitive traditionalist and great melodist, achieved some superb results in his Verlaine settings, in a smaller, more restricted sphere, Debussy's art could encompass the complex spirit of Baudelaire or could enhance and add a new dimension to the delicately contrived eroticism of Louÿs's *Chansons de Bilitis*.

Not all the early 20th-century French songwriters felt so close and penetrating an identification with the poetry. Jean Rivier (*b* 1896), in settings ranging from 16th-century poems to Apollinaire, showed fine craftsmanship, an approachable style and beautiful singable vocal lines. Albert Roussel combined many different influences – impressionism, neo-classicism, d'Indy, German composers, oriental music – in a wide range of songs of marked individuality. Florent Schmitt's songs achieve a distinctive synthesis of German and French sympathies. Georges Migot (1891–1976), in his 'vocal chamber music', used original polyphonic textures with decorative and striking effect. Lili Boulanger was already following her own lyrical path at the time of her early death in 1918; her cycle *Clairières dans le ciel* is an important achievement in French song.

The influence of the other arts is strongly felt in the work of the Parisian group Les Six, which came into existence after World War I under the leadership of Cocteau and Satie. All six (Auric, Durey, Honegger, Milhaud, Poulenc, Tailleferre) wrote songs. The aesthetic climate was clearly set out in Cocteau's little book *Le Coq et l'Arlequin* (sub-titled *Notes autour de la musique*): enough of clouds, waves, aquariums, undines and perfumes of the night; what was wanted was a music with its feet firmly planted on the ground, a music for every day, made to man's measurements. Their ideals, anti-Wagner and anti-Debussy, were in many ways similar to those of groups in painting and literature who were reacting against various forms of Romanticism and impressionism. The combination of gaiety, clowning, sophistication and surrealism found musical reflection in extreme dissonances, banal 'wrong notes' and polytonality, and in the abrupt changes from a slapdash 'classicism' of empty 18th-century figuration to jazz and music-hall style. The superficial gaiety, however, often masked deeper feelings, as in many of the songs of Poulenc and Milhaud, who at their best both made an important contribution to the *mélodie*. Poulenc's style was a surrealistic mixture of contradictory elements, for he drew inspiration as easily from 16th-century polyphony as from popular song and the music-hall. His wit, irony and directness often recall Satie. In Poulenc's *mélodies* the influence of Chabrier, Ravel and Stravinsky contrast with passages of Schumann-like dreaminess or classical detachment: the mixture includes seriousness, impudent *gaminerie*, ingenuousness, sophistication, the lyrical, the extremely *sec*, the vulgar and the fastidious. Among his best song cycles are *Le bestiaire*, polished settings of humorous animal poems by Apollinaire, and *Tel jour telle nuit*, a set of nine poems by Paul Eluard, at times impassionedly lyrical, at times presenting musical images that follow the patterns of Eluard's free association of ideas. Milhaud, whose prolific output is very uneven, also brought together the most diverse elements in his predominantly lyrical songs: jazz, polytonality, folksong, harmonic and contrapuntal freedom. There is genuine poignancy in *Alissa*, settings of fragments from André Gide's *La porte étroite*; and in his *Quatre chansons de Ronsard* the vocal style is beautifully flexible and expressive. There is also a hilarious setting, in pastoral style, of passages from a catalogue of agricultural machinery, *Machines agricoles*. Most notably, there was the intimate and passionate assertion of personal religious feeling in the justly famous *Poèmes juifs*, a work of real distinction. Of the other Les Six composers, Auric, like Satie, found inspiration in popular music; much is very trivial, but his *Quatre chants de la France malheureuse* and *Six poèmes de Paul Eluard* show a composer of intelligence and depth of feeling.

Of composers born in the 20th century, Henri Sauguet has had an individual outlook on tradition, and has shown the direct influence of Satie in his song-cycle *Cirque*. Henri Barraud, very mixed in style, has effectively explored neo-classicism in settings of Victor Hugo. Jean Françaix, with his lightness, gaiety and polish, seems to personify the Gallic spirit in his Marot settings, *L'adolescence clémentine*, while his Charles d'Orléans songs of 1950 go back in spirit to 17th-century courtly music. When a group known as 'La Jeune France' was formed in 1936, its avowed aim was to compose in a lyrical style with a personal message. The leader of the group was then Olivier Messiaen. In his important song-cycles *Poèmes pour Mi* and *Chants de terre et de ciel*, both settings of his own texts, the meaning and purpose derive from a fervent Catholicism. They are clothed in a highly symbolic and personal musical language, elaborately calculated modally and rhythmically, and bold in chordal structure. Much of the style of *Harawi* (songs of love and death), for 'grande soprano dramatique' with a virtuoso piano part, derives from Indian music. There has been more spontaneous lyrical quality in the styles developed by other members of that group, notably Daniel Lesur and Yves Baudrier; and André Jolivet has written songs in a magical incantatory style related to primitive religion. More recent styles in French song have become ever more eclectic, and 12-note techniques have extended to athematic serialism.

BIBLIOGRAPHY

C. Bellaigue: 'Les mélodies françaises', *Revue des deux mondes*, liii (1919), 448

C. Laforêt: *La vie musicale au temps romantique* (Paris, 1929)

J. Tiersot: *La musique aux temps romantiques* (Paris, 1930)

J. d'Udine: *L'art du Lied et les mélodies de Massenet* (Paris, 1931)

E. Lockspeiser: 'The French Songs in the 19th century', *MQ*, xxvi (1940), 192

S. Northcote: *The Songs of Henri Duparc* (New York, 1950)

E. Reuter: *La mélodie et le Lied* (Paris, 1950)

H. Schouten: *Drei Franse Liederencomponisten: Duparc, Fauré, Debussy* (Amsterdam, 1950)

M. Cooper: *French Music from the Death of Berlioz to the Death of Fauré* (London, 1951)

J. Hall: *The Art Song* (Norman, Oklahoma, 1953)

F. Noske: *La mélodie française de Berlioz à Duparc: essai de critique historique* (Paris, Amsterdam, 1954; rev.2/1970 with R. Benton, Eng. trans. R. Benton) [incl. bibliography and song catalogue]

D. Cox: 'France', *A History of Song*, ed. D. Stevens (London, 1960), 194–227

C. Panzera: *50 mélodies françaises: leçons de style et d'interprétation* (Brussels, 1964)

P. Bernac: *The Interpretation of French Song* (London, 1970)

RITA BENTON, FRITS NOSKE (1)
DAVID COX (2)

**Melodik** (Ger.). The approach to or study of MELODY and melodic construction; the melodic resources of a composer or school, piece or set of pieces etc.

**Melodists' Club.** London concert organization founded in 1825; see LONDON, §VI, 4.

**Melodrama** (from Gk. *melos*, *drama*; Fr. *mélodrame*; It. *melologo*; Ger. *Melodram*). A kind of drama, or a part of a drama, in which the action is carried forward by the protagonist speaking in the pauses of, and later commonly during, a musical accompaniment. (It is distinct from the Italian *melodramma*, meaning simply 'musical drama', or opera.) The brief orchestral passages that separate the dialogues are clearly related to, and presumably in a sense derived from, those in accompanied operatic recitative (just as the pantomimic movement and gesture of a scene like Beckmesser's discovery of the song manuscript in *Die Meistersinger von Nürnberg*, Act 3, has its antecedents in the ballet-pantomime). The term 'melodrama' is also used in a less specifically musical sense to denote a kind of play, particularly popular in the 19th century (more commonly without a musical accompaniment) in which romantic and frequently sensational happenings that follow certain conventions are carried through until at the end Good triumphs and Evil is frustrated. This article is concerned almost entirely with the first of these definitions.

Although there is good reason for dating the invention of melodrama to J.-J. Rousseau's *Pygmalion*, probably written in 1762, J. E. Eberlin used the speaking voice against a musical accompaniment in his Latin drama *Sigismund* (Salzburg, 1753), and indeed the use of music as an adjunct to dramatic action is probably almost as old as drama itself. It is more fruitful to consider melodrama as a technique that seeks a particular kind of balance between words and music than to look upon it as an independent dramatic genre, since many of the best-known examples – the dungeon scene in *Fidelio*, the scene at the Wolf's Glen in *Der Freischütz*, or the part of the Majordomo in the revised version of Strauss's *Ariadne auf Naxos* – are effective by reason of the contrast they provide with the rest of the work.

Problems of nomenclature existed from the beginning. Rousseau subtitled *Pygmalion* a 'scène lyrique'; often used the term 'mélodrame', but always as a synonym for opera, like the Italian *melodramma*. Although Rousseau's text of *Pygmalion* probably dates from 1762, it was Easter 1770 before, at Lyons, he asked Coignet to set it to music. The work was given at Lyons in November of that year, the overture and an Andante probably composed by Rousseau himself, the rest by Coignet. The text was published in January 1771 in the *Mercure de France* and the *Nouveau journal helvétique*, and at about the same time as a slender separate publication at Geneva and Lyons; other editions and translations were not long in following. The work was probably staged in Paris (at the Opéra) in March 1772, and was frequently given by the Comédiens Français between 30 October 1775 and the early 19th century. Grimm wrote (*Correspondances littéraires*) of the 'effet surprenant' that the work made, and Rousseau (who refused to acknowledge the work in the 1775 production) summed up his achievement in the piece when he wrote (*Fragments d'observations sur l'Alceste italien de M. le Chevalier Gluck*) that in his conception 'la phrase parlée est de quelque sort annoncée et préparée par la phrase musicale'. This clause indeed may further be taken as indicating the principal difference between the French and the German melodrama: the former is divided into a number of generally short, independent musical numbers, to be played between the passages of spoken text, whereas the preferred German form tended towards continuity of musical thought, even where the spoken text interrupted, rather than was accompanied by, the flow of the music.

Despite the popularity in France of the Coignet–Rousseau setting, the influence of *Pygmalion* must be seen as largely theoretical and textual. Asplmayr set Rousseau's text to music in 1772; the wording of the title-page of the libretto makes it clear that the work was intended for performance at the Vienna court opera (*Pygmalion de J.-J. Rousseau, scène lyrique exécutée sur le Théâtre Imperial de Vienna avec la musique du Sieur Aspelmayer*); it was performed there in January 1772. The libretto contains timings of the musical numbers, as well as pantomimic directions, indicating that the work would have lasted some nine or ten minutes. The score does not seem to have survived. Another setting of the Rousseau text, by Anton Schweitzer, was given at Weimar in 1772; Goethe wrote admiringly of it in *Dichtung und Wahrheit* (iii, 2). Rousseau's text was known in Italy by 1771; it enjoyed considerable success there and also, from 1788, in Spain. The most famous *Pygmalion*, the setting of Georg Benda (Gotha, 20 September 1779), used an almost literal translation of the French original, with just one sizable cut, and a few minor alterations and misunderstandings.

In spite of the priority of Asplmayr's and Schweitzer's *Pygmalion* settings, the perfecter of the melodrama in Germany was Georg Benda. If chance dictated that he should set J. C. Brandes's version of Gerstenberg's *Ariadne auf Naxos* in place of Schweitzer (who abandoned work on the project in favour of Wieland's opera libretto *Alceste*), he succeeded brilliantly in his task. His melodrama scores show remark-

*Madame Brandes as Ariadne in Georg Benda's 'Ariadne auf Naxos': engraving from the Gotha 'Theater-Kalender' (1776)*

able flexibility and sustained musical invention. *Ariadne* was first given at Gotha (where the Seyler company had removed to after the Weimar theatre had burnt down in May 1774) on 27 January 1775, two months after the same company had given Schweitzer's *Pygmalion*. Benda's *Ariadne* was immediately successful with public and professional musicians alike (it reached Paris in 1781, translated by Dubois and subtitled *mélodrame*); it was followed by *Medea* (text by Gotter) on 1 May of the same year, and his *Pygmalion* four years later. *Theone* also dates from 1779 (it was later revised as *Almansor und Nadine*); in it Benda used the singing voice (solo and chorus) as well as the speaking voice. Although he never again achieved quite the mastery or the success of *Ariadne*, and indeed wrote more operas and Singspiels than melodramas after *Ariadne* (as before), the genre he had perfected was eagerly taken up by a host of contemporary and later composers, including Neefe, Reichardt, Zumsteeg, Iriarte and many of the Mannheim musicians. Goethe's *Proserpina* (1775), set by Seckendorff, is a well-known literary example. Some such works were called 'monodramas' (with one speaking part) or 'duodramas' (with two).

The first great composer to take up the melodrama was Mozart, whose enthusiastic comments on the Benda 'duodramas' he had heard (*Ariadne* and *Medea*) are to be found in his letters to his father from Mannheim of 12 and 24 November and 3 and 10 December 1778, and from Kaisheim on 18 December. Nothing survives of the full-length melodrama *Semiramis* that Mozart was to write in collaboration with Gemmingen (the repeated inclusion of it in the Gotha *Theater-Kalender* – in 1779 and 1780 as a work in progress, in 1781 and 1782 as a completed work – is almost certainly just one of the many mistakes contained in that publication). Despite his comment of 3 December 1778 that he was at work on it, he may not have progressed very far, once the chance of a specific performance had passed. Mozart did however write two fine and expressive examples of melodrama in the incomplete Singspiel *Zaide* of 1779–80, and included one in the contemporaneous music to *Thamos, König in Ägypten* (no.4). The two *Zaide* examples are among the most striking and extensive numbers in the score; the second leads into an aria.

Most 18th-century melodramas were serious in tone and classical in subject; by the early 19th century the range of subject matter was widening to include biblical and more general dramatic subjects, and comic melodramas began to be popular. In Vienna Kotzebue parodied Benda's *Ariadne*, and Wenzel Müller included comic melodramas, as well as more traditional serious examples, in some of his stage scores.

Beethoven's interest in the melodrama extended beyond the familiar example of the dungeon scene in *Fidelio*. There are melodramas in the incidental music to *Die Ruinen von Athen* and *König Stephan*, and it is the form he chose for Egmont's farewell to life, the penultimate number of the *Egmont* incidental music (which also includes pantomimic passages). Weber used melodrama in *Der erste Ton* of 1808 and in *Preciosa* as well as in *Der Freischütz*, and Schubert's *Die Zauberharfe* (D644, begun 1820) is an interesting large-scale venture which includes half-a-dozen melodramatic scenes, seven choruses and a romance that exists in two tenor versions and one for orchestra alone. Schubert also used melodrama in *Des Teufels Lustschloss* and in a sequence of three numbers near the close of Act 2 of *Fierabras*; and he also wrote a lied-like melodrama for piano and speaking voice, *Abschied von der Erde* (D829, 1826). The genre was indeed particularly popular in Vienna, where examples from the works of Starzer, Paradis, Eberl and Winter may be adduced in addition to those already mentioned.

More generally, Berlioz's *Lélio* is an ambitious if diffuse example; Marschner included a particularly striking example in Act 2 of *Hans Heiling* (1833) in Gertrude's spinning-song, which progresses from melodrama, via wordless humming, to the song proper ('Des Nachts wohl auf der Heide', no.12). Mendelssohn, Schumann, Liszt, Wagner and Humperdinck all tried their hand. Indeed, there can hardly be a 19th-century opera composer who did not. It had been a feature of much French *opéra comique* of the Revolution period, used in works by Méhul, Isouard, Boieldieu and others, and notably Cherubini (*Les deux journées*, 1800). Verdi found it convenient for the letter scenes in Act 1 of *Macbeth* and Act 2 of *La traviata*, as did Smetana similarly in Act 2 of *The Two Widows*.

The genre thrived in the 19th century in the lands that are now Czechoslovakia. Fibich was perhaps the most important and ambitious of all composers of melodrama, his *Hippodamia* of 1889–91 being a trilogy of full-length works; he had earlier written smaller examples for voice and orchestra or piano. For the use of leitmotifs as an aid to dramatic and stylistic cohesion he needed to look back no further than Wagner, though it is interesting to note that the very first important composer of melodramas, Fibich's compatriot Benda, had used an elementary form of leitmotif in his works. Čelansky, better remembered as the founder of the Czech Philharmonic Orchestra, wrote several melodramas.

There has perhaps been an increase in the use of melodrama in the 20th century, by such varied composers as Schoenberg and Stravinsky, Milhaud with Claudel in *Le livre de Christophe Colomb*, Honegger in *Jeanne d'Arc au bûcher*, Puccini (the end of *La bohème*), Berg, Busoni, Strauss (*Enoch Arden*, and passages in several of the operas), Walton (*Façade*), Britten, Henze and many more. Early this century a large selection of melodramas was readily available, published for domestic performance mainly with piano accompaniment, but some also with orchestra or chamber ensemble. The desire for experiment is constantly producing fresh ways (or the return to old ways) of combining the spoken voice with music (*see also* SPRECHGESANG).

BIBLIOGRAPHY

[? J. F.] Schink: 'Ueber das musikalische Duodrama, mit und ohne Gesang', *Theater-Kalender auf das Jahr 1778* (Gotha, 1778), 60

E. Istel: *Studien zur Geschichte des Melodramas, i: Jean-Jacques Rousseau als Komponist seiner lyrischen Scene 'Pygmalion'* (Leipzig, 1901) [continued in *Annales de la Société J. J. Rousseau*, i–iii (1905–7)]

F. Brückner: 'Zum Thema "Georg Benda und das Monodram" ', *SIMG*, vi (1904–5), 496

E. Istel: *Die Entstehung des deutschen Melodramas* (Berlin, 1906)

A. Pitou: 'Les origines du mélodrame français à la fin du XVIIIe siècle', *Revue d'histoire littéraire en France*, xviii (1911), 256–96

M. Steinitzer: *Zur Entwicklungsgeschichte des Melodrams und Mimodrams* (Leipzig, c1919)

E. C. van Bellen: *Les origines du mélodrame* (Utrecht and Paris, c1927)

H. Martens: *Das Melodram* (Berlin, 1933)

L. Gramisch: *Die Erscheinungsformen des melodramatischen Stils im 19. Jahrhundert* (Vienna, 1936)

G. Crocioni: *L'Alidoro o dei primordi del melodramma* (Bologna, 1938)

J. Subirá: *El compositor Iriarte (1750–1791) y el cultivo español del melólogo (melodrama)* (Barcelona, 1949–50)

J. van der Veen: *Le mélodrame musical de Rousseau au romantisme: ses aspects historiques et stylistiques* (The Hague, 1955)

J. Subirá: 'Melologo', *ES*

J. L. Smith: *Melodrama* (London, 1973)

E. F. Kravitt: 'The Joining of Words and Music in Late Romantic Melodrama', *MQ*, lxii (1976), 571

PETER BRANSCOMBE

**Melodramma** (It.). A dramatic text written to be set to music (*see* DRAMMA PER MUSICA), or the resultant opera. Verdi's second opera, *Un giorno di regno*, with a libretto by Felice Romani, was termed a *melodramma giocoso*; its successors were variously described as *tragedia lirica*, *dramma lirico*, *dramma tragico* and so on, but the term reappeared on two librettos of some literary pretension, *I masnadieri* and *Macbeth*. Each was described as a *melodramma*, as were *Rigoletto*, *Un ballo in maschera* and the revised *Simon Boccanegra*. It is hard to attach any special significance to the term; it alternated freely, often in successive editions of the same work, with the other terms mentioned above and also with *dramma* and *libretto composto per musica*. There is perhaps some slight evidence to suggest that, unlike 'melodrama' in the popular English sense, *melodramma* was regarded as one of the more distinguished terms for a librettist's work.

ANDREW PORTER

**Melody.**

1. Definition and origins. 2. Early history. 3. General concepts. 4. Structure and design. 5. Sacred monophony. 6. Metre and tonality. 7. Harmonic melody: instrumental-vocal. 8. Melody and scale. 9. Style and function. 10. Melodic texture. 11. Absolute melody?

1. DEFINITION AND ORIGINS. Melody, defined as pitched sounds arranged in musical time in accordance with given cultural conventions and constraints, represents a universal human phenomenon traceable to pre-historic times; in some cultures, however, rhythmic considerations may always have taken precedence over melodic expression, as in parts of Africa where percussive sounds of undetermined pitch are employed in lieu of semantic communication, or as pacemakers for systematic forms of physical effort (whether in daily work or ritual dance), or both. Primary concerns with melody appear to have been related more specifically to verbal, in some instances pre-verbal, modes of social intercourse.

While the exact causal relationships between melody and language remain to be established, the broad cultural bases of 'logogenic melody' are no longer in question. Nor are some of its widely shared characteristics. Certain universal manifestations of the melodic impulse, for example, appear to be centred intervallically on the descending minor 3rd. Children's singsongs are a case in point, as are the calls and responses of Alpine shepherds. The most universal instance of pitch modification is, needless to say, the infant's first cry; and recent research in infant behaviour has shown to what extent pitch-differentiated pre-verbal utterances are employed systematically and effectively by infants to communicate physiological needs as well as affective states. If natural phenomena, such as birdsong and other forms of animal communication, are any indication at all, it should be possible in time to arrive at meaningful concepts concerning an evolutionary continuum from pathogenic to logogenic forms of pitched vocal behaviour.

2. EARLY HISTORY. The pre-history of melody, however, though of unquestioned scientific interest, in no way affects the phenomenology of melody as it emerges from the annals of recorded history, both written and oral. Historically, the early development of melody may well have proceeded, as Szabolcsi suggested, from simple one-step voice inflections via conjunct trichordal patterns to intervallic combinations of minor 3rds and major 2nds. The superimposition of two such patterns would account for the countless pentatonic melodies found geographically from China to Appalachia and historically from Gregorian chant to Debussy. In all probability, the combination of the simplest one-step inflection with the basic singsong interval owes its broad appeal not only to the fundamental qualities of its pitch components but also, and more decisively, to its potential for variation through configurational rotation of its pitch content. The 3rd-cum-2nd, after all, lends itself to retrograde and mirror inversion without sacrifice of its quartal contour. When two such quartal patterns are joined disjunctively or conjunctively, i.e. either separated by a 2nd or in such a way that the highest note of the lower and the lowest note of the upper trichord overlap, the motivic possibilities are maximized to the point where pure pentatonicism can provide an adequate scalar framework for some rather sophisticated melodic manipulations. Indeed, if a motif is defined as a minimum of melodic substance susceptible to creative manipulation in a given aesthetic context, then pentatonicism would seem to offer matchless opportunities for motivic elaborations of the 4th, the acoustically 'perfect' interval that determines the tuning of so many instruments as well as the structural division of the octave. Empirically speaking, it is clear that pentatonicism satisfies a broad range of musical needs from basic logogenic progressions to the most varied treatments of motivic nuclei in sacred monophony, in Renaissance polyphony and beyond, wherever and whenever purely melodic forces have prevailed. The underlying pentatonicism of such music is admittedly not always easily recognized, if only because it often affects the melodic infra-structure more directly than the surface design. It nevertheless remains true that, in the absence of Western tonal harmony, quartal melodic patterning, with or without subdivisions of the 3rd-cum-2nd variety, has spawned the bulk of melodic activity from the dawn of history and the four corners of the earth.

Ever since Hornbostel, Sharp, Kodály and Bartók suggested early in the 20th century that quartal, if not always outright pentatonic, thinking may be a worldwide phenomenon, pertinent data have been collected among the most 'primitive' of tribes as well as in the most complex of musical cultures and sub-cultures. Wiora, who has attempted to document music in the late palaeolithic hunting civilizations, pointed to melodies based on disjunct 4ths with an occasional passing or auxiliary note among ethnic groups as disparate as Bushmen, Lapps and Menominee Indians. The descending trichord bounded by the interval of a 4th appears in the musical recitations of the ancient Hebrew community of Djerba between Passover and the Feast of Weeks (Pentecost) and, almost identically, in the Kyrie of the Roman Easter Vigil, one of the oldest of plainchant melodies. In Hungary, even relatively extended folksongs belonging to the 'oldest layer' favour the descending pentatonic 4th. The Hungarian case, which has been particularly well researched thanks to the work of Kodály and Bartók, also illustrates the effective interaction of linguistic and purely 'musical' considerations in the formation of characteristic melodies. The declining pitch lines, both sudden and gradual, so typical of the spoken language, are reflected in the motivic and structural tendencies of Hungarian melody from ancient times to the present.

Melodic descent, to be sure, is among the most

'natural' of musical procedures because it requires no 'artificial' generation of melodic energies. Its pathogenic archetype, as Sachs has shown, is the 'tumbling strain' where an initial high pitch provides a melodic diving-board, as it were, permitting melodic gravity to take charge. Given the law of melodic gravity, extensions of the 'tumbling strain' into relatively complicated anti-climactic melodies are understandably rare. By the same token, it may well have been an awareness of 'natural' melody that caused the ancients to think of musical systems as descending rather than rising. Whatever the case, melodic descent permeates much of the oldest known music irrespective of geographic origin. It would almost seem that, wherever music became an intrinsic condition of life, certain common melodic procedures were necessarily adopted, because they satisfied basic physiological and biological requirements, if not the aesthetic imagination *per se*.

3. GENERAL CONCEPTS. Etymologically, melody combines the ancient Greek terms for poetic order and song (*melos*, *ōtē*). That *melos* had early physiological associations, before it entered the realm of aesthetics, is quite in line with the characteristically Greek conception of music and poetry as organic mirrors of human, indeed cosmic existence. It was during the European Middle Ages that the Latin adaptation *melodia* assumed the specifically musical connotations which it retains in modern vernacular usage. Tinctoris, in the mid-15th century, no longer hesitated to identify *melus* with *cantus*, and most subsequent definitions similarly associated melody with song, though inevitably from varying stylistic perspectives. Rameau, in the 18th century, regarded melody as a product of harmony; but Rousseau claimed priority for autonomous melody. Hegel, in the early 19th century, thought of harmony and melody 'as one compact whole, and a change in the one necessarily involves a change in the other'. For the acoustician Helmholtz, melody was the incarnation of motion in music, expressed 'in such a manner that the hearer may easily, clearly, and certainly appreciate the character of that motion by immediate perception'. Perception was also the principal concern of Hanslick who saw in melody the 'archetypal configuration of beauty' ('Grundgestalt der Schönheit'). Hanslick's Apollonian viewpoint was, of course, diametrically opposed to the Dionysiac ideal of 'unending melody', expounded by Wagner, who postulated 'an ordered series of quasi-intellectual, unfulfilled speech-sounds – indirectly representative, concentrated as image but not yet as immediate, inevitably true expression ... directly addressed to feeling, unerringly vindicated and fulfilled'. When, in the mid-1920s, Watt applied Helmholtzian physics to a comparative study of the intervallic properties of selected Schubert songs and American Indian melodies, he reached the post-Wagnerian conclusion that there was

no reason why a melody should ever stop. Every interval carries its motion farther along, so that another group of conditions must exist which modify and arrest its motion. One very natural condition of arrest is the ordinary limit of memory. No doubt the lengths of primitive melodies, if not of all melodies, are largely determined by this. But this is a condition of ending, not of arrest of motion in the musical sense.

A few years earlier Thurstone, another student of non-Western music searching for universal answers, had defined 'the essence of melody' as 'unity in the perception of pitch variation'. Consonance and dissonance, those perennial bones of theoretical contention, were ruled out as criteria for 'melodic unity'. The same could

be said up to a point for harmonic considerations generally. For even in the essentially triadic melodies associated with functionally tonal music, harmony provides at most 'an inner skeleton on which varying contours may be draped' (Watt). Anyone attempting to appreciate the mono-rhythmic oboe melody in the Andantino of Tchaikovsky's Fourth Symphony in terms of its harmonic infra-structure would not only miss the point of its finely chiselled phrasing; seduced by its seeming simplicity he might well misunderstand the composer's rather complex harmonic intent. 'Melodic unity' is configurationally speaking an intrinsic psycho-acoustical function of melodic generation in a given historic–cultural context and must in the end be experienced as such.

4. STRUCTURE AND DESIGN. The character of a given melody is determined by its range or relative position within the total pitch continuum, its ambitus or pitch spread, its contour or linear design, and its syntactic structure with respect to elements of contrast and repetition, variation and development. The smallest melodic-rhythmic unit, the motif, requires a minimum of two distinct pitch levels. Syntactically, motivic materials are arranged in phrases, the general characteristics of which are determined by the specific melodic idiom. Thus, in contrast to the larger, songlike melodic entities, which as a rule eschew a great deal of motivic differentiation, instrumental themes of the type associated with Western music from the middle of the 18th century onwards favour sharply profiled, contrasting motifs arranged in an open-ended fashion to allow for their subsequent structural development. As Schoenberg once put it, 'a melody can be compared to an "aperçu", an "aphorism", in its rapid advance from problem to solution ... a theme resembles rather a scientific hypothesis which does not convince without a number of tests, without presentation of proof'. A properly conceived melody is thus by and large self-sufficient, whereas a good theme generates energies needed for the formation of larger entities that exceed structurally and expressively the apparent potential of its motivic substance. But self-sufficiency is not necessarily bound to sectional repetition, as has often been asserted. None would wish to deny that note-for-note repeats of structural sub-units have been characteristic of Western song at least since medieval times. Such perennial patterns as *AAB* and *ABA* furnish ample evidence to this effect. By the same token, there is nothing to justify sectional repetition as an absolute criterion of melodic design. Schoenberg's work alone offers ample proof to the contrary, while demonstrating at the same time the structural importance of transposed or varied recurrences, or both, of motivic materials of the kind that animate so much of plainchant or, for that matter, any number of non-Western repertories. In Western composition, sectional repetition became virtually identified with melody conceived in harmonic tonal terms. It is, therefore, a hallmark of the Classical–Romantic era. But already Berlioz, not to speak of Wagner, avoided untransposed sectional repetition in some of his most haunting melodies, perhaps because he, more than any of his contemporaries, had begun to think of melody more as a reflection of a psychological 'stream of consciousness' than of man's rational perception of 'reality'.

As for thematic matter, the multi-motivic designs of Haydn, Mozart and Beethoven, geared to dramatic conflict, superseded more than a century of mono-motivic incipits ('developmental themes' in Kurth's terminology) that provided the decisive initial spark for considerable amounts of Baroque instrumental music. But if the early 18th century had thus managed to imbue even the most innocuous melodic–rhythmic stuff with a salutary dose of kinetic energy, the Romantic reaction to the dialecticism of the Classical masters offered entirely new mono-motivic opportunities. The cello melody in the Intermezzo movement of Schumann's Piano Concerto, not to speak of the closely related opening subject of Brahms's Fourth Symphony, reveals the previously unsuspected affective and structural potential of a single iambic two-note motif at the behest of lyrical genius. Such uniquely 'stripped' tunes notwithstanding, the harmonic age generally practised the art of melodic 'drapery' with a gusto exceeded only by that which inspired certain 17th-century keyboard works or that with which South Asian musicians go about their ever surprising raga improvisations. Meanwhile, monophonic chant and modal polyphony, the largest and most influential Western reservoirs of pure melody, were waiting in the wings of history, ready to burst on to a musical scene that sought melodic salvation increasingly from 'exotic' sources, including the quartal and modal folktunes of Russia.

5. SACRED MONOPHONY. Theoretically at least, the dogged adherence of plainchant to its ancient roots must have been the motivating force behind the plagal modes centred on a *finalis* a 4th above the lowest pitch in the scalar order. Similarly, the prevalence of recitation tones (tenors) a 3rd above the *finalis* suggests the genetic significance of the descending 3rd in the melodic practices of early European Christendom. Where, as in the case of the 4th, or Hypophrygian, mode, the tenor occurs instead a 4th above the *finalis*, the mode may have been generated by two conjunctive pentatonal 4ths. The 'authentic' recitation pitch, on the other hand, generally a 5th above the *finalis* (except for the 3rd mode, where practical considerations dictated a minor 6th), points to disjunct quartal origins. Quartal movement as a fundamental melodic resource is illustrated by the antiphonal rendition of Psalm cxlvii, where the recitation pitch is brought into focus by lower and upper auxiliary notes, then confirmed configurationally by a rapid descent to the *finalis* a 4th below (ex.1).

Ex.1 Psalm cxlvii (LU, p.202)

Lau-da  Je-ru-sa-lem Do-mi-num: lau-da De-um tu-um  Si - on.____

Careful analysis is likely to dispel any lingering doubts concerning the pentatonal foundations of plainchant. The Easter sequence *Victimae paschali laudes*, based on a metrical text from the first half of the 11th century, supplies a perfect model for the sophisticated manipulation of the 3rd-cum-2nd motif (ex.2). Its opening phrase features in typical chant fashion the minor 3rd flanked by upper and lower auxiliary notes. The penultimate E, which poses at first as a mere passing note, assumes structural functions in the second phrase, where it anchors the trichord A–G–E. The transposition of the original pattern to the upper 5th is followed by a move in the opposite direction to the 4th below, in conformity with a prominent melodic procedure that recalls the gradual descent of a glider released in mid-air: taking full advantage of air currents it manages to

Ex.2 Sequence *Victimae paschali laudes* (LU, p.780)

Vic - ti-mae pas-cha - li   lau-des  im-mo-lent Christ-ti - a - ni.

A-gnus  re - de - mit  o - ves: Chris-tus  in - no-cens  Pa - tri

re - con - ci - li - a - vit  pec - ca - to - res

rise above the point of release; only then, lacking propulsive power, it descends gently but inevitably to the take-off level or lower altitudes.

The third section, starting at the lowest pitch level, telescopes two occurrences of the rising 3rd-cum-2nd motif, and in so doing regenerates a goodly amount of melodic energy. This ingenious, intensely dynamic procedure receives further impetus from a device that is common to a wide variety of melodic styles, because it effectively restores pitch balance in the wake of a more or less drastic drop: once the downward leap has 'hit bottom', an immediate directional reversal propels the melodic line up and well beyond the original jump-off point, much as a skilful trampoline gymnast is projected ever higher. In the realm of melody even the law of gravity bows to aesthetic priorities. As the trampoline effect shows, any sudden change in direction must be quickly redressed if melodic unity is not to suffer.

By the end of the first millennium, plainchant melody had evidently recognized the structural weight of the melodic *finalis* in a manner comparable only to the magnetic force of the harmonic tonic centuries later. Tentatively at first, but soon inescapably, Western goal-orientation led to directional diatonicism. In the Easter sequence, the final complete section summarizes, as it were, all the basic melodic forces at work in this seemingly simple yet compositionally intricate tune. After an initial repeat of the second verse, the melody ascends once more to the high C in dramatic preparation for the trampoline jump from low C to the recitation pitch A just before the final decline. A last allusion to the initial motif reconfirms the *finalis* in the 'Amen Alleluia' coda.

With respect to total structure, the gradual rise of the first verse is properly balanced by the anti-climactic design of the second section with its elaborate descent from the highest point of the melody, which in turn prepares the subsequent trampoline effect. In these and many other ways the Easter sequence is the acme of melodic efficiency and effectiveness, as is plainchant at large, perhaps because it feeds on melodic energy unadulterated by strong rhythmic intervention and unencumbered by harmonic commitments. Though necessarily emphasizing conjunct motion in keeping with its contemplative aesthetic, plainchant demonstrates melodic principles as valid in the 20th century as they were at a time when the church controlled virtually all learned European music. The principle of melodic compensation by contrary conjunct motion, for one, has never ceased to affect melodic phraseology at all levels. The contingent primacy of the structural arch, on the other hand, is in no way obviated by the many melodic elaborations of the 'tumbling strain' or, for that matter, a number of climactic melodies with *finales* well above the initial pitch. In liturgical practice, such relatively infrequent types will on occasion form sub-divisions of larger melodic complexes which, as cumulative entities, display features that clearly comply, at least in general terms, with the law of directional compensation.

Unlike the syllabic Easter sequence, the melismatic gradual *Haec dies* gives full rein to pathogenic melodic energies, though inevitably within the confines of sacred aesthetic convention (ex.3). Structurally unfettered by definition, such compositions sacrifice motivic tightness at the altar of vocal virtuosity, thriving instead on ornamental devices, including scalar and sequential passages, that tend to obscure any pentatonal remnants. But if the virtuosity of solo singers was a contributing factor in the promotion of medieval diatonicism, its principal source of encouragement was no doubt secular practice, especially in dance music, where choreographic considerations dictated rhythmic regularity from the start and with such marked consequences for all aspects of melodic articulation.

6. METRE AND TONALITY. Nowhere is this more evident than in the monophonic secular dance music of the outgoing Middle Ages, as represented by the well-known *Estampie Kalenda maya* or a typical dance-song like Moniot d'Arras' *Ce fut en mai*. Both are clearly in the major mode, the *modus lascivius* of medieval theory; both favour the tonic major triad and generally betray harmonic tendencies that are strengthened by rhythmic periodization which in turn is mandated by the underlying dance figures. Periodization of one sort or another was also a feature of the dance-determined polyphony of the same period, specifically the 12th-century clausula and the 13th-century French motet. And if melismatic organum can be said to reflect, like melismatic chant, the pathogenic 'outpouring of the soul' that characterizes, for example, the freely unfolding *taqāsīm* of Middle Eastern music, then the measured or discant style may well have been suggested by the strictly metric portions which follow the *taqāsīm* and provide often long delayed, and hence welcome, kinetic relief. The celebrated rhythmic modes, in turn, may have been the outcome of classicistic rationalization on the part of Christian apologists embarrassed by the veritable dance mania that swept through Europe in the later Middle Ages. From then on, at any rate, rhythmic forces, whether metrical or not, left their lasting imprint on any number of melodic types, and there can be no doubt that the seesaw relationship of rhythmic–harmonic and rhythmic–melodic factors vying for priority was a

crucial factor at every stage of eight centuries of stylistic transformation. After all, the late medieval predilection for metrical organization, though seemingly superseded by the overriding melodic concerns of modal polyphony, remained alive in the Italian frottola as well as the French chanson and other dance-conditioned vocal and instrumental forms.

The prolonged struggle between these two basically antagonistic melodic–rhythmic orientations was stalemated throughout much of the 17th century. But before long, rationalistic criteria began to affect aspects of melodic organization no less than the continuing debate about melody in the hierarchy of musical values. Viewed in this light, Rousseau's promotion of popular melody, especially of the Italian variety, and Rameau's discovery of the 'natural' laws of functional harmony appear anything but incompatible. On the contrary, together they provided the intellectual underpinning for the harmonically conceived, periodically structured melodies of the so-called Classical era. The polyphonic heritage of the Renaissance, as codified in Zarlino's rules for composition based on melody, characteristically assumed a central position in the systematic teachings of 18th-century theorists from Fux and Martini to Albrechtsberger, the tutor of Beethoven; and Beethoven could say of himself that, unlike his predecessors, he had been born with the obbligato accompaniment. Significantly, it was Beethoven who, in his last quartets, unleashed once again the full force of pure melody as the prime carrier of musical structure and in a manner that conveys the spirit, if not always the letter, of the principles of motivic manipulation in plainchant and modal polyphony. Beethoven's ever-expanding musical universe, to be sure, reflected more directly a lasting preoccupation with J. S. Bach. Whatever his principal inspiration, the later Beethoven refined earlier methods of motivic recycling in ways that were to revolutionize the ecology of music, if only because the melodic materials saved served to generate ever new melodic energies. In this respect Wagner approached the ideals of the later Beethoven more closely than Brahms, who responded more readily to the homophonic 'middle period' Beethoven. By the same token, it was because he could not and would not abandon the basically triadic–metric traditions of Italian folk music that Verdi emerged as Wagner's natural opponent.

7. HARMONIC MELODY: INSTRUMENTAL-VOCAL. The harmonic era, which gave birth to musical drama and to instrumental music as a functionally autonomous art, unwittingly came to rely heavily on melodic figuration, Watt's 'drapery', i.e. the melodic tissue that connects and covers the intermittent supports furnished by the harmonic substructure. Figuration had been a favourite device of early organists who developed the idiomatic 'coloration' techniques that typify the 15th-century Faenza Codex, Conrad Paumann's *Fundamentum organisandi* and many 16th-century keyboard tablatures. The history of vocal music, too, is replete with characteristic instances of melodic coloration, from the more florid types of plainchant and early polyphonic genres, especially those of the Italian trecento, to the sacred polyphony of the late 16th century – which was often rendered with improvised figurations as a concession to contemporaneous monodic practices involving diminution, whether in the melodic enhancement of an extended pitch or elaborate melodic fillers bridging the

Ex.3 Gradual *Haec dies* (LU, p.778)

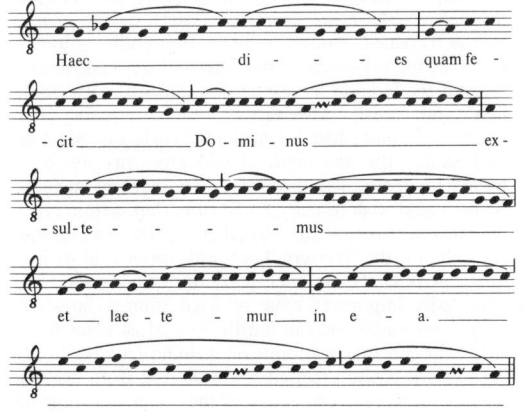

outer limits of large intervals. With the development of 'florid song' in Italian opera, improvised figuration became the special province of the virtuoso singers who thus adorned the da capo portions of late 17th- and early 18th-century solo arias.

The essentially decorative function of so much vocal music inspired by the Italian Baroque inevitably required outright logogenic complementation, at least in opera, if any plot continuity was to be maintained. Bel canto melody, therefore, produced its logogenic counterpart in the form of recitative, both simple and accompanied. Simple (*semplice*; or 'dry', *secco*) recitative reduced the pitch substance by and large to what was needed to render musically the most typical of speech inflections. Accompanied (or obbligato) recitative, on the other hand, assumed increasingly dramatic stances, as attempts were made to compensate for the largely lyrical nature of the vocal display pieces. In so doing, accompanied recitative developed an often highly expressive melodic idiom that was to have considerable influence on both instrumental music and musical drama, culminating in the work of Wagner. In accordance with its dramatic function, accompanied Italian recitative was characterized by intervallic leaps and generally unpredictable melodic behaviour. Structurally, it remained open-ended, like most of the action it related, in contrast to the closed, for the most part ternary, forms of the intervening arias. Moods and reflections that were not easily rendered in either recitative or aria style, were relegated to an intermediary style, the arioso, which combined features of the logogenic and pathogenic or decorative types of melody. At the same time, the growing desire for 'natural' musical expression, which caused the 18th-century enthusiasm for comic opera, also produced song types that eschewed the decorative element altogether in favour of an often folksy tunefulness. By the time Mozart achieved his unique operatic synthesis, he was able to draw not only on various Italian conventions but also on *tragédie lyrique* as transformed by Gluck with due regard to its deeply ingrained logogenic traditions – a rich melodic palette indeed, embracing the 'driest' of recitatives as well as the most florid of figurated song (as in the Queen of Night's aria in *Die Zauberflöte*).

Instrumental figuration has been a perennial favourite of composers of variation sets, particularly for keyboard, since the 16th century. The melodies underlying such variation sets are often referred to as 'themes'. But if Schoenberg was correct in his proposition that 'a theme is not at all independent and self-determined . . . it is strictly bound to consequences which have to be drawn, and without which it may appear insignificant', such careless usage can hardly be said to benefit conceptual clarity. Variation themes, after all, must be perfectly balanced, self-sufficient melodies tending almost by definition 'toward regularity, simple repetition and even symmetry' (Schoenberg). In fact, composers of variations could indulge their taste for figuration and coloration only as long as they were able to rely on a firm melodic frame of reference. Generally speaking, the 'theme and variation' issue is typical of the terminological confusion that has always surrounded melodic matters. During the Middle Ages such Latin terms as *harmonia*, *cantus* and *melodia*, even *modulatio*, were used interchangeably; the same holds for motif, phrase and theme in more recent times. Mozart was no longer alive when Galeazzi in his otherwise important description of the sonata form could declare with impunity that

'the motif is nothing but the principal idea of melody, the subject, the theme, one might say, of the musical discourse, and the whole composition must revolve upon it'.

A subject, to be sure, is not necessarily a theme, even though an entire composition may indeed revolve upon it. About the middle of the 16th century Zarlino could say with good cause that 'in every musical composition, what we call the subject is that part from which the composer derives the invention to make the other parts of the work, however many they may be'. He went on to explain that such a subject may be the composer's own or somebody else's invention 'that it may be a tenor or some other part of any composition you please, whether of plainsong or of figured music', and that it may be taken over in its original form or in a novel adaptation. But a polyphonic subject, treated in accordance with the rules of modal counterpoint, by necessity had qualities that were incompatible with the requirements of an 18th-century theme designed not only to raise compositional problems but to ensure their resolution. If the head-motif of a late 15th- or early 16th-century motet can be said to behave at all thematically, it does so at most in the sense of an instrumental incipit, like the rising triad in long note values which sparks off the first movement of Bach's E major Violin Concerto.

In the absence of intrinsic motivic dialectics of the dramatic type, thematic development of the Classical variety was precluded in either case. That is not to say, of course, that the nature of motivic relationships, let alone of motivic substances, has remained unaffected by the stylistic vicissitudes of a world dedicated to 'progress'. The opening bars of Mahler's Second Symphony syncretize the incipit and dramatic types in a manner that echoes the 'Sturm und Drang' rhetoric of some of the keyboard works of C. P. E. Bach, composed nearly a century and a half earlier. After 1900, rhetorical gestures became identified not only with the melodic idiom of 'expressionism' but, in association with neo-Baroque motoric energies, also of the 'neo-classicism' of the early 1920s.

8. MELODY AND SCALE. The systematic investigation and discussion of melodic phenomena has inevitably been affected over the centuries by sundry historical perspectives and changing stylistic contexts. Still, surprisingly little has been done to sort out a host of conceptual ambiguities and vague definitions in the 40 years since an alarmed Paul Hindemith decried the longstanding systematic neglect of melody, the element through which, in his view, the Western composer had always revealed himself most meaningfully. Already Parry, at the beginning of the 20th century, had warned 'against the familiar misconception that scales are made first and music afterwards'. A few years later Hornbostel published his brilliant article on 'Melodie und Skala'. But the myth of scalar priority has continued to distort the theoretical treatment of melody. None would wish to deny, to be sure, that certain types of musical instruments, whether of the Indonesian gamelan or the Western keyboard variety, have had prescriptive effects on pitch selection. Leaving aside the admittedly important issue of fixed tuning, however, scalar considerations can hardly be said to place more than very general constraints on melodic activity, if only because the scales themselves are derived from existing melodic practices. The image of the scalar tail wagging the melodic dog would seem grotesque, were it not for

the implied reminder of the extent to which musical notation, with all its blessings, has narrowed Western man's understanding of a cultural phenomenon that is always aural in essence and rarely if ever graphic.

9. STYLE AND FUNCTION. Broadly speaking, melodic styles are identifiable, like spoken languages, by their vocabulary, grammar and syntax, as well as idioms related to function and social class. Structurally, melody may be akin to freely evolving prose or the measured balance of poetry. It may comply with harmonic requirements or obviate them. It may suggest certain forms of physical behaviour or, for that matter, rational thought; then again, it may reflect the affective complexities of the subconscious. Above all, as a social product, melody is part and parcel of the culture or sub-culture to which it owes its existence. Melodic styles, therefore, share not only specific national characteristics; they also respond to a variety of social and functional needs, as Johannes de Grocheo observed some 700 years ago when he divided 13th-century French practice into *musica vulgaris*, the popular monophonic music of his time, *musica mensurabilis*, the measured learned music of the intelligentsia, and *musica ecclesiastica*, the music of the church, which drew upon elements of both the popular and learned genres. More recently, Mozart (in the ballroom scene of *Don Giovanni*) and Berg (in the tavern scene of *Wozzeck*) have dealt with different social classes in characteristic melodic–rhythmic terms.

Melodic expression, in the sense of melodic associations with non-musical subject matter, whether purely emotional, physical or 'natural', has been an intrinsic (though by no means uncontroversial) feature of Western music at least since the early Renaissance, when so many ancient concepts, the Platonic notion of ethos included, re-entered the secular consciousness of Europe. Textual allusions of a directional nature thus found literal melodic representation both in Renaissance polyphony and the monodic art that took its place precisely for the sake of ever greater melodic expressiveness. Programmatic symbolism accounts for triadic lines in the battle and hunting chansons of Janequin and for chromatic alterations in late 16th-century Italian madrigals, for the siciliana movements in 18th-century Christmas concertos and for fanfare patterns in the symphonies of Beethoven. In the 19th century some historical references to older melodic styles were allowed to shape the 'contemporary' idiom. The late 17th-century passion for affective–rhetorical minutiae produced a whole array of appropriate melodic formulae as well as a complex set of rules for their 'correct' application, codified most successfully by Mattheson and known in Germany as the 'doctrine of the Affections'. By the same token, if Monteverdi defended his *stile concitato* with the words of Plato, calling for melodies worthy of 'the utterances and the accents of a brave man who is engaged in battle', Mendelssohn thought of his celebrated Songs without Words as fit only for ladies.

But political movements, too, have left their imprints on specific types of melody. The tunes of the Geneva Psalter and the chorales of Martin Luther and his followers did not merely have religious connotations; their measured rhythms and sharp melodic profiles also mirror the sense of dignity with which the 16th century reformers pursued political goals of well-nigh universal significance. Similarly, the songs of the French Revolution, exemplified by the *Marseillaise*, with their dotted rhythms and rising triadic patterns, not only sparked the enthusiasm of the thousands who placed their trust in the new republicanism; they also became cherished models for the fighting-songs of international socialism which produced a repertory recognized as such all over the world. And in the USA the hymn tunes of the pioneers who settled the West generations later inspired the hopeful songs of the Civil Rights movement. In other words, melodic styles have rarely been mere figments of the abstract aesthetic imagination. In Western civilization, no less than in Africa and elsewhere, melodic idioms have often been functionally determined and associated with clearly defined ideas and concrete activities. Surely, when Beethoven decided to open his violin concerto with a march tune supported by military drum rhythms, he did so with the knowledge that such an obvious reference to the Napoleonic war machine and the mental anguish it caused would be clearly understood, if only because the general procedure had by then become familiar through the violin concertos of some of his immediate French predecessors.

Similar considerations pertain, needless to say, in the folk realm as well, where songs of mourning, spinning-songs, and others associated with typical activities or social functions, may actually be members of distinctive tune families. At the very least, their functional intent is reflected in identifiable melodic terms, if not always common structural characteristics. The outside observer, however, is bound to think of folksong by and large in geographic–cultural terms. Thus he will recognize that central Europe and parts of France and Italy represent triadic strongholds, while Russia is attached to quartal melodic patterns. In southern Europe, including Spain and Sicily as well as Albania and parts of Greece and Yugoslavia, he will sense a common Mediterranean heritage in the prevailing taste for augmented 2nds, not to speak of the general predilection for descending melodic patterns or, for that matter, intonational idiosyncracies that would be considered intolerable in the triadic north.

10. MELODIC TEXTURE. A given melodic style, let alone the texture of a specific tune, necessarily involves every aspect of musical order, not merely single pitch arrangements. Thus periodic structure, or melodic patterning in terms of properly balanced sub-units, was conditioned as much by textual requirements as by kinetically determined dance rhythms and the rise of functional harmony. Typically the melodic root interval, the 4th, was forced to surrender to the harmonically derived 5th, once melodic tension *per se* had begun to yield to harmonic concepts of consonance and dissonance. Neither was the 3rd-cum-2nd motif capable, under the circumstances, of withstanding the frontal assault of thirdal chains. To compensate for the resulting decline in pure melodic energy, rhythmic devices assumed unprecedented powers of motivic definition. The beginning of Beethoven's Fifth Symphony is often cited in this connection, and there can be no question but that during his 'middle period' Beethoven pushed the rhythmic potential of functionally harmonic melody to unsuspected extremes, indeed beyond the point of no return, considering the pre-eminence of melodic–polyphonic textures in his last quartets. Historically, however, the Beethovenian phenomenon, though unique within the specific context of early 19th-century music, was but one of many recurring manifestations of the funda-

mental dichotomy of melody and harmony – a traumatic issue in Western music that has elicited the very best from superior musicians ready to meet the challenge as a unique opportunity to achieve the well-nigh impossible yet, by the same token, has played perpetual havoc among those who have brought mere talent to their tasks. The history of music is staked out by the stylistic landmarks left behind by the few who thus survived the long trek from medieval monophony to 20th-century serialism.

Among the exceedingly limited number of modern scholars devoted to the historical or the cross-cultural study of melody, or both, Lach, in a pioneering dissertation published shortly after World War I, relied heavily on visual, especially architectural, analogies. Mindful of the age-old technique of melodic–rhythmic diminution or coloration, he distinguished between major structural (architectonic) components and ornamental 'melic' forces, corresponding to the weight-carrying structural skeleton of a building as opposed to its readily accessible surface characteristics. Lach also felt that certain types of 'primitive' melodic patterning reflected mental processes akin to those which may, in the visual domain, account for the more elementary combinations of such primary elements as dots, dashes and circles. The complex musical structures identified with at least 1000 years of Western composition, on the other hand, reminded him of the great mosques of Persia and Turkey as well as the Gothic and Baroque churches of Europe, where intricate design and sophisticated engineering went so happily hand in hand.

Whatever the merits of some of his more eccentric points, at least by implication Lach focussed long overdue attention on the crucial analytical problems of melody as form in relation to structure as process. That he should have conceived his theory of melodic infra- and super-structures at a moment in history when non-Western, particularly Asian music in all its splendid variety, had begun to penetrate the aesthetic consciousness of the European vanguard (*Der blaue Reiter* appeared in 1912), was anything but accidental. By 1913, closed forms had become vestiges of the past, melodically, rhythmically, even harmonically. Gregorian chant, as restored by the monks of Solesmes, was not only the subject of a papal *motu proprio*, it had long since been recognized as the ultimate source of pure melody by an entire generation of French composers identified with the Paris Schola Cantorum. Debussy, for his part, had jettisoned the harmonic strictures of the musical academic world in favour of a freely evolving melodic flow inspired by the literary orientalism of symbolist poetry no less than the musical exoticism of Balakirev and Rimsky-Korsakov and the Javanese and Annamite revelations of the Paris exhibition of 1889. In central Europe, 'open' melodic patterning was a conditioning factor in Schoenberg's 'emancipation of dissonance' as well as his abiding concern for musical cohesiveness, stimulated, interestingly enough, by intensive studies of Bach and Mozart. With melody thus restored to its once dominant position in European compositional practice, reassessments from different analytical–historical perspectives were merely a matter of time. Four years after Lach, Kurth came forth with his epochal treatise on the foundations of linear counterpoint which draws general conclusions regarding the laws of melody from the specifics of Bach's style. Eventually, in his last major work, *Musikpsychologie* (1931), Kurth made configurational perception the ultimate touchstone of melodic experience.

In contrast to Lach's visual–architectonic approach, which emphasized the static–structural aspects of melody, Kurth found analogies in the discoveries of modern science for his discussion of melodic energy; and unlike Lach, who documented his theories with melodic excerpts from non-Western cultures on the one hand and, on the other, variation-prone eras and styles in the history of Western music, Kurth based his observations on music that represents Western teleology at its motoric musical best. Artistically, his ideas about musical energy generation had contemporaneous parallels in the neo-Baroque works of Stravinsky, Schoenberg and Hindemith, who emulated Scarlatti and Bach with melodic incipits designed to project tightly controlled groups of closely related ideas into the musical time-space continuum where they are sustained and if necessary reinforced by recurring motivic boosts, emanating as a rule from transposed restatements of the incipit or an appropriate variant. The resulting melodic lines typically reach their climax about three-quarters of the way along, when their energies begin to be spent. The completed melodic course of such motoric music is reminiscent of the well-known projectile curve where a forceful yet smooth ascent is followed by a rather rapid decline. Melodic projectile curves of this sort retain a certain expressive neutrality. They are neither dramatic nor specifically lyrical. Instead, they appeal to one's inherent sense of musical movement, especially when, as in Bach's music, rhythm and metre are perfectly synchronized to avoid any suspicion of periodicity. Periodization, of course, had sacrificed freely unfolding rhythm to the mandates of dance and metrical poetry, and had done so justifiably also in the interest of rational organization conducive to immediate appeal and ease of perception. 19th-century textbook writers, unfortunately, made periodization the principal basis for their broad generalizations concerning the essence of melody at large, the growing testimony of history to the contrary notwithstanding. Composers of the first rank, though, were quick to recognize the 'tyranny of the bar-line' as an additional threat to melody struggling against the paralysing effects of tonal harmony. Responding with alacrity to the rediscovery of Bach and Palestrina, among other masters of the past, they proceeded to balance periodic and non-periodic elements in their melodic idiom to the point where, in Beethoven's last quartets, polyphonic–kinetic forces take hold of the harmonic–metric sub-structure in a manner that anticipates not only the mature Wagner but also Schoenberg.

Prose-based music for the stage, meanwhile, required strong motivic contrasts if it was to do justice to swift dramatic change. The German lied, on the other hand, favoured the use of motivic variants or, at the very least, motivic family relationships in keeping with its subtle poetic moods. Lyrical melody caters to conjunct motion, just as its dramatic counterpart thrives on the sensation of tension associated with intervallic leaps. Dramatic idioms are also marked by higher degrees of rhythmic irregularity, since rhythmic analogy and metric equivalence tend to convey a sense of repose.

The opening theme of Mozart's Haffner Symphony, no.35 in D (ex.4), furnishes an excellent example, because it mirrors in instrumental terms the same kind of dramatic situation that motivates the first duet in the opera *Don Giovanni*. Here as there, three basic moods are represented by three sharply differentiated melodic

Ex.4 Mozart: Symphony in D K385, first movt

patterns heard in immediate succession. In the symphony the first idea takes up the initial five bars, while the second idea occupies the next four, and the third concludes what is, oddly enough, a 13-bar melody. These three components do, however, share a march-like rhythm first heard in bar 4. Thanks to the ingenious use of this persistent motivic pattern, which undergoes significant changes in meaning as its relative position shifts within the melody as a whole, contrast and continuity are kept in perfect balance. The explosive energy emanating from the long initial low D prepares the startling effect of the octave leap, but it also accounts for the irregular completion of the melody in bar 13. The opening note thus fulfils a multiple function like that of the motivic incipit of Bach's E major concerto. But Mozart's theme is instructive in other ways as well. The melodic infra-structure of the first five bars consists of a conjunct descending 4th. This ubiquitous pattern is, of course, equally familiar from lyrical compositions like the celebrated 'Largo' in Handel's *Serse*. But there the conjunct descent is solemnly straightforward and immediately followed by an equally unadorned retrograde. That this directional reversal manages to overshoot the original pitch level is due to a combination of the law of melodic compensation and the 'trampoline effect'. Mutual reinforcements of this sort can trigger even more drastic reactions to a relatively rapid descent. Handel, anxious to maintain a lyrical mood, prolonged the retrograde motion but slightly. Mozart's dramatic leap, on the other hand, unleashes compensatory forces that are further energized by the ever-so-brief shortening of the long note values. Instead of pursuing the sequential descent of the melodic line all the way, he inserted the march motif just ahead of the long trill which prepares the half-close on the dominant, perhaps because he wished to underscore the heroic implications of his work. The second thematic component picks up that same motif but softly and in conjunction with an upward leap to a long appoggiatura that lends this fragment a reflective, if not melancholy flavour. Finally, the same dotted pattern reappears at the higher octave from where it skips gaily down to the opening note, like Leporello, the *buffo* character, returning to his stern master.

Structurally, the Haffner theme illustrates both Lach's notion of architectonic infra-structures and Kurth's laws of musical energy. Moreover, since Mozart made the most of a simple descending 4th and did so for primary melodic reasons, one of Szabolcsi's most cherished postulates is also upheld. The general validity of these basic concepts, whatever the exact harmonic or textural context, will be confirmed by a brief examination of the first bars of Wagner's *Tristan* (ex.5). Here the upward leap of a minor 6th finds immediate conjunct compensation in keeping with the rules laid down by Zarlino and other early theorists. While the cellos pursue the descending line a semitone further, the oboes mirror the chromatic descent of the cellos with a semitone rise to the tonic. In essence, if not note-for-note, this procedure corresponds to the manner in which Mozart complemented the appoggiatura in bar 7 of his Haffner Symphony with a semitone rise in bar 9. Wagner, however, went two chromatic steps further to the supertonic, whereas Mozart called a dramatic halt with a three-quaver rest before moving to the minor 3rd above, as if nothing had happened. The *Tristan* Prelude as a whole offers a veritable compendium of melodic procedures in a chromatic–harmonic context. The cello melody beginning in bar 17 is a poignant instance, since it generates tremendous energies with a single motivic idea spurred by strict adherence to the law of directional compensation.

Ex.5 Wagner: *Tristan und Isolde*

(a) Langsam und schmachtend

(b)

The remaining examples, taken from the string quartets of Schoenberg, may serve to demonstrate that the abandonment of functional tonality, far from impeding melodic forces, actually restored the well-nigh absolute rule in all matters of musical texture they had enjoyed in the final quartets of Beethoven. The soprano melody in Schoenberg's Second Quartet (ex.6) is composed almost entirely of minor 2nds. But the law of directional compensation is scrupulously observed. The appoggiatura treatment of 'Kreisend, webend' is in fact strik-

Ex.6 Schoenberg: String Quartet no.2, 4th movt

ingly similar to Mozart's and Wagner's manner, while the words 'mich in tönen' are actually set to the 'Jupiter' motif. That ever popular variant of the 3rd-cum-2nd idea re-surfaces in Schoenberg's Fourth Quartet, a work based coincidentally on the same melodic materials as Beethoven's String Trio op.9 no.3, the thematic precursor of the late quartets. By the same token, the recitative-like opening of Schoenberg's Largo (ex.7) demonstrates Lach's 'melic' concept even more forcefully than its apparent model, the Hebrew *Kol nidrei*, a melody which, as Schoenberg himself observed, is not so much a tune in the Western sense as a quasi-oriental series of related and interlocking 'melodicles'.

Ex.7 Schoenberg: String Quartet no.4, 3rd movt

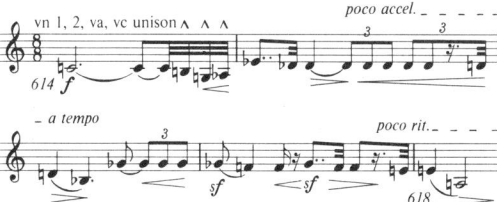

11. ABSOLUTE MELODY? Unlike Schoenberg, who placed himself squarely in the European tradition, as represented by Bach, Mozart and Wagner, Webern favoured octave transposition to an extent that placed the age-old laws of melodic design under severe strain. A serial work like the Symphony op.21 abandons the last vestiges of vocal constraint for the seemingly limitless possibilities of advanced instrumental techniques. A quarter of a century later musical synthesizers, computers and machines of all sorts managed to achieve what the mere serial treatment of conventional pitch materials had left unfinished. Busoni (1922) uttered indeed prophetic words when he attempted to define 20th-century melody as follows:

A row of repeated (1) ascending and descending (2) intervals which (3) organised and moving rhythmically (4) contains in itself a latent harmony and (5) which gives back a certain atmosphere of feeling; which can and does exist (6) independent of accompanying voices for form; and in the performance of which (7) the choice of pitch (8) and of instrument (9) exercise no change over its essence . . .

This 'absolute' melody, at first a self-sufficient formation, united itself subsequently with the accompanying harmony, and later melted with it into oneness; out of this oneness the continually progressive polyharmony aims to free and liberate itself.

It must be asserted here, in contradiction to a point of view which is deeply-rooted, that melody has expanded continuously, that it has grown in line and in capacity for expression, and that it must succeed in attaining universal command in composition.

In this sense, Webern emerged as the supreme master of 'absolute melody'. But paradoxically, the 'melodic rhythm', created by the conspicuous peaks and low points of his intricate textures, recalls very similar aspects of a much simpler medieval monophony, while the spatial metaphors he employed for his essentially elliptical musical ideas recall the non-teleological music of the orient he so admired. More specifically, the disembodiment of traditional melodic continuity at the behest of the 'tone-colour melody', postulated by Schoenberg as early as 1911, appears to be a function of omnidirectional sonorous forays that issue from and return to a small number of stable pitch centres, not unlike the circular harmonic excursions of the mature Wagner. By assigning unprecedented aesthetic significance to single pitches as well as selected intervallic relationships, moreover, Webern accomplished for

traditional melody what Wagner had done for tonal harmony. Inevitably, his unrestrained explorations of musical space at the expense of temporal factors raised serious questions about the very future of melody. It was one of the more ironic quirks of history which turned the herald of 'absolute melody' into the revered godfather of an avant garde that has decreed the virtual demise of melody as a primary factor in musical experience.

But melody will not die that easily. After surviving handily in eastern Europe in the name of socialist realism, it has reasserted its strength in the West under the guise of an ideologically motivated folksong revival as well as in elaborate concert pieces relying on outright quotation or, at the very least, unqualified imitation of the past. During the decades of melodic drought, popular music of the commercial variety had been the only persistent and pervasive source of melodic inspiration. Some of the best tunes of the post-World War II era issued from the pens of the Beatles, just as those of the interwar period had been written by the Gershwins, the Cole Porters and the Irving Berlins. In the mid-1970s, the melodic circle appeared to be closing once again. For with its devotion to small, often descending and pentatonically conditioned melodicles, Afro-American rock music has returned melody, quite unwittingly, to its very beginnings.

BIBLIOGRAPHY

G. Zarlino: *Le istitutioni harmoniche* (Venice, 1558/*R*1965, rev. 3/1573/*R*1966; Eng. trans. of pt.ii, 1968 as *The Art of Counterpoint*)
J.-P. Rameau: *Traité de l'harmonie* (Paris, 1722/*R*1967; Eng. trans., 1971)
J. Mattheson: *Kern melodischer Wissenschaft* (Hamburg, 1737)
J.-J. Rousseau: *Essai sur l'origine des langues* (Paris, 1753)
J.-P. Rameau: *Observations sur notre instinct pour la musique* (Paris, 1754/*R*1967)
C. Nichelmann: *Die Melodie nach ihrem Wesen sowohl als nach ihren Eigenschaften* (Danzig, 1755)
J.-J. Rousseau: *Dictionnaire de musique* (Paris, 1768/*R*1969; Eng. trans., 1771, 2/1779/*R*1975)
A. Reicha: *Traité de melodie* (Paris, 1814)
H. Helmholtz: *Die Lehre von den Tonempfindungen* (Brunswick, 1863)
L. Bussler: *Elementarmelodik* (Leipzig, 1879)
F. A. Gevaert: *Mélopée antique dans le chant de l'église latine* (Ghent, 1895)
H. Riemann: 'Die musikalische Phrasierung', 'Was ist ein Motiv?', *Präludien und Studien*, ii (Leipzig, 1895), 67, 137
S. Jadassohn: *Das Wesen der Melodie in der Tonkunst* (Leipzig, 1899)
C. Sharp: *English Folk Song* (London, 1907)
A. Schoenberg: *Harmonielehre* (Vienna, 1911, rev. 3/1922; Eng. trans., abridged, 1948)
E. M. von Hornbostel: 'Melodie und Skala', *JbMP 1912*, 11
L. R. Lach: *Studien zur Entwicklungsgeschichte der Ornamentalen Melopoie* (Leipzig, 1913)
A. Z. Idelsohn: *Hebräisch-orientalischer Melodienschatz* (Leipzig, 1914–42)
O. Bie: 'Melody', *MQ*, ii (1916), 402
E. Kurth: *Grundlagen des linearen Kontrapunkts* (Berne, 1917)
L. L. Thurstone: 'The Problem of Melody', *MQ*, vi (1920), 426
F. Busoni: *Gesammelte Aufsätze: von der Einheit der Musik* (Berlin, 1922; Eng. trans., 1957, 2/1965 as *The Essence of Music*)
A. H. Fox Strangways: 'Tune', *ML*, iii (1922), 90
K. Huber: *Der Ausdruck musikalischer Elementarmotive* (Leipzig, 1923)
H. G. Watt: 'Melody', *ML*, v (1924), 272
J. Handschin: 'Zur Frage der melodischen Paraphrasierung im Mittelalter', *ZMw*, x (1927–8), 513
F. Blume: 'Fortspinnung und Entwicklung', *JbMP 1929*, 51
E. Kurth: *Musikpsychologie* (Berlin, 1931)
P. Ferretti: *Estetica gregoriana* (Rome, 1934)
G. Herzog: 'Speech-melody and Primitive Music', *MQ*, xx (1934), 452
P. Hindemith: *Unterweisung im Tonsatz* (Mainz, 1937–9; Eng. trans., 1941–2 as *Craft of Musical Composition*)
Z. Kodály: *A magyar népzene* (Budapest, 1937, rev. 5/1969; Eng. trans., 1960, 2/1965 as *Folk Music of Hungary*)
C. Sachs: *The Rise of Music in the Ancient World East and West* (New York, 1943)
B. Szabolcsi: 'Five-tone Scales and Civilization', *AcM*, xiv (1943), 24
E. Toch: *The Shaping Forces in Music* (New York, 1948)

K. von Fischer: *Die Beziehungen von Form und Motiv in Beethovens Instrumental-Werken* (Strasbourg, 1949)

J. Smits van Waesberghe: *Melodieleer* (Amsterdam, 1950; Eng. trans., 1954 as *A Textbook of Melody*)

B. Szabolcsi: *A melódia története* (Budapest, 1950, 2/1957; Eng. trans., 1966 as *A History of Melody*)

R. Steglich: 'Über Mozarts Melodik', *MJb 1952*, 47

T. Georgiades: *Musik und Sprache* (Berlin, 1954)

A. C. Edwards: *The Art of Melody* (New York, 1956)

B. Nettl: 'Infant Musical Development and Primitive Music', *Southwestern Journal of Anthropology*, xii (1956), 87

——: 'Notes on Infant Musical Development', *MQ*, xlii (1956), 28

——: *Music in Primitive Culture* (Cambridge, Mass., 1956)

W. Apel: *Gregorian Chant* (Bloomington, Ind., 1957, 3/1966)

W. Wiora: *Europäische Volksmusik und abendländische Tonkunst* (Kassel, 1957; Eng. trans., 1966 as *European Folk Song*)

K. Reinhard: 'On the Problem of Pre-pentatonic Scales, particularly the Third-Second Nucleus', *JIFMC*, x (1958), 15

E. Werner: *The Sacred Bridge* (New York, 1959)

C. Dahlhaus: 'Melodie', *MGG*

W. Wiora: *Die vier Weltalter der Musik* (Stuttgart, 1961; Eng. trans., 1965)

C. Sachs: *The Wellsprings of Music* (The Hague, 1962)

R. Sessions: *The Musical Experience* (New York, 1962)

M. Kolinski: 'The General Direction of Melodic Movement', *EM*, ix (1965), 240

A. Schoenberg: *Fundamentals of Musical Compositions*, ed. L. Stein (New York, 1967)

B. Churgin: 'Francesco Galeazzi's Description (1796) of Sonata Form', *JAMS*, xxi (1968), 181

M. Schneider: *Geschichte der Mehrstimmigkeit* (Tutzing, 1969)

J. Blacking: *How Musical is Man* (Seattle, 1973)

C. Brailoiu: *Problèmes d'ethnomusicologie* (Geneva, 1973)

J. H. K. Nketia: *The Music of Africa* (New York, 1974)

A. L. Ringer: 'Musical Composition', *Encyclopedia Britannica* (Chicago, 15/1974)

——: 'Islamic Civilization and the Rise of European Polyphony', *Studia instrumentorum musicae popularis*, iii (Stockholm, 1974), 189

P. Sassu: 'Le strutture musicali', *La musica Sarda* (Milan, 1974), 36

C. R. Adams: 'Melodic Contour Typology', *EM*, xx (1976), 179

ALEXANDER L. RINGER

**Melody type.** A term used in literature on Gregorian chant to describe melodies adapted to new texts; *see* CENTONIZATION.

**Melograph.** An electronic instrument used in musicological research for the continuous graphic representation of melody. It is particularly important in the analysis of those melodic elements which cannot be expressed in traditional notation, such as intonations based on systems other than those of Western music, microtonal intervals, glissandos, the attack and decay of notes individually and in relation to adjacent notes, vibrato and relationships between pitch and loudness. Such elements are important mostly in the study of non-Western music, but also in that of certain Western folk musics and in the performance style of Western art melodies (*see* UNITED STATES OF AMERICA, §II, 1(ii)). The melograph is also an aid to research into musical aspects of speech and birdsong.

The melograph displays acoustical information in the form of a melogram, which generally shows pitch and loudness in relation to time. Although some melographs also analyse and display the spectrum of sounds, this is usually recorded by other instruments, such as the sonagraph, which is used mainly for spectral analysis of speech. The melograph analyses music and speech either live or from a tape recorder and usually displays two simultaneous graphs, as in fig.1: here the graph above the notated melody shows the fundamental frequency of the melody and its change with time; the graph below the notation is of the relative amplitude. The first quality, fundamental frequency, is the main factor determining pitch and, when the scale is logarithmic, equal vertical distances on the graph represent equal musical intervals. The second quality, relative amplitude or intensity, is the main factor determining relative loudness: a graph showing this is relatively simple to obtain, and many machines besides the melograph can supply one. Obtaining a pitch graph is more complicated. The melograph is not concerned with the shape of sound vibrations (which may be seen on an oscilloscope), but has to extract the magnitude of the frequencies of these vibrations. One way of doing this is as follows: each time a vibration passes the zero point an electric pulse is produced, the number of pulses per time unit being proportional to the frequency of the vibration. The combined pulses form an electric current with an intensity proportional to the frequency of the original vibration. A stronger current indicates a higher frequency, and vice versa. Fig.2*a* demonstrates schematically a sequence of four different pure vibrations (A, B, C and D) as they would appear on an oscilloscope and, in the graph below (fig.2*b*), how they would be registered by the melograph. Since only fundamental frequencies are to be measured, the melograph incorporates a filter unit to suppress the upper partials, which are often of

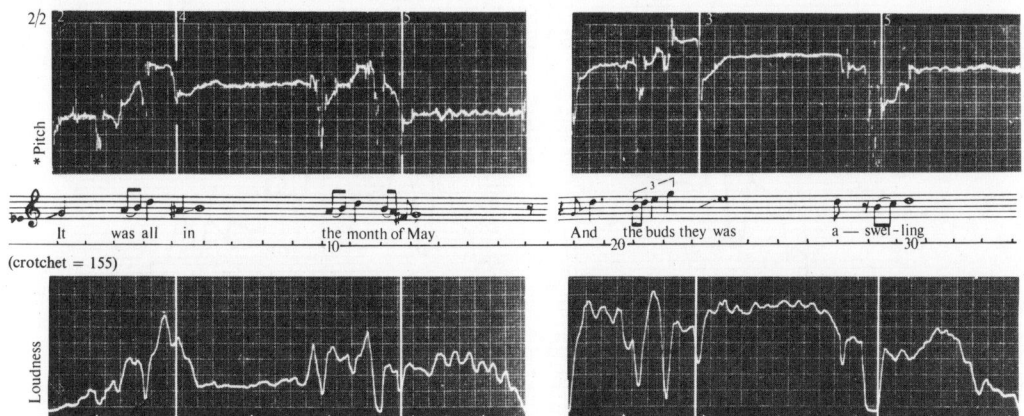

*1. Melogram of the beginning of 'Barbara Allen' (Child no.84) showing pitch and loudness in relation to time; made on melograph model B at the Institute of Ethnomusicology, UCLA, from a recording (1935) by A. Lomax and M. E. Barnicle of the singing of Molly Jackson of Kentucky*

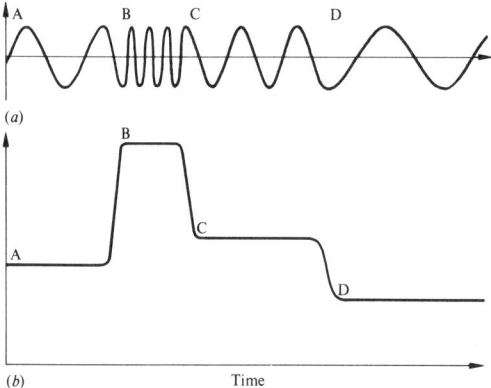

*(a)*

*(b)*                    Time

2. (a) *Schematic representation of four different pure vibrations as they would appear on an oscilloscope;* (b) *the same vibrations as they would be registered by a melograph*

high intensity. Sounds of indefinite pitch ('noise'; for example, the sound of breathing) cannot be recorded on this graph and their existence may be indicated in various ways, as a break in the graph or as some schematic symbol.

The Seeger melograph model C incorporates the function of the sonagraph so that the melogram includes a sonagram which supplies information about the spectrum of the examined material (see Crossley-Holland, p.11). In this sonagram the vertical axis designates the

distribution of spectral energy over seven octaves (100 Hz–15,000 Hz). The relative intensity at any given moment is indicated by the intensity of the appropriate line or band on the sonagram, which can be compared with a 'grey scale' if one wishes to quantify the data. Thus changing spectral content can be noted visually. The melograph model C therefore simultaneously produces three graphs (pitch, amplitude and spectrum). The actual registration of the graphs may be carried out in various ways: by a mechanical needle, which notates in ink on paper; by light-beams striking light-sensitive paper; by photographing from a cathode ray tube, etc. The scales of the axes of frequency, amplitude and time may be contracted or expanded to suit the analysis. From the graphs it is possible to measure each of the components – pitch, interval, loudness and duration – and study their interrelation. When a great deal of material is to be analysed a computer can be used. The date obtained by the melograph may be stored directly in the computer and the computer can be programmed for searches and analysis.

Before the invention of the melograph in the 1950s, intonation was determined with the aid of the simple monochord. The pitches of notes were compared by ear to the pitches of the monochord, the frequencies of which were known. From the 1920s researchers used electronic devices such as the oscilloscope, the pitch of the fundamental being determined from the wave-form obtained. The monochord had many shortcomings: it could only measure pitch; it relied on the keenness of the ear of the researcher; only one note could be measured at a time; it was impossible to examine variations within

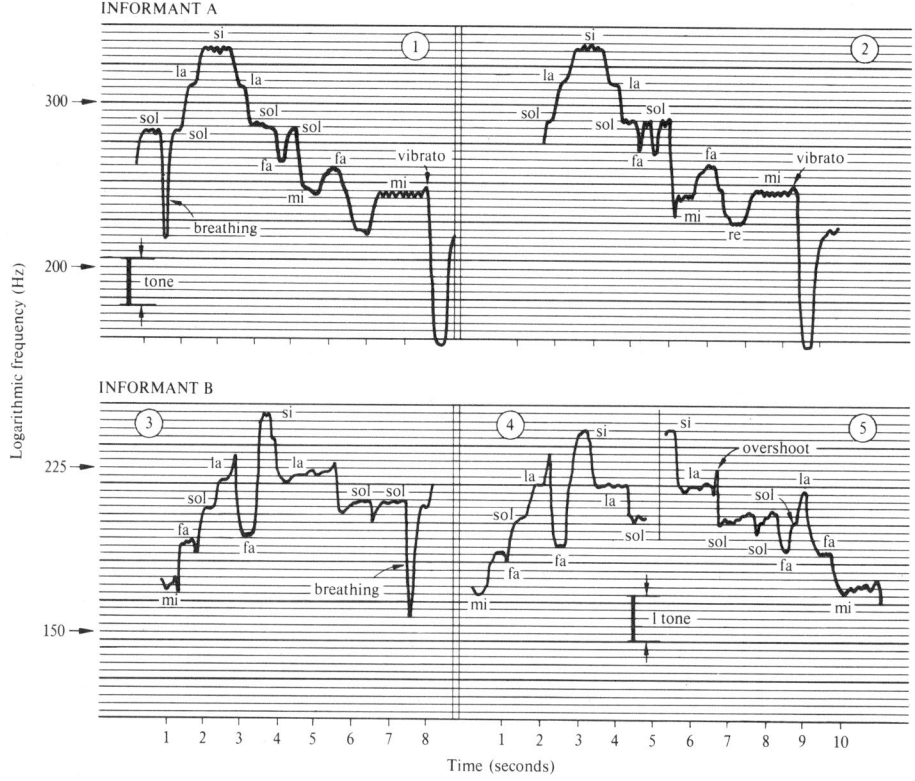

3. *Recurrent musical motifs from the same song, 'Indama', sung by two Israeli Arabs (after Cohen and Katz)*

a note, for the pitch was related to a single point in time; rapid notes could not be isolated; and the work was very slow. The deficiency of early electronic instruments designed to replace the monochord lay in the detailed calculations involved and in their inconvenience when examining a large body of material.

The melograph has opened up the field for accurate, reliable and convenient analysis of many details important in determining melodic style, and, because it can handle large quantities of material, it is useful for statistical analysis. For instance, it is now possible to determine the rules of intonation in different types of music and styles of performance, whereas previously these subjects had been a matter for speculation without a sound empirical basis.

Melographs have been developed and used at the following centres: at the University of California at Los Angeles (under the direction of Charles Seeger); in Norway (where Olav Gurvin pioneered development of 'melody writers' during the early 1950s); in Jerusalem (Cohen and Katz) from 1957; and in Uppsala, Sweden from 1966. In each of these places the melograph underwent several different stages of development to improve convenience, efficiency and precision (although in musical analysis there is little point in developing instrumental accuracy greater than the sensitivity of the human ear). Researches with Seeger's successive models have encompassed many areas of vocal and instrumental music (particularly oriental music) and heightened speech (some of this work is discussed by Crossley-Holland). In Norway a team at the Institute of Folk Music in Oslo examined the differences noted in various folksingers' performances of a single 'control' melody, as well as the characteristics of modern performances of melodies collected 100 years earlier by Ludwig Lindeman and published in his *Aeldre og nyere norske fjeldmelodier* ('Old and more recent Norwegian mountain melodies', Christiania, 1853–67/ R1963), and the study of *lokk* (cattle calls) and lullabies (see Dahlback). During the 1970s Anna Johnson was carrying out similar research at the University of Uppsala, Sweden. Several models were developed in Jerusalem: the first resembled the Norwegian 'melody writer' and the most recent is designed for use with a computer. They have aided research into the intonation of the music of several communities – Samaritans, Syrian Jews, and the secular and sacred music of Arabs (see fig.3) – and more recently into the musical parameters of the Hebrew language. All the machines discussed above were constructed individually; today the melograph is manufactured commercially.

BIBLIOGRAPHY

M. E. Metfessel: *Phonophotography in Folk Music* (Chapel Hill, 1928)
C. E. Seashore: *Psychology of Music* (New York and London, 1938)
O. Gurvin: 'Photography as an Aid in Folk-music Research', *Norveg*, iii (1953), 181
C. Seeger: 'Towards a Universal Music Sound-writing for Musicology', *JIFMC*, ix (1957), 63
K. Dahlback: *New Methods in Vocal Folk Music Research* (Oslo, 1958)
C. Seeger: 'Prescriptive and Descriptive Music-writing', *MQ*, xliv (1958), 184
D. Cohen and R. T. Katz: 'Explorations in the Music of the Samaritans: an Illustration of the Utility of Graphic Notation', *EM*, iv (1960), 67
P. A. Tove, B. Norman and others: 'Direct-recording Frequency and Amplitude Meter for Analysis of Musical and other Sonic Waveforms', *Journal of the Acoustical Society of America*, xxxix (1966), 362
D. Cohen and R. Katz: 'Remarks Concerning the Use of the Melograph in Ethnomusicological Studies', *Yuval*, i (1968), 155
D. Cohen: 'Patterns and Frameworks of Intonation', *JMT*, xiii (1969), 66
P. Crossley-Holland, ed.: *Selected Reports*, ii/1 (Los Angeles, 1974) [on Seeger melograph model C and its uses]

DALIA COHEN

**Melologo** (It.). MELODRAMA.

**Melophone.** A portable accordion with a keyboard, shaped like a guitar, harp or cello (see illustration). It is 80 to 130 cm high and 32 to 65 cm wide, and is played

*Melophone, French, after 1842 (Museum of Fine Arts, Boston)*

resting on the right thigh; the right hand works the handle (*archet*) of the bellows, which can produce a vibrato effect on all notes and a trumpet-like tone in certain registers. The left hand works the 40 to 84 keys, some with octave couplings, controlling a range of three to five octaves. The melophone was invented in 1837 by a Parisian watchmaker, Leclerc, whose instruments were made in Paris by A. Brown. In 1842 C. A. Pellerin and François Durbain obtained licences to manufacture it; Durbain subsequently developed the harmonium, which eventually superseded the melophone. According to Galpin (*Grove 5*) the melophone was 'introduced by Halévy into one of his operas'. Examples of the instrument are in the Instruments Museum of the Brussels Conservatory and the Boston Museum of Fine Arts.

STEPHEN BONNER

**Melopiano** (It.). *See* SOSTENENTE PIANO, §4.

**Méloplaste.** A chart showing a vacant staff. It was used to point out intervals in the GALIN-PARIS-CHEVÉ METHOD of teaching sight-singing.

**Melos Ensemble** (of London). English ensemble. It was formed in 1950 by Cecil Aronowitz (viola) and Gervase de Peyer (clarinet), with the flautist Richard Adeney and the cellist Terence Weil, as a variable group of up to 12 players (string quintet, wind quintet, harp and piano). Their original purpose was to rehearse and perform the larger chamber works (such as the Schubert and Mendelssohn octets, the Beethoven and Ravel septets) under better conditions than generally obtained at that time, and the ensemble soon gained a reputation for style and artistry which set new standards for the performance of this repertory. The personnel remained unchanged until the death in 1972 of Ivor McMahon, the second violinist, and the departure shortly afterwards of Emanuel Hurwitz, the first violinist, and two other players.

During this time, in addition to the repertory of chamber music classics, the ensemble gave numerous first performances, and took part as the separate chamber group at the première, and in many later performances, of Britten's *War Requiem* (1962). Besides giving concerts and BBC broadcasts, it has appeared frequently at principal festivals in Britain and elsewhere (including Venice, Warsaw, Zagreb, Holland and Iran), and first toured the USA in 1966. The ensemble has made over 50 records, several of which have received international awards. After a period of inactivity in 1973–4 it was re-formed with eight of the original players, and gave a 25th-anniversary concert (Elizabeth Hall, 20 January 1975) as a prelude to renewed regular performances. The ensemble's character is achieved by the sum of the individual talents of its members, each a distinguished solo player, together with the responsiveness derived from their mutual respect and friendly rapport.

NOËL GOODWIN

**Melos Quartet** (of Stuttgart). German string quartet. It was formed in 1965. The members are Wilhelm Melcher (*b* Hamburg, 5 April 1940), Gerhard Ernst Voss (*b* Burscheid, 17 Dec 1939), Hermann Voss (*b* Brünen, 9 July 1934) and Peter Buck (*b* Stuttgart, 18 May 1937). All four players had established careers as soloists and orchestral musicians before the quartet was formed. Melcher studied in Hamburg and Rome, won the 1962 International Chamber Music Competition in Venice, and became leader of the Hamburg SO in 1963; Gerhard and Hermann Voss studied in Düsseldorf (with Maier) and Freiburg (with Végh), Gerhard also at Cologne (with Marschner); Buck studied at the Stuttgart Conservatory with Ludwig Hölscher. Between 1960 and 1967 Hermann Voss was solo violist of the Stuttgart Chamber Orchestra; his colleagues were members of the Württemberg Chamber Orchestra until 1967, when they left their orchestras to concentrate on quartet playing. The quartet had already won the Geneva International Competition (with the prize for the best quartet) and an award at the Villa-Lobos String Quartet Competition in Rio de Janeiro, both in 1966. Its first concert tours were sponsored by the Deutsches Musikleben foundation and it represented West Germany at the 1966 Jeunesses Musicales in Paris. From 1967 it embarked on extensive international concert tours and made a complete recording of Beethoven's quartets (1968–70). Other notable recordings include an outstanding collaboration with the guitarist Narciso Yepes in quintets by Boccherini. The members' chamber orchestral experience, individual maturity and collective excellence have combined to ensure the development of a style that is consistently warm and romantic without undue sentiment, totally secure and assured. They play, respectively, violins by Domenico Montaguana (1731) and Carlo Tononi (Bologna, n.d.), a viola by C. F. Landolfi (Milan, 18th century) and a cello by Francesco Ruggieri (Cremona, 1682).

BIBLIOGRAPHY
E. Schwarz: 'Analyse eines Karrierebeginns', *Das Orchester*, xv (1967), 393

LESLIE EAST

**Melpomene.** The Muse of tragedy, Aeolic poetry and songs of mourning; *see* MUSES.

**Meltzelius, Jiří.** *See* MELCELIUS, JIŘÍ.

**Meltzer, Adam** (*b* Neustadt an der Heide, nr. Coburg; *d* Dillingen an der Donau, 1609). German printer. In 1587 he was a journeyman at Frankfurt an der Oder; subsequently he moved to Dillingen an der Donau (1591) to work for Johann Meyer, and in 1603 he established his own business. After his death his widow ran the press until 1610, when she sold it to the printer Gregor Haenlin. Meltzer's publications consist mainly of music, and he was responsible for disseminating the works of such Swabian composers as Erbach, Aichinger, Klingenstein and Jacob Reiner.

BIBLIOGRAPHY
O. Bucher: 'Adam Meltzer (1603–1610) und Gregor Haenlin (1610–1617) als Musikdrucker in Dillingen/Donau', *Gutenberg Jb 1956*, 216

THEODOR WOHNHAAS

**Mely, Pietro Paolo.** *See* MELLI, PIETRO PAOLO.

**Membranophone.** General term for musical instruments that produce their sound from tightly stretched membranes. Membranophones form one of the four main classes of instruments (along with idiophones, chordophones and aerophones – to which a fifth, electrophones, has recently been added) in the system of classification devised by C. Sachs and E. M. von Hornbostel and published by them in *Zeitschrift für Ethnologie* in 1914 (Eng. trans. in *GSJ*, xiv, 1961, p.3). Their system, the one most commonly used today, is based on Victor Mahillon's division of instruments according to the nature of their vibrating bodies, which he devised for his catalogue of the instruments in the Royal Conservatory in Brussels. Membranophones are subdivided according to whether they are struck drums, plucked drums, friction drums or singing membranes. Struck drums can be struck directly (as with timpani, side drums, tambourines and so on), or indirectly (as with rattle drums). Plucked drums have a string knotted below the centre of the membrane; when the string is plucked its vibrations are transmitted to the membrane (as with the *gopi yantra* and *ānanda laharī* of India). Friction drums are made to vibrate either by means of a stick (*Rommelpot*), a cord or the hand. Singing membranes are those which are made to vibrate by speaking or singing into them, as with the kazoo. Each category may be further subdivided according to the more detailed characteristics of an instrument. To each category, Sachs and Hornbostel gave a number derived from the Dewey decimal library classification system.

*See also* INSTRUMENTS, CLASSIFICATION OF.

HOWARD MAYER BROWN

**Membre** (Fr.). Term used by A. Reicha and others to denote a small unit of melodic construction; *see* ANALYSIS, §II, 2.

**Memo** [Memmo], **Dionisio** (*fl* 1507–39). Italian musician, organist and, according to his contemporary, Marino Sanuto, a Crutched friar. He was a pupil of Paul Hofhaimer and became first organist of St Mark's, Venice, from 1507 to 1516. With the doge's permission, he left Venice for London in September 1516, bringing with him 'a most excellent instrument', presumably an organ. The reports of the Venetian ambassador, Giustiniani, contain several references to Memo and his triumphs at the English court: that through the offices of Henry VIII, he was released from his monastic vows, given a chaplaincy by the king and made 'chief of his instrumental musicians'; how he was required to play frequently at court, often before foreign ambassadors, and once for four hours at Windsor, where the king had gone to escape the plague. Memo appears to have acted as an agent for the Venetians: in one of his reports to the signory, Giustiniani mentions asking Memo 'to make his report'. Such political activities may have led to his sudden departure from England ('for fear of his life', according to Sanuto) sometime before 24 December 1525. Memo appears to have gone, first to Portugal, then to Santiago de Compostela, where in 1539 he was mentioned as organist in the cathedral. Even the little we know about his career well illustrates the important role played by peripatetic virtuosos in the diffusion of musical styles in the 16th century. Of Memo's compositions, including the setting of *Memor esto verbi tui* which he played before Henry, nothing remains.

BIBLIOGRAPHY

C. de Villalón: *Ingeniosa comparación entre lo antiguo y lo presente* (Valladolid, 1539); ed. M. Serrano y Sanz (Madrid, 1898)
S. Giustiniani: *Four Years at the Court of Henry VIII* (Eng. trans., London, 1854)
F. Stefani and others, eds.: *I diarii di Marino Sanuto*, xl (Venice, 1894), 534
H. J. Moser: *Paul Hofhaimer* (Stuttgart, 1929)

JOHN M. WARD

**Memory.** *See* PSYCHOLOGY OF MUSIC, §III.

**Memphis Minnie** [Douglas, Minnie] (*b* Algiers, Louisiana, 3 June 1896; *d* Memphis, 6 Aug 1973). Black American blues singer and guitarist. At the age of eight she went to Memphis, where she was a street musician. In 1928 she moved to Chicago, and with her first husband, the Mississippi blues guitarist and mandolin player Joe McCoy, began a highly popular series of blues recordings. After their divorce in 1935, she recorded instead with Black Bob (piano), her second husband Casey Bill Weldon (guitar) and Ernest 'Lil Son' Lawler, her third husband, also a blues guitarist. With Lawler she recorded her popular *Me and my Chauffeur Blues* in 1941. For nearly 30 years her 'Blue Monday' parties in Chicago were celebrated among blues singers. In 1957 she returned to Memphis and five years later had a stroke which ended her singing career. Memphis Minnie enjoyed unequalled stature among women country blues singers. Her performances were greatly admired by male blues artists, and she was the only significant female blues instrumentalist, playing the guitar with the forceful, swinging rhythm characteristic of many Memphis-based musicians. Her voice was strong, with breadth in the middle range, and her guitar playing well phrased, as for example on her best-selling *Bumble Bee* (1930). Among her finest recordings were the guitar duets with McCoy, including the exceptional *Let's Go to Town* (1931).

PAUL OLIVER

**Mena, Gabriel** (*fl* 1511–16). Spanish poet and composer. He was a singer in the court chapel of Ferdinand V of Aragon in 1511, and may have been identical with Gabriel de Texerana, who was a member of the chapel as early as 1500. In 1516 he entered the service of Fadrique Enríquez, Admiral of Castile. In a poem printed in 1554 but written a generation earlier, Mena asked the admiral for a pack-horse and described himself as a married man living at Torrelobatón, near Valladolid. Of Mena's 19 villancicos in the *Cancionero musical de palacio* (MME, v and x) at least two, *La bella malmaridada* and *Aquella mora garrida*, quote folktunes. These fresh and charming compositions reveal Mena as a man of considerable poetic and musical gifts.

BIBLIOGRAPHY

R. Stevenson: *Spanish Music in the Age of Columbus* (The Hague, 1960)

ROBERT STEVENSON

**Mena'anim** (Heb.). Ancient Jewish instrument, possibly a rattle; *see* JEWISH MUSIC, §I, 4(i).

**Menalt, Gabriel** (*b* Martorell, nr. Barcelona; *d* Barcelona, 1687). Spanish composer and organist. Accounts exist of his competing for the posts of organist at the Barcelona churches of SS Justo y Pastor in 1678 and S María del Mar in 1679; he won the latter position and held it until his death, which apparently occurred when he was still young. All his known works are for the organ and are contained in two MSS (*E-Bc* M. 729 and M. 751.21); they include six pieces of the tiento type (some termed 'gaytilla' or 'partido'; five are in H. Anglés, ed.: *Antología de organistas españoles del siglo XVII*, i–ii, Barcelona, 1965–6), two sets of versets, and several settings of *Sacris solemniis* and the Spanish *Pange lingua*. One set of versets for the eight psalm tones treats the plainsong in each of the four voices in turn amid imitative counterpoint. The other set, as well as most of the larger pieces, is less contrapuntal. Several are for divided register – a Spanish tradition – and feature lively figuration in the solo register against a relatively static accompaniment; those for single register tend to pursue lengthy sequences in a somewhat homophonic texture.

BIBLIOGRAPHY

F. Pedrell: *Catàlech de la Biblioteca musical de la Diputació de Barcelona*, ii (Barcelona, 1909)
J. Soler y Palet: 'La música a Catalunya: a Santa María del Mar', *Revista musical catalana*, xviii (1921), 19
H. Anglés: 'Els organistes i la música d'orgue a Catalunya en els segles XVIIè i XVIIIè', *Revista catalana de música*, i (1923), 29
F. Baldelló: 'La música en la basílica parroquial de Santa María del Mar de Barcelona', *AnM*, xvii (1962), 209
H. Anglés: 'Supervivencia de la música de Cabezón en los organistas españoles del siglo XVII', *AnM*, xxi (1966), 87

ALMONTE HOWELL

**Menander** [Menandros] (*b* Athens, 342 BC; *d* Athens, *c*290 BC). Greek comic poet. The most famous playwright of Greek New Comedy, he wrote over 100 plays, domestic comedies in which intrigues, reversals and recognition scenes abound. The plays, of which few survive, have little metrical variety, being mostly in iambic trimeters. However, in a long scene (ll.880–958) from the *Dyskolos* ('Misanthrope') Menander changed the metre to the 15-syllable catalectic iambic tetrameter which was recited to an aulos accompaniment. Two brief fragments of another play, the *Theophoroumenē* ('Possessed girl'), contain an invocation to Cybele and a corybantic dance and song in hexameters. For the latter the aulos modality would almost certainly have been Phrygian. A mosaic (100 BC) from the Villa of Cicero at Pompeii shows three actors in this comedy playing (or pretending to play) the double aulos, small cymbals and hand-held drum or tambourine (auloi, kymbala, tympanon).

The characters represented as musicians in these comedies were usually young women of slave status skilled in playing the double aulos or *psaltērion* (a harplike instrument). Apparently the *psaltria* was more respectable than the *aulētris*, who was often a prostitute. One *psaltria*, Habrotonon, had a major role in the *Epitrepontes* ('Arbiter'). Phanias, the main character of the *Citharistes*, was apparently a successful concert performer, freeborn and wealthy. One fragment of this play (no.7, ed. Sandbach) refers to someone (presumably not Phanias) who through instruction (*paideuesthai*) is acquiring or perhaps imparting an affected taste for music; but little more than 100 lines have survived.

The male aulete who provided the accompaniment played the music that was supposedly being performed by an *aulētris* but his principal task was to accompany the chorus (by convention a group of drunken revellers, votaries of Pan, huntsmen etc), who were irrelevant to the plot. Only their initial appearances were even acknowledged in dialogue; otherwise a mere stage direction 'chorus' (*chorou*) sufficed, or occasionally 'aulos music' (*aulei*, '[someone] plays the aulos'), as in the manuscripts of Aristophanes. These entr'acte performances were probably a combination of song, dance and mime.

BIBLIOGRAPHY

F. G. Allinson, ed. and trans.: *Menander: the Principal Fragments* (London and Cambridge, Mass., 1921, 5/1964)

E. W. Handley, ed.: *The Dyskolos of Menander* (London, 1965), esp. 171ff, 210f, 282ff

A. D. Trendall and T. B. L. Webster: *Illustrations of Greek Drama* (London, 1971), 145

F. H. Sandbach, ed.: *Menandri reliquiae selectae* (Oxford, 1972)

A. W. Gomme and F. H. Sandbach: *Menander: a Commentary* (Oxford, 1973)

WARREN ANDERSON

**Menantes.** Pseudonym of CHRISTIAN FRIEDRICH HUNOLD.

**Menasce, Jacques de** (*b* Bad Ischl, 19 Aug 1905; *d* Gstaad, 28 Jan 1960). American composer and pianist of Franco-Egyptian and German descent. He graduated from the Schotten-Gymnasium in Vienna in 1924. His first piano teacher was Emil Friedberger, and at the age of 14 he began work with Emil von Sauer. After some years of travel he went to the Vienna Music Academy to study the piano and composition; later he was a composition pupil of Pisk and Berg. From 1932 he appeared widely in Europe and the USA as a pianist, notably in performances of his own and other modern chamber music. His activities were centred in New York from the 1940s; he became an American citizen, and he took part in the work of the League of Composers and other organizations promoting new music. His music is not easy to classify: structurally it bears some relation to impressionism, while its sombreness and its vivid, crisp chromaticism recall late Bartók.

WORKS
(*selective list*)

Ballets: The Fate of my People, dancer, pf, 1945; Status quo, 1947

Orch: 2 pf concs., 1935, 1939; Divertimento on a Children's Song, pf, str, 1940

Vocal: Le chemin d'écume, song cycle, S, orch, 1940; 3 Romantic Songs, 1943; 2 Poems (H. Wolfe), 1v, pf, 1944

Inst: Sonata, vn, pf, 1940; Hebrew Melodies, vn, pf; Sonata, va, pf, 1955

Pf: Variations, 1933; Visionen, 1934; 3 sonatinas, 1934, 1942, 1945; Toccata, 1935; 2 sonatas, 1936, 1947; Improvisations on a Chorale

Theme, 1937; 5 Fingerprints, 1943; Perpetuum mobile, 1944; Pour une princesse, 1947; Romantic Suite, 1950

PEGGY GLANVILLE-HICKS/R

**Menault, Pierre-Richard** (*b* Beaune, shortly before 1644; *d* Dijon, 1694). French composer. From the title-pages of his published works it can be established that in 1676 he was choirmaster of Ste Marie, Beaune, in 1686 a canon at Châlons-sur-Marne and in 1691 choirmaster of the collegiate church of St Etienne, Dijon. He competed for one of the four positions of *sous-maître* at the royal chapel in 1683 but was eliminated in the first round. He was over 50 years old at his death. His compositions are in a simple, contrapuntal style, largely syllabic, and rather thick in texture. Imitation is frequently rhythmic rather than melodic; in spite of the five- or six-part texture, true imitative counterpoint is confined to four (occasionally five) parts. The Vespers are said to have been dedicated to Père Lachaise, Louis XIV's confessor; there may be some truth in this, since, though there is actually no written dedication, the movements are those of second Vespers for a confessor other than a bishop.

WORKS
(*all published in Paris*)

Missa 'O felix parens', 6vv (1676)
Missa 'Tu es spes mea', 6vv (1686)
Missa 'Ave senior Stephane', 5vv (1687)
Missa 'Ferte rosas', 6vv (1691)
Missa 'Date lilia', 6vv (1692)
Vespres à deux choeurs avec symphonies (1693)

BIBLIOGRAPHY

*FétisB*

P. Papillon: *Bibliothèque des auteurs de Bourgogne* (Dijon, 1745/R1970)

C. Poisot: *Les musiciens bourguignons* (Dijon, 1854)

F. Zobeley: *Die Musikalien der Grafen von Schönborn-Wiesentheid* (Tutzing, 1967)

WILLIAM HAYS

**MENC.** *See* MUSIC EDUCATORS NATIONAL CONFERENCE.

**Menckin, Thomas.** *See* MANCINUS, THOMAS.

**Mendel, Arthur** (*b* Boston, Mass., 6 June 1905; *d* Newark, NJ, 14 Oct 1979). American musicologist. From Harvard University (AB 1925) he went to the Ecole Normale de Musique in Paris, where he studied music theory and composition with Nadia Boulanger (1925–7). He was music critic of the *Nation* (1930–33), literary editor for G. Schirmer, Inc. (1930–38), editor of the American Musicological Society's journal (1940–43) and editor for Associated Music Publishers (1941–7). In addition he was also an active translator (of Bekker, Hindemith and Alfred Einstein) and from 1936 to 1953 he was the conductor of the Cantata Singers, one of the first choral groups in the USA to give authentic performances of Baroque music. He taught at the Dalcroze School of Music and the Diller-Quaile School in New York from 1938 to 1950, serving as president of the former (1947–50).

In the late 1940s Mendel gained recognition as a musicologist (self-taught). He held lectureships at Columbia University (1949) and at the University of California, Berkeley (1951), and was appointed professor of music at Princeton University (1952), where he was department chairman (1952–67) and held the Henry Putnam University Professorship from 1969 until his retirement in 1973. In 1976 he was awarded the honorary doctorate from Brandeis University. He was a member of the editorial boards of the Neue Bach-

Ausgabe and of the new Josquin edition.

Mendel published some editions in vocal score of works by Schütz and Mozart and studies in the history of musical pitch and on the rhythmic structure of Renaissance and Baroque music. He also examined the basic assumptions of musicological method and wrote on the goals and tasks of higher musical education. His editions and studies of Bach's life and works, most notably the documentary biography *The Bach Reader* (with Hans T. David), and his practical and critical editions of the *St John Passion*, have brought him recognition as the foremost American Bach scholar of his generation. In his later years he investigated the music of Josquin and the possible applications of computer technology to musicological problems.

WRITINGS

'Spengler's Quarrel with the Methods of Music History', *MQ*, xx (1934), 131–71

*The Changing Opera* (New York, 1935) [trans. of P. Bekker: *Wandlungen der Oper*, Zurich, 1934]

'The Changing Audience of the Composer', *MTNA Proceedings*, xxxii (1937), 21

*The Craft of Musical Composition: Theoretical Part* (New York, 1942) [trans. of P. Hindemith: *Unterweisung im Tonsatz: theoretischer Teil*, Mainz, 1937]

with N. Broder: *Mozart: his Character, his Work* (New York, 1945) [trans. of A. Einstein: *Mozart*, Stockholm, 1947]

ed., with H. T. David: *The Bach Reader* (New York, 1945, rev. 2/1966)

'More for The Bach Reader', *MQ*, xxxvi (1950), 485

'On the Keyboard Accompaniments to Bach's Leipzig Church Music', *MQ*, xxxvi (1950), 339

'The Services of Musicology to the Practical Musician', A. Mendel, C. C. Pratt and C. Sachs: *Some Aspects of Musicology: Three Essays* (New York, 1957/R1977), 1

'Recent Developments in Bach Chronology', *MQ*, xlvi (1960), 283

'Evidence and Explanation', *IMSCR*, viii *New York 1961*, ii, 3

'The Doctorate in Composition', *College Music Symposium*, iii (1963), 53

'Traces of the Pre-history of Bach's St. John and St. Matthew Passions', *Festschrift Otto Erich Deutsch* (Kassel, 1963), 31

'More on the Weimar Origin of Bach's "O Mensch bewein" (BWV 244/35)', *JAMS*, xvii (1964), 203

'Some Ambiguities of the Mensural System', *Studies in Music History: Essays for Oliver Strunk* (Princeton, 1968), 137

*Studies in the History of Musical Pitch: Monographs by Alexander J. Ellis and Arthur Mendel* (Amsterdam, 1968) [incl. 7 articles by Mendel from *MQ* and *AcM*]

'Some Preliminary Attempts at Computer-assisted Style-analysis in Music', *Computers and the Humanities*, iv (1969), 41

'Towards Objective Criteria for Establishing Chronology and Authenticity: What Help can the Computer give?', *Josquin des Prez: New York 1971*, 297

'Pitch in Western Music since 1500: a Re-examination', *AcM*, l (1978), 1–93; pubd separately (Kassel, 1979)

EDITIONS

*J. S. Bach: The Passion According to St John*, vocal score (New York, 1951); *Ich liebe den Höchsten von ganzem Gemüthe*, BWV 174, Neue Ausgabe sämtlicher Werke, i/14 (Kassel, 1962–3); *Johannes-Passion*, ibid, ii/4 (Kassel, 1974)

*H. Schütz: A German Requiem (Musicalische Exequien)* (New York, 1957)

BIBLIOGRAPHY

R. L. Marshall, ed.: *Studies in Renaissance and Baroque Music in Honor of Arthur Mendel* (Kassel and Hackensack, NJ, 1974) [incl. R. L. Marshall: 'Arthur Mendel: a Portrait in Outline', p.9 and list of writings, p.376]

ROBERT L. MARSHALL

**Mendelsohn, Alfred** (*b* Bucharest, 4 Feb 1910; *d* Bucharest, 9 May 1966). Romanian composer and conductor. He studied composition with F. Schmidt and Marx at the Vienna Academy of Music (1927–31), where he was also a pupil of Wellesz and Lach in music history; he continued his composition studies under M. Jora at the Bucharest Conservatory (1931–2). After a period as a harmony teacher at the E. Massini Conservatory in Bucharest (1932–6), he directed that institution from 1936 until 1940; later he was assistant director of music and conductor at the Romanian Opera (1945–54). He held the posts of secretary (1946–9, 1954–63) and vice-chairman (1963–6) of the Romanian Composers' Union, and taught counterpoint and composition at the Bucharest Conservatory (1949–66). Mendelsohn made his mark both as an exceptional teacher and as a prolific composer of wide culture, working in a great diversity of styles, forms and genres. He had a propensity for the monumental and grandiose, particularly in his cantatas and oratorios on patriotic historical subjects. His dramatic temperament is evident in the operas *Meşterul Manole* ('Master Manole') and *Michelangelo*, but even more so in the oratorios *Horia* and *1907* and in the Symphony no.3. The basis of his style evolved from Regerian late Romanticism to serialism in the manner of the Second Viennese School; his final mature manner was realized in several works of a nationalist spirit written during the period 1950–66.

WORKS

(*selective list*)

Stage: Harap Alb, ballet, 1948; Meşterul Manole [Master Manole], opera, 1949; Călin, ballet, 1956; Anton Pann, musical comedy, 1961; Michelangelo, opera, 1964

Orch: 3 suites, 1937–43; 9 syms., 1944–64; 2 sym. poems, 1949, 1953; 3 vn concs., 1953, 1957, 1963; Org Conc., 1960

Choral: Poemul păcii [Poem to peace], 1952; Cantata Bucureştiului, 1953; Horia, oratorio, 1955; '1907', oratorio, 1957; Sub cerul de vară [Summer sky], sym.-cantata, 1959; Pentru marele octombrie [For the great October], oratorio, 1960

10 str qts; 3 vn sonatas; Vc Octet

Principal publishers: ESPLA (Bucharest), Editura muzicală (Bucharest)

BIBLIOGRAPHY

G. Breazul: 'Mendelsohn, Alfred', *MGG*

G. W. Berger: *Ghid pentru muzica instrumentală de cameră* [Guide to instrumental chamber music] (Bucharest, 1965), 368ff

V. Cosma: *Muzicieni români* (Bucharest, 1970), 295ff

VIOREL COSMA

**Mendelssohn, Arnold (Ludwig)** (*b* Ratibor [now Racibórz], Silesia, 26 Dec 1855; *d* Darmstadt, 19 Feb 1933). German teacher, composer and organist, son of a second cousin of Felix Mendelssohn. After studying law at Tübingen (1877), he pursued a musical education at the Institute für Kirchenmusik in Berlin (1877–80), where his teachers included Haupt for the organ, Loeschhorn for the piano and Grell, Kiel and Taubert for composition. In the 1880s he occupied in rapid succession a number of increasingly important posts: music director and organist of Bonn University (1880–82) where he made friends with P. Spitta; music director in Bielefeld (1882–5); teacher of composition at the Cologne Conservatory (1885–90); and finally Hessian master of church music and professor at the conservatory in Darmstadt (1891–1912). From 1912 he taught at the Frankfurt am Main Conservatory where one of his pupils was Hindemith. He was also the recipient of numerous honorary degrees and titles, as well as other awards.

Mendelssohn contributed significantly to the renewal of interest in Lutheran church music both by his promotion of the works of Bach and Schütz and through his own compositions, which began to chart a new course that Distler, Pepping, Raphael and others would later follow. Rejecting the romanticized style of his contemporaries, he evolved a purer and more appropriate polyphonic liturgical idiom. The influence of Bach is strongest in such early works as the *Abendkantate* (1881); Mendelssohn later showed considerable individuality in his incidental music to Goethe's *Paria* (1906) and *Pandora* (1908) and in his

*Geistliche Chormusik* (1926). In his operatic works he avoided Wagnerian influences and accordingly chose a fairytale subject and a folklike musical setting for *Der Bärenhäuter* (1897); many of his later lieder are in a similar vein, while his earlier ones, more complex in style, betray the influence of Hugo Wolf, whom he met in 1890.

A man of impressive cultural breadth, Mendelssohn wrote essays (*Gott, Welt und Kunst* is the best-known), edited music by Hassler, Schütz and Monteverdi, and was well-versed in literature, theology and philosophy. He was also widely respected as a sensitive judge and source of encouragement to talented young musicians.

WORKS

At least 219 items, prints and MSS, all in *D-Bds*; complete list compiled by F. Noack in *D-DS*; all printed works published in Leipzig, unless otherwise stated

STAGE

Elsi, die seltsame Magd (opera; H. Wette, after J. Gotthelf), op.8, Cologne, 1896 (Berlin, 1896)
Der Bärenhäuter (opera; H. Wette), op.11, Berlin, 1900 (Berlin, 1897)
Paria (incidental music; Goethe), op.36 (Berlin, 1906)
Pandora (incidental music; Goethe), op.37 (Berlin, 1908)

OTHER VOCAL

Sacred choral works incl. Abendkantate (Berlin, 1881); Das Leiden des Herrn, solo vv, chorus, org, orch, op.13 (1900); Auferstehung, A, chorus, org, orch, op.17 (Berlin, 1900); Aus tiefer Not, S, chorus, org, orch, op.54 (1912); Auf meinen lieben Gott, solo vv, chorus, org, orch, op.61 (1912); Zagen und Zuversicht, 3 solo vv, chorus, orch, op.84 (1920); Deutsche Messe, 8vv chorus, op.89 (1923); Geistliche Chormusik, 14 motets for the liturgical year, op.90 (1926)
Secular works incl. Zehn Volkslieder, 3–4 male vv, op.99 (1929); lieder comprising 4 collected vols. and individual op. nos.

INSTRUMENTAL

Orchestral works incl. 3 syms., E♭, C and a (all MS); vn concerto, op.88 (Berlin, 1922); 3 str qts, incl. no.2, D, op.67 (Leipzig, 1916) and no.3, B♭, op.83 (Leipzig, 1926); trio, a, 2 vn, pf, op.76 (Leipzig, 1916); sonata, f♯, vc, pf, op.70 (Leipzig, 1916); sonata, C, vn, pf, op.71 (Leipzig, 1916); 2 sonatas, c and e, op.66, both (1916)

WRITINGS

'Allerlei', *Die Musik*, vii (1907–8), 214
ed. W. Ewald: *Gott, Welt und Kunst* (Wiesbaden, 1949)

BIBLIOGRAPHY

E. O. Nodnagel: *Jenseits von Wagner und Liszt* (Königsberg, 1902), chap. 'Arnold Mendelssohn'
W. Nagel: *Arnold Mendelssohn* (Leipzig, 1906)
——: 'Arnold Mendelssohn', *Monographien moderner Musiker*, ed. C. F. Kahnt, i (1906), 96
——: 'Arnold Mendelssohn', *Die Musik*, vii (1907–8), 199
H. Hering: *Arnold Mendelssohn: die Grundlagen seines Schaffens und seine Werke* (diss., U. of Marburg, 1927; Regensburg, 1930)
K. Holzmann: 'Pädagogen von einst: Arnold Mendelssohn als Lehrer Paul Hindemiths', *Musik im Unterricht*, xliii (1952), 112
A. Werner-Jensen: *Arnold Mendelssohn als Liederkomponist* (Winterthur, 1976)

EDWARD F. KRAVITT

**Mendelssohn(-Bartholdy)** [Hensel], **Fanny (Cäcilie)** (*b* Hamburg, 14 Nov 1805; *d* Berlin, 14 May 1847). German pianist and composer, sister of Felix Mendelssohn. Her early childhood in Hamburg was overshadowed by the years of Napoleonic oppression, which in 1811 caused the family to flee to Berlin; she grew up, however, in the security of the Mendelssohn home in Berlin. Fanny is said to have been as musically gifted as her brother; she was apparently an excellent pianist, and composed in the same style as he did. However, her historical importance consists in her having provided, both in her diary and in her correspondence, much essential source material for the biography of Felix, to whom she was very close.

Fanny received her first instruction in music from her mother, who commented on her 'Bach-fugue fingers' at her birth. She studied the piano with Ludwig Berger and composition with Zelter; in 1816 the family went to stay in Paris for a time, where she received tuition from Marie Bigot. She is said to have been able to play Bach's *Wohltemperirtes Clavier* from memory at the age of 13. In 1822 she travelled to Switzerland with her family, and in 1825 attended Alexander von Humboldt's lectures on physical geography and Holtei's lectures on experimental physics at the Berlin Singakademie. In 1829 she married the painter Wilhelm Hensel; the diary which she kept until then formed the main source for the family biography, written by her son Sebastian. The year 1839–40 marked the high point of her life, when she travelled with her husband and son throughout Italy, staying for some time in Milan, Venice, Naples and Genoa. After the death of her mother Lea (12 December 1842) she became the central figure of the Mendelssohn household and led the Sunday morning concerts at the Elternhaus in Berlin. She also occasionally made public appearances as a pianist in Berlin. She died during a rehearsal of her brother's *Walpurgisnacht* for one of the Sunday concerts.

Six of her songs were published under her brother's name in his opp.8 and 9 (*Heimweh, Italien, Suleika und Hatem, Sehnsucht, Verlust* and *Die Nonne*). Works published under her own name, some posthumously, include songs (opp.1, 9 and 10), *Lieder ohne Worte* (opp.2, 6 and 8), *6 Gartenlieder* op.3 for four-part mixed choir, a Piano Trio op.11 and a few piano works without opus numbers. Most of her compositions, however, including cantatas, oratorios and dramatic scenas, were never printed; some of her unpublished works are in the collections of the New York Public Library, the Bodleian Library in Oxford, the Library of Congress in Washington and the Mendelssohn-Archiv in West Berlin.

BIBLIOGRAPHY

S. Hensel: *Die Familie Mendelssohn 1729–1847, nach Briefen und Tagebüchern* (Berlin, 1879, 18/1924, rev., abridged 19/1959; Eng. trans., 1882/R1969)
J. Werner: 'Felix and Fanny Mendelssohn', *ML*, xxviii (1947), 303
F. Schnapp: 'Felix Mendelssohn-Bartholdys Brief an seine Schwester Fanny Hensel', *SMz*, xcix (1959), 85
*Fanny Hensel: Dokumente ihres Lebens*, Ausstellungskatalog der Staatsbibliothek Preussischer Kulturbesitz, ii (Berlin, 1972)

KARL-HEINZ KÖHLER

**Mendelssohn(-Bartholdy), (Jakob Ludwig) Felix** (*b* Hamburg, 3 Feb 1809; *d* Leipzig, 4 Nov 1847). German composer. One of the most naturally gifted musicians of the 19th century, he developed his talent to a high degree while still a boy. Although he grew up surrounded by Romantic influences, his inspiration was essentially Classical and his musical ideals were embodied in the works of Bach, Handel and Mozart rather than those of his contemporaries. He was a Romantic chiefly in his skilful use of literary and other extra-musical stimuli, and his Classical inclinations led him to embody these in music of traditional form and elegance, expressed with an individual melodic grace and brilliance.

1. Family and childhood. 2. The young composer in Berlin, 1825–9. 3. European travels, 1829–35. 4. Leipzig and the Gewandhaus, 1835–40. 5. Hope and disappointment in Berlin, 1841–2. 6. The Leipzig Conservatory. 7. Last years. 8. The work: basic concepts, trends and influences. 9. Singspiels and operas. 10. Incidental music. 11. Oratorios. 12. Other vocal works. 13. Symphonies. 14. Overtures. 15. Concertos. 16. Chamber and solo instrumental music. 17. The heritage.

1. FAMILY AND CHILDHOOD. Felix Mendelssohn's paternal grandfather was the philosopher of the Enlightenment, Moses Mendelssohn (1729–86, originally Moses Dessau), whose characteristic philosophical and

literary views played a significant part in the education and thought of young Felix. Together with his friends Gotthold Ephraim Lessing and Friedrich Nicolai, he laid the foundation stone of German national literature. He fought against religious intolerance and the anti-semitic excesses of 18th-century Prussia. His methodology follows classical models in its use of dialogue in order to approach the truth by the dialectic confrontation of opposing viewpoints. Lessing raised an enduring monument to him as the eponymous *Nathan der Weise*.

The civil rights that had extended to Germany after the French Revolution were an essential precondition for the development of the Mendelssohn family; in particular, the attainment of social equality by citizens of the Jewish faith was a consequence of the Enlightenment and the political movements of the second half of the 18th century. Moses Mendelssohn's son Abraham (1776–1835) worked in Paris as a banker in 1803–4; there he met his lifelong companion Lea Salomon (1777–1842), whom he married in 1804. Her grandfather, as financial adviser to Friedrich II, was a factory and property owner who, as one of the most affluent citizens of Berlin, enjoyed special privileges. His family lived in a cultured environment, in which music played a prominent part; Felix's maternal inheritance was especially conducive to his cultural and artistic development. After their marriage Abraham Mendelssohn moved to Hamburg, where he went into partnership with his brother Joseph in a family banking business. There were four children by his marriage to Lea Salomon: Fanny Cäcilie (1805–47), an excellent pianist who married the painter Wilhelm Hensel; Felix; Rebekka (1811–58), who married Peter Dirichlet, a professor of mathematics; and Paul (1813–74), a financier.

To force England to her knees, Napoleon had decreed a trade blockade of the Continent in 1810. The bankers and merchants of Hamburg, who were particularly hard hit, sought to circumvent the decree by contraband. The French occupying forces then retaliated with a regime of terror, which many of the victims sought to evade by flight. Abraham Mendelssohn and his family were among those who fled to Berlin in 1811 to escape persecution by Maréchal Davout. In 1813 Abraham Mendelssohn equipped a volunteer armed force at his own expense and gave money for a military hospital in Prague. After the victory against the Napoleonic alliance he became a town councillor in Berlin and enjoyed a rapidly advancing social position.

The flowering of Berlin as an intellectual and artistic metropolis, together with the upper middle-class environment of his parental home, formed the essential foundation upon which Felix Mendelssohn's prodigious talent could be developed still further. At first he was educated by his parents. His father taught him arithmetic and French and his mother instructed him in German, literature and the fine arts; no doubt he also received his first piano lessons from her. A family journey to Paris in 1816 (Abraham Mendelssohn had been entrusted by the Prussian government with the collection of French reparations) remained no more than an episode in Felix's artistic development, although during this stay he took piano lessons from Marie Bigot, who was highly esteemed by Haydn and Beethoven.

In the same year Abraham Mendelssohn followed his brother's advice and had his children baptized; he was himself converted to Christianity six years later. This was of course partly to help give real effect to the promised pledge of emancipation, but still more in the genuine conviction of being able to reconcile the moral content and ethical essence of Christianity with the specific inclinations of the Enlightenment philosophy – a reconciliation that was to prove a vital component of Felix's later religious attitude and convictions. As an outward sign of Christian conversion, the family added the name of Bartholdy (after the former owners of a garden site purchased by his mother's elder brother Jakob Lewin Salomon).

In 1819 Felix's education in general subjects and classical languages was entrusted to Carl Wilhelm Ludwig Heyse, a considerable philologist and the father of the poet and short-story writer Paul Heyse. His instruction in the piano had been taken over in 1815 by Ludwig Berger, an admired pianist and teacher of his time, and the nine-year-old Felix made an extremely successful private début with a *Concert militaire* by F. X. Dušek. In 1819 Carl Friedrich Zelter, friend of Goethe and principal of the Berlin Singakademie, began Mendelssohn's instruction in theory and composition. Among his other teachers were the violinist Carl Wilhelm Hennig and the landscape painter Johann Gottlob Samuel Rösel. The artistic talents of young Felix were manifest not only in musical achievements, but also in notable drawings and poems. The earliest extant attempt at composition is a piano piece entitled *Recitativo* and dated 7 March 1820 (fig.1). In that first year as a composer there followed in quick succession a profusion of small-scale works in which the boy sought to master the world of musical form. His main

1. *Autograph MS of Mendelssohn's earliest surviving composition, a piano piece entitled 'Recitativo' (7 March 1820) (D-Bds Mendelssohn I)*

*2. Felix Mendelssohn: drawing (14 November 1822) by his brother-in-law, Wilhelm Hensel (D-B Mendelssohn-Archiv)*

influences were the contrapuntal techniques of Bach and the Classical style of Mozart. In addition, the earliest Singspiels, *Die Soldatenliebschaft* and *Die beiden Pädagogen*, show a penchant for the dramatic style of Mozart's works of that genre.

The next phase of the young Mendelssohn's development as a composer, up to the end of his 13th year, is marked by an increased mastery of counterpoint and Classical forms, especially sonata form. From June to August 1821 he wrote the G minor Sonata, which was first published posthumously as op.105. The early works, in particular the first Singspiels, were performed in the parental home for the approval and entertainment of invited guests. In November 1821 Zelter took his pupil to see Goethe in Weimar. The resulting relationship with Goethe, which deepened in succeeding years, was of fundamental significance for the young Mendelssohn in that aspect of his creative work related to the Classical period of German literature. Between 1821 and 1830 Mendelssohn paid five substantial visits to Goethe, whose philosophical emphasis on the dynamic and productive aspects of art proved an enriching influence. Mendelssohn for his part increased Goethe's understanding of the music of the Classical period and attempted (though unsuccessfully) to foster an appreciation of Beethoven. Among other Weimar acquaintances were Mozart's pupil Hummel and the writer and music critic Ludwig Rellstab.

A third phase in Mendelssohn's youthful development began soon after his first meeting with Goethe. He began to compose in the larger forms, above all concertos (e.g. the Piano Concerto in A minor and the D minor Violin Concerto in the style of Mozart) and

preparatory studies for symphonies. Then came larger-scale sacred works (a setting of Psalm lxvi and the D major *Magnificat*). His exceptional dramatic gifts were manifest in the Singspiels *Die wandernden Komödianten* (1821–2) and *Der Onkel aus Boston oder Die beiden Neffen* (1822–3), the spoken dialogues of which are lost. From July to October 1822 the family travelled to Switzerland by a route from Berlin by way of Potsdam, Brandenburg, Magdeburg, Göttingen, Kassel (where Mendelssohn met Ludwig Spohr), Frankfurt am Main (where he met the pianist Aloys Schmitt), Darmstadt, Stuttgart and Schaffhausen into the Alpine region of the Gotthard, by way of Interlaken to Lake Geneva and Lausanne, into the Valais, to the Simplon, thence to Lake Maggiore and back via Berne and Frankfurt to Weimar (and a further meeting with Goethe). Soon afterwards Swiss folksongs were woven into two of the early symphonies. The fruits of the Swiss journey include the C minor Piano Quartet op.1. Immediately Mendelssohn underwent a fourth and final phase in his youthful development as a composer, making rapid progress towards complete maturity and laying the foundation of a personal style. He composed four more string symphonies, the F minor Violin Sonata op.4, the F minor Piano Quartet op.2 and the C minor Symphony op.11, a double concerto for violin and piano and two for two pianos.

Mendelssohn's childhood years were rounded off by further travels with his father, to Silesia in August 1823 and in summer 1824 to Doberan (near Rostock), where he composed the Overture for wind instruments op.24. It fell to Luigi Cherubini to decide Mendelssohn's future as a musician by pronouncing favourably on the Piano Quartet in B minor op.3 (dedicated to Goethe) during a visit to Paris in March 1825 (where Mendelssohn also met Hummel, Kalkbrenner, Moscheles, Rode, Baillot, Boucher, Rossini, Meyerbeer and Kreutzer).

2. THE YOUNG COMPOSER IN BERLIN, 1825–9. In summer 1825 Abraham Mendelssohn acquired the Berlin house and grounds at 3 Leipziger Strasse. The cultural atmosphere of upper middle-class prosperity was of far-reaching significance for Mendelssohn's young manhood. With its theatrical performances, literary readings and regular Sunday concerts, this house developed into the most important salon in Berlin. Among the foremost guests were the natural scientist Alexander von Humboldt and the philosopher Hegel. Here too the young Mendelssohn formed important friendships with Karl Klingemann, later a diplomat; the orientalist Friedrich Rosen; the music editor and critic Adolf Bernhard Marx; the violinist Eduard Rietz; the actor Eduard Devrient and his wife the actress Theresa; Ferdinand David, later Mendelssohn's Konzertmeister in Leipzig; Julius Schubring, the theologian who compiled the texts of Mendelssohn's oratorios; and the philologist Gustav Droysen.

Next to the writings of Jean Paul it was above all the Schlegel translations of Shakespeare and the poetry of Goethe that exerted a decisive influence on Mendelssohn's circle. Possibly Hegel's aesthetic influenced the young Mendelssohn, who later attended his university lectures. In his *Vorlesungen über die Ästhetik* (Berlin, 1836), Hegel stipulated 'that even in instrumental music the composer should devote equal attention to two aspects – musical structure, and the expression of an admittedly indeterminate content'.

Inspired by the classical poetry of Goethe, Mendelssohn composed the String Octet op.20 (October 1825), in which his thoroughly individual maturity is recognizable for the first time. On the composer's testimony the scherzo is indebted to the final lines of the *Walpurgisnacht* from the first part of *Faust* (see fig.8 below). Soon afterwards appeared Mendelssohn's most popular work, the overture to Shakespeare's *A Midsummer Night's Dream* op.21; its first public performance was in Stettin in April 1827 at a concert given by Carl Loewe. The last of Mendelssohn's early operas, *Die Hochzeit des Camacho*, was given its première shortly afterwards in the Berlin Schauspielhaus (29 April 1827). Intrigues were staged against the performance. The choice of theme, a socio-critical satire based on episodes from the adventures of *Don Quixote*, was ill-suited to Berlin audiences and the work itself had weaknesses, not least the dramatic construction of Klingemann's libretto; the result was no more than a *succès d'estime*.

In summer 1827 there followed more travels, which took Mendelssohn into the Harz, then to Thuringia and Franconia and to the south of Germany. In Heidelberg he met Justus Thibaut who, in his book *Über die Reinheit der Tonkunst* (1825), had campaigned for a revival of 17th- and 18th-century music, especially the work of Handel. Thibaut aroused Mendelssohn's interest in early Italian music.

Mendelssohn's translation of Terence's Latin comedy *The Woman of Andros*, published by his teacher Heyse, secured him a place at the University of Berlin in autumn 1827. There he attended Hegel's lectures in aesthetics, Carl Ritter's in geography and Eduard Gans's on the history of the liberation movement and on the French Revolution. A crisis in the 19-year-old Mendelssohn's artistic development was ended by the composition of the overture *Meeresstille und glückliche Fahrt* op.27, based on two poems by Goethe. The early creative years in Berlin were rounded off by a cantata commemorating the tricentenary of the death of Albrecht Dürer (April 1828) and another celebrating a convocation of natural scientists and doctors summoned by Humboldt.

In the Berlin Singakademie as early as 1819 Mendelssohn had been in contact with the works of Bach, at a time when the large-scale works were considered impossible to perform. Mendelssohn and his friends in the domestic circle had come to know the *St Matthew Passion* from a manuscript copy. A plan for its revival matured and was put before Zelter by Mendelssohn and Eduard Devrient; after some hesitation Zelter agreed. The performance under the direction of the 20-year-old Mendelssohn that followed at the Singakademie on Unter den Linden was a great achievement of musical history, ushering in the modern cultivation of Bach's music. (For an illustration of Mendelssohn's markings in the score, *see* BACH REVIVAL.) Two more performances followed in quick succession, the proceeds of which were devoted to social purposes, in particular the founding of two schools of needlework for girls 'of lower social position'.

3. EUROPEAN TRAVELS, 1829–35. At the insistence of his parents Mendelssohn set out for several years of travel abroad. On 10 April 1829 he accepted an invitation to London from Klingemann, who lived there as a diplomat and who, together with the pianist Ignaz

Moscheles and his wife, introduced him into London salons and social life. Thus the way was prepared for him to appear before the London public in four large-scale concerts. Among other works, his Symphony op.11 and his E major Double Concerto for two pianos were performed (Mendelssohn and Moscheles were the soloists in the latter work); Mendelssohn also played Beethoven's Emperor Concerto. After the concert season he travelled to Edinburgh (30 July 1829), where the first ideas for the Scottish Symphony came to him. On the way to the Scottish highlands he visited Sir Walter Scott in Abbotsford. On 7 August came the stormy crossing by steamship to the island of Staffa with its 'Fingal's Cave', to which Mendelssohn owed the inspiration of his overture *Die Hebriden* op.26 (originally called *Die einsame Insel*). The final stage of the journey was a visit to Coed Du, the estate of the Taylor family, who were business connections of Mendelssohn's father. The journey back to London began on 10 September. Soon afterwards Mendelssohn injured his knee in a coach accident and this delayed his planned return home. After a sojourn at the country home of Thomas Attwood, a former pupil of Mozart, on 7 December he returned to Berlin, where he staged the Liederspiel *Die Heimkehr aus der Fremde* for the silver-wedding anniversary of his parents.

At the beginning of 1830 Mendelssohn, then just 21 years old, was offered the chair of music at the University of Berlin; he declined, however, recommending his friend Adolf Bernhard Marx instead. In winter 1829–30, while at work on the Reformation Symphony, he had had an attack of measles, but by May was ready to begin an Italian journey, which had been suggested by Goethe. (A volume of letters recounts the experiences of this journey in brilliantly entertaining style.) In Weimar Mendelssohn saw Goethe for the last time and played his own works, pieces by Bach and Weber and

*3. Durham Cathedral: drawing (1829) by Mendelssohn (D-B Mendelssohn-Archiv)*

Beethoven's Fifth Symphony. Early in June he arrived in Munich and then proceeded through Salzburg, Linz, Vienna, Pressburg (for the coronation of Ferdinand V as King of Hungary) via Graz to Venice (18 October). At the end of October Mendelssohn went by way of Florence to Rome, where he met the music collector Fortunato Santini, the papal choirmaster and Palestrina scholar Giuseppe Baini, Berlioz, and the painter and sculptor Wilhelm Schadow.

In Rome Mendelssohn completed the overture *Die Hebriden*, began composing the Italian Symphony and sketched a setting of Goethe's ballad *Die erste Walpurgisnacht*. Early in 1831 he travelled with Schadow to Naples and Pompeii, whose artistic treasures and natural surroundings much impressed him; he was also deeply moved by the poverty of the Neapolitans. At the end of July 1831 he continued his travels by way of Florence and Genoa to Milan, where he sought out the company of the pianist Dorothea von Ertmann, an admired friend of Beethoven's. He travelled during the next two months through Switzerland, arriving back in Germany in October. On 17 October 1831 he gave a concert in Munich that included the Symphony op.11, the overture to *A Midsummer Night's Dream* and the completed G minor Piano Concerto. In Düsseldorf Schadow arranged Mendelssohn's first introduction to the dramatist Karl Immermann, though negotiations for an opera libretto were unsuccessful. Mendelssohn passed the second winter of his great journey in Paris, where he renewed his acquaintance with Baillot, Cherubini and Heine (who had taken part in the revival of the *St Matthew Passion*), met Chopin and the writer Ludwig Börne, and gave successful concerts at the Conservatoire.

Deeply distressed by the news of the death of Goethe and Zelter, Mendelssohn made another visit to London in spring 1832; during the season he took part in five concerts that included performances of the *Hebriden* and *Midsummer Night's Dream* overtures and the G minor Piano Concerto. At the end of June he returned to Berlin to apply, at his father's urging, to succeed Zelter as director of the Singakademie. The election was contested and in a ballot among members of the Singakademie Mendelssohn lost to Zelter's deputy, Carl Friedrich Rungenhagen. From November 1832 to January 1833 he gave four concerts in the Berlin Schauspielhaus; in the last of these, *Die erste Walpurgisnacht* was given its first performance.

Early in 1833 Mendelssohn accepted two important invitations. The Philharmonic Society of London had asked him to conduct the Italian Symphony on 13 March, and at the end of that month he was invited to conduct at the Lower Rhine Music Festival in Düsseldorf. In preparation for these events he travelled on 14 April by way of Düsseldorf to London, where the triumphant successes of the previous visits were repeated. A performance of *Israel in Egypt* in Düsseldorf on 26 May 1833 inaugurated a series of Handel oratorio performances in Mendelssohn's own arrangements; they proved an important contribution to Handel's popularity in Germany. On this occasion, stage spectacle was afforded by the background presentation of *tableaux vivants*. After the successful completion of the music festival, which included performances of Beethoven's Pastoral Symphony and *Leonore* Overture no.3, Mendelssohn received a promising commission that required his services in Düsseldorf for two

years as city music director, at an annual salary of 600 thaler with three months' leave of absence. His duties consisted in directing Catholic church music and organizing the city music society, which was to give from four to eight concerts a year. A recuperative holiday in England with his father (who had an accident that delayed their return until the end of August) and a short visit to Berlin bridged the gap until he took up his appointment in Düsseldorf. At the beginning of his stay there a meeting with the Crown Prince of Prussia (later King Friedrich Wilhelm IV) resulted in Mendelssohn's nomination as a member of the musical section of the Berlin Academy of the Arts.

At Düsseldorf Mendelssohn concentrated on the cultivation of Handel's oratorios. Within two years five more oratorios were performed in his own arrangements: *Alexander's Feast* (22 November 1833), *Messiah* (Elberfeld, 8 March 1834), the Dettingen *Te Deum* (August 1834), *Judas Maccabaeus* (16 December 1834) and *Solomon* (Cologne, May 1835). He also worked in close collaboration with Immermann to found a theatre in Düsseldorf along the lines of Goethe's reforms in Weimar. Increased prices of admission levied in order to prepare exemplary performances provoked a demonstration during the performance of Mozart's *Don Giovanni* under Mendelssohn's direction. After productions of Goethe's *Egmont*, Cherubini's *Les deux journées* and Marschner's *Hans Heiling*, the formal opening of the theatre was on 28 October 1834. Mendelssohn conducted noteworthy works from the opera repertory, including *Oberon*, *Der Freischütz*, *Fra Diavolo*, *Die Entführung aus dem Serail* and *Die Zauberflöte*. But he was plagued by administrative difficulties, which led to an untimely breach with Immermann and ultimately his departure from Düsseldorf. Among the important works he composed during this period are the overture *Die schöne Melusine* op.32, inspired by Conradin Kreutzer's opera (which Mendelssohn saw in Berlin in 1833) and first performed in London on 7 April 1834, and *St Paul*, an oratorio in the tradition of Handel, first performed at the Lower Rhine Music Festival in Düsseldorf on 22 May 1836. The text of the oratorio was freely adapted from the *Acts of the Apostles* by Mendelssohn's friend Julius Schubring. Otherwise, it was the smaller forms that prevailed – lieder and genre pieces for the piano, appropriately entitled *Lieder ohne Worte* – composed mainly for the salon of the hospitable music-loving family of Woringen, the Düsseldorf city president.

4. LEIPZIG AND THE GEWANDHAUS, 1835–40. At the beginning of 1835, after successful negotiations with the lawyer Konrad Schleinitz (who was acting on behalf of Leipzig's town council), Mendelssohn was named the fifth conductor of the Leipzig Gewandhaus orchestra. Following his departure from Düsseldorf after the final concert (2 July 1835) Mendelssohn returned to Berlin, where he witnessed the uprising of 3 August 1835, directed against the despotism of the military regime, and reported its events in detail in a letter to Klingemann. The first concert season began on 4 October with the overture *Meeresstille und glückliche Fahrt* and Beethoven's Symphony no.4. His activities as conductor in Leipzig developed into what must be regarded overwhelmingly the most far-reaching achievement of his life, sustained by his determination to secure a continuing improvement in the standards of orchestral

performance, to advance the social position of its members, to plan programmes consisting of items of special historical interest as well as contemporary music, and to invite leading soloists to perform with the orchestra. During the winter concert season, from October to March, some 20 subscription concerts were organized. In addition there were chamber music performances, quartet evenings, and performances of cantatas and oratorios. Mendelssohn acted not only as conductor but also as a soloist, especially as pianist and organist. The contract agreed with the Leipzig town council assured him an annual income of 1000 thaler with permission to leave Leipzig for six months a year. He also received an honorary doctorate from the University of Leipzig.

On 19 November Mendelssohn was shattered by the death of his father. After directing the Lower Rhine Music Festival in Düsseldorf (May 1836) in the first performance of *St Paul*, a performance of Beethoven's Ninth Symphony and the first concert performance of the *Leonore* Overture no.1, Mendelssohn deputized for his friend J. N. Scheible in summer 1836 as director of the Cäcilienverein, an amateur choral society in Frankfurt am Main. During this time he lived with relatives of his Leipzig friend Schleinitz. His hostess, the widow of a minister of the Reformed Church, lived with her two daughters in Frankfurt. After a brief visit to Scheveningen with Schadow in September 1836 he became engaged to one of the daughters, Cécile Charlotte Sophia Jeanrenaud (1817–53), and the wedding was on 28 March 1837 in Frankfurt. On the honeymoon journey (to Freiburg and the Black Forest) and during the following summer sojourn in Bingen am Rhein, he composed the String Quartet in E minor op.44 no.2, the D minor Piano Concerto and a setting of Psalm xlii. After directing the Birmingham Music Festival (19–22 September 1837) in another performance of *St Paul*, Mendelssohn moved to Leipzig with his young wife and took up residence in Lurgensteins Garten. There were three sons and two daughters of this happy marriage.

In the decade of his activity in Leipzig Mendelssohn campaigned for the recognition of forgotten 18th-century works. He introduced Bach's orchestral suites into the civic concert hall. His performance, with Clara Wieck and Louis Rakemann, of Bach's Concerto in D minor for three pianos and orchestra (9 November 1835) was a sensational success. He fostered an increasing interest in Mozart's symphonies, as well as in the symphonies and concertos of Beethoven; Beethoven's Ninth Symphony was performed at the Gewandhaus six times in just ten years. Mendelssohn was also an enthusiastic supporter of Weber's concertos, overtures and operas (scenes from which were frequently given in concert performances). One of the great events of the day was the première of Schubert's C major Symphony (21 March 1839). Schumann had located the manuscript on New Year's Day 1839, at the home of Schubert's brother Ferdinand, and had sent it to Mendelssohn for performance at the Gewandhaus; Mendelssohn conducted it 12 times in all.

To arouse and cultivate the general musical appreciation of his audiences, Mendelssohn introduced in the winter season 1837–8 the so-called 'historical concerts', a kind of history of music in sound. In four concerts he introduced listeners to music from the time of Bach to their own day: works by Handel, Viotti, Haydn, Cimarosa, Naumann, Righini, Mozart, Salieri, Méhul,

B. H. Romberg, Beethoven and the Abbé Vogler. Not only was forgotten music revived but contemporary composers were encouraged. Above all, Schumann owed a large measure of his development and fame to the help and sponsorship of Mendelssohn, who conducted the premières of his first two symphonies (31 March 1841 and 5 November 1846) and Piano Concerto (22 January 1846). Others whose cause he advanced by performing their works were Ferdinand David, Niels Gade, Ferdinand Hiller and Julius Rietz.

Not only notable composers but eminent executants appeared in the Gewandhaus concerts. Clara Schumann gave 21 performances with Mendelssohn as conductor. In March 1840 Liszt gave three special concerts in the Gewandhaus. The programmes contain the names of other well-known performers whom Mendelssohn encouraged: Thalberg, Alexander Dreyschock, Raimund Dreyschock (later leader of the Gewandhaus orchestra), Moscheles, Anton Rubinstein, Vieuxtemps and Joachim, who as a 13-year-old prodigy was recommended by Mendelssohn to London concert promoters. Eminent singers also took part in the concerts: from Sweden came Jenny Lind, who made a triumphantly successful appearance in December 1845 (for illustration of the programme, *see* CONCERT); from England Clara Novello, who sang under Mendelssohn's direction in the winter season 1837–8; and from Leipzig itself Livia Frege, to whom Mendelssohn dedicated some of his songs.

Such programmes, with their emphasis on outstanding works of the past and serious contemporary works, together with the recruitment of outstanding performers, pointed the way to the future. There was also an improved standard of orchestral playing, which Mendelssohn brought about by a radical change in leadership at the outset of his Leipzig activities. The direction of symphonies, previously entrusted to the leader of the orchestra, was taken over by the conductor. An added stimulus to the orchestra's achievement was Mendelssohn's passionate and successful intervention on behalf of the players for increases in salary. With these outstanding achievements as conductor, performer and music organizer, the years of Mendelssohn's Leipzig activities count among the most significant of his life.

The summer holidays allowed by the contract were usually spent travelling, composing and directing music festivals. In April 1838 Mendelssohn went with his family to Berlin. At the beginning of July he once again undertook the direction of the Lower Rhine Music Festival in Cologne (including a performance of Handel's *Joshua*) and then spent the rest of the summer in Berlin. The family spent the next summer in Frankfurt am Main, though Felix again assumed the directorship of the Lower Rhine Music Festival in Düsseldorf from 19 to 21 May (this time performing Handel's *Messiah* and Beethoven's Mass in C) and, before the start of the Leipzig concert season, conducting *St Paul*, the D minor Piano Concerto and Beethoven's fifth and seventh symphonies at the Brunswick Music Festival (6–8 September). During the summer recess of 1840 *St Paul* was performed in Weimar on 15 April and the family spent a two-month holiday in Berlin. But the main event was the Leipzig Festival on 25 June celebrating the 400th anniversary of the invention of the printing press. Mendelssohn was commissioned to write the festival music. His second symphony, the symphonic cantata *Lobgesang* op.52, was performed on 25 June at the Thomaskirche in Leipzig, together with Weber's *Jubelouvertüre* and Handel's Dettingen *Te Deum*. At the North German Music Festival in Schwerin (8–10 July) Mendelssohn once again conducted *St Paul*. On 6 August he inaugurated with a concert of organ music the raising of funds for the erection of a Bach memorial in front of the Thomaskirche; the unveiling of this memorial was not until 23 April 1843. On 18 September Mendelssohn stayed in London for the sixth time, and at the Birmingham Music Festival (22–5 September) he again conducted the *Lobgesang*.

5. HOPE AND DISAPPOINTMENT IN BERLIN, 1841–2. The death of Friedrich Wilhelm III, King of Prussia, on 7 June 1840 was of great significance for Mendelssohn's career. Far-reaching reforms and basic changes were expected from his son and successor, Friedrich Wilhelm IV. Plans for reform were extended to include the arts, thus affecting the musical life of Berlin. The Academy of the Arts was to be reconstituted to include a section for music, as well as for painting, sculpture and architecture. A new conservatory and a new concert organization were to be associated with the music section of the Academy, and the king wanted the energetic Mendelssohn to move to Berlin to be in charge of the whole enterprise. Through the agency of the court official Massow, Friedrich Wilhelm established contact with Paul Mendelssohn, who in November 1840 informed his brother of the ambitious plans. Mendelssohn's protracted correspondence with the king was of little practical result. To begin with, he found himself required to go to Berlin for a year, at three times his salary in Leipzig, but without defined duties except to be in readiness for special employment. He retained his Leipzig position and some of his conducting duties (Ferdinand David acted as deputy conductor in the winter season 1841–2). During summer 1841 he conducted *St Paul* in Weimar (again on 15 April) and in the following months visited Berlin once and Dresden several times, finally arriving at Berlin again at the end of July to take up his new post.

Mendelssohn's first duty was to assist the king in accomplishing the task of ushering in a renaissance of Greek tragedy with incidental music. For this purpose the writer Ludwig Tieck, who had shown himself worthy to take over from Schlegel the task of translating Shakespeare into German, was summoned from Dresden to Potsdam as theatre expert; August Böckh acted as linguistic adviser. The first choice was Sophocles' *Antigone*: it was decided to set the choruses of the classical drama in a modern musical style, with due attention to rules of poetic metre. The composition of the incidental music was completed within 11 days and on 28 October 1841 the first performance took place under Mendelssohn's direction in the small theatre of the Neuer Palais, Potsdam, with an audience of court officials and university professors. On 13 April 1842 *Antigone* was performed at the Berlin Schauspielhaus and was repeated five times in the next three weeks. The setting made a substantial contribution to the popularization of Greek tragedy; the success was sensational and was considered epoch-making.

But despite this success Mendelssohn had not found the field of activity that had been promised him in Berlin. The reforms had not been carried through.

The winter season of 1841–2 in Berlin afforded Mendelssohn only one opportunity of public appearance, that of conducting performances of *St Paul* (10 January and 17 February), with only moderate contributions from his collaborators. The king's inability to carry out the promised reforms, deeply rooted in the backward social circumstances in Prussia, were denounced above all in the literature of political reform. In 1843 appeared Bettina von Arnim's book *Dies Jahr gehört dem König*, which advocated the idea of a republican people's monarchy. In 1841 the physician Johann Jacoby published his pamphlet *Vier Fragen* calling for the establishment of a parliament, a share in government for the people, the dismantling of official power and general freedom of thought. Disappointment with the Berlin circumstances induced in him an ever deeper resignation. This is partly reflected in the Scottish Symphony op.56, with which he was occupied in 1841–2, 12 years after the earliest inspiration, and which was first performed at the Gewandhaus under his own direction on 3 March 1842. During winter 1841–2 Mendelssohn travelled to Leipzig many times to fulfil his concert obligations. Summer 1842 was occupied with a further visit to Düsseldorf, where Mendelssohn and Julius Rietz together directed the Lower Rhine Music Festival; Mendelssohn conducted the *Lobgesang* and Handel's *Israel in Egypt* and performed Beethoven's 'Emperor' Concerto at very short notice in place of an indisposed soloist.

At the end of May Mendelssohn paid his seventh visit to England. The climax of his stay in London was the performance of the Scottish Symphony at the Philharmonic Society on 13 June. The composer was twice received by Queen Victoria and the Prince Consort Albert, on 20 June and 9 July, and in gratitude Mendelssohn dedicated the Scottish Symphony to the queen.

On 27 September he returned to Leipzig via Frankfurt am Main and on 2 October conducted the first concert of the season in the Gewandhaus. The next day he returned to Berlin. As no attainment of the promised reforms was in prospect, Mendelssohn decided to withdraw from his Berlin obligations, and only the moderating influence of his mother prevented a complete breach with the Prussian king. Mendelssohn waived half his salary. Friedrich Wilhelm IV appointed him general music director and entrusted him with the supervision and direction of sacred music. This meant that Mendelssohn, though still in the king's service, had no binding duties and could instead devote himself entirely to the Gewandhaus orchestra.

The death of his mother on 12 December 1842 caused an emotional crisis that Mendelssohn overcame by undertaking a complete revision of the cantata *Die erste Walpurgisnacht*. The first performance of the new version followed on 2 February 1843 at the Gewandhaus; among those present was Berlioz, who expressed great enthusiasm for the work. Berlioz, whose acquaintance Mendelssohn had made 12 years earlier in Rome, was at the time on a concert tour of Germany during which he had failed to make any great impression; Mendelssohn's selfless assistance in the preparation of the Leipzig concerts helped to make Berlioz recognized for the first time in Germany. Mendelssohn gave similar support to the Danish composer Niels Gade, whose Symphony no.3 was performed on 3 March 1842.

*4. Mendelssohn with Queen Victoria and the Prince Consort: engraving by H. Hannal after G. Durand*

6. THE LEIPZIG CONSERVATORY. On 13 February 1839 the lawyer Heinrich Blumner died, leaving a bequest of 20,000 thaler for 'the founding of a new or the support of an existing all-purpose national institute for the arts or science'. The bequest left the disposition of the sum at the discretion of King Friedrich August II of Saxony. Mendelssohn intervened and in April 1840 submitted to Falkenberg, the district director, a petition giving reasons for the need for a music academy in Leipzig. In March 1841 the petition was granted, and after an interval for intensive preparation the new institute was ceremonially opened on 2 April 1843. In the courtyard of the Gewandhaus the city council had a two-storey house built and placed at the disposal of the conservatory. Mendelssohn then devoted himself intensively to the work of organizing the teaching arrangements. His far-reaching ideas included the division into several teaching faculties, the requirement that students practise ensemble playing, the institution of regular, main and auxiliary examinations as well as evening recitals by the students. He laid special emphasis on the maintenance of discipline in teaching and the active encouragement of outstanding talents. He was successful in engaging well-known representatives of special subjects as teachers, among them the choirmaster of the Thomaskirche, Moritz Hauptmann, for harmony and counterpoint; Schumann for the piano, composition and score-reading; Ferdinand David for the violin; and Carl Ferdinand Becker for the organ, music history and theory. Later they were joined by Clara Schumann, Ferdinand Hiller, Gade and Moscheles, who succeeded Mendelssohn in 1847 as director of the conservatory. Among the earliest of the outstanding pupils whom Mendelssohn taught there were the composer and aesthetician Emil Naumann and the violinist and historian Joseph von Wasielewski.

In summer 1843 the boundaries of Mendelssohn's Berlin duties seemed to be more clearly defined. He was entrusted with the direction of the newly formed male-voice cathedral choir and of the symphony concerts given by the opera orchestra in the 1843–4 season. The king also asked that the series of dramatic productions with incidental music should be continued. Among the plans under consideration, Mendelssohn chose to provide music for *A Midsummer Night's Dream*. In some of the 11 numbers of the incidental music he used themes from the overture written 17 years before. The first complete performance of the incidental music was on 14 October 1843 at the Neuer Palais; the first public performance was four days later at the Berlin Schauspielhaus. Its success was overwhelming. After fulfilling some concert obligations in October and November in Leipzig, Mendelssohn moved with his family to Berlin and occupied apartments in the parental home at 3 Leipziger Strasse.

In his work with the cathedral choir, for which he composed four cantatas to psalm texts (nos.2, 22, 43, 98), Mendelssohn showed a preference for the *a cappella* style of the early Italian masters. His activity as choirmaster, however, was impeded by differences with the choir authorities, especially with the senior court chaplain Strauss. Similar difficulties occurred in planning and rehearsing the ten Berlin symphony concerts, the conducting of which Mendelssohn shared with the opera director Wilhelm Taubert. Mendelssohn concluded the concert season with a performance of Beethoven's Ninth Symphony (27 March 1844) and in April returned to Leipzig. Discouraged again by the circumstances in Berlin, he concentrated on the idea of composing an opera. The plan of collaborating with his friend Eduard Devrient in writing a libretto on a subject from the period of the German peasant revolt took definite shape but was ultimately abandoned. After the summer recess of 1844, when there still seemed no possibility of a change in Berlin, Mendelssohn took steps to release himself almost completely from his obligations there. His salary was further abated on the understanding that for the future he was to continue in the royal service solely as a composer. He furnished two more plays with incidental music, composed early in 1845 but not performed until late autumn. The première of *Oedipus at Colonos* op.93 was on 1 November 1845 at the Neuer Palais; a private performance of Racine's *Athalie* op.74 followed on 1 December at Schloss Charlottenburg. Other similar commissions were refused by Mendelssohn, so that a final breach with the Prussian monarch became inevitable.

In the summer recess of 1844 (May to July)

Mendelssohn paid his eighth visit to England, conducting six Philharmonic concerts in performances of his own works as well as those of Bach and Beethoven. On 10 July he returned to Soden, near Frankfurt am Main, where he relaxed with his family except for a brief interruption by the music festival in Zweibrücken (31 July–1 August); Mendelssohn conducted *St Paul* and *Die erste Walpurgisnacht* and had friendly encounters with the poets Lenau, Hoffman von Fallersleben and Freiligrath. During this holiday in Soden he composed the Violin Concerto op.64, which was first performed in the Leipzig Gewandhaus on 13 March 1845 with Ferdinand David as soloist and Gade conducting. After a short stay in Berlin, from October to November, during which he conducted a symphony concert on 15 November of Beethoven's Fifth Symphony, *Coriolanus* Overture, and Weber's Overture to *Euryanthe*, he spent the following months in Frankfurt am Main and travelling with his brother and sisters on holiday to Freiburg and Soden.

7. LAST YEARS. In August 1845, at the request of the Saxon minister Falkenstein, he resumed his earlier activities at the Gewandhaus, and on 13 August he moved into his last home in Leipzig, at 3 Königstrasse. That summer he completed the Quintet in B♭ op.87. When he resumed the direction of the Gewandhaus concerts on 5 October 1845 he was no longer in full command of his powers. He shared his duties with his deputy Gade. The highpoints of the concert season were the second performance of his Violin Concerto (on 23 October), the concert with the Swedish soprano Jenny Lind (4 December), and the first performance of Schumann's Piano Concerto, with Clara Schumann as soloist (1 January 1846). During the first part of the season Mendelssohn also performed as a pianist, but on medical advice he appeared only as a conductor in the Gewandhaus from early 1846 onwards. At the request of Albert Lortzing he set Schiller's poem *Der Sänger* as a contribution to the festival programme of the Leipzig Schiller Society (10 November). Throughout spring and summer 1846 Mendelssohn's activities were taxing and unremitting. He was committed to several important engagements that involved travelling. He had again been commissioned to take over the direction of the Lower Rhine Music Festival in Aachen (31 May to 2 June); he conducted Haydn's *The Creation*, Handel's *Alexander's Feast* and Beethoven's Fifth Symphony. On 11 June he travelled to Liège for the sexcentenary of the feast of Corpus Christi for which he had set a passage from Thomas Aquinas's *Lauda Sion Salvatorem*. From 14 to 16 June Mendelssohn took part in the German–Flemish choral festival in Cologne, for which he had set Schiller's *An die Künstler* as the *Festgesang* op.68. After a stay in Leipzig he went on his journey to England on 18 August 1846 to rehearse the oratorio *Elijah*, which he had composed in a single creative outburst in spring and summer 1846 for the first performance at the Birmingham Music Festival (26 August 1846; for illustration, *see* BIRMINGHAM). Soon afterwards he returned to Leipzig via London, Ramsgate, Ostend, Cologne and Frankfurt am Main, where in the autumn he undertook a thorough revision of the score of *Elijah* for publication by Simrock in July of the following year. During winter 1846–7 he again conducted the Gewandhaus concerts.

Mendelssohn, who had long been in search of a suit-

*5. Felix Mendelssohn: portrait (1845) by Eduard Magnus (D-B Mendelssohn-Archiv)*

able opera subject, finally settled on the Rhine legend of the Loreley. In collaboration with Eduard Devrient he tried to remedy the defects of a libretto by Emanuel Geibel. This last dramatic composition by Mendelssohn remained fragmentary. (In 1863 Geibel's text was set by Max Bruch, though without lasting success.) Nor was he able to complete his attempt to write a third oratorio, *Christus*. On 18 March 1847 he conducted one of his historical concerts for the last time; and on 2 April, with a performance of his *St Paul* in the Paulinerkirche, he conducted for the last time in Leipzig and in Germany. Soon afterwards he visited England for the tenth and last time, conducting several brilliantly successful performances of *Elijah* (16, 23, 28 and 30 April in London, 20 April in Manchester and 27 April in Birmingham). His symphony and chamber concerts also received a tumultuous reception. On 8 May 1847 he began his final journey home, arriving at Frankfurt am Main on 12 May. There he learnt the shattering news of the death of his sister Fanny. In June he sought to recover in Baden-Baden, and at the end of June he travelled with his Berlin relatives via Schaffhausen to Thun. In mid-July he went to Interlaken, where his last great work, the String Quartet in F minor op.80, was composed as a 'Requiem for Fanny'.

On 17 September he returned to Leipzig, where his friends found that he appeared to have changed, looking pale and tired. A week's journey to Berlin to visit his sister's grave brought on a condition of strange perturbation; he became seriously ill and could not conduct even the first of the Gewandhaus concerts. At the end of October he had a slight stroke. Then the attacks became more frequent, leading to a crisis on 3 November. On 4 November, at 9.24 p.m., he died. In his funeral procession to the Paulinerkirche, the pallbearers were Schumann, David, Gade, Hauptmann, Rietz and Moscheles. After the mourning ceremony the coffin was taken by special train to Berlin, where on the following day Mendelssohn was buried near the grave of his sister Fanny in the Trinity Cemetery. Mourning and memorial concerts were given in several cities in Germany and England until the end of the year.

8. THE WORK: BASIC CONCEPTS, TRENDS AND INFLUENCES. The catalogue of Mendelssohn's published compositions, issued by Breitkopf & Härtel (Leipzig, 3/1882), lists 121 works with opus numbers. The first 72 were published in Mendelssohn's lifetime and numbered according to his wishes; the sequence of these works affords a conspectus of the chronological order only of publication, not of composition. Opp.73–121, first published posthumously in the Gesamtausgabe (1874–7), were numbered by Julius Rietz, the general editor of the Gesamtausgabe. In addition some 100 early works, 1821–4, including 13 string symphonies called 'sinfonie', were rediscovered in 1960 and have in part been published in the Leipzig collected edition of Mendelssohn's works. There is as yet no definitive catalogue of Mendelssohn's work as a whole, though by a careful estimate it comprises about 250 individual items.

Mendelssohn's creative work was moulded by a variety of experiences, trends and influences. It is salutary to distinguish between musical reactions, basic aesthetic concepts and extra-musical influences derived from poetry and emotions which, though subjectively expressed, represent tangible experiences of art, nature, religion, people, society and history. Two principles stand out from the evidence of the compositions themselves, namely the emphasis on clarity and the adherence to the Classical tradition. The young Mendelssohn was guided by Classical and pre-Classical techniques and forms, his first model being the contrapuntal style, in particular the fugal technique, of Bach, whose music he copied out as a boy. Among other examples one may point in particular to the convincing chromatic fugal introduction of the Sinfonia no.12 of August 1823. The early work also demonstrates his intensive study of Handel's instrumental technique, which is often apparent in the introductions to the string symphonies, with their typically Handelian rhythms and harmonic progressions.

Mendelssohn's indebtedness to the music of Mozart and his time is no doubt of greater consequence, being perceptible in nearly all the string symphonies written between the ages of 12 and 14, the D minor Violin Concerto of 1822 and the early Singspiels. In the closing bars of Die beiden Pädagogen Mendelssohn quoted from the 'Jupiter' Symphony, which he had begun transcribing for piano the same year. The instrumental technique of Beethoven was a formative influence in the early works for full symphony orchestra, especially in the two concertos for two pianos and orchestra. The towering achievement of the young prodigy consists above all in having outgrown a reliance on Classical models and developed a personal style in only four years, between the ages of 11 and 15. His individual stylistic traits include characteristic small-scale rhythmic figures, melodies incorporating a variety of motifs, harmonies intensified by cadential 7th chords, and a freer adaptation of Classical forms. The strikingly individual style of the Mendelssohn of 1825–6, the composer of the String Octet and the overture to A Midsummer Night's Dream, proved hardly capable of further change or development during his life. Yet he was able to put his stylistic methods to good effect in a broader thematic application and thus achieved a creative freshness later in such works as the Violin Concerto in E minor (1844) and the Piano Trio in C minor (1845).

The extra-musical influences are shown by a frequent programmatic underlining of musical material. The relationship between content and import can be traced back to the demands of the Hegelian aesthetic, which attributes to music an 'indeterminate content' together with an independently formed musical structure; it is perhaps more than a coincidence that Mendelssohn's acquaintance with the philosopher in his family home was concurrent with the ripening of his style and the interrelationship of his music and the literature with which he was familiar: the Octet, for instance, has a documented connection with lines from the Walpurgisnacht scene from the first part of Faust. The literary influences were indeed the strongest; they determined the composer's choice and treatment of subject. After Schlegel's Shakespeare translations, Goethe's poetry was the dominant factor, followed by other contemporary German poetry. The influences of art and nature crystallize mainly in the Italian Symphony; emotions from the sphere of personal human relationships are encapsulated in lieder and choruses, and the Scottish Symphony suggests the influence of history as well as of nature. The contrasting feelings of acquiescence and strong protest aroused by his disappointments in Berlin were, on Mendelssohn's own testimony, expressed in Elijah, and they are also perceptible in the Scottish Symphony.

Neither these various influences nor the composer's own comments about his music permit any definitive classification of Mendelssohn into the mode of thought of any particular period. Least of all is it tenable to call him a Romantic; on the contrary, his affiliations with the 18th century, especially the music of Mozart, make him if anything a neo-classicist.

9. SINGSPIELS AND OPERAS. Mendelssohn showed an early gift for the dramatic. For his first Singspiel he chose surprisingly realistic subjects related to his immediate surroundings. True, the trend towards the increasing romanticization of opera subjects inhibited Mendelssohn's later development from the boyhood Singspiel composer who had promised such great success for the future, and this may be reflected in his long, fruitless search for a suitable and above all realistic opera subject. He required of such a subject that it should be drawn from a national event, story or popular legend, and that it should be elevated and serene in style or else should embody a real basic character on the model of Fidelio.

The librettist of the early Singspiels, Johann Ludwig Casper (1796–1864), was a friend of the Mendelssohn family. In 1819 he travelled and studied in France, where he came into contact with the critical thought in French vaudeville theatre and translated and made imitations of some of these plays for the young Mendelssohn. Die Soldatenliebschaft is set in Countess Elvira's castle and grounds during the French occupation of Spain at the beginning of the 19th century. Mendelssohn obtained striking contrasts by juxtaposing arias, ariettas and ensembles with sharply distinctive rhythms and skilful introduction of different vocal ranges. The psychological relationships are vividly personified in the music, and it is not difficult to recognize the influence of Mozart in the art of characterization as well as in general stylistic features. *Die beiden Pädagogen* also takes place at the beginning of the 19th century, when Pestalozzi's ideas were first beginning to filter through. The play is based on a comedy by Eugène Scribe written in 1817 and called *Les deux précepteurs, ou Asinus asinum fricat*. The musical characterization in this Singspiel is already extended further, especially that of Herr von Robert, a member of the landed gentry, and his rebellious son Carl, whose emotions, views and resolve are depicted in two trios; the typical pedantry of the village schoolmaster is strikingly satirized in the aria 'Probatum est' and in the duet 'Ei, da möchte man ersticken'. And Mendelssohn, then scarcely 12 years old, achieved a masterpiece in a quartet whose middle section incorporates the differences of opinion about the ideas of Pestalozzi and Basedow. The dramatic finale 'Reichen Segen gab der Himmel', with a quartet of soloists, chorus, dance and violin solo, also shows Mendelssohn's striking dramatic talent, even though Mozart's influence is again palpable.

The subject of Mendelssohn's early and only completed opera, *Die Hochzeit des Camacho*, is based on a socio-critical satire from *Don Quixote*. The ballet entr'actes for the wedding celebrations in Act 2, in which Cupid's warriors defeat the champions of wealth, allude to the social criticism underlining the plot, which may well have been one of the causes of the demonstrations staged against the first performance on 29 April 1827. The dramatic construction of the opera (the dialogue of which is attributed to Karl Klingemann) shows undeniable weaknesses – the climax of the action, Basilio's feigned death, is not set to music at all – to which the opera's failure can be attributed.

The Liederspiel *Heimkehr aus der Fremde* op.89 (1829) was written in the simplest of musical styles and remains unrelated to Mendelssohn's work as a whole. Among further opera plans, a work based on Shakespeare's *The Tempest* (in collaboration with Karl Immermann) took firm shape in 1831 and so in 1834 did *Pervonte* (from a Kotzebue comedy adapted by Klingemann); but neither achieved completion. Nor did plans to write an English opera with James Robinson Planché, the librettist of *Oberon*, come to fruition. The romanticization of opera subjects after 1830 and, most probably, Mendelssohn's premature breach with the operatic stage in Düsseldorf, did not permit his operatic and dramatic gifts to achieve their full development; his only late attempt at opera, *Die Loreley* (1847), amounted to no more than a fragment.

10. INCIDENTAL MUSIC. The overture and romance written in Leipzig in 1839 for Hugo's drama *Ruy Blas* were a consequence of the Berlin commissions. Hugo's tragedy treats of the rise and fall of Ruy Blas in the Spain of Charles II, although the main theme in the tragedy is less the political scene than a lackey–hero's love for his queen. At first Mendelssohn refused the commission (which reached him in March 1839) for an overture for a performance of the play in aid of the Leipzig theatre's pension fund. Instead he set the romance *Wozu der Vöglein Chöre belauschen fern und nah* for a chorus of six to eight sopranos and strings. He pleaded lack of time to write the overture, but the truth was that he found the play 'entirely repulsive, and beneath all dignity'. But eventually he became unable to endure the accusations that he was taking too much time

to compose the overture and despite the heavy burden imposed by his concert duties at the Gewandhaus he finished it in three days, with plenty of time for rehearsal. It was intended as an independent concert overture; its dynamics convey a sense of tension by juxtaposing sharp contrasts between the powerful, thrice-repeated wind chords of the introduction and the main theme with which they are contrasted. With its tragic content, it is numbered among the more significant of Mendelssohn's dramatic compositions.

The incidental music to Sophocles' *Antigone*, the result of a personal commission from Friedrich Wilhelm IV of Prussia, was undertaken in collaboration with the philologist August Boeckh and the writer Ludwig Tieck. Classical Greek tragedy is confined to a few actors who describe the action in brief dialogues and a chorus that observes and interprets the events; the ancients used music as a symbol of contemplation. Mendelssohn set the choruses with all the modern musical resources at his command, yet in conformity with the ancient Greek manner (i.e. closely observing the metrical rules of the poetry). For this purpose he followed the precedent of Gluck's operas. The philologist Jacob Christian Donner's translation was chosen as a basis for the adaptation. While this attempt did not escape criticism in philological circles, its aim of popularizing classical Greek tragedy in Berlin was completely successful.

Mendelssohn's most popular work is rightly held to be the overture and incidental music to Shakespeare's *A Midsummer Night's Dream*. He had already written the overture at the age of 17, strongly influenced by Shakespeare's plays in the translations of Schlegel, which he had come to know as a boy through readings or performances in his family home. 17 years later, in 1843, he composed incidental music to the play, 13 numbers in all, as one of the commissions from Friedrich Wilhelm IV; in doing so, he relied to a considerable extent on motifs from the overture. The correspondence of the thematic material in the overture with the various dramatic levels of Shakespeare's play is made clear by verbal correspondences within the incidental music. The following dramatic levels may be identified: (*a*) the figures of popular legend Oberon and Titania, together with (*b*) their subordinate spirits, elves and fairies; (*c*) the realistic dramatic level of the classical pairs of lovers Theseus–Hyppolita (the nobility) and Lysander–Hermia and Demetrius–Helena (the gentry), which is shown as a different world in which the dynamics of decisive complications and conflicts is set in motion; and, as an amusing counterpoint to this level, (*d*) the amateur dramatics of the artisans. In the incidental music Mendelssohn used several themes from his overture as leitmotifs for the dramatic levels. Thus he linked the introductory chords of the overture (ex.1) with the entry of Oberon and Titania in the finale of the incidental music, while the ensuing themes in smaller rhythmic units and played by the upper strings (ex.2)

Ex.1 *A Midsummer Night's Dream*, overture

Ex.2 ibid

are allotted to the song of the spirits, elves and fairies. A third thematic complex of the overture defines the realistic level of the drama, although only the hunting motif (ex.3) is quoted literally in the incidental music (no.8). Variants of other motifs, however, are easily detectable and are invariably associated with the middle dramatic levels. The main theme of the Wedding March, for example, can be understood as a variant of ex.4, while the chromatically falling line of ex.5a finds its application at least as an allusion in the thematic material of no.5, where it is associated with Hermia's renunciation (ex.5b). The markedly slower variant of ex.4 in the coda

Ex.3 ibid

Ex.4 ibid

Ex.5
(a) Overture

(b) No. 5 (Intermezzo)

of the overture, which has often been compared with the theme of the Mermaid's Song from *Oberon* (which Mendelssohn could not have known at the time he composed the overture), is used in the finale of the incidental music to unite the dramatic levels of the fairy world with the human world. The use of the theme given in ex.6, with its characteristic falling 9th (Bottom's 'hee-haw'), is entirely unequivocal; it appears in *A Dance of Clowns* (no.11), the dance of the artisan mummers.

These themes and their associated motifs in the exposition of the overture provide a basis for the transpar-

Ex.6 Overture

ent clarity of the twofold form and structure of the incidental music. The individual themes are changed with each new presentation, transposed to other keys, varied harmonically or contrapuntally, and this musical variability is the essential dynamic element of the work. In its beauty and simplicity it demonstrates Mendelssohn's principles of composition more clearly, perhaps, than any other of his compositions: lucidity in the coordination of intelligible themes, the classic unity of form and structure based on a free use of Classical models, and the connection between music and great poetry, a context in which Mendelssohn's dramatic gifts again become apparent in the construction and interweaving of thematic material.

11. ORATORIOS. In Mendelssohn's oratorios the musical inspiration is derived in great part from those of Handel, and content derives from his own code of ethics. The relevance of *St Paul* as an allegory of Mendelssohn's own family history and as a profession of his own religious faith may have been the deciding factors in his choice of subject. The idea of writing an oratorio on the story of the apostle began to mature during his stay in Paris early in 1832, but the plan could not be carried out until after he had made his intensive study of Handel's oratorios in Düsseldorf.

Mendelssohn composed *St Paul* between early 1834 and the spring of 1836. The dramatic tension of the subject is matched musically primarily by the inclusion of large-scale choruses. These are allotted partly to the blind rage of the adherents of the old idolatries and partly to the victorious followers of the new faith. In its attack on intolerance and fanaticism the work proclaims a central doctrine of that faith, 'How lovely are the messengers that preach us the gospel of peace!', which Mendelssohn symbolically set as a spacious choral fugue. He matched the symbolic content of individual situations by distinct but easily comprehensible musical symbols. For example, the descriptive passages treated as recitative are assigned to various voices, and are thus wholly depersonalized, a procedure unthinkable in Bach but frequent in Handel. Similarly, the voice of God is presented impersonally, by four women's voices. Mendelssohn drew freely on Handelian models; the overture is based on the chorale *Wachet auf, ruft uns die Stimme*, and the same theme, treated as a powerful choral movement, dominates the central part of the oratorio. Dramatic choruses, contemplative arias, narrative recitative passages alternate with one another. At pauses in the action, Mendelssohn inserted chorales with simple accompaniments, after the model of Bach's Passions and cantatas.

In summer 1844, after the years of dissension in Berlin (and doubtless motivated by them), Mendelssohn was again seized by the idea of writing an oratorio. This time his subject was the legend of the prophet Elijah (*1 Kings* xvii–xix) and the world of the religious dissension in Israel and Judaea over the divinities Jehovah and Baal. He had written to his librettist Julius Schubring on the subject six years earlier, in a letter of 2 November 1838:

In fact I imagined Elijah as a real prophet through and through, of the kind we could really do with today: strong, zealous and, yes, even badtempered, angry and brooding – in contrast to the riff-raff, whether of the court or of the people, and indeed in contrast to almost the whole world – and yet borne aloft as if on angels' wings.

The work begins with a brief prologue announcing

the prophecy of drought and the advent of Elijah. Then follows the overture, which begins with the sonorities of lower strings and rises to the brilliance of the upper strings and wind, epitomizing the musical symbolism of the work as a whole. A chorus and a duet, a recitative and an aria followed by a second chorus testify to the people's alarm about the onset of drought and the approach of famine. The excitement of these events is contrasted with the restrained musical evocation of the isolated prophet. The dramatic musical climax of the first part of the oratorio is set on Mount Carmel; the firmness of purpose in Elijah's bass aria is set off against the despairing cries of the chorus, 'Hear and answer, Baal'. The leading part in the action, however, is played by the chorus, which embodies the people just as in Handel's oratorios. Here it provides the symbolism for the climax of this part of the work ('The fire descends'). The second part, containing the indictment, escape and ascension of the prophet, unfolds no less dramatically. There are programmatic elements in the presentation of the tempest, the ocean, the earthquake and the fire during Elijah's sojourn on Mount Horeb. The oratorio ends with the sound of choruses in dramatic triumph.

12. OTHER VOCAL WORKS. The cantatas include occasional works – commissioned pieces and festival music – as well as works written independently of commissions and psalm settings for liturgical use. Significant among the commissioned works is the cantata *Begrüssung*, a festival piece composed for the assembly of natural scientists convened in Berlin in 1828 by Alexander von Humboldt, to whom the work is dedicated. The text, which celebrates Man's conquest of the forces of nature, is by Ludwig Rellstab.

*Die erste Walpurgisnacht* op.60, based on one of the preliminary studies for *Faust*, is an outstanding cantata.

6. *Frontispiece* (*second title*) *to the first edition of the full score of 'Elijah', published by Simrock in 1847*

Its theme is the old folk custom of greeting May and springtime. In his reply to Mendelssohn's announcement of his intention to set the poem, Goethe observed:

This poem is in a very real sense highly symbolic in its intention. For it must repeatedly happen in the course of world history that something old, established, tested, and reassuring is probed, harassed and oppressed by the emergence of new ideas and if not destroyed is at least entirely hemmed in and immobilized. The Middle Ages, when hatred could and did evoke such reactions, are here effectively epitomized, and a joyful serene enthusiasm flares out once more in all its pristine fire and brightness.

Mendelssohn was wholly faithful to Goethe's interpretation; he set the two basic ideas of the work by contrasting musical means. The spring festival is presented nobly and with stateliness; but the work as a whole is intensified to a pitch of Bacchantic frenzy in the scene depicting the uproar of the simulated witch-dances that drive away the dogmatic and prejudiced adversaries whose inflexibility threatens their old ways of life. The cantata was composed in 1831 and revised in 1843. Berlioz, who heard the revised version, said in his memoirs:

I was at once quite astounded by the quality of the voices, the responsiveness of the singers, and above all by the grandeur of the work. . . . One must hear Mendelssohn's music to realize what scope the poem offers a skilful composer. He has made admirable use of his opportunities. The score is of impeccable clarity, notwithstanding the complexity of the writing. Voices and instruments are completely integrated, and interwoven in an apparent confusion which is the perfection of art.

In comparison with the splendid achievement of this highly dramatic work, the settings of psalms for liturgical use show a decline in musical quality. In form and structure they recall Bach's cantatas, but without attaining the dramatic effect of their antecedents. In the Leipzig psalm settings, on the other hand, Mendelssohn was able to extract a rich variety of form and expression from the genre. While Psalm cxiv op.51 is laid out as a through-composed work for double chorus, the other cantatas are framed by opening and final choruses and are mainly dominated by solo voices. The cantatas of opp.78 and 91 were written for the Berlin Cathedral choir, and of necessity were scored for restricted forces. This hampered Mendelssohn and eventually led to disputes with Berlin theologians; the use of the harp in op.91 caused a quarrel because it was a profane instrument.

Among Mendelssohn's best-loved church music is his setting of Psalm c. Occasional pieces such as the early *Magnificat* written for the Berlin Singakademie (1822), the *Te Deum* (1826) or the *Lauda Sion* (1846) are, however, among his less significant works. Likewise, the secular 'Dürer' Cantata (1828) and the festival chorus *An die Künstler* op.68 (1846) are relatively unimportant.

The often-heard reproach that Mendelssohn was a sentimental Romantic and insipid artist usually derives from misinterpretation of the stylistic resources of his choral songs. Barely half his works in this genre were intended for publication, and were only for social purposes; without exception they were occasional pieces written to grace the social gatherings of choral singers after taxing oratorio performances. The singers went for long walks together and, while resting, sang these choral songs 'in the open air', according to the sub-title of the cycle op.41. A few were commissioned for almanacs or special festivals. At all stages of his life Mendelssohn had occasion to write short community songs, whether in Berlin for the Singakademie, for the participants in the Lower Rhine Music Festival or for the choral singers who helped to give the Leipzig concerts.

Among the finest examples is the setting of Goethe's *Frühzeitiger Frühling*, with its unobtrusive humming of bees in the middle section, and *Die Nachtigall*, with its heartfelt folksong style and magical sonorities. The settings of Eichendorff include the warm *Abschied vom Wald* and the ingenious and fiery *Jagdlied*. The choral songs were popular throughout the composer's lifetime, and have lost none of their power to delight; they cannot be considered in the context of the Romantic song cycle, nor should they be, in the words of Ernst Wolff, 'transplanted to the concert hall, where they are like wild flowers in a hot-house'.

Even as a child Mendelssohn turned to the form of art song, but he was 18 before he published his first set of songs, op.8. These are a crystallization of his carefree boyhood years among his friends in the talented Berlin circle. The main literary inspiration in those years came from Shakespeare and Goethe. The masterly style of the setting of Hölty's *Hexenlied* is akin to that of *Die erste Walpurgisnacht* and also the mood of the Octet. Mendelssohn's art songs were not originally intended for the large concert hall but for the small circle of intimate music-making, as found in the family, among friends and in middle-class drawing-rooms in the towns where he was professionally active – Berlin, Düsseldorf and Leipzig; they were the result of special suggestions or occasions. If the op.9 set (1830) remains all too evidently the reflection of personal experience, that is, the emotional expression of young love (no.1, *Frage*, later became a theme of the String Quartet op.13), Mendelssohn strove in his next set (op.19a) to create something more than a melodic line with a piano accompaniment; he attempted to enhance the meaning of the poem through the music. The piano accompaniments were themselves made into self-contained character-pieces, a development that led to the *Lied ohne Worte* for solo piano. This connection was underlined by Mendelssohn himself in the dual function of op.19 as lieder or as piano pieces.

Mendelssohn's lieder differ widely in form. Together with virtuoso character-pieces there are simple popular melodies. Among the lyrics are pieces from folksong collections like the *Minnelied* op.34 no.1. Many have even become popular songs in their own right (e.g. *Gruss* op.19a no.5, to words by Heine). Mendelssohn favoured the strophic song, and in composing musical material appropriate to the content he shaped the melodic line as well as fashioning a characteristic instrumental accompaniment; the demand for singability was also a factor. In these features Mendelssohn showed a kinship with his predecessors in the Berlin lieder school – Reichardt, J. A. P. Schulz, Zelter and Klein – but at the same time his towering superiority.

13. SYMPHONIES. Mendelssohn wrote 13 early symphonies for string orchestra (no.8 in D also exists in a version with wind) and five symphonies for full orchestra, three of which were published in his lifetime (the Italian Symphony and the Reformation Symphony were first published in the Gesamtausgabe). The early sinfonias demonstrate the composer's development and his links with tradition perhaps better than any other genre. Those composed as exercises for his teacher Zelter were numbered 1–10; two of them and an isolated movement were left unnumbered but are now commonly referred to as 11–13. The first six are the work of a 12-year-old and clearly show the influence of the Viennese Classical style; the first movements of nos.3 and 4 bear the contrapuntal imprint of Bach and Handel.

The influences of both Bach and Handel, and of the Viennese Classics, were even more clearly perceptible in the later string symphonies, which already show traces of a personal style combined with Classical and pre-Classical traits. The emphasis on counterpoint in the first movement of no.7 is continued in the introduction to no.8, whose second theme is constructed within the limitations of a fugue subject. The addition here of wind instruments indicated the completion of Mendelssohn's first real symphony, but he continued to experiment with string symphony writing. No.9 in C represents a splendid achievement in the mastery of the Classical style. A sprightly virtuoso development of a simple and tuneful first theme determines the course of the first movement (Mozartian antecedents are unmistakable here), and the fairy-like atmosphere of the overture to *A Midsummer Night's Dream* is anticipated in the scherzo and the finale; the trio of the scherzo is an elaboration of a Swiss folksong. In the scherzo of no.11 another Swiss folksong *Bin alben e wärti Tächter gsi* is used, as a memento of the family's summer holiday in Switzerland. No.12 offers a masterly confrontation with the principles of fugue; a complex, chromatically descending fugue subject is used as a means of developing a symphonic form from the contrapuntal stimulus of Bach via the polyphonic world of Mozart to a personal mode of expression. In the symphonic movement in C minor (now referred to as no.13) Mendelssohn similarly sought to unite triple fugue with the technique of symphonic development. This last symphonic study was immediately followed by Mendelssohn's first published symphony, op.11 in C minor (1824). In form, structure and melodic invention it is akin to the attempts of the previous year, and its autograph, owned by the London Philharmonic Society (to which the work was dedicated), bears the number 13, thereby linking it to the earlier creative period of the string symphonies.

It is perhaps surprising that some five years elapsed before Mendelssohn, who had meanwhile been strongly influenced by Hegel's ideas, continued his symphonic work. This time he turned to a programmatic vein and composed a work for the celebrations planned in remembrance of the Reformation and commemorating the Augsburg Confession. In the event, the celebrations planned for Berlin did not take place, but the stimulus gave Mendelssohn the occasion to formulate the concept of the Reformation in symphonic terms. Noble in character, the symphony begins with a contrapuntal treatment of the psalmodic incipit D–E–G–F♯, which is also a transposition of the main motif of the finale of Mozart's 'Jupiter' Symphony, and leads to a statement of the so-called Dresden Amen. Powerful trumpet motifs usher in the main theme of the Allegro con fuoco (ex.7), which recalls the opening of Haydn's 'London' Symphony; the movement is based on a contrast of exultation and suffering. In the second movement the cheerful strains of band music, which have been said to be an expression of the simple and powerful feelings of joy, belong to an entirely different world, one suggesting

Ex.7 Reformation Symphony, 1st movt

7. Autograph MS of the opening of Mendelssohn's 'Italian Symphony', first performed in London, 13 March 1833 (D-Bds Mendelssohn 27)

the countryside and its people. After the sustained recitative movement the finale introduces a set of variations, laid out on broad lines, on Luther's confessional chorale *Ein feste Burg ist unser Gott*. Thus the music is linked with the idea behind the work. The closing movement is also thematically related to the opening of the symphony by the recurrence of the Dresden Amen.

The Italian Symphony was completed in Berlin after Mendelssohn's return from Italy in winter 1832. It was successfully first performed in London on 13 March 1833 and has remained Mendelssohn's most popular symphony. According to his own account, a wide range and variety of impressions were concentrated in it, not only from art and nature but also from the realm of personal experience and contact with the vitality of the Italian people. The guiding main theme of the opening Allegro is energetic and concise; two more themes add variety to the musical continuity of the first without detracting from its clarity. The Andante breathes a restrained quietude and nobility; according to Moscheles the composer used the theme of a Czech pilgrim song in this movement. The third movement (Con moto moderato) may have been inspired by his study of Goethe's *Lilis Park*, a humorous poem written for Goethe's friend Lili Schönemann, for he wrote to Fanny on 16 November 1830: 'I want to turn *Lilis Park* into a scherzo for a symphony'. A Neapolitan saltarello forms the basis of the Presto finale.

The *Lobgesang* op.52 (1840) was written for the Leipzig celebrations of the 400th anniversary of the invention of printing. In its external form the work bears a general resemblance to Beethoven's Ninth Symphony. The instrumental opening consists of three movements played without a break and the opening movement is ceremonial in character, with dotted rhythms in the manner of Handel. The folksong-like theme of the Allegretto breathes relaxed enjoyment. It is followed by a variation movement also with songlike melody (Andante religioso) that concludes the instrumental section, constituting about one third of the work. The rest is a great cantata for solo voices, chorus and orchestra and ends triumphantly with a spacious choral fugue.

The first inspiration for the Scottish Symphony op.56 dates back to 1829, the year of Mendelssohn's first visit to England. His letter of 30 July 1829 from Edinburgh suggests a musical transformation of historical events (he had visited Holyrood, the palace of Mary Queen of Scots). His mood of resignation soon gave way to optimism, and he laid the work aside as new plans for composition took shape; it was not until after the disappointments of 1841 that his mood predisposed him to resume work on the score. This symphony extends far beyond the programmatic poetic description of landscape and allowed Mendelssohn to attain artistic freedom on a number of emotional levels. It is noteworthy that he added to the tempo indications further directions that stress the meaningful and conceptual side of the work and make his intentions clear, as follows:

| Tempo indication | Character indications |
|---|---|
| I. Andante con moto — | Introduction |
| Allegro un poco agitato — | Allegro agitato |
| Assai animato | |
| II. Vivace ma non troppo | Scherzo assai vivace |
| III. Adagio | Adagio cantabile |
| IV. Allegro vivacissimo | Allegro guerriero |
| | Finale maestoso |

The introduction to the first movement is restrained and resigned; the main theme in its Allegro section treats the opening idea in variation style. Dynamic intensifications lead to gripping dramatic scenes in which the experience of nature (depiction of the storm and the sea) mingle with the world of emotions. The mood now declines to melancholy, now builds up a resistance to it, until these conflicts finally give way to the elegiac opening theme. In complete contrast, the cheerful dance-like character of the scherzo is derived from Scottish folk idioms. The third movement is again imprinted with resignation and yearning, strongly prophetic of Brahms. The militant mood of the last movement is new and surprising in Mendelssohn; its purposeful energy, interspersed with folktunes, finally gives way to the sombre opening idea of the introduction, treated once again in variation style, but, released from its elegiac mood, ultimately brought to a triumphant close. In its structure, too, the Scottish Symphony stands apart from the earlier symphonic works, with the individual movements joined to one another much as in the piano concertos and the Violin Concerto op.64. Thus one of Mendelssohn's least resolved instrumental works may at the same time be regarded as the summit of his achievements as a symphonist.

14. OVERTURES. Like his symphonies, Mendelssohn's overtures emphasize the programmatic and may be regarded basically as one-movement symphonic poems. The main works in the genre were preceded by the Overture for wind instruments op.24 (1824), written for the court orchestra of Bad Doberan near Rostock, and the Trumpet Overture op.101 (1826), so called because of its introductory fanfares; both are in C. In the overture to *A Midsummer Night's Dream* op.21, word-painting had progressed to the point where ideas could be identified with specific musical motifs (see also §10 above).

The overture *Meeresstille und glückliche Fahrt* op.27 is of central importance, representing the young composer's breakthrough from a crisis in his development. The work is based on two poems by Goethe that describe the external events of nature, the first depicting the obstinate stillness of the sea during a lull, the second the rushing power of waves in motion. As well as this description of natural forces the poems contain allegorical allusion to human behaviour in general: they contrast the unremitting and despairing inertia of the mere observer with the life-enhancing dynamism of the active participant. Mendelssohn depicted the content of the poems in two musically contrasted halves.

A musical interpretation of an experience at sea also determines the course of the B minor overture *Die Hebriden*. Four years later Mendelssohn composed the overture *Die schöne Melusine* op.32. Grillparzer had adapted the Romantic legend of the mermaid Melusine as an opera subject for Beethoven, who eventually decided against setting it. After Beethoven's death Conradin Kreutzer took up the libretto and set it as an opera commissioned by the Königstädtisches Theater in

Berlin. Mendelssohn saw a performance there in spring 1833. He disliked Kreutzer's work but expressed the wish to write his own overture based on the subject; in it he combined a penchant for depicting moods aroused by the sea with the expression of lovers' joy and sorrow, all within the broad framework of the legendary subject.

15. CONCERTOS. Mendelssohn's concerto writing covers all periods of his life; he wrote three concertos for the piano, two for two pianos, two for the violin and one for violin and piano. If the early concertos of 1822–3 are, like most of the string symphonies, akin to Viennese Classical models in their form, structure and thematic material, the two double piano concertos of 1823 and 1824 evince an amazing maturity.

Mendelssohn continued his series of larger-scale piano compositions with the Piano Concerto in G minor op.25 (1831); it was conceived completely in his head during the Italian journey, and set down on paper in three days in Munich, where it was first performed in 1832. Although inferior in content to the Italian Symphony, the concerto is planned economically and bears some resemblance to the fantasia form: the first two movements run together and the finale is improvisatory in style. Thus the piece goes beyond the conventional concerto form, a trend that Mendelssohn continued in the next two works in the genre. The Piano Concerto in D minor op.40, written during the honeymoon journey of summer 1837, is dominated by Mendelssohn's joyous emotions of that period and is relatively straightforward; Schumann called it a 'fleeting, carefree gift'. To enhance the virtuoso element in the work, Mendelssohn used techniques introduced by Thalberg, such as transferring the melody to an inner part and decorating it with figurations in both hands.

The summit of Mendelssohn's concerto writing is undoubtedly the Violin Concerto in E minor op.64, which he composed while on a recuperative holiday in Soden near Frankfurt am Main in September 1844. A completely carefree mood permeates the work. The passionately sustained first movement, in sonata form, takes its melodic substance from its urgent initial impulse (ex.8) and a more reflective idea. A transitional section

Ex.8 Violin Concerto, 1st movt, main theme
Allegro molto appassionato

joins the first movement to a songlike Andante. In the last movement Mendelssohn demonstrated the virtuoso possibilities of violin technique, at the same time recalling the atmosphere of *A Midsummer Night's Dream*. But the most significant features of the concerto are formal innovations. Not only are the first two movements joined, but the introduction to the finale (ex.9), beginning on the minor subdominant, recalls the opening theme of the first movement in addition to providing an ingenious link with the finale. The first movement, too, has important formal innovations, notably in the omission of the orchestral exposition and in the placing of the cadenza at the end of the develop-

*8. Autograph MS of the opening of the Scherzo from Mendelssohn's Octet in E♭ op.20, composed 1825 (US-Wc)*

ment section and the beginning of the recapitulation. One of the most lyrical of Mendelssohn's instrumental compositions, this concerto stands beside those of Beethoven and Brahms as one of the most significant works in the genre.

Ex.9 Violin Concerto, introduction to finale

16. CHAMBER AND SOLO INSTRUMENTAL MUSIC. Like his solo works for individual instruments, Mendelssohn's chamber music plays a relatively small part in his output; yet its importance for his development should not be underrated. Even as a boy he set himself impressive tasks. Next to the remarkable Sextet in D op.110 (1824) comes the outstanding Octet in E♭ op.20 for strings (1825), written for the 23rd birthday of the violinist Eduard Rietz, one of the closest friends of Mendelssohn's family circle. After five years' development of his compositional technique Mendelssohn created his own musical idiom in the Octet. The first movement begins with a wide-ranging theme that rises from the depths and soars up to radiant heights, followed by a simpler theme that maintains the forward impulse. The independent character of the movement, marked 'con fuoco', is underlined by its rhythm and dynamics. This contrasts with the simple melody of the Andante, whose folksong-like quality is soon quickened in an enlivened variation form and then immersed in a wonderful stream of animated flowing polyphony. The spirit of the 'Walpurgisnacht Scherzo', as the third movement is sometimes known, is shared and enhanced by the finale with its eight-part fugato, in which the theme of the scherzo returns, interacting with the themes of the finale to bring the work to its Bacchantic close.

Like the string quintets op.18 and op.87, Mendelssohn's string quartets have until recently been unjustifiably neglected. One could say that in the early symphonies he was already trying out string quartet ideas, admittedly with more emphasis on orchestral sound than on the independence of the four parts; his development in quartet writing in the Haydnesque sense, however, was comparatively late. The Quartet op.13 (1827) suggests a reflection of the emotions of an early love affair; the piece develops its thematic substance from a love-song with the text: 'Is it true that you are waiting for me in the arbour by the vine-clad wall?'. The Quartet in E♭ op.12 (1829), on the other hand, suggests a musical confrontation with Beethoven. The initial idea suggests the basic contours (and an inversion) of the themes of Beethoven's 'Harp' Quartet, also in E♭, and these permeate the first movement.

The Three Quartets op.44 (1837–8) are Mendelssohn's masterpieces in the genre, and the second, in E minor, has claims to be considered the best. Its elegiac opening theme gives the first movement its care-free yet noble character; the thematic material is distributed among all four parts, in a filigree technique that Mendelssohn also acquired from Beethoven's quartet style. The short rhythmic units of the scherzo recall the realm of elves and fairies in the works of the early period, particularly the overture to *A Midsummer Night's Dream*. After a songlike Andante comes a playfully passionate finale with many formal contrasts. In Mendelssohn's last quartet, in F minor, grief for his sister Fanny is musically expressed as a pessimistic departure from Classical form. Painful despair, wild yearning, dramatic urgency and spectral unrest dominate the thematic ideas, which suggest no optimistic solution to the problems of the composer, who was himself not far from death.

The piano quartets opp.1–3, all written in childhood, were Mendelssohn's first published works and are comparable to Beethoven's first publication, the Three Piano Trios op.1. The third quartet, in B minor, which decided Mendelssohn's choice of career, is outstanding among the early works, and is dedicated to Goethe. Together with the Octet, the two late piano trios op.49 in D minor and op.66 in C minor represent the peaks of Mendelssohn's achievement in chamber music. Schumann made a striking comment in his discussion of op.49: 'Mendelssohn is the Mozart of the 19th century, the most illuminating of musicians, who sees more clearly than others through the contradictions of our era and is the first to reconcile them'.

Mendelssohn's solo instrumental works are dominated by piano pieces. Apart from the three large-scale sonatas, a fantasia and a variation set, he cultivated the smaller, more intimate form, derived from the song and produced in profusion from 1830 onwards under the title *Lieder ohne Worte*. Six cycles of these partly lyric, partly virtuoso pieces were published in his lifetime; two were published posthumously. He also wrote virtuoso works, fully exploring the artistic possibilities of the instrument in free form and characterization. The outstanding examples of these are the F♯ minor Fantasia op.28, to which he gave the title 'Sonate écossaise', and the *Variations sérieuses* in D minor op.54, probably his most successful solo piano work. Building on an ingeniously constructed theme that offers a wide range of harmonic interpretations, he used every device of virtuoso thematic transformation.

Though primarily a pianist, Mendelssohn was also an excellent violinist and organist and wrote equally gratefully for these instruments. The Violin Sonata op.4 (1825) is akin to the early piano quartets in its form and structure though it is certainly overshadowed by the F major Violin Sonata of 1838, which is an immensely virtuoso work, especially the last movement. It is interesting that only one of Mendelssohn's early works belongs to this genre, an F major sonata for the violin written in 1820 as an exercise. The Viola Sonata and the two cello sonatas are also typical of their genres. Lyricism prevails in the earlier cello sonata, op.45 in B♭ (1838). The later sonata, op.58 in D (1843), was written for Paul Mendelssohn and manifests spirited passion and brilliant sonorous effects; it was conceived during the tense period between Mendelssohn's artistic disappointments in Berlin and the wide-ranging opportunities offered in Leipzig (the conservatory was inaugurated in 1843) and, like the Scottish Symphony, communicates a concentrated impression of the dramatic tensions and contradictions through which he lived during those years.

Mendelssohn departed from the Classical tradition in his piano writing, but in his organ Preludes and Fugues op.37 (1837) and the noteworthy organ sonatas op.65 (1844–5) he reverted to the contrapuntal style of Bach, as he did also in the numerous early works for organ, mostly fugal exercises.

17. THE HERITAGE. For nearly a generation immediately after his death, Mendelssohn's formative influence and popularity continued as an active force in the 19th century. But the memorial tributes of friends and relatives were hardly suited to the process of an objective, scientific and lasting assessment. The 41-volume Gesamtausgabe prepared by Julius Rietz was the most important achievement in Mendelssohn scholarship in the 19th century; but the short time it took to produce (it appeared in its entirety between 1874 and 1877) gives rise to doubts about its textual reliability. The anti-semitic trends that were already perceptible in the middle of the 19th century had a powerfully inhibiting effect on the spread of Mendelssohn's music, and they proliferated in the German writings of the generation that followed Wagner. The main musical factor that inhibited Mendelssohn's popularity was an enhanced Romanticism in performance, with considerable broadening of tempos and fluctuations in phrasing, especially at cadences. This led to interpretations of Mendelssohn's music that tended towards the sentimental, and an exaggeration of chromatic melody and harmony. A misunderstanding of his music, attributable to this sentimentalizing, permeated the music criticism in the later part of the 19th century. This was especially widespread at the turn of the century (in the writings of Riemann, for example) and has still not been wholly overcome. But many eminent musicians were the most enthusiastic admirers and defenders of Mendelssohn, among them Bülow, Brahms and Reger. Ernst Wolff's documentary biography (1906), which is still unsurpassed, was written 'in order to reaffirm decisively Mendelssohn's greatness and originality, in opposition to those superficial and vindictive judgments to which he . . . is still exposed'.

The racial persecutions of the Fascist era led to the destruction of the Mendelssohn memorial in Leipzig in 1936 and the complete suppression of his music everywhere within Hitler's sphere of influence. An intensification of Mendelssohn studies, which had been recommended by Alfred Einstein in his book *Greatness in Music* as early as 1941, has led to a reappraisal. After World War II there were three commemorative years (1947, 1959 and 1972) with numerous exhibitions that led to a further consideration of Mendelssohn's work and personality. Rediscovery and publication of the early works in the new Leipzig edition has measurably increased the music available for performance and has influenced revivals, as well as more Classically orientated interpretations, of his forgotten mature works. Most significantly, these have enabled a truer, more informed assessment to be made of Mendelssohn's development as an accomplished composer.

## WORKS

Editions: *F. Mendelssohn-Bartholdy: Werke: kritisch durchgesehene Ausgabe*, ed. J. Rietz (Leipzig, 1874–7) [R]
*Leipziger Ausgabe der Werke Felix Mendelssohn Bartholdys*, ed. Internationale Felix-Mendelssohn-Gesellschaft (Leipzig, 1960–) [L]

*(printed works published in Leipzig unless otherwise stated)*

\* – autograph

STAGE

| op. | Title | Genre, Text | Completion | Production | Publication or MS | Edition |
|---|---|---|---|---|---|---|
| — | Ich, J. Mendelssohn . . . | Lustspiel, 3, Mendelssohn | 1820 | — | *D-Bds | — |
| — | Die Soldatenliebschaft | comic opera, 1, J. L. Casper | 1820 | Wittenberg, 28 April 1962 | *Bds | — |
| — | Die beiden Pädagogen | Singspiel, 1, Casper, after Scribe | 1821 | Berlin, 27 May 1962 | L | L v/1 |
| — | Die wandernden Komödianten | comic opera, 1, dialogue lost | 1822 | — | *Bds | — |
| — | Der Onkel aus Boston oder Die beiden Neffen | comic opera, 3, dialogue lost | 1823 | Berlin, 3 Feb 1824 | *Bds | — |
| 10 | Die Hochzeit des Camacho | opera, 2, K. Klingemann, after Cervantes: Don Quixote (dialogue lost) | 10 Aug 1825 | Berlin, 29 April 1827 | vocal score, 1829 | R xv/7 |
| 89 | Die Heimkehr aus der Fremde | Liederspiel, 1, Klingemann | 1829 | Berlin, 26 Dec 1829 | n.d. | R xv/8 |
| — | Der standhafte Prinz | incidental music, Calderón | 18 March 1833 | Düsseldorf, ?1833 | *Bds | — |
| — | Trala. A frischer Bua bin i | Schnadahüpferl | 9 Dec 1833 | — | *Bds | — |
| — | Ruy Blas: Romance (ov.: see orchestral works, op.95) | incidental music, V. Hugo | 8 March 1839 | — | R | R xviii |
| 55 | Antigone | incidental music, Sophocles | 10 Oct 1841 | Potsdam, 28 Oct 1841 | 1841 | R xv/1 |
| 61 | A Midsummer Night's Dream (ov.: see orchestral works, op.21) | incidental music, Shakespeare | 1842 | Potsdam, 14 Oct 1843 | 1842 | R xv/4 |
| 93 | Oedipus at Colonos | incidental music, Sophocles | 25 Feb 1845 | Potsdam, 1 Nov 1845 | n.d. | R xv/3 |
| 74 | Athalie | incidental music, Racine | 12 Nov 1845 | Berlin-Charlottenburg, 1 Dec 1845 | n.d. | R xv/2 |
| 98 | Loreley, frag. (finale of Act 1 and Vintners' Chorus) | opera, 3, E. Geibel | 1847 | Birmingham, 8 Sept 1852 | R | R xv/9 |

ORATORIOS

| op. | Title | Text | Completion | Performance | Publication | Edition |
|-----|-------|------|-----------|-------------|-------------|---------|
| 36 | St Paul (Paulus) | J. Schubring, after the *Acts of the Apostles* | 18 April 1836 | Düsseldorf, 22 May 1836 | Bonn, 1836 | R xiii/1 |
| 70 | Elijah (Elias) | Schubring, after *1 Kings* xvii–xix | 11 Aug 1846 | Birmingham, 26 Aug 1846 | Bonn, 1847 | R xiii/2 |
| 97 | Christus, inc. | — | — | — | R | R xiii/3 |

ORCHESTRAL

op.
— Sinfonia no.1, C, str, 1821; L i/1
— Sinfonia no.2, D, str, 1821; L i/1
— Sinfonia no.3, e, str, 1821; L i/1
— Sinfonia no.4, c, str, 5 Sept 1821; L i/1
— Sinfonia no.5, B♭, str, 15 Sept 1821; L i/1
— Sinfonia no.6, E♭, str, aut. 1821; L i/1
— Sinfonia no.7, d, str, ?1821–2; L i/1
— Sinfonia no.8, D, str, 27 Nov 1822, arr. orch, 30 Nov 1822; L i/2
— Violin Concerto, d, str, 1822, ed. Y. Menuhin (New York, 1952); L ii/6
— Piano Concerto, a, str, 1822, *Bds
— Sinfonia no.9, C, str, 12 March 1823; L i/3
— Concerto, d, vn, pf, str, 6 May 1823; L ii
— Sinfonia no.10, b, str, 18 May 1823; L i/3
— Sinfonia no.11, F, str, 12 July 1823; L i/3
— Sinfonia no.12, g, str, 17 Sept 1823; L i/3
— Concerto, E, 2 pf, 17 Oct 1823, perf. Berlin, 14 Nov 1824, edn. (Leipzig, 1960); L ii/4
— Sinfonia no.13, c, str, 1 movt only, 29 Dec 1823; L i/3
11 Symphony no.1, c, 31 March 1824 (Berlin, 1828); R i
— Concerto, A♭, 2 pf, 12 Nov 1824, perf. Stettin, 20 Feb 1827, edn. (Leipzig, 1961); L ii/5
24 Overture for wind instruments, C, 1824 (Bonn, 1832); R vii
22 Capriccio brillant, b, pf, ?1825–6 (1831); R viii
101 Overture ('Trumpet Ov.'), C, 4 May 1826, rev. 10 April 1833 (n.d.); R ii
21 Ein Sommernachtstraum, ov., after Shakespeare: A Midsummer Night's Dream, 6 Aug 1826, perf. Stettin, 29 April 1827 (1830); R ii
27 Meeresstille und glückliche Fahrt, ov., after Goethe, 1828, perf. Berlin, 18 April 1828 (1833); R ii
26 Die Hebriden ('Fingals Höhle'), ov., 16 Dec 1830, rev. 20 June 1832 (1832), based on 1829 version entitled Die einsame Insel; R ii
25 Piano Concerto no.1, g, 1831 (1832); R viii
107 Symphony no.5 'Reformation', D, 1832, perf. Berlin, 1832 (1868); R i
90 Symphony no.4 'Italian', A, 13 March 1833 (n.d.); R i
32 Die schöne Melusine, ov., after Grillparzer, 14 Nov 1833, perf. London, 7 April 1834 (1835); R ii
29 Rondo brillant, E♭, pf, 29 Jan 1834 (1835); R viii
103 Trauermarsch, a, wind, c8 May 1836 (1868); R vii
40 Piano Concerto no.2, d, 5 Aug 1837 (1838); R viii
43 Serenade and Allegro giocoso, b, pf, 11 April 1838 (Bonn, 1839); R viii
95 Ruy Blas, ov., after V. Hugo, March 1839, perf. Leipzig, March 1839 (n.d.); R ii
52 Symphony no.2 ('Lobgesang'), symphony-cantata, B♭, last movt with solo vv, chorus, org, perf. Leipzig, 25 June 1840, rev. 27 Nov 1840 (1841); R vi/A2
108 March, D, April 1841, perf. Dresden, 1841 (1868); R iii
56 Symphony no.3 'Scottish', a, 20 Jan 1842, perf. Leipzig, 3 March 1842 (1843); R i
64 Violin Concerto, e, 16 Sept 1844, perf. Leipzig, 13 March 1845 (1845); R iv

CHAMBER

— Trio, c, vn, va, pf, 9 May 1820, *Bds
— Presto, F, vn, pf, 1820, *Bds
— Violin Sonata, F, 1820, *Bds
— Fifteen Fugues, str qt, spr. 1821, *Bds
— Piano Quartet, d, 1822, *Bds
1 Piano Quartet no.1, c, 18 Oct 1822 (Berlin, 1823); R ix
— String Quartet, E♭, 30 March 1823, edn. (Berlin, 1879)
2 Piano Quartet no.2, f, 3 Dec 1823 (Berlin, 1824); R ix
— Viola Sonata, c, 14 Feb 1824, edn. (Leipzig, 1966)
110 Sextet, D, vn, 2 va, vc, db, pf, May 1824 (n.d.); R ix
— Clarinet Sonata, E♭, 1824, *Bds
3 Piano Quartet no.3, b, 18 Jan 1825 (1825); R ix
4 Violin Sonata, f, 1825 (1825); R ix

20 Octet, E♭, 4 vn, 2 va, 2 vc, 1825 (1830); R v
18 Quintet no.1, A, 2 vn, 2 va, vc, 1826, rev. 1832 (Bonn, 1832); R v
13 String Quartet no.2, A, 26 Oct 1827 (1830); L iii/1
— Fugue, E♭, str qt, 1 Nov 1827, *Bds
81/4 Fugue, E♭, str qt, 1 Nov 1827 (1849); R vi
17 Variations concertantes, vc, pf, 30 Jan 1829 (Vienna, 1830); R ix
12 String Quartet no.1, E♭, 14 Sept 1829 (1829); R vi, L iii/1
— The Evening Bell, harp, pf, Nov 1829, pubd in *Musical Haunts in London* (London, 1830)
113 Concert Piece, F, cl, basset-hn, pf/orch, 19 Jan 1833, pf version (Offenbach, n.d.); R vii [pf version]
114 Concert Piece, d, cl, basset-hn, pf, Jan 1833 (Offenbach, n.d.); R vii
44 String Quartets nos.3–5 (1838): D, 24 July 1838, e, 18 June 1837, E♭, 6 Feb 1838; R vi, L iii/2
— Violin Sonata, F, 15 June 1838, ed. Y. Menuhin (New York, 1953)
45 Cello Sonata no.1, B♭, 13 Oct 1838 (1839); R ix
49 Piano Trio no.1, d, 23 Sept 1839 (1840); R ix
81/3 Capriccio, e, str qt, 5 July 1843 (1849); R vi
58 Cello Sonata no.2, D, 1843 (1844); R ix
87 Quintet, no.2, B♭, 8 July 1845 (n.d.); R v
66 Piano Trio no.2, c, 1845 (1845); R ix
109 Lied ohne Worte, D, vc, pf, ?1845 (n.d.); R ix
80 String Quartet no.6, f, Sept 1847 (1849); R vi
81/1 Andante, E, str qt, 1847 (1849); R vi
81/2 Scherzo, a, str qt, 1847 (1849); R vi

PIANO SOLO

— Andante, F, 1820, *Bds
— Piano piece, e, 1820, *Bds
— Two little pieces, 1820, *Bds: Andante, C, Presto, C
— Two little pieces, 1820, *Bds: Largo, d, untitled, f
— Five little pieces, 1820, *Bds: Allegro, C, Allegro, g, Andante, A, untitled, b, untitled, a
— Largo–Allegro, c, 1820, *Bds
— Recitativo ('Largo'), d, 1820, *Bds
— Sonata, f, 1820, *Bds
— Sonata, a, 12 May 1820, *Bds
— Presto, c, 1 July 1820, *Bds
— Sonata, e, 13 July 1820, *Bds
— Two studies, d, a, 28 Dec 1820, *Bds
— Allegro, a, 5 Jan 1821
— Study, C, 30 March 1821, *Bds
105 Sonata, g, 18 Aug 1821 (1868); R xi/3
— Largo–Allegro molto, c/C, ?1821–2, *Bds
— Three Fugues, d, d, b, ?1822, *Bds
— Allegro, d, 19 Feb 1823, *Bds
— Fantasia ('Adagio'), c, ?1823, *Bds
14 Rondo capriccioso, E, 1824 (Vienna, 1827); R xi/1
5 Capriccio, f♯, 23 July 1825 (Berlin, 1825); R xi/1
— Fugue, c♯, 5 Jan 1826, *Bds
6 Sonata, E, 22 March 1826 (1826); R xi/1
7 Sieben charakteristische Stücke, e, b, D, A, A, e, E (1827); R xi/1
15 Fantasia, E, on 'The Last Rose of Summer', 1827 (Vienna, 1833); R xi/1
106 Sonata, B♭, 31 May 1827 (1868); R xi/3
— Fugue, e, 16 June 1827, added to Prelude of 13 July 1841
— Scherzo, b, 12 June 1829, pubd in *Berliner allgemeine musikalische zeitung*, vi (1829)
16 Trois fantaisies ou caprices (Vienna, 1829): a, 4 Sept 1829, e, 13 Nov 1829, E, 5 Sept 1829; R xi/1
— Andante, A, 13 June 1830, *Bds
19 Lieder ohne Worte, i, orig. pubd as Melodies for the Pianoforte (London, 1830): E, a, 'Jägerlied', A, A, 14 Sept 1829, f♯, 'Venezianisches Gondellied', g, 16 Oct 1830; R xi/4
28 Fantasia ('Sonate écossaise'), f♯, 29 Jan 1833 (Bonn, 1834); R xi/1
30 Lieder ohne Worte, ii (Bonn, 1835): E♭, b♭, E, b, 30 Jan 1834, D, 12 Dec 1833, 'Venezianisches Gondellied', f♯; R xi/4

33      Three Caprices (1836): a, 9 April 1834, E, 12 Sept 1835, b♭, 25 July 1833; R xi/2
—       Scherzo a capriccio, f♯, ?1835–6, pubd in L'album des pianistes (Bonn, n.d.); R xi/1
—       Study, f, 13 March 1836, pubd in Moscheles and Fétis's Méthode des méthodes (Berlin, 1840); R xi/1
—       Andante, A♭, 27 June 1836, *Bds
—       Lied, f♯, 16 Oct 1836, *Bds, arr. 2vv, pf as Herbstlied op.63 no.4
—       Prelude, f, 13 Nov 1836, *Bds
104a    Three Preludes (1868): B♭, 9 Dec 1836, b, 12 Oct 1836, D, 27 Nov 1836; R xi/3
35      Six Preludes and Fugues (1837): e/E; D, prelude 8 Dec 1836; b, fugue 21 Dec 1832; A♭, fugue 6 Jan 1835; f, prelude 19 Nov 1836, fugue 3 Dec 1834; B♭, prelude 3 Jan 1837, fugue 27 Nov 1836; R xi/2
38      Lieder ohne Worte, iii (Bonn, 1837): E♭, c, E, A, a, 6 April 1837, 'Duetto', A♭, 27 June 1836; R xi/4
—       Gondellied ('Barcarole'), A, 5 Feb 1837 (Dresden, 1838); R xi/1
—       Lied ohne Worte, A, 22 April 1837, *Bds
118     Capriccio, E, 11 July 1837 (1872); R xi/3
117     Albumblatt ('Lied ohne Worte'), e, ?1837 (1872); R xi/3
—       Andante cantabile and Presto agitato, B, 22 June 1838, pubd in Musikalisches Album (1839); R xi/1
104b    Three Studies: b♭, 9 June 1836. F, 21 April 1834, a, ?1838; R xi/3
—       Lied ohne Worte, f♯, 5 April 1839
53      Lieder ohne Worte, iv (Bonn, 1841): A♭, E♭, g, 14 March 1839, F, 'Volkslied', a, 30 April 1841, A, 1 May 1841; R xi/4
—       Prelude and Fugue, e, pubd in Notre temps (Mainz, 1842): prelude 13 July 1841, added to fugue of 16 June 1827; R xi/3
54      Variations sérieuses, d, 4 June 1841 (Vienna, 1842); R xi/2
82      Variations, E♭, 25 July 1841 (1849); R xi/2
83      Variations, B♭, ?1841 (1850); R xi/2
72      Kinderstücke ('Christmas Pieces') (1847): G, 24 June 1842, E♭, G, D, g, F; R xi/2
—       Lied ohne Worte, D, 18 March 1843, *Bds
62      Lieder ohne Worte, v (Bonn, 1844): G, 12 Jan 1844, B♭, 29 July 1843, 'Trauermarsch', e, 16 March 1843, G, 'Venezianisches Gondellied', a, 'Frühlingslied', A, 1 June 1842; R xi/4
—       Lied ohne Worte ('Allegro marcato alla marcia'), d, 12 March 1844, *Bds
67      Lieder ohne Worte, vi (Bonn, 1845): E♭, 29 June 1843, f♯, 3 May 1845, B♭, 'Spinnerlied', C, 5 May 1845, b, 12 Jan 1844, E; R xi/4
85      Lieder ohne Worte, vii (Bonn, 1850): F, a, 9 June 1834, E♭, D, 6 May 1845, A, 7 May 1845, B♭, 1 May 1847; R xi/4
102     Lieder ohne Worte, viii (Bonn, n.d.): e, 1 June 1842, D, 11 May 1845, C, 12 Dec 1845, g, 'Kinderstück', A, 12 Dec 1845, C; R xi/4
—       Two Piano Pieces, B♭, g (1860); R xi/3
119     Perpetuum mobile, C (1873); R xi/3
—       Con moto, b♭, *Bds
—       Study, F, *Bds
—       Two Piano Pieces: Andante, E, Allegro, e: *Bds
—       Lied ohne Worte ('Andante tranquillo'), D, *Bds

PIANO DUET

—       Lento–Vivace, g, 1820, *Bds
—       Fantasia, d, 15 March 1824, *Bds
92      Allegro brillant, A, 23 March 1841 (n.d.); R x
83a     Variations, B♭, ?1841 (1850), based on op.83 for pf solo; R x

TWO PIANOS

—       Duo concertant, variations on march from Weber's La preciosa, ?1833, collab. Moscheles [pubd as Moscheles's op.87b], orig. with orch

ORGAN

—       Six little pieces, *Bds: Fugue, d, Fugue, g, Minuet, d, all 3 Dec 1820, Fugue, d, 6 Jan 1821, untitled, d, Dec 1820, Prelude, d, 28 Nov 1820
—       Fantasia, g, ?1822–3, *Bds
—       Wie gross ist des Allmächt'gen Güte, chorale-prelude, 3 variants, 30 July–2 Aug 1823, *Bds
—       Two little pieces, *Bds: Andante, D, 9 May 1823, untitled, c, ?1823
37      Three Preludes and Fugues (1837): c, prelude 2 April 1837; G, prelude 4 April 1837, fugue 1 Dec 1837; d, prelude 6 April 1837; R xii
—       Fugue, e, 13 July 1839, *Bds
—       Fugue, f, 18 July 1839 (London, n.d.)
—       Prelude, c, 9 July 1841; R xii
—       Four little pieces, *Bds: Andante, F, 21 July 1844, Allegretto, d, 22 July 1844, Andante, D, 23 July 1844, Allegro, d, 25 July 1844
—       Two Pieces (London, n.d.): Andante with variations, D, 23 July 1844, Allegro, B♭, 31 Dec 1844
—       Chorale, A♭, 10 Sept 1844, *Bds

—       Allegro, B, 31 Dec 1844, *Bds
65      Six Sonatas (1845): f/F, 18 Dec 1844, c/C, 21 Dec 1844, A, 17 Aug 1844, B♭, 2 Jan 1845, D, 9 Sept 1844, d/D, 27 Jan 1845; R xii
—       Andante alla marcia, B, 2 Jan 1845
—       Andante sostenuto, D, 26 Jan 1845
—       Fugue, B, 2 April 1845
—       Chorale, D, *Bds

PSALMS, SACRED CANTATAS

—       Psalm lxvi, double female chorus, bc, 1822, *Bds
—       Magnificat, D, chorus, orch, 31 May 1822, *Bds
—       Salve regina, E♭, S, str, ?1824, pubd in R. Werner (1930)
—       Two sacred pieces, chorus, *Bds: Wie gross ist des Allmächt'gen Güte, ?1824, Allein Gott in der Höh' sey Ehr, 10 Sept 1824
—       Te Deum, D, double chorus, bc, 5 Dec 1826, edn. (Leipzig, 1972)
—       Jesu, meine Freude, chorale cantata, double chorus, str, facs. ed. O. Jonas (Chicago, 1966)
31      Psalm cxv, solo v, chorus, orch, 15 Nov 1830 (London, 1830); R xiv/A1
—       Verleih uns Frieden, chorus, orch, 10 Feb 1831; facs. in AMZ, xli, suppl. for 5 June 1839; R xiv/A3
—       Te Deum, A, double chorus, org, 1832 (London, 1832); R xiv/B
121     Responsorium et Hymnus, male vv, vc, org, 5 Feb 1833 (n.d.); R xiv/A3
42      Psalm xlii, solo vv, chorus, orch, 22 Dec 1837 (1838); R xiv/A1
46      Psalm xcv, T, chorus, orch, 6 April 1838, rev. 3 July 1841 (1841); R xiv/A1
—       Psalm v 'Lord hear the voice', chorus, 26 Feb 1839, *Bds
—       Psalm xxxi 'Defend me, Lord', chorus, 27 Feb 1839, *Bds
51      Psalm cxiv, double chorus, orch, 9 Aug 1839 (1841); R xiv/A1
—       Geistliches Lied, E♭, solo v, chorus, org, 12 Dec 1840
—       Psalm c, 'Jauchzet den Herrn', chorus, ?1842
91      Psalm xcviii, double chorus, orch, 27 Dec 1843 (n.d.); R xiv/A1
73      Lauda Sion, chorus, orch, 10 Feb 1846, perf. Liège, 11 June 1846; R xiv/A3
78      Three psalms, solo vv, double chorus (1848): Psalm ii, 15 Dec 1843, Psalm xliii, 3 Jan 1844, Psalm xxii, 1844; R xiv/C
—       Ach Gott vom Himmel sieh darein, chorale cantata, solo vv, chorus, orch, *Bds
—       Christe, du Lamm Gottes, chorale cantata, chorus, orch, *Bds
—       Vom Himmel hoch, chorale cantata, solo vv, chorus, orch, *Bds
—       Er wird öffnen die Augen der Blinden, chorus, orch, *Bds, intended for Elijah
—       Gloria, E♭, solo vv, chorus, orch, inc., *Bds
—       Kyrie, chorus, orch, *Bds

MOTETS, ANTHEMS, OTHER SHORTER SACRED PIECES

—       Die Himmel erzählen, 5vv, 16 June 1820, *Bds
—       Gott, du bist unsre Zuversicht, 5vv, ?1820, *Bds
—       Ich will den Herrn nach seiner Gerechtigkeit preisen, 4vv, ?1820, *Bds
—       Tag für Tag sei Gott gepriesen, 5vv, ?1820, *Bds
—       Das Gesetz des Herrn ist ohne Wandel, 5vv, ?1821–2, *Bds
—       Er hat der Sonne eine Hütte gemacht, 5vv, ?1821–2, *Bds
—       Jube Domine, solo vv, double chorus, 25 Oct 1822, *Bds
—       Kyrie, c, solo vv, chorus, 12 Nov 1823, *Bds
—       Jesus, meine Zuversicht, solo vv, chorus, pf, 9 June 1824, *Bds
111     Tu es Petrus, chorus, orch, 14 Nov 1827; R xiv/A3
—       Ave maris stella, S, orch, 5 July 1828, *Bds
—       Hora est, 16vv, org, 1828, *Bds
23      Three sacred pieces, T, chorus, org (Bonn, 1830): Aus tiefer Not, Ave Maria, Mitten wir; R xiv/B
—       Zum Feste der Dreieinigkeit ('O beata et benedicta'), 3 S, org, 30 Dec 1830, *Bds
39      Three Motets, female chorus, org, 31 Dec 1830 (Bonn, ?1831): Hear my prayer, O Lord ('Veni, Domine'), O praise the Lord ('Laudate pueri'), O Lord, thou hast searched me out ('Surrexit Pastor'); R xiv/B
—       Lord have mercy upon us, chorus, 24 March 1833 (n.d.); R xiv/C
115     Two sacred choruses, male chorus, ?1833; R xiv/C
96      Hymn, A solo, chorus, orch, 14 Dec 1840, org acc. arr. 1841, 3 choruses added 5 Jan 1843 (Bonn, n.d.)
—       Herr Gott, dich loben wir, solo vv, chorus, orch, org, 16 July 1843, *Bds
—       Ehre sei dem Vater, 8vv, 17 Jan 1844, *Bds
—       Hear my prayer, hymn, S, chorus, org, 25 Jan 1844 (Berlin, n.d.); R xiv/B
—       Ehre sei dem Vater, C, 4vv, 5 March 1845, *Bds
—       Er kommt aus dem kindlichen Alter der Welt, 6vv, ?25 Jan 1846, *Bds
—       Die deutsche Liturgie, 8vv, 28 Oct 1846: Kyrie, Heilig, Ehre sei dem Vater, all pubd (Berlin, n.d.), Und Friede auf Erden, Wir loben dich, Denn du allein bist heilig, Amen, all unpubd, *Bds; R xiv/C

69  Three English Church Pieces, solo vv, chorus, 1847 (?1847):
    Nunc dimittis, 12 June 1847, Jubilate, 5 April 1847,
    Magnificat, 12 June 1847; R xiv/C
79  Six Anthems double chorus (1848): Rejoice, O ye people; Thou,
    Lord, our refuge hast been, 25 Dec 1843; Above all praises, 9
    Oct 1846; Lord, on our offences, 14 Feb 1844; Let our hearts
    be joyful, 5 Oct 1846; For our offences, 18 Feb 1844;
    R xiv/C
—   Cantique pour l'Eglise wallonne de Francfort ('Venez chantez'),
    4vv, *Bds
—   Gloria patri ('Ehre sei dem Vater'), 4vv, *Bds
—   Glory be to the Father, 4vv, *Bds
—   Kyrie, A, 8vv
—   Three sacred pieces: Ehre sei Gott, 8vv; Heilig, 8vv; Ps c, mixed
    vv; R xiv/C

SECULAR CANTATAS

—   In feierlichen Tönen, wedding cantata, S, A, T, chorus, pf, 13
    June 1820, *Bds
—   Grosse Festmusik zum Dürerfest (K. Levezow), solo vv, chorus,
    orch, 1828, perf. Berlin, 18 April 1828, *Bds
—   Begrüssung (' "Humboldt" Cantata') (L. Rellstab), festival
    music, solo male vv, male chorus, wind (with timp, vc and
    db), 12 Sept 1828, perf. Berlin, 18 Sept 1828
60  Die erste Walpurgisnacht (Goethe), cantata, chorus, orch, 13 Feb
    1832, perf. Berlin, Jan 1833, rev. 1843, perf. Leipzig, 2 Feb
    1843 (1844)
—   Gott segne Sachsenland, male vv, wind, 2 June 1843, perf. Dres-
    den, 7 June 1843, *Bds
68  An die Künstler (Schiller), festival song, male vv, brass, 19 April
    1846, perf. Cologne, June 1846 (Bonn, 1846)

CHORAL SONGS

—   Einst ins Schlaraffenland zogen, 4 male vv, 1820, *Bds
—   Lieb und Hoffnung, male vv, 1820, *Bds
—   Jägerlied ('Kein bess're Lust in dieser Zeit') (L. Uhland), 4 male
    vv, 20 April 1822, *Bds
—   Lob des Weines ('Seht, Freunde, die Gläser'), solo male vv, male
    chorus, 1822, *Bds
—   Lass es heut am edlen Ort (Goethe), 4 male vv, 19 May 1828,
    *Bds
—   Worauf kommt es überall an, 4 male vv, 23 Feb 1837, *Bds
41  Im Freien zu singen, mixed vv (1838); R xvi
    1  Im Walde (A. von Platen)
    2  Entflieh mit mir (Heine)
    3  Es fiel ein Reif (Heine)
    4  Auf ihrem Grab (Heine), 22 Jan 1834
    5  Mailied (L. Hölty)
    6  Auf dem See (Goethe)
48  Der erste Frühlingstag, mixed vv, 1839 (1840); R xvi
    1  Frühlingsahnung (Uhland), 5 July 1839
    2  Die Primel (N. Lenau), 1839
    3  Frühlingsfeier (Uhland), 28 Dec 1839
    4  Lerchengesang, canon, 15 June 1839
    5  Morgengebet (Eichendorff), 18 Nov 1839
    6  Herbstlied (Lenau), 26 Dec 1839
—   Ersatz für Unbestand (F. Rückert), 4 male vv, 22 Nov 1839
    (n.d.); R xvii
—   Festgesang [for the Gutenberg Festival] (A. E. Prölss), male vv,
    1840, perf. Leipzig, 25 June 1840 (n.d.); R xv [no.2 adapted
    by W. H. Cummings as 'Hark! the Herald Angels Sing']
50  Six Male Choruses (1842); R xvii
    1  Türkisches Schenkenlied (Goethe), ?1839–40
    2  Der Jäger Abschied (Eichendorff), 4 hn, b trbn acc.,
       6 Jan 1840
    3  Sommerlied (Goethe), 1839–40
    4  Wasserfahrt (Heine), ?1839–40
    5  Liebe und Wein, 7 Dec 1839
    6  Wanderlied (Eichendorff), 6 Jan 1842
—   Nachtgesang, 4 male vv, 15 Jan 1842 (n.d.); R xvii
—   Die Stiftungsfeier, 4 male vv, 15 Jan 1842 (n.d.); R xvii
59  Im Grünen, mixed vv (1844); R xvi
    1  Im Grünen (H. von Chezy), 23 Nov 1837
    2  Frühzeitiger Frühling (Goethe), 17 Jan 1843
    3  Abschied vom Wald (Eichendorff), 4 March 1843
    4  Die Nachtigall (Goethe), 19 June 1843
    5  Ruhetal (Uhland), 4 March 1843
    6  Jagdlied (Eichendorff), 5 March 1843
116 Sahst du ihn hernniederschweben, funeral song, mixed vv, 8 July
    1845 (n.d.); R xiv
—   Der Sänger (Schiller), 30 Oct 1845, perf. Leipzig, 10 Nov 1846
75  Wandersmann, male vv (1848); R xvii
    1  Der frohe Wandersmann (Eichendorff), 8 Feb 1844
    2  Abendständchen (Eichendorff), 14 Nov 1839
    3  Trinklied (Goethe)
    4  Abschiedstafel (Eichendorff), 29 Aug 1844

76  Four Male Choruses (1848); R xvii
    1  Das Lied vom braven Mann (Heine)
    2  Rheinweinlied (G. Herwegh), 8 Feb 1844
    3  Lied für die Deutschen in Lyon (F. Stoltze), 8 Oct 1846
    4  Comitat (Hoffmann von Fallersleben)
88  Six Choruses, mixed vv (n.d.); R xvi
    1  Neujahrslied (J. P. Hebel), 8 Aug 1844
    2  Der Glückliche (Eichendorff), 20 June 1843
    3  Hirtenlied (Uhland), 14 June 1839
    4  Die Waldvögelein (Schütz), 19 June 1843
    5  Deutschland (E. Geibel), ?1839–43
    6  Der wandernde Musikant (Eichendorff), 10 March 1840
100 Four Choruses, mixed vv (n.d.); R xvi
    1  Andenken, 8 Aug 1844
    2  Lob des Frühlings (Uhland), 20 June 1843
    3  Frühlingslied, ?1843–4
    4  Im Wald, 14 June 1839
120 Four Male Choruses (n.d.); R xvii
    1  Jagdlied (W. Scott), 27 Nov 1837
    2  Morgengruss des Thüringischen Sängerbundes, 20 Feb
       1847
    3  Im Süden
    4  Zigeunerlied (Goethe)
—   Lob der Trunkenheit ('Trunken müssen wir alle sein'), 4 male vv,
    *Bds
—   Musikantenprügelei ('Seht doch diese Fiedlerbanden'), 2 male vv,
    *Bds

CONCERT ARIAS

—   Che vuoi mio cor?, Mez, str, *Bds
94  Infelice, S, orch, 3 April 1834, rev. 15 Jan 1843 (n.d.); R xv

SOLO SONGS
(all with pf acc.)

—   Ave Maria, 1820, *Bds
—   Raste Krieger, Krieg ist aus, 1820, *Bds
—   Die Nachtigall ('Da ging ich hin'), ?1821–2, *Bds
—   Der Verlassene ('Nacht ist um mich her'), ?1821–2, *Bds
—   Von allen deinen zarten Gaben, 18 Sept 1822, *Bds
—   Wiegenlied ('Schlummre sanft'), 18 Sept 1822, *Bds
—   Sanft weh'n im Hauch der Abendluft, 28 Dec 1822, *Bds
—   Der Wasserfall ('Rieselt hernieder'), ?1823, *Bds
8   Twelve Songs (Berlin, 1828); R xviii [no.12], xix [nos.1–11]
    1  Minnelied (Hölty)
    2  Das Heimweh (F. Robert) [by Fanny Mendelssohn]
    3  Italien (F. Grillparzer) [by Fanny Mendelssohn]
    4  Erntelied (trad.)
    5  Pilgerspruch (P. Flemming)
    6  Frühlingslied, 2 April 1824
    7  Maienlied
    8  Andres Maienlied ('Hexenlied') (Hölty)
    9  Abendlied (J. H. Voss)
    10 Romanze (Sp.)
    11 Im Grünen (Voss)
    12 Suleika und Hatem (Goethe), 2vv [by Fanny
       Mendelssohn]
—   The Garland (Der Blumenkranz) (T. Moore), 2 May 1829
    (London and Brunswick, n.d.); R xix
9   Twelve Songs (Berlin, 1830); R xix
    1  Frage (Voss)
    2  Geständnis
    3  Wartend, romance
    4  Im Frühling, 3 April 1829
    5  Im Herbst (K. Klingemann)
    6  Scheidend (Voss)
    7  Sehnsucht (J. G. Droysen) [by Fanny Mendelssohn]
    8  Frühlingsglaube (Uhland), 19 Jan 1830
    9  Ferne (Droysen)
    10 Verlust (Heine) [by Fanny Mendelssohn]
    11 Entsagung (Droysen)
    12 Die Nonne (Uhland) [by Fanny Mendelssohn]
—   Four Songs, 1 May 1830, *Bds
    1  Der Tag ('Sanft entschwanden mir')
    2  Reiterlied ('Immer fort')
    3  Abschied ('Leb wohl mein Lieb')
    4  Der Bettler ('Ich danke Gott dir')
—   Seemanns Scheidelied (Hoffmann von Fallersleben), 1831, in
    Musikalisches Souvenir (Berlin, 1831); R xix
—   Weihnachtslied ('Auf schicke dich recht feierlich'), 2 versions,
    19–20 Dec 1832, pubd in H. Gerber: Albert Baur (Freiburg,
    1971)
19a Six Songs (1834); R xix
    1  Frühlingslied (U. von Lichtenstein), 21 Feb 1830
    2  Das erste Veilchen (E. Ebert)
    3  Winterlied (Swed.)
    4  Neue Liebe (Heine)
    5  Gruss (Heine)
    6  Reiselied (Ebert), 16 Oct 1830

— Mailied ('Ich weiss mir'n Mädchen'), 14 May 1834, *Bds
— Two Romances (Byron) (n.d.): There be none of beauty's daughters, ?1833, Sun of the Sleepless, 31 Dec 1834; R xix
— Two Songs (Eichendorff) (Elberfeld, 1835): Das Waldschloss, 17 Aug 1835, Pagenlied, ?1835; R xix
34 Six Songs (1836); R xix
    1 Minnelied (Old Ger.), 11 May 1834
    2 Auf Flügeln des Gesanges (Heine)
    3 Frühlingslied (Klingemann)
    4 Suleika (Goethe)
    5 Sonntagslied (Klingemann), 28 Dec 1834
    6 Reiselied (Heine)
— Lied einer Freundin ('Zarter Blumen leicht Gewinde') (Goethe), 13 July 1837 (Düsseldorf, 1960)
— Im Kahn (Heine), 12 Dec 1837, *Bds
— O könnt ich zu dir fliegen, 15 Aug 1838, *Bds
47 Six Songs (?1840); R xix
    1 Minnelied (L. Tieck)
    2 Morgengruss (Heine)
    3 Frühlingslied (Lenau), 17 April 1839
    4 Volkslied (E. von Feuchtersleben), 18 April 1839
    5 Der Blumenstrauss (Klingemann), May 1832
    6 Bei der Wiege (Klingemann)
— Two Songs (n.d.): Todeslied der Bojaren (K. Immermann), Ich hör ein Vöglein (A. Böttger), 20 April 1841 [no.1 orig. pubd Düsseldorf, before 1841]
57 Six Songs (1843); R xix
    1 Altdeutsches Lied (H. Schreiber)
    2 Hirtenlied (Uhland), 20 April 1839
    3 Suleika (Goethe)
    4 O Jugend (Rhenish folksong)
    5 Venetianisches Gondellied (after Moore), 17 Oct 1842
    6 Wanderlied (Eichendorff), 29 April 1841
71 Six Songs (?1847); R xix
    1 Tröstung (Hoffmann von Fallersleben), 22 Dec 1845
    2 Frühlingslied (Klingemann), 3 April 1845
    3 An die Entfernte (Lenau), 22 Sept 1847
    4 Schilflied (Lenau), 3 Nov 1842
    5 Auf der Wanderschaft (Lenau), 27 July 1847
    6 Nachtlied (Eichendorff), 1 Oct 1847
84 Three Songs, low v (1850); R xix
    1 Da lieg' ich unter den Bäumen, 5 Dec 1831
    2 Herbstlied (Klingemann), 26 Feb 1839
    3 Jagdlied (from Des Knaben Wunderhorn), 25 May 1834
86 Six Songs (1851); R xix
    1 Es lauschte das Laub (Klingemann)
    2 Morgenlied
    3 Die Liebende schreibt (Goethe), 10 Aug 1831
    4 Allnächtlich im Traume (Heine)
    5 Der Mond (E. Geibel)
    6 Altdeutsches Frühlingslied (F. Spee), 8 Oct 1847
99 Six Songs (n.d.)
    1 Erster Verlust (Goethe), 9 Aug 1841
    2 Die Sterne schau'n (A. von Schlippenbach)
    3 Lieblingsplätzchen (from Des Knaben Wunderhorn)
    4 Das Schifflein (Uhland), 6 June 1841
    5 Wenn sich zwei Herzen scheiden (Geibel), 22 Dec 1845
    6 Es weiss und rät es doch keiner (Eichendorff)
112 Two Sacred Songs: Doch der Herr, er leitet die Irrenden recht; Der du die Menschen lässest sterben; R xiv [intended for St Paul]
— Des Mädchens Klage (Schiller) (n.d.); R xix
— Warnung vor dem Rhein (C. Simrock) (Bonn, n.d.); R xix
— Der Abendsegen (The Evening Service), *Bds
— Gretchen ('Meine Ruh ist hin') (Goethe), *Bds
— Lieben und Schweigen ('Ich flocht ein Kränzlein schöner Lieder') (K. Tischendorf)
— Es rauscht der Wald, *Bds
— Vier trübe Monden sind entfloh'n, *Bds
— Weinend seh' ich in die Nacht, *Bds
— Weiter, rastlos atemlos vorüber, *Bds
— Erwartung ('Bist auf ewig du gegangen'), frag.

VOCAL DUETS
(all with pf acc.)

— Ein Tag sagt es dem andern, S, A, 1821, *Bds
63 Six Duets (1845); R xviii
    1 Ich wollt' meine Lieb' (Heine), Dec 1836
    2 Abschiedslied der Zugvögel (Hoffmann von Fallersleben)
    3 Gruss (Eichendorff)
    4 Herbstlied (Klingemann)
    5 Volkslied (R. Burns), 17 Oct 1842
    6 Maiglöckchen und die Blümelein (Hoffmann von Fallersleben), 23 Jan 1844
77 Three Duets (1848); R xviii
    1 Sonntagsmorgen (Uhland), 3 Dec 1836

    2 Das Aehrenfeld (Hoffmann von Fallersleben), 18 Jan 1847
    3 Lied aus 'Ruy Blas' (Hugo), 14 Feb 1839
— Three Folksongs (Berlin, n.d.); R xviii
    1 Wie kann ich froh und lustig sein (P. Kaufmann)
    2 Abendlied (Heine)
    3 Wasserfahrt (Heine)

CANONS

— Der weise Diogenes, 2 male vv, 11 Feb 1833, *Bds
— Und ob du mich züchtigst, 5vv, 24 Dec 1835, *Bds
— Two-part canon, b, pf, 24 Sept 1837, *Bds
— Two-part canon, c, pf, Jan 1838, *Bds
— Three-part canon, 8 Sept 1839, *Bds
— Two-part canon, 14 Feb 1840, *Bds [solution by F. Möhring]
— Two-part canon, 7 April 1841, ? ded. R. Lepsius, *Bds
— Two-part canon, pf, 22 April 1841, ded. V. Carus, *Bds
— Canon, f♯, 2 Nov 1844, ded. L. Lallemant, *Bds
— Four-part double canon, *Bds

TRANSCRIPTIONS AND ARRANGEMENTS
Bach

Organ Compositions on Chorales, i–iv (London and Leipzig, 1845–6)
44 kleine Choralvorspiele für die Orgel (Leipzig and London, 1845)
15 grosse Choral-Vorspiele für die Orgel (Leipzig and London, 1846)
6 Variations on the Chorale 'Christ der du bist der helle Tag – Christ who art the brightest day' (Leipzig and London, 1846)
11 Variations on the Chorale 'Sey gegrüsset Jesu gütig – All hail good Jesus' (Leipzig and London, 1846)
Chaconne, vn, pf (London and Hamburg, 1847; Fr. edn., Paris and elsewhere, 1848) [pf acc. for the Chaconne in D minor for vn solo]
Suite, D, orch, ed. F. David (Leipzig, 1866) [Mendelssohn's performing edn. for the Gewandhaus concerts]

Handel

Israel in Egypt (London, 1846) [Handel Society edn.]
Dettingen Te Deum (Leipzig, n.d.)
Acis and Galatea (London, n.d.)
org parts for Solomon, 1834, and two choruses from Messiah, all unpubd, *Bds

other

6 schottische National-Lieder, Ger. and orig. Eng. texts (Leipzig, 1839); ed. R. Elvers (1977)

WRITINGS

*Das Mädchen von Andros, eine Komödie des Terenz, in den Versmassen des Originals übersetzt* (Leipzig, 1826) [trans. of Terence: The Woman of Andros]

BIBLIOGRAPHY
CATALOGUES OF WORKS
'Felix Mendelssohn-Bartholdy', *AMZ*, xxxix (1836–7), 845
*Vollständiges Verzeichnis im Druck erschienener Compositionen von . . . Felix Mendelssohn Bartholdy* (Leipzig, 1841)
A. J. Becher: 'Vollständiges Verzeichnis der Compositionen von Felix Mendelssohn Bartholdy', *Orpheus-Almanach*, iii (Vienna, 1842), pp.iii–viii
*Thematisches Verzeichnis im Druck erschienener Compositionen von Felix Mendelssohn Bartholdy* (Leipzig, 1846; new edn., 1853, 2/1873, 3/1882/R1966 and 1973)
'Systematisches Verzeichnis der in Deutschland im Druck erschienenen Compositionen von Felix Mendelssohn Bartholdy', *Musikalisches Wochenblatt*, i (1870), suppl.

COLLECTIONS AND EXHIBITIONS
G. Kinsky: *Erstlingsdrucke der deutschen Tonmeister der Klassik und Romantik* (Vienna, 1934), 16 [on opp.1–3]
Y. Rokseth: 'Manuscrits de Mendelssohn à la Bibliothèque du Conservatoire', *RdM*, xv (V 1934), 103
E. Walker: 'An Oxford Collection of Mendelssohniana', *ML*, xix (1938), 426
M. F. Schneider: 'Eine Mendelssohn-Sammlung in Basel', *Der Amerbach Bote: Almanach* (Basle, 1947), 200
E. Werner: 'Mendelssohn Sources', *Notes*, ii (1954–5), 201
*Mendelssohn-Festwoche aus Anlass der 150. Wiederkehr des Geburtstages am 3. Februar 1959* (Leipzig, 1959)
R. Elvers: 'Verzeichnis der von Felix Mendelssohn Bartholdy herausgegebenen Werke J. S. Bachs', *Gestalt und Glaube: Festschrift für Oskar Söhngen* (Witten and Berlin, 1960), 145
A. H. King: *Some British Collectors of Music c.1600–1960* (Cambridge, 1963), 86f
M. F. Schneider: *Mendelssohn-Archiv der Staatsbibliothek Stiftung Preussischer Kulturbesitz* (Berlin, 1965)
——: *Die Wach'sche Mendelssohn-Sammlung auf dem Ried in Wilderswil bei Interlaken* (Berlin, 1966)
R. Elvers: 'Neuerwerbungen für das Mendelssohn-Archiv der Staatsbibliothek 1965–69', *Jb der Stiftung Preussischer Kulturbesitz 1969*, 308

E. F. Flindell: 'Ursprung und Geschichte der Sammlung Wittgenstein im 19. Jahrhundert', *Mf*, xxii (1969), 300 [with list of Mendelssohn's letters]

R. Elvers: *Felix Mendelssohn Bartholdy: Dokumente seines Lebens: Ausstellung zum 125. Todestag*, Staatsbibliothek Preussischer Kulturbesitz, Ausstellungskataloge, iii (Berlin, 1972)

P. Krause: *Autographen, Erstausgaben und Frühdrucke der Werke von Felix Mendelssohn Bartholdy in Leipziger Bibliotheken und Archiven* (Leipzig, 1972)

B. Richter: 'Das Mendelssohn-Zimmer in Leipzig', *Musik und Gesellschaft*, xxii (1972), 646

ICONOGRAPHIES

M. F. Schneider: *Felix Mendelssohn im Bildnis* (Basle, 1953)

——: *Ein unbekanntes Mendelssohn-Bildnis von Johann Peter Lyser* (Basle, 1958)

LETTERS

F. Mendelssohn: *Reisebriefe aus den Jahren 1830 bis 1832*, ed. P. Mendelssohn Bartholdy (Leipzig, 1861, 2/1870; rev., enlarged P. Hübner, Bonn, 1947; Eng. trans., 1862, 2/1865/*R*1970) [vol.i of *Briefe aus den Jahren 1830 bis 1847*, compiled J. Rietz (Leipzig, 1861–3, 8/1915)]

——: *Briefe aus den Jahren 1833 bis 1847*, ed. P. and C. Mendelssohn Bartholdy (Leipzig, 1863; Eng. trans., 1863, 4/1864/*R*1970) [vol.ii of *Briefe aus den Jahren 1830 bis 1847*]

*Pis'ma Mendel'sona-Bartol'di* [Mendelssohn's letters] (St Petersburg, 1863)

L. Nohl: *Musiker-Briefe* (Leipzig, 1867; Eng. trans., 1867), 297–346 [30 letters of Mendelssohn]

F. Mendelssohn: *Acht Briefe* (Leipzig, 1871; Eng. trans. in *Macmillan Magazine*, London, 1871, June) [letters to Henriette Voigt]

F. Hiller: *Felix Mendelssohn Bartholdy: Briefe und Erinnerungen* (Cologne, 1874, 2/1878; Eng. trans., 1874) [see also R. Sietz: *Aus Ferdinand Hillers Briefwechsel* (Cologne, 1958), 31ff]

F. Mendelssohn: *Letters*, ed. J. Sime (Cambridge, 1887)

——: *Briefe an Ignaz und Charlotte Moscheles*, ed. F. Moscheles (Leipzig, 1888/*R*1976; Eng. trans., 1888/*R*1970)

M. Friedländer, ed.: 'Felix Mendelssohn Bartholdy: Briefe an Goethe', *Goethe-Jb*, xii (1891), 77

F. Mendelssohn: *Briefwechsel mit Julius Schubring*, ed. J. Schubring (Leipzig, 1892/*R*1973)

W. F. Alexander, ed.: *Selected Letters of Mendelssohn* (London, 1894)

E. Schirmer, ed.: 'Briefe Felix Mendelssohns an Johann Wilhelm Schirmer', *Die Musik*, ii (1902–3), 83

H. B. and C. L. E. Cox: *Leaves from the Journals of Sir George Smart* (London, 1907) [incl. letters from Mendelssohn]

J. R. Sterndale Bennett: *The Life of William Sterndale Bennett* (Cambridge, 1907) [incl. correspondence with Mendelssohn]

E. Wolff, ed.: *Meister-Briefe* (Berlin, 1907)

K. Klingemann [jr], ed.: *Felix Mendelssohn Bartholdys Briefwechsel mit Legationsrat Karl Klingemann in London* (Essen, 1909)

M. Unger: *Von Mendelssohn Bartholdys Beziehungen zu England: fünf englische Briefe des Meisters* (Langensalza, 1909)

E. Wolff: 'Briefe von Felix Mendelssohn Bartholdy an seine rheinischen Freunde', *Rheinische Musik- und Theaterzeitung*, x (1909), 86, 104, 121, 136, 149, 163, 182

L. Dahlgren, ed.: *Bref till Adolf Fredrik Lindblad från Mendelssohn, . . . och andra* (Stockholm, 1913)

A. Mendelssohn Bartholdy: 'Felix Mendelssohn Bartholdy und Richard Wagner', *Programmbuch des 1. Fränkischen Musikfestes zu Würzburg* (Feb 1914) [incl. 4 letters from Wagner to Mendelssohn]

G. Fischer: 'Ein Brief des 15-jährigen Felix Mendelssohn Bartholdy', *Kleine Blätter* (Hanover, 1916), 9 [letter to Friedrich Voigts]

A. Mendelssohn Bartholdy: 'Erinnerungen an Felix Mendelssohn: aus alten Familienbriefen', *Neue freie Presse* (19 April 1925), suppl.

R. Hübner: *Johann Gustav Droysen: Briefwechsel*, i (Berlin, 1929) [see also Wehmer (1959) below]

R. B. Gotch: *Mendelssohn and his Friends in Kensington: Letters from Fanny and Sophy Horsley* (London, 1934)

F. Mendelssohn: *Letters*, trans. G. Selden-Goth (New York, 1945/*R*1969)

H. Weiss: *Felix Mendelssohn Bartholdy: ein Lebensbild in Briefen und zeitgenössischen Urteilen* (Berlin, 1947)

K. Lindholm, ed. and trans.: *Mendelssohns breve* (Odense, 1949)

H. Erdmann and H. Rentzow: 'Mendelssohns Oratorien-Praxis: ein bisher unbekannter Brief', *Musica*, vi (1952), 352 [letter to Julius Stock]

C. Wehmer, ed.: *Ein tief gegründet Herz: der Briefwechsel Felix Mendelssohn Bartholdys mit Johann Gustav Droysen* (Heidelberg, 1959)

E. Werner: 'The Family Letters of Felix Mendelssohn Bartholdy', *Bulletin of the New York Public Library*, lxv (1961), 5

R. Elvers: 'Ein Jugendbrief von Felix Mendelssohn', *Festschrift für Friedrich Smend* (Berlin, 1963), 95 [letter to Rudolph Gugel]

'Ein unbekannter Brief Felix Mendelssohn Bartholdys', *BMw*, v (1963), 69 [letter to N. Simrock]

D. Schmidt: 'Felix Mendelssohn Bartholdy, ein Helfer der Abgebrannten von 1842', *Hamburgische Geschichts- und Heimatblätter*, viii (1967), 30

F. Mendelssohn: *Briefe*, ed. R. Elvers (Berlin, 1968–)

*Briefe von Felix Mendelssohn Bartholdy, 1833–1847* (Leipzig, 1968) [facs. edn. of 10 letters from *D-LEsm*]

G. Schulz: *Glückliche Jugend: Briefe des jungen Komponisten Felix Mendelssohn Bartholdy* (Bremen, 1971)

W. Anacker: 'Zwei Briefe von Felix Mendelssohn Bartholdy', *Musik und Gesellschaft*, xxii (1972), 654 [letters to A. F. Anacker]

H. J. Rothe and R. Szeskus, eds.: *Felix Mendelssohn Bartholdy: Briefe aus Leipziger Archiven* (Leipzig, 1972)

FACSIMILE EDITIONS OF DOCUMENTS

F. Mendelssohn: *'Die Hebriden'*, ed. M. F. Schneider (Basle, 1947) [autograph of 1st version]

M. F. Schneider: *Felix Mendelssohn Bartholdy: Denkmal in Wort und Bild* (Basle, 1947) [autographs of opp.30, 48/4, 88/3 and 100/4]

F. Mendelssohn: *Reisebilder aus der Schweiz 1842*, ed. M. F. Schneider (Basle, 1954)

K. H. Köhler, ed.: *Die Frauen und die Sänger nach dem Gedicht 'Die vier Weltalter' von Friedrich Schiller für gemischten Chor komponiert* (Basle, 1959)

M. F. Schneider, ed.: *Lied einer Freundin: Zarter Blumen leicht Gewinde, ein bisher ungedrucktes Goethe-Lied von Mendelssohn* (Düsseldorf, 1960)

F. Mendelssohn: *Aquarellenalbum*, ed. M. F. Schneider and C. Hensel (Basle, 1968) [13 watercolour sketches in *D-B*]

R. Elvers, ed.: *Endreim-Spiele mit Felix Mendelssohn, Weimar, November 1821* (Berlin, 1970)

MEMOIRS, RECOLLECTIONS

L. Rellstab: *Aus meinem Leben* (Berlin, 1861), ii, chap.11

A. B. Marx: *Erinnerungen* (Berlin, 1865)

J. Schubring: 'Erinnerungen an Felix Mendelssohn Bartholdy', *Daheim*, ii (1866), 373; Eng. trans. in *Musical World*, xxxi (1866), 12 and 19 May

E. Polko: *Erinnerungen an Felix Mendelssohn Bartholdy* (Leipzig, 1868; Eng. trans., 1869)

E. Devrient: *Meine Erinnerungen an Felix Mendelssohn Bartholdy und dessen Briefe an mich* (Leipzig, 1869, 3/1891; Eng. trans., 1869)

H. F. Chorley: *Autobiography, Memoir and Letters*, ed. H. G. Hewlett (London, 1873) [incl. correspondence with Mendelssohn]

C. Moscheles: *Aus Moscheles Leben* (Leipzig, 1872–3; Eng. trans., 1873) [incl. correspondence with Mendelssohn]

J. Eckardt: *Ferdinand David und die Familie Mendelssohn Bartholdy* (Leipzig, 1888)

H. S. Holland and W. S. Rockstro, eds.: *Memoir of Mme Jenny Lind-Goldschmidt* (London, 1891, abridged 2/1893) [incl. letters from Mendelssohn]

H. Devrient, ed.: *Briefwechsel zwischen Eduard und Therese Devrient* (Stuttgart, 1909)

H. Davison: *Music during the Victorian Era: from Mendelssohn to Wagner* (London, 1912) [incl. letters of Mendelssohn]

R. Schumann: *Erinnerungen an Felix Mendelssohn Bartholdy*, ed. G. Eismann (Zwickau, 1947, enlarged 2/1948)

BIOGRAPHY, LIFE AND WORKS

W. A. Lampadius: *Felix Mendelssohn Bartholdy: ein Denkmal für seine Freunde* (Leipzig, 1848; Eng. trans., 1876; Eng. trans. with suppl. sketches by J. Benedict, H. F. Chorley, L. Rellstab and others, ed. W. L. Gage, New York, 1865/*R*1978, 2/1866, and Boston, 1872, 2/1887)

L. Stierlin: *Biographie von Felix Mendelssohn Bartholdy* (Zurich, 1849)

J. Benedict: *A Sketch of the Life and Works of the late Felix Mendelssohn* (London, 1850, 2/1853)

W. H. Riehl: 'Bach und Mendelssohn aus dem socialen Gesichtspunkte', *Musikalische Charakterköpfe*, i (1853), 65–107

H. F. Chorley: 'The Last Days of Mendelssohn', *Modern German Music: Recollections and Criticisms* (London, 1854), ii, 383–418

W. Neumann: *Felix Mendelssohn Bartholdy: eine Biographie* (Kassel, 1854)

A. Reissmann: *Felix Mendelssohn Bartholdy: sein Leben und seine Werke* (Berlin, 1867, rev., enlarged 3/1893)

C. Selden: *La musique en Allemagne: Mendelssohn* (Paris, 1867)

H. Barbedette: *Felix Mendelssohn Bartholdy: sa vie et ses oeuvres* (Paris, 1868)

T. Marx: *Adolf Bernhard Marx' Verhältnis zu Felix Mendelssohn Bartholdy* (Leipzig, 1869)

C. Mendelssohn Bartholdy: *Goethe und Felix Mendelssohn Bartholdy* (Leipzig, 1871; Eng. trans. with addns by M. E. von Glehn, London, 1872, 2/1874/*R*1970)

S. Hensel: *Die Familie Mendelssohn 1729–1847, nach Briefen und Tagebüchern* (Berlin, 1879, 18/1924; Eng. trans., 1882/*R*1969)

J. Sittard: *Felix Mendelssohn Bartholdy* (Leipzig, 1881)

W. S. Rockstro: *Mendelssohn* (London, 1884, 2/1911)

G. von Loeper: 'Mendelssohn Bartholdy', *ADB*

E. David: *Les Mendelssohn Bartholdy et Robert Schumann* (Paris, 1886)

W. A. Lampadius: *Felix Mendelssohn Bartholdy: ein Gesamtbild seines Lebens und Wirkens* (Leipzig, 1886)

J. C. Hadden: *Mendelssohn* (London, 1888, 2/1904)

S. S. Stratton: *Mendelssohn* (London, 1901, 6/1934)

V. Blackburn: *Mendelssohn* (London, 1904)

E. Wolff: *Felix Mendelssohn Bartholdy* (Berlin, 1906, enlarged 2/1909)

C. Bellaigue: *Mendelssohn* (Paris, 1907, 4/1920)

J. Hartog: *Felix Mendelssohn Bartholdy en zijne werken* (Leiden, 1908)

P. de Stoecklin: *Mendelssohn* (Paris, 1908, 2/1927)

A. Mendelssohn Bartholdy: 'Felix Mendelssohn Bartholdy: Beitrag zur Geschichte seines Lebens und seiner Familie', *Frankfurter Zeitung* (31 Jan 1909), literary suppl.

W. Altmann: 'Mendelssohns Eintreten für Händel', *Die Musik*, xii (1912–13), 8, 79

F. Iribarne: *Mendelssohn: su vida y sus obras* (Paris, 1914)

M. Jacobi: *Felix Mendelssohn Bartholdy* (Bielefeld, 1915)

W. Dahms: *Mendelssohn* (Berlin, 1919, 9/1922)

A. Hillman: *Felix Mendelssohn Bartholdy* (Stockholm, 1919)

J. Esser: *Felix Mendelssohn Bartholdy und die Rheinlande* (diss., U. of Bonn, 1923)

W. H. Fischer: 'Felix Mendelssohn Bartholdy: sein Leben und Wirken in Düsseldorf', *Niederrheinisches Musikfest, Düsseldorf*, xcv (1926), 9–43

C. Winn: *Mendelssohn* (London, 1927)

J. F. Cooke: *Felix Mendelssohn Bartholdy* (Philadelphia, 1929)

E. Vuillermoz: *Une heure de musique avec Mendelssohn* (Paris, 1930)

S. Kaufman:. *Mendelssohn: 'a Second Elijah'* (New York, 1934, 2/1936/R1971)

G. Mariotti: *Mendelssohn* (Rome, 1937)

J. Petitpierre: *Le mariage de Mendelssohn 1837–1847* (Lausanne, 1937; Eng. trans., 1947, as *The Romance of the Mendelssohns*)

B. L. Richmond: *Felix Mendelssohn* (Molenbeek and Brussels, 1946)

B. Bartels: *Mendelssohn Bartholdy: Mensch und Werk* (Bremen, 1947)

J. Werner: 'Felix and Fanny Mendelssohn', *ML*, xxviii (1947), 303

K. H. Wörner: *Felix Mendelssohn Bartholdy: Leben und Werk* (Leipzig, 1947)

G. Grove: *Beethoven–Schubert–Mendelssohn*, ed. E. Blom (London, 1951) [repr. from *Grove I*]

A. Koole: *Felix Mendelssohn Bartholdy* (Haarlem, 1953)

P. Radcliffe: *Mendelssohn* (London, 1954, rev. 2/1967)

R. Sterndale Bennett: 'The Death of Mendelssohn', *ML*, xxxvi (1955), 374

E. Werner: 'New Light on the Family of Felix Mendelssohn', *Hebrew Union College Annual*, xxvi (Cincinnati, 1955), 543

U. Galley: 'Bilder aus Düsseldorfs musikalischer Vergangenheit', *Niederrheinisches Musikfest, Düsseldorf*, cx (1956), 33 [on Mendelssohn and K. Immermann]

H. C. Worbs: *Felix Mendelssohn Bartholdy* (Leipzig, 1956, 2/1957)

S. Jemnitz: *Felix Mendelssohn Bartholdy* (Budapest, 1958)

H. C. Worbs: *Felix Mendelssohn Bartholdy: Wesen und Wirken im Spiegel von Selbstzeugnissen und Berichten der Zeitgenossen* (Leipzig, 1958)

F. H. Franken: *Das Leben grosser Musiker im Spiegel der Medizin: Schubert, Chopin, Mendelssohn* (Stuttgart, 1959)

H. E. Jacob: *Felix Mendelssohn und seine Zeit: Bildnis und Schicksal eines Meisters* (Frankfurt am Main, 1959–60; Eng. trans., 1963)

M. F. Schneider: 'Mendelssohn und Schiller in Luzern', *Die Ernte*, xli (Basle, 1960), 125

——: *Mendelssohn oder Bartholdy? Zur Geschichte eines Familiennamens* (Basle, 1962)

——: 'Felix Mendelssohn Bartholdy: Herkommen und Jugendzeit in Berlin', *Jb der Stiftung Preussischer Kulturbesitz 1963*, 157

E. Werner: *Mendelssohn: a New Image of the Composer and his Age* (New York, 1963)

E. Rudolph: *Der junge Felix Mendelssohn: ein Beitrag zur Musikgeschichte der Stadt Berlin* (diss., Humboldt U., Berlin, 1964)

K.-H. Köhler: *Felix Mendelssohn Bartholdy* (Leipzig, 1966, rev. 2/1972)

A. S. Kurtsman: *Mendel'son* (Moscow, 1967)

S. Grossmann-Vendrey: *Felix Mendelssohn Bartholdy und die Musik der Vergangenheit* (Regensburg, 1969)

M. Hurd: *Mendelssohn* (London, 1970)

W. Reich: *Felix Mendelssohn im Spiegel eigener Aussagen und zeitgenössischer Dokumente* (Zurich, 1970)

H. Kupferberg: *The Mendelssohns: Three Generations of Genius* (New York, 1972)

G. R. Marek: *Gentle Genius: the Story of Felix Mendelssohn* (New York, 1972)

P. Ranft: *Felix Mendelssohn Bartholdy: eine Lebenschronik* (Leipzig, 1972)

Y. Tiénot: *Mendelssohn: musicien complet* (Paris, 1972)

D. and M. V. Jenkins: *Mendelssohn in Scotland* (London, 1978)

### WORKS

O. Jahn: *Über Felix Mendelssohn Bartholdys Oratorium Paulus* (Kiel, 1842)

J. J. Bussinger: *Über Felix Mendelssohn und seine Musik zur Antigone* (Basle, c1862)

F. Zander: *Über Mendelssohns Walpurgisnacht* (Königsberg, 1862)

G. A. Macfarren: *Mendelssohn's Antigone* (London, 1865)

F. Chrysander: 'Mendelssohns Orgelbegleitung zu Israel in Ägypten', *Jahrbücher für musikalische Wissenschaft*, ii (Leipzig, 1867), 249

A. M. Little: *Mendelssohn's Music to the Antigone of Sophocles* (diss., U. of London, 1893)

F. G. Edwards: 'Mendelssohn's Organ Sonatas', *PMA*, xxi (1894–5), 1

——: *The History of Mendelssohn's Oratorio 'Elijah'* (London, 1896/R)

J. W. G. Hathaway: *An Analysis of Mendelssohn's Organ Works: a Study of their Structural Features* (London, 1898)

O. A. Mansfield: *Organ Parts of Mendelssohn's Oratorios and other Choral Works Analytically Considered* (London, 1907)

W. Kahl: 'Zu Mendelssohns Liedern ohne Worte', *ZMw*, iii (1920–21), 459

G. Schünemann: 'Mendelssohns Jugendopern', *ZMw*, v (1922–3), 506

J. Koffler: *Die orchestrale Koloristik in den symphonischen Werken von Mendelssohn* (diss., U. of Vienna, 1923)

H. Mandt: *Die Entwicklung des Romantischen in der Instrumentalmusik Felix Mendelssohn Bartholdys* (diss., U. of Cologne, 1927)

C. W. Wilkinson: *How to Interpret Mendelssohn's 'Songs without Words'* (London, 1930)

T. Armstrong: *Mendelssohn's 'Elijah'* (London, 1931)

K. G. Fellerer: 'Mendelssohns Orgelstimmen zu Händelschen Werken', *HJb*, iv (1931), 79

G. Wilcke: *Tonalität und Modulation im Streichquartett Mendelssohns und Schumanns* (diss., U. of Rostock, 1932)

T. L. Buick: *Elijah: the Story of Mendelssohn's Oratorio* (New Plymouth, New Zealand, 1935)

L. Hochdorf: *Mendelssohns 'Lieder ohne Worte' und der 'Lieder-ohne-Worte'-Stil in seinen übrigen Instrumentalwerken* (diss., U. of Vienna, 1938)

J. Horton: *The Chamber Music of Mendelssohn* (London, 1946)

L. W. Leven: 'An Unpublished Mendelssohn Manuscript', *MT*, lxxxix (1948), 361

A. van der Linden: 'Un fragment inédit du "Lauda Sion" de Felix Mendelssohn', *AcM*, xxvi (1954), 48

E. Werner: 'Two Unpublished Mendelssohn Concertos', *ML*, xxxvi (1955), 126

J. Werner: 'The Mendelssohn Cadence', *MT*, xcvii (1956), 17

K.-H. Köhler: 'Zwei rekonstruierte Singspiele von Felix Mendelssohn Bartholdy', *BMw*, ii/3–4 (1960), 86

D. M. Mintz: *The Sketches and Drafts of Three of Mendelssohn's Major Works* (diss., Cornell U., 1960) [on *Elijah*, the Italian Symphony and the D minor Trio]

M. Rasmussen: 'The First Performance of Mendelssohn's Festgesang "An die Künstler" op.68', *BWQ*, iv (1961), 151

M. Geck: 'Sentiment und Sentimentalität im volkstümlichen Liede Felix Mendelssohn Bartholdys', *Hans Albrecht in memoriam* (Kassel, 1962), 200

D. Siebenkäs: 'Zur Vorgeschichte der "Lieder ohne Worte" von Mendelssohn', *Mf*, xv (1962), 171

K.-H. Köhler: 'Das Jugendwerk Felix Mendelssohns: die vergessene Kindheitsentwicklung eines Genies', *DJbM*, vii (1962), 18

P. Mies: 'Über die Kirchenmusik und über neu endeckte Werke bei Felix Mendelssohn Bartholdy', *Musica sacra*, lxxxiii (1963), 212, 246

S. Vendrey: *Die Orgelwerke von Felix Mendelssohn Bartholdy* (diss., U. of Vienna, 1964)

J. Werner: *Mendelssohn's 'Elijah': a Historical and Analytical Guide to the Oratorio* (London, 1965)

H. C. Wolff: 'Zur Erstausgabe von Mendelssohns Jugendsinfonien', *DJbM*, xii (1967), 96

G. B. Friedrich: *Die Fugenkomposition in Mendelssohns Instrumentalwerk* (Bonn, 1969)

R. Gerlach: 'Mendelssohns Kompositionsweise: Vergleich zwischen Skizzen und Letztfassung des Violinkonzerts op.64', *AMw*, xxviii (1971), 119

F. Krummacher: *Mendelssohn – der Komponist: Studien zur Kompositionsweise am Beispiel der Kammermusik für Streicher* (Habilitationsschrift, U. of Erlangen, 1972)

M. Thomas: *Das Instrumentalwerk Felix Mendelssohn Bartholdys: eine systematisch-theoretische Untersuchung unter besonderer Berücksichtigung der zeitgenössischen Musiktheorie*, Göttinger musikwissenschaftliche Arbeiten, iv (Kassel, 1972)

R. Elvers: 'Auf den Spuren der Autographen von Felix Mendelssohn Bartholdy', *Beiträge zur Musikdokumentation: Franz Grasberger zum 60. Geburtstag* (Tutzing, 1975)

B. W. Pritchard: 'Mendelssohn's Chorale Cantatas: an Appraisal', *MQ*, lxii (1976), 1

R. L. Todd: 'Of Sea Gulls and Counterpoint: the Early Versions of Mendelssohn's Hebrides Overture', *19th Century Music*, ii (1979), 197

OTHER STUDIES

A. B. Smith: 'The Workmanship of Mendelssohn', *ML*, iv (1923), 18
L. Leven: *Mendelssohn als Lyriker unter besonderer Berücksichtigung seiner Beziehungen zu Ludwig Berger, Bernhard Klein und Adolph Bernhard Marx* (diss., U. of Frankfurt am Main, 1926)
R. Werner: *Felix Mendelssohn Bartholdy als Kirchenmusiker* (diss., U. of Frankfurt am Main, 1930)
L. H. and H. Tischler: 'Mendelssohn's Style', *MR*, viii (1947), 256
P. M. Young: *Introduction to the Music of Mendelssohn* (London, 1949)
R. Sterndale Bennett: 'Mendelssohn as Editor of Handel', *MMR*, lxxxvi (1956), 83
H. C. Wolff: 'Mendelssohn and Handel', *MQ*, xlv (1959), 175
D. Mintz: 'Mendelssohn's Water Color of the Gewandhaus', *Notes*, xviii (1960–61), 211
W. Vetter: 'Die geistige Welt Mendelssohns', *Vermächtnis und Verpflichtung: Festschrift für Franz Konwitschny* (Leipzig, 1961), 83
N. Temperley: 'Mendelssohn's Influence on English Music', *ML*, xliii (1962), 224
D. Mintz: 'Mendelssohn and Romanticism', *Studies in Romanticism*, iii (1964), 216
G. Schuhmacher: 'Mendelssohn heute oder seine Wiederentdeckung durch die Schallplatte', *Schallplatte und Kirche*, i (1969), 3
G. Hendrie: *Mendelssohn's Rediscovery of Bach* (London, 1971)
C. Lowenthal-Hensel, ed.: *Beiträge zur neueren deutschen Kultur- und Wirtschaftsgeschichte*, Mendelssohn-Studien, i (Berlin, 1972)
E. Werner: 'Mendelssohn–Wagner: eine alte Kontroverse in neuer Sicht', *Musicae scientiae collectanea: Festschrift Karl Gustav Fellerer* (Cologne, 1973), 640
C. Dahlhaus, ed.: *Das Problem Mendelssohn* (Regensburg, 1974)
J. Godwin: 'Early Mendelssohn and Late Beethoven', *ML*, lv (1974), 272
T. Stoner: 'Mendelssohn's Lieder not included in the Werke', *FAM*, xxvi (1979), 258

KARL-HEINZ KÖHLER (text)
EVELINE BARTLITZ (work-list, bibliography)

**Mendelssohn Glee Club.** New York choral society founded in 1866; see NEW YORK, §7.

**Mendelssohn societies.** Although attempts were made in Germany soon after Mendelssohn's death to form a musical fund in his memory, the first successful venture was the founding in England of a fund to endow a scholarship for composers and performers. The fund was launched in 1848 and the first Mendelssohn Scholarship was awarded in 1856, to Arthur Sullivan; it was restricted to composers in 1890 and is still in existence. No comparable body emerged in Germany until 1878 when the Felix Mendelssohn-Bartholdy-Stiftung was founded. With the annual revenue paid by the Prussian government for the receipt of Mendelssohn's manuscripts, the heirs of Mendelssohn established two annual scholarships and provided other support for music. The foundation was active until 1934 when political pressure caused its closure; the scholarships were revived in 1962 by the Preussischer Kulturbesitz, Berlin, and since 1963 Mendelssohn prizes have been awarded annually.

In 1958 Hugo von Mendelssohn Bartholdy and Max Friedrich Schneider founded in Basle the Internationale Felix-Mendelssohn-Gesellschaft; its activities centred on a research institute with a special library containing autograph and unpublished works, letters, pictures and newspapers. The society edited the first volumes of the Leipziger Ausgabe der Werke Felix Mendelssohn Bartholdys devoted to hitherto unpublished works. In 1964 the Basle collection was transferred to the Preussischer Kulturbesitz in the Staatsbibliothek, Berlin, where it now forms part of the Mendelssohn-Archiv. The Mendelssohn-Gesellschaft Eingetragener Verein, founded in Berlin in 1967, quickly grew into an international society. It has collected and made available to the Mendelssohn-Archiv a number of letters and autograph manuscripts, as well as documents and other material concerning the Mendelssohn family; it publishes *Mendelssohn-Studien* (1972–).

BIBLIOGRAPHY

J. Marshall: 'Mendelssohn Scholarship', *Grove 5*
M. F. Schneider: 'Eine Mendelssohn-Stätte in Basel', *CIBA-Blätter* (1962), July–Aug, 35
R. Elvers: 'Zur Geschichte der Felix Mendelssohn-Bartholdy-Stiftung', *Jb der Stiftung Preussischer Kulturbesitz 1972*, 147
*Verzeichnis der Autographen, die von der Mendelssohn-Gesellschaft e.V. seit ihrer Gründung im Jahr 1967 erworben und als Deposita in das Mendelssohn-Archiv der Staatsbibliothek Preussischer Kulturbesitz gegeben wurden* (Berlin, 1976)

based on *MGG* (xvi, 1264–6) by permission of Bärenreiter
FRANZ KRAUTWURST

**Mendès, Catulle** (*b* Bordeaux, 20 May 1841; *d* St Germain-en-Laye, Paris, 8 Feb 1909). French writer. His excellent education and considerable talents helped him, while still a youth, to make his way to Paris. Encouraged by Hugo, De Banville and Gautier, he became friendly with Baudelaire, Coppée, Heredia and Villiers de l'Isle-Adam, some of the poets who contributed to *Le Parnasse contemporain*. After the *Tannhäuser* débacle at the Opéra in 1861, the discerning Mendès, eager to demonstrate his faith in Wagner, invited the composer to contribute an article to *La revue fantaisiste*, the journal founded and edited by Mendès. In 1866 Mendès married a fellow Wagnerite, JUDITH GAUTIER; they separated in 1874. Mendès later established a liaison with AUGUSTA HOLMÈS, by whom he had three daughters.

In 1873 Wagner published the crude anti-French parody *Eine Kapitulation* and consequently lost favour with several of his French supporters, among them Mendès. Nevertheless, and in spite of a novel *Le roi vierge* mocking the relationship between Wagner and Ludwig II, Mendès published in 1886 the first full-length biography of Wagner. The book's epilogue reprinted an article, published in the *Revue Wagnérienne* the previous year, in which Mendès urged his countrymen to practise what Wagner preached, and to seek their musical inspiration from within their own country and its literary and historical heritage rather than to imitate Wagner slavishly. Mendès's championing of French nationalism and native composers brought him into contact with the young Debussy in 1889. He paid for the engraving of Debussy's *Fantaisie* and the composer agreed to his proposal that they work together on *Rodrigue et Chimène*, Mendès's adaptation of Corneille's *Le Cid*. Two years later, when Debussy discovered Maeterlinck, their collaboration was abandoned: Debussy let it be known that the score had gone up in flames when the table on which he had been working overturned near his fireplace. Sketches for the almost completed work were found, however, in Cortot's library after his death.

WRITINGS

*Le roi vierge* (Paris, 1881)
[Obituary of Wagner], *Le Gil Blas* (16 Feb 1883)
'Le jeune Prix de Rome et le vieux Wagnériste', *Revue Wagnériste* (8 June 1885)
*Richard Wagner* (Paris, 1886)
*L'homme orchestre* (9/1896) [tales]
*L'art du théâtre* (Paris, 1897–1900)
*L'oeuvre wagnérienne en France. Pages nouvelles. Tristan et Iseult* (Paris, 1899)

WORKS SET TO MUSIC

(*theatrical works first produced in Paris, unless otherwise indicated*)
Le capitaine Fracasse (after T. Gautier), opéra comique by Pessard, 1878
Penthésilée, sym. poem by Bruneau, 1884
Gwendoline, opera by Chabrier, Brussels, 1886
Isoline, fairy opera by Messager, 1888
Le colliers de saphirs, ballet by Pierné, 1891

Les joyeuses commères de Paris (collab. G. Courteline), ballet by Pierné, 1892
Le docteur Blanc, ballet by Pierné, 1893
Medée, incidental music by d'Indy, 1898
La reine Fiammette, incidental music by P. Vidal, 1898; opéra comique by X. Leroux, 1903
Briseïs (collab. E. Mikhaël), opera by Chabrier, Berlin, 1899
Le cygne, ballet by Lecocq, 1899
La Carmélite, opéra comique by Hahn, 1902
Le fils de l'étoile, opera by E. Erlanger, 1904
Ariane, opera by Massenet, 1906
La fête chez Thérèse, ballet pantomime by Hahn, 1910
L'amoureuse leçon, ballet by Bruneau, 1913

Lieds de France, songs by Bruneau (1892)
12 songs by Paderewski, op.22 (1903)
Other songs by Bizet, Chabrier, Fauré, Messager, Pierné, Roussel, Saint-Saëns and others

BIBLIOGRAPHY
W. Festerling: Catulle Mendès' Beziehungen zu Richard Wagner (Greifswald, 1913)
J. F. Herlihy: Catulle Mendès: critique dramatique et musical (Paris, 1936)
G. Samazeuilh: Musiciens de mon temps (Paris, 1947)
L. Guichard: La musique et les lettres en France aux temps du Wagnérisme (Paris, 1963)
E. Brody: 'La famille Mendès: a Literary Link between Wagner and Debussy', MR, xxxiii (1972), 177
ELAINE BRODY

**Mendes, Gilberto (Ambrósio García)** (b Santos, 13 Oct 1922). Brazilian composer. He studied harmony with de Benedictis and the piano with Rudge at the Santos Conservatory (1941–8). After a period of independent composition study he had lessons with Santoro (1954) and Olivier Toni (1958–60). He also took part in the Darmstadt summer courses of 1962 and 1968, attending classes given by Boulez, Pousseur and Stockhausen. While in Europe on various occasions he visited the electronic music studios of West German Radio, the ORTF and Karlsruhe University. He has taught new musical techniques in Santos at the Clube de Arte (1956), the Escola de Jovens (1966) and the Colégio Vocacional Stella Maris (from 1968). In 1962 he took charge of the annual New Music Festival of the Santos Ars Viva Society, and from the late 1950s he has been a member of the Santos Musica Nova group, whose aim, as announced in their manifesto of 1963, is to promote 'a new Brazilian music ... according to the modern theories of cybernetics, information, probability, quanta, semantics and semiotics, structuralism and human communication'.

Mendes has created highly individual works to texts by Brazilian concrete poets, among them Décio Pignatari and José Lino Grunewald. His choral piece Beba Coca-Cola (after Pignatari, 1967) achieved outstanding popularity for an avant-garde composition. He has also been strongly influenced by developments in the visual arts of the 1960s: the pop art of Rauschenberg, Lichtenstein and Oldenburg, the films of Godard, and conceptual art. These interests stimulated his exploration of visual aspects in such works as Cidade, Vai e vem, Son et lumière, Asthmatour and Pausa e meno-pausa, where there is an obvious affinity with the indeterminacy and music-theatre of Cage.

WORKS
(selective list)
Fuga dupla a 4 vozes, pf, 1957; Piece, cl, pf, 1957; 7 Pieces, cl, 1957; Ricercare, 2 hn, str, 1960; Music for 12 Insts, 1961; Rotationis, 13 insts, 1961; Música para piano no.1, 1962; nascemorre, vv, perc, 2 typewriters, tape, 1963; Cidade (A. de Campos), mixed media, 1964; Blirium a-9, 12 str, 1965; Blirium b-9, 12 inst, 1965; Blirium c-9, 1/2/3 kbd, 1965; Beba Coca-Cola (Pignatari), 4vv, 1967; Son et lumière, 2 photographers, player pf, tape, 1968
Vai e vem (Grunewald), 1969; Santos Football Music, 12 insts, tape,

audience, 1969; Asthmatour, 1971; O objeto musical, elec fan, elec shaver, 1972; Omaggio a de Sica, tpt, trbn, 1972; Pausa e meno-pausa, coffee cups, spoons, medicine dropper, 1972

Principal publisher: Ricordi (São Paulo)

WRITINGS
with others: 'Música nova', Revista musical chilena (1963), no.86, p.30 [repr. from Invenção (São Paulo, 1963)]
'Música nuova brasiliana: dati e problemi', Aut aut (Milan, 1969), nos.109–10, p.206

BIBLIOGRAPHY
M. Lozano: 'El grupo brasileño Música nova', Sonda (1968), no.1, p.37 [Ger. trans. in Melos, xxxv (1968), 141]
C. Filho: A aventura da música (São Paulo, 1970)
GERARD BÉHAGUE

**Mendes, Manuel** (b Lisbon, c1547; d Évora, 24 Sept 1605). Portuguese composer. He received his musical training at Évora Cathedral, where Cosme Delgado (b 1530) was mestre de capela from 1555 to 1596. After serving as mestre de capela at Portalegre Cathedral he returned to Évora, became a bachelor of arts of the university on 15 March 1575, and was named bacharel da Sé (bachelor of the cathedral) on 16 August 1585. He entered the priesthood on 24 September 1575 and that same year became master of the cathedral choirboys; among his students of the following 20 years were Anjos, Duarte Lobo, Filipe de Magalhães and Manuel Rebelo. Another pupil, Thomé Álvares, negotiated unsuccessfully in 1610 with Balthasar Moretus, representative of the Plantin firm, for the publication of a volume of works by his former teacher.

Mendes's works survive only in MS; some travelled widely, notably an alleluia which survives in four MSS, including a Mexican source. A generation after Mendes's death Manuel de Faria e Sousa mentioned him in Fuente de Aganipe (Madrid, 1644), octavas 72–3 (poema x), among the principal Portuguese composers, as a master to be compared to Morales and Guerrero. An MS appendix to the copy of Morales's Missarum liber secundus (1551) at the Paço de Lamego contains a four-voice Missa pro defunctis by 'Emanuelis Lusitani' (Emanuel of Portugal).

BIBLIOGRAPHY
DBP
J. Mazza: Dicionário biográfico de músicos portugueses (Lisbon, 1945), 90
M. de Sampayo Ribeiro: Sete 'alleluias' inéditos (dum códice do Mosteiro de Aronca) (Oporto, 1949), 20f
M. Joaquim: Vinte livros de música polifónica do Paço Ducal de Vila Viçosa (Lisbon, 1953), 164, 170f
R. Stevenson: Renaissance and Baroque Musical Sources in the Americas (Washington, 1970), 209, 215
ROBERT STEVENSON

**Mendoza (Gutiérrez), Vicente T(eódulo)** (b Cholula, Mexico, 27 Jan 1894; d Mexico City, 27 Oct 1964). Mexican folklorist. He was born of a musical family (his great-grandfather was an organist, his grandfather a tenor and his father a piano teacher) and he began his studies at home at a very early age. When his family moved to Mexico City in 1906, Mendoza began working as a barber while continuing his music instruction; this lasted for 12 years. At the same time he also worked as a draughtsman and as a pianist for silent films. In 1916 he entered the National Conservatory, where he studied under Lauro Beristáin and Rubén M. Campos, and until 1925 he studied intermittently with Julián Carrillo.

After four years working in state schools, he took a post in 1936 at the Institute of Aesthetic Investigations at the University of Mexico which he held until his death. He was founder and president of the Sociedad Folklórica de México from 1938, editor and a principal contributor to its *Anuario*, and participated in many congresses in Latin America, Europe, Japan and the USA. In 1946 he studied at Indiana University and the University of North Carolina (with Ralph Steele Boggs); he received his master's degree at the University of Mexico in 1955.

His first wife, Virginia Rodríguez Rivera, was herself a prominent folklorist, and with her he carried out his most important field work and produced the significant *Folklore de San Pedro Piedra Gorda, Zacatecas* (1952). The aim of his life's work was to make folklore a scholarly discipline in Mexico.

### WRITINGS

with D. Castañeda: *Instrumental precortesiano* (Mexico, 1933–9)
*El romance español y el corrido mexicano* (Mexico, 1939)
with J. Fernández: *Danzas de los concheros en San Miguel de Allende* (Mexico, 1940)
*Lírica infantil de México* (Mexico, 1951)
with V. Rodríguez Rivera: *Folklore de San Pedro Piedra Gorda, Zacatecas* (Mexico, 1952)
*El corrido mexicano* (Mexico, 1954)
*Panorama de la música tradicional de México* (Mexico, 1956)
*Glosas y décimas de México* (Mexico, 1957)
*La canción mexicana* (Mexico, 1961)

### BIBLIOGRAPHY

G. Chase: *A Guide to the Music of Latin America* (Washington, 1962)

E. THOMAS STANFORD

**Mendoza-Nava, Jaime** (*b* La Paz, 1 Dec 1925). Bolivian composer and conductor. A graduate of the Juilliard School, he won the 1950 Premio de Madrid by completing the conservatory curriculum in a few months; later he studied in Paris with Boulanger and Honegger. In 1952 he was appointed conductor of the Bolivian National SO, whose standards he brought to a professional level. He settled in Los Angeles, California, in the following year. Works composed before this move include the orchestral *Don Alvaro*, the *Preludio sinfónico* and the *Suite andina* for wind trio; his Los Angeles compositions include *Estampas y estampillas* for cello ensemble, a Sonata for horn and piano, and many film scores. Several of his scores are published by G. Schirmer.

CARLOS SEOANE

**Mene.** See MEANE.

**Menehou, Michel de** (*fl* Paris, 1557–68). French theorist and composer. In 1558 he was *maître de chapelle* at the abbey church of St Maur-des-Fossés and enjoyed the patronage of Cardinal Guillaume de Bellay, the dedicatee of his *Nouvelle instruction familière, en laquelle sont contenues les difficultés de la musique*. According to Du Verdier and La Croix du Maine, and Draud, the treatise was reissued in 1571 under the title *Nouvelle instruction contenant en brief les preceptes ou fondemens de musique tant pleine que figurée*; an edition with this title was published at Paris in 1582. The book responded to contemporary demand for vernacular treatises on music, but it differs from similar works by Loys Bourgeois, Maximilien Guilliaud, Philibert Jambe de Fer and Claude Martin in devoting much space to elementary harmony; the full title referred to 'concordances et accords' (concordances and intervals) and their use in two- to five-part writing, while Menehou's prologue mentioned young people's desire to learn 'la maniere de pratiquer les accords affin de coucher quelque chose par escript'. He accordingly included chapters on three-,

four- and five-part harmonization, counterpoint, canons and cadences, as well as the usual ones on rudiments (mode, mutation, time, prolation and proportion) which paraphrase Latin authorities (Gaffurius, Frosch, Lampadius and Glarean). The treatise ends with a four-voice chanson, *Le souvenir de ma dame jolie*. Du Chemin printed eight more chansons by Menehou between 1557 and 1568. All but one are courtly *épigrammes* set in a predominantly homophonic style with occasional imitative entries; their rhythm and musical form reflect the decasyllabic metre and structure of the texts.

### WORKS

*Nouvelle instruction familière, en laquelle sont contenues les difficultés de la musique, avecques le nombre des concordances et accords: ensemble la maniere d'en user* (Paris, 1558, 2/1582 as *Nouvelle instruction contenant en brief les preceptes de musique tant pleine que figurée*) (incl. chanson, 4vv); ed. H. Expert, *Les théoriciens de la musique au temps de la Renaissance*, i (Paris, 1900)

8 chansons, 4vv, 1557⁹, 1557¹², 1560³ᵃ, 1560³ᵇ, 1568¹⁰ᵃ

### BIBLIOGRAPHY

G. Draudius: *Bibliotheca exotica* (Frankfurt, 1610), 210
A. Du Verdier and F. La Croix du Maine: *Bibliothèques françaises*, ed. R. Juvigny (Paris, 1772), ii, 127; iv, 63
F. Lesure and G. Thibault: 'Bibliographie des éditions musicales publiées par N. du Chemin (1549–1576)', *AnnM*, i (1953), 277–345

FRANK DOBBINS

**Menestrier, Claude-François** (*b* Lyons, 9 March 1631; *d* Paris, 21 Jan 1705). French Jesuit and savant. Menestrier studied at the Jesuit Collège de la Trinité in Lyons and subsequently taught rhetoric there, having joined the Jesuit order in 1646. He later taught at Chambéry, Vienne (Isère) and Grenoble before being recalled to the college at Lyons. It was during this latter stay there that he developed the special interest in the history and organization of public festivals and ceremonies that occupied him for most of his life. This interest resulted not only in his organizing such events (for example on the occasion of the visit of Louis XIV to Lyons in 1658, an event which is known to have included student performances of ballets devised by Menestrier) but especially in his publishing a series of works dealing with their details: his studies in heraldry, in imagery and decoration, in stage design and construction, in the writing of occasional poetry and ballets and in the theatrical use of music and dance are all notable. In 1667 he was named librarian of his college, but he left shortly afterwards for a period of travel in Europe (notably to Italy, Germany, Flanders and England). Finally, in 1670, he made his home in Paris, where he remained for the rest of his life except for occasional trips undertaken as a preacher for the Jesuit order.

The four works by Menestrier that have particular relevance to music are among the earliest publications to combine what was, for the time, a thorough study of the history and aesthetics of theatrical performance with practical and detailed descriptions of actual events (chiefly ballet and opera in France and Italy). As such they are valuable documents bearing on the development of theatre and dance, as well as of music, from the time of the ancient Hebrews and Greeks to that of Louis XIV. His works in general remained current through much of the 18th century.

### WRITINGS

*(only those on music)*

'Remarques, pour la conduite des ballets', *L'Autel de Lyon* (Lyons, 1658), 50–56 [repr. in Christout, 221ff]
'De l'harmonie', *Traité des tournois, joustes, carrousels et autres spectacles publics* (Paris, 1669), 167

*Des représentations en musique anciennes et modernes* (Paris, 1681/*R*1972, 3/1685)
*Des ballets anciens et modernes selon les règles du théâtre* (Paris, 1682/*R*1972, 4/1686)

BIBLIOGRAPHY
*HawkinsH*
L. C. Mizler: *Musicalische Bibliothek*, ii/3 (Leipzig, 1742), 39ff
J.-B. Montfalcon: 'Menestrier, Claude-François', *Nouvelle biographie générale*, xxxiv (Paris, 1861)
G. Tani: 'Le Comte d'Aglié et le ballet de cour en Italie', *Les fêtes de la Renaissance*, ed. J. Jacquot (Paris, 1956), 222ff
M. M. McGowan: *L'art du ballet de cour en France, 1581–1643* (Paris, 1963)
A. Cioranescu: *Bibliographie de la littérature française du dix-septième siècle*, ii (Paris, 1966), 1401ff
M.-F. Christout: *Le ballet de cour de Louis XIV, 1643–1672* (Paris, 1967), esp. chap.5

ALBERT COHEN

**Mengal, Martin-Joseph** (*b* Ghent, 27 Jan 1784; *d* Ghent, 4 July 1851). Belgian composer and horn player. He studied the horn with his father, and by the age of 13 was playing at the theatre in Ghent. He entered the Paris Conservatoire in 1804 and after playing the horn in the orchestra at the Odéon he became principal horn at the Opéra-Comique and remained there for 13 years. He studied composition with Reicha and wrote a number of operas and instrumental works; three of his *opéras comiques* were produced in Paris in 1818–23. In 1825 he was appointed director of the theatre in Ghent but soon resigned and after the 1830 Revolution became a conductor in Antwerp and The Hague. Finally, in 1835, he obtained the directorship of the new conservatory in Ghent, where his pupils included Gevaert and Van Duyse. His brother Jean-Baptiste (*b* Ghent, 21 Feb 1792; *d* Paris, 19 Dec 1878) was also a distinguished horn player and one of the founders of the Paris Société des Concerts du Conservatoire.

WORKS
*(selective list, all MSS at B-Gc)*
THEATRICAL
Une nuit au château (1, P. de Kock), Paris, Feydeau, 5 Aug 1818 (Paris, 1818)
L'île de Babilary (3, de Kock), Paris, Feydeau, 27 March 1819
Les infidèles (1, de Kock), Paris, Feydeau, 2 Jan 1823
Le vampire (3), Ghent, 1826
Apothéose de Talma, Ghent, 1826
Un jour à Vaucluse (1), Ghent, 1 May 1830

OTHER WORKS
Requiem; Salve regina; Tantum ergo
Concertante, ob, hn, bn; concertante, 2 fl, ob, cl, hn (both Ghent, n.d.)
Symphonie concertante, 2 hn, orch
3 concs., hn, orch
Chamber music; songs and choruses

BIBLIOGRAPHY
*FétisB*
E. Fétis: 'Martin Joseph Mengal', *Annuaire de l'Académie royale de Belgique*, xxv (Brussels, 1859), 167
P. Bergmans: 'Mengal, Martin-Joseph', *BNB*

JOHN LADE

**Mengelberg.** Dutch family of musicians.

**(1) (Josef) Willem Mengelberg** (*b* Utrecht, 28 March 1871; *d* Zuort, Switzerland, 22 March 1951). Conductor. His musical training was at Utrecht and at the Cologne Conservatory. In 1891 he became conductor of the municipal orchestra of Lucerne. In 1895 he returned to Holland to take up an appointment which was to last for the rest of his working life. As conductor of the Amsterdam Concertgebouw, Mengelberg brought the orchestra into the front rank of European ensembles. Although famous for his annual Palm Sunday performances, which started in 1899, of the *St Matthew Passion*, he was first and foremost an orchestral virtuoso with special sympathy for Strauss and Mahler.

Strauss dedicated *Ein Heldenleben*, which was to become one of Mengelberg's favourite warhorses, to him and to his orchestra. Mengelberg did the initial preparation for Mahler's concerts at the Amsterdam Concertgebouw from 1903. In 1920 his 25th year with the orchestra was celebrated with, among other things, a complete Mahler cycle. He was much in demand abroad. He directed the Museum Concerts at Frankfurt am Main from 1907 to 1920. His London appearances included concerts for the Royal Philharmonic Society between 1911 and 1914. His duties in Amsterdam were so arranged that he could make annual visits to the New York PO from 1921 to 1929. He also toured at the head of his orchestra.

*Willem Mengelberg*

Mengelberg was small and dynamic, a forceful interpreter of the Romantic repertory (notably Tchaikovsky), a martinet addicted to meticulous and voluble rehearsals (Bernard Shore gave a long description of the BBC SO's first experience of his methods). He had no scruples about making what he used to call 'changements' in a composer's markings where he considered that sound and meaning would benefit. Mengelberg was not only concerned with interpretative detail. He did much in the Netherlands to introduce good music to popular audiences, to secure better conditions for the players and wider recognition for Dutch composers. The end of his career was sad. During the Occupation he accepted invitations to conduct in Germany, and his conciliatory attitude to the Nazis induced a resentment the more bitter because of his eminence and his achievements. He was forbidden to conduct in Holland after 1945, and spent his last years in retirement in Switzerland.

BIBLIOGRAPHY
B. Shore: *The Orchestra Speaks* (London, 1938)
H. C. Schonberg: *The Great Conductors* (London, 1968)
J. Wouters: 'Gramophone Records and the Concertgebouw Orchestra', *Recorded Sound*, xxxvi (1969), 524
D. Wooldridge: *Conductor's World* (London, 1970)
R. Wolf: 'The Mengelberg Recordings', *Grand baton*, viii (Cleveland, 1971), 41
R. Hardie: *The Recordings of Willem Mengelberg* (Nashville, Tenn., 1972)

**(2) (Curt) Rudolf Mengelberg** (*b* Krefeld, 1 Feb 1892; *d* Monte Carlo, 13 Oct 1959). Musicologist and composer of German origin, a nephew of (1) Willem Mengelberg. He studied law at the universities of Geneva and Munich, took piano lessons from Neitzel in Cologne and read musicology at Leipzig under Riemann. Then in Amsterdam he studied composition under Dopper and his uncle, and in 1917 he was appointed artistic assistant to the Concertgebouw Orchestra, later becoming artistic manager (from 1925) and director (1935–54). In 1920 he organized the Concertgebouw Mahler Festival, during which all Mahler's works were performed in nine concerts. Mengelberg's compositions are predominantly vocal, this preference being expressed at first in romantic songs and later in large-scale sacred pieces, sometimes drawing on Gregorian chant.

### WORKS
*(selective list)*

Orch: Vn Conc., 1930; Capriccio, pf, orch, 1936; Fl Concertino, 1943
Choral: Weinlese, T, chorus, orch, 1928; Requiem, solo vv, chorus, orch, 1924; Stabat mater, solo vv, chorus, orch, 1940; Victimae paschali laudes, solo vv, chorus, orch, 1946

### WRITINGS

*G. A. Ristori* (diss., U. of Leipzig, 1915; Leipzig, 1916)
*Das Mahler-Fest Amsterdam, Mai 1920* (Vienna, 1920)
*Gustav Mahler* (Leipzig, 1923)
*Holland als kulturelle Einheit* (Leipzig, 1928)
*50 jaar Concertgebouw* (Amsterdam, 1938)
*Muziek, spiegel des tijds* (Rotterdam, 1949)

### BIBLIOGRAPHY

W. Paap: 'Dr Rudolf Mengelberg zestig jaar', *Mens en melodie*, vii (1952), 34

**(3) Karel (Willem Joseph) Mengelberg** (*b* Utrecht, 18 July 1902). Conductor and composer, a nephew of (1) Willem Mengelberg. He studied composition with Pijper and later at the Berlin Hochschule für Musik, and was a conducting pupil of Scherchen. After some years as a choral and opera conductor in Germany, he was attached to the theatre in Greifswald (1927–30). From 1930 to 1933 he was music adviser to the Reichsrundfunk and chief sound producer for the Deutschlandsender in Berlin. He held contracts in Barcelona and Kiev, made many European concert tours, and in 1938 settled in Amsterdam. Thereafter he appeared as a conductor with Dutch orchestras, and from 1945 established a reputation as a music critic. He composed orchestral and chamber music, choral, piano and carillon pieces in a conventional style, as well as numerous scores for plays, films and radio dramas; Donemus published his works. The ballet *Signalen* (1935) and the Horn Concerto (1950) each won a City of Amsterdam Prize.

**(4) Misha** [Misja] **Mengelberg** (*b* Kiev, 5 June 1935). Pianist and composer, a son of (3) Karel Mengelberg, he studied composition with Van Baaren at the Conservatory of The Hague, where he took a final examination in theory in 1964. He became well known as a jazz pianist and improviser, playing with Eric Dolphy and other leading musicians, and in 1967 he was a founder-member of the Instant Composers' Pool, a group formed to perform and record improvised music, often of a theatrical nature.

### WORKS
*(selective list)*

Musica per 17 strumenti, 1959; Medusa, str qt, 1962; Commentary, orch, 1965; Exercise, fl, 1966; Omtrent een componistenactie, wind qnt, 1966; 4 Pf Pieces, 1966; Amaga, gui, Hawaiian gui, b gui, elec, 1968; Anatoloose, orch, 1968; Hello Windyboys, 2 wind qnts, 1968; Met welbeleefde groet van de kameel, orch, 1971–3; Onderweg, orch, 1973

Principal publisher: Donemus

### BIBLIOGRAPHY

E. Vermeulen: 'Misha Mengelberg: Anatoloose', *Sonorum speculum* (1971), no.48, p.9
RONALD CRICHTON (1), ROGIER STARREVELD (2–4)

**Menges, (Siegfried Frederick) Herbert** (*b* Hove, 27 Aug 1902; *d* London, 20 Feb 1972). English conductor and composer, brother of Isolde Menges. He was the son of a German father and a British mother, both violinists who ran a music school in Brighton. He studied at the Royal College of Music, where he worked with Holst and Vaughan Williams. Much of his career was spent in the London theatre but he also maintained a connection with Brighton as founder and director of the Brighton PO from 1925 until his death. In 1931 he became musical director of the Old Vic Theatre and composed or arranged and conducted incidental music for most of Shakespeare's plays. He served Sir John Gielgud in all his productions from *Richard of Bordeaux* in 1933 to the end of World War II. He conducted most of the principal British orchestras. For these services, and especially for his sustained influence on the musical life of the south-east, he was made an OBE in 1963.

FRANK HOWES

**Menges, Isolde (Marie)** (*b* Hove, 16 May 1893; *d* Richmond, Surrey, 13 Jan 1976). English violinist, sister of Herbert Menges. After a start with her parents, both violinists, she had lessons from Sauret, and studied for three years with Auer in St Petersburg and Dresden from 1910. Her London concerto début was in February 1913. In May she played the Brahms and Glazunov concertos under Mengelberg, and continental engagements began. In 1916 she was invited to the USA, and in 1922 was the first to make a complete recording of the Beethoven concerto with orchestra (under Landon Ronald). An expressive player of deep insight, she had a classical style of great purity and a range of interest that made her a world soloist in considerable demand. A natural chamber musician, in the late 1920s she played piano trios with Ivor James and Harold Samuel. In 1931 she founded the Menges Quartet and began her teaching activities at the Royal College of Music.

ROBERT ANDERSON

**Mennin, Peter** (*b* Erie, Penn., 17 May 1923). American composer and teacher. He studied at Oberlin College under Normand Lockwood and, after military service, at the Eastman School under Hanson and Rogers (BMus 1945, MMus 1945, PhD 1947). In 1945 he won the first Gershwin Memorial Award with the Symphony no.2, subsequently performed by Bernstein and the New York PO and later awarded the Bearns Prize of Columbia University. He spent the year 1957–8 in Europe. Back in the USA he was appointed director of the Peabody Conservatory (1958–62) and then president of the Juilliard School. Mennin has received commissions from leading American orchestras and foundations; awards have been made to him by the American Academy of Arts and Letters, the Guggenheim Foundation and other bodies. He has served as chairman of the board of the National Music Council and president of the Naumburg Foundation, besides numerous other administrative positions. His music is conservative, marked by sound form and orchestration and by romantic melody; he belongs essentially to the American symphonic tradition.

## WORKS
*(selective list)*

Orch: 8 syms., 1941, 1944, 1946, 'The Cycle' 1948, 1950; 1958, 1963, 1973; Concertino fl, str, perc, 1944; Folk Ov., 1945; Sinfonia, chamber orch, 1946; Fantasia (Canzona and Toccata), str, 1947; Canzona, band, 1951; Concertato 'Moby Dick', 1952; Vc Conc., 1956; Pf Conc., 1958; Canto, 1963; Sinfonia, 1971

Vocal: Alleluia, chorus, 1941; 4 Songs (Dickinson), S, pf, 1941; A Song of the Palace, Crossing the Han River, The Gold-Threaded Robe (Kiang Kang-Hu, trans. W. Bynner), chorus, 1948; Tumbling Hair (Cummings), chorus, pf, 1949; Bought Locks (Martial, trans. J. Harington), chorus, pf, 1949; The Christmas Story, S, T, chorus, brass qt, timp, str, 1949; Cantata de virtute, solo vv, narrator, chorus, children's chorus, orch, 1969; Voices, 1v, pf, harp, hpd, perc, 1976

Inst: 2 str qts, 1941, 1951; Org Sonata, 1941; 5 Pf Pieces, 1949; Sonata concertante, vn, pf, 1959; Pf Sonata, 1967

JAMES G. ROY JR

**Meno** (It.: 'less'). A word used both adjectivally and adverbially as an adjustment to a tempo or expression mark. *Meno mosso*, normally found in the middle of a movement, indicates a change to a slower tempo. Occasionally it comes at the beginning: the most famous case is Schoenberg's Second String Quartet which opens with the instruction *etwas langsamer anfangend* ('beginning a little more slowly').

**Menologion** (Gk.). MARTYROLOGY.

**Menon, Tuttovale** [Tuttualle, Tutval] (*b c*1510; *fl c*1545–52). Italian composer of French origin. If he was the 'Tutval' who was the 'peritevole guida' in music to Gaspare Stampa, the noted Paduan poet and singer, he must have been living in Venice or Padua from 1545 to 1547. By 1547 he must have left Venice, for a dedication by Antonio Barges in 1547 refers to Menon in the past tense. In 1546 he was the subject, together with other musicians, of poems by Girolamo Fenaruolo published that year in Padua. In 1548 his *Madrigali d'amore*, dedicated to Renée of France, Duchess of Ferrara, were published in Ferrara. One of these, *Non fu giamai ne fia*, actually names Renée and another, *Un giglio d'or*, probably refers to her. Menon's dedication refers to France as 'that homeland which . . . made me a faithful subject of Your Excellency'. In 1552 he was definitely in Correggio, as he was described by Ortensio Landi as 'habitatore di Correggio huomo singolare'. He was probably one of the teachers there of Claudio Merulo. In 1588 a piece by 'Menon' was published by the Veronese composer Paolo Bozi, in *Giardinetto de madrigali e canzonette a tre* (Venice, 1588).

The bulk of his surviving work consists of the 45 *Madrigali d'amore* (Ferrara, 1548, reprinted in truncated form in 1549 in Venice). This is probably the collection to which Doni referred in *La libraria* (Venice, 1550, 2/1557), naming the composer as 'Tutuual' or 'Tuduual'. Some of the madrigals may have circulated earlier, for Fenaruolo spoke of Menon's madrigals in 1546, hinting that some were so amorous as to 'make short work of honour'. Some may be much older, as they employ the under-6th cadence. If Menon is the composer of some or all of the pieces ascribed to TUDUAL then his activity as a composer may well date back to 1538 or earlier.

### BIBLIOGRAPHY

*FétisB*

O. Landi: *Sette libri di cathaloghi a varie cose appartenenti* (Venice, 1552), 512

R. Giazotto: *La musica a Genova* (Genoa, 1951), 129ff

———: *Harmonici concenti in aere veneto* (Rome, 1954), 19f, 27f

J. Haar: 'The *Libraria* of Antonfrancesco Doni', *MD*, xxiv (1970), 108

THOMAS W. BRIDGES

**Menon, V(atakke) K(urupath) Narayana** (*b* Trichur, 27 June 1911). Indian music administrator, writer and composer. After early vocal training he studied the *vīṇā* under Appu Bhagavathar of Trivandrum and later under K. S. Narayanaswami, giving his first major recitals at the Travancore Arts Festival (1930 and 1931). He took the MA at Madras University and, with a dissertation on Yeats's poetry (1939, published 1942), a doctorate at Edinburgh University, where his interest in Western music was first stimulated by Tovey's concerts at the Usher Hall. He was a Carnegie Scholar (1939–41) and Senior Carnegie Scholar (1941–2) in English at Edinburgh University. As music adviser and producer of the BBC Eastern Service (1942–7) he became known for his understanding (rare at that time) of both Indian and Western art music. He was subsequently director of staff training (1948–63) and director general (1965–8) of All India Radio and secretary of the National Academy of Music, Dance and Drama, New Delhi (1963–5). He was also appointed a member of the faculty of music and fine arts, University of Delhi.

As an administrator Menon has been influential in creating links between Indian and Western national and international music organizations. He was a member of the executive board of the International Music Council, UNESCO, serving twice as vice-president and later as president (1966–8); his other positions include executive director of the National Centre for the Performing Arts, Bombay (1968), chairman of the Asian Music Rostrum (1969, 1971, 1973) and vice-president of the International Institute for Music, Dance and Theatre. His compositions include dance and ballet music, arrangements of Indian and Western music, and music for documentary films.

MANTLE HOOD

**Menotti, Gian Carlo** (*b* Cadegliano, 7 July 1911). American composer of Italian birth. The sixth of ten children, Gian Carlo Menotti was born in a country town on Lake Lugano. His father was a prosperous businessman and his mother a talented amateur musician. He had already written two operas when he entered the Milan Conservatory at the age of 13. In 1928 he began studies with Rosario Scalero at the Curtis Institute of Music in Philadelphia, where a close friendship with his fellow student Samuel Barber began. The two spent several summers in Europe attending opera performances in Vienna and in Italy. It was in Vienna, having received his diploma with honours from the Curtis Institute in 1933, that Menotti began the libretto for an *opera buffa*, *Amelia al ballo*. He completed the orchestration on his return to the USA in 1935; the opera received its première in an English translation by George Mead as *Amelia Goes to the Ball*. A few days later it was performed in New York with such success that the Metropolitan Opera accepted it for the following season.

The success of *Amelia* brought Menotti a commission from NBC for a radio opera. Using the *opera buffa* tradition of set numbers, Menotti wrote his first libretto in English, *The Old Maid and the Thief*. His next opera, *The Island God*, was poorly received. Menotti remained in the USA but retained his Italian citizenship during World War II. There he wrote the Piano Concerto in F and a dramatic ballet, *Sebastien*, set in 17th-century Venice.

*Gian Carlo Menotti*

A commission by the Alice M. Ditson Fund led to the very successful opera *The Medium*, a tragedy in two acts for five singers, a dance-mime role and a chamber orchestra of 14 players. The melodramatic story is the 'tragedy of a person caught between two worlds, the world of reality which she cannot comprehend, and the supernatural world in which she cannot believe'. The work is theatrically effective and the music, often quite dissonant, conveys an eerie, morbid atmosphere. Typical of the Italian operatic tradition, *The Medium* has memorable melodies such as the folksong-like 'O, black swan'. The opera had a run of 211 performances during 1947–8 at the Ethel Barrymore Theatre on Broadway. As a curtain-raiser for these performances of *The Medium* (and a striking contrast), Menotti wrote a light one-act comedy, *The Telephone*, sub-titled *L'amour à trois*. The State Department organized a European tour of these works in 1955. In 1951 Menotti directed a successful film version of *The Medium*.

Menotti's versatile dramatic skills, as director, librettist and composer, brought him a contract from Metro-Goldwyn-Mayer to write film scripts. Although his scripts were never filmed, one contained the seeds of his first full-length opera, *The Consul*, considered by many to be his greatest work. It uses the verismo of Puccini's day to treat a contemporary situation: the impossibility of obtaining a visa to leave a police state. Music and stage techniques combine to communicate strongly and directly. The New York première at the Ethel Barrymore Theatre on 15 March 1950 was a great success and performances continued there for about eight months. The work received the Pulitzer Prize and the Drama Critics Award. It has been translated into 12 languages and has been performed in over 20 countries. With *The Consul* and his next two operas, Menotti seemed at the height of his powers and of public acclaim.

*Amahl and the Night Visitors*, commissioned by NBC, was the first opera written expressly for television. In writing it, Menotti was influenced by *The Adoration of the Magi* of Hieronymus Bosch. The work was first televised on Christmas eve 1951 and has been broadcast annually. The roles, particularly the main part for boy soprano, are skilfully conceived so that the work can be performed by amateurs. The charm and clear diatonicism of the work have helped to make it one of the most frequently performed operas of the 20th century. Menotti's next opera, *The Saint of Bleecker Street*, is a full-length piece in the broad and serious style of *The Consul*. It is an effective drama set in contemporary New York and concerned with the conflict of the physical and spiritual worlds. Again a contemporary plot is set in a Puccinian manner. The opera received the Drama Critics Circle Award for the best play, the Music Critics Circle Award for the best opera and the Pulitzer Prize in music for 1955.

Choral music was an important element in *Amahl* and *The Saint of Bleecker Street*; it is basic to the 'madrigal fable' *The Unicorn, the Gorgon and the Manticore*. Commissioned by the Elizabeth Sprague Coolidge Foundation, it is one of Menotti's most charming works. The model was the late Renaissance madrigal comedy (such as Vecchi's *L'amfiparnasso*), and the work consists of an introduction, 12 madrigals (some *a cappella*) and six instrumental interludes. At about the same time Menotti wrote the text for Samuel Barber's opera *Vanessa*.

Menotti's next opera, *Maria Golovin*, was again commissioned by NBC. It was performed in New York in November of 1958, but with little success, and later broadcast by NBC. From 1958 much of Menotti's time was taken up by the Spoleto Festival of Two Worlds, which he founded and directed. Thomas Schippers became music director of this major summer festival in 1967, but Menotti continued as president of the organization. However, new works began to appear again in 1963: *Labyrinth*, written for NBC television, exploits the possibilities of special camera techniques. A cantata *The Death of the Bishop of Brindisi* (concerning the Children's Crusade of 1212) was commissioned by the Cincinnati Musical Festival Association; and *Le dernier sauvage* was written for the Paris Opéra. The première of the latter work in fact occurred at the Opéra-Comique and it was later given a lavish production at the Metropolitan Opera in New York.

A CBS commission for the 1964 Bath Festival was fulfilled by a church opera in one act, *Martin's Lie*, which was broadcast in the USA in the following year. More recent works include *Canti della lontananza*, a cycle of seven songs on Menotti's own texts written for Elisabeth Schwarzkopf; *Help, Help, the Globolinks!*, a 70-minute 'opera in one act for children and those who like children' commissioned by the Hamburg Staatsoper; and an opera commissioned by the New York City Opera, *The Most Important Man*. A drama without music, *The Leper*, was first performed in Tallahassee, Florida, on 22 April 1970.

Menotti cares about his audience and about the human voice. He has written: 'There is a certain indolence towards the use of the voice today, a tendency to treat the voice instrumentally, as if composers feared that its texture is too expressive, too *human*' (1964). Like Puccini he is sensitive to new musical techniques that will serve his dramatic purpose: a high, sustained dissonant chord in *The Consul* as Magda turns on the gas stove to commit suicide; the 12-note music used to parody contemporary civilization (and indirectly the avant-garde composer) in Act 2 of *Le dernier sauvage*; or electronic tape music to represent the invaders from outer space in *Help, Help, the Globolinks!* Also like Puccini he gives first place to the human voice and the effective theatrical moment. Menotti's melodies are tonal, sometimes with a modal flavour, and often easily remembered. Sequence and repetition are common, but aria-like passages tend to be brief so as not to interrupt the dramatic flow. The continuous, recitative-like passages set the text with naturalness and clarity. His harmony is tonal, sometimes using parallel chords over a clear and simple tonal basis. Many of his more commanding musical gestures, like the opening of *The Medium*, reflect his avowed fondness for Musorgsky. His orchestration tends to be light and open and he writes particularly well for small instrumental ensembles. His rhythms, even when metrical irregularities are used, are natural and easily grasped by performer and listener.

Critical appraisal of Menotti's works has ranged from sincere appreciation (Sargeant) to bitter denunciation (Kerman). His techniques are traditional and conservative, and while some have faulted his style as sentimental or even dull, his best works can be powerful (*The Consul*) or charming (the Scarlattian Piano Concerto, or *Amahl and the Night Visitors*). The best summary of his achievement is by Hitchcock: 'Menotti combined the theatrical sense of a popular playwright and a Pucciniesque musical vocabulary with an Italianate love of liquid language and a humane interest in characters as real human beings; the result was opera more accessible than anyone else's at the time'.

## WORKS
*(all texts by Menotti unless otherwise stated)*

OPERAS, BALLETS, CANTATAS

Amelia al ballo (opera buffa, 1), 1936; Philadelphia, 1 April 1937
The Old Maid and the Thief (radio opera, 1), 1939; NBC, 22 April 1939; stage, Philadelphia, 11 Feb 1941
The Island God (opera, 1), 1942; New York, Metropolitan, 20 Feb 1942
Sebastian (ballet, 1), 1944; New York, 31 Oct 1944
The Medium (tragedy, 2), 1945; New York, 8 May 1946
The Telephone (opera buffa, 1), 1946; New York, 18 Feb 1947
Errand into the Maze (ballet), 1947; New York, 2 Feb 1947
The Consul (musical drama, 3), 1949; Philadelphia, 1 March 1950
Amahl and the Night Visitors (television opera, 1), 1951; NBC-TV, 24 Dec 1951; stage, Bloomington, Illinois, 21 Feb 1952
The Saint of Bleecker Street (opera, 3), 1954; New York, 27 Dec 1954
The Unicorn, the Gorgon and the Manticore, or The Three Sundays of a Poet (madrigal ballet or madrigal fable), chorus, 10 dancers, 9 insts, 1956; Washington, 21 Oct 1956
Maria Golovin (music drama, 3), 1958; Brussels, 20 Aug 1958
Labyrinth (television opera, 1), 1963; NBC-TV, 3 May 1963
The Death of the Bishop of Brindisi (cantata), S, B, children's chorus, chorus, orch, 1963; Cincinnati, 18 May 1963
Le dernier sauvage (opéra-bouffe, 3), 1963; Paris, Opéra-Comique, 21 Oct 1963
Martin's Lie (church opera, 1), 1964; Bristol (England), 3 June 1964
Help, Help, the Globolinks! (opera, 1), 1968; Hamburg, Staatsoper, 21 Dec 1968
Landscapes and Remembrances (cantata); Milwaukee, 14 May 1976
The Hero (comic opera); Philadelphia, 1 June 1976
The Egg (church opera); Washington, DC, Cathedral, 17 June 1976
The Most Important Man (opera), 1971; New York, 12 March 1971
Tamu-Tamu (opera, 2), 1973; Chicago, Studebaker Theatre, 5 Sept 1973

ORCHESTRAL

Piano Concerto, F, 1945
Sebastian, suite from the ballet (1947)
Apocalypse, 1951
Violin Concerto, a, 1952

Triplo Concerto a tre, 9 soloists forming 3 trios (pf, harp, perc; ob, cl, bn; vn, va, vc), orch, 1970
Sym. no.1 'The Halcyon', 1976

MISCELLANEOUS

Variations on a Theme of Schumann, pf, 1931, MS
Six Compositions for Carillon, 1934, MS
Pastorale and Dance, pf, str orch, 1934, MS
Trio for a House-warming Party, pf, vc, fl, 1936, MS
Four Pieces, str qt, 1936, MS
Poemetti per Maria Rosa, 12 pieces for children, pf, 1937
The Hero (R. Horan), v, pf, 1952
Ricercare and Toccata on a Theme from The Old Maid and the Thief, pf, 1953
Canti della lontananza, cycle of 7 songs, S, pf, 1967; New York, E. Schwarzkopf, 18 March 1967
Suite, 2 vc, pf, 1973; New York, G. Piatigorsky, L. Parnas, C. Wadsworth, 20 May 1973
The Trial of the Gypsy, tr vv, pf; New York, 24 May 1978

Principal publishers: G. Schirmer, Ricordi

WRITINGS

'Notes on Opera as Basic Theatre', *Perspectives USA*, xii (1955), 5
*A Hand of Bridge* [libretto for opera by Barber] (New York, 1960)
*Introductions and Goodbyes* [libretto for opera by Foss] (New York, 1961)
*Vanessa* [libretto for opera by Barber] (New York, 1964)
'I am the Savage', *Opera News*, xxvii/13 (1964), 8

BIBLIOGRAPHY

W. Sargeant: 'Orlando in Mount Kisco', *New Yorker*, xxxix/11 (1963), 49–89
R. Tricoire: *Gian Carlo Menotti: l'homme et son oeuvre* (Paris, 1966)
D. Ewen: 'Gian Carlo Menotti', *The World of Twentieth-century Music* (Englewood Cliffs, NJ, 1968), 481ff
H. Wiley Hitchcock: *Music in the United States: a Historical Introduction* (Englewood Cliffs, NJ, 1969), 211f
L. Grieb: *The Operas of Gian Carlo Menotti, 1937–1972: a Selective Bibliography* (Metuchen, NJ, 1974)

BRUCE ARCHIBALD

**Mensur** (Ger.). SCALING.

**Mensuratio morosa, media, cita, citissima** (Lat.). Four levels of tempo, reflecting stylistic categories of music, formulated by Jacques de Liège; they are similar to the *mores* of PETRUS LE VISER.

**Mensuration.** The late medieval system governing the relationships between long, breve and semibreve. See NOTATION, §III.

**Mensurstrich** (Ger.). A vertical line drawn between (not through) the staves to show the metrical division in editions of early music; *see* STRICH.

**Menta, Francesco** (*b* Brussels, *c*1540; *fl* 1560–77). Italian composer of South Netherlands birth. In the dedication of his *Il primo libro de madrigali a cinque voci* (Venice, 1564) Menta stated that he went to Italy in his youth. It can be deduced from the dedication of *Madrigali a quattro voci* (Rome, 1560) that he lived and studied at Naples; and these madrigals are described as his first compositions. He also contributed a setting of Petrarch's *Padre del ciel* to *Aeri racolti insieme* (*RISM* 1577[8]).

BIBLIOGRAPHY

G. Gaspari: *Catalogo della Biblioteca del Liceo musicale di Bologna*, iii (Bologna, 1893/R1961), 111f

PIER PAOLO SCATTOLIN

**Mentalism.** See PSYCHOLOGY OF MUSIC, §I, 3(i).

**Mentionnière** (Fr.). CHIN REST.

**Mento.** An indigenous Jamaican folk form in which music, words and movement are closely linked. Mento

(Old Sp. *mentar*, 'to mention') is sung in the Jamaican vernacular, and covers a wide range of subjects expressed in humorous satirical style. When the songs are used to ridicule or censure, personal references are veiled in symbols to avoid undue embarrassment or offence.

*Mento* is similar to the Afro-Cuban rumba but sung at a slower tempo (see ex.1). It is characterized by

Ex.1 transcr. O. Lewin

strong accents on the last beat of the four-beat bar; accents sometimes occur not in the melody but in the supporting percussion rhythms, clapping and stamping (ex.2). *Mento* involves group participation, although a soloist often leads vocally or instrumentally and improvises.

Ex.2 transcr. O. Lewin

*Mento* is accompanied by ensembles of four to ten instrumentalists playing various combinations of flute, fiddle, harmonica, penny whistle, accordion, home-made clarinets and trumpets (for the melody); guitars, banjos, bass fiddles (with one, three or four strings) and rumba boxes (for the harmony); drums, sticks, maracas, triangles, tambourine, jawbone of a horse or ass (used as a rattle), grater stroked with a nail or other metal object (percussion).

The *mento* is danced either independently or as the fifth figure of Jamaican quadrille sets; the hips move circularly in a horizontal plane while the feet cover a small area in backwards, sideways and turning steps. *Mento* music largely depends on the virtuosity and improvisatory skill of musicians who have often had no formal training. Unlike calypso it has never enjoyed great commercial popularity, but the political independence of Jamaica (1962) created renewed interest in the genre.

OLIVE LEWIN

**Mentoniera** (It.). CHIN REST.

**Menuet** (Fr.; Ger. *Menuett*). MINUET.

**Menuetto, tempo di menuetto.** Title used for minuet-style movements in instrumental works of the later 18th century. It seems to be a mixture of the German word 'Menuett' and the Italian 'minuetto' and is used only in non-Italian works (*see* MINUET).

**Menuhin.** American family of musicians of Ukrainian origin.

**(1) Yehudi Menuhin** (*b* New York, 22 April 1916). Violinist. He had his first lessons in San Francisco from Sigmund Anker a few months after his fourth birthday. He continued his studies with Persinger and his progress was so rapid that he appeared professionally in San Francisco in 1924 and in New York in 1926 with considerable success. He made a sensational début in Paris in February 1927 and thereafter studied with Enescu. When he played the Beethoven Concerto under Fritz Busch in New York in November 1927 he became a world celebrity overnight. These concerts were followed by tours throughout the USA and Europe (débuts in Berlin, 1928, and London, 1929), and he began making his first gramophone records in 1928. Further periods of study with Enescu (whose musical personality has been a lasting influence on Menuhin) and Adolf Busch alternated with many enormously successful concert appearances. The dominant characteristics of Menuhin's playing during this period, apart from his remarkable technical ability, were the maturity and depth of his musical understanding and his spontaneity and freshness. These qualities enabled the 12-year-old boy to play works of the stature of the Beethoven Concerto and Bach's Chaconne with absolute conviction, and Mozart's concertos with a completeness of identification that has seldom been equalled. One of the notable events of his youth was the performance and gramophone recording, in 1932, of Elgar's Violin Concerto conducted by the composer, then aged 75.

Menuhin has rarely been absent for any length of time from the international concert platform. During World War II he gave over 500 concerts for American and Allied troops in many theatres of war. He was the first artist to appear in the reopened Paris Opéra immediately after the German occupation, and the first Jewish artist to play with the Berlin PO under Furtwängler after the overthrow of the Nazi regime (an action for which he was much criticized, especially among Jewish communities, but which he defended with courage and conviction). On his reappearances under more normal conditions, it was noted that his playing, while it had maintained many of its old qualities and added thereto a further nobility and depth, had at times lost something in spontaneity and technical reliability. Menuhin has indeed made no secret of the fact that he has gone through periods during which he has had to rethink the whole basis of his approach to violin technique.

In 1959 Menuhin made his home in London. He has directed several musical festivals, notably the Bath Festival (1958–68), the Windsor Festival (1969–72), and the Gstaad Festival (from 1956). He has given many concerts playing with and conducting his own chamber orchestra, founded in 1958, during tours throughout the world. He has also conducted many of the leading symphony orchestras in Europe and America, and encouraged and collaborated in the performance of Indian music in Western culture. In 1962 he started a board-

*Yehudi Menuhin*

ing-school for musically talented children at Stoke d'Abernon, near London.

Menuhin has achieved a remarkable position as a world citizen with diverse interests apart from music; and as a violinist the purity of style and depth of interpretative power that he displays in his finest performances place them in the highest category. He has edited Bartók's Sonata for solo violin (London, 1947), one of the many works written for him; Walton's Sonata for violin and piano (London, 1950), written for him and his brother-in-law Louis Kentner; and Mendelssohn's early Concerto in D minor (New York, 1952). He is a Commander of the Légion d'honneur, a Knight of the Dutch Order of Oranje Nassau, an Hon. KBE and, among his many other honours and awards, he received the Nehru Award for International Understanding.

WRITINGS
*Six Lessons with Yehudi Menuhin* (London, 1971)
*Theme and Variations* (London, 1972)
*Violin: Six Lessons with Yehudi Menuhin* (London, 1975)
with W. Primrose: *Violin and Viola* (London, 1975)
*Unfinished Journey* (London, 1977) [autobiography]
with C. W. Davis: *The Music of Man* (London, 1980)

BIBLIOGRAPHY
R. Magidoff: *Yehudi Menuhin, the Story of the Man and the Music* (Garden City, NY, 1955, 2/1973) [with discography]
N. Wymer: *Yehudi Menuhin* (London, 1961)
J. Hartnack: *Grosse Geiger unserer Zeit* (Munich, 1967), 223ff
E. Fenby: *Menuhin's House of Music* (London, 1969)
R. Daniels: *Conversations with Menuhin* (London, 1979)

**(2) Hephzibah Menuhin** (*b* San Francisco, 20 May 1920). Pianist, sister of (1) Yehudi Menuhin. After study in San Francisco, she worked with Marcel Ciampi in Paris. In 1934 she made her début there with her brother, thus starting a partnership in sonata recitals that has seldom been broken for long. She has also made many appearances as a soloist throughout the world but particularly in Australia, where she lived for some years. She combines her musical career with an active interest in social problems.

**(3) Yaltah Menuhin** (*b* San Francisco, 7 Oct 1922). Pianist, sister of (1) Yehudi Menuhin. She studied in Paris with Marcel Ciampi, in Rome, and in New York with Carl Friedberg. She has appeared in many countries as a soloist and has collaborated in chamber music with a number of distinguished colleagues.

**(4) Jeremy Menuhin** (*b* San Francisco, 2 Nov 1951).

Pianist, son of (1) Yehudi Menuhin. He studied in Paris, Vienna and Italy and made his début at the Gstaad Festival in 1965. He has often played as a soloist under his father's baton and independently in Europe and America.

RONALD KINLOCH ANDERSON

**Menzingen, Mauritius von.** *See* MAURITIUS VON MENZINGEN.

**Meo, Ascanio** (*b* *c*1570–80; *d* ?Naples, after 1608). Italian composer. In Venice on 10 January 1601 he dedicated his *Terzo libro de madrigali* for five voices to Francesco Domingo Ruiz de Castro y Portugal, Count of Castro, who in October 1601 succeeded his father as viceroy of Naples. In 1608 Meo was *maestro di cappella* of S Giacomo degli Spagnuoli, Naples, a church particularly noted for its music. On 1 January 1608 in Naples he dedicated his *Quinto libro de madrigali* to Cardinal Montalto. His 1601 book which is incomplete is rather old-fashioned: the poems, including sonnets by G. Mozzarella, B. Tasso and others, are set in a style influenced by A. Gabrieli, Primavera and Felis, rather than by the composers of the *seconda prattica* madrigal. The 1608 book is more modern in its preference for madrigal and canzonetta texts over sonnets or *stanze*, but the musical style remains old-fashioned; pervasive counterpoint and imitation are rarely interrupted by cadences or chordal phrases, chromaticism is absent and the rhythms are square and inflexible. One five-voice madrigal was printed in *RISM* 1609[16].

KEITH A. LARSON

**Merbecke** [Marbeck], **John** (*b* ?Windsor, between *c*1505 and *c*1510; *d* *c*1585). English composer and writer. He is chiefly remembered as the composer of *The Booke of Common Praier Noted* (1550).

1. LIFE. The date of Merbecke's birth is generally estimated as about 1510, on the basis of his son Roger's birth in 1536, although Bergsagel suggested that the inclusion of Merbecke's mass in the early 16th-century Forrest–Heyther partbooks (*GB-Ob* Mus.Sch.E.376–80) indicates that he was born substantially earlier than 1510. His name heads the list of clerks of St George's Chapel, Windsor, for 1531. Also at this time he held one of the two organist's posts at the chapel, apparently continuing to hold it (apart from a period of imprisonment) until he died. In 1543 he was arrested for heresy: it seems that he had favoured Calvinism for a considerable period before his arrest, for he had already completed a substantial portion of his concordance of the English Bible as well as other theological writings and studies of Calvinism, and on 16 March these manuscripts were seized, and Merbecke was arrested shortly afterwards with two of his colleagues from Windsor. At his trial he was accused of expressing contempt for the Mass, and of writing and possessing heretical documents. All the accused were sentenced to death at the stake, and shortly afterwards this sentence was carried out on the others. Merbecke, however, was reprieved by Henry VIII, thanks to the intercession of Stephen Gardiner, Bishop of Winchester, and Sir Humphrey Foster, both of whom had initially been among his accusers. After his release from the Marshalsea prison, Merbecke was reinstated as organist at Windsor, although judging by his own account he had lost all interest in this aspect of church music. He may have been responsible for the musical setting of

Archbishop Cranmer's English Litany published in 1544.

For the rest of his life Merbecke devoted himself solely to the study and dissemination of Protestantism. On his return to Windsor he at once began work on compiling another concordance, to replace the one confiscated on his arrest. He was unable to find a publisher willing to accept it, however, owing to its great length and consequent expense. As a result, he compiled a third, shortened version which nevertheless consists of 900 folio pages, each of three columns, and this version, the first complete concordance of the English Bible to be published, appeared in 1550. In its preface, dedicated to Edward VI, Merbecke stated that he considered the early part of his life a waste, because he had been trained solely as a church musician, a vocation which he had now virtually renounced. The preface goes on to describe his efforts on the first concordance, his trial and pardon and the circumstances leading to the final published version of the work.

With the accession of Edward VI in 1547 Calvinist views became acceptable and Merbecke was no longer under threat of punishment. He may have received the degree of BMus at Oxford University in 1549. The Act of Uniformity (1549) made the use of English services in the first Book of Common Prayer mandatory throughout the country. Merbecke was called on to provide a musical setting within the highly restrictive limitations imposed on church music by Archbishop Cranmer, and the result was *The Booke of Common Praier Noted* (1550). His setting became obsolete in 1552 with the introduction of the second Book of Common Prayer, which incorporated several changes incompatible with Merbecke's music.

In 1550 Merbecke was exempted from duty as organist at St George's Chapel, although he still held the post nominally and received a stipend. From 1571 he also received a stipend as chantry priest at Windsor, a further nominal appointment carrying no duties. As far as is known he wrote no music after 1550. Between 1574 and 1584 he published several prose works, in which he opposed the use of even the simplest choral and instrumental music in church. In 1579 he published a history in verse of King David; he died presumably in 1585, when John Mundy succeeded to the post of organist.

2. WORKS. Merbecke's *The Booke of Common Praier Noted* (1550) was the first musical setting of services in the 1549 Prayer Book. It consists of simple monodic settings designed for use in parish churches rather than in cathedrals. The Book of Common Prayer enforced by the Act of Uniformity (1549) had given no guidance on the use of music in services, and therefore Merbecke's setting, which had official approval, established a plan for subsequent settings by other composers. He provided music for the Preces and responses, Matins, Evensong, *Benedicite*, *Quincunque vult*, Communion and Burial of the Dead. Some movements are given two settings. The music consists partly of adaptations by Merbecke of plainsong from the Latin rites, and partly of tunes in a similar style by Merbecke himself. The underlay is syllabic throughout, and phrase climaxes are typically reserved for important words. He adopted a special form of rhythmic notation, probably with the aim of achieving speech rhythm in the music: he used only four note shapes, 'strene note' (breve),

'square note' (semibreve), 'pycke' (minim) and 'close' (breve with pause, for cadences). He also used the 'prycke', a dot lengthening the preceding note by half. Merbecke explained the system in his preface, and it is clear that he intended the note values to be interpreted exactly, rather than in the freer manner associated with plainsong (see illustration).

It is highly unlikely that *The Booke of Common Praier Noted* passed through more than a single edition. Conjecture that there were two separate editions in 1550 seems to be based on misleading evidence from the printing techniques used. The appearance of a revised Book of Common Prayer (1552), the reversion to Roman Catholicism under Mary Tudor and the use of newly prepared English liturgies after the accession of Elizabeth I caused Merbecke's setting to fall into disuse. Several Tudor composers, however, used Merbecke's melody for the Preces and responses as part of their own polyphonic settings of the same text. Apart from such settings, Merbecke's work remained forgotten until the mid-19th century, when it was revived as part of the Oxford High Church Movement. Since then numerous editions and arrangements of sections of *The Booke of Common Praier Noted* have been published. Merbecke's music (in particular his Communion setting) is still sung in Anglican churches throughout the world, as well as in Methodist, Presbyterian and other Protestant churches. It has even been adopted by the Roman Catholic Church as a setting for the Mass in English.

Only four polyphonic works by Merbecke survive. Of these, it is certain that the three Latin works, at least, date from his early years; all three display considerable variety of texture. Merbecke frequently used different groups of voices as the means of contrast between successive sections within the music. The vocal lines are characteristically wide-ranging, with long melismas on individual syllables. However, he sometimes introduced chordal writing, particularly to stress an important word such as 'Jesu'.

The unique source of the Mass *'Per arma justiciae'* dates from about 1530, and also contains masses by

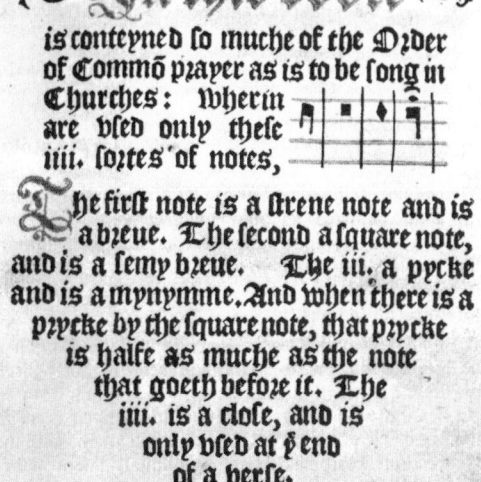

*The four note shapes explained in the preface to Merbecke's 'The Booke of Common Praier Noted' (1550)*

Fayrfax, Taverner and Tye. Merbecke's mass is a large-scale setting based on the first antiphon at Lauds and Vespers on Trinity Sunday, and is typical of the pre-Reformation English mass. The Kyrie is not set polyphonically, and part of the Credo is omitted. The remaining movements combine cantus firmus and paraphrase techniques with freer writing. Imitation does not predominate, and tends to occur during the course of a section rather than at its outset. Although confined mostly to the tenor, the cantus firmus occurs in all four upper voices, and in the Agnus Dei it migrates five times between three voices. The sole surviving sources of the extensive motets *Ave Dei patris filia* and *Domine Jesu Christe* date respectively from before 1550 and 1585. Both works are similar in style to Merbecke's mass, with occasional use of word-painting and intentionally abrupt harmonic changes. The source of the anthem *A virgin and mother* dates from about 1600. Merbecke treated the brief, versified English text simply in comparison with his treatment of Latin: the style is more closely imitative, the phrases shorter, some words are repeated, and although short melismas occur, syllabic writing predominates, suggesting that Merbecke may have composed this much later than his Latin works.

### WORKS

The Booke of Common Praier Noted (London, 1550, facs. 1939): Preces and responses; Matins (Ven, ps, TeD, Bs); Evensong (ps, Mag, Nunc); Benedicite; Quincunque vult; Communion (Ky, Gl, Cr, San, Bs, Ag, post-communion, offs); Burial of the Dead (Ky, San, Ag)
Mass 'Per arma justiciae', 5vv, *GB-Ob*; ed. in TCM, x (1929)
Ave Dei patris filia, 5vv, *Cu* (T missing); ed. in TCM, x (1929)
Domine Jesu Christe, 5vv, *Ob*; ed. in TCM, x (1929)
A virgin and mother (anthem), 3vv, *Lbm*; ed. in TCM, x (1929)

### BIBLIOGRAPHY

J. Foxe: *Acts and Monuments*, ii (London, 1576)
J. Jebb: *Three Lectures on the Cathedral Service of the Church of England* (Leeds, 1841, 3/1860)
R. R. Terry: 'John Merbecke: 1523?–1585', *PMA*, xlv (1918–19), 75
——: *A Forgotten Psalter and Other Essays* (London, 1929)
J. E. Hunt: *Cranmer's First Litany: 1544, and Merbecke's Book of Common Prayer Noted: 1550* (London, 1939) [facs.]
E. H. Fellowes: *English Cathedral Music* (London, 1941, rev. 5/1969 by J. A. Westrup)
A. Hughes: *Medieval Polyphony in the Bodleian Library* (Oxford, 1951)
R. Stevenson: 'John Marbeck's "Noted Book" of 1550', *MQ*, xxxvii (1951), 220
J. Stevens: *Music and Poetry in the Early Tudor Court* (London, 1961)
J. D. Bergsagel: 'The Date and Provenance of the Forrest–Heyther Collection of Tudor Masses', *ML*, xliv (1963), 240
P. le Huray: *Music and the Reformation in England 1549–1660* (London, 1967)
H. Byard: 'Farewell to Merbecke?', *MT*, cxiv (1973), 300
N. Sandon: 'Merbecke', *MT*, cxiv (1973), 597 [letter to the editor]
H. Benham: *Latin Church Music in England, 1460–1575* (London, 1977)
R. A. Leaver: *The Work of John Marbeck* (Oxford, 1978)

JUDITH BLEZZARD

**Mercadante, (Giuseppe) Saverio (Raffaele)** (*b* Altamura, nr. Bari, baptized 17 Sept 1795; *d* Naples, 17 Dec 1870). Italian composer and teacher, the most important among those Italian opera composers contemporary with Donizetti, Bellini and Verdi whose works are no longer in the repertory.

1. LIFE. He was an illegitimate child. In later life (when he had become the accepted figurehead of Neapolitan music) he himself insisted that he had been born in Naples, but in fact he apparently first arrived there at the age of 11, when his father took employment with the Neapolitan customs. His exceptional talent early indicated a musical training and in 1808, to obtain a free place at the conservatory (the Collegio di S Sebastiano), being over age and not a Neapolitan, his first Christian name and the place and date of his birth

were falsified. As a result, some early reference works date his birth at Naples in 1797 or even 1798, and the statue erected to him there in 1876 perpetuates the incorrect first name of Francesco.

At the Collegio Mercadante studied *solfeggio*, the violin and flute, also figured bass and harmony with Furno and counterpoint with Tritto (both of whom taught Bellini a few years later). From 1816 to 1820 he studied composition with the director, Zingarelli, whose favourite pupil he became. Having already composed marches and other small pieces for a band that he organized among his fellow students, by 1817 he was entrusted with the direction of the Collegio orchestra, for which he wrote a number of compositions, including several sinfonias: it was probably one of these that Rossini heard on a visit to the Collegio at about this time which prompted his remark in a letter to Zingarelli, 'My compliments – your young pupil Mercadante begins where we finish'. Other works from these years include instrumental duets, trios and quartets, and concertos for flute and other instruments. In 1818 he composed a cantata in honour of the ex-King Charles IV of Spain, and Florimo mentions a four-part mass with orchestra, but in general (and unusually for an Italian composer at this period) Mercadante's predominant interest until the age of 23 was instrumental music. In the same year, however, he produced the music for three ballets at the Teatro S Carlo; the third of these, *Il flauto incantato*, met with such success that at least one Neapolitan critic urged the young composer to abandon his 'sterile symphonies' in favour of vocal music, and in 1819 (no doubt with the encouragement of Rossini, then musical director of the S Carlo) he was invited to compose his first opera, *L'apoteosi d'Ercole*, for that theatre. It was enthusiastically received and in 1820, the year he completed his studies with Zingarelli, he produced four more, two in Naples and two in Rome. From then on he concentrated exclusively on operatic composition. His fame spread rapidly through Italy and during the seven years that followed he turned out an average of three operas a year, at one point actually producing five within 11 months.

Mercadante's first really big success came in 1821 with his seventh opera, *Elisa e Claudio*, given at La Scala, Milan, on 30 successive nights and repeated six months later for a further 28. With this work he established a European reputation: it was performed in London, Barcelona and Paris in 1823, and Vienna in 1824. Mercadante himself directed the Viennese performances, and remained in Vienna to write three further operas for the Kärntnertor-Theater, but these were poorly received and the composer returned at the end of the year to Italy, where a new triumph followed with *Caritea, regina di Spagna* (more often known as *Donna Caritea*) at Venice in 1826. At about this time he was offered a contract to write two operas a year, over a period of seven years, for the Italian opera in Madrid; he arrived there later in 1826, but the contract fell through and he returned to Turin for a new opera in the following February. A few months later he was in Spain again: the details of his life at this period are not clear, but it seems probable that one opera, *I due Figaro*, was written for performance in Madrid in 1827, only to be banned on political grounds shortly after his arrival. (It was eventually given there in 1835.) By August the composer had moved on to Lisbon, where he produced three or possibly four operas during the next 12 months; of these, *Gabriella di Vergy* later had considerable success in Italy. By the autumn of 1829 he was in Cádiz, where he interested himself in the Italian opera and produced two comic operas of his own. There is some evidence that he revisited Italy at about this time, to engage artists for his Spanish companies, but later in 1830 he was in Madrid again as director of the Italian Opera, and by November was 'in the process of composing' *Francesca da Rimini* (which opera was therefore given, or intended to be given, at Madrid during the Carnival of 1830–31, not in 1828 as often stated).

In spite of various negotiations no solid contract materialized in Spain, and at the beginning of 1831 Mercadante finally returned to Italy. This was the period of Bellini's greatest Italian successes and of Donizetti's first fame: after so long an absence from the Italian scene Mercadante seems to have felt the need to reconsider his style, and though *Zaïra*, his first work at Naples for over six years, had only a moderate reception, he scored a triumph at Turin in 1832 with *I normanni a Parigi*. On 9 July of that year he was married at Genoa to a young widow, Sofia Gambaro, by whom he subsequently had a daughter and two sons. At the beginning of 1833 he succeeded Pietro Generali as *maestro di cappella* at Novara Cathedral; this appointment lasted for seven years and occasioned the composition of much church music (as well as a *fantasia funebre* in memory of Generali) but did not interrupt his operatic career. The famous *Sette ultime parole di Nostro Signore* belong to this period.

In 1835 Rossini, from Paris, invited Mercadante (as he had already done Bellini and Donizetti) to write an opera for the Théâtre-Italien. Mercadante arrived in Paris in September, but the libretto, which Romani was to provide, had not arrived by the end of November and he was obliged to accept another, of inferior quality, and set it to music in a hurry. In spite of the singing of Grisi, Rubini, Tamburini and Lablache, *I briganti* was a failure. Nevertheless, Mercadante's Paris visit was of decisive importance for the contact it gave him with a new and more sophisticated musical world, and for the music he heard there – particularly that of Meyerbeer, whose *Les Huguenots* had its first performance at the Opéra during February 1836.

The example of Meyerbeer is evident in Mercadante's next opera, *Il giuramento*, which was produced at La Scala 11 months after his return from Paris. It was received with enthusiasm and has remained his best-known work ever since. With *Il giuramento* Mercadante finally broke away from his earlier style and began the programme of operatic reform with which his name has been chiefly associated in the history of Italian opera. The four operas that followed, *Le due illustri rivali*, *Elena da Feltre*, *Il bravo* and *La vestale*, maintained and developed the ideals of this reform and are all among his best works. By this time conditions in Italy were more favourable to Mercadante than ever before: Rossini's operatic career was over, Bellini was dead, and Donizetti, though still active, was being increasingly drawn to Paris and Vienna for his best works; at home, among a mass of minor figures, only Pacini (though an altogether less substantial composer) was a serious rival, and by 1840 Mercadante was certainly the most respected figure on the purely Italian operatic scene.

In 1839 Rossini offered Mercadante the post of director of the Liceo Musicale in Bologna (in preference to Donizetti and Pacini; both were offered it afterwards); Mercadante accepted, only to turn it down without warning a few months later when he was invited to

*1. Saverio Mercadante*

succeed his former teacher, Zingarelli, as head of the more important conservatory in Naples. He took up this appointment in October 1840 and retained it until his death 30 years later. His theatrical career continued, however: another important opera, *Il reggente*, followed at Turin in 1843; in August 1844 he made a ceremonial visit to his birthplace at Altamura, where he was received with great honour, returning to Naples for another success with *Leonora* at the end of the year; and in 1846 he scored a spectacular triumph at the S Carlo with *Orazi e Curiazi*.

But with the passing of the years Mercadante's operatic output began to slow down. One reason was certainly his position at the conservatory and his growing preoccupation, in that capacity, with instrumental works, church music and teaching. But another may well have been jealousy of the young Verdi. At an early stage in their relations Verdi seems to have respected Mercadante, and trusted him enough to ask him to supervise the choice of artists for the first Neapolitan *Macbeth* in 1848. But later Mercadante became outspokenly critical of this dangerous new rival and fought bitterly to block Verdi's success in Naples. At the time of the first performance of *Il trovatore* at the S Carlo in 1853 he is said to have used all his considerable influence with the Neapolitan authorities to get only the first two acts of the opera allowed – though in the end without success. Relations between the two men were eventually patched up, and in 1868, when Mercadante was old and blind, Verdi put him 'even for a few bars' at the head of his list of contributors to the projected composite Requiem in memory of Rossini.

The last complete opera certainly composed by Mercadante was *Pelagio* (Naples, 1857). *Virginia*, which followed in 1866, was an earlier work that had been refused performance by the censor; it gave him his last great public success. By this time he had become a venerable figurehead in Italian musical life. While he

*2. Part of the finale to Act 1 of 'Il giuramento', from the first edition of the vocal score published by Ricordi (Milan, 1837)*

was at Novara he had lost the sight of one eye, and about the middle of 1862 he became completely blind; yet in the same year he managed to compose, by dictation to pupils, a full-scale orchestral piece with the evidently autobiographical title *Il lamento del bardo*. In his last years he wrote, by the same method, an immense hymn for the inauguration of Rossini's statue at Pesaro, as well as symphonic works in memory of Pacini and Rossini and a number of other instrumental pieces; at his death he left the manuscript of yet another opera dictated as far as the middle of the finale of the first act.

2. WORKS. Mercadante's 60 operas span an active half century of Italian operatic history: the first was performed only three years after *Il barbiere di Siviglia* and the last a year before *Don Carlos*. In the early part of his career, like most of his contemporaries, he was a follower of Rossini, and of this period *Elisa e Claudio* is the outstanding example, a neat and brilliantly written *opera buffa* in a style that was sure of success. But Mercadante's temperament was more naturally drawn to serious subjects. Many of his earlier librettos are based on classical themes redolent of 18th-century *opera seria* (four are actually by, or after, Metastasio), giving way, as his dramatic instinct developed, to the Romantic melodramas of Romani (17 librettos) and Cammarano (nine). Here, too, Rossini was the point of departure: although his last opera for the Italian stage, *Semiramide*, dates from as early as 1823, it was not until the mid-1830s that Mercadante really began to shake off the florid manner of Rossinian lyric drama. *Donna Caritea* in 1826 shows an early tendency in this direction: the vocal writing is simpler than in the works around it, and there is more of the lyrical pathos that is associated with Bellini or Donizetti rather than Rossini (though in fact *Donna Caritea* antedates all the characteristic works of both these composers). But by 1832, after Mercadante's return from Spain, the boot was on the other foot, and it was certainly the examples of Donizetti's *Anna Bolena* and Bellini's *Norma* that prompted the new seriousness of purpose that can be glimpsed in *I normanni a Parigi*.

Besides much that is conventional and frankly banal, there are new touches of harmony and orchestration, freer treatment of declamation and a sense of dramatic intention which represent an advance, however primitive, on his earlier works.

But it was *Il giuramento* that marked the turning-point of Mercadante's career. In Italy this work has usually been regarded as his masterpiece. Its libretto, after Hugo's *Angelo* (the same subject as Ponchielli's *Gioconda*), is a good one, and the composer made a genuine attempt to set it as a drama rather than a theatrical entertainment, discarding conventions where he felt it necessary to do so and creating a real interplay of characters in a seriously considered, if not always consistent, musical framework. That much of the improvement is due to the example of Meyerbeer can hardly be doubted; but it remains an example, and not an influence, and there is little or no direct trace of the Meyerbeerian idiom (as there is, for example, in certain of Verdi's later operas) to dilute the essentially Italian quality of Mercadante's melodic style.

*Il giuramento* and the best of the operas that follow it are of great interest and significance in the history of 19th-century Italian music; more than any others of the period, they provide the link between Rossini, Bellini and Donizetti on the one hand, and Verdi and the later 19th-century melodrama on the other. Mercadante himself was quite aware of what he was doing. In a much quoted letter written to Florimo during the composition of *Elena da Feltre* he put it clearly:

I have continued the revolution I began with *Il giuramento*; forms varied, trivial cabalettas banished, crescendos out, vocal lines simplified, fewer repeats, more originality in the cadences, emphasis on the drama, orchestra rich but not so as to swamp the voices, no long solos in the ensembles – which force the other parts to stand coldly by to the detriment of the action, not much bass drum, and a lot less brass band.

Besides eliminating the external weaknesses of the earlier lyric drama, he deliberately attempted to loosen its basic schematic patterns in a new approach, combining musical intelligence and greater dramatic fluency with the powerful melodic impulse that is the motive power behind all 19th-century Italian opera. With varying success he tried to balance the claims of music and drama in a way that not even Donizetti had done before him, using calculated repetition to weld whole scenes into dramatic unity (the opening scene of Act 1 of *Il bravo* is an example), and strengthening and unifying the action by means of recitatives that are genuinely compelling, with sudden lyrical phrases for the voice and melodious (as well as dramatic) orchestral writing – very much in the manner that Verdi was later to develop. The harmonic interest and range of modulation in these scores are well ahead of anything else in the period: the treatment of the orchestra is imaginative – sometimes almost over-elaborate; accompaniments are varied and the ensemble writing is masterly (*Le due illustri rivali* offers some fine examples). He could not always keep it up. In every opera there are lapses into rhetoric and convention, particularly in the arias (where he still had to content his singers); and the melodic ideas, though carefully worked out, are not always characteristic or memorable in themselves. But the general level is still far above that of his Italian contemporaries, as Liszt noted in an otherwise critical account of the current Italian scene:

Exception must always be made for Mercadante. He has the wisdom to write slowly, and revises his compositions with care ... Several of the ensemble pieces are really remarkable. The latest works of Mercadante are without question the most seriously thought out of the contemporary repertory.

The role of these works in the development of Verdian melodrama was crucial. Mercadante had written 45 operas and was at the height of his fame when Verdi opened his career: at the very time when the younger composer was struggling to get *Oberto* put on at La Scala, *Il bravo* was receiving its brilliantly successful first performance at the same theatre. Verdi had many opportunities of seeing Mercadante's works on the stage, and their influence on his operatic thinking extended in some cases even to literal echoes. In 1841 he witnessed the triumph at Genoa of Mercadante's next opera, *La vestale*, an impressive and unusually consistent work on the grand scale which some authorities consider his masterpiece. The parallels between this opera and *Aida* were pointed out by Frank Walker (*Grove 5*): both are set against a priestly background, contain a spectacular triumph scene and end with the entombment alive of the chief character; not only did the general style of Mercadante's work recur to Verdi's subconscious mind, but even some individual phrases – as, for instance, the Chief Vestal's 'Decio ritorna, de' Galli vincitor' to a rising phrase virtually identical, even in key, to the famous 'Ritorna vincitor' of Amneris (and Aida) in the first act of Verdi's opera.

The last of Mercadante's operas which can properly be said to fall into the 'reform' group is *Il reggente*, a finely written opera on the same subject as Verdi's *Un ballo in maschera*, with a greater sense of personal intimacy than many of Mercadante's works. But in the operas that follow the ideals of reform tended to get forgotten. The forms are more conventional, with much repetition; vocalization reappears as an end in itself, the scoring is heavy, and there is a tendency to deploy great energy for little result. Even so, a work like *Orazi e Curiazi*, where the power of the scoring and the heroic scale of the vocal writing are justified by the subject, must certainly be counted among his best: the magnificent finale of Act 1 is a worthy summing up of all that is finest in the ensemble writing of the period. The last two

operas, *Virginia* and *Pelagio*, both contain fine music, and the latter at least one aria (for Bianca in Act 4) of an almost Verdian intensity and pathos.

Mercadante's considerable output of church music resulted mainly from his professional appointments at Novara and Naples. In general it is either academic or semi-operatic in style, or mixes the two with an easy emotionalism that is not always acceptable to modern ears. The *Christus e Miserere*, written for the pupils of the Naples Conservatory, is an extended and serious piece of unusual design, but his most celebrated sacred work is the *Sette ultime parole di Nostro Signore*, which tends in the operatic direction and achieves moments of touching sincerity. The substantial list of his instrumental compositions reflects a lifelong interest in the orchestra that dates from his earliest years and provides one of the most characteristic features of his operas. His sinfonias, however, bear no relation to the classical symphony, being simply free variations of the overture form, and the various works in memory of other composers are mostly fantasias on themes of theirs. There are one or two chamber works for unusual combinations, including a sombre quartet for four cellos and a *decimino* in four movements, probably inspired by the popularity of Beethoven's Septet. Among the usual romances and salon pieces, a number of delightful and characteristic Neapolitan songs are also noteworthy.

After Mercadante's death his reputation suffered a rapid decline. By the standards of his time his best work had been serious and thoughtful, producing its effect by technical skill and controlled vigour rather than by any very immediate lyrical impulse: its weaknesses, at least from *Il giuramento* onwards, are not the negative ones of so many of his contemporaries, but rather a tendency to over-elaboration and too much care, so that vocal lines and harmonic progressions sometimes seem almost wilfully contorted in order to avoid the obvious. As a result his operas can be impressive, beautiful, passionate and physically exciting, but seldom spontaneous or directly personal – and beside the powerful, comprehensive genius of Verdi they inevitably appeared old-fashioned and lacking in human appeal. This change of attitude took an extreme form in the writings of Francesco Florimo, whose *Cenno storico sulla scuola musicale di Napoli* (1869–71) was originally written while Mercadante was director of the conservatory where Florimo was librarian. His praise of Mercadante was expressed in superlatives. But in the second edition, revised ten years after Mercadante's death, Florimo quite startlingly changed his attitude, sharply curtailing his admiration and sometimes simply inserting the word 'not' in order to reverse the meaning of his original text.

Florimo's *volte face*, whatever its true cause, gave rise in the 1940s to a violent polemic in defence of Mercadante by a fellow Altamuran, Biagio Notarnicola, whose wild and ill-informed claims that Verdi stole his ideas from Mercadante, and then brought pressure to bear on Florimo to discredit him, are as false as they are absurd. Nevertheless it has for too long been an easy commonplace of Italian musical history that Mercadante's sole importance was having, in Amintore Galli's phrase, 'served as a footstool [sgabello] for Verdi'. The fact that he contributed to the development of a very much greater composer does not invalidate his own intrinsic qualities, and if these have been temporarily exaggerated in certain quarters that is an understandable reaction. The revivals of his operas in connection with the centenary of his death in 1970 have shown that, with all his faults, Mercadante clearly demands consideration as a composer in his own right.

## WORKS

### OPERAS

References to *I-Nc* are from Florimo (1869–71); though uniformly given here as full scores, the exact nature of the material is not always certain; some is autograph. Scores in *I-Mr* are copyists' MSS: the existence of such scores, even when not indicated, may be assumed where the autograph is in Ricordi's possession, but the firm's own copies of much stock material were destroyed in 1943.

L'apoteosi d'Ercole (dramma per musica, 2, G. Schmidt), Naples, S Carlo, 19 Aug 1819; *F-Pn*, *I-Fc*, *Mr*, *Nc*, *US-Bp*, *Wc*, vocal score, excerpts (Milan, c1821; Naples, n.d.)

Violenza e costanza, ossia I falsi monetari (dramma giocoso, 2, A. L. Tottola), Naples, Nuovo, 19 Jan 1820; *I-Bc*, *Fc*, *Mr*, *Nc*, vocal score, excerpts (Naples, 1822); also as Il castello dei spiriti (Lisbon, 1825)

Anacreonte in Samo (dramma per musica, 2, Schmidt, after J.-H. Guy: Anacréon chez Polycrate), Naples, S Carlo, 1 Aug 1820; *F-Pn*, *I-Fc*, *Mr*, *Nc*

Il geloso ravveduto (melodramma buffo, 2, B. Signorini), Rome, Valle, Oct 1820; *Fc*

Scipione in Cartagine (melodramma serio, 2, J. Ferretti), Rome, Argentina, 26 Dec 1820; *Fc*, *Mr*, *US-Wc*, vocal score, excerpts (Milan, 1821)

Maria Stuarda regina di Scozia (Maria Stuart) (dramma serio, 2, G. Rossi), Bologna, Comunale, 29 May 1821; *I-Mr*

Elisa e Claudio, ossia L'amore protetto dall'amicizia (melodramma semiserio, 2, L. Romanelli, after F. Casari: Rosella), Milan, La Scala, 30 Oct 1821; autograph *Mr*; copies *B-Bc*, *GB-Lbm*, *I-Bc*, *Fc*, *Nc*, *US-Bp*, *Wc*; vocal scores (Milan, 1821 or 1822; Paris, 1823; excerpts, Vienna, 1824)

Andronico (melodramma tragico, 2, Dalmiro Tindario P. A. [G. Kreglianovich]), Venice, La Fenice, 26 Dec 1821; *I-Mr*, vocal score, excerpts (Milan, 1821–4)

Il posto abbandonato, ossia Adele ed Emerico (melodramma semiserio, 2, F. Romani), Milan, La Scala, 21 Sept 1822; autograph *Mr*, vocal score, excerpts (Milan, 1823); rev. 1828 or 1829, ? for perf. in Spain

Amleto (melodramma tragico, 3, F. Romani, after Shakespeare), Milan, La Scala, 26 Dec 1822; autograph *Mr*; copy *Nc*

Alfonso ed Elisa (melodramma serio, 3, after Alfieri: Filippo), Mantua, Nuovo, 26 Dec 1822; lib rev. as Aminta ed Argira, Reggio Emilia, 1823

Didone abbandonata (dramma per musica, 2, Metastasio), Turin, Regio, 18 Jan 1823; *F-Pn*, *I-Fc*, *Mr*, *Nc*, *US-Wc*, vocal score, excerpts (Milan, 1823)

Gli sciti (dramma per musica, 2, Tottola), Naples, S Carlo, 18 March 1823; vocal score, excerpts (Milan, 1823 or 1824)

Costanzo ed Almeriska (dramma per musica, 2, Tottola), Naples, S Carlo, 22 Nov 1823; *I-Nc*, vocal score, excerpts (Naples, ?1824)

Gli amici di Siracusa (melodramma eroico, 3, Ferretti), Rome, Argentina, 7 Feb 1824

Doralice (dramma ?semiserio, 2), Vienna, Kärntnertor, 18 Sept 1824

Le nozze di Telemaco ed Antiope (azione lirica, 3, C. Bassi), Vienna, Kärntnertor, 5 Nov 1824; collab. other composers

Il podestà di Burgos, ossia Il signore del villaggio (melodramma semiserio, 2, Bassi), Vienna, Kärntnerthor, 20 Nov 1824; under 2nd title, in Neapolitan dialect, Naples, Fondo, 28 May 1825; *Nc*

Nitocri (melodramma serio, 2, Conte Prosasco, after Zeno), Turin, Regio, 26 Dec 1824; *Mr*, vocal score, excerpts (Milan, 1826)

Ipermestra (dramma tragico, 2, L. Ricciuti, after Metastasio), Naples, S Carlo, Carn. 1824–5; autograph *Mr*; copy *Nc*; probably rev., ? Spain, c1828–30, perf. ? Genoa, Carlo Felice, 26 Dec 1832; vocal score, excerpts (Milan, ?1833)

Erode, ossia Marianna (dramma tragico, 2, Ricciuti), Venice, La Fenice, 27 Dec 1825; autograph *Mr*; copy *Vt*

Caritea, regina di Spagna (Donna Caritea), ossia La morte di Don Alfonso re di Portogallo (melodramma serio, 2, P. Pola), Venice, La Fenice, 21 Feb 1826; autograph *Mr*; copies *GB-T*, *I-Bc*, *Fc*, *Nc*, *Vt*, *US-Wc*; vocal scores (Milan, ?1828; Paris, n.d.)

Ezio (dramma per musica, 2, Metastasio), Turin, Regio, 2 Feb 1827; vocal score, excerpts (Milan, 1827)

Il montanaro (melodramma comico, 2, F. Romani), Milan, La Scala, 16 April 1827; *I-Mr*

La testa di bronzo, ossia La capanna solitaria (melodramma eroico comico, 2, F. Romani [1816]), Lisbon, private theatre of Barone di Quintella at Laranjeiras, 3 Dec 1827; *GB-Lbm*, *I-Mr*, vocal score (Paris, ?1828), excerpts (Milan, ?1833)

Adriano in Siria (dramma serio, 3, A. Profumo, after Metastasio), Lisbon, S Carlos, 24 Feb 1828

Gabriella di Vergy (melodramma serio, 2, Profumo, partly after Tottola), Lisbon, S Carlos, 8 Aug 1828; rev. (E. Bidera), Genoa, spr. 1832; autograph *Mr*; copy *Nc*, vocal scores (Milan, n.d; Naples, n.d.)

La rappresaglia (opera buffa, 2, Romani), Cádiz, Principal, ? 20 Nov 1829; *US-Wc*

Don Chisciotte [alle nozze di Gamaccio] (opera buffa, 2, ? orig. in Sp.), Cádiz, Principal, ? carn. 1829–30, *I-Nc* [apparently no connection with Les noces de Gamache, see below]

Francesca da Rimini (melodramma, 3, Romani [1823]), Madrid, Principe, ? carn. 1830–31

Zaïra (melodramma tragico, 2, Romani [1829, for Bellini], after Voltaire), Naples, S Carlo, 31 Aug 1831; autograph *Nc*, copy *F-Pn*, vocal score, excerpts (Milan, c1831)

I normanni a Parigi (tragedia lirica, 4, Romani), Turin, Regio, 7 Feb 1832; *I-Bc*, *Fc*, *Mr*, *Nc*, *US-Bp*, vocal score (Milan, 1832)

Ismalia, ossia Amore e morte (melodramma serio fantastico, 3, Romani), Milan, La Scala, 27 Oct 1832; autograph *I-Mr*, vocal score (Milan, c1832)

Il conte di Essex (melodramma, 3, Romani), Milan, La Scala, 10 March 1833; autograph *Mr*, copy *Mc*, vocal score, excerpts (Milan, ?1833)

Emma d'Antiochia (tragedia lirica, 3, Romani), Venice, La Fenice, 8 March 1834; autograph *Mr*; copies *Nc*, *Vt*, vocal score, excerpts (Milan, 1835)

Uggero il danese (melodramma, 2, Romani), Bergamo, Riccardi, 11 Aug 1834; *Mr*, vocal score (Milan, 1839)

La gioventù di Enrico V (melodramma, 4, Romani, partly after Shakespeare), Milan, La Scala, 25 Nov 1834; autograph *Mr*, vocal score, excerpts (Milan, ?1835)

I due Figaro (melodramma buffo, 2, Romani [1820], after Martelly), probably composed c1827–9; 1st known perf. Madrid, Principe, 26 Jan 1835

Francesca Donato, ossia Corinto distrutta (melodramma semiserio, 3, Romani, after Byron), Turin, Regio, 14 Feb 1835; rev. (S. Cammarano), Naples, S Carlo, ? Jan 1845; autograph *Nc*, copy *Mr*, vocal score, excerpts (Milan, ?1845)

I briganti (melodramma, 3, J. Crescini, after Schiller: Die Räuber), Paris, Théâtre-Italien, 22 March 1836, *Fc*, *Mr*, vocal score, excerpts (Milan, 1838); rev. with adds, apparently Naples, S Carlo, 1853, autograph *Mr*; copy *Nc*

Il giuramento (melodramma, 3, G. Rossi, after V. Hugo: Angelo), Milan, La Scala, 11 March 1837; as Amore e dovere, Rome, 1839; autograph *Mr*; copies *Fc*, *Nc*, *US-Wc*, vocal scores (Milan, 1837, 2/1860; Paris, 1859)

Le due illustri rivali (melodramma, 3, Rossi), Venice, La Fenice, 10 March 1838; *I-Nc*, *Vt*, vocal scores (Milan, ?1838; Leipzig, c1840); adds Milan, La Scala, 26 Dec 1839, vocal score (Milan, 1839)

Elena da Feltre (dramma tragico, 3, Cammarano), Naples, S Carlo, 26 Dec 1838; *Fc*, *Mr*, *Nc*, vocal scores (Milan, 1839; Naples, n.d.)

Il bravo (La veneziana) (melodramma, 3, Rossi and M. Marcello), Milan, La Scala, 9 March 1839; autograph *Mr*; copies *F-Pn*, *GB-Lbm*, *I-Nc*, vocal scores (Milan, 1839, 2/?1888; Naples, n.d.; Paris, n.d.)

La vestale (tragedia lirica, 3, Cammarano), Naples, S Carlo, 10 March 1840; *Fc*, *Mr*, *Nc*, vocal scores (Milan, 1840; Paris, n.d.); as Emilia (title changed by censor), Rome, aut. 1842; as San Camillo (azione sacra), Rome, 1851

La solitaria delle Asturie, ossia La Spagna ricuperata (melodramma, 5, Romani), Venice, La Fenice, 12 March 1840; autograph *Mr*; copy *Vt*

Il proscritto (melodramma, 3, Cammarano, after F. Soulié), Naples, S Carlo, 4 Jan 1842; *Nc*, vocal score, excerpts (Milan, 1842)

Il reggente (dramma lirico, 3, Cammarano, after Scribe: Gustave III), Turin, Regio, 2 Feb 1843; autograph *Mr*, vocal score (Milan, n.d; Paris, n.d.); rev. with addns Trieste, 11 Nov 1843

Leonora (melodramma semiserio, 4, M. D'Arienzo), Naples, Nuovo, 5 Dec 1844; autograph *Mr*; copy *Nc*, vocal scores (Milan, n.d; Paris, n.d.) [see also I cacciatori delle Alpi]

Il Vascello de Gama (melodramma romantico, prol, 3, Cammarano), Naples, S Carlo, 6 March 1845; autograph *Mr*; copy *Nc*, vocal score, excerpts (Milan, 1845)

Orazi e Curiazi (tragedia lirica, 3, Cammarano), Naples, S Carlo, 10 Nov 1846; autograph *Mr*; copies *Bc*, *Nc*, vocal scores (Milan, c1846; Naples, n.d.)

La schiava saracena, ovvero Il campo di Gerosolima [orig.: Il campo de' crociati] (melodramma tragico, 4, F. M. Piave), Milan, La Scala, 26 Dec 1848, rev. Naples, S Carlo, ?1850; autograph *Mr*; early draft *US-NYpm*, ov. *STu*; copy *I-Nc*, vocal score (Milan, c1849–51)

Medea (tragedia lirica, 3, Cammarano, after Romani [1813]), Naples, S Carlo, 1 March 1851; autograph *Mr*, copy *Nc*, vocal scores (Milan, ?1864; Rome, n.d.)

Statira (tragedia, 3, D. Bolognese, after Voltaire: Olimpie), Naples, S Carlo, 8 Jan 1853; *Nc*, vocal scores (Paris, 1853; Naples, n.d.)

Violetta (melodramma, 4, D'Arienzo), Naples, Nuovo, 10 Jan 1853; autograph *Nc*, copy *Mr*, vocal score (Milan, n.d.)

Pelagio (tragedia lirica, 4, D'Arienzo), Naples, S Carlo, 12 Feb 1857; autograph *Nc*, copy *Mr*, vocal score (Milan, n.d.)

Virginia (tragedia lirica, 3, Cammarano, after Alfieri), Naples, S Carlo, 7 April 1866 (composed 1845 or ?1851, perf. not allowed); autograph *Nc*, copy *Mr*, vocal scores (Milan, ?1845; Naples, n.d.)

L'orfano di Brono, ossia Caterina dei Medici (Cammarano), inc., unperf., autograph *Nc* (MS dictated to middle of Finale, Act 1)

Giovanna I (scene i), autograph *Nc*

*(doubtful)*

Les noces de Gamache (opéra bouffon, 3, J. H. Dupin and T. Sauvage), Paris, Odéon, 9 May 1825; music arr. by Guénée; full score (Paris, ?1825) from which all details taken [presumably pasticcio or other adaptation]

Pietro il grande, Lisbon, 1827 [mistaken reference to Vaccai's opera]

Eduardo ed Angelica; de Napoli cited announcement of benefit perf. of Act 1, Naples, Nuovo, 9 Aug 1828

Parisina, presumably a confusion with Donizetti's opera

I cacciatori delle Alpi (?1), Mantua, 1859; de Napoli gave Ferrara, Buonacossi, 12 Oct 1859, stating that lib is extract, with changed names, etc, of Leonora (see above, 1844)

### BALLETS

*(choreographers given in parentheses)*

Il servo balordo o La disperazione di Gilotto (S. Taglioni), Naples, S Carlo, 1 Feb 1818

Il califfo generoso (A. Vestris), Naples, Fondo, spr. 1818

Il flauto incantato o Le convulsioni musicali (Taglioni), Naples, S Carlo, 19 Nov 1818; rev. Milan, La Scala, 12 Jan 1828; excerpts arr. 2 fl (Naples, n.d.)

I portoghesi nelle Indie o La conquista di Malacca (5 pts., Taglioni), Naples, S Carlo, 30 May 1819, collab. Gallenberg; excerpts arr. 2 fl (Naples, n.d.)

### SACRED

Le sette [ultime] parole di Nostro Signore, S, S, T, Bar, SSTB, 2 va, vc, db, Novara, Lent 1838, *I-NOVd* (Milan, ?1840); Mass, TTB, org (Milan, ?1840); Mass, ATTB, org, *Nc* (Milan, n.d.); De profundis (It. trans. Tommaseo), SATB, orch, *Nc* (Milan, *c*1844); Christus e Miserere, A, T, B, eng hn, hn, bn, harp, SATB unacc., Naples, Conservatory, 19 March 1856, *Nc* (Milan, 1856); Mass no.3, TTB, org (Milan, ?1861); Gran messa, solo vv, ATTBarB, orch, ?1868, *Nc*; 2 Tantum ergo: Bar, orch, *Nc*, vocal score (Milan, n.d.); 3vv, orch, *Nc*; Salve regina, S, female vv, org, harp, vc; [Dixit] Dominus, vv, orch, *Nc*; Salve Maria, S, pf (Milan, *c*1864)

*c*17 masses, *c*13 motets, 3 Domine [? ad adiuvandum], 3 Dixit Dominus, 2 Laudate pueri, 2 Nisi Dominus, Lauda Jerusalem, 8 Magnificat, ?5 Salve regina, 4 Regina coeli, ?2 Tantum ergo, Litany, Responses for Rogationtide and Holy Week, others, all composed Novara, 1833–40, *NOVd*

Giaele (azione sacra), Rome, Oratorio dei Filippini, 2 Feb 1855; mentioned by de Napoli, ? adapted from an opera

### CANTATAS AND HYMNS WITH ORCHESTRA

Cantata in honour of Charles IV of Spain, Naples, Villa Reale, 1818, Naples, Fondo, 1818, as L'unione delle belle arti; Coro dedicato all'illustrato pubblico di Cadice (Sp. text), vv, orch, *c*1829; L'inaugurazione, 3 solo vv, vv, orch, in cantata: In morte di Maria Malibran (A. Piazza), Milan, La Scala, 17 March 1837, vocal score (Milan, 1837); Cantata in honour of Felice Romani (R. Genovese), Novara, July 1838; Inno a Santa Irene, Altamura, Aug 1844; Inno a Pio IX, 5vv, Naples, 1850, *I-Nc*; Un sospiro sulla tomba di Monsignor Scotti, cantata, 5vv, Naples, 1850, *Nc*; Inno funebre in memoria di Monsignor Somma, 4vv, Naples, 1851, *Nc*; Inno alla vergine immacolata, 5vv, Naples, 30 Dec 1854, *Nc*; La danza augurale, cantata (N. Sole), Naples, S Carlo, for the accession of Francis II, 26 July 1859, *Nc*; Inno a Vittorio Emanuele re d'Italia (L. Tarantini), 4vv, Naples, 1860, *Nc* (Milan, n.d.); Inno guerriero dedicato a Garibaldi, unison vv, Naples, 1861, *Nc* (Milan, n.d.); Inno popolare dedicato a Dante, unison vv, Naples, 1863, *Nc*; Inno all'armonia, 5vv, Naples, for the 1st musical congress, Sept 1864, *Nc*; Inno a Rossini, 4 male vv, orch, Pesaro, for the inauguration of the statue to Rossini, 21 Aug 1864, *Nc* (Milan, ?1865); Hymn for the Accademia di S Cecilia, 4 solo vv, vv, Rome, *c*1868, mentioned by Notarnicola

### ORCHESTRAL

Concs. d, hn, B♭, cl, ?others, all composed ? 1817–20; 6 fl concs. (Naples, *c*1819), 1 ed. A. Girard (Milan, 1973); Sinfonia caratteristica napoletana no.1, *I-Nc*; Sinfonia caratteristica napoletana no.2, autograph *US-STu*, copy *I-Nc*; Lo zampognaro, sinfonia caratteristica napoletana no.3, *Nc*; L'aurora, sinfonia, autograph *US-STu*, copy *I-Nc*; Il lamento dell'arabo, sinfonia, autograph *US-STu*, copy *I-Nc*; La religione, sinfonia, autograph *US-STu*, copy *I-Nc*; Sinfonia caratteristica (on Sp. themes), *GB-Lbm* [2 mentioned by Florimo]; Sinfonia [fantasia] funebre, Novara, for the inauguration of the statue to Generali, 1836, *I-Fc*, *Nc*; Sinfonia sopra i motivi dello Stabat mater di Rossini, *Nc*, arr. pf (Milan, ?1843); La rimembranza, sinfonia fantastica, composed June, 1849, *Nc*; Omaggio a Donizetti, sinfonia (on themes of Donizetti), autograph *US-STu*, copy *I-Nc*; Omaggio a Bellini, fantasia (on themes of Bellini), ?1860, *Fc*, *Nc*, arr. pf (Milan, 1861); Il lamento del bardo, sinfonia, 1862, *Nc*, arr. pf (Milan, *c*1865); Sinfonia dedicata a Rossini, composed 1864, *Nc*;

Sinfonia fantastica (Milan, 1865); Omaggio a Pacini, fantasia, Naples, 6 Dec 1868, *Nc*, arr. pf (Milan, n.d.); Omaggio a Rossini, fantasia (on themes by Rossini), written for Rossini's memorial service, Naples, Conservatory, 22 Dec 1868, *Nc*, arr. pf (Milan, n.d.); Sinfonia marcia, Naples, for the birth of the Prince of Naples, 1869, *Nc* [Mercadante's last composition, perf. by 12 regimental bands]; 3 divertimenti, *Nc*; Elegia, vn, orch, *Nc*; La malinconia, mazurka di concerto, *Nc*, arr. pf (Milan, 1865); various marches, occasional pieces, some pubd; arrs. of operatic excerpts for solo insts, orch, etc

### OTHER VOCAL

Duet for opera Olimpiade (composer unknown) (Naples, *c*1823); 8 notturni, 4vv, bc, *I-Nc* (Rome, *c*1824); Cantata: Sorge invan per me l'aurora, A, pf (Milan, *c*1824); [6 or 12] Ariette per camera, pubd in 2 pts. (Vienna, *c*1824); Aria for Meyerbeer's opera Il crociato in Egitto (Milan, ?1830); Tema e variazioni: Sento brillarmi in seno, for Pucitta's opera I due prigionieri (Milan, 1833); Soirées italiennes (Serate italiane) (Crescini and Pepoli), 8 ariettas, 4 duos, solo vv, pf (Paris, *c*1836; Milan, n.d.); 4 canzoni napoletani (Milan, 1849, 2/1878 in V. de Meglio: Eco di Napoli); L'araba, romanza, Mez, pf (Milan, *c*1858); Il sogno, melodia, Bar, pf, vv (Milan, n.d.); Il sogno di Torquato, romanza, T, pf (Milan, n.d.); La tradita, romanza, Mez, pf (Milan, n.d.); Nol sai, romanza, Mez, pf, composed 1860 (Milan, n.d.); A mia figlia, romanza, Bar, pf, composed 1862 (Milan, 1865); T'amo, romanza, S/T, pf (Milan, 1865); Un'estate a Sorrento, 5 songs, various solo vv, pf (Milan, 1865); La stella, romanza, Mez, pf (Milan, 1865); Giovanottino che di qua passate, stornello, S, pf (Milan, 1865); La fidanzata del demonio, romanza, S, pf (Milan, 1865); La mesta tacente, romanza, S, pf (Milan, 1865); T'amo, romanza [different setting], S, pf (Milan, 1865); L'abbandonata, romanza, S/T, pf, composed 1869, for an album for F. M. Piave (Milan, *c*1870); many other romanze, ariettas, stornelli etc, with pf, some pubd (Milan, Naples, Florence, London), many in MS

Pedagogical: Esercizi di canto, i–iii (Vienna, *c*1828); 24 melodie preparatorie al canto drammatico, with pf, i–ii (Milan, ?1864)

### CHAMBER

3 melodie, 4 vn, Terzettino 3 hn, 2 duets, 2 hn, 2 qts, 4 hn, all *I-Nc*, mentioned by Florimo; 3 serenatas, 3 fl (Milan, 1823); Divertissement, pf, vc (Vienna, ?1820s); 3 qts, fl, str; La poesia, qt, 4 vc, *Fc*; Decimino, E♭, fl, ob, bn, pf, 2 vn, 2 va, vc, db; Elegia, d, vc, pf (Milan, 1865); concert studies for various insts; duets, solos etc, fl; polkas and other salon pieces, pf

## BIBLIOGRAPHY

*FétisB*

J. Sainsbury, ed.: *A Dictionary of Musicians* (London, 2/1825/*R*1966)

W. Neumann: *Saverio Mercadante* (Kassel, 1855)

R. Colucci: *Biografia di Saverio Mercadante* (Venice, 1867)

F. Clément: *Les musiciens célèbres* (Paris, 1868)

F. Florimo: 'Saverio Mercadante', *Cenno storico sulla scuola musicale di Napoli* (Naples, 1869–71, rev. and enlarged 2/1880–83/*R*1969 as *La scuola musicale di Napoli e i suoi conservatorii*)

O. Chilesotti: *I nostri maestri del passato* (Milan, 1882)

O. Serena: *I musicisti altamurani . . . in occasione del centenario di S. Mercadante* (Altamura, 1895)

G. Bustico: 'Saverio Mercadante a Novara', *RMI*, xxviii (1921), 361–96

A. Pomè: *Saggio critico sull'opera musicale di S. Mercadante* (Turin, 1925)

G. Pannain: 'Saggio su la musica a Napoli nel sec. XIX, da Mercadante a Martucci', *RMI*, xxxv (1928), 198, 331; rev. and abridged as 'Saverio Mercadante', *Ottocento musicale italiano* (Milan, 1952), 114

G. de Napoli: *La triade melodrammatica altamurana: Giacomo Tritto, Vincenzo Lavigna, Saverio Mercadante* (Milan, 1931), 67–256

G. Solimene: *La patria e i genitori di Mercadante* (Naples, 1940)

Comitato 'Pro Mercadante' di Altamura: *Saverio Mercadante, note e documenti* (Bari, 1945)

F. Schlitzer: *Mercadante e Cammarano* (Bari, 1945)

B. Notarnicola: *Saverio Mercadante, biografia critica* (Rome, 1945; rev. and enlarged 2/1948 as *Saverio Mercadante nella gloria e nella luce*)

F. Walker: 'Mercadante and Verdi', *ML*, xxxiii (1952), 311; xxxiv (1953), 33

A. R. Sardone: *Mercadante, le due patrie e 'La gran madre Italia'* (Naples, 1954)

G. Roncaglia: 'Il giuramento', *La Scala*, lxi (1954)

B. Notarnicola: *Verdi non ha vinto Mercadante* (Rome, 1955)

F. d'Amico: 'Il Ballo in Maschera prima di Verdi', *Verdi: bollettino dell'Istituto di studi verdiani*, i/3 (1960), 1251–328

M. Rinaldi: 'Mercadante, Saverio', *ES*

E. Brizio: 'Saverio Mercadante: cause e rimedi di una ingiustizia', *Altamura: bolletino dell'archivio* (Jan 1967)

F. Lippmann: 'Vincenzo Bellini, und die italienische Opera Seria seiner Zeit', *AnMc*, vi (1969), esp. 328ff

G. Carli Ballola: 'Incontro con Mercadante', *Chigiana*, xxvi–xxvii (Florence, 1969–70), 465–500

——: 'Le due illustri rivali: un positivo ricupero di valori musicali', *Teatro la Fenice* (1970), Dec, 3

M. Rinaldi: 'Significato di Mercadante', *Ritratti e fantasie musicali* (Rome, 1970)

G. Carli Ballola: 'Mercadante e *Il bravo*', *Il melodramma italiano dell'ottocento: studi e ricerche per Massimo Mila* (Turin, 1977)

MICHAEL ROSE

**Mercator** [Krämer], Sir **Michael** (*b* Venlo, 1491; *d* 1544). Dutch or German harpsichord maker. He was a maker of virginals to Floris, Count of Egmont. In 1526 he was in England and was included in a list of the musical establishment of Henry VIII and between 1529 and 1532 made 'virginals' for both Henry VIII and Cardinal Wolsey. In 1539 a medal was struck in his honour (perhaps by Hagenauer); an example is in the Department of Coins and Medals at the British Museum.

BIBLIOGRAPHY

A. J. Hipkins: *Musical Instruments, Historic, Rare, and Unique* (Edinburgh, 1887, 2/1921/R1945), v [photograph of the medal]

GUY OLDHAM

**Merceur, John.** *See* MERCURE, JOHN.

**Mercher, Matthias.** *See* MERCKER, MATTHIAS.

**Merchi** [Merchy, Merci], **Joseph Bernard** (*b* Naples, *c*1730; *d* Paris, 22 May 1793). Italian instrumentalist and composer, active in France. Together with his brother Giacomo, with whom he is often confused, he first appeared in France at Rennes on 25 May 1751; the two brothers posed as Venetians and chamber musicians to the King of Sardinia, and further pretended to have invented an instrument called the 'calissonciny', which (to judge from a later description in the *Mercure de France*) was clearly a colascione, known for more than a century and typically Neapolitan. They soon became known for their performances on this instrument and on the guitar, mandolin and lute. In August and September 1752 they gave five concerts in Frankfurt am Main and on 31 May 1753 they performed a concerto of their own composition (for two 'calissonciny') at the Concert Spirituel in Paris. After this success one of the brothers (probably Joseph Bernard) settled in Paris and began a remarkable career as a guitar and mandolin teacher and as a composer. Every year from 1760 to 1780 he published from his own establishment one or more guitar books; these usually consisted of airs and currently popular melodies with guitar accompaniment, and apparently enjoyed considerable vogue. The other brother may have moved to England and written some collections for the guitar which were printed 'for the author' in London.

The Merchi brothers were concerned with building up a fashionable repertory for the guitar, which was somewhat neglected at the time; they also attempted vocal works, which suffered from their deplorable French prosody. In addition to his compositions Joseph Bernard wrote two guitar methods including a noteworthy *Traité des agréments* (1777).

WORKS

All published in Paris unless otherwise indicated; London publications are probably by Giacomo.

INSTRUMENTAL

op.
3   4 duetti, 2 gui, e 6 minuetti . . . con variazione, gui (n.d.)
5   6 trio, 2 vn, b (*c*1755)
9   Trios, 2 vn/mand, vc (n.d.)
12  6 duos, gui, muted vn (1764)
15  6 duetti, 2 mand/vn/tr viol (1766)
16  12 suonate, 6 for gui, 6 for 2 gui/gui, vn (London, 1766)
21  Pièces, gui, vn acc. (1769)
21  12 divertimentos, 2 gui/gui, vn (London, n.d.)
28  Pièces et duos, gui, vn (n.d.)
33  6 duetti, 2 gui/gui, muted vn, XXIX<sup>e</sup> livre de guitare (1775)

VOCAL
—   6 barcaroles italiennes, 1v, gui (1755)
4   Raccolta d'ariette francesi ed italiane, 1v, gui (?1760)
—   Ariettes et vaudevilles nouveaux, 1v, gui (1760), ?identical to op.4
15  Scelta d'arietta francesi, italiane ed inglesi, 1v, gui (London, 1766)

Livre[s] de guitare, opp.6, 8, 10–11, 13–14, 18–20, 22–4, 26–7, 29–31, 34, 36 (1761–1780), incl. La guitare de bonne humeur, Les soirées de Paris, Recueil d'airs avec accompagnement de guitare

Various pieces, *F-Pc*

PEDAGOGICAL WORKS
op.
7   *Le guide des écoliers de guitare ou Préludes aussi agréables qu'utiles . . . V<sup>e</sup> livre de guitare* (*c*1761, 2/1761 as *Instructions préliminaires ou Méthode*)
35  *Traité des agréments de la musique exécutés sur la guitare* (1777)

BIBLIOGRAPHY
*Mercure de France* (June 1753), 163
J.-B. de La Borde: *Essai sur la musique ancienne et moderne* (Paris, 1780/R1972), i, 291
A. Choron and F. Fayolle: *Dictionnaire historique des musiciens* (Paris, 1810–11/R1971)
Comte de Palys: Communication, *Bulletin de la Société archéologique d'Ille et Vilaine*, xxvii (1898), p.xiii

ROGER COTTE

**Merck, Daniel** (*b* Augsburg, *c*1650; *d* Augsburg, 1713). German composer, musician, teacher and writer on music. He spent his life in his native city. He received his musical education at the Protestant Gymnasium and college of St Anna and sang in the choir in the production of a play there in 1671. His teacher was Tobias Kriegsdorfer. From about 1678 he was Kantor of the Barfüsserkirche and from 1686 an instrument teacher. In 1697 he is recorded as a city wait. In the same year, on the death of Georg Schmezer, he succeeded him as Kantor and director of music at St Anna, and he held these posts until 1712. He published *Compendium musicae instrumentalis Chelicae, das ist: kurtzer Begriff, welcher Gestalten die Instrumental-Music auf der Violin, Pratschen, Viola da Gamba, und Bass gründlich und leicht zu erlernen seye* (Augsburg, 1695). This short volume is the first German tutor for string instruments. In addition Merck is said to have composed two funeral songs and the music for the play *Cevilinda*, produced in 1702 in the mastersingers' hall at Augsburg.

BIBLIOGRAPHY
K. Koeberlin: 'Beiträge zur Geschichte der Kantorei bei St. Anna in Augsburg', *Zeitschrift des Historischen Vereins für Schwaben und Neuburg*, xxxix (1913), 89
J. W. von Wasielewski: *Die Violine und ihre Meister* (Leipzig, 8/1927), 285
L. Gerheuser: 'Jacob Scheiffelhut und seine Instrumentalmusik', *Zeitschrift des Historischen Vereins für Schwaben und Neuburg*, xlix (1933), 21
D. D. Boyden: *The History of Violin Playing from its Origins to 1761* (London, 1965), 245
*Augsburger Barock* (Augsburg, 1968), 463f

ADOLF LAYER

**Mercker** [Maercker, Merkher, Mercher], **Matthias** (*b* Amsterdam; *fl c*1600–22). Netherlands composer and instrumentalist. He was probably taught by Cornelius Conradus, a pupil of Sweelinck. His first known activity was as a cornett player in Lüneburg in about 1600, where he worked for about a year before entering the service of King Christian IV of Denmark. In 1602 he travelled to Russia as leading instrumentalist to the younger brother of Christian IV. After his return to Copenhagen in 1603 he discovered that his post had been filled by someone else and so left the country. Four years later he became organist in Franeker (Netherlands), but by Christmas eve 1608 had taken up a post as cornett player to the Duke of Holstein. Because of financial difficulties he was forced to leave in 1615, after which he almost certainly went into the service of Eberhard Otto von Münchhausen for three years, as suggested by the dedication in *Musica instrumentalis*. From 1618 to 1622 he was organist of the St Nicolaus Church in Strasbourg. The last mention of his name is found in a document dated 1622 recommending his appointment as director of an instrumental ensemble.

Mercker seems to have been a very skilful musician and was versed both in composition and the playing of several instruments. According to Tobias Speccerus (in the 1620 archives of the St Nicolaus Church in Strasbourg), Mercker played the organ, trombone, cornett, flute and viol. His works show a thorough knowledge of musical theory and good craftsmanship; he often exploited harsh sonorities, and in the *Odae spirituales binae* made effective use of contrasting homophonic and polyphonic textures. Among his compositions instrumental dances are in the majority.

## WORKS

Musica instrumentalis (n.p., n.d.)
Wir wünschen frölich jederman, 5vv; 3 Fugen, Pavana, a 5 (n.p., n.d.)
Fantasie seu cantiones gallicae, 4vv, accomodatae cymbalis (Frankfurt am Main, 1604), lost
20 neue ausserlesene Padouane und Gaillard, 5vv (Helmstedt. 1609)
Matthie Merckeri belgae concentus harmonici, varii generis, instrumentis quibusuis congruentes, 2–6vv (Frankfurt am Main, 1613), lost
Newe künstliche musikalische Fugen, Pavanen, Galliarden und Intraden, 2–6vv (Frankfurt am Main, 1614), lost
Odae spirituales binae, 5vv (Strasbourg, 1619)

Further works in 1607[28], 1609[30]

Christ, Gottes und Mariae Sohn, 5vv, 1599, *D-B*
Harmonia musica, 4, 5vv, 1609, *Kl*
41 sacred pieces, formerly Breslau, lost, doubtful

## BIBLIOGRAPHY

M. Vogeleis: *Quellen und Bausteine zu einer Geschichte der Musik und des Theaters im Alsass 500–1800* (Strasbourg, 1911)
M. Seiffert: 'Matthias Mercker, ein ausgewanderter holländischer Musiker', *Gedenkboek aangeboden aan Dr. D. F. Scheurleer* (The Hague, 1925), 291

F. J. DE HEN

**Mercure** [Merceur, Mercoeur, Mercury], **John** (*fl* 1640–50). Composer and lutenist, probably of French origin. During the reign of Charles I he established himself at the English court, becoming a musician for the lutes and voices in ordinary on 1 December 1641; he died before the Restoration, when his place was taken by Stephen Nau. He is important chiefly for having helped to introduce the *style brisé* of French lute music to English lute and harpsichord music. He has sometimes been confused with Mercure d'Orléans, a shadowy figure who composed lute music in France around the beginning of the 17th century. Dances for lute, harpsichord and viols (principal sources: *GB-Lbm, Ob, Och, US-NYp*, 1658[4]) by both composers have been edited by M. Rolland and J.-M. Vaccaro in *Oeuvres des Mercure* (Paris, 1977).

B. A. R. COOPER

**Mercure, Pierre** (*b* Montreal, 21 Feb 1927; *d* Avallon, 29 Jan 1966). Canadian composer. He studied theory, composition (with Champagne) and several instruments at the Quebec Conservatory with the intention of becoming a conductor. However, he quickly showed considerable creative gifts in various incidental scores, a few songs, the orchestral pieces *Kaléidoscope* (1947–8) and *Pantomime* (1949), and in three ballet scores written for Françoise Sullivan. These initiated a constant preoccupation, the fusion and integration of different art forms; he also associated with a group of painters, writers, actors and dancers centred on Paul-Emile Borduas, an artist whose manifesto *Refus global* (1948) was an indictment of conservative middle-class society and a call for the liberation of creative man.

In the autumn of 1949 Mercure travelled to Europe and joined Boulanger's class in Paris. His interests, however, were increasingly in new music, and he stayed with his teacher for only a few months before leaving to work assiduously with Gabriel Charpentier, Jocelyne Binet and Clermont Pépin on improvisation, superimposed forms and collective composition. At the same time he studied orchestration with Hoérée and conducting with Fournet. His choral work *Ils ont détruit la ville* (1950), later incorporated as one of the movements of *Cantate pour une joie*, won him first prize in a Canadian Broadcasting Corporation (CBC) International Service competition.

After a year's absence Mercure returned to his post as bassoonist in the Montreal SO (1947–52); later he also played at the Théâtre des Variétés Lyriques (1951). He studied with Dallapiccola at Tanglewood in 1951 and there discovered the principles of 12-note serialism – which he almost immediately rejected. Instead he went on to develop his poetic manner, hesitantly but surely, in more Charpentier settings, the *Divertissement* for strings (1957) and *Triptyque* for orchestra (1959). Throughout this early period (1948–59) he had been looking for new sonorities. Failing to find them, he had turned to a spontaneous lyrical expression in traditional forms, influenced by Stravinsky, Milhaud and Honegger, and also by popular American music and jazz (several of his themes are from Glenn Miller numbers). The rhythms are explicit, the orchestration shimmers. All this while Mercure had continued his association with artists in other media, particularly during his period of service in the music department of the CBC French television network (1952–66). He was the first Canadian producer of music on television, and his programmes included performances of *Oedipus rex*, *Jeanne d'Arc au bûcher* and *Wozzeck*.

After this period Mercure was impelled above all by the desire to align himself with the most modern forms of art. He spent the years 1959–62 seeking a new language in electronic music, stimulated by his contacts with Schaeffer and the Groupe de Recherches Musicales. The works he produced include *Répercussions*, *Structures métalliques*, *Incandescence* and *Improvisation*, most of them involving dance and/or film projections. He also organized the Semaine Internationale de Musique Actuelle (1961) in Montreal, presenting music by Cage, Stockhausen, Wolff, Xenakis and others. This single festival, which he had intended should be the first of an annual series, prepared the way for the Société de Musique Contemporaine du Québec, founded in 1966 and devoted to promoting new music.

Mercure returned to Europe in the summer of 1962 to familiarize himself with new developments in electronic and other music in Paris, Darmstadt and Dartington. He then undertook a cantata for radio, *Psaume pour abri* (1963), the first of three works combining electronic with live music, in this case synthetic sounds, transformed sounds from three brass quintets and four string quartets, singing and speaking choruses, a reciter and seven instrumentalists. The work is a 'cry against barbarism, atrocity, absurdity' in seven parts, of which the last three are varied versions of the first three, the whole moving away from and back to the human element. Following this, in *Tétrachromie* for instruments and electronic sounds (1963), Mercure produced a work on the four seasons and the four ages of man, symbolically represented by the colours green, yellow, red and white. It was commissioned by the Compagnie des Grands Ballets Canadiens for the inaugural festival at the Place des Arts, but the performance did not take place because of a labour dispute. *Lignes et points* for orchestra (1963–4) has links with both of the preceding works; indeed, the same melodic cells of three, four or five notes occur in all three. The piece, a set of variations on a theme, attempts to reproduce electronic sounds in the orchestra.

Two film scores for Jacques Giraldeau, *Formes 64* and *Elément III*, were Mercure's last works, though the latter generated a by-product in *H₂O per Severino* (1965), a sequence of eight serial improvisations for flutes and/or clarinets sparked off by Severino Gazzelloni's recording of music for the film. Before his death as a result of a car accident, Mercure prepared for CBC a television production of Schafer's opera *Loving/Toi*, whose performance, a few days after the event, made an entirely appropriate tribute.

### WORKS
(*selective list*)

BALLETS

Dualité (F. Sullivan), tpt, pf, 1949; Montreal, Compagnons, 8 May 1949
La femme archaïque (pantomime, Sullivan), va, pf, perc, 1949; Montreal, Compagnons, 8 May 1949
Lucrèce Borgia (Sullivan), tpt, pf, perc, 1949; Montreal, Compagnons, 8 May 1949
Emprise, cl, bn, vc, pf, 1950; Paris, American Club, 1950
Structures métalliques I (F. Riopelle), metal sculptures, tapes, 1961; Montreal, L'Egrègore, 6 June 1961
Incandescence (Riopelle), tapes, 1961; Montreal, Comédie Canadienne, 6 Aug 1961
Structures métalliques II (Riopelle), metal sculptures, tapes, 1961; Montreal, Comédie Canadienne, 6 Aug 1961
Improvisation (Riopelle), prepared pf on tape, 1961; Montreal, Studio Françoise Riopelle, Dec 1961
Manipulations (J. Renaud), tapes, 1963; Quebec, L'Estoc, 8 May 1964
Tétrachromie, cl, b cl, sax, perc, tape, 1963; unstaged
Surimpressions (Riopelle), prepared pf on tape, 1964; Montreal, Studio Françoise Riopelle, 16 Dec 1964

ORCHESTRAL AND VOCAL ORCHESTRAL

Kaléidoscope, 1947–8; version for small orch, 1949
Pantomime, 1948; versions for 14/18 wind, perc, 1949
Cantate pour une joie (G. Charpentier), S, chorus, orch, 1955
Divertissement, str qt, str, 1957, rev. 1958
Triptyque, 1959
Psaume pour abri (F. Ouellette), reciter, choruses, 7 insts, tapes, 1963
Lignes et points, 1963–4

OTHER WORKS

Vocal: Colloque (Valéry), 1v, pf, 1948; Dissidence (Charpentier), S/T, pf, 1955
Inst: Pantomime, vc, pf, 1949, inc.; H₂O per Severino, 4–10 fl and/or cl, 1965
Tape: Répercussions, Japanese bell sounds, 1961; Jeu de hockey, 1961; Structures métalliques III, 1962, inc.; see also ballets
Film scores: Formes 64, ou La forme des choses (J. Giraldeau), brass qnt, tape, 1965; Elément III (J. Giraldeau), fl, 1965

Principal publisher: Ricordi

### BIBLIOGRAPHY

R. Duguay: 'Pierre Mercure', *Musiques du Kébèk* (Montreal, 1971), 115
J. Maillard: 'Pierre Mercure (1927–1966): Psaume pour abri (1963)', *Education musicale* (1971), no.179, p.23
P. Mercure: 'Commentaires', *Musiques du Kébèk*, ed. R. Duguay (Montreal, 1971), 121

LYSE RICHER-LORTIE

**Mercurio, Vecchio.** Copyist of *GB-Lbm* Add.30342, a companion manuscript to that copied by JACQUES CELLIER.

**Mercury.** Ancient Roman god, possibly to some extent identifiable with the Greek god HERMES.

**Mercy [Merci], Lewis** (*b* *c*1695; *d* ?London, *c*1750). English composer and recorder player of French origin. He was in the service of James Brydges, Earl of Caernarvon and 1st Duke of Chandos, probably before 1720. A notice in the *Daily Courant* records that on 13 February 1719 he played a recorder solo in a benefit concert for Dahuron at Hickford's Room. His opp.1 and 2, both sets of six flute solos, were published by Walsh in 1718 and 1720 and reprinted in 1730; only the reprint of op.1, dedicated to the Earl of Caernarvon, is extant; if this dedication was in the lost 1718 edition, it would refer to Mercy's patron James Brydges; if it occurs only on the 1730 title-page, it would be Brydges's son Henry. Two different works were published as Mercy's op.3, a set of flute sonatas (on the title-page the composer is styled 'di nazione inglesa') and a set of bassoon sonatas. On 18 July 1730, while lodging in the parish of St Paul's, Covent Garden, Mercy married Ann Hampshire at St Vedast, Foster Lane; from 1733 to 1736 he lived in Orange Court, Castle Street.

According to Hawkins, who described him as 'a celebrated performer on the flute abec and an excellent composer for that instrument', Mercy was concerned about the decline in popularity of the recorder in face of competition from the transverse flute: as a result, he collaborated in about 1735 with the instrument maker Thomas Stainsby jr on a new system for the recorder. In an unsuccessful attempt to promote this modified instrument, he apparently published 12 solos,

the first six whereof are said to be for the Traverse-flute, Violin, or English Flute, according to Mr. Stanesby's new system, with a preface in recommendation of it in which he refers to Mersennus, de Instrumentis Harmonicis; and asserts that Stanesby's is in truth the ancient system of the flute.

An earlier footnote about Stainsby, however, states that Mercy published 'six solos for the flute, three whereof are said to be accommodated to Mr Stanesby's new system'. Any such sonatas are now lost: the six of op.3 have no such preface, and the preface to the op.1 reprint makes no reference to Stainsby but discusses performing techniques ('divisions' resembling double stops) designed to prove that the flute is 'as capable of doing as hard things as the Violin'. Hawkins ranked Mercy's flute solos 'among the best compositions for that instrument extant'. They are Italianate in style: the two sets of flute solos follow the normal four-movement plan; the flute writing is idiomatic and demands considerable virtuosity. The bassoon or cello sonatas of op.3 are in three movements; several, including an allemande and a Larghetto, are marked 'ala Scotseza'.

### WORKS

6 solos, fl, hpd/vc, op.1 (London, 1718, 2/1730)
Solos, fl, bc, op.2 (London, 1720, 2/1730), lost
VI Sonate, bn/vc, bc, op.3 (London, *c*1735)
VI Sonate, fl, vc/hpd, op.3 (London, *c*1745)

### BIBLIOGRAPHY

HawkinsH
C. H. C. and M. I. Baker: *The Life and Circumstances of James Brydges, First Duke of Chandos* (London, 1949)

MAURICE BYRNE

**Méreaux.** French family of musicians.

**(1) Nicolas-Jean Le Froid de Méreaux** (*b* Paris, 1745; *d* Paris, 1797). Organist and composer. He was educated in Paris under various French and Italian musicians. By 1767 he was organist at St Sauveur, Paris, and later organist of the Petits Augustins and of the royal chapel. He was described by Gerber as one of the best-liked French composers of both church and theatre music. In a series of works composed between the ages of 27 and 32 for the *opéra comique* players and for the Concert Spirituel, he achieved particular recognition for the oratorio *Samson*. This was given four times, attracting listeners who found it both noble and picturesque. *Samson* and the oratorio *Esther* placed emphasis on choral writing, while *La Résurrection* contained comparatively more soloistic writing and was the 'only Parisian oratorio of the period dealing with the life of Christ apart from the Christmas story' (Foster); the figure of Christ does not appear, and the story is told by observers. A letter by Méreaux, describing the current state of church music in France, was published by his friend Martin Gerbert in *De cantu et musica sacra* (1774).

*Alexandre aux Indes*, Méreaux's first full-length opera, seems to have been his most successful one, although *Oedipe et Jocaste* enjoyed some popularity. In the latter he scored for the newly reconstructed neoclassical instruments, the tuba curva and buccin, to add impact in the final conflagration scene. Méreaux played the organ in various Revolutionary ceremonies.

WORKS

OPERAS

*(all performed in Paris unless otherwise stated)*

La ressource comique (1, L. Anseaume), Comédie-Italienne, 22 Aug 1772 (Paris, n.d.)
Le retour de tendresse (1, Anseaume), Comédie-Italienne, 1 Oct 1774 (Paris, n.d.)
Laurette (1, Danzel de Malzeville), Comédie-Italienne, 23 July 1777 (Paris, n.d.)
Alexandre aux Indes (3, E. Morel de Chédeville), Opéra, 26 Aug 1783 (Paris, n.d.)
Oedipe et Jocaste (Oedipe à Thèbes) (3, P. A. Duprat de la Touloubre), Opéra, 30 Dec 1791, *F-Pn*, *Po*
Fabius (3, J.-M.-D.-M. Barouillet), Opéra, 9 Aug 1793, *Po*
Le duel comique, Comédie-Italienne, 1776 [arr. and rev. of music by Paisiello]
Unperf.: Les Thermopyles, *Pc*; Scipion à Carthage

VOCAL

Aline reine de Golconde, cantata (Paris, 1767); Ariettes de la feste donnés à Monsieur de La Garde (Paris, 1770); Motet, 1v, 1773; Motet, 3vv, 1773; Samson (after Voltaire), oratorio, 1774, *Po*; Esther (after Racine), oratorio, 1775, *Po*; Laudate Dominum, motet, 1775; La Résurrection (P.-L. Moline), oratorio, 1780, *Pn*; Laudate pueri, motet, 1781; Ode sur la naissance du dauphin (Moline), 1781; Te Deum, 1789; Cantique française, 1789

**(2) Jean-Nicolas Le Froid de Méreaux** (*b* Paris, 22 June 1767; *d* Paris, 6 Feb 1838). Organist, pianist, teacher and composer, son of (1) Nicolas-Jean Le Froid de Méreaux. He was taught music by his father and, although remaining a Roman Catholic, became organist of the Protestant church of St Louis-du-Louvre in 1791. He remained in this post until 1811 when the church was demolished, thereafter being transferred to the Chapelle de l'Oratoire St Honoré. He produced an unofficial hymn for solo voices, choir and orchestra for Napoleon's coronation in 1804. According to Fétis, he published flute sonatas, piano sonatas and piano fantasias. In 1828 he edited a French psalter, *Les pseaumes de David mis en vers français*.

**(3) Jean-Amédée Le Froid de Méreaux** (*b* Paris, 17 Sept 1802; *d* Rouen, 25 April 1874). French musicologist, pianist and composer, son of (2) Jean-Nicolas Le Froid de Méreaux. He was given piano lessons by his father, but was sent to university to pursue a legal career. Instead, he took lessons from Reicha in counterpoint and concentrated on becoming a pianist and composer for the piano. After 1830 he travelled in France and went to London in 1832–3, giving concerts and teaching. In 1835 he settled in Rouen, where he combined teaching with the publishing of music and musical articles. Curiosity about music of the past led him to mount 'historical concerts' in Rouen in 1842 and in Paris the following year; later he confessed that his performances on these occasions of early keyboard music were insufficiently based on precise knowledge, especially of the interpretation of ornaments. Contact with early music had awakened an intellectual interest, however, which was later to prove fruitful in the longer term.

Permanent reminders of his keyboard teaching appeared in 1855 with the 60 *Grandes études pour piano*. These were officially adopted by the Paris Conservatoire, and the fact advertised. Three years later Méreaux was elected to the Académie Impériale of Rouen. As a pianist he continued to appear occasionally in Paris; in 1855 (according to Fétis) he gave with a pupil the first performance in Paris of Mozart's double piano concerto K365/316a.

The double talent of composer and musicologist recognized by Comettant in his obituary was most completely realized in Méreaux's *Les clavecinistes de 1637 à 1790* (1864–7), an edition of a large collection of keyboard music, with full introductory essays on the composers, the problems of their keyboard music and on early instruments. The earliest composers dealt with are Frescobaldi, Chambonnières, Purcell, the Couperins and the Bach family; the emphasis is on the 18th century, and a sonata by Steibelt was considered historically justified for inclusion. The editorial outlook was, however, a scholarly one: 'It is necessary to study the theory and meaning of ornaments in order to discover the composer's intentions'. Accordingly, comparative tables of explanation are given and in the music itself the ornaments are all written out in modern notation. This, and the many dynamic markings, make Méreaux's edition seem clumsy. But the importance of the collection was recognized at the time, and is valuable in the history of 19th-century musicology. Méreaux's compositions for piano appear unoriginal; they are predominantly influenced by Chopin and at times approach salon music. The trio, quartet and second mass represent a late, more ambitious flowering.

WORKS

*(selective list, most pubd Paris, n.d.)*

VOCAL

Messe solenelle, 4vv, orch, Rouen, c1852
Second mass, 4vv, orch, 1866
2 cantatas; 2 idylls, male vv; romances

ORCHESTRAL AND CHAMBER

Grand concerto symphonique, pf, orch
2 duets, pf, vc; Cantilènes concertants, pf, vn
Grand trio, pf, vn, vc, op.102, 1873
Str Qt, 1877
Hymne du matin and Hymne de la nuit, vn, pf/org, 1877

PIANO

Grandes études pour piano en 60 caprices (1855)
Ballade, op.60; Addio, elegy, op.71; Boléro, op.72; Inquiétude
Au bord de la mer, barcarolle; Une chanson d'autrefois, arabesque
Le départ des pèlerins; Souvenir de la Bastide
Variation sets

Many transcrs. for pf and for chamber ensembles of operatic and chamber works by Handel, Mozart and Beethoven; vocal score of Berlioz's L'enfance du Christ (1855), collab. J. Ritter

### WRITINGS

Les clavecinistes de 1637 à 1790 (Rouen, 1864–7)
Biographies musicales (Rouen, n.d.)
Esquisse de l'histoire du chant en France (Rouen, n.d.)
Articles in Moniteur universel and Journal de Rouen, many collected in Variétés littéraires et musicales (Paris, 1878)

### BIBLIOGRAPHY

FétisB; GerberL
M. Gerbert: De cantu et musica sacra, ii (St Blasien, 1774), 362f
A. Choron and F. Fayolle: Dictionnaire historique des musiciens (Paris, 1810–11/R1971)
O. Comettant: Obituary, Art musical (30 April 1874), 141
A.-F. Marmontel: 'Notice biographique', in Méreaux: Variétés littéraires et musicales (Paris, 1878)
G. Servières: Documents inédits sur les organistes français (Paris, ?1923)
J. G. Rushton: Music and Drama at the Académie royale de musique (Paris) 1774–1789 (diss., U. of Oxford, 1969)
D. H. Foster: 'The Oratorio in Paris in the 18th Century', AcM, xlvii (1975), 84
C. Pierre: Histoire du Concert spirituel 1725–1790 (Paris, 1975)

DAVID CHARLTON

**Merelli, Bartolomeo** (b Bergamo, 19 May 1794; d Milan, 3 or 4 April 1879). Italian librettist and impresario. The son of Count Moroni's agent, he was originally intended for law, but preferred to devote himself to music and literature. He studied privately with Mayr, at whose instance he wrote verses for the young Donizetti to set to music. From 1818 to 1824 Merelli was active as a professional librettist, providing opera texts for Mayr, Vaccai and Donizetti: these included Enrico di Borgogna (1818), Donizetti's first opera to be given on a public stage, and Zoraide di Granata (1822), his first real success. The next few years in Merelli's life are obscure (Monaldi's story of a theft from Count Moroni's household, banishment to Milan and meteoric rise to fame in Vienna is now discredited). During the later 1820s he appears to have been a theatrical agent. His first appointment as impresario was at Varese in 1830; in 1835 he managed short seasons at Cremona and Como. The following year he became joint lessee of the Kärntnertor-Theater in Vienna and succeeded Visconti as impresario of La Scala, Milan. The revolution of 1848 caused the Italian season in Vienna to be suspended, whereupon, according to one source, Merelli consented to act as a spy for Radetzky and became so unpopular that for years afterwards he dared not stir out of Austrian Italy. His lease of La Scala expired in 1850 and was renewed from 1853 to 1855 and from 1861 to 1863. Some time afterwards he retired to Bergamo, where his name appears as a member of the Consultative Commission of the School of Music in 1871.

Merelli is best remembered as the man who launched Verdi on his operatic career in 1839, and whose faith in him remained unshaken by the fiasco of Un giorno di regno and was rewarded two years later with the success of Nabucodonosor. He rarely retained the good opinions of those whom he befriended. Verdi, Donizetti and many others had harsh things to say about his management. Bellini and Nicolai doubted his honesty; however, the legend that he was the protector of Giuseppina Strepponi (later Verdi) and the father of her illegitimate children has been effectively disposed of by Frank Walker.

### BIBLIOGRAPHY

R. Wallaschek: Das k.k. Hofoperntheater (Vienna, 1909)
A. Cametti: Donizetti a Roma (Rome, 1917)
G. Monaldi, Impresari celebri del secolo XIX (Rocca S Casciano, 1918)
L. Miragoli: Il melodramma italiano nel ottocento (Rome, 1924)
——: 'Bartolomeo Merelli', Musica d'oggi, vi (1924), 232
C. Gatti: Verdi (Milan, 1931)
F. Abbiati: Giuseppe Verdi (Milan, 1959)
F. Walker: The Man Verdi (London, 1962)

JULIAN BUDDEN

**Merengue.** A dance of Venezuela, Haiti and the Dominican Republic of both folk and urban popular traditions. While exhibiting the influences of Afro-Cuban dance forms and responsorial singing practices, its song texts, often regional in subject matter, are in typical Spanish copla (four-line stanza) and estribillo (refrain) form. The guitar, cuatro (small guitar), charrasca (metal scraper), tambora (double-headed drum) and bajo (single-headed drum) provide accompaniments that combine duple and triple metres, sometimes creating 5/8 effects. Afro-Cuban cinquillo and tresillo rhythmic figures are predominant.

WILLIAM GRADANTE

**Mergot, Franciscus** [Francisco de Novo Portu] (fl 1560–76). Singer and composer of ?Spanish birth, resident in Austria. He was known by the sobriquet 'de Novo Portu', but recent research has shown that his surname was Mergot. He may have come from Spain, as Eitner said. In the court records of Archduke Maximilian of Austria his name first appears in 1560, when he was a court chaplain with a monthly stipend of ten guilders. When his employer became Emperor Maximilian II in 1564, he became a bass singer in the Vienna Hofkapelle at a salary of 15 guilders plus allowances. In 1576 he received a honorarium in recognition of his long and faithful service at court. After Maximilian's death on 12 October 1576 and the consequent dissolution of the court all trace of him is lost. He may be the Franciscus Portu who had a five-part madrigal included in a collection by the Milanese composer Antonio Martorello (RISM 1547[17]). He was, however, definitely the composer of two three-part motets (in 1567[2]) and of four motets in 1568[2] and 1568[4-5] (one five-voice motet ed. W. Pass, TM, xxxiv, 1974).

### BIBLIOGRAPHY

EitnerQ ('Francisco de Novo Portu')
W. Pass: Musik und Musiker am Hof Maximilians II (diss., U. of Vienna, 1972)

WALTER PASS

**Merian, Wilhelm** (b Basle, 18 Sept 1889; d Basle, 15 Nov 1952). Swiss musicologist and critic. He studied classical philology, and then musicology with Resniček, Kretzschmar and J. Wolf in Berlin and with K. Nef at the University of Basle. In 1915 he took the doctorate with a dissertation on Hans Kotter's organ tablature. He became a critic and later music editor (1920–51) of Basler Nachrichten. In 1921 he was appointed lecturer at the University of Basle and completed his Habilitation with a study of the keyboard music of the German colourists; he was subsequently appointed reader (1930) and full professor (1935). He was the secretary of the IMS (1927–48) and president of the Schweizerische Musikforschende Gesellschaft (1935–46); later he became an honorary member of both societies. In 1933 with Paul Sacher he founded the

Schola Cantorum Basiliensis.

Merian is important for his studies of 16th-century organists, particularly those associated with Basle. In his dissertation, *Habilitationsschrift* and in several articles (e.g. those on Amerbach and Meyer) he drew on archival evidence and letters for biographical information. In *Der Tanz in den deutschen Tabulaturbüchern* he traced the development of a keyboard style through the intabulation practices of the 16th century.

WRITINGS

'Felix Platter als Musiker', *SIMG*, xiii (1911–12), 272

*Die Tabulaturen des Organisten Hans Kotter: ein Beitrag zur Musikgeschichte des beginnenden 16. Jahrhunderts* (diss., U. of Basle, 1915; Leipzig, 1916/R1973)

ed.: *Gedenkschrift zum 50jährigen Bestehen der Allgemeinen Musikschule in Basel*-(Basle, 1917)

'Bonifazius Amerbach und Hans Kotter', *Basler Zeitschrift für Geschichte und Altertumskunde*, xvi (1917), 140–206

'Johann Friedrich Reichardt und Isaac Iselin', *ZMw*, i (1918–19), 698

*Basels Musikleben im XIX. Jahrhundert* (Basle, 1920)

*Die Klaviermusik der deutschen Koloristen* (Habilitationsschrift, U. of Basle, 1921)

'Gregor Meyer', *Schweizerisches Jb für Musikwissenschaft*, i (1924), 138

*Der Tanz in den deutschen Tabulaturbüchern mit thematischem Verzeichnis, Beispielen zur Intavolationspraxis und einer Studie über die Anfänge des Klavierstils* (Leipzig, 1927/R1968)

ed. with E. Refardt and H. Ehinger: *Festschrift Karl Nef zum 60. Geburtstag* (Zurich and Leipzig, 1932) [incl. 'Mozarts Klaviersonaten und die Sonatenform', p.174]

*Hermann Suter* (Basle, 1936)

EDITIONS

*Geistliche Werke des 16. Jahrhunderts*, Musikalische Werke schweizerischer Komponisten, i (Geneva, 1927)

BIBLIOGRAPHY

A. Geering: 'Wilhelm Merian zum 60. Geburtstag', *SMz*, lxxxix (1949), 333

K. Jeppesen: 'Wilhelm Merian in Memoriam', *AcM*, xxiv (1952), 220

W. Nef: 'Wilhelm Merian zum Gedächtnis', *Mf*, vi (1953), 143

M. E. C. BARTLET

**Méric-Lalande, Henriette (Clémentine)** (*b* Dunkirk, 1798; *d* Chantilly, 7 Sept 1867). French soprano. The daughter of J.-B. Lamiraux-Lalande, the director of a provincial operatic company, she made her début in 1814 at Nantes and appeared with success in French provincial towns until 1822. Though Ebers attempted to engage her for London, she joined the Théâtre du Gymnase Dramatique in Paris, and took lessons from Garcia before making her first appearance on 3 April 1823 in *Les folies amoureuses*, a pasticcio arranged by Castil-Blaze. About this time she married Jules Méric, a horn player at the Opéra-Comique. On Garcia's advice she went to Italy, where she received additional training from Bonfichi and Banderali at Milan. She took part in the première of Meyerbeer's *Il crociato in Egitto* (Venice, 26 December 1824) and later appeared with success at Munich, Naples, Vienna and Milan, where she sang in the premières of Bellini's *Il pirata* (1827) and *La straniera* (1829): Bellini himself had told Florimo in 1828 that she was 'incapable of delicate sentiment'. Méric-Lalande made her London début at the King's Theatre on 17 April 1830 in *Il pirata* but, according to Chorley, her voice was past its best and given to 'trembling'. Later that year she appeared at the Théâtre-Italien in Paris (2 October), and in 1831 she again sang in London and Paris, where she was admired as Rossini's Semiramis. She continued to sing in Italy and Spain, but retired shortly after singing the title role in the première of Donizetti's *Lucrezia Borgia* (Milan, 26 December 1833). In her prime she was a brilliant dramatic singer, with an admirable technique and a

powerful theatrical presence, the original exemplar of the *soprano drammatica d'agilità*. A biography, with a portrait, was published in the musical journal *Teatro della Fenice* (Venice, 1826).

JULIAN MARSHALL/PHILIP ROBINSON

**Mericocke, Thomas** (*fl c*1550–70). English composer. A five-part In Nomine attributed to him is in *GB-Ob* Mus.Sch.C.212–16; in style it is not dissimilar to those in the same MS by Tye, and both composers may well have been of the same generation. Mericocke was probably also the composer of the English settings of *Te Deum*, *Magnificat* and *Nunc dimittis*, attributed simply to 'Merricock', of which a single (alto) part survives in *Lbm* Add.29289. Although, like the MS in *Ob*, this partbook dates from the early 17th century, the texts set are not later than 1552.

In *Lbm* R.M.24.d.2 there is a three-part setting, attributed to 'mr. moorecocke', of *Gloria, laus et honor*, the hymn sung in the Sarum rite during the procession before Mass on Palm Sunday. In this case, however, a more plausible candidate for identification with the composer would be ROBERT MORECOCK.

ROGER BOWERS

**Merighi, Antonia Margherita** (*fl* 1717–40; *d* before 1764). Italian contralto. She came from Bologna and was for long in the service of the Dowager Grand Duchess Violante Beatrice of Tuscany. She sang regularly in Venetian theatres (1717–21, 1724–6 and 1732–3), appearing altogether in 19 operas there, the first of them being Vivaldi's *Tieteberga*. In June 1719 she had a great success at Bologna in F. Gasparini's *Sesostri*. She sang in 14 operas at Naples (1721–4, 1728–9). In many of them, as sometimes in Venice and London, she played male roles. She sang at Parma and Florence in 1725, Turin in 1726 and Bologna again in 1727. In summer 1729 Handel engaged her for London, and she was advertised as 'a Woman of a very fine Presence, an excellent Actress, and a very good Singer – A Counter Tenor'. The fact that her salary was £800 (Rolli in a letter to Riva put it even higher) – considerably more than those of Strada and Fabri, and second only to Bernacchi – is a sufficient pointer to her reputation at this date. Quadrio wrote that she was universally and rightly applauded. She remained at the King's Theatre for two seasons, singing in eight Handel operas and the pasticcio *Ormisda*. She created the parts of Matilde in *Lotario* (her début in December 1729), Rosmira in *Partenope* and Erissena in *Poro*, and was also heard as Cornelia in *Giulio Cesare*, Elisa in *Tolomeo*, Armira in *Scipione*, Armida in *Rinaldo* (April 1731) and probably Eduige in *Rodelinda*. Elisa, Armira and Armida were originally soprano parts, which Handel adapted for Merighi partly by transposition and partly by transference of arias from other operas, with a little new composition. That the singer stood high in Handel's favour is clear from the size of all her parts in these seasons, as well as the quality of the three specially written for her. Rolli paid tribute to her intelligence in *Lotario*, and told Riva that 'Merighi is really a perfect actress and that is the general opinion'. Mrs Pendarves wrote that 'her voice is not extraordinarily good or bad, she is tall and has a very graceful person, with a tolerable face; she seems to be a woman about 40, she sings easily and agreeably'. In *Poro* she (and Handel) had such a success with the aria 'Son confusa pastorella' that it was taken up by other singers, including the future Mrs Clive at Drury Lane, as 'Signora Meriggi's Favourite Song'. Burney, who dismissed her quite wrongly as 'a singer of the second or third class', said that her 'voice, though a female, was a low contralto'. In fact her tessitura was fairly high for a contralto; her compass in Handel parts extended from $ab$ to $f''$.

Merighi was singing at Florence in 1732 and at Modena in December 1735. In November 1736 she returned to London for the unsuccessful final season of the Opera of the Nobility. She sang with Francesina and Chimenti before the royal family at Kensington Palace on the 15th and at the King's Theatre in operas by Hasse, Riccardo Broschi, Pescetti, Veracini and Duni. The following season she was a member of Heidegger's company, appearing in two pasticcios, further operas by Pescetti and Veracini, and in Handel's *Faramondo* and *Serse*, in which she was the original Gernando and Amastre. Mrs Pendarves had written of her in Hasse's *Siroe* in November 1736 that there was '*no sound* in her voice, but thundering action – a beauty with *no other merit*'; her last two Handel parts confirm that she had indeed declined. Her compass had narrowed (in *Serse* it

*Antonia Margherita Merighi: caricature by Anton Maria Zanetti (1680–1767) in the Fondazione Giorgio Cini, Venice*

was no more than $c'$ to $d''$), and she was given few divisions. She is last heard of at Munich, where she sang in two operas during the carnival season of 1740, before retiring to Bologna. She married the tenor Carlo Carlani (1716–76), who must have been considerably her junior; she was dead by 1764, when he married again. There is a caricature of her by A. M. Zanetti, reproduced here, in the Cini collection (*I-Vgc*).

WINTON DEAN

**Merikanto, Aarre** (*b* Helsinki, 29 June 1893; *d* Helsinki, 29 Sept 1958). Finnish composer and teacher, son of Oskar Merikanto. He studied composition at the Helsinki Music Institute with Melartin, at the Leipzig Conservatory with Reger (1912–14) and in Moscow with Vasilenko (1915–16). He worked at the Sibelius Academy, Helsinki, as a teacher of theory and analysis (1936–51) and as professor of composition (1951–8). Using unorthodox methods he was responsible for the training of many Finns who became well-known composers.

Merikanto was brought up in a highly musical home and he began to improvise and to compose as a very young child. When he was 18 his one-act opera *Helena* was performed. In Leipzig he developed his contrapuntal technique, but it was in Moscow that he was most decisively influenced – by the harmonic and orchestral effects of Skryabin. His mature style may be seen as a fusion of chromatic polyphony, Russian 'mystical' colour and Finnish folkdance rhythms; he was one of the pioneers of highly chromatic, and highly coloured, writing in Finland, and for years, even decades, his endeavours were not understood. Many works remained unperformed at his death: the Second Violin Concerto, for example, was composed in 1925 and unheard until 1959; and the opera *Juha* (1922) was neglected – partly as a result of personal conflicts within the Finnish National Opera, partly through its novel style – until Finnish radio gave a concert performance in December 1958, and it received its stage première in 1963. This was the period when Merikanto's music was rediscovered, and *Juha* was soon regarded as the best Finnish, and probably the best Nordic, opera. Stylistically comparable with Janáček, the opera describes with dramatic power and strong colour the conflict between the inflexibility of the Finnish character and the liveliness of the east Karelian milieu. Merikanto's adventurous period lasted from the orchestral songs *Syyssonetti* ('Autumn sonnet') and *Ekho* (both 1922) to the symphonic suite *Kyllikin ryöstö* ('The abduction of Kyllikki', 1935). Thereafter, perhaps responding to the neglect of his work, he turned more towards the national romantic style, developing at the same time a mature and classically balanced expression.

### WORKS
*(selective list)*

Opera: Juha (3, A. Ackte, after J. Aho), 1922

Orch: 3 pf concs., 1913, 1937, 1955; 3 syms., 1914–16, 1918, 1953; 4 vn concs., g, 1916, 1925, n.d., 1954; 2 vc concs., 1919, D, 1941–4; Lemminkäinen, 1916; Fantasy, 1923; Pan, sym. poem, 1924; Partita, 1927–31; 10 Pieces, 1930; 4 Compositions, 1932; Dance Suite, 1934; Kyllikin ryöstö [The abduction of Kyllikki], sym. suite, 1935; Intrada, 1936; 5 Ugrian Folk Melodies, 2 suites, 1937, 1938; Olympic Hymn, 1952–4; Andante, str, 1956

Vocal: Syyssonetti [Autumn sonnet], Ekho, S, orch, 1922

Chamber: Conc., vn, cl, hn, str sextet, 1925; Nonetto, fl, eng hn, cl, pf, str qnt, 1926; Str Sextet, 1932

Principal publishers: Fazer, Schott
MSS in *SF-Hr*

BIBLIOGRAPHY
K. Maasalo: *Suomalaisia sävellyksiä*, ii (Borgå and Helsinki, 1969), 209–49
T. Teerisuo: *Aarre Merikannon ooppera Juha* (diss., U. of Helsinki, 1970)
ERKKI SALMENHAARA

**Merikanto, (Frans) Oskar** (*b* Helsinki, 5 Aug 1868; *d* Oitti, 17 Feb 1924). Finnish composer and organist. He studied at the Leipzig Conservatory (1887–8) and in Berlin (1890–91). His activities in church music education and in initiating professional opera performances were of great importance in the development of Finnish musical life in the early 20th century; he also appeared as an opera conductor and as an excellent accompanist. *Pohjan neiti* was the first opera in Finnish, but he owed his wide popularity to his numerous folksong-influenced salon romances.

WORKS
*(selective list)*
Operas: Pohjan neiti [The maid of the north], 1899; Elinan surma [Elina's death], 1910; Regina von Emmeritz, 1920
Incidental music: Tukkijoella [Log river], several other scores
Choral orchestral: Kesäillan valassi [Summer evening waltz], Merellä [At sea]
Many solo songs

Principal publishers: Fazer, Westerlund
ERKKI SALMENHAARA

**Meriläinen, Usko** (*b* Tampere, 27 Jan 1930). Finnish composer. He studied at the Helsinki Academy of Music (1951–6), taking diplomas in conducting under Funtek and composition under Merikanto, and in 1958 he learnt 12-note technique from Vogel in Ascona. After work as a conductor and teacher in Kuopio (1956–7) and as a theatre conductor in Tampere (1957–60) he remained in the latter city as a theory teacher at the music institute (1961–6) and the university (from 1965). Among the awards he has received are first prize in a national competition for ballet scores (1958, with *Arius*), first prize in the AIDEM competition at Florence (1963, with the Chamber Concerto) and in 1965 the Sibelius Prize of the Wihuri Foundation.

The conception of tonality and the use of polymodal counterpoint in Meriläinen's early music indicate the influences of Hindemith, Bartók and Stravinsky. Many sections of the Partita for brass (1954) are very Stravinskian: its opening, for example, resembles that of *Agon*. He was one of the first Finnish composers to use the 12-note method, and serial thinking led to an enrichment of texture in such works as *Arius* (1958–60) and the First Piano Sonata (1960), but the rational control inherent in serial writing proved alien to his aspirations. In subsequent works, such as *Epyllion* for orchestra (1963), he returned to the idea that perceptible 'Gestalten' should be the starting-point for a composition, and he developed a technique he terms the 'metamorphosis of musical characters'. These characters, as Heininen has pointed out, are 'ideas or embryos, the identity of which is directly recognizable but not dependent on definite rhythmic or intervallic structure'; thus they can develop in any direction. The key works of this period are the Second Symphony (1964) and the Second Piano Sonata (1966), both rich and complex in structure. The characters of the sonata are the point, the line and the plane, familiar from Euclidean geometry or Kandinsky's abstract paintings, but seldom treated in music so naturally as here. It seems that Meriläinen has developed a technique that suits a composer who believes in, and depends on, the unconscious structuring capacities of the mind. His later works, among them the Piano Concerto no.2 (1969), the Symphony no.3 (1971) and the Piano Sonata no.4 (1974), exhibit no fundamental change in orientation, but rather develop the metamorphosis technique within a wider span. These pieces have a rhythmic elasticity, a warmth and continuity of sound, and a structural coherence rare in new Finnish music.

WORKS
*(selective list)*
Stage: Arius, ballet, 1958–60; Psykhe, ballet, tape, 1973; Alasin [The anvil], dance pantomime, tape, 1975, concert version = Elec Sym.; incidental music and film scores
Orch: 4 syms., 1953, 1964, 1971, 1976; 2 pf concs., 1955, 1969; Conc. for Orch, 1956; 2 suites from Arius, 1960, 1962; Chamber Conc., vn, 2 str orchs, perc, 1963; Epyllion, 1963; Musique de printemps, 1969; Conc. for 13, str, 1971; Vc Conc., 1975
Chamber: Partita, 12 brass, 1954; 4 Bagatelles, str qt, 1962; Arabesques, vc, 1963; Str Qt, 1965; Opusculum, vn, 1965; Impression, wind qnt, pf, perc, va, vc, db, 1965; Hommage à Jean Sibelius, vn, pf, 1965; Divertimento, wind qnt, harp, va, vc, 1968; Metamorfora per 7, cl, bn, tpt, trbn, harp, vn, db, 1969; Conc., db, perc, 1973; Aspects of Psykhe, wind qnt, tpt, trbn, perc, harp, vn, db, 1973; Meditatio, vc, pf, 1975
Pf: 4 sonatas, 1960, 1966, 1972, 1974; Suite, 1955; Sonatina, 1958; Riviravi, children's pieces, 1962; 3 notturni, 1967; Papillons, 2 pf, 1969
Songs: 4 Love Songs (P. Lounela), S, pf, 1961
Tape: Sym. no.4 (Elec Sym.), 1975

Principal publishers: Bote & Bock, Fazer, Finnish Broadcasting Co., King, Westerlund

BIBLIOGRAPHY
A. Kinnunen: 'Usko Meriläinen', *Suomen säveltäjiä*, ed. E. Marvia, ii (Borgå, 2/1966), 503
P. Heininen: 'Usko Meriläinen', *Musiikki*, ii/2 (1972), 67–99
ILKKA ORAMO

**Mérimée, Prosper** (*b* Paris, 28 Sept 1803; *d* Cannes, 23 Sept 1870). French novelist and writer. His works inspired two famous operas, *Carmen* and *Les Huguenots*, the latter taken from his novel *Chronique du règne de Charles IX* (1829) which also gave rise to Hérold's *Le pré aux clercs*, and one celebrated operetta, *La périchole*, derived from his comedy *Le carrosse du Saint-Sacrement* (1829): besides Offenbach's setting (1874) three others exist – by Théaulon and Desforges (1835), Berners (1924) and Büsser (1948). His *La Guzla* (1827) inspired Gérard de Nerval to prepare the libretto for Limnander's *Les Monténégrins* (1849).

Though his own works for the theatre failed, Mérimée's short stories were a source of opera plots and scenes throughout the 19th century. His *Vision de Charles XI* (1829), in which he projects the conspiracy of the Swedish nobility against Gustavus III and that monarch's eventual murder in 1792, furnished the plot of *Un ballo in maschera*. After a brilliant final performance of *Don Giovanni* at the Théâtre-Italien on 31 March 1833, Mérimée wrote *Les âmes du purgatoire* (1834), which in turn contained what was destined to become another celebrated operatic scene, the duelling sequence at the close of *La forza del destino*, though in Mérimée's story it is the friar who challenges the brother of the seduced heroine. This came to Verdi through the Spanish dramatization of *Les âmes du purgatoire* by the Duke de Rivas's *Don Alvaro o la fuerza del sino* (1835).

Mérimée followed Stendhal's taste for Italian opera, preferring Rossini's first manner, but without Stendhal's deep love of music (see his essay on Stendhal in his *Portraits* in which he claimed Stendhal 'discovered' Rossini and the Italian opera and had the courage to defend them in 1818). Similarly, his addiction to opera was based on his attachment for his *Inconnue*. As a man of the world he felt it necessary to make deprecatory remarks about Verdi: 'Tout ce que font Verdi et ses consorts ressemble à un habit d'arlequin' (*Lettres à une inconnue*, clxxxi); and about Wagner (*Tannhäuser*; Opéra, 1861) '. . . on nous a envoyé Wagner pour nous forcer d'admirer Berlioz . . . Il me semble que je pourrais écrire demain quelque chose de semblable, en m'inspirant de mon chat marchant sur le clavier d'un piano . . . Auber dit que c'est du Berlioz sans mélodie' (letter, 21 March 1861).

His translations from the Russian inspired Scribe to do a libretto for Halévy on *La dame de pique* (1849; Opéra-Comique, 8 December 1850). He also appreciated Glinka's *A life for the Tsar* in his *Lettres sur la Russie* (*La vie pour le Czar*; 16 April 1845). Other works of his that furnished opera librettos are *Colomba* (Pacini, 1842), Mackenzie (1883), Büsser (1921); *La Vénus d'Ille* (Schoeck, 1922), Wetzler (1928); *Matteo Falcone* (Cui, 1907).

Named 'rapporteur de la loi sur la fabrication des instruments de musique mécaniques', he made one far-reaching decision: that no work still in copyright should be adapted to piano rolls, hand-organs and other mechanical devices for reproducing music.

### WRITINGS
*Lettres à une inconnue* (Paris, 1874)
*Lettres sur la Russie* (Macon, ?1904)
*Oeuvres* (Paris, 1929), especially 'Stendhal', in vol.iv, *Portraits historiques et littéraires*, pp. 153–92

### BIBLIOGRAPHY
A. Jullien: *Paris dilettante au commencement du siècle* (Paris, 1884), 337–67
E. J. N. Piñeyro: *El Romanticismo en España* (Paris, 1904; Eng. trans., 1934), 53f
P. Trahard: *La jeunesse de Mérimée* (Paris, 1925), 334
R. L. Evans: *Les Romantiques français et la musique* (Paris, 1934), 38ff
                                        A. RICHARD OLIVER

**Merkel, Gustav Adolf** (*b* Oberoderwitz, nr. Zittau, 12 Nov 1827; *d* Dresden, 30 Oct 1885). German organist and composer. The son of a teacher and organist, he studied at the teacher's college in Bautzen from 1844, becoming 'Musikpräfekt' there. From 1848 to 1853 he was a schoolteacher in Dresden. He then earned a living as a piano teacher while studying the piano with Friedrich Wieck, music theory with Ernst Julius Otto (Kantor at the Kreuzkirche), the organ with Johann Schneider and composition with Schumann and K. G. Reissiger. From 1858 until his death, Merkel worked as an organist in Dresden, first at the orphanage church, from 1860 at the Kreuzkirche and from 1864 at the Catholic court church. He taught the organ at the Dresden Conservatory from 1861 and directed the Dreyssig Singakademie from 1867 to 1873.

A world-famous organist and highly regarded composer, Merkel wrote organ music whose great popularity in Germany in the second half of the 19th century spread to America, England and elsewhere. He continued the Bach tradition which his teacher Schneider had helped to preserve; his concert works for organ also have a pleasing style, using the rich tone-colouring of the 19th-century organ. His organ tutors and studies are intelligently arranged for didactic purposes and include exercises for cantus firmus pedalling and for pedalling simultaneously with both feet. Merkel also wrote compositions for harmonium and piano, instrumental pieces and solo songs with piano or organ accompaniment, motets and choral songs.

### BIBLIOGRAPHY
P. Janssen: *Gustav Merkel* (Leipzig, 1886) [with complete list of works]
O. Schmid: 'Gustav Merkel', *Blätter für Haus- und Kirchenmusik*, xiv (1909–10), no.11, p.163
L. Finzenhagen: 'Gustav Merkel: ein Bild seines Lebens und Schaffens', *Kirchenmusikalische Blätter*, ii (1921), 242
M. Schneider: *Die Orgelspieltechnik des frühen 19. Jahrhunderts, dargestellt an den Orgelschulen der Zeit* (Regensburg, 1941)
F. Blume: *Geschichte der evangelischen Kirchenmusik* (Kassel, 2/1965), 257, 267; Eng. trans., enlarged, 1974 as *Protestant Church Music: a History*
                                        KARL-ERNST BERGUNDER

**Merklin, Joseph** (*b* Oberhausen, 17 Jan 1819; *d* Nancy, 16 June 1905). German organ builder. He studied under his father, an organ builder in Freiburg, and under Walcker and Korfmacher. He set up a firm in Brussels in 1843, and in 1853 formed Merklin, Schütze & Cie. Two years later he bought the Ducroquet firm in Paris (*see* DAUBLAINE & CALLINET) and enlarged the organization, with its main office in Lyons from about 1870 (he sold the Lyons firm to Kuhn in 1894, as Michel, Merklin & Kuhn, which after Kuhn's death in 1925 continued as a limited company: *see* KUHN, THEODOR). Merklin was a prolific builder, and a rival to Cavaillé-Coll; but his organs were designed to suit current taste, and many have since been rebuilt. Notable instruments include at Paris St Eugène (1855, 33 stops) and St Eustache (1879, 72), and several at French cathedrals (Bourges, 1860; Arras, 1862; Clermont-Ferrand, 1878; Strasbourg, choir organ, 1878) as well as others abroad. He wrote *Notice sur l'électricité aux grandes orgues* (1887).

**Merkù, Pavle** (*b* Trieste, 12 July 1929). Yugoslav composer. He graduated in Slavonic studies at Ljubljana University in 1950 and at Rome University in 1960; his music studies were undertaken privately in Trieste under Ivan Grbec and V. Levi. Merkù taught in schools in Ljubljana (1950–51) and Trieste (1952–64), and in 1965 he was appointed to the staff of Italian radio and television in Trieste. He also writes on music. A prolific composer, he always aims for a refined and delicate style, particularly in his chamber music. He has little interest in folk music and has investigated new techniques, choosing only those elements that are compatible with clarity of expression and beauty of sound, and preferring a moderate approach. After his early essays in orchestral music, he turned almost exclusively to smaller scale music. His outstanding vocal work is the extended expressionist cantata *Von der Kindermörderin Maria Farrar*, which uses recitative and unusual tonal progressions to great dramatic effect. Much of his later music is 12-note, and there are many miniatures of great subtlety and delicacy.

### WORKS
*(selective list)*

CHAMBER AND INSTRUMENTAL WORKS
Romanca, pf, 1948; Balada, pf, 1948; Introduzioni e allegro, pf trio, 1950–51; Drobnice, pf, 1951; Quartetto breve, str, 1952; Romanca, bn, pf, 1952; 2 glasbeni vezili, pf, 1953; Lahke skladbice, vn, pf, 1953–4; Ricercare e allegro, str trio, 1954; Suita, fl, ob, cl, pf, 1954; Divertimento, fl, 2 cl, bn, 1954; Sonata, ob, pf, 1954; Varijacije na temo Primoža Ramovša, ob, pf, 1955; Preludium i fuga br. 1 i 2, pf, 1955–6

Astrazioni, cl, vc, pf, 1956; 3 uspavanke za Jasno, cl, pf, 1958; Diversione e melodia, pf, 1958; 3 skladbice za Evico, pf, 1959; 2 skladbi, fl, gui, 1960; 2 Mood Songs, vn, pf, 1961; Canto popolare Croato, gui, 1962; Canto popolare Slavacco, gui, 1962; Phillobolia, pf, 1963; Corale e toccata, pf, 1964; Invocazioni: no.1, 2 pf, metallophone; no.2, harp, pf, metallophone, 1966; Str Qt no.2, 1968; Epistola à Lojze Lebič, pf, 1969; Epistola à Giampaolo de Ferra, vc, cl, hn, tpt, perc, pf, 1973; Metamorfosi di un canto popolare, hn, 1973

OTHER WORKS

Orch: Baroque Ov., str, 1950; Concertino, chamber orch, 1954–7; Conc. lirico, cl, orch, 1959; Musica per archi, str, 1962; Vn Conc., 1970; Tpt Conc., 1974

Vocal: 2 pesmi na besedilo Alojzija Rebule, T, pf, 1952; Von der Kindermörderin Maria Farrar (cantata, Brecht), Bar, chorus, 2 pf, perc, 1957–8; Kadar gre Romar (Kosovel), Bar, str, 1959–60; Vezilo Srečku Kosovelu [Homage to Srečko Kosovel], chorus, 1961; Prijazna smrt [Kind Death], B, pf, 1960–64; Ex Alchuini carminibus, conc., hn, chorus, 1962; Eno besedo (cantata, Kosovel), reciter, chorus, orch, 1964; Divertimento (M. Kravos), T, chamber orch, 1965; Oj ptički, children's chorus, 1965; Tri majne kantate (Kosovel), chorus, wind insts, org, 1967; Qui od altrove, Bar, str qt, 1971–3; Vojskin čas ('War Time'), A, chamber ens, 1974

Incidental music: Ta vesili dan ali Matiček se ženi (A. T. Linhart), 1958; Zločin i kazna [Crime and Punishment] (Dardi, after Dostoyevsky), 1958; Pekel je vender pekel (J. Tavčar), 1959; Antigona (Anouilh), 1960; Hamlet (Shakespeare), 1961; Na velikom drumu [On the great road] (Babić, after Chekhov), 1961; Po brezkončni poti (B. Kreft), 1964; O les beaux jours (Beckett), 1964; Mrtvi kanarček (Tavčar), 1966

Principal publishers: Društvo slovenskih skladateljev (Ljubljana), Suvini Zerboni, Gerig

NIALL O'LOUGHLIN

**Merli, Francesco** (*b* Milan, 27 Jan 1887; *d* Milan, 11 Dec 1976). Italian tenor. He studied in Milan with Negrini and Borghi, and in 1914 won second prize in a competition for tenors organized by the conductor Campanini; Gigli won first prize. He began his career as a second tenor in Buenos Aires, and at La Scala in 1916, but was soon singing larger roles, and in 1918 he sang Elisero in *Mosè* and created Fausto in Favara's *Urania* at La Scala, where he continued to appear until 1942, sharing the dramatic tenor roles in the repertory with Pertile. He sang at Covent Garden between 1926 and 1930 and was the first London Calaf in *Turandot*. His appearances at the Metropolitan Opera in 1931–2 were dogged by ill-health and he was never re-engaged. He participated in numerous revivals of works by Franchetti, Gomez, Catalani and Zandonai and continued to sing until 1948. Merli had a powerful and resonant voice and his feeling for words in operas like *Otello* was notable. His acting was never less than adequate and often in roles congenial to him, like Don José, Dick Johnson and Samson, rather more than that.

BIBLIOGRAPHY

R. Celletti: 'Merli, Francesco', *Le grandi voci* (Rome, 1964) [with opera discography by R. Vegeto]

——: 'Francesco Merli', *Discoteca* (1967), no.71, p.35 [with discography by R. Vegeto]

HAROLD ROSENTHAL

**Merlin, John Joseph** (*b* Huys, nr. Liège, 1735; *d* Paddington, London, 1803). Flemish instrument maker and inventor. He came to England in 1760, and in 1774 patented a 'compound harpsichord' which included a piano action. He also made pianos, besides various inventions including an invalid chair (which is still used today). A 'compound harpsichord' dated 1780 is in the Deutsches Museum, Munich.

The patent of 1774 claimed that the piano action could be applied to 'an harpsichord of the common kind already made', but the instrument now in Munich is anything but 'common'. From its single manual are played four sets of strings (16′, 8′, 8′ and 4′) carried on three bridges; the harpsichord can activate 16′, 8′ and 4′ strings, and the piano (with its action above the strings) 16′, 8′ and 8′. One row of 8′ strings can be undamped; a 'Welsh harp' buffs the 16′; two pedals affect the 16′ and pedal action respectively. In addition, the instrument carries a recording device: a clockwork-

activated roll of paper may be pricked by the 4′ jacks.

Merlin's extravagance of invention should not detract from his positive contribution to the more important basic elements of piano making. The six-octave (*C*′ to *c*′′′′) piano ordered from him by Burney in 1777 shows that he had a realistic idea of the instrument's future requirements; if only for this reason he should not be considered purely as a dynamic-obsessed inventor.

BIBLIOGRAPHY

R. E. M. Harding: *The Piano-forte: its History traced to . . . 1851* (Cambridge, 1933, rev. 2/1978)

R. Russell: *The Harpsichord and Clavichord* (London, 1959, rev. 2/1973)

F. Hubbard: *Three Centuries of Harpsichord Making* (Cambridge, Mass., 1965)

DONALD HOWARD BOALCH, PETER WILLIAMS

**Merline** (Fr.). A type of bird flageolet; *see* BIRD INSTRUMENTS.

**Merlo** [Merlus, Merulus, Romano, della Viola], **Alessandro** [Alexander] (*b* Rome, *c*1530; *d* ?Rome, after 1594). Italian composer, singer and viol player. On the title-pages of his published works he consistently called himself Alessandro Romano, but he has nevertheless been confused with Giulio Cesare (sometimes called Romano), Alexandrino Venitiano (represented by one piece in *RISM* 1557[17]) and G. A. Merlo (a singer in the Sistine Chapel between 1555 and 1588). In the dedication to *Le sirene* (1577) Alessandro Merlo indicated that he had studied with Willaert and Rore; there is no documentary evidence for his claim, but his first publication, *Le vergini* (1554), includes texts already set by Rore (e.g. *Alla dolce ombra* and *Vergine bella*). In 1553 he was for three months *maestro di musica* at the Accademia Filarmonica, Verona. It is known that he was a member of the Sistine Chapel for much of his career, but there is disagreement over the date of his entry there: a composer listed as 'Merlus' first appears in the Sistine Chapel diaries on 13 May 1559, but that may refer to G. A. Merlo or to G. A. Latino (both often listed as 'Giovanni'), and some scholars maintain that Alessandro Merlo was not admitted as a singer until 20 December 1561. He probably remained there until 1594 (except for a three-week period in 1585 when he was dismissed and subsequently readmitted), but he was again at the Accademia Filarmonica, Verona, in 1566–7. The name 'Alexander Romanus', which may refer to him, appears in the records of St John Lateran for 1571, 1573 and 1576.

Merlo was probably best known to his contemporaries as a singer. In a letter to Cardinal Guglielmo Sirleto from Naples (10 December 1579), Tommaso Cimello, who had spent the preceding decade in Rome, commended Merlo's ability to rhythmicize chant melodies and begged Sirleto to request him to try out the motet included in the letter. In his *Discorso sopra la musica* (1628), Vincenzo Giustiniani recalled that in his youth (about 1575) he had greatly enjoyed hearing homophonic *villanelle alla napoletana* performed by solo voices and instruments, and he particularly mentioned Merlo, whom he referred to as a Roman with a vocal range of three octaves. In his polyphonic madrigals Merlo clearly showed himself a disciple of Rore and Willaert; his pieces in the lighter genres, on the other hand, have treble-dominated textures and use melodic and rhythmic motifs associated with regional song.

## WORKS
(all published in Venice)

SECULAR VOCAL

Le vergini con la gionta di alcuni altri madrigali, 4vv (1554)

Il primo libro de madrigali, 5vv, con doi dialoghi, 7vv (1565) [incl. 2 madrigals by Rore]

Il primo libro delle canzoni alla napoletana, 5vv (1570)

Il secondo libro delle canzoni alla napoletana, con una canzone . . . nel fine, 5vv (1571)

Le sirene . . . secondo libro de madrigali, 5vv (1577)

Il primo libro delle villanelle et secondo suo, 4vv (1579)

2 madrigals, 5 lute intabulations, 1561[10], 1563[23], 1600[6]

SACRED VOCAL

Lamentationi, libro primo, 5vv (1582)

Works in GB-Lbm, I-CMac, VEaf

### BIBLIOGRAPHY

V. Giustiniani: Discorso sopra la musica de' suoi tempi (MS, 1628); Eng. trans., MSD, ix (1962), 69

G. Baini: Memorie storico-critiche della vita e delle opere di Giovanni Pierluigi da Palestrina (Rome, 1828/R1966), i, 21

F. X. Haberl: 'Giovanni Maria Nanino', KJb, vi (1891), 85

A. Solerti: Le origini del melodramma (Turin, 1903/R1969), 107

A. Celani: 'I cantori della Cappella Pontificia nei sec. xvi–xiii', RMI, xiv (1907), 754

R. Casimiri: 'Lettere di musicisti (1579–1585) al Cardinal Sirleto', NA, ix (1932), 103

P. Guerrini: 'Frammenti bibliografici delle opere di Luca Marenzio', NA, ix (1932), 280

G. Turrini: 'Catalogo descrittivo dei mss musicali antichi della Soc. Accademia filarmonica di Verona', Atti e memorie dell'Accademia di agricoltura, scienze e lettere di Verona, 5th ser., xv (1937), 168

R. Casimiri: 'I "Diarii Sistini" ', NA, xvi (1939), 75; xvii (1940), 66

——: 'Annibale Zoilo (1540?–1592) e la sua famiglia', NA, xvii (1940), 4

N. Fortune: 'Solo Song and Cantata', NOHM, iv (1968), 143

PATRICIA ANN MYERS

**Merlotti, Claudio.** See MERULO, CLAUDIO.

**Merlus, Alessandro** [Alexander]. See MERLO, ALESSANDRO.

**Mermet, Auguste** (b Brussels, 5 Jan 1810; d Paris, 4 July 1889). French composer. His father was a colonel in Napoleon's army and he was himself destined for a military career. But he abandoned this for music, having studied first the flute and later composition privately with Le Sueur and Halévy. Most of his small output was for the stage. His first opera, La bannière du roi, was performed at Versailles in 1835 and his Le roi David was staged at the Paris Opéra in 1846 with Rosine Stoltz singing David's part. A long gap intervened before Roland à Roncevaux in 1864 and yet another between that and Jeanne d'Arc in 1876. Roland à Roncevaux enjoyed considerable if short-lived success (65 performances by 1867) owing to its patriotic tone and appeal to the spectacular. Mermet's Napoleonic connections served him well under the Second Empire and he exploited the same patriotic vein, with less success, in Jeanne d'Arc, the first new work presented at Garnier's Opéra (opened in 1875). Both of these works told of stirring episodes in French history; the music was modelled closely on Meyerbeer and Halévy, and his own librettos were modelled on those of Scribe, but Mermet lacked their imaginative sweep. His music is direct, attractive, unadventurous and noisy. He filled canvases too large for his slender musical skills but knew how to make a direct appeal to certain sectors of Parisian taste, with a special fondness for martial and rousingly rhythmic music. The failure of Jeanne d'Arc has been seen as the close of Meyerbeer's domination of French opera. Two further operas were never performed: Pierrot pendu, a comic opera, and Bacchus dans l'Inde.

## WORKS
(selective list)

La bannière du roi (opéra comique, 2, P.F.A. Carmouche), Versailles, April 1835

Le roi David (opera, 3, A. Soumet and F. Mallefille), Paris, Opéra, 3 June 1846

Roland à Roncevaux (opera, 4, A. Mermet), Paris, Opéra, 3 Oct 1864 (Paris, ?1865)

Jeanne d'Arc (opera, 4, Mermet), Paris, Opéra, 5 April 1876, vocal score (Paris, 1876)

### BIBLIOGRAPHY

FétisBS

H. Blanchard: 'David de M. Mermet', Revue et gazette musicale, xiii (1846), 177

P. Smith: 'Théâtre Imperial de l'Opéra: Roland à Roncevaux', Revue et gazette musicale, xxxi (1864), 321

A. Dupeuty: 'A. Mermet (notes intimes)', Chronique musicale, xi (1876), 57

A. Jullien: 'Théâtre National de l'Opéra: Jeanne d'Arc', Revue et gazette musicale, xliii (1876), 113

HUGH MACDONALD

**Merques, Nicolas** [Nicholas de, C., C. de] (fl 1433–6). French composer. The names 'Nicholas' and 'C. Merques' appear in 15th-century music manuscripts; the name 'K. Merques' appears only in modern musicological literature, and has arisen owing to a misreading of the index of the inventory of the Trent manuscripts (in DTÖ, xiv–xv, Jg.vii/1–2, 1900) where the first composition listed under the surname Merques is a Kyrie, abbreviated K. Nicolas and C. Merques may be the same, since 'C.' could mean either Colin, the diminutive, or Claus, the German equivalent of Nicolas, as was suggested by Van den Borren. A singer and cleric from Arras named Nicolas de Merques entered the chapel of the Council of Basle in November 1433 and remained until at least 1436. The style of the 14 works attributed to him or to C. Merques suggests that they were composed in the mid-1430s, and there is no stylistic reason to doubt that anything under the surname Merques, including works attributed to C. Merques, is by Nicolas Merques of Arras.

His liturgical works include Kyries, antiphons, hymns and an introit. In all he employed the treble-dominated style with cantus firmus appearing in the superius in ornamented form. An exception is found in the Kyries where fauxbourdon sections alternate with sections in three voices where the cantus firmus lies in the tenor. All these works are rather small-scale and functional liturgical works.

The five chansons are similar to other works of the 1430s in their use of perfect time and in the application of text to either the superius alone or to the superius and tenor. The motet is somewhat archaic in its use of separate texts in the three voices.

In addition to the above-mentioned works, six antiphons and an incomplete Kyrie in I-TRmn 92 can be attributed to Merques on stylistic, liturgical and palaeographical grounds. The antiphons belong to the same service as those actually ascribed to him, they are identical in style, and each group was copied into the manuscript by a single scribe who added no other music. The manner in which the Kyrie is entered in the original index suggests that Merques was the composer and in its treatment of the cantus firmus the work is very similar to his other Kyries. If these attributions are correct, he ranks after only Dufay and Binchois in the number of his works found in the first section of I-TRmn 92.

## WORKS

All 3vv; precise ascriptions added because of the possible confusion of authorship.

LITURGICAL

Kyrie, *I-TRmn* 92, f.12v–13 (no.1373), C. Merques
Kyrie, *TRmn* 92, f.101v (no.1454), Merques
Audi benigne conditor (hymn), *TRmn* 92, Merques
Da pacem Domine (introit), *TRmn* 92, C. Merques
Pange lingua (hymn), *TRmn* 92 (twice) and *D-Mbs* 14,274 (twice), Merques; ed. in DTÖ, liii, Jg.xxvii (1920/*R*), 84
Regali ex progenie (antiphon), *I-TRmn* 92, N. de Merques
Ut queant laxis (hymn), *TRmn* 92, Merques
Vidi turbam (antiphon), *TRmn* 92, Merques

MOTET

Castrum pudicitie/Virgo viget/Benedicamus, *TRmn* 92 and *AO* Al° D 19, Merques; ed. in DTÖ, lxxvi, Jg.xl (1933/*R*), 84

RONDEAUX

Adieu Apurille, *F-Sm* 222, Nicolas de Merques
Amors forga, *Sm* 222, Nicolas de Merques
Las comment porray je, *Sm* 222 and *E-E* V.III.24, Nicolas de Merques
Volés scavoir, *F-Sm* 222, Merques
Vos soyez, *I-TRmn* 92 and *Bu* 2216, C. de Merques; ed. in DTÖ, xxii, Jg.xi (1904/*R*), 91

ANON. WORKS POSSIBLY ATTRIBUTABLE TO MERQUES

Kyrie, *TRmn* 92, f.44
Benedicite Dominum (antiphon), *TRmn* 92, f.127
Cum jocunditate (antiphon), *TRmn* 92, f.122
Et omnes angeli (antiphon), *TRmn* 92, f.126v
Hymnus omnibus sanctis (antiphon), *TRmn* 92, f.143v
Nativitas gloriose (antiphon), *TRmn* 92, f.122
Redemisti nos (antiphon), *TRmn* 92, f.127

BIBLIOGRAPHY

J. Haller: *Concilium basiliense* (Basle, 1896–1926)
C. van den Borren: *Le manuscrit musical 222 C 22 de la Bibliothèque de Strasbourg* (Antwerp, 1924)
K. Mixter: 'Johannes Brassart: a Bio-bibliographical Study', *MD*, xviii (1964), 47
T. R. Ward: 'The Structure of the Manuscript Trent 92-I', *MD*, xxix (1975), 127

TOM R. WARD

**Merriam, Alan P(arkhurst)** (*b* Missoula, Montana, 1 Nov 1923; *d* nr. Warsaw, 14 March 1980). American ethnomusicologist. He took the BA at Montana in 1947, then began studies in anthropolgoy under Melville J. Herskovits and Richard A. Waterman at Northwestern University (MM 1948, PhD 1951). He taught anthropology at Northwestern University (1953–4; 1956–62) and at the University of Wisconsin (1954–6). In 1962 he became professor of anthropology at Indiana University, where he was chairman of the department from 1966 to 1969. In spring 1976 he was senior scholar in anthropology at Sydney University. He died in an air crash.

Merriam conducted field research among the Flathead Indians in the USA (1950, 1958) and among the tribes of Zaïre (formerly the Congo; 1951–2, 1959–60, 1973). His approach to ethnomusicology as the study of music in culture is reflected in *The Anthropology of Music*. This stresses the importance of cultural and social factors in any discussion of the process of creation within a culture, its musical aesthetics and the training of its performers. The principles of this book are applied in *Ethnomusicology of the Flathead Indians*, one of the most exhaustive studies of an individual musical culture. Merriam is also the co-author of *A Bibliography of Jazz*.

WRITINGS

'Flathead Indian Instruments and their Music', *MQ*, xxxvii (1951), 368
with R. Benford: *A Bibliography of Jazz* (Philadelphia, 1954/*R*1970)
'Some Texts of the Bashi (Congo)', *African Music*, i (1954), 44
with S. Whinery and B. G. Fred: 'Songs of a Rada Community in Trinidad', *Anthropos*, li (1956), 157
'Characteristics of African Music', *JIFMC*, xi (1959), 13
'An Annotated Bibliography of Theses and Dissertations in Ethnomusicology and Folk Music accepted at American Universities', *EM*, iv (1960), 21
'Ethnomusicology: Discussion and Definition of the Field', *EM*, iv (1960), 107
'The Word Jazz', *Jazz Review*, iii (1960), no.3, p.39; no.4, p.40; no.5, p.40; no.6, p.40; no.7, p.36
*A Prologue to the Study of African Arts* (Yellow Springs, Ohio, 1962)

Review of J. S. Laurenty: *Les cordophones au Congo Belge et du Ruanda-Urundi* (Tervuren, 1960), *EM*, vi (1962), 47
'The African Idiom in Music', *Journal of American Folklore*, lxxv (1962), 120
'The Epudi – a Basongye Ocarina', *EM*, vi (1962), 175
'Songs of the Gêge and Jesha Cults of Bahia, Brazil', *Jb für musikalische Volks- und Völkerkunde*, i (1963), 100–35
*The Anthropology of Music* (Evanston, Ill., 1964)
Review of F. Harrison, M. Hood and C. Palisca: *Musicology* (Englewood Cliffs, NJ, 1963), *EM*, viii (1964), 179
with F. Gillis: *Ethnomusicology and Folk Music: an International Bibliography of Dissertations and Theses* (Middletown, Conn., 1966)
*Ethnomusicology of the Flathead Indians* (Chicago, 1967)
'Music and the Origin of the Flathead Indians: a Problem in Culture History', *Music in the Americas*, ed. G. List and J. Orrego-Salas (The Hague, 1967), 129
with F. Garner: 'Jazz: the Word', *EM*, xii (1968), 373
'Ethnomusicology Revisited', *EM*, xiii (1969), 213
'The Ethnographic Experience: Drum-making among the Bala (Basongye)', *EM*, xiii (1969), 74
*African Music on LP: an Annotated Discography* (Evanston, Ill., 1970)
Review of recordings *Musique du Burundi* and *Musique du Gabon* (1968), *EM*, xv (1971), 302
Review of recordings *Musique Gouro de Côte d'Ivoire* (1969) and *Musique guéré: Côte d'Ivoire* (1971), *EM*, xvi (1972), 145
*The Arts and Humanities in African Studies* (Bloomington, Ind., 1972)
'The Bala Musician', *The Traditional Artist in African Societies*, ed. W. L. d'Azevedo (Bloomington, Ind., 1973), 250
*An African World: the Basongye Village of Lupupa Ngye* (Bloomington, Ind., 1974)
'Anthropology and the Dance', *New Dimensions in Dance Research*, ed. T. Comstock (New York, 1974), 9
'Change in Religion and the Arts in a Zairian Village', *African Arts*, vii (1974), 46, 95
'Social and Cultural Change in a Rural Zairian Village', *African Studies Review*, xvii (1974), 345
*Culture History of the Basongye* (Bloomington, Ind., 1975)
'Ethnomusicology Today', *CMc* (1975), no.20, p.50

PAULA MORGAN

**Merrick, Frank** (*b* Clifton, Bristol, 30 April 1886). English pianist, composer and teacher. He came of musical parents (his father of the same name was a Doctor of Music), who taught him music until in 1898 he went to study with Leschetizky. He made his London début in 1903, and then toured with Clara Butt. He taught at the RMCM (1910–29), the RCM (1929–56) and from 1956 at Trinity College of Music.

Merrick was the winner of one of the prizes offered by the Columbia Graphophone Company for two movements (which were recorded) to complete the 'Unfinished' Symphony of Schubert in the year of the Schubert centenary (1928). His other compositions include two piano concertos, a symphony, and songs (some in Esperanto). As a pianist, while showing a fine grasp of the Classics and a far-ranging taste, he has been an enthusiastic champion of John Field and Prokofiev. Long, taxing recitals at the Wigmore Hall (where he gave his first London recital) on his 75th and 80th birthdays showed that his powers were little diminished. He is editor of the Students' Edition of Chopin's works and of the first three Field piano concertos (MB, xvii). He published *Practising the Piano* (London, 1958) and, with M. C. Butler, *Muzika terminaro* (Rickmansworth, 1944). His recordings include concertos and other works by Field and his own Piano Sonata.

BIBLIOGRAPHY

A. Alexander: 'Frank Merrick', *RCM Magazine*, lii (1956), 64
Discography, *Recorded Sound*, xviii (1965), 340

H. C. COLLES/FRANK DAWES

**Merricocke, Thomas.** See MERICOCKE, THOMAS.

**Merrill, Robert** (*b* Brooklyn, NY, 4 June 1919). American baritone. He was trained first by his mother, Lillian Miller Merrill, a concert singer, then by Samuel

Margolis in New York. Although he occasionally appeared in Europe and South America, he preferred to base his career at the Metropolitan Opera where he has sung all the major baritone roles of the Italian and French repertories. In terms of vocal endowment, technical security, and longevity, he is unequalled among baritones of his generation at the Metropolitan, where he made his début as Germont in *La traviata* on 15 December 1945 and where he celebrated his 500th operatic performance on 5 March 1973, still singing with undiminished vigour. He has made numerous complete opera recordings (Toscanini chose him as his Germont and Renato), one film, and he often sings on radio and television and in musical comedy. In 1975 he made his London concert début, winning praise for the generosity, if not the subtlety, of his singing. For all the natural beauty and healthy resonance of his voice, he has never been highly regarded as an imaginative interpreter or a compelling actor.

BIBLIOGRAPHY
L. Riemens: 'Merrill, Robert', *Le grandi voci* (Rome, 1964) [with discography by S. Smolian]
R. Merrill: *Once More from the Beginning* (New York, 1965)
PETER G. DAVIS

**Merriman, Nan** [Katherine-Ann] (*b* Pittsburg, 28 April 1920). American mezzo-soprano. She studied in Los Angeles with Alexia Bassian, and began her career singing background music for Hollywood films. In 1940 she toured the USA with Olivier and Vivien Leigh in *Romeo and Juliet*, singing music by Palestrina and Purcell during scene changes. In 1942 she made her operatic début at the Cincinnati Summer Opera as La Cieca in *La Gioconda*; the following year she won a singing competition which resulted in a 15-minute NBC broadcast. It was heard by Toscanini, who engaged her for his broadcasts and recordings of Gluck's *Orfeo*, *Falstaff* (Meg), *Rigoletto* (Maddalena) and *Otello* (Emilia). She was seen as Dorabella at Aix-en-Provence (1953, 1955, 1959), La Piccola Scala (1955–6) and Glyndebourne (1956), and she took part in Karajan's recording. She played Baba the Turk in the British première (Edinburgh Festival, 1953) of *The Rake's Progress*, and Laura in Dargomïzhky's *The Stone Guest* at La Piccola Scala (1958). Merriman undertook many recitals and orchestral concerts, but decided to retire in 1965 while her appealingly vibrant mezzo-soprano was still at the height of its powers.

HAROLD ROSENTHAL

**Merritt, A(rthur) Tillman** (*b* Calhoun, Missouri, 15 Feb 1902). American musicologist. He graduated from the University of Missouri with a BA in 1924 and received a BFA there in 1926. The following year he took an MA at Harvard University. After studying in Paris with Nadia Boulanger and Paul Dukas, he taught at Trinity College in Hartford, Connecticut, from 1930 to 1932. From 1932 he was professor of music at Harvard University, where he served as chairman of the department from 1942 to 1952 and 1968 to 1972. Since his retirement in 1972 he has been curator of the Isham Memorial Library at Harvard.

Merritt specializes in the music of the Renaissance, particularly the 16th-century chanson. He has co-edited the complete secular works of Janequin, a major chanson composer of the period, and has edited several volumes of motets originally published by Attaingnant. His widely used textbook on counterpoint includes a thorough discussion of 16th-century contrapuntal practice and offers a useful alternative to the study of the subject by species.

WRITINGS
*Sixteenth-century Polyphony: a Basis for the Study of Counterpoint* (Cambridge, Mass., 1939)
'A Chanson Sequence by Fevin', *Essays on Music in Honor of Archibald Thompson Davison* (Cambridge, Mass., 1957), 91
'Undergraduate Training in Music Theory', *College Music Symposium*, v (1965), 21
'Janequin: Reworkings of Some Early Chansons', *Aspects of Medieval and Renaissance Music: a Birthday Offering to Gustave Reese* (New York, 1966), 603

EDITIONS
*Treize livres de motets parus chez Pierre Attaingnant*, viii–xiv (Paris, 1962–4)
with F. Lesure: *C. Janequin: Chansons polyphoniques* (Monaco, 1965–71)

BIBLIOGRAPHY
*Words and Music: the Scholar's View; a Medley of Problems and Solutions Compiled in Honor of A. Tillman Merritt by Sundry Hands*, ed. J. M. Coopersmith (Cambridge, Mass., 1972)
PAULA MORGAN

**Merro, John.** 17th-century copyist of a manuscript containing six partbooks; *see* SOURCES OF INSTRUMENTAL ENSEMBLE MUSIC TO 1630, §7.

**Merseburger.** German firm of music publishers. It was founded in Leipzig on 21 September 1849 when Carl Merseburger (1816–85) purchased the C. F. Meusel publishing house in Weissenfels. From 1885 to 1898 Carl's brother Otto Merseburger (1822–98) directed the business, followed until 1918 by Otto's son Max Merseburger (1853–1935) with Georg Merseburger (1871–1958); by 1904 Georg had founded his own book publishing concern in Leipzig. In 1944 the firm in Leipzig was destroyed, but it was re-established in Berlin in 1951 by Georg's son Karl Merseburger (1905–78), with temporary subsidies in Heidelberg and Darmstadt. In 1956 Adolf Strube acquired the firm, which became a limited company in 1964. Wolfgang Mattei (*b* 1925) became principal shareholder in 1972.

Carl Merseburger was also a writer on music (*Taschenbüchlein des Musikers*, 1858, 31 editions; *Kleines Tonkünstlerlexikon*, 1860, 14/1936). He established his firm as publishers of educational music, founding an educational periodical *Euterpe* (1851–94, ed. E. J. Hentschel and Ludwig Erk); Strube, an author for the firm from 1924, followed the same policy. The firm is one of the principal Protestant church music publishers in Germany; it also issues musicological literature, new editions of old masters, and the periodicals *Der Kirchenmusiker* (1950) and *Ars organi* (1952).

BIBLIOGRAPHY
*Katalog der Bücher und Musikalien . . . welche in den 50 Jahren 1849–1899 erschienen sind* (Leipzig, 1899)
*Festgabe des Pädagogischen Verlages C. Merseburger zum 75. Gründungsgedenktage* (Leipzig, 1924)
*100 Jahre im Dienste der Musik: aus der Arbeit des Verlages C. Merseburger* (Leipzig, 1949)
K. Merseburger and R. Elvers, eds.: *Adolf Strube zum 60. Geburtstag* (Berlin and Darmstadt, 1954)
*Musikverlage in der Bundesrepublik Deutschland und in West-Berlin* (Bonn, 1965)
RUDOLF ELVERS

**Mersenne, Marin** (*b* La Soultière, nr. Oizéî, Maine, 8 Sept 1588; *d* Paris, 1 Sept 1648). French mathematician, philosopher, music theorist and savant. He was one of the leading French thinkers of the 17th century, and his work is central to the academic and scientific movements of the second quarter of the century; an important part of it is devoted to the science, theory and practice of music. He was a transitional figure at a crucial confluence of Renaissance and Baroque ideas in France, summing up the accomplishments of the past and posing the difficult questions for the future inherent in the new attitudes of his own time.

1. LIFE. Mersenne studied first at the college at Le Mans and from 1604 at the newly established Jesuit school at La Flèche, where he trained in logic, physics, metaphysics, mathematics and theology. He left for Paris in 1609 to complete his studies at the Collège Royal and the Sorbonne. In 1611 he joined the Order of Minims, beginning his novitiate at the monastery at Nigeon, near

*Marin Mersenne: engraving by Claude Duflos*

Paris, and completing it at St Pierre de Fublaines, near Meaux, where he received his holy orders on 17 July 1612. Thereafter he served the Minim monastery in the Place Royale, Paris, and was named deacon and priest. In 1614 he was sent to the monastery near Nevers as teacher of philosophy (1615–17) and theology (1618), after which he was designated corrector. In 1619 he returned to Paris as conventual of the order, and he remained there for the rest of his life except for occasional trips to the Low Countries, the French provinces and Italy.

2. WORKS. Mersenne's output reflects a neo-Platonic, encyclopedic outlook, in which science is at first used in defence of religion. His later thinking is dominated by the concept of the universality of knowledge and the development of scientific methodology based on experimentation and the principles of mechanics. He strongly believed in the reason of Man and in the order of the universe, and he fostered co-operative ventures and the dissemination of scientific knowledge, championing the establishment of an international academy. His cell in Paris became a meeting place for the intellectually curious, and he maintained an immense correspondence with leading thinkers of the day, including Descartes,

Gassendi, Hobbes, Constantijn Huygens, Fermat, Roberval, Galileo, Doni, Arnauld and Peiresc; many of the ideas exchanged therein found their way into his published works.

Although his interests ranged widely, Mersenne's work has particular import in several specific areas of learning: in philosophy he served as an intermediary between Descartes and other thinkers of the time, in mathematics his name is specially associated with research on cycloid curves and on the theory of numbers, in astronomy his writings helped establish a modern science, and in physics he made remarkably original contributions to acoustical theory.

It is notably through mathematics and physics that music is assigned an important role in Mersenne's writings. For him music was capable of being analysed and rationally explained, and it took its place along with other disciplines as an area for scientific pursuit. Six of his 24 published works are devoted either entirely or in large part to music. He raised fundamental acoustical questions even in the earliest of them, *Quaestiones celeberrimae in Genesim* (1623) – notwithstanding the general exegetical and polemical nature of the tract, in which music is treated in a humanistic way and special emphasis is placed on the nature and power of ancient music. By the 1630s his writings on music took on a new scientific interest and format: this is the period of his most indispensable published work, the *Harmonie universelle*, which in spite of its characteristic digressiveness and occasional uncritical reporting, contains his most developed and perceptive ideas on music, both theoretical and practical.

Mersenne's derivation of the basic principles of the behaviour of sound, which are the foundation of the science of acoustics in later times, is central to his contributions to musical knowledge. On the basis of observations derived from experimentation and the study of natural phenomena he discerned sound as pure motion rather than as substance, and he accurately described the method of sound transmission. He is credited with being the first to formulate rules governing vibrating strings, based on an understanding of the variable factors on which pitch depends (length, diameter, tension and mass of the vibrating body), and the first to discern the nature of partials (harmonics) related to a fundamental note. He contributed to the theory of tuning and temperament through a synthesis of knowledge of earlier systems, and he advocated an equal temperament intended for practical application in the construction of certain instruments. He also inquired into the nature of the speed of sound, the phenomena of echo and resonance and the character of a vibrating column of enclosed air: in all of these areas again his work was important for later developments.

Questions of speculative theory are raised throughout Mersenne's work, yet he clearly favoured a theory based on practice, even though he himself was not a performer or composer. He gave wide coverage to practical subjects and sought advice and compositional models from leading musicians of the day, including Mauduit, Titelouze, Du Caurroy, Le Jeune, Antoine Boësset, Moulinié and Charles Racquet. His description of the compositional practice of the early 17th century, though based in large part on the work of Zarlino, provides a view of the effect that new attitudes had on such practice, particularly in France. The nature of consonance and dissonance is reassessed in the light of the laws of vibrating bodies and the nature of partials; but there is a new awareness of the psychological factor in a listener's comprehension of a musical event (a question also discussed by Descartes), and he allowed a certain freedom in the interests of a pleasurable sound or desired effect. For Mersenne consonance provided the basis of a composition, and dissonance served an ornamental function.

In developing rules for the construction of melodies Mersenne stressed the relationship of music to rhetoric and recommended use of the practice of *ars combinandi* in seeking an acceptable solution to a given problem. He contributed to rhythmic theory through a study of Greek metrics and their emotional content and of the oratorical qualities of rhythm. His work provides a virtual compendium of modal systems advocated and used at the time, but he suggested a reduction in the number of such systems, recommending that they be based squarely on the octave species (rather than on finals) and that a seven-syllable solmization procedure be adopted to eliminate mutation.

Mersenne distinguished between national styles of performance. He also showed practical concern about pedagogical techniques in the teaching of children and beginners. He recommended alternative methods of notation with the aim of simplifying the learning and performance of music. He reviewed ornaments and methods of ornamental elaboration and found room for definitions of terminology. His classification of musical instruments (partly indebted to the earlier work of Michael Praetorius) and his extensive presentation of the structures and capabilities of both occidental and oriental instruments then known to him are of particular importance to organology.

WRITINGS
(only those on music)

Quaestiones celeberrimae in Genesim (Paris, 1623)
La verité des sciences (Paris, 1625)
Livre de la nature des sons (MS, F-Pa 2884)
Traité de l'harmonie universelle (Paris, 1627) [Eng. trans. of book 2 with commentary in Egan]
Les préludes de l'harmonie universelle (Paris, 1634)
Les questions théologiques, physiques, morales, et mathématiques (Paris, 1634)
Questions harmoniques (Paris, 1634/R1972)
Questions inouyes ou Récréation des sçavans (Paris, 1634)
Harmonicorum libri, in quibus agitur de sonorum natura (Paris, 1635–6)
Harmonicorum instrumentorum libri IV (Paris, 1636); pubd with Harmonicorum libri (1635–6) as Harmonicorum libri XII (Paris, 1648, 2/1652/R1972)
Harmonie universelle (Paris, 1636–7/R1963; Eng. trans. of the book on instruments, 1957)
Cogitata physico-mathematica (Paris, 1644)
Novarum observationum physico-mathematicarum III (Paris, 1647)
Letters, ed. C. de Waard and B. Rochot, as Correspondance du P. Marin Mersenne (Paris, 1932–)

BIBLIOGRAPHY

H. Ludwig: Marin Mersenne und seine Musiklehre (Halle and Berlin, 1935)
R. Lenoble: Mersenne ou la naissance du mécanisme (Paris, 1943)
F. Yates: The French Academies of the Sixteenth Century (London, 1947)
Revue d'histoire des sciences et de leur applications, ii/1 (1948) [devoted to articles on Mersenne on the occasion of the tercentenary of his death]
F. B. Hyde: The Position of Marin Mersenne in the History of Music (diss., Yale U., 1954)
J. B. Egan: Marin Mersenne, Traité de l'harmonie universelle: Critical Translation of the Second Book (diss., Indiana U., 1962)
P. J. S. Whitmore: The Order of Minims in Seventeenth-century France (The Hague, 1967), pt.iii, chap.4
A. Gruber: 'Mersenne and Evolving Tonal Theory', JMT, xiv (1970), 36–67
H. Schneider: Der französische Kompositionslehre in der ersten Hälfte des 17. Jahrhunderts (Tutzing, 1972)
D. P. Walker: 'Joan Albert Ban and Mersenne's Musical Competition', ML, lvii (1976), 233

ALBERT COHEN

**Merseyside Symphony Orchestra.** Orchestra formed by Louis Cohen during World War II; *see* LIVERPOOL, §2.

**Mersmann, Hans** (*b* Potsdam, 6 Oct 1891; *d* Cologne, 24 June 1971). German musicologist and journalist. He studied musicology with Sandberger and Kroyer, history, art history, German and archaeology at Munich (1910–12), and musicology with Riemann and Schering for one term in Leipzig and with Kretzschmar and Wolf in Berlin (1912–14); he also had some practical training at the Stern Conservatory. He took his doctorate in 1914 with a dissertation on Christian Boxberg and the music history of Ansbach, and then as assistant to Kretzschmar at the musicology institute of Berlin University he catalogued old music in archives and libraries in Germany and Italy (1915–17); he was subsequently the first director of the Musikarchiv Deutscher Volkslieder (1917–34). In 1921 he completed his *Habilitation* at the Berlin Technische Hochschule with a study of new musical methods of research into folksong, and in 1927 he became a reader at the Technische Hochschule. During his years (1924–34) as editor of *Melos* he secured its international standing. In this period he became one of the leading apologists for new music; he began broadcasting in 1930, and in 1932 became director of German Radio's music department. The Nazis stripped Mersmann of all his posts, and from 1933 to 1945 he could work only in a private capacity.

In 1946 he held a teaching post at the Munich Musikhochschule, and then directed the Staatliche Hochschule für Musik, Cologne (1947–58). Mersmann held many honorary offices: he was a founder-member of the Institut für Neue Musik und Musikerziehung at Bayreuth and later at Darmstadt, in 1947, director of the governing body of the Max-Reger-Institut, 1948, and took part in the music report of the Ministry of Culture in North Rhine and Westphalia, 1948–56. As a founder-member, chairman (1953–64) and honorary president (1964–8) of the Deutscher Musikrat he laid down and helped realize many of its aims: the publication of the periodical *Musikalische Zeitfragen*, the encouragement of young musicians and the organization of international exchange concerts.

All Mersmann's work as a scholar, journalist and organizer was marked by a vigorous and practical understanding of art, as are his compositions and writings. His central interests – folksong research, performing practice, music teaching and analysis, musical aesthetics, modern music, German and Western music – were closely linked with each other in the context of a creative and humane approach to central problems of history and philosophy.

WRITINGS

Christian Ludwig Boxberg und seine Oper 'Sardanapalus' (Ansbach 1698), mit Beiträgen zur Ansbacher Musikgeschichte (diss., U. of Berlin, 1914; extracts in Beiträge zur Ansbacher Musikgeschichte, Leipzig, 1916)
'Beiträge zur Aufführungspraxis der vorklassischen Kammermusik in Deutschland', AMw, ii (1919–20), 99–143
Grundlagen einer musikalischen Volksliedforschung (Habilitationsschrift, Berlin Technische Hochschule, 1921; AMw, iv (1922), 141; v (1923), 81–135; vi (1924), 127–64; pubd separately, Leipzig, 1930)
Kulturgeschichte der Musik in Einzeldarstellungen (Berlin, 1921–5)

[i, *Beethoven: die Synthese der Stile*; ii, *Das deutsche Volkslied*; iii, *Musik der Gegenwart*; iv, *Mozart*]
'Mahlers Lied von der Erde', *Melos*, ii (1921), 131, 154
'Zur Stilgeschichte der Musik', *JbMP 1921*, ii, 67
'Versuch einer Phänomenologie der Musik', *ZMw*, v (1922–3), 226–69
*Angewandte Musikästhetik* (Berlin, 1926)
'Archaismus im gegenwärtigen Schaffen', *Melos*, vi (1927), 190
*Bericht über die Arbeitsgemeinschaft 'Einführung in das Verstehen von Musik'* (Quakenbrück, 1928)
*Die Tonsprache der neuen Musik* (Mainz, 1928, 2/1930)
*Einführung in die Musik* (Berlin and Schöneberg, 1929; Jap. trans., 1930)
*Musiklehre* (Berlin, 1929)
'Sonatenformen in der romantischen Kammermusik', *Musikwissenschaftliche Beiträge: Festschrift für Johannes Wolf* (Berlin, 1929), 112
*Die Kammermusik*, ii–iv (Leipzig, 1930); i (Leipzig, 1933)
'Zeit und Musik', *4. Kongress für Ästhetic und allgemeine Kunstwissenschaft: Hamburg 1930* [*Zeitschrift für Ästhetic und allgemeine Kunstwissenschaft*, xxv (1931), 216]
'Zur Geschichte des Formbegriffs', *JbMP, 1930*, 32
*Das Musikseminar* (Leipzig, 1931)
*Eine deutsche Musikgeschichte* (Potsdam and Berlin, 1934; enlarged 2/1952 as *Musikgeschichte in der abendländischen Kultur*, 3/1973)
'Versuch einer musikalischen Wertästhetik', *ZMw*, xvii (1935), 33
*Volkslied und Gegenwart* (Potsdam, 1937)
*Musikhören* (Potsdam and Berlin, 1938, 2/1952)
'Das Erbe der neuen Musik', *Neue Musik-Zeitschrift*, i (1946), 7
'Paul Hindemith', *Die Schule: Monatsschrift für geistige Ordnung*, ii (1947), 169
'Musik und Bildkunst in unserer Zeit', *Musica*, ii (1948), 301
'Schau und Ordnungen der Musikgeschichte', *Musik-Almanach*, i, ed. V. Schwarz (1948), 143–86
*Neue Musik in der Strömungen unserer Zeit* (Bayreuth, 1949)
'Neue Musik – junge Musik', *Junge Musik* (1952), 112
'Der Spätstil Bartóks', *Musik der Zeit*, ed. H. Lindlar (Bonn, 1953), no.3, p.60
'Neue Musik als gemeinschaftsbildende Kraft', *Musik im Unterricht*, xliv (1953), 193
'Soziologie als Hilfswissenschaft der Musikgeschichte', *AMw*, x (1953), 1
'Strawinsky', *Musik der Zeit*, ed. H. Lindlar (Bonn, 1953), no.1, p.65
'Mensch und Mikrophon', *Musikalische Zeitfragen*, iii (1957), 57
*Deutsche Musik des 20. Jahrhunderts im Spiegel des Weltgeschehens* (Rodenkirchen, 1958)
'Freiheit und Bindung im künstlerischen Schaffen', *Musikalische Zeitfragen*, viii (1960) [collection of essays]
*Stilprobleme der Werkanalyse* (Neuss, 1963)
*Lebensraum der Musik: Aufsätze – Ansprachen* (Rodenkirchen, 1964)
'Der Orchestermusiker als Interpret im Wandel der Zeiten', *Philharmonische Blätter* (Berlin, 1967–8), no.1, p.2
'Haydns historische Sendung', *Philharmonische Blätter* (Berlin, 1968–9), no.7, p.4
'Die Symphonie im Spiegel der Zeiten', *Philharmonische Blätter* (Berlin, 1969–70), no.7, p.2
'Strawinskys Oedipus Rex', *Philharmonische Blätter* (Berlin, 1969–70), no.2, p.10
'Relativität von Fortschritt und Tradition in der Musik', *Philharmonische Blätter* (Berlin, 1970–71), no.1, p.7

FOLKSONG EDITIONS
*Handwerkslieder aus dem Archiv deutscher Volkslieder Berlin* (Potsdam, 1935)
*Volksbrauch im Liede: eine Sammlung herausgegeben vom Archiv deutscher Volkslieder Berlin* (Potsdam, 1936)

BIBLIOGRAPHY
T.-M. Langner: 'Hans Mersmann 60 Jahre alt', *Melos*, xviii (1951), 315
W. Wiora, ed.: *Musikerkenntnis und Musikerziehung: Dankesgaben für Hans Mersmann* (Kassel and Basle, 1957) [incl. list of writings and works]
H. Mersmann: 'Mersmann, Hans', *Rheinische Musiker*, ii, ed. K. G. Fellerer (Cologne, 1962), 55 [incl. list of poems, compositions, editions and writings]
G. Hausswald: 'Hans Mersmann 75 Jahre', *Musica*, xx (1966), 294
T.-M. Langner: 'Apologet der neuen Musik: zum Tode von Hans Mersmann', *Musica*, xxv (1971), 500
O. Schreiber: 'Hans Mersmann zum Gedächtnis', *Mitteilungen des Max-Reger-Instituts* (1971), no.18, p.1
W. Wiora: 'Hans Mersmann', *Mf*, xxiv (1971), 365
THOMAS-M. LANGNER

**Mertel** [Mertelius, Martelius], **Elias** (*b* Wangen, nr. Molsheim, Lower Alsace, *c*1561; *d* Strasbourg, 21 July 1626). German lutenist, composer and intabulator. The dedication of his *Hortus musicalis* (1615) indicates that he was in the service of the Elector Palatine Friedrich IV until 1595, but was summoned to Heidelberg to play at celebrations there in November 1600, October 1601, August 1605 and May 1606. On 27 January 1596 he married at Strasbourg, and on 23 December became a citizen of the city. He later became treasurer of the Strasbourg academy. Gumpelzhaimer named him as one of the best-known lutenists in Germany.

An assessment of the importance of Mertel's *Hortus musicalis*, which contains 235 preludes and 120 fantasies and fugues, is hindered by the fact that no composers' names appear on the pieces; it is doubtful whether any of the works are his own. J. D. Mylius included nine preludes and six fantasies from *Hortus musicalis* in his *Thesaurus gratiarum* (1622). Of Mertel's few surviving original compositions, most are dances. These are usually rambling movements in variation form, only occasionally enlivened by imitations and sequences; the textures are thin, though, where possible, chords are spread in various ways and the bass notes are played before the beat so that there is some movement in all the parts. However, in the vocal arrangements, many of which are also variations, the notes of the chords are usually plucked simultaneously.

WORKS
*(all for lute)*

Hortus musicalis novus . . . testudine carpendis atque delibandis consitus: in cuius hac parte prima continentur praeludia, variis ex tonis plusquam ducenta phantasiae item & fugae complures . . . ex optimis quibusque authoribus Germanicis, Italicis, Gallicis, Anglicis, constructus (Strasbourg, 1615)
[Hortus musicalis novus, part II], announced but probably never pubd
Allemande, balletto, 4 galliards, 2 passamezzos, prelude, Spectri cujusdam sonus nocturnus, 4 vocal intabulations, untitled piece: 1603[15], 1615[24]

2 ballettos, in J. D. Mylius: *Thesaurus gratiarum* (Frankfurt am Main, 1622), lost
Balleto, 2 galliards, *D-Ngm, W*

BIBLIOGRAPHY
G. Gumpelzhaimer: *Gymnasma: de exercitiis academicorum* (Strasbourg, 1621)
M. Vogeleis: *Quellen und Bausteine zu einer Geschichte der Musik und des Theaters im Elsass 500–1800* (Strasbourg, 1911)
K. Dorfmüller: 'Mertel, Elias', *MGG*

HANS RADKE

**Meruco, Johannes de.** *See* JOHANNES DE MERUCO.

**Merula, Tarquinio** (*b* Cremona, 1594 or 1595; *d* Cremona, 10 Dec 1665). Italian composer, organist and violinist. He was one of the finest and most progressive Italian composers of his generation, and excelled in both vocal and instrumental music.

1. LIFE. The suggested years for Merula's birth derive from the fact that he was confirmed on 23 April 1607, probably at the customary age of 12. His earliest post was probably as organist of S Bartolomeo, the church of the Carmelite Fathers, at Cremona. On 22 October 1616 he signed a three-year contract to serve as organist of S Maria Incoronata, Lodi. He was re-engaged on 8 February 1620 but appears to have left Lodi at the end of January 1621. He probably went directly to his next known position, in Poland, since in a letter of Anton Neunhaber of about that time he is mentioned as being in Warsaw. In 1624 the nature of his position is made explicit: he was serving as 'organista di chiesa e di camera' to Sigismund III, King of Poland.

Returning to Cremona, Merula was elected on 18 February 1626 provisional *maestro di cappella* for the Laudi della Madonna, which took place at the main altar in the cathedral on Saturdays and on vigils of Marian feasts. A regular appointment followed on 13 January 1627. In 1628 he was also holding the position of organist of the collegiate church of S Agata. His next move was to Bergamo, where on 12 April 1631 he signed a three-year contract to serve as *maestro di cappella* of S Maria Maggiore. As successor to Alessandro Grandi (i), who had died in the plague of 1630, Merula began the work of rebuilding the *cappella*. In his first year G. B. Buonamente was one of its members. Merula was, however, dismissed on 29 December 1632 for 'indecency manifested towards several of his pupils'. Threatening a lawsuit to recover his lost salary he was in turn faced with the prospect of a criminal complaint lodged by the governing body of S Maria Maggiore. On 11 April 1633 the matter was resolved by a statement from him in which he apologized and relinquished all claim to his salary. He again returned to Cremona and at his own request and by prior agreement was reinstated on 19 August 1633 as *maestro di cappella* for the Laudi della Madonna in the cathedral, thereby displacing G. B. Minzio, *maestro* at the time. Disagreements with the governing body there over matters of salary and responsibilities, however, led to his resignation in 1635. He is next heard of in 1638 at Bergamo, this time as *maestro di cappella* and organist at the cathedral, adjacent to S Maria Maggiore. Further problems with his former employers at S Maria Maggiore prompted them on 14 April 1642 to forbid any of their musicians to perform under his direction, thus disrupting the customary exchange of musicians between the two churches. He appears to have remained at Bergamo Cathedral until his final return to Cremona, which resulted from his appointment on 25 August 1646, in succession to Nicolò Corradini, as organist of the cathedral and as organist and *maestro di cappella* for

the Laudi della Madonna. He thus held the last of these posts for the third time, and he now held all three until his death. In 1643 he collaborated with five others in composing music for *La finta savia*, performed in Venice. He was a member of the Accademia dei Filomusi of Bologna and a Knight of the Golden Spur.

2. WORKS. Merula was particularly responsive to Venetian stylistic developments, and his sacred music is thoroughly progressive. The sacred concertos for few voices resemble Monteverdi's in their skilfully wrought lines, often richly embellished, as can be seen in ex.1. He was one of the first to write solo motets with string accompaniment. His sacred concertos for more voices are in the style of Giovanni Gabrieli, with harmonically conceived lines, strong tonal movement and formal clarity. In the mid-1630s Merula turned to writing mass and vesper psalm settings, several of which use ostinato basses. One setting of *Beatus vir* uses the romanesca, and an entire mass is said to be built on the *Aria del Gran Duca*, though in fact it is on the Ruggiero (see Kirkendale, p.41). Other formal schemes encountered in his music include the ritornello principle and the *ABB* design common throughout Italy until the 1680s.

Merula's secular music comprises monodies, dialogues and accompanied madrigals and includes some of the finest settings of his day. His arias are in the Venetian style of Berti and Grandi and are usually in triple metre. In numerous accompanied madrigals from the 1630s he adopted ostinato bass patterns, and in several the division into recitative and aria, characteristic of the mature Baroque cantata, is clearly recognizable. The title piece of his op.13 includes elements of Monteverdi's *stile concitato*. His instrumental music comprises works for both keyboard and ensemble. The ensemble canzonas are among his most significant works and trace the development of the form up to the 1650s, including the gradual fusion with the sonata that led to the *sonata da chiesa*. The earliest, like those of his north Italian contemporaries, use four-part writing and are divided into contrasting sections, which are often repeated. In his second book he adopted three-part textures, specified the violin (using notably idiomatic writing) and often re-used opening material at the end of a work. In his later canzonas the influence of violin technique is more marked, so they are indistinguishable from the early church sonatas subsequently produced by such composers as Cazzati and Legrenzi. In the 1630s and later he wrote several canzonas based on ostinatos, variations on popular tunes, chamber sonatas, sinfonias and a number of dances. He also wrote several sonatas similar to those of Buonamente and G. B. Fontana. His surviving keyboard works show similarities to those of Frescobaldi and Michelangelo Rossi. Several pieces use subjects found in his ensemble canzonas.

Ex.1 *Cantate Domino* from *Il primo libro de motetti e sonate* (1624)

WORKS

Edition: *T. Merula: Opere complete*, I/i, ed. A. Sutkowski (Brooklyn, 1974) [S]

OPERAS

La finta savia (Giulio Strozzi), Venice, 1643, collab. Filiberto Laurenzi, Arcangelo Crivelli, Alessandro Leardini, Vincenzo Torri and Benedetto Ferrari

SACRED

op.
6    Il primo libro de motetti e sonate concertati, 2–5vv (Venice, 1624)
?8   Libro secondo de concerti spirituali con alcune sonate, 2–5vv (Venice, 1628)
11   Pegaso . . . salmi, motetti, suonate . . . 2–5vv, libro terzo (c1633–7, Venice, 2/1640)

15 Concerto . . . messi, salmi . . . concertati, 2–8, 12vv, insts (Venice, 1639)
16 Arpa Davidica . . . salmi, et messe, a 4 (Venice, 1640)
18 Il terzo libro delle salmi et messa concertati, a 3–4 (Venice, 1652)
Pieces in 1620² (2 motets), 1624² (1), 1641² (1), 1641³ (1), 1642⁴ (3), 1646⁴ (1), 1649¹ (5), 1649⁶ (1), 1651² (2), 1657¹ (1); *D-Aa, I-Bc, Rli*

SECULAR VOCAL

4 Il primo libro de madrigaletti, 3vv, bc (Venice, 1624)
5 Il primo libro de madrigali concertate, 4–8vv, bc (Venice, 1624)
?7 Satiro e Corisca dialogo musicale, 2vv, bc (Venice, 1626)
10 Madrigali et altre musiche concertate a 1–5, libro secondo (Venice, 1633, 2/1635 as Musiche concertante et altri madrigali, libro secondo)
13 Curtio precipitato et altri capricii, libro secondo, 1v (Venice, 1638)
?14 Canzonette a 3 et 4 (before 1649); lost, mentioned in A. Vincenti's catalogue of 1649 (see *MMg*, xv, 1883, p.22)

INSTRUMENTAL

[1] Il primo libro delle canzoni, a 4 (Venice, 1615); S
9 Il secondo libro delle canzoni da suonare, 3 insts, bc (*c*1631–3, Venice, 2/1639)
12 Canzoni overo sonate concertate per chiesa e camera, a 2–3, libro terzo (Venice, 1637)
17 Il quarto libro delle canzoni da suonare, a 2–3 (Venice, 1651)
Pieces in 1646¹² (1), 1650¹⁰ (2), 1652⁴ (2), 1655⁴ (1)
Keyboard works: Canzon, Capricio, Sonata cromatica, Toccata del secondo tono, Un cromatico overo Capricio primo tuono per le semituoni; ed. A. Curtis, MMI, 1st ser., i (1960)

BIBLIOGRAPHY

J. W. von Wasielewski: *Die Violine im 17. Jahrhundert* (Bonn, 1874)
M. Seiffert: 'Paul Seiffert: biographische Skizze', *VMw*, vii (1891), 401
E. Schmitz: *Geschichte der weltlichen Solokantate* (Leipzig, 1914, rev. 2/1955)
H. A. Sander: 'Beiträge zur Geschichte der Barockmesse', *KJb*, xxviii (1933), 77
E. van der Straeten: *The History of the Violin* (London, 1933)
E. C. Crocker: *An Introductory Study of the Italian Canzona for Instrumental Ensembles* (diss., Radcliffe College, 1943)
R. Monterosso: 'Mostra bibliografica dei musicisti cremonesi', *Annali della Biblioteca governativa e Libreria civica di Cremona*, iii (1949), 50
N. Fortune: *Italian Secular Song from 1600 to 1635: the Origins and Development of Accompanied Monody* (diss., U. of Cambridge, 1954)
L. F. Tagliavini: 'Un musicista cremonese dimenticato', *CHM*, ii (1956), 419
W. S. Newman: *The Sonata in the Baroque Era* (Chapel Hill, 1959, 2/1966/R1972)
A. Curtis: 'L'opera cembalo-organistica di Tarquinio Merula', *L'organo*, i (1960), 141
J. Roche: 'Music at S. Maria Maggiore, Bergamo, 1614–1643', *ML*, xlvii (1966), 296
D. Arnold and N. Fortune, eds.: *The Monteverdi Companion* (London, 1968), 126
C. V. Palisca: *Baroque Music* (Englewood Cliffs, NJ, 1968), 136f, 139
J. L. A. Roche: *North Italian Liturgical Music in the Early 17th Century* (diss., U. of Cambridge, 1968)
A. Colzani: 'La cappella della Laudi a Cremona fino al servizio di Tarquinio Merula', *Contributi e studi di liturgia e musica nella regione padana* (Bologna, 1972), 342
W. Kirkendale: *L'Aria di Fiorenza, id est Il ballo del Gran Duca* (Florence, 1972), 41, 65, 69
M. Padoan: 'Tarquinio Merula nelle fonte documentarie', *Contributi e studi di liturgia e musica nella regione padana* (Bologna, 1972), 231
W. Apel: 'Studien über die frühe Violinmusik', *AMw*, xxx (1973), 153; xxxi (1974), 185
E. Ferrari Barassi: 'Tarquinio Merula i jego dialog "Satiro e Corisca" ', *Pagine* (1974), 149

STEPHEN BONTA

**Merulo [Merlotti], Claudio** (*b* Correggio, 8 April 1533; *d* Parma, 5 May 1604). Italian composer, organist and publisher.

1. Life. 2. Musical works. 3. Publishing and editing.

1. LIFE. Merulo is the Latin form of the Italian Merlotti, which is sometimes found in archival references and on title-pages of 16th-century publications of his music. He was a pupil of Tuttovale Menon and Girolamo Donato, and obtained the post of organist at Brescia Cathedral

on 21 October 1556, succeeding Vincenzo Parabosco. On 2 July of the following year he was appointed organist at St Mark's, Venice, succeeding Girolamo Parabosco after a competition in which Andrea Gabrieli was one of the unsuccessful candidates. He remained in the service of the doge's chapel for nearly 30 years, composing music for many official occasions, including that for *intermedi* to Lodovico Dolce's play *Le troiane* in 1566 and to Frangipane's *Tragedia*, written for the state visit of Henry III of France in 1574. He was one of the composers who wrote music for the marriage celebrations of Francesco de' Medici and Bianca Cappello in Florence in 1579. In 1584 he resigned his post; it is unknown precisely where he was during the next two years, although it is possible he was briefly in the service of the Duke of Mantua. In 1586 he became the organist to the Duke of Parma, the following year adding similar duties at the cathedral. In 1591 he was made organist to the wealthy company of the Steccata, where he remained until his death. He was married twice: his first wife had a daughter, Antonia; his second wife was Amabile Banzola, whom he married in 1588. Merulo was engaged during part of his Venetian period as a music publisher, an organ consultant and a teacher. Among his pupils were several well-known composers including Giovanni Battista Mosto, Florentio Maschera and Vincenzo Bonizzi. He was buried next to Cipriano de Rore in Parma Cathedral, where there is a memorial to him.

Many of his contemporaries called Merulo the greatest organist of his period. His pupil Girolamo Diruta in his treatise *Il transilvano* described Merulo's performing methods. He played with arched fingers and gave much attention to acquiring a good legato touch. Although the actual fingering that he advocated is not more advanced than others of the time, restricting the use of thumb and little finger to the extremities of scale passages, the attention that he gave to relative strengths of fingers, acknowledging the necessity to use the stronger ones on accented notes, was an important step in keyboard technique.

2. MUSICAL WORKS. Merulo's compositions for organ show both his dexterity as a player and considerable imagination in developing a distinctive keyboard idiom. Like most of his contemporaries, Merulo based much of his music on vocal models, his technique at its simplest being largely a transcription of works for ensemble. But these are nearly all enlivened by a use of embellishment which is different from the customary rather mechanical making of divisions in two respects. First, there is more rhythmic variety in the figuration, although it is never complex in the way advocated by some of the less practical theorists of the earlier 16th century. Secondly, there is the ability to invent a short, memorable ornament which may be consistently used throughout a piece, to give a sense of musical development. Such ornaments are often variants of either a trill or a mordent, which are nearer to the 17th-century concept of keyboard embellishment than to that of other Venetians such as Andrea Gabrieli and Annibale Padovano.

Merulo's finest works are probably his toccatas, which take this principle of ornamentation still further. In these, contrapuntal sections in a somewhat old-fashioned style are juxtaposed with free, improvisatory passages during which virtuosity predominates. Again the use of short motifs gives shape to a genre which had previously tended to be amorphous, but it is the freedom from an ensemble texture which gives a new, more idiomatic style for the instrument. Held chords in one hand are common while the other displays the figuration. Dissonance is taken more freely, without consideration of the rules of part-writing, sometimes anticipating the kinds of effects that the advanced madrigalists achieved about 1600. Such freedom gives a distinctly romantic flavour unique in 16th-century keyboard music, although it was to lead to a similar attitude in the works of Frescobaldi, and to a lesser extent Sweelinck, both of whom knew Merulo's toccatas.

Merulo was also a more than competent madrigalist and composer of church music. In both he belonged to the Venetian school. His madrigals are mainly in a semi-serious vein, as were Andrea Gabrieli's, with the same bright sonorities and diatonicism as prominent features. There is the same attention to word-setting and perhaps a slightly more modern attitude to underlay, so that the text can be heard distinctly. His motets for single choir are more massive than are those of his colleague, and less affected by the more intimate madrigal style. Those for double choir are less adventurous than Gabrieli's in their exploitation of combinations of instruments and voices, but have many of the same traits of harmony and form.

3. PUBLISHING AND EDITING. Merulo's career as a music printer, from 1566 to 1570, was brief but productive, and his editorial activities continued until 1575. In 1566 he and his partner, Fausto Bethanio, printed several first editions, including music by Primavera, Wert, Merulo himself and Porta, whom Merulo called 'carissimo amico mio'. The partnership was apparently very short-lived; a reprint of Verdelot for 1566 is signed by Merulo alone, and, in an arbitrator's ruling of the following year, he, although assigned complete control of the firm, was required to compensate Bethanio with both equipment and a part of the stock.

Merulo continued to bring out reprints and new volumes, including his own *Ricercari d'intavolatura d'organo . . . libro primo* (1567) and *Messe d'intavolatura d'organo . . . libro quarto* (1568). The numbering of these volumes conforms to a programme laid out in the 1567 *Ricercari*. Merulo planned editions of organ music by himself and others, including Andrea Gabrieli, in 12 volumes; although these two are the only ones extant from his press, book 7 (*Toccatas*) survives in an edition by Verovio (1598 and 1604) and books 8 (*Canzoni*) and 12 (Gabrieli's *Ricercari*) from the Gardane press.

Merulo's printer's mark was a woodcut representing Proserpina's golden bough and the motto 'Simili frondescat virga metallo' ('Let a bough put forth leaves in the same metal'), a variation of the phrase from the Aeneid (iv, 144). The presence of Merulo's mark and the phrase 'per Claudio Merulo . . . corretti' in Roccia's *Madrigali* (1571) show that he acted as its editor, and he apparently also edited editions of Arcadelt, Lassus and Rore. In some volumes, notably the 1566 collection of Verdelot and the 1572 Arcadelt edition, he made many musical changes. Systematic changes of underlay and alterations in the music to remove tritones and consecutive octaves, to complete chords by adding thirds, or to alter the modal pattern by changing accidentals, were evidently all within the scope of what Merulo considered the duties of an editor.

## WORKS

Editions: *C. Meruli musica sacra*, ed. J. Bastian, CMM, li/1– (1970–) [B]

　　*L'arte musicale in Italia*, i, ed. L. Torchi (Milan, 1897/*R*) [contains 6 madrigals]; iii (Milan, 1899/*R*) [contains 4 toccatas]

　　*C. Merulo: Toccate per organo*, i–iii, ed. S. Dalla Libera (Milan, 1959/*R*) [DL]

### SACRED

Missarum liber primus, 5vv (Venice, 1573), B i
Misse due, 8, 12vv, org (Venice, 1609), B ii

Liber primus sacrarum cantionum, 5vv (Venice, 1578), B iii
Liber secundus sacrarum cantionum, 5vv (Venice, 1578), B iii
Il primo libro de mottetti, 6vv (Venice, 1583)
Il secondo libro de motetti, 6vv (Venice, 1593)
Il terzo libro de mottetti, 6vv (Venice, 1605)
Il primo libro de mottetti, 4vv (Venice, 1584)
Sacrorum concentuum, 5, 8, 10, 12, 16vv (Venice, 1594)

2 magnificat in 1600[1]
29 motets in 1586[1], 1590[4], 1590[5], 1598[2], 1600[2], 1604[11], Il secondo libro della musica di C. Monteverdi e d'altri autori, 5vv (Milan, 1608), 1609[15], 1610[10], 1613[1], 1613[2], 1618[1]

### SECULAR

Il primo libro de madrigali, 5vv (Venice, 1566)
Il primo libro de madrigali, 4vv (Venice, 1579)
Il primo libro de madrigali, 3vv (Venice, 1580)
Il secondo libro de madrigali, 5vv (Venice, 1580)
49 Madrigals in 1560[22], 1561[15], 1562[6], 1564[16], 1567[13], 1567[18], 1568[16], 1570[15], 1570[17], 1576[5], 1577[7], 1578[22], 1579[2], 1579[3], 1582[5], 1583[12], 1584[4], 1584[5], 1586[11], 1586[12], 1588[17], 1588[21], 1589[8], 1589[12], 1590[11], 1591[10], 1592[15], 1592[17], 1593[3], 1593[5], 1596[8], 1596[11], 1597[13], 1605[9]
Intermedi for Le troiane, 1566, Tragedia, 1574; lost

### INSTRUMENTAL

Ricercari d'intabolatura d'organo . . . libro primo (Venice, 1567)
Messe d'intavolatura d'organo (Venice, 1568)
Il primo libro de ricercari da cantare a 4 (Venice, 1574)
Canzoni d'intavolatura d'organo a 4 fatte alla francese (Venice, 1592), ed. P. Pidoux, *C. Merulo: Canzonen (1592)* (Kassel and Basle, 1941)
Toccate d'intavolatura d'organo, libro primo (Rome, 1598), DL i
Toccate d'intavolatura d'organo, libro secondo (Rome, 1604), DL ii
Libro secondo di canzoni d'intavolatura d'organo a 4 fatte alla francese (Venice, 1606)
Ricercari da cantare a 4 . . . libro secondo (Venice, 1607)
Ricercari da cantare a 4 . . . libro terzo (Venice, 1608)
Terzo libro de canzoni d'intavolatura d'organo a 5 fatte alla francese (Venice, 1611)

2 toccatas in 1593[9], 1607[29]
18 canzonas in 1588[31], 1593[11], 1608[24], 1617[24]
8 motet arrs. in 1593[11], 1599[19], 1617[24]

9 toccatas, org, *I-Tn* Intavolatura ms. tedesca; DL iii

### BIBLIOGRAPHY

F. Caffi: *Storia della musica sacra nella già cappella ducale di San Marco in Venezia dal 1318 al 1797* (Venice, 1854–5, repr. 1931)
A. Catelani: 'Memorie della vita e delle opere di Claudio Merulo', *Gazzetta musicale di Milano*, xviii (1860)
Q. Bigi: *Di Claudio Merulo da Correggio* (Parma, 1861)
P. de Nolhac and A. Solerti: *Il viaggio di Enrico III re di Francia* (Turin, 1890), 133
A. Einstein: 'Claudio Merulo's Ausgabe der Madrigale', *SIMG*, viii (1906–7), 220–54, 516
N. Pelicelli: 'Musicisti in Parma nel sec. 15–16', *NA*, viii (1931), 213, 278; x (1933), 36
G. Benvenuti: Preface to *Andrea e Giovanni Gabrieli e la musica strumentale in San Marco*, IMi, ii (1943), xliii f
A. Einstein: *The Italian Madrigal* (Princeton, 1949/*R*1971)
G. Reese: *Music in the Renaissance* (New York, 1954, 2/1959)
C. Sartori: *Dizionario degli editori musicali italiani* (Florence, 1958)
L. H. Debes: *Die musikalischen Werke von Claudio Merulo (1533–1604)* (diss., Julius-Maximilians U., Würzburg, 1964)
J. G. Bastian: *The Sacred Music of Claudio Merulo* (diss., U. of Michigan, 1967)
D. Kämper: 'Studien zur instrumentalen Ensemblemusik des 16. Jahrhunderts', *AnMc*, no.10 (1970) [whole vol.]

　　DENIS ARNOLD (1, 2, work-list), THOMAS W. BRIDGES (3)

**Merulo, Giacinto** (*b* S Giovanni Evangelista, nr. Parma, ? 13 Jan 1595; *d* Parma, 23 Feb 1650). Italian composer and organist, probably a great-nephew of Claudio Merulo. The date of birth is given by Pelicelli, although it must be considered doubtful since in his dedication of his uncle's third book of ricercares (1608) Giacinto stated that he was ten years old. On 1 July 1630 he succeeded Bonizzi as the organist of Parma Cathedral, a post that he retained until his death. His only publication, *Madrigali a quattro voce in stile moderno, libro primo* (Venice, 1623), survives in an incomplete form.

BIBLIOGRAPHY

N. Pelicelli: 'Musicisti in Parma nel sec. 15–16', *NA*, viii (1931), 213, 278; x (1933), 36

DENIS ARNOLD

**Merulus, Alessandro** [Alexander]. *See* MERLO, ALESSANDRO.

**Mesangeau** [Mezangeau, Mesangio, Mésengeot, Mesengé, Meziniot, Meschanson, Messangior], **René** (*b* late 16th century; *d* Paris, 1638). French lutenist, lute teacher and composer; 'Mesangeau' is the spelling he used in his signature. He is known to have been in Cologne before 1617, and in 1619 he was described as an equerry at the French court. In 1621 he was 'musicien ordinaire du Roi' (Louis XIII), a position he held until his death. During his highly successful career he moved in high court circles and was a 'bourgeois de Paris'. He was one of the greatest lutenists of the 17th century, and the friend and possibly the teacher of Ennemond Gaultier, who dedicated to him a *tombeau* that is considered one of his finest compositions. For one of his students, an Englishman named B. Reymes, Mesangeau wrote out some pieces in tablature in 1632.

Mesangeau was highly regarded by his contemporaries; Besard, in his anthology of 1617, described him as a most skilful musician. Gumpelzhaimer's *Gymnasma* (Strasbourg, 1621) mentioned Mesangeau along with Ennemond Gaultier, Robert Ballard and Mercure as one of the most famous lutenists in France. Pierre Ballard considered him one of the foremost innovators of new lute tunings, and gave him a prominent place in his anthologies of 1631 and 1638. One of his allemandes was used by Mersenne in 1636 to demonstrate these new tunings.

WORKS

Edition: *Oeuvres de René Mesangeau*, ed. A. Souris and M. Rollin, Corpus des luthistes français (Paris, 1971)

Courante in 1617[26]

12 dances in 1631[6]

17 dances, 2 preludes, chanson intabulation, in 1638[7]

Allemande in M. Mersenne: Harmonie universelle (Paris, 1636/R1963)

5 courantes, *CS-Pu* IV G 18; courante, *F-Pn* Vm[7] 6211; sarabande, *F-Pn* Barbe; 3 courantes, prelude, *CH-Bu* 53; 3 allemandes, sarabande, courante, *F-Pcrs* (holograph), *GB-En* 9452 (holograph), duplicates works in prints and other MSS

BIBLIOGRAPHY

L. de La Laurencie: 'Quelques luthistes français du XVIIᵉ siècle: Michel de Béthune, les Dubut et René Mesangeau', *RdM*, iv (1923), 145

M. le Moël: 'Pour une meilleure biographie de Mesangeau', *RMFC*, iii (1963), 21

MONIQUE ROLLIN

**Mesmes Chansonnier.** *See* SOURCES, MS, §III, 4.

**Mesōdos** (Gk.). In antiquity, a section of a choral lyric setting intervening between strophe and antistrophe. The term *mesōdion* from the 7th century AD similarly referred to a Byzantine chant intervening between the *staseis* of the psalter; *see* CANTICLE, §2.

**Mesomedes** (*b* Crete, *fl* early 2nd century). Greek kitharode and lyric poet. He was a freedman and favourite of the emperor Hadrian, who made him his chief musician; he also served under Hadrian's successor, Antoninus Pius (*Suda*; Jerome, *Chronicle*, in *PL*, xxvii, p.469; Julius Capitolinus, *Historia Augusta*; vii, chap.8). It was probably he whom the emperor Caracalla honoured with a cenotaph a century later (Dio Cassius, lxxvii, chap.12[13], §7) and not a successor who had taken as his own a famous name from the past, although this practice is attested for some kitharodes.

13 poems by him, five with musical notation, survive. Except for two occurrences of an accidental (*c♯*) borrowed from the chromatic Hypolydian, the *tropos* or pitch-scale is Lydian (with a range *e–g′*) in the diatonic genus. Melodic and accentual pitch usually coincide. Although the degree of correspondence cannot be determined with absolute precision because of variant readings, it appears to be clearly less than in the Delphic Hymns (2nd century BC). Pöhlmann (p.30) has countered Henderson's arguments questioning the authenticity of the musical notation.

The manuscript tradition represented the poems by Mesomedes with musical settings as three hymns, addressed to the Muses, to Helios and to Nemesis. This erroneous division has been under attack since 1877, and the correct division is now established beyond dispute. There are actually three prooimia (literally 'preludes') – brief hymns to an unnamed Muse, to Kalliope and Apollo and finally to Apollo alone – and two full-scale compositions, the hymns to Helios and to Nemesis (ex.1). In 1906, eight poems almost certainly

Ex.1 *Hymn to Nemesis*

1 Ne - me - si  pte - ro - es - sa  bi - ou  rho - pa,

2 ky - an - ō - pi  the - a,  thy - ga - ter  Di - kas,

3 ha  kou - pha  phry - ag - ma - ta  thna - tōn

4 ep - ech - eis  a - da - man - ti  cha - li - nō,

5 ech - thou - sa  d'hu - brin  o - lo - an  bro - tōn

6 me - la - na  phtho - non  ek - tos  e - lau - neis.

by Mesomedes and one by the 4th-century lyric poet Ariphron were discovered. The manuscript contained the compiler's comment that the music had been deliberately left out, although the tropos for three settings is identified. The loss may be thought especially regrettable in the case of the hymn to Isis. As Horna (the discoverer of the manuscript) pointed out, it was the last pagan cult song. Here the modality has been given as Hypolydian; for two other poems it was Lydian. Ariphron's paean to the goddess Hygieia, written about 400 BC, was still sung as late as the 4th century, possibly in a new setting composed by Mesomedes. Later still, the Christian philosopher Synesius of Cyrene (*d* AD 430) spoke of the hymn to Nemesis as 'sung to the lyre' in his own time (*Epistle* lxxv).

The metrical and stylistic influence of Mesomedes seems to be discernible in the earliest known Christian hymn (Oxyrhynchus Papyrus 1786; Pöhlmann, 1970, no.34), which dates from the end of the 3rd century BC. The use of semiquavers, however, sets this work quite apart from all other surviving examples of Greek music. Wellesz has even sought to detach it completely from Hellenic musical tradition, associating it instead with early Byzantine hymnody. The metrical evidence, in particular, hardly permits this. Mesomedes must be accorded, however tentatively, a place of some importance in the transition to Christian hymnography. It is all the more to be regretted, therefore, that neither his poetry nor his melody suggests any ability to rise beyond mediocrity.

BIBLIOGRAPHY

C. von Jan, ed.: *Musici scriptores graeci* (Leipzig, 1895–9/*R*1962), 454ff, suppl., 40ff

J. U. Powell, ed.: *Collectanea alexandrina* (Oxford, 1925), 197f

K. Horna: 'Die Hymnen des Mesomedes', *Sitzungsberichte der Akademie der Wissenschaften in Wien, philosophisch-historische Klasse*, ccvii/1 (Vienna and Leipzig, 1928), 3–45

G. Martellotti: *Mesomede* (Rome, 1929)

W. Vetter: 'Mesomedes', *Paulys Realencyclopädie der classischen Altertumswissenschaft*, xv/1 (Stuttgart, 1931), 1103

R. P. Winnington-Ingram: *Mode in Ancient Greek Music* (Cambridge, 1936/*R*1968), 41ff

E. Wellesz: *A History of Byzantine Music and Hymnography* (Oxford, 1949, 2/1962), 152ff

I. Henderson: 'Ancient Greek Music', *NOHM*, i (1957), 371

E. Heitsch: 'Die Mesomedes-Überlieferung', *Nachrichten der Akademie der Wissenschaften in Göttingen, philologisch-historische Klasse*, iii (1959), 35

——, ed.: *Die griechischen Dichterfragmente der römischen Kaiserzeit*, i (Göttingen, 1961, 2/1963), 24ff

E. Pöhlmann, ed.: *Denkmäler altgriechischer Musik* (Nuremberg, 1970), 13ff

WARREN ANDERSON

**Mesonyktikon.** The Byzantine midnight office which begins the daily cycle of Orthodox services. It consists mostly of readings from the psalms and the chanting of several troparia. *See* TROPARION.

**Mesopotamia.** This article deals with the music of the nations between the Tigris and Euphrates rivers – Sumeria, Akkadia, Babylonia and Assyria – from the period of the earliest surviving evidence in the 3rd millennium BC until late antiquity.

1. Periods of western Asiatic history. 2. Sumerian instruments (3rd millennium BC). 3. Babylonian instruments (2nd millennium BC). 4. Assyrian and neo-Babylonian instruments (1st millennium BC). 5. Nomenclature of instruments. 6. Religious significance of music. 7. Music in worship. 8. Performing practice. 9. Musical education. 10. Musical theory.

1. PERIODS OF WESTERN ASIATIC HISTORY. Western Asiatic history may be divided into periods with the following approximate dates (all BC).

3100–2800: Uruk VI–IV period
2800–2700: Jamdat Nasr period
2700–2600: early Dynastic period I (Mesilim period)
2600–2350: early Dynastic period II–III (Ur I period)
2350–2150: Akkadian period
2150–1850: neo-Sumerian period (Ur III period)
1850–1600: old Babylonian (old Assyrian) period
1600–1000: middle Babylonian (middle Assyrian) period
1000–500: neo-Babylonian (neo-Assyrian) period.

2. SUMERIAN INSTRUMENTS (3RD MILLENNIUM BC). Since western Asia lacks the favourable climate which in Egypt aided the preservation of numerous musical instruments from antiquity, it is necessary to resort to iconographical and, to a lesser extent, literary evidence. The earliest surviving representations of Sumerian instruments occur on tablets of the Uruk IV period. One of the characters used shows a short form of a curved or bow-shaped harp with three strings, a resonator and a neck (see fig.1); it represents the sound 'balag' or

*1. Sumerian characters, representing boat-shaped harps, copied from stone tablets of the Uruk IV period (c2800 BC)*

'balang'. A drawing of the same period scratched on stone may represent this instrument, but the shape of the Sumerian harp becomes clear only in cylinder seals dating from the Jamdat Nasr to the Mesilim period, and in reliefs from the Mesilim period. The instruments had an asymmetrical parabolic shape with an oblong, probably keel-shaped, soundbox; they were made in various sizes and might have up to six strings.

The harps of the Ur I period (see fig.2), remains of which have been excavated in the Royal Cemetery at Ur, are similar in appearance, but had 11 to 15 strings. The neck also had copper or gold pegs to secure the strings, and a mushroom-shaped cap of silver or gold to round off the end. These harps were of a considerable size and, like their predecessors, were played in an upright position, with the fingers.

The Sumerians' other important string instrument was the lyre, which was associated with the bull, a symbol of fertility and divine power. There are numerous illustrations of lyres on cylinder seals from the Jamdat Nasr period to the Ur I period, and parts of lyres from the Royal Cemetery at Ur have been identified and restored. The soundbox, originally modelled on the body of a bull, became increasingly stylized; eventually only the bull's head remained as an embellishment (see fig.3a). Both small portable lyres (*see* LYRE, fig.4), and larger ones that rested on the ground, are found (see fig.3b); all of them, however, were held in a vertical position and played with the fingers. One special feature of Sumerian lyres was small tuning-sticks (levers) placed through the knots where the strings were attached to the cross-post; slight upward or downward movement of these altered the tension and, accordingly, the tuning of the strings. During the Ur I period the number of strings was increased to 11. After the Sumerian period, bow-shaped harps and bull's-head lyres gradually disappeared from Mesopotamia, and only in the Akkadian period did some of these types reappear (see §3 below).

The oldest percussion instruments were clappers, used by dancing girls to provide a rhythmic accompaniment to their dance. These can be seen on Mesilim inlaid work and Ur I cylinder seals, and actual examples have also been excavated. They were 15 to 30 cm long and 4 cm wide, and shaped like a crescent or an 'S'; the dancer held one in each hand and struck them together. A fragment of inlaid work of the Mesilim period shows a type of clappers held in one hand only – an early version of the crotala, or hinged clappers later used all over Greece.

During the neo-Sumerian period the small frame drum or tambourine first appeared. Dancers used it instead of clappers in the performance of ritual dances, and from that time it remained in constant use in western Asia. From the same period there is pictorial evidence of a giant frame drum: one player stood at either side, beating the skin with both hands.

Wind instruments were used in ancient Egypt, and would therefore probably have been known in western Asia, but the evidence is too scanty for certainty: fragments of tubes from the tombs at Ur cannot be positively identified as wind instruments, still less as flutes or reed instruments.

3. BABYLONIAN INSTRUMENTS (2ND MILLENNIUM BC). The Babylonian period brought changes in practically all the instruments of western Asia. The lyre, which the Sumerians had held upright, plucking the strings with their fingers, and which even in its portable form had been relatively large and ornate, now became a small, easily portable instrument without a bull's head. It was held more or less tilted, occasionally even horizontal, so that the player could pluck the strings with a plectrum while touching the strings with the fingers of the other hand. This technique of playing the lyre spread from Mesopotamia to Egypt, Greece and Rome. Although the lyre had originally been simple in design, the arms in time became beautifully arched, and the yoke set more or less obliquely.

The angled harp now appeared. There were various playing techniques depending on the position in which the harp was held. If the strings were vertical the soundbox would lie against the body of the player, who would pluck the strings with the fingers of both hands (see HARP, fig.5). If the strings were horizontal, the player would clasp the soundbox horizontally under his left arm, pluck the strings with a plectrum held in his right hand, and extend the fingers of his left hand to reach the strings (see fig.4). The technique was therefore the same as for the lyre. These harps had between four and eight strings, most commonly seven; those of the vertical harp were attached by means of leather pads.

A round harp, to be played in a horizontal position, again with the soundbox clasped under the left arm, appears as a separate variety on a fragmentary shard from Adab (Bismāya), dating from the first half of the 3rd millennium BC; another example of the same instrument dates from the beginning of the 2nd millennium. The origin of this instrument is uncertain.

In the 2nd millennium, the long-necked lute (tanbūr) appeared in Mesopotamia and became highly popular; it was soon found in Egypt and elsewhere. Its existence is attested even in the second half of the 3rd millennium, but it came into widespread use only during the Babylonian period, as is shown by numerous contemporary terracotta reliefs. The soundbox of this lute was

small and round or oval, and skin was stretched over it. The fingers of the left hand were used to stop the strings (between one and three in number), while the right hand plucked them. In the early stages of the instrument's development a plectrum was invariably used.

The small tambour became common in Mesopotamia during the Babylonian period. For centuries it was the most important percussion instrument of western Asia, and it flourished there to the end of the ancient era. It was soon adopted by the Egyptians, and later also by the Greeks and Romans. The drum was clasped from beneath against the left shoulder or side of the body, while the skin was beaten with the right hand. The drum could also be held out in front of the player. At first it was played on its own, especially as an accompaniment to the dance; later it appeared in instrumental ensembles.

A relief of the Babylonian period depicts for the first time a sizable goblet-shaped drum that remained an important cult instrument until the late Babylonian era. A table of sacerdotal instructions from Uruk, dating from the Seleucid period, gives precise details for making these sacred drums (lilissu) from the hide of a bull. The large frame drum continued to flourish at this time.

The earliest certain evidence of wind instruments in western Asia dates from the 2nd millennium. Chief of these instruments were double-reed double-pipes; isolated examples existed from the Akkadian period, but they now became the principal wind instruments. They

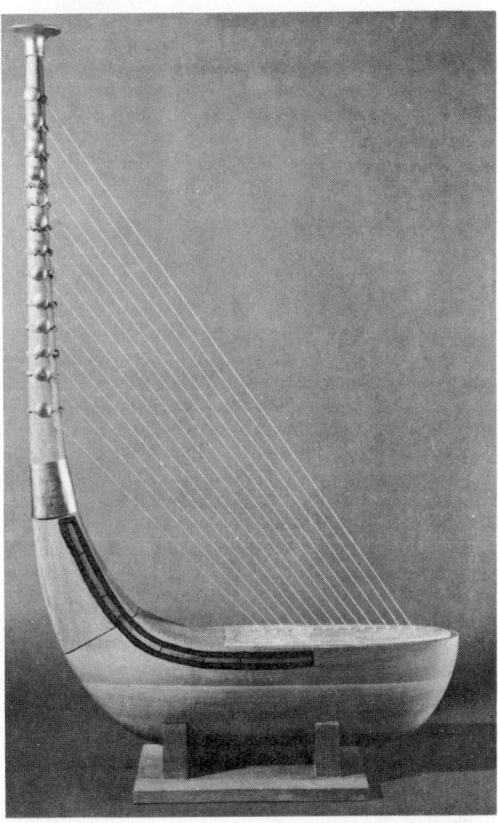

2. Reconstruction of a boat-shaped harp from the Royal Cemetery at Ur (Ur I period, 2600–2350 BC) (British Museum, London)

(a)

(b)

3. (a) Reconstruction of a silver Sumerian lyre from the Royal Cemetery at Ur (Ur I period, 2600–2350 BC) (British Museum, London); (b) detail of inlay work on a similar Sumerian lyre of the same period, showing a large standing lyre and single clapper (University Museum, Philadelphia)

were subsequently adopted by the Egyptians and, still later, by the Greeks (see AULOS). Like the frame drum, it became a standard instrument in western Asia.

4. ASSYRIAN AND NEO-BABYLONIAN INSTRUMENTS (1ST MILLENNIUM BC). Almost all the instruments of the 1st millennium appear in the wall-reliefs of the Assyrian kings. Harps, both vertically and horizontally angled, had developed into large instruments with from 8 to 22 strings. The two types of harp were no longer inter-changeable, however, as those of the Babylonians had been; they were designed specifically for one position or the other. Like earlier harps, vertical harps were plucked with the fingers; horizontal harps were played with a plectrum sometimes of considerable size.

The lyre (fig.5) was held horizontally or at an angle, and was played with or without a plectrum. It had between five and seven strings, and came in a variety of sizes and shapes (with a horizontal or inclined yoke, with straight or curved arms, etc). The long-necked lute in common use at this time differed little from earlier instruments.

Besides the shallow frame drum, two types of drum were found, both played with the hands. One was a medium-sized cylindrical drum, probably with two skins, which was fastened to the player's body; the other was a long quiver-shaped instrument of small diameter; it had only one skin.

Cymbals, found occasionally in the Babylonian peri-od, now took two different forms. Some were pairs of flat, plate-like objects of moderate size, grasped by

looped straps and struck against each other (see fig.5). Others were almost conical in shape, with long handles, and these, too, were used in pairs and struck against each other.

Besides these percussion instruments, there were also clay and metal bells of various shapes and sizes. These possessed a primarily magical significance.

Wind instruments included the double-reed instru-ments already mentioned. Instruments of the horn and trumpet types are also occasionally found (fig.6), but nothing definite is known about their use.

Musical instruments were used chiefly to accompany song and ritual dancing. Nevertheless, even in the Sumerian period, there had been small instrumental groups, and larger ensembles followed in the Assyrian period (see fig.7).

5. NOMENCLATURE OF INSTRUMENTS. It is extremely difficult to identify the instruments known in western Asiatic depictions by the names which occur in the written sources. First, only a few different types of instrument are found, but there are a large number of names of musical instruments. Secondly, the Akkadian nomenclature differs considerably from the Sumerian, and one Akkadian term frequently corresponds to several Sumerian terms, and vice versa. It would appear that there was no strict system of naming instruments in ancient western Asia, and no classification according to the criteria which are now taken for granted, such as form, material and manner of tone production. The names appear to follow the function of the instruments

and the manner in which they were used, or they may signify the manner of musical performance, or the melodic formulae or modes to be used. The study of instrumental terminology is assisted, however, by multi-lingual Babylonian lists that set the Sumerian and Akkadian terms side by side; these lists often give information about the material from which particular instruments were normally made (e.g. wood, copper, bronze, hide or reed). It is therefore possible to classify most of the names of Sumerian and Akkadian instruments in broad groups – chordophones, membranophones and aerophones – although the terminology for idiophones remains obscure.

6. RELIGIOUS SIGNIFICANCE OF MUSIC. Music in ancient western Asia served primarily to honour God and to accompany prayers; it was an essential part of worship, and making music was a religious activity. Musical instruments were sacred and might themselves be objects of veneration. Nothing is known of any organized popular or secular music; depictions of shepherds or herdsmen playing instruments and corresponding cuneiform signs have frequently been misunderstood. They were symbolic and often connected with Tammuz, the god of plant life.

This basic conception of music altered little through the 3000-year history of western Asiatic civilization, and even left clear traces of its influence on later cultures. Despite the fact that the peoples who entered Mesopotamia during this time did enrich its music, the new elements were always absorbed smoothly into the existing musical tradition; even the Assyrians added little to earlier ideas, but simply codified and organized earlier learning.

7. MUSIC IN WORSHIP. Music accompanied Man from birth to death, and even beyond, as the traditional funeral rites and the excavations of the Royal Cemetery at Ur show. Music was performed in the daily liturgy of the temple, in annual festivals, at special occasions, such as the building of a temple, and during burial rites, and precise rules governed its performance. In the Babylonian period particularly, the new year festival (*akitu*), an annual celebration of plant life and fertility, was of great importance. It extended over a number of days, and was usually associated with a wedding of the gods that had its origin in the early Sumerian period. Musical performance was specifically mentioned in connection with an epic of the creation of the world, recited on the fourth day of the festival.

8. PERFORMING PRACTICE. Oriental music in antiquity was found only in conjunction with religious texts, which were spoken, sung or intoned, and might also be accompanied by instruments. Nothing is known of independent instrumental music which may have been restricted to brief preludes, interludes or postludes. There is little evidence about performing style or the criteria governing the choice of different instruments; special instructions frequently appear at the ends of texts, but their meaning is still unknown. Certain inferences may be drawn from the forms of the texts, however, and from pictorial representations. Solo and choral singing were widely practised, the latter in both responsorial and antiphonal styles; there was also psalmodic recitation, with accompaniment by various solo instruments or ensembles. The religious texts performed either entirely or in part with music included songs, hymns, laments and prayers; myths or epics were also recited to music.

The use of instruments was determined largely by the ritual occasion; certain instruments were excluded at certain times, and instruments might be changed in the course of a performance. Often one instrument accompanied a whole piece or long sections of the liturgy. From the very earliest times, singing and dancing were accompanied by hand-clapping and various instruments. Ensembles of several instruments existed as early as the Ur I period, but instrumental ensembles were especially varied in the Assyrian period: there were combinations ranging from groups of four or five players to large ensembles of orchestral proportions. It should not be thought, however, that these ensembles performed polyphony: they are likely to have been restricted to doubling the melody at the unison or octave, with occasional melodic decoration.

4. *Horizontal arched harp: terracotta relief (2100–1800 BC) found at Tell Asmar (Musée du Louvre, Paris)*

5. *Assyrian musicians playing cymbals, lyres and small frame drum: relief (7th century BC) from the palace of Ashurbanipal, Nineveh (British Museum, London)*

*6. Musicians playing a horn and large frame drum: relief (beginning of the 1st millennium BC) from Carchemish (British Museum, London)*

9. MUSICAL EDUCATION. The melodies that were sung and played were transmitted orally, as there was no need to record them in writing. Since music was so closely associated with worship, the melodies were regarded as priestly secrets, and were not made generally accessible. The many attempts that have been made in modern times to identify and transcribe cuneiform musical notation have therefore met with no success. In any case, it was foreign to the ways of those early oriental civilizations to make fixed definitive versions of their melodies.

Oral tradition and the memorization of melodies presuppose some systematic training. Since music was invariably associated with worship and was therefore taught with particular emphasis on its liturgical functions, musical education was originally provided, together with other subjects relevant to the training of

*7. Assyrian musicians with double reed pipes (partly visible extreme left), harp, lyre and double end-blown pipes: relief (7th century BC) from the palace of Ashurbanipal, Nineveh (British Museum, London)*

priests, in the temple schools, which had existed from the earliest stages of Sumerian and Babylonian civilization.

There were at first no specialized music schools, but in time schools arose within the royal palaces, and often developed further into academic institutions where all the major disciplines of the time were taught including music and its theory. The training of a musician was rigorous; for a temple musician, it lasted about three years and concluded with an examination. The subjects of instruction included the sacred texts that had to be spoken, recited or sung, as well as performance on a number of instruments. Sumerian remained the cult language until a late stage, when it had long been obsolete in everyday usage.

10. MUSICAL THEORY. The Babylonians were excellent mathematicians with a talent for observation, and string instruments had been played in Mesopotamia from the earliest period for which evidence survives. Thus the Babylonians were well acquainted with the relationship between the length of a string and its pitch, and with the connection between numerical ratios and musical intervals, which obviously provided the starting-point for Pythagorean numerical speculation.

The temple schools taught their pupils not only to memorize melodies, but also to understand the theory of music, which itself would facilitate the understanding of practical music. Scales may already at this period have been calculated mathematically; some mathematical work was expressly concerned with the strings and pitches of musical instruments.

Cosmology played an important part in musical theory: the identification of gods with stars and numbers led to the formulation of the most important numerical proportions in music. The introduction of the long-necked lute must have been of particular significance for the calculation of pitch, since relationships between pitch and string length could easily be demonstrated on it, and pitches could easily be compared on the two strings. Indeed, it is probable that scales were mathematically determined on the lute.

Cuneiform texts indicate that the Babylonians had a tonal system based on an octave with seven divisions, that they used seven different scales defined as different sections of the same octave and which may therefore be regarded as modes, and that they knew the principle of the cycle of 5ths. Research is still in progress on the pitches and methods used in tuning string instruments. A comparison of the lengths of strings in depictions of Assyrian angled harps would suggest that these instruments had a total range of two to two and a half octaves.

BIBLIOGRAPHY

F. W. Galpin: *The Music of the Sumerians and their Immediate Successors the Babylonians and Assyrians* (London, 1937, 2/1955)
H. G. Farmer: *The Musical Instruments of the Sumerians and Assyrians* (London, 1953)
W. Stauder: *Die Harfen und Leiern der Sumerer* (Frankfurt am Main, 1957)
H. G. Farmer: 'The Music of Ancient Mesopotamia', *NOHM*, i (1957), 228
H. Hartmann: *Die Musik der sumerischen Kultur* (diss., U. of Frankfurt, 1960)
A. D. Kilmer: 'Two New Lists of Key Numbers for Mathematical Operations', *Orientalia*, new ser., xxix (1960), 273–308
——: 'The Strings of Musical Instruments: their Names, Numbers and Significance', *Assyriological Studies*, xvi (1965), 261
M. Duchesne-Guillemin: 'A l'aube de la théorie musicale: concordance de trois tablettes babyloniennes', *RdM*, lii (1966), 147
O. R. Gurney: 'An Old Babylonian Treatise on the Tuning of the Harp',

*Iraq*, xxx (1968), 229

D. Wulstan: 'The Tuning of the Babylonian Harp', *Iraq*, xxx (1968), 215

M. Duchesne-Guillemin: 'La théorie babylonienne des métaboles musicales', *RdM*, lv (1969), 3

J. Rimmer: *Ancient Musical Instruments of Western Asia in the British Museum* (London, 1969)

H. G. Güterbock: 'Musical Notation in Ugarit', *Revue d'assyriologie et d'archéologie orientale*, lxiv (1970), 45

H. M. Kümmel: 'Zur Stimmung der babylonischen Harfe', *Orientalia*, new ser., xxxix (1970), 252

W. Stauder: 'Die Musik der Sumerer, Babylonier und Assyrer', *Orientalische Musik*, Handbuch der Orientalistik, *Abt.* I, suppl. iv (Leiden and Cologne, 1970), 171–243

A. D. Kilmer: 'The Discovery of an Ancient Mesopotamian Theory of Music', *Proceedings of the American Philosophical Society*, cxv (1971), 131

W. Stauder: *Alte Musikinstrumente in ihrer vieltausendjährigen Entwicklung und Geschichte* (Brunswick, 1973)

WILHELM STAUDER

**Mesplé, Mady** (*b* Toulouse, 7 March 1931). French soprano. She studied the piano and singing at the Toulouse Conservatory, and in 1953 joined the Liège Opera, making her début as Lakmé. After three seasons she was contracted by La Monnaie, Brussels, playing Lucia and the Queen of Night. In 1956 she first appeared at the Opéra-Comique, in 1958 at the Opéra, in such roles as Sister Constance (Poulenc's *Les dialogues des Carmélites*), Oscar, Gilda, Sophie, and the Fire, Princess and Shepherdess in Ravel's *L'enfant et les sortilèges*. She has sung throughout Europe and the USA, as well as at Edinburgh (in 1962, as Lucia with the Covent Garden company) and frequently at Aix-en-Provence. A high soprano of unusual distinction, with an individuality of timbre and a refinement of phrase beyond the usual coloratura singer, she is also a noted concert performer and recitalist, including in her adventurous 20th-century repertory Webern's cantatas. She has recorded Satie's *Socrate* and Madame Herz in Mozart's *Der Schauspieldirektor*, in addition to several French operatic roles.

MAX LOPPERT

**Mesquita, Henrique Alves de** (*b* Rio de Janeiro, 15 March 1836; *d* Rio de Janeiro, 12 July 1906). Brazilian composer. He acquired his training at the Imperial Conservatory of Music where he received the gold medal in 1856 on completion of the counterpoint course under Gioacchino Giannini. He was granted a government scholarship for further studies in Europe; at the Paris Conservatoire he studied harmony with Bazin. His symphonic overture *L'étoile du Brésil* was performed in Paris (1861), as was his comic opera *Une nuit au château* (Portuguese version *Noivado em Paquetá*). His most important work was the opera *O vagabundo* produced on 24 October 1863 at the Teatro Lírico Fluminense (Rio). This was the last work by a Brazilian composer to be presented by the Imperial Academia de Música e Opera Nacional, founded in 1857. In 1869 Mesquita became the regular conductor of the Teatro Fénix Dramática, which specialized in operettas, and for which he wrote some successful pieces including *Ali Babá* and *Coroa de Carlos Magno*. He also composed salon music. In 1891 he was appointed professor of brass instruments at the Instituto Nacional de Música.

BIBLIOGRAPHY

L. H. C. de Azevedo: *150 anos de música no Brasil (1800–1950)* (Rio de Janeiro, 1956)

A. de Andrade: *Francisco Manuel da Silva e seu tempo*, ii (Rio de Janeiro, 1967)

GERARD BÉHAGUE

**Mesquita, José Joaquim Emerico Lôbo de** (*b* between 1730 and 1745; *d* Rio de Janeiro, 1805). Brazilian composer and organist. He was active in the province of Minas Gerais during the latter part of the 18th century, spending most of his life at Arraial do Tejuco (now Diamantina) and Villa Rica (Ouro Prêto). He entered the brotherhood of Nossa Senhora das Mercês dos Homens Crioulos in Arraial do Tejuco, which indicates that he was a mulatto. Mesquita was apparently the first organist of the Irmandade do Ss Sacramento in the same city, working concurrently at the Irmandade da Ordem Terceira do Carmo. He moved to Villa Rica in about 1795, where he worked for about a year and a half as a composer, conductor and organist of the same Ordem Terceira brotherhood. He then moved to Rio de Janeiro, but his professional activities there have not been determined.

Mesquita was the most prolific composer of the Brazilian captaincy. The oldest manuscripts bear the date 1779 (*Antiphona regina coeli laetare* and *Antiphona zelus domus tuae*), but many works were copied throughout the 19th century in Minas Gerais and São Paulo as well. Works available in modern editions (published or unpublished) include a mass in E♭, a mass in F, a *Te Deum*, several litanies, motets and offices for the dead, and an *Antiphona de Nossa Senhora* (*Salve regina*) of 1787, for chorus, strings and organ, edited by F. C. Lange in *Archivo de música religiosa de la capitania geral das Minas Gerais*, i (Mendoza, 1951). Mesquita cultivated an individual homophonic concertante style whose components often recall some European Classical practices.

BIBLIOGRAPHY

F. C. Lange: 'La música en Villa Rica (Minas Gerais, siglo XVIII)', *Revista musical chilena* (1967), no.102, p.8; (1968), no.103, p.77

GERARD BÉHAGUE

**Mesrop-Mashtots** (*d* 440). Monk and possibly a hymnographer of the Armenian Church; *see* ARMENIAN RITE, MUSIC OF THE.

**Messa** (It.). MASS.

**Messa di voce** (It.: 'placing of the voice'). The singing or playing of a long note so that it begins quietly, swells to full volume, and then diminishes to the original quiet tone. The *messa di voce* was at first looked upon as an ornament, and was described by Caccini in his *Le nuove musiche* (1601/2) as 'il crescere e scemare della voce'. P. F. Tosi (*Opinioni de' cantori antichi e moderni*, 1723) defined *messa di voce* briefly and advised that it should be used sparingly. Mancini (*Pensieri, e riflessioni pratiche sopra il canto figurato*, 1774), on the other hand, devoted a short chapter to the subject, specifying that the *messa di voce* should be used 'at the beginning of an aria and on any note with a fermata. Similarly it is necessary at the beginning of a cadenza. A truly accomplished singer, however, will use it on every long note that occurs in a cantilena'. During the 18th century the *messa di voce* acquired such importance in Italian singing that it was turned into a vocal exercise. Domenico Corri, the principal transmitter of the pedagogical method of his teacher, Nicola Porpora, set forth as the first lesson in his *The Singer's Preceptor* (1810) the singing of the *messa di voce* on different notes of the scale with piano accompaniment. The term is also found in 19th-century scores, for example in Act 1 scene vi of Bellini's *Norma* (1831), where the first note of Adalgisa's phrase, 'Lo, l'obbliai', is to be sung 'con messa di voce assai lunga'. Although originally part of vocal technique, the *messa di voce* has also been used in instrumental music. Several treatises, including those for trumpet by Fantini (1638), for flute by Quantz (1752) and for violin by North (1728), Geminiani (1751) and L'Abbé *le fils* (1761), contain descriptions of the *messa di voce*, often (though not always) using the actual term.

OWEN JANDER

**Messager, André (Charles Prosper)** (*b* Montluçon, Allier, 30 Dec 1853; *d* Paris, 24 Feb 1929). French composer, conductor, opera administrator, pianist, organist and critic. His father was a prosperous revenue collector, and his mother came from a military family. Although his family was not particularly musical, he learned the piano from an early age. He was an unruly child, and at the age of seven was sent to boarding school in Montluçon, where he received his first real musical tuition. His parents' reduced income forced him to take steps towards earning a living, and he gained admission to the Ecole Niedermeyer, Paris, in 1869. There he practised the organ and composed much religious music, and was taught by Fauré and Saint-Saëns, who were to remain his close friends. On leaving the Ecole Niedermeyer in 1874 he succeeded Fauré as organist at St Sulpice, where Widor was chief organist. In 1876 Messager won first prize in a competition organized by the Société des Auteurs et Compositeurs de Musique with a symphony which was performed at the Concerts Colonne in 1878; a cantata, *Prométhée enchaîné*, later won him second prize in the same competition. He also conducted at the Folies-Bergère, where some of his ballets were performed, and was for a short time in 1880 conductor at the Eden-Théâtre in Brussels. In 1881 he became organist at St Paul-St Louis and from 1882 to 1884 he was *maître de chapelle* at Ste Marie-des-Batignolles. While in Le Havre, replacing Saint-Saëns as pianist at a series of concerts, he met Edith Clouet, whom he married in 1883 (Fauré played the organ at the ceremony); they were later divorced.

In 1883 he had his first opportunity in the field of composition in which he was later to excel, when his publisher Enoch commissioned him to complete Firmin Bernicat's unfinished operetta *François-les-Bas-Bleus*. This was followed by further operettas of his own and also by the ballet score *Les deux pigeons*, which Saint-Saëns was instrumental in getting performed at the Opéra in 1886. His operettas also achieved popularity in England, and a production of the *opéra-comique La basoche* (1890) as successor to Sullivan's *Ivanhoe* at Richard D'Oyly Carte's Royal English Opera House in 1891 led to the composition of *Mirette* for the Savoy Theatre in 1894, assisted by the Irish composer Hope Temple (pseudonym of Dotie Davies, 1859–1938), who became his second wife in 1895. Messager's work as a composer of operetta reached a peak with *Les p'tites Michu* (1897) and *Véronique* (1898), both of which have remained classics of the French operetta repertory.

Thereafter his work as a composer decreased as other commitments grew. He appeared more and more as conductor in the concert hall and opera house, particularly as a conductor of Wagner, who had influenced him during the 1880s. In 1898, when his friend Albert Carré became manager of the Opéra-Comique, Messager became musical director and held this position until 1903. He was also manager for the Grand Opera Syndicate at Covent Garden (1901–7), director of the Opéra (1907–14) and musical director at the Opéra-Comique again (1919–20). In addition he was conductor of the Concerts Lamoureux in 1905 and of the Société des Concerts du Conservatoire from 1908 to 1919. With the latter orchestra he toured Argentina in 1916, conducting his *Béatrice* at the Teatro Colón, and also the USA in 1918. His insistence on conducting the works of Wagner in wartime during the Argentinian tour provoked criticism in France. After the war he was again able to devote more time to operetta composition. After *Monsieur Beaucaire* (1919), written to an English libretto and starring Maggie Teyte, he replaced Ivan Caryll as the composer of *L'amour masqué* (1923) for Sacha Guitry and Yvonne Printemps, and followed this with further works in similar style. In 1923 he became the first musician to be elected president of the Société des Auteurs; in 1926 he was elected a member of the Institut; and in 1927 he was appointed a Commandeur de la Légion d'honneur.

In this age of increasing musical specialization, Messager's continuing fame as a composer of light music has tended to obscure his considerable standing in contemporary serious musical circles. His friendship and advice were prized by the leading composers of the time, and Fauré himself acknowledged his comprehensive ability: 'familiar with everything, knowing it all, fascinated by anything new . . . one of the first pilgrims to Bayreuth and [able] to play Wagner by heart at a time when the latter was still unknown in Paris'. He was also noted for his performances of Mozart's operas, and in the concert hall for his performances of Russian works. As a music critic he wrote for several papers, including *Le Figaro*. As an orchestrator he was called on by Saint-Saëns to orchestrate the first act of *Phryné* (1892), and for Marguerite Long he reorchestrated Chopin's Piano Concerto in F minor. Although he did not persevere with a career as concert pianist, he was noted in Paris salons for his performances with Fauré of their jointly composed quadrille for piano duet *Souvenirs de Bayreuth* on themes from Wagner's *Ring*. As opera conductor and administrator he is particularly remembered for encouraging Debussy with *Pelléas et Mélisande* and eventually conducting its first performance at the Opéra-Comique in 1902. He also introduced Charpentier's *Louise* and Massenet's *Grisélidis*, as well as being responsible at various times for revivals of works by Gluck and Rameau. His first seasons as manager at Covent Garden (1901–3) were somewhat undistinguished, and he himself appeared as conductor only for the world première of Herbert Bunning's *Princesse Orsa* (1902); but from 1904 operatic activity at Covent Garden picked up, and Messager conducted *Carmen*, *Faust*, *Roméo et Juliette*, *Don Giovanni*, *Orphée* and *Armide*, British premières of Saint-Saëns' *Hélène* and Massenet's *Le jongleur de Notre-Dame* and the world première of Franco Leoni's *L'oracolo*. He also introduced to Covent Garden in 1906 his ballet *Les deux pigeons*.

Even as a composer of operetta Messager displayed unusual versatility, achieving success both in the classical French operetta of the 1890s and in the more intimate style of the 1920s based on the popular chanson. Although a few more ambitious stage works have failed to remain in the repertory, *Véronique* in particular has given him a place with Offenbach and Lecocq as one of the leading composers of French operetta. *Les deux pigeons* has also remained familiar as a ballet score of rare distinction. His work was always that of a craftsman, with a spontaneous flow of melody supported with harmonic freshness, shapely construction and fine orchestration. Reynaldo Hahn declared that neatness was Messager's most distinctive characteristic, particularly on the rostrum, but also in all he did.

### WORKS

Unless otherwise indicated, all published in Paris, all theatrical works first performed in Paris and published at time of first production.

#### OPERETTAS AND OPÉRAS COMIQUES
*(in 3 acts unless otherwise indicated)*

François-les-Bas-Bleus (E. Dubreuil, E. Humbert, P. Burani), Folies-Dramatiques, 8 Nov 1883; completion by Messager of work begun by F. Bernicat
La fauvette du temple (Humbert, Burani), Folies-Dramatiques, 17 Nov 1885
La béarnaise (E. Leterrier, A. Vanloo), Bouffes-Parisiens, 12 Dec 1885
Le bourgeois de Calais (Dubreuil, Burani), Folies-Dramatiques, 6 April 1887
Isoline (C. Mendès), Renaissance, 26 Dec 1888
Le mari de la reine (Grenet-Dancourt, O. Pradels), Bouffes-Parisiens, 18 Dec 1889
La basoche (A. Carré), Opéra-Comique, 30 May 1890
Miss Dollar (C. Clairville, A. Vallin), Nouveau Théâtre, 22 Jan 1893
Madame Chrysanthème (G. Hartmann, A. Alexandre, after P. Loti), Renaissance, 26 Jan 1893
Mirette (M. Carré, F. E. Weatherly, A. Ross), London, Savoy, 3 July 1894 (London, 1894)
La fiancée en loterie (C. de Roddaz, A. Douane), Folies-Dramatiques, 15 Feb 1896; collab. P. Lacome
Le chevalier d'Harmental (5, P. Ferrier, after A. Dumas, A. Maquet), Opéra-Comique, 5 May 1896
Les p'tites Michu (Vanloo, G. Duval), Bouffes-Parisiens, 16 Nov 1897; rev. London
Véronique (Vanloo, Duval), Bouffes-Parisiens, 10 Dec 1898; rev. London
Les dragons de l'impératrice (Vanloo, Duval), Variétés, 13 Feb 1905
Fortunio (5, G. A. de Caillavet, R. de Flers, after A. de Musset: Le chandelier), Opéra-Comique, 5 June 1907
Béatrice (4, de Caillavet, de Flers, after C. Nodier), Monte Carlo, 21 March 1914
Cyprien, ôte ta main d'là (1, M. Hennequin), Concert Mayol, 1916 (Paris, 1936)
Monsieur Beaucaire (F. Lonsdale, Ross, after B. Tarkington), Birmingham, Prince of Wales, 7 April 1919 (London, 1919; Paris, 1926)
La petite fonctionnaire (X. Roux, after A. Capus), Mogador, 14 May 1921 (Paris, 1930)
L'amour masqué (S. Guitry), Edouard VII, 13 Feb 1923
Passionément (Hennequin, A. Willemetz), Michodière, 19 Jan 1926
Coups de roulis (Willemetz, after M. Larrouy), Marigny, 28 Sept 1928

#### INCIDENTAL MUSIC

Le Petit Poucet (E. Mortier, Leterrier, Vanloo), Gaîté, 28 Oct 1885, selections pubd
Colibri (L. Legendre), Vaudeville, 12 June 1889, 1 serenade
Hélène (P. Delair), Vaudeville, 15 Sept 1891
La montagne enchantée (A. Carré, E. Moreau), Porte-Saint-Martin, 12 April 1897; collab. X. Leroux
Debureau (Guitry), Sarah Bernhardt, 9 Oct 1926

#### BALLETS
*(in 1 act unless otherwise indicated)*

Fleur d'oranger (Dreyfous), Folies-Bergère, 1878
Les vins de France (Dreyfous), Folies-Bergère, 1879
Mignons et vilains (Dreyfous), Folies-Bergère, 1879
Les deux pigeons (2, H. Régnier, L. Mérante), Opéra, 8 Oct 1886
Les bleuets (?after Hugo), 1889, not pubd, lost
Scaramouche (2, M. Lefèvre, H. Viragneux), Nouveau Théâtre, 17 Oct 1891; collab. G. Street
Amants éternels (Corneau, Gerbault), Théâtre Libre, 26 Dec 1893
Le procès des roses (Mendès), Marigny, 6 June 1896, not pubd, lost
Le chevalier aux fleurs (A. Silvestre), Marigny, 15 May 1897, choruses pubd; collab. R. Pugno
Une aventure de la guimard (H. Cain), Opéra-Comique, 8 Nov 1900

#### VOCAL

Prométhée enchaîné (G. Clerc), cantata, solo vv, 4vv, orch, c1877
Don Juan et Haydée (Byron), cantata, 3vv, c1880
Nouveau printemps (Clerc, after Heine), 5 songs, 1v, pf acc. (1885)
Amour d'hiver (A. Silvestre), 6 songs, 1v, pf acc. (1911)
21 singly pubd songs, 1v, pf acc.:
(1882–9): À une fiancée (V. Hugo); Chanson de ma mie (T. de

Banville); Chanson mélancolique (C. Mendès); Gavotte, danse chantée (de Banville); La chanson des cerises (Silvestre); Mélodies, sérénade from Colibri (Legendre); Mimosa (Silvestre); Neige rose (Silvestre); Regret d'avril (Silvestre)
(1890–c1922): Chanson d'automne (P. Delair); Chant d'amour (Silvestre); Curly Locks (F. E. Weatherly); Douce chanson (E. Blémont); Fleurs d'hiver (Silvestre); La paix de blanc vêtue (Lahovary); Le bateau rose (J. Richepin); Notre amour (Silvestre); Pour la patrie (Hugo); Ritournelle (H. Gauthier-Villars); Si j'avais vos ailes, valse chantée (Grenet-Dancourt, O. Pradels); Va chercher quelques fleurs (L. Aufauvre)

#### INSTRUMENTAL

Symphony, A, 1875, perf. Concerts Colonne, 1878 (1948)
Loreley, ballade, orch, c1880
Trois pièces, vn, pf (1897): Barcarolle, Mazurka, Sérénade
Solo de concours, cl, pf (1899)
3 valses, pf 4 hands (1884)
Souvenirs de Bayreuth, pf 4 hands, collab. G. Fauré, c1880–99 (1930)
Impromptu, op.10; Habañera, op.11; Menuet, op.12; Mazurka, op.13; Caprice polka, op.14; Valse, op.15; Pavane des fées: all pf (1889)
Many pf arrs., 2–4 hands, incl. Chabrier's España and Gwendoline, Charpentier's Impressions d'Italie, Holmès' Au pays bleu, Lalo's Namouna, Saint-Saëns' Etienne Marcel, Phryné, Requiem and Symphony no.2
Messager also orchd Act I of Saint-Saëns' Phryné

### WRITINGS

'André Messager par . . . André Messager', *Musica*, lxxii (1908)
Other articles for *La grande revue* (1903–4), *Musica* (1902–8), *Le gaulois* (1919), *Comoedia* and *Le Figaro*

### BIBLIOGRAPHY

*Musica*, lxxii (1908) [special Messager number]
O. Séré: *Musiciens français d'aujourd'hui* (Paris, 1911, 2/1921)
J. Brindejont-Offenbach: 'Cinquante ans de l'operette française', *Cinquante ans de musique française*, ed. L. Rozhinsky (Paris, 1925), 199–322
O. Samazeuilh: *Musiciens de mon temps* (Paris, 1947)
H. Février: *André Messager, mon maître, mon ami* (Paris, 1948)
M. Augé-Laribé: *André Messager, musicien de théâtre* (Paris, 1952)
G. Hughes: *Composers of Operetta* (London, 1962)

ANDREW LAMB

**Messangior, René.** *See* MESANGEAU, RENÉ.

**Messaus [Messeaux], Guillaume (van)** (*b* Antwerp, baptized 2 July 1589; *d* Antwerp, 8 March 1640). Flemish composer. He spent his life at Antwerp. In 1610 he was sacristan of St Joris and in 1613 became schoolmaster and sacristan at St Willibrordus. Before 1620 he became choirmaster of St Walburgis, and held this position until his death: in 1620, however, he was suspended for a time because of his extreme stubborness and harshness after refusing to perform a Gregorian mass instead of a polyphonic 'missa de angelis' for a dead child. He wrote at least 15 masses, including the unpublished *Missa Victorius Fernandus*, which was found in his estate and was also in the library of King John IV of Portugal. In addition 55 motets and Flemish carols, a canon and three secular Flemish songs by him are known. It is possible that a number of partbooks listed under his name in inventories of St Jacob, Antwerp (1677), and St Salvator, Ghent (1754), can be traced back to his printed collections of 1633 and 1635.

#### WORKS
*(all printed works published in Antwerp)*

Missae 5, 6, 8, 10, 12vv [bc (org)] . . . quibus inserta sunt moteta aliquot 10, 12vv (1633)
[27] Cantiones sacrae praecipuis anni festis accommodatae 8vv cum Missa Maiali, 2vv/insts, bc (org) (1635)
About 20 motets and carols, 1629², 1648²; 2 ed. in F. Noske, *Six Seventeenth-century Carols from the Netherlands for Mixed Voices* (London, 1965); 5 ed. A. Bank (Amsterdam, n.d.)
1 motet, 3vv, in Luscinia sacra (1633)
2 motets, 2, 3vv, 1634²
3 Flemish songs, 4vv, in Livre septième des chansons vulgaires de diverses autheurs (5/1636)

Missa Victorius Fernandus, MS, now lost

BIBLIOGRAPHY
L. de Burbure: MS notes, *B-Aa*
A. de la Fage: *Extraits du catalogue critique et raisonné d'une petite bibliothèque musicale* (Rennes, n.d.), 34
E. vander Straeten: *La musique aux Pays-Bas avant le XIXᵉ siècle*, i (Brussels, 1867/*R*1969), 103; v (Brussels, 1880/*R*1969), 32, 233, 265; viii (Brussels, 1888/*R*1969), 491
A. Goovaerts: *Histoire et bibliographie de la typographie musicale dans les anciens Pays-Bas* (Antwerp and Brussels, 1880/*R*1963), 348, 360, 362
——: 'Messaus, Guillaume', *BNB*
L. Willems: 'Vlaamsche polyphonische kerstliederen van Willem van Messaus', *Verslagen en mededeelingen van de Koninklijke Vlaamsche academie voor taal- en letterkunde* (Ghent, 1934), 387
R. Vannes: *Dictionnaire des musiciens (compositeurs)* (Brussels, 1947), 276
F. Noske: 'The cantiones natalitiae', *Essays in Musicology: a Birthday Offering to Willi Apel* (Bloomington, 1968), 123
GODELIEVE SPIESSENS

**Messchaert, Johannes (Martinus)** (*b* Hoorn, 22 Aug 1857; *d* Zurich, 9 Sept 1922). Dutch baritone and singing teacher. He studied with Karl Schneider at Cologne, Franz Wüllner at Munich and Julius Stockhausen at Frankfurt am Main. A celebrated concert and oratorio singer, he specialized in lieder and the music of Bach, and was a noted interpreter of Jesus in the *St Matthew Passion*. As a teacher he held posts in Amsterdam, Wiesbaden, Frankfurt and Berlin, where in 1911 he was appointed professor of singing at the Königliche Hochschule für Musik. In 1920 he moved to Zurich, where he taught at the conservatory.

BIBLIOGRAPHY
F. Martienssen: *Johannes Messchaert* (Berlin, 1914, 2/1920 as *Die echte Gesangskunst*)
ELIZABETH FORBES

**Messe** (Fr., Ger.). MASS.

**Messiaen, Olivier** (*b* Avignon, 10 Dec 1908). French composer. Messiaen is one of the most important composers of the 20th century. He is totally independent of all schools or any other groupings but has nevertheless played an essential part in the development of modern music from before World War II up to the present, both by his works and by his teaching.

1. Life. 2. Language. 3. Works.

1. LIFE. His musical vocation became evident at a very early age, thanks to the encouragement of his father, Pierre Messiaen, who taught English and translated the complete works of Shakespeare, and also his mother, the poet Cécile Sauvage. Messiaen began to compose when he was seven years old. In 1918 in Nantes, J. de Gibon, who taught him elementary harmony, gave him the score of *Pelléas et Mélisande*. The discovery of Debussy strengthened his determination to become a composer, a determination which was unusually firm for one so young. Messiaen entered the Paris Conservatoire when he was 11 (1919); there he studied harmony, counterpoint and fugue (*premier prix* in 1926), piano accompaniment (*premier prix* in 1928), the history of music (*premier prix* in 1929) and composition (*premier prix* in 1930). His teachers were J. and N. Gallon, Caussade (counterpoint and fugue), Dupré (improvisation and organ), Maurice Emmanuel (history of music) and Dukas (composition). His Preludes for piano date from his last years at the Conservatoire (1929). Immediately after finishing his studies, Messiaen became the principal organist at La Trinité in Paris (1930), a position which he continued to hold for more than 40 years. In 1936 he joined the staff of the Ecole Normale de Musique in Paris and also of the Schola Cantorum. In the same year, together with Lesur, Baudrier and Jolivet, he founded the group La Jeune France (a group which depended on ties of friendship between the four composers rather than on any particular aesthetic or common ideology). The group did not exist for very long, as the war interrupted its activities. Messiaen was taken prisoner in 1940 and while captive in a Silesian camp he composed the *Quatuor pour la fin du temps*; in 1941 the work was performed before 5000 prisoners. After his liberation in the same year, Messiaen became professor of harmony at the Paris Conservatoire. His *Visions de l'amen* for two pianos (1943) and his *Vingt regards sur l'enfant Jésus* date from this period. In 1944 Messiaen published a theoretical work, *Technique de mon langage musical*, which sums up his musical ideas at that time.

From 1943 to 1947 he gave semi-private lessons in the home of Guy-Bernard Delapierre; these seminars for analysis and composition brought together a group of young composers among whom were Boulez, Yvonne Loriod (later his wife), Yvette Grimaud, Jean-Louis Martinet and Maurice Le Roux. These disciples called themselves 'les flèches' (the arrows) as a symbol of their avant-garde spirit. It was in these courses that Messiaen first used his analysis of Stravinsky's *The Rite of Spring* in his teaching. From that time he began to teach outside France: he taught for periods in Budapest (1947), Tanglewood (1948), Darmstadt (1950–53), Saarbrücken and elsewhere. In France his activity as a teacher was crowned by his appointment to a class of musical analysis at the Paris Conservatoire, specially created for him in 1947 by the far-seeing director, Claude Delvincourt. Here, for nearly 20 years, Messiaen's teaching went beyond the traditional Conservatoire courses, ranging from Greek metres and Hindu rhythms to birdsong. He analysed Beethoven's quartets with the same passionate lucidity as Debussy's *Pelléas et Mélisande* or the serial works of the Second Viennese School. Indeed, this analysis class gained a reputation with young musicians from all over the world; it was viewed as a 'super-composition' class, giving a unique musical education. The *Turangalîla-symphonie*, commissioned by Koussevitzky, dates from 1946–8; it was given its first performance in Boston in 1949 with Bernstein conducting. During the 1950s Messiaen strengthened his contacts with the important younger composers, most of them his own pupils, but this time as a composer rather than as a teacher. He was a constant supporter of the concerts of the Domaine Musical, founded in 1954 by Boulez, and these concerts provided the occasion for the first performances of several of Messiaen's works, including the *Catalogue d'oiseaux*, played by Loriod in celebration of Messiaen's 50th birthday.

From his youth Messiaen had been passionately fond of birdsong and spent much of his time in the wild noting down their dictation (using conventional notation, with no tape recorder). He is a member of several ornithological societies. Birdsong was a direct source for *Réveil des oiseaux* (1953), *Oiseaux exotiques* (1955–6) and the *Catalogue d'oiseaux*, as well as for most of Messiaen's later works. In 1962 the composer visited Japan with Loriod, and this visit led to the composition of his *Sept haïkaï* (first performed in 1963 at the Domaine Musical); he then visited Bulgaria and Argentina, where he gave a course on rhythm in Buenos Aires (1964). Official recognition came in 1965, when the French Government commissioned his *Et exspecto resurrectionem mortuorum*, dedicated to the dead of the two world wars; this was performed in the Sainte-Chapelle in Paris, and then in Chartres Cathedral on 20 July 1965 in the presence of General de Gaulle. It was later performed at the Domaine Musical with Boulez conducting. Following a trip to Finland in 1966, Messiaen was appointed professor of composition at the Paris Conservatoire, and in 1967 he was elected a member of the Institut. An international piano competition bearing his name was established in 1967 as part of the Royan Festival. In 1971 he won the Erasmus Prize.

*1. Olivier Messiaen at Rocamadour in 1961*

2. LANGUAGE. Messiaen has described himself as 'compositeur et rythmicien', which underlines the dominant importance played by rhythm in his musical language. Messiaen's rhythmic imagination was stimulated by a number of influences: ancient Greek metres, medieval rhythms and western developments. He met Greek rhythm through his teachers Dupré and Emmanuel; subsequently he continued to study it on his own, although without understanding the Greek language. He was particularly interested in rhythms using odd numbers (such as the Cretic based on 5), as well as in the symmetrical and asymmetrical combination of different rhythms, with permutation and overlapping (e.g. the anaklasis) which Messiaen discovered while analysing Le Jeune's *Printemps*, a work which uses '*vers mesurés à l'antique*' in its 39 choruses. A number of Messiaen's works use complex rhythmic structures derived from Greek rhythm and metre.

In the field of Hindu rhythm, Messiaen's main source was the 13th-century *Salgîta-Ratnâkara* by Carnagadeva, which contains a list of 120 deçî-tâlas (rhythms from the different provinces). Messiaen spent a great deal of time in the study of this list in order to determine the general rules governing its rhythmic elements and their possible uses, as well as to clarify their religious and philosophical symbolism. He gave particular attention to ways of altering rhythms; his methods include augmentation and diminution (both of which may be constant or varying), the addition or subtraction of elements, and combining rhythms or splitting them into components. The 'added value' technique (adding the same duration to each element of a rhythm) is an example of constant augmentation. It was in applying these methods that Messiaen came across the non-retrogradable rhythms which play a very important part in his own work. These are rhythms made up of two symmetrical wings, and so no different retrograde form can be obtained (see ex.1). Few of Messiaen's works use

Ex.1 from the *Quatuor pour la fin du temps*

Hindu rhythm unaltered: the main examples are to be found in the *Cinq rechants* and the *Livre d'orgue*, one of the composer's most daring works, in which the sections entitled 'Pièce en trio' (no.5) and '64 durées' are remarkable examples of experiment with durations. But we find the influence of the deçî-tâlas in Messiaen's whole concept of rhythm – assimilated, developed and used with great imagination. The *Technique de mon langage musical* contains an explanation of the ways in which he employs non-retrogradable rhythms and rhythms of Hindu origin.

Messiaen studied western rhythm in the works of Le Jeune, Mozart, Beethoven, Chopin (for irrational values) and, most importantly, Stravinsky and Debussy. In his analysis of Stravinsky's *The Rite of Spring* Messiaen found what he calls 'personnages rythmiques' – that is rhythmic structures which remain recognizable although they may be augmented or diminished in symmetrical or asymmetrical manner. The final 'Sacrificial Dance' gives particularly clear examples. (Boulez also described the rhythmic structure of the 'Sacrificial Dance' from a new point of view, but his analysis clearly springs from Messiaen's earlier study.) Debussy's rhythm seems to have influenced Messiaen's progress even more deeply than did Stravinsky's. In Debussy's music, rhythm is freed from its dependence both on tonality and on pulse: the rhythmic function of the bar-line and of strong beats is greatly reduced, and this permits an abundance of rich and independent rhythmic figures which cannot be fitted into a basic pulse. This is particularly evident in Debussy's piano compositions. In many works by Messiaen the rhythmic function of the bar-line is completely abandoned, opening up a great range of possibilities for using different durations and rhythmic cells or themes, which are then developed in independent structures and in complex contrapuntal forms. Rhythmic pedals and canons form a polyrhythmic texture as rich as it is strictly controlled. In works for instrumental ensembles, bar-lines may be written merely for the guidance of the conductor.

Messiaen's harmony is equally individual (the term 'harmony' includes here the principles governing all pitch relationships and not only the vertical ones). Taking Debussy's wider conception of tonality as his starting point, Messiaen swiftly developed a system of modes. Serial technique, which he has used, particularly in the *Livre d'orgue*, came to enrich this greatly, but did not take its place. In a totally personal way, Messiaen's harmonic language combines tonality, atonality, modality and serialism. Central to Messiaen's harmonic technique are the modes of limited transposition (see ex.2). These modes may be transposed by a semitone

Ex.2

only a limited number of times, after which the original set of notes reappears. It will be noted that the symmetry of the non-transposable mode is comparable with that of the non-retrogradable rhythm. The most important aspect of his harmonic language is that the modes govern both the vertical and the horizontal dimensions of a work to the extent that a horizontal line will be harmonized exclusively with the notes of the mode. This allowed Messiaen to enter all the more easily into the world of serialism, which developed his harmonic style, subduing a number of traits which still owed their existence to a dualist vertical-horizontal way of thinking. In Messiaen's harmony (using the term in its traditional academic sense) elements such as the addition of the augmented 4th or 6th to the perfect triad, as well as certain procedures such as chord-chains, disappeared under the immediate influence of serialism. Nevertheless, such harmonic structures reappeared in later works, notably *La Transfiguration* (1969), marking Messiaen's wish to integrate all the stages of his evolution. Messiaen has been able to create new harmonies capable of encompassing even birdsong.

This concept of colour too is completely unique. He has often stated that he sees colours when writing or listening to music. The analogies which Messiaen makes between some types of music and specific colours (e.g. a page of one of his works may be described as 'violet' or 'milk-white') may be purely subjective and therefore of limited value. It is nonetheless true that he composes sounds just as a painter mixes his colours, and he is aware of the importance of both instrumentation and harmonic structure in producing his colours. Messiaen often produces tone-colours by a process analogous to that of organ mixtures: pitches are written in vertical combinations which correspond either with the natural harmonic series or with what Messiaen calls 'effects of pure fantasy, very distantly analogous to the phenomenon of natural resonance'. These may be used with or without a fundamental. This technique gives Messiaen's writing for the piano a completely new range of colour, a 'rainbow' as he calls it. In his works for organ, and above all for orchestra, Messiaen makes original use of stops and instruments and their combinations to produce sounds of great harmonic complexity. But the functional aspect of timbre in Messiaen's music is most important. Like Debussy, Messiaen uses timbre for essential structural purposes: tone-colour is as important as pitch and duration. *Chronochromie* gives the best possible example of the functional role of timbre, for it is based, as the title indicates, on the equal importance of timbre and duration in its architecture.

3. WORKS. Messiaen's work may be divided into four 'periods': (1) up to the *Turangalîla-symphonie* (1946–8), (2) *Cantéyodjayâ* to the *Livre d'orgue* (1951), (3) *Réveil des oiseaux* to *Sept haïkaï* (1962) and (4) *Couleurs de la cité céleste* onwards. In his first period Messiaen's personal style and principal discoveries in rhythm, harmony and tone-colour are already evident. The style is rich, even baroque, and is perfectly adapted to the forces it employs. The eight Preludes are among the few works of this period which have no connection with religion; their titles, for example 'La colombe', 'Chant d'extase dans un paysage triste' or 'Un reflet dans le vent', look back to Debussy and to a neo-romanticism that strives both to paint a picture and express a sentiment. But the language here is already new, with much use of modes of limited transposition and added rhythmic values. In organ works like *La Nativité du Seigneur* (1935), and in the *Poèmes pour Mi* (1936) for voice and piano, the style is perfectly integrated. The *Quatuor pour la fin du temps* (1940) for violin, clarinet, cello and piano, represents the high peak of this style and demonstrates both complexity and great refinement. Messiaen's techniques of rhythmic variation, together with occasional quotations of birdsong, emerge triumphant in a score whose titles refer to the Apocalypse ('Danse de la fureur pour les sept trompettes', 'Fouillis d'arcs-en-ciel pour l'ange qui annonce la fin du temps', etc). Descriptive and expressive writing here take their place in a mystical perspective where the now terrible, now merciful features of Messiaen's God are captured in an amazingly precise architectural outline.

Two great keyboard works followed the *Quatuor*: *Visions de l'amen* (1943) and *Vingt regards sur l'enfant Jésus* (1944). *Visions de l'amen*, for two pianos, consists of seven sections whose titles all contain the word 'Amen'. One of the most remarkable innovations in this work is the use of the keyboard registers: outbursts, leaps and contrasts, and long passages in extreme registers where the music seems to be imprisoned, particularly in the extreme upper range. Such 'ostinatos of registers' (Liszt's *Totentanz* offers a rare anticipation of them) recur in the second book of Boulez's *Structures*; here, as in so many other ways, it is possible to detect the strength of Messiaen's influence on his most famous pupil. *Vingt regards*, with its 'rainbow' sonorities, forms one of the great peaks of 20th-century piano writing. In the period immediately following the war Messiaen again participated fully in the new explorations of possible piano techniques.

The preceding works were religious, but *Harawi* (1945) for dramatic soprano and piano, *Cinq rechants* (1949) for small choir and the *Turangalîla-symphonie* (1946–8) are all poems of love. The text of *Harawi*, 'song of love and of death', is by Messiaen himself; it combines elements from Peruvian folklore with surrealist tendencies, adding some onomatopoeic embellishments. Goléa described one of the poems of this work as 'the most divine surrealist romance', and its quality cannot be better described. Particularly noteworthy among the musical features of this cycle, based on Messiaen's own innovations in rhythm and harmony, is the use of the rising 6th in cadential formulae. This type of melodic writing vanished from Messiaen's style after his contact with serialism. *Cinq rechants* also celebrates love as it is symbolized in the legend of Tristan and Isolda. Side by side with his poetic text in French, Messiaen used an invented language: he composed the timbre in his choice of phonemes. The rhythm of *Cinq rechants* is most important. It is a homage to Le Jeune's *Printemps* and, as in that work, the form falls into couplets ('chants') with refrains ('rechants'). The rhythms are mainly Hindu and these are elaborately developed with non-retrogradable patterns, expansion of central or end elements, augmentation and diminution. *Cinq rechants* was first performed by the Couraud choir and is one of the most frequently heard of Messiaen's works. The title of the *Turangalîla-symphonie* was deliberately chosen for its euphony: it is a compound Sanskrit word which symbolizes for Messiaen vitality and life (one of the meanings of 'lîla' is 'game'). Divided into ten sections, it lasts nearly an hour and a half. This work represents a synthesis of Messiaen's first-period style. Rhythmic counterpoints are employed on a considerably expanded time-scale. The harmony expands over vast fields, both horizontal (very progressive developments and transformations) and vertical (a considerably widened instrumental vocabulary). In the luxuriant orchestration, the 'mixture' technique produces unusual sonorities, to which the ondes martenot makes an important contribution. The flamboyant style of this work, and its immediate impact make it one of Messiaen's most popular works, despite its complexity. It was used as a ballet score in 1968 at the Paris Opéra.

Radically opposed to the baroque characteristics of the *Turangalîla-symphonie* are Messiaen's second-period works: the piano pieces *Quatre études de rythme* (1949) and *Cantéyodjayâ* (1948), and the *Livre d'orgue* (1951). These works have had a profound influence. The *Quatre études de rythme*, entitled *Ile de feu* 1 and 2, *Neumes rythmiques* and *Modes de valeurs et d'intensités*, show a sudden paring down in Messiaen's pianistic writing; it is as if all the special features of his style were laid bare. Manipulations of rhythms become extremely clear, and the contrasts of registers and densities are brutal, so as to be as obvious as possible. This is true of the first three pieces in particular. As for the fourth piece, *Modes de valeurs et d'intensités*, it displays some most important musical innovations which led to total serialism. In a long passage in *Cantéyodjayâ* Messiaen had already associated each pitch in a mode with a particular duration and intensity, each sound thus possessing a complete identity from the outset. During the previous year Babbitt had already tried a strict application of serialism to all musical parameters. A short time after Messiaen's piece, Boulez extended the use of serial technique to duration, intensity and attack in his first book of *Structures* for two pianos. These preoccupations show how pressing the problem of subordinating all musical parameters to a general system had become and in this Messiaen may be seen as a pioneer.

*Mode de valeurs et d'intensités* is entirely built on four 'modes', each of which governs a particular parameter: thus there is a mode containing 36 pitches, another of 24 durations, a third of 12 types of attack and a fourth of 7 different degrees of intensity; each is independent of the others and all four unfold in a field divided into three registers (high, medium and low). Each register uses a particular type of duration (short, medium and long), and if a certain pitch changes register, it also changes in duration. Therefore the four 'modes' appear subordinate to a more general relationship between tempo and register. This means that the piece deliberately introduced a notion of structural relativity in music, far in advance even of the problems

of serialism which were occupying the youngest generation at the time. This work, the archetype of total serialism, was understood in different ways by the younger composers close to Messiaen. Boulez saw it as the model for total serialism. Stockhausen first listened to a recording of the piece for about 30 times, with no score, and discovered in it new perspectives of sound opened up by the possibility of dissociating the various parameters. This led to important thoughts on the dependence of timbre on time (see Karlheinz Stockhausen, 'How Time Passes', *Die Reihe* (English translation), iii (1957), 10–41 and 'The Concept of Unity in Electronic Music', *PNM*, i/1 (1962), 39). Finally, the anti-serialist Xenakis saw in this piece a positive example of combinatory musical thought, vitally important for his own mathematical conception of music (see Iannis Xenakis, *Musiques formelles*, Paris, 1963).

Messiaen has always refused to adopt a single system in his music, but he has paid serialism an occasional – and brilliant – tribute. In the *Livre d'orgue* his serial writing is of exceptional virtuosity and elegance and his use of rhythm attains an unprecedented richness, particularly in the 'Pièce en trio' (no.5). Messiaen could never have remained for long in such a world of abstraction. His deep love of nature took him to birdsong, which he had always admired, and which became a major source of material from 1953. *Le réveil des oiseaux* (1953) and *Oiseaux exotiques* (1955), both for piano and orchestra, usher in a third period. The monumental *Catalogue d'oiseaux* (1956–8) for piano solo, contains in each of its 13 pieces voices of different birds from the provinces of France. Here Messiaen solves in masterly fashion the double problem of making a faithful transcription of birdsong and then integrating it into his musical language.

*Chronochromie* (1960), for large orchestra, is the masterpiece of this period. The title derives from two Greek words – 'chronos' (time) and 'chrōma' (colour) – which emphasizes the importance of these elements in the work. The treatment of time involves the principle of interversion. A 'chromatic scale' of durations from a demisemiquaver to a semibreve is numbered from 1 to 32. The 32 durations are then reordered according to the composer's choice. A first interversion is obtained by applying the same process of reordering to this chosen sequence. Then a second interversion may be obtained by another identical reordering of the first, and so on. Colour is used to underline these processes, and in this work Messiaen attempts to reconstruct the sounds of Alpine torrents, as well as his more usual birdsongs. The section entitled 'Epode' is one of the most remarkable in the work. It is written for 18 strings, each playing a different birdsong (see fig.2). In *Sept haïkaï* (1962), written after Messiaen's trip to Japan, and *Couleurs de la cité céleste* (1963), the solo piano and the xylophones play an important part, whereas wind instruments with six percussionists are used in Messiaen's most dramatic work, *Et exspecto resurrectionem mortuorum* (1964). It is an impressive synthesis of Messiaen's language. Here too we find the birds: the Amazon uirapuru, for example, and a very rare kind of lark. Theologically the work has to do with the Apocalypse, death and resurrection; it is the most forceful expression of the composer's Catholic faith. Messiaen's treatment of religion remains extremely personal, even subjective. It is utterly different from the religious quality in Stravinsky, who rejected all subjec-

2. *Part of the autograph MS of Messiaen's 'Chronochromie', composed in 1960*

tivity in sacred works.

Messiaen's later keyboard works – the *Méditations sur le mystère de la Sainte Trinité* (1969) for organ, and *La fauvette des jardins* (1972) for piano – attempt to synthesize the composer's different styles from the first period, with its idiosyncratic harmonic system, to seri-

alism and the imitation of birdsong. Both works are long and elaborately wrought; they require great virtuosity from the performer. Another later work, *La Transfiguration de notre Seigneur Jésus-Christ* for a choir of 100 voices, seven instrumental soloists and a large orchestra, was commissioned by the Gulbenkian

Foundation and composed between 1965 and 1969. The Latin texts were selected by the composer from the Bible, the Missal and the *Summa theologiae* of St Thomas Aquinas. The work is in two parts ('septenaires'), each containing seven sections organized as follows: 1. Gospel narrative, 2 and 3. Meditations, 4. Gospel narrative, 5 and 6. Meditations, 7. Final chorale.

With this work (and to a certain extent in his other music since *Couleurs de la cité céleste*) Messiaen appears to have abandoned the highly speculative musical ideas he had developed, to return, in what may be called a fourth period, to a greater simplicity of language, with clear structures and even stylistic traits which had been given up in the preceding works. This less hermetic music is enriched with the fruits of long experience; its great clarity and expressive force have reached a large audience.

## WORKS

### ORCHESTRAL

Fugue, d, 1928, unpubd; Le banquet eucharistique, 1928, unpubd; Simple chant d'une âme, 1930, unpubd

Les offrandes oubliées, méditation symphonique, 1930; cond. W. Staram, Paris, Champs-Elysées, 19 Feb 1931; red. pf, 1930

Le tombeau resplendissant, 1931; Paris SO, cond. Monteux, Paris, Salle Pleyel, 1932

Hymne au Saint Sacrement, 1932

L'ascension: Majesté du Christ demandant sa gloire à son Père, Alléluias sereins d'une âme qui désire le ciel, Alléluia sur la trompette, alléluia sur la cymbale, Prière du Christ montant vers son Père, 1933; cond. R. Siohan, Paris, Feb 1935; arr. org, 1934

Turangalîla-symphonie: Introduction, Chant d'amour I, Turangalîla I, Chant d'amour II, Joie du sang des étoiles, Jardin du sommeil d'amour, Turangalîla II, Développement de l'amour, Turangalîla III, Final, pf, ondes martenot, orch, 1946–8; Loriod, Boston SO, cond. Bernstein, Boston, 2 Dec 1949

Réveil des oiseaux, pf, orch, 1953; Loriod, South West German RSO, cond. Rosbaud, Donaueschingen, Oct 1953

Oiseaux exotiques, pf, 11 winds, xyl, glock, 2 perc, 1955–6; Loriod, Domaine Musical, cond. R. Albert, Paris, Petit Marigny, 10 March 1956

Chronochromie: Introduction, Strophe I, Antistrophe I, Strophe II, Antistrophe II, Epode, Coda, 1960; South West German RSO, cond. Rosbaud, Donaueschingen, 16 Oct 1960

Sept haïkaï: Introduction, Le parc de Nara et les lanternes de pierre, Yamanaka-cadenza, Gagaku, Miyajima et le torii dans la mer, Les oiseaux de Karuizawa, Coda, pf, 13 winds, xyl, mar, 4 perc, 8 vn, 1962; Loriod, Domaine Musical, cond. Boulez, Paris, Odéon, 30 Oct 1963

Couleurs de la cité céleste, pf, 13 winds, xyl, xylorimba, mar, 4 perc, 1963; Loriod, Domaine Musical, cond. Boulez, Donaueschingen, 17 Oct 1964

Et exspecto resurrectionem mortuorum, 5 sections, 18 ww, 16 brass, 3 perc, 1964; Domaine Musical, cond. S. Baudo, Paris, Sainte-Chapelle, 7 May 1965

Des canyons aux étoiles, pf, hn, orch, 1970–74; Loriod, S. Moe, Musica Aeterna, cond. Waldman, New York, 20 Nov 1974

### VOCAL

Deux ballades de Villon, 1v, pf, 1921, unpubd

Trois mélodies: Pourquoi? (C. Sauvage), Le sourire (Messiaen), La fiancée perdue (Messiaen), S, pf, 1930

La mort du nombre (Messiaen), S, T, vn, pf, 1930

Mass, 8 S, 4 vn, 1933, unpubd

Vocalise, S, pf, 1935

Poèmes pour Mi (Messiaen): Action des grâces, Paysages, La maison, Epouvante, L'épouse, Ta voix, Les deux guerriers, Le collier, Prière exaucée, S, pf, 1936; M. Bunlet, Messiaen, Paris, 28 April 1937; orchd 1937, Bunlet, Orch National de l'ORTF, cond. Désormière, Paris, Champs Elysées, 1946

O sacrum convivium!, SATB/S, org, 1937

Chants de terre et de ciel (Messiaen): Bail avec Mi, Antienne du silence, Danse du bébé-Pilule, Arc-en-ciel d'innocence, Minuit pile et face, Résurrection, S, pf, 1938

Choeurs pour une Jeanne d'Arc, large chorus, small chorus, 1941, unpubd

Trois petites liturgies de la Présence Divine (Messiaen): Antienne de la conversation intérieure, Séquence du verbe, cantique divin, Psalmodie de l'ubiquité par amour, 18 S, pf, ondes martenot, cel, vib, 3 perc, str, 1944; Loriod, G. Martenot, Conservatoire Orch, cond. Désormière, Paris, 21 April 1945

Harawi, chant d'amour et de mort (Messiaen): La ville qui dormait, toi, Bonjour toi, colombe verte, Montagnes, Doundou tchil, L'amour de

Piroutcha, Répétition planétaire, Adieu, Syllabes, L'escalier redit, gestes du soleil, Amour oiseau d'étoile, Katchikatchi les étoiles, Dans le noir, S, pf, 1945; Brussels, 1946

Cinq rechants (Messiaen), 3 S, 3 A, 3 T, 3 B, 1949; Marcel Couraud Chorale, cond. Couraud, Bordeaux, 1950

La Transfiguration de Notre Seigneur Jésus-Christ (Bible, Missal, St Thomas Aquinas), 14 sections, SSMezAATTBarBB (100vv), pf, vc, fl, cl, vib, mar, xylorimba, orch, 1965–9; Loriod, cond. Baudo, Lisbon, 7 June 1969

### PIANO

La dame de Shalott, 1917, unpubd

La tristesse d'un grand ciel blanc, 1925, unpubd

Preludes: La colombe, Chant d'extase dans un paysage triste, Le nombre léger, Instants défunts, Les sons impalpables du rêve, Cloches d'angoisse et larmes d'adieu, Plainte calme, Un reflet dans le vent, 1929

Fantaisie burlesque, 1932

Pièce pour le tombeau de Paul Dukas, 1935

Rondeau, 1943

Visions de l'amen: Amen de la création, Amen des étoiles, de la planète à l'anneau, Amen de l'agonie de Jésus, Amen du désir, Amen des anges, des saints, du chant des oiseaux, Amen du jugement, Amen de la consommation, 2 pf, 1943; Loriod, Messiaen, Paris, 10 May 1943

Vingt regards sur l'enfant Jésus: Regard du Père, Regard de l'étoile, L'échange, Regard de la vierge, Regard du Fils sur le Fils, Par lui tout a été fait, Regard de la croix, Regard des hauteurs, Regard du temps, Regard de l'esprit de joie, Première communion de la Vierge, La parole toute-puissante, Noël, Regard des anges, Le baiser de l'enfant Jésus, Regard des prophètes, des bergers et des mages, Regard du silence, Regard de l'onction terrible, Je dors, mais mon coeur veille, Regard de l'église d'amour, 1944; Loriod, Paris, Salle Gaveau, 26 March 1945

Cantéyodjayâ, 1948

Quatre études de rythme: Ile de feu I, Ile de feu II, Mode de valeurs et d'intensités, Neumes rythmiques, 1949

Catalogue d'oiseaux: Le chocard des alpes, Le loriot, Le merle bleu, Le traquet stapazin, La chouette hulotte, L'alouette lulu, La rousserolle effarvatte, L'alouette calandrelle, La bouscarle, Le merle de roche, La buse variable, Le traquet rieur, Le courlis cendré, 1956–8; Loriod, Paris, 15 April 1959

La fauvette des jardins, 1972

### ORGAN

Esquisse modale, 1927, unpubd

Variations écossaises, 1928, unpubd

Le banquet céleste, 1928

L'hôte aimable des âmes, 1928, unpubd

Diptyque, essai sur la vie terrestre et l'éternité bienheureuse, 1930

Apparition de l'église éternelle, 1932

L'ascension [version of orch work, 1933, 3rd movt rewritten as Transports de joie d'une âme devant la gloire du Christ qui est la sienne], 1934

La nativité du Seigneur: La vierge et l'enfant, Les bergers, Desseins éternels, Le verbe, Les enfants de Dieu, Les anges, Jésus accepte la souffrance, Les mages, Dieu parmi nous, 1935

Les corps glorieux, sept visions brèves de la vie des ressuscités: Subtilité des corps glorieux, Les eaux de la grâce, L'ange aux parfums, Combat de la mort et de la vie, Force et agilité des corps glorieux, Joie et clarté des corps glorieux, Le mystère de la Sainte Trinité, 1939

Messe de la Pentecôte: Entrée (Les langues de feu), Offertoire (Les choses visibles et invisibles), Consécration (Le don de sagesse), Communion (Les oiseaux et les sources), Sortie (Le vent de l'Esprit), 1950

Livre d'orgue: Reprises par interversion, Pièce en trio, Les mains de l'abîme, Chants d'oiseaux, Pièce en trio, Les yeux dans les roues, 64 durées, 1951; Messiaen, Stuttgart, Villa Berg, 1952

Verset pour la fête de la dédicace, 1960

Méditations sur le mystère de la Sainte Trinité, 9 sections, 1969; Messiaen, Washington, DC, Basilica of the Immaculate Conception, 20 March 1972

### INSTRUMENTAL AND TAPE

Thème et variations, vn, pf, 1932

Fantaisie, vn, pf, 1933, unpubd

Fête des belles eaux, 6 ondes martenot, 1937, unpubd

Deux monodies en quart de ton, ondes martenot, 1938, unpubd

Quatuor pour la fin du temps, cl, pf, vn, vc, 1940; Silesia, Stalag 8A, 15 Jan 1941

Music de scène pour un Oedipe, ondes martenot, 1942, unpubd

Le merle noir, fl, pf, 1951

Timbres-durées, tape, 1952, collab. Henry

Le tombeau de Jean-Pierre Guézec, hn, 1971; Royan, 6 April 1971

Principal publishers: Leduc, Durand

## WRITINGS

with others: *Vingt leçons de solfège moderne* (Paris, 1933)

'Ariane et Barbe-bleue de Paul Dukas', *ReM* (1936), no.166

'Le rythme chez Strawinsky', *ReM* (1939), no.191, p.331

*Vingt leçons d'harmonie* (Paris, 1939)
*Technique de mon langage musical* (Paris, 1944; Eng. trans. 1957)
Preface to A. Jolivet: *Mana* [score] (Paris, 1946)
'Maurice Emmanuel: ses 30 chansons bourguignonnes', *ReM* (1947), no.206
*Conférence de Bruxelles* (Paris, 1958)
Preface, *La prophétie musicale dans l'histoire de l'humanité précédée d'une étude sur les nombres et les planètes dans leur rapports avec la musique*, A. Roustit (Roanne, 1970)

BIBLIOGRAPHY
J. Bruyr: *L'écran des musiciens* (Paris, 1933)
P. Landormy: *La musique française après Debussy* (Paris, 1943)
P. Messiaen: *Images* (Paris, 1944)
B. Gavoty: *Musique et mystique: le 'cas' Messiaen* (Paris, 1945)
M. Frémiot: 'Le rythme dans le langage d'O. Messiaen', *Polyphonie* (1949)
V. Zinke-Bianchini: *Olivier Messiaen* (Paris, 1949)
C. Rostand: *La musique française contemporaine* (Paris, 1952, 2/1961)
J.-E. Marie: *Musique vivante* (Paris, 1953)
J. Barraqué: 'Rythme et développement', *Polyphonie*, ix–x (1954), 47
D. Drew: 'Messiaen: a Provisional Study', *Score* (1954), no.10, p.33; (1955), no.13, p.59; no.14, p.41
J. J. Brothier: *La 'Jeune France'* (Paris, 1956)
C. Rostand: *Olivier Messiaen* (Paris, 1957)
P. Boulez, A. Goléa, C. Rostand and others: *Melos*, xxv/12 (1958) [Messiaen issue]
D. Bourdet: *Visages d'aujourd'hui* (Paris, 1960)
A. Goléa: *Rencontres avec Olivier Messiaen* (Paris, 1961)
A. Hodeir: *La musique depuis Debussy* (Paris, 1961; Eng. trans. 1961)
J. Roy: *Présences contemporaines: musique française* (Paris, 1962)
C. Samuel: *Panorama de l'art musical contemporain* (Paris, 1962)
P. Mari: *Olivier Messiaen* (Paris, 1965, 2/1970)
W. Mellers: *Caliban Reborn* (New York, 1967)
C. Samuel: *Entretiens avec Olivier Messiaen* (Paris, 1967; Eng. trans., 1976)
P. Schaeffer: *La musique concrète* (Paris, 1967)
S. Ahrens and H.-D. Möller: *Das Orgelwerk Messiaens* (Duisburg, 1968)
R. Smalley: 'Debussy and Messiaen', *MT*, cix (1968), 128
B. D. Adams: *The Organ Compositions of Olivier Messiaen* (diss., U. of Utah, 1969)
L. R. Garrett: *Melodic and Harmonic Style in the Organ Works of Olivier Messiaen from 1928 to 1939* (diss., Indiana U., 1969)
S. Waumisley: *The Organ Music of Olivier Messiaen* (Paris, 1969)
H. Heiss: 'Struktur und Symbolik in "Reprises par interversion" und "Les mains de l'abîme" aus Olivier Messiaens "Livre d'orgue"', *Zeitschrift für Musiktheorie*, i/2 (1970), 32
G. Tremblay: 'Oiseau-nature, Messiaen, musique', *Cahiers canadiens de musique*, i (1970), 113
T. Hold: 'Messiaen's Birds', *ML*, lii (1971), 113
R. S. Johnson: *Messiaen* (London, 1975)
R. Nichols: *Messiaen* (London, 1975)
P. Griffiths: 'Catalogue de couleurs: Notes on Messiaen's Tone Colours on his 70th Birthday', *MT*, cxix (1978), 1035

ANDRÉ BOUCOURECHLIEV

**Messina.** Italian city, in Sicily. The city dates from about 2169 BC when it was called Zancle. A musical tradition noted in Greek times did not survive in the Roman period; Byzantine liturgical music flourished during the Middle Ages. The most important monastery was S Salvatore, a cultural centre which reached its peak in the 12th century. Its flourishing musical activity was closely linked to that of the *scriptorium* of the monastery, as is indicated by the 27 manuscripts with Byzantine notation (in *I-ME*) and other manuscripts from Messina surviving elsewhere. The activity of the *scriptoria* encouraged the importation of troubadour songs, such as the *chansons courtoises* and the *chansons de geste*. During the 15th century there was renewed interest in humanistic studies in Messina; a public Greek school was founded and in 1473 Arrigo Alding introduced printing. From 1551 the Jesuits presented tragedies, comedies and sacred dramas with an ever increasing number of sung parts in the Teatro del Collegio Mamertino. Most of the works staged up to the end of the 16th century had texts written by Stefano Tuccio, Bartolomeo Petraccio and Girolamo Cariddi. Local performers seem to have been unsatisfactory; in 1549 and 1552 the senate engaged foreign musicians to perform at all religious and secular occasions, both in the cathedral and in the piazzas. The Messina Cathedral *cappella* was established in 1558; it was employed by the senate and soon attained fame throughout Italy, attracting musicians from elsewhere in Italy to become *maestro di cappella*: Heliseo Ghibel (1558–61), Bartolomeo Lombardo (1561–4 and 1567–95), Filippo Bonaffino and Gerolamo Lombardo (1614). Bartolomeo Lombardo's compositions were performed with notable success in Italy and in the royal chapel of Spain. Later *maestri* included Ottavio Catalani (1621–*c*1644), Vincenzo Tozzi (1653–74), Paolo Lorenzani (1675–8) and Domenico Scorpione (1680–81). Between the mid-16th century and the mid-17th the choir's numbers increased from eight (in 1564) to over 20.

In the same period polyphonic music was developed in Messina and throughout Sicily. Most of the *maestri di cappella* published religious and secular polyphonic music, as did Vincenzo Gallo, G. P. Flaccomio and P. M. Marsolo, all of whom were madrigal composers. This activity had a great impact on music publishing; the printing firms of Fausto Bufalini (1589–93) and of Pietro Brea ed Eredi (1594–1671) achieved a standard of production which could compete with that of their Venetian counterparts. The elder Antonio Ruffo was an important 17th-century patron of the arts; his collection became the most important in southern Italy. He had transformed his palazzo in Regio Campo into an academy, and between about 1662 and 1725 scholars gathered there, and devoted much of their time to music: musicians were invited from outside the town and several members of the Ruffo family were accomplished instrumentalists and composers.

Other academies flourished in the 17th century and became famous throughout Italy: the 'Radicati', or 'Abbarbicati' (1653–78), one held in the house of the La Rocca family (where the first comedy was staged in Messina in 1575) and, most outstanding, the Accademia della Fucina (1639–78), the centre of the intellectual and political life of the city. Many of its members wrote texts for music, others were musicians, but the most famous were the poets Errico Scipione (1592–1670), author of the music drama *Deidamia*, performed in Venice in 1644, and Carlo Musarra, who probably introduced the melodrama to Messina several years before it reached other Sicilian cities. His dramatic poem *Eneidem*, or *Eneide di Virgilio*, with music by either Ottavio Catalani or Vincenzo Tozzi was performed before the Prince of Castile and Viceroy of Sicily, probably in January 1652. The heroic drama *Il ratto d'Elena*, by Bernardo Morando with music by Tozzi, dates from 1657; it was performed by musicians hired by the city *cappella* who had formed a society which had an oratory in the church of S Gioacchino. In 1716 the society obtained the church of S Cecilia, transferring in the mid-19th century to that adjoining the former convent of S Agostino, where it remained until the earthquake of 1908, after which it moved to the church of S Antonio Abbate.

Both before and after the rise of the melodrama, other forms of music and music drama such as miracle plays, sacred dramas, oratorios, serenades, cantatas and musical intermezzos were popular, particularly for use at special occasions. Performances were given in the theatres and churches of the religious orders, on parade floats, in the Teatro alla Marina built by the clergy, but especially in the theatre of the royal palace and of the senate. Messina acquired a proper theatre only in 1724 with the conversion of a large 14th-century warehouse known as the 'Munizione'; it had already been used for theatrical performances, including opera.

The cultural development of the 16th and 17th centuries was halted after the failure of the anti-Spanish revolt of 1674–8. The senate, the university (founded 1596), the order of the Cavalieri della Stella (1595) and the Academy of Letters (whose members were sent into exile) were all abolished. Later, the plague of 1743 and the 1783 earthquake had disastrous effects on the cultural life of the city, which had seen the foundation of several new academies: that of the Clizia (1701), the Accorti (1725) and, the most important and long-lasting, the Peloritana dei Pericolanti, founded in 1728. In the 18th century the Teatro della Munizione had engaged as designers Filippo Juvarra, Pietro Cirino and Quagliata, and Neapolitan opera had gained a strong hold, stimulated by the presence of the *opera buffa* composer Nicola Logroscino. The theatre was restored many times (1747–54, 1777, 1876, 1895), and engaged such outstanding singers as Luigi Lablache and Teresa Brambilla; it was destroyed in the earthquake of 1908.

Cultural life was renewed by the middle of the 19th century: the Accademia Peloritana enjoyed a period of great distinction (1827–47), the university was reinstated in 1838 and new libraries were opened – the Gabinetto Letterario (1839–47) and the Gabinetto di Lettura (from 1860). In 1852 the spacious Teatro S Elisabetta (renamed Teatro Vittorio Emanuele II in 1860) was officially inaugurated with Donizetti's *Marino Faliero* under the title *Il pascià di Scutari*. The theatre attracted many famous singers and conductors. Antonio Laudamo (1813–84), the most important local musician during the 19th century, was conductor at the theatre, *maestro di cappella* at the cathedral and a composer of operas and sacred music. A second theatre, the Arena Peloro, was opened in 1882. Concerts also became popular and several concert societies were founded: the Accademia Filo-Armonica di Messina (1833), which merged in 1840 with the Reale Accademia Filodrammatica to become the Accademia Filodrammatica e Filo-Armonica (later Filodrammatica Pietro Cossa); the Melopea Accademia Filarmonico-Drammatica (1868); the Società del Quartetto (1880); the Filarmonica Verdi (1880); the Società Orchestrale l'Avvenire (1886); and the Società del Circolo Musicale. Their concerts presented works by Haydn, Mozart, Beethoven, Mendelssohn, Schubert and Liszt, as well as arrangements of chamber and symphonic music for piano (or other instruments) and for brass band. The concerts were given in the Teatro della Munizione, the Teatro Vittorio Emanuele, the Arena Peloro, the Sala Comunale, Coglitore, Sala Mola and elsewhere. The Banda Cittadina, the Banda Militare and the Banda delle Società Operaia also gave concerts.

The earthquake of 28 December 1908 destroyed all the city's cultural institutions. The void was only partly filled by the establishment of the Sezione di Messina della Federazione Orchestrale Italiana (1921) and the Filarmonica 'Antonio Laudamo' (1922). The Accademia Filarmonica e Filodrammatica was re-established in 1948, and in the same year two new institutions were established in anticipation of the reopening of the Teatro Vittorio Emanuele: the Scuola di Danza Classica, and the Istituto Musicale 'A. Corelli'. The Teatro Vittorio

Emanuele, however, had not been restored by 1975; musical activities are organized by the Associazione 'V. Bellini', the Filarmonica 'Laudamo' and the Accademia Filarmonica.

BIBLIOGRAPHY

G. Oliva: *Memorie storiche e letterarie della Reale accademia peloritana di Messina dal tempo della sua fondazione fino al presente* (Messina, 1884, 2/1916)

L. Perroni-Grande: *Uomini e cose messinesi de' secoli XV e XVI* (Messina, 1903)

B. Soldati: *Il Collegio mamertino e le origini del Teatro gesuitico* (Turin, 1908)

F. Mazziotta: 'Il teatro messinese: una rappresentazione a Messina il 4 dicembre 1539', *Archivio storico messinese*, xviii (1917), 122

L. Nicotra: 'I musicisti messinesi', *Archivio storico messinese*, xix–xxi (1918–20), 155–91

N. Scaglione: *La vita artistica del Teatro Vittorio Emanuele dal 12 gennaio 1852 al 28 dicembre 1908* (Messina, 1921)

E. Mauceri: *Messina nel settecento* (Milan and Palermo, 1924)

——: 'Appunti per una storia della musica in Messina', *Atti della Regia accademia peloritana*, xxxii (Messina, 1926), 260

O. Tiby: 'Antichi musicisti siciliani', *Archivio storico siciliano*, new ser., liv (1934), 1–75

N. Scaglione: *Bellini a Messina* (Messina, 1935)

F. Mompellio: *Pietro Vinci madrigalista siciliano* (Milan, 1937)

O. Tiby: 'I codici musicali italo-greci di Messina', *Accademie e biblioteche d'Italia*, xi (1937), 65

N. Scaglione: *Antonio Laudamo* (Messina, 1939)

O. Tiby: 'The Polyphonic School in Sicily of the Sixteenth–Seventeenth Century', *MD*, v (1951), 203

*Accademia filodrammatica e filoarmonica di Messina: calendario musicale messinese e le prime del Teatro Vittorio Em.II dalle sue origini al suo silenzio* (Messina, 1956)

S. Pugliatti: *Le 'Musicae traditiones' di Francesco Maurolico* (Messina, 1968)

*Accademia filarmonica, Messina: vent'anni di attività: 1948–1968* (Messina, 1969)

R. Pagano: 'La vita musicale a Palermo e nella Sicilia del seicento', *NRMI*, iii (1969), 439

O. Tiby: *I polifonisti siciliani del XVI e XVII secolo* (Palermo, 1969)

L. Bianconi: 'Sussidi bibliografici per i musicisti siciliani del cinque e seicento', *RIM*, vii (1972), 3–38

G. La Face: 'Beethoven a Messina nell'ottocento', *NRMI*, viii (1974), 36

G. Donato: *La musica a Messina nel seicento* (in preparation)

GIUSEPPE DONATO

**Messner, Joseph** (*b* Schwaz, Tyrol, 27 Feb 1893; *d* Salzburg, 23 Feb 1969). Austrian organist, conductor and composer. After studies in Innsbruck University and his ordination in 1918, he studied the organ and composition at the Akademie der Tonkunst in Munich. In 1922 he returned to Salzburg Cathedral, where he had been a choirboy, and assumed the duties of organist. Messner became Kapellmeister in 1926 and for many years conducted concerts in the cathedral as a part of the Salzburg Festival. He also led the seminar on church music at the Mozarteum. His honours included election to the Académie des Beaux Arts (1931), Austrian honorary professorship (1932) and the Austrian State Prize (1936). He was distinguished both as an improviser on the organ and as a composer. His compositions, particularly his numerous church works, are in the tradition of Bruckner, although his songs show the influence of Mahler.

WORKS
(*selective list*)

VOCAL

Operas: Hadassa (after Bible), perf. 1925; Ines, op.35 (after T. Körner), *c*1933; Agnes Bernauer, op.39 (after Hebbel), *c*1935

Mass, D, op.4, solo vv, chorus, wind, org (1920); Missa poetica, op.9 (von Stach), 1v, org (1923); Das Leben, op.13 (after Novalis), S, female chorus, str orch, harp, pf (1925); 5 symphonische Gesänge, op.24 (after W. Hendel), S, orch (1928); Die vier letzten Dinge, op.27 (after A. Selesius), chorus, orch, 1936; Mass, B♭, op.29, S, chorus, wind (1931); Vater, deine Kinder treten, op.34, male chorus 4vv (1933); Te Deum, op.38, S, Bar, chorus, wind, org ad lib (1935); Marien Messe, op.40, S, chorus 5vv, org/str orch, *c*1935; Festliche Messe, C, op.42, chorus 5vv (1935)

3 Songs, op.43 (L. Maasfeld), Bar, orch, *c*1936; Mass, g, op.46, chorus, org (1937); Der Himmel hängt voller Geigen, op.48 (Des Knaben

Wunderhorn), boys' chorus, orch (1939); Fröhliche Weisheit, op.49 (W. Busch), Mez, male chorus, ob, (c1941); Schicksal der Deutschen, op.56 (H. Lersch), Bar, male chorus 4vv, orch (1943); Mass, E, solo vv, chorus, orch, org, 1959; Erfüllung, op. 64, S, str qt (1960); Mass, A, op.66, chorus, str (1960)

INSTRUMENTAL

Orch: Sym. no.1, c, op.5, c1920; Scherzo fugato, op.6 (1939); Sinfonietta, op.10, pf, orch, c1922; Sym. no.2 'Savonarola', f, op.25, c1928; Symphonische Festmusik, op.45, 1937; Salzburger Suite, op.51, c1940; Rondo giocoso, op.54, 1942; Sinfonietta, op.55, pf, orch, c1942; Sym. no.3, A, op.58, c1950; Vn Conc., op.61, c1955 Phantasie-Fuge, op.14, pf (1924); Improvisation on a Theme of Anton Bruckner, op.19, org (1925); Suite, op.33, org (1932)

Principal publishers: Böhm, Leuckart, Universal

EDITIONS

Alte Salzburger Meister, i–xix (Augsburg, 1927–37)
A. Bruckner: Mass, C (Augsburg, 1950); Mass, F (Augsburg, 1950)

WRITINGS

Das Salzburger Glockenspiel und das Hornwerk auf Hohensalzburg (Salzburg, 1936)
'Die Musik am Salzburger Dom', Oesterreichische Musik- und Sängeralmanach, 1937, 138f

BIBLIOGRAPHY

H. Jancik: 'Messner, Joseph', MGG

WILLIAM D. GUDGER

**Mester, Jorge** (b Mexico City, 10 April 1935). American conductor of Hungarian parentage and Mexican birth. At the Juilliard School he concentrated on conducting, principally with Jean Morel; he also worked with Bernstein (Tanglewood, 1955) and Albert Wolff. He made his début in 1955 with the Orquesta Sinfónica Nacional de México, and his operatic début in Salome at the 1960 Spoleto Festival. He has conducted most major orchestras and several opera companies in the USA as well as the BBC SO and the RPO in London, and worked with leading dance companies. In 1967 he became music director of the Louisville Orchestra, and in 1969 of the Aspen Festival; in 1971 he was also musical adviser and principal conductor of the Kansas City PO. At Juilliard, where he taught until 1967, he conducted the American premières of Hindemith's Long Christmas Dinner, Henze's Elegy for Young Lovers and Cavalli's L'Ormindo. His association with Louisville has made him one of the most recorded conductors of his generation. Blacher, Cowell, Crumb, Dallapiccola, Ginastera, Koechlin, Penderecki, Petrassi, Schuller, Schuman and Shostakovich are among the composers whose works he has been the first to record. He has also made first recordings of music as unusual and interesting as Dante by Granados, Bruch's Symphony no.2 and (with Charles Treger) Joachim's Hungarian Concerto. More an intuitive than an intellectual musician, Mester has nonetheless conducted brilliantly works as difficult as Sessions's Trial of Lucullus, and though the projection of colour and temperament is his particular strength, he has also given notably effective performances of Haydn and Mozart.

MICHAEL STEINBERG

**Mesto** (It.: 'sad', 'sorrowful', 'dejected'). A tempo or mood designation used primarily in the 19th century. The word itself was used in musical contexts by Zarlino (1558) and by Bernardino Bottazzi (1614), as well as by Monteverdi in a celebrated direction in Il ritorno d'Ulisse: 'Finita sinfonia in tempo allegro, si incomincia la seguente mesta, alla bassa sia che Penelope sarà gionta in scena per dar principio al canto'. But this did not bring the word into current musical vocabulary. The most famous uses are probably by Beethoven, who marked the slow movement of his Piano Sonata op.10

no.3 largo e mesto and that of his String Quartet op.59 no.1 adagio molto e mesto. Bartók's Sixth Quartet opens mesto.

For bibliography see TEMPO AND EXPRESSION MARKS.

DAVID FALLOWS

**Mestral, Patrice (Jean Serge)** (b Paris, 7 Aug 1945). French composer and conductor. He studied the piano and aesthetics (with Beaufils) at the Paris Conservatoire and conducting (with Dervaux) at the Ecole Normale de Musique. Though he had no composition teacher, his association, beginning in 1961–2, with Eloy, Amy and others was of decisive importance: through them he came to a knowledge of the Boulezian techniques he has used in his work. His first commission came in 1966 when Petit asked for a ballet score; Les affinités electives was produced the same year with choreography by Blaska. Since that time Mestral has appeared with increasing frequency as a conductor for the ORTF and the Domaine Musical.

WORKS
(selective list)

Pf Sonata, 1962; Périodes I, 9 insts, 1965; Les affinités electives (ballet), 1966; Relations, 17 insts, 1967; Alliages, tpt, 10 insts, 1969; Blocs lumineux, 32vv, 15 insts, 1969; Eléments, orch, 1969; Unité, coloratura S, 9 insts, 1971; Bimorphie, vc, 17 insts, 1972; Bloc I, brass qnt, 1972; Bloc II, fl, hpd, vc, 1972; Dessensions insertions, orch, 1973

PAUL GRIFFITHS

**Mestre de capela** (Port.). The musician in charge of a CHAPEL.

**Mestres-Quadreny, Josep (Maria)** (b Manresa, Barcelona, 4 March 1929). Spanish composer. He studied music in Barcelona with Maria-Rosa Kucharsky, Taltabull and Sigg. His first compositions, dating from the late 1950s, show the use of serialism, to which aleatory techniques were added in 1960. In 1968 he began work in the newly founded Electronic Music Laboratory of Barcelona, and he subsequently became interested in the use of computers in composition; Ibemia for chamber orchestra is the most outstanding of his works produced in this way. He has also collaborated with Spanish writers and visual artists in the creation of theatre pieces, sculptures with sound and other events.

WORKS
(selective list)

Music-theatre: Concert per a representar (J. Brossa), vv, fl, cl, tpt, trbn, perc, db, tape, 1964; Suite bufa (Brossa), Mez, pf, elec, 1966; Homenatge a Joan Prats, 6 actors, elec, fl, cl, tpt, 2 tromb, tuba, str qt, 4 perc, 1972
Orch: Antiodas, 1964; Ibemia, chamber orch, 1968; Double Conc., ondes martenot, perc, orch, 1970
Chamber: Invenciones moviles nos.1–3, 1960–61; Tramesa a Tàpies, vn, va, perc, 1962; Quartet de Catroc, 1962; 3 cànons en homenatge a Galileu, pf/perc. elec, 1965; Str trio, 1968; Frigoli-Frigola, any insts, 1969; Variacions essencials, str trio, perc, 1970; Micos i Papellones, gui, perc, 1970; Aronada, any insts, 1972
Kbd: Pf Sonata, 1957; Org Sonata, 1960

Principal publisher: Moeck

BIBLIOGRAPHY

W.-E. von Lewinski: 'Vier katalanische Komponisten in Barcelona', Melos, xxxviii (1971), 92
D. Gojowy: 'Spanien rückt ins Blickfeld', Melos, xli (1974), 271

MANUEL VALLS

**Mestrino, Nicola** (b Milan, 1748; d Paris, July 1789). Italian violinist and composer. He entered the service of Prince Esterházy in November 1780 and played in the orchestra under Haydn. In 1785 he became chamber musician of Count Erdödy in Pressburg (now

Bratislava). The following year he travelled to Brussels and proceeded from there to Paris. There he made his début at the Concert Spirituel during the Christmas season 1786 and his style was warmly acclaimed as 'new, full of expression and sensitivity' (*Mercure de France*). Soon he became one of the city's most popular performers, rivalling Lolli and Giornovichi. Viotti thought highly of him and engaged him as leader of the Théâtre de Monsieur from its opening in January 1789.

Mestrino's compositions bear traces of his years in Austria and his association with Haydn. Established in Paris, he developed his style and virtuosity to match the high level of the French school, particularly in his concertos. His works, mainly published in Paris, were soon forgotten, except for the *Caprices*, which are still used for study purposes.

WORKS
(*all published in Paris, n.d., unless otherwise stated*)
12 vn concs.
Duos, 2 vn, opp.2–4, 7
Sonates, vn, bc, op.5
Fantasie, Theme varié, vn, and Capriccio, 2 vn (after 1793); fantasy ed.
  F. David: Die hohe Schule des Violinspiels (Leipzig, 1868)
Caprices ou études, vn, dédiés aux amateurs (Vienna, n.d.)
Modulations ou exemples pour passer d'un ton à l'autre (Vienna, n.d.)
12 grands solos ou études, vn, choisies dans les ouvrages de Mestrino
  (extracts, mainly 1st movts, from the vn concertos)

BIBLIOGRAPHY
*FétisB*
M. Pincherle: *Les violonistes compositeurs et virtuoses* (Paris, 1922)
A. Moser: *Geschichte des Violinspiels* (Berlin, 1923, rev. 2/1966)
A. Schering: *Geschichte des Instrumental-Konzerts* (Leipzig, 2/1927)
BORIS SCHWARZ

**Mesuré** (Fr.: 'measured'). In time. Couperin (1716) described it as an instruction to play regularly, not freely, and thus as the equivalent of *tempo giusto*. For Rousseau (1768), however, it was the French equivalent of *a tempo* or *a battuta*, an indication to return to the correct tempo after a deviation or specifically at the end of a recitative. Both uses are found in French music of the 18th century.

For bibliography *see* TEMPO AND EXPRESSION MARKS.
DAVID FALLOWS

**Metabolē** (Gk., from *metaballesthai*: 'to change [behaviour, etc]', 'exchange'; plural *metabolai*). A term referring to changes within a piece from one mode – pitch-key or genus (*tonos, genos*) – to another; it has often been imperfectly translated as 'modulation'. So far as scales underlying melodic structure are concerned, Aristoxenus and Ptolemy (see below) furnished some support to the hypothesis of equivalence between ancient *metabolē* and modern modulation, but the vertical dimension of harmony, essential to modern conceptions of modulation, formed no part of ancient Greek music.

Probably *metabolē* had been practised since the early 5th century BC; the early modes, the true *harmoniai*, had been kept distinct and did not admit of modulation. By the late 5th century, the melodic sequences used in dithyrambs by Cinesias and Timotheus were termed *exarmonios*, 'extra-modal' (in the comedy *Chiron*, attributed to Pherecrates). 12 years later, Aristophanes attacked certain unidentified dithyrambists as 'song-twisters' (*aismatokamptai; Clouds*, l.333); the term 'kampē' ('twist' or 'bend') embodied here had already been applied to Cinesias in the *Chiron*. Its precise meaning remains uncertain, but *metabolē* was evidently a prominent part of the radical movement now termed the

'new music'. One of the Pseudo-Aristotelian *Musical Problems* (§xix, problem 15, p.86, ll.10–12, ed. Jan) reflects the earlier situation with the comment that dithyrambic choruses had once sung melodies in a single mode (*enarmonia*).

In the early 4th century BC, Plato twice condemned what he called 'panharmonic' or 'polyharmonic' music (*Republic*, 399c, 1.7; *d*, ll.1, 4; 404*d*, 1.12). He used *metabolē* solely in its original sense of 'change' or 'variation' to describe the plain and the florid styles of oral delivery (397*b*, ll.6, 9; *c*, l.5); but by adding the hypothesis of a musical setting he provided a precedent for later theorists, many of them followers of Aristoxenus, who used *metabolē* as an established technical musical term.

It is chiefly through the works of these theorists that the views of Aristoxenus on *metabolē* have survived; specifically Aristoxenian elements, however, are difficult to isolate. The surviving portions of his *Harmonics* contain a brief definition of *metabolē* as alteration of melodic order, *taxis* (p.38, l.6, ed. Meibom). This agrees with the description by Ptolemy (2nd century AD): for him *metabolē* was not a change of pitch for its own sake, the shift upwards or downwards of an entire transposition scale; rather, it involved a departure from the original melodic sequence, thus producing 'a sense of change affecting the ethos' (*Harmonics*, ii, chap.55, ll.3–7, ed. Düring; see Winnington-Ingram, p.66).

Other writers enumerated additional varieties of *metabolē*, and their comments help to explain the emphasis on melodic order. Thus Cleonides spoke of *metabolē* affecting system and melodic composition (*systēma, melopoiïa*) as well as key (*tonos*) and genus (*Isagoge*, chap.13, p.204, l.19 – p.206, l.18, ed. Jan). If it affects the *systēma*, it has to do with the transition between disjunct and conjunct tetrachords; here the reference is to the Greater or Lesser Perfect Systems, based on tetrachordal groups (*see* GREECE, §I, 7). *Metabolē* affecting *melopoiïa* had to do with shifts among three types of ethos, but Cleonides offered no explanation of this type of *metabolē* in practice. By the mid-1st century BC, some writers had gone so far as to transfer the idea of *metabolē* to ethical rather than musical processes. Thus the Epicurean philosopher Philodemus of Gadara scoffed at the belief that there could be a *metabolē* concerned not with musical elements but with emotions 'modulated', through the supposed power of music, to form character in a certain way (*De musica*, iii, §54, ll.6–9; p.44, ed. Kemke). This belief almost certainly represents a late Stoic doctrine.

Aristides Quintilianus offered accounts of *metabolē*, including *metabolē* of rhythms (*De musica*, i, chap.11, p.22, ll.11–26; chap.19, p.40, ll.1–7, ed. Winnington-Ingram), which in some respects are clearer than those of Cleonides; and Bacchius (*Isagoge*, §§50–57; p.304, l.6 – p.305, l.4, ed. Jan) distinguished seven types of *metabolē*, discussed in detail by Vetter. Many problems, however, remain unsolved.

BIBLIOGRAPHY
W. Vetter: 'Metabole', *Paulys Realencyclopädie der klassischen Altertumswissenschaft*, xv (Stuttgart, 1932), 1313
R. P. Winnington-Ingram: *Mode in Ancient Greek Music* (Cambridge, 1936/R1968), 53, 66f
W. D. Anderson: *Ethos and Education in Greek Music* (Cambridge, Mass., 1966, 2/1968), 49ff, 64f, 171
WARREN ANDERSON

**Metacrusis.** *See* FEMININE ENDING.

**Metallo, Grammatio** [Grammatico, Graminazio] (*b* Bisaccia, nr. Naples, 1539 or 1540; *d* ?Venice, after 1615). Italian composer. His birthplace is known from the dedication of his second book of *Canzoni* (1577), and he was probably a pupil of Tommaso Cimello in Naples. In 1582 he competed unsuccessfully for the position of *maestro di cappella* of Aquileia Cathedral. According to Fétis, the title-page of his now lost *Canzoni alla napolitana* (1594) stated that he was then *maestro di cappella* of Bassano Cathedral. Some time before 1602 he journeyed to the Holy Land, Crete and Egypt. As he recorded in his later publications, he composed many of his motets during his travels. He was imprisoned for a time in Crete; and in Egypt, to quote the dedication of his *Primo libro de motetti* (signed from Alexandria on 15 September 1601), he was 'stripped of his clothes, tortured and ruined'.

On 2 February 1602 he completed his volume of *Magnificat* settings in Cairo and returned to Venice the same year to assume the post of *maestro di cappella* at S Marcuola, which he still held in 1610. His portrait in the 1614 edition of his *Ricercari* gives his age as 74, and according to Romano Micheli's *Musica vaga et artificiosa* he was still living in Venice in 1615.

Metallo composed mainly lighter music and instrumental works during his early years; only later did he turn exclusively to sacred music. Judging from the number of reprints, his *Ricercari* was his most popular publication. Each ricercare carries a text incipit; the title-page states that the pieces are 'to sing and play', and these opening words are those of proverbs to be completed by the performers. Metallo was particularly adept at the composition of canons, and Micheli admired his skill sufficiently to add parts to 15 of them in his *Musica vaga et artificiosa*, a compendium of contrapuntal dexterity. His sacred music is rather conservative and recalls the stylistic trends current in Rome at the time rather than the more progressive Venetian church music.

WORKS

Il secondo libro de canzoni . . . con una moresca, a 3, 4 (Naples, 1577⁹)
Villanelle alla napolitana con una moresca, 3vv (Venice, 1592¹⁹)
Canzoni alla napolitana con 2 canzoni alla francese per sonare, a 4, 5 (Venice, 1594); lost, 13 pieces transcr. org in *CH-Bu*
Messe comodissime, libro sesto, 4 equal vv (Venice, 1602)
Il primo libro di motetti . . . con una messa, 3, 4vv (Venice, 1602)
Ricercari per sonare et cantare, 2vv (Venice, 1603)
Magnificat con le 4 antifone, hymno et un motetto con diversi canoni, 4, 5vv (Venice, 1603)
Motetti, 6vv, con una Magnificat, messa e motetti, 8vv, libro secondo (Venice, 1604)
Messe con 2 motetti, 5vv, bc, org, op.17 (Venice, 1610)
Motetti con una Magnificat, 5, 10vv, bc, org, op.18 (Venice, 1610)
Motetti, per tutte le solennità dell'anno, 4vv, opp.19, 20 (Venice, 1610)
Messa, motetti et un Magnificat . . . et un circolo musicale, 5vv, op.21 (Venice, 1611)
Epistola, introiti, offertorii, passii, improperii, et messa, 4vv, op.24 (Venice, 1613)
Motetti, Magnificat et madrigali spirituali, 3vv, bc, op.25 (Venice, 1613)
Motet: Sanctus Dominus, canon, 3vv, *D-Bds*
19 villanelle, 3vv, in 1590²⁴; 15 canons in 1615³, with add. parts by Micheli; 1 canon in Cerone: El melopeo y maestro (Naples, 1613)

BIBLIOGRAPHY

*BrownI; FétisB*
G. Vale: 'Vita musicale nella chiesa metropolitana di Aquileja', *NA*, ix (1932), 210
N. Pelicelli: 'Musicisti in Parma', *NA*, x (1933), 317
E. Ferrari Barassi: 'La tradizione della moresca e uno sconosciuto ballo del cinque-seicento', *RIM*, v (1970), 37
D. Kämper: 'Studien zur instrumentalen Ensemble-musik des 16. Jahrhunderts', *AnMc*, no.10 (1970) [whole vol.]

DAVID NUTTER

**Metallophone.** A percussion instrument consisting of a series of tuned metal bars which are arranged in a single or a double row. Musical instruments made of metal slabs were known in China by AD 700. An instrument of Turkish origin consisting of 16 slabs of metal suspended in an upright frame is said to have been introduced into China in the 7th century. Bronze slabs came two centuries later in the form of the Javanese *saron*. This bronze metallophone differs from the earliest instruments in that the slabs are suspended horizontally over a cradle of wood similar to the trough xylophone. The *saron* and a similar instrument, the *gĕnder*, have distinctive roles in the gamelan ensemble. In the *gĕnder* the tone of each bar is enriched by means of bamboo tubes which are placed in the framework in a vertical position under the slabs. Each bar is tuned by adjusting its length to sound in unison with its corresponding slab. (For illustrations *see* INDONESIA, figs.3 and 4.)

The Far Eastern metallophones have influenced certain of the present-day orchestral percussion instruments such as the glockenspiel and vibraphone. In modern compositions the term 'metallophone' is applied to a series of alloy bars suspended over a resonance box. The bars are arranged in a single row or in keyboard fashion. A damping mechanism is incorporated in certain models. In some cases the sustaining power is controlled by a magnetized strip of metal which is moved towards or away from the nodal points.

Carl Orff scored for metallophones in a number of his compositions, and in a simple form metallophones are included in 'school percussion'.

JAMES BLADES

**Metallov, Vasily Mikhaylovich** (*b* Saratov govt., 13 March 1862; *d* Moscow, 1 June 1926). Russian musicologist and composer. He studied theology in Moscow, and taught at the Synodal School there from 1894. In 1901 he was appointed professor of the history of church music at the Moscow Conservatory, and he also lectured at the Institute of Archaeology. He was for many years an active member of the Russian Academy of Sciences. Metallov made a study of the neumatic notion of the early Russian Church, and transcribed pieces from service books dating from the 11th to the 14th centuries. He published two useful textbooks on notation, and also wrote books and articles dealing with the history of the Russian Church and with the development of early Russian music in general. He also composed some sacred music.

WRITINGS

*Ocherk istorii pravoslavnovo tserkovnovo peniya v Rossii* [A study of the history of Orthodox Church singing in Russia] (Saratov, 1893, 3/1900)
*Strogiy stil' garmonii: opït izlozheniya osnovaniya strogovo i strogo-tserkovnovo stilya garmonii* [The strict style of harmony: an attempt to describe the principles of strict church harmony] (Moscow, 1897)
*Sinodal'nïye, bïvshiye patriarshiye pevchiye* [The Synodal, formerly the Patriarchal, Choristers] (Moscow, 1898)
*Azbuka tserkovnovo peniya: opït sistematicheskovo rukovodstva k chteniyu kryukovoy semiografii pesnopeniy znamennovo rospeva perioda kinovarnïkh pomet* [The alphabet of church singing: an attempt at a systematic guide to the reading of *kryuki* in the singing of *znamennïy* chant in the period of the *kinovarnïye pometi*] (Moscow, 1899)
*Osmoglasiye znamennovo rospeva: opït rukovodstva k izucheniyu osmoglasiya znamennovo rospeva po glasovïm popevkam* [The *osmoglasiye* of *znamennïy* chant: an attempt at a guide to the study of the *osmoglasiye* of *znamennïy* chant in vocal *popevki*] (Moscow, 1900)
*Bogosluzhebnoye peniye russkoy tserkvi: period domongol'skiy* [Divine singing in the Russian Church: pre-Mongol period] (Moscow, 1906)
*Sinodal'noye uchilishche tserkovnovo peniya v evo proshlom i nastoyashchem* [The Synodal Academy of church singing past and present] (Moscow, 1911)

ed.: *Russkaya semiografiya* [Facsimiles of Russian chant manuscripts] (Moscow, 1912)

BIBLIOGRAPHY

A. K. [K. A. Kuznetsov]: Obituary, *Muzïkal'noye obrazovaniye* (1926), nos.3–4

G. B. Bernandt and I. M. Yampol'sky: *Kto pisal o muzïke* [Writers on music], ii (Moscow, 1974)

JENNIFER SPENCER

**Metamorphosis, thematic.** *See* TRANSFORMATION, THEMATIC.

**Metaphor aria.** *See* SIMILE ARIA.

**Metastasio, Pietro** [Trapassi, Antonio Domenico Bonaventura] (*b* Rome, 3 Jan 1698; *d* Vienna, 12 April 1782). Italian poet and librettist. His librettos were set over 800 times by different composers during the 18th and early 19th centuries and acquired a reputation unmatched in the history of opera.

1. LIFE. As a child, Antonio Trapassi was adopted by the Roman jurist and classicist, Gian Vincenzo Gravina, who changed his name to Pietro Metastasio and educated him with a view to guiding him into the legal profession. He also encouraged his remarkable ability at written and extemporary verse. Gravina died in January 1718, and his will gave Metastasio the financial means to be independent. He soon decided to give up the legal profession and become a poet. Among those who encouraged him to follow a literary career was the singer Marianna Benti-Bulgarelli, called 'La Romanina', with whom he became associated in the early 1720s and who sang in many premières of his work during that decade. He began his career as music poet writing wedding serenatas and other laudatory poems for members of the Neapolitan aristocracy. In 1723 he moved into the field of opera, revising an old text of D. David called *La forza della virtù* (performed that year in Naples with the new title of *Siface re di Numidia*) and afterwards writing his first original operatic libretto *Didone abbandonata* (Naples, 1 February 1724, with music by Domenico Sarro). The success of *Didone* established his name throughout Italy. Between 1724 and 1730 he lived chiefly in Rome and Venice. During that period he wrote six librettos of major importance. Competition arose between Roman and Venetian impresarios over who should be the first to present them, with the result that more than once near-contemporary first productions of new texts, with music by different composers, were given in the two cities.

On 31 August 1729 Metastasio received an invitation from the Austrian court to take up the post of court poet in Vienna in succession to Apostolo Zeno. Because of commitments to complete works for the forthcoming Roman carnival, Metastasio could not leave for Vienna until the following spring. He arrived in Vienna about 17 April 1730 and found lodgings there in the house of Niccolò Martinez, master of ceremonies to the papal nuncio. Henceforth he had to satisfy all requests for new poetry made by the court, so he was less free to write what he chose. Emperor Charles VI often asked for a new oratorio in Lent and a new opera for the birthday of the empress (28 August); the empress in turn sometimes required a new opera for the name day of the emperor (4 November). Because of these and other demands, Metastasio's first years in Vienna were among his most productive. After the death of Charles VI in autumn 1740 the situation changed, for Metastasio's new

patroness, Empress Maria Theresia, was less interested than her father had been in costly court ceremonial and made fewer demands on Metastasio for elaborate librettos. From then on he was normally called upon to write shorter, more intimate works for the pleasure of the court. Nonetheless, the empress was prepared on occasion to order a full-scale opera for some particularly important family event. During the 1740s and 1750s the poet wrote several texts to be acted and sung by her daughters in private; and during the 1760s and early 1770s he completed some further librettos to honour important family occasions such as the marriages of her children or the birth of a grandchild.

*Pietro Metastasio: engraving by Caronni after Johann Steiner*

Throughout his many years in Vienna Metastasio kept up a voluminous correspondence with friends and acquaintances in Italy, but he never returned there. He was well liked at the Austrian court because of his gentle nature, and had some firm friends in Vienna including Marianna Pignatelli Belmonte, Countess d'Althann (*d* 1759), and members of the Martinez family.

2. WORKS. Metastasio wrote librettos for 27 three-act heroic operas, several short dramatic works of the *azione teatrale* type, eight oratorios, and many serenatas, lyrical poems and canzonettas. He was sufficiently skilled in music to be able to set some of his own verses as well. Of his many works the heroic opera librettos were the most widely known and the most often set to music by the great composers of the period. He accepted the generally held view that heroic opera should demonstrate on stage cases of upright, noble behaviour in the face of adversity, and provoke some kind of cathartic response from the audience sympathetically drawn to the chief character because of his sufferings. At the same time he was not generally in favour of tragic endings; in only two of his librettos, *Didone abbandonata* (1724) and *Catone in Utica* (first version, 1728), does the

action terminate with the death of the hero or heroine. It was his aim to show how reason should so conduct the affairs of men that it can prevent tragedy leading to ultimate disaster. Thus the 'happy ending' of many Metastasian operas was not just a way of pleasing audiences; it was a demonstration of how circumstances may be changed for the better by the force of reason. Metastasio often showed reason in conflict with human desire and passion, the clash either personified by different characters or occurring within the mind and soul of the hero himself. The tug-of-war between reason and passion produces a constant debate within the hero that often effectively deters him from action. It is clear from the poet's letters that he regarded the psychological dilemmas and consequent inaction of his heroes as among the most interesting features of his dramas, though many of his 19th- and 20th-century critics have attacked him on precisely this point, saying that his handling of the debate within the hero creates the effect of a weak, unheroic personality that is out of place or alternatively produces unintentionally comic results.

When Metastasio moved to Vienna, he found it necessary to write librettos supporting the institution of Absolutist monarchy (an institution in which he anyway firmly believed). From then on he added *licenze* (i.e. epilogues) praising the member of the imperial family for whom the libretto was written, and, for the remainder of the reign of Charles at least, saw to it that the plots were allegories of Absolutist kingship in its best possible guise. In some of his Viennese operatic librettos he demonstrated how reason prevents passion from destroying social and political institutions like the monarchy. Thus in *Demetrio*, the first of his Viennese operas (1731), the queen, Cleonice, falls in love with a shepherd but then increasingly doubts the wisdom of accepting him as husband. Reason is therefore shown supporting the institution of the throne and enhancing the figure of the queen in control of her irrational passion. Alternatively, Metastasio showed the hero or heroine unyielding in his or her intention to proceed in the morally correct direction. Attilio Regolo, the Roman hero in the opera of that name (text written 1740, first performed 1750) who determined to sacrifice his life for the sake of his country, is the epitome of this type of character.

The role of music in Metastasian opera raises many complicated issues. The poet himself always regarded music as pleasurable accessory to his dramas, but the fact that his texts were afterwards to be set to music had a profound effect on their style and structure. The customary division of opera into recitatives and arias predetermined the verse metre to a large extent. The mellifluous quality of his verse was in part the result of his sympathetic understanding of what composers and singers found agreeable. The structure of his plots was affected by the convention that leading singers were entitled to more arias than subordinate singers and, furthermore, that each singer left the stage after his aria. This meant that the position and allocation of arias (and therefore the position and number of characters' exits) had to be carefully considered while the plot was being worked out.

It might be said with justification that Metastasio's success cannot be isolated from the success of the composers and other musicians with whom he worked. The sort of cantabile, affecting but not over-violent vocal music written by Italian composers of the 1720–40

period well suited, as it happened, the type of affecting, cathartic, but not over-passionate dramas he was writing. Furthermore, his dramas appeared at a time when demand for Italian heroic opera was high in many parts of Europe, owing mainly to the popularity and competence of Italian singers. The chief problem of Italian heroic opera was, however, that singers became less and less prepared to respect all parts of the drama. There is plenty of evidence that many of them performed the recitative scandalously and reserved their skill for the arias, which gradually became mere showpieces for the enjoyment of the public. It is clear from Metastasio's correspondence that his attitude towards music became increasingly ambivalent. On the one hand the performance of his librettos in opera houses throughout Europe made them well known to an extent they would not have been had they been acted as spoken plays; on the other hand the manner in which they were set and, more especially, the thoughtless manner in which they were acted and sung produced results on stage that were increasingly different from what he intended.

The new political and social ideas current during the age of Enlightenment did not find favour with Metastasio, whose faith in the older, Absolutist order remained unshakeable. His last operatic librettos continued to demonstrate the same virtues of princely heroes, tragic and Caesar-like, in a polite, courtly society, that his earlier librettos had demonstrated, and it is not surprising that some of these last librettos made little headway with the public. Paradoxically, esteem for Metastasio as a public figure reached its zenith during the 1770s and 1780s when the literary climate was turning against him. In many tributes he was likened to the greatest tragedians of all time. During the period of the French Revolution and beyond his reputation slumped, and though there was a temporary revival of interest during the second and third decades of the following century it never recovered. Throughout most of the 19th and first half of the 20th centuries, Metastasian opera was considered a decadent genre; only in recent years has it been re-evaluated in a more positive light. His collected writings were published in his lifetime and there have been many editions since, notably by B. Brunelli, *Tutte le opere di Pietro Metastasio* (Milan, 1943–54).

For a discussion of Metastasio's influence on musical forms *see* ARIA and OPERA, §II, 2.

## WRITINGS

Each work is followed by the composer of the first setting and the place and date of the first performance; other important settings are also given.

### DRAMMI PER MUSICA

*(all in 3 acts)*

*Siface re di Numidia* (rev. of D. David: *La forza della virtù*), Feo, Naples, S Bartolomeo, 13 May 1723; also: Porpora, Milan, 1725; G. Sellitto and others, Naples, 1734; Hasse [with title Viriate], Venice, 1739; I. Fiorillo, Brunswick, 1752; D. Fischietti, Venice, 1761; Galuppi [as Viriate], Venice, 1762

*Didone abbandonata*, Sarro, Naples, S Bartolomeo, 1 Feb 1724 (text rev. Metastasio, 1751); also: Albinoni, Venice, 1725; Porpora, Reggio Emilia, 1725; Vinci, Rome, 1726; Lampugnani, Padua, 1739; Galuppi, Modena, 1741; Hasse, Hubertusburg, 1742; Jommelli, Rome, 1746; Traetta, Venice, 1757; Sarti, Copenhagen, 1762; Schwanenberger, Brunswick, 1765; G. di Majo, Venice, 1769; Piccinni, Rome, 1770; Insanguine, Naples, 1772; G. Colla, Turin, 1773; D. Mombelli, Crescentino, 1775; A. Sacchini, London, 1775; P. Anfossi, Venice, 1775; Schuster, Naples, 1776; B. Ottani, Forlì, 1779; G. Andreozzi, Pisa, 1785; G. Gazzaniga, Vicenza, 1787; G. Paisiello, Naples, 1794; F. Paer, Parma, 1817; Mercadante, Turin, 1823

*Siroe re di Persia*, Vinci, Venice, S Giovanni Grisostomo, Jan 1726;

also: Porpora, Rome, 1727; Sarro, Naples, 1727; Vivaldi [as pasticcio], Reggio Emilia, 1727; Handel, London, 1728; A. S. Fiorè, Turin, 1729; Hasse, Bologna, 1733; G. Scarlatti, Florence, 1742; Wagenseil, Vienna, 1748; Lampugnani, London, 1755; G. B. Borghi, Venice, 1771; Sarti, Turin, 1779

*Catone in Utica*, Vinci, Rome, Delle Dame, 19 Jan 1728 (text rev. Metastasio, 1729); also: Leo, Venice, 1729; Hasse, Turin, 1731; Vivaldi, Verona, 1737; Rinaldo da Capua, Lisbon, 1740; Graun, Berlin, 1744; Jommelli, Vienna, 1749; Ciampi, Venice, 1757; Gassmann, Venice, 1761; J. C. Bach, Naples, 1761; di Majo, Turin, 1762; Ottani, Naples, 1777; Andreozzi, Cremona, 1786; Paisiello, Naples, 1789; Winter, Venice, 1791

*Ezio*, Porpora, Venice, S Giovanni Grisostomo, aut. 1728; also: Auletta, Rome, 1728; Hasse, Naples, 1730; Handel, London, 1732; Jommelli, Bologna, 1741; Sarro, Naples, 1741; Lampugnani, Venice, 1743; G. Scarlatti, Lucca, 1744; Gluck, Prague, 1750; Graun, Berlin, 1755; Galuppi, Milan, 1757; Traetta, Rome, 1757; F. Alessandri, Verona, 1767; Bertoni, Venice, 1767; Sacchini, Naples, 1771; Gazzaniga, Venice, 1772; J. Mysliveček, Naples, 1775; Anfossi, Venice, 1778

*Semiramide* [*Semiramide riconosciuta*], Vinci, Rome, Delle Dame, 6 Feb 1729, and Porpora, Venice, S Giovanni Grisostomo, carn. 1729 (text rev. Metastasio, 1752/3); also: Lampugnani, Rome, 1740; Jommelli, Turin, 1741; Hasse, Venice, 1744; Gluck, Vienna, 1748; Galuppi, Milan, 1749; G. di Majo, Naples, 1751; Sarti, Copenhagen, 1762; Sacchini, Rome, 1763; Traetta, Venice, 1765; A. Bernasconi, Munich, 1765; Salieri, Munich, 1782; Meyerbeer, Turin, 1819

*Alessandro nell'Indie*, Vinci, Rome, Delle Dame, 26 Dec 1729 (text rev. Metastasio, 1753/4); also: Porpora [as Poro], Turin, 1731; Handel [as Poro], London, 1731; Hasse [as Cleofide], Dresden, 1731; F. Mancini, Naples, 1732; Sarro, Naples, 1736; Galuppi, Mantua, 1738; Gluck [as Poro], Turin, 1744; Wagenseil, Vienna, 1748; G. Scarlatti, Reggio Emilia, 1753; Araja, St Petersburg, 1755; Piccinni [1st version], Rome, 1758; Holzbauer, Milan, 1759; Scolari, Venice, 1759; Jommelli, Stuttgart, 1760; J. C. Bach, Naples, 1762; Traetta, Reggio Emilia, 1762; Sacchini, Venice, 1763; di Majo, Mannheim, 1766; Gatti, Mantua, 1768; Bertoni, Genoa, 1769; Anfossi, Rome, 1772; Paisiello, Modena, 1773; Piccinni [2nd version], Naples, 1774; Rust, Venice, 1775; Cimarosa, Rome, 1781; Cherubini, Mantua, 1784; F. Bianchi, Venice, 1785; Sarti, Palermo, 1787; Guglielmi, Naples, 1789

*Artaserse*, Vinci, Rome, Delle Dame, 4 Feb 1730, and Hasse, Venice, S Giovanni Grisostomo, Feb 1730; also: Lampugnani, Milan, 1738; Gluck, Milan, 1741; Graun, Berlin, 1743; G. Scarlatti, Lucca, 1747; Jommelli, Rome, 1749; Galuppi, Vienna, 1749; Pampani, Venice, 1750; J. C. Bach, Turin, 1761; di Majo, Venice, 1762; Arne [as Artaxerxes], London, 1762; Piccinni, Rome, 1762; Fiorillo, Kassel, 1765; Sacchini, Rome, 1768; Paisiello, Modena, 1771; T. Giordani, London, 1772; Mysliveček, Naples, 1774; Bertoni, Forlì, 1776; Caruso, Florence, 1780; Cimarosa, Turin, 1784; A. Tarchi, Mantua, 1788; Anfossi, Rome, 1788; Zingarelli, Trieste, 1789; Andreozzi, Livorno, 1789

*Demetrio*, A. Caldara, Vienna, name day of Emperor Charles VI, 4 Nov 1731; also: Hasse, Venice, 1732; A. Giai, Rome, 1732; Leo, Naples, 1732; Leo and others (pasticcio), Naples, 1738; Gluck [as Cleonice], Venice, 1742; Wagenseil, Florence, 1746; Galuppi, Vienna, 1748; G. Scarlatti, Padua, 1752; Jommelli, Mannheim, 1753; N. Sala, Naples, 1762; Paisiello, Modena, 1765; Piccinni, Naples, 1769; Bernasconi, Munich, 1772; Guglielmi, London, 1772; Mysliveček, Pavia, 1773; F. Bianchi, Venice, 1780; Mayr, Turin, 1824

*Issipile*, F. Conti, Vienna, 7 Feb 1732; also: G. Porta, Venice, 1732; Galuppi, Turin, 1738; Gluck, Prague, 1752; Holzbauer, Mannheim, 1754; P. Errichelli, Naples, 1754; Gassmann, Venice, 1758; G. Scarlatti, Vienna, 1760; Anfossi, London, 1784

*Adriano in Siria*, Caldara, Vienna, name day of the emperor, 9 Nov 1732 (text rev. Metastasio, 1752/3); also: Pergolesi, Naples, 1734; Veracini, London, 1735; Duni, Rome, 1736; Giai, Venice, 1740; Lampugnani, Vicenza, 1740; Galuppi, Turin, 1740; Graun, Berlin, 1745; A. G. Pampani, Milan, 1751; G. Scarlatti, Venice, 1752; Hasse, Dresden, 1752; Rinaldo da Capua, Rome, 1758; Colla, Milan, 1763; J. C. Bach, London, 1765; Guglielmi, Venice, 1766; Holzbauer, Mannheim, 1768; di Majo, Rome, 1769; Sacchini, Venice, 1771; Insanguine, Naples, 1773; Mysliveček, Florence, 1776; Anfossi, Padua, 1777; Sarti, Rome, 1778; Alessandri, Venice, 1778; Cherubini, Livorno, 1782; S. Nasolini, Milan, 1789; Mayr, Venice, 1798

*Olimpiade*, Caldara, Vienna, birthday of the empress, 30 Aug 1733; also: Vivaldi, Milan, 1734; Pergolesi, Rome, 1735; Leo, Naples, 1737; Galuppi, Milan, 1747; Wagenseil, Vienna, 1749; Lampugnani, Florence, 1748; Logroscino, Rome, 1753; Hasse, Dresden, 1756; Traetta, Verona, 1758; Jommelli, Stuttgart, 1761; Guglielmi, Naples, 1763; Bernasconi, Munich, 1764; Gassmann, Vienna, 1764; Bertoni, Venice, 1765; Arne, London, 1765; Piccinni, Rome, 1768; P. Cafaro, Naples, 1769; Piccinni [2nd version], Naples, 1774; Anfossi, Venice, 1774; Gatti, Salzburg, 1775; Mysliveček,

Naples, 1778; Bianchi, Milan, 1781; Sarti, Rome, 1783; Cimarosa, Vicenza, 1784; Borghi, Florence, 1785; Paisiello, Naples, 1786; Tarchi, Rome, 1792

*Demofoonte*, Caldara, Vienna, name day of the emperor, 4 Nov 1733; also: Leo, Sarro and Mancini, Naples, 1735; Gluck, Milan, 1742; Jommelli [1st version], Padua, 1743; Graun, Berlin, 1746; Hasse, Dresden, 1748; Galuppi, Madrid, 1749; Traetta, Mantua, 1758; Piccinni, Reggio Emilia, 1761; di Majo, Rome, 1764; Guglielmi, Treviso, 1766; Mysliveček, Venice, 1769; Jommelli [2nd version], Naples, 1770; Anfossi, Rome, 1773; Paisiello, Venice, 1775; Alessandri, Padua, 1783; Prati, Venice, 1786; Gatti, Salzburg, 1787; G. Pugnani, Turin, 1787

*La clemenza di Tito*, Caldara, Vienna, name day of the emperor, 4 Nov 1734; also: Leo, Venice, 1735; Hasse [as Tito Vespasiano], Pesaro, 1735; Veracini, London, 1737; Wagenseil, Vienna, 1746; Pampani, Venice, 1748; Gluck, Naples, 1752; Jommelli, Stuttgart, 1753; G. Scarlatti, Venice, 1757; Holzbauer, Mannheim, 1757; Galuppi, Turin, 1760; Bernasconi, Munich, 1768; Naumann, Dresden, 1769; Sarti, Padua, 1771; Mozart, Prague, 1791; Ottani, Turin, 1798

*Achille in Sciro*, Caldara, Vienna, wedding of Archduchess Maria Theresia to Duke Francis of Lorraine, 13 Feb 1736; also: Sarro, Naples, 1737; Leo, Turin, 1740; Jommelli, Vienna, 1749; Hasse, Naples, 1759; J. F. Agricola, Berlin, 1765; Gassmann, Venice, 1766; P. P. Sales, Munich, 1774; Paisiello, St Petersburg, 1778; Sarti, Florence, 1779; Pugnani, Turin, 1785

*Ciro riconosciuto*, Caldara, Vienna, birthday of the empress, 28 Aug 1736; also: Rinaldo da Capua, Rome, 1737; Galuppi and others, Venice, 1737; Leo, Turin, 1739; Jommelli, Bologna, 1744; Duni, Genoa, 1748; Hasse, Dresden, 1751; Sarti, Copenhagen, 1754; Piccinni, Naples, 1759; Tarchi, Piacenza, 1796

*Temistocle*, Caldara, Vienna, name day of the emperor, 4 Nov 1736; also: G. A. Ristori, Naples, 1738; Porpora, London, 1743; Bernasconi, Venice, 1744; Jommelli, Naples, 1757

*Zenobia*, L. A. Predieri, Vienna, birthday of the empress, 28 Aug 1740; also: Porpora [as Tiridate], Naples, 1740; G. Latilla, Turin, 1742; Piccinni, Naples, 1756; Sala, Naples, 1761; G. B. Pescetti, Padua, 1761; Hasse, Warsaw, 1763

*Attilio Regolo* (1740), Hasse, Dresden, 12 Jan 1750; also: Jommelli, Rome, 1753

*Antigono*, Hasse, Hubertusburg, 10 Oct 1743; also: Galuppi and others, London, 1746; Wagenseil, Vienna, 1750; Sarti, Copenhagen, 1754; Gluck, Rome, 1756; Piccinni, Naples, 1762; Traetta, Padua, 1764; Guglielmi, Milan, 1767; di Majo, Venice, 1767; Sales, Munich, 1769; Cafaro, Naples, 1770; Anfossi, Venice, 1773; Giordani, London, 1774; Latilla, Naples, 1775; Gazzaniga, Rome, 1779; Mysliveček, Rome, 1780; Gatti, Milan, 1781; Paisiello, Naples, 1785; Zingarelli, Mantua, 1786; Caruso, Rome, 1788

*Ipermestra*, Hasse, Vienna, private perf. at court, 8 Jan 1744; also: Gluck, Venice, 1744; Jommelli, Spoleto, 1751; Cafaro, Naples, 1751; Galuppi, Milan, 1758; Sarti, Rome, 1766; di Majo, Naples, 1768; Piccinni, Naples, 1772; V. Martín y Soler, Naples, 1780; S. Rispoli, Milan, 1785; Paisiello, Padua, 1791; Mercadante, Naples, 1825

*Il re pastore*, G. Bonno, Vienna, Schönbrunn, 27 Oct 1751; also: Sarti, Venice, 1753; Hasse, Dresden, 1755; Gluck, Vienna, 1756; Lampugnani, Milan, 1758; Galuppi, Milan, 1758; Piccinni, Florence, 1760; Jommelli, Ludwigsburg, 1764; Mozart, Salzburg, 1775

*L'eroe cinese*, Bonno, Vienna, Schönbrunn, 13 May 1752; also: Galuppi, Naples, 1753; Hasse, Hubertusburg, 1753; N. Conforto, Madrid, 1754; Sacchini, Munich, 1770; Colla, Genoa, 1771; Bertoni [as Narbale], Venice, 1774; Cimarosa, Naples, 1782

*La Nitteti*, Conforto, Madrid, Buen Retiro, 23 Sept 1756; also: Traetta, Reggio Emilia, 1757; Holzbauer, Turin, 1758; Hasse, Venice, 1758; Jommelli, Stuttgart, 1759; Sarti, Copenhagen, 1761; Mysliveček, Bologna, 1770; Anfossi, Naples, 1771; Sacchini, London, 1774; Paisiello, St Petersburg, 1777; Gatti, Mantua, 1779; Rispoli, Turin, 1783; Nasolini, Trieste, 1788; Bianchi, Milan, 1789; Bertoni, Venice, 1789

*Il trionfo di Clelia*, Hasse, Vienna, birth of child to Archduke Joseph and Archduchess Isabella, 27 April 1762; also: Gluck, Bologna, 1763; Mysliveček, Turin, 1767; Bertoni, Padua, 1769; J. K. Vanhal, Rome, 1770; Borghi, Naples, 1773; Jommelli, Lisbon, 1774; Tarchi, Turin, 1787; M. Portugal, Lisbon, 1803

*Romolo ed Ersilia*, Hasse, Innsbruck, wedding of Archduke Leopold to Princess Marie Luise of Spain, 6 Aug 1765; also: Mysliveček, Naples, 1773

*Ruggiero ovvero l'eroica gratitudine*, Hasse, Milan, wedding of Archduke Ferdinand to Princess Maria Beatrice d'Este, 15 Oct 1771

ORATORIOS

*Componimento sacro per la festività del SS Natale*, G. B. Costanzi, Rome, Cancelleria, 2 Jan 1728; also: A. Mazzoni, Bologna, 1735; P. Chiarini, Venice, 1744; Sales, Augsburg, 1756

*La passione di Gesù Cristo*, Caldara, Vienna, 1730; also: Sarro, Bologna, 1738; Jommelli, Rome, 1749; Naumann, Padua, 1767; Salieri, Vienna, 1776; Mysliveček, Bologna, 1777; Schuster,

Dresden, 1778; Paisiello, St Petersburg, 1783; F. Morlacchi, Dresden, 18Î1

*Sant'Elena al Calvario*, Caldara, Vienna, 1731; also: Leo, Bologna, 1734; Hasse, Dresden, 1746; Naumann, Dresden, 1775; A. Tozzi, Madrid, 1790; Sales, Koblenz, 1791

*La morte d'Abel* [*Abele*], G. Reutter, Vienna, 1732; also: Leo, Bologna, 1738; Arne [as The Death of Abel], Dublin, 1744; Piccinni, Naples, 1758; Costanzi, Rome, 1758; Naumann, Dresden, 1790; Morlacchi, Dresden, 1821

*Giuseppe riconosciuto*, G. Porsile, Vienna, 1733; also: D. Terradellas, Naples, 1736; Hasse, Dresden, 1741; A. Accorimboni, Rome, 1757; L. Boccherini, Lucca, 1765; Bonno, Vienna, 1774; Anfossi, Rome, 1776; J. von Pasterwitz, Kremsmünster, 1777; Prati, St Petersburg, 1783

*Betulia liberata*, Reutter, Vienna, 8 April 1734; also: Jommelli, Venice, 1743; Bernasconi, Munich, 1754; Holzbauer, Mannheim, 1760; G. Calegari, Padua, 1771; Mozart, completed 1771; Gassmann, Vienna, 1772; Sala, Naples, 1780; Sales, Ehrenbreitstein, 1783; Schuster, Dresden, 1796

*Gioas re di Giuda*, Reutter, Vienna, 1735; also: Costanzi, Rome, 1748; J. Ritschel, Mannheim, 1763; Boccherini, Lucca, 1765; J. C. Bach, London, 1770; Schuster, Dresden, 1803

*Isacco figura del Redentore*, Predieri, Vienna, 12 Feb 1740; also: Jommelli, Rome, 1750; Holzbauer, Mannheim, 1757; Bonno, Vienna, 1759; K. D. von Dittersdorf, Grosswardein, 1766; Naumann, Dresden, 1772; Morlacchi, Dresden, 1817

FESTE TEATRALI, COMPONIMENTI, SERENATE

*Angelica* (serenata, 2), Porpora, Naples, 1 Oct 1720; also: J. de Sousa Carvalho, Lisbon-Queluz, 1778

*Endimione* (azione teatrale, 2), Sarro, Naples, 30 May 1721; also: D. Alberti, Vienna, 1737; Bernasconi, Venice, 1742; Jommelli, Genoa, 1756; Fiorillo [as Diana ed Endimione], Kassel, 1763

*Gli orti esperidi* (azione teatrale, 2), Porpora, Naples, Royal Palace, 28 Aug 1721; also: Conforto, Naples, 1751, according to Apollonio; L. X. dos Santos, Lisbon-Queluz, 1764; G. F. Lima, Lisbon, 1779

*La Galatea* (azione teatrale, 2), Naples, Palace of Duke of Monteleone, 1722; also: Alberti, Vienna, 1738; F. A. Uttini, Stockholm, 1754; Schwanenberger, Brunswick, 1763

*La contesa dei numi* (festa teatrale, 2), Vinci, Rome, Palace of Cardinal Polignac, birth of the dauphin, 26 Nov 1729; also: Gluck, Copenhagen, 1749

*Enea negli Elisi ovvero Il tempio dell'eternità* (festa teatrale, 1), Fux, Vienna, birthday of the empress, 28 Aug 1731; also: G. Liverati, Vienna, 1810

*L'asilo d'amore* (festa teatrale, 1), Caldara, Linz, birthday of the empress, 28 Aug 1732, as Il trionfo dell'onore, Vienna, 1765; also: Pescetti, London, 1738; Hasse, Naples, 1742; Jommelli, Stuttgart, 1758; Gassmann [as Il trionfo dell'onore], Vienna, 1765

*Le cinesi* (azione teatrale, 1), Caldara, Vienna, carn. 1735 (text rev. Metastasio, 1751); also: Conforto, Aranjuez, 1751; Gluck, Schlosshof, 1754; Sales, Augsburg, 1757; G. Astaritta, Florence, 1773

*Le grazie vendicate* (azione teatrale, 1), Caldara, Vienna, birthday of the empress, 28 Aug 1735

*Il Palladio conservato* (azione teatrale, 1), Reutter, Vienna, birthday of the emperor, 1 Oct 1735; also: dos Santos, Lisbon-Queluz, 1771

*Il sogno di Scipione* (azione teatrale, 1), Predieri, Vienna, ?6 Oct 1743; also: C. Nichelmann, Berlin, 1746; Bonno, Vienna, 1763, ? unperf.; Uttini, Stockholm, 1764; Mozart, Salzburg, 1772

*Il Parnaso accusato e difeso* (componimento drammatico, 1), Reutter, Vienna, birthday of the empress, 28 Aug 1738; also: Schwanenberger, Brunswick, 1768

*La pace fra la virtù e la bellezza* (azione teatrale, 1), Predieri, 1738, unperf.; also: Galuppi, St Petersburg, 1766; D. Perez, Lisbon, 1777

*Astrea placata ovvero La felicità della terra* (componimento drammatico, 1), Predieri, Vienna, birthday of the empress, 28 Aug 1739, ? unperf.; also: J. G. Schürer, Dresden, 1746; Sarti, Copenhagen, 1760

*Il natal di Giove* (azione teatrale, 1), Bonno, Vienna, birthday of the emperor, 1 Oct 1740; also: Hasse, Hubertusburg, 1749

*L'amor prigioniero* (componimento drammatico, 1), Reutter, Vienna, aut. 1741; also: Araja, Oranienbaum, 1755

*Il vero omaggio* (drammatico componimento, 1), Bonno, Vienna, Schönbrunn, birthday of Archduke Joseph, 13 March 1743

*La danza* (cantata a 2vv, 1), Bonno, Vienna, 1744; also: Gluck, Laxenburg, 1755; F. H. Himmel, Berlin, 1792

*L'augurio di felicità* (cantata a 3vv, 1), Reutter, Vienna, Schönbrunn, 28 Aug 1749

*La rispettosa tenerezza* (componimento drammatico, 1), Reutter, Vienna, Schönbrunn, 15 Oct 1750

*L'isola disabitata* (azione teatrale, 1), Bonno, Madrid, 31 May 1753; also: Holzbauer, ?Schwetzingen, 1754; Uttini, Stockholm, 1755; Sales, Augsburg, 1758; Jommelli, Ludwigsburg, 1761; Perez, Lisbon, 1767; Traetta, Bologna, 1768; Calegari, Padua, 1770;

Naumann, Venice, 1773; Astaritta, Florence, 1773; Haydn, Eszterháza, 1779

*Il Ciclope* (cantata a 2vv, 1), Vienna, April 1754

*Tributo di rispetto e d'amore* (componimento drammatico, 1), Reutter, Vienna, birthday of Emperor Franz I, 8 Dec 1754

*La gara* (componimento drammatico, 1), Reutter, Vienna, birth of Archduchess Maria Antonia, 18 Dec 1755

*Il sogno* (componimento drammatico, 1), Reutter, Vienna, carn. 1756

*La ritrosia disarmata* (componimento drammatico, 1), sent by Metastasio to Spain, 1756

*L'ape* (componimento drammatico, 1), sent by Metastasio to Spain, 1756

*Complimento per il giorno onomastico dell'imperatore d'Austria* (1), Hasse, Vienna, 13 May 1760

*Il quadro animato* (cantata a 2vv, 1), Wagenseil, Goldegg, 18 Aug 1760

*Alcide al bivio* (festa teatrale, 1), Hasse, Vienna, marriage of Archduke Joseph to Princess Isabella of Bourbon, 7 Oct 1760; also: Conforto, Madrid, 1765; Paisiello, St Petersburg, 1780; V. Righini, Mainz, 1790

*Complimento per il giorno onomastico dell'imperatrice d'Austria* (1), Hasse, Vienna, 8 Dec 1760

*L'Atenaide ovvero Gli affetti generosi* (azione teatrale, 2), Bonno, 1762, unperf.

*Egeria* (festa teatrale, 1), Hasse, Vienna, coronation of Archduke Joseph as King of the Romans, 24 April 1764

*Il Parnaso confuso* (festa teatrale, 1), Gluck, Vienna, Schönbrunn, marriage of Archduke Joseph to Princess Maria Josepha of Bavaria, 24 Jan 1765

*La corona* (azione teatrale, 1), Gluck, 1765, unperf.

*La pace fra le tre dee* (festa teatrale, 1), ?Conforto, ?Madrid, marriage of Carlos of Bourbon to Luisa, Princess of Parma, 1765

*Partenope* (festa teatrale, 2), Hasse, betrothal of King Ferdinand IV of Naples to Archduchess Maria Josepha, 9 Sept 1767; also: Martín y Soler, Naples, 1782

OTHER WORKS

Various Strofe per musica da cantarsi a canone, incl. 36 vocal canons set by Metastasio (Vienna, 1782)

Groups of canzonette: La libertà a Nice, 1733; Palinodia a Nice, 1746; La partenza, 1749: all set by Metastasio

34 poems of cantata type: settings of individual poems by Hasse, G. D. Apell, Wagenseil and others; 12 set by Porpora (London, 1735)

Works not intended for musical setting: Giustino (tragedia), 1712; various canzonette, terzine, epitalamii, idillii, stanze, sonetti, etc; prose writings and letters

DOUBTFUL WORK

*Dorina e Nibbio* (intermezzi, 2), Sarro, perf. with Didone abbandonata, Naples, S Bartolomeo, 1 Feb 1724; also: Albinoni [as L'impresario delle Canarie], Venice, 1725; Leo [as L'impresario delle isole Canarie], Venice, 1742

BIBLIOGRAPHY

R. da Calzabigi: 'Dissertazione su le poesie drammatiche del Signor Abate Pietro Metastasio', *Poesie del Signor Abate Pietro Metastasio*, i (Paris, 1755)

C. Cristini: 'Vita dell'Abate Pietro Metastasio', *Opere di Pietro Metastasio*, i (Nice, 1785)

S. Mattei: *Memorie per servire alla vita di Metastasio* (Colle, 1785)

C. Burney: *Memoirs of the Life and Writings of the Abate Metastasio* (London, 1796/R1971)

F. de Sanctis: 'Pietro Metastasio', *Nuova antologia*, xvi (1871), 807; also in Storia della letteratura italiana (Naples, 1872) and many subsequent edns.

J. M. Baroni: 'La lirica musicale di Pietro Metastasio', *RMI*, xii (1905), 383

A. Wotquenne: *Alphabetisches Verzeichnis der Stücke in Versen aus den dramatischen Werken von Zeno, Metastasio, und Goldoni* (Leipzig, 1905)

M. Callegari: 'Il melodramma e Pietro Metastasio', *RMI*, xxvi (1919), 518; xxvii (1920), 31, 458

L. Russo: *Pietro Metastasio* (Pisa, 1915, rev. 2/1921–45 as *Metastasio*)

A. della Corte: *L'estetica musicale di Pietro Metastasio* (Turin, 1922) [pt.ii of bk incl. *Paisiello: con una tavola tematica*]

R. Giazotto: *Poesia melodrammatica e pensiero critico nel settecento* (Milan, 1952)

B. Brunelli, ed.: *Tutte le opere di Pietro Metastasio* (Milan, 1943–54) [incl. bibliography of writings on Metastasio, vol.v, and fuller list of his writings]

H. Kunz: 'Höfisches Theater in Wien zur Zeit der Maria Theresia', *Jb der Gesellschaft für Wiener Theaterforschung 1953–4* (1958), 3

M. Apollonio and others: 'Metastasio, Pietro', *ES* [incl. fuller list of writings]

A. A. Abert: 'Metastasio, Pietro', *MGG*

W. Binni: *L'Arcadia e Metastasio* (Florence, 1963)

——: 'Pietro Metastasio', *Storia della letteratura italiana*, vi (Milan, 1968), 461

F. Gavazzeni: Introduction to *Opere scelte di Pietro Metastasio* (Turin, 1968) [bibliography of writings on Metastasio, 67ff]

K. Hortschansky: Introduction to J. A. Hasse: *Ruggiero ovvero L'eroica gratitudine*, Concentus musicus, i (Cologne, 1973), p. ix

E. Paratore: 'L' "Andromaque" del Racine e la "Didone abbandonata" del Metastasio', *Scritti in onore di Luigi Ronga* (Milan and Naples, 1973), 515–48

D. Heartz: 'Hasse, Galuppi and Metastasio', *Venezia e il melodramma nel settecento: Venezia 1975*

R. Monelle: 'The Rehabilitation of Metastasio', *ML*, lvii (1976), 268

H. E. Smither: *A History of the Oratorio*, i: *The Oratorio in the Baroque Era: Italy, Vienna, Paris* (Chapel Hill, 1977)

MICHAEL F. ROBINSON

**Methodius** [Methodios] (*b* Sicily; *d* 846). Greek patriarch of Constantinople, saint and composer of Byzantine chants; *see* BYZANTINE RITE, MUSIC OF THE, §10.

**Methven Simpson.** Scottish firm of music publishers established in Dundee in 1851 by William Methven (*d* 1886) and Alexander Simpson. In 1887 they took over the Edinburgh firm founded by ROBERT PURDIE and continued by his son John.

**Metner** [Medtner], **Nikolay Karlovich** (*b* Moscow, 5 Jan 1880; *d* London, 13 Nov 1951). Russian composer and pianist. Both his parents were of German descent, though their families had lived in Russia for several generations. Metner received his earliest piano lessons from his mother and also studied as a child with his uncle, F. K. Gedike. At the age of 12 he entered the junior classes of the Moscow Conservatory, where he was a pupil of Galli and Pabst. When Pabst died in 1897 Metner continued his studies first with Sapelnikov and then, for his last three years at the conservatory, with the brilliant pianist and teacher, Safonov. He also studied under Arensky and, outside of the conservatory, with Taneyev, but as a composer he was to a large degree self-taught. Metner left the conservatory in 1900 with a gold medal for piano playing but soon decided, with Taneyev's encouragement, to devote himself mainly to composition. He nevertheless continued to play a good deal in public, and achieved recognition among connoisseurs as one of the finest pianists of his generation. He returned to the Moscow Conservatory to teach the piano in 1909, but the pressure of other work forced him to resign his appointment after only a year. In 1910 Koussevitzky invited him to join the advisory panel of the newly formed Edition Russe and shortly afterwards the writer Marietta Shaginian introduced him to Rakhmaninov, with whom he was later on very close terms.

Metner resumed his teaching at the conservatory in 1914, but in 1921 he felt it necessary to follow Rakhmaninov and other compatriots into exile and, apart from a single concert tour in 1927, he did not see Russia again. With his wife, Anna (née Bratenshi), whom he had married in 1919 and who had previously been the wife of his brother, Emil, he went first to Germany and then, after a period of travel in Europe and the USA, settled near Paris in 1925. Despite the presence there of an important Russian community, Metner found himself largely out of sympathy with Parisian musical life, and he expressed his misgivings about modern trends in composition in a book, *Muza i moda* ('The muse and fashion'), which Rakhmaninov published in Paris in 1935. As might be expected, his own musical works were largely neglected there, though they found wide acclaim in other European capitals and also in the USA and Canada, which he toured in 1929–

30. English critics and audiences were at this time particularly receptive to his music; in 1928 the Royal Academy of Music made him an honorary member and he was also fêted by the Royal Philharmonic Society. He made many friends in England who finally persuaded him to leave Paris in winter 1935 and settle in Golders Green, London, where (except for a brief wartime period in Warwickshire) he remained until his death. Illness forced Metner to give up public concert work in 1944, but the formation two years later of a Medtner Society, with the financial support of the Maharajah of Mysore and the cooperation of the Gramophone Co., allowed him to make recordings of a substantial number of solo piano works, as well as the three concertos and several songs. Though he was by this time past his best as a pianist and already ill with thrombosis, these recordings bear eloquent testimony to his outstanding keyboard technique and are invaluable for their authoritative interpretations.

Apart from about 100 songs and a small quantity of chamber music, Metner's compositions are exclusively for the piano. This absorption with the piano places Metner in the long line of Romantic composer-pianists, but his own style of piano writing owed less to this tradition than to Schumann and Brahms. Schumann's influence is particularly evident in the early works, where it extends even to such external features as titles and notation. The textures of these early pieces (and of the early songs) are often rather overladen, but after about 1906 Metner's piano style became gradually more refined, while remaining always Romantically full-blooded and virtuoso. Darkly coloured harmonies in the lower part of the keyboard (often directed to be played *tenebroso*) lend a characteristic touch to an idiom that stems basically from the 19th-century German masters, but which also derives certain melodic and harmonic inflections from Russian folk music. Indeed the interaction of Metner's German blood with his Russian environment contributed in no small measure to his individual style. The two different traditions are more than usually distinct in the many settings of his two favourite poets, Goethe and Pushkin, settings which are among the finest songs of the 20th century.

Metner's music is most sharply distinguished from Rakhmaninov's, which it often superficially resembles, by a strong vein of classicism apparent in its tightly controlled structures and its contrapuntal textures. The ingenuity in combining different themes and constructing all kinds of effortless-sounding canons contributes immeasurably to the intellectual appeal of Metner's music, and his rhythmic inventiveness goes further than Rakhmaninov's (or for that matter Brahms's) in the direction of intricate cross-rhythms and syncopation. A progressive feature that has been overlooked is the degree of thematic integration achieved even in the longest of the sonatas and concertos. Nearly every one of the major works might have been written to satisfy analytical concern for the unity of contrasting themes; Metner's own interest in thematic unity resulted in some remarkably integrated single-movement structures (e.g. those of the First Piano Concerto and the Piano Sonata op.22). A similar integrity and sense of purpose informs the expressive content of the music seen as a whole, for all its variety of mood. Metner's dedication to what he considered the immutable laws of his art was such that for him composition amounted almost to a profession of faith, and despite its strong appeal to the emotions his music has a priestly quality to which not everyone can respond.

## WORKS

Published parallel titles in different languages are given in brackets after the principal title. The final roman numeral for each entry indicates the volume number in the collected edition, *N. Metner: Sobraniye sochineniy* (Moscow, 1959–63).

op.

### PIANO AND ORCHESTRA

—   Kontsertshtyuk, d, n.d., inc., unpubd
33   Piano Concerto no.1, c, 1914–18, x; also arr. 2 pf, ix
50   Piano Concerto no.2, c, 1920–27, xi; also arr. 2 pf, ix
60   Piano Concerto no.3, e, c1940–43, xii; also arr. 2 pf, ix

### PIANO

—   Adagio funèbre (cacofoniale), 1894–5
—   Muzïkal'nïy moment, 1896
—   Pastoral, C, 1896
—   Yumoreska, 1896
—   Shest' prelyudiy, 1896–7
1   8 Stimmungsbilder: Prolog – Andante cantabile, Allegro con impeto, Maestoso freddo, Andantino con moto, Andante, Allegro con humore, Allegro con ira, Allegro con grazia, 1896–7, i
2   3 Improvisations: Nixe, Eine Ball – Reminiscenz, Scherzo infernale, 1896–1900, i
4   4 morceaux: Etude, Caprice, Moment musical, Prélude, 1897–1902, i
5   Sonata, f, 1896–1903, rev. (1955), i
—   Impromptu alla mazurca, 1897
—   P'yesa, 1897
—   Sonata, f♯, 1897, inc.
—   Sonatina, 1898
—   Ekspromt, 1898
10   3 Dithyramben (3 dithyrambes), D, E♭, E, 1898–1906, i
—   Listok iz alboma, 1900
—   Sonata, b, n.d., unpubd
—   Marsh, n.d., unpubd
—   Postlyudiya, c, n.d., unpubd
—   Postlyudiya, b, n.d., unpubd
—   Façon de parler, n.d., unpubd
—   Moderato – con molto tenerezza, a, n.d. unpubd
7   3 Arabesken: Ein Idyll, Tragoedie-Fragment, a, Tragoedie-Fragment, g, ?1904, i
8   2 Märchen (2 Fairy Tales), c, c, 1905, i
9   3 Märchen (3 contes, 3 Fairy Tales), f, C, G, 1904–6, i
11   Sonaten-Triade, A♭, d, C, 1904–8, i
14   2 Märchen (2 Fairy Tales): f, Ritterzug (March of the Paladin), e, 1906–7, i
17   3 novellï (3 Novellen, 3 novelles): G, c, E, 1908, ii
20   2 skazki (2 Märchen, 2 contes, 2 Fairy Tales), b♭, b, 1909, ii
22   Sonata, g, ?1909–10, ii
—   2 cadenzas for Beethoven: Piano Concerto no.4, ?1910, ii
23   4 liricheskikh fragmenta (4 lyrische Fragmente, 4 fragments lyriques): c, a, f, c, ?1910–11, ii
25/1   Sonata-Skazka (Märchen-Sonate, Sonate-Conte), c, ?1910–11, ii
25/2   Sonata, e, 1911, ii
—   Etyud, c, ?1912, ii
26   4 skazki (4 Märchen, 4 contes, 4 Fairy Tales): E♭, E♭, f, f♯, ?1912, ii
27   Sonata-Ballada (Sonate-Ballade), F♯, ?1912–14, ii
30   Sonata, a, ?1914–15, ii
31   3 p'yesï (3 morceaux): Improvizatsiya (Improvisation), Traurnïy marsh (Marche funèbre), Skazka (Conte, Fairy Tale), ?1914–15, ii
—   Skazka (Conte, Fairy Tale), d, 1915, ii
34   4 skazki (4 Märchen, 4 Fairy Tales): Volshebnaya skripka, b, e, a, d, ?1916–17, iii
35   4 skazki (4 Märchen): C, G, a, c♯, ?1916–17, iii
38   Zabïtïye motivï (Vergessene Weisen, Forgotten Melodies), i: Sonata reminiscenza, Danza graziosa, Danza festiva, Canzona fluviale, Danza rustica. Canzona serenata, Danza silvestra, alla Reminiscenza, ?1918–20, iii
39   Zabïtïye motivï (Vergessene Weisen, Tanzweisen, Forgotten Melodies), ii: Meditazione, Romanza, Primavera (Fruhlingsmärchen), Canzona matinata, Sonata tragica, ?1918–20, iii
40   Zabïtïye motivï (Vergessene Weisen, Forgotten Melodies), iii: Danza col canto, Danza sinfonica, Danza fiorita, Danza jubilosa, Danza ondulata, Danza ditirambica, ?1918–20, iii
42   3 skazki (3 Märchen, 3 Fairy Tales): Russkaya skazka (Russisches Märchen, Russian Fairy Tale), f, c, g♯, ?1921–3, iii
47   2ya improvizatsiya (2te Improvisation), 1926, iii
48   2 skazki (2 Märchen, 2 Fairy Tales): C, Skazka el'fov (Elfenmärchen) g, ?1926, iv
49   3 gimna trudu (3 Hymnen an die Arbeit, 3 Hymns in Praise of Toil): Gimn pered rabotoy (Hymne vor der Arbeit, Before Work), Gimn 'U nakoval'ni' (Hymne 'Am Amboss', At the Anvil), Gimn posle rabotï (Hymne nach der Arbeit, After Work), ?1926–7, iv
51   6 skazok (Märchen, Fairy Tales, Contes): d, a, A, f♯, f♯, G, ?1928, iv
53/1   Sonata romantica, b♭, ?1931–2, iv
53/2   Sonata minacciosa, f, ?1931–2, iv
54   Romantische Skizzen für die Jugend (Esquisses romantiques pour la jeunesse, Romantic Sketches for the Young): i, Prélude (Pastorale), Vögleins Märchen (Conte d'oiseaux, Bird's Tale); ii, Prèlude (Tempo di sarabanda), Märchen (Conte, Tale); iii, Prélude (Zarter Vorwurf, Tendre reproche, Tender Reproach), Märchen (Der Leierkastenmann) (Conte, Le joueur d'orgue de Barbarie; Tale, the Barrel-organ-player): iv, Prélude (Hymne), Märchen (Der Bettler) (Conte, Le mendiant; Tale, the Beggar), ?1932, iv
55   Tema s variatsiyami (Tema con variazioni), ?1933, iv
56   Sonate-Idylle, G, ?1937, iv
59   2 elegii (2 Elegien): a, e♭, ?1938, iv
—   Marsh, C, 2 pf, 1897
58/1   Russian Round Dance (A Tale), 2 pf, c1940, ix
58/2   Knight Errant, 2 pf, c1940, ix

### CHAMBER

—   Skazka, pf trio (1923) [from op.9, no.2]
16   3 Noktyurna: d, g, c, vn, pf, 1908, vii
21   Sonata no.1, b, vn, pf, 1909–10, vii
43   2 kantsonï t tantsami: C, b, 1924, vii
44   Sonata no.2, G, vn, pf, 1926, vii
57   Sonata no.3 'Epica', e, vn, pf, 1938, vii
posth.   Piano Quintet, C, 1904–49, viii

### SONGS

1a   Angel (Der Engel) (Lermontov), ?1908, v
3   3 romansa (3 Lieder): U vrat obiteli svyatoy (Vor einer heiligen Pforte stand) (Lermontov), Ya perezhil svoi zhelan'ya (Ich überlebte mein Verlangen) (Pushkin), Na ozere (Auf dem See) (Fet, after Goethe), 1903, v
6   9 Goethe-Lieder (9 pesen V. Gyote): Wandrers Nachtlied (Nochnaya pesn' strannika), Mailied (Mayskaya pesn'), Elfenliedchen (Pesenka el'fov), Im Vorübergehn (Mimokhodom), Aus 'Claudine von Villa-Bella' (Pesnya iz 'Klaudinï', Liebliches Kind), Aus 'Erwin und Elmire' I (Iz 'Ervina i El'mirï I, Himmlisch), Aus 'Erwin und Elmire' II (Iz 'Ervina i El'mirï II, Sieh mich, Heil'ger wie ich bin) Erster Verlust (Pervaya utrata), Gefunden (Epitalama), 1904–5, v
12   3 Gedichte von Heine: Lieb Liebchen (Day ruchku mne), Lyrisches Intermezzo (Sosna), Bergstimme (Gornïy golos), 1907–8, v
13   2 stikhotvoreniya (2 Gedichte): Zimnïy vecher (Winterabend) (Pushkin), Epitafiya (Das Epitaph) (Belïy), 1903–7, v
15   12 pesen Gyote (12 Goethe-Lieder): Wandrers Nachtlied I (Nochnaya pesn' strannika, Der du von dem Himmel bist), Aus 'Wilhelm Meister' (Iz Vil'gelma Meystera, An die Türen will ich), Selbstbetrug (Samoobman), Aus 'Erwin und Elmire' (Da, lyubit ona, Sie liebt mich), Aus 'Lila' (Iz Lilï, So tanzet), Vor Gericht (Pered sudom), Meeresstille (Tish' na more), Glückliche Fahrt (Schastlivoye plavaniye), Nähe des Geliebten (Blizost' milago), Der untreue Knabe (Nevernïy Yunosha), Gleich und Gleich (Drug dlya druga), Geistergruss (Privet dukha), 1907–8, v
18   6 Gedichte von W. Goethe (6 stikhotvoreniy V. Gyote): Die Spröde (Nedostupnaya), Die Bekehrte (Obrashchennaya), Einsamkeit (Odinochestvo), Mignon (Pesnya Min'yonï), Das Veilchen (Fialka), Jägers Abendlied (Vechernyaya pesn' okhotnika), 1908–9, v
19   3 Gedichte von Nietzsche: Gruss (Privet rodine), Alt Mütterlein (Starushka), Heimweh (Toska po otchizne), ?1910
19a   2 Gedichte von Nietzsche: Heimkehr (Vozvrashcheniye na rodin), Verzweiflung (Otchayaniye), ?1910
24   8 stikhotvoreniy (8 poèmes, 8 Poems) (Tyuchev, Fet): Den' i noch' (Day and Night), Chto tï klonish' nad vodami (Willow, why for ever bending?), Duma za dumoy, volna za volnoy (Sea-swell and Memories), Sumerki (Twilight), Ya potryasen kogda krugom (O'er thee I bend), Tol'ko vstrechu ulïbku tvoyu (When my glances thy smile chance to meet), Shopot, robkoye dïkhanye (Whisp'ring, Nature faintly stirring), Ya prishel k tebe s privetom (Greeting), 1911, v
28   7 stihotvoreniy (7 Gedichte): Nezhdannïy dozhd (Der ungeahnte Regen) (Fet), Ne mogu ya slïshat etoy ptichki (Jedes Mal hör' ich dies Vöglein singen) (Fet), Babochka (Der Schmetterling) (Fet), Tyazhela, bestsvetna i pusta (Auf dem Kirchhof, da es) (Bryusov), Vesennee uspokoyeniye (Der Frühlingsberuhigung) (Tyutchev, after Uhland), Sizhu zadumchiv i odin (Ich sitz' so einsam am Kamin) (Tyutchev), Poshli,

gospod', svoyu otradu (Gott, sende jedem seine Labe) (Tyutchev), 1913–14, v

29    7 stikhotvoreniy Pushkina (7 poèmes de Pouchkine): Muza (The Muse, La muse), Pevets (The Singer, Le chanteur), Stikhi, sochinennïye noch'yu vo vremya bezsonnitsï (Lines written during a sleepless night, Vers composés par une nuit d'insomnie), Kon' (The Horse, Le cheval), Elegiya: Ya perezhil svoi zhelan'ya (Gone are my heart's desires, J'ai survécu à tous mes rêves), Roza (The Rose, La rose), Zaklinani'e (The Call, Evocation), 1913, v

32    6 stikhotvoreniy Pushkina (6 poésies de Pouchkine): Ekho (Echo, Echo), Vospominanïye (Ressouvenir, Remembrance), Pokhoronnaya pesnya (Chant funéraire, Funeral Song), Ya vas lyubil (Je vous aimais, I loved thee well), Mogu l' zabït to sladkoye mgnoven ye (Vals, The Waltz) (Delvig), Mechtatelyu (A un rêveur, To a Dreamer), 1915, vi

36    6 stikhotvoreniy A. Pushkina (6 Gedichte von A. Puschkin): Angel (Der Engel), Tsvetok (Die Blume), Lish' rozï uvyadayut (Kaum welken hier die Rosen), Ispanskiy romans (Spanische Romanze), Noch' (Nachts), Arion (Arion), 1918, vi

37    5 stikhotvoreniy Tyutcheva i Feta (5 Gedichte von Tjutschew und Foeth): Bezsonnitsa (Schlaflosigkeit), Slyozï (Tränen), Impromptu, Val's (Walzer), O chem tï voyesh' vetr nochnoy? (Was heulst du, Wind, um Mitternacht?), 1918, vi

41/1  Sonate-Vocalise mit einem Motto 'Geweihter Platz' (Goethe), ?1922–3, vi

41/2  Suite-Vocalise, ?1926, vi

45    4 pesni (4 Lieder): Elegiya (Elegie) (Pushkin), Telega zhizni (Der Karren des Lebens) (Pushkin), Pesn' nochi (Das Nachtlied) (Tyutchev), Nash vek (Unsere Zeit) (Tyutchev), 1923–4, vi

46    7 Lieder (7 Songs): Praeludium (Goethe), Geweihter Platz (The Sacred Grove) (Goethe), Serenade (Eichendorff), Im Walde (In the Forest) (Eichendorff), Winternacht (Winter Night) (Eichendorff), Die Quelle (The Fountain) (Chamisso), Frisch gesungen (Gaily Singing) (Chamisso), 1925–6, vi

52    7 pesen na stikhotvoreniya A. Pushkina (7 Lieder nach Dichtungen von A. Puschkin): Okno (Das Fenster), Voron (Der Rabe), Elegiya (Elegie), Primetï (Zeichnen), Ispanskiy romans (Spanische Romanze), Serenada, Uznik (Der Gefangene), 1929–30, vi

59/1  Polden' (Midday) (Tyutchev), 1946, vi

61    7 hinterlassene Lieder (7 pesen): Reiselied (Pesn' strannika, Traveller's Song) (Eichendorff), Nachtgruss (Nochnoy privet, Night's Revelation) (Eichendorff), Chto v imeni tebe moyom? (Was fragst du nach dem Namen mich?, What means to thee my humble name?) (Pushkin), Esli zhizn' tebya obmanet (Wenn du eines Tags enttäuscht bist, If one day you're disillusioned) (Pushkin), Molitva (Gebet, The Prayer) (Lermontov), O, veshchaya dusha moya (Sei stille, mein verzagtes Herz, Behold my visionary soul) (Tyutchev), Kogda, chto zvali mï svoim (Unwiederbringlich ist dahin, We lost all that was once our own) (Tyutchev), ?1940–50, vi

Principal publishers: Editions russes, Jurgenson, Novello, Zimmermann

### WRITINGS

Muza i moda [The muse and fashion] (Paris, 1935; Eng. trans., 1951)
ed. M. Gurvich and L. Lukomsky: *Povsednevnaya rabota pianista i kompozitora: stranitsï iz zapisnïkh knizhok* (Moscow, 1963)
ed. Z. A. Apetian: *N. K. Metner: pis'ma* [Letters] (Moscow, 1973)

### BIBLIOGRAPHY

G. Prokof'yev: 'O Metnere', *RMG*, iii (1913), 65
M. Montagu-Nathan: 'The Violin Music of Nicholas Medtner', *The Strad*, xxv (1915), 356
E. Newman: 'Medtner', *MT*, lvi (1915), 9
H. S. Gerstlé: 'The Piano Music of Nicolai Medtner', *MQ*, x (1924), 500
L. Sabaneyev: 'Two Critiques: II Medtner', *ML*, viii (1927), 328
A. J. Swan: 'Medtner and the Music of our Time', *ML*, viii (1927), 46
V. Yakovlev: *Nikolaj Medtner* (Moscow, 1927)
A. J. Swan: 'Nicholas Medtner', *The Chesterian*, x (1928), 77
W. Lyle: 'Medtner and his Music', *Sackbut*, xi (1931), 260
O. von Riesemann: *Rachmaninoff's Recollections* (New York, 1934)
S. Miller: 'Medtner's Piano Music', *MT*, lxxxii (1941), 361
R. Holt: *Medtner and his Music* (London, ?c1948)
A. Alexander: 'Nicolas Medtner', *Tempo* (1951–2), no.22
V. I. Seroff: *Rachmaninoff* (New York, 1951)
M. Boyd: 'Medtner Reconsidered', *MMR*, lxxxii (1952), 260
R. Holt, ed.: *Nicolas Medtner (1879–1951): a Tribute to his Art and Personality* (London, 1955)
B. Pinsonneault: *Nicolas Medtner: pianiste, compositeur 1879–1951* (Montreal, 1956)
G. Shneyerson: 'Novoye o Metnere', *SovM* (1956), no.7, p.139
H. Truscott: 'Nicolas Medtner', *The Chesterian*, xxxi (1956), 1
Z. Apetian, ed.: *Vospominaniya o Rakhmaninove* (Moscow, 1957, enlarged 4/1974)
J. Frank: 'Rachmaninov and Medtner: a Comparison', *MO*, lxxxi (1958), 387
P. Vasilyev: preface to *N. Metner: Sobraniye sochineniy* [Collected works], i (Moscow, 1959)
I. Zetel': 'N. K. Metner (materialï i zametki o zhizni i kontsertnoy deyatelnosti)', *Nauchnometodicheskiye zapiski Ural'skoy konservatorii*, ii (1959), 240
——: 'Iz perepiski N. Metnera i S. Rakhmaninova', *SovM* (1961), no.11, p.76
H. Truscott: 'Medtner's Sonata in G minor, op.22', *MR*, xxii (1961), 112
P. I. Vasil'yev: *Fortep'yannïye sonatï Metnera* (Moscow, 1962)
M. Boyd: 'The Songs of Nicolas Medtner', *ML*, xlvi (1965), 16
E. B. Dolinskaya: *Nikolay Metner: monograficheskiy ocherk* (Moscow, 1966)
T. Malikova: 'Original'nïye chertï u garmonii Metnera' [Original traits in Metner's harmony], *Teoreticheskiye problemï muzïki XX veka*, ed. I. N. Tyunlin (Moscow, 1967)
A. J. Swan: 'Das Leben Nikolai Medtners', *Musik des Ostens*, iv (1967), 65–116
O. Sokolov: 'Forma v tvorchestve Metnera' [Form in Metner's work], *Voprosï teorii muzïki*, ed. S. Skrebkov (Moscow, 1968)
A. Alexeyev: *Russkaya fortepiannaya muzïka: konets XIX – nachalo XX veka* (Moscow, 1969)
B. H. Loftis: *The Piano Sonatas of Nicolai Medtner* (diss., U. of West Virginia, 1970)
I. Zetel': *Nikolay Metner* (diss., Moscow Conservatory, 1970)
C. W. Keller: *The Piano Sonatas of Nicolas Medtner* (diss., Ohio State U., 1971)
Yu. Tyulin, A. Swan and P. Vasil'yev: 'Iz vospominaniy o N. K. Metnera', *SovM* (1972), no.7, p.112
C. C. Elmore: *Some Stylistic Considerations in the Piano Sonatas of Nikolai Medtner* (diss., U. of North Carolina, 1972)
E. Hughes, B. Martyn and G. Stonehill: 'Medtner Recordings', *Recorded Sound* (1978), nos.70–71, p.794
E. Iles: 'Medtner, Friend and Master', *Recorded Sound* (1978), nos.70–71, 791
M. Boyd: 'Metner and the Muse', *MT*, cxxi (1980), 22
H. Milne: 'Nicholas Medtner: a Centenary Appraisal', *Music and Musicians*, xxviii/5 (1980), 20

MALCOLM BOYD

**Métra, (Jules Louis) Olivier** (*b* Le Mans, 2 June 1830; *d* Paris, 22 Oct 1889). French composer. He was the son of an actor and appeared in his father's touring company as a child. At the age of 11 he joined the company of the Théâtre Comte in Paris, where he received his initial musical training from Edmond Roche. He played the violin, the cello and the double bass in various theatre orchestras. In January 1849 he entered Elwart's harmony class at the Conservatoire (gaining first prize in harmony in 1854) and he also attended the composition classes of Ambroise Thomas. He became conductor at the Théâtre Beaumarchais and at various dance halls and music halls, including the Athénée Musical and the Elysée-Montmartre. His waltzes, quadrilles, polkas and other dance music enjoyed considerable vogue and established him in the line of leading French dance composers represented by Musard, Isaac Strauss and, later, Waldteufel. From 1871 he conducted the masked balls at the Opéra-Comique, in 1874 and 1876 the balls at the Théâtre de la Monnaie in Brussels, and then those at the Paris Opéra, where his Japanese ballet *Yedda* was given in 1879. From 1872 to 1877 he was conductor at the Folies-Bergère, for which he composed a number of operettas and ballets. One of these ballets, *Les volontaires*, contains the *Marche des volontaires*, which became one of his most popular compositions. During the last years of his life he worked little, but was always ready to perform for charity. His last work was an operetta, *Le mariage avant la lettre*, for the Bouffes-Parisiens (1888). He died a week after suffering a stroke. His music has not enjoyed great posthumous currency, but he and his most celebrated waltz, *Les roses*, are featured in Hahn's operetta *Ciboulette*.

WORKS

Selective list; unless otherwise indicated, all first perf., and published (mostly pf/vocal score) at same time, in Paris.

OPERETTAS

Le valet de chambre de Madame, 1872
Un soir d'orage, Folies-Bergère, 21 April 1874
La fée aux perles, 1880, ?unpubd
Le mariage avant la lettre, Bouffes-Parisiens, 5 Dec 1888, ?unpubd
A few others, apparently unpubd

BALLETS

Yedda (3, P. Gille, A. Mortier, L. Mérante), Opéra, 17 January 1879
Several ballet-divertissements, mostly Folies-Bergère, 1872–7

DANCE MUSIC

Many waltzes, orch 1856–89, incl. Le tour du monde; Les roses; La vague; La sérénade, valse espagnole; Gambrinus; L'orient; Les faunes; over 100 others, many on themes from contemporary stage works
Les volontaires, polka-marche, several hundred other polkas, galops, quadrilles, etc, often on themes from contemporary stage works

BIBLIOGRAPHY

FétisB
E. Nick: 'Métra, Jules-Louis-Olivier', MGG

ANDREW LAMB

**Metre.** The organization of the notes in a composition, or a section thereof, with respect to time, in such a way that a regular pulse made up of beats (*see* BEAT) can be perceived and the time span occupied by each note can be measured in terms of these beats; in addition, the beats are grouped into larger units called bars (*see* BAR), within which the number of beats is always the same. Metre is the means by which rhythm can be perceived and described. It is therefore analogous to the measurement of distance; this analogy becomes especially clear if one compares measurement by quarter-inches with so-called common time, in which there are four crotchets in a bar and each crotchet is given one beat (see fig.1). *See also* NOTE VALUES.

Fig.1

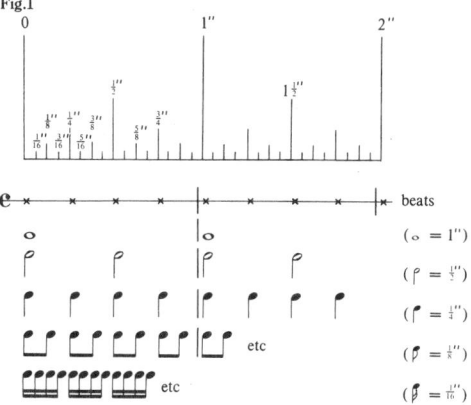

Metre is identified at the beginning of a composition, or at any point within the composition where it changes, by a TIME SIGNATURE, which is usually a fraction indicating the number of beats per bar (numerator) and the note value that is accorded one beat (denominator); thus a time signature of 3/8 means that there are three beats in each bar and that an 'eighth-note' (i.e. a quaver) is given one beat.

*See also* COMPOUND TIME.

**Metrical psalm.** See PSALMS, METRICAL, and PSALM.

**Metronome** (from Gk. *metron* 'a measure' and *nomos* 'a law'; Fr. *métronome*; Ger. *Metronom, Taktmesser*). An instrument for determining the pace of performance for a musical work. The earliest method of measuring small

intervals of time used the beat of the human pulse, but by the end of the 16th century Galileo had determined the laws of vibration of pendulums and realized the possibilities of some form of pendulum as a time-keeper. He established the so-called isochronism of the pendulum (i.e. that if the arc of swing is not too great, a pendulum of invariable length accomplishes equal swings in equal times until its motion is reduced to rest by friction with the air) and also the important law that the times of vibration of different simple pendulums are proportional to the square roots of their lengths. After his death his scheme for a pendulum time-marker was discovered among his papers.

The possibilities of the pendulum as a time-marker in music seem to have been envisaged first by Thomas Mace; in *Musick's Monument* (London, 1676) he suggested that one could keep time by means of a 'bullet or any round piece' attached to a thread. Etienne Loulié in *Elémens ou principes de musique, mis dans un nouvel ordre* (Paris, 1696) attempted to improve on this by giving instructions for shortening or lengthening the cord to produce different degrees of velocity, but his work did not attract much attention. During the next 50 years similar suggestions were made by, among others, the French physicist Joseph Sauveur and the Englishman Joseph Tans'ur, whose treatise *A New Musical Grammar* (1746) contains a section of 'the doctrine of pendulums applied to music'.

Gottfried Weber advocated carrying a simple pendulum with different tempos indicated by knots along the cord, the whole being small enough when coiled up to go into a pocket. When extended, however, such a pendulum was inconveniently long (one to beat seconds, for example, had to be over 100 cm) and inventors were led to consider some form of compound pendulum as an alternative.

While in a simple pendulum (to which Galileo's law applies) the mass of the system must be concentrated in the bob (the cord being without mass and exerting no constraint), a compound pendulum conforms to other principles. It commonly takes the form of a supported steel bar, near one end of which a sphere of metal is attached. The time of swing about one point along the bar depends on a number of factors, the principal one being the distance of the point of suspension from the system's centre of gravity. At the beginning of the 19th century Captain Kater performed his renowned experiments on such a pendulum, with two masses attached to the beam on opposite sides of the centre of gravity, one fixed and the other capable of being set along a range of positions by a fastening screw. Whether this was the inspiration for the form the metronome finally took is uncertain, but Kater's pendulum and the metronome of JOHANN NEPOMUK MAELZEL are remarkably similar in physical form though different in size.

On a visit to Amsterdam in 1815, Maelzel was struck by the ingenuity of Winkel's compound pendulum for musical time-marking. In Paris, he made a copy of the instrument he had seen, merely adding a scale of divisions, and patented the device under the name 'metronome' (see illustration). The following lawsuit finally gave the credit to Winkel, but Maelzel had already set up a factory and sold many instruments under his own name. (In fact, though the patent has long lapsed, the apparatus still bears Maelzel's name.)

The metronome (still manufactured in its original form) is a pendulum formed of a flat steel shaft about 18 cm long with a pivot that carries a fixed mass of lead about 4 cm from its lower end. The pivot and lead mass are inside the lower section of a pyramidal case that also contains the clockwork and escapement by which the pendulum, set in motion, is maintained against friction without its natural time of swing being interfered with, in the same fashion as a pendulum clock. The escapement also provides the tick by which one can count the pendulum beats. The adjustable weight (made of brass) is at the upper end and is equipped with a spring which grips the shaft and comes to rest on it at places determined by notches along its length. The number of beats per minute for each position (the range covered is from 40 to about 200) is indicated on the case behind the corresponding notch. Composers indicate the desired tempo by a symbol for a note value and then a figure indicating the number of such notes per minute; this is sometimes preceded by 'M.M.' (Maelzel's metronome). Beethoven was the first important composer to use Maelzel's metronome, but his markings are not reliable tempo indications as he frequently changed his mind about them and his publishers often misprinted or altered his instructions.

Modifications of the metronome have been patented from time to time. Electric ones, without a pendulum, are often equipped with a blinking light to operate simultaneously with, or instead of, the tick.

BIBLIOGRAPHY
J. T. Harrison: 'A New Metronome', *PMA*, xx (1893–4), 23

*Prototype of the modern metronome, made by Maelzel in 1815 (Gesellschaft der Musikfreunde, Vienna)*

Z. Drechsel: 'Geschichte des Taktmessers', *Zeitschrift für Instrumentenbau*, xlvi (1926), 948
E. Borrel: 'Les indications métronomiques laissées par les auteurs français du XVIIIe siècle', *RdM*, ix (1928), 149
R. E. M. Harding: 'The Metronome and its Precursors', *Origins of Musical Time and Expression* (London, 1938)
W. Georgi: 'Das Metronom als Freund', *Klavierspielerbüchlein* (Zurich and Freiburg, 1953)
F. Goebels: 'Vom sinnvollen Gebrauch des Metronoms', *Musik im Unterricht*, xlix (1958), 5
P. Stadlen: 'Beethoven and the Metronome – I', *ML*, xlviii (1967), 330
H. C. Wolff: 'Das Metronom des Louis-Léon Pajot 1735', *Festskrift Jens Peter Larsen* (Copenhagen, 1972), 205

E. G. RICHARDSON/R

**Metrophonia.** The method by which Byzantine musical neumes are read note-for-note without any additional vocal realization. *See* PARALLAGĒ and PHTHORA.

**Metropolitan College of Music.** London conservatory founded in 1889 and amalgamated with the London Academy of Music in 1904; *see* LONDON, §VII, 3.

**Metropolitan Conservatory.** New York conservatory established in 1886, renamed the Metropolitan College of Music in 1891 and the American Institute of Applied Music in 1900; *see* NEW YORK, §10.

**Metropolitan Opera House.** The most important New York opera house, opened in 1883; a new house opened in Lincoln Center in 1966. *See* NEW YORK, §2.

**Métru, Nicolas** (*b* Bar-sur-Aube, ?*c*1610; *d* after 1663). French composer, organist, teacher and music publisher. He was living in Paris by 1631, when he was referred to as a 'maître compositeur de musique'. In 1642 he was organist of St Nicolas-des-champs. He was highly thought of as a teacher, for in 1643 Gantez spoke of 'Vincent, Métru and Massé, the three most celebrated teachers in Paris'; he also stated that Métru was *maître de musique* to the Jesuits. A document of 1692 (*Mémoire des compositeurs*), corroborated by La Borde, states that, together with Roberday and Gigault, he was one of Lully's teachers. He also tried his hand at music publishing: on 21 June 1633 he obtained official permission 'to print, sell and distribute, through any printer or bookseller he may choose, every kind of music he has produced or may produce in the future'. To this end he took on a printer from Pierre Ballard, who at the time had a monopoly of music publishing and now used his influence in high places to suppress his rival. On 7 April 1635 he managed to get Métru's privilege withdrawn; however, a judgment of 3 July 1635 obliged him to print all of Métru's works from then on and 'to provide him with 100 copies' of each.

Métru's earliest known music, which appeared in 1628, just after the capture of La Rochelle, was composed to celebrate this event and was sung before Louis XIII. In 1632 he was well enough known for the author of *La Philomèle séraphique* to convert some of his *airs*, together with some by Guédron and other composers, into sacred songs. His two-part fantasies for viols are in a lively, rhythmic chanson style, with a strong sense of key. His books of *airs* (as far as can be judged) and his mass are notable for their precise word-setting and melodic grace.

WORKS

Recueil des vers du Sr. G. de Baïf, mis en musique par N. Métru, chantez en l'alégresse de l'heureux retour du roy, 4, 5vv (Paris, 1628) [Quinta pars pubd Fontainebleau]
Fantaisies, 2 viols (Paris, 1642)

Premier livre d'airs, ?4vv (Paris, ?1646), lost
Deuxième livre d'airs, 4, 5vv (Paris, 1646)
Troisième livre d'airs, 4vv (Paris, 1661)
Missa, 4vv, ad imitationem moduli Brevis oratio (Paris, 1663)
Contrafacta in 1632³

BIBLIOGRAPHY
A. Gantez: *L'entretien des musiciens* (Auxerre, 1643); ed. with commentary by E. Thoinan (Paris, 1878/*R*1971)
*Mémoire des compositeurs, clavecinistes et luthiers, lors du procès contre les ménestriers et joueurs d'instruments* (Paris, 1692)
J.-B. de La Borde: *Essai sur la musique ancienne et moderne* (Paris, 1780/*R*1972)
E. Socard: *Biographie des personnages de Troyes et du département de l'Aube* (Troyes, 1882)
D. Launay: 'La fantaisie en France jusqu'au milieu du XVIIème siècle', *La musique instrumentale de la Renaissance: CNRS Paris 1954*, 327
DENISE LAUNAY

**Metrum** (Lat.). The principal break, or mediation, in a simple Gregorian reciting tone; *see* INFLECTION, §(1).

**Mettenleiter.** German family of church musicians.

**(1) Johann Georg Mettenleiter** (*b* St Ulrich, Lohntal, Württemberg, 6 April 1812; *d* Regensburg, 6 Oct 1858). Intended by his father for the teaching profession, he went in 1824 to his uncle, choirmaster in Wallerstein, who instructed him in practical music, among other subjects. In 1837 he was appointed choirmaster of the parish church of Oettingen and two years later choirmaster and organist at Regensburg.

Mettenleiter's most extensive work is the *Enchiridion chorale, sive selectus locupletissimus cantionum liturgicarum* (Regensburg, 1853; org acc., 1854–69), along with the *Manuale breve cantionum ac precum liturgicarum* (Regensburg, 1852), adapted for student use. At the recommendation of the Regensburg bishop, Riedel, the *Enchiridion* came to be a foundation of the sacred music restoration movement, its harmonic practice becoming a model for Cecilian chant harmonizations. As a conductor, Mettenleiter performed early polyphonic works in services of the Alte Kapelle, carrying out the church music reform plans of Proske. Most of his own compositions, sacred choral works, remain in manuscript (*D-Rp*).

**(2) Dominicus Mettenleiter** (*b* Thannhausen, 20 May 1822; *d* Regensburg, 2 May 1868). Brother of (1) Johann Georg Mettenleiter. He was also educated and taught music by his uncle in Wallerstein. In 1835 he went to Regensburg, where in 1846 he was ordained. Four years later he was appointed vicar of the collegiate monastery of the Alte Kapelle. Through his association with Proske, active at the same institution, he acquired a broad musicological knowledge. A member of many learned societies and a contributor to numerous German and foreign music journals, he is perhaps best known for his music histories of Regensburg and the Upper Palatinate.

WRITINGS
*Aus der musikalischen Vergangenheit bayrischer Städte: Musikgeschichte der Stadt Regensburg* (Regensburg, 1866)
*Johann Georg Mettenleiter: ein Künstlerbild* (Brixen [Bressanone], 1866)
*Musica* (Brixen, 1866–8)
*Philomele*, i (Regensburg, 1866); ii (Brixen, 1868)
*Musikgeschichte der Oberpfalz* (Amberg, 1867)
*Karl Proske: ein Lebensbild* (Regensburg, 1868, 2/1895)
*Orlando di Lasso: Registratur für die Geschichte der Musik in Bayern* (Brixen, 1868)

**(3) Bernhard Mettenleiter** (*b* Wallerstein, 25 April 1822; *d* Marktheidenfeld, 14 Jan 1901). Cousin of (1) Johann Georg and (2) Dominicus Mettenleiter. The son of the prince's secretary and choirmaster Johann

Michael Mettenleiter in Wallerstein, he took up the post of teacher and choirmaster at Memmingen in 1848 and in 1856 became choirmaster and music teacher at the royal Gymnasium in Kempten. From 1871 to 1894 he was president of the Cecilian society of the Augsburg diocese, and he was a member of the Referentenkollegium of the Allgemeiner Deutscher Cäcilienverein.

Among the earliest and most ardent members of the German Cecilian movement, Mettenleiter was also known as an organist and music pedagogue. His church compositions are distinguished by their aptness to the solemnity of the sacred service; those published include eight masses, a requiem, a *Te Deum*, five Vespers, four *Pange lingua*, Marian antiphons and two Good Friday settings. He also wrote *Die Behandlung der Orgel* (Regensburg, 1869, 3/1886) and *Das Harmoniumspiel*, i (Kempten, 1880, 5/1904), ii (1882, 2/1892), iii (1899).

BIBLIOGRAPHY
D. Mettenleiter: *Johann Georg Mettenleiter* (Brixen, 1866)
Obituary, *Fliegende Blätter für katholische Kirchenmusik*, iii/5 (1868), 39 [Dominicus Mettenleiter]
R. Schlecht: *Geschichte der Kirchenmusik* (Regensburg, 1871), 154, 194, 195
G. Jakob: 'Johann Georg Mettenleiter: eine Skizze seines Lebens und Wirkens', *Caecilien-Kalender*, iii (1878), 5 [incl. a 4-pt. Adoramus]
U. Kornmüller: *Lexikon der kirchlichen Tonkunst* (Regensburg, 2/1895)
Obituary, *Caecilienverein-Organ*, xxxvi/3 (1901), 25 [Bernhard Mettenleiter]
based on *MGG* (ix, 239–41) by permission of Bärenreiter
AUGUST SCHARNAGL

**Metzger, Ambrosius** (*b* Nuremberg, 31 Jan 1573; *d* Nuremberg, 1632). German composer and mastersinger. His family came from Swabia. He attended the grammar school of St Sebald at Nuremberg for five years from 1586. After travels which took him to Regensburg and Linz he completed his education at Steyr and stayed there for a year and a half as a teacher and finally as tutor to an aristocratic Austrian family. After his father's death he returned to Nuremberg and in 1600 went to the university at nearby Altdorf to study theology. In 1604 at the latest he took his master's degree. As there was no position as a priest available to him he obtained a post, which he held until his death, as a teacher at the school of St Egidien, Nuremberg. His only known music from these years is *Venusblümlein: 1. Theil Neuer, lustiger, welticher Liedlein* for four voices and *Ander Theil Neuer, lustiger, welticher Liedlein* for five voices (Nuremberg, 1611–12); a third part was never printed. This work was probably modelled on Hans Leo Hassler's *Lustgarten neuer teutscher Gesäng* (1601).

An ailment of the eyes, which eventually led to blindness, prevented Metzger from continuing with composition; he devoted himself instead to the art of the mastersinger. Of his works from his later years only *Der Psalter David, in der gebräuchlichsten Kirchengesänge Melodeyen gebracht, mit hundert neuen Melodeyen geziert* (Nuremberg, 1630) was printed; everything else remained in MS. In an MS curriculum vitae of 1620 (in *D-Nst*), which is a valuable source of information about the later mastersingers, he prided himself on having composed more than 3000 poems and 340 melodies in less than seven years. In the Nuremberg Stadtbibliothek there is also a paraphrase of Ovid's *Metamorphoses* 'in Meister Tönen' and other mastersinger poetry by him, together with a careful list of his poetry, including both sacred and secular songs (which he did not, however, compile himself). The phrase 'in Meister Tönen' refers to the melodies that he took over as well as to those of his own composition, which can be ascertained with the help of the psalter of 1630. He certainly appears to be an interesting figure among later mastersingers.

BIBLIOGRAPHY

J. Zahn: *Die Melodien der deutschen evangelischen Kirchenlieder*, iv–vi (Gütersloh, 1891–3/R1963)
H. Zirnbauer: 'Zwei autobiographische Gedichte von Ambrosius Metzger', *Mitteilungen aus der Stadtbibliothek Nürnberg*, ix/2 (1960)

WALTER BLANKENBURG

**Metzger, Heinz-Klaus** (*b* Konstanz, 6 Feb 1932). German writer on music and music theorist. He studied at the Staatliche Musikhochschule in Freiburg (1949–52) and then studied composition with Max Deutsch in Paris and musicology in Tübingen (1952–4). He qualified in 1956 at the Akademie für Tonkunst, Darmstadt. He also received a lasting stimulus from the Darmstadt summer courses and, starting with Webern's music, was a champion of serial and electronic music. As a writer on music he has adhered to Hegel and Marxist philosophy; stylistically he was influenced by Adorno, who was quick to recognize his talents. His articles deal with 12-note music, Webern, Varèse, Cage, Hans-Joachim Hespos and theoretical, aesthetic and philosophical problems in avant-garde music.

HANSPETER KRELLMANN

**Metziltayim** (Heb.). Ancient Jewish cymbals; *see* JEWISH MUSIC, §I, 4(i).

**Metzler.** English firm of instrument dealers and music publishers, established in London. The founder was Valentin Metzler, a native of Bingen am Rhein who opened a shop in London for the sale of instruments in 1788. The name Metzler first appears in the London directories in 1812, and about four years later, when the publishing side of the business was apparently started, Metzler was joined by his son George Richard Metzler (1797–1867) to form the firm Metzler & Son. In 1833, presumably the year of the elder Metzler's death, the firm became G. Metzler & Co.; by 1838 they were advertising its 'improved Seraphines', early precursors of the harmonium. George Richard Metzler retired in 1866 in favour of his son George Thomas (1835–79), a well-known writer of song lyrics. In 1867 a partnership was established with Frank Chappell, who remained with the company until his death in 1886 and who formed a connection with the firm of Mason & Hamlin of Boston, Massachusetts, through which they effectively introduced the American organ into Britain. Their publishing activities covered all fields; many of the songs of Sullivan and Goring Thomas were published by the firm, and keyboard music was especially prominent in its catalogue. Among its operatic successes were Sullivan's *The Sorcerer* and *HMS Pinafore*, and it held the British rights for Bizet's *Carmen* and French songs and piano music by Gounod, Bizet, Godard and others. The firm became a limited company in 1893, and was taken over by J. B. CRAMER in 1931.

BIBLIOGRAPHY

C. Humphries and W. C. Smith: *Music Publishing in the British Isles* (London, 1954, 2/1970)

PETER WARD JONES

**Metzler & Söhne.** Swiss organ builders. The firm was founded in 1890 in the Swiss canton of Graubünden by Jakob Metzler. In 1930 his son Oscar moved the company to Dietikon (Zurich). In 1968 the direction was taken over jointly by his sons, Oskar and Hansueli. Although always craftsmanlike, the work of the firm was without special distinction until the mid-1950s when, on the insistence of the family's younger generation, it became more closely allied with the European organ reform movement. It did not achieve outstanding success, however, until its instruments in Schaffhausen and the Grossmünster, Zurich, were built in consultation with the distinguished Danish organ builder and designer Poul Gerhard Andersen. An enlightened tonal design and 'reformed' voicing techniques joined with the firm's traditional precision of workmanship to produce a general excellence which established it as Switzerland's most important builder. A new organ in 1965 for the Cathedral of St Pierre in Geneva (also in collaboration with Andersen) reinforced the firm's position of leadership and its international reputation dates from the completion of that instrument. The firm now specializes in the construction of organs in a severe, neo-classical style more reminiscent of the north German style than is generally typical of Swiss builders. The stop action, as well as the key action, is mechanical, and all casework is designed on strictly Baroque lines. Unlike most modern builders, Metzler does not use any electric or electronic playing aids, such as combination pistons or crescendo pedal. The instruments are noted for their traditional stop-lists, cohesive and well-balanced ensembles, responsive key action and perfection of construction. Fine examples are those at Netstal, Frauenfeld (Stadtkirche) and Brugg (Evangelische Kirche). Metzler is also known for its meticulous restoration and reconstruction of historical instruments, as at Muri (Aargau), where the two choir organs dating from 1743–4 were restored and the 1628 organ rebuilt.

GILLIAN WEIR

**Meulemans, Arthur** (*b* Aarschot, 19 May 1884; *d* Etterbeek, Brussels, 29 June 1966). Belgian conductor and composer. He studied under Tinel at the Lemmens Institute, Mechelen (1900–1906), where he was a professor until 1914. From 1916 to 1930 he was director of the organ and song school at Hasselt; he was then made conductor, and later director, of Belgian radio. He left this position in 1942 to devote his time to composition. The numerous awards made to him include the Flemish Academy's Boury Prize for his songs, the prize for a symphony awarded by the SABAM (the Belgian composers' union) in 1947, the Noordstar-Boerhave Prize in 1950 and the Jef Denijn Prize (1950) for his Serenata for carillon. The Arthur Meulemans Foundation was established in Antwerp in 1956 for the publication of scores and discs of his music. Meulemans' most important work was for the orchestra. He wrote a great deal and demonstrated a brilliant orchestral technique considerably influenced by French impressionism, although there is individuality in the descriptive nature of some of the symphonic poems that were stimulated by the naturalism of Flemish Renaissance painters. He wrote the music for a play, *Sanguis Christi*, which is given every five years before the Belfry of Bruges.

WORKS
*(selective list)*

Orch: Dance Suite, 1943; De witte, 1949; Meteorologisch instituut, 1951; Peter Bruegel Suite, 1952; Hertog Jan van Brabant Suite,

1953; Sinfonietta, 1959; Middelheim, 1961; Het zwin, 1963; Torenhof, 1963; concs. for vc, 1920, 1944; pf, 1941, 1956; vn, 1942, 1946, 1950; va, 1942; harp, 1953; 2 vn, 1954; hpd/pf, 1958; org, 1958

Operas: Vikings, 1919; Adriaan Brouwer, 1925; Egmont, 1944

Choral: Sacrum mysterium, 1916; De zeven weeën, 1920; Sanguis Christi, solo vv, chorus, orch, 1938; Kinderen van deze tijd (H. R. Horst), 1957; cantatas, masses, etc

Chamber pieces incl. Aubade, pf, wind qnt, 1934; pf works; songs

Principal publishers: Arthur Meulemans Fonds, Schott (Brussels)

### WRITINGS

'Moderne muziek', Katholieke Vlaamse hogeschooluitbreiding, xxix/2 (1930), 279

'Aspecten van het moderne orkest', Mededelingen van de Koninklijke Vlaamse academie voor wetenschappen, letteren en schone kunsten van België, xv/3 (1953)

### BIBLIOGRAPHY

M. Boereboom: Arthur Meulemans (Kortrijk, 1951)

Aan Meester Arthur Meulemans bij zijn tachtigste verjaardag (Antwerp, 1964)

CORNEEL MERTENS

**Meulen** [Muelen, Mülen], **Servaes** [Servais] **vander** (b 1525; d after 1592). Flemish organist and composer. He was probably born in Antwerp or Mechelen. In 1556 he was organist at St Gertrud's, Bergen op Zoom, and in 1557 of the Lady Chapel in Antwerp Cathedral. He was involved in examination of two organs built by Gilles Brebos in 1561 and was a witness when Brebos was given contracts for a new pedal organ in the cathedral (1567–8) and the rebuilding of the Lady Chapel organ in 1573 (it had been damaged during religious riots in 1566). His career was greatly affected by the religious unrest of the time: in 1581 Calvinists took over all the Catholic churches in the city and in 1582 Alexander Farnese, Prince of Parma, asked for his dismissal 'for having served heretics and made a public scandal in the said church'. The cathedral authorities acceded to this request on condition that Meulen continued to have half his salary; Meulen took up his post again for a while but relinquished it at Farnese's insistence. He continued to receive half his former salary. No other details of his career are known (it is not certain whether he became court organist at Brussels; the last mention of him is dated 1592. Only one piece by Meulen is known: a four-part song (Altijt so moet ic trueren) in Jacob Baethen's Dat ierste boeck van den nieuwe duytsche liedekens (RISM 1554³¹).

### BIBLIOGRAPHY

P. Bergmans: 'Muelen, Servais vander', BNB

G. Persoons: De orgels en de organisten van de O. L. Vrouwkerk te Antwerpen 1500–1650 (Louvain, 1968), i, 187ff

R. B. LENAERTS

**Meursius, Johannes** (b Loosduinen [now part of The Hague], 9 Feb 1579; d Sorø, Denmark, 20 Sept 1639). Dutch classical philologist and historian. He studied classical languages at Leiden. After receiving a doctorate in law at Orleans in 1608, he was appointed professor of history (later of Greek philology) at Leiden University. In 1625 Christian IV called him to Sorø to become professor of history and politics, a position he held until his death.

Meursius published much in the fields of history, politics and philology; his two musical tracts were products of this last interest. His work on Aristoxenus, Nicomachus and Alypius is, despite debatable additions and interpretations, a valuable presentation of Greek musical theory that broke the ground for later scholars such as Marcus Meibom. The Orchestra is a lexicon of old Greek and Roman dances.

### WRITINGS

(only those relating to music)

Aristoxenus, Nicomachus, Alypius, auctores musices antiquissimi, hactenus non editi Ioannes Meursius nunc primus vulgavit, et notas addidit (Leiden, 1616) [based on an MS in NL-Lu, now lost, it contains the following treatises in Greek, with translations and copious notes in Latin: Aristoxenus, Harmonic Elements; Nicomachus, Handbook of Harmonics; Alypius, Introduction to Music]; edn. Ioan. Meursi opera omnia, ed. J. Lamius (Florence, 1741–63), v, 189 (Orchestra); vi, 335 (Auctores, with additions by Meibom); xiii (4 plates for Auctores)

Orchestra, sive De saltationibus veterum (Leiden, 1618)

### BIBLIOGRAPHY

'Meursius, Johannes', NNBW

RANDALL H. TOLLEFSEN

**Meuschel.** See NEUSCHEL family.

**Mewton-Wood, Noel** (b Melbourne, 20 Nov 1922; d London, 5 Dec 1953). Australian pianist. After studying at the Melbourne Conservatory under Seidel, he entered the RAM in London at the age of 14 and later took lessons from Schnabel. He made his London début at the Queen's Hall in 1940, playing Beethoven's First Concerto under Beecham. His success was immediate, and older musicians who heard him at that time were quick to compare him with the greatest pianists of the past. His technique and his musical intellect alike were comprehensive. In his short career (he committed suicide at 31) he mastered a wide repertory which included such formidable and dissimilar works as Busoni's Concerto and Fantasia contrappuntistica, Bliss's Concerto, Tippett's First Sonata and Stravinsky's Concerto for piano and wind (which he recorded), as well as the more regular classics and Weber's sonatas. Also a distinguished chamber pianist and accompanist, he is remembered for his playing of Tippett's The Heart's Assurance and Boyhood's End for Peter Pears (both recorded). In 1944 he composed music for the film Tawny Pipit.

### BIBLIOGRAPHY

Anon.: 'Noel Mewton-Wood, Gifted Young Pianist', The Canon, iv (1951), 401

A. Porter: 'Noel Mewton-Wood', Gramophone, xxxi (1954), 279

FRANK DAWES

**Mexico.** North American federal republic.

I. Art music. II. Folk music.

### I. Art music

1. Colonial period, 1521–1821. 2. 19th and 20th centuries.

1. COLONIAL PERIOD, 1521–1821. There were remarkable achievements in the organization of musical life around the church and in the repertories performed, as the large number of extant works in Mexican archives confirms. At the outset of the Spanish Conquest church officials emphasized music in worship. Missionaries were instructed by Juan de Zumárraga, first Bishop of Mexico, to use and teach music as 'an indispensable aid in the process of conversion', and the admirable aptitude and talent of the Indians in learning the European musical system was constantly discussed in 16th-century missionary chronicles. In 1523 the first three Franciscan missionaries arrived in Mexico, of whom one, Pedro de Gante (1480–1572), a member of Charles V's private chapel, opened the first music school where Indians were taught plainchant and instrument making. Gante's pupils spread his instruction through the colony; Franciscans and missionaries of other orders, as well as the secular clergy who came later,

adopted his educational methods. Missionary work continued throughout the colonial period.

Documentary evidence (e.g. Juan de Torquemada's *Monarquía indiana*, Seville, 1615) points to remarkable musical accomplishments among Indian populations, including the foundation of libraries of church music by copying materials brought from Europe. As early as 1539 there was a printing press in Mexico; it produced 13 liturgical books with music during the 16th century. An *Ordinarium* of 1556 is the first book with music printed in the New World; the other 12, published between 1560 and 1589, contain portions of the Ordinary and Proper of the Mass, hymns, antiphons, psalms and Passion music. Indian choirs did not limit their repertory to these books: they also learnt non-liturgical music, such as villancicos and *coplas*, as well as Spanish religious plays with music about the Nativity and Passion.

Polyphony in the best Spanish tradition was practised early in Mexico, at first in the form of villancicos, motets and psalms and then as settings of the Mass, *Magnificat*, *Te Deum* and Passion. Works of the Spanish polyphonists Morales, Guerrero and Victoria were sent to New Spain soon after their publication. The Mexico City and Puebla cathedrals received copies from the Seville and Toledo cathedral archives, which indicates the importance attached to partsinging. The most substantial Mexican archives are those of the Mexico City and Puebla cathedrals, Tepotzlán and Morelia, which contain many copies and originals of European and Mexican music from the 16th to 19th centuries.

The first *maestro de capilla* of Mexico City Cathedral was Canon Juan Xuárez (appointed 1539); Hernando Franco (1532–85) occupied the post during the last ten years of his life. His seven settings of the *Magnificat*, the Franco Manuscript, are considered the most important examples of Mexican 16th-century polyphony. Other works by Franco are contained in various manuscripts (Valdés MS, Carmen MS, and the six volumes of Mexican and Spanish polyphony in *US-Cn*), which also include the extant compositions of Juan de Lienas (*fl* late 16th century) and those of Pedro Bermúdez, *maestro de capilla* at Puebla during the first decade of the 17th century.

The musical development of Puebla in the 17th century was remarkable, particularly during the reign (1639–53) of Bishop Juan de Palafox y Mendoza (1600–59), because of his devotion to music and the city's considerable wealth. Puebla Cathedral's large choir stalls made possible the performance of polychoral music, as is evident in the extant works of Bernardo de Peralta (*fl* 1640), and especially of Juan Gutiérrez de Padilla (*maestro de capilla*, 1629–64), the most important 17th-century composer working in Mexico. In his music for double choir, including masses, motets, hymns and Lamentations, he used imitative techniques and antiphonal effects with considerable diversity; his villancico cycles also deserve special attention. Other renowned composers active at Puebla by the middle and late 17th century were Francisco López Capillas and Miguel Mateo Dallo y Lana, who made polyphonic settings of Sor Juana Inés de la Cruz's villancicos (Mexico, 1690).

The growth of music in the province of Michoacán was due to the Cathedral of Morelia (formerly Valladolid) and the convent of S Rosa de S Maria de Valladolid, where the Franciscan monk Juan Navarro wrote his *Quatuor Passiones* (Mexico City, 1604). The convent established a music school for orphan girls by the mid-18th century which became the most famous conservatory of music in the colony, known as the Las Rosas Conservatory. The archives of Morelia Cathedral and the conservatory contain an impressive number of Gregorian choirbooks, sacred and secular polyphonic works and instrumental pieces, from the 16th century to the 19th.

Several composers active at Mexico City Cathedral as *maestros de capilla* during the 18th century contributed greatly to the city's musical life. Antonio de Salazar, *maestro de capilla* from 1688 to 1715, wrote Latin hymns and villancicos. Manuel Zumaya (*fl* 1720), a native of Mexico, composed the second opera known to have been produced in the New World, *La Parténope* (1711). Some of José de Torres's works are in the cathedral archive but there is no definite evidence that he held the post. The Italian composer Ignacio Jerusalem, *maestro de capilla* 1749–69, introduced the prevailing operatic style; he was succeeded by Matheo Tollis de la Roca. During Antonio Juanas's appointment José Maria Aldana (*d* 1810) was considered the most prominent musician of the time, but his liturgical and instrumental works clearly indicate the decline of neo-Hispanic music in Mexico. The fact that Manuel Arenzana, an opera composer, was *maestro de capilla* at Puebla at the turn of the 19th century similarly indicates the secularization of sacred music, following the concurrent European tendency.

2. 19TH AND 20TH CENTURIES. During the 19th century Italian opera dominated the Mexican musical scene. At first the cultivated genres were of Spanish origin: zarzuela, *tonadilla escénica*, *sainete*. But the Coliseo Nuevo theatre, which had been functioning from 1735, became bankrupt during the revolutionary period, and Mexican operas began to be produced only after independence. In the meantime José Mariano Elízaga (1786–1842) exerted an important influence in music education. He founded a conservatory of music in 1825 which flourished briefly, and wrote two influential theoretical treatises, the second, *Principios de la armonía y de la melodía* (1835), being an introduction to four-part harmony. His compositions are mostly sacred and adhere to the Classical style. Later attempts to create a regular school of music in Mexico City resulted in the foundation of a privately maintained conservatory (1866), which eventually became the government-subsidized Conservatorio Nacional de Música (1877).

The better-known Mexican opera composers of the 19th century were Luis Baca (1826–55), Cenobio Paniagua (1821–82) and Melesio Morales (1838–1908). The opera *Guatimotzin* by Aniceto Ortega (1823–75), first performed in 1871 with the Mexican soprano Angela Peralta, is considered the first serious attempt to incorporate some elements of indigenous music within the framework of prevailing Italian models.

A large number of pianist–composers who cultivated salon-music genres and European Romantic piano music were active during the last three decades of the 19th century. The most popular composer of salon music was Juventino Rosas (1868–94), who wrote a set of waltzes in the purest Austrian tradition, *Sobre las olas*, which became famous throughout the world. The

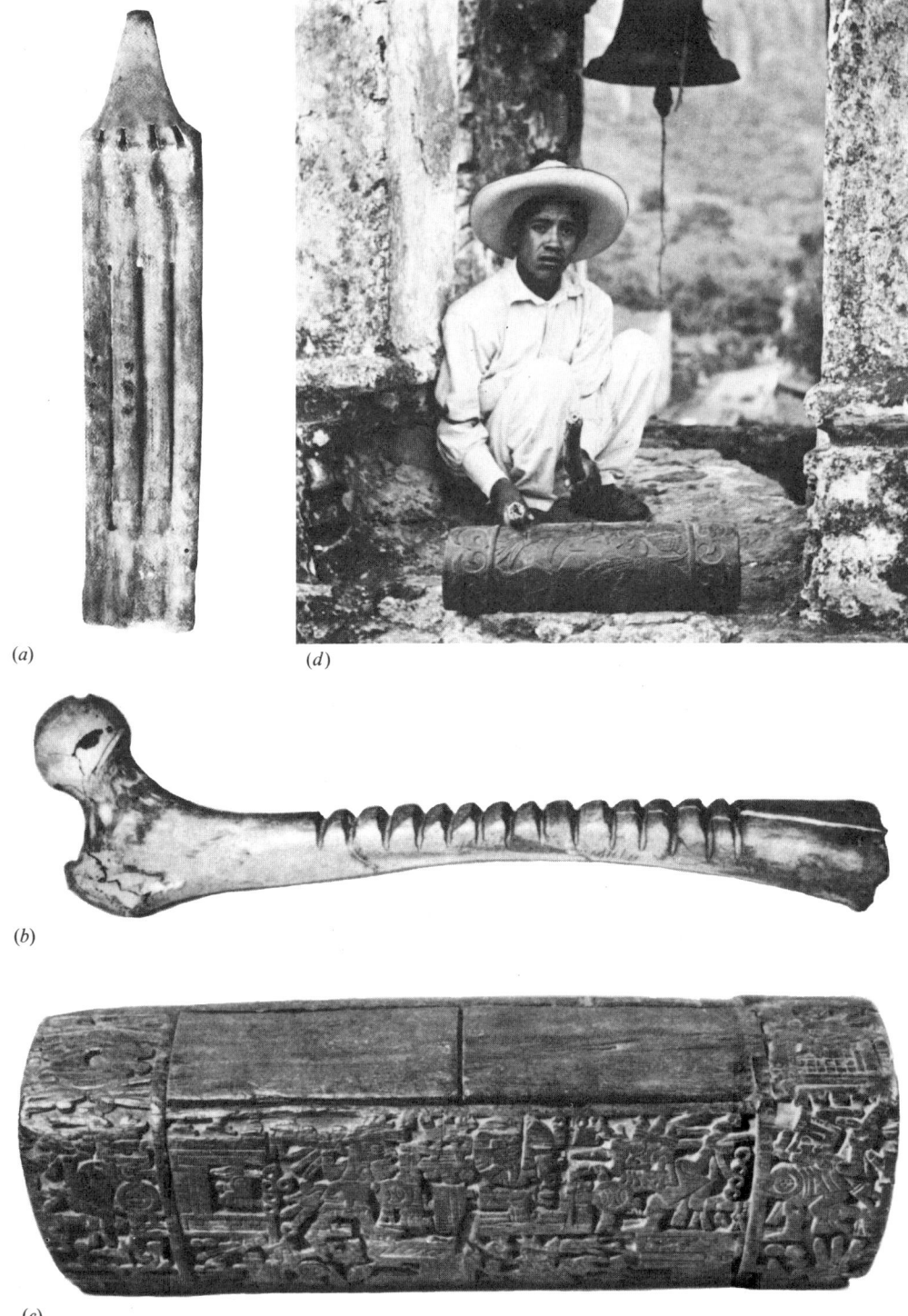

1. (a) *Quadruple flute made of clay* (AD *c500*) *of the Teotihuacán culture, in the Museo Nacional de Antropología e Historia, Mexico City;* (b) *omichicahuaztli* (*serrated bone scraper*), *Aztec culture* (AD *c1350–1521*), *in the Museum of the American Indian, New York;* (c) *teponaztli* (*slit-drum*) *of the Mixtekische culture* (AD *c12th–15th century*), *in the British Museum, London;* (d) *modern copy of a teponaztli, played by a Mexican boy on the roof of La Santísima church*

piano virtuosos of the time included Tomas León (1826–93), Julio Ituarte (1845–1905), Ernesto Elorduy (1853–1912) and Felipe Villanueva (1862–93). The last two cultivated the *danza mexicana*, following the model of Ignacio Cervantes's Cuban *contradanzas*. Ricardo Castro (1866–1907), who had some success in Europe, wrote piano and orchestral works and two operas, *Atzimba* (1901) and *La légende de Rudel* (1906). Gustavo E. Campa (1863–1934) wrote piano music and an opera *Le roi poète* (1901), strongly influenced by Saint-Saëns and Massenet.

An exceptional case in Mexican music history is the prophetic theoretical work of the composer Julián Carrillo (1875–1965), who from 1895 elaborated a microtonal system known as *sonido trece* ('13th-tone'), using up to 16th-tones. He wrote orchestral and chamber works according to this system and also in more conventional genres.

The Mexican Revolution (1910) made a deep impression on the country's artistic life. Musicians gave expression to their patriotic fervour in nationalist music which drew on Indian and mestizo cultures. The composer Manuel M. Ponce (1882–1948), considered the pioneer of nationalism in Mexico, systematically investigated and used all types of mestizo folk music (*corrido*, *jarabe*, *huapango son* etc). His large output reveals a nationalist orientation which implies a greater autonomy of the popular elements integrated within a generally neo-Romantic or neo-classical style. This tendency was followed by most composers of Ponce's generation, such as José Rolón (*b* 1883) and Candelario Huízar (*b* 1889).

In the so-called 'Aztec Renaissance' of the post-revolutionary period the attempted return to pre-Conquest Indian musical practices was less an authentic reconstruction of those practices than a subjective evocation of the remote past, or of the character and physical setting of ancient and contemporary Indian culture. Carlos Chávez (*b* 1899), the most influential early 20th-century Mexican composer, has been particularly successful in assimilating elements of music. In his works of Indian character, such as *Los cuatro soles*, *Sinfonía India*, or in his most abstract compositions, such as his last three symphonies, his highly personal style and Mexican identity appear so intimately connected that his music has been described as 'profoundly non-European'. Chávez has also had a brilliant career as a conductor; he founded the Orquesta Sinfónica de México in 1928, and directed it for over 18 years. The orchestra has given the first performances of many 20th-century Mexican symphonic works.

Silvestre Revueltas (1899–1940), another nationalist composer of international fame, drew on contemporary Mexican popular and folk music to evolve his own style. Many of his works, such as *Ocho por radio* (1933) and *Sensemayá* (1938), reveal his spontaneous and good-humoured temperament.

Nationalist feeling is also evident in the works of Daniel Ayala Pérez (*b* 1908), Salvador Contreras (*b* 1912), José Pablo Moncayo (*b* 1912), Blas Galindo (*b* 1910) (all students of Chávez and at one time known as El Grupo de los Cuatro), Luis Sandi (*b* 1905) and Miguel Bernal Jiménez. While they attempt to integrate Mexican subjects and musical elements within traditional large forms (operas, symphonies), these composers are not exclusively nationalist.

As a teacher of composition at the Conservatorio Nacional the Spanish-born Rodolfo Halffter (*b* 1900) has exerted a decisive influence on the younger generation of Mexican composers. His style, at first a form of neo-classical nationalism, gradually evolved towards atonality and serialism. Musical nationalism began to decline in Mexico only in the 1960s, largely through the work of a dynamic group of avant-garde composers which includes Manuel Enríquez, Héctor Quintanar and Mário Kuri-Aldana.

*See also* MEXICO CITY; MORELIA; PUEBLA.

BIBLIOGRAPHY
L. M. Spell: 'The First Music Books Printed in. America', *MQ*, xv (1929), 50
M. Galindo: *Nociones de historia de la música mejicana* (Colima, 1933)
G. Saldívar: *Historia de la música en México (épocas pre-cortesiana y colonial)* (Mexico City, 1934)
O. Mayer-Serra: *Panorama de la música mexicana desde la independencia hasta la actualidad* (Mexico City, 1941)
——: *The Present State of Music in Mexico* (Washington, DC, 1946)
L. M. Spell: 'Music in the Cathedral of Mexico in the 16th Century', *Hispanic American Historical Review*, xxvi (1946), 293
I. Pope: 'Documentos relacionados con la historia de la música en México', *Nuestra música*, vi (1951), 5, 245
J. Bal y Gay, ed.: *El códice del convento del Carmen*, Tesoro de la música polifónica en México, i, (Mexico City, 1952)
R. Stevenson: *Music in Mexico: a Historical Survey* (New York, 1952)
——: 'Sixteenth and Seventeenth Century Resources in Mexico', *FAM*, i (1954), 69; ii (1955), 10
S. Barwick, ed.: *The Franco Codex* (Carbondale, 1965)
R. Stevenson: *Music in Aztec and Inca Territory* (Berkeley, 1968)
L. B. Spiess and E. T. Stanford: *An Introduction to Certain Mexican Musical Archives* (Detroit, 1969)
F. Antúnez: *La capilla de música de la catedral de Durango* (Mexico City, 1970)
R. Stevenson: *Renaissance and Baroque Musical Sources in the Americas* (Washington, DC, 1970)
J. Estrada: *Música y músicos de la época virreinal* (Mexico City, 1973)
D. Malmström: *Introduction to 20th Century Mexican Music* (Uppsala, 1974)

For further bibliography *see* LATIN AMERICA; MEXICO CITY; PUEBLA.

## II. Folk music

1. History. 2. Mestizo forms. 3. Indigenous forms.

### 1. HISTORY.

(*i*) *Pre-Columbian cultures*. Knowledge of music before the Conquest derives from three main sources: archaeology, testimony of observers during the initial period of contact, and analysis of vocabularies and grammars of Indian languages. These allow a detailed reconstruction of the instrumentation of Indian music.

There were many types of wind instrument, including fipple flutes and end-blown flutes made of clay, jadeite, reed, bone and metal, conch trumpets (sometimes of clay, and often with inserted clay mouthpieces) and perhaps double-reed wind instruments. There is no evidence of indigenous string instruments, and when they were introduced by the Spaniards, the Indians classified them as drums – a reflection both on the Indian classification system and on the contemporary Spanish style of guitar playing.

Maracas and *omichicahuaztli* (a long serrated stick or bone scraped with a smaller stick, fig.1*b*) were widely used instruments, the latter especially for funeral music. Conch shells and their clay replicas (exactly reproduced in all internal and external detail) were greatly esteemed, and ceremonially associated with the god of rain. Among the many types of flutes two were distinctive. The triple and quadruple flutes of the Teotihuacán culture, dating from the period AD 400–600 (fig.1*a*), were tuned to play untempered triads and 6-3 chords, which suggests that their music incorporated a concept of harmony. A second type, dating from the period just preceding the Conquest, is a double flute, with similar placement of finger-holes on both tubes; it was apparently tuned to produce a beating effect between the near-unison pitches of the two tubes. It was also frequently perforated as if to be hung on a string and might have been used for signalling in combat, especially as it produces a tremendous volume of sound.

The two most important instruments were the drums *huehuetl* and *teponaztli*, named after demigods of Aztec legend. *Huehuetl* incorporated the name of the tree *ahuehuete* which supplied the wood from which the instrument was made; it normally grows near water, and ceremonial sites, town markets and plazas were (and are) found in its shade. Moreover *huehue* is the root of several words with connotations of esteem and value ('town elder', 'ancient' etc). The instrument is a single-headed three-footed drum, with a jaguar skin or deer-skin fixed to its upright end; it was tuned by heating the interior with live coals which dried and tautened the head (for illustration, *see* AZTEC MUSIC).

The *teponaztli*, a slit-drum, was made of a section of tree-trunk, as thick as the body of a man and about a metre long, hollowed out through a rectangular opening in its side (fig.1c and d). Opposite this opening, on the other side of the cavity, an H-shaped incision formed two tongues of wood which were tuned to harmonics of the resonant pitch of the drum cavity – most commonly an interval of a minor 3rd or major 2nd. According to 16th-century writers the sound of this instrument was doleful and carried a great distance.

At pre-Columbian festivities the *teponaztli* and *huehuetl* were usually placed on a grass mat at the centre of the dancing area, the dancers – often hundreds – moving round them in concentric circles. The nobility danced in the inner circles, and, to synchronize with the dancers in the outer circles, abbreviated their steps, while those in the outermost circles danced at twice the speed; thus all the circles completed a revolution in the dance at the same time. Choreography, melodic shape and drum rhythms were so coordinated that the rise and fall of the dancers' arms and feet matched the rise and fall of the melody in the song and the pitches of the drums. A drum terminology based on four syllables and a suffix (*ti*, *to*, *ki*, *ko*, and *-n*) must therefore, besides indicating drum rhythms, have related to choreography and song pitch. A noteworthy feature of this system is its duality of consonant and vowel (*t* versus *k*, *i* versus *o*), which possibly relate to the high or low drum pitch, positions of arms and feet in the dance, the two pitch levels of the Náhuatl language, or to the left as opposed to the right hand. Most instruments found at archaeological sites – flutes, whistles, ocarinas, conch shells – produce only two notes (usually a minor 3rd or major 2nd, like the *teponaztli*).

High-pitched and metallic timbres were highly esteemed by Mexican Indians in festivities, a fact reflected in the roots of their words. *Náhuatl*, as well as being the name of the language of the Aztecs, means 'sonorous, audible, council, law; to dance embraced at the neck'. In Mixtec, *huij* means 'agreeable, polished, gentle; clear, high, clean, pretty'; and the radical *kaa* or *saa* means 'to roar' (especially a jaguar, one of the forms of a principal native god); 'to sound high, clear, loud and metallic'; 'to whistle, to sigh, to jump in dance, to throw a certain clay piece in a ceremonial game'; 'metal' (especially gold, metal of the sun god); 'to cast metal'. According to one 16th-century chronicle the vocal

quality of the Indians when singing amused the Spaniards, sounding somewhat out of tune and thin. An analysis of Indian musical terminology suggests that this thinness was a preferred musical quality, associated with gold, the metal of the sun god (the principal Indian deity), and the roar of the jaguar. In festivities the dances gradually progressed from a low pitch and slow tempo to a higher pitch and much faster tempo at the culmination of the celebration; this is reflected in the Mixtec word *saa-nino* (literally 'high–low', meaning 'a festivity, to celebrate').

To err in the dance was expressed with the words *tlakoa* ('to sin, to lie') and *tlako'tli* ('slave'); dancers who so 'sinned' were summarily executed. Cortés was so impressed with the precision and beauty of Aztec dance that he returned to the court of Charles V in 1527 with Indian entertainers who later performed for the pope.

Before the Conquest music was closely related to the dance, ceremonial, drama and poetry; there was no abstract music. Songs were probably differentiated more by text than by melody. The *cuicacalli* ('house of song') was described in Spanish as 'school of dance'. A high regard for song, however, is revealed in Aztec literature, which continually reiterates that the two most precious things in life are flowers and song. Musicians were members of the élite and enjoyed considerable social prestige.

At least four types of dance and song were taught and practised in the schools of dance attended by all Indian youths, male and female, as well as at the courts of the nobility, for whom there were separate schools. The first type, possibly generic and still encountered among the Yaquis, Mayos, Tarahumaras and other tribes in northern Mexico, was called *mitote* (from *itotia*: 'to dance'), a large communal celebration. The second, which also survives, was a penitential which subsequently merged with Catholic tradition and gave rise to the modern *concheros* (dance depicting Indian converts on a religious pilgrimage). The term for this type of dance, *macehua*, also means 'to obtain, to be meritorious, to do penitence'; 'merit, humble person, peon'. A third type, practised in the schools of dance during the morning and early afternoon before the youths arrived for their classes, was by all accounts high-pitched and lascivious, associated with certain 'public' women allotted to principal warriors in reward for their valour. This type, too, has survived as a bar-room song form. For the fourth type, practised by musicians at the courts of the nobility, singers with deep bass voices were particularly prized. Ceremonial wailing for dead relatives, chiefs or friends, a widespread pre-Conquest tradition, may not have been considered song at all as the same word is used for singing and crying. It has survived in some parts of southern Mexico and is noteworthy for its relaxed vocal quality – a unique trait in the indigenous repertory.

*See also* AZTEC MUSIC and MAYA MUSIC.

(ii) *Cultural transition.* The social prestige of the musician in native society greatly encouraged the considerable growth of musical activities during the 16th century. Spanish friars began giving formal instruction in music to Indians in 1527, with such success that the first pupils from influential families immediately began teaching others. This process of dissemination, which probably employed an established method, resulted in the rapid and widespread assimilation of Spanish songs by the Indian populace. This response initially led the Spaniards to encourage Indian involvement in musical activities, as they felt that music, more than anything else, attracted the natives to Christianity. Subsequently, however, they decided that Mexico was overpopulated with musicians.

Mid-16th-century decrees attempting to limit musical activity ordered that no church should have more than one orchestra; the use of most instruments except the organ was restricted, the size of Indian choirs was reduced, and the qualifications necessary for natives involved in musical activities were made more stringent. Within 20 years of the Conquest, however, Indians were already composing in the European idiom, copying manuscripts and manufacturing their own instruments (except organs, which were built under Spanish supervision). There were said to be more flutes, sackbuts, trumpets and drums in Mexico than in all the rest of Christendom.

The first known Indian composition is a mass by an Indian singer from the city of Tlaxcala (1540). Following missionary practices of the time, a local liturgical repertory was created employing indigenous melodies. However, the only identified Indian compositions (dating from the last quarter of the 16th century) are two hymns by an Indian namesake of the Mexico City Cathedral *maestro de capilla*, Hernando Franco. It is not known if these two pieces make use of native melodies; indeed no pre-Columbian melodies are identifiable, even if they have survived in 16th-century manuscript.

(*iii*) *The colonial period.* Catholic priests built churches on the ruins of pagan temples; they also instituted Christian celebrations on the dates of pre-Conquest ceremonies, for example the celebration of Corpus Christi in Mexico City was a substitute for the pagan celebration dedicated to the god of music, Huitzilopochtli. As most Indian celebrations were associated with the agricultural calendar before the Conquest, so most of the Christian celebrations are connected with the blessing of crops.

Indian music changed rapidly during the 16th century to conform with Catholic dogma and adjust to changes in function, but did not completely lose its native identity in the process. Certain elements conspicuous at the time of the Conquest have been retained: the blackening of the dancers' faces; the predominance of flutes and drums; ceremonies connected with the propitiation of crops and penance; street decorations of paper; bonfires and general public drunkenness after the observances; the use of high-pitched falsetto in ceremonial song; the prominent use of feathers in head-dresses (a stock way of portraying Indians); dancers costumed as tigers, deer, coyotes (or dogs) and other animals, as well as men dressed as women, soldiers, hunters and savages (in costumes made of paper, feathers and leather); and the use of masks, props (including stuffed animals), jingles, rattles (seashells, gourds, cocoons, metal etc) and canes.

The villancico is an important source of information on 17th-century rural dance. The form represents an emulation of peasant music by contemporary *maestros de capilla* and professional musicians, whose manuscripts are the most direct evidence of the peasant tradition of that period. Varying types of this form that have contributed to the development of Mexican popular music include the *negrilla* (blackface minstrelsy), the

*jácara* (especially with *corrido* guitar accompaniment) and the *tocotín*, an Aztec villancico usually sung in Náhuatl. The *tocotín* was thought to have developed from pre-Conquest traditions, as linguistic evidence would also suggest (its name derives from the drum terminology referred to above).

Touring theatrical groups popularized music and dance forms during the 18th century. The *son*, which appeared during the 17th century as a generic type of all popular song and dance forms (including the villancico), continued to contribute new variants; those considered native were called *sones de la tierra*, one of particular significance being the *jarabe* (see below).

Colonial dance-dramas usually included processions, elaborate costumes, armies of soldiers (Christians and infidels – frequently negroes), elaborate props such as fireworks castles ('burnt' at nightfall), papier mâché figures etc. The most frequent theme was conquest – the Conquest of Mexico, and the struggle between Moors and Christians in the re-Conquest of Spain (see §3(ii) below). Carnival themes became common in the theatre in the 18th and 19th centuries with the introduction of masked balls; the public could watch these fêtes from balconies and thus learn the latest European vogues. But Carnival celebrations, first mentioned in Mexico about 1544, were always popular. They were characterized by people in disguise (to avoid being recognized) behaving with moral abandon, by men dressed as women and by processions in which the populace participated. Celebrations were numerous, as Carnival formerly extended from early January to Ash Wednesday.

(*iv*) *Independence.* The Mexican movement for independence espoused a musical form, the *jarabe*. Couples in this exhibition dance are properly attired as Mexican peasants in gala dress. It was frequently prohibited during Mexico's last decades as a colony, presumably as much because of its association with the insurgents as for the official reason, its immorality (it imitates the courtship of hen and cock). A century later the *corrido* was similarly associated with the Mexican Revolution of 1910; being a narrative ballad, it reputedly served to spread news of revolutionary exploits.

Independence from Spain led to a reaction against everything Spanish during the 19th century. Paris became the cultural focus; new dance forms were introduced, including the *cuadrilla, mazurca, polca, vals* and *chotis*. After the first few decades of independence, when a lack of law and order inhibited public celebrations in cities, Carnival and church celebrations reassumed their former importance. Public balls in large dance halls characterized secular and religious observances from the late 19th century to the 1930s. The costumes of mid-20th-century rural groups in such dances as *las cuadrillas* (indigenous or mestizo) recall the elegant attire proper to the dances of these occasions, including the masks which conceal the identities of participants in Carnival debaucheries.

American influences were evident during the period of the Revolution of 1910, perhaps because of the contact of rebel groups with arms suppliers in the USA. These groups adopted the one-step and the *paso doble* (two-step) as well as the *corrido*; most of the *canciones revolucionarias* used their rhythms and styles.

## 2. MESTIZO FORMS.

(*i*) *The son.* The generic term for peasant or rural music is the *son*. The difference between this term and the

Spanish *música* roughly parallels the distinction between the Spanish *danza* and *baile*, the former implying a rural dance form and the latter an urban or court form (cf English 'ball'). The villancico (itself a generic type) was a common type of *son*, as also were many other dances at different periods. The *contradanza* (country dance) has been a common variant since the mid-18th century.

A form represented in music, song and dance, the most prominent trait of the *son* is its unequal triple rhythm based on patterns of six beats, described in Spanish as *sesquialtera*, which has been associated with the form since at least the beginning of the 17th century. Verses alternate with refrains, sometimes vocal and sometimes instrumental. Final cadences are often stereotyped. Instrumental ensembles vary regionally, as do most of the details of performance – dance steps, song texts, patterns of verse repetition, etc; but the combinations seem to suggest origins before the mid-18th century. The harp, for instance, common in 20th-century and particularly in 19th-century ensembles, was seldom used in theatres and large churches after about 1720 in Latin America, apparently becoming an exclusively rural instrument. Instruments of the guitar family in these ensembles are normally played in the strumming style known as RASGUEADO.

Song texts are always in couplets, usually octosyllabic. Involving neither pathos nor sentimentality, they almost always deal, directly or indirectly, with women and love; the stereotyped woman is often called María (a Spanish saying has it that *toda mujer es María*: 'all woman is Mary'). In other characteristic texts the verses may be dedicated to spectators, women or important people in attendance or may extol the beauties of a town or region; imagery is drawn from nature (animals, trees, birds, fruit, colours etc), and symbolism, characteristically involving women and love, from objects and colours. Final verses are often called *despedidas* ('leave-takings').

The *son* is danced by independent couples, and is characterized by sections executed in *zapateado*, a rapid movement of the dancer's feet against the ground or a *tarima* (raised wooden platform), producing a percussive accompaniment to the music. The *zapateado* is normally performed during instrumental interludes so as not to drown the singing during the verses when melody instruments, such as the violin, are also inactive.

The most common *son* ensemble in urban centres is the *mariachi*. An unlikely derivation is frequently given for this name, the French 'mariage'; it is more probably derived from the name María with the Náhuatl diminutive 'chi', particularly as Náhuatl was widely spoken in the area where the ensemble evolved. Its characteristic instruments were two violins, a vihuela (regional name for a small five-course guitar, also known locally as *guitarra de golpe*), a *jarana* (a slightly larger five-course guitar) and a harp; but several changes have taken place in the 20th century. The *guitarrón* (a large bass guitar with four strings) has been substituted for the harp, which was more awkward to transport. In the 1930s in Mexico City two trumpets were added, and the resultant ensemble became popularized through films, radio and the gramophone. During the same period a female soloist was introduced, normally with a husky, somewhat masculine voice and dressed like a *soldadera* (a woman who followed her husband into combat during the Mexican Revolution), although singing the customary couplets about women. The *mariachi* is indigenous to the region south of the city of Guadalajara; the original form of *mariachi* is however still found in the coastal plains of the state of Michoacán. Instruments of the guitar family in these ensembles frequently have lute-shaped bodies with rounded backs.

An important type of *son*, the Mexican *chilena*, occurs on the Pacific coast of Mexico in an area just southeast of the port of Acapulco extending to the town of Tututepec in the state of Oaxaca. Its name derives from that of the *cueca chilena* introduced into the region by Chilean sailors during the Californian gold rush in the mid-19th century. The form, however, became assimilated into the general *son* repertory, having lost its division into two parts (known as *primerita* and *segundita* in the Andean region of South America). The original ensemble for the *chilena* was apparently a violin, *jarana* and harp, a fourth musician frequently adding a percussive accompaniment on a wooden box or the soundboard of the harp with his hands. The harp is now rare, and the violin and *jarana* occur only in local Indian groups. When singing *chilenas* as serenades, mestizos employ a guitar and a *requinto* (a smaller guitar tuned a 4th higher). When it is danced, the *chilena* is usually accompanied by an ensemble consisting mainly of wind and brass instruments with percussion and a string bass (see fig.2); it is followed by a faster dance known locally as a *son*, reminiscent of the *fuga* section which concludes many Andean *sones*. Mexican *chilenas* often shift between minor and major, a characteristic feature of many *sones* of the Caribbean and Andean areas of Latin America and especially common at the beginning of the refrain.

The *huapango* is both another type of *son*, and a widespread Mexican term for a type of *son* accompaniment pattern executed *rasgueado* on instruments of the guitar family in much of Latin America. The rhythm of this pattern has a number of variants and is normally heard in the bass. As a musical form the *huapango* is indigenous to the Huastec region, which extends from the Gulf Coast south of Tampico into the highlands. The word *huapango* itself derives from a Náhuatl word for the raised wooden platform on which the dance may be executed (Sp: *tarima*). The normal ensemble consists of one violin, a *jarana* and a *huapanguera* (large five-course guitar with eight or ten strings; see fig.3). Ex.1 illustrates the lively style of violin playing reminiscent of fiddle playing in the southern USA, the singer's frequent use of falsetto, and the type of variation that occurs from verse to verse. The articulation above the middle staff is that of the *jarana*; that below the staff is for the *rasgeo* of the *huapango*. An asterisk indicates a prolonged *rasgeo* called 'abanico' ('fan', since the player's hand is extended in a fan-shape). The sign – above or below a note indicates a prolongation of the duration of it; the sign (·) indicates a shortening (not a staccato). No attempt has been made to measure the intonation of the half-sharp with very great precision, but it is apparent that there are two intonations present for F♯ in this selection, at times appearing even simultaneously in the same harmony.

The *son jarocho* is found in the Jarocho region of Mexico, which centres round the port of Veracruz, and extends southwards to the isthmus of Tehuantepec. This region and the music from it have a particular affinity with the Caribbean area, especially the coastal regions of Venezuela. The regional ensemble consists of a harp,

Ex.1 *El Fandanguito, huapango* form, Veracruz; rec. and transcr. E. T. Stanford

a *jarana* (somewhat longer and thinner bodied than elsewhere) and a *cuatro* (small four-course guitar with four strings). Both the harp and the *cuatro* are melody instruments, the latter played with a pick in the PUN-TEADO style with rapid scales and arpeggios. This *son* is thought to show considerable black influence and is performed by many black groups where it is indigenous. In Venezuela (but not in Mexico) maracas, sometimes considered black instruments, are added to the (similar) ensemble. However the *son jarocho* shows no more black influence than most other *son* types. It is probably second only in popularity to the *mariachi* in Mexican urban centres; the repertoire includes the famous *La bamba*.

The *jarana* is a *son* type from the peninsula of Yucatán which appears to have been common in the early 20th century, but is performed mostly by folk-dance groups. The instrument called *jarana*, a member of the guitar family, may have been so named on account of its association with this *son*.

*Zapateado*, apart from denoting one of the universal traits of the *son*, often refers to a specific *son* or type of *son*. Conversely, in the valley of the Río Balsas in central Guerrero, *son* denotes a piece danced entirely *zapateado* (i.e. not sung, as is also the case with the *son* that follows the orchestral version of the *chilena*), the remainder of the repertory being labelled *gusto*. *Zapateado* is also the generic name for many south Mexican *sones* performed on the marimba, of which some belong to a repertory of *sones istmeños* or *sones de marimba*. A *son* designated *zapateado* is danced entirely or mainly with a *zapateado* step.

A considerable number of *son* forms are distinguished not by form, rhythm or choreography, but by textual content, and are called *cuando, gusto, malagueña indita* etc according to which word occurs in their texts. The *malagueña* and the *petenera* usually deal with sailing and the sea, the *indita* with a passion for Indian women.

*(ii) The jarabe.* Although properly another *son* type, the

2. Ensemble of saxophones, trumpet, violin, percussion and string bass used to accompany the danced chilena, Pinotepa Nacional, Oaxaca

3. Ensemble of violin, huapanguera (large five-course guitar) and jarana (small five-course guitar) used to accompany the huapango dance, Tamazunchale

*jarabe* is sufficiently atypical of the *son* repertory to justify separate treatment. It is mentioned as a *son de la tierra* in theatrical annals of the second half of the 18th century, and seems to retain traces of its theatrical origins as it is still an exhibition dance. It consists of a series of musical sections, many of which have their own names, such as *la paloma*, *la diana* (the final section of most *jarabes*), *la iguana* (many have names of animals, which are mimicked in the accompanying dance) and *los machetes*; each has a contrasting characteristic rhythm. Each phrase of music is normally repeated once before proceeding to the next, but no whole section of music is repeated, except the sung sections which are performed while the dancers rest. The first two sung sections repeat the lines of one couplet so as to deploy it over two verses in the following way:

> Al pie de un encino roble
> me dio sueño y me dormí;
> me dio sueño y me dormí
> al pie de un encino roble.
>
> Me despertó un gallito
> cantando quiquiriquí
> al pie de un encino roble
> me dio sueño y me dormí.

The couple in the dance should be attired as *charro* (a Mexican cowboy with chaps and a wide-brimmed hat) and *china* (with a full, sequinned skirt of bright colours, and a hand-woven shawl) that is, in the national costume. Despite popular theories of Far Eastern origin, the term 'china' (a household servant of the lower classes) in this context is probably derived from the same word in Quechua, the language of the Incas.

(*iii*) *The corrido*. In 20th-century Mexico the term means either a type of dance generally performed in two lines with a *corrido* dance step (in north-eastern Mexico), or, more commonly, a narrative ballad accompanied by one or more guitars. Ex.2 shows the first verse of the 12-verse ballad *El capitán de ladrones*, illustrating its strophic form and the simple rhythmic and chordal accompaniment. The term 'corrido' in 17th- and 18th-century Spanish was used for a special kind of accompaniment for the *jácara* (a type of villancico), usually performed on the guitar and so-called for its light, running style. The *jácara* shares several traits with the 20th-century *corrido*: it is usually narrative, dealing with violent or unusual events, and often uses a variant of the stepwise ascending and descending melodic idea shown in ex.3 (which in the 16th century employed enharmonic alterations, according to whether ascending or descending). Further traits of the modern form are the simple duple-time *paso doble* type of accompaniment or the similar but more common triple-time accompaniment typified in ex.2 and the usual strophic ballad structure beginning with an instrumental statement of the strophe (this introduction is only occasionally musically unrelated), which is also interspersed through the *corrido* to give the singer an occasional rest. The instruments are usually either a single six-string guitar, or the guitar with a *requinto* which plays the melody in the interludes and doubles with the guitar during the verses. The *corrido* is sung and played by the characteristic ensemble of the *canción ranchera* (see §2(iv) below) when performed in mass entertainment media, and is sometimes sung by a female soloist with a masculine voice. This type of ensemble frequently performs a *corrido* which is atypical in that it has a refrain and is not

Ex.2 *El capitán de ladrones, corrido* ballad, Oaxaca; rec. and transcr. E. T. Stanford

narrative; its accompaniment, however, is of the *corrido* type.

The text of the *corrido* begins with a couplet (usually octosyllabic) setting the scene and frequently giving the time and place of the event to be narrated, and ends with a *despédida* which customarily identifies the singer or author or both. The *décima*, which was apparently the 19th-century literary antecedent of the *corrido*, almost always ended with a moral; early *corridos* in *décima* verse form retain this trait. The usual *corrido* contains a statement like: 'he died like a *valiente*'. The word 'valiente' appears to have survived from the 17th-century *jácara*; and like that form, the *corrido* sometimes deals with 'underworld' figures (bandits, revolutionaries etc). The *corrido* and *jarabe* are found throughout Mexico because they are national forms associated with nationalist sentiments.

Ex.3 *Jácara* motif

(*iv*) *The canción*. The term 'canción' denotes a musical form not intended to be danced, with a text characterized by Romantic sentimentality and pathos, and which makes considerable use of rubato – traits which are rare in other types of Mexican popular music. The Caribbean connections of some types of canción are evident in the use (particularly prominent in the bolero) of maracas, which do not occur in any other Mexican forms. The *canción yucateca*, *canción habanera*, *bambuco* and bolero (the last three differentiated by distinctive rhythms) all have such links, the *bambuco* being the national dance of Colombia and the *habanera* (formerly also known as *danza*) having evolved in the port of Havana during the early 19th century.

The *canción ranchera* developed in the early 20th century and was associated with the Mexican Revolution of 1910. It is usually accompanied by a *mariachi* ensemble in *corrido* style, the musicians dressed like dancers of the *jarabe*. The song texts frequently deal with *soldaderas* (soldiers), the stereotyped man abandoned by his woman, and patriotic subjects. As in *son* texts the style is devoid of pathos but the musical metre is often duple.

(v) *19th-century dance forms and música norteña.* The *polca*, *mazurca*, *redova* (*redowa*), *vals* and *chotís*, with the *paso doble* and *corrido* (20th-century forms), are especially prominent in northern Mexico, where final settlements were established mostly in the 19th century. The characteristic instruments of this repertory, called *música norteña*, are the accordion and the *bajo sexto* (large 12-string guitar), which were widespread during the same period. Accompaniment patterns generally resemble those associated with the *canción ranchera* and *canciones revolucionarias*; the repertory overlaps to a large extent and is mostly differentiated by instrumental usage.

(vi) *Bands and regional orchestras.* These exist in many of the smaller towns throughout Mexico, and are famous in such larger places as the city of Oaxaca and Culiacán, Sinaloa. They are supposedly a heritage of the French Empire in Mexico (1863–7), but the fact that a large proportion of the earlier instruments still in use by these groups, although French, date from around 1850, suggests that they have earlier antecedents. These were possibly church ensembles, as traditional orchestras in a few isolated regions formerly played 18th-century church music, and as in colonial Mexico church and state were not separate. In the isthmus region the ensemble incorporates a marimba, and is called *marimba-orquesta*: such groups are widely popularized in Mexican tourist centres. In north-western Mexico, from Mazatlán northwards, the orchestras are called *tamboras*, because the large bass drum (*tambora*) is featured prominently. Both the *tambora* and the *marimba-orquesta* normally play *sones*, and make constant use of *corrido* accompaniments. The instruments are frequently municipal property, and musicians may be exempt from certain other civic responsibilities by virtue of their service in these groups. The *chile frito* of central Guerrero (south of Mexico City) is an indigenous ensemble which plays imitation band instruments made of assembled sections of gourds.

3. INDIGENOUS FORMS. Scholars have extensively debated the ethnic identity of Indian music in Latin America, some maintaining that it is predominantly indigenous and others that it is fundamentally Hispanic. The characteristics of 20th-century Mexican ceremonial traditions are generally survivals from pre-Conquest times, transformed by the assimilation of similar Hispanic cultural traits. Mestizo and indigenous musical and ceremonial traditions are fairly close, and traditional bases for defining indigenous culture, such as language, dress or life style, are unsatisfactory. However,

most of the distinctions between Indian and mestizo musical institutions can be explained in terms of economics, since economic conditions are a major determinant of Indian patterns of culture.

The Indians' musical resources are restricted by the isolation of the areas they live in and by their barter economy. They can rarely acquire goods sold only for money and musical instruments are usually inherited, obtained through barter, or home-made. The absence of such commodities as electric power, television and films compels them to invent their own forms of entertainment; indigenous musical expression is extremely varied, being determined by the different physical and economic conditions of each group.

Inventiveness plays a large role in indigenous ceremonial. The task of the investigator is made more difficult by the fact that a popular tune becomes transformed almost beyond recognition when it has been adapted to a local flute and drum repertory, and it is often difficult to establish common elements between indigenous dances such as *los voladores*, the deer dance and *los matachines*. Most accounts of Mexican dance-dramas dwell on relatively insignificant traits, which vary widely from town to town, or even from occasion to occasion within the same community. Such accounts often show a tendency to assume that all details have been preserved from antiquity. Indians deliberately attempt to maintain a cultural identity, but do not necessarily consider all elements of the culture equally important. Those which they value usually involve ceremonial and civic organization, objects with religious and/or ceremonial significance, or ceremonial itself. Varied and unpredictable detail delights Indian spectators.

Virtually all Indian dance-dramas are supported by ceremonial organizations (some specifically dance societies) descended from colonial brotherhoods, unions and guilds (*gremios*). They are financially based on the *mayordomía*, headed by *mayordomos* (lay officials in a semi-religious organization) who, as part of their civic responsibility, pay for and organize certain church celebrations, dedicated at least ostensibly to a Christian saint. Dance groups within the *mayordomía* have a quasi-military structure with *caporales* and *capitanes*. Dancers are usually life members of the organizations, often promised when children by their parents; commonly if a child has an apparently serious illness, its mother vows that when it recovers it will dance to the society's patron saint for life. Some members serve only for a limited number of years (as among the *concheros*) as a penance. These societies, as well as performing in church celebrations, attend their members on such occasions as baptism, marriage and burial. Their musicians are the closest equivalents to professionals in the Indian communities, though they are never salaried (they are compensated for time lost from their normal occupations with food and drink for them and their families for the duration of the celebrations in which they participate).

In nearly all indigenous dance-dramas, the dancing takes place during interludes. The usual dance formation is two parallel lines, either facing each other or in one direction. The most experienced dancers are in front, and the *capitán* (whether or not he is part of the formation) leads the line; newcomers and children take positions at the end of the lines where they can watch and imitate the movements of the experienced. The groups rehearse for months before a celebration, and during all rehear-

4. *Diatonic marimba in three sections, covered by four players, probably Tzeltal or Tzotzil Indians from the highlands, early 1900s*

sals the captain pays for food and drink.

The dances are usually called *contradanzas* or *cuadrillas*, *son* being their generic name. As might be expected, Indian informants usually describe them as *bailes*, mestizos as *danzas*. Although the dancers are usually paired, the dances are not true couple dances except when some of the participants are dressed as women. The only common dances involving women are the *concheros*, songs of praise to the Virgin (*alabanzas*, *alabados*), and the *pastoras*, in which young virgins take flowers to the Virgin at the local church, dancing to the accompaniment of a violin. In all other contexts Indian communities disapprove of women who dance. Few dances, except for *los concheros*, involve any significant amount of singing.

Ex.4 *Danza de la pluma, xililo*, Zaachila, Oaxaca; rec. and transcr.
E. T. Stanford

The indigenous *son* generally consists of two short phrases of music, each repeated once before proceeding to the other (see ex.4). The first phrase usually leads to the dominant, and the second back to the tonic. This short structure may be repeated strophically for half an hour or more. The usual instrumental ensemble is the flute and drum (or drums); or, more rarely, a violin with or without some type of guitar (or guitars) and occasionally a harp. The latter is apparently based on typical mestizo *son* instrumentation. Regional mestizo ensembles, such as orchestras and the violin, mandolin and *guitarra séptima* ensemble in southern Mexico, have become part of local Indian traditions. Tunes acquired from transistor radios or local mestizo groups are transformed as they are assimilated and so gain an indigenous quality.

(ii) *Conquest dances*. These have always depicted the 'pacification' of infidels, their repentance for godless behaviour and subsequent vows never to revert to their sinful ways. At a symbolic level they portray the victory of good over evil, which is viewed as inevitable. Nearly all Mexican Indian dances belong to this category; there are numerous variants although certain elements recur continually. One Conquest dance, *los concheros*, is exceptional for its consistency over a relatively large geographical area in the central highlands, a result of the 'unionization' of the *conchero* brotherhoods (*cofradías*, *sindicatos*) which form its ceremonial base. This dance, however, is not strictly Indian, but rather a form of dance cultivated by the lower economic classes on the outskirts of large towns and in small rural communities. In the Aztec tradition it is nonetheless a dance for penitence.

In rural areas the most common type of Conquest dance depicts the recapture of Spain from the Moors. It involves at least two groups of dancers (*comparsas*), generally three: the Christians and infidels (Moors, Turks, Jews etc) are invariable, but the third group, *los negros*, is the most popular. In earlier versions of the drama this third group apparently consisted of actors portraying Moorish slaves, but now usually portrays local heathen Indians before their conversion to Christianity. The blackening of faces, or the use of black masks, is no longer a sign of racial identity, but an indication that the dancers are infidels. Fertility sym-

(a)　　　　　　　　　　　　　　　　　　　　　　　　　(b)

5. (a) Yaqui Indians assembled for the 'los matachines' dance, holding sonajas (rattles), with the accompanying ensemble of two violins and guitar; (b) another form of sonaja (rattle)

bolism resulting from the association of the celebrations with the agricultural cycle is apparent in the mischievous behaviour of the *negritos*, full of sexual allusion. They sin, symbolically; hence, for all these dances, the groups must first obtain permission from the local authorities before appearing in the streets of town.

Where the *negros* are not part of the dance-drama, the Moors, Turks or Jews are the sinners, and the dance is reduced to a series of battles between Christians (kings) and infidels. Santiago, the patron saint of Spain, is the most popular Christian; he often has a kind of hobby horse. The dance called *los santiagueros* sometimes depicts only one episode, a battle between Santiago and his knights and the infidels. A common infidel, usually a Moor or a Turk, is Pontius Pilate. Several other dances may also be considered Conquest dances, including *los matachines* (fig.5a), *los sonajeros* (so-called for an unusual rattle that the dancers carry, made of metal discs in a wooden handle: fig.7), and dances involving the use of whips (identified with serpents, reminiscent of the pre-Columbian god Quetzalcoatl, the Plumed Serpent).

Another type of Conquest dance-drama depicts the Conquest of Mexico by Cortés. The large cast includes Cortés, Montezuma, *la reina Xochitl*, *la Malinche* (historically, Cortés's mistress, but here depicted as an Aztec monarch) and Cortés's captain Pedro de Alvarado. In all Conquest dramas, and here especially, the players and the public side with the infidels, to the extent that the final victory of good over evil seems unexpected. Most of the action centres round the infidels. The vessel in which Cortés sailed to Mexico is commonly represented by an oxcart with mast and sail.

All dances depicting Indians use feathers to identify the infidels, as in the *concheros* and the *danza de la pluma* (ex.4), which spread from the highlands north of

Mexico City to the state of Oaxaca during the mid-20th century, apparently partly through folkdance educational programmes. The *concheros*, named after their large guitars made from armadillo shells, represent Chichimec Indians from the north-east on a pilgrimage to pay homage, most often to the Virgin of Guadalupe. They are unusually represented as converts, and the dance is entirely pious.

A final type of Conquest dance depicting the symbolic victory of good over evil associates good with a deer and evil with a tiger (*tigre, gato, jaguar*). The main examples are the deer dance of many of the Indian groups of north-western Mexico, especially the Yaquis (in which, atypically, the deer, symbolizing good, is killed; see fig.6), and the tiger dance found among several Indian groups west and south of Mexico City in the states of Mexico, Guerrero and Oaxaca: in this dancers enact a tiger hunt, representing the hunter, the old fool (*el viejo loco*), dogs, domestic animals etc. The tiger is a precocious character, with many wives, much material wealth, and extremely mischievous. He is shot by the hunter at the conclusion of the dance. The jaguar was one of the forms of a principal Indian god before the Conquest.

(*iii*) *Chirimía music and Holy Week processions.* In many parts of Mexico processions are customary during Holy Week, enacting each event of the Passion. Sometimes Christ, the disciples, and the other principals in the drama are represented by live actors, and sometimes by images taken from church and chapel altars and carried in processions through the streets. The church bells are silenced, and drums replace them for the duration of Lent. In many parts of Mexico a *chirimía* (shawm) is played from the church tower in alternation with strokes on a drum played in the atrium below; this also accompanies the Roman soldiers in the procession representing Christ's march to Calvary. The shawm music is unique in that it retains elements of the microtonal structure of Arab music. Shawms are no longer generally made in Mexico, and when existing instruments become unplayable flutes or some sort of trumpet usually replace them, but the substitute instrument often retains the name 'chirimía' when employed in this context. Ex.5 shows part of a processional melody from Venustiano Carranza, in which six different motifs are introduced, repeated and extended in various ways.

The *chirimía* is also used to announce bullfights and to convene musicians and dancers for rehearsals, the repertory consisting of standard bullfight fanfares and popular tunes such as revolutionary songs.

Ex.5 Passion music, processional melody, Venustiano Carranza, Chiapas; rec. and transcr. E. T. Stanford

(*iv*) *Personal music*. 'Personal' music here means all music performed by an individual member of an Indian society without official sanction. Ceremonial music performed out of its proper context is believed to be highly perilous, endangering crops, causing droughts, or provoking retribution against offenders and the community as a whole. Virtually all members of the Indian community perform music for purely personal motives, on almost any occasion, although invariably while drinking. Texts are improvised – often amorous, though sometimes devotional – and sung in a high-pitched, strained voice; accompanying instruments are high-pitched, such as the harmonica, concertina, *jarana* or, rarely, one of the larger guitars. Some groups sing unaccompanied (most Náhuatl-speaking groups, Amuzgos and Otomies); among the Mayo and Yaqui unaccompanied duets, mostly in 3rds and 6ths, are common.

Melodic and/or harmonic formulae in this repertory are usually peculiar to each hamlet. Neither texts nor melodies are strictly metrical, and the number of notes in each phrase is determined by the number of syllables in the text. Generally, all the songs of a given community conform to a single formula, or at most two or three. The concept of song here is mainly textual, and each new text is considered as constituting an entirely new song. Possibly some melodic formulae carry verbal associations, established by analogy with the tonal patterns of the Indian and Spanish languages.

6. *Participants in the deer dance of the Yaqui Indians, with* (*right to left*) *drum, water-drum, two raspadores* (*scrapers*), *'deer' man holding sonajas* (*rattles*), *'tiger' man holding raspador* (*scraper*), *harp and violin; a flute would normally complete the ensemble*

7. *Procession including (foreground) a group of sonajeros dancers with long wooden rattles, accompanied by pipes and tabors, Tuxpan, Jalisco*

BIBLIOGRAPHY

R. M. Campos: *El folklore y la música mexicana* (Mexico City, 1928)
——: *El folklore musical de las ciudades* (Mexico City, 1930)
D. Castañeda and V. T. Mendoza: *Instrumental precortesiano: instrumentos de percusión* (Mexico City, 1933)
G. Saldívar: *Historia de la música en Mexico* (Mexico City, 1934)
V. T. Mendoza: *El romance español y el corrido mexicano* (Mexico City, 1939)
J. C. Romero: *Música precortesiana* (Mexico City, 1947)
F. Toor: *A Treasury of Mexican Folkways* (New York, 1947)
R. Stevenson: *Music in Mexico* (New York, 1952)
V. T. Mendoza: *Panorama de la música tradicional de México* (Mexico City, 1956)
T. Stanford: 'A Linguistic Analysis of Music and Dance Terms from Three Sixteenth-century Dictionaries of Mexican Indian Languages', *Yearbook, Inter-American Institute for Musical Research*, ii (1966), 101–59
R. Stevenson: *Music in Aztec and Inca Territory* (Berkeley, 1968)
G. Orta Velázquez: *Breve historia de la música en México* (Mexico City, 1970)
S. Martí: *La música precortesiana – Music before Cortés* (Mexico City, 1971, rev. 2/1978 by G. Nilsson as *Música precolombina – Music before Columbus*)
C. af Segerstam: *Popular Music in Mexico* (Albuquerque, 1976)
J. Koetling: 'The *son jalisciense*: Structural Variety in Relation to a Mexican Mestizo *forme fixe*', *Essays for a Humanist: an Offering to Klaus Wachsmann* (New York, 1977), 162
        GERARD BÉHAGUE (I), E. THOMAS STANFORD (II)

**Mexico City.** Capital of Mexico.

1. Before 1800. 2. 19th and 20th centuries.

1. BEFORE 1800. Tenochtitlán, the Aztec capital built where central Mexico City now stands, was founded, according to legend, in 1325 by a nomadic warrior tribe from the north. At the consecration ceremonies for the new great temple, erected at the centre of the city between 1482 and 1485 in honour of the heart-hungry deity Huitzilopochtli, 20,000 captives had their chests cut open by priests wielding sharp obsidian blades amid the din of *huehuetl* (an upright wooden cylinder drum covered with jaguar skin, beaten with bare hands), *teponaztli* (a two-keyed wooden slit-drum, beaten with rubber-tipped mallets) and other percussion instruments.

Among Spanish annalists of the final siege that preceded the fall of Tenochtitlán, Bernal Díaz del Castillo (c1492–c1581) best described the eerie throb of the *tlalpanhuehuetl* and other drums pounded during human sacrifices at this temple in July 1521. The Aztecs played no string instruments (none was known before the European invasion); instead, their highly trained musicians and priests played conch shell trumpets, metal trumpets, notched bone rasps, shrill clay whistles, vertical flutes, ocarinas, tortoise shells struck with antler prongs, rattles of different kinds, and especially the several varieties of *huehuetl* and *teponaztli*.

In the opinion of the invaders, Aztec music, whether heard during Montezuma's repasts or during sacrifices in the lofty terraced temples, faithfully mirrored the fierce and rigidly ritualistic Aztec religion. Drummers who missed a beat during their rituals were summarily withdrawn from their ensembles and executed. To sing from memory the lengthy hymns honouring their gods, young acolytes spent years in a special priests' seminary at Tenochtitlán (called *calmécac*). Every three-hour interval day and night had its own blood-letting ceremonies accompanied by appropriate music. But with their onerous responsibilities the court and temple musicians also enjoyed considerable social prestige, exemption from tribute, and constant contact with the mighty.

After 1521 these musicians, who under Aztec law had enjoyed privileges because they preserved community lore and morale, passed easily into the service of the scores of churches that Franciscans, Dominicans and Augustinians began planting over the former Aztec realm. Because the Indian populace assimilated European music more readily than any other facet of imported culture the cathedrals at Mexico City, Puebla and elsewhere could boast of music that rivalled the best in Spain only a half-century after the Conquest. As early as 1530 an Indian choir trained by Pedro de Gante (c1480–1572, a Franciscan from Ghent) sang every Sunday and feast day at Mexico City Cathedral (founded 1528). Only a year later Bishop Juan de Zumárraga (1468–1548) praised the skill of Indian polyphonic singers and in 1532 lauded the deft Indian copyists who transcribed European part music. In 1539, nine years after arriving in Mexico, Canon Juan Xuárez was appointed *maestro de capilla* of the cathedral and Antonio Ramos cathedral organist.

Lázaro del Álamo followed Xuárez in 1556, the year in which the first music book was published in the New World, an Augustinian 80-page *Ordinarium* printed at Mexico City by Giovanni Paoli (Juan Pablos), a native of Brescia, containing plainsong (copies in the British Museum and the New York Public Library at 42nd Street). Within the next 33 years 12 more lavish liturgical music books were printed at Mexico City. A 354-page *Manuale sacramentorum* printed in 1560 was followed by a 660-page *Missale Romanum Ordinarium* in 1561 (copy at *US-SM*) that has been justly called the handsomest New World book of its century; the music is printed on 52 pages in black notes over a five-line red staff. The other books printed before 1600 include four graduals, two psalters, two antiphoners, a Passion-book, and a new edition of the 1560 manual to conform with revisions of the sacramentary authorized by the Council of Trent. In 1604 a Franciscan, Juan Navarro from Cádiz, published at Mexico City *Quatuor Passiones* (copies at *GB-Lbm*, *US-SM*, *BLl*), which in contrast with the previous imprints consists of 105 leaves entirely of music (for the four Passions, Lamentations, and the Prayer of Jeremiah). Nowhere in the colonial Americas was any similar succession of plainsong imprints published.

Polyphony continued to flourish in the Mexico City Cathedral under the direction of such distinguished *maestros de capilla* as Hernando Franco (1575–85), Juan Hernández (1586–1620), Antonio Rodríguez de Mata (1625–43), Luis Coronado (1643–8), Fabián Pérez Ximeno (1648–54), Francisco López Capillas (1654–73), José de Loaysa y Agurto (1676–88), Antonio de Salazar (1688–1715) and Manuel de Zumaya (1715–39). They were all proficient composers with (except Hernández) an extant body of polyphony to prove their worth and also ran choir schools, superintended the purchase and care of large choral libraries, and conducted permanent paid choirs and professional instrumental ensembles that were equalled elsewhere in the New World only at Puebla, Lima and from time to time Bogotá, La Plata (now Sucre, Bolivia), Guatemala and Oaxaca.

Zumaya composed the music for the first North

American opera, *La Parténope*, mounted in the viceroyal palace 1 May 1711 (Silvio Stampiglia's libretto in Italian and Spanish on facing pages is in the Mexican National Library). After an interregnum the cathedral music was directed by the native of Lecce, Ignacio Jerusalem (1749–69), who was concurrently director of the theatre orchestra at the imposing Coliseo Nuevo (inaugurated 23 December 1735; the old Teatro Coliseo built in 1670 burnt down on 19 January 1722). The cathedral orchestra in the 16th century consisted of brass and woodwinds supported by organs, in the 17th century of the same forces augmented by harps, and in the 18th century predominantly of strings. The large surviving output of Jerusalem and his successors Matheo Tollis de la Roca and Antonio Juanas, the last colonial *maestros de capilla*, faithfully reflects the successive influences of the church music of Leo, Jommelli and Paisiello.

2. 19TH AND 20TH CENTURIES. During the 19th century Mexico City Cathedral music lost stature because of the curtailing of funds. The focus of musical life was the theatre until 1900 and then the concert hall. A typical season at the Coliseo Nuevo towards the end of the viceroyalty (1821) contained Cimarosa's *zarzuela bufa El Filósofo Burlado* (*Diario de México*, i, 100, 25 October 1805), and three theatre pieces by composers from nearby Puebla, Manuel Arenzana's *El Extrangero* billed as a two-act comedy with music, his *Los Dos Ribales en amor* billed as a new duo (*Diario*, i, 236 and 264, 25 November and 2 December 1805), and a sung-and-danced *bailete Siana y Silvio* in which the two daughters of the guitar-playing composer Luis Medina (1751–1806) took the parts of a shepherd and shepherdess driven into each other's arms by a sudden storm (*Diario*, i, 264, 2 December). The climax of the 1806 season at the Coliseo Nuevo was the première (4 December) of Paisiello's *Il barbiere di Siviglia* translated into Spanish and given as an 'opera bufa en cuatro actos'. The interludes between the four acts consisted of short Mexican dances ('bailes del país'). Five days later it was repeated, again with popular Mexican interludes ('sonecitos del país'). Native contributions to the Mexico City lyric stage were generally limited to the popular interludes in this way until well into the 19th century.

Between 1790 and 1810 the Coliseo orchestra was conducted by José Manuel Aldana, a native of Mexico City, who was however cynically urged in 1805 to change his name to something Italian. In 1813 the orchestra included strings, a flute, a bassoon, two trumpets and kettledrums. A singer's salary averaged three times that of an instrumentalist; star singers earned more than twice as much as less famous singers. However it was only after independence that opera sung in Italian became a matter of course at Mexico City: Manuel García, fresh from New York triumphs, inaugurated the custom on 29 June 1827 with Rossini's *Il barbiere di Siviglia*. From 1831 the Teatro Principal, newly refurbished, housed a regular annual season of Italian opera, and even native-born composers, including Cenobio Paniagua (1821–82) and Melesio Morales (1838–1908) had to compose their operas in Italian to get them produced at Mexico City. Aniceto Ortega first broke this rule with his one-act opera *Guatimotzín* (13 September 1871), in which the princess's part was sung by the chief Mexican-born prima donna of the century,

Angela Peralta (1845–83), and the last Aztec ruler's role by the celebrated Italian tenor Enrico Tamberlik. The Italian opera company contracted for the 1852–3 season advertised as its star the *prima donna assoluta* Balbina Steffennone who gave the official première of the Mexican national anthem on 16 September 1854 in the Gran Teatro de Santa Anna (music by the Catalan Jaime Nunó, 1824–1908).

The Conservatorio Nacional de Música grew out of an earlier conservatory organized under the auspices of the Sociedad Filarmónica Mexicana; it opened in 1866 with 14 instructors directed by Agustín Caballero, whose private academy (founded 1838 in cooperation with Joaquín Beristáin, 1817–39) provided the nucleus of the new conservatory. In 1877 it was nationalized. It was at Calle de la Moneda 16 in central Mexico City until 1950, when it moved to an attractive site in the suburbs, Avenida Presidente Masaryk 582.

Construction of the Carrara marble National Palace of Fine Arts was started in 1900 according to plans drawn by the Italian Boari, but after various intermissions and changes of plans was not finished until 1930, and so, like Mexico City Cathedral, it is in diverse styles. The concert hall (seats 3500) houses annual seasons of opera, symphony, ballet and large recitals; chamber concerts are given in the small adjacent hall named after Manuel M. Ponce. As in all other Latin American capitals, visiting musical celebrities perform frequently at the cultural institutes subsidized by the large European nations and the USA.

The National Institute of Fine Arts formerly located in upper floors of the Palace of Fine Arts was set up by President Miguel Alemán in 1946. In 1972 President Luis Echeverría decreed a new National Plan of Music Action headed by Carlos Chávez, the composer-conductor who founded the Orquesta Sinfónica de México in 1928. The composer Manuel Enríquez headed the National Conservatory from 1972 to August 1974 when he was succeeded by the organist Victor Urbán.

BIBLIOGRAPHY

A. Herrera y Ogazón: *El arte musical en México* (Mexico City, 1917)
G. Saldívar: *Historia de la música en México, épocas precortesiana y colonial* (Mexico City, 1934)
L. M. Spell: 'Music in the Cathedral of Mexico in the Sixteenth Century', *Hispanic American Historical Review*, xxvi (1946), 293
O. Mayer-Serra: 'México', *Música y músicos de Latinoamérica*, ii (Mexico City, 1947), 622
S. Barwick: *Sacred Vocal Polyphony in Early Colonial Mexico* (diss., Harvard U., 1949)
J. Bal y Gay: *Tesoro de la música polifónica en México*, i (Mexico City, 1952)
R. Stevenson: *Music in Mexico* (New York, 1952/*R*1971)
——: 'Mexico City Cathedral Music 1600–1750', *The Americas*, xxi/2 (1964), 111
——: *Music in Aztec and Inca Territory* (Berkeley and Los Angeles, 1968)
——: 'Mexico City', *Renaissance and Baroque Musical Sources in the Americas* (Washington, 1970), 131–80
D. Malmström: *Introduction to Twentieth Century Mexican Music* (Uppsala, 1974)

ROBERT STEVENSON

**Meyer, André(-Charles)** (*b* Colombes, 5 July 1884; *d* Paris, 10 May 1974). French collector. Having taken a degree in English literature at the Sorbonne (1904), he became an industrialist. When he was 15 he began an eclectic collection of considerable musical interest. Its most unusual section consists of drawings and engravings relating to music and musicians; its most important part comprises printed scores from the 17th century to the 19th, especially 18th-century instrumental music, chiefly French. Meyer always opened his collection to interested students. He was treasurer of the Société Française de Musicologie from 1945 to his death. There are two published catalogues of the collection. The first (1961), listing autograph manuscripts, printed and manuscript music, theoretical, historical and educational works, librettos, iconography and musical instruments, contains descriptions of the documents and about 300 illustrations; it was compiled by François Lesure and Nanie Bridgman. A supplement (1963) marks the acquisition of the sketches for *The Rite of Spring*. The second catalogue (1973, autograph manuscripts and iconography) consists of illustrations (251 plates) of the items described in the 1961 catalogue, and of later acquisitions. It was published under the direction of Fromrich-Bonéfant.

BIBLIOGRAPHY

*Collection musicale André Meyer* (Abbeville, 1961, suppl. 1963)
*Collection musicale André Meyer* (Abbeville, 1973)

CHRISTIANE SPIETH-WEISSENBACHER

**Meyer, Berta.** *See* MORENA, BERTA.

**Meyer, Conrad** (*b* Marburg; *d* Philadelphia, 1881). American piano maker of German origin. He emigrated to Baltimore in 1819, subsequently working for the piano maker Joseph Hisky. In 1829 he settled in Philadelphia where he started his own firm, and in 1833 exhibited one piano with 'shifting or transposing action' and another with an iron frame at the Franklin Institute. He later claimed that this square was made in 1832 and was unique in the USA for its single cast-iron frame. He did not patent it, and was in fact preceded by ALPHEUS BABCOCK, who patented a similar frame in 1825. But Meyer was often credited with this clever design, which permitted greater string tension and consequently a more resonant tone. Spillane wrote that Meyer made excellent pianos and that on Meyer's death the firm passed to his sons. The firm continued into at least the 1890s.

BIBLIOGRAPHY

D. Spillane: *History of the American Pianoforte* (New York, 1890/*R*1969)
*The Crosby Brown Collection of Musical Instruments of all Nations: Catalogue of Keyboard Instruments* (New York, 1903)

MARGARET CRANMER

**Meyer, Ernst Hermann** (*b* Berlin, 8 Dec 1905). German composer and musicologist. His father was a physician and his mother an artist. Brought up in a cultured environment, he showed early promise as a violinist and pianist, and by the age of seven he had already begun to compose. After a general education in a grammar school Meyer went in 1924 into an office, where he remained in uncongenial employment for three years. For the next few years, supporting himself by playing in dance bands and taking other jobs, he studied at the university and the Hochschule für Musik in Berlin, and in 1930 took a PhD at Heidelberg. His teachers included Hirschberg, Eisler, Butting, Schering, Sachs, Besseler and Hindemith, and his studies were wide-ranging – from the early instrumental music which formed the subject of his dissertation to the new compositional techniques of the day, particularly those relating to film music.

Having completed his formal studies with distinction, Meyer went into a world in which fascism and antisemitism were rampant. He courageously associated himself with those who opposed and, despite the hazards, illegally worked against Nazism. In 1933 he was obliged to emigrate to England, where he remained for 15 years. During the war years, under conditions of hardship, Meyer took various musical and non-musical jobs to aid the country in which he had found refuge. He was active as a choral conductor, as a university extra-mural and Workers' Educational Association lecturer, and as a composer, especially of music for documentary films; while his pioneer researches into old English chamber music (summarized in his important study of 1946) were a seminal influence on English musicology. In London Meyer was politically active and was among those who helped to establish the Free German League of Culture, an anti-Nazi organization of artists, scientists and writers.

In 1948 Meyer was invited back to Berlin as professor and director of the institute for musicology at the Humboldt University, an appointment he retained until his retirement in 1970. During this period he served as president of the East German Association of Composers and Musicologists, president of the Handel Society, and vice-president of the Academy of Arts, as well as holding other offices and membership of international organizations. Always deeply convinced of the necessity for the artist to be an active agent in the reform of society and the propagation of humanist ideals, Meyer threw himself wholeheartedly into the affairs of the newly formed state. His list of compositions rapidly lengthened according to the requirements of the times, and he was awarded national prizes in 1950, 1952 and 1963; he published many essays and gave many lectures on music and its social purposes as well as on musicological themes, and he educated a whole new generation of musicologists; he travelled extensively to give encouragement to professional and amateur musicians alike.

The leading musician of the German Democratic Republic, Meyer has exerted a profound influence on the general musical life of that state since its inception, and has consistently acted according to the Marxist-Leninist philosophy that was his early inspiration. His attitudes were also shaped by the tragic events and persecutions of the 1930s which were part of his own experience and which have given his works a particular passionate quality.

Meyer's public career has been entirely consistent and has embodied a coherent philosophy of life, evident both in his writings and compositions. A craftsman who exemplifies the virtues of the tradition in which he was brought up, with an unerring ear for the requirements of ensemble or occasion, and respectful of the Baroque and Classical heritage, Meyer informs his larger works with a distinctive intensity. His urgency of rhythmic drive is controlled by architectonic clarity, while the whole structure of the major work is marked by brilliant colour in instrumentation. His major works represent the deliberations of many years. The powerful Symphony for strings, for instance, was conceived when the composer was in exile, but was not ready for a first performance until 1957. There followed further revisions before the final version was published three years later. The Symphony in Bb, which grew out of a Sinfonietta, also had a long period of gestation. Like other works of Meyer this is patently referential and thematically recalls the *Mansfelder Oratorium*, the Symphony for strings, and the Goethe Lieder. In the Violin Concerto ideas from L. Fürnberg are acknowledged as implicit. In

film music of the London period Meyer experimented with considerable success, and the real-life noises imposed on to the soundtrack of, for example, *Roadways* were a new departure and an example for younger composers. Meyer's political faith went into settings of such poets as John Heartfield and have the character of similar settings by Eisler. But in settings of Fürnberg and J. R. Becher, free rein is given to a strong sense of lyricism also to be encountered in Meyer's choral works and children's music. He sometimes used the pseudonym Peter Baker.

## WORKS
*(for fuller list see the Festschrift, whose numbering is used here)*

### VOCAL ORCHESTRAL

| | |
|---|---|
| 186 | Now, Voyager (Whitman), 1946 |
| 201–4 | Vier Goethe Chöre, 1949 |
| 215 | Mansfelder Oratorium (S. Hermlin), 1950 |
| 238 | Der Flug der Taube (1952) |
| 241 | Des Sieges Gewissheit (J. R. Becher), 1952, rev. 1953 |
| 246 | Ein Lied für ihn (J. Fefer) (1953) |
| 248 | Ein Leben wahrhaft lebenswert (Becher) (1953) |
| 287 | Gesang von der Jugend (L. Fürnberg), 1957–8 |
| 290 | Du Mutter der Freien (Neruda), 1957–8 |
| 302 | Das Tor von Buchenwald (N. Bush, trans. P. Wiens), 1959 |
| 334 | Jahrhundert der Erstgeborenen (Fürnberg), 1961 |
| 352 | Rote Fahnen auf die Universität tät (R. Reinsch), 1962 |
| 371 | Der Staat (Becher) (1964) |
| 435 | Lenin hat gesprochen, cantata, 1970 |

### ORCHESTRAL

| | |
|---|---|
| 106 | Open Air Suite, 1934 |
| 130 | Three Tunes, 1939 |
| 188 | Symphony, str, 1947, rev. 1957–8 |
| 198 | Den Freiheitskämpfern zum Gedächtnis, sym. prol, 1949 |
| 275 | Musik für Postsportler I, 1956 |
| 278 | Musik für Postsportler II, 1956 |
| 298 | Sportmusik, 1959 |
| 305–8 | Orchestersuiten 1–4 [partly based on film music], 1959 |
| 341 | Konzertante Sinfonie, pf, orch, 1961 |
| 349 | Musik für Sportvereinigung Dynamo, 1962 |
| 353 | Poem, vn, orch (1964) |
| 357 | Festliche Ouvertüre, 1963, rev. 1965 as Sinfonisches Vorspiel |
| 369 | Violin Concerto, 1963–4 |
| 383 | Serenata pensierosa, 1965 |
| 390 | Concerto grosso, 1966, rev. 1969 |
| 391 | Rhapsodie élégiaque, mand, fl, str, 1966 |
| 398 | Symphony (originally Sinfonietta), Bb, 1967–8 |
| 415 | Concerto, harp, chamber orch, 1968 |
| 421 | Einleitungsmusik für Sportschau 69, 1969 |
| 422 | Leinefelder Suite, 1969, rev. 1971 as Leinefelder Divertimento |
| 445 | Toccata, 1971 |
| — | Divertimento concertante, 1973 |

### STAGE AND CINEMA

| | |
|---|---|
| 297 | Rostokker Hafen (ballet), 1958–9 |
| — | Reiter der Nacht (opera, G. Deicke, after P. Abraham: The Path of Thunder), 1970–71; Berlin, Staatsoper, 17 Nov 1973 |

Film scores: Roadways, 118, 1937; Lubricating Oil, 119, 1937; Oil from the Earth, 120, 1937; North Sea, 121, 1938; D.10, 122, 1938; The Londoners, 124, 1938; Why Make-up, why not?, 125, 1938–9; Guns or Butter, 126, 1939; British Made, 129, 1939; Collective Adventure, 133, 1940; A Few Ounces a Day, 139, 1941; When the Pie was Opened, 1941; Ship Control, 1941; Mobilise your Scrap, 1941; Fire Fighting, 146, 1941; Documentaries, 149–58, 160, 1942; Subject for Discussion, 162, 1943; Cameramen at War, 170, 1943–4; Spirit of Speed, 182, 1946; Water for Fire Fighting, 190, 1947; Switch Control, 192, 1948; Die Auftrag Höglers, 205, 1949; Von Hamburg nach Stralsund, 206, 1950; Chronik des Aufstiegs, 214, 1950; Roman einer jungen Ehe, 226, 1951; Wo du hingehest, 284, 1957; Solange Leben in mir ist (Karl Liebknecht I), 379, 1964–5; Trotz alledem (Karl Liebknecht II), 447, 1971

### UNACCOMPANIED CHORAL

| | |
|---|---|
| 113 | Labour's Marching Song (H. Farley) (?1936), as Peter Baker |
| 114 | The Final Struggle (G. Atterbury) (1936), as Peter Baker |
| 116 | We are the Men (R. Swingler), 1936–7 |
| 145 | For Cooperation (E. Ganley), 1941 |
| 172 | Our Life (after N. Ostrovsky), 1943 |
| 199 | Maientag (W. Dehmel), 1949 |
| 253–5, 261, 264–8 | Landschaftsbilder aus Deutschland (Becher, W. Layh), female vv, 1954 |
| 273 | Unserem Präsident (Layh), children's/mixed vv, 1955 |
| 274 | Vorspruch (Layh), 1955 |
| 276 | Sommernacht (Fürnberg), 1956 |
| 329 | Hütet nun ihr die Wissenschaften Licht (Brecht), 1960 |

362–4  Drei Lieder für Frauenchor (Fürnberg)
381    Drei Leipziger Kanons (Meyer), children's vv, 1965
Numerous unison and partsongs with kbd or other inst acc.

CHAMBER

1      String Quartet, g, 1916
10     Piano Trio, 1922
108    Sechs Flötenstücke, fl/rec, 1935
109    Trio, fl, ob, harp, 1935, rev. 1965–6
176    Clarinet Quintet (1970)
191    Piano Trio 'Reflections and Resolution', 1948
194    Movement, 2 vn, hn, 1948
259    Melodie [after Irish folksong], vn/cl, pf, 1954
279    String Quartet no.1, G, 1956
301    String Quartet no.2, 1959
384    Preludio alla ciacona, str qt, 1965
397    String Quartet no.3 [incl. 384 as last movt], 1966–7
411    Intermezzo, wind qnt, 1968
414    Kleine Eröffnungsmusik, cl qnt, 1968
—      String Quartet no.4, 1974
Many other early chamber pieces

OTHER WORKS

The most important solo songs with pf are collected in 10 Lieder (1922–3), 12 Lieder (1923–4), 6 Lieder (1924–5), 12 Lieder (1952), [63] Lieder und Gesänge (1961), [10] Pesni i romansï (Lieder und Gesänge) (1966), [40] Lieder und Gesänge, ii (1971)
Pf: 6 Pf Pieces, 68–73, 1929; 4 Pf Pieces, 183–5, 272, 1946, 1955, 1956; Aus dem Tagebuch eines kleinen Mädchens, 187, 1946; Toccata appassionata, 386, 1966; 2 Klavierstücke für Sylvia, 436, 1950; Allegro presto, 439, 1970

EDITIONS AND ARRANGEMENTS

J. Vaet: Sechs Motetten zu 4–6 Stimmen, Cw, ii (1929)
J. Pezel: Turmmusik: Auswahl von 18 Stücken (1930)
with K. Schleifer and W. Weismann: Neues Volksliederbuch für gemischten Chor (n.d.)
Numerous folksong arrs., 300–400 inst pieces of 1550–1700

WRITINGS

Die mehrstimmige Spielmusik des 17. Jahrhunderts in Nord- und Mitteleuropa (diss., U. of Heidelberg, 1930; Kassel, 1934)
English Chamber Music: the History of a Great Art from the Middle Ages to Purcell (London, 1946, 2/1951; Ger. trans., rev., 1958)
Musik in Zeitgeschehen (Berlin, 1952)
with H. Goldschmidt and G. Knepler: Musikgeschichte im Überblick (Berlin, 1956)
Aufsätze über Musik (Berlin, 1957)
'Hanns Eisler, der Lehrer', Musik in der Schule, ix (1958), 289
'Hanns Eisler – Kämpfer – Schöpfer – Vorbild', Musik und Gesellschaft, xii (1962), 587
'Concerted Instrumental Music', The Age of Humanism 1540–1630, NOHM, iv (1968)
Musik der Renaissance – Aufklärung – Klassik (Leipzig, 1973)
Numerous other articles, forewords, speeches, lectures

BIBLIOGRAPHY

J. Huntley: British Film Music (London, 1947)
F. K. Prieberg: Musik im anderen Deutschland (Cologne, 1968)
G. Knepler, ed.: Festschrift für Ernst Hermann Meyer (Leipzig, 1973)
K. Niemann: Ernst Hermann Meyer: für Sie porträtiert (Leipzig, 1975)

PERCY M. YOUNG

**Meyer, Johann David.** See MAYER, JOHANN DAVID.

**Meyer, Kathi.** See MEYER-BAER, KATHI.

**Meyer, Kerstin (Margareta)** (b Stockholm, 3 April 1928). Swedish mezzo-soprano. She studied in Stockholm with Arne Sunnegaardh and Andreyeva von Skoldonz, and then at the Salzburg Mozarteum, in Siena, Rome and Vienna. Her début in Stockholm was in 1952, as Azucena, and she became permanently associated with that company. She sang Carmen in Wieland Wagner's controversial 1959 production at Hamburg, where she also created Mrs Claiborne in Schuller's The Visitation (1966), Alice Arden in Goehr's Arden Must Die (1967) and Gertrude in Searle's Hamlet (1968). In 1960 she sang Dido in Les troyens (in English) at Covent Garden, later appearing as Octavian and Clytemnestra. After her début as Carolina in the first English-language performances of Henze's Elegy for Young Lovers (1961), she became a favourite at

Glyndebourne; her many roles there include Debussy's Geneviève, Monteverdi's Octavia, Clairon (Capriccio), Elisabeth in the première of Maw's The Rising of the Moon (1970) and the title role in the first British performances of Einem's Der Besuch der alten Dame (1973). At Salzburg she created Agave in Henze's The Bassarids (1966); she has also appeared at the Metropolitan Opera (1960–63) and Bayreuth (1962–5). A frequent performer in recital and concert, she often sings in duo with Elisabeth Söderström. Her voice is not large, and although its tendency to unsteadiness has become more pronounced, is used with skill; of strikingly handsome presence, she exhibits a remarkable dramatic flair. Meyer translated Einem's Der Besuch der alten Dame into Swedish for its production in Stockholm in 1976 and sang the title role.

HAROLD ROSENTHAL

**Meyer, Krzysztof** (b Kraków, 11 Aug 1943). Polish composer. He studied theory and composition with Wiechowicz and Penderecki in Kraków (where he returned to teach at the Conservatory), and took lessons with Boulanger in Paris. Among the awards he has received are a prize in the 1968 Fitelberg Competition for the Symphonie d'Orphée and a Prince Rainier III Prize (1970) for Cyberiada. The principal influences on his work are those of Lutosławski and Penderecki, but, particularly in chamber compositions, he has followed international avant-garde techniques.

WORKS

(selective list)

Stage: Cyberiada (comic opera, Meyer, after S. Lem), 1967–70
Orch: Conc. da camera, fl, perc, str, 1964; Sym. no.1, 1964; Sym. no.2, 1967; Symphonie d'Orphée (Sym. no.3) (Valéry), chorus, orch, 1968; Conc. da camera, ob, perc, str, 1972; Vn Conc., Vc Conc., Tpt Conc., 1975; Sym. no.4, 1975; Sym. no.5, 1978–9
Vocal chamber (J. Szczeblowska, J. Tuwim), 1963–7: Lyrics, S, ens; Songs of Resignation and Denial, S, vn, pf; Quartettino, S, fl, vc, pf; 5 Chamber Pieces, S, cl, vn, va; Lyric Triptych (Ander), T, chamber orch, 1976; 9 Epigrams, S, pf, 1979
Inst: Quattro colori, cl, trbn, vc, pf, 1970; Hommage à Nadia Boulanger, fl, harp, 1971; Sonata, hpd, 1973; 5 str qts; 5 pf sonatas; Interludio statico, cl, 4 vc; Conc. retro, fl, vn, vc, hpd, 1976; 24 Preludes, pf, 1978
Principal publishers: Moeck, Polskie Wydawnictwo Muzyczne

BIBLIOGRAPHY

A. Walaciński: 'Il kwartet smyczkowy Meyera', Ruch muzyczny (1965), no.17, p.10

MIECZYSŁAWA HANUSZEWSKA

**Meyer, Leonard B(unce)** (b New York, 12 Jan 1918). American musicologist and writer on aesthetics. Meyer studied philosophy and music at Columbia University (MA in music, 1948) and the history of culture at the University of Chicago (PhD, 1954), and studied composition privately with Stefan Wolpe and others. In 1946 he became a member of the department of music at the University of Chicago (professor, 1961–75; chairman, 1961–70) and in 1975 was appointed professor of music and the humanities at the University of Pennsylvania. He is best known for the theory of musical meaning expounded in Emotion and Meaning in Music, which develops in psychological terms a dynamic view of musical significance derived from Heinrich Schenker. He interprets musical forms and styles as historically evolving systems of expectations. The confirmations and frustrations of these expectations give rise to patterns of tensions aroused, sustained, and finally resolved, which musicians experience primarily as musical order and laymen primarily as a source of affect. Meyer's theory thus contrives a fusion of formal and expressive properties, which other aestheticians find it necessary to contrast. In *Music, the Arts, and Ideas* he reformulates his theory in terms of the mathematical theory of information, and predicts a situation in which radically divergent musical arts, derived from different world-views, will co-exist without mingling in a pluralistic civilization. *Explaining Music* explores the principles of structure in tonal music, and its relation to criticism. Meyer's was the most widely accepted account of music in America in the 1960s.

*See also* ANALYSIS, §§II, 7 and III, 1.

WRITINGS

*Emotion and Meaning in Music* (Chicago, 1956)
with G. Cooper: *The Rhythmic Structure of Music* (Chicago, 1960)
*Music, the Arts, and Ideas: Patterns and Predictions in Twentieth Century Culture* (Chicago, 1967)
*Explaining Music: Essays and Explorations* (Berkeley, 1973)
ed., with E. Zonis: *Improvisation in Music: East and West* (Chicago, 1973)
'The Sciences, the Arts – and the Humanities', *Critical Inquiry*, i 1974–5), 163–217
'Grammatical Simplicity and Relational Richness: the Trio of Mozart's G minor Symphony', *Critical Inquiry*, ii (1975–6), 693–761

BIBLIOGRAPHY

E. A. Lippman: Review of *Emotion and Meaning in Music*, *MQ*, xliii (1957), 553
R. C. Marsh: 'Analyst of the Muse', *High Fidelity*, vii (1957), May, 45–6, 118–20
H. Tischler: Review of *The Rhythmic Structure of Music*, *JAMS*, xvi (1963), 270
R. Woodham: Review of *Music, the Arts, and Ideas*, *ML*, xlix (1968), 238
L. Plantinga: Review of *Music, the Arts, and Ideas*, *JMT*, xiii (1969), 141

F. E. SPARSHOTT

**Meyer, Philippe-Jacques** [Philipp Jakob; Philip James] (*b* Strasbourg, 1737; *d* London, 1819). Alsatian harpist and composer who worked in Paris and London. He originally studied theology but soon devoted himself to the harp. He became a pupil of Christian Hochbrucker in Paris, then the centre of harp playing; his first solo appearance at the Concert Spirituel was in 1761 and he performed there for three more years, often playing his own compositions. He established himself as a teacher and published a harp method in 1763 (*Essai sur la vraie manière de jouer de la harpe* op.1). After marrying in his homeland he was again active in Paris after 1765 as a teacher and composer. He introduced the new pedal harp to England during his first visit there in 1772. For the next eight years he travelled between London, Paris and Strasbourg until he settled in London in 1784.

Meyer's harp method is important as the first historical survey of harps and as one of the earliest specialist tutors. In it he discussed both the old hook harp and the new pedal harp, gave the correct tuning of both, dealt with the positioning of the hands, elaborated on *agréments* and recommended the arpeggio; the wording is expressly for beginners and laymen. He published many works for solo harp and harp with other instruments in Paris and London. The setting of *Apollon et Daphné*, 1782, attributed to him by Sainsbury, is by the Bohemian stage composer Anton Mayer (*b* Libicz, *c*1750; *d* after 1793).

Meyer's sons, Philippe-Jacques Meyer jr (*d* London, 1841) and Frédéric-Charles Meyer, were harpists, teachers and composers in England. Each published light music for the harp such as lessons, arrangements of songs, variations, divertimentos and sonatas; Frédéric-Charles also wrote a harp method (*A New Treatise on the Art of Playing upon the Double Movement Harp*,

*c*1825). It is doubtful whether the harpists Johann Bernhard Meyer and Johann Baptist Meyer were related to Philippe-Jacques Meyer, although both were active in Paris and London and both published harp compositions and methods.

WORKS

*(only those extant)*

Pedagogical: Essai sur la vraie manière de jouer de la harpe, avec une méthode de l'accorder, op.1 (Paris, 1763, 2/1772); Nouvelle méthode pour aprendre à jouer de la harpe avec la manière de l'accorder, op.9 (Paris, 1774)
Solo harp: 6 sonate, op.3 (Paris, 1768); 6 sonates, op.4 (Paris, 1770); 4 Original Lessons, i–ii (London, n.d.); Favorite Lesson (Dublin, n.d.)
Other: 6 divertimenti, harp, vn, op.2 (Paris, 1767); 8 divertissements, harp, vn, b, op.6 (Paris, 1771); 6 sonate, harp, vn ad lib, op.7 (Paris, 1773); Divertissement (2 harps)/(harp, pf/hpd), vn, fl (Kehl, 1782); 6 divertimentis, pf/harp, vn, fl (London, n.d.); 2 Sonatas, harp, pf/(2 vn, va, vc) (London, n.d.); A Sonata, harp/pf, vn (London, n.d.); 2 Duets, harp, pf/hpd (London, n.d.); 2 Duets, 2 harps/harp, pf, 2nd Set (London, n.d.); An Original Theme and a Favourite Scotch Air with Variations, harp, pf/fl ad lib (London, n.d.)
Many arrs. of songs and variations for harp/kbd pubd in London and Paris

BIBLIOGRAPHY

*EitnerQ*; *FétisB*; *GerberL*; *GerberNL*
J. Sainsbury, ed.: *A Dictionary of Musicians* (London, 2/1825/*R*1966)
F. Vernillat: 'Littérature de la harpe en France au XVIIIe siècle', *RMFC*, ix (1969), 165

HANS J. ZINGEL

**Meyer-Baer** [née Meyer], **Kathi** (*b* Berlin, 27 July 1892). American musicologist and librarian of German birth. She studied musicology at Berlin under Kretzschmar, Riemann and Johannes Wolf, and obtained her PhD in 1916. She has had a varied and distinguished career as scholar, as music librarian in many different capacities, and as critic. From 1922 onwards she worked mainly as assistant to Paul Hirsch in his music library at Frankfurt for nearly 14 years, during which period she was also research librarian at the Berlin State Library in 1928, and from 1927 to 1929 worked on the organization of the music department in the city library at Frankfurt. She supervised various important exhibitions, including the international music exhibition at Frankfurt in 1927, the 'Goethe and music' exhibition of 1932 and the Wagner Memorial Exhibition of 1933. From 1923 to 1932 she was a music critic on the *Frankfurter Zeitung* and, for a shorter period, on the *Neue Musik-Zeitung* of Stuttgart. After emigrating to the USA in 1939 she became a member of the editorial board of Schirmer in 1941 and joined the music department of the New York Public Library (1942–3).

Meyer-Baer's personal research has produced important work in four main fields: the aesthetic aspects of music, liturgical music, musical bibliography and music printing. In the last of these, her long research culminated in *Liturgical Music Incunabula* which was the first thorough study of the subject. This, though an invaluable book, should be used with caution because of certain basic inadequacies in identifying printers and presses. Her other outstanding achievement was the four volumes of the Hirsch Library catalogue which she edited in conjunction with Paul Hirsch. Her studies in musical iconography are the product of keen observation and fine critical judgment, and like so much of her work reflect a wide-ranging and thoughtful mind.

WRITINGS

*(those before 1947 appeared under her maiden name Kathi Meyer)*
*Der chorische Gesang der Frauen* (diss., U. of Berlin, 1916; Leipzig, 1917)

'Das "Amptbuch" des Johannes Meyer: ein Beitrag zur Geschichte des Musikbetriebes in den Klostern des Mittelalters', *AMw*, i (1918–19), 166
'Ein historisches Lied aus dem Frauenkloster zu St.-Gallen', *ZMw*, i (1918–19), 269
'Das Offizium und seine Beziehung zum Oratorium', *AMw*, iii (1921), 371–404
'Der Einfluss der gesanglichen Vorschriften auf die Chor- und Emporenanlagen in den Klosterkirchen', *AMw*, iv (1922), 155
*Das Konzert* (Stuttgart, 1925)
*Katalog der internationalen Ausstellung 'Musik im Leben der Völker': Frankfurt am Main 11. Juni–28 August 1927* (Frankfurt, 1927)
'Die Musikbibliothek Paul Hirsch in Frankfurt a.M.', *Taschenbuch für Büchersammler*, ii (1927), 10
'Ein Musiker des Göttinger Hainbunds, Joseph Martin Kraus', *ZMw*, ix 1926–7), 468
with P. Hirsch: *Katalog der Musikbibliothek Paul Hirsch* (Frankfurt, 1928–36; Eng. trans., 1947)
*Bedeutung und Wesen der Musik* (Strasbourg, 1932)
'Die Musikdrucke in den liturgischen Inkunabeln von Wenssler und Kilchen', *Gutenberg Jb* (1935), 117
with E. J. O'Meara: 'The Printing of Music 1473–1934', *The Dolphin*, ii (1935), 171–207
'Was sind musikalische Erstausgaben', *Philobiblon*, viii (1935), 181
'Die Illustrationen in den Musikbüchern des 16–17 Jahrhunderts', *Philobiblon*, xii (1939), 205, 278
with I. M. Christensen: 'Artaria Plate Numbers', *Notes*, 1st ser., no.15 (1942), 1
'Early Breitkopf und Härtel Catalogues', *MQ*, xxx (1944), 163
'Michel de Toulouse: the First Printing of Measured Music', *MR*, vii (1946), 178
'Nicolas de Cusa on the Meaning of Aesthetics', *Journal of Aesthetics and Art Criticism*, v (1946–7), 301
'Musical Iconology in Raphael's Parnassus', *Journal of Aesthetics and Art Criticism*, viii (1949–50), 87
'Classifications in American Music Libraries', *MR*, xii (1951), 76
'The Eight Gregorian Modes on the Cluny Capitals', *Art Bulletin*, xxxiv (1952), 75
'Psychologic and Ontologic Ideas in Augustine's De Musica', *Journal of Aesthetics and Art Criticism*, xi (1953), 224
'St. Job as a Patron of Music', *Art Bulletin*, xxxvi (1954), 21
'Saints of Music', *MD*, ix (1955), 11
'Some Remarks on the Problems of the Basse-dance', *TVNM*, xvii/4 (1955), 251
'Der Musikdruck in Inkunabeln: ein übersehenes Hilfsmittel zur Beschreibung', *Libri*, x (1960), 105
*Liturgical Music Incunabula: a Descriptive Catalogue* (London, 1962)
*Music of the Spheres and the Dance of Death: Studies in Musical Iconography* (Princeton, 1970)

EDITIONS
E. Bottrigari: *Il Desiderio, 1594* (Berlin, 1924)
C. Stieler: *Die geharnischte Venus, 1660* (Munich, 1925)
ALEC HYATT KING

**Meyerbeer** [Meyer Beer], **Giacomo** [Jakob Liebmann] (*b* Vogelsdorf, nr. Berlin, 5 Sept 1791; *d* Paris, 2 May 1864). German composer, the central musical figure in French grand opera after 1831.

1. Education and early career. 2. Italy and Paris (1816–29). 3. 'Robert le diable' and 'Les Huguenots' (1831–6). 4. From 1836 to the première of 'Le prophète'. 5. Final years. 6. Meyerbeer's concept of grand opera. 7. Other works.

1. EDUCATION AND EARLY CAREER. Meyerbeer came from a wealthy Jewish merchant family in Berlin. His father Jakob (Juda) Herz Beer (1769–1825) was licensed as an army contractor in Berlin in 1794 and owned sugar refineries in Berlin and Gorizia in north-eastern Italy. His mother Amalia (1767–1854) was a daughter of Liebmann Meyer Wulf (1740–1812), who became general concessionaire of the Prussian lottery in 1794, held licences as contractor to both the army and the postal service and was also a banker. He was a highly respected elder of the Jewish community and took a leading part in the struggles for emancipation from the French in 1812. Amalia Beer was awarded the Order of Luisa for her work with the wounded during the 1813–15 war. From 1800 Meyerbeer's parental home was a favourite meeting-place of Berlin's cultural élite, particularly its musical members, and although Amalia did not belong to the upper middle class she knew how to create an interesting and stimulating circle, so that even members of the court frequented her house, including the future King Friedrich Wilhelm IV, whom Meyerbeer therefore met during his childhood. Men like Iffland and Alexander von Humboldt were among the Beer family's long-standing friends, and the Prussian royal house took a continual interest in its fortunes.

Franz Lauska, piano teacher to the royal princes, gave Meyerbeer his first music lessons, and at the age of 11 he appeared in Berlin as a pianist. From 1805 to 1807 he studied composition with Zelter, and then with B. A. Weber, who had considerable theatrical experience and who recommended him to his own former teacher, Abbé Vogler in Darmstadt. Vogler, the leading music theorist in Germany, carefully analysed a fugal exercise of Meyerbeer's and wrote an elaborate commentary on it; both were published as *System für den Fugenbau* (Offenbach, ?1811). While studying with Weber, Meyerbeer wrote his first stage work, a ballet-pantomime, from an outline by Lauchery, the head ballet-master of the Royal Opera. It was called *Der Fischer und das Milchmädchen* and was performed in Berlin early in 1810.

On 1 April 1810 Meyerbeer, accompanied by his tutor Aron Wolfssohn and his brother Heinrich (known as Hans), went to Darmstadt to complete his musical education under Vogler, who had assured Meyerbeer's parents that his teaching method avoided any undue effort 'because it is conducted through an exchange of multifarious and exhaustive artistic conversations'. Vogler wrote to them on 3 May 1810 of Meyerbeer's 'excellent talent', stressing his 'rare perseverance and industriousness'. Among Meyerbeer's fellow pupils were C. M. von Weber, J. B. Gänsbacher and, for a time, Gottfried Weber and Alexander Dusch from Mannheim; several lifelong artistic friendships were formed at this time. These like-minded young men, led by C. M. von Weber, founded the so-called Harmonischer Verein (1810–13) whose members (using pseudonyms) published reviews of each others' works to further their artistic ends. During the next few years Meyerbeer wrote a number of such reviews under the names Julius Billig and Philodikaios.

During his two years with Vogler, Meyerbeer made great progress with his piano playing and also wrote many small, unpublished works, as well as two operas, *Der Admiral* (never performed) and *Jephtas Gelübde*. At the end of 1811 he left his teacher, whose great fame had begun to irritate his ambitious nature, and in March 1812 embarked on an independent artistic career. From Darmstadt he went to Munich, where he stayed nine months; during this time he met the clarinettist H. J. Baermann, for whom he drafted several clarinet works. *Jephtas Gelübde* was performed there on 23 December 1812 without apparent success, and Meyerbeer composed the little comic opera *Wirth und Gast*, which was equally unsuccessful when performed in Stuttgart on 6 January 1813. Even in its revised version, *Die beyden Kalifen* (later *Alimelek*), its Viennese première on 20 October 1814 was a failure. On arriving in Linz on his way to Vienna, Meyerbeer learnt that on 12 February 1813 he had been named court composer to the Grand Duke of Hesse, an appointment secured for him by Vogler, who felt that an official title would help his pupil's career.

Meyerbeer's success as a pianist was as great as his failure as a composer of German opera. In Darmstadt he had already written for his own use several piano works that were never published and have since disappeared. He wrote of them to Fétis on 17 April 1838: 'They are not worth mentioning. But my playing is quite another matter'. In fact, he was at this time acclaimed in private circles as a virtuoso whose playing even Ignaz Moscheles found 'unsurpassed' and of which Gänsbacher said that he 'had never heard the like'.

In spring 1814 Meyerbeer wrote a Singspiel *Das Brandenburger Tor* for the coming entry of the victorious Prussian troops into Berlin (3 August), but it was not performed because the score reached Berlin too late. In mid-November 1814 he left Vienna for Paris, travelling via Munich, where he appeared as a pianist; he already regarded Paris as the 'first and most important stage' for his musical–dramatic development, as he wrote to his father in the same month, but his idea of composing a small work for the Théâtre Feydeau was not realized. At the beginning of December 1815 Meyerbeer, who had not yet abandoned the idea of a career as a pianist (*Briefwechsel*, i, 307), went to London to hear J. B. Cramer play. There he also met Kalkbrenner, Ivan Müller and Ferdinand Ries.

2. ITALY AND PARIS (1816–29). Early in 1816 Meyerbeer visited Italy for the first time. In March he met Baermann and the singer Helene Harlas in Genoa and composed the monodrama *Gli amori di Teolinda* for them. He left shortly after for Rome, in June arrived in Naples and sailed to Palermo, where he stayed three months collecting national folksongs, an idea conceived in London (see Bose, 1970).

*1. Giacomo Meyerbeer: portrait (1802) by Friedrich Georg Weitsch in the Staatliches Institut für Musikforschung Preussischer Kulturbesitz, Berlin*

This stay in Italy, planned as a study tour, gradually extended itself to nine years, broken by several trips to Germany and Austria. While in Italy Meyerbeer met the foremost artists, won the interest of leading librettists and impresarios and was more successful as an opera composer than he had ever hoped. The six operas performed there – *Romilda e Costanze* (1817), *Semiramide riconosciuta* (1819), *Emma di Resburgo* (1819), *Margherita d'Anjou* (1820), *L'esule di Granata* (1821) and *Il crociato in Egitto* (1824) – so increased his reputation that in Italy he was even placed on the level of Rossini. The reserve with which he was greeted in his native country, however, soon dispelled his idea of simply adapting his Italian operas for the German stage. He wrote later to Count Moritz of Dietrichstein in Vienna that his time in Italy had been a 'period of seduction' in which his own 'artistic self . . . was unfaithful' to him (*Briefwechsel*, ii, 368).

The great success of *Il crociato* gave Meyerbeer the confidence to confront Paris. On 23 July 1825 the King's Theatre, London, staged the work in the impresario Barbaia's original production, and the Théâtre-Italien in Paris followed suit on 25 September. Its brilliant success in Paris, which was witnessed by Friedrich Wilhelm III, turned Meyerbeer overnight into a composer of European standing, and Spontini was instructed to persuade him to compose an opera for Berlin. His most important encounter in Paris was with Eugène Scribe, who at that time dominated the French theatre.

Although from 1825 Meyerbeer often spent several months a year in Paris, he never settled there nor acquired a permanent home, but rented hotel suites or private lodgings for each visit. After his appointment in 1842 as Generalmusikdirektor in Berlin his visits to Paris became rarer, though he was only occasionally in Berlin. Always on the move, he was in every sense an international man, whose real home was Europe. There were three main reasons for his journeys: medical orders to take cures at Ems, Baden-Baden, Ischl or Spa (both he and his wife Minna suffered from ill-health), productions of his operas in major European cities and, not least, the auditioning of new singers. His interest in hearing little-known singers was a continual incentive to embark on spontaneous and unexpected journeys. He was rarely if ever attracted to premières of new operas, and would attend them only if the principal singers interested him.

Meyerbeer knew that he could risk an assault on the Paris Opéra only if he had an outstanding libretto and time enough to compose a score that would appeal to French taste. First, however, he exploited the impressive success of *Il crociato*, so that his current popularity should not fade. He secured the collaboration of an experienced French playwright, Thomas Sauvage, to adapt the text of another of his Italian operas, *Margherita d'Anjou*. Its première on 11 March 1826 at the Odéon was followed by 36 more performances. It is not clear what part the conductor Pierre Crémont played in reworking the score, but his name appeared in one newspaper as 'author'. In 1826 Sauvage also wrote for Meyerbeer the libretto of a fairy opera, *La nymphe de Danube*, which was to be a pasticcio of the most popular numbers of his Italian operas; however, the work was eventually put aside.

When Weber died (1826) his heirs, in accordance with his wishes, gave Meyerbeer the sketches for his

*2. Autograph score of part of the Page aria from Act 1 of Meyerbeer's opera 'Les Huguenots', first performed Paris 1836 (D-Bim Meyerbeer Archive); this autograph is a later, German version with transposition to F major*

unfinished opera, *Die drei Pintos*, in the hope that he would complete it and have it produced in Paris. In repeated attempts Meyerbeer found it impossible to do anything with the rough and sketchy material, and as he could not accept Weber's libretto, he put off completing the opera from year to year, for which he was repeatedly attacked in the German and French press. On 27 January 1852 he settled the matter with Weber's heirs by handing over to them copies of Weber's music prepared by F. W. Jähns and by compensating them with a payment of 4000 thalers.

Meyerbeer's high opinion of *Il crociato* is shown by his decision to revise it as a grand opera for the Opéra. In 1826 he agreed with the Opéra's director, the

Viscount de la Rochefoucauld, to shelve the Italian version so that comparisons should as far as possible be avoided. By 1828 he had composed a new overture, much ballet music and other new numbers. *Robert le diable*, the *opéra comique* on which he had agreed in 1827 to collaborate with Scribe, was evidently not representative enough for him. These somewhat frenetic projects demonstrate Meyerbeer's determination to overcome any obstacles to his success in the Paris opera world. This is all the more remarkable because these very years were beset by various developments and calamities in his private life: on 27 October 1825 his father died unexpectedly; on 25 May 1826 he married his cousin Minna Mosson, the daughter of his mother's younger sister; and in 1827 and 1829 his children Eugénie and Alfred died in infancy.

3. 'ROBERT LE DIABLE' AND 'LES HUGUENOTS' (1831–6). The production of Auber's *La muette de Portici* (1828) and Rossini's *Guillaume Tell* (1829) may have convinced Meyerbeer that he would never reach the first rank of Paris composers simply by revising old scores. He therefore gave up all his previous projects and, instead of adapting *Il crociato*, turned *Robert le diable* from an *opéra comique* into a grand opera. The success of its première on 21 November 1831 was greater than any that Meyerbeer or the Opéra itself had known before and placed him unchallenged at the head of European opera composers. Rossini, his most important rival, definitively renounced the stage, and Fétis wrote in the *Revue musicale* (1831, 366): 'The score of *Robert le diable* is not just M. Meyerbeer's masterpiece; it is a work remarkable in the history of art ... it incontestably places M. Meyerbeer at the head of the present German school and makes him its chief'. Within three years it had been performed in 77 theatres in ten countries. Ten years later Wagner wrote in the Dresden *Abendzeitung*: '*Robert le diable* has a wonderful, almost sinister atmosphere. ... It is deathless!' (*Briefwechsel*, iii, 619). (For Cicéri's original setting for Act 3, *see* OPERA, fig.11).

Many composers, including Chopin, Thalberg, Herz, Adam, Kalkbrenner, Liszt and Strauss sought to take advantage of the new opera's success through producing countless arrangements, variations and fantasias; Meyerbeer himself was faced with the prospect of not merely maintaining the same standard of success, but surpassing it, and within a short period of time – a virtually impossible task, of which he remained conscious even later in life. He felt that he must continually compete with his own increasing fame, which began to bring him a series of honours: in 1832 he was made a Chevalier of the Légion d'honneur and a Prussian Hofkapellmeister, on 2 May 1833 a member of the senate of the Prussian Academy of Arts and in December 1834 a member of the French Institute.

In January 1831, even before the première of *Robert*, Scribe and Meyerbeer had discussed the libretto of *Le portefaix*, an *opéra comique* originally intended for Hérold, and on 1 February 1831 a contract was signed, Meyerbeer undertaking to write the score by October that year. The success of *Robert* decided Meyerbeer, who had not completed *Le portefaix*, to give this opera to the Opéra as a through-composed work. However, the Opéra director Véron insisted on a five-act work, and as Scribe was not willing to extend the three of *Le portefaix*, the contract was terminated in 1834.

Scribe was meanwhile busily seeking a new subject; in 1832 he and Dumas discussed with Meyerbeer a libretto called *Les brigands*, but this came to nothing through a quarrel between the two writers. On 23 October 1832 a contract was signed for *La St Barthélemy* (also known as *Léonore*, *Valentine* and eventually *Les Huguenots*), the music for which was to be ready by 15 December 1833. This early deadline shows that Meyerbeer let himself make commitments that he could not meet, though he did initially plan his grand operas on much more modest lines than those they eventually assumed. Véron had insured himself against non-fulfilment of the contract with a penalty clause of 30,000 francs. The composition of the opera dragged on as the work grew larger. When the deadline arrived and Meyerbeer had not finished it, he claimed that he had to accompany his sick wife to Italy. Véron nevertheless foolishly insisted on his paying the fine, which he did promptly.

It seemed to Meyerbeer a shortcoming in the libretto that many sections contained no female voices, and as Scribe would make no alterations, Meyerbeer had some parts of Act 4 modified by his former Italian collaborator, Gaetano Rossi in Verona. He told Scribe, however, that he had written them himself, and when Scribe refused to translate them into French, Emile Deschamps did so. Véron paid Meyerbeer back his fine on 30 October 1834; however, his position as director of the Opéra had become untenable, and *Les Huguenots* had its première – one of the most memorable in opera history – on 29 February 1836 under the directorship of Duponchel, who had succeeded Véron on 16 August 1835. Only shortly before, Meyerbeer had had to alter the scene of the blessing of the daggers (inspired by Bellini's *Norma*), because the censors had forbidden the representation of Catherine de' Medici on stage. The scene with the monks (one of the most famous in opera) was also condemned, but saved through Scribe's intervention; this act (the fourth) underwent a further change in December 1835 with the insertion of the celebrated love-duet, on which the tenor Adolphe Nourrit had been insisting since August.

4. FROM 1836 TO THE PREMIÈRE OF 'LE PROPHÈTE'. When the vocal score and excerpts of *Les Huguenots* were on sale (the publisher Schott in Mainz had offered 24,000 francs for the score even before it was finished) Meyerbeer once again started negotiations with Scribe for a new subject. By the end of the year they were conferring over *Le prophète*; the first scenic heading for it in Meyerbeer's 1836 pocket diary reads 'Coronation'. In March 1835 he had received the libretto of *Cinq mars* (Henry Saint-Georges), which he envisaged as an *opéra comique* for Crosnier, director of the Théâtre Porte St Martin; after several false starts he eventually abandoned working on this on 5 December 1837, the reason probably being a new Scribe libretto, *L'africaine*. In accordance with a contract signed on 24 May 1837, he had received *L'africaine* at the end of August 1837; he was to complete the music by 24 August 1840, and he paid Scribe 5000 francs for the text.

The principal role of *L'africaine* was written, dramatically and musically, for Mlle Falcon and it was the loss of her voice and the absence of a comparable artist to take her place that decided Meyerbeer to stop work on it, not a growing distaste for the libretto, as has occasionally been suggested. On 1 August 1838 the contractual deadline was provisionally extended to 24

August 1842 and on 2 August a contract for *Le pro-phète* was drawn up. *Le prophète* was intended for the new tenor at the Opéra, Gilbert Duprez, who was at this time enjoying tremendous success as Arnold in *Guillaume Tell*, which he was the first to sing with a full chest voice in the upper range. The exceptional tenor role in *Le prophète* was conceived for his type of voice, though later modified for Gustave Roger.

Meyerbeer's memorable first encounter with Wagner took place on 20 August 1839 at Boulogne, where Meyerbeer was taking a cure. Wagner asked for help, which Meyerbeer gave him both financially and through professional recommendations. Only when he learnt that Wagner, discontented with the slow progress of his career, was speaking ill of him behind his back did he withdraw his help, but without his previous assistance *Rienzi* and *Der fliegende Holländer* would not have been mounted on the German stage so soon.

With Gaspare Spontini's dismissal as Prussian Generalmusikdirektor in 1842 after the death of Friedrich Wilhelm III, new forces in Berlin put an end to cultural bigotry, and Meyerbeer was unanimously chosen as his successor. He was now not merely the only German opera composer of international standing, but indisputably the leading active opera composer in the world. The first result was that *Les Huguenots*, which had been banned by the late king on the recommendation of the Prussian censorship office, was at last performed in Berlin (20 May 1842). Its success was outstanding, despite some opposition (including that of Berlin's most powerful critic, Ludwig Rellstab), and on 31 May 1842 Meyerbeer was the first composer to receive a newly created award of the Order of Peace. This was followed on 11 June by his installation as

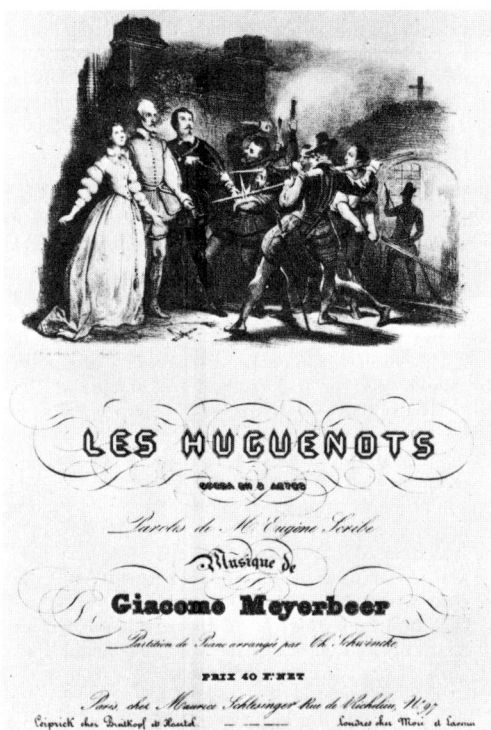

*3. Title-page of the first edition of the vocal score of 'Les Huguenots', published by Schlesinger (Paris, 1836)*

Prussian Generalmusikdirektor, for which no less a figure than Alexander von Humboldt had energetically canvassed. The intendant, Count Redern, was simultaneously promoted to Generalintendant and a newcomer, Karl Theodor von Küstner, took his place. Meyerbeer and Küstner were soon in conflict over demarcation of authority, since Küstner regarded himself as Meyerbeer's superior, while the latter considered him an equal. This growing controversy came to a head on 26 November 1848 with Meyerbeer's dismissal, though he had in effect already resigned from this onerous post because of his prolonged absence without pay. He remained director of the royal court music until his death. As court composer Meyerbeer produced works for royal family occasions and official court entertainments, including several Fackeltänze for royal weddings and *Das Hoffest von Ferrara*, written for a masked ball on 28 February 1843. The grand opera *Ein Feldlager in Schlesien*, written for the reopening on 7 December 1844 of the opera house, which had been destroyed by fire, should also be counted among these occasional compositions. The principal role was sung by Jenny Lind, whom Meyerbeer discovered. The fact that he asked Scribe to write a full scenario for this work, although his name could not appear, shows how much Meyerbeer cared about his success at the Berlin Opera. Through Liszt's mediation a reconciliation was effected between Meyerbeer and Rellstab, who now agreed to write the German text in verse. Nevertheless, the parochial Prussian patriotism of the libretto and Meyerbeer's 'simple, warmhearted, German' music (Hanslick) gave the work little chance of a place in the international repertory. The final *tableaux vivants* were a trite concession to a passing fashion and were soon replaced by a new finale. For the Viennese production in 1847 Meyerbeer, with the help of Charlotte Birch-Pfeiffer, moved the scene of the action to Bohemia, and under its new name, *Vielka*, this opera had a great success. Meyerbeer himself, with astute realism, saw this as solely of nationalist origin and obstinately refused to bring this version to Paris.

For years Meyerbeer had been exposed to ironical innuendos in Paris about the delay over *Le prophète* and *L'africaine*. Now in his own interest he wanted to prepare a new première, his first there for over ten years. On 15 January 1846 he signed a contract with Scribe and Saint-Georges for *Noëma, ou Le repentir*, intending its première to take place in April 1849, but for personal reasons he gave up this work after he had already started composing it. He then returned seriously to *Le prophète*, the score of which had been finished since 1840 and deposited with a Paris lawyer, as the Opéra director Léon Pillet would not engage a suitable tenor. In the meantime Meyerbeer composed incidental music for a Berlin production of the play *Struensee*, by his brother Michael Beer (d 1833), but only the overture survived its shortlived success. Attacks in the press, instigated by Heinrich Laube, whose own *Struensee* had been unfavourably compared with Beer's, showed Meyerbeer clearly that he had more enemies than supporters in Germany.

The emergence of the contralto Pauline Viardot-Garcia, whose voice fascinated Meyerbeer, and the hopelessness of finding an outstanding tenor for *Le prophète* led the composer to reduce the importance of its tenor part in favour of the alto part of Fidès. When the incumbent director was replaced on 31 July 1847 by Nestor Roqueplan and Duponchel, the new directors quickly engaged Viardot-Garcia. Meyerbeer totally revised the score and added some completely new sections, particularly for Fidès, and in this version it was first performed on 16 April 1849, with Gustave Roger and Viardot-Garcia in the leading roles. The enthusiastic reception of the work, attributed by Meyerbeer to Viardot-Garcia's performance, confirmed his position in grand opera. Leading Paris critics, among them Berlioz and Théophile Gautier, described this success as unparalleled and Meyerbeer became the first German musician to receive the award of Commandeur of the Légion d'honneur. Publishers fought over the score and theatres all over Europe competed to stage it. Meyerbeer received 44,000 francs for the publishing rights in France, England and Germany, and in the following year *Le prophète* was produced in 40 theatres and on 14 July 1851 had its 100th performance at the Opéra.

5. FINAL YEARS. Immediately after the première of *Le prophète* Meyerbeer started discussions with Scribe about a revision of the libretto of *Ein Feldlager*. Whether they originally envisaged a new opera or simply an adaptation of the *Feldlager* music to a new libretto is uncertain. At first Meyerbeer described *La cantinière*, which Scribe had adapted from an earlier ballet scenario, as his 'new opera'; only later, after he had changed the title to *L'étoile du nord*, did it become clear that he intended using music from *Ein Feldlager*. He prepared so-called 'monstres', or metric patterns, to which Scribe was to write his verse. In this work for the first time he consciously used a leitmotif. As before, he did not work steadily, but kept breaking off on the pretext of outside pressures. He again took up *L'africaine*, for which Scribe sent him a new scenario on 1 December 1851, and wrote several pieces for it at the beginning of 1853. On 16 February 1854 *L'étoile du nord* had its première at the Opéra-Comique in the presence of the emperor and empress, and its brilliant success served once more to underline his supremacy as an opera composer. He chose the biblical story of Judith for his next work, again in collaboration with Scribe, but after a number of false starts he abandoned it.

On 27 June 1854 Jules Barbier gave Meyerbeer the synopsis of a one-act comic opera *Le chercheur du trésor*. Meyerbeer liked it and asked Barbier and Michel Carré to write it as a three-act *opéra comique*. As *Le pardon de Ploërmel* it had a particularly successful première on 4 April 1859; within a few days 1500 copies of the extracts had been sold, these having been prepared in time for the première, contrary to usual practice. The German première on 21 December 1859 in Stuttgart, conducted by the composer, was one of the high points of Stuttgart's opera history. On 31 August 1860 Meyerbeer agreed to write incidental music to Henri Blaze's play *La jeunesse de Goethe* by 10 May 1861. He composed and orchestrated *Der König von Thule, Mignon, Faust, Der Erlkönig* and several passages of melodrama, but the play was never performed, and the music was lost along with his other manuscripts after his death.

At the end of 1860 Meyerbeer continued with his interrupted work on *L'africaine*, at that time still entitled *Vasco da Gama*, and in the middle of January 1861 wrote two songs as incidental music for Charlotte Birch-Pfeiffer's *Goldbauer*. On 24 January 1861 his *Krönungsmarsch* was performed at the coronation of Wilhelm I at Königsberg. Further work on *L'africaine* was threatened when Scribe died on 20 February 1861.

4. *Giacomo Meyerbeer*

'Who will undertake the textual alterations while the opera is in production?' Meyerbeer wrote in his diary. Although he and Scribe had often differed in their dramatic concepts, Meyerbeer valued Scribe's ingenious and wide-ranging inventive talent and described him as 'unequalled among writers of comic opera'.

In 1862 Meyerbeer produced the *Fest-Ouverture im Marschstyl* for the World Exhibition in London, which he agreed to compose only because Verdi, whose rivalry he feared, had also undertaken to write a work for the exhibition. When rumour reached him that Verdi was himself to rehearse his work in London, he pulled himself together in spite of physical weakness and went to London in April 1862 for the celebrations. He refused Cambridge University's offer of a MusD on 9 June because he was committed to taking a cure at that time. When in September 1862 the agreed period for completing *Judith* expired, he paid Scribe's widow the contractual penalty of 10,000 francs (he had already paid Scribe the same amount on 13 September 1857 for extending the contract for *L'africaine*). A month later Napoleon III sent him word that he expected the new opera to be performed in Paris that winter and held out to him the prospect of becoming a grand officer of the Légion d'honneur. Although Meyerbeer settled down to diligent composition, he still did not finish *L'africaine* until April 1864. Once the vexed questions of casting were settled, the rehearsals began, with Meyerbeer tirelessly in attendance, but in the night of 2 May, after a brief indisposition, he died. After grand official obsequies at the Gare du Nord on 6 May 1864, of a sort hardly ever accorded a musician before, his body was taken by special train to Berlin, where he was buried in the family vault at the Jewish cemetery on 9 May, in the presence of the court, leading citizens and a large number of the general public. The première of *L'africaine*, Fétis having taken charge of the final revisions, became a brilliant posthumous tribute to its composer. Leading theatre directors and producers from all over Europe came to Paris to study the effect of the new work in its

5. *Finale of Act 3 of 'L'africaine', first performed at the Paris Opéra on 28 April 1865: engraving from 'L'Illustration' (6 May 1865); the sinking of the ship on stage caused a sensation*

original presentation before staging their own productions (see fig.5).

The countless honours conferred on Meyerbeer included an award of the Order of the Red Eagle in 1842, the Knight's Cross of the Saxon Order of Merit and an honorary doctorate of philosophy of the University of Jena in 1850, the Commander's Cross of the Württemberg Order of the Crown, along with membership of the Württemberg nobility in 1852 and the Commander's Cross of the Ernestine House Order in 1855.

6. MEYERBEER'S CONCEPT OF GRAND OPERA. Meyerbeer's artistic activity developed between the extreme admiration aroused in France by his grand operas and the contemptuous rejection with which they were often met in Germany. In later critical appraisals it was often suggested that he appealed to the lowest common denominator in his audience, but in fact he did not embody the taste of the petite bourgeoisie or lower classes, but was rather the composer of high society. His operas were not tailored to the artistic interests of the masses: their contemporary social content fulfilled the cultural demands of the progressive aristocracy of his time.

Grand opera, as Meyerbeer moulded it, was an integrated whole. Like Berlioz in instrumental music, he developed a style that can be called 'expressive monumentalism'. Schumann's reproach that the horrific was Meyerbeer's element correctly identifies an essential aspect of his method of dramatic expression; but Schumann did not recognize the innovatory stylistic elements that Meyerbeer was introducing. Meyerbeer cultivated a consistently realistic style and was always seeking unexplored combinations of sounds. Together with Beethoven in his last years, Meyerbeer and Berlioz were among the first composers to create a deliberately 'unbeautiful' sound. Marcel's Piff-Paff aria in *Les Huguenots*, whole scenes in *Le prophète* and the role of Nelusko in *L'africaine* were composed with unusual orchestration designed to express their content rather than to produce a sensuous sound. This accounts for the criticism often voiced in Germany of the studied element in Meyerbeer's musical language.

Meyerbeer's instrumental technique was unanimously praised by his contemporaries, and an important aspect of it was his love of experimentation. Trying out new types of instrument, such as the bass clarinet or the saxophone, was as relevant to his work as his indefatigable efforts to escape from the customary opera orchestra layout by moving groups of instruments and even putting the trumpets in the prompter's box. Wagner learnt much from Meyerbeer's experiments, but these innovations also reappeared and were further developed in the works of many later composers who tried to free themselves from Wagner's musical style, among them Eugen d'Albert, Schreker, Brüll and Korngold.

Meyerbeer's attitude to his works and to collaboration with his librettists was determined by the primary importance he gave to his singers. He worked with more than 20 librettists, but only Scribe could claim to have been a real collaborator. Gaetano Rossi, who wrote most of his Italian texts, was only a makeshift whose ideas did not really correspond to Meyerbeer's. Meyerbeer's Italian operas were important to him as studies in Italian vocal style and, consequently, of vocal technique in general. In later life he repeatedly insisted that it was essential for an opera composer to work in Italy, because only there could he learn to write for the voice. Since childhood Meyerbeer's model had been Mozart, not Rossini, but in Italy as in France, he could not avoid conforming to the firmly established national operatic styles and conventions.

From early in his Paris period onwards, Meyerbeer

laid stress on originality in the material he chose for operatic treatment. Although the subject of *Robert le diable* was not new, it had not been used operatically before. *Les Huguenots* was a decisive step towards historical opera, and the story of the St Bartholomew's Eve massacre had never been treated dramatically. *Les Huguenots* was historic as well as historical, for Meyerbeer was one of the first opera composers to do research into music history for a composition. With the help of Bottée de Toulmon, he studied Maraut's Psalter and French 16th-century instrumental music in the Bibliothèque Nationale, and he used the Jewish hymn of thanksgiving on the eve of the Sabbath (the Yigdal) for the nightwatchman's scene. This care over detail in his work, which his contemporaries emphasized and admired in him, was particularly evident in his creation of local colour, which he himself considered an important attribute of a good opera composer.

The singers were always the central factor in Meyerbeer's conception of an opera. This is not to say that he gave no regard to the dramatic concept, but that he saw it from the point of view of his singers' capabilities. His continual journeys to hear and come to know singers helped him in this regard. His experiences with representatives of the classical school of singing in Italy (among them Velluti, the last of the great castratos, for whom he wrote the principal role in *Il crociato*) were useful to him in France, where he worked closely with Marco Bordogni, who coached most of the principal singers of the Paris Opéra, and whose teaching methods find their echo in the music for his leading roles.

While working on his operas Meyerbeer frequently kept specific interpreters in mind, and he carefully considered the vocal nuances and technical capabilities of the singers whom his contracts obliged the opera director to engage. If a singer cancelled before the opera was completed, he re-tailored the role to the replacement; if none was available, he abandoned the whole project. This method partly explains the long delays in staging *Le prophète* and *L'africaine* and also, to some extent, the breaking off of several planned works. A further concern was to distribute the soloists in each act so that their scenes built towards a climax and so that they had enough time to rest between them. Meyerbeer was particularly drawn to massive choral crowd scenes and refused librettos offering little opportunity for such 'tableaux', as he called them. These he constructed with block orchestration and rhythmic uniformity, building up a grandiose volume of sound. Together with the exorbitant technical demands of his solo roles, these were perhaps the most remarkable characteristic of his operas. It must, however, be remembered that in Paris he had the requisite stage resources.

Strauss's motto for *Ariadne auf Naxos* – 'Give the aria its due by keeping the orchestra quiet' – admirably describes one of the aesthetic principles of Meyerbeer's operas. Not only did he never drown his singers, but he occasionally even removed their orchestral support altogether over long passages, thus cultivating the pure solo; he always reserved massive orchestration for choral scenes. His themes, which often have heavy downbeats and insistent rhythms, are predominantly dance-like in character, sometimes causing rather restricted phrasing. Instead of developing themes, Meyerbeer often broke off the melodic line (the 'ligne brisée') so as to introduce new thematic material. Meyerbeerian grand opera lives, like Baroque opera, on a succession of inventions; if the invention fails in any

one piece, that number is irretrievably lost. This chain-like construction is especially observable in the ballet scenes, as they depend entirely on melodic invention: Meyerbeer therefore composed them with immense care and assiduously tested their effectiveness in rehearsal. If the orchestra and dancers were not satisfied, he threw away the music and started again, for he saw his operas as artistic entertainment and not as high art.

The eclipse of Meyerbeer's operas in popularity and critical esteem was to some extent due to Wagner's attacks but more to the novel approach to drama developing at the time. Wagner's idea of 'music drama' was originally developed by way of grand opera, which he greatly admired, but his ideas could never have been realized in their particular form without the pioneering development of orchestral technique and instrumentation and the high level of vocal prowess that Meyerbeer's operas were the first to demand.

Although he knew all Wagner's works up to *Tristan und Isolde* and was very interested in his work, Meyerbeer obstinately refused to conduct his operas in Berlin. He did not express his opinions of Wagner's music in public but occasionally noted his impressions in his diaries, such as 'very beautiful passages' in the second act of *Der fliegende Holländer*; on 28 May 1855 he noted that *Tannhäuser* was a 'highly interesting piece of musical art' but he criticized it for 'lack of melody, clarity and form', while acknowledging 'great flashes of genius in conception, orchestral colour, sometimes even in the music of its instrumental passages'. In December 1860 he studied the piano score of *Tristan* very thoroughly.

Meyerbeer was one of the richest men in Europe. He could be sure of the support of the press so long as he was prepared to offer financial inducement, but he could be equally sure of attack as soon as he refused. A clear example was Heine, who first supported him in long essays, but later, when revising them for publication in book form, changed them into often bitingly ironic attacks. Wagner became a direct opponent in 1846, when Meyerbeer withdrew his financial support. It is often maintained that Meyerbeer bribed the press, but in fact he had no need to. Journalists like Fiorentino, Scudo and Spazier, who were usually in financial difficulties, put themselves in his power by their persistent demands for loans. Naturally Meyerbeer's financial independence affected the public's view of him as an artist. Many press opinions of him must be read differently from those of less wealthy composers. His skilful manipulation of the press shows him to have been a worthy pupil of Weber, who had founded the Harmonischer Verein for that purpose. The modern press conference with refreshments was Meyerbeer's invention.

7. OTHER WORKS. Meyerbeer's instrumental works take second place to his operas. He himself later dismissed as negligible his youthful unpublished piano compositions, but they served to show off his piano playing, which he used in turn to further his claim to be taken seriously as an artist. However, once he had had his first operatic success in Italy, his career as a pianist was over, though he subsequently accompanied singers at court concerts and even late in life was famed for the reliability of his technique and his skill in accompaniment, which, in the tradition of an earlier age, he improvised. His piano playing was also useful for coaching singers in their roles, for he turned these sessions into singing lessons.

Meyerbeer's numerous orchestral compositions were

written for special occasions, but he ranked them higher than his piano works. The Fackeltanz no.1 remains a popular number at open-air concerts and in the light repertory of radio orchestras. As in his vocal writing, Meyerbeer considered the particular capabilities of the performers of his instrumental works and of the orchestral scores of his operas. The viola d'amore accompaniment to Raoul's romance in Act 1 of Les Huguenots was inspired by the presence of a first-class soloist in Chrétien Urhan.

Meyerbeer's excellent work as an orchestral coach, in particular the care with which he rehearsed and the extra sessions he held, is little known. When he was conductor of the Prussian court orchestra he particularly favoured the works of Mozart and Gluck, both of whom he deeply revered, but also performed works by living composers, especially Spohr. Meyerbeer's sacred works are equally unfamiliar though he worked on them very seriously. Their style was soon outdated by the revival of Baroque church music, but he nevertheless wrote some impressive pieces, for example his setting of Psalm xci.

Meyerbeer has been underrated as a song composer. He developed the unpretentious drawing-room romance into a little dramatic scene, as with the much-imitated Le moine, Rachel à Nephtali and La mère grand. These songs were very popular in drawing-rooms of the time, and even Fétis acknowledged them as 'a mode of expression to which German Romanticism gives a very special character'. Meyerbeer also composed lieder, but his settings of Heine's Die Rose, die Lilie, die Taube and Komm du schönes Fischermädchen and of Müller's Der Garten des Herzens are virtually unknown, yet they can be favourably compared with works by important German lieder composers and hardly betray their social salon origin. Fétis called Der Garten des Herzens 'an emanation of German genius'. Meyerbeer also captured the subtle nuances of the Italian canzonetta, as in the little song for Rubini Soave l'istante. These compositions were not intended for concert halls or bourgeois gatherings, but for the salon. They require a first-class, trained virtuoso singer who could also set the scene dramatically. The importance of this side of the performance is shown in Fétis's remarks about Meyerbeer as a composer of 'mélodies': 'for he alone possesses these shapes, these details, these little touches that complete and breathe creative life into a thought' (Revue et gazette musicale, viii, 1841, p.166).

## WORKS

### OPERAS

*(for facsimiles of scores see Gossett and Rosen)*

| Title and genre | Acts and librettist | First performance | Sources and remarks |
|---|---|---|---|
| Jephtas Gelübde, opera | 3, A. Schreiber | Munich, Court, 23 Dec 1812 | GB-Lbm, duet (Munich, ?1812) |
| Wirth und Gast, oder Aus Scherz Ernst, Lustspiel | 2, J. G. Wohlbrück | Stuttgart, 6 Jan 1813 | as Die beyden Kalifen, 1814; as Alimelek, 1820, arr. pf 4 hands (Milan, n.d.) |
| Das Brandenburger Tor, Singspiel | E. Veith | not perf. | composed for Berlin, 1814 |
| Romilda e Costanza, melodramma semiserio | 2, G. Rossi | Padua, Nuovo, 19 July 1817 | I-Bc, Fc, Mr; excerpts (Milan, n.d.) |
| Semiramide riconosciuta, dramma per musica | 2, Rossi, after Metastasio | Turin, Regio, March 1819 | excerpts pubd |
| Emma di Resburgo, melodramma eroico | 2, Rossi | Venice, S Benedetto, 26 June 1819 | as Emma di Leicester, 1820; I-Fc, Mr, vocal score (Berlin, ?1820) |
| Margherita d'Anjou, melodramma semiserio | 2, F. Romani, after Pixérécourt | Milan, La Scala, 14 Nov 1820 | rev. Paris, 1826; I-Mr, vocal score (Paris, 1826) |
| L'Almanzore | Rossi | not perf. | intended for Rome, Argentina, carn. 1821; probably unfinished |
| L'esule di Granata, melodramma serio | 2, Romani | Milan, La Scala, 12 March 1821 | I-Mr, excerpts (Milan, n.d.) |
| Il crociato in Egitto, melodramma eroico | 2, Rossi | Venice, La Fenice, 7 March 1824 | rev. Paris, 1826; GB-Lbm, I-Bc, Mr, US-Bp, Cu, Wc, vocal score (Milan, 1824; Bonn and Cologne, 1824; Paris, 1826) |
| Robert le diable, grand opéra | 5, Scribe and G. Delavigne | Paris, Opéra, 21 Nov 1831 | (Paris, 1831); scene and prayer added for Mario's début, 1839; rondo for Mme Alboni added to It. version |
| Les Huguenots, grand opéra | 5, Scribe and E. Deschamps | Paris, Opéra, 29 Feb 1836 | (Paris, 1836) |
| Ein Feldlager in Schlesien, Singspiel | 3, Scribe, L. Rellstab and C. Birch-Pfeiffer | Berlin, Court, 7 Dec 1844 | As Vielka, 1847; US-Wc |
| Le prophète, grand opéra | 5, Scribe | Paris, Opéra, 16 April 1849 | begun 1836; (Paris, 1849); Ov., Berthe's cavatina and barcarolle added c1850 |
| L'étoile du nord, opéra comique | 3 Scribe, partly after his ballet La cantinière | Paris, Opéra-Comique, 16 Feb 1854 | based on the music of Ein Feldlager in Schlesien; (Paris, ?1854) |
| Le pardon de Ploërmel, opéra comique | 3, J. Barbier and M. Carré | Paris, Opéra-Comique, 4 April 1859 | also known as Le chercheur du trésor and as Dinorah, oder Die Wallfahrt nach Ploërmel; Paris, ?1859) |
| L'africaine, grand opéra | 5, Scribe and F. J. Fétis | Paris, Opéra, 28 April 1865 | also known as Vasco da Gama; begun 1837; final revisions by Fétis; (Paris, 1865), 22 pieces and frags. not used in final version, ed. Fétis in vocal score (Paris, 1865) |

Opera frags.: Abu Hassan, Darmstadt, 1810, not perf.; Der Admiral, oder Der verlorene Prozess, Darmstadt, 1811, not perf.; Le bachelier de Salamanque, ?1815, not completed; Ines de Castro (G. Rossi), 1824, not completed; Malek Adel (Rossi), 1824, not completed; La nymphe de Danube (T. Sauvage), 1826, not completed; Le portefaix (Scribe), 1831, not completed; Les brigands (Dumas), planned 1832, not begun; Cinq mars (H. Saint-Georges and Planard, after A. de Vigny), Dec 1837, not completed; Noëma, ou Le repentir (L'ange au exil) (Scribe and Saint-Georges), contract signed 15 Jan 1846, not completed; Judith (Scribe), 1854, not completed

### OTHER DRAMATIC

Der Fischer und das Milchmädchen, oder Viel Lärm um einen Kuss (Le passage de la rivière, ou La femme jalouse; Le pêcheur et la laitière) (divertissement, 1, E. Lauchery), Berlin, Royal Theatre, 26 March 1810

Gli amori di Teolinda (Thecelindens Liebschaften) (monodrama, G. Rossi), S, cl, orch, Genoa, 1816; A-Wgm

Das Hoffest von Ferrara (masque, E. Raupach, after Tasso), Berlin, 28 Feb 1843; excerpts pubd

Struensee (incidental music, M. Beer), Berlin, Schauspielhaus, 19 Sept

1846 (Berlin, n.d.)

Ballade in the play Murillo, ou La corde du pendu (Aylic-Langlé [M. A. F. Langlois]), Paris, Comédie-Française, 18 Oct 1853 (Paris, n.d.)

La jeunesse de Goethe (L'étudiant de Strasbourg) (incidental music, H. Blaze de Bury), Nov–Dec 1860, Aug 1862, not perf., lost [incl. scenes to Faust, Der Erlkönig (after Schubert), Mignon, Der König von Thule, Iphigenie]

OCCASIONAL AND CHORAL

Zur Feier des 15ten Juni 1810, solo vv, vv, pf, for Vogler's birthday, collab. J. Gänsbacher; autograph *US-STu*

Bayerischer Schützenmarsch (King Ludwig I of Bavaria), cantata, 4 solo vv, male vv, wind insts, 1829

Festgesang zur Errichtung des Guttenbergischen Denkmals in Mainz (C. Rosenberg), T, T, B, B, TTBB, pf ad lib, 1834 (Mainz, ?1835)

Freundschaft, TTBB, for foundation festival of the Friends of the Berliner Singakademie, 1842 (Berlin, n.d.; Fr. trans., Paris, 1862)

Dem Vaterland, TTBB, Berlin, 1842 (Berlin, n.d.; Fr. trans., Paris, 1861)

Die lust'gen Jägersleut, TTBB (Berlin, n.d.; Fr. trans., Paris, 1861)

Dem Meister deutschen Lieds ein Lied, TTBB, Berlin, for reception of Spohr, 1845

Le voyageur au tombeau de Beethoven (M. Bourges), solo B, SSAA, unacc., 1845 (Paris, n.d.)

Festhymne (C. G. T. Winkler), solo vv, vv, pf ad lib, for 25th wedding anniversary of king and queen of Prussia, 1848 (Berlin, 1854)

Ode an [Christian] Rauch (A. Kopisch), solo vv, SATB, orch, vocal score (Berlin, 1851); as Opferhymne an den Zeus (L. Rellstab) (Berlin, 1854)

Maria und ihr Genius (Goldtammer), cantata, S, T, SATB, pf, Berlin, for 25th wedding anniversary of Prince and Princess Carl, 1852 (Berlin, 1852)

Brautgeleite aus der Heimat (Adieux aux jeunes mariés), serenade, SSAATTBB, unacc., Berlin, for wedding of Princess Luise, 1856 (Berlin and Posen, 1856; Fr. trans., Paris, 1857)

Choeur des sybarites, Lyons, 1857

Nice à Stephanie, S, 3vv, pf, for birthday of Grand Duchess Stephanie of Baden, 1857 (Paris, 1858)

Festgesang zur Feier des 100 jährigen Geburtsfestes von Fr. Schiller (L. Pfau), S, A, T, B, SATB, orch, 1859 (Berlin, ?1860)

Bundeslied (Invocation à la terre), TTBB, Berlin, 1861 (Berlin, n.d.; Paris, 1861) [on 'God Save the King']

Festhymnus, solo vv, vv, pf ad lib, Königsberg, for coronation of Wilhelm I, 1861 (Berlin, n.d.)

Das Lied vom blinden Hessen (Altmüller), T, 4 male vv, pf, for the Schwalbacher Liedertafel, 1862 (Berlin, ?1863; Fr. trans., Paris, 1863)

SACRED

Gott und die Natur (A. Schreiber), oratorio, Berlin, Singakademie, 8 May 1811; *F-Pn*

Geistliche Gesänge (Klopstock), S, A, T, B, *c*1811 (Leipzig, 1817 or 1818): 1 Wenn ich einst von jenem Schlummer, 2 Preis ihm, 1st pubd in *AMZ*, xv (1813), suppl.2, 3 Erheb' uns zu dir, du, 4 Auf ewig ist der Herr mein Theil; repr. (Paris, 1841) with 3 added nos.: 5 Müde sündevolle Seele, 6 Wach auf mein Herz und singe, 7 Jesus Christus wir sind hier

An Gott (F. W. Gubitz), hymn, S, A, T, B, pf, 1814 (Leipzig, ?1817)

Hallelujah (E. Kley), cantatine, 4 male solo vv, vv ad lib, org, before 1815, autograph *US-Wc*

2 religiöse Gedichte von Jakob Neus, SSA, org (Mainz, *c*1891): Glorie in der Höhe, Halleluja, der Herr ist da

Psalm xci, S, A, T, B, double chorus SATB, unacc., Berlin, 1853 (Berlin, 1853; Paris, 1858)

Pater noster, off, SATB, unacc., in *La maîtrise*, i (15 Nov 1857), also (Berlin, n.d.)

Busslied (Qui sequitur me) (Corneille and Rellstab, after Thomas à Kempis), solo B, SSATTB, org, Berlin, 1859, in *La maîtrise*, iii (1859)

Prière du matin (E. Deschamps), 2 choirs, pf ad lib, Paris, 1864 (Paris, n.d.)

Prière, 3 female vv, unacc. (Paris, n.d.)

SONGS

6 élégies et romances (Leipzig, 1839) [A]

12 mélodies (Paris, 1839 or 1840) [B]

40 mélodies (Paris, 1849) [C]

6 canzonettes italiennes (Metastasio), 1810, autograph *D-Dlb*; Der Traumgeist (L. Robert), 1824; Ballade de la reine Marguerite de Valois (Marguerite de Valois), 1829, in *Hommage aux dames* (Paris, 1829), C; La barque légère (Naudet) (Paris, 1829), C; Le voeu pendant l'orage (A. Betourné) (Paris, 1830), C; Au revoir, ?1833 (Paris, 1833); L'absence (M. Desbordes-Valmore), 1833 (Paris, 1833); Le miroir magique, 1833 (Paris, 1833); Soave l'istante, 1833, autograph in Floersheim Collection, Switzerland; Le ricordanze (G. Rossi), 1833 (Paris, 1834; Milan, 1834); L'enlèvement, 1834; Le moine (E. Pacini), 1834, in *Keepsake lyrique* (Paris, 1834), C; Rachel à Nephtali (E. Deschamps), 1834, in *Keepsake lyrique* (Paris, 1834), C; Sie und ich (F. Rückert), 1835, B, C; Le poète mourant (C.

Millevoye), élégie, 1836 (Paris, 1836), A, C

Fantaisie (H. Blaze), 1836, in *Revue de Paris* (4 Sept 1836), A, B, C; Hör ich das Liedchen klingen (De ma première amie) (Heine), 1837 (Paris, 1837), B; Komm du schönes Fischermädchen (Guide au bord ta nacelle) (Heine), 1837 (Paris, 1837), B, C; La fille de l'air (Méry), 1837 (Leipzig, 1837), A, C; La folle de St Joseph (Marquis de Custine), 1837 (Paris, 1837; Leipzig, 1837), A, C; Scirocco (M. Beer), 1837 (Paris, 1837), B, C; Lied des venezianischen Gondoliers (Mina) (Beer), ?1837, in *Album für Pianoforte und Gesang für das Jahr 1839* (Leipzig, 1838), C; Chant de mai (Blaze), 1837, in *Revue de Paris* (25 June 1837), A, B, C

Menschenfeindlich (Seul) (Beer), 1837, in *Revue de Paris* (25 June 1837), B, C; La Marguerite du poète (Blaze), 1837, in *Europa*, ii (1838), A, B, C; Die Rose, die Lilie, die Taube (C'est elle) (Heine), 1838, in *Album für Pianoforte und Gesang für das Jahr 1839* (Leipzig, 1838), C; Die Rosenblätter (Müller), in *Album für Pianoforte und Gesang für das Jahr 1839* (Leipzig, 1838); Chant des moissoneurs vendéens (Blaze), 1839 (Paris, 1839), B, C; Nella (Deschamps), chansonette, *c*1839 (Paris, 1840); Suleika (Goethe), 1838 (Paris, 1839), C; Der Garten des Herzens (W. Müller), 1839 (Paris, 1839), B, C

Le baptême (M. de Flassan), 1839, as Magdalena (W. von Chézy), in *Europa* (1841), C; La chanson de Maître Floh (Blaze), 1839 or 1840, B, C; A une jeune mère (Durand), by 1839 (Paris, n.d.), C; De miei giorni (Délire) (N. del Santo Mano), canzona, 1840, in *Le ménestrel*, v (1840), C; Le repos du gondolier, 1840, in *Le ménestrel*, v (1840), C; Ständchen (G. Seidel), 1840 in *Orpheus*, ii (1841), C; La luna in ciel risplende (?Rossi), canzona, ?1841; Sonntagslied (Kletke), 1841, in *Le ménestrel*, viii (15 Jan 1843), C; Gottergebenheit (Mahlmann), 1841, in *Wiener allgemeine Musik-Zeitung* (1842); Luft von Morgen (Le pénitent) (Knapp), 1841 (Paris, 1842), C; Gebet am Donnerstag Morgen, 1841, in *Wiener allgemeine Musik-Zeitung* (1842); Au victoire (Am Rhein) (K. Kaskel), 1842

Hirtenlied (Des Schäfers Lied) (L. Rellstab), T, cl, pf, 1842 (Paris, 1857); Cantique du trappiste, 1842, in *France musicale*, vi (13 Nov 1842), C; Reue (Oft muss ich weinen) (Gottschalk), geistliches Lied, in Album für Gesang, ii (Leipzig, 1843); Siciliene (Méry), ?1845 (Paris, 1849), C; Sur le balcon (E. Thierry), romance, 1845 (Paris, 1845), C; La dame invisible (Thierry), chanson persane, 1845 (Paris, 1845), C; An den Neugeborenen, 1846; Aimez (Aufforderungen zur Liebe), chansonette, 1846 (Paris, 1847); Frühling im Versteck (Lua), 1847 (Paris, 1848), C; Drei Küsse (Klein), 1847

Confidences (Liederbothe), ?1851 (Paris, 1851); Les plus beaux jours (Crével de Charlemagne), arioso, 1852 (?Paris, 1853); Les fleurs de la vie (Crével de Charlemagne), 1853 (?Paris, 1853); Se per tutte ordisce amore (Metastasio), canzonetta, 1855 (Florence, 1866); La lavandière (M. Carré), ballade, in *Messager des dames et des demoiselles* (15 Oct 1855); A Venezia (P. Beltrame), barcarolle, 1856 (Paris, 1856); Près de toi (Roger and Duisberg), T, vc, *c*1857 (Paris, 1857); Le revenant du vieux château de Bade (Méry), ballade, 1858 (Paris, 1859); Die helle Sonne leuchtet (Mirze-Schaffy), 1860; Le retour (Millevoye); Giuseppe in carcere monologue lyrique, lost

Le ranz-des-vâches d'Appenzell (Scribe), chanson suisse, 2vv, pf, 1828, rev. 1846 (Paris, 1828), C; La mère grand (Betourné), nocturne, 2vv, pf, 1830 (Paris, 1830); Kindergebet, SSA, unacc, autograph facs. in *AMZ*, xli (1839), suppl.6

INSTRUMENTAL

4 Fackeltänze, military band, for Prussian royal weddings: 1, B♭, for Princess Marie, 1844 (Berlin, ?1854), 2, E♭, for Princess Charlotte, 1850 (Berlin, ?1854), 3, c, for Princess Anna, 1856 (Berlin, n.d.), 4, C, for welcome of newly married Prussian crown prince, 1858 (Berlin, n.d.)

Festmarsch, orch, Vienna and Paris, for centenary of Schiller's birth, 1859 (Berlin, ?1860; Paris, 1860)

Krönungsmarsch, 2 orchs, Königsberg, for coronation of Wilhelm I, 1861 (Berlin, ?1861; Paris, 1862)

Fest-Ouverture im Marschstyl, orch, for inauguration of London World Exhibition, 1862 (Paris, 1862; Berlin and Posen, 1863)

Sym., E♭, 1811; Conc., pf, vn, orch, 1812

Pf: Conc., 1811; Concert Piece, with orch; Variations, with orch; Sonata; Fugues; Dances; Variations, all early, unpubd; Page d'album inédite, in *L'illustration* (1897), suppl. to no.2832

BIBLIOGRAPHY

A. Morel: *Le prophète: analyse critique de la nouvelle partition de Giacomo Meyerbeer* (Paris, 1849)

E. O. Lindner: *Meyerbeers 'Prophet' als Kunstwerk beurtheilt* (Berlin, 1850)

J. Schladebach: *Meyerbeers Prophet (unter besonderer Berücksichtigung der Dresdner Aufführung)* (Dresden, 1850)

E. de Mirecourt: *Meyerbeer* (Paris, 1854)

E. Pougin: *Meyerbeer: notes biographiques* (Paris, 1864)

H. Blaze de Bury: *Meyerbeer et son temps* (Paris, 1865)

H. Mendel: *Giacomo Meyerbeer* (Berlin, 1868)

J. Schucht: *Meyerbeers Leben und Bildungsgang* (Leipzig, 1869)

A. Body: *Meyerbeer aux eaux de Spa* (Brussels, 1885)

A. Kohut: *Meyerbeer* (Leipzig, 1890)

E. Destranges: *L'oeuvre théâtral de Meyerbeer* (Paris, 1893)

J. Weber: *Meyerbeer* (Paris, 1898)

H. Tardel: 'Die Sage von Robert dem Teufel in neueren deutschen Dichtungen und in Meyerbeers Oper', *Forschungen zur neueren Literaturgeschichte*, xiv (1900)

J. G. Prod'homme: 'Die Hugenotten-Premiere', *Die Musik*, iii/1 (1903–4), 187

L. A. Bourgault-Ducoudray: 'Meyerbeer: souvenirs d'autrefois', *RHCM*, iv (1904), 452

F. Brückner: 'Meyerbeer en Allemagne', *RHCM*, iv (1904), 455

J. Combarieu: 'Meyerbeer', *RHCM*, iv (1904), 434

C. Ettler: 'Bibliographie des oeuvres de G. Meyerbeer', *RHCM*, iv (1904), 436 [incl. MSS, then in possession of Raoul Richter, Leipzig]

G. R. Kruse: 'Das Brandenburger Tor von J. Meyerbeer', *Berliner Tageblatt* (3 May 1904), no.222, suppl.2

H. de Curzon: *Meyerbeer* (Paris, 1910)

H. Eymieu: *L'oeuvre de Meyerbeer* (Paris, 1910)

L. Dauriac: *Meyerbeer* (Paris, 1913, 2/1930)

L. Hirschberg: 'Meyerbeers religiöse Tonwerke', *Die Musik*, xiii/3 (1914), 146

G. R. Kruse: 'Meyerbeers Jugendopern', *ZMw*, i (1918–19), 399

H. Strelitzer: *Meyerbeers deutsche Jugendopern* (diss., U. of Münster, 1920)

A. E. Brent Smith: 'The Tragedy of Meyerbeer', *ML*, vi (1925), 248

E. Istel: 'Meyerbeer's Way to Mastership', *MQ*, xii (1926), 72–109

G. Servières: 'Les transformations et tribulations de *L'africaine*', *RMI*, xxxiv (1927), 80

R. Haudek: *Scribes Operntexte für Meyerbeer: eine Quellenuntersuchung* (diss., U. of Vienna, 1928)

H. Abert: 'Giacomo Meyerbeer', *Gesammelte Schriften und Vorträge*, ed. F. Blume (Halle, 1929), 397

J. Kapp: *Giacomo Meyerbeer* (Berlin, 8/1932)

E. Istel: 'Act IV of *Les Huguenots*', *MQ*, xxii (1936), 87

J. G. Prod'homme: 'Meyerbeer à Paris avant "Robert le diable", d'après son journal inédit', *Mercure de France* (14 April 1936), 275

W. L. Crosten: *French Grand Opera: an Art and a Business* (New York, 1948)

H. Becker: 'Meyerbeers Ergänzungsarbeit an Webers nachgelassener Oper "Die drei Pintos" ', *Mf*, vii (1954), 300

F. Noske: *La mélodie française de Berlioz à Duparc* (Amsterdam and Paris, 1954; Eng. trans., rev., 1970)

M. Cooper: 'Giacomo Meyerbeer', *Fanfare for Ernest Newman* (London, 1955), 38

H. Becker: 'Meyerbeers Beziehungen zu Louis Spohr', *Mf*, x (1957), 479

——: *Der Fall Heine–Meyerbeer* (Berlin, 1958)

——: 'Meyerbeers erstes Bühnenwerk "Der Fischer und das Milchmädchen" ', *Kleine Schriften der Gesellschaft für Theatergeschichte*, xvi (1958), 26

H. Becker, ed.: *Giacomo Meyerbeer: Briefwechsel und Tagebücher* (Berlin, 1960–) [with additional bibliography in each vol.]

M. T. Mann: *Heinrich Heines Musikkritiken* (diss., Harvard U., 1962)

H. Becker: 'Giacomo Meyerbeer', *Leo Baeck Institute: Yearbook*, ix (London, 1964), 178

M. Brod: 'Some Comments on the Relationship between Wagner and Meyerbeer', *Leo Baeck Institute: Yearbook*, ix (London, 1964)

H. Kirchmeyer: 'Psychologie des Meyerbeer-Erfolges', *NZM*, 125 Jg. (1964), 471

J. W. Klein: 'Giacomo Meyerbeer (1791–1864)', *MR*, xxv (1964), 142

J. Meyerowitz: 'Giacomo Meyerbeer', *Musica*, xix (1965), 9

S. Dohring: *Formgeschichte der Opernarie* (diss., U. of Marburg, 1969)

H. Frederichs: 'Das Rezitativ in den Hugenotten G. Meyerbeers', *Beiträge zur Geschichte der Oper*, ed. H. Becker (Regensburg, 1969), 55

H. Becker: 'Giacomo Meyerbeers Mitarbeit an den Libretti seiner Opern', *GfMKB, Bonn 1970*, 155

F. Bose, ed.: *Meyerbeer: sizilianische Volkslieder* (Berlin, 1970)

C. Frese: *Dramaturgie der grossen Opern Giacomo Meyerbeers* (Berlin, 1970)

H. Kirchmeyer: 'Ein Kapitel Meyerbeer', *Das zeitgenössische Wagner-Bild*, i (Regensburg, 1972), 51

A. Edler: ' "In ganz neuer und freier Form geschrieben": zu Liszts Phantasie und Fuge über den Choral "Ad nos ad salutarem undam" ', *Mf*, xxv (1972), 249

S. Döhring: 'Les oeuvres tardives de Meyerbeer', *SMz*, xcv (1975), 57

M. Loppert: 'An Introduction to "L'étoile du nord" ', *MT*, cxvi (1975), 130

J. L. Thomson: 'Giacomo Meyerbeer: the Jew and his Relationship with Richard Wagner', *Musica judaica*, i (1975–6), 55–87

H. Becker: 'Die Couleur locale als Stilkategorie der Oper', *Die Couleur locale in der Oper des 19. Jahrhunderts*, ed. H. Becker (Regensburg, 1976), 23

P. Gossett and C. Rosen, eds.: *Early Romantic Opera*, xviii–xxiv (Garden City, NY, 1977) [facs. of 7 opera scores]

H. Becker: *Meyerbeer: Bild-Monographie* (Reinbek, nr. Hamburg, 1980)

HEINZ BECKER

**Meyerowitz, Jan** (*b* Breslau [now Wrocław], 23 April 1913). American composer of German birth. He studied at the Hochschule für Musik, Berlin, with Gmeindl and Zemlinsky; and at the Accademia di S Cecilia, Rome, with Respighi, Casella, and Molinari. A strong believer in the role of music in education, Meyerowitz has held teaching positions at the opera department of Tanglewood (1948–51), Brooklyn College (1954–61) and City College of the City University of New York (since 1962). He has also lectured frequently for German radio services and has written two books. He has appeared as a pianist and conductor, mainly in Italy. As a composer, he has adhered to tonality and attempted to build his own style within that tradition. Occasionally the impact of Schoenberg and Berg becomes noticeable, but Meyerowitz himself considers Italian neo-classicism the principal influence of his formative years. The lyrical expressionism found in his operas conforms to the ideals of 19th-century opera. Without abandoning the European basis of his style, he has employed typically American idioms in his operas on American topics. His early opera, *The Barrier*, on a libretto by Langston Hughes dealing with the Black problem in the South, was performed on Broadway (1950) and revived by the Teatro San Carlo in Naples (1971).

### WORKS
*(selective list)*

OPERAS

Simoon (Strindberg), 1949; The Barrier (L. Hughes), 1950; Eastward in Eden (D. Gardner), 1951; Esther (Hughes), 1957; Godfather Death (P. Stephens), 1961; Winterballade (G. Hauptmann), 1967

VOCAL

Missa Rachel plorans, S, T, chorus, org ad lib, 1954; The Glory around his Head (L. Hughes), B, chorus, orch, 1955; Hebrew Service, T, Mez, chorus, org, 1962; Cantata on poems by Platen, 1v, 5 insts, 1963; I rabbini, solo vv, chorus, orch, 1965

INSTRUMENTAL

Midrash Esther, sym., 1957; Ob Conc., 1963; 6 Pieces for Orch, 1967; 7 Pieces for Orch, 1974; 4 Sym. Movts, band, 1974

Sonatas and chamber music

Principal publisher: Broude Brothers

### WRITINGS
*Arnold Schönberg* (Berlin, 1967)

*Der echte jüdische Witz* (Berlin, 1970)

### BIBLIOGRAPHY
F. Greissle: 'Current Chronicle', *MQ*, xliii (1957), 233

Broadcast Music Inc.: *Catalogue of works* (New York, 1958)

SIEGMUND LEVARIE

**Meyer-Siat, Pie** (*b* Ribeauvillé, Haut-Rhin, 15 Oct 1913). French musicologist and authority on organs. At the University of Strasbourg he took a degree in philosophy (1937), the agrégation in German (1948) and, with a dissertation on the Callinets, the doctorate in musicology (1962). From 1948 he taught German at the Lycée Kléber in Strasbourg. He has devoted his research to the study of organ building in Alsace, in particular organ building at the end of the classical period which, in Alsace, extended into the mid-19th century. At first he was interested in the Callinets; the best-preserved organ by Joseph Callinet is in Mollau, a village in the Haut-Rhin at the bottom of the Thur valley where Meyer-Siat's father was a schoolteacher. He has extended his research to other 19th-century Alsatian builders, and produced an exhaustive work on the most important of them, the Stiehr-Mockers. His articles in *Les cahiers de la Société d'histoire de Saverne* are concerned with lesser builders (the Sauers, N. A. Lété, the Moellers, P. Rivinach, L. Geib, S. Krämer, N. Hellé, J. Gottlob Sachse, A. and A. Meyer, J. Henn, J. N. Hesse, J. and J. Erckmann and G. Wegmann).

Meyer-Siat's work is characterized by its pioneering approach (the Callinets, now a familiar subject, were scarcely known when he became interested in them) and its soundness, the product of limitless dedication, a rigorous method of investigation and perfect knowledge of the subject.

#### WRITINGS

*Les Callinet, facteurs d'orgues à Rouffach, et leur oeuvre en Alsace* (diss., U. of Strasbourg, 1962; Strasbourg, 1965)
*L'orgue Callinet de Masevaux* (Mulhouse, 1962)
'Claus Reinbolt und die Orgel', *Petite revue du nouvel Alsacien* (18 Dec 1963)
*L'orgue Joseph Callinet de Mollau* (*Haut-Rhin*) (Strasbourg, 1963)
'Albert Schweitzer zum Gedächtnis', *Das Musikinstrument*, xiv (1965), 900
'La facture d'orgues en Alsace au XIXe siècle', *Artisans d'Alsace*, ed. F. Kniffke (Strasbourg, 1965), 237
'La réforme alsacienne de l'orgue', *Bulletin des professeurs de Mulhouse*, iii (1965), 13
Preface to J. Goebel: *Theorie und Praxis des Orgelpfeifenklangs* (Frankfurt am Main, 1967)
Preface to W. Kwasnik: *Emile Rupp als Orgelreformer* (Frankfurt am Main, 1967)
'Die Orgelbauer-Familie Callinet', *Acta organologica*, ii (1968), 82
'Le projet d'orgue Callinet pour la cathédrale de Metz', *Annuaire de la Société d'histoire de Metz* (1968), 189–229
'Antoine Herbuté', *Archives de l'église d'Alsace*, new ser., xvii (1969), 159–241; xviii (1970), 350
'Die Orgelbauer-Familie Sauer', *Acta organologica*, iii (1969), 100–32; iv (1970), 206
'L'orgue Silbermann de St-Georges de Sélestat', *Annuaire de la Société d'histoire de Colmar* (1969), 96
'Les projets d'orgues pour la cathédrale de Metz au XIXe siècle', *Annuaire de la Société d'histoire de Metz* (1969), 215
'Administration et musique au milieu du XIXe siècle: I: L'élaboration d'une "doctrine" sur la facture d'orgues: le devis d'orgue Zégowitz'; 'II: La doctrine officielle de la préfecture du Bas-Rhin dans le domaine de la facture d'orgues vers 1860', *La musique en Alsace hier et aujourd'hui* (1970), 197; 217
'L'orgue Konrad Sauer de Kolbsheim', *Annuaire de la Société d'histoire de Molsheim* (1970)
Preface to H. G. Klais: *Die Würzburger Domorgeln* (Frankfurt am Main, 1970)
'Walbourg', *Archives de l'église d'Alsace*, new ser., xviii (1970), 346
'Die Orgeln zu St-Nicolas, Strassburg', *Acta organologica*, v (1971), 140
'L'église St-André d'Andlau et d'Eichhoffen au XIXe siècle', *Annuaire de la Société d'histoire de Barr* (1971), 82
*Les orgues de Niedernai et d'Obernai* (Colmar, 1972)
'Les orgues de Westhoffen', *Cahiers de la Société d'histoire de Saverne*, lxxix–lxxx (1972), 37
'L'orgue dans les synagogues d'Alsace', *Archives juives*, i (1972), 7
'L'orgue Silbermann de Marmoutier menacé en 1805', *Cahiers de la Société d'histoire de Saverne*, lxxvii (1972), 23
*Stiehr-Mockers, facteurs d'orgues* (Hagenau, 1972) [incl. list of publications]
'Les orgues de Breitenbach (Hohwald)', *Annuaire de la Société d'histoire de Barr*, vii (1973), 121
'Les orgues de Dorlisheim', *Annuaire de la Société d'histoire de Molsheim* (1974), 37
'Georg Wegmann: facteur d'orgues', *Archives de l'église d'Alsace*, new ser., xxiii (1975), 272–322
'Orgue et musique à Andlau', *Annuaire de la Société d'histoire de Barr*, x (1976), 57
'Quelques orgues d'Outre-Forêt', *Saisons d'Alsace* (1976), no.59, p.171

CHRISTIANE SPIETH-WEISSENBACHER

**Meyer von Schauensee, Franz Joseph Leonti** (*b* Lucerne, 10 Aug 1720; *d* Lucerne, 2 Jan 1789). Swiss organist and composer. He was a member of an aristocratic Lucerne family, the son of Joseph Leonti and his wife Cäcilia (née Rusconi). He was taught the organ, cello and violin (the last by Galimberti in Milan 1740–

42). In 1738 he entered the Cistercian monastery of St Urban but left after a year. In 1742–4 he served in a mercenary regiment in Sardinia and on his return, in keeping with his aristocratic background, worked in public life in Lucerne from 1744 to 1752, while also following his musical interests. Having already taken minor orders, he became organist at the seminary of St Leodegar in Lucerne (1752), and rose to become successively titular chaplain (1760), minor canon (1764) and prebendary (1765). In 1760 he established a public college of music, and in 1768 founded the Helvetische Konkordiagesellschaft, remaining its president until 1783. In his last years he was active as an organist.

Meyer von Schauensee was one of the first Swiss musicians to become known beyond the boundaries of his own country. According to Koller his works show him to be a representative of a late Neapolitan style, revealing many points of contact with Hasse, Sammartini and Pergolesi, as well as Handel's influence.

#### WORKS

*(for complete list with thematic index see Koller)*

Stage: Die Parnassische Gesandschaft (operetta), 1746; Hans Hüttenstock (opera buffa), 1769; Angenehmer und wohllautender Streit dreyer Polizeiständen (Singspiel), 1773; Die Engelbergische Talhochzeit (opera buffa), 1781; Heli (Singspiel), 1785, Iphigenie (Singspiel), 1785, Lucerne, Allgemeine Musikgesellschaft; incidental music
Sacred: De semine bono flos vernans, 40 arias, op.1 (Unterammergau, 1748); Obeliscus musicus, 16 offs, op.2 (Unterammergau, 1752); Ecclesia triumphans, op.3 (Unterammergau, 1753); Pontificale Romano-Constantiniense, 7 masses, op.4 (Augsburg, 1757); Cantica Doctoris Melliflui Mariano dulcisona, op.5 (Augsburg, 1757); Omne Trinum perfectum, op.6 (Zug, 1763); Par nobile fratrum, op.7 (Zug, 1764); others, lost or MS
Various inst works, lost or MS

#### BIBLIOGRAPHY

E. Koller: *Franz Joseph Leonti von Schauensee* (Frauenfeld and Leipzig, 1922)
J. E. Saladin: *Die Musikpflege am Stift St. Leodegar in Luzern* (Stans, 1948)
W. Jerger: 'Zur Musikgeschichte der deutschsprachigen Schweiz im 18. Jahrhundert', *Mf*, xiv (1961), 303
M. Vogt: 'Unbekannte Briefe Meyer von Schauensees', *Neue Zürcher Zeitung* (14 Feb 1971), 51

WILHELM JERGER

**Meylan, Pierre** (*b* Lucens, Vaud, 22 Oct 1908; *d* Morges, 7 May 1974). Swiss musicologist and critic. After studies in Lausanne, Halle and Leipzig, where he took a degree in social sciences and literature, he taught at Vevey and Lausanne (1940–70). In 1954 he became editor of the *Revue musicale de Suisse romande* (formerly *Feuilles musicales*) and director of the Editions du Cervin at Morges; he was one of the authors of the *Schweizer Musiker-lexikon*. As a musicologist he was interested essentially in the relationship between music and literature, and in the musical history of the Suisse Romande. He wrote opera librettos for Sutermeister, Schibler and Kelterborn.

#### WRITINGS

*Les écrivains et la musique* (Lausanne, 1944–51)
*Une amitié célèbre: C.-F. Ramuz et Igor Stravinsky* (Lausanne, 1962)
*René Morax et Arthur Honegger au Théâtre du Jorat* (Lausanne, 1965)
*Arthur Honegger: humanitäre Botschaft der Musik* (Frauenfeld, 1970)

#### BIBLIOGRAPHY

*SML* [contains complete list of writings up to 1964]

ETIENNE DARBELLAY

**Meylan, Raymond** (*b* Onex, Geneva, 22 Sept 1924). Swiss flautist and musicologist. During his school studies he had flute lessons in Geneva with Marcel Moyse and after taking a degree in mathematics and physics at Lausanne (1947), he continued his flute studies in Paris (diploma, 1948) and with Ruggero Gerlin at Siena (1949–51). He then became second flute in the Winterthur Stadtorchester (1948), soloist in the Associazone Alessandro Scarlatti of Naples (1951), in the Pomeriggi Musicale of Milan (1954), and in the Radio Beromünster Orchestra at Zurich (1958–70), at the same time giving numerous performances on both modern and original instruments throughout Europe. He has made many recordings. He has been equally involved in musicology, obtaining a doctorat ès lettres in musicology from Zurich University under Kurt von Fischer in 1967 with a dissertation on the basse danse, since when he has been lecturer in musicology at Zurich University. Head of the Orchestre Académique of Zurich (from 1969), he is a member of the team researching into the analysis and transcription of tablature by computers at the CNRS, Paris, and solo flute in the Basle Orchestra (from 1971). His principal fields of research are the editing of early music, mensural notation, Renaissance instruments and the use of computers. Meylan has edited for performance numerous works mainly by 18th-century composers.

### WRITINGS

. 'La collection Antonio Venturi, Montecatini-Terme (Pistoia), Italie', *FAM*, v (1958), 31
'Documents douteux dans le domaine des concertos pour instruments à vent au XVIIIᵉ siècle', *RdM*, xlix (1963), 47
'Utilisation des calculatrices électroniques pour la comparaison interne du répertoire des basses danses du quinzième siècle', *FAM*, xii (1965), 128
'Recherche de parenté parmi les basses danses du XVᵉ siècle', *AcM*, xxxviii (1966), 46
'Symbolisierung einer Melodie auf Lochkarten', *Elektronische Datenverarbeitung in der Musikwissenschaft*, ed. H. Heckmann (Regensburg, 1967), 21
*L'énigme de la musique des basses danses du quinzième siècle* (diss., U. of Zurich, 1967; Berne, 1968)
'Théorie de la centonisation', *IMSCR, x Ljubljana 1967*, 427
'A propos du développement de l'instrumentation au début du dix-neuvième siècle', *AcM*, xlii (1970), 70
'La technique de transcription au luth de Francesco Spinacino', *Schweizer Beiträge zur Musikwissenschaft* (Berne, 1972), 83
*La flûte* (Lausanne, 1973)
'Limites de l'objectivité dans les écritures instrumentales de la Renaissance', *Journées d'étude informatique musicale: ERATTO Paris 1973*, 1
Articles in *BordasD*

### EDITIONS

*A. Scarlatti: Sinfonien für Kammerorchester*, HM, xlviii (1950); cxvi (1952); cxxv (1954); cxlvi (1957); clxviii (1960)
*D. Mazzocchi: Sechs Madrigäle*, Cw, xcv (1965)
*P. Attaingnant: Danserie à 4 parties, second livre (1547)*, Le pupitre, xix (Paris, 1968)
*Polyphonic Basse Dance*, CMM (in preparation)

### BIBLIOGRAPHY

E. Refardt, ed.: *Historisch-biographisches Musiker-Lexikon der Schweiz* (2/in preparation) [contains complete discography]
ETIENNE DARBELLAY

**Meyland, Jacob** [Jakob]. *See* MEILAND, JACOB.

**Meyner, Giorgio.** *See* MAINERIO, GIORGIO.

**Meytus, Yuly Sergeyevich** (*b* Elizavetgrad [now Kirov̌grad], 28 Jan 1903). Russian composer and pianist. He graduated from Bogatïryov's composition class at the Kharkov Music and Drama Institute in 1931, having been one of the founders of the Association of Revolutionary Composers of the Ukraine (ARKU) in 1926. From 1938 he took a leading part in the Ukrainian Composers' Union, though he was in Turkmenia during the war. An Honoured Art Worker of the Turkmen SSR (1944) and of the Ukrainian SSR (1948), he also holds the USSR State Prize and the title People's Artist of the Ukrainian SSR. He made an important contribution with the percussion piece *Na Dneprostroye* ('On the Dnieper dam', 1929–32), a suite in machine-like style. Later works also show a tendency to the mechanical, laconic and simple.

### WORKS

*(selective list)*

Operas: Perekop [The trench] (V. Bichko, B. Shelontsev), 1939, collab. V. Ribalchenko, M. Tits; Gaydamaki [Ukrainian Cossacks] (Bichko, after T. Shevchenko), collab. Ribalchenko, Tits; Abadan (B. Kerbabayev), 1943, rev. 1946–7, collab. A. Kuliyev; Leili i Medzhnun (K. Burunov), 1946, collab. D. Ovezov; Molodaya gvardiya [The young guard] (A. Malïshko, after A. Fadeyev), 1947, rev. 1950; Zarya ad Dvinoy [Dawn over the Dvina] (Severnïye zor [Northern lights]) (V. Rozhdestvensky, after N. Nikitin), 1952–4; Ukradennoye schast'ye [Stolen happiness] (M. Rïlsky, after I. Franko), 1958; Makhtumkuli (A. Karliyev, Kerbabayev), 1961; Doch' vetra [Daughter of the wind] (A. Vasilyeva, V. Zubar), 1963–4; Bratzy Ulyanovï [The brothers Ulyanov] (Vasilyeva, D. Pavlïchko), 1965–6, rev. 1970; Anna Karenina (Vasilyeva, L. Smirnov), 1969–70; Yaroslav mudrïy [Yaroslav the wise] (Vasilyeva, after I. Kochberg), 1970–71
Orch: 5 suites, 1928; 'Na Dneprostroye' [On the Dnieper dam], perc, 1929–32; 1939; 1942; 1944; Turkmenian Sym. (1946); other pieces
Vocal: Klyatva [The oath] (V. Bazhan) cantata, solo vv, chorus, orch (1941); several other choral works, c200 solo songs, solo and choral folksong arrs.
Instrumental pieces, 30 incidental scores, film music

### BIBLIOGRAPHY

Yu. Malïshev: *Ocherk tvorchestva Yu. S. Meytusa* [Sketch of Meytus's work] (Moscow, 1962)
——: *'Ukradene shchastya' opera Yu. Meytusa* (Kiev, 1964)
L. Bas: *Yuly Meytus* (Kiev, 1973)
DETLEF GOJOWY

**Mezangeau** [Meziniot], **René.** *See* MESANGEAU, RENÉ.

**Mezari, Maddalena.** *See* CASULANA, MADDALENA.

**Mező, László** (*b* Szeghalom, 27 April 1939). Hungarian cellist. He studied at the Bartók Conservatory, then at the Budapest Academy with Antal Friss, 1954–62. One of the founders of the Bartók String Quartet in 1957, he was a member until 1960 and again from 1976. After winning prizes in several international competitions, including the first prizes at Helsinki and Budapest in 1963, he took further studies with Eisenberg at the Juilliard School, New York, 1965–6, and on a Ford Foundation scholarship with Casals and Piatigorsky. He has toured widely in Europe, was appointed a professor at the Budapest Academy in 1970, and in 1972 joined the Budapest Chamber Ensemble. His repertory includes music by Britten, Penderecki and Shostakovich which he introduced to Hungarian audiences, and a number of contemporary Hungarian works, most of them dedicated to him. He plays a cello by Alessandro d'Espini, dated 1830. Apart from splendour of tone, his playing is characterized by rhythmical force and a sense of contemporary style. He received the Liszt Prize in 1968.

PÉTER P. VÁRNAI

**Mezza voce.** *See* MEZZO, MEZZA.

**Mezzo, mezza** (It.: 'half', 'medium'). A word used in several different musical contexts, one of the commonest of which is the MEZZO-SOPRANO voice. In current Italian *mezza manica* means the half-position in string playing, *mezza cadenza* a half-cadence or half-close and *mezzotono* a semitone. In addition the following universally used technical meanings appear.

(1) *Mezza voce, mezzavoce* ('half-voice'). A direction

in both vocal and instrumental music to produce a quiet, restrained tone, found as early as Tosi's *Opinioni* (1723, pp.20f), where it is recommended that ascending appoggiaturas, especially those involving chromatic intervals, be performed *mezza voce*. This very specific direction is most often found in operatic scores of the 19th century: in the second act of Verdi's *Otello*, for example, Iago's narration of Cassio's dream ('Era la notte, Cassio dormiva') is marked *mezza voce*; and the opening scene of *Simon Boccanegra* is marked 'tutta questa scena a mezzavoce'. It appears also in instrumental music, for example in the slow movements of Beethoven's opp.106, 109, 125 and 131; in very similar circumstances he also used *sotto voce* (*see* SOTTO). The French equivalent in the 18th century, *à demi* or *à demi voix*, also applied to both vocal and instrumental music. *Mezza voce* is entirely different from MESSA DI VOCE.

(2) *Mezzo carattere*. A term sometimes applied in operatic parlance to a character part-serious, part-comic, as for example Susanna in *Figaro*.

(3) *Mezzo-forte*, *mezzo-piano* (*mf*, *mp*). Dynamic indications implying moderation. Thus *mezzo-forte* is less loud than *forte*; and *mezzo-piano* is less soft, therefore louder, than *piano*.
*See also* TEMPO AND EXPRESSION MARKS.

(4) *Mezzo-legato*, *mezzo-staccato* (and *legato-staccato*). Articulations normally designated by a slur with staccato dots beneath it; *see* ARTICULATION.

**Mezzo, Pietro de.** *See* DEMEZZO, PIETRO.

**Mezzo-contralto** (It.). A voice of contralto timbre but with the compass of a mezzo-soprano. This recherché term, a product of the mid-19th-century French penchant for classifying every variety of voice, was used to describe that of the great tragédienne Rosine Stoltz (1815–1903). Among the several roles she created was that of Léonore in Donizetti's *La favorite* (1840), which extends to *a''* but quite frequently sweeps down to *b*.

OWEN JANDER

**Mezzogorri** [Mezzogori], **Giovanni Nicolò** (*b* Comacchio, late 16th century; *d* ?Comacchio, in or after 1623). Italian composer. He was a pupil of Girolamo Belli at nearby Argenta. He was a beneficed priest and was *maestro di cappella* at Comacchio Cathedral in 1611; he was still there in 1623. He must have been on good terms with the town authorities, for in 1614 (according to the title-page of his *Cantilene ecclesiastiche*) Lorenzo Ferrucci, the governor of Comacchio, defended him against wrongful accusations, ordering that all 'foolish rumours' should cease. Mezzogorri probably spent his entire life in modest surroundings in his native town. He may have had connections with nearby Ravenna, for his *La celeste sposa* is dedicated to the Archbishop of Ravenna. His output consists almost entirely of sacred music for two to four voices; in the four-voice works he favoured low voice-groupings, making particular use of combining one alto, two tenors and a bass.

WORKS
*(all published in Venice)*

Del primo libro de sacri concerti, 2, 3vv, bc (1611)
La citara sacra: secondo libro degli ecclesiastici concerti, 2, 3vv, bc (1612)
La celeste sposa: terzo libro de gli ecclesiastici concerti, 2–4vv, bc (1613)

Cantilene ecclesiastiche, varie messe, mottetti, e un Miserere intiero, libro quarto, 4vv, bc (1614)
Il pastor fido armonico, in due parti diviso, parte prima, secondo libro de [21] madrigali, 5vv, bc (hpd/spinet/chit) (1617)
Cantico della beatissima vergine sopra gli otto toni . . . con l'inno Ave maris stella, 4vv, bc (org) [op.8] (1622)
Salmi festivi vespertini intieri, 4vv, bc (1623)
Works in 1616², 1623², 1627¹, 1627², 1628², 1638⁵

JUDITH NAGLEY

**Mezzo-soprano** (It.). A female voice, normally written for within the range *a* to *f♯''*, which may be extended at either end, particularly in solo writing. The distinction between soprano and mezzo-soprano became common only towards the middle of the 18th century. In the 17th century most music for 'soprano' had a range *c'* to *g''*, which by later criteria would be deemed appropriate for a mezzo-soprano. During the first half of the 18th century, however, composers of operas and cantatas began writing soprano parts that not only slightly extended the upper range (frequently reaching *a''*) but used a somewhat higher tessitura, and were particularly characterized by lengthy *fioriture* in the range *g'* to *g''*. Along with this trend towards more characteristic writing for the soprano voice came an awareness of the somewhat weightier mezzo-soprano voice, which was unsuited to the new soprano roles. This awareness was well expressed by the discriminating J. J. Quantz in his autobiography in Marpurg's *Historisch-kritische Beyträge zur Aufnahme der Musik* (1755, v, pp.213, 240f). The castrato Senesino, 'who was always regarded in England as a contralto' (Burney: *History*, iv, 1789, p.275), was described by Quantz as having 'a penetrating, clear, even, and pleasant deep soprano voice (mezzo Soprano)' which he rarely used above *f''*. In comparing the soprano Cuzzoni (whose range was *c'* to *c'''*) with Faustina Bordoni, Quantz (quoted in Burney, iv, 318ff) similarly reported that the latter had 'a less clear than penetrating mezzosoprano voice' with the range *b* to *g''*.

The distinction between the soprano and mezzo-soprano voices was more keenly sensed by composers in the 19th century. Paradoxically, in this same period it became common to extend the mezzo-soprano range as high as *b♭''* (even higher in the roles of Eboli and Amneris); and at the same time many sopranos cultivated their voices so as to be highly effective in producing the rich timbre required for mezzo-soprano roles. Mezzo-sopranos with an extended upper range tackled with increasing frequency the lower of two soprano roles in such operas as Bellini's *Norma* (Adalgisa) and Donizetti's *Anna Bolena* (Jane Seymour); and the mid-century singers at the Paris Opéra such as Rosine Stoltz, Cornélie Falcon and Pauline Gueymard (for whom the roles of, respectively, Léonore in Donizetti's *La favorite*, Valentine in Meyerbeer's *Les Huguenots* and Eboli in Verdi's *Don Carlos* were composed) resist any strict classification as either dramatic sopranos or dramatic mezzos. Wagner's Ortrud, Fricka (described by Wagner as 'Sopran' in *Das Rheingold* and as 'tiefer Sopran' in *Die Walküre*) and Kundry are roles equally difficult to categorize; both sopranos and mezzo-sopranos sing them.

The mezzo-soprano has frequently been cast in the role of nurse or confidante (e.g. Brangäne in *Tristan und Isolde*, Magdalena in *Die Meistersinger*, Emilia in Verdi's *Otello* and Suzuki in Puccini's *Madama Butterfly*) or of the mature married woman (e.g. Herodias in Strauss's *Salome*, Adelaide in *Arabella* and Kate Pinkerton in *Madama Butterfly*). Saint-Saëns'

*Samson et Dalila* is one of the few exceptions to the general rule that the heroine (particularly the beautiful maiden) is cast as a soprano.

BIBLIOGRAPHY

*RicordiE*

R. Celletti: 'Mezzosoprani e contralti', *Musica d'oggi*, new ser., v (1962), 110

OWEN JANDER

**mf.** *Mezzoforte* (It.: 'moderately loud'); *see* MEZZO, MEZZA.

**MG.** *Main gauche* (Fr.: 'left hand'); *see* ABBREVIATIONS.

**Mi.** The third degree of the Guidonian HEXACHORD; *see also* SOLMIZATION, §I. In French, Italian and Spanish, the note E; *see* PITCH NAMES.

**Míča** [Micza, Mischa, Mitscha], **František Adam** [Jan Adam František de Paula] (*b* Jaroměřice nad Rokytnou, Moravia, 11 Jan 1746; *d* Lwów, 19 March 1811). Czech composer, nephew of František Antonín Míča. He studied music probably with his father Karel Antonín Míča (1699–1784), a Kammerdiener (valet) and musician of Count Questenberg at Jaroměřice, later a door-keeper and musician to the imperial court at Vienna. After law studies at Vienna (completed 1767), he became a government official there, and later in Styria (*c*1786–96) as well as in the Austrian provinces of Poland (from May 1796). He devoted himself to music as an amateur, mostly while in Vienna (to December 1785). He played several instruments, and his compositions enjoyed considerable esteem, notably with W. A. Mozart and Emperor Joseph II. His symphonies (of which the earliest manuscript is dated 1771) and string quartets (manuscripts dated 1786) use the general expressive techniques of the period. They consist of three or four movements, the first two sometimes being reversed (slow–fast); the movements in sonata form usually have two contrasting themes. A manuscript biography of Míča, including a detailed though incomplete list of his works, is in the library of the Gesellschaft der Musikfreunde in Vienna, and was partly published in Veselý (1968).

WORKS

INSTRUMENTAL

Orch: 27 syms., some in *CS-Bm*, *Pnm*, *I-MOe*, 1 in *D-Bds*, 4 listed in Breitkopf catalogues (1776–8), 1 attrib. Haydn in 6 Sinfonie . . . par G. Hayden, op.14 no.3 (Paris, 1772), 1 in E♭ ed. E. Hradecký (Prague, 1958), 1 in D ed. J. Racek (Prague, 1946) also attrib. F. Antonín Míča; 4 vn concs., 1777–81; Hpd Conc.; dances, incl. *c*40 minuets, 12 German dances, krakowiak (lost)

Chamber: 12 str qts: all *A-Wn*, 6 also in *CS-Bm*, no.2 ed. in MAB, vi (1949, 2/1965), nos.8–9 ed. A. Bílková (Prague, 1968–9); 6 qts, fl, str; 3 qts, ob, vn, va, b, *Pnm*, 1 ed. in Diletto musicale, cclviii (Vienna and Munich, 1967); Trio, 2 vn, vc; 4 sonatas, harp, 1781; 6 notturnos, 2 vn, 2 va, 2 hn, b, 1 in *CS-K*; Notturno, vn solo, 2 vn, 2 ob, 2 hn, 2 bn, 2 va, b, ed. in MAB, xix (1953, 2/1964); Divertissement, pf, 2 vn, 2 va, 2 ob, 2 hn, b; Sextet, fl, ob, 2 vn, va, b, *Pnm*

VOCAL

Adrast und Isidore, oder Die Nachtmusik (Singspiel, 2, C. F. Bretzner, after Molière), Vienna, Burg, 26 April 1781, lib pubd
Bernardon, die Gouvernante (Singspiel, 2, J. Kurz-Bernardon)
Der 50ste Psalm Davids, oratorio, 1810, perf. Lwów, 16 April 1813
Arias, ariettas, duets, serenades (Studenten-Cassation), incl. Memento homo, sacred duetto, S, A, 2 vn, org, *CS-Bm*, doubtful

BIBLIOGRAPHY

*ČSHS*; *EitnerQ*

'Nachricht vom Leben des Franz Adam von Mitscha', *Monatbericht der Gesellschaft der Musikfreunde* (1829), no.8, p.113

C. von Wurzbach: *Biographisches Lexikon des Kaiserthums Oesterreich*, xviii (Vienna, 1868), 373ff

H. C. R. Landon: *The Symphonies of Joseph Haydn* (London, 1955), 3

J. Racek: 'František Adam Jan Míča', *Zprávy Bertramky* (1961), no.25 [with bibliography]

A. Bílková: *Smyčcové kvartety Františka Adama Míči: rozbor z hlediska tektoniky* [Míča's string quartets: a structural analysis] (diss., U. of Prague, 1968) [with thematic catalogue of string quartets]

O. Veselý: 'Rod Míčů' [Míča family], *HV*, v (1968), 264

O. Michtner: *Das alte Burgtheater als Opernbühne* (Vienna, 1970), 97f, 117, 373, 466

MILAN POŠTOLKA

**Míča** [Micza, Mitscha], **František Antonín (Václav)** (*b* Třebíč, 5 Sept 1694; *d* Jaroměřice nad Rokytnou, 15 Feb 1744). Czech composer. He was the son of Mikuláš Ondřej Míča (1659–1729) and was taken as a child to Jaroměřice, where his father had been appointed organist to Count Questenberg. After studying music as the count's page in Vienna (1711), he was Kammerdiener (valet) and Kapellmeister of the count's orchestra from about 1722. He conducted performances of operatic works by Caldara, F. B. Conti, I. M. Conti, D. N. Sarro, Vinci, Leo, Hasse and others, occasionally with insertions and adaptations of his own, and frequently sang the tenor parts.

Míča's compositions date from about 1723 to 1738. They are in a late Baroque operatic idiom close to that of Caldara. The overtures (sinfonias) of his secular cantatas and of his only extant opera belong to the Italian type, with a tripartite fast–slow–fast order, the first allegros including elements of the pre-Classical sonata form. His authorship of a Sinfonia in D (Prague, 1946) is refuted by stylistic factors; it is now ascribed to his nephew František Adam Míča, but on slim evidence.

WORKS

Complete list in Helfert (1916), 158ff; first performed at Jaroměřice, unless otherwise stated.

DRAMATIC

L'origine di Jaromeriz in Moravia (opera, 2, It. text N. Blinoni; Cz., A. F. Dubravius; 3, Ger., H. Rademin), with 2 intermezzos (Bonlini), Dec 1730; score, *A-Wn*; 1 recit and aria, ed. in DČHP (1958), no.122
Other intermezzos, arias, operas (some Cz.), ballets, 1723–38, lost

OTHER VOCAL

Cantatas, solo vv, chorus, insts: Bellezza e decoro (D. Blinoni), 17 Jan 1729, score, *Wgm*; Nel giorno natalizio, 1732, score, *Wgm*; Der glorreiche Nahmen Adami (J. Želivský), 24 Dec 1734, score, *CS-Pu*, pt.2 ed. H. Krupka as Quatuor elementa (Prague, 1960, 2/1966); Operosa terni colossi moles (Želivský), 23 or 24 Dec 1735, score, *A-Wgm*
Easter oratorios (sepolcri), solo vv, chorus, insts, some also perf. Brno, Olomouc, music lost (under otherwise stated), pubd libs extant: Abgesungene Betrachtungen, 11 April 1727, score, *Wn*; Krátké rozjímání (Dubravius), 26 March 1728; Obviněná nevinnost (Dubravius), 15 April 1729; Öfterer Anstoss (Dubravius), 7 April 1730; Die heilige Helena, 1733

BIBLIOGRAPHY

*ČSHS*; *EitnerQ*

V. Helfert: *Hudební barok na českých zámcích* [Musical Baroque in Bohemian castles] (Prague, 1916) [with list of works]

——: *Hudba na jaroměřickém zámku* [Music in the Jaroměřice castle] (Prague, 1924)

J. Bužga: 'Míča, František Václav', *MGG*

O. Veselý: 'Rod Míčů' [Míča family], *HV*, v (1968), 264

V. Telec: 'Stará libreta a míčovská otázka' [Old librettos and the Míča problem], *OM*, ii (1970), 239

T. Straková: 'Jaroměřice nad Rokytnou', *OM*, v (1973), 57

J. Trojan: 'Jak to dopadlo v Jaroměřicích: německý tisk libreta opery *L'origine di Jaromeriz in Moravia*' [A German print of the libretto of the opera *L'origine di Jaromeriz in Moravia*], *OM*, vi (1974), 82

MILAN POŠTOLKA

**Michael.** German family of composers and musicians. (1) Rogier Michael was a notable late representative of the Netherlands school, and (2) Tobias Michael was also a notable composer and as Kantor of the Thomaskirche, Leipzig, between Schein and Knüpfer held one of the principal musical posts in Germany.

(1) **Rogier Michael** (*b* Mons or Bergen op Zoom, *c*1552; *d* Dresden, after 25 Jan 1619). Composer and singer of Netherlands birth, father of (2) Tobias, (3) Christian and (4) Samuel Michael. His father was a tenor in the Vienna Hofkapelle, where Rogier became a choirboy. In 1564 he was transferred to the Graz Hofkapelle of Archduke Karl II, where the Kapellmeister was first Johannes de Cleve and then Annibale Padovano and where the boys were taught from 1567 by Jacob de Brouck. In 1569 he was given a three-year scholarship and may have studied in Italy. He was a tenor in the Hofkapelle of Margrave Georg Friedrich von Onolzbach at Ansbach from 1572 to 1574, when he went to the Dresden Hofkapelle as singer and musician. He remained there until his death, serving four electors during this 45-year period. From 12 December 1587 he was Hofkapellmeister, but because of increasing infirmity he was assisted from 1613 by Michael Praetorius and later by Schütz, who was appointed his successor in 1619. Apart from his sons his pupils included Schein (from 1599 to 1603).

The basically late Netherlands style of his music was doubtless modified to some extent by contact with more recent Italian music through his teachers in Vienna and Graz, his residence at Dresden and, if he went there, his experiences in Italy. Italian influences appear clearly in *Introitus dominicorum dierum ac praecipuorum festorum* (1603), a collection of 52 five-part motets, 49 of his own composition and one each by Andrea Gabrieli, Lassus and Padovano. None of the motets is based on a cantus firmus, and motet-like writing is fused with madrigalian elements, producing simple melodies and a good deal of homophony. In historical terms Michael's volume of chorale settings (1593) is more significant. Placing the melody in the descant, as Lucas Osiander did in his collection of 1586, he tried to combine a feeling for a type of melody appropriate to a prominent top part with the polyphonic style of the older type of chorale setting of Luther's day as represented by the work of Johann Walter (i). More important still are his two sacred histories of 1602, *Die Empfängnis unseres Herrn Jesu Christi* and *Die Geburt unseres Herrn Jesu Christi*. They are similar in layout: the recitation tone of the Evangelist is unaccompanied (in the former it is based on the *Canticum Mariae*, in the latter on the *Canticum Simeonis*), the turbae and the parts of the individual characters are for two to four voices, and the works are framed by an exordium and conclusion for six voices, and a *Magnificat* and *Nunc dimittis* for four and five voices respectively, with the psalm tones used as cantus firmi in the descant. The two works are interesting links in the tradition of sacred histories at Dresden between those by Michael's predecessors, Matthaeus Le Maistre and Antonio Scandello, and those by his successor Schütz. What was probably his last work, the five-part psalm in *RISM* 1623[14], shows that he remained faithful to the traditions of the *prima prattica* and shunned up-to-date styles and techniques.

WORKS

Der ander Theil: die gebräuchlichsten und vornembsten Gesenge D. Mart. Luther und anderer frommen Christen: itzo auffs neue mit fleis componieret und den Choral durchauss in Discant geführet, 4vv (Dresden, 1593) [pt ii of Dresden Gesangbuch]

Hochzeit Gesang (Drei schöne stück sind) zu Ehren dem ... Herrn Iohanni Georgi Gödelman ... und ... der Frauen Katharina Unwirdt, 6vv (Dresden, 1602)

Introitus dominicorum dierum ac praecipuorum festorum, in Electoratus Saxonici ecclesiis usitatissimorum, iuxta seriem totius anni, ad modum sacrarum cantionum, 5vv (Leipzig, 1603[5])

[Hochzeits-Gesang], 6vv (Dresden, 1611), lost

Qualis uvidulis brasilica jurgera ... serenissimis principis ... Joannis Georgii ... filio Johanni Georgio, 31. Maji nato et 27. Junii 1613 ... venato (Dresden, 1613), lost

Psalm, 5vv, 1623[14]

Te Deum, 6vv, *c*1595; 3 Lat. motets, 4, 6, 8vv (incl. 1 *c*1593–6); 3 wedding motets (2 Ger., 1 Lat.), 8, 12vv, 1604–7; Ger. work, 6vv: *D-Dla, Dla, FBo, Z, PL-GD*

Die Empfängnis unseres Herrn Jesu Christi, 6vv, 1602; Die Geburt unseres Herrn Jesu Christi nach ... Lukas und Matthaeus, 6vv, 1602: lost, formerly Bibliothek der Regierungspräsidenten, Stettin (Szczecin); both ed. in *Handbuch der deutschen evangelischen Kirchenmusik*, i/3–4 (Göttingen, 1933); Die Geburt ... Jesu Christi, ed. H. Osthoff (Kassel, 1937)

Ger. mass, 6vv, 2 Passions, lost (cited in R. Kade)

Madrigal, 5vv, 1589[15]

(2) **Tobias Michael** (*b* Dresden, 13 June 1592; *d* Leipzig, 26 June 1657). Composer, second son of (1) Rogier Michael, brother of (3) Christian and (4) Samuel Michael. He was a pupil of his father. In 1601 he became a treble in the Dresden Hofkapelle and was thus also taught by Andreas Petermann, *Präzeptor* to the choirboys. On 8 May 1609 he was admitted to Schulpforta, the electoral school near Naumburg that specialized in music and the humanities, and at about the same time, together with his brother Christian, he matriculated at the University of Leipzig. From 1613 to 1618 he studied theology and philosophy at the University of Wittenberg and shortly before he left he founded a collegium musicum practicum. In 1619 he was appointed Kapellmeister of the Neue Kirche at Sondershausen, Thuringia, by the Counts of Schwarzburg and Hohenstein. When fire destroyed both the castle and the church he remained at Sondershausen for a few years as an official in the government offices. After the death of Schein on 16 November 1630, he applied to succeed him as Kantor of the Thomaskirche, Leipzig. He was chosen on 29 December, his appointment was confirmed as from 26 April 1631, and he took it up on 2 June. A letter from him to the Leipzig city council in 1633 (printed in La Mara) reveals something about his duties as a teacher at the Thomasschule and about the difficulties he encountered in trying to maintain the high standards of the choir during the Thirty Years War. He supported Marco Scacchi in his dispute with Paul Siefert, and a letter from him to this effect was printed by Scacchi in his *Judicium cribri musici* (*c*1649). He enjoyed friendly relations with several other musicians and scholars, including Scheidt, and wrote a number of occasional works for civic and university personalities in Leipzig; they included three works in 1650 celebrating the official ending of the war. At his funeral on 30 June 1657, Martin Geyer, professor of theology at the University of Leipzig and preacher at the Thomaskirche, delivered the oration, and the service also included a work Michael had written shortly before, *In Angst und Noth*.

Michael's principal achievements as a composer are the two volumes of *Musicalische Seelenlust* (1634–7), which were influenced by Italianate models. The first volume comprises 30 motets for five voices and continuo to German biblical texts, which in their 'singularly delightful madrigalian manner' are clearly reminiscent of the pieces in Schein's *Israelis Brünlein* (1623). The second volume contains 50 Italianate sacred concertos of various kinds: the first 12 comprise three solo concertos each for soprano, alto, tenor and bass, the next 12 comprise three duet concertos each for sopranos, altos, tenors and basses, and the last 26 are concertos for various solo voices with obbligato instruments, some with symphonies and ritornellos. The preface to the second volume includes useful information on performing practice, especially the embellishment of the voice parts: in this regard Michael stated that as far as possible he had followed Kapsperger's method. He added separate decorated parts which the singer could use or take as models. The style and techniques in his concertos derive to some extent from Michael Praetorius, for example in the contrast between solo and choral voices and in the use of contrasted tempo and dynamic markings.

### WORKS
*(published in Leipzig unless otherwise stated)*

#### SACRED VOCAL
Musicalischer Seelenlust, erster Theil, darinnen ausserlesene . . . Glaubens-Seufftzerlein, Andacht und Freude, 5vv, bc (1634–5); 2 ed. in *Handbuch der deutschen evangelischen Kirchenmusik*, ii/1 (Göttingen, 1935)
Musicalischer Seelen-Lust ander Theil, darinnen, gleichermassen, ausserlesene . . . Glaubens-Seufftzerlein, 1–6 and more vv, insts, bc (1637); 2 ed. in Wustmann; 1 ed. in Mw, xii (1956; Eng. trans., 1961)
5 chorales, 5vv, in J. H. Schein: Cantional (Leipzig, 2/1645), J. Frentzel: Seraphischer Engels-Chor (Leipzig, 1652); 2 sacred songs, 1v, bc, in J. Frentzel: 10 andächtige Bussgesänge (Leipzig, 1650), 1653⁵, ed. in Wustmann; Ger. psalm, 3–5vv, 1623¹⁴

Ger. sacred work, 1v, chorus 6vv, bc, *D-GRH*

#### OCCASIONAL
Der 127. Psalm (Wo der Herr nicht das Haus bauet): in ein musicalisch Concert gebracht zu hochzeitlichen Ehren H. Christian Michaels . . . Organisten zu St Nicolai und Pauli . . . und . . . Frauen Susannen . . . Beumels, 4vv, bc (1635)
Gedächtnüss-Mahl (O liebe Lyr) . . . zu . . . Ehren . . . Thomae Leonhard Schwendendörffern . . . welcher das Ziel seines Lebens . . . beschlossen . . . den 25 . . . Decembr . . . anno 1635, 2vv, bc (1635)
Klaglied (Siehe, der Gerechte kömpt), über das unverhoffte . . . Ableiben der . . . Frauen Susanna geborne Euringin, 5vv, bc, in Leich-Predigt . . . bey . . . Leichbestattung . . . Frauen Susannen (Leipzig, 1635)
Aller frommen Christen Ruhe . . . auf . . . H. Leonhard Hermans . . . Leichenbegängnüss, in die Music . . . gesetzet . . . den 16. Decembr. anno 1646, 8vv, bc (1647)
Sehnlicher Nachklang (So kans nicht anders seyn) betrübter Eltern, welche ihrem lieben Kinde . . . zu dessen . . . Cämmerlein folgen müssen, 5vv, in Weiber-Schmuck . . . bey . . . Leichen-Bestattung . . . Fr. Claren Magdalenen gebohrnen Michaelin . . . Lanckisch . . . 1649 . . . am 30. Sept. (Leipzig, 1649)
Christliche Gedancken (In Angst und Noth) über den mühseligen Lebenslauff Hn. Tobias Michael . . . welche er . . . mit eigener Hand gesetzt und bey seiner Beerdigung zu musiciren begehret, welches geschehen den 30. Iunii 1657, 5vv (1657)

#### LOST WORKS
[Komm, mein Freund] Melos novis honoribus viri Jac. Edelmanni . . . nuptias celebrantis . . . anno 1617, 21. Febr., 6vv (Wittenberg, 1617)
[Ich liege und schlafe] Ewige Seelen-Ruhe, der Frawen Johannae, geb. Crefftin . . . zu dero Leichbegängnis . . . 21. Aug. anno 1631, 5vv, bc (1631)
Applausus musico-gratulatorius (n.p.), 1641)
Glückwünschungs-Gesang für Dr. Theol. Joh. Hülsemann, 14. Mai 1646, 5vv (1646)
Gottes Güte, Huld und Treu . . . Glückwunsch zur Hochzeit Fr. Lancke, 15. Febr. 1648 (1648)

3 Ger. motets, 7, 8vv, bc, perf. Leipzig, 7 Sept 1650, for end of war, formerly Königsberg Universitätsbibliothek; 1 motet ed. in Wustmann
Other works, formerly at *D-Bds*, *NAUw* (12 pr. works, 15 others, all 5–8vv, bc, see Werner), Breslau

### (3) Christian Michael (*b* Dresden, *c*1593; *d* Leipzig, 29 Aug 1637). Composer and organist, son of (1) Rogier Michael and brother of (2) Tobias and (4) Samuel Michael. Together with Tobias he matriculated at the University of Leipzig in 1609. In 1613 he was given a scholarship by the Saxon Elector Johann Georg I. In 1633, after the death of his brother Samuel, he succeeded him as organist of the Nicolaikirche, Leipzig,

and held this position until his early death. His *Tabulatura, darinnen etzliche Praeludia, Toccaten und Couranten uff das Clavier Instrument gesetzt* (Brunswick, 1639, 2/1645; 14 preludes and toccatas ed. P. Rubardt, Leipzig, 1940), published posthumously, is among the last printed German organ tablatures. It contains nine three-part and nine four-part preludes (arranged, as the preface points out, according to the cycle of 5ths), six four-part toccatas and ten courantes. Three manuscript vocal concertos by Christian Michael, two for five voices, the other for eight and 16 voices, seem now not to be extant. Like his father and his brother Tobias, he had a psalm published in *RISM* 1623¹⁴; it is in three sections and is for three and five voices. Daniel Michael, who is represented in the same volume by a similar work, seems to have been Christian's twin brother. Apart from the fact that he matriculated with Samuel Michael at Leipzig University in the summer of 1613, nothing is known about him.

### (4) Samuel Michael (*b* Dresden, *c*1597; *d* Leipzig, between 14 and 17 Aug 1632). Composer and organist, son of (1) Rogier Michael and brother of (2) Tobias and (3) Christian Michael. He matriculated at the University of Leipzig in 1613. From 1617 to 1621 he held a scholarship from the Saxon Elector Johann Georg I similar to that held from 1613 by his brother Christian. He was organist of the Nicolaikirche, Leipzig, from 1628 until his early death. He died of the plague, and Paul Fleming commemorated him in a Latin elegy. Two collections published by him are extant: *Neue Paduanen, Intraden, Balletten, Allemanden, Auffzüge, Galliarden, Volten, Couranten und Schertzi* (Leipzig, 1627), for three to five instruments and organ continuo, and *Psalmodia regia, das ist Ausserlesene Sprüche aus den ersten 25. Psalmen*, i (Leipzig, 1632), for two to five voices and continuo, which can also be performed on instruments. He also published several funeral motets, of which only one survives, the five-part *Christliches Trost-Lied (Die mit Thränen seen) . . . über den Hintritt . . . der Frauen Catharinen . . . Hans Behrs* (Leipzig, 1632). There are also four pieces by him in the *Cantionale sacrum* (Gotha, 1646–7).

### BIBLIOGRAPHY
*EitnerQ*; *GerberNL*; *WaltherML*
J. Mattheson: *Grundlage einer Ehren-Pforte* (Hamburg, 1740); ed. M. Schneider (Berlin, 1910/R1969)
O. Kade: 'Rogier Michael, ein deutscher Tonsetzer des 16. Jahrhunderts', *MMg*, ii (1870), 3
P. Spitta: 'Leichensermone auf Musiker des XVI. und XVII. Jahrhunderts, iii: Tobias Michael', *MMg*, iii (1871), 24
La Mara: *Musikerbriefe*, i (Leipzig, 1886)
R. Kade: 'Der Dresdener Kapellmeister Rogier Michael, c. 1550–1619: unbekanntes Aktenmaterial über ihn aus dem Kgl. Sächs. Hauptstaatsarchiv', *VMw*, v (1889), 272
R. Wustmann: *Musikgeschichte Leipzigs*, i: *Bis zur Mitte des 17. Jahrhunderts* (Leipzig and Berlin, 1909/R1975)
A. Schering: *Musikgeschichte Leipzigs*, ii: *Von 1650 bis 1723* (Leipzig, 1926)
A. Werner: 'Die alte Musikbibliothek an St. Wenzel in Naumburg a.d. Saale', *AMw*, viii (1926), 406
W. Dane: 'Briefwechsel zwischen dem landgräflich hessischen und dem kurfürstlich sächsischen Hof um Heinrich Schütz (1614–1619)', *ZMw*, xvii (1935), 343
H. J. Moser: *Heinrich Schütz: sein Leben und Werk* (Kassel, 1936, rev. 2/1954; Eng. trans., 1959)
J. Franck: *Die Introitus-Kompositionen von Rogier Michael (ca. 1550–1619)* (Giessen, 1937)
H. Osthoff: 'Die Historien Rogier Michaels: ein Beitrag zur Geschichte der Historienkomposition', *Festschrift Arnold Schering* (Berlin, 1937/R1973), 166
——: *Die Niederländer und das deutsche Lied (1400–1640)* (Berlin, 1938/R1967)

H. Federhofer: 'Etats de la chapelle musicale de Charles V et de Maximilien', *RBM*, iv (1950), 176

——: 'Jugendjahre und Lehrer Rogier Michaels', *AMw*, x (1953), 221; see also *RBM*, viii (1954), 135

J. K. Munson: *The 'Musicalischer Seelenlust' of Tobias Michael* (diss., U. of Rochester, 1953)

H. Federhofer: Introduction to DTÖ, xc (1954)

E. Kapst: *Tobias Michael und seine 'Musicalische Seelenlust'* (diss., U. of Halle, 1955)

A. Adrio: 'Tobias Michaels *Musicalische Seelenlust* (1634–1637): über einige Fragen der musikalischen Aufführungs- und Editionspraxis im frühen 17. Jahrhundert', *Festschrift Helmuth Osthoff* (Tutzing, 1961), 115

W. Apel: *Geschichte der Orgel- und Klaviermusik bis 1700* (Kassel, 1967; Eng. trans., rev., 1972)

BERND BASELT

**Michael, Daniel.** German musician, brother of Christian Michael; *see* MICHAEL family, (3).

**Michael, David Moritz** (*b* 1751; *d* 1827). American Moravian musician and composer; *see* MORAVIANS, AMERICAN.

**Michaele, Antoninus de.** *See* DI MICHELI, ANTONIO.

**Michaelides, Solon** (*b* Nicosia, 12 Nov 1905; *d* Athens, 9 Sept 1979). Greek composer. He studied at Trinity College, London (1927–30), where he was made an honorary fellow in 1952. In Paris he was a pupil of Boulanger (harmony, counterpoint and fugue) and of Maize and Cortot (piano) at the Ecole Normale de Musique (1930–34) and of Lioncourt (composition) and Labey (conducting) at the Schola Cantorum. He then took a leading part in promoting musical life and music education in Cyprus and Salonica. He was director of the Limassol Conservatory (1934–56) and professor of music at the Lanitis Communal High School in that city (1941–56). On moving to Salonica he was appointed director of the state conservatory (1957–70) and director-general and principal conductor of the state orchestra. He also appeared as a guest conductor in Europe and the USA, and lectured on Greek music for the BBC (1946–8) and at American universities (1963). A composer of the national school, he made use of modal cantilena and folk or Byzantine elements, soberly harmonized in a manner slightly suggestive of Franck, Fauré or Vaughan Williams. His orchestration includes impressionist touches.

WORKS

(*selective list*)

Stage: Nausicaa, ballet, 1950; Ulysses (opera, 3, Michaelides), 1951, rev. 1972–3; 3 incidental scores for Greek tragedies

Orch: De profundis, 1933, rev. 1949; 2 Byzantine Sketches, str, 1934; Cypriot Wedding, fl, str, 1935; 2 Greek Sym. Pictures, 1936; Byzantine Offering, str, 1944; Archaic Suite, fl, ob, harp, str, 1954; Kypriaka eleftheria [To Cypriot freedom], 1959; Pf Conc., 1966; In memoriam, str, 1974 [from Pf Sonata, 1934]

Choral: O táfos [The tomb] (Palamas), Mez, Bar, chorus, orch, 1936; I hara [The joy] (Michaelides), female vv, 1946; I itia [The poplar] (A. Theros), 1947; Crux fidelis, 1949; Ave Maria, male vv, 1950; Prosefhi [Prayer] (Michaelides), 1952; I eleftheroi poliorkimenoi [The free besieged] (D. Solomos), S, Bar, chorus, orch, 1955; Hymnos stin eleftheria [Hymn to freedom] (Cypriot national anthem, Solomos), 1962

Inst: Prelude, harp, 1933; Str Qt, 1934; Pf Sonata, 1934; Pf Trio, 1946; Sappho's Lyre, pf, 1948; I lambri [Easter], pf, 1956; Greek Suite, pf, 1966

Songs: La flûte (Chénier), Mez, pf, 1934; Ta mavra matia [The black eyes] (D. Libertis), S/T, pf, 1935; I prosefhi tou tapeinou [The prayer of the humble one] (Z. Papantoniou), Mez/Bar, pf, 1953; Ta matia sou [Your eyes] (N. Kranidiotis), S/T, pf, 1965

Principal publishers: Greek Ministry of Education, Gwynn (Llangollen), Union of Greek Composers

WRITINGS

*Synchroni angliki moussiki* [Modern English music] (Nicosia, 1939)

*I kypriaki laiki moussiki* [Cypriot folk music] (Nicosia, 1944, 2/1956)

*Harmonia tis synchronis moussikis* [Modern harmony] (Limassol, 1945)

*The Neo-Hellenic Folk-music* (Limassol, 1948)

*I neo-elleniki moussiki* [Modern Greek music] (Nicosia, 1952)

*The Music of Ancient Greece: an Encyclopaedia* (London, 1978)

Articles on Greek composers in *Grove 5*

BIBLIOGRAPHY

A. S. Theodoropoulou: 'Synchronoi ellenes moussikoi: 6. Solon Michaelides', *Anglo-elleniki epitheorissi*, iii/6 (1947), 179

F. Anoyanakis: 'I moussiki stin neoteri Ellada', in K. Nef: *History of Music* (Gk. trans., Athens, 1958), 598f

GEORGE S. LEOTSAKOS

**Michaelis, Zanetto de.** *See* ZANETTO DI MONTICHIARO.

**Michael Modrekili** (*fl* 10th century). Hymnographer of the Georgian Church; *see* GEORGIAN RITE, MUSIC OF THE.

**Michael Scotus** (*b* ?Scotland, ?1175; *d* 1235). Theorist, possibly Scottish. He probably studied at Oxford and Paris, and he worked at Toledo and Bologna. From 1220 he was in Sicily at the imperial court of Frederick II. Music is discussed in two chapters of his principal work, the *Liber introductorius*, which is a compendium of astronomy for the use of students. One chapter deals with the relationships between music and astronomy, and expounds the traditional theory of the harmony of the spheres. The other chapter comprises musical definitions and the classification of music, the division of the monochord and rules for the liturgical chant. Of particular interest are the analogies he drew between the elements of astronomy and those of music (sun and moon correspond respectively to the red and yellow lines of Guidonian notation, and the firmament corresponds to the cantus firmus), and the references to contemporary musical practice in Italy (*cantus fractus* and organum).

BIBLIOGRAPHY

L. Thorndike: *Michael Scot* (London, 1965)

F. A. Gallo: 'Astronomy and Music in the Middle Ages: the *Liber introductorius* by Michael Scot', *MD*, xxvii (1973), 5

F. ALBERTO GALLO

**Michałowski, Aleksander** (*b* Kamieniec Podolski, 5 May 1851; *d* Warsaw, 17 Oct 1938). Polish pianist, composer and teacher. He studied with Reinecke and Moscheles at the Leipzig Conservatory and with Tausig in Berlin. He made his début in Leipzig in 1869 and lived in Warsaw from 1874, giving concerts mainly in Poland and Russia. Though possessing a vast repertory, he concentrated on Chopin and was notable for his delicacy of touch. Between 1891 and 1917 he held piano classes at the Warsaw Music Institute and then at the school of the Warsaw Music Society, establishing a school of his own in the Polish piano tradition. His pupils included Wanda Landowska. Michałowski composed a few dozen piano miniatures; they are influenced by Chopin and not unlike works by Moszkowski and Anton Rubinstein. He also made some virtuoso arrangements of works by Chopin, and prepared for publication a collected edition of Chopin's works; the études, waltzes, ballades and impromptus were published by Gebethner & Wolff, Warsaw.

BIBLIOGRAPHY

*SMP* [incl. list of works]

J. Kleczyński: 'Aleksander Michałowski', *Echo muzyczne, teatralne i artystyczne* (1887), no.172, p.25

Z. Drzewiecki: 'Aleksander Michałowski: nestor pianistów', *Muzyka polska*, x (1938), 423
Z. Romankówna: *Aleksander Michałowski: utwory fortepianowe* [Piano works] (MS, *PL-Kj*)
W. Poźniak: 'Muzyka fortepianowa po Chopinie' [Piano music after Chopin], *Z dziejów polskiej kultury muzycznej*, ii, ed. A. Nowak-Romanowicz and others (Kraków, 1966), 527

ZOFIA CHECHLIŃSKA

**Michałowski, Kornel** (*b* Poznań, 23 Feb 1923). Polish musical bibliographer and librarian. He studied musicology under Chybiński at the University of Poznań (1947–51). In 1950 he was made head of the music section at the University Library in Poznań, and in 1967 chairman of Polish National Committee of RILM. Michałowski is the author and the editor of most of the basic Polish music bibliographies. He is also the author of the Szymanowski thematic catalogue, which is the first publication of this type in Poland. In it he applied a new methodological approach which goes beyond schemes usually employed in such works.

WRITINGS
*Opery polskie* [Polish operas: a bibliography and catalogue] (Kraków, 1954)
ed.: *Bibliografia polskich czasopism muzycznych* [Bibliography of Polish music periodicals] (Kraków, 1955)
*Bibliografia polskiego piśmiennictwa muzycznego* [Bibliography of Polish music literature] (Kraków, 1955–64)
*Gazeta teatralna 1843–1844* (Kraków, 1956)
with W. Bogdany: *Ruch muzyczny 1857–1862* (Kraków, 1957)
ed.: *Bibliografia muzyczna polskich czasopism niemuzycznych* [Music bibliography of Polish non-musical periodicals] (Kraków, 1962–)
*Karol Szymanowski 1882–1937: katalog tematyczny dziel i bibliografia* (Kraków, 1967)
'Uwagi o bibliografii muzycznej' [Remarks on music bibliography], *Muzyka*, xii/1 (1967), 79
*Bibliografia chopinowska 1849–1969* (Kraków, 1970)
*Wprowadzenie do bibliografii muzycznej* [Introduction to music bibliography] (Kraków, 1976)
with E. Dziębowska: *Mieczysław Karłowicz 1876–1909: katalog tematyczny dziel i bibliografia* (Kraków, in preparation)

ZYGMUNT M. SZWEYKOWSKI

**Micheau, Janine** (*b* Toulouse, 17 April 1914; *d* Paris, 18 Oct 1976). French soprano. She studied in Toulouse and at the Paris Conservatoire and made her début in 1933 as La Plieuse in *Louise*. In 1935 in Amsterdam she sang the part of Mélisande, which she was to sing all over the world (San Francisco in 1938, after the Maggio Musicale, and Amsterdam in 1935–7). Her French roles at the Paris Opéra-Comique between 1933 and 1956 included Mireille, Olympia and Bizet's Léïla; she was the first French Zerbinetta in 1943 and Anne Trulove in 1953. Her roles at the Opéra, where she sang between 1940 and 1956, included Juliet, Gilda, Violetta and Pamina, as well as Sophie, a role which she sang under Kleiber at the Colón, Buenos Aires, in 1939. She made her Covent Garden début as Micaëla in 1937 and at the Paris Opéra created the roles of Creusa in Milhaud's *Médée* (1940) and Manuela in the same composer's *Bolivar* (1950). In 1947 she sang in the BBC's broadcast of Cherubini's *Les deux journées*. In all her roles Micheau was admired for the care, skill and taste with which she used a characteristically French voice, light and flexible with a wide range and conspicuously even production.

MARTIN COOPER

**Michel.** *See* MICHL family.

**Michel, Arthur.** *See* SAINT-LÉON, ARTHUR.

**Michel, Guillaume** (*fl* Paris, 1636–56). French composer. He was a popular composer of dance chansons at the French court in the mid-17th century and composed four collections of them. The first (Paris, 1636) includes duets as well as solo songs. The remainder (Paris, 1641, 1647, 1656) are all for solo voice; the second also contains a few drinking-songs. He modelled his *chansons pour danser* on those of François de Chancy (to whom he dedicated the first book). They are all strophic and in duple metre and move almost exclusively in syllabic crotchets. Nearly all consist of eight bars followed by a repeated four-bar refrain. Only seldom is there rhythmic variety, such as the hemiolas at the end of *Robin est d'humeur gentille*, or thematic development, as in *A vos pieds je viens*. The overriding simplicity of these songs was no doubt the secret of their success among the pleasure-loving amateurs for whom they were written. A wider popularity is indicated by the reprinting of all four books in 1699, by the appearance of six of them translated into German and arranged for three voices by the leading German song composer of the time, Heinrich Albert, in his *Arien*, vii (Königsberg, 1648; edn., DDT, xiii, 1904/*R*), and by the survival of one chanson in a *Recueil d'airs sérieux et à boire* (Paris, 1720). One *air* appeared as a sacred contrafactum in *La Philomèle séraphique* (Tournai, 1640).

JOHN H. BARON

**Michel, Paul** (*b* Greiz, 8 Oct 1918). German musicologist and educationist. He studied music education with Reuter and musicology with Siegmund-Schultze at Jena University (1936–9); he took the doctorate in 1957 at the Humboldt University, Berlin, with a dissertation on the training of the orchestral musician in the 19th century, and completed his *Habilitation* in 1965 at Halle University with a work on the psychological foundations of music education. His first post was as a teacher at Greiz. After an appointment as adviser in teacher training to the Thuringian Ministry of Education (1945) he became assistant director of the Pädagogisches Zentralinstitut at Weimar (1949); he then joined the Weimar Hochschule für Musik as prorector and lecturer in musical psychology (1951), later becoming professor (1959) and director of the Institut für Pädagogik und Methodik (1960). In 1976 he was appointed director of research at the Liszt Academy, Weimar. In his extensive work on problems in music psychology he has studied musical talent, musical development in children, pre-school instrument teaching and the psychological bases of music education. He has been largely responsible for the establishment of uniform standards in the training of young musicians in East Germany.

WRITINGS
*Die Ausbildung des Orchestermusikers im 19. Jahrhundert* (diss., Humboldt U. of Berlin, 1957)
'Die Bedeutung musikpsychologischer Forschungen für die Entwicklung der Musikästhetik', *Musik und Gesellschaft*, viii/4 (1958), 22
ed. with G. Kraft: *Festschrift Louis Spohr* (Weimar, 1958) [incl. 'Die pädagogischen Ansichten Louis Spohrs und ihre Beziehungen zum Philanthropismus', 26]
*Über musikalische Fähigkeiten und Fertigkeiten* (Leipzig, 1960, 2/1962 as *Musikalische Fähigkeiten und Fertigkeiten*, 4/1971)
'Franz Liszt als Lehrer und Erzieher', *Liszt-Bartók: 2nd International Musicological Conference: Budapest 1961* [*SM*, v (1963)], 105
*Psychologische Grundlagen der Musikerziehung* (Habilitationsschrift, U. of Halle, 1965; Leipzig, 1968, 2/1973)
'Richard Wagners musikpädagogische Reformideen', *BMw*, vii (1965), 2
'Zum Problem des inneren musikalischen Hörens und seiner Entwicklung', *Wissenschaftliche Zeitschrift der Humboldt-Universität Berlin*, xv/3 (Berlin, 1965), 84

'Max Regers musikpädagogische Auffassungen', *BMw*, viii (1966), 136–65

'Musikpsychologische Untersuchungen über die optimale Entwicklung musikalischer Fähigkeiten in den ersten Lebensjahren', *GfMKB, Leipzig 1966*, 510

'Researches on the Optimal Development of Musical Capacities of the Child in Different Age Levels', *XVIII. Internationaler Kongress für Psychologie: Moskau 1966*, ii, 212

*Musik und Hörer in unserer Zeit* (Berlin, 1967)

'Ergebnisse musikpsychologischer Forschungen über den Einfluss von Rundfunk und Fernsehen auf die musikalische Entwicklung von Kindern und Jugendlichen', *Musik in der Schule*, xix (1968), 452

'Akzeleration und Mutation', *Sborník pedagogické fakulty university Jana Evangelista Purkyně k šedesátým pátým narozeninám Prof. Dr. Františka Lýska* (Brno, 1969), 81

'Musik und Musikunterricht im Urteil der Schüler', *Musik in der Schule*, xx (1969), 391

'Geschichte der Musikhochschule Weimar', *Festschrift zum 100jährigen Bestehen der Hochschule für Musik 'Franz Liszt' in Weimar* (Weimar, 1972), 10, 50

'On Physical and Psychological Acceleration: Effects on the Musical Development during Childhood and Adolescence', *New Patterns of Musical Behaviour of the Young Generation in Industrial Societies: Vienna 1972*, 183

'Psychologische und methodische Grundfragen der Werkbetrachtung im Fach Musikerziehung', *Forum. Musik in der DDR*, ed. D. Brennecke and M. Hansen (Berlin, 1972), 52–94

'Zur Problematik des Instrumentalunterrichts im Vorschulalter', *Musik in der Schule*, xxiii (1972), 430, 469

*Musikerziehung in der DDR* (Berlin, 1973)

'Zum Problem der musikalischen Begabungsdiagnostik', *Musik in der Schule*, xxiv (1973), 474; xxv (1973), 10

'Zur Funktion des musikalischen Voraushörens (Antizipation)', *Festschrift für Ernst Hermann Meyer* (Leipzig, 1973), 97

'Music Education in the GDR as a Means of an All-round and Harmonious Development of Personality', *Music Education in the Modern World: ISME*, ix *Moscow 1974*, 83

'Results of Psychological Research into the Instrumental–musical Development of Children and Adults and Conclusions for the Training of Future Professional Musicians', *International Music Education: ISME Yearbook*, ii (1974), 131

'The Necessity for an Early Development of Musical Talents at Preschool Age and the Problem of Aptitude Diagnosis', *Music Education for the Very Young Child: International Seminar in Research of Music Education*, iv *Wellington 1975*, 26

'The Need for Close Interdisciplinary Co-operation between Music Education and Psychology', *Challenges in Music Education: ISME*, xi *Perth 1976*, 98

HORST SEEGER

**Michelangeli, Arturo Benedetti** (*b* Brescia, 5 Jan 1920). Italian pianist. He learnt the violin from the age of three, but abandoned it when he entered the Milan Conservatory at the age of ten to study the piano with Giuseppe Anfossi; in 1933 he graduated with honours. Six years later, having meanwhile begun, but not finished, a course in medicine, he won the Geneva International Piano Competition, and was invited to become principal professor of the piano at the Martini Conservatory in Bologna, where for two years he devoted himself to teaching and to an increasingly successful concert career. During the war he served first as a pilot in the Italian Air Force and then in the underground anti-fascist resistance. In 1945 he returned to the concert platform, visiting London for the first time to play at the Albert Hall in 1946; within a few years he established a worldwide reputation as one of the outstanding pianists of his (or, as many admirers would declare, of any) generation.

Michelangeli has cancelled nearly as many recitals and concerts as he has performed, but those who have heard him play have been rarely disappointed. He is a consummate technician, renowned for his fine control of colour and counterpoint, for the perfect clarity in his playing of outline and detail, and for a very characteristic blend, instantly recognizable, of romantic fervour and classical poise. He has a relatively small repertory:

*Arturo Benedetti Michelangeli*

but his achievements within such self-imposed limits are perfect models of their kind.

In 1952 serious illness forced Michelangeli to interrupt a series of successful concert tours which had taken him through Europe and the USA (where he first played in 1948) to South America, South Africa, the Lebanon, Italy and Japan. He settled in northern Italy, teaching and giving master classes in Bolzano, Arezzo, Siena and Lugano, and in 1964 founded the International Pianists' Academy in Brescia, of which he was the artistic director until 1969. In 1964 he made his first concert tour of the USSR, and the next year he moved to Switzerland. In 1973 he began to teach at a summer school in the Villa Schifanoia near Florence.

BIBLIOGRAPHY

J. Kaiser: *Grosse Pianisten in unserer Zeit* (Munich, 1965; Eng. trans., 1971, with enlarged discography)

M. Meyer: '. . . und leben über ihr Verhältnisse', *Fonoforum* (1975), no.6, p.528

DOMINIC GILL

**Michel Angelo del Violino.** See ROSSI, MICHELANGELO.

**Michel de Toulouse** [Toulouze] (*fl* 1496–1505). French printer. He was presumably from Toulouse, and may have been the first to print mensural music using movable type; his *L'art et instruction de bien dancer* uses type and is earlier than Petrucci, though in many respects rather crude. He was not the earliest music printer in Paris, though his predecessors had printed only liturgical volumes. He was living there in 1496, close to Guerson, who also printed and sold music. They seem to have collaborated, for Michel printed a volume of Guerson's and also used some of his type. He is mentioned in Guerson's will of 1503, and was last referred to in 1505.

None of Michel's four musical books is dated, although 1488 has been added by hand to *L'art*. This is certainly too early: it was probably printed about 1496. All Michel's other known prints (nearly 20) date from after this. *L'art et instruction de bien dancer* is an important collection of melodies for the basse danse, with instructions. It is closely related to a Brussels manuscript of dance tenors (*B-Br* 9085).

BIBLIOGRAPHY

V. Scholderer: Introduction to facs. edn. of *L'art et instruction de bien dancer* (London, 1936)

M. Dean-Smith: 'A Fifteenth Century Dancing Book', *JEFDSS*, iii (1936–9), 100
K. Meyer: 'Michel de Toulouze', *MR*, vii (1946), 178
F. Crane: *Materials for the Study of the Fifteenth Century Basse Danse* (New York, 1968)
R. Rastall, ed.: *L'art et instruction de bien dancer* (Wakefield, 1971) [facs. and edn.]

STANLEY BOORMAN

**Micheletti, Gioseffo** (*fl* 1683–92). Italian music publisher. He was active in Bologna, keeping his printing establishment on the Pavaglione. He published sacred music by Cazzati (op.19, 1687), Cavanni (op.1, 1689) and Albergati (op.7, 1691), chamber cantatas by G. F. Tosi (op.2, 1688) and instrumental music by G. B. Degli Antoni (opp.1 and 3–6, 1687–90), G. Torelli (opp.1–3 and 5, 1686–92), Gaspardini (op.1, 1683), Clemente Monari (op.1, 1686), Mazzolini (op.1, 1687), Berri (op.1, 1688), Elia Vannini (op.1, 1691) and Belisi (op.1, 1691). Micheletti's publications are characterized by neatness and elegance; his typographical mark is an angel with a cornucopia filled with flowers, a crown or a noble coat-of-arms.

BIBLIOGRAPHY
F. Vatielli: 'Editori musicali dei secoli XVII e XVIII', *Arte e vita musicale a Bologna* (Bologna, 1927/*R*1969), 239
L. Gottardi: *La stampa musicale in Bologna dagli inizi fino al 1700* (diss., U. of Bologna, 1951)
C. Sartori: *Dizionario degli editori musicali italiani* (Florence, 1958)

ANNE SCHNOEBELEN

**Micheli, Antonino di.** *See* DI MICHELI, ANTONINO.

**Micheli, Benedetto** (*b* Rome, ?*c*1700; *d* after 15 Sept 1784). Italian composer, poet and painter. The principal source of biographical information is his own preface to an unpublished epic poem (reproduced by Narducci). There he said that he studied painting 'under excellent masters' from the age of eight until he was 15; then his attention turned to music, where it remained until at least 1739. As a young man he appears to have enjoyed the patronage of Cardinal Alvaro Cienfuegos, who between 1722 and 1734 ordered five *Componimenti* to celebrate the name day of the Empress Elisabetta Cristina; during that period he also wrote a few serious operas, which, however, cannot have been greatly successful, for no further commissions ensued. His main interest to music history derives from his activities in about 1736–8. By his own recollection early in 1736 he was requested to compose a *farsetta* 'ad uso d'Intermezzi . . . in una Tragicomedia' for the Teatro di Valle, which met with such applause that two more were commissioned for the autumn season, and another pair, now to his own librettos, for Carnival 1737. Similar work followed for the Teatro di Torre Argentina; there he introduced characters speaking Roman dialect, a novelty that captured the local fancy. Thereafter, he said, he worked for some time in the Roman theatres, writing other such intermezzos and adapting *opere buffe* by such composers as Gaetano Latilla, Rinaldo da Capua, Pietro Auletta and Nicolò Conforti to meet the new taste (Narducci suggested that the Roman production of Latilla's popular *La finta cameriera*, Teatro di Valle, spring 1738, may have been one of these). This represents the northern adaptation of a comic device which, though it continued for many years to have a following in Naples, had already passed its peak of popularity there.

In 1740 Micheli became a member of the Accademia di S Cecilia as 'organista e maestro'; elsewhere in the Accademia archives he is called 'Professore di Organo', suggesting that he made part of his living by teaching. Meanwhile, he had maintained relationships with the world of art and composed several occasional pieces for the Festa del Concorso of the Accademia del Disegno di S Luca (later to become the Rome Accademia di Belle Arti), and conducted others; at the 1732 Concorso he performed the solo part of a flute concerto. By 1749 misfortune had overtaken him (the suggestion is of some chronic illness); no further music is known from him; and he became a pensioner of the musical Accademia, from 4 June of that year receiving several payments per year of two scudi from a fund established for distressed musicians. During that period he turned his hand to literature and in 1756 produced the curiosity of a 12-canto epic poem in Roman dialect, dealing with Rome's early history, *La libbertà romana* (*D-WRtl*). The last disbursement to him from S Cecilia was on 15 September 1784 (the last receipted one, 25 January 1783); presumably he died shortly thereafter.

WORKS
*(lost unless otherwise stated; all first performed in Rome)*

DRAMATIC
L'Oreste (opera seria, G. Bartolucci), Sala Capranica, 1723
La virtù trionfante dell'amore, e dell'odio, ovvero Il Tigrane (opera seria), Capranica, carn. 1724; Act 1 and intermezzos by Micheli, Act 2 by Vivaldi, Act 3 by Romaldi
S Cotardo (dramma sacro, A. Ruspoli), 1725

OCCASIONAL WORKS
Componimento for the name day of the Empress Elisabetta Christina (S. Stampiglia), 1722
Componimento for the name day of the empress (Tiberio Pulci [D. Pietrosellino]), 1724
Componimento for the name day of the empress (G. B. Pontici), 1727
Componimento for the name day of the empress (Pontici), 1728
Cantata (B. Bucci), Palazzo Apostolico, Christmas 1731
Componimento for the name day of the empress (Pietrosellino), Piazza for Cardinal Cienfuegos, Festa di SS Pietro e Paolo, 1734
Componimento, Campidoglio, Accademia del Disegno, Festa del Concorso 1738
Componimento, Palazzo Colonna di Sciarra, carn. 1739
Componimento Campidoglio, Accademia del Disegno, Festa del Concorso 1739
?Componimento, *D-MÜp*
Several sinfonie and arias, *B-Bc*, *D-SWl*, *E-Bc*, *GB-Lbm*

BIBLIOGRAPHY
*FétisB*
L. Allacci: *Drammaturgia . . . continuata fine all'anno MDCCLV* (Venice, enlarged 2/1755/*R*1961), 208
J.-B. de La Borde: *Essai sur la musique ancienne et moderne* (Paris, 1780/*R*1972), iii, 204
Abbate Cancellieri: *Le due nuove campane di Campidoglio* (Rome, 1806), 124f
E. Narducci: 'Di Benedetto Micheli, poeta, musico e pittore romano del secolo XVIII e di un suo poema inedito in dialetto romanesco intitolato *La libbertà romana*', *Reale Accademia dei lincei*, cclxxv, 3rd ser., *Memorie della Classe di scienze morali, storiche e filologiche*, ii (Rome, 1878)
G. Pittrè and F. Sabatini: 'Due manoscritti inediti in dialetto romanesco del secolo XVIII esistenti nella Biblioteca granducale di Weimar', *Rivista di litteratura popolare*, i (Rome, 1878), 145

JAMES L. JACKMAN

**Micheli, Domenico** (*b* Bologna, *c*1540; *d* ?Bologna, *c*1590). Italian composer. He received his early musical training at S Petronio in his native city. In 1564 he signed the dedication of his first book of madrigals from Bologna; he succeeded Gabriele Martinengo as *maestro di cappella* at Udine Cathedral in April 1567, but resigned in September. In 1577 he was in the service of the Malvasia family at Cesena; from there he applied unsuccessfully for the then vacant post of *maestro di cappella* at S Petronio. In 1580 he applied for a similar position at Padua Cathedral, but was turned down in favour of G. B. Mosto. By 1581 he had moved to Ravenna, where he was employed as a private musician in the household of Innocenzo Malvasia. He was appointed singing master at the cathedral of S Pietro, Bologna, in 1588, and in 1589 assumed full duties there as *maestro di cappella*.

Although Micheli was a priest, his secular output considerably exceeds his sacred. In general he set poems of a serious nature, and was one of the few 16th-century composers to set a passage from Dante (*Quivi sospiri*, from *Inferno*, iii.22). Exceptional is the one *giustiniana* which survives in G. Policreti da Treviso's *Secondo libro delle giustiniane* (*RISM* 1575¹⁴). Micheli was especially skilful at handling large vocal compositions of many parts; his dialogue madrigals for ten voices (1569) and 12 voices (1567) are the earliest examples for these numbers of parts to appear in print. The *Quinto libro* seems to be retrospective, since it includes a sonnet, also set by Wert, on the battle of Lepanto (1571). Stylistically Micheli belongs to the north Italian school of madrigalists, and he was particularly indebted to the experiments of Rore and to the sonorous polychoral style of the Venetians.

### WORKS
(*all published in Venice*)

Il primo libro de madrigali, 5vv (1564)
Il secondo libro de madrigali, 5vv (1564)
Madrigali, libro terzo, 6, 12vv (1567)
Il quarto libro de madrigali, 5–7vv, con uno dialogo, 8vv, et uno, 10vv (1569)
Il quinto libro de madrigali, 5vv, con uno dialogo, 10vv (1581)
Missarum quinque, liber primus, 5vv (1584)
Works in 1570¹⁵, 1575¹⁴, 1577⁷, 1586⁹, 1600⁸, 1616⁸

### BIBLIOGRAPHY
G. Gaspari: 'Memorie risguardanti la storia dell'arte musicale in Bologna al XVI secolo', *Atti e memorie della R. deputazione di storia patria per le provincie della Romagna*, i (1875),79
G. Vale: 'La cappella musicale del duomo di Udine', *NA*, vii (1930), 114
R. Casimiri: 'Musica e musicisti nella cattedrale di Padova', *NA*, xviii (1941), 112

DAVID NUTTER

**Micheli, Romano** (*b* Rome, *c*1575; *d* Rome, after 1659). Italian composer and music polemicist. He learnt the art of counterpoint from Soriano and G. M. Nanino. After a brief period serving the Duke of S Giovanni in Rome about 1593, he spent some time in various Italian cities, engaging the composers he met in friendly competition in contrapuntal writing. Among the cities he visited were Venice, Naples (where he was in the service of Gesualdo from about 1596 to 1598), Ferrara, Bologna and Milan. He became *maestro di cappella* at Tivoli Cathedral in June 1609 but left under duress in January 1610. He later held similar posts at the Cathedral of Concordia, near Udine, in 1616 and at the Metropolitan Church, Aquileia, near Venice, from 1618 to 1621. Returning to Rome he was offered the position of *maestro di cappella* at the church of the Gesù but was unable to take it up because the choir refused to sing under him. However, he successfully assumed a similar position at S Luigi dei Francesi in 1625. In 1636 he received a canonicate in Naples and remained there for several years. By 1644 he had returned to Rome, possibly in the hope of regaining his former position at S Luigi dei Francesi. His attempt failed, and in his later works he designated himself simply 'prete sacerdote' or 'musico di Roma' without naming a position.

As a composer Micheli devoted himself to the writing of various types of canon thereby contributing to a flourishing of the art of canonic composition in 17th-century Rome. Although his works include examples of enigma and polymorphous canons, as well as canons with basso continuo, he prided himself particularly on the writing of canons according to *obblighi* (pre-compositional restrictions) and canons *sopra le vocali di più parole* ('on the vowels of several words') – a type he claimed to have invented. One such canon, to the text 'LUDOVICUS, Rex defensor omnium Christianorum', for 36 voices in nine choirs, was given the text 'Sanctus' and shown in the frontispiece of Kircher's *Musurgia universalis* (Rome, 1650). The distinction that Kircher thus accorded this canon and its composer was instrumental in establishing Micheli's reputation in the later 17th century.

Throughout his career Micheli was active as a polemicist, challenging others to compositional tests and boasting of his own prowess and that of other Roman composers. His conduct alienated him from many of his contemporaries and embroiled him in several disputes, most notably in that between Marco Scacchi, Paul Siefert and Kaspar Förster (i). Responding to Siefert's claim that Italians could write nothing but 'comedie, ariette, canzonette' and similar trifles, Micheli sent copies of his *Canoni musicali* (1645) to the three parties to the dispute. Förster replied in February 1647 with a complimentary letter and Siefert remained silent, but Scacchi launched a vigorous attack on Micheli, accusing him of not inventing *canoni sopra le vocali di più parole* and criticizing his relentless pursuit of canonic artifice. Undaunted, Micheli rebuffed him in his *Avviso inviato da me* (1650) and defiantly continued to proclaim himself the inventor of *canoni sopra le vocali di più parole*.

### WORKS

Psalmi ad officium Vesperarum, 3vv, org, lib.I (Rome, 1610)
Musica vaga et artificiosa (Venice, 1615)
Salmi per i Vesperi, 3vv, bc, lib.II, op.3 (Venice, 1615)
Compieta, 6vv, bc, op.4 (Venice, 1616)
Madrigale, 6vv, in canone (Rome, 1621)
Dialogus annuntiationis BVM, 20vv (Rome, 1625)
Specimina musices magis recondita, op.5 (Rome, 1633)
Vivit Deus: canones super plurium verborum vocalibus (Rome, 1644)
Canoni musicali composti sopra le vocali di più parole (Rome, 1645)
Canone musicale, 4vv, ad honore della concettione della BVM (Rome, 1650)
In honore del nome di Giesu e di Maria: canone musicale, 5vv (Rome, 1652)
Hic finis: (non) plus ultra . . . canon super vocalibus, 12vv in 3 choirs (Rome, 1655)
Virtutes theologales (Rome, 1658)

### POLEMICAL WRITINGS

*Alli molt'illustri . . . musici della Cappella di N.S.* (Venice, 1618) [contains 2 canons by Micheli to be sung with 1 by Willaert]
*All'illustri & eccellentissimi signori . . . Francesco Soriano . . . et Gironimo Frescobaldo* (Venice, 1619) [contains 1 canon by Micheli based on 1 by G. P. Cima]
*All'illustrissimo . . . Sig. Cardinal Borghese: 10 obligationes* (Venice, 1619)
*Certezza d'artificii musicali* (Venice, 1621)
*Copia di lettera con manoscritta, mandata dal Sig. Abundio Antonelli* (Venice, 1621)
*Virtuoso manifesto sopra li piu dotti studi della musica* (Rome, 1624)
*Virtuoso aviso sopra li più dotti studi della musica* (Rome, 1633)
*Virtuoso avviso . . . sopra la nuova, e facile maniera d'imparare à cantare* (Naples, 1636)
*Virtuoso, et publico invito, che si fà alli . . . musici di questa città di Napoli* (Naples, 1636)
*Virtuoso risposta . . . alla virtuosa curiosità d'un musico peritissimo in Roma* (Rome, 1645)
*Virtuoso, e publico esperienza, che si fà in Roma, nell'insegnare di cantare in breve tempo* (Rome, 1647)
*Avviso di una virtuosa, e publica esperienza, che s'è fatta in Roma nell'insegnare di cantare in breve tempo* (Rome, 1647)
*Avviso inviato da me* (Rome, 1650)
*Alli peritissimi signori musici compositori d'Italia* (Rome, c1659)

### BIBLIOGRAPHY
G. Baini: *Memorie storico-critiche della vita e delle opere di Giovanni Pierluigi da Palestrina* (Rome, 1828/R1966), ii, 34

G. Radiciotti: *L'arte musicale in Tivoli nei secoli XVI, XVII, e XVIII* (Tivoli, 1907, enlarged 2/1921), 59
A. Cametti: 'La scuola dei pueri cantus di S. Luigi dei Francesi in Roma (1591–1623)', *RMI*, xxii (1915), 593
R. Casimiri: 'Romano Micheli (1575–1659) e la Cappella Sistina del suo tempo', *NA*, iii (1926), 233
G. Vale: 'Vita musicale nella chiesa metropolitana di Aquileia', *NA*, ix (1932), 213
——: 'Memorie musicali della cattedrale di Concordia', *NA*, x (1933), 133
W. Krüger: 'Ein neunchöriger Sanctus-Kanon', *Musik und Kirche*, xxv (1955), 180
H. Smither: 'Romano Micheli's "Dialogus Annuntiationis" (1625): a Twenty-voice Canon with Thirty "Obblighi"', *AnMc*, no.5 (1968), 34–91
C. Palisca: 'Marco Scacchi's Defense of Modern Music (1649)', *Words and Music: the Scholar's View . . . in Honor of A. Tillman Merritt* (Cambridge, Mass., 1972), 189–235
CHARLES M. ATKINSON

**Michi** [Mihi; Dell'Arpa; Michi dell' Arpa], **Orazio** [Horatio] (*b* Alife, nr. Caserta, 1594–5; *d* Rome, 26 Oct 1641). Italian harpist and composer. He probably studied music in Naples, which was a centre of skilled harpists and composers. At an early age, however, he settled in Rome. There he was in the service of Cardinal Montalto from February 1614 at the latest to June 1623, when the cardinal died. Later he served Cardinal Maurizio of Savoy from about July 1623 to February 1630. He left his service partly because he was dissatisfied at having to make frequent journeys from Rome to Turin, though he may have served Maurizio again from 1635 to 1638. He seems to have had additional patrons in the Cardinals Pallotta, Bernardino Spada and Antonio Barberini. He acquired wealth enough to own a carriage and horses as well as a large house richly furnished and to employ a coachman and two other servants. When he died, at the age of 46, he was buried in the place he had reserved at S Maria in Vallicella, with which he was closely associated, and he left the bulk of his sizable estate to the Congregation of the Oratory there.

Michi's fame as a player of the double harp is cited by Vincenzo Giustiniani in 1628, André Maugars in 1639, Pietro della Valle in 1640 and Severo Bonini towards 1650. Because of his virtuosity the sobriquet 'Dell'Arpa' was often added to his name. About 60 compositions by him survive. The majority are spiritual cantatas for solo voice and continuo to Italian texts which were very likely performed in the oratory at S Maria in Vallicella. Some are strophic songs; others, also short, contain sections in the styles of recitative, aria and arioso. They are among the finest cantatas produced in Rome at the time.

WORKS
56 cantatas: 42 for 1v, bc; 7 for 2vv, bc; 7 for 3vv, bc: *CS-Pnm*, *F-Pn*, *I-Bc*, *Rc*, *Rvat*; 1 ed. in AMI, v (n.d.); 1 ed. in Cametti
5 cantatas, 1v, bc, in 1640²

BIBLIOGRAPHY
A. Cametti: 'Orazio Michi "dell'Arpa"', *RMI*, xxi (1914), 203–77
S. Cordero di Pamparato: 'I musici alla corte di Carlo Emanuele I di Savoia', *Biblioteca della Società storica subalpina*, cxxi (1930), 120
J. Rimmer: 'Harps in the Baroque Era', *PRMA*, xc (1963–4), 65
GLORIA ROSE

**Michigan, University of, School of Music.** A state university was established at Ann Arbor in 1837. The Ann Arbor School of Music, founded in 1880 and from 1892 called the University School of Music, was at first administered by the University Musical Society and directed by Calvin B. Cady (1851–1928). From 1929 to 1940 it was run jointly by the society and the university's regents, and in 1940 it became an integral unit of the university. In the 1970s it enrolled about 900 students, including over 300 graduate students and over 200 students at the National Music Camp (established 1942) run by the university at Interlochen, Michigan, in the summer. The faculty numbers 97 full-time and 110 part-time instructors. BM, BA, MM and MA degrees are offered as well as the DMA in composition and performance, and the PhD in musicology, music theory and music education. In 1973 a BMA degree course was initiated. Reports on graduate courses have been published in *Current Musicology*: (1965), no.2, p.149; (1966), no.3, p.14; (1967), no.5, p.37; (1968), no.7, p.30; (1970), no.10, p.14; (1971), no.11, p.27; (1974), no.18, p.27.

The school has a very wide range of facilities, including the Stearns Collection of Musical Instruments (1899), the Charles Baird Carillon (1935), an electronic studio (1965) and a Javanese gamelan (1966). The resident Stanley Quartet, founded in 1949, has commissioned works from many American composers. The Symphony Band makes regular concert tours of the USA and performs abroad, and the Marching Band is one of the most famous in the country. The music library contains 50,000 books, manuscripts and scores as well as 14,000 recordings, and includes the Stellfeld Collection, much American sheet music and the Eva Jessye Afro-American Music Collection. The university's Clements Library of Early Americana contains many musical items including the papers of Andrew Law; both libraries are described in *Current Musicology* (1974), no.17, p.20.

The University Musical Society also founded the annual Ann Arbor May Festival in 1894. Participants include leading composers and orchestras and international soloists as well as the University Choral Union; they have included the Boston Festival Orchestra conducted by Mollenhauer (1894–1904), the Chicago SO conducted by Stock (1905–35) and the Philadelphia Orchestra conducted by Stokowski in 1936 and by Ormandy from 1937. Copland, Enescu, Holst and Stravinsky have been guest conductors at the festival.

A group of progressive young artists called the ONCE organized a series of annual festivals in the 1960s in Ann Arbor. Among its founders were the avant-garde composers Roger Reynolds, Robert Ashley and Gordon Mumma, and the film maker George Manupelli.

BIBLIOGRAPHY
'The University Musical Society and the School of Music', *The University of Michigan: an Encyclopedic Survey* (Ann Arbor, 1953), iii, 1121
L. Cuyler, G. Sutherland and H. David: 'The University of Michigan's Purchase of the Stellfeld Music Library', *Notes*, xii (1954–5), 41
S. L. Schrader: *A History of the University Musical Society . . . 1879–1892* (diss., U. of Michigan, 1968)
BRUCE CARR, RITA H. MEAD

**Michl** [Michel]. German family of musicians.

(1) **Johann Joseph Ildefons Michl** (*b* Neumarkt, Upper Palatinate, 1708; *d* Regensburg, 1770). Composer, son of the choirmaster and organist Anton Michl. He studied for four years with Wagenseil in Vienna, then became Kapellmeister at Sulzbach during the brief reign of Duke Johann Christian Joseph (1732–3). After the duke's death Michl worked in Regensburg as, among other things, a composer for the embassies; in 1738 he became Kapellmeister at the cathedral. He composed

some music (now lost) for sacred dramas, including a Lenten meditation for the Congregatio Latina Major in Munich (1739) and others for the Jesuits in Ingolstadt. Apart from six masses printed in Augsburg (op.1, 1744) his many liturgical works remained in manuscript and are now lost (see Mettenleiter).

(2) **Ferdinand Michl** (*b* Neumarkt, 1723; *d* Munich, 23 March 1754). Organist and composer, brother of (1) Johann Joseph Ildefons Michl. He was educated at the electoral Gymnasium in Munich. In 1740–41 he was organist at the Jesuit church of St Michael, and in 1745, through the influence of Duke Clemens Franz of Bavaria, he also became the organist for vocal music at the electoral court. In 1748, while retaining both posts as organist, he was named deputy Konzertmeister for court instrumental music. Between 1740 and 1754 Michl composed 16 Lenten meditations for the Congregatio Latina Major in Munich and numerous school comedies for the Gymnasium in Munich and Ingolstadt (all lost). The organ part of his *XII symphoniae* op.1 (Augsburg, 1740) survives (*A-Gmi*); perhaps his only complete extant works are two organ preludes attributed to a composer of this surname (in *D-Mbs*).

(3) **Melchior Virgil Michl** (*b* Munich, *c*1735; *d* Munich, 8 Sept 1795). Cellist and singer, son of (2) Ferdinand Michl. By 1764 at the latest he was a supernumerary cellist in the Munich court orchestra, where in January 1765 he was fully installed. At times he was also principal of a German theatrical troupe which played in Salzburg (winter 1778) and, newly organized, in the Faberbräutheater, Munich (1785). No works by him, not even the lost opera *Marcio Coriolano* (Munich, 1786) sometimes attributed to him, have been authenticated.

(4) **Joseph (Christian) Willibald Michl** [Michelini] (*b* Neumarkt, 9 July 1745; *d* Neumarkt, 1 Aug 1816). Double bass player, publisher and composer, son of (1) Johann Joseph Ildefons Michl. He studied at the electoral Gymnasium and Lyceum in Munich, and was an accomplished double bass player in the Jesuit church of St Michael until about 1767. In the 1760s Elector Maximilian III Joseph sent him to Freising to study for two years under Placidus von Camerloher. By the beginning of 1771 at the latest Michl was named a composer to the electoral chamber, and in 1774 he travelled to Italy at the elector's expense. In 1776 he wrote the Carnival opera *Il trionfo di Clelia* for the Munich court. With the succession of the new elector, Carl Theodor, in 1778 Michl was dismissed with a pension of 125 florins (which he did not receive until 1780), raised to 240 florins in 1790. In July 1779 he was granted a privilege to publish music in manuscript; he seems however to have restricted this activity to his own works. From about 1784 to 1 September 1803 he lived with his brother-in-law, Johann Baptist Moser, a judge at the Augustinian prebendary institute at Weyarn, and wrote sacred works as well as symphonies and school dramas for the monastery. In 1786 he also taught composition at the Benedictine abbey at Tegernsee.

Michl was a talented composer, known particularly for his sacred works. These include numerous extant liturgical works as well as six Lenten meditations, performed at the Congregatio Latina Major in Munich between 1768 and 1772, which are now lost. Also lost

are numerous works for school theatres, though several larger stage and vocal works remain, some of which were possibly composed by Johann Michael Michl, the musical director of F. J. Moser's theatrical troupe. Michl's instrumental output includes a wide range of orchestral and chamber works, and his abilities as a composer are attested by Burney, who, having heard a quintet performed in Munich (1772), wrote that few works showed more genius and invention or demanded more skill in performance.

WORKS

Stage (first perf. Munich unless otherwise stated): Il barone di Torre Forte (opera buffa, 2), March 1772, *D-Rtt*; L'amante deluso (opera buffa), 27 Nov 1773, lost; Il trionfo di Clelia (opera seria, 3, Metastasio), 8 Jan 1776, *Mbs*; Johann Faust (incidental music), 31 May 1776, lost; Das Urtheil des Paris (ballet, C. Legrand and P. Constant), after 1777, lost; L'isola disabitata (azione teatrale, ?Metastasio), 1780, lost; Regulus, der Patriot (opera seria), Weyarn, 3 Sept 1781, frag. *WEY*; Milton und Elmire (Singspiel), 6 June 1785, lost; Der König auf der Jagd (Singspiel), 8 Aug 1785, lost; Fremor und Meline, Der König und der Pachter, Der Jahrmarkt, mentioned in Lipowsky (1811)

Secular vocal: Zephiro et Flora, cantata, Munich, 1776, lost; Il trionfo della gloria, cantata, Munich, before 1778, *Dlb*; Wohin krochst du, cantata, *WEY*; Il re alla caccia, Il cacciatore deluso, cantatas, mentioned in Lipowsky (1811)

Sacred vocal (mostly *BB*, *Mbs*, *WEY*, some autograph): masses; Gioas, re di Giuda, oratorio, Munich, Lent 1772, lost; Ich warne dich, oratorio, ?Munich, *Mbs*; 2 Requiem, 1815; vespers; litanies; many shorter works

Inst: 6 syms., *WEY*; 5 syms., *Rtt*; 1 sym., *Mbs*; 8 serenades, *Rtt*; Bn Conc., *B*; 6 sonatas, pf, vn, bn, *B*; qt, 2 vn, bn obbl., vc, *B*; others, listed in Breitkopf catalogues (1773–87)

BIBLIOGRAPHY

F. J. Lipowsky: *Baierisches Musik-Lexikon* (Munich, 1811/*R*1971)
D. Mettenleiter: *Musikgeschichte der Stadt Regensburg* (Regensburg, 1866)
P. Legband: *Münchner Bühne und Literatur im 18. Jahrhundert* (Munich, 1904)
A. Zehelein: *Joseph Michl* (Munich, 1928)
A. Scharnagl: 'Michl', *MGG*
R. Münster: *Oberpfälzische Komponisten zur Zeit Mozarts* (Regensburg, 1963)
R. Münster and R. Machold: *Thematischer Katalog der Musikhandschriften der ehemaligen Klosterkirchen Weyarn, Tegernsee und Benediktbeuern* (Munich, 1971)
R. Münster and others: *Thematischer Katalog der Musikhandschriften der Benediktinerinnenabtei Frauenwörth und der Pfarrkirchen Indersdorf, Wasserburg am Inn und Bad Tölz* (Munich, 1975)
G. Haberkamp: *Thematischer Katalog der Musikhandschriften der Fürstlich Oettingen-Wallerstein'schen Bibliothek Schloss Harburg* (Munich, 1976)

ROBERT MÜNSTER

**Michna, Adam Václav** (*b* ?Jindřichův Hradec, *c*1600; *d* Jindřichův Hradec, 2 Nov 1676). Czech composer. Michna's father was bailiff of Jindřichův Hradec castle and reputedly town organist and leader of the castle trumpeters. Adam probably received his early musical training from his father. Later he studied at the town's Jesuit Gymnasium. The Jesuits were the leading musical force in the Czech lands in the 17th and 18th centuries and Michna seems to have become one of their favoured composers, a fact attested to by the striking number of his compositions printed, mostly by the Jesuit Academic Press in Prague. Around 1633 Michna became town organist of Jindřichův Hradec, his only official musical appointment. He divided his time between music and commerce. A licensed wine vault brought him considerable revenue, he was a substantial property owner and prominent in local affairs. In 1673 he established an endowment for talented young musicians in his area. He was twice married but there are no records of any children.

It is estimated that only about a third of Michna's compositions survive. They are all for the church and are of two distinct types: simple vernacular hymns and elaborate Latin concertato works. The hymns are clearly influenced by the strong and long-established tradition of congregational singing in the Czech lands, but nothing discoverable in his background fully accounts for the marked, and contemporary, Italian influence in his Latin church music. His two hymnals, *Česká mariánská muzika* ('Czech Marian music') and *Svatoroční muzika* ('Music for the liturgical year'), were specifically compiled for the use of churches with limited musical resources. They contain simple four- and five-part homophonic settings of his own religious poetry, and the melodies have a decided folk character. Each hymn is provided with a simple continuo part. Several of the pieces from these two books have remained in popular use in Czechoslovakia to this day. Michna also wrote the words for *Loutna česká* ('The Czech lute'), which is also technically a hymnbook but which, in musical style, provides a bridge between his two extremes of composition. The hymns are set as arias for solo voices with accompanying strings and organ, the instruments providing short ritornellos. Both *The Czech lute* and *Officium vespertinum*, his earliest surviving concertato music, are now incomplete. Of the latter only one partbook remains.

Of his works in the Italianate style, the most notable are those in *Sacra et litaniae* (1654). They employ between four and six solo voices with chorus, and sometimes two choirs. The instrumentation is varied but relies on permutations of violins, violas, trombones and cornetts with organ continuo. Even in such elaborate music there is still a strong folk admixture, partly through the modality of the harmony and partly through the brief melodic motives on which his counterpoint is built. In the second mass of *Sacra et litaniae* Michna actually used the opening of a Czech Christmas carol, which recurs as a linking motif. In the third mass he created an extended passacaglia, the whole mass consisting of variations over an eight-bar bass. Michna's music is notable for its colour and its attractive melodic qualities. He was the outstanding composer in the Czech lands during the 17th century, dominating his contemporaries.

WORKS

Česká mariánská muzika, 4, 5vv, bc (Prague, 1647); ed. J. Sehnal and L. Štukavec (Prague, 1974)
Officium vespertinum, op.3, 5vv, insts (Prague, 1648), inc.
Loutna česká, v, str, org (Prague, 1653); inc., reconstruction ed. E. Trolda (Prague, 1943)
Sacra et litaniae (Prague, 1654), 6 masses, Requiem, 2 litany settings, Te Deum, 4–8vv, insts (vns, vas, trbns, cornetts), bc (org); part of the Requiem, ed. J. Pohanka in DČHP, no.107 (1958), 77
Svatoroční muzika, 4, 5vv, bc (Prague, 1661)
Missa Sancti Wenceslai, 6vv, 2 vn, 4a, 2 tpt, org, CS-KRa; ed. J. Sehnal, MAB, 2nd ser., i (1966)
Tantum ergo, vv, insts, org, lost
Magnificat 1 toni, 12vv, Municipal Library, Wrocław

BIBLIOGRAPHY

E. Trolda: 'Neznámé skladby Adama Michny' [Michna's unknown compositions], Sborník prací k padesátým narozeninám professora Dra Zdeňka Nejedlého (Prague, 1929), 69–101
——: 'Loutna česká Adama Michny z Otradovic' [Michna's Czech lute], Vlast (1930), i, 392; ii, 465
——: 'Michnova Mše sv. Václava po stránce hudební' [The musical aspects of Michna's St Wenceslas Mass], Našinec, lxvi (1930), nos.117, 119
——: 'Česká církevní hudba v období generálbasu' [Czech sacred music in the figured bass period], part iii 'Adam Michna', Cyril, lx (1934), 103
J. Muk: 'Adam Michna z Otradovic, básník a skladatel českého baroku' [Michna: poet and composer of the Czech Baroque], Ohlas od Nežárky, lxx–lxxi (1941), 1–70
A. Buchner: 'Hudební sbírka Emiliána Troldy' [The musical collection

of Emilian Trolda], Sborník Narodního musea v Praze, viii/A (1954), 77
J. Bužga: 'Zur musikalischen Problematik der alttschechischen Kantionalien', Mf, xii (1959), 13
——: 'Der tschechische Barockkomponist Adam Michna z Otradovic', Festschrift für Heinrich Besseler (Leipzig, 1961), 305
J. Sehnal: 'Adam Michna of Otradovice, a Master of Czech Baroque Music', Programme Book of the Second Brno International Music Festival (Brno, 1967), 26
A. Škarka, ed.: 'Das dichterische Werk', Slavische Propyläen, xxii (Munich, 1968) [contains all song texts set by Michna, with critical commentary]
J. Sehnal: 'Renaissanceerbe und neues Denken in den Kirchenmelodien von Adam Michna mit Bezug auf die dichterisch-metrische Vorlage', Music and Word: Brno IV 1969, 81
——: 'Die Entwicklungstendenzen und Stilschichten im tschechischen barocken Kirchenlied', Musica antiqua Europae orientalis: Bydgoszcz 1972, 127
——: 'Písně Adama Michny z Otradovic (1600–1676)', HV, xii (1975), 3–43 [incl. list of songs and Ger. résumé]

ADRIENNE SIMPSON

**Micho, Richard.** *See* MICO, RICHARD.

**Micieres** [Micieces, Mizieres], **Tomás** (*b* Villaescusa de Ecla, nr. Palencia, baptized 22 Dec 1624; *d* Toledo or Madrid, after 1662). Spanish composer. He studied at Palencia with the choirmaster of the cathedral, Cristóbal de Isla, through whose efforts he became *maestro de capilla* of León Cathedral in 1646. On 22 November 1650 he became *maestro* of Toledo Cathedral, where Juan de Padilla succeeded him on 19 January 1664. He excelled in the composition of Christmas villancicos, booklets of which he published at Toledo in 1651, 1653 and 1660. A 12-part Latin Lamentations (in *E-CU* and *CO-B*), like numerous other works (in various sources, such as *E-Bc* and *E-PAp*), may be by him, but they could also be by a musician of the same name (*b* Toledo, *c*1656; *d* Salamanca, 17 May 1718), who was probably his son (but is referred to also as his nephew) and who after ordination became in 1680 *maestro de capilla* at S Esteve de Castellar, in June 1685 at Burgo de Osma, from 1 June 1692 at La Seo, Saragossa, and finally, from 12 November 1694 until his death, at Salamanca, where on 26 October 1700 he also became professor of music at the university.

BIBLIOGRAPHY

E. Esperabé Arteaga: Historia de la Universidad de Salamanca, ii (Salamanca, 1917), 661
F. Rubio Piqueras: Música y músicos toledanos (Toledo, 1923)
R. Stevenson: 'The Bogotá Music Archive', JAMS, xv (1962), 306
L. Siemens Hernández: 'La Seo de Zaragoza, escuela de órgano en el siglo XVII', AnM, xxiii (1968), 140
——: 'Datos sobre el nacimiento y muerte de Miguel Gómez Camargo (*1618 †1690)', AnM, xxvi (1971), 114

ROBERT STEVENSON

**Micinella.** Term which appears at the head of a four-part Gloria by Zacar (in *I-Bc* 15; ed. in Günther). Like analogous terms, it may denote a composition forming a basis for the piece, in parody fashion; certainly this Gloria resembles a four-part Gloria by Ciconia (ed. in Clercx) based on the motet *Regina gloriosa* in its two-voice opening, its repeat of tenor and contratenor, its duple rhythms and the alternating motifs in the upper voices. The word 'Micinella' may also, however, be related to the title of Antonio Zacara's ballata *Ciaramella*, which resembles the Gloria (e.g. in the opening and conclusion of the upper voice of the ballata). The Gloria is also related to a third work, an anonymous three-part Gloria (at the end of *GB-Lbm* Add.29987; ed. in Reaney), whose opening and concluding sections are based on the opening and conclusion of Zacar's Gloria, and which may also owe something to Ciconia's Gloria.

BIBLIOGRAPHY

G. Reaney: 'The Manuscript London, British Museum, Additional 29987 (Lo)', *MD*, xii (1958), 88 [incl. edn. of the anon. Gloria]
S. Clercx: *Johannes Ciconia*, ii (Brussels, 1960), 102ff, 157ff [incl. edns. of the Gloria by Ciconia and its underlying motet]
B. J. Layton: *Italian Music for the Ordinary of the Mass 1300–1450* (diss., Harvard U., 1960), 251ff
U. Günther: 'Quelques remarques sur des feuillets récemment découverts à Grottaferrata', *L'ars nova italiana del trecento II: Certaldo 1969*, 315 [incl. edn. of the Gloria by Zacar]

GILBERT REANEY

**Mico** [Micoe, Micho, Meco, Myco], **Richard** (*b* Taunton, *c*1590; *d* London, buried 10 April 1661). English composer. His family, originally named Micault, came from northern France some time before 1509; several of his near relations were merchants, including his cousin Sir Samuel Mico, an alderman of London. In 1608 Richard Mico was appointed resident musician at Thorndon Hall, Essex, the seat of John, first Lord Petre, whose son Sir William Petre was Mico's employer. His wages, £10 a year, were above average for the period, suggesting that he was already regarded as a musician of promise. He took charge of the household instruments, and in 1611 was teaching one of William Petre's daughters the virginals. John Petre was patron of William Byrd, who lived nearby, and the household music books in Mico's charge included much of Byrd's Latin church music. Mico remained in Essex after William Petre succeeded to the title in 1613; he evidently became, like Byrd, an intimate of the family, since in 1627 he was chosen to escort one of Lord Petre's younger sons to school abroad. The Petres were Catholics, and Mico, though born of Protestant parents, had become a Catholic by 1614. In 1628 he married a Catholic, and their only son became a Jesuit. In 1631 Mico moved to London, where in 1634 he registered a coat-of-arms (derived from the Micaults), and in 1639 he was referred to as 'Richard Mico of London gent'. In 1658 he was receiving an annuity of £20 per annum from the 4th Lord Petre. He was buried at St Paul's, Covent Garden, on 10 April 1661.

Mico's surviving compositions comprise fantasias, pavans and an In Nomine, all for two to five viols. The absence of six-part works may perhaps be linked with the fact that the Petre chest of viols lacked a second bass. None of his works was published during his lifetime, although they evidently circulated quite widely in manuscript, and one manuscript is devoted solely to all his four-part works. Stylistically Mico's music stands between that of Alfonso Ferrabosco (ii) and John Jenkins. At its best it displays deep feeling coupled with lyrical freshness. Both Simpson (1665) and Roger North (1728) ranked him among leading composers of consort music.

WORKS

4 fantasias, 2 viols, org, *GB-Ckc*
7 fantasias, 3 viols, org, *EIRE-Dm, GB-Lbm, Ob, Och*
17 fantasias, 4 viols, *Lbm, Lcm, Och*
2 fantasias, 5 viols, *Och*
4 pavans, 4 viols, *Lbm, Lcm*
3 pavans, 5 viols, org, *EIRE-Dm, GB-Ckc, Lbm, Ob, Och*
In Nomine, 5 viols, org, *Lbm, Och*
'Latral, part 2', 5 viols, org, *Lbm, Ob, Och*

For complete thematic index with comments on attributions see *Chelys*, ii (1971)

BIBLIOGRAPHY

C. Simpson: *The Principles of Practical Musick* (London, 1665, rev., enlarged 2/1667 as *A Compendium of Practical Musick*); ed. P. J. Lord (Oxford, 1970)
*The Visitation of London 1633–35*, ed. Harleian Society (London, 1880)
*Registers of St. Paul's, Covent Garden*, ed. Harleian Society (London, 1908)
J. Wilson, ed.: *Roger North on Music* (London, 1959)
N. Briggs: 'William, 2nd Lord Petre (1575–1637)', *Essex Recusant*, x (1968), 51
J. Bennett and P. Willetts: 'Richard Mico', *Chelys*, vii (1977), 24

J. S. BENNETT

**Micronesia.** One of the three groups of the PACIFIC ISLANDS.

1. Introduction. 2. Caroline Islands: (i) Ifaluk, a Carolinian atoll (ii) Palau Islands (iii) Ponape (iv) Truk Islands (v) Yap Islands. 3. Kiribati (Gilbert Islands). 4. Mariana Islands: (i) Chamorro music and dance (ii) Guam. 5. Marshall Islands.

1. INTRODUCTION. Micronesia (from Gk. *micro*: 'small'; *nesos*: 'island') comprises more than 2000 small islands with a total land area of about 2800 sq km lying mostly north of the equator, east of island south-east Asia, west of northern Polynesia and north of Melanesia, in an ocean area of about 7·7 million sq km (for map, *see* PACIFIC ISLANDS, fig.1). Geographically the major divisions are the Mariana Islands, including Guam and islands north of it; the Caroline Islands, a broad arc north of the equator; the Marshall Islands, two parallel chains in a north–south direction east of the Carolines; the Gilbert Islands, south of the Marshalls; and the separate islands of Nauru and Ocean (Banaba). Micronesia appears to have been settled both eastward, probably from the Philippines into the high islands of Palau, Yap and Guam, and northward, probably from the Solomon Islands into the eastern part of Micronesia. There are important cultural distinctions between the high islands (mostly volcanic in origin) and the low islands (coral atolls) because of the difference in resources available for cultural use. The peoples speak 12 (sometimes listed as 15) different major Micronesian languages and many dialects; first Japanese and later English became the lingua franca. Foreign powers – Spain, Germany, England, Japan and the USA for the United Nations – have, where possible, established their administrative districts to centre on a high island and to include its neighbouring low islands. Culturally, however, many of the low islands have more in common with each other than with their high-island district centres (see §2). From 1915 to 1975 the Gilbert Islands and the (culturally Polynesian) Ellice Islands were administered as a unit, and interesting modern accommodations in music and dance styles resulted (see §3). In 1975 the Ellice Islands became an independent state called Tuvalu (*see* POLYNESIA, §8).

Most of the available early information about Micronesian music derives from explorers' accounts, anthropological studies and missionaries' descriptions. Traditional Micronesian music is predominantly vocal. There are accounts of both solo and group singing, the latter being both in unison and in parts (the notion that partsinging did not exist before the introduction of Western music is false). In most Micronesian societies, music was – and, except for church music, still is – associated intimately with dance, the same participants performing the vocal (chant or song) component, the rhythmic accompaniment (using body percussion or idiophones, mostly sticks) and the dance movements. A few instruments have been noted in some areas but these are no longer played, partly because of direct missionary influence, and partly because of a general change in cultural values. Christian hymns, and in some areas secular songs in hymn tune style, are widely sung. Other introduced Western music includes songs brought by sailors. But now the popular urban styles are far more prevalent and are heard, even on small islands, on transistor radios from district-centre broadcasting stations. The main introduced instruments are the guitar, ukelele, mandolin, harmonica, accordion, a few reed organs, a few brass-band instruments and some varieties of drum (although most percussion instruments, especially on islands far from the district centres, are made from locally available materials).

2. CAROLINE ISLANDS. The 963 Caroline Islands are divided into four administrative districts. The cultures of the low atolls throughout the archipelago have more in common with each other than with their high-island district centres of Palau, Ponape, Truk and Yap; their cultural variation could be compared to dialects of a language, whereas the cultures of the high islands from which they are administered are as varied as different languages. Thus the concept of a 'Carolinian' culture excluding the high islands is useful. Of the many musical 'dialects' of low-island Carolinian culture, that of Ifaluk is used as an example here; the high islands' music is also discussed. Those who inhabit the low Caroline Islands sail extensively throughout the islands. Navigation is related to both the content of songs and the performing style. In Ulithi atoll, for example, the same text can be sung in different locations and circumstances (e.g. while sitting on a beach, while paddling a canoe, or while under sail), but must be performed with the specifically designated tempo, rhythmic pulse, melodic contour and vocal production appropriate to the situation.

(i) Ifaluk, a Carolinian atoll. Ifaluk (sometimes spelt Ifalik), a typical low coral island of the central Caroline Islands, lies between the high islands of Truk and Yap. Traditionally Ifaluk, as a member of the Yap 'empire', recognized the overlordship of Yap and its people could perform their songs and dances as part of their duties to Yap.

The chants, songs and dances of Ifaluk are similar to those of neighbouring atolls and are important both in ceremonies and as entertainment during the day or evening. Typically, young men gather in the canoe house in the evening and among other activities sing *bwarux* (love-songs, with text composed by a woman in praise of a man she loves, sung with or without stylized body movements). Women also sing and dance *bwarux*, but men and women do not perform them together – in fact, traditionally neither should even use the word *bwarux* in the presence of the other. *Arüerü* are laments sung to a dying person, after the death, and still later in remembrance. *Arüerü* may also be sung in praise of a good chief or fisherman, for a construction project, and for other purposes. The *gapengapeng* is an invocation to the god Tilitr during which the singers swing trimmed half-leaves of the coconut tree. The *ur* is the formal, ceremonial dance and its song is performed to entertain the gods; men spend many evenings rehearsing it. The *laūra*, a stick dance performed to a song, is easily recognizable as a characteristically Carolinian dance.

Ifaluk song – and the Carolinian style in general – is characterized by a very small number of notes (often only two or three), a narrow range (a 2nd, at most a 3rd), many phrases ending in a terminal glide that spans about an octave, and strict, marked rhythm. Several types of song and chant have certain melodic contours

specifically associated with them. Multi-part singing is mostly in parallel movement, with the voices at any of several intervals, but most characteristically at 4ths. On Ifaluk, as elsewhere in the Caroline Islands, heavy pulling or hauling is performed to a leader–chorus chant, with the group doing the strenuous work during its response.

Sound-producing instruments include the conch-shell trumpet for signalling and a double-reed instrument, used either informally or as a children's toy, made from a wound strip of coconut leaf. A police whistle is now sometimes used by Ifaluk islanders because its sound is so similar to the trilled whistle required at some phrase endings.

(ii) *Palau Islands.* Palau comprises a cluster of high islands in the south-western Caroline Islands including Koror (the district centre), Babelthuap, Peleliu and Angaur, as well as the Kayangel atoll and over 300 mostly uninhabited rock islets. Some small atolls to the south, with closer cultural affinity to the central Carolines than to Palau, are also in the administrative district. Of the foreign administrations since 1886 the Japanese have had most influence; Christian missionaries had less than in northern and eastern Micronesia.

There are two major musical styles in Palau: traditional and modern. The classical tradition was flourishing at the end of the 19th century when foreign influences began to disrupt the traditional social structure and values. In the traditional milieu music and dance had political and economic, as well as personally communicative, psychological and perhaps other functions. Contemporary genres are used principally for entertainment, school activities and religious services.

Two forms current during the heyday of the classical tradition, *klou chesols* (devout song in ensemble) and *derebesbes*, were sung by groups of older men in connection with council activities in and around the *bai* (community house). *Derebesbes*, a solo sung either entirely by one person or a verse at a time by each member of a council (in either case with yells between strophes by the whole group), includes a variety of song forms: *ulengokl chesols* (heroic song), *demalasoi chesols* (communicative song with a text ascribed to the fictitious character Damalasoi) and *rederad ra chesols* (miscellaneous songs). At funerals *kelloi* and *eldolem* (dirges) were sung by women. During festivals, usually held in clan-affiliated villages, both *ruk* (men's dances) and *ngloik* (women's dances) were performed; these consisted of introductory, standing, sitting, stick and stamping dances. Men also performed war dances on a triumphal return from battle. Children sang their own festival songs, visiting every house in the vicinity.

Most types of song were performed by both sexes but, except in *alall* (mock quarrel song exchanged between pubescent male and female groups), performance was differentiated. Other group songs included *keredekill* (occasional and topical song), *derebesiil* (sincere love-song), and *kerekord* (harmonious song in which the singers lean towards each other, slightly covering their ears with their hands). Other solo songs included *rebetii* (a love-song referring to well-known historical events) and *kesekes* (a lullaby in epic style recounting the deeds of a legendary or historical hero of the village). Genres employing speech-song styles included *ongurs* (for work), *klaiskurs* (for racing), *dalang* (sarcastic recitation) and *ollai* (incantation). Children accompanied their games with songs and recitations.

Each genre of classical Palauan music has its own characteristic tonal and rhythmic configuration, with prescribed phrases for different musical functions varying in length, melodic contour, rhythmic figure, dynamic design and sometimes agogic change (e.g. an introductory phrase characterized by a sustained note; a penultimate phrase introducing the highest note; a final phrase with a terminal crescendo). Strophic form predominates, but sequences of phrases are also used. There are usually between three and seven notes, adjacent notes being from 50 to 300 cents apart; the melodic range is narrow, usually no more than a 5th (400 to 700 cents), and the tessitura varies according to the requirements of the genre or sometimes personal preference. Melodies commonly move conjunctly. In polyphonic ensembles the roles were differentiated: *mesuchokl* (textual prompter), *mengiidr* (starter), *meliikes* (chorus leader), *mengesbch* (second soloist using falsetto and head tone) and *rokui* (chorus). The polyphonic progressions were both parallel and oblique.

Indigenous instruments (generally called *tumtum*) were the *ngaok* (reed or bamboo fipple flute with four finger-holes) played as a solo instrument and to accompany *derebesiil*; *tumtum ra lild* (bamboo jew's harp); *debusch* (conch-shell trumpet) for signalling; and dance sticks. These instruments are no longer appreciated by the majority of the population. Foreign instruments – primarily the guitar, ukelele and harmonica, and to some extent the mandolin and accordion – have become popular, especially with the younger generation.

Although the classical repertory is performed infrequently, some traditional stylistic elements survive through incorporation into new songs. For example, some aspects of the structure of classical *keredekill* are perpetuated in *boid*, *beches keredekill*, and even in *kesekes ra Modekngei* (a song for the modern local religion Modekngei). Some modern dances also use traditional stylistic elements. Other contemporary pieces are composed in essentially foreign styles – both other Micronesian styles and Japanese, European, American and Hawaiian styles. Both the text and music of *beches chelitakl* (new song) show the influence of *kayōkyoku* (Japanese popular song) and American popular music. *Matmatong* (marching music and dance) reveals a more complex mixture of traditional Palauan, other Micronesian and foreign elements: it consists of a series of line-dances in which boys and girls dance together, and incorporates harmonica music, songs with foreign influence, yells by the leader, and stamping and body-slapping. It is often performed for tourists and outside Palau as representative of Palauan culture. Christian church music, apart from its voice production technique, is essentially European in style.

(*iii*) *Ponape*. Ponape (from Pohnpei: *pohn*, 'on top of'; *pei*, 'stone altar') is a high volcanic island in the eastern Caroline Islands. It was discovered by Europeans in the 16th century but was relatively isolated until 1852, when American Protestant missionary schools were established which had a great and continuing influence on Ponapean music. Ponape has been the headquarters of all foreign administrations of the eastern Caroline Islands, which lie from a few to several hundred kilometres distant and are significantly different in language and culture, including music. They include the sizable island of Kusaie, several atolls with cultural affinity to the central Carolines, and two atolls (Kapingamarangi and Nukuoro) that are culturally Polynesian. People from these islands (and from Truk) travel to Ponape regularly and many settle there, some in enclaves perpetuating their own traditions and styles. In 1973 the population of the entire Ponape administrative district numbered approximately 23,700, of whom over 17,000 lived on Ponape. The following discussion concerns only specifically Ponapean music and dance.

The Ponapean word for music, song or singing is 'kaul'. Ponapeans distinguish between two styles: *kaul en kawa*, the older traditional style, and *kaul en sarawi*, the newer style resulting from the influence of Western hymn singing. Few of the love-songs, dance-songs, feast songs, children's songs and lullabies in the traditional style are still sung; most have been replaced by songs in modern styles. On special occasions fragments of old rhythmic chants commemorating events in the island's history are performed. They are now called *ngis* and are scarcely known except by old people; listeners must be familiar with the story to understand the highly metaphorical language and archaic words. The surviving traditional songs, however, give young Ponapeans an important link with their past.

Songs in the traditional style have a limited number of notes, often only two or three, and are characterized by a conjunct melodic movement. The rhythm of most songs is complex because the metre of the text does not correspond with the underlying metre of the music (ex.1). Partsinging, usually in two parts and sometimes in three, is common; polyphonic intervals approximating to the 2nds and 3rds of Western music predominate.

Instruments associated with music in the traditional style are mostly obsolete but the *sowi* (shell trumpet) is still occasionally used. The reed-grass or bamboo nose flute and the side-blown arrowroot mouth flute were formerly popular instruments; no one on the island can now play or even remember them. The *aip*, an hourglass drum covered with the bladder or skin of a fish, was played during festive occasions for signalling, and reportedly in connection with dancing. It resembled that used in the Marshalls, but on Ponape it was beaten both with a hibiscus stick and with the hand; only a few islanders remember it. Ponapeans also had a type of jew's harp, but the instrument now played is imported from Pingelap atoll (see fig.1).

On Ponape the flat basalt slabs used for preparing the ceremonial beverage *sakau* (kava) are specially selected for their metallic sounds. Squatting in front of them, men pound the roots of the *Piper methysticum* with smaller stones. At frequent intervals they take turns to produce, on the edge of the slabs, specific rhythms

Ex.1 *Kaul en kawa*, Ponapean traditional song, Uh district, Ponape; transcr. R. Kennedy

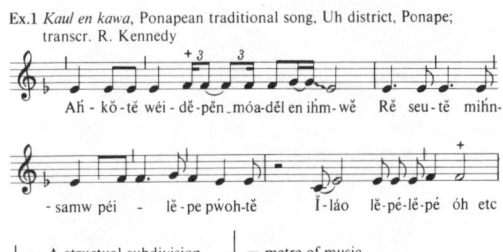

Añ – kŏ-tĕ wéi – dĕ-pĕn—móa-dĕl en ihm-wĕ    Rĕ seu-tĕ mihn-

- samw péi  –  lĕ-pe pẅoh-tĕ    Ï-láo  lĕ-pé-lĕ-pé óh etc

| = A structural subdivision    ⌐ = metre of music
+ = Tone somewhat higher than written
♭ = Pitch indefinite, but approximately where the stem ends

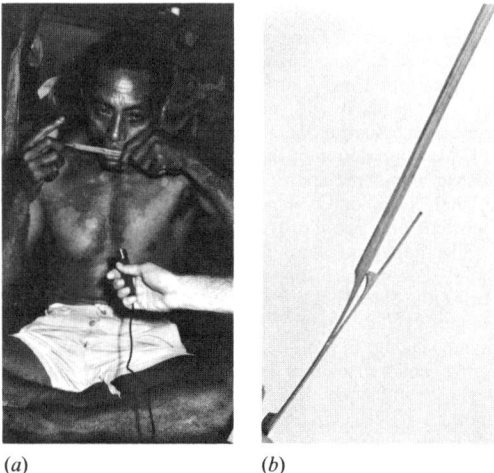

(a)                    (b)

*1. Jew's harp of Pingelap Island: (a) played by the late Makis Ohsai; (b) detail of the instrument*

which indicate stages in the preparation of the beverage (ex.2), and then unite in a special rhythm when it is finished. It was formerly common for certain women to dance during the final stage of preparation.

On special occasions (e.g. after a feast and ceremonial *sakau*) four Ponapean traditional dances are sometimes performed simultaneously on tiered platforms. The *wen*, which involves hand and leg movements, is performed by a row of young men standing on the top tier. The *kepir*, which incorporates stylized paddle movements, is performed by a row of young men standing on the second tier from the top. The *dukia* is performed by a row of young women seated on the tier below, holding a short stick in each hand which they strike together, against their neighbour's, and on a long board laid across their laps in prescribed rhythms. The *sapei*, in which hand and head movements are important, is performed by a row of young women seated on the lowest tier. The dancers sing a *kaul en kawa* while performing the dance

*2. Nose flute player, Truk Islands, 1910*

movements; each dance may also be performed separately.

*Lehp* (the Ponapean pronunciation of 'left') is an adaptation of a Western military drill that incorporates some traditional dance movements; the accompanying music is a Ponapean adaptation of Western music.

Ponapean authorities encourage the native arts. But most traditional music and dance is neglected, because the associated culture is becoming extinct; it has been superseded by hymns (*kaul en sarawi*) and various forms of American, other Micronesian and Polynesian music. Hymn singing is especially popular in the Ponape district, where many Western hymns have been translated and some new hymns composed by islanders. Hymn singing in four-part harmony is common and arrangements in eight parts have been reported. Hymns are sung at both religious and secular occasions, often to the accompaniment of the guitar or ukelele.

Ex.2 *Sakau* pounding rhythm, Uh district, Ponape; transcr. R. Kennedy

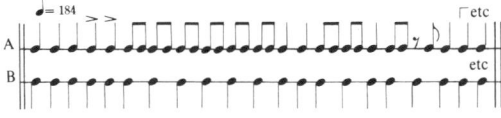

A = Special rhythm played on the edge of the basalt slab signalling a stage of the sakau preparation.
B = *Sukusuk* (pounding of the sakau) (steady pounding)
⌐ = ♩ notes continued for a variable length, depending on the maceration of the sakau.

(*iv*) *Truk Islands*. Truk is a cluster of high islands encircled by a great reef. Trukese people are credited by other Micronesians with being very musical, their songs being noted for flowing tunefulness and their choral singing for vitality. Singing by large groups is predominantly in four-part hymn tune style (both Catholic and Protestant). The songs are settings of translations of introduced hymns, other religious texts composed in Trukese and secular texts. Singing in small groups (e.g. by three or four singers accompanied by a guitar) of secular Trukese songs stylistically influenced by Indonesian, Japanese or American song, and of imported songs, is especially popular among young people. Solo singing is also enjoyed (performed mostly by young people). According to reports in the early 20th century, dance festivals preceded by months of rehearsal were among the most important occasions of the year (in contrast to the custom of the Yap Islands, there was no dancing at the time of burial). Both gesture dances and stick dances were reported. Song types included the chants accompanying breadfruit dances and war dances, and many types of chant related to canoe-building, children's songs, lullabies and songs for hauling and food-carrying.

In analysing music recorded in Micronesia between 1908 and 1910 George Herzog differentiated two styles, western and eastern Carolinian. Both styles represented in the Trukese recordings. The western Carolinian style – essentially chant (also found on Yap, see (v), and Ifaluk, see (i)) – was characterized by two principal notes in a narrow range, duple rhythms in irregular metres, an introductory phrase and a terminal 'glide' (downward glissando); intonation was not precise. The eastern Carolinian style – more tune-like – was characterized by more notes (pentatonic, organized in tetrachords) in a wider range (up to an 11th), flowing triple-metre rhythms, no introductory phrase but a common cadential formula and shouted endings; intonation was well focussed. In the 1960s the traditional western Carolinian style was perpetuated in some canoe songs and stick-dance chants (and perhaps other types); the traditional eastern style survived in songs with *itang* words (the *itang*, a prestigious class of war leaders with a knowledge of traditional lore and magic power, used a special language or vocabulary for certain songs). The exhibitionist character of some traditional dances was decried by missionaries; the sexual aspect of song texts is of considerable interest to some folklorists and social psychologists. In contrast to those of Yap, love-songs – with foreign (Japanese or English) and Trukese texts – are openly and frequently sung in Truk.

Musical instruments reportedly included both mouth and nose flutes (made from the aerial roots of mangrove) used primarily in courting; after World War II (and perhaps earlier) these were largely replaced by the harmonica. Other instruments reported in Truk are the rolled-leaf double-reed aerophone, the shell trumpet (for signalling, used only by chiefs) and carved wooden rods (later bamboo) used for the *dukia* or *tukija* (stick dance).

(*v*) *Yap Islands*. Chant and its associated dance were traditionally a central feature of village life in Yap. *Tagum* ('village ceremonies'), *mitmit* (inter-village ceremonial feasts) and *guyuwol* (dance contests) were im-

concern mythological historical events; new texts and dances are also composed, including some based on the Bible.

In contrast to the dance-chants, which are public, a love-song should not be performed in the hearing of anyone except one's lover; thus little is known of them. Work songs for hauling and canoe-lashing were noted in the early 1900s.

Traditional Yapese instruments included the *ngal* (bamboo flute, fig.3, of the same type as the *ngaok* in Palau; see (ii)), *yubul* (conch trumpet) and *uchif* (rolled-leaf whistle); but, as elsewhere in Micronesia, bamboo dance sticks are the principal traditional instruments. Foreign music in Yap is predominantly Japanese and American.

3. KIRIBATI (GILBERT ISLANDS). This archipelago of 16 low coral islands (many are atolls) is in south-east Micronesia. The islands became independent in 1979 as the Republic of Kiribati. The total land area of 686 sq km is spread over more than 2·5 million sq km of ocean.

For the evidently introverted Gilbertese, dance is less an expression of enjoyment of life than it is for Polynesians. The traditional dances resemble rather ritual performances, but the dance-songs now performed with fervour in the islands are only to a limited extent specifically magic songs (e.g. to sway spirits, entice schools of fish to the fishing grounds or make European

*3. Ngal (external duct flute), Yap Islands*

portant events, and dance was also essential for funerals. *Tagum* fell into disuse before World War II when the Yapese were forced to labour for the Japanese. Since the establishment of the United Nations trusteeship the *mitmit* continue to take place and the most important *guyuwol* is that of the celebration for United Nations day (24 October). High school graduation and (with increasing self-rule in the 1970s) the opening of the Yap legislature and visits by dignitaries are also occasions for dance. When the dance to be performed at an event has been decided upon, there is a *pilig e churu* ('bringing-down ceremony' – figuratively from the rafters of the community house where all valuables are stored). After the dance has been practised and performed at the *mitmit* or *guyuwol*, it is performed again in the village in full costume at a *penga lan e churu* ('hanging-up ceremony').

Yapese dance-chants are strophic. The dance begins with an introductory solo call followed by a strophe of chant and ends with a shout by all the dancers. The chant has a small number of notes with a narrow range and a strong sense of tonic. Traditional dances – standing, sitting and stick dances – are performed by men or women (but not both together). The texts of the most highly valued dance-chants are said by the Yapese to be in the language of Ulithi (a neighbouring atoll) whence the Yapese received them as tribute payments. However, many of them probably originated in atolls further east (e.g. Ifaluk and especially Woleai) and had been taken to Ulithi in a previous step of the chain of obligations in the Yap 'empire'. Texts of the most highly valued chants

ships turn back). A few songs deal with mythological events, but most are about events in everyday life; they are mainly love-songs, although some have a magical character. These songs are, however, performed in the same ceremonial style as dance-songs which have actual magical or mythological subject matter. All traditional dance-songs originate from magic ceremonies; belief in the power of the spirits of ancestors, and in their ability to give magic power, largely governs the daily existence of the Gilbertese.

The complex of *ruoia* dances (most performed while standing) is an important element of traditional Gilbertese culture. The dance-song *kawawa* is performed by a small group of men and women already in the *maneaba* ('assembly house') in order to summon other groups to participate. An analogous, but longer, starting dance is the *wa ni banga*; the song *arira* ('song for the tying on of clothing mats') is also part of the opening of the *ruoia* complex. The main dance of the *ruoia* group is the *kamei*, considered the 'real *ruoia*'. Its performance requires a woman dance leader (there may however be as many as six women leading). There is usually a contest, within each settlement or between individual settlements, to choose the best woman dance leader. The *kamei* includes the usual slow arm movements interrupted by pauses and small steps forwards and backwards. Although the *ruoia* complex consists mainly of standing dances, it also contains some sitting dances (e.g. the *bino*, which resembles the *kamei* in its arm movements and in the fact that it requires a woman dance leader), in some of which (e.g. the *tirērē*) each participant holds two sticks and hits them together in the rhythm of the song. The *ruoia* complex also includes some newly introduced dances such as the *batere*, derived from the Ellice Islands *fatele* but adapted to Gilbertese style. According to an old rule, individual dances of the same type had distinctive melodies; nevertheless some melodies, for example of a few *kamei*, are very similar.

The Gilbert Islands originally had no instruments, and even now traditional dances are performed without instrumental accompaniment. For the *batere*, however, the Gilbertese use a borrowed instrument, the box drum.

Traditional *ruoia* are no longer composed; those still known and danced were composed in the 1920s or

Ex.3 *Kawawa*, transcr. D. Christensen (Koch, 1969)

[O kati e]
You will not tie on your dance mat as well as I will tie mine! So beautiful, so beautiful, and it will be carefully tied. How well I do it, I prepare you, I prepare you, my dance mat. O men! But Burebure says, Ten Tabuariki will place a symbol on my boat. The woman is very good in the dance. I recognize the ship of the White one, which is travelling there with your eldest daughter Nei Kate. E a ao aei!

1930s at the latest. According to the old custom the composer (*tia kario* or *tia ototo*) of a *ruoia* also led it, if possible. He was believed to have composed the song (or songs) with the help of spirits; according to accounts of the old men, the texts of dance-songs were given 'from the *anti*', that is, from the spirits of ancestors. The words were dictated in a trance, to assistants, at the *nikawewe* ('composer's place'); then the composer returned to full consciousness and, ascertaining the words from each assistant in turn, combined them into a song text, for which he instantly 'knew' (i.e. spontaneously composed) the melody; actually, however, new texts could be created for an already known melody, and old texts could be fitted with new melodies. When the composition was complete, the composer taught his assistants to sing and dance it; later, in a public performance, the new dance-song was made known to the entire clan who learnt to perform it, without necessarily understanding (or having explained) the meaning of the text. There seems to have been no special proprietary interest attached to any dance-song. The songs were allowed to be copied by other family groups without restriction; indeed, the composer was proud if his songs were imitated. Although large *ruoia* were basically conceived at the *nikawewe*, a good composer, according to Gilbertese opinion, could compose a small love-*ruoia* at his own home for a paying customer, and *katake* ('individual songs') originated solely at home.

The musical style of *ruoia* dance-songs such as the *kawawa* (ex.3) belongs to Gilbertese tradition dating from before European contact. An individual man sings the introductory call 'O kati e' and then the actual song begins. At first a few men join in, followed later by women, who double the men's voices at the upper octave. The two parts – marked by a few heterophonic deviations – run in parallel octaves. The text of the song is through-composed. It is recited syllabically and unmetred, using the degrees of a tetratonic scale. The slow, rhythmically unarticulated recitation becomes stricter only in the short sections which are accompanied by choral hand-clapping. The form of the text is closely related to that of the music: a textual phrase is fitted with a comparably proportioned musical phrase, which closes with a cadential formula – frequently with a melisma. The intimate connection of the textual and musical forms, and the fact that text and melody share certain important predefined aspects, are evident in the extended repeat at the beginning of the *kawawa*: except for a small degree of variation which seems to result only from the uncertainty of individual singers, the repeat is the same note for note as the first statement.

4. MARIANA ISLANDS. The group of Micronesian islands closest to the continent of Asia is the Mariana Islands, an archipelago of volcanic islands extending from Guam northwards for about 670 km. Guam, the largest island in Micronesia (its area is about 540 sq km), became a port of call for the Spanish Manila Galleon (an annual expedition from 1565 to 1815 between the Philippines and Mexico). In 1899, after the end of the Spanish colonial administration, Guam became a naval base and later a territory of the USA, while Saipan, Rota, Tinian and the other 11 Mariana Islands were administered by the same foreign governments as were the Caroline and Marshall Islands. In October 1975 the Marianas became a commonwealth 'in

free association' with the USA. The name 'Mariana Islands' (or 'the Marianas') still excludes Guam in a political context but includes it in a geographical context. The population of Guam (approximately 100,000) consists of inhabitants of indigenous extraction, many Americans from the mainland and Hawaii, Filipino and Korean workers, refugees from Vietnam, and a smaller number of Carolinians and Marshallese. The population of the Mariana Islands excluding Guam (over 12,000) includes inhabitants of indigenous extraction, a significant proportion of Carolinians, Americans, Filipinos and Koreans.

Chamorro is the name of the indigenous people and language of the Mariana Islands (including Guam), although the Chamorro population was almost annihilated through war and disease during the 17th century. This demise was accompanied by the growth of a new hybrid population, in which Chamorros intermarried primarily with Spaniards and Filipinos, and of a hybrid culture including Roman Catholicism and some Hispanic elements. Modern inhabitants resemble Spaniards or Filipinos – or Japanese, American or other more recent immigrants – but in language and culture they differ from them and from their Micronesian neighbours. They are, and should be recognized as, neo-Chamorros.

(i) *Chamorro music and dance.* Little is definitely known of the indigenous music of the Marianas. The only available documents concerning music for over 150 years after the discovery of the islands (by Ferdinand Magellan in 1521) are fragmentary accounts in the journals of early voyagers and missionaries. These are brief, superficial and frequently contradictory; but they record that on the death of a friend or relative the Chamorros expressed their sorrow by wailing and singing dirges. On festive occasions men and women assembled and, forming semicircles, sang and chanted their history and legends, sometimes in three-part harmony. The songs were accompanied by hand and body movements, the women often playing a container rattle filled with shells. Women also wore shell ornaments which acted as strung rattles while they danced. Competitive dancing in which men exercised their strength was also popular; such dancing finds expression today during the fandango (wedding feast).

Accounts of Chamorro musical instruments are rare. The bamboo flute was used, and the conch-shell trumpet was sounded as a symbol of peace. Two instruments still played on Guam in the 20th century may be replicas of ancient prototypes: the *belembaupachot* (*belémban-bátchot*), a bamboo jew's harp resembling those in other parts of Micronesia, the Philippines and Asia, and the *belembautuyan* (*belenbaotuyan*, *belémban-túyan*), a musical bow (fig.4). The *belembautuyan* is especially important to the people of Guam as it has become a symbol of their earlier Chamorro culture. As late as 1968 there were two active players of the instrument who performed at various political and social functions. The main stick of the *belembautuyan*, made of a supple native wood (usually hibiscus), is about two metres long. A string made from wild pineapple fibre (wire in later forms) is stretched across the stick and fastened at both ends (when wire is used, protective lead cylinders are worn on the fingers of the left hand). A half gourd (or two half coconut-shells, one inside the other) is attached about midway between the two ends of the stick on the side opposite the string. The player reclines or sits, the gourd resting against his stomach, and fingers the string with his left hand while striking it with a piece of sword-

4. *Chamorro belembautuyan* (musical bow)

*5. Jobwa stick dance, Marshall Islands, 1962*

grass held in his right hand. Freely translated, *belembautuyan* means 'vibrations of the stomach'; *belembaupachot* means 'vibrations of the mouth'.

The *chamorita* (*tsamorita*) and similar strophic folk-songs also persist in the 20th century. Most *chamorita* melodies are of Spanish or American origin, but they are melodically altered when Chamorro texts are fitted to them. The *chamorita* is sung as a solo or chorus; harmony parts are usually improvised. The *chamorita* pattern is used in many types of song: love-songs, lullabies, fishing songs, work-party songs, teasing songs and songs of farewell. The intricate play on words and allusions can be appreciated fully only by those conversant with the Chamorro language.

Rapid Americanization of the Marianas following World War II further reduced the importance of much Chamorro culture. Although the *chamorita* is still sung, and at some novenas elderly women sing what may be an archaic polyphonic style, the indigenous music of the islands has mostly been supplanted by various Western forms of music.

(*ii*) *Guam*. In the mid-1970s modern Guamanian music – primarily vocal – was flourishing locally and beginning to be exported. In style it is a synthesis of Chamorro, Filipino, Latin American and other genres adopted and adapted throughout many years of cultural contact. Most song texts are in Chamorro; some are in English. A few Japanese popular songs translated into Chamorro and English are treated by Guamanian musicians as part of this repertory. The accompaniment is played sometimes on a single guitar (as in Saipan and other Mariana islands) but more characteristically on a band of percussion and plucked string instruments with electronic amplification. A saxophone or other wind instrument from the jazz band tradition is sometimes added.

Each resident cultural group enjoys its own music and dance at social events. For the rapidly expanding tourist industry and the commercial entertainment of residents, hotels import Hawaiian, Filipino and Korean bands, and pan-Polynesian and pan-Micronesian shows. Community activities include orchestral, oratorio and other programmes by amateur groups. The armed

forces band contributes to both military and civilian (including school) activities. Music taught in schools is essentially Western with a few items from the local cultures. The College of Guam has begun a programme for the study and preservation of Micronesian performing arts and offers some training in Western art music.

5. MARSHALL ISLANDS. The Marshall Islands lie in two parallel chains called Ratak and Ralik (usually referred to as the sunrise and sunset chains), about 1280 km long, in north-eastern Micronesia. Together they comprise 20 atolls with more than 1000 islets, and five raised coral islands. The total land area is about 180 sq km, the population about 25,000.

The first European discovery was by Spanish navigators in 1526. Among the later navigators was the British Captain John Marshall (after whom the archipelago was named), who sailed in company with Captain Gilbert along the Ratak chain in 1788. In 1888 Germany took administrative control, followed by Japan; after World War II the Marshall Islands became part of the United Nations Trust Territory administered by the USA.

The most revealing information about music and dance in pre-missionary times occurs in journals from two Russian expeditions led by Otto von Kotzebue between 1815 and 1826. One entry states that the boat and the drum were the Ratak islanders' favourite possessions, and that their principal pastimes were navigation and singing; another records that through dancing and singing every evening the islanders learnt their history and preserved their traditions in a very pleasant manner.

In the 20th century the most important indigenous vocal genres have included navigation chants, *eb* (legends recounted in chant and dance, with some pantomime) and chants for tattooing. Chants for harvesting, food preparation, canoe making and fishing, lullabies and prayers for a safe voyage and good weather were still performed in the early 1960s, but tattoo chants and perhaps some of the others are becoming extinct.

The *eb* chant believed to have the oldest musical style and text is *Jobwa*, a legendary story that supposedly originated on Ebeju in the Ujae atoll, from which it spread through appropriate channels of the traditional pre-missionary social structure to many other atolls. Although its text is archaic and not all the words are understood, Marshallese opinions about the chant's origin, meaning and performing practice are remarkably consistent. The text is chanted by a group of women (as late as the early 20th century, accompanied by a drum); the dancing (with sticks – formerly wooden, now bamboo; fig.5) and shouted responses are performed by men of high rank. (The requirement of rank is now being relaxed, and schoolboys learn at least part of the dance.) Although the length both of textual lines and of musical phrases is irregular, form is readily apparent through the repetition and recurrence of textual and melodic contours, cadential formulae and sectional divisions. The range is narrow, the melodic progression is mostly stepwise (and often sliding), the intervallic relations of principal tones is microtonic, and the rhythm is simple but has no fixed pattern. *Jobwa* is highly valued for maintaining cultural identity and is often chosen for performance to distinguished visitors.

Of all the foreign contacts – explorers, traders, whalers, administrators and missionaries – the missionaries had the greatest impact on Marshallese music and dance. Missionaries (including some recently converted Hawaiians) of the American Board of Commissioners for Foreign Missions began establishing missions in 1857. As elsewhere they sought to replace chants and dances associated with traditional beliefs with hymn tunes. Texts were translated into Marshallese and new texts were written in the vernacular; in both cases musical phrases were extended to accommodate the textual sense, and the musical style of adapted hymn tunes with characteristic phrase extensions is now used for both religious and secular songs. Christmas is an important occasion musically: members of the church from all the islets of an atoll come together for the whole day, and groups sing both old and newly composed Christmas songs to each other. There is no formal competition, but each group's concern to achieve recognition stimulates excellence both in performance and in the creation of new songs. Favourite Christmas and Easter songs are performed not only at the appropriate season but on any occasion for singing. Singing in the hymn tune style is usually in four parts, but doubling of any or all parts, to make the sound rich and full, is common. Marshallese choir conductors, like some in other Pacific islands, often move in an almost dance-like manner besides using the Western conductor's standard arm movements.

The range of instruments at the time of European contact was small. The *aje* drum was hourglass-shaped, and most descriptions indicate that it was single-headed. It was introduced from Melanesia, directly or through Ponape, where the *aip* resembles it in structure (see §2 (iii) above). It was held on the lap or under the arm. Finger and hand strokes, and centre and rim positions, were differentiated. One, two or three *aje* (apparently different numbers on different islands or atolls) were played by women to accompany chanting or singing, sometimes with dance or pantomime. The *aje* was also beaten by women as a signal and behind battle lines. It was not played after the early 20th century (as a result of Christian missionary work) and no extant specimens are known in the Marshalls.

The *jilel* (shell trumpet) was primarily a signalling instrument: there are numerous accounts of its being carried and blown in battle, by the highest ranking man in a canoe, to sound the alarm and to call people together. It was also blown during dance activities: at the beginning of an event or major section of a dance-pantomime; extensively during a vigorous men's dance; and with the *aje* to accompany a vocal duet. There is also a report of its being blown at the water's edge during a chant intended to calm high waves endangering a low coral islet. The *jilel* is still used, especially in outlying atolls. Dance sticks were of two types: short wooden sticks (*jimokmok*) for a women's sitting dance and long wooden staffs or spears (*made*), some with decorative plaiting, for men's standing dances. Bamboo, which was introduced after written records began to be kept, is now used for men's dance sticks. The guitar, ukelele and harmonica are now considered by the Marshallese to be their principal *kojangjang* (musical instruments).

BIBLIOGRAPHY

W. E. Safford: 'Guam and its People', *American Anthropologist*, iv (1902), 707

W. Müller: *Yap*, Ergebnisse der Südsee-Expedition 1908–1910, ed. G. Thilenius, IIB/2/i (Hamburg, 1917)

P. Hambruch and A. Eilers: 'Musik und Tanz', *Ponape*, ii: Ergebnisse der Südsee-Expedition 1908–1910, ed. G. Thilenius, IIB/7/ii (Hamburg, 1936), 184–225

G. Herzog: 'Die Musik der Karolinen-Inseln (aus dem Phonogramm-Archiv, Berlin)', *Westkarolinen*, Ergebnisse der Südsee-Expedition 1908–1910, ed. G. Thilenius, IIB/9/ii (Hamburg, 1936), 263–351

H. Hijikata: 'Palao no odori' [Dance of Palau], *Nanyō Guntō* (1941), June, p.22

L. M. Thompson: *Guam and its People* (Princeton, NJ, 1941, rev. 3/1947)

E. G. McClain and R. W. Clopton: 'Guamanian Songs: a Collection of Songs Commonly Sung on Guam and Not Hitherto Notated', *Journal of American Folklore*, lxii (1949), 217

S. H. Riesenberg: *The Cultural Position of Ponape in Oceania* (diss., U. of California, Berkeley, 1950)

J. L. and A. M. Fischer: *The Eastern Carolines* (New Haven, 1957)

E. G. Burrows: 'Music on Ifaluk Atoll in the Caroline Islands', *EM*, ii (1958), 9

J. L. Fischer: 'Meter in Eastern Carolinian Oral Literature', *Journal of American Folklore*, lxxii (1959), 47

O. Yamaguchi: *The Music of Palau: an Ethnomusicological Study of the Classical Tradition* (diss., U. of Hawaii, 1967)

G. and S. Koch and D. Christensen: 'Mikronesier (Gilbert-Inseln, Tabiteuea) "ruoia"-Tanz "kawawa" ', *Encyclopaedia cinematographica*, ed. G. Wolf (Göttingen, 1968), 3 [rev. and enlarged as 'Tänze', in G. Koch: *Kultur der Gilbert-Inseln* (Göttingen, 1969), 277–319]

O. Yamaguchi: 'The Taxonomy of Music in Palau', *EM*, xii (1968), 345

L. M. Thompson: *Archaeology of the Marianas Islands* (New York, 1971; orig. in *Bishop Museum Bulletin*, c (1932), 1–82)

——: *The Native Culture of the Marianas Islands* (New York, 1971; orig. in *Bishop Museum Bulletin*, clxxxv (1945), 1–48)

O. Yamaguchi: 'Music as Behavior in Ancient Palau', *Kikkawa Festschrift* (Tokyo, 1973), 547

BARBARA B. SMITH (1, 2: i, iv, v, 4: ii, 5)
OSAMU YAMAGUCHI (2: ii)
RAYMOND F. KENNEDY (2: iii, 4: i)
GERD KOCH, DIETER CHRISTENSEN (3)

**Microtone.** Any musical interval or difference of pitch distinctly smaller than a semitone. Some writers restrict the term to quantities of less than half a semitone; others extend it to refer to all music with intervals markedly different from the (logarithmic) 12th part of the octave and its multiples, including such scales with fewer than 12 pitches as are used, for example in south-east Asia.

Microtones encountered in music theory include the tiny enharmonic melodic intervals of ancient Greece, the several divisions of the octave into more than 12 parts, and various discrepancies among the intervals of just intonation or between a sharp and its enharmonically paired flat in various forms of mean-tone temperament. The Indian concept of a *śruti* might also belong in this list (*see* INDIA, SUBCONTINENT OF, §II, 1). Theoretical divisions of the octave into equal microtones have included the 19 division employed by late Renaissance and early Baroque musicians including Costeley and Titelouze; the 31 division calculated by Christiaan Huygens in the 1660s (often dubiously attributed to Nicola Vicentino); the 55 division discussed by Joseph Sauveur in 1701 and attributed by G. A. Sorge in 1748 to Telemann; and the 53 division implicit in the Renaissance concept that the Pythagorean whole tone (monochord ratio 9:8) could be divided into nine equal parts, four of which would comprise a Pythagorean diatonic semitone (ratio 256:243): thus the octave, consisting of five whole tones and two semitones, would implicitly contain $5 \times 9 + 2 \times 4$ equal microtones. Theorists of the 17th century showed that the 53 division contains virtually pure 3rds as well as 5ths (*see* INTERVAL, Table 1), and later R. H. M. Bosanquet (1875) built a harmonium tuned to this scale.

The use of microtones in Western art music is essentially a 20th-century phenomenon, though Julian Carillo had experimented with his 'sonido 13' system (of equal-tempered quarter-tones) in the 1890s. Ives began his *Three Quarter-tone Pieces* for two pianos early in the century, using a pair of instruments tuned a quarter-tone apart. In Europe, however, there was little quarter-tone music until Alois Hába and Ivan Vishnegradsky composed their first such pieces, both in the 1920s. Hába also used finer divisions, particularly the sixth-tone, and wrote a great deal of microtonal music, from piano pieces and string quartets to a full-scale opera. He was also able to found a Czech school of microtonal composition. Vishnegradsky, a Russian émigré in Paris, made less of an impact, though it was probably through the influence of his music that Pierre Boulez came to write the first quarter-tone serial music, in his *Le visage nuptial* (1946). Carillo, who was also active in Paris between the wars, extended his interests to the construction of quarter-tone pianos and to the use of eighth- and 16th-tones.

Other composers have used microtones not as additions to the 12-semitone equal-tempered system but rather as basic intervals in other tunings. Of those who have used non-tempered systems the most successful was Harry Partch. He employed a 43-interval octave which made available every rational fraction involving the numbers 1–12, and he built special instruments to play his music. Just natural intervals have also been used by, for example, Eiving Groven, Ben Johnston and LaMonte Young.

Most microtonal composers, however, have developed alternative equal temperaments in their search for closer approximation to just intervals. Joseph Yasser has argued for a 19-interval system as a logical evolution from the conventional 12-interval one, the addition of seven new notes being analogous to the addition of the five chromatic degrees to the diatonic scale. Groven and Johnston have used the 53-interval equal temperament favoured by earlier theorists. However, the most widely advocated and frequently employed microtonal equal temperament is that which divides the octave into 31 intervals. Adriaan Fokker commissioned the construction of a pipe organ in that system, whose accurate renderings of the just major 3rd and natural 7th have appealed to many, as has its integral relation to mean-tone temperament. It has continued to be used in the Netherlands, by Henk Badings, Hans Kox and others.

A major problem in microtonal music has been the construction of instruments and of means for tuning them. This difficulty can, of course, be overcome with ease in the electronic studio, and it is there that most microtonal music has been created. Only in a few cases, however, have composers set out to explore a microtonal universe, as Stockhausen did with the system of 25 equal-tempered intervals to two and a half octaves in his *Studie I* (1953). Much more often microtones arise as a by-product of electronic manipulation, or from the use of unconventional sound-generating media.

*See also* INTERVAL; TEMPERAMENTS; THEORY, THEORISTS.

MARK LINDLEY, PAUL GRIFFITHS

**Miculi, Karol.** See MIKULI, KAROL.

**Micza, František Adam.** See MÍČA, FRANTIŠEK ADAM.

**Micza, František Antonín.** See MÍČA, FRANTIŠEK ANTONÍN.

**Middle C.** A colloquial name for the note whose pitch is 256 Hz. It is probably so called because it is written on

a leger line midway between two staves bearing a treble and bass clef respectively. It is also placed roughly at the middle of the keyboard; further, it is near the top of the male vocal range and near the bottom of the female range.

**Middle East.** The coverage of music of the Middle Eastern countries is discussed under the heading NEAR EAST.

**Middleground** (Ger. *Mittelgrund*). In Schenkerian analysis (*see* ANALYSIS, §III) the region between the background and foreground layers of a tonal piece or movement, consisting of one layer or more of part-writing, linking the background to the foreground (*see* LAYER).

**Middle Temple.** One of the London Inns of Court; *see* LONDON, §III.

**Midzahket.** Sign marking a secondary pause and lowering of the voice in Armenian EKPHONETIC NOTATION.

**Miechura, Leopold Eugen.** See MÉCHURA, LEOPOLD EUGEN.

**Miedke, Karl August.** See KREBS, KARL AUGUST.

**Mieg, Peter** (*b* Lenzburg, canton of Aargau, 5 Sept 1906). Swiss composer, critic and painter. He studied the history of art and music, archaeology and literature at the universities of Zurich, Basle and Paris (1927–33), graduating with a dissertation on contemporary watercolours. His music teachers were C. Richter (theory) in Lenzburg, H. Münch in Basle and E. Frey (piano) in Zurich; later he was a composition pupil of Martin (1942–5). As an art critic for Swiss and foreign publications he worked in Basle from 1933, and from 1938 in Lenzburg, where he was also active as a painter. It was the collaboration with de Stoutz and Baumgartner in the early 1950s that decisively turned him towards composition. Influenced by Stravinsky, Bartók and Martin, he developed a style marked by the paramountcy of singable melody, with condensed structures and a transparent sound. This style is based on conventional means, but the content is individual and the effect unusual. The harmony is veiled: tonality is enriched with polytonality, and a fluctuating modality is common; chromaticism and whole-tone scales are used coloristically. The element of rhythm is accentuated.

WORKS

(*selective list*)

Vocal: Wie es euch gefällt (incidental music, Shakespeare), 1935; An die Leier Apollons (Pindar, Hölderlin), Bar, 1946; 4 chansons (A. Narakas), S, pf, 1949; 3 Duette (Baroque verse), S, Bar, pf, 1955; Der Frühling (Claudius), unison children's vv, str, 2 tpt, timp, org, 1956; Die mit Schiffen auf dem Meer (Ps cvii), chorus, 1956; Mit Nacht und Nacht (C. Atabay), T, orch, 1962; 3 Gesänge (Hofmannsthal), T, pf, 1968

Orch: Daphne, ballet (M. von Meyenburg), chamber orch, 1945; Vn Conc., 1949, rev. 1959; Conc. da camera, str, pf, timp, 1952; Hpd Conc., 1953; Conc. veneziano, str, 1955; Ob Conc., 1957; Sym., 1958; Toccata-Arioso-Gigue, 1959; Pf Conc. no.2, 1961; Conc., fl, str, 1962; Rondeau symphonique, 1964; Vc Conc., 1966; Meilener Ballette I–III, 1967; Harp Conc., 1970; Conc., 2 fl, str, 1973

Inst: Sonata, vn, pf, 1937; Divertimento, ob qt, 1950; Pièce, org, 1951; Musik, 2 wind, 4 str, hpd, 1954; Pour le clavecin, 1956; Variations, ob, pf, 1963; Sonata, fl, pf, 1963; Sur les rives du lac Léman, vn, pf, 1968; Qnt, fl, 2 vn, vc, db, 1969; Morceau élégant, fl, harp, 1969; Canto lirico, eng hn, 1970; La sombre, vc, 1970; Les jouissances de

Mauensee, 3 fl, 1971; Les plaisirs de Rued, fl, 1971; Les charmes de Lostorf, 2 fl, 1971; Les humeurs des Salis, fl, hpd, 1971; Konzertstück, 2 harps, 1973
Pf: Conc., 2 pf, 1934; Lettres à Goldoni, 3 sonatas, 1944, 1959, 1971; 5 mouvements, duet, 1947; La passeggiata, duet, 1968

Principal publishers: Bote & Bock, Henn, Schott

### WRITINGS
'Betrachtungen zu Ravels Klaviermusik', *SMz*, lxxxv (1945), 116
'Zu Strawinskys Klavierwerk', *SMz*, lxxxvii (1947), 227
'Tschaikowskys Klaviermusik', *SMz*, lxxxviii (1948), 377
'Blick auf das neuere kompositorische Schaffen in Zürich', *SMz*, xc (1950), 230
'Autobiographische Skizze', *SMz*, cvi (1966), 267

### BIBLIOGRAPHY
H. Gattiker: 'Peter Mieg', *SMz*, lxxxviii (1948), 382
W. Schuh: 'Kammermusik von Peter Mieg', *SMz*, xciii (1953), 39
F. Muggler: 'Peter Mieg', *SMz*, ciii (1963), 64

PETER ROSS

**Mielczewski** [Milchevsky, Myltzewski], **Marcin** (*d* Warsaw, Sept 1651). Polish composer. He is first heard of in 1638 as a musician of the royal chapel in Warsaw, where he had probably been active for a number of years, mainly as a composer. Before this he is supposed to have been a member of the primatal chapel at nearby Łowicz. From 1645 until his death he was director of music to the king's brother, Karol Ferdynand Waza, Bishop of Płock (the bishop's court stayed mostly in Warsaw and at his residences nearby). His Polish contemporaries recognized Mielczewski as a composer of the front rank. Although only two of his works were printed in the 17th century, they were performed abroad, as is proved by manuscripts containing some of them in archives in Czechoslovakia and Germany. Matthias Schacht included an entry on him in his *Musicus danicus* (completed 1687), and Nikolay Diletsky, probably one of his pupils, also referred to him and quoted extracts from his works in his treatise *Musikiyskaya grammatika*.

Mielczewski was indeed one of the leading Polish composers of his time, and his output was large and varied. The concertato principle dominates his entire corpus of accompanied vocal works, and homophonic and polyphonic writing alike are subordinated to it. He composed a wide variety of sacred concertatos for both a few and many voices, and he was the first to introduce the Venetian rondo concertato into Polish music. The style of his small-scale concertatos, in which the words are given full expression, suggests that he must also have composed secular vocal and instrumental pieces, such as madrigals, which have not survived. The accompanied masses for large numbers of performers continued the polychoral tradition of the Venetian school and also include virtuoso solo passages in contrast to the tutti. His instrumental canzonas are clearcut in form and include arch structures. He also wrote variation canzonas, one of which is particularly characteristic; in every other section there is an exact or slightly modified quotation of a Polish folktune, some in dance rhythms – the mazurka is found here for the first time in Polish art music. Mielczewski also quoted popular Polish religious songs in his sacred works, thus giving them a specific local character: for instance, his *Missa super 'O gloriosa domina'* is based on the tune of the song named in the title which is known only from Polish sources. He wrote other masses, and motets too, in a *prima prattica* style reminiscent of the Roman school in their textures but more modern in their strong sense of tonality: the plainsong cantus firmus is generally placed in the bass as a harmonic foundation.

### WORKS
Edition: *M. Mielczewski: Opera omnia*, ed. Z. M. Szweykowski, MMP (1976–) [S]

#### SACRED VOCAL
Missa 'O gloriosa domina', 6vv, bc, *PL-Wu*, S iii
Benedictio et claritas, 6vv, 2 vn, 4 trbn, bc, ed. in WDMP, lxvi (1969); S ii
Deus in nomine tuo, 1v, 2 vn, bn/vc, bc (org), 1659³; ed. in WDMP, ii (2/1961); S ii
Gaude Dei genetrix, 5vv, *Kk*
Veni, Domine, 3vv, bc (org), ed. in WDMP, xxxviii (2/1972); S ii
Vesperae dominicales, 4vv, chorus, 2 vn, bn, bc (org), ed. in WDMP, xlii (1962); S ii
Triumphales dies, 2 choirs, insts, ed. H. Feicht, *Muzyka staropolska* (Kraków, 1966); S ii

Missa Cerviensiana, 12vv, insts, S iii; Missa 'Nun bitten wir', S iii; Missa Sancta Anna, 12vv, insts, S iii; Missa triumphalis, 2 choirs, insts, S iii; Anima mea in aeterna, S ii; Audite et admiramini, S ii: formerly *GD*, now extant only in photocopies (some inc.), *Kj*
Benedicam Dominum, Cantabo Domine, Confitemini Domino, Gaudeamus omnes, Maria Magdalena et altera Maria, Nobis est natus: formerly *D-Lm*, now lost

#### INSTRUMENTAL
7 canzoni, a 2, 3, bc, ed. in WDMP, vi (2/1961); xxix (2/1962); lxi (1966); S i
Double canon, a 4, in M. Scacchi: Cribrum musicum (Venice, 1643)

For complete list of works see *SMP*

### BIBLIOGRAPHY
*SMP*
A. Chybiński: 'O koncertach wokalno-instrumentalnych Marcina Mielczewskiego', *KM*, i (1928–9), 34, 144, 246; ii (1929–30), 10, 306
H. Feicht: 'Przyczynki do dziejów kapeli królewskiej w Warszawie za rządów kapelmistrzowskich Marka Scacchiego' [Contribution to the history of the royal chapel in Warsaw under the musical directorship of Marco Scacchi], *KM*, i (1928–9), 125
——: 'Marcin Mielczewski – "Missa super O gloriosa domina"', *Księga pamiątkowa ku czci Prof. Adolfa Chybińskiego w 70-lecie urodzin* (Kraków, 1950), 218
O. Petraš: 'Kompozycje Marcina Mielczewskiego w archiwum arcybiskupim w Kromieryżu', *Sobótka*, vi (1951), 157
Z. M. Szweykowski: 'Nowe canzony Marcina Mielczewskiego', *Ruch muzyczny*, ii/17 (1958), 5
D. Lehmann: 'Mikołaj Dylecki a muzyka polska w XVII wieku' [Nikolay Diletsky and Polish music in the 17th century], *Muzyka*, x/3 (1965), 38
J. Stęszewski: 'Marcina Mielczewskiego Canzon prima a 2 na tle rękopisu Biblioteki Jagiellońskiej Sygn.127/56', *Muzyka*, xii/1 (1967), 27

ZYGMUNT M. SZWEYKOWSKI

**Mielorth.** *See* RÖMHILD, JOHANN THEODOR.

**Mierzwiński, Władysław** (*b* Warsaw, 21 Oct 1850; *d* Paris, ?14 July 1909). Polish tenor. He studied singing at the Warsaw Institute of Music and later in Italy, at the Naples Conservatory with Guercia and Scafati and at the Milan Conservatory. He made his début at the Paris Opéra as Raoul in *Les Huguenots*. His appearance in opera in London (1880) marked the beginning of a great career. He appeared on all the leading opera stages of Europe and the USA with enormous success, singing the leading roles in *Guillaume Tell*, *Les Huguenots*, *Robert le diable* and *Il trovatore*. His voice was distinguished by its wide range, great strength and fine sound, and Mierzwiński was considered one of the most outstanding tenors of his time. His career was short-lived: a throat disease forced him to abandon performances, and he died in poverty as a hotel porter, completely forgotten.

### BIBLIOGRAPHY
'Władysław Mierzwiński i jego występy na scenie warszawskiej w Hugonotach, Robercie Diable i Wilhelmie Tellu' [Władysław Mierzwiński and his performances on the Warsaw stage in *Les Huguenots*, *Robert le diable* and *Guillaume Tell*], *Echo muzyczne*, xvii (1881), 130
Z. Noskowski: 'Władysław Mierzwiński', *Echo muzyczne, teatralne i artystyczne* (1892), no.431, p.1

A. Dobrowolski: 'Władysław Mierzwiński: wspomnienie pośmiertne' [Władysław Mierzwiński: posthumous recollections], *Tygodnik ilustrowany*, xxx (1909), 598
R. Koczalski: 'Wspomnienie o Władysławie Mierzwińskim' [Recollections of Władysław Mierzwiński], *Scena i sztuka* (1911), no.8, p.4; no.9, p.3

ZOFIA CHECHLIŃSKA

**Mies, Paul** (*b* Cologne, 22 Oct 1889; *d* Cologne, 15 May 1976). German musicologist. He studied musicology with Leonhard Wolff as well as mathematics and physics at the University of Bonn, where he took a doctorate in 1912 with a dissertation on tone painting in music. He taught in Cologne from 1919 to 1939 except for a brief period of further study (1925–7), and in the late 1920s and early 30s he supervised several radio broadcasts for high schools. From 1946 to 1954 he was professor and director of the Institut für Schulmusik at the Staatliche Hochschule für Musik, Cologne. In 1946 he became a member of the board of directors of the Beethovenhaus, Bonn. In addition to his studies of the history of music in Cologne, Mies is known for his work on musical style and analysis (particularly of Beethoven's compositions) in which he attempts to describe the process of composition as well as assessing the music's effect.

WRITINGS

*Über die Tonmalerei* (diss., U. of Bonn, 1912; extracts in *Zeitschrift für Ästhetik und allgemeine Kunstwissenschaft*, vii (1912), 397–450, 578–618)
with E. Bücken: 'Grundlagen, Methoden und Aufgaben der musikalischen Stilkunde', *ZMw*, v (1922–3), 219
*Stilmomente und Ausdrucksstilformen im Brahms'schen Lied* (Leipzig, 1923)
ed.: *M. G. Nottebohm: Zwei Skizzenbücher von Beethoven aus den Jahren 1801 bis 1803* (Leipzig, 1924)
*Die Bedeutung der Skizzen Beethovens zur Erkenntnis seines Stiles* (Leipzig, 1925; Eng. trans., 1929/*R*1969)
*Musik im Unterricht der höheren Lehranstalten* (Cologne, 1925–6)
*Das romantische Lied und Gesänge aus Wilhelm Meister* (Berlin, 1926)
*Skizzen aus Geschichte und Ästhetik der Musik* (Cologne, 1926)
*Schubert, der Meister des Liedes: die Entwicklung von Form und Inhalt im Schubertschen Lied* (Berlin, 1928)
*Johannes Brahms: Werke, Zeit, Mensch* (Leipzig, 1930)
*Der Charakter der Tonarten: eine Untersuchung* (Cologne, 1948)
*Von Sinn und Praxis der musikalischen Kritik* (Krefeld, 1950)
with N. Schneider: *Musik im Umkreis der Kulturgeschichte: ein Tabellenwerk aus der Geschichte der Musik, Literatur, bildenden Kunst, Philosophie und Politik Europas* (Rodenkirchen, 1953)
*Franz Schubert* (Leipzig, 1954)
*Textkritische Untersuchungen bei Beethoven* (Munich and Duisburg, 1957)
*Die geistlichen Kantaten Johann Sebastian Bachs und der Hörer von heute* (Wiesbaden, 1959–60, 2/1964/*R*1967)
'Quellenbewertung bei den Werken Ludwig van Beethovens', *BeJb 1959–60*, 72
*Bilder und Buchstaben werden Musik* (Rodenkirchen, 1964)
with H. Grundmann: *Studien zum Klavierspiel Beethovens und seiner Zeitgenossen* (Bonn, 1966, 2/1970)
*Die weltlichen Kantaten J. S. Bachs und der Hörer von heute* (Wiesbaden, 1967)
*Das instrumentale Rezitativ: von seiner Geschichte und seinen Formen* (Bonn, 1968)
'Beethoven–Collin–Shakespeare: zur Coriolan-Ouvertüre, op. 62'; 'Einige allgemeine und spezielle Beispiele zu Beethovens Notation', *BeJb 1965–8*, 260; 215
'Zu Werdegang und Strukturen der Paganini-Variationen op.35 für Klavier von Johannes Brahms', *SM*, xi (1969), 323
*Die Krise der Konzertkadenz bei Beethoven* (Bonn, 1970)
*Das Konzert im 19. Jahrhundert: Studien zu Kadenzen und Formen* (Bonn, 1972)
Many articles in *AMf*, *BeJb*, *BMw*, *Gregoriusblatt*, *Halbmonatsschrift für Schulmusikpflege*, *Haydn-Jb*, *Kölnische Volkszeitung*, *Jung-Köln*, *MMR*, *Musica sacra*, *Die Musik*, *Mf*, *Musikhandel*, *Neues Beethoven-Jb*, *NZM*, *Zeitschrift des deutschen Sängerbundes*, *ZfM*, other periodicals and Festschriften

EDITIONS

*Das kölnische Volks- und Karnevalslied: ein Beitrag zur Kulturgeschichte der Stadt Köln von 1823 bis 1923 im Lichte des Humors*, Denkmäler rheinischer Musik, ii (Cologne and Krefeld, 1951)

*C. Leibl: Fest-Kantate zur Feier der Grundsteinlegung für den Fortbau des Kölner Doms 1842*, Denkmäler rheinischer Musik, v (Düsseldorf, 1955)
*J. Haydn: Mehrstimmige Gesänge*, Werke, xxx (Munich and Duisburg, 1958)
*L. van Beethoven: Streichquartette*, Werke, Abt.6, iii–iv (Munich and Duisburg, 1962–8)

BIBLIOGRAPHY

I. Geipel: 'Paul Mies 70 Jahre', *Musikhandel*, x (1959), 303
P. Mies: 'Mies, Paul', *Rheinische Musiker*, i, ed. K. G. Fellerer (Cologne, 1960), 168 [with complete list of writings to 1960]
——: *Bilder und Buchstaben werden Musik* (Rodenkirchen, 1964) [incl. list of writings, 1960–64]

M. E. C. BARTLET

**Mi fiolo.** *See* RANIERI, GIOVANNI SIMONE.

**Mignon, Jean** (*b* ?Paris, *c*1640; *d* ?Paris, *c*1707). French composer. He was the son of Pierre Mignon, cobbler and valet to the Prince of Condé. He was educated as a choirboy at Notre Dame, Paris, and later at the College of Fortet. At an unknown date he became choirmaster of Senlis Cathedral. In 1663, despite the attempted influential intervention of his father, he applied unsuccessfully for one of the choirmasterships at the royal chapel. On 30 August 1664 he succeeded Pierre Robert, a successful applicant at the royal chapel, as choirmaster of Notre Dame, Paris. There he was made sub-deacon of St Denis-du-Pas on 3 June 1682; sub-deacon (canon according to the title-page of his mass of 1686) of St Jean-le-Rond some time between 1682 and 1686; and vicar of St Aignan on 5 February 1687. In 1683 he tried again for a choirmastership at the royal chapel and survived the first elimination only to be defeated in the second. On 21 June 1694 he retired from his position at Notre Dame and was succeeded by Campra. On the same date he was made canon of St Aignan, an honour reserved for those with whom the cathedral chapter had been specially well pleased; he was the last choirmaster of Notre Dame to be so honoured. He was highly regarded in his day as composer and musician. His masses were reprinted as late as 1744. His musical opinion was valued: for example, he was one of the judges for the celebrated musical competitions held at Caen from 1669. He also had some skill at poetry; in 1682 he sponsored a contest to write a sonnet in praise of the king using specified rhymes, and according to contemporary sources this kept everyone busy for the whole season. His music, although contrapuntal, is in a simple, largely chordal and syllabic style, often with sparse imitation and square phrases and with angular melodic lines and little affective response to the words. Its interest depends almost entirely on the drive of its dotted, dance-like rhythms.

WORKS

*(all published in Paris)*

Airs à quatre parties (1664)
Missa 'Iterum dico, gaudete', 4vv (1676)
Missa 'Gaudete in Domino semper', 4vv (2/1678; 1st edn. lost)
Missa 'Vinea nostra floruit', 6vv (1678)
Missa in honorem Divi Joannis Baptistae 'Joannes est nomen ejus', 5vv (1682); facs. extracts in Chartier
Missa 'Psallite sapienter', 4vv (1686)
Missa 'Laetitia sempiterna', 4vv (1707); facs. extract in Chartier
7 airs, a 2, 1660[1]
Missa 'Magnificate Dominum mecum', 5vv, 2 choirs ad lib; lost, cited in Ballard catalogue of 1707
Psalms, motets, Te Deum settings: lost, cited in *Mercure galant* (1679–83)

BIBLIOGRAPHY

*EitnerQ*; *GerberNL*; *WaltherML*
A. du Pradel: *Le livre commode des adresses de Paris pour 1692* (Paris, 1692, repr. 1878)

J. Carlez: 'Le puy de musique de Caen', *Réunion des sociétés des beaux-arts de départements*, ix (1885), 99

F. L. Chartier: *L'ancien chapitre de Notre-Dame de Paris et sa maîtrise* (Paris, 1897/R1971)

M. Barthélemy: *André Campra: sa vie et son oeuvre (1660–1744)* (Paris, 1957)

L. E. S. J. de Laborde: *Musiciens de Paris, 1535–1792*, ed. Y. de Brossard (Paris, 1965)

M. Benoit: *Versailles et les musiciens du roi, 1661–1773* (Paris, 1971)

D. Taitz-Desouches: 'Jean Mignon (1640–1710): maître de chapelle de Notre Dame de Paris', *RMFC*, xiv (1974), 82–153

M. Benoit and N. Dufourcq: 'Les musiciens de Versailles', *RMFC*, xv (1975), 155–90, esp. 158

WILLIAM HAYS

**Mignone, Francisco (Paulo)** (*b* São Paulo, 3 Sept 1897). Brazilian composer and conductor. A son of an Italian immigrant musician, he began flute and piano studies with his father, continuing his piano training from 1907 under Silvio Motto. At an early age he played both of his instruments in local dance orchestras. He studied the piano, the flute and composition at the São Paulo Conservatory, where he was a pupil of Cantù and where he graduated in 1917; although Mário de Andrade was his teacher for history and aesthetics, it was only later that Mignone came under Andrade's influence. By 1920, when he left for Europe, Mignone had composed and conducted several orchestral pieces. He studied under Ferroni at the Milan Conservatory, and there he wrote the opera *O contratador de diamantes* (1921), first performed in Rio de Janeiro in 1924; *Congada*, taken from the second-act ballet, achieved great popularity. A second opera, *L'innocente*, was presented in Rio with great success in 1928, and in the following year Mignone returned to the São Paulo Conservatory as a harmony teacher. In 1933 he moved to Rio and was appointed official conductor and conducting teacher at the National Music School; he also taught privately for many years. After a European conducting tour (1937–8) he visited the USA for the first time in 1942. In New York the League of Composers had some of his works performed, and he conducted the NBC and CBS orchestras in concerts of his music. During the next two decades he held many different appointments, among them the music directorships of the Teatro Municipal, Radio Ministério da Educação e Cultura and Radio Globo.

In the first (*c*1917–28) of the three periods that may be distinguished in Mignone's output, his Italian background and training are evident in the Romantic structure and harmony of such pieces as the *Suite campestre*, the *Paráfrase sobre o hino dos cavalheiros da Kirial*, and the tone poems *Festa dionisíaca*, *Momus* and *No sertão*, the last a fantasy suggested by the work of Euclides da Cunha. At the same time, an interest in national idioms may be perceived in *Maxixe* and *Congada*, both based on Brazilian popular rhythms.

Mignone was strongly attracted by the ideals of musical nationalism eloquently propounded by Andrade, and about 1929 he began a new period of intensive creativity drawing on all manner of Brazilian folk and popular traditions, a period that lasted until around 1959–60. Typical of this nationalist style are the ballets *Maracatu de chico rei* and *Leilão*, the orchestral *Batucajé* and *Babaloxá*, and the four *Fantasias brasileiras* for piano and orchestra. The first ballet and the two orchestral pieces are on Afro-Brazilian subjects and use almost exclusively Afro-Brazilian themes, or themes akin to them in rhythm and melody. Nearly all

of the collective numbers of *Maracatu* are stylized folk-or popular dances, and the orchestration is given individuality by the inclusion of popular percussion instruments. The *Fantasias* epitomize Mignone's style better than any other works of the period; all are rhapsodic pieces with a piano part recalling the captivating, spontaneous, virtuoso style of such popular pianist-composers as Nazareth. In a 1939 newspaper article Andrade mentioned the third *Fantasia*, *Babaloxá* and *Maracatu* as 'monumental landmarks', recognizing their importance in contemporary Brazilian music. The symphonic 'impressions' *Festa das igrejas*, which received international recognition after a Toscanini NBC SO performance in 1944, take some thematic material from the mestizo *caboclo* music.

In the 1930s and 1940s Mignone had most success in Brazil with solo songs and piano pieces. His first nationalist song, *Quando na roça anoitece*, is characteristic in its melody and guitar-like accompaniment; and the best of these songs are the *Seis líricas*, *Dentro da noite* and *Dona Janaína* from the cycle *Quatro líricas*, and *Pousa a mão na minha testa*. Of the piano pieces, the most overtly nationalist are the *Lendas sertanejas*, the *Quatro peças brasileiras*, *Cucumbizinho*, *Cateretê*, *Dança do Botocudo* and *Quase modinha*. Lyrical melodies, some taken from folksongs, within a prevailingly tonal harmony and frequent syncopated rhythms (as in *Nazareth* from the *Quatro peças*) point to a heavy dependence on urban popular music. Two sets of very romantic waltzes, *Valsas de esquina* and *Valsas choros*, attempt to recreate the style of the improvised waltzes of early-20th-century strolling serenaders, of the popular piano pieces of such composers as Nazareth, and, in their melody, of the popular *modinhas*. These persistent references to national music were to some extent transcended in the Piano Sonata no.1 (1941).

Writing six years later in *A parte do anjo*, Mignone decided that 'my music will have to be gradually more refined technically, but clear, honest and easily understandable to the majority'. Such an intention appears to underlie the Piano Concerto (1958), a Romantic piece with colourful orchestration and brilliant bravura solo passages. Other orchestral and chamber pieces of the late 1950s indicate a turning away from direct preoccupation with national sources in favour of an attitude of such eclecticism that it is difficult to isolate constant features, although there has been a tendency to polytonality, tone clusters, atonality and serialism. Indeed, the *Variações em busca de um tema* (1972) were designed to accommodate 'all present-day compositional processes'.

### WORKS

STAGE

O contratador de diamantes (opera, 3, G. Bottoni, after A. Arinos), 1921, Rio, Municipal, 20 Sept 1924; L'innocente (opera, 3, A. Rossato), 1927, Rio, 5 Sept 1928; Maracatu de chico rei, ballet, Andrade, 1933; Leilão, ballet, 1941; O espantalho, ballet, 1941; Iara, ballet, 1942; O guarda chuva, ballet, 1953; Sugestões sinfónicas, tone poem-ballet, 1969

ORCHESTRAL

Suite campestre, 1918; Paráfrase sobre o hino dos cavalheiros da Kirial, 1919; Congada (from opera O contratador), 1921; Festa dionisíaca, sym. poem, 1923; Elegia, str, 1924; Momus, poema humorístico, 1925; No sertão, fantasia, 1925; Maxixe, 1925; Suite asturiana, 1928; Fantasias brasileiras nos.1–4, pf, orch, 1929, 1931, 1934, 1936; Variações sobre um tema brasileiro, vc, orch, 1935; Babaloxá, 1936; Batucajé, 1936; Sinfonia do Trabalho, 1939

Festa das igrejas, 1940; 4 amazônicos, 1942; Burlesca e toccata, pf, orch, 1956; Bn Concertino, 1957; Cl Concertino, 1957; Lenda sertaneja, str, 1957; Pf Conc., 1958; Sinfonia tropical, 1958; Vn Conc., 1961; Conc. duplo, vn, pf, orch, 1966; Canto seresteiro, str,

1972; Sinfonia transamazônica, 1972; Variações em busca de um tema, 1972

### CHAMBER

Sonata, A, vn, pf, 1919; Gavota all'antica, vn, pf, 1930; Berceuse, vn, pf, 1930; Noturno sertanejo, vn, pf, 1931; Canção sertaneja, pf trio, 1932; Sexteto no.1, fl, ob, cl, bn, tpt, pf, 1935; Variações sobre um tema brasileiro, vn, pf, 1935; Oteto, str, 1956; 2 peças, str qnt, pf, 1956; Str Qts nos.1–2, 1957; Andantino, str qnt, 1958; 2 sonatas, 2 bn, 1960, 1965; 3 sonatas, vn, pf, 1964, 1965, 1966; Tetrafonia, 4 bn, 1967; 4 sinfonias, ob, cl, bn, 1968
Sexteto no.2, wind qnt, pf, 1969; Sonata a 3, fl, ob, cl, 1970; Str Qt no.3, 1970; Serenata a Dulcinéa, str sextet, 1972; Preludio, coral para uma fuga, pf qnt, 1973

### CHORAL

Cateretê, SATB, 1930; Menina Bonita, SSA, 1932; Papai, eu quero me casar, SSA, 1932; Sonhei que Sinhá tinha morrido, SSA, 1932; Hino do Colégio Bennett, SATB, 1938; Meu São Benedito, TTBB, 1941; Folga nêgo, TTBB, 1941; Enquanto morrem as rosas, SSAA, 1948; Samba-lelê, SATB, 1951; Seresta, SATB, 1951; Baianinha, SATB, 1951; Jura de ioiô, SATB, 1951; Despacho de Iemanjá, SATB, 1951
14 cânones, 1954; Oratorio de S Clara, solo vv, chorus, orch, 1962; 7 masses, SATB, 1962, 1963, 1963, 1965, 1966, 1967, 1968; Belém! verde Belém!, SATB, 1970; 16 cantos escolares, 2vv, 1970 .

### PIANO

Lendas sertanejas nos.1–9, 1923, 1923, 1928, 1930, 1930, 1932, 1934, 1938, 1940; Maxixe, 1928; 4 peças brasileiras, 1930; 6 estudos transcendentais, 1931; Cucumbizinho, 1931; Cateretê, 1931; Valsas de esquina nos.1–12, 1938–43; Quase modinha, 1940; Dança do Botocudo, 1940; Sonata no.1, 1941; Valsas choros no.1, 1946, nos.2–5, 1950, nos.6–12, 1955; Sonatinas nos.1–14, 1949; Samba ritmico, 2 pf, 1953; Sonatas nos.2–4, 1962, 1964, 1967; Sonata humoristica, 2 pf, 1968; 6½ preludios, 1972

### SONGS

Morena, morena (C. da Paixão Cearense), 1925; Las mujeres son las moscas, 1928; Quando na roça anoitece (R. Guimarães), 1930; Luar do Sertão (Paixão Cearense), 1931; 6 líricas, 1932; Cânticos de Obaluaiê, 1934; Trovas de amor, 1936; 4 líricas (M. Bandeira), 1938; Berimbau (Bandeira), 1942; Pousa a mão na minha testa (Bandeira), 1942; Ruda! ruda! (Andrade), 1947; Cantiga do ai (Andrade), 1947; Violão do capadócio, 1953; Modinha, 1959; Poema para Manuel Bandeira, 1964; 7 líricas, 1967

### BIBLIOGRAPHY

F. Mignone: *A parte do anjo: autocrítica de um cinqüentenário* (São Paulo, 1947)
*Composers of the Americas*, iv (Washington, DC, 1958)
V. Mariz: *A canção brasileira* (Rio de Janeiro, 1959)
M. de Andrade: *Música, doce música* (São Paulo, 1963)
M. Verhaalen: 'Francisco Mignone: his Music for Piano', *Inter-American Music Bulletin* (1970–71), no.79, p.1

GERARD BÉHAGUE

**Mignot, de la Voye.** *See* LA VOYE-MIGNOT, DE.

**Migot, Georges** (*b* Paris, 27 Feb 1891; *d* Levallois, nr. Paris, 5 Jan 1976). French composer. His father was a pastor and doctor, and Migot's concern for spiritual and humane values was instilled from his earliest years. In 1909 he entered the Paris Conservatoire, studying composition with Widor, orchestration with d'Indy and music history with Emmanuel. Badly wounded at the outset of World War I, he resumed his studies after a long convalescence; he won three successive composition prizes (1918–20). In 1921 he won the Blumenthal Foundation Prize for French Thought and Art for a body of work that was already considerable and showed great originality. At the same time he was producing remarkable paintings (exhibitions of his work were held at the Georges Petit Gallery in 1917 and at the Marcel Bernheim Gallery in 1919); he also published a volume of *Essais* (1920) and two volumes of *Poèmes* (1950–51). The years 1920–39 were ones of constant struggle – in music, writings and discussion – against the neo-classical aesthetic which was dominating music in Paris. Always an independent, Migot took nothing from this or any other fashionable movement; instead he continued to pursue his own ideas, steadily adding to his monu-mental oeuvre. From 1949 to 1961 he was keeper of the Museum of Instruments at the Conservatoire. He was an Officer of the Légion d'honneur.

His earliest works, possibly influenced by Fauré's late music, show a trend from harmonic writing to the linear style of such pieces as the Trio (before 1919) for violin, viola and piano. What distinguishes him from his contemporaries – Hindemith or Les Six, for example – is the uncompromisingly polyphonic manner which he progressively evolved. In his mature works he achieved a line which is completely free from rigid metrical restriction and from tonal function, as in the Requiem (1953). While the melody is strictly diatonic, Migot avoided any suggestion of definite tonality; he used the term 'permodality' for this technique. This melodic style is one of the most characteristic features of Migot's music, but his use of timbre is also highly individual, whether in the unusual combinations of his chamber music (e.g. the *Deux stèles* for solo voice, harp, celesta, tam-tam, cymbal and double bass), the subtlety of his orchestral scoring (most notable in the three concertante suites, 1924–6) or the adventurous sonorities of his piano works (e.g. *Le zodiaque*).

The flowing quality of Migot's music sets it in the tradition of Couperin, Rameau and Debussy. However, the visionary imagination displayed in such works as *Le sermon sur la montagne* and *La passion* is essentially original. Migot moulded his thought on biblical philosophy, particularly that of the New Testament: he wrote six oratorios on the life of Christ, as well as other religious works (*Le petit évangéliaire*, *De Christo*, etc), sometimes using his own texts based on the Gospels. His independent poetry, too, is concerned principally with spiritual themes. He insisted on a close spiritual link between text and music, scorning simplistic word-painting, but even in his secular and instrumental works the loftiness of thought is unmistakable.

### WORKS

*(selective list)*

#### STAGE

Hagoromo (symphonie lyrique et chorégraphique, Laloy and Migot), 1920–21; La fête de la bergère (ballet), 1924; Le rossignol en amour (chamber opera, Migot), 1926; Les aveux et les promesses (ballet), 1935; La belle et la bête (opéra chorégraphique, Migot), 1938; Mystère orphique (polyphonie chorégraphique, Migot), 1948; Le zodiaque (chorégraphie lyrique, 4, Migot), 1958–60

#### CHORAL

Le cortège d'Amphitrite (A. Samain), chorus, str orch, 1923; Psaume xix, chorus, orch, 1925; 2 Pieces, pf, chorus, orch, 1934; Le sermon sur la montagne, 5 solo vv, chorus, str orch, 1936; La Passion, solo vv, chorus, orch, 1941–2; L'Annonciation, 2 solo vv, female chorus, str orch, 1945–6; Saint Germain d'Auxerre (Migot), 4 solo vv, 3 choruses, 1947; Suite (Concerto), pf, chorus, 1947–8; La mise au tombeau, chorus, wind qnt, 1949; 10 Vocal Quartets (Migot), chorus, 1949
Cantate d'amour (Migot), 2 solo vv, chorus, orch, 1950; Les Nativités (Migot), chorus, str orch, 1951; Le petit évangéliaire (Migot), 9 choruses, 1952; Psaume cxviii, chorus, wind qnt, timp, 1952; 10 Noëls anciens, chorus, 1952; Requiem, chorus, 1953; La Résurrection, 3 solo vv, chorus, chamber orch, 1953; La Nativité de Notre Seigneur (Migot), 3 solo vv, chorus, fl, bn, str qt, 1954; Cantate pascale (Nuit pascale et Résurrection), 5 solo vv, chorus, chamber orch, 1954
Cantate de la vie meilleure (Migot), children's chorus, youth chorus, chorus, orch, 1956; Du ciel et de mer (Migot), children's chorus, SA, 10 insts, 1961; L'ecclésiaste, Bar, chorus, orch, 1963; In memoriam (Migot), chorus, orch, 1963; La sulamite, 2 solo vv, chorus, chamber orch, 1969; L'arche (Migot), 3-part female chorus, orch, 1971; De Christo (Migot), Bar, chorus, fl, org, 1971–2; Okeanos (Migot), chorus, 1972

#### ORCHESTRAL

Le paravent de laque aux 5 images, before 1917; Sym. no.1 'Les Agrestides', 1919–20; Premier dialogue, vc, orch, 1922; Suite, vn, orch, 1924; Suite, pf, orch, 1925–6; Suite en concert, harp, orch,

1926; Sym. no.2, 1927; Prélude, salut et danse, str, 1927; Prélude pour un poète, 1928; La jungle, org, orch, 1928; Le livre des danceries, 1929

Sym. no.3, 1946; Sym. no.4, 1947; Sym. nos.7–9, 1948–54; Sym. no.6, str, 1951; Sym. no.5 'Sinfonia da chiesa', wind, 1955; Phonie sous-marine, 1960; Sym. no.10, 1962; Pf Conc., 1962; Sym. no.11, wind, 1963; Sym. no.12 'Les nombres', 1964; Conc., hpd, chamber orch, 1964; D'un cercle de l'Enfer du Dante, 1966; Sym. no.13 'Du temps et de l'espace', 1966–7; Little Sym., str, 1970

CHAMBER

Str Qt no.1 '5 mouvements d'eau', before 1917; Le paravent de laque aux 5 images, 2 vn, va, pf, before 1917; Pf Trio, before 1919; Les Agrestides, pf qnt, 1919–20; 3 Pastorales, fl, ob, cl, bn, 1922–3; Qt, fl, vn, cl, harp, 1924; Le premier livre de divertissements français, fl, cl, harp, 1925

Conc., fl, vc, harp, 1929; Le livre des danceries, fl, vn, pf, 1929; Trio [Suite for 3], pf trio, 1935; Wind Trio, 1943–4; Wind Qnt, 1954; Saxophone Qt, 1955; Str Qt no.2, 1957; Qt, fl, vn, vc, pf, 1960; Pf Qt, 1960–61; Trio no.2, fl, vc, harp, 1965; Str Qt no.3, 1966; Trio, fl, vn, hpd, 1968

VOCAL

*(for 1v, pf, unless otherwise stated)*

7 petites images du Japon, before 1917; 4 Songs (G. Kahn), 1917; 3 Songs (T. Derême), 1922; 3 Songs and a Vocalise (A. Spire), 1v, str qt, before 1923; Hommage à Thibaut de Champagne, 1924; 2 stèles (V. Segalen), low v, harp, cel, tam-tam, cymbal, db, 1925; Elégie à Clymène (Derême), 1926; La surprise amoureuse, 1926; 3 monodies (T. Klingsor), 1927; Les chrysanthèmes d'or (J. Bruyr), 1928

3 chants pour 3 poètes, 1929; 3 Poems (G. Normand), 1930; 2 Songs (G. Ville), 1932; Reposoir grave, noble et pur (C. de Saint-Cyr), 1v, fl, harp, 1932; 3 chansons de Margot (P. Lebesgue), 1932; Les poèmes de Brugnon (Klingsor), 17 songs, 1933; 3 berceuses chantées (M. Gevers), 1934–5

Vini vinoque amor (Migot), Mez, T, fl, vc, pf, 1937; 2 Songs (J. Pourtal de Ladevèze), 1938; La retraite ardente (Migot), 1v, fl, vn, vc, 1945; 12 chansons de bord (Migot), 1950; 5 Songs, 1v, str qt, 1951; 3 Songs (Migot), 1v, 2 fl, 1953; 5 quatrains (A. M. Oddo), 1957; 6 Poems (P. Moussarié), 1962

3 sonnets funéraires (A. Lebois), 1965; 5 monodies (Moussarié), 1968; 3 chansons de joie et de souci (Moussarié), 1v, gui, 1969; 2 Songs (Migot), 1v, tpt, vc, org, 1972; 2 dialogues (Migot), 1v, vc, 1972; 5 chants initiatiques (Migot), 1973

KEYBOARD

8 Preludes, pf, 1925; Ad usum delphini, pf, 1927–8; Le petit fablier, pf, 1927; Prélude, salut et danse, pf, 1927; Le zodiaque, pf, 1931–2; Le calendrier du petit berger, pf, 1932; 3 nocturnes dantesques, 1933–4; La nimura, pf, 1934; Premier livre, org, 1937; Le livre d'Anne-Marie, pf, 1939; Sonata 'Polonia', pf, 1939; 5 études en forme de suite, pf r.h., 1941

4 Nocturnes, pf, 1945–6; 12 Préludes, pf, 1946–7; Sonate fuguée, org, 1948; Sonata no.2 'D'octaves', pf, 1951–2; 8 préludes hors du temps, 2 pf, 1957; 10 Variations, pf, 1963; Sonata, 2 pf, 1964–5; Déploration, org, 1965; Deuxième livre, org, 1954–71; Rhapsody, pf duet, 1972; Dialogue, 2 pf, 1973

OTHER INSTRUMENTAL

Dialogue no.1, vn, pf, 1922; Dialogue no.1, vc, pf, 1922; Hommage à Claude Debussy, gui, 1924; Dialogue no.2, vn, pf, 1925–7; 6 Little Preludes, 2 fl, 1927; Dialogue no.2, vc, pf, 1929; Suite, vn, vc, 1929; Suite, fl, 1931; Prélude a 2, hpd, harp, 1931; 3 Pieces, vc, pf, 1932; Suite, fl, 1945; Sonata, fl, pf, 1945; Sonate à danser 'La malouve', vn, pf, 1948; Sonate luthée, harp, 1949; Pastorale, 2 ob, 1950

Sonata no.1, vn, 1951; Sonata, cl, 1953; Sonata, bn, 1953; Sonata, vc, 1954; Suite, 2 rec, 1957; 2 Sonatinas, rec, pf, 1957, 1959; Sonata, vc, pf, 1958; Sonata no.2, vn, 1959; 3 petites prières, harp, 1960; Sonata, gui, 1960; 2 Preludes, 2 gui, 1961; Sonata, 2 gui, 1962; Sonatine en duo, ob, cl, 1962; Suite, 2 vc, 1962; Suite, eng hn, vc, 1963; 3 Nocturnes, harp, 1965

Sonata, fl, gui, 1965; Grave, vn, pf, 1965; Fantaisie 1, fl, pf, 1968; Fantaisie 2, ob, pf, 1968; Fantaisie 3, cl, pf, 1968; Le mariage des oiseaux [28 pieces], fl, 1970; Prélude et choral, trbn, pf, 1970; Epithalame, tpt, org, 1971; 4 Preludes, Celtic harp, 1971; 5 Pieces, fl, org, 1972

Principal publisher: Leduc

WRITINGS

*Essais pour une esthétique générale* (Paris, 1920, 2/1937)
*Appoggiatures résolues et non résolues* (Paris, 1922–31)
*J. Ph. Rameau et le génie de la musique française* (Paris, 1930)
ed. J. Delaye: *Les écrits de G. Migot* (Paris, 1932)
*Lexique de quelques termes utilisés en musique* (Paris, 1947)
*Kaléidoscope et miroirs ou les images multipliées et contraires* (Toulouse, 1970)
*Matériaux et inscriptions* (Toulouse, 1970)

BIBLIOGRAPHY

L. Vallas: *Georges Migot* (Paris, 1923)

E. Vuillermoz: *Musiques d'aujourd'hui* (Paris, 1923)
I. Schwerke: *Kings Jazz and David* (Paris, 1927)
——: 'Georges Migot', *The Dominant*, ed. E. Evans (London, 1928)
P. Wolff: *La route d'un musicien: Georges Migot* (Paris, 1933)
*Quelques extraits critiques consacrés au Zodiaque de Georges Migot* (Paris, 1934)
M. Honegger: 'Georges Migot', *SMz*, xciv (1954), 329
——: 'Georges Migot et la musique religieuse', *Revue d'histoire et de philosophie religieuse*, xxxix (1959), 361
M. Pinchard: *Connaissance de Georges Migot* (Paris, 1959)
G. Leblond and A. Surchamp: 'Saint Germain d'Auxerre', *Zodiaque*, xlv (1960), 1–48
M. Honegger: 'Georges Migot', *Réforme* (25 Feb 1961)
J. Roy: *Présences contemporaines* (Paris, 1962)
M. Honegger: 'Introduction à Georges Migot, musicien', *Profils*, iii (1963), 42 [repr. in *SMz*, cv (1965), 348]
H. Morissette: *L'oratorio français des origines à Georges Migot* (diss., U. of Montreal, 1970)
A. Surchamps: 'Georges Migot ou la foi vécue et contemplée', *Encyclopédie des musiques sacrées*, ii, ed. J. Porte (Paris, 1970), 123
M. Honegger: 'Georges Migot et le chant choral', *Le chef de choeur*, xxxi (1971), 21 [repr. in *Revue musicale de Suisse romande*, xxv/4 (1972), 3]
L. Poirier: 'Georges Migot et la musique d'orgue' (diss., U. of Strasbourg, 1972)
*Georges Migot* (Besançon, 1973) [Musée des Beaux-Arts exhibition catalogue]
J. Viret: 'Mélodie et polymélodie dans l'oeuvre de Georges Migot', *Chant choral* (1976), no.9, p.4
M. Honegger, ed.: *Catalogue des oeuvres musicales de Georges Migot* (Strasbourg, 1977)

MARC HONEGGER

**Migret, Giacomo.** Composer, probably not identifiable with ROBERT MEIGRET.

**Miguel, Mariano Tafall y.** *See* TAFALL Y MIGUEL, MARIANO.

**Miguez, Leopoldo (Américo)** (*b* Niterói, Rio de Janeiro, 9 Sept 1850; *d* Rio de Janeiro, 6 July 1902). Brazilian composer and conductor of Spanish descent. His first music studies were under Nicolau Ribas in Oporto, Portugal, where his father, a businessman, had settled. He returned to Brazil in 1871 and became associated in 1878 with the publishing firm Artur Napoleão. In 1882 his Symphony in B♭ was performed with considerable success. That same year he travelled to Brussels, where he had wanted to study since childhood and where he came under the influence of Wagnerian ideals; upon his return to Rio in 1884 he became the chief advocate of Wagner in Brazil. He served as conductor and director of an opera company for several years. After the proclamation of the Republic (15 November 1889), a hymn of his won first prize in the contest for selecting a new national anthem, but it became simply the *Hino à proclamação da República*. He was appointed director of the newly created National Institute of Music (1890), establishing and implementing new educational policies, and visited several European conservatories in 1895 to obtain ideas and suggestions for the betterment of the institute.

Miguez's works were strongly influenced by the philosophies and musical languages of Wagner and Liszt. He wrote the dramatic poem *Pelo amor!* (1897) and the opera *Os saldunes* (1901), both on librettos by Coelho Neto, the latter 'conceived in the most orthodox Wagnerian spirit', according to Corrêa de Azevedo. The symphonic poems *Parisina*, *Ave, libertas* and *Prometeu* rely on thematic transformation and exhibit the composer's efficient handling of development techniques and of the orchestral palette. His contributions to musical education and concert life in Rio in the last two decades of the 19th century were remarkable.

## WORKS

*(selective list)*

Stage: Pelo amor! (dramatic poem, 2, Coelho Neto), 1897; Os saldunes (opera, 3, Coelho Neto), 1901

Orch: Sym., B♭, 1882; Parisina, sym. poem, op.15, 1888 (Leipzig, 1895); Ave, libertas, sym. poem, op.18, 1890 (Leipzig, 1895); Prometeu, sym. poem no.3, op.21, 1892 (Leipzig, 1895); Suite à l'antique and Ouverture dramática, both 1890s

Pf: Noturno, op.10; Souvenirs, op.20; Scènes intimes, op.24

Other: Vn Sonata; Oda à Benjamin Constant; Hino à proclamação da República, 1890

### BIBLIOGRAPHY

O. Bevilacqua: 'Leopoldo Miguez e o Instituto nacional de música', *Revista brasileira de música*, vii (1940), 10

G. de Melo: *A música no Brasil* (Rio de Janeiro, 1947)

L. H. Corrêa de Azevedo: *150 anos de música no Brasil* (1800–1950) (Rio de Janeiro, 1956)

GERARD BÉHAGUE

**Mihalovich, Ödön Péter József de** (*b* Feričance, Slovenia [now in Yugoslavia], 13 Sept 1842; *d* Budapest, 22 April 1929). Hungarian composer and educationist. While still at school he began to take private music lessons with Mihály Mosonyi in Pest, but it was the influence of Wagner, whose first concert in Pest he attended, that finally decided him on a musical career. He wrote his earliest works, such as the overture to *Timon of Athens*, in about 1860; the first to be published was a *Faust Overture* for piano duet, which already showed the Wagnerian influence that was to characterize his later music. After reading philosophy in Pest, he went to Leipzig in 1865 to study composition under Moritz Hauptmann and completed his education in Munich under Peter Cornelius in 1866.

At about that time he met Wagner and Bülow, whose friend he was to remain; their correspondence provides valuable glimpses into the music and musical life of the day. Mihalovich made his public début as a composer in 1865 when his march for orchestra was played by the Philharmonic Society of Leipzig, and in 1867 the revised version of his *Timon of Athens* overture was performed in Meiningen. The first complete concert of his orchestral works was given in Pest on 6 April 1870. In 1872 he became president of the Wagner Society in Pest, and in 1881 director of the Szinitanoda (drama school). In 1887, shortly after the publication of his important essay on the country's system of musical education, he was appointed principal of the academy of music in Budapest, succeeding Liszt as head of the most important musical institute in the country. In more than 40 years in this post, he greatly contributed to the school's attaining an international reputation and to the general development of Hungarian musical life.

Mihalovich was not only gifted with outstanding organizing and administrative talent, but also with fore-sight, as shown by his role in securing Mahler's ap-pointment at the Royal Hungarian Opera House. More-over, he was an active writer on music, and contributed to the country's earliest musical periodical, *Zenészeti lapok*. As a creative musician, Mihalovich's signific-ance was, as he recognized, minor; yet apart from its profound technical competence, his work shows an aristocratic sensibility. Many of his compositions are wholly under the influence of the New German School; and although his music bears little trace of a Hungarian nationalist idiom, his aversion to new music of the 20th century and even his rejection of the contemporary style of the Hungarian school did not prevent him from sup-porting the most talented figures of the younger genera-tion: Bartók, Kodály and Weiner.

## WORKS

*(principal MS source: H-Bl)*

### OPERAS

Hagbart und Signe (3, A. Stern, after A. Oehlenschläger), 1867–74, Dresden, 12 March 1882

Wieland der Schmied (3, Stern, after R. Wagner), 1876–8

König Fjalar (O. Schlemm), 1880–84, inc.

Eliane (3, H. Herrig, after Tennyson), 1885–7, Budapest, 16 Feb 1908 (Budapest, 1908)

Toldi szerelme [Toldi's Love] (3, G. Csiky and E. Ábrányi, after J. Arany), 1880–90, Budapest, 18 March 1893; rev. 1893–4, Budapest, 28 Feb 1895 (Budapest, 1895)

A tihanyi visszhang [The Echo of Tihany] (G. Moravcsik), 1903, inc.

### ORCHESTRAL

4 syms.: no.1, d, 1879 (Leipzig, c1880); no.2, b, 1892; no.3, a, 1899–1900; no.4, c, 1901–2

Ov. to Timon of Athens, 2nd version, ?1866–7

Das Geisterschiff, ballad (after Count Strachwitz), ?1870–71 (Mainz, 1879)

A sellő [The Naiad], ballad (after P. Gyulai), 1874 (Mainz, 1879)

Hero und Leander, ballade, 1875 (Mainz, 1879)

La Ronde du Sabbat, sym. poem (Mainz, 1879)

Gyász hangok (Trauerklänge), 1876 (Mainz, 1879)

Faust-Fantasie, 1880 (Leipzig, c1880)

Pán halála [Death of Pan] (after G. Reviczky), 1897–8

### OTHER WORKS

Choral: Sturmesmythe (N. Lenau), male vv, orch, 1870; Csatadal [Battle song] (S. Petőfi), male vv, orch, 1871 (Pest, 1873); other choruses for unacc. mixed and male vv

Lieder: c35, incl. settings of Lenau, J. Kerner, Hoffmann von Fallersleben, O. Sternau, Uhland, M. Wesendonck

Chamber: Sonata, E♭, vn, pf, 1861; Ov. to Timon of Athens, pf 4 hands, 1st version, 1860; Faust Ov., pf 4 hands (Pest, 1864); Epithalame pour la noce de la Princesse Paola Borghese, pf 4 hands, 1899; Fantaisie pour piano (Pest, 1870); Nocturne (Pest, 1872)

### WRITINGS

'Franz Liszt und die Beethoven-Feier in Pest', *Pester Lloyd* (25 Dec 1870)

'Der Tannhäuser im Nationaltheater', *Ungarischer Lloyd* (14 March 1871)

'Reformplan des ungarischen Musikunterrichts', *Nemzet* (17 Dec 1887)

'Nemzeti opera- és zeneviszonyainkról' [On the situation of our national opera and music culture], *Zenevilág* (15 Feb 1901)

### BIBLIOGRAPHY

E. Haraszti: *Wagner Richard és Magyarország* [Richard Wagner and Hungary] (Budapest, 1916)

*Zenei szemle*, i/10 (1917) [special Mihalovich number]

E. Major: 'Mihalovich Ödön: tanulmány' [Mihalovich: a study], *Muzsika*, i/5 (1929)

K. Isoz: 'Liszt Cosima levelei Mihalovich Ödönhöz' [Cosima Liszt's letters to Mihalovich], *Énekszó*, xvii/5 (1950)

M. Prahács: 'Kiadatlan és ismeretlen Liszt-levelek a Zeneművészeti főiskola levéltárában' [Unpublished and unknown Liszt letters in the archives of the High School of Music], *Zenetudományi tanulmányok*, ed. D. Bartha and B. Szabolcsi, iii (Budapest, 1955)

'A Zeneművészeti főiskola Liszt-hagyatéka' [The Liszt Bequest in the High School of Music], *Zenetudományi tanulmányok*, ed. D. Bartha and B. Szabolcsi, vii (Budapest, 1959)

H.-L. de Lagrange: *Mahler*, i (London, 1974)

JOHN S. WEISSMANN

**Mihalovici, Marcel** (*b* Bucharest, 22 Oct 1898). French composer of Romanian origin. He studied in Bucharest (1908–19) with Bernfeld (violin), Cuclin (harmony) and Cremer (counterpoint), and at the Schola Cantorum, Paris (1919–25) with d'Indy (composition), Saint Réquier (harmony), Gastoué (Gregorian chant) and Lejeune (violin). In Paris he also had advice from his compatriot Enescu. Mihalovici remained in the French capital, drawing in his music on a wide range of current trends. He married the French pianist Monique Haas.

## WORKS

*(selective list)*

### STAGE

Une vie de Polichinelle (ballet, M. Sauvage), 1922; Le postillon du roy (ballet), 1924; Karageuz (ballet), 1926; L'intransigeant Pluton (opera, Regnard), 1928; Phèdre (opera, Goll, after Racine), 1949; Die Heimkehr (opera, K. H. Ruppel), 1954, rev. 1955; Thésée au labyrinthe (ballet, Ruppel), 1956; Alternamenti (ballet, Rostand), 1957;

Krapp (opera, Beckett), 1960; Les jumeaux (opera buffa, Rostand), 1962; Héracles (incidental music to Euripides: Heraclidae), 1975

ORCHESTRAL

Le cortège des divinités infernales, 1928; Chindia, 1929; Vn Conc., 1930; Caprice romanien, 1936; Toccata, pf, orch, 1938, rev. 1940; Symphonies pour le temps présent, 1944; Variations, brass, str, 1946; Séquences, 1947; Rhapsodie concertante, pf, orch, 1951; Sinfonia giocosa, 1951; Etude en 2 parties, pf, orch, 1951; Sinfonia partita, 1952; Elégie, 1955; Ouverture tragique, 1957
Esercizio, str, 1959; Sinfonia variata, 1960; Nocturne, cl, orch, 1963; Prétextes, ob, cl, bn, chamber orch, 1968; Sym. no.5, 1966–9; Refrains, 1969; Chant premier, ten sax, pf/orch, 1973; Follia, 1976–7

VOCAL AND CHAMBER

3 poèmes chinois, 1918–20; Chansons et danses, 1924; 3 romances (Hugo), 1929; Abendgesang (Goll), 1957; Sinfonia cantata, Bar, chorus, orch, 1953–63; Stanzas (M. Dumitrescu), 1967; Cantilène (Y. Sandro), Mez, chamber orch, 1972; Prétextes, 1974
Pf Sonatina, 1923; 3 str qts, 1923, 1931, 1946; Sonatina, ob, pf, 1924; 2 sonatas, vn, pf, 1927, 1941; Str Trio, 1929; Sonata, 3 cl, 1933; Ricercari, pf, 1941; Sonata, va, pf, 1942; Sonata, vn, vc, 1944; Sonata, vc, 1949; Sonata, vn, 1949; Wind Trio, 1955; Sonata, bn, pf, 1958; Sonata, cl, pf, 1958; Dialogues, cl, pf, 1964; Pf Sonata, 1964; Cantus firmus, 2 pf, 1970; Variantes, hn, pf, 1970; Serioso, b saxhn, pf, 1971; Récit, cl, 1973; Mélopée, ob, 1973; Passacaille, pf, left hand, 1975

Principal publishers: Amphion, Billandot, Bote & Bock, Editions Françaises de Musique, Eschig, Heugel, Leduc, Mogador, Muzicală, Pro musica

BIBLIOGRAPHY

G. Beck: *Marcel Mihalovici: esquisse biographique* (Paris, 1952)
M. Deutsch: 'Phèdre de Marcel Mihalovici', *Revue de musique* (1952)
*Marcel Mihalovici: catalogue de l'oeuvre* (Paris, 1968) [incl. preface by C. Rostand]
Z. Vancea: *Creaţia muzicală românească* (Bucharest, 1968), 396ff
V. Cosma: *Muzicieni români* (Bucharest, 1970), 307ff

VIOREL COSMA

**Mihály, András** (b Budapest, 7 Nov 1917). Hungarian composer, conductor and teacher. He entered the Budapest Academy of Music in 1934 as a cello pupil of Schiffer, and he also studied in the chamber music class of Waldbauer and Weiner. Although he began his career as a cellist, he took private lessons in composition with Kadosa and Strasser. His artistic development was greatly affected by World War II and the political struggles of the period. In 1941 he joined the illegal communist party; he directed workers' choirs and propagated new music (chiefly the works of Bartók, Schoenberg, Berg and Hindemith) within the framework of private concerts given by his own string quartet. His own compositions of the period, such as the Piano Trio and the First Quartet, came about under the influences of Bartók and the Second Viennese School. At the same time he became concerned with the problems of educating, and communicating with, a larger audience, and his first cantata, *Szabadság és béke* ('Freedom and peace'), was composed for a Petőfi festival organized in 1942 to unite anti-fascist forces. In 1944 Mihály was arrested for his activities in the resistance movement.

After the liberation, in 1946, he composed his first symphony, subtitled 'Sinfonia da requiem', in memory of those killed as a result of war and persecution. Mihály became solo cellist at the State Opera, general secretary of the Philharmonia Society and general secretary of the State Opera (1948–50). In 1950 he was appointed professor of chamber music at the Budapest Academy. As a summary of his evolution until then, he composed the Cello Concerto in 1953, mainly under the influence of Kodály. After this Mihály set himself to follow and assimilate the example of Bartók. The first works resulting from this intention were the Piano Concerto (1954) and the Fantasie (1955) for wind quintet and orchestra. These pieces exhibit a rather direct dependence on

Bartók that was overcome in the Violin Concerto (1959), which incorporates neo-Baroque ideas.

In 1962 Mihály was appointed music adviser to the music section of Hungarian broadcasting. He received the Erkel Prize in 1964 for the third time; he had already been awarded the Kossuth Prize in 1955. A group of elaborate chamber pieces was succeeded by the Third Symphony (1962), constructed as a fresco of isolated points and close, in technique and aesthetic, to pre-serial Schoenberg. In 1964–5 Mihály composed a three-act opera to his own text, *Együtt es egyedül* ('Together and alone'), drawing on his wartime experiences. From 1965 he became more closely connected with avant-garde music. He founded the Budapest Chamber Ensemble in 1968 for the performance of new Hungarian and foreign works. Concurrently his own music grew more widely known internationally with performances in Zagreb, Darmstadt, Warsaw and London. Works written during this period, such as the Three Movements (1969) for ensemble and the orchestral *Monodia* (1970), show Mihály employing clusters, controlled aleatory writing and other novel developments.

WORKS

(selective list)

Opera: Együtt es egyedül [Together and alone] (3, Mihály), 1964–5
Orch: 3 syms., 1946, 1950, 1962; Vc Conc., 1953; Pf Conc., 1954; Fantasia, wind qnt, harp, cel, perc, orch, 1955; Festive Ov., 1959; Vn Conc., vn, obbl. pf, chamber orch, 1959; Monodia, 1970
Chamber: Pf Trio, 1940; 2 str qts, 1942, 1960; Rhapsody, va, pf, 1947; Serenade, wind trio, 1956; 3 Movements, ens, 1969
Vocal: Chamber Music (Joyce), 1v, pf, 1958; Attila József Songs, 1v, pf, 1961; 3 Apocrypha, 3 female vv, cl, perc, 1962; Az áhitat zsoltárai [Psalms of rapture] (M. Radnoti), 1v, pf; 5 cantatas, 3 choral pieces
Inst pieces, pf works, incidental music for the theatre and cinema

Principal publisher: Editio Musica

BIBLIOGRAPHY

J. Kárpáti: *Mihály András* (Budapest, 1965)
P. Várnai: 'The Middle Generation', *Tempo* (1969), no.88, p.25
*Contemporary Hungarian Composers* (Budapest, 1970), 90f
G. Kroó: *A magyar zeneszerzés 25 éve* [25 years of Hungarian music] (Budapest, 1971), 68f, 114ff

JÁNOS KÁRPÁTI

**Mihi, Orazio.** See MICHI, ORAZIO.

**Mijwiz.** Double clarinet with six paired finger-holes and with idioglott reeds, played mainly in Syria (*see* LEBANON, fig.3). An instrument of this type is more widely known throughout the Middle East as MIZMĀR.

**Mikeš, Adolf** (b Hradec Králové [Königgratz], 23 Dec 1864; d Prague, 26 May 1929). Czech piano teacher. After preliminary musical education at Hradec Králové, he studied law and painting in Prague and later in Vienna. On his return to Prague he continued music studies with Josef Klička and Jindřich Kàan, becoming the latter's assistant at the conservatory. Unsuccessful in his pursuit of a solo career, he turned to teaching and founded his own piano school, first in Plzeň and later in Prague. He carefully studied the Deppe piano method which, in combination with Batka's principles of music education, he elaborated as the basis of his own method. Harmony, music history, theory and aesthetics were also taught at his school. When he refused to submit the school to an official inspection he was obliged to retire and hand it over to his pupils; after 1918 he was professor at the Prague Conservatory.

Mikeš made a valuable contribution to the Czech school of piano playing, both by broadening its range through his introduction of the Deppe method and by teaching many distinguished players, a number of whom later became professors at the Prague Conservatory. His importance goes beyond his pedagogical activities; he was also an enlightened musical personality, who published many articles in newspapers and music journals and gathered round him a group of progressive musicians, among them the composer Vítězslav Novák.

BIBLIOGRAPHY

ČSHS

H. Jonášová: 'Adolf Mikeš', Sborník na paměť 125 let konservatoře hudby v Praze [Commemorative volume for the 125th anniversary of the Prague Conservatory] (Prague, 1936), 220

Z. Böhmová: 'Adolf Mikeš', HRo, i (1948–9), 237

MIROSLAV K. ČERNÝ

**Mikhaylov, Maxim (Dormidontovich)** (b Koltsovka, nr. Kazan, 25 Aug 1893; d Moscow, 30 March 1971). Soviet bass. He sang in a church choir from the age of nine and studied singing with F. Oshustovich in Kazan and V. Osipov in Moscow. He was a soloist with the All-Union Radio from 1930 to 1932 and at the Bol'shoy Theatre from 1932. He sang mainly in Russian operas, his great parts being Susanin, Konchak, Pimen (which he sang in the film of Boris Godunov, 1955), and the Viking Guest (Sadko). The rare power and tonal beauty of his voice were impressive in heroic-epic roles, while in a part such as Chub (Tchaikovsky's The Slippers) he displayed a sharp sense of comedy. He was made People's Artist of the USSR in 1940.

BIBLIOGRAPHY

V. Endrzheyevsky and E. Osipov: M. Mikhaylov (Moscow, 1957)

I. M. YAMPOL'SKY

**Mikhaylova, Maria (Alexandrovna)** (b Kharkov, 3 June 1866; d Molotov [now Perm], 18 Jan 1943). Russian lyric soprano. She studied in St Petersburg, Paris and Milan, and made her début in 1892 as the Queen (Les Huguenots) at the Imperial Opera, St Petersburg; she remained there until 1912, apart from frequent tours in Russia, one to Prague and its neighbouring region (1903) and one to Tokyo (1907). She was the first Electra in Taneyev's Oresteia (1895); and her repertory included Mozart's and Auber's Zerlina, Aennchen (Der Freischütz), Carolina (Matrimonio segreto), Berthe (Le prophète), Juliette, Nanetta (Falstaff), Gilda, Lakmé, Micaela, Tamara (The Demon) and Glinka's Lyudmila and Antonida. With a pure, musical voice, she was the first singer to achieve world fame, from 1900, through the gramophone alone. By 1913 she had made over 320 recordings.

BIBLIOGRAPHY

E. Stark: Peterburgskaya opera i eyo mastera [The St Petersburg opera and its stars] (Leningrad, 1940)

A. Favia-Artsay: 'Marie Michailowá', Hobbies (1954), June, 22

H. Barnes: 'Maria Michailova', Recorded Sound (1969), no.33, p.354 [with discography]

HAROLD BARNES

**Mikhaylov-Stoyan, Konstantin Ivanovich** (b Golyam Boyalak, Bessarabia, 25 March 1853; d Sofia, 13 June 1914). Bulgarian tenor. He was the first Bulgarian opera singer and producer, and one of the founders of Bulgarian opera. Born Konstantin Ivanovich Mikhaylov, the son of Bulgarian emigrants to Bessarabia, he adopted the typically Bulgarian name Stoyan in order to stress his origins. He studied in Odessa, sang in a choir as soloist, worked as a teacher and studied for several months at the St Petersburg Conservatory. He also toured Russia in various opera companies, and in 1888 became soloist at the Bol'shoy

Theatre in Moscow. There he sang until 1899, when he went for the first time to Bulgaria to give concerts. He returned to Russia as guest artist in different opera houses (in 1902 together with Shalyapin) and in Helsinki; he was also lecturer at the music school in Vilnius, and in 1905 became headmaster of the music school at Rostov-na-Donu. In 1907 Mikhaylov-Stoyan gave successful concerts in Bulgaria with two other Bulgarian opera singers from Bessarabia (Ivan Vulpe and Bogdana Gyuzeleva-Vulpe). This led to the foundation in the same year of the Operna Druzhba (Opera Association) which marked the beginning of opera performances in Sofia. Mikhaylov-Stoyan's repertory included many leading tenor parts from operas by Verdi, Wagner, Gounod, Mascagni and above all by Russian composers, and a large number of Bulgarian folksongs. He staged several operas in Sofia and wrote many articles in Bulgarian and Russian as well as a book, Po vaprosa za osnovavaneto na Balgarskata narodna opera ('On the foundation of the Bulgarian National Opera', Sofia, 1907).

LADA BRASHOVANOVA

**Miki, Minoru** (b Tokushima, Shikoku, 16 March 1930). Japanese composer. He was brought up in a musical household, several members of his family being accomplished performers on Japanese instruments. At high school he had his first encounters with European music as a member of a choral group, and at the age of 20 he began to study the piano and harmony with the aim of becoming a professional musician. He studied composition with Ifukube and Ikenouchi at the Tokyo Geijutsu Daigaku (National University of Fine Arts and Music) from 1951 to 1955. In 1953 he won second prize in the Japanese radio competition for orchestral works with Kōkyōteki sangakushō (or Trinità sinfonica), and after graduating he continued to write large works for European orchestra while supporting himself by composing for films, particularly documentary and educational ones. Around 1960 he turned his attention to choral music. He joined the Tokyo Liedertafel in 1961 and wrote many pieces for it; in 1963 the group gave a concert entirely of his works. Meanwhile, in 1962, he had composed his first piece for traditional Japanese instruments, Sonnet for three shakuhachi. Together with a number of players on Japanese instruments he organized the Ensemble Nipponia in 1964; the group had given seven official concerts by 1967, when it received the government-sponsored Art Festival Prize, and Miki established himself as a leading composer for traditional forces. In 1968 he took the Tokyo Liedertafel to Europe and gave a series of concerts in West Germany. Two years later an anthology of his music, including a specially commissioned work, was issued on disc, winning the grand prix at the Art Festival of the same year. Miki was appointed general secretary of the Japanese section of the ISCM in 1972, and in the autumn of that year he led the Ensemble Nipponia on a European tour, the first of several foreign visits.

Miki mastered the techniques of European art music with astonishing rapidity; his command is displayed fully in the early expressionist orchestral works, which already show a sensitivity to instrumental timbre and a fascination with extra-European music. His early instrumental works and a large number of choral pieces of 1960–63 demonstrate his attempts to combine European and oriental features in his own style. However, the formation of the Ensemble Nipponia marked a turning-point: from then on he gradually departed from the European tradition and began to explore original techniques appropriate to Japanese instruments. In doing so he depended a great deal on effective combinations of timbre and a strong sense of rhythm; his rhythms may be determinedly violent, irregular in beat or completely free and improvisatory, while he has benefited from his close contact with performers in developing music requiring a high degree of virtuosity. Indeed, much of his music since 1960 has been written for specific artists, in particular the Tokyo Liedertafel and the Ensemble Nipponia. In 1968 he met the koto virtuoso Keiko Nosaka, for whom he has written a series of pieces; and he has also composed for the marimba virtuoso Keiko Abe.

## WORKS
*(selective list)*

Stage: Mendori teishu [Husband the hen] (operetta), Tokyo, 1963; Kikimimi (children's musical play), 1967; Shunkin shō (opera), Tokyo, 1975

Choral: Mittsu no Awa no warabe-uta [3 children's ballads from Awa], 1960; Hikari o otte [Chasing the light], 1961; Furuki Indoshina no uta [Old songs from Indochina], 1961; Umi no sei [Ode to oceanid], 1962; Awa, choral poem, 1962; Mogura no monogatari [Mole's tale], 1966; Habataki no uta [Ballad for winging], 1968; Gaki [Hungry devil], 1970; Dansei banka-shū [Barbaric glees], 1971

Other vocal works: Shunrai [Spring thunder], Bar, pf, 1960; Kurudando, cantata, 1963; Requiem, 1963; Sōmon II, 1v, koto, 1972; Muma no shirabe, 1v, koto, db, 1974

Orch: Kōkyōteki sangakushō (Trinità sinfonica), 1953; Gamulan kōkyōkyoku (Sinfonia Gamula), 1957; Joya [New Year's eve], sym., 1960; Mar Conc., 1969; Ha no kyoku, koto, orch, 1974

Chamber: Osabai, wind, perc, 1955; Natsu no jojishi (Poema estiva), pf, 1958; Sonnet, 3 shakuhachi, 1962; Sextet, wind, pf, 1965; 2 Eclogues, shino-bue, noh-kan, 3 perc, 1966; Kodai bukyoku ni yoru parafurēzu [Paraphrase after ancient Japanese dances], Japanese ens, 1966; Yongun no tame no keishō [Figures for 4 groups], Japanese ens, 1967–9; Marimba no toki [Time for mar], mar, 1968; Sō tanshi-shū [Ballads], koto, 1969; Jo no kyoku, shakuhachi, koto, sangen, str, 1969; Tennyo, koto, 1969; Kokyō, shakuhachi, 1970; Totsu [Convexity], 3 Japanese ens, perc, 1970; Saho no kyoku [The Venus in spring], koto, 1971; Tatta no kyoku [The Venus in autumn], koto, 1971; Miyabi no uta, shakuhachi, jūshichigen, 1971; Hakuyō vn koto, 1973; Ne-tori, Japanese ens, 1973; Participation, Japanese ens, 1973; 3 festal ballades, 4 koto, 1975; Hinaburi, jūnigen, fl, 1975; Kagura 1976, Japanese ens, 1976; Wa, Japanese ens, 1976; Hote, Japanese ens, 1976

Principal publishers: Kawai Gakufu, Ongaku-no-Tomo Sha, Zen-on Gakufu

MASAKATA KANAZAWA

**Mikley-Kemp, Barbara.** *See* KEMP, BARBARA.

**Mikołaj z Krakowa** [Nicolaus Cracoviensis] (*fl* 1st half of the 16th century). Polish composer and organist. He is known from works signed N. C. or Nicolai Crac. in two Kraków keyboard tablatures: the Jan z Lublina tablature (in *PL-Kp*) and the Kraków Tablature (now lost) formerly in the Monastery of the Holy Ghost. The two manuscripts have 40 compositions in common including two ascribed to N. C. Some works signed N. Z. in the Kraków Tablature may also be by this composer (see White). The works, many bearing dates (from 1537 to 1546) include some pieces specifically for keyboard, and also intabulations of vocal works. Some of the vocal pieces signed N. C. may be transcriptions of unidentified compositions by other composers. It is uncertain how many of the dances following 'Sequuntur coree' (*Kp* Jan z Lublina tablature, ff.213v–224r) are attributed to N. C.

The composer is of great importance for his contribution to the development of polyphony in Poland: his works illustrate the process of transition from three- to four-part polyphonic textures, and the transcriptions of contemporary popular dances and dance-songs are the oldest Polish examples of this type of composition.

## WORKS
*(all intabulated for kbd, in Jan z Lublina tablature, PL-Kp)*

Editions: *36 tańców z tabulatury organowej Jana z Lublina*, ed. A. Chybiński, WDMP, xx (1948) [C]
    *Jan z Lublina: Tablature of Keyboard Music*, ed. J. R. White, CEKM, vi/1–6 (1964–6) [W i–vi]
    *Tabulatura organowa Jana z Lublina*, facs. ed. K. Wilkowska-Chomińska, MMP, ser. B, i (1964)

2 mass movements: Kyrie 'Lux et origo', 4vv, W i, 63; Patrem per octavas, 4vv, W i, 35

4 introits: Benedicta sit Sancta Trinitas, 4vv, W ii, 21; Cibavit eos, 4vv, W ii, i; Gaudeamus omnes, 4vv, W ii, 11; Resurrexi et adhuc tecum sum, 4vv, W ii, 15

6 motets: Ave ierarchia, 4vv, W iii, 90; De sancto Johanne Baptista, 4vv, W iii, 72; Muteta Philipe qui videt me resolutum, 5vv, W iii, 49; Nunc rogemus, 5vv, W iii, 95; Quem preces, 4vv, W iii, 82

1 Salve regina, 4vv, W iii, 80

2 Pol. sacred songs: Nasz Zbawiciel, W v, 54; Wesel się polska corona, W v, 44

1 Ger. song: Ach hilph mich laith, 4vv, W iv, 12

Dance compositions: Aleć nade mną Wenus, W v, 46; ?others, W v, 22, C

3 praeambula, F (f.91v), D, F: Wi, 7, 9, 15

1 untitled work: Resolutum, W v, 69

## BIBLIOGRAPHY

A. Chybiński: 'Tabulatura organowa Jana z Lublina (1540)', *KM*, i (1911), 9, 122, 217–52, 297–340

Z. Jachimecki: *Wpływy włoskie w muzyce polskiej* [Italian influences in Polish music] (Kraków, 1911), 1–41

——: *Tabulatura organowa z biblioteki klasztoru Św. Ducha w Krakowie z r. 1548* (Kraków, 1913)

J. R. White: 'The Tablature of Johannes de Lublin', *MD*, xvii (1963), 137

K. Wilkowska-Chomińska: *Twórczość Mikołaja z Krakowa* (Kraków, 1967) [with full work-list]

B. Brzezińska: 'W kwestii autorstwa motetu *Date siceram moerentibus*', *Muzyka*, xxi/2 (1976), 53

ZYGMUNT M. SZWEYKOWSKI

**Mikuli, Karol** [Miculi, Carol (Carl)] (*b* Czernowitz [now Chernovtsy], 20 Oct 1819; *d* Lwów, 21 May 1897). Polish pianist, composer, conductor and teacher of Moldavian origin. From 1839 to 1844 he studied medicine in Vienna, then moved to Paris, where until 1847 he was a pupil of Chopin. At the same time he studied composition under N. H. Reber. As a pianist he made successful tours of France, Austria, Russia and Romania. In 1858 he settled permanently in Lwów and became artistic director of the Galician Music Society, whose symphony orchestra and chorus he conducted. He was also director and professor of the Lwów Conservatory, where he taught the piano, composition and theory. After 1887 he opened a separate piano school which he ran with his wife. In the last years of his life he suffered from a persecution mania and withdrew from active musical life.

Mikuli composed a large number of piano works (for two and four hands) as virtuoso practice pieces, often in the form of lyrical miniatures and dances. He also wrote chamber music, songs and choral works, such as the mass composed for the consecration of Czernowitz Cathedral. The chamber music includes numerous paraphrases and arrangements of popular works; all his music is in an early Romantic style. His textbook *Der Canon* remains unpublished, but his Chopin edition (Leipzig, 1879) long enjoyed wide circulation. As a pupil for whom Chopin had a high regard, and whom he made his assistant, Mikuli was able to take into account the directions and remarks of the composer himself.

## BIBLIOGRAPHY

*SMP*

M. Biernacki: 'Karol Mikuli', *Echo muzyczne, teatralne i artystyczne*, (1897), no.713, p.353

M. Sołtys: 'Karol Mikuli', *Wiadomości artystyczne*, xi (1897), 13

R. Koczalski: 'Jak grał i uczył Karol Mikuli' [How Karol Mikuli played and taught], *Muzyka*, vii–viii (1937), 216

O. Beu: 'Carol Mikuli, un prieten romîn al lui Chopin' [Karol Mikuli, Chopin's Romanian friend], *Studii muzicologice*, vi (1957), 43

Z. Vancea: 'Der Chopin-Schüler Carol Mikuli, ein Bindeglied zwischen rumänischer und polnischer Musikkultur', *Chopin Congress: Warszawa 1960*, 410

H. Federhofer: 'Der Chopin-Schüler Carl Mikuli in Rom und Graz', *DJbM*, x (1965), 82

JERZY MORAWSKI

**Mila, Massimo** (*b* Turin, 14 Aug 1910). Italian music critic and writer. At Turin University he studied art with Lionello Venturi, French literature with Ferdinando Neri and music with Alberto Gentili; for his arts degree he wrote a thesis on Verdi (1931). In all his work he has been much influenced by studies in Croce's aesthetics. He was arrested for anti-fascist activities in 1929 and again in 1935, and given a seven-year prison sentence which he served until 1940; after the war he helped in reorganizing the government. He has taught music history at Turin Conservatory (1953–73) and University (appointed 1960) and worked as music critic of the prestigious Turin weekly *L'espresso* (1955–68) and the daily *La stampa* (1968–74). His theory of 'espressione inconsapevole', explained in *L'esperienza musicale*, suggests that an artist may achieve the highest possible aesthetic expression (in Croce's sense) even though his aims may be only technical; such composers as Stravinsky are analysed in this light. His *Breve storia della musica* offers the only compact yet comprehensive account of the subject in Italian. He has also written extensively on Verdi and Mozart. As a critic he is generally conservative towards avant-garde music, responding chiefly to Italian composers. He became a member of the S Cecilia Academy in 1956. His work outside music has included translations of Goethe, Schiller, Hesse and Wiechert, criticism (e.g. on his friend Pavesi), novels and articles on mountain climbing.

### WRITINGS

*Il melodramma di Verdi* (Bari, 1933/*R*1958 as *Verdi*)

'Musica e ritmo nel cinematografo', *I° congresso internazionale di musica: Firenze 1933*, 209

*Cent'anni di musica moderna* (Milan, 1944)

*Saggi mozartiani* (Milan, 1945)

*W. A. Mozart* (Turin, 1945)

*Breve storia della musica* (Milan, 1946, 2/1963)

'La melurgia bizantina', *RMI*, xlviii (1946), 193

'Sul carattere inconsapevole dell'espressione artistica', *6° congresso internazionale di musica: Firenze 1949*, 87

*L'esperienza musicale e l'estetica* (Turin, 1950, 3/1965)

'La natura e il mistero nell'arte di Béla Bartók', *RaM*, xxi (1951), 95; enlarged in *Chigiana*, xxii (1965), 147

'*La carriera d'un libertino*' di Strawinsky (Milan, 1952)

'Razionalismo di "Così fan tutte" ', *Mozart: la vita e le opere*, ed. F. Armani (Milan, 1956), 195

*Cronache musicali 1955–1959* (Turin, 1959)

*La mia vita* (Turin, 1959) [trans. of R. Wagner: *Mein Leben*, Munich, 1911]

'La linea Nono', *RaM*, xxx (1960), 297

'La dialogizzazione dell'aria nelle opere giovanili di Verdi', *I° congresso internazionale di studi verdiani: Venezia 1966*, 222

'"Il turco in Italia", manifesto di dolce vita', *NRMI*, ii (1968), 857

'La fortuna di Rossini', *Bollettino del Centro rossiniano*, new ser., ii (1968), 1

'Bartók–Webern 25 Years Later: their Place in Today's Music', *World Music*, xii/3 (1970), 32

'Fétis e Verdi, ovvero Gli infortuni della critica', *3° congresso internazionale di studi verdiani: Milano 1972*, 312

'Casorati e la musica', *Quadrivium*, xiv (1973), 65

'*I vespri siciliani*' di Verdi (Turin, 1973)

'Lettura della "Grande fuga" op.133', *Scritti in onore di Luigi Ronga* (Milan and Naples, 1973), 345

'Piero Gobetti e la musica', *RMI*, x (1976), 91

*Il posto della musica* (in preparation)

BIBLIOGRAPHY

G. Pestelli, ed.: *Il melodramma italiano dell'ottocento: studi e ricerche per Massimo Mila* (Turin, 1977)

CAROLYN M. GIANTURCO

**Miładowski, Florian Stanisław** (*b* Minsk, 4 May 1819; *d* Bordeaux, 8 July 1889). Polish pianist, conductor, teacher and composer. He was the son of Fabian Miładowski, a music teacher who gave him his first piano instruction. Later he studied under Thiebe in Vilnius. Further study followed at the Gesellschaft der Musikfreunde in Vienna under Joseph Fischof (counterpoint), Franz Hauser (singing), Simon Sechter and F. S. Hölzl (composition). After a short stay in Berlin, and a visit to France, he returned to his own country, where he taught music and conducted the then celebrated orchestra of Benedykt Count Tyszkiewicz at the Czerwony Dwór (Red Manor), near Kaunas. He next moved to Vilnius, where he taught music. In 1854 he and Moniuszko founded the Society of St Cecilia, the aim of which was the cultivation of church music. He then spent some time at his estate in Macki, near Minsk, but in 1862 left for France, where he worked in Metz, Nancy and Bordeaux. Miładowski composed a number of orchestral works, some chamber music (a string quartet and three piano trios) and pieces for piano (three sonatas, lyrical miniatures and dances). He also wrote an operetta *Konkurenci* ('The Rivals'), to a libretto by M. Łapicki and W. Syrokomla (Minsk, 12 Feb 1861), and numerous religious works. During the period 1857–60 he also published reviews and articles in *Ruch muzyczny*.

BIBLIOGRAPHY

*SMP*

'Florian Miładowski', *Echo muzyczne, teatralne i artystyczne* (1889), no.312, p.449

JERZY MORAWSKI

**Milan** (It. *Milano*; Ger. *Mailand*; Lat. *Mediolanum*). Italian city, capital of Lombardy.

1. Up to 1500. 2. 1500–1700. 3. 18th century. 4. 19th century. 5. 20th century.

1. UP TO 1500. Milan probably existed before the invasion of the Gauls or the Celts, to whom the foundation of the city in the late 5th century BC is attributed. The political and economic importance of Milan grew further in the 3rd century AD, and in 313 Constantine promulgated the famous edict favouring Christianity there; with Constantium II (352) Milan became the effective capital of the Roman Empire. Soon afterwards AMBROSE, who came to be the symbol of Milan, arrived in the city; at first he was consular governor (*c*370), and he was elected bishop by the people in 374. Milanese (also called Ambrosian) chant is the earliest Western repertory of liturgical music to have survived parallel to the Gregorian repertory, and only in the 20th century has it begun to be undermined as a result of liturgical reforms. The independence of the Milanese rite was due to the political and ecclesiastical authority commanded by the city during the Middle Ages, and it was reinforced by the prestige associated with Ambrose, to whom the Milanese chant and liturgy had been traditionally attributed, together with the introduction of antiphonal singing from the East. It is certain only that he wrote the texts for four or six hymns. Milanese chant is characterized by a strong Eastern influence (Byzantine and Graeco-Syrian) but built on a nucleus apparently of local origin. The long tradition of

Milanese chant was fostered and maintained through the establishment of a *schola cantorum* conducted by a *magister chori puerorum*, which may have been founded by Ambrose. His successor, Simpliciano, is said to have enlarged the *schola* and appointed at least three *magistri cum ferulis*. The Milanese chronicler Landolfus the Elder reported that Archbishop Ariberto d'Intimiano (1018–45) reorganized the *schola* and the children were taught in the cathedral by four priests, including Arialdo and Azzone in the first half of the 12th century, and Eriprando and Ogero in 1144. Perhaps during Ariberto's tenure, but at least in the first half of the 12th century, the practice of two-voice polyphony was known at the cathedral.

The only Ars Nova composer connected with Milan appears to have been Jacopo da Bologna, who was at the Visconti court during the reign of Luchino (1339–49) and after 1352. The Milanese were always specially inclined towards religious music, about which the first official document was issued by the provincial council in 1311. When it was decided that a new cathedral be built, Gian Galeazzo Visconti, in his proclamation establishing the prerogatives of the deputies entrusted with its construction (1394), included regulations for the cathedral's music. In the same year the first organist was appointed, magister Montus a Prato, and the cathedral *cappella* was essentially established. Matteo da Perugia was appointed *biscantor* in 1402, remaining until 1407 and later returning in 1414 for two years; from 1411 the post was held by Ambrogio da Pessano. Matteo was in effect the first of a long series of outstanding *maestri di cappella* and was followed by Beltrame Feragut (1425–30), Ambrosius da Pessano (appointed 1430) and Santino Taverna.

There is evidence of only limited musical activity in the Duchy of Milan under the rule of the Visconti (to 1447) and during the short-lived Ambrosian Republic (1447–50). This changed with the advent of the Sforza family, which began in 1450 with Francesco I (*see* SFORZA). Under Francesco, who had married Bianca Maria Visconti, but especially under his son and successor, Galeazzo Maria, sacred and secular music reached its greatest splendour. The cathedral *cappella* grew to include 12 first-rate singers (Josquin among them, 1459–72) with Giovanni Molli and Gaffurius (1484–1522) as *maestri*, and in 1491 Bartolomeo Antegnati built a fine organ in the cathedral. Galeazzo Maria Sforza established a court ensemble in 1473, recruiting the best French and Flemish singers and composers, which by 1474 included 18 *cantori di camera* and 22 *cantori di cappella*, and which became one of the most important ensembles of the period; Weerbeke (?1471–80), Josquin (?1473–?1479), Johannes Martini (1474) and Compère (1474–5) were among the members of the *cappella* at its height. But many musicians began to leave the Sforza court after the murder of Galeazzo Maria in December 1476. Under Galeazzo's brother Ludovico il Moro, who seized power from his brother's widow in 1479, splendid musical festivities, some with sets and machinery designed by Leonardo da Vinci, were organized at court; Bellincioni's *Festa del Paradiso* with music by Gaffurius was staged for the wedding festivities of Gian Galeazzo Sforza and Isabella of Aragon in 1489. The high level of musical life at court was largely due to Beatrice d'Este, Ludovico's wife. Ludovico also established a Gymnasium in Milan in 1492 at which Gaffurius lectured on music; other professors included Luca Pacioli and Facius Cardanus. During his 38 years in Milan, Gaffurius established a reputation as one of the leading musical figures of the time; he wrote his major theoretical treatises and composed most of his music there. Although the cathedral *cappella* was dominated by Italians and the court *cappella* by Netherlanders, the relationship between the two was cordial and there were frequent interchanges of musical forces.

2. 1500–1700. In 1535 Sforza rule ended, and for nearly two centuries Milan came under Spanish rule; a long period of general decadence began, which had repercussions in musical development and inhibited the development of an autonomous tradition. Nevertheless religious music, fostered in particular in the cathedral, maintained its traditionally high standards. Gaffurius was succeeded as *maestro di cappella* by Mathias Werrecore (1522–50), Olivero de Phalanis (1550–51), Simon Boyleau (?1557–63 and 1572–4), Ruffo (1563–72) and Bartolomeo Torresani. The Council of Trent and the Counter-Reformation had considerable consequences for the city's musical life, mainly because of Cardinal Carlo Borromeo, Archbishop of Milan from 1560 until 1584: interpreting the recommendations of the Council, he established a more rigorous code affecting both the character of religious music and the discipline of the musicians who performed it. One of the new rules banned all instruments except the organ in church; Ruffo wrote a series of masses accordingly in 1570, and many of his later masses were written to render the text as intelligible as possible in accordance with the wishes of Cardinal Borromeo.

During the early 16th century secular music continued to be practised even if it had lost the splendour that had characterized the Sforza court. The Spanish governors also employed musicians at their court; Ferrante Gonzaga (in Milan from 1546) had an instrumental and a vocal *cappella*, with the madrigalist Hoste da Reggio as *maestro*, and among his musicians was a cornett virtuoso, Moscatello, and the young Lassus, who was probably there in 1547–9. There was no shortage of festivities or sumptuous performances accompanied by music; notable ones took place in 1548 on the occasion of the visit to Milan of Philip of Spain and in 1559 to celebrate the peace of Cateau-Cambrésis. In 1563 Giaches de Wert was *maestro di cappella* to Governor Gonzalvo Fernandez de Cordova; in 1573 Giovan Leonardo Primavera was *maestro* to Luis de Requesens. Outside the court, music was practised by many accomplished noble amateurs; preference was given to the lute by most players and composers, and a Milanese school of composers of lute music centred on Francesco Canova da Milano (including Joan Ambrosio Dalza, Marco Dall'Aquila, P. P. Borrono, Alberto da Ripa, G. G. Albuzio, G. P. Paladino and Perino Fiorentino) began to develop. Madrigals were also greatly favoured and were published in costly editions by such composers (many of them *maestri* in Milan) as Lassus, Hoste da Reggio, Wert, Primavera, Ruffo, Boyleau, Pietro Taglia, Giuseppe Caimo, Maddalena Casulana, Vicentino and Michele Varotto, printed in Milan by Castiglione, Moscheni, Ponzio, Piccaglia and Pontano; these printers also published editions of canzonettas and villanellas by such composers as Vecchi and Giovanelli.

The violin and viol families were also popular in

instrumental music, Milan being the centre of the region most important in the early history of the violin; the first use of the term *violino* appears in 1538 in a document describing some of the musicians brought by Pope Paul III to the peace conference at Nice in 1538 as *violini Milanesi*. Virtuoso players became famous outside Italy; for example, by 1590 almost all the players of violins and viols employed by Queen Elizabeth I of England were Italian, including various members of the Lupo family headed by Ambrose Lupo of Milan. The Milanese Riccardo Rognoni was the author of one of the early important violin methods (1592). This predilection for instrumental music was noticeable in the 16th century and continued in the 17th; many canzonas (the *canzon francese* was much favoured) and instrumental capriccios were composed by musicians employed in the city churches, for instance Florentio Maschera and Francesco Rognoni Taeggio. Such compositions were often performed in patricians' houses and dedicated to noble patrons, often taking their title from a patron's name ('La Brasca', 'L'Aresa' etc). The most notable among the noble amateurs to hold academies in their palazzos were the Brivio brothers, and the Arese and Valera families.

The first known sonata *per violino e basso continuo* and the first *sonata a tre* were published in the collection *Concerti ecclesiastici* (Milan, 1610), composed by G. P. Cima, a local musician who became the leading composer of the Milanese instrumental school in the early 17th century. These two musical forms were substantially developed in the 17th century by Lombard composers, mainly from Brescia and Bergamo, rather than Milan; similarly, Lombards from Cremona and Brescia became the outstanding lute and violin makers at that time. Biagio Marini, *maestro di cappella* at S Maria della Scala (1649–52), published his op.16 of three- to six-part chamber pieces at Milan in 1649.

A considerable number of organ works (ricercares and canzonas) were also published by such composers as Gian Paolo and Andrea Cima, and Francesco and Gian Domenico Rognoni. The end of the 16th century marked a decline in the popularity of the lute, which was increasingly replaced by the harpsichord or the Spanish guitar. The Milanese school of dancing-masters, including Pompeo Diobono and Virgilio Braccesco, became established around Cesare Negri and attained international fame. Negri was the author of the dance treatise *Le gratie d'amore* (1602), dedicated to Philip III of Spain, which is illustrated with dance figurations (fig.1) and their music, and provides a comprehensive record of the social and theatrical dance music of the period.

During the 17th century the results of the rigorous restrictions imposed by the Counter-Reformation became increasingly extensive, so that religious music became almost totally predominant. Musicians had to compose madrigals of a religious character (such as Orfeo Vecchi's *La donna vestita di sole*, 1602); secular madrigals were often presented in sacred guise – Monteverdi's madrigals, for example, were mainly known in Milan in a religious arrangement by Coppini (1607–11). Collections of vocal music by Milanese composers were also published in the early 17th century, such as the *Concerti de diversi eccellentissimi autori* (*RISM* 1608[13]), published by Lomazzo and edited by Francesco Lucino, a musician at the cathedral; it included concertante pieces by such composers as G. C. Gabussi, Gastoldi, G. D. Rognoni and G. P. Cima.

After the departure of Vincenzo Ruffo (*maestro di cappella*, 1563–72), the cathedral *cappella* continued its tradition of excellent *maestri*, most of whom were also prolific composers of sacred music. Carlo Borromeo and, later, his cousin Cardinal Federico devoted their personal attention to the *cappella* which was in turn entrusted to Boyleau (1572–4), Pietro Ponzio, Gabussi (1582–1611), Vincenzo Pellegrini (1612–30), Ignazio Donati (1631–8), G. B. Crivelli (1638–42), A. M. Turati (1642–50), Michel'Angelo Grancini (1650–69), G. A. Grossi (1669–84), C. D. Cossoni (1684–93) and G. M. Appiani (1693–1714). Grancini was outstanding among these *maestri*; he was active in Milanese churches from 1622 and was renowned for the expressive singing style of his polyphonic writing, clearly influenced by Monteverdi. Polyphony also flourished during the 16th century in other Milanese churches with musical establishments, among them S Maria della Scala, S Ambrogio, S Marco, S Simpliciano, S Celso and S Eufemia, and in the convents. The strict polyphonic style gave way to a more expressive style using a few voices and continuo. Among local composers was the nun Caterina Assandra, who published a collection of motets in the new concertato style in Milan in 1609.

In so austere a climate there was little opportunity for the development of opera. However, some public festivities with music were arranged when distinguished visitors came to the city. The first drama with music in the recitative style staged in Milan was the pastoral fable *Armenia*, with the customary *intermedii*, performed on 5 July 1599 for the visit of the Infanta Isabella and her husband Archduke Albert of Austria. These performances were generally given in the Salone Margherita, the theatre in the ducal palace named after Archduchess Margherita of Austria, wife of Philip III of Spain, and opened in her presence in 1598. The ducal palace also contained the small Teatrino della Commedia (from 1686 the Regio Nuovo Teatro; closed 1729) used by touring theatrical companies, among them the famous

*1. Woodcut of two dancing couples from Cesare Negri's 'Le gratie d'amore' (1602)*

2. Interior of the Regio Ducal Teatro during the ball in celebration of the birth of Peter Leopold, Archduke of Austria, 1747: engraving by Marc'Antonio Dal Re

'Fedeli' of G. B. Andreini, which included his wife Virginia Ramponi, creator of the title role in Monteverdi's *Arianna* in Mantua.

Opera gradually acquired greater status in Milan. The first opera performed there was Manelli's *L'Andromeda*, to a libretto by Benedetto Ferrari, brought to Milan by its authors in 1644. They had been instrumental in establishing the tradition of public opera in Venice with a performance of *L'Andromeda* to inaugurate S Cassiano (1637), the first public opera house; the contemporary Venetian repertory long dominated Milanese operatic activity. Among the operas by Cavalli performed there, *L'Orione* was composed for Milan and had its première at the Teatro Regio (Salone Margherita) in 1653. After 1670 the dependence on Venice decreased and a certain amount of local operatic production began to take shape, in part because of the local librettists Count Francesco Lemene and Carlo Maria Maggi, also a vernacular poet. In 1686 the Teatrino della Commedia was restored and adapted exclusively to opera by the Milanese impresarios Lonati and the Piantanida brothers. Local productions entered a repertory that had been almost completely dominated by works imported from other Italian centres.

3. 18TH CENTURY. The end of the Spanish domination of Lombardy and the advent of Austrian rule in 1708 heralded a new era, no longer characterized by religious austerity but by enjoyment, entertainment and a general intellectual broadening. This favoured the development and popularity of opera; it also reflected a general shift in power throughout Europe towards France. The Salone Margherita had been restored in 1696 but was burnt down in 1708, and a new theatre, the Regio Ducal Teatro (sometimes called 'Teatro Regio Ducale') was built on that site and opened in 1717 with Francesco Gasparini's *Costantino*. A number of intermezzos were staged in the intervals of the operas, introducing to Milan the comic genre with local vernacular texts; the first printed anthology of intermezzos, *Raccolta copiosa d'intermedi* (Amsterdam, 1723), contains several texts in Milanese dialect. Milan soon became an active centre in the growth of *opera buffa*. From 1745 comic opera in the full sense had its own season in the spring while Carnival (at the end of the year, and into the new year) was reserved for *opera seria*. As in other operatic centres, the public was becoming less concerned with the musical value of the operas than with the virtuosity of the singers, and the impresarios who took over the management of the Regio Ducal Teatro responded by engaging the most celebrated singers of the day. The eclectic operatic repertory included works by composers from all parts of Italy as well as some foreigners, but many were Milanese, the most distinguished being G. B. Lampugnani (ii).

The 18th-century Milanese musical scene, closely linked with that of Vienna, was of a high standard, due, in particular, to the presence of G. B. Sammartini, who spent his entire life in Milan. Gluck probably studied with Sammartini during the period 1737–41 when he was in Milan in the service of Count Antonio Melzi; many of his early works were influenced by the Milanese composer (indeed he borrowed movements from two Sammartini symphonies for his operas *Le nozze d'Ercole e d'Ebe* and *La contesa de' numi*); and four of his early operas had premières at Milan at the Regio

*3. Interior of the Regio Ducal Teatro, with a sonnet to Violante Vestri in honour of her performance as Apamia in J. A. Hasse's opera 'Tigrane' in 1750: engraving by Marc' Antonio Dal Re*

Ducal Teatro (*Artaserse*, 1741; *Demofoonte*, 1742; *La Sofonisba*, 1744; *Ippolito*, 1745). J. C. Bach went in 1754 to Italy, where he had a patron, Count Agostino Litta, in Milan, and a teacher, Padre Martini, in Bologna. His style was influenced by that of Sammartini and other Milanese symphonists, and this in turn had some influence on Mozart's style. By 1760 Bach was appointed one of two organists at Milan Cathedral and his opera *Catone in Utica*, written for Naples in 1761, was revived at the Regio Ducal Teatro the next year.

Sammartini was *maestro di cappella* in several Milanese churches and he took a leading role in the city's musical life, composing and conducting music for religious and state occasions. He composed and conducted vocal and especially instrumental music, notably his symphonies – the first examples of the genre in Europe – in which harmonic and thematic relationships clearly indicate the emerging Classical style; they soon became recognized outside Italy, and he was considered the leading figure in a Milanese symphonic school, including Brioschi, Galimberti, Giorgio Giulini, G. B.

Lampugnani (ii) and Melchiorre Chiesa. During Lent, when the theatres were closed, private concerts 'di sinfonia e di canto' continued, while in the churches, especially the Jesuit church of S Fedele, sacred cantatas were performed, many of them by Sammartini, who from 1728 was *maestro di cappella* of the Congregazione del Ss Entierro which met at S Fedele.

The Milanese of the mid-18th century had a keen interest in orchestral music, and concerts were organized on the ramparts of the Castello Sforzesco, where a large orchestra gave open-air performances several times a week. The vogue of instrumental and symphonic music was such as to encourage the establishment of the Accademia Filarmonica (1758), whose members were primarily noblemen, but whose musical backbone was formed by Sammartini and other musicians. Those seeking admission to the Accademia were required to pass stringent tests and each member was obliged to compose a sonata or overture annually. The government of Maria Theresia, particularly through Chancellor von Kaunitz and the Plenipotentiary

Minister Firmian, gave substantial encouragement to cultural and musical development. The enlightened cultural atmosphere in Milan in the second half of the 18th century made it unlike any other Italian centre; typical of the time were such influential writings as Cesare Beccaria's *Dei delitti e delle pene*, denouncing capital punishment and torture and advocating prevention of crime by education. Milan was noted for its enlightened milieu, typified by the important patron Firmian and the poet Parini, both of whom had contact with Mozart during his visits there. The young Mozart first went to Milan early in 1770, when he was warmly received and met several musicians, including Sammartini; he returned at the end of the year to direct performances of his new opera *Mitridate, rè di Ponto*, which he had written for the Regio Ducal Teatro. He again visited Milan in 1771 for the first performance of *Ascanio in Alba*, a *festa teatrale* to a text by Parini (commissioned for the wedding of Archduke Ferdinand of Austria and Maria Ricciarda Beatrice, at which Hasse's *Ruggiero* was the main operatic event), and in 1772–3 for the première of *Lucio Silla*; both works were given at the Regio Ducal Teatro.

The cathedral *cappella* continued to flourish and musicians of high repute competed for the posts of organist and *maestro di cappella*, though the Enlightenment had brought about a general decline in liturgical music. The *maestri* were Carlo Baliani (1714–47), G. A. Fioroni (1747–78), Giuseppe Sarti (1778–87), Carlo Monza (1787–93) and N. A. Zingarelli (1793–4), all of whom were active in other Milanese musical institutions and as composers.

Opera, however, remained the main attraction. At the Regio Ducal Teatro the ballets that followed the operas grew in proportion; choreographers included Le Pic, Favier, Noverre and Angiolini. Splendid sets were specially designed by the Galliari brothers. In February 1776 the theatre burnt down; while a new and bigger theatre was being built it was replaced by the provisional Teatro Interinale (designed by Giuseppe Piermarini). The initiative was taken by the box holders of the Regio Ducal Teatro and was granted Maria Theresia's approval in 1776. The new theatre, the Teatro alla Scala, was built by Piermarini and opened on 3 August 1778 with Salieri's *L'Europa riconosciuta*, specially written for the occasion, with sets by the Galliaris, followed by two ballets. The theatre took its name from the site previously occupied by the church of S Maria della Scala (named after Bernabò Visconti's wife Beatrice della Scala), and soon became one of the most famous in Italy; it represented one of the main centres of development of Italian opera, the genre that dominated Italian musical life in the 19th century. It also became a centre of Italian social and political history: in 1793 it was the scene of festivities for the coronation of Emperor Joseph II; in 1797 the end of Austrian domination and the advent of Napoleonic rule was celebrated by the performance of a tragedy-ballet, where the royal box was divided into six smaller boxes reserved for the 'liberated people'; also in 1797 the revolutionary opera *La congiura pisoniana* was first performed there; and in 1805 impressive performances for the coronation of Napoleon as King of Italy were given there. During the Napoleonic period of transition, operas from the old repertory were staged alternately with cantatas and other works. (For the theatre plan and interior, *see*

ACOUSTICS, fig.22.)

The Teatro della Cannobiana (or Canobbiana), also designed by Piermarini, was built on a site next to La Scala and opened in 1779 with two ballets as well as *Il talismano* (written specially for the opening) and *La fiera di Venezia*, both by Salieri (who was then court composer and conductor of the Italian opera in Vienna). It gave primarily drama, but included a summer season of opera and ballet when La Scala was closed.

4. 19TH CENTURY. At the turn of the century Milan began to develop into a modern city based on the activity of a prosperous middle class, which eventually turned it into the most important industrial centre of Italy. Lombardy was returned to Austrian control in 1815 and renewed Viennese connections resulted in a large patrician and upper class supporting cultural life.

A new era of Italian opera began with the success of Rossini (*La pietra del paragone*, 1812), who quickly came to dominate Italian opera along with Donizetti and Bellini; from then on, Milan's musical history became virtually identified with that of Italian opera, of which La Scala was perhaps the most notable centre (it was also at that time that cycles of Mozart operas began to be mounted there). Important operas had their premières at La Scala and helped to establish the theatre's reputation: Rossini's works dominated the period 1812–20 (including *Aureliano in Palmira*, 1813; *Il Turco in Italia*, 1814; *La gazza ladra*, 1817; and *Bianca e Faliero*, 1819); Meyerbeer had successes with *Margherita d'Angiò* (1820) and *L'esule di Granata* (1823); Mercadante with *Elisa e Claudio* (1821), *Il giuramento* (1837) and *Il bravo* (1839); Donizetti with *Lucrezia Borgia* (1833) and others; and Bellini had three successes particularly important for the theatre, *Il pirata* (1827, commissioned by Barbaia and initiating the composer's fruitful collaboration with the librettist Romani), *La straniera* (1829) and, after an initial failure, *Norma* (1831).

By the 1830s La Scala was one of the leading opera houses in Europe; 40 premières were given in that decade and in 1839 Verdi's first opera, *Oberto, Conte di San Bonifacio*, was performed there. Ricordi bought the publishing rights, and the theatre's director, Bartolomeo Merelli, commissioned three more operas from the young composer. The first, *Un giorno di regno*, was a failure and was withdrawn after its first performance in 1840, but *Nabucco* (1842) and *I lombardi alla prima crociata* (1843), were great successes; in fact, *I lombardi* came to represent the drive towards unification and the patriotic choruses often incited demonstrations in the theatre. Although Verdi is closely associated with La Scala, his career there was chequered, and his works until *Otello* in 1887 had their premières elsewhere (with the exception of revisions); there was hissing and chatter during the Milan performances of *La forza del destino*, *Un ballo in maschera* and *Aida*, and Milanese critics accused Verdi of not knowing how to write for singers and of imitating Wagner. The Requiem, written for Manzoni, was given at La Scala in 1874 only a few days after its first performance at S Marco (see fig.4), and Verdi did return to La Scala with the premières of his last two operas, *Otello* (1887) and *Falstaff* (1893). Many other Italian composers were presented at La Scala during the second half of the 19th century, including Petrella, Faccio, Marchetti, Boito, Ponchielli

*4. Verdi conducting his Requiem at La Scala, 1874: engraving by Baldi after Oswaldo Tofani from 'Nuova illustrazione universale'* (*14 June 1874*)

and Catalani. The works of foreign composers were also brought to the theatre and, after initial failure, Wagner's operas were enthusiastically received under Franco Faccio's direction.

The best Italian singers performed at La Scala throughout the century, while the most notable conductors were Alberto Mazzucato (1859–68), Faccio (1871–91) and Toscanini (1898–1903). Alessandro Sanquirico was the theatre's leading stage designer and scene-painter from 1817 to 1832; besides setting new standards of design in Rossini's *opere serie* and the operas of Mozart, Bellini, Donizetti and Meyerbeer, he influenced opera stage design throughout the 19th century and into the 20th. Carlo Ferrario, who was the leading Milanese scene-painter of the second half of the 19th century, worked at other theatres as well as at La Scala, making a return to more realistic design. Ballets were produced there by such great choreographers as Salvatore Viganò, Gaetano Gioia and Salvatore Pallerini.

Throughout the 19th century alterations and improvements were made to the theatre, the most important of which were the enlargement of the stage in 1807, the overall restoration in 1838, and the removal in 1857 of the tall houses that had made it impossible to have a perspective view of the façade. Gas lighting was installed in 1860 and electric lighting in 1883. There have traditionally been four annual seasons: Carnival to Lent (initially reserved for *opere serie*), and autumn, spring and summer, when *opere buffe* were mounted. The administration of La Scala had at first been supported by the proceeds of the dramatic company which used the theatre until 1803, but from 1806 to 1918 the theatre was supported, with varying success, by its joint owners: the state, then the city, box holders, impresarios

and patrons. During the Austrian Restoration, the administration was in the hands of the government, but afterwards the theatre attracted such adventurous impresarios as Domenico Barbaia (1826–32) and Bartolomeo Merelli (1835–50 and 1861–3). In 1897 the city withdrew its subsidy and Duke Guido Visconti di Modrone formed a syndicate to take over the theatre's management, appointing Toscanini artistic director in 1898, with Giulio Gatti-Casazza as manager.

There were several minor Milanese theatres that mounted opera during the 19th century. Despite several substantial interruptions the Teatro della Cannobiana continued its activities, particularly when La Scala was closed. Many works by second-rate composers had their premières there, as did Donizetti's *L'elisir d'amore* (1832). In 1894, under the ownership of the publisher Sonzogno, the theatre was renamed the Teatro Lirico Internazionale and opened with the Greek composer Spiro Samara's *La martire*; it was later known simply as the Teatro Lirico and passed into other hands. In 1897 Caruso made his Milan début there in the première of Cilea's *L'arlesiana*. The Teatro Carcano, modelled on La Scala, was built by Giuseppe Carcano in 1803 and opened that year with Vincenzo Federici's *La Zaira*. Of the operas that had their premières there, few were memorable, though Donizetti's *Anna Bolena* (1830) and Bellini's *La sonnambula* (1831) were notable exceptions. In 1882 the first concert of Wagner's music in Milan was given there by Faccio. The Carcano had largely lost its importance by the mid-century and by 1900 it was no longer used for music. The Teatro di S Radegonda was opened in 1803 in a Benedictine convent, remodelled to accommodate drama and opera; it was demolished in 1882. The Teatro Lentasio opened in 1801 as a marionette theatre, but also presented opera and drama from 1805 to 1853. The Teatro Re was built by Carlo Re, opening in 1813 with Rossini's *Tancredi*; after the 1848 revolution it was used primarily for drama, though operas were occasionally mounted until its demolition in 1872, the final performance being Rossini's *Il barbiere di Siviglia*. In 1815 the Teatro Fiando was opened, offering a variety of entertainments including marionette plays, drama, opera and ballet; the building was demolished in 1868, rebuilt and renamed the Teatro Gerolamo. The Teatro Manzoni (so-called from 1873) was built in 1872 as the Teatro della Commedia to replace the Teatro Re. It initially concentrated on performances of drama and music, particularly *opere buffe* and operettas, and over the next 50 years gradually raised its standards to occupy an important place in the city's theatrical life; however, soon after 1900 its musical activity ceased. The Politeama Ciniselli, a private theatre, was acquired by Count Francesco Dal Verme, demolished and rebuilt, reopening in 1872 with Meyerbeer's *Les Huguenots* as the Teatro Dal Verme. The most modern theatre of its time, it primarily gave drama and grand opera; first performances there included Puccini's first opera *Le villi* (1884) and Leoncavallo's *Pagliacci* (1892).

One of the city's most important institutions, the Milan Conservatory, was founded during the Napoleonic era; from 1803 there had been attempts to establish a residential conservatory based on the traditional Italian model, and in 1807 the conservatory, partly modelled on the Paris Conservatoire, was instituted by Napoleonic decree, principally to train musicians for the city's main musical institution, La Scala. The conservatory was housed in the convent attached to the church of S Maria della Passione, where it has remained, and all the students were resident. Simon Mayr was asked to take up the post of director in 1808, but he preferred to remain in Bergamo and it was subsequently offered to Bonifazio Asioli, *maestro di cappella* and music director at the court of Viceroy Eugène de Beauharnais (Napoleon's stepson); he accepted, and held the post until the fall of the Kingdom of Italy in 1814. Among the first professors were the violinist Alessandro Rolla, the horn player Luigi Belloli and the pianist Piantanida. The founding of the Milan Conservatory initiated the founding of a series of conservatories all over Italy. Under Austrian rule the conservatory underwent some changes; literary and historical studies were added to the teaching of music and it was opened to non-resident students. Outstanding 19th-century directors were Francesco Basili (1827–37), who refused admission to Verdi in 1832, Nicola Vaccai (1837–44), Alberto Mazzucato (1872–7) and Antonio Bazzini (1882–97). The conservatory soon became the most important music school in Italy, attracting such pupils as Puccini and Catalani to study with professors of the stature of Ponchielli (1880–86).

5. *Teatro alla Scala, built by Piermarini: painting (1852) by Angelo Inganni in the Museo Teatrale alla Scala, Milan*

During the 19th century Milan became one of the most important centres of Italian publishing, dominated by the firm of Ricordi; it was established in 1808 by Giovanni Ricordi, a modest artisan, typographer and copyist, and developed by his descendants, who turned it into a flourishing and powerful business, also serving as a patron to support and stimulate composers. By 1811 Giovanni Ricordi was appointed publisher to the Milan Conservatory; in 1814 he was prompter and exclusive copyist to La Scala, which gave him rights to publish the music performed there, and in 1825 he bought its musical archives. Ricordi absorbed Artaria in 1837, further consolidating its power, and in 1839 the firm published Verdi's first opera; with the exception of three operas published by Lucca in 1846–8, Ricordi published all his subsequent operas and most of his other works. Lucca had been established in 1825 and became Ricordi's chief rival from about 1840. In 1842 Ricordi initiated the *Gazzetta musicale di Milano*, Italy's first regular musicological and critical journal, with Lucca issuing the rival publication *Italia musicale* (1847–59). From 1874 the firm of Sonzogno began to specialize in music under Edoardo Sonzogno; in 1888, when Ricordi absorbed Lucca (which had taken over Canti and several other smaller music publishers), Sonzogno proved to be Ricordi's main rival, being the publishers of many *verismo* composers, for instance Mascagni and Leoncavallo. Ricordi, however, published all but one of Puccini's operas and, with the absorption of Lucca, had gained Italian rights to publish those of Wagner.

Although the tradition of instrumental music began to wane with the rise of opera, Milan remained one of the most important centres for its cultivation. During the first half of the 19th century instrumental music was performed in Milan more than in any other Italian centre, partly because the tradition established during the previous century was continued by such figures as Rolla and other professors at the conservatory, and partly because of the presence of the occupying Austrian nobility, who were directly connected with the musical activity at Vienna. This resulted in the foundation of several circles for amateur performances, for example the Società Filarmonica conducted by Pietro Massini (a friend and mentor of Verdi); such works as Haydn's *The Creation* and Beethoven's *Christus am Ölberg* were translated into Italian, performed, and their scores published. A detailed picture of this concert activity can be drawn from the correspondence in the Leipzig *Allgemeine musikalische Zeitung* of Peter Lichtenthal, a Hungarian established in Milan, an ardent proponent of the works of Mozart, and the author of the *Dizionario e bibliografia della musica* (1826), the first music dictionary in Italian. The decade 1850–60 was almost devoid of instrumental music, but thereafter it started to revive. The court *cappelle* were dissolved with the establishment of the Kingdom of Italy and were replaced throughout Italy by philharmonic societies and other private associations founded by members of the aristocracy and wealthy middle class. The Società del Quartetto was founded in Milan in 1864 (similar organizations were established in other Italian cities) with members like Mazzucato and Boito as its intellectual backbone. Boito was actively associated with the 'Scapigliatura', a mainly literary movement which aimed at revitalizing and reforming the arts. The group reflected, in part, the disillusionment that followed the enthusiasm of unification. Boito published music criticism in the *Giornale della Società del quartetto*, promoting greater simplicity in art. From 1872 the orchestra of La Scala gave concerts under Faccio for the Società del Quartetto and in 1878 it took part in the Paris Exhibition; its success was so great that the following year the Società Orchestrale della Scala was formed with Faccio as director, giving two annual seasons of concerts in the spring and autumn. The orchestra played an important role in renewing interest in instrumental music and Faccio did much to establish high standards. Of lesser importance was a short-lived society founded in 1863 by Gustavo Adolfo Noseda on the model of the Concerts Populaires de Musique Classique initiated by Pasdeloup in Paris in 1861.

5. 20TH CENTURY. Milan continued to grow as a thriving industrial city supporting a wide range of musical activity. La Scala further expanded its prestige and in addition to presenting the standard repertory and works by Puccini, Franchetti, Leoncavallo and Giordano, mounted the first Italian productions of many foreign works, including Tchaikovsky's *Eugene Onegin* (1900), Strauss's *Salome* (1906), *Elektra* (1908) and *Rosenkavalier* (1911), Debussy's *Pelléas et Mélisande* (1908), Musorgsky's *Boris Godunov* (1909) and Falla's *La vida breve* (1934). After World War II several important works had their premières there, for instance Milhaud's *David* (first staged performance, 1955), Poulenc's *Dialogues des carmélites* (1957), Pizzetti's *Assassinio nella cattedrale* (1957) and Falla's cantata *Atlántida* (first staged performance, 1962, completed by Ernesto Halffter); many works were given their Italian premières there, for example Britten's *Peter Grimes* (1947), Prokofiev's *The Love of Three Oranges* (1947), Walton's *Troilus and Cressida* (1956) and Janáček's *The Cunning Little Vixen* (1958). However, J. J. Castro's *Proserpina y lo extranjero*, which won the International Verdi Prize in 1952, was banned from performance at La Scala.

In 1920 the theatre became a self-governing body, 'Ente Autonomo del Teatro alla Scala'; Toscanini was then appointed artistic director and established a reputation for consistent excellence in performances during what was called 'the great Toscanini period'. He formed a new orchestra of 100 players and a chorus of 120; while the stage and auditorium were being reconstructed he took the company on a tour of Italy, the USA and Canada. His regime culminated in the company's visit to Vienna and Berlin in 1929. His eventual resignation had many causes, including political ones. Artistic directors succeeding him have included Erardo Trentinaglia (appointed 1931), Jenner Mataloni (1935), Carlo Gatti (1941), Gino Marinuzzi (1944), Antonio Ghiringhelli (1948), Victor De Sabata (1953) and Francesco Siciliani (1957), while conductors have included De Sabata, Giulini and Abbado. The La Scala company has also toured to Munich (1937), London (Covent Garden, 1950 and 1976), Johannesburg (1957), Edinburgh (1957), Brussels (1958), Moscow (1964), Montreal (1967) and Washington, DC (1976). After being seriously damaged by bombing in 1943, La Scala was one of the first buildings in Milan to be rebuilt after the war. It was reconstructed to its original designs (capacity now 3000) and was reopened on 11 May 1948 with a concert conducted by Toscanini containing works by Rossini, Verdi, Boito and Puccini. In 1955 the

Piccola Scala (capacity 600) was built next to La Scala for performances of early opera and small-scale contemporary works, opening with Cimarosa's *Il matrimonio segreto*.

There is little opera activity in Milan outside La Scala. The Teatro Nuovo was built in 1938 and has always alternated productions of drama and opera; it has a permanent orchestra and since World War II has played a particularly important role in the dissemination of new music, and in giving young singers performing opportunities during its Stagione Sperimentale.

Concert life revolves largely round La Scala's orchestra, which has continued to give two annual series of orchestral concerts, in spring and autumn, usually conducted by the resident conductor. In addition, from 1959 the Milan radio orchestra of the RAI has given public orchestral concerts in the conservatory, with Bruno Maderna as permanent conductor from 1971 to 1973. The Teatro Angelicum was built in 1939 specially for concerts of sacred music; its regular chamber orchestra, which gives an annual winter series of concerts, was founded in 1941 primarily to present Italian instrumental music of the 17th and 18th centuries. The orchestra of the Società dei Pomeriggi Musicali aims to bring artists and audiences up to date with new works. The Polifonica Ambrosiana, founded in 1947 by Giuseppe Biella, devotes many of the programmes it organizes to medieval, Renaissance and Baroque music. There are many solo and chamber concerts given under the auspices of the Società del Quartetto, the Associazione Riunite Concerti (formed in 1948 from the merger of the Amici della Musica and the Associazione Milanese per la Musica da Camera), the Teatro del Popolo and many other groups.

The Studio di Fonologia Musicale was opened in 1955 at the Milan branch of the RAI on the initiative of Berio and Maderna, and was directed by Berio until 1961. This electronic studio gave rise to a vigorous promotional and organizing activity, attracting composers of every tendency, from Pousseur to Cage. It also resulted in the publication of the magazine *Incontri musicali* (1956–60) and the establishment of a concert series, run by Berio and Maderna, under the same title; among the musicians who took part in the series were Scherchen, Boulez and Cage.

After the unification of Italy (1870) the conservatory came under state control, and in 1901 it was named after Verdi, becoming the Conservatorio di Musica 'G. Verdi'; it continued to be one of the most important music conservatories in Italy. 20th-century directors have included Pizzetti (1924–34), G. F. Ghedini (1951–62) and Jacopo Napoli (1962–72). Most of the conservatory buildings were destroyed in the 1943 bombing, but have since been reconstructed. The conservatory has a large library of over 250,000 volumes, including rare manuscripts and early editions, the collection that Noseda bequeathed to the library and the musical archives of the Church of S Barbara in Mantua, as well as a collection of instruments. Other schools of music are the Scuola di Musica di Milano and the Civica Scuola di Musica, while the University of Milan has a music department.

Publishing in Milan remains centred on Ricordi, which began opening branches elsewhere from the beginning of the 20th century. After World War I the firm began to publish new editions of works by earlier composers; while it also continued to publish contemporary Italian works, this was done less energetically than in the 19th century. The Milanese firms of Carisch, Curci and Suvini Zerboni (founded 1930) are among the leading publishers of contemporary Italian music.

In addition to the library at the conservatory there is an important archive at Ricordi which includes all Verdi's autographs. The Museo Teatrale alla Scala (opened 1913) has a large collection of musical autographs and manuscripts, letters and portraits of composers, opera librettos and drawings and etchings by important stage and set designers. The Castello Sforzesco has a music library as well as a museum of instruments, containing about 650 instruments from the Renaissance to the 20th century; the Civica Raccolta delle Stampe Bertarelli holds 11,000 illustrations of musicians and other theatrical personalities. The Ufficio per la Ricerca dei Fondi Musicali Italiani, founded in 1965, contains the union catalogue of manuscript and printed music (up to 1900) in Italian libraries.

## BIBLIOGRAPHY

G. Chiappori: *Serie cronologica delle rappresentazioni . . . dei principali teatri di Milano dall'autunno 1776 sino all'intero autunno 1818* (Milan, 1818–25)

L. Romani: *Teatro della Scala* (Milan, 1862)

P. Cambiasi: *Rappresentazioni date nei Reali Teatri di Milano 1778–1872* (Milan, 2/1872)

L. Melzi: *Cenni storici sul Reale Conservatorio di Musica* (Milan, 1878)

G. Porro: 'Lettere di Galeazzo Maria Sforza, duca di Milano', *Archivio storico lombardo*, v (1878), 107, 254, 637–68; vi (1879), 250

G. Martinazzi: *Cenni storici dell'Accademia dei filodrammatici di Milano (già Teatro Patriottico)* (Milan, 1879)

D. Muoni: 'Gli Antegnati organari insigni e serie dei maestri di cappella nel duomo di Milano', *Archivio storico lombardo*, x (1883), 211

E. Motta: 'Musica alla corte degli Sforza', *Archivio storico lombardo*, xiv (1887), 29–64, 278–340, 514–61; pubd separately (Geneva, 1977)

A. Paglicci-Brozzi: *Contributo alla storia del teatro: il teatro a Milano nel secolo XVII* (Milan, 1892)

——: *Il R. Ducal Teatro di Milano nel secolo XVIII* (Milan, 1894)

V. Rossi: 'Per la storia dei cantori sforzeschi', *Archivio storico lombardo*, xxviii (1901), 150

P. Cambiasi: *La Scala* (Milan, 1906)

G. de Saint-Foix: 'Les débuts milanais de Gluck', *Gluck-Jb*, i (1913), 28

B. Gutierrez: *Il Teatro Carcano (1803–1914)* (Milan, 1914)

G. Marangoni and E. Vanbianchi: *La Scala* (Bergamo, 1922)

G. Cesari: *Musica e musicisti alla corte sforzesca* (Milan, 1923)

G. Macchi: *La Scala, dalle origini all'ordinamento attuale* (Milan, 1927)

V. Ramperti: *Per la storia del teatro milanese* (Milan, 1929)

G. M. Ciampelli and B. Gutierrez: *La Scala nel 1830 e nel 1930* (Milan, 1930)

A. De Gani: *I maestri cantori e la cappella musicale del duomo di Milano, 1395–1930* (Milan, 1930)

G. Morazzoni: *I palchi del Teatro alla Scala* (Milan, 1930)

L. Parigi: *La musica nelle Gallerie di Milano* (Milan, 1935)

F. Mompellio: *Il R. Conservatorio di Musica 'G. Verdi'* (Florence, 1941)

F. Abbiati and others: *La Scala (3. 8. 1778–11. 5. 1946)* (Milan, 1950)

E. Cattaneo: *Note storiche sul canto ambrosiano* (Milan, 1950)

F. Armani and G. Bascapé: *La Scala: breve biografia 1778–1950* (Milan, 1951)

C. Sartori: 'Monteverdiana', *MQ*, xxxviii (1952), 399

——: 'The Scala Under Toscanini', *Opera*, v (1954), 266

G. Barblan: 'Le orchestre in Lombardia all'epoca di Mozart', *Kongressbericht: Wien Mozartjahr 1956*, 18

G. Barblan and A. Della Corte: *Mozart in Italia* (Milan, 1956)

F. Fano: *Le origini e il primo maestro di cappella: Matteo da Perugia*, La cappella musicale del duomo di Milano, i, IMi, new ser., i (Milan, 1956)

C. Sartori: 'Josquin des Près, cantore del duomo di Milano (1459–1472)', *AnnM*, iv (1956), 55

——: 'Matteo da Perugia e Bertrand Feragut, i due primi maestri di cappella del duomo di Milano', *AcM*, xxviii (1956), 12

——: *Catalogo delle musiche della cappella del duomo di Milano* (Milan, 1957)

——: 'Organs, Organ-builders and Organists in Milan', *MQ*, xliii (1957), 57

G. Barblan: 'Il teatro musicale in Milano nei secoli XVII e XVIII', *Storia di Milano*, xii (Milan, 1958), 947–96

——: 'Sammartini e la scuola sinfonica milanese', *Musicisti lombardi e emiliani*, Chigiana, xv (1958), 21

——: 'Sulla tracce di un'espressione musicale "padana" ', *Musicisti lombardi ed emiliani*, Chigiana, xv (1958), 9

——: 'Boccheriniana', *RaM*, xxix (1959), 123, 322; xxx (1960), 33

R. Allorto: *La musique sacrée à Milan à la moitié du XVIIIe siècle* (Paris, 1960)

C. Sartori: 'G. B. Sammartini e la sua corte', *Musica d'oggi*, new ser., iii (1960), 106

——: 'Mailand', *MGG*

G. Barblan: 'Vita musicale alla corte sforzesca'; 'La vita musicale in Milano nella prima metà nel Cinquecento', *Storia di Milano*, ix (Milan, 1961), 787–852; 853–95

M. Donà: *La stampa musicale a Milano fino all'anno 1700* (Florence, 1961)

C. Sartori: 'La musica nel duomo e alla corte sino alla seconda metà del '500', *Storia di Milano*, ix (Milan, 1961), 723

R. Allorto: 'La musica sacra a Milano', *La Scala*, xiv (1962), July, 9

G. Barblan: 'I Rognoni, musicisti milanesi tra il 1500 e il 1600', *Anthony van Hoboken: Festschrift zum 75. Geburtstag* (Milan, 1962), 19

——: 'La musica strumentale e cameristica a Milano dalla seconda metà del Cinquecento a tutto il Seicento'; 'La musica strumentale e cameristica a Milano nel Settecento'; 'L'Ottocento e gli inizi del secolo ventesimo', *Storia di Milano*, xvi (Milan, 1962), 589–618; 619–660; 661–771

F. Mompellio: 'La cappella del duomo dal 1573 al 1714'; 'La cappella del duomo dal 1714 ai primi decenni del '900', *Storia di Milano*, xvi (Milan, 1962), 506–552; 553–88

*Annuario dell'anno accademico 1962–1963 e sguardo storico dal 1917 al 1962*, ed. Conservatorio di Musica 'G. Verdi' (Milan, 1963)

G. Confalonieri, ed.: *Cento anni di concerti della Società del Quartetto di Milano* (Milan, 1964; Eng. trans., 1965)

C. Gatti: *Il Teatro alla Scala nella storia e nell'arte (1778–1963)* (Milan, 1964)

*Il Museo teatrale alla Scala 1913–1963* (Milan, 1964)

F. Armani, ed.: *La Scala 1946–1966* (Milan, 1966)

G. Barblan: 'Beethoven in Lombardia nell'Ottocento', *NRMI*, vi (1972), 3–63

L. Rossi: *Il ballo alla Scala, 1778–1970* (Milan, 1972)

A. Basso and G. Barblan, eds.: *Storia dell' opera* (Turin, 1977–)

MARIANGELA DONÀ

**Milán, Luis de** [Milan, Luys] (*b* c1500; *d* c1561 or later). Spanish musician and writer. He apparently spent most of his life in Valencia, associated with its ducal court at least until 1538. His published works, all issued in Valencia, span 26 years, from a parlour-game book, *El juego de mandar* (1535), to *El cortesano* (1561). The latter, dedicated to Philip II of Spain, provides an attractive picture of the social and cultural ambience of the Valencia court. His most important book, *Libro de música de vihuela de mano intitulado El maestro* (Valencia, 1536/R1978; ed. R. Chiesa, Milan, 1965, and C. Jacobs, University Park, Penn., 1971; extracts ed. L. Schrade, Publikationen älterer Musik, ii/1, Leipzig, 1927), was dedicated to John III of Portugal, the musical activity of whose court Milán admired.

*El maestro* is distinguished not only as the first collection of vihuela and therefore guitar music, but also as the earliest source employing verbal indications of tempo. Such phrases as 'ni muy apriessa ni muy a espacio sino con un compás bien mesurado' (neither very quickly nor very slowly, but with a moderate measure), 'algo apriessa' (somewhat quickly), 'compás batido ... apressurado' (agitated measure ... rushed) and 'compás a espacio' (slow measure) are used. In addition, Milán, using the expression 'tañer de gala', called unequivocally for the use of rubato in the performance of specific compositions. The tablature is similar to that found in most Spanish vihuela sources except that the lowest (rather than the highest) line of the tablature is used to represent the lowest-pitched course of the instrument. The vocal line of the many songs is printed in red within the tablature. It is not clear whether these notes were to be played as well as sung, though this seems more likely.

*El maestro* contains 40 fantasias, formally free with a typical blend of homophony and polyphony. Some are characterized by free polyphony; imitation appears in others. A number feature virtuoso passage-work, principally in the form of runs or ornamental turns. Sequential, chordal and arpeggiated passages are common. Little difference can be observed between the four *tentos* and the several fantasias in the 'tañer de gala' style; evidently, for Milán, rubato was a necessary element in the *tento*. 'Fantasia' had a fairly broad meaning in the 16th century: introducing the six pavans contained in *El maestro*, Milán described them as 'fantasias', for to him the word apparently implied only solo instrumental music. The pavans, in duple or triple metre, are all in a moderately fast tempo. Milán suggested that the pavan originated in Italy and stated that the 'sonada' (sound) of his pavans nos.5 and 6 is Italian. The melody of the Pavan no.6 in the 8th tone is found again in Antonio Valente's *Intavolatura de cimbalo* (Naples, 1576), in his *Gagliarda lombarda*. Milán's use of 'sonada' is one of the earliest references to the term 'sonata'.

In addition to its instrumental music, *El maestro* contains a rich repertory of vocal music. There are six villancicos in Castilian and six in Portuguese. The form of Milán's villancicos is invariably *ABBA*. Ten are given in two musically similar versions; in five of these double versions the *vuelta* (the B section) is identical. In the initial, rather simple versions, the vocalist is expected to ornament the vocal line. Regrettably, Milán did not provide examples of the ornamentation, which he described as 'hacer garganta' (to involve the throat), 'quiebro' (a kind of ornament, possibly not specific at the time), and 'glosa' (gloss). In the second version of these double villancicos, the singer is instructed to sing without ornamentation, while the vihuela part is considerably more elaborate than in the initial versions. The vocal pieces also include four *romances*, of which three concern the Moorish occupation of Spain, and the fourth the fall of Troy. *El maestro* also contains six *sonetos*, settings of Italian poetry by Petrarch, Sannazaro and others.

Exact performing directions for individual compositions support the impression that *El maestro* was meticulously prepared. Several bars of the villancico *Perdida teñyo la color* may be omitted at will by performers, and vihuela passage-work in the *soneto Madonna per voi ardo* may be ignored.

Milán's treatment of the modes in *El maestro* merits careful scrutiny. Not only did he transpose the modes and use a superabundance of certain accidentals with several of them (B♭ with the 1st, 2nd, 5th and 6th modes or F♯ with the 7th and 8th modes), he claimed to have mixed modes in a number of works (e.g. Fantasia no.14 in the 3rd and 4th tones, Pavan no.3 in the 5th and 6th tones, etc).

Unusual chromatic writing is found in Fantasia no.27 in the 3rd tone, where an augmented unison occurs on several occasions and augmented triads twice. The motion of an augmented unison is also used in the *romance Durandarte, Durandarte* as a cogent element in a modulatory progression. In Milán's setting of Petrarch's *Nova angeleta* a simultaneous cross-relation (*e'* against *e♭''*) emphasizes the word 'ordiva' (woven) from the phrase of the poem 'a snare of woven silk', and a similar cross-relation may be found in Milán's setting of Sannazaro's *O gelosia d'amanti*.

For an illustration from *El maestro*, see VIHUELA, fig.2; for an extract *see* TABLATURE, fig.6.

BIBLIOGRAPHY

*BrownI*

L. de Milán: *Libro de motes* (Valencia, 1535); facs. repr. in *Colección de libros españoles raros ó curiosos*, vii (Madrid, 1874)

——: *Libro intitulado El cortesano* (Valencia, 1561); facs. repr. in *Colección de libros españoles raros ó curiosos*, vii (1874)

A. Paz y Mélia: 'Coplas de Juan Fernández contra D. Luis de Milán', *Revista de archivos, bibliotecas, y museos*, vi (1876), 258, 275

T. F. Crane: *Italian Social Customs of the Sixteenth Century and their Influence on the Literatures of Europe* (New Haven, 1920)

J. B. Trend: *Luis de Milán and the Vihuelists* (Oxford, 1925)

J. Ward: *The Vihuela de Mano and its Music (1536–1576)* (diss., New York U., 1953)

F. Almela i Vives: *El duc de Calàbria i la seua cort* (Valencia, 1958)

J. Romeu Figueras: 'Mateo Flecha el Viejo, la corte literariomusical del duque de Calabria y el Cancionero llamado de Upsala', *AnM*, xiii (1958), 25–101

I. Pope: 'La vihuela y su música en el ambiente humanístico', *Nueva revista de filología hispánica*, xv (1961), 364

J. Moll Roqueta: 'Notas para la historia musical de la corte del Duque de Calabria', *AnM*, xviii (1963), 123

J. Romeu Figueras: 'Una nueva versión de la ensalada "El Toro"', *AnM*, xxiv (1969), 153–90

CHARLES JACOBS

**Milanese rite, music of the.** *See* AMBROSIAN RITE, MUSIC OF THE.

**Milani, Francesco** (*b* Bologna; *fl* 1630–38). Italian composer. In 1630 he was appointed *maestro di cappella* at S Petronio in Bologna, where, under the name 'Il Solitario', he was a member of the Accademia dei Filomusi. His small output of sacred music shows a bias towards the *stile antico*, particularly in the case of functional liturgical music such as psalms and hymns. That his vesper psalms for four voices, published as *Vespri per tutto l'anno* (Venice, 1635), can be performed 'con l'organo e senza' indicates this; the pieces are all *alla breve*, and some are written for the old 'high clef' combination. The hymn settings seem to have been written in accordance with a new reform by Urban VIII, the pope at that time: they were published in 1635 under the title *Hymnorum Urbani VIII* (even though the extant MS copy in *I-Bc* dates from 12 years later). In the double-choir *Letanie e motetti* (Venice, 1638), the old style contrasts with a more up-to-date one; the second choir is sometimes lower in range, and some pieces (e.g. *Dilecta mea*) have much dance-like triple time. The best work in the set, however, is not a double-choir one but the very attractive and expressive *Ave verum* for five voices and organ.

JEROME ROCHE

**Milano, Francesco Canova da.** *See* FRANCESCO CANOVA DA MILANO.

**Milanollo, Maria.** Italian violinist, sister of TERESA MILANOLLO.

**Milanollo, (Domenica Maria) Teresa** (*b* Savigliano, nr. Turin, 28 Aug 1827; *d* Paris, 25 Oct 1904). Italian violinist and composer. She learnt solfège from her father and studied the violin with Giovanni Ferrero, Mauro Caldera and Giovanni Morra. She made her début on 17 April 1836 in the theatre of Mondovi before moving with her family to France. After giving five concerts in Marseilles, she went to Paris and met Lafont, who recognized her talents and took her with him on tours to The Hague, Amsterdam and elsewhere in the Netherlands. In December 1836 she gave a benefit concert in Brussels which marked the beginning of her lifelong concern for the poor.

Early in 1837 the Milanollo family went to England.

Teresa performed with Johann Strauss (i) and was for a time the protégée and pupil of Francis Mori. In 1838 she toured Wales with the harpist Charles Bochsa, giving 40 concerts within a month. She then returned with her family to France and began teaching music to her younger sister Maria (*b* Savigliano, 19 July 1832; *d* Paris, 21 Oct 1848) before both completed their violin training with Bériot. In 1840–41 Teresa studied with Habeneck in Paris, and in 1842 the sisters began a series of extended European concert tours which took them to England, Belgium, France, Germany, Bohemia, Switzerland and northern Italy, rivalling Paganini in artistic and financial success. For a time they settled in Brussels, where Teresa studied composition with Ferdinand Kufferath. During their second visit to England, in 1845, they appeared at the Philharmonic Concerts; their benefit concerts and quartet performances in Lyons surpassed the earlier successes of Thalberg, H. W. Ernst and even Liszt in that city.

In autumn 1848 Maria died suddenly of tuberculosis; Teresa went into mourning for two months before giving a concert in Paris for the benefit of the Association des Artistes Musiciens. She virtually retired for the next two years, giving only benefit concerts. In 1852 she resumed full-time playing, touring France, Switzerland, Germany and Austria; she interrupted this tour only once, to recover from an injury to her thumb. From 1855 to 1857 she made few appearances. The day of her last public concert, on 16 April 1857, she married Théodore Parmentier, a military engineer and an amateur musician of some repute, who wrote for the *Revue et gazette musicale*.

The high point of Milanollo's career was her six-year period of concert tours with her sister. Teresa's playing was said to be full of warmth and feeling, while Maria's was brilliant and sparkling; to these characteristics they owed their respective nicknames, Mlle Adagio and Mlle Staccato. A Frankfurt critic wrote of them: 'Maria plays like a prodigy, Teresa like an angel'. But the most eloquent praise of Teresa's playing came from Joachim who, according to Moser, said that

he had hardly ever heard then, or since, such accurate or charming violin playing; her technique was secure in every respect, and even in very difficult passages, her bow moved fluently and her tone was full of inner warmth. She was for him, in short, one of the most delightful and sympathetic artists that he had ever met.

The sisters were known particularly for their benefit concerts for the poor, in Savigliano and throughout France; when Teresa had recovered from her sister's death she established the Concerts des Pauvres in Lyons.

Milanollo's compositions include opera transcriptions for two violins and orchestra, numerous pieces for solo violin (including a *Fantaisie élégiaque*, written in memory of her sister in 1853) and an Ave Maria for male chorus.

BIBLIOGRAPHY

*FétisB*

A. Pougin: 'Les soeurs Milanollo', *RIM*, xxiii (1916), 345–89

A. Moser: *Geschichte des Violinspiels* (Berlin, 1923, rev., enlarged 2/1966–7)

E. van der Straeten: *The History of the Violin* (London, 1933/R1968), ii, 32ff

E. HERON-ALLEN/ALBERT MELL

**Milanov [Kunc Milanov Ilić], Zinka** (*b* Zagreb, 17 May 1906). Yugoslav soprano. She used her maiden name, Kunc, until her first marriage, in 1937, to Pedrag Milanov, a Yugoslav actor. She studied at the Zagreb

Academy of Music, and with Milka Ternina, Maria Kostrenčić and Fernando Carpi. Her operatic début was as Leonora (*Il trovatore*) at Ljubljana in 1927; from 1928 to 1935 she was the leading soprano at the Zagreb Opera, where she gave more than 350 performances in such roles as Sieglinde, the Marschallin, Rachel (*La juive*) and Minnie (*La fanciulla del West*), all sung in Serbo-Croat. After appearances at the German Theatre, Prague, in 1936, she was engaged by Toscanini for Verdi's Requiem at the 1937 Salzburg Festival. On 17 December 1937 in *Il trovatore* she began a long association with the Metropolitan Opera, appearing every season (except for 1941–2 and 1947–50) until her farewell performance as Madeleine de Coigny in *Andrea Chénier* on 13 April 1966; with the company, in New York and on tour, she gave 424 performances in 14 works – notably as the principal Verdi and Puccini heroines, but also as Norma, Donna Anna in Bruno Walter's revival of *Don Giovanni* (1941), and Gioconda. She appeared at the Teatro Colón, Buenos Aires (1940–42), San Francisco and Chicago, but her European performances after 1939 were few: in *Tosca* at La Scala (1950) and Covent Garden (1956 and 1957), and *Il trovatore* at Covent Garden (1957).

Milanov's voice was one of translucent beauty as well as great power, and she was able to spin out the most exquisite *pianissimo* phrases with little or no apparent effort. Even at the peak of her career, however, she was not a perfect vocalist, and an impeccable performance on one evening could be followed by an erratic one on the next. A certain unsteadiness of tone, noticeable in some of her recordings, at times marred her performances, while in the theatre uncertainties of pitch were not unknown. In the 1940s and 1950s, however, she had few equals in Verdi roles, as her recording of *Il trovatore* demonstrates. She was a handsome and even stately figure on the stage, relying mostly on her voice to achieve dramatic effects: by postwar standards her acting was old-fashioned.

BIBLIOGRAPHY
L. Riemens: 'Milanov, Zinka', *Le grandi voci* (Rome, 1964) [with opera discography by S. Smolian]
E. K. Einstein: 'Zinka Milanov Discography', *Grand baton*, v/2 (1968), 7

HAROLD ROSENTHAL

**Milanova, Stoika** (*b* Plovdiv, 5 Aug 1945). Bulgarian violinist. She studied with her father until the age of 18, winning competition prizes in Bulgaria and Helsinki, and in 1964 became a pupil in Moscow of David Oistrakh, with whom she worked for five years. After gaining a second prize in the 1967 Queen Elisabeth of the Belgians competition, she won the first in the 1970 Carl Flesch international competition organized by the City of London Festival. Her British concert début followed during the same festival at Southwark Cathedral, and she later toured Britain and other European countries with developing success. Her outstanding qualities are an unusual purity of tone and a mature musicianship in the major works of the violin repertory, some of which she has recorded. She has given duo recitals with Radu Lupu and Malcolm Frager, and made a number of gramophone records with the latter. Milanova plays a 1733 Guarneri 'del Gesù'.

NOËL GOODWIN

**Milanta, Giovanni Francesco** (*b* Parma, 1 March 1607; *d* after 1651). Italian composer and organist. He was born into an influential family living near to what is now the Oratorio of S Lucia at Parma. In 1651 he was organist and choirmaster at the royal fortress of Asola, near Mantua.

WORKS
Misse, salmi e motetti con sinfonie, 1–5, 8vv, bc, op.1 (Venice, 1649)
Il secondo libro de motetti, 2–5vv, vns, et le Letanie, 4vv, bc, della BVM et in fine 4 Tantum ergo sacramentum (Venice, 1651)
Il primo libro de madrigali, 2–4vv, con alcune canzonete, sonetti in genere rappresentativo, 1v, bc, op.3 (Venice, 1651)
Salve Regina and several litanies, cited in *LaMusicaD*
BIBLIOGRAPHY
*EitnerQ*; *WaltherML*
N. Pelicelli: 'Musicisti in Parma nel secolo XVII', *NA*, x (1933), 321

JOHN WHENHAM

**Milanuzzi** [Milanuzii], **Carlo** (*b* Sanatoglia [formerly S Natoglia], nr. Camerino; *d* c1647). Italian composer, organist and poet. Though born in central Italy he spent much of his life in the north. He became an Augustinian monk and was possibly in Venice by 1615, working at S Stefano. In 1619 he was organist of the Augustinian church at Perugia and returned north by 1622 to be *maestro di cappella* at S Eufemia, Verona. From 1623 to 1629 he was organist at S Stefano, Venice, and from 1629 to c1634 at Finale di Modena. In 1636 he was *maestro di cappella* at Camerino Cathedral, and his last known appointment, in 1643, was once more in the Venetian area, as *maestro* and organist at S Mauro, Noventa di Piave. He was also known as a preacher.

For a priest and church musician, Milanuzzi wrote a surprisingly large number of secular monodies, mainly in his at least nine books of 'ariose vaghezze', eight of which survive. They are mostly short arias in a tuneful style that was rapidly gaining popularity in northern Italy in the 1620s; many are very charming. No doubt aiming at as wide an audience as possible he included

*Zinka Milanov as Madeleine de Coigny in Giordano's 'Andrea Chénier'*

letters for the guitar, and there are some Spanish dances for guitar in op.9, among them a very early example of the *folia* melody. He was one of the most progressive secular monodists of his day, and forward-looking developments in the strophic aria in the 1620s and 1630s are clearly reflected in his output. Op.11 includes monodies by Monteverdi, Berti and Miniscalchi. The earlier concerted secular pieces for two to four voices in op.3 have gracefully ornamented melodies, and some are in a simple binary form.

Milanuzzi's preference for monody is paralleled in his sacred output, which is very largely for the *concertato* medium of a few voices with continuo. Though he published no collections of solo motets he drew special attention to the six motets for bass solo in op.13, and in the litanies of op.5 he adopted the cantilena style, in which there are extended solo passages unified by a tutti. The influence of the aria is felt in the 'walking' crotchet bass figures of op.19 which become like ground basses when, as sometimes occurs, they are repeated often enough (even in different keys). A genuine ground bass does indeed appear in parts of a psalm from op.14, an indication that in setting long psalm texts Milanuzzi felt that some kind of repeated material would help to unify a work: in several pieces he brought back his opening theme at the words 'Sicut erat', while once he brought back the opening text as well, just as Monteverdi did in some of his Venetian psalms. Milanuzzi was certainly one of the foremost minor composers to experiment with the unifying of psalm settings: since his psalms are for more modest forces than those of most other Italian composers of the period, such structural interest was all the more necessary to prevent monotony. Even his masses (op.16) are basically for only three soloists and organ, though there are optional parts for ripieno and instrumental ensemble that make them more like the festive orchestral masses of the time.

### WORKS
*(all published in Venice)*
#### SACRED

op.
1  Sacri rosarum flores, 2–4vv, liber I (1619)
2  Vespertina psalmodia, 2vv, org, liber I (1619)
5  Letanie della beata vergine, 4, 8vv, parte sono in cantilena, parte correnti, et parte in concerto . . . bc (1622)
6  Armonia sacra di concerti, messa et canzoni, 5vv, bc (1622⁶)
13  Sacra cetra concertata con affetti ecclesiastici, 2–5vv. Con l'aggiunta di 6 motetti, ariosi, e commodi per un basso solo, libro II (1625)
14  Concerto sacro di salmi intieri, 2–3vv, comodi, vaghi, et ariosi . . . bc (org),liber I (1629)
16  Messe a 3 concertate che si possono cantare a 7, 11, aggiuntovi 4vv, et 4 stromenti ad lib, bc, libro I (1627)
19  Hortus sacer deliciarum . . . 1–3vv . . . una cum missa 2, ac Litaniis BVM, 3vv, org, liber III (1636)
21  Concerto sacro di salmi intieri, 2–3vv, bc (org) . . . aggiuntovi 2 vn, libro II (1643)
23  Compieta intiera concertata con le antifone, e Litanie BVM di Dio . . . bc (org), 1–4vv (1647)

1 motet in 1625²

#### SECULAR

3  Aurea corona de scherzi poetici, 2–4vv, bc, libro I (1620)
7  Primo scherzo delle ariose vaghezze, 1v, hpd/chit/double harp/other inst con le littere del alfabetto, con intavolatura, e con la scala di musica, gui (1622)
8  Secondo scherzo delle ariose vaghezze, 1v, bc, aggiuntevi . . . alcune sonate facili intavolate (1622)
9  Terzo scherzo delle ariose vaghezze, 1v, bc, con l'aggiunta . . . di alcuni balletti, sarauende, spagnolette, gagliarde, follie, ciaccone, et altre sonate intavolate, gui (1623)
11  Quarto scherzo ariose delle vaghezze, 1v, bc, con una cantata, altre arie del Signor Monteverdi . . . aggiuntovi . . . 2 arie dall'autore (2/1624)
15  Sesto libro delle ariose vaghezze, 1v, bc (1628)

17  Settimo libro delle ariose vaghezze, 1v, bc, aggiuntavi un'arietta, 2vv, con sinfonie di 2 vn (1630)
18  Ottavo libro delle ariose vaghezze, 1v, bc (1635)
20  Nono libro delle ariose vaghezze, commode da cantarsi, 1, 2vv, bc (1643)

2 arias in 1634⁷
Bc to Pomponio Nenna's Il primo libro de madrigali, 4vv (2/1621)
#### LOST WORKS
*(cited in the appendix to Messe a 3 concertate op.16)*
Primo e secondo libro di motetti, 1–5vv. Libro primo de madrigali concertati, 2–4vv. Le musice moderne, 1, 2vv. Il primo libro de motetti, 1v. Il primo libro de salmetti, 2vv, spezzati
Il primo, e secondo libro de salmi concertati con voci, e con stromenti, 4 chori. Una copia di salmi in tripla, 3 chori. Un'altra copia di salmi à 8 correnti. Le messe con alcuni motetti, 8vv. Una copia di messe concertati à 14 con voci, e stromenti; un altra copia à 12, concertate. Il primo libro delle messe, 4vv da capella. Una terza in tripla, 8vv. Una copia di compiete, 5vv, con sinfonie di 2 vn, e 1 bn. Un'altra compieta, 5vv, corrente intiera. Un altra, 8vv. Due altre copie di compiete, 4, 5 chori concertate. Il secondo libro de madrigali concertati, 2–4vv. Un'altra copia di madrigali, 4vv, non concertati. Una messa, 6 chori concertata. Gl'improperii della settimana santa, 4vv. Un corpo di salmi, 4–6 chori, concertati. Altri salmi, 5vv, concertati, e correnti. Il settimo libro delle ariette, 1v. Diverse correnti, capricci sonate, balletti, e stravaganze da sonare. Il terzo libro de motetti, 1–4vv
Corenti baletti mentioned in Vincenti's *Indice*
Balletti, saltarelli, e corretine alla francese, 1v, libro I, et salmi, 2 vn, bc mentioned in *WaltherML*

### BIBLIOGRAPHY
*WaltherML*
A. Vincenti: *Indice di tutte le opere di musica che si trovano nella Stampa della Pigna di Alessandro Vincenti in Venezia* (Venice, 1619–49); ed. F. X. Haberl, *MMg*, xiv–xv (1882–3/R), suppl.
E. Schmitz: *Geschichte der weltlichen Solokantate* (Leipzig, 1914, rev. 2/1955), 39, 47, 49, 68f
S. L. Astengo: *Musici agostiniani anteriori al secolo 19* (Florence, 1929), 32ff
N. Fortune: *Italian Secular Song from 1600 to 1635: the Origins and Development of Accompanied Monody* (diss., U. of Cambridge, 1954)
——: 'A Handlist of Printed Italian Secular Monody Books, 1602–1635', *RMARC*, iii (1963/R1970), 27
J. L. A. Roche: *North Italian Liturgical Music in the Early 17th Century* (diss., U. of Cambridge, 1968)
——: 'Giovanni Antonio Rigatti and the Development of Venetian Church Music in the 1640s', *ML*, lvii (1976), 256
JEROME ROCHE

**Milashkina, Tamara (Andreyevna)** (*b* Astrakhan, 13 Sept 1934). Soviet soprano. Until 1959 she studied under Elena Katul'skaya at the Moscow Conservatory; in 1958, while still a student, she was engaged as a soloist at the Bol'shoy Opera. She became the first Soviet singer to appear at La Scala when she made her début there in 1962, as Lida in Verdi's *La battaglia di Legnano*. One of the leading singers of the Bol'shoy Opera, Milashkina has a voice of distinctive timbre and unusual warmth and beauty; reserve and emotional depth combine to lend her stage portrayals particular sensitivity. Notable among her many roles are the Tchaikovsky heroines Tatyana, Lisa and Mariya (*Mazepa*), Fevroniya (Rimsky-Korsakov's *The Legend of the City of Kitezh*, filmed in 1966), Prokofiev's Natasha (*War and Peace*) and Lyubka (*Semyon Kotko*), Leonora (*Il trovatore*), Elisabeth de Valois, Aida and Tosca. She has sung throughout Europe, and appeared at the Metropolitan Opera during the Bol'shoy company's visit in 1975. In 1973 she was made a National Artist of the USSR.

### BIBLIOGRAPHY
B. Pokrovsky: 'Tamara Milashkina', *Teatr* (1961), no.1, p.70
I. Tumanov: 'Chetire goda spustya' [Four years later], *Teatr* (1965), no.1, p.85
G. Baranova: 'Solistka Bol'shovo: Tamara Milashkina', *Molodiye golosa* [Young voices] (Moscow, 1966), 26ff
I. M. YAMPOL'SKY

**Milchevsky, Marcin.** *See* MIELCZEWSKI, MARCIN.

**Mildenburg, Anna von.** *See* BAHR-MILDENBURG, ANNA.

**Milder-Hauptmann, (Pauline) Anna** (*b* Constantinople, 13 Dec 1785; *d* Berlin, 29 May 1838). German singer and tragedienne. The daughter of a Viennese courier, she studied with Tomaselli and Salieri (on Schikaneder's recommendation) and also had instruction from Neukomm (on Haydn's advice). She made her début as Juno in Süssmayr's *Der Spiegel von Arkadien* (1803). Beethoven wrote for her the part of Leonore (1805), which she later told Schindler led to some 'hard fights' over passages in the 'Komm Hoffnung' section of 'Abscheulicher!' that she found inimical to her voice: she was able to persuade him to alter them in 1814 only by refusing to sing them. Her voice had previously been described by Haydn as 'like a house' and by Griesinger as 'like pure metal'; but her first performances of *Fidelio* seem to have been tentative (because of inexperience) beside her later ones.

In 1808 she made a successful tour, and was admired by Napoleon, among others; on her return she was appointed court *prima donna assoluta* in Berlin. In 1810 she married a jeweller, Hauptmann, whose difficult personality seems to have lain behind a later faltering in her career. But she achieved her greatest triumph in 1812 in Gluck's *Iphigénie en Tauride*, which she performed again in Berlin four years later. Gluck's heroines suited her imposing presence and her magnificent full, rich and flawless voice; though less successful with Donna Elvira and Susanna, she made Weigl's *Das Waisenhaus* and *Die Schweizerfamilie* famous. Cherubini wrote *Faniska* for her, and Schubert *Der Hirt auf dem Felsen* and the second *Suleika* song. In 1829 she left Berlin over a quarrel with Spontini and visited Russia, Sweden and Denmark; in the same year she sang in Mendelssohn's historic revival of Bach's *St Matthew Passion*. Her last public appearance was in Vienna in 1836.

BIBLIOGRAPHY

G. Griesinger: *Biographische Notizen über Joseph Haydn* (Leipzig, 1810; Eng. trans., 1963); ed. F. Grasberger (Vienna, 1954)
A. F. Schindler: *Biographie von Ludwig van Beethoven* (Münster, 1840, 3/1860; Eng. trans., 1966 as *Beethoven as I Knew him*)
L. Eisenberg: *Grosses biographisches Lexicon der deutschen Bühne im XIX Jh.* (Leipzig, 1903)
O. E. Deutsch: *Schubert: die Dokumente seines Lebens* (Munich and Leipzig, 1914, rev. 2/1964; Eng. trans., 1947)
E. Forbes, ed.: *Thayer's Life of Beethoven* (Princeton, 1964)
F. A. MARSHALL/JOHN WARRACK

**Mildmay, (Grace) Audrey (Louise St John)** (*b* Herstmonceux, 19 Dec 1900; *d* London, 31 May 1953). English soprano. She studied in London with Johnstone Douglas and in Vienna with Jani Strasser, later touring Canada and the USA as Polly Peachum (*The Beggar's Opera*) in 1927–8. On her return to England she joined the Carl Rosa Opera, playing such roles as Zerlina, Gretel, Micaela, Olympia, Musetta and Nedda, and remaining a member until her marriage to John Christie in 1931. With her husband she helped found the Glyndebourne Festival and then, with Rudolf Bing, the Edinburgh Festival. Except for the 1937 season, she sang at Glyndebourne each summer from 1934 to 1939, her Susanna, Zerlina and Norina being much admired. In 1940 she sang Polly Peachum in Glyndebourne's wartime tour. She appeared as guest artist at Sadler's Wells in 1939 as Susanna, and in the same role under Beecham at Montreal (1943), after which she sang no more in opera. Carl Ebert called her

'an unforgettable Susanna and Zerlina as well as the heart and spirit of Glyndebourne'; her performances of those roles in the Glyndebourne recordings give an incomplete impression of her vivacity and charm on stage.

BIBLIOGRAPHY

S. Hughes: *Glyndebourne* (London, 1965)
HAROLD ROSENTHAL

**Miles, Jane Mary.** *See* GUEST, JANE MARY.

**Miley, 'Bubber'** [James Wesley] (*b* Aiken, South Carolina, ?19 ?Jan 1903; *d* New York, ?24 May 1932). Black American jazz trumpeter. He moved to New York at the age of six, and studied the trombone before learning the cornet. He was active professionally from 1920 with Willie Gant, Mamie Smith and others, and in 1923 joined Elmer Snowden's Washingtonians, who soon afterwards came under the leadership of Duke Ellington. Miley remained with Ellington until early 1929, and then worked with Noble Sissle (touring to Paris in 1929), Zutty Singleton and others. In the last months of his life he led his own orchestra.

Miley's melodic and rhythmic styles were influenced by King Oliver and the trumpeter Johnny Dunn. But he is noted for having begun the practice of using a 'wah-wah' tone modifier on an already muted trumpet, thus combining two techniques employed separately by Oliver. His 'growl' effect was adopted by Sidney de Paris, Cootie Williams, Ray Nance and many other jazz trumpeters, and formed an important element of Ellington's style. He was the most impressive of the early Ellington soloists, and collaborated on or strongly influenced many of Ellington's early compositions; the better sections of *Black and Tan Fantasy*, *East St Louis Toodle-oo* and *Doin' the Voom-voom* are thought to be Miley's work.

BIBLIOGRAPHY

R. Dodge: 'Harpsichords and Jazz Trumpets', *Frontiers of Jazz*, ed. R. de Toledano (New York, 1947), 13
G. Schuller: *Early Jazz* (New York, 1968), 320ff
D. Ellington: *Music is my Mistress* (New York, 1973), 106ff
J. R. TAYLOR

**Milford, Robin (Humphrey)** (*b* Oxford, 22 Jan 1903; *d* Lyme Regis, Dorset, 29 Dec 1959). English composer. He was the son of Sir Humphrey Milford, formerly head of Oxford University Press, and he was educated at Rugby and the RCM, where he studied under Holst, Vaughan Williams and R. O. Morris. Able to devote himself almost entirely to composition, Milford soon developed into a prolific composer in all genres. He made his first impact with a Double Fugue for Orchestra, published in 1927 by the Carnegie Collection of British Music, and the oratorio *A Prophet in the Land*, performed at the 1931 Gloucester meeting of the Three Choirs Festival. Despite successful first performances, many of his more ambitious orchestral works, including the Violin Concerto in G minor (1937), have remained in manuscript and it is through his choral works, songs and smaller essays in chamber music that he reached his widest audience. A full-scale opera, *The Scarlet Letter* (1958–9), to an adaptation by D. S. Savage of the novel by Hawthorne, has remained unpublished and unperformed. This partial neglect is not perhaps unjustified, for Milford's talent found its happiest expression in writing for the voice on a small scale. Thus the collection *A Book of Songs* (Oxford, 1926) gives a fair view of his creative gifts which, though slight, were genuine and not without individuality. His style is simple, diatonic and much influenced by folksong. Economical and always practical in layout, his music has been of particular service to amateurs.

BIBLIOGRAPHY
S. Goddard: 'Milford, Robin', *Grove 5*

MICHAEL HURD

**Milhaud, Darius** (*b* Aix-en-Provence, 4 Sept 1892; *d* Geneva, 22 June 1974). French composer.

1. LIFE. He came of a well-to-do Jewish family long settled in Aix and closely in touch with the cultural life of that area. Milhaud began to study the violin at the age of seven and started composing soon after; he entered the Paris Conservatoire primarily as a violin student, but gradually became convinced that composing was his true vocation. His teachers included Leroux, Dukas, Gédalge and Widor; but the many friends he made among writers and painters, especially Jammes and Claudel, influenced him as much as, if not more than, his musical contemporaries. At this time he began to travel widely, a habit which remained with him throughout his life despite the severely disabling rheumatoid arthritis which eventually confined him to a wheelchair.

Milhaud's first major works were the incidental music to Claudel's *Protée* (composed in three different versions, 1913–19) and the opera *La brebis égarée* (composed 1910–15, produced 1923) to a libretto by Jammes. He was at work on the latter when war broke out, but was rejected for military service on medical grounds. The following year he composed *Les choëphores*, the work in which he established polytonality as the norm of his harmonic language. In 1913 he had begun his settings of the *Oresteia* in Claudel's translation with *Agamemnon*, in which he shunned traditional techniques of incidental music and effected a novel type of transition from speech to song; he employed the same basic procedures in *Les choëphores* and later in *Les euménides* (1917–22), of which the former also contains the fruits of his research into every aspect of polytonality. He sub-titled his manuscript 'harmonic variations', following for each strophe and anti-strophe a definite line of harmonic research, applying variation technique to sequences of chords. In two scenes Milhaud employed a large battery of pitchless percussion as background to a woman narrator who declaims the text in strict synchronization with the 'music', and the chorus is required to whistle, groan and shriek; its parts are notated in rhythm but not pitch. *Les euménides* marked a further step forward in the same direction, and the polytonal elements in Milhaud's harmony and the personal use to which he put them are responsible above all else for the distinctive profile of his music. They are present in one form or another throughout his work, although once the initial novelty had worn off there was some abatement in the intellectual rigour and consistency with which he applied them.

Although the outbreak of war prevented Milhaud from competing for the Prix de Rome, he lost nothing thereby, for in 1916 Claudel, then better known as a diplomat than as a poet, was appointed French minister to Brazil, and invited Milhaud to accompany him to Rio de Janeiro as his secretary. They spent nearly two years in South America, whose atmosphere and native music made an indelible impression on the young composer. To this the ballet *L'homme et son désir* (1918), the two

dance suites *Saudades do Brasil* (1920–21) and random reminiscences in many later works all bear witness.

On his return to Paris in November 1918 Milhaud was drawn into the Cocteau circle of writers, artists and composers and became one of Les Six. There was however insufficient unanimity of temperament and aesthetic to bind the members together as a unit for very long, and eventually they all went their separate ways; but not before works such as *Le boeuf sur le toit* (1919) and *Les mariés de la tour Eiffel* (1921, jointly composed by the group) had successfully branded Milhaud in the public mind as an unprincipled exploiter of fashionable oddities. Nor did the *Rite of Spring*-like reception accorded the first performances of the *Protée* symphonic suite under Pierné in 1920 and of the *Cinq études* for piano and orchestra the following year in any way redeem his standing. Even *La brebis égarée*, a relatively conventional piece, caused a riot when staged at the Opéra-Comique in 1923, and critics firmly refused to take the song cycles *Machines agricoles* (settings of descriptions of farm machinery in agricultural catalogues) and *Catalogue de fleurs* (to poems by Lucien Daudet inspired by a florist's catalogue) in the perfectly serious spirit in which they had been conceived.

During a visit to London in 1920 for a performance of *Le boeuf sur le toit*, Milhaud first heard jazz played by Billy Arnold and his band. On his return he began steeping himself in all the American popular music he could find, *très à la mode* as it then was with his friends Jean Wiener and Clément Doucet, who played all the latest transatlantic import of blues and ragtime. In 1922 Milhaud went on a tour of the USA and in 1923, fired by his first experience of authentic black jazz in Harlem, he composed the ballet *La création du monde* to a scenario by Cendrars. The next year saw the production of two new ballets almost simultaneously: *Le train bleu* for Dyagilev and *Salade* (choreographed by Massine); the latter eventually became *Le carnaval d'Aix* for piano and orchestra. Then in 1925, to a libretto by Armand Lunel, Milhaud composed *Les malheurs d'Orphée*, the first of his several chamber operas (counterparts to the six chamber symphonies of 1917–23), each relatively short in duration and scored for a minimum of singers and instrumentalists; the others were the popular *Le pauvre matelot* (1926, libretto by Cocteau), a piece of great melodic spontaneity and directness, and the trilogy of one-acters to librettos by Henri Hoppenot: *L'enlèvement d'Europe*, *L'abandon d'Ariane* and *La délivrance de Thésée*, all written in 1927. On the other hand the most imposing of the Milhaud–Claudel collaborations, *Christophe Colomb* (1928), is an opera on the grandest scale, part symbolic, part expressionist; it incorporates references to the Greek chorus, the medieval mystery, the Wagnerian leitmotif; it calls for an army of executants including 45 vocal soloists, an offstage orchestra, non-singing actors and a huge chorus; and it experiments with film inserts. The opera was successfully produced in Berlin in 1930 but not taken up by other theatres for over 30 years; for the 1969–70 stage representations in Graz and Wuppertal the composer drastically revised the structure of the work. All the facets of Milhaud's polymorphous musical personality are in some measure therein represented; none of his later large-scale stage works (*Maximilien*, 1930; *Bolivar*, 1943; *David*, 1952) exhibits the same concentrated musical vitality.

*Darius Milhaud*

All through the 1920s and 1930s Milhaud combined a high rate of composition with extensive travelling in Russia, Syria, Sardinia, Spain and elsewhere. He made frequent appearances at, for example, the Venice and Florence festivals, both as conductor and pianist, and in 1932 participated in a critics' congress organized by the Portuguese Government. His musical horizons continued to broaden: he began to write scores for children and amateurs (*A propos de bottes*, 1932; *Un petit peu de musique*, 1932; *Un petit peu d'exercice*, 1934), for the cinema (Renoir's *Madame Bovary*, 1933; *Tartarin de Tarascon*, 1934; *La citadelle du silence*, 1937), and for the stage (*L'annonce faite à Marie*, 1932; *Le château des papes*, 1932; *Le trompeur de Séville*, 1937). His *Introduction et marche funèbre* was originally written for Rolland's *Le quatorze juillet* together with music by seven other French composers and produced at the Paris Arena in 1936; the following year Milhaud made a number of contributions to the International Exhibition, including music for Claudel's *Fête de la musique*, a 'spectacle de lumière et d'eau'.

In 1940 the fall of France drove the Milhauds from their home, but not before the composer, bedridden in Aix, had made a start on the first of a series of 12 symphonies for full orchestra, of which no.3 (*Te Deum*, 1946) is a choral hymn of thanksgiving for victory, no.4 (1947) an epic of the 1848 Revolution, and no.8 (1957) a portrait of the Rhône. On arrival in the USA Milhaud was offered a teaching post at Mills College, Oakland, California, and spent the war years there, composing prolifically the while. After his return to France in August 1947 he combined his Mills College post with that of professor of composition at the Paris Conservatoire, and also established a long-lasting connection with the music school at Aspen, Colorado. In 1952 he composed the opera *David* to a libretto by Armand Lunel for the Festival of Israel in honour of the 3000th anniversary of King David and of the founda-

tion of Jerusalem, making a special journey to Israel to steep himself in its atmosphere. Despite his disabilities he maintained a full and active schedule of teaching and composing until long after his 70th birthday, which was marked by widespread celebrations in France and a spate of new recordings. In 1971 ill-health finally forced him to resign from his post at Mills College and to move to Geneva. On his 80th birthday tribute was paid him in Rome, Nice, Aix, Brussels and elsewhere. His last work was a cantata, *Ani maamin, un chant perdu et retrouvé*, written for the 1973 Festival of Israel.

2. WORKS. With this final work Milhaud reached his op.441. He was one of the 20th century's most industrious composers, impelled to expend himself in unceasing productivity in such a way that his creativity diffused itself over a vast area of heterogeneous works. Potentially he was one of the best composers of his generation: there are few pieces that do not contain something of value, though not many people have the time or energy to sift through vast quantities of chaff in quest of the isolated grain of wheat.

Much the larger part of Milhaud's most durable music was written while he was still a comparatively young man. Certainly his best work was done by the outbreak of World War II. The distinct falling-off in quality (if not in quantity) perceptible thereafter may be attributable partly to increasing age and infirmity, professorial commitments and other extra-musical impediments; but the real cause of the trouble was surely the war, which cut Milhaud off from his homeland and from one of the two prime sources of his inspiration. For he neatly isolated both mainsprings when he declared in the opening words of his autobiography 'I am a Frenchman from Provence, and by religion a Jew'. The experience of Aix, his exposure in youth to the Provençal landscape and its popular music, remained central to his creativity, and much of his best music is that which, often unconsciously, attempts to recapture the spirit of 'dandelion days' in Provence, the happiest time of an unusually rich and happy life (for despite great physical adversity Milhaud always retained his serenity). Of course, he early acquired a patina of urban sophistication in Paris, and was happy enough to allow himself to be swept along by the currents of contemporary musical thought; his contacts with Cocteau, Satie and Stravinsky and the formation of Les Six encouraged his natural iconoclasm in harmonic and structural matters (his waywardness in respect of the latter is frequently the result either of a desire to allow the music to find the form best suited to its own expression, as in the perfectly proportioned *Concertino de printemps* of 1934, or of an impulsiveness that casts aside the predictable in favour of the unexpected, regardless of context), his bias towards popular music, even that of 'low life', his delight in the refurbishing of old music in present-day garb, and the sometimes rather selfconscious cleverness of his own technical facility, as in the oft-quoted case of those two of his 18 string quartets which can be played separately or together. But like Chabrier, with whom he had many affinities, Milhaud remained a countryman at heart, a 'français de Provence' whose style, soaked in the sun and the folk-melos of the region, set early and evolved hardly at all. This quite spontaneous and unselfconscious use of folk materials brought into his best work precisely that freshness and element of 'Mediterranean lyricism' elsewhere conspicuously absent. In this he resembled d'Indy for, despite his abhorrence of Wagner and oft-professed allegiance to Debussy, the temper of much Milhaud is Teutonic rather than Gallic; his sympathies often lay more with central European expressionism (he was one of the earliest champions of *Pierrot lunaire*) than with the fastidiousness and formal intellectualism of Latin artists. It is significant that Honegger, much the most Germanically-biassed of Les Six, was greatly influenced by Milhaud, particularly in the *Chant de joie*, the *Pastorale d'été* and *Le roi David*.

As a folklorist, however, Milhaud successfully crossed the borderline between popular culture and high art. His aim in so doing may have been to find a broader, less exclusive and inhibiting framework within which to work than that postulated by Hindemith or Schoenberg; but more probably the Provençal vernacular was so deeply ingrained in the rhythms and cadences of his everyday musical speech that to write in any other way would have been tantamount to denying his birthright. The pastoral note is all-pervasive, as in *Protée*, the First String Quartet, the six chamber symphonies, the First Piano Sonata, the *Suite française* for band, the *Catalogue de fleurs*, and the song cycles *Alissa* and *Le voyage d'été*; and the twin themes of spring and rebirth are favourites (*Le printemps* was the title of a set of six piano pieces, a work for violin and piano which later became the Nocturne in *Protée*, and the First Chamber Symphony; see also the *Concertino de printemps* for violin and chamber orchestra and the ballet *Jeux de printemps*). Many of these works bear the outline and imprint of folksong, which occasionally becomes crossed with nursery jingles (as in the First Chamber Symphony, *L'homme et son désir,* and *Scaramouche* for two pianos). The *Suite française*, *Suite provençale* and other works which draw on actual folk or traditional sources serve to emphasize Milhaud's indebtedness in those which do not. Nor was his response to folk cultures restricted to those of France. He paid tribute to North American folk music in *Kentuckiana, Carnaval à la Nouvelle-Orléans, Le bal martiniquais* and *La création du monde*; and to that of the Piedmont in the *Suite cisalpine* for cello and orchestra. But whereas many of his compatriots looked to Spain, Milhaud was forever haunted by memories of Latin America; his *Saudades do Brasil* have none of the air of arty condescension or wryly amused detachment often perceptible in the Les Six treatment of extra-curricular material, but are poetic, sensitive mood-evocations in the manner of Albeniz's and Debussy's *Ibéria*. Milhaud's use of bitonality in both melody and harmony achieves that strange and subtle distancing wherein lies the potency of the music's nostalgia.

To understand the true origin and purpose of Milhaud's use of bitonality, as exemplified in the *Saudades* and *L'homme et son désir*, one should first consider his affinities with Cézanne. For both artists wanted to integrate impressionist concepts of light and coloured shadow with cleaner-cut and more substantial formal designs. Neither was enamoured of atmospheric abstractions; but to return to the statuesque, heavily stylized scene-painting methods of former years was similarly out of the question. In Cézanne's Provençal landscapes, no less than in Milhaud's (*La cueillette des citrons*, the *Ouverture méditerranéenne*, the *Suite campagnarde*, the *Suite provençale*, the *Symphonie rurale*), are imprinted the familiar features of the Provençal

scene: the harsh light, the dry air, the jagged shapes of rocks and trees, the noisy blend of colours. The realism and naturalness are those striven for by the impressionists; but the compositions have volume and consistency, architectural sharpness, linear definition. The burning southern light is used not to soften outlines but to throw them into clear relief. Milhaud's language is no more primitive than Cézanne's; both are on the contrary highly sophisticated. But both achieved a remarkable combination of rustic simplicity and earthy solidity. In Milhaud's case this would have proved impossible but for the new dimension he added to the harmonic language of his age, and his harmonic explorations may be viewed at least partly as a means to this end. He gave two accounts of the origin of his interest in polytonality, which he saw as a tonal, 'melodic' antidote to the disintegration of the diatonic system. One was the study of a Bach duet in which the initial entries of the two voices appeared to be in different keys. The other – more fanciful, but in fact probably much nearer the mark – was a recurrent, quasi-mystical experience at night in the country, when he felt rays and tremors converging on him from all points of the sky and below ground, 'a thousand simultaneous musics rushing towards me from all directions'. This suggests that the composer to whom Milhaud owed the most in this area was not Bach or Stravinsky but Koechlin, whose early reading of Verne bred in him a strain of nature mysticism which later (but before Milhaud) sought expression in polychordal complexes. Milhaud's great admiration for the bitonal opening of Roussel's *Pour une fête de printemps* adduces further evidence. It was when he approached polychords and bitonality not as ends in themselves but as a means to the creating of a unique atmosphere that Milhaud made his best music.

Less significant perhaps in the overall perspective of his achievement, yet a potent force to be reckoned with, was Milhaud's awareness of his Jewish heritage. Among his finest scores must certainly be numbered the *Service sacré* (1947), parts of the ballet *Moïse* (*Opus americanum no.2*, 1940), the *Liturgie comtadine* (1933) and above all the magnificent *Poèmes juifs* (1916). All are imbued with an emotional intensity and undercurrent of lament unmistakably Jewish in character. Lambert in *Music Ho!* quoted Cendrars on the Jews' almost masochistic passion for lamentation, and perhaps this may be related to Milhaud's predilection for librettos based on Greek tragedy: the *Oresteia*, *Les malheurs d'Orphée*, *Médée*, even *Le pauvre matelot*, which falls into the same category by virtue of its core of tragic inevitability. This throws another light on his attempts, notably in *Les choëphores*, to intensify the expressive power of harmony with polychords, a polychord being to his ears 'more subtly sweet and more violently potent' than diatonic harmony. In their baroque expressionism and violent, impulsive lyricism, these works approximate to what Cézanne familiarly termed his 'couillarde' period, but for Milhaud a more fruitful expressive outlet in this area was New Orleans jazz. Since jazz was the music of one dispossessed and persecuted race it was likely to appeal strongly to another; in any event, *La création du monde* commands respect when other similar hybrids have been forgotten. Yet the oboe solo just before the coda, with its triplet falling through a sharp 4th, is a reminder that even in the frenzy of a Harlem jam session Milhaud never lost sight of the 'exquisite blue lines of the horizon' of Aix; and the coda itself ultimately dissolves in the mists of a Provençal spring. For Milhaud all roads led back to Aix; and no composer has captured its Mediterranean spirit in music more persuasively.

For a design for *La création du monde*, see FRANCE, fig.7.

## WORKS

### OPERAS

La brebis égarée, op.4 (3, Jammes), 1910–15; Paris, Opéra-Comique, 1923
Les malheurs d'Orphée, op.85 (3, A. Lunel), 1925; Brussels, Monnaie, 1925
Esther de Carpentras, op.89 (comic opera, 2, Lunel), 1925; Paris, Radio Rennes, 1937
Le pauvre matelot, op.92 (3, Cocteau), 1926; Paris, Opéra-Comique, 1927
L'enlèvement d'Europe, op.94 (1, H. Hoppenot), 1927; Baden-Baden, 1927
L'abandon d'Ariane, op.98 (1, Hoppenot), 1927; Wiesbaden, 1928
La délivrance de Thésée, op.99 (1, Hoppenot), 1927; Wiesbaden, 1928
Christophe Colomb, op.102 (2 parts, Claudel), 1928; Berlin, 1930 ·
Maximilien, op.110 (3, Werfel, Hoffman, Lunel), 1930; Paris, Opéra, 1932
Médée, op.191 (1, M. Milhaud), 1938; Anvers, Opéra Flamand, 1939
Bolivar, op.236 (3, M. Milhaud, J. Supervielle), 1943; Paris, Opéra, 1950
David, op.320 (5, Lunel), 1952; Jerusalem, 1954
Fiesta, op.370 (1, Vian), 1958; Berlin, Staatsoper, 1958
La mère coupable, op.412 (3, M. Milhaud, after Beaumarchais), 1964; Geneva, 1965
Saint Louis, roi de France, op.434 (opera-oratorio, 2 parts, Claudel, M. Doublier), 1970; RAI, 1972

### BALLETS

L'homme et son désir, op.48 (Claudel), 1918
Le boeuf sur le toit, op.58 (Cocteau), 1919
La création du monde, op.81 (Cendrars), 1923
Salade, op.83 (Flament), 1924
Le train bleu, op.84 (Cocteau), 1924
Polka for L'éventail de Jeanne, op.95, 1927
La bien-aimée, op.101 [after Schubert and Liszt], pleyela, orch, 1928
Les songes, op.124 (Derain), 1933
Moyen âge fleuri, op.152, 1936
Moïse (Opus americanum no.2), op.219, 1940
Jeux de printemps, op.243, 1944
Les cloches, op.259 (after Poe), 1945
'Adame Miroir, op.283 (Genet), 1948
La cueillette des citrons, op.298, 1949–50
Vendanges, op.317 (Rothschild), 1952
La rose des vents, op.367 (Vidalie), 1957
La branche des oiseaux, op.374 (Chamson), 1958–9

### OTHER DRAMATIC WORKS

Incidental music: Agamemnon, op.14 (Claudel, after Aeschylus), 1913–14; Protée, op.17 (Claudel), 1913–19; Les choëphores, op.24 (Claudel, after Aeschylus), 1915; Les euménides, op.41 (Claudel, after Aeschylus), 1917–22; L'annonce faite à Marie, op.117 (Claudel), 1932; Le château des papes, op.120 (Richaud), 1932; Se plaire sur la même fleur, op.131 (Moreno), 1934; Le cycle de la création, op.139 (L. Sturzo), 1935; Le faiseur, op.145 (Balzac), 1935; Bolivar (Supervielle), 1935–6; Bertran de Born, op.152a (Valmy, Baisse), 1936; Le trompeur de Séville, op.152c (Obey), 1937; Le quatorze juillet (Rolland), Introduction et marche funèbre for finale of Act 1 only, op.153, 1936; Le conquérant, op.154 (Mistler), 1936; Amal, ou La lettre du roi, op.156 (Tagore, Gide), 1936; Le voyageur sans bagages, op.157 (Anouilh), 1936; Jules César, op.158 (Shakespeare), 1936; La duchesse d'Amalfi, op.160 (Webster), 1937; Roméo et Juliette, op.161 (Shakespeare), 1937; Le médecin volant, op.165 (Molière), 1937; Macbeth, op.175 (Shakespeare), 1937; Hécube, op.177 (Richaud, after Euripides), 1937; Plutus, op.186 (Jollivet, after Aristophanes), 1938; Tricolore, op.190 (Lestringuez), 1938; Le bal des voleurs, op.192 (Anouilh), 1938; La première famille, op.193 (Supervielle), 1938; Hamlet, op.200 (Laforgue), 1939; Un petit ange de rien du tout, op.215 (Puget), 1940; L'annonce faite à Marie, op.231 (Claudel), 1942; Lidoire, op.264 (Courteline), 1946; Shéhérazade, op.285 (Supervielle), 1948; Le conte d'hiver, op.306 (Shakespeare), 1950; Christophe Colomb, op.318 (Claudel) [new incidental music for stage play with only 1 reference to opera], 1952; Saül, op.334 (Gide), 1954; Protée, op.341 (Claudel), 1955; Juanito, op.349 (Humblot), 1955; Mother Courage, op.379 (Brecht), 1959; Judith, op.392 (Giraudoux), 1961; Jerusalem à Carpentras, op.419 (Lunel), 1966; Tobie et Sarah (Claudel), 1968

Film scores: Actualités, op.104, 1929; La p'tite Lilie, op.107 (dir. Cavalcanti), 1929; Hallo Everybody, op.126 (dir. Richter), 1933; Madame Bovary, op.128 (dir. Renoir), 1933; L'hippocampe, op.137 (dir. J. Painlevé), 1934; Tartarin de Tarascon, op.138 (dir. R. Bernard), 1934; Voix d'enfants, op.146 (dir. Reynaud), 1935; The

Beloved Vagabond, op.150, 1936; Mollénard, op.174 (dir. Gilbert), 1937; La citadelle du silence, op.176 (dir. L'Herbier, collab. Honegger), 1937; Grands feux, op.182 (dir. Alexeiev), 1937; La conquête du ciel, op.184 (dir. Richter), 1937; Tragédie impériale, op.187 (dir. L'Herbier), 1938; Les otages, op.194 (dir. Bernard), 1938; Islands, op.198 (dir. Cavalcanti), 1939; Espoir, op.202 (Malraux), 1939; Cavalcade d'amour, op.204 (dir. Bernard, collab. Honegger); Gulf Stream, op.208 (dir. Alexeiev), 1939; The Private Affairs of Bel Ami, op.272 (dir. Lewin, after Maupassant), 1946; Dreams that Money can Buy, Man Ray sequence only, op.273, 1947; Gauguin, op.299 (dir. Resnais), 1950; La vie commence demain, op.304 (dir. N. Vedres), 1950; Ils étaient tous des volontaires, op.336, 1954; Celle qui n'était plus (Histoire d'une folle), op.364 (dir. Gerard, Colpi), 1957; Péron et Evita, op.372, 1958; Burma Road, op.375, 1959

Radio scores, unpubd: Voyage au pays du rêve, op.203 (J. Ravenne), 1939; Le grand testament, op.282 (N. Franck), 1948; La fin du monde, op.297 (Cendrars), 1949; Le repos du septième jour, op.301 (Claudel), 1950; Samaël, op.321 (Spire), 1953; Le dibbouk, op.329 (Anski), 1953; Etude poétique, op.333 (C. Roy), 1954

Miscellanea: Les mariés de la tour Eiffel (ballet-show, Cocteau), Marche nuptiale and Fugue du massacre only, op.70, 1921; La sagesse, op.141 (stage spectacle, Claudel), 1935; Fête de la musique, op.159 (light and water spectacle, Claudel), 1937; Vézelay, la colline éternelle (son et lumière, M. Druon), 1967

### ORCHESTRAL

Sym. Suite no.1, op.12, 1914; Poème sur un cantique de Camargue, op.13, pf, orch, 1913; Chamber Sym. no.1 (Le printemps), op.43, 1917; Chamber Sym. no.2 (Pastorale), op.49, 1918; Sym. Suite no.2 (Protée), op.57, 1919; Ballade, op.61, pf, orch, 1920; Serenade in 3 Parts, op.62, 1920–21; 5 études, op.63, pf, orch, 1920; Chamber Sym. no.3 (Serenade), op.71, 1921; Chamber Sym. no.4 (Ov., Chorale, Etude), op.74, 1921; Chamber Sym. no.5, op.75, 1922; Chamber Sym. no.6, op.79, 1923; Le carnaval d'Aix, op.83b [after ballet Salade], pf, orch, 1926

2 hymnes, op.98, 1925; Vn Conc. no.1, op.93, 1927; Va Conc. no.1, op.108, 1929; Conc., op.109, perc, chamber orch, 1929–30; Pf Conc. no.1, op.127, 1933; Concertino de printemps, op.135, vn, chamber orch, 1934; Vc Conc. no.1, op.136, 1934; Suite provençale, op.152b, 1936; Le carnaval de Londres, op.172, 1937; L'oiseau, op.181, 1937; Fantaisie pastorale, op.188, pf, orch, 1938; Conc., op.197, fl, vn, orch, 1939; Cortège funèbre, op.202 [after film score Espoir], 1939; Fanfare, op.209, 1939; Sym. no.1, op.210, 1939; Indicatif et marche pour les bons d'armement, op.212, 1940

Introduction et allegro, op.220 [after Couperin: La sultane], 1940; Mills Fanfare, op.224, str, 1941; Pf Conc. no.2, op.225, 1941; 2 Pf Conc. op.228, 1941; Cl Conc., op.230, 1941; Suite in 3 Parts, op.234, vn/harmonium, orch, 1942; Fanfare de la liberté, op.235, 1942; Sym. no.2, op.247, 1944; Vc Conc. no.2, op.255, 1945; 2 marches, op.260, 1945–6; Vn Conc. no.2, op.263, 1946; 7 danses sur des airs palestiniens, op.267, 1946–7; Pf Conc. no.3, op.270, 1946; Conc., op.278, mar, vib, orch, 1947; Suite concertante, op.278a [after op.278], pf, orch, 1952; Sym. no.4, op.281, 1947; Kentuckiana, op.287, 1948, arr. 2 pf

Pf Conc. no.4, op.295, 1949; Suite, op.300, 2 pf, orch, 1950; Concertino d'automne, op.309, 2 pf, 8 insts, 1950; Concertino d'été, op.311, va, chamber orch, 1950; Sym. no.5, op.322, 1953; Harp Conc., op.323, 1953; Concertino d'hiver, op.327, trbn, str, 1953; Suite campagnarde, op.329, 1953; Ouverture méditerranéenne, op.330, 1953; Suite cisalpine, op.332, vc, orch, 1954; Va Conc. no.2, op.340, 1954–5; Pensée amicale, op.342, str, 1955; Sym. no.6, op.343, 1955; Sym. no.7, op.344, 1955; Pf Conc. no.5, op.346, 1955; Les charmes de la vie (Hommage à Watteau), op.360, 1957

Aspen Serenade, op.361, 1957; Sym. no.8 'Rhodanienne', op.362, 1957; Symphoniette, op.363, str, 1957; Ob Conc., op.365, 1957; Vn Conc. no.3 (Concert royal), op.373, 1958; Sym. no.9, op.380, 1959; Sym. no.10, op.382, 1960; Sym. no.11 'Romantique', op.384, 1960; Les funérailles de Phocion (Hommage à Poussin), op.385, 1960; Aubade, op.387, 1960; Sym. no.12 'Rurale', op.390, 1961; Conc., op.394, 2 pf, 4 perc, 1961; Ouverture philharmonique, op.397, 1962; A Frenchman in New York, op.399, 1962; Meurtre d'un grand chef d'état, op.405, 1963; Ode pour les morts des guerres, op.406, 1963

Hpd Conc., op.407, 1964; Music for Boston, op.414, 1965; Music for Prague, op.415, 1965; Elégie pour Pierre, op.416, va, perc, 1965; Music for Indiana, op.418, 1966; Music for Lisbon, op.420, 1966; Music for New Orleans, op.422, 1966; Promenade concert, op.424, 1967; Musique pour l'univers claudélien, op.427, 1968; Music for Graz, op.429, 1968–9; Suite, op.431, 1969; Music for Ars Nova, op.432, 1969; Music for San Francisco, op.436, 1971; Ode pour Jerusalem, op.440, 1972

Brass band: Suite française, op.248, 1944, also for orch, additional movts for ballet, op.254, 1945; West Point Suite, op.313, 1951; Fanfare, op.396, 4 hn, 3 tpt, 3 trbn, tuba, 1962; Fanfare, op.400, 2 tpt, trbn, 1962; Musique de théâtre, op.334b [after incidental music Saül], 1954–70

Also orchestrations of pf works

#### CHORAL

Psalm cxxxvi, op.53 (trans. Claudel), Bar, chorus, orch, 1919
Psalm cxxvi, op.72 (trans. Claudel), male vv, 1921
Cantate pour louer le Seigneur, op.103, solo vv, chorus, org, orch, 1928
La mort du tyran, op.116 (Lampride, Diderot), chorus, wind, perc, 1932
Devant sa main nue, op.122 (Raval), female vv/vocal qt, 1933
Les amours de Ronsard, op.132, chorus/vocal qt, small orch, 1934
Cantique du Rhône, op.155 (Claudel), unacc., 1936
Cantate de la paix, op.166 (Claudel), children's vv, male vv, 1937
Main tendue à tous, op.169 (Vildrac), unacc., 1937
Les deux cités, op.170 (Claudel), unacc., 1937
Quatre chants populaires de Provence, op.194, chorus, orch, 1938
Incantations, op.201 (Aztec poems, Carpentier), male vv, 1939
Quatrains valaisans, op.206 (Rilke), unacc., 1939
Cantate de la guerre, op.213 (Claudel), unacc., 1940
Bolechou-schema, op.239, 1v, chorus, org, 1944
Prière pour les morts, op.250, 1v, chorus ad lib, org, 1945
Sym. no.3, op.271 (Te Deum), chorus, orch, 1946
Service sacré, op.279, Bar, reciter, chorus, orch/org, 1947
L'choh dodi, op.290, 1v, chorus, org, 1948
Naissance de Vénus, op.292 (Supervielle), cantata, unacc., 1949
Barba Garibo, op.298 (trad., Lunel), chorus, orch, 1949–50
Cantate des proverbes, op.310, female vv, harp, ob, vc, 1950
Les miracles de la foi, op.314 (Bible), cantata, T, chorus, orch, 1951
Le château de feu, op.338 (Cassou), cantata, chorus, orch, 1954
Trois psaumes de David, op.339, unacc., 1954
Deux poèmes de Louise de Vilmorin, op.347, chorus/vocal qt, 1955
Le mariage de la feuille et du cliché, op.357 (Gerard), solo vv, chorus, orch, tape, 1956
La tragédie humaine, op.369 (d'Aubigné), chorus, orch, 1958
Huit poèmes de Jorge Guillen, op.371, unacc., 1958
Cantate de la croix de charité, op.381 (Masson), solo vv, chorus, children's vv, orch, 1959–60
Cantate sur des textes de Chaucer, op.386, chorus, orch, 1960
Cantate de l'initiation, op.388 (Bar Mitzvah Israel), chorus, orch, 1960
Traversée, op.393 (Verlaine), unacc., 1961
Invocation à l'ange Raphael, op.395 (Claudel), female vv (2 groups), 1962
Caroles, op.402 (Charles d'Orléans), cantata, 4 solo groups, chorus, 1963
Pacem in terris, op.404 (Pope John XXIII), choral sym., Bar, chorus, orch, 1963
Cantate de Job, op.413, 1v, chorus, org, 1965
Promesse de Dieu, op.438 (Bible), unacc., 1971–2
Les momies d'Egypte, op.439 (Regnard), choral comedy, unacc., 1972
Ani maamin, un chant perdu et retrouvé, op.441 (Elie Wiesel), cantata, S, 4 reciters, chorus, orch, 1972

#### SOLO VOCAL

Alissa, op.9 (Gide), cycle, S, pf, 1913, rev. 1931; 2 poèmes de Gardener, op.35 (Tagore), 2vv, pf, 1916–17; 3 poèmes, op.37 (Rossetti, Meynell), 1v, pf/small orch, 1916; No.34 of L'église habillée de feuilles, op.38 (Jammes), vocal qt, pf 6 hands, 1916; 2 poèmes, op.39 (Saint Léger, Chalupt), vocal qt, 1916–19; Le retour de l'enfant prodigue, op.42 (Gide), cantata, 5vv, 21 insts, 1917; 2 poèmes tupis, op.52, 4 female vv, hand-clapping, 1918; Psalm cxxix, op.53 (trans. Claudel), Bar, orch, 1919; Machines agricoles, op.56, 1v, 7 insts, 1919; Catalogue de fleurs, op.60 (L. Daudet), 1v, pf/7 insts, 1920
4 poèmes de Catulle, op.80, 1v, vn, 1923; 6 chants populaires hébraïques, op.86, 1v, pf/orch, 1925; 2 poèmes de Cendrars, op.113, vocal qt/SATB, 1932; 2 élégies romaines (Goethe), (2S, 2A)/SSAA, 1932; Liturgie comtadine, op.125, 1v, pf/small orch, 1933; Panet Syrinx, op.130 (Piis, Claudel), S, Bar, vocal qt, 5 insts, 1934; Cantate pour l'inauguration du Musée de l'Homme, op.164 (Desnos), vocal qt, reciter, 6 insts, 1937; Cantate nuptiale, op.168 (after the Song of Songs), 1v, orch, 1937; Prends cette rose, op.183 (Ronsard), S, T, orch, 1937; Cantate de l'enfant et de la mère, op.185 (Carême), speaker, str qt/orch, 1938; Les quatre éléments, op.189 (Desnos), cantata (S, T)/S, orch, 1938
3 élégies, op.199 (Jammes), S, T, str, 1939; Couronne de gloire, op.211 (Gabirol, Lunel), 1v, pf/(str qt, fl, tpt), 1940; 4 chansons de Ronsard, op.223, 1v, pf/orch, 1940; 5 prières, op.231c, 1v, org, 1942; Cain et Abel, op.214, reciter, orch, 1944; Le jeu de Robin et de Marion (Adam de la Halle), 1v, 5 insts, 1948; Fontaines et sources, op.352 (Jammes), 1v, pf/orch, 1956
Suite de quatrains, op.398 (Jammes), reciter, 8 insts, 1962; Suite de sonnets, op.401 (du Bellay, Jodelle, de Magny, Jamin), cantata, vocal qt, 6 insts, 1963; Adieu, op.410 (Rimbaud), cantata, 1v, fl, va, hp, 1964; Adam, op.411 (Cocteau) S, 2T, 2Bar, 1964; Hommage à Comenius, op.421 (Comenius), cantata, S, Bar, orch, 1966; Cantate de psaumes, op.425 (trans. Claudel), Bar, orch, 1967

#### SONGS

Poèmes de Francis Jammes, op.1, 2 sets, 1910–12; 3 poèmes de Léo Latil, op.2, 1910–16; Poèmes de Francis Jammes, op.6, 1912; 7 poèmes de la connaissance de l'est, op.7 (Claudel), 1912–13; 3 poèmes de Lucile de Chateaubriand, op.10, 1913; 3 poèmes romantiques, set 1, op.11, 1913–14, set 2, op.19, 1914; 4 poèmes de Léo Latil, op.20, 1914; Le château, op.21 (Lunel), 1914; 4 poèmes pour baryton, op.26 (Claudel), 1915–17; D'un cahier inédit du journal d'Eugène de Guérin, op.27, 1915
2 poèmes d'amour, op.30 (Tagore), 1915; 2 poèmes de Coventry Patmore, op.31, 1915; Poèmes juifs, op.34, 1916; Child poems, op.36 (Tagore), 1916; Chansons bas, op.44 (Mallarmé), 1917; 2 poèmes de Rimbaud, op.45, 1918; Poèmes de Francis Jammes, op.50, 1918; 2 petits airs, op.51 (Mallarmé), 1918; Les soirées de Pétrograd, op.55, 1919; 3 poèmes de Jean Cocteau, op.59, 1920; Feuilles de température, op.65 (Morand), 1920; Poème du journal intime de Léo Latil, op.73, 1921
Prières journalières à l'usage des juifs du Comtat Venaissin, op.96, 1927; 5 chansons, op.167 (Vildrac), 1937; Le voyage d'été, op.216 (Paliard), 1946; Rêves, op.233, 1942; Chants de misère, op.265 (Paliard), 1946; 6 sonnets composés au secret, op.266 (Cassou), 1946; 3 poèmes, op.276 (Supervielle), 1947; Petites légendes, op.319 (Carême), 1952; Tristesse, op.355 (Jammes), 1956
Numerous single songs

#### CHAMBER

Str qts: no.1, op.5, 1912; no.2, op.16, 1914–15; no.3 (Latil), op.32, 1v, str qt, 1916; no.4, op.46, 1918; no.5, op.64, 1920; no.6, op.77, 1922; no.7, op.87, 1925; no.8, op.121, 1932; no.9, op.140, 1935; no.10, op.218, 1940; no.11, op.232, 1942; no.12, op.252, 1945; no.13, op.268, 1946; nos.14–15, op.291 [playable separately or together as octet], 1948–9; no.16, op.303, 1950; no.17, op.307, 1950; no.18, op.308, 1950
Other works: Sonata, op.47, pf, fl, cl, ob, 1918; Pastorale, op.147, ob, cl, bn, 1935; Suite d'après Corrette, op.161 [after incidental music Jules César], ob, cl, bn, 1937; La cheminée du roi René, op.205, suite, wind qnt, 1939; Sonatine à 3, op.221b, str trio, 1940; Str Trio, op.274, 1947; L'apothéose de Molière, op.286, suite, hpd, fl, ob, cl, bn, str, 1948; Les rêves de Jacob, op.294, dance suite, ob, str trio, db, 1949; Divertissement, op.299b [after film score Gauguin], wind qnt, 1958; Qnt no.1, op.312, pf qnt; Qnt no.2, op.316, str qt, db, 1952; Qnt no.3, op.325, va, str qt, 1953; Qnt no.4, op.350, vc, str qt, 1956; Str Sextet, op.368, 2 vn, 2 va, 2 vc, 1958; Concert de chambre, op.389, pf, wind qnt, str qnt, 1961; Str Septet, op.408, 2 vn, 2 va, 2 vc, db, 1964; Pf Qt, op.417, 1966; Pf Trio, op.428, 1968; Stanford Serenade, op.430, chamber orch, 1969; Hommage à Igor Stravinsky, op.435, str qt, 1971

#### INSTRUMENTAL

Sonata no.1, op.3, vn, pf, 1911; Sonata, op.15, 2 vn, pf, 1914; Le printemps, op.18, vn, pf, 1914; Sonata no.2, op.40, vn, pf, 1917; Sonatina, op.76, fl, pf, 1922; Sonatina, op.100, cl, pf, 1927; Sonatina, op.221, 2 vn, 1940; Sonatina, op.226, vn, va, 1941; 4 visages, op.238, va, pf, 1943; Sonata no.1, op.240, va, pf, 1944; Sonata no.2, op.244, va, pf, 1944; Elégie, op.251, va, pf, 1945; Danses de Jacaremirim, op.256, vn, pf, 1945; Sonata, op.257, vn, hpd, 1945; Duo, op.258, 2 vn, 1945; Farandoleurs, op.262, vn, pf, 1946; Sonatina, op.324, vn, vc, 1953; Sonatina, op.337, ob, pf, 1954; Duo concertante, op.351, cl, pf, 1956; Ségoviana, op.366, gui, 1957; Sonata, op.377, vc, pf, 1959; Sonatina, op.378, va, pf, 1959; Sonatina pastorale, op.383, vn, 1960; Sonata, op.437, harp, 1971

#### KEYBOARD

Pf: Suite, op.8, 1913; Variations sur un thème de Cliquet, op.23, 1915; Le printemps [I], op.25, 1915–19; Sonata no.1, op.33, 1916; Le printemps [II], op.66, 1920; Saudades do Brasil, op.67, 1920–21, arr. orch/(vn/vc), pf; Caramel Mou, op.68, 1920, arr. 1v, jazz band; 3 rag caprices, op.78, 1922, orchd; L'automne, op.115, 1932; 4 esquisses, op.227, 1941, arr. orch/wind qnt; La libertadora, op.236, pf/2 pf, 1943; La muse ménagère, op.245, 1945; Une journée, op.269, 1946; L'enfant aimé, op.289, 1948; Sonata no.2, op.293, 1949; Candélabre à sept branches, op.315, 1951; Hymne de glorification, op.331, 1953–4; La couronne de Marguerite, op.353, 1956, orchd; Sonatina, op.354, 1956; Le globe-trotter, op.358, 1956, orchd
2 pf: Scaramouche, op.165b [after incidental music Le médecin volant], 1937; Songes, op.237, 1943; Le bal martiniquais, op.249, 1944, orchd; Carnaval à la Nouvelle-Orléans, op.275, 1947; 6 danses en 3 mouvements, op.433, 1969–70
4 pf: Paris, op.284, 1948, orchd
Org: Pastorale, op.229, 1941; 9 Preludes, op.231b [after incidental music L'annonce faite à Marie, op.231], 1942; Petite suite, op.348, 1955

#### CHILDREN'S WORKS

A propos de bottes, op.118 (Chalupt), 1v, pf/(vns, vcs), 1932; Un petit peu de musique, op.119 (Lunel), 1v, pf/(vns, vcs), 1932; Un petit peu d'exercice, op.133, 1v, pf/(vns, vcs), 1934; Récréation, op.195 (Krieger), 1v, pf, 1938; Sornettes, op.214 (Mistral), 2vv, 1940; Cours de solfège, op.217, 1v, pf, 1940; Touches noirs, touches blanches, op.222, pf, 1941; Acceuil amical, op.326, pf, 1944–7; Service pour la veille du sabbat, op.345, vv, org, 1955

ARRANGEMENTS

G. Auric: *Adieu New York*, pf 4 hands
F. Poulenc: *Sonata*, pf 4 hands; *Finale*, orch
E. Satie: *5 grimaces*, pf; *Gymnopédie*, vn, pf; *Jack-in-the-Box*, orch; *Relache: Entr'acte*, pf 4 hands; *Suite after 3 morceaux en forme de poire*, vn, pf

Principal publishers: Associated, Durand, Elkan-Vogel, Eschig, Heugel, Leeds, Salabert, Universal

### WRITINGS

*Etudes* (Paris, 1927)
*Notes sur Erik Satie* (New York, 1946)
*Notes sans musique* (Paris, 1949, rev., enlarged 2/1974 as *Ma vie heureuse*; Eng. trans., 1952) [autobiography]

### BIBLIOGRAPHY

P. Collaer: *Darius Milhaud* (Antwerp and Paris, 1948)
G. Beck: *Darius Milhaud* (Paris, 1949)
*Entretiens avec Claude Rostand* (Paris, 1952)
*Correspondance Paul Claudel–Darius Milhaud*, Cahiers Paul Claudel, iii (Paris, 1961)
J. Roy: *Darius Milhaud* (Paris, 1968)
R. Crichton: Obituary, *MT*, cxv (1974), 684
E. Helm: 'Darius Milhaud und seine moderne Musik südlicher Impressionen', *Universitas*, xxix (1974), 1177
M. J. Rupert: *The Piano Music of Darius Milhaud: a Survey* (diss., Indiana U., 1974)
C. Palmer: *Milhaud* (London, 1976)

CHRISTOPHER PALMER

**Milhouse** [Millhouse]. English family of woodwind makers. Richard Millhouse (*b* Newark, *c*1725) married in 1753 in Fledborough, when he was described as a turner. The few surviving instruments stamped 'Millhouse Newark', including a fine bassoon dated 1763 in the Sheffield Museum, may confidently be ascribed to him; the attribution of those stamped 'Milhouse Newark' is uncertain. His son William Milhouse (*b* Newark, after 1753) moved to London and had opened a shop at 100 Wardour Street by mid-1787, moving at the end of 1797 to 337 Oxford Street. For the next 40 years he enjoyed the highest reputation as a busy maker of woodwind instruments. His trade cards describe him as 'Manufacturer to their Royal Highnesses the Dukes of Kent & Cumberland'; he stamped his instruments 'W. Milhouse/London'. Of his oboes, *The Harmonicon* (1830) wrote: 'Great improvements have been made on this instrument by Millhouse, the only maker in England of any celebrity'. He is especially noted for his excellent bassoons, which have survived in comparatively large numbers; he also published some music. In 1828 he was joined by his son Richard Milhouse, who ran the business alone from 1836 to 1840. (For Milhouse instruments *see* OBOE, figs.6 and 13.)

An R. Milhouse, described in a directory as a maker at Market Place, Newark, before 1804, and a Richard Millhouse at Middlegate, Newark, 1829–36, may be presumed descendants of Richard Millhouse.

H. Milhouse & Sons are mentioned in directories of 1788 and 1794 as instrument makers at Pratt Street, Lambeth, London. None of their instruments has survived and their relationship to the above is not known.

### BIBLIOGRAPHY

'On the Oboe and Bassoon', *The Harmonicon*, viii (1830), 192
L. G. Langwill: *An Index of Musical Wind-instrument Makers* (Edinburgh, 1960, rev. 4/1974)    WILLIAM WATERHOUSE

**Milikit.** Interlinear signs of Ethiopic notation; *see* ETHIOPIAN RITE, MUSIC OF THE.

**Milioni** [Millioni], **Pietro** (*fl* 1st half of the 17th century). Italian guitarist and composer. He probably lived in Rome, where the first editions of all his works were published. He was the author of six instruction books for five-course Baroque guitar and one collection of villanellas with guitar accompaniment. The fact that five of his books were reprinted at least once attests to their great popularity and to the immense public interest in the instrument; Mersenne, in his *Harmonie universelle*, quoted from two of his pieces to illustrate his discussion of Italian guitar notation.

Milioni's didactic works are concerned solely with the *battute* or strummed style of guitar playing. In them he expanded the alphabet system of chord notation introduced in 1606 by Girolamo Montesardo to include dissonant chords (*lettere tagliate*), more advanced fingerings for the basic chords (*lettere false*) and a system of transposition for barred chords. In *Vero e facil modo*, written in collaboration with LODOVICO MONTE and reprinted at least 11 times, he introduced a special 'alfabeto straordinario' for a scordatura tuning of the instrument (*G/g–B/b–e/e–b/b–d'/d'*), and his *Corona del primo, secondo e terzo libro* contains an alphabet for the four-course guitar or chitarrino. His books instruct the reader in the proper right-hand technique for the *battute* style, describing basic strums such as the *trillo* and *repicco*, and also include chordal accompaniments to popular Italian songs and dances of the early 17th century, such as the ciaccona, passacaglia, gagliarda, romanesca, *aria di Fiorenza* and *monica*.

### WORKS

Il primo, secondo, et terzo libro d'intavolatura (Rome, 1627; Mersenne mentions an earlier edn., 1624); later edn. as Corona del primo, secondo e terzo libro d'intavolatura di chitarra spagnola (Rome, 1631)
Quarto libro d'intavolatura, gui (Rome, 1627)
Quinto libro d'intavolatura, gui (Rome, 1627)
Prima scielta di villanelle accomodate con l'intavolatura per cantare sopra la chitarra spagnola (Rome, 1627)
Vero e facil modo d'imparare a sonare et accordare da se medesimo la chitarra spagnuola (Rome and Macerata, 1637), with L. Monte
Nuova corona d'intavolatura di chitarra spagnola (Rome, 1661), wrongly attributed to Milioni, is actually a reprint of F. Pico: Nuova scelta di sonate per la chitarra spagnola (Naples, 1608)

### BIBLIOGRAPHY

J. Wolf: *Handbuch der Notationskunde*, ii (Leipzig, 1919), 173ff, 207
R. Hudson: *The Development of Italian Keyboard Variations on the Passacaglio and Ciaccona from Guitar Music in the Seventeenth Century* (diss., U. of California, Los Angeles, 1967), 70ff
S. Murphy: 'Seventeenth-century Guitar Music: Notes on Rasgueado Performance', *GSJ*, xxi (1968), 27f, 30f
W. Kirkendale: *L'aria di Fiorenza, id est Il ballo del Gran Duca* (Florence, 1972)
ROBERT STRIZICH

**Militär Glockenspiel** (Ger.). BELL-LYRA.

**Militärkapell** (Ger.). MILITARY BAND.

**Militärtrommel** (Ger.). Side drum; *see* DRUM, §3.

**Military band** (Fr. *harmonie*; Ger. *Militärkapell, Musikkorps*; It. *banda, corpo di musica*). The expression dates from the late 18th century and denoted at that time a regimental band composed of woodwind, brass and percussion. During the next century it became applied as well to civilian bands of similar constitution.

In the later Middle Ages, bands of shawms, bagpipes, trumpets and drums, broadly on the Muslim patterns witnessed in the crusades, performed at tournaments, were taken on campaigns and were employed on naval vessels. During the Renaissance outdoor combinations of wind instruments, though consistently maintained for royal and civilian purposes, ceased to serve the armed forces, which confined themselves to trumpets for the cavalry, and drum, or drum and fife, for the foot (*see* MILITARY CALLS). The modern era of the military band began in the 17th century. Towards the end of the Thirty Years War (1646) the Brandenburg Dragoon Guards had a music of shawms (two treble and one tenor schalmeien) with a dulcian for the bass. This type of combination seems not to have continued in military use after the war, but was revived in Germany towards the end of the century, using instruments of a later type described as 'deutsche Schalmeyen', also with the dulcian.

Meanwhile in France the Mousquetaires, who had previously used the fife (or, when mounted, the trumpet), were equipped in 1663 with three oboes and drums, soon increased to four, namely, two oboes, third oboe (*taille des hautbois*, 'tenor oboe', written down to *g*) and bassoon; other French regiments followed. Many of their marches and the *airs* performed as routine calls with the drums, written by Lully, André Philidor *l'aîné*, Martin Hotteterre and others from c1670, are in the Philidor Manuscripts of 1705 in the Bibliothèque Municipale, Versailles (ex.1; most of the pieces are printed in Kastner, *Manuel général*). England followed

Ex.1 MOUSQUETAIRES: L'assemblée

with the appointment of 'hautboys' to the Horse Grenadier Guards in 1678 and to the Foot Guards soon afterwards, while in Germany replacement of the 'deutsche Schalmeyen' by the French *hautbois* had begun by the beginning of the 18th century. Johann Philipp Krieger's *Lustige Feldmusik* of 1704 is an early example of German music for the new combination. Krieger advised certain doublings of the four parts in the open air, and around 1720 such a group typically had six members. Hans F. von Fleming in *Der vollkommende teutsche Soldat* (Leipzig, 1726) told how in Saxony they played in the mornings a march, an entrée and a couple of the colonel's favourite minuets.

By Fleming's time the Saxon infantry were adding to the band two horns (in Prussia replaced by a single trumpet on foot). The first date in England for a military oboe band with horns or trumpet has not been accurately established, but horns were usual there by the

mid-18th century, and in the Netherlands. Handel's Fireworks Music shows how the instrumentation could be scaled up (here including serpent) to celebrate a special occasion. Clarinets began to be introduced in Germany about the time of the Seven Years War. In 1762 the English Royal Artillery raised a 'Band of Music' in emulation of what had been seen in Germany. It consisted of eight men provided by the regiment playing ten instruments: pairs of trumpets, horns and bassoons, and 'four hautbois or clarinetts'. In the same year in France the Swiss Guards had duplicate pairs of oboes, clarinets, horns and bassoons. Such an eight-part ensemble was later used in private wind music of the Austrian emperor and others (*see* HARMONIEMUSIK). The 'Turkish music' had meanwhile been introduced, first in Austria and Prussia in the second decade of the 18th century; in its most developed form it consisted of bass drum, cymbals and triangle or tambourine, in England played by black men. The drumstick display and leopard-skin apron of these bands remain with us today (*see* JANISSARY MUSIC).

Very many military bands of the second half of the 18th century were maintained unofficially at the officers' expense, which kept their numbers small. In England the raising of volunteer regiments at the end of the century much increased the number of such small bands, which usually consisted of two clarinets (optionally oboes), two horns, two bassoons (often played from one part), one trumpet and commonly a serpent. Their repertory comprised marches and quicksteps, varied by an occasional military rondo, often composed by local bandmasters. Much of this music was published at the time. Haydn wrote marches for this combination on his first visit to London. Sometimes there were extra parts for small flutes in B♭ or for flutes in F, and for a small Turkish music of long drum and cymbals (see fig.1). Established bands, however, had by then grown chiefly through an increase in the number of clarinets: there were six in the Grenadier Guards in 1794 and in the bands provided from 1795 in Paris by the Conservatoire for the Garde Nationale. The French bands were assembled on special occasions, with the addition of trombones, to perform overtures and symphonies by such composers as Gossec and Méhul. By about 1810 the larger European military bands had reached their present size, having further increased the number of clarinets (which, as subsequently, took orchestral violin and viola parts in transcriptions) and added small clarinets and in Germany often basset-horns; the brass regularly included trombones, while extra pairs of horns and trumpets made different crookings simultaneously available. In England the serpent was supported by bass horn and in Germany by the double bassoon (ex.2). A fine civilian band of this description, the Prince Regent's Band at Brighton, had been developed from the band of the Tenth Hussars; in 1818 it had 34 players, many of them German, including Christian Kramer, the master of the band, who also made the opera selections and transcribed symphonies including Beethoven's Fifth and Mozart's 'Jupiter' (see Carse).

Though cavalry regiments in the 18th century, particularly light cavalry, occasionally employed a band of woodwind and horns, they did not forsake the traditional corps of trumpets and kettledrums, which has survived in many countries to the present day. It also formed the nucleus of the true cavalry band, instituted in France under Napoleon but developed with

Ex.2 Anon.: *Ungarischer Grenadier Marsch* (Berlin, c1822)

greater enthusiasm in Germany and Austria. Natural trumpets in Eb, played with traditional 'schmetternd' double tonguings, dominated such *Trompetenmusik*, but the introduction of a trombone or serpent for a diatonic bass and of horns to enrich the middle harmony brought it closer to the sound of a conventional ensemble. The ophicleide made its début in Paris as bass to a stage cavalry band in Spontini's *Olimpie*, while the British keyed bugle met success in Germany from 1815 as an additional treble voice in this early type of brass band. Stölzel's new valve trumpets and valved *Tenorhorn* and *Basshorn* were reported by Sundelin in *Instrumentierung für sämmtliche Militär-Musik-Chöre* (Berlin, 1828) specifically as instruments for cavalry music in Prussia. This grew under WILHELM WIEPRECHT to combinations of the kind illustrated in ex.3; Gungl's 'Cornett in B' denotes the Berlin species, almost indistinguishable from a flugelhorn, and 'Piccolo' is its smaller size; 'Cornett in Es' is the bell-to-front alto, horns and the 'Tenorbass' the baritone in the same pitch. The 'Trombe', the heart of the band, are all valved; their *fff* against *dolce* for the rest and the quotation from the old cavalry code in the third bar are typical. 'Bassi' would have included bass trombones on the upper line and the new Moritz tuba on the lower.

Cavalry bands elsewhere varied the pattern, in Austria and Italy stressing the trumpet element and in some cases retaining this music and its special band journals for regiments with mounted traditions after the demise of the cavalry itself; in some cases they became mere brass bands, and in England approximated to the infantry band. Another special type of 19th-century military music, analogous to and as old as the 'trumpet music' of the cavalry, was the 'horn music' of the German *Jäger* and French *chasseurs*: a brass combination with a preponderance of the valved successors of the horn and bugles traditional in light infantry. Such bands are now sometimes led by *trompes de chasse* (hunting horns), a practice now popular in civilian band music as well.

Valve instruments share a basic technique which can up to a point be quickly learnt; they are unaffected by bad weather and can be played by a person wearing gloves. As they became everywhere procurable from the late 1830s they were incorporated into the existing infantry and other woodwind-based bands, often to replace the woodwind partly or even, as in British workmen's bands, entirely (*see* BRASS BAND). Today by far the commonest small band, regimental or civilian, and confined by no means to Europe, has an economical base of brass instruments, self-sufficient in harmony, with clarinets (in B♭ and E♭), perhaps a piccolo and in the Latin countries a saxophone or two. Though its sound in, for example, the Tyrol may differ from that in the Pampas, the same printed editions can be used everywhere. This type of military band is the closest to a standard combination yet evolved; only in Britain, where it is called a 'brass and reed' band, is it rare, and now possibly extinct since the Burwash Brass and Reed Band in Sussex disbanded.

French infantry bands of the 1830s were organized on a more extravagant scale; they included full wood-wind and the classic brass, strengthened by cornets, keyed bugles, alto ophicleides or clavicors, and bass ophicleides (the first edition of Kastner's *Cours d'in-strumentation* includes an example in score). The addi-tion of a 'bande turque' must have made a colourful effect; however, it was usually 'improved' by the mass of very efficient saxhorns and 'bugles' (flugelhorns) with which Sax and others smothered the old nucleus, producing a densely homogenous, rather bland sonority. In France leading bands built up their woodwind for concert performance by adding every sort of wind instrument that manufacturers could produce, even in some cases two desks of cellos to warm the lower regis-ter. The French model, which grew to enormous proportions, was largely followed in Italy and Spain as well. The 'banda municipale' of a major Italian city with its brilliance of tone-colour, excellent players and reper-tory of orchestral transcriptions perhaps marks the high-point of the military band's history. The following list of instruments specified in a 'transcrizione libera' (1927) of Puccini's *Turandot* illustrates the maximum instrumen-tation found in such music.

Ottavino; 2 Flauti; 2 Oboi; Corno inglese; 2 Clarinetti piccoli in La♭; 2 Clarinetti piccoli in Mi♭; Clarinetti soprani in Si♭ I.; Clarinetti soprani in Si♭ II.; Clarinetti contralti in Mi♭; Clarinetti bassi in Si♭; Sarrusofono baritono in Mi♭; Sarrusofono basso in Si♭; Saxofono soprano in Si♭; Saxofoni 2 contralti in Mi♭; Saxofoni tenori in Si♭; Saxofono baritono in E♭; Saxofono basso in Si♭; Sarrusofono contrabasso, Contrabasso ad ancia, Contrabassi a corda, 4 Corni in Fa; 2 Cornette in Si♭; 2 Trombe in Fa; 2 Trombe in Si♭ basso; 2 Tromboni tenori; Trombone basso in Fa, Trombone contrabasso in Si♭; Timpani; Triangolo–Tamburo; G. C. Piatti–Tam-tam; Glockenspiel–Xilofono; Xilophono basso – Gong Chinesi; Celeste; 2 Flicorni soprani in Mi♭; 2 Flicorni soprani in Si♭; 2 Flicorni contralti in Mi♭; 2 Flicorni tenori in Si♭; 2 Flicorni baritoni in Si♭; 2 Flicorni bassi in Si♭; 2 Flicorni bassi gravi in Fa-Mi♭; 2 Flicorni contrabassi in Si♭.

(*Contrabasso ad ancia:* double-reed instrument of brass, different from the sarrusophones which in this example replace bassoons; *Flicorni:* generic title covering flugelhorns, alto and tenor horns, baritone and the brass basses; the deeper trombones are valved, sometimes the tenors as well; *G. C. Piatti:* one player, cymbal attached to bass drum.)

Infantry bandmasters in Germany and Britain – and in the USA where bands similar to those in England were in existence at the end of the 18th century – have from the onset of the valve era, out of conservative feeling and practical consideration, generally kept to the well-balanced instrumentation advocated by military band journals of the mid-19th century (in England, for example, C. Boosé's *Military Journal* from c1845). As shown in ex.2 this consists of a contemporary orchestral wind and percussion group augmented to fulfil band requirements and filled out with a few extra instruments. Saxophones, invented for the band, were freely used only in America; in Germany they were ignored until recently, and in England resisted at first, then limited to two. The brass is led by cornets, flugelhorns or (increasingly) trumpets, and the bass is supplied by valved basses (in America sousaphones); a string bass is often added in concert performance. The only other instrument foreign to the orchestra is the euphonium

Ex.3 J. Gungl: *Parade Marsch* (Berlin, c1850)

*1 Military band at the Changing of the Guard at St James's Palace: engraving (c1790)*

*2. Band of the Royal Marines, with (left to right) bass drum, fife, side drum, trumpet, horn, bass and side drums, serpent, trombone and bassoon: watercolour (1825) by an unknown artist, in the Royal Military School of Music, Kneller Hall*

*3. Band of the Grenadier Guards, with woodwind and brass, at the Lord Mayor's Show, London, 1941*

(baritone) which helps with nearly everything prominent in the tenor and bass registers. The scoring of a march is illustrated in ex.4. Miller (a Berliner) gave the following rules of thumb for arranging orchestral works (they cannot of course always be followed in detail): violins to clarinets; violas to clarinets and alto clarinets or saxophone, or to horns; cello to bassoon, bass clarinet or euphonium; flute and oboe parts are unchanged, supported in loud passages by clarinets in Eb; clarinets to cornets; bassoons to trombones; horn parts unchanged or given to saxophones; other brass parts are not changed (this last rule has priority).

With small variations this combination has ruled at the Royal Military School of Music (*see* LONDON, §VII, 4(ii)) since the days of its early directors from Germany, and in British and Commonwealth service bands and the civilian military bands which were popular institutions up to the 1930s and which are having a revival thanks to the flourishing teaching of wind instruments in schools. Sousa's band, although much larger, used the same instrumentational practice for most of its career from 1892. American service and

Ex.4 K. J. Alford: *March: 'Colonel Bogey'*

college bands follow its tradition; in their semi-standardized printed editions certain 19th-century anomalies have been ironed out: flute parts are no longer written for flute in D♭ (an extinct instrument pitched a semitone higher than normal and better suited for flat tonalities than the eight-keyed flute in C); the old parts for trumpets in E♭ and two cornet parts have been abolished in favour of three parts for trumpets in B♭; and the formerly variable saxophone group has stabilized at two altos and a tenor, with an optional part for the increasingly popular baritone. The repertory has changed little; it comprises marches, selections, transcribed overtures and specially composed works among which those of light character are the general favourites. The 'wind symphony' is a recent American modification dedicated to the performance of weightier compositions and transcriptions, and giving equal opportunities to players of each orchestral wind instrument: the flutes and double reeds are matched in strength to the clarinets and saxophones; the heavy brass is deprived of the spectacular prominence accorded them in the marching band; and extra clarinettists are easily switched to alto, bass and contrabass clarinets.

BIBLIOGRAPHY

G. Kastner: Cours d'instrumentation (Paris, 1837)
——: Manuel général de musique militaire (Paris, 1848/R1973-4)
C. Mandel: Treatise on the Instrumentation of Military Bands (London, c1859)
A. Kalkbrenner: Wilhelm Wieprecht: sein Leben und Wirken (Berlin, 1882)
H. G. Farmer: Memoirs of the Royal Artillery Band (London, 1904)
——: The Rise and Development of Military Music (London, 1912/R1970)
G. Miller: The Military Band (London, 1912)
P. Panoff: Militärmusik in Geschichte und Gegenwart (Berlin, 1938)
H. E. Adkins: Treatise on the Military Band (London, 1945)
A. Carse: 'The Prince Regent's Band', ML, xxvii (1946), 147
H. G. Farmer: Military Music (London, 1950)
K. Berger: The March King and his Band (New York, 1957)
R. F. Goldman: The Wind Band (Boston, 1961/R1974)
A. Rose: Talks with Bandsmen (London, n.d.)
S. Strand: Militärmusikern i svenskt musikliv (Stockholm, 1974)

See also BANDMASTER; HARMONIEMUSIK; MARCH.

HAROLD C. HIND/ANTHONY C. BAINES

**Military calls.** Signals played on various musical instruments to give information, commands or encouragement to an army during battle or in camp.

1. Origins (to 1700). 2. Germany. 3. France. 4. Great Britain. 5. USA. 6. Use by composers.

1. ORIGINS (TO 1700). Melodic or rhythmic 'calls' to convey information were used by the Greeks and Romans, who sounded them on the tuba, cornu and bucina. There is little evidence of such usage in the European Middle Ages until the time of the crusades, when Europeans came in contact with Middle Eastern cultures. From Saracen practices of military music, Europeans adopted the nafīr, tabl and naqqāra as, respectively, the anafil (straight trumpet), tabor (small drum, sometimes with a snare) and naker (kettledrum). The Saracen custom of using instrumental 'calls' seems also to have been taken up, along with the notion of the noisy military band as a weapon of 'fear and affray', as Bartholomaeus Anglicus (13th century) described it, and as the centre of resistance. A contemporary account of the third crusade provides an early reference to trumpet calls being used by a European army to signal a charge (Galfridus de Vinosalvo, Itinerarium regis Anglorum Richardi I (1684), referring to a battle near Arsuf, Syria, in 1191). Although no early trumpet sig-

nals are known to survive, an idea of their intervallic range can be obtained from Johannes de Grocheo (c1300), who indicated that the medieval trumpet did not play higher than the 4th harmonic partial. In all probability the earliest (Western) trumpet signals came from Italy, whence they were carried throughout Europe by mercenaries and modified by the different troops that adopted them.

By the late 15th century the Swabian and Swiss Landsknechte were also using the side drum for military calls. Early 16th-century use of the trumpet, drum and flute was described by Machiavelli in his Libro della arte della guerra (1521), where he stated that during battle the trumpet, as it could be heard above all, should give the officer's commands, followed by drums and zufoli (flutes). He further advised that the cavalry trumpets should be of a different and lesser sound from those of the infantry, and that military music was a valuable aid for marching. Italian use of trumpets and drums was also mentioned by Zarlino (Le istitutioni armoniche, i, 1558, chap.2): 'Such a custom is still observed in our time, so that one of two fighting forces does not assault the enemy unless urged by the sound of the trumpets and kettledrums, or by some other kind of musical instrument'. The illustrations to the 1566 edition of L. Fronsperger's Kriegsbuch show several examples of the use of kettledrums and trumpets by German cavalry. A French source, Thoinot Arbeau's Orchésographie (Langres, 1588), also mentions that among certain German troops the cavalry used kettledrums. Rabelais (1494–1553/4) fashioned a description of the Andouille folk attacking Pantagruel and his company to the sound of 'joyous fifes and tabours, trumpets and clarions'.

Early references to the use of trumpet signals by the British army are found in Rules and Ordynaunces for the Warre, published for the French campaign of 1544:

After the watche shal be set, unto the tyme it be discharged in the mornynge, no maner of man make any shouting or blowing of hornes or whisteling or great noyse, but if it be trumpettes by a special commaundement. Euery horseman at the fyrst blaste of the trumpette shall sadle or cause to be sadled his horse, at the seconde to brydell, at the thirde to leape on his horse backe, to wait on the kyng, or his lorde or capitayne.

The Venetian Daniele Barbaro, reporting from England, wrote that the cavalry used trumpets and the infantry drums (Calendar of State Papers: Venetian, v, 1534–54, no.703); and a set of rules for drummers and fifers by Ralph Smith (c1557) mentions such 'callings' as 'Marche', 'Allarum', 'Approache', 'Assaulte', 'Battaile', 'Retreate' and 'Skirmishe'. Which instruments were used, and by which army groups, was not standardized in 16th-century England (or in the rest of Europe) to judge from the varied references in military treatises. For example, Peter Whitehorne (Certaine Wayes for the Ordering of Souldiours, 1573) advised the captain that it is 'with sounde of the Trompette' that he 'shall cause the Souldiour to be advertised and taughte to know', while in Robert Barret's The Theorike and Practike of Modern Warres (1598) the soldier was told to learn the 'severall soundes of the Drum whereby to obey to that which is commaunded', and Digges's Arithmetical Warlike Treatise (1590) says 'they are to learne of the Dromme Maior'.

In the 17th century the use of drum, fife and trumpet was specified by Lawes and Ordinances of Warre (1639), issued by the Earl of Arundel and Surrey: 'Every soldier shall diligently observe and learne the distinct and different sounds of Drums, Fifes, and

*Trumpets*, that he may know to answer and obey each of them in time of service'. Francis Markham in his famous *Five Decades of Epistles of Warre* (1622) precluded the fife: 'It is to the voice of the Drum the Souldier should wholly attend, and not the the aire of the whistle'.

Numerous military manuals and other works published during the 17th century include allusions to and descriptions of the signals in use. Markham's book was the first to describe the different ones. In Decade I, Epistle 5, 'Of Drummes and Phiphes', he specified drum signals as follows:

First in the morning the discharge or breaking up of the *Watch*, then a

preparation or Summons to make them repaire to their colours; then a beating away before they begin to march; after that a *March* according to the nature and custom of the country (for diuers countries have diuers Marches), then a *Charge*, then a *Retrait*, then a *Troupe*, and lastly a *Battalion* or a *Battery*, besides other sounds which depending on the phantasttikenes of forain nations are not so useful.

Markham was no less explicit with regard to trumpet signals (III/1):

In Horse-Troupes ... the *Trumpet* is the same which the *Drum* and *Phiph* is, only differing in the tearmes and sounds of the Instrument: for the first point of warre is *Butte sella*, clap on your saddles; *Mounte Cauallo*, mount on horseback; *Tucquet*, march; *Carga, carga*, an Alarme to charge: *A la Standardo*, a retrait, or retire to your colours;

Ex.1

*Auquet*, to the Watch, or a discharge for the watch, besides diuers other points, as Proclamations, Cals, Summons, all which are most necessary for euery Souldier both to know and obey.

It is noticeable in this list that the names of the trumpet sounds suggest an Italian origin, while those of many subsequent drum signals are clearly English. The signals mentioned in English works include: 'Reliefe', 'Parado', 'Tapto' (*Count Mansfields Directions of Warre*, translated 1624); 'March', 'Alarm', 'Troop', 'Chamadoes and answers thereunto', 'Reveills', 'Proclamations' (Du Praissac's *Art of Warre*, trans. J. Cruso, 1639); 'Call', 'Preparative', 'Battle', 'Retreat' (Bariffe's *Military Discipline, or The Young Artillery Man*, 2/1639, and Elton's *Compleat Body of the Art Military*, 1650); 'Take Arms', 'Come to Colours', 'Draw out onto the Field', 'Challenge', 'General', 'Parley' (*English Military Discipline*, 1680); 'Watch', 'To Saddle', 'To Horse', 'Charge', 'Retire' (James Turner's *Pallas Armata*, 1683); and 'Gathering', a Scottish call (Acheson's *The Military Garden*, 1629, and Turner's *Pallas Armata*).

The first military signals to have survived in notation are in Janequin's remarkable composition *La bataille* (Paris, 1528), which may depict the French victory at Marignano in 1515. The second section (of which the first ten bars are given as ex.1) includes two trumpet calls, 'Le boute-selle' and 'A l'étendart', along with effects imitative of drums and the noise of battle. Janequin's chanson was one of the earliest of a genre of vocal and instrumental 'battle pieces'. The English keyboard manuscript collection *My Ladye Nevells Booke* (1591) includes a 'Battell', attributed to Byrd, with several sections containing evident imitations of trumpet sounds that were probably English military signals of the period.

About 1600, military trumpet calls appeared in notation in music instruction books for the first time. These sources include the notebooks of two German trumpeters at the Danish court, Hendrich Lübeckh (notated about 1596–1609) and Magnus Thomsen (1598), Bendinelli's *Tutta l'arte della trombetta* (1614, the first known trumpet method), the fifth book of Mersenne's *Harmonie universelle* (1636–7), and Fantini's *Modo per imparare a sonare di tromba* (1638). (It should be mentioned that Schünemann's transcription of Lübeckh's and Thomsen's tablature is in many cases one note too high in the harmonic series.) According to Bendinelli, 'the military calls . . . are to be performed gaily, lightly and without a definite beat, but well articulated'. Ex.2 shows a section of 'La butta sella' from each of these four sources, showing the low register of the medieval

trumpet. Mersenne's version is the simplest and probably the oldest; the differences between Thomsen and Fantini, in spite of the short time separating them, show a marked tendency towards codification and increased rhythmic exactitude. The syllables under the versions by Bendinelli and Fantini were provided as an aid to memory and only as an approximate indication of the actual articulation.

2. GERMANY. Fronsperger's classic *Kriegsbuch* (1566), although it details the duties of military musicians and provides fine plates showing trumpeters, drummers and fifers, only alludes to the military calls used by the Germans. Information from other sources and early examples of signals in notation are similarly scarce. Kastner (1848), for instance, gave no German signals from earlier than the 1820s, though notations for French and Belgian signals of the 1700s are included. A possible reason for the scarcity of early collections of signals in Germany is that trumpeters formed a close and strict guild. The Holy Roman Emperor Ferdinand II granted them in 1632 a set of imperial privileges, confirmed and revised by emperors until 1810, when Friedrich Wilhelm III dissolved the guild. Its chief functions had been to maintain the quality of playing and the instrument's status; another was to ensure that pupils, who studied for a period of two years with an acknowledged 'field trumpeter' before his release from apprenticeship, learnt thoroughly the five principal military calls or 'field pieces'. These, according to J. E. Altenburg (1795), were 'Boute-selle', 'A cheval', 'Le marche' (or 'Cavalquet'), 'La retraite', and 'A l'étendart'; he described their use in his famous treatise (pp.89f) and printed 'Le marche' (p.143). Other trumpet calls from the 17th and 18th centuries are 'Ingangk' ('L'entrée'), 'Ughetto' ('Auged', 'Guet'), 'Ban' (to call attention to a proclamation), 'Charge', 'Butta la tenda' (take down tents), 'Chamade' (invitation to negotiations), 'Alarme' and 'Apell' (cavalry retreat).

3. FRANCE. The 17th-century tendency towards codification continued for the next two centuries, especially in France. From the time of Louis XIV onwards, numerous government orders regulated the different trumpet and drum signals. (Many of the signals were printed by Kastner.) In 1705 André Philidor inserted in his immense autograph collection many of the *batteries et sonneries* that he and Lully had composed for the French army. From this time, the number and diversity of the French signals increased enormously, as may be seen from Lecocq Madeleine's *Service ordinaire et jour-*

Ex.2

Mersenne: *Boute-selle*

Thomsen: *Pottesella*

Bendinelli: *Butasella*

dran   da ten te na da te da ten te na da ten te ne da te da ten te na da ten te ne da te da ten te na da ta dran

Fantini: *Butta sella*

ta dra da ton del la da ton da ton del la [da ton del la] da ton da ton del la [da ton del la] da ton da ton     del la *nalier de la cavalerie en abrégé* (1720) and Marguery's *Instructions pour les tambours*. Under the consulate and empire the military calls received some additions from David Buhl, who prepared (from 1803 onwards) different sets of trumpet, drum and fife *ordonnances*, adopted by successive French governments during the first half of the 19th century. The extent of his revision can be seen from a comparison of the beginning of Philidor's and Buhl's versions of 'A cheval', a signal still extant in England in the calls 'To horse' and 'General parade' (see ex.3). The 1825 *ordonnance* by Buhl still forms the principal body of French army signals.

Ex.3

4. GREAT BRITAIN. After the Rebellion, the English army underwent many changes, influenced by association with foreign allies during the continental wars of the 18th century. The fife, which had fallen into disuse at the close of the 17th century, was reintroduced in Flanders in 1745–7. Regiments of horse used trumpets for their calls; horse grenadiers, dragoon guards and foot regiments had used side drums only. But from this time marching regiments and occasionally even cavalry used fife and drum to give the signals. Fife and drum calls appear in manuals from the second half of the 18th century, notably *A Compleat Tutor for the Fife* (c1750–55) and R. Spencer's *The Drummers Instructor: with English and Scotch Duty* (c1760). Two distinct systems – 'English Duty' and 'Scots Duty' – were followed until 1816, when by war office orders 'Scots Duty' was abolished and a system set out by Samuel Potter in *Art of Playing the Fife* and *Art of Beating the Drum* (1815) was adopted throughout the army.

In 1766 trumpets were substituted for side drums in the horse grenadier guards and dragoons. Light dragoons were already using 'horns like post boys' in 1761 for certain calls. This custom soon spread; Robert Hinde (*Discipline of the Light Horse*, 1778) described a horn of semicircular shape that was adopted by the light infantry, artillery and regiments of foot. In 1798 the war office employed James Hyde to 'revise the trumpet and bugle soundings'; his versions were issued in *The Sounds for Duty & Exercise for the Trumpet & Bugle Horns of His Majesty's Regiments, & Corps of Cavalry* under authority dated 29 December 1798, and in 1799

Hyde corrected errors of notation in the original work with a publication of his own, *A New and Complete Preceptor for the Trumpet and Bugle Horn*. These were the first books of their kind, although James Gilbert, in his *Bugle Horn Calls for Riflemen* (1804), stated that he had been 'the First that Arranged and Published the compleat Duty for the Trumpet and Bugle Horn for the Light Horse Regiments and Associations throughout Great Britain' in 1795. Bugle calls also appeared in T. R. Cooper's *Practical Guide for the Light Infantry* (1806).

In 1812 the bugle appeared in a new shape, with a single coil in its tube. Originally pitched in C and issued with a B♭ crook, orders of 1835 specified that it be built in B♭. During the 1800s it gradually replaced the drum and fife. Drum signals were used in the artillery until 1856, but the fife continued to display a few of the routine calls as late as the 1890s (the last war office issue of *Drum and Fife Duty*, apparently, was published in 1887). The trumpet (in E♭) continued in use; regimental trumpet calls were introduced by Sir Hussey Vivian in 1835. In 1858 a new type of bugle, with a double coil in its tube and therefore a more compact and handier instrument, was issued.

Up to the close of the 19th century there were two sets of calls, the *Trumpet and Bugle Sounds for Mounted Services and Garrison Artillery* and *Infantry Bugle Sounds*; in addition there was *The Regulation Bugle Calls as used by the Volunteer Rifle Corps and Light Infantry*. In 1902 all service calls were assimilated into one manual, *The Trumpet and Bugle Sounds for the Army*, which however maintained an old anomaly – that although calls for trumpet and bugle might be rhythmically identical, they were often harmonically different because of their scales (see ex.4). The British Army now divides calls

Ex.4

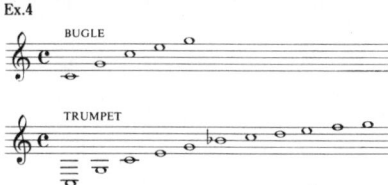

into three categories: regimental calls, field calls and routine calls. Soldiers have set many of the British calls to doggerel verses that have been part and parcel of military life for at least a century; probably they originated in the tonguing syllables that Bendinelli claimed to have invented in 1614. Five minutes after the sounding of the 'Dinner' comes the 'Vegetables' call, to which is sung ex.5.

Ex.5

Oh, offi - cers' wives have pud-dings and pies, but sol - diers' wives have skil - ly.

5. USA. At the start of the American War of Independence the Continental Army patterned its organization after British military custom, with which it was familiar. Although the earliest American military manuals contain no notation for military calls, it is reasonable to suppose that the majority were drawn from those of the British duty. The *Regulations for the*

*Order and Discipline of the Troops of the United States*, compiled by Friedrich von Steuben in 1778, lists and describes the beats and signals ordered into use for the Continental Army: 'The General', 'The Assembly', 'The March', 'The Reveilly', 'The Troop', 'The Retreat', 'The Tattoo', 'To Arms' and 'The Parley'. American regiments of foot recruited drummers and fifers to play the signals; light dragoons used trumpeters and fifers; companies of riflemen included a drummer or a trumpeter; and light infantry units used the bugle horn. William Duane's *A Military Dictionary* (1810), based on an 1802 British dictionary by Charles James, specified that 'the trumpet is always to be considered as the principal military instrument ... particularly belonging to the line; the bugle horn to riflemen and detached parties'. Although in the USA, as in England, the bugle replaced fife and drum towards the end of the 19th century, numerous drum and fife tutors appeared during the 1800s, among them *The Fifer's Companion* (1805), J. L. Rumrille and H. Holton's *The Drummer's Instructor* (1817), a *Fife Instructor ... to which is prefixed Instructions for the Drum, including the Principal Duties of the Camp* (c1830) and *Strube's Drum and Fife Instructor* (1870). The old American bugle calls laid down by Scott and Casey were largely derived from the French (e.g. 'Retreat' and 'Tattoo'), but in 1867 General Upton appointed Truman Seymour to revise and assimilate the calls, and it is his work that laid the foundation for the present system. Reminders of both British and French calls can be heard; for example, the opening of 'Tattoo' is from a French call, the conclusion from the British version. 'Boots and Saddles' is also French (a corruption of 'boute-selle'), but 'Stables' is British. In the USA as in Britain soldiers have set certain calls to doggerel verse. Ex.6 shows the first four bars of such a setting of 'Reveille' (whose music is borrowed from the French).

Ex.6

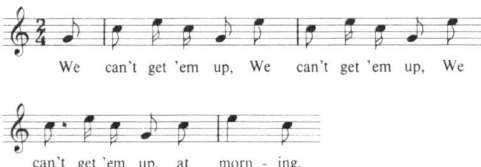

We  can't get 'em up, We  can't get 'em up, We

can't get 'em up, at  morn - ing.

6. USE BY COMPOSERS. Bach, in the bass aria 'Grosser Herr, o starker König' of his *Christmas Oratorio*, employed a trumpet signal used earlier by H. I. F. Biber (ex.7); both composers probably drew on 'A cheval'. Berlioz, in *La damnation de Faust*, used the French 'Retraite'; Suppé used the Austrian cavalry 'Retreat' for the opening of his overture *Leichte Kavallerie* and

Auber's overture to *Fra Diavolo* presents the French 'boute-selle'. Another such use is in *Carmen*: Bizet probably did not know a Spanish call, and was in any case writing for a French audience, so he borrowed for his purpose the French cavalry 'A cheval'.

BIBLIOGRAPHY

C. Bendinelli: *Tutta l'arte della trombetta* (1614), DM, 2nd ser., *Handschriften-Faksimiles*, v (1975)
M. Mersenne: *Harmonie universelle*, v (Paris, 1636–7/R1963; Eng. trans., 1957), 267
G. Fantini: *Modo per imparare a sonare di tromba* (Frankfurt am Main, 1638/R1972) (Milan, 1934; Eng. trans., 1976) [facs. edns.]
J. E. Altenburg: *Versuch einer Anleitung zur heroisch-musikalischen Trompeter- und Pauker-Kunst* (Halle, 1795; Eng. trans., 1973)
G. Kastner: *Manuel général de musique militaire* (Paris, 1848/R1973–4)
J.-B. Weckerlin: *Musiciana* (Paris, 1877)
J. A. Kappey: *Military Music* (London, 1894)
G. Kobbe: 'The Trumpet in Camp and Battle', *Century Magazine*, i (1898)
H. G. Farmer: *The Rise and Development of Military Music* (London, 1912/R1970)
M. Brenet: *La musique militaire* (Paris, 1917)
G. Schünemann, ed.: *Trompeterfanfaren, Sonaten und Feldstücke*, EDM, 1st ser., *Reichsdenkmale*, vii (1936)
P. Panoff: *Militärmusik in Geschichte und Gegenwart* (Berlin, 1938)
*Trumpet and Bugle Sounds for the Army, with Words; also Bugle Marches* (Aldershot, 1941)
W. C. White: *A History of Military Music in America* (New York, 1944)
H. G. Farmer: *Handel's Kettledrums: Papers on Military Music* (London, 1950)
———: *Military Music* (London, 1950)
H. Heyde: *Trompete und Trompeteblasen im europäischen Mittelalter* (diss., U. of Leipzig, 1965)
E. Tarr: 'Monteverdi, Bach und die Trompetenmusik ihrer Zeit', *GfMKB, Bonn 1970*, 592
D. Altenburg: *Untersuchungen zur Geschichte der Trompete im Zeitalter des Clarinblasens* (Regensburg, 1973)
R. F. Camus: *The Military Music of the American Revolution* (Chapel Hill, 1976)
D. Altenburg: 'Zum Repertoire der Hoftrompeter im 17. und 18. Jahrhundert' (in preparation)

WILLIAM BARCLAY SQUIRE,
H. G. FARMER/EDWARD H. TARR

**Military School of Music.** London conservatory established in 1857 and renamed the Royal Military School of Music in 1865; *see* LONDON, §VII, 3(ii).

**Milkina, Nina** (*b* Moscow, 27 Jan 1919). British pianist of Russian birth. She studied with Leon Conus in Paris and Harold Craxton in London and made her début with the Lamoureux Orchestra when she was 11. She has won a particular reputation for her clear-textured, neat playing of Mozart; she has broadcast all his sonatas, and in his bicentenary year she gave the solo recital of his piano music at the Edinburgh Festival. Also at Edinburgh she took part in a rare performance of Strauss's *Enoch Arden* (1956) and in the first performance of Donald Swann's *London Sketches* (1958). Her recording of all Chopin's mazurkas was praised for its freshness and, within her own range, her playing is poetic and vivacious. She has published some piano works and has performed her own cadenza for Mozart's Concerto in D K537.

FRANK DAWES

**Millán, Francisco** (*fl* early 16th century). Spanish composer. In 1501 and 1502 he was a chaplain and singer in the chapel of Queen Isabella. 24 settings by him are contained in the Cancionero Musical de Palacio; the music of three, however, is included twice. Millán's works appear in the later part of the manuscript or were added in spaces left blank by earlier scribes. In the

Ex.7

Biber: [*Sonata*] *A.M.D.G.B.M.V. et S. Josephi*
Intrada
TROMBA. *udite in violino solo*
tr   tr   tr

1

Bach: *Christmas Oratorio* Part 1, no.8
TRUMPET IN D
tr

15

collection more works are attributed to Millán than to any other composer with the exception of Encina. All his compositions are secular; the great majority being villancicos on the conventional theme of courtly love. This subject is treated in an exaggerated, highly stylized manner, characterized by intellectual conceits, plays on words and sharp juxtaposition of contrasting emotions.

These melancholy love-songs were evidently composed for solo voice with instrumental accompaniment: only the superius carries text, and the movement of the lower voices suggests instrumental rather than vocal performance. Three pieces, however (*Mios fueron mi coraçon, O dulce y triste memoria, Sy no piensas remediar*), have texts in all parts. The simple, grave melodies move smoothly in a fairly narrow range. Sometimes repeated notes are used for a declamatory effect. The predominant mode is Mixolydian; a few pieces cadence on C, others on E or F. The middle section, as well as the final, regularly cadences on the tonic. The style is generally note against note and homorhythmic with brief ornamentation at the cadence, but frequent use of imitation is a characteristic of Millán's music. Normally it occurs only at the beginning but occasionally it opens inner phrases as well. Usually the imitation involves only two voices, but sometimes all three participate. Metre is regularly duple. However, in three courtly villancicos (*Porque de ageno cuidado, Señora, después que os vi, Temeroso de sufrir*) ¢3 alternates with ¢. In *Ved, comadres, que dolencia* the two lower voices anticipate the change to triple metre while the upper two briefly maintain duple measure.

Millán set two famous traditional ballads: *Durandarte, Durandarte*, for four voices, and *Los braços trayo cansados*. The broad, stately melodies have instrumental accompaniments which may have been for vihuela or clavichord. The versions of these ballads by Luis de Milan and Enriquez de Valderrábano both stem from a different tradition, both musical and poetic. In *Serrana del bel mirar* Millán sets a little dramatic scene to music. A herdsman encounters a pretty mountain maid and is enamoured by her singing. The two stanzas of the narrative *villancico* are separated by the maiden's song and at the end the maiden again sings a villancico. Both are traditional female laments. The composition, in the 7th mode, is chordal and in triple metre, opening with the brief imitation so characteristic of Millán.

### WORKS
*(for 3vv unless otherwise indicated)*

Edition: *La música en la corte de los reyes católicos: Cancionero musical de palacio*, ed. H. Anglès, MME, v, x (1947, 1951) [A i, ii]

Al dolor que siento estraño, A ii, no.457; Aunque no spero gozar, A ii, no.366; Durandarte, Durandarte, 4vv, A ii, no.445; Es de tal metal mi mal, A ii, no.334

Los braços trayo cansados, A ii, no.446; Maravilla es como bivo, A ii, no.368; Mios fueron mi coraçon, A i, no.185; No husies de buen tempero, A ii, no.295

O dulce y triste memoria, A ii, no.452; O vos omnes qui transistes, A ii no.232 (macaronic love-song); ¿Para que mi pensamiento? A i, no.195; Porque de ageno cuidado, A ii, no.319; Pues la vida en mal tan fuerte, A ii, no.333; Que mas bien aventuransa, A i, no.147

Señora, después que os vi, A ii, nos.339, 450; Serrana del bel mirar, A i, no.71; Si el dolor sufro secreto, A ii, no.367; Si ell esperança es dudosa (= Pues la vida en mal tan fuerte), A ii, no.351; Sufriendo con fe tan fuerte, A ii, no.323; Sy no piensas remediar, A i, no.194

Temeroso de sufrir, A ii, no.448 (music of Porque de ageno with added contra); Ved, comadres, que dolencia, 4vv, A i, no.122, ii, no.449

### BIBLIOGRAPHY
R. Stevenson: *Spanish Music in the Age of Columbus* (The Hague, 1960), 272ff

ISABEL POPE

**Millar, Edward** (*fl* 1624–43). Scottish musician. He graduated MA from Edinburgh University in 1624 and probably subsequently taught music in Edinburgh. His MS collection of psalm settings dated 1626 was known and described as recently as 1911 by Cowan, but has since disappeared. After Charles I's coronation at Holyrood in 1633, regular choral services were re-established at the Scottish Chapel Royal; Millar was appointed Master of the Choristers in 1634 and in 1635 his fine edition of psalm settings was printed in Edinburgh. In this collection the 104 anonymous settings of the Proper Tunes are by Scottish composers of the late 16th century. Millar wrote in his preface: 'I acknowledge sinceerely the whole compositions of the parts to belong to the primest Musicians that ever this kingdome had, as Deane John Angus, Blackhall, Smith, Peebles, Sharp, Black, Buchan and others famous for their skill in this kind . . .'. Some of these settings can be identified from other sources as wholly the work of Peebles, Buchan and Kemp. In many cases, however, Millar seems to have made 'composite' pieces by taking phrases from different settings and fitting them together (sometimes even transposing the parts) to form a more or less pleasing whole. In other sections of the book, certain settings of Common Tunes and psalms 'in reports', new to the 1635 Psalter, may be Millar's work. A musical commonplace-book (otherwise known as the MacAlman MS; ed. in MB, xv, 1957) containing psalmody, Scottish Renaissance partsongs and cittern music in Millar's hand is signed and dated 1643.

### BIBLIOGRAPHY
W. Cowan: 'A Bibliography of the Book of Common Order', *Proceedings of the Edinburgh Bibliographical Society*, x (1911–13), 53–100
K. Elliott: *Music of Scotland, 1500–1700* (diss., U. of Cambridge, 1960), i, 327ff
——: 'Scottish Music of the Early Reformed Church', *Transactions of the Scottish Ecclesiological Society*, xv/2 (1961), 18
R. E. White: *Aspects of Scottish Church Music, 1560–1645* (diss., U. of St Andrews, 1972), i, 100ff

KENNETH ELLIOTT

**Miller, Dayton C(larence)** (*b* Strongsville, Ohio, 13 March 1866; *d* Cleveland, 22 Feb 1941). American acoustician. He studied at Princeton (DSc 1890) and held appointments there before becoming head of the physics department at the Case School of Applied Science, Cleveland. He was an accomplished flautist, and wrote extensively about the instrument, provided a catalogue of literature on the flute, and gathered an important collection of flutes (now in the Library of Congress, Washington, DC). His most important contribution as an acoustician was the development in 1909 of the 'phonodeik', which incorporated a diaphragm of thin glass closing the end of a receiving horn; this allowed him to analyse waveforms of various instruments – by means of a thin wire attached to the centre of the diaphragm, which passed over a spindle pulley, the rotation of the spindle (due to movement of the diaphragm) was recorded by light reflected from a mirror affixed to the spindle. He also carried out experiments on organ pipes and trumpets having walls of different thicknesses, and produced results suggesting that desirable physical qualities for the containing walls of an instrument, for the maximum fullness of the partials, were softness, thinness, flexibility and high density. He became an expert on engineering acoustics and was responsible for the design of many concert halls. His 32-element harmonic synthesizer won him a medal from the Franklin Institute.

Miller's *The Science of Musical Sounds* (New York, 1916) incorporates the results of his charting of instrument waveforms; his *Anecdotal History of the Science of Sound* (New York, 1935), if it leaves something to be desired as a historical work, is the first broad history of acoustical studies.

*See also* PHYSICS OF MUSIC, §6.

JAMES F. BELL, R. W. B. STEPHENS

**Miller, Edward** (*b* Norwich, 30 Oct 1735: *d* Doncaster, 12 Sept 1807). English organist, composer and historian. His father was a paviour, and he was apprenticed to that trade but absconded and studied music under Charles Burney. He is said to have played the flute in Handel's oratorio orchestra during the 1750s. On 15 July 1756 he was elected organist of Doncaster, in succession to John Camidge, on the recommendation of James Nares. In Doncaster he came to know Herschel, later the astronomer royal, and helped bring him out of obscurity. He played an active part in musical life in his native East Anglia and in the Doncaster region, and directed the Sheffield Festival of 1788. He took the MusD degree at Cambridge in 1786. According to Southey (*The Doctor*), the Marquis of Rockingham applied on his behalf for the post of Master of the King's Band of Musicians on Boyce's death in 1788, but John Stanley was appointed. Miller was first married in 1763; his wife died ten years later, and he remarried in 1796. He was said to be a simple and warmhearted man, with generous philanthropic tendencies.

Of his publications, *Elements of Thorough Bass and Composition* is a practical work containing examples for performance, and *Institutes of Music* is a book of rudiments for beginners. In *The Psalms of David* he attempted a reform of metrical psalmody; this volume includes the tunes 'Rockingham' and 'Galway', and had what has been claimed as the largest number of subscribers for any musical publication in England. In *David's Harp* he collaborated with his son, a Methodist clergyman, in adapting and composing about 300 tunes to Wesley's selection of hymns. His best instrumental works, the six flute solos, are reminiscent of Arne in style. The harpsichord sonatas are of slighter content, and the 'easy voluntaries' for organ are ephemeral works; Miller also 'adapted' Corelli's sonatas opp.1–4 for the organ and harpsichord. His *History of Doncaster* (1804) is a work of substance and scholarship.

### WORKS

*(all printed works published in London)*

VOCAL

A Collection of New English Songs and a Cantata (*c*1755)
Elegies, Songs and an Ode, op.3 (1770)
Anthem and Hymn, op.6 (1789); anthem autograph *GB-Lbm*
The Psalms of David for the Use of Parish Churches (1790)
12 Canzonets, v, pf, op.10 (*c*1800)
Sacred Music, containing 250 of the most Favourite Tunes (*c*1800)
David's Harp (with W. E. Miller) (*c*1803), 100 of the 300 tunes are by E. Miller
Dr Watts's Psalms and Hymns set to new Music, 3, 4 vv (1802; with second pt., 2/*c*1805; ed. for choirs as Psalm Tunes composed in 4 parts, *c*1805)
Te Deum, Jubilate, Magnificat and Nunc dimittis (org pt. only), *GB-Cu*
Various songs, glees, etc

INSTRUMENTAL

6 Solos, fl, bc, op.1 (*c*1760)
6 Sonatas, hpd, 3 with vn/fl, op.2 (*c*1765)
12 Progressive Lessons, pf/hpd, with fl/vn, op.8 (1791)
16 Easy Voluntaries, org, op.9 (1797)

### WRITINGS

*(only those pertaining to music)*

Institutes of Music, or Easy Instructions for the Harpsichord, op.4 (London, 1783)
Letters on Behalf of Professors of Music . . . to the . . . Directors and Managers of the . . . Commemoration of Handel (London, 1784)
Elements of Thorough Bass and Composition, op.5 (London, 1787)
Thoughts on the Present Performance of Psalmody (London, 1791)
The New Flute Instructor . . . also a Dictionary (London, *c*1800)

### BIBLIOGRAPHY

E. Jackson: *The History and Description of St George's Church Doncaster* (Doncaster, 1855)
E. H. Allen: 'Miller, Edward', *DNB*
'The Tune Rockingham', *MT*, xlii (1901), 736
E. M. Lockwood: 'Edward Miller', *ML*, ix (1928), 67
C. Cudworth: 'Miller, Edward', *MGG*
M. Frost, ed.: *A Historical Companion to Hymns Ancient and Modern* (London, 1962)
A. H. Mann: Notebooks on East Anglian musical life (MS, *GB-NWr*)

J. M. BLACK

**Miller, Ernest Louis.** *See* MÜLLER, ERNEST LOUIS.

**Miller, (Alton) Glenn** (*b* Clarinda, Iowa, 1 March 1904; *d* between London and Paris, *c*15 Dec 1944). American band-leader, trombonist, arranger and composer. He played in groups led by Boyd Senter (1921), Ben Pollack (1926) and Smith Ballew (1932–4) before joining the Dorsey Brothers' Orchestra in 1934; thereafter he studied with Joseph Schillinger and arranged scores for the Casa Loma Orchestra and Ozzie Nelson. While with Ray Noble's group (1935) he conceived his characteristic reed-section sound of a clarinet over four saxophones. He formed his first big band in 1937, but without success. Having reassembled in 1938 the Glenn Miller Orchestra rapidly became the most popular 'sweet' swing band through its recordings *Moonlight Serenade*, *Little Brown Jug* and *In the Mood* as well as two very successful films, *Sun Valley Serenade* and *Orchestra Wives*. In these years Miller rarely played the trombone or arranged, but dedicated himself to reaching an ever-widening audience for his band, from which he demanded, and obtained, superb precision. He disbanded the group in 1942 to join the US Army, and there assembled a service band which in 1944 was posted to England. A certain mystery surrounding his death (he was declared missing after an aeroplane flight) helped to translate his former international fame into near legend, and his service band remained active under various leaders, most notably Ray McKinley (1956–65) and Buddy DeFranco (from 1966), performing and recording much of Miller's repertory.

### BIBLIOGRAPHY

J. Flower: *Moonlight Serenade: a Bio-discography of the Glenn Miller Civilian Band* (New Rochelle, 1972)
G. Simon: *Glenn Miller and his Orchestra* (New York, 1974)

JOSÉ HOSIASSON

**Miller, Silverius** [Franz]. *See* MÜLLER, SILVERIUS.

**Milleran, René** (*fl* late 17th and early 18th centuries). French grammarian and amateur lutenist. He lived in Paris, taught German and English and was an interpreter in the service of Louis XIV. Charles Moon and Louis la Bolle taught him to play the lute. About 1690 he compiled an anthology of the lute music of his time: *Livre de lut de M. Milleran, interprète du roy . . . recueil des plus belles pièces de lut des meilleurs maîtres, sur les 14 modes de la musique, savoir 7 en bémol et 7 en bécarre* (*F-Pn* Rés.823). It contains pieces by Charles

Bocquet, Delaunay, the Dubuts, Dufaut, Dupré d'Angleterre, Emont, the Gallots, the Gaultiers, Gomprecht, Kremberg, Charles Mouton, Esaias Reusner (ii) and Valentin Strobel (ii), as well as several anonymous pieces. Milleran gave a list of the principal lutenists of his time, including Mouton and Jacques Gallot. He also wrote several works on the grammar and orthography of the French language.

BIBLIOGRAPHY
M. Brenet: 'Notes sur l'histoire du luth en France', *RMI*, vi (1899), 1
JOËL DUGOT

**Millet, Jean** (*b* Montgesoye, Doubs, 1618; *d* Besançon, 10 Feb 1684). French musician and ecclesiastic. He served the two principal churches of the metropolitan chapter of Besançon as *enfant de choeur*, singer, organist, canon and, most notably, as *sur-chantre*. He was responsible for several books relating to music in the service in Besançon, but his most significant work is *La belle méthode*, a vocal tutor concerned with ornamentation of *airs*, which contains his only known surviving music – four *airs* and two motets.

WRITINGS
*Directoire du chant grégorien* (Lyons, 1666)
*La belle méthode, ou l'art de bien chanter* (Besançon, 1666/R1973)
ed.: *Antiphonarium bisuntinum* (Besançon, 1681)
ed.: *Graduale bisuntinum* (Besançon, 1682)

BIBLIOGRAPHY
A. Cohen: 'Jean Millet "de Montgesoye" (1618–1684)', *RMFC*, viii (1968), 15
——: '*L'art de bien chanter* (1666) of Jean Millet', *MQ*, lv (1969), 170
ALBERT COHEN

**Millet, Luis Maria** (*b* Barcelona, 21 June 1906). Spanish choirmaster, composer and teacher. He studied at the Barcelona Municipal Music School with his father, Luis Millet (composition and harmony), Gibert (organ, fugue and counterpoint) and Canals (piano). In 1925 he joined the Orfeó Català as a baritone; with this choir he was successively appointed teacher (1931), assistant conductor (1941) and conductor (1945). He has also taught at the Barcelona Municipal Music School (solfège, history and aesthetics) and the Seminario Conciliar (piano), and has been choirmaster of S Felipe Neri, Barcelona. An honorary member of the Spanish Institute of Musicology and a corresponding member of the San Fernando Academy, he holds the silver medal of the province of Barcelona. His compositions include many choral pieces, both sacred and secular (among them a mass and the *Poema nadalenc* for solo voice, chorus and orchestra, *La reliquia*, *Chora* and *Agar*), as well as works for piano and organ.

A. MENÉNDEZ ALEYXANDRE

**Milleville.** French family of musicians from Paris, largely active in Ferrara.

**(1) Pierre [Pierreson] Milleville** (*fl* Ferrara and Rome, 1504–19). He was the first professional musician of this family and is first heard of as a singer in the ducal chapel at Ferrara in August 1504. He remained at Ferrara until the temporary dissolution of the chapel in 1510. He is mentioned as being among the singers in the private chapel of Pope Leo X in 1518 and 1519. According to Ferrarese chroniclers, Duke Alfonso d'Este I, after a visit to France and England in spring and early summer 1504, brought back to Ferrara a remarkable 12-year-old boy, who was gifted both as a singer and as a composer. This report is supported by Pierre

Milleville's presence in the chapel from 1504, but no compositions by him are known.

**(2) Jean Milleville** (*b* before *c*1500; *d* ?after 1573). Music teacher. According to Fétis he went to the Ferrarese court in about 1530 at the request of Renée of France, the daughter of Louis XII, who had married Duke Ercole II of Ferrara in 1528. According to Weyler, he was a singer at the court of Ferrara from 1534 to 1550 and was perhaps already in service there in 1530. Although Valdrighi stated that the teacher of the Princesses of Modena from 1544 to 1573 was Alessandro Milleville, Solerti and Campori gave the entire document from the account books of the Duchess of Ferrara from which this notice seems to have been taken: it mentions paying a sum 'A milleville chantre' for teaching the princesses, presumably the duchess's daughters. It seems likely, then, that Valdrighi confused Alessandro with his father, Jean, and that the princesses were of Ferrara, not of Modena, and were taught by Jean. In locating a motet by Jean in a book by Attaingnant, Fétis identified Jean with Maistre Jhan of Ferrara, but this was probably an error since Maistre Jhan seems to have been at Ferrara from at least 1522.

**(3) Alessandro Milleville** (*b* Paris, ?1521; *d* Ferrara, 8 Sept 1589). Organist and composer, son of (2) Jean Milleville. That Milleville was born in Paris is reported only by Fétis, who did not give his source. Although Fétis derived Alessandro's birthdate from the assertion that he went to Ferrara in 1530 at the age of nine (for which assertion no source is given), this birthdate is probably correct, for Superbi said that Milleville died at the age 68 and Borsetti said that he died in 1589. He was a tenor in the papal chapel from January 1553 to June 1558. From April 1560 until his death he was second organist (under Luzzaschi) at the Ferrarese court. He was the teacher of Ercole Pasquini, of Vittoria Aleotti and, presumably, of his own son Francesco. He is said to have been a fine organist and may have been an important figure in the Ferrarese organ school, which included Luzzaschi and reached its height in Pasquini and Frescobaldi. No organ music by him survives. His madrigals of the 1580s do not indicate that he had a strongly individual personality as a composer of secular music. His madrigal books appear to have circulated only locally, and, with one exception, his pieces appeared only in specifically Ferrarese anthologies.

WORKS
Libro primo de' madrigali, 5vv (Venice, 1575)
Madrigali libro secondo, 5vv (Ferrara, 1584)
Madrigali, 6vv (Ferrara, 1584)
Sacrarum cantionum liber primus, 5vv (Ferrara, 1584)
Le vergine con 10 altre stanze spirituali, 4vv (Ferrara, 1584)
4 madrigals, *I-MOe* Mus.F.1358
Further madrigals, 1581[5], 1582[5], 1583[10], 1586[10], 1591[9], 1593[3]

**(4) Francesco Milleville** [Padre Barnabá, Milleville Ferrarese] (*b* ?Ferrara, ?*c*1565; *d* after 1639). Composer and organist, son of (3) Alessandro Milleville. Fétis, the only source of information concerning Milleville's birthdate, said that he was organist to the King of Poland and to Emperor Rudolf II before going to Rome in 1614. After going to Italy Milleville became *maestro di cappella* of Volterra Cathedral, according to Sartori. The title-pages of his publications show that he held numerous posts in Italy between 1616 and 1628: in 1616 he was at Gubbio, in 1619–20 at Chioggia, in 1622 at S Giorgio, Ferrara, and in 1627–8 at S Benedetto, Siena. In 1632, according to Sartori, he was organist of Arezzo Cathedral. The dedication of op.20

to the abbot of the monastery of S Giorgio, Ferrara, may indicate that Milleville had returned to Ferrara by that time.

## WORKS
### (all published in Venice)

Una messa in concerto, 1 motet. 2 Dixit Dominus, 1 Magnificat, op.5 (1616)
Concerti, 2–4vv, bc (org), op.2 (1617)
Il secondo libro delle messe, 4, 8vv, op.6 (1617)
Il primo libro de' madrigali in concerto, 1, 5, 8vv, bc, op.3 (1617)
Letanie della B. Vergine con le sue antifone, 8vv, bc (org), op.8 (1619)
Il terzo libro de' motetti, 1–3vv, op.9 (1620)
Sacre gemme legate nell'oro, 1v, op.10 (1622)
Pompe funebri nel mortorio di Cristo, Responsori, op.14 (1624)
Il quinto libro delli motetti, 2–5vv, op.17 (1627)
Mazzo d'armonici fiori, 3vv, bc, op.18 (1628)
Letanie della Beatissima Vergine, 3vv, op.20 (1639)
2 motets, 2vv, 1624[2]

### BIBLIOGRAPHY
FétisB; RicordiE
A. Superbi: Apparato degli uomini illustri di Ferrara (Ferrara, 1620), 130
F. Borsetti: Historia almi ferrariae gymnasii (Ferrara, 1735)
L. F. Valdrighi: 'Cappella, concerti, e musiche di casa d'Este', Atti e memorie ... per le provincie modenesi e parmensi, 3rd ser., ii (1884), 417; iii (1885), 507
A. Solerti and G. Campori: Luigi, Lucrezia e Leonora d'Este (Turin, 1888)
W. Weyler: 'Documenten betreffende de Muziekkapel aan het hof van Ferrara', Vlaams jaarboek voor muziekgeschiedhis, i (1939), 81
A. Newcomb: The 'Musica secreta' of Ferrara in the 1580's (diss., Princeton U., 1969)

ANTHONY NEWCOMB

**Millhouse.** See MILHOUSE family.

**Millico, (Vito) Giuseppe** (*b* Terlizzi, nr. Bari, 19 Jan 1737; *d* Naples, 2 Oct 1802). Italian soprano castrato, composer and singing teacher. He was active as an opera singer in all the principal European musical centres, from St Petersburg and Berlin to London, and in the south from Vienna to Parma and Naples. After being at the Russian court from 1758 to 1765 he returned to Italy; at Parma in 1769 he sang Orpheus in *Le feste d'Apollo* by Gluck, who befriended him and took him to Vienna, where he taught Gluck's niece and created the role of Paris in Gluck's *Paride ed Elena* (3 November 1770). Two years later he went to London, and in 1773 again appeared as Orpheus. In autumn 1774 he was with Gluck in Paris and went with him to Zweibrücken and Mannheim. He was in Berlin before his final return to Italy in 1780, when he was appointed 'virtuoso di camera e della Regia Cappella' in Naples; while there he composed the operas *Le cinesi* and *L'isola disabitata* for the Bourbon princesses Teresa and Luisa. The score of his opera *La pietà d'amore* was published in Naples in 1782, with an acknowledgment to Gluck and his ideals in the foreword, addressed to the opera's librettist, Antonio Lucchesi. In addition to at least half a dozen operas, Millico composed several cantatas and, more importantly, numerous arias, canzonettas and duets, often with harp accompaniment. The fact that many of these works were published individually and in collections, along with the extraordinarily wide circulation in manuscript of the smaller vocal and instrumental compositions, thought to be late works, testifies to their popularity and to Millico's reputation as a singer, composer and teacher. His portrait appears in Antonio Fedi's *Parnaso* (*c*1790), and as Orpheus in an illustration for the libretto of *Le feste d'Apollo* (Parma, 1769).

### BIBLIOGRAPHY
BurneyH; GerberL; GerberNL; RiemannL 12
F. Haböck: Die Kastraten und ihre Gesangskunst (Stuttgart, 1927)

R.-A. Mooser: Annales de la musique et des musiciens en Russie au XVIIIme siècle, i (Geneva, 1948), 309f
M. Belluci La Salandria: Vito Giuseppe Millico (Bari, 1951)
H. Kühner: 'Millico, Giuseppe', MGG
L. Finscher: 'Der Opernsänger als Komponist: Giuseppe Millico und seine Oper La pietà d'amore', Opernstudien: Anna Amalie Abert zum 65. Geburtstag (Tutzing, 1975), 57–90

GERHARD CROLL

**Milligen, Simon van** (*b* Rotterdam, 14 Dec 1849; *d* Amsterdam, 11 March 1929). Dutch teacher, critic, conductor and composer. He was an organ pupil of J. A. Klerk and Samuel de Lange (i) and a composition pupil of Bargiel and Nicolaï. In 1871 he was a piano teacher in Middelburg and in 1873 he was an organist in Groningen, where he continued his studies with Worp. From 1875 to 1888 he was director of the music school in Gouda, leaving his post to complete his study of composition in Paris. After returning to Holland in 1890, he settled in Amsterdam, working as a newspaper critic until 1906, and from 1902 editing the monthly *Caecilia*; he also gave lessons and was conductor of several choirs with whom he promoted modern French music. In 1913 he was appointed professor of music history at the Amsterdam Conservatory, a post he held until his death. As a result of his teaching work, he wrote a comprehensive history of music, *Ontwikkelingsgang der muziek* (Groningen, 1912), based on an earlier work by Worp, and a study of early Christian church music, *De kerkzang van de eerste christelijke periode tot onzen tijd* (Groningen, 1908). His compositions include two operas, choral works in the style of Massenet, cantatas and a cycle of Romanian songs.

### BIBLIOGRAPHY
A. Averkamp: 'In memoriam S. van Milligen', TVNM, xiii/2 (1929), 101

JAN TEN BOKUM

**Millioni, Pietro.** See MILIONI, PIETRO.

**Millner, Silverius** [Franz]. See MÜLLER, SILVERIUS.

**Millöcker, Carl** (*b* Vienna, 29 April 1842; *d* Baden, nr. Vienna, 31 Dec 1899). Austrian composer. The son of a goldsmith, he studied the flute at the Vienna Conservatory (1855–8) and theory with F. J. Zierer and Laimegger. In 1858 he played at the Theater in der Josephstadt and in 1864, on the recommendation of Suppé (from whom he had received some practical tuition), he became conductor at the Thalia-Theater in Graz. There his first one-act pieces, somewhat in the style of Offenbach, were produced in 1865; and there he also married one of the theatre's singers. In 1866 he obtained a position as conductor at the Theater an der Wien, but because of the lack of opportunities he moved to the Harmonie-Theater, where a further one-act operetta *Diana* was produced.

In 1868 Millöcker was appointed conductor at the Deutsches Theater in Budapest and then in 1869 returned to the Theater an der Wien as second conductor. In the course of his duties there he composed songs and incidental music for many short theatrical pieces, first gaining attention with his score for *Drei Paar Schuhe* (1871). From 1873 to 1876 he edited the *Musikalische Presse*, a monthly magazine of piano music and articles. He also tried writing full-length operettas, his first successes being *Das verwunschene Schloss* (1878) and *Apajune der Wassermann* (1880), which like his later major works starred the leading Viennese operetta singer of the time, Alexander Girardi. His greatest success came with *Der Bettelstudent* (1882), and in 1883 he was able to give up his conducting position to concentrate on composition. *Gasparone* (1884) was almost as well received, but thereafter his success declined. The most successful of his later operettas was *Der arme Jonathan* (1890): set partly in the USA, it was performed in London (with some additional numbers by Isaac Albéniz) and in the USA, where it was particularly popular. In 1894 Millöcker suffered the first of several strokes which partly paralysed him and eventually led to his death. He was twice married.

Millöcker's successes in the 1880s established him with Johann Strauss and Suppé as one of the three leading exponents of Viennese operetta of the time. Though his music lacked the vigorous appeal of Suppé's and the melodic facility of Strauss's (as a result of which he remained less well known abroad) he was technically the most proficient of the three. *Der Bettelstudent*, based on Sardou's *Les noces de Fernande* (in turn derived from Bulwer-Lytton's *The Lady of Lyons*), is still frequently performed in Austria and Germany and admirably displays Millöcker's expressive and essentially theatrical vocal writing and part-writing. Several numbers from other operettas remain well known, notably the waltz songs written for Girardi and especially 'Er soll dein Herr sein' from *Gasparone* which also became popular in Germany in bastardized form as 'Mutter der Mann mit dem Koks ist da'. Millöcker's music was also used for several pastiche operettas, including Mackeben's *Die Dubarry* (1931) which used music from the unsuccessful *Gräfin Dubarry* (1879) and other pieces.

WORKS
*(many MSS at A-Wst)*

OPERETTAS

Most operettas published in Vienna (vocal score) about date of first performance. Unless otherwise indicated, first performed in Vienna, Theater an der Wien.

Der tote Gast (1), Graz, Thalia-Theater, 21 Dec 1865
Die lustigen Binder (1), Graz, Thalia-Theater, 21 Dec 1865
Diana (1, J. Braun), Vienna, Harmonie-Theater, 2 Jan 1867
Die Fraueninsel (3), Budapest, Deutsches Theater, 1868
Abenteuer in Wien (3, A. Berla), 20 Jan 1873
Das verwunschene Schloss (3, Berla), 30 March 1878
Gräfin Dubarry (3, F. Zell, R. Genée), 31 Oct 1879
Apajune der Wassermann (3, Zell, Genée), 18 Dec 1880
Die Jungfrau von Belleville (3, Zell, Genée), 29 Oct 1881
Der Bettelstudent (3, Zell, Genée after Sardou: Les noces de Fernande), 6 Dec 1882
Gasparone (3, Zell, Genée), 26 Jan 1884
Der Feldprediger (3, H. Wittmann, A. Wohlmuth), 31 Oct 1884
Der Vice-Admiral (3, Zell, Genée), 9 Oct 1886
Die sieben Schwaben (3, Wittmann, J. Bauer), 29 Oct 1887
Der arme Jonathan (3, Wittmann, Bauer), 4 Jan 1890
Das Sonntagskind (3, Wittmann, Bauer), 16 Jan 1892
Der Probekuss (3, Wittmann, Bauer), 22 Dec 1894
Nordlicht, oder Der rote Graf (3, Wittmann), 22 Dec 1896

OTHER WORKS

c40 other theatrical pieces, mostly for Theater an der Wien, incl. Drei Paar Schuhe (1871), Die schlimmen Töchter (1876), Ein Blitzmädel (1878), Ihr Korporal (1878), Die Näherin (1880), Ihre Familie (1881): for detailed list see *ES*
6 heitere Lieder, Bar/B, pf (Vienna, 1872)
Lebensphasen, quodlibet, v, pf (Vienna, 1872)
Miscellaneous songs and dances

BIBLIOGRAPHY

C. Preiss: 'Versuch einer Biographie Carl Millöckers', *Wochenschrift für Kunst und Musik*, iii (1905), 18
E. Nick: *Vom Wiener Walzer zur Wiener Operette* (Hamburg, 1954)
F. Racek: 'Das Tagebuch Carl Millöckers', *Wiener Schriften*, iii (1969), 137–230

ANDREW LAMB

**Millot, Nicolas** (*fl* Paris, 1556–86). French composer. In December 1559 Noel Millot was registered as one of the 12 clerks at the Sainte-Chapelle, Paris; this was probably Nicolas Millot, since the records are known to have cited incorrect christian names in a number of cases. His four-voice settings of Accace d'Albiac's *Proverbes de Salomon* were published in 1567 with a dedication to Charles IX who in 1572 sent him from Chambord to Tours to find two boy choristers. In 1575 he won the silver lyre prize in the St Cecilia competition at Evreux for his chanson *Les espis sont à Ceres*, and was described as 'one of the *maîtres de chapelle* to King Henri III'; when he resigned this post to the castrato Estienne le Roy in March 1585, he was reported to have been 'sous-maître de la chapelle de musique du Roy' for over 20 years. In 1578 he was also referred to as a singer ('haute-contre') and composer at the royal chapel. His last recorded appointment was as *sous-maître* in the queen's chapel in 1586.

30 chansons by Millot were printed at Paris between 1556 and 1578. They include settings of poems by François I, Eustorg de Beaulieu, Guillaume Guéroult and Ronsard, as well as popular verse (e.g. *J'ay l'alouette* which is related to the folksong *L'alouette, gentille alouette*). His musical style is predominantly old-fashioned, resembling that of the Parisian chansons of Sandrin, Janequin and Arcadelt; the courtly pieces are generally homophonic with occasional imitative passages, and the rustic songs are more syllabic and contrapuntal. Only occasionally does the contemporary tendency towards a treble melody and homophonic harmony appear. The 20 *Proverbes* do not use Gindron's Huguenot melodies, as Janequin's settings do, but are freely composed.

WORKS

Les [20] proverbes de Salomon mis en musique, 4vv (Paris, 1567)
30 chansons, 3–5vv, 1556[20], 1556[21], 1557[15], 1559[10], 1559[13], 1567[11], 1569[10], 1569[17], 1570[4], 1570[9], 1572[2], 1578[14], 1578[15]; 1 ed. M. Cauchie, *15 chansons françaises du XVIe siècle* (Paris, 1926); 1 ed. in Thibault and Perceau; 1 ed. F. Lesure, *Anthologie de la chanson parisienne au XVIe siècle* (Monaco, 1953)

BIBLIOGRAPHY

G. Thibault and L. Perceau: *Bibliographie des poésies de P. de Ronsard mises en musique au XVIe siècle* (Paris, 1941)
F. Lesure and G. Thibault: *Bibliographie des éditions d'Adrian le Roy et Robert Ballard (1551–1598)* (Paris, 1955), 23–198

FRANK DOBBINS

**Mills.** Welsh family of musicians and pioneers in congregational singing.

(1) **Henry Mills** (*b* Llanidloes, 1757; *d* Llanidloes, 28 Aug 1820). Minister. His singing impressed the celebrated preacher Thomas Charles of Bala during a Methodist revival in 1780 and made him responsible for improving congregational singing in the district, despite the opposition of some of the elders who objected to his youth and his ability to play several instruments.

(2) **James Mills** (*b* Llanidloes, 1790; *d* Llanidloes, 1844). Conductor, son of (1) Henry Mills and his first wife. Continuing his father's activities, he attracted as many as 70 students to his weekly classes in the rudiments of music – a surprisingly high figure for the size of the district. He composed several anthems and hymn tunes.

(3) **Richard Mills (i)** [Rhydderch Hael] (*b* Llanidloes, March 1809; *d* Llanidloes, 24 Dec 1844). Composer and lecturer, son of (1) Henry Mills and his second wife. His collections of hymn tunes *Caniadau Seion* (1840,

suppl. 1842) and *Yr Arweinydd Cerddorol* (1842–5) greatly influenced congregational singing in Wales and were landmarks in its improvement. He composed about half the tunes in these books; the latter contains a 78-page introduction to rudiments, and advice on singing and interpretation. Mills followed the general practice of printing in open score with the melody in the line above the bass. Most tunes were in four parts although there was much controversy over whether tunes should be sung in harmony at all, or in three parts instead of four.

**(4) John Mills** [Ieuan Glan Alarch] (*b* Llanidloes, 19 Dec 1812; *d* London, 28 July 1873). Minister, writer and musician, grandson of (1) Henry Mills and his first wife. In 1838 he travelled throughout Wales lecturing on music and temperance and founding music societies. His 'grammar of music' (*Gramadeg Cerddoriaeth*) published in the same year ran to several editions. Ordained a Calvinistic Methodist minister in 1841, he took charge of a church in Ruthin but moved to London in 1846 to pursue missionary work among the Jews. In 1863 he became pastor of the Welsh church in Nassau Street. He published many theological works in Welsh and English. His music books waged an active campaign for better congregational singing, better metrical consistency between hymns and tunes and a wider general knowledge of musical rudiments. With (3) Richard Mills (i) he was particularly influential in the admission of congregational singing as an essential part of Welsh nonconformist worship, which made possible the choral movement of the later 19th century. His other books include *Y Salmydd Eglwysig* (1847), *Elfennau Cerddoriaeth* (1848), *Y Canor* (1851), *Yr Athraw Cerddorol* (1854, with Thomas Williams 'Hafrenydd') and *Y Cerddor Dirwestol* (1855). He published *Y Cerddor Eglwysig* (1846, suppl. 1847) and a second edition of *Y Canor* (1859) with his brother, another Richard Mills.

**(5) Richard Mills (ii)** (*b* Llanidloes, 1 Oct 1840; *d* Rhosllanerchrugog, 18 May 1903). Musician and printer, son of (3) Richard Mills (i). Trained as a staff-notation compositor, he supervised the music publishing of Hughes & Son in Wrexham to 1877, then established his own press in Rhosllanerchrugog. In 1894 he started the *Rhos Herald*, which he edited until his death. Throughout his life he conducted various choral societies in Denbighshire. His partsongs were popular and a few of his hymn tunes are still remembered.

BIBLIOGRAPHY

R. D. Griffith: *Hanes canu cynulleidfaol Cymru* (Cardiff, 1948)

G. P. Ambrose: 'Mills, Henry', 'Mills, John', 'Mills, Richard', *Dictionary of Welsh Biography* (London, 1959)

R. B. Jones, ed.: *Anatomy of Wales* (Cardiff, 1972), chap.11

OWAIN EDWARDS

**Mills, Charles (Borromeo)** (*b* Asheville, North Carolina, 8 Jan 1914). American composer. He was musically self-taught until the age of 19, when he began studies in New York with Max Garfield, going on to take composition lessons from Copland, Sessions and Harris. For eight years he was radio critic of *Modern Music* and he headed the composition department of the Manhattan School of Music in 1954–5, but he has concentrated on composition, particularly in later years. Among the awards he has received was a Guggenheim Fellowship (1952). His compositional style reflects his belief in the continued validity of traditional forms (fugue and sonata) and the diatonic system. There are often perceptible

influences from his experience, both musical (the spirituals and folksongs heard during his childhood in South Carolina, and the jazz music of the dance orchestras in which he played as a young man) and spiritual: he was a convert to Roman Catholicism in 1944, and his work carries a sense of piety and contemplation.

WORKS

*(selective list)*

Orch: Sym. no.1, e, op.15, 1940; Sym. no.2, C, op.20, 1942; Sym. no.3, d, op.55, 1946; 'Crazy Horse' Sym., op.71, 1958; Pf Conc., op.75, 1948; Conc. grosso, op.78, small orch, 1949; Theme and Variations, 1951; Toccata, 1951; Prelude and Fugue, 1952; Prologue and Dithyramb, str, 1954; Concertino, ob, str, 1957; Serenade, 1960; In a Mule Drawn Wagon, str, 1969

Choral: Festival Ov., op.8 (McLeish), vv, orch, 1940; Ars poetica, op.10 (McLeish), unacc., 1940; The Dark Night, op.59, female vv, str, 1946

Chamber: Chamber Sym., op.6, 11 insts, 1939; 5 str qts, F, op.7, 1939, D, op.22, 1942, f, op.31, 1943, C, 1952, 1958; Sonatine, op.9, fl, str sextet, 1940; Chorale Fantasia, op.11, str trio, 1940; 3 sonatas, vn, pf, c1940, 1942, 1948; Pf Trio, d, op.18, 1941; Chamber Conc., op.26, 10 insts, 1942; Serenade, op.69, fl, hn, pf, 1946; Conc. sereno, op.77, 8 ww, 1948; Duo Fantasie, vc, pf, 1953; Brass Qnt, 1963; Breezy Point Pipings, 1963; The Brass Piano, 6 brass, 1964; Paul Bunyan Jump, jazz qnt, 1964; many sonatas and suites

Other works: ballet, 4 film scores, songs

BARBARA HAMPTON

**Mills, Richard** (*b* ?1798; *d* London, 28 Nov 1870). English music publisher, successor to ROBERT BIRCHALL.

**Mills Music.** Part of the BELWIN-MILLS Publishing Corporation.

**Milne, Peter** (*b* Kincardine-O'Neil, Aberdeenshire, 30 Sept 1824; *d* Aberdeen, 11 March 1908). Scottish composer and violinist. His early education was scanty and his first job that of a farm labourer; it is not known how he came to learn music and acquire a violin. He was musician enough to lead the orchestra at the Theatre Royal, Aberdeen, and to go on, after some years, to similar appointments in Edinburgh. But he drifted from one job to another, until finally he earned his living by playing on the ferries and pleasure-boats of the River Forth, at Edinburgh, Queensferry, Granton and Burntisland. He returned in his later years to Tarland, Aberdeenshire, later moving to Aberdeen, where he taught intermittently. He died in the Aberdeen poorhouse of Oldmill.

Milne composed numerous fine dance tunes, some of which (*Aboyne Brig*, *The Brig o' Teuch*) are still warmly alive to Scottish fiddlers. They were published, with those of other players, and edited by him in a collection entitled *Selections of Strathspeys, Reels, etc.* (Keith, Banffshire, 1870), which reached five editions. A monument in his honour was placed in the wall above his grave in Tarland churchyard near Aberdeen.

JEAN MARY ALLAN

**Milner, Anthony (Francis Dominic)** (*b* Bristol, 13 May 1925). English composer and teacher. He was educated at Douai School, Woolhampton, and at the Royal College of Music, where he studied piano with Herbert Fryer and composition with R. O. Morris. He also studied privately with Seiber. He joined the teaching staff of Morley College in 1947 and became a London University extension lecturer in 1954. In 1965 he was appointed lecturer in music at King's College, London, and in 1971 senior lecturer in music at Goldsmith's College, London. He is a professor of composition at the RCM, and has often visited America as lecturer or as visiting composer at summer schools or music workshops.

Milner has written much choral music, mostly to religious texts. His dramatic oratorio *The Water and the Fire* was first performed at the Three Choirs Festival at Hereford in 1964; most of his later music has been written to commission. His instrumental works include the Variations for Orchestra (first performed at the Cheltenham Festival in 1959) and a symphony, begun in 1964 in response to a commission from the LSO, but brought to performance only in January 1973, after the BBC had taken over the commission. He has written a textbook on the teaching of harmony, and has contributed chapters on 16th-century and Baroque music to symposia on music history.

Milner, a practising Roman Catholic, is strongly motivated in his work by his religious beliefs. He is deeply involved with the words he chooses to set, seeing music as 'part of the great act of praise we should all be giving'. Even his Variations for Orchestra have symbolic meaning, being based on the Rosary: the 15 movements, in three groups of five, represent the Joyful, the Sorrowful and the Glorious Mysteries.

He is always careful not to allow the meaning of texts to be obscured, often allowing music to follow the rhythms and inflections of speech, and setting words generally syllabically. He makes use of such familiar symbolizations as falling semitones for grief, or clear diatonic harmony and rising 4th or 5ths for affirmation and belief. Melodically, his music shows considerable subtlety and a traditional restraint; tunes tend to proceed by step, avoiding leaps that could be considered awkward, and to be compact rather than straggling. The same type of restrained melodic line, vocal in derivation, appears in much of his instrumental writing.

Milner is an outstandingly resourceful contrapuntist. His intimate acquaintance with medieval music is reflected in melodic figurations reminiscent of plainsong, and in occasional uses of isorhythm and hocket. Textures remains clear even when processes of great complexity are at work; the fugal finale of the Variations for Orchestra is a most remarkable example of unlaboured contrapuntal ingenuity. But the vocal works tend to be more freely and personally expressive, and it is in these that the most striking and imaginative uses of instruments are to be found.

In two articles written in 1956, Milner criticized the computational approach of 12-note composers and the 'anti-melodic' vocal writing of Webern and Stravinsky. Yet there is some similarity between his own uses of medieval methods of note manipulation and the methods of serial composers. *Roman Spring* uses 12-note themes melodically, but not in the organization of harmony, and individual notes may undergo octave transposition, as in serial music. Though Milner upholds traditional values, in words and in music, he rarely repeats old formulae, and almost every new work shows signs of change and progress. While he remains always a conscientious and skilled craftsman, in full control of his material, there is often, in his best works, a suggestion of spiritual and emotional forces operating at deeper levels of consciousness.

## WORKS

op.
1    Salutatio angelica (Angelus, Regina coeli, Psalm cxxx), A, chorus, orch, 1948
3    Mass, SATB chorus, 1951
4    Oboe Quartet, 1953
5    The Song of Akhenaten, S, chamber orch, 1954
6    Rondo saltato, org, 1955
7    The City of Desolation (Bible trans. Knox), S, chorus, orch, 1955
8    St Francis (J. A. Cuddon), T, chorus, orch, 1956
9    The Harrowing of Hell, B, chorus, 1956
10/1  Benedic anima mea Dominum, SSAATTBB, 1954
10/2  Christus factus est, SSAATTBB, 1959
—    Corfu, suite, 2 tr rec, a rec, 1957
11    Our Lady's Hours, S, pf, 1957
14    Variations, orch, 1958
15    Peacock Pie (de la Mare), SSA, pf, 1959
16    The Water and the Fire (Bible, St John of the Cross), S, T, B, chorus, orch, 1960–61
17    April Prologue, ov., orch, 1961
18    Divertimento, str, 1961
20    Break to be Built, O Stone, ceremonial ode, chorus, orch, 1962
21    Sinfonia pasquale, str, wind ad lib, 1963
22    Wind Quintet, 1964
—    Festival Te Deum, chorus, orch, 1967
—    Chamber Symphony, chamber orch, 1968
27    Roman Spring (Horace, Lucretius, Catullus, anon.), S, T, chorus, orch, 1969
28    Symphony no.1, 1972
29    Motet for Peace, TTBB, 9 brass, 1973
30    The Leaden Echo and the Golden Echo, partsong, 1974
31    Midway, Mez, chamber orch, 1974
32    Cantata for Christmas 'Emanuel', Ct, SATB, chamber orch, 1974–5
33    String Quartet no.1, 1975
34    Festival Anthem, S, A, T, B, chorus, org, 1976
35    Symphony no.2 (G. M. Hopkins, St Francis, Bible), S, T, chorus, orch, 1977–8

Principal publishers: Novello, Universal

### WRITINGS
'The Vocal Element in Melody', *MT*, xcvii (1956), 128
'The Lunatic Fringe Combed', *MT*, xcvii (1956), 516
'English Music', *European Music of the Twentieth Century*, ed. H. Hartog (Harmondsworth, 1957)
with A. Harman: *Man and his Music*, ii, (London, 1959/*R*1962)
'Radio and Gramophone', *Twentieth Century Music*, ed. R. Myers (London, 1960, 2/1968)
'Sixteenth Century Music', *The Pelican History of Music*, ed. A. Robertson and D. Stevens (Harmondsworth, 1963)
'The Sacred Capons', *MT*, cxiv (1973), 250

### BIBLIOGRAPHY
A. Jacobs: 'The Music of Anthony Milner', *MT*, xcix (1958), 482
D. Stevens: 'Anthony Milner's Variations for Orchestra', *MT*, c (1959), 384
E. Bradbury: 'The Progress of Anthony Milner', *MT*, civ (1963), 405
F. Routh: 'Anthony Milner', *Contemporary British Music* (London, 1972)

HUGO COLE

**Milnes, Sherrill (Eustace)** (*b* Downers Grove, Ill., 10 Jan 1935). American baritone. After studies at Drake University with Andrew White and Northwestern University under Hermanus Baer, he made his début with the Margaret Hillis Choir in Chicago. He also sang in the chorus of the Santa Fe Opera, augmenting ensemble duties with occasional appearances in small roles. His first important engagement was as Masetto in *Don Giovanni* with Boris Goldovsky's touring Boston Opera company in 1960. In 1961 he sang Gérard (*Andrea Chénier*) for Rosa Ponselle's Baltimore Civic Opera. In 1964 he was Rossini's Figaro at the Teatro Nuovo in Milan. He made his New York City Opera début the same year as Valentin in *Faust*, the role that took him to the Metropolitan with Caballé in 1965. Since then he has appeared with extraordinary success in Mexico City, Santiago, Barcelona, Vienna, San Francisco, London (Covent Garden début, Renato, 1971), Buenos Aires, Chicago and Hamburg, and he has become one of the most prolific recording artists of his time. His repertory includes all the leading Verdi baritone roles, Escamillo, Tonio, Don Giovanni, and Barnaba in *La*

*Gioconda* (which, in the London Opera Society's performance, introduced him to England in 1969). In 1967 he created Adam Brant in Marvin David Levy's *Mourning Becomes Elektra* at the Metropolitan Opera. Milnes's brilliant top voice, general fervour and extraordinary command of legato have occasioned credible comparisons with such predecessors as Lawrence Tibbett, Leonard Warren and Robert Merrill. He married the soprano Nancy Stokes.

BIBLIOGRAPHY
S. Milnes: 'A Role in Hand', *Opera News*, xxxvi/2 (1971), 12
W. Sargeant: 'Sherrill Milnes', *New Yorker* (29 March 1976), 36
MARTIN BERNHEIMER

**Milojević, Miloje** (*b* Belgrade, 28 Oct 1884; *d* Belgrade, 16 June 1946). Yugoslav composer, musicologist and conductor. He studied at the Serbian School of Music, Belgrade, with Mokranjac and then at the Munich Academy (1910) with Klose (composition), Mayer G'schray (piano) and Mottl (conducting). In addition he studied musicology at the University of Munich with Sandberger and Kroyer, and with Nejedlý at Prague University (DMus 1925). Milojević engaged himself actively in Belgrade musical life as a choirmaster, as conductor of the Collegium Musicum, the university chamber orchestra (1925–41) and as music critic for the review *Književni glasnik* (1908–14, 1920–41) and for the daily paper *Politika* (1921–41); he was also editor of *Muzika* (1928–9). Within the Collegium Musicum organization he gave a series of lectures, and he held teaching positions successively at a secondary school, at the school of music, at the university as professor of music history and at the academy of music as professor of composition (1939–46). While in France during World War I he published in Paris a series of Oeuvres des Compositeurs Serbes. In his own work he passed through several stylistic phases, from the late-Romanticism of the piano *Miniature* ('Miniatures') and the C minor Quartet to impressionism (as in the French songs and the *Quatre morceaux* for piano) and expressionism, as in the choral cycle *Pir iluzije* ('The feast of illusion') and the *Ritmičke grimase* for piano. But he retained a link with Yugoslav folk music, a heritage from his studies with Mokranjac and the direct result of his own researches; the peasant influence is most marked in the folksong arrangements and in several piano cycles. It was in the fields of song and piano music that he made his major contribution, though his partsongs for children were very successful.

WORKS
(*selective list*)
Chamber: 2 str qts, G, c; 2 sonatas, fl, pf, f♯, f♯; La légende de Yéphimia, vc, pf; other pieces
Pf: Miniature [Miniatures]; Dans mons pays: airs et danses; 4 morceaux; Ritmičke grimase; Kameje [Cameos], 2 sets; Melodije i ritmovi sa Balkana, 2 sets; Kosovska svita; Povardarska svita; Sonata ritmica in modo balcanico; other pieces
Songs: Pred veličanstvom prirode [Before nature's majesty], cycle; Mélodies populaires serbes; 5 mélodies; La chanson du vent de mer; Haikai; other pieces
Choral: Many songs for male/female/mixed/children's chorus, sacred music

Principal publishers: Collegium Musicum, Prosveta, Rouart

WRITINGS
*Osnovi muzičke umetnosti* [Elements of music] (Belgrade, 1922, 1927)
*Smetana* (Belgrade, 1924)
*Smetanin harmonski stil* (Belgrade, 1926)
*Muzičke studije i članci* [Music studies and articles] (Belgrade, 1926, 1933, 1953)
Ethnomusicological articles in Yugoslav periodicals

BIBLIOGRAPHY
M. Vukdragović: 'Miloje Milojević', *Glasnik muzičkog društva Stanković*, ix (1929)
S. Osterc: 'Dr. Miloje Milojević', *Zvuk* (1935), no.1
P. Konjović: *Miloje Milojević: kompozitor i muzički pisac* (Belgrade, 1954)
STANA ĐURIĆ-KLAJN

**Milonga.** A song genre of Uruguay, Paraguay, Argentina and Chile. It is the vehicle of expression in *payas* or *payadas* (vocal duels). Lighthearted in mood, the texts are in *corrido*, *romance*, *décima* or *verso* structures, and in a question-and-answer format. Melodies tend to descend scalewise and are in duple metre, contrasting with the guitar accompaniment in 6/8 metre. When *estribillos* (refrains) are added they are commonly harmonized in parallel 3rds.

WILLIAM GRADANTE

**Milošević, Predrag** (*b* Knjaževac, 4 Feb 1904). Yugoslav conductor, composer and pianist. He studied at the Belgrade School of Music, at the Munich Academy with E. Bach (piano), and then at the Prague Conservatory with Křička (composition) and Procházka (piano), where he completed his training in the master classes of Suk (composition) and Dědeček (conducting). After returning to teach at the Belgrade School of Music, he was made professor of composition and conducting at the academy (1939); he was rector there from 1960 to 1967. He began his conducting career with the Union and Hlahol choirs in Prague; in Yugoslavia he conducted the Belgrade Choral Society (1932–47), the Belgrade Opera (1932–55) and the Novi Sad Opera (1955–60), which he also directed for the first two years of his appointment. In addition, he has been active as an orchestral conductor, broadcaster, administrator and writer on music. Most of his output has been of incidental music for the theatre, which reveals a talent for illustration and for the grotesque. His concert pieces are neo-classical; they include a Sinfonietta (1930), chamber and piano pieces, songs and choruses. Scores have been published by Collegium Musicum and Prosveta.

STANA ĐURIĆ-KLAJN

**Mil'shteyn, Yakov Isaakovich** (*b* Voronezh, 4 Feb 1911). Soviet musicologist, pianist and teacher. In 1932 he graduated from Igumnov's piano class at the Moscow Conservatory and in 1942 was awarded the doctorate for his dissertation on Liszt. In 1935 he joined the teaching staff of the Conservatory as Igumnov's assistant; he was appointed senior lecturer in 1948 and professor in 1963. Mil'shteyn's writings are concerned mainly with the history of piano music, in particular the music of Liszt. He has edited the collected piano works of Liszt, Skryabin, Chopin, Brahms, Schubert and Tchaikovsky, and has written a number of articles on piano music and the history of instrumental teaching and performance.

WRITINGS
*Frants List i evo pianizm* [Liszt and his pianism] (diss., Moscow Conservatory, 1942)
'Ispolnitel'skiye i pedagogicheskiye printsipī K. N. Igumnova' [Igumnov's principles of teaching and performance], *Mastera sovetskoy pianisticheskoy shkolï*, ed. A. A. Nikolayev (Moscow, 1954, 2/1962), 40–114
*F. List* (Moscow, 1956, rev. 2/1971)
'K istorii izdaniy sochineniy Shopena' [The history of the publication of Chopin's works], *Friderik Shopen: stat'i i issledovaniya sovetskikh muzïkovedov*, ed. G. Ya. Edel'man (Moscow, 1960), 323–60
*Vïdayushchiyesya pianistï proshlovo* [Distinguished pianists of the past] (Moscow, 1963)
ed.: *A. Korto: Ratsional'nïye printsipï fortepiannoy tekhniki* (Moscow,

1966) [incl. 'Al'fred Korto i evo *Ratsional'nïye printsipï fortepiannoy tekhniki*' [Cortot and his *Principes rationnels de la technique pianistique*], p.97]
'O vospitanii tekhniki pianista' [The training of a pianist's technique], *Metodicheskiye zapiski po voprosam muzïkal'novo obrazovaniya*, ed. N. L. Fishman (Moscow, 1966), 181ff
*Sovetï Shopena pianistam* [Chopin's advice to pianists] (Moscow, 1967)
*Khorosho temperirovannïy klavir I. S. Bakha i osobennosti evo ispolneniya* [Bach's *Das wohltemperierte Clavier* and features of its performance] (Moscow, 1968)
*Vospominaniya o Sofronitskom* (Moscow, 1970) [incl. 'O Vladimire Vladimiroviche Sofronitskom', p.3]
'O nekotorïkh tendentsiyakh razvitiya ispolnitel'skovo iskusstva' [Some trends in the development of the art of performing], *Masterstvo muzïkanta-ispolnitelya*, ed. T. Gaydamovich and others (Moscow, 1972), 3–56
'Vsevolod Buyukli', *Muzïkal'noye ispolnitel'stvo*, vii, ed. G. Ya. Edel'man (Moscow, 1972), 195ff
'Fransua Kuperen: evo vremya, tvorchestvo, traktat *Iskusstvo igrï na klavesine*' [Couperin: his times, works and treatise *L'art de toucher le clavecin*], *Fransua Kuperen: Iskusstvo igrï na klavesine*, ed. D. M. Serov (Moscow, 1973), 76–118 [with commentary, 119–57]
*Konstantin Nikolaevich Igumnov* (Moscow, 1975)

LEV GINZBURG

**Milstein, Nathan (Mironovich)** (*b* Odessa, 31 Dec 1904). American violinist of Russian birth. At the age of seven he began to study with Pyotr Stolyarsky and remained with him until 1914. (At the final student concert that year, he shared the stage with five-year-old David Oistrakh.) Milstein made his official début in Odessa in 1920; that same year he played Glazunov's Concerto under the composer. For the next five years he enjoyed growing success in Russia. He often appeared in joint recitals with Vladimir Horowitz, when his accompanist was Vladimir's sister, Regina. In 1925 Milstein and Vladimir Horowitz left Russia on a concert tour and decided to remain abroad. Occasionally they were joined for trio concerts by Pyatigorsky, also a recent émigré. In 1926 Milstein went to Brussels, where he received artistic advice from Ysaÿe. He made his début with the New York Philharmonic in 1929 and settled in the USA, becoming an American citizen in 1942. After World War II, Milstein re-established his European reputation. Among his honours is that of Officier de la Légion d'honneur (1968).

Milstein is, perhaps, the least 'Russian' among Russian violinists because his violinistic instincts are so controlled by intellect. He began his career as a virtuoso and matured into a most individual interpreter. His fiery temperament is firmly disciplined, his line classically pure. His tone, though not large, has great carrying power: he changes his bowing frequently to produce power through sweep rather than by pressure. His intonation is incomparably true because his vibrato never becomes too wide or cloying. His interpretations of the great concertos are full of nobility and reveal a stimulating mind. It is clear that he can be a dazzling technician when he plays his own *Paganiniana* (New York, 1954), or his cadenza to Beethoven's Violin Concerto. He ranks among the foremost violinists of his generation.

BIBLIOGRAPHY
B. Gavoty: *Nathan Milstein* (Geneva, 1956) [with discography]
L. Raaben: *Zhizn' zamechatelnï'kh skripachey* [The lives of famous violinists] (Leningrad, 1967)
J. Hartnack: *Grosse Geiger unserer Zeit* (Gütersloh, 1968)

BORIS SCHWARZ

**Milton, John** (*b* Stanton St John, nr. Oxford, *c*1563; *d* London, buried 15 March 1647). English amateur composer, father of the poet. In 1572 he was sent to Christ Church, Oxford, by his father, an affluent local yeoman and a fervent Roman Catholic. Prince Albertus Alasco visited Oxford in 1583, and it may have been for this occasion that Milton composed the 40-part In Nomine (John Aubrey in his *Brief Lives* described it as an 80-part work) of which Edward Philips (his son's nephew and biographer) wrote with admiration in 1694. Milton left Oxford for London in 1585, having been disowned by his father 'for abjuring the popish tenets', and by 1595 he had become apprenticed to James Colbron, a member of the Scriveners' Company. He was admitted to the freedom of the company on 27 February 1600; he married and settled in Bread Street, off Cheapside. His professional work and amateur pursuits from 1601 to 1621 laid the foundations of a good musical reputation, future prosperity and a stable family life. The value of his property (£358 in 1627 and £560 in 1629) was the basis of the considerable fortune with which he retired to Horton, Buckinghamshire, in 1632.

He was elected to the Mastership of the Scriveners' Company in 1634, but did not serve in that office. His wife died on 3 April 1637, after which he lived with his son Richard. He moved back to London in 1639 but later went with Richard to Reading, where they stayed until it was captured by the royalists in 1643. Once more he returned to London and lived first with his son John in Aldersgate Street and then in a house in the Barbican, where he died. He was buried in the chancel of St Giles', Cripplegate.

Milton's music has been considered principally in relation to its influence on his son John, whose praise of his father's musical achievements can be read in his poem *Ad patrem*. But his music was obviously highly regarded by his contemporaries: Morley included a madrigal in *The Triumphes of Oriana*, Sir William Leighton invited him to contribute to his collection of *Teares or Lamentacions*, and Ravenscroft included his work in his 1621 psalter. Milton's tune 'York' was described by Hawkins in his *General History*, and was still popular in 1680. His anthems are in the 'full' style, and their sources suggest that they were written for domestic rather than liturgical performance. Little of his consort music remains; the 40-part In Nomine may never have existed, but his six-part In Nomine (virtually a consort song, since the cantus firmus has the text 'If that a sinners' sighs' added to it) and other fantasias testify to his ability in this area of composition.

WORKS
Editions: *J. Milton: Six Anthems*, ed. G. E. P. Arkwright, Old English Edition, xxii (London, 1900) [A]
    *Sir William Leighton: The Tears or Lamentations of a Sorrowful Soul*, ed. C. Hill, EECM, xi (1970) [H]
8 anthems, 4–6vv (1 with broken consort), *GB-Lbm*, *Ob*; 2 in A, 4 in H, 2 ed. in Brennecke
Motet, 6vv, *Lbm*
7 psalm settings, 1621[11]; 'York' tune, 1680[5]
2 madrigals, 5vv, *Lbm*, 1601[16]; 1 ed. in EM, xxxii (2/1962)
In Nomine a 6, 4 fantasias a 5, a 6, *Och* 423–8; 1 ed. in MB ix (1955, 2/1962)

BIBLIOGRAPHY
D. Masson: *The Life and Times of John Milton* (London, 1858–79, rev. 2/1881) [on his son, the poet]
S. G. Spaeth: *Milton's Knowledge of Music* (Princeton, 1913/R1973)
E. Brennecke: *John Milton the Elder and his Music* (New York, 1938)

NORMAN JOSEPHS

**Miltou.** See DANIEL, JEAN.

**Milveden, (Jan) Ingmar (Georg)** (*b* Göteborg, 15 Feb 1920). Swedish musicologist and composer. He was taught music first by his father Werther Carlsson and then at Uppsala University, where he studied counterpoint and composition with S. E. Svensson and musicology with Moberg (graduated 1945, Fil. lic. 1951); he took the doctorate there in 1972 with a dissertation on the music of the liturgical *historia* in Sweden. As well as lecturing in musicology at the universities of Stockholm (1970–73) and Uppsala (assistant professor from 1972), he became organist of St Per's Church, Uppsala, in 1967. His predominating scholarly interest is Gregorian chant and he continues the distinguished tradition of research in Swedish medieval liturgical music begun by Moberg; of particular importance are the studies from his doctoral thesis and his contributions to the *Kulturhistoriskt lexikon*.

As a composer Milveden has written vocal and instrumental music in a variety of forms, including a Sonatina for piano (1943), Serenade for string orchestra (1944), Duo for violin and piano (1947), *Pezzo concertante* (1970), *Concerto al Fresco* for clarinet and orchestra (1971), *Nu* (1974) and *Gaudeat Upsalia* (1976); his main interest, however, as in his musicological work, is in church music (e.g. *Mässa i skördetid*, 1969; a church opera *Vid en korsväg*, 1971; *Fem orgelkoraler*, 1973; *Magnificat*, 1973; *Tre motetter*, 1973). He is a member of the Royal Academy of Arts and Sciences, Uppsala (1974) and of the Royal Swedish Academy of Music (1975), as well as being chairman of the Musikaliska Konstförening (from 1975) and of the Upplands Musikstiftelse (from 1976).

### WRITINGS
'Gregoriansk koral (Sverige)', 'Notskrift', 'Organum', 'Rimofficium', 'Sekvens', 'Tractus', 'Trop', 'Versus' and other articles in *Kulturhistoriskt lexikon för nordisk medeltid* (Malmö and Copenhagen, 1956–)
'Fragment av en hittillis ok ånd Historia de BMV in Visitatione', *Svenskt gudstjänstliv*, xxxviii (1963), 23
'Manuskript, Mönch und Mond: ein Hauptteil des Cod. Upsal. C 23 in quellenkritischer Beleuchtung', *STMf*, xlvi (1964), 9
'Neue Funde zur Brynolphus-Kritik', *STMf*, liv (1972), 5–51
*Zu den liturgischen 'Hystorie' in Schweden: Liturgie- und choralgeschichtliche Untersuchungen* (diss., Uppsala U., 1972)

JOHN BERGSAGEL

**Milwid, Antoni** (*fl* late 18th century). Polish composer. He worked at a church at Czerwińsk, near Warsaw. A national element is pronounced in his compositions, especially his sacred music: it appears principally in the use of Polish dance melody (mainly in polonaise and mazurka rhythms), traditional church songs and carols in his compositions. His sacred music shows both Baroque and Classical features; the cantata *Semper mi Jesu* employs techniques appropriate to the Baroque style, but in the cycle of 12 cantatas *Sub tuum praesidium* residual features of the concertato style are combined with early Classical elements, influenced by sonata form, and in his masses these last elements are combined with the *galant* style. His music is unusually lyrical in character.

### WORKS
*(all vocal works in monastery archives in Czerwińsk, Poland)*
4 masses, 2vv, 2 vn, 2 cl, 2 hn, bc
Sub tuum praesidium (cycle of 12 cantatas), 2vv, 2 vn, fl, cl, bc, ed. in ZHMP, xxvi (1977)
2 Litanie (C, F), 2vv, vn, cl, 2 hn, bc; Dixit Dominus, 2vv, 2 vn, 2 cl, 2 hn, bc; Semper mi Jesu, 1v, vn, bc
Fragments of 2 symphonies, *PL-Wtm*

### BIBLIOGRAPHY
J. Reiss: 'Dzieje symfonii w Polsce' [A history of the symphony in Poland], *Muzyka polska*, ed. M. Gliński (Warsaw, 1927), 131ff
T. Strumiłło: 'Do dziejów symfonii polskiej', *Muzyka*, iv/5–6 (1953), 26
A. Nowak-Romanowicz: 'Muzyka polskiego oświecenia i wczesnego romantyzmu' [Music of the Polish Enlightenment and early

Romantic period], *Z dziejów polskiej kultury muzycznej*, ii (1966), 9–152

ZYGMUNT M. SZWEYKOWSKI

**Milyutin, Yury Sergeyevich** (*b* Moscow, 18 April 1903; *d* Moscow, 10 June 1968). Russian composer. He studied with Vasilenko and Alexandrov at the Moscow Municipal Technical School. An actor in his youth, he composed principally for the theatre; he was one of the masters of Soviet operetta, and his works have been staged both in the USSR and in many east European countries. Milyutin was equally well-known for his vocal pieces, particularly for the songs to texts by Viktor Mikhaylovich Gusev and Vasily Ivanovich Lebedev-Kumach. He received the State Prize and the title Honoured Art Worker of the RSFSR.

### WORKS
*(selective list)*
Operettas: Zhizn' aktyora [The life of an actor], 1940; Devichiy perepolokh [Girlish commotion], 1944; Bespokoynoye schast'ye [Unsettled happiness], 1947; Trembita, 1949; Pervaya lyubov' [First love], 1950; Lyubushka, 1952; Potseluy Chanitï [Chanita's kiss], 1956; Fonari–fonariki [Lamps–little lamps], 1958; Tsirk zazhigayet ogni [The circus lights fires], 1961; Anyutinï glazki [Anyutina's eyes], 1964; Tikhaya semeyka [The quiet little family], 1968
Songs, 1930s: Nas ne trogay [Do not touch us], Mï – vesolïye rebyata [We are gay lads], Chayka [The seagull], Na vostok mï zavtra uletayem [We will fly off to the east tomorrow]
Songs, 1940s–1950s: Morskaya gvardiya [Sea guard], Vozle goroda Kronshtadta [Around the town of Kronstadt], Siren'-cheremukha [Lilac-bird cherry], Leninskiye gorï [The Lenin hills], Provozhayut garmonista [They accompany the harmonist], Sineglazaya [Blue-eyed]

Principal publishers: Muzïka, Sovetskiy Kompozitor

### BIBLIOGRAPHY
K. Petrova: 'Operettï Yu. Milyutina', *SovM* (1951), no.8, p.23
'Nash kalendar' ', *Muzïkal'naya zhizn'* (1963), no.5, p.19
O. Fel'tsman: 'Yu. S. Milyutin', *SovM* (1963), no.4, p.142
Obituary, *Izvestiya* (12 June 1968)
Obituary, *Sovetskaya kul'tura* (13 June 1968)

GALINA GRIGOR'YEVA

**Mimaroğlu, Ilhan (Kemaleddin)** (*b* Istanbul, 11 March 1926). Turkish composer. He studied law at Ankara University while working as a music critic and broadcaster. In 1955 he travelled to the USA on a Rockefeller Fellowship, and in 1959 he settled in New York, where he studied at Columbia University with Ussachevsky, Beeson, Chou, Lang and Wolpe, also receiving advice from Varèse. He taught at the teacher's college of Columbia University in 1970–71 and received a Guggenheim Fellowship in 1971–2. In his works he has developed an approach which he likens to that of a film director: the composer transmits his ideas to the performer in a variety of ways ranging from conventional notation to verbal instruction; the performance is recorded; and the work takes its final shape in the electronic studio. His music began to show a growing commitment to new left politics in the early 1970s.

### WORKS
*(selective list)*
Parodie sérieuse, str qt, 1947; Cl Conc., 1950; 4 Pieces, cl, pf, 1952; Metropolis, orch, 1955; Pièces sentimentales, pf, 1957; Pièces futiles, cl, vc, 1958; Bagatelles, pf, 1959; Epicedium, Mez, ens, 1961; Trio 1961, cl, vn, pf, 1961; 2 × e.e. (Cummings), 4 solo vv, 1963; Rhapsody, 2 cl, 1963; Conjectus I, 3 insts, 1964; Intermezzo, tape, 1964; Le tombeau d'Edgar Poe, tape, 1964; Music, 4 bn, vc, 1964; Pf Sonata, 1964; Anacolutha, tape, 1965; Trenodia, pf, 1965; Visual Studies, tape, 1964–6
12 Preludes, tape, 1966–7; September Moon, orch, 1967; Wings of the Delirious Demon, tape, 1969; Music plus One, vn, tape, 1970; Cristal de Bohème, perc ens, vn, vc, hpd, 1971; Sing me a Song of Songmy, tape, 1971; Coucou Bazar (incidental music, Dubuffet), tape, 1973; Tract, tape, 1972–4; To Kill a Sunrise, tape, 1974

Principal publishers: Cotillion, MCA, Okra

**Mime** [mimos, mimus]. In classical antiquity, an imitative performer or performance. In Greece almost all dancing was regarded as mimetic, and mimetic dances were often performed by itinerant groups of singers (*mimōdoi*) and dancers. A mimic actor accompanied by the aulos was a *mimaulos*.

**Mimesis** (Gk. *mimēsis*: 'imitation', 'representation'). A term found in Greek literature from the final years of the 5th century BC referring to an aesthetic ideal underlying music and art (see Aristophanes, *Thesmophoriazusae*, l.156; *Frogs*, l.109). From the beginning it was used primarily in relation to art and dramatic poetry, but it came to be employed also in discussions of music and particularly of musical ETHOS, with reference to modes (*harmoniai*) and rhythms. Damon and Plato showed particular interest in such questions; the comments on music as mimesis which most influenced subsequent writers were those of Aristotle (*Poetics*, §1447a). Varying translations of the term illustrate the difficulties of interpretation associated with it. 'Imitation' stresses the concept of copying; the preference for 'representation' emphasizes instead that of creative involvement. Many 18th-century English writers on music, notably Burney and Avison, rejected the first of these (inherited from French and Italian Aristotelians), partly because it could not be reconciled with a belief in 'pure music'.

*See also* GREECE, §I.

WARREN ANDERSON

**Mimos** [mimus]. *See* MIME.

**Mimra.** Verse or prose Syriac sermon, the former originally sung; *see* SYRIAN CHURCH MUSIC.

**Minagawa, Tatsuo** (*b* Tokyo, 25 April 1927). Japanese musicologist. After graduating in European history at Tokyo University in 1951, he took a two-year postgraduate course in aesthetics. In 1955 he went to New York, where he studied with Sachs and Reese, and in 1958 he spent several months in Europe studying musical sources. He returned to Europe four years later to study musicology with Osthoff in Frankfurt and Schrade in Basle (1962–4). He began teaching musicology at St Pauls University, Tokyo, in 1958, becoming a professor in 1964; he also lectures regularly at Tokyo University and Tokyo Geijutsu Daigaku (Tokyo National University of Fine Arts and Music). His work centres on medieval and Renaissance music, with special emphasis on the history of music theory, notation, the history of the cyclic mass and the 16th-century chanson. (He is the director of an amateur choral group which specializes in the performance of choral music up to 1600.) He is also an accomplished performer of noh plays and has written articles on the subject.

WRITINGS

'The Japanese Noh Music', *JAMS*, x (1957), 181

'Sento Marsharu gakuha' [St Martial school], *Ongakugaku*, v (1959), 14 [with Eng. summary]

'Iburea shahon ni kansuru komonjogaku-teki kōsatsu' [Palaeographic problems in the Ivrea MS], *Ongakugaku*, x (1964), 75 [with Eng. summary]

*Gasshō ongaku no rekishi* [History of choral music] (Tokyo, 1965)

'Junkan misa ni kansuru shomondai' [The problems of the cyclic mass], *Ongakugaku*, xiii (1967), 33 [with Eng. summary]

*Gakufu no rekishi* [History of music notation] (Tokyo, 1970)

*Gakki* [Musical instruments] (Osaka, 1970)

*Barokku ongaku* [Baroque music] (Tokyo, 1972)

MASAKATA KANAZAWA

**Minas Gerais.** A mining region for gold and precious stones in east-central Brazil, discovered in the late 17th century and exploited throughout the next century, during which an important musical life developed. Its population at first included Indians (pure blood or mestizos), Portuguese and Brazilian colonizers, and negro slaves. By the mid-18th century mulattos and negroes formed the majority of the population in spite of intensive migration from Portugal and other areas of the colony itself. Soon a large number of free mulattos held important positions among the clergy and became craftsmen and artists, and the splendid development of local Baroque architecture, sculpture and music was due largely to them. The musicologist Francisco Curt Lange, who first uncovered the musical history of this area, referred to this phenomenon as *mulatismo musical*. Since the mid-1940s Lange has found substantial documentary evidence of a unique musical development which reached its peak during the last two decades of the 18th century, and has edited some MSS of a large corpus dating from this period.

Musical life in Minas Gerais was organized after the Portuguese example in and around the various brotherhoods (*irmandades*) and not the church; all practising musicians belonged to a music brotherhood. Such corporations included the Irmandade de S Cecilia, Irmandade do Ss Sacramento, Irmandade da Ordem Terceira do Carmo, Irmandade da Ordem Terceira de S Francisco etc. These brotherhoods supplied music for the Church or the municipality, which generally commissioned specific works, or simply performances for religious festivities.

The most active music centres in colonial Minas Gerais were the capital Vila Rica (now Ouro Prêto), Sabará, Mariana, Arraial do Tejuco (now Diamantina), São João del Rei and São José d'el Rei. In spite of the relative isolation of these centres, there is evidence of local organ builders (e.g. Manuel de Almeida Silva), and the use of the harpsichord in church, and extant MS copies and prints of contemporary European music (Haydn, Boccherini, Mozart, Pleyel, Beethoven) indicate acquaintance with current European styles. Almost all *mineiro* composers cultivated a particular homophonic style which drew on characteristics of pre-Classical styles. Compositions of the 'Minas School' are in general liturgical works for four-part mixed chorus with orchestral accompaniment. The most important composers were José Joaquim Emerico Lôbo de Mesquita (*c*1740–1805), Marcos Coelho Netto (*d* 1806), Francisco Gomes da Rocha (*d* 1808), and Ignacio Parreiras Neves (*c*1730–*c*1793). But (according to Lange) there were about 1000 musicians active in this vast region during the latter part of the century. The oldest known MSS are dated 1779, but the repertory was copied as late as the 1880s for use in Minas Gerais and the neighbouring captaincies. Theatre life is well documented but no work produced in Vila Rica is extant.

BIBLIOGRAPHY

F. C. Lange: 'La música en Minas Gerais: un informe preliminar', *Boletín Latino-Americano de Música*, vi (1946), 408

——, ed.: *Archivo de música religiosa de la 'Capitania Geral das Minas Gerais' (Siglio XVIII), Brasil* (Mendoza, Argentina, 1951)

——: 'La música en Minas Gerais durante el siglo XVIII', *Sodre*, v (1957), 47

——: 'La Opera y las Casa de Opera en el Brasil colonial', *Boletín Interamericano de Música*, xlix (1964), 3

——: 'Os compositores na Capitania Geral das Minas Gerais', *Revista de Estudos Históricos* (Marília, Brasil), iii–iv (1965), 33

——: 'Sobre las difíciles huellas de la música antigua del Brasil: la "Missa abreviada" (1823) del Padre José Mauricio Nunes Garcia', *Yearbook, Inter-American Institute for Musical Research*, i (1965), 15

——: *A organização musical durante o período colonial brasileiro* (Coimbra, 1966)

——: 'A música na Vila Real de Sabará', *Revista de Estudos Históricos* (Marília, Brasil), v (1966), 97–198

——: 'La música en Villa Rica (Minas Gerais, siglo XVIII)', *Revista musical chilena* (1967), no.102, p.8; (1968), no.103, p.77

G. Béhague: 'Música "barrôca" mineira: problemas de fontes e estilística', *Universitas* (Revista de Cultura da Universidade Federal da Bahia), ii (1969), 131

——: 'Música colonial mineira à luz de novos manuscritos', *Barroco* (Revista de Ensaio e Pesquisa, Universidade Federal de Minas Gerais), iii (1971), 6

For further bibliography *see* LATIN AMERICA.

GERARD BÉHAGUE

**Minato,** Count **Nicolò** (*b* Bergamo, *c*1630; *d* Vienna, 1698). Italian librettist, impresario, poet and lawyer, later resident in Austria. His prodigious career as a librettist, attested to by an extant output of over 200 works, began in 1650 with *Orimonte* and continued until the year of his death, which is established in the publisher's preface to a revival of *L'esclamar à gran voce* (1698), a *rappresentazione sacra*. His activity fell into two distinct periods: the Venetian years, from 1650 to 1669, and the longer Viennese period, from then until his death. In Venice he belonged to the Accademia degli Imperfetti, formed in 1649 and dedicated to the study of jurisprudence, history and the classics; Giacomo dall' Angelo, Aurelio Aureli and G. F. Busenello were other librettists who belonged to it. Two poems by Minato appeared in a volume published by the academy in 1651, *La gloria dell'armi venete celebrate nell'Accademia de' Signori Imperfetti*. The prefaces to his earliest librettos indicate that he was a lawyer by profession and that he initially viewed his writing as an avocation. By the mid-1660s, however, he was fully committed to the theatre as both librettist and impresario, a combination characteristic of the careers of several other Venetian librettists, including Giovanni Faustini and Aureli. By 1665 he was involved in the management of the Teatro di S Salvatore, an involvement reaffirmed by a three-year contract in 1667. His departure for Vienna in 1669 to become court poet to the Emperor Leopold I thus provoked a lawsuit for breach of contract by the Vendramin family, owners of the theatre. In the dedication of *Il ratto delle Sabine* (1674) Minato mentioned nine librettos that he had written for Venice, but he actually wrote at least 11. His chief musical collaborator there was Cavalli, though Antonio Sartorio provided the music for his last three Venetian librettos.

Minato's duties in Vienna included the provision of texts for a wide range of theatrical events, sacred as well as secular, on the occasion of weddings, royal visits, royal birthdays and name days, Carnival and the important Lenten celebrations. During his 29-year period at the Viennese court he wrote more than 170 secular librettos (variously labelled 'dramma per musica', 'festa teatrale', 'invenzione', 'introduzione ad un balletto' or 'serenata') and approximately 40 sacred texts (labelled 'rappresentazione sacra' or 'oratorio'). He averaged about five texts a year and occasionally – in 1678, for example – produced as many as ten. Most of his Viennese works were collaborations with the court composer Antonio Draghi and the court designer Ludovico Burnacini. His election to the exclusive Italian Academy of Vienna and the posthumous republication in 1700 of two volumes of his sacred texts indicate the high esteem in which he was held. Revived throughout Italy, as well as in France and Germany, his works were set by many composers, among them Leopold I himself, Pederzuoli, Sances, Pistocchi, Legrenzi, Giovanni Bononcini, M. A. Ziani, Albinoni, Hasse and Telemann.

Most of Minato's texts, like those of such contemporaries as Aureli and Matteo Noris – but unlike the pseudo-historical and mythological librettos of Giovanni Faustini, his chief predecessor in Venice – exploit and embroider events of ancient history, with particular emphasis on the military and moral stature of the hero. Although these subjects suggested parallels between the virtues of ancient Rome and those of the Venetian republic, political symbolism became more overt in the Viennese librettos, many of which contain detailed allegorical elucidations identifying the hero with the Emperor Leopold I. Unlike those of his contemporaries, Minato's multi-act librettos contain an equal number of scenes in each act, 20 in the Venetian texts, usually fewer in those written for Vienna. The growing public demand for arias in Venice after about 1650 is reflected in the increased formal and functional distinction he made between recitative and aria as well as in his ingenious manipulation of situations and characters to create plausible opportunities for arias. Although they afforded a means of integrating both arias and scenic display within the drama, his elaborate secondary plots and mixture of comic and serious elements earned him the scorn of late 17th-century opera reformers.

BIBLIOGRAPHY

Archivio Vendramin, 42 F 6/2 (*I-Vcg*) [papers concerning Minato's relationship to the Teatro di S Salvatore]

M. Maylender: *Storia delle accademie d'Italia*, ii (Bologna, 1929), 175f

E. E. Salzer: 'Il teatro italiano in Vienna barocca', *Rivista italiana del dramma*, ii (1938), 47

——: 'Il teatro allegorico italiano a Vienna', *Rivista italiana del dramma*, iii (1939), 65

A. A. Abert: *Claudio Monteverdi und das musikalische Drama* (Lippstadt, 1954)

S. T. Worsthorne: *Venetian Opera in the Seventeenth Century* (Oxford, 1954/*R*1968)

F. Hadamowsky: 'Barocktheater am Wiener Kaiserhof', *Jb der Geschichte für Wiener Theaterforschung 1951–2* (1955)

A. della Corte: 'Il Serse', *Drammi per musica dal Rinuccini allo Zeno*, i (Turin, 1958), 579–760

A. Limentani: 'Minato, Nicola', *ES*

H. S. Powers: 'Il Serse trasformato', *MQ*, xlvii (1961), 481; xlviii (1962), 73

M. Dietrich: 'Le livret d'opéra et ses aspects sociaux à la cour de Léopold I', *Dramaturgie et société aux XVI^e et XVII^e siècles: CNRS Paris 1967*, 203

R. Freeman: 'Apostolo Zeno's Reform of the Libretto', *JAMS*, xxi (1968), 321

R. Schnitzler: *The Sacred Dramatic Music of Antonio Draghi* (diss., U. of North Carolina, 1971)

H. S. Powers: 'Il "Mutio" tramutato, Part I: Sources and Libretto', *Venezia e il melodramma nel Seicento: Venezia 1972*, 227–58

N. Hilte: *Die Oper am Hofe Kaiser Leopolds I. mit besonderer Berücksichtigung der Tätigkeit von Minato und Draghi* (diss., U. of Vienna, 1974)

N. Mangini: *I teatri di Venezia* (Milan, 1974), 48ff

ELLEN ROSAND

**Minchejmer** [Münchheimer], **Adam** (*b* Warsaw, 23 Dec 1830; *d* Warsaw, 27 Jan 1904). Polish conductor, teacher and composer. He studied music in Warsaw under S. Niedzielski and J. Hornziel (violin), A. Tausig (piano), A. Freyer (composition) and also, briefly, in Berlin (composition with A. B. Marx). At the Wielki Theatre, Warsaw, he was first violin (1850–64), music director and manager of the ballet (1858–72), conductor (1872–82), director of the opera (1882–90) and librarian (1890–1902). He taught at the Warsaw Music Institute (1861–4), the Aleksandryjski Institute (1864–72) and the music and drama school of the Warsaw Music Society (1895–1902); he also performed with the society (1876–1902) and conducted many other choral and instrumental ensembles. Warsaw's musical life was much enriched through his efforts: for instance, he organized symphony concerts, and performed a number of major works by Polish and foreign composers. His own compositions include four operas, in the manner of Meyerbeerian grand opera. He also composed many solo songs, piano pieces, orchestral works and incidental music; and he reorchestrated Chopin's E minor Piano Concerto (MS in *PL-Wtm*).

## WORKS
### STAGE
Otton łucznik [Otto the archer] (opera, 5, J. Chęciński, after Dumas), Warsaw, 1864, *Pl-Wtm*
Figle szatana [Satan's tricks] (ballet, 6 scenes), collab. Moniuszko, Warsaw, 1870, *Wtm*
Stradiota (opera, 5, J. S. Jasiński), Warsaw, 1876, *Wtm*
Mazepa (opera, 4, M. Radziszewski, after J. Słowacki), Warsaw, 1900
Mściciel [The avenger] (opera, W. Miller), Warsaw, 1910

### VOCAL
Choral: 3 masses (grad from Missa solemnis in *Echo muzyczne, teatralne i artystyczne*, vii, 1890, no.339, appx); Requiem; 4 cantatas: Pomnik Mickiewicza [In memory of Mickiewicz] (Warsaw, 1861); Hymn do mistrzów sztuki [Hymn to the masters of art]; Powitanie słońca [Greeting of the sun], *Wtm*; Sprawa Clemenceau [The Clemenceau affair] (after A. Dumas *fils*), *Wtm*; works for 1v, chorus, orch: Flisaki [The bargemen] (Warsaw, n.d.); Marsz żałobny [Funeral march]; Pieśń pochodu Litwinów [Song about the Lithuanian march]; Pieśń przy kielichu [Drinking-song]; Polonez weselny [Wedding polonaise] (Poznań, 1913); Świteżianka [The water-nymph]; Góral [The mountaineer] (Warsaw, 1890); Nasz mazur [Our mazurka] (Warsaw, 1905); Wisełka (Warsaw, 1888); other choral works
Solo songs: Bławatek [The blue cornflower] (Warsaw, n.d.); Czarny krzyżyk [The little black cross] (Warsaw, n.d.); Jej usteczka [Her lips], in *Nowości muzyczne* (Warsaw, 1910), no.6, p.5; Już nie powróci [Never to return] (Warsaw, 1860); Moja kochanka [My sweetheart], in *Echo muzyczne* (Warsaw, 1879), no.7, appx; Z nową wiosną [With the new spring], in *Echo muzyczne, teatralne i artystyczne*, viii (1891), no.391, appx; Wieczór i ranek [Evening and morning] (Warsaw, 1888); other solo songs and folksong arrs.

### INSTRUMENTAL
Orch: Mistrz Twardowski [Master Twardowski], sym. legend; Marche héroïque polonaise; 2 polonaises; Scherzo; Suita koncertowa; Uwertura dramatyczna, c, *Wtm*; Les sons mystérieux, concert ov., *KA*; Ov. to Tasso's La Gerusalemme liberata; Ov., wind insts; incidental music; other works and arrs.
Chamber: Ballada, str, pf; Barkarola, str, pf (Leipzig, 1861); Mazurek, str, pf; Nokturn, hn/vc, pf
Pf: Kontredans, in *Ruch muzyczny* (1857), no.14, appx; Marsz żałobny [Funeral march], in *Echo muzyczne, teatralne i artystyczne* (1886), no.139, appx; Les deux styles; Nocturne; Polonez elegijny; Pieśni bez słów [Songs without words]; Romance; other works

### BIBLIOGRAPHY
*Album Münchheimera* (MS, *PL-WRol* 5836) [collection of press cuttings, photographs and other documents]
'Śp. Adam Münchheimer', *Echo muzyczne, teatralne i artystyczne*, xxi/3–4 (1904), 76
T. R. Bartkiewicz: 'Adam Minchejmer', *Śpiewak* (1909), no.7, p.12
T. Joteyko: 'Adam Minchejmer', *Przegląd muzyczny* (1931), nos.2–3, p.6
L. T. Błaszczyk: *Dyrygenci polscy i obcy w Polsce działający w XIX i XX wieku* [Polish and foreign conductors working in Poland in the 19th and 20th centuries] (Kraków, 1964)
A. Nowak-Romanowicz and others, eds.: *Z dziejów polskiej kultury muzycznej* [From the history of Polish musical culture], ii (Kraków, 1966), 275ff, 360f, 428f

KATARZYNA MORAWSKA

**Minchi, John** (*fl* 1st half of 10th century). Hymnographer of the Georgian Church; *see* GEORGIAN RITE, MUSIC OF THE.

**Minghino dal violoncello.** Nickname of DOMENICO GABRIELLI.

**Mingotti, Pietro** (*b* Venice, *c*1702; *d* Copenhagen, 28 April 1759). Italian opera impresario. He is first heard of in 1736 in Graz, where he and his brother Angelo Mingotti (*b* *c*1700; *d* after 1767) ran an opera troupe. Angelo had had such a troupe from at least 1732, principally in Brno, and it is possible that Pietro had been connected with it. In following years the names of the two appeared separately and together in similar ventures in many cities of Germany and the Austrian possessions. The company usually consisted of three male and five female singers and performed both *opera buffa* and *seria* with an orchestra hired on the spot. From at least 1742 its music director was Paolo Scalabrini. In 1747 the company performed at Dresden for a royal wedding. This occasion marked the first appearance of Gluck with the troupe as conductor and composer (with his *festa teatrale Le nozze d'Ercole e d'Ebe*) and the rise to fame of Pietro's wife Regina, who then left the troupe to enter the royal service. Also in 1747, the new King of Denmark, who had heard the company in Hamburg in 1743, invited it to perform under royal auspices in Copenhagen, which became its base of operations until 1756. Gluck was also with it there and in Hamburg in 1748. After 1756 Angelo seems to have continued alone, being last heard of at Bonn in 1764–7.

### BIBLIOGRAPHY
E. H. Müller von Asow: *Die Mingottischen Opernunternehmungen: 1732 bis 1756* (Leipzig, 1915)
——: *Angelo und Pietro Mingotti* (Dresden, 1917)
——: 'Gluck und die Brüder Mingotti', *Gluck-Jb*, iii (1917), 1
V. Mackeprang: 'Pietro Mingotti's operaopførelser i København', *Historiske meddelelser om København*, iv/2 (1949)

**Mingotti** [née Valentin], **Regina** (*b* Naples, 16 Feb 1722; *d* Neuburg an der Donau, 1 Oct 1808). Austrian opera singer. The daughter of an Austrian officer, she was taken by him to Graz in 1722 and educated in a convent there after his death. In 1743 she joined the Mingotti opera troupe, which was then in Graz, made her début in Hamburg and in 1746 married Pietro Mingotti. In 1747 she had great success when the troupe performed at Dresden. She was engaged at the court opera there and became a pupil of Porpora at royal expense. She later sang in Naples, Prague (1750) and Madrid (1751–3) and then went to Paris and London, where she made her very successful début at the King's Theatre in November 1754. In the 1756–7 season, after the previous manager had gone bankrupt, partly because of disagreements with her, she was co-manager of the theatre with Giardini, the orchestra director. The season not proving a great success financially, the pair gave up the management at its end. Mingotti, according to Burney 'in the decline of her favour' and of her voice, next sang at the King's Theatre in the 1763–4 season, when she was again manager as well. (She had sung in London in May 1759 at a concert at Covent Garden.) She also sang in Italy before retiring to Dresden. In 1772 she was living in Munich, where Burney met her and reported that her voice was in better condition than on her last London appearance.

Burney described Mingotti as 'a perfect mistress of her art' and her style of singing as 'always grand'. Martinelli considered that she owed to her study with Porpora 'that propriety, delicacy and expression' in rendering the passions that characterized the Porpora school and contrasted with the more ornate and artificial style of singing that came into vogue about the middle of the century. Yet the cantabile, pathetic style was not her forte, and early in her career, Hasse, whose wife Faustina had been made intensely jealous by Mingotti's success in Dresden, composed for her a setting of the pathetic aria 'Se tutti i mali miei' in his *Demofoonte* (Dresden, 1748), intended to demonstrate her inadequacy in this regard. Mingotti determinedly overcame the challenge and triumphed in the aria, which she later sang in London with equal success. Even so, Burney wrote that 'her greatest admirers allowed that her voice and manner would have been still more irresistible, if she had had a little more female grace and softness'. Highly admired as an actress, she occasionally turned her lack of grace and softness to advantage by appearing to great effect in male parts.

### BIBLIOGRAPHY

BurneyH
V. Martinelli: *Lettere familiari e critiche* (London, 1758), 135, 159, 362
C. Burney: *The Present State of Music in Germany, the Netherlands and United Provinces* (London, 1773, 2/1775); ed. P. Scholes as *Dr. Burney's Musical Tours* (London, 1959)
E. H. Müller von Asow: 'Regina Mingotti', *Musikblätter* (1950)

**Minguet y Yrol, Pablo** (*fl* Madrid, 1733–75). Spanish writer, engraver and publisher. He was active in Madrid for over 40 years, publishing popular manuals on a variety of subjects from religion to magic tricks; among them are two series of self-instruction books on music, one on instruments and theory and the other on dancing. Their bibliographical aspect is exceptionally complex; they were available in separate parts, some of which were published in several editions, various additions were incorporated through the years, and no two copies seem exactly identical. The series on instruments devotes most space to the guitar, but covers a total of 13 instruments, including the psaltery and the bandurria. The dance series surveys both French and Spanish styles and the art of choreography. The author claims to be first in the field in Spain, having allegedly brought out the earliest dance manual in 1733. The texts consist of series of elementary rules; of greater interest are the engravings, charts and musical examples. The books contain illustrations of musical instruments, various dancing positions and movements, diagrams of tablatures, keys and chords, and examples of popular tunes – the minuet, passepied, fandango, jota and others, with instrumental tablatures or diagrammed dance steps.

### WRITINGS
*(only those relating to music)*

*Reglas, y advertencias generales que ensenan el modo de tañer todos los instrumentos mejores* (Madrid, n.d.)
*Reglas . . . para tañer la guitarra, tiple y vandola, con variedad de sones, danzas y otras cosas semejantes . . . por música, y cifra, al estilo castellano, italiano, catalán y francés* (Madrid, 1752, rev. 2/1774)
*Reglas . . . para acompañar sobre la parte con la guitarra, clavicordio, órgano, arpa, cithara o qualquier otro instrumento* (Madrid, n.d.)
*Reglas . . . para tañer el psalterio* (Madrid, 1754)
*Reglas . . . para tañer la bandurria* (Madrid, n.d.)
*Reglas . . . para tañer al violín* (Madrid, n.d.)
*Reglas . . . para tañer la flauta traversa, la flauta dulce y la flautilla* (Madrid, 1754)
*El noble arte de danzar a la francesa y española* (Madrid, 1755)
*Papelito nuevo que contiene un laberyntho de laberynthos, a siete voces* (Madrid, 1755) [rev. version of part of *Reglas . . . para acompañar*]
*Arte de danzar a la francesa* (Madrid, 3/1758)
*Breve tratado de los passos del danzar a la española* (Madrid, 2/1764)
*Cuadernillo nuevo que en ocho láminas finas demuestran y explican el arte de la música* (Madrid, 1773)

*Breve explicación de diferentes danzas y contradanzas demonstradas con media choreographia* (Madrid, n.d.)
*Explicación y demonstración de los bayles que mas se usan en las cortes de Europa* (Madrid, n.d.)

### BIBLIOGRAPHY

B. Saldoni: *Diccionario biográfico-bibliográfico de efemérides de músicos españoles*, iv (Madrid, 1881)
F. Pedrell: *Catàlech de la Biblioteca musical de la Diputació de Barcelona*, i (Barcelona, 1908), 190ff
R. Mitjana y Gordón: 'La musique en Espagne', *EMDC*, I/iv (1920), 2187, 2191, 2194
H. Anglès and J. Subirá: *Catálogo musical de la Biblioteca nacional de Madrid*, iii (Barcelona, 1951), 68ff
J. Subirá: *Historia de la música española e hispanoamericana* (Barcelona, 1953)
A. Palau y Dulcet: *Manual del librero hispanoamericano*, ix (Barcelona, 2/1956)
F. J. León Tello: *La teoria española de la música en los siglos XVII y XVIII* (Madrid, 1974)

ALMONTE HOWELL

**Mingus, Charles** (*b* Nogales, Arizona, 22 April 1922; *d* Cuernavaca, Mexico, 8 Jan 1979). Black American jazz composer, double bass player and pianist. After formal study in the Los Angeles area, he played with Louis Armstrong (1941–3) and then worked with Kid Ory before joining Lionel Hampton (1946–8). In 1950–51 he toured with the Red Norvo Trio, and later worked with Billy Taylor. In 1952 he founded his own record company, named Debut, but although it produced several important records, it was commercially unsuccessful. A brief association with certain experimental jazz composers, including Teddy Charles and John LaPorta, was followed by work with groups led by Charlie Parker, Bud Powell, Stan Getz and Art Tatum. With his own Jazz Workshop group, founded in New York about 1953, Mingus established himself over the next few years as a unique composer and bandleader, though his volatile temperament provoked frequent changes in the group's personnel. Afterwards he led a variety of groups, appearing in clubs and at jazz festivals in the USA and Europe, and maintained his position as a leading jazz composer.

*Charles Mingus*

Mingus's early reputation derived chiefly from his virtuoso bass playing, especially as a member of the Norvo group. Possibly because jazz composition depends so much on the maintenance of a regular ensemble, his first compositions, though innovatory, were inconsistent. The turning-point came with the title-piece of his *Pithecanthropus erectus* (1956), which broke away from the conventional repeating chorus structure of jazz and encompassed an unusually wide range of instrumental sonorities. Further works in a similar vein followed on records dating from 1957 to 1960; despite the wide-ranging character of these pieces, they all show Mingus's gift for inspiring improvisation from his bandsmen, both through the concentration his material imposes and the stimulus of his own virtuoso bass playing. His music remained expressionistic, but the use of collective improvisation became increasingly dominant, so that *The Black Saint and the Sinner Lady* (1963), a rare example of successful sustained composition in jazz, has a compactness that makes it his most intricate and demanding work.

BIBLIOGRAPHY
L. Gushee: 'Three by Mingus', *Jazz*, i (1958), aut., 55
N. Hentoff: 'Function Before Form', *These Jazzmen of our Time*, ed. R. Horricks (London, 1959), 176
B. Coss: *Charles Mingus: a List of Compositions Licensed by B.M.I.* (New York, 1961)
N. Hentoff: *The Jazz Life* (New York, 1961), 157ff
J. Goldberg: *Jazz Masters of the 50s* (New York, 1965), 132ff
C. Mingus: *Beneath the Underdog* (New York, 1971)
E. Jost: *Free Jazz* (Mainz, 1975), chap.2
MICHAEL JAMES

**Mini, Alessandro** (*b* Padua, *c*1756; *d* Padua, 27 June 1825). Italian organist, composer and theorist. He studied the organ and composition with Ferdinando Turrini and Gaetano Valeri; he replaced Valeri as organist of Padua Cathedral on 29 January 1803. He enjoyed a local reputation as an outstanding organist, theorist and composer. Although he is said to have composed several masses, only manuscript copies of mass movements for three voices and organ survive, in the cathedral library, Padua. In 1825 Mini was succeeded by his most famous student, Melchiorre Balbi.

BIBLIOGRAPHY
N. Pietrucci: *Biografia degli artisti padovani* (Padua, 1859), 11
A. Garbelotto: 'Piccola enciclopedia musicale padovana', *Padova e la sua provincia*, xix (May 1973), 23
SVEN HANSELL

**Minim** (Fr. *blanche*; Ger. *Halbe-Note*; It. *bianca*; Lat. *minima*; Sp. *blanca*). The note that is half the value of a semibreve and twice the value of a crotchet. In American usage it is called a half-note. It was the shortest of the five notes of early medieval music, hence its name. It is first found in early 14th-century music. Before about 1600 its value was a half or a third of a semibreve. The minim was shown as a semibreve with a stem. Some Italian and Spanish sources use the alternative terms *bianca* and *blanca* respectively. The minim is still in regular use, although in common with other notes it now has a round note head. Its various forms and the minim rest are shown in ex.1*a–d*.

Ex.1

(a)        (b)        (c)   (d)

$\downarrow$ or $\downarrow$        $\equiv$        $\downarrow$   $\equiv$

*See also* NOTATION, §III, 3(iii–iv), 4(ii), (vii), and NOTE VALUES.
JOHN MOREHEN

**Minimal music.** *See* SYSTEM (ii).

**Miniscalchi, Guglielmo** (*b* Venice; *fl* 1622–30). Italian composer. He was an Augustinian monk who in 1622 was *maestro di cappella* of S Stefano, Venice. In that year he published at Venice *Il salmo 'Miserere mei Deus' concertato a tre voci con sinfonie . . . et in fine doi motetti a duo voci*, but he was most popular for his secular solo songs contained principally in three books of *Arie* (Venice, 1625, 2/1627; 1627; 1630; one from each of the first two in G. Benvenuti, ed.: *35 arie di vari autori del secolo XVII*, Milan, 1922). Symmetrically, each book contains 20 unpretentious strophic songs clearly catering for the market for this sort of simple music for the home; indeed the publisher, Alessandro Vincenti, who collected the contents of the second book, claimed in his dedication that Miniscalchi's style 'in this particular form [is] sought after and embraced by all'. There are two further songs by Miniscalchi in Milanuzzi's *Quarto scherzo delle ariose vaghezze* (Venice, 2/1624). Miniscalchi kept abreast of developments in Venetian song, though only in a modest way; far more of his later songs are in the increasingly popular triple time, the melodies in his third book in particular are much more long-breathed than those of, for example, the first book, and there is some contrast between recitative and aria-like writing (see *Gia che per hor intenerir*). But even this music is less interesting formally and less forward-looking than many of the songs that Berti was writing in Venice at the same period. However, several of Miniscalchi's tunes are catchy and agreeable, and his songs are generally well shaped. Some are dance-songs (two in the third book are labelled 'corrente'). Nearly every song in the first book has a ritornello, but there are none in the other two books.

NIGEL FORTUNE

**Minkus, Léon (Fyodorovich)** [Alois; Aloysius Ludwig] (*b* Vienna, 23 March 1826; *d* Vienna, 7 Dec 1917). Composer and violinist of Czech or Polish origin. He worked in Russia and probably studied in Vienna. He collaborated with Delvedez on the music for the ballet *Paquita*, which was performed in Paris with choreography by Mazillier (1846). In the early 1850s he went to Russia, where he directed Prince N. B. Yusupov's serf orchestra in St Petersburg (1853–6). He had some success as a concert soloist, and later gave private violin lessons. He was engaged as a soloist at the Bol'shoy Theatre in Moscow in 1861, and the following year was appointed to the conductorship of the orchestra, a post he held until 1872. He taught the violin at the Moscow Conservatory from 1866, and was also inspector of the orchestras to the Moscow imperial theatres. At the same time he maintained a connection with Paris, writing several ballets, performed there in collaboration with the choreographer and musician Saint-Léon and, in 1866, with Delibes; but it was generally agreed that Delibes' contribution to their score for the ballet *La source* was far superior to Minkus's. However, he made an auspicious début as a composer in Russia: his ballet *Don Quixote*, with a scenario by Petipa and choreography by Gorsky, was well received in Moscow in 1869, and remained in the repertory for many years; it has been revived occasionally by Soviet companies. On the strength of this success, Gedeonov invited Minkus in 1872 to write most of the ballet music for an opera-ballet, *Mlada*, the rest of the score being allotted to

Borodin, Cui, Musorgsky and Rimsky-Korsakov. Although Gedeonov's project was never realized, it seems that Minkus fulfilled his part of the contract, and, like Rimsky-Korsakov, found a use for the music that was left on his hands: his ballet *Mlada* was eventually performed in St Petersburg in 1879. He was appointed to the important post of ballet composer to the imperial theatres in St Petersburg in 1872, and continued his association with Petipa in a long series of ballets, popular in their day but now completely forgotten. He retired from the imperial theatres in 1891; it seems likely that he returned to Vienna and died there in obscurity. As a composer Minkus has been the subject of much adverse criticism. It is true that he never aspired to the highly developed symphonic techniques which distinguish the ballet scores of Tchaikovsky from those of his lesser contemporaries, but his music is agreeably tuneful and tailor-made for conventional choreographic treatment. He is perhaps typical of that large band of composers who have carried out their professional duties competently, without ever achieving more than a routine level of inspiration.

WORKS

*(ballets first performed in St Petersburg unless otherwise stated)*
c20 ballets, incl. Paquita, collab. Delvedez, Paris, 1846; Néméa, collab. Saint-Léon, Paris, 1864; La source, collab. Delibes, Paris, 1866, arr. pf (Paris, 1884); Le poisson d'or, collab. Saint-Léon, Paris, 1867; Le lys, Paris, 1869; Don Quixote, Moscow, 1869; Camargo, 1872; Les brigands, 1875, place unknown; Les aventures de Pelée, 1876; La bayadère, 1877; Roxana, 1878; Mlada, 1879; Nuit et jour, 1882; Les pillules magiques, 1886; L'offrande à l'Amour, 1886

Vn works, incl. concs., études and teaching pieces; pf music

BIBLIOGRAPHY

L. S. Popova: 'Don Quixote', *Bol'shoy teatr SSSR: opera, balet* (Moscow, 1958)
A. Bonkowska: '*Don Quixote* w Teatrze Wielkim', *Ruch muzyczny*, viii/10 (1964), 14

JENNIFER SPENCER

**Minneapolis and St Paul.** American twin cities, on the Mississippi River, in Minnesota. In the westward expansion of the 1850s Minneapolis and St Paul attracted immigrants to the fertile upper Midwest. Apart from appearances by the Hutchinson family in 1855 and by Ole Bull with the 13-year-old Adelina Patti a year later, home entertainment and singing schools – the beginning of a choral tradition enriched by German and Scandinavian settlers – marked the decade in which the state of Minnesota was founded. By 1863, however, the St Paul Musical Society had played the first symphony heard in Minnesota, and three years later the city built an opera house to accommodate burgeoning local events and European artists who came on American tours.

Spurred by the example of St Paul, Minneapolis inaugurated in 1867 the Pence Opera House, boasting the only grand piano in the city. With the founding of instrumental and choral groups the building soon proved inadequate, and a new Academy of Music was opened in 1871; at its opening concert the St Paul Musical Society played the first symphonic music heard in Minneapolis. This exchange between the cities' instrumental ensembles has continued; for example, the Minneapolis-based Minnesota Orchestra and the St Paul Chamber Orchestra offer seasons in each other's cities.

With expanded facilities and the growing population (particularly German and Austrian musicians eager to teach and perform), the range of musical activities grew more diversified, partly through the pioneering work of

the Hamburg musician Ludwig Harmsen. The first conductor and full-time professional musician in Minneapolis, Harmsen conducted the Minneapolis Musical Society and its successor, the Orchestral Union. In the 1880s, when both St Paul and Minneapolis had become major commercial cities, opera, choral societies and festivals flourished. In 1881 Minneapolis engaged Franz Danz, a German immigrant musician, to form an instrumental ensemble to match the Great Western Band and Orchestra in St Paul. Two years later Danz's son, Frank Danz jr, came from the Theodore Thomas Orchestra to become Director of Professor Danz's Orchestra, which formed the nucleus of the Minnesota Orchestra, known as the Minneapolis SO on its foundation 20 years later. Emil Oberhoffer was appointed musical director, with Frank Danz becoming leader. The inaugural concert was given on 5 November 1903, and two years later the orchestra moved into a new auditorium, the site of which was used in 1974 for its new hall.

In its fifth season (1907) the orchestra embarked on the first of several tours that soon took it to both coasts, and later to Canada, Mexico, Cuba and the Middle East. As early as 1914 a St Paul series was added, but it was abandoned during most of the orchestra's 43 years (1931–74) at the University of Minnesota's Northrop Auditorium (capacity 4800). The St Paul series was reinstated in 1970 on the opening of the I.A. O'Shaughnessy Auditorium (capacity 1800) at the College of St Catherine. By 1922 Oberhoffer had inaugurated youth concerts and established extensive tour routes, especially throughout the north-west and Canada. After a season of guest conductors, including Walter Damrosch and Bruno Walter, in 1922–3, Henri Verbrugghen (1922–31) succeeded him, and added to the repertory works by Bach as well as introducing Delius, Elgar and Vaughan Williams. The long history of the orchestra's recordings began in 1923; with the recordings issued during the conductorship of Eugene Ormandy (1931–6), the orchestra acquired an international reputation that Dimitri Mitropoulos (1937–49) brought to fruition; he risked his popularity by championing the works of Schoenberg, Berg, Krenek (resident in St Paul 1942–7) and Shostakovich, and by giving the premières of such works as Hindemith's Symphony in E$\flat$ (1941). He created a climate for new music that was expanded by his successors: Antal Dorati (1949–60), who introduced works by Bartók, and the Polish-born Stanislaw Skrowaczewski, whose extended tenure (1960–79) witnessed not only the growth of the orchestra but also several USA premières including Penderecki's *St Luke Passion* (1967). He was succeeded by Neville Marriner in 1979. In 1968 the Minneapolis SO changed its name to the Minnesota Orchestra as a sign of its expanded activities. In 1974 the new Orchestra Hall (capacity 2543) was completed; it has been widely acclaimed for its acoustics. A wide variety of musical events is organized there by the Minnesota Orchestral Association.

The Twin Cities now have two full-time professional orchestras as well as many civic and student ensembles. The St Paul Chamber Orchestra was founded in 1959, and was directed by Leopold Sipe who was succeeded in 1972 by Dennis Russell Davies. From 1968 to 1978 it was the only full-time professional chamber orchestra in the USA. It gives annual concert series in St Paul and

Minneapolis, and also plays throughout the region. It tours nationally each year and has performed in western and eastern Europe and in the Soviet Union. It is noted for its innovatory programming, and includes works for full ensemble and smaller groups, ranging over four centuries. It has commissioned works from Dominick Argento, William Bolcom and Hans Werner Henze among others.

Opera in Minneapolis and St Paul is dominated by two complementary seasons: that of the Minnesota Opera, a resident ensemble company founded in 1962 as the Center Opera under the auspices of the Walker Art Center (which promotes contemporary music as well as art), and the annual spring visit of the Metropolitan Opera. Like the Minnesota Orchestra, the Minnesota Opera's change in name reflects its service to the state; the company has also earned national recognition, and has commissioned works from Dominick Argento (1964, 1971, 1976) and Conrad Susa (1973, 1975) among others. Until 1973 the St Paul Opera, founded to encourage local musical theatre during the Depression, also presented an annual season.

Since 1919 the University of Minnesota has presented international musicians and dance companies. The St Paul Schubert Club, prominent since 1882 and one of the few American organizations of its kind to survive and develop after World War II, sponsors some 50 recitals annually, including international artists, local professional and amateur musicians and students. The Schubert Club offers student scholarships and master classes, a music therapy project and a commissioning programme, and has a musical instrument collection. Like other local musical institutions, it is supported partly by the St Paul–Ramsey Arts and Science Council, an agency designed to support and develop cultural organizations.

Chamber music is provided by the members of the St Paul Chamber Orchestra and has been encouraged by the Schubert Club, the Walker Art Center (which has its own recital hall) and New Friends of Chamber Music (1955–78). The Thursday Musical (formed as the Lorelei Club in 1892) focusses on musicians resident in Minneapolis and on scholarship awards. Post-graduate music degrees are offered by the University of Minnesota Department of Music, which was formally instituted in 1903, the same year as the Minnesota Orchestra.

BIBLIOGRAPHY
J. K. Sherman: *Music and Maestros* (Minneapolis, 1952)
B. Flanagan: *Ovation* (Minneapolis, 1977)

MARY ANN FELDMAN

**Minnesang.** The German tradition of courtly lyric and secular monophony that flourished particularly in the 12th, 13th and 14th centuries. Though it is in many ways merely the German branch of the genre represented by the troubadours and trouvères in France, it has substantial independent features. The musical history of Minnesang is a particularly controversial subject because the melodies survive largely in manuscripts from the 14th and 15th centuries (*see* SOURCES, MS, §III).

1. Introduction. 2. Origins and courtly love. 3. Genres, prototypes, forms. 4. Historical development. 5. The melodies and their sources. 6. Evidence for performing practice. 7. Transcription problems.

1. INTRODUCTION. The name 'minnesinger' appears for the first time in the work of Hartmann von Aue (*Minnesangs Frühling*, 218.21; *c*1189); the word 'minnesanc' is substantially later, being first found in Walther von der Vogelweide (W 66.31; *c*1230); and 'minneliet' is used by Neidhart von Reuental (85.33; after 1230). Reaching its peak in the years of the Hohenstaufen emperors, the tradition grew alongside early Gothic architecture, the great religious movements of the time (particularly the Albigensians) which culminated in the crusades, and the brilliant rise of scholasticism. Just as in France, German Minnesang was cultivated by the travelling musicians but particularly by the nobility; and the intensity of the tradition shows the central role it must have played in the cultural and social life at court. This could happen only with the rise of a separate, carefully cultivated life style and new social obligations among the nobility coming together with the ethical duty to provide guidelines for their secular existence.

The *Minnedienst* – servitude to love – is the central motif of this aristocratic poetry and must be understood in terms of the feudal system. Alongside the inevitable components, the inferior social position in court of the professional singers as well as of the noble *ministeriales* among whose ranks most Minnesinger were found, there is the knight's courteous striving for the grace and favour of a lady, one who is a respected (and unreachable) member of the courtly society to whom the singer fully yields himself – at least in the fiction created by the ideology and poetic conventions of *Minne*. Within this concept of an inferior position is mirrored the idea of feudal dependence to which even the nobility were subject. *Ministeriales*, the vassals of the king and the great landlords, were bound to faithfulness, to service and to military duty; the fief they held in return for this was hereditary from the time of Konrad II. And it is perhaps from that context that many of the fundamental motifs of Minnesang – *dienen*, *triuwe*, *zuht* and *staete* – take their full meaning. Equally, the repertory contains many concepts taken from religious contexts – *hulde*, *genade* – thus emphasizing also the musical connection of Minnesang with the church.

Music and dancing were important components of courtly life, and the performance of epics and songs played a major role. The performer had normally created both the poetry and the music which he sang to the assembled company with instrumental accompaniment. But although this is one of the earliest repertories in which the poet is regularly named, the poetry is well separated from biographical detail: it takes place largely in the imagination, in a generalized fiction, and it is only after the factually documentable political songs of Walther von der Vogelweide that it becomes possible, in the more derivative later Minnesang, to begin to read biographical or historical fact in the poetry. Therefore many historical questions such as chronology, particularly of Walther's or Reinmar's poetry, and the mutual influences of single poets or groups of poets must remain unresolved. Further questions are made difficult by the nature of the sources: the earlier manuscripts tend to contain poetry alone; and it is therefore possible to overestimate the value of the few scattered early musical fragments as well as the much later large manuscripts with music.

2. ORIGINS AND COURTLY LOVE. Although the German Minnesang tradition contains indigenous features and

characteristic forms, its dependence on other western European song is predominant. The search for its origin is no longer limited to Provence and northern France since *jarchas* have been found in Cairo, at the extreme edge of the Romanic area (see Stern, 1953); but even so Provençal lyric poetry is still unquestionably the oldest vernacular tradition of its kind in Europe. It had an exceptionally strong effect over the whole West, and much in the German Minnesang is nothing more than a direct imitation of this art. From the beginning of the 12th century there was a fully formed tradition; for the various hypotheses as to its further courses and origins see TROUBADOURS, TROUVÈRES, §I, 4.

Central to the German tradition is the idea of *Minne*, a word coming from the Old High German *minna* and including the concepts of 'mindfulness' and 'remembrance' but best translated in English with the much contested but useful phrase 'courtly love'. It corresponds also to the late classical Latin *amor*. The verb *minnen* (Old High German *minnôn*) means 'to love' or 'to be complaisant' in both religious and secular senses. *Minne* therefore has both spiritual and sensual qualities, and it is possible to see within Middle High German literature a development from the earlier primarily spiritual and emotional use to a more sensual one in the later Middle Ages.

During the peak era of Minnesang *Minne* represented an ideal spiritual relationship between the man (*ritter*, *man*) and the lady (*frouwe*, *wîp*), also called *hôhiu minne* (high *Minne*), first by Friedrich von Hûsen (before 1190) and later also by Walther von der Vogelweide; it was a sensual force determined by the nature of courtly society and culture. By contrast, *nideriu minne* (low *Minne*) was the more outright demand by a man for physical possession of a woman. But the spiritual nature of earlier Minnesang makes it impossible to inflict the widely accepted characterization of 'low *Minne*' on, for example, Walther von der Vogelweide's *Mädchenlieder* (girls' songs).

*Liebe* ('love') represents fulfilment, acceptance, but normally includes the spiritual as well as the physical relationship of man and woman, though it can stand for the spiritual alone; it is, however, a less common word. A constantly repeated fundamental motif in Minnesang is the knight's longing for an unreachable woman, the lament over this unbridgeable chasm, and at the same time the spiritual optimism (*vröide*) which results in the sensual character-developing force of *Minne*, service of a woman without any reward.

3. GENRES, PROTOTYPES, FORMS. Of the three main categories of Minnesang, the *Lied*, the *Spruch* and the *Leich*, only the *Leich* is clearly identifiable in formal terms: it is not strophic but a through-composed form with a highly developed and complex metrical structure, containing repetition either in pairs of lines (*AABBCC* ...) or in groups of lines (*AABBCC ... AABBCC ...*), often framed by individual opening and closing lines (*ABBCCDDEE ... X*). The earliest known example in German seems to be the *Kreuzleich* of Heinrich von Rugge (c1190), but the form remained in use throughout the Minnesang era and beyond (see LAI). In the 13th century it reached full flowering with such poets as Ulrich von Winterstetten (five), Tannhäuser (six), Konrad von Würzburg (two), etc, while later figures representing the transition to Meistergesang, such as Hadlaub (three) and Frauenlob (three), also fully ex-

ploited the form.

*Lied* and *Spruch* are closer to one another, however: modern scholarship largely accepts but continues to discuss the received distinction according to content and form (*see* SPRUCH). A social division whereby the travelling musician sang *Spruch* whereas the nobleman sang *Minnelied* is valid for the early period but ceases to hold towards the end of the 12th century with Walther von der Vogelweide, who was a master of both genres. On the other hand the most useful division of Walther's extensive lyric output seems to be between the single stanzas in *Spruch* form with elements of the travelling musician and the more noble multi-stanza *Minnelieder*. Hugo Kuhn has been followed by many modern scholars in considering a series of *Spruch* stanzas to the same melody (the so-called *Spruchlied*) as having been written a stanza at a time over a period of years. Several later poets wrote both *Minnelied* and *Spruch*, among them Neidhart von Reuental, Frauenlob and Wizlâw, while Reinmar von Brennenberg even wrote examples of both to a single melody.

Compact four-line stanzas or stanzas with four long lines more in the manner of epic poetry (Kürnberger) are characteristic of early Minnesang; in the subsequent era of classic Minnesang canzone form (otherwise called bar form) was preferred for both *Lied* and *Spruch*, though other types of stanza existed; finally, in the course of the 13th century there was an astonishing expansion of forms and formal techniques with refrains, internal rhyme, linking rhyme and other features to which the melody could add a further structural dimension. In particular the canzone form was developed in many varied ways (*see* BAR FORM); it should however be emphasized that the presence of canzone form in the poetry did not necessarily imply music in the same form (see Paul and Glier, 1961, esp. p.88) so it is important to qualify all formal descriptions as being musical or poetic. In this, as in so much else, the lack of melodies in many cases and the lack of metre for the melodies that do survive have tended to focus metrical research onto the text and many of the received formal categories were devised by modern scholarship on the basis of textual form alone; and while a fuller knowledge of Minnesang music together with its context within early European secular monophony in general has brought some perspective to the subject, it remains true that questions concerning upbeats to lines, line ends, rests and so on remain entirely unresolved.

In terms of their content the songs can be classified as follows. *Spruch* poetry divides into two main groups, the religious and the political; further there is a group of social criticism, often commenting on the generosity of a patron; and others may be classified as ethical and philosophical.

Minnesang proper is normally categorized according to content: (1) the strict *Minnelied* is normally the song of a man, describing his own happiness, sadness or longing in love, and is often introduced by a description of nature and the time of year; (2) the *Frauenstrophe* or *Frauenlied*, the song of a woman, belongs particularly to the early years of Minnesang but is otherwise found in many parts of the world (*cantigas d'amigo*) portraying the woman's longing; in the (3) *Wechsel* ('exchange') stanzas from the man and the woman alternate, not in dialogue, but rather explaining to the listener their respective views of a situation; (4) the *Tagelied*, closely related to the Provençal ALBA and many similar types across the world describing the parting of lovers at dawn, awoken by the watchman's warning, is the only genre within Minnesang that enabled an apparently objective description of sensual love; (5) the *pastourelle* of Latin and French medieval poetry is relatively rare in its purest form in Minnesang, but appears in Walther von der Vogelweide's *Under der linden*; (6) the *Tanzlied* (dance-song, round-dance) is most clearly represented in songs of Neidhart von Reuental but appears in songs of different content; finally (7) the *Kreuzlied* (crusade song), found particularly in the work of Hartmann von Aue, Friedrich von Hûsen, Walther von der Vogelweide and others, describes the experience of renunciation of the world on a crusade but contains rich overtones of other genres.

4. HISTORICAL DEVELOPMENT. The development of Minnesang may perhaps be followed in terms of five very approximate chronological periods.

(1) According to the earliest evidence of Minnesang (c1150–70) the tradition began with simple straightforward love-songs in a folksong-like manner. Based on dance-songs and other types of folksong with unconventional and directly experienced content, this earlier phase from the area round the Danube remains quite different from the Provençal model later adopted and is therefore independent of the strict stylization of high Minnesang. *Frauenstrophe*, *Tagelied* and *Wechsel* are common in these years. Long poetic lines after the manner of the epic and rhyming lines with four main accents are common, often with freer metre and assonance. The poems are for the most part single stanzas and are anonymous: the most famous names are Kürnberger and Dietmar von Aist – yet the latter has only two poems from this early date and they are quite different from the rest of his work in both style and content.

(2) Romanic influence characterizes the next generation (c1165–1200): the impact of the growing troubadour and trouvère traditions is first clearly recognizable in the dactylic verses surviving under the name of 'Heinrich' (VI) (fig.1), but is more traditionally associated with the wedding of Heinrich's father, Emperor Friedrich Barbarossa, to Beatrice of Burgundy (9 June 1156), who had the trouvère GUIOT DE PROVINS in her retinue. An important symptom of the change is the position of the man (rather than the woman) as the longing, yearning partner; and the love becomes less overtly sensual, more contemplative. Bar form seems also to grow at this point and to have been borrowed from the troubadours with a carefully differentiated rhyme scheme and form in the Abgesang. This new artistic, rhetorical and musical impulse from the west evidently created stylistic ideas of a hitherto unimagined range. Earlier representatives of this generation, whose music must largely be reconstructed from contrafacta, are RUDOLF VON FENIS-NEUENBURG from Switzerland (then the kingdom of Arelat), FRIEDRICH VON HÛSEN from the lower Rhineland and HENDRIK VAN VELDEKE.

(3) The golden age of German Minnesang is generally agreed to belong to those years (c1180–1230) when the influence of the new Romance poetries was united with the indigenous tradition in a courtly art – a development sometimes related to Friedrich Barbarossa's international festival in 1184 at Mainz. Bar form and dactylic rhythm became the most common technical features; but the whole form was now more varied and complex. Pure (exact) rhyme was now required, and the anacrusis was no longer added spasmodically but became a regulated part of the metre; syllabic lines became predominant. The content, motifs and metaphors were now largely romanic; and knightly *Minne* was the central theme. REINMAR VON HAGENAU, HEINRICH VON MORUNGEN and HARTMANN VON AUE were the most important poets; in addition Albrecht von Johannsdorf from Bavaria, Heinrich von Rugge from Swabia, Ulrich von Gutenburg from Rhenish Franconia, BERNGER VON HORHEIM and Bligger von Steinach should also be mentioned. But WALTHER VON DER VOGELWEIDE represents the very peak of Minnesang, his all-embracing, superbly independent invention being conceptually, stylistically and formally beyond any classification and standing as a model for subsequent generations.

(4) The following years (c1220–1300) show an extraordinary expansion of Minnesang with the *Spruch* also being cultivated more systematically. Two main traditions may be identified: many poets continued the courtly tradition, albeit in a more mannerized style, following Walther von der Vogelweide. These included ULRICH VON LIEHTENSTEIN, REINMAR VON BRENNENBERG, REINMAR VON ZWETER, Friedrich von Suonenburg and MEISTER ALEXANDER. On the other hand NEIDHART VON REUENTAL (d c1250), though a contemporary of Walther, led towards a new realism with his pointed style, often using rustic wit with positively coarse undertones and ironic parody. The use of a highly idealized fiction based on the courtly classical Minnesang is characteristic of this generation; it need on no account be considered derivative for it was a

*1. Keiser Heinrich: miniature from the Manessische Liederhandschrift, c1320 (D-HEu pal.germ.848, f.6r)*

thoroughly creative transitional era also characterized by a return to realism and to parody as well as a retreat from the Romance influences of the preceding generation and a stronger alliance with indigenous traditions. DER TANNHÄUSER, Geltar and Der von Scharfenberg are the prime representatives of this second group. Poets who occupy a position between the two extremes include Burkhard von Hohenfels, Gottfried von Neifen, Ulrich von Winterstetten and WIZLÂV III VON RÜGEN. This generation closes impressively with the comprehensive and productive FRAUENLOB (see fig.2).

(5) With the 14th century, in a changed political and social ambience with growing national consciousness and the rise of the towns and of the bourgeoisie, Minnesang finally retreated from its courtly idealism while still retaining much of its traditional sense. So the learned but not particularly gifted HUGO VON MONTFORT (d 1423), whose poems were set to music by BURK MANGOLT, sang no more of unattainable women but of his own wife. Spiritual and didactic material came to the forefront, as did the *geblümte Stil* (florid style) that had already been cultivated by Burkhard von Hohenfels and Wizlâv von Rügen and was further developed by Heinrich von Mügeln (d after 1371): the transition to MEISTERGESANG was inevitable. The musically important songs of the MONK OF SALZBURG (c1400) owe only a small part of their range to Minnesang. A century after the end of Minnesang OSWALD VON WOLKENSTEIN (d 1445), the 'last courtly singer', continued the tradition, but he must be considered the herald of a new epoch in musical and literary history.

5. THE MELODIES AND THEIR SOURCES. No certain information survives as to the earlier scribal stages that led to the relatively late manuscripts for the texts and the music of Minnesang. Presumably the poets themselves or other singers and musicians collected repertory on single leaves or in volumes that were circulated and copied. Yet oral transmission must also have been extremely important. Only about 1300 did the literary era begin owing to the initiative of collectors, amateurs and patrons, such as the Zurich town councillor Rüedeger Manesse. But even then texts were copied much more than music, as in the three major manuscripts, A (Kleine Heidelberger Liederhandschrift, *D-HEu* pal.germ.357, late 13th century), B (Weingartner Liederhandschrift, *D-Sl* HB XIII, 1, early 14th century with 25 illustrations) and C (Grosse Heidelberger Liederhandschrift, or Manessische Handschrift, *D-HEu* pal.germ.848, c1320, with 138 magnificent illustrations) as well as E (Würzburger Handschrift, *D-Mu* 2° cod.ms.731, mid-14th century); in addition there is a large number of smaller manuscripts, equally without music.

By contrast with the text transmission and with the rich legacy of trouvère melodies, the musical transmission of early and high Minnesang (c1150–1300) is extremely slender except for the songs of Neidhart von Reuental; only with the latest representatives of Minnesang such as Hugo von Montfort, the Monk of Salzburg and Oswald von Wolkenstein, who were conscious of standing at the end of a vanishing tradition and concerned to preserve their art, were melodies regularly written down, often in manuscripts prepared by the poets themselves. Subsequently, in the Meistersinger guilds it became a regular practice to write down songs.

Apart from the non-diastematic neumes for a few

*2. Frauenlob (Heinrich von Meissen) and musicians with (from left to right) tabor, straight cornett, shawm, fiddles and bagpipe: miniature from the Manessische Liederhandschrift, c1320 (D-HEu pal.germ.848, f.399); see also FLUTE, fig.8*

Middle High German poems in the *Carmina burana* manuscript (*D-Mbs* Clm 4660), for a single song of Walther von der Vogelweide in *A-KR* 127.VII.18 and for the anonymous *Rôsen ûf der heide* in *D-ERu* 1655 – all of which are only subjectively transcribable – there are essentially three groups of musical sources for Minnesang:

(1) The musical manuscripts of Minnesang, mostly from the 14th and 15th centuries. Music from the earlier generation (before c1230) appears only in the Münster fragment (*D-MÜsa* VII.51), with one complete melody for Walther von der Vogelweide, and in the Neidhart sources, particularly *D-B* germ.fol.779, *A-Wn* suppl.3344, *D-F* germ.oct.18 and the lost manuscript from Sterzing; but even among these the 55 Neidhart and pseudo-Neidhart songs represent a new departure from the courtly Minnesang in both poetic and musical respects for they have a dancing, folksong-like style. The four major manuscripts, the Jenaer Liederhandschrift (*D-Ju* E 1.f. 101), the Wiener Leichhandschrift (*A-Wn* 2701), the Colmar manuscript (*D-Mbs* Cgm 4997) and its sister manuscript at Donaueschingen (*D-DO* 120), are largely taken up with Meistergesang and in any case do not always seem entirely reliable. Further manuscripts include fragments related to the Jenaer Liederhandschrift at Basle (*CH-Bu* N.I.3, 145), a fragment with the anonymous spring song *Ich sezte minen vuz* (*D-B* germ.qu.981; see fig.3, p.342) and perhaps also some of the 12 anonymous folksong-like melodies in *D-B* germ.qu.922. (For a table summarizing

the sources and their notation, see Kippenberg, 1962, p.46; *see also* SOURCES, MS, §III, 4.)

(2) A substantial body of indirect musical transmission appears among the 'inferred melodies' (*erschlossene Melodien*): a number of texts are related to troubadour or trouvère songs in their form and content and seem to be contrafacta, so it is possible to take the original melody which the poet perhaps also used and to give it to the German poem. As a result of the energetic and thorough work of Spanke, Frank, Gennrich and Aarburg among others, over 30 cases of such contrafacta have been produced with greater or lesser degrees of certainty.

(3) Of questionable value for the study of this early period are manuscripts of Meistergesang from the 16th and 17th centuries which often contain melodies ascribed to earlier poets, among them Walther von der Vogelweide, Wolfram von Eschenbach, Tannhäuser, Marner, Reinmar von Zweter and Konrad von Würzburg. But the melodies are apparently changed and provided with new texts. Minnesang scholarship can use them only with the utmost caution.

6. EVIDENCE FOR PERFORMING PRACTICE. Any attempt to imagine the performance of Minnesang must begin by considering the rich instrumental practice of minstrelsy as recorded in a profusion of visual representations, in legal or administrative documents and within the poetry. This vital tradition must inevitably have affected the daily life of all classes in spite of the social disadvantage under which the performers laboured. Minstrels, jongleurs and travelling clerics with a variegated range of instruments and sometimes with extreme virtuosity took part in all kinds of festivities at court, in the countryside and at other secular occasions. The rondeau, the virelai and the *estampie* all contain some evidence of their music-making which did not care much for theories and rules or for written records, but exerted a strong influence over courtly song forms in France and Germany as a result of its example and of the active and varied part it took in those song forms.

Textual evidence suggests that the vocal and instrumental abilities of the troubadours, trouvères and Minnesinger were often very good, sometimes excellent. Often additional musicians were employed to sing the song or to accompany it on instruments (see fig.2); and it is recorded that Rumzlant, for example, had his songs performed by a *singerlîn*. Sometimes instrumentalists were sent to other courts in order that they might spread knowledge of their patron's creations.

For the accompaniment all kinds of instruments seem to have been used. Here virtuosity was presumably important and the most varied performing styles may have been exploited. Thus GOTFRID VON STRASSBURG praising Walther von der Vogelweide's singing drew attention to his skill in diminution (*wandelieren*) and in instrumental accompaniment (*organieren*). Equally he made the mythical figure Tristan accompany his *schanzune* (chanson) on the harp, showing how at that time a singer who was also a practised musician would master various styles:

> er sanc diu leichnotelin
> britunsche und galoise,
> ltinsche und franzoise
> so suoze mit dem munde,
> daz nieman wizzen kunde,
> wederez süezer waere
> oder bas lobebaere
> sin harpfen oder sin singen

('He sang the *Leich* melodies in Breton and Gaelic, Latin and French [styles] so sweetly with his voice that nobody could tell which of the two was sweeter or more praiseworthy: his harp playing or his singing.' *Tristan*, ll.3626–33.) And Isolde had mastered the playing of bowed instruments in the French fashion:

> si videlt ir stampenie,
> leiche und so vremediu notelin,
> diu niemer vremeder kunden sin,
> in franzoiser wise
> von Sanze und San Dinise

('She fiddled her *estampies*, *Leichs* and melodies so strange that they could never be stranger; and she followed the French manner of Saintes and St Denis'. *Tristan*, ll.8058–62.) Normally the melody covered a 10th or an 11th, only rarely reaching two octaves. But the notation is sometimes in a relatively high tessitura: Ulrich von Liehtenstein even wrote that many fiddlers would thank him for choosing such high pitches (*Frauendienst*, l.1373).

Eustache Deschamps, writing much later (*L'art de dictier*, 1392), distinguished *musique naturelle* ('leiz, sirventois de Nostre Dame, chançons royaulx, pastourelles, ballades, virelais, rondeaux') from *musique artificielle* (mensural polyphony), emphasizing that *musique naturelle* had no fixed rules and could not be learnt but depended entirely on natural talent. This seems to reflect the commonly made distinction between *cantor* and *musicus*, between *ars* (music according to the schools) and *usus* (practical music). Courtly singers on the whole were probably more practitioners, but may have had varied theoretical backgrounds: Gotfrid praised Tristan's *hantspil* (playing ability with his hands) as well as his ability as a *schuollist* (theoretician); on the other hand Ulrich von Liehtenstein, when he had been sent melodies by a lady with the request that he should write new poems for them, first had them sung to him by a musician, and afterwards the songs he had composed for the lady had to be written down, both text and melody, by an expert. But many of the surviving Minnesang melodies, particularly the through-composed *Leichs*, bear witness to considerable technical skill. The representatives of the less regulated Minnesang had various attitudes towards church music: Rumzlant and Gervelin, representing an older and less sophisticated tradition in northern Germany, expressed disapproval of the south German Marner who probably had church training and of the middle German Meissner whose singing they found strange because of its reliance on solmization and church modes.

Various notational problems present both palaeographical and historical difficulties. Not only individual copying errors, but also frequent changes of tonality (major to minor, leading note to *finalis* or *confinalis*) and suggestions and changes of mode, imply that all the manuscripts were copied partly by ear. Yet the parallel existence of several versions of melodies (rather more in the French repertory than in the German) can not always be explained in terms of errors or limitations in the notation; they can also be seen as a normal and perhaps thoroughly legitimate symptom of largely oral transmission in which a song is performed by several singers and variants could arise in performance, or even be added by the individual artist. Repeatedly these questions make it important to bear in mind that the relationship of notation to musical reality was then rather different from what it is today. In the same way, a

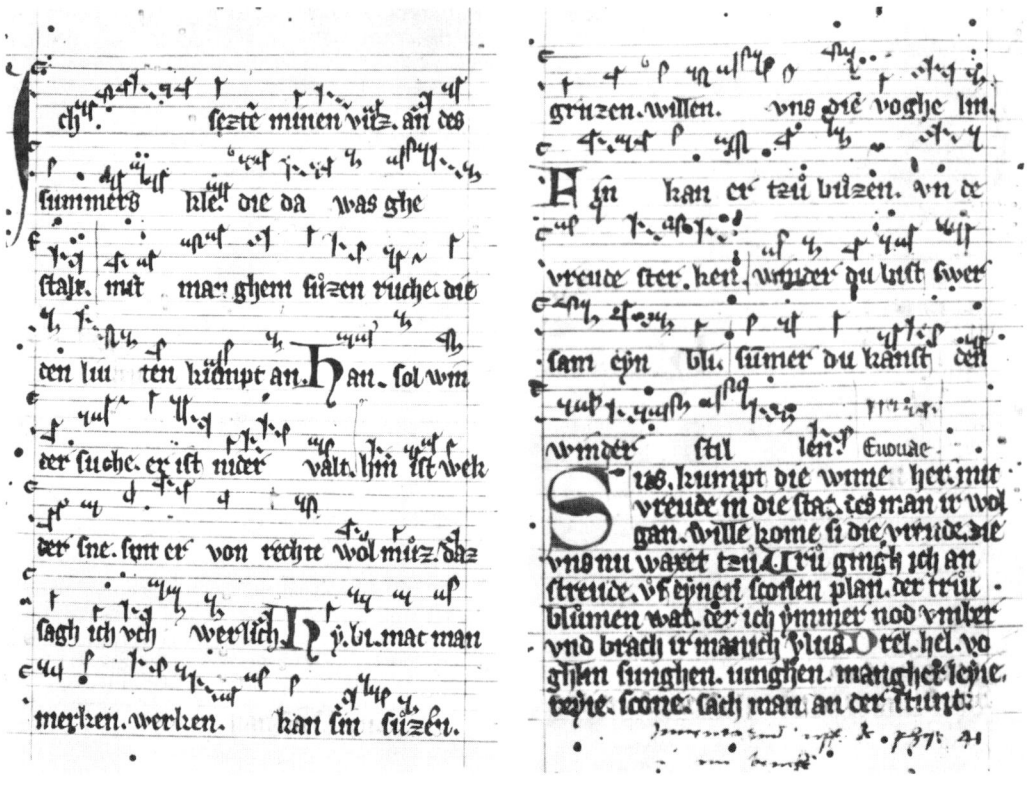

*3. Anonymous spring song 'Ich sezte minen vuz', 14th century (D-B germ.qu.981, f.1r and v)*

variable instrumental accompaniment could have caused this, because it was doubtless natural for the instrumentalist to show his skill with devices and embellishments that were quite independent of any musical notation.

So it is impossible to say how far the occasional appearance of melismas, for example in Wizlâv or Meister Alexander, and the later increase of melismatic melodies with Hugo von Montfort and the early Meistersinger are really a new development of the 'florid' style or whether they are rather – at least in part – a different, more detailed approach to notation (and to notational technique). It seems likely that the earliest Minnesang notation, before the big collective manuscripts, used extremely varied techniques, some of them considerably simplifying the music. There was probably a certain degree of freedom not visible in the notation inasmuch as the close interchange of vocal practice and instrumental sound has always been one of the determining factors in the development of stylistic tendencies. In this context one may note the anonymous spring song in the fragment *D-B* germ.qu.981 (fig.3), remarkable because of its rich melismas but perhaps only a special case of more fully written-out notation which, copied by an experienced copyist, could well give a more reliable record of the musical reality of Minnesang.

7. TRANSCRIPTION PROBLEMS. The surviving notation for Minnesang is extremely varied and sometimes changes even within a single manuscript. Yet there is another reason why no uniform transcription technique

can be established; the question of rhythm is still unsolved and will probably remain so.

The earliest sources in non-diastematic neumes (*D-Mbs* Clm.4660, *ERu* Kremsmünster) do not even give clear information as to pitch, so no transcription can reasonably hope to be more than approximate. In the remaining sources the melodic shape is usually unambiguous; but there are variant readings in different manuscripts. This results partly from the chronological distance between the composition of the original and the copying of it, partly from the inherent variability within a primarily oral tradition, and partly from the incompatibility of that notation and ours. The principle of 'musical textual criticism' (*musikalische Textkritik*, Gennrich) which reconstructs an 'original form' from the various surviving versions of a melody (as has been done successfully with literary texts) must be considered highly questionable for this branch of medieval monody.

One must, for instance, consider conscious changes made by the scribes who mostly belonged to a later generation, were instructed in musical theory and may therefore themselves have produced a 'critical' edition. More recent scholarship sees only a limited relationship between text and melody, with a certain freedom to vary or even exchange the melodies (Räkel).

Embellishment, particularly as concerns the plica, is still little understood. Riemann's idea of replacing plicas and melismas with embellishment signs from the Baroque is now considered historically misleading; but his error led Runge to transcribe all the *puncta* as plicas in his edition of the Colmar manuscript, which is notated entirely in *virgae* and *puncta*.

The rhythm is not specified in the notation of Minnesang. This has caused considerable polemic and controversy among scholars. For primarily syllabic melodies editors have tended to adopt the principle that speech rhythm (of the verse metre) should provide the basis for an interpretation of the musical rhythm. But for poetry with alternating accented and unaccented syllables this amounts basically to the possibility of either duple or triple time (spondee, trochee or iamb). Even dactylic verses allow of a duple interpretation, although by analogy with certain mensural pieces in the trouvère repertory one could perhaps accept a dotted triple rhythm in some cases. But a particular problem lies in finding an appropriate rhythm for line ends and melodic cadences.

In discussions of rhythm it is obvious that one must consider not only the structure of the text but the shape of the melody, particularly its melismatic sections. Beginning with a consideration of both, musicologists and literary historians have been striving since the 1950s to join forces in reaching an understanding of Minnesang that is free from the dogmas of earlier years. So scholars have agreed, for instance, that the categories of line and line ends put forth in Andreas Heusler's *Deutsche Versgeschichte* (1925–9) cannot simply be applied to the rhythmic interpretation of the melodies as well.

Modern scholarship is inclined to give the melismas a much stronger melodic importance and even to give them a structural function, which can be seen in their regular appearance on accented syllables at particular places in the line. This discovery supports other arguments against a strictly uniform rhythmic structure in the music. And in these melismatic outgrowths, which represent independent elements in the strict structure of the line, some scholars have seen the influence of Gregorian chant, particularly where it consisted of a festive elaboration of a cadence. Direct evidence for some connection between Minnesang and the liturgy may be found in the addition 'EVOVAE' at the end of the melody of the anonymous song *Ich sezte minen fuoz* (see fig.3) and in *Leichs* of Frauenlob.

It is often difficult to decide whether such melismas are vocal or instrumental preludes and interludes; and the problem is not always solved for the editor by the appearance of a continued text syllable beneath such apparently instrumental sections (e.g. in *D-B* germ. qu.922 or in Hugo von Montfort's manuscript at Heidelberg). Further difficulties arise in text underlay when the melody is written down apart from the text (e.g. in the Neidhart manuscript *D-B* germ.fol.799).

Reviewing the history of Minnesang scholarship from the viewpoint of the constantly controversial question of its rhythm, one can see that it is clearly characterized by a change in evaluation of the sources: the first editors (von der Hagen, 1838; K. K. Müller, 1896; Mayer and Rietsch, 1896) were concerned primarily to produce an accurate reproduction of the written signs (facsimile). After early unsuccessful attempts to interpret the rhythms (Burney, Forkel, Fétis, Coussemaker) scholars began from 1900 to see the transcription of medieval monody into modern notation as their main aim, tacitly transferring contemporary notation and barring into the Middle Ages and attempting to close the 'information gap' in the sources with rhythmic theories. One of these theories attempted a free chant-like 'rhetorical' rhythm (Molitor, 1910–11). Another followed the metre of the

text: Runge first publicized this theory (*Die Sangesweisen der Colmarer Handschrift*, 1896), and was followed by Saran (*Die Jenaer Liederhandschrift*, 1901), who expanded the idea with his exclusively metrical scheme and stated that his transcriptions were intended primarily to reproduce the metrical scheme of the poetry but not necessarily the musical results. Riemann also attempted to work from the poetic metre, but in his attempts to subject the melodies to his theories of *Vierhebigkeit* often overruled the facts of literary scansion; yet his exaggerated theories were limited to theoretical publications, not included in actual editions. Then the theories of 'modal rhythm' arose, transcribing the melodies according to the medieval teaching of the six rhythmic modes, following the lead set by Aubry and Beck with troubadour and trouvère melodies; for Minnesang this theory influenced practically all publications from about 1925 to 1960. Yet more recently (and following a lead already clear in Schmieder's edition of Neidhart in 1930) scholarship has largely discarded the schematic use of modern notation with barring, time signatures and modern note values, seeing the unqualified use of modal theory with more and more scepticism (Reichert, Anglès, Kippenberg, Jammers etc).

Rejection of the earlier and sometimes rather dogmatically held theories admittedly brings with it a realization that very little is known about the rhythm of Minnesang: so the transcriber must limit himself carefully to a notation that is fundamentally neutral in rhythm (either simple note heads or a series of crotchets or quavers without precise values), adding signs to mark the poetic accents, the cadences, the ligatures, etc (Jammers).

### BIBLIOGRAPHY

#### MAJOR TEXT EDITIONS

F. H. von der Hagen, ed.: *Minnesinger: deutsche Liederdichter des 12., 13. und des 14. Jahrhunderts* (Leipzig, 1838/*R*1962–3)

K. Lachmann and M. Haupt, eds.: *Des Minnesangs Frühling* (Leipzig, 1857, rev. 30/1950 by C. von Kraus)

K. Bartsch: *Meisterlieder der Kolmarer Handschrift*, Bibliothek des Literarischen Vereins in Stuttgart, lxvii (Stuttgart, 1862/*R*1962)

——: *Die Schweizer Minnesänger* (Frauenfeld, 1886/*R*1964)

H. Brinkmann, ed.: *Liebeslyrik der deutschen Frühe in zeitlicher Folge* (Düsseldorf, 1952)

C. von Kraus, ed.: *Deutsche Liederdichter des 13. Jahrhunderts* (Tübingen, 1952–8)

O. Sayce, ed.: *Poets of the Minnesang* (Oxford, 1967)

U. Müller, ed.: *Die grosse Heidelberger 'Manessische' Liederhandschrift* (Göppingen, 1971) [facs.]

#### MAJOR MUSIC EDITIONS

K. K. Müller, ed.: *Die Jenaer Liederhandschrift* (Jena, 1896) [facs.]

P. Runge, ed.: *Die Sangesweisen der Colmarer Handschrift und die Liederhandschrift Donaueschingen* (Leipzig, 1896/*R*1965)

F. A. Mayer and H. Rietsch, eds.: *Die Mondsee-Wiener Liederhandschrift und der Mönch von Salzburg* (Berlin, 1896)

G. Holz, F. Saran and E. Bernoulli, eds.: *Die Jenaer Liederhandschrift* (Leipzig, 1901/*R*1966)

R. Molitor: 'Die Lieder des Münsterischen Fragmentes', *SIMG*, xii (1910–11), 475

H. Rietsch, ed.: *Gesänge von Frauenlob, Reinmar von Zweter und Alexander*, DTÖ, xli, Jg.xx (1913/*R*)

I. Frank and W. Müller-Blattau, eds.: *Trouvères und Minnesänger* (Saarbrücken, 1952–6)

H. Kuhn: *Minnesang des 13. Jahrhunderts* [with melodies ed. G. Reichert] (Tübingen, 1953, rev. 2/1962)

F. Gennrich: *Mittelhochdeutsche Liedkunst: 24 Melodien zu mittelhochdeutschen Liedern*, Musikwissenschaftliche Studienbibliothek, x (Darmstadt, 1954)

——: *Die Jenaer Liederhandschrift: Faksimile-Ausgabe ihrer Melodien*, SMM, xi (1963)

E. Jammers: *Ausgewählte Melodien des Minnesangs: Einführung, Erläuterung und Übertragung* (Tübingen, 1963)

F. Gennrich, ed.: *Die Colmarer Liederhandschrift: Faksimile-Ausgabe ihrer Melodien*, SMM, xviii (1967)

H. Moser and J. Müller-Blattau: *Deutsche Lieder des Mittelalters: von Walther von der Vogelweide bis zum Lochamer Liederbuch: Texte und Melodien* (Stuttgart, 1968)

R. J. Taylor, ed.: *The Art of the Minnesinger* (Cardiff, 1968)

H. Müller: *Die Jenaer Liederhandschrift in Abbildung, mit einem Anhang: die Basler und Wolfenbüttler Fragmente*, Litterae, x (Göppingen, 1972)

H. Brunner, ed.: *Minnesang und Spruchdichtung*, Monumenta musicae medii aevi, xv (in preparation)

GENERAL

A. E. Schönbach: *Die Anfänge des deutschen Minnesanges: eine Studie* (Graz, 1898)

P. S. Allen: 'The Origins of German Minnesang', *Modern Philology*, iii (1905), 411

J. Schwietering: 'Einwirkung der Antike auf die Entstehung des frühen deutschen Minnesangs', *Zeitschrift für deutsches Altertum*, lxi (1924), 61

K. Burdach: 'Über den Ursprung des mittelalterlichen Minnesangs, Liebesromans und Frauendienstes', *Vorspiel: gesammelte Schriften zur Geschichte des deutschen Geistes*, i/1 (Halle, 1925), 235–333

H. Brinkmann: *Entstehungsgeschichte des Minnesangs* (Halle, 1926/R1971)

F. Gennrich: 'Zur Ursprungsfrage des Minnesangs: ein literarhistorisch-musikwissenschaftlicher Beitrag', *Deutsche Vierteljahrsschrift für Literaturwissenschaft und Geistesgeschichte*, vii (1929), 187–228

L. Ecker: *Arabischer, provenzalischer und deutscher Minnesang: eine motivgeschichtliche Untersuchung* (Berne and Leipzig, 1934)

K. J. Heinisch: *Antike Bildungselemente im frühen deutschen Minnesang* (diss., U. of Bonn, 1934)

H. Spanke: *Deutsche und französische Dichtung des Mittelalters* (Stuttgart and Berlin, 1943)

T. Frings: *Minnesinger und Troubadours*, Vorträge und Schriften der Deutschen Akademie der Wissenschaften zu Berlin, xxxiv (Berlin, 1949); repr. in Fromm (1961)

H. Kuhn: 'Die Klassik des Rittertums in der Stauferzeit', *Annalen der deutschen Literatur*, ed. H. O. Burger (Stuttgart, 1952, 2/1961), 99–177

L. Spitzer: 'The Mozarabic Lyric and Theodor Frings' Theories', *Comparative Literature*, iv (1952), 1

H. de Boor: *Die höfische Literatur: Vorbereitung, Blüte, Ausklang, 1170–1250*, Geschichte der deutschen Literatur, ed. H. de Boor and R. Newald, ii (Munich, 1953, 8/1969)

P. F. Ganz: 'The "Cancionerillo Mozarabe" and the Origin of the Middle High German "Frauenlied" ', *Modern Language Review*, xlviii (1953), 301

R. Kienast: 'Die deutschsprachige Lyrik des Mittelalters', *Deutsche Philologie im Aufriss*, ed. W. Stammler, ii (Berlin, 1954, rev. 2/1960), 1–132

H. Kuhn: *Dichtung und Welt im Mittelalter* (Stuttgart, 1959)

T. Frings: *Die Anfänge der europäischen Liebesdichtung im 11. und 12. Jahrhundert*, Sitzungsberichte der Bayerischen Akademie der Wissenschaften, Philosophisch-historische Klasse, ii (Munich, 1960); repr. in *Beiträge zur Geschichte der deutschen Sprache und Literatur*, xci (Halle, 1969–71), 473

H. Fromm, ed.: *Der deutsche Minnesang: Aufsätze zu seiner Erforschung*, Wege der Forschung, xv (Darmstadt, 1961, 4/1969)

R. W. Linker: *Music of the Minnesinger and Early Meistersinger: a Bibliography*, University of North Carolina Studies in the Germanic Languages and Literatures, xxxii (Chapel Hill, 1962)

A. T. Hatto: 'Folk Ritual and Minnesang', *Modern Language Review*, lviii (1963), 196

P. Kesting: *Maria-Frouwe: über den Einfluss der Marienverehrung auf den Minnesang bis Walther von der Vogelweide* (Munich, 1965)

J. Bumke: *Die romanisch-deutschen Literaturbeziehungen im Mittelalter* (Heidelberg, 1967), esp. 41ff, 94ff [incl. bibliography]

H. Tervooren: *Bibliographie zum Minnesang und zu den Dichtern aus 'Des Minnesangs Frühling'* (Berlin, 1969)

H. Moser, ed.: *Mittelhochdeutsche Spruchdichtung*, Wege der Forschung, cliv (Darmstadt, 1972)

LITERATURE

L. Uhland: 'Der Minnesang', *Schriften zur Geschichte der Dichtung und Sage*, v (Stuttgart, 1870), 111–282

F. Grimme: 'Freiherren, Ministerialen und Stadtadelige im XIII. Jahrhundert: mit besonderer Berücksichtigung der Minnesinger', *Alemannia*, xxiv (1897), 97–141

P. Kluckhohn: 'Der Minnesang als Standesdichtung', *Archiv für Kulturgeschichte*, xi (1914), 389

K. Korn: *Studien über 'Freude und Trûren' bei mittelhochdeutschen Dichtern: Beiträge zu einer Problemgeschichte*, Von deutscher Poeterey, xii (Leipzig, 1932)

F. R. Schröder: 'Der Minnesang: I die Forschung, II das Problem', *Germanisch-romanische Monatsschrift*, xxi (1933), 161, 257

M. Ittenbach: *Der frühe deutsche Minnesang: Strophenfügung und Dichtersprache* (Halle, 1939)

M. F. Richey: *Essays on the Mediaeval German Love Lyric* (Oxford, 1943, 2/1969)

A. Moret: *Les débuts du lyrisme en Allemagne, des origines à 1350*, Travaux et mémoires de l'Université de Lille, xxvii (Lille, 1951)

H. Thomas: 'Die jüngere deutsche Minnesangforschung', *Wirkendes Wort*, vii (1956–7), 269

G. Jungbluth: 'Neue Forschungen zur mittelhochdeutschen Lyrik', *Euphorion*, li (1957), 192

W. Salmen: *Der fahrende Musiker im europäischen Mittelalter*, Die Musik im alten und neuen Europa, iv (Kassel, 1960)

P. Wapnewski: *Deutsche Literatur des Mittelalters: ein Abriss* (Göttingen, 1960, 2/1968)

J. Bumke: *Studien zum Ritterbegriff im 12. und 13. Jahrhundert* (Heidelberg, 1964)

P. Dronke: *The Medieval Lyric* (London, 1968)

THE CONCEPT OF 'MINNE'

E. Wechssler: *Das Kulturproblem des Minnesangs: Studien zur Vorgeschichte der Renaissance*, i: *Minnesang und Christentum* (Halle, 1909/R1966)

A. T. Hatto: 'Gallantry in the Mediaeval Germanic Lyric', *Modern Language Review*, xxxvi (1941), 480

A. Moret: 'Qu'est-ce que la Minne? contribution à l'étude de la terminologie et de la mentalité courtoises', *Etudes germaniques*, iv (1949), 1

A. Closs: 'Minnesang and its Spiritual Background', *Medusa's Mirror: Studies in German Literature* (London, 1957), 43

H. Kolb: *Der Begriff der Minne und das Entstehen der höfischen Lyrik*, Hermaea, new ser., iv (Tübingen, 1958)

W. Spiewok: 'Minneidee und feudalhöfisches Frauenbild: ein Beitrag zu den Massstäben literarhistorischer Wertung im Mittelalter', *Wissenschaftliche Zeitschrift der Universität Greifswald, gesellschafts- und sprachwissenschaftliche Reihe*, xii (1963), 481

D. Wiercinski: *Minne: Herkunft und Anwendungsgeschichte eines Wortes* (Cologne and Graz, 1964)

H. Wenzel: *Frauendienst und Gottesdienst: Studien zur Minne-Ideologie* (Berlin, 1974)

FORMS AND GENRES

K. Bartsch: 'Der Strophenbau in der deutschen Lyrik', *Germania*, ii (1857), 257–98

R. M. Meyer: *Grundlagen des mittelhochdeutschen Strophenbaus*, Quellen und Forschungen, lviii (Strasbourg, 1886)

R. Weissenfels: *Der daktylische Rhythmus bei den Minnesängern* (Halle, 1886)

W. Wilmanns: *Untersuchungen zur mittelhochdeutschen Metrik* (Bonn, 1888)

K. Plenio: 'Bausteine zur altdeutschen Strophik', *Beiträge zur Geschichte der deutschen Sprache und Literatur*, xlii (1917), 411–502; lxiii (1918), 56–99

A. Heusler: *Deutsche Versgeschichte* (Berlin and Leipzig, 1925–9, 2/1956)

H. Brinkmann: *Zu Wesen und Form mittelalterlicher Dichtung* (Halle, 1928)

W. Bücheler: *Französische Einflüsse auf den Strophenbau und die Strophenbindung bei den deutschen Minnesängern* (Dillingen, 1930)

F. Gennrich: 'Das Formproblem des Minnesangs: ein Beitrag zur Erforschung des Strophenbaues der mittelalterlichen Lyrik', *Deutsche Vierteljahrsschrift für Literaturwissenschaft und Geistesgeschichte*, ix (1931), 285–349

W. Fischer: *Der stollige Strophenbau im Minnesang* (diss., U. of Göttingen, 1932)

F. Gennrich: *Grundriss einer Formenlehre des mittelalterlichen Liedes* (Halle, 1932)

H. de Boor: 'Langzeilen und lange Zeilen in Minnesangs Frühling', *Zeitschrift für deutsche Philologie*, lviii (1933), 1–49

M. Ittenbach: *Der frühe deutsche Minnesang: Strophenfügung und Dichtersprache* (Halle, 1939)

C. von Kraus: *Des Minnesangs Frühling: Untersuchungen* (Leipzig, 1939)

H. Kuhn: *Minnesangs Wende* (Tübingen, 1952, rev. 2/1967)

S. M. Stern: *Les chansons mozarabes: les vers finaux (kharjas) en espagnol dans le muwashshahs arabes et hébreux* (Palermo and Oxford, 1953)

H. Moser: 'Minnesang und Spruchdichtung? über die Arten der hochmittelalterlichen deutschen Lyrik', *Euphorion*, l (1956), 370

——: 'Die hochmittelalterliche deutsche "Spruchdichtung" als übernationale und nationale Erscheinung', *Zeitschrift für deutsche Philologie*, lxxvi (1957), 241

U. Pretzel: 'Deutsche Verskunst: mit einem Beitrag über altdeutsche Strophik von H. Thomas', *Deutsche Philologie im Aufriss*, ed. W. Stammler, iii (Berlin, 1957, 2/1962), cols.2357–546 [incl. bibliography]

F.-W. Wentzlaff-Eggebert: *Kreuzzugsdichtung des Mittelalters: Studien zu ihrer geschichtlichen und dichterischen Wirklichkeit* (Berlin, 1960)

O. Paul and I. Glier: *Deutsche Metrik* (Munich, 1961)

K. H. Bertau: *Sangverslyrik: über Gestalt und Geschichtlichkeit mittelhochdeutscher Lyrik am Beispiel des Leichs*, Palaestra, ccxl (Göttingen, 1964)

H. Tervooren: *Einzelstrophe oder Strophenbindung? Untersuchungen zur Lyrik der Jenaer Handschrift* (diss., U. of Bonn, 1967)

K. Ruh: 'Mittelhochdeutsche Spruchdichtung als gattungsgeschicht-liches Problem', *Deutsches Vierteljahrsschrift für Literatur-wissenschaft und Geistesgeschichte*, xlii (1968), 309
A. H. Touber: *Deutsche Strophenformen des Mittelalters* (Stuttgart, 1975)
S. Ranawake: *Höfische Strophenkunst* (Munich, 1976)

MUSIC

G. Jacobsthal: 'Über die musikalische Bildung der Meister-sänger', *Zeitschrift für deutsches Altertum*, xx (1876), 69
J. Sittard: 'Jongleurs und Menestrels', *VMw*, i (1885), 175
H. Riemann: 'Die Melodik der (deutschen) Minnesänger', *Musikalisches Wochenblatt*, xxviii (1897), 1, 17, 33, 45, 61, 389, 401, 413, 425, 437; xxix (1898), 353; xxxi (1900), 285, 309, 321, 333, 345; xxxiii (1902), 429, 441, 457, 469
F. Ludwig: 'Zur "modalen Interpretation" von Melodien des 12. und 13. Jahrhunderts', *ZIMG*, xi (1909–10), 379
H. Rietsch: 'Einige Leitsätze für das ältere deutsche einstimmige Lied', *ZMw*, vi (1923), 1
H. J. Moser: 'Musikalische Probleme des deutschen Minnesangs', *Kongressbericht: Basel 1924*, 259
W. Lipphardt: 'Neue Wege zur Erforschung der linienlosen Neumen', *Mf*, i (1948), 121
H. Anglès: 'Der Rhythmus der monodischen Lyrik des Mittelalters und seine Probleme', *IMSCR, iv Basle 1949*, 45
B. Nagel: 'Das Musikalische im Dichten der Minnesinger', *Germanisch-romanische Monatsschrift*, xxxiii (1951–2), 268
W. Bittinger: *Studien zur musikalischen Textkritik des mittelalterlichen Liedes* (Würzburg, 1953)
H. Husmann: 'Das Prinzip der Silbenzählung im Lied des zentralen Mittelalters', *Mf*, vi (1953), 8
F. Gennrich: 'Grundsätzliches zur Rhythmik der mittelalterlichen Monodie', *Mf*, vii (1954), 150
H. Husmann: 'Das System der modalen Rhythmik', *AMw*, xi (1954), 1–38
J. A. Westrup: 'Medieval Song', *NOHM*, ii (1954), 220–69
R. J. Taylor: 'The Musical Knowledge of the Middle High German Poet', *Modern Language Review*, xlix (1954), 331
——: 'Zur Übertragung der Melodien der Minnesänger', *Zeitschrift für deutsches Altertum*, lxxxvii (1956–7), 132
U. Aarburg: 'Muster für die Edition mittelalterlicher Melodien', *Mf*, x (1957), 209
B. Kippenberg: *Der Rhythmus im Minnesang* (Munich, 1962)
R. J. Taylor: 'Minnesang – wort unde wîse', *Essays in German Literature*, i, ed. F. Norman (London, 1965), 1
U. Aarburg: 'Probleme um die Melodien des Minnesangs', *Das Deutschunterricht*, xix/2 (1967), 98
W. Lipphardt: 'Über die Begriffe: Kontrafakt, Parodie, Travestie', *Jb für Liturgik und Hymnologie*, xii (1967), 104
H.-H. S. Räkel: 'Liedkontrafaktur im frühen Minnesang', *Probleme mittelalterlicher Überlieferung und Textkritik*, ed. P. F. Ganz and W. Schröder (Berlin, 1968), 96
B. Kippenberg: 'Die Melodien des Minnesangs', *Musikalische Edition im Wandel des historischen Bewusstseins*, ed. T. Georgiades, Musikwissenschaftliche Arbeiten, xxiii (Kassel, 1971), 62–92
H. Brunner: *Die alten Meister: Studien zur Überlieferung und Rezeption der mittelhochdeutschen Sangspruchdichter im Spätmittelalter und in der frühen Neuzeit*, Münchener Texte und Untersuchungen, liv (Munich, 1974)
E. Jammers: *Aufzeichnungsweisen der einstimmigen ausserliturgischen Musik des Mittelalters*, Palaeographie der Musik, i/4 (Cologne, 1975)
B. Stäblein: *Schriftbild der einstimmigen Musik*, Musikgeschichte in Bildern, iii/4 (Leipzig, 1975)

BURKHARD KIPPENBERG

**Minoja, Ambrogio** (*b* Ospitaletto Lodigiano, nr. Piacenza, 22 Oct 1752; *d* Milan, 3 Aug 1825). Italian composer and teacher. According to Choron and Fayolle, he began musical studies at 14, but did not make music his profession until much later, having been born into a life of ease. He studied with Secondo Anselmi in Lodi and with Nicola Sala in Naples. He was *maestro al cembalo* at La Scala and the Teatro Canobbiana in Milan from 1780 until 1802. While at La Scala, he represented his colleagues in negotiations with impresarios and was secretary-general of a musicians' union, the Pio Istituto de' Professori di Musica, which sponsored Lenten concerts at La Scala. According to Choron and Fayolle, in 1789 Minoja was appointed *maestro di cappella* for the priests of S Maria della Scala; however, this probably refers to S Fedele,

where the priests had been transferred by Marie Therese. A Signora Minoja, whom Gerber described as a musical dilettante and harpist of Milan, has not been identified.

Although Minoja's two operas for Milan and Rome (1786–7) brought no commissions from other cities, he was called upon to compose for state occasions in Milan. During the French occupation of the city, he wrote a *Sinfonia funebre* (1798) on the death of the French general Lazare Hoche, and a hymn (1799) to commemorate the decapitation of Louis XVI. However, barely a month after the Austrians retook Milan (27 April 1799), Minoja directed a performance of a cantata praising the defeat of the French forces by General Suvorov. In 1805, when Napoleon was crowned King of Italy in Milan Cathedral, Minoja again provided special music, conducting 250 musicians in a *Te Deum* and *Veni Creator Spiritus*. When Napoleon named Eugène Beauharnais Viceroy of Italy, Minoja composed a cantata to celebrate his marriage to Augusta Amalia of Bavaria and their arrival in Milan (1806).

Minoja's remarkable ability to function under different regimes was again demonstrated in 1814 when Milan passed into the hands of Emperor Francis I of Austria. At that time Minoja replaced Bonifazio Asioli as censor of the Milan Conservatory. Although he could not match Asioli as composer or administrator, he tried to equal him as a teacher; his treatise on singing, *Lettera sopra il canto* (Milan, 1812; Ger. trans., 1815) gained recognition and was favourably reviewed in the *Allgemeine musikalische Zeitung* (xv, 1813, cols.448–9). He held the post of censor, the highest teaching position at the conservatory, until his death.

WORKS

VOCAL

Operas: Tito nelle Gallie (after P. Giovannini: Giulio Sabino), Milan, La Scala, 26 Dec 1786, *F-Pn, P-La* [Act 1]; Olimpiade (Metastasio), Rome, Argentina, 26 Dec 1787
Occasional works: Il sogno (festa teatrale), Milan, 1776, *F-Pc*; Inno per l'anniversario della caduta di Luigi XVI (V. Monti), Milan, La Scala, 21 Jan 1799; Cantata (L. Ciceri), Milan, La Scala, 25 May 1799; L'arrivo in Milan degli sposi (cantata, L. Rossi), Milan, La Scala, 13 Feb 1806
Sacred: Mass, 4vv, orch, *D-MÜs*; 2 Gloria, D, *CH-E*, Bb, *I-MZ*; 2 Credo, C, G, *CH-E*; Requiem, mentioned by Fétis; Te Deum, Veni Creator, both 3vv, orch, for coronation of Napoleon, 1805; Cantico primo di Mosè, S, B, vv, orch, *F-Pc*; Canone, 1818, 4vv, orch, ?*D-Bds*; De profundis (It., S. Mattei), SSB, orch (Milan, n.d.); Eructavit cor meum, 4vv, *I-Md*; Hostias et preces, SAT, bc, *Tn*; Laudate pueri, 4vv, orch, *Td*; Lessons of Job, STB, 3 va, b, *D-MÜs, GB-Lbm*, S, male vv, orch, *D-MÜs*; Stabat mater, 3vv, orch, *CH-E*
Other vocal: La distruzione di Gerusalemme, oratorio, Milan, Conservatory, Lent 1820, collab. C. Soliva; Smarrito in rea foresta, trio, S, S, B, orch, *I-Mc*; Taccuini nuovi: schiribizzo musicale, 3vv, hpd (Milan, n.d.); arias, *CH-E*, *I-Tn*; solfeggi, 1–2 S, bc (Milan, n.d.)

INSTRUMENTAL

Orch: Sinfonia funebre, 1798, *I-BGc*; syms., sym. movts, C, *I-Mc*, D, *GB-Lbm*, *I-Gi(l)*, Mc, Eb, *GB-Lbm*, *I-Mc*, Bb, *GB-Lbm*, *I-Mc*, ?others, *CH-E*
Chamber: 6 sonatine, hpd, vn (Milan, 1793); Divertimento no.1, Bb, hpd, vn (Milan, 1799); Divertimenti della campagna, 6 str qts, *I-Mc*, *OS*; 12 qts, hpd, 2 vn, vc, *GB-Lbm*; 6 duets, 2 vn, *I-Mc*; Minuet with variations, Bb, hpd, vn, *GB-Lbm*; Sonata, Bb, hpd, vn, *I-Mc*; Minuetto, Bb, harp, *Tn*
Hpd: Battaglia, D, *I-A*, *Bsf*; La caccia, *Tn*; Sinfonia, D, *GB-Lbm*; 2 sonatas, C, *I-OS*, F, *Mc*

BIBLIOGRAPHY

*EitnerQ; FétisB; GerberNL*
C. Gervasoni: *Carteggio musicale* (Milan, 1804) [incl. letter by Minoja]
A. Choron and F. Fayolle: *Dictionnaire historique des musiciens* (Paris, 1810–11/R1971)
P. Cambiasi: *Rappresentazioni date nei reali teatri di Milano, 1778–1872* (Milan, 2/1872/R1969), 115
F. Florimo: *La scuola musicale di Napoli e i suoi conservatorii*, ii (Naples, 1882/R1969), 14

F. Mompellio: *Il R. Conservatorio di musica 'G. Verdi' di Milano* (Florence, 1941), 100, 322

A. Loewenberg: 'Minoia, Ambrogio', *Grove 5*

G. Barblan: 'La musica strumentale e cameristica a Milano nel '700', *Storia di Milano*, xvi (1962), 654, 662, 669, 672

G. Grigolato: 'I primi saggi di studio degli allievi (1809–13)', *Conservatorio di musica, Milano: annuario 1966–67* (Milan, 1967), 207

SVEN HANSELL

**Minor.** (1) The name given to a SCALE whose octave species, in its natural form, is built of the following ascending sequence of intervals: T–S–T–T–S–T–T (T = tone, S = semitone). The note chosen to begin the sequence, called the key note, also becomes part of the name of the scale; a D minor scale, for instance, consists of the notes D–E–F–G–A–Bb–C–D. In practice, however, some notes of the scale are altered chromatically to help impart a sense of direction to the melody. The harmonic minor scale has a raised 7th, in accordance with the major triad on the fifth step (the dominant). The melodic minor scale has a raised 6th and a raised 7th when it is ascending, borrowing the leading-note function of the seventh step from the major scale; in descending, though, it is the same as the natural minor scale.

(2) Any INTERVAL that is a semitone smaller than a major interval (*see* MAJOR, §2) but contains the same number of diatonic scale steps: minor 2nd (S), minor 3rd (S + T), minor 6th (2S + 3T), minor 7th (2S + 4T), minor 9th (octave + S = 5T + 3S). A minor triad is a three-note chord which, reckoned from the lowest note, is built of a minor 3rd and a perfect 5th; a D minor triad, for instance, consists of the notes D–F–A.

(3) The name of the mode of a piece, or a part thereof, having as its melodic basis a minor scale, and as its harmonic basis the minor triad built on the key note of that scale; if the key note is D, the piece is said to be in D minor. A piece described as 'in d' is normally taken to be in D minor. *See also* TONALITY.

(4) The term used to denote the size (rather than function) of an ORGAN STOP.

WILLIAM DRABKIN

**Minor canon.** A member of the Anglican Church clergy; *see* CATHEDRAL MUSIC AND MUSICIANS, ANGLICAN, §2.

**Minore** (It.: 'minor'). A term used, as was its French equivalent, *mineur*, to denote a change to the minor tonality – generally the tonic minor – in a work or movement written predominantly in the major key, no doubt serving as a warning to the performer in addition to that usually already provided by the change of the key signature. It makes an early appearance in the first of François Couperin's *Leçons de ténébres* (1713–17) where, following the setting of 'Beth' in the major key, the section 'Plorans ploravit in nocte' bears the rubric *Mineur et mesuré lent*. From the mid-18th century to the early 19th it was most frequently used to mark a change of mode in three contexts: in the central episode of a rondeau (e.g. the finale of J. C. Bach's Sinfonia concertante in A for violin, cello and orchestra, *c*1770, and Mozart's Rondo in F for piano K494); in sets of variations – one or more of the variations were usually in the minor key at this period (e.g. the finale of Mozart's Clarinet Quintet and Beethoven's Variations on a Russian Dance WoO71, where no fewer than three variations are marked *minore*); and in ternary movements such as the minuet and trio or its equivalent

(examples in Haydn's B minor Piano Sonata H XVI:32, Beethoven's Sonata in Eb op.7). In a few cases, such as the trio of the second minuet of Beethoven's String Trio in Eb op.3, the change is to the relative rather than to the tonic minor. After Beethoven the term was little used; two of its few later occurrences are in Schumann's *Arabesque* op.18 (1838), with its contrasting *minore* sections in the mediant and relative minor keys respectively. The resumption of the major key was usually indicated by the word MAGGIORE.

MICHAEL TILMOUTH

**Minoret, Guillaume** (*b* ?Paris, *c*1650; *d* Paris, 1717). French composer and ecclesiastic. According to Rouxel, Minoret received his early training in Paris at one of the choir schools. At some date before 1679 he was appointed *maître de musique* at Orléans Cathedral, and on 5 September that year he accepted a similar position at St Germain-l'Auxerrois, Paris. In 1683 he was one of four winners of the competition held to nominate *sous-maîtres* to the royal chapel. There is evidence that he was a protégé of Maurice Le Tellier, Archbishop of Rheims and *maître* of the chapel. Minoret's position at the court was undoubtedly much less influential than that of his more famous colleague Lalande: in 1693, when Goupillet was dismissed, Lalande was assigned his quarter of chapel duties, while Minoret was to take complete charge of the choirboys, a duty he had hitherto shared with Goupillet. He retired from the chapel in September 1714.

Minoret composed more than 50 motets, most of which are lost. Those that survive, all composed before 1697, resemble in style the earlier motets of Robert and Du Mont rather than those of his more progressive contemporary Lalande. He used polychoral techniques extensively, but his style is devoid of contrapuntal sophistication, and generally declamatory treatment of the texts is at times perfunctory.

WORKS

6 grands motets: Ad te Domine clamabo; Currite, populi; Deus docuisti-me; Prope es tu, Domine; Usquequo, Domine; Venite exultemus, soloists, 2 choirs (4vv, 5vv), str orch, bc, *F-Pc*, *Pn*, T

2 petits motets: Misericordia Domine; Sancti Spiritus; 2vv, bc; *LYm*

Missa pro tempore Nativitatis, 1694 (symphony added by Brossard), *Pn*

Lost works including the grands motets: Beati quorum, composed for competition, 1683; Te Deum, performed at St Victor Abbey, 1682; Lauda Jerusalem Dominum; Nisi Dominus; Quaemamodum desiderat (the last 3 mentioned in *FétisB*)

BIBLIOGRAPHY

*Nouveau Mercure galant* (April 1683), 310

*Etats de la France* (Paris, 1702)

S. de Brossard: *Catalogue des livres de Musique* (1724, MS, *F-Pn*), 451

E. Titon du Tillet: *Le Parnasse françois* (Paris, 1732/*R*1971), 561

A. Rouxel: *Guillaume Minoret* (Paris, 1879)

C. Masson, ed.: 'Dangeau Journal extraits', *RMFC*, ii (1961–2), 193–223

M. Benoit: *Musiques de cour, chapelle, chambre, écurie, 1661–1773* (Paris, 1971)

——: *Versailles et les musiciens du roi, 1661–1773* (Paris, 1971)

JOHN H. HAJDU

**Minshull, Richard.** *See* MYNSHALL, RICHARD.

**Minstrel.** A professional entertainer of any kind from the 12th century to the 17th, juggler, acrobat, story-teller etc; more specifically, a professional secular musician, usually an instrumentalist. This article is concerned chiefly with the period *c*1250–*c*1500, the heyday of minstrelsy.

1. Terminology. 2. Early history. 3. Minstrel instruments and ensembles. 4. Minstrels' music. 5. The minstrel in society. 6. Court minstrels. 7. Minstrel schools. 8. Conclusion.

1. TERMINOLOGY. Etymologists agree that the Latin *ministerialis*, meaning office-holder or functionary, is the source of the Old French 'menestrel' and of the English 'minstrel'. By the 9th century the Latin word had also come to mean craftsman or handworker (cf the French *métier* from the Latin *ministerium*). Thus it is not known whether instrumentalists and other musicians came to be called minstrels because of their official or unofficial connections with noble courts or because of their virtuosity and technical specialization. At any rate both the Latin and the French terms were used in fiscal records and literary sources of the first half of the 13th century to designate either craftsmen or musicians, but this ambiguity disappeared by the end of the century. The former sense persisted in the 14th century in countries, such as Spain, which were slow in using the Latin word to indicate musical performers.

Slightly before 'menestrel' (later 'ménétrier') came into general use, the French term used to describe secular musicians was 'jogleor' ('jogleur', later 'jongleur', in English 'jogelour'). It may be that the change in nomenclature (in the early 14th century) reflected a change in function, from the jack-of-all-trades entertainer to the specialist in playing a single instrument. In other Romance languages the Latin *ministerialis* did not give way to a vernacular equivalent; the Spanish 'joglar' and Italian 'gioccolatore' remained in use into the 15th century.

The troubadour Guiraut Riquier (*c*1275) claimed, however, that, whereas in Provence 'joglars' covered a number of different types of musician, in Spain their functions were distinguished by different terms: instrumentalists (*juglares*), imitators of animal sounds etc (*remedadores*), troubadours who travelled from court to court (*segrieres*) and street musicians (*cazurros*). In a reply no doubt written by Riquier but attributed to Alfonso X of Castile, his patron, it is suggested that street entertainers and the like should be called *bufones*; that he who could comport himself among the rich with *cortesia* and *ciencia* in playing instruments, reciting narratives and singing songs and verses made by others should be called *juglar*; that he who could make (*trovar*) words and melody should be called *trovador*; and that he who could do it with mastery and with an ethical or moral message should be called *don doctor de trobar*. Germanic languages generally used the word 'Spielmann', though forms of the French word (e.g. 'minstreel') are frequent in Flemish and Dutch records.

At all times and in all languages the naming of the player after his instrument was common, but there is some confusion over the nomenclature for secular singers. Although most references to minstrels appear to indicate instrumental performance only, there is no reason to suppose that the instrumentalists did not also sing; nor should the possibility be ruled out that, in some cases, 'minstrel' means 'singer'. In the second half of the 14th century the confusion is somewhat mitigated by the use of such terms as 'menestrel de bouche' or 'juglar de boca'.

Although even in the 14th century the word 'musician' (or its cognates) could, in addition to its traditional sense of judge and theorist of music, refer to performers, it was not until the 16th century that it began to offer serious competition to 'minstrel', by which time 'jongleur' seems virtually to have vanished. By the end of the 16th century, 'minstrel' had come to designate wretched mendicants, capable only of croaking or scratching out old-fashioned songs. An analogous shift can be observed in French, in which 'ménétrier' had come to mean village and country musicians. With the Romantic reawakening of interest in the culture of the Middle Ages, 'minstrel' became frequent in the special sense of wandering poet-musician, and to this day the word evokes the image of the itinerant singer accompanying himself on a plucked string instrument before an audience of knights and their ladies – a real enough phenomenon but only one among many in the range of medieval secular music. (In English the terms 'minstrel' and 'minstrelsy' have a broader meaning than their equivalents in other languages, and their use in this article is merely a convenience.)

2. EARLY HISTORY. There is no reason to suppose that at any time during the Middle Ages secular musicians were absent from western Europe. One difficulty in interpreting the historical documents is that wherever records are kept in Latin the same terms, chiefly 'histrio' and 'mimus', serve to designate entertainers of all sorts, including musicians, from the 9th century to the end of the 14th. All were tarred with the same brush by the ecclesiastical authorities, who as a rule deplored their mode of life or even forbade it: the *Commemoratio brevis* (*c*900; *GS*, i, 213) is unusual in its partly respectful attitude. Some modern scholars view the secular musician-entertainers of this early period as a continuation of the entertainer class of late Roman culture, but such an abstraction tells nothing of their specific functions, nor does it rule out the existence of other social or ethnic traditions.

One traditional role that has fascinated scholarship since the 18th century is that of the bard or epic poet–singer. He is usually supposed to have recited his lengthy tales to simple melodic formulae corresponding in their articulation and repetitions to the half-lines, lines and couplets of epic or narrative verse; he is also thought to have supported his song with an instrument such as the harp or fiddle. An image of this kind of verse- and music-making can be formed on the one hand from scattered documents of the Middle Ages up to about 1300 (*see* CHANSON DE GESTE) and on the other from still extant or only recently extinct practices in non-literate cultures. Questions of individual or so-called collective creation and composition, textual variation and improvisation, mnemonic schemes and oral transmission have been intensively studied in the last 60 years by historians of literature and folklore.

If such poet-singers can be thought with good reason to form a class distinct from entertainers with skills in non-verbal domains (instrumentalists, dancers, acrobats, prestidigitators, animal trainers and the like), the position of the 12th- and 13th-century creators and performers of lyric or didactic stanzaic poetry in the vernacular is not so clear. Whereas there is every reason to date the development of epic narrative poetry well before the beginning of written records and to see it as an essentially non-literate art, the various schools of Romance and Germanic poetry appear to be literary in every sense. But although there is a considerable corpus of French and Provençal poetry dating from before 1300, very little of it was transmitted with music, and such music as there is bears the signs of oral transmission. The nature of the relationship between poets and instrumentalists or singers, or the combination of these

C ar bien mouftra quamoes eft tedens li efmue
f oztune fait que tout autte poot fefnue

v n bzieuet faquerai fans riulle z fans auis
a ais que te uoftre affens/i foie fi commis

*1. Minstrels with (left to right) bagpipes, hurdy-gurdy (*symphonia*), shawm, portative organ, nakers, mandore, harp, fiddle and psaltery: miniatures from the Romance of Alexander, believed to have been copied in Bruges, 1338–44 (GB-Ob Bodley 264, f.180v); the only major instrumental types of the period missing from this group are trumpet, bells, cymbals and transverse flute*

functions in one individual, has often been discussed in connection with the Provençal troubadours.

A number of 13th-century French poets are also known to have been musical performers or composers: Adenes (often called Adenes le roi), was a *menestrel* in the employ of the Count of Flanders from about 1270 to 1300; another, Adam de la Halle, belonged to the retinue of the Count of Artois. These poet-composers and their music are interesting in view of the special character of bourgeois society and culture in the Low Countries and the close relations between the feudal nobility and the bourgeoisie.

3. MINSTREL INSTRUMENTS AND ENSEMBLES. There are two major sources of facts and impressions concerning the varied roles and functions of medieval minstrels: literature, in which, especially in poetry, the symbolic element often outweighs the descriptive; and financial records, which only now are beginning to be explored systematically. While 13th- and 14th-century poetry mentions many instruments by name, financial records are less specific, and neither source gives much information as to what exactly the instruments were, how they were played (in terms enlightening to a 20th-century musician) or how they sounded. How instruments were held and typical groupings of minstrels can sometimes be seen in manuscript and easel painting from the early 15th century on, but the pictorial record before that is thin and frequently ambiguous. There is also very little evidence concerning regional differences or the development of performing practice.

The records are equally ambiguous concerning the size and composition of ensembles; it is possible that both polyphonic and monophonic works were performed by more than one musician to a part. Payments for solo minstrelsy on every sort of instrument were frequent, as were those for two minstrels, often fiddlers. One can rarely be sure that simultaneous payment to several musicians meant that they played together, but in those accounts that permit such interpretation a great variety of trio combinations is found, and occasionally quartets (often trumpets and pipes). Larger groups also appear, mostly in connection with urban processions. The division of instruments into *haut* and *bas* groups seems to have been common in the 15th century and relatively so in the 14th, though it is difficult to identify undesignated pipes and the 'ghiterne', which may be found in the company of both *haut* and *bas* instruments. The so-called *alta capella*, a trio or quartet of shawms and sackbuts (sometimes including the S-shaped slide

trumpet), was also a 15th-century development. The chief percussion instrument was the nakers, usually found with trumpets or pipes but occasionally with a *bas* instrument such as the psaltery.

4. MINSTRELS' MUSIC. Little is known of the repertory performed by the minstrels. The various scraps that seem to be dance music (the *estampies* of *F-Pn* fr.844, the pieces of *GB-Lbm* Harl.978 or the *istanpitte* and saltarellos of *Lbm* Add.29987) are so diverse in date, style and probable geographical origin that no coherent picture appears. Nor is it clear what place notated pieces occupied in a musical practice that was predominantly unwritten and to some extent extemporized. Certainly the ESTAMPIE must have been the leading kind of dance, and if it followed the pattern of many later dances it must have progressed by the mid-14th century some way beyond its beginnings as functional dance music; its characteristic structure – progressive repetition with *ouvert* and *clos* endings – seems specially well adapted to duet playing, particularly by similar instruments. The existence of this practice is corroborated by Raimbaut de Vaqeiras, who composed the poem *Kalenda maya* to an *estampie* that he first heard played by two fiddlers from France. From the end of the 14th century the basse danse also entered the minstrels' repertory, though its structure, and the ensemble of two shawms and slide trumpet or trombone frequently associated with it, sharply contrast with what is known of the *estampie*. As well as accomplished dance music, minstrels seem to have played the tenor and contratenor parts of the standard three-voice polyphonic chanson of the 14th century; Johannes de Grocheo (c1300) singled out fiddle players as particularly skilled in this practice. In the generations after Machaut, and perhaps during his lifetime, minstrels are even supposed to have composed such works.

5. THE MINSTREL IN SOCIETY. The chief difficulties in comprehending the social functions of the minstrels stem from the absence of a comprehensive repertory of written music and the failure of medieval writers on music to devote any attention to them. Salmen (1960) singled out four factors contributing to this lack of critical attention: vagueness in systematic sociological foundations; lack of a complete view of European historical sources; failure to look to surviving traditions for parallels with extinct practices; and a lack of comparative studies of non-European cultures in which travelling musicians lived in similar circumstances. The role of the minstrels is deeply involved with the

sociology of medieval musical life, which can only be fully understood from a systematic analysis of non-musical sources and an understanding of the musical characteristics and artistic possibilities of largely illiterate musical cultures. Granted such general considerations, knowledge of minstrelsy is also very uneven according to country or geographical area. In France and Burgundy, noble and royal minstrels held the centre of the stage; in the Low Countries, urban or bourgeois instrumentalists; and in Spain, poet-musicians. Of the position in some countries (e.g. Italy) virtually nothing is known. Although this diverse picture is partly due to real regional differences, it is also the result of unevenness in the historical records and of the varying interests – often motivated by patriotism – of the few modern scholars who have worked on the subject.

While the organization of musical life and therefore the social status of the minstrel differed from one region to another, it is clear that some secular musicians of the later Middle Ages were completely outside the predominant social structure; along with entertainers generally and others (e.g. wandering clerks) they had no fixed abode and owed allegiance to no civil or ecclesiastical authority. In the absence of historical records it is impossible to describe the musical life of the vast rural majority (85–95%) of the medieval population of Europe; it is not known whether musicians providing music for rural populations were called minstrels, what proportion of instrumental to vocal music there was or how it was performed. Moreover, the music of the medieval church has no demonstrable direct relationship to minstrels or minstrelsy, although bishops who were also temporal lords supported minstrels, and minstrels were often essential in urban religious processions and sometimes participated in church services. Necessarily, then, the two main divisions of inquiry are the courts and cities of medieval Europe. In both cases, accounts and other records providing names and numbers of musicians, dates and places are virtually non-existent before about 1200, rare until about 1300, sporadic but significant until 1350 and increasingly common thereafter. Although the pattern of documentary evidence is partly due to the loss of older records, it also reflects social changes in which book- and record-keeping went hand in hand with increasingly regulated and normalized forms of feudal and municipal government; this development had a direct bearing on the social context of music-making.

6. COURT MINSTRELS. The chief sources of information concerning court minstrels are household accounts of the monarchs and noblemen of medieval Europe; these are sometimes quite full, as in the case of the Household and Wardrobe Accounts of Edward I of England (see Rastall, 1964), sometimes vexingly skimpy, as in the case of the French Valois kings (largely because the archives of the Chambre des Comptes at Paris were destroyed in 1737). In addition there sometimes exist

*2. Urban procession accompanied by minstrels playing harps, lutes, shawms and trumpet; miniature from a copy of the Romance of Alexander, English, c1380 (F-Pn fr.22547, f.245v)*

ordinances specifying the size of the household and its administrative subdivisions, along with the duties and perquisites of the retinue. The accounts often furnish names, dates, places and precise sums of money given as regular wages, gifts, liveries or extraordinary expenses, and they sometimes specify the instruments played by a minstrel – though it is doubtful whether such designations needed, or were intended, to be precise – but they do not usually provide direct evidence for the size or composition of ensembles or the nature of the repertory.

In the earlier part of the period under consideration, a noble household – though it might range from 30 or 40 to several hundred – did not always include minstrels on the payroll. For example, while Robert, Count of Artois (1250–1302), appears to have had up to half a dozen minstrels in his regular employ, none are found in the accounts of his daughter and successor, Mahaut (1302–29). Philip VI of France (1328–50), in a household of at least 140, had only two minstrels, according to an ordinance of 1355; but 13 years later his son John, Duke of Normandy, employed at least 12 instrumentalists. In particular it is not at all clear that there was a general increase through the 14th century in the numbers of minstrels employed. To find no minstrels on regular wages in a sizable household is unusual, but the number employed seems to have borne little relationship to the size of the household as a whole. The development of French secular polyphony during the 14th century may well have been influenced by the assiduous patronage of minstrels by John the Good of France (1350–64) and his sons, Charles V (1364–80) and the Dukes of Berry, Burgundy and Anjou.

It is not certain that only minstrels designated as such could provide court music on a regular basis. A number of court posts are frequently cited in close proximity to that of minstrel in the records, for example fools, heralds, waits, waiters, bodyguards, justicers or waferers, who were variously responsible for entertainment, protocol, procurement of prostitutes and guarding the gates and doors and who on occasion may also have provided music. The records also testify to a constant traffic of minstrels from other courts, as well as common minstrels with no designated status. Normally, court minstrels did not receive wages significantly higher than those of other lesser personnel of the household, nor did they enjoy social privileges; they were not badly paid and they received many occasional and extraordinary gifts. Players of the *trompe* or *trompette* were distinguished from other minstrels and were paid higher wages at some courts.

It has often been stated that minstrels frequently achieved a relationship of special intimacy and trust with their noble employers. This undoubtedly happened at times, particularly with harpers and other chamber musicians, but the fact that minstrels were often entrusted with messages and more devious political missions such as espionage may only reflect their mobility as an occupational group. In the 14th century particularly, minstrels often moved from court to court, were sometimes lent by their employers and seem often to have travelled independently of their masters. Two sorts of occasion – noble weddings, and ceremonies of knighthood which frequently took place at Pentecost – attracted vast assemblies of minstrels; in a few instances several hundred gathered, and the payroll of one such ceremony, at Westminster in 1306, lists over 150 names.

Minstrels sometimes remained associated with a court for many years, often surviving their original employer to serve his successor. There are no women on the rosters of court musicians, though they were sometimes remunerated as the wives of regularly employed minstrels. Present knowledge of the records permits no general conclusions as to the minstrel's status in the occupational or class structures of the later Middle Ages. But it is extremely rare for the term 'magister' (i.e. the holder of a university degree) to be applied to a minstrel and the term 'clerk' is rarer still. Nor are there cases of the same person exercising the functions of minstrel and chapel clerk (or chapel singer) either simultaneously or at different times and places.

7. MINSTREL SCHOOLS. During the 14th century and the early 15th, annual assemblies of minstrels took place, chiefly in the Low Countries and at Beauvais, in the week before Laetare Sunday in Lent. They seem to have involved both city and court minstrels, some of whom came from as far away as Aragon and Navarre. The earliest known gathering of this sort was in 1318 at Bruges (though there may have been one at Ieper in 1313) and the last was in 1447 at Damme. They were usually called 'escoles' or 'scoelen' – i.e. schools in the sense of a large group – but there is evidence from the second half of the 14th century that there were also schools in the more usual modern sense, in which musical instruction was offered (for example at Paris). Little is known of the duration of the *escoles*, the numbers of musicians present or the purposes for which they met, though a few records state that they learnt new songs and purchased instruments. There may have been several concurrent regional meetings in a single year. Such gatherings can be regarded as contributing to a supra-regional musical culture and to the musical predominance of the Low Countries as early as the 14th century.

8. CONCLUSION. There is no distinct line of demarcation between an era of minstrels and minstrelsy and a subsequent one, unless it is that provided by the appearance of an extensive body of written instrumental music composed on polyphonic choral models and by the elevation of the status of the minstrel to a *musico*. This took place during a lengthy period from about 1500 to about 1650 or even later. Another principal factor in the disappearance of the minstrel may have been the increasing synthesis of sacred and secular and vocal and instrumental styles from the second half of the 15th century onwards.

*See also* GUILDS.

BIBLIOGRAPHY

E. vander Straeten: *Les ménestrels aux Pays-Bas du XIIIe au XVIIIe siècles* (Brussels, 1878/R1969) [repr. of extracts from *La musique aux Pays-Bas avant le XIXe siècle*]

E. K. Chambers: *The Medieval Stage* (Oxford, 1903)

E. Faral: *Les jongleurs en France au moyen âge* (Paris, 1910/R1964)

J. Wolf: 'Die Tänze des Mittelalters: eine Untersuchung des Wesens der ältesten Instrumentalmusik', *AMw*, i (1918–19), 10–42

L. Schrade: *Die handschriftliche Überlieferung der ältesten Instrumentalmusik* (Lahr, nr. Strasbourg, 1931/R1968)

R. Morgan jr: 'Old French *jogleor* and Kindred Terms', *Romance Philology*, vii (1953–4), 279–325

E. Bowles: ' "Haut" and "Bas": the Grouping of Musical Instruments in the Middle Ages', *MD*, viii (1954), 115

R. Menéndez Pidal: *Poesia juglaresca y origenes de las literaturas romanicas* (Madrid, rev. 6/1957)

W. Salmen: *Der fahrende Musiker im europäischen Mittelalter* (Kassel, 1960)

E. Bowles: 'Musical Instruments in Civic Processions during the Middle Ages', *AcM*, xxxiii (1961), 147

U. Günther: 'Die Musiker des Herzogs von Berry', *MD*, xvii (1963), 79

R. Rastall: 'The Minstrels in the English Royal Households, 25 Edward I – 1 Henry VIII: an Inventory', *RMARC*, iv (1964), 1–41

F. Idoate: *Rincones de la historia de Navarra*, iii (Pamplona, 1966)

L. M. Wright: 'Misconceptions concerning the Troubadours, Trouvères and Minstrels', *ML*, xlviii (1967), 35

K. Polk: *Flemish Wind Bands in the Late Middle Ages: a Study in Improvisatory Performance Practices* (diss., U. of California, Berkeley, 1968)

——: 'Wind Bands of Medieval Flemish Cities', *BWQ*, i (1968), 96

R. Rastall: *Secular Musicians in Late Medieval England* (diss., U. of Manchester, 1968)

K. Polk: 'Municipal Music in Flanders in the Late Middle Ages', *BWQ*, ii (1969), 1

J. Spruit: *Van vedelaars, trommers en pijpers* (Utrecht, 1969)

C. Wright: *Music at the Court of Burgundy, 1364–1419* (diss., Harvard U., 1972)

R. Rastall: 'Some English Consort-groupings of the Late Middle Ages', *ML*, lv (1974), 179

LAWRENCE GUSHEE

**Minstrelsy, American.** A type of 19th-century popular entertainment that featured impersonation of the Negro by white performers in song, dance and speech. Minstrelsy took the theatrical productions of the Englishman Charles Mathews as one point of departure. Negro music and dialect greatly attracted Mathews during his visit to the USA in 1822 and he incorporated these elements in his skits and sketches, stump speeches and songs. Before Mathews, Charles Dibdin had used Negro elements in his musical extravaganzas, which began in 1768 and were still popular well into the first decade of the 19th century. Southern plantation and frontier songs, Negro tunes patterned on English musical models, English plays and operas with Negro subjects and plots, and British dance types and tunes constituted other sources for early minstrelsy.

By the end of the 1820s there evolved, from the convergence of the various lines of interest in the Negro, an indigenous and novel American, or blackface, minstrelsy. The performances of George Washington Dixon and of Thomas Dartmouth ('Daddy' or 'Jim Crow') Rice represented the incipient stages of the form. The performer blackened his face with burnt cork and wore costumes that represented, to the white audience, the typical Negro: the uncouth, naive, devil-may-care Southern plantation slave (Jim Crow) in his tattered clothing, or the ludicrous Broadway dandy (Zip Coon or Dandy Jim) complete with blue coat and tails. These

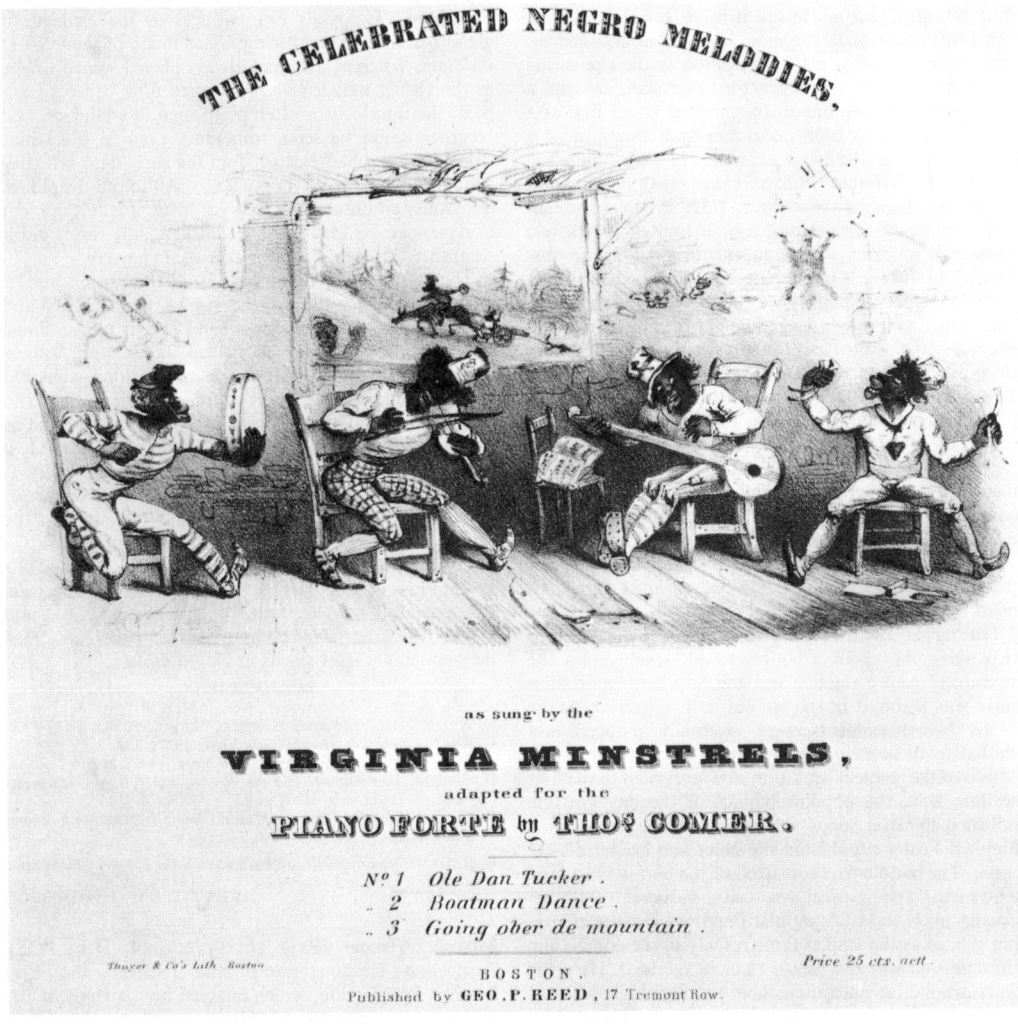

*The Virginia Minstrels: title-page of a song collection published in 1843*

two exaggerated stereotypes persisted in minstrelsy for the next several decades. Rice developed the minstrel show, or 'Ethiopian opera', expanding the roles played by the Negro dialect plantation songs, virtuoso dancing, banjo and fiddle music and crude humour, and providing the whole with a greater degree of organization. Nevertheless its place was still primarily that of an entr'acte in the theatre or in the circus ring.

The classic age of blackface minstrelsy ($c$1840–70) drew appreciably closer by the late 1830s when a modicum of dramatic continuity was introduced and as performers joined together to form duos (most frequently a banjoist and a dancer), trios and finally quartets. The instruments used were the banjo, the tambourine, the violin, bone castanets and sometimes the accordion, all except the last-named associated with the Southern plantation Negro. At least one musician in the group doubled as a dancer. The Virginia Minstrels (see illustration) presented the first show of this new type, performing initially with a circus at the Bowery Amphitheatre in New York on 6 February 1843 and soon afterwards in solo appearances. The group consisted of Daniel Decatur Emmett, who played the violin, Billy Whitlock (banjo), Frank Brower (bones) and Dick Pelham (tambourine). Emmett, who had established his reputation as a banjo player and singer in the circus ring and who was a versatile, practical musician, enjoyed a long and productive life on the minstrel stage, first as a performer, then as both performer and composer of a large number of the finest examples of classic minstrel music. The Virginia Minstrels met with spectacular success in cities of the eastern USA in the spring of 1843 and in concerts during a brief tour of the British Isles that summer. Although the original group disbanded in July 1843, Emmett re-established it on his return to the USA, replacing Pelham, who had chosen to remain permanently in England. The Virginia Minstrels provided the prototype for the instrumentation and stage action of the many troupes that were formed in the 1840s. They arranged themselves in a semicircle with bones and tambourine at either end as focusses of attention. One of these players would serve as master of ceremonies, a role later assumed by an interlocutor at the centre of the band. While minstrelsy still retained its connections with the theatre and circus as an entr'acte, those associations became increasingly attenuated as the show gained in scope and content; more and more it stood by itself as a fully developed form of entertainment.

During the 1840s the minstrel show was divided into two parts; the opening concentrated largely upon the Broadway Negro dandy, and the Southern plantation slave was featured in the second half. However by the 1850s Negro elements were gradually reduced and shifted to the concluding part of a tripartite structure. Music of the 'genteel' tradition now prevailed in the first section; here, the popular ballads of the day and the polished minstrel songs written by such composers as Stephen Foster supplanted the older and cruder dialect tunes. The middle part consisted of the olio, a potpourri of dancing and musical virtuosity, parodies of Italian operas, plays and such popular imported European singing groups as the Rainer family. Only in the concluding third section was the Negro element retained. Here the walk-around, at once the conclusion and high point of the show, took on primary importance. This was an ensemble finale in which members of the troupe participated in various combinations in song, instrumental and choral music and dance. Although examples of the walk-around performed by a solo dancer exist from the late 1840s, the ensemble finale dates from only around 1858. *Dixie*, composed by Emmett in 1859 for the Bryant Minstrels, is the best-known example of this genre, although it soon lost its original function. Emmett, whose finales enjoyed an enormous popularity, described his walk-arounds as an attempt to imitate 'the habits and crude ideas of the slaves of the South' whose 'knowledge of the world at large was very limited'.

The inclusion of genteel-tradition music and of the olio began a movement away from the primitive quality of early minstrelsy towards a more sophisticated and standardized variety show. From 1857 to 1866 the Bryant Minstrels, led by Dan Bryant, slowed this trend with their productions of a rejuvenated minstrel show, full of the vitality so characteristic of the period of the 1840s. The Bryants' performances were unqualified financial successes even during the Civil War (1861–5), but this older classic type of minstrelsy fell from fashion by 1870 and was replaced by a variety show of increasing proportions. Leavitt's Gigantean Minstrels and Cleveland's Colossals bear witness to the element of gigantism that so greatly impressed much of the USA at the time. Whereas men had always played wench's roles in the classic minstrel show, women now began to appear; the interlocutor often performed in whiteface, and Negroes could be seen, sometimes even in blackface. (Black troupes had existed from the early days but they were not considered important.) Although blackface minstrelsy continued as a popular form of entertainment in American life into the 20th century, only rarely did it recapture the vigour and quality of its heyday.

The animated rhythmic element of the banjo tunes or jigs composed for the minstrel shows between 1840 and 1890 greatly influenced American popular music. Some of the jigs rely heavily on British dance types; others illustrate irregular rhythmic accentuations achieved through phrasing, rests, textures, ornamentation and metrical shifts. These patterns of syncopation served as rhythmic models for ragtime, blues and early jazz. Most tunes have a relatively narrow compass and there is frequent reiteration of brief melodic segments. Modality, especially pentatonicism, prevails in the earlier tunes, evidently influenced by folk music.

From 1840 to 1870, when minstrelsy was at its height, composers borrowed freely from British and European folk models, theatre and plantation music, and a body of earlier popular and minstrel tunes, to which they added cheerful words in Negro dialect.

BIBLIOGRAPHY

*Minstrel Songs: Old and New* (Boston, 1882, 6/1919)

C. Wittke: *Tambo and Bones* (Durham, North Carolina, 1930)

C. Rourke: *American Humor* (New York, 1931), 78ff

——: *Roots of American Culture* (New York, 1942), 262ff

H. Nathan: *Dan Emmett and the Rise of Early Negro Minstrelsy* (Norman, Oklahoma, 1962)

R. C. Toll: *Blacking Up: the Minstrel Show in Nineteenth-century America* (New York, 1974)

Important collections of documents are at *US-Cn*, *CA*, *Wc* and the State Library of Ohio in Columbus.

CLAYTON W. HENDERSON

**Minton, Yvonne (Fay)** (*b* Sydney, 4 Dec 1938). Australian mezzo-soprano. She received the Elsa Strahlia Scholarship, which enabled her to study at the Sydney Conservatory. After winning the 1960 Canberra opera aria competition she moved to Europe, and in 1961 she won a Kathleen Ferrier Prize.

Minton began a concert career in England before making her first operatic appearances in London, notably as Britten's Lucretia (City Literary Institute, January 1964), as Maggie Dempster in the 1964 première of Nicholas Maw's *One Man Show*, and in the title role of *Rinaldo* with the Handel Opera Society in 1965. In 1965 she joined the Royal Opera, her first important role being Marina (*Boris Godunov*) that December; her many Covent Garden parts have included Ascanio (*Benvenuto Cellini*), Gluck's Orpheus, Dorabella, Cherubino, Debussy's Geneviève, Marfa (*Khovanshchina*), a noble Sextus (*La clemenza di Tito*), Waltraute and the Composer, in addition to Thea in the first performances of Tippett's *The Knot Garden* (1970). She has regularly visited the Cologne Opera since her first Sextus there in September 1969; as Octavian, one of her most praised roles (later recorded under Solti), she made her débuts at Chicago (September 1970), the Metropolitan (March 1973) and the Paris Opéra (January 1976). Her first Bayreuth appearance was as Brangäne in 1974; she sang Waltraute and Fricka in Chéreau's 1976 production of the *Ring*. Her voice is an even, supple instrument, used with warmth, smoothness and vivid intelligence, and enhanced by her striking appearance; she is a dignified and commanding actress. In concert she embraces a wide repertory, much of which she has recorded, including works by Bach, Berlioz, Elgar and Mahler, Schoenberg's *Gurrelieder*, Boulez's *Le marteau sans maître* and Maw's *Nocturne*. She was made CBE in 1980.

ALAN BLYTH

**Minuet** (Fr. *menuet*; Ger. *Menuett*; It. *minuetto*; Sp. *minuete, minué*). A French dance in a moderate or slow triple metre, the most popular social dance in aristocratic society from the mid-17th century to the late 18th. It appeared as a movement in some Baroque suites and became one of the standard movements of late 18th-century multi-movement forms like the sonata, the string quartet, and the symphony, where it was usually paired with a TRIO (*see also* SCHERZO).

1. The dance. 2. Minuets in Baroque instrumental music. 3. Classical and neo-classical minuets.

1. THE DANCE. The origin of the minuet is unknown, but it seems to have appeared in the court of Louis XIV during the 1660s. Praetorius (*Terpsichore*, 1612) is now thought to have erred in claiming it to be a descendant of the *branle de Poitou*, a claim that was nonetheless repeated over a century later by Pierre Rameau (*Le maître à danser*, 1725), with the addition of the plausible detail that Pierre Beauchamp, Louis XIV's dancing-master, had effected the transformation. There is virtually no point of resemblance between the two dances; some of the minuets included in the Philidor Collection consist of the three-bar phrases characteristic of the BRANLE, however, so the theory cannot be entirely discounted. The name 'menuet' may have derived from the French 'menu' (slender, small), referring to the extremely small steps of the dance, or from the *branle à mener* or *amener*, which, like the *branle de Poitou*, were popular group dances in early 17th-century France.

As an aristocratic social dance the minuet was dignified, graceful, relaxed and unaffected, unlike some modern re-creations in which exaggerated postures are used. The attention of both dancers and spectators was directed to the elegant and seemingly effortless perform-

*1. Minuet at a formal court ball: engraving from Pierre Rameau's 'Le maître à danser' (1725); for an illustration of the 17th-century minuet, see* DANCE, *fig.11*

ance of complex step patterns, and, secondarily, to the movement of the dancers in particular floor patterns. In France the minuet was performed in a moderately slow tempo (which placed greater emphasis on the execution of individual steps than, for example, in the related but more rapid PASSEPIED) and it was universally recognized as the most elegant of social dances. There is some evidence that Italians danced the minuet at a faster tempo (Brossard, *Dictionaire de Musique*, 1703, 'Minuetto': 'On devroit à l'imitation des Italiens se servir du signe 3/8 ou 6/8 pour en marquer le mouvement, qui est toujours gay et fort vite'). Specific information on the actual steps and movements is not extant from before 1700, when the publication of the Beauchamp–Feuillet system of dance notation (*see* BEAUCHAMP, PIERRE, and FEUILLET, RAOUL-AUGER) made it possible to record dance steps in their proper relationship to the accompanying music. At least 23 early 18th-century choreographies survive, showing floor patterns as well as steps and music, and two treatises by Pierre Rameau (Paris, 1725) supply additional information on practices at the French court. According to Rameau, each formal ball conformed to a pre-arranged ritual establishing the seating arrangement in the salon and indicating when, how and by whom each dance would be performed. Ordinarily the minuet was danced by one couple at a time while the rest of the company watched and appraised their accomplishments (see fig.1). After making honours to the Présence (the king or someone else designated to preside for the evening) and to each other, the dancers moved through a series of prescribed step patterns to diagonally opposite sides of a rectangular area. From there they moved, again in the typical minuet step patterns, along an imaginary letter Z (see fig.2) so that they passed each other in the middle and finished the figure in opposite positions (before 1700 the figure of the floor pattern was a letter S, the sign for the

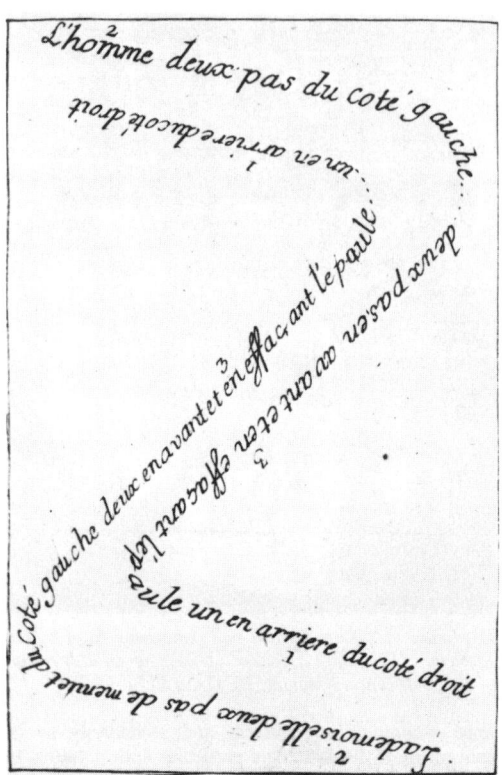

*2. 'Z' pattern in the minuet, showing the path travelled by the dancers, with the verbal instructions for the steps to use, from Pierre Rameau's 'Le maître à danser' (1725)*

Sun King, Louis XIV). After several Z figurations, the dancers presented their right hands to each other in the middle of the rectangle, and turned a full circle before retreating to diagonally opposite corners. Then they advanced again for a similar presentation of left hands, followed by more letter Z figurations. The climax of the dance was the presentation of both hands, during which the dancers turned several circles before retreating together to make honours to each other and to the Présence (see fig.3).

The basic step pattern of the minuet consisted of four small steps taken to six crotchets (two bars in 3/4 or 3/8), beginning always on the right foot. A number of different step patterns were used, all but a few ornamental ones made up of combinations of *demi-coupés* (rises from previous bends during the transfer of weight from foot to foot), *demi-jettés* (small leaps from one foot to the other) and *pas marchés* (plain steps on to the ball of the foot), all steps that end with the dancer's weight on the ball of the foot. Most step patterns can be taken in any direction, and all four-step complexes are tiny, covering a distance of about a metre, or perhaps 1·5 metres for tall dancers. Two of the most popular patterns were the *pas de menuet à deux mouvements*, consisting of two *demi-coupés* and two *pas marchés* with the steps falling on the first, third, fourth and fifth crotchets of a two-bar unit (see Table 1) and the *pas de menuet à trois mouvements*. The latter, more difficult to execute, consists of two *demi-coupés*, a *pas marché* and either another *demi-coupé* or a *demi-jetté*, with steps falling on the first,

third, fourth and sixth crotchets of a unit. Gentle accents in the music accompanying the dance are always implied by the *demi-coupé* and the *demi-jetté*. Thus, musicians accompanying dancers or playing stylized minuets should realize that the basic unit of the dance is two bars long (not one or four), and that while the dancers' movements always imply an accent on the first beat of a unit, strong secondary accents would not necessarily fall on the second downbeat. Further, the letter Z floor design ordinarily took six step patterns to execute, thus best fitting a musical strain 12 bars long. Although many of the minuets in Lully's ballets, for example, have such strains, most minuets are made of strains eight or 16 bars long, suggesting that some tension may have arisen from the lack of coincidence between music and dance, presumably resolved by the end of the 100 to 120 bars usually required for a complete minuet performance.

One reason for the minuet's remarkable longevity as a social dance may have been the considerable variety of steps it could absorb into the basic pattern. The 'minuet hop' or *contretemps*, the *balancé*, the *tems de courante* and the *fleuret* were among the most common interpolated steps in France (see treatises by Rameau and Feuillet). GOTTFRIED TAUBERT, writing in 1717, described four step patterns for the minuet, in different relationships to music and in eight different rhythmic-

TABLE 1: Two common minuet patterns

| | | ♩ | ♩ | ♩ | ♩ | ♩ | ♩ |
|---|---|---|---|---|---|---|---|
| ¾ | | 1 | 2 | 3 | 4 | 5 | 6 |
| pas de minuet à deux mouvements | v | ∧ | v | ∧ | ǀ | ǀ | |
| | | R | | L | | R | L |
| pas de minuet à trois mouvements | v | ∧ | v | ∧ | ǀ | v | j |
| | | R | | L | | R | | L |

v = plié [bend knee(s)];      R = right foot   L = left foot
j = demi-jetté [small leap on to ball of foot];
∧ = élevé [rise to straightened knee(s) on ball of foot];
v∧ = demi-coupé [bend and rise];
ǀ = pas marché [step on ball of foot]

metrical configurations. Dufort, writing in Italian in 1728, mentioned three possible step patterns with other relationships to the accompanying music. In 1767 C. J. von Felsenstein described a pattern with accents on the first, fourth, fifth and sixth beats (see Table 1). The French minuet apparently formed a point of departure for varied practices in different countries and social settings. Minuet steps were adopted into the CONTREDANSE, for example, creating a set of dances for two or four couples using repetitive step patterns and a variety of floor designs. Later in the 18th century steps from other triple-metre dances like the waltz and the ländler were introduced into the minuet, resulting in a juxtaposition of styles. In Spain and Portugal, where the minuet was a popular court dance, native dance styles infiltrated, as in the 'minuet afandangado' (see Minguet e Yrol and Hatchette).

2. MINUETS IN BAROQUE INSTRUMENTAL MUSIC. Early examples of minuets apparently intended to accompany

dancing survive in the Kassel Manuscript (c1660, ed. J. Ecorcheville, *Vingt suites d'orchestre*, Paris, 1906/R1970) and in the Philidor Collection. The two minuets in the former source both consist of two unrelated strains, each eight bars long; those in the Philidor Collection consist of phrases three bars long, resembling the characteristic phrases of the *branle à mener* and suggesting an elegant cross-rhythm of music and dance resolved at the end of the strain. Many printed and manuscript collections of music to accompany dancing remain unedited (particularly rich holdings exist in France and England), and study of these sources may shed light on the early development of the minuet as a musical form. The earliest significant corpus of minuets comes from the theatrical works of Lully: 92 titled minuets appear in his ballets and operas from 1664 to 1687, and several of his overtures include minuet movements (e.g. *Armide*), presumably not intended to accompany the dance. The 'Menuet pour les faunes et les dryades' from *Les amants magnifiques* (*Oeuvres complètes*, ix/3, p.200) is cast in two strains, each 12 bars long and, therefore, each perfectly tailored to accompany the execution of one Z floor pattern. Not all Lully's minuets conform so strictly to the phrases of the dance, however; the fifth entrée of his *Ballet des nations* (*Oeuvres complètes*, ix/3, p.142, 'Les français'), including two instrumental minuets separated by a vocal reprise of the first, consists of two-, four- and ten-bar phrases, thus creating some tension between music and dance. Significantly, the entire entrée is 124 bars long when the indicated repeats are taken, almost exactly the prescribed length for a complete minuet performance. Ex.1, from the 'Menuet des Thébains' (*Entr'acte*

Ex.1 Lully: *Entr'acte d'Oedipe* (1664), Menuet des Thébains

*d'Oedipe*, 1664), shows a five-bar minuet strain, which, though unorthodox, would not necessarily preclude social dancing, since with the repeat an even number of bars would result. It should be remembered that theatrical dancing in general was more elaborate and virtuoso than contemporary social dancing, permitting and even encouraging considerable freedom in the accompanying musical structures.

Like most 17th-century dances, the minuet was included in French keyboard and ensemble suites, usually (along with other still-popular dances like the bourrée and gavotte) appearing after the sarabande, and many composers included minuets among their independent keyboard pieces (e.g. Chambonnières, Lebègue, Louis Marchand, and the minuets in Bach's Anna Magdalena notebook). In addition, many minuets were included in manuscript collections of music for guitar and lute (most of them still unedited), and minuet-like movements (usually without the dance title), occurred in collections of organ music (e.g. by Guillaume-Gabriel Nivers, Gilles Jullien and Nicolas de Grigny) and were incorporated into songs (*see* BRUNETTE). Usually, the minuet received a rather straightforward treatment, with its characteristic clarity of rhythm and phrase preserved. Even the occasional DOUBLE of a minuet was likely to be free from the complex texture and rhythmic ambiguities that otherwise fascinated instrumental composers of the French Baroque period, probably because the minuet was still a familiar social dance. Some composers experi-

(a)

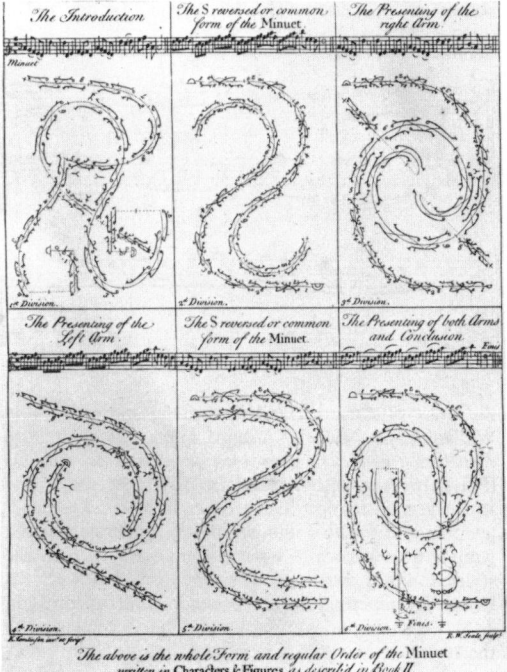

(b)

3. Engravings from Tomlinson's 'The Art of Dancing' (1735) showing (a) presentation of the right hand, and (b) the 'whole form and regular order of the minuet'

mented with irregular phrase structure: Louis Marchand's second minuet in the collection *Pièces de clavecin* (Paris, 1702) consists of a ten-bar strain divided into five-bar phrases: at least one of Louis Couperin's minuets retains the three-bar phrase structure of the minuets in the Philidor Collection.

The minuet was a popular social dance in 17th-century England, where it also appeared in stylized forms (see the keyboard pieces in *The Second Part of Musick's Hand-maid*, London, 1689) and in music for the theatre. Purcell set minuets more often than any other dance in his stage works and incidental music, including movements marked 'minuet' or 'tempo di minuetto' in the overtures to *The Double Marriage* (*c*1682), *The Old Bachelor* (1693) and *Bonduca, or The British Heroine* (1695); his minuets, like those of his French contemporaries, are in binary form, usually consisting of no more than two eight-bar strains. German composers of the Louis XIV era, like Georg Muffat, Pachelbel and J. C. F. Fischer, also wrote minuets in the French style, adding more contrapuntal and motivic interest than the French while retaining the clear phrasing and unambiguous rhythms of the original dance.

As with other Baroque dance forms like the allemande, courante and gigue, Italian minuet style differed from the mainstream of European taste in a preference for faster tempos, implied by the prevalent use of 3/8 or 6/8 as the ordinary time signature. Melodic movement in the Italian minuet was carried over a longer phrase than in the French dance (usually eight bars rather than two or four), and more use was made of both melodic and harmonic sequence to sustain a clear sense of direction. Examples of the Italian-style minuet may be found in some of the opera overtures of Alessandro Scarlatti and Handel (ex.2), in some of Handel's keyboard suites, and in

Ex.2 Handel: *Rodelinda* (1725), menuet from the overture

the music of some of Handel's contemporaries, notably William Boyce. Michel L'Affilard, in his valuable treatise *Principes très-faciles pour bien apprendre la musique* (Paris, 1694), gave two examples of minuet songs, one with the mensuration 3, the other in 6/8 and a faster tempo, indicating that minuets in both moderate and fast tempos were known to French composers; in fact, the stylized dance music of French composers such as François Couperin, Rameau, Boismortier, Hotteterre and J.-M. Leclair includes examples of minuets influenced by the Italian style within a repertory that generally caters more for French taste. Similarly, Telemann and Bach wrote minuets of both kinds, Bach restricting himself to the time signature 3/4, regardless of tempo. His minuets occur in the keyboard partitas and suites, in chamber music for solo and accompanied violin, cello and flute, in

three of the four orchestral suites, and in the First Brandenburg Concerto. This last minuet has been described as being in the form of a RONDEAU (ii), because it forms a sort of ritornello to three successive sections, a trio in the relative minor, a lively POLACCA, and a second, duple-metre trio in the tonic. Many dancers who have practised Pierre Rameau's minuet directions insist that Bach's minuets are extremely well suited to dance accompaniment, both in their aptness of phrase structure and tempo and in their feelings of elegant ease, suggesting that Bach had a practical knowledge of both the dance movements themselves and the requirements of good dance accompaniment.

3. CLASSICAL AND NEO-CLASSICAL MINUETS. Minuets remained among the most popular social dances of aristocratic Europe throughout the 18th century, exerting a continuing influence on stylized dance music. The restrained yet complex elegance of the dance itself appealed to the requirements of the developing aesthetic of the Rococo period, and the relative simplicity of its phrases and harmonic movement made it an admirable vehicle for experiments with large structures based on contrasting harmonic and tonal plateaux, while permitting the introduction of other triple-metre styles and learned contrapuntal devices. By the mid-18th century, in fact, the minuet was the only important Baroque dance surviving as a popular form, and thus it seems only logical that it should have been the dance usually included in the sonata, the string quartet and the symphony, the large multi-movement forms then becoming fashionable.

The minuet was probably first included in symphonies by Italian composers in the early 18th century, as movements labelled 'tempo di minuetto' often closed opera overtures which, like that to Domenico Scarlatti's *Narciso*, for example, were sometimes later published independently as 'sinfonias' (London, 1720). Scarlatti's minuet movement, typical of its time and in the binary form typical of late Baroque dance movements, consists of two eight-bar strains based on a single rhythmic motif; many of Sammartini's symphonies end with similar minuet movements, as do the symphonies of C. F. Abel, Johann Stamitz, M. G. Monn, and some of the early keyboard sonatas of Haydn.

Rather different minuet finales became fairly frequent in the symphonies, concertos and sonatas of English-influenced composers during the third quarter of the 18th century. These movements, generally headed with the rubric 'tempo di minuetto' or the hybrid Italian–German word 'menuetto', often applied some of the principles of so-called SONATA FORM to a movement having the characteristic metre, tempo and phrasing of the minuet. The third movement of Thomas Arne's Symphony no.3 in E♭ (1767, ed. in Musica da Camera, iii, London, 1973), for example, marked 'tempo di minuetto', has an opening section presenting two distinct themes in contrasting keys; after repetition of that section, a brief development combines motivic transformation of the opening theme with a series of rapid modulations, followed by a full recapitulation of the opening without the change of key. J. C. Bach's Sinfonia concertante in E♭ (*c*1775, ed. J. A. White, *The Concerted Symphonies*, Tallahassee, 1963) includes a slightly more complex minuet finale: the sonata-like minuet section (the first modulation to the dominant occurs after the double bar, followed by intense motivic development of the first section's theme, a long dominant pedal, and a full recapitulation) is paired with a short trio in ternary form, and then repeated da capo. Later and perhaps clearer examples of sonata principles applied to minuet movements (other than finales) can be found in the works of both Mozart (e.g. K387, which lacks motivic development but has a sharply defined contrast of tonality and theme in the 'exposition', and K464) and Haydn (piano sonatas HXVI:25 in Eb, HXVI:35 in C). Minuet finales, whether or not they use formal procedures derived from the sonata, occur fairly often in Haydn's piano sonatas and piano trios and in several of Mozart's concertos (e.g. K271 and K482 for piano, K190/186E for two violins, K191/186e for bassoon and K313/285c for flute).

Other formal schemes used for such movements included the rondeau-like alternations of one minuet with several trios seen in the minuet movement of Bach's First Brandenburg Concerto, commonly used in divertimentos and serenades (e.g. Mozart's Serenade in D K185/167a, the second minuet, and Haydn's piano sonatas HXVI:22 in E and HXVI:29 in F), variations of a binary minuet theme (Haydn's piano sonatas HXVI:30 in A and HXVI:33 in D), and, most familiarly, the common stereotype of a minuet paired with a single trio contrasting in key, thematic material, scoring and general mood. The last form, which came to be the standard third of four movements in symphonies and string quartets written after about 1770, typically consisted of a ternary minuet section (about 24 bars long without repeats) and a shorter ternary trio, the minuet being repeated da capo (see TERNARY FORM). About midcentury the trio was normally in a closely related key, usually either the tonic minor or the relative minor of the minuet, but in many of Haydn's later string quartets the tonal contrast was made considerably more striking: in op.77 no.2, for example, the minuet is in F major, the trio in Db. Sometimes the characteristically simple and elegant style of the minuet was infused with elements from more 'serious' kinds of music, often with quite dramatic effects. The minuet of Haydn's piano sonata HXVI:26 in A, for example, is cast in the typical minuet and trio form, but, as indicated by its heading 'menuet al rovescio', the second half of each section is an exact retrograde of the first. Haydn's Symphony no.44 ('Trauer') and String Quartet op.76 no.2 both include minuet and trio movements which employ strict canon and irregular phrases to lend an unaccustomed seriousness to the form, as does the use of both canon and double counterpoint in the minuet of Mozart's Symphony no.40 (K550).

All the forms applied to minuet movements in Classical symphonies and chamber works probably derived from the actual practice of dance accompaniment. Most surviving functional minuets are quite short, often no more than 16 or 32 bars, and indeed the instructions for composing minuets given by such theorists as Brossard (1703), J.-J. Rousseau (1768) and Honoré Compan (1787) specified that the individual strains of a minuet ought to be only eight or 16 bars long, divided into phrases of two or four bars. Contemporary descriptions of the dance, however, indicate that a complete performance would have taken at least 100 bars. Thus musicians apparently improvised embellishments to the successive repetitions of strains, creating variation forms, or performed several contrasting minuets in succession. The minuet and trio stereotype seems

to have been the most common such practice to be transferred to stylized music by composers who, for the most part, had contributed many minuets for ballroom use at various times in their careers. As an aristocratic dance, the minuet continued throughout the 18th century to hold its place in opera and ballet as well as in the ballroom and concert hall, especially in France, and several theatrical minuet choreographies have survived. Grétry included a minuet in his Céphale et Procris (1773), as did Gluck in the Paris version of his Orphée (1774), Sacchini in his opera Chimène ou Le Cid (1783) and Salieri in his Tarare (1787). Probably the most famous appearance of the minuet on stage, however, was in Mozart's Don Giovanni (1787), where, in the finale of Act 1, Don Ottavio and Donna Anna dance a minuet while Leporello and Masetto perform the comparatively plebeian German dance and Don Giovanni and Zerlina the middle-class contredanse, a scene in which the dances serve as labels of social standing and cultural values.

18th-century theorists such as J. P. Kirnberger (Der allezeit fertige Polonoisen- und Menuettenkomponist, Berlin, 1757) used the minuet as an elementary composition exercise, and the process was even reduced to methods used in games of chance such as the throwing of dice: the clear implication is that the melodic and harmonic patterns of the standard eight-bar minuet could be so standardized that arbitrary arrangements of them could be made without incongruity (see Ratner, 1970), despite the sophistication that had been brought to the form by some composers. Interestingly enough, minuet movements seldom appeared in Italian symphonies and concertos after the mid-18th century, and, in fact, the standard minuet and trio movement was increasingly often replaced by a similarly structured movement called 'scherzo' (It.: 'joke'). Haydn was apparently the first to substitute movements with this heading for the minuets in his string quartets op.33 (the set is sometimes called 'Gli scherzi'). It is not clear exactly why Haydn labelled the triple-metre movements thus in op.33, however, for while at least one such movement, the scherzo of no.5, does include several humorous elements such as unpredictable phrasing, some of the other movements are quite serious. Beethoven seems to have preferred the title 'scherzo' to 'minuet' in most of his works, using it to indicate a more vigorous, robust movement than that implied by the minuet's associations with elegant court pastimes. He used the minuet, however, in a number of his piano sonatas, including op.2 no.1, op.10 no.3 and op.49 no.2, in the String Quartets op.18 nos.4 and 5, in the Septet op.20, and in Symphonies nos.1 and 8. Twice, in the Violin Sonata in G op.30 no.3 and the Piano Sonata op.31 no.3, a movement entitled 'tempo di minuetto' actually takes the place of the slow movement.

19th-century composers were less interested in the minuet, an attitude which may have been influenced by political as well as musical considerations; nonetheless, Schubert (some of his piano works) and Brahms (Serenade op.11, 1857–8) included minuets in a number of their works, and Bizet used the form in his music for L'arlésienne (1872) and in the Symphony in C (1860–68). Early 20th-century neo-classicism led to a revival of interest in the minuet, evidenced by its appearance in Fauré's Masques et bergamasques (1919), Debussy's Suite bergamasque (c1890), Jean Françaix's Musique de cour (1937), Bartók's Nine Little Pieces (1926) and the second book of Mikrokosmos, Schoenberg's Serenade op.24 (1920–23) and Suite for piano op.25 (1921–3) and Ravel's *Sonatine* (1903–5), his independent *Menuet antique* (1895) and *Menuet* (on 'Haydn', 1909).

BIBLIOGRAPHY

DANCE INSTRUCTION

R.-A. Feuillet: *Chorégraphie* (Paris, 1700, 2/1701/*R*1968; Eng. trans., 1706)

I. H. P. [Johann Pasch]: *Maître de danse oder Tantz-Meister* (Glückstadt and Leipzig, 1705)

L. Bonin: *Neueste Art zur galanten und theatralischen Tantz-Kunst* (Frankfurt and Leipzig, 1711, 2/1712)

G. Taubert: *Rechtschaffener Tanzmeister* (Leipzig, 1717/*R*1976)

P. Rameau: *Le maître à danser* (Paris, 1725; Eng. trans., 1931/*R*1970)

——: *Abrégé de la nouvelle methode* (Paris, 1725)

G. Dufort: *Trattato del ballo nobile* (Naples, 1728)

K. Tomlinson: *The Art of Dancing* (London, 1735)

G. Bickham: *An Easy Introduction to Dancing or, The Movements in the Minuet Fully Explained* (London, 1738)

C. G. Hänsel: *Allerneueste Anweisung zur äusserlichen Moral* (Leipzig, 1755)

P. Minguet e Yrol: *Arte de danzar a la francesa* (Madrid, 1758)

Magny: *Principes de chorégraphie, suivis d'un traité de la cadence* (Paris, 1765)

C. I. V. F. [C. J. von Felsenstein]: *Die Kunst nach der Choreographie zu Tanzen* (Brunswick, 1767)

J. M. de Chavanne: *Principes du menuet* (Luxembourg, 1767)

C. J. von Felsenstein: *Erweiterung der Kunst nach der Choreographie zu Tanzen* (Brunswick, 1772)

G. Gallini: *A Treatise on the Art of Dancing* (London, 1772/*R*1967)

STUDIES OF MUSIC AND DANCE

A. Adam: 'Menuett und Scherzo', *Der Musikerzieher*, xxxv (1940)

E. Blom: 'The Minuet-trio', *ML*, xxii (1941), 162

S. Poladian: *Handel as an Opera Composer* (diss., Cornell U., 1946)

J. Guthrie: *Historical Dances for the Theatre* (Worthing, Sussex, 1950)

H. Goldmann: *Das Menuett in der deutschen Musikgeschichte des 17. und 18. Jahrhunderts* (diss., U. of Erlangen, 1956)

I. Hermann-Bengen: *Tempobezeichnungen: Ursprung, Wandel im 17. und 18. Jahrhundert* (Tutzing, 1959)

G. Tani: 'Minuetto', *ES*

G. Massenkeil: *Untersuchung zum Problem der Symmetrie in der Instrumentalmusik W. A. Mozarts* (Wiesbaden, 1962)

P. Nettl: *The Dance in Classical Music* (New York, 1963)

H. M. Ellis [Little]: *The Dances of J.-B. Lully (1632–1687)* (diss., Stanford U., 1967)

K. Padrta: 'Die Menuett-Typen im Werke des Komponisten Kramár-Krommer', *Sborník prace filosofické fakulty brněnské university*, H2 (1967), 31

K. H. Taubert: *Höfische Tänze* (Mainz, 1968)

L. Ratner: 'Ars combinatoria, Chance and Choice in 18th-century Music', *Studies in Eighteenth-century Music: a Tribute to Karl Geiringer* (New York and London, 1970), 343

C. Zachariassen: 'Om menuetten', *Musik*, iv/8 (1970), 16

M. F. Hatchette: *Forty-nine Lisbon Minuets by Pedro Antonio Avondano* (diss., Tulane U., 1971)

W. Steinbeck: *Das Menuett in der Instrumentalmusik Joseph Haydns* (diss., U. of Freiburg, 1972; Freiburg, 1973)

MEREDITH ELLIS LITTLE

**Mioduszewski, Michał Marcin** (*b* Warsaw, 16 Sept 1787; *d* Kraków, 31 May 1868). Polish priest and editor of religious songs. He was educated at the seminary of the Kościół św. Krzyża (Church of the Holy Cross) in Warsaw (1804–10), and then worked as a teacher in similar establishments in Warsaw (1810–14), Włocławek (1814–20) and Kraków (1820–68). He collected and edited several volumes of Polish religious songs, and also left extensive manuscript collections; until 1939 these were in the Biblioteka XX Misjonarzy in Kraków, but their whereabouts are now unknown.

SONG EDITIONS

*Śpiewnik kościelny bez melodyj* [Church songbook without music] (Kraków, 1838)

*Śpiewnik kościelny czyli pieśni nabożne z melodiami w kościele katolickim używane* [Church songbook, or prayer songs with music for use in the Catholic Church] (Kraków, 1838, rev. 2/1842, Leipzig, 1853)

*Pastorałki i kolędy z melodiami* [Pastoral songs and carols with music] (Kraków, 1843, rev. 2/Leipzig, 1853)

*Pastorałki i kolędy bez melodyj* [Pastoral songs and carols without music] (n.p., n.d.)

BIBLIOGRAPHY

H. Feicht: 'Michał Marcin Mioduszewski (1787–1868)', *Księga pamiątkowa ku czci profesora dr Adolfa Chybińskiego* (Kraków, 1930), 67

KATARZYNA MORAWSKA

**Miolan, Marie.** *See* CARVALHO, CAROLINE.

**Mion, Charles-Louis** (*b* 1698; *d* Versailles, 12 Sept 1775). French composer and teacher. He was a great-nephew of Michel-Richard de Lalande, who was among his early teachers. From 1709 to July 1718 he was a choirboy at the Sainte-Chapelle, and in 1727 was a singer in the royal chapel. Subsequently he taught music to Mme de Pompadour, whose protection he enjoyed. On 15 March 1747 Mion was granted a royal pension of 2000 livres a year in appreciation of various compositions, and in particular the ballet *L'année galante*. In 1750 he was referred to as 'composer of the royal ballets', and on 24 January 1755 became music master to the children of the royal family. By August 1765 he was unable to write, owing to paralysis. From then onwards his name is absent from the pension lists, though he was still described as a royal pensioner at his death.

Mion had three motets performed at the Concert Spirituel, but the stage works, which dominate his output, were almost all intended for the court circle where he spent his working life. Notably, the ballet *Julie et Ovide* was written for the marriage celebrations of the Prince de Condé in 1753. The exception is his only *tragédie lyrique*, *Nitétis*, performed at the Paris Opéra in 1741.

The mistaken forenames Jean-Jacques-Henri and the year of birth 1702 seem to have originated with Fétis.

WORKS
*(? music lost unless otherwise stated)*

SECULAR VOCAL

Bouquets de Mlle de G*** à sa mère (idylle, 3, Morand), Versailles, 12 Dec 1735

Nitétis (tragédie lyrique, prol, 5, J. L. I. de La Serre), Paris, 11 April 1741 (Paris, 1741)

Les quatre parties du monde (opéra-ballet, P. C. Roy), Versailles, 1745

Bouquet (romance, L. Fuzelier), pubd in *Mercure de France* (1746), July

L'année galante (opéra-ballet, prol, 4, Roy), Versailles, 13 Feb 1747 (Paris, 1747)

Julie et Ovide (ballet héroïque, Fuzelier: Les amours déguisez), Paris, 11 June 1753

SACRED VOCAL

Motets, all perf. Paris, Concert Spirituel: Magnus Dominus, 7 Feb 1728; Beatus vir, 30 March 1735; De profundis, 13 April 1753

Te Deum, chorus, orch, *F-Pc*

BIBLIOGRAPHY

*FétisB*

*Mercure de France* (1728), Feb, 386; (1753), June, 164

C. P. d'Albert: *Mémoires du Duc de Luynes* (Paris, 1860–65), viii, 116

N. Dufourcq, ed.: *Notes et références pour servir à une histoire de Michel-Richard Delalande* (Paris, 1957)

ANTHONY BENNETT

**Mira, Leandro** (*b* probably in Sicily; *fl* north Italy, 1566–92). Italian composer. His first published compositions, two madrigals and a motet, appeared in two Venetian collections edited by Giulio Bonagionta (*RISM* 1566[23], 1567[3]). Four more madrigals for four and six voices were published in madrigal books by Maddalena Casulana and Pietro Vinci (1570[24], 1571[13]); a further five madrigals for three, five and six voices, composed in a style resembling Vinci's, are scattered through four printed collections (1583[10], 1586[12], 1591[23], 1592[15]), and two intabulations survive, one printed (1600[5a]) and one in manuscript (in *I-Tn*). Mira published, at his own expense, Monte's *Terzo libro di madrigali a cinque* (Venice, 1570).

BIBLIOGRAPHY

O. Tiby: 'The Polyphonic School in Sicily of the 16th–17th Century', *MD*, v (1951), 203

O. Mischiati: 'L'intavolatura d'organo tedesca della Biblioteca Nazionale di Torino', *L'organo*, iv (1963), 1–154, esp. 89

O. Tiby: *I polifonisti siciliani del XVI e XVII secolo* (Palermo, 1969), 52, 70

L. Bianconi: 'Sussidi bibliografici per i musicisti siciliani del cinque e del seicento', *RIM*, vii (1972), 3–38

PAOLO EMILIO CARAPEZZA

**Miracle** [miraculum]. (1) A generic title for medieval mystery plays, i.e. the vernacular English religious cycles (*see* CORPUS CHRISTI PLAYS).

(2) More strictly, a narrative or dramatic presentation of a miraculous action, or miracle, performed in most cases by the Virgin Mary or by one of the saints. Four Latin plays with music in the FLEURY PLAYBOOK deal with the miracles of St Nicholas. Another well-known group is the 14th-century French *Les miracles de Notre Dame* (*see* MEDIEVAL DRAMA, §III, 3(ii)). The influence of Gautier de Coinci (*c*1177–1236) is evident; his narrative miracles, intercalated with pious songs, survive in numerous manuscripts.

JOHN STEVENS

**Mirecki, Franciszek Wincenty** (*b* Kraków, baptized 31 March 1791; *d* Kraków, 29 May 1862). Polish composer, conductor and teacher. When he was four he began learning music from his father, also named Franciszek, organist of the Church of Our Lady in Kraków, and sang in the church choir. At the age of nine he gave his first public concert as a pianist. In 1810 he began to study classics at the Jagiellonian University, specializing in Greek. In 1814 he went to Vienna, where he studied the piano with Hummel, while acting as secretary and librarian to Count Joseph Maximilian Ossolinsky (until 1816). In Vienna Mirecki met Beethoven and presented him with some Polish folk themes. He then visited Venice and Milan (1816–17), afterwards moving to Paris, where he became a composition pupil of Cherubini. From 1822 to 1838 he was active as a composer, conductor and singing master in Milan and (from 1826) Genoa. He conducted an Italian opera company (1825–6), visiting Lisbon, England and France. In 1838 he returned to Kraków, where for two years he had his own private singing school. From 1841 he taught singing in the reorganized music school, and from 1844 to 1847 was artistic director of the Kraków Opera, which he provided with several singers from his own school. His composition pupils included Władysław Żeleński.

Mirecki was the first Polish composer to have a work produced in an Italian theatre, with his operas *Evandro in Pergamo* (Genoa, 1824) and *I due forzati* (Lisbon, 1826 and Florence, 1831). His five Polish operas, including *Nocleg w Apeninach* ('A night in the Appenines') (Kraków, 1845), were composed between 1882 and 1860. Between 1841 and 1844 he wrote his opera *Cornelio Bentivoglio*, which was performed with success at La Scala in 1844. He arranged for orchestra Marcello's 50 two-part psalms (published jointly with Cherubini in 1830), and wrote an admired treatise on instrumentation, the first in Italian in the 19th century, *Trattato intorno agli stromenti ed all'istromentazione* (Milan, 1825). In his operas, he was a follower of

Rossini, while his instrumental output (chiefly for the piano) is in the Viennese Classical tradition.

BIBLIOGRAPHY

Z. Jachimecki: *Muzyka polska w rozwoju historycznym* (Kraków, 1948–51)

W. Sandelewski: 'Francesco Mirecki, campione polacco del melodramma italiano', *RMI*, lv (1953), 426

K. Herman: 'Franciszek Mirecki w setną rocznicę śmierci', *Ruch muzyczny*, xviii/11 (1962), 1

TADEUSZ PRZYBYLSKI

**Miremont, Claude-Augustin** (*b* Mirecourt, 1827; *d* Pontorson, 1887). French violin maker. He was a pupil of his father Sebastien, a little-known and unexceptional craftsman who worked at Mirecourt all his life. After working for Claude Collin he moved to Paris in 1844 and was employed by Lafleur and Bernardel *père*. In 1852 he moved to New York, where he worked for nine years before returning to Paris to establish his own shop at 20 rue Faubourg-Poissonnière. There his intimate contact with the work of Stradivari and Guarneri 'del Gesù' inspired him to make instruments that at times rival those of his great competitor J.-B. Vuillaume. The workmanship is refined and delicate, the varnish often of good substance and attractive appearance. The tone of his instruments is remarkably fine, his best-known advocate being the cellist Pierre Fournier, who has used his Miremont in preference to Italian instruments for most of his career.

BIBLIOGRAPHY

R. Vannes: *Essai d'un dictionnaire universel des luthiers* (Paris, 1932, 2/1951/R1972 as *Dictionnaire universel des luthiers*, suppl. 1959)

CHARLES BEARE

**Miristus.** See MURISTUS.

**Mirliton.** A group of acoustic devices, probably of folk origin, which modify the tonal characteristics of vocal or instrumental sounds fed into them. They are not musical instruments in the strictest sense as they do not actually generate sounds. Marcuse, following Galpin, adopted the word 'mirliton', of French origin, as a generic term to cover all such musical auxiliaries whose behaviour depends on the forced vibration of a thin membrane. This membrane may be free, as in the 'comb-and-paper', or may form part of the wall of a tube or vessel containing an air column; its general effect is to add a buzzing or nasal quality. In certain primitive mirlitons the membrane may be derived from the wall of a vegetable stem by scraping a thin area, as in a form of *trombetta di cana* mentioned by Bonanni in 1722, but commonly it is made of parchment, treated paper or silk, or even onion skin (whence the name 'onion flute').

Although associated today mainly with trivial music (it is the basis of such toys as the kazoo and bigophone) the mirliton principle is of considerable antiquity and has at times been treated seriously. In the Middle Ages the onion flute or *flûte-eunuque* (*see* EUNUCH-FLUTE) was evidently well esteemed, and Mersenne wrote of performances in four- or five-part harmony. A few examples of the eunuch flute survive and show that it was sometimes made to look like a true musical instrument, even to the provision of (non-functional) finger-holes. That the principle can be used indirectly as well as directly is shown by the Indian *nyastaranga*, a brass trumpet closed near the narrow end by a membrane and applied to the side of the larynx while the musician hums or vocalizes.

A few true musical instruments incorporate the vibrating membrane, notably the classical Chinese flute *ti-tzu*, the *flauto di voce* of Wigley and McGregor (*c*1810), and the SUDROPHONE.

BIBLIOGRAPHY
M. Mersenne: *Harmonie universelle* (Paris, 1636–7/*R*1963)
F. Bonanni: *Gabinetto armonico* (Rome, 1722/*R*1964)
T. S. Wotton: *A Dictionary of Foreign Musical Terms* (Leipzig, 1907)
F. W. Galpin: *Textbook of European Musical Instruments* (London, 1937, 2/1944)
C. Sachs: *The History of Musical Instruments* (New York, 1940)
N. Bessaraboff: *Ancient European Musical Instruments* (New York, 1941, 2/1964)
S. Marcuse: *Comprehensive Dictionary of Musical Instruments* (New York, 1964)
A. C. Baines: *European and American Musical Instruments* (London, 1966)

PHILIP BATE

**Miroglio, Francis** (*b* Marseilles, 12 Dec 1924). French composer. He attended the conservatories of Marseilles (1945–7) and Paris (1951–2), studying composition with Milhaud at the latter. From 1959 to 1961 he worked in the electronic music studios of the ORTF, and his work began to be recognized with prizes from the Gaudeamus Foundation (1960) and the Paris Biennale (1961). He also secured performances at the Darmstadt summer courses, which he attended several times during the early 1960s, and the Domaine Musical. In 1965 he founded and assumed the artistic direction of the Nuits de la Fondation Maeght at St Paul de Vence, an annual summer festival which has sponsored highly distinguished presentations of contemporary art music, jazz, painting and sculpture. He has also organized concerts elsewhere and has appeared widely within France as a lecturer. Many of his compositions are mobile in form, variable in instrumentation and ornately fashioned. The virtuoso harp piece *Réseaux*, for example, exists in three versions, one solo and two accompanied, and if playing in ensemble the harpist is required to produce a whole range of imitations of other instrumental sounds. All are, however, successfully accommodated into a style of great smoothness and sophistication.

WORKS
*(selective list)*
Stage: Il faut rêver dit Lénine (opera), Avignon, 1972; Reflex (music-theatre), 1973
Orch: Allotropie, str, perc, 1954; Divertimento, cl, orch, 1955; Espaces, 1961–2; Espaces II, wind, perc, 1962; Espaces III, str, 1962; Extensions, 6 perc, orch, 1970; Extensions 3, 1970; Eclipses, 1972
Vocal: Magies (Miroglio), S, 10 insts, 1960; Tremplins (Dupin), 4 solo vv ad lib, 13 insts ad lib, 15 insts, 1968–9
Chamber: Sonata, vc, pf, 1952; Pierres noires, ondes martenot, 2 perc, 1958; Choréiques, gui, 1958; Fluctuances, fl, harp, 2 perc, 1961; Espaces IV, 9 insts, tape, 1962; Espaces V, 9 insts, 1962; Soleils, pf, 1962; Réseaux, harp/(harp, str qt)/(harp, 9 insts), 1964; Phases, (fl, pf)/(fl, pf, str trio)/(fl, pf, 3 perc)/(fl, pf, str trio, 3 perc), 1965; Projections, str qt, slides of Miró paintings, 1966–7; Refractions, fl, pf, perc, vn, 1968; Insertions, hpd, 1969; Masques, 3–9 wind, 1971

Principal publishers: Heugel, Peters, Suvini Zerboni, Universal

BIBLIOGRAPHY
J.-P. Garnier: 'Entretien avec Francis Miroglio', *Courrier musical* (1967), no.17, p.4
F. Miroglio: 'Ad libitum', *The World of Music*, i (1967), 23

PAUL GRIFFITHS

**Miroglio, Jean-Baptiste** (*b* Piedmont, ? *c*1725; *d* Paris, *c*1785). Italian composer, violin and viola teacher and music publisher, active in Paris. He called himself 'le cadet' or 'le jeune' until 1763–4, when his elder brother probably died. Three of his first four published works were dedicated to Parisians who apparently were his patrons or pupils. In 1765 he began an enterprise which was to be much more important than his compositions or teaching: he and the German painter Johann Anton de Peters (1725–95) founded the first Parisian musical subscription and lending establishment, the Bureau d'Abonnement de Musique. For two years La Chevardière and other publishers fought the new Bureau in court, involving hundreds of musicians on either side; the decision in 1767 was in favour of the Bureau, which continued in operation until at least 1789. Miroglio was listed in periodicals as a composer and teacher up to 1785. His compositions are competent but unremarkable; their style is a mixture of the Italian, French and Mannheim characteristics typical of Paris in that period.

Miroglio had two brothers, Joseph-Antoine, of whom nothing musical is known, and Pierre (*b* Piedmont, *c*1715; *d* Paris, *c*1763–4). Pierre was in Paris by 1738, when he was mentioned in the *Mercure de France* as an Italian violinist of distinction; he was in the retinue of Prince Carignan and later that of La Pouplinière. Pierre and his famous compatriot in Carignan's orchestra, Guignon, had been violin pupils of Miroglio's uncle, G. B. Somis. His only known works are six *Sonate a violino e basso* op.1, published in Paris in 1741 and dedicated to Geminiani, Italian in style and requiring considerable technical facility.

WORKS
*(all published in Paris)*
[6] Sonates, vn, b, op.1 (before 1750)
[6] Sonates, vn, b, op.2 (1750)
[6] Ovs. a 4, 2 vn, va/vn, bc, op.3 (1751)
[6] Sonatas, 2 vn, op.4 (1753)
Les amusements des dames [suites 1–10], 2 vn/tr viols/mand (1760–68); all lost
Ariettes, all lost: L'art de plaire (1763); Amar e un piacer (1767); Vous qui cherchez une femme, 1v, 2 vn, bc (1772)
le suitte de menuets en trio, 2 vn/tr viols, bc (*c*1763)
[6] Simphonies à grand orchestre, 2 vn, va, bc, 2 hn, op.10 (1764)
? [12] Duos, 2 vc (*c*1773–4), lost; see Johansson and Brook (*MGG*)
Les amusements des dames [suite 11: 6 divertissements], harp/pf/hpd, vn ad lib, ?op.12 (1776); lost
Recueil d'ariettes, avec paroles françaises et italiennes, lost; see Brenet

BIBLIOGRAPHY
M. Brenet: 'Les débuts de l'abonnement de musique', *Mercure musical*, ii (1906), 256
L. de La Laurencie and G. de Saint-Foix: 'Contribution à l'histoire de la symphonie française vers 1750', *Année musicale*, i (1911), 1–123
L. de La Laurencie: *L'école française de violon de Lully à Viotti* (Paris, 1922–4/*R*1971)
C. Hopkinson: *A Dictionary of Parisian Music Publishers 1700–1950* (London, 1954)
C. Johansson: *French Music Publishers' Catalogues of the Second Half of the Eighteenth Century* (Stockholm, 1955)
B. S. Brook: 'Miroglio', *MGG*
——: *La symphonie française dans la seconde moitié du XVIIIe siècle* (Paris, 1962)

PEGGY DAUB

**Miroglio, Pierre.** Brother of JEAN-BAPTISTE MIROGLIO.

**Miron, Issachar** (*b* Kutno, 5 July 1920). Israeli composer of Polish birth. He graduated from the Warsaw Conservatory in 1938 and the following year, having obtained a master's degree, settled in Palestine. After periods in the British (1940–44) and Israeli (1948–50) armies he served in a variety of administrative capacities before accepting, in 1967, the post of associate professor and chairman of the music department at the Jewish Teachers' Seminary and People's University, New York. His compositions include concert pieces (chiefly for chorus or piano), liturgical music and over 1000 songs, most of them in a popular vein, the most famous being *Tzena, tzena*.

WILLIAM Y. ELIAS

**Miroshnichenko, Evgeniya (Semyonovna)** (*b* Kharkov district, 12 June 1931). Soviet soprano. She studied with Mikhail Donets-Tesseir at the Kiev Conservatory, graduating in 1957, the year she joined the Kiev Opera. She won second prize at the 1958 Toulouse Competition. Her voice is of light and beautiful timbre, particularly clear in the upper register, and aided by a sparkling coloratura technique. In a repertory of roles including Violetta, Gilda, Rosina, Musetta, Venera (Lysenko's *Eneida*), Yolan (Mayboroda's *Milana*) and Stasya (Zhukovsky's *First Spring*), her performances are distinguished by their liveliness of musical colour and dramatic expression. She was made People's Artist of the USSR in 1965.

I. M. YAMPOL'SKY

**Mirror canon, mirror fugue.** The use of inversion or retrograde motion, or both, in conjunction with the direct version of the material. In mirror canon the consequent may be the inversion, the retrograde or the retrograde inversion of the antecedent. In mirror fugue the second section (which may be a separate fugue) is normally a wholesale inversion of the first (e.g. Bach's *Art of Fugue*, Contrapunctus 12 and 13, each two separate fugues, and his English Suite in D minor BWV811, Gigue, where the second half is virtually a mirror image of the first).

*See also* CANON (i) and FUGUE.

**Miry, Karel** (*b* Ghent, 14 Aug 1823; *d* Ghent, 3 Oct 1889). Belgian composer. He studied the violin with Jean Andries and harmony and composition with Martin Joseph Mengal at the Ghent Conservatory; subsequently he studied at the Brussels Conservatory, where he was a fellow pupil of Gevaert. In 1845 he composed *De vlaamse leeuw* to words by his uncle, H. van Peene; the song became popular immediately, and remains today the national hymn of the Flemish people. In 1857 Miry succeeded Andries as professor of harmony and counterpoint at the Ghent Conservatory, where he also conducted the orchestra. In 1871 he became its assistant director, under Adolphe Samuel. From 1875 he was inspector of music at the municipal schools of Ghent, and six years later he became the inspector of state-aided schools of music; his influence greatly helped to raise the musical standards of these institutions.

Miry was one of the first Belgian composers to set Flemish texts. Of his 18 operas and operettas, most of them based on librettos by van Peene, *Bouchard d'Avesnes* was a great success when it was first produced in Ghent in 1864. From 1853 to 1863 Miry composed four symphonies, which reveal more his professional skill than any marked originality. He also composed ballets, sacred music, chamber music and works for wind instruments. But his most important works are his choral music and songs, especially children's songs.

BIBLIOGRAPHY
C. Bergmans: *Le Conservatoire Royal de Musique de Gand* (Ghent, 1901)
A. Corbet: 'De musicologische betekenis van "De vlaamse leeuw" ', *De toerist*, xxx/24 (1951)
J. Maertens: *De structuuronleding van de symfonieën van Karel Miry (1823–1889)* (diss., U. of Ghent, 1968)
ANNE-MARIE RIESSAUW

**Mir y Llussá, José** (*d* c1784). Catalan composer. About 1755 he succeeded Pedro Rodrigo as *maestro de capilla*

of the Royal Incarnation Convent at Madrid. He was one of the three chief Catalan composers at Madrid invited to contribute introductions to Antonio Soler's *Llave de la modulación* (1762) and the only one to show his wide learning with a quotation from Augustine's *Epistola 104*. Soler responded by soliciting many of Mir's works for El Escorial, the earliest of which is dated 1757. These are mostly Latin double-choir compositions with either two obligatory organs or orchestral accompaniment; they were still being recopied in 1803. He is also heavily represented by double-choir Latin music at Montserrat, and was widely performed in the Americas; a mass written in 1754, surviving at Lima, was still performed as late as 1810, when the Peruvian organist Melchor Tapia added flute and horn parts to it.

WORKS
Mass; 8 vesper psalms; Magnificat quarti toni; 2 Litanies of Our Lady: all 8vv, 2 org, all in *E-E*
Compline, vv, vns, hns, bc, 1758; 6 villancicos, 4–8vv, vns, hns/obs, bc: all in *E*
3 masses; Salve regina; 6 vesper psalms; Christmas responsories; responsories for the Office of the Dead; numerous motets: most 8vv, all in *MO*; villancicos, *MO*
Mass (Ky-Gl-Cr), 4vv, orch, Archivo Arzobispal, Lima, Peru; Mass, F [without Agnus], 4–8vv, orch, Mexico City Cathedral; Envozado Dios mio reduces (villancico), 4vv, vns, hns, bc, Colegio de S Rosa, Morelia, Mexico

BIBLIOGRAPHY
*LaborD*
C. J. de Benito: *Catálogo por orden alfabético de los autores de obras musicales, y de número que hay de éstas en los archivos del Real Monasterio de San Lorenzo del Escorial* (MS, *E-Mn* M.1281, 1875)
R. Stevenson: *Renaissance and Baroque Musical Sources in the Americas* (Washington, 1970), 123, 158, 190
ROBERT STEVENSON

**Mirzoyan, Edvard Mik'aeli** (*b* Gori, Georgia, 12 May 1921). Armenian composer and teacher. A son of the composer M. Mirzoyan (1888–1958), he studied composition under Talyan at the Erevan Conservatory (1936–41); his studies were continued at the House of Armenian Culture in Moscow (1946–8) under Litinsky and Peyko. In 1957 he was made head of the Armenian Composers' Union, and he is a People's Artist of the Armenian SSR and professor of composition at the Erevan Conservatory. His music has been greatly influenced by the Armenian tradition and by the work of Prokofiev, Shostakovich and Bartók. He has developed a dramatic style of great intensity, but there is also a lyricism springing from Armenian folksong. These qualities are treated with freshness in the Symphony, a work bordering on the neo-classical tendency in contemporary Armenian music; the first part is a double fugue on a peasant song theme, and the second and fourth movements have a dynamic rhythmic pulse.

WORKS
(*selective list*)
Cantatas: Hayastan, 1948; Tonakan kantat [Festival cantata], 1949; Sovetskaya Armeniya, 1950
Orch: Loretsi Sak'o, sym. poem, after H. T'umanyan, 1941; Hayrenakan paterazmi herosnerin [To the heroes of World War II], sym. poem, 1944; Simfonicheskiye tantsï [Symphonic dances], 1946; Uvertyura, 1947; Simfonicheskaya poema, 1955; Introduktsiya i perpetuum mobile, vn, orch, 1957; Sym., str, timp, 1962
Inst: Str Qt, 1947; Sonata, vc, pf, 1967; Poema, pf, 1970
Songs, folksong arrs., film scores

BIBLIOGRAPHY
T. Arazyan: *E. Mirzoyan* (Erevan, 1963)
M. Ter-Simonyan: *Edvard Mirzoyan* (Moscow, 1969)
SVETLANA SARKISIAN

**Misa** (Sp.). MASS.

**Misch, Ludwig** (*b* Berlin, 13 June 1887; *d* New York, 22 April 1967). American musicologist, conductor and critic of German birth. He studied musicology with Friedlaender at the University of Berlin and law at the University of Heidelberg, where he received a doctorate in 1911. From 1913 to 1921 he worked as an operetta conductor in Osnabrück, Essen, Strasbourg, Bremen and elsewhere; later (1921–3) he was music director of the Berlin Kammeroper. In the 1920s and 30s he was a critic for the *Lokalanzeiger* and other newspapers (including a few Jewish ones) and a writer of programme notes for the Berlin Philharmonic Orchestra. He taught music theory and history at the Stern Conservatory and conducted several madrigal choirs. After a period of imprisonment he again taught at the conservatory before emigrating to the USA in 1947. In New York he was a synagogue organist and music director as well as a teacher. As a musicologist, Misch is known for his analyses of form and melody in Beethoven's works.

WRITINGS

*Johannes Brahms* (Bielefeld, 1913, 2/1922)
ed., with W. Klatte: *Das Sternsche Konservatorium der Musik zu Berlin 1850–1925* (Berlin, 1926)
*Beethoven-Studien* (Berlin, 1950; Eng. trans., 1953)
'Der persönliche Stil in Beethovens Erster Symphonie: Organismus und Idee des ersten Satzes', *BeJb 1955–6*, 55–101
ed., with D. W. MacArdle: *New Beethoven Letters* (Norman, Oklahoma, 1957)
*Die Faktoren der Einheit in der Mehrsätzigkeit der Werke Beethovens: Versuch einer Theorie der Einheit des Werkstils* (Bonn, 1958)
'Beethovens "Variierte Themen": op.105 und op.107', *BeJb 1959–60*, 102–42
'Eine problematische Aufzeichnung Beethovens', *BeJb 1961–4*, 80
*Neue Beethoven-Studien und andere Themen* (Bonn, 1967)

BIBLIOGRAPHY

*RiemannL 12*
P. Mies: 'Zum Gedenken an Ludwig Misch', *Mf*, xx (1967), 243
F. A. Kuttner: 'Ludwig Misch (1887–1967)', *JAMS*, xxi (1968), 409
M. E. C. BARTLET

**Mischa, František Adam.** See MÍČA, FRANTIŠEK ADAM.

**Mischa, František Antonín.** See MÍČA, FRANTIŠEK ANTONÍN.

**Mischakoff, Mischa** (*b* Proskurov, Ukraine, 16 April 1896). American violinist of Russian birth. He studied with S. Korguyev at St Petersburg and made his début in Berlin in 1912. After various teaching and orchestral posts he settled in the USA in 1921. There he chose the career of an orchestral leader: 1924–7 with the New York SO (when Damrosch was conductor), 1927–30 with the Philadelphia Orchestra (under Stokowski), 1930–37 with the Chicago SO (under Stock), 1937–52 with the NBC SO in New York (under Toscanini) and 1952–68 with the Detroit SO (under Paray). In 1968–9 he was the guest-leader of the Baltimore SO. For 40 summers, 1925–65, he served as leader and soloist of the Chautauqua SO. Mischakoff was on the faculty of the Juilliard School in New York (1941–52) and, from 1952, of Wayne University in Detroit; he was also frequently a guest professor. For many years he led the Mischakoff String Quartet.

Mischakoff's style was ideally suited to his career. His tone was strong yet beautiful, and his rhythm robust. Untroubled by nerves, he conveyed his rock-like assurance to the orchestra, yet was always sensitive to the conductor's wishes. His experienced advice was highly prized, especially by Toscanini. In spite of his years of orchestral playing, Mischakoff never lost the refinement necessary for solo and chamber music. A connoisseur of fine instruments, he owned at one time two Stradivari violins known as the 'Booth' and the 'General Kyd', as well as a Guarneri 'del Gesù'. Later he played the 'Adam' Stradivari.

BORIS SCHWARZ

**Mischiati, Oscar** (*b* Bologna, 11 July 1936). Italian musicologist. For his degree in philosophy at the University of Bologna he wrote a thesis on Baroque musical aesthetics (1960). He then became a lecturer in poetry and drama at the Conservatory of Bolzano (1960–63) and assistant in music history at the University of Bologna (1961–3); in 1964 he was appointed librarian at the Bologna Conservatory. His two main interests, arising from his informal studies as a boy with Tagliavini, have been music bibliography and organs. At the beginning of his career he wrote articles on some 80 Italian composers for *MGG*. He has made the Bologna library into one of the few comprehensive centres of secondary sources in Italy. He is honorary inspector for a city committee formed to save works of art in Bologna and a member of the government commission for the preservation and restoration of organs in Emilia and Lombardy: he has organized research all over the country towards the preparation of a list of all early organs, with a view to saving the instruments and publishing the catalogue. With Tagliavini he edits *L'organo*, the journal founded by Lunelli to investigate the history and literature of the organ; he is co-editor of *Monumenti di Musica Italiana* and a member of the editorial board for the Catalogus Musicus series of the International Association of Music Libraries. He is also a council member of the Società Italiana di Musicologia. In 1961 he was awarded the A. T. Davison Memorial Medal for Musicology by the Harriet Cohen International Music Award Foundation.

WRITINGS

'L'organo della basilica di S. Martino di Bologna capolavoro di Giovanni Cipri', *L'organo*, i (1960), 213–56
with V. Giacolli: 'Gli antichi organi del Cadore', *L'organo*, iii (1962), 3–58
'Per la storia dell'oratorio a Bologna: tre inventari del 1620, 1622 e 1682', *CHM*, iii (1962), 131–70
with L. F. Tagliavini: 'Appunti di organaria in un manoscritto del XVII secolo della Biblioteca comunale di Siena', *L'organo*, iv (1963), 201
'L'intavolatura d'organo tedesca della Biblioteca Nazionale di Torino: catalogo ragionato', *L'organo*, iv (1963), 1–154
'Studenti ultramontani di musica a Bologna nella seconda metà del secolo XVI', *AnMc*, iii (1966), 1–42
'Un'inedita testimonianza su Bartolomeo Ramis de Pareia', *FAM*, xiii (1966), 84
'Uno sconosciuto frammento appartenente al codice Vaticano Rossi 215', *RIM*, i (1966), 68
'Aspetti dei rapporti tra Corelli e la scuola bolognese', *Studi corelliani: 1° congresso internazionale: Fusignano 1968*, 23
'Le terza nel ripieno italiano', *L'organo*, vi (1968), 3
*L'organo della chiesa del carmine di Lugo di Romagna* (Bologna, 1968)
with L. F. Tagliavini: 'La situazione degli antichi organi in Italia: problemi di censimento e di tutela', *L'organo*, vii (1969), 3–61
'L'organo del Santuario di Tirano: le vicende storiche e i lavori di restauro dell'insigne strumento', *Basilica Santuario di Tirano: numero unico per la inaugurazione del restaurato organo monumentale – 10 ottobre 1970*, 5
'Adriano Banchieri (1568–1634): profilo biografico e bibliografia delle opere, *Annuario 1965–1970 del Conservatorio di musica 'G. B. Martini' di Bologna* (Bologna, 1971), 39–201
with G. Cattin and A. Ziino: 'Composizioni polifoniche del primo quattrocento nei libri corali di Guardiagrele', *RIM*, vii (1972), 153
ed.: *I cataloghi originali degli organi Serassi* (Bologna, 1973)
ed., with L. F. Tagliavini: *Un anonimo trattato francese di arte organaria del sec. XVIII* (Bologna, 1974)
'Un'antologia manoscritta in partitura del secolo XVI: il MS Bour-

deney della Bibliothèque Nationale di Parigi', *RIM*, x (1975), 265–328

EDITIONS

*G. M. Trabaci: Composizioni per organo e cembalo*, MMI, i/3 (1964–9)
*C. Porta: Missa 'La Sol Fa Re Mi'*, Cw, xciii (1965)
with others: *G. Frescobaldi: Opere complete*, Monumenti musicali italiani (Milan, 1975–)    CAROLYN M. GIANTURCO

**Mise en bouche** (Fr.). EMBOUCHURE.

**Miserere** (Lat.: 'have mercy'). The first word of Psalms l, lv and lvi, as well as of a number of liturgical texts. Of the former, Psalm l (li in the Hebrew numbering followed in the Authorized Version and Prayer Book translations) is the most important in the history of polyphonic composition. In the Roman rite it is sung at Lauds in the Office for the Dead and at TENEBRAE, and it is also one of the seven penitential psalms. Its first verse and *Gloria Patri* are also sung with the antiphon *Asperges me* at the principal Mass on Sundays, except during Eastertide: four anonymous polyphonic settings occur in an English source of the mid-16th century (*GB-Lbm* 17802–5). Polyphonic settings of the complete psalm for use at Tenebrae (when the *Gloria Patri* is not sung) are usually in simple *falsobordone* style, alternating with the plainchant, a tradition that may have been initiated under Pope Leo X in 1514. A pair of manuscripts in the Vatican (*I-Rvat* C.S.205–6) includes a set of 12 such works for alternating choirs of four and five voices (the choirs themselves alternating with the plainchant) by Fabrizio Dentice, Palestrina, Gagari, G. F. Anerio and his brother Felice, Domenico Nanino, Giovannelli and anonymous composers, ending with the celebrated work by Gregorio Allegri. (The attribution by some modern authors of the first work in this set to Costanzo Festa, with the date 1517, appears to be unjustified.) Palestrina's work is compounded of a four-part setting, published with his Lamentations (1588) and also included as the first of a set of three in Guidetti's *Cantus ecclesiasticus officii majoris hebdomadae* (1587), and a five-part work printed as the second of Guidetti's set. Nine-part settings were evidently popular: one by Lassus and numerous examples by minor composers are in the library of the Sistine Chapel. Other noteworthy settings in a simple style are those of Victoria (1581) and Gesualdo (1611), printed in their collections of Holy Week music. There are more elaborate and very beautiful works by Lassus (*Psalmi Davidis poenitentiales*, 1584) and Giovanni Gabrieli (a setting of the first four verses in *Sacrae symphoniae*, 1597). Tye's *Miserere* is a setting of Psalm lv. Josquin's extended setting of Psalm l (425 bars) is particularly noteworthy. The refrain 'Miserere mei Deus', heard after each verse, is based on a short phrase in the second tenor sung on successive degrees of the scale in turn: from $e'$ to $e$ in part i, from $e$ to $e'$ in part ii and from $e'$ to $a$ in part iii. The tonality of the work thus strongly suggests the E-modes, though it comes to rest on a chord of A minor.

Several texts from the Roman psalter or other old Latin versions begin with the words 'Miserere mihi Domine'; these are taken not only from the psalms mentioned above, but from verses of Psalms iv, vi, xxx and lxxxv. In the English tradition the most important is undoubtedly the short compline antiphon which continues and concludes with the words 'et exaudi orationem meam' (from Psalm iv, second part of v.2, in the Roman psalter). The plainchant is a simple two-phrase melody in the 8th mode. This gave rise to vocal settings (e.g. anonymous liturgical settings in *GB-Cmc* Pepys 1236, a liturgical setting by John Norman in *GB-Lbm* Add.5665 and an elaborate non-liturgical canon by Byrd in his *Cantiones sacrae*, 1575, perhaps written in rivalry to Tallis's canonic *Miserere nostri* in the same publication) as well as to a whole repertory of instrumental works. 18 liturgical settings of the plainchant for the organ survive by Kyrton, John Redford, Philip ap Rhys, William Shelbye, E. Strowger and 'Wodson' (possibly Thomas Woodson). After the Reformation the genre attracted such composers as Bull, Byrd, Benjamin Cosyn, John Lugge, Tomkins and Thomas Woodson. In these compositions liturgical conventions are subordinated to increasing virtuosity, the possibility of stating the cantus firmus more than once (resulting in a miniature set of variations) and canonic treatment. The 20 surviving settings, out of a supposed 40, by Thomas Woodson, illustrate canonic technique; and Tomkins's eight works, all probably dating from the late 1640s and early 1650s, are a remarkable testimony to the resilience of the form in the hands of a master of the traditional style.

There are a few settings of the plainchant for lute by such composers as Alfonso Ferrabosco (ii), and ensemble settings by Tye, Byrd and others. According to Morley, Byrd and Alfonso Ferrabosco (i) each wrote 40 canonic settings in friendly rivalry. They were apparently printed in 1603 under the title *Medulla Musicke* (i.e. *musicae*), of which no copy survives; but the 19 canonic works of Byrd which survive in manuscript may represent part of his contribution. Morley also mentioned that George Waterhouse had composed 1000 or more settings, and R. A. Harman (in his edition of Morley's *Plaine and Easie Introduction*) referred to '1163 strict canons on the "Miserere" plainsong in the manuscripts at Oxford and Cambridge'. Some of the six-part canons that follow keyboard works by Bull and others in *A-Wn* 17771 are based on the 'Miserere' plainsong, but the printed collections of canons by John Farmer (i) (1591) and Elway Bevin (1631) are based on other plainchants.

BIBLIOGRAPHY

E. H. Meyer: *English Chamber Music* (London, 1946, 2/1951)
J. Noble: 'Le répertoire instrumental anglais (1550–1585)', *La musique instrumentale de la Renaissance: CNRS Paris 1954*, 91
G. Reese: *Music in the Renaissance* (New York, 1954, rev. 2/1959)
W. Boetticher: *Orlando di Lasso und seine Zeit* (Kassel and Basle, 1958)
F. Ll. Harrison: *Music in Medieval Britain* (London, 1958, rev. 2/1963)
K. Jeppesen: 'Palestriniana', *Miscelánea en homenaje a Monseñor Higinio Anglés*, i (Barcelona, 1958), 417
J. M. Lloréns Cisteró: *Capellae Sixtinae codices musicis notis instructi sive manu scripti sive praelo excussi* (Vatican City, 1960)
J. Caldwell: 'Keyboard Plainsong Settings in England, 1500–1660', *MD*, xix (1965), 129
——: *English Keyboard Music before the Nineteenth Century* (Oxford, 1973)    JOHN CALDWELL

**Miskiewicz [Miśkiewicz], Maciej Arnulf** (*d* between 1682 and 1685). Polish musician and composer. From 1651 he was a substitute in the Cappella Rorantistarum of Kraków Cathedral. In 1653 or 1654 he became a full member and shortly afterwards its director, a position that he held until 1682. In this capacity he produced for the chapel a number of copies of vocal works by Polish composers of the time (particularly Pękiel) and also adapted some 16th-century partbooks. These copies, which bear the signature MMPR ('Mathias Miskiewicz Praepositus Rorantistarum') and survive in three libraries (Kraków City Archive, *PL-Kk* and *Pu*), are very important for the documentation of Polish music in the 17th century. Only one composition certainly by Miskiewicz is known, the four-part *Jesu, dulcis memoria* (in *Kk* and dated 3 June 1668), which is in the traditional contrapuntal style typical of sacred music. Another work among the manuscripts from the Cappella Rorantistarum is a *Missa 4 vocum pro nativitate D. N. Jesu Christi* bearing the initials M.M.; it is more likely to be by him than by the other possible candidate, Marcin Mielczewski.

BIBLIOGRAPHY

A. Sowiński: *Les musiciens polonais et slaves* (Paris, 1857; Pol. trans., 1874)
A. Chybiński: 'Notatki biograficzne o przełożonych kapeli rorantystów w XVII stuleciu' [Biographical notes about the leaders of the Cappella Rorantistarum in the 17th century], *KM* (1911), no.1
Z. Jachimecki: *Muzyka polska w rozwoju historycznym* [Polish music in its historical development], I/i (Kraków, 1948), 192, 220f
A. Chybiński: *Słownik muzyków dawnej Polski* [Dictionary of early Polish musicians] (Kraków, 1948–9), 85
H. Feicht: 'Muzyka w okresie polskiego baroku' [Music in the Baroque period in Poland], *Z dziejów polskiej kultury muzycznej, i: Kultura staropolska* [From the history of Polish musical culture, i: Early Polish culture], ed. Z. M. Szweykowski (Kraków, 1958), 213
J. Kłobukowska: 'Msze francuskie w repertuarze kapeli rorranckiej' [French masses in the repertory of the Cappella Rorantistarum], *Muzyka*, xvi/3 (1971), 85
E. Głuszcz-Zwolińska: 'Zbiory muzyczne proweniencji wawelskiej' [The collection of music originally from Wawel Castle archives], *Musicalia vetera: katalog tematyczny rękopiśmiennych zabytków dawnej muzyki w Polsce* [Thematic catalogue of manuscript treasures of early Polish music], ed. Z. M. Szweykowski, i/2 (Kraków, 1972), 19, 21
——: 'W sprawie repertuaru kapel wawelskich' [Concerning the repertory of the Wawel Castle chapels], *Muzyka*, xvii/4 (1972)

MIROSŁAW PERZ

**Misón** [Missón], **Luis** (*b* ? Barcelona; *d* Madrid, 13 Feb 1766). Spanish composer. He became a flautist and oboist in the Madrid royal chapel on 27 June 1748 and conductor in 1756. He also worked for the Teatro del Buen Retiro. From a very early time he was called the inventor of the *tonadilla* (his earliest known piece of that kind dates from 1757) but, although he was one of the most important composers in the first period of this genre's history, he at most only standardized the format of the solo *tonadilla*. More than 80 of his *tonadillas* (for which he sometimes wrote the text himself), along with *sainetes*, *entremeses* and comedies are in the Madrid National Library. An Italian intermezzo, *La festa chinese*, was performed at the Buen Retiro in 1761 and a zarzuela, *El tutor enamorado*, written in collaboration with Ramón de la Cruz, was seen at the French ambassador's in 1764. Misón's flute playing was praised by the poet Samaniego in his *El tordo flautista*. 12 sonatas for flute, viola and bass, written for the Duke of Alba, are in the Alba archives (lacking the viola part).

BIBLIOGRAPHY

J. Subirà: 'Vida y obras de Don Luis Misón', *La música en la casa de Alba* (Madrid, 1927), 191
——: *Tonadillas teatrales inéditas* (Madrid, 1932)
——: *La tonadilla escénica* (Barcelona and Buenos Aires, 1933)

**Misonne** [Myssonne, Missonne, Mizonne], **Vincent** (*b* ?Cambrai, *c*1490, *d* Cambrai, 7 April 1550). ?Franco-Flemish composer. Letters sent by Pope Leo X in 1515–19, granting him benefices in the diocese of Cambrai, name him as a member of the papal chapel. He appears to have moved to Cambrai by 1523–4, when he was *magister parvorum vicariorum*. In 1524 he received a leave of absence to procure singers for the pope, and must have returned to the papal chapel at this time, for

he signed two receipt lists, one dated December 1526, the other dating from between 1524 and 1527, and he is listed in a Roman census of late 1526 or early 1527. He may have left as a result of the Sack of Rome (6 May 1527), for in 1527 he was back in his old position in Cambrai. Other references in the Cambrai archives show him there in 1528–9, 1532, 1538–9 and 1547. He apparently retained links with the papal chapel, however: a document of 1531 allowed him the privileges of a papal singer *in absentia*.

Misonne wrote a small number of sacred works, contained mostly in the manuscripts of the Cappella Sistina. He seems to have found favour with Leo X, who made him an apostolic notary, and he was in a position of some authority in Cambrai, for a notice of August 1529 stated that no masses could be sung without his permission.

WORKS

Missa de beata virgine, 4vv, *D-Bds* 40091, *I-Rvat* C.S.13
Missa 'Gracieuse plaisant', 4vv, *Rvat* C.S.26
Missa 'Que nay je marion', 4vv, *CMac* P(E), *Rvat* C.S.26
Regina caeli, 4vv, *Rvat* C.S.26; Salve regina, 4vv, *Rvat* C.S.26

BIBLIOGRAPHY

D. Gnoli: 'Descriptio urbis o Censimento della popolazione di Roma avanti il Sacco Borbonico', *Archivio della R. Società romana di storia patria*, xvii (1894), 439
H.-W. Frey: 'Regesten zur päpstlichen Kapelle unter Leo X und zu seiner Privatkapelle', *Mf*, viii (1955), 178, esp. 195ff
R. Sherr: 'New Archival Data concerning the Chapel of Clement VII', *JAMS*, xxix (1976), 472

RICHARD SHERR

**Missa.** The Latin term for the principal service of the Roman Catholic Church and the music used for it. *See* MASS.

**Missa brevis** (Lat.: 'short mass'). (1) In the 15th and 16th centuries this term denotes a complete setting of the Ordinary of the Mass in which all movements are short. The term was in use by about 1500 in Italy, as is shown by two masses by Gaffurius entitled *Missa primi toni brevis* and *Missa brevis octavi toni*. It was used more widely after 1560, for example by Palestrina, at a time when a general tendency towards shorter mass settings prompted greater recognition of the *missa brevis* as a distinct type of mass. A number of works that actually fit the category were not designated in this way, however, since the term was reserved for short masses that had no antecedent from which they could be named: thus Josquin's *Missa D'ung aultre amer*, based on a chanson by Ockeghem, is in its proportions a *missa brevis*.

(2) In the 17th and 18th centuries the term came to mean principally a setting of the Kyrie and Gloria only, usually intended for use in the Lutheran service (*missa* alone sometimes signified the same). Less commonly *missa brevis* refers to a four- or five-movement setting of the Ordinary that was highly abbreviated. Abbreviation was sometimes achieved by the exclusion of portions of the text or by the simultaneous presentation of successive clauses. In the 20th century the term has been used for masses of modest proportions, very often with accompaniment for organ only (Kodály, Britten). *See also* MASS, §§I and II.

LEWIS LOCKWOOD

**Missa dominicalis** (Lat.: 'Lord's Day mass'). The term normally designates a 'mass for Sunday use', that is, in the traditions of Catholic plainsong, a mass using the plainsongs brought together in the Roman Gradual as

Mass XI ('In dominicis infra annum') and using one of several Credo melodies. In the polyphonic tradition the *missa dominicalis* was a setting of the Ordinary that paraphrased several or all of these plainsongs and normally alternated sections of text sung in plainsong with sections sung in polyphony. An early example using chants from Mass XI is the *Missa dominicalis* by Johannes Martini (*d* 1497), while the first one to be published seems to be the one by Marbrianus de Orto (1505). German composers of the period especially favoured this type of mass, and important settings were made by Heinrich Finck and Senfl, among others. Palestrina wrote a setting on Mantuan plainsongs which was published in 1592 together with other masses of the same kind by Italian contemporaries. A *Missa dominicalis* by Viadana for solo voice and basso continuo alternating with plainsong is in Wagner (p.534ff).

*See also* MASS, §§I and II.

BIBLIOGRAPHY
P. Wagner: *Geschichte der Messe* (Leipzig, 1913)
O. Strunk: 'Guglielmo Gonzaga and Palestrina's *Missa dominicalis*', *MQ*, xxxiii (1947), 228

LEWIS LOCKWOOD

**Missal** (from Lat. *missale, liber cantus missae*). A liturgical book of the western Church containing all the material necessary for the celebration of Mass.

1. General. 2. Evolution. 3. 11th–20th centuries.

1. GENERAL. The missal is composite, a collection of material from various liturgical books in which all the pieces necessary for the solemn celebration of Mass are brought together: the prayers and preface chanted by the priest; lessons read by the deacon and sub-deacon; and the chants of the Proper and Ordinary performed by the choir or soloists. The missal unites in a single book elements formerly dispersed in several books: the sacramentary (for the priest); the lectionary or the epistolary and the evangeliary (for the deacon and sub-deacon); the gradual and troper-proser (for the singers); and the ordinal, which gave directory rubrics for the manner of performance of the liturgical rites.

Surviving documents indicate that the various attempts to bring together the different books that resulted in the missal were usually carried out on the basis of the sacramentary, more rarely the lectionary, and pursued very different courses. This survey of the evolution of the books leading to the noted missal will be pursued through groupings which illustrate the progressive inclusion of sung pieces with the other elements of the Mass.

2. EVOLUTION.

(*i*) *Sacramentaries with marginal chant text incipits.* The sacramentary, which usually began with the feast of Christmas (25 December), contained only prayers, the preface and the *Canon missae*, the chanted recitation of which is the task of the celebrant, bishop or priest. In several ancient sacramentaries, chant incipits for each feast, taken from the gradual, were added opposite the first collect of the corresponding Mass, in minuscule script. The incipits were generally given without music, as one would expect bearing in mind the antiquity of the books. Manuscripts with such chant indications in the margin are: *F-AN* 102 (94) (end of 10th century, from Angers); *BS* 37 (end of 12th century, from St Bertin; introits only); *B-Br* 2034–5 (12th century, Saxon sacramentary passed into use at Stavelot; see F. Masai, *Scriptorium*, xiii, 1959, pp.22ff, pl.5); *D-DÜl* D1

(10th century, from Corvey); *DÜl* D2 (10th century, from Corvey); *GB-Ob·* Bodley 579 ('The Leofric Missal', 10th century, a Cambrai missal passed into England; ed. in Warren, 1883); *Ob* Rawl.lit.C1 (12th century, from St Albans; introits only); *F-Pn* lat.821 (11th century, from Limoges); *Pn* lat.9430 and *TO* 184 (end of 11th century, from Tours); *Pn* lat.9432 (second half of 11th century, from Amiens); *Pn* lat.11589 (11th century, from Brittany); *Pn* nouv.acq.lat.1589 (end of 11th century, from Tours); *RSc* 213 (second half of 11th century, from Noyon); *RSc* 214 (10th century, from St Thierry, Rheims); *I-Rvat* Ottob.313 (11th century, from Paris; chant text incipits included in edn. by H. A. Wilson, Henry Bradshaw Society, xlix, 1915); and *VEcap* LXXXVI (81) (11th century, from Verona).

(*ii*) *Sacramentaries with gradual chants in full* (*text and music*). The sacramentary was here transformed into a sacramentary-gradual: for each Mass, first the five chants from the Proper (sometimes simply a cue), then the three prayers and preface were given. Manuscripts arranged thus are: *F-AN* 91 (83) (10th century, possibly from St Pierre, Angers); *A* 220 (12th century, from St Pierre, Apt); Archives nationales, Paris, AB XIX 1742–3 (10th–11th century; fragments with transitional notation, perhaps of Poitevin origin); *Pn* lat.9439 (11th–12th century, from St Etienne, Limoges); *TO* 184 (11th century, from Tours); *I-TRmd* 43 (10th–11th century, from Austria).

The insertion of prayers in the middle of the pieces of chant (i.e. a missal without readings) is much rarer. This arrangement is found in two Paris missals: *F-Pn* lat.12054 (11th century) and *Pn* lat.9441 (13th century). In the latter, the readings are indicated by a cue, the full text being written out further on, as in the sacramentary-gradual.

A conflict was inherent in such 'half-missals' between the different calendars of each component part: the sacramentaries began from the Vigil of Christmas, whereas the graduals started with the first Sunday in Advent (introit *Ad te levavi*). In order to align the two books it was therefore necessary for the calendar of one to give way to that of the other: in the missal, it was the gradual order that usually prevailed. Furthermore, the separation of the Proper of the Time from that of the Saints was achieved very early, and led to the creation of a Common of Saints, which did not exist in the ancient graduals (the singer was simply directed back to a previous feast of the same class).

(*iii*) *Missals created by the juxtaposition of component books.* The gradual, containing the chants for Mass, did not remain isolated: it might be coupled to a sacramentary, a lectionary or both.

Gradual-sacramentary: the gradual, containing the chants for the Proper of the Mass, preceded the sacramentary of the Gregorian type; the same copyist transcribed both books and the same artist drew the initials. This juxtaposition occurs in very ancient books. From the 8th century: *CH-Zz* Rheinau 30 (from Nivelles; see Hesbert, 1935, pp.xii ff, and A. Hänggi and A. Schönherr: *Sacramentarium rhenaugiense*, Fribourg, 1971). From the 11th century: *F-Pn* lat.2291 (from St Amand; gradual ff.9–15, with some added Paleofrankish neumes, ed. in Netzer, 1910, pp.283–355); *Pn* lat.12050 (gradual, slightly later than sacramentary, ed. Hesbert, 1935, pp.xxi ff, cxxiii; for the tonal indications in the margin see M. Huglo: *Les tonaires*, Paris, 1971, pp.91ff); *Psg* 111 (9th–10th century, from St Denis); *GB-Ob* Can.lit.319 (*c*997, from Reichenau; see D. H. Turner, *Revue bénédictine*, lxxxv, 1965, pp.255ff); *CH-SGv* 295 (10th–11th century, from St Gall). This arrangement, which explains why the gradual also benefited from the attribution of the sacramentary to GREGORY THE GREAT, enjoyed wide popularity in the German-speaking regions of eastern Europe at the same time as the other, three-book, arrangement (see below). Of the 57 manuscripts of the 11th century or later that use the two-book juxtaposition, only three are from Romance-language countries (*F-AM* 155, from Corbie; *Pn* lat.2293, from Figeac or Moissac; *Pn* lat.9434, from Tours).

Gradual-lectionary: this juxtaposition is very rare. It is found in only three manuscripts (St Omer, B.Mun.252, 10th–11th century, from St Bertin; *I-Rvat* Borg.lat.359, 11th century, from St Etienne, Besançon; *CH-SGs* 374, 11th century from St Gall).

Gradual-sacramentary-lectionary: this arrangement does not seem to be as old as the two-book juxtaposition. It appears in the 11th century in a manuscript written at Gembloux for Stavelot (*B-Br* 2031–2; see *Scriptorium*, xiv, 1960, p.86), but it is found most frequently in manuscripts of the Lake Constance region: from Zwiefalten (*D-Sl* HB I 236), St Gall (*CH-SGs* 342–3), Rheinau (*Zz* 14, 71, 75), although also in a Cologne manuscript (*D-DÜl* D3). The juxtaposition of three liturgical books in a single volume has serious practical disadvantages: it results in a very thick 'missal by juxtaposition' that is not easy to handle. It survived, nevertheless, until the 14th–15th century in the east (13 manuscripts), which was more conservative than the west (two manuscripts).

*(iv) Full missals created by the amalgamation of component books.* The collection of the diverse component elements of the Mass (prayers, chants and readings) into a single book sufficient for the complete celebration of Mass seems to have been achieved first in Italy, possibly northern Italy. The oldest complete missals that include musical notation over the chant texts originate in Italy and belong to the 10th century: *US-BAw* M.6 (votive and festal masses, from St Michael, Monte Gargano; the manuscript is very rich in liturgical texts, see for instance the ancient offertory for Pentecost *Factus est repente*, ed. in *Organicae voces: Festschrift J. Smits van Waesberghe*, Amsterdam, 1963, pp.62f; see also A. Doherty: *A Romano-Beneventan Missale plenum in the Walters Art Gallery*, diss., Princeton U., 1974); *I-BV* VI 33 ('Missale Antiquum' of Benevento, with Beneventan neumatic notation; see PalMus, xiv, 1931, pl.i–vii; the manuscript has several archaisms, some liturgical, see K. Gamber, *Ephemerides liturgicae*, lxxiv, 1960, pp.428f, and some scriptural, see M. Huglo, *Vigiliae Christianae*, viii, 1954, pp.83ff); *Bu* 2217, ff.158–61 (10th–11th century) and *Bu* 2679 (11th century; fragments of missals with neumatic notation); Archives de l'Etat, Lausanne (fragments of missals from the Bari region, second half of 10th century, other leaves of which are at Lucerne, Peterlingen and Zurich; see bibliography in *Le graduel romain*, ii, 1957, p.57); *I-Ma* L 77 sup. (10th century; missal with neumes from north Italy); *D-Mbs* lat.3005 (11th century, taken in 11th century to Wessobrunn, then to Andechs where it was noted and modified; see *Le graduel romain*, ii, 1957, p.77); Hauptstaatsarchiv, Munich (fragment of a

missal from St Christina, near Olonna, second half of 11th century, later taken to Wessobrunn; see *Le graduel romain*, ii, 1957, p.83); *F-Pa* 610 (10th century, from Worms; votive missal); *I-PAVs* (fragments of a 10th-century missal, from ?Pavia).

3. 11TH–20TH CENTURIES. In the 11th and 12th centuries complete missals with neumatic notation proliferated: about 50 from the 11th century and about 40 from the 12th century are known, almost all of west European origin. In the 13th century missals with neumes decreased in favour of missals with music on lines, which flourished until the end of the 14th century. The actual use to which these noted missals were put is not always clear, but many were no doubt used in small parishes or small monasteries with limited financial resources; a single book thus served the celebrant and his ministers, who would read the lessons of the Mass of the Catechumens from one and the same missal, while the singer also used the book, before the Offices, for *recordatio*, that is, to remind himself of the melodies to be performed.

Thus, from the 11th century, although sacramentaries sometimes remained in use at the same time as the other mass books, a 'missal' was formed in each church and was passed on with all its local peculiarities from one set of copies to another. In certain churches a modification was made during the Middle Ages. At Salisbury, Richard Poore, even before being elected head of the diocese in 1217, began the restoration of the liturgy with the help of Edmund Rich, the treasurer, thus establishing the Use of Sarum for Mass and Office; it spread through most of the kingdom, displacing nearly all local uses (except those of York, Westminster etc). At Rome at about the same time, a reorganization of liturgical books was undertaken by Pope Innocent III (1198–1216), and a complete missal 'secundum consuetudinem romanae curiae' was established (see van Dijk, 1956). The new Roman missal spread to several churches in central Italy from the 13th century, for example to Todi (*GB-Lbm* 14793) and to Assisi. The new Franciscan order adopted the missal from the Curia, inserting their own festivals (12 August, 17 September, 4 October) which were introduced into the universal Roman missal by Franciscan popes such as Nicholas IV (1288–92), or Sixtus IV (1471–84) under whose pontificate the first Roman missal was printed (1474). In 1570 Pius V, a Dominican, made a new version of the missal which remained the basis of the *Missale romanum* until the Second Vatican Council. (For the missal since the Second Vatican Council *see* ORDO CANTUS MISSAE.)

In 15th-century missals very little music was noted: the liturgical recitatives belonging to the celebrant (preface, *Pater noster*) and the intonations of the Ordinary (*Gloria in excelsis Deo*, *Credo in unum Deum*); and sometimes also the *Ite missa est*, sung by the deacon. These pieces were reproduced from 1476 onwards in the first printed missals with music (see Meyer-Baer, 1957, p.17, and 1962, no.119).

Even when not noted, a missal is always of interest for the study of the ordering of chants in diverse local liturgies, at least before the Council of Trent (22nd session, September 1562) which resulted in the progresssive 'Romanization' of the ancient local liturgies. Sometimes pieces peculiar to one church survive only in a printed 16th-century source, and certain sequences and rhythmic alleluias are known only from printed missals.

*See also* GRADUAL (ii); for illustration *see* SOURCES, MS, fig.17.

BIBLIOGRAPHY

HISTORY

H. Netzer: *L'introduction de la messe romaine en France* (Paris, 1910)

A. Gastoué: *Musique et liturgie: le graduel et l'antiphonaire romains* (Lyons, 1913)

F. Cabrol: 'Missel', *Dictionnaire d'archéologie chrétienne et de liturgie*, xi/2 (1933–4), 1431–68

——: 'Missel romain', *Dictionnaire d'archéologie chrétienne et de liturgie*, xi/2 (1933–4), 1468ff

R.-J. Hesbert: *Antiphonale missarum sextuplex* (Brussels, 1935)

J. A. Jungmann: *Missarum sollemnia* (Freiburg, 1948–9, rev. and enlarged 5/1962; Eng. trans., 2/1951)

A. Chavasse: 'Les plus anciens types du lectionnaire et de l'antiphonaire romains', *Revue bénédictine*, lxii (1952), 3–94

S.-R. Marosszeki: *Les origines du chant cistercien*, Analecta sacri ordinis Cisterciensis, viii (Rome, 1952)

S. J. P. van Dijk and J. H. Walker: *The Origins of the Modern Roman Liturgy* (London, 1960)

SOURCES

L. Delisle: 'Mémoires sur d'anciens sacramentaires', *Mémoires de l'Académie des inscriptions et belles-lettres*, xxxii (1886), 57–423

W. H. Frere: *Bibliotheca musico-liturgica* (London, 1894–1932/R1967)

A. Ebner: *Quellen und Forschungen zur Geschichte und Kunstgeschichte des Missale Romanum im Mittelalter: Iter Italicum* (Freiburg, 1896)

V. Leroquais: *Les sacramentaires et les missels manuscrits des bibliothèques publiques de France* (Paris, 1924)

W. H. J. Weale and H. Bohatta: *Catalogus missalium ritus latini ab anno MCCCCLXXIV impressorum* (London and Leipzig, 1928)

*Le graduel romain*, ii: *Les sources* (Solesmes, 1957)

K. Meyer-Baer: *The Printed Note* (Toledo, 1957)

——: *Liturgical Music Incunabula* (London, 1962)

P. Salmon: *Les manuscrits liturgiques latins de la Bibliothèque Vaticane*, Studi e testi (Rome, 1968–72), nos.251, 253, 260, 267, 270

For brief descriptions and bibliography for over 50 missals containing music see SOURCES, MS, §II.

MODERN EDITIONS OF NOTED MISSALS

F. E. Warren: *The Leofric Missal as Used in the Cathedral of Exeter during the Episcopate of its First Bishop* (Oxford, 1883) [*GB-Ob* Bodley 579]

J. W. Legg: *Missale ad usum ecclesiae Westmonasteriensis*, Henry Bradshaw Society, i, v, xii (London, 1891–7) [*GB-Lwa* 'Lytlington Missal']

R. Lippe: *Missale romanum: Mediolani, 1474*, Henry Bradshaw Society, xvii, xxxiii (London, 1899–1907)

J. W. Legg: *The Sarum Missal edited from Three Early Manuscripts* (Oxford, 1916) [*GB-Mr* lat.24, *I-Bu* 2565, *F-Pa* 135]

D. H. Turner: *The Missal of the New Minster, Winchester: Le Havre, Bibliothèque Municipale, MS 330*, Henry Bradshaw Society, xciii (London, 1962)

A. Hughes: *The Bec Missal*, Henry Bradshaw Society, xciv (London, 1963) [*F-Pn* lat.1105]

M. Parvio: *Missale aboense secundum ordinem Fratrum Praedicatorum* (Helsinki, 1971) [facs.]

S. Rehle: *Missale beneventanum von Canosa*, Textus patristici et liturgici, ix (Regensburg, 1972)

STUDIES OF INDIVIDUAL MISSALS

O. Gatzweiler: *Die liturgischen Handschriften des Aachener Münsterstifts* (Münster, 1926)

R. Bauerreis: 'Die geschichtlichen Einträge des Andechser Missale', *Studien und Mitteilungen zur Geschichte des Benediktinischen Ordens*, xlvii (1929), 52–90, 433

L. F. Miller: 'Missal W.11 of the Walters Art Gallery in Baltimore', *Traditio*, ii (1944), 123–54

E. Omlin: 'Beneventanisches Missale von Zürich und Payerne aus dem beginnenden XI. Jahrhundert', *Innerschweizerisches Jb für Heimatkunde*, viii–x (1944–6), 39

R.-J. Hesbert: *Les manuscrits musicaux de Jumièges*, Monumenta musicae sacrae, ii (Mâcon, 1954)

S. J. P. van Dijk: 'The Legend of the "Missal of the Papal Chapel"', *Sacris erudiri*, viii (1956), 76–142

M. Huglo: 'Un missel de St.Riquier (Wien, Ö.N.B. 1933)', *Ephemerides liturgicae*, lxxiii (1959), 402

H. Reifenberg: *Messe und Missalien im Bistum Mainz seit dem Zeitalter der Gotik*, Liturgiewissenschaftliche Quellen und Forschungen, xxxvii (Münster, 1960)

M. Huglo: 'Un missel d'Annet Régin, chantre de la cathédrale de

Clermont', *Bulletin historique et scientifique de l'Auvergne*, lxxxiii (1964), 27

R. Amiet: 'Le missel du prieuré bénédictin de St. Sauveur en Rue au diocèse de Vienne', *Scriptorium*, xix (1965), 42

A. Oliver: 'Sobre un missal manuscrito procedente de Santes Creus', *Analecta sacra tarraconensia*, xxxviii (1965), 211

G. Baroffio: 'Il messale di Boccioletto', *Rivista di storia della Chiesa in Italia*, xx/1 (1966), 34

M. Huglo: 'Un missel noté de Fleury', *Scriptorium*, xx (1966), 275

N. J. Weyns: 'Een Antwerps missaal uit de XII eeuw', *Bijdragen tot de geschiedenis, bijzonderlijk van het oud-hertogdom Brabant*, xviii (1966), 5–42

H. Platelle: 'Un missel du XVe siècle à l'usage de l'abbaye de St. Amand (Valenciennes, Ms. no.118): le donateur, l'enlumineur, le contenu', *Littérature et religion: mélanges J. Coppin* (Lille, 1967), 119–55

M. Gros: 'El "Missale Parvum" de Vic', *Hispania sacra*, xxi (1968), 313–78

M. Bernard: 'Un missel manuscrit de S. Nizier de Lyon (Ecole des Beaux Arts, Collection Masson 121, fin XVe siècle)', *Études grégoriennes*, x (1969), 117

C. de Clercq: 'Deux missels enluminés peu connus: le ms. 138 du Musée Calvet à Avignon et le ms. 86 de Lisbonne', *Gutenberg Jb 1969*, 32

K. Gamber: 'Das Reichsmessbuch der Langobarden', *4° congresso internazionale sull'alto Medioevo, Spoleto 1969*, 421–6

N. K. Rasmussen: 'Une "cartula missalis" retrouvée', *Ephemerides liturgicae*, lxxxiii (1969), 482

J. O. Braganca: 'O missal votivo de Santa Cruz de Coïmbra', *Didaskalia*, i (1971), 363

K. G. Roth: 'Zum Schicksale eines handschriftlichen Missale der Kölner Pfarrkirche St. Aposteln', *Scriptorium*, xxv (1971), 290

A. G. Martimort: 'Missels incunables d'origine franciscaine', *Mélanges liturgiques offerts au Rév. Père Dom B. Botte* (Louvain, 1972), 359

A. Nocent: 'Un missel plénier de la Bibliothèque Vallicelliana', *Mélanges liturgiques offerts au Rév. Père Dom B. Botte* (Louvain, 1972), 417

K. Gamber: 'Fragmenta liturgica, V', *Sacris erudiri*, xxi (1972–3), 241

S. Rehle: 'Ein Plenarmissale des IX. Jhdts. aus Oberitalien, zuletzt in Regensburg (Clm. 23281)', *Sacris erudiri*, xxi (1972–3), 291–321

——: 'Missale beneventanum (Codex VI 33 des Erzbischöflichen Archivs von Benevento)', *Sacris erudiri*, xxi (1972–3), 323–405

V. Saxer: 'Le missel du Cardinal Bessarion', *Scriptorium*, xxvi (1972), 302

H. Hauke: 'Das Isingrim Missale von Ottobeuren', *Studien und Mitteilungen zur Geschichte des Benediktinischen Ordens*, lxxxiv (1973), 151

K. Gamber: 'Fragmente eines Missale beneventanum als Palimpsestblätter des Cod.Ottob. lat. 576', *Revue bénédictine*, lxxxiv (1974), 367

MICHEL HUGLO

**Missa lecta** (Lat.: 'spoken mass'). A mass in which none of the liturgy is sung, although hymns may be interpolated during the service; *see* MASS, §I.

**Missa solemnis** (Lat.: 'solemn mass'). A MASS in which all sections except readings (i.e. Epistle and Gospel) are sung, whether in plainchant or polyphony. The term can also be applied to extended, ceremonious settings.

**Missinai melodies.** A category of medieval Ashkenazic Jewish chant; *see* JEWISH MUSIC, §I, 10.

**Missón, Luis.** *See* MISÓN, LUIS.

**Missonne, Vincent.** *See* MISONNE, VINCENT.

**Misticanza** [mistichanza]. A term used by Praetorius (*Syntagma musicum*, 2/1619) to refer to the Italian QUODLIBET; he also used the term 'messanza'. *Misticanza* is an archaic form of the modern Italian words 'misto' and 'mescolanza' ('mixture'), but the derivation of *messanza* is obscure. From Praetorius's definition it is clear that *misticanza* and *messanza* represented the Italian counterparts of the German quodlibet in the Renaissance, and thus belong to that genre of combinative composition that Italian scholars call the INCATENATURA. The two examples mentioned by

Praetorius, *Mirami vita mia* and *Nasce la pena*, are both six-voice choral works combining fragments from famous Italian madrigals and a few German lieder; they were included in Kaufmann's *Musikalischer Zeitvertreiber* (1609). The term 'misticanza' also appeared in G. B. Fasolo's *Misticanza di vigna alla bergamasca* (1627), a collection of solo songs with guitar accompaniment; here it simply means potpourri or miscellany, although one song combines different languages and Italian dialects for comic, quodlibet-like effect. The term 'messanza' was also used by W. C. Printz (*Compendium musicae*, 1688) to describe a particular ornamental figure.

For bibliography *see* QUODLIBET.

MARIA RIKA MANIATES

**Misura** (It.: 'measure', 'time', 'bar'). A word found in music primarily in the direction *senza misura*: 'without barring' (in the case of recitative sections with only declamatory rhythm), or 'freely', 'without strict regard for the metre'. Where *misura* is used in this last sense (as particularly often by Liszt, for example) the return to strict time is marked by *a tempo*, or simply *giusto*. Within the Italian language *misura binaria* means 'duple time', *misura composta* 'compound time', etc.

**Misura vuota.** *See* VUOTA.

**Mitantier.** *See* MITTANTIER.

**Mitchell, Donald (Charles Peter)** (*b* London, 6 Feb 1925). English writer on music and critic. He studied at Dulwich College (1939–42) and from 1945 taught in London. He is largely self-taught in music, though he spent one year at Durham University (1949–50), where he studied with Arthur Hutchings and A. E. F. Dickinson. In 1947 he founded *Music Survey* and edited it (from 1949 with Hans Keller) until it ceased publication in 1952. From 1953 to 1957 he wrote regularly for the *Musical Times*, and from 1958 to 1962 edited *Tempo* for Boosey & Hawkes, for which firm he was music adviser in 1963–4. He was on the music staff of the *Daily Telegraph* (1959–64), and in 1964 music critic for *The Listener*. In 1958 he was appointed head of the music department of Faber & Faber and in 1965 managing director of Faber Music, its subsidiary. In 1970 he became a visiting fellow at Sussex University, was professor of music there (1971–6) and visiting professor from 1976. He joined the board of Faber & Faber in 1973 and is a director of the Performing Rights Society and of the English Music Theatre (formerly the English Opera Group); he is also chairman of the education committee of the Snape Maltings Foundation. He became vice-chairman of Faber Music in 1976 and chairman in 1977. He was made an honorary MA at Sussex in 1973 and took the doctorate with a dissertation on Mahler at Southampton University in 1977.

Mitchell's writings have been almost exclusively concerned with 20th-century music, and he has written cogently and perceptively on a wide range of composers and styles. His more general essays, of which his short book *The Language of Modern Music* is the most important, are informed by a wide range of references from other disciplines, especially the visual arts. He has identified particularly with the music of Mahler and Britten, though the insights contained in his article on Elgar (1957) show how acutely he can write on a major figure in a different tradition. His principal achievement,

still in progress, is his multi-volume work on Mahler, a highly detailed undertaking that involves the examination of all extant sketches and documents as well as a broader discussion of the composer's chronological development.

WRITINGS

'Max Reger', *Mandrake*, i/2 (Oxford, 1946), 25
'Music and the Literature of Childhood', *Music Survey*, i (1947–9), 108
'Gustav Mahler and Hugo Wolf', *Chord and Discord*, ii/5 (1948), 40
'A Note on St. Nicolas: some Points of Britten's Style', *Music Survey*, ii (1949–50), 220
'Britten's "Let's Make an Opera", op.45', *Music Survey*, ii (1949–50), 86
'Schoenberg the Traditionalist', *The Chesterian*, xxiv (1949–50), 1
'Kurt Weill's "Dreigroschenoper" and German Cabaret-opera in the 1920's', *The Chesterian*, xxv (1950–51), 1
'Max Reger (1873–1916): an Introductory Musical Portrait', *MR*, xii (1951), 279
'More off than on "Billy Budd" ', *Music Survey*, iv (1951–2), 386
'Some Observations of William Walton, i: Point of Departure – "Façade"; ii: Walton and Conservatism: Attractions and Revulsions (a Partly Psychological Analysis)', *The Chesterian*, xxvi (1951–2), 35; 67
ed. with H. Keller: *Benjamin Britten: a Commentary on his Works from a Group of Specialists* (London, 1952/*R*1972) [incl. 'The Musical Atmosphere', 9–58]
'Delius: the Choral Music', *Tempo*, no.26 (1952–3), 8
'The Later Development of Benjamin Britten', *The Chesterian*, xxvii (1952–3), 1, 35
'Bartók, Stravinsky and Schoenberg: Periods: Early, Middle and Late', *The Chesterian*, xxviii (1953–4), 9
'Some Observations on "Gloriana" ', *MMR*, lxxxiii (1953), 255
'The World of Paul Hindemith', *The Chesterian*, xxviii (1953–4), 35
'Bohuslav Martinů (b. 1890)'; 'Hans Pfitzner (1869–1949)'; 'Max Reger (1873–1916)', *The Music Masters*, iv, ed. A. L. Bacharach (London, 1954), 205; 227; 281
'The Character of Lulu: Wedekind's and Berg's Conceptions Compared', *MR*, xv (1954), 268
'Malcolm Arnold', *MT*, xcvi (1955), 410
' "The Turn of the Screw": a Note on its Thematic Organization', *MMR*, lxxxv (1955), 95; see also *MO*, lxxviii (1954–5), 219, 221, 279, 281
'Prokofieff's "Three Oranges": a Note on its Musical Dramatic Organization', *Tempo* (1956), no.41, p.20
ed. with H. C. R. Landon: *The Mozart Companion* (London, 1956, 2/1965) [incl. 'The Serenades for Wind Band', 66]
'Some Thoughts on Elgar (1857–1934)', *ML*, xxxviii (1957), 113
*Gustav Mahler: the Early Years* (London, 1958, rev. 2/1980)
'Mahler and Freud', *Chord and Discord*, ii/8 (1958), 63
'Gustav Mahler: Prospect and Retrospect', *PRMA*, lxxxvii (1960–61), 83; also in *Chord and Discord*, ii/10 (1963), 138
'In and out of Britten's "Dream" ', *Opera*, xi (1960), 797
'A Suggested Anatomy of Twentieth-century Art', *MR*, xxiii (1962), 89
'Stravinsky and Neo-classicism', *Tempo* (1962), nos.61–2, p.9
'Britten's Revisionary Practice: Practical and Creative', *Tempo* (1963), nos.66–7, p.15
*The Language of Modern Music* (London, 1963, 2/1966)
'The Truth about Così', *Tribute to Benjamin Britten on his Fiftieth Birthday* (London, 1963), 95
'Public and Private Life in Britten's "Gloriana" ', *Opera*, xvii (1966), 767
ed.: *Gustav Mahler: Memories and Letters* (London, enlarged 2/1968, further enlarged 3/1973 [with K. Martner]) [trans., 1946 by B. Creighton of *Gustav Mahler: Erinnerungen und Briefe*, Amsterdam, 1940]
'Owen Wingrave and the Sense of the Past: some Reflections on Britten's Opera', SET 501–2 [disc notes]
'Double Portrait: some Personal Recollections'; 'Britten's Church Parables'; 'Shostakovich and his Symphonies'; 'A Second Renaissance for English Music', *Aldeburgh Anthology*, ed. R. Blyth (Aldeburgh, 1972), 431; 251; 215; 88
'An Introduction to Death in Venice', SET 581–3 [disc notes]
*Gustav Mahler: the Wunderhorn Years* (London, 1975)
with J. Evans, ed.: *Benjamin Britten, 1913–1976: Pictures from a Life* (London, 1978)
'Mahler, Gustav', §§10–15, Grove 6
Further articles in *The Chesterian*, *The Listener*, *MMR*, *MO*, *MT*, *Music Survey*, *Tempo*, *Times Literary Supplement*

DAVID SCOTT

**Mitchell, Howard** (*b* Lyons, Nebraska, 11 March 1911). American conductor and cellist. As a child he studied the piano and trumpet in Sioux City, Iowa, his family's home, before moving to Baltimore, where he took up the cello at the Peabody Institute. He then went to the Curtis Institute of Music in Philadelphia as a pupil of Felix Salmond (1930–35), and while still a student he was engaged as principal cellist of the National SO of Washington, DC. He held this position from 1933 until 1941, when he was appointed assistant conductor to Hans Kindler, whom he succeeded as principal conductor in 1949. He gave the premières of Paul Creston's fourth and fifth symphonies (1952, 1956), Quincy Porter's *New England Episodes* (1958), and Villa-Lobos's Symphony no.12 (1958). He resigned from the National SO in 1969, becoming music director emeritus, and was appointed principal conductor of the SODRE SO in Montevideo. Repeatedly honoured for his services to American music, he received the Ditson Award of Columbia University, a citation of merit from the National Association for American Composers and Conductors, and an award for distinguished services from the National Music Council. Conservative in his musical tastes and competent as a conductor, he brought the National SO to the brink of becoming a first-rate orchestra before leaving it for his work in Uruguay.

GEORGE GELLES

**Mitchell, William John** (*b* New York, 21 Nov 1906; *d* Binghamton, NY, 17 Aug 1971). American musicologist. He studied in New York at the Institute for Musical Art (1925–9) and at Columbia University (BA 1930, MA 1938), where he was a Clarence Barker Fellow and won the Joseph H. Bearns Prize in composition. After spending two years in Vienna (1930–32) he returned to Columbia University, where he was successively an assistant (1932), lecturer (1933), instructor (1934), assistant professor (1941), associate professor (1947) and professor (1952), as well as chairman of the music department (1962–7). Concurrently he lectured at Mannes College, New York (1957–68), and subsequently at the State University of New York at Binghamton; he was also a visiting lecturer at the University of California (1950, 1957). In 1949 he became secretary of the American Musicological Society, of which he was later president (1965–6). His main area of interest was music theory; he devised the curriculum in this subject as an academic discipline at Columbia University, and wrote a wide variety of works on the theory and historical practice of harmony and structure.

WRITINGS
ed. and trans.: *The Life and Times of Beethoven* (New York, 1935) [trans. of E. Herriot: *La vie de Beethoven*, Paris, 1929]
*Elementary Harmony* (New York, 1939, 3/1965)
'Heinrich Schenker's Approach to Musical Detail', *Musicology* (1946)
'C. P. E. Bach's Essay: an Introduction', *MQ*, xxxiii (1947), 460
ed. and trans.: *Essay on the True Art of Playing Keyboard Instruments* (New York, 1949) [trans. of C. P. E. Bach: *Versuch über die wahre Art das Clavier zu spielen*, Berlin, 1753–62]
Review of H. J. Moser: *Bernhard Ziehn der deutsch-amerikanische Musiktheoretiker* (Bayreuth, 1950), *MQ*, xxxvii (1951), 435
'The Study of Chromaticism', *JMT*, vi (1962), 2
'Chord and Context in 18th-century Theory', *JAMS*, xvi (1963), 221
'The Tristan Prelude: Techniques and Structure', *Music Forum*, i (1967), 162–203
'Giuseppe Sarti and Mozart's Quartet, K.421', *CMc* (1969), no.9, p.147
'A Hitherto Unknown . . . or . . . a Recently Discovered . . .', *Musicology and the Computer*, ed. B. S. Brook (New York, 1970), 1
'Modulation in C. P. E. Bach's *Versuch*', *Studies in Eighteenth-century Music: a Tribute to Karl Geiringer* (New York and London, 1970), 333
'The Prologue to Orlando di Lasso's *Prophetiae Sibyllarum*', *Music Forum*, ii (1970), 264

'Beethoven's *La malinconia* from the String Quartet, opus 18, no. 6: Techniques and Structure', *Music Forum*, iii (1973), 269

BIBLIOGRAPHY
P. H. Lang: Obituary, *JAMS*, xxiv (1971), 503

**Mithou.** (1) *See* DANIEL, JEAN.
(2) [Mitou] *See* CHAMPION family, (3) Thomas.

**Mitjana y Gordón, Rafael** (*b* Málaga, 6 Dec 1869; *d* Stockholm, 15 Aug 1921). Spanish musicologist. A diplomat by profession, he served in Spanish embassies in Russia, Turkey, Morocco and Sweden. Composition was his first musical interest, and he studied in Málaga with Eduardo Ocón, in Madrid with Felipe Pedrell, and in Paris with Saint-Saëns. Although he composed various works, including an opera *La buena guarda*, he eventually devoted himself exclusively to musicology and in particular to the study of Spanish music. His writings have dealt with many of the seminal figures of Spanish music including Juan del Encina, Francisco Guerrero, Cristóbal de Morales and Don Fernando de las Infantas; he also compiled the catalogue of the printed music of the 16th and 17th centuries at Uppsala University, and discovered the important collection *Villancicos de diversos autores* (Venice, 1556[30]), the music of which was later published by J. Bal y Gay as the *Cancionero de Upsala* (Mexico, 1944). Mitjana himself published an important study of the texts and musical forms of these pieces. His article 'La musique en Espagne', contributed to Lavignac's encyclopedia (1920), is one of the most comprehensive surveys of Spanish music history. Mitjana is a transitional figure in Spanish musicology between the 19th-century school of Pedrell and Barbieri and the modern school of Anglès; his work is more thorough than that of the former two, but retains their elegant and personal style of writing.

WRITINGS
*Sobre Juan de Encina, músico y poeta* (Málaga, 1895)
*La música contemporánea en España y Felipe Pedrell* (Madrid, 1901)
*Ensayos de crítica musical*, i (Madrid, 1904); ii (Madrid, 1922)
*Discantes y contrapuntos: estudios musicales* (Valencia, 1905)
*Histoire du développement du théâtre dramatique et musical en Espagne depuis ses origines* (Uppsala, 1906)
*L'orientalisme musical et la musique arabe* (Uppsala, 1907)
*Cinquenta y cuatro canciones españolas del siglo XVI. Cancionero de Upsala, ahora de nuevo publicadas, acompañadas de notas y comentarios* (Uppsala, 1909)
*El maestro Rodríguez de Ledesma y sus lamentaciones de Semana Santa* (Málaga, 1909)
*Claudio Monteverdi y los origines de la ópera italiana* (Málaga, 1911)
'El Padre Francisco Soto de Langa (1534–1619)', *Músico sacro-hispana* (1911)
*Catalogue critique et descriptif des imprimés de musique des 16e et 17e siècles, conservés à la Bibliothèque de l'Université d'Upsala* (Uppsala, 1911)
*Don Fernando de las Infantas, teólogo y músico* (Madrid, 1911)
*Estudios sobre algunos músicos españoles del siglo XVI* (Madrid, 1918)
*Cristóbal de Morales: estudio crítico biográfico* (Madrid, 1920)
'La musique en Espagne', *EMDC*, I/iv (1920), 1913–2351
*Francisco Guerrero* (Madrid, 1922)
*¡Para música vamos!; estudios sobre el arte musical contemporáneo en España* (Valencia, n.d.)

JOSÉ LÓPEZ-CALO

**Mitropoulos, Dimitri** (*b* Athens, 1 March 1896; *d* Milan, 2 Nov 1960). American conductor, pianist and composer of Greek birth. He intended to enter the Orthodox Church, in which his grandfather and others of his family had been ordained, but his studies at the Athens Odeion Conservatory under Wassenhoven (piano) and Marsick (harmony) brought him a gold medal for piano playing in 1918, and two years later the production at the conservatory of his opera based on

Maeterlinck, *Soeur Béatrice*. This engaged the interest of Saint-Saëns, who suggested that Mitropoulos should have further studies in Paris. He went instead to Brussels, for composition studies with Gilson (1920–21), and was accepted for Busoni's piano master class at the Berlin Hochschule für Musik, 1921–4, while working as répétiteur at the Staatsoper there. Returning to Athens in 1924 he began to conduct the conservatory orchestra, becoming joint musical director with Boutnikoff, 1927–9, then the principal conductor. He was appointed a professor of composition at the Odeion Conservatory from 1930. His work in raising orchestral standards and widening the repertory brought him more than local attention, and in 1930 he was engaged to conduct the Berlin PO. Here the pianist Egon Petri failed to appear for one concert, and Mitropoulos successfully took the role of pianist-conductor in Prokofiev's Third Concerto, a practice he repeated on later tours in Europe and the USSR. He was engaged by Koussevitzky as guest conductor for the Boston SO in 1936, his American début, and thereafter he settled in the USA, taking American nationality in 1946.

Mitropoulos first succeeded Ormandy in 1937 as conductor of the Minneapolis SO, remaining for 12 years, then shared the direction of the New York PO with Stokowski for a few weeks in 1949 before Stokowski resigned and Mitropoulos became sole conductor until 1958 (when he resigned and was succeeded by Bernstein). During these years he much improved the Minneapolis SO standards; devoted much care and effort to enriching the American concert repertory with works by Berg, Krenek, Schoenberg and others at a time when they were considered avant garde; received the medal of the American Mahler Society in 1940 for his promotion of Mahler's music; and gave concert performances of such operas as *Elektra*, *Erwartung*, *Wozzeck* and *Arlecchino* when they were seldom seen on the stage. With the New York PO he appeared at the 1951 and 1955 Edinburgh Festivals, and in 1955 in London, where he was otherwise a rare visitor. Mitropoulos seldom worked in the opera house until his début at the Metropolitan Opera in 1954 with *Salome*. He returned each season until his death, and gave the première there of Barber's *Vanessa* (1958), which he introduced to Europe at the Salzburg Festival the same year. An ascetic by temperament, he was an unorthodox conductor, preferring no baton and no score (but having a total command of the music's detail), using jerky and imprecise gestures which were sometimes found to vary an interpretation between rehearsal and performance. He obtained performances of an impassioned intensity that at times put severe strain on the structure of Classical and Romantic works. His Edinburgh performances of the Fourth Symphonies of Beethoven and Vaughan Williams were described (in *The Times*) as 'hateful' and 'revelatory' respectively, but it was also well said of him (in *The Observer*) that when it came to more problematic music, he was 'not one of those who pass by on the other side'. He died after a heart attack while rehearsing Mahler's Third Symphony with the orchestra of La Scala. An international conductors' competition bearing his name was established in New York in 1961. His compositions, besides *Soeur Béatrice*, include a symphonic poem *La mise au tombeau de Christ* (1916), a Concerto grosso (1929), a Piano Sonata (1919) and *Fête crétoise* (1928), orchestrated by Skalkottas, a song

cycle *Hedonica* (1927; poems by Cavafy), incidental music for plays, other piano and chamber music, and orchestrations of organ works by Bach.

BIBLIOGRAPHY
'Dimitri Mitropoulos', *The Observer* (2 Sept 1951)
D. Brook: *International Gallery of Conductors* (London, 1951), 121ff
W. S. Meadmore: 'Dimitri Mitropoulos', *Gramophone*, xxxiii (1956), 344
H. Stoddard: *Symphonic Conductors of the USA* (New York, 1957), 126ff
R. Leibowitz: 'L'eredità di Dimitri Mitropoulos', *L'approdo musicale* (1960), July–Sept, 192
R. Breuer: 'Mitropoulos: Mystiker und Moralist', *Melos*, xxviii (1961), 113
U. Bonafini: 'Mitropoulos fra Mahler & Verdi', *Discoteca* (1976), no.157, p.12 [with discography by M. Vicentini]
NOËL GOODWIN

**Mitscha, František Adam.** See MÍČA, FRANTIŠEK ADAM.

**Mitscha, František Antonín.** See MÍČA, FRANTIŠEK ANTONÍN.

**Mitsukuri, Shūkichi** (*b* Tokyo, 21 Oct 1895; *d* Chigasaki, 10 May 1971). Japanese composer. He studied chemistry at Tokyo University and, from 1921, in Berlin, where he also went to Georg Schumann for harmony lessons. In 1925 he returned to Tokyo and there became a pupil of Ikenouchi, König and Rosenstock. He made his début as a composer with the *Two Dances* for orchestra in 1926, and in 1930 he was a founder of the Shinkō Sakkyokuka Renmei. His *Shō-kōkyōkyoku* (or *Sinfonietta classica*) won a prize at the Japan Music Contest (1934) and the Weingartner Prize (1939). In the latter year Mitsukuri took a doctorate of science, but from 1945 he limited himself to musical activities. His style is strongly tonal and follows the German Romantic tradition, though in some works he made use of pentatonic scales and oriental harmonies. In *Ongaku no toki* ('Moment of music', Tokyo, 1948) he discussed an original tonal system based on the 5th; he also published an article, 'Japanese scales and their harmonic treatment' (*Japanese Music*, Tokyo, 1967, p.1).

WORKS
*(selective list)*
2 Dances, orch, 1926; Bashō kikō-shū [10 haikai of Bashō], 1v, pf/orch, 1931, rev., orch, 1947; Shō-kōkyōkyoku (Sinfonietta classica), orch, 1934; Sonata, vn, chamber orch, 1935; 2 syms., 1949, 1963; Nihon min'yō-shū [Japanese folksongs], 3 vols., 1950, 1954, 1955; Pf Concertino, 1953; Pf Qnt, 1955; Gendai shi-shū [Anthology of contemporary poems], nos 1–5., S, pf, 1931–60; 3 Movts, orch, 1968

Principal publisher: Ongaku-no-Tomo Sha
MASAKATA KANAZAWA

**Mittantier** [Mitantier] (*fl* 1536–47). French composer. He wrote 22 chansons which were published in Paris by Pierre Attaingnant. Two bicinia printed by Georg Rhau at Wittenberg in 1545 are also (dubiously) ascribed to Mittantier. His works are typical of the Parisian polyphonic chanson of Sermisy's generation. The majority are settings of courtly *épigrammes*, each line of poetry corresponding with a musical sentence which may be repeated for another line with or without symmetrical correspondence with the rhyme scheme. The music is generally homophonic, but opening or intermediate phrases occasionally have brief points of imitation. Just one chanson, *Amours si m'ont cousté*, is of the salacious anecdotal type, set in rapid syllabic counterpoint.

WORKS

Edition: *Mittantier: Opera omnia*, ed. A. Seay, CMM, lxvi (1974)

(*all 4vv unless otherwise indicated*)

Amours si m'ont cousté cent livres, 1538[10]; Celluy qui fust du bien et du tourment, 1538[10]; Ce n'est sans tort que me plains, 1547[12]; En esperant espoir me désespere (Marot), 1538[13]; Jamais amour ne peult si fermement, 1538[14]; J'ay tant chassé que la proye m'a pris, 1536[5]; Layssons amour qui nous faict tant souffrir, 1539[15–16]; Le rossignol plaisant et gracieulx, 1539[15–16]

Moins je la veulx plus m'en croist le désir, 1540[14]; O que je tiens celle la bien heureuse, 1539[15–16]; Par ton parler n'auras sur moy puissance, ed. in PÄMw, xxiii (1899); Pauvre et loyal trompé par l'espérance, 1540[14]; Plus je la voys moins y treuve à redire, 1539[15–16]; Puis que fortune a sur moy entrepris, 1542[14–15]; Si bon vouloir méritoit récompense, 1547[11]; Si j'eusse esté aussi prompte à donner, 1539[17]; Si l'amytié porte la suffisance, 1538[12]; Si tu voulois accorder la demande, 1538[13]

Tant est l'amour de vous en moy empraincté (Marot), 1538[13]; Tant seullement ton amour je demande (Marot), 1543[7–8]; Tel en mesdit qui pour soy la desire, 1543[7], ed. in PÄMw, xxiii (1899); Tel en mesdit qui pour soy la desire, 2vv, 1545[7] (parody of 4-voice version); Ung doulx baiser je prins subtilement, 1539[17]; Vous perdez temps de me dire mal d'elle, 2vv, 1545[7] (Marot; parody of 4-voice model by Sermisy, 1538[12])

FRANK DOBBINS

**Mittelgrund** (Ger.). MIDDLEGROUND; *see also* LAYER.

**Mitteltönige Temperatur** (Ger.). MEAN-TONE temperament.

**Mitzler de Kolof** [Koloff], **Lorenz Christoph.** *See* MIZLER VON KOLOF, LORENZ CHRISTOPH.

**Mixolydian.** The common name for the seventh of the eight church modes, the authentic mode on G. In the Middle Ages and Renaissance the Mixolydian mode was described in two ways: as the diatonic octave species from *g* to *g'*, divided at *d'* and composed of a fourth species of 5th (tone–tone–semitone–tone) plus a first species of 4th (tone–semitone–tone), thus *g–a–b–c'–d' + d'–e'–f'–g'*; and as a mode whose FINAL was *g* and whose AMBITUS, or range, was *f–g'*, with extensions 'by licence' up to *a'* and even down to *e*. In addition to the final, the note *d'* – the tenor of the corresponding seventh psalm tone – was regarded as having an important melodic function in the fifth church mode.

For the early history of 'Mixolydian' and the other Greek-derived modal names, *see* DORIAN.

*See also* MODE.

HAROLD S. POWERS

**Mixture stop.** An ORGAN STOP composed of several ranks of pipes at various pitches, most often octaves and 5ths. The term is both generic, referring to compound stops in general, and specific, in that Mixture (*Mixtur, mixtuur, mixtura*) is also the name used in some areas and periods for the chief mixture of the Diapason chorus or *pleno* (*lleno, plein jeu, ripieno*). The history of mixture stops is the history of the organ itself, from the big *pleno* at Winchester (10th century) through the medieval *Blockwerke* and Renaissance Mixtura (Barcelona, 1480), Locatio (A. Schlick, 1511), Hintersatz, Zimbel and Fourniture to the 19th-century Compensation mixture, Progressio Harmonica, etc. The chief Baroque additions to the chorus mixtures are the wider-scaled solo or colour mixtures, often with a Tierce rank included, such as Cornet, Hörnli, Sesquialtera, Terzian and Carillonmixtur. Some mixtures, such as Rauschpfeife, were chorus stops at one period, solo at another. The term 'mixture' appeared late in England (Father Smith's Temple organ, 1688); in his MS of

*c*1695 Talbot used it to include solo mixtures. The contents, planning, voicing and scaling of the various mixture stops distinguish national organ schools and test the skill of both ancient and modern builders more than any solo reed or Principal stop.

PETER WILLIAMS

**Miyagi** [Wakabe; Suga], **Michio** [Nakasuga Kengyō] (*b* Kobe, 7 April 1894; *d* Kariya, 25 June 1956). Japanese player of the *zoku-sō* (the 13-string koto) and composer. A son of Kunijirō Wakabe, he was given the family name of Suga as an infant. By the age of seven he was totally blind. He became in 1902 a disciple of Nakajima Kengyō II, a koto master of the Ikuta Shool; in 1903 he made his début as a solo performer, and in 1905 he received a certificate of highest proficiency in koto playing, earning the professional name of Nakasuga. Two years later he went to Korea, where he taught the koto and *shakuhachi* in Jinsen (Inchon) and then in Keijō (Seoul). In 1909 he wrote his first composition, *Mizu no hentai* ('Metamorphosis of water'), a song with koto solo which won considerable fame. He received the professional title of Kengyō in 1912; and in 1913, when he married Nakako Kita, he assumed the surname Miyagi, after which he became best known as Michio Miyagi. In 1914 he met Seifū Yoshida, who became a lifelong friend and with whom he began in 1920 the Shin Nihon Ongaku (New Japanese Music Movement), aimed at adapting elements of European music to composition for Japanese instruments. Meanwhile he had returned to Japan in 1917 and settled in Tokyo. The first concert devoted to his music was given successfully on 16 May 1919 and was followed by more in 1920 and 1921.

Although Miyagi sometimes composed in a purely traditional style, as in *Yosamu no kyoku* ('Music on a cold night', 1920) or *Tsuki no kagami* ('The moon mirror'), his works more often incorporate European features, in harmony, form or instrumental combination (he occasionally used mixed ensembles of Western and Japanese instruments); the influence of French impressionism is particularly prominent. In 1921 he introduced the newly invented *jūshichigen* (a 17-string variant of the koto), used for the first time in his *Ochiba no odori* ('Dance of falling leaves'). His less important innovations include the *hachijūgen* (an 80-string koto) and the bass *kokyū* (a large bowed instrument), while he also experimented in other directions: *Kairo-chō* (1923) was written for a group of seven Japanese instruments in emulation of European chamber music; *Sakura hensōkyoku* ('Variations on "Sakura"', 1923) adapts a Western form to Japanese instruments; and *Etenraku hensōkyoku* (1928) is virtually a concerto for koto and Western orchestra.

In 1929 Miyagi composed his most celebrated work, *Haru no umi* ('The sea in spring') for koto and *shakuhachi*; the piece was later arranged for koto and violin, and in this version became an extraordinary international success through performances by Stern and others. Miyagi took appointments as lecturer (1930) and professor (1937) at the Tokyo Music School. His activities were interrupted by the war, but in 1946 he resumed teaching and in 1950 was appointed lecturer at the Tokyo Geijutsu Daigaku (National University of Fine Arts and Music). In 1948 he was made a member of the Japan Art Academy, in 1950 he received the Broadcasting Cultural Prize sponsored by

Japanese radio, and in 1951 the Miyagi Kai, an association of his supporters, was formed. He visited Europe in 1953 to take part in the International Festival of Folk Music at Biarritz and Pamplona.

Miyagi was a prolific composer as well as a gifted essayist. His compositions are in the main for koto or for an ensemble including the koto, and most of them follow Japanese custom in having a text, even where the instrumental parts are primary. He also left solely instrumental pieces and made numerous arrangements of pieces from the traditional koto repertory.

### WORKS
(selective list)

#### STAGE AND CHORAL
Opera: Kariteibo, 1924
Incidental music: Takiguchi Nyūdō, 1946; Genji monogatari [Tale of Genji], 1951–4
Cantata: Nichiren, 1953; Matsu [Pine], 1955
Choral: Tennyo bukyoku [Heavenly maiden's dance], vv, wind, str, 1927; Aki no hibiki [Sounds of autumn], vv, 5 Jap. insts, perc, 1931; Sakura ni yoseru iwai [Celebration with cherry blossom], vv, wind, str, 1940

#### SOLO VOCAL
Mizu no hentai [Metamorphosis of water], 1v, koto, 1909; Haru no yo [Spring night], 1v, 2 koto, 3 shakuhachi, 1913; Hatsu uguisu, 1v, 2 koto, 3 shakuhachi, 1914; Aki no shirabe [Autumn music], 1v, koto, shakuhachi, 1919; Aki no yo [Autumn night], 1v, koto, 1919; Benisōbi, 1v, koto, 1920; Cosmos, Sekirei [Wagtail], 1v, koto, 1921; Hira, 1v, Jap. ens, 1923; Noki no shizuku [Raindrops on eaves], 1v, Jap. ens, 1926; Hana momiji, 1v, Jap. ens, 1927
Tō-ginuta, 1v, Jap. ens, 1929; Mushi no Musashino [The Musashino with its insects], 1932; Shun'yōraku, 1v, wind, str, 1933; Ochiba [Falling leaves], 1v, koto, 1933; Miyo no iwai [Celebration of the generation], 1v, koto, 1934; Uteya tsuzumi [Play the hand drum], 1v, koto, 1935; Dōkan, 1v, koto, wind, str, 1936
Yumedono, 1v, ens, 1940; Yamato no haru [Spring in Yamato], 1v, koto, ens, 1940; Shiki no yanagi [Willows in four seasons], 1v, Jap. ens, 1954; Nara no shiki [Four seasons in Nara], 1v, 2 koto, 1955; Hamayū, 1956

#### INSTRUMENTAL
For koto/zoku-sō, orch: Etenraku hensōkyoku [Variations on 'Etenraku'], 1928; Shinsen-chō kyōsōkyoku [Conc. in shinsen mode], 1933; Hyōjō kyōsōkyoku, 1936; Ichikotsu-chō kyōsōkyoku, 1937; Shukuten sō kyōsōkyoku [Festival conc.], 1940; Banshiki-chō kyōsōkyoku, 1953, collab. Y. Matsudaira
For ens: Kara-ginuta, 2 koto, 2 shamisen, 1914; Fubuki no hana [Flower drift], 4 koto, 1919; Higurashi, koto, shakuhachi, kokyū, 1920; Ochiba no odori [Dance of falling leaves], koto, shamisen, jūshichigen, 1921; Hanamibune, ens, 1921; Kairo-chō, ens, 1923; Tanima no suisha [Watermill in a valley], koto, shakuhachi, 1923; Sakura hensōkyoku [Variations on 'Sakura'], 3 koto, 1923; Seoto, koto, jūshichigen, 1923; Haru no otozure [Arrival of spring], koto, shakuhachi, 1924; Kohen no yūbe [An evening by a lake], koto, shakuhachi, kokyū, 1925; Seisui-raku, koto, shakuhachi, 1925; Wafū-raku, ens, 1926; Kimigayo hensōkyoku [Variations on the Jap. national anthem], 3 koto, 1927; Suzumushi, koto, shakuhachi, 1927; Kinuta, 2 koto, 1928; Kotori no uta [Song of birds], koto, shakuhachi, 1928; Haru no umi [The sea in spring], koto, shakuhachi/vn, 1929; Kōrogi, koto, shakuhachi, 1930; Shin-en no asa [Morning in the holy ground], ens, 1937; Uguisu, koto, shakuhachi, 1939; Mura no haru [Spring in villages], ens, 1941; Gyōshun [Arrival of spring], koto, shakuhachi, 1950; Sarashi-fū tegoto, 2 koto, 1952; Izumi [Fountain], koto, shakuhachi, 1954; Kiku no sakae [Prosperity for chrysanthemum], ens, 1956
For koto: Kazoe-uta hensōkyoku [Variations on 'Kazoe-uta'], 1934; Isuzu-gawa [Isuzu river], 1947; Rondon no yoru no ame [Evening rain in London], 1953

Principal publisher: Hōgaku Sha

#### BIBLIOGRAPHY
*The Complete Works of Michio Miyagi* (Tokyo, 1957–8, rev. 2/1972) [collected essays, with list of compositions, vol.iii, pp.390ff]
E. Kikkawa: *Miyagi Michio den* [The life of Miyagi] (Tokyo, 1962)

MASAKATA KANAZAWA

**Miyoshi, Akira** (*b* Tokyo, 10 Jan 1933). Japanese composer. He played the piano from an early age and took private composition lessons with Kōzaburō Hirai and Tomojirō Ikenouchi. In 1953 he won first prize at the Japan Music Competition for his Sonata for clarinet,

bassoon and piano, and in 1954 the Sinfonia concertante won him the Odaka Prize. A French government scholarship enabled him to study with Gallois-Montbrun at the Paris Conservatoire (1955–7). On his return to Japan he entered Tokyo University to study French literature and graduated in 1960. Meanwhile his compositions received further awards, notably the Italia Prize for *Ondine*. The most significant influence on his work has been that of Dutilleux.

### WORKS
(selective list)
Orch: Sinfonia concertante, pf, orch, 1954; Torse I, chamber orch, 1960; 3 mouvements symphoniques, 1960; Pf Conc., 1962; Conc. for Orch, 1964; Vn Conc., 1965; Odes métamorphosées, mar, vib, cel, pf, harp, orch, 1968; Conc., mar, str, 1969; Ouverture de fête, 1969; Leos, 1976; Noesis, 1978
Chamber: Sonata, cl, bn, pf, 1953; Vn Sonata, 1955; Pf Sonata, 1958; Str Qt no.1, 1962; Conversation, mar, 1962; Torse III, mar, 1964; Etudes en forme sonate, pf, 1967; Str Qt no.2, 1967; 8 poèmes, fl ens, 1969; Transit, perc, kbds, tape, 1970; Hommage à 'Musique de chambre '70' nos. 1–4, fl, vn, pf, 1970, 1971, 1972, 1974; Torse IV, 4 Jap. insts, str qt, 1972; Prelude chaîne, pf, 1973; Nocturne, fl, cl, db, mar, perc, 1973; Torse V, 3 mar, 1973; Litania, db, perc, 1975; Epitase, gui, 1975; Un deuil, fl, vn, pf, 1976; Concert étude, 2 mar, 1977
Vocal: Ondine, radio score, 1959; Torse II, chorus, pf, tape, 1961; En blanc, S, pf, 1962; Verre, S, pf, 1963; 3 occasions, male chorus, pf, 1963; Duel, S, orch, 1964; Saisons d'enfants, chorus, 1965; A quatre saisons, chorus, 1966; 5 images enfantines, chorus, pf, 1968; Requiem, 1972; Mittsu no umi no uta [3 sea songs], chorus, 1974; Kitsune no uta [Song of the fox], chorus, 1975

Principal publishers: Kawai Gakufu, Ongaku-no-Tomo Sha

MASAKATA KANAZAWA

**Mizieres, Tomás.** *See* MICIERES, TOMÁS.

**Mizler von Kolof** [Mitzler de Kolof, Koloff], **Lorenz Christoph** (*b* Heidenheim, Franconia, 25 July 1711; *d* Warsaw, March 1778). German writer on music, physician and mathematician. He was the son of Johann Georg Mizler, court clerk to the Margrave of Ansbach at Heidenheim, and Barbara Stumpf of St Gall. Most of his early life is chronicled in his autobiography published by Mattheson in *Grundlage einer Ehren-Pforte* (Hamburg, 1740). According to this, he first studied in Heidenheim with N. Müller, minister from Obersulzbach. At 13 he entered the Ansbach Gymnasium where for six years his teachers were Rector Oeder and Johann Matthias Gesner, subsequently director of the Leipzig Thomasschule, 1731–4, and professor at the university. Gesner's move to Leipzig may have led Mizler to enter Leipzig University on 30 April 1731, where he studied theology. In Ansbach he had had music lessons with the music director Ehrmann and learnt the violin and the flute. Mizler recorded that he had studied composition by reading the best books on the subject, hearing performances by good musicians, looking at the scores of the best masters, and through his association with J. S. Bach, whom he said he had the honour to call 'his good friend and patron'. The nature and duration of Mizler's association with Bach remains unknown. At Leipzig his teachers included such distinguished German intellectuals as Gesner, J. C. Gottsched and Christian Wolff. After an illness which required convalescence in Altdorf, Mizler returned to Leipzig to complete a bachelor's degree in December 1733 and a master's on 4 March 1734. His thesis, *Quod musica ars sit pars eruditionis philosophicae*, was later published, dedicated to Mattheson.

After a journey through Germany 'to visit various men of learning' he settled in Wittenberg in 1735 to study law and also medicine 'so that he could better care for his own health'. He returned to Leipzig in 1736 where he presented a disputation *De usu atque praestantia philosophiae in theologia, jurisprudentia, medicina* (Leipzig, 1736, 2/1740). In May 1737 he began lecturing on Mattheson's *Neu-eröffnete Orchestre* and music history at the university; he was the first to lecture on music at a German university for 150 years. In the same year he established a monthly publication, *Neu eröffnete musikalische Bibliothek*, which became the official periodical of the Korrespondierenden Sozietät der Musicalischen Wissenschaften that he founded in 1738 with the support of Count Giacomo de Lucchesini and the Ansbach court Kapellmeister G. H. Bümler. At the same time Mizler began his own music publishing business. In 1743 he entered the service of the Polish Count Malachowski of Konskie as secretary, resident teacher, librarian and court mathematician, taking up with enthusiasm the learning of the Polish language, history and literature. In 1747 he returned to his earlier interest in medicine, taking the doctorate of medicine at Erfurt University. In the same year he moved to Warsaw, turning his attention largely to the natural sciences and becoming court physician in 1752. He established a publishing house in Warsaw in 1754, became a member of the Erfurt Academy of Sciences in 1757, and received Polish nobility in 1768.

Mizler was a major figure in the history of German music in the 18th century. Although never more than an amateur composer, he commanded an extraordinary range of knowledge about music, mathematics, philosophy, theology, law and the natural sciences. He advocated what he felt was still an unattained goal: the establishment of a musical science based on mathematics and philosophy. His philosophical outlook was based largely on the writings of Christian Wolff (see Birke) and Gottfried Leibnitz, and much of his aesthetic doctrine, including his advice to imitate nature in music, was the result of his intimate association with the ideas of Gottsched. Mizler's most significant contribution was the publishing of the *Musikalische Bibliothek* between 1736 and 1754, a rich document of contemporary musical life in Germany as well as a review of many important books on music, largely from the period 1650–1750. He contributed wide-ranging commentaries on and criticisms of works by such Baroque writers as Printz, Gottsched, Mattheson, Euler, Scheibe, Schröter and Spiess. The works of Gottsched and Mattheson are particularly prominent in the pages of the *Musikalische Bibliothek*. There are several large excerpts from Gottsched's *Critische Dichtkunst*, including the sections on opera and cantata. More than 200 pages are devoted to the *Vollkommene Capellmeister* and, while often genuinely impressed by Mattheson's ideas, Mizler criticized him for failing to create a systematic ordering of musical materials and a methodical presentation of the basic principles of part-writing (see Federhofer). In his detailed and perceptive essays Mizler formulated an invaluable musical philosophy and a musicological resource for Baroque music history that has not as yet been digested by musical scholarship nor recognized in contemporary studies of music history. Equally significant was Mizler's organization of a corresponding society of musical scholars. The society was established to enable members to circulate by mail theoretical papers on various aspects of musical science and to further musical understanding by encouraging discussions of these papers by correspondence. Many of these theoretical statements appear in the *Musikalische Bibliothek*. The membership, limited to 20, comprised: 1738: 1. G. de Lucchesini; 2. Mizler (permanent secretary); 3. G. H. Bümler. 1739: 4. C. G. Schröter; 5. H. Bokemeyer; 6. G. P. Telemann; 7. G. H. Stölzel. 1742: 8. G. F. Lingke. 1743: 9. M. Spiess; 10. G. Vensky. 1745: 11. G. F. Handel; 12. U. Weiss. 1746: 13. C. H. Graun. 1747: 14. J. S. Bach; 15. G. A. Sorge; 16. J. P. Kunzen. 1748: 17. C. F. Fischer. 1751: 18. J. C. Winter. 1752: 19. J. G. Kaltenbeck. 1755: 20. L. Mozart (invitation apparently declined). Another important contribution by Mizler was his translation into German of Fux's *Gradus ad Parnassum*; in Mizler's judgment 'this methodical guide to musical composition [is] among all such works the best book that we have for practical music and its composition'.

## WRITINGS
*(only those pertaining to music included)*

*Dissertatio quod musica ars sit pars eruditionis philosophicae* (Leipzig, 1734, 2/1736 as *Dissertatio quod musica scientia sit et pars eruditionis philosophicae*, 3/1740)

*Lusus ingenii de praesenti bello* (Wittenberg, 1735); Ger. trans. in *Neu eröffnete musikalische Bibliothek* i/3, 65

*Neu eröffnete musikalische Bibliothek oder Gründliche Nachricht nebst unpartheyischem Urteil von musikalischen Schriften und Büchern*, i (Leipzig, 1739) [i/1 (1736), i/2–3 (1737), i/4–6 (1738)]; ii (Leipzig, 1743) [ii/1–2 (1740), ii/3 (1742), ii/4 (1743)]; iii (Leipzig, 1752) [iii/1–2 (1746), iii/3 (1747), iii/4 (1752)]; iv (Leipzig, 1754)

*Musikalischer Staarstecher, in welchem rechtschaffener Musikverständigen Fehler bescheiden angemerket, eingebildeter und selbst gewachsener sogenannter Componisten Thorheiten aber lächerlich gemachet werden* (Leipzig, 1739–40)

*Anfangs-Gründe des General-Basses nach mathematischer Lehr-Art abgehandelt* (Leipzig, 1739)

Preface to J. C. Voight: *Gespräch von der Musik, zwischen einem Organisten und Adjuvanten* (Erfurt, 1742)

*Gradus ad Parnassum oder Anführung zur regelmässigen Composition, aus dem Lateinischen ins Deutsche übersetzt, und mit Anmerkungen versehen* (Leipzig, 1742) [trans. of J. J. Fux: *Gradus ad Parnassum* (Vienna, 1725)]

## WORKS

Musikalisches Vergnügen, bestehend in einer Sammlung von verschiedenen Oden und einer moralischen Cantate, announced 1737, not pubd

Sammlung auserlesener moralischer Oden, zum Nutzen und Vergnügen der Liebhaber des Claviers, i (Leipzig, 1740), ii (Leipzig, 1741), iii (Leipzig, 1743), iv, announced, not pubd [facs. edn. of i–iii, ed. D. Plamenac (Leipzig, 1971); ode 24 from vol.i, *D-Bds*]

4 Sonatinen, fl/ob/vn (Leipzig, 1754), lost

Corrections to G. Lucchesini's Fl Conc., 1741, *D-Dlb*

## BIBLIOGRAPHY

*WaltherML*

J. Mattheson: *Grundlage einer Ehren-Pforte* (Hamburg, 1740); ed. M. Schneider (Berlin, 1910/R1969)

F. Wöhlke: *Lorenz Christoph Mizler: ein Beitrag zur musikalischen Gelehrtengeschichte des 18. Jahrhunderts* (Würzburg, 1940)

J. Birke: *Christian Wolffs Metaphysik und die zeitgenössische Literatur- und Musiktheorie: Gottsched, Scheibe, Mizler* (Berlin, 1966)

H. Federhofer: 'Johann Joseph Fux und Johann Mattheson im Urteil Lorenz Christoph Mizlers', *Speculum musicae artis: Festgabe für Heinrich Husmann* (Munich, 1970), 111

GEORGE J. BUELOW

**Mizmār.** A term used in the Islamic world at different times to denote various reed-vibrated instruments. Up to the 10th century *mizmār* (plural *mazāmīr*) referred to any reed instrument; it is now used primarily for a type of idioglott double clarinet. The pipes are of equal length and made from wood, reed, ivory or bone, bound together with string, wax, metal or pitch; pipes made from the thigh-bones of eagles are particularly prized. The pipes have an equal number of paired stops, usually six (but ranging from four to seven). The reeds are each made by cutting upwards into a separate short length of cane; they are attached to the instrument by a small piece of cord, and are fitted into the top of each pipe.

Both mouthpieces are held entirely within the player's mouth and circular breathing is used to produce continuous sound. Variant names include *zamr* (an instrument of north Africa, particularly Morocco, which often has a horn bel), *mijwiz*, *mizweg* and *mizmar* (Syria), *mutbej* (Iraq), *mazaamir* (Yemen), *çifte* (Turkey) and *zummāra* (Jordan). In all areas the *mizmār* is primarily a folk instrument played by nomads and at village dances and gatherings.

BIBLIOGRAPHY

S. Marcuse: *A Survey of Musical Instruments* (Newton Abbot and London, 1975), 702f

L. Picken: *Folk Musical Instruments of Turkey* (London, 1975), 514ff

J. Jenkins and P. Rovsing Olsen: *Music and Musical Instruments in the World of Islam* (London, 1976), 58

WILLIAM J. CONNER, MILFIE HOWELL

**Mizonne, Vincent.** *See* MISONNE, VINCENT.

**Mizuno, Shūkō** [Nobutaka] (*b* Tokushima, 24 Feb 1934). Japanese composer. He studied with Shibata and Hasegawa at the Tokyo Geijutsu Daigaku (National University of Fine Arts and Music) from 1958 to 1963. Together with Takehisa Kosugi he organized in 1958 the Group Music for improvisation, and he used improvisatory playing in *Three Dimensions* (1961) for three brass groups, each with a separate conductor. He adopted more conventional materials in the *Nihon no senritsu ni yoru composition* ('Composition based on Japanese melodies') series for orchestra (1962–6), but at the same time he began to use graphic notation in the *Autonomy* series. Another graphic piece, *Orchestra 1966*, makes extensive use of clusters, and in *Provisional Color* for piano (1967) only pitches are stipulated. In subsequent works he has drawn on jazz, an increasingly strong influence in his compositions from *Jazzy Work* for chorus and orchestra (1967) to *Jazz Orchestra '73*. He was appointed to teach at Chiba University in 1968 and Tokyo Geijutsu Daigaku in 1971.

WORKS
*(selective list)*

3 Dimensions, 3 brass ens, 1961; Gyomon, tape, 1962; Remote Control, tape, 1962; Nihon no senritsu ni yoru composition [Composition based on Japanese melodies], nos.1–5, 1962–6; Autonomy of Strings, 1963; Autonomy of Voice, 1964; Autonomy of Insts, 1964; Orch 1966, 1966; Jazzy Work, chorus, orch, 1967; Provisional Color, pf, 1967; Original, nos.1–2, jazz orch, 1968, 1970; Cross Talk 1969, insts, tape, elec, 1969; Provisional Color, jazz ens, 1969; Autonomy for Chorus, 1972; Dies irae, chorus, elec, 1972; Jazz Orch '73, 1973; Spring!, harp, 1973; Maboroshi [Phantom], chorus, 1975; Jazz Orch '75, 1975; Joya no tame no etude [Etude for New Year's eve], pf, 1976; Tenshukaku Monogatari (TV drama), 1977

Principal publisher: Ongaku-no-Tomo Sha

WRITINGS

'Ongun-teki sahō eno shikō' [The theory of composition dealing with the *ongun*], *Ongaku geijutsu*, xxv/11 (1967), 12; xxvi/11 (1968), 50

MASAKATA KANAZAWA

**MLA.** MUSIC LIBRARY ASSOCIATION.

**Młynarski, Emil** (*b* Kibarty, nr. Suwałki, 18 July 1870; *d* Warsaw, 5 April 1935). Polish conductor, violinist and composer. He studied at the St Petersburg Conservatory under Auer (violin) and Lyadov (composition); while a student he led the Imperial Musical Society orchestra and was a member of Auer's quartet. In 1894 he settled in Odessa where until 1897 he taught at a music school attached to the Imperial Musical Society. There he discovered Kochański and also taught Luboszyc. He returned to Poland in 1898 and was the first to organize regular orchestral concerts in the capital. In 1903 he organized in Paris the first festival of Polish music in connection with a series of Colonne concerts. He was director of the Warsaw Conservatory (1904–7) and permanent conductor of the Scottish SO (1910–16), also appearing as a guest conductor in London during this period. From 1914 to 1917 he was active in Moscow, conducting the Bolshoy Theatre orchestra. He returned to Warsaw in 1918 and was again director of the conservatory (1919–22) and of the opera (1919–29). His conducting activities abroad included another festival of Polish music in Paris (1925), while at home he was responsible for the premières of several important Polish stage works, among them Szymanowski's *Hagith* and *King Roger*. He was in Philadelphia (1929–31) as a conductor and teacher of conducting at the Curtis Institute, but ill-health forced his return to Warsaw where he conducted the Philharmonic, opera and radio orchestras. Although he was active in the promotion of new Polish music, his own work follows the traditions of Moniuszko, Wieniawski and Paderewski, combining Romantic traits with folksong elements. The style is somewhat academic but the instrumentation is very colourful. Among his best works are the Symphony 'Polonia', the Second Violin Concerto and the violin miniatures.

WORKS
*(selective list)*

Vocal: Noc letnia [Summer night] (opera, 3, H. Fried), 1914; songs, other vocal pieces

Orch: 2 vn concs., d, op.11, 1897, D, op.16, 1914–17; Sym. 'Polonia', F, op.14, 1910; Cradle Song (1954)

Inst: 3 Pieces, op.4, vn, pf (*c*1892); 3 Pieces, op.6, vn, pf (*c*1893); 2 Mazurkas, G, A, op.7, vn, pf (*c*1895); pf sonata; miniatures

BIBLIOGRAPHY

*SMP*

J. W. Reiss: *Statkowski-Melcer-Młynarski-Stojowski* (Warsaw, 1949), 16ff

A. Wach: *Życie i twórczość Emila Młynarskiego* [Life and works of Emil Młynarski] (diss., U. of Kraków, 1953)

J. Mechanisz: *Emil Młynarski: w setną rocznicę urodzin (1870–1970)* (Warsaw, 1970)

TERESA CHYLIŃSKA

**MM.** *Metronom Maelzel* (Ger.); *see* METRONOME; MAELZEL, JOHANN NEPOMUK; TEMPO AND EXPRESSION MARKS.

**Moberg, Carl-Allan** (*b* Östersund, 5 June 1896; *d* Uppsala, 19 June 1978). Swedish musicologist. He began his musicological studies under Tobias Norlind (1917–24). From 1924 he studied counterpoint in Vienna with Berg, and medieval music with Peter Wagner in Fribourg until 1927 and with Handschin in Basle (1934–5). He achieved an international reputation as a medievalist with his doctoral thesis of 1927 on Swedish sequences; in 1928 he became reader at Uppsala University and was professor there, 1947–61.

With his research and teaching from the 1920s following on Norlind's pioneering work, Moberg must be considered the founder of Swedish musicology. Though his output as a scholar lies mainly in the history of Swedish music, he also did important ethnomusicological research. A distinctive feature of his work is his critical approach to source material and his keen interest in aspects of cultural and social history. Besides medieval church music, Moberg made a particular study of Swedish 17th-century music, the history of ideas in music and Swedish folk music, carrying out field work in different parts of Sweden. For some decades he was involved in popular education, especially in Uppsala and with the Swedish Broadcasting Corporation. He was a member of the board of Svenska Samfundet för Musikforskning from 1943 and in 1945 was elected president and editor-in-chief of its periodical, *Svensk tidskrift för musikforskning*, positions which he held until 1961. He was also the editor of *Studia musicologica upsaliensia* (1952–61) and a member of the editorial staff (1947–52) of *Sohlmans musiklexikon*. He was made an honorary doctor of theology in 1945. A member of the Swedish Royal Academy of Music from 1943, he was its president from 1960 to 1963.

### WRITINGS

'Lully-skolan i Uppsala universitetsbibliotekets handskriftsamlingar', *STMf*, vii (1925), 64, 113

*Über die schwedischen Sequenzen: eine musikgeschichtliche Studie* (diss., U. of Uppsala, 1927)

'Om flerstämmig musik i Sverige under medeltiden', *STMf*, x (1928), 5–92

'Musik und Musikwissenschaft an den schwedischen Universitäten', *Mitteilungen der Internationalen Gesellschaft für Musikwissenschaft*, i (1929), 54; ii (1930), 10, 34

'Tobias Norlind och svensk musikhistorisk forskning', *STMf*, xi (1929), 5

'Eine vergessene Pseudo-Longinusstelle über die Musik', *ZMw*, xii (1929–30), 220

'Un compositeur oublié de l'école de Lully: Jean Desfontaines', *RdM*, x (1929), 5

'Kleine Bemerkungen zum Codex Upsal. C 23', *STMf*, xii (1930), 37

'Zur Geschichte des schwedischen Kirchengesangs', *IMSCR, i Liège 1930*, 184

'Olof Rudbeck d.ä. och musiken', *Rudbecksstudier* (Uppsala, 1930), 176–210

*Kyrkomusikens historia* (Stockholm, 1932)

'Der gregorianische Gesang in Schweden während der Reformationszeit', *KJb*, xxvii (1932), 84

'Essais d'opéras en Suède sous Charles XII', *Mélanges de musicologies offerts à M. Lionel de La Laurencie* (Paris, 1933), 123

'Från Abbé Vogler till John Morén', *Kyrkohistorisk årsskrift*, xxxv (1935), 217–72

*Tonkonstens historia i västerlandet* (Stockholm, 1935)

'Die neue musikwissenschaftliche Forschung in Schweden', *AMf*, ii (1937), 361

'De folkliga koralvarianterna på Runö', *STMf*, xxi (1939), 9–47

*Från kyrko- och hovmusik till offentlig konsert: studier i stormaktstidens svenska musikhistoria* (Uppsala, 1942/*R*1970)

*Dietrich Buxtehude* (Hälsingborg, 1946)

*Die liturgischen Hymnen in Schweden*, i (Uppsala, 1947)

'Richard Dybeck och svensk folkmusik', *Arv*, iv (1948), 1

*Bachs passioner och höga mässa* (Stockholm, 1949)

'The Function of Music in Modern Society', *STMf*, xxxvi (1954), 84

'Drag i Östersjöområdets musikliv på Buxtehudes tid', *STMf*, xxxix (1957), 15–88

'Kühreigen, Lobetanz und Galder', *DJbM*, iii (1958), 98

'Die Musik in Guido von Arezzos Solmisationshymne', *AMw*, xvi (1959), 187

'Zur Melodiegeschichte des Pange-Lingua-Hymnus', *Jb für Liturgie und Hymnologie*, v (1960), 46

'Gregorianische Reflexionen', *Miscelánea en homenaje a Monseñor Higinio Anglés*, ii (Barcelona, 1961), 559

'Vincenzo Albrici und das Kirchenkonzert: ein Entwurf', *Natalicia musicologica Knud Jeppesen* (Copenhagen, 1962), 199

'Fistula und Fidhla: zur Kritik altschwedischer Musiknotizen', *SMw*, xxv (1962), 369

*Studien zur schwedischen Volksmusik* (Uppsala, 1971) [articles on Swedish folk music from *STMf*, 1950–59]

*Musikens historia i västerlandet intill 1600* (Stockholm, 1973)

### BIBLIOGRAPHY

'Studier tillägnade Carl-Allan Moberg 5 juni 1961', *STMf*, xliii (1961) [incl. M. Tegen: 'Carl-Allan Mobergs Skrifter: en förteckning' (complete list of writings to 1961), 403]

INGMAR BENGTSSON

**Mobile form.** See ALEATORY, §4.

**Mocke, Antoine.** See MOUQUÉ, ANTOINE.

**Mockridge, Cyril** (*b* London, 6 Aug 1896). American composer of English birth. He studied at the Royal Academy of Music and, after war service, settled in the USA in 1922 where he worked on Broadway before joining the Fox Film Corporation in 1931. Among his notable film scores were *The Ox-Bow Incident*, *My Darling Clementine*, *Nightmare Alley*, *Where the Sidewalk Ends* and the theme music for the TV series 'Laramie'.

*See also* FILM MUSIC.

CHRISTOPHER PALMER

**Mock trumpet.** A term which seems to have been used about 1700 for an undeveloped CHALUMEAU. The mock trumpet has been confused with the trumpet marine, with which it has no connection. Dart (*GSJ*, vi, 1953, 35) described a book of instructions for playing the mock trumpet, as well as a 'Variety of new Trumpet Tunes Aires Marches and Minuets' for the instrument. This was clearly the chalumeau before its improvement by Denner; it carried three finger-holes for each hand, one thumb-hole, and had no keys. Such an instrument is illustrated as no.221 in the *Catalogue of the Royal Military Exhibition* (ed. C. R. Day, London, 1890), where its length is said to be $8\frac{1}{4}$ inches (*c*23 cm). Its range was $g'$ to $g''$ and its tone may be assumed to have been strident. The copy described by Dart seems to have been printed in about 1707, but he showed that an earlier edition was printed in 1698. No other music for the chalumeau before its improvement is known.

NICHOLAS SHACKLETON

**Mocqué, Antoine.** See MOUQUÉ, ANTOINE.

**Mocquereau, André** (*b* La Tessoualle, Maine-et-Loire, 6 June 1849; *d* Solesmes, 18 Jan 1930). French scholar of plainchant. He took his vows as a Benedictine monk at Solesmes on 9 April 1877, was ordained priest on 28 December 1879 and was prior at Solesmes from 1902 to 1908. His musical education allowed him soon to become Pothier's assistant; he worked with him for 13 years and eventually replaced him as choirmaster at Solesmes in 1889. From 1887, in order to defend the *Liber gradualis* (1883), which was attacked by the supporters of official editions of chants (Pustet, Regensburg), Mocquereau began to conceive the idea of a monumental work entitled Paléographie Musicale containing facsimile reproductions of Gregorian MSS as well as commentaries on them; the first volume appeared in 1889. From 1888 to 1891 he went on several journeys within and outside France, bringing back much information and numerous photographs of musical MSS. This was revised and expanded on several occasions by his associates until 1914, by which time a valuable collection had been gradually compiled in the palaeographic centre at Solesmes. Many synoptical tables of different readings of the MSS were prepared from this collection. With such material Mocquereau was appointed a member of the commission formed in 1904 at the instigation of Pope Pius X to bring out a new official Vatican edition of chant and he was given the task of drawing up the musical text to be put forward for discussion. This text, based on what was thought to be the oldest and most authentic tradition, was often criticized and modified by Pothier, who believed in the 'living tradition' and in its modern variants. The association of the two men soon came to an end. It was only in 1913 that Solesmes was again given the task of preparing forthcoming official editions.

Mocquereau had the insight to realize that our comprehension of Gregorian chant is to be gained above all from the MSS. The objective method which he was the first to apply in this field has still to be developed since Mocquereau himself, much to his regret, had neither the time nor the possibility of carrying it through completely. In the first volumes of the Paléographie Musicale, of which he edited the first 13 volumes, he examined the relation between the Latin accent and Gregorian melody; this study is the basis of a true understanding of the aesthetics of Gregorian chant. In volume vii (1901) he discussed the connection between accent and rhythm, an argument which Mocquereau took much further than the simple study of Gregorian chant and its MSS and which he dealt with more fully in the *Nombre musical grégorien*. From the beginning of his analysis, by means of the binary and tertiary subdivisions marked by the *ictus* (as by the alternation of the *arsis* and *thesis*), Mocquereau first wanted to specify the rhythm of Gregorian chant in an exact way. This precision he was then able to modify in practice through a flexible understanding of dynamic and agogic values acquired during his early musical training.

WRITINGS

*Paroissien romain: Liber usualis* (Tournai, 1903, 5/1905) [with oriscus and rhythmic signs]

*Le nombre musical grégorien*, i (Tournai, 1908; Eng. trans., 1932–51); ii (Tournai, 1927)

Articles in *Rassegna gregoriana* and Solesmes publications, *Monographies grégoriennes* and *Revue grégorienne*

BIBLIOGRAPHY

N. Rousseau: *L'école grégorienne de Solesmes* (Tournai, 1910)

P. Combe: 'Bibliographie de Dom André Mocquereau', *Etudes grégoriennes*, ii (1957), 189 [gives list of writings]

——: *Histoire de la restauration du chant grégorien d'après des documents inédits* (Solesmes, 1969)

EUGÈNE CARDINE

**Moda** (Sp.: 'fashion', 'style'). A narrative song genre related to the Iberian ballad; *see* BRAZIL, §II, 1(ii, iv), 3(ii, iv), and MODINHA.

**Modal jazz.** A term applied to certain jazz techniques of the late 1950s and early 1960s, notably associated with the work of the tenor and soprano saxophonist John Coltrane. Its origin is usually traced to Miles Davis's record *Kind of Blue* (1959), in which Coltrane and the archetypal 'modal' pianist Bill Evans took part. In this work the soloists, supported by harmonically ambiguous accompaniment (e.g. parallel 4th chords) from Evans, based their improvisations on pre-established series of modes instead of the complex harmonic patterns favoured by the bop and 'hard bop' schools; *Flamenco Sketches*, for example, used five modes, each on a different tonic, and *So What* two Dorian modes separated by a semitone (see ex.1). In the same year

Ex.1

etc

Charles Mingus independently applied similar techniques to the collectively improvised passages of his *Mingus-Ah-Um*. The technique of modal jazz received its fullest expression a few years later in the work of Coltrane. By simplifying harmony and emphasizing freedom of line it stimulated many of the advances of free jazz.

BIBLIOGRAPHY

E. Jost: 'John Coltrane und die modale Spielweise', *Free Jazz* (Mainz, 1975)

BRADFORD ROBINSON

**Modal rhythm.** *See* RHYTHMIC MODES.

**Mode** (from Lat. *modus*: 'measure', 'standard'; 'manner', 'way'). A term in Western music theory with three main applications, all connected with the above meanings of *modus*: the relationship between the note values *longa* and *brevis* in late medieval notation; interval, in early medieval theory; most significantly, a concept involving scale type and melody type. The term 'mode' has always been used to designate classes of melodies, and in this century to designate certain kinds of norm or model for composition or improvisation as well. Certain phenomena in folksong and in non-Western music are related to this last meaning, and are discussed below in §§IV and V. The word is also used in acoustical parlance to denote a particular pattern of vibrations in which a system can oscillate in a stable way; *see* SOUND, §5.

I. The term. II. Medieval modal theory. III. Modal theories and polyphonic music. IV. Modal scales and folksong melodies. V. Mode as a musicological concept.

*I. The term*

1. Mensural notation. 2. Interval. 3. Scale or melody type.

1. MENSURAL NOTATION. In this context the term 'mode' has two applications. First, it refers in general to the proportional durational relationship between *brevis* and *longa*: the *modus* is *perfectus* (sometimes *major*) when the relationship is 3:1, *imperfectus* (sometimes *minor*) when it is 2:1. (The attributives *major* and *minor* are more properly used with *modus* to distinguish the relation of *longa* to *maxima* from the relation of *brevis* to *longa*, respectively.)

In the earliest stages of mensural notation, the so-called Franconian notation, 'modus' designated one of five to seven fixed arrangements of longs and breves in particular rhythms, called by scholars rhythmic modes. In these stylized patterns both long and breve could have two possible durations: if the shortest breve is assigned the value 1, the breve could be 1 or 2, the long 2 or 3; for example: B L + B L (12 + 12), L + L (3 + 3), B B + L (12 + 3) and B B B + B B B (1 1 1 + 1 1 1).

*See also* NOTATION, §III, 2(vii), 3, and RHYTHMIC MODES.

2. INTERVAL. Hucbald (*c*840–930) listed nine 'modes' in his *De harmonica*, ranging from semitone to major 6th by semitonal increments, giving examples from the chant repertory for each (*GS*, i, 105). His discussion was transmitted verbatim through Berno of Reichenau (*d* 1048; *GS*, ii, 64). In chapter 4 of his *Micrologus* (*c*1026) Guido of Arezzo gave six 'modes' 'by which the scale degrees are linked' from the semitone to the 5th with the exception of the tritone. He then mentioned an expansion to eight, adding the major and minor 6ths, and to nine, including the octave. Wilhelm of Hirsau (*d* 1091; *GS*, ii, 173f) reported both traditions – Guido's six 'modes' and Berno's nine – replacing the word 'modes' with 'intervals', and he added examples from plainchant for the minor 7th and the unison. (Further references to early traditions for *modus* meaning 'interval' may be found in Vivell's edn. of Frutolfus of Michelsberg's *Breviarium*, p.64, n.11.) The designation of interval by *modus* was repeated in manuals and treatises of later times, especially in Germany. In book 1 of Ornithoparchus's *Musicae activae micrologus* (1517) chapter 7 is entitled 'De modis seu intervallis', which in Dowland's translation of 1609 became 'Of Moodes, or Intervals'. As late as 1716 J. H. Buttstett, objecting

to calling the unison an interval, repeated an old tradition that 'The unison is not a *mode* but rather the first foundation of other *modes*, as [is] unity of the numbers' (*Ut, mi, sol, re, fa, la*, p.29).

3. SCALE OR MELODY TYPE. It is essential to distinguish between 'mode' as a concept in the history and theory of European music and 'mode' as a modern musicological concept, though the latter naturally grew out of the former. As an indigenous term in Western music theory the term is applicable in three separate successive historical stages: to Gregorian chant, to Renaissance polyphony, and to tonal harmonic music of the 17th century to the 19th. These three stages of modality in European music were historically continuous in the higher levels of a single musical culture.

The nucleus of the concept of mode in its basic Western form may be illustrated in two early 11th-century Italian formulations: 'A tone or mode is a rule which distinguishes every chant in its final [scale degree]' (*Dialogus de musica, GS*, i, 257); and 'The first degree A and the fourth, D, are alike and are designated "of a single mode" because both have a tone beneath and [have] tone–semitone–tone–tone above. And this is the first "similarity in the scale degrees", that is, the first mode' (Guido: *Epistola de ignoto cantu, GS*, ii, 47). The famous definition from the anonymous *Dialogus* emphasized both the classificatory function of mode and the primacy of the final scale degree; Guido here stressed the scalar–melodic environment of any given scale degree, thus providing a structural definition for mode. These and other elements of mode and modality had a considerable earlier and subsequent history in medieval theory and practice, but they epitomize the two most important features: classification, and tonal structure.

In the first part of the 16th century theorists began to use first the eight medieval modes of Gregorian chant and then also an extended system of 12 modes to account for such features of polyphonic music as the choice of cadential pitches and of pitches for the opening imitative entries, as well as to specify aspects of range and contour in individual melodic lines. How real these theories of polyphonic modality were for 15th-century musicians is moot; but from the mid-16th century until well into the 17th polyphonic modality was a central feature of many repertories as well as of many theories. Finally, during the 17th century various systems of polyphonic modes played complex roles in the development of theoretical systems made up of pairs of major and minor keys in what has come to be called tonal HARMONY or harmonic TONALITY.

All three stages of European modal theory emphasized the classificatory and scalar aspects of mode, though one can observe or infer important melodic and motivic features that may be called 'modal' in some phases of medieval and Renaissance theory and practice. But in the 20th century the use of the term 'mode' in English has been broadened to the extent that melodic type and motivic features are now given equal weight with scale type in musicological parlance. The broader concept came into the scholarly literature during the first quarter of the 20th century in studies of eastern Mediterranean musical styles and Eastern Christian liturgical music, from which it has become the basis of the common understanding of 'mode'. A new basic definition from Idelsohn's *Jewish Music* (1929) was given wide currency in the English-speaking world when it was taken over by Reese for his *Music in the Middle Ages* (1940, p.10): 'A MODE . . . is composed of a number of MOTIVES (i.e. short music figures or groups of tones) within a certain scale'. In Winnington-Ingram's *Mode in Ancient Greek Music* (1936) both the scalar and the melodic aspects of mode are summarized, in a broad geographical and cultural context that includes both the historical Western definition and the then new aspects proposed by Western scholars of Eastern music:

Mode is essentially a question of the internal relationships of notes within a scale, especially of the predominance of one of them over the others as a tonic, its predominance being established in any or all of a number of ways: e.g., frequent recurrence, its appearance in a prominent position as the first note or the last, the delaying of its expected occurrence by some kind of embellishment. [p.2]

Mode may be defined as the epitome of stylized song, of song stylized in a particular district or people or occupation; and it draws its character partly from associations contracted in its native home, reinforced perhaps by the sanctions of mythology. This is true of the Chinese *tyao*, the Indian *rāg*, and the Arabian *maqam*; and probably of the [ancient] Greek [*harmonia*]. [p.3]

To the terms above, for which 'mode' is used as a translation, should be added 'echos', used in medieval Greek Christian music theory to describe the direct model for what became the mode of Gregorian chant theory. To the oriental technical terms one might add Persian *dastgāh* or *āvāz, paṭet* in Javanese gamelan music, and Japanese *chō* – with its usual enclitic, *chōshi* – a word cognate with Chinese *tyao*, and written with the same ideograph.

Taking the term in the modern, twofold sense, mode can be defined as either a 'particularized scale' or a 'generalized tune', or both, depending on the particular musical and cultural context. If one thinks of scale and tune as representing the poles of a continuum of melodic predetermination, then most of the area between can be designated one way or another as being in the domain of mode. To attribute mode to a musical item implies some hierarchy of pitch relationships, or some restriction on pitch successions; it is more than merely a scale. At the same time, what can be called the mode of a musical item is never so restricted as what is implied by referring to its 'tune'; a mode is always at least a melody type or melody model, never just a fixed melody. This polarity of scale and tune is an instance of the familiar opposition of general to specific, which in music is often thought of as a contrasting of theory with practice. When modes (or their equivalents) are construed as primarily scalar, they tend to be used for classifying, for grouping musical entities into ideal categories. When the melodic aspects of modality are its predominant features, then modes are seen as guides and norms for composition or improvisation.

The opposition of mode as class and mode as musical function is reflected in contrasts of emphasis observed in other aspects of modality. Modal systems used for classification are closed and often symmetrical in some way as well; they are constructions used for ordering purposes, and may well have origins and associations that have nothing essentially to do with any musical properties of the repertory to which they are actually applied. Musically functional modal systems, on the other hand, have to be open-ended and capable of making room for new musical modes, which may come into the system through borrowing, variation, proliferation, inspiration, and in many other ways. In this same vein, a modal system may be a rational construction, devised or revised by the learned; or it may be a traditional assemblage of musical entities used and retained by the working musician. And further, the possession of modality may be construed as a natural musical property, inevitably inherent in all music of the culture; or modality may be regarded as a property of a particular repertory, not necessarily applicable to other kinds of music in the culture.

***II. Medieval modal theory.*** Medieval Christian music of the West is the oldest musical style from which theory and repertory survive in sufficient quantity for comparative examination over time. Gregorian chant is a body of monophonic music melodically characterized by general open-ended modality and theoretically classified into a closed symmetrical system – the eight church modes. For ripeness of age combined with richness of intelligible sources, both musical and theoretical, it is unmatched. For these reasons, as well as because they are the ultimate source of all later Western notations of mode, chant theory and Gregorian chant provide the best paradigm for study and illustration of most aspects of mode and modality, both historically and systematically.

1. The elements: (i) The Hellenistic model: tone, mode, trope (ii) The Byzantine model: oktōēchos. 2. Carolingian synthesis, 9th–10th centuries: (i) The Boethian double octave and the modes (ii) Octave species and the Hellenistic names (iii) Melodic types and modal orientation. 3. 11th-century syntheses: (i) Italian theory of modal functions (ii) Reichenau theory of modal species and locations (iii) Authentic–plagal distinctions. 4. Mode in the later Middle Ages: (i) Modal quality and hexachord syllables (ii) Italian modal theory in the 14th and 15th centuries (iii) Expansion of the tonal system.

1. THE ELEMENTS. Modal theories in the West originated in a confluence of the Western chant repertory that had already existed in oral tradition in pre-Carolingian times with two main strands of theory imported during the 8th and 9th centuries from outside the practical traditions of that time. The first strand and the fundamental component of Western modal theory was a system of eight modes borrowed from Eastern Christianity, as reported in the earliest Carolingian sources. The rest of the theory was erected on this foundation with the aid of a congeries of patterned schemes and abstract terms originating with the musical systematists of the Hellenistic era – Ptolemy of Alexandria and others – and transmitted to the medieval West by Martianus Capella, Cassiodorus, Isidore of Seville and especially Boethius. The essential contributions to modal theory of this second strand were: (*a*) a precise means of measuring and demonstrating intervals of the diatonic scale using the monochord, a one-string instrument of ancient repute with a movable bridge; (*b*) a system of names for the resulting pitches, based on the diatonic tetrachord, along with the notion of using letter designations of some sort for the pitches of the whole system; (*c*) the idea of scale types, the species of the octave, along with a set of Greek names for them; and (*d*) the species of the smaller perfect consonances, the 4th and 5th.

(*i*) *The Hellenistic model: tone, mode, trope.* Making distinctions among various aspects of the modal continuum in the sources of chant theory is complicated by the use of three different terms that came to cover more or less the same phenomena: 'tone', 'mode' and 'trope'. 'Tone' and 'trope' are Latinized Greek, 'mode' is pure Latin. These terms are often found in pairs or as a set, in contexts implying synonymity, as well as alone; and each of them has not only one or more significances in the realm of modality, depending on the source, but also at least one other, quite different meaning in medieval theory.

The Greek terms 'tone' and 'trope' occur Latinized in the writings of Martianus Capella and Cassiodorus, respectively; the three terms appear together, and synonymously, in book 4 chapter 15 of Boethius's *De institutione musica* (early 6th century). For Boethius, as for his Hellenistic sources, tones or modes were simply devices for transposition; they had nothing whatsoever to do with the church modes:

From the 'species' of the 'consonance' of the 'octave' arise what are called 'modes', which same they call 'tropes' or 'tones'. 'Tropes', moreover, are 'constitutions' differing by lowness or height in the entire dispositions of the pitches. A 'constitution' in fact is, so to speak, a whole framework for melody [*modulationis corpus*] consisting of a linking together of the [fixed ends of the] 'consonances' – that is, of either the octave, the 11th, or the double octave – . . . with the interstitial pitches . . . which are interposed in between. If then one makes the 'constitutions' all higher or all lower, following the aforesaid 'species' of the 'consonance' of the octave, one gets seven 'modes', whose names are: Hypodorian, Hypophrygian, Hypolydian, Dorian, Phrygian, Lydian, Mixolydian.

Ex.1 is a translation into modern staff notation of Boethius's instructions for deriving his 'modes', 'tropes' or 'tones'. The (diatonic) species of the octave to which he referred is the distribution of tones and semitones filling in an octave consonance by step. The (diatonic) 'constitution' – a translation of the Greek *systēma* – of the double octave can be thought of as transposed to seven different relative pitch levels in such a way as to generate the seven possible diatonic octave species at the same relative pitch level, here shown as the octave *e–e'*. In terms of the staff notation, as the movable double octave shifts its position here and there against the stationary 'characteristic' octave span *e–e'*, some of the interstitial degrees of the scale between *e* and *e'*, though they can keep their letter names, have to be sharpened or flattened, shown here by a modern key signature. (In ex.1 round semibreves show the 'characteristic' octave containing the octave species with the same name and number as the key of transposition, square breves show the movable 'dynamic *mesē*', with which other note names also move, and the diamond-shaped semibreves on *a* and *a♯* show the fixed 'thetic *mesē*'.)

There was of course no implication in Boethius's description of any actual musical function. Neither *mesē* nor boundary notes nor any other note was deputed to a musical role such as tonic or final. There was on the other hand a necessary connection between the particular transposition of the movable double octave and the particular distribution of tones and semitones within the stationary characteristic octave; this was indeed the whole purpose of the scheme. In book 4 chapter 15 Boethius had already listed and numbered the seven diatonic octave species; transposition keys were modes that generated those octave species within the characteristic octave and were named for them.

(*ii*) *The Byzantine model: oktōēchos.* From the 6th century to the 9th, when the repertory of Western liturgical song achieved its basic forms, there is no record of descriptive or theoretical sources, and of course no notated music. During this period a system of eight modal categories, for which there was no genuine precedent in Hellenistic theory, came to be associated with the rapidly stabilizing repertory of Western liturgical song. This system was proximately of medieval Greek origin,

Ex.1

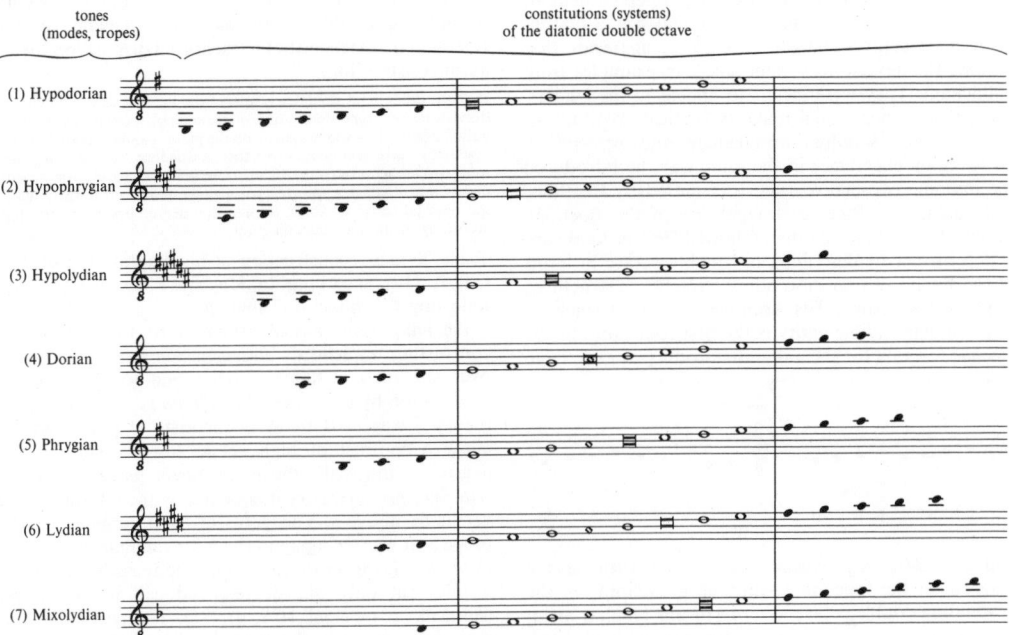

tones
(modes, tropes)

constitutions (systems)
of the diatonic double octave

(1) Hypodorian

(2) Hypophrygian

(3) Hypolydian

(4) Dorian

(5) Phrygian

(6) Lydian

(7) Mixolydian

as indicated by the non-Hellenistic Greek names of the modes in the earliest Western sources from about 800.

The origins of the Eastern Christian system of eight modes – usually called *oktōēchos* – are not entirely clear; but it seems more than probable that it was not delimited purely or even primarily by musical criteria. In any case, the octenary property of the modal system of Latin chant in the West was of non-Latin origin; the idea of an eightfold system of modes in a four-by-two matrix was adopted by Carolingian theorists to an existing body of traditional liturgical song with which it had not originally been associated. The eightfold system was of Eastern provenance, originating probably in Syria, and was transmitted from Byzantine sources to the Carolingian clergy during the 8th century.

Looked at in this way, that which is musically consistent between the modal system and the repertory of medieval Latin liturgical song is not to be explained as the natural reflection of an inherent homology (with minor inconsistencies) between a natural melodic modality in the chant and the closed and symmetrical system of the eight modes. The consistencies, rather, are the result of medieval classification, adaptation and adjustment, which took full advantage of existing modalities of the chant repertory, and brought the borrowed eightfold system into as much harmony as possible with existing melodies, melody types and psalmodic practices. The result was on the whole successful but there were numerous discrepancies; in most cases these were easily managed, but there were many cases in Latin liturgical song where a satisfactory fit was never really achieved. Attempts by medieval theorists to deal with conflicts between chant practice and modal theory furnish essential insights into the processes of medieval musical thought; the dozens of discussions and analyses of individual items provided by the theorists embody useful paradigms for modal analysis in general.

'Tone' was defined and a system of eight tones outlined by the beginning of the 9th century, in the first part of 'De octo tonis', incorporated in chapter 8 of the *Musica disciplina* of Aurelian of Réôme. Presumably the 8th-century or earlier Greek model for the Carolingian system was ordered like the Byzantine *oktōēchos*, that is, the four principal modes first, then the four plagals. The Latin modes, however, from the outset were grouped the other way, with the authentics and plagals paired (see Table 1).

TABLE 1: The modal system of Latin chant

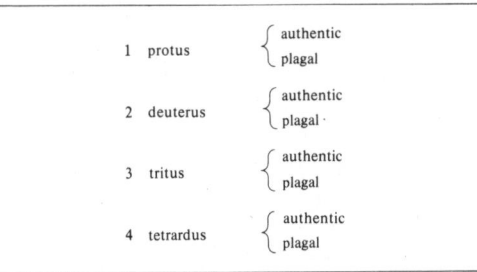

| 1 | protus | { authentic |
|   |        | { plagal    |
| 2 | deuterus | { authentic |
|   |        | { plagal ·  |
| 3 | tritus | { authentic |
|   |        | { plagal    |
| 4 | tetrardus | { authentic |
|   |        | { plagal    |

2. CAROLINGIAN SYNTHESIS, 9TH–10TH CENTURIES. The writings of later 9th-century theorists brought back Boethius's terms 'trope' and 'mode', but now (like 'tone') to designate members of the system of church modes. First and foremost among these writings is the treatise *De harmonica* attributed to Hucbald (*GS*, i, 104–21; see Weakland, 1956). This work brought together in a brilliant synthesis the three fundamental and, so far as the sources indicate, previously disparate strands of modal theory: the chant, the *oktōēchos* and Hellenistic theory (after Boethius).

*(i) The Boethian double octave and the modes.*

(a) The systems of tetrachords. The opening demonstrations in Hucbald's treatise – interval size, a diatonically filled octave, and even a diatonic aggregate that became the hexachord – refer solely to examples from plainchant. They were meant to appeal to his readers' experience, which would make theoretical distributions of tones and semitones immediate and perceptible. Drawing on experience in the same way, he introduced the diatonic two-octave scale transmitted by Boethius. First listing the tones and semitones of the Boethian double octave, Hucbald then followed Hellenistic theory a step further by describing his double octave in terms of the system of four descending tetrachords structured tone–tone–semitone. His example for this tetrachord as a familiar audible entity is the first four notes of the *Noeane* formula for the authentic protus (see ex.2, from

Ex.2

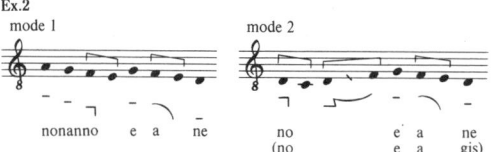

Aurelian, *Musica disciplina*, chap.9). He then gave a diagram of the tone–tone–semitone tetrachords of the descending double octave in terms of this familiar melodic figure, as shown in Table 2a (from Weakland, 1956, fig.iv – the Latin letter names are not Hucbald's): two pairs of conjunct tetrachords separated by a tone and

with a tone added at the bottom.

Hucbald showed (*GS*, i, 112) that the framework behind the double octave does not depend on the Boethian (i.e. Hellenistic) tetrachordal disposition for its aural construction:

If on the other hand, completely apart from the first set of tetrachords [tone–tone–semitone descending or ascending], you should wish to build up [a double-octave system] on the place *'Venite'*, taken from the invitatory *Christus natus est nobis*, then you deduce, by tone–semitone-tone [two tetrachords from 'A'], up to the seventh [degree], where, with disjunction of a degree upwards, you arrange two [more] tetrachords on the path [already] set forth, adding one degree besides at the top, according to the subjoined diagram.

Table 2b is a reconstruction of his diagram (garbled in *GS*, i, 112) according to Hucbald's instructions and following the model of Table 2a.

Hucbald drew special attention to the use of the contrasting tetrachords *diezeugmenōn* and *synēmmenōn* over the *mesē*. Changing from one to the other – modulation by system (*metabolē kata systēma*) in Greek theory – was used by early theorists of plainchant to allow a contrast of high versus low varieties in the degree of the scale above the *mesē*: *paramesē* versus *tritē synēmmenōn*, later designated by the contrast of b♮ versus b♭ above *a*. Theogerus of Metz summed up the usage as it was changing to the more familiar one: 'Some musicians however do not apply the tetrachord *synēmmenōn*, but only one degree, and call it soft [*unam chordem . . . mollem*]' (*GS*, ii, 187). The particular and predominant use in the tritus modes of the tetrachord *synēmmenōn* to which Hucbald drew attention (*GS*, i, 114) is a reference to what in later times was considered

TABLE 2

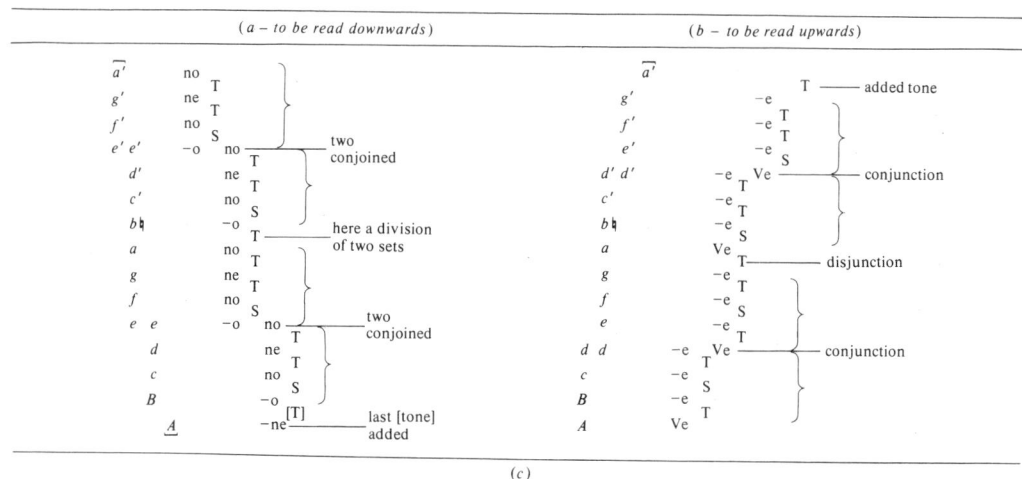

the particular and predominant importance of *b♭* in the F modes 5 and 6. Hucbald's adaptation of the Boethian double octave and tetrachord is shown in Table 2c (after *GS*, i, 112, 115, 119, with Roman letters for degrees of the scale and Latin names for tetrachords added in square brackets, taken from later authors).

(*b*) *Tetrachordal degrees and modal quality.* The Boethian double octave plus the tetrachord *synēmmenōn* is now set forth as a descriptive foundation for modal theory (*GS*, i, 119), and its systemic assumptions and properties endured for hundreds of years:

The four [degrees] after the first three, that is *d, e, f, g* [after *A, B, c*] are appropriate for ending the four modes or tropes, which they now call 'tones' – that is, protus, deuterus, tritus and tetrardus – so that each of these four degrees may govern a pair of tropes subject to it: a principal, which is called authentic, and a collateral, called plagal:

| | | |
|---|---|---|
| lichanos hypatōn [*d*]: | authentic/plagal protus: | [modes] 1 and 2 |
| hypatē mesōn [*e*]: | authentic/plagal deuterus: | [modes] 3 and 4 |
| parhypatē mesōn [*f*]: | authentic/plagal tritus: | [modes] 5 and 6 |
| lichanos mesōn [*g*]: | authentic/plagal tetrardus: | [modes] 7 and 8 |

– so that every song, whatever it may be, however it may be twisted this way and that, necessarily may be led back to one of these four. And thence they are denoted 'final', because all things which are sung may take an ending in [one or another of] them. We notate them briefly, put into the notation already at hand [Boethius's letters]: in descent [*g, f, e, d*]; in ascent [*d, e, f, g*].

On their pattern [four] other tetrachords bring forth no less the intervals or quality of the sounds: of these [tetrachords] one comes out below [the finals] and three above. The addition of the examples shows all these sufficiently [i.e. the tetrachord demonstrations, and especially the demonstration represented by Table 2*b*].

Table 2c follows Hucbald's diagram in marking the 'tetrachord of the finals', and in labelling each final degree according to its assigned modal quality of protus, deuterus, tritus or tetrardus. The fifth tetrachord *synēm-menōn*, though it had a Latin translation 'coniunctarum', continued to bear its Greek name as a rule.

Hucbald drew attention (*GS*, i, 119) to the parallel modal quality of equivalent degrees in the tetrachord of the *finales* and the one above it:

The fifth steps above [i.e. *a, b♮, c′, d′*, above *d, e, f, g*] are always linked to these four [finals] by a sort of connective bond, such that most melodies may be found leaving off in them quite as though by the rule [i.e. as well as in the 'regular' finals] – contravening neither reason nor perception on this account, and going on correctly under the same mode or trope. In this way, therefore, are associated together [*socialiter continentur*] *d* with *a*, *e* with *b♮*, *f* with *c′*, which are distant one from the other in the fifth place.

The relationship of modal equivalence between *d* and *a, e* and *b♮, f* and *c′* was described again in the 11th century in chapter 8 of Guido's *Micrologus*: '*d, e, f* take *a, b♮, c′*, which are of the same mode', and the notes *a, b♮* and *c′* were designated 'affinals'; later still the term 'confinal' was used in the same way.

Having discussed how the three lower degrees of the *finales* and the *superiores* 'are associated together', Hucbald (*GS*, i, 119) went on to the uppermost degrees in the central tetrachords of his system, whose mutual orientation is not the same as the others:

*g* and *d′* should be deputed as much as possible not to the end but to beginnings. They maintain a somewhat similar relationship also with the 4ths below, and certain 5ths, for in commencing they bend down towards them as a limit. These [lower 4ths] are *A* with respect to *d*; *B* with respect to *e*, but this rarely; *c* with respect to *f*; [and] *d* with respect to *g*, but in this latter it goes down sometimes to *c*, that is, to the [lower] fifth place; in the others this happens very rarely.

Hucbald here observed that while *d′* and *g*, like the three pairs *c′–f, b♮–e*, and *a–d*, occupy parallel positions in their respective tetrachords, *d′* is not likely to serve as a secondary final (Guido's 'affinal') in place of *g*; on the contrary, *d′* and *g* have their affinity in downward-tending lines at beginnings.

(*ii*) *Octave species and the Hellenistic names.* After Hucbald's *De harmonica* the most important surviving source for the introduction of Boethius's terms 'mode', 'tone' and 'trope' in connection with the eightfold system is the 9th-century treatise that Gerbert called *Alia musica*. Chailley has reconstructed, edited, analysed and annotated it, and shown it to consist of three layers, all anonymous. The putative Model Treatise, like Aurelian's *Musica disciplina*, used only 'tone' to refer to a member of the eightfold system. The Principal Treatise, a reprise of and commentary on the Model Treatise, retained 'tone' in this sense and added 'trope' as well. The third layer of the *Alia musica*, a summary and correction of the Principal Treatise by means of a 'New Exposition', used only the word 'trope'.

The most lasting contribution of the *Alia musica* to modal theory was the integration of the seven species of the octave with the eight church modes. The octave species were given the Greek names not of Boethius's octave species but rather of his transposition keys – Hypodorian, Hypophrygian etc – which he had called 'modes'. Thus the term 'mode' came to mean not only the modal quality of protus, deuterus, tritus or tetrardus – the sound of a prominent pitch against its intervallic background – but also sometimes 'octave species', a distribution of tones and semitones within the extremes of an octave consonance. Modal qualities in turn were then attributed to either the lower terminus (in authentics) or to one of the medians of the octave species (in plagals), making the octave species into a modal octave.

The crucial passage in the Principal Treatise (ed. Chailley, p.107) begins:

The first mode therefore will be the lowest of all, namely the Hypodorian, from the first octave species, and it is terminated [at the top] by the middle degree [of the Boethian double octave], which is called *a* [*mesē*]. The second octave species produces the second, Hypophrygian mode, which is ended in *b♮* [*paramesē*].

The above was continued by order number, name and upper terminus of each octave species: 3, Hypolydian, *c′*; 4, Dorian, *d′*; 5, Phrygian, *e′*; 6, Lydian, *f′*; 7, Mixolydian, *g′*.

At this point the author of the Principal Treatise had run out of octave species, but had one church mode left, the eighth. In his individual treatment of the church modes he treated the eighth trope (church mode) as a mere appendage of the seventh (p.163), saying: 'it is of course called Hypermixolydian that transcends the Mixolydian; according to Ptolemy it traverses an eighth octave species higher than all the rest', which is no new octave species at all but simply a replication of the first octave species *A–a* an octave higher, *a–a′*.

The difficulty was resolved by the third author of the *Alia musica* in his New Exposition (pp.198f):

All octave species can begin either above or below, e.g. first, *a–A* or *A–a*; second, *b♮–B* or *B–b♮*; third, *c′–c* or *c–c′*; fourth, *d′–d* or *d–d′*; fifth, *e′–e* or *e–e′*; sixth, *f′–f* or *f–f′*; seventh, *g′–g* or *g–g′*. There are accordingly four higher [limits], that is *a, b♮, c′, d′* and four lower, that is *d, e, f, g*. The four higher end [*finiunt*] the Hypodorian, Hypophrygian, Hypolydian, and Hypermixolydian in the higher section, while the four lower end [*finiunt*] the Dorian, Phrygian, Lydian, and Mixolydian in the lower section. Hence they are called 'finals'.

Ex.3*a* illustrates the above with a visual model based on Chailley's. The word 'finiunt' in the text of the New Exposition means 'end' in the sense of 'make a terminus' or 'limit', confused (perhaps intentionally) with Hucbald's sense of 'end' as 'make a termination' or 'conclude'.

Ex.3
(a)

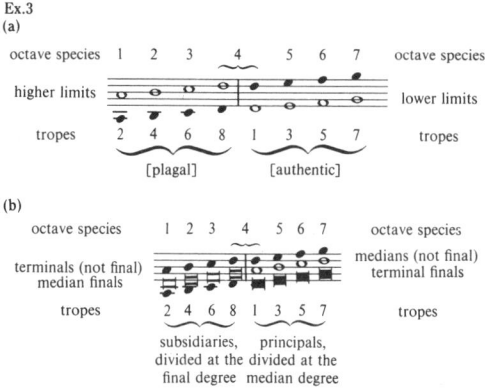

[plagal]     [authentic]

(b)

subsidiaries,     principals,
divided at the     divided at the
final degree     median degree

Ex.3*b* illustrates the way in which the New Exposition later divides each octave species into species of the 4th and 5th by a single median (pp.200f):

let the Dorian either descend from *a* to *d* or ascend to *d'*, and let it have these [*d'*, *d*] above and below for its limits. Likewise from *b♮* let the Phrygian either descend to *e* or ascend to *e'*; in the same way the Lydian from *c'* descends to *f* or ascends to *f'*, [and] no less the Mixolydian from *d'* either descends to *g* or ascends to *g'*. And always any principal trope whatsoever has a 5th below the median degree and a 4th above it . . . and in fact any subsidiary trope has a 5th above the final degree and a 4th below it.

The author of the New Exposition went on to apply a doctrine from the Principal Treatise allowing the addition of an auxiliary note to the smaller consonances, as well as to upper and lower termini of the octaves (p.201):

And if a note is added on to some trope, above or below the species of the octave, it will not be out of place to include this as *emmelis* [*aptus melo*, i.e. 'included in the tune', after a Boethian term]; wherever it adjoins the aforesaid medians, here or there, it may be a 5th plus a tone, or a 4th plus a tone.

Later writers retained the concept of the added note but applied it largely to the modal octave, using terms like *subfinalis* or *subtonium* for a one-note extension at the lower end of an authentic modal octave, and terms like *licentia* for a one- or two-degree extension at either end of any modal octave.

The New Exposition further explained the numerical discrepancy between the seven species of the octave and the eight tropes by invoking the concept of modal quality (p.202): 'Finally, the eighth trope has the same octave species [*d–d'*] as the first, but differs in that it has *g* as the preserver of its quality [*sue qualitatis custodem*], while the other [has] *a* under the name of protus'. With this work the members of the eightfold system, and their modal qualities, are joined to Boethius's seven species of the octave, with the Greek names of his seven transposition keys; Hypermixolydian became Hypomixolydian, consistent with the new names of the other three plagal modes.

### (iii) Melodic types and modal orientation.

(*a*) *Modal beginnings and modal endings.* A clear distinction can be made between the practical and theoretical aspects of the church modes. For the sake of theoretical consistency virtually every item in the entire repertory of plainchant was assigned to one of the eight modes in the closed system. But for certain kinds of items the modal system was made to serve a practical end as well. Antiphons of the Office and of the Mass (introits, communions, and probably originally offer-

tories) were sung in what amounts to a special kind of refrain–verse pattern; a large number of independent songs serving as refrains were coupled with verses from the psalms sung to a relatively small number of musical recitation formulae. Making an immediate juncture of two separate melodic entities, such as psalm tone (i.e. music for the verse) and antiphon (music for the refrain), so as not to fall into ugly inconsistencies of pitch or pattern later on, is a formidable difficulty in a purely vocal, purely oral tradition.

The Carolingian clergy regulated the relationship in the Franco-Roman Gregorian chant by using the borrowed system of the *oktōēchos*. In the compilations known as tonaries (practical manuals useful in an era when chant was transmitted orally, *see* TONARY) every antiphon was assigned to one of the eight modes. Within each mode the antiphons were again divided into subgroups, from one to as many as 13 per mode, depending on the mode and the usage at the time and place to which the tonary belonged. The rubric for each such subgroup of antiphons was a numbered 'difference' (or 'variety' or 'division' or 'definition'), which meant that the antiphons of each mode were subclassified according to variable endings for the psalm tone associated with the mode. This was done so that singers could learn to make the return from a psalm tone ending to the beginning of an antiphon in terms of some general feature of the antiphon beginning, rather than having to handle independently each link between psalm tone and antiphon. Sometimes the general feature at the beginning of the antiphon was no more than the initial pitch, but often it was a typical opening gesture. At the same time the endings of the antiphons were deemed protus, deuterus, tritus or tetrardus; they were also classed as authentic or plagal according to tessitura, and thus assigned to one of the eight modes. This classification of antiphons first by mode and then by psalm-tone difference can be construed as a kind of two-level scheme comprising closed systematic modes based on the endings of the antiphons, and open melody-type modes based largely on their beginnings.

A consequence of the identification at different levels of two areas of modality was that a number of antiphons seemed to belong to difference-classes of one mode according to the opening of the melody and of another mode according to the end. Conflict of modal assignment between one source and another sometimes arose as a result of this. In Regino of Prüm's tonary (*CS*, ii, 1–73) and chapter 2 of his *Epistola* (*GS*, i, 231) ambiguities of beginning and end are noted for many specific antiphons; melodies with this ambiguity are called 'illegitimate chants' or 'hybrid songs' (*cantus nothi*). Some other writers before 1100 who commented on this are Berno of Reichenau, in chapters 9–11 of the prologue to his tonary (*GS*, ii, 72–6); the anonymous author of the Reichenau Tonary (ed. H. Sowa, pp.81–154); and Johannes Afflighemensis, chapters 14–16 of his *De musica* (*CSM*, i; *GS*, ii).

Conflict of modal assignment from source to source may of course arise simply as a result of the melodies' being different; but often the same melody only slightly changed, or even unchanged, may quite legitimately be assigned to one mode or another. These variously ambiguous pieces and the theorists' attempts to deal with them indicate just what difficulties, both in theory and in practice, there must originally have been in fitting the vast body of plainchant to the closed eightfold system.

At the same time, by focussing attention on the modality of musical sequences smaller than whole pieces, the multimodal attributions provide the best approach to melodic modality itself in the plainchant repertory.

Lists of ambiguous pieces and discussions of particular cases are given by Lipphardt (1965, pt.iii, esp. chap.6) and Huglo (1971, esp. chaps.1, 2 and 12). Gevaert's *La mélopée antique* (1895), based on a study of Regino's tonary, is the seminal analytical study, even though its historical premises have long been discredited. And although his tonary can no longer be thought of as reflecting the most ancient state of chant modality, Regino was so generous with his annotations of ambiguities and his explicit recognition of modality in openings that Gevaert's analysis seems almost inevitably to follow. This analysis demonstrated for the antiphoner the existence of an open-ended modality behind the closed eightfold system; it is in fact paradigmatic for such analyses. Gevaert's two levels of classification – 47 melodic *thèmes* grouped into a much smaller number of fixed modes – embody a hierarchical contrast of free melody versus bound class, of flexible compositional (or improvisational) norms and models versus controlled aggregates of pitch relationships, which is characteristic of more than one musical culture of the past and present.

(*b*) An instance of modal ambiguity. The mode at the end of an antiphon is established by the final degree and the manner in which it is approached; at the beginning a mode is often strongly suggested by some characteristic opening gesture. Hence conflicting assignments and bimodal antiphons arise from a similarity in opening phrases between two melodies or melody types whose continuations or conclusions are dissimilar. Concomitant contradictions in scale type, or implied chromatic inflections, either of which may lead to the transposition of a melody to its affinal position a 5th higher in the double octave, or to its projection a 4th higher, are a frequent but secondary result; the primary phenomenon is the accidental confusion or deliberate admixture of phrases, motifs and configurations.

In Regino's tonary several antiphons assigned to mode 3, the authentic deuterus, are annotated 'can be in mode 1' (authentic protus). They are all tunes with a mode 3 opening (Gevaert's *thème* 35) which strongly resembles the most common of all mode 1 openings (Gevaert's *thème* 6). This particular ambiguity is also described by Johannes Afflighemensis at the end of chapter 15 of his *De musica*. The antiphons in question are given in mode 1 in most readable medieval sources (see Lipphardt, 1965, p.262, for other mode 3 attributions); but sources of the hymn tune *Pange lingua* can be used to illustrate the relationship.

Ex.4*b* gives the tune of *Pange lingua* in its familiar mode 3 form (as used, for instance, in Josquin's paraphrase mass); ex.4*d*, the hymn *Urbs beata*, begins like dozens of mode 1 antiphons. Ex.4*c* gives the *Pange lingua* text to the *Urbs beata* tune, projected one degree higher in the double octave, with final at *e* instead of *d*; this has the effect of replacing the tone *e–d/d–e* in the fourth and fifth phrases with a semitone *f–e/e–f*. In terms of scale type reckoned from a tonic final degree, this constitutes a change of mode; yet the tune, as represented in ex.4*c*, *d*, is effectively unchanged. (In ex.4, *a*, *c* and *d* are after Wagner, 1921, pp.477f, and *b* from Glarean, *Dodecachordon*, chap.36.)

Ex.4

The standard version of ex.4*b* differs from 4*c* in two essential particulars: there is an upper semitone inflection of the first note in the opening gesture; and in the opening gesture and elsewhere *b*♮ is replaced by *c'* when approached by step from below (a feature of the so-called German chant dialect, but here modally significant as well). These differences, unlike the differences in interval structure in the fourth and fifth phrases, bring about a clear contrast in melodic features between 4*b* and 4*d*. The opening gesture now brings forward the minor 6th above the final instead of the 5th, and this degree, especially as it is handled in the second and third phrases, is characteristic not only of this tune but of mode 3 tunes in general. In mode 1 tunes, conversely, the minor 6th above the final is an upper auxiliary inflection incidental to the 5th, as often notated by *b*♮ or *c'* as by *b*♭. So melodically, the second and third phrases of the *Urbs beata–Pange lingua* tune are not at all mode 1, no matter where they are projected on to the double octave.

Ex.4*a* is the *Pange lingua* tune projected a 4th higher, so as to end at *a* instead of *e*. The availability of both *b*♮ and *b*♭ above *a* makes possible the transformation of *a* protus at the affinal position with *b*♮ into *a* deuterus with *b*♭. For instance, the relationship between the mode 1 and mode 3 versions of the tune can be visualized most easily by supposing a transposition of ex.4*d* up a 5th to its affinal position; this would be an *a* protus version of the tune to contrast with the *a* deuterus version of ex.4*a*, and either could be considered a modal transformation of the other.

### 3. 11TH-CENTURY SYNTHESES.

(*i*) *Italian theory of modal functions*. The two works on plainchant theory that had both the widest circulation in manuscripts and the most frequent appearance in commentary and quotation were produced in Italy in the late 10th century or early 11th. They were the *Micrologus* by Guido of Arezzo (*c*1026) and the *Dialogus de musica*, formerly attributed to one or another Odo, now established by Huglo as the work of an anonymous Lombard monk in the years not long before the appearance of Guido's work. (The *Micrologus* and its commentaries have been extensively studied by Smits van Waesberghe, and a comparative study of the *Micrologus* and *Dialogus* appears in Oesch's biography of Guido; the *Dialogus* itself is almost completely translated in Strunk, 1950, pp.103ff – only the portions dealing with the specific characteristics of each mode have been omitted.)

These two works, especially the *Dialogus*, are characterized by their practical approach to modal theory. Learned reference to Boethius and other ancient authors is eschewed, and the elegant Greek note names for the double octave are replaced by the simple and familiar Latin letters *A–G*, *a–g*, *aa*, with the Greek gamma added at the bottom; the available musical space was soon extended upwards to *dd* and later *ee*. The aim was not so much to make or remake new theory as to preserve and clarify traditional practices. Modal theory, especially in the *Dialogus*, is presented as simple truth, needed to help resolve confusions in the practice, with minimal recomposition according to theory in the most extreme cases. The Italian theorists were dealing in synthesis and didactic theory, not in new theoretical discovery and analysis.

The discussion of chant modes and modality in the

*Dialogus*, the *Micrologus*, and their many followers is based on the definition of modal functions, which are segmental and suprasegmental; that is, they apply to single pitches in critical positions or to ranges and successions of pitches. The modal functions are basically three: final, initial and medial. In the 'classical' modal theory from the 11th century onwards final and initial functions are treated as segmental, applied to single pitches, though these functions were occasionally also thought of in terms of characteristic phrases. The medial functions are of both kinds, having to do with range and register on the one hand, and individually important medial pitches on the other.

(*a*) *Final*. The classic definition of the final as modal function in the *Dialogus* (quoted in §I, 3, above), is: 'A tone or mode is a rule which distinguishes every chant in its final'. This famous dictum recurs in dozens of theoretical works over the next six or seven centuries; it is indeed part of the ultimate origin of the conventional notion of the 'tonic', current since the 18th century, which is almost inseparable in textbooks from the notion of 'finishing'.

After the *Dialogus* few objections were ever entered against the idea that the modal quality of the last note of a song should override all other considerations in melodic classification and orientation in the modal system. The doctrine had the virtues of simplicity and clarity, and it was soon buttressed by powerful logical arguments. Guido gave five in chapter 11 of his *Micrologus*, which are elaborated in Vivell's Anonymous, pp.36ff (*Commentarius . . . in Micrologum*; Smits edn., pp.132ff) and thence in book 6 chapter 40 of the 14th-century *Speculum musice* of Jacques de Liège (*CS*, ii, 246–8). Two versions of Guido's third argument may be seen in translation in Apel, 1958, p.175; but the second argument (a restatement of *Dialogus*, chap.8, see Strunk, 1950, p.113f) is the most important. It provides a two-stage rule whereby notes within a phrase are restricted to certain intervallic relationships with the note ending the phrase; the phrase-final notes in turn are restricted to the same set of intervallic relationships with the final:

With the degree which terminates a phrase [*neuma*], the rest of the degrees [in the phrase] ought certainly to agree, through the aforesaid six consonances [semitone, tone, minor 3rd, major 3rd, 4th, 5th]. To the degree which terminates a song, its beginning and the ends and also the beginnings of all its medial sections [*distinctionum*] have the duty to adhere.

Degrees rightly 'are suited to the final', so that they are 'coloured' by it . . . for they concord to a medial cadence [*distinctioni*] by the aforesaid consonances, and the medial cadence [*distinctio*] to the final through the same consonances.

(*b*) *Ambitus*. With the modal quality of a song residing only in the final, to which all other degrees were made directly or indirectly subordinate, the course of a liturgical song from incipit to final was necessarily governed in its internal pitch relationships by that final. The main independent function that was still to be determined in the domain of pitch was the registral area, the boundaries between which those relationships could exist. These boundaries were located in the double-octave system with respect to the final. Guido summarized (*Micrologus*, chap.13):

as is sustained by the evidence of liturgical songs [*usualium cantuum attestatione*], authentics hardly ever descend more than one degree from their final; [and] of these the authentic tritus seems to do so very rarely, on account of the imperfection beneath of the semitone. The authentics rise, however, to the eighth and ninth [degrees above the final], and even the tenth. Plagals, to be sure, fall and rise to the fifth [degree on either

Ex.5

side of the final], but the sixth or seventh [degree] is authoritatively granted in the ascent, like the ninth and tenth in the authentics. The plagals of the protus, deuterus and tritus sometimes necessarily finish in the upper *a*, *b♮*, *c′* [respective affinals, by the process of transposition].

Ex.5 summarizes the classical doctrine of the ambitus of the eight church modes. The doctrine began with the *Dialogus* (*GS*, i, 259–63), but was repeated in many later works. Ex.5 is based ultimately on the *Dialogus*, but in the light of later commentary, particularly the *Questiones in musica* (ed. Steglich, pp.45ff), which was the principal source in turn for book 6 chapters 42–9 of *Speculum musice* (*CS*, ii, 251–63). The several ambituses are abstractly measured by systems of perfect consonances – an octave in mode 5, three conjunct 4ths in modes 2 and 4, and two conjunct 5ths elsewhere. (In modes 1 and 8 the note *e′* is regarded as extra, though legitimate, because the span *c*–*e′* cannot be contained within a system of three perfect 4ths or two perfect 5ths.) These systems are merely measuring devices: they are part of the doctrine and have nothing to do with the internal structure of the modal scales. They are not to be confused with the species of consonances adumbrated in the *Alia musica* (see §2(ii) above) which were developed by the Reichenau theorists and later by Marchetto and his followers up to Tinctoris (see §4(ii–iii) below), and on into the 16th century. (In ex.5 square notes indicate modal finals, parentheses enclose notes that are 'incorrect' according to the texts, and square brackets enclose notes theoretically available but rarely found; although the note *b♭* is not mentioned in the standard theoretical summary for modes 3, 7 and 8, it appears often in graduals and in a few anomalous tetrardus antiphons.)

(*c*) Initials and medials. After the 11th century, ambitus and final were normally considered necessary and sufficient to determine the mode of a piece. To go be-

yond the mere determination of a mode, however, and to deal with melodic relationships in more analytical detail, other modal functions besides final and ambitus were required. The older and more abstract suprasegmental functions dealing with aggregates of pitches and intervals, such as modal quality and the modal species of the consonances, were to be developed as tools for analysis of chant by the 11th-century Reichenau theorists; more concrete and practical single-pitch segmental functions were developed largely as a consequence of the doctrines of the *Dialogus* and *Micrologus*. For each mode certain specific degrees could take on important secondary functions that were derived from the practice of liturgical music itself, and were determined in two ways: from the initial notes of songs in the several modes, particularly of Office chants with verse formulae, namely antiphons and responsories; and from the verse formulae themselves, particularly the psalm tones for the antiphons.

In Guidonian theory initial notes were taken as important guides to modal structure in connection with the doctrine of the supremacy of the final, and strictly as single pitches. Beginnings were obviously likely to be in the forefront of consciousness (Hucbald used them wherever possible in his practical demonstrations of the intervals). Furthermore, none of the modes had chants beginning on all seven degrees of the scale (given octave equivalence), and the number of possibilities in any one mode ranged from one (mode 6 in some descriptions) to seven pitches at the most (mode 8 in some descriptions, with octave duplication of *c* and *c′*). Since they were easily identified, and yet were restricted to fewer than all the possibilities, those degrees in any mode that had chants beginning on them were believed to be a sure guide to the degrees allowable at the beginnings and endings of the medial phrases in that mode.

The tradition linking initials with the beginnings and ends of medial phrases – 'distinctions' – antedates the Guidonian school; but the author of the *Dialogus* was the first to link the theory and the practice by citing an example for each modal initial. Many of his citations, particularly of course for the less frequently used initials, were repeated down to Jacques' *Speculum musice* in the 14th century, and beyond.

Characteristic expressions of the connection between initial and medial functions in each mode may be found in the anonymous *Musica* (*GS*, i, 337f) and Berno (*GS*, ii, 70f), whence they were taken over by Frutolfus of Michelsberg as part of the descriptive headings for each mode in his tonary. His heading for mode 1 reads, in part: 'Its singing begins in six degrees, *c d e f g a*, in which are comprised also the "colons" and "commas", that is, parts and sections [*membra et incisiones*], which we call the "distinctions" of the song' (*Breviarum*, ed. Vivell, p.113). The equivalence of song initials with medial initials and medial cadences ('distinctions') is perhaps not always as close in practice as it is in theory, at least in terms of frequency of distribution. Rare beginnings may make fairly frequent medial cadences, such as *g* in mode 1, while some beginnings are never used as medial cadence points, such as *e* in mode 1. But on the whole the lists of modal initials so often provided by chant theorists can be used as a rough guide to the important secondary melodic nodes in each chant mode, as the theorists intended them. More than that, the very idea of secondary strong points in each mode played a central role in some of the later elaborations of the eightfold system as a theory for the structuring of polyphonic music between the 15th and 17th centuries.

(*d*) Tenor. The other main source for secondary modal functions was the psalmody of the Office. The most important borrowing was the designation of the tenor of the psalm tone associated with a given mode as a modal degree second in importance only to the final of its antiphons. For it is indeed the case that the reciting pitch of each psalm tone, the tenor, is among the pivotal degrees of many melodies in each mode. The incorporation of psalm tones and especially psalm-tone tenors as aids in the understanding of chant modality was a natural consequence of both liturgical association and musical similarities.

In chapter 13 of the *Micrologus* Guido suggested that the upper pitch limit for the beginning of a liturgical song coincides with and thus in a sense is set by the psalm-tone tenors. Part of the passage is quoted below with the commentary of Vivell's Anonymous (p.46); Guido's own words are in quotation marks:

'For there', that is, in these formulae like *seculorum amen*, 'we see in which degrees of the individual modes a song may be begun more often or more rarely, and in which it' – that is, the beginning – 'may never occur'. For every song, plagal as well as authentic, can begin – or any medial phrase [*distinctio*] can begin or end – as high above the final as the place where the *seculorum amen* and the tenor of the whole psalm appropriate to any authentic or plagal mode rises.

Here the tenor is merely set as a guide to the upper limit for initials and for medial cadences. But by the end of the 11th century, in a passage at the beginning of chapter 11 of the *De musica* of Johannes Afflighemensis, the practical distinction of mode and psalm tone is obliterated even with respect to the tenor. Even the chapter title itself – 'On the tenors of the modes and their finals' – attributes the psalm-tone element to the mode. The chapter begins:

As there are eight tones, moreover, so there are eight tenors. . . . And in music we say tenor just where the first syllable of the *seculorum amen* of any tone begins, for it is as though they hold the keys of the melody [*claves modulationis tenent*] and give us access to an understanding of the chant [*ad cantum cognoscendum*]. . . . Moreover it is to be noted that, as the ends [*fines*] of the eight tones are disposed on four notes, which on that account are called finals, so also four notes are attributed, but in a different way, to the eight tenors . . . the tenor of the second tone is on *f*; of the first, fourth and sixth on *a*; of the third, fifth and eighth on *c′*; of the seventh on *d′* [see Table 3]. Nor is it unsuitable that the tenor of the second and seventh claim solitary places for themselves, because the second descends the furthest, to the 4th [below *d*], and the seventh rises above all the others.

Johannes specifically pointed to the tenor as a guide to something outside the psalm tone, in the song itself, for while 'modulatio' frequently refers to a psalm-tone configuration, 'cantus' never does. His observations mingle aspects of psalm tone and mode as concepts. He compared and contrasted psalm-tone tenors and modal finals in the same context; and his accounting for the singularity of the psalm-tone tenors *f* and *d′* is on the grounds of the ranges of their correlated modes, for it is not the second psalm tone that 'descends . . . to the 4th'. The psalm tones here are not merely indicators of the mode of their associated antiphons; rather, they have in themselves properties that can be attributed to the mode of the refrains, the liturgical songs, to which they pertain. Table 3 shows the relation of psalm-tone tenors and modal finals, as described by Johannes.

TABLE 3: Psalm-tone tenors and modal finals

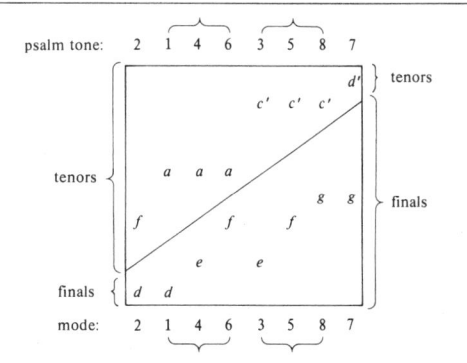

The addition of the tenor to the final and the initials further refines the hierarchy of single-pitch modal functions, for it implies that one among the secondary strong points has a certain limiting power and governance over the others; it is the one which in fact is the upper limit of the theoretical possibilities for a resting point, and it is to be established by reference to the psalm-tone tenor. A four-tiered system of modal pitch functions results: at the first level the final, at the second level the tenor, at the third level the other initial–medial strong points, and at the lowest level the remaining degrees of the scale.

(*ii*) *Reichenau theory of modal species and locations.* In Guido's references to mode, whether in connection with the eightfold system or as the quality of a note in its melodic environment, no mention is made of one of his two lasting inventions, the didactic syllables *ut re mi fa sol la* (not yet called HEXACHORD), the device which by the mid-13th century had become indissolubly associated with the idea of modal quality. Nor is there any treatment of species of the modal octave or of the smaller consonances. The aspect of modal theory first seen in the work of the Reichenau theorists was a coordination of four hitherto independent elements: the eightfold system; the species of the 4th, 5th and octave; Hucbald's Boethian double octave as constructed in tetrachords; and modal quality. Its culmination was Hermannus Contractus's scheme of hexachordal 'seats of the tropes' (*sedes troporum*).

(*a*) Modal species of the consonances. Guido's contemporary Berno of Reichenau built up the species of the consonances on the abstract description of an anonymous earlier work (*GS*, i, 313), designating specific locations in the double octave for their primary positions. The three species of the 4th are differentiated according to the position of the tones and the semitone: tone–semitone–tone; semitone–tone–tone; and tone–semitone (placed *d–e–f–g*, *e–f–g–a* and *g–a–b♮–c'* by Berno). (The first species of 4th is clearly to be distinguished from the 'tetrachord of the finals' first described by Hucbald. Species of the 4th, with all possible positions of the semitone, are used in the description of modes; tetrachords are invariant in form and are simply the elements used for building the background system of pitch relationships, the Boethian double octave.)

The four species of the 5th were generated by adding tones above and below the three species of 4th; Berno's placement is shown in ex.6a (from *GS*, ii, 67, after *GS*, i, 313). In ex.6b (from *GS*, ii, 69f, after *GS*, i, 313) are shown his constructions of the eight modal octave species, analogously generated by adding species of the 4th above and below the four species of the 5th. (Numbers above the staff indicate which species of 4th,

circled numbers which species of 5th.) To the abstract intervallic descriptions in his source (*GS*, i, 313) Berno added not only specific placement (in terms of the usual Boethian Greek note names) but also some explanation in his own words (*GS*, ii, 69):

What I am saying is this: the first tone has the liberty of rising from its final, that is from [*d*], up in a [first species] 5th, that is to [*a*], and from [*a*] to [*d'*], which is the first species of the 4th. The second tone, however, which is called its subsidiary, rises to the same 5th, but by the same species of the 4th descends from [*d*] to [*A*], by tone, semitone, and again tone.

The theoretical contributions of Berno's younger colleague Hermannus Contractus originated as improvements on Berno's *Musica* and Guido's *Micrologus*; though neither author is mentioned by name, the doctrines criticized are unmistakable. Hermannus's new theory began from a more elegant systematization of the modal species of 4th, 5th and octave, which were generated from the four fixed tone–semitone–tone tetrachords of Hucbald's Boethian double octave. He then made each of the four tetrachords the nucleus of a hexachordal module linking melodic configuration and modal quality together, and both to the background double octave. Hermannus's *De musica*, unlike the *Musica* of Berno, was not circulated widely in manuscript, however. Despite the elegance of his system and the resemblance of some of its most novel features to central features of later theory, there is no clear evidence that this work directly influenced hexachordal and modal theory after the 11th century.

Modal quality pertains to all degrees in Guidonian theory, though it is only the modal quality of the final that can determine the mode of a chant. There is a theoretical inelegance in the Guidonian scheme, however, visible in the diagrams shown in Table 4. It is most evident in the failure of *g*, the seventh degree of the system – 'te'/IV, tetrardus, in Table 4a, modal pair 7–8 in Table 4b – to have any parallel or affinity elsewhere in the system comparable with those for the protus–deuterus–tritus qualities (4a) or the modal pairs 1–2, 3–4, 5–6 (4b).

TABLE 4

|  | (*a*) | | | | | | | | | |
|---|---|---|---|---|---|---|---|---|---|---|
| *A* | *B* | *c* | *d* | *e* | *f* | *g* | *a* | *b♮* | *c'* |
| pro | de | tri | pro | de | tri | te | pro | de | tri |
| I | II | III | I | II | III | IV | I | II | III |

|  | (*b*) | |
|---|---|---|
| DIATESSARON | // | DIAPENTE |

| [authentic]: | 1 | 3 | 5 | 1 | 3 | 5 | 7 | 1 | 3 | 5 |
|---|---|---|---|---|---|---|---|---|---|---|
|  | *A* | *B* | *c* | *d* | *e* | *f* | *g* | *a* | *b♮* | *c'* |
| [plagal]: | 2 | 4 | 6 | 2 | 4 | 6 | 8 | 2 | 4 | 6 |

Hermannus's rectification of this inconsistency, arising originally out of his criticism of Berno's derivation of the species, led him into a new doctrine of great significance: in different contexts certain degrees of the scale can have different modal qualities. Specifically, the degrees *d* and *d'* can have either protus

Ex.6

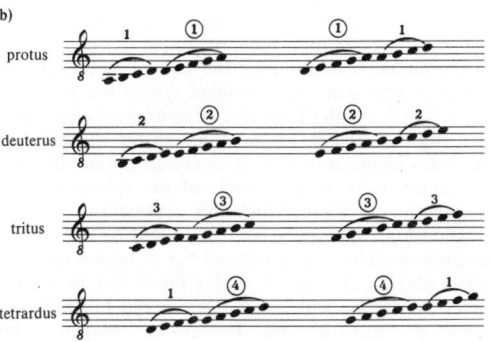

(a)

①    4th + tone
1 — T S T +T

② 
2 — S T T +T

③    tone + 4th
3 — T+ T T S

④ 
1 — T+ T S T

(b)

protus   ① ① 1

deuterus   2 ② ② 2

tritus   3 ③ ③ 3

tetrardus   1 ④ ④ 1

or tetardus quality; and it follows as a corollary that the tone–semitone–tone species of the 4th is also twofold when it is located on *d–e–f–g* in the double octave system (ed. Ellinwood, p.27):

Let us denote the degrees of the tetrachords... by their own letters. One [note] in the middle is enumerated (not measured) twice [*d/d*].... The *graves* or *principales*, then, are *A, B, c, d*, the *finales d, e, f, g*. The first species of 4th [*diatessaron*] is necessarily then *A–d*, consisting of tone–semitone–tone, enclosed by its own letters; the second *B–e*, consisting of semitone–tone–tone, [is] bounded by its own letters this side and that; the third *c–f*, consisting of tone–tone–semitone, [is] secured on both sides by its own letters. The fourth species *d–g* – first [species] in disposition [of intervals] but fourth in the system and in power [*constitutione et potestate*] – delimits the seven intervals of the degrees [*septena vocum discrimina*] in this way [see ex.7].

Hermannus objected that his predecessors 'did not attend to the oft-mentioned double form of *d*, and erred [in] withholding recognition of the fourth trope in the fourth place' (ed. Ellinwood, p.59).

Just as the species of 4th are constructed by linking the melodic functions I, II, III, IV in the tetrachords of the *graves* and *finales*, the species of 5th are based on the modal affinities of I, II, III, IV in the *finales* and *superiores* (ex.7). And so the whole system of conjunct and disjunct tetrachords is built up on the basis of replication of the four modal qualities and the assignment of both protus and tetardus potential quality to *d* and *d'*.

way usable as a description of diatonic scale type in the octave species. And it was, in fact, the seven species of the octave, as integrated with the eightfold system in the New Exposition of the *Alia musica* and transmitted to and by Berno's *Musica*, which continued as the basis of the doctrine of modal octaves.

(*b*) Modes of the degrees and the 'sedes troporum'. In both chapter 7 of the *Micrologus* and the letter to Michael *De ignoto cantu*, Guido discussed the modal qualities of the degrees of the diatonic system under the name 'modes of the degrees' (*modi vocum*) (ex 8*a*; protus, deuterus, tritus and tetardus are marked I, II, III and IV, the last being shown in two versions – IV-A from *De ignoto cantu*, IV-B from *Micrologus*). The fuller explanation is in *De ignoto cantu* (GS, ii, 47):

Degrees are alike and make similar sounds and concordant phrases [*concordes neumas*] only insofar as they are raised and lowered similarly with regard to the disposition of tones and semitones. So the first degree *A* and the fourth, *d*, are alike and are designated 'of a single mode' because both have tone in descent and tone–semitone–tone–tone in ascent, and this is the first similitude in degrees, that is, the first mode. The second mode is in the second [degree] *B* and the fifth [degree] *e*, for they both have tone–tone in descent and semitone–tone–tone in ascent. The third mode is in the third [degree] *c* and the sixth [degree] *f*, for both descend semitone–tone–tone and ascend tone–tone. But the seventh [degree] *g* makes the fourth mode alone; it has tone–semitone–tone–tone in descent and tone–tone–semitone in ascent.

Ex.7

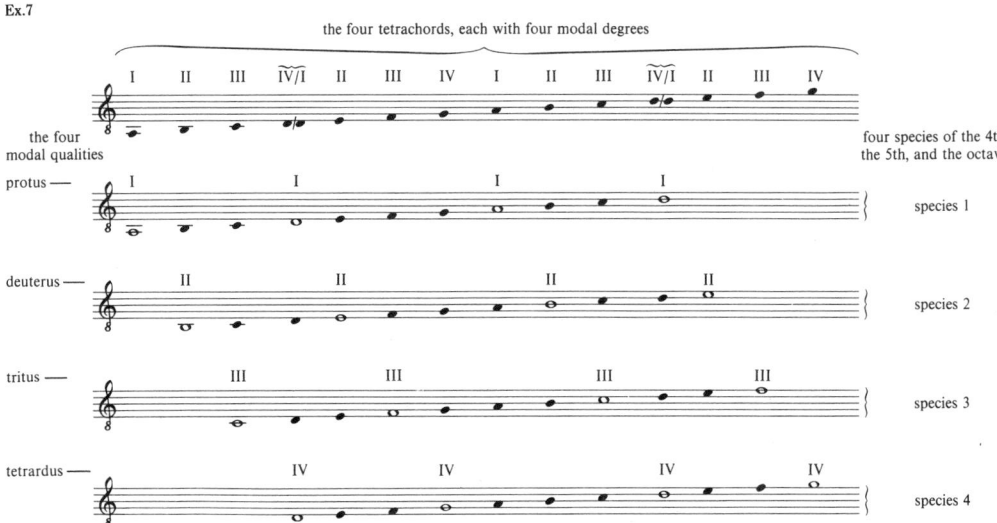

The build-up of modal octave species is also based on the presence of the same modal quality – I, II, III or IV – on degrees an octave apart in the system. Hermannus's system has the advantage of bringing everything – modal quality, position within the structural tetrachord, and species of 4th, 5th and octave alike – under the same set of numbers. Its one serious inconsistency arises if one tries to connect his modal octaves with the scale types of the seven octave species. If octave species are to be derived only by filling in between modal qualities an octave apart in the system, there can of course be only four of them, and Hermannus duly allotted both the octaves *A–a* and *d–d'* to the first species, *B–b♮* and *e–e'* to the second, *c–c'* and *f–f'* to the third, and of course *d–d'* as well as *g–g'* to the fourth (ed. Ellinwood, pp.30ff). From a modal point of view this is eminently satisfactory, but of course it is in no

In chapter 7 of the *Micrologus*, the version of Guido's *modi vocum* known to Hermannus and later writers, a more limited descent is ascribed to the fourth mode of the degrees: 'but the fourth [mode] is lowered by a tone, and rises through tone, tone, semitone, like *g*'.

Hermannus's solution for the lack of modal affinity for the degree *g* in the Guidonian system was corollary to his doctrine of the 'biformity' of *d* and *d'*. His 'modes of the degrees' (*modi vocum*), though in all but the tetardus identical in form with Guido's, were different in nature. Hermannus completed his system symmetrically, by developing Hucbald's treatment of the *g–d'* relationship, whereby '*g* and *d'* should be deputed as much as possible not to the end but to beginnings' (see §2(*ib*) above). He did not derive his modes of the degrees by starting with single degrees and building outwards as far as possible. Rather, he began with his

Ex.8

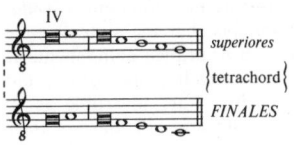

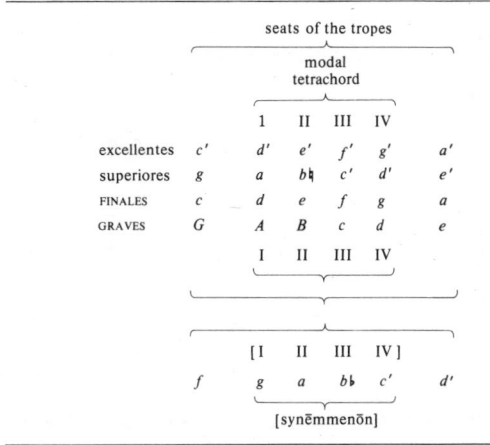

existing cluster of four modal degrees in the tetrachord, modified to allow for melodic extension to the limits possible for parallel modal degrees everywhere in the diatonic double octave; thus he arrived at the modal aggregate of six degrees which he called the 'seat of the tropes' (*sedes troporum*). Hermannus described its construction: 'Take any tetrachord you want, for instance the *graves*, and having added a tone on both sides, you have the limits of the modes, which makes the seat of the tropes' (ed. Ellinwood, p.57). Ex.8*b* shows Wilhelm of Hirsau's version of the modes of the degrees (*GS*, ii, 175, 178f) after Hermannus (ed. Ellinwood, pp.58f).

Table 5 shows Hermannus's construction of the *sedes troporum* from the modal tetrachords, with the additional tetrachord appended after Wilhelm of Hirsau. Hermannus's discussion of the individual *modi vocum* ('modes of the degrees') is given below in the version transmitted through Wilhelm, which supplies brief but significant additional detail both in the theory and in the practical examples cited (*Musica*, chap.38). Wilhelm's additions are set off in diamond brackets; those of Hermannus's words that Wilhelm omitted are supplied in brackets and identified.

I. The first *modus vocum* appears wherever a degree can be lowered by a tone and raised by a first species of 5th [tone–semitone–tone–tone], as can be recognized in *A.d.a.d'*, the principal degrees of the protus; and therefore this mode is ⟨indifferently⟩ [as to authentic or plagal] suited to the protus, as the ⟨authentic⟩ antiphon *Prophete predicaverunt* [see ex.9*a*] shows [Hermannus: and in *In tuo adventu*, and in similar ones that do not exceed six degrees].

Wilhelm's 'indifferently' emphasized an important aspect of the *modus vocum* of the protus, to wit, that it may shape the nuclear structure of either authentic or plagal antiphons. The versions of *Prophete predicaverunt* in ex.9*a* are in fact in mode 1 in the Worcester

Antiphoner (WA) and mode 2 in the Lucca Antiphoner (LA).

II. A degree shows the second mode [when it is] lowered by a ditone [tone–tone] and raised by a second species 4th [semitone–tone–tone], which appears in *B.e.b♮.e'* the principal degrees of the deuterus ⟨to which this mode is related⟩. The ⟨plagal⟩ antiphon *Gloria hec est* [see ex.9*b*; PA–Petershausen Antiphoner] shows this [Hermannus: and similar ones, either authentic or subsidiary, which do not exceed six degrees].

Hermannus's reference to authentic deuterus is curious. A deuterus composition strictly within the limits of the *sedes troporum* can either reach only to a 4th above the modal degree, in which case it would be plagal, or never get down to its final at all; if the modal degree is *e*, for example, the *sedes troporum* can be only *c–a* (plagal) or *g–e'* (without the final beneath).

III. The third mode is lowered by the third species of 4th [tone–tone–semitone] and raised by a ditone [tone–tone], as the principal degrees of the tritus *c.f.c'.f'* show, of which this is the mode. Evidence of this ⟨mode⟩ is in the ⟨plagal⟩ antiphon *Modicum et non videbitis* [see ex.9*c*].

Ex.9

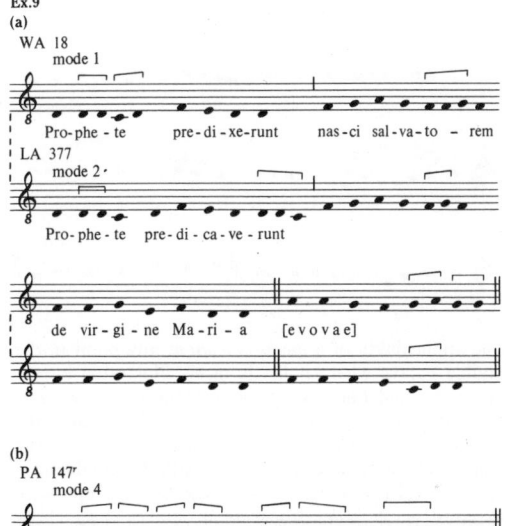

(c)

WA 143
mode 6

Mo - di - cum et non vi - de - bi - tis     me di - cit do - mi - nus

LA 236
mode 6

i - te - rum mo - di -     cum et     vi - de - bi -     tis     me

qui-a va - do ad pat - rem     al - le - lu - ia al - le - lu - ia

[e v o v a e]

(d)

WA 79
mode 7

Si     ve - re frat - res     di - vi - tes es - se cu - pi - tis

ve - ras di - vi - ti - as     a - ma - te     [e v o v a e]

PA 34ᵛ
mode 8

Mul-ti     ve - ni - unt ab o - ri - en - te     et recumbent cum

ab - ra - ham et i - sa - ac     et ia - cob in reg - no ce -

- lo - rum     al - le - lu - ia     [e v o v a e]

The applicability of a *modus vocum* at any point in the double octave where it fits is nicely illustrated by the Worcester and Lucca versions of *Modicum et non videbitis*, at *f* and *c'* respectively. This *modus vocum*, like that for the deuterus, is again only applicable here to the plagal. The authentic tritus sung with *b♭* would be a hypothetical possibility for a *modus vocum* if one were to construct a *sedes troporum* around *g–a–b♭–c'* by adding *f* and *d'* at the extremes. Though Hermannus did not use this tetrachord, the tetrachord *synēmmenōn* was

mentioned by Wilhelm (*Musica*, chap.38) as the basis of a *sedes troporum* (Table 5).

IV. We set up the fourth mode of the degrees raised by a tone and lowered by a fourth species of 5th [tone–tone–semitone–tone] [Hermannus: in the tetrardus] since its principal degrees produce that. ⟨This mode has the speciality among the others that⟩ you can recognize ⟨not only the authentic⟩ antiphon *Si vere fratres* ⟨but also the plagal⟩ antiphon *Multi veniunt* [see ex.9d] [Hermannus: and the like].

Hermannus's tetrardus *modus vocum*, as exemplified in *Multi veniunt*, was built from *g*, the final of mode 8, downwards. There are perhaps only half a dozen antiphons that would fit into this pattern used in this way, but this part of mode 8 is an important element in many antiphons with a higher reach. Since a *modus vocum* can be built around any modal degree, not necessarily just a final, Hermannus was able to follow up Hucbald's hint to attend 'not to the end but to beginnings' in *d'* and in *g*, and use the same *modus vocum* from *d'* as a module for the authentic tetrardus mode 7, even though mode 7 ends on *g*. *Si vere fratres* represents a common melody type in mode 7 (discussed by Apel, 1958, pp.400ff). This and several other mode 7 types begin on *d'*, or move up to *d'* rapidly, and then work their way down through the fourth species of 5th to the final *g*.

An elegant theoretical feature in Hermannus's *modus vocum* and *sedes troporum* was that the systems were completely symmetrical in terms of their components as described. That is, the *modi vocum* in pairs – protus and tetrardus, deuterus and tritus – are invertible as to pitch, as are the species of 4th and 5th that are their greater components; their lesser components, the tone and ditone, are of course self-inverting. This symmetry was noticed and elaborated by a few other writers, notably Aribo (*GS*, ii; *CSM*, ii), where it was likened to symmetries in other domains.

(iii) *Authentic–plagal distinctions.* Hermannus's *modus vocum* of the protus could refer to authentic or plagal, 'indifferently', as Wilhelm added. But of course any particular antiphon in a particular liturgy would be assigned one way or the other, since one or the other psalm tone had to be chosen for the psalm verses. For Hermannus's first example, *Prophete predicaverunt* (or *predixerunt*), the choice could go either way, as ex.9a shows. A number of medieval treatises included discussions of how to make the choice of authentic or plagal in such cases. Both Guidonian and Reichenau theorists discussed modal features that might be relevant to the choice, and both their points and their examples give excellent insights into the medieval sense of mode and modality. These discussions were most extensive regarding the protus, as was the case with most medieval essays on the specific details of modal theory.

(a) *Repercussion.* The *Dialogus* gives rationalized guidance on making such choices. The discussion begins and ends with two criteria: if it falls short of the 5th, it is plagal; if all else fails, judge by the traditional psalm tone. But in between there are clear instructions for making the choice on the basis of the modal structure of the antiphon (*GS*, i, 260):

There are, however, many songs among them which are neither lowered to G, A or B, nor raised to the 10th or 11th [scale-steps *c'* or *d'*]. The discrimination [*discretio*] for them is this:
[A] if they do not reach the 8th or 9th [*a* or *b♭*], they are certainly in the second tone;
[B] the 8th and 9th [*a* and *b♭*] are common to both [authentic and plagal]; when the song rises up to them it will be of the first mode if:
[1] it dwells in them at length, or

[2] it strikes [*repercutiat*] them three or four times, or

[3] it begins in the 8th [*a*].

[C] If, however, it begins in lower [notes] and reaches to them [*a* and *b♭*] infrequently (according to the size of the antiphon) it will be of the second mode.

[D] Otherwise, they are discriminated according to the varieties and differences of their formulae [i.e. of their psalm tones].

The rule labelled '[B2]' above particularly reverberates through the literature on mode through Marchetto to Tinctoris and beyond. A note that is *repercussa* several times becomes a single-note medial function of a mode, like the tenor of the psalm tone, with which it is usually identical in fact and confused in principle.

(*b*) Mechanical measurement of average tessitura. In the 13th-century scholastic *Summa musicae* a mechanical routine for distinguishing authentic from plagal was suggested (*GS*, iii, 225f):

as there are four final degrees [*claves finales*], so there are four discriminatory degrees [*claves discretive*]. . . . Each discriminatory degree effects the distinction of two tones, for *f fa ut* discriminates the first [tone] from the second, *g* the third from the fourth, *a* the fifth from the sixth, and hard *b* [*b♮*] the seventh from the eighth. . . . If a protus song has more notes above *f fa ut*, to that extent [*quantum ad hoc*] it is authentic and of the first [tone]; if more beneath, to that extent it is plagal and of the second. [And so forth, for *g*, *a*, and *b♮* in deuterus, tritus, and tetrardus.]

The 'discriminatory degree' midway between the modal final and its upper 5th became an important part of the modal doctrine of Marchetto and Tinctoris, under the name of 'chorda'; as *chorda mezana* it was later developed in a different direction by Zarlino.

### 4. MODE IN THE LATER MIDDLE AGES.

(*i*) *Modal quality and hexachord syllables.* The existence of modal qualities in parallel places in the Boethian double octave had been stipulated by Hucbald; the tetrachords embodying the set of four such modal qualities had been expanded to hexachordal *sedes troporum* by Hermannus and Wilhelm. The other 11th-century hexachord was the set of 'Guidonian' solmization syllables *ut re mi fa sol la*; but Guido himself connected his syllables neither with his own doctrine of affinities – *d* with *a*, *e* with *b♮*, *f* with *c'*, and so on – nor *a fortiori* with modal theory. It can be shown that by the end of the 11th century the 'Guidonian hexachord' must have been conceived as fully transferable to any place in the system where its stepwise successions would fit, that is, where there were affinities (see *Commentarius anonymus*, ed. Smits van Waesberghe, p.120). Yet there is no documentary evidence for what would seem to have been the obvious connection between the Guidonian *ut re mi fa sol la* transferable according to intervallic affinity and the Reichenau *sedes troporum* transferable according to modal quality. Hermannus's passage explicating his hexachordal *modi vocum* and *sedes troporum* appears in only a few other 11th-century works, notably Wilhelm of Hirsau's *Musica*. Another passage in Wilhelm's work summarizing the structure of each of the four *modi vocum* as the property of a trope is paraphrased in turn by Aribo (*GS*, ii, 217; *CSM*, ii, 32); and this is recast in the treatise of Engelbert of Admont (*GS*, ii, 348), who died in 1331. Apart from this no direct transmission of the Reichenau hexachord has been traced.

(*a*) *Regular finals and transposed affinals.* It is only in treatises from the second half of the 13th century that the connection between hexachordal syllables and modal quality is documented. Yet the treatise of the

Dominican Jerome of Moravia, the earliest fully to explain the modal quality of hexachord syllables, makes no more claim than any other 13th-century writing to be presenting original doctrine in this area. The source is almost certainly not Reichenau; but whatever it is, the connecting of the hexachord syllables with the modal qualities of the four tetrachordal degrees united the functional approach of the 11th-century Italian writers with the structural analysis of their northern contemporaries. Jerome's explanation of the location of modal finals and affinals in the hexachords follows below and is illustrated in Table 6 (A): 'the first and second tone end in *d* or in *a*, with *re*. The third and fourth tone end in *e* or in *a*, with *mi*, or in *b♮*. . . . The fifth and sixth tone end in *f* or in *c'*. The seventh and eighth end only in *g*' (*CS*, i, 77f; ed. Cserba, pp.159ff). The hexachordal syllables for the tritus and tetrardus finals, which Jerome neglected to mention, are given in a similar passage from the *Speculum musice* of Jacques de Liège (early 14th century). Table 6 (B) illustrates 'chants ending in *fa* are of the fifth or sixth tone, and in fact chants ending in *sol* are of the seventh or eighth' (*CS*, ii, 313). The association of the four central hexachord syllables with the four pairs of authentic–plagal modes was simply the final stage in the evolution of a constant symmetry extending back through the four positions in the structural tetrachord and four modal qualities: *re*, modes 1 and 2, I, protus; *mi*, modes 3 and 4, II, deuterus; *fa*, modes 5 and 6, III, tritus; *sol*, modes 7 and 8, IV, tetrardus.

Some necessary substitutions for convenience of solmization at the approach to the tritus and tetrardus finals is supplied here from an anonymous treatise on the eight tones 'by some Chartist monk', and illustrated

TABLE 6

| Mode | Function | c | d | e | f | g | a | b♭ | b♮ | c' | d' | e' | |
|------|----------|---|---|---|---|---|---|----|----|----|----|----|---|
| I 1/2 | FINAL | ut | [re] | mi | fa | sol | la | | | | | | |
| | affinal | | | | | | ut | | (re) | | mi fa sol la | | |
| II 3/4 | FINAL | ut | re | [mi] | fa | sol | la | | | | | | |
| | (transformed) | | | ut | re | ⟨mi⟩ fa | | sol | la | | | | A |
| | affinal | | | | | | ut | | re | (mi) fa sol la | | |
| III 5/6 | FINAL | | | | [f] | | | | | | | | |
| | affinal | | | | | | | | | (c') | | | |
| IV 7/8 | FINAL | | | | | [g] | | | | | | | |
| | | c | d | e | f | g | a | b♭ | b♮ | c' | d' | e' | |
| III {5/6 | FINAL | ut | re | mi | [fa] | sol | la | | | | | | |
| | affinal | | | | | | ut | | re | mi (fa) sol | la | | B |
| {5/6 | | ut | re | mi | [fa] | sol | la | | | | | | C |
| | FINAL | | | [ut] | re | mi fa | | sol | la | | | | |
| IV 7/8 | FINAL | ut | re | mi | fa | [sol] | la | | | | | | B,C |
| | | | | [ut] | re | mi fa | sol | la | | | | | C |
| | | c | d | e | f | g | a | b♭ | b♮ | c' | d' | e' | |
| I 1/2 | (transformed) | | | ut | ⟨re⟩ | mi fa | | sol | la | | | | D |

□ – regular final   ◯ – affinal (final in a transposed mode)   ◇ – final in a transformed mode in Table 6 (C): 'The fifth and sixth [tones] in *f fa ut* are also ended in *ut* when the hexachord [*cantus*] is soft and . . . descends to the final. Similarly the seventh and eighth [tones] are ended in *ut* when their chant [*cantus*] descends to the final' (*CS*, ii, 442).

(*b*) Transformed finals. The use of *a*, *b♮* and *c'* as protus, deuterus and tritus at the upper 5th had been recognized in Hucbald's 'associated together' and Guido's doctrine of affinity and term 'affinal'. But the conjunct tetrachord *synēmmenōn* (*a–b♭–c'–d'*), which made the 'second 9th degree' *b♭* of the *Dialogus* available, was regarded at the outset as auxiliary to the system rather than essential; the same in principle remained true of its *b♭* taken alone, which was considered merely a variant for *b♮* despite its early and continuous recognition as essential in the tritus modes. Hence theoretical recognition of the projection of the finals at the upper 4th rather than the upper 5th was long in coming. A corollary of this projection, that one note could serve as modal final for two different scale types, caused particularly keen theoretical discomfort in the case where the note was a regular final, namely *g*. The process of turning *g* tetrardus into *g* protus (or for that matter *a* protus into *a* deuterus) by using *b♭* was called 'transformation', and was not considered quite respectable by theorists until the full integration of the hexachords with the modal system. Jacques de Liège drew attention to the hexachordal orientation of the protus on the tetrardus final *g* in the course of objecting to the use of a tetrardus–protus transformation within a mode 8 antiphon, one also discussed in the *Questiones in musica* (ed. Steglich, p.51); Table 6 (D) illustrates Jacques' location of the *g* protus final (*CS*, ii, 316):

every regular or irregular chant, if it terminates suitably and finally in *re*, is of the first or second tone wherever it may be found or with whatever letter of the monochord it may be joined. For that [*re*] is the final degree [*vox finalis*] of the first and second tone, and it begins the first species of 5th, which is common to those two tones. Moreover I said 'if . . . suitably' on account of those [mode 8] chants which have their final in *g* with *b♭* . . . such as the [mode 8] antiphon *Magnus sanctus Paulus*.

(*ii*) *Italian modal theory in the 14th and 15th centuries.* The last phase of medieval modal theory developed in Italy; the seminal work was the *Lucidarium* of Marchetto da Padova (*GS*, iii), completed by 1318, a few years before the *Speculum musice* of Jacques de Liège. Aspects of the tradition for modal description and classification established by Marchetto endured for two and a half centuries. One of the lasting features of the theory was in itself not new: the formal disposition of the scale structure of the modes according to species of the 4th and 5th. A second feature was the classification of the modal ambitus and melody into five categories: perfect, imperfect, mixed, pluperfect (some later writers preferred the term 'superfluous') and commixed. A third feature of the theory was a functional ordering of the species of 4th and 5th 'as they may be named when positioned in the tones' (*GS*, iii, 114). The first four among these functional species were named 'principal' (or 'initial'), 'terminal', 'common' and 'proper'; also included were commixed species, conjunct and disjunct species (*aggregata*, *disgregata*), species rising or falling, and species with all possible interruptions (i.e. omissions of one or more notes between the outer tones of the consonance).

Up to the 16th century this theory was transmitted in Italy itself, where it is first documented over a

century after the *Lucidarium*, in book 1 of the *Declaratio musice discipline* of Ugolino of Orvieto, written in the 1430s (CSM, vii). Much of Ugolino's treatment is an enormously expanded and rationalized commentary on Marchetto's work. (This work should be added to those discussed by K. W. Niemöller in *KJb*, xl, 1956, 23.) Several writers of northern origin working in Italy were influenced by the theory, such as Johannes Legrense (Gallicus) (*CS*, iv, 345–69), the teacher of Nicolaus Burtius. Tinctoris, whose *Liber de natura et proprietate tonorum* was written in 1476 in Naples, was a Fleming much in the centre of this Italian tradition. His exposition is the most complete of any and his work is characterized even more than Marchetto's by the use of examples composed to illustrate the points.

Franchinus Gaffurius's exposition of the doctrine is in book 5 chapters 6–8 of his *Theorica musicae* (Milan, 1492), and book 1 of the *Practica musicae* (Milan, 1496, first draft before 1487). Gaffurius's *Practica musicae* was the principal vehicle for aspects of the theory outside Italy (see Cochlaeus, 1511, bk.2 chaps.2–3, and Wollick, 1509, bk.3 chap.3). Pietro Aaron also belongs to the tradition, and part iii of Lanfranco's *Scintille di musica* (Brescia, 1533) should be included. As late as 1588 Pietro Pontio used and cited Gaffurius (*Practica musicae*, bk.1 chap.8) for the five categories of modal ambitus and melody.

Marchetto's approach was implicitly scholastic, and Ugolino's *Declaratio* explicitly so. The first stage in the process of modal differentiation was a threefold classification of intervals; they were called conjunctions, and Marchetto defined them as 'disposition or arrangement [*ordinatio*] of sounds' (*GS*, iii, 92). Tone, semitone, major and minor 3rds were 'syllable conjunctions', which were in turn the immediate constituents of 'species conjunctions', the consonances of the 4th, 5th and octave (plus the 11th, 12th and double octave). Ugolino defined this relationship metaphysically: 'Since there is no giving form without material . . . we claim the tones, semitones, ditones and other conjunctions of the degrees, from which the species of 5th and 4th are fitted together, to be the material for the form' (CSM, vii, 92). Marchetto's third class of conjunctions comprised the 6ths and the other intervals from diminished 5th and tritone to major 7th and diminished octave. The species of 4th exhibited the familiar structure tone–semitone–tone, semitone–tone–tone and tone–tone–semitone; three of the species of 5th were derived from them by adding a tone at the upper end, but the tone–tone–tone–semitone species of 5th 'arises from itself' (Marchetto, *Lucidarium*, *GS*, iii, 97f; Ugolino, *Declaratio*, bk.1 chap.29). These species were then summed in pairs to form the eight modal octaves, as they had been by Berno and his sources three and more centuries earlier (see ex.6*b*).

The passages in Marchetto's *Lucidarium* (*GS*, iii, 114–17) and Ugolino's *Declaratio* (bk.1 chap.46) that classify the species according to function rather than structure are close in both text and illustrations. Their first two types of functional species – initial and terminal – are yet another representation of the importance of opening gesture and cadential approach. Ugolino's illustrations, shown in ex.10*a*, are not labelled as to mode, but they hardly need to be. The first 'initial' is Gevaert's *thème* 6, and the other is as clearly mode 3, from the final *e* up to the tenor *c'*. The first 'terminal' can be cadential in either protus mode, but is more frequent in mode 2, and is evidently so intended since the second

Ex.10

(a)

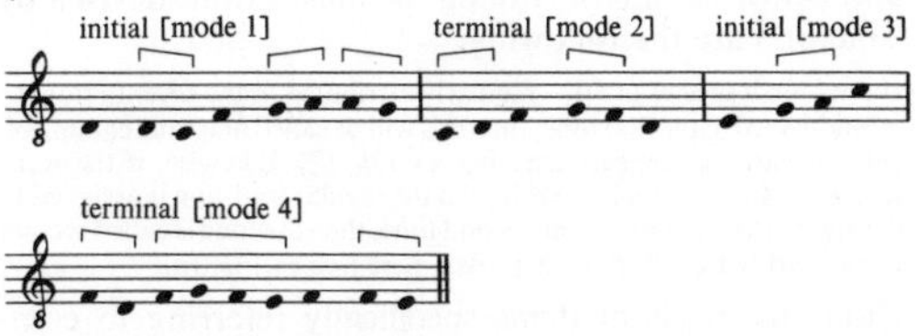

initial [mode 1]    terminal [mode 2]    initial [mode 3]

terminal [mode 4]

(b) 'proper [4th and common 5th] of [each] tone'

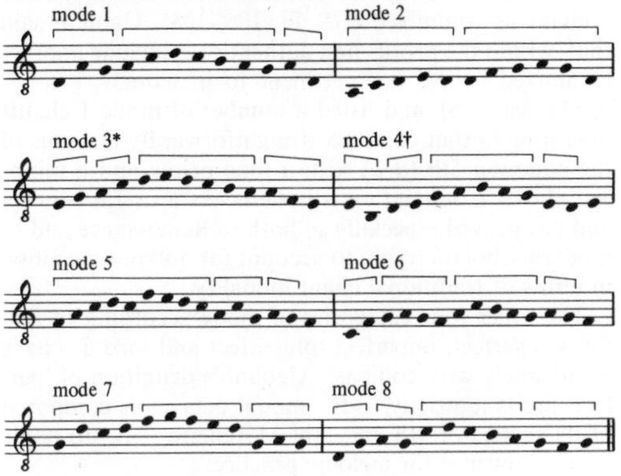

mode 1      mode 2

mode 3*      mode 4†

mode 5      mode 6

mode 7      mode 8

*'... to its prescribed ascent, which is c'...,' although 'the third tone is
formed from the II. species of fifth and the II. species of fourth..'
(GS, iii, 109)

†'even though the lower fourth may be rarely used' (loc. cit.)

(c) 'common [species of 4th] of the tones'

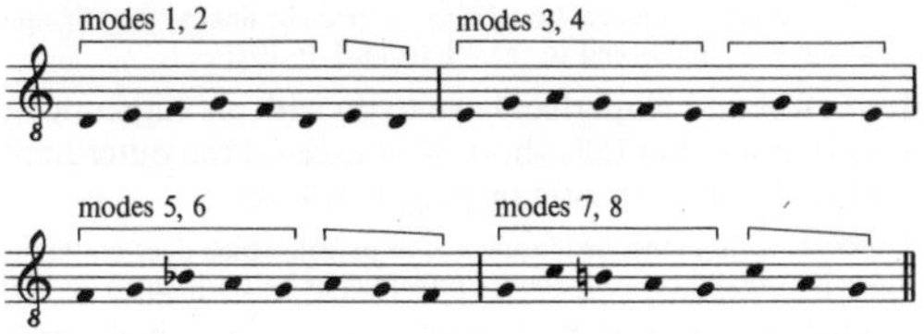

modes 1, 2      modes 3, 4

modes 5, 6      modes 7, 8

Ex.11

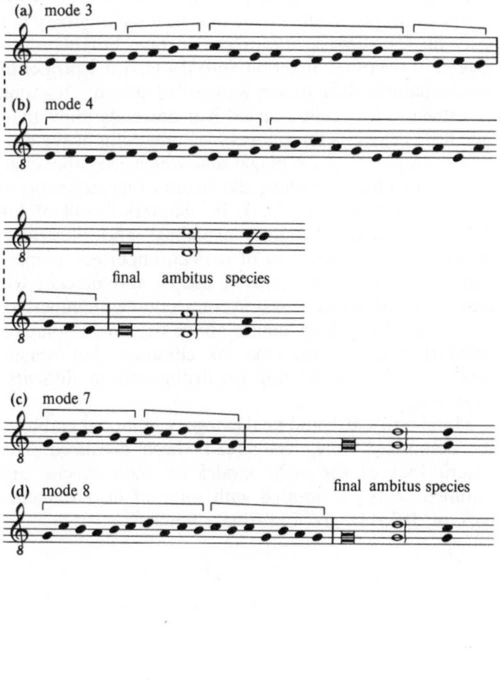

(a) mode 3

(b) mode 4

final   ambitus   species

(c) mode 7

final ambitus species

(d) mode 8

final ambitus species

'terminal' is unmistakably mode 4, a deuterus plagal.

The species of 5th common to each authentic–plagal pair of modes reaches from final up to fifth. The species proper to each individual authentic or plagal is the species of 4th conjoined above or below the common 5th, respectively, to form the mode, that is, the modal octave. Ex.10b gives Ugolino's unambiguously composed illustrations showing the conjoining of proper 4th and common 5th in each mode. Appropriate cautionary footnotes are added from Marchetto's *Lucidarium*.

The doctrine also includes a 'common species' of 4th (*GS*, iii, 108):

In any of the tones, that species [of 4th] is called common which begins ... where the tone has to end, and rises upwards; this species of course is used in [both] authentics and plagals, although it can be put more often in plagals. For if in a chant [lying] high this species is struck [*repercussa*] several times, [provided] the chant does not rise beyond the 6th, the tone will be judged plagal.

Ex.10c is the illustration given by Marchetto and Ugolino for the species of 4th common in each authentic–plagal pair. In his *Practica musicae* (bk.1 chap.9; trans. Miller, p.53) Gaffurius misunderstood this notion of Marchetto's. Tinctoris, however, used it cogently in his *Liber ... tonorum* (*CS*, iv):

If the tone rises above its final to the 5th plus a tone or semitone and descends a tone or semitone below, it will still be called authentic, as is proven here [see ex.11a] ... [but if] common species of 4th are struck [*repercutiantur*] several times, it will be judged plagal, as appears here [see ex.11b]. [p.32]

If a tone not descending beneath its final does not rise above the 5th, and [if it] frequents the 5th as much or more than the common 4th, it is authentic; otherwise, [it is] plagal, as is proven here [see ex.11c, d]. [p.33]

The contrast between common species of 5th as a mark for authentics and common species of 4th as a mark for plagals is thus both assimilated to and developed from the notion of repercussion, as first expounded in the *Dialogus*. The repercussion – or common 5th/common 4th – coincides with the corresponding psalm-tone tenor for three of the four authentics and for two of the plagals; neither historically nor musicologically have the distinctions between repercussion and tenor been observed as scrupulously as is sometimes necessary. Ex.12 shows a mnemonic verse found in several 16th-century German works in which in effect the common 5th of the authentics and the tenor

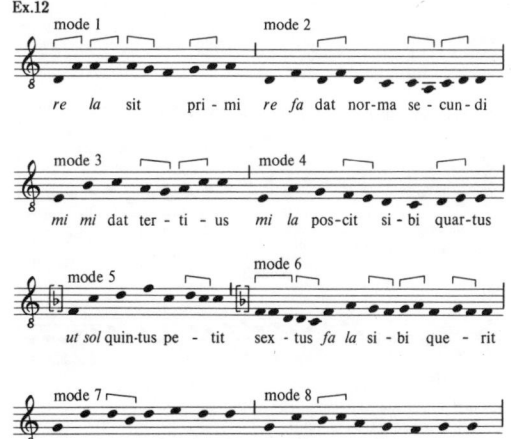

Ex.12

mode 1      mode 2

*re la* sit pri - mi *re fa* dat nor-ma se - cun-di

mode 3      mode 4

*mi mi* dat ter - ti - us *mi la* pos-cit si - bi quar-tus

mode 5      mode 6

*ut sol* quin-tus pe - tit sex - tus *fa la* si - bi que - rit

mode 7      mode 8

*ut sol* im - par te-trar-dus *ut fa* pos - tre-mus ha - be - bit.

of the plagals has been combined, to form a consistent pattern of repercussions. In the third part of Lanfranco's *Scintille di musica* (p.117, *recte* p.107) the same pattern may be found, making explicit the connection of repercussion with (common) species, as well as with the term 'melodia' (which sometimes also means psalm-tone tenor, or psalm-tone difference, or the whole psalm tone): 'The repercussion, which is the *melodia* or interval proper to each chant . . . all of which repercussions are called species of chant'.

The confinal too is occasionally taken not as the final of the whole piece projected on the system a 5th higher but rather simply as the conclusion of a piece on the note a 5th above what would normally have constituted its final. This is Gaffurius's interpretation of the antiphon *Nos qui vivimus* 'which ends on the *confinalis* . . . [in] a very old antiphoner . . . it ends on its untransposed *confinalis d la sol re*' (*Practica musicae*, bk.1 chap.14; trans. Miller, pp.60f).

When a species of 4th or 5th that was neither proper nor common to the mode of a melody was introduced, it was called 'commixed' with respect to the species of the mode in question. Marchetto illustrated this by devising commixtures of the common species of 5th for mode 1 (*d–a*) with species common or proper to every other mode except 2 and 8 (the former shares the same final, the latter the same octave species), as may be seen in ex.13*a*.

Commixture of species produced commixture of modes, the most novel of Marchetto's five categories of mode with reference to ambitus (which in this category

was not confined merely to the sense of compass above and below the final). Among the illustrations devised by Tinctoris are the following:

If the fourth species of 5th – regularly attributed to the seventh [tone] – is established in the first tone, then this will be called first tone commixed with seventh, as appears here [see ex.13*b*, (i)]. Likewise, if the third species of 4th . . . which according to the regular tradition is assigned to the eighth [tone], is put in the second tone, then the tone is called second commixed with eighth, as is proven here [see ex.13*b*, (ii)].

Citations of chant items specifically referring to commixture were infrequent. Marchetto (and others including Gaffurius after him) referred to an initial *e* in a mode 1 chant as commixed (*GS*, iii, 106, 108). Ugolino said that 'within the protus first authentic we include another commixed octave not pertinent to it, namely, *c* to *c′*' (*CSM*, vii, 186), and listed a number of mode 1 chants operating in that compass straightforwardly in terms of the common 5th (*d–a*) with a tone below and a minor 3rd above. Commixture is nonetheless a useful concept and has proved especially so both to Renaissance and to modern scholars trying to account for polyphonic music in terms of traditional chant modality.

The other four categories of mode according to ambitus – perfect, imperfect, pluperfect and mixed – have to do solely with compass. Ugolino's definition of 'perfect' limits it strictly to the modal octave, as composed of its species of 4th and 5th; Marchetto (*GS*, iii) made some allowance for melodic practice:

That tone is called perfect which fills its mode [i.e. modal octave] above and below. Now to fill its mode in an authentic [tone] is to rise from its final to the octave and not beyond, and to descend from the same final by a tone, excepting the tritus [authentic], which has a semitone below the final [p.101]

[and] the fifth tone very seldom descends below its final [p.112]

To fill its mode in a plagal [tone] is to rise from its final to the 6th, and from the final to descend to the 4th [below]. [p.102]

Imperfect and pluperfect have to do with an authentic or plagal mode that falls short of or exceeds the outer limit that makes it authentic or plagal (*GS*, iii):

Imperfect is that tone, be it authentic or plagal, which does not fill its mode [i.e. modal octave], above [authentic] or below [plagal]. [p.102]

The authentic tone which rises beyond the octave from its final, namely to the 9th or 10th, is called pluperfect. The plagal tone which descends below the 4th under its final is [also] called pluperfect. [p.103]

Either authentic or plagal can also encroach upon the compass proper to the other; that is, a melody may not only fill (or surpass) its 'proper' octave but may also extend in the other direction, into the territory proper to its companion. Such modes were called 'mixed'. 'If a tone is authentic it is called mixed if it descends more than one note below its final, touching something of the descent of its plagal. . . . A plagal tone which rises above the 6th from its final, touching the ascent of its authentic, is called mixed' (*GS*, iii, 103). In chapters 28–48 of his *Liber . . . tonorum* Tinctoris explained and illustrated the possible combinations of perfect, imperfect, pluperfect (superfluous), and mixed ascent and descent for authentic and plagal. It was in connection with imperfection – in effect, small ranges above the final – that he invoked the repercussions to common 5th versus common 4th as a criterion for distinguishing authentic from plagal.

Marchetto's fifth and final category of modal ambitus, the commixed tone, has already been discussed. His descriptions of the eight modes by their species are outlined below, annotated with some of his comments (*GS*, iii, 103–14), given in square brackets:

Ex.13

(a) commixture of species, after Marchetto (*GS*, iii, 115f)

mode 1: 5th
modes 6 and 4: common species of 4th
modes 3, 5 and 7: 5th

(b) commixture of modes, after Tinctoris (*CS*, iv, 24)

modes 1 and 7: 5th

mode 2: proper and common species of 4th
mode 8: common species of 4th

(i) Species I 5th (*defga*) + species I 4th above (*abᵇc′d′*) + tone below (*c*) [either it ascends beyond its first species only as far as *c′* [!] and no further, and then it ought to be sung always with *b♭*, and may be said to be common with the 6th [mode], . . . or it ascends to the aforesaid *c′* [or *a fortiori* beyond it] several times . . . before it descends to *f*, and then it will be sung with *b♮*].

(ii) Species I 5th (*defga*) + species I 4th below (*dcBA*) and common (*defg*).

(iii) Species II 5th (*efgab♮*) + species II 4th (*b♮c′d′e′*), + tone below (*d*) [such a chant may want to rise to its prescribed ascent, which is upper *c′*].

(iv) Species II 5th (*efgab♮*) + species II 4th below (*edcB*) and common (*efga*) [even though the lower 4th may be rarely used].

(v) Species III 5th (*fgab♮c′*) + species III 4th above (*c′d′e′f′*) in ascent [when it rises from the final to the 5th above in whatever way, the extension through these notes passes more sweetly and smoothly to the ear . . . so that we may use the third species of 5th, which can be used in no other tone but this and its plagal]; in descent species IV 5th (*fgab♭c′*) [so that when it wants to come from the 5th above to the final, it may avoid the harshness of the tritone] + species III 4th above.

(vi) Species III 5th (*fgab♮c′*) + species III 4th below (*fedc*) in ascent; species IV 5th (*fgab♭c′*) + species III 4th below (*fedc*) and common (*fgab♭*) in descent [Why it is so formed, and how it ought to be sung with *b♭* or *b♮*, is the same reason as was said of its authentic].

(vii) Species IV 5th (*gab♮c′d′*) + species I 4th above (*d′ e′ f′ g′*) + tone below (*f*).

(viii) Species IV 5th (*gab♮c′ d′*) + species III 4th [common] (*gab♮c′*) [which begins in high *c′* tending downward; though this species is in common with its authentic, yet it should be put more often in the eighth]; also, species IV 5th (*gab♮c′d′*) + species I 4th below (*gfed*).

Like his contemporary, Jacques de Liège, Marchetto (*GS*, iii) accepted with only *pro forma* reservations the projection of the modes anywhere they could fit on the system:

The first tone and its plagal can be ended in any part of the [Guidonian] hand where the species which form it above and below can be arranged. [p.104]. . . . Such a tone is called 'proper' in terms of composition but 'improper' in terms of location, because it is settled in a place other than its own. [p.108]. . . . And we claim the same for any other tone, authentic as well as plagal. [p.104]

The principle was to cover projections of modal degrees both at the upper 5th, to the affinal (or confinal), and at the upper 4th. First, 'if any tone finishes in its confinal, it is because of accidence [*propter accidens*]' (*GS*, iii, 105). Marchetto used accidence in contradistinction to substance or essence. He took as his example the gradual *Nimis honorati* (*GR*, 391), one of the so-called 'Justus ut palma' type. These graduals are in mode 2 ending on the affinal *a*, a projection required because of two 'accidentals' (*GS*, iii, 105); regularly in mode 2 there was neither a semitone above the final nor a major 3rd below it. Second, 'there are also some chants which can finish neither in the final nor in the confinal on account of some inconvenient accidentals falling in them, such as the communion *Beatus servus*. . . . Such a note is called "acquired" [*tonus . . . acquisitus*]' (*GS*, iii, 105f). *Beatus servus* (*LU*, 1203) is discussed at length in Jacobsthal, *Die chromatische Alteration* (pp.99ff), although his constructions can be considerably improved with the better text of chapter 21 of Johannes Afflighemensis's *De musica* (CSM, i). It is a mode 3 piece that also must finish on *a*; it uses *b♭* in mode 3 phrases at the beginning and end, but there are two medial phrases reflecting mode 1 that use *b♮*.

(*iii*) *Expansion of the tonal system*. The freedom to claim the species of the 5th and 4th as modal, no matter where they might fall in the system, had radical implications. The soft hexachord provided a protus final on *g*, but to use it 'suitably' in the sense meant by Jacques de Liège entailed a consistent use of *fa* on *b♭* along with the protus final *re* on *g*. Hence the soft hexachord *f–g–a–*

*b♭–c′–d′* became a *sedes tonorum* encompassing *g* protus modes, and *b♭* became an essential degree, no longer accidental, just as the natural hexachord *c d e f g a* was the *sedes tonorum* encompassing the regular *d* protus modes, which use *b♮* of the hard hexachord as the essential sixth degree and *b♭* of the soft hexachord as the accidental. The acceptance of *g* protus modes with an essential *b♭* as their third degree further entailed a new accidental sixth degree, *e♭′*, solmized *fa* in a new soft hexachord *b♭–c′–d′–e♭′–f′–g′*. The *b♮* of the original system was reduced to the status of an alteration for approaching *c′* in cadences. By the 16th century the new system came to be called *cantus mollis*, because *b♭ mollis* is essential, as opposed to the traditional system where *b♮ durus* is essential, which thereby came to be called *cantus durus*.

Ex.14*a* illustrates what became the most conventional 16th-century usages of the *cantus mollis* system, in which all voices had a signature of B♭. The hexachordal and species patterns of the protus and deuterus modes (1, 2, and 3, 4) are identical with those of the traditional system – that is, *cantus durus* – but the letter names are different, so that protus finals are on *g* (solmized *re*) and deuterus finals are on *a* (solmized *mi*). For the tritus modes, conversely, the *cantus mollis* was used for the regular final *f*. For these two modes, from Hucbald (9th century) to Guido (11th century) to Marchetto (14th century), *b♭* was recognized as at least as powerful as *b♮*, in practice and in theory; the *cantus mollis b♭* signature simply recognized the fact. (However, the acquisition by the system as a whole of a soft hexachord *b♭–c′–d′–e♭′–f′–g′* made available to the tritus on *f* the same *subtonium* that all the other regular modes had always had.)

Once *b♭* as *fa* of the soft hexachord could be considered an essential rather than an accidental degree in the system as a whole – a possibility not readily open to *b♭* as a member of the extra tetrachord *synemmenon* (see §2(i) above) – the same principle could be extended to *e♭′*, the *fa* of the new soft hexachord: it could be seen as the essential third degree in a new protus first species of 5th *re–mi–fa–sol–la*, *c′–d′–e♭′–f′–g′*. Since this extension provided for an essential note name (E♭) that had not formed even an accidental part of the traditional system, it was regarded as musically contrived, or somehow not quite real – *musica ficta* or *musica falsa* as opposed to *musica vera* – and the system of hexachordal relationships providing for it came to be called *cantus fictus*, as opposed to *cantus durus* and *cantus mollis*. The protus species of *cantus fictus* are shown in ex.14*b* (see also MUSICA FICTA).

*Cantus mollis* tetrardus modes on *c* had been theoretically available in chant theory as transformations at the tritus affinal *c*, but they were extremely rare. The more common orientation for a *c* mode was the traditional tritus affinal, much in evidence as a *sedes* for mode 6 (Hypolydian). Also in frequent use were the protus modes at the affinal position with the *sedes a*, especially the plagal protus.

Ex.14*c* shows the *cantus durus* interpretation of the species in *a* protus, and *c* and *c′* tritus. For the protus modes there is an essential difference between the *cantus mollis* 'transpositions' (in the modern sense) and the *cantus durus* transpositions, which continue in the medieval sense. The medieval transposition simply projected the melody against a different segment of the double octave, with no effect on the background system. A protus melody with its final set at *a* could thereby have a major 3rd below its final (*f*) and the minor 6th above its final (*f'*) as logically essential notes; it also gained the option of using an accidentally lowered second degree (*b♭*), and it lost altogether the possibility of using a major 6th above the final. In terms of the hexachordal species shown in ex.14c, the common species of 5th for the protus *re–mi–fa–sol–la* (as in *a–b♮–c'–d'–e'*) dominated, but the conjoined species of 4th (below for plagal, above for authentic) was *mi–fa–sol–la* (as in *e–f–g–a*), which was proper to the deuterus rather than to the protus. A protus using its confinal *a*, then, was a commixed protus. In the tritus modes, on the other hand, both the common 5th *ut–re–mi–fa–sol* (as in *c'–d'–e'–f'–g'*) and the proper 4th *ut–re–mi–fa* (as in *g–a–b♭–c'*) had the same hexachordal syllables as those for the species of the tritus in *cantus mollis* at the regular final *f*. The only tritus species unavailable as a modal element in *c*-final projections was the third species of 5th *fa–sol/re–mi–fa*, with its internal mutation between natural and hard hexachord, which could only be projected at *f–g–a–b♮–c'*.

The extension of the hexachord system in such a way as to provide modal species and modal finals in unaccustomed places was a part of the development of polyphonic music, that is, 'composed songs, in primary attention to which', Tinctoris stated, 'I have principally undertaken this treatise' (*Liber de natura et proprietate tonorum, CS,* iv, 27). He concluded his treatise in fact with a discussion (with his usual ad hoc illustrations) of what he designated as 'irregular finals'. These included any final other than the regular finals *d, e, f, g,* and the confinals *a, b♮, c'*. These last three involved transposition only in the medieval sense and did not involve the transformation of the whole system effected by changing *b♭* from accidental to essential; in that sense Tinctoris had chosen to consider the three confinals as regular also. So, for example, the medieval tritus confinal at *c'* was not represented among his 'transpositions'. An octave lower, however, *c* was an 'irregular' tritus final, as shown in ex.15a. Also shown in ex.15a are the irregular tritus modes on *B♭* and *b♭*, along with Tinctoris's earlier examples for the regular tritus at *f*. It should be noted of the regular tritus at *f* and the irregular tritus at *b♭* that express provision was made for the perfect 4th above the final, *fa* as *b♭* or *e♭'*, respectively. Conversely, *fa* occurred naturally as *f* in the irregular tritus at *c*, which passed without any comment, indicating that the fourth degree above this tritus final *c* would never occur otherwise than as *f*.

Ex.15b shows two of Tinctoris's illustrations for irregular protus modes. One pair is *g* protus, in *cantus mollis*; the other is *c* protus, in *cantus fictus*.

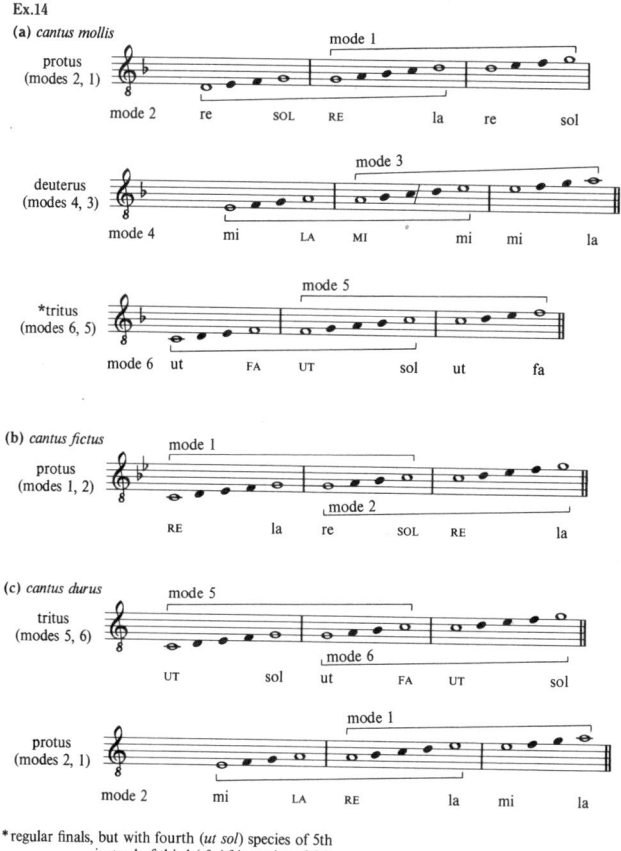

Ex.14

(a) *cantus mollis*

protus (modes 2, 1)

(b) *cantus fictus*

protus (modes 1, 2)

(c) *cantus durus*

tritus (modes 5, 6)

protus (modes 2, 1)

\* regular finals, but with fourth (*ut sol*) species of 5th instead of third (*fa/fa*) species of 5th

Ex.15

(a) tritus

regular *f* tritus
*mode 5                    *mode 6

*'either of these two tones can be formed from the fourth species of 5th (*f, g, a, b♭, c'*) ... by reason of perfect concords ... in composed song ... or ... to avoid the tritone' (*CS*, iv, 21)

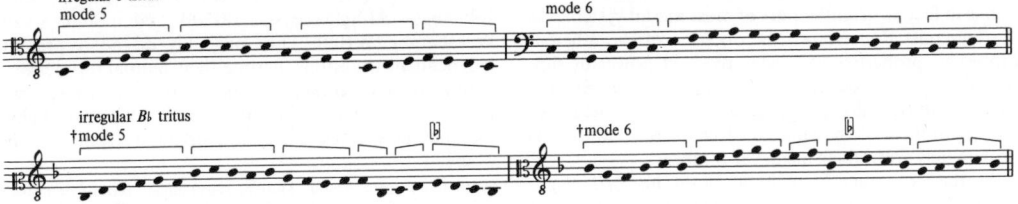

irregular *c* tritus
mode 5                    mode 6

irregular *B♭* tritus
†mode 5                    †mode 6

†'with altered *e* when it is necessary' (*CS*, iv, 38)

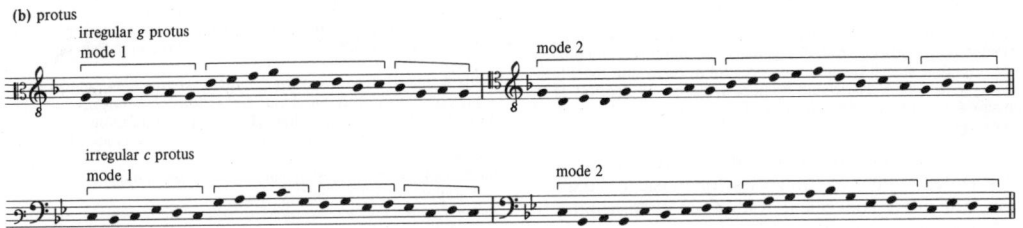

(b) protus

irregular *g* protus
mode 1                    mode 2

irregular *c* protus
mode 1                    mode 2

## III. Modal theories and polyphonic music

1. Elements of polyphonic modal theory: (i) The poetic function of the modes (ii) Modality in a polyphonic texture. 2. Polyphonic modal functions: (i) Cadences and openings (ii) The integration of modality and polyphony. 3. Polyphonic modal theory and the eightfold system: (i) Aaron and the psalm-tone differences (ii) Composite modes (iii) Modal cadences and polyphonic psalmody. 4. Systems of 12 modes: (i) The 12 modes before Glarean (ii) Glarean's 12 modes (iii) Zarlino's synthesis of modality and polyphony. 5. Transition to major and minor keys: (i) The 12 modes in the late 16th century (ii) The modes in the 17th century (iii) The modal triad.

1. ELEMENTS OF POLYPHONIC MODAL THEORY. Between the 13th century and the 15th modal theory was rationalizing and integrating an edifice of doctrine and analysis whose elements and concepts had been largely worked out two centuries earlier, initially to deal with a repertory yet more ancient. During the same period, while creative musicians were devising artistic forms of polyphony, theory too was attending with greater interest to the problems of rhythm and proportion in durations, and structure and succession of simultaneities – in short, to mensural notation and to discant and counterpoint. Johannes de Grocheo, writing about 1300, specifically excluded mode from polyphony (trans. Seay, p.31):

Certain people describe a tone by saying that it is a rule that judges every song by its end [*regulam quae de omni cantu in fine iudicat*]. But these men seem to err in many ways, for when they speak of 'every song' they seem to include popular and measured song [*cantum civilem et mensuratum*]. This kind of song does not perhaps proceed through the rules of a tone, nor is it measured by them. Further, if it is measured by them, they do not speak of the method by which it is used nor do they make mention about it.

Earlier Grocheo had specifically included organum, conductus, and motet in the category of measured song,

so the presence or absence of a plainchant tenor as the basis for a polyphonic composition had no bearing on the question of whether or not it ought to be considered modal.

Well over two centuries later Sebald Heyden asked 'Why is it necessary to pursue religiously the ranges of authentic and plagal tones, as they are called, and the *differentiae* added to them, when we know that they have almost no meaning in figural music?' (MSD, xxvi, 113). Heyden was chiefly interested in *tactus* and proportions. Nonetheless, such a statement is surprising, for it came at a time when secular polyphonic collections ordered according to the eight modes were beginning to make an appearance. Moreover, immediately following Heyden's own summary and examples for the traditional modes and psalm tones he himself printed polyphonic compositions illustrating each of the eight modes. The question draws attention to the fact, however, that between modes and modal theory on the one hand and the actual composition of polyphony on the other there was no necessary connection either in theory or in practice. Between counterpoint – the rules governing simultaneities and their successions – and modality there was nothing comparable to the indissoluble link between harmony and tonality that prevailed from Rameau's *Traité de l'harmonie* to Schoenberg's *Harmonielehre*.

(i) *The poetic function of the modes.* During the period 1450–1600 musicians increasingly came to feel that polyphonic music must somehow be modal. But a mode, unlike a key in 18th- and 19th-century music, was not an abstract general pattern of tonal relationships inherent in the grammar and syntax of the musical language. It was, rather, a part of musical style. Musicians believed that the modes furnished a number of differently structured sets of coherent musical relationships each of which had its own set of expressive characteristics that could naturally and of themselves reinforce the affective sense of a verbal text.

(a) Modal ethos in the Middle Ages. The tradition that a mode has inherent expressive properties and extramusical associations was of classical origin; this notion is in fact an essential part of most modal systems. In the humanist Renaissance the doctrine of the inherent expressive properties of modes received powerful support from direct reference to classical sources. But the tradition of modal expressivity as well as the details of the eightfold system came to Renaissance musicians proximately from their medieval forebears.

At the beginning of chapter 14 of his *Micrologus* Guido had proposed that 'the diversity of tropes is suited to the diversity of mentalities' and had described four of the eight modes briefly. Engelbert of Admont reported the tradition as follows (*GS*, ii, 340):

Guido says that the third tone has broken leaps, and so its song is impetuous. The sixth in truth has gentle leaps, and this is voluptuous. The seventh is indeed garrulous, on account of many and short turnabouts [*reflexiones*]. The eighth is more agreeable on account of its lingering and less frequent turnings [*propter morosos et pauciores reflexus*].

Seen in this way, the modes are not merely members of a closed system of categories for musical classification, nor just a convenient traditional code helping to link a handful of recitation formulae with a galaxy of separate songs, nor only a collection of scales or melody types. Guido's tropes are depicted as real, individual entities, with characters identified as 'impetuous . . . voluptuous . . . garrulous . . . agreeable'. Such characters as these are ethic; they have to do with the expressive and even the moral power of a musical entity to act on a human spirit.

For the most part, the general idea of modal ethos was accepted in medieval theory without question (where it appeared at all), and specific doctrines regarding one mode or another are ad hoc, and purely traditional. Like many other usages in medieval musical theory the notion of ethos (though not the term) was borrowed ultimately from classical antiquity. A characteristic instance is a story about the ethos of the Phrygian *harmonia* whose name had become attached to the authentic deuterus by the end of the 9th century. This story is retold after Boethius (see Strunk, 1950, p.82) by medieval and Renaissance theorists from Regino in the 9th century (*GS*, i, 235) to Glarean in the 16th (bk.2 chap.23). Engelbert's version reads (*GS*, ii, 340):

Boethius tells in the prologue of his *De musica* that the Phrygian tone, that is, the third, sung to a musical instrument, aroused one young man listening, the suitor of a certain girl, and provoked him to such rashness that he wanted to break into the girl's room at once, by force. And when the Phrygian tone was changed to Hypophrygian, that is, the third to the fourth tone, the young man calmed down, appeased by the gentleness of the tone.

While modal ethos plays a smaller role in Western modal theory than it does in modal systems in some other cultures, there are ample listings of modal affect among medieval and Renaissance sources to illustrate the phenomenon. These lists are by and large in agreement as to the general character of an authentic as

against its corresponding plagal, in that in each pair the plagal is almost always darker or softer than its corresponding authentic; beyond this there is only partial agreement. There follows below a compilation of modal affects from three 11th-century sources, as an illustration of the kinds of similarities and differences that can exist in the ascription of ethos to the members of a modal system. The sources are Hermannus Contractus (mid-11th century, ed. Ellinwood, p.65), Frutolfus of Michelsberg (before 1100, ed. Vivell, p.105), and Johannes Afflighemensis (c1100, ed. Smits van Waesberghe, p.109). They probably do not represent independent traditions, despite their mutual differences. Frutolfus and Johannes knew Guido's work, and Hermannus must have also; and Frutolfus knew Hermannus's work since he borrowed from it elsewhere.

mode 1, authentic protus, Dorian: Hermannus, 'serious or noble'; Frutolfus, 'mobile because it is capable of all affects'; Johannes, 'lingering and courtly meanderings'.

mode 2, plagal protus, Hypodorian: Hermannus, 'agreeable'; Frutolfus, 'mournful, because its melody seems more suitable to sad and unhappy things'; Johannes, 'deep-voiced seriousness'.

mode 3, authentic deuterus, Phrygian: Hermannus, 'excited or leaping'; Frutolfus, 'excitable'; Johannes, 'harsh and rather indignant leaping about'.

mode 4, plagal deuterus, Hypophrygian: Hermannus, 'moderate or lingering'; Frutolfus, 'moderate and serious'; Johannes, 'adulatory'.

mode 5, authentic tritus, Lydian: Hermannus, 'voluptuous'; Frutolfus, 'joyful'; Johannes, 'moderate wantonness and a sudden fall to the final'.

mode 6, plagal tritus, Hypolydian: Hermannus, 'mournful'; Frutolfus, 'voluptuous'; Johannes, 'lacrymose'.

mode 7, authentic tetrardus, Mixolydian: Hermannus, 'garrulous'; Frutolfus, 'joyful and merry'; Johannes, 'theatrical leaps'.

mode 8, plagal tetrardus, Hypomixolydian: Hermannus, 'joyful or exultant'; Frutolfus, 'agreeable and sweet'; Johannes, 'seemly and rather matronly'.

An anonymous *Tractatus de natura et distinctione octo tonorum musice* (*CS*, ii, 434ff, from a 16th-century manuscript at Ghent) makes an effort to illustrate and justify ascriptions of ethos to church modes by choosing chant examples whose texts are congruent in some way to the traditional ethos of the mode of their traditional melodies. Though the demonstration is necessarily specious, it was of course possible to find texts in the enormous liturgical corpus with the right affect in the right mode. Perhaps the most difficult case would have been mode 3, the Phrygian, whose ascribed ethos lends itself ill to liturgical texts; but the author found an ingenious rationalization. Since this mode is 'harsh and inciting to wrath and war, it is suitably applied to those matters where something of bravery or power is shown, such as [the Responsory] for the mystery of the Holy Cross, *O crux gloriosa* [*Variae preces* (Solesmes, 5/1901), 151]' (p.446). The verbs in the *repetendum* of the respond warrant the affect: '[O glorious cross . . . wonderful sign] Through which the devil was conquered, and the world was rescued through the blood of Christ'.

The system of modes was also correlated with extramusical octenary, quaternary and binary systems. Near the very outset of the medieval development Aurelian began his own supplement to the 'De octo tonis' that begins chapter 8 of *Musica disciplina* with a comparison of the eight modes to the motions of the seven planets (the moon, Mercury, Venus, the sun, Mars, Jupiter, Saturn) plus the zodiac. In the Guidonian tradition the eight modes were likened to the Beatitudes and also the parts of speech. Johannes reported the last congruence, and added another (*De musica*, chap.10):

It seems very fitting that as all that is said is contained in eight parts [of speech] so all that is sung may be governed [*moderetur*] by eight modes. But though they are now eight they were once only four, probably in imitation of the four seasons. For as the ages are diversified by the four seasons, so all song is diversified by the four modes.

In chapter 14 of the anonymous 13th-century *Summa musicae* (*GS*, iii) the eightfold system is correlated with the macrocosmic elements of the universe and the human microcosm of bodily fluids and temperaments. Authentic and plagal were more often than not called principal and subordinate, or master and disciple or servant; Aribo (*GS*, ii, 205, late 10th century) expanded the roster of dichotomies to include not only rich and poor but also male and female, which was further elaborated by Johannes de Grocheo (*c*1300): 'Just as the masculine universally exceeds the female in skill and virtue, so it seems appropriate that the principal modes exceed their plagals in ascent' (trans. Seay, p.33).

(*b*) Modal ethos for polyphony. Renaissance notions of textual expressiveness and the humanists' recovery of more and better classical authorities stimulated great interest in the idea of modal ethos as an aid to the musically expressive setting of a text. Chapter 5 of Nicolaus Burtius's counterpoint treatise (1487, pt.ii) is entitled 'How chansons [*cantilenae*] ought to be composed'. After recommending that a composer be thoroughly familiar with repertory and acquire experience through practice in his art, Burtius continued: 'most important of all, let him be familiar with the tropes, or (to use the term of practising [musicians]), the tones; for some of these induce joy, others rather sadness, while others [are] holding to a mean' (ed. Massera, p.124). The ethic properties of the eight modes, according to Burtius 'as found in documents of the musicians', are:

(1) '. . . induces happiness . . . capable of producing all affects'; (2) '. . . heavy and pitiable . . . suitable for lamentations'; (3) '. . . provoking to anger'; (4) '. . . inciting to pleasure and tempering wrath'; (5) '. . . delightful, modest, and cheerful'; (6) '. . . pious and lacrymose'; (7) '. . . partly . . . playful and pleasant . . . partly . . . inciting, and having a variety of leaps'; (8) '. . . more gladdening . . . and stimulates pleasantness'.

Hermann Finck (1556, bk.4) drew attention to the difficulties of applying the traditional stipulations for the eight modes in composition, given the needs of the contemporaneous method of setting a text, for while a plainsong mode (Rr iv–Rr iir):

is recognized according to the ordinary precepts, with almost no difficulty by [even] the moderately erudite, polyphonic [music] does not follow the ordinary rules [of the modes]. . . . The chief reasons are [1] the observation of affects in the text, and according to that [2] the [textually] appropriate variation of the points of imitation and of the cadences [*fugarum ac clausularum conveniens variatio*]. . . . Hence . . . the limits of the tones cannot be observed strictly in polyphonic music.

Notwithstanding the variety of affect within a piece, a single mode will probably predominate, 'For the song as a whole is to be ascribed to the tone to which the greater part of its points of imitation and cadences can be referred' (Rr ii). So even though the method of recognizing a mode may be completely different, a predominant affect will be established, and Finck concluded the fourth book with a list giving the property (*proprietas*) of each tone, that is, its ethic affect. Along with traditional attributes Finck included the seven planets (no mention is made of the zodiac for the eighth mode); the authentics are deputed to the unwavering sun and outer planets, the plagals to the moon and inner planets

with their variable phases. Authentic–plagal pairs are male–female, in one case master–servant.

(1) 'Dorian . . . has the liveliest melody of all, arouses the somnolent, refreshes the sad and disturbed . . . [it is] like the Sun, who is deemed first among the planets . . . the foremost musicians today use this tone the most'. (2) 'Hypodorian . . . is diametrically opposed to the former . . . produces tears, makes [one] morose . . . pitiable, heavy, serious, most subdued of all . . . [like] the Moon'. (3) 'Phrygian . . . not wrongly attributed to Mars . . . moves to choler and biliousness . . . loud words, hideous battles, and bold deeds suit this [tone]'. (4) 'Hypophrygian . . . represents the parasite, who caters to the passions of his master . . . is assigned to Mercury on account of the likeness in nature'. (5) 'Lydian . . . not unlike the sanguine [temperament] . . . corresponds with cheerfulness, friendliness, the gentler affects . . . since it pleases most of all, it averts quarrels, calms agitation, fosters peace, and is of a jovial nature . . . [it is] the joy of the sorrowful, the restoring of the desperate, the solace of the afflicted'. (6) 'Hypolydian . . . [is] contrary to the former . . . not infrequent in prayers . . . by others attributed to Venus'. (7) 'Mixolydian . . . has more in common with Saturn . . . shows itself with stentorean voice and great shouts, so as to be a terror to all'. (8) 'Hypomixolydian . . . is not unlike an honest matron, who tries to soften and calm the wrath and turmoil of [her] husband with agreeable discourse . . . studiously avoids offence . . . pacific'.

To what extent Renaissance composers of polyphonic music concerned themselves with the expressive possibilities of modal ethos is moot. That polyphonic modalities based on the eightfold system came to be used by the greatest masters of the 16th century is beyond question. From the 1540s onwards polyphonic collections fully or partly ordered with the eight modes in succession were published, from Rore's first book of five-part madrigals (1542), nos.1–17 to Palestrina's offertories (1594), nos.1–32. Such regularity might seem incompatible with the notion that the mode of a composition was determined by the principal affect of its text. In Palestrina's settings of the offertories for the Sundays from Advent to Trinity in chronological and modal order there is of course no question of choice of modal ethos. Nonetheless, the general theory of modal affect as well as the specific affects of individual modes were expounded with enthusiasm by Renaissance theorists. These included the classicizing humanists who propounded the 12-mode system, Glarean and Zarlino. Among modern scholars Bernhard Meier has argued that consideration of modal ethos played a central role in the musical setting of textual affects with such composers as Rore and Lassus.

(*ii*) *Modality in a polyphonic texture.* Until the middle of the 15th century modal theory remained completely separate from theories of counterpoint. This is not to say that independent sections dealing with each could not appear in a single work; indeed, hardly any discant treatise is without an inserted or appended chapter 'on the eight tones'. But the connection between the two was made only in about 1450, and at that rather tentatively. For instance, Guillelmus Monachus (*c*1480) concluded with a section on the modes (not printed in *CS*, iii). He began almost as though he had intended to contradict Johannes de Grocheo. 'A tone, as it may be summarized here, is a certain rule [*regula*] which judges in every song [*in omni cantu dijudicat*], and I say "in every song" rightly, either plain [song] or polyphonic [*sive firmo sive figurato*]'. But the rest is exclusively a discussion of chant mode criteria: 'ascent–descent', psalm-tone intonations and mediations, finals and tenors. Only one more passing reference to polyphony occurs, in a discussion of extended compasses in authentics, which 'can be comprised in measured or polyphonic music [*in* *cantu figurato sive organico*] or in . . . the music . . . of sequences, but not in Gregorian plainsong', (CSM, xi, p.55).

Johannes de Grocheo's objection that 'if [measured music] is measured by [modes], [the writers] do not speak of the method' began to be met when the late medieval Italian concepts of 'commixture' and 'mixture' came to be spoken of as applicable to contrapuntal voices in simultaneous combination as well as to single melodic lines. A rapprochement of commixture with counterpoint is mentioned by Johannes Legrense: 'What then are "commixed voices" or what "counterpoint"? Certainly nothing more than just simple song [*cantus simplex*] in duplicate or triplicate, and so *in infinitum*' (*CS*, iv, 383). His student Nicolaus Burtius called the second part of his *Opusculum musices* (1487) 'Rules of commixed song [*cantus commixti*] or counterpoint'. In Tinctoris's *Liber . . . tonorum* (written in 1476 in Naples) both commixture and mixture are applied to counterpoint and to mode together (*CS*, iv, 29):

it is to be noted that commixture and mixture of tones are made not only in plainsong but also in composed [song], so that if the music [*cantus*] be composed with two, three, four, or more parts, one part will be of one tone, another of another – one authentic, another plagal – one mixed, another commixed.

(*a*) The modal voices. If a mixed mode can be authentic and plagal combined contrapuntally as well as melodically, it would seem to follow that a polyphonic composition would most naturally be assignable as a whole to a mixed mode according to final, without distinction as to authentic or plagal – to a *maneria* (Gaffurius, 1496, bk.1 chap.7 has 'maneries'). For some time it was the common practice of modern scholars to do just that: to refer to any polyphonic *g* protus piece as '*g* Dorian', or to any *f* tritus piece as '*f* Ionian' or '*f* Lydian', and so on; the term 'maneria' has been used more in modern times than it ever was in the Middle Ages or Renaissance. But in fact, the authentic–plagal distinction was as scrupulously maintained in the Renaissance as in the Middle Ages, beginning with Tinctoris in the continuation of the above passage:

Hence, when some mass or chanson [*cantilena*] or whatever other composition you like is made from different parts carried through in different tones, if anyone asks of what tone such a composition may be, he [who is] interrogated ought to reply, for the whole, according to the quality of the tenor, because that is the chief part and the foundation of the whole relationship [*fundamentum totius relationis*]. And if one be asked in particular, about some part, of what tone it may be in a composition of this sort, he will reply, this [tone] or that. For, if anyone were to say to me, 'Tinctoris, I ask you, of what tone is the song [*carmen*] "Le Serviteur"?' [by Dufay], I would reply 'in general, of an irregular first tone [*c* protus authentic], because the tenor, the principal part of the song, is of such a tone'. If however he were to ask in particular, of what tone the superius or contratenor might be, I would reply in particular, [that] the one and the other were of the second tone, also irregular [*c* protus plagal].

In Tinctoris's famous dictum the tenor is to be taken as the 'chief part' only in the contrapuntal sense. As Gaffurius put it, 'since the tenor [1] supports the cantus and [2] is supported by the *baritonans*, it is called the foundation of the relationship' (1496, bk.1 chap.15). There is no necessary implication either that the tenor is the chief melodic part, though it may be so, or that it has the 'chief part' because it was there first, though it may have been. Nicolaus Burtius (1487) described two ways of composing a chanson (*cantilena*; cf Tinctoris's dictionary *Terminorum musicae, diffinitorium* written *c*1475); both methods result in a 'discant–

tenor framework' with added contratenor (ed. Massera, pp.124ff):

you may compose first the *cantus*, or as they say, soprano, after careful consideration [*investigatione premissa*, presumably of the text]; then the tenor, corrected in all rigour; and finally the *contra*[*tenor*] *bassus*, producing no dissonances with the others. . . . Having shown the fabrication of a [free] polyphonic song, it [remains] only to be told how [one] is to be arranged on a plainchant . . . it is necessary that the plainchant have been made first. Next then, let the soprano be produced or composed with great ingenuity, having regard to the tenor (which is the plainchant), thence arriving at a *contra*[*tenor*] *bassus* [which is] to be completed, rooting out with mind, eyes, and reason whatever will have stood in the way of the sweetness of the harmony.

In both Burtius's methods the composer's primary imaginative effort is directed to the soprano; in the second not only 'careful investigation' but also 'great ingenuity' is required because of the pre-existing tenor. Given Burtius's previously quoted exhortation to the composer that he be familiar with the modes and their affects above all else, the inference that the soprano is the modal voice is inescapable. Meier's modal analysis of a number of chansons by Dufay and others in a Ferrarese manuscript of about 1450 has shown the primacy of the upper voice, and Meier proposed that the compositions demonstrate conscious use of modal affect (1953).

In the *Opus aureum* (Cologne, 1501), freedom to choose a modal voice freely is specifically stipulated: 'Therefore, desiring to compose something, first it is necessary that one put a tenor – or indeed another part [*chorum*] if desired – yet such that it be well formed according to the requirements of the tone under which it is ruled' (Schanppecher, 1501, ed. Niemöller). A decade later one begins to read that the voices should be taken in pairs, in what was rapidly becoming the standard distribution: 'The tenor [*media vox*] produces the soprano part [*supremam vocem*] and the bass [*gravis*] the alto [*acutam*]; and in the way in which the soprano seems subject to the tenor, so let the alto be subject to the bass' (Philomathes, 1512).

From this time on, though most writers continued to mention the tenor as the principal modal voice (Vicentino, 1555, f.48, proposed the bass), the soprano and tenor pair in fact functioned together in this role. Principal cadences in the four-part distribution were mostly formed by the tenor and soprano, with the bass and alto providing harmonic support and filling, respectively. A complete summary of the functions of the four 'primary voices' is in Burmeister (1606, p.11):

Discant . . . because it is the highest in the system [*temperamentum*] of [paired authentic and plagal] modes, it is defined by the diapason or octave above the tenor.
Alto . . . its limit is set in the octave which is median in the system of modes, between the discant and the tenor.
Tenor . . . the nearest to the foundation of the harmony [i.e. the bass], suitable for maintaining the status of the mode by which the harmony or melody is defined.
Bass . . . the lowest among the primary voices, carrying out the duties of fulcrum or foundation in the harmony.

Burmeister's useful term for the functionally paired voices – the modal tenor–soprano, the supportive bass–alto – was 'conterminous' (because their respective highest and lowest points just meet), while adjacent pairs of voices were 'disterminous' (because their registers overlap rather than conjoin).

(*b*) The modal ensemble. Though the tenor or soprano, or both, might be designated as the chief modal parts, the fully imitative musical style of 16th-century polyphony went far to obfuscate any distinctive type of line, pace or registral position that could mark one voice as modal and its neighbour as merely supporting. Gallus Dressler (1563) explained the matter with his wonted explicitness (ed. Engelke, p.229):

in free counterpoint account is taken not only of the tenor but of all the other voices ... the ambitus of the tones, which is shown by the customary cadences and repercussions, is observed, by which means account is taken of all the voices ... in songs which consist of points of imitation [*quae ex fuga constant*] the voice beginning the point is primary and pre-eminent.

As musicians came consciously to think of the modes of the eightfold system as essential to the full enrichment of their art they began to favour particular modal complexes of voices selected from the expanded tonal system. Such a complex could be designated through the particular choice of *cantus durus* versus *cantus mollis* combined with a higher as against a lower general disposition of the clefs for the voices.

One of the earliest polyphonic collections showing a consistent combining of clefs and systems for modal purposes is Rore's first book of madrigals for five voices (1542). Nos.1–17 constitute a modally ordered set. They are disposed in a conventional pattern of systems and clefs which was the preferred norm until into the 17th century: *g* protus and *f* tritus modes were set in *cantus mollis*, *e* deuterus and *g* tetrardus modes in *cantus durus*: the authentic modes (1, 3, 5, 7) were set in high clefs (*chiavette*) and the plagals (2, 4, 6, 8) in 'normal' clefs. Ex.16 shows the convention as reported in 1595 (see Meier, 1959); Rore's dispositions in 1542 differ from these only in that he distinguished plagal from authentic deuterus by using *c′*2 *c′*4 *c′*4 *f*3 *f*5 clefs for mode 4. The systems and clefs of Palestrina's second book of spiritual madrigals (1594) are disposed exactly as in ex.16 (with the normal *cantus mollis* protus modes). To avoid making a distinction between modes 3 and 4 is a common usage. Glarean observed that 'it often

happens ... among *symphonetae* [polyphonic composers] that [Hypophrygian] songs rise to small *d* [i.e. *d′*] and do not descend below *D* [i.e. *d*], which range the Phrygian, its principal mode, also has' (MSD, vi, 254). Since contrast of high clefs and low clefs is merely the polyphonic equivalent of the traditional contrast of authentic and plagal, the common clef disposition for both modes 3 and 4 is perfectly consistent.

2. POLYPHONIC MODAL FUNCTIONS. Modal prescriptions and the rules for the formation and succession of simultaneities came together only very gradually, and in some respects never completely. There was no real need to try to link the fields of modal theory and counterpoint so long as it was felt that mode belonged only to the chant, or even that mode could be understood in terms of a single newly composed voice; given one modally correct voice, the rules of counterpoint would handle the rest of the polyphonic texture automatically. Of nearly 70 concocted illustrations in Tinctoris's *Liber ... tonorum*, only five are in two voices, even though Tinctoris proclaimed the work as largely in the interests of polyphony (*cantus compositus*); and his five two-voice examples are all concerned with the tritone. But the change from composing predominantly on a tenor to composing free imitative counterpoint gradually made some inroads into modal theory.

(*i*) *Cadences and openings*. The first of the modal functions to be accommodated to counterpoint was the cadence, final and medial alike. In 1490 Adam von Fulda wrote, as the first of his ten counterpoint rules (*GS*, iii, 352, with emendations from Riemann, *Geschichte der Musiktheorie*, 2/1920, p.321):

In every song at least one voice is appointed to be adapted to a correct tone. Moreover, to adapt to a tone (namely, of the eight tones) is this: it is to place cadences beautifully and appositely, for as the rise and fall of speech (*accentus prosae*) is set off by the period, so the tone by a perfection.

In his *Liber ... contrapuncti* written 13 years earlier Tinctoris (MSD, v, 135) had phrased it negatively (and he supplied two pieces in illustration): 'The fifth rule [of counterpoint] is that above absolutely no note, be it medium, superior, or inferior, should a perfection be taken by which a removal from its mode [*distonatio*] can happen'. A 'perfection', according to Tinctoris's dictionary, 'designates ... the conclusion of a whole piece or of any of its sections' (p.48); under 'clausula', the cadence is defined as 'a small part of some section of a piece, at the end of which ... is found a perfection'.

To make a cadence function modally in counterpoint, however, raises hardly any question for traditional modal theory. Cadences were of two voices (other voices when present being treated as accompanying) and were normally led to the perfection of an octave or unison, thus merely doubling the letter name and hexachord syllable alike of the modal degree. Even though medially 'an imperfect one is inserted from time to time' (Tinctoris, MSD, v, 136), the modal voice is not thereby affected. As for the course of the music between perfections, which most sets of counterpoint rules allowed to be filled with imperfect consonances if desired, only one voice is relevant to the mode.

Changes in compositional technique during the 16th century did not affect the fundamental structure of the cadence as a two-voice progression with accompaniment, and the general principle established in the later

Ex.16

†mode 1    mode 1

†mode 2    mode 2

modes 3, 4

mode 5

mode 6

mode 7

†rarely used

mode 8

15th century by Tinctoris and his contemporaries, that the making of a cadence established a modally significant degree, continued to be valid. Beginnings, however, were more of a problem. As long as the counterpoint rule 'begin with a perfect consonance' reflected a practice of beginning all the parts together – as in Tinctoris's examples for his fifth rule (MSD, v, 135f) – no question about the modal voice need in principle arise. But the great variety of possible starting pitches stipulated in chant theory was drastically reduced, according to Tinctoris, even for the one modal voice (*CS*, iv, 27): 'any tone can begin in any place in its ambitus. Nonetheless, there are some places more suitable than others . . . and out of 50 composed songs there may be hardly a one which does not begin in the place where it finishes'. Such a neat formal link between the opening and closing notes of a piece – making the final the initial – was often wistfully mentioned by chant theorists, but no fixed rule could be made in the face of the enormous variety of chant initials in every mode. The anonymous 11th-century Italian *Dialogus* put it, 'the beginnings, too, are found most often and most suitably on the sound which concludes the melody' (Strunk, 1950, p.113).

In the 1470s and 1480s the imitative style was well on the way to achieving the pre-eminent status it was to enjoy in the 16th century, and to make a simple analogy of an opening perfection with the modally significant cadential perfection could hardly have sufficed, nor does it seem to have been suggested. It was the point of imitation, the *fuga*, that developed a modal significance. Like other contrapuntal and compositional devices imitation was not linked to modality when its descriptions first began to appear in the literature. One of its essential features, however, ensured that in time it would be so linked.

Tinctoris defined 'fuga' in his dictionary (written *c*1475, printed 1495) as: 'the identity in a song of the notes and rests of the parts as to [1] value, [2] name, [3] shape, and sometimes as to [4] location'. Under 'solfisatio' Tinctoris confirmed that 'name' (*nomen*) referred to the hexachord syllables.

Bartolomeo Ramos de Pareia (1482) also described imitation. The same passage appears in substance and partly verbatim in Burtius (1487), though this was a work directed against Ramos; as had Ramos, Burtius appended the passage as a supplement to the counterpoint rule recommending contrary motion. Ramos's passage (p.68), with Burtius's important changes (ii, ed. Massera, p.122), reads as follows:

The best fashion of making organum [*modus organizandi*], however, is when the organum [Burtius added 'or "soprano", to use the common term'] imitates the tenor in ascent or descent. It begins making the same melody at the same degree [*eundem cantum* – Burtius had *eandam melodiam – in eadem voce*], not at the same time, but after one or more notes. Or [it makes] a similar melody at the 4th or 5th or even octave, or in their replications below or above [Burtius omitted this sentence]. This fashion practising [musicians] call *fuga*.

Ex.17 shows Ramos's illustration, with one subject imitated at the 4th below and the 5th above, and another at the octave above.

Burtius's omission of Ramos's list of intervals of imitation, seen in the light of Tinctoris's definition, goes to the heart of the matter. Ramos had discarded the traditional system of hexachords, replacing it with an octave solmization system of his own, and he was thereby forced to name the 4th and 5th as intervals of imitation. Burtius, who defended the traditional hexachord system, was

Ex.17

under no such constraint. As Tinctoris made clear, it was enough that the points of imitation use the same hexachord syllables, whose location in hard, natural or soft hexachord automatically designates Ramos's intervals of imitation. Ramos's imitations at the lower 4th and upper 5th (ex.17a) would be solmized *re fa mi re fa mi sol* in all locations. This is of course the first species of the 4th, and since it occurs with *re* at *a'* and *a* as well as at *d'*, it is a modal species of the protus, in terms of the late medieval Italian theory. The leading voice (*dux*) works in the common species of 4th *re–sol* (*d'–g'*) while the answering voice (*comes*) exploits the proper species *re–sol* (*a–d'* or *a'–d''*).

The connection of the modes with the intervals of imitation was not explicitly to be made for several decades, though there are passages implying such a connection. In his *Compendium musices* (1537) Lampadius gave three 'rules' for imitative beginnings and for cadences. The first warned not to let the parts of a composition 'wander outside the regular tone, otherwise the melody will be corrupted'; the second warned not to exceed the double octave; the third stated that 'Josquin, who in this art is deemed most experienced [and] to be emulated, was the most distinguished of all in forming cadences and points of imitation'. There follow cadences combined with points of imitation (p.89), made, however, not with modal species but with the intonation plus the principal difference of each of the eight psalm tones, or as Lampadius and numerous other German writers called them, 'the tropes of the tones, with which psalms conclude'. The confounding of tone as church mode with tone as psalm tone is as old as the modal system in the West. In Finck's *Practica musica* (1556) they are so confounded, and claimed for polyphonic music as well: 'A trope is a brief phrase beginning in the repercussion of each tone which is added at the end of the individual verses of psalms and responsories . . . [these are] the differences, an understanding of which is as necessary as the knowledge of their tones, especially in polyphonic music' (p.iii). It was of course necessary for a church composer to know how to set psalms and canticles polyphonically, and their recitation tones were often used as subjects; but a psalm tone as subject is modal only in the sense that any plainchant subject is modal, and in certain respects it is less so, for a psalm-tone difference taken out of context can be strikingly at variance with the structure – in terms of species, or as final with ambitus – of its corresponding mode.

Where Lampadius left connection of the modes with imitation and cadences implicit, Finck stated it very pointedly, as quoted earlier, and stated it again in almost the same words: 'a song is referred to the tone which has the most cadences and points of imitation relating to it [*plures clausulae ac fugae sibi familiares*]' (Rr ii). This statement is a curiously apt transformation into indigenous polyphonic terms of one of the oldest doctrines of chant theory: 'A melody . . . belongs most to the mode in which a majority of its distinctions lie' (anonymous *Dialogus*, *c*1000; Strunk, 1950, p.113).

(*ii*) *The integration of modality and polyphony.* That composers were consciously considering the modes in their work is established at the latest by the 1540s, when the ordering of pieces within collections according to the order of the modes can sometimes be confirmed by the objective evidence of orderly clef and system combinations. Modern scholars have tried to demonstrate that older composers were also consciously applying the modes in their compositions, irrespective of any modal assignment that might arise from a plainchant tenor or model. Perkins (1973) has investigated the possibility for two generations earlier; Treitler (1965), Meier (1953) and Reichert (1951) raised the question for two and more generations earlier still. But all these studies are necessarily based on the scholar's own analysis of the music, based on more or less compelling inferences drawn from theorists like Tinctoris. Until the mid-16th century, direct assistance from contemporaneous writers is available only in the form of general directives in the areas just considered: a modal voice might or must be chosen, and cadences (and latterly points of imitation) had to reflect and not distort the mode.

In chapter 7 of his *Isagoge* (1516) Glarean expressed a discomfort with traditional modal theory which he exorcized by radical means in his *Dodecachordon*, by incorporating traditional modal theory into a more comprehensive new system that he believed to be founded on both classical authority and reason. The inability of modal theory satisfactorily to account for polyphonic practices was dealt with in another way by 16th-century German theorists who stressed *musica poetica* – the art of composition – as a third and culminating branch added to the traditional branches of musical doctrine, *theorica* and *practica*. *Musica poetica* offered a natural disciplinary forum for combining traditional modal theories and the teaching of counterpoint.

The clear and thoughtful manuscript treatise of Gallus Dressler (1563) brings the doctrines of modality and counterpoint into as close a symbiosis as they were ever to achieve. His manuscript is annotated with references to a few compositions; his lectures must have been replete with them. The work is one of a few sources fully discussing the art of polyphonic composition in terms of the traditional eightfold system; Dressler himself adopted Glarean's 12 modes in his own *Musicae practicae elementa* (1571), and was followed in this by numerous German theorists of the next half-century, most of whom cited or supplied profuse illustrations of the modes in polyphonic music.

Chapters 1–8 of Dressler's *Praecepta musicae poeticae* make up a well-ordered conventional treatise on counterpoint, divided into *simplex* (note-against-note), *floridus* or *fractus* (smaller values over a cantus firmus) and *coloratus* (free counterpoint); chapters 7 and 8 are on the traditional construction of four-voice sonorities and cadences by means of adding to the soprano–tenor framework. Chapters 9–14 describe the proper use of counterpoint for developing modal structures and thereby compositions – that is, for *musica poetica*.

Chapter 15 contains a summary of the method, and recommendations to study four generations of masters, from Josquin to Lassus, each in terms of special characteristics of compositional style.

Like his immediate predecessors, Dressler stressed the importance of controlling contrapuntal beginnings and cadences through the modes; he also specified how it ought to be done (ed. Engelke, p.239):

What the period and comma are in speech the cadences are in *poetica musica* . . . it is not enough therefore to know only the composition of cadences, but students are to be taught in what rank order the cadences are joined together so that they may render a correct *harmonia* to the ear. . . . First, they ought to correspond to the words . . . whatever *virgula*, comma, or period there may be, to them are cadences designated. Second, in what rank order the music may admit cadences is known from the doctrine of the tones . . . we may make three kinds of cadence . . .

[1] principal . . . in which the chief foundation of the tone consists . . . the cadences . . . are built on the [notes bounding the] species of 4th and 5th, or on the [notes of the] repercussions.

[2] secondary [*minus principales*] . . . which do not flow from the special sources [of the tone] but which can be inserted without offence in the middle part of the song.

[3] foreign [*peregrinae*] . . . which have no proper place but rather invade from another tone.

In showing the cadences for each mode Dressler listed its (unfilled) species of 4th and 5th, and its repercussion, in hexachord syllables. The interval of the repercussion was simply that of the final of the mode and the tenor of the psalm tone, but in his work on *musica poetica* there was no reason for Dressler to allude to psalm tones, and the repercussion was treated as a purely modal function. The term 'repercussion' could refer to the single note or to the interval formed with the final, with or without other notes between.

The principal cadential degrees are listed, clearly in rank order of their importance, and then the secondary cadential degrees (if any); remaining degrees are classed

Ex.18

as foreign. Dressler's species, repercussions and principal and secondary cadences are shown in ex.18 (after *Praecepta*, ed. Engelke, pp.239ff).

After describing three types of imitation (*fuga integra, semifuga, fuga mutillata*), Dressler wrote that imitations that initiate phrases, like cadences that conclude phrases, arise from the species and the repercussions; he divided them into four types (p.243):

(1) The foundations of imitations are taken from the species of 4th or 5th . . .
(2) The foundations of imitations are taken from the repercussions of the tones which [and this will apply to species too] are made not only empty [*nudae*] but also with many other intervals intervening.
(3) Imitations may arise out of cadences in the musical tones [i.e. modes], so that we may get from one cadence to another.
(4) 'Mixed' imitations are made partly from the repercussions and partly from the species of 4th and 5th; thus the *exordium* in Crequillon's *Deus virtutum* is made partly from the species of 4th *fa ut* and partly from the repercussion *fa la*, for it is of the sixth tone.

The touchstone of *musica poetica* is its parallel with the language arts. The use in a composition of a number of musical units one after another, each demarcated by imitation at the opening (or simultaneous entry) and cadence at the close, is conceived in terms of *exordium, medium* and *finis*. About the modality of the regular final ending Dressler said little, but he warned the student (p.248) that 'an irregular [final] is not to be introduced without an instance from an acknowledged composer [*sine probati authoris exemplo*] . . . and is mostly to be given to the first part of a song, where a second part is expected; rarely, however, [is it] to be regularly constructed as a final ending'.

The middle, between *exordium* and *finis*, can be composed with or without imitation. Four general rules are suggested, of which the first is a summary list of Dressler's modal affects: 'First of all, a tone suitable to the matter [of the text] is to be chosen: for some tones are joyful, like 1, 5, and 8; some are sad, like 2, 4, and 6; and some are captious and harsh [*morosi et austeri*], like 3 and 7'.

The *exordium* is crucial, compositionally, modally and aesthetically (p.244):

*Exordia* are taken moreover from the chief sources of the tones, namely [1] from the species of 4th and 5th, or [2] from the repercussions and [3] the principal cadences . . . as we see the poet put forth his proposition in the *exordium* and the first lines . . . so we in music – whose alliance with poetry is very close – should express the tone in the *exordium* itself.

*Exordia* are of two types: ' "Full" [*plenum*] is when all the voices begin at the same time [*uno tempore ictu*]: "bare" [*nudum*] . . . when they come in one after another. *Exordia* of this type are mostly constructed of imitations'.

The beginning of Lassus's *In me transierunt* (*Sacrae cantiones*, 1562, no.14) is an imitative *exordium* made with the repercussion. Though all the deuterus pieces in this collection are set in the same modal complex – low clefs in *cantus durus* – this one at least is unmistakably announced as authentic by its opening subject, the repercussion for mode 3; the solmization is *mi, mi/fa, mi/ la, sol*. The piece is attributed to mode 3 by a number of writers, including Dressler himself in a marginal note (ed. Engelke, p.239). It was analysed in detail by Burmeister (1606), and the analysis is discussed by Palisca (1972).

3. POLYPHONIC MODAL THEORY AND THE EIGHTFOLD SYSTEM. Most of the inconsistencies and anomalies of polyphonic modal theory arose from incompatibilities between *a priori* systems of modes and compositional practice. In contrast to the casual attitude of composers towards particular aspects of modality, polyphonic modal theorizing – Renaissance and modern alike – tends towards the universal. It is assumed on historical, traditional, humanistic or analogical grounds that there has to be an inherent system of modalities in polyphonic music; that this system can be deduced or induced with the help of a proper understanding of the medieval tradition, or with the help of classical authority, or through systematic and rational analysis; and that the system can then be demonstrated in the repertory.

*(i) Aaron and the psalm-tone differences.* Pietro Aaron was the first theorist to undertake a thorough-going study of polyphonic repertory in modal terms. His theoretical premises were those of chant theory as formulated in the late medieval Italian tradition; they were set forth in his *De institutione harmonica* (1516), i.26–35, and appear in summary form in his *Compendiolo di molti dubbi* (*c*1550), i.29–50. Aaron referred many times both to Gaffurius and to Marchetto; though he usually took issue with Marchetto, for example in *Lucidario* (1545), i.4,7, it was only in matters of detail, while the theoretical concepts of Marchetto's doctrine were taken for granted (the relationship being much like that of Kirnberger and Rameau).

Aaron (1525) cited a substantial number of polyphonic pieces, almost all taken from Petrucci prints, in exemplification of his modal assignments, which are made according to the eightfold system. Criteria for determining the mode of a composition are its final and its species of 4th and 5th; medial cadence points must be in support of the other two.

Voices are governed modally by their courses of motion through the species of 4th and 5th; Aaron's term is 'procedure' (*procedere, processo*), a sometime synonym for 'ambitus' (cf Jacques de Liège, *Speculum musice*, CS, ii, 246, 315). Long before Aaron's time the word 'ambitus' had come to refer to the 'Guidonian' ambitus, which was not controlled by modal species; at the same time the term had lost any implication of motion implicit in its etymology and had acquired a purely static sense of compass. On both counts Aaron's choice of 'procedure' was apt. To refer simply to compass he used 'ascent' and 'descent'.

Aaron's doctrine of the finals is at once the most ingenious and the most specious aspect of his work. There are three kinds of finals: regular finals *d, e, f* and *g*; irregular finals, which can refer both to *a, b♮* and *c'* (which he also called confinals) and to any other concluding degree found in a composition; and the concluding notes of psalm-tone differences. The differences are needed not because Aaron wished to include psalm-tone functions by right; conspicuously absent from his list of functions is the psalm-tone tenor (or its equivalent the modal repercussion). He invoked the differences to account for the combined procedure and final of most works ending with *a* or *c'/c*; indeed Aaron usually preferred to cite psalm-tone differences as modal finals even where confinals were available for the purpose.

Psalm-tone differences were originally of the essence of movement and continuity, in their role as adjustable melodic links between psalm verse and antiphon. It is ironic that they should have taken on the function of pseudo-finals; it is not, however, unprecedented. The 12th-century Cistercian radical reformers of the chant had considerably reduced the number of psalm-tone differences, and for the introit verse tones they not only confirmed them at one per mode but also recomposed those of modes 3, 5 and 7 to bring them down to a conclusion on the modal final (see Huglo, 1971, pp.365f, and Sweeney, 1975).

Aaron's principles for assigning a mode to a given piece turn on a hierarchical authority of modal functions. Regular finals *d, e, f* and *g* prevail in determining a mode except in the case of *g* protus modes in *cantus mollis*, where the species govern (*g* being otherwise the regular tetrardus final). The modes of both *f*-final and *d*-final pieces in *cantus mollis*, however, are determined by the final, since there is no question of a conflict of two modes sharing one regular final; Aaron did mention *f* and *g* as possible pseudo-finals for those modes where they occur as differences in the corresponding psalm tones, but he had no occasion actually to use them in that way. The pseudo-final differences he needed were those on *a* and *c'*.

For pieces ending elsewhere than on one of the regular finals the species and procedure prevail. For example (*Trattato*, after Strunk, 1950):

Certain other [presumably mode 1 or 2] tenors end on *a la mi re*; here you will need to consider and examine whether their procedure is suited and rational to such an ending, for if a tenor end irregularly in the first or second tone, not proceeding with its proper form, it may easily not belong to it, even though this step [*a*] is one of its irregular finals and an ending of its *Saeculorum* or difference. As you will understand from what follows, this is because the third and fourth tones also use this step [*a*] as a difference. For this reason, then, you will assign such a tenor to the first or second tone only when you find the proper form, as in *La plus de plus* by Josquin, which is of the first tone in view of the course of its diapente [5th] and its upward range. [p.213]

You will also find certain other compositions ending on *a la mi re*; when these observe the appropriate procedure they will be assigned to the third tone, for example, *Miserere mei Deus* by Josquin. [p.215]

The compositional difference between *a* modes that Aaron's distinction reflects is a real one, and it is not that of the *a* protus and *a* deuterus of chant theory, the former in *cantus durus*, the latter transformed by the *cantus mollis*. It has to do rather with a property of the tonal system itself making the modal quality of *a* ambiguous. In §II, 3(ii*b*) above, Guido's passage on the *modi vocum* was quoted; it included a description of the affinity of *A* and *d* in the melodic environment of what would come to be called a rising first species of 5th, *re mi fa sol la*, plus the tone beneath. In his next chapter Guido dealt with 'other affinities of the degrees', and began by showing that 'A and E agree in descent, which with both is made by two tones and a semitone', that is, by a descending second species of 4th *la sol fa mi* (*a g f e = e d c B*).

In both pieces that Aaron cited the first species of 5th *a–e'* in the hard hexachord dominates the music. In *La plus de plus* the *a–e'* in both superius and tenor is joined with the first species of 5th, *d–a*, in the tenor, so that the piece works with the protus species of 5th in two positions. Hence the piece is indeed 'proceeding with the proper form of the first tone', and it ends 'on one of its irregular finals'.

In the *Miserere*, on the other hand, the 5th *a–e'* is joined with the second species of 4th *a g f e* (*la sol fa mi*) in the bass, so that the structural voices exploit the octave *e–e'* divided at *a*. The ascent and descent between *e* and *e'* call for assignment to mode 3; the conclusion on *a* is accounted for by invoking the third psalm-tone difference ending at *a*.

Aaron's reliance on the difference as a pseudo-final led him into a novel explanation for pieces having irregular finals at *c'* and *c*. He granted (Strunk, 1950, p.216) that pieces ending with *c'* may be said 'to be of the fifth tone, both with and without the flat signature, for example, *Si sumpsero* by Obrecht; this is solely in view of the [psalm-tone] difference which the plainsong sometimes exhibits here'. For Aaron the existence of a psalm-tone difference was decisive: the credentials of a note existing in a mode as a confinal but not at the same time as a difference were insufficient to permit it to serve as an irregular final if any explanation for such a final invoking a difference could be found. Thus despite the chant tradition for transposing mode 6 to the position with *c'* as final, for Aaron 'The sixth tone is lacking on this step [*c'*], even though it is the confinal of the fifth and sixth tones regularly ended, for the step [*c'*] can bear no form or difference appropriate to it'. The curious consequence of this doctrine is that no *cantus durus* *c*-mode piece is assigned to the tritus modes. Obrecht's *Si sumpsero* is a *cantus mollis f*-mode piece which happens to end at *c'*; Aaron's classification of it as mode 5 ending at the psalm-tone difference is appropriate. But a piece like Josquin's *Comment peult avoir joye*, a setting of a popular or courtly tune, published by Glarean as *O Jesu fili David*, cannot by Aaron's criteria be considered as in mode 6, despite its overwhelmingly preponderant composition with the species *ut–sol* (*c'–g'*) and *ut–fa* (*g–c'*) – not to mention the constant repercussion of *fa* and *la*, *c'* and *e'*. He had to call it mode 7, since it is in the octave *g–g'*, with a pseudo-final at one of the mode 7 psalm-tone differences, *c'*.

Similarly, pieces ending at low *c* are not considered to be mode 5 irregular, as Tinctoris would have considered them (see ex.15*a*). On the contrary (Strunk, 1950, p.217):

Those ending on *c fa ut*, for the reason given above [. . . we see them clearly continue in what the proper and regular tones naturally need and require . . .] and also because they do not have the proper diatessaron [4th], I assign to the eighth tone and not the seventh.

Aaron appears to be saying that pieces ending on *c* have at least a perfectly normal tetrardus species of 5th (*ut–re–mi–fa–sol = c–d–e–f–g*), as used in both tetrardus modes, but that the species of 4th set above it (*ut–re–mi–fa = g–a–b♮–c'*) is not, however, that of mode 7, the authentic tetrardus. That assignment thereby being eliminated, only mode 8 remains. As far as the 'ascent and descent' of such tenors are concerned, from *c* up to *d'* or even *e'* or *f'*, it is perfectly appropriate for mode 8, but not at all for mode 7.

For each mode Aaron listed internal cadence points both appropriate (chaps.9–12) and inappropriate (chaps.13–20), followed by listings of initials (see Strunk, 1950, p.208, n.4). But since four of the modes have five or more allowable cadential degrees, only one as few as three, and no criteria for their applications, Aaron's general admonition about cadences and species seems a more useful guide (Aaron, 1525, chap.13):

It is necessary that the composer take care to proceed in his music with [the correct] species or form, through which the movements will seem pleasing and harmonious. But if you proceed in some other way in the tone, the tonally discordant path will always appear [*nascera sempre il distonata via*], and so also if you use contradictory cadences.

(*ii*) *Composite modes*. The most elaborate exposition of the eightfold system as a theory for polyphonic music was that of Aiguino (1581), who referred to Aaron as his 'maestro irrefragibile'. This treatise, the last in the long series beginning with Marchetto's *Lucidarium*, considers the species of 4th and 5th in as many combinations as possible within the diatonic systems. The traditional plainchant mode 2 at the affinal position is regarded as a composition of species from two modes; ex.19a shows Aiguino's composite forms for modes 1 and 2 (*Il tesoro*, ff.77v–8). Aiguino's term is 'mixed modes' (obviously not in Marchetto's and Tinctoris's sense, though he also used the term 'commixture'). Though the 4ths are of the second species, and thus pertain to modes 3 and 4, 4ths are the 'minor species' in a mode, according to Aiguino. Here the 'major species' is the protus first species of 5th, which determines the modes as 1 and 2.

Ex.19

Aiguino argued that this construction made it unnecessary to add to the eightfold system the separate authentic and plagal modes on *a* proposed by Glarean and Zarlino. Neither this construction of 'mixed modes' nor this usage of the term originated with Aiguino, however. Tinctoris had already given an instance (ex.19b from *CS*, iv, 26, corrected after Seay translation) of the 'second tone commixed with the fourth, so as to make *fa* against *mi* into a perfect consonance' – that is, to avoid a diminished 5th; as a result, 'the B♭ put against *f* creates the second species of the 4th in the fourth tone [in the lower voice]'. Vicentino called the combination of *d–e–f–g–a* with *a–b♭–c'–d'* (ex.19c, from *L'antica musica*, f.51r) a 'mode mixed from the first [species of] 5th from mode 1 and the second [species of] 4th from mode 3'. In Bermudo's *Declaración* (iv, 40) the same combination of 5th and 4th – the authentic *d* mode in *cantus mollis* – is called a 'mingling [*mezclan*] of the first tone with the fourth'.

The concept of modal 'mixture' is also used by Vicentino and Bermudo to account for the traditional *f* tritus in *cantus mollis*. Vicentino called it a mode-7 5th (*ut re mi fa sol*) with a mode-5 4th (*ut re mi fa*), as in ex.19c (ii). Bermudo said that 'always playing the sixth

[mode] with flat sign is similar to the eighth [mode] in its [species of] 5th' (iv, 23), and later, 'the mode which is played as the sixth is composed of the eighth and the sixth' (iv, 40).

(*iii*) *Modal cadences and polyphonic psalmody*. Pietro Pontio (1588, bk.3) gave a full account of the application of cadential degrees in modal polyphony, an account based not only on the theory of the modal species but even more on his observations of compositional practice. Principal and obvious cadential degrees are mentioned without much elaboration, but for all other cadential degrees Pontio provided not only comment but also precise references to cadences in compositions by Rore, Giaches de Wert, Morales and himself, and many others.

Besides this Pontio made a clear distinction between modal cadences 'as in motets, masses, madrigals, and the like' and 'in psalms, because the psalms have different cadences, proper and separate from those of motets, and different composition, and they have their own endings' (p.101). This distinction was by no means always carefully made, and Pontio drove the point home by supplying an illustrative duo not only for each mode (except mode 4) but also for each of the eight psalm tones.

Pontio was anxious to isolate polyphonic psalmody from polyphonic modality; but in analysing distributions of modal cadences he was quite ready to recognize influences from the corresponding psalm tones, to which more often than not his comments attributed subtle but important elements for distinguishing authentics from plagals, especially in the deuterus and tetrardus modes where transposition is less easily available for the task.

Table 7 is a conspectus of Pontio's discussion of modal cadences (iii, pp.94ff), showing cadential degrees in the eight modes. As in Dressler, so also in Pontio the eightfold system found an intelligent and gracious pragmatic spokesman, a composer, in an age when speculative rational theorizing about the modes was bringing them to utter confusion.

TABLE 7

| MODE | CADENCES | | | |
| | Primary | Secondary | Transitory | Inimical |
|---|---|---|---|---|
| 1, 2 | *d    a* | *f* | *g    c* | *e    b♮* |
| 3, 4 | *e    a* | *c'* | *g    b♮* | *f* |
| 5 | *f    c'* | *a* | *d'    g* | *e    b♮* |
| 6 | *f    c'* | *a    b♭* | *d'    g* | *e    b♮* |
| 7 | *g    d'* | – | *c' f a e* | – |
| 8 | *g    c'd'* | – | *f    a* | – |

4. SYSTEMS OF 12 MODES.

(*i*) *The 12 modes before Glarean*.

(*a*) Four extra melodic types. At the end of the Carolingian 'De octo tonis' (in chapter 8 of Aurelian's *Musica disciplina*) the author related that 'there were some singers who claimed that there were certain antiphons which could in no way be adapted to their rule; hence your pious and august ancestor Charles ordered four [tones] to be added'.

Though *Noeane* syllables are named, no antiphons for the extra modes are mentioned. In a number of later sources, however, there are citations of chants (see Huglo, 1971, pp.35ff, 79ff and 156f for sources and references). In some of the sources the extra modes are called *mesi*, in others *parapteres* (or *paracteres*) and *circumaequales*. Though the sources are by no means in full concord in their choice of chant citations, three relevant facts do come out: the extra modes were never more than a curiosity; but the tradition of their existence was fairly widely known; and the antiphons cited were indeed anomalous.

In Berno of Reichenau's *Musica* the tradition is reported for the last time, applied now to melodies anomalous only in that they are confined to the common 5th, making it difficult to fix them definitely as authentic or plagal: 'Some are accustomed to call these medial tones [*tonos medios*], and because they can be put between the four individual authentics and plagals, they add these four to those eight, and claim to have demonstrated twelve tones' (*GS*, ii, 73).

(*b*) Modal divisions of the octave. The integration of eight modes with seven octave species was achieved in the 9th century in the New Exposition of the *Alia musica* (see §II, 2(ii) above), through the device of modes 1 and 8 sharing the octave species *d–d'* mediated in two positions (see ex.3*a*). The 11th-century *Questiones in musica* points out how the operation of transposition brings about a similar pairing of modes in two other modal octaves: modes 3 and transposed 2, sharing the octave *e–e'*, modes 7 and transposed 6, sharing the octave *g–g'* (ed. Steglich, 1911, p.55). A logical completion of this pattern would try to divide every modal octave by two medians. Such a division was described by Wilhelm of Hirsau, in the latter half of the 11th century (*Musica*, chap.37).

(*ii*) *Glarean's 12 modes*. Glarean's *Dodecachordon* is the product of an extraordinary synthesis of medieval tradition, both practical and theoretical, with Renaissance classicizing humanism, original system building and musical analysis. The publication of writings on ancient Greek music, including sources both of musical theory (such as Valla's 1497 edition of Cleonides' Aristoxenian *Eisagōgē*) and of musical anecdotes (the Aldine edition of Athenaeus's *Deipnosophistae*, 1524) ensured Glarean a supply of classical authority when he needed it. Glarean was also a lifelong admirer of Boethius, whose doctrines he always preferred as the source for his own. Finally, he was devoted to the church and its traditional music; his analyses of plainsong in *Dodecachordon* (Book 2, §§36–7) show an enthusiasm for the beauty of the chant matched only by the perspicacity with which its musical properties are expounded.

The synthesis of classical authority and medieval tradition shows itself in all phases of Glarean's study of the modes save one: for analysis of the structure of actual music, plainsong or polyphony, he could have no classical models. But he hoped to bring order and reason to existing modal theory, to reconcile it with classical sources wherever possible, and through it to provide a uniform doctrine to guide his readers to an understanding of the wonders of both kinds of music.

(*a*) The 12 modal octave species and their Greek names. Apart from classical writings there were four main sources for Glarean's theory: Gaffurius, Cochlaeus, Boethius and 11th-century chant theory. Gaffurius's work (1518), upon which Glarean drew heavily, was itself under the influence of rediscovered classical writings on music. It is brought into the *Dodecachordon* at a crucial juncture, in the last chapter

of Book 1, as a preparation for Book 2 which has no separate introduction. In the introduction to Book 3 Gaffurius is lauded again, along with Cochlaeus, Glarean's teacher at Cologne, 1507–10. Cochlaeus's teaching on mode, as reflected in Tract iii of his *Tetrachordum musices* (1511), was a combination of the late medieval Italian theories of species conjunction and five types of modal ambitus (perfect to commixed) with a German version of the repercussion doctrine and emphasis on the psalm tones. And finally, in the dedicatory preface, Glarean concluded (after references to Plato, Aristoxenus and Boethius) by alluding to a number of writers he had studied at a Benedictine monastery near Freiburg not long after he went there from Basle in 1529. The manuscripts he saw contained two further kinds of sources: a better text for Boethius than he had seen before, and a group of six 11th-century chant theorists. Three of these were 'Guidonian': Guido himself, 'Otto' (certainly the author of the *Dialogus*) and Johannes (like other writers of his time Glarean identified him with Pope John XXII). The other three are of the Reichenau school: Berno, Wilhelm (of Hirsau), and his disciple Theogerus (of Metz).

That the 11th-century writers had some influence on Glarean's thinking seems more than probable. Glarean was anxious that his 12-mode system be taken as a reconstruction, not a new creation, and he was quite ready to invoke medieval authority when it suited him, as well as classical. In justifying his six principal modes as six he cited Plato's *Republic* (MSD, vi, 38; cf Strunk, 1950, pp.4f) and Aristoxenus (p.102, presumably after Cleonides; cf Strunk, p.44). But no classical source could give him the number 12 for his modes, so he also reported that 'Berno . . . says there had been some who devised four other modes, so that there were twelve modes in all; so far has the truth about the 12 modes left some trace even among the men of so barbarous an age' (MSD, vi, 197). And in arguing the logical case for dividing every octave at both the 4th and the 5th, Glarean observed (p.115) that:

since they [the early church musicians] could not separate the eighth mode from the first mode . . . they were forced by necessity to have recourse to the inversion of a system [*d–a–d'* into *d'–g–d*]. When they saw that this turned out successfully, they also considered the arithmetical and harmonic interchange of the other modes. Thus, after these eight modes, they invented four besides, [each of] which still remained in the same system [as one of the others].

Since Glarean knew of Wilhelm of Hirsau's work it seems more than likely that the above refers to the first part of chapter 37 of Wilhelm's *Musica*, as Gerbert pointed out (*GS*, ii, 54). Glarean continued: 'these last four modes . . . seem to have been neglected . . . either because they were not known to all or because the first eight seemed enough'.

Glarean's own construction of the 12 modes is based on a consistent rule differentiating the seven diatonic octave species according to combinations of the species of 4th and 5th (pp.104ff). Each one of the four species of 5th is combined in turn with each one of the three species of 4th above, making 12 species of octave, and with each of the three species of 4th below, making another 12. Of these 24 octave species, however, 12 are rejected on the ground that they have either fewer than two or more than three whole-tone steps between the two pairs of semitones. Of the 12 octave species then remaining, five have the same pattern of tones and semitones as another five, differing from them only in the way the 4th and 5th are disposed; these five plus the two unduplicated octave species make seven, which encompass the 12 legitimate combinations of the 4th and 5th. Table 8 and ex.20 show the seven octave species (*a*), Glarean's modal names and numbers for their harmonic and arithmetic divisions (*b*), the modal divisions of the octave (*c*), and Zarlino's renumbering (1571, 1573) and rearrangement of the names (*d* and *e*). Note that Glarean's first eight numbers and the associated names and species are those of the eightfold system. For modes 11, 12 and 8 Glarean also used the names Iastian, Hypoiastian and Hyperiastian, since these names were said to be in Aristoxenus (along with Aeolian and Hypoaeolian); on his retention of old names and assignment of new, see *Dodecachordon* Book 1, §21, and Book 2, §§4, 7, 9, 10.

TABLE 8

| (a) | (b) | | (c) | (d) | (e) | (a) |
|---|---|---|---|---|---|---|
| $A-a$ | Aeolian | 9 | $A-e, e-a$ | 11 | Aeolian | $A-a$ |
| | Hypodorian | 2 | $A-d, d-a$ | 4 | Hypophrygian | |
| $B-b\flat$ | (Hyperaeolian) | – | – | – | – | $B-b\natural$ |
| | Hypophrygian | 4 | $B-e, e-a$ | 6 | Hypolydian | |
| $c-c'$ | Ionian | 11 | $c-g, g-c'$ | 1 | Dorian | $c-c'$ |
| | Hypolydian | 6 | $c-f, f-c'$ | 8 | Hypomixolydian | |
| $d-d'$ | Dorian | 1 | $d-a, a-d'$ | 3 | Phrygian | $d-d'$ |
| | Hypomixolydian | 8 | $d-g, g-d'$ | 10 | Hypoionian | |
| $e-e'$ | Phrygian | 3 | $e-b\natural, b\natural-e'$ | 5 | Lydian | $e-e'$ |
| | Hypoaeolian | 10 | $e-a, a-e'$ | 12 | Hypoaeolian | |
| $f-f'$ | Lydian | 5 | $f-c', c'-f'$ | 7 | Mixolydian | $f-f'$ |
| | (Hyperphrygian) | – | – | – | – | |
| $g-g'$ | Mixolydian | 7 | $g-d', d'-g'$ | 9 | Ionian | $g-g'$ |
| | Hypoionian | 12 | $g-c', c'-g'$ | 2 | Hypodorian | |

With his modes firmly rooted in mediated octave species, Glarean was forced to maintain that distribution of the semitones is the essential feature of a mode. He argued that if replacing $b\natural$ with $b\flat$ in a mode with $g$ final changes it from mode 7 to mode 1, replacing $b\natural$ with $b\flat$ in a mode with $f$ final should change the mode also. He claimed that Lydian and Hypolydian (modes 5 and 6) if performed with $b\flat$ throughout are really Ionian and Hypoionian (modes 11 and 12), transposed so that their finals are at $f$. Indeed, Glarean referred to Ionian and Hypoionian many times as 'new mode 5' and 'new mode 6' – whether $f$-final in *cantus mollis* or $c$-final in *cantus durus* – in contrast with 'old' modes 5 and 6 (that is, $f$-final modes in *cantus durus*, which he presumed to have been the original condition of Lydian and Hypolydian melodies).

By the same token, Dorian and Hypodorian (modes 1 and 2) with $b\flat$ throughout must be redesignated Aeolian and Hypoaeolian – or rather restored to their putative rights, for Glarean supposed that his Aeolian was 'old indeed, but deprived of a name for many years' (p.142); or conversely, as he observed, 'one rarely finds a song in the Dorian which they have not somewhere turned into the Aeolian through the *synemmenon* tetrachord [that is, by using $b\flat$], which I do not condemn if it is done with good judgment' (p.157). One such piece is the mode 1 antiphon *Ave Maria* (Gevaert's *thème* 5) which Glarean wished to call Aeolian.

Glarean's synthesis of medieval and ancient sources is also demonstrated in his method for assigning names to his new modes. He retained Boethius's names for the

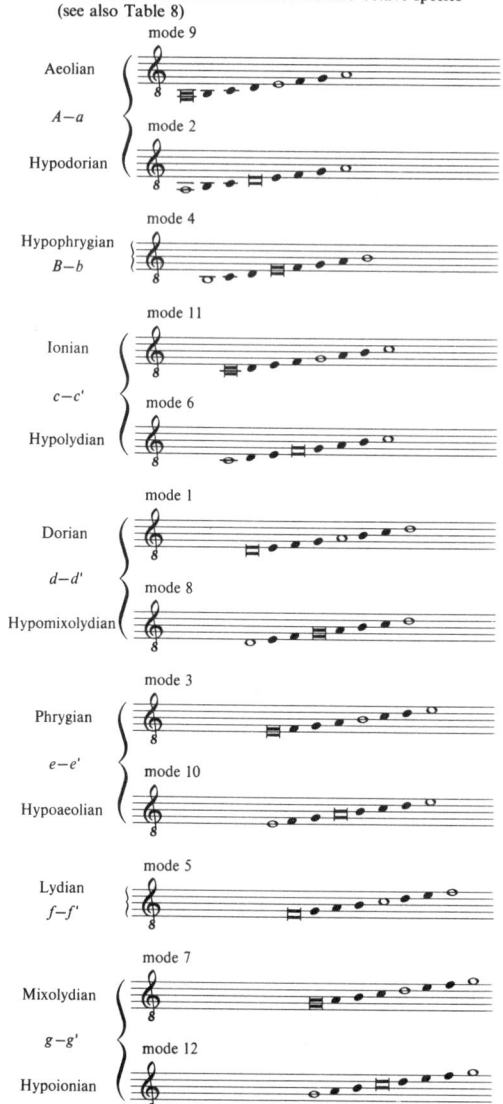

Ex.20 Glarean's 12 modes from seven mediated octave species (see also Table 8)

Aeolian   $A-a$    mode 9 / mode 2   Hypodorian

Hypophrygian   $B-b$    mode 4

Ionian   $c-c'$    mode 11 / mode 6   Hypolydian

Dorian   $d-d'$    mode 1 / mode 8   Hypomixolydian

Phrygian   $e-e'$    mode 3 / mode 10   Hypoaeolian

Lydian   $f-f'$    mode 5 / mode 7

Mixolydian   $g-g'$    mode 7 / mode 12   Hypoionian

seven 'modes or tones or tropes' in the sense in which they had come to be understood in the Middle Ages, as octave species; he retained the medieval usage of 'hypo-' meaning 'plagal' when prefixed to a principal modal name; and he ransacked classical authorities for a set of five names that might be made to fit the modal scales left over. Glarean was quite frank in saying, after a great deal of discussion of the 'more than twenty names by which the seven octave species are designated' (p.101), that 'we shall now attempt to fit these names of modes into a definite form which is appropriate to the art and also adhered to by us in the following, howsoever the names may have occurred among writers' (p.117). Table 8(*b*) shows his final results. Boethius's seven names having been given to their customary medieval modal scales, 'the remaining five modes in the writings of Aristoxenus, as Valla reports [cf Cleonides; Strunk, 1950, p.44], are named ... Hypoiastian, Hypoaeolian, Iastian, Aeolian, and Hyperiastian' (pp.115f).

To distribute these five names among the five remaining modal scales Glarean had recourse to a passage in Athenaeus in which the Aeolian and Hypodorian are equated (p.116; Strunk, pp.48f); Glarean took the equation as meaning that they share the same octave species. With the Aeolian placed in the octave *A–a*, divided *A–e* and *e–a*, its plagal the Hypoaeolian reverses the species of 4th and 5th and occupies the other form of the Phrygian octave, *e–e'* divided into *e–a* and *a–e'*. This leaves only one pair of similarly related modal scales, *c–g–c'* and *g–c'–g'*, for the Iastian–Hypoiastian pair. From other classical sources Glarean (p.116) got the equation of Iastian with Ionian, which he preferred as being a Greek tribal name more on a par with Dorian and Aeolian. Hyperiastian – '[one degree] above the Iastian' – occupies the position of the plagal form of mode 7, the Hypomixolydian. The two 'rejected' scales are given names with the 'hyper-' prefix by analogy. Taken as a whole, the confection is as brilliant as it is specious; with very few loose ends and inconsistencies several classical authorities are adduced to justify an *a priori* construction improving upon and extending a purely medieval tradition.

(*b*) Modal function and non-modal consonance species. Classical authority, however, could give Glarean no direct support for analysis of repertory, and his musical discussions reflect the influence of traditional modal theory as he must have learnt it from Cochlaeus at Cologne. Book iii.1–4 of the latter's *Tetrachordum musices* deals with non-psalmodic aspects of the eightfold system. Chapters 1 and 4, as Miller has shown (MSD, xxiii, Preface), are modelled on Wollick (1501), but Cochlaeus replaced Wollick's 'Guidonian' doctrine of measuring modal ambitus solely by its extent above and below the final; in chapter 2 the finals, confinals, and systems of modal species of the 4th and 5th are described, surely under the influence of Gaffurius's *Practica musicae*, from which Cochlaeus borrowed directly elsewhere. In chapter 3 Cochlaeus discussed the five types of ambitus (perfect to commixed) of the Italian theory, also doubtless after Gaffurius.

Cochlaeus's teaching on the species of the smaller

consonances may well have predisposed Glarean towards a construction based on those species along with the octave, reinforced as it would have been by the species doctrines of Boethius and Berno. But *Tetrachordum musices*, iii.4, reflecting the same doctrines as Wollick (1501), seems the clearest influence of the Cologne theorist on Glarean. For while Glarean proposed 'that modes are recognized principally by the octave division, which is made through the fourth and fifth consonances' (p.194), he also stressed 'that modes do not always fill out the outermost strings, but are recognized partly by *phrasis* and also partly by the final key' (p.197).

Glarean nowhere defined the term 'phrasis', but at one point he referred it back to 'certain rather easy and relatively common rules which . . . certainly should not be neglected' (pp.195, 71). The rules turn out to be a form of the familiar list of eight pairs of characteristic modal intervals, those pairs consisting of the final and one other note, a note variously derived from (psalmtone) tenor or (modal) repercussion, called *melodia* by Cochlaeus, Wollick, and other writers in the German orbit, and now *phrasis* by Glarean. Ex.21 is a composite reference list of all the modal pairs in *cantus durus* (two hexachordal positions where relevant) and in *cantus mollis*, which is the norm for the regular *f*-final modes (note that as usual in their case the use of *cantus mollis* effects no transposition).

Wollick (1501, ii.9) gave a diagnostic definition of *melodia* in which the psalm-tone tenor and the modal melodic function are completely amalgamated (ed. Niemöller):

it is necessary to distinguish authentics from plagals . . . considering thereunder two things: (1) the *melodia* itself, that is, its nature or essence, of which more later; (2) the ambitus. . . . [p.56]
The *melodia* infallibly leads us to recognition of the tone. Every chant finishing in *re*, taking the beginning of its 'seculorum amen' [that is its psalm-tone tenor] in *la* of the first tone. . . . To put it another way: . . . in every chant often attaining to *la* [and] recurring to *fa* above [i.e. *b♭* over *a*, *f'* over *e'*, or *e♭'* over *d'*], if a chant of this kind finishes in *re*, it is of the first tone. . . . [p.58]

Cochlaeus's wording of the doctrine emphasizes further the melodic aspect of the two notes in the pair, and separates this aspect of *melodia* from the sense of *melodia* as psalm-tone tenor (which he mentioned briefly

Ex.21 *Melodia* (Cochlaeus, Wollick)/*repercussa*/*phrasis* (Glarean)

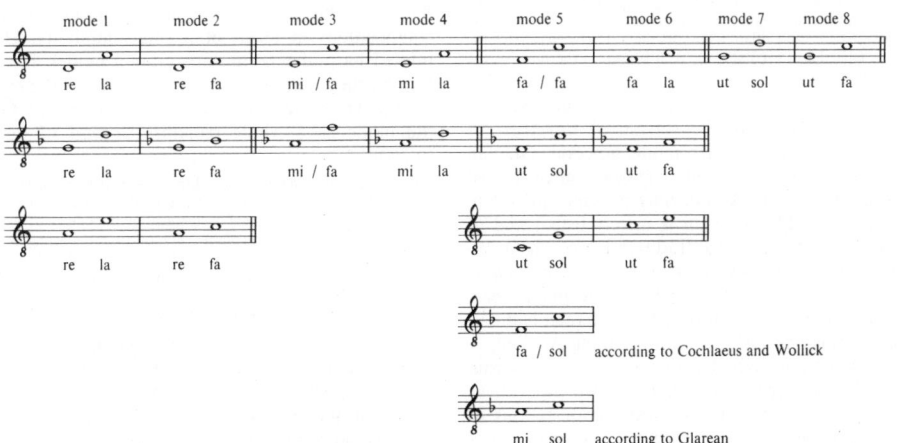

at the beginning of iii.5): 'The *melodia* of a tone is a conventional progression of notes, according to fixed intervals, which is more common to one tone than to another. For its recognition there are four rules, according to the [four] finals of the tones'. Following his list of four (pairs of) rules Cochlaeus gave an ad hoc formula or progression to demonstrate the role of the *melodia* in the course of each of the eight modes.

In Glarean (1547) the equivalent term 'phrasis' occurs constantly, and in contexts where it implies both a still greater generality in melodic emphasis and at the same time a still greater specificity as motivic nucleus. The variant for mode 5 in Glarean's list (see ex.21) demonstrates an evident desire to turn the traditional *melodia* of his Cologne mentor into a unique definition of the mode. The traditional *cantus mollis melodia* for mode 5 is the third species of 5th *ut sol* (or *fa/sol*); *ut sol* is also the *melodia* for mode 7. Glarean's substitution of *mi sol* as the characteristic interval for mode 5 has two effects. First, by dispensing with the final of the mode as a member of the pair, Glarean showed that he conceived the *phrasis* as a melodic interval, not a pair of modal functions or a single prominent note to complement the final. Second, the substitution eliminates the one duplication of intervals in the traditional list, *ut sol* in both modes 5 and 7. Now every modal pair is intervallically unique: one minor 6th (*mi/fa*); two 5ths differently composed (*re la* and *ut sol*); two 4ths likewise (*mi la* and *ut fa*); one major 3rd (*fa la*); and two minor 3rds differently composed (*re fa* and *mi sol*).

In Book 2, §§36–7, Glarean discussed the species of consonances as non-modal boundaries of pitch areas in which melodies operate – melodies whose true modality is determined by their finals and *phrasis*. Non-modal use of the consonances was of course not new: it was part of the 11th-century Italian theory of the ambitus, and the consonances were used as registral boundaries in the 9th-century *Alia musica* (see, for example, Chailley ed., pp.121ff, for an analysis by non-modal consonances of the Advent introit *Rorate coeli*).

(c) Mode as ethos, category, and inherent property. As a humanist Glarean was fully committed to the doctrine of modal ethos, and here too his work reveals his synthesis of the classical revival with the medieval heritage. The two modes of the Phrygian octave species (*e–e′*) are particularly revealing (p.160):

The Phrygian is commonly called the third mode, a particularly famous and ancient mode ... Horace calls it '*barbarus*' ... Lucian calls it 'divinely inspired', Apuleius, 'religious' ... some say that it evokes the harsh reviling of the indignant [cf Johannes in §1(i) above], others say that it incites to battle and inflames the appetite of a frenzied rage [cf, the anonymous Chartist in §1(i) above]. Well known is the fable of the Tauromenian youth...

Glarean then retold the Phrygian story from Boethius, quoted in §1(i) above in the version of Engelbert of Admont. For the Hypoaeolian mode, however, Glarean could report no ethos; the only classical source he had for the name was the Aristoxenus passage quoted in Cleonides, where Hypoaeolian is merely listed, and of course there was no medieval tradition for it. The arithmetically mediated octave *e–a–e′* got the name Hypoaeolian solely by virtue of being the plagal rearrangement of the *A–e–a* octave, which Glarean had had an excellent classical justification for calling Aeolian.

Glarean must have felt that the contrast in surviving richness of ethic attributions for these two modes was paralleled in their surviving musical manifestations in the chant. For the Phrygian, 'since it is known to every-

one we shall be content with one example' (p.160); but the Hypoaeolian 'is infrequently used in our time, and one finds few songs in choirs [i.e. chant] according to it' (p.162). Yet as his only plagal *a* mode the Hypoaeolian is necessarily his category for two of the most provocative melody types in the repertory, probably very ancient, with apparent calendaric associations. First, there are 'some Graduals, as they are called, many of which are sung in Advent, and in Easter time, also some at other times' (p.167). These are the *Tollite portas–Haec dies* mode 2 transposed graduals (see Apel, 1958, 357ff, and PalMus, ii, iii; also G. M. Suñol y Baulenas, *Introduction à la paléographie musicale grégorienne* (1935), Plate F, for a tabular analysis). Glarean went on to observe that 'this [Hypoaeolian] mode is also found between small *e* and large *F* [i.e. *e′* and *f*] ... within the same range as the Lydian ... yet it ends on its proper final, small *a* [i.e. *a*], while the Lydian ends on large *F* [i.e. *f*]. We shall present an example of this ...', and he printed the antiphon *Exaltata est* (*Liber responsorialis*, p.374, 'mode 4 transposed') – Gevaert's *thème* 29 – cited two more of the same melody type, and went on: 'Similar also are many used in Advent and other times, especially during Lent' (pp.162f). (For a brief discussion of this melody type see Apel, 1958, pp.398ff.) Glarean also used the Hypoaeolian as he did the Aeolian, as a modal assignment for protus melodies that use the flat 6th degree exclusively, as do many mode 2 responsories (see Apel, pp.332ff, for discussion of the type and references).

In applying his system to polyphony Glarean was limited in three ways. First, for him as for others the modes were monophonic, and a principle for integrating the voices was needed. Second, though the *Dodecachordon* includes a discussion of mensuration and proportion (Book 3, §§1–12), there is no treatment at all of counterpoint or of the composition of the sonorities, and thus no doctrine of polyphonic cadences or beginnings. Third, Glarean the humanist was committed to the integrity of the octave species; though he was aware of the potential modality of the smaller species he mentioned them only incidentally in his analyses, normally preferring rather vague invocations of *phrasis* when reference to a modal element of narrower compass was needed (though he often also used *phrasis* in a context implying the full span of a modal octave).

Glarean's examples are modally labelled according to the tenor, but in no sense did he discuss polyphonic compositions in terms of a single modality. He postulated natural relationships among modes as entities; though these relationships in fact turn on the existence of smaller species common to two modes, for Glarean the mode as a whole remains the unit of discourse (p.250):

There is a certain hidden relationship of the modes and a generating of one from the other, certainly not acquired through the ingenuity of *symphonetae*, but determined in this way by the nature of the modes. For we see this happen whenever a Hypodorian tenor [e.g. *a–d′–a′*] is arranged so that its bass is Dorian [*d–a–d′*], often also Aeolian [*A–e–a′*].... Contrariwise, whenever the tenor is Phrygian [*e–b♮–e′*], the bass and cantus often fall into the Aeolian [*A–e–a*, *a–e′–a′*].... Sometimes the cantus comes into the Hypophrygian [*b♮–e′–b♮*].

Glarean's 'hidden relationship of the modes' is nowhere better illustrated than in his own observations on the combinations of the Aeolian modes with the Dorian modes on the one hand and the Phrygian on the other. This relationship of modal systems is the equivalent, in

Glarean's terms, of Aaron's distinction between final *a* as mode 1 confinal and final *a* as mode 3 difference. Looked at yet another way, the relationship of Glarean's Aeolian to both Dorian and Phrygian reflects the mixed composition of the *a* modes, which consist of the *re la* mode 1 (protus) species of 5th and the *mi la* mode 3 (deuterus) species of 4th.

As an example of the Aeolian mode Glarean quoted the 'Pleni sunt coeli' from Josquin's *Missa sine nomine*, 'in which the higher voice begins, and after two *tempora* the lower voice follows at the fourth below, as they usually say. But its system is truly Aeolian, not Dorian as some have written, and also ends on the lowest string [i.e. degree] of the [Aeolian] fifth'. This canon is constructed on the same tonal principle as Bartolomeo Ramos de Pareia's little demonstration *fuga* in ex.17*a*: each voice lies within a single hexachord, natural (*c′–a′*) in the upper voice and hard (*g–e′*) in the tenor, and hence would be solmized with the same syllables. In terms of modal species of 5th both voices are protus, set at two positions a 4th apart.

Josquin's five-voice *Miserere* was one of Aaron's examples for mode 3 ending at its difference on *a*; Glarean said of the same piece, referring like Aaron to the pattern of its ostinato tenor, 'One truly sees here the Hypoaeolian from small *e* to large *E* [i.e. *e′* to *e*], indeed divided arithmetically at small *a* [i.e. *a*], on which it also ends, namely on the lowest string [i.e. degree] of the [Hypoaeolian] fifth [*a–e′*]' (p.260).

The relationship of Glarean's Ionian and Hypoionian to the rest of his system is of a different kind. First, *c*-mode pieces, otherwise considered secondary forms of members of the eightfold system, could now be supposed to have separate modes of their own. For instance, Josquin's *Comment peult avoir joye*, which Aaron had assigned to mode 7 ending on its difference *c*, naturally became Hypoionian when Glarean printed it with the words *O Jesu fili David*. Second, Glarean's insistence on the integrity of the semitone distribution in his modal octaves required him to consider *f*-mode pieces in *cantus mollis* as transpositions of his Ionian or Hypoionian mode because they had the same intervallic structure. This made the *cantus mollis f* modes systematically consistent with the other *cantus mollis* modes (p.256): ·

Ionian . . . all the examples of this mode are transposed from the proper tonic by a fourth . . . which change usually occurs in most other modes, as in the Dorian and Hypodorian, its plagal, and in the Hypoionian, the plagal of this [Ionian] mode. . . . Moreover, a beautiful five-voice example of this mode is the *Stabat mater dolorosa* of Josquin des Prez.

Aaron had also cited the Josquin *Stabat mater*, an *f*-final *cantus mollis* composition, as one of his instances for mode 5 with the regular final, Glarean's 'old' Lydian; in so doing he was following the centuries-old tradition of considering *b♭* – from the *synēmmenōn* tetrachord – a co-equal member of the tonal system when it occurred in tritus modes.

The simple and logical symmetries of Glarean's system eliminated cumbrous lucubrations over modal assignments for pieces ending with *a* or *c′*; it also eliminated the apparent inconsistency by which *f* modes were considered to be modes 5 or 6 in *cantus durus* and *cantus mollis* alike, while *g* modes in *cantus durus* were modes 7 or 8 but in *cantus mollis* they were modes 1 or 2. On the other hand, the 12-mode system also logically eliminated important and by no means over-subtle distinctions, such as those between the two

kinds of *a* modes in *cantus durus*. Of course such distinctions could continue to be made on a secondary level, as Glarean and some of his immediate successors made them. But those who took up the 12-mode system, whether directly from Glarean or from Zarlino, eventually lost sight of such distinctions in their enthusiasm for the simple, rational and universal paradigm that the system provided.

*(iii) Zarlino's synthesis of modality and polyphony.* The modal doctrine of Zarlino is expounded in detail in Part iv of his *Istitutioni harmoniche* (1558, rev. 3/1573); important concepts are also found in Part iii, on counterpoint. Zarlino adopted Glarean's system in its entirety; he added to it the polyphonic modal functions that had been creeping into the literature since the 15th century; and more than that, he succeeded in bringing polyphonic texture, modal structure and modal ethos under the rule of a single unifying musical principle.

In the 1558 edition Zarlino kept Glarean's 12 modes as Glarean had ordered and named them. In the 1573 edition, however, he renumbered the modes to begin with the authentic and plagal *c* modes as modes 1 and 2, the *d* modes as 3 and 4, and so through the hexachord up to the *a* modes as 11 and 12 (see Table 8(*d*)). The reordering followed on some conclusions published in his *Dimostrationi harmoniche* (1571, pp.270ff); in this work he reordered the names of the modes along with their numbers (Table 8 (*e*)) but in the revised *Istitutioni* he used the new numbers alone, without names, on the grounds that though the old names had been wrongly used it would be too confusing to insist on a new usage. Of the six reasons offered for the reordering the most important was that his tuning was based on just intonation of the (C) major scale (for which his classical warrant was Ptolemy's syntonic diatonic); he also believed, wrongly, that the names in his new ordering represented the correct interpretation of the 'modes or tones or tropes'.

Zarlino often adopted Glarean's comments on the ethos of one or another mode. For instance, he said that mode 9/11 – Glarean's Aeolian – is 'very old, yet it has long been deprived of its name and proper place' (1573, p.411), and shortly thereafter he listed several epithets translated from Glarean's classical sources. Zarlino's musical comments on individual works are not unlike Glarean's, but with regular reference to the smaller species of consonances, especially in cases where his new doctrine of modal structure produces something flagrantly at variance with what he knew to be the practice. On the Phrygian, for instance, whose regular cadence points he required to be *e*, *g*, *b♮* and *e′*, he observed (1573, p.401):

If this mode had not been mixed . . . with [the Aeolian], and if it were heard plain, it would have had a harmony rather harsh. But because it is tempered by the 5th of mode [9/11, Glarean's Aeolian, namely *a–b♮–c′–d′–e′*] and by the cadence that is made on *a* which is so greatly used, some have thought on that account that it has the character of moving to tears; therefore they set it freely to words that are tearful and full of laments. It has great conformity to the aforesaid [Aeolian], because they have the [*mi fa sol la*] species of 4th in common.

In the treatise on counterpoint (Part iii), Zarlino introduced polyphonic modal functions. The fifth of his six general rules for composition requires that 'a composition be ordered under a prescribed and determined mode, or tone, as we like to call it' (trans. Marco and Palisca, p.52). He went on to require that imitative voices enter on modal degrees (p.55):

the interval between the initial notes of the two voices should be one of the perfect consonances named above [. . . unison, fifth, octave, or compound . . .], or a 4th. This is not unreasonable, for one begins on the extremes or the middle points of the modes on which the melody is founded.

The cadences are to be on the modal degrees also (p.42):

The cadence has a value in music equivalent to the period in prose and could well be called the period of musical composition. . . . The end of a sentence in the text should coincide with the cadence, and this should not fall on an arbitrary tone but on the proper and regular steps of the mode used.

In its details Zarlino's counterpoint treatise is a summary, extension and codification of existing doctrine. But permeating the polyphonic web Zarlino saw the same 'sonorous numbers' that he had used for his tuning system, those perfect and imperfect consonances of just intonation which he had measured in the simple ratios of the numbers one to six. The small-number ratios of just intonation now allowed the 5th easily to be conceived as harmonically and arithmetically mediated into major and minor 3rds with simple ratios, just as the octave had always been simply mediated into a perfect 5th and a perfect 4th. As a consequence, the general bilateral pattern of both structural and ethic contrast that had been associated with the harmonically mediated authentic octave versus the arithmetically mediated plagal octave could be claimed as well for the harmonically versus the arithmetically mediated 5th.

The 5th and its 3rds now became the sonorous glue of the contrapuntal texture. Zarlino portrayed them in their new role as follows:

The variety of the harmony . . . results from the position of the note that divides the fifth. . . . On this variety depend all the diversity and perfection of harmonies. [p.69]

Since harmony is a union of diverse elements, we must strive . . . to have those two consonances [the third and the fifth] or their compounds sound in our compositions as much as possible. [p.188]

Zarlino was of course quite ready to recognize the existence of other consonances in the texture, but he regarded them as substitutes for the 3rd or 5th (p.188):

True, musicians often write the sixth in place of the fifth, and this is fine. . . . Especially in three-voice writing the octave may be used in place of one of them to preserve a beautiful, elegant, and simple voice line. To want to use those consonances constantly in such pieces would be impossible.

The consonances that dominate the contrapuntal composition of the texture were also invoked to govern the modal disposition of the structure, establishing the final, its upper 5th, and its mediating 3rd (major or minor) as the proper scale degrees for beginnings and cadences: 'The true and natural beginnings not only of this but of any mode you like should be at the boundary degrees [chorde estreme] of their fifths and fourths, and on the median degree [chorda mezana], which divides the 5th into major 3rd and minor 3rd' (1573, iv.18, p.392). And again Zarlino recognized the realities of practice, though in this case he attempted no explanations: 'All the same, many compositions that have their beginnings on other degrees are to be found'.

To allow for anomalous cadence points is both prudent and customary, and Zarlino did so; what is new is his prescription of a uniform basis for fixing cadential norms, the same for all 12 modes (1573, iv.18):

Cadences are found to be of two kinds, 'regular' and 'irregular'. Regular are those which are always made on the boundary notes or degrees of the modes. (Where the octave in each mode is harmonically or arithmetically mediated or divided by a median degree, those degrees are the boundaries . . . likewise where the 5th is divided by a median degree into a major 3rd and minor 3rd.) Any other [cadences] then may be made wherever you like; they are called irregular.

The intervals that permeate the contrapuntal texture and regulate the modal structure are also said to determine the general ethos of a mode (pp.21f):

the fifth, sixth, seventh, eighth, eleventh and twelfth [modes, numbered as in 1558, see Table 8 (b), (c)] . . . are very gay and lively, because in them the consonances are frequently arranged [in an order] according to the nature of the sonorous number, that is, the fifth is harmonically divided into a major and minor third which is very pleasing to the ear. . . . In the other modes, which are the first, second, third, fourth, ninth, and tenth, the fifth is arithmetically divided by a middle note, in such a way that one often hears the consonances arranged [in an order] contrary to the nature of the sonorous number. Whereas in the first group [of modes] the major third is often placed beneath the minor, in the second [group of modes] the opposite is true, with a result I can only describe as sad or languid.

This theory of a bipolar modal ethos based on the harmonic or arithmetic division of the modal 5th in Part iii is a generalization; in Part iv specific, usually traditional, affects are attributed to each mode individually. Zarlino's recognition of the realities of compositional practice regarding 'irregular' cadences in the Phrygian has been quoted. Finally, his recommendations for a predominant use of 3rds and 5ths in the texture did not prevent him from providing for the actual construction of simultaneities through the conventional rules for adding first the bass and then the alto to a principal interval in soprano and tenor (see trans., pp.178ff, and especially the table on pp.182f). Nonetheless, his synthesis of texture, mode and affect through their joint participation in a background ambience of major 3rds, minor 3rds and 5ths, was an enduring contribution, and it had a devastating effect on polyphonic modality. The essence of all traditional modal theory, as applicable to polyphonic music, had been that the tonal relationships specific to each mode were treated as completely independent of the general tonal relationships governing vertical sonorities and their successions. Zarlino's construction on Glarean's 12 modes broke down the barrier between modal structure and chord structure and left them wholly dependent on each other.

5. TRANSITION TO MAJOR AND MINOR KEYS.
(i) The 12 modes in the late 16th century. The new and systematically conceived theory of 12 modes was promulgated with both sets of names and numbers. One was Glarean's, and Zarlino's 1558 version as well: modes 1 (Dorian) to 8 (Hypomixolydian) – the old eightfold system – and modes 9 (Aeolian) to 12 (Hypoionian) as authentic–plagal pairs of a-final (9, 10) and c- or c'-final (11, 12) modal octaves. The other set of numbers and names was Zarlino's second version from 1571 and 1573: six pairs of authentic–plagal modal octaves, with finals in order of the natural hexachord, c d e f g a; c authentic (mode 1) to f plagal (mode 8) were now called by the old names, Dorian to Hypomixolydian; the g-final modal octaves became Ionian and Hypoionian, and only the names Aeolian and Hypoaeolian (modes 11 and 12) referred to the same modal octaves as they had in Glarean's system. (See Table 8 (e).)

In the later 16th century and early 17th the 12-mode system was taken up enthusiastically, by composers as well as by theorists. In Germany at first Glarean was the source, so that mode 1 (Dorian) continued to be d authentic in cantus durus with b♮, or g authentic in cantus mollis with b♭. The earliest large-scale musical embodiment of Glarean's new system was a setting of the Gospel texts for the whole year, published in 1565, in four cycles of the 12 modes, by Glarean's student Homer Herpol. Alexander Utendal's 1570 settings of the seven penitential psalms (plus five texts from the Prophets) in the 12 modes, along with Herpol's works, were among those often cited as examples for the 12 polyphonic modes in music textbooks for the German Lateinschulen well into the 17th century. The 1570 *Cantiones* of Eucharius Hoffmann is another 12-mode collection, and in Hoffmann's 1582 treatise *Doctrina de tonis seu modis* Lutheran chorale tunes were added to the recurrent roster of citations exemplifying the 12 modes. Andreas Raselius also wrote about the 12 modes and illustrated them in his *Hexachordum seu questiones musicae practicae* (1591) and published two collections of motets on German Gospel texts, one set for Sundays and the other for important feasts, 'in which living examples of Glarean's *Dodecachordon* in both scales [*cantus durus, cantus mollis*] have been invented' (*Teutsche Sprüche*, 1594–5).

In Italy too the earlier 12-mode system was preferred, not because musicians were unaware of Zarlino's new scheme, but because it was easier in a liturgical context if the first eight modes could be associated directly with the traditional eightfold system; organists had not only to play independent pieces during the service but also to collaborate with both the polyphony and the plainchant of the choir. Organ compositions keyed to the 12 modes proliferated in the late 16th century and early 17th. Andrea Gabrieli's *Ricercari* of 1595 form a full set of extended compositions in all 12 modes. Table 9*a* lists their modes (called 'tones') along with their scales (*cantus durus* unmarked, *cantus mollis* designated by a flat sign), their endings

and their putative transpositions from the abstract system.

In France, conversely, Zarlino's second scheme was generally accepted in principle, with the *c* authentic modal scale being mode 1, or Dorian. (Conflicts that arose in liturgical situations were accepted, though they had to be explained.) In Le Jeune's *Octonaires* (1606; ed. in MMFTR, i, viii) each of the 12 modes has two chansons for four voices and one for three; the *c*-final and *d*-final authentic–plagal modal pairs – modes 1 (Dorian) to 4 (Hypophrygian) – are set in *cantus mollis*, to end with *f* and *g*. Table 9*b* lists the modes, scales, endings and putative transpositions for this collection.

The potential for confusion in two co-existing sets of names is only terminological; in any specific circumstance one set of names or the other will be found. But the 12 modes and the eightfold system were two genuinely competing theories, one rational and unified, the other traditional and diverse. Coupled with that source of confusion was the matter of transposition (in the modern sense) of modes. Even considering only the traditional overlapping systems of *cantus durus* and *cantus mollis* – the scale with *b♮* and the scale with *b♭* – the number of octave scales of potential modal legitimacy was doubled without there being much increase in the number of finals in the system as a whole. From Table 9 two preliminary illustrations may be extracted.

The Gabrieli *Ricercari* (see Table 9*a*) include two *f* modes, one authentic and one plagal, both with the *b♭* scale; one of these, however, is called mode 11 (Glarean's Ionian) transposed down a 5th while the other is the traditional mode 6 of the eightfold system, the ancient tritus plagal mode with its traditional *b♭*. A similar coupling occurs with the *c* and *c'* modes: one is in principle a transposition of the traditional mode 5 (with its traditional *b♭*) into *cantus durus*, down a 4th to *c*; the *c'* mode is called mode 12 (Glarean's Hypoionian). Finally, the set includes two *d*-final authentic modes, mode 1 in its regular position and mode 9 a 5th lower. They differ in their sixth degrees, but the distinction is minimized by the normal practice of using *b♭* over *a* (*fa* over *la*) in the authentic protus at *d*. (The downward transposition of mode 9, like the transposition of mode 5 down to *c* and mode 2 up to *g*, is ultimately a reflection of systematic adjustment of the organ to a convenient pitch level for the choir in the musical liturgy: see §5(ii*b*) below.)

Quite different instances of two modes sharing the same final due to the overlapping *cantus durus* and *cantus mollis* systems are furnished by Le Jeune's scheme for the *Octonaires* (see Table 9*b*). The collection includes two sets of plagal–authentic *f* modes, and two sets of plagal–authentic *g* modes: in each set with common final one pair uses *b♮*, the other *b♭*, like Gabrieli's mode 1 and mode 9. In the *f* modes the contrast in scale system comes in their fourth degrees, the old question of theoretical tritus versus practical tritus. The contrast in the third degrees of the *g* modes, *b♮* and *b♭*, is also reminiscent of an old modal contretemps, the transformation of mode 7 tetardus on *g* to mode 1 protus on *g* (see §II, 4(i), above); but here it is not a question of changing modes in one piece but of the existence of whole pieces in different modes with the same final. This is the converse of the situation illustrated in the Gabrieli *Ricercari* by the first two pieces, which are both in the authentic protus mode but with

TABLE 9

| Tone | Scale | Final | (a) Putative transposition | 'Natural' final |
|---|---|---|---|---|
| 1 | – | d | – | |
| 1 | ♭ | g | ↑4 | d |
| 2 | ♭ | g | ↑4 | d |
| 3 | – | e | – | |
| 4 | – | e | – | |
| 5 | – | c | ↓4 | f (in B♭ scale) |
| 6 | ♭ | f | – | |
| 7 | – | g | – | |
| 8 | – | g | – | |
| 9 | ♭ | d | ↓5 | a |
| 10 | – | a | – | |
| 11 | ♭ | f | ↓5 | c' |
| 12 | – | c' | – | |

| | | | (b) | Name of mode |
|---|---|---|---|---|
| 1 | ♭ | f | ↑4 | c Dorian |
| 2 | ♭ | f | ↑4 | c Hypodorian |
| 3 | ♭ | g | ↑4 | d Phrygian |
| 4 | ♭ | g | ↑4 | d Hypophrygian |
| 5 | – | e | | Lydian |
| 6 | – | e | | Hypolydian |
| 7 | – | f | | Mixolydian |
| 8 | – | f | | Hypomixolydian |
| 9 | – | g | | Ionian |
| 10 | – | g | | Hypoionian |
| 11 | – | a | | Aeolian |
| 12 | – | a | | Hypoaeolian |

different finals – *g* (in the *b♭* system) and *d* (in the *b♮* system).

These collections between them embody three elements of disorder for polyphonic modality: the existence of a new modal theory in conflict with the traditional eightfold system; systemic ambiguities arising ultimately from the practical requirements of transposition; and contrasts in scale type over common finals arising out of two parallel systems of scales, *cantus durus* and *cantus mollis*.

*(ii) The modes in the 17th century.*

*(a) Transposition of modal scales.* Before the humanists with their classical authority came to rationalize the eightfold system and make it more consistent it had been an essential part of the Catholic liturgy, and so it continued. An ever more important part in both Mass and Office was played by the organ, and in performing *alternatim* mass sections and *Magnificat* verses with the choir the organist had to be ready to accommodate his music to pitch levels comfortable to the choir. This meant that the whole complex of modes and psalm tones had to be available in practice at pitch levels on the keyboard other than those embedded in the traditional system of note names, out of which the design of that keyboard had developed. The background diatonic assemblage of course already provided for one substantial and useful shift in relative pitch level through the two parallel systems of *cantus durus* and *cantus mollis*, the scales with *b♮* and *b♭*. *Cantus fictus*, with its two flats, was a way of considering transpositions by a whole step downward as only slightly contradicting the conception of a single diatonic framework with exchangeable ancillary notes. Practical transpositions to other parts of the keyboard further augmented both the number of places a given mode could be projected and the number of modal scales that could be projected at a given place. This process, accompanied by necessary acoustic refinements, led in time to the abandonment of the extended double octave coupled with hexachord syllables as the model for the background assemblage of pitches and pitch relationships available for music.

*(b) The eightfold system and the 12 modes.* The organist's need to transpose arose from his interaction with the choir; a considerable share in the confusions of later polyphonic modality in Catholic countries is due to the intersection of the practical need for transposition with conflicting systems of 12 modes, eight modes and eight psalm tones.

Pietro Pontio had made a clear and emphatic distinction between the eight tones used for motets, masses, madrigals and the like, and the eight tones used for the psalms, which, he rightly observed, have their own cadences and even their own endings (see §3(iii) above). Those adhering in principle to the new 12-mode systems generally made this same distinction; Zacconi, for instance, distinguished 12 'tuoni harmoniale' from eight 'aeri di salmeggiare' (*Prattica di musica*, ii, 1622, p.43), and proposed that in any case the latter are derived from the former.

Others, especially those inclined to prefer the traditional eightfold system as the basis for tonal distinctions, were not ready to build a wall between tone (for psalms) and mode (for everything else). Banchieri (1614) gave a thorough, fully illustrated account of a kind of conglomerate modal system that was typical in Catholic usage well past the first half of the 17th cen-

tury, with some local variations. Basically these systems were developed in three stages. First, members of the two eightfold systems – like Pontio's tones for motets and tones for psalms – were mingled together in theory, as in liturgical performing practice, into a single eightfold system. Second, the conglomerate eightfold system was compared and correlated with the 12 modes in *cantus durus* and *cantus mollis*. The third stage then either recognized the systems as separate in function or derived one of the systems from the other, implying or stating that there was only one true system of modes. The organist's practical experience with transposition played a leading role in the construction of the conglomerate system, but only *cantus durus* and *cantus mollis* were originally drawn on to provide theoretical scales for constituent modes in a closed system.

Banchieri began his discussion with a list of the traditional eight modes, illustrated however not by stepwise species or final–ambitus but by modal degrees within their octaves, in the manner of Zarlino (ex.22a); this is followed immediately by the eight psalm tones illustrated by the ancient and familiar couple of modal final with psalm-tone tenor (ex.22b – both from 1614, p.68). Shortly thereafter follows the principal demonstration, in which Banchieri depicted an eightfold system of polyphonic modes based on the psalm tones (see ex.23, from 1614, pp.70f). He began with the 'intonation, middle, and end of the plainchant' for each of the

Ex.22

(a) the eight modes

● = final

(b) the eight tones

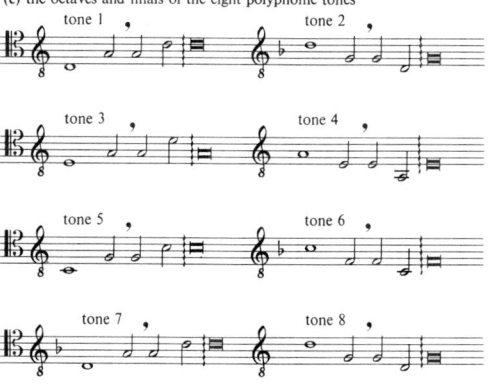

(c) the octaves and finals of the eight polyphonic tones

Ex.23

eight psalm tones at its regular position, ending each with its principal difference. They are all then shown again, each one 'transposed for compositions in polyphony for the choir' (*trasportato alle compositioni coriste del figurato*); following their transposed forms their modal degrees are shown as 'cadences', on a pattern like that shown in ex.22a.

The transpositions that are made all occur within the parallel systems of *cantus durus* and *cantus mollis*. Tones 2 and 7 go from *cantus durus* into *cantus mollis*, up a 4th and down a 5th, respectively. Tone 5 appears as though it were merely transposed down within the *cantus durus* system, but Banchieri's tone 5 at the f-final position would have had its usual b♭ in practice (see ex. 22b); tone 5 is in fact transposed the other way, from *cantus mollis* at f to *cantus durus* at c.

The practical aim of these transpositions was to reduce the range needed for the choir's psalmody. This is seen clearly in the 'middle' notes of Banchieri's formulation, which represent the recitation pitch of the psalm-tone tenor, on which the bulk of a psalm verse was chanted. Column 1 in ex.23 shows that in the pure diatonic double octave the psalm-tone tenors are spread between f and d'; their equivalents in the partly transposed system drawing from both b♮ and b♭ scales cover only g to c'. The lowest psalm tone (2), with its equivalent polyphonic tone, has been brought up, the two highest (5 and 7) have been brought down. In the alternative use of a *cantus mollis* transposition by downward whole step suggested by Banchieri for the otherwise untransposed tones 3 and 8, the range of recitation pitches is still further contracted. In the *Cartella musicale* no explanation is offered for these alternative sets of cadence points, but in his *L'organo suonarino* (1605) Banchieri at one point outlined soprano and bass parts for the polyphonic verses of an *alternatim Magnificat* for each

of his eight tones, and tones 3 and 8 have indeed been set 'a tone lower for the convenience of the choir' (pp.94, 104), bringing the tenors from c' down to b♭, thereby compressing the range of recitation tones to a minor 3rd, g, a and b♭.

It may be observed that a systemic effect of the mixed pattern of transposition is to subvert one of the fundamental premises of the traditional eightfold system. Instead of sharing a common final in a single diatonic system and being contrasted by higher and lower ambitus, three of the four authentic–plagal pairs – 1 and 2, 5 and 6, 7 and 8 – keep the octave span constant, and it is the final and scale system that change. This may be seen in ex.22c (from 1614, pp.84–7) which shows the prescribed intervals of imitation and the last notes in the tenor part for each of Banchieri's eight tones (the points of imitation are assigned to the extremes and the mean of each modal octave).

Tones 3 and 4 also have different finals, but both are in *cantus durus* and they have different octave spans as well. Tone 3, like all the others, is a psalmodically engendered polyphonic mode, and a is the last note of its most prominent difference. The emphasis on a and c' in mode 3 is of course nothing new, but using a as the final of mode 3 is only justifiable when the psalm tone is the model for the mode. In a system of polyphonic modes avowedly derived from psalm tones there is no reason to call particular attention to this final in tone 3, and there is nothing inconsistent in Banchieri's taking it for granted. What is inconsistent is the treatment of mode 4. In his model for the derivation of the system (ex.23) he assigned two sets of modal degrees to tone 4, as he did for tones 3 and 8. The basis for the substitution – borrowed from Zarlino – is entirely different, and has to do neither with psalm tones nor with the convenience of the choir (p.75):

Because the degree *b♮* does not have an upper [perfect] 5th, and so much the less a [perfect] 4th below, imitations by the 5th from *e* to *A* responding [to those] by the 4th from *a* to *e* are permitted. The proper cadences in two voices are *c′* [upper] terminal, *b♮* median, *g* indifferent, and *e* final; but with more voices, because of the aforesaid impediments [arising] from the note *b♮*, cadences on the two notes contiguous to the *b♮* are permitted, that is, the note *c′* [as] median cadence and *a* as indifferent, or *a* as median and *c′* as indifferent, as you wish.

After a detailed exposition and correlation of Zarlino's 12 modes in both scale systems and his own eight polyphonic tones Banchieri revealed himself as in the end rather partial to the claims of the two-scale eightfold system (p.136):

It has already been said how much to be esteemed are the 12 modes, on their own degrees or transposed, as learnedly expounded by Gioseffe Zarlino. . .but it seems right to me to warn the novice composer of the difficulties, found on closer examination, that pervade them: [1] that really in every composition [i.e. worldly as well as churchly] the eight or nine ecclesiastical tones [the ninth being the *misto tuono*, that is, *tonus peregrinus*] come into the 12 modes; and [2] that the 12 modes do not exceed the eight (or nine) tones if they are desired to be usable in more than two parts.

(*c*) The eightfold system and the 24 major and minor keys. The conception that 12 modes in each of two scales, 24 in all, should be compressed into a combined system of eight modes, some using one scale and some the other, continued in Italy for several generations. A succinct report appears in Bononcini's *Musico prattico* (1673), ii.17. 'Of the 12 tones . . . there are seven that are normally used' (pp.121f): see ex.24*a* (based on pp.137–47). The reduction of 12 modes to seven rather than eight devolves from the correlation of mode 10 with both tone 3 and tone 4: Bononcini distinguished them only by their endings. Ex.24*b* (based on pp.148–53) is Bononcini's demonstration of how a melody can be converted from its 'natural' mode to any other mode by changing the key signature.

By a circuitous but traceable route through French- and German-speaking Catholic countries, what had begun as Banchieri's eight 'psalm-tone keys' were finally incorporated into the system of 24 major and minor keys in Mattheson's *Das neu-eröffnete Orchestre* (1713). After a discussion of the '12 *modi*, or Greek manners of singing' (p.57), Mattheson described the final stage of the eight 'psalm-tone keys' (p.60): 'The Italians and the present-day composers employ another fashion of differentiating their *modulationes*' (shown in Table 10). As his source for this set of eight tones Mattheson

Ex.24
(a) modes and psalm-tone keys

○: the mediated octaves    ●: finals

(b) modes and key signatures
modes: 1   9   7   11

modes: 7   1   11   9

in Heinichen's *Neu erfundene und gründliche Anweisung . . . des General-Basses*, recommending the more familiar approach: 'There are just the 12 semitones of the chromatic octave, each of which can be differentiated once, through the major or through the minor 3rds; thus the aforementioned 24 arise, and so it remains' (Mattheson, 1713, p.63).

A few traces of the heterogeneously agglomerated major–minor key system can be observed in early 18th-century musical practice. Most conspicuous are the key signatures with one flat or one sharp too few or one sharp too many, representing transpositions of mode 1 or mode 2 (minor keys with one flat too few or one sharp too many), transpositions of mode 8 (major keys with one sharp too few), or use of a one-flat or two-flat signature as though it were *cantus mollis* or *cantus fictus* (major keys with one flat too few). Certain details of early 18th-century harmonic movement or aspects of

TABLE 10

| tone 1 | D | F | A | or D minor |
|---|---|---|---|---|
| 2 | G | B♭ | D | G minor |
| 3 | A | C | E | A minor |
| 4 | E | G | B♮ | E minor |
| 5 | C | E | G | C major |
| 6 | F | A | C | F major |
| 7 | D | F♯ | A | D major |
| 8 | G | B♮ | D | G major |

must have used the 'regular tones or modes' in Georg Falck's *Idea boni cantoris* (1688), since he continued with a second eightfold set of four major and four minor keys corresponding to Falck's *fictus* or transposed modes, observing that they are 'no less usable and customary'. Mattheson concluded 'Whoever is desirous of knowing all tones must include the following', and completed the 24 by adding the remaining four major and four minor keys (cf Riemann, *Geschichte der Musiktheorie*, 2/1920, pp.454f). But shortly thereafter he returned to the 24 major and minor keys, first set out as a whole in 1711, only two years earlier, tonal relationships also represent vestiges of polyphonic modality; familiar and obvious is the IV(6-3)–V half-cadence in minor keys, a survival of the mode 4 cadence to the final with an upper leading note in the lower voice.

*(iii) The modal triad.* In his *Cartella musicale* Banchieri listed the cadential degrees for his eight modes (ex.22*a*) and his eight psalm-tone keys (ex.23). His cadential degrees, however, are not those of a partly traditional, partly empirical scheme of species boundary tones and repercussions; rather they follow Zarlino's doctrine stipulating the same three cadential degrees for each and every mode, regardless of its diatonic species: the final, the upper 5th, and the mediating 3rd. A set of any three things is called a 'triad', and the set of three modal cadential degrees may be called a 'modal triad'.

Claiming the degrees of the modal triad as the regular cadence points in every mode eliminated in theory (though by no means in practice) the variable distribu-. tions of cadential degrees that had differentiated polyphonic modes based on the eightfold system. Furthermore, just as an octave cannot be mediated in perfect consonances in more than two ways, which had always distinguished authentic modes from plagal modes, so a 5th cannot be mediated into 3rds in more than two ways, which came to distinguish major keys from minor keys. Granting overriding importance to the final, upper 5th, and mediant 3rd in all modes alike had the effect of calling attention to the modal triad common to all modes mediating their 5ths in the same way; concomitantly subordinated were most of the theoretically decisive modal distinctions supposed to arise from varying placements of the semitones in the modal octave.

Around 1600 German theorists began to manipulate simultaneities comprising three pitch classes as single entities, that is, as chords. Burmeister (1606, p.22) called them 'conjugate' and named the pitches *basis*, *media* and *suprema*. Harnisch (1608) offered for the first time a description of 6-3 chords as though they were inversions of 5-3 chords; his term for them is 'composite consonance', 'imperfect' and 'perfect' respectively, and he also discussed both doubling and open spacing in terms of octave duplication of chordal degrees (see Lester, 1974, p.110).

In the writings of Calvisius's student Johannes Lippius (published 1609–12), appears the expression 'harmonic triad' (*trias harmonica*), along with 'monad' (a single note in a melodic context) and 'dyad' (a two-note interval). Lippius not only defined 5-3, 6-3 and 6-4 chords as triads, however; he also defined each of the 12 modes in terms of the triad of its final, third and fifth degrees, defined the general 'lively' or 'sad' affect of each mode by the affect of its modal triad, and then finally listed the cadential degrees of modes in terms of that same modal triad, thus making the modal triad the single foundation of melodic identity, poetic affect and formal structure in each of the 12 modes.

Lippius's theories were transmitted to later generations through the publications of Johann Crüger, whose first significant work, *Synopsis musicae* (1630), borrowed not only its title but most of its language from Lippius's *Synopsis musicae novae* of 1612, simplifying or eliminating the theology and numerology and also expanding and clarifying the explanations. The *trias musica* is made up of three sounds, and (chap.8):

this harmonic Trinity is the true and correct root of the *unitrisona* [one sound in three pitches] . . . it is twofold. One is natural, perfect, noble, and suave [and Crüger added] having the major 3rd below the minor 3rd. . . . The other is imperfect and soft [*mollior*]. . . . Each harmonic triad has its species, now native, now fictive through chromatic notes. [see ex.25*a* and *b*]. . . . Other species of triad . . . [see ex.25*c*].

Ex.25

(a) natural triad, native and fictive species

(b) soft triad

(c) other species of triad

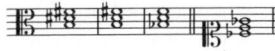

(d) the modal triad and authentic and plagal modes

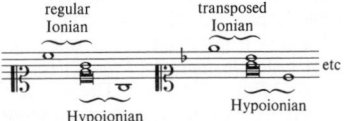

Crüger grouped the modes by the species of triad:

The modes, because of the proper and individual harmonic triad that each has, are either natural, consisting of a natural harmonic triad, or soft [*molliores*], consisting of a soft triad. Ionian, Lydian, Mixolydian are natural; Dorian, Phrygian, Aeolian are soft.

They are either authentic and primary, or plagal and secondary, by virtue of the 4th conjoined to the harmonic triad. . . . If the 4th is placed above the harmonic triad to complete the ambitus of an octave it will represent an authentic and primary mode . . . if below, a plagal and secondary mode [see ex.25*d*].

Crüger then ascribed poetic content to each mode according to two hierarchic criteria, the modal triad and the scale type (chap.11):

The nature of each mode follows the nature of its fundamental triad [*naturam radicis unitrisonae*], and of its intervals – tones and semitones disposed in the ambitus of an octave – by which the modes are distinguished from each other.

Thus the one is vigorous and cheerful – Ionian extremely so, Lydian enchantingly, Mixolydian moderately – and the other is soft, weak, sad, serious – Dorian moderately so, Aeolian less so, Phrygian completely.

The primary, secondary and tertiary cadential functions handed down from the latter part of the 16th century are now mechanically assigned (as in Zarlino) to the lowest (and 'final degree'), the highest and the median parts of the harmonic triad; the foreign cadences (*peregrinae*) 'arise irregularly, from the harmonic triad of another mode' (chap.15).

Varying combinations of elements from Glarean's modal doctrines and Lippius's doctrines as promulgated by Crüger continued to appear in German textbooks throughout the 17th century. The 12-mode doctrine, however, was never amalgamated with any other theory of modal or tonal structure; unlike the Italian modal theories it was not gradually transformed and merged into an evolving tonal theory. It survived as an antiquarian anachronism – but it also survived as well in one kind of musical practice, the Lutheran service, as can be observed in many of Bach's chorale settings and elaborations. Both the doctrine and the practice of Glarean's 12 modes at that time are summarized in J. G. Walther's

*Musicalisches Lexicon* (1732, p.409):

Modus musicus is the way of beginning a song, continuing it correctly within fixed limits, and ending it suitably. The Greeks principally had 12, namely six chief and as many collateral modes . . . only the Greek names survived, and they are applied to the diatonic melodies placed on the following six keys: D, E, F, G, A, and C . . . to know this doctrine is indispensable particularly to organists, since they have mostly to do with chorale songs, among which ever so many have been set and handed down in those old modes.

Walther listed five to ten familiar German chorale tunes under ten of Glarean's modes; he rejected Lydian and Hypolydian, quoting Glarean at length on the point.

*See also* HARMONY, § 3.

### IV. Modal scales and folksong melodies

1. Modal scales as a new musical resource. 2. Modal scales and melody types in Anglo-American folksong: (i) Folksong scholarship and the modes (ii) Melody type in Anglo-American folksong (iii) Mode as musical property versus mode as category.

1. MODAL SCALES AS A NEW MUSICAL RESOURCE. To musicians in the early 19th century mode meant chiefly the major or minor scale; otherwise 'mode' could designate a 'Greek mode', which meant one of Glarean's 12 authentically or plagally mediated octave species. The German term for mode and key alike was *Tonart*; to distinguish Greek modes from major keys one used Glarean's names, for example *Ionische Tonart* ('Ionian mode') as opposed to *C Dur* ('C major'). The distribution of semitones in Glarean's Ionian (or Iastian) mode is the same as that in the major scale, and his Aeolian coincides with the minor mode of tonal music with the sixth and seventh degrees lowered, as they normally were in descent. By 1800 it had come to be believed that the major and minor modes were the result of historical reduction of a primitive welter of scales to their purified essences. Koch's *Musikalisches Lexikon* (1802) concludes a discussion of 12 modes with the observation that 'our two modern modes are the descendants of the old Ionian and Aeolian'. A century later Heinrich Schenker attributed 'the reduction of those many systems to only two' to the 'instinct and experience' of 'the artist' (*Harmonielehre*, 1906, Eng. trans., ed. O. Jonas, 1954/R1973, p.45).

The teachings of 19th-century theory on the whole began with the diatonic major and minor scales as their didactic foundation. Composers too thought in terms of scales when – under the influence of Romantic fashions – they wanted to evoke a Gothic atmosphere and antique mystery. Beethoven, expressing his thanks to God for a recovery from illness in the String Quartet op.132, set a churchly, prayerful mood by composing a four-part chorale-like movement 'in the Lydian mode'. But strange scales were useful not only for local colour; they also provided novelty. Beethoven's composition was an experiment as well as an evocation.

Another 19th-century Romantic fashion that led ultimately in the direction of strange scales was a yearning after the state of nature as expressed in 'the folk'. In its earliest French and German phases the concomitant interest in folksong added little to the purely tonal resources of the urban composer, but with the growth of nationalist enthusiasm, internationally known musicians originally from outlying European regions began to think of native rural and archaic musical practices in their homelands with an ear attuned not just to their patriotic virtue but to their novelty as well. Exotic scales could be made to generate flamboyant harmonies. The

occasional melodies with raised fourth degrees or lowered supertonics in Chopin's (Polish) mazurkas, the use of gypsy-like melodies with exotic scales in Liszt's *Hungarian Rhapsodies* come easily to mind as instances of patriotism and piquancy combined. But the experimental utility of strange scales went deeper than patriotism with Liszt. In an abstract work like the Sonata in B minor, for example, Liszt's technique of thematic transformation was consistently and rigorously applied. The opening notes of the sonata comprise simply a descending octave scale; throughout the work Liszt made use of a half dozen different transformations of the descending scale idea, which of course produce a half dozen different scale types, from which he realized every drop of potential for novel harmonizations.

With the emancipation of Russian and Scandinavian composers from the domination of Italian and German musicians, added to the continuing desire for national musical expression in the eastern European empires of Russia and Austria, the fondness for 'modal' harmonies made available by ethnic scales grew apace. To the repertory of modal novelties arising from European sources were eventually added new sounds from oriental outposts of European imperialism like Russian Turkestan and Dutch Indonesia, as well as from the Ottoman Levant. The enthusiasm for exotic scales as a new musical resource in time led to an eclectic attitude welcoming creolization and homogenization of musical styles. The preface to a collection of harmonizations of *Mélodies populaires de Grèce* by Bourgault-Ducoudray is quoted approvingly by Cecil Sharp (1907, p.52):

we have forced ourselves to preserve in the accompaniment the character of the mode in which the melody is cast . . . we have directed our efforts to enlarge the circle of the modalities of polyphonic music. . . . Eastern music, till now exclusively melodic, will start upon a new harmonic career; Western harmonic music, hitherto restricted to the use of two modes, the major and minor, will escape at last from its long confinement.

Throughout the 19th century experimentation with so-called modal scales and modal harmonies remained firmly based on the assumption that successions of simultaneously sounding notes were the basic building-blocks of art music, whether those harmonies were the simple consonant triads of Beethoven's op.132 'Song of thanks' or the strange harmonies of Musorgsky's *Boris Godunov* which Rimsky-Korsakov tried to correct. The coherence of 'classical' European ensemble music depends on certain quasi-linguistic conventions of harmonic succession – fundamental part-writing connections and cadential relationships – which governed structural relationships on the largest scale and in detail alike. Whether coherence in the large could or should survive an onslaught of exotic 'modal' harmonies in the small was moot. Two conflicting comments on Beethoven's 'Song of thanks in the Lydian mode' epitomize the relationship of exotic scales to European art music as it was seen at the turn of the 20th century. Schenker (1906) said no such relationship was possible (ed. Jonas, pp.60f):

He attacked his task in a spirit of orthodoxy, and, in order to banish F major once and for all from our perception, he carefully avoided any B-flat, which would have led the composition into the sphere of F major. He had no idea that behind his back there stood that higher force of Nature and led his pen, forcing his composition into F major while he himself was sure he was composing in the Lydian mode.

The English folksong collector Cecil Sharp applauded Beethoven's experiment, which he saw as a model for composers (1907, p.48):

The melody is harmonized exclusively with diatonic chords of the mode and without, of course, modulation. This is a typical example of genuine modal writing, and one which musicians would do well to study.

2. MODAL SCALES AND MELODY TYPES IN ANGLO-AMERICAN FOLKSONG. During the second half of the 19th century, while continental composers were becoming ever more interested in native peasant musical sources, English and American professional musicians remained dependent on the mainstream style as taught in continental conservatories. A few collections of British peasant songs with their melodies were published during this period by educated amateurs; one of the first was *Sussex Songs*, collected from farm people and privately printed in 1843 by John Broadwood, a grandson of the founder of Broadwood, the piano manufacturers. His niece Lucy Broadwood was one of the founders of the English Folk Song Society. Although notated tunes had occasionally appeared with the literary collections of ballads and popular lyrics that began to be published in the mid-18th century, it was with the publication of the *Journal of the Folk Song Society* from 1899 that extensive tune collections made by the members of the society began to provide sufficient material for serious musical study.

(*i*) *Folksong scholarship and the modes.* Professionally trained musicians and scholars were associated with the society from the outset. J. A. Fuller Maitland was one of the founders, and both Vaughan Williams and Percy Grainger published collections in its journal. For Vaughan Williams the contact with native folksong released a pent-up compositional creativity, as it had for other composers. Grainger, for his part, made the first attempt at a really precise notation of performing practice. His elaborately detailed transcriptions, made from wax cylinders, were published in no.12 of the journal in 1908.

(*a*) *Folksong and pseudo-Greek modes.* Grainger's preface to his transcriptions included a section on 'Folksong scales in the phonograph' in which he made some analytical observations about the modality of the songs: 'Of seventy-three tunes phonographed in Lincolnshire, forty-five are major and twenty-eight modal. . . . Most [of the latter] are in a mongrel blend of Mixolydian and Dorian' (p.156). Grainger summed up his observations by saying that (pp.158f):

the singers from whom I have recorded do not seem to me to have sung three different and distinct modes (Mixolydian, Dorian, Aeolian), but to have rendered their modal songs in *one single loosely-knit modal folksong scale* . . . consisting of:
Firstly – the *tonic, second, major and minor (or unstable) third, fourth, fifth, and flat seventh* . . .
Secondly – the *sixth*, which is generally major, though sometimes minor . . . and the *sharp, or mutable seventh*; which intervals do not, as a rule, form part of the bed-rock of tunes, but act chiefly as passing and auxiliary notes.

Grainger's grouping of his repertory into two basic classes, major as against modal, accords well with the fact that rural American singers even in much more recent times used to sing major tunes with instrumental accompaniment – 'chording' – and other tunes without. But Grainger's theory was very much at variance with the by then already conventional modal doctrines of the society – so much so that the editorial committee of the journal responded to his 'mongrel blend' observation in an editorial footnote. These doctrines are summed up in chapter 5, 'The Modes', of Cecil Sharp's *English Folk-song: some Conclusions* (1907). On the tunes of Grainger's second class, Sharp wrote (pp.36f):

The scales, upon which many English folk-tunes are constructed . . . are generally known as the Greek modes. . . . It has been customary to look upon the ancient modes as mere relics of a bygone day . . . but the recent discoveries of English folk-song have thrown a fresh flood of light upon the matter . . . for here are scores of melodies cast, it is true, in the old despised modes, yet throbbing with the pulse of life . . . such melodies as these cannot be quietly dismissed as archaic survivals. . . . Nor, again, are they to be confounded with the music of the church. Except for the fact that they happen to be cast in the same scales, they have but little in common with the melodies of plain-song.

Sharp continued with a summary exposition of the diatonic species of the octave, concluding with Glarean's modal names and the observation that 'amongst secular musicians the old scales are known by the pseudo-Greek names' (p.44). To the diatonic modal scales Sharp added the five octave species of the anhemitonic pentatonic scale (the general scale made up of minor 3rds separated alternately by one tone and a pair of tones). He observed that the anhemitonic pentatonic collection: 'is still used by the peasant-singers of Scotland and Ireland, and also by the natives of New Guinea, China, Java, Sumatra, and other Eastern nations. It is occasionally used in English folk-music' (p.44). In contradistinction to Grainger's modal theory, which was derived largely from observation, however limited, the modal theories of the Folk Song Society were at first based entirely on the conception of a set of pre-existing 'old scales . . . known [amongst secular musicians] by the pseudo-Greek names'. This of course accorded well with the Romantic idea of a living survival of some older and purer pre-Raphaelite music in what was left of the as yet uncorrupted rural countryside, and this flavour of quaintly antique peasant modalism is still very much a part of the folk music cult.

(*b*) *A new modal theory for Anglo-American folksong.* A truly creative contribution to the theory of modality in folk music of the United Kingdom was made by Annie Gilchrist in a brief 'Note on the Modal System of Gaelic Tunes' (*JFSS*, iv, p.150; and see ex.26). Gilchrist's scheme is based on the set of five anhemitonic pentatonic octave species, which she expanded to hexatonic and heptatonic octave species by filling in the minor 3rds. Her attitude towards modalism in general was fully rooted in the late 19th-century presuppositions embodied in Sharp's chapter on 'The Modes' in that the pentatonic scales are regarded as more 'primitive' (p.150) and the hexatonic scales 'form a convenient index to the modifications of the pentatonic scale on its way towards a seven-note system' (p.153). Nonetheless her scheme is in no way *a priori* but rather is empirically founded on the specific collection to which her 'Note' is appended. Furthermore, she made a point of the necessary distinction between 'tonic' and 'final'. At the same time she drew attention to the musical uncertainties inherent in this kind of modal theory, uncertainties consequent on its need to make an assignment of tonic function to some one degree of every tune, whether or not the 'true tonic' can be established (p.153):

No doubt there will be differences of opinion regarding classification in some of these tunes, especially those in which the modes are mixed, and certain others in which it is difficult to believe that the last note of the tune is the true tonic. . . . In examining the tunes in MS., there was also some uncertainty in certain cases as to where the tune really ended, owing to the fact of the song beginning with the chorus or refrain. [footnote] Some of these tunes, being of the 'circular' class, have *no* definite ending.

Gilchrist did not go so far as to suggest that some tunes might not have any definite tonic either, but she came closer here than any of those who followed her. The annotations to her table of modes (facing p.152; see ex.26) regarding strong and weak notes also testify to an extraordinary appreciation of the subtle importance of strong and weak degrees in a melody. She commented on modes 1-A, 2-A and 3-A that 'the E [marked *] is sometimes flattened in these three modes, more especially when occurring as the 7th degree of mode 3'. She also commented that 'The distinction between mode 1-A and mode 3-B, which appear to correspond in scale, lies in whether the 3rd or the 4th degree of the mode be an essential note, belonging to the original pentatonic framework'; and 'Similarly, in the case of mode 2-A and mode 4-B, the distinction lies in whether the 2nd or 3rd degree be the imported note'. Also 'The characteristic Highland mode formed by the filling-up of the gaps in mode 1 by E♮ and B♭ is distinct in tonality from the Mixolydian mode, whose scale it resembles; it corresponds more nearly to the Hypo-Ionian, owing to the prominence of F and A, its 4th and 6th degrees'.

Ex.26

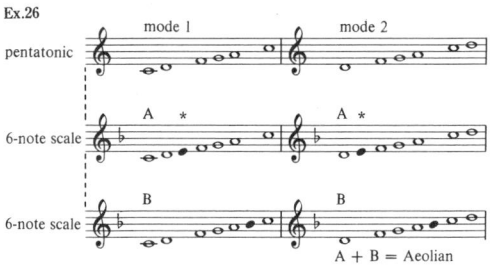

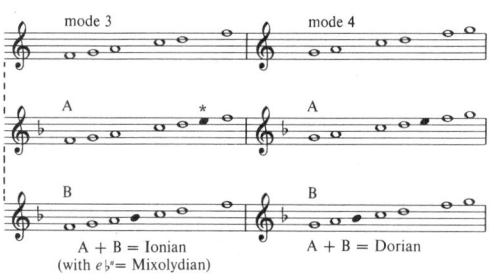

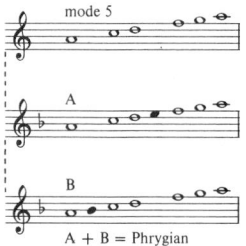

Gilchrist's modal scheme was adapted by Sharp for *English Folk Songs from the Southern Appalachians* in 1917 (see pp.xxx–xxxiv of the 'Introduction to the First Edition' in the second edition of 1932); the scheme thus adapted was thereafter cited or used by other studies, for instance Buchanan in 1939. The youngest descendant of

Gilchrist's combined pentatonic–hexatonic–heptatonic scheme is the 'modestar' of Bertrand Bronson (*The Traditional Tunes of the Child Ballads*, ii, pp.xi–xiii, first described in his article 'Folksong and the Modes', 1946; repr. in Bronson, 1969). Bronson's diagram is a seven-pointed star schematically representing the connections of pentatonic, hexatonic, and heptatonic scale types, in terms of contrasting or overlapping scale degree content, by means of interior angles and intersections.

*(ii) Melody type in Anglo-American folksong.*

*(a) Mode as a musical property.* Bronson's modal designation for the tunes in *The Traditional Tunes of the Child Ballads* (1959–72, i) and his description of the system (p.xxviii) were, as he put it, 'generally either ignored or charged a little impatiently with being rather cryptic, or "fuzzy", or imperfectly described' (ii, p.xi). Whether such criticisms are apt or otherwise, there is one thing that Bronson did not attempt to do with his modes, and that is to use them as a basis for classification of the melodies. Kolinski (1968), opening with the words 'Bronson's classification of tonal structures' (p.208), merely criticized the modestar's pentatonically based system for failing to be arranged like his own pentatonically based system for ordering and classifying notated melodies (Kolinski, 1961). Cazden (1971) at one point referred to the 'imaginative epicycles of Bronson' (p.47) along with Sharp's 'church-mode plan' (p.57), and both are taken as being among the 'accepted mode classifications'. Yet neither for Sharp nor for Bronson was 'mode' a tool for classifying melodies, as is for instance Kolinski's congeries of modal 'tint-complexes' (Kolinski, 1961 and elsewhere).

Scholars have usually failed to make a clear distinction between mode in connection with melodic type and mode as a classifying rubric. Herzog (1937), observing that 'typology and classification are merely different facets of the same procedure', nonetheless warned against confusing them. In Bronson's monumental collection of ballads the hundreds of tunes that there are for some of the ballads are grouped and subdivided not according to modes but according to the tune families to which they belong. Bronson's modal theories have not prevented him from ordering the tunes with the greatest sensitivity to their melodic typology. The only claim he made for his cyclic formulation of modal scales is that 'the solid connections of the whole system show us how, in the chances of oral transmission, the same basic tune may pass from mode to mode almost imperceptibly' (ii, p.xiii). For Bronson, as for Sharp before him, 'mode' was an inherent musical property. As Sharp put it: 'Each of the modes has its own set of intervals from which it derives an individuality as characteristic and distinct as that of the major or minor. . . . The character of every melody is, in part, derived from the mode in which it is cast' (1907, p.47).

*(b) Tune families.* Like the construction of modal theory, the consciousness of tune relationship has its roots in the work of the English Folk Song Society. Samuel P. Bayard observed of Gilchrist that she 'has, almost uncannily, the faculty that discerns the basic tune in its persistent phrasal pattern, contour, intervals, and diagnostic formulae' (1953, p.128). The collectors were well aware that the existence of different tunes for the same text and the singing of different texts to very

similar tunes betokened tune 'types' or 'styles' at several levels of resemblance, and the pages of the *Journal of the Folk Song Society* are replete with references to such tune resemblances by the name of some particularly well-known tune of the kind. More recently the writers most concerned with the theory of tune relationships have been Bronson and, above all, Bayard.

The term 'tune family' was first used consistently by George P. Jackson, but it is indelibly associated with Bayard's name as a result of a series of papers on tune families stretching over three decades. From the outset Bayard dealt with no abstractions not inferable from the tunes. His intention was 'to identify specific melodies in as many of their variant forms as possible' (1950). In the process of attempting to isolate factors common to tunes that singers, collectors and scholars with a wide acquaintance with folksong tunes agree to be related, he arrived at a certain number of important factors, no one of which is universally consistent in tunes of the same family, but many of which can be observed to cluster and form melodic prototypes. Among his observations on the relatedness of tunes is that 'the mode in which an air happens to be cast of course means nothing' (1939, p.125). In the same paper he asserted that 'the number of separate tunes is not large . . . the well-known tunes in the British folk repertory [are] about fifty-five in number' (p.124), and he suggested three central factors in tune resemblance, namely, contour, important degrees of the scale, and stereotypical motifs (pp.125f):

[1] consistently parallel melodic lines . . . are much more important than any similarity in modal or rhythmic features
[2] strongly accented . . . diagnostic tones
[3] closely related melodic formulae of progression and cadence

He went on to observe in more general terms that:

the problems of variation can never be solved by thinking in terms either of independently composed tunes in great numbers, falling into similar conventional lines or of mere rearrangements and recombinations of stock musical phrases. . . . The versions resemble each other in ways too deep and too intricately detailed to be accounted for in either manner.

Over the subsequent decades Bayard refined, elaborated, and demonstrated the theoretical premises here set forth, without needing to modify them in any essential way. The specific number of tune families suggested varies trivially; in 1953 he wrote that 'over forty such tune-families are current' (1953, p.132), and went on to discuss seven of them thoroughly. In his 'Prolegomena to a Study of the Principal Melodic Families of Folksong' (1950, repr. 1961) Bayard developed his 1939 outline of the principal factors in tune resemblance in great detail, and mentioned yet another number of tune families: 'no fewer than thirty-five' (p.115). In the same article he referred to three hierarchical levels of tune relationship: 'tunes, tune-versions, and tune-families' (p.118). Bayard's one really extensive comparative analysis, 'Two Representative Tune Families of British Tradition' (1954), is a full and convincing demonstration of his command.

Another study dealing directly with tune families is Bronson's 'Some Observations about Melodic Variations' (1950; rewritten in 1954 and so repr. in Bronson, 1969), and of course Bronson's grouping of tunes under each ballad in *The Traditional Tunes of the Child Ballads* is an epic demonstration of results of the tune family approach. Charles Seeger's 'Versions and Variants of the Tunes of "Barbara Allen"' (1966) is a sophisticated discussion and analysis of two of the tune families associated with this ballad. (In Bronson, ii, four tune families for 'Barbara Allen' are represented by over 200 individual tunes.) The 30 notated tunes analysed by Seeger are transcriptions from the holdings of the Archive of American Folk Song (Library of Congress) and may be heard on their recording AAFS L54.

Ex.27 shows skeleton outlines of six versions of the tune 'Demon Lover', taken from among those included by Sharp for two Child ballads in his *English Folk Songs from the Southern Appalachians* (2/1932). Versions of this tune sung to some other Child ballads may be seen in the same collection: 4-F, H, I ('Lady

Ex.27

(a) 94-F

(b) 94-A

(c) 35-R

(d) 35-P

(e) 35-L

(f) 35-C

Isabel'), 7-H ('Earl Brand'), 13-G ('Edward'). Despite the apparent variety in scale type and several striking deviations of contour and emphasis they are patently the same tune in all but the narrowest sense.

(*iii*) *Mode as musical property versus mode as category*. Bayard's '35' or 'over 40' or '55' tune families are certainly comparable in order of magnitude with Gevaert's 47 *thèmes*, in contrast to the fixed number of modes in Gilchrist's, Sharp's or Bronson's systems, or in the eightfold system. But even Bronson has not proposed his system of modes as a set of superordinate categories for the tune families corresponding to the role of the eightfold system for Gevaert's *thèmes*. So far the modes of Anglo-American folksong, whatever they may be, have been treated by most of those who know the repertory best more as properties of individual items than as universal categories. All the same, there is a constantly recurring and obviously powerful urge to imbue all items believed to have a common mode with a common musical property so distinctive or so fundamental that it warrants claiming all those items as members of a modal category.

In the 20th-century interest in systematic modal order set alongside ever changing congeries of melodic types it is certainly not going too far to see a parallel to similar relationships that have arisen at least twice before: between the eightfold system and the antiphons in the 9th century; and between the eight or the 12 modes and vocal polyphony in the 16th century. The same kinds of musical results also seem to ensue: modern professional folksingers compose 'in the modes', as had the late medieval composers of tropes and rhymed offices, or the late 16th- and 17th-century composers of collections ordered by the eightfold system or by Glarean's or Zarlino's 12 modes.

### V. Mode as a musicological concept

1. Expansion and internationalization of the concept. 2. Modal entities in western Asia and south Asia: (i) Maqām (naghmah–gusheh–āvāz) (ii) Raga. 3. Modal entities in south-east and east Asia: (i) Paṭēt (ii) Chōshi.

1. EXPANSION AND INTERNATIONALIZATION OF THE CONCEPT. By the mid-18th century, 'mode' in European languages meant a collection of degrees of a scale (and its aggregate intervallic content) being governed by a single chief degree: a mode was a scale with a tonic, which was the last note of a melody or the root of a final triad. This is the sense in which the major and minor scales, as well as the so-called 'church modes', are still deemed 'modes', and it is with this sense that application of the term 'mode' to phenomena and practices in other musical cultures first appeared.

The earliest full-scale attempt to deal with a modal system in a living non-European musical culture was Sir William Jones's 'On the Musical Modes of the Hindoos', first published in 1792, translated into German in 1802 by Dalberg, and reprinted several times since then. He gave a systematic exposition, in terms of:

the variety of modes, or manners, in which the seven harmonic sounds [diatonic degrees of the scale] are perceived to move in succession, as each of them takes the lead, and consequently bears a new relation to the six others. . . . [Since] we find twelve semitones in the whole series, and, since each semitone may, in its turn, become the leader of a series formed after the model of every primary mode [diatonic octave species] we have seven times twelve, or eighty-four, modes in all.

Jones observed further that 'the Persians and the Hindoos (at least in their most popular system) have exactly eighty-four modes, though distinguished by different appellations and arranged in different classes'. As the last words imply, however, the number 84 is not necessarily obtained by multiplying the seven diatonic octave species by the 12 semitonal degrees of the total chromatic. That process may be seen as the theoretical basis of a Chinese system of 84 *diaw* (see §3(ii) below). The Persian theoretical 84 was merely one of a number of Perso-Arabic schemes, this one comprising the sum of 'twelve *makams* or *perdahs*, [plus] twenty-four *shobahs*, and forty-eight *gushas*' (p.134), a scheme partly related to older Perso-Arabic theories, and dimly reflected in present Persian practice. The Hindu 'most popular system' is arrived at through the 'families of the six rāgas . . . each of whom is . . . wedded to five rāginīs . . . and father of eight . . . sons' (p.146), so that the Hindu 84 arises from six groups of 14 'modes' each, each group of 14 comprising one raga plus five raginis plus eight sons. But this too was only one of many such symmetrical classification schemes, by no means the most widespread, and it is the only one that adds up to 84.

In any case, individual Persian '*makams* or *perdahs*' and Hindu 'rāgas and rāginīs' in musical practice do not fit the 18th-century European abstract scale type 'mode' well. In fact almost a century earlier Jean Chardin had located the Persian entity at the melodic rather than the scalar end of the spectrum: '*Perdah* is the Persian term which means "[the] tune of [a] song" [*air de chanson*], and they distinguish the tunes by the names of their ancient kings, and by names of provinces' (*Voyages*, 1711, ii, p.114). Jones (see Tagore) himself was well aware that: '*rāga*, which I translate as mode, properly signifies a *passion* or *affection* of the mind' (p.142), and he knew of more specific ethic attributes as well.

It seems to have been Willard who first perceived the incompatibility of the standard European conception of 'mode' with the phenomenon of raga in Indian practice, in a perceptive discussion at the beginning of the chapter 'Of Rags and Raginees' in his *Treatise on the Music of Hindustan* (1834). The review in the *Journal of the Asiatic Society*, xxv (1834) sums it up: 'The author [Captain Willard] corrects Sir William Jones' rendering of *Rág* by the expression "*mode*" or "*key*" for which the Hindus have the distinct word t'hat [*thāt*]: *Rág* signifies rather "*tune*" or "*air*" '. But Willard in fact had not moved 'raga' quite wholly to the melodic end of the scale–tune spectrum: 'It is not strictly a tune . . . it is likewise not a raga, for able performers can adapt the words of a song to any Raginee; nor does a change of time destroy its inherent quality' (p.65). In short, Willard saw 'raga' as falling between the 19th-century European conceptions of 'mode' and 'tune', and he almost always left it untranslated.

The grey area between a comparatively undifferentiated scale type 'mode' and a comparatively precisely determined 'tune' became a matter of continuing interest for European musicological scholarship only in this century, at first as a result of greatly intensified work in the music of Eastern Christianity and Judaism. In the year before the outbreak of World War I a seminal article, 'L'octoëchos syrien' by the Benedictines Jeannin and Puyade in *Oriens christianus*, radically extended the scope of what had come to be understood as modal (p.277):

The modality of a musical item is principally determined by the arrangement of intervals on the scale. But in the case where the arrangement of intervals is the same for several modes, there are other empirical means for distinguishing the modality of a particular melody: return of certain cadences or of certain melodic formulae, preponderance of certain dominant degrees, and lastly, the final note.

In the same year an article along similar lines was published by Idelsohn, who devoted his life to the collection and study of Jewish music. He defined the Arabic term *maqām*, as he had come to understand it from his vantage-point in Jerusalem in the closing years of the Ottoman Empire:

In the musical sense, *maqām* is now used for 'tone'. . . . In the wider sense *maqām* in music signifies in effect *Musikweise*, that is, a musical type [*Musikart*] which makes use of its own proper degrees of the scale [*Tonstufen*] and motivic groups [*Motivgruppen*]. In no way may the concept *maqām* be identified with 'church mode' [*Kirchenmodus*] or even 'tonality' [*Tonart*]. For while these latter merely denote the scale in which tunes [*Weisen*] can be sung as desired, in *maqām* both scale type and melody type [*Tonleiter und Tonweise*] are comprised, and pre-eminently the latter. For in *maqām* the main emphasis is laid on the melody type [*Tonweise*], that is, on the organization and articulation of the tones [*Tongruppierung und Tongefüge*].

The definition of 'mode' that Idelsohn gave in 1929 is given earlier in this article; it differs in no essential particular from his definition of *maqām* in 1913.

In 1920 Egon Wellesz introduced Idelsohn's contrast into an article on the Serbian eightfold system (*osmoblasnyk*) (*ZMw*, ii, 1919–20, p.141):

Now if one examines the eight groups of songs according to the characteristics of the church tones [*Kirchentöne*], one concludes that no differentiation seemingly conformable to the nature of the eight modes can be worked out. On the contrary, it turns out that in each group of songs certain formulae appear which in turn are lacking in the other groups, and that the presence of just these formulae is the essential characteristic for whatever group a melody is to be assigned to. This however leads us on to the path that Idelsohn and Jeannin–Puyade have shown for the analysis [*Erschliessung*] of Arabic and Syrian songs.

Here the new notion of melodic type and the traditional notion of church mode are still thought of as separate, even opposed. But an increasing awareness of the importance of melodic formula in Byzantine chant in time led Wellesz to equate the individual members of the (Byzantine) eightfold system with their melody types (1961, p.326): 'The mode, we may therefore conclude, is not merely a "scale" but the sum of all the formulae which constitute the quality of an Echos'. The melody type phenomena observed in *maqām* and echos are proposed as members of a larger metacultural musical entity (p.325):

this principle of composition is of far greater importance than was at first thought. Further investigations have shown that it was not confined to the melodies of a few areas, but was the ruling principle of composition in Oriental music and, with the expansion of Christian music, spread over the whole Mediterranean basin.

The Indian raga and Perso-Arabic *maqām*, as well as the Byzantine echos, thus independently came to be seen by European musicians and musicologists as falling between or combining together, or both, scale type and melody type. Furthermore, each term has had its own musicological history of association with the term 'mode' of European languages.

Similar associations of the European term 'mode' with technical terms in Asian musical cultures still farther east are now widely accepted. For instance: '*Paṭĕt* is the Javanese system of classifying gamelan pieces, usually translated as mode' (Becker, 1972, p.160); 'these modes, or *chōshi* as they are known in Japanese' (Garfias, 1975, p.61). The association of such culturally and linguistically diffused terms as echos (Greek),

*maqām* (Arabic), *rāga* (Sanskrit), *paṭĕt* (Javanese), and *chōshi* (Japanese) with the much expanded European concept of mode has naturally led to an almost unquestioned assumption of some minimal underlying metacultural or scientific category 'modality', to which concepts and phenomena of specific musical cultures might be referable as special cases. For example, Mantle Hood, in *The Ethnomusicologist* (1971), wrote that:

in considering existing definitions of 'mode'. . . . We discovered that there were quite a few in print . . . [but] none of them could be applied on an international level. In fact, all of them taken together, contradictions aside, could not account for Indian raga, Javanese patet, Persian dastgah, and modal practices of other musical cultures. . . . After spending four or five months examining modal practices in various parts of the world, the Seminar was able to construct a definition . . . that rests on the assumption that mode itself is a continuum. [p.57]

Basic features of Mode seem to include the following: (1) a gapped scale . . .; (2) a hierarchy of principal pitches; (3) the usage of . . . ornamental pitches; and (4) extra-musical associations. [p.324]

It is not clear, however, here or elsewhere, whether 'mode' in such a broad sense is an ontological or merely an epistemological object, an inherent musical property or a scientific paradigm. In the following sections several terms in Asian languages that have been associated with 'mode' and 'modality' are discussed with the aim of highlighting the similarities and, even more, the differences in the musical phenomena to which they refer in the different cultures.

The four kinds of modal entity to be compared are not only drawn from four different Asian musical cultures or genres but also represent four different points on the modal spectrum between abstract scale and fixed tune. The Middle Eastern *maqām* and particularly the Indian raga are nearer the tune end; the *paṭĕt* of Javanese gamelan music and particularly the *chōshi* of Japanese court music (gagaku) are nearer the scale end. But they differ strikingly in some much less abstract aspects of their performing practice. First, most obviously and most significantly, the art of western Asian and south Asian musical high cultures is pre-eminently the art of the virtuoso vocal or instrumental soloist, while the gamelan music of Java and the gagaku of Japan are for ensembles including many different types of melody instrument (sometimes including solo or choral vocal parts), performing simultaneously most of the time. Second, the number of named modal entities in the western and south Asian spheres, the number of *maqām* or ragas, runs to many dozens, even hundreds; the sets of central Javanese *paṭĕt* or Japanese *chōshi* number fewer than ten entities each. Finally – and perhaps subsuming the dichotomies of tune versus scale, solo versus ensemble, and many versus few – the western Asian and Indian modal entities are primarily compositional–improvisational models, while the south-east and east Asian modal entities are primarily categories of a repertory.

## 2. MODAL ENTITIES IN WESTERN ASIA AND SOUTH ASIA.

(i) *Maqām* (*naghmah–gusheh–āvāz*).

(*a*) The basic terms. *Maqām* (plural *maqāmāt*) is an Arabic word meaning 'place'. Its modal meanings ultimately derive from a basic meaning of 'tone' or 'degree of the scale' – that is, a particular place in the general scale of all pitches available in the system. In Arabic-speaking countries of the eastern Mediterranean, *maqām* has become the technical term for 'modal entity', but the word *naghmah* ('tune', 'voice') is also used in this sense (D'Erlanger, v, pp.69ff). In Persia the operative terms for a modal entity are *gusheh* (plural *gusheh-hā*) or *āvāz*, depending on the scope and systematic importance of the modal entity in question; *maqām*, and the word 'mode' as well, refer only to scale type (Farhat, 1965, pp.37f). *Naghmah* is sometimes used as equivalent to *gusheh* (Khatschi, 1962, pp.87–116), or to *āvāz*. The Persian word *perdeh* has passed out of use as a term for modal entity; it means literally 'curtain' or more generally 'partition', and from this last comes its continuing musical sense of 'fret' and now 'key' (of a piano). *Perdeh* in this sense parallels the basic meaning of *maqām*, both of them referring to a determined position in an overall background system of available pitches.

(*b*) Modal entities and the general scale. In Arab, Turkish and Persian musical cultures alike the modal entities are made up of a limited number of degrees of the scale which are seen as being drawn out of a general background collection (D'Erlanger, v, p.99):

> The general scale [*échelle générale*] of sounds of Arabic music is capable of giving rise to an infinitude of particular complexes [*gammes particulières*]. The sounds which compose each of these complexes constitute the material substance of a particular melody. The intervallic relationships which separate the sounds in their natural succession constitute the physical form of this substance, and the procedures of melodic succession [*processus du mouvement*, i.e. *ṭawr al-naghmah*] across the scale whose sounds form the degrees of the scale constitute the animating principle which enlivens that form. Each of these complexes [*gammes*] – composed of a succession of sounds linked by predetermined melodic [i.e. intervallic] relationships and ruled by a predetermined motion – constitutes for the Arabic musicians of our time a special mode, a *naghmah*. [See also Touma (1976), pp.88ff.]

In Arabic and Turkish usage every degree of the general scale has its own name. The fundamental collection comprises two octaves, from *yakāh* to *ramal tūtī*, which can be extended outwards. Within any octave are 14 separately named degrees of the scale, which correspond roughly to the 12 semitones of the European chromatic plus two 'neutral' degrees. Most octave-equivalent degrees have different names; for instance, the upper octaves of the degrees in the perfect 4th span *'irāq, kawāsht, rāst, zirkūlah, dūkāh, kurdī* and *sikāh* – *b-½♭, b, c', d♭', d', e♭', e-½♭'* – are called *'awj, hihuft, māhūr* (or *kardan*), *shāhnāz, muḥayyir, sunbulah* and *buzurk*. In addition to these 14 separately named principal degrees, up to as many as ten auxiliary modifications (named as 'low' or 'high' plus one of the standard names) are deemed to be possible within an octave span.

Not only in Turco-Arabic but also in Persian usage European note names and note symbols, with modifications, have come into use; in Iran the traditional Arabic note names (most of which are Persian words) have passed out of use altogether (but see Huart in *EMDC*, I/v). Arabic usage equates the global collection from *yakāh* to *ramal tūtī* with the double octave *g–g''*, while the Turkish notational convention makes it *d'–d'''*. Persian conventions are of the same order, but the actual letter notes used depend on the instrument and its tuning. In no case do the European names imply any exterior absolute pitch standard; like the Guidonian diatonic, the general scale is the total background from which any particular foreground modal complex is conceived to have been drawn.

(*c*) Modal nucleus and modal complex. The ambitus of a *naghmah, maqām* or *gusheh* is variable, even ambiguous. D'Erlanger (v, pp.69ff) complained that:

> The Arabic musicians of our time seem to confound the idea of genus [*genre*, Arabic *jins*, by which D'Erlanger meant the span of a tetrachord

or pentachord] with that of mode: the same term *naghmah* serves them, in effect, to denote either the one or the other. ... Every melodic succession, whatever its scope, is for these musicians a *naghmah* ... this term *naghmah* (melody or emission of the voice), employed in our time to denote any melodic conglomeration [*toute ensemble mélodique*] must originally have denoted genus, and by extension it would subsequently have been attributed to the modal complexes [*gammes modales*] of which the genera are the constituent elements.

It is indeed the case that single modal nuclei of fairly limited scope are combined together into composite modal complexes of much greater scope, and that a modal composite may have the same name as one of its modal units. To the acculturated ear, however, any musical entity with a recurrently recognizable individuality has an identity and can have a modal name. Complexes of three or four notes may be so characterized by intervallic configuration and melodic direction alone that they are easily recognized and hence named. Ex.28 illustrates the modal entity *segāh* (Arabic *sikāh*) as heard in each of the three musical cultures. The

Ex.28
(a) Arabic (D'Erlanger, v, p.307)
*taqsīm* in [*naghmah*, i.e. *maqām*] *sikāh*

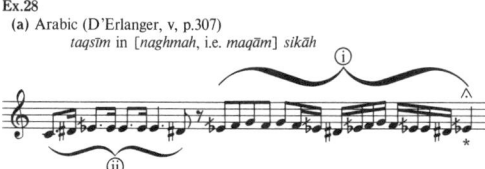

(b) Turkish (Bey, in *EMDC*, I/v, 3042; signature modernized after Signell, 1977, p.74a)
*aksak-semái* in *makam segāh*

(c) Persian (Farhat, 1965, p.104)
formula for a *darāmad* in [*dastgāh*] *segāh*

modal entity is named for the degree *sikāh* (marked *) of the general scale, which characterizes it, and with which any presentation of it must conclude; the degree of the scale *segāh* is written as *e-½♭', b-½♭'* and *e-½♭'* (or *a-½♭'*) in the Arabic, Turkish and Persian staff notations respectively. This particular degree is one of the 'neutral' degrees, forming intervals of roughly three-quarters of a tone with its adjacent upper note in Arabic and Persian music; it forms roughly a quarter-tone interval with its adjacent lower note in the Arabic example (*d♯'* to *e-½♭'*); in Turkish music this interval is roughly a semitone (*a♯'* to *b-½♭'*). In the Persian modal nucleus *segāh*, the adjacent lower note to the final is often omitted, as in ex.28. A general characteristic for *segāh* is variability of pitch level, both within and across musical cultures, vis-à-vis system-framing notes such as *yakāh*, *rāst* and *nawā* (*g–c'–g'* in ex.28*a*, *c*; or *d'–g'–d''* in ex.28*b*). Turkish *segāh* (*b-½b'*) is a just major 3rd above *rāst* (*g'*), while in Arabic styles the interval *rāst-sikāh* (*c'–e-½b'*) is neither major nor minor. The same interval in Persian music is also always a 'neutral' 3rd, but with noticeable differences from performer to performer.

The unusual intervallic complex in Arabic and Persian music formed by the degree *segāh* and the two degrees of the scale above it – a neutral step and a whole step – is sufficient to identify the modal entity *segāh*. In the Arabic *naghmah* of *sikāh* the tiny fluctuations between the degree *sikāh* and its adjacent lower note confirm the identification, as do the corresponding full semitone fluctuations in the Turkish *makam segâh*. Also characteristic of the latter is the 'stereotyped motif' (*g'–a♯'–b-½b'*) connecting the degrees *rāst* and *segāh* (ex.28*b* (ii), and cf Signell, 1977, p.127); this figure is also found in the Arabic *naghmah sikāh* (ex.28*a* (ii), *c'–d♯'–e-½b'*). The comparable element in the Persian *segāh* is *c'–e-½b'*, *c–e-½b'*, *e-½b'* (ex.28*c* (ii)); this is the *forūd* of *segāh*, the cadential motif, which is used to conclude presentations of the modal nucleus *segāh*, and to mark returns to it when it forms a part of a larger modal complex.

In addition to intervallic structure and occasional use of a stereotyped motivic tag, a modal entity such as *sikāh/segâh* in Arabic and Turkish music is also distinguished from other modal entities by its position in the system at large. The only other places where the unusual intervallic configuration of *sikāh/segâh* can occur are at the 4th below and 5th above, around the degree *'irāq/irak* (*b-½b'* Arabic, *f♯'* Turkish) or its upper-octave equivalent *'awj/eviç*. But when a given scalar type is developed in performance at another place in the general scale it is usually heard as another modal entity, with another name. The general term for a new (Turkish) *makam* generated by transposition of a modal complex to another position in the general scale is *şet* (Arabic *shaṭṭ*, 'being distant'). In D'Erlanger (v, pp.158ff) scale types and sample *taqsīm* for *maqām 'irāq* and *maqām 'awj* are shown; Signell (1977, pp.180, 179) defines *makam irak* and *makam eviç* as '*segâh*-on-F♯'. In ex.30*a* Turkish and Arabic *irak/'irāq* (as part of a composite *maqām*) are also shown as a transposition of *segâh/sikāh*. Two modal entities transpositionally related as *'irāq* and *sikāh* are called in Arabic *maqāmāt mutashābihah* ('conformable' *maqām*).

For a detailed study of the Arabic modal entity *sikāh*, showing how the three-note modal nucleus *e-½b'–f'–g'* is expanded into a composite modal complex, see Reichow (1971). Good recordings illustrating the modal entity *segāh* in each of the three cultures are *UNESCO Tunisia* (Bärenreiter BM 30 L 2008, Arabic, side A, band 3); *Musique traditionelle turque* (OCORA OCR 56, all four items on side B, Turkish); *Musique persane* (OCORA OCR 57, all of side B, Persian), and see the supplementary analysis in Sadeghi's review (1973, p.356).

(*d*) Turco-Arabic simple and mixed modal complexes. In Turkish usage, as in Arabic, the term *makam* (plural *makamlar*) designates any recognizable modal entity, whether a nuclear modal complex or a composite of several such nuclear complexes. For instance, ex.29 is a schematic outline of Turkish *makam sabâ* (reduced

from Signell, 1977, pp.62f). Ex.29*a* (i) shows the modal nucleus of *sabâ* (marked \*): (ii) and (iii) are the upward extensions of *sabâ* (note that the upward extension does not produce octave equivalents of the modal nucleus). Ex.29*b* is a further reduction of the *makam* structure, showing only component degrees of the scale, with prominent degrees singled out. Both the simple modal nucleus (which appears often in mixtures with other named *makam*) and the composite modal entity are designated by the same name, *sabâ* (see also D'Erlanger, v, pp.282f).

Ex.29

(a) modal composition of *makam sabâ*
   (i) *sabâ*        (ii) extension        (iii) optional further extension

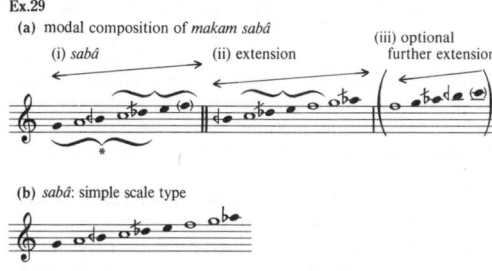

(b) *sabâ*: simple scale type

Turkish *makam* (and their Arabic equivalents) can be mixed together, in two different ways. A *makam* in either kind of mixture need not be 'complete'; it is sufficient that enough motivic or intervallic individuality, or both, be present for a modal nucleus to be identified. Ex. 30*a* (after Signell, 1977, p.108) illustrates the last line of a *şarki* of the Turkish *makam beste-nigâr* (*sabâ* plus

Ex.30

(a) Turkish: *makam beste-nigâr*
   voice

   instrument

\**makam sabâ*   †*makam irak*      *makam segâh*, see ex.28*b*

= common scale degrees
↓ *karar* (final)

(b) Arabic: *taqsīm* in *bastah-nigâr*

\**şabā*    †*'irāq*

= common scale degrees
↓ *qarār* (final)

*irak*); illustrations from the Arabic equivalent, the beginning and end of *taqsīm* in *bastah-nigār*, appear in ex.30*b* (after D'Erlanger, v, p.171). (In Persian music *basteh-negâr* is not a modal entity but an item characterized by its performing style.) The Turco-Arabic *makam beste-nigâr* is composed of the modal nucleus of *makam sabâ* placed above that of *makam irak*, with which *sabâ* has three degrees of the scale in common. A *makam* of this sort is called in Turkish *mürekkep* (Arabic *murakkab*) 'composed, compounded'. The more common Arabic term is *tarkīb*, 'composition, mixture'.

Ex.31 (after Signell, 1977, p.83) is a Turkish instance for another kind of combination of modal nuclei. The *makam* is *sabâ*, but in the third line the modal nucleus is changed to that of *makam hicaz*, which normally appears at the same pitch level as *sabâ* but has a completely different intervallic structure. In Arabic the word *tarkīb* ('composition, mixture') is also used for this kind of modal change; the Turkish term is *geçki* (Signell, 1977, p.179).

Jürgen Elsner (1973) fully discussed *maqām* as scale step, modal nucleus and what are here called simple and composite *maqām*. Elsner used 20th-century Arabic theorists as the basis for discussing general principles and illustrated with published and recorded examples of *maqām bayyātī*. His examples extend from a piece using the modal nucleus *bayyātī* only minimally to compositions and improvised *taqsīm* of *maqām bayyātī* as a composite *maqām* using several other modal nuclei in the course of its development. Touma (1976) took a different approach to the *maqām* phenomenon, but also used *bayyātī* as his point of reference.

*See also* ARAB MUSIC, §I, and TURKEY. For the influence of *maqām* on Syrian Orthodox, Assyrian, Chaldean and Maronite modal systems *see* SYRIAN CHURCH MUSIC, §3.

(*e*) Modal nucleus and modal complex in Persian music. In the limited sense of modal nucleus the Turkish *makam*, Arabic *maqām* or *naghmah*, and Persian *gusheh* are all equivalent. But *makam* (*maqām*) and *naghmah* also refer to larger modal complexes, simple or compound, while in Persian the term *gusheh* ('corner') can refer modally only to a unitary modal nucleus. A larger complex of such modal nuclei is best designated in Persian by the term *āvāz* ('voice' or 'note', hence linguistically equivalent to Arabic *naghmah*).

However, both *gusheh* and *āvāz* have formal as well as modal senses, and the senses are easily and naturally confused.

*Gusheh* (plural *gusheh-hā*) can refer to any item in one of the traditional series (*radīf*) of musical items called a *dastgāh* ('organization, system'). Some *gusheh* names denote modal structures (see below), some denote fixed compositions in a particular style of performance; in short, the term *gusheh* can mean any item in a traditional series, as well as a nuclear modal entity.

*Āvāz*, though it refers to a composite modal complex of several unitary modal nuclei, is at the same time often synonymous with *dastgāh*, while *dastgāh* in turn is sometimes conceived as a modal entity. Hence the expressions *dastgāh-e chahārgāh* and *āvāz-e chahārgāh* both mean either the major unitary modal complex *chahārgāh*, or a whole set of *gusheh* traditionally performed with *chahārgāh* at their head as the principal modal nucleus. The expression *gusheh-e chahārgāh* would designate any *gusheh* (either modal nucleus or item of performing style) belonging to the *dastgāh* dominated by the modal nucleus *chahārgāh*, but it would not mean *chahārgāh* itself.

The dominant modal nucleus of a *dastgāh*, such as *segāh* or *chahārgāh*, is developed in its fullest form in unmeasured improvisatory items called *darāmad* ('introduction, entrance, prelude') which are presented at or near the beginning of the performance. The *darāmad* corresponds in style and developmental technique to the Turco-Arabic *taqsīm*; therefore *darāmad-e chahārgāh* is a *gusheh* of *dastgāh-e chahārgāh*, showing the modal nucleus *chahārgāh* in a quasi-improvisatory and freely pulsed guise. After one or more *darāmad* in the dominant modal complex, and perhaps after several minor *gusheh* – items in other performing styles but using the same modal complex – a shift is made to a new modal nucleus at a higher pitch level, which will also be a named *gusheh*. This second modal *gusheh* may be concluded by a return to the *forūd* (cadential formula, cadential degree) of the *āvāz*, or may move still higher into yet another modal *gusheh*. This procedure of ordering *gusheh* at successively higher levels of register is generally followed, though many deviations and interruptions are possible.

Ex.32 gives a conspectus of most of the principal modal nucleus *gusheh* of *dastgāh-e chahārgāh*, the

Ex.31

lines 1, 2, 4: *makam sabâ*    line 3: *makam hicaz*

'system of [the dominant modal complex] *chahārgāh*', based on Farhat (1965, pp.115ff), Nettl (1972, *Daramad* and 'Notes'), and where relevant (marked *) the *santūr* performance by Nasser Rastegar-Nejad (Lyrichord LLST-7165). The *gusheh* are aligned to show the nuclei in overlapping registers. Also marked are the modal functions: Ā = *āqāz* ('initial'), F = *forūd-e kāmel* ('final'), S = *shāhed* ('predominant'), and Ī = *īst* ('temporary stopping-note'). Two alterations of the basic scale type can occur, in the *gusheh mūyeh* and *hesār*; these are usually described as a transposition of the *chahārgāh* scale type a 4th and 5th higher respectively. This is intervallically correct, but in fact the altered degrees of the scale work rather as variant ancillary degrees in the same register; there is no return of *chahārgāh* motivic material in a higher register. In the *gusheh hesār* there is great variability of tuning of the putative altered degrees (Nettl, 'Notes', 1972, pp.177f), and in Nasser Rastegar-Nejad's *santūr* version the degrees e♮′ and f♮′ of the principal scale type (as in *chahārgāh*) continue unaltered (and cf Nettl, 'Notes', 1972, pp.180, 192).

Ex.32

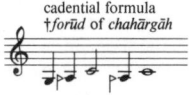

cadential formula
†*forūd* of *chahārgāh*

(*f*) Modulation. The term 'modulation' sometimes occurs in the literature on western Asian music; it is used in three different, often insufficiently distinguished, senses. All three senses can entail a change of *maqām/naghmah/gusheh*. (*i*) A modal nucleus is transposed as a whole to another pitch level in the general scale where it can fit (Arabic *shaṭṭ*, Turkish *şet*) without any internal changes of either intervallic structure or melodic emphasis. In effect, the key only has been changed, as in ex.30*a*, where *irak* is a transposition downward by a 4th of *segâh*. (*Irak* is notated for the instrumental echo as though it were an octave higher.) (*ii*) Both the inter-

vallic structure of a modal nucleus and its position in the general scale remain substantially the same but there is a change in melodic emphasis. This is a change of melody type (in Persian music it entails a change of *gusheh*), as in ex.32, *mokhālef* and the version of *hesār* with f♮′ and e♮′. In that case the modal individuality turns most obviously on the replacement of g′ as predominant and final with a-½b′. (*iii*) One modal nucleus is replaced by another with a different aggregate interval structure but spanning the same segment of the general scale and with the same principal degree. This is a change in scale type, a transformation, as in ex.31 where in the third line makam sabâ on a′ is replaced by makam hicaz on a′. In Arabic this process is designated by the general term *tarkīb*, whose Turkish equivalent is *geçki*; in the Persian system it is simply a change of *gusheh*. Any of these three procedures normally entails a change of modal name, but not always. The upward extension of makam sabâ shown in ex.29*a* (ii) involves changes of pitch level, scale type, and necessarily melody type, yet it is simply part of the larger domain of makam sabâ.

(*g*) Modal functions. Western Asian modal entities on the whole seem more easily viewed from the end of the scale–tune spectrum which concerns degrees of the scale than from that which concerns tune. To be sure, characteristic motifs often play identifying and formal roles: there is often an initial 'stereotyped motif', such as that heard at or near the beginning of *segāh* (see ex.28*a*, *c*, and Signell, 1977, pp.126f, g′-a♯′-b-½b′); the cadential *forūd* of a Persian *āvāz* is a vital element of large-scale formal shape. But on the whole, the pivotal notes of the modal nucleus, the directions of their stepwise connections, and their ornamenting arabesques play the major characterizing role.

Table 11 shows a comparative listing of some terms for the principal modal functions in Arabic, Turkish and Persian music. Note that a 'final' note ought no more than a 'predominant' note to be assumed to be a 'tonic'.

TABLE 11

|  | Arabic | Persian | Turkish |
|---|---|---|---|
| initial | āghāz mabdā' | āqāz | agaz giriş |
| predominant | ghammāz | shāhed | güçlü |
| medial stop | markaz | īst | muvakkat kaliş |
| subfinal | ẓahīr |  | yeden |
| final | qarār | [forūd-e kāmel] | karar |

The term 'tonic' normally implies that the degree in question has some sort of pitch-related governance over other degrees, a governance that goes beyond mere weight of recurrence ('predominance') or temporal position ('finality'). Words like 'repose' or 'termination' (*qarār*), or 'descent' or 'bottom' (*forūd*), do not of themselves suggest 'tonic'. They suggest, rather, that the modal function designated by them is determined by form and register, and not necessarily by constraints based on pitch relationships. A 'final' may in fact be harmonically stable and central, as it is in Persian *chahārgāh*, but it may also be weak and unstable, as it is in Persian *segāh*, where the 'predominant' function is prominent, and is not assigned to the same degree as the 'final' function.

(*h*) Modal systems. The Turkish *makam* now form an open-ended system of several dozen modal entities.

Signell (1977, p.16) suggested '60–70 makams recognized today'; Oransay (1966, p.91) cited a 19th-century Turkish source claiming 92 *makam* in common currency and 62 more not in common use. D'Erlanger (v, p.111) described and later exemplified 119 Arabic *naghmah* obtained and verified in 1932, but said that only 30 were well known, and still fewer in popular café music.

D'Erlanger's classification of his 119 modal entities follows a traditional procedure of grouping the *maqām* simply by their finals. He provided nine groups based on finals, but contemporary Arab theorists use only eight finals (Faruqi, 1974, p.94), from *g* up to *f'*. Another classification system was proposed in a report published by an Egyptian Government Committee in 1964 (see Faruqi, 1974, pp.86ff, 94ff). 46 basic *maqām* are grouped into 11 categories, according to the intervallic structure of the lowest tetrachord (*jins*); these categories in turn are divided in two according to *dalīl* ('method'), that is, according to whether the basic tetrachord has only tones, semitones, and augmented seconds (method I) or uses also 'neutral' tones (method II) (see Table 12).

TABLE 12

| 2 dalīl | I | | | | | II | | | | | |
|---|---|---|---|---|---|---|---|---|---|---|---|
| 11 jins | 1 | 2 | 3 | 4 | 5 | 1 | 2 | 3 | 4 | 5 | 6 |
| 46 maqām | (4) | (5) | (4) | (4) | (7) | (9) | (7) | (1) | (2) | (1) | (2) |

This three-level system has three significant characteristics: its primary level of 46 *maqām* comprises phenomena of actual practice; the criteria for distinguishing its categories at both superordinate levels are purely musical (albeit rather mechanical or even arbitrary); as a result, the system is on the whole non-symmetrical, and remains musically open-ended not only at the primary level but also potentially at the secondary level as well. One cannot be sure about the criteria for categorizing in older *maqām* systems, but the fact that most of the systems reported are wholly or partly symmetrical and evidently closed suggests that the classifying began with the system rather than with the phenomena, and that phenomena which did not fit well were sometimes either forced in or left out. The system reported by Jones (see §V, 1, above) is an extreme case: 12 *maqām*, 24 *shu'ba*, 48 *gusheh*, with each level double the previous level. Another one cited in Khatschi (1962, pp.46f) is symmetrical at the two superordinate levels of 12 *maqām* and 24 *shu'ba*, but the number of *naghmah* assigned to each *shu'ba* varies from two to ten, amounting to 139 in all, which suggests that empirical modal entities were involved at the primary level of the system.

12 entities in the highest category was the norm for Arabic-based theory, beginning with Ibn Sīnā in the 10th century, and bearing a set of names which remained constant as a whole, though with some variants and order changes. The set of 12 was handed on through Safi al-Dīn and his followers after the 13th century (when the term *maqām* was first attached to them) and on into the 18th century (Oransay, 1966, p.91). Both emotional affects and suitable times of day for performance are attributed to the 12 from the beginning. The 12 *maqām* of Al-Lādhiqī in the 15th century are further correlated not only with three general ethical categories (of Platonic origin) but also with the 12 zodiac signs and the four elements; his secondary *āvāz* are seven in number, one for each planet; his four *shu'ba* have only

the four elements, one each. At the primary level, though, there are evidently again real musical entities; the number of *tarkīb* ('mixtures') is said to be infinite in principle: 'in our time however there are about 30' (D'Erlanger, iv, pp.428ff).

While Arab and Turkish theorists in this century have tried to organize existing modal entities in rational categories, those who reconstituted Persian music in the first decades of the century preferred to rebuild and work from traditional assemblages of *gusheh* of all kinds, performing-style *gusheh* as well as modal nuclei. Their prime concern has been to assemble authoritative sequences of *gusheh* into larger systems, that is, to determine one or more series (*radīf*) for a small number of *dastgāh*. Present feeling about the standardized number of 12 *dastgāh* systems – seven primary and five secondary (called *āvāz* or *naghmeh*) – seems uncomfortably poised between adherence to an important traditional number, thus keeping the system closed, and allowing one or two important *gusheh* such as *shushtārī* to break away and perhaps begin to accrete secondary *gusheh* and ultimately form new *dastgāh* systems of their own, thus opening the system and breaking up its exterior symmetry. But at any rate there has as yet been no serious attempt actually to reclassify the over 200 *gusheh* of the various present-day traditions by scale type, or by any other arbitrary or logical criterion.

*See also* IRAN, §I.

(*i*) The central Asian systems. Similar to the 20th-century Persian set of 12 *dastgāh* are the remnants of central Asian court music suites going by the name of *shashmakom* ('six *maqām*'). The word *makom* here has the same sense as Persian *dastgāh*, that is, it designates a series of items called *shuba*. *Shu'ba* of course designates *makom* has two main divisions, a set of instrumental items followed by a set of vocal items. The second (instrumentally accompanied) vocal set comprises a series of items called *shuba*. *Shu'ba* of course designates in many traditional Perso-Arabic systems a modal entity or complex that is found on the classificatory level below *maqām* and *āvāz*; here the term *shuba* corresponds in form and function to the modern Persian *gusheh*. Some are chiefly characterized by performing style, but melodic recognizability is fundamental. A *shuba* is a melodic entity – and in some sense, then, a modal entity – but now a *shuba* is a fixed composition and no longer improvised. The characteristic beginning of a *shuba* from one of the six *makom* systems may well turn up as a subsequent subdivision of a *shuba* in another *makom*, or even elsewhere in the same *makom*. Such a quotation from a melodic entity normally belonging elsewhere is designated by the Persian word *namud* ('appearance'). For instance, there is a *shuba* in the Uzbek *makom dugāh* which is called *chārgāh*; most of it appears a 5th higher, modified in detail but clearly the same configuration, as the registral climax of the first vocal item in the *makom buzruk*. In this alien context the *shuba chārgāh* is referred to as a *namud-e-mukhayyar-e-chārgāh*: 'appearance of an excerpt of *chārgāh*' (Radjabī and Karamatov, 1966, pp.18ff, 52ff).

*See also* UNION OF SOVIET SOCIALIST REPUBLICS, §XI, 6.

(*ii*) Raga.

(*a*) The basic terms. The two art musics of the south Asian subcontinent, Hindustani music and Carnatic music, are similar and dissimilar in roughly the same degree as western Asian musics. Of the span of the scale–tune spectrum covered in western Asia by the Arabic word *maqām*, the major part, stretching towards the tune end, is designated in south Asia by the Sanskrit word *rāga* (pronounced *rāg* in north Indian languages like Hindi and Bengali, *rāgam* in south Indian languages like Tamil and Telugu). The feminine derivative *rāginī*, regularly found along with *rāg* in north Indian sources from the 16th century to the 19th, is identical with *rāg* in musical meaning.

The basic meaning of the Sanskrit word *rāga* is 'emotion, affect, passion'. Like the Arabic word *maqām* ('position, place') and the Persian word *dastgāh* ('system'), *rāga* is used widely in its common-language senses as well as in its musical sense. The strikingly different semantic fields of the musical terms *rāga* and *maqām* suggest that their musical senses may have less in common than at first appears. The cognizable identity of a raga seems ultimately to devolve from the associative and expressive effects of its tonal configurations, while the identity of a *maqām* seems to depend more on the means of producing those configurations, ultimately on the position of the *maqām* in and its relationship to an instrumentally definable scale. This is not to say that a raga cannot be discussed in terms of its scale. On the contrary, for several hundred years Indian theory has had precise, instrumentally determined means for describing intervallic structures and scale types. But from the outset a clear distinction has been made between a raga and its scale type.

As Willard pointed out in 1834, the Hindustani word *ṭhāṭ* ('framework, arrangement') is used in the north precisely to denote 'scale type'. The *ṭhāṭ* – the scale type of a modal entity – of a raga was originally simply that 'arrangement' of frets that would produce the intervals needed for the raga. The word *ṭhāṭ* first appears in the commentary of a musical treatise of 1609, where it is offered as the vernacular equivalent of the Sanskrit *mela* ('assembly'), that is, an assembly of degrees of a scale (Somanātha, *Rāga-vibodha*, iii, 1). The word *melam* is still used in the sense of scale type in south Indian theory; another 17th-century term *melakarta* – 'that which produces a *mela*' – is also used (and helps to prevent confusion with other musical senses of the word *melam*).

The terms *mūrcchanā* and *jāti*, long obsolete but once theoretically connected with the idea of mode, are often encountered in the literature on Indian music. *Mūrcchanā* once signified the sets of octave species (actually heptads) drawn from background pitch collections (a pitch collection is called *grāma*); the word *mūrcchanā* is not in current usage, and its sporadically occurring senses differ widely in their meanings. *Jāti* – literally 'genre' or 'type' – is now used in only one restricted musical sense. It denotes the type of a raga in terms of the number of scale degrees it includes within an octave: the *jāti* of a raga can be *auḍava*, *ṣāḍava*, or *sampūrūa*, as it allows five, six or seven different scale degrees.

It is believed that the melodic types (*jāti*) first described in Chapters 28–9 of the *Nāṭya-śāstra* must have had musical structures and functions corresponding to those of ragas; the word *rāga* is not used as a technical musical term in the *Nāṭya-śāstra* and appears for the first time only in about the 8th century.

(*b*) Modal entities and the general scale. There are a few evident parallels between south Asian and western Asian orderings of modal complex and general scale. For instance, in both cases a given modal entity will use only some of whatever pitch positions an octave span of the general scale makes available – in principle seven – and normally no more than two intervals of the semitone class will occur in succession in a single modal complex. But the designation of degrees of a scale in Indian music, their organization into modal complexes, and above all the relationship of modal complex to general scale – of *gamme particulière* to *échelle générale* – are very different from western Asian conceptions.

The underlying point of reference in Indian pitch nomenclature is melodic function rather than intervallic structure. The basic note names are vocal solmization syllables that were only secondarily adapted to the designation of measured intervals. An octave span in the centre of the Indian general scale provides only seven independent note names – *sa ri ga ma pa dha ni* – as compared with the 14 in the central octave of the western Asian general scale. Extension to registers above or below produces replications of note names in the central octave. In other words, the basic set of western Asian note names denotes in principle a general scale of all available pitches, while the basic set of Indian note names denotes degrees of the scale of any possible modal entity but without specifying precise pitch relationships.

To provide for more precise description, Indian theory declares that some one particular scale type, some particular intervallic arrangement of seven pitch positions, is to be deemed 'basic' and that any pitches other than those occurring in the defined 'basic' scale will be considered as having been 'altered', much like the post-Scholastic European modal theorists' distinction of 'essential' and 'accidental'. 'Altered' scale degrees have the same names as 'essential' ones, but with an attributive term added.

The term denoting a degree of a solmization scale is *svara*. A *svara* in the 'basic' scale is called 'pure' (*śuddha*); any alteration of its pitch makes it 'modified' (*vikṛta*), and different terms for designating the 'modified' degrees came into use. By the 17th century the nomenclature of pitch as 'pure' or 'modified' had been adapted to the designation of fret positions on the contemporary *vīṇā*. The frets provided for 12 semitone positions in an octave. Note names of the seven 'pure' solmization degrees (*svara*) plus from five to ten 'alterations' of them (including enharmonic equivalents) were assigned to the semitone positions determined by the frets, each of which was called *svarasthāna* ('position for the solmization degrees'). From the general scale of 12 such positions to the octave various systems of seven-degree scale types were extracted. These systems were based on intervallic structures found in ragas of the current practice, and named for them; each of these was known as a *mela* or *ṭhāṭ*.

The distinction between a general scale of available pitches and numerous particular scale types is an important part of Indian scale theory today, for both Hindustani and Carnatic music. The particular scale types may be considered either as abstractions from ragas (modal entities) or as selected subsets of all the available pitch positions.

(*c*) The system tonic. The emphasis in modern Indian theory on an abstract scale type (*mela* or *ṭhāṭ*) intervening between the general scale (the whole set of pitch positions) and the specific modal complex (the raga) is directly related to a basic feature of Indian music that radically differentiates it from western Asian music. Every Indian raga has a tonic, the *svara* named *sa*, which occurs in every raga and which has only one *svarasthāna*, that is, no higher or lower varieties. In terms of the Indian general scale all ragas have the same tonic, unlike the Turkish, Arabic or Persian *maqām*. (The scale degree *pa*, a perfect 5th above *sa*, also has no higher or lower varieties, but it is omitted altogether in some ragas, such as those illustrated in exx.33 and 34.) All the abstract seven-degree scale types (*thāṭ* and *mela*) are reckoned as including *sa* for the first degree. The pitch frequency used by a performer for *sa* is the system tonic for every item he may render. In Hindustani music it is his *sur*, in Carnatic music his *śruti* or *ādhāra-ṣaḍja*.

Note that 'tonic' does not mean 'final' nor 'predominant' nor any other modal function. The tonic in Indian music belongs to the system as a whole, not to individual modal complexes. Every raga, like every *maqām*, has its own set of modal functions and its own internal melodic and harmonic relationships, motif to motif as well as note to note. But beyond and in addition to all that, every note and every motif and every relationship is additionally related to the system tonic. In normal performance the system tonic is constantly present as an unchanging drone, in contrast to the sporadic drones of western Asian music, which may change pitch not only from one modal entity to another but also between one part and another in the same modal entity. Of course *sa* as a degree of the scale in this raga or that raga may well have a modal function specific to the raga as well, but that is not the same as its general function as tonic for the whole system.

As a rule a performer at the end of an item will indeed subside to the system tonic; but this is 'repose' not in the sense of 'finality' for the particular raga being performed but in a universal sense. In the Hindustani *rāg mārvā*, for example (see ex.33a, after Omkarnāth Ṭhākur, *Saṅgītâñjalī*, iv, p.134), the degree *sa* is mostly avoided, and this avoidance is a most essential element in the individuality of the *rāg*. When *mārvā* finally subsides to *sa*, with no more motions towards other degrees, it is the system tonic, not a modal tonic, that has emerged; the *rāg mārvā* is not just concluded, it is annihilated. The system tonic, in short, pervades and overrides all ragas; by being a required part of each it is a definitive part of none.

The system tonic in Indian music, then, is part of the *échelle générale*. There is no tonic of this kind in western Asian music. If one chooses to take 'tonic' as synonymous with the modal function *qarār* ('final, repose') or with *shāhed–ghammāz* ('predominant'), or any other modal function, then western Asian modal entities have different tonics, in terms of the background system. So for example simple melodies in the Arabic *maqām sikāh* and *maqām rāst* work with the same basic aggregate of intervals – the nucleus may be written *c′–d′–e-½♭′–f′–g′*– and are distinguished sometimes only by whether they cadence finally to *e-½♭′* (*sikāh*) or *c′* (*rāst*), as shown in Reichow (1971, pp.13ff). In Indian music the system tonic and the *échelle générale* are inseparable, and together they provide the frame of reference for the individual modal entities, the ragas. In western Asian music there is an *échelle générale* as frame of reference, but no system tonic.

There is a real and necessary distinction between the notion of a tonic common to a system of modes and the notion of a system of modes each having a tonic, just as there is a real and necessary distinction between the notions 'tonic' and 'final'. Failure to recognize these distinctions has engendered much confusion and misunderstanding. It is not to be supposed *a priori* that the function of system tonic so central to modern Indian music is necessarily valid for other Asian musics, such as those of south-east or east Asia, or for the much more readily comparable musical modalities of western Asia, or even for the earlier phases of Indian music itself. Transcriptions that suppose a system tonic where none is evident from the performing practice are all too fre-

Ex.33

(a)

(i) procedure (*calan*) in *rāg mārvā*

[1] [2]

[3]

[4] [5]

(ii) chief component (*mukhyāṅga*)

(iii) ascent–descent (*āroha–avaroha*)

(b)

(i) procedure (*calan*) in *rāg pūriyā*

[1] [2]

[3] [4]

[5] [6]

[7]

(ii) chief component (*mukhyāṅga*)

(iii) ascent–descent (*āroha–avaroha*)

quent in musicological literature. Such transcriptions are not only spurious in themselves, but are also likely to hide genuine relationships among modal entities based on other kinds of pitch connections.

(*d*) Modal nucleus and modal entity. An Indian raga in performance is developed in the same general way as a Persian *āvāz* (see ex.32): low-register modal nuclei are brought in first; then the general tessitura moves up through ever higher-pitched modal nuclei (with occasional *forūd*-like gestures back to the original cadential material); after the highpoint has been established a return to the original register is made. (Ex.33*a* (i), *b* (i), after Omkarnāth Ṭhākur, iv, pp.109f, shows typical though compressed sequences of phrases in two Hindustani ragas.)

The characteristic Persian use of separate names for different levels of register of the same modal complex, however, has no counterpart in Indian music. Instead a general term *aṅga* – 'limb (of the body), member, component' – is coupled with various attributives to designate different 'components' of a raga. The compounds *pūrvâṅga* and *uttarâṅga* designate formal and registral components or both, *mukhyâṅga* and *rāgâṅga* designate thematic or motivic components, which are referred to specific ragas by compounds with the raga names, such as *kānaḍâṅga* or *bihāgâṅga*. All these compounds extend the basic term *aṅga* in many different directions but all convey the fundamental sense of a distinctive yet fully integrated part of some larger whole.

The two principal components of a raga are the *pūrvâṅga* 'prior component' and *uttarâṅga* 'higher component', to give *pūrva* and *uttara* their primary meanings. Actually two contrasts are implied in the dichotomy between *pūrva* and *uttara*: prior–subsequent (temporal) and lower–higher (registral). These contrasts are of course mutually consistent, since in a typical presentation of a raga the lower-pitched material is in

fact supposed to appear first, the higher-pitched afterwards as a 'response' (another meaning of *uttara*). Ex.34*a*, *b*, shows three registrally delineated components (*aṅga*) of Hindustani *rāg mārvā* and *rāg pūriyā*, based on the epitomes in ex.33*a* (i), *b* (i). The first *aṅga* to be fully developed in performance, even before the full elaboration of the *pūrvâṅga*, is the *mandra* ('low [register]'); in a full rendition there would also be an extension of the *uttarâṅga* into the *tāra saptaka* ('high heptad') before the return to the *pūrvâṅga*. (In ex.34 T = *sa* ('system tonic'), V = *vādī* ('predominant'), S = *samvādī* ('secondary predominant').)

The registral components of an Indian raga contrast with their western Asian counterparts in yet another way. In addition to other features, a raga is almost always characterized by one or more striking motivic tags, by recognizable thematic elements. Such 'stereotyped motifs' are not merely ancillary to the raga system, they are its central feature. One term for such an element is *mukhyâṅga*, 'chief component'. Ex.33*a* (ii), *b* (ii), show *mukhyâṅga* for Hindustani *rāg mārvā* and *rāg pūriyā*. Emphasis on their modal degrees is of course part of the identity of each raga, but in *pūriyā* particularly there are characteristic melodic ideas dominating every stage of the proceedings (see ex.33*b* (i)). In the *pūrvâṅga* of *pūriyā* the last two segments of units [4] and [7] represent a characteristic rising contour followed by the cadential figure; unit [2] is another version of the same sequence, and unit [3] is a less characteristic form of the rising figure (as before, ending with *e'* resolved from a long held *f♯'*). In the *uttarâṅga* the configuration *f♯'–a'–c''* establishing the upper tonic is striking, but this motif is found in a number of other Hindustani ragas. Absolutely characteristic for *pūriyā*, though, is the way of making the descent from *b'* down to *e'* that is shown in unit [6]. In any rendition (improvised or otherwise) of a raga some such absolutely characteristic phrases, or group of phrases, of the raga must be heard first, before anything else, so that the identity of the raga is unmistakably clear.

A glance through the sample procedures (*calan*) for *mārvā* and *pūriyā* shown in ex.33 will illustrate how each thematic–registral component is fully developed in both rising and falling configurations before a shift is made to the next level. In *pūriyā*, for instance, units [1–2], [3–4], [5–6] and [7] are each self-contained cycles within *mandra*, *pūrvâṅga*, *uttarâṅga* and return to *pūrvâṅga*, respectively. Yet the levels can be bridged by a wide-ranging flourish across two or more registers, as in the *mārvā calan* in the middle segment of unit [4], or in the *pūriyā calan* at the beginning of unit [5]. To run through such a full sweep of a raga is to show its *āroha* and *avaroha*, its ascent and descent. Indian theoretical descriptions tend to summarize ragas in terms of a full scalar ascent and descent – *āroha* and *avaroha* – across the registers, showing in the process both which degrees in the *mela* or *ṭhāṭ* (abstract scale type) are to be omitted (*varjya*), and which degrees (if any) occur out of straight ascending or descending order (*vakra*) as a result of required motivic configurations. Ex.33*a* (iii), *b* (iii) shows the *āroha* and *avaroha* for *mārvā* and *pūriyā* as given by Omkarnāth Ṭhākur. In the *pūriyā āroha–avaroha* the suggested ascent–descent is so characterized by out of order scale degrees (*vakra svara*) as to be no 'ascent–descent' at all but rather an abbreviated *calan* ('procedure'). His ascent–descent for *mārvā* is a more straightforward scale pattern, though it does show how

Ex.34

(a) *rāg mārvā*

[1, 2, 5]    T   V        *mandra*

[3]    V   S        *pūrvâṅga*

[4]    V   S   (V)        *uttarâṅga*

(b) *rāg pūriyā*

[1, 2]    T        *mandra*

[3, 4, 7]    (S) T   V        *pūrvâṅga*

[5, 6]    V   S   (T)        *uttarâṅga*

the system tonic *sa* (C) is characteristically omitted (*varjya*) in the ascent.

The conventional type of ascent–descent description adds yet another stage to the progressive crystallization of modal individuality from *échelle générale* through *gamme particulière*. The points on the scale–tune continuum for a Hindustani *rāg* can be summed up as in Table 13, reading from top to bottom. The same scheme would apply to the description of a Carnatic *rāgam*, substituting the words *mela* for *ṭhāṭ*, *sañcāra* for *calan* and *śruti* for *sur*.

TABLE 13

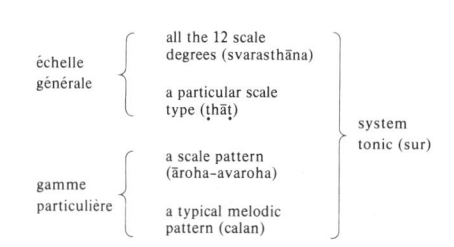

(*e*) Simple and complex modal entities. An old tripartite classification divides ragas into *śuddha* ('pure'), *chāyālaga* ('[with] tinges added' from other ragas), and *saṅkīrṇa* ('mixed'). This appears not unlike the distinction of simple and compound *maqām* in Turco-Arabic music, but there are significant differences. The underlying conception of 'pure' (*śuddha*) in this context has nothing to do with the mechanics of mixed versus unmixed scale types, but rather with how a given raga is directly apprehended. 'Pure' means uncontaminated by melodic configurations audibly reminiscent of other ragas. As explained by Somanātha in 1609, 'pure [*śuddha*] is what is pleasing by itself, that is of its own accord, and without resorting to other tinges [*chāyā*]' (*Rāga-vibodha*, iv, 3, commentary). He was paraphrasing the 15th-century theorist Kallinātha (see *Saṅgīta-ratnākara*, ii.133) and, like him, then cited a much earlier authority.

This conception is still current. Omkarnāth Ṭhākur (ii, 1954, p.1) began by defining 'purity' of raga the same way. Then, however, he speculated that a concomitant feature of 'pure' ragas may be parallel tetrachords, but he returned to the direct perception of melodic resemblance from which he began:

A *rāg* in which there is no tinge or mixture [*chāyā yā miśraṇ*] of another *rāg* is regarded as a pure [*śuddha*] *rāg*. But there is another key for

Ex.35

(a) 'in the *pūrvâṅg* and *uttarâṅg* . . . the same motif'

(b) 'ascent–descent'

(c) 'ascent–descent . . . in high-speed passage-work'

understanding pure *rāg*, arising from experience. . . . In the pure *rāg* the same [intervallic] structure of degrees of the scale is found in the *pūrvâṅg* and *uttarâṅg* [lower and upper sections of the central octave]. There are even some *rāg* of this sort in which the same motif is found in both components [*aṅga*]. *Bihāg* is one such *rāg*; the [parallel] motifs in *bihāg* are like this: [ex.35*a*].

Paṇḍit Ṭhākur then showed an *āroha–avaroha* ('ascent–descent') incorporating these figures (ex.35*b*), and a simple rising–falling scale (ex.35*c*).

The conception of *chāyālaga* – 'a tinge [of another raga] added' – is the clearest illustration of the difference between the Turco-Arabic and the Indian approaches to mixture of modal entities. Since the *chāyā* – 'shadow, image, reflection, tinge' – of a raga is produced whenever a particular melodic configuration brings that raga to mind, there need be neither a change of register nor a change of scale type for the *chāyā* of an extraneous raga to be evoked. A characteristic motif from the other raga, or even an emphasis on one of its modal degrees (if that contrasts with those of the established raga) is sufficient.

Ex.36*a* (after Omkarnāth Ṭhākur, i, 39) shows a few configurations illustrating the pentatonic Hindustani *rāg* *sāraṅg*. A *chāyā* ('tinge') of this raga in turn strongly permeates a large and important group of ragas of which one, *darbārī-kānaḍā*, may be the most widely performed and recorded of all Hindustani ragas.

Ex.36

(a)

(i) 'ascent–descent'

(ii) 'these note groups are taken repeatedly'

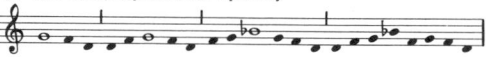

(iii) '*sārang* comes into view in just these notes'

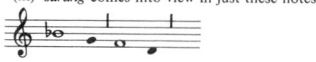

(b)

'Every Kanhada variety must have this passage'

The link among all ragas of the *kānaḍā* class is a recognizable melodic configuration with several elements (Ratanjankar, 1951, p.103):

The mark of Kanhada *anga* [component] is an oscillating Komal Gandhara [*eḇ′*], Komal Ni-Pancham Swara Sangati [*bḇ′–g′* interval] and Vakra Gandhara in the *avaroha* [out-of-order *eḇ′* in the descent]. To illustrate: [see ex.36*b*]. Every Kanhada variety must have this passage, whatever else it may have.

Ex.37*a* is a *calan* for the *rāg* *darbārī-kānaḍā*. The *kānaḍā* component appears in full in the final descent at the end, and elements of it appear separately earlier; all are marked *.

The *chāyā* ('tinge') of *sārang* permeates the *rāg* *darbārī-kānaḍā* because of the prominence of two of its principal elements as parts of the *kānaḍā* component (Omkarnāth Ṭhākur, v, 122):

The very sustenance of this *rāg* [*darbārī-kānaḍā*] is coming onto these *sārang* notes *bḇ′–g′* and *f′–d′*; . . . taking these two intervals in the descent is unavoidable because from them the *rāg* is manifested. It is true what the learned say, that the *kānaḍā* component is formed by the use of out-of-order *eb′* and *ab′* in the *sāraṅg* degrees of the scale [i.e. *bb′–g′* and *f′–d′* become *ab′–bb′–g′* and *eb′–f′–d′*]. These *sāraṅg* elements are found in almost all *rāg* of the *kānaḍā* type.

The addition of *ab′* in the *bb′–g′* *sāraṅg* component to make the *uttarâṅga* descent in *darbārī-kānaḍā* is not a matter of a different scale type for *darbārī* than for *sāraṅg*. The *rāg* *sahānā* (ex.37d) uses *ab*, and *nāyakī* (ex.37c), like *sāraṅg* itself, has no sixth degree at all. Nonetheless, all three are clearly *kānaḍā* melodic types, and *a fortiori* all three show a *chāyā* ('tinge') of *sāraṅg* in the *uttarâṅga* because of the *bb′–g′*.

Ex.37
(a) *darbārī-kānaḍā*

(b) *aḍānā*

(c) *nāyakī*

(d) *sahānā*

The *kānaḍā* component, as a whole or in part, provides much of the descent material for the ragas in the *kānaḍā* group, as may be seen in the four ragas illustrated in ex.37a–d; the *kānaḍā* component is marked *. Each has its own melodic individuality as well as its own *rāgâṅga* – raga component – that is, its characteristic motivic configurations. (The word *rāgâṅga* is used in Carnatic music with a very different meaning, where it signifies a raga which is used as a scale type, a *melakarta*.) Characteristic components (*rāgâṅga*) of each individual raga in ex.37 are marked with daggers.

The melodic contrasts among these four related ragas in some cases also entail registral emphasis or pace, or both. For instance, a pseudo-ethic contrast of serious and stately (*gambhīr*) versus playful and wild (*cancal*) in *darbārī* versus *aḍānā* is a reflection of the rather faster than average performing tradition of *aḍānā* as well as of its characteristic emphasis on a higher tessitura.

Thus the *kānaḍā* ragas illustrated in ex.37 show a twofold layering of purely melodic allusion. All the

ragas have the elements of the *kānaḍā* component, a common *rāgâṅga*; but in addition the *kānaḍâṅga* in all its contexts incorporates a shading, a 'tinge', of the 'pure' *rāg* *sāraṅg*.

None of these *kānaḍā* ragas, however, would be called *saṅkīrṇa*, that is 'mixed', since none of the individuating non-*kānaḍā* components by itself suggests any different raga. It is quite otherwise with another much-performed and recorded Hindustani raga, a *bihāg* variety called *māru bihāg*, in which virtually every element is also an element in another fully independent raga. The configurations of *māru bihāg* are illustrated in ex.38; bracketed numbers in ex.38a are keyed to Omkarnāth Ṭhākur's analysis (v/2, p.15):

This *rāg* [*māru bihāg*] has obtained a widespread currency these days. Going *sarinisa*, *ga–ma* [1] and then back to *ga* [*e′*] is quite like *bihāg*; but if one makes a pause on *ma* [*f′*] it [*bihāg*] is suppressed and the *chāyā* of *nand* is shown. Having shown its *chāyā* to that extent, then do *pa ma ma ga–sa* and again *bihāg* is manifested [2]. And from then doing *sa–ga–ma♯ pa gama♯–pa* [3], at that point comes a view of *suhāg*.

In the *uttarâṅg*, show the *chāyā* of *nand* [with] *pa dha ni pa, dha ♯ma, pa ga* [4] for the *bihāg* component [i.e. instead of using the *uttarâṅg* in the *bihāg* fashion, as in the second unit of ex.35a, do the same notes in such a way as to call to mind the *rāg nand*]. Then couple this with the *kalyāṇ* motif *♯ma ga gari–sa* [5]. From these gestures collectively a complete form of the *rāg* [*māru bihāg*] stands forth.

Remember that showing any one component repeatedly in the whole structure of this *rāg* will be a mistake. The *rāg* arises from the mingling of the components indicated above. Therefore when singing this mixed [*saṅkīrṇa*] *rāg* one has to develop it keeping in mind the varying movements in its assorted components.

In ex.38b a typical *calan* of *māru bihāg* is shown. Of the elements not already identified in the above analysis only the *c′–e′–f♯′–e′* in the last segment is special to *māru bihāg*. The approach to and descent from the upper tonic (*c″*) are found in the already mentioned *rāg nand*, which is itself a mixed raga; the upper register descent, considered separately, shows a *chāyā* ('tinge') of *kalyāṇ*. Ex.38c is a less elaborate form of the first three segments of ex.38b, the *rāgâṅga* or *pakaḍ* ('catch') for *māru bihāg*.

Ex.38
(a)
[1] *nand*    *bihāg*    [2] *bihāg*    [3] *suhāg*

[4] *nand*    [5] *kalyāṇ*

(b)

(c)

(*f*) Modal functions. Modal functions in Indian music have been defined in two ways: according to general tonal function; and according to phrase structure. Sets of terms for each exist in traditional music theory, both originating from lists in the *Nāṭya-śāstra*, where they are applied to *jāti*; hence the names of modal functions antedate the appearance of the word *rāga* in the meaning of modal entity: *vādī*: 'sonant' (i.e. sounding out); *saṃvādī*: 'consonant'; *anuvādī*: 'assonant' (i.e. auxiliary); *vivādī*: 'dissonant'. These four terms originally designated interval classes (*vādī* being unison and octave), but by an easy transition came to be applied to individual degrees of the scale as well. The last two terms are obsolete, but *vādī* and *saṃvādī* are important in Hindustani terminology, where they designate the 'predominant' and 'secondary predominant' degrees in a raga. In exx.34 and 37 – the *mārvā* and *pūriyā* registral segmentations and the outline of four *kānāḍā* type ragas – these two modal functions are marked 'V' and 'S'. *Vādī* is analogous to Persian *shāhed*; *saṃvādī* would be analogous to the *shāhed* of a principal *gusheh* in another register (see §2(i) (*e*) above and ex.32).

Two things may be observed of the *mārvā* and *pūriyā* modal functions (and compare also the melodic outlines in ex.33). First, the two ragas share the same scale type exactly, and a contrast in the *vādī-saṃvādī* pair is a major aspect of their modal differentiation. *Mārvā* stresses the degrees D♭ and A. The chief degrees of *pūriyā* are E – the normal phrase final in both *pūrvâṅga* ascent and *uttarâṅga* descent, in both cases usually following a prolonged F♯ – and B at phrase beginnings, and often sustained. Second, while the *vādī-saṃvādī* degrees are normally mutually separated by 4th or 5th, the 4th or 5th is not necessarily perfect (though it almost always is); in *mārvā* the augmented 5th or diminished 4th interval of *vādī* and *saṃvādī* is due to the retention of the traditionally predominant pair even after the original scale type of *mārvā* had undergone a change.

The registral placement of predominant and secondary predominant degrees – *vādī* and *saṃvādī* – in the four *kānāḍā* ragas illustrated in ex.37 suggests the enormous range of contrasting possibilities available even to melodically related modal entities. Four different predominant pitches (*vādī*) are represented: one is high (*aḍāṇā*) and the others are low; two are established in descent (*nāyakī* and *sahānā*), one is established in the ascent (*aḍāṇā*), and the oscillating *e♭′* of *darbārī* is approached freely from both sides.

The other way of characterizing the function of a single degree of the scale in a modal entity is according to registral or temporal position. The various forms of the rather longer list of such terms differ slightly in different sources and at different times or places. The following list of raga characteristics – *rāga-lakṣaṇa* – is typical; it is taken proximately from Śārṅgadeva (ii.23f), where it is said that the degrees of the scale exhibiting these features of a raga must be made manifest in an *ālāpa*, that is, in an improvised exposition:

1. *graha*: initial
2. *aṃśa*: predominant
3. *mandra*: low point
4. *tāra*: high point
5. *nyāsa*: final
6. *apanyāsa*: secondary final
7. *alpatva*: weakness: a degree of the scale either appears rarely (*anabhyāsa*), or is always moved through quickly (*laṅghana*), as a passing note
8. *bahutva*: strength: a degree of the scale either appears repeatedly (*abhyāsa*), or is capable of being prolonged to any extent (*alaṅghana*)

9. *ṣāḍava*: hexatonic (one of seven possible degrees of the scale is wholly absent)
10. *auḍava*: pentatonic (two degrees of the scale are wholly absent)

The purely negative property of complete absence – today called *rarjatva* – is covered by characteristics 9 and 10. The two selectional subcategories in characteristics 7 and 8, the strength–weakness field, are frequent–infrequent and prolongable–transitory; they were traditionally associated with the basic *bahutva–alpatva* opposition (see for example Śārṅgadeva 1.7, 49ff and Kallinātha's commentary, pp.189f). The *mandra–tāra* 'low point–high point' couple – *lakṣaṇa* no.3 and no.4 above – is associated in ancient and modern times alike with the registers below and above the central operating register. The simple designation of specific degrees of the scale as outer limits is not common, though it is easy in almost any raga to see points where to go beyond a certain degree of the scale entails a completion of some gesture thereby begun. For instance, in the Hindustani *rāg pūriyā* illustrated in exx.33*b* and 34*b*, the note E is a phrase ending in descent. To go below a low *e* in the *mandra* register would require continuing through low *d♭* to low *c*, with the sequence *f♯–e–d♭–c*, since D♭ can neither begin nor end a phrase in *pūriyā*; hence, low *e* is an effective lower limit to a rendition of *pūriyā* for most singers.

The remaining four modal functions – nos.1, 2, 5 and 6 – are analogous to the four principal modal functions in the modal entities of medieval Europe or of modern western Asia, as suggested in Table 14.

TABLE 14

| Gregorian | Sanskrit | Persian |
|---|---|---|
| initial | graha | āqāz |
| tenor | aṃśa | shāhed |
| final | nyāsa | forūd[-e kāmel] |
| medial | apanyāsa | īst |

In the older Sanskrit technical literature there is some argument about whether there is any difference between the terms *graha* and *aṃśa* – initial and predominant – in this list, but the distinction was well expressed quite early in terms of the relation of each to the *vādī* ('predominant') of the other list: 'Matanga says that only the *vādī* [pitch predominant] is the *aṃśa* [formal predominant], but any of the fourfold varieties of *vādī* [i.e. *vādī*, *saṃvādī*, *anuvādī*, or *vivādī*] may be a *graha* [initial]' (Kallinātha in *Saṅgīta-ratnākara*, ALS edn., i.183). This illuminates the distinction between what were two aspects of modal predominance. The *aṃśa* was a temporal–formal predominant, marked by highest frequency or most extensive prolongation, or both. *Vādī* was originally a tonal way of emphasizing the structural *aṃśa*, probably by unison and octave doubling; in time the terms became effectively synonymous.

Another historical confusion around the terms *graha–aṃśa–nyāsa* (initial–predominant–final) anticipates the present-day ambiguities regarding the system tonic. The group of 16th- and 17th-century treatises in which the notion of scale type – *mela* or *ṭhāṭ* – was first developed also report the degree *sa* as initial, predominant and final for almost all ragas; only in a few evidently exceptionally striking cases are other degrees of the scale reported as having any modal function.

Other than the *vādī-saṃvādī* couple in Hindustani music, few terms for modal functions are used consistently by practising musicians, north or south. In Carnatic music the term corresponding to the Hindustani *vādī* is *jīva-svara*, meaning 'life[-giving] degree of the scale'. The Tamil *eṭuppu* 'taking up' is used for the initial note of a phrase; it is a translation of *graha* ('taking, seizing'). The term *nyāsa* is much used, but in the sense of a mid-phrase note sustained without oscillation, as well as in the sense of a phrase-final degree of the scale: it can mean a note to finish with, but it can also mean a note to pause upon, a function also conveyed by the term *viśrānti-svara* ('resting degree'). The common Hindustani expression for sustaining a tone in this way is *mukām karnā* ('to make a halt').

(*g*) Modal systems. In the oldest sources of Indian music theory modal entities are associated with performance in the theatre, and the systematizations of them reflect this connection in various ways. But well before the 13th century (when the treatise *Sangīta-ratnākara* was written) music theory was quite independent of dramaturgy, and post-13th-century kinds of modal systems are clearly akin to modern approaches to the matter.

The number of ragas current in either Hindustani or Carnatic music is indeterminate. It is of an order of magnitude ranging between the 60 to 70 Turkish *makam* reported in Signell (1977) and the close on 300 *gusheh* in the current Persian *radīf*. Some of the systematizations of Indian modal entities have been symmetrical and closed, others have been open-ended and asymmetrical. Sometimes the criteria for structuring a system have been musical, sometimes extra-musical. Sometimes systems are closed at superordinate levels but open at the primary level.

An idea of the diversity of past Indian modal systems may be gleaned from Gangoly's *Rāgas and Rāginīs* and Bhatkhande's *Some...Leading Music Systems*. An outline of three models still current will indicate the range of possibilities:

(*1*) A traditional group of ragas still respected by some older musicians is called the 'Hanuman doctrine'. It is a closed symmetrical system of 36 entities comprising six ragas personified as male, to each of which are assigned five raginis as wives. This system is known with two slightly differing distributions of raginis. The one reported by both Jones and N. A. Willard is attested in a number of musical treatises; the other form is widely represented in numerous sets of 36 miniature paintings in which each personified raga or ragini is depicted in some stylized indoor or outdoor setting (see Ebeling, 1973, for an extensive bibliographical and iconographical inventory). There are several older schemes which also have superordinate classification levels of six ragas; in some the six ragas are specifically assigned to the six seasons of the year in north India: cold season, spring, summer, rainy season, autumn, winter (see for instance Bake, 1930, pp.42f). Beyond this extra-musical association there is no certain iconographical or musical basis for the grouping in these symmetrical systems, though an argument can be made for an original pentatonicism of the six superordinate ragas. The systems are purely traditional associations of raga names and iconographies, found together long before any record of their musical properties exists. In some cases, in fact, differences over time or geography, or both, in both melodic type and scalar type in particular ragas can be demonstrated to have taken place during the long period over which the names of these ragas have been classed

together. The earliest fully comprehensible source for both scale type and melody type for a complete set of 36 ragas and raginis is Chapter 7 of the treatise *Saṅgīt-sār* (Poona, 1910–12). It was compiled some time before 1805, and there was then no more musical basis for the classification than there is now; indeed, some of the 36 are unmistakably the same musically as their modern embodiments.

(*2*) The present south Indian system is closed and symmetrical in its superordinate levels but open-ended at the level of the modal entities themselves. The closed system is a symmetrical arrangement of 72 scale types (*melakarta*) whose generating algorithm was devised by Venkaṭamakhi of Tanjore in the 17th century. In his time only between 12 and 23 scale types had been inferred from existing ragas (he himself mentioned 19). Venkaṭamakhi proposed a method for providing scale types for any and all modal entities that might evolve in the future, based on systematic permutation of the variable pitches of the five degrees of the scale subject to 'modification' – that is, all but the system tonic and its invariant upper 5th. With the lower variety of scale degree, the fourth kept constant, the pitches of the variable second, third, sixth and seventh degrees within the two tetrachords are permuted so as to obtain six groups of six scale types per group; the whole pattern is then duplicated with the higher fourth degree, making 72 scale types (*see* INDIA, SUBCONTINENT OF, Table 10). Within each scale type, however, an infinite number of ascent–descent patterns are possible, since in actual ragas one or two degrees may be omitted (*varjya*), one or more degrees may be taken out of order (*vakra*) and this sometimes more than once, or an altered variety (*anya-svara*) of one or more of the variable degrees of the scale may be used in some contexts. Ragas showing any of these three 'deviations' from scalar regularity are often said to be *janya* ('born, generated') of their superordinate scale type, called *janaka* ('giving birth, generator'). Early in this century V. N. Bhatkhande, after investigating the southern system of scale types and its historical prototypes, devised his own system of ten scale types (*ṭhāṭ*) for Hindustani music. He chose to follow the principle of Venkaṭamakhi's predecessors and contemporaries, however, using the fewest scale types possible that might still be made to accommodate modal entities existing in musical practice.

(*3*) In south India the term for a raga whose degrees are taken as representing one of the 72 scale types is *rāgāṅga-rāga*. In north Indian usage, however, the word *rāgāṅga* means the *aṅga* – melodic 'component' – that characterizes a raga, as the *kānadāṅga* (ex.36*b*) characterizes the *rāg darbārī-kānaḍā* and a number of other ragas (ex.37), or as the *bihāgāṅga* (ex.35*a*, first unit) characterizes a small group of ragas including *māru bihāg* (ex.38).

Musicians and theorists (including V. N. Bhatkhande) often draw attention to the fact that there are many clusters of ragas like the *kānaḍā* and *bihāg* groups in Hindustani music (see also Kaufmann, 1968, pp.394–531; Powers, 1970, pp.15–45; Powers, 1976). Ratanjankar (1951, p.100) observed that:

distinctions in the swara sancharas [scale degree patterns] have given rise to classifications and groupings of ragas from an aspect totally different from the Janya Janaka [modal entity–scale type] aspect. There are about 20 such ragangas [generalized nuclear motifs] which have given rise to as many groups of ragas, whatever melakartas [scale types] they might belong to as regards their flats and sharps.

He went on to list some *rāgâṅga*, and discussed five of them, including the *kānaḍâṅga* (see above and ex.37*c*).

A number of motivically characterized components (*rāgâṅga*), each dominating a group of its own, is of course as much a two-layer modal system as any formally symmetrical *rāg–rāginī* system or any rationally ordered *ṭhāṭ–rāg* system. Being open-ended and asymmetrical at all levels it has many more loose ends. On the other hand it also has the same expanding–contracting capacity as any of the innumerable modal entities, the ragas themselves, whose separate individualities emerge into musical practice or are submerged by it as the passing of years and the tenacity of tradition continue their endless conflict.

*See also* INDIA, SUBCONTINENT OF, §§I, 5(i–iii), II, 1–2, and (for bibliographical details of treatises), §§I–II, bibliography.

3. MODAL ENTITIES IN SOUTH-EAST AND EAST ASIA. What have been deemed to be modes and modal systems in south-east and east Asia contrast strikingly with the raga and *maqām* systems. In heterophonic ensemble music such as that of the Javanese gamelan or of Japanese ceremonial court music (gagaku), factors such as instrumental tone colour and range, as well as potentialities, conventions and limitations of instrumental technique, may make the same underlying melodic, modal or scalar structure sound very different when it is actually performed. In a composition played by a Javanese gamelan the same structural notes are approached not only with different melodic lines but even in different styles: with flowing and pulsed melodic patterns (*cengkok*) in the multi-octave *gambang* (xylophone) and *gĕnder* (metallophone) parts; with floating and unpulsed melodic formulae (*cengkok*) in the *pasinḍen* (female solo voice) or flute (*suling*) or spike fiddle (*rĕbab*) parts; and with stately and regular successions of four-beat 'nuclear motifs' (*gatra*) in the single-octave metallophone *saron* parts. The various lines can differ considerably among themselves without violating the integrity of the composition, and the two styles of elaborating patterns and formulae (*cengkok*) and the 'nuclear motifs' (*gatra*) alike are cumulatively associated with the *paṭĕt*, the modal categories.

In Japanese gagaku music too a 'nuclear theme' is variously rendered by different instruments of the ensemble, although isolated single notes of that nuclear theme do not appear in any one of the instrumental parts. Rather, the pitch content of each instrumental version of the melody is related to the technique of the instrument: chords on the *shō* (mouth organ); blowing and fingering articulation on the other two wind instruments, the cylindrical-bore double-reed *hichiriki* and the flute (*ryūteki* or *fue*); plucking patterns of the 13-string half-tube zither *gakusō* (usually called by its modern name koto); and plucking and strumming on *biwa* (large four-string pear-shaped lute). The different 'tonalities' or 'modes' – the *chōshi* – differ not only in register but also according to the effects of instrumental tuning and technical considerations, particularly in the *hichiriki* part, the dominating melodic line.

(i) *Paṭĕt*.

(*a*) South-east Asian modal systems. There are generally at least two basic modal levels in south-east Asian musics, as in south Asian and western Asian, but the numbers of named entities involved, and even to some extent the relationship of the hierarchic levels, are very different. In Burma, for instance, over a dozen basic named song types are grouped into four superordinate named categories; for each of these four 'modes' some of the strings of the Burmese bow harp *saùng-gauk* have to be retuned. In traditional Vietnamese music there are two modal categories called *diêu* – named *bac* 'north', *nam* 'south' – and each *diêu* has three or four subordinate 'nuances' appended; *diêu* and 'nuance' alike are mutually distinguishable on the basis of pitch content and organization, as well as by circumstances of performance or type of ensemble, or both.

(*b*) Modes and scales in Javanese gamelan music. There are two different tunings for the fixed-pitch instruments of Javanese gamelans, called *laras pelog* and *laras slendro*. The two *laras* are similar to the two *diêu* of Vietnam in that the contrast in their intervallic structuring involves much more than a mere choice of different degrees or intervals from a common stock; *pelog* and *slendro* are altogether different from each other. The difference has nothing to do with the fact that interval sizes differ from one gamelan to another in any case; the basic contents and even concepts of the two tunings differ. *Slendro* is always an anhemitonic pentatonic tuning, with only five named degrees of the scale. *Pelog* is always a heptatonic tuning of seven named degrees of the scale, with two conjunct intervals somewhat smaller than the others; (in any specific musical context only five degrees of the scale are prominent, but at least one 'semitone' must be among them). The degrees of these two tunings are listed in Table 15, as though naming the keys of two single-

TABLE 15

| Pelog | | | Slendro | | |
|---|---|---|---|---|---|
| barang | 7 | B | C | 1 | barang alit ('high') |
| nĕm | 6 | A | A+ | 6 | nĕm |
| lima | 5 | G♯ | G | 5 | lima |
| pelog | 4 | F♯+ | | | |
| ḍaḍa | 3 | E | E+ | 3 | ḍaḍa |
| gulu | 2 | D | D | 2 | gulu |
| bĕm | 1 | C♯ | C | 1 | barang |

octave metallophones *saron* (one tuned for *pelog* and one for *slendro*), with Indonesian names and modern cipher equivalents, to which are added Western equivalents. The Roman letter D is arbitrarily set as though it were a common pitch (*tumbuk*) for the degree *gulu*/2 between a set of paired gamelan; all other apparent pitches are necessarily approximate and the intervals would differ widely from one gamelan to another in either system. The pitches most ill-represented by Western equivalents are those marked with plus signs. Degree 4 (*pelog*) is normally much closer to 5 (*lima*) than to 3 (*ḍaḍa*). Likewise, degree 3 (*ḍaḍa*) in *slendro* is as likely as not to be closer to 5 (*lima*) than to 2 (*gulu*) in any given gamelan. In short, the note *pelog* might as well have been represented by F𝄪 and *ḍaḍa* (degree 3) in *slendro* by F♮; the same applies with only slightly less force to other scale degrees, and instruments not having pre-set tunings (including the human voice) seem to be inflected one way or another, according to *paṭĕt* ('mode') even within a single gamelan ensemble.

In the central Javanese gamelan, traditional repertory items in each *laras* are assigned to one of three *paṭĕt*; *paṭĕt* is the term customarily rendered as 'mode'. To consider each *laras* – *slendro* and *pelog* – as a 'mode' with several subdivisions would make the word 'mode' merely synonymous with 'scale type'. Therefore it seems quite natural to think of the relationship of *laras* and *paṭĕt* as analogous rather to the relationship of *échelle générale* and *gamme particulière*. In that case, however, there would be two *échelles générales*, not one. At the same time, for each of the two *échelles générales*, *slendro* and *pelog*, there are only three *gammes particulières*, the three *paṭĕt*. Furthermore, each of the three *slendro paṭĕt* uses all the degrees of the *laras*, so there is no question of *gammes particulières* using particular degrees selected from a larger stock contained in an *échelle générale*. At the same time, in *laras pelog* just such selections of *gammes particulières* are made: *pelog paṭĕt barang* uses scale degree 7 (*barang*/B) to the virtual exclusion of scale degree 1 (*bĕm*/C♯); the latter is featured in the other two *pelog paṭĕt*, where degree 7 plays a subsidiary role, normally being omitted altogether. Degree 4 (*pelog*/F♯+) is an 'exchange note' (*sorogan*), normally for degree 3 (*ḍaḍa*/E) in two *pelog paṭĕt* and normally for degree 5 (*lima*/G♯) in the third *pelog paṭĕt*. Thus in *pelog* several different pentatonic *gammes particulières* are selected from a heptatonic *échelle générale*, by selecting either 1 or ,7, and exchanging 4 for 3 or 5; in *slendro*, on the other hand, each *gamme particulière* is coextensive with the *échelle générale*.

(*c*) *Paṭĕt versus raga*. Both the number of entities – six *paṭĕt* divided between two *laras* – and their hierarchic relationship contrast strongly with the multiplicities of modal entity versus singular *échelle générale* of western and south Asia. But in addition to numbers and systems, there is a difference in the way modal entities are related to the repertory in performance and to what is expected of the performer. For a Javanese musician the closest quantitative equivalent to the dozens of *ragas* an Indian musician must control is not the six *paṭĕt* but the one or two hundred *gĕnḍing* – gamelan compositions – that he knows and can play. An Indian musician must know compositions too, but they are conceived as the embodiments of ragas, and any major performance is dominated by the artist's own ad hoc elaborations in the raga, attached to a composition only as to a convenient peg. Thus, for example, the improvised *ālāpana* of a south Indian artist in a major *rāgam* could be followed by any of several dozen *kīrtanam*.

The opening solo *bubuka* of a Javanese *gĕnḍing*, conversely, is a fixed pattern attached to that particular *gĕnḍing*; it foreshadows not so much the *paṭĕt* in general but rather specific passages of the *gĕnḍing* itself. A musician is not at liberty to transfer a *bubuka* belonging to one piece to some other piece in the same *paṭĕt*. So too the closing soloistic *paṭĕtan* after a *gĕnḍing* is an instrumental elaboration not on the *paṭĕt* as an abstract modal entity but rather on a specific vocal composition in that *paṭĕt*, traditionally attached to the *gĕnḍing*. In short, where a raga is one of hundreds of more or less sharply defined musical entities, under the direct control of the artist and in the forefront of his consciousness, a *paṭĕt* is one of a tiny handful of musical categories embodying in the most general kind of way features of hundreds of individual and distinct traditional compositions.

(*d*) *Modal entity and modal functions*. Indeed, questions of how the *paṭĕt* are to be recognized and what their distinguishing characteristics may be form a major

research area in Indonesian musicology. Since there are no obvious melodic formulae deliberately used to announce *paṭĕt* and *paṭĕt* alone, earlier studies concentrated more on its scalar aspects and tried to establish modal functions for the degrees of the *paṭĕt*, recognizing thematic significance only in cadential formulae (Hood, 1954; Kunst, 1949). More recent work has drawn attention to the melodic aspects of the question (Becker, 1972; Walton, 1974; Sumarsam, 1975; McDermott and Sumarsam, 1975).

Clear and distinct separate modal functions like predominant, final and the like cannot be established for the *paṭĕt*. The notion of modal 'tonic' (Javanese *bakuswara*, 'basic note') is more plausible, and the word *tonika* has been borrowed in modern Indonesian (McDermott and Sumarsam, 1975, p.236; see also Hood, 1954). The 'tonic' or 'tonics' of a *paṭĕt*, however, are neither finals nor necessarily predominants; they are simply those degrees of the scale that tend to occur more often at important structural positions. Of equal or greater importance in *paṭĕt* recognition, however, is the general avoidance in each *paṭĕt* of a particular degree of the scale at important positions.

The pivotal positions in the structure of gamelan music are the goal notes of the largest divisions: those divisions are called *gongan* because their goal notes are marked by a stroke of the hanging *gong agung* ('great gong'), and their goal notes are *gong* notes. Each *gongan* in turn is divided into two or more *kĕnongan*, whose goal notes are marked by strokes on a gong called *kĕnong*; less important formal positions are sometimes marked by the gong *kĕmpul*. The fourth and last of every group of four *saron* beats (every *gatra*) is the goal note for the three that lead up to it. The more important the structural position, the more likely in any given *paṭĕt* that certain degrees will occur with significant frequency at that position and that others will not be heard there.

The predominant usage for degrees of the scale in the three *pelog paṭĕt* is summarized in Table 16, with comments following. (For Indonesian note names and approximate intervals, see above.) Degree 1 (*bĕm*/C♯) in

TABLE 16

| Paṭĕt | Basic pentatonic (strong) | (others) | With 4 (pelog) substituted | Weak/absent |
|---|---|---|---|---|
| lima | 1,5 | 2,3,6 | 1 2 4 5 6 | 7 |
| nĕm | 6,5 | 1,2,3 | 1 2 4 5 6 | 7 |
| barang | 6,2 | 3,5,7 | 2 3 4 6 7 | 1 |

effect is omitted in *paṭĕt barang*; degree 7 (*barang*/B) does occur in *paṭĕt lima* and *paṭĕt nĕm*, but rarely, and in *paṭĕt lima* only in passing. Degree 4 (*pelog*/F♯+) in place of 3 or 5 occurs most significantly in *paṭĕt nĕm*, least significantly in *paṭĕt barang*.

*Paṭĕt barang* is the most easily distinguishable of the three *pelog paṭĕt*. Not only is its pitch content unique – it has its own fixed-pitch idiophones – but also it has a significantly higher tessitura in vocal music and a different pair of open strings on the *rĕbab*. *Paṭĕt lima* and *paṭĕt nĕm*, on the other hand, are identical in pitch content and similar in other respects; for example, the contour 2 1 7 5 is a characteristic cadential approach to degree 5 (*lima*/G♯) in both. They seem so much alike that they are sometimes paired into a mediate category, *paṭĕt bĕm*, so named for the degree (1/C♯) which distinguishes them as a pair from *paṭĕt barang*. Still, the relative structural prominence of degree 6 (*nĕm*/A) in *paṭĕt nĕm* helps to distinguish it from *paṭĕt lima*, where degree 1 (*bĕm*/C♯) is more probable at points of structural weight.

It must be stressed that relative strength of degrees as structural goal notes is only one factor in *paṭĕt* individuation – manner of approach is significant – and strength itself is a matter of probability: any note may occur, but some are more likely than others. This is all the more the case for the three *slendro paṭĕt*, where there is no pre-selection of a subset of pitch classes less than those of the *laras* as a whole (see Table 17). Strength and avoidance is noted particularly with respect to *gong* and *kĕnong* tones, but in some cases – 3 (*ḍaḍa*/E+) in *manyura* particularly – it is also meant to reflect prominence in the approach to structural strong points.

TABLE 17

| Paṭĕt | Avoided | 'Tonic' | Also strong |
|---|---|---|---|
| nĕm | – | 2,6 | 5 |
| sanga | 3 | 5 | 1 |
| manyura | 5 | 6 | 3,2 |

The strongest contrast is between *paṭĕt sanga* and *paṭĕt manyura*. *Sanga* is in fact the most distinct of the *slendro paṭĕt*, and a great frequency of degree 5 (*lima*/G) at the goal tones of *gongan* and *kĕnongan* contributes most strongly to this distinctiveness. *Paṭĕt manyura* by contrast avoids degree 5 at strong goal notes; strong positions in *sanga* in turn avoid showing 3 (*ḍaḍa*/E+), a note correspondingly emphasized in *manyura*.

Distinctions between *paṭĕt nĕm* and *paṭĕt manyura* are much hazier. These two *paṭĕt* share strong degrees 2 and 6 (as well as many configurations approaching them). They are distinguished most strongly by a noticeably higher tessitura for *paṭĕt manyura* in all multi-octave instruments and by the fact that *paṭĕt nĕm* has degree 5 (*lima*/G) as an occasional goal note in *kĕnongan*, while *paṭĕt manyura* generally avoids it in structural positions.

(*e*) Goal notes and melodic elaboration in the *slendro paṭĕt*. The characteristic feature of gamelan music is the superimposition of many different parts whose relationship is one of increasing subdivision of a long, fundamental time span. Each *gongan* is divided into *kĕnongan*; each *kĕnongan* contains a set of two, four, or eight *gatra*. 'The unit of measurement of *gamelan* pieces is the *gatra*. One *gatra* consists of four *saron* strokes [original has "four beats of the *balungan*", that is, of the so-called "nuclear theme"] and is the smallest meaningful unit' (Sindusawarno, *Ilmu karawitan*, after Becker, 1972, p.21). Just as the goal note of a *kĕnongan* or *gongan* subsumes and completes everything that has led up to it since the last goal note at that level appeared, so the pitch at the last position of the *gatra* is the goal note subsuming the three previous beats. *Gatra* are reckoned in pairs, the second (even-numbered) *gatra* of each pair being strong (*ulihan*) while the first (odd-numbered) *gatra* is weak (*padang*).

Judith Becker (1972) has established significant correlations between (even-numbered) strong *gatra* and *paṭĕt* in a large repertory of *gĕnḍing*. On the significance for *paṭĕt* of four-stroke *gatra* she observed that 'a patet is the profile of the use of particular contours on par-

ticular pitch levels (patterns) in particular positions within a composition' (p.187). 'Contour' is an abstract arrangement of pitches (such as four adjacent descending notes, her contour no.2), used to establish the pitch level of a goal note (such as 2, 5 or 6) resulting in a pattern, such as 6 5 3 2, or 3̇ 2̇ 1 6, or 2̇ 1̇ 6 5. The more important the structural position on which such patterns end, the more likely the patterns are to be specifically correlated with *paṭĕt*. The three patterns mentioned are in fact Hood's 'tonic cadential formula' in the *balungan* (*saron* part and 'nuclear theme') for *paṭĕt nĕm*, *paṭĕt sanga* and *paṭĕt manyura*, respectively (Hood, 1954, p.124). Note again that these patterns are not exclusive, as they would have to be if they were modal identifying tags like a north Indian *pakaḍ* or a south Indian *piṭuppu* ('catch'). The *gatra* 6 5 3 2, for instance, the 'tonic cadential formula' for *paṭĕt nĕm*, happens to appear in ex.39a as part of a piece in *paṭĕt manyura*, and appears in the *balungan* in ex.40a, b, illustrating both *paṭĕt* (*nĕm* and *manyura*). The *gatra* 6 5 3 2 also appears in *paṭĕt sanga*, but not in strong positions.

Strong-position *gatra* are often more characteristic of *paṭĕt* if their associated preceding weak-position *gatra* are taken into account. For instance, the *gatra* 6 5 3 2 forms part of an overwhelmingly probable *paṭĕt manyura* formula if preceded by the weak-position (odd-numbered) *gatra* 3 3 . . (two strokes on degree 3, the second being undamped and dying away over three counts, with silence at the goal note): 3 3 . . 6 5 3 2 (McDermott and Sumarsam, 1975, p.238). Strong emphasis on degree 3 in any context is associated with *paṭĕt manyura*.

The four-beat *gatra* is the basic melodic unit of the *balungan*, Hood's 'nuclear theme'. It is also the unit controlling not only the elaborating subdivisions provided by multi-octave fixed-pitch instruments like *gĕndèr* (metallophone) and *gambang* (xylophone) but also the free-floating elaborations of the spike-fiddle, end-blown flute, and solo female voice (*rĕbab*, *suling* and *pĕsinḍen*). The pitch of the fourth stroke of a four-note *gatra* is not only the goal note for the *gatra* of the 'nuclear theme' itself; it also stabilizes the goal for each layer of the filling-in parts (*panerusan*). A stretch of music in a filling-in part is denoted by two closely related terms, *cengkok* and *wilĕt* (Kunst, 3/1973, i, p.334):

*wilĕt . . . is the piece of melody, the melodic turn, between two given points . . . the piece of melody between two interpunctuating tones . . . [but] whereas wilĕt refers to the fragment of melody as it is being sung, or played on the rebab [or gendèr, etc], at a given moment, including all variations and fioriture added by the player, the meaning of chèngkok is exclusively the sequence of the essential, so to speak, 'compulsory' tones, i.e. those which give the melody its specific character. One might say, therefore 'Niyaga A plays a different wilĕt from that of niyaga B; but the chèngkok of both their performances is the same'.*

It is *cengkok* – 'standard' fragments of melody leading up to a given structural point – that are of concern in the matter of *paṭĕt*. It should be noted also that the *cengkok* used in a given *gĕnḍing* are indeed 'compulsory', as Kunst has it (and see also McDermott and Sumarsam, 1975, pp.234f). A *cengkok* may be locally embellished or varied by the musician, and there may be ample occasions to substitute one *cengkok* for another (*santun cengkok*, see Kunst, 3/1973, p.127, n.2); nonetheless a basic sequence of *cengkok* appropriate to the elaborating parts is specific to each *gĕnḍing*. Current research is trying to establish that the traditional *cengkok* for a given *gĕnḍing* are in addition independently specific to paṭět, that is, that they are not just governed by the individual *gatra* or pair of *gatra* with which they occur, nor by the goal notes alone. Research emphasis up to 1978 has been on *cengkok* in the three *slendro paṭět*.

Ex.39*a* shows three different vocal *cengkok* associated with the same place in the same *gěnḍing* in *slendro paṭět manyura* (after Walton, 1974, pp.6, 8, 75, 93). Each comprises a standard initial formula and a standard final formula; the final one in each case establishes the goal note of the *gatra*. In the vocal and end-blown flute parts in the gamelan (*pěsinḍen* and *suling*), the free-flowing, unpulsed lines begin late in the time span – sometimes they do not appear with odd-numbered weak-position *gatra* at all – and characteristically spill over the time point of the goal note's appearance. Note that initial and final formulae are separable: ex.39*a* (ii), (iii) have the same opening but different conclusions.

**Ex.39**

**(a)**

**(i)**

**(ii)**

**(iii)**

*balungan*

(b) same melodic formula (*cengkok*) in a different context

*balungan*

Ex.39*b* illustrates the independence of *cengkok* from specific *gatra* contours. The vocal *cengkok* is that of ex.39*a* (iii), but it accompanies a different *gatra* (the approach in the *gatra*, however, is still from above, with the penultimate degree one key above the goal note).

Ex.40 (after McDermott and Sumarsam, 1975, p.238) illustrates the proposition that choice of *cengkok* is connected with *paṭět*. The two *cengkok* for *gěnder* accompany the same *gatra* occurring in compositions in different *paṭět*. The *paṭět manyura cengkok* typically and characteristically lies much higher than the *paṭět něm cengkok*; moreover the approach independently emphasizes degree 3 (*ḍaḍa*/E+) and even seems to suggest the *manyura* descent 3 2 1̣ 6, while the *paṭět něm cengkok* hovers around degree 2 (*gulu*/D) and uses 3 largely as an upper auxiliary to 2. But more than that, the *gěnder* intervals at the goal note of a *cengkok* are said to be specific to the *paṭět* (McDermott and

Sumarsam, 1975, pp.235ff). *Slendro* simultaneities where degrees are separated by two keys on the *gěnder* – 'slendro 5ths' – are called *kěmpyung*, and octaves are *gěmbyang*. The low-lying *gěmbyang* octave 2–2̣ (*gulu-gulu/d'–d*) as the concluding arrival interval of a full *cengkok* (ex.40*a*) is claimed as exclusive to *paṭět něm*, while the final higher-lying *kěmpyung* '5th' 6–2 (*něm-gulu/a+'–d'*) that occurs in ex.40*b* is claimed for *paṭět manyura* or *paṭět sanga* and excluded from *paṭět něm*.

**Ex.40**

(a) *paṭět něm*

*gěnder*

*balungan*

(b) *paṭět manyura*

*gěnder*

*balungan*

barang–gulu–ḍaḍa–lima–něm = 1 2 3 5 6 = C–D–E+–G–A +

One of the few features distinguishing *paṭět manyura* from *paṭět něm* is that its melodic formulae by and large lie noticeably higher on multi-octave instruments, as was noted above for ex.40. The same registral contrast is of course also embodied in the *gěnder* intervals claimed as exclusive to the one *paṭět* or the other at goal points. The distinctions between *paṭět manyura* and *paṭět sanga*, on the other hand, do not depend on distinctions of general tessitura. Distinctions between these two *paṭět* are, rather, a matter of differently emphasized structural scale degrees and correspondingly different choices of formula, even on multi-octave instruments.

Ex.41 is based on the *gatra* 5 3 2 1. This *gatra* occurs indifferently distributed over all three *slendro paṭět* (with a slight preference for *paṭět sanga*), without playing a significant structural role in any. Along with

**Ex.41**

(a) *paṭět manyura* (from *ladrang Pangkur*)

(b) *paṭět sanga* (from *gěnḍing Gambirsawit*)

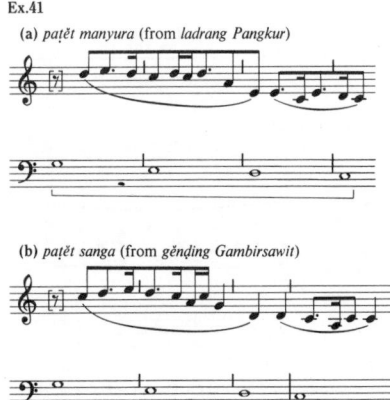

Ex.42

(a) ending on the fifth $a+'-d'$ (kĕmpyung nĕm–gulu)

(i) paṭĕt manyura

(ii) paṭĕt sanga

(iii) paṭĕt manyura

(b) ending on the octave $a+'-a+$ (gĕmbyang nĕm –nĕm)

(i) paṭĕt manyura

(ii) paṭĕt sanga

(iii) paṭĕt manyura

barang–gulu–ḍaḍa–lima–nĕm = 1 2 3 5 6 = C–D–E+–G–A+

the 5 3 2 1 gatra are shown vocal cengkok (sinḍen cengkok by Wasitodipuro, after Walton, 1974, pp.83, 102) accompanying it as it occurs in two well-known gĕnḍing in paṭĕt manyura and paṭĕt sanga, respectively. The goal note is of course degree 1 (barang/C), and it is established in both cengkok, but the manner of establishing it is quite different. The paṭĕt manyura cengkok stresses degree 3 (ḍaḍa/E+), and in the closing formula particularly brings out the line 3 2 1 (ḍaḍa–gulu–barang/E+–D–C) of the gatra. The paṭĕt sanga cengkok, conversely, stresses degree 2 (gulu/D), and its closing formula brings out the cadential weak–strong descent 2 1 (gulu–barang/D–C). The initial formulae likewise emphasize degrees 3 and 2 (ḍaḍa/E+, and gulu/D) for paṭĕt manyura and paṭĕt sanga respectively.

But more than that, the opening of the paṭĕt sanga cengkok in ex.41b seems to be only a trivially varied transposition down one slendro step of the opening of the paṭĕt manyura cengkok (in ex.41a). And indeed, Javanese musicians believe that many aspects of paṭĕt sanga can be explained as the shifting of paṭĕt manyura down one slendro step. Ex.42 (after Sumarsam, 1975, p.169) illustrates this theory. Ex.42a (i), (ii), and ex.42b (i), (ii), show cengkok leading to the same simultaneity in the two paṭĕt: the kĕmpyung 6–2 (nĕm-gulu/a+'–d') in ex.42a, and gĕmbyang 6–6̣ (nĕm–nĕm/a+'–a+) in ex.42b. The cengkok in ex.42a (i), b (i), are for paṭĕt manyura: the paṭĕt sanga cengkok are in ex.42a (ii), b (ii). The two paṭĕt sanga cengkok, however, have been derived merely by downward of one position from paṭĕt manyura cengkok as shown in ex.42a (iii), b (iii).

On the gĕnḍer of course such a downward shift is an extremely easy and natural process, involving only a slight shift of the hands towards the left, with not the slightest difference in playing technique. But the same

Ex.43

*pĕsinḍen

†gĕnḍer

balungan

barang–gulu–ḍaḍa–lima–nĕm = 1 2 3 5 6 = C–D–E+–G–A+

transposition relationship has been claimed for the free-floating vocal *cengkok* as well: '*cengkok* [original has *wilĕt*] of *slendro paṭĕt sanga = cengkok* [*wilĕt*] of *slendro paṭĕt manyura* lowered one note' (Walton, 1974, p.13, after Sulaiman Gitosaprodjo). Whether the primary factor is indeed only transposition of whole patterns, or whether it also entails rather subtle matters of adjusting initial and final formulae to emphasize different structural degrees seems still open; the opening formulae in ex.41*a*, *b*, are near enough to pattern transposition – and others are nearer still – but the closing formulae have been adjusted so much that they are distinctive in contour emphasis as well as in pitch level.

Nonetheless, pattern shifting is near enough the truth to allow the aurally evident distinction between the two *slendro paṭĕt*, *manyura* and *sanga*, to be characterized in terms of a contrast in degrees of the scale with associated melodic patterns bringing out degrees 6, 3 and 2 in *paṭĕt manyura*, as against degrees 5, 2 and 1 one step away in *paṭĕt sanga*. For the *cengkok* of *paṭĕt nĕm* a different derivation is proposed: 'In practice, the *cengkok* or melodies [original has *wilĕt-wilĕt* (*melodi*)] for *slendro paṭĕt nĕm* are a combination of *cengkok* of *paṭĕt sanga* and *paṭĕt manyura*' (Walton, 1974, p.13, after Gitosaprodjo). For the *gĕnder* too, *slendro paṭĕt nĕm* is said to comprise *cengkok* from *paṭĕt sanga* and *paṭĕt manyura*, with a few of its own (Sumarsam, 1975, pp.169ff).

Ex.43 is from the modally ambiguous *ladrang Remeng*, classified in *slendro paṭĕt nĕm*. It shows vocal and *gĕnder cengkok* accompanying the two pairs of 'nuclear-theme' *gatra* in the strong (i.e. second) half of one *gongan*. The second *gatra* shown in the example closes the third *kĕnongan*, the fourth *gatra* closes the *gongan*. The female voice (*pĕsinḍen*) is from Walton, 1974, p.142, after Wasitodipuro; the *gĕnder* is from Sumarsam, 1975, p.170. Both parts alike have a *cengkok* in each of the four *gatra* (the vocal *cengkok* of the second *gatra* runs over into the third in a technique called *plèsèdan*). The second and fourth *gatra* in the example (sixth and eighth of the whole *gongan*) are characteristic cadential formulae for *paṭĕt sanga* ([2] 1 6̣ 5̣) and *paṭĕt manyura* (3̣ 2̣ 1̣ 6) respectively; 3̣ 2̣ 1̣ 6 is also used in *paṭĕt nĕm*, but rarely in *paṭĕt sanga*, and . 1̣ 6̣ 5̣ is very uncommon for *paṭĕt manyura*, more likely in *paṭĕt nĕm*. The use of mutually contradictory . 1̣ 6̣ 5̣ in a *kĕnong* position immediately preceding 3̣ 2̣ 1̣ 6 in *gong* position strongly suggests *paṭĕt nĕm*.

The first three *gĕnder cengkok* belong to *paṭĕt sanga*, the fourth to *paṭĕt manyura*; the fourth vocal *cengkok* is *paṭĕt manyura*, and the second vocal *cengkok* ends with a *paṭĕt sanga* formula. In this example the *gatra* and *cengkok* alike illustrate the notion that *paṭĕt nĕm* is readily heard as a combination of the other two *slendro paṭĕt*; at any rate it is aurally the least distinctive of the three *slendro paṭĕt*.

(*f*) Transposition and transformation. Ex.44 illustrates the relatively uncommon case of a *gĕnḍing* which exists in both transposed and transformed versions. *Pangkur* is one of the most familiar *ladrang* in the repertory, and is well known in all three of the *paṭĕt* shown (the *slendro paṭĕt sanga* and *pelog paṭĕt barang* versions are from Gitosaprodjo, 1972; for the two *slendro* versions see also Sumarsam, 1975).

Ex.44
(a) *umpak, irama II*
(i) *slendro paṭĕt sanga*
(ii) *slendro paṭĕt manyura*
(iii) *pelog paṭĕt barang*

(b) *ngelik, irama III*
(i) *slendro paṭĕt sanga*
(ii) *pelog paṭĕt barang*

The *manyura* version can be made from the *sanga* version by simply shifting up one degree in *laras slendro* (for *gĕnder* parts for both *slendro* versions of *Pangkur* see Sumarsam, 1975, pp.171ff). The *slendro paṭĕt manyura* version can in turn be transformed into *pelog paṭĕt barang* by playing it in the same position on instruments tuned in *laras pelog*. Ex.44*b* shows the 'nuclear theme' of the second section of *Pangkur* in *slendro paṭĕt sanga* and *pelog paṭĕt barang*. Note how in *pelog* the note *lima* (5/G♯) of the (written) lower register is replaced by the note *pelog* (4/F♯+) in the (written) upper register. Both correspond with the note *ḍaḍa* (3/E+) of the *slendro paṭĕt sanga* version (which becomes 5/G in the *slendro paṭĕt manyura* version).

*(ii) Chōshi.*

*(a)* A term for mode in east Asia: *tiao–diêu–chō*. The Japanese word *chōshi* means 'note', 'key', 'mode' or 'tuning' in differing musical contexts. *Chō* is sometimes softened to *jō* in compounds (e.g. *hyōjō, hira-jōshi*); it is an *onyomi* word, that is, a loan word from Chinese in pronunciation as well as in using a Chinese ideogram. The modern Chinese pronunciation is *diaw* (*tiao⁴*); the Vietnamese is *diêu*. If east Asia as a cultural area is defined by the use of Chinese ideograms, then the one for *diaw–diêu–chō* is in fact the general east Asian equivalent for mode, with as widely varying contexts and ranges of meaning as the words 'mode' and '*maqām*'. The Vietnamese contrast of *diêu bac* and *diêu nam* – 'northern mode' as against 'southern mode' – refers to a contrast of style, function and pitch content easily comparable with the contrast between *slendro* and *pelog* in Javanese music. At the other extreme, Japanese *honchōshi* simply means 'standard tuning' for the shamisen, as opposed to 'second [string] up' (*niagari*) or 'third [string] down' (*sansagari*).

The original Chinese term *diaw* (*tyao, tiao⁴* etc) appears first in sources from the T'ang and Sung dynasties (Courant, 1921, pp.96ff, 114ff; Picken, 1957, pp.93ff; Pian, 1967, chap.2). As Picken put it, 'The term "system" (*diaw*) includes both mode and key in the Western sense'. The Chinese system of modes incorporated three aspects:

*(1)* a set of 12 pitch classes theoretically generated through the circle of 5ths – six female *leu* (*lü³*) alternate with six male *liuh* (*lü⁴*), known collectively as the 12 *liuh* (*lü⁴*) – on each one of which can be constructed either:

*(2)* five anhemitonic pentatonic octave species or seven diatonic octave species, comprising either the five different five-note segments from the intervallic succession: ... |T|T|m3|T|m3|T|T|m3| ... or the seven different seven-note segments from the intervallic succession: ... |T|T|T|S|T|T|S|T|T|T|S|T|T| ... and

*(3)* one degree of each pentatonic or diatonic sequence is in turn the principal note.

Such systems can be grasped in several different ways depending on the order in which the three criteria are applied. One method is to confine all the 12 pitch classes within a single octave and to make from these all 12 of the possible pentatonic or diatonic series; in modern staff notation this amounts to 12 different key signatures, producing 12 different pentatonic or diatonic collections. Each degree of such a collection in turn is designated as principal degree, making 12 × 5 pentatonic 'systems' or 12 × 7 diatonic 'systems'. The diatonic result of this process is illustrated in Pian (1967, table 2 and pp.43f.)

The system of 7 × 12 modal systems was probably only theoretical. In late T'ang and Sung sources, however, systems of 28 'popular' modes are reported; their names are different from the names of the 84 but each of the 28 is equated with one of the 84. Courant (1921, pp.117f) gave a list of those 60 modes out of the 84 which arise from degrees of the basic pentatonic collections, including equivalent names for the 28, after northern Sung sources. Pian (1967, p.54) gave a slightly different list of the 28, after southern Sung sources.

*(b)* Scales and modes in Japanese gagaku music. During the Nara (710–84[94]) and Heian (794–1185) periods Japan was saturated with influences from the China of the T'ang dynasty (618–907); among the surviving phenomena is the repertory of the dominant division of gagaku, the imperial court music. This repertory goes by the name of *tōgaku*, which means 'T'ang music'. By the end of the Heian period at the latest, however, gagaku as a whole had ceased to play any role outside the ceremony of the court and of a few temples. After the Meiji restoration (1868) different gagaku traditions were brought together and some standardization was attempted. Although it remains an isolated, somewhat esoteric, branch of Japanese music, it has been preserved, and gagaku embodies in some form an audible ancient system of east Asian ensemble modalities, the *chōshi*.

The theoretical basis of *tōgaku*, including the *chōshi*, is from T'ang China, but much modified. The 12 pitch classes are recognized as the *échelle générale* but only one of them, conventionally notated and played A, has the same name as one of the 12 Chinese *liuh* (Japanese *ōshiki* is Chinese *hwang jong*, the first *liuh*). Furthermore, *tōgaku* uses only nine of the 12 pitch classes. Equivalents of D♯, F, and A♯ are not found among pipes of the 'mouth organ' *shō* nor in any koto tuning (though playing techniques of the double-reed *hichiriki* and flute *ryūteki* add these and other pitch inflections in performance).

The Chinese terms *leu* and *liuh*, read in Japanese as *ryō* and *ritsu*, retain their female–male associations, but now denote two anhemitonic pentatonic scale types rather than denoting types of pitch class. The *ryō* and *ritsu* scale types each have two additional 'exchange notes', similar to the *sorogan* in Javanese *laras pelog*, whereby five of the five degrees of the scale have alternative degrees which may be and often are substituted. These exchange notes are called *hennon*, equivalent to Chinese *biann-in* (*pien⁴-yin*) (exchange notes in a pentatonic scale are in fact sometimes called '*pièn*-tones' in musicological writings).

Ex.45 shows the theoretical *ritsu* and *ryō* scales for the principal *tōgaku chōshi*. The five principal degrees of the scales are numbered 1, 2, 3 or 4, 5, and 6. In both *ritsu* and *ryō* scales (with one exception) the theoretical sixth degree can be exchanged for the degree a semitone above (exchange notes are shown as solid note heads). In *ryō* scales the third degree may be exchanged with the degree a semitone above, in *ritsu* scales it is the second degree that has an exchange degree a semitone above it. Ex.45a illustrates a *ritsu chōshi* and a *ryō chōshi* with the same 'tonic' degree, E. In terms of the apparent heptatonic collection of pitches they differ only in that *hyōjō* has G (*sōjō*) versus *taishikichō*'s G♯ (*fūshō*), but in fact there is a noticeably greater stress on a stable second degree – F♯ (*shimomu*) – in *taishikichō* compositions. Ex.45b shows the theoretical scales for a *ritsu* and a *ryō chōshi* using the same collection of pitch classes, exchangeable degrees included, falling at different places in the *échelle générale*.

Ex.45c shows the theoretical scales of the remaining *ryō* and *ritsu chōshi*. The exchange tone F♯ (*shimomu*) in *sōjō* is anomalous both in that it is exchanged within the modal degree itself, *sōjō*, and in that it is a semitone below it whereas all the other exchange notes are semitones above the degrees they can replace. The theoretical pitch class F (*shōsetsu*), which would have been expected as an exchange degree for E (*hyōjō*), is not part of the nine-pitch *échelle générale* theoretically available for *tōgaku*.

*Suichō* has a *ryō* scale sharing its 'tonic' degree A with the *ritsu* scale of *ōshikichō*, the two thus being

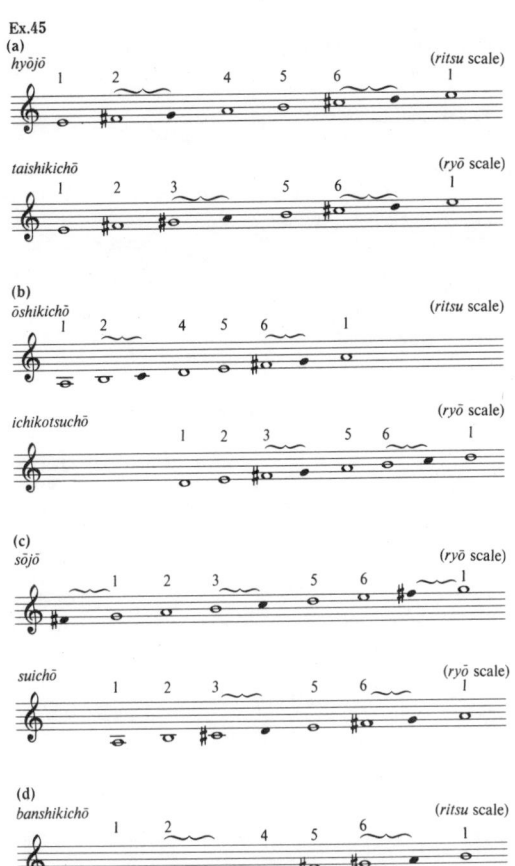

Ex.45

(a) hyōjō (ritsu scale)

taishikichō (ryō scale)

(b) ōshikichō (ritsu scale)

ichikotsuchō (ryō scale)

(c) sōjō (ryō scale)

suichō (ryō scale)

(d) banshikichō (ritsu scale)

related as are *hyōjō* and *taishikichō* in ex.45*a*. Banshikichō (ex.45*d*) is the third *ritsu*-scale *chōshi*.

These seven *chōshi* are the principal modes of the *tōgaku* repertory. They are almost certainly surviving descendants of the 28 'popular modes' of T'ang court music. Their names at least, or sufficiently close equivalents, may be found among the northern Sung version of the late T'ang 28-mode system (Courant, 1921, pp.117f, nos.2, 5, 23 and/or 30, 38 and/or 72, 40, 51 and 75).

The assignment of only five numbers to the scale degrees of individual scales in ex.45 is in accordance with the koto tunings (see below and cf ex.48*a*) and it corresponds to Sino-Japanese patterns of pentatonic nomenclature. It also represents audible musical reality in that the degree numbered 1 for each *chōshi* is indeed a tonic in every sense of the word, as well as being a final. The *chōshi* really are tonalities – 'keys' – in addition to whatever else they may embody. The tonic of a composition in *hyōjō* will be the degree E of the *échelle générale*, whose name is *hyōjō*; it will be a 4th higher (or 5th lower) than the tonic of a piece in *banshikichō*, represented as B in the *échelle générale*, named *banshiki*; and it will be a 5th higher (or 4th lower) than the tonic degree A (*ōshiki*) or *ōshikichō*. To translate *hyōjō*, *oshikichō* and *banshikichō* by 'the key of E', 'the key of A' and 'the key of B' would be correct, though also insufficient (especially with respect to the melodic wind parts).

The *tōgaku chōshi*, then, form a system of *gammes*

*particulières* grouped into two general scale-type classes *ritsu* and *ryō*, and they are projected at different places on an *échelle générale* of nine pitch classes. Five pitch classes – equivalent to G, D, A, E and B – can serve as tonics of a *ryō* tonality (G, D, A and E) or a *ritsu* tonality (A, E and B). Three of the remaining pitch classes – equivalent to F♯, G♯ and C♯ – can serve only as secondary degrees. *Shinsen* – equivalent to C – can only be an exchange note. Of the primary or secondary degrees G, D, A and F♯ also serve as exchange notes, and are variously inflected in the melodic wind parts. Only *hyōjō* (E) is never inflected and is never either an exchange note or subject to being exchanged. In this sense *hyōjō* is the one fixed note of the system, though in no sense is it a system tonic.

(*c*) Modal individuality and transposition in the three *ritsu chōshi*. The *tōgaku chōshi*, though they incorporate the notion of 'key', are something more than simply equivalent entities projected at different places in the background system. Even apart from any differences reflecting *ryō* and *ritsu* scale types, the requirements of the melodic instruments ensure a distinctive character for each *chōshi*. The distinctions are most easily seen through comparison of transposed versions of *tōgaku* compositions.

There exist versions of the *shōkyoku* ('little piece') *Etenraku* in each of the three *ritsu chōshi*. The *banshikichō* version is believed to be the original. The *hyōjō* version of *Etenraku* is the one item of gagaku that could be considered familiar, even 'popular'. Recorded performances of all three may be heard on Everest Record 3322, side A. Ex.46 (reduced after Shiba, 1969, pp.161f, 155f, 111f) shows the basic shape, the 'nuclear theme', for all three versions of *Etenraku*, with each note head corresponding to one 'bar' of the actual music. The design of the piece is *ABCAB* (the *tomede* – final close or coda – are not included). The modal degree numbers and the staff notes alike represent an abstraction; they happen to be derived from the koto parts, but the lowest and principal note of each chord of the 'mouth organ' *shō* might have been used, or a reduced version of the part

Ex.46

*banshikichō* ('B mode')

modal degrees   6  5  1  1  6  2  1  1      5  4  5  6  2  5  1  1

*ōshikichō* ('A mode')

modal degrees   6  5  1  1  6  2  1  1      5  4  5  6  2  5  1  1

*hyōjō* ('E mode')

modal degrees   6  5  1  1  6  2  1  1      5  4  5  6  2  5  1  1

1  1  2  4  5  5̂  4  4  4   6  5  1  1  6  2  1  1      5  4  5  6  2  5  1  1

1  1  2  4  5  5̂  4  4  4   6  5  1  1  6  2  1  1      5  4  5  6  2  5  1  1

1  1  2  4  5  5̂  4  4  4   6  5  1  1  6  2  1  1      5  4  5  6  2  5  1  1

Ex.47
*banshikichō*

Ex.48
(a) *ritsu*-scale tunings for the *gakusō* (koto) in gagaku

(i) *banshikichō*

(ii) *ōshikichō*

(iii) *hyōjō*

(b) *in*-scale tunings for the koto (17th century and later)

(i) *hira-jōshi*

(ii) *hon-kumoi-jōshi*

(iii) *nakazora-chōshi*

(transposed down a 4th from Adriaansz, 1973)

Ex.49
(a) *banshikichō*

(b) *ōshikichō*

(c) *hyōjō*

*da capo al* 𝄐

*da capo al* 𝄐

for *biwa* (large four-string, pear-shaped lute).

Each melodic instrument has a highly stylized, even stereotyped, conventional manner of presenting its version of the basic shape. Ex.47 (from Shiba, 1969, pp.161, 155, 111) shows the end of the koto part in each transposition of *Etenraku* – the last four bars, equivalent to the last four note heads of the abstracted basic shapes. The two-bar plucking pattern named *shizugake* (appearing twice in each example) goes all through the piece, with a variant only in the fifth bar of the contrasting *C* section. For each of the three transpositions the player's physical motions are identical; the same koto strings are plucked each time, as shown in the numbers under the staff notation, and differences of pitch content result only from different tunings of the open strings. Ex.48a (after Shiba, 1955, p.4) shows the tunings of the 13 strings of the koto for each of the three *ritsu chōshi*. Substituting the designated pitches (or their exchange tones) for the string numbers in ex.47 will produce the figuration shown in the staff notation.

The realization of the abstract pattern on the double-reed *hichiriki* or the flute *ryūteki* is a much more complex affair, depending on wind pressure, fingering and oddities of instrumental construction, all leading to a complicated oral performing tradition of only slightly less complicated notated parts. Garfias (1975, pp.47ff, 68ff) gave a full account of the technique and notation of the two instruments; a pale reflection of what the *hichiriki* does to those abstract *Etenraku* melodies so simply touched up by the koto can be gleaned from Shiba's transcriptions into staff notation, shown in ex.49a, b, c (after Shiba, 1969, pp.161f, 155f, 111f). The wonderfully raucous tone, the correlated changes of pitch and dynamics, the hiccoughing breaks of register, cannot be shown (though semi-attack has been shown with a cross); but even the outline of pitches – many penetratingly stable, others approximate and shifting, a few merely quick flickers of articulation (such as the semiquavers, which are articulations rather than pitches) – suggests vast differences between the three versions.

Some of the differences in the three *hichiriki* melodies reflect different inflections of the same pitch in different *chōshi*, and others are functions of the technique and tradition of the instrument itself; a detailed description of many subtleties of *hichiriki* and *ryūteki* figures in the three *ritsu chōshi* is given by Garfias (1975, pp.135ff). Some grosser modal distinctions of the three versions of the melody can be seen in the transcribed examples. The *hichiriki* has a limited range of effectively an octave, with a downward extension by one degree, that is, by one fingering, which here (as in most cases) can produce more than one pitch.

Ex.50 illustrates the effect on the *hichiriki* part of its limited range. Ex.50a gives the three theoretical *ritsu* scales, each with the range of one degree beyond the octave needed for the basic shape of *Etenraku*. Ex.50b gives the same degrees of the scale but compressed within the single octave *a–a′*, as though within the effective range of the *hichiriki*. Ex.50c gives scale types extracted from the actual *hichiriki* parts of ex.49, omitting note heads that only indicate articulations. Sounding all three *chōshi* in a single common register does not suppress but rather highlights individual melodic differences, emphasizing that a difference in *chōshi* is not only a difference in 'key'.

Comparing ex.50b and c, one also observes that the

basic pentatonic structure of the theoretical *ritsu* scales is maintained in the *hichiriki* melodies, along with the exchange notes (see particularly the complementary distribution of C and B♭ in the *ōshikichō* version). Certain of the actual pitches, however, fairly regularly conflict with those of the two string instruments in being altered downward: G♯ > G♮, C♯ > C♮, and F♯ > F♮ (except in *banshikichō* where F♯ generally holds its proper pitch level to provide the 5th above the tonic B). In other words, in the linear wind parts a secondary degree 2 or 6 of a *chōshi* is usually transformed so as to make a semitone above a primary degree 1 or 5, instead of the whole tone/minor 3rd called for by the theoretical *ritsu* scale, and actually present in the koto tunings.

**Ex.50** Transformation of *ritsu* scales in *hichiriki* performing practice
(a) *ritsu* scales
*banshikichō*

(b) *ritsu* scales in one octave
*banshikichō*

*ōshikichō*

*hyōjō*

(c) scales of *hichiriki* part in *Etenraku*
*banshikichō*

*ōshikichō*

*hyōjō*

There are, then, three basic elements endowing each *hichiriki* melody in the three transpositions of *Etenraku* with a distinct modal character: the transformation of secondary degrees to upper-auxiliary semitones; the compression of melodic motion into one octave plus a 'degree' below; and blowing and fingering traditions of the instrument. Allowing for these three factors, the basic shapes of *Etenraku* in *banshikichō*, *ōshikichō* and *hyōjō* – realized so regularly and mechanically in the koto part – can almost as easily be matched to the *hichiriki* parts, one bar in ex.49 to each note head in ex.46. Yet the *hichiriki* music is in fact different in each version; such differences make a *chōshi* a modal entity and not just a tonality.

(*d*) Transformation and transposition: modes, scales and tunings. The *hichiriki* parts whose scales are summarized in ex.50*c* are in effect using transformed versions of the three *ritsu chōshi*: the anhemitonic pentatonic scale structure of tones and minor 3rds that arises from the koto part becomes a hemitonic pentatonic with a skeleton of semitones and major 3rds.

In later Japanese theory the scale types are no longer discussed in terms of *ritsu* and *ryō*. The male–female dichotomy is now presented in the much more obvious and familiar opposition of *yō* and *in* (equivalent of Chinese *yang* and *yin*), as illustrated in ex.51*a* (after Kishibe, 1969, p.12). A *ritsu* type of scale structure is seen in the *yō* scale; the opposed *in* scale is also a *ritsu* type, transformed by a lowering of the second degree of the scale and the sixth (or its exchange note) from tones or minor 3rds above the first and fifth to semitones above the first and fifth – the same difference that the *hichiriki* intonations produce in the *chōshi* of *tōgaku*. The *in* scale provides a semitone–major 3rd division of the 4th which is characteristic of the bulk of Japanese traditional music from the 16th century onwards, and is apparently of ancient and indigenous provenance. Ex.51*b* (after Malm, 1963, p.61) shows the five forms of the *in* scale used for the shamisen in *nagauta*.

It has been suggested that this characteristically Japanese *in* scale may have influenced the intonations of the *hichiriki* to bend in its direction over the centuries (but cf Garfias, 1975, pp.135f). Be that so or otherwise in principle, it has been shown that just such a transformation of a *ritsu*-scale tuning into an *in*-scale tuning in practice was responsible for the composition effectively launching the modern koto traditions. Willem Adriaansz, after relating the story of the origin of the first *kumiuta* (koto with voice) – that it was developed during the 16th and 17th centuries from the koto part of *Etenraku* – showed how it was done (Adriaansz, 1973, pp.147ff). It involves a chain of tuning transformations

Ex.51

and structural elaborations, leading from the *ritsu*-scale *hyōjō* version of *Etenraku* to the *in*-scale form of *Fuki* as it existed in the late 17th century. Ex.52 shows the first part of Adriaansz's demonstration (pp.270f, together with Shiba, 1969, p.111) written out in staff notation, with the koto string numbers from his table underneath; two bars of *Fuki* correspond to one measure of *Etenraku*. It may be observed that every string number of *Etenraku* is matched by a string number in *Fuki*; there are also extra actions in *Fuki* filling the pauses, with the single-note bars in *Etenraku* being treated especially elaborately (string numbers for these bars are omitted in ex.52*b*).

Ex.52

Note that it is not the background basic shape of *Etenraku* that was used but the koto's particular version of it. The pitch content of the original, and hence the scale or mode, has been transformed, again simply by retuning the koto. There is no sure way of knowing from which *ritsu chōshi* version of *Etenraku* the *in*-scale *Fuki* ultimately descended; from ex.48*a* (iii), *b* (i), can be seen how the *hyōjō* tuning of the koto might have been modified from a *ritsu* tuning to an *in* tuning to produce the tuning used for *Fuki*, and indeed for the bulk of traditional koto music. This tuning is called *hira-jōshi* (ex.48*b* (i)); *hira* is the *kunyomi* (Japanese) word written with the same ideogram as *hyō* (both words meaning 'plain, level, peaceful, ordinary'), a probably more than coincidental reflection of the transformation of *ritsu*-scale types to *in*-scale types.

Two other Edo-period (1603–1868) koto tunings are shown in ex.48*b* (ii), (iii); like the shamisen scales of ex.51*b*, all three koto tunings can be thought of as simply making available different transpositions of the *in* scale (Adriaansz, 1973, pp.115, 475). Of course the same can be said of the *ritsu*-scale tunings of the *gakusō*, the koto played in the *tōgaku* ensemble. And indeed, compared with the flamboyant modal individuation of the *hichiriki*, the koto parts seem hardly more than transpositions of one another. Yet they do differ slightly, if only by registral dislocations in the lower strings (ex.47). Perhaps the combination of changing tessituras of the different *in* scales and the constant strings 1 and 2 (ex.48*b*) provide a difference in orientation from one koto *chōshi* to another that is more than just a change in the register – a change of 'key' – of the *in* scale. But on the whole, to compare the *hira-jōshi* and *kumoi-jōshi* of the koto and voice ensemble with the comparably transposed *hyōjō* and *ōshikichō* of the *hichiriki* in the *tōgaku* ensemble is to know the difference between *chōshi* as a mere tuning pattern and *chōshi* as a unique modal entity.

See also JAPAN, §§III, 1, and IV, 2, 4.

### BIBLIOGRAPHY

For fuller information on editions and reprints, *see* THEORY, THEORISTS, and articles on individual theorists.

MEDIEVAL THEORY AND PRACTICE: PRIMARY SOURCES

Anonymous: *Alia musica*; ed. J. Chailley (Paris, 1965)
Anonymous: *Commemoratio brevis*; GS, i, 213–29
Anonymous: *Commentarius anonymus in Micrologum Guidonis Aretini*; ed. C. Vivell (Vienna, 1917); ed. J. Smits van Waesberghe, *Expositiones in Micrologum* (Amsterdam, 1957), 95–172
Anonymous: *Commentum super tonos*; ed. J. Smits van Waesberghe, *Divitiae musicae artis*, 1st ser., i (Buren, 1975)
Anonymous: *Dialogus de musica*; GS, i, 251–64; part trans. O. Strunk, *Source Readings in Music History* (New York, 1950/R1965), 103 [attrib. Odo]
Anonymous: *Musica*; GS, i, 330–38
Anonymous: *Musica enchiriadis* (F-Pn lat.7202); GS, i, 152–73
Anonymous: *Questiones in musica*; ed. R. Steglich, *Die quaestiones in musica* (Leipzig, 1911)
Anonymous: *Summa musicae*; GS, iii, 189–248
Anonymous: *Tractatus cuiusdam monachi de musica*; ed. J. Wolf, 'Ein anonymes Musiktraktat des elften bis zwölften Jahrhunderts', *VMw*, ix (1893), 186–234
Anonymous: *Tractatus de natura et distinctione octo tonorum musice*; CS, ii, 434–49
Aribo: *De musica*; GS, ii, 197–230; ed. J. Smits van Waesberghe, CSM, ii (1951)
Aurelian of Réôme: *Musica disciplina*; GS, i, 27; ed. L. Gushee, CSM, xxi (1975)
Bernard of Clairvaux: *Tonale*; GS, ii, 265–77
Berno of Reichenau: *Prologus in tonarium cum tonario [Musica Bernonis]*; GS, ii, 61–117
Boethius: *De institutione musica*; trans. C. Bower (diss., George Peabody College, 1967)
*Corpus antiphonalium officii*, ed. R. Hesbert, Rerum ecclesiasticarum documenta, main ser., Fontes, vii–xi (Rome, 1963–75)
Engelbert of Admont: *De musica*; GS, ii, 287–369
Frutolfus of Michelsberg: *Breviarum de musica et tonarius*; ed. C. Vivell (Vienna, 1919)
Guido of Arezzo: *Epistola de ignoto cantu*; GS, ii, 43
——: *Micrologus*; ed. J. Smits van Waesberghe, CSM, iv (1955); Eng. trans. W. Babb (New Haven, Conn., 1979)
Guy d'Eu: *Regulae de arte musica*; CS, ii, 150–91
[Hartker Antiphoner]; PalMus, 2nd ser., i, (1900, 2/1970)
Hermannus Contractus: *De musica*; ed. L. Ellinwood (Rochester, 1936)
Hucbald: *De harmonica institutione*; GS, i, 104–21
Jacques de Liège: *Speculum musice*; CS, ii, 193–433 [attrib. Jehan des Murs]
Jerome of Moravia: *Tractatus de musica*; ed. S. Cserba (Regensburg, 1935)
Johannes Afflighemensis: *De musica*; ed. J. Smits van Waesberghe, CSM, i (1950); Eng. trans. W. Babb (New Haven, Conn., 1979)
[Lucca Antiphoner]; PalMus, ix, (1905–9)
[Petershausen Antiphoner] (*D-KA* 60)
Regino of Prüm: *Epistola de armonica institutione* and *Octo toni de musicae artis*; ed. M. P. Le Roux (Ann Arbor, 1970) (*D-LEu* Rep. I.8.93 [169]); CS, ii, 1–73 (*B-Br* 2750–65) [*Octo toni* only]; GS, i, 230–47 [*Epistola* only]
[Reichenau Antiphoner] (*D-Kl* Cod.Aug.LX)
[Reichenau Tonary]; ed. H. Sowa, *Quelle zur Transformation der Antiphonen* (Kassel, 1935)
[Sarum Antiphoner]; ed. W. H. Frere, *Antiphonale sarisburiense*, Plainsong Medieval Music Society (London, 1901–25/R1967)

Theogerus of Metz: *Musica*; GS, ii, 182–96
Wilhelm of Hirsau: *Musica*; GS, ii, 154–82
[Worcester Antiphoner]; PalMus, 1st ser., xii (1922–5)

MEDIEVAL THEORY AND PRACTICE: SECONDARY SOURCES

M. Gerbert: *Scriptores ecclesiastici de musica* (St Blasien, 1784) [GS]
C.-E.-H. de Coussemaker: *Scriptorum de musica medii aevi nova series* (Paris, 1864–76) [CS]
F. A. Gevaert: *La mélopée antique dans le chant de l'église latine* (Ghent, 1895)
G. Jacobsthal: *Die chromatische Alteration im liturgischen Gesang der abendländischen Kirche* (Berlin, 1898)
H. Abert: *Die Musikanschauung des Mittelalters und ihre Grundlagen* (Halle, 1905)
P. Wagner: *Einführung in die gregorianischen Melodien* (Leipzig, 1895–1921/R1962)
U. Bomm: *Der Wechsel der Modalitätsbestimmung in der Tradition der Messgesänge im IX. bis XIII. Jahrhundert und sein Einfluss auf die Tradition ihrer Melodien* (Einsiedeln, 1928)
P. Wagner: 'Zur mittelalterlichen Tonartenlehre', *Studien zur Musikgeschichte: Festschrift für Guido Adler* (Vienna, 1930/R1971), 30
E. Omlin: *Die Sankt Gallischen Tonarbuchstaben* (Regensburg, 1934)
P. Ferretti: *Esthétique grégorienne* (Paris, 1938)
O. Gombosi: 'Studien zur Tonartenlehre des frühen Mittelalters', *AcM*, x (1938), 149; xi (1939), 28, 128; xii (1940), 21–52
J. Smits van Waesberghe: 'Some Music Treatises and their Interrelation: a School of Liège (c. 1050–1200)?', *MD*, iii (1949), 25, 95
S. R. Marosszéki: *Les origines du chant cistercien* (Rome, 1952)
K. Meyer: 'The Eight Gregorian Modes on the Cluny Capitals', *Art Bulletin*, xxiv/2 (1952), 75
J. Smits van Waesberghe: 'La place exceptionelle de l'Ars Musica dans le développement des sciences au siècle des Carolingiens', *Revue grégorienne*, xxxii (1952), 81
H. Hucke: 'Musikalische Formen der Officiumsantiphonen', *KJb*, xxxvii (1953), 7
H. Potiron: *La composition des modes grégoriens* (Tournai, 1953)
H. Oesch: *Guido von Arezzo: Biographisches und Theoretisches unter besonderer Berücksichtigung der sogenannten odonischen Traktate* (Berne, 1954)
K. G. Fellerer: 'Zum Musiktraktat des Wilhelm von Hirsau', *Festschrift Wilhelm Fischer* (Innsbruck, 1956), 61
K. W. Niemöller: 'Zur Tonus-lehre der italienischen Musiktheorie des ausgehenden Mittelalters', *KJb*, xl (1956), 23
R. Stephan: 'Aus der alten Abtei Reichenau', *AMw*, iii (1956), 61
R. Weakland: 'Hucbald as Musician and Theorist', *MQ*, xlii (1956), 66
W. Apel: *Gregorian Chant* (Bloomington, Ind., 1958, 3/1966)
K. G. Fellerer: 'Untersuchungen zur Musica des Wilhelm von Hirsau', *Miscelánea en homenaje a Monseñor Higinio Anglés* (Barcelona, 1958), i, 239
K. W. Gümpel: *Zur Interpretation der Tonus-Definition des Tonale Sancti Bernardi* (Wiesbaden, 1959)
H. Oesch: *Berno und Hermann von Reichenau als Musiktheoretiker* (Berne, 1961)
J. Ponte: *The 'Musica disciplina' of Aureliani Reomensis* (diss., Brandeis U., 1961)
H. Hüschen: 'Regino von Prüm, Historiker, Kirchenrechtler, und Musiktheoretiker', *Festschrift Karl Gustav Fellerer* (Regensburg, 1962), 205
W. Lipphardt: *Der karolingische Tonar von Metz* (Münster, 1965)
R. Monterosso: 'Un compendio inedito del *Lucidarium* di Marchetto da Padova', *Studi medievali*, 3rd ser., vii (1966), 914
M. Huglo: 'L'auteur du dialogue sur la musique attribué à Odon', *RdM*, lv (1969), 119–71
J. Smits van Waesberghe: *Musikerziehung: Lehre und Theorie der Musik des Mittelalters* (Leipzig, 1969)
M. Huglo: *Les tonaires* (Paris, 1971)
T. Connolly: 'Introits and Archetypes: some Archaisms of the Old Roman Chant', *JAMS*, xxv (1972), 157
R. Crocker: 'Hermann's Major Sixth', *JAMS*, xxv (1972), 19
F. A. Gallo: 'Philological Work on Musical Treatises of the Middle Ages', *AcM*, xliv (1972), 78
L. Gushee: 'Questions of Genre in Medieval Treatises on Music', *Gattungen der Musik in Einzeldarstellungen: Gedenkschrift für Leo Schrade*, i (Berne and Munich, 1973), 365–433
T. Seebass: *Musikdarstellung und Psalterillustration im früheren Mittelalter* (Berne, 1973)
T. Bailey: *The Intonation Formulae of Western Chant* (Toronto, 1974)
L. Treitler: 'Homer and Gregory: the Transmission of Epic Poetry and Plainchant', *MQ*, lx (1974), 333
H. Hucke: 'Karolingische Renaissance und Gregorianischer Gesang', *Mf*, xxviii (1975), 4
C. Sweeney: 'John Wylde and the *Musica Guidonis*', *MD*, xxix (1975). 43
L. Treitler: 'Centonate Chant', *JAMS*, xxviii (1975), 1
P. Cutter: 'Oral Transmission of the Old-Roman Responsories', *MQ*,

lxii (1976), 182

M. Markovits: *Das Tonsystem der abendländischen Musik im frühen Mittelalter* (Berne, 1977)

MODAL THEORIES AND POLYPHONIC MUSIC: PRIMARY SOURCES

Adam von Fulda: *De musica*; *GS*, iii, 329–81

Johannes de Grocheo: *De musica*; trans. A. Seay (Colorado Springs, 1967)

J. Legrense: *Vera quamque facilis ad cantandum atque brevis introductio*; *CS*, iv, 345–95

Marchetto da Padova: *Lucidarium in arte musicae planae*, 1309–18; *GS*, iii, 64–121

Ugolino of Orvieto: *Declaratio musice discipline*, c1430–35; ed. A. Seay, CSM, vii (1960–62)

J. Tinctoris: *Terminorum musicae diffinitorium*, written c1475 (Treviso, 1495); ed. and trans. C. Parrish (New York, 1963)

——: *Liber de natura et proprietate tonorum*, 1476; *CS*, iv, 16–41; trans. A. Seay (Colorado Springs, 1967)

——: *Liber de arte contrapuncti*, 1477; *CS*, iv, 76–153; trans. A. Seay, MSD, v (1961)

Guillelmus Monachus: *De preceptis artis musicae*, c1480; ed. A. Seay, CSM, xi (1965)

B. Ramos de Pareia: *Musica practica* (Bologna, 1482); ed. J. Wolf (Leipzig, 1901/R1968)

N. Burtius: *Opusculum musices* (Bologna, 1487/R1969); ed. G. Massera, *Florum libellus* (Florence, 1975)

F. Gaffurius: *Theorica musicae* (Milan, 1492)

——: *Practica musicae* (Milan, 1496); trans. C. Miller, MSD, xx (1969)

Bonaventura da Brescia: *Breviloquium musicale* (Brescia, 1497)

G. Valla: *Harmonicorum introductorium* (Venice, 1497) [Lat. trans. of Gk. treatises, incl. Cleonides: *Eisagōgē harmonikē*]

M. Schanppecher: 'De musica figurativa', pts.iii–iv of N. Wollick: *Opus aureum* (Cologne, 1501); ed. K. W. Niemöller (Cologne, 1961)

N. Wollick: *Opus aureum* (Cologne, 1501); ed. K. W. Niemöller (Cologne, 1955)

——: *Enchiridion musices* (Paris, 1509)

J. Cochlaeus: *Tetrachordum musices* (Cologne, 1511); ed. and trans. C. Miller, MSD, xxiii (1970)

W. Philomathes: *Musicorum libri quatuor* (Vienna, 1512)

P. Aaron: *Libri tres de institutione harmonica* (Bologna, 1516/R1971)

H. Glarean: *Isagoge* (Basle, 1516); trans. F. B. Turrell, *JMT*, iii (1959), 97–139

A. Ornithoparchus: *Musicae activae micrologus* (Leipzig, 1517; trans. J. Dowland, London, 1609; both R1973)

F. Gaffurius: *De harmonia musicorum instrumentorum opus* (Milan, 1518)

J. Galliculus: *Isagoge de compositione cantus* (Leipzig, 1520)

P. Aaron: *Trattato della natura et cognitione di tutti gli tuoni di canto figurato* (Venice, 1525); chaps.1–7 trans. O. Strunk, *Source Readings* (New York, 1950/R1965), 205

G. M. Lanfranco: *Scintille di musica* (Brescia, 1533)

A. Lampadius: *Compendium musices* (Berne, 1537)

N. Listenius: *Musica* (Wittenberg, 1537)

S. Heyden: *De arte canendi* (Nuremberg, 1540); trans. C. Miller, MSD, xxvi (1972)

P. Aaron: *Lucidario* (Venice, 1545)

H. Glarean: *Dodecachordon* (Basle, 1547); trans. C. Miller, MSD, vi (1965)

P. Aaron: *Compendiolo di molti dubbi* (Milan, c1550)

A. P. Coclico: *Compendium musices* (Nuremberg, 1552/R1954)

J. Bermudo: *Declaración de instrumentos musicales* (Osuna, 1555)

N. Vicentino: *L'antica musica* (Rome, 1555/R1959)

H. Finck: *Practica musica* (Wittenberg, 1556)

G. Zarlino: *Le istitutioni harmoniche* (Venice, 1558/R1965, rev. 3/1573/R1966; Eng. trans. of pt.iii, 1968, by G. A. Marco and C. V. Palisca, as *The Art of Counterpoint*)

G. Dressler: *Practica modorum explicatio* (Jena, 1561)

L. Lossius: *Erotemata musicae practiae* (Nuremberg, 1563)

G. Dressler: *Praecepta musicae poeticae*, 1563; ed. B. Engelke, *Geschichts-Blätter für Stadt und Land Magdeburg*, xlix–l (1914–15)

——: *Musicae practicae elementa* (Magdeburg, 1571)

G. Zarlino: *Dimostrationi harmoniche* (Venice, 1571)

E. Hoffmann: *Musicae practicae praecepta* (Hamburg, 1572)

C. Praetorius: *Erotemata musices* (Wittenberg, 1574)

I. Aiguino: *Il tesoro illuminato di tutti i tuoni di canto figurato* (Venice, 1581)

E. Hoffmann: *Doctrina de tonis seu modis musicis* (Greifswald, 1582)

J. Yssandon: *Traité de la musique pratique* (Paris, 1582)

P. Pontio: *Ragionamento di musica* (Parma, 1588)

A. Raselius: *Hexachordum seu questiones musicae practicae* (Nuremberg, 1591)

C. Schneegass: *Isagoges musicae libri duo* (Erfurt, 1591)

S. Calvisius: *Melopoeia* (Erfurt, 1592)

L. Zacconi: *Prattica di musica*, i (Venice, 1592); ii (Venice, 1622)

V. Bona da Brescia: *Regole del contraponto et compositione* (Casale,

1595)

J. Magirus: *Artis musicae* (Frankfurt am Main, 1596); ed. E. Nolte (Marburg, 1971)

T. Morley: *A Plaine and Easie Introduction to Practicall Musicke* (London, 1597); ed. R. A. Harman (London, 1952, 2/1963)

S. Calvisius: *Exercitationes musicae duae* (Leipzig, 1600)

P. Eichmann: *Praecepta musicae practicae* (Stettin, 1604)

J. Burmeister: *Musica poetica* (Rostock, 1606/R1955)

O. S. Harnisch: *Artis musicae delineatio* (Frankfurt am Main, 1608)

A. Banchieri: *Cartella musicale* (Venice, 1614)

J. Titelouze: *Magnificat pour l'orgue* (Paris, 1626); ed. A. Guilmant and A. Pirro, *Archives des maîtres de l'orgue*, i (1898/R1972)

J. Crüger: *Synopsis musicae* (Berlin, 1630)

G. G. Nivers: *Traité de la composition de musique* (Paris, 1667); ed. and trans. A. Cohen, Music Theorists in Translation, iii (Brooklyn, 1961)

G. M. Bononcini: *Musico prattico* (Bologna, 1673)

G. Falck: *Idea boni cantoris* (Nuremberg, 1688)

J. Mattheson: *Das neu-eröffnete Orchestre* (Hamburg, 1713)

J. Buttstett: *Ut, mi, sol, re, fa, la, tota musica et harmonia aeterna* (Erfurt, 1716)

MODAL THEORY AND POLYPHONIC MUSIC: SECONDARY SOURCES

O. Strunk: *Source Readings in Music History* (New York, 1950/R1965)

G. Reichert: 'Kirchentonart als Formfaktor in der mehrstimmigen Musik des 15. und 16. Jahrhunderts', *Mf*, iv (1951), 35

B. Meier: 'Die Handschrift Porto 714 als Quelle zur Tonartenlehre des 15. Jahrhunderts', *MD*, x (1956), 67–105

M. Ruhnke: *J. Burmeister: ein Beitrag zur Musiklehre um 1600* (Kassel, 1955)

B. Meier: 'The Musica Reservata of Adriann Petit Coclico and its Relationship to Josquin', *MD*, x (1956), 67–105

K. W. Niemöller: *Nicolaus Wollick (1480–1541), und sein Musiktraktat* (Cologne, 1956)

B. Meier: 'Bemerkungen zu Lechners Motetae Sacrae von 1575', *AMw*, xiv (1957), 83

A. C. Howell: 'French Baroque Organ Music and the Eight Tones', *JAMS*, xi (1958), 106

B. Meier: Foreword to *C. de Rore: Opera omnia*, CMM, xiv: i (1959), pp.i–vi; ii (1963), pp.i–vii; iii (1961), pp.i–viii; iv (1969), pp.i–ix

S. Hermelink: *Dispositiones modorum: die Tonarten in der Musik Palestrinas und seiner Zeitgenossen* (Tutzing, 1960)

C. B. Miller: *Chiavette: a new Approach* (diss, U. of California, Berkeley, 1960)

G. Reichert: 'Tonart und Tonalität in der älteren Musik', *Musikalische Zeitfragen*, x (1962), 97

B. Meier: 'Wortausdeutung und Tonalität bei Orlando di Lasso', *KJb*, xlvii (1963), 75–104

E. P. Bergquist: *The Theoretical Writings of Pietro Aaron* (diss., Columbia U., 1964)

L. Treitler: 'Tone System in the Secular Works of Guillaume Dufay', *JAMS*, xvii (1965), 131–69

C. Dahlhaus: *Untersuchungen über die Entstehung der harmonischen Tonalität* (Kassel, 1968)

K. G. Fellerer: 'Die kölner musiktheoretische Schule des 16. Jahrhunderts', *Renaissance-muziek 1400–1600: donum natalicium René Bernard Lenaerts* (Louvain, 1969), 121

B. Meier: 'Alte und neue Tonarten, Wesen und Bedeutung', *Renaissance-muziek 1400–1600: donum natalicium René Bernard Lenaerts* (Louvain, 1969), 157

——: 'Modale Korrektur und Wortausdeutung im Choral der Editio Medicaea', *KJb*, liii (1969), 101–32

C. Palisca: 'Ut oratoria musica: the Rhetorical Basis of Musical Mannerism', *The Meaning of Mannerism*, ed. F. Robinson and S. Nichols (Hanover, 1972), 37

H. Schneider: *Die französische Kompositionslehre in der ersten Hälfte des 17. Jahrhunderts* (Tutzing, 1972)

W. Atcherson: 'Key and Mode in 17th-century Theory Books', *JMT*, xvii (1973), 205

L. Perkins: 'Mode and Structure in the Masses of Josquin', *JAMS*, xxvi (1973), 189–239

J. Lester: 'Root-position and Inverted Triads in Theory around 1600', *JAMS*, xxvii (1974), 110

B. Meier: *Die Tonarten der klassischen Vokalpolyphonie* (Utrecht, 1974)

H. S. Powers: 'The Modality of "Vestiva i colli" ', *Studies in Renaissance and Baroque Music in Honor of Arthur Mendel* (Kassel and Hackensack, 1974)

R. G. Luoma: 'Aspects of Mode in Sixteenth-century Magnificats', *MQ*, lxii (1976), 395

J. Lester: 'Major–minor Concepts and Modal Theory in Germany: 1592–1680', *JAMS*, xxx (1977), 208

MODAL SCALES AND FOLKSONG MELODIES

C. Sharp: *English Folk-song: some Conclusions* (London, 1907)

P. Grainger: 'Collecting with the Phonograph', *JFSS*, iii (1908–9), 147

A. Gilchrist: 'A Note on the Modal System of Gaelic Tunes', *JFSS*, iv (1910–13), 150

C. Sharp and M. Karpeles: *English Folk Songs from the Southern Appalachians* (London, 1917, 2/1932)

P. Barry: 'The Music of the Ballads', *British Ballads from Maine*, ed. P. Barry, F. H. Eckstrom and M. W. Smyth (New Haven, Conn., 1929), xxi–xxxvii

——: 'American Folk Music', *Southern Folklore Quarterly*, i (1937), 29

G. Herzog: 'Musical Typology in Folksong', *Southern Folklore Quarterly*, i (1937), 49

H. Reichenbach: 'The Tonality of English and Gaelic Folksong', *ML*, xix (1938), 263

S. P. Bayard: 'Aspects of Melodic Kinship and Variation in British–American Folk-tunes', *PAMS 1939*, 122

A. M. Buchanan: 'Modal and Melodic Structure in Anglo-American Folk Music: a Neutral Mode', *PAMS 1939*, 84

B. H. Bronson: 'Folksong and the Modes', *MQ*, xxxii (1946), 37

S. P. Bayard: 'Prolegomena to a Study of the Principal Melodic Families of Folksong', *Journal of American Folklore*, lxiii (1950), 1–44; repr. in *The Critics and the Ballad*, ed. M. Leach and T. P. Coffin (Carbondale, Ill., 1961)

B. H. Bronson: 'Some Observations about Melodic Variations in British–American Folktunes', *JAMS*, iii (1950), 120 [see also 'Habits of the Ballads', in Bronson, 1969]

S. P. Bayard: 'American Folksongs and their Music', *Southern Folklore Quarterly*, xvii (1953), 122

——: 'Two Representative Tune Families of British Tradition', *Midwest Folklore*, iv (1954), 13

——: 'A Miscellany of Tune Notes', *Studies in Folklore*, ed. W. E. Richmond (Bloomington, Ind., 1957), 151

D. K. Wilgus: *Anglo-American Folksong Scholarship since 1898* (New Brunswick, 1959)

B. H. Bronson: *The Traditional Tunes of the Child Ballads* (Princeton, 1959–72)

M. Kolinski: 'Classification of Tonal Structures', *Studies in Ethnomusicology*, i (1961), 38–76

C. Seeger: 'Versions and Variants of the Tunes of "Barbara Allen" ', *Selected Reports*, i/1 (1966), 120–67

J. M. Ward: 'Apropos *The British Broadside Ballad and its Music*', *JAMS*, xx (1967), 28–86

R. P. Abrahams and G. Foss: *Anglo-American Folksong Style* (Englewood, 1968)

M. Kolinski: 'Barbara Allen: Tonal versus Melodic Structure', *EM*, xii (1968), 208; xiii (1969), 1–73

B. H. Bronson: *The Ballad as Song* (Berkeley, 1969)

N. Cazden: 'A Simplified Mode Classification for Traditional Anglo-American Song Tunes', *YIFMC*, iii (1971), 45–78

MODE AS A MUSICOLOGICAL CONCEPT

W. Jones: 'On the Musical Modes of the Hindoos', *Asiatick Researches*, iii (1792), 55–87; repr. in Tagore (1875); repr. in S. Gupta, *Music of India* (Calcutta, 1962)

N. A. Willard: *Treatise on the Music of Hindustan* (Calcutta, 1834); repr. in Tagore (1875); repr. in S. Gupta, *Music of India* (Calcutta, 1962)

S. M. Tagore, ed.: *Hindu Music from Various Authors* (Calcutta, 1875) [incl. W. Jones: 'On the Musical Modes of the Hindoos', N. A. Willard: *Treatise on the Music of Hindustan*]

V. N. Bhatkhande: *Hindustānī-saṅgīta-paddhati* (Bombay, 1910–32; Hindi trans., 1951–7)

J. Jeannin and J. Puyade: 'L'octoëchos syrien', *Oriens christianus*, new ser., iii (1913)

A. Z. Idelsohn: 'Die Maqamen der arabischen Musik', *SIMG*, xv (1913–14), 1–63

M. Courant: 'Chine et Corée', *EMDC*, I/i (1921), 77–241

R. Yekta Bey: 'La musique turque', *EMDC*, I/v (1922), 2945–3064

J. Rouanet: 'La musique arabe', *EMDC*, I/v (1922), 2676–812

A. A. Bake: *Bydrage tot de kennis der voor-indische muziek* (Paris, 1930) [edn. and Eng. trans. of *Saṅgīta-darpaṇa*, chaps. 1–2]

V. N. Bhatkhande: *A Comparative Study of the Leading Music Systems of the 15th, 16th, 17th and 18th Centuries* (n.p., n.d.) [written 1930]

R. d'Erlanger: *La musique arabe*, i [Al-Fārābī], ii [Al-Fārābī and Ibn Sīnā]; iii [commentaries on Ṣafi al-din]; iv [anon. and Al-Lādhiqī]; v [scales and modes]; vi [rhythm and form] (Paris, 1930–59)

N. Peri: *Essai sur les gammes japonaises* (Paris, 1934)

O. C. Gangoly: *Rāgas and Rāginīs* (Bombay, 1935, repr. 1948)

N. S. Ramachandran: *The rāgas of Karnatic Music* (Madras, 1938)

Omkarnāth Ṭhākur: *Saṅgītāñjalī*, i (Lahore, 1938, 2/1959); ii (Hathras, 1954); iii–vi (Benares, 1955–62); vii–viii (MSS, unpubd) [Hindi]

J. Kunst: *Music in Java* (The Hague, 2/1949; 3/1973, ed. E. L. Heins)

K. Ramachandran: *Śrī dakṣiṇarāga ratnākaram* (Madras, 1949) [Tamil]

S. N. Ratanjankar: 'Ragas in Hindustani Music', *Journal of the Music Academy, Madras*, xxii (1951), 97

A. Daniélou: *Northern Indian Music*, ii: *The Main ragas* (London, 1954, 2/1968)

M. Hood: *The Nuclear Theme as a Determinant of paṭet in Javanese Music* (Groningen, 1954)

S. Shiba: *Ga-gaku*, i (Tokyo, 1955)

Sindusawarno: *Ilmu karawitan* (Surakarta, n.d. [1955]; Eng. trans., M. Hatch, in preparation)

B. Subba Rao: *Raganidhi: a Comparative Study of Hindustani and Karnatak Ragas*, i (Nagpur, 1956); ii–iv (Madras, 1964–6)

L. Picken: 'The Music of Far Eastern Asia, i: China', *NOHM*, i (1957), 83–134

W. P. Malm: *Japanese Music and Musical Instruments* (Rutland and Tokyo, 1959)

E. Wellesz: *A History of Byzantine Music and Hymnography* (Oxford, 2/1961)

K. Khatschi: *Der Dastgāh: Studien zur neuen persischen Musik* (Regensburg, 1962)

Trân van Khê: *La musique vietnamienne traditionelle* (Paris, 1962)

M. Ma'aroufi: *Les systèmes de la musique traditionelle de l'Iran (radif)* (Teheran, 1963)

W. P. Malm: *Nagauta: the Heart of kabuki Music* (Rutland and Tokyo, 1963)

H. Farhat: *The Dastgāh Concept in Persian Music* (diss., U. of California, Los Angeles, 1965)

N. Caron and D. Safvate: *Les traditions musicales: Iran* (Paris, 1966)

G. Oransay: *Die melodische Linie und der Begriff Makam der traditionellen türkischen Kunstmusik vom 15. bis zum 19. Jahrhundert* (Ankara, 1966)

Y. Radjabi and F. Karamatov: *Shashmakom*, i (Tashkent, 1966), preface; abridged Ger. version, *BMw*, xi (1969), 91

E. L. Heins: 'The Music of serimpi "Anglir mendung" ', *Indonesia* (April 1967), 135 [with music exx.]

Rulan Chao Pian: *Soṇǵ Dynasty Musical Sources and their Interpretation* (Cambridge, Mass., 1967)

W. Kaufmann: *The ragas of North India* (Bloomington, Ind., 1968)

M. T. Massoudieh: *Āwāz-e-Šur: zur Melodiebildung in der persischen Kunstmusik* (Regensburg, 1968)

E. L. Heins: 'Tempo (Irama) in de M.-Javaanse gamelanmuziek', *Kulturpatronen*, nos.10–11 (1968–9), 30

J. Becker: 'The Anatomy of a Mode', *EM*, xiii (1969), 267

S. Kishibe: *The Traditional Music of Japan* (Tokyo, 1969)

S. Shiba: *Gosenfu ni yoru gāgaku sofu*, ii (Tokyo, 1969) [Jap.]

J. Kuckertz: *Form und Melodiebildung der karnatischen Musik Sudindiens* (Wiesbaden, 1970)

H. S. Powers: 'An Historical and Comparative Approach to the Classification of ragas', *Selected Reports*, i/3 (1970), 1–78

J. Spector: 'Classical 'Ud Music in Egypt with Special Reference to Maqamat', *EM*, xiv (1970), 243

N. A. Jairazbhoy: *The Rāgs of North Indian Music* (Middletown, Conn., 1971)

J. Reichow: *Die Entfaltung eines Melodiemodells im Genus Sikāh* (Regensburg, 1971)

H. H. Touma: 'The *Maqam* Phenomenon: an Improvisation Technique in the Music of the Middle East', *EM*, xv (1971), 38

J. Becker: *Traditional Music in Modern Java* (diss., U. of Michigan, 1972)

S. Gitosaprodjo: *Titilaras gending* (Malang, 1972)

B. Nettl: *Daramad of Chahargah: a Study in the Performance Practice of Persian Music* (Detroit, 1972)

——: 'Notes on Persian Classical Music of Today: the Performance of the Hesar Section as Part of Dastgāh Chahārgāh', *Orbis musicae*, i (1972), 175

Gen'ichi Tsuge: 'A Note on the Iraki *Maqam*', *Asian Music*, iv (1972), 59

W. Adriaansz: *The kumiuta and danmono Traditions of Japanese koto Music* (Los Angeles, 1973)

K. Ebeling: *Ragamala Painting* (Paris and New Delhi, 1973)

J. Elsner: *Der Begriff des Maqām in Ägypten in neuerer Zeit* (Leipzig, 1973)

M. Kartomi: *Matjapat Songs in Central and West Java* (Canberra, 1973)

B. Nettl and R. Riddle: 'Taqsim Nahawand: a Study of Sixteen Performances by Jihad Racy', *YIFMC*, v (1973), 11–50

M. Sadeghi: Review of Persian music records, *EM*, xvii (1973), 354

E. Zonis: *Classical Persian Music: an Introduction* (Cambridge, Mass., 1973)

L. Ibsen al Faruqi: *The Nature of the Musical Art of Islamic Culture: a Theoretical and Empirical Study of Arabian Music* (diss., Syracuse U., 1974)

B. Nettl: 'Aspects of Form in the Instrumental Performance of the Persian *āvāz*', *EM*, xviii (1974), 405

S. P. Walton: *Sindèn and paṭet* (diss., U. of Michigan, 1974)

R. Garfias: *Music of a Thousand Autumns: the tōgaku Style of Japanese Court Music* (Los Angeles, 1975)

V. McDermott and Sumarsam: 'The paṭet of laras slendro and the gendèr barung', *EM*, xix (1975), 233

Martopangrawit: *Pengetahuan karawitan* (Surakarta, 2/1975) [vol.1, Indonesian; vol.2, Javanese]
Sumarsam: 'Gendèr barung, its Technique and Function in the Context of Javanese gamelan', *Indonesia* (October 1975), 161
M. Hatch: 'The Song is Ended: Changes in the Use of Macapat in Central Java', *Asian Music*, vii (1976), 59
H. S. Powers: 'The Meaning of Musical Discourse: a View from Banaras', *PNM*, xiv–xv (1976), 308
Sumarsam: 'Inner Melody in Javanese gamelan Music', *Asian Music*, vii (1976), 3
H. H. Touma: *Die Maqam Bayati im arabischen Taqsim* (Hamburg, 2/1976)
K. Signell: *Makam: Modal Practice in Turkish Art Music* (Seattle, 1977)
R. A. Sutton: 'Notes toward a Grammar of Javanese *gender* Playing', *EM*, xxii (1978), 275
O. Wright: *The Modal System of Arab and Persian Music* (Oxford, 1978)
A. Templeton: 'An Informational Analysis of paṭet', appx to J. Becker: *Traditional Music in Modern Java* (Honolulu, in preparation)
                                        HAROLD S. POWERS

**Modena.** Italian city. Although of modest size and until the 17th century lacking a local court to patronize music, Modena has long maintained a lively musical tradition supported by the cathedral and the city government.

The earliest musical source, dating from the 9th century (*I-MOd* Cod.O.I.4), contains a nightwatchman's song (in diastematic notation), *O tu qui servas armis*, celebrating the unsuccessful siege of the city by foreign invaders. After the translation in 1106 of the body of S Geminiano, Modena's patron saint, the musical life of the city centred mainly on the Romanesque cathedral (1099). Two 14th-century plainchant sequences written in honour of the saint survive (*I-MOd* Cod. O.I.16, *Glorietur letabunda* and *Haec sunt sacra festa*). Only from 1453, however, do the *Atti della fabbrica di S. Geminiano* record the musicians attached to the cathedral's *cappella musicale*. In that year Alessandro de Galvan was appointed first organist, a post he held for 20 years; in 1463 Zohane de Marchatelo completed the construction of a new organ, installed next to the old one built by Giacomo Guidini da Regio in 1438. About 1530 Cardinal Morone, one of the main 'reformers' of sacred music at the Council of Trent and then Bishop of Modena, made the first attempt to reform polyphony there; he aimed to make the text better understood and focus the attention of the congregation on the liturgy rather than the music. During the first four decades of the 16th century the cathedral's polyphonic repertory (*I-MOd* Cod.I–XIII) reflected the styles of internationally renowned composers, and Modena maintained strong ties with Rome and Ferrara (Modena became part of the Este domain in 1336 and became a duchy in 1543 under Duke Borso d'Este). During these decades about ten professional singers and instrumentalists were active in the cathedral in addition to the organist. However, the focus of the city's musical affairs moved from the cathedral to the local court after Duke Cesare d'Este moved the family seat from Ferrara to Modena in 1598.

*Maestri di cappella* at the cathedral included Jacopo Fogliani (1505–20), Vecchi (1583–6, 1593–1604), Capilupi (1604–14), Stefanini (1615–26), Bravusi (1626–30), Uccellini (1647–65), Agatea (1665–73), G. M. Bononcini (1673–8), Giuseppe Colombi (1678–94), Pacchioni (1694–1738) and Catelani (1848–66); renowned organists were Fogliani (1498–97, 1504–48), Lodovico Casali (1638) and Cornetti (1639–43, 1646–8).

In the early 17th century the status of Modena's musical activities was raised through the patronage of the Este family. The reputation of the musical establishment of the Este court was sufficient to attract significant composers and artists both from nearby areas and from other parts of Italy. The virtuoso cornettist Nicolò Rubini and the harpsichordist Michelangelo Rossi held court positions in 1610 and 1614 respectively. Sigismondo d'India was there in 1623–4 and again in 1626, and composed his eighth book of madrigals for the Este court, 'a gathering . . . of the best singers to be heard in Europe' (preface, *Ottavo libro di madrigali*, Rome, 1624). Throughout the 17th century Modena vied with other centres to attract the most celebrated singers.

The court helped to establish a local tradition of string playing and composition which antedated comparable developments in nearby Bologna. Although it is not possible to determine the size of the court orchestra in the second half of the 17th century (it varied with the importance of the functions, as is suggested by the many ad lib parts in works written for the court), its high level of performance attracted significant artists, particularly from Bologna. This vitality was stimulated by the violinist Marco Uccellini during his stay in Modena (1641–65); his novel treatment of violin playing (with scordatura, double stopping and highly embellished passages) and use of instrumental puzzle canons remained characteristic features of the Modenese school, later continued by Giuseppe Colombi, G. M. Bononcini, G. B. Vitali, Domenico Gabrielli and T. A. Vitali. The marriage in 1665 of Alfonso IV d'Este to Laura Martinozzi, niece of Mazarin, opened the Modenese court to French influences, demonstrated not only in the works labelled 'in the French style', but also in the fusion of Italian and French elements in dance forms and in the *sonata da camera*.

During the two decades of Francesco II d'Este's reign (1674–94) music at the court reached its most splendid phase. The young duke stimulated many musical performances, mostly of oratorios and sacred and instrumental music; from 1680 to 1691 about 100 oratorios, many of them dedicated to Francesco II, were performed at Modena. He also made efforts to establish a good library and university there, and played a part in the founding (c1683) of the Accademia de' Dissonanti, which held most of its meetings at the court and whose repertory emulated the experiments in novel concerto grosso instrumentation influenced by contemporary Roman practice. The academy became federated with Messina's Accademia Peloritana in 1728, and was renamed Ducale Accademia dei Dissonanti in 1752 and Regia Accademia di Scienze, Lettere ed Arti di Modena in 1817; it is still active, maintaining a sizable library.

Under Francesco II the court *cappella musicale* was led by two *maestri* (Benedetto Ferrari and Giuseppe Paini), two *sottomaestri* (Colombi and G. B. Vitali) and one *capo degl'istromentisti* (G. M. Bononcini), thus providing an exceptional environment for the cultivation of the current instrumental forms. The increasing demand for music during this period also stimulated the activity of many printers, the most representative being those of the Cassiani family, the Soliani family, Cristoforo Canobi, Gasparo Ferri and Antonio Vitaliano.

Among the directors of the *cappella musicale* (a complete list can be found in *I-MOe* Misc.It.L.9.27, f.405–8) were Cornetti (1633–5, 1643–8), Ferrari (1653–62, 1674–81), Colombi (*sottomaestro*, 1674–92), G. B.

Vitali (*sottomaestro*, 1674–92), Antonio Gianettini (1686–1721), Pacchioni (*sottomaestro*, 1699–1720, and *maestro*, 1722–38) and A. M. Bononcini (1721–6).

Francesco II was succeeded by his uncle Rinaldo d'Este in 1694, and musical life at Modena entered a period of decline, particularly with regard to instrumental music, although operatic performances increased. During the French occupation of Modena (1702–7) all musical activities at court were suspended while the duke lived at Bologna. On his return the *cappella musicale* was reduced in size and by 1713 it included only four instrumentalists, seven singers and two *maestri*; a further reduction to a total of nine members was made in 1734.

In 1771 the Accademia Filarmonica Modenese was founded, and by 1777 supported a chorus and orchestra. In 1780 it was renamed the Accademia Ducale dei Filarmonici and from 1817 it was known as the Società Filarmonica Modenese. It was dissolved in 1845.

The Società Artistico-Filarmonica was instituted in 1881 with the aim of promoting all artistic activities, including public and private concerts, particularly during Holy Week. A choral society, the Corale Rossini, was founded in 1887 and remained active until 1937. A music school supported by city funds was instituted in 1864; it was renamed the Scuola Comunale di Musica 'Orazio Vecchi' in 1914, and in 1950 came under state control.

The earliest theatre in Modena, the Sala or Teatro della Spelta, was in the Palazzo Comunale, and dramatic and musical performances were held there from 1539. Vecchi's madrigal comedy *L'Amfiparnaso* was given there in 1594, but no reports of subsequent musical performances remain from before 1654, when Duke Francesco I d'Este rebuilt the old hall into a large theatre with graded seating, columns and galleries (capacity 3000). It was named the Teatro Ducale di Piazza and inaugurated in 1656 with a performance of Francesco Manelli's *Andromeda*. After 1710 the theatre mounted comedies, served as a site for 'azioni accademiche' and eventually became a warehouse; it was demolished in 1769.

A smaller theatre, the Teatro di Corte (also known as the Teatro Ducale), was built in 1669 and inaugurated in 1686 with *L'Eritrea o Gl'inganni della maschera* (composer unknown) and was used irregularly, mostly for courtly events. Renovated and enlarged in 1749 and 1768, it was renamed Teatro Nazionale in 1796, Teatro Regio in 1806 and again Teatro Ducale in 1815. It was closed in 1848 and demolished in 1862; a new theatre, the Teatro Aliprandi, was built on the site and used mostly for performances of comedies and musical comedies until it burnt down in 1881.

The Teatro Valentini, which staged comedies from 1643, likewise burnt down, in 1681. It was reconstructed and renamed the Teatro Fontanelli (after its new owner) in 1683. During its short autumn season a few operatic performances were given there such as Carlo Pallavicino's *Il Vespasiano* in 1685. It was renamed Teatro Rangoni in 1705, Teatro di via Emilia in 1807, Teatro Comunale in 1816 and Teatro Vecchio in 1845. The city administration built a larger theatre, the Teatro Comunale Nuovo, which was inaugurated in 1841 with Alessandro Gandini's *Adelaide di Borgogna*.

A small but elegant and comfortable theatre used at Modena during the 18th century was the Teatro Molza,

built next to the Teatro della Spelta in the ducal palace and inaugurated in 1713 with F. Gasparini's *La fede tradita e vendicata*; it staged performances (supervised by A. M. Bononcini, 1718–21) until 1764.

The court's music library formed the bulk of the musical collection of the Biblioteca Estense (*I-MOe*), which also contains the music library of Maximilian, youngest son of Maria Theresa. The collection of the Modenese musicologist L. F. Valdrighi is in the Modena Museum.

BIBLIOGRAPHY

A. Gandini: *Cronistoria dei teatri di Modena dal 1539 al 1871* (Modena, 1873/R1969)

L. F. Valdrighi: 'Di Bellerofonte Castaldi e per incidenza di altri musicisti modenesi dei secoli XVI e XVII: annotazioni biobibliografiche', *Atti e memorie delle RR. Deputazioni di storia patria per le provincie dell'Emilia*, new ser., v/1 (1880), 89

——: *Musurgiana* (Modena, 1881–94)

G. Ferrari Moreni and V. Tardini: *Cronistoria dei teatri di Modena dal 1873 a tutto il 1881* (Modena, 1883)

L. F. Valdrighi: 'Cappelle, concerti e musiche di case d'Este (dal sec. XV al XVIII)', *Atti e memorie delle RR. Deputazioni di storia patria per le provincie modenesi e parmensi*, 3rd ser., ii (1883), 415–94; iii (1885), 507

A. Restori: 'Il canto dei soldati di Modena', *RMI*, vi (1899), 742

V. Tardini: *I teatri di Modena* (Modena, 1899–1902)

G. Roncaglia: 'Di insigni musicisti modenesi (documenti inediti)', *Atti e memorie della R. Deputazione di storia patria per le provincie modenesi*, 7th ser., vi (1930), 7

E. J. Luin: 'Antonio Giannettini e la musica a Modena alla fine del secolo XVII', *Atti e memorie della R. Deputazione di storia patria per le provincie modenesi*, 7th ser., vii (1932), 145–230

——: 'La musica sacra alla fine del secolo XVII a Bologna e Modena', *Musica d'oggi*, xiv/4 (1932), 151

G. Roncaglia: 'L. A. Muratori, la musica e il maggior compositore del suo tempo', *Atti e memorie della R. Deputazione di storia patria per le provincie modenesi*, 7th ser., viii (1933), 277–318

E. J. Luin: 'Repertorio dei libri musicali di S. A. S. Francesco II d'Este nell'Archivio di Stato di Modena', *La bibliofilia: rivista di storia del libro*, xxxviii (1936), 418

G. Roncaglia: 'Di J. Fogliani e G. Segni: documenti', *RMI*, xlvi (1942), 294

G. Vecchi: 'Il "Canto delle scolte modenesi": la notazione musicale', *Cultura neolatina*, x (1950), 49

E. Schenk: 'Osservazioni sulla scuola istrumentale modenese nel Seicento', *Atti e memorie dell'Accademia di scienze, lettere e arti, Modena*, 5th ser., x (1952), 3

G. Roncaglia: 'Giuseppe Colombi e la vita musicale modenese durante il regno di Francesco II d'Este', *Atti e memorie dell'Accademia di scienze, lettere e arti, Modena*, 5th ser., x (1952), 31

A. Torelli: *Notizie storiche, documenti, cronache sul Liceo musicale 'Orazio Vecchi' nel 90° della istituzione (1864–1954)* (Modena, 1954)

G. Roncaglia: 'La scuola strumentale modenese nel secolo XVII', *Musicisti della scuola emiliana*, Chigiana, xiii (1956), 69

——: *La cappella musicale del duomo di Modena* (Florence, 1957)

G. Cavazzuti: *I duecentosettantacinque anni della Accademia di scienze, lettere e arti, Modena* (Modena, 1958)

G. Roncaglia: 'Gli Ambreville, musicisti modenesi (con documenti inediti)', *Atti e memorie della Deputazione di storia patria per le antiche provincie modenesi*, 8th ser., xi (1959), 126

——: 'La musica alla Corte Estense dal 1707 alla costituzione del Regno d'Italia', *Atti e memorie della Deputazione di storia patria per le antiche provincie modenesi*, 10th ser., i (1966), 259

——: 'Un capitolo di antica storia musicale modenese ed estense (con notizie e documenti inediti)', *CHM*, iv (1966), 255

D. E. Crawford: *Vespers Polyphony at Modena's Cathedral in the First Half of the Sixteenth Century* (diss., U. of Illinois, Urbana, 1967)

O. Jander: 'The Cantata in Accademia: Music for the Accademia de' Dissonanti and their Duke, Francesco II d'Este', *RIM*, x (1975), 519

ELVIDIO SURIAN

**Modena, Julio da.** *See* SEGNI, JULIO.

**Modena, Leo [Leone] da.** *See* LEO DA MODENA.

**Moderato** (It.: 'moderate', 'restrained'). A direction used either alone as a tempo designation or as a qualification to some other direction. It is sometimes abbreviated to *mod.to*. Because verbal directions appeared in 17th-century music only to tell the musician something that his sense of tradition would not tell him, *moderato* did not appear until the very end of the century, when certain composers began marking everything they wrote. Thus François Couperin, who marked everything but his sacred pieces, made considerable use of the French adverbial form *modérément*; and his contemporaries in France also used the adjectival form *modéré*, which has remained in common usage ever since. *Moderato* itself was included in Brossard's *Dictionaire* (1703) as meaning 'with moderation, discretion, wisdom, etc, neither too loud, nor too soft, nor too fast, nor too slowly, etc' – a definition which is in itself a sign of a new generation in tempo and expression marks, one in which for the first time even the ordinary had to be explained. Rousseau (1768) gave *modéré* as the equivalent of the Italian *adagio*, the second of his five main degrees of movement in music. Since the early 19th century, *moderato* has most often appeared either alone or in the compounds *allegro moderato* (a little slower than *allegro*) and *andante moderato* (a little faster than *andante*). For a curious usage in J. S. Bach *see* LENTO.

For bibliography *see* TEMPO AND EXPRESSION MARKS.

DAVID FALLOWS

**Moderator pedal** [muffler pedal, celeste]. A pedal that introduces a strip of cloth between the hammers and strings of a piano to produce a muted effect. It is still occasionally provided as a middle pedal on upright pianos. The same device, sometimes operated by a knee lever instead of a pedal, was commonly found on German and Austrian grand pianos of the late 18th century and the early 19th, sometimes apparently as a substitute for a true UNA CORDA but more frequently to provide special tone-colour in addition to that provided by the normal 'loud' and 'soft' pedals. Some instruments by Conrad Graf of Vienna have the added refinement of two moderator pedals, one of which inserts the muting cloth farther than the other.    EDWIN M. RIPIN

**Modéré** (Fr.). *See* MODERATO.

**Moderne, Jacques** (*b* Pinguente, *c*1495–1500; *d* Lyons, in or after 1562). French music printer of Italian birth. He was the second printer to publish music on a large scale in France. The first was Pierre Attaingnant of Paris, who began issuing his music books in 1528, using a practical and relatively inexpensive single-impression method which he had just developed. Moderne was one of the first (along with Christian Egenolff independently in Frankfurt) to adapt this new method for his own use. He began music printing in 1532 and continued to be Attaingnant's only rival in France for 15 years.

From the identification on his early books as 'Jacobus Modernus de Pinguento' we know that Moderne was born in the village of Pinguente (now Buzet, Yugoslavia) on the Istrian peninsula. Whether he spent some apprentice years in Venice cannot be determined. He appeared on the tax rolls of Lyons for the first time in 1523 as a

1. *Superius voice of the first part of the motet 'Laetare nova Sion' by Andreas de Silva, from 'Motteti del fiore' printed by Jacques Moderne (Lyons, 1532)*

bookseller and regularly thereafter in the Lyons archives until the early 1560s. According to a contract dated 28 May 1562 he rented out a room in his house, but in 1568 his widow is listed in the tax records.

He is identified in the archives and frequently on his title-pages as 'grand Jacques', no doubt because of his girth or his height, or both. His social stature must have been substantial as well, since the Lyons records show him to have been a modest landowner and an official in various Lyons activities, as well as a neighbour to some of that city's most prominent citizens.

Moderne's publishing activity was by no means restricted to music. He was an active printer of several types of popular books – on religion, home remedies, emblems and palmistry among others – in Latin and in French. Though some undated ones were undoubtedly printed before, the earliest dated one appeared in 1529. He continued printing these books throughout his career.

Music is the part of his production that brought him the greatest renown. Masses, motets, chansons and instrumental music are well represented in his books. He published a series of eight motet anthologies from 1532 to 1542, four called *Motteti del fiore* because of the woodcut of a thistle (see fig.2). A similar series of 11 (or perhaps more) chanson collections, named *Le parangon des chansons*, was issued between 1538 and 1543. Later several books were devoted to the music of single composers. There were also two books of plainsong masses, some monophonic noëls and two treatises on music theory reprinted from earlier sources. There is no evidence that Moderne was a musician himself. He is never so described in the contemporary records, nor has any music written by him turned up in MSS or printed editions.

Moderne was probably persuaded to try his hand at music printing by FRANCESCO DE LAYOLLE, a Florentine composer and the organist at Notre Dame de Confort in Lyons. He acted as editor for Moderne's first musical publication, *Liber decem missarum* of 1532, as Moderne acknowledged in the dedication. He probably continued as Moderne's editor, especially since the greater part of the musical output was published or prepared for publication before Layolle's death around 1540. After that the originality of the repertory declined.

Moderne printed about 50 music books, which contain over 800 pieces. More than half are unique to Moderne's prints. Many of the rest were frequently reprinted later by others but made their first printed appearance here. These books are a particularly important source for the music of Layolle and of Pierre de Villiers, who seems to have lived in Lyons and perhaps also offered musical assistance to Moderne. Besides Layolle and Villiers, Henry Fresneau and G. Coste are other probable Lyonese composers in these collections. Most of the composers best represented here are international figures like Gombert, Willaert, Arcadelt, Lhéritier and Jacquet of Mantua, or members of the Parisian school like Claudin de Sermisy, Maillard, Sandrin, Certon and the ubiquitous Janequin. In contrast to Attaingnant who confined himself for the most part to French and Netherlands composers, Moderne also included works by composers from Italy, Spain and Germany. He devoted entire books to Italian canzoni by Layolle and Matteo Rampollini and to lute music by Francesco Bianchini and Giovanni Paolo Paladino. The

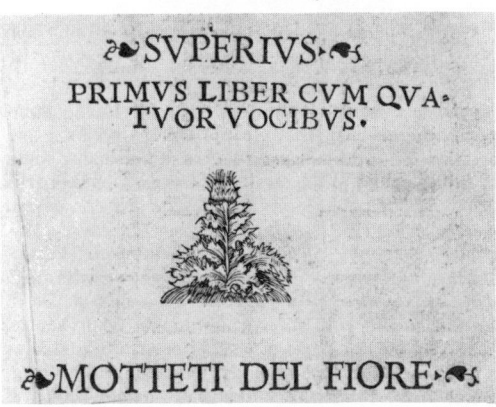

*2. Title-page of the superius partbook of 'Motteti del fiore', printed by Moderne (Lyons, 1532)*

first part of *Musique de joye*, reprinted from a Venetian source, contains ricercares by a number of other Italians. Morales, Mateo Flecha and Luys de Narváez represented Spain, and Leonhard Paminger and Mathias Eckel were from Germany. Moderne was the first to print the lute music of the Hungarian Bálint Bakfark.

Some explanation for the variety in Moderne's repertory lies in the character of the place where he worked. In the first half of the 16th century Lyons was a cosmopolitan city with large Italian and German colonies, an important centre of the new printing trade and a meeting ground for intellectuals. Its position on the border between France and Savoy and at the confluence of the Saône and Rhône rivers made it a crossroads. Fairs four times a year brought traders from as far away as Lebanon in the east and Portugal to the west. Thus Moderne had access to music of varied origins and a ready market to disseminate his music books throughout Europe.

BIBLIOGRAPHY

F. Lesure: 'Moderne, Jacques', *MGG*

J. Vial: 'Un imprimeur lyonnais méconnu, Jacques Moderne', *Gutenberg-Jb* (1962), 256

S. F. Pogue: *Jacques Moderne: Lyons Music Printer of the Sixteenth Century* (Geneva, 1969)

D. Heartz: *Pierre Attaingnant: Royal Printer of Music* (Berkeley and Los Angeles, 1969), 144ff

SAMUEL F. POGUE

**Modern Jazz Quartet.** American jazz ensemble. Its original members were MILT JACKSON (vibraphone), JOHN LEWIS (piano and music director), KENNY CLARKE (drums) and Percy Heath (double bass); in 1955 Clarke was replaced by Connie Kay (*b* 1927). The group made its first recording in 1951, and another under its own name in 1952, but was not established on a permanent basis until 1954. Jackson, an outstanding soloist, dominated the quartet's early recordings, but it later became noted for its collective improvisation and jazz composition, this being primarily Lewis's achievement. The group toured Europe in 1957–8 and yearly in the 1960s; until it disbanded in 1974, after an unusually long and stable career, it was among the most creative and highly regarded small jazz groups.

For photograph *see* JAZZ, fig.12.

BIBLIOGRAPHY

M. Harrison: 'Looking Back at the Modern Jazz Quartet', *The Art of Jazz*, ed. M. Williams (New York, 1959), 219

——: 'Modern Jazz Quartet', *Jazz Journal*, xiv (1961), Nov, 5

J. Goldberg: *Jazz Masters of the Fifties* (New York, 1965), 113ff

BRADFORD ROBINSON

**Moderno, stile** (It.). A term used in opposition to STILE ANTICO.

**Modiana, Orazio** [Horatio] (*fl* 1623–5). Italian composer. He was a priest who in 1625 was a canon and choirmaster of the collegiate church at Guastalla, south of Mantua, and in the service of Cesare Gonzaga. His two surviving publications are *Primitie di sacri concerti a voce sola, con il basso per sonar l'organo, clavicembalo, chitarone, ò altra sorte di stromenti* (Venice, 1623) and *Filomenici concenti di madrigali concertati a due, tre, quattro e cinque voci: da cantarsi con il clavicembalo, ò altro stromento musicale*, op.3 (Venice, 1625). On the title-pages of both he described himself as a member of the Accademia de' Filomeni at Casalmaggiore, near Parma, his academic name being 'Il Pellegrino'. In the preface to his 1623 book he directed the singer to vary the tempo of the music according to the nature of the words being sung.

BIBLIOGRAPHY
E. Bohn: *Bibliographie der Musik-Druckwerke bis 1700, welche . . . zu Breslau aufbewahrt werden* (Berlin, 1883/*R*1969), 286
H. Goldschmidt: *Die italienische Gesangsmethode des XVII. Jahrhunderts* (Breslau, 1890), 34
N. Fortune: 'Italian Seventeenth-century Singing', *ML*, xxxv (1954), 206, 218

JOHN WHENHAM

**Modinha.** A Portuguese and Brazilian sentimental art song cultivated in the 18th and 19th centuries. *Moda* is a generic term applied vaguely to any song or melody. Particularly common in the 18th century were the *modas a duo*, for two sopranos, sung in parallel motion with harpsichord accompaniment and a possible doubling of the bass line by a low string instrument. In practice most printed *modinhas* in Portugal were accompanied by the guitar. During the Second Empire in Brazil the *modinha* acquired the character of the Italian opera aria, while in Portugal the same occurred about 1800. Under such influences the *modinha* began to lose its original simplicity, acquiring elaborate melodic lines with typically superficial ornamentation. Aspects of the opera aria were retained in the popularization of the *modinha* and came to be identified later in the 19th century as 'national' traits. Eventually the Brazilian *modinha* became a strongly lyrical folksong. As a love-song it was closely related to another popular genre, the *lundu*, a song and dance born of African origin which, together with the *modinha*, became the most important salon genre in Portugal and Brazil.

BIBLIOGRAPHY
M. de Andrade: *Modinhas imperiais* (São Paulo, 1930)
B. Siqueira: *Modinhas do passado* (Rio de Janeiro, 1956)
M. de Araújo: *A modinha e o lundu no século XVIII* (São Paulo, 1963)
G. Béhague: 'Biblioteca de Ajuda (Lisbon) MSS 1595/1596: Two Eighteenth-century Anonymous Collections of Modinhas', *Yearbook, Inter-American Institute for Musical Research*, iv (1968), 44

GERARD BÉHAGUE

**Mödl, Martha** (*b* Nuremberg, 22 March 1912). German soprano (for a period, mezzo). She studied at the Nuremberg Conservatory, made her début as Hansel at Remscheid in 1942 and was then engaged by the Düsseldorf Opera from 1945 to 1949, singing Dorabella, Octavian, the Composer in *Ariadne auf Naxos*, Clytemnestra, Eboli, Carmen and Berg's Marie. In 1949 she joined the Hamburg Staatsoper and soon found her voice changing to a dramatic soprano. In 1950–51 she appeared as Lady Macbeth in Berlin, and

then added Kundry, Venus, Isolde and the *Walküre* Brünnhilde to her repertory. In 1951 she sang Kundry at the first postwar Bayreuth Festival and returned regularly there until 1967; her Kundry, Isolde, Brünnhilde, Sieglinde and Gutrune became outstanding features of the Wieland and Wolfgang Wagner productions. She acknowledges her success as a Wagnerian artist to the careful coaching and musical inspiration of Wagner's grandsons.

Mödl's first appearance in England was in the 1949–50 Covent Garden season, when she sang Carmen in English. She was heard with the Hamburg company at Edinburgh in 1952, and as Isolde with the Stuttgart Opera at the Festival Hall, London, in 1955 and at Edinburgh in 1958. She sang Leonore in *Fidelio* at the reopening of the Vienna Staatsoper in 1955, Brünnhilde at Covent Garden in 1959, Clytemnestra in *Elektra* in 1966, and the Housekeeper in *Die schweigsame Frau* with the Bayerische Staatsoper in 1973.

Martha Mödl's approach to her art typifies the ideas of operatic interpretation current in postwar Germany. These stress the importance of acting, and encourage intensity in portraying the emotions. It has an invigorating effect on the audience, but also its dangers, for, after a series of performances such as those at Bayreuth, the voice is apt to tire more quickly than is the case with more restrained singers. Her voice, with its warm and beautiful lower register, an inheritance from her mezzo-soprano days, is, however, always at the service of this highly individual and intelligent singer.

BIBLIOGRAPHY
H. Rosenthal: 'Martha Mödl', *Sopranos of Today* (London, 1956)
A. Natan: 'Mödl, Martha', *Prima donna* (Basle and Stuttgart, 1962) [with LP discography]
G. Gualerzi: 'Mödl, Martha', *Le grandi voci* (Rome, 1964) [with opera discography by R. Vegeto]
H. Rosenthal: 'Martha Mödl', *Great Singers of Today* (London, 1966)
W. E. Shäfer: *Martha Mödl* (Hanover, 1967)

HAROLD ROSENTHAL

**Modrekili, Michael** (*fl* 10th century). Hymnographer of the Georgian Church; *see* GEORGIAN RITE, MUSIC OF THE, §III.

**Modulation (i).** In tonal music the movement out of one key into another as a continuous musical process. The chief importance of modulation is the articulation of harmony in large-scale structures: harmonic interest could not be maintained without a clear contrast of key, and modulation gives meaning to this contrast by showing a relationship between keys as an integral part of the composition itself.

One of the most common types of modulation involves the pivot chord, which is related both to the key already established and to the key to which the modulation is to be made. It may be only lightly touched on, resulting in an easy move into the new key, for example in Beethoven's Pastoral Symphony, first movement, bars 57–60, where a D minor chord functions as VI of F and as II of C; or it may be enlarged to make an entire subsidiary section before the new key is approached – for example in Mozart's Sonata in F K332/300*k* the same D minor chord, again VI of F and II of C, is expanded to an 18-bar section with its own theme. These examples illustrate the diatonic pivot chord, which belongs to the tonalities of both the original key and the key to which the modulation is made. A pivot chord may, however, be chromatic, in which case it belongs to one of the keys or the other, or to neither. Three examples in which the chord of the Neapolitan 6th (i.e. the major triad based on the flattened 2nd degree) is used illustrate each of these cases. In ex.1, from the first movement of Schubert's Quartet in A minor D804, the pivot chord, a first-inversion B♭ major triad, is approached as the tonic chord of the established key; it then functions as a Neapolitan 6th chord in A minor, the modulation being completed by a perfect cadence in the new key. In ex.2, from Schubert's *Erstarrung* (*Winterreise*, no.4), the pivot chord is approached as the Neapolitan 6th chord of the established key and functions as a first-inversion subdominant of the new key. In ex.3, from the Scherzo of Beethoven's Quartet in F op.59 no.1, the pivot chord

Ex.1

Ex.2

Ex.3

is a major triad on the flattened submediant of the established key and at the same time a Neapolitan chord in root position of the new key, to which it resolves normally. Pivot chords can also effect modulations by enharmonic reinterpretation. That is, one spelling of a chord seems to belong more to the established key, and a different spelling of the same chord tends towards the new key. As with the chromatic type, enharmonic pivot chords can belong to the established key by the first spelling, or to the new key by the second spelling, or they can belong to neither key by either spelling. The kinds most susceptible to this enharmonic modulation are the augmented 6th and diminished 7th chords, as well as chords having an augmented 5th.

It is possible to effect a modulation to the dominant of the established key simply by passing into it after an imperfect cadence, as in the first movement of Mozart's Sonata in C K545 (bars 12–13). Although no actual modulation takes place, the new key is prepared – by its own tonic. This is actually a special case of modulation by a pivot chord, one in which the arrival in the new key requires no more than a restatement of that chord.

Modulation by a pivot note is usually more direct than modulation by a pivot chord. A note that is an important melodic degree of the established key – the tonic, mediant or dominant – becomes an important melodic degree in the new key. A number of possible modulations from C major by a pivot note are illustrated in ex.4. Sometimes the pivot note is changed enharmonically to give the impression of modulation to a more remote key, as in the modulation from D♭ major (i.e. C♯) to A major in Chopin's Second Scherzo op.31 (ex.5). This type of modulation presupposes not only an equal-tempered intonation but also complete equality of the keys, and is a feature of 19th-century chromaticism, particularly in the work of Schubert, Chopin, Liszt and Wagner.

Ex.4 Modulation by pivot note, with respect to C major

I   V(♭)   I   III   I   ♭III   I   III(♯)   I   VI(♯)   I   VI

I   ♭VI   I   IV(♭)

Ex.5

Finally, one may speak of modulation by direct leap, from the tonic of the established key to the tonic of the new key. Such a move would appear to contradict the principle that modulation is the joining as a continuous process of two key centres and that there should be some territory that the two key centres share, however briefly or tentatively. But certain direct moves from one key centre to another actually give evidence of a functional relationship between the two centres, for example the move from E to F in the middle section of the slow movement of Schubert's Quintet in C D956, given in ex.6a. The 'modulation' is achieved simply by moving in unison from the established tonic to the new tonic. But this shows an inherent leading-note relationship between the two keys, E♮ being the raised seventh degree of F minor. This relationship, merely implied here, is made explicit in the coda of the movement, where there is barely an echo of the middle section, but where the relationship of E to F, as part of its dominant chord, is nevertheless made unmistakable (ex.6b).

Ex.6

H. K. ANDREWS/WILLIAM DRABKIN

**Modulation (ii).** A term originating in telecommunications usage describing the superimposition of characteristics of one signal ('programme') upon another ('carrier'); it later entered the terminology of electronic music where it is frequently used in a broader sense, sometimes as unspecific as 'a process of change'. Many characteristics of signals may be modulated. In frequency modulation the frequency of the carrier is made to conform to the wave shape of the programme: for example, if the programme is a sine wave of frequency 6 Hz and low amplitude, the audible result of modulation will resemble the carrier in all respects except that a vibrato (small variation of pitch) will be superimposed upon it. Alterations in the wave form, frequency, or amplitude of the programme will produce results more complex and less easily described; in particular, as its frequency enters the audio range (approximately 18 Hz–22 kHz), distinct new 'sideband' frequencies will be produced. In amplitude modulation it is the amplitude of the carrier that is made to conform to the wave shape of the programme: here the same sine wave of 6 Hz as programme will have the effect of superimposing a tremolo (small variation of dynamic) upon the carrier. Again, more complex results may be produced by changing the programme.

In contrast to these two types of modulation, the distinction between programme and carrier is of less significance for ring modulation, the effect of which is symmetrical. The output from a RING MODULATOR consists of the sum and difference of the frequencies of the inputs: for example, the result of ring modulating two sine waves of 400 Hz and 500 Hz will be two sine waves of 100 Hz and 900 Hz. However, if either or both of the input signals is more complex than a sine wave, as is likely to be the case in a musical context, then the output will be even more complicated since each partial of the one input will be added to and subtracted from each partial of the other. (This is necessarily a simplified description as the amplitudes of each

partial also affect the result.)

Frequency, amplitude and ring modulation are the oldest and most familiar modulation processes used in electronic music. However, with the development of voltage control systems the number of devices based on the programme–carrier principle has proliferated: all of these perform operations that may legitimately be described as modulations. Pulse modulation, for example, is the modification by control voltage of the length of individual pulses from a pulse generator. Phase modulation is produced by the superimposition of a signal upon itself after an extremely short but continually changing time delay regulated by a control voltage; with a slow rate of change in the time delay the effect upon a complex signal will be of a band of noise sweeping through the signal.

This extension of applications has encouraged a looser use of the term. For instance, location modulation is a variation in the apparent spatial location of a sound (pitch and timbre may also be affected); this may or may not be governed by a control voltage. The term has even been extended beyond the boundaries of electronic music to describe any continuous change in timbre, rhythm or other parameters.

DAVID ROBERTS

**Modulator.** (1) A device used in ELECTRONIC MUSIC to modulate sound signals; *see also* MODULATION (ii) and RING MODULATOR.

(2) A chart showing the initials of the sol-fa syllables arranged vertically and adapted by John Curwen from Sarah Glover's NORWICH SOL-FA LADDER. (*See also* TONIC SOL-FA.)

**Modulus** (Lat.). Synonym for AMBITUS in the treatise *Questiones in musica*.

**Modus** (Lat.: 'mood'). In the system of mensural notation of the late Middle Ages, the relationship between long and breve; see MODE, §I, 1, and NOTATION, §III.

**Modus lascivus** (Lat.). The medieval name for the IONIAN mode.

**Moeck.** German firm of music publishers and instrument makers. Founded by Hermann Moeck (i) (*b* Elbing, 9 July 1896) in 1925 at Celle, it soon devoted itself to promoting recorders and their music in particular. The journal *Der Blockflötenspiegel* (1931–4), partly in conjunction with Nagels Musikverlag) contributed much to the revival of recorder playing by the clarification and discussion of technical questions. The journal *Celler Spielmann* appeared between 1938 and 1948; the *Zeitschrift für Spielmusik*, issued monthly (in three languages) from 1932, contains articles on music history, folk and contemporary music. The firm has published the series Moecks Gelbe Musikhefte (1934–) and Moecks Kammermusik (1938–), including many new editions of early music for school and practical use, as well as the series Der Bläserchor (1965–), which includes Renaissance music for large ensembles.

In 1948 Hermann Moeck (ii) (*b* Lüneburg, 16 Sept 1922), son of the founder, became a partner in charge of the publishing. In 1956 Moeck purchased the Chrysander publishing firm of Bergedorf; this added to the firm's catalogue the *Aufführungsmaterialien zu Handel Oratorien* and Chrysander's complete Handel edition. In the same year the firm became actively involved with modern music and in 1958 it began to represent Polskie Wydawnictwo Muzyczne; from then on it has promoted such contemporary Polish composers as Lutosławski, Penderecki and Serocki.

Herbert Höntsch (*b* 1917) joined the firm in 1959; Hermann Moeck (i) retired in 1960 and was succeeded by his son, who also took charge of the instrument making. In the early 1970s 180 employees were making some 350,000 instruments annually. The aim is to combine the craftsman's skill with the techniques of precision engineering to produce a flow of high-quality early instruments of almost every kind. The firm is known for viols and the Krefeld *Quintfidel*; the tradition of promoting recorders has also been maintained, from 1967 partly in cooperation with FRIEDRICH VON HUENE. In 1964 OTTO STEINKOPF, whose contribution to the revival of many early wind instruments has been unique, joined the firm and the production of those instruments has been rapidly extended. The firm maintains its own instrument museum (founded 1930) as well as a programme of systematic research; it also runs instruction courses on early instruments.

CHRISTOPHER MONK

**Moench von Salzburg.** *See* MONK OF SALZBURG.

**Moennig.** American family of violin dealers. William Heinrich Moennig (*b* Markneukirchen, Saxony, 29 June 1883; *d* Philadelphia, 1962) trained as a violin maker with an uncle in Budapest before going to work with his brother-in-law Julius Guetter in Philadelphia at the beginning of the 20th century. (The family firm, now specializing in the repair and sale of all bowed musical instruments, was founded in 1909.) William Heinrich's son, William Herrman Moennig jr (*b* Philadelphia, 21 July 1905) grew up in an atmosphere of violins and music (the Moennig home was above the business). He became a pupil of his father, who then sent him to study in Markneukirchen and Mittenwald. He qualified as a master violin maker under the auspices of the German Guild.

After World War II William Moennig jr built up a business with a fine reputation among musicians and teachers all over the USA for fair dealing in old instruments. He is one of the leading experts on fine old violins and was the first American member of the International Society of Violin and Bow Makers. His son William Harry Moennig (*b* Philadelphia, 28 Aug 1930) is an excellent craftsman. He trained with Dieudonné in Mirecourt, France, and at the violin making school in Mittenwald under Leo Aschauer, before studying repairing in Philadelphia. In 1975 he took over the running of the business from his father.

CHARLES BEARE

**Moer, de.** *See* MOORS family.

**Moeran, E(rnest) J(ohn)** (*b* Heston, 31 Dec 1894; *d* nr. Kenmare, Ireland, 1 Dec 1950). English composer of Anglo-Irish descent. He was the son of a Norfolk clergyman and was educated at Uppingham School, where he learnt the violin and played in a quartet. He entered the Royal College of Music in 1913, but after 18 months his studies were interrupted by World War I; he joined up as a despatch rider and was commissioned, but after being severely wounded in the head was de-

clared unfit for further active service. On demobilization in 1919 he returned to his old school as music master, but he soon decided to continue his studies and worked under John Ireland until 1923.

It was after this period with Ireland that Moeran's music began to receive public performances. The First Rhapsody for orchestra was played several times before it was given by the Hallé Orchestra in 1924 under Harty, and a series of his programmes was given at the Wigmore Hall in 1925. At this time his music was dominated by the influences of Ireland and of Delius, whose chromatic harmony was always to colour Moeran's work, while his intimacy with the folksongs of his native East Anglia strongly affected his melodic style. Throughout the 1920s and early 1930s Moeran concentrated on the smaller genres which seemed to suit his lyrical and harmonic gifts. Among the earliest and most attractive pieces of the period are the Three Piano Pieces, the Theme and Variations for piano, the String Quartet, the Piano Trio and the Violin Sonata. Although their gestures are broader, the two orchestral rhapsodies of 1922 and 1924 are loosely episodic, and it is significant that Moeran found himself unable to fulfil a commission from the Hallé Orchestra for a symphony in 1926.

Nevertheless, he had achieved considerable technical fluency, and the bounds of his style were firmly established when he wrote the String Trio (1931), his outstanding chamber work. That style places him definitively among his more eminent contemporaries: Delius, Vaughan Williams, Holst, Bax, Ireland and Warlock. Indeed, his music may be criticized as too reliant on the work of these composers, but Moeran's individuality had continued to develop after the frankly Delian references of the Piano Trio. The influence of Warlock is still present in the Seven Poems of James Joyce (1929), among Moeran's many early songs, written shortly after the period when he and Warlock shared a house in Eynsford. But if this stylistic dependence robs his work of a strong personal identity, such pieces as *Whythorne's Shadow* (1931) and *Lonely Waters* (1932) have a distinctive quality that resides primarily in their characteristic harmony, although Moeran's was but a limited area lying narrowly between Delius's chromaticism as transformed by Warlock, and Vaughan Williams's modality or, more importantly, his bimodality.

At this time Moeran retired to the Cotswolds, and set out to review his achievement and expand his style and technique. Although there was no immediate major change in his music, this period of self-criticism eventually produced a series of large-scale works, and his output of songs, piano pieces and chamber music was greatly reduced. The first fruit was the Symphony in G minor (1934–7), a remarkable accomplishment for a man who, until then, had conceived music lyrically, drawing heavily on his immediate responses to nature. Nature remained the foremost spur to his invention, however, and he stated that the symphony was imagined 'among the mountains and seaboard of County Kerry' and 'around the sand-dunes and marshes of East Norfolk' (Westrup) – a reflection of his twin heritage. But the symphony is far more than a record of his impressions of the landscape, and the time he took to complete it may indicate the struggle to change his approach to composition. The lyricism is still there, as in the first movement's second subject, and themes in folksong style supply the basic material. However, Moeran was now capable of sustaining much wider spans, and his style extended to include vigorous fugato writing and a Sibelian thematic growth – the opening theme, for instance, is reconstituted at each appearance. Only in the finale does invention flag, and here the references to Sibelius are most overt. But the work has a strong vitality and nobility; the grandly proportioned first movement and the variegated textures of the Scherzo are possibly Moeran's finest achievements. The Symphony was first performed in January 1938 under Leslie Howard.

This work encouraged Moeran to develop the energetic side of a character that had previously given rise principally to wistful introverted moods. The outgoing quality was most brilliantly expressed in the Sinfonietta (1944), whose first and last movements are conceived in terms of sparkling virtuosity with vigorous contrapuntal writing and luminous orchestration. But before this piece Moeran completed a work which achieves a paradigmatic balance between poetic dreaming and dashing vitality: the Violin Concerto. Of its three movements, only the central rondo scherzo provides fully worked quick music, the outer movements sharing slow, meditative material. In 1945 Moeran composed the Cello Concerto for Peers Coetmore, whom he married in the same year. This concerto is formally more conventional and its ideas are less striking, while his last orchestral work, the Serenade in G, includes elements of pastiche, which are not completely convincing although they are handled delightfully. The Serenade and the sombre Cello Sonata were Moeran's last major works: in December 1950 he was found dead in the River Kenmare, having fallen after a heart attack. He was then working on a Second Symphony and was probably going through another transitional stage, with bitonal elements becoming increasingly important.

Moeran occupied a minor place in the British music of the time, but his meticulously polished and ready technique is matched only by Holst and Bridge among his British contemporaries. This craftsmanship is evident in the tidy textures and in the aptness of his writing for whatever forces he had chosen.

### WORKS
*(selective list)*

#### ORCHESTRAL

Symphonic Impression, In the Mountain Country, 1921; Rhapsody no.1, F, 1922; Rhapsody no.2, E, 1924, rev. 1941; Whythorne's Shadow, 1931; Lonely Waters, 1932; Symphony, g, 1934–7; Vn Conc., 1942; Rhapsody, F♯, pf, orch, 1943; Overture to a Masque, 1944; Sinfonietta, 1944; Vc Conc., 1945; Serenade, G, 1948

#### CHAMBER AND INSTRUMENTAL

3 Pf Pieces, 1919; Theme and Variations, pf, 1920; Pf Trio, D, 1920; Str Qt, a, 1921; On a May Morning, Stalham River, Toccata, pf, 1921; Fancies, pf, 1922; Vn Sonata, e, 1923; Bank Holiday, Summer Valley, pf, 1925; Sonata, 2 vn, 1930; Str Trio, 1931; Berceuse, pf, 1933; Prelude, g, pf, 1933; Fantasy Qt, ob, vn, va, vc, 1946; Vc Sonata, 1947; Prelude, vc, pf, 1948; Str Qt, E♭, n.d.

#### VOCAL

Ludlow Town, 1v, pf, 1920; 6 Norfolk Folksongs, 1v, pf, 1923; 7 Poems of James Joyce, 1v, pf, 1929; 6 Suffolk Folksongs, 1v, pf, 1931; 4 English Lyrics, 1v, pf, 1933; Nocturne, Bar, chorus, orch, 1934; Songs of Springtime, chorus, 1934; Phyllida and Corydon, chorus, 1934; 4 Shakespeare Songs, 1v, pf, 1940; 6 Songs of Seumas O'Sullivan, 1v, pf, 1944

Principal publishers: Novello, Augener, Chester, Oxford University Press, Schott

### BIBLIOGRAPHY

H. Statham: 'Moeran's Symphony in G minor', *MR*, i (1940), 245
E. Evans: 'Moeran's Violin Concerto', *MT*, lxxxiv (1943), 233
J. A. Westrup: 'E. J. Moeran', *British Music of our Time*, ed. A. L. Bacharach (Harmondsworth, 1946), 175
H. Foss: *Compositions of E. J. Moeran* (London, 1948)
A. Bax; 'E. J. Moeran 1894–1950', *ML*, xxxii (1951), 125
H. Foss: 'Ernest John Moeran', *MT*, xcii (1951), 20
W. Mann: 'Some English Concertos', *The Concerto*, ed. R. Hill (Harmondsworth, 1952), 418
W. J. Mitson: 'Moeran', *Cobbett's Cyclopedic Survey of Chamber Music* (London, 2/1963), 146
S. Wild: *E. J. Moeran* (London, 1973)

ANTHONY PAYNE

**Moeschinger, Albert** (*b* Basle, 10 Jan 1897). Swiss composer. He studied in Berne, Leipzig and Munich (with Walter Courvoisier) during the years 1917–23, and taught the piano and theory at the Berne Conservatory from 1937 to 1943. After this he retired to Saas Fee in the mountains of Valais to devote himself undisturbed to composition in a diversity of genres; he moved to the canton of Ticino in 1956. His orchestral music was played from the 1930s under such conductors as Sacher, Schaichet, Ansermet, Rosbaud and Scherchen, and Walther Frey and Franz Josef Hirt have been among the interpreters of his virtuoso chamber music. He wrote the cantata *Tag unsres Volks* op.46 for the opening of the Swiss Fair in 1939; his awards include the Basle Arts Prize (1953) and the Swiss Musicians' Union composition prize (1957).

Moeschinger brought about a distinctive and personal synthesis of German and French elements: his extensive oeuvre, numbering more than 200 works, is rooted in the chromaticism of Reger and also in the sound world of Debussy. Although his First String Quartet (1921) shows the influence of Schoenberg, Moeschinger made no closer approach to that composer, not even when, from 1956, he began to make an independent use of 12-note procedures. These made it possible for him to control and objectify his athematic writing more thoroughly; throughout his career, his music has increasingly stretched the boundaries of tonality. The French element is asserted in varying degree in Moeschinger's work; another abiding characteristic is his rich harmony and complex rhythm, comparable with that of Stravinsky and Bartók.

### WORKS
*(selective list)*

Vocal: Mass, op.59, chorus 4vv, org, 1943; Der Herbst des Einsamen, op.69 (Trakl), female chorus, str, 1934–45; Die kleine Seejungfrau, op.75 (radio opera, after Andersen), 1947; Miracles de l'enfance, op.92, Mez, 2 fl, 2 cl, ob, harp, db, perc, 1961; Labyrinth, op.94 (after Dante: Il paradiso), 3 female vv, orch, 1962–3

Orch: Amor und Psyche, op.79, ballet, 1955; Ballade symphonique, op.82, 1957; Fantaisie concertante, op.95, fl, cl, bn, orch, 1963; Extra muros, op.97, wind, harp, pf, perc, 1964; Toccata cromatica, op.100, wind, pf, perc, 1965; Ignis divinus, op.101, 1966; Erratique, 1969; On ne traverse pas la nuit, after C. Mauriac, 1969–70; Blocs sonores, 1977; Variations mystérieuses, chamber orch, 1977; 5 syms., 5 pf concs., concs. for vn, sax, tpt

Chamber: 8 soldats armés d'instruments, ww qt, str qt, 1971; 6 str qts, 3 str trios, 2 pf trios, 3 pf qnts, 1 pf sextet, 6 wind trios

Pieces for pf, org

### BIBLIOGRAPHY

J. Handschin: 'Neues von Albert Moeschinger', *SMz*, lxxxv (1945), 424 [incl. list of works]
W. Schuh: *Schweizer Musik der Gegenwart* (Zurich, 1948)
E. Mohr: 'Albert Moeschinger: Werk und Persönlichkeit', *SMz*, xciii (1953), 153
H. Oesch: 'Albert Moeschinger', *SMz*, xcvii (1957), 169 [incl. list of works]
——: 'Was hat uns Albert Moeschinger zu sagen?', *SMz*, cvii (1967), 2 [incl. list of works]
——: 'Albert Moeschingers Briefwechsel mit Thomas Mann', *SMz*, cxii (1972), 3 [incl. list of works]

HANS OESCH

**Moevs, Robert (Walter)** (*b* La Crosse, Wisc., 2 Dec 1920). American composer. He gave his first piano recital in La Crosse, Wisconsin, in 1929 and has remained active as a concert and ensemble pianist. After studying music at Harvard College (AB 1942), he entered the US Air Force and served as a pilot and later as an officer in the US Military Mission to the Allied Control Commission in Romania until 1947. Moevs resumed his musical studies at the Paris Conservatoire (1947–51), and then returned to Harvard (AM in 1952); his principal teachers were Piston at Harvard and Nadia Boulanger in Paris. For the next three years he was at the American Academy in Rome as a Rome Prize Fellow in Music. He taught in the music department of Harvard University from 1955 to 1963 and at Rutgers, the State University of New Jersey, from 1964. He was composer-in-residence at the American Academy in Rome in 1960–61 and a Guggenheim Fellow in 1963–4. Awards made to him include one of the National Institute of Arts and Sciences in 1956 and several from ASCAP. His broad musical structures are logical and balanced, with an extremely impassioned content; he is a master of the orchestra, and writes particularly skilfully for percussion.

### WORKS
*(selective list)*

INSTRUMENTAL

Orch: Endymion, ballet, 1948; Introduction and Fugue, 1949; Ov., 1950; 14 Variations, 1952; 3 Sym. Pieces, 1955; Conc., pf, orch, perc ens, 1960; In festivitate, wind, perc, 1962

Sonatina, pf, 1947; Sonata, pf, 1950; Spring, 4 vn, tpt, 1950; Pan, fl, 1951; Fantasia sopra una motivo, pf, 1951; Duo, ob, eng hn, 1953; Sonata, vn, 1956; Str Qt, 1957; Variazioni sopra una melodia, va, vc, 1961; Musica da camera, 9 insts, 1965; Fanfara canonica, 6 tpt, 1966; Piece for synket, 1969; Heptachronon, vc, 1969; B-A-C-H Es ist genug, org, 1970; Paths and Ways, dancer, sax, 1970; Phoenix, pf, 1971; Musica da camera II, ens, 1972

VOCAL

Choral: Peace (Moevs), female chorus, 1942; The Bacchantes (after Euripides), 1947; Cantata sacra (Easter liturgy), Bar, male chorus, fl, 4 trbn, timp, 1952; Attis (Catullus), S, T, chorus, orch, 1958–63; Et nunc, reges, female chorus, fl, cl, b cl, 1963; Et occidentem illustra (Dante, etc), chorus, orch, 1964; Ave Maria, 1966; Alleluia for Michaelmas, congregation, org, 1967; A Brief Mass, chorus, org, vib, gui, db, 1968

Songs: Youthful Song (Moevs), 3 songs, 1940–51; Villanelle (Desportes), 1950; Time, Mez, pf, 1969

Principal publishers: Belwin Mills, Eschig, Harvard University, Piedmont, E. C. Schirmer

MS (14 variations) in *US-Wc*

### WRITINGS

'Some Observations on Instruction in Music Theory', *College Music Symposium*, vi (1966), 69

'Music and the Liturgy', *Liturgical Arts*, xxxviii/1 (1969), 4

'Intervallic Procedures in Debussy: Serenade from the Sonata for Cello and Piano, 1915', *PNM*, viii/1 (1969), 82

'Mannerism and Stylistic Consistency in Stravinsky', *PNM*, ix/2 (1971), 92

### BIBLIOGRAPHY

B. Archibald: 'Composers of Importance Today: Robert Moevs', *Musical Newsletter*, ii/1 (1971), 19

BRUCE ARCHIBALD

**Moffat, Alfred (Edward)** (*b* Edinburgh, 4 Dec 1866; *d* London, 9 June 1950). Scottish music editor and collector. He studied compostion for five years in Berlin under Ludwig Bussler and remained there for another five years working for most of the large music publishers. On his return to London in the late 1890s he devoted himself to the rediscovery of British violin composers of the 18th century and earlier. He was general editor of Schott's Kammersonaten series and Simrock's Meisterschule der alten Zeit; he later induced Novello to embark on his Old English Violin Music series. Though modern scholarship has condemned his heavy and elaborate continuo parts, his pioneering work in this field

was of great importance. Moffat was also active as collector and arranger of traditional music of the British Isles. His fine library of early violin music was dispersed before his death and bought mostly by the Library of Congress and the British Museum.

FOLKSONG EDITIONS

*The Minstrelsy of Scotland* (London, 1895, 2/1896)

*The Minstrelsy of Ireland* (London, 1897, 3/1905)

*The Minstrelsy of England* (London, 1901)

with J. D. Brown: *Characteristic Songs and Dances of all Nations* (London, 1901)

*The Minstrelsy of Wales* (London, 1906)

*The Minstrelsy of the Scottish Highlands* (London, 1907)

*Melodious Scotland* (London, 1924–5)

FRANK KIDSON/PETER PLATT

**Moffo, Anna** (*b* Wayne, Penn., 27 June 1935). American soprano. She studied at the Curtis Institute, Philadelphia, with Eufemia Giannini-Gregory, and in Rome with Luigi Ricci and Mercedes Llopart, making her début in 1955 at the Teatro Sperimentale, Spoleto, as Norina. For Italian television she played Cio-cio-san (1956), and subsequently Nannetta, Amina, Lucia and Marie (*La fille du régiment*). In 1956 she sang Zerlina at Aix-en-Provence, and appeared throughout Italy, making her American début the following year, as Mimì in Chicago. She joined the Metropolitan Opera in 1959, making her début there as Violetta; she appeared regularly in New York during the 1960s and early 1970s in such roles as Pamina, Norina, Gilda, Luisa Miller, the four heroines of *Les contes d'Hoffmann*, Juliette, Gounod's Marguerite, Massenet's Manon, Mélisande, and the title role in *La Périchole*. She sang Gilda at Covent Garden (1964), and has appeared in Vienna, Salzburg, Berlin and elsewhere. A lyric soprano of warm, full, radiant tone, she was capable of undertaking coloratura parts. As Violetta, a role in which she was internationally acclaimed, notably on film and record, and as a guest artist in Felsenstein's production at the Komische Oper, Berlin, the range and versatility of her voice, and her charming stage presence, were put to particularly good use. Unfortunately her musical and dramatic talent was exploited, and she appeared in the theatre and on record in unsuitable roles. This led to a vocal breakdown in 1974–5, but in 1976 she made a fresh start.

HAROLD ROSENTHAL

**Mogavero, Antonio** (*b* Francavilla Fontana, nr. Brindisi; *fl* 1590–1600). Italian composer. Although he was born in southern Italy, he seems to have been active, at least in the late 1590s, in the Venetian area; the dedication to Archduke Ferdinand of Austria of his third book of madrigals for five voices, entitled *Vezzi amorosi*, suggests a northern connection. He is represented, moreover, in a collection of settings of poems by the abbot Angelo Grillo, who was Prior of S Giuliano in Genoa (*RISM* 1598⁶); most of the other composers whose works appear in the volume are northerners. A substantial portion of Mogavero's output, including the first two books of madrigals for five voices, is now lost. His surviving work consists entirely of secular compositions, although he also wrote and published sacred music. Some of the lost works were formerly in the library of King John IV of Portugal (destroyed in 1755).

### WORKS

Canzonette alla napolitana . . . libro primo, 3, 4vv (Venice, 1591)

Il primo libro delle canzonette, 4vv (Venice, 1596)

Il terzo libro de madrigali intitolato Vezzi amorosi, 5vv, con un dialogo, 8vv (Venice, 1598)

Partitura Lamentationum Jeremiae prophetae in maiori hebdomada, 6vv, bc. . .canticum vero Zacchariae & Miserere, 8vv (Venice, 1623)
1 madrigal, 1598[6]

LOST WORKS
1 book madrigals, 5vv; 1 book madrigals, 4vv; 1 book motets, 5–8vv; 2 motets, 6vv; 1 book masses, 8vv; all cited in catalogue of King John IV library, Portugal

STEVEN LEDBETTER

**Mogilevsky, Evgeny (Gedeonovich)** (*b* Odessa, 16 Sept 1945). Soviet pianist. He studied the piano with his mother, S. E. Mogilevskaya, at the Stolyarsky music school in Odessa. In 1963 he entered Heinrich Neuhaus's class at the Moscow Conservatory, and after Neuhaus's death, studied with his son Stanislav Neuhaus and then with Yakov Zak, from whose class he graduated in 1969; he completed his postgraduate studies in 1971. In 1964 he won the Queen Elisabeth Competition in Brussels, and in 1966, as best performer of the year, was presented with a Harriet Cohen Medal. Mogilevsky has toured the USSR and abroad and is one of the distinguished representatives of the younger generation of Soviet pianists. Vividness, depth and feeling of interpretation, and remarkable virtuoso skill are the distinctive features of his style. In 1972 he began to teach at the Moscow Conservatory.

BIBLIOGRAPHY
Yu. Zvereva: 'Talant, est' strast' plyus intellekt' [Talent: passion plus intellect], *SovM* (1972), no.5, p.70

I. M. YAMPOL'SKY

**Mohaupt, Richard** (*b* Breslau, 14 Sept 1904; *d* Reichenau, Austria, 3 July 1957). German composer. After music studies under Prüwer and Bilke at Breslau University, he worked as a vocal coach and as a conductor at the opera houses of Weimar, Breslau and Aachen. In 1931–2 he toured as a pianist and conductor, then settled in Berlin, where he spent several years as a composer and pianist for a film company. His opera *Die Wirtin von Pinsk* (1937) was banned after two performances and continuing conflicts with the Nazi regime led to his emigration to New York in 1939. There he worked as a music teacher and composed the greater part of his serious compositions, including the frequently performed *Stadtpfeifermusik*, based on the *Nürnberger Stadtpfeifer* mural of Dürer. Mohaupt received several commissions, and he was highly successful as a composer for the cinema and broadcasting, as well as producing popular children's pieces. In 1955 he moved to Semmering in Austria. His music shows great technical facility and a distinctly progressive tendency combined with the simplicity developed in his popular music. Among his most interesting works are the stage works, most of them comic.

WORKS
(*selective list*)

Operas: Die Wirtin von Pinsk (after Goldoni: Mirandolina), 1937, Dresden, 1938; Die Bremer Stadtmusikanten, 1944, Bremen, 1949; Double Trouble (Zwillingskomödie) (after Plautus), 1954, Louisville, Kentucky, 1954; Der grüne Kakadu (after Schnitzler), 1956, Hamburg, 1958
Ballets: Die Gaunerstreiche der Coursache, 1935, Berlin, 1936; Lysistrata, dance-comedy, solo vv, chorus, orch, 1941, rev. as Der Weiberstreik von Athen, orch, 1955, Karlsruhe, 1957; Max und Moritz, dance-burlesque, 1945, Karlsruhe, 1949; The Legend of the Charlatan, mimodrama, 1949
Orch: Die Gaunerstreiche der Coursache, suite, 1935; Pf Conc., perf. 1938, rev. 1942; 3 Episoden, perf. 1938; Stadtpfeifermusik, 1939, rev. wind, 1953; Sym. 'Rhythmus und Variationen', 1940; Conc. for Orch, 1942; Vn Conc., 1945; Lysistrata, choreographic episodes, 1946; Max und Moritz [after ballet], narrator, orch, 1946; Banchetto musicale, 12 inst, orch, 1955; Offenbachiana, 1955

Vocal: Trilogy (Euripides, Sappho, Aristophanes), A, orch, 1951; Das goldene Byzanz, dramatic cantata, chorus, ens, 1954; Bucolica, 4 solo vv, chorus, orch, 1955; lieder, children's songs
Chamber and pf pieces, music for the cinema and broadcasting, arrs.

Principal publishers: Associated, Universal

BIBLIOGRAPHY
R. Bilke: 'Richard Mohaupt', *Musica*, iv (1950), 324

JOSEPH CLARK

**Mohler, Philipp** (*b* Kaiserslautern, 26 Nov 1908). German composer and teacher. After studies in Kaiserslautern at the conservatory and at the Ober-Real Schule, from which he graduated in 1928, he went to Munich to attend the university and the academy, where his principal teachers were Haas (composition), Härtl (violin) and von Waltershausen (dramatic music). He continued his training in Haas's master classes (1931–4) while beginning a career as a music teacher and conductor in Munich (1933) and in Nuremberg and Landau, Rhineland (1934–9). In 1940 he succeeded Distler as instructor in conducting and composition at the Staatliche Hochschule für Musik, Stuttgart, where he was appointed professor (1943–59). He also directed the Stuttgart Orchester-Verein (from 1940) and the Stuttgart Lehrergesangverein (from 1955). In 1958 he was appointed director of the Staatliche Hochschule für Musik, Frankfurt. Among the honours he has received are the Stamitz Prize (1944), the Rhineland-Palatinate Arts Prize (1961) and first-class membership in the Bundesverdienstkreuz (1968).

WORKS
(*selective list*)

Orch: Pf Conc., op.16 (1937); Fantasiestück, op.17, vc, orch (1960); Sinfonisches Vorspiel, op.18 (1939); Sinfonische Fantasie, op.20 (1941); Heitere Ouvertüre, op.27, str (1951); Concertino, op.28, fl, str (1955); Sinfonisches Capriccio, op.40 (1957)
Choral: Leben, op.5 (J. Linberg), male vv, brass, timp (1936); Vergangen ist die Nacht, op.14, female vv, fl, str orch (1943); Nachtmusikanten, op.24 (A. a S Clara), T, chorus, orch (1943); Laetare, perf. 1968
Solo vocal: Rilke-Lieder, op.2, S/T, pf, perf. 1932; Geistliche Solokantate, op.10 (J. Langbehn), S, pf qt, perf. 1933; Vagabundenlieder, op.36 (Hesse), Bar, pf (1957); Cantata domestica, 1v, 2 vn, vc, unpubd
Inst: Divertimento, op.13, vn, va (1947); 3 Konzertstücke, op.21, pf (1951); 2 Canzonen, org, perf. 1941

Principal publishers: Gerig, Hochstein, Müller, Schott, Sikorski

BIBLIOGRAPHY
O. Riemer: 'Bodenständige Musik', *Musica*, vi (1952), 104
G. Schweizer: 'Philipp Mohler-Feier in Frankfurt', *Musik im Unterricht*, iv (1959)
——: 'Philipp Mohler 60. Jahre', *Musikalische Jugend*, xvii (1968)

JOHN MORGAN

**Mohr, Ernst (Werner)** (*b* Basle, 4 March 1902). Swiss musicologist. He started to study natural sciences, but then studied musicology at the universities of Basle under Karl Nef, Berlin under Abert, Sachs and Wolf, and Paris under Pirro, while also studying theory at Basle Conservatory. In 1927 he took his doctorate at Basle University with a dissertation on the allemande. He taught theory, history of music and literature at Basle Conservatory (1928–69) and he was also reader in theory of music at Basle University (1946–70). Between 1933 and 1959 he was president of the Basle section of the Schweizerische musikforschende Gesellschaft, and from 1949 to 1974 he was president of the society. He began acting as chief examiner for the Schweizerischer musikpädagogischer Verband in 1943, and from 1952 to 1972 he was general secretary of the IMS, in succession to Merian; in 1972 the IMS made him an honorary member.

When Mohr became general secretary he had the task of reviving international cooperation among musicologists, and he won world-wide recognition for his sustained ability to remove obstacles with diplomatic finesse and patience. He has worked equally for musicology in Switzerland: he instigated the Schweizerische Musikdenkmäler, the *Schweizer Beiträge zur Musikwissenschaft* and the 25 volumes of publications of the Schweizerische musikforschende Gesellschaft, whose *Mitteilungsblatt* he started editing in 1945. He was an influential teacher at both conservatory and university and has published a large number of studies of modern German–Swiss musical history, among which the biography of Willy Burkhard is particularly important.

WRITINGS

*Die Allemande: eine Untersuchung ihrer Entwicklung von den Anfängen bis zu Bach und Händel* (diss., U. of Basle, 1927; Zurich, 1932)
'Karl Nef und sein Werk, eine Zusammenstellung [Bibliographie]', *Festschrift Karl Nef zum 60. Geburtstag* (Zurich, 1932), 10
'Die Orchester [in der Schweiz]', *Schweizer Musikbuch* (Zurich, 1939), i, 235
'Neuere und neueste Debussy-Literatur', *SMz*, lxxxi (1941), 257
'Das Problem der Form in Schoecks Liederzyklen', *SMz*, lxxxiii (1943), 85
'Richard Strauss als Dirigent in der Schweiz', *SMz*, lxxxiv (1944), 236
'Ältere Schweizer Musik in Neuausgaben', *SMz*, lxxxvii (1947), 333
'Das Werk Walther Geisers', *Musica*, iii (1949), 259
ed., with H. Ehinger: E. Refardt: *Musik in der Schweiz, ausgewählte Aufsätze* (Berne, 1952)
'Albert Moeschinger: Werk und Persönlichkeit', *SMz*, xciii (1953), 153
'Walther Geiser: Persönlichkeit und Werk', *SMz*, xcvii (1957), 174
*Willy Burkhard: Leben und Werk* (Zurich, 1957)
'Walter Müller von Kulms Weg als Musiker und Komponist', *SMz*, c (1960), 76
'Zur Kompositionstechnik, Rudolf Kelterborns', *Musica*, xiv (1960), 281
'Zum Kompositionsstil von Conrad Beck', *SMz*, ci (1961), 6
'Rudolf Kelterborn: analytische Hinweise zu seiner Missa für Sopran, Tenor, Chor und Orchester', *Musica*, xvi (1962), 232
'Über einige neue Werke von Rudolf Kelterborns', *SMz*, cii (1962), 201
Articles in *MGG*

BIBLIOGRAPHY

F. Blume: 'Ernst Mohr siebzigjährig', *AcM*, xliv (1972), 29
K. von Fischer: 'Laudatio zum 70. Geburtstag von Dr Ernst Mohr', *Schweizerische musikforschende Gesellschaft: Mitteilungsblatt* (1972), no.45, p.14
W. Schuh: 'Ernst Mohr siebzig Jahre alt', *SMz*, cxii (1972), 95

JÜRG STENZL

**Mohrhardt, Peter.** *See* MORHARD, PETER.

**Moire, Ephrem** (*d c*1100). Hymnographer of the Georgian Church; *see* GEORGIAN RITE, MUSIC OF THE, §3.

**Moisai** (Gk.). MUSES.

**Moiseiwitsch** [Moyseivich], **Benno** (*b* Odessa, 22 Feb 1890; *d* London, 9 April 1963). British pianist of Russian birth. In Odessa he studied at the Imperial Music Academy with Dmitry Klimov, winning the Rubinstein Prize when he was nine. At 14 he went to Vienna (where he adopted the German transliteration of his name) to study with Leschetizky but his family settled in England and he made his official début at Reading in 1908, and his first London appearance a year later (in 1937 he took British nationality). After 1919 he toured Europe and the USA regularly, later the Antipodes, the Far East, Africa and South America. His daughter Tanya became a stage designer.

Moiseiwitsch's playing was marked by a semblance

*Benno Moiseiwitsch*

of utter impassivity, possibly modelled on his friend and musical idol Rakhmaninov, though Moiseiwitsch was himself a passionate and expert poker player. His interpretations, notwithstanding, were essentially fiery, effortlessly brilliant and powerful, with singing tone, firmly controlled yet subtle rhythm, and a strong vein of elegant poetic expression. 'Moiseiwitsch double octaves', thumbs louder than fifth fingers, became a household word among pianists. He excelled in Rakhmaninov's music (Rakhmaninov often complained with feigned envy that Moiseiwitsch played his works better than he did), but was as cogent in that of Metner, whom he constantly championed, and in Tchaikovsky. His repertory, formerly extensive, really began with Beethoven, like that of other Leschetizky pupils (earlier works were played in Romantic arrangements), and extended to Poulenc, though he sometimes gave first performances of newer music. In later years he played Beethoven often but drily, without much charm or brilliance; yet those were two principal characteristics of Moiseiwitsch the man (but he also had a dry, leisurely sense of humour), as of his interpretation in Chopin, Schumann and Liszt, and of his instant appeal to audiences everywhere. He was a scrupulous and warm-hearted partner in chamber music, for example Brahms's Quintet or Rakhmaninov's Elegiac Trio and Cello Sonata.

WILLIAM S. MANN

**Mojiganga** (Sp.). (1) A short theatrical piece of grotesque, comic or satirical nature, popular in Spain during the 17th and early 18th centuries as the conclusion to a dramatic production. Songs and dances such as *canarios*, *chaconas*, *zarambeques* and, later, fandangos and arias, were included, sometimes with loud instrumental accompaniments. Calderón, Avellaneda, Marchante and other notable poets of the period wrote *mojigangas*, but most of the music is lost.

(2) A public outdoor festival, usually held at carnival time, with participants on horseback wearing masks and strange costumes; these burlesque entertainments involved flutes, castanets and side drums.

### BIBLIOGRAPHY
*LaborD*
E. Cotarelo y Mori: *Colección de entremeses, loas, bailes, jácaras y mojigangas*, xvii (Madrid, 1911), p.ccxci

**Mojsisovics(-Mojsvár), Roderich** Edler von (*b* Graz, 10 May 1877; *d* Graz, 30 March 1953). Austrian composer. He studied theory and composition with Degner in Graz (1896–9), also taking a doctorate in law at the university (1900). In 1901 he studied with Wüllner and Klauwell at the Cologne Conservatory, and in 1901–2 with L. Thuille and E. Bach at the Music Academy in Munich. He worked variously as a choral conductor, teacher and writer on music until 1912, when he was appointed director of the Steiermärkische Musikverein (Conservatory from 1920) in Graz. He remained there until 1931, teaching Max Schönherr among others. His subsequent career was again varied: he taught music history at Graz University (1932–5), worked in Munich as a teacher at the Trapp Conservatory and as a music critic (1935–41), joined the staff of the Mannheim Musikhochschule (1941–4) and returned to Graz to teach operatic dramaturgy at the conservatory (1945–8). His style belongs to the tradition of Reger, though his main interest was in opera.

### WORKS
*(selective list)*

Stage: Ninion, op.19 (melodrama, 1, E. Mayer, A. Weissmann), Pressburg, 1907; Die roten Dominos, op.20 (opera, 2, Mojsisovics, after H. Hopfen: Zehn oder elf), Graz, 1907; Messer Ricciardo Minutolo, op.50 (music-comedy, Mojsisovics); Der Zauberer, op.60 (opera, 1, Mojsisovics, after Cervantes), Gera, 1926; Madame Blaubart, op.62 (opera, 3, K. Mayer, E. Meier-Hahn), inc. radio perf., Breslau, 1934; König Mensch, op.63 (marionette play, 2, W. Illing), Graz, 1922; Die Locke, op.72 (opera, 1, Mojsisovics), Knittelfeld, 1927; Anno domini, op.75 (opera, 2 scenes, Mojsisovics); Phantastisches Tanzspiel, op.76, Graz, 1929

Orch: 5 syms., opp.15, 25, 61, 65, 86; Vn Conc., f♯, op.40 (1931); 2 pf concs., opp.55, 57; 2 ovs., 2 serenades

Other works: 3 str qts, other chamber music, pf and org works, choral pieces, songs

Principal publishers: M. Hieber (Munich), F. Schuberth jr (Leipzig), Serano (Zurich), F. Zierfuss (Munich)

### WRITINGS
'Ein wiederaufgefundenes Ballett Mozarts', *ZMw*, xii (1929–30), 472; repr. in *MJb* (1957), 150
*Bach-Probleme* (Würzburg, 1930)

### BIBLIOGRAPHY
M. Morold: 'Roderich von Mojsisovics', *ZfM*, xcix (1932), 661
F. Stichtenoth: 'Roderich von Mojsisovics', *ZfM*, cix (1942), 202
K. Haidmayer: *Roderich von Mojsisovics: Leben und Werk* (diss., U. of Graz, 1951)
based on *MGG* (ix, 429–30) by permission of Bärenreiter

RENATE FEDERHOFER-KÖNIGS

**Mokranjac, Stevan (Stojanović)** (*b* Negotin, 9 Jan 1856; *d* Skopje, 28 Sept 1914). Serbian composer, musicologist and conductor. From 1879 he studied at the Munich Conservatory with Sachs (harmony) and Rheinberger (composition); he also studied with Parisotti in Rome (1884–5) and with Reinecke, Jadassohn and Brodsky in Leipzig (1885–7). In 1887 he returned to Serbia to become conductor and lifelong director of the Serbian Choral Society in Belgrade, for which he wrote many works. Two years later he founded a string quartet, in which he played second violin. He made numerous tours of Slav territories, notating folksongs as he heard them. In 1893 he visited

Dubrovnik and Cetinje, in 1894 Skopje and Budapest; in 1896 he toured Macedonia extensively and in 1910–11 visited Bosnia, Herzegovina, Montenegro, Dalmatia and Croatia. He incorporated many of the folksongs he collected into his own compositions. In 1899, with K. Manojlović and S. Binički, he founded the Serbian School of Music in Belgrade (now the Mokranjac School of Music), remaining its director until his death.

Had Mokranjac accomplished nothing more than the establishment of the Belgrade String Quartet and the Serbian School of Music, he would nevertheless have been assured a place in history. But by his training and development of the Serbian Choral Society into a group of international standard, which toured Russia, Germany, Austria and Hungary, he set a standard of choral singing that is still emulated. Even more important was his work in collecting folksongs from Serbia, Macedonia, Montenegro, Bosnia and other Slav territories. He notated many of them in their original form (published in 1966), also making a scientific analysis of their musical content. Among his most noteworthy collections are 160 folk melodies from Kosovo (1896) and about 300 Serbian melodies.

Folksong naturally inspired Mokranjac's own compositions. Wishing to liberate Serbian music from its primitive inheritance, he believed that by studying with the best teachers in Europe and by basing his own music on national melodies he could achieve this aim. Apart from a few instrumental works, his music is all vocal (predominantly choral), divided nearly equally between secular and sacred. The most famous of his secular pieces are the 15 *Rukoveti* ('Bouquets') or choral rhapsodies that incorporate some 90 folksongs, arranged and harmonized in a vivid, imaginative and varied manner. He was a deeply religious man and contributed abundantly to church music, notably with two settings of the Serbian Orthodox Requiem, various services (including the large-scale *Božestvenaja služba* ('Liturgy' of 1894–5) and a manual of Orthodox church singing (*Opšte pojanje*, Belgrade, 1935).

### WORKS
SACRED CHORAL
*(all for mixed vv unless otherwise stated)*

Tebe boga hvalim [Lord, we give thee thanks], 1882; Opelo [Requiem], no.1, g, 1883, no.2, f♯, 1888; Svjati Bože i Alliluja [Sacred service and Alleluia], 1883; Akatisti Bogorodici [Prayers for the Virgin], 1892; Tebe odjejuščagosja [Songs for Good Friday], 1892; Veličanije Sv. Savi [The glorification of St Sava], male vv, 1893, rev. for mixed vv, 1906; Božestvenaja služba [Liturgy], 1894–5

Crkveno pojanje [12 sacred songs], 3 children's vv, 1901–2; Ps cxxxvi 'Na rjekah Vavilonski' [On the waters of Babylon], male vv, 1908; 24 other works (incl. 1 for male vv)

SECULAR VOCAL

[15] Rukoveti [Bouquets], on folksongs from various regions, all with chorus: 1 with T, B, 1884; 2 with T, 1884; 3 with T, B, 1888; 4 Mirjano, B, pf, 1890; 5 with S, T, 1892; 6 Hajduk Veljko, T, 1892; 7 Iz Stare Srbije i Makedonije [From Old Serbia and Macedonia], T, 1894; 8 Sa Kosova [From Kosovo], 1896; 9 Iz Crne Gore [From Montenegro], 1896; 10 Sa Ohrida [From Ohrid], 1901; 11 Iz Stare Srbije, 1905; 12 Sa Kosova, 1906; 13 Iz moje domovine [From my homeland], 1907; 14 Iz Bosne [From Bosnia], 1908; 15 Iz Makedonije, 1909

Ivkova slava (S. Sremac and D. Brzak), 8 dramatic scenes, S, A, T, chorus, orch, 1901

Other: 36 songs, mixed vv, incl. Jadna draga [Unfortunate sweetheart], S, 1887, Primorski napjevi [Coastal songs], 1893, Kozar [The goatherd], 1904; 5 songs, male vv; 21 folksongs and ballads, 1v, pf; 1 song, 1v, orch; 10 songs, children's vv

INSTRUMENTAL

Sanjarije [Reveries], on a Serbian folksong, str qt, 1877; 5 fugues, str

### BIBLIOGRAPHY
T. M. Bušetić: *Srpske narodne pesme i igre . . . musički priredbe S. S. Mokranjac* [Serbian folksongs and dances . . . musical arrangements

by Mokranjac] (Belgrade, 1902)
K. P. Manojlović: *Spomenica St. St. Mokranjcu* [Memorial to Mokranjac] (Belgrade, 1923)
M. Milojević: 'Umetnička ideologija Stevana St. Mokranjca' [The artistic ideology of Mokranjac], *Srpski književni glasnik*, liii/3 (1938), 192
V. Vučković: 'Muzički realizam Stevana Mokranjca' [The musical realism of Mokranjac], *Slavenska muzika*, i (1940), no.5, p.36; no.6, p.43; no.7–8, p.59
P. Bingulac: 'Stevan Mokranjca i njegove Rukoveti' [Mokranjac and his *Rukoveti*], *Godišnjak Muzeja grada Beograda*, iii (1956)
P. Konjović: *Stevan St. Mokranjac* (Belgrade, 1956)
M. Živković: *Rukoveti St. St. Mokranjca* (Belgrade, 1957)
I. I. Martuinov: *Stevan Mokranjac* (Moscow, 1958)
S. S. Mokranjac: *Zapisi narodnih melodija* (Belgrade, 1966)
V. Peričić: 'Stevan Mokranjac', *Muzičke stvaraoci u Srbiji* (Belgrade, 1969), 303
M. Vukdragović, ed.: *Zbornik radova o Stevanu Mokranjcu* [Anthology of works on Mokranjac] (Belgrade, 1971)

NIALL O'LOUGHLIN

**Mokrý, Ladislav** (*b* Topolčany, 2 June 1932). Slovak musicologist. He studied musicology and history at Bratislava University (graduated 1955) and was librarian (from 1953) and assistant lecturer (1954–9) at its musicology institute. In 1963 he became a research fellow at the Musicology Institute of the Slovak Academy of Sciences, part-time lecturer in musicology at the Bratislava Academy of Music and secretary of the musicology section of the Slovak Composers' Union; between 1957 and 1971 he also served on the editorial board of *Slovenská hudba*. His particular interests are early music (notably palaeography and Slavonic chant) and musical sociology, whose position he has defended within the Marxist concept of musicology; his article on the subject (1962) shows considerable historical awareness and made it a viable study in Czechoslovakia. He was the co-author of a history of Slovak music (1957) and helped to edit the first Slovak music encyclopedia; he also made Slovak translations of Siegmund-Schultze's *G. F. Händel* (Bratislava, 1959) and Stokowski's *Music for all of us* (Bratislava, 1963).

WRITINGS

with J. Tvrdoň: *Dejiny slovenskej hudby* [History of Slovak music] (Bratislava, 1957)
'Die slowakische Oper', *Musica*, xi (1957), 529
*Hudobná paleografia* [Musical palaeography] (Bratislava, 1957)
'Pestrý sborník: Levočská tabulaturná kniha z konca 17. storočia' [The coloured codex: Levoča tablature book from the end of the 17th century], *Hudobnovedné štúdie*, ii (1957), 106–66
with L. Burlas: '40 rokov slovenskej hudby' [40 years of Slovak music], *SH*, i (1957), 245
'Poznámky k súčasnej seriálnej hudbe' [Remarks on contemporary serial music], *SH*, ii (1958), 461
'Otázky renesančnej hudby a súčasná hudební historiografia' [Questions of Renaissance music and contemporary musical historiography], *Slovenská hudba 1959*, 55
'Zu den Anfängen der Mehrstimmigkeit bei den Westslawen', *Chopin Congress: Warszawa 1960*, 567
'O hudební sociológii' [Musical sociology], *HV 1962*, 159
'Z československo-sovietskych hudobných vztahov poroku 1945' [Czech-Soviet musical contacts after 1945], *Slovanské štúdie*, v (1962), 205
*Hudba pre všetých* (Bratislava, 1963) [trans. of L. Stokowski: *Music for all of us*, New York, 1943, 2/1947]
'Soziologie und Marxismus', *I. Internationale Seminar marxistischer Musikwissenschaftler: Prague 1963* [*BMw*, v (1963)], 307
'Der Kanon zur Ehre des hl. Demetrius als Quelle für die Frühgeschichte des kirchenslavischen Gesanges', *Anfänge der slavischen Musik: Symposia I: Bratislava 1964*, 35
'Hudba na Slovensku v rokoch 1945–1965' [Music in Slovakia 1945–65], *Slovenská kultúra 1945 až 1965*, ed. K. Rosenbaum (Bratislava, 1965), 75
'Počiatky hudobného baroka na Slovensku' [The beginnings of musical Baroque in Slovakia], *Hudobnovedné štúdie*, vii (1966)
'Die musikalischen Interessen der Pubeszenten und deren Motivation', *Sborník prací filosofické fakulty brněnské university*, H3 (1968), 21
ed., with M. Jurík and others: *Malá encyklopédia hudby* [Small encyclopedia of music] (Bratislava, 1969)

'Sociológia a historiografia' [Sociology and historiography], *Musicologica slovaca*, iv (1973), 253

**Molaines, Pierre de.** *See* PIERRE DE MOLINS.

**Molchanov, Kirill Vladimirovich** (*b* Moscow, 7 Sept 1922). Russian composer. He graduated from Alexandrov's class at the Moscow Conservatory in 1949. Active in the Moscow section of the Composers' Union, he is also director of the State Academic Bol'shoy Theatre of the USSR, and he holds the title Honoured Art Worker of the RSFSR. Chief among his works are the operas, which reveal an outstanding feeling for the stage and for vivid theatrical effect, together with a moving lyricism. The subjects range from the fantasy of *Kamenniy tsvetok* ('The stone flower'), based on tales from the Urals (the piece is close to the Rimsky-Korsakov tradition), to the historical revolutionary themes of *Zarya* ('Daybreak'). Molchanov's operas have been produced in the USSR and abroad, and his expressive and accessible songs have also achieved popularity.

WORKS
*(selective list)*

Operas: Kamenniy tsvetok [The stone flower] (after N. Bazhov), 1950; Zarya [Daybreak] (after B. Lavrenyov), 1956; Ulitsa del corno [Del corno street] (after V. Pratolini), 1960; Romeo, Dzhulyetta i t'ma [Romeo, Juliet and the darkness] (after J. Otčenášek), 1963; Neizvestniy soldat [The unknown soldier] (Brestskaya krepost' [The Brest fortress]) (Molchanov), 1967; Russkaya zhenshchina [The Russian woman] (Molchanov, after Yu. Nagibin), 1969; Odissey, Penelopa i drugiye [Odysseus, Penelope and others], musical comedy, 1970; Zori zdes' tikhiye [The dawns are quiet here] (Molchanov, after B. Vasnetsov), 1973
Songs: Pesni (N. Gil'yen), 1956; 4 romansa (L. Hughes), 1958; Romansï (Smelyakov, Tyomin, Prokofiev), 1961; Iz ispanskoy poezii (Lorca), 1963; Pesni Khirosimï [Songs of Hiroshima] (Jap.), 1964; Chornaya shkatulka [The black box] (L. Ashkenazi), 1967; Lyubov [Love] (Khikmet, Karasïmovich, Kallau, Voznesensky, Keno), 1971
Pf: Russkiye kartinï [Russian pictures], 1953
22 film scores, 33 incidental scores

BIBLIOGRAPHY

Yu. Korev: 'Pesni K. Molchanova', *SovM* (1960), no.7, p.30
V. Shmelyov: 'Tret'ya shkatulka' [The third box], *SovM* (1968), no.7, p.32 [on Molchanov's romances]
Yu. Korev: *Kirill Molchanov* (Moscow, 1971)

GALINA GRIGOR'YEVA

**Moldavia.** Region in south-east Europe, partly a constituent republic of the USSR; *see* UNION OF SOVIET SOCIALIST REPUBLICS, §VIII, and ROMANIA.

**Moldenhauer, Hans** (*b* Mainz, 13 Dec 1906). American musicologist of German birth. He graduated from the Musikhochschule in Mainz, where he was a pupil of Hans Rosbaud. He emigrated to America in 1938 and took the BA at Whitworth College, Spokane, in 1945 and the DFA in musicology at Chicago Musical College of Roosevelt University in 1951. In 1942 he founded the Spokane Conservatory, of which he has been president since 1946. He also taught at the University of Washington from 1961 to 1964, and he has lectured at colleges and universities throughout Europe and America.

Moldenhauer is the founder and director of the Moldenhauer Archive, which contains autograph musical manuscripts, letters and documents; most of the archive is located in Spokane, Washington, with parts housed at Northwestern University. An important section of this collection is the Webern Archive; Moldenhauer's long-standing interest in the composer is reflected in this compilation of manuscripts and memorabilia and in his many articles about Webern. Moldenhauer has published a number of Webern Archive music manuscripts, including the sketches, in facsimile or practical editions.

WRITINGS

*Duo-pianism* (Chicago, 1950)

'Ein neu entdecktes Mozart-Autograph', *MJb 1953*, 143; Eng. trans. in *JAMS*, viii (1955), 213

'From my Autograph Collection: C. Ph. E. Bach–Dittersdorf–Mozart', *Kongressbericht: Wien Mozartjahr 1956*, 412

'Übersicht der Musikmanuskripte W. A. Mozarts in den Vereinigten Staaten von Amerika (1956)', *MJb 1956*, 88

*The Death of Anton Webern; a Drama in Documents* (New York, 1961; Ger. trans., 1970)

ed. with D. Irvine: *Anton von Webern: Perspectives: 1st Webern Festival: Seattle 1962* [incl. 'A Webern Archive in America?', 117]

'Unbekannte Briefe Gustav Mahlers an Emil Hertzka', *NZM*, cxxxv (1964), 544

'Das Webern-Archiv in Amerika', *ÖMz*, xx (1965), 422

'Paul Amadeus Pisk and the Viennese Triumvirate', *Paul A. Pisk: Essays in his Honor* (Austin, Texas, 1966), 208

'A Webern Pilgrimage', *MT*, cix (1968), 122

'Webern's Projected Opus 32', *MT*, cxi (1970), 789

'Weberns letzte Gedanken', *Melos*, xxxviii (1971), 273

'Anton von Webern: neue Sichten über einige posthume Werke', *ÖMz*, xxvii (1972), 114

*Anton von Webern: Chronicle of his Life and Work* (New York and London, 1978; Ger. trans., 1979)

BIBLIOGRAPHY

P. Nettl: 'Hans Moldenhauer, Pionier der Musikwissenschaft', *Festschrift Alfred Orel* (Vienna, 1960), 133

PAULA MORGAN

**Mole, 'Miff'** [Irving Milfred] (*b* Roosevelt, NY, 11 March 1898; *d* New York, 29 April 1961). American jazz trombonist. He played the violin and piano before learning the trombone. Based in New York, he made hundreds of recordings with many groups, the most influential being those with the Original Memphis Five and with Red Nichols's innovatory groups in the 1920s. In these years he fashioned the first distinctive and influential jazz trombone style, free from the glissandos and rudimentary bass-line paraphrases of 'tailgate' playing and characterized by precise execution, wide leaps and short rhythmic values. This style was already formed by the time he recorded his own composition *Slippin' Around* with Nichols (1927). In 1929 he joined the NBC radio orchestra, where he remained for most of the 1930s. After playing briefly with Paul Whiteman (1938–40) and Benny Goodman (1943) he returned to small group jazz, sometimes with Muggsy Spanier, until the mid-1950s, when illness prevented him from playing.

BIBLIOGRAPHY

N. Shapiro and N. Hentoff, eds.: *Hear me talkin' to ya* (New York, 1955), 244ff

J. Grunnet Jepsen: *Jazz Records: 1942–1962*, v (Copenhagen 1963)

B. Rust: *Jazz Records, 1897–1942* (London, 1965, rev. 2/1969)

A. McCarthy: *Jazz on Record* (London, 1968), 200f

M. Harrison: *A Jazz Retrospect* (Newton Abbot, 1976), 190ff

JAMES DAPOGNY

**Molière** [Poquelin, Jean-Baptiste] (*b* Paris, baptized 15 Jan 1622; *d* Paris, 17 Feb 1673). French playwright and actor. Musically he is important for his *comédies-ballets*, which date from the last 12 years of his life, when he also wrote most of his most famous plays; he was living in Paris at this period after being away for some years. The *comédie-ballet*, which incorporated elements of the *ballet de cour* into spoken comedy, came into existence almost accidentally. For festivities at the court of Louis XIV in August 1661 both a play by Molière and a ballet were planned. However, only a small number of dancers were available, and in order to give them time for costume changes it was decided to place the ballet entrées between the acts of the play (*Les fâcheux*); then, as Molière explained in his preface, 'in order not to break the thread of the play by these *intermèdes*, we decided to link them with its subject as best we could and to make a single thing of the ballet and the play'.

Following *Les fâcheux* (with music partly by Lully), Molière and Lully collaborated in a number of other *comédies-ballets*: *Le mariage forcé* (1664), *La princesse d'Elide* (1664), *L'amour médecin* (1665), *Pastorale comique* (1667), *Le sicilien* (1667), *George Dandin* (1668), *Monsieur de Pourceaugnac* (1669), *Les amants magnifiques* (1670), *Le bourgeois gentilhomme* (1670) and *La comtesse d'Escarbagnas* (1671). Molière also wrote with Lully the *tragédie-ballet Psyché* (1671). After becoming estranged from Lully he asked Marc-Antoine Charpentier to revise parts of Lully's scores for *La comtesse d'Escarbagnas*, *Le mariage forcé* and *Les fâcheux* (summer and autumn 1672) and to compose the music for his last *comédie-ballet*, *Le malade imaginaire* (1673).

Besides ballet entrées and entr'acte *intermèdes* set to music, many of these works include songs and other musical divertissements within the play proper. The dramatic and musical components are integrated to varying degrees. They are most inseparably intertwined in *La princesse d'Elide*, *Les amants magnifiques*, *Le bourgeois gentilhomme* and *Le malade imaginaire*; the last two in fact culminate in farcical final *intermèdes* absolutely essential to the comedy.

Molière had no immediate successors in the genre of *comédie-ballet*, mainly because the king came to prefer Lully's operas to spoken plays. But the nature of Quinault's verse in his *tragédies lyriques* for Lully owes something to Molière; Lully had devised and perfected his recitative in his earlier work with Molière; and the first real opera of Lully and Quinault, *Cadmus et Hermione* (1672), bears in general plan a considerable resemblance to the *comédie-ballet*.

For good texts of Molière's *comédies-ballets*, see the edition of his works by E. Despois and P. Mesnard (Paris, 1873–1900); relevant music by Lully appears in his *Oeuvres complètes*, ed. H. Prunières: *Les comédies-ballets* (Paris, 1931–8).

BIBLIOGRAPHY

Castil-Blaze: *Molière musicien* (Paris, 1852)

V. Fournel: *Les contemporains de Molière* (Paris, 1862–75)

A. Pougin: *Molière et l'opéra-comique* (Paris, 1882)

L. de La Laurencie: *Lully* (Paris, 1911)

M. Pellisson: *Les comédies-ballets de Molière* (Paris, 1914)

F. Böttger: *Die 'Comédie-ballet' von Molière–Lully* (Berlin, 1931)

H. C. Lancaster: *A History of French Dramatic Literature in the Seventeenth Century* (Baltimore, 1936)

R. Brancour: 'Molière et la musique', *RMI*, xli (1937), 446

A. R. Oliver: 'Molière's Contribution to the Lyric Stage', *MQ*, xxxiii (1947), 350

M.-F. Christout: *Le ballet de cour de Louis XIV, 1643–1672* (Paris, 1967)

H. W. Hitchcock: 'Marc-Antoine Charpentier and the Comédie-Française', *JAMS*, xxiv (1971), 255

——: 'Problèmes d'édition de la musique de Marc-Antoine Charpentier pour *Le malade imaginaire*', *RdM*, lviii (1972), 3

H. Purkis: 'Les intermèdes musicaux de George Dandin', *Baroque*, v (1972), 63

E. B. Lance: 'Molière the Musician: a Tercentenary View', *MR*, xxxv (1974), 120

H. WILEY HITCHCOCK

**Molière, Louis de.** *See* MOLLIER, LOUIS DE.

**Molina, Antonio (Jesus)** (*b* Manila, 26 Dec 1894). Filipino composer and conductor. He studied at the S

Juan de Letran College (BA) and the University of the Philippines Conservatory (teacher's cello diploma 1933); his composition teacher was Abelardo. Later he joined the staff of the University of the Philippines, where he was secretary of the conservatory until 1941. He taught and lectured outside the university as well, also conducting choral groups, church choirs, opera and orchestral concerts. In 1956 he was made director of the Cosmopolitan Academy of Music, and he directed the Centro Escolar University Conservatory (1948–71); from that university he received an honorary doctorate in 1953, and he was made dean emeritus of the conservatory on his retirement. Among other honours he has received are the Republic Cultural Heritage Award (1965, 1972), the Araw ng Maynila Award (1969), the Civic Assembly of Women of the Philippines Citation of Merit (1962), the University of the Philippines Conservatory Alumni Award, the Phi Kappa Beta Award (1972) and the National Artist Award (1973), the last being the highest state recognition ever accorded a Philippine musician. His compositions show a daring departure from the traditional Romantic style of his colleagues: he employed the whole-tone scale, augmented 4ths, unresolved dissonances, parallel 5ths and Debussian progressions, all with a meticulous care for detail.

### WORKS
*(selective list)*

Choral: 5 Philippine Folksongs, 1933; The Living Word, Christmas cantata, 1936; Misa antoniana, chorus, orch, 1964; Ang batingaw [The bells], choral sym., 1972
Chamber: Hating gabi [Midnight], vn, pf, 1915; Pf Qnt, C, 1929; Trio, F, 1931; Marian Ricercata, pf, str, 1956
Songs: Amihan [North breeze], 1923; Kung sa iyong gunita [In your memory], 1925; Oras ng gabing mangitngit [Hours of dark night], 1937; Kundiman-kundangan [Love-song – uncertainty], 1938; Awit ni Maria Clara [Song of Maria Clara], 1944
Pf: Malikmata [Transformation], 1939; A Dove came down in Sunshine, 1941; We were Moonlight, 1941; Dancing Fool, 1942; Toccata in Blue, 1958

LUCRECIA R. KASILAG

**Molina, Bartolomé de** (*fl* early 16th century). Spanish theorist. He was a member of the Franciscan order and a Bachelor of Theology. He published a brief treatise on plainsong entitled *Arte de canto llano Lux videntis dicha* (Valladolid, 1504), dedicating it to the Bishop of Lugo and explaining his choice of title by saying that 'those who would like to see and read by it will, in a very short time, be taught, illuminated and removed from error'. It is similar to Duran's *Lux bella* and expounds without originality the essentials of the subject, with a study of the manner of writing chants in different modes when using a single line instead of a staff.

### BIBLIOGRAPHY
F. Valverde: *Colección de los bibliófilos gallegos* (Santiago de Compostela, 1949)
R. Stevenson: *Spanish Music in the Age of Columbus* (The Hague, 1960)
F. J. León Tello: *Estudios de historia de la teoria musical* (Madrid, 1962)

F. J. LEÓN TELLO

**Molinari, Bernardino** (*b* Rome, 11 April 1880; *d* Rome, 25 Dec 1952). Italian conductor. He studied at the Rome Liceo di S Cecilia with Renzi and Falchi, graduating in 1902, and first attracted attention when he prepared the Augusteo Orchestra in Rome for a concert of Richard Strauss works conducted by the composer in 1909. Molinari was appointed artistic director of the Augusteo in 1912, and he devoted his energies

primarily to this organization until his retirement in 1943. He conducted its orchestra on tour in Italy and abroad and, with the support of Mussolini as head of state and the Governor of Rome, he obtained a permanent basis for the orchestra from 1937. Meanwhile, he initiated popular open-air summer concerts from 1929, and in that year set up a reading commission to examine works by younger composers; it brought to light Petrassi, among others. At the Accademia di S Cecilia in 1936 he established an advanced course for conductors, a position that developed into a professorship in 1939; his students included Gavazzeni, Molinari Pradelli, Pedrotti, Petrassi and Rossellini. In a period of renewed Italian interest in symphonic music, Molinari wielded much influence through his performances of new works by such composers as Alfano, Casella, Malipiero, Perosi, Pizzetti and Respighi, and contemporary music by other composers, in particular Debussy, Strauss and Stravinsky, with whom he was on friendly terms. His activities had strong government backing, which brought about his 1937 tour of Germany, but otherwise he made only rare guest appearances abroad (including those in Britain, the USA and South America), and occasional appearances conducting opera in Rome, Florence, Buenos Aires, Vienna and Prague. With Debussy's approval he transcribed *L'isle joyeuse* for orchestra, but his transcriptions of 17th- and 18th-century Italian music (such as 'The Four Seasons' and other concertos by Vivaldi, and Monteverdi's *L'incoronazione di Poppea* and *Sonata sopra Sancta Maria*) are stylistically free.

### BIBLIOGRAPHY
E. Mucci: *Bernardino Molinari* (Lanciano, 1941)
M. Labroca: 'Ricordo di Bernardino Molinari', *RaM*, xxiii (1953), 38

CLAUDIO CASINI

**Molinari, Pietro** (*b* Murano, Venice, *c*1626; *d* Murano, 8 Oct 1679). Italian composer. He was parish priest at S Stefano, Murano, from 1671. With Aurelio Aureli he was a charter member of the Accademia degli Angustiati and in 1664 supplied music for the prologue and other parts of Domenico Gisberti's *La barbarie del caso*, the inaugural (and only) drama presented by the academy. For Carnival 1660 he composed all or part of *Hipsicratea* (to a text by G. M. Milcetti), the first opera performed at Murano. Molinari's only surviving work is a cantata (in *D-Kl*).

### BIBLIOGRAPHY
*EitnerQ*
E. A. Cicogna: *Delle inscrizioni veneziane*, vi (Venice, 1853), 366, 464, 474f, 477
F. Caffi: *Storia della musica sacra nella già cappella ducale di San Marco in Venezia dal 1318 al 1797* (Venice, 1854–5, repr. 1931), i, 376
L. N. Galvani [pseud. of G. Salvioli]: *I teatri musicali di Venezia nel secolo XVII (1637–1700): memorie storiche e bibliografiche* (Milan, 1879/R1969), 157f
M. Maylender: *Storia delle accademie d'Italia*, i (Bologna, 1926), 184ff

LORENZO BIANCONI

**Molinari Pradelli, Francesco** (*b* Bologna, 4 July 1911). Italian conductor and pianist. He studied the piano with Ivaldi and composition with Nordio at Bologna, then conducting with Bernardino Molinari at the Accademia di S Cecilia in Rome, graduating in 1938. He made his début the same year as a concert conductor but has concentrated almost exclusively on opera since 1939, when he conducted *L'elisir d'amore* at Bologna, Bergamo and Brescia. Since his first appearance at La Scala in 1946, he has conducted regularly at leading

Italian opera houses as well as making frequent tours in other countries. He first appeared at Covent Garden in 1955, conducting *Tosca* (with Tebaldi), and returned to conduct the new production of *Macbeth* in 1960. From 1957 he was a regular conductor at San Francisco, and from 1959 at the Vienna Staatsoper; he made his début at the Metropolitan Opera in 1966, and has returned there often. His records include notable versions of *La forza del destino*, *La traviata* and *Manon Lescaut* (all with Tebaldi), *Turandot* (with Nilsson) and the first complete *La rondine*. He has continued to perform as a pianist, exploring lesser-known works; a record made with Suzanne Danco of album pieces by Rossini and his contemporaries was a collectors' item in the 1950s.

BERNARD JACOBSON

**Molinaro, Simone** (*b* *c*1565; *d* Genoa, 1615). Italian composer. He was a nephew and pupil of G. B. de la Gostena, whom he succeeded as *maestro di cappella* of S Lorenzo, Genoa, no later than 1602. Several of his publications include works by Gostena, and his own compositions, typical of the best Genoese music of the day, were widely disseminated. His lute compositions reveal melodic and rhythmic gifts and a sure sense of his instrument. They include eight saltarellos, 11 passamezzos, each with its own galliard, 15 fantasias, a *Ballo detto Il Conde Orlando* (arranged for orchestra by Respighi in his first set of *Antiche danze e arie*, 1971) and intabulations of pieces by Crecquillon, Clemens non Papa and Gioseffo Guami. In the passamezzos and galliards his control of variation technique is demonstrated in the use of sequences, echo effects and ornamental elaborations. The fantasias are more virtuoso and daring than the dance pieces, and in his celebrated 12th fantasia his fluent sense of modulation leads to remote areas unusual for the time. His use of chromaticism is only occasional, and contrary to expectation shares none of the audacity or harmonic sureness of Gesualdo, whose music he admired. As a madrigalist, too, he was skilful but unadventurous, and *Baci amorosi e cari* and *Cantiam Muse cantiamo*, the two pieces which appeared in the *Giardino nuovo bellissimo* (*RISM* 1605[7]), are among his best. His basically conservative and smoothly lyrical style is perhaps most suited to the requirements of sacred music, yet even in his sacred works his potential as a harmonic colourist is sometimes realized, as in *Domine convertere* from the *Motectorum* of 1597. His reputation as a connoisseur of contemporary music is demonstrated in *Fattiche spirituali*, his collections of sacred contrafacta of madrigals by Andrea Gabrieli, Alessandro Striggio (ii), Macque, Marenzio, Monte and Orazio Vecchi, as well as in his edition of Gesualdo's six books of five-voice madrigals.

WORKS<br>SACRED

Motectorum, 5vv, et missa, 10vv, liber primus (Venice, 1597)
Fattiche spirituali ossia Motteti, libro primo, 6vv (Milan, 1599, lost; 2/1610[2])
Fattiche spirituali ossia Motteti, libro secundo, 6vv (Milan, 1599, lost; 2/1610[3])
Secondo libro de motetti, 8vv (Milan, 1601)
Primo libro de Magnificat, 4vv, bc (Milan, 1605[4])
Concerti ecclesiastici, 2–4vv (Venice, 1605)
Terzo libro de motetti, 5vv, bc (Venice, 1609[6]); 10 ed. F. Commer, Musica sacra, xv, xvi (Berlin, 1840)
Concerti, 1, 2vv, bc (org) (Milan, 1612[11])
Passio domini nostri Jesu Christi secundum Matthaeum, Marcum, Lucam, et Joannem (Loano, 1616)
17 motets, 1598[2], 1600[2], 1605[6], 1610[10], 1611[1], 1612[2], 1612[3], 1613[2]

SECULAR

Primo libro di canzonette, 3, 4vv (Venice, 1595)

Intavolatura di liuto libro primo (Venice, 1599[18])
Primo libro de madrigali, 5vv (Milan, 1599[15])
Secondo libro delle canzonette, 3vv (Venice, 1600)
Madrigali con partitura, 5vv (Loana, 1615)
6 madrigals, 1589[13], 1605[7], 1624[16]

BIBLIOGRAPHY

A. A. Abert: *Die stilistischen Voraussetzungen der 'Cantiones sacrae' von H. Schütz* (Wolfenbüttel and Berlin, 1935)
G. Roncaglia: 'Simone Molinaro', *RMI*, xlv (1941), 184
T. Dart: 'Simone Molinaro's Lutebook of 1599', *ML*, xxviii (1947), 258
R. Giazotto: *La musica a Genova nella vita pubblica e privata dal XIII al XVIII secolo* (Genoa, 1951), 149ff, 166ff
E. Pohlmann: *Laute, Theorbe, Chitarrone* (Bremen, 1968, enlarged 4/1976)

GLENN WATKINS

**Moline, Pierre Louis** (*b* Montpellier, *c* 1740; *d* Paris, 19 Feb 1821). French writer. Moline studied arts at Avignon and law in Paris, but adopted literature as a profession. With deplorable fecundity, he contributed to every fashionable stage genre including tragedy, comedy of manners, bourgeois drama and Revolutionary *sans-culottide*. He was advocate to the *parlement*, then secretary to the Convention (1792–4). Among his few, generally poor, librettos, two were outstandingly successful at the Opéra: the adaptation of Calzabigi for Gluck's *Orphée* (1774), and the most important stage work of J. F. Edelmann, *Ariane dans l'isle de Naxos* (1782). He also wrote the texts for Edelmann's *L'Amour enchaîné par Diane* (1783) and Candeille's pastoral *Laure et Pétrarque* (1778); he adapted Vadé's text for a revision of Gluck's *L'arbre enchanté* (Versailles, 1775), and translated Paisiello's *Le Roi Théodore à Venise* for the Opéra (1787). He contributed to the Gluckist controversy a *Dialogue entre Lully, Rameau, et Orphée dans les Champs Elysées* (Amsterdam, 1774).

BIBLIOGRAPHY

[?F.] Fayolle: 'Moline, (Pierre-Louis)', *Biographie universelle*, ed. L. G. Michaud (Paris, 1843–65)
'Moline, (Pierre-Louis)', *Nouvelle biographie générale*, ed. J. C. F. Hoefer (Paris, 1852–66)

JULIAN RUSHTON

**Molinié, Etienne.** *See* MOULINIÉ, ÉTIENNE.

**Molino, Antonio** [Burchiella; Blessi, Manoli] (*b* *c*1495–7; *d* ?Venice, in or after 1571). Italian actor, poet and musician. In a sonnet that he set in his 1568 volume he stated that he was then over 70. He lived in Venice. According to the dedicatory letter by Lodovico Dolce in *I fatti, e le prodezze di Manoli Blessi strathioto di M. Antonio Molino detto Burchiella* (Venice, 1561) he was educated in all the attributes of a gentleman, including dancing, singing and the playing of instruments. He travelled in the Levant and on his return to Venice founded an academy of music with Brother Armonio, who was the organist of St Mark's. Molino was one of the first to recite comedies in a variety of dialects, including those of Venice and Bergamo, in a mixture of Greek and Italian, and in the jargon of soldiers ('stil strathiotesco'). In the introduction to the 'third night' of *Le notti piacevoli* by Straparola there is a reference to his abilities on the viol. Molino is regarded, along with ANDREA CALMO and ANGELO BEOLCO as one of the seminal figures in the early history of the *commedia dell'arte*. He was closely associated with some of the best-known composers of his day, and Andrea Gabrieli and Monte dedicated madrigal books to him. The print *Di Manoli Blessi il primo libro delle greghesche* (*RISM* 1564[16], ed. S. Cisilino, Padua, 1974), for four to eight voices, consists of settings of his poetry by Andrea

Gabrieli, Merulo, Padovano, Porta, Rore, Wert, Willaert and others, among them a setting by Gabrieli of a lament on the death of Willaert. Gabrieli's *Greghesche et iustiniane* for three voices (1571) includes 15 settings of texts by him. Molino also published two books of madrigals, *I dilettevoli madrigali* (Venice, 1568, inc.), for four voices, and *Il secondo libro de madrigali ... con uno dialogo* (Venice, 1569, inc.), for four and eight voices.

BIBLIOGRAPHY
A. d'Ancona: *Origini del teatro italiano* (Florence, 1877, 2/1891), ii, 112
A. Einstein: 'The Greghesca and the Giustiniana of the Sixteenth Century', *JRBM*, i (1946–7), 191
——: *The Italian Madrigal* (Princeton, 1949/R1971)
S. Cisilino: Introduction to edn. of *RISM* 1564[16] (Padua, 1974)
P. Fabbri: 'Fatti e prodezze di Manoli Blessi', *RIM*, xi (1976), 182
CHARLES WARREN

**Molins, P. des** (*fl* mid-14th century). French composer. The most likely identification of Molins (proposed by Günther) is with a Philippe de Moulins who was chancellor of the Duke of Berry in 1368 and received a pension in 1371. Other identifications have been suggested by Anglès and Clercx-Lejeune.

His two extant compositions were extremely popular. *De ce que fol pensé*, a three-voice ballade, is in many MSS, occasionally with a fourth voice (a triplum), and also has a decorated two-part keyboard version. The opening of the cantus even appears in a tapestry, in which a lady plays a harp while a servant holds the roll of music. *Amis, tout dous vis*, a three-voice rondeau, is known with two different contratenors and two different but related ornamental versions of the top voice. Such ornamented, probably instrumental versions of the piece caused the Flemish form of the composer's name to be interpreted by medieval performers as a programme for the work: 'Die Molen van Pariis' as 'the mill of Paris'.

BIBLIOGRAPHY
F. Kammerer: *Die Musikstücke des Prager Kodex XI E 9* (Brno, 1931), 56
H. Anglès: 'La musica en la corte del rey Alfonso V de Aragon (1413–1420)', *Spanische Forschungen der Görresgesellschaft*, 1st ser., viii (1939), 349
R. H. Hoppin and S. Clercx-Lejeune: 'Notes biographiques sur quelques musiciens français du XIV° siècle', *L'ars nova: Wégimont II 1955*, 75
U. Günther: 'Die Musiker des Herzogs von Berry', *MD*, xvii (1963), 85
W. Apel, ed.: *French Secular Compositions of the Fourteenth Century*, CMM, liii/1 (1970), 84f
GILBERT REANEY

**Molins, Pierre de.** See PIERRE DE MOLINS.

**Molique, (Wilhelm) Bernhard** (*b* Nuremberg, 7 Oct 1802; *d* Cannstadt, nr. Stuttgart, 10 May 1869). German violinist and composer. His father, a musician in the municipal band, was his first teacher, and he performed in public at the age of six. In November 1815 Spohr passed through Nuremberg and agreed to give him a few lessons because 'the lad performed excellently for his age'. He completed his studies in Munich under Pietro Rovelli (1816–17) and travelled with his master to Vienna, where he made a successful début on 28 December 1817 and joined the orchestra of the Theater an der Wien. In January 1820 he was recalled to Munich to succeed Rovelli; from 1826 to 1849 he served as royal music director and orchestra leader in Stuttgart. The excellence of the Stuttgart orchestra (attested to by Berlioz) was largely due to Molique's

teaching skill. At the same time he undertook extensive concert tours throughout Europe, including Russia. He was particularly well received in London where he first appeared at the Philharmonic on 14 May 1840 playing his own Concerto no.5 in A minor. Further successful visits to England in 1842 and 1848 led to his decision to settle in London in 1849, where he was highly acclaimed as a performer (particularly in chamber music), teacher and composer. His oratorio *Abraham* was given at the Norwich Festival of 1860. In 1861 he was appointed professor of composition at the RCM. After a farewell concert in London's St James's Hall on 3 May 1866, he retired to Cannstadt. His eldest daughter Caroline became known as an accomplished pianist.

Molique was an impressive violinist of sound musicianship and masterful technique but lacked the flair of a true virtuoso. Berlioz described his playing as 'vigorous, broad and severe, though lacking in nuance'. Mendelssohn and Schumann admired his extraordinary technical dexterity but found his playing cold. Joachim, a friend and admirer, praised his infallible intonation while criticizing his angular bowing. Molique's violin style was influenced by German and French models, particularly Spohr and Lafont. As a composer, he was closer to Mendelssohn and disliked the modernism of the 'new German school'. His conservative leanings are also evident in his somewhat old-fashioned *Studies in Harmony* (London, 1862). Of his six violin concertos the fifth enjoyed great popularity and was considered by Joachim to be a mainstay of the violin repertory. Equally popular was his Cello Concerto, which Riemann compared with that of Schumann. The Piano Trio op.27 was a favourite work of Hans von Bülow, and he wrote the Concertina Concerto specially for the virtuoso Giulio Regondi. Molique's numerous compositions, which also include much chamber music and many songs, are now almost forgotten.

WORKS
Orch: 6 vn concs., E, op.4 (Leipzig, 1827), A, op.9 (Leipzig, 1831), d, op.10 (Leipzig, 1832), D, op.14 (Vienna, 1839), a, op.21 (Leipzig, 1841), e, op.30 (Vienna, 1846); Vc Conc., op.45 (Leipzig, 1853); Concertina Conc., op.46 (London, 1853); Fl Conc., op.69 (London, n.d.); Vn Concertino, op.1 (Mainz, 1822); Cl Concertino, arr. J. Michaels for cl, pf (Kassel, 1970); Ov., f, 1827, Sym., 1837–42, Ob Concertino: all unpubd
Chamber: Qnt, fl, vn, 2 va, vc, op.35 (London, 1848); Pf Qt, op.71 (Leipzig, 1870); 8 str qts, G, op.16 (Vienna, 1841), c, op.17 (Vienna, 1841), F, a, Eb, op.18 (Leipzig, 1843), f, op.28 (Leipzig, 1847), Bb, op.42 (London, 1854), A, op.44 (Leipzig, 1853); 2 pf trios, op.27 (Vienna, 1846), op.52 (Mainz, 1858); Grand Duo, vn, pf, op.24 (Hamburg, 1845); 2 duos concertants, vn, pf, op.20 (Hamburg, 1844), op.33 (Hamburg, 1857); 3 Duos, 2 vn, op.2 (Mainz, 1824)
Vocal: Abraham, oratorio, op.65 (London, 1861); 2 masses, f, op.22 (Vienna, 1843), c, 1864, lost; numerous songs, 1v, pf, incl. Sacred Songs, op.48 (London, 1854)

BIBLIOGRAPHY
H. Berlioz: *Mémoires* (Paris, 1879; Eng. trans., 1969), 336
F. Schröder: *Bernhard Molique und seine Instrumentalkompositionen* (Stuttgart, 1923) [with list of works]
BORIS SCHWARZ

**Molitor, Alexius** [Müller, Johann Adam] (*b* Simmershausen, nr. Rhön, 19 Nov 1730; *d* Mainz, 16 June 1773). German musician and cleric. He was a pupil of Georg Joachim Josef Hahn from 1743 to 1749 at the Gymnasium at Münnerstadt, Lower Franconia, where, after the completion of his studies, he entered the Augustinian order as a novice. After a short stay at Oberndorf he moved to the Augustinian monastery at Mainz where he completed his theological and canonical studies at the university. After his ordination in about 1752 Molitor worked as a preacher, father confessor and composer; from 1761 he was also *Director chori musici*. The monastery organ, built in 1775 by the Stumm brothers from Rhaunen-Sulzbach, Johann Philipp and Johann Heinrich, was no doubt planned with his help.

In his treatment of the orchestra and his general style Molitor is a representative of early Classicism in Mainz. His works are distinguished by their pleasing Italianate melody. Choral fugues occur seldom in the Kyrie and Credo sections of his masses, but more often in the Gloria. The 'Dona nobis' section is sometimes based on the Kyrie, and the solo passages in the Benedictus and Gloria are especially lovingly handled; the fugues are capably written, sometimes on scale-wise and sometimes on triadic, striding subjects. His interest in dramatic characterization is seen in the quartet from the oratorio *Daniel in der Löwengrube* where Daniel prays, the two Babylonians babble and the king rages in *buffo* style.

### WORKS

Daniel in der Löwengrube (oratorio), Mainz, Good Friday 1765, *D-B*; Esther (oratorio), Mainz, Good Friday 1766, music lost, lib extant; another oratorio, Mainz, music lost, lib extant
3 Missa solemnis, *EB* (1 also in *F*)
3 Missa solemnis, *F*, *AR*, *Tmi*
Requiem, 3 masses, D: *F*; 2 masses, 4vv; 1 other mass: *EB*
Missa pastoralis, Domchorbibliothek, Würzburg (? destroyed in World War II)

### BIBLIOGRAPHY

A. Gottron: 'Die Pflege der Kirchen-Musik bei den Mainzer Augustinern im 17. und 18. Jahrhundert', *Mainzer Zeitschrift*, Jg.xli–xliii (1946–8), 121
——: *Mainzer Musikgeschichte von 1500 bis 1800* (Mainz, 1959), 120ff
——: 'Der Komponist P. Alexius Molitor O. Er. S. Aug. ein Student der Mainzer Universität', *Jb der Vereinigung der Freunde der Universität Mainz*, ix (1960), 48ff [incl. 2 music exx.]
reprinted from *MGG* (ix, 437) by permission of Bärenreiter
ADAM GOTTRON

**Molitor** [Müller], **Fidel** (*b* Wil, canton of St Gall, 13 June 1627; *d* Magdenau, canton of St Gall, 3 Oct 1685). Swiss composer. His original name was Müller. He was first of all Kantor, then Kapellmeister, of the Cistercian monastery at Wettingen. He was later prior and father confessor at the nunneries at Feldbach and Magdenau in eastern Switzerland. Like J. M. Gletle, Berthold Hipp, Martin Martini and Valentin Molitor, he was one of the most important Swiss church composers of the second half of the 17th century. Two of his three volumes contain solo motets with instruments. In the 17 pieces in the third volume soloists are pitted against a chorus in the manner of the double concerto; the homophonic tuttis are somewhat primitive, but in the solo parts Molitor often showed himself capable of stronger melodic expression.

### WORKS

Praegustus musicus, seu cantiones, 1v, 2 vn (Konstanz, 1659)
Cantionum sacrarum . . . liber secundus, 1v, 2 insts (Innsbruck, 1664)
Mensa musicalis quam apparatu piarum cantionum, op.3 (Innsbruck, 1668)

### BIBLIOGRAPHY

E. Refardt: *Historisch-biographisches Musikerlexikon der Schweiz* (Leipzig and Zurich, 1928)
P. Vetter: 'Von alten Schweizer Kirchenkomponisten', *Chorwächter*, lxx (1945), 19
HANS PETER SCHANZLIN

**Molitor** [Müller], **Valentin** (*b* Rapperswil, canton of St Gall, 15 April 1637; *d* Weingarten, Württemberg, 4 Oct 1713). Swiss composer and organist; his original name was Müller. In 1656 he took his vows at the monastery at St Gall and in 1662 was ordained priest.

After working in various monasteries as organist and organ teacher he became Kantor at the monastery at St Gall in 1683 and in 1685 Kapellmeister. He spent his last years at the monastery at Weingarten, Württemberg. His works display characteristic features of the concerted style of church music, but in his melodious *Odae* simple songlike forms predominate. The mass and motets have rich textures, sometimes reinforced by clarinos, but they lack impetus since their form is so disjointed. He was commissioned by the Swiss Benedictine congregation to edit the second edition of the *Directorium*.

### WORKS

Odae genethliacae ad Christi cunas, 1–3, 5vv, 2 vn (Kempten, 1668)
Missa una cum tribus motettis in solemni translatione Ss et martyrum (St Gall, 1681)
Epinicion marianum (St Gall, 1683)

### EDITIONS

Directorium seu cantus et responsoria in processionibus ordinariis per annum (St Gall, 2/1692)

### BIBLIOGRAPHY

E. Refardt: *Historisch-biographisches Musikerlexikon der Schweiz* (Leipzig and Zurich, 1928)
R. Henggeler: *Professbuch der fürstlichen Benediktinerabtei . . . zu St. Gallen* (Zug, 1929), 323
W. Vogt: *Die Messe in der Schweiz im 17. Jahrhundert* (diss., U. of Basle; Schwarzenburg, 1940), 54ff, 106f, 131
HANS PETER SCHANZLIN

**Moll** (Ger., from Lat. *mollis*: 'soft'). Minor, as in *A moll* (A minor), *Mollklang* (minor triad), *H-moll Messe* (Mass in B minor), etc.

For the origins of the term, *see* DUR. *See also* MINOR.

**Moll** (**Roqueta**), **Jaime** (*b* Barcelona, 15 Feb 1926). Spanish musicologist. He studied history at the University of Barcelona (1946–52) and then became secretary and research assistant at the Institute of Musicology in Barcelona (1952–4) and Madrid (1954–5) before being appointed director of the Spanish Royal Academy Library, Madrid (1955). In 1975 he took his doctorate in history at the University of Barcelona with a dissertation on Visigoth-Mozarabic musical notation. He has lectured on music history at the Escuela de Documentalistas, Madrid, and discussed musical topics on the radio and in the press. His main interest is the subject of his dissertation, particularly the Toledan repertory: he has worked extensively on a bibliography of its surviving manuscripts in Spanish and foreign libraries. He has also worked from documentary sources on Spanish music and musicians from the 16th century to the 18th.

### WRITINGS

'Nuevos hallazgos de manuscritos mozárabes con neumas musicales', *AnM*, v (1950), 11
'Músicos de la corte del Cardenal Juan Tavera (1523–1545): Luis Venegas de Henestrosa', *AnM*, vi (1951), 155
'Cristóbal de Morales en España (notas para su biografía)', *AnM*, viii (1953), 3
'Un villancico de Morales y otro de Cárceres en el cancionero español de Upsala', *AnM*, viii (1953), 167
'Documentos para la historia de la música de la catedral de Toledo', *AnM*, xiii (1958), 159
'Nuevos datos para la biografía de Juan Hidalgo, arpista y compositor', *Miscelánea en homenaje a Monseñor Higinio Anglés* (Barcelona, 1958–61), 585
'Notas para la historia musical de la corte del Duque de Calabria', *AnM*, xviii (1963), 123
'La Princesa Juana de Austria y la música: notas para su estudio', *AnM*, xix (1964), 119
'Libros de música e instrumentos musicales de la Princesa Juana de Austria', *AnM*, xx (1965), 11
'El estatuto de maestro cantor de la catedral de Avila del año 1487', *AnM*, xxii (1967), 89

'Una bibliografía musical periódica de fines del siglo XVIII', *AnM*, xxiv (1969), 247
'Los villancicos cantados en la capilla real a fines del siglo XVI y principios del siglo XVII', *AnM*, xxv (1970), 81
'La notación visigótico-mozárabe y el origen de las notaciones occidentales', *I congreso internacional de estudios mozárabes: Toledo 1975*
*Un scandicus de significación melódica en la notación visigótico-mozárabe* (diss., U. of Barcelona, 1975)

JOSÉ M. LLORENS

**Moll, Kurt** (*b* Buir, 11 April 1938). German bass. He studied at the Cologne Hochschule für Musik, then privately with Emmy Mueller. He made his début as Lodovico (*Otello*) at Aachen, where he was engaged from 1961 to 1963, and then sang at Mainz and Wuppertal before joining the Hamburg Staatsoper in 1970. From 1972 he has been a regular guest at Munich, Vienna and Paris, and has also appeared at Salzburg and Bayreuth. His roles include most of the leading bass parts in Wagner's operas, his King Marke and Pogner being particularly vivid portrayals, and he uses his true, strong and flexible bass equally well in less serious roles such as Osmin, which he recorded with considerable success under Böhm. In 1975 he created the King in Bialas's *Der gestiefelte Kater* at the Schwetzingen Festival in the Hamburg Staatsoper's production, and the same year added the title role in Massenet's *Don Quichotte* (given with the same company) to his repertory. He made his Covent Garden début as Kaspar in Götz Friedrich's production of *Der Freischütz* in 1977.

ALAN BLYTH

**Molle, Henry** (*b* Leicester, *c*1597; *d* Cambridge, 10 May 1658). English composer. He was the son of John Molle, a prisoner of the Inquisition in Rome from 1608 to 1638. He went to Eton College (*c*1608–12) and then to King's College, Cambridge, in 1612, taking the BA in 1617 and the MA in 1620. He was elected a Fellow of King's in 1615, and public orator to the university in about 1635. At this time he may have been acting as organist of Peterhouse. He was dismissed from his fellowship in 1650, but this was restored to him by Cromwell in 1653. A Henry Molle was headmaster of the King's School, Worcester, and the dedicatee of a piece in Thomas Tomkins's *Songs* of 1622. All his music is liturgical and most is for full choir.

WORKS

First Service (Mag, Nunc), verse, *GB-Cp*
Second Service (Mag, Nunc), *Cp*, *Lbm*
Magnificat, *Lbm*
Nunc dimittis, *Lbm*
Te Deum, Litany (both Lat.), *Cp*
Litany 'made for Dr Couzens' (Eng.), *Cu*
Great and marvellous, verse anthem, *Cp*, *US-NYp*
God the protector, ?anthem, inc., *NYp*
Thou art my portion, music lost

BIBLIOGRAPHY

J. Morehen: *The Sources of English Cathedral Music 1617–1644* (diss., U. of Cambridge, 1969)

PETER LE HURAY

**Mollenhauer.** German family of woodwind instrument makers. The Mollenhauers were a well-known family active in Hesse from the early 19th century. Johannes Andreas Mollenhauer (*b* Fulda, 31 Aug 1798; *d* Fulda, 30 Aug 1871), who probably learnt instrument making in Vienna, set up his business in 1822. His elder son Gustav (*b* Fulda, 7 Feb 1837; *d* Kassel, 18 Dec 1914), after working for his father, founded in 1864 an apparently independent firm at Kassel, which passed in turn to his two sons, Thomas (ii) (*b* Kassel, 21 Feb 1867; *d* Kassel, 10 July 1938) and Johannes (*b* Kassel, 20 April

1875; *d* Kassel, 22 Feb 1952). The firm's title was Gustav Mollenhauer, Kassel, and in 1900 it became G. Mollenhauer & Söhne; in 1958 the proprietorship passed to Karl Schaub.

Thomas Mollenhauer (i), younger son of Johannes Andreas (*b* Fulda, 22 Feb 1840; *d* Fulda, 1 July 1914), is recorded as having worked for Boehm and Mendler from 1862 to 1864; correspondence dated 1865 suggests that Boehm tried to persuade Mollenhauer to build piccolos on his system, as he did not wish to undertake further experimental work at his advanced age. A letter dated 1878 mentions both alto flutes in F and piccolos on the Boehm system but examples from this period seem to be rare. Between 1865 and 1866 Thomas (i) also worked for Ottensteiner of Munich. His elder son Josef Nikolaus (*b* Fulda, 20 July 1875; *d* Friesenhausen, 12 Oct 1964) worked with Heckel and was later head of the firm J. Mollenhauer & Söhne, Fulda. The younger son Conrad (*b* Fulda, 10 Sept 1876; *d* Friesenhausen, 12 Oct 1943) worked with Rittershausen of Berlin and then Adler of Markneukirchen and established his own business in 1912. His son was Thomas (iii) (*b* Fulda, 17 July 1908; *d* Fulda, 8 Feb 1953), after whose death the firm continued as Conrad Mollenhauer, Fulda, under the direction of his widow.

The Mollenhauers produced a full range of woodwind instruments, together with certain specialities. C. Mollenhauer, Fulda, embarked on a revival of the recorder and in 1954 introduced the Jugendoboe or Choroboe, a simplified oboe conceived by Arnold Klaes for group playing, particularly in schools.

BIBLIOGRAPHY

G. Antoni and E. Stein, eds.: *Die Stadt Fulda*, Monographien Deutscher Städte, xxxiv (Berlin, 1930)
A. Klaes: 'Mollenhauer', *MGG*

PHILIP BATE

**Moller.** *See* MALER.

**Moller, Joachim.** *See* BURCK, JOACHIM A.

**Möller, Johann** (*b* Alsfeld, Hesse, *c*1570; *d* Darmstadt, 6 Jan 1617). German composer and organist. After receiving a master's degree he became a teacher at Darmstadt court school in 1593; his pupils included Ludwig, the heir-apparent, and Philipp, the future Landgrave of Hessen-Butzbach. In 1597 he was appointed organist of the court church and soon afterwards carried out the duties of Kapellmeister too. When Ludwig became landgrave in 1596 Möller's opportunities for composition increased: as well as writing sacred music he supplied music for ballets and carousels performed to mark baptisms, weddings and visits from other rulers. Of his secular output only two books of pavans and galliards survive. Following earlier practice, each galliard is a rhythmic variation of the preceding pavan, a procedure by which Möller, together with composers such as Christoph Demantius and Johann Groh, laid the foundations of the later orchestral suite.

WORKS

Newe Paduanen und darauff gehörige Galliarden, 5vv, sampt einem newen Quodlibet, insts (Frankfurt am Main, 1610) [quodlibet also pubd separately as Ein new Quodlibet zu unterhänigen Ehren, 4vv]
Newe teutsche muteten, 5–8vv (Darmstadt, 1611)
Andere noch mehr newe Paduanen und darauff gehörige Galliarden, 5vv, sampt eins, 3vv, insts (Darmstadt, 1612)

Es wolt gut Jager jagen, 4vv, in Biblioteca Legnica (according to *EitnerQ*)
2 sacred works destroyed by fire in 1944: Vater unser; Psalm cxxi

ELISABETH NOACK

**Möller** [Müller], **Johann Patroklus** (*b* Soest, Westphalia, 1697 or 1698; *d* Lippstadt, 24 July 1772). German organ builder. His father, Martin, was a cabinet maker in Soest. Johann Patroklus was possibly taught by P. H. Varenholt; he settled in Lippstadt in 1720 and became one of the leading organ builders of the region, supplying instruments in the southern part of the Münster district, the northern part of the Sauerland, and in the Detmold district. He was concurrently organist of the Grosse Marienkirche in Lippstadt. His organs included that for St Thomae, Soest (1720; two manuals, 26 stops); the rebuilding (1734) of the organ at the Grosse Marienkirche, Lippstadt; and organs for Marienmünster Abbey (1736–8; three manuals, 34 stops; still extant); Böddeken Abbey (1744; three manuals, 43 stops; now in Büren); Münster Cathedral (1752–5; three manuals, 55 stops); and Paderborn Cathedral (1754–6; three manuals, 42 stops). The organ built about 1735 for Dahlheim Abbey (three manuals, 45 stops; now in Borgentreich) is also attributed to Möller. He developed the characteristics of the typical 17th-century Westphalian organ, with its rich tone-colour, in an apt and logical manner. In all his organs each manual was provided with a complete Principal chorus (including 5⅓′, 3⅕′, Sesquialtera, Mixtur and Zimbel in the Hauptwerk; and in the Positiv 2⅔′ as well as Sesquialtera and Mixtur or 1⅓′ and Mixtur) and a respectable group of foundation stops (including Quintaden, Gemshorn, Salicional, Transverse flute and Viola da gamba), in addition to reeds (Trumpet 8′ and 4′, Fagott and Rankett 16′ and Krummhorn and Vox humana 8′) and flute upperwork (2⅔′, 2′, 1⅓′, 1′ and Kornett III). His pedal-boards usually had 16′ and 8′ foundation stops, a 2′ or 1′ flute, and reeds (Posaune 16′, Trumpet 8′, Schalmei 4′ and Kornett 2′). The synthesis of the styles of NIEHOFF and BECK, already vigorously pioneered by the Bader family, was perfected by Möller in accordance with the needs of his age. Like his predecessors in Westphalia he remained partial to the spring-chest, continuing to incorporate it in his new organs. Möller may be regarded as one of the leading masters of the classical German organ.

BIBLIOGRAPHY
G. Schwake: *Forschungen zur Geschichte der Orgelbaukunst in Nordwestdeutschland* (Münster, 1923)
H. Linssen: 'Die Domorgel zu Münster in Westfalen', *Die Kirchenmusik*, ii (1939), 5, 28
H. Böhringer: *Untersuchungen zum Orgelbau im Hochstift Paderborn* (Cologne, 1949)
R. Reuter: 'Johann Patroklus Müller, Westfalens bedeutendster Orgelbauer im 18. Jahrhundert', *Westfalen*, xxxvii (Münster, 1959)
——: 'Müller', *MGG*
——: *Orgeln in Westfalen* (Kassel, 1965)
U. Wulfhorst: *Der westfälische Orgelbauer Johann Patroklus Möller 1698–1772* (Kassel, 1967)

HANS KLOTZ

**Moller, John Christopher** [Möller, Johann Christoph] (*b* Germany, 1755; *d* New York, 21 Sept 1803). British-American composer, organist, concert manager and music publisher. After about a decade in London, where his major works were published, he moved to the USA. He was prominent in the musical life of Philadelphia (October 1790–November 1795) as organist of the Zion Lutheran Church and co-manager (with Reinagle) of the City Concerts (1790–93), performing as a pianist, harpsichordist and violist. In New York he was organist at the Trinity Episcopal Church and concert manager at fashionable summer pleasure gardens.

Moller's and Capron's press (established in March 1793) was probably the first in the USA for printing exclusively music, and Moller alone issued over 40 publications.

WORKS
Six Quartettos, str (London, c1775)
Six Sonatas, fortepiano/hpd, vn, vc (London, c1775)
Six Sonatas, op.4, hpd/pf, vn, vc ad lib (London, c1782)
Eight Easy Lessons . . . for young practioners, op.5, pf/hpd (London, c1784)
A Sett of [10] Progressive Lessons . . . particularly calculated for the use and improvement of young practitioners, op.6, hpd/pf (London, 1785/*R*1795); reprinted as A Compleat Book of instructions . . ., op.6, pf/hpd, org (London, c1803)
Sinfonia from the Moller & Capron First [Monthly] Number, kbd (Philadelphia, 1793); ed. W. T. Marrocco and H. Gleason in Music in America (New York, 1964)
Rondo from Third Number, kbd (Philadelphia, 1793/*R*1798–1804)
Favorite la chasse, kbd (Philadelphia, 1793–4)
Sonata VIII (Philadelphia, 1793–4) [same as Lesson, op.5/8]
Dank und Gebet, cantata, solo vv, chorus (Philadelphia, 1794)
Meddley with the most favorite Airs and Variations, kbd (Philadelphia, c1796)
March by Moller, kbd (New York, c1800)
A Favorite New German Waltz and Admiral Nelson's March, pf (Philadelphia, 1802–3)
2 concertos, kbd, small orch, *D-MGs*, *US-Wc*
MSS mainly in *GB-Lbm*, *US-NYp*, *Wc*

BIBLIOGRAPHY
O. G. T. Sonneck: *Early Concert Life in America (1731–1800)* (Leipzig, 1907/*R*1949)
E. C. Wolf: *Lutheran Church Music in America during the Eighteenth and Early Nineteenth Centuries* (diss., U. of Illinois, 1960) [incl. text and music of *Dank und Gebet*]
R. D. Stetzel: *John Christopher Moller (1755–1803) and His Role in Early American Music* (diss., U. of Iowa, 1965) [incl. complete list of works with incipits and several complete compositions]
E. C. Wolf: 'Music in Old Zion, Philadelphia, 1750–1850', *MQ*, lviii (1972), 622–52

RONALD D. STETZEL

**Möller, M. P.** American firm of organ builders. It was founded at Warren, Pennsylvania, in 1875 by Mathias Peter Möller (*b* Denmark; 1854–1937). After training as a mechanic Möller emigrated to the USA in 1872 and worked for Derrick & Felgemaker, organ builders, of Erie, Pennsylvania, developing there an improved windchest. In 1880 he moved his business to Hagerstown, Maryland, where it has remained to the present day, and is now the largest manufacturer of organs in the USA. On Möller's death, his son, M. P. Möller jr became president of the firm, and upon the latter's death in 1961, his brother-in-law, W. Riley Daniels, became president.

The first Möller organs had mechanical action, but Möller soon developed a reliable pneumatic action which was used until electro–pneumatic action was adopted in 1923. Although Möller was responsible for some of the largest organ installations in the USA, the firm is also known for its pioneering work in the development of small self-contained organs, sold originally under the name of 'Möller Artiste' but now known as 'Series 70' after revision along more classic lines. Their important installations include those in St George's Church, New York City (1958), the Cathedral of Mary Our Queen, Baltimore (1959), the National Shrine of the Immaculate Conception, Washington (1965), and Heinz Chapel at the University of Pittsburgh (1970).

BARBARA OWEN

**Möller, Wolfgang Michael.** *See* MYLIUS, WOLFGANG MICHAEL.

**Mollica, Giovanni Leonardo.** *See* ARPA, GIOVANNI LEONARDO DELL'.

**Mollier [Molière], Louis de** (*b c*1615; *d* Paris, 18 April 1688). French dancer, composer, poet, lutenist and lute teacher. He was director of entertainments for the Countess of Soissons from at least 1636 until her death in 1644; it was her patronage which enabled him to enter the court. He became a royal lutenist in 1644 and was still playing the lute at court in 1673. He was named a royal dancer in 1644, and it is in this capacity that he achieved his greatest renown. He danced in nearly every *ballet de cour* from then until 1665, often alongside the young Louis XIV and his favourite, Lully. He composed music for at least four ballets between 1651 and 1657. His greatest success came on 6 September 1656, when he directed the dancing and danced in a ballet presented before Queen Christina of Sweden of which he had written both text and music. The following February the musicians at court tried to prevent any further increase in Lully's power at court by excluding him from a ballet that they presented with music by Mollier, but the plan miscarried owing to the inferior music, and Lully became more solidly entrenched. Lully bore no grudge against Mollier, who continued to dance, compose *airs* and accompany singers on the lute and theorbo. From 1650 until his death he was lute teacher to the children of the court; his most important pupil was the dauphin. From 1665 to 1673 he composed songs for Marais' theatre, and he wrote music (which is lost) for two operas when opera replaced the *ballet de cour* as the most important form of court entertainment in the 1670s.

It is uncertain if Mollier was related to his colleague and good friend, the playwright MOLIÈRE, but it is likely that the latter assumed this alias from Mollier. Since both men wrote poetry at the court at the same time, there is some difficulty in distinguishing between them.

Mollier's daughter Marie-Blanche (1644–1733) was a famous singer and dancer at court.

WORKS

Les chansons pour danser, 1v (Paris, 1640)
1 air de cour in Airs de différents autheurs, 2vv (Paris, 1658³)
3 airs in *F-Pn* 854 Rés Vma
Dance music from ballets de cour (including Ballet du roy des festes de Bacchus, May, 1651) in Philidor Collection, *F-Pc*, iv, vii
2 operas (lost): Les amours de Céphale et d'Aurore, 1677; Andromède, 1678
Other lost stage works for which Mollier possibly wrote music include: Ballet de l'oracle de la Sibylle de Pausoust, 1645; Les amours de Jupiter et Sémélé, 1666; Les amours du Soleil, 1671; Le mariage de Bacchus et Ariane, 1672

BIBLIOGRAPHY

C. I. Silin: *Benserade and his 'ballets de cour'* (Baltimore, 1940, 2/1970)
E. Maxfield-Miller: 'Molière and his homonym Louis de Mollier', *Modern Language Notes*, lxxiv (1959), 619
——: 'Louis de Mollier, musicien, et son homonyme Molière', *RMFC*, iii (1963), 25
M.-F. Christout: *Le ballet de cour de Louis XIV, 1643–1672* (Paris, 1967)
M. Benoit: *Musiques de cour: chapelle, chambre, écurie, 1661–1733* (Paris, 1971)

JOHN H. BARON

**Mollo, Eduard.** Proprietor of Austrian music publishing company, 1837–42; *see* CAPPI.

**Mollo, Tranquillo** (*b* Bellinzona, 10 Aug 1767; *d* Bellinzona, after 1837). Italian music publisher active in Vienna. He was first employed by the firm of ARTARIA in Vienna and in 1793 was made a partner. After leaving Artaria, he and Domenico Artaria (iii) founded the firm of T. Mollo & Co. in July 1798. In October 1802 Mollo purchased Carlo Artaria's firm which Domenico Artaria then directed while Mollo remained at the parent firm. In 1804 Domenico Artaria broke with Mollo and reactivated the family firm in the Kohlmarkt; Mollo continued to run his business under his own name as a map, art and music publishing firm. The firm's basic stock consisted of the material taken over from Artaria in the years 1798 and 1804; thus the works published up until that time bear the imprint of Artaria or Mollo, but often with the plate numbers altered. Production begun after 1804 brought a confusing amount of altered plate and edition numbers which have still not been clarified; current works from the old stock were also reprinted when necessary.

Music publishing, somewhat neglected during the troubled years of war in favour of map production, began to flourish again after 1815. Under Mollo's direction his sons Eduard (1799–1842) and Florian (*b* 1802) worked in the firm. On 1 January 1832 Tranquillo announced his official retirement in a printed advertisement, and on 17 February of that year the publishing house was renamed Kunsthandlung der Tranquillo Mollo's Söhne. A division soon followed: Eduard retained his father's shop, while Florian founded his own firm on 4 July 1834, which existed until June 1839. Eduard joined G. Cappi's firm in 1837 and worked there until his death. The final fortunes of the firm are reported in a contract between Mollo's sons and Tobias Haslinger, by which 630 publications on 11,348 plates were transferred to the latter. Haslinger wrote the document on 24 May 1832; it lists each work with the sum of the plates and plate numbers, providing valuable material for research into both Mollo's and Haslinger's publishing firms. Written five months after Mollo's retirement, the contract gives a detailed account of his sons' plans as well as information on Haslinger.

The output of the publishing house T. Mollo & Co. and later T. Mollo alone (after 1804) shows a wide variety of composers (most of them represented by a few works only) including Cherubini, Clementi, Fiorillo, Gyrowetz, Kreutzer, J. B. Cramer, Eberl, G. G. Ferrari, Krommer, G. J. Vogler and Vanhal. Works by Haydn and Mozart are chiefly from the Artaria period while Beethoven's (including 19 original pieces) come from both periods. After 1804 music by new and less important composers was published, including Bevilacqua, L. von Call (*c*100 works), Carulli, Diabelli, J. L. Dussek, Josef Gelinek, Mauro Giuliani, E. von Lannoy, Adolf Müller, Paer, Payer, Pleyel, Ries, Rossini, Steibelt and Zumsteeg. On 30 December 1828 the first edition of Franz Schubert's choral work *Glaube, Hoffnung und Liebe* (D954) was published.

BIBLIOGRAPHY

F. Gräffer: *Kleine Wiener Memoiren und Dosenstücke*, i (Munich, 1917), 292, 549f
G. Gugitz: *Von Leuten und Zeiten im alten Wien* (Vienna and Leipzig, 1922), 139
A. Weinmann: *Vollständiges Verlagsverzeichnis Artaria & Comp.* (Vienna, 1952)
——: *Verlagsverzeichnis Tranquillo Mollo* (Vienna, 1964)
——: *Ergänzungen zum Verlagsverzeichnis Tranquillo Mollo* (Vienna, 1972)

ALEXANDER WEINMANN

**Molnár, Albert Szenczi.** *See* SZENCI MOLNÁR, ALBERT.

**Molnár, Antal** (*b* Budapest, 7 Jan 1890). Hungarian musicologist, composer and violist. After studying composition with Herzfeld at the Budapest Academy of Music (1907–10), he made expeditions collecting folk music in Transylvania and northern Hungary (1910–12), played the viola in the Waldbauer String Quartet (1910–13) and the Dohnányi-Hubay Piano Quartet (1915–17) and taught music history and solfège at the Municipal Music School (1912–18). In 1919 he was appointed professor at the Budapest Academy of Music, where he remained until his retirement in 1959, teaching music history, theory, solfège (a subject he introduced at the academy) and chamber music; he also served in the 1930s as vice-president of the Hungarian Association of Music Teachers. He published the series Népszerü Zenefüzetek ('Popular musical pamphlets'), which included studies by Bartók and Szabolcsi, and his own *Kodály Zoltán* (the first monograph on the composer). Later he was editor of the series Kis Zenei Könyvtár ('Little library of music'), composer monographs which appeared from 1957. He was awarded the Haynald Prize for his *Missa brevis* (1910), the Franz Joseph Prize for composition (1914), the Baumgarten Prize for his literary activity (1938, which enabled him to publish his *Zeneesztétika*, 'Musical aesthetics', i) and the Kossuth Prize (1957); on his 80th birthday (1970) he received the title of Eminent Artist.

Molnár is one of the founders of modern Hungarian musicology. His comprehensive knowledge of all periods of music and his thorough insight into musical aesthetics, which draws on psychology and sociology (his chief works on musical aesthetics in 1938 and 1971 illuminate the matter from philosophical and analytical points of view), have enabled him to write authoritatively on a wide range of subjects. As early as 1912 he was able to assign Bartók and Kodály to their proper place in music history, being one of the first to recognize their achievement. Several of his books were directed to amateurs and contributed greatly to music education in Hungary.

Molnár's compositions include chamber music (notably three string quartets and a flute quartet), orchestral works (e.g. the Variations on a Hungarian Theme, the Hungarian Comedy Overture and the Budapest Overture), works for piano and organ, sacred and secular vocal music, and many pieces for teaching purposes. In 1934 the Greenwich Symphony Orchestra gave an entire concert of his works in New York.

WRITINGS

'Bartók kvartettje' [Bartók's quartets], *Zeneközlöny*, ix (1911), 275
*A zenetörténet szelleme* [The spirit of the history of music] (Budapest, 1914)
*Bartók Béla – táncjátéka alkalmából* [Bartók – on the occasion of his ballet] (Budapest, 1917)
'Bartók operája: A kékszakállu herceg vára' [Bartók's opera: *Bluebeard's Castle*], *Zenei szemle*, ii (1918), 115, 148
*Az európai zene története 1750–ig* [History of European music until 1750] (Budapest, 1920)
*Bach és Händel zenéjének lelki alapjai* [Spiritual basis of Bach's and Handel's music] (Budapest, 1920)
'Bartók Béla és a kultura-történet' [Bartók and the history of culture], *Magyar irás* (1921), 36
*Bartók Két elégiájának elemzése* [Two elegies – an analysis] (Budapest, 1921) [first analytical study on Bartók]
*A zenetörténet szociológiája* [The sociology of music history] (Budapest, 1923)
*Az uj zene* [New music] (Budapest, 1925)
*Az uj magyar zene* [The new Hungarian music] (Budapest, 1926)
'Bartók: I. Konzert für Klavier und Orchester', *Melos* (1927), enlarged version pubd separately (Vienna, 1927)

*Bevezetés a zenekulturába* [Introduction to musical culture] (Budapest, 1928)
'Esquisse d'un portrait de Liszt', *ReM*, ix/7 (1928), 101
*Bevezetés a mai muzsikába* [Introduction to contemporary music] (Budapest, 1929)
*Fizika és muzsika* [Physics and music] (Budapest, 1930)
*A gyermek és a zene* [The child and music] (Budapest, 1931)
'Die Bedeutung der neuen osteuropäischen Musik', *Archiv für die gesamte Psychologie*, no.81 (1931), 160
*A zenetörténet megvilágitása* [Light on musical history] (Budapest, 1933)
*Zeneesztétika és szellemtudomány* [Musical aesthetics and 'Geisteswissenschaft'] (Budapest, 1935)
*A ma zenéje* [Music today] (Budapest, 1936)
*Az óvodáskoru gyermek zenei nevelése* [Musical education in the nursery school] (Budapest, 1936)
'Die Bedeutung der Cantata Profana von Bartók', *Pester Lloyd* (15 Nov 1936)
*Kodály Zoltán* (Budapest, 1936)
Introductions to *Don Juan*, *Rigoletto* and *Il trovatore* (Budapest, 1937)
*Zeneesztétika*, i [Musical aesthetics, i] (Budapest, 1938)
'Bartók Béla hegedüversenye' [Bartók's Violin Concerto], *A zene*, xx (1939), 41
*Népszerü zeneesztétika* [Popular musical aesthetics] (Budapest, 1940)
*Az uj muzsika szelleme* [The spirit of the new music] (Budapest, 1948)
*Bartók müvészete, emlékezésekkel a müvész életére* [The art of Bartók with reminiscences of his life] (Budapest, 1948)
'Nyugatias magyar dallamok a XVIII. század végén és a XIX. század elsö felében' [Western-type Hungarian melodies at the end of the 18th century and in the first half of the 19th], *Zenetudományi tanulmányok*, iv (1955), 103
'Az ifju Kodály [The young Kodály], *Zenetudományi tanulmányok*, vi (1957), 9
*Repertórium a barokk zene történetéhez* [Repertory of the history of Baroque music] (Budapest, 1959)
'Die Persönlichkeit Chopins', *Chopin Congress: Warszawa 1960*, 701
'Emlékezés Weiner Leóra' [Commemoration of Leó Weiner], *Magyar zene*, i/1–6 (1960–61), 267
'Az uj magyar zene kibontakozása' [The development of new Hungarian music], *Magyar zene*, i/1–6 (1960–61), 400, 489, 588; xiv (1973), 339; xv (1974), 3
*Irások a zenéről* [Writings on music] (Budapest, 1961)
'Über Transkriptionen and Paraphrasen von Liszt', *SM*, v (1963), 227
*A Léner-vonósnégyes* [The Léner Quartet] (Budapest, 1968)
*A zeneszerző világa* [The world of the composer] (Budapest, 1969)
*Gyakorlati zeneesztétika* [Practical musical aesthetics] (Budapest, 1971)
*Magamról – másokról* [On myself – on others] (Budapest, 1974) [memoirs]

BIBLIOGRAPHY

M. D. Calvocoressi: 'Hungarian Music of To-day', *MMR*, lii (1922), 30
J. S. Weissmann: 'The Contemporary Movement in Hungary', *Music Today*, i (1949), 81
Articles on Molnár's 80th birthday, *Muzsika*, xiii/1 (1970), 7

PÉTER P. VÁRNAI

**Molnar, Josef** (*b* Gänsendorf, 7 Sept 1929). Austrian harpist. A member of the Vienna Boys Choir, he later trained as a harpist at the Vienna Academy of Music. Settling in Japan, he was responsible for the creation of a school of Japanese harp playing, introducing the European repertory to that country, encouraging Japanese composers to write for the harp, and publishing the first harp method to have been written in Japanese.

ANN GRIFFITHS

**Molt, Theodore Frederic** [Johann Friedrich] (*b* Gschwend, Baden-Württemberg, 13 Feb 1795; *d* Burlington, Vermont, 16 Nov 1856). Canadian music teacher of German birth. The son of a schoolteacher and Lutheran organist, he studied music under his father and an older brother, interrupting his studies briefly to serve in the Napoleonic army. Possibly Molt came to the Philadelphia region in the early 1820s; in 1823 he taught music and formed a Juvenile Harmonic Society in Quebec. He returned to Europe in the spring of 1825. In the autumn he visited Beethoven who gave him as a souvenir the canon *Freu dich des Lebens* (WoO195; autograph in the L. Lande Collection of Canadiana at McGill University, Montreal). He also met Czerny and Moscheles, both of whom may have taught him, and, according to Converse, Schubert. In 1826 Molt returned to North America and for the next 30 years taught music in Quebec, Montreal and at the Burlington Female Seminary (1833–c1837 and from 1849). From 1840 to 1849 he was organist at the Roman Catholic Cathedral in Quebec. Molt's setting of I. Bédard's *Sol canadien, terre chérie* was one of the first patriotic songs composed in Canada. Of his compilation *La lyre sainte* (Quebec, 1844–5) only two instalments appeared. A hard-working and respected teacher, Molt published a number of instruction books for piano and for voice (Quebec, 1828 and 1845; Burlington, 1835 and 1836; Boston, 1855).

BIBLIOGRAPHY

J. K. Converse: 'Burlington Female Seminary', *Vermont Historical Gazetteer*, i (1868), 531
A. W. Thayer: *The Life of Ludwig van Beethoven* (New York, 1921, rev. 2/1964)
*Beethoven & Quebec* (Montreal, 1966)

HELMUT KALLMANN

**Molteni, Benedetta Emilia.** *See* AGRICOLA, BENEDETTA EMILIA.

**Molter, Johann Melchior** (*b* Tiefenort, nr. Eisenach, 10 Feb 1696; *d* Karlsruhe, 12 Jan 1765). German composer. Like many German musicians of the first half of the 18th century, he came from the Thuringian-Saxon area. His father, Valentin Molter, was a teacher and Kantor in the village of Tiefenort, and Johann Melchior probably received his earliest musical education from him. Later he attended the Gymnasium in Eisenach, where J. S. Bach had earlier been a student; he also belonged to the Chorus Symphoniacus under the directorship of Kantor Geisthirt, which brought him into contact with the music currently cultivated in Thuringia. He apparently left Eisenach in 1715; about 1717, as a violinist, he entered the service of the Margrave Carl Wilhelm of Baden-Durlach who in 1715 had moved from Durlach to the newly-built and rapidly growing city of Karlsruhe. There, in 1718, Molter married Maria Salome Rollwagen; they had eight children.

The young *Hof-musicus* rapidly won the margrave's favour and he was sent to Italy with full salary to study the Italian style. Molter spent 1719–21 in Venice and Rome, and may have come into contact with such artists as Vivaldi, Albinoni, the Marcello brothers and Alessandro Scarlatti. In 1722, after his return to the Baden residence, the margrave appointed him court Kapellmeister in succession to Johann Philipp Käfer. His varied duties included the direction of the court chapel and the provision of music at table, for balls and various other occasions; he also directed performances in the margrave's theatre, where German opera was cultivated. Numerous compositions date from that period, including oratorios, cantatas, orchestral works, chamber music and perhaps even operas. This activity came to an abrupt end in 1733 when, at the outbreak of the War of the Polish Succession, the margrave dissolved his Kapelle and fled to Basle in exile. Molter was dismissed but retained his title.

The next year, however, he obtained the post of Kapellmeister at the court of Duke Wilhelm Heinrich of Saxe-Eisenach, which had fallen vacant on the death of Johann Adam Birckenstock. His duties in Eisenach were the same as those in Karlsruhe except that there were no opera productions. The many works of these years include sacred and secular vocal compositions.

Molter's wife died in 1737, and a second visit to Italy later that year may be connected with this; artistically, the reason for the journey lay in Molter's wish to acquaint himself with the new developments in Italian music, associated with such composers as Pergolesi, Leo and Sammartini. He visited Venice, Ancona, Foligno, Rome and Bologna; he probably also stayed in Naples and Milan. While in Italy, in 1738, Molter received news of the Margrave Carl Wilhelm's death, and hurried to Karlsruhe where he honoured his former patron with a performance of funeral music. He returned to Eisenach, and during the next few years he probably remarried. In 1741, Duke Wilhelm Heinrich died without issue (Molter supplied the funeral music) and Saxe-Eisenach passed to the Duke of Saxe-Weimar, who dissolved the Eisenach Kapelle. Molter went to Karlsruhe in 1742 and obtained employment there the next year, with the additional obligation to teach music at the Gymnasium. Financial conditions, however, were less good than before 1733: the small orchestra was appropriate only for modest undertakings. Molter overcame this situation by composing many chamber works.

No change occurred until Carl Wilhelm's grandson and successor, Margrave Carl Friedrich (1728–1811), reached his majority and assumed government. He ruled his small country with justice and moderation, and was an educated man with an interest in the arts and sciences which subsequently allowed him contact with Gluck, Klopstock and Goethe, among others. In 1747 he commissioned Molter to develop a plan for the reorganization of the court's musical establishment, with which he subsequently agreed in most respects. Molter was given a suitable salary, and had at his disposal about 20 instrumentalists as well as singers, the number being increased as necessary by various servants and retired musicians. Besides strings and harpsichord (or organ), the orchestra included two oboes (doubling flutes), two bassoons, two horns, two or three trumpets and timpani. Molter could now perform any kind of music, especially as several musicians were not only virtuosos on their own instruments but also played a second (among them the clarinet and viola da gamba). In the following years, Molter wrote a vast quantity of cantatas, symphonies, concertos and chamber music. Works of other composers, German, Italian and French, were also performed. Court music at Karlsruhe flourished, though opera production was not resumed.

Molter occupied this post until his death; his second wife survived him by only two years, and it may have been as a tribute to Molter that the margrave left his post vacant for a whole year despite the existence of a suitable candidate.

Molter's surviving body of work is comprehensive and includes all contemporary genres; it reflects the many influences to which he was exposed. A steady development may be traced from the late Baroque style to the *galant*, as in the work of his contemporaries Hasse, Quantz and the Graun brothers. During his first period at Karlsruhe (1722–33) his style was affected by his studies in Italy and his encounter with the music of the Venetian masters, but French elements are also recognizable. In the Eisenach years (1734–41) he drew nearer to Telemann's manner of writing, through contact with the work of his central German colleagues, including J. C. Hertel, J. B. Bach and G. H. Stölzel; but after his second Italian journey (1737–8) he completed the transition to the *galant* style under the influence of the Neapolitans and Sammartini, and this was carried further during his second Karlsruhe period (1742–65) through familiarity with the flourishing Mannheim school. Throughout these stylistic changes, Molter remained bound to the central German tradition of Kantor and organist; and this must be viewed as the basis of his style.

Although the occasional dullness of invention, the generally small dimensions and the routine, schematic use of familiar models show the hand of a minor master, that is not the entire story. His interest in sonorities, and thus in instruments and their acoustic and technical possibilities, is particularly notable; he followed attempted advances in this direction, for example (like Graupner and Endler) using five timpani instead of the usual two. He also experimented on his own account. He not only used familiar instruments in new ways (among them the trumpet and the horn) but also gave preference to new or unusual instruments like the clarinet, the chalumeau, the flauto d'amore, the flauto cornetto and the harp. He combined the most diverse instruments and put them to singular uses with great taste, particularly showing a feeling for wind instruments. Timbre gradually became a structural element in his music. The combination of this understanding of instrumentation with a marked melodic gift produced some charming chamber works – he called them 'concertinos' – whose small dimensions give them the character of miniatures. His clarinet concertos also owe their existence to his interest in instrumental problems, and have more than once been assigned a special historical importance: but they were written less because of Molter's desire to experiment than to provide a repertory for the Karlsruhe flautist, oboist and clarinetist Johann Reusch.

Some of his concertos and symphonies have music of unusual animation; in the overtures, on the other hand, there is French pomp mixed with French grace, elegance and delicacy. His 'Sonate grosse' represent a bold experiment: these are an entirely new kind of orchestral composition in their cyclic construction and type of movement. No other composer, however, followed up that development. These works include some polyphonic writing, which usually remains in the background in Molter's music, even in the vocal works. Most of his vocal music is lost; there is reason to believe that some of it was particularly important. Despite his limitations, Molter was an artistic personality well above the average level of the 18th-century German minor master.

## WORKS

All surviving works are in *D-KA* unless otherwise stated. They form the composer's MSS legacy, donated by his son Friedrich Valentin Molter, a former director of the Library. A complete catalogue of works is found in Häfner; the following is a summary list (see also Eitner).

### VOCAL

Schertzt und lacht, vergnügte Sinnen (drama per musica for Margrave Carl Friedrich's birthday), 5vv
Oratorio for Good Friday, *D-SHs*, same as Passion cited in Eitner
7 Italian cantatas: 5 for S, orch; 1 for S, bc; 1 fragment for B, orch
2 Italian arias, S, orch
Fragments of oratorios, funeral music, cantatas, arias, etc.

### INSTRUMENTAL

Esercizio studioso, continente 6 sonate, vn, bc, op.1 (Amsterdam, 1723)
170 sinfonias, 2 in *D-SWl*; 14 ovs, 1 inc.; Musica turchesa [suite]; 21 sonatas, 2 inc.; 20 concertos, 12 formerly *KA*, destroyed; ballet music: all for orch
44 concertos for solo inst, orch: 6 for vn, 1 lost, 1 inc.; 1 for vc; 10 for fl; 1 for fl d'amore; 5 for ob; 3 for bn, 1 inc.; 5 for 2 tpt; 3 for tpt; 1 for hn in D; 6 for cl; 1 for kbd; 2 fragments for unspecified inst(s)
Chamber music for winds: 1 sinfonia, 4 hn; 3 sinfonias, tpt, 2 hn, 2 ob, bn; 3 concertinos, tpt, 2 ob, bn; 6 concertinos, 2 fl, 2 hn, bc; 2 concertinos, 2 hn, 2 chalumeaux, bn, 1 inc.; 2 concertinos, 4 fl, bc
*c*100 other chamber works incl. sonatas and concertinos à 4 and à 3; sonatas, vn/fl, bc; minuets with variations, va da gamba, bc; duets, 2 fl; marches and single pieces for wind insts
Chorale preludes, org; other pieces and exercises, kbd

## BIBLIOGRAPHY

*EitnerQ*
L. Schiedermair: 'Die Oper an den badischen Höfen des 17. und 18. Jahrhunderts', *SIMG*, xiv (1912–13)
E. W. Böhme: *Die frühdeutsche Oper in Thüringen* (Stadtroda, 1931)
H. Becker: Preface to *Klarinetten-Konzerte des 18. Jahrhunderts*, EDM, xli (1957)
F. Längin: 'Johann Melchior Molter, der Markgräflich Baden-Durlachische Kapellmeister und Hofkompositeur', *Badische Heimat: Jb für das Badner Land 1965* (Freiburg, 1965)
N. O'Loughlin: 'Johann Melchior Molter', *MT*, cvii (1966), 110
K. Häfner: *Johann Melchior Molter (1696–1765): Leben und Werk* (in preparation)
                                                    KLAUS HÄFNER

**Molto** (It.: 'much', 'very'). A word used to qualify tempo and expression marks in music: *molto piano*, *molto grazioso*, *molto andante* (*see* ANDANTE), etc. It is also found in such contexts as *allegro di molto* (given by Koch, 1802, as the equivalent of *allegro assai*).

For bibliography *see* TEMPO AND EXPRESSION MARKS.

**Möltzel, Jiří.** *See* MELCELIUS, JIŘÍ.

**Molu, Pierre.** *See* MOULU, PIERRE.

**Molza, Tarquinia** (*b* Modena, 1542; *d* Rome, 8 Aug 1617). Italian virtuoso singer and poet. She was the niece of the poet Francesco Maria Molza. Tributes to her singing appear in both literary and musical prints from the early 1570s onward. She was a member of the famous group of singing ladies at Ferrara from 1583 until October 1589, when the impropriety of her relationship with the composer and Mantuan *maestro di cappella* Wert caused her dismissal.

## BIBLIOGRAPHY

P. Ferri: *Biblioteca femminile italiana* (Padua, 1842) [contains list of Molza's published literary works]
A. Solerti: *Ferrara e la corte estense* (Città di Castello, 1891), p.lxvii in
A. Newcomb: *The 'Musica secreta' of Ferrara in the 1580's* (diss., Princeton U., 1969)
P. di Pietro: 'La biblioteca di una lettera a modenese del cinquecento, Tarquinia Molza', *Atti e memorie della Deputazione di storia patria per le antiche provincie modenesi*, 10th ser., viii (1973), 55
                                                ANTHONY NEWCOMB

**Mombelli, Luisa.** *See* LASCHI, LUISA.

**Moment form.** A concept introduced by Stockhausen in which individual passages of a work are regarded as experimental units; *see* STOCKHAUSEN, KARLHEINZ, §1.

**Moment musical.** A term invented in the spring of 1828 by Maximilian Josef Leidesdorf, a publisher in Vienna, to describe each of six piano pieces by Schubert when they were published as his op.94 (D780), under the title *Momens musicals*. The faulty French (*recte* 'moments musicaux') has frequently been attributed to Schubert. The origin of the name seems to lie in the fact that just before their publication Leidesdorf had composed a set of pieces that he published under the name *Momens mélancoliques*. Schubert wrote his *Moments musicaux* at various times: no.6 probably in 1818, no.3 in 1823 and the rest in 1827. All are delightful examples of his lyric genius. Outside Schubert there are very few examples, but Paderewski wrote one (op.7, 1884) and Rakhmaninov wrote six (op.16, 1896).

MAURICE J. E. BROWN

**Momigny, Jérôme-Joseph de** (*b* Philippeville, Namur, 20 Jan 1762; *d* Charenton, 25 Aug 1842). Belgian theorist and composer. By the age of 12 he had progressed sufficiently to hold one of the appointments of organist in the town of St Omer. He later settled in Lyons as a music teacher and as organist at St Pierre. He played a political role in Lyons during the Revolution, and several years later settled in Paris where he founded a music publishing house in 1800. It was his goal to reformulate the principles of music theory entirely, and to replace textbooks used at the time with his own. In 1828 he was driven into bankruptcy and forced to sell his publishing house but through the good offices of Cherubini he obtained an annual pension of 400 francs. Momigny's last years were marked by a progressive mental decline; he spent several periods in the asylum at Charenton, where he died.

It is primarily for his writings that Momigny is of interest to scholars today; the theories he developed were very advanced for his time, and in a certain sense ingeniously anticipate modern music theory. Except for certain preliminary comments of a distressingly childish nature – Momigny always presented his ideas as if they were the only ones which were valid – the modernity of some of his ideas on rhythm and harmony is striking. Fundamentally convinced of the relationship between musical phenomena and human physiological functions, he established a link between a man's walking pace, his rate of heartbeat and the musical measure. His basic principle, that music proceeds from the upbeat to the downbeat, adumbrated the idea of the *mesure à cheval*, formulated by Mathis-Lussy in 1883. 'The real rhythmic unit', Momigny wrote, 'is therefore not imprisoned: it should not be considered as enclosed within two barlines, as it does not start with the downbeat and end with the upbeat. Rather, it straddles the bar-line, with its first beat to the left and its second to the right.' This theory led him to distinguish the *mesure auriculaire*, the measure as it is heard, from the *mesure oculaire*, the measure as it is written down.

In the field of harmonic theory, Momigny worked to expand the concept of tonality. Like Rameau, he accepted resonance as the starting-point of his theory; but he did not limit himself to a fundamental concord based on three pitches. Instead, he constructed a seven-note chord built in 3rds, which is what modern French 12-note theorists refer to as *le total diatonique*. Momigny, however, went even further: to the seven diatonic notes he added the five chromatic and the five enharmonic notes, so that 17 notes, not seven, belonged to the same tonality. The enharmonic notes were as much a part of the tonality as the others; it was only from their context that one could determine whether or not they would lead to a modulation. It is plain how daring this new theory must have seemed in the early 19th century; the elaborations it underwent a century later, when Ravel and Stravinsky introduced the concept of polytonality, are equally striking. (*See also* ANALYSIS, §II, 2, and fig.6.)

Momigny's compositions, which never enjoyed much of a reputation outside the fashionable salons, include a few pieces of chamber music, numerous songs, various arrangements and transcriptions, and three operas: *Le Baron de Felsheim* (Lyons, before 1800), *La nouvelle laitière* (before 1811) and *Arlequin Cendrillon* (Paris, 1800).

WRITINGS

*Méthode de piano* (Paris, 1802)
*La première année de leçons de pianoforte* (Paris, 1802–3)
*Cours complet d'harmonie et de composition* (Paris, 1803–6, 2/1808)
*Exposé succinct du seul système musical qui soit partout d'accord avec la nature, avec la raison et avec la pratique* (Paris, 1808)
*Le nouveau solfège* (Paris, 1808)
*La seule vraie théorie de la musique* (Paris, 1821)
*A l'Académie des Beaux-Arts* (Paris, 1831)
*Cours général de musique* (Paris, 1834), inc.

BIBLIOGRAPHY

A. Morel: *Observations sur la seule vraie théorie de la musique de M. de Momigny* (Paris, 1822) [see also J.-J. de Momigny: *Réponse aux observations de M. Morel* (Paris, 1822)]
A. Mocquereau: 'Jérôme de Momigny et le rythme musical', PalMus, 1st ser., vii (1901), 355
H. Riemann: 'Ein Kapitel vom Rhythmus', *Die Musik*, iii/3 (1903–4), 155
A. Palm: *J.-J. de Momigny* (diss., U. of Tübingen, 1957)
J. Chailley: 'Un grand théoricien belge méconnu de la musique, J.-J. de Momigny', *Académie royale de Belgique: bulletin de la classe des beaux-arts*, xlviii/2–3 (1962)
A. Palm: 'Contribution à la connaissance de J.-J. de Momigny', *RMFC*, vii (1967), 127
——: 'Neue Dokumente zur Lebensgeschichte Momignys', *Mf*, xx (1967), 393
M. Cole: 'Momigny's Analysis of Haydn's Symphony no.103', *MR*, xxx (1969), 261
A. Palm: *Jérôme-Joseph de Momigny: Leben und Werk: ein Beitrag zur Geschichte der Musiktheorie im 19. Jahrhundert* (Cologne, 1969)

JEAN MONGRÉDIEN

**Mompellio, Federico** (*b* Genoa, 9 Sept 1908). Italian musicologist. He studied the piano at Genoa with Lifschitz and composition with Barbieri and took diplomas in both subjects at the Conservatory of Parma (1926, 1928). He also has an arts degree from Genoa University (1932), where he studied musicology with Torrefranca. He began his career teaching music history at Palermo Conservatory (1933) and then taught both music history and composition at Parma Conservatory (1934). From 1938 to 1949 he was librarian of Milan Conservatory and was responsible for saving much of the collection during the war. In 1949 he became professor of music history and later also vice-director of the conservatory, where he remained until 1968; in the years 1965–7 he gave a musicology course there. From 1950 he taught music history at the universities of Pavia, Milan and Parma and in 1954 joined the staff of the advanced Scuola di Paleografia e Filologia Musicale of the University of Pavia, becoming professor there in 1968. He was vice-president of the Società Italiana di Musicologia (1964–8) and is a member of the Accademia di S Cecilia. Mompellio's research has dealt mainly with 15th-century and later Italian music; he is known particularly for his editions and biography of Sigismondo d'India.

WRITINGS

ed.: G. C. Conestabile: *Vita di Niccolò Paganini* (Milan, 1936)
*Pietro Vinci: madrigalista siciliano* (Milan, 1937)
*Marco Enrico Bossi* (Milan, 1952)
'Sigismondo d'India e il primo libro di *Musiche da cantar solo*', *CHM*, i (1953), 113
'Un *grillesco capriccio* di A. Banchieri', *RMI*, lx (1953), 371–403
*Sigismondo d'India: musicista palermitano* (Milan, 1957)
'La Cappella del Duomo da M. H. di Vercore ai primi decenni del '900', *Storia di Milano*, ix (1961), 749; xvi (1962), 507
'Musica provvisoria nella prima *Forza del destino*', *Bollettino* [quadrimestrale] *dell'Istituto di studi verdiani*, ii (1961–6), 1611–80
'Critiche di Verdi ai critici', *A Ettore Desderi nel suo 70. compleanno* (Bologna, 1963), 97–150
'San Filippo Neri e la musica "pescatrice di anime"', *Chigiana*, xxii (1965), 3–33

*Lodovico Viadana: musicista fra due secoli* (Florence, 1967)
'Premessa all'opera di Leoš Janáček da una casa di morti', *Conferenze dell'Associazione amici della Scala 1966–1967*, 51–88
'Valori cromatici nel quintetto di César Franck', *Quadrivium*, xii/2 (1971), 311
'Un certo ordine di procedere che non si può scrivere', *Scritti in onore di Luigi Ronga* (Milan and Naples, 1973), 367
'Il quinto concerto di Paganini: un'avventura orchestrale ieri e oggi', *Quaderni dell'Istituto di studi paganiniani* (Genoa, 1974), no.2, p.3

EDITIONS
S. d'India: *Madrigali a cinque voci, libro I*, CMI, x (1942); *Il primo libro di musiche da cantar solo* (Cremona, 1970)
N. Paganini: *Quartetti per archi*, PIISM (1975)

CAROLYN M. GIANTURCO

**Mompfort, Hugo von.** See HUGO VON MONTFORT.

**Mompou, Federico** (*b* Barcelona, 16 April 1893). Spanish (Catalan) composer. He began to study the piano at the Conservatorio del Liceo and gave his first public concert at the age of 15. Hearing Marguerite Long play Fauré in Barcelona fired him to go to Paris where in 1911, armed with a recommendation from Granados, he studied the piano with Ferdinand Motte-Lacroix and harmony with Marcel Samuel-Rousseau; but his abnormally shy and retiring disposition led him to give up any idea of a concert career and to devote himself to composition. By temperament and birth (his mother was of French descent) he was much attracted to Debussy and the new French school, and the influence of Satie in particular is evident in the ideal of primitivism he set himself, and which he termed 'Recomençament'. (An echo of Satie is also to be observed in such occasional directions in his music as 'Chantez avec le fraîcheur de l'herbe humide' or 'Donnez des excuses'.) His aim, maximum expressiveness through minimum means, involved the adoption of popular themes and a virtual renunciation of modulation and development; side-effects were the intermittent dropping of key signatures and bar divisions and the insertion of an accidental at each appearance of an affected note. At the outbreak of war in 1914 he went back to Barcelona, but in 1921 returned to Paris, where he was championed by the critic Vuillermoz and where he stayed for 20 years. From 1941 he again lived in Barcelona. He was elected a member of the Royal Academy of San Jorge in Barcelona and of San Fernando in Madrid, and made a Chevalier des Arts et des Lettres by the French government; but he has chosen to live out of the public eye, playing his compositions only among friends.

The naivety of his music, his almost complete self-restriction to intimate piano miniatures or to predominantly slow songs of very similar style, his predilection for 'black-note' keys and the limitations of his technical invention combine to suggest a salon dilettantism based on keyboard improvisation. Nevertheless many of his pastels are of an extraordinarily haunting, exquisitely melancholy elegance; and a fondness for ostinato figures and bell sounds often lends a static, incantatory quality to his poetic evocations. These – as hinted by his use of *Música callada* as a title – sometimes approach the 'voice of silence' apostrophized by St John of the Cross. Various arrangements and orchestrations of Mompou's pieces – as for the Royal Ballet's *House of Birds* and the de Cuevas Ballet's *Don Perlimplin* – have been made by other hands.

WORKS
(*selective list*)
PIANO
Impresiones intimas, 1911–14; Pessebres, 1914–17; Suburbis, 1916–17; Scènes d'enfants, 1915–18; Cants magics, 1917–19; Fêtes loin-

taines, 1920; Charmes, 1920–21; 3 variations, 1921; Dialogues I–II, 1923, III–IV, 1941–62; Cançons i dansas I–IV, 1921–8, V–XII, 1942–62; Préludes I–VI, 1927–30, VII–X, 1943–51; Souvenirs de l'exposition, 1937; La canción que más amaba, 1944; Canción de cuna, 1951; Variaciones sobre un tema di Chopin, 1938–57; Paisajes, 1942–60; Música callada, 1959–67

OTHER WORKS
Songs: L'hora gris (Blancafort), 1915; Cançoneta incerta (Carner), 1926; 4 mélodies (Mompou), 1926–8; Le nuage (Pomés), 1928; Comptines I–III (1931), IV–VI, 1943; Llueve sobre el rio, Pastoral (J. R. Jiménez), 1945; Combat del somni (J. Janés), 1942–8; Cançó de la fira (Garcés) (1949); Aureana do sil (Cabanillas), 1951; Cantar del alma (St John of the Cross) (1961); Sant Marti (Ribot), 1962; Primeros pasos (C. Janés), 1964
Choral: Improperios, chorus, orch, 1963; Cantar del alma (St John of the Cross), chorus, 1962–6
Gui: Suite compostelana, 1962

Principal publishers: Eschig, Salabert, Unión Musical Española

BIBLIOGRAPHY
S. Kastner: *Federico Mompou* (Madrid, 1946)
S. Moreux: 'Federico Mompou', *Revue française* (1950), Christmas
W. Starkie: 'Homenaje a Federico Mompou', *Revista musical*, no.26
F. Sopeña: *Historia de la música española contemporánea* (Madrid, 1958), 256ff
M. Valls: *La música catalana contemporània* (Barcelona, 1960), 113ff
A. Iglesias: *Federico Mompou* (Madrid, 1977)

LIONEL SALTER

**Monaca, Riccardo la.** Italian composer, possibly identifiable with MICHELE MALERBA.

**Monachus, Guillelmus.** See GUILLELMUS MONACHUS.

**Monaco.** Independent European principality in an enclave on the French Mediterranean coast. At the end of the 12th century it came under Genoese control, and from the 13th century the Grimaldis (Guelphs) fought for its independence; but they were successively dominated or protected by the counts of Provence, the dukes of Milan, the Genoese, the Spanish, the dukes of Savoy and the French. There were consequently many influences on Monaco's cultural life. Some surviving folksong texts indicate Provençal influence in the 18th century; sea songs show Italian, Spanish and French features.

As early as 1406 the Avignon Pope Benedict XIII and his court stayed in Monaco and had music performed there. During the Renaissance, when Italian influence was predominant, the Genoese lords commissioned music, had manuscripts copied and protected printers. Music also flourished in the mid-17th century, when as a result of the Treaty of Péronne (1641), Prince Honoré II of Monaco passed from Spanish to French protection, and during visits to Paris (1642–3, 1646–7, 1651) acquired a taste for court songs and ballet and made the acquaintance of some composers. Freed from the cares of war, Monaco mounted entertainments in imitation of Versailles, with French dancing-masters, music masters and performers. For the Carnival in 1654 the court presented the first work known to have been written in Monaco, *Les entretiens de Diane et d'Apollon*, a sumptuous *ballet de cour* initiated by the Duchesse de Valentinois, Honoré's daughter-in-law, on a text by Sir Charles Ferriol. In 1655 there followed *Le vittorie de Minerva*, on a libretto by F. F. Frigoni and with music by F. Gropallo, Honoré's *maître de chapelle*. Liturgical music was performed in the church of St Nicolas, where a new organ was installed in 1638.

Music was even more prominent at the court of Honoré II's grandson, Antoine I (reigned 1701–31). He was a favourite pupil of Lully, who had given him his conducting stick, and was active as composer, conductor and producer. He corresponded with Couperin and Destouches, was a patron of the local composer, a 'sieur David', sent his musicians to study in Paris or Turin and encouraged them to perform outside Monaco. At that time the repertory of dramatic, symphonic and chamber music performed in Monaco consisted of works by the leading French and Italian composers. Subsequent princes were less enthusiastic about music, although Honoré III sponsored the Monaco-born Honoré Langlé, who later became a theorist and music teacher in Paris. With the French Revolution and the Empire, Monaco's sovereignty was suspended and significant artistic activity ceased.

Prince Florestan, who reigned in the mid-19th century, was fond of the theatre, and music reappeared in vaudeville and comic opera, notably in the works of Dalayrac, a pupil of Langlé. In the late 19th century cultural life revived with a favourable economic situation, and Monte Carlo (founded 1858) became a popular resort and the main town of Monaco. Entertainments and concerts were given at the new casino (1862–3), concert hall (1872) and playhouse (1878). Leading performers appeared there, including Léon Carvalho (1879), Adelina Patti (from 1881), Caruso (1904) and Mary Garden (1905). The Monte Carlo Opera Orchestra was founded in 1863 by E. Lucas who was its conductor until 1876; important subsequent conductors have been Paul Paray (1928–44) and Louis Frémaux (1956–65), who introduced a series of concerts at the Monaco Royal Palace from 1959, as well as many internationally known guest conductors. The orchestra has made many recordings of orchestral music. A series of outstanding artistic directors (including Raoul Gunsbourg from 1893 to 1951) have mounted many performances of opera and ballet at the casino; among the many first performances were Berlioz's *La damnation de Faust* (first staged production, 1893), Franck's *Hulda* (1894), Saint-Saëns' *Hélène* (1904) and *L'ancêtre* (1906), Fauré's *Pénélope* (1913), Puccini's *La rondine* (1917) and Ravel's *L'enfant et les sortilèges* (1925).

BIBLIOGRAPHY

P. Casimir: 'Le théâtre dans la principauté de Monaco depuis le XVIIe siècle', *Journal de Monaco* (1915–17)
L.-H. Labande: *Inventaires du Palais de Monaco (1604–1731)* (Paris, 1918)
——: *La bibliothèque musicale du Prince Antoine I de Monaco* (Paris, 1925)
A. Tessier, ed.: 'Correspondance entre le Prince Antoine I et François Couperin', *RdM*, vi (1925), 169
L.-H. Labande: *Histoire de la principauté de Monaco* (Paris, 1934)
G. Favre: 'Un prince mélomane au XVIIIe siècle: la vie musicale à la cour d'Antoine I Prince de Monaco (1663–1731)', *RdM*, lvii (1971), 134
——: *Histoire musicale de la principauté de Monaco du XVIe au XXe siècle* (Monaco and Paris, 1974)
T. J. Walsh: *Monte Carlo Opera, 1879–1909* (Dublin, 1975)
G. Favre: *Etudes musicales monégasques: notes d'histoire (18e–20e siècles)* (Paris, 1976)

MARCEL FRÉMIOT

**Monacordio** (Sp.). CLAVICHORD.

**Monagas, Natalie.** *See* HINDERAS, NATALIE.

**Monari, Bartolomeo** ['Monarino'] (*fl* Bologna, ?1670–1707). Italian composer and organist. From the use of the diminutive 'Monarino' it has been supposed that he was the younger brother of Clemente Monari, though their respective periods of activity suggest otherwise. He seems to have spent his whole career at Bologna. According to Fétis he was organist of S Petronio in 1670 and studied with Agostino Filipucci, whom he succeeded as *maestro di cappella* of S Giovanni in Monte (?1679). He was admitted to the Accademia Filarmonica in 1679 and in 1689 was elected *principe*. In 1687 he was involved in a quarrel between his protector Filippo Bentivogli and the Malvezzi family over whether he or G. A. Perti should compose music for the feast of the convent of S Lorenzo (see Ricci). From 1693 to 1697 he was *coadiutore* to G. C. Arresti, organist of S Petronio. The organ pieces heavily edited by Piccioli (supposedly in manuscript in *I-Bc* but not traceable in Gaspari's catalogue) are well-crafted one-movement works of medium length, mostly fugal in style.

WORKS

SACRED

Agare (S. Gualchieri), oratorio, Church of S Filippo Neri, Bologna, 1685, lost
L'enigma di Sansone (A. A. Sacco), oratorio, house of Marquis G. F. A. Spada, Bologna, 1690, lost
Missa brevis, 4vv, 1679, composed for admission to Accademia Filarmonica, score *I-Baf*
Laudate pueri, A, T, B, vns, 14 July 1707, score *Bc*
Miserere, 4vv, ripieno, attrib. only to 'Monari', score *A-Wn*

OTHER WORKS

Catone il giovane (G. B. Neri), opera, Teatro Formagliari, Bologna, lost
8 cantatas, *I-Nc*; 1 cantata, *MOe*
1 cantata, 1685[1]
2 sonatas, org, [c1697][8]
6 sonatas, 1 gigue, orig. org, ?*I-Bc*; ed. G. Piccioli (Bologna, 1933)

BIBLIOGRAPHY

*EitnerQ*; *EitnerS*; *FétisB*; *RicordiE* ('Bologna'); *SchmidlD*
C. Ricci: *I teatri di Bologna nei secoli XVII e XVIII* (Bologna, 1888/*R*1965)
G. Gaspari: *Catalogo della biblioteca del Liceo musicale di Bologna*, v, ed. U. Sesini (Bologna, 1943/*R*1970)

THOMAS WALKER

**Monari, Clemente** (*b* Bologna, ?c1660; *d* ?Forlì, in or after 1729). Italian composer and violinist, probably the younger brother of Bartolomeo Monari. He began his career as 'musico di violone' to Marquis Guido Rangoni of Modena, as indicated in his op.1 (1686), containing 'the first works of a young man'. By 1692 he was in the service of Duke Anton Ulrich at Brunswick, where he probably remained until 1703 or shortly before and where he had three operas performed in 1692. From 1703 to at least 1706 he was *maestro di cappella* of Reggio Emilia Cathedral, and he held a similar position at Forlì Cathedral from 1713 to 1729.

WORKS

OPERAS

*(lost unless otherwise stated)*

Il Pirro, ?Venice, *D-SHsk*; Act 1 by Monari, Act 2 by A. Fiore, Act 3 by A. Caldara
Gl'amori innocenti, Brunswick, 1692
La Libussa, Brunswick, 1692
Il Muzio Scevola, Brunswick, 1692
L'Aretusa (P. d'Averara), Milan, 1703
L'amazzone corsara (G. C. Corradi), Milan, 1704
Il Teuzzone (A. Zeno), Milan, 1706; Act 1 by P. Magni, Acts 2, 3 by Monari
L'Atalanta (Zeno), Modena, 1710
I rivali generosi (Zeno), Reggio Emilia, 1710, collab. F. A. Pistocchi, G. M. Cappelli
Arias, some probably from Il Teuzzone, *E-Mn*

ORATORIOS

*(lost unless otherwise stated)*

La lite de' fiori, Cremona, 1691
Il fasto depresso, Modena, 1692, *I-MOe*
La Purità trionfante, Modena, 1711
S Cecilia, Forlì, 1713

La Clotilde, Forlì, 1721; Bologna, 1722, as La conversione di Clodoveo
Il ripudio di Vasto, Bologna, 1724
La fuga gloriosa di S Pellegrino Lazioso, Forlì, 1728
Il Beato Stanislao Kostka, Bologna, 1729

OTHER WORKS

Balletti e correnti da camera, 2 vn, bc, op.1 (Bologna, 1686)
Sonate, 2 vn, vle/hpd (Modena, c1705)
8 cantatas, 1v, bc (incl. 1 perf. 1728), *D-B*, *Bds*, *GB-Ob*
Mass, 7 other sacred works, 3–5vv, str, org, bc, *D-Bds*
Mass, 3 other sacred works, 4–8vv, wind, str, bc; single parts of 6 other
sacred works: *I-Baf*

BIBLIOGRAPHY

*EitnerQ*; *FétisB*; *LaMusicaD*; *SchmidlDS*
F. S. Quadrio: *Della storia e della ragione d'ogni poesia*, v (Milan,
1744), 512, 519

ELVIDIO SURIAN

**Monarino.** *See* MONARI, BARTOLOMEO.

**Monasterio, Jesús** (*b* Potes, Santander, 21 March 1836;
*d* Potes, 28 Sept 1903). Spanish violinist and composer.
He studied the violin, first with his father and then in
Valladolid. A child prodigy, in 1843 he played in
Madrid before Queen Isabel II, who became his
patron, and then in many Spanish towns. In 1851 he
was awarded a grant to go to Brussels, where he completed his studies with Bériot at the conservatory, and
where he won the *prix extraordinaire*. After several
highly successful concert tours of Europe, he returned
to Madrid and was named honorary violinist of the
royal chapel in 1854. He became professor of the violin
in the Madrid Conservatory in 1857 and director in
1894. In the meantime he made several concert tours in
Europe, always with acclaim. On the death of Bériot in
1870, he was offered the post of professor of the violin
at the Brussels Conservatory, but did not accept it,
preferring to remain in Spain. In Madrid he contributed
greatly to the diffusion of chamber and orchestral
music, founding in 1863 the Quartet Society, which for
a number of years put on regular concerts of chamber
music. In 1864 he began conducting, becoming in 1869
conductor of the Concert Society, in which he promoted
orchestral works of the great Romantic and neo-
classical composers, until then almost unknown in
Spain. His compositions are mostly for violin or for
orchestra, but also include a few religious works for
voices. The best known is *Adiós a la Alhambra* (for
violin and piano), about which Meyerbeer was
enthusiastic when he heard it in 1862 in Berlin. In
general, however, Monasterio was less important as a
composer than as a soloist and, above all, as an organizer and promoter of instrumental music in Madrid,
which at that time was overshadowed by Italian opera.

BIBLIOGRAPHY

SAJ [J. Alarcón]: *Un gran artista* (Madrid, 1910)
L. Villalba: *Ultimos músicos españoles del siglo XIX*, i (Madrid, 1914),
63ff
J. A. Ribó [pseud. of J. Subirá]: 'El archivo epistolar de don Jesús de
Monasterio', *Academia* (Madrid, 1961)
J. Subirá: 'Don Jesús de Monasterio: novísimos apuntes biográficos',
*Academia* (1972), 13

JOSÉ LÓPEZ-CALO

**Moncada (Garcia), Francisco** (*b* Indaparapeo, 18 Jan
1922). Mexican musicologist and folklorist. He studied
music with Miguel Bernal Jiménez, Blas Galindo and
José Pablo Moncayo and folklore with Vicente T. Mendoza and Virgina Rodríguez at the Mexican National
Conservatory, graduating as Maestro de Música. Later
he held appointments as professor of solfège at the
conservatory (from 1949) and professor of music at the
National University (1966–7), and also taught music in

state schools (1944–70). He has worked as a choral
conductor (1956–63) and on cultural television programmes (1967–8). His writings include a collection of
60 biographies of Mexican musicians, an analysis of
song from historical, geographical, literary and musical
angles, and a collection of traditional children's games;
he has also written a textbook on music theory and
composed some popular and instructional music.

WRITINGS

'Recolección folklórica', *Anuario de la Sociedad folklórica de México*,
vii (1951), 73
'Cómo Juegan los Niños', *Previsión y seguridad*, xxiii (Monterrey,
1959)
'Necesidad de crear en México un Instituto de folklore musical', *IV
Congreso nacionale de música: México 1964*
*Asi juegan los niños* (Mexico City, 1966, rev. 4/1974 as *Juegos infant-
iles tradicionales*)
*Las mas sencilla, util y practica: teoria de la música* (Mexico City,
1966, 5/1974)
*Pequeñas biografias de grandes músicos mexicanos* (Mexico City, 1966)
*Los magueyes* (Mexico City, 1971) [analytical study of the song]

CARMEN SORDO SODI

**Moncayo García, José Pablo** (*b* Guadalajara, 29 June
1912; *d* Mexico City, 16 June 1958). Mexican composer. He studied the piano with Hernández Moncada
and composition with Huízar and Chávez at the Mexico
City Conservatory, where he joined Ayala, Contreras
and Galindo in a 'Group of Four' dedicated to propagat-
ing new Mexican music. Chávez appointed him pianist
(1932), percussionist (1933), subdirector (1945) and
artistic director (1946–7) of the Mexico SO, and he
was conductor of the National SO (1949–52). His
*Huapango*, a colourful, orgiastic piece mixing three
folkdances of that name, was introduced by Chávez in
1941 and frequently conducted by him thereafter. Moncayo's major triumph, however, was the opera *La
mulata de Córdoba*, a reworking of the Mexican legend
of the black enchantress who, when called before the
Inquisition in late colonial times, vanished in a puff of
smoke.

WORKS
(*selective list*)

Opera: La mulata de Córdoba (1, A. Lazo, X. Villarrutia), Mexico City,
Palace of Fine Arts, 23 Oct 1948
Orch: Huapango, 1941; Sym., 1944; Sinfonietta, 1945; 3 piezas, 1947;
Sym. no.2, inc.; Simiente, pf, orch, inc.

Principal publishers: Ediciones Mexicanas de Música

BIBLIOGRAPHY

S. Moreno: 'José Pablo Moncayo García', *Enciclopedia universal illus-
trada: supplemento annual, 1957–1958* (Barcelona, 1959), 241f

ROBERT STEVENSON

**Mönch von Salzburg.** *See* MONK OF SALZBURG.

**Monckton, (John) Lionel (Alexander)** (*b* London, 18
Dec 1861; *d* London, 15 Feb 1924). British composer
and music critic. He was educated at Charterhouse and
Oriel College, Oxford, where he did much acting and
wrote incidental music for the University Dramatic
Society productions, but he took up law as a career and
was called to the Bar in 1885. After writing dramatic
and musical criticism for the *Pall Mall Gazette* he later
joined the *Daily Telegraph* as an assistant to Clement
Scott and Joseph Bennett. A song submitted to George
Edwardes was used in the burlesque *Cinder-Ellen up too
late* (1891), and he continued to contribute numbers to
Edwardes's productions, collaborating with Ivan Caryll
on early musical comedy scores. These works often
owed much of their success to Monckton numbers such
as 'Jack's the boy' (*The Geisha*), 'A Simple Little String'

(*The Circus Girl*), which was popularized in Paris by Yvette Guilbert, and 'Soldiers in the Park' (*A Runaway Girl*). The first score that was predominantly his own was *A Country Girl* (1902), and he subsequently wrote music for the most successful Edwardian musical comedies, including *The Arcadians* and *The Quaker Girl*. He was married to Gertie Millar, for whom he wrote some of his best numbers, including 'Keep off the Grass' (*The Toreador*), 'Moonstruck' (*Our Miss Gibbs*) and 'Chalk Farm to Camberwell Green' (*Bric-à-brac*). As a writer of gay and striking melodies he stood out from the other musical comedy composers of the time; his light and unpretentious results were often achieved with a good deal of self-criticism and reshaping.

WORKS

(*selective list*)

MUSICAL COMEDIES

The Circus Girl (2, J. T. Tanner, W. Palings, H. Greenbank, A. Ross), 1896, collab. I. Caryll; A Runaway Girl (2, S. Hicks, H. Nicholls, A. Hopwood, H. Greenbank), 1898, collab. Caryll; The Messenger Boy (2, Tanner, A. Murray, Ross, P. Greenbank), 1900, collab. Caryll; The Toreador (2, Tanner, Nicholls, Ross, P. Greenbank), 1901, collab. Caryll; A Country Girl (2, Tanner, Ross, P. Greenbank), 1902; The Orchid (2, Tanner, Ross, P. Greenbank), 1903, collab. Caryll; The Cingalee (2, Tanner, Ross, P. Greenbank), 1904

The Spring Chicken (2, G. Grossmith, Ross, P. Greenbank), 1905, collab. Caryll; The Girls of Gottenberg (2, Grossmith, L. E. Berman, Ross, B. Hood), 1907, collab. Caryll; Our Miss Gibbs (2, Tanner, Ross, P. Greenbank), 1909, collab. Caryll; The Arcadians (3, M. Ambient, A. M. Thompson, A. Wimperis), 1909, collab. Talbot; The Quaker Girl (3, Tanner, Ross, P. Greenbank), 1910; The Mousmé (3, A. M. Thompson, R. Courtneidge, Wimperis, P. Greenbank), 1911, collab. Talbot; The Dancing Mistress (3, Tanner, Ross, P. Greenbank), 1912; The Boy (2, F. Thompson, Ross, P. Greenbank), 1917, collab. Talbot

OTHER WORKS

Contributions to The New Aladdin (1906), Bric-à-brac (1915), We're all in it (1916), Airs and Graces (1917)

Numbers for musical comedies incl. Caryll: The Shop Girl, Felix: Les merveilleuses, Jones: The Geisha, Jones: A Greek Slave, Jones: San Toy, Roger: Topsy-Turvy Hotel [after L'auberge du Tohu-Bohu], other songs

ANDREW LAMB

**Moncrieff, Gladys** (*b* Bundaberg, Queensland, 13 April 1892; *d* Brisbane, 8 Feb 1976). Australian soprano. She began singing at the age of six, toured with her parents' musical company and established an early local reputation. Moving to Sydney in 1912 she was employed by the theatrical entrepreneurs J. C. Williamson as a chorus girl, but soon played small parts and was given her first leading roles during a 1916 South African tour. Her association with the Williamson firm continued for 36 years, with successes in *Maytime*, *The Merry Widow*, *The Chocolate Soldier*, *Kissing Time*, and Gilbert and Sullivan operettas. Her most famous role was Teresa in *Maid of the Mountains*, which, after the 1921 Melbourne opening season of 27 weeks, travelled the Australian theatre circuit continuously for two and a half years; she played Teresa 2500 times in 25 years. Although Moncrieff appeared outside Australia, notably in London in *Riki-tiki* and *The Blue Mazurka* in the 1920s, her greatest popularity was in Australia and New Zealand, where she toured in 1928 with *Rio Rita*. Affectionately known as 'Our Glad' and 'Australia's Queen of Song', she was the best-loved star in the heyday of Australian musical comedy, much praised and admired during a career of 50 years for her warmth of personality and for a quality of singing described by Fritz Kreisler as 'soul in her voice'. She sang for troops in two world wars and in Korea. After her retirement reissues of early recordings ensured her continued fame

and popularity. She wrote an autobiography *My Life of Song* (Rigby, 1971).

ANN CARR-BOYD

**Monday, John.** *See* MUNDY, JOHN.

**Monday, William.** *See* MUNDY, WILLIAM.

**Mondéjar, Alonso de** (*fl* 1502–5). Spanish composer. In January 1502 he entered the chapel of Queen Isabella as a singer, according to an order signed by her at Toledo on 17 August 1502. After the queen's death in November 1504 he entered the royal chapel of Ferdinand V. From 1505 he received an annual salary of 25,000 maravedís. A *Magnificat*, three motets and 12 secular pieces by Mondéjar are extant. 11 villancicos are contained in the Palacio Cancionero; all are late additions to the manuscript. They are set to poems on the theme of courtly love and the unrequited lover's tragic condition. All are for three voices except *Oyan todos mis tormentos*, a public proclamation of the poet's sorrows. The *estribillo* twice has brief imitation, while the stanza is chordal. In *Mios fueron, mi coraçon* Mondéjar rearranged for three trebles Millan's setting of the same text. After the opening imitation Mondéjar's version proceeds quite differently and uses a more felicitous stanza text. In general, Mondéjar's pieces are terse with fluent movement of the parts and frequent imitation.

WORKS

(*all for 3vv unless otherwise stated*)

Edition: *La música en la corte de los Reyes Cátolicos: Cancionero musical de Palacio*, ed. H. Anglès, MME, v, x (1947, 1951) [A i–ii]

SACRED

Magnificat, *E-Bc* 454

Ave rex noster, 4vv, *SE* 203; Ave verum corpus in ara crucis, 4vv, *Bc* 454; Textless motet, *Bc* 454

SECULAR

Amor quiso cativarme, A ii; Camino de Santiago, Bc 454; No desmayes, coraçon, A ii; Mios fueron, mi coraçon, A ii; No penséis vos, pensamiento, A ii; No podrán ser acavadas, A ii; No teneis la culpa, vos, A ii; Oyan todos mis tormentos, 4vv, A ii; Remedio para bevir, A ii; Sospiros, pues que descansa, A ii; Tales son mis pensamientos, A i; Un solo fin de mis males, A i

BIBLIOGRAPHY

F. A. Barbieri: *Cancionero musical de los siglos XV y XVI* (Madrid, 1890), 40

R. Stevenson: *Spanish Music in the Age of Columbus* (The Hague, 1960), 183, 294

ISABEL POPE

**Mondolfi-Bossarelli, Anna** (*b* Pisa, 13 July 1907). Italian musicologist. She studied the piano with Ernesto Consolo, composition with Vito Frazzi and musicology with Arnaldo Bonaventura at the Florence Conservatory. She began her career as a concert pianist (1928–35) and then became piano professor at the Istituto Musicale, Lucca (1935–8). Fascist racial laws forced her to retire from all musical activity until the end of the war when she returned to musicology and music bibliography. In 1947 she was appointed director of the conservatory library, Naples, and began to investigate the music history of the city and conservatory. With Guido Pannain, Vincenzo Vitale and Renato Parodi she founded the *Gazzetta musicale di Napoli* in 1955.

WRITINGS

*L'anima di Macbeth da Shakespeare a Verdi* (Bologna, 1951)

'Il fondo musicale cinquecentesco della Biblioteca Nazionale di Napoli', *CHM*, ii (1957), 277

*Aspetti e caratteri livornesi in un capolavoro napoletano* (Livorno, 1958)

*Autografi di Giordano in San Pietro a Majella* (Foggia, 1959)
'Vita e stile di Francesco Provenzale', *Annuario del Conservatorio di Napoli* (1962–3), 15
'Ancora intorno al codice napoletano dell'*Incoronazione di Poppea*', *RIM*, ii (1967), 294
'Due varianti dovute a Mozart nel testo del "Matrimonio segreto" ', *AnMc*, iv (1967), 124
'La biblioteca del conservatorio di Napoli', *Accademia e biblioteche d'Italia*, xxxviii (1970), 286
'Carattere didascalico della musica a Napoli fino alla fine del XVI° secolo', *Archivio storico per la provincia napoletana*, x (1971), 205
'Mario Savioni e la duplice veste musicale assunta dal testo *Occhi ardenti*', *Rassegna dell'istruzione artistica* (in preparation)
'Riesumazione di uno sconosciuto Scarlatti', *Annuario del Conservatorio di Napoli* (in preparation)
Further articles in *La Scala, Gazzetta musicale di Napoli, Annuario del Conservatorio di Napoli* and *Rassegna dell'istruzione artistica*
CAROLYN M. GIANTURCO

**Mondondone, Girolamo da.** *See* FERRARI, GIROLAMO.

**Mondonville, Jean-Joseph Cassanéa de** (*b* Narbonne, baptized 25 Dec 1711; *d* Belleville, 8 Oct 1772). French violinist, composer and conductor. He was one of two brothers; Jean Cassanéa de Mondonville (called 'le jeune' or 'cadet'; *b* Narbonne, 15 April 1716) was a violinist of the royal chapel, and published *Six Sonates à violon seul et basse continue* in 1767 (previously ascribed to the son of his elder and more famous brother).

Jean-Joseph Cassanéa de Mondonville was one of the most important and most active musicians in Paris in the middle of the 18th century. It may be presumed that he studied with his father, organist of the Maîtrise de St Just at Narbonne. The son is first known of in 1733–4 in Paris, where he published his first volumes of instrumental music and appeared at the Holy Week programme of the Concert Spirituel. The *Mercure de France* of April 1734 (p.796) reported that he performed 'in a very brilliant manner'.

After a spell at the Concert de Lille, Mondonville returned to Paris in 1739 as violinist of the royal chapel and chamber. His performance at the Concert Spirituel on Passion Sunday of 1739 was reviewed as being 'as admirable as it was singular' (*Mercure de France*, March 1739, p.590), a reference to the use of harmonics, doubtless in sonatas from his op.4, *Les sons harmoniques*, which contains as an introduction the first known manual on the playing of harmonics on the violin. Later that season the *Mercure de France* (April 1739, p.803f) reported that on three days different *grands motets* by Mondonville were featured at the concerts, and stated that the 'young master' had already established a reputation as both composer and violinist. In 1739 records show that he received payment for about 100 concerts at Versailles, Compiègne, Fontainebleau and Marly.

From that time, Mondonville was an important figure in Paris musical life. His career as a violinist continued through the 1740s, when he performed both as soloist and with the flautist Michel Blavet, the 'roi des violons' Jean-Pierre Guignon, and the famous soprano Marie Fel. From 1740 Mondonville was associated with the royal chapel as *sous-maître*; in 1744 he succeeded Gervais as *intendant*. He was associated with the Académie Royale de Musique in connection with both the Opéra and the Concert Spirituel, producing operas at the former and *grands motets* at the latter, as well as appearing in chamber music of his own composition. He was also associated with the Théâtre des Petits-Cabinets.

In 1748 Mondonville married Anne-Jeanne Boucon,

*Jean-Joseph Cassanéa de Mondonville: pastel portrait by Maurice Quentin de la Tour (1704–88) in the Musée Antoine Lécuyer, St Quentin*

a well-known harpsichordist (a pupil of Rameau) and a wealthy woman in her own right; she was three years his senior. The marriage was a happy one: at his death his widow said that in 25 years he had not revealed a single fault to her. Their son, Maximilien-Joseph (*c*1749–1808), was an amateur musician who played the violin and the oboe.

Mondonville was not a prolific composer. Certain of his works ranked in popularity with any of his day. The *grands motets* were universally admired; in this genre Mondonville must be considered the principal successor to Lalande. His operas too were popular: *Le carnaval du Parnasse* was performed 35 times in 1749 and was revived in 1750, 1759 and 1767, while *Titon et l'Aurore*, along with Rameau's *Castor et Pollux*, became a chief rallying-point of the French in the Querelle des Bouffons. His lively and resourceful style informed these works; others manifested a certain character, an interest in accommodation and interaction between instruments and types of music. His solo and trio sonatas explored instrumental quality at the expense of virtuosity (three of the latter specify flute and violin, exploiting the idioms of those instruments); his opera *Daphnis et Alcimadure* introduced the Gascon dialect, in a libretto of the composer's authorship; and his oratorio *Les Israélites à la Montagne d'Horeb* revived a type in which the French had lost interest for over half a century.

Mondonville is best known, however, for his *Pièces de clavecin en sonates* (op.3, 1734) and *Pièces de clavecin avec voix ou violon* (op.5, 1748), both of which resulted from his desire to combine the personalities of different media at their most idiomatic. In op.3 the harpsichordist needed the full technique implied by the title 'pièces de clavecin', while the violinist needed that of the solo sonata: it is the simultaneous appearance of these two techniques to which the title refers. In op.5

the voice is added (the parallel title would have been 'Pièces de clavecin en motets'); in spite of the option in the title, both voice and violin are required in all but one of the ten pieces. The music is vigorous, clear, and various in textural deployment. The slow movements in particular display a diversity of formats, from a violin aria accompanied by a highly original keyboard figuration, to a treble aria in the keyboard with counterparts exchanged between the keyboard left hand and the violin, and an Andantino with one instrument in 2/4 and the other in 6/8. Their originality lies in the ingenuity with which Mondonville devised textural variety; his actual ideas, though virile and effective, are less original than their combination.

### WORKS

#### DRAMATIC
*(music lost unless otherwise stated)*

Isbé (pastorale-héroïque, prol, 5, La Rivière), Paris, 10 Oct 1742 (Paris, 1742)
Bacchus et Erigone (opera, 1, La Bruère), Versailles, 1747
Le carnaval du Parnasse (ballet-héroïque, prol, 3, L. Fuzelier), Paris, 23 Sept 1749 (Paris, 1749)
Vénus et Adonis (ballet-héroïque, C. de Messine), Paris, 1752
Titon et l'Aurore (opera, La Marre, Voisenon), Paris, 1753
Daphnis et Alcimadure (pastorale languedocienne, prol, 3, Mondonville), Fontainebleau, 4 Nov 1754; as op.9 (Paris, 1754); rev., Fr. trans., Paris, 1768
Les fêtes de Paphos (ballet-héroïque, 3, Collé, La Bruère, Voisenon), Paris, 9 May 1758; as op.10 (Paris, 1758)
Psyché (ballet entré, 1, Voisenon), Paris, 1762
Thésée (opera, 5, Quinault), Fontainebleau, 1765
Les projects de l'Amour (ballet-héroïque, Voisenon), Paris, 1771

#### SACRED VOCAL

Dates taken from ascriptions by Hellouin [H]; Fétis [F]; La Laurencie [L] or F. Michaud, *Biographie universelle* [M]

Oratorios, music lost: Les Israëlites à la Montagne d'Horeb, 1758, M; Les fureurs de Saül, 1758, M. 1759, H; Les Titans, 1758, M, 1761, H
Grand motets, principal sources *F-A, Pc, Pn*: Dominus regnavit, 1734, H, 1737, F; Jubilate Deo omnis terra, 1734, H, 1737, F; Magnus Dominus, 1734, H, 1737 F; Lauda Jerusalem, 1739, L; Cantate Domino, 1743, L; Nisi Dominus, 1743, H; Venite exultemus, 1743, H; Bonum est, 1745, L; Omnes gentes, 1745, L; Qui confidunt, 1745, L; Laudate Dominum omnes gentes, 1747, H; De profundis, 1748, H; Coeli enarrant, 1750, H; Quam dilecta, 1753 [*Mercure de France*]; In exitu, 1755, H; Laudate Dominum quoniam bonus, 1756, H; Exultate justi, 1758, H
Solo motets: Regina coeli, 1755, H; Simulacra gentium, 1759 [B. Schwarz, *MGG*]

#### INSTRUMENTAL

Sonates, vn, bc, op.1.(Paris, 1733)
Sonates en trio, 2 vn/fl, bc, op.2 (Paris, 1734); ed. R. Blanchard (Paris, 1967)
Pièces de clavecin en sonates, hpd, vn, op.3 (Paris and Lille, 1734), ed. M. Pincherle (Paris, 1935); arr. as 6 sonate a 4, 2 vn, 2 ob, bn, bc [perf. Concert Spirituel, 1749, according to La Laurencie, i, 385], *F-Pn*
Les sons harmoniques, sonates, vn, bc, op.4 (Paris and Lille, 1738)
Pièces de clavecin, hpd, vn/lv, op.5 (Paris, 1748), ed. in Borroff (1958)
Lost works cited in *Mercure de France*: vn concs., 1739 and later; Concert à 3 choeurs (1738); Concert de violon avec chant (1747); Concert de violon, avec voix, orchestre et choeurs (1752); some org arrs. of Ouvertures

### BIBLIOGRAPHY

*FétisB*
N. A. Pluche: *Le spectacle de la nature* (Paris, 1751; Eng. trans., 10/1766)
J.-J. Galibert: *Jean-Joseph Cassanéa de Mondonville* (Narbonne, 1856)
F. Hellouin: *Mondonville: sa vie et son oeuvre* (Paris, 1903)
L. de La Laurencie: *L'école française de violon de Lully à Viotti* (Paris, 1922–4/R1971)
E. Reeser: *De klaviersonate met vioolbegeleiding* (Rotterdam, 1939)
E. Borroff: *The Instrumental Works of Jean-Joseph Cassanéa de Mondonville* (diss., U. of Michigan, 1958)
——: 'The Instrumental Style of Jean-Joseph Cassanéa de Mondonville', *RMFC*, vii (1967), 165
C. Pierre: *Histoire du Concert spirituel 1725–1790* (Paris, 1975)

EDITH BORROFF

**Mondstein, Christian.** Pseudonym of HEINZ KIESSLING.

**Mone, Franz Joseph** (*b* Mingolfsheim, nr. Bruchsal, Baden, 12 May 1796; *d* Karlsruhe, 12 March 1871). German historian. He studied at Heidelberg where he later taught and served as librarian; he taught at Louvain, 1827–31, and was director of the archives at Karlsruhe, 1835–68. He worked on north European paganism, and published documents on Latin and Greek religious services; musicologically he is notable for his text edition *Lateinische Hymnen des Mittelalters* (Freiburg, 1853–5); from his references here to Greek hymns he seems to have been aware of the verse structure of Greek medieval liturgical poetry, the discovery of which is usually credited to JEAN BAPTISTE PITRA. In this matter see W. Myer: 'Pitra, Mone und die byzantinische Strophik', *Gesammelte Abhandlungen zur mittellateinischen Rhythmik*, ii (Berlin, 1905), p.287.

MILOŠ VELIMIROVIĆ

**Monet, Jean.** See MONNET, JEAN.

**Monetarius** [Münzer], **Stefan** (*b* Kremnica, Slovakia; *fl* 1490–1525). Slovak theorist. He studied at Kraków and probably in Vienna, where he may have taught; he published his *Epithoma utriusque musices practice* in Kraków in 1515–20, dedicated to his patron Jerzy Turzon, a member of a family that had served the cause of humanism. Its first part deals with chant, its second with mensural theory (largely based on Gaffurius). In his treatise Monetarius quotes a poem by the German humanist Walter Eck, who was in Kraków 1511–17.

### BIBLIOGRAPHY

R. Rybaric: *Stephan Monetarius a jeho hudobná teória* (Bratislava, 1960)

ELŻBIETA WITKOWSKA-ZAREMBA

**Monferrato, Natale** (*b* Venice, *c*1603; *d* Venice, before 23 April 1685). Italian composer and organist. He was a priest and was probably a pupil of Giovanni Rovetta. He took part in the competition for the second organist's post at St Mark's, Venice, in January 1639 (not 1640, as Caffi and others stated), when Cavalli was appointed, but the following month he became a singer there at the modest annual salary of 60 ducats. On 20 January 1647 he was made vice-*maestro di cappella* at a salary of 120 ducats, which was raised in 1650 to 160 ducats and three years later to 200. The dedication of his op.4 of 1655 reveals that he was teaching at the Conservatorio dei Mendicanti, although no details of his appointment there are known. On the death of Rovetta he was again passed over in favour of Cavalli, for the post of *maestro di cappella* of St Mark's in 1668, but he finally obtained it in April 1676 following Cavalli's death and held it until his death. He was an energetic director: he attempted to raise the standards of the choir by re-auditioning the older singers and by reducing its numbers, thus allowing higher salaries to be paid, though he met with bureaucratic difficulties in carrying out this policy. He was much appreciated by the procurators, who twice (in 1670 and 1682) awarded him a special grant for dedicating compositions to them. His successor was Legrenzi, whose appointment from 23 April 1685 indicates that Monferrato died shortly before this. In his later years he was a partner with Giuseppe Sala in the ownership of a publishing house. His will shows that he was a reasonably wealthy man; he left various musical instruments to G. B. Volpe and Pietro Varalli, while the residue went to the Scuola del

Sacramento in the church of S Bartolomeo di Rialto, where a marble bust of him was erected in the sacristy.

Monferrato's works for St Mark's seem mainly to have been in the *stile antico*, of which documentary evidence also suggests he was much in favour. His masses are very austere examples of this manner, displaying few of the expressive devices of chromaticism and dissonance that other composers used to modify its traditional basis. His motets and psalms, by contrast, show the influence of his teaching at the Mendicanti, especially the solo motets of op.4, which he wrote for its pupils. These are attractive works, displaying elements of both the melodious arias and expressive recitative found in the Venetian operas of the mid-17th century. They are not quite so clearly diatonic as those of the Bologna school, but with their harmonic sequences and regular rhythms they approach the idiom of the Italian sacred cantata, especially as individual sections within them are often expansive and highly developed.

WORKS
*(all printed works published in Venice unless otherwise stated)*

Salmi concertati, 5–8vv, 2 vn, org, op.1 (1647)
Salmi, 8vv, org, op.2 (1653)
[20] Motetti concertati . . . lib.I, 2, 3vv, op.3 (1655)
[21] Motetti . . . lib.I, 1v, op.4 (1655)
Motetti . . . lib.III, 1v, op.6 (1666)
[21] Motetti concertati, 2, 3vv (1669)
Salmi concertati . . . lib.II, 3–8vv, 2 vn, va, org, op.8 (1671)
Salmi brevi, 8vv, org, op.9 (Bologna, 1675)
[9] Salmi concertati, 2vv, 2 vn, va, org, op.11 (1676)
[6] Missae, 4, 5vv, org, op.13 (1677)
Salmi concertati, 3, 4vv, 2 vn, va, org, op.16 (1678)
Antiphonae, 1v, op.17 (1678)
Motetti . . . lib.III, 2, 3vv, op.18 (1681)
Missae et Magnificat, op.19 (1681)

2 motets, 1656[1]; Dulce sit, 2vv, bc, 1688[2]; Exaltabo te Deus, 1v, 1670[1]

Magnificat, 8vv, org; 2 Magnificat, 4vv: *D-Bds, Dlb*
Salve regina, 3vv, bc, 1655, *Bds*
1 cantata, 1v; 2 motets, 3vv, insts: *Kl*

BIBLIOGRAPHY
F. Caffi: *Storia della musica sacra nella già cappella ducale di San Marco in Venezia dal 1318 al 1797* (Venice, 1854–5, repr. 1931)
G. Fantoni: 'Scoperta e ricupero di musiche autografe ed inedite dei veneziani maestri N. Monferrato e G. F. Brusa', *Gazzetta musicale di Milano* (1877), 147, 166

DENIS ARNOLD

**Monferrina.** A country dance, Piedmontese in origin, popular in England in the early 19th century (sometimes called 'monfrina', 'monfreda' or 'manfredina'). Typical examples, in 6/8 metre, appear in *Wheatstone's Country Dances for 1810* and *Companion to the Ballroom* (c1816). Clementi composed two sets, of 12 (op. 49, 1821) and six (wO15–20).

**Mongini, Pietro** (*b* Rome, 1830; *d* Milan, 27 April 1874). Italian tenor. He started his career as a bass, but by 1853 was singing tenor roles at Genoa. In 1855 he made his Paris début at the Théâtre-Italien as Edgardo in *Lucia di Lammermoor*, and in 1857 sang at Reggio Emilia in the first performance of Achille Peri's *Vittor Pisani* and in Donizetti's *Anna Bolena*. He first appeared at La Scala on 11 March 1858 as Arnold in *Guillaume Tell*, and made his London début on 25 April 1859 as Elvino in *La sonnambula* at Drury Lane, where he also sang Arrigo in the first London performance of Verdi's *Les vêpres siciliennes* (in Italian, 27 July). In 1860 he sang Manrico in *Il trovatore* at La Scala and Huon in Weber's *Oberon* at Her Majesty's Theatre. He returned to London every year from 1862 to 1873, appearing either at Her Majesty's, where his many roles included Don Alvaro in the first London performance of

*La forza del destino* (22 June 1867), or at Covent Garden, where he made his début as Gennaro in *Lucrezia Borgia* (24 October 1868). On 24 December 1871 he created the role of Radamès in the first performance of *Aida*, at the Cairo Opera House. According to contemporary reports, his genuinely heroic tenor voice was not used with much subtlety or intelligence, but in such roles as Arnold, Manrico and Alvaro the sheer brilliance of sound and the excitement of his performances compensated for any lack of artistry.

BIBLIOGRAPHY
J. H. Mapleson: *The Mapleson Memoirs* (London, 1888); ed. H. Rosenthal (London, 1966)
C. Gatti: *Il Teatro alla Scala nella storia e nell'arte 1778–1963* (Milan, 1964)

ELIZABETH FORBES

**Mongolia.** *See* MONGOL MUSIC.

**Mongol music.** The geographical areas in which Mongols live fall into three political divisions: the People's Republic of Mongolia (which is inhabited by about 1,250,000 Mongols); the USSR (Buryats and Kalmyks); and China, where the majority of Mongols are found. This article concerns the music of all these Mongol peoples, although the examples quoted are taken from the People's Republic of Mongolia.

1. History. 2. Musical concepts. 3. Musical and textual characteristics. 4. Traditional music. 5. Instruments. 6. Shamanic and Lamaist music. 7. New music.

1. HISTORY. The earliest references to Mongol music date from the 13th century. Joannes de Plano Carpini, the first European traveller to Mongolia (1246), spoke of 'saddle songs' (warrior songs); William of Rubrouk and Marco Polo both remarked on the originality of the instruments they saw at the court of the nobles. The earliest Mongol source on music, the *Secret History of the Mongols* (13th century), testifies to the existence of a sung literature, the function of the drum at gatherings, the efficacy of shamanic singing and the political role of the bards: for example, Genghis Khan entrusted political missions to his favourite fiddle player, Arghasun; it was also a bard who was sent by Arghun Khan, regional ruler of Persia, with a message to Philip the Good of France (1289).

Gmelin, who made an expedition to Siberia (1735–45), was responsible for the first published transcription of Mongol music. Collections of text and music have appeared since the end of the 19th century, and the earliest sound recordings were made in the early 20th century (37 Kalmyk songs, recorded in 1910 by Ochirov; 24 Oirat Mongol songs, recorded by Vladimircov, 1912–13; both in the folklore archives of the Academy of Sciences, USSR). However, only the recordings made by Haslund-Christensen of Mongol music in Inner Mongolia have resulted in a substantial publication which is considered authoritative.

2. MUSICAL CONCEPTS. Despite the antiquity of certain instruments, Mongol music is predominantly vocal; instruments have only an accompanimental role, faithfully following the voice in unison, although they have an autonomous function in religious music. Instrumental ensembles traditionally were found only in court music, a practice which declined with the collapse of the Mongol empire and had disappeared by the beginning of the 20th century, since when they have been found only in folk ensembles.

The Mongols conceive of music as a means of communication. It is regarded as a vehicle (the traditional instruments are 'mounts', as reflected in their zoomorphic design, their use and their nomenclature) and a language (the verbs meaning 'to sing' are etymologically derived from the terms 'vowel', 'summons', 'manner of speaking', which reflects the linguistic nature and function of singing). Harmony as a concept implies the presence of an instrument. The Mongols' concept of rhythm does not seem inherent in that of music: the rhythm reflects the pace of the 'mount instrument', being frequently designated by the term *zhoroo* ('to amble'). Mongols do not consider music an appropriate accompaniment to labour (the work song as such is rare and non-traditional, and should not be confused with the propitiation which is recited or sung before work). Musical activity is accessible to everyone; formerly, anyone who at a festive time was unable either to sing or to play the fiddle was severely reproached and penalized with such punishments as slaps administered with sheep's ribs, or having to swallow enormous cupfuls of fermented mare's milk. The actions of festivity, singing and milking are interrelated. Certain musical genres (e.g. epic and shamanic songs) are performed exclusively by professional bards, who come from all levels of society and do not form a separate group.

3. MUSICAL AND TEXTUAL CHARACTERISTICS. On the threshold of music Mongols use certain quasi-musical vocal registers which are reserved for a given genre: for example, the nasal recitation of counting-rhymes, the high-pitched rapid utterance of blessings, the murmuring of maledictions, and the imitation of hunted animals' cries. This concern with imitating natural sounds, such as birdcalls, the gushing of springs or the galloping of horses (the young bard's ability to perform these is tested before his apprenticeship), is related to the Mongols' concept of music as a symbolic journey to the supernatural world. Since birds are able to join the sky and springs able to join the underworld, since in general nature itself is inhabited and governed by spirits, then by imitating these natural sounds one can communicate with both the natural sounds and the supernatural.

Every song text obeys the laws of Mongol poetry, comprising alliteration, assonance, initial rhyme, phonetic and semantic parallelism of the lines or groups of lines, and the addition of meaningless syllables which balance and link the lines, serving as a support to the melodic form. Vocalises are highly developed and seem to be greatly valued. Parallel to the close relationship between music and phonetics, the link between music, literature and poetry is closer than with any other form of expression or communication. Traditionally, bardic recitation constitutes the only form of dramatic performance (apart from the noble courts, where dramatic art and choreography were commonly found). Similarly, dance is known in only two forms: those that are individual and performed by women who move only the upper part of the body (a type of dance particularly developed in western Mongolia); and those that are collective, sung round-dances, performed in connection with socio-economic activity, found especially among the Buryats.

Mongol music is anhemitonic pentatonic. There is no indigenous musical notation, although in certain Mongol collections of texts from the beginning of the 20th century references to 'high register' or 'low register' appear to indicate ornamentation.

4. TRADITIONAL MUSIC. Vocal music, whether accompanied or solo, may be grouped into three broad categories: the epic genre, song, and specialized vocal techniques.

(*i*) *Epic song*. The Mongol epic (*tuul'* in the west, *ülger* elsewhere) belongs to the great heroic tradition of Central Asia. A noble and exclusively masculine genre, formerly highly developed, it survives only in fragmentary or reduced forms. It consists of narrative song, sometimes more than 20,000 verse lines long, in which spoken passages may be inserted. The verse form is not fixed, and there is a rough correspondence of one syllable to one note. The rhythm and melody vary according to the episode being described, such as combat, sorrow, riding or the appearance of spirits. The same melodic phrase is repeated for the duration of the episode. Ornamentation is minimal and the intervals are restricted, with improvisation an important aspect: in a fixed framework, which is at once textual, stylistic, rhythmic and melodic, the bard gives free rein to his gifts and to the inspiration of the moment. He is sensitive to the nature and reactions of his listeners as well as to current news, which can lead him to modify the content and to integrate new elements with the mythological and fantastic and with the warrior tradition of the epic. The instrumental accompaniment, which is optional, is provided by the lute in western Mongolia, and by the fiddle elsewhere. All aspects of the performance – singing, narrative and accompaniment – are the responsibility of the same bard. Epic singing is prohibited in summer but considered indispensable in autumn before hunting, and also takes up winter evenings. About 20 Khalkha epics (central Mongolia), about 50 Oirat epics (western Mongols) and about two dozen Buryat epics are known. The best known are *Gesar* (*see* TIBET, §4), *Zhangar* and *Khan Kharanguj*. There are no more than a handful of expert performers left.

Two song genres may be considered the living representatives of the epic: the historical type, which includes the *domog* (legend, i.e. epic fragment or summary) and the *tüükhen duu* (historical song, elaborated on the basis of real events); the second is the glorification type, which includes the *magtaal* (hymn, in praise of heroes, places or sacred objects, including horses, springs, fiddles, bows etc) and the *tsol* (in praise of a title, e.g. of the victorious wrestler or racehorse).

(*ii*) *'Long' and 'short' song*. The song is the most widespread genre, accessible to all. It is sung solo, sometimes accompanied in unison on the fiddle. Two categories may be distinguished: the *urtïn duu* (long song) and the *bogïno duu* (short song).

The Mongol *urtïn duu* is, like the Romanian *hora lunga*, 'an infinite melody of which the performer improvises the architecture with the aid of a play with constant formulae which he blends, repeats or evades at his pleasure' (Brăiloiu). It is a strophic song without a real refrain, performed with the full voice. The voice production, which is strained and guttural, is so distinctive that the song is immediately recognizable as Mongol; breath is taken freely, but as seldom as possible, in order not to interrupt the ornamentation. The ornaments are largely improvised, but they always occur at the same point in each melodic strophe. The longer and more plentiful the vocalises, the greater the admiration of the audience. The range (up to three octaves) and the size of intervals may be considerable, and this is emphasized by the frequent passage from throat voice to falsetto (which is more pronounced in men than in women). As a general rule text and melody are not inseparable: it is possible to vary infinitely any single melody, just as the same melodic variant can be sung to different words.

For the Mongol, the long song evokes the steppe; vast and drawn out like the steppe, it generates nostalgia – hence the preference for slow tempos, long melodic lines, wide intervals and the absence of measured rhythm other than that dictated by the singer's breath. The adjective *urtīn* (long) indicates that this genre lays emphasis on the musical rather than the textual aspect, and the long song is absolutely incompatible with work. With regard to the function and content of the long song, one can distinguish 'context-free' and 'context-bound' songs. The context-free songs may be performed in a variety of situations, for example as entertainment after festivities, as companionship for the rider, as a means of expression, or of teaching or relaying information. According to their content they may be grouped in cycles, such as young married women's laments and songs praising the nomad's virtues; their tone is inclined to be lyrical. Love, the underlying theme of these songs, is considered from three inseparable aspects – human love, love of the horse and love of the country. The context-bound songs form part of certain rituals, and as such are considered necessary to the correct execution of the ritual and are endowed with symbolic efficacy. The more specific their function, the more they are bound by a specific form. Some are introductory songs

*Mongol street musician with morin khuur (spike fiddle)*

to family or public ceremonies, with long texts, sometimes sung antiphonally by two groups; others accompany certain traditional activities, such as sports (archery, races) or husbandry (preparation of a horse for a race, taming a mare for milking). These are designated by specific terms that safeguard the symbolic value of the texts, which have since been forgotten.

The *bogīno duu* (short song) differs in form from the *urtīn duu* by precise rhythm, reduction of ornamentation and extreme vivacity of performance. Range and intervals remain wide. Easier and freer than the long song, this genre also flourishes to a greater extent. Originally satirical in essence, the *bogīno duu* covers increasingly diverse themes. Drinking-songs belong to this category as well as the work songs which have appeared.

*(iii) Specialized vocal techniques.* Imitative vocal techniques, which are disappearing, are an exclusively male repertory. The most notable of these, *khöömiy* (pharynx), designates the simultaneous emission of two notes by one singer; one note provides the fundamental and the other is a harmonic resulting from a modification of the mouth cavity without moving the lips, which stay half-open. The upper partial varies according to the mouth formation of either a back vowel (a, o, u), which gives a low partial, or a front vowel (e, ö, ü), which gives a high partial. The cheek and tongue muscles are taut. The performance is short. The possible relationship between this technique, known also among the Tuvan and Buryats in the USSR (*see* CENTRAL ASIA, §I, 5), and the divinatory use of the jew's harp, remains to be explored. *Limbedekh* (derived from the *limbe*-flute) designates the imitation 'through the nose' of the flute, obtained by a process analogous to that which produces the upper partial in the *khöömiy* technique (ex.1).

5. INSTRUMENTS. The *khuur*, a term which covers both string and lamella (i.e. jew's harp) instruments, constitutes the most indigenous Mongol category of instruments. They have in common the facts that they are performed by men only, that they symbolize mounts, that they play a divinatory role and that they accompany recitatives of a more or less magical character. The best known is the *morin khuur* (horse-head fiddle, also called *khil-khuur*; see illustration), a spike fiddle with a trapeziform body consisting of a wooden frame and a goatskin soundboard and back; at the top of the wooden pegbox the head of a horse (or of a dragon) is carved, with two long lateral pegs, the animal's 'ears' (*chikhe*). The two strings, one 'thick' or low, the other 'thin' or high, are of horsehair, as is the bow (see illustration).

Carrying less prestige but easier to play is the *dörvön chikhtey khuur* or *khuuchir* (spike fiddle). Widespread in the east, it has rear pegs and two or four strings of goat gut imprisoning the bow (cf Chinese *hu-ch'in*); the body is small and cylindrical. The plucked lute, *tobshuur*, with two strings and trapeziform body, is the equivalent of these fiddles among the western Mongols. *Amankhuur*, 'mouth' *khuur*, designates the shamanic jew's harp.

Apart from the many types of whistles, reeds and pipes used in hunting, the best-known wind instrument is the bamboo *limbe* (transverse flute, cf Tibetan *glingbu*), which has at least eight holes and a mirliton, and is played by shepherds.

The majority of instruments performed at spectacular displays are of Chinese origin, or are widely known in

Ex.1 *Khöömiy*, vocal harmonics (Vargyas, 1968)

The music of the Mongol Lamaist monasteries is a faithful reproduction of the Tibetan model. The songs, which are in Tibetan, are characterized by the same low-pitched tones; the temple orchestra instruments are identical with those of the Tibetan service and are played in an analogous fashion. Mongol Lamaist chant is sometimes notated according to the Tibetan *dbyangs-yig* system (*see* TIBET, §2(ii)).

7. NEW MUSIC. 20th-century song composers use the short song as a model, playing with its formal suppleness and diversifying the textual themes to include such subjects as the glories of the revolution and the benefits of the cooperative. Performers of the long songs and the fiddle are becoming fewer, but small amateur groups who perform the traditional songs are numerous. The national folklore orchestra is composed of two *morin khuur*, a *shandz*, a *khuuchir*, a *yoochin*, an elaborated *limbe*, a drum and a pair of cymbals of the lamaic type. Along with a style of music inspired by the Soviet model, a new genre (comparable to opera) is developing, a modern variant of the epic, in which traditional songs are integrated and the pentatonic scale retained. The best known of these 'opera' composers is B. Damdinsüren, the author of *Uchirtay gurvan tolgoy*. Other noteworthy operas are *Khan bürged* ('The king eagle') and *Sharay golïn gurvan khaan* ('The three kings of the river Sharay'), which revive the epic of Gesar.

BIBLIOGRAPHY

J. G. Gmelin: *Reise durch Sibirien*, iii (Göttingen, 1752), 370
A. M. Pozdneyev: *Obraztsy narodnoy literaturï mongol'skikh plemen* [Examples of folk literature of Mongol tribes], i (St Petersburg, 1880)
C. Stumpf: 'Mongolische Gesänge', *VMw*, iii (1887), 2
A. D. Rudnev: 'Melodii mongol'skikh plemen [Melodies of the Mongol tribes], *Zapiski Imperatorskovo russkovo geograficheskovo obshchestva po otdelu etnografii*, xxxiv (1909), 395
A. D. Rudnev and T. Zhamcarano: *Obraztsy narodnoy slovesnosti mongol'skikh plemen* [Examples of folk literature of Mongol tribes] (Petrograd, 1913–18)
B. Krasin: '24 Melodii s mongol'skim tekstom sobrannïye v severnoy Mongolii'v 1910–14 gg.' [24 melodies with Mongol texts, collected in northern Mongolia in 1910–14], *Prilozheniye k Zhivoy Starine*, i (1914), 20
J. van Oost: 'La musique chez les Mongols des Urdus', *Anthropos*, x–xi (1915–16), 358–96
I. Krohn: 'Mongolische Melodien', *ZMw*, iii (1920–21), 65
P. Berlinsky: *Mongol'skiy pevets i muzïkant Ul'dzuy-Lubsan-Khurchi: opït analiza mongol'skovo ustnovo muzïkal'no-poeticheskovo tvorchestva* [The Mongol singer and musician Ul'dzuy-Lubsan-Khurchi: an attempt to analyse the oral art of music and poetry in Mongolia] (Moscow, 1933)
M. Trituz: *Khal'mg dun* [Kalmyk songs] (Moscow, 1934)
N. de Tourhout: *Dix-huit chants et poèmes mongols* (Paris, 1937)
E. Emsheimer and H. Haslund-Christensen: *The Music of the Mongols* (Stockholm, 1943)
C. Brăiloiu: 'Musique populaire roumaine', Musée de l'Homme MH 49 [disc notes]
S. Lkhamsüren: *Duunï tüüver* [Collection of songs] (Ulan Bator, 1957)
N. Nadmid and S. Tsoodol: *Mongol ardïn duunuud* [Mongol folksongs] (Ulan Bator, 1959)
B. Rintchen: *Folklore mongol* (Wiesbaden, 1960)
D. Luvsansharav: *Duunï tüüver* [Collection of songs] (Ulan Bator, 1960)
P. Aalto: 'The Music of the Mongols: an Introduction', *Aspects of Altaic Civilization*, ed. D. Sinor (Bloomington, 1963), 59
L. Vargyas: 'Performing Styles in Mongolian Chant', *JIFMC*, xx (1968), 70
P. Donner: 'Mongolia', LREP 113 [disc notes]
G. Kara: *Chants d'un barde mongol* (Budapest, 1970)
*Urtïn duu* [Long song], ed. Ulsïn khevleliyn gazar (Ulan Bator, 1970)
B. F. Smirnov: *Mongol'skaya narodnaya muzïka* [Mongol folk music] (Moscow, 1971)
L. Vargyas: 'Mongol nepzene' [Mongol folk music], Hungaroton LPX 18013–14 [disc notes]
R. Hamayon: 'Chants mongols et bouriates', Musée de l'Homme LDM 30 188 [disc notes]

ROBERTE HAMAYON

Asia; played by women, they frequently accompany dancing. The most notable examples are the *yatag* (board zither; cf Chinese *cheng*), which was in favour at the Kublai court and consists of a long wooden rectangular body with a slightly curved soundboard over which 10 to 14 strings are stretched across movable bridges; the *yoochin* (dulcimer; cf Chinese *yang ch'in*), in which 14 double metal courses are stretched over the flat trapeziform body and are struck with two beaters; and the *shudraga* or *shandz* (long-necked lute; cf Chinese *san-hsien*), which has three plucked or bowed strings.

6. SHAMANIC AND LAMAIST MUSIC. Music is an integral part of shamanic ritual among Mongols, expressing one aspect of the communication with the supernatural which the shaman conducts. The songs, which are little ornamented and restricted in range and interval, are close in form to the epic genre. *Duudlaga* (invocations) relate the progress of contact with the spirit: thus a gradual acceleration of rhythm is found, with sharp breaks, sighs, sobs or sounds imitative of birdcalls; whereas the *tamlaga* are recitations by the shaman of the spirits' speech.

The shaman accompanies himself on the *khets*, a round frame drum with a single skin made of deer hide. He holds it by a grip running across the inside of the frame, equipped with metal jingles, in which musical expression is united with magical function. The shaman strikes the skin with a beater, using variable force and rhythm according to the stage in the ritual. The drum contributes towards inducing a state of trance and serves as the shaman's mount (a ceremony 'animates' the drum; the beater is the whip and the drumstrokes imitate the gallop). On occasion the drum also functions as a divinatory instrument, but this role falls more properly to the jew's harp. These traditions, however, seem to have disappeared.

**Monica** [monicha, monaca] (It.). A song popular in Italy during the first half of the 17th century and sometimes used for sets of instrumental variations. The keyboard version in ex.1 shows the musical scheme and the opening line of the text, the lament of a young girl forced to become a nun. This single line of text was cited by Pazio in a manuscript dated 1610 (*I-BRq*), by Benedetto Sanseverino in his *Intavolatura facile* for guitar (1620) and by Matteo Coferati in *Corona di sacre canzoni* (1675). The chordal accompaniment for the music appears in almost all 17th-century Italian tablatures for the five-course guitar; often two standard *riprese* or ritornellos were added at the end (*see* RIPRESA, ex.1*a*). One guitar example (in *I-Fr* 2804) is called 'Aria venetiana da. la monica', and the same music appears in another manuscript with the title 'Aria Venetia che cantava Scappino' (*I-Fr* 2793).

Ex.1 *Madre mia non mi far monaca, US-LAu* 51/1

Versions of the song for keyboard, for discant and bass and for lute have survived in various manuscripts (*I-Fn* Magl.XIX 115 and 138, *Bc* Q34 and *Fn* Magl.XIX 179 respectively). Frescobaldi composed two sets of keyboard variations called *Parte sopra lamonicha* (1615, six variations; 1637, 11 variations, including some from the earlier set), as well as a *Missa sopra l'Aria della monaca* (*I-Rsg*). Other keyboard variations appear in Bernardo Storace's publication of 1664 and in the Chigi manuscripts (CEKM, xxxii/3). Biagio Marini wrote a *Sonata sopra la monica* (1626) for instrumental ensemble.

The *monica* melody appears in the *Neder-landtsche Gedenck clanck* of Adriaen Valerius (1626) with the title *Almande nonette* or *Une jeune fillette*; the former title had appeared earlier in a Phalèse collection (1568), the latter in a collection of French chansons (1576) and in Vallet's lutebook (1615). A similar melody occurs in the chorale *Von Gott will ich nicht lassen* and in the noël *Une vierge pucelle* by Lebègue.

BIBLIOGRAPHY
R. Casimiri: 'Girolamo Frescobaldi, autore di opere vocali sconosciute, ad otto voci', *NA*, x (1933), 1–31
C. van den Borren: 'A proposito de l'Aria della monicha', *NA*, x (1933), 200
R. Casimiri: 'Un antico *noel* du l'*aria de la monicha*', *NA*, xi (1934), 211
F. B. Pratella: 'Ancora dell'*Aria della monicha* e dell'*Aria di Fiorenza*', *NA*, xi (1934), 214
L. H. Moe: *Dance Music in Printed Italian Lute Tablatures from 1507 to 1611* (diss., Harvard U., 1956), 184ff
J. M. Ward: 'Music for *A Handefull of Pleasant Delites*', *JAMS*, x (1957), 175
G. Reese: 'An Early Seventeenth-century Italian Lute Manuscript at San Francisco', *Essays in Musicology in Honor of Dragan Plamenac* (Pittsburgh, 1969), 253
J. Wendland: *La monica: the History of a Migrating Melody* (diss., Duke U., 1974)
——: '"Madre non mi far monaca": the Biography of a Renaissance Folksong', *AcM*, xlviii (1976), 185

RICHARD HUDSON

**Moniglia, Giovanni Andrea** (*b* Florence, 22 March 1624; *d* Florence, 21 Sept 1700). Italian librettist and personal physician to Cardinal Gian Carlo de' Medici. Moniglia, despite lack of appreciation on the part of the academic reformers of the early 18th century, must be reckoned among the most original librettists of the 17th century. His comic libretto, of which the most famous is *Il potestà di Colognole*, better, though incorrectly, known as *La Tancia* (Florence, 1657, music by Jacopo Melani), established a genre that continued unbroken into the next century. His *Ipermestra* (Florence, 1658, music by Cavalli) and *Ercole in Tebe* (Florence, 1660, music by Melani) set a standard for the *festa teatrale*. *Il ritorno d'Ulisse* (Pisa, 1669, music by Melani) and *Enea in Italia* (Pisa, 1670, music by Melani) anticipate in many respects Quinault's librettos for Lully, and the signs of reform are clearly visible in *Il tiranno di Colco* (Pratolino, 1688, music by Pagliardi).

His librettos were published under the title *Poesie dramatiche* (3 vols., Florence, 1689–90, 2/1698). The great majority were written for Florence with music by Jacopo Melani and Lorenzo Cattani, but they were also much in demand in Venice and Vienna. Other composers who set them include Cesti, Legrenzi, Pasquini and Pietro Andrea Ziani.

BIBLIOGRAPHY
H. Goldschmidt: *Studien zur Geschichte der italienischen Oper im 17. Jahrhundert*, i (Leipzig, 1901)
R. L. Weaver: *Florentine comic operas of the 17th century* (diss., U. of North Carolina, 1958)

ROBERT LAMAR WEAVER

**Moniot d'Arras** (*fl* 1213–39). French trouvère. ('Moniot' is an Old French diminutive for 'monk'.) According to *Amours, s'onques en ma vie* his given name was Perron, but the authorship of this work has been questioned. The Moine d'Arras who appears as respondent to Guillaume li Vinier in the jeu-parti *Moines, ne vous anuit pas* is assumed to be the same; Moniot was probably at one time associated with the Abbey of St Vaast in Arras. Poems by him are apparently addressed to Robert III, Count of Dreux, to his brother, Jehan de Braine, to Gérard III, Seigneur of Picquigny and Vidame of Amiens, and to Alphonse of Portugal, Count of Boulogne. Two quotations from Moniot's poems appear in the *Roman de la violette*, written by Gerbert de Montreuil *c*1230. The charming pastourelle *Ce fut en mai* was used by Hindemith in his *Nobilissima visione*. Its attribution has also been questioned.

Moniot wrote in a variety of genres and forms. In addition to the pastourelle and jeu-parti and the customary *chansons courtoises* he wrote two religious poems, both based on earlier models and their melodies, both apparently youthful works. The two initial and two concluding lines of the first strophes of *Bone amour* and *Li dous termines* form the opening and close of two *motets entés* (Motets 593 and 668 in Ludwig). The authorship of the Motet 528c is credited to Moniot in the Vatican Chansonnier, where it appears in monophonic form. While six chansons employ bar form, *Dame, ains que je voise* and *Quant voi les prés* use the repeat of the initial phrase that is characteristic of many rotrouenges. *Bone amour* is non-repetitive. *A ma dame, Chançonete a un chant* and *Nus n'a joie* begin in this fashion, but they each repeat one or more early phrases towards the end of the melody. *Amours n'est pas* and *Amours, s'onques en ma vie*, which share the same poetic form and melody, display the unusual structure *ABA¹A²ACDEFG*. The same melody appears also as one of three settings of *Qui bien aime*, a poem of different form requiring the merging of the third and fourth phrases into one.

A comparatively large amount of information regarding rhythmic structure is available for Moniot's melodies. The motet quotations of *Li dous termines* and *Bone amour* indicate the 1st and 2nd modes respectively, while the 1st mode is indicated for large portions of *Ne me dones pas talent* in *F-Pn* fr.846. Passages exhibiting regular disposition of ligatures occur in *A l'entrant de la saison, Amours n'est pas, Chançonete a un chant, Dame, ains que je voise* and *Quant voi les prés*, while the modal transcription proposed for *Ce fut en mai* seems quite apt. *Bone amour* apparently enjoyed extraordinary popularity, since it served as the model for four later works. *Chançonete a un chant* and *Li dous termines* were each imitated in one later poem and *Ne me dones pas talent* in two.

## WORKS

Editions: *Grundriss einer Formenlehre des mittelalterlichen Liedes*, ed. F. Gennrich (Halle, 1932) [F]
  *Troubadours, Trouvères, Minnesang und Meistergesang*, ed. F. Gennrich, Mw, ii (1951; Eng. trans., 1960) [G]

Abbreviations:
(R, a) etc  MS (using Schwan sigla – see SOURCES, MS) in which a late setting of a poem occurs
(nm)  No music

A l'entrant de la saison, R.1896
A ma dame ai pris congié, R.1087 (R)
Amours me fait renvoisier et chanter, R.810 = 796 (nm)
Amours n'est pas, que c'on dit, R.1135 [model for: Anon., 'Toi reclaim, vierge Marie', R.1183; contrafactum: Amour, songues, Qui bien aime], chanson couronée (R, V)
Amours, s'onques en ma vie, R.1231 [contrafactum: Amours n'est pas] (V)
Bone amour sans tricherie, R.1216 [model for: Anon., 'Qui a chanter veut entendre', R.631; Anon., 'Por ce que verité die', R.1136; Anon., 'C'est en mai quant reverdie', R.1203; Anon., 'De la vierge nete et pure', R.2114], F 238
Ce fut [=L'autrier] en mai, R.94, F 208, G 31 (V)
Chançonete a un chant legier, R.1285 [model for: Anon., 'Talent me rest pris de chanter', R.793]
Dame, ains que je voise en ma contree, R.503
De haut lieu muet la chançon que je chant, R.304 [?modelled on: Robert de Reins, 'Plaindre m'estuet', R.319 = 320] (nm)
Encor a si grant poissance, R.242 (V)
L'autrier [=Ce fut] en mai, R.94 (V)
Li dous termines m'agree, R.490 [model for: Gillebert de Berneville, 'Thumas Herier, j'ai partie', R.1191] (R)
Ne me dones pas talent, R.739 [model for: Thibaut IV, 'Phelipe, je vous demant/Dui amant', R.334; Richart de Fournival, 'Mere au roi comnipotent', R.713] (R)
Nus n'a joie ne soulas, R.382 (R, V)
Plus ain que je ne soloie, R.1764
Quant voi les prés flourir et blanchoier, R.1259 = 1318
Qui bien aime, a tart oublie, R.1188 [probably modelled on: Anon., 'Quant voi venir la gelee', R.518 = 516 (without music); music in MS i model for: Anon., 'De chanter m'est pris envie', R.1140a; music in MSS P and X adapted from Amours n'est pas] (a)

DOUBTFUL WORKS
Compaignon, je sais tel chose, R.1939
De joli cuer enamouré, R.430 [model for: Anon., 'Au dous comencement d'esté', R.435; Anon., 'Au partir d'esté et de flours', R.2033]

WORKS OF PROBABLE JOINT AUTHORSHIP
Moines, ne vous anuit pas, R.378 (with Guillaume li Vinier)
Par main s'est levee, Motet 528c

BIBLIOGRAPHY
F. Ludwig: *Repertorium organorum recentioris et motetorum vetustissimi stili* (Halle, 1910)
H. P. Dyggve: 'Moniot d'Arras et Moniot de Paris', *Mémoires de la Société néo-philologique de Helsinki*, xiii (1938), 3–252
For further bibliography *see* TROUBADOURS, TROUVÈRES.
THEODORE KARP

**Moniot de Paris** (*fl* mid-13th century). French trouvère poet and composer. He may be identifiable with the Monniot who was the author of a *Dit de Fortune* written in 1278, but is not to be confused with Moniot d'Arras (*fl* 1213–39). Nine songs without conflicting attributions are ascribed to Moniot de Paris in a group of MSS that represents the main tradition of trouvère song. In these sources he is usually grouped with trouvères who were active in the mid- and late 13th-century; this fact tends to reinforce Dyggve's estimate that he was active at about the middle of the century.

Moniot's works are of interest largely because of the prevalence of relatively simple forms with refrain. Particularly prominent is the rotrouenge; the four examples are invariably of the utmost simplicity in musical construction, and their melodies show none of the sophistication of the *chanson courtoise*. An extreme illustration of this tendency is *Lonc tens ai mon tens usé* with its 'vadu, vadu, vadu, va' refrain; its melody, made up of four phrases, is restricted almost entirely to repeated notes beginning on C, progressing to B, A, and finally cadencing on G. Other songs, not of the rotrouenge type, are also characterized by simple melodies. *Au nouvel tens*, for instance, has three basic melodic phrases which together do not exceed the range of a major 6th. The pastoral character of this song is also found in several others; their musical simplicity and rustic themes are probably not coincidental. Evidence for the popularity of these melodies is provided by the fact that we have contrafacta for no fewer than four (*Au nouvel tens, Je chevauchoie l'autrier, Li tens qui reverdoie* and *Qui veut amours*). *Je chevauchoie* was used twice by Moniot himself.

## WORKS

A une ajournee, R.492 (rotrouenge)
Au nouvel tens que nest la violete, R.987 [model for: Anon., 'Au renouvel du tens que la florete', R.980; Anon., 'Mainte chançon ai fait de grant ordure', R.2111]
Je chevauchoie l'autrier, R.1255 [= Pour mon cuer] (rotrouenge)
L'autrier par un matinet, R.965
Li tens qui reverdoie, R.1756 [model for: Anon., 'Fou est qui en folie', R.1159]
Lonc tens ai mon tens usé, R.475 (rotrouenge)
Pour mon cuer releecier, R.1299 [= Je chevauchoie] (rotrouenge)
Quant je oi chanter l'alouete, R.969
Qui veut amours maintenir, R.1424 [model for: Moine de Saint-Denis or Guiot de Dijon, 'D'amour me doit souvenir', R.1468; Richart de Semilli, 'Pars amours ferai chanson', R.1860]

BIBLIOGRAPHY
F. Gennrich: *Die altfranzösische Rotrouenge* (Halle, 1925) [incl. four edns.]
H. Spanke: *Eine altfranzösische Liedersammlung* (Halle, 1925) [incl. edn. *Au nouvel tens*]
H. P. Dyggve: 'Moniot d'Arras et Moniot de Paris', *Mémoires de la Société néo-philologique de Helsinki*, xiii (1938), 3–252
For further bibliography *see* TROUBADOURS, TROUVÈRES.
ROBERT FALCK

**Moniuszko, Stanisław** (*b* Ubiel, nr. Minsk, 5 May 1819; *d* Warsaw, 4 June 1872). Polish composer.

1. LIFE. He came from a patriotic family of Polish landowners. From his earliest years he showed an interest in music, and when his family settled in Warsaw (1827) he began to learn the piano and rudiments of music from August Freyer, also taking private lessons in general subjects. In 1830 the Moniuszko family moved to Minsk, where the boy attended the Gymnasium (until 1837) and studied music with Dominik Stefanowicz, a local pianist. His first compositions date from this time: two mazurkas written in an album of Aleksandra Müller, his future wife. These were still the music of an amateur, but in autumn 1837 he began to study composition in Berlin with C. F. Rungenhagen, who also instructed him in choral conducting. A year later the firm of Bote & Bock published three of his songs to words by Adam Mickiewicz, soon favourably received by Polish music critics. In 1840 he returned to Poland and, after his marriage, obtained a post as organist at St John's, Vilnius, also giving piano lessons and occasionally conducting the theatre orchestra. He became closely acquainted with the novelist Józef Ignacy Kraszewski and corresponded with the humorist Aleksander Fredro, contacts which stimulated his interest in dramatic music. He began to compose intensively, writing his first operas and several other stage works, as well as sacred music (*Litanie Ostrobramskie* ('Ostra Brama litanies') and secular cantatas (*Milda* and *Nijoła*). It was at this period that he first conceived the idea of writing a collection of songs that would have a universal appeal: in 1842 the *Tygodnik Petersburgski* carried an announcement for *Śpiewnik domowy* ('Songbook for home use'), the first volume of which was published the following year. This collection aroused a lively response from writers on music and much interest among the public.

Moniuszko's visit to Warsaw in 1846 was of crucial importance; he met Józef Sikorski, an influential writer on music and the future editor of the journal *Ruch muzyczny*, Oskar Kolberg, a well-known folksong collector, and Włodzimierz Wolski, a poet and the future librettist of Moniuszko's opera *Halka*. On 1 January 1848 a concert performance of the first (two-act) version of *Halka* was given in Vilnius; the same year saw the first performance of the cantata *Milda* and the symphonic overture *Bajka* ('The fairy tale'). Shortly afterwards two other works were performed in St Petersburg, where Glinka and Dargomïzhsky showed appreciation of Moniuszko's talent. Even in later years Moniuszko maintained a friendly relationship with both these composers, and with Cui, who had been his own pupil. In the same period further *Songbooks for Home Use* appeared, contributing to his popularity. After a staged performance of *Halka* in Vilnius in 1854, he began to press for a performance of the opera in Warsaw. He went there in 1857 and, together with Wolski, made substantial alterations to the work, expanding it to four acts and adding the music which has become best known, the arias of the main characters (Halka and Jontek) and the ballet movements.

On 1 January 1858 the première of the new version of *Halka* took place in Warsaw and was received by the public with great enthusiasm. Polish reviewers recognized the importance of the event and stressed the originality of Moniuszko's style, also appreciated by

Hans von Bülow (*NZM*, 12 November 1858). Moniuszko became known as the foremost Polish composer of opera; performances of *Halka* began to take place not only in Polish cities, but also in Prague (1868), Moscow (1869) and St Petersburg (1870). When the opera *Flis* ('The raftsman', 1858) also met with success, he moved with his family to Warsaw (1859), where he was engaged as opera conductor at the Grand Theatre. Musical conditions at the theatre allowed Moniuszko's style to develop in his next operas, *Hrabina* ('The countess'), *Verbum nobile*, *Straszny dwór* ('The haunted manor'), and in further cantatas and sacred

Stanisław Moniuszko

music. Wishing to improve his material situation, a continual problem with ten children, from 1864 he taught harmony and counterpoint at the Music Institute, where he also conducted a choral ensemble. One of the fruits of his work as a teacher was the *Pamiętnik do nauki harmonii* ('Textbook on harmony'), published in 1871. Large crowds attended his funeral, which became the equivalent of a national demonstration.

2. WORKS. Moniuszko is the most representative opera composer of the Polish 19th-century national school, and his historical role is comparable to that of Smetana, Glinka, The Five, Weber, Rossini and Auber. In spite of stylistically distinctive features, the works of these composers are linked by strongly marked national traits. In Moniuszko's operas this tendency is apparent in the librettos, whose plots represent the typically Polish world of nobility and of gentry in the knightly tradition (*The Haunted Manor*, *The Countess*, *Verbum nobile*, the unfinished *Rokiczana*), an anachronistic world in 19th-century Europe. Particularly in the oper-

ettas, common people are also introduced as characters; the plot of *Halka* reveals dramatic analogies with Auber's *La muette de Portici*, with their common Romantic subject of a simple girl (Halka is a young woman from the mountains), seduced and abandoned by a powerful lord. The apparently banal story was able to arouse in the audience associations with the peasants' revolt in southern Poland in 1846 and with the European revolutionary movement of 1848; and in this respect, too, there is an analogy with *La muette de Portici*. In *The Haunted Manor*, the plot, naive though touched with humour, became a pretext for presenting the splendid customs and traditions of Polish chivalrous nobility; after the tragic failure of the January revolt in 1861 the performance thus had a decidedly political accent and fostered patriotic feeling. In a country deprived of statehood, the audience interpreted the artist's intention clearly; *The Haunted Manor* became associated with Poland's aspirations to such an extent that after the third performance the tsar's censor removed the work from the repertory of the Grand Theatre.

Stylistically, Moniuszko may be linked with both Italian (notably Rossini) and French composers, particularly those of *opéra comique*, whose features may be seen in his operettas. He was especially fond of Auber's music and introduced his works to the Warsaw stage, conducting them himself and adding his own interludes. In Moniuszko's operas arias, recitatives and ensembles predominate, typical of 19th-century opera, but in *The Haunted Manor* there is a greater use of choral writing, testifying to his technical command of writing for many voices. The national element is seen above all in the use of typical Polish dances; for instance he often used the mazurka for ballet music (as in *The Haunted Manor* and *Halka*) and the rhythms of the polonaise in vocal parts (*The Haunted Manor*, *Halka*, *The Countess*, *Verbum nobile*). There is also sporadic use of the rhythms of other folkdances: the krakowiak (*The Haunted Manor*, *The Raftsman*) and kujawiak (*The Raftsman*).

Moniuszko was also the foremost Polish 19th-century composer of song, a form preferred when political and economic conditions made symphony orchestras, concert halls and professional performances impossible; further, the song was the only form which could be developed freely and universally, and performed in the home to serve as testimony to the 'Polishness' of society. In these conditions Moniuszko resolved to enrich the Polish vocal repertory and began to issue his *Songbooks for Home Use*. Of his 12 songbooks (267 songs with piano accompaniment), only six appeared during the composer's life. The songs are simple, usually strophic, although there are also ballads and dialogues. The texts are treated mainly syllabically, with melodies based on a single rhythmic pattern, often drawn – as in the operas – from folkdances: the krakowiak, mazurka, kujawiak and oberek, as well as the polonaise. In spite of their simplicity the songs bear witness to the composer's great melodic inventiveness, the most distinctive evidence of his talent and artistic individuality; and his works became a model for later Polish composers. His songs were enormously popular in 19th-century Poland and his more important works have maintained a place in the concert repertory, bearing out the composer's own words: 'that which is national, indigenous, local, that which is an echo of our childhood memories, never ceases to please the inhabitants of the country'.

Among Moniuszko's most important cantatas are those with texts by Adam Mickiewicz – *Widma* ('Phantoms') and *Sonety krymskie* ('Crimean sonnets'). The latter is remarkable for its expressive melody; some parts of the cantata take the form of variation and reprise. His sacred works were generally intended for performance by amateurs. Instrumental music occupies only a marginal place in his output.

After Moniuszko's death the collection of his manuscripts (compositions, documents, letters) was charged to a special committee formed in 1891 by the Warsaw Music Society, which also initiated the publication of his works. Polskie Wydawnictwo Muzyczne began an Urtext edition of all his works in 1965.

## WORKS

Edition: *S. Moniuszko: Dzieła* [Works], ed. W. Rudziński (Kraków, 1965–) [MD]

All manuscripts are in *PL-Wtm*; printed works were published in Warsaw unless otherwise stated.

### OPERAS

Halka (2, W. Wolski, 1846–7, concert perf., Vilnius, 1 Jan 1848; rev. (4, Wolski), 1857, staged perf., Warsaw, 1 Jan 1858 (1861)
Sielanka [Idyll] (2, W. Marcinkiewicz), ?1848, lost
Bettly (comic opera, 2, Scribe and A. H. J. Mélesville: Le chalet, trans. F. Schober), 1852, Vilnius, 20 May 1852
Flis [The raftsman] (1, W. Bogusławski), 1858, Warsaw, 24 Sept 1858, vocal score (1902)
Rokiczana (3, J. Korzeniowski), 1858–9, inc., Ballada o Florianie Szarym [Ballad of Florian the Grey], Bar, chorus, orch (1913)
Hrabina [The countess] (4, Wolski), 1859, Warsaw, 7 Feb 1860 (1889)
Verbum nobile (1, J. Chęciński), 1860, Warsaw, 1 Jan 1860 (Kraków, 1953)
Straszny dwór [The haunted manor] (4, Chęciński), 1861–4, Warsaw, 28 Sept 1865 (1937)
Paria (prol, 3, Chęciński, after C. Delavigne), 1859–69, Warsaw, 11 Dec 1869, vocal score (1913)
Trea (2, J. S. Jasiński), 1872, inc.
Undated: Biuraliści [The bureaucrats] (comic opera, 1, F. Skarbek); Cudowna woda [Water of life] (comic opera, 2), lost except ov.; Sen wieszcza [The seer's dream] (Rosier, de Leuven: Le songe d'une nuit d'été, trans. W. Syrokomla), lost except song in Śpiewnik domowy [Songbook for home use], vii (1877), 2 other frags.

### OPERETTAS

Nocleg w Apeninach [A night's lodging in the Apennines] (A. Fredro), Vilnius, 1839
Ideał czyli Nowa Preciora [Ideal or The New Preciosa] (O. Milewski), 1840, Vilnius, 1840
Karmaniol czyli Francuzi lubią żartować [Carmagnole or The French like joking] (Milewski, after Théaulon de Forges and Jaime), 1841
Żółta szlafmyca [The yellow nightcap] (F. Zabłocki), 1841, lost except Kolęda, 4vv, *Kalendarz wydawany przez Warszawskie towarzystwo dobroczynności* (Warsaw, 1863)
Nowy Don Quichot czyli Sto szaleństw [The new Don Quixote or 100 follies] (Fredro), 1841, Lwów, 1849, vocal score (1927)
Loteria [The lottery] (Milewski), 1842 or 1843, Minsk, Nov 1843 (1908)
Cyganie [The gypsies] (F. D. Kniaźnin), 1850, Vilnius, 20 May 1852, rev. as Jawnuta, Warsaw, 5 June 1860
Beata (Chęciński), 1870 or 1871, Warsaw, 2 Feb 1872
Undated: Nowy dziedzic [The new landlord] (M. Radziszewski); Walka muzyków [The musicians' struggle] (W. Marcinkiewicz), lost; Pobór rekrutów [Conscription] (Marcinkiewicz), lost except song in Śpiewnik domowy [Songbook for home use], viii (1908)

### OTHER STAGE

Incidental music: Kupiec wenecki [The Merchant of Venice] (Shakespeare), perf. 1870–71; Zbójcy [The robbers] (Schiller), 1870–71; Hamlet (Shakespeare), Warsaw, 24 March 1871; music to 11 other plays
Ballets: Monte Christo (after Dumas), Warsaw, 27 Aug 1866; Na kwaterze [In the quarters], Warsaw, 6 Sept 1868; Figle szatana [The Devil's jokes], Warsaw, 1 Dec 1870, collab. A. Münchheimer

### SACRED VOCAL

[4] Litanie Ostrobramskie [Ostra Brama litanies], solo vv, chorus, orch, 1843, 1849, before 1854, 1855; MD D/v/30
7 masses: d (Funeral), 1850 (1862); e, 1855 (1860); Eb, 1865 (1874); a (1870); Bb, Warsaw, 19 May 1872 (1873); g (Funeral) (1873); Db (1874)
Requiem aeternam, solo vv, chorus, orch (1890)
Other works: mass frags., smaller choral and solo works

SECULAR VOCAL

Milda (after J. I. Kraszewski: Witolorauda), cantata, solo vv, chorus, orch, Vilnius, 18 Dec 1848 (1909)

Nijoła (after Kraszewski: Witolorauda), cantata, Vilnius, 8 March 1852

Madonna (Petrarch: Sonnets), B solo, chorus, orch, St Petersburg, 20 March 1856 (Kraków, 1961)

Ballada o Florianie Szarym [Ballad of Florian the Grey] (J. Korzeniowski), Bar, chorus, orch, 1858–9 (1913) [from Rokiczana, opera]

Widma [Phantoms] (after A. Mickiewicz: Dziady), cantata, solo vv, chorus, orch, before 1859, Warsaw, 1865 (1900)

Sonety krymskie [Crimean sonnets] (Mickiewicz), cantata, solo vv, chorus, orch, 1867, Warsaw, 16 Feb 1868 (1901)

Pani Twardowska (Mickiewicz), ballad, solo vv, chorus, orch, Warsaw, 8 Dec 1869

4 other cantatas

360 songs, MD A/i–vi, 267 orig. pubd in Śpiewnik domowy [Songbook for home use], i–vi (Vilnius, 1843–59), vii–xii (Warsaw, 1877–1910)

INSTRUMENTAL

Orch: Bajka [The fairy tale], ov., Vilnius, 1 May 1848 (Kraków, 1949); Kain, ov., St Petersburg, March 1856; Polonaise de concert, arr. pf (1866); Uwertura wojenna [Military overture], Vilnius, 19 March 1857

Chamber: 2 str qts, no.1, d, 1839, no.2, f, before 1840, both MD E/ii/33; mazurkas, polonaises and other pieces, pf, MD E/iii/34

PEDAGOGICAL

Pamiętnik do nauki harmonii [Textbook on harmony] (1871)

BIBLIOGRAPHY

A. Walicki: Stanisław Moniuszko (Warsaw, 1873)

J. Karłowicz: 'Rys żywota i twórczości Stanisława Moniuszki' [Account of Moniuszko's life and creative work], Echo muzyczne, teatralne i artystyczne, ii (1885), nos.66–8, 70, 72, 74, 76, 78

A. Poliński: Moniuszko (Kiev, 1914)

Z. Jachimecki: 'S. Moniuszko and Polish Music', Slavonic Review, ii (1924), 533

——: Moniuszko (Warsaw, 1924, enlarged edn., 1961)

H. Opieński: S. Moniuszko: życie i dzieła [Moniuszko: life and works] (Lwów, 1924)

Z. Jachimecki: 'Stanislaus Moniuszko', MQ, xiv (1928), 54

S. Niewiadomski: Stanisław Moniuszko (Warsaw, 1928)

H. Feicht: 'Pamiętnik do nauki harmonii S. Moniuszki' [Moniuszko's textbook on harmony], PRM (1936), 45

F. Kęcki: A Catalogue of Musical Works of M. Karłowicz and S. Moniuszko (Warsaw, 1936)

Z. Jachimecki: Muzyka kościelna Moniuszki [Moniuszko's church music] (Warsaw, 1947)

I. Belza: 'Monyushko v Rossii', SovM (1952), no.6, p.73; Pol. trans., Muzyka, iii/9–10 (1952), 30

W. Rudziński and J. Prosnak: Almanach Moniuszkowski: 1872–1952 (Warsaw, 1952)

E. Nowaczyk: Pieśni solowe S. Moniuszki: katalog tematyczny [Moniuszko's solo songs: thematic catalogue] (Kraków, 1954)

W. Rudziński: Stanisław Moniuszko (Kraków, 1954, 4/1972)

——: Stanisław Moniuszko (Kraków, 1955–61)

J. Prosnak: Stanisław Moniuszko (Kraków, 1964, 2/1969)

T. Kaczyński: Dzieje sceniczne 'Halki' Stanisława Moniuszki [Performance history of Moniuszko's Halka] (Kraków, 1969)

W. Rudziński and M. Stokowska, eds.: Stanisław Moniuszko: listy zebrane [Moniuszko: collected letters] (Kraków, 1969)

K. Mazur: Pierwodruki Stanisława Moniuszki [The first editions of Moniuszko's works] (Warsaw, 1970)

ELŻBIETA DZIEBOWSKA

**Monk, Christopher (William)** (b Delhi, 28 Dec 1921). English cornett maker. Monk studied history at Lincoln College, Oxford, from 1940 to 1944; from 1942 to 1945 he studied the trumpet with George Eskdale. He is now a full-time maker and player of the cornett, sackbut and serpent. His first cornett was completed in March 1955, and his first cornettino in 1956; he first broadcast as cornett player (with Brian Baker) on 25 April 1958. In 1968, with Len Ward, he devised an inexpensive system of manufacturing resin cornetts; thousands of them have since gone to all parts of the world, doing much to stimulate the modern revival of this difficult instrument.

WRITINGS

'The Older Brass Instruments: Cornett, Trombone, and Trumpet', Musical Instruments through the Ages, ed. A. Baines (Harmondsworth, 1961), 277

EDWARD H. TARR

**Monk, Edwin George** (b Frome, 13 Dec 1819; d Radley, nr. Oxford, 3 Jan 1900). English organist and composer. After studying in London with Hullah, Henry Phillips and Macfarren, he became organist and music master at St Columba's College, Stackallan, in 1844. In 1847 he settled in Oxford, where he helped to found the University Motet and Madrigal Society and became its first conductor. He graduated BMus in 1848 and proceeded DMus in 1856. In 1847 he was one of the four founder members of staff at Radley College where he developed a fine tradition of choral worship. He was appointed organist of York Minster in 1859, retiring in 1883. One of the original members of the Musical Association (1874), he was also an amateur astronomer (elected FRAS, 1871) and a Bible scholar, and compiled the librettos for Macfarren's oratorios St John the Baptist, The Resurrection and Joseph. Monk's most important work was his editing; his compositions are of little value.

EDITIONS

The Order of Chanting the Daily Prayer and the Litany as used in the College of St. Columba (1845)

Novello's Partsong Book (London, 1850)

The Anglican Chant Book (London, 1850)

The Anglican Choral Service Book (London, 1858)

Chants for the Daily Psalms, as used in York Minster (London, 1859)

with F. A. G. Ouseley: The Psalter and Canticles Pointed for Chanting (London, 1862)

with R. Corbet Singleton: The Anglican Hymn Book (London, 1868)

Unison Chants for the Psalter (London, 1892)

BIBLIOGRAPHY

J. D. Brown and S. S. Stratton: British Musical Biography (London, 1897/R1971)

B. Rainbow: The Choral Revival in the Anglican Church, 1839–1872 (London, 1970)

STEPHEN BANFIELD

**Monk, Thelonious (Sphere)** (b Rocky Mount, North Carolina, 10 Oct 1920). Black American jazz pianist and composer. In the early 1940s he took part in the jam sessions at Minton's Playhouse, New York, where he is said to have contributed significantly to the harmonic idiom of the 'bop' style. He played briefly in the bands of Lucky Millander (1942) and Coleman Hawkins (1944), but principally led his own small groups. He made recordings (1947–54), but remained in relative obscurity, though at the height of his creativity as a composer; later recordings (1955–62) brought him considerable praise. He continued to lead small groups in the 1960s and 1970s, reaching a peak of popular acclaim with his recordings of the mid-1960s.

Early 'location recordings' from Minton's show that Monk had mastered the fluent Hines style, but by the late 1940s and early 1950s he had evolved an unorthodox approach to the piano, involving a heavy attack and distinctive 'clanging' timbre, crushed notes and clusters, and left-hand chords made up of 2nds and 6ths instead conventional triadic jazz harmonies. This economical approach emphasized his unique, often humorous sense of rhythmic anticipation and delay, tempo suspension and silence, and allowed him when improvising to explore different aspects of themes with unusual rigour, extending even to his accompaniment of soloists. His concern with structure and free variation of motif presented a strong challenge to his sidemen, many of whom, such as Sonny Rollins, Max Roach and John Coltrane, were greatly influenced by his method, as were the pianists Mary Lou Williams and, in his later work, Bud Powell. Monk's jazz compositions frequently used unconventional chord progressions and melody, and include such standard jazz pieces as *Criss-Cross,* *Epistrophy, Round about Midnight, Straight no Chaser* and *Misterioso,* as well as music for the film *Les liaisons dangereuses* (1959). (*See* JAZZ, fig.10.)

BIBLIOGRAPHY

G. Schuller: 'Thelonious Monk', *Jazz Review,* i (1958), Nov, 22; iii (1960), June, 26
M. Harrison: 'Thelonious Monk', *Just Jazz 3,* ed. S. Traill (London, 1959), 14
N. Hentoff: *Thelonious Monk: a List of Compositions Licensed by B.M.I.* (New York, 1961)
——: *The Jazz Life* (New York, 1961), 178ff
A. Hodeir: *Toward Jazz* (New York, 1962), 156ff
J. Grunnet Jepsen: *Jazz Records: 1942–1962,* v (Copenhagen, 1963)
J. Goldberg: *Jazz Masters of the Fifties* (New York, 1965), 24ff
M. Williams: *The Jazz Tradition* (New York, 1970), 138ff
V. Wilmer: *Jazz People* (London, 1970), 41ff
M. Harrison: *A Jazz Retrospect* (Newton Abbot, 1976), 28ff

RAN BLAKE

**Monk, William Henry** (*b* London, 16 March 1823; *d* London, 18 March 1889). English church musician and composer. He was a pupil of Thomas Adams, J. A. Hamilton and G. A. Griesbach, and began his career in 1841 as organist of St Peter's, Eaton Square. After holding similar posts at St George's, Albemarle Street (1843), and St Paul's, Portman Square (1845), he was appointed choirmaster (1847) and organist (1849) at King's College, London. While at King's he came under the influence of William Dyce, professor of fine arts, whose recent scholarly investigation of the principles of plainchant had prepared the way for its use in the Anglican service. Monk assisted in that development by contributing the first articles on the subject to the journal of the Tractarian Society for Promoting Church Music, the *Parish Choir* (1846–51), of which he later became musical editor.

As organist and choirmaster of the new church of St Matthias, Stoke Newington (1852), Monk established daily choral services that presented a unique model of the Tractarian ideal – the choir leading the people, the music chosen to suit the calendar, the psalms chanted to plainsong. At the same time he was professor of vocal music at King's College, London (1874), at the National Training School for Music (1876) and at Bedford College, London (1878).

In 1857 Monk was made musical editor of *Hymns Ancient and Modern* (1861) for which he wrote 'Eventide', his famous tune for *Abide with me.* He wrote many other popular hymn tunes as well as anthems and service music, and edited several collections of hymns and metrical psalms. He was awarded an honorary MusD at Durham in 1882.

BIBLIOGRAPHY

B. Rainbow: *The Choral Revival in the Anglican Church, 1839–1872* (London, 1970)

BERNARR RAINBOW

**Monke, Josef** (*b* Elberfeld, 18 March 1882; *d* Cologne, 17 Nov 1965). German brass instrument maker. From 1896 to 1900 he studied instrument making with Mitsching, and trumpet playing with Liebe, in Elberfeld. He then began a series of visits destined to make him one of the best-informed makers of his time: to Knoth (not Kuth) in Danzig (1900), Moritz in Berlin (1901–2), Enders in Mainz (1902), where he worked on the Alschausky trombone (in Bb, with F valve), and to Markneukirchen (1903). In 1904 he became first assistant to Leopold August Schmidt in Cologne (successor to his father, F. A. Schmidt, who had succeeded a

certain Schröder in 1848). In 1922, the year following Schmidt's death, Monke opened his own shop, later employing up to 16 workers. Although the firm now makes all brass instruments, their trumpets in particular represent the culmination of the development of the so-called 'Cologne' models, with a wider bore and larger bell than those of HECKEL, their chief rivals.

Among Monke's innovations, starting while he was working for Schmidt, were the double-cone mouthpipe (it had formerly been cylindrical); the expanded bore of the valve slides (formerly cylindrical), the slight expansion at the bends allowing a freer air-flow; the refinement of the former Cologne rotary valve mechanism from a single to a double joint system, with open spiral springs instead of the former enclosed 'drum' springs; and the shortening of the third valve slide (*c*1926–7) – a trigger mechanism was added in 1950. In addition he made two important contributions to brass mouthpiece making by introducing standard tools, which guarantee uniformity, and (in 1908) by inventing the screw rim mouthpiece. (P. Bate, *The Trumpet and Trombone* (London, 1966), erroneously attributed this innovation to Vincent Bach.) Since Monke's death, the firm has been directed by his daughter Liselotte (*b* Cologne, 9 June 1923). Wilhelm Monke (*b* Cologne, 27 Nov 1913), Josef's son, studied instrument making with his father from 1928 and, simultaneously, trumpet playing with Ludwig Werle; he passed his *Meisterprüfung* with distinction in 1937. He continued to work for his father until 1945. After that, he not only continued to make brass instruments, but also expanded his business to include sales and service of all other types of musical instruments. He has filled various posts in professional organizations.

Wilhelm's son Friedrich Wilhelm Monke (*b* Cologne, 19 Feb 1943) received his training with his grandfather from 1957 to 1960; his journeyman's examination piece received local and national prizes (1960–61) and he became a master in 1966. Today he is the director of the wind instrument department of his father's firm.

BIBLIOGRAPHY

K. Körner: 'Monke, Josef', and 'Monke, Wilhelm', *Rheinische Musiker,* v, ed. K. G. Fellerer (Cologne, 1967), 110
W. Monke and H. Riedel, eds.: *Lehrbuch des Musikalienhandels* (Bonn, 1971)

EDWARD H. TARR

**Monk of Bristol.** *See* TUNSTEDE, SIMON.

**Monk of Salzburg** (*fl* late 14th century). German poet and composer. 49 sacred and 57 secular songs, all with music, appear in manuscripts of the 15th and 16th centuries and of the era of the Meistergesang. Although his works are to be found in more than 90 manuscripts, his identity, like that of most medieval German poets, has never been documented. The introduction to the manuscript A (*D-Mbs* cgm 715) mentions the name Herman, but manuscripts C (*Mbs* cgm 528) and E (*A-Wn* 4696) call him Johanns or Hanns (Spechtler, 9ff); manuscript A makes him a Benedictine and C a Dominican while E and the other manuscripts give no such description; but they all agree that he was a learned monk who wrote sacred and secular songs, many of which are attributed to him as 'Mönch', not only in the introductions to manuscripts but even singly (e.g. in D, *Wn* 2856, 'Mondsee–Wiener Liederhandschrift').

The manuscripts also unanimously name as his patron the Archbishop of Salzburg, Pilgrim II von

Puchheim (1365–96), at whose magnificent court the Monk wrote his songs, some of them at his lord's express command (A, f.1r, E, f.107r). The acrostic in song G 2 (see Spechtler) 'Pylgreim Erczpischof Legat' (contrafactum of *Lauda Sion Salvatorem*) is a tribute to his patron. Pilgrim was trained as a priest at the papal court of Avignon. As Archbishop of Salzburg he had under him the suffragan bishops of Brixen, Freising, Regensburg, Passau, Gurk, Chiemsee, Seckau and Lavant. In international politics he attempted successfully to mediate between the pope and King Wenceslaus in the great western schism of 1386–7, and as a temporal landowner he achieved the largest territorial expansion of Salzburg and concluded alliances with the Swabian league against the neighbouring Bavarian dukes in the Nuremberg Reichstag of 1387, though these eventually proved ineffectual. The secular songs MR 18 and 30 (1392 and 1387) mention Pilgrim's travels and the court he paid to King Wenceslaus in Prague. The foundation of more than 100 endowments for the cathedral (1393) gives an idea of the archbishop's standing.

Other names mentioned in manuscripts and in the songs themselves reveal a circle around the author. A alludes to a priest named Martin who 'supported' the Monk in some unspecified manner; the acrostic in G 3 refers to Pilgrim's court chaplain, Richerus von Radstadt, the foreword to G 5 names the scholar Jakob von Mühldorf as author of its Latin source and that to G 9 (a Latin song) states that the original German song was written by Peter von Sachsen, who had sent it to the Monk.

The 49 sacred songs can be subdivided into 20 songs to the Virgin (G 1–20), 24 songs to the Trinity (G 21–44) with invocations, and 5 songs to the saints (G 45–9). The songs to the Virgin praise her in rich imagery, calling on her especially as intermediary; and except for G 1–9 they are designated for specific feasts – Christmas, New Year, the Annunciation, the Assumption and the birth of the Virgin. G 1–9 stand out in being based on acrostics or otherwise independent of the liturgical year.

The second group includes a Christmas carol still sung today – *Josef, lieber neve mein* (G 22), to the tune of *Resonet in laudibus*; it also includes hymns for Passiontide, Easter, Whitsun and Corpus Christi and even a mealtime grace (G 42). The first hymn to the saints is a calendar song (*Cisiojanus*, G 45), followed by one each for Epiphany, the feast of St John, the sending-out of the apostles and St Elizabeth. The Monk wrote his own words and music and also translated or adapted many Latin hymns and sequences.

His secular songs comprise all the genres of late medieval lyric poetry. The ALBA scheme is varied, as the song titles imply: if the 'Taghorn' (MR 12) describes the characteristic call to awaken in the morning, the 'Nachthorn' (MR 11) represents the man bidding goodnight to his beloved, whereas the 'Trumpet' (MR 15) is a night-time dialogue in which the watchman sings the second voice; MR 14 represents a return welcome (*Ain enpfahen*) and 'Das Kühhorn' (MR 13) parodies the *alba* in that the lovers are a servant and maid awakening from their midday rest. The Monk also wrote New Year songs, love-letters, songs attacking the 'Klaffer' (court enemies of the lovers), love-songs on every theme (a hawking song, farewell, longing, etc) and even a *Leich* (MR 44). Autumn songs and canons to St Martin

(drinking-songs) are also represented and courtly forms like those found in 15th-century songbooks may be found, e.g. in the 'Rosenlied' (MR 49).

The melodic style of the sacred songs is essentially close to that of Latin hymns and sequences (G 22, *Josef, lieber neve mein*, to the tune of *Resonet in laudibus*, is an exception, with its 3rds and 5ths). The texts and melodies of his secular songs do follow medieval tradition, but also herald a new departure, both in introducing major modality (MR 49 and 13) and because they include the first recorded examples of polyphonic, and therefore rhythmically notated, tunes in the history of German song. For 'Pumhart' (MR 11; D, f.186r), a primitive bass (unisons and 5ths) in precise rhythm has been written in. The superscription to MR 12 indicates a similar case and in MR 15 (also an *alba*) the upper part is sung in alternating dialogue by a man and a woman, while the watchman sings the lower part. His Martincanon (E, f.170v) is the earliest surviving canon *a 3* in German (E: 'Radel von drein stimmen').

BIBLIOGRAPHY

F. A. Mayer and H. Rietsch: *Die Mondsee-Wiener Liederhandschrift und der Mönch von Salzburg* (Berlin, 1896) [MR] [texts and melodies for the secular works]

F. V. Spechtler, ed.: *Die geistlichen Lieder des Mönchs von Salzburg* (Berlin and New York, 1972) [G] [incl. texts and further bibliography]

G. F. Jones, F. V. Spechtler and U. Müller, eds.: *Verskonkordanz zu den Geistlichen Liedern des Mönchs von Salzburg* (Göppingen, 1975)

For further bibliography *see* MINNESANG and MEISTERGESANG.

FRANZ VIKTOR SPECHTLER

**Monmart, Berthe** (*b* c1924). French soprano. She made her début at the Paris Opéra in 1951 as Gerhilde (*Die Walküre*) and first appeared at the Opéra-Comique the same year as Mozart's Countess; for 20 years she sang in Paris and the French provinces. Her repertory, which ranged from Mozart (Fiordiligi, Donna Anna) to Wagner (Senta, Elsa), and from Verdi (Aida, Desdemona) to Strauss (Ariadne, the Marschallin), also included many French works: *Les Indes galantes, Numance, Werther*, Gounod's *Faust, La damnation de Faust, Béatrice et Bénédict, Le roi d'Ys, Dialogues des Carmélites* and Fauré's *Pénélope*. Later in her career, as her lyric soprano voice grew darker in tone, she took more dramatic parts such as Judith (*Bluebeard's Castle*), Marina (*Boris Godunov*), Kabanicha (*Kat'á Kabanová*), the Woman in *Erwartung* and the title role of Milhaud's *Medée*, which she sang in Lisbon in 1971.

ELIZABETH FORBES

**Monn, Johann.** See MONN, MATTHIAS GEORG.

**Monn [Mann], Johann Christoph** (*b* 1726; *d* Vienna, 24 June 1782). Austrian pianist and composer, brother of Matthias Georg Monn. He was a music teacher in the employ of Count Kinsky in Prague in autumn 1750. J. A. Hiller reported him to be flourishing in Vienna in 1766 as a freelance musician, teaching keyboard students 'with much success and acclaim'. His only work known to have been published in his lifetime, a piano sonata, appeared in a 1765 collection in which he was recognized as a 'Virtuoso di musica in Vienna'. He died in impoverished circumstances.

An evaluation of Monn's music has been hindered by the confusion of his works with those of his brother, whose style his resembles. Less prolific than Matthias, he composed some orchestral and chamber music, but was best known for his keyboard works, of which eight sonatas, 20 minuets and trios, and a 'ballo' survive. The sonatas surpass those of his brother in variety and virtuosity; they are in three to five movements, some with characteristic titles, though the typical sonata has four movements, including a minuet and quick finale. Attractive themes and short phrases contribute to the *galant* character of Monn's music, but his predominantly motivic treatment of material (producing related figures instead of contrasting themes) lends a conservative air to his style surprising for his time.

## WORKS

*(numbers in square brackets refer to Fischer's thematic catalogue)*

Insts: 6 syms., *A-ST*, *CS-Pnm*; 10 divertimentos, a 3 [80–89], *A-M*, *Wgm*, 1 ed. in DTÖ, xxxix, Jg.xix/2 (1912/R); Divertimento, vn, b [90], *Wgm*; 3 pf concs. [123–5], *D-B*, attrib. M. G. Monn, probably by J. C. Monn

Pf: 8 sonatas [91–8], *A-Wgm*, *D-B*, 1 in J. Haffner: *Oeuvres mêlées*, xi (Nuremberg, 1765); 20 minuets and trios [99–109, 111–19], *A-Wgm*, *D-B*; Ballo [110], 1766, *A-Wgm*

### BIBLIOGRAPHY

J. Hiller: *Wöchentliche Nachrichten und Anmerkungen, die Musik betreffend*, i (Leipzig, 1766/R1970), 97

K. Horwitz and K. Riedel: Foreword, *Wiener Instrumentalmusik vor und um 1750*, i, DTÖ, xxxi, Jg.xv/2 (1908/R)

W. Fischer: Foreword, *Wiener Instrumentalmusik vor und um 1750*, ii, DTÖ, xxxix, Jg.xix/2 (1912/R)

I. Kollpacher: 'Monn', *MGG*

W. S. Newman: *The Sonata in the Classic Era* (Chapel Hill, 1963, rev. 2/1972)

G. Henrotte: *The Ensemble Divertimento in Pre-Classic Vienna* (diss., U. of North Carolina, 1967)

JUDITH LEAH SCHWARTZ

**Monn** [Mann], **Matthias Georg** [Johann; Georg Matthias] (*b* Vienna, 9 April 1717; *d* Vienna, 3 Oct 1750). Austrian composer and organist. The elder son of a coachman, Jakob Mann, he changed his name from Johann to Matthias possibly to avoid confusion with his younger brother JOHANN CHRISTOPH MONN. The spelling 'Monn', preferred by the composer, may be understood as a Lower Austrian dialect version of the original family name Mann. He apparently sang in the choir at Klosterneuburg monastery in 1731–2 and at an early age (but not before 1738) became organist at the newly built church of St Charles in Vienna. There is little to support Gerber's assertion that Monn was 'Hoforganist' at Melk Abbey or that he gave J. G. Albrechtsberger his first lessons in thoroughbass there. Albrechtsberger's alleged reverence for Monn as a teacher (described by Sonnleithner) has not been proved, but a surviving set of thoroughbass exercises by Monn (*A-Wn* 19101) suggests that he devoted part of his career to teaching.

As a composer, Monn ranked with Wagenseil as the leading Viennese counterpart to Johann Stamitz in Mannheim. Although he never attained wide European recognition his local reputation was substantial, as shown by performances of his music at the imperial court of Joseph II and in monasteries in Austria and Slovakia. Described by biographers as a temperate and economical person, Monn apparently never married, and died at the age of 33. Although he composed much music none was published during his short lifetime.

Monn is noted for having composed the first known four-movement symphony with a third-movement minuet (1740); however, he did not adopt this pattern in his other symphonies, all of which are in three movements. A more significant contribution was his handling of form in fast movements: his clear development sections and full recapitulations in the tonic heralded the emergence of sonata form in the symphony. Possessing the most subtle musical technique of the early Viennese

symphonists, Monn showed his originality in effective harmonic detail, striking thematic development, and a well-developed sense of melodic line. In other respects however his style remained conservative, owing to the motivic nature of his themes, frequent use of sequences and a lack of strong thematic contrast. Moreover small proportions, trio sonata textures (without viola) and occasional church sonata designs suggest the strong influence of chamber music on Monn's symphonic writing.

Monn's concertos were the first by a Viennese composer to show elements of Classical style in their thematic structure. Ritornello form persists, but extraordinary modulations in the second solo section enhance the developmental character of the solo part (cf the keyboard concerto in E♭, Fischer no.44, with the modulations e♭–c♯–f♯–b–e♭). Tutti interjections and dialogue passages between solo and orchestra enliven the solo sections – a prediction of textures in Mozart's concertos. The Cello Concerto, a fine work, exploits the technical possibilities of the instrument to a surprising extent, making especially good use of the low register. Schoenberg made an edition of it in 1911–12.

In contrast the chamber music appears conservative in style. The six string quartets each consist of a slow movement and a fugue, suggesting church sonata origins. (Two of these two-movement quartets are simply transcriptions of opening movements from Monn's four-part string symphonies in *sinfonia da chiesa* style.) The eight partitas for two violins and cello follow in the *da camera* tradition with their greater number and variety of movements, including minuets and trios. Here too, however, a taste for counterpoint is in evidence. The 18 fugues found in Monn's chamber music are in many respects models of fugal composition. Nevertheless the fugues as well as the binary and ternary movements combine Baroque melodic lines with the broadly conceived harmonic plans characteristic of the Classical period.

Monn's keyboard sonatas resemble the French suite and the Scarlatti sonata. Consisting of one to seven binary movements, they usually combine suite dances with movements identified only by tempo. Within a predominantly two-part texture, the sonatas offer a continuous unfolding of motivic material, not aspiring to the neat regularity of phrase structure found in *galant* keyboard music. Monn's idiomatic and demanding use of the keyboard contributes to the attractiveness of these works, which, if not as brilliant as those of Scarlatti, still reveal high musicianship and originality.

*See also* SYMPHONY, §I, 6.

## WORKS

*(numbers in square brackets refer to Fischer's thematic catalogue)*

Editions: *Wiener Instrumentalmusik vor und um 1750*, i, ed. K. Horwitz and K. Riedel, DTÖ, xxxi, Jg.xv/2 (1908/R) [H]
  *Wiener Instrumentalmusik vor und um 1750*, ii, ed. W. Fischer, DTÖ, xxxix, Jg.xix/2 (1912/R) [F]

### ORCHESTRAL

21 syms.: 2 for str, ww [1–2], 1 dated 1740, *A-Wn* (autograph), H, Minuet ed. in Mw, vi (1953), 1 in *Wgm*, *F-Pc*, *H-Gk*, F; 12 a 4, str [4, 7–13, 15–17], *A-M*, *Wgm*, *Wm*, *Wn* [Sym. in D, MS 2952, not in Fischer], *B-Bc*, 4 in F, 1 in H; 3 a 3 [24, 27–8], *A-M*, *Wm*; 4 dated 1759, 1765, formerly *GÖ*, now lost; 1 in E♭ [120], *D-Rtt*, H, probably by F. X. Pokorny

Other orch: 7 hpd concs. [35–6, 40–44], *B*, 1 in F; Vc Conc. [39], *A-Wgm* (also in hpd arr.), F; Divertimento, hpd, str [38], *Wgm*; Concertino fugato, vn, str [37], 1742, *Wgm*

### CHAMBER

2–4 insts: 6 str qts [3, 5–6, 11a, 13a, 14] (Vienna, 1808), 2 arr. from syms., see *AMZ*, x (1808), 433; Divertimento, str [20], *D-B*; 8

partitas, 2 vn, b [18–19, 21–2, 25–6, 29–30], *A-Wgm, Wn, H-Gk*, 1
in H; 2 trios [23, –], *A-Wn, H-Gk*; 2 sonatas, 2 allegros, vn, b
[31–4], *D-B*
Kbd (all *D-B*): 14 sonatas [45–7, 49–55, 57–9, 61]; 6 preludes and
fugues [66–71]; 2 capriccios [56, 60], 4 minuets [62–5], 2 fugues,
partita; 8 sets of preludes and versetti, org [72–9]

### VOCAL

Masses: Missa solemnis, 4vv, orch, org, *A-Wgm, Wn*; 3 for 4vv, orch,
org, *GÖ, Wn*
Other vocal: Magnificat, 4vv, orch, *Wn* (autograph); Fuga cum sancto
spiritu, 4vv, *Wn*; Motetto de tempore, B, chorus, orch, *Wgm*; 2
Deutsche Marienlieder, A solo, vn, org, *SE*, ed. R. Moder (Vienna,
1955)

### THEORETICAL

*Theorie des Generalbasses in Beispielen ohne Erklärung* (MS, *A-Wn*)

### BIBLIOGRAPHY

*GerberNL*
Review of six published string quartets, *AMZ*, x (1808), col.433
J. Sonnleithner: 'Biographische Notizen über G. M. Monn aus dem
    Munde seines Schülers Georg Albrechtsberger', *Monatsbericht der
    Gesellschaft der Musikfreunde*, vi (1830), 88
H. Riemann: 'Stamitz oder Monn?', *Blätter für Haus- und
    Kirchenmusik*, xii/7–8 (1907–8)
K. Horwitz and K. Riedel: Foreword, *Wiener Instrumentalmusik vor
    und um 1750*, i, DTÖ, xxxi, Jg.xv/2 (1908/R), p.xv
W. Fischer: Foreword, *Wiener Instrumentalmusik vor und um 1750*,
    ii, DTÖ, xxxix, Jg.xix/2 (1912/R), p.vii
K. Nef: *Geschichte der Sinfonie und Suite* (Leipzig, 1921/R1970), 145f
G. Frotscher: *Geschichte des Orgel-Spiels und der Orgel-Komposition*, i
    (Berlin, 1935, enlarged 3/1966)
R. Philipp: *Die Messenkomposition der Wiener Vorklassiker G. M.
    Monn und G. Chr. Wagenseil* (diss., U. of Vienna, 1938)
I. Kollpacher: 'Monn', *MGG*
W. S. Newman: *The Sonata in the Classic Era* (Chapel Hill, 1963, rev.
    2/1972)
J. Vinton: 'The Development Section in Early Viennese Symphonies: a
    Revaluation', *MR*, xxiv (1963), 13
W. Kirkendale: *Fuge und Fugato in der Kammermusik des Rokoko und
    der Klassik* (Tutzing, 1966), 29f, 60, 89f, 101ff
G. Henrotte: *The Ensemble Divertimento in Pre-Classic Vienna* (diss.,
    U. of North Carolina, 1967)
H. Engel: *Das Instrumentalkonzert: eine musikgeschichtliche
    Darstellung* (Wiesbaden, 1971), i, 215f, 311

JUDITH LEAH SCHWARTZ

**Monnet** [Monet], **Jean** (*b* Condrieu, 7 Sept 1703; *d*
Paris, 1785). French impresario, writer and composer.
Son of a baker, he was orphaned at an early age but
received a good education under the patronage of the
Duchess of Berry in Paris. After his benefactress's death
in 1719 he was a librarian, an editor, and an author until
he was thrown into jail in 1741 for the anonymous
publication of his *Annales amusantes*. Soon afterwards
he developed a passion for the theatre, and in 1743
acquired the *privilège* to the Opéra-Comique for six
years. Favart and Boucher were recruited for this enterprise, and the orchestra, under Rameau, was expanded
to 18 players; the conductorship soon passed to Blaise,
and later to Boismortier. In 1745 Berger, director of the
Opéra, closed the Opéra-Comique because of the competition it offered with the Comédie-Française and the
Comédie-Italienne.

Monnet then went to Lyons and became the director
of the Opéra there. A troupe was formed, but its initial
success was not followed through. He was back in Paris
early in 1749, serving as manager to the actress Mlle de
Navarre. His next venture was an attempt to set up a
French theatre in London. After only four performances
at the Little Theatre in the Haymarket in November and
December 1749, the troupe returned to France, leaving
Monnet behind in a debtors' prison. A benefit performance was given at the Theatre Royal, Drury Lane, in
May 1750 to relieve him of his debts.

In December 1751 Monnet again acquired the
*privilège* to the Opéra-Comique, and remained its director until 1758; he was then at the height of his fame and

career. The Opéra-Comique achieved enormous
success, and he himself was referred to as the 'grand
prophète Monnet' in the Querelle des Bouffons. Thereafter, however, his importance faded. About 1766 he published *Projet pour l'établissement d'un opéra italien
dans la ville de Londres*, the result of another visit to
London. He participated in 1769 in the enterprise of the
Colisée at the Champs Elysées, modelled on the London
pleasure gardens.

Monnet's significance lies in his substantial contribution to the development of *opéra comique* (*see* OPERA,
§III, 2), beside which his own compositions and librettos
are of small importance. His edition of the *Anthologie
françoise* (1765) is of historical value to the study of
French folklore; he also published *Supplément au
roman comique, ou Mémoires pour servir à la vie de
Jean Monnet* (London, 1772–7).

### WORKS

Le chirurgien anglais (C. Collé), Etiolles, 7 Sept 1750 (Paris, 1750)
Le prologue des amours des dieux (L. Fuzélier), Paris, Opéra, Oct 1787
14 airs, solo v, in *Tribut*, viii–x (Paris, ?1759)
Airs pubd in 18th-century anthologies

### EDITIONS

Anthologie françoise ou Chansons choisies depuis le XIIIe siècle
    jusqu'à présent, i–iii (Paris, 1765), iv as Chansons joyeuses
    (Paris, 1765)

### WRITINGS

Librettos: ? La fausse turque (opéra comique by P.-C. Gibert), Paris,
    Foire St Laurent, 3 July 1761, doubtful, attrib. P.-N. Brunet by
    Brenner; L'inconsequence ou Le fat dupé (opéra comique), Paris,
    Théâtre des Variétés-Amusantes, 20 Aug 1787
Projet pour l'établissement d'un opéra italien dans la ville de Londres
    (Paris, c1766)
Supplément au roman comique, ou Mémoires pour servir à la vie de Jean
    Monnet, ci-devant directeur de l'Opéra-Comique à Paris, de l'Opéra
    de Lyon, et d'une Comédie françoise à Londres, écrits par lui-même
    (London, 1772–7)

### BIBLIOGRAPHY

*FétisB*
*Almanach des spectacles* (1754–61)
J. Bonnassies: *Les spectacles forains et la Comédie française* (Paris,
    1875)
A. Heulhard: *J. Monnet, vie et aventures d'un entrepreneur de spectacles
    au XVIIIe siècle* (Paris, 1884)
G. Cucuel: *Les créateurs de l'opéra-comique français* (Paris, 1914)
L. Vallas: *Un siècle de musique et de théâtre à Lyon 1688–1789*
    (Lyons, 1932)
C. Brenner: *A Bibliographical List of Plays in the French Language
    1700–1789* (Berkeley, Calif., 1947)
M. Briquet: 'Monnet, Jean', *MGG*
C. Barnes: 'Instruments and instrumental music at the Théâtres de la
    Foire (1697–1762)', *RMFC*, v (1965), 142
P. Letailleur: 'Jean-Louis Laruette, chanteur et compositeur: sa vie et
    son oeuvre', *RMFC*, viii (1968), 161
*The London Stage, 1660–1800*, iv (Carbondale, Ill., 1972)
J. R. Anthony: *French Baroque Music from Beaujoyeulx to Rameau*
    (London, 1973)
D. Launay: *La Querelle des Bouffons* (Paris, 1973)
G. Sadler: 'Rameau, Piron and the Parisian Fair Theatres', *Soundings*,
    iv (1974), 13

VIVIEN LO

**Monnikendam, Marius** (*b* Haarlem, 28 May 1896; *d*
Heerlen, 22 May 1977). Dutch composer, critic and
teacher. He studied with De Pauw (piano and organ) and
Dresden (composition) at the Amsterdam Conservatory,
and then received a state grant for study in Paris with
d'Indy and Aubert. He then taught composition and analysis for several years at the Rotterdam Conservatory
and at the Amsterdam Muzieklyceum. Prolifically
active as a newspaper critic, he was appointed music
editor for the *De tijd–Maasbode* group in 1960. As a
composer he developed a conventional style with certain
innovations. The first of his works to attract notice was
the symphonic movement *Arbeid* (1931), which was
followed by the Symphonic Variations on the Dutch

folksong *Merck toch hoe sterck*, a piece typical of his rhythmic and dynamic style. His numerous church works include the *Te Deum* (1945), *Klaagzangen van Jeremias* (1962), the *Magnificat* (1966), *Via sacra* for speaker, chorus, organ, percussion and projector (1969) and *Elckerlijc* for chorus, children's voices, chamber orchestra and organ (1975). He also composed oratorios, secular choral pieces, concertos and incidental music; his many organ works include a Concerto (1968), the Toccata no.2 (1971) and the Toccata concertante (1976). Scores are published by Donemus. He wrote books on Stravinsky (Haarlem, 1951), César Franck (Haarlem, 1966) and Netherlands composers (Amsterdam, 1968).

BIBLIOGRAPHY
H. Nolthenius: 'Het jongste werk van Marius Monnikendam', *Mens en melodie*, i (1946), 240 [on the *Te Deum*]
W. Paap: 'Marius Monnikendam 70 jaar', *Mens en melodie*, xxi (1966), 134

ROGIER STARREVELD

**Monochord.** An ancient single-string instrument first mentioned in Greece in the 5th century BC, and said to have been an invention of Pythagoras. The monochord remained a viable musical device, used mainly for teaching, tuning and experimentation, until the advent of more accurate instruments in the late 19th century.

In its earliest form the monochord's single string was stretched across two fixed bridges which were erected on a plank or table. A movable bridge was then placed underneath the string, dividing it into two sections. The marks indicating the position of the fixed bridge were inscribed on the table beneath the string. The resonating box, seen in drawings after the 12th century, was a late medieval addition which increased the portability in addition to enhancing the tone of the monochord. After 1500 one of the end bridges was replaced with a nut, the attendant lowering of the string enabling the user to press it directly on the belly of the instrument. Although simple to use, this modified monochord was considerably less accurate. The name monochord was usually retained for multi-string instruments when the strings were tuned in unison or when the instrument was used for the same purposes as a monochord. The medieval instrument varied from about 90 to 122 cm in length. During the Middle Ages the selection of a monochord's basic pitch was influenced by its size and by the voice range of the user rather than by any existing standards.

1. Acoustical systems. 2. System of string lengths. 3. Division of the chromatic scale. 4. Uses.

1. ACOUSTICAL SYSTEMS. The divisions of the monochord are usually presented in terms of proportions, string lengths or cents. A fourth method, that of expressing string lengths by means of logarithms, was often used in the 18th century, but this system, like the cents system derived from it, is not proportional and cannot be used on the instrument without further calculation. The first two can be directly applied and are the only kinds of division to have attained any practical significance before the 20th century; this kind of division is designated a manual division.

The Pythagorean concept of division by proportions is based on the relationship of the harmonic and arithmetic means as they are represented by the numbers 6, 8, 9 and 12. The ratio 12:6 produces the octave; 9:6 and 12:8, the 5th; 8:6 and 12:9, the 4th; and 9:8, the major 2nd. Reduced to their lowest terms these ratios are dupla (2:1), sesquialtera (3:2), sesquitertia

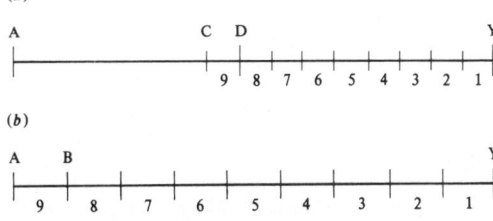

*1. Diagrams showing divisions of the monochord*

(4:3) and sesquioctava (9:8). They can be applied to a string in two ways. For example, in fig.1*a*, one whole tone (D down to C) can be produced by dividing half the string length (AY) into eight parts (DY) and then adding an equal ninth portion (sesquioctava) to form the second pitch (CY). Conversely (fig.1*b*) a subsesquioctava proportion (8:9) can be used if the string length AY is divided into nine parts and the second is sounded with only eight of them (BY).

In fig.1*a* the monochord is divided in a descending manner, i.e. from the higher pitches to the lower. The second division (1*b*), moving from the lower to the higher pitches, is an ascending division. It is of course possible to use both techniques alternately in one division. The more complex ratio, like that of the Pythagorean semitone (256:243), can be determined by calculation with simple intervals, e.g. the sum of two whole tones $(9/8 \times 9/8 = 81/64)$ is subtracted from the fourth $(4/3 - 81/64 = 256/243)$ – an extremely simple manoeuvre when done on the instrument.

*2. Monochord from 'De musica' by Boethius, Canterbury, 1150 (GB-Cu Ii.3.12, f.61v) (for a further illustration of the monochord see* GUIDO OF AREZZO, *fig.1)*

The completion of either of the above divisions in the manner of the Middle Ages would give a two-octave scale in the Pythagorean tuning whose lowest note would be given by the entire length of the string. In general it may be said that the Greek writers up to AD 500 utilized the descending division. Medieval scholars began with the descending division and subsequently adopted the ascending division. The technique of the latter, originally attempted by Boethius, was first successfully described by Odo of St Maur (Cluny) in c1000. Writers of the Renaissance and the post-Renaissance eras preferred the ascending division.

The selection of the technique to be used in working out a specific division was often dependent on its intended usage. Although all medieval divisions achieve the same end and utilize the same four proportions the method of division selected depended on whether it was for a speculative (descending division) or a practical (ascending) treatise. The popularity of the ascending division parallels the rise of the practical treatise in the late Middle Ages.

2. SYSTEM OF STRING LENGTHS. The cumbersome nature of the proportional system together with the difficulty of using a compass to divide the string caused some investigators to adopt the system of string lengths, an accurate and simple method of proportional pitch representation. The only problem with the string lengths lies in the number of units encountered. For example Johann Neidhardt in 1706 specified a string length of 1781·82 units for the second step of his scale. Other advocates, like Marpurg, suggested the use of only three digits to represent the total length of the string; however, this was a compromise rarely admitted by the users of the technique.

3. DIVISION OF THE CHROMATIC SCALE. Semitones can be determined on the monochord by three methods: by extending the superparticular divisions, arithmetically dividing the tone, or by mean-proportional division. In superparticular divisions two complete and different (different even for notes which are enharmonically equivalent) sets of chromatic notes are available. These may be obtained by the successive application of the sesquialtera proportion (beginning with the note F) or of the subsesquialtera proportion (beginning with B). The former will produce a series of perfect 5ths in descending order (called 'flat semitones'), and the latter a set of ascending perfect 5ths ('sharp semitones'). Arithmetical semitones are determined by an equal division of the difference between the string lengths of two pitches a step apart. This method was frequently used in post-medieval times even though the semitones are of unequal size. The mean proportional string lengths necessary for single equal semitones are usually determined by means of the Euclidean construction (a perpendicular erected at the juncture of two string lengths which are used as the diameter of a semicircle will equal the proportional length). To determine two or more mean-proportionals, a mechanical device like the mesolabium (a series of overlapping square frames) can be used to substitute for the mathematical function of the cube root; multiple mean-proportionals can also be formed by means of the sort of geometrical figures used by Lemme Rossi in the 17th century.

4. USES. In addition to its value as an experimental device, the monochord served throughout the Middle Ages as a teaching instrument. Monochord-based diagrams and sets of directions for determining the consonances abound in both speculative and practical treatises of this era. Until the adoption of sight-singing methods based upon the hexachord system, the monochord was used to produce pitches for rote singing; from then until the 13th century it was used mainly to check correct reproduction of intervals. The decline of its pedagogical use after this time is probably due to the introduction of keyboard instruments. The use of the monochord by teachers in the Renaissance was restricted to those few who rigidly maintained the Pythagorean scale as the basis of their musical instruction.

Because so much of the early use of the monochord was didactic, its users attempted to make the division as efficient and accurate as possible. The efficiency of a monochord division depends on the relation between the number of separate measurements and the number of notes produced. The results of these efforts are particularly noticeable after 1450 because after this date each new division often produced a new variation of a given tuning. Often the musician wished to change the tuning but not infrequently he was only seeking a simpler method of division. It would seem that the appearance of an altered tuning bothered the Renaissance musician little, for because of the monochord's inaccuracy, a variation of a few cents (in some cases as much as 22 cents) was a small sacrifice to pay for a more efficient division. A case in point is the division of Ramos de Pareia whose monochord tuning varied widely from the accepted Pythagorean standard. Ramos, however, was apparently not bothered by the pitch deviation as long as he was able to simplify the division. To this end he stated: 'So therefore we have made all of our division very easy, because the fractions are common and not difficult'. In many cases this desire is not stated expressly, as it was by Ramos, but it may be suspected that it served as an underlying cause of many tuning variations in the Renaissance and later eras.

The other areas in which the influence of the monochord is evident are in its instrumental applications and its use as a symbolic device. In the former instance the use of the monochord in ensembles is cited in both Greek and medieval writings. In later times, however, the descendants of the monochord, the clavichord, hurdy-gurdy and trumpet marine, were more frequently used. Throughout the late Middle Ages and the Renaissance the monochord is often mentioned as a basic tool in the design or measurement of bells and organ pipes. Finally, until about 1700, the monochord was commonly used to show the unity existing between man and the universe. It is represented as a divided string whose pitches may represent the solar system (*musica mundana*), the muses, the zodiac, or even bodily functions; often this is being tuned by the hand of God.

For Jacques de Liège's division of the monochord, *see* THEORY, THEORISTS, fig.4.

BIBLIOGRAPHY

S. Wanlztoeben: *Das Monochord als Instrument und als System* (Halle, 1911)
J. M. Barbour: *Tuning and Temperament* (East Lansing, 1951)
L. W. Gümpel: 'Das Tasten-Monochord Conrads von Zabern', *AMw*, xii (1955), 143
C. Adkins: *The Theory and Practice of the Monochord* (diss., U. of Iowa, 1963)
——: 'The Technique of the Monochord', *AcM*, xxxix (1967), 34
T. J. Mathiesen: 'An Annotated Translation of Euclid's Division of a Monochord', *JMT*, xix (1975), 236
CECIL ADKINS

**Monocordo** (It.; Fr. *monocorde*). An instruction to a string player to execute a passage or piece on one string. The effect was first used by Paganini in his *Sonata Napoleone* (1807).

**Monod, Jacques(-Louis)** (*b* Asnières, Paris, 25 Feb 1927). French conductor, composer and pianist. He entered the Paris Conservatoire below the official age of nine, taking courses in various disciplines, and in 1944 attended Messiaen's seminars, his fellow students including Boulez and Yvonne Loriod. His crucial teachers, however, were René Leibowitz, with whom he studied theory, composition and analysis from 1944 to 1950, and his godfather, Paul-Silva Hérard, organist at St Ambroise, Paris. In 1951 Leibowitz took him to the USA, where he studied at the Juilliard School (composition with Bernard Wagenaar) and Columbia University (conducting with Rudolf Thomas). At the Juilliard he was also a teaching assistant to Richard Franko Goldman, in whose class Monod prepared and directed the first all-Webern concert ever given, on 8 May 1951. Later he studied with Blacher and Rufer in Berlin. Monod made his piano début in a Schoenberg 75th birthday concert conducted by Leibowitz in Paris in 1949. He was subsequently active as a pianist, in many song recitals with the American soprano Bethany Beardslee (then his wife) and as a conductor. He played or conducted the premières of Schoenberg's Songs op.48, Webern's Songs opp.17 and 25, the two versions of Berg's *Schliesse mir die Augen beide*, Babbitt's *Widow's Lament* and *Du* (written for him and Beardslee). Between 1960 and 1966, when he conducted regularly for the BBC Third Programme, he gave the first European performances of several American works and he has made the first recordings of much 20th-century music.

Monod's compositions (published by Boelke–Bomart, New York; he became chief editor in 1952) include many settings of texts by Eluard, Valéry, Renard and René Char, chamber and solo works, two chamber cantatas and works for orchestra. He has taught at the New England Conservatory, Hunter College, Princeton, Harvard, Columbia and Queens College, New York.

MICHAEL STEINBERG

**Monodrama.** A MELODRAMA (i.e. a work with spoken text and musical accompaniment) for one character. The term is not strictly applied: Rousseau's *Pygmalion* (*c*1762) and Benda's setting of the same text (1779) are reckoned as monodramas, although Galatea speaks a few words at the close. Schoenberg called *Erwartung* (1909) a monodrama; despite the use of Sprechgesang, however, the notated vocal line and continuous score hardly accord with the original juxtaposition of speaking voice and orchestral commentary.

PETER BRANSCOMBE

**Monody.** (1) Term applied to music consisting of a single line; see MONOPHONY.

(2) Accompanied Italian solo song, especially a secular one, of the period *c*1600–40. The term can either denote an individual song or define the entire body of such songs (and solo recitatives in operas and other works can also be described as monodic). Its use in these senses is a product of modern scholarship, now generally accepted; the word was certainly never used by the composers themselves. The songs that it embraces are those for solo voice and continuo dating from the inception of the medium at the close of the 16th century to the emergence of the chamber cantata. Most are for high voice. The accompanying instruments most frequently used were the lute, chitarrone, theorbo, harpsichord and, for lighter songs, guitar. Obbligato instruments occasionally appear, but there is no evidence that a bass viol doubled the continuo bass.

The medium to some extent grew out of late 16th-century solo arrangements of ensemble music, but the vast majority of monodies were composed as such. The main forms are broadly the madrigal and the aria. Monodic madrigals essentially continued the tradition of ensemble madrigals in a new guise (*see* MADRIGAL, §III, 3). There is a marked polarity between the bass and the vocal line, which is often embellished with quite elaborate ornamentation, some of it written out, some of it improvised according to tried formulae. The arias are more varied in form and style (*see* ARIA, §2). They include examples of strophic bass (*see* STROPHIC VARIATIONS), with the earliest pieces called 'cantata', by composers such as Alessandro Grandi (i) and G. P. Berti, which are distinct from later chamber cantatas. Most arias, however, are strophic songs, usually in triple time and with very little ornamentation, ranging from trifling canzonettas to longer, more serious pieces out of which grew the arias of chamber cantatas. Strophic arias gradually became more popular and began to supplant madrigals from about 1618; by the early 1630s the madrigal was virtually dead. Some monodies also include passages of recitative. Many favourite poems of the past were set, particularly as madrigals, but much contemporary verse was used too, especially for arias; much of this verse is anonymous, and a good deal of it must have been written for musical setting.

The terms 'madrigal' and 'aria' were established for monodies by Caccini in his *Le nuove musiche* (Florence, 1601/2), an epoch-making collection from which it is plausible and convenient to date the inception of genuine monody. The success of Caccini's songs was undoubtedly a major factor in establishing the popularity of monodies, through which in turn – possibly more than through any other medium – the new Baroque style based on the continuo was quickly disseminated throughout Italy; it took several years longer to become accepted in other countries. Florence was the main centre of monody up to about 1620, after which the initiative passed to Venetian composers; but monodies were written in many other places, especially in Rome and at courts and cathedral cities in northern Italy, by both professional and amateur composers. A very high proportion were published. Volumes of monodies, some including one or two by other composers as well as pieces for two or more voices, were produced by over 100 composers, of whom Caccini, Grandi, Berti, Peri, Marco da Gagliano, Sigismondo d'India and Claudio Saracini are among the most interesting and important; some produced single volumes, others as many as half a dozen in the space of a few years. Monodies are relatively unimportant in the work of the two greatest Italian composers of the period, Monteverdi and Frescobaldi. Nevertheless the quality of their finest examples and of the best songs of the other composers named, together with the sheer quantity of songs written over a comparatively short period, makes Italian monody the most important body of solo song of its time and established the fruitful tradition of solo vocal chamber music that lasted throughout the Baroque period in Italy.

The term may also be applied to Italian solo motets of the same period (*see* MOTET, §III, 2(i)). They were less assiduously cultivated than were secular songs, but there are a few fine examples by Monteverdi, and composers such as Barbarino and Ignazio Donati published collections of them that show that such pieces were prompted and influenced by the popularity of secular monodies, many of whose most characteristic features inform them also.

BIBLIOGRAPHY

N. Fortune: 'Italian Secular Monody from 1600 to 1635: an Introductory Survey', *MQ*, xxxix (1953), 171

——: *Italian Secular Song from 1600 to 1635: the Origins and Development of Accompanied Monody* (diss., U. of Cambridge, 1954)

——: 'A Handlist of Printed Italian Secular Monody Books, 1602–1635', *RMARC*, iii (1963/*R*1970), 27

J. Racek: *Stilprobleme der italienischen Monodie* (Prague, 1965)

N. Fortune: 'Solo Song and Cantata', *NOHM*, iv (1968), 140–80

NIGEL FORTUNE

**Monogammique** (Fr.). *See* NOTATION MONOGAMMIQUE.

**Mononen, Sakari (Tuomo)** (*b* Korpiselkä, now in USSR, 27 July 1928). Finnish composer. He studied the organ and composition with Fougstedt and Englund at the Helsinki Academy (diploma 1962). Thereafter he took a post as organist in Kuopio and lecturer in theory at the music institute there, where he became head of the church music department (1970) and prorector (1976). A 'moderate modernist' composer, he achieves a considerable freedom of expression, ranging from the serious organ sonatas to the sarcastic and humorous song cycle *Souvenirs*.

WORKS
(*selective list*)

Orch: Prelude, 1961; Sym., 1962; Conc. grosso, 1968; Divertimento, 1971; Legenda con espressione, 1971; Perspectives, 1972

Choral: 3 Motets, 1971; Vuorela Suite, 1972

Song cycle: Souvenirs (E. Karjalainen), 1v, pf, 1972

Org: 3 sonatas

Principal publisher: Fazer

ERIK WAHLSTRÖM

**Monophony** (from Gk. *monos*: 'single', and *phōnē*: 'voice'). Music for a single voice or part, for example plainsong and unaccompanied solo song. The term is contrasted with 'polyphony' (music in two or more independent parts) and HOMOPHONY (which implies rhythmic similarity in a number of parts).

**Monopoli, Giacomo.** *See* INSANGUINE, GIACOMO.

**Monosoff** [Pancaldo], **Sonya** (*b* Cleveland, 11 June 1927). American violinist. After training at the Juilliard School, where her instrumental teacher was Louis Persinger and her chamber music coaches were Felix Salmond and Hans Letz, she became a founding member of the New York Pro Musica under Noah Greenberg. In 1963 she founded and directed the Baroque Players of New York, later called the Chamber Players. An advocate of Baroque and Classical music played on original instruments, she has increasingly devoted her energies to early music. Included in her repertory are Heinrich Biber's Mystery Sonatas, Bach's sonatas for violin and harpsichord, and Corelli's Sonatas op.5, all of which she has recorded. A former Fellow of the Radcliffe Institute and a research associate of the Smithsonian Institution, she was appointed associate professor at Cornell University in 1972 and full professor in 1974. She plays with Malcolm Bilson (fortepiano) and John Hsu (cello) in the Amadé Trio.

GEORGE GELLES

**Monothematic.** Term used to describe a piece of music constructed on a single theme, either in one movement or in several, throughout which that theme is used; any incidental material that may appear would be of little structural importance.

The point is an example of monothematicism from the 16th century; others are the instrumental fantasia and vocal motet, though in both of these forms multi-sectional structures are found coupled with plurality of themes. In the variation canzonas and ricercares of the 17th century, however, one theme was modified rhythmically to provide the basis of each section, and a genuine monothematicism results. The concept was revived in Bach's *Kunst der Fuge* and *Das musikalische Opfer*. The 18th-century fugue, provided that it is based on a single subject and uses no prominent counter-subject, may also be said to be monothematic. A stretto fugue like the one in C♯ from book 2 of Bach's '48' is of this kind; the G minor fugue of book 1 is monothematic by virtue of the fact that its counter-subject is derived by inverting and reversing the order of the two figures of the subject. Bach's Inventions were specifically designed to show young composers how to manipulate a single theme; many of his binary dance movements are also entirely derived from the opening theme by a process of continuous extension and elaboration (e.g. the Allemande of English Suite no.3).

Monothematicism is perhaps a more remarkable feature in music conceived in forms normally exhibiting thematic plurality, such as the sonata or rondo. Many of Haydn's mature sonata first movements derive the opening of their second group material from the first group either in a very evident way (Symphony no.104) or with more concealed art (String Quartet op.77 no.2). Such movements are said to be in monothematic sonata form though material of a contrasting nature almost inevitably makes its appearance later in the second group. Mozart's melodic prodigality and his different approach to development made him less inclined to use such forms, though they appear in several mature works (e.g. the first movements of the Piano Trio in B♭ K502, the String Quintet in D K593 and the finale of Symphony no.39 K543). A particularly interesting example is the Rondo in D for piano K485, which is in fact a sonata-form movement deriving nearly all its themes from the main subject; the resulting frequent occurrence of this idea together with its tuneful character doubtless accounts for Mozart's choice of title.

With the more extended structures of the period of Beethoven and Schubert, monothematic sonata-form movements are comparatively rare (though the influence of Haydn in this respect is evident in Clementi's work, e.g. op.39 no.2). 19th- and 20th-century composers seeking to achieve thematic unity in extended works have often resorted to thematic transformation similar to the kind used in the 17th-century variation canzona. Music adhering rigorously to the principles of 12-note composition is monothematic if theme and note row can be equated, but in many instances rhythm and other factors create thematic contrasts which are more apparent to the ear than the basis provided by the note row.

MICHAEL TILMOUTH

**Monotone** (from Gk. *monos*: 'single', and *tonos*: 'note'). A single unvaried tone, or a succession of sounds at the same pitch. Prayers, psalms, lessons and other portions of the Divine Office, when declaimed on a single note, are said to be monotoned or recited in monotone. The device is often used for special effects in opera (for example the Notary's utterances in the Act 2 finale of Mozart's *Così fan tutte* or the taking of the oath in the opening scene of Britten's *Peter Grimes*).

**Monpou, (François Louis) Hippolyte** (*b* Paris, 12 Jan 1804; *d* Orleans, 10 Aug 1841). French composer. At the age of five he became a choirboy at St Germain l'Auxerrois; when he was nine he went to Notre Dame, where his precociously able music reading and organ playing attracted attention. At 13 he was one of the first students in Choron's Ecole Royale et Spéciale de Chant. Choron sent the boy to study the organ at Tours Cathedral, where in 1819 he became organist; but he was recalled to be master accompanist at the Académie Royale.

At this time Fétis called Monpou 'a mediocre reader, an incompetent pianist, ignorant of harmony', but he worked to acquire practical knowledge and to correct faults instilled by his earlier musical education. In 1822 he began to take harmony lessons from Fétis at Choron's academy. In 1825 he taught singing and was *maître de chapelle* at the College of St Louis. He accompanied Choron's public concerts, and acquired the poise he had lacked. Two years later he became organist at St Thomas d'Aquin, St Nicolas des Champs and the Sorbonne. In 1829 he was appointed to the highly reputed Abbaye aux Bois.

Escudier suggested that, had not the Revolution of 1830 moved to close Choron's school, Monpou might never have considered 'a dramatic career where struggle and suffering are the conditions for success'. As it happened, Monpou was among the first composers who set the new works of poets such as Victor Hugo and Alfred de Musset. His success began with a collection, based on Béranger's words 'Si j'étais petit oiseau', of piquant little songs, sentimental and gay. In September 1830 he set Musset's *L'Andalouse* to music; it was an instant success, as was his *Le lever*. Then followed such settings as *Sara la baigneuse*, *Madrid*, *Les deux archers* and *Gastibelza* all showing his taste for 'Spanish' sounds reminiscent of guitars and castanets.

In 1833 Monpou began writing comic operas. The *Gazette musicale* praised the Opéra-Comique for staging his *Les deux reines* (6 August 1835). The same magazine recognized the quality of Dumas *père*'s libretto and Monpou's score of *Piquillo* (5 November 1837). In 1839 Monpou created for Jenny Colon the role of Miss Jenny in *Le planteur*, which was a triumphant success. To establish his reputation he now needed a libretto from Scribe, whose librettos had made fortunes for many composers; and Monpou succeeded in acquiring his three-act play *Lambert Simnel*. However, the Opéra-Comique imposed a penalty of 20,000 francs if Monpou could not produce the score by 6 August 1841. He became ill; his doctors ordered rest and a change of climate. Exhausted and suffering from a heart ailment, he left for his daughter's home in Orleans, where he died.

Monpou, in the judgment both of his contemporaries and of subsequent critics, was an innovator, not an imitator; his songs show true originality and sympathy for the Romantic poets. Further years of composing might have matured his natural talent.

WORKS
*(all printed works published in Paris)*
OPERAS
*(all first performed in Paris, Opéra-Comique, unless otherwise indicated)*

Les deux reines (1 act, F. Soulié, Arnould), 6 Aug 1835, vocal score (?1840)
Le luthier de Vienne (1 act, H. de St Georges, de Leuven), 30 June 1836 (1836)
Le Piquillo (3 acts, A. Dumas père), 31 Oct 1837, vocal score (?1845)
Un conte d'autrefois (1 act), 28 Feb 1838
Perugina (1 act), 20 Dec 1838
La chaste Suzanne (4 acts, Carmouche, de Couray), 27 Dec 1839 (1840)
Le planteur (2 acts, St Georges), 1 March 1839 (1839)
La reine Jeanne, 13 Oct 1840
Lambert Simnel (3 acts, Scribe, Mélesville), 1 Sept 1843; completed by A. Adam, vocal score (1843)
L'orfèvre, not completed

SONGS
Si j'étais petit oiseau (Béranger), 3vv (1828); several other pubd duets and trios
76 singly pubd songs, 1v, pf acc:
(1830): Chauvin et Jeanneton; Fauvette; Il était trois chasseurs; Joli coeur; La milice; L'Andalouse (A. de Musset); Marie (Naudet); Vous vous trompez, grand-mère
(1834): Enfant, dis-moi ta romance (Schoeppers); Il ne faut pas rire des sorciers; La juive (Hugo); Le beau moine (B. Lopez); Le noir (R. de Beauvoir); Les colombes de Saint-Marc (Beauvoir); Les deux archers (Hugo); Le soulier dans la cheminée (Thierry); Les résurrectionnistes (F. Soulié); Le voeu sur mer (Beauvoir); Mignon (Goethe); Sara la baigneuse (Hugo); Si j'étais ange (A. de Kermainguy); Un clair de lune; Vite, aimez-moi (M. Aumassip)
(1835–8): Addio Teresa (Dumas); A genoux (Hugo); Hélène (Danglemont); La chanson de la nourrice; La chanson du fou (Hugo); La gitana (Soulié); Lamento (T. Gautier); L'espignole; Les trois marteaux; L'étoile disparue (E. Plouvier); Madrid (Musset); Paroles d'un croyant (Lamennais); Si je mourais! (A. Vanauld); Simple amour (Mme H. Lesguillon); Une sérénade (M. de Forges); Vieux sergent, jeune soldat (E. Barateau)
(1840–44): Dans ma gondole de Venise (Plouvier); Exil et retour (Plouvier); Gastibelza, le fou de Tolède (Hugo); La captive (Hugo); La chanson de triboulet (Plouvier); L'âme du bandit (A. Richomme); La Psyché (Plouvier); Le mal d'amour (Plouvier); L'enfant perdu (Plouvier); Les deux étoiles (Plouvier); Les larmes du départ (Plouvier); La voile blanc (Abbé de Lécluse); Mon fils charmant (Plouvier); Pauvre Hélène (A. Gourdin); Pour un sourire (Plouvier)
(undated publications): C'est tout mon bien (H. L. Guerin); Je ne réponds de rien (Robillard); La femme changée en pierre (M. Waldor); La fille de Gentilly; La glaneuse; La madonna col bambino (A. Vannault); La tour de Nesle; Le capitaine négrier (R. de Fobriant); Le lever (Musset); Lénore (Bürger); Les clocheteurs des trépassés; Les jolis tambours; Le soulier de la liberté; Les yeux noirs (C. Dovalle); L'oiseau de Cèdre; L'onde et les beaux jours (Romagnési); Pastourelle (M. de Manchange); Prière pendant l'orage; Rosa (Waldor); Une marine; Une nuit sur l'eau; Venise (Musset)

BIBLIOGRAPHY
G. Grand: 'Hippolyte Monpou', *Revue de Paris*, ix (1868), 297
H. Bachelin: 'Hippolyte Monpou', *Le ménestrel*, xc (1928), 205, 217
P. Rossillion: 'Un romantique oublié: le "Berlioz de la ballade": Hippolyte Monpou', *Guide musical*, iii–iv (1930), 265
F. Noske: *La mélodie française de Berlioz à Duparc: essai de critique historique* (Amsterdam, 1954)

DELBERT R. SIMON

**Monroe, Bill** [William] **(Smith)** (*b* nr. Rosine, Kentucky, 13 Sept 1911). American country music performer and composer. He learnt music from his uncle Pen (Pemberton) Vandiver, a fiddler with whom he lived for several years, and from local black musicians. In 1929 he moved to Chicago where, with two older brothers, he joined an exhibition square dance team sponsored by the radio station WLS (1932). From 1934 to 1938 he and his brother Charlie Monroe were professional 'hillbilly' radio singers, gaining national popularity through broadcasts, appearances in the south-east, and recordings. In 1938 Bill Monroe formed the Blue Grass Boys; the group joined the 'Grand Ole Opry' radio programme in 1939 and made numerous lastingly popular recordings. Monroe's compositions include instrumental works and religious and secular songs. He plays the mandolin and sings in a distinctive high tenor voice. During the 1940s he developed an innovatory ensemble style based on earlier string-band music of the southeastern USA; the sound was copied during the late 1940s and by the mid-1950s had become known as BLUEGRASS MUSIC. In the 1960s Monroe was the central figure in the appearance of bluegrass festivals and in 1971 he was elected to the Country Music Hall of Fame.

BIBLIOGRAPHY
R. Rinzler: 'Bill Monroe: the Daddy of Blue Grass Music', *Sing Out*, xiii/1 (1963), 5
J. Rooney: *Bossmen: Bill Monroe & Muddy Waters* (New York, 1971)
N. V. Rosenberg: *Bill Monroe and his Blue Grass Boys: an Illustrated Discography* (Nashville, 1974)

NEIL V. ROSENBERG

**Mons, Philippe de** [Filippo di, Philippus de]. *See* MONTE, PHILIPPE DE.

**Monsardus, Hieronymus.** *See* MONTESARDO, GIROLAMO.

**Monserrate** [Montserrat], **Andrés de** (*b* Codalet, Catalonia; *fl* 1614). Spanish theorist. He served as precentor (*capiscol*) of the church of S Martín, Valencia. His brief plainsong treatise, *Arte breve, y compendiosa de las dificultades que se ofrecen en la música practica del canto llano* (Valencia, 1614), is among the very few works on music theory published in Spain in the first half of the 17th century. Although intended as a practical guide, its approach is learned, and it is solidly based on past authorities, ancient and modern, who are listed at the beginning and cited throughout. In his second prologue Monserrate described the place of music among the arts and echoed Bermudo in his scorn of the practical musician ignorant of the foundations of the art. His work is divided into two parts, the first concisely summarizing the fundamentals, the second expanding them with quotations and musical examples. He included the customary topics: notation, solmization, mutation, accidentals, cadences and the modes. He dwelt on certain controversial topics at some length – for example the use of sharps and flats in plainsong and the reasons in favour of the use of B♭ in the 5th and 6th modes. His work was often cited by later Spanish theorists. A tiento and several villancicos by one 'Montserrat' are known; it is uncertain if some of these are by the theorist.

BIBLIOGRAPHY
F. Pedrell: 'Andreu de Montserrat', *Revista musical catalana*, iv (1907), 45
H. Collet: *Le mysticisme musical espagnol* (Paris, 1913)
H. Anglés and J. Subirá: *Catálogo musical de la Biblioteca nacional de Madrid*, ii (Barcelona, 1949)
J. Subirá: *Historia de la música española e hispanoamericana* (Barcelona, 1953)
F. J. León Tello: *La teoría española de la música en los siglos XVII y XVIII* (Madrid, 1974)

ALMONTE HOWELL

**Monsigny, Pierre-Alexandre** (*b* Fauquembergues, nr. St Omer, 17 Oct 1729; *d* Paris, 14 Jan 1817). French composer. Born into an impoverished noble family on his father's side he received a classical education at the Jesuit college in St Omer, where he also learnt to play the violin. When his father died in 1748, he had to provide for his mother, his sister and his four brothers, and to this end he took up employment the following year in Paris in the offices of M. de Saint-Julien, the receiver-general of the Clergé de France. A few years later he came into contact with the Duke of Orleans, grandson of the regent and a great lover of the theatre, who had a stage fitted out in each of his residences. It was through the duke that Monsigny met Collé, his future collaborator, and Carmontelle, who were in charge of organizing the entertainments. Feeling that his technique lacked a solid basis, however, he became for five months the pupil of Gianotti, a double bassist in the orchestras of the Opéra and the Concert Spirituel who was about to publish *Le guide du compositeur* (1759), based on Rameau's theories. Under Gianotti, after a few uncompleted attempts, Monsigny wrote the score of *Les aveux indiscrets*, which was successfully mounted in February 1759. After two further successes he had the good fortune to become associated with Sedaine, one of Philidor's librettists. *On ne s'avise jamais de tout* (1761) marked the beginning of a long series of successful collaborations between the two.

The fusion of the Comédie-Italienne and the Théâtre de la Foire in 1762, and the success of the Forains, increased the popularity of theatre pieces with ariettes; yet though quite a number of works by Duni and

*1. Title-page of the first edition of the full score of Monsigny's 'Le roy et le fermier', published by Hérissant (Paris, 1762)*

Philidor were put on within the next few years, Monsigny was less prolific, and seemed to stand aside while working out a fresh approach to the genre. His next work, *Le roy et le fermier* (November 1762), surprised the audience by its depth and originality; abandoning conventional subjects, it was based on a work from English literature, and brought new political and social overtones to French comic opera. After the lighter *Rose et Colas* (1764) and two other works Monsigny produced his only work for the Opéra – *Aline, reine de Golconde* (1766).

In 1768 Monsigny entered the service of the Duke of Orleans by purchasing the lucrative position of *maître d'hôtel*. The next year *Le déserteur* appeared, an *opéra comique larmoyant* dedicated to the duke. The humanity of its subject, drawn from the Flemish war, and the union of its music and drama marked a decisive step away from the conventional *comédie à ariettes*. Several more works appeared, but after the immense success of *Félix ou L'enfant trouvé* (1777) he gave up composition for unknown reasons, although he was to live another 40 years. In 1784 he declined to compose the score of *Richard Coeur-de-Lion* and advised Sedaine to turn to Grétry.

In 1784 Monsigny married a woman 25 years his junior; she bore him several children, of whom two survived. In the following year the duke died and the post of *maître d'hôtel* was abolished, but the new duke, who held Monsigny in high esteem, appointed him inspector of the canals of Orleans and he was able to continue living in the royal palace. Unfortunately the Revolution deprived him of his means, and Monsigny's financial situation became increasingly difficult. It was somewhat alleviated by a pension from the Opéra-Comique in 1798, and greatly improved in 1800 when he succeeded Piccinni as Inspector of Musical Education. Two years later this post was abolished, but he was later awarded a number of pensions. Finally, from 1810, after nearly two decades of obscurity, his works returned to the stage. He became a Chevalier of the Légion d'honneur in 1804 and took Grétry's place as a member of the Institute in 1813. He had, however, been infirm since 1809, and was unable to take part in the work of the Academy.

Like Sedaine, Monsigny had a feeling for the theatre, and devoted all his artistic efforts to the stage. He took pains to match his music to the subject and to the action, and was personally involved with the *mise en scène*. Though he never achieved the fluency of Grétry, nor the technique of Philidor, Monsigny nevertheless showed a remarkable feeling for melody (Grétry considered him 'the most tuneful of all musicians') and a freshness of inspiration which is always attractive, despite its limitations. The technical imperfections in his works are the result of his desultory formal training; he relied on instinct rather than acquired technique. Apart from the use of diminished 7th chords at moments of high drama, a practice which became common only later in the century, and some examples of unusual but apposite part-writing, his harmonic idiom has scarcely anything original to offer. His instrumental writing, however, rivals that of Philidor and Méhul in its modernity, and is richer than that of Grétry, whose poverty in this respect was often emphasized by Berlioz. The striking combination of flutes and piccolos in *Aline* (prelude to Act 2, 'Lever de l'Aurore', and finale of Act 3) and the use of

2. *Pierre-Alexandre Monsigny: portrait (1812) by Charles Thévenin in the Bibliothèque et Musée de l'Opéra, Paris*

the drum in *Le déserteur* (Act 3 scene iv) show his awareness of the colouristic and dramatic potential of the orchestra. These qualities, allied with his melodic gift and his instinct for dramatic truth, have secured him a place among the creators of French comic opera, and make him a precursor of Boieldieu, Auber, Bizet and Massenet.

## WORKS

*(all published in full score in Paris, unless otherwise indicated)*

Les aveux indiscrets (opéra comique, 1, La Ribardière), Paris, Foire St-Germain, 7 Feb 1759

Le maître en droit (opéra comique, 2, P.-R. Lemonnier), Paris, Foire St-Germain, 23 Feb 1760

Le cadi dupé (opéra comique, 1, Lemonnier), Paris, Foire St-Germain, 4 Feb 1761

On ne s'avise jamais de tout (opéra comique, 1, M.-J. Sedaine), Paris, Foire St-Laurent, 14 Sept 1761

Le roy et le fermier (comédie, 3, Sedaine, after Dodsley: The King and the Miller of Mansfield), Paris, Théâtre-Italien, 22 Nov 1762

Le nouveau monde (divertissement, C.-S. Favart, after S.-J. Pellegrin), 1763, unperf., lost

Rose et Colas (Comédie, 1, Sedaine), Théâtre-Italien, Paris, 8 March 1764

Le bouquet de Thalie (prol, C. Collé), Bagnolet, Theatre of Duke of Orleans, 25 Dec 1764, lost

Aline, reine de Golconde (ballet héroïque, 3, Sedaine), Paris, Opéra, 15 April 1766

Philémon et Baucis (comédie, 1, Sedaine), Bagnolet, theatre of Duke of Orleans, 1766, unpubd, lost

L'isle sonnante (opéra comique, 3, Collé), Bagnolet, theatre of Duke of Orleans, 5 June 1767

Le déserteur (drame, 3, Sedaine), Paris, Théâtre-Italien, 6 March 1769

La rosière de Salency (comédie, 3, Favart), Fontainebleau, 25 Oct 1769, collab. Philidor, Blaise, Swieten, ?Duni

Pagamin de Monègue (opéra comique, 2, Sedaine), c1770, unperf., accepted by Opéra 1782, unperf., score, F-Pn

Le faucon (opéra comique, 1, Sedaine), Fontainebleau, 2 Nov 1771

La belle Arsène (comédie féerie, 4, Favart), Fontainebleau, 6 Nov 1773: rev. Paris, Théâtre-Italien, 14 Aug 1775

Félix ou L'enfant trouvé (comédie, 3, Sedaine), Fontainebleau, 10 Nov 1777

Robin et Marion (?Sedaine), unperf., score, Po

Le rendez-vous bien employé (parade, 1, L. Anseaume) is by J. P. A. Martini

O ma tendre musette (La Harpe), ariette, is probably by La Pouplinière

Exercises, vn, b, sur la manière de lier les sons, *F-Pc*

BIBLIOGRAPHY

A.-J. Desboulmiers: *Histoire du Théâtre de l'Opéra-Comique* (Paris, 1769)

L. Petit de Bachaumont: *Mémoires secrètes* (London, 1780–89)

A. C. Quatremère de Quincy: *Institut . . . de France: funérailles de M. de Monsigny* (Paris, 1817)

——: *Notice historique sur la vie et ouvrages de M. de Monsigny* (Paris, 1818)

A. Alexandre: 'Eloge historique de P.-A. Monsigny', *Mémoires de la Société royale d'Arras*, ii (1819), 37

P. Hédouin: *Notice historique sur P.-A. de Monsigny* (Paris, 1821)

C. Collé: *Journal et mémoires* (Paris, 1868)

F. M. Grimm: *Correspondance littéraire*, ed. M. Tourneux (Paris, 1877–82)

F. de Ménil: *Les grands musiciens du Nord: Monsigny* (Paris, 1893)

A. Pougin: *Monsigny et son temps* (Paris, 1908)

G. Cucuel: *Les créateurs de l'opéra-comique français* (Paris, 1914)

H. Abert: *W. A. Mozart*, i (Leipzig, 1919, 3/1955), esp. 654ff

M. Pincherle: *Musiciens peints par eux-mêmes* (Paris, 1939), 43

P. Druilhe: 'Une lettre inédite de Monsigny', *RdM*, xxix (1950), nos.93–4, 53

——: *Monsigny* (Paris, 1955)

L. Fox: ' "La belle Arsène" by P.-A. Monsigny', *RMFC*, ix (1969), 141

PAULE DRUILHE

**Montagnana, Antonio** (*b* Venice; *fl* 1730–50). Italian bass. In 1730 he sang at Rome and in 1731 at Turin in operas by Porpora, who is said to have been his teacher. He was a member of Handel's company at the King's Theatre between 1731 and 1733 and may have made his début as Leone in *Tamerlano* on 13 November 1731. During that season he sang in revivals of *Poro* (Timagene), *Admeto* (Meraspe), *Flavio* (Ugone, originally a tenor part) and probably *Giulio Cesare* (Achillas), and in the first productions of *Ezio* (Varo) on 15 January and *Sosarme* (Altomaro) on 15 February; also in Ariosti's *Coriolano* and the pasticcio *Lucio Papirio dittatore*. In the following year he was in Leo's *Catone*, revivals of Handel's *Alessandro* (Clito), *Tolomeo* (Araspe) and probably *Floridante* (Oronte), and the first production of *Orlando* (Zoroastro). He sang Haman in *Esther* and Polyphemus in *Acis and Galatea* during Handel's first London oratorio season in May and June 1732, and Abinoam and the Chief Priest of Israel in the first performance of *Deborah* on 17 March 1733. Handel composed the part of Abner in *Athalia* for him and cast him as Emireno in a planned revival of *Ottone*, but in the early summer he left the company with Senesino and Bertolli to join the Opera of the Nobility. The anonymous pamphlet *Harmony in an Uproar*, published in February 1734, implies that he broke a formal contract to do so. Montagnana remained with the Opera of the Nobility throughout its four London seasons (1733–7) and sang in at least 15 operas at Lincoln's Inn Fields and the King's Theatre, including Porpora's *Arianna in Nasso*, *Enea nel Lazio*, *Polifemo*, *Ifigenia in Aulide* and *Mitridate*, Hasse's *Artaserse* and *Siroe*, Veracini's *Adriano* and *La clemenza di Tito*, Bononcini's *Astarto* and Handel's *Ottone* (Emireno). In 1737–8 he was a member of Heidegger's company at the King's, appearing in two pasticcios, Pescetti's *La conquista del vello d'oro*, Veracini's *Partenio* and two new Handel operas,

*Cello by Domenico Montagnana, Venice, 1710 (private collection)*

*Faramondo* (3 January 1738) and *Serse* (15 April), in which he sang Gustavo and Ariodate. For ten years from 1740 he was attached to the royal chapel at Madrid. He sang there in many operas and cantatas, chiefly at the palace of Buen Retiro. He retired in 1750 or soon after.

When he arrived in London Montagnana was a remarkable singer. Unlike Boschi, he was a genuine bass, with powerful low notes, considerable agility and a compass of more than two octaves (*E* to *f'*). The parts Handel composed for him in his first two seasons, Varo, Altomaro and Zoroastro, bear ample witness to his gifts. Burney, with reference to his first aria in *Sosarme*, 'Fra l'ombre', singled out his voice's 'depth, power, mellowness and peculiar accuracy of intonation in hitting distant intervals'. In *Ezio* he was required to trill on the bottom A, and Zoroastro's music is at once solemn, sonorous and full of taxing divisions. Handel regularly expanded the parts he sang in revivals, giving him three extra arias in *Poro* and *Admeto*. In *Flavio* he sang the two arias composed for Boschi in a different part. By 1738 his powers were on the wane. In his last two Handel parts his compass shrank to *G* to *eb'*, and he was given little music and of much less striking quality. This is particularly evident in *Serse*, where he had the smallest part in the opera.

WINTON DEAN

**Montagnana, Domenico** (*b* Lendinara, *c*1687; *d* Venice, 7 March 1750). Italian string instrument maker. He went to Venice about 1699 and probably in due course became the pupil and assistant of Matteo Goffriller; in about 1711 he opened his own shop, though at this time he may also have been associated with Francesco Gobbetti. Surviving instruments seldom date from earlier than about 1720, but from then on his reputation grew fast and his output was considerable.

Montagnana's violins were made on a number of different patterns. The standard sized flat models make first-rate solo instruments, but others are now less suitable because of their small dimensions or a tendency towards the higher build favoured by Stainer, whose instruments were popular in Venice as elsewhere in Italy. Only one viola has been attributed to Montagnana: the instrument used for many years by Tertis. Its shape, though altered from the instrument's original form, was the inspiration for the 'Tertis' model adopted by many modern makers.

Montagnana is especially famed for his cellos. Encouraged by the cello's particular popularity in Venice, and perhaps commissioned by the four music conservatories, he produced cellos that are regarded by many of today's soloists as ideal. Bold, sometimes massive in appearance, they have much of the quality of sound of the great Cremonese instruments and a greater volume when forcefully played. The novelist Charles Reade dubbed Montagnana 'the mighty Venetian', and all familiar with his work acknowledge its power.

BIBLIOGRAPHY
C. Beare: *The Venetian Violin Makers* (in preparation)

CHARLES BEARE

**Montagnana, Rinaldo da** (*b* Montagnana; *fl* 1558–73). Italian composer and priest. It is likely that he spent his whole life in the Veneto. His first book of canzoni is unusual in that it contains multi-strophic settings of five of Petrarch's most popular canzoni and sestinas, four by Montagnana and one by Daniele Vicintino. Two works attributed to 'Rinaldo' (in *GB-Lbm* Add.30491) are probably the work of Rinaldo del Mel.

WORKS
Delle canzone, con alcuni madrigali aierosi . . . libro primo, 4vv (Venice, 1558[17])
Il primo libro di motetti . . . per tutte le feste dell'anno, 5vv (Venice, 1563[5])
Il primo libro di motetti, 4vv (Venice, 1573)

PATRICIA ANN MYERS

**Montagney, Joseph.** *See* ARTÔT, ALEXANDRE.

**Montagu-Nathan, M(ontagu)** (*b* Banbury, 17 Sept 1877; *d* London, 15 Nov 1958). English violinist and writer on music. He was educated at King Edward's School, Birmingham, and studied at the Brussels Conservatoire as a violin pupil of Ysaÿe and at the Hoch Conservatory, Frankfurt am Main. He also had private lessons with Wilhelmj in London. He appeared frequently at the Belfast University Chamber Concerts between 1900 and 1905, and joined the teaching staff of the Leeds Municipal School of Music about 1907. He played violin concertos at the Leeds municipal concerts and acted as music critic to the *Yorkshire Observer*. He learnt Russian and made his name as a writer and lecturer chiefly as a specialist in Russian music, of which he gave pioneer concerts at Steinway Hall, London, in 1913–14. His writings include biographies of the major Russian composers as well as general histories of Russian music, which he continued to write about to an advanced age. He was secretary of many musical and other organizations in London, notably the Camargo Ballet Society.

WRITINGS
'Moussorgsky', *ZIMG*, xv (1913–14), 194
*A History of Russian Music* (London and New York, 1914, 2/1918/R1973)
'Russian Literature and Russian Music', *PMA*, xli (1914–15), 113
*An Introduction to Russian Music* (London and Boston, 1916)
*Glinka* (London, 1916, 2/1921/R)
*Moussorgsky* (London, 1916/R)
*Rimsky-Korsakof* (London, 1916/R)
*Contemporary Russian Composers* (London, 1917)
*Handbook to the Piano Works of A. Scriabin* (London, 1917)
*The Orchestra and how to Listen to it* (London, 1920)
'Eugène Ysaye: some Personal Reminiscences', *MT*, lxxii (1931), 593
*Mlle. Camargo* (London, 1932)
Articles on Arensky, Balakirev, Cui, Glazunov, Grechaninov, Khachaturian, Lyadov, Shaporin and Shostakovich in *The Music Masters*, ed. A. L. Bacharach (London, 1948)
'The Function of Music in Ballet', *MMR*, lxxx (1950), 265
'Gogol and Music', *MMR*, lxxxi (1952), 92
'Shaliapin's Precursors', *ML*, xxxiii (1952), 232
'Stasov in London', *MMR*, lxxxiii (1953), 126
ed. and trans.: 'Balakirev's Letters to Calvocoressi', *ML*, xxxv (1954), 347
'The Origin of "The Golden Cockerel" ', *MR*, xv (1954), 33
'A. T. Grechaninov, 1864–1956', *MMR*, lxxxvi (1956), 52
'The Strange Case of Professor Assafiev', *ML*, xxxviii (1957), 335

ERIC BLOM/R

**Montalbano** [Mont'Albano], **Bartolomeo** (*b* Bologna, ?*c*1600; *d* Venice, 1651). Italian composer. On 20 October 1619 he entered the Franciscan order and settled at the monastery of S Francesco, Bologna. After a journey to Rome, he was taken to Palermo by Bonaventura Arezzo, head of the order in Sicily. When he published his only known music in 1629 he was *maestro di cappella* of S Francesco there. From 1642 until his death he was *maestro* of S Francesco, Bologna. In 1647 he directed the music for the general chapter of his order, held at Ss Apostoli, Rome. In 1650 he was sent to Venice, where he died soon after.

He published two volumes of music at Palermo in 1629: *Sinfonie ad uno, e doi violini, a doi, e trombone, con il partimento per l'organo, con alcune a quattro viole*, and *Motetti ad 1, 2, 3, 4, et 8 voci, con il partimento per l'organo, et una messa a 4 voci*. The latter appeared twice in the same year as opp.2 and 3, with different dedications; despite the title-page neither edition includes any three-part motets. The former volume comprises four pieces for solo violin, two for two violins, two for two violins and trombone, and four for four viols, all with continuo; they are named after prominent citizens or Sicilian places. The three- and four-part sinfonias are modest examples of the instrumental canzona. Those for two violins and especially those for solo violin are more interesting (one solo piece is in Mw, xv, 1959; Eng. trans., 1960). They are structurally free and give the impression of being written-down virtuoso improvisations, with contrasts of presto and adagio and of *forte* and *piano* in echo, and detailed indications of phrasing. The figuration, which is purely instrumental in conception, derives from the tuning of the violin in 5ths. Montalbano is thus, together with men such as Biagio Marini, G. B. Fontana and Camillo Cortellini (with whom he probably studied at Bologna), one of the founders of modern violin technique. In the mass of opp.2–3, he said, 'the Sanctus and Agnus are short in order to allow room for a motet or sinfonia'. Of the motets, two are for solo voice, six for two voices, one for four and one for eight (this last is in praise of St Bonaventure and was no doubt intended as a homonymous tribute to Father Arezzo). Montalbano's vocal style is to some extent an adaptation of his instrumental style; the music is fluent and serviceable in an idiom that can be seen as a stylized, debased simplification of the sacred concerto established by Giovanni Gabrieli and Monteverdi.

BIBLIOGRAPHY

*EitnerQ; SchmidlD*

L. Torchi: 'La musica istrumentale in Italia nei secoli XVI, XVII e XVIII', *RMI*, iv–viii (1897–1901); pubd separately (Turin, 1901/R1969), 42f

A. Schering: 'Zur Geschichte der Solosonate in der ersten Hälfte des 17. Jahrhunderts', *Riemann-Festschrift* (Leipzig, 1909), 309

F. Vatielli: 'Primizie del sinfonismo', *RMI*, xlvii (1943), 124; Ger. trans., ed. F. Giegling, *SMz*, xci (1951), 341

W. Apel: 'Studien über die frühe Violinmusik, ii', *AMw*, xxxi (1974), 212

PAOLO EMILIO CARAPEZZA

**Montanari, Francesco** [Antonio] (*b* Padua; *d* Rome, 1730). Italian composer. He was a pupil of Corelli and established himself in Rome, where he became a member of the orchestra of St Peter's in 1717 as principal violinist and, according to Burney, died of a broken heart when Pasquale Bini went to Rome and proved himself to be the finest performer of the period. Montanari composed 12 sonatas for violin which were published in Bologna. Four of his violin concertos survive (*D-Dlb*) under the name by which he was known to Hawkins and Gerber: Antonio Montanari.

E. HERON-ALLEN/R

**Montanos, Francisco de** (*b* c1528; *d* after 1592). Spanish theorist and composer. He was *maestro de capilla*, presumably at Valladolid, from 1551, according to a note at the end of his treatise *Arte de musica* (1592). Two of the epigrams included in this work imply that he came from a wealthy family. On 24 September 1564

Montanos, already *maestro de capilla* of the collegiate church of S Maria la Mayor in Valladolid, was granted the revenues of a half-prebend. The chapter instructed him on 8 June 1571 to give daily group music lessons to the 55 adults and choirboys of the procathedral chapel, threatening to fine him if he should be absent. On 13 June 1572 the choirboys were removed from his charge and on 2 April 1576 he was relieved of the post of *maestro de capilla*. He continued to receive the revenues of his half-prebend and by 1587 was again *maestro de capilla*. He dedicated *Arte de musica*, begun in 1576, to Fernando Ruiz de Castro Andrade y Portugal (c1548–1601), Count of Lemos. The count married the granddaughter of S Francis Borgia at Valladolid on 28 November 1574, and it was probably about this time that Montanos spent several years in the household of his patron.

Montanos's *Arte de musica theorica y pratica* (Valladolid, 1592; part published separately as *Arte de canto llano con intonaciones communes*, Salamanca, 1610, enlarged 4/1648, enlarged 12/1734) consists of six books on musical topics: *canto llano* (plainsong), *canto de órgano* (measured music), *contrapunto*, *compostura* (composition), *proporcione*, and *lugares comunes* (commonplace examples). The first of these was repeatedly reprinted, sometimes with additions, up to the mid-18th century. Montanos claimed in his treatise to have 'communicated with the best composers of Spain and viewed a large number of works by the finest foreigners of our time and of the past'. He was the first theorist from the Iberian peninsula to show familiarity with the music of Palestrina, and also knew the works of Lassus and Phinot. He followed Martínez de Bizcargui in judging the 'sung' semitone (*mi, fa*) larger than the 'unsung' semitones (e.g. *c, c♯*).

Cerone, in *El melopeo y maestro* (Naples, 1613), quoted Montanos extensively, including a four-part canon in which each successive voice enters a 5th higher than the last. He likened it to one in the final Agnus Dei of Palestrina's canonic *Missa sine nomine* (printed 1599), a comparison which would have pleased Montanos. Cerone reproduced without acknowledgment 46 examples from the last book of *Arte de musica*. He printed from Montanos's fifth book, also without acknowledgment, the four-voice *Diffusa est gratia* as an example of the chromatic genus. This brief chromatic motet, full of progressions which suggest Gesualdo (E♭-a, A♭-F, c♯-F), is only 32 breves long. Cerone smoothed its harmonic clashes and abbreviated it by a third. Two four-voice motets in modern edition show Montanos to have been concerned more with the spirit of the text than with technical ingenuity.

BIBLIOGRAPHY

A. Palau y Dulcet: *Manual del librero hispanoamericano*, x (Barcelona, 1957), 77

R. Stevenson: *Spanish Cathedral Music in the Golden Age* (Berkeley and Los Angeles, 1961), 318f

D. M. Urquhart: *Francisco de Montanos's 'Arte de musica theorica y pratica': a Translation and Commentary* (diss., U. of Rochester, 1969)

ROBERT STEVENSON

**Montanus.** *See* BERG, JOHANN.

**Montbuisson** [Montbuysson], **Victor de** [Bergwald, Victor von] (*b* Avignon, c1575; *d* after 1638). French lutenist. From 1598 to 1627 he was employed by the Landgrave Moritz of Hesse at the Kassel court. He then apparently settled at The Hague as a teacher until 1638.

Denss, in his *Florilegium* (1594), listed Montbuisson as the composer of three courantes (probably those which were in *D-Dlb*, now lost). In Besard's *Thesaurus* of 1603, where he is identified as 'Avenionensis', three galliards are ascribed to him. There is also an MS (in *D-Kl*) described on its 54th folio as 'Livre de tableture de lhut pour Madame Elisabeth princesse de Hessen commencé par Victor de Montbuysson, le dernier janvier 1611'. In French tablature, it contains about 80 dance pieces and over 50 vocal pieces. The majority of the dance pieces are courantes, which include the only one actually inscribed with Montbuisson's name. Most of the vocal pieces are intabulations; only a few include voice parts. Several others appear in two- or three-voice versions in score with no lute part. Other composers listed include Moritz of Hesse ('M.L.H.'), Hassler, Dowland, Philips, Vallet (a number of concordances exist with his *Le secret des muses* of 1615 and 1616), Besard, Gautier and Mercure. Concordances also exist with Fuhrmann's *Testudo gallo-germanica* (1615). The main interest in the pieces known to be by Montbuisson is harmonic and rhythmic rather than melodic; changes of metre from 3/4 to 6/8 are common. He sometimes used a two-part texture characterized by scale passages which feature unexpectedly free treatment of accidentals. Some of his works are edited in Souris, Rollin and Vaccaro.

BIBLIOGRAPHY
A. Arnheim: 'Ein Beitrag zur Geschichte des einstimmigen weltlichen Kunstliedes in Frankreich im 17. Jahrhundert', *SIMG*, x (1908–9), 399
A. Souris, M. Rollin and J.-M. Vaccaro, eds.: *Oeuvres de Vaumesnil, Edisthon, Perrichon, Rael et Montbuysson* (Paris, 1974)
H. B. LOBAUGH

**Monte, Cola Nardo de** (*fl* Bari, *c*1570–80). Italian composer. He was probably employed in Bari since a villanella by him was published in a collection (*RISM* 1574⁵) devoted to musicians from Bari. The only volume of his own music is *Il primo libro de madrigali con le parole di vilanelle* (Venice, 1580; examples in *Villanelle alla napolitana a tre voci di musicisti baresi del secolo XVI*, ed. S. A. Luciani, Rome, 1941). It consists of 24 four-part pieces. Although they are called madrigals most of the texts are in the sectional form of the villanella, with one or both of the outer sections repeated. Only the alto part is extant, but it appears from it that word-painting is limited to rapid upward scales and occasional chromatic inflections.

DONNA G. CARDAMONE

**Monte, Lodovico** (*b* Bologna; *fl* mid-17th century). Italian guitarist, composer and music editor. He seems to have lived for a time in Rome. He was co-author with PIETRO MILIONI of *Vero e facil modo d'imparare a sonare et accordare da se medesimo la chitarra spagnuola* (Rome and Macerata, 1637, and many times reprinted), an instruction book for the *battute* (strummed) style of playing the guitar which shares several features with Milioni's other volume. Monte also edited a similar volume on his own, *Vago fior di virtù, dove si contiene il vero modo per sonare la chitarriglia spagnuola* (Venice, n.d.). Again it comprises an explanation of the alphabet tablature, tuning instructions, and *battute* accompaniments to songs and dances.

BIBLIOGRAPHY
J. Wolf: *Handbuch der Notationskunde*, ii (Leipzig, 1919/*R*1963), 173f
S. Murphy: 'Seventeenth-century Guitar Music: Notes on Rasgueado Performance', *GSJ*, xxi (1968), 28

W. Kirkendale: *L'Aria di Fiorenza, id est Il ballo del Gran Duca* (Florence, 1972), 25, 27, 65f, 78
ROBERT STRIZICH

**Monte, Philippe de** [Filippo di, Philippus de] (*b* Mechlin [now Mechelen], 1521; *d* Prague, 4 July 1603). Flemish composer. He was one of the most renowned and prolific composers of the 16th century and is particularly important for his secular works.

1. Life. 2. Sacred works. 3. Secular works.

1. LIFE. Monte was probably trained as a choirboy at St Rombaut, Mechlin, and while young went to Italy. He made his living there as a singer, teacher and composer, and adopted an italianized form of his name, Filippo di Monte. In the preface to his 19th book of five-voice madrigals he referred to 'the many years of my youth' that he had spent in the service of the Pinelli family of Naples; he is now known to have been there from 1542 to 1551. His first published music appeared in 1554 in Rome, where he seems to have attracted the attention of Cardinals Aldobrandini and Orsini. In the same year he returned to the north, first to Antwerp, and then to England, where he served as *chorus praefectus* in the private chapel of Philip II of Spain, husband of Mary Tudor. He was evidently unhappy in England, and left in 1555. His immediate movements are unknown, but on 22 September 1555 Georg Seld, who had been sent to Brussels by Archduke Albrecht V of Bavaria to recruit musicians, recommended Monte for the post of court composer, describing him as 'a quiet, reticent person, modest as a girl, who has spent the greater part of his life in Italy, speaks Italian like a native, and also Latin, French and Flemish'. But despite Seld's praise Monte was not engaged.

After the death on 8 January 1567 of Jacobus Vaet, court Kapellmeister to the Emperor Maximilian II, attempts to engage Palestrina as his successor were unsuccessful, and the position was offered to Monte, then in Rome and probably in the service of Cardinal Orsini. After some negotiations over salary, he assumed his duties in Vienna on 1 May 1568. This marked a turning-point in his career, for it evidently stimulated his creativity and between 1569 and 1600 hardly a year passed without the publication of at least one volume of his works. In 1570 Maximilian sent him to the Low Countries to recruit musicians for the chapel. Two years later he was appointed treasurer of Cambrai Cathedral, and in 1577 Rudolf II, Maximilian's successor, appointed him a canon there – neither benefice carried any obligation of residence, but both augmented his income. He spent the rest of his life at the Habsburg court at Vienna or Prague; in his will, drawn up at Prague on 15 January 1603 (now in *A-Wst*), he expressed a wish to be buried in St Jakub, Prague.

Monte's circle of friends was wide. The English poet Elizabeth Weston studied under him in Prague and later honoured him with a lengthy eulogy, and he was on intimate terms with the botanist Charles de l'Ecluse. His cordial relationship with Lassus probably dates from their youth, for their paths had crossed in Italy and at Antwerp. During his period in England Monte became acquainted with the Byrd family and later exchanged compositions with William. His pupils included Regnart, Luython, G. B. della Gostena and Macque. Two portraits of him are known: a medallion by Conrad Bloc pictures him at the age of 63 (see illustration), and an engraving by Raphael Sadeler shows him at 73; since both are dated, they serve to determine his date of birth. A number of his letters are also extant (see Bergmans).

2. SACRED WORKS. Monte's sacred output is large, though he was not as prolific here as in his secular music. Apart from approximately 40 masses, most of which remain in manuscript, the majority of his sacred works, numbering about 260 pieces, were published during his lifetime. In his masses he displayed a mastery of traditional parody techniques, which he treated with considerable variety. The seven masses of his first book (1587) are all based on motets; elsewhere he used chansons and madrigals as parody material, drawing not only on his own compositions, but also on those by Jacquet of Mantua, Josquin, Lassus, Palestrina, Rore, Alessandro Striggio (i), Verdelot and Wert. In his masses and motets he preferred a contrapuntal texture, reserving homophonic passages for variety and special effect. His melodies are often enlivened with lengthy melismas, which may well represent a notated equivalent of vocal improvisation; they recall the references in Georg Seld's letters to the 'art des colorierens' practised in Flanders. Although the part-writing in the motets is generally smooth, many passages contain angular melodies of almost instrumental character; in this respect Monte's style differs sharply from that of Palestrina. A melodic peculiarity is his occasional use at cadences of a formula that lacks the resolution of the leading note to the tonic but is otherwise conventional.

The technical features of Monte's sacred works range from the use of puzzle canons and cantus firmi to polychoral writing. Some of his polychoral motets are for seven voices, divided into choirs of three and four, instead of the more conventional eight or 12 voices. Unusual from the formal standpoint is the extensive repetition of text and music in some of his motets, so that a single *pars* may be patterned *ABB* or *ABCB* (e.g. in the *secunda pars* of *Exsurge Deus* from book 5, 24 of the 60 bars are repeated, producing an *ABB* form). His music is well supplied with specified accidentals, but he did not indulge in chromatic experiments, notwithstanding Cerone's statement (*El melopeo y maestro*, 1613) that 'Filippo de Monte and Luca Marenzio like to use very pleasant and very sweet chromatic progressions, or, to put it more appropriately, soft, sensuous and effeminate ones'. As far as the sacred music is concerned, no doubt Cerone was thinking of passages like that in *O suavitas et dulcedo*, where Monte used successive F♯'s and G♯'s in flowing melismas on the opening syllable, in order to evoke a mood of mystic exaltation (ex.1).

Ex.1 *O suavitas et dulcedo: Libro quarto de motetti*

3. SECULAR WORKS. Monte's secular works represent the largest part of his output and most of them are madrigals. He wrote over 1100 (compared with fewer than 50 chansons), published in 34 books spanning his entire career, and he also produced five books of *madrigali spirituali*. Many of his pieces were widely disseminated in collections and manuscripts. (Copies of the third seven-voice book of madrigals, mentioned by Einstein, and the ninth six-voice book, printed in 1603 and formerly in the Heyer Collection, Cologne, are lost.) Before his appointment in 1568 as imperial court Kapellmeister, Monte had proved himself a progressive, using many techniques that are typical of his style as a whole, such as mild, though sometimes striking, chromaticism, and a tendency to homophonic text treatment. It seems characteristic of his quiet and reserved personality that, even after his late start as a composer in 1554 at the age of 33, he took his time in producing the four works that pre-date his period of Habsburg service. After his appointment to the Habsburg court, the subsequent 35 years represent his most productive and successful period.

The texts of Monte's madrigals often dictate the musical forms. The early works are mostly drawn from Petrarch and the Petrarchists, but after the mid-1570s, during Rudolf II's reign, he turned to the pastoral poetry of his own time, particularly G. B. Guarini's *Il pastor fido*. This trend reached its climax in his madrigals for seven voices, *La fiammetta* (1599) and *Musica sopra Il pastor fido* (1600), which are settings of texts from Guarini's play. These two books show a late expansion of Monte's style, with greater use of short motifs, probably a result of Venetian influence. They are the only works with titles, thus suggesting a possible connection with court spectacle or theatrical performance. The *madrigali spirituali*, direct offshoots of the Counter-Reformation, differ from his other madrigals only in their texts. The chansons are mostly settings of Ronsard. The musical style of Monte's madrigals shows his mastery in counterpoint, but also his willingness to

*Philippe de Monte: medallion by Conrad Bloc (showing the composer at the age of 63) in the Bibliothèque Royale de Belgique, Brussels*

transgress strict contrapuntal rules in the search for effect. He frequently used cross-relations and other chromatic devices, but usually disguised them by making the alterations in different voices (ex.2). Towards the end of his career, a formal simplification, caused by the repetition of the last section of a piece, often led to an *ABB* form (this can also be found in the sacred works: see §2). Apart from a tendency towards homophonic writing, other important aspects of his style are subtle groupings of voices for creating certain effects, and frequent melismas, usually used in connection with word-painting.

Ex.2 *Hor che'l ciel: Il terzo libro de madrigali a sei voci* (Petrarch)

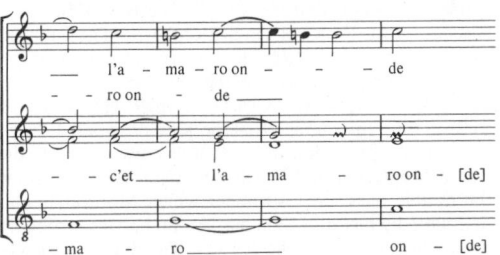

Monte's secular music was sung and admired across Europe, as is attested by the widespread distribution of his works in printed volumes and manuscripts. His length of service at the Habsburg court, the numerous reprints of his madrigal volumes and the frequent inclusion of his pieces in anthologies are all marks of his success and of the respect and esteem that he commanded. But a full evaluation of his work and influence must await the completion of a modern edition of his music.

## WORKS

Editions: *Trésor musical*, ed. R. van Maldeghem (Brussels, 1865–93) [M]

P. de Monte: *Opera*, ed. C. van den Borren and G. van Doorslaer (Bruges, 1927–39/*R*1965) [B]

P. de Monte: *New Complete Edition*, ed. R. B. Lenaerts and others (Louvain, 1975–) [L]

(*printed works published in Venice unless otherwise stated*)

### MASSES

Missa ad modulum 'Benedicta es', 6vv (Antwerp, 1579); M, and ed. in UVNM, xxxviii (1920)

Liber primus [7] missarum, 5, 6, 8vv (Antwerp, 1587); M, 2 in B xxiv, xxvii, 4 in L iii

Mass, 5vv, 1590[1]

Anchor che col partire, 4vv, *B-Bc*, *D-B*, *YU-Lu* (inc., T only), B viii; Aspice Domine, 6vv, *A-Wn*, *D-Mbs*, *Z*, *H-Bn*, B xxvi; Cara la vita mia, 5vv, *A-Wn*, *YU-Lu*, B xxi; Inclina cor meum, 5vv, *B-Bc*, B i; La dolce vista, 8vv, *A-Wn*, *B-Bc*, B xiv; Nasce la pena mia, 6vv, *A-Wn*, *B-Bc*, *D-B*, *PL-WRu*, Kaplanské Knihovny, B x; O altitudo divitiarum, 5vv, *B-Bc*, B iv; Missa pro defunctis, 5vv, *A-Wn*, B xiii; Quando lieta speray, 5vv, *Wn*, B xxiii; Reviens vers moi, 4vv, *B-Bc*, B ix; Ultimi miei sospiri, 6vv, *A-Wn*, *B-Bc*, B v

Missa sexti toni, 6vv, *PL-WRu*; Missa septimi toni, 5vv, *WRu*; Missa septimi toni, 6vv, *WRu*; Missa ad tonum peregrinum, 6vv, *WRu*

5 untitled, 4vv, *B-Bc*, Cologne, Chapel of St Maria im Kapitol, 3 in B iii, xi, xvi; 4 untitled, 5vv, *D-B*, *PL-WRu*, 1 in B xxviii; 5 untitled, 6vv, *A-Wn*, *CS-Pnm*, *D-B*, *Nla*, *PL-WRu*, 4 in B vii, xviii, xxx, xxxi; 1 untitled, 8vv, *A-Wn*, B xxix

### MOTETS

Sacrarum cantionum ... liber primus, 5vv (1572); L i
Sacrarum cantionum ... liber secundus, 5vv (1573); L ii
Sacrarum cantionum ... liber tertius, 5vv (1574)
Libro quarto de motetti, 5vv (1575); B xxii
Sacrarum cantionum ... liber quintus, 5vv (1579)
Sacrarum cantionum ... liber sextus, 5vv (1584), lost
Sacrarum cantionum ... liber primus, 6, 12vv (1585)
Sacrarum cantionum ... liber secundus, 6vv (1587)
Sacrarum cantionum ... liber primus, 4vv (1596) [B only]
Sacrarum cantionum ... liber septimus, 5vv (1600); B xvii

28 motets, 3–6vv, 3 odes, 2 litanies, 1564[3], 1580[3], 1583[2], 1590[5], 1591[2], 1596[2], 1598[2], 1600[2], 1605[1], 1609[15], c1610[18], 1611[1], 1621[2], Florilegium musicum motectorum (Bamberg, 1631)

Asperges me, 5vv, *A-Wn*, B xv; Ave regina coelorum, 4vv, *E-Bc* (doubtful); Beati omnes, *CS-Pnm* (inc., A only); Expurgate vetus, *Pnm* (inc., A only); Laudate Dominum, 8vv, *D-B*, B xv; Magnificat, 4vv, *A-Gmi*, *D-As*, B xii; Salve regina, 5vv, *YU-Lu* (anon., inc., A only); Super flumina Babylonis, 8vv, *CS-Pnm* (inc., A II only); *GB-Lbm*, *T* (inc., A I only), B xv

### MADRIGALI SPIRITUALI

Il primo libro de madrigali spirituali, 5vv (1581); ed. in Nuten (1958), ii
Il primo libro de madrigali spirituali, 6vv (1583/*R*1972); B vi
Il secondo libro de madrigali spirituali, 6, 7vv (1589/*R*1972); ed. in Nuten (1958), iii
Il terzo libro de madrigali spirituali, 6vv (1590)
Eccellenze di Maria vergine, 5vv (1593) [B only]
1 madrigale spirituale, 6vv, *I-Rsc* (inc.)

### MADRIGALS

Madrigali ... libro primo, 5vv (Rome, 1554)
Il primo libro de madrigali, 4vv (1562)
Il secondo libro de madrigali, 5vv (1567); 1 ed. in DTÖ, lxxvii, Jg.xli (1934/*R*)
Il primo libro de' madrigali, 6vv (before 1569, lost; 2/1569)
Il secondo libro delli madrigali, 6vv (1569)
Il secondo libro delli madrigali, 4vv (1569)
Il terzo libro delli madrigali, 5vv (1570)
Il quarto libro delli madrigali, 5vv (1571)
Madrigali ... libro quinto, 5vv (1574)
Il sesto libro delli madrigali, 5vv (1575)
Il terzo libro de madrigali, 6vv (1576)
Il settimo libro delli madrigali, 5vv (1578)
Il quarto libro de madrigali, 6vv (1580)
L'ottavo libro delli madrigali, 5vv (1580)
Il nono libro de madrigali, 5vv (1580)
Il terzo libro de madrigali, 4vv (before 1581, lost; 2/1585)
Il decimo libro delli madrigali, 5vv (1581)
Il quarto libro de madrigali, 4vv (1581); B xix
Il primo libro de madrigali, 3vv (1582)
Il quinto libro de madrigali, 6vv (1584)
L'undecimo libro delli madrigali, 5vv (1586)
Il duodecimo libro delli madrigali, 5vv (1587)
Il terzodecimo libro delli madrigali, 5vv (1588)
Il quartodecimo libro delli madrigali, 5vv (1590)
Il sesto libro de madrigali, 6vv (1591)
Il settimo libro de madrigali, 6vv (1591)
Il quintodecimo libro de madrigali, 5vv (1592)
Il sestodecimo libro delli madrigali, 5vv (1593)
L'ottavo libro de madrigali, 6vv (1594)
Il decimosettimo libro delli madrigali, 5vv (1595)
Il decimottavo libro de madrigali, 5vv (1597)
Il decimonono libro delli madrigali, 5vv (1598)
La fiammetta ... libro primo, 7vv (1599); 2 ed. in DTÖ, lxxvii, Jg.xli (1934/*R*)

Musica sopra Il pastor fido . . . libro secondo, 7vv (1600)

Madrigals, ?incl. some reprints, in 1558[13], 1561[15], 1562[7], 1567[15], 1568[12], 1570[25], 1573[16], 1576[5], 1577, 1579[3], 1583[10], 1583[14], 1583[15], 1584[4], 1585[17], 1585[19], 1586[11], 1588[19], 1589[12], 1590[11], 1591[18], 1591[23], 1592[11], 1593[3], 1593[5], 1596[8], 1601[7]

Madrigals, 3rd book, 7vv, lost (cited in Einstein, 1949)
Madrigals, 9th book, 6vv, lost (formerly Heyer Collection, Cologne)

CHANSONS

Sonetz de P. de Ronsard mis en musique, 5–7vv (Paris and Louvain, 1575)
22 chansons, 4–6vv, 1567[11], 1570[6], 1570[7], 1570[9], 1572[2], 1575[4], 1576[4], 1577[6], 1583[8], 1597[10]

BIBLIOGRAPHY

E. van der Straeten: *La musique aux Pays-Bas avant le XIXe siècle* (Brussels, 1867–88/*R*1969)
V. Ebenstein: *Die Messen Philippe de Montes, mit besonderer Berücksichtigung seiner Parodietechnik* (diss., U. of Vienna, 1912)
C. van den Borren: *Les musiciens belges en Angleterre à l'époque de la Renaissance* (Brussels, 1913)
P. Wagner: *Geschichte der Messe* (Leipzig, 1913)
A. Smijers: 'Die kaiserliche Hofmusik-Kapelle von 1543–1619', *SMw*, vi (1919); vii (1920); viii (1921); ix (1922); pubd separately (Vienna, 1922)
P. Bergmans: *Quatorze lettres inédites du compositeur Philippe de Monte* (Brussels, 1921)
G. van Doorslaer: *La vie et les oeuvres de Philippe de Monte* (Brussels, 1921)
A. Smijers: *Karl Luython als Motetten-Komponist* (Amsterdam, 1923)
G. van Doorslaer: *Deux lettres nouvelles de Philippe de Monte* (Mechelen, 1927)
A. Einstein: 'Filippo di Monte als Madrigalkomponist', *IMSCR*, i *Liège 1930*, 102
G. van Doorslaer: 'Die Musikkapelle Kaiser Rudolfs II. im Jahre 1582 unter der Leitung von Philippe de Monte', *ZMw*, xiii (1930–31), 481
——: 'La chapelle musicale de l'empereur Rudolph II en 1594, sous la direction de Philippe de Monte', *AcM*, v (1933), 148
A. Einstein: 'Italienische Musik und italienische Musiker am Kaiserhof', *SMw*, xxi (1934), 3
M. van Crevel: *Adrianus Petit Coclico* (The Hague, 1940)
P. Oberg: *The Sacred Music of Philippe de Monte* (diss., U. of Rochester, 1944)
A. Einstein: *The Italian Madrigal* (Princeton, 1949/*R*1971)
R. B. Lenaerts: 'The 16th-century Parody Mass in the Netherlands', *MQ*, xxxvi (1950), 410
M. Antonowytsch: *Die Motette Benedicta es von Josquin des Prez und die Messen Benedicta von Willaert, Palestrina, de la Hêle und de Monte* (Utrecht, 1951)
H. C. Wolff: *Die Musik der alten Niederländer* (Leipzig, 1956)
P. Nuten: *De madrigali spirituali van Filip de Monte* (Brussels, 1958)
G. Michael: *The Parody Mass Technique of Philippe de Monte* (diss., New York U., 1959)
W. Elders: 'Enkele aspecten van de parodie-technik in de madrigaal-missen van Philippus de Monte', *TVNM*, xix/3–4 (1962–3), 131
A. vander Linden: 'Note sur les dédicaces de Philippe de Monte', *Bulletin de la classe des beaux-arts de l'Académie royale de Belgique*, l (1963)
P. Nuten: 'Enkele stijlkritische beschowingen over de Franse chansons van Filip de Monte', *Renaissance-muziek 1400–1600: donum natalicium René Bernard Lenaerts* (Louvain, 1969), 195
W. Pass: 'Die originelle Ansicht des Unendlichen: die Madrigali spiri-tuali von Philippo de Monte und der Manierismus', *Musica bohemica et europaea: Brno V 1970*, 145
R. M. Lindell: *Die sechs- und siebenstimmige Madrigale von Filippo di Monte* (diss., U. of Vienna, 1977)
——: 'Filippo di Montes Widmungen an Rudolf II.', *Musicologica aus-triaca*, ii (1978)
I. Bossuyt: 'Newly-discovered Part Books of Early Madrigal Collections of Philippus de Monte (1521–1603)', *FAM*, xxvi (1979), 295

MILTON STEINHARDT (1, 2), ROBERT M. LINDELL (3)

**Monte Carlo.** Town in the principality of MONACO.

**Monte Carmelo, Pater a.** *See* SPIRIDION.

**Montecino, Alfonso Montalva** (*b* Osorno, 28 Oct 1924). Chilean pianist and composer. Having begun his music studies in Osorno, in 1938 he entered the Santiago Conservatory, where he studied the piano with Spivkin and composition with Santa Cruz and Urrutia. He remained at the conservatory until 1945, and from 1947 to 1948 studied composition with Thompson at Princeton University; among his other teachers at this time were Martinů, Varèse and Sessions, the last-named at the Juilliard School (1948–50). He continued piano studies, from 1948 to 1957, with Arrau and Silva. Known for his interpretations of the music of Bach and Beethoven, he was awarded the Bach Medal of the Harriet Cohen Foundation in 1954. In 1964 he joined the staff of Indiana University. His compositions are neo-classical in style. He has written an article on the interpretation of the '48' (*Revista musical chilena* (1975), nos.129–30, p.41).

WORKS
(*selective list*)

Orch: Obertura concertante, 1948; Concertino, 1965
Chamber: Str Qt, 1945; Trio, ob, cl, bn, 1948; Wind Qnt, 1960
Pf: Sonata, 1946; Suite, 1948; Composición, left hand, 1951; 5 piezas, 1960; 4 Inventions, 1965

BIBLIOGRAPHY
J. Orrego-Salas: 'Alfonso Montecino y las sonatas de Beethoven', *Revista musical chilena* (1973), nos.121–2, p.126

JOHN M. SCHECHTER

**Montéclair, Michel Pignolet** [Pinolet] **de** (*b* Andelot, Haute-Marne, baptized 4 Dec 1667; *d* Aumont, 22 [not 27] Sept 1737). French composer, theorist and teacher. Michel Pignolet was the youngest of seven children born to the weaver Adrien Pignolet and Suzanne Galliot. On 27 January 1676 he entered the choir school at the Cathedral of Langres where he studied under Jean-Baptiste Moreau, director of the choir from October 1681 to February 1682. He added the name of 'Montéclair' (a fortress in Andelot) to his own some time after his arrival in Paris in 1687, but signed himself 'Pignolet dit Montéclair' as late as 1724. From the title-page of his *Nouvelle méthode pour apprendre la musique* (1709), we learn that he was 'formerly *maître de la musique* for the Prince of Vaudémont', whom he followed to Italy. Details of his Italian sojourn are unknown.

Montéclair performed on the *basse de violon* in the Paris Opéra orchestra as early as 1699. He played so well on this instrument that he was designated 'symphoniste du petit choeur'. It is well known that at the Opéra Montéclair and Fedeli were the first to introduce the double bass, an instrument which Montéclair had undoubtedly heard in Italian opera orchestras, probably soon after the turn of the century. The double bass was possibly used as early as Gatti's *Scylla* in 1701 and certainly by the time of Campra's *Tancrède* in 1703.

Montéclair, whose pupils included the daughters of François Couperin, was highly regarded as a teacher. His pedagogical approach was non-doctrinaire ('It is very difficult to give general principles on the *égalité* and the *inégalité* of notes') and at times quite modern ('The surest way of all is to make them [children] think of the lessons as something amusing'). In 1721 he and his nephew, François Boivin, founded a music shop on the rue St Honoré in the parish of St Eustache. In 1728, after François' marriage, Montéclair sold his interest for 9000 livres. After François' death in 1733, the shop, directed by his widow, became one of the most important in Paris. Montéclair gave up teaching about 1735 but retained his position in the Opéra orchestra until 1 July 1737. He never married. At the time of his death he lived with a niece and nephew at 16 rue des Marmousets (now rue Chanoinesse) on the Ile de la Cité.

Although not prolific, Montéclair wrote in most of the genres cultivated during the early 18th century in France, excepting only the keyboard. He was one of the most versatile of the generation between Lully's death (1687) and Rameau's advent as a stage composer (1733); composers of this 'préramiste' period are often described as 'imitators of Lully', but Montéclair and Campra are among those who influenced Rameau's dramatic music. In his stage works, Montéclair was particularly sensitive to the dramatic function of orchestral colour. His operatic scores are much clearer than those of his contemporaries in giving directions for specific instruments, like the off-stage horns 'played very softly to simulate the hunt in the distance' in the second *entrée* of *Les festes de l'été* (Montéclair added that 'if no *cors de chasse* are available, oboes and violins may play the following and remain in the orchestra'). In the same work, a 'Prélude à trois basses' introduces the first scene of the third *entrée*, where the main roles are sung by basses; the prelude to the second scene, whose main roles are sung by sopranos, is scored for violins and violas without continuó. The parts enter in reverse order, and the melodic material is derived from the earlier prelude (ex.1). *Les festes de l'été* and *Jephté* both contain an *a cappella* chorus and the former has a large-scale double chorus – an operatic counterpart to the choruses in Lalande's *grands motets*.

Ex.1(a) from the Prelude to Act 3 scene i of *Les festes de l'été*

*Basses   du   côté droit*

*Basses   du   côté gauche*

*Contre-basses, basses d'accompagnement et bassons*

(b) from the Prelude to Act 3 scene ii of *Les festes de l'été*

*Premier dessus de violons*

*Second dessus de violons*

*Haute-contres, tailles et quintes de violons*

Rameau particularly admired the chorus 'Tout tremble devant le Seigneur', from the first act of *Jephté*, a 'Tragedy taken from Holy Scripture', whose prologue is set on the stage of the Académie Royale de Musique itself, and which was very successful in spite of its condemnation by the Archbishop of Paris. Its music was considered difficult; D'Aquin observed that 'several pieces from this Opera could not have been performed at the time of Lully because of their difficulty' (*Siècle littéraire de Louis XV*, Paris, 2/1753).

Montéclair's contribution to the development of the French cantata has been little studied. His *Adieu de Tircis à Climène* appeared in October 1695 in the Ballard *Recueil d'airs sérieux et à boire*. This little scene expands the dialogues by Richard, La Barre, Lambert and others found in earlier collections. Its musical components are organized as follows: (1) Recitative of Tircis; (2) Air of Climène; (3) Recitative of Tircis; and

(4) Duo (in da capo form). This cantata-like dialogue was composed at least 11 years before J.-B. Morin set the cantata texts of J.-B. Rousseau to music, thereby earning the title of 'first composer of French cantatas'. The story of Tircis and Climène served Montéclair for a true cantata in 1728, in his third book of *Cantates*.

The 20 French and four Italian cantatas by Montéclair ill deserve their neglect. Like Clérambault and Campra, he borrowed liberally from operatic sources; his cantatas include a *tempête* (*La mort de Didon*), a *bruit de guerre* (*Le retour de la paix*) and a *sommeil* (*La bergère*). *Le retour de la paix* is an impressive study in contrast of textures, moods, tempos and tonalities (D major frames the cantata, which moves through B minor, G major, E minor, A minor, F major and D minor). The longest and most dramatic cantata is *Pyrame et Thisbé* (four *airs*, two *ariettes*, ten recitatives and three duos). In Montéclair's words, it is 'half Epic, half Dramatic. What is Epic is sung by a baritone who represents the narrator, and what is Dramatic must be performed by a soprano and countertenor who are the protagonists'. The characterization is achieved in the opening bars of the first duo (ex.2) through the delayed resolution of the 9th chords in bars eight and 12 and through representation of 'allarmes' by a fanfare motif.

For Montéclair, only French composers 'possessed true taste for writing small pieces that other nations call Bagatelles' (preface to *Brunètes anciènes et modernes*). Most of Montéclair's instrumental music reflects this point of view, such as the three suites that comprise his *Sérénade ou concert* of 1697. The sub-title informs us that this music is 'suitable for dancing', and the preface suggests that the 'violons, flûtes & hautbois' called for

Ex.2 opening of the duo 'Que d'allarmes' from *Pyrame et Thisbé*

(*Cantates à une et à deux voix*, book 2)

could be reduced to 'just one treble and one bass instrument'. Each suite is built around a particular instrumental colour: the first, 'Airs de fanfare', uses the French 'trio des hautbois'; the second, 'Airs tendres', is 'night music' filled with the poetry of flutes and violins; and the third, 'Airs champêtres', exploits musettes and a 'Tambour de Basque'.

As a theorist, Montéclair was less systematic and abstract than Rameau, with whom he quarrelled in an exchange of eight anonymous articles in the *Mercure de France*. He was concerned mostly with the practical application of theory, as exemplified by his *Petite méthode pour apprendre la musique aux enfans* and his *Méthode facile pour apprendre à jouer du violon* (the first violin method in France). The pages of his *Nouvelle méthode pour apprendre la musique* are filled with musical examples illustrating 'Airs de dance sur toutes sortes de mouvements'. The carefully illustrated section on the '18 principal ornaments in singing' in his *Principes de musique* makes this one of the most important sources on French vocal ornamentation of the early 18th century.

### WORKS
*(all printed works published in Paris unless otherwise stated)*

#### AIRS
*(published in the following books)*

Nouvelles poésies morales sur les plus beaux airs de la musique françoise et italienne (1737)
Nouvelles poésies spirituelles et morales sur les plus beaux airs de la musique françoise et italienne (1730–37)
Les parodies du nouveaux théâtre italien (1731–8)
Les parodies nouvelles et les vaudevilles inconnus (1731–6)
Recueil d'airs sérieux et à boire (1695³, 1696², 1697², 1698¹, 1713, 1716)
Recueil de pièces, petits airs, brunettes, menuets ... pour les flûtes traversières, violons, pardessus de viole (c1755)
Second recueil des nouvelles poésies spirituelles et morales (1731)
Le tribut de la toilette. Mélanges lyriques (c1744)
1 air in J. B. de La Borde: *Essai sur la musique ancienne et moderne*, ii (Paris, 1780/R1972), 55

#### CANTATAS

Cantates, 1v, insts, premier livre (c1709): La fortune, extract ed. J. Arger (Paris, n.d.); Le triomphe de la constance, extract in H. Prunières: *Les maîtres du chant*, ii (Paris, 1925); La badine, extract ed. J. Arger (Paris, 1913); Le dépit généreux, extract ed. J. Arger (Paris, n.d.); Godimento e pena in amore; La mort de Didon; Amante di bella donna; Le retour de la paix, extract ed. J. Arger (Paris, 1913, 2/1945)
Cantates, 1–2vv, insts, second livre (c1716): L'amour vangé; Les syrènes, extract ed. J. Arger (Paris, n.d.); Le triomphe de l'amour; Pan et Syrinx, extract ed. J. Arger (Paris, 1910); L'enlèvement d'Orithie; Pyrame et Thisbé; Il dispetto in amor
Cantates, 1–2vv, insts, troisième livre (1728), ed. J. Anthony and D. Akmajian, *RRMBE*, xxix–xxx (1978): Les délices champestres (Dejan); L'heureux moment; Ariane et Bachus; Sur un arbrisseau (Rousseau); La bergère; Tircis et Climène; Le songe; Europe; Morte di Lucretia
Les vendanges, cantata, in Recueil de cantates françoises et italiennes (Amsterdam, 1726)

#### THEATRICAL WORKS
*(all first performed at Paris Opéra)*

Les festes de l'été, opéra ballet (S. J. Pellegrin), prol, 4 entrées: Les jours d'été, Les soirées d'été, Les nuits d'été, Les matinées d'été (added later, 1716); 12 June 1716 (1716; 2/1716 avec une entrée ajoutée); last revival (prol only), 1752
Jephté, tragédie lyrique (Pellegrin), prol, 5 acts, 28 Feb 1732 (c1732, 2/c1733); last revival 1761

#### SACRED MUSIC

Messe de Requiem, 1736; lost, mentioned in Titon du Tillet
Diligam Te, 2 S; In choris, 2 S: both in Principes de musique
O sacrum convivium, 2 S, bc; Properate huc, o populi, 2 S, B, chorus, bc: both *F-Pn*
In exitu Israel, for large choruses; Credidi propter, for 2 choruses: both lost, mentioned in Principes de musique
Exaltabor, motet, lost
Motets, 16vv, lost, mentioned in preface to Brunètes anciènes et modernes
Canons, 8vv, lost

#### INSTRUMENTAL MUSIC

Sérénade ou concert divisez en 3 suites, vns, recs, obs (1697)
Contre-dances et branles, i (?before 1709); ii, lost
Pieces in Menuets tant anciens que nouveaux (?before 1709); Deuxième recueil (?before 1709); 3e–6e recueils (?before 1709), lost
Recueil de trio italiens et françois, 2 fl/vn, bc (n.d.), lost
[6] Concerts, 2 fl, no b (n.d.); ed. R. Viollier (New York and Locarno, 1962–4)
Concerts, fl, bc (n.d.)
Brunètes anciènes et modernes, fl/vn (n.d.)

### WRITINGS
#### TREATISES
*(all published in Paris)*

*Nouvelle méthode pour apprendre la musique* (1709)
*Leçons de musique divisées en quatre classes* (c1709)
*Méthode facile pour apprendre à jouer du violon* (1711–12)
*Petite méthode pour apprendre la musique aux enfans et même aux personnes plus avencées en âge* (c1735)
*Principes de musique* (1736/R1972)

#### ARTICLES
*(all in Mercure de France)*

'Conférence sur la musique' (June 1729), 1281
'Réponse du second musicien au premier musicien, auteur de l'examen inséré dans le Mercure d'octobre 1728' (May 1730), 880
'Réponse du second musicien au premier musicien sur les deux écrits qui concernent l'accompagnement du clavecin' (June 1730), 1079

#### BIBLIOGRAPHY

E. Titon du Tillet: *Le Parnasse françois* (Paris, 1743/R1971)
J. A. L. de La Fage: 'Michel Montéclair', *Revue et gazette musicale de Paris*, xxiv (1857), 250, 259
J. Carlez: 'Un opéra biblique au xviiie siècle', *Mémoires de l'Académie des sciences, arts et belle-lettres de Caen* (Caen, 1879), 364
E. Voillard: *Essai sur Montéclair* (Paris, 1879)
M. Pincherle: 'La technique du violon chez les premiers sonatistes français', *BSIM*, vii (1911), 1–32; viii (1912), 19
L. de La Laurencie: *L'école française de violon de Lully à Viotti* (Paris, 1922–4/R1971)
M. Pincherle: 'Elementary Musical Instruction in the 18th Century: an Unknown Treatise by Montéclair', *MQ*, xxxiv (1948), 61
E. Borrel: 'Notes sur l'orchestration de l'opéra *Jephté* de Montéclair (1733) et de la symphonie des *Elémens* de J. F. Rebel (1737)', *ReM*, no.226 (1955), 105
M. Briquet: 'Deux motets inédites de Montéclair', *IMSCR, vii Cologne 1958*, 75
R. Viollier: 'Trois Jephté, trois styles', *RdM*, xliii (1959), 125
S. Milliot: 'Le testament de Michel Pignolet de Montéclair', *RMFC*, viii (1968), 131
J. R. Anthony: *French Baroque Music from Beaujoyeulx to Rameau* (London, 1973, rev. 2/1978)
D. Tunley: *The Eighteenth-century French Cantata* (London, 1974)
J. R. Anthony: 'French Binary Air within Italian Aria da capo in Montéclair's Third Book of Cantatas', *PRMA*, civ (1977–8), 47
J. A. Sadie: 'Montéclair, the Viol Player's Composer', *Journal of the Viola da Gamba Society of America*, xv (1978), 330
JAMES R. ANTHONY

**Montella** [Montelli], **Giovanni Domenico** [Mico] (*b* Naples, *c*1570; *d* Naples, before 2 July 1607). Italian composer, lutenist and organist. He was a lutenist in the academy of Don Fabrizio Gesualdo in the late 1580s and at this period worked in close association with his teacher, Giovanni de Macque. In 1591 Montella became a lutenist in the chapel of the Spanish viceroy in Naples, where from 1599 he again served under Macque, not only as a lutenist but also as an organist. He worked alongside Trabaci and Mayone as well as Macque, an association that seems to have stimulated him to exceptional productivity, for all but two of his 19 publications appeared between 1600 and 1607. He had died by 2 July 1607, the date of dedication of his posthumously published eighth book of five-part madrigals.

In 1599 Ancina included six three-part *laude* by 'Mico Montelli' in his *Tempio armonico*. They resemble villanellas in style: occasional imitative passages with the upper voices in 3rds against the bass enliven a basically homophonic texture. His four-part *lauda Se mai vergine pia*, which appeared in 1600 in *Nuove laudi ariose*, sounds a more personal note, expressed through chromaticism and experimental harmonies. The latter tendency is also present in the eight-part polychoral motets and masses of 1600, whose more lyrical aspects set Montella apart from Trabaci and Mayone. The five-part motets of 1603, while more conservative in style, show him to be a master of contrapuntal techniques: in *Terribilis est locus* the outer voices sing a double canon against the cantus firmus in the tenor, and *Ad Dominum cum tribular clamavi* is a strict triple canon. The *Lamentationes* (1601) combines contrapuntal ingenuity with expressive, roving harmonies and appropriate chromaticism.

The texts that Montella chose for his madrigals have a popular, villanella-like flavour. Tasso and Macedonio di Mutio are the only poets who can be identified. The madrigals can be divided into three distinct groups: the two early books (1595–6); the experimental madrigals of 1602–4 (five books); and the last three books (1605–7). In the second group Montella developed his roving harmonies more extravagantly and many passages are in the *durezze e ligature* style. In the later books this highly personal style subsided in favour of a more pastoral type of piece, usually with long homophonic passages incorporating contrasting metres.

WORKS
*(all published in Naples unless otherwise stated)*

SACRED

Motectorum et missarum, liber primus, 8vv (1600); a few ed. in IMi, v (1934)
Lamentationes et alia ad officium Hebdomadae, 4vv (1601)
Responsoria Hebdomadae Sacrae, 4vv (1602)
Motectorum, liber primus, 5vv (1603)
Psalmi, 4, 8vv (1605)

SECULAR

Primo libro de madrigali, 5vv (1595)
Secondo libro de madrigali, 5vv (Venice, 1596)
Terzo libro de madrigali, 5vv (1602)
Quarto libro de madrigali, 5vv (1602)
Primo libro de villanelle, 3, 4vv (2/1602)
Quinto libro de madrigali, 5vv (1602)
Sesto libro de madrigali, 5vv (1603)
Primo libro de madrigali, 4vv (1604)
Secondo libro de villanelle, 2, 4vv (1604)
Settimo libro de madrigali, 5vv (1605)
Terzo libro de villanelle, 2, 4vv (1605)
Quarto libro de villanelle, 2, 4vv (1606)
Ottavo libro de madrigali, 5vv (1607)
Secondo libro de madrigali, 4vv (1607)

6 laude, 3vv, in 1599[6]; 1, 4vv, in 1600[5]; Ferrabosco's Io mi son giovinetta, arr. Montella for kbd, ed. in CEKM, xxiv (1967)

BIBLIOGRAPHY

U. Prota-Giurleo: 'La musica a Napoli nel seicento', *Samnium*, iv (1928), 72
G. Pannain: Introduction to IMi, v (1934), xxv
M. Reimann: 'Ein italienisches Pasticcio von 1609', *Mf*, xix (1966), 289
W. RICHARD SHINDLE

**Montelli, Giovanni Domenico.** *See* MONTELLA, GIOVANNI DOMENICO.

**Montemezzi, Italo** (*b* Vigasio, nr. Verona, 31 May 1875; *d* Vigasio, 15 May 1952). Italian composer. He began studying engineering before entering the Milan Conservatory, where he took a diploma in 1900 and then taught harmony for a year. Thereafter he was able to live entirely as a composer, and he never again held an official teaching post. From 1939 to 1949 he resided mainly in California. His reputation rests largely on *L'amore dei tre re*, which has been persistently successful in the USA – far more so, indeed, than in Italy. But his best qualities were already evident in *Giovanni Gallurese*: sound craftsmanship, a theatrical instinct, appropriate touches of local colour (in this case Sardinian) and, above all, a judicious use of Wagnerian

harmony and orchestration within a framework that is still traditionally Italian and voice-centred – a compromise at times reminiscent of Catalani. Wagnerian tendencies became more pervasive in *Hellera* and *L'amore dei tre re*; there are even parallels of plot between the latter work and *Tristan*. The opera contains moments of real tragic power, as in Archibaldo's formidable cry of desperation at the end of Act 1. Yet even in this, Montemezzi's most celebrated work, it is hard to discover an individual personality; indeed, compared with *Giovanni Gallurese*, there is already some loss of melodic spontaneity. *L'amore dei tre re* was the last of his compositions to win enduring success: *La nave*, though forceful enough in some scenes and enriched with occasional Straussian devices, is laboured and uneven. Montemezzi then lapsed into a long silence, broken only by a few minor pieces, in which he showed no further interest in broadening his language.

WORKS

Operas: Bianca (Z. Strani), early, unpubd, unperf.; Giovanni Gallurese (F. d'Angelantonio), Turin, 1905; Hellera (L. Illica), Turin, 1909; L'amore dei tre re (S. Benelli), Milan, 1913; La nave (D'Annunzio), Milan, 1918; La notte di Zoraima (M. Ghisalberti), Milan, 1931; L'incantesimo (Benelli), NBC, 1943, staged Verona, 1952, unpubd; at least 1 other, inc.

Other works: Cantico dei cantici, chorus, orch, 1900; Per le onoranze ad Amilcare Ponchielli, chorus, orch, 1911; Paolo e Virginia, orch, 1929; Elegy, vc, pf, 1932; Italia mia, nulla fermerà il tuo canto, orch, 1944

Principal publisher: Ricordi

BIBLIOGRAPHY

L. Gilman: 'A Note on Montemezzi', *Nature in Music and Other Studies* (New York, 1914), 155
U. Navarra: *Noterelle critiche sulla tragedia . . . La nave . . .* (Milan, 1918)
A. Lualdi: 'L'amore dei tre re di Montemezzi alla Scala', *Serate musicali* (Milan, 1928), 237
L. Tomelleri: 'La nave (D'Annunzio e Montemezzi)', in L. Tomelleri, I. Pizzetti and others: *Gabriele d'Annunzio e la musica* (Milan, 1939), 40; repr. in *RMI*, xliii (1939), 200
D. J. Grout: *A Short History of Opera* (New York, 1947), 444; (2/1965), 509
L. Tretti and L. Fiumi, eds.: *Omaggio a Italo Montemezzi* (Verona, 1952)
T. Serafin: 'Italo Montemezzi', *Opera News*, xvii/12 (New York, 1952–3), 10, 31
A. Toni: 'Italo Montemezzi', *Ricordiana*, new ser., ii (Milan, 1956), 229
JOHN C. G. WATERHOUSE

**Montenelli, Bernardo.** *See* HALTENBERGER, BERNHARD.

**Montero.** Venezuelan family of musicians.

**(1) José María Montero** (*b* 1782; *d* 1869). Composer and violinist. He studied with J. Luís Landaeta and from 1816 worked with the Venezuelan musicians José de Jesús Alas and Manuel Peña. From 1822 to 1851 his name appeared in account books indicating his service to churches and confraternities in Caracas, such as the Church of Altagracia (1822), S Mauricio (1824, 1826, 1842) and Divina Pastora (1842). At Altagracia he worked with the musicians Josef Marquez and Ramón Lozano. In 1824 he was employed by the Confraternity of the Holy Rosary for the important feast of Naval. He also worked for the confraternities Blessed Sacrament (1822) and S Juan Bautista (1824, 1826, 1842).

WORKS

Trisagio, 3vv, 1814; 2nd Lesson of the Dead, in honour of Bolívar, 1842; Tono, 3vv, for the Society of S José; Vexilla regis; O sacrum convivium; Pange lingua (Sp.), 3vv; Tono para le fiesta de Nuestra señora de Candelaria; Libera me; Quae est ista, gradual; Salve; Canto a María; Versos a Jesús crucificado; Versos a la virgen del Carmen; Aria a la virgen (?spurious); Versos a la virgen para la pesta (?spurious)

**(2) José Lorenzo Montero** (*b* ?Caracas, *fl* 1842–5). Composer, teacher and music director, son of (1) José María Montero. He formed and directed a music group that was first announced in *El venezolano* on 17 December 1844 and 7 January 1845. The group was qualified to play for churches, theatres, dances and other occasions. He also collected newly composed Venezuelan music and foreign works. His own compositions are both lyrical and dramatic. He had a penchant for melodic variation, chromatic word-painting and madrigalisms. His works are formally well structured, and there are many points of imitation within the sections. Soloistic writing and pairing of voices contrast with homophonic blocks, and he favoured elided resolutions and mediant shifts.

WORKS

Sacred: Tantum ergo; 3rd Lesson of the Dead, in memory of Bolívar, 1842; Funeral March; Mass of the Dead; Pange lingua; Trisagio; Tollite portes, gradual; Ave Maria, offertory; Credo; Gradual for the Holy Cross; Jerusalem; O María, soberana reina del cielo; Salve; Gozos a San Francisco de Paula; Benedicta, gradual; Ave maris stella
Other works: March, F; Himno for 5 July; Andante; Patriotic Song for 19 April

**(3) Ramón Montero** (*b* ? Caracas, early 19th century; *d* after 1878). Composer, son of (1) José María Montero. He is mentioned in a document of 17 February 1851. Among the musicians who knew him were Manuel Peña and José de Jesús Alas. His most active years musically were 1863–79, when he was in the employ of Caracas Cathedral as a church musician, receiving payments in 1863–4, 1868, 1875 and 1877–9. It is likely that he was also employed by various confraternities, as he was recompensed in 1875 for music he provided at the feast of Minerva.

WORKS

Sacred: Invitatory and Office of the Dead; Office of the Dead; Magnificat; Tantum ergo; Versos para el Santo niño de Atocha; Gozos a San Juan Nepomuceno; Letrilla al corazón de Jesús; Stabat mater; Gozos del Trisagio; Canticos a María; Música para cuadros biblicas; Oh reina del Carmelo; Pange lingua
Other works: Canción andaluza

**(4) José Angel Montero** (*b* 1839; *d* 1881). Composer, singer, flautist and educator, son of (1) José María Montero. His earliest dated composition is a zarzuela, *Colegiales son colegiales*, of 5 March 1868. Other stage works, *El charlatan mudo*, *Diomira* and *Virginia*, date from 1873. In 1875 he became *maestro de capilla* of Caracas Cathedral and presided over feasts such as Corpus Christi, S Pedro and Holy Week. On 20 April 1876 he presented to the Venezuelan ministers a proposal for a national musical institute to educate musicians, print Venezuelan compositions and reprint foreign music. He further proposed a musical periodical, the *Gazeta musical*. Among his board of directors he mentioned the musicians José de Jesús Alas, Rogerio Caraballo and S. Talavera. The President of Venezuela decreed that the institute be created to accommodate 45 students.

The style of Montero's sacred compositions is rhythmically versatile, dynamic, yet fluid and graceful. His orchestration is dense, with sudden changes in dynamics. He often favoured a homophonic declamatory style and used major–minor shifts and effective word-painting.

WORKS
(*selective list*)

Stage: Colegiales son colegiales (zarzuela), 1868; El charlatan mudo, 1873; Diomira (lyric tragedy), 1873; Virginia, 1873; La curiosidad de las mujeres (zarzuela); Los alemanes in Italie (opera, 4); Quiero ser ministro (zarzuela)

Sacred: 8 masses, incl. 1 dated 1855, 1 for 2vv, insts, 1874, 4 in D, d, e, F; Org mass; Benedicta es venerabilis, gradual; Gradual and Offertory for Holy Thursday; Requiem with response, 4vv, 16 June 1880; Requiem, 1v, org; Libera me; 2 Third Lessons of the Dead, incl. 1 for Bar, vv, vc, orch, June 1880; 3 psalms for the Vigil of the Dead; 2 graduals and Offices of the Blessed Sacrament, incl. 1 dated 1875; Gradual and Office of S Rafael; Gradual and verses to the Sacred Heart; Versos to Our Lady and canticles, 1856; Invitatory for Matins of the Holy Virgin, 4vv; Vespers, 7 Dec 1876; 2 Pange lingua; Tantum ergo; Miserere, C; Popule meus; 3 Te Deum; 2 Salve; Litany; St John Passion; Salve, oh Virgen; Domine salvum me fac; Hymn to Pius IX
Other works, incl. ovs., sinfonias, waltzes, marches and songs; harmony method; arrs. of other composers' works

BIBLIOGRAPHY
*Instituto musical venezolano* (Caracas, 1876)
*El siglo* (24–5 Aug 1881)
R. de la Plaza: *Ensayos sobre el arte en Venezuela* (Caracas, 1883)
J. A. Calcaño: *La ciudad y sa música* (Caracas, 1958)
SHARON E. GIRARD

**Montero, Atanasio Bello.** *See* BELLO MONTERO, ATANASIO.

**Montero, Joaquin** (*fl* 1764–1815). Spanish composer. He was organist of the parish church of S Pedro el Real in Seville. He published a *Compéndio armónico* (Madrid, 1790) and *Seis sonatas para clave y fuerte piano* op.1 (Madrid, 1790; ed. L. Powell, Madrid, 1977); he also published sonatas and minuets for harpsichord (1796). A treatise by him, *Tratado teórico-práctico sobre el contrapunto*, dated 1815, is also extant (*E-Bc, Sco*).

To judge from a dated manuscript (*E-Mn* M2810), Montero was active as a composer as early as 1764. The manuscript contains, among other works, ten minuets for harpsichord and piano, possibly the earliest Spanish keyboard works to indicate specifically the piano as well as the harpsichord (ed. A. Ruiz-Pipó, Madrid, 1973). Montero's *Seis sonatas para clave y fuerte piano* represent his best surviving works. Almost all of the movements of his sonatas approximate to sonata-allegro form and show a very lucid melodic organization, with a good sense of phrase balance, and many have Alberti basses or similar accompaniment patterns.

BIBLIOGRAPHY
J. Gillespie: *Five Centuries of Keyboard Music* (Belmont, Calif., 1965), 110
B. Saldoni: *Diccionario biográfico-bibliográfico de efemérides de musicos españoles*, iv (Madrid, 1881), 215f
LINTON POWELL

**Monterosso, Raffaello** (*b* Cremona, 18 Jan 1925). Italian musicologist. He studied the piano and composition with Federico Caudana and musicology with Giusto Zampieri and took an arts degree in music history at the University of Pavia (1947). His main area of research is the theory and history of medieval music, especially its notation (e.g. *La notazione modale di transizione* and *Sacre rappresentazioni nel manoscritto 201 della Bibliothèque municipale di Orléans*). From 1950 he taught the subject at the Scuola di Paleografia e Filologia Musicale, University of Pavia (Cremona), being appointed full professor there in 1968. He has also taught music history at the University of Pavia (1952–8) and at various conservatories (1960–68). Monterosso is active as an orchestral conductor.

WRITINGS

*La musica nel Risorgimento* (Milan, 1948)
*I musicisti cremonesi: catalogo storico-critico* (Cremona, 1951)
Critical commentary to *Le frottole nell'edizione principe di Ottaviano Petrucci*, IMa, 1st ser., i (1954)
*Musica e ritmica dei trovatori* (Milan, 1956)

*La notazione modale di transizione* (Cremona, 1956–8)
'Gasparo Visconti, violinista cremonese del secolo XVIII', *SMw*, xxv (1962), 378
*Il linguaggio musicale della lauda dugentesca* (Perugia, 1962)
*Il culto dei Santi nella tradizione musicale medievale liturgica ed extraliturgica* (Todi, 1963)
'L'ornamentazione nella monodia medievale', *Rivista di cultura classica e medievale*, vii (1965), 7
'Musica e poesia nel De Vulgari Eloquentia', *Dante: giornata internazionale di studio per il VII centenario: Ravenna 1965*, 83
'Un "auctoritas"·dantesca in un madrigale dell'Ars Nova', *CHM*, iv (1966), 185
'Un compendio inedito del *Lucidarium* di Marchetto da Padova', *Studi medievali*, 3rd ser., vii (1966), 914
*Tecnica ed espressione artistica nella musica del secolo XII* (Cremona, 1967)
ed.: *Congresso internazionale sul tema Claudio Monteverdi e il suo tempo: Venezia, Mantova e Cremona 1968* [incl. 'Claudio Monteverdi e il suo tempo', 17]
'La tradizione melismatica sino all'Ars Nova', *L'ars nova italiana del trecento II: Certaldo 1969*, 29
'L'oratorio musicale in Bologna nel secolo XVIII', *Convegno internazionale di studi: Perugia 1969*, 99
'Per un'edizione di "Norma" ', *Scritti in onore di Luigi Ronga* (Milan and Naples, 1973), 415

EDITIONS

with G. Tintori: *Sacre rappresentazioni nel manoscritto 201 della Bibliothèque municipale di Orléans*, IMa, 1st ser., ii (1958) [facs. edn.]
A. Vivaldi: *La fida ninfa*, IMa, 1st ser., iii (1964)
*Tecnica ed espressione artistica nella musica del secolo XII*, IMa, 2nd ser., i (1964)
T. Massaino: *Liber primus cantionum ecclesiasticarum*; 3 instrumental canzonas in DTÖ, cx (1964)

CAROLYN M. GIANTURCO

**Montesano, Alfonso** (*b* ?Maida, ?1595–1605; *d* ?Naples, ? after 1624). Italian composer. He dedicated his only extant music, *Madrigali a cinque voci . . . libro primo* (Naples, 1622¹³), to Marc'Antonio Loffredo, Prince of Maida, and one madrigal in the book to Loffredo's son Francesco. The 18 pieces, which include settings of poems by Guarini, Marino, G. B. Strozzi and Petrarch, have the usual features of the Neapolitan *seconda prattica* madrigal – chordal declamatory phrases, points of close imitation and slow *durezze e ligature* – but Montesano combined them in a less disjunct, contrasting and expert manner than did, for example, Lacorcia or Agresta. The three madrigals by Francesco Genuino also in the book only heighten the impression of Montesano's compositional inexperience suggested by occasional awkward, inexpressive clashes of seconds, maladroit harmonic progressions (both the result of inexpert partwriting) and trite imitative motifs. There are a few effective examples of chromaticism in the manner of Gesualdo. A list appended to a letter of Schütz's mentions a second and third book of five-part madrigals by Montesano (see E. H. Müller, ed.: *Heinrich Schütz: Gesammelte Briefe und Schriften* (Regensburg, 1931), 117f), but they cannot now be traced.

KEITH A. LARSON

**Montesardo** [Muscarini], **Girolamo** [Monsardus, Montisarduus, Hieronymus] (*b* ?Naples; *fl* 1606–*c*1620). Italian composer and singer. He was a member of the clergy. In 1606 his first surviving (though surely not his first) work was published in Florence, and on 11 April 1607 he was engaged at S Petronio, Bologna, as a singer. From 16 January to 16 November 1608 he served as *maestro di cappella* at Fano and by 1611 was living at Naples. He is remembered for having devised (according to his claim) a simple alphabet notation of chords for use in RASGUEADO playing of the five-course

guitar, probably based on a similar system already in use in Spain (*see* GUITAR; TABLATURE; JOAN CARLOS AMAT). This notation was popular in Italy through much of the 17th century and was used for song accompaniments as well as for solo playing. The *Nuova inventione*, in which Montesardo's system is presented, contains such popular dances and harmonic patterns as the Ruggiero, *bergamasca*, folía and *ballo del gran duca*. It is the first Italian publication to include ciacconas and passacaglias; the latter are equated in meaning with ritornellos. Although Montesardo seems to have composed mostly polyphonic church music and madrigals, he also tried his hand at monody. *I lieti giorni di Napoli* shows strong Florentine connections in its prologue, which is similar in poetry and music to those of the earliest operas, and in its settings of poems by Chiabrera; it also contains, among a variety of pieces, an echo song and three puzzle canons.

WORKS

Nuova inventione d'intavolatura per sonare li balletti sopra la chitarra spagnuola senza numeri e note (Florence, 1606)
Ecclesiastici concentus, 1–8vv, bc, op.8 (Venice, 1608)
L'allegre notti di Fiorenza . . . dove intervengono i più eccellenti musici di detta città, 1–5vv (Venice, 1608)
I lieti giorni di Napoli: concertini italiani in aria spagnuola con le lettere dell'alfabeto par la chitarra, 2, 3vv, op.11 (Naples, 1612)
Amphiteatrum angelicum divinarum cantionum, 1–8vv, op.12 (Venice, 1612)
Motetti, 2–4vv; lost, listed in *Indice* (1649)
Vespri, 4vv; lost, listed in *Indice* (1649), probably the work mentioned by Walther as pubd before 1653
2 motets, 8vv, 1613²; Puer qui natus es nobis, mentioned by Eitner as MS at Breslau, is probably the first of these
2 motets, 3vv, 1616²; 1 each repr. in 1623² and 1627¹

BIBLIOGRAPHY

EitnerQ; WaltherML
*Indice di tutte le opere di musica che si trovano nella Stampa della Pigna di Alessandro Vincenti in Venetia* (Venice, 1619–49); repr. in *MMg*, xiv–xv (1882–3/R), suppl.
R. Paolucci: 'La cappella musicale del duomo di Fano', *NA*, iii (1926), 100
R. A. Hudson: *The Development of Italian Keyboard Variations on the Passacaglio and Ciaccona from Guitar Music in the Seventeenth Century* (diss., U. of California, Los Angeles, 1967)
T. Walker: 'Ciaccona and Passacaglia: Remarks on their Origin and Early History', *JAMS*, xxi (1968), 300
R. A. Hudson: 'Further Remarks on the Passacaglia and Ciaccona', *JAMS*, xxiii (1970), 302

THOMAS WALKER

**Monteux, Claude** (*b* Brookline, Mass., 15 Oct 1920). American conductor and flautist, son of Pierre Monteux. He first studied the flute with Georges Laurent and made his solo début with an orchestra at the age of 20. In 1946 he joined the Kansas City PO and three years later began his conducting career with the itinerant Ballets Russes. He has been a guest conductor of the LSO, and of orchestras in Germany, France, the Netherlands and Scandinavia. In 1959 he became music director of the Hudson Valley PO in Poughkeepsie, New York. He has given master classes for conductors with the Canadian National Youth Orchestra and has directed the conducting department of the Peabody Institute. As a flautist he is admired for his clean technique and charm of manner. He and his father collaborated as soloist and conductor in some recordings.

GEORGE GELLES

**Monteux, Pierre** (*b* Paris, 4 April 1875; *d* Hancock, Maine, 1 July 1964). American conductor of French birth, father of Claude Monteux. He began learning the violin when he was six and at the age of nine entered the

Paris Conservatoire, where he studied the violin with Maurin and Berthelier, harmony with Lavignac and counterpoint with Lenepveu, and shared with Thibaud a *premier prix* for violin in 1896. When he was 12 he conducted an orchestra in Paris and elsewhere with Cortot as soloist, and in 1890, while still a student, he was engaged as violist at the Opéra-Comique (where he led his section at the première of *Pelléas et Mélisande*), and for the Concerts Colonne, of which he became

*Pierre Monteux*

assistant conductor and choirmaster in 1894. That year he also joined the Quatuor Geloso as violist, remaining with it until 1911; he took part in a performance of a Brahms quartet in the composer's presence. He was conductor of the Orchestre du Casino at Dieppe, 1908–14. In 1911, as well as founding the Concerts Berlioz, Monteux was appointed conductor of Dyagilev's Ballets Russes, and thereby became responsible, between 1911 and 1914, for the premières of *Petrushka*, *The Rite of Spring* and *The Nightingale*, *Daphnis et Chloé* and *Jeux*. Each was an outstanding contribution to 20th-century music and dance, and brought Monteux into close contact with Debussy, Ravel, Stravinsky and other composers, giving him the basis of his lifelong support and understanding of their music in particular, as well as of French music in general.

Recalled from wartime military service, Monteux went in 1916 to the USA and took up a post at the Metropolitan Opera (1917–19) in charge of the French repertory. Among other works he conducted the American première of *The Golden Cockerel*. He moved to the Boston SO in 1920, where he introduced a number of contemporary works to the repertory – mostly French (Debussy, Chausson, Milhaud and others), but also including Bliss, Bridge, Falla, Malipiero, Schreker

and Szymanowski. In 1924 he returned to Europe as second conductor (under Mengelberg) of the Amsterdam Concertgebouw Orchestra, and remained with the orchestra for ten years. In addition, he formed the Orchestre Symphonique de Paris in 1929 and conducted it until 1938, giving a large number of first performances, including Prokofiev's Symphony no.3 (1929) and Honegger's Cello Concerto (1930). Always concerned with young talent, he founded the Ecole Monteux at Paris in 1932 for the coaching of conductors, and continued this work later at his American home at Hancock, Maine (his pupils included Neville Marriner and André Previn). He had returned to the USA in 1936 as conductor of the San Francisco SO, a post he held until 1952, and during this period he raised the standard of the orchestra to an international level. He took American nationality in 1942. In the 1950s he again appeared frequently with the Boston SO, but in spite of many gramophone records made with both these and other orchestras, which were widely praised, he once said that he hated all the records he made because of the lack of spontaneity in the technique of recording. He preferred live concerts and remained active to an advanced age, accepting his final appointment in London in 1961 as chief conductor of the LSO at the age of 86, on a contract for 25 years. In this capacity he conducted *The Rite of Spring* in London in 1963 on the 50th anniversary of its Paris première, and gave noble performances of the German repertory, especially Brahms, and a varied selection of English works.

Monteux was never an ostentatious conductor, preparing his orchestra in often arduous rehearsal and then using small but decisive gestures to obtain playing of fine texture, careful detail and powerful effect, retaining to the last his extraordinary grasp of musical structure and a faultless ear for sound quality. He was a Commandeur of the Légion d'honneur and a Knight of the Order of Oranje Nassau.

BIBLIOGRAPHY

'Conductor of 102 Orchestras', *The Times* (31 March 1959)
M. Rayment: 'Pierre Monteux', *Audio & Record Review*, ii/5 (1963), 20 [with discography by F. F. Clough and G. J. Cuming]
D. Monteux: *It's All in the Music* (New York and Toronto, 1965) [with discography by E. Kunzel]

MARTIN COOPER

**Monteverdi** [Monteverde], **Claudio (Giovanni** [Zuan] **Antonio)** (*b* Cremona, 15 May 1567; *d* Venice, 29 Nov 1643). Italian composer. Although he has often been called a revolutionary, he was in fact less an inventor of forms and techniques than one who refined them and made them viable for lesser men. He did so throughout a long life, in which he showed an astonishing capacity for keeping abreast of the latest ideas. His major achievement lay in his penetrating expression of human psychology. The early madrigals can be considered as studies of emotions more varied and powerful than those of any other composer. His first opera, *L'Orfeo*, was the earliest to reveal the potential of this then novel genre, while his second, *L'Arianna*, may well have been responsible for its survival; the refinement of psychological attitudes in his late operas meant that the form became capable, like all great drama, of creating a new and satisfying world. In his sacred works, notably the famous Vespers, he brought a secular, up-to-date manner into church music. He can, in sum, be justly appraised as one of the most powerful figures in the history of music.

1. Early years at Cremona. 2. Mantua. 3. Venice. 4. Theoretical basis of works. 5. Madrigals and related genres. 6. Early dramatic works. 7. Later dramatic works. 8. Sacred music. 9. Historical position.

1. EARLY YEARS AT CREMONA. Monteverdi commonly used in letters the form of his name shown here, but the variant 'Monteverde' frequently appeared on title-pages whose production he may well have supervised. He was born in the parish of SS Nazaro e Celso, Cremona, where his father was living at the time and was eventually to be buried. His father Baldassare (*b* c1542) was a chemist, who practised medicine in the way of barber surgeons, even though this was not strictly legal. Claudio's mother, Maddalena (née Zignani), gave birth to a daughter and two boys. She died probably before 1576. His father remarried and had three more children, the eldest of whom was born in 1579; but his second wife, Giovanna Gadio, also died young, in 1583, and in the following year he married for a third time. His circumstances during Claudio's formative years seem to have been modest. Until 1566 he carried on his business in a small shop or stall rented from the chapter of Cremona Cathedral in the square in front of the cathedral; he then transferred it to his own parish. As late as 1582 he needed time to find a comparatively small sum that he owed the cathedral authorities. Nevertheless the two sons of his first marriage were given a good musical education under Marc'Antonio Ingegneri, *maestro di cappella* of the cathedral; the lessons seem to have been private, since there is no evidence that either brother sang in the choir. Claudio was clearly precocious, for in 1582 he published a volume of three-part motets with the famous Venetian printing house of Gardane and in 1583 a book of sacred madrigals, a more local enterprise with a publisher in nearby Brescia. Within a year a further volume, of canzonettas, appeared under the imprint of another leading Venetian publisher, the house of Amadino and Vincenti, who were to publish much of his later music. The cost of printing these volumes must have been borne to some extent by the Cremonese patrons to whom they were dedicated, and Baldassare may have been gaining some useful social acquaintances, since in 1583 he was involved in negotiations with the health authorities in Milan to legalize the practice of medicine by the chemists of Cremona, on the grounds that there was no college of surgeons there. These negotiations took some three years to complete, and from 1587 he was allowed to call himself 'dottore'. In the same year Claudio produced a book of madrigals, on whose title-page he still acknowledged Ingegneri as his teacher, but it is clear that now he was looking for work outside Cremona. In 1589 he visited Milan, and it seems likely that about then he was obtaining engagements, probably as a player of string instruments, at the court of the Gonzaga family at Mantua. He published a second book of madrigals in 1590, and before a third appeared two years later he was in full-time employment at Mantua.

2. MANTUA. Duke Vincenzo I maintained a comparatively small but virtuoso group of musicians at his court at Mantua, augmenting it for special occasions. Monteverdi held a post as 'suonatore di vivuola', which could mean a player of either a viol (viola da gamba) or a violin (viola da braccio) or both. His duties included taking part in weekly concerts given in the ducal palace, and it was probably for these that he produced a new set of madrigals soon after his appointment. These pieces show such a strong influence of Giaches de Wert, the

*maestro di cappella* to the court, that he must be assumed to have replaced Ingegneri as Monteverdi's spiritual master, though nothing is known of their formal relationship. This third madrigal book was popular enough to be reprinted in 1594. Although he did not assemble another collection for publication until 1603, it is clear that Monteverdi quickly became one of the leading musicians at Mantua, since he was included in the train of courtiers accompanying the duke on his expedition to Austria and Hungary against the Turks in 1595. Wert died in 1596, and though Monteverdi expected to succeed him (as is apparent from a letter he wrote in 1601), the post went to a senior colleague, Benedetto Pallavicino. Monteverdi's reputation was spreading, however, and he was known at the court of Ferrara, for he was about to dedicate a book of madrigals to Duke Alfonso d'Este when the duke died in 1597. On 20 May 1599 he married Claudia de Cattaneis, one of the court singers, but almost immediately he again had to accompany his employer abroad, this time to Flanders, where the duke went for a cure at Spa. Claudia bore him three children, Francesco (Baldassare) (baptized 27 August 1601), Leonora (Caiulla) (baptized 20 February 1603) and Massimiliano (Giacomo) (baptized 10 May 1604). The daughter died shortly after she was born; for the sons see §3 below.

Monteverdi's reputation as a composer was firmly established by 1600. In that year the first attacks by G. M. Artusi on his supposed harmonic innovations appeared, though the works Artusi discussed had not yet been published; henceforward Monteverdi was considered a leading exponent of the modern approach to text expression. In 1601 he was appointed *maestro di cappella* at Mantua on the death of Pallavicino. In 1603 he published his fourth book of madrigals, which was followed in 1605 by the fifth, the two together forming a retrospective collection of his work over more than ten years and including pieces already known to Artusi. In the fifth book he included the outline of a reply to Artusi, which was amplified by his brother Giulio Cesare in the famous *Dichiaratione* in the *Scherzi musicali* (1607). Such public discussion did even more to promote Monteverdi's music, and both the latest and earlier madrigal books quickly went into new editions. In February 1607 his first opera, *L'Orfeo*, was produced before the Accademia degli Invaghiti of Mantua. Little is known about this production, but some at least of the singers and players were brought from Florence and elsewhere, and it may be assumed that it was given on a substantial scale. During August of the same year Monteverdi was made a member of the Accademia degli Animosi, Cremona, and some of his music, possibly part of *L'Orfeo*, was performed at one of its meetings. But his main reason for being in his home town at this time was probably the illness of his wife, who had been unwell since the previous year and who was being cared for by his father. She died on 10 September and was buried at SS Nazaro e Celso (her grave does not survive).

After Claudia's death Monteverdi refused at first to return to his duties at Mantua, but by October it became expedient for him to do so since another opera by him, *L'Arianna*, was planned for production. It proved impossible, however, to adhere to the original date during Carnival, and Marco da Gagliano's *La Dafne* was substituted. It was decided to stage it instead as part of the celebrations marking the homecoming of the Gonzaga heir-apparent, Francesco, with his bride, Margaret of Savoy, after their marriage at Turin in May 1608. There was thus plenty of time for rehearsal, though the preparations were complicated by the death from smallpox of the singer engaged for the title role, Caterina Martinelli; this was another great sadness for Monteverdi, for she had been living in his house for several years, possibly as a pupil of his wife. Her part was taken at short notice by Virginia Andreini, a member of the Comici Fedeli, a troupe then in Mantua. *L'Arianna* was given on 28 May and was enthusiastically received. Andreini scored a big success in the famous and influential lament, on which the opera's reputation largely rested. Monteverdi contributed to two further events in the nuptial celebrations: the music for the prologue to the pastoral play *L'Idropica*, performed by the Comici Fedeli, and a full-length French-style ballet, *Il ballo delle ingrate*.

After this period of intensive work Monteverdi returned to Cremona in a state of virtual collapse and depression that lasted for over a year. His father was alarmed enough in the autumn of 1608 to ask for his son's release from the service of the Gonzaga family, and when this was denied, Monteverdi himself wrote a bitter letter that showed his complete disenchantment with Mantua. He accused the authorities of the duke's household of meanness and insulting behaviour towards him, and although he was granted a pension in return for his recent labours he continued to feel unhappy and by 1610 was looking for a new post. This was probably the main reason for his visiting Rome during that year, though a subsidiary reason was to try to obtain a place in the papal seminary for his elder son. He seems also to have gone to Venice to supervise the printing of a large volume of his church music, dedicated to Pope Paul V and significantly containing a type of music that might prove attractive to the authorities of St Mark's, Venice. At this time he was planning another madrigal book, to include three extended laments, but before it was completed his employer, Duke Vincenzo, died, and his successor, Francesco, dismissed him, together with a number of other artists, in July 1612, apparently without warning. He went back to Cremona and seems to have done little for about a year, although he gave a concert in Milan. Then, on the death of the *maestro di cappella* of St Mark's, G. C. Martinengo, he was invited to Venice, where on 19 August he performed some of his church music as a test in front of the procurators. He was appointed to the post at an annual salary of 300 ducats and given an immediate present of 50 ducats to cover his expenses. He returned to Cremona to make arrangements for moving. On his way back to Venice he was robbed by highwaymen.

3. VENICE. Since the *cappella* of St Mark's was at a low ebb, Monteverdi's first few years there were largely concerned with its reorganization. He seems to have been an efficient and energetic administrator: he brought the choir up to strength, found new virtuoso singers, transferred the instrumental ensemble from a per diem basis to the full-time payroll, bought new music and reintroduced the custom of singing masses on ferial days as well as festivals, using works by 16th-century composers such as Lassus and Palestrina. He must also have composed some large-scale works for use at St Mark's, but none of them was published at this time; the works that did appear were either motets for small forces,

which were included in several anthologies from 1615 onwards, or, like the pieces in the sixth book of madrigals (1614), had been written at Mantua. During his early years at St Mark's little music was published by his colleagues, but gradually he appointed younger men, among them Cavalli, Alessandro Grandi (i) and Giovanni Rovetta, who took some of the burden off him.

Monteverdi was thus able to accept commissions from elsewhere, notably from Mantua, where he was again persona grata, Duke Francesco having died and been succeeded by his brother Ferdinando, whom Monteverdi had known well. He composed a ballet, *Tirsi e Clori*, which was produced at Mantua in 1616. In the same year he began work on a *favola marittima* called *Le nozze di Tetide*, though he was unhappy with the libretto and never completed the music, even when it transpired that the work was intended simply as a set of *intermedi*, not as a continuous, unified whole. In 1618 he began composing another dramatic work, *Andromeda*, which he also left unfinished, after two years of intermittent work. In letters to Mantua his main excuses for his slow progress on these commissions refer to his duties in St Mark's, for which the procurators raised his salary in 1616 to the unique height of 400 ducats. There can be no doubt, however, that he was also composing for secular academies, since his ample seventh book of madrigals (1619) is full of concertato music in an up-to-date style. In 1620 there was some discussion of a revival of *L'Arianna* at Mantua. It was also in 1620 that he received an offer to return to Mantuan service; in his indignant refusal of it he catalogued all his old grievances, which clearly were still alive in his mind. In doing so he revealed that his income in Venice was much augmented by commissions from the religious confraternities, a fact confirmed by the accounts of the Scuola Grande di S Rocco, for which he wrote music for the day of its patron saint in 1623 and 1628. Other works from the 1620s include the dramatic dialogue *Combattimento di Tancredi e Clorinda*, which was staged in the home of a Venetian nobleman, Girolamo Mocenigo, in 1624. But the most important is a full-length opera, *La finta pazza Licori*, about which his long correspondence with the Gonzagas' court chancellor, Alessandro Striggio (ii), survives. It was intended for performance at Mantua in 1627 (with a well-known opera singer, Margherita Basile, in the title role), probably to celebrate the succession of Vincenzo II on the death of Duke Ferdinando; but Vincenzo was constantly ill, and the work was never performed. Immediately after completing it, Monteverdi was asked to write music for *intermedi* and a torneo to be given at the Farnese court at Parma, and the procurators gave him leave of absence to go there.

During this period of activity there was worrying news of his younger son, Massimiliano, who was studying medicine at Bologna. In 1627 he was arrested on the orders of the Inquisition for reading forbidden books. He was acquitted in 1628 but only after a short period in prison, during which his father had to raise bail for his release. He eventually became a fully qualified doctor and practised at Cremona, where he died in 1661. Monteverdi's elder son, Francesco, after briefly studying, probably law, at the universities of Padua and Bologna, entered the Carmelite order shortly after 1620. In 1623 he became a singer at St Mark's, Venice. He was still included in a list of singers drawn up in 1677, but he probably died shortly after this, since in

1678 several new appointments were made to fill unspecified places in the choir. He sang at Padua in 1636 in *Ermiona*, an 'introduction to a torneo' by Pio Enea degli Obizzi, with music by G. F. Sances. There are two typically Venetian ariettas by him in Carlo Milanuzzi's *Quarto scherzo delle ariose vaghezze* (Venice, 2/1624).

After about 1629 Monteverdi seems to have become less active as a composer. This was probably because of external circumstances. In 1628, on the death of Vincenzo II, Mantua was left without a male heir and promptly became the cause of a major war, during which it was sacked by imperial troops. He thus received no further commissions from there. Venice itself suffered from a disastrous attack of plague in the winter of 1630–31, which caused a complete cessation of activity for several months and a noticeable diminution of music publishing for several years. In 1630, before the arrival of the plague, Monteverdi set Giulio Strozzi's drama *Proserpina rapita* for a wedding of nobility (Mocenigo–Giustinian). He composed the mass of thanksgiving for deliverance from the plague in November 1631. In 1632 he published a slim volume of pieces for one and two voices under the title *Scherzi musicali* and was away from Venice for a while, probably at Cremona seeing to family affairs; at about this time he took holy orders. Little is heard of him during the next few years, although it is known that he was considering the completion of a book explaining his basic principles of composition that he had promised some 30 years earlier. He published a grand retrospective collection of his secular music in 1638 and a similar volume of church music in 1641. Yet his life's work was by no means over. Following the opening of public opera houses in Venice from 1637, he was much sought after as a composer of operas. In 1640 *L'Arianna* was revived, and in the following two years three new works, *Il ritorno d'Ulisse in patria*, *Le nozze d'Enea con Lavinia* and *L'incoronazione di Poppea*, were given first performances. The first of these was also performed in Bologna with certain Venetian singers, and he wrote a ballet, *La vittoria d'Amore*, on a commission from Piacenza. In 1643 he was given leave to visit Cremona. He died shortly after returning to Venice. He was buried in the church of the Frari, where a commemorative plaque was erected; a copy still exists in the chapel to the north of the high altar.

4. THEORETICAL BASIS OF WORKS. Throughout the greater part of his mature working life Monteverdi consciously strove to achieve certain intellectual concepts common during the High Renaissance, and it is impossible to understand his stylistic development without taking them into account. Although it is unlikely that he read Greek, at least with any fluency, he held, like many musicians and theorists of his time, that the highest achievement of the artist was the Platonic goal of moving the affections, which can be translated less literally but more cogently as 'affecting the whole man'. His lack of Greek, and probably his lack of mathematical training too, inclined him against the interest, current in his youth, in acoustical experiments that attempted to revive the temperament of ancient music. He therefore turned to Plato's general artistic ideas, the most important of which seemed to him to be one discussed by Zarlino that Ficino had rendered from the Greek as 'melodia ex tribus constare, oratione, harmonia, rhythmus'. Mon-

teverdi's interpretation of this influential concept insisted on the order in which Plato mentioned the three elements of music – the text ('oratio'), the combination of notes ('harmonia') and rhythm. In his view, therefore, the music should be second in importance to the words. Not all commentators of the time considered that this order was of supreme significance. Caccini was one who did, but unlike him and other members of the Florentine school, Monteverdi, thoroughly grounded in traditional techniques, believed that Plato's ideal could be realized within the framework of polyphony. Certainly some elements in the generally accepted procedure of polyphonic composition would have to be modified, notably those relating to harmony, and he was convinced too that the modal structure as explained and defended by Artusi was completely outdated. He also saw the necessity for a wider use of dissonance. Although he found analogies in current methods of improvised ornamentation to explain his own free use of dissonance, there can be no doubt that he sought to make it a much more significant means of expression.

Later in his life Monteverdi turned his attention to the interpretation of Plato's idea of rhythm. Whereas in his earlier attempts at recreating ancient concepts by modern means he had left the technical terms distinctly vague, he here accepted the direct correlation between certain rhythmic patterns and certain emotional states. Influenced, perhaps, by his family's medical background, he believed that the emotions could be divided in the manner of the humours of the body and that music might follow these divisions. He worked out this idea in some detail in certain pieces in the *stile concitato*, but in general he remained a pragmatist and never allowed his natural musicality to be overruled by academic ideas, even when these were at their most influential in his work. This pragmatism is shown at its best in his avowed acceptance of a completely different style of music that was absolutely traditional and needed no explanation by reference to the Greek philosophers. While his views on dissonance and modality can be found in other writers of the time, the crystallization of his idea of two 'practices' – the one based on the purity of the style developed from the Netherlands school, the other a modern one based, paradoxically, on ancient principles – was unique. Though not directly responsible for the way in which later Baroque composers were to use this division, Monteverdi himself clearly derived great benefit as a composer from his theoretical thinking, even if much of it was imprecise.

5. MADRIGALS AND RELATED GENRES.
(*i*) *Books 1–6*. Monteverdi wrote music in most of the madrigalian genres current between about 1580 and 1640. Those that he ignored were largely of no emotional weight, such as the mascherata or the villanella, even though they offered opportunities for caricature, in which he showed some interest in his last operas. It is difficult to date many of his pieces because of the long gaps between some of the publications in which they appeared, but evidence from his letters and occasionally from the texts he set enables the continuity of his stylistic development from 1584 until the late 1630s to be charted with some certainty. It is thus possible to assert that he worked almost continuously throughout his life in this medium. His earliest published madrigals were a set of *madrigali spirituali*, which appeared in 1583, his 17th year, and obviously

*1. Claudio Monteverdi: portrait by Bernardo Strozzi (1581–1644) in the Tiroler Landesmuseum Ferdinandeum, Innsbruck*

followed a fashion for such pieces that was also exploited by Marenzio, the Gabrielis and several other composers in the mid-1580s. Only the bass part of Monteverdi's volume survives, but it is enough to show that the music was rather old-fashioned, as might be expected from a pupil of Ingegneri, whose own madrigal style was typical of the early 1570s. Monteverdi's canzonettas for three voices (1584) equally show Ingegneri's influence, for instead of the very simple homophonic textures of most examples of the genre there is a certain amount of genuine polyphony that is not always suitable for the small-scale proportions of the bipartite form. Also unusual for canzonettas is Monteverdi's marked interest in word-painting, another feature that seems to stretch beyond the confines of a strophic genre. At the same time, the need for compactness in working on a small scale made him appreciate two main ideals of such music: crisp rhythmic motifs based on the natural accentuation of the words, and short singable phrases rather than the extended vocal lines of the larger contrapuntal forms.

This mixture of old and new informs Monteverdi's first secular madrigal book (1587), which appeared after the vogue of the Marenzian madrigal style had become well established. He seems at times a shade unsure in the handling of five voices, some parts being not well integrated into the texture, but on the whole he again shows the soundness of Ingegneri's tuition in counterpoint, many of the madrigals being written in a manner not far from that of his teacher. Yet several contain hints of the newer style, setting the fashionable pastoral verse in a more obviously melodious way and underlining the text with the musical images of the Marenzian school. The texture in these pieces is not strictly contrapuntal but rather a quasi-polyphonic interweaving of motifs giving a lighter feeling and a brighter sound. Two further traits that assume importance in later works are a distinct interest in the deriving of formal patterns from musical motifs with similar rhythms, as in the cycle *Ardo, sì, ma non t'amo*, where the opening lines of the two succeeding madrigals, *Ardi o gela a tua voglia* and *Arsi e alsi a mia voglia*, provide obvious material for such integration; and the use of dissonance, treated with perfect circumspection according to Zarlino's practice but nonetheless extended in places to some length.

The second book of madrigals (1590) is much more assured in technique, with no signs of weakness in the counterpoint and a better sense of proportion in setting the words, so that important phrases are given ample development. There are still a few pieces in the manner of Ingegneri, but most are now in the Marenzian style. The chosen verse is in the courtly pastoral tradition of Tasso (and Guarini), and the musical setting is based on the detailed expression of rich imagery. Monteverdi had not only mastered conventional devices, such as a broken melody for 'sospiri' (sighs) and scales for the ideas of ascending and descending, but was full of original imaginative ideas, such as that at the beginning of *Non si levav'ancor*, where the idea of the sun having not yet risen is expressed by simultaneous motifs, one rising, the other falling, and in the 'mirror' image to convey the reflection of the dawn on the sea in *Ecco mormorar l'onde*. To the crispness of rhythm suggested by a syllabic word-setting is added a more brilliant sound than formerly, largely based on the upper voices of the ensemble. A few madrigals show a knowledge of the school of composers at Ferrara; they wrote for an ensemble of virtuoso women singers, and Monteverdi imitated the florid style of their soprano parts. This volume represents the zenith of his work at Cremona, forward-looking but never going beyond the technical limits of the amateur circle of a provincial town academy.

Though a few numbers in the third madrigal book (1592) are also in this style and may therefore be assumed to have been written for Cremona, the volume as a whole represents a major change in direction. For now, after cultivating the popular manner of Marenzio, Monteverdi adopted a distinctly modern approach. Although this new style was to become fashionable in the 1590s, it is significant that Monteverdi was among the first to adopt it. The effect of Platonic thinking is evident in several ways. In contrast to the essentially hedonist attitude of the Marenzian style, the progressive traits are revealed in a greater seriousness, obviously with the intention of moving the affections. To this end the Tasso-like verse of the second book, with its tendency towards concrete images allowing obvious equivalents in the music, was supplanted by the more introverted poems of Guarini, which needed a new kind of interpretation. This interpretation was obviously based on that of Wert, who had been attempting something of the kind for several years. Since the words were of the greatest importance in this new approach, Wert tried both to make them audible and to express their emotional meaning, rather than just their external images. In ensuring audibility Wert created melodies that approached rhythms of spoken declamation both in their frequent eliding of syllables and in the use of very short notes, often repeated on a monotone, giving the effect of quasi-recitative. While the logic of this was to be followed by the monodists, Wert attempted to work within a conventional framework by simplifying the textures of the madrigal ensemble to produce virtual homophony, thus effectively abolishing counterpoint, though since he did not pursue his principles to their logical extreme there are still conventional sections even in his most unusual works. For the purposes of expression Wert abandoned the usual confines of singable melody, writing angular lines sometimes of great difficulty, with wide or awkward leaps to underline the astringencies of the verse. Noticeably he did not go beyond the normal handling of dissonance, and his basic sonorities were those derived from his experience with the Ferrarese ensemble. Monteverdi followed him very closely in certain respects and took up his general attitude in several works in his third book. Much of the

volume consists of settings of Guarini, though there are two Tasso cycles. He came nearest to Wert's style in one of these, *Vattene pur, crudel*, which contains a great deal of choral recitative, whose monotoned melody is broken by expressive intervals pointing emotional words. Using predominantly homophonic textures he sought variety by using different combinations of voices, which resulted in a series of trio sections clearly related to those of the Ferrara school. As with Wert, his music assumes virtuosity on the part of the performers, and, as adumbrated in certain pieces in the second book, the upper voices especially are treated in a florid manner. Monteverdi was, however, less consistent than Wert in this respect, for he periodically broke into his former style to express the concrete images of the verse. He also made much greater use of dissonance than Wert. In its details it still obeys the criteria of the conservatives, but in a piece such as *Stracciami pur il core* (which Martini and Burney were to use in the 18th century to prove Monteverdi's revolutionary nature) it is extended to such a degree as to make it the most noticeable feature of the madrigal, especially since the discords are made harsher by double suspensions and by including the note of resolution simultaneously with the actual dissonant note. There are signs that Monteverdi had not completely assimilated this new idiom, largely in the imbalance between sections and in the extreme nature of the difficult passages. These signs may well have been the result of his quick production of these more modern madrigals, which he must have composed soon after arriving at Mantua.

The fact that his next madrigal book did not appear until 11 years later, in 1603, suggests that it took Monteverdi some time to integrate the various new elements in his style. There seems to have been no practical reason for the long wait, since the third book achieved a second edition within two years, indicating a certain popularity, as does the inclusion of a number of canzonettas in an anthology assembled by Antonio Morsolino in 1594. These light works are much more up-to-date than the similar essays of ten years earlier. In them Monteverdi put aside counterpoint in favour of the trio textures current in his colleague Gastoldi's three-part ballettos of the same period, which are the main influence on these canzonettas. The madrigals included in the fourth and fifth books (which are best considered together since between them they represent the work of the 13 years from 1592) show a greater maturity in every way than anything that had gone before and must be considered the peak of the music that Monteverdi produced in the first half of his life. The verse that he set is nearly all by Guarini (more than half of the poems in the fifth book come from *Il pastor fido*) and often has a strongly erotic flavour more intense than that of the usual pastoral verse. The musical style is an extension of that of the third book, with a deep concern for the audibility and expression of the words. Again it is the madrigal cycles, *Ecco Silvio* in five sections and *Ch'io t'ami* in three, that use the Wertian chordal recitative most extensively; indeed in *Ecco Silvio* there is little relief from it. There are many passages of it in the single madrigals, but they are integrated into a more normal texture to form a smaller part of the whole than is usual in the third book. The manner can be seen at its most imaginative in *Sfogava con le stelle*, where the recitative is actually notated in the manner of psalmodic chanting so that the declamation can be exactly as in speech.

These passages occur several times and on each occasion give rise to extensive free counterpoint, using expressive harmony and melody which are thrown into strong relief by their recitative context. More often still, the recitative in these madrigals is felt to be part of a normal motif, as in *A un giro sol*, where there is extensive use of the monotone; yet the phrases are completed with figuration completely in a 16th-century idiom, so the parlando writing becomes no more than incidental. Expressiveness is achieved without the extreme awkwardness of melody of the third book. The wide leaps of Wert are rare, though diminished and augmented intervals are common, as is the downward minor 6th, which from now on was a hallmark of Monteverdi's melodic style. Such difficulties as do exist for the singers come largely from the way in which major and minor are juxtaposed, for they are presented with an unpredictable freedom that is untypical of the formal chromatic writing of the late 16th century. This results in an unusually rich harmony, which, without seeming extravagant in Gesualdo's later manner, completely breaks with the rules laid down by Zarlino.

As Artusi found, Monteverdi's use of dissonance is highly original, although in several respects it is based on the common practice of the period. First, he wrote down ornaments that would previously have been improvised. These are much less revolutionary than those suggested by Caccini, for they were culled from such treatises on embellishment as those by Bassano, Bovicelli and Conforti. But Monteverdi's application of them seems at times deliberately to flout the methods of those writers by making the discords appear in their harshest form. Secondly, he extended the idea of passing notes by missing out the consonances from and to which the dissonance should proceed, thus making the discord more prominent, even though in itself it could well have been found in works by very conservative composers. Thirdly, suspensions are irregularly resolved, so that instead of proceeding by step they leap on to a consonant note of the succeeding chord. This procedure is not strictly original, since Vincenzo Galilei had advocated it about 1590, but it too is used in a such a way as to intensify the dissonant feeling. Finally, there is a frequent holding of bass notes to give the effect of a pedal, which appears to increase the actual number of passing notes and chords, even if all the details lie within the conventions codified by 16th-century theorists. By such extensions of previous practice, Monteverdi appeared to have invented a completely revolutionary idiom, in which chords of the 7th and 9th could be treated freely; it was this that gave him the reputation of being a progressive composer. The remarkable feature of this novelty is less its supposed originality than the purposes to which it is put. There is a vast range of emotion within these madrigals: some are tragic in the sustained use of dissonance, others are playful by virtue of the lightly touched discords, while the richness of the integrated chromaticism conveys the eroticism of Guarini's verse with uncanny exactness. Achieving a nice balance between the painting of the concrete image and the introverted intensity that is the basic feature of the poetry, Monteverdi's middle-period madrigals are never merely clever or shocking in the mannerist way, for they show acute psychological penetration allied to a sense of proportion whereby the musical material never seems under-developed and is thus wholly appropriate to the terseness of the verse.

The fifth book was published with the addition of a basso continuo part. For all except the last six numbers this is virtually a *basso seguente* and is unnecessary in performance. A harmony instrument is an essential ingredient in the other six madrigals, where it is largely used instead of a third voice as the bass in the trio sections derived from the earlier madrigal style. It therefore provides a new freedom in the handling of sonorities, since a solo voice could now be used to contrast with the tutti without complete disruption of the harmony. The immediate effect of the innovation on Monteverdi's style was that it made for greater contrasts. The vocal lines of the solo sections (including duets) have more elaborate embellishments, while the instrumental bass tends to move quite slowly, to allow a feeling of improvisation suggested by the rhythmically more irregular ornaments he now used. The tutti sections usually have very plain melodies, with a simple homophonic texture. To give a sense of shape, Monteverdi replaced the contrapuntal devices of previous madrigals by rondo patterns in which the tutti sing the recurrent refrain and the soloists provide the episodes. Emotionally these works are less sophisticated than the others in the volume, though they have a new charm resulting from their concentration on melody rather than on rich harmony and textures.

The same can be said of the *Scherzi musicali* (1607). His brother's *Dichiaratione* in explanation of Monteverdi's principle of two 'practices' mentions that Monteverdi had imported a 'canto alla francese' into Italy, and this has been taken by some scholars to mean that in this volume he was experimenting with *musique mesurée*. There are certain points of resemblance: the metrical novelties of Chiabrera's strophic verse reflect a knowledge of Ronsard and the French classicizing lyric (see Pirrotta, *NRMI*, 1968), and the regularity of the contents of the *Scherzi musicali* derives from its patterns. Nonetheless they are really hemiola songs – a genre that was to become extremely fashionable in the first two decades of the 17th century – which are given a texture very similar to that of Gastoldi's three-part balletti already mentioned in connection with Monteverdi's canzonettas of 1584. In such respects these pieces are forward-looking, for regular rhythmic patterns and simple textures are the main features of the monodic arias that were now replacing polyphonic madrigals in public esteem.

Monteverdi's sixth book of madrigals (1614) seems retrogressive since in it he reverted to the mannerist style, which he now took to a new extreme point. It consists chiefly of two extended cycles, both laments dating from the period 1608–10 (a third was planned but was apparently not completed). The first of these is an arrangement of the climactic scene of the opera *L'Arianna*. The scene does not survive in its original form, but the extant versions and the libretto show that it was an extended arioso with choral interjections. Monteverdi clearly reworked it extensively in his madrigalian version for five voices, which highlights the close relationship between his monodic style and that of his Wertian recitative ensemble madrigals, both in the nature of the melody and in the expressive dissonance that is amply used throughout. Unity between the sections is achieved by a subtle repetition of thematic fragments, and the first part is virtually a rondo, with the episodes providing an imaginative concept of surprise in their novel development of material. Although there are few signs that the *Lamento d'Arianna* is an arrangement, a comparison with the other cycle, the threnody for Caterina Martinelli, *Incenerite spoglie*, shows that the textures and sonorities of a work originally designed for ensemble can be more varied. This is the finest work of Monteverdi's mannerist period, with the recitative style thoroughly integrated into the madrigal idiom. The verse, by a Mantuan poetaster, is bad, offering few concrete images but a plethora of emotional words, which Monteverdi set in an austere melodic style. The harmony is highly expressive, extreme dissonance being saved for the climaxes in a restrained manner, which makes the cry of despair in the final section seem, in its astringency, even more moving. The sixth book includes two other, shorter works in this vein, and the remainder of the volume consists of madrigals of the newer, continuo type, among them the joyous *Qui rise, O Tirsi*, in which the duet texture possible in this idiom is used to the utmost advantage.

*(ii) Book 7 onwards.* The sixth book was the last of Monteverdi's madrigal books to persist with forms directly related to those of the 16th century, for the seventh book (1619), entitled *Concerto* (perhaps in deference to a Venetian tradition dating back to Andrea Gabrieli's similarly-named volume of 1587), is entirely devoted to genres developed since 1600. It is an unusual collection in displaying a great variety of works; it is virtually a retrospective view of his secular oeuvre over several years. It may owe this pattern to Marco da Gagliano's *Musiche* (1615), but it contains an even greater diversity of means and idiom than that widely ranging volume. Surprisingly little of Monteverdi's book is given over to purely monodic genres. The two pieces that can be described unequivocally as monodies both seem to be essays in the Florentine manner of recitative. They are *lettere amorose* and consist of syllabic declamation over a narrow range, obviously in imitation of speech inflection. Expressiveness is achieved by the use of ornaments and occasionally by raising the voice above this narrow range. By contrast Monteverdi's usual harmonic style is totally lacking, the basso continuo being given simple consonances in slow motion. While they are not ineffective in the hands of a dramatic singer, these pieces are so unlike Monteverdi's operatic recitative that they seem to have been experiments in an academic manner that he quickly abandoned. A third work for solo voice, *Tempro la cetra*, is more characteristic. It is a sonnet, divided into a set of strophic variations for tenor, preceded by a short overture whose last phrase is used as a ritornello and followed by a dance for instrumental ensemble. This seems to be part of a dramatic entertainment of some kind, possibly a prologue to a play or an *intermedio*, as it closely resembles the prologue to *L'Orfeo* in the expressiveness of both melody and harmony and in its realization of the potentialities offered by the variation form. The fourth work for a single voice, *Con che soavità*, is completely *sui generis*. Related less to monody than to the Venetian concertato motet, it is written for three groups of musicians, two of string and keyboard instruments, the third a soprano with continuo instruments. The interest lies less in the vocal line than in the kaleidoscope of sonorities, which are conceived as a variety of pastel shades rather than in terms of strong contrasts. The other work written for a large concerted ensemble is *A quest'olmo*, for six voices with violins and recorders, which in spite of the presence of instruments is essentially in the idiom of previous madrigal books.

The bulk of the seventh book consists of duets, which now succeeded the five-part madrigal in Monteverdi's work as the medium for the sophisticated psychological expression of a wide range of emotions. The duets divide into three main types, one derived from the solo madrigal with continuo, another from the aria (in the early 17th-century meaning of the word), while the third is a set of variations over a stock bass such as the romanesca. The relationships between the older madrigal and the first type is seen in the seventh book in *O come sei gentile*, a setting of Guarini including a great deal of detailed word-painting and displaying the virtuosity of the singers very much in the manner of the Ferrarese madrigals of the previous century. There are also echoes of Wertian melody in the awkward melodic leaps of *Ah, che non si conviene*; but it is the word-setting in these duets that gives the feeling of continuity from Monteverdi's earlier work. The intensity of *Interrotte speranze*, created largely by harmonic means, resembles that of several madrigals from the fourth book, and the close way in which the varying emotions of the verse are reflected achieves the same degree of subtlety. The aria-type duets are essentially projections of the canzonetta, although the simple strophic patterns of that genre are modified by the introduction of ritornellos and by making the succeeding verses different in detail. Although not as popular a melodist as some of his younger contemporaries, Monteverdi shows an appreciation of current tastes in the regular phrasing and harmonic changes and the strongly diatonic melody of a piece such as the well-known *Chiome d'oro*. The type of duet in which variations unfold over a bass reveals his

2. *Title-page, with portrait of Monteverdi, from G. B. Marinoni's 'Fiori poetici' (1644)*

craftsmanship in the new medium, which is seen at its best in *Ohimè, dov'è il mio ben?*, where the recurring bass suggests an ample variety of harmony and does not impede his imagination in allowing the melody to express the words in considerable detail. In all the duets he achieved a relationship between the voices like those in the former madrigalian idiom, not despising homophonic euphony but often suggesting contrapuntal interplay, with motifs passed freely between the voices. The fact that the bass rarely takes its part in such quasi-polyphony emphasizes the fact that the modern idiom dominates these works.

The few pieces that appeared in the 1620s in anthologies persist in the same vein. Two duets (in *RISM* 1624[11]) are excellent examples of their kind; one of them, *O come vaghi*, is a re-creation for the smaller ensemble of the spirit of a madrigal in the fourth book, *A un giro sol*. Three ariettas for solo voice also published in 1624 were Monteverdi's first pieces in this popular genre to be printed. Interestingly he differed from his younger contemporaries in his liking for word-painting even within the very restricted scope of the light strophic genre, though the songs are not less attractive melodically on that account. His liking for the greater possibilities in this direction offered by variation form is plain in the *Scherzi musicali* of 1632, where the most ambitious works use a repeated bass pattern rather than a simple melodic repetition. The three sections of *Quel sguardo sdegnosetto* are specially masterly because of Monteverdi's capacity for finding seemingly new harmonic progressions from the same bass notes, while the almost madrigalian imagery through which he ennobled trivial verse is even more remarkable. The masterpiece of the volume is again a duet, *Zefiro torna*, set as a chaconne. A two-bar pattern is repeated exactly many times, while the voices are manipulated to form differing phrase lengths; there is thus not a hint of monotony. Monteverdi's penchant for word-painting again results in a highly imaginative setting of the detail of the poem, a sonnet by Rinuccini similar in its use of concrete imagery to the poems by Tasso that he had set earlier. *Zefiro torna* is the first great vocal chaconne, and it heralded a tradition that was to last until the middle of the 18th century.

The final book of madrigals produced under Monteverdi's supervision is unusual not only for its large size and because it seems to have been designed as a grand retrospective collection of music that he had composed over some 30 years, but mainly because it appears to be a manifesto for his theories of the three styles of humours. It is divided into two parts, 'Canti guerrieri' and 'Canti amorosi'. The volume includes *Il ballo delle ingrate*, first performed at Mantua in 1608 but here revised with adaptations probably made for a later performance in Vienna; *Combattimento di Tancredi e Clorinda* (1624); and a ballet probably written for the festivities celebrating the coronation of Ferdinand III as Holy Roman Emperor in 1636. The dating of these works (which are discussed in §§6–7 below) suggests equally wide dating for the other pieces, which show an equal diversity of manner. The earliest of these are probably two pieces 'in the French style', *Dolcissimo uscignolo* and *Vago augelletto*. These have little, if any, relationship with the *Scherzi musicali* of 1607 previously mentioned in this connection except that they too adopt a metrical rhythmic pattern rather than one based on Italian speech rhythms; but their

connection with the writers of *musique mesurée* is strengthened by the alternation of solo sections and tuttis that are full harmonizations of them, a feature known in France about 1600. The cycles of concerted madrigals for a few voices and continuo seem to belong to the period 1620–35, the duets in particular developing the techniques of those in the seventh book. Of these, *Ardo e scoprir* has the sexual passion associated with Monteverdi's Mantuan works, though the continuo technique belongs to the 1620s; while the equally fine *O sia tranquill'il mare* is a study in loneliness and tries to reflect the mood of Penelope in *Il ritorno d'Ulisse*. The greatest of the pieces requiring small forces, the *Lamento della ninfa*, develops this same mood. It is a triptych whose main central section, a soprano lament over a four-note ground bass, is framed by an introduction and conclusion that set the scene. The harmonic resource in this section is astonishing, the dissonances normal in Monteverdi's tragic music made more prominent by the use of three male voices as a background to the soprano's melody. Another remarkable feature is the instruction that the soprano must use tempo rubato while the remainder of the ensemble keep in strict time, thus accentuating the dissonance while underlining the emotional separation of the lovelorn nymph from the rest of the world. In its use of the ostinato this extraordinary work acts as a link between the earlier monodic laments following the vogue set by that in *L'Arianna* and those in later operas, by Cavalli, Cesti, Purcell and others, which usually employ some repeated bass formula.

If few of these works show much sign of Monteverdi's theorizing, the large-scale pieces show more obvious connection with it. His invention of the *stile concitato* was ostensibly the outcome of his reflections on Plato's concept of arousing the warlike or agitated state in Man. Monteverdi interpreted this to mean that a semibreve should be divided into 16 semiquavers repeated on a single note. This clearly could not be done to any great extent in voice parts whose words are sung, so it is mainly given to string instruments, where the effect can be achieved by bowing. This isolating of a rhythm tends to make the harmony static, since the repetition of the single note allows for little variety, and much of Monteverdi's *stile concitato* music is from this point of view rather dull. His natural pragmatism, however, tends to cause an integration of other elements into the style, notably those associated with the realism of the earlier madrigals. He had several times set texts including references to battle and in doing so had used quasi-fanfare motifs probably borrowed from the battaglia and deriving ultimately from Janequin's *La bataille de Marignan*. He now adapted these to this new context. The avowed new style thus has a number of older traits within it. The realistic word-painting of *Altri canti d'amor*, probably written for the Emperor Ferdinand III, is thus in many ways nearer to the madrigal style of the 1580s, in spite of external features that point to an appreciation of the newer sonorities available with modern string playing. More interesting emotionally are the works in which the *stile concitato* is an incidental ingredient rather than the raison d'être. Such a work is the excellent setting of Petrarch's sonnet *Hor ch'el ciel e la terra*, in which the three humours, 'molle', 'temperato' and 'concitato', are contrasted in music that succeeds not only in painting the words but in expressing their inner meaning with the sophistication of the great psychological madrigals of the fourth book.

A third of the contents of the posthumous ninth book consists of previously published music, the remaining pieces being largely trios of a lighter kind, attractively written in the regular triple rhythms fashionable in the 1620s though not attempting the intensity of Monteverdi's grand manner. One of these, *Come dolce hoggi l'auretta*, is from the opera *Proserpina rapita*. From this it may be deduced that all the music that Monteverdi wished to preserve had already been printed under his own auspices and that we thus possess the entire corpus of his music in madrigalian genres.

(*iii*) *Summing-up*. Some scholars have viewed the later works not as truly madrigalian pieces but as incipient cantatas. The sectional structure of such a work as *Ninfa che scalza il piede*, in which each *parte* is written for a different combination of voices, may lead to this conclusion. Yet in spite of its formal variety Monteverdi's secular chamber music all belongs to the tradition he inherited in the 16th century. It is significant that at a time when solo music was predominating he preferred to write for an ensemble, if only of two or three voices. This allowed him a greater variety of texture, enhanced by the possibilities of the loose counterpoint that after the 1580s was all that conventional madrigals contained. It is also significant that even when he did write solo pieces the principles of word-painting, learnt from the Marenzian madrigal, still informed his approach to the madrigalian genre. The roots of the real developments in 17th-century music must therefore be sought elsewhere. Monteverdi's madrigals, however, form the finest corpus of work by any composer working in this sphere. He was as technically accomplished as Marenzio but had a much greater emotional range. He was as speculative as Gesualdo, but his much greater compositional skill means that his experimental writing is better integrated into his works and is of greater value in expressing emotion. If he lacked the lightness of touch of Vecchi, this is essentially because, as an 'academic' composer, his main preoccupation was with realizing the Greek concept of 'affecting the whole man'. He was also writing, after his Cremona years, for professional performers of great skill. Thus virtually all his 250 works in this genre are of some interest, a high proportion are masterly and some are masterpieces.

6. EARLY DRAMATIC WORKS. Monteverdi was probably engaged in the production of various kinds of theatrical entertainment from his earliest years at Mantua. It is unlikely that he had a chance to gain such experience at Cremona. His models for dramatic works were thus those of his colleagues in the service of the Gonzaga family. Their activities undoubtedly included the provision of music for ballets, a favourite amusement of Vincenzo I, who had probably acquired some knowledge of it from the court at Ferrara. Monteverdi's participation in dance music is made the more probable by virtue of his employment as a string player, as it was the five-part ensemble of viols and violins that was used in such entertainments. He must also have performed in *intermedi* and music for plays, notably Guarini's celebrated pastoral comedy *Il pastor fido*, originally planned for 1591 but finally produced early in 1598. The music for 1591 was probably by Wert and Gastoldi, but the production of 1598 may well have included some by Monteverdi. Cavicchi (*Congresso internazionale . . .1968*) has pointed out that in the preface to a volume of

contrafacta including some taken from the Guarini settings in the fifth book of madrigals the editor, Aquilino Coppini, referred to 'La Musica rappresentata del Quinto libro de' Madrigali del Signor Claudio Monteverdi' and that this, taken literally, would imply that they were originally monodic theatre music, for which five-part versions had been made later in the manner of the *Lamento d'Arianna*. Whether or not this is true, it is certain that Monteverdi's experience of stage music began well before he could have become acquainted with the Florentine operatic experiments and that it is an important factor in the consideration of his stylistic development.

The first knowledge of Monteverdi's working in this area comes in a letter dating from 1604, while he was awaiting details of choreography from the Mantuan dancing-master before writing the music for a ballet. This shows a concern for practical matters that was to prove typical of his approach to later projects for theatre music. It may be assumed that he was involved in similar works for Mantua during the next two years, since one of the reasons given by Giulio Cesare Monteverdi for writing his *Dichiaratione* of 1607 was that his brother was too busy 'ora in Tornei, ora in Balletti, ora in Commedie'. The first score to survive, however, is that for an opera, *L'Orfeo*, called a 'favola in musica' and produced at Mantua in 1607. Where exactly the production took place is unknown, since the Accademia degli Invaghiti, before whom it was given, had no permanent premises at this time, and speculation that it was in the Galleria dei Fiumi in the Palazzo Ducale is so far unproven. It seems likely that the ambience was a relatively small hall, where the grand effects customary in productions of pastorals had to be reduced to modest proportions. Although both Monteverdi and his librettist, Alessandro Striggio (ii), almost certainly knew Peri's *Euridice*, there are notable differences between the two. In both works the classical story is treated as a pastoral, with the usual semi-happy conclusion, but the printed libretto of *L'Orfeo* shows that either composer or poet intended an ending closer to the myth, with Orpheus menaced by the Bacchantes. Why this was put aside is unknown, but it indicates an altogether grander conception than that of *L'Euridice*, and helps to explain the greater length of *L'Orfeo*, with its five acts demanding different scenes, whereby the classical concept of unity of place is abandoned. In addition to pastoral there are strong elements of the *intermedi*, notably in the scene depicting Orpheus's descent to Hades, for which precedents can be found in several 16th-century entertainments. Opportunities for dancing are also included, both in the first act and at the conclusion of the opera. Thus elements from the genres in which Monteverdi had been working for at least a decade were present to allow him to move away from recitative-dominated drama in the Florentine pattern.

The music of *L'Orfeo* is therefore a mixture of monody, madrigal, and instrumental music of various kinds. Since it derived from *intermedi* and ballet music, Monteverdi demanded an instrumental ensemble of a similar kind to those used in such entertainments. It is accordingly larger and more varied than that of *L'Euridice* and includes the trombones traditionally used in infernal scenes, and recorders and strings for pastoral scenes. It is somewhat smaller than the largest ensemble used in 16th-century *intermedi*, and a new feature is the great variety of harmony instruments accompanying the voices. It is exceptional in deliberately demanding virtuosity from several players, especially those of cornettos, small violins (dancing-masters' kits) and harp, the player of the last-named at the first performance probably being a famous harpist from Naples. On the other hand, its deployment to gain dramatic atmosphere was not very unusual, except perhaps in the simultaneous use of various continuo instruments, which is sometimes highly imaginative in its exploration of sonorities.

The individual items from which the opera is built are also largely traditional. The pastoral first act includes a choral canzonetta which in style derives from Gastoldi's ballettos and the large-scale chorus lamenting the death of Eurydice in Act 2 is a homophonic madrigal whose rich harmony is typically Monteverdian. The instrumental pieces in the body of the opera are mostly short and in five parts, and they are often based on dance rhythms such as that of the pavan. They resemble similarly short pieces by Monteverdi's colleague Salamone Rossi, another string player, which apparently were written for dramatic entertainments of some kind. The toccata for the total ensemble, including trumpets, that begins the opera is a military fanfare, which could well have been played *al fresco* by the town musicians; again this was not an unusual prelude to a play or *intermedi*. The greatest stylistic variety in *L'Orfeo* is to be found in the monodic music, in which Monteverdi shows a flair beyond the reach of the Florentines. Comparatively little of it is recitative, but the narration of the messenger describing Eurydice's death clearly owes much to Peri, whose expressive power and interesting harmonies in a similar style furnished an inviting model. Monteverdi preferred more organized patterns of solo music such as strophic variation, which he used most effectively for the Prologue; the duet, used less as dialogue than as the expression of two shepherds or of Apollo and Orpheus, who voice the same emotions simultaneously; and the continuo madrigal after the manner of the last six numbers of his fifth book, duet sections alternating with tuttis which often repeat the same material to give an elementary rondo form. Thus much of the music is based on the madrigalian style, the melody having a shape similar to that in the fourth and fifth books. The harmony is equally expressive, with a great deal of dissonance brought about by a melodic anticipation of a succeeding chord or by the irregular resolution of passing notes. The desire for organization informs the structure both of the individual acts and of the work as a whole. Ritornellos occur frequently to provide small-scale patterns, but Act 1 is conceived virtually as an arch, an example of large-scale planning unprecedented at this epoch. Even more remarkable is the fact that the opera has a grand, carefully placed climax, Orpheus's great aria in Act 3, 'Possente spirto', which, with its display of vocal and instrumental virtuosity, has something of the role of a grand scena in later operas. (For illustration, *see* AMADINO, RICCIARDO.)

From the point of view of drama *L'Orfeo* belongs to the tradition of the late Renaissance and thus does not pretend to depict rounded human characters. The only role aspiring to such a condition is that of Orpheus himself, but even he is seen more as an allegorical figure representing the power of music. On the other hand, there are many touches of excellent theatrical effect in the music: the unexpected breaking off of the Prologue to allow the drama to begin; the simple style of the last

verse of 'Possente spirto' after the previously embellished melody, to show that Orpheus's increasing desperation results in a human rather than a virtuoso plea to be allowed to cross the Styx; the use of sinfonias to change the mood between scenes. It is such things, not to mention the excellence of the music itself, that made *L'Orfeo* the first viable opera in the repertory.

Only the libretto and several versions of the lament survive from *L'Arianna*. These, together with the sketchy description of its first performance by the Mantuan court chronicler Follino, suggest a somewhat more ample scale of production than in *L'Orfeo*, as would be expected for such a formal occasion. Monteverdi maintained, however, the general approach of the earlier opera. The monodic versions of the lament reveal the same expressive, malleable melodic style, based on his madrigalian experience, while the libretto shows that this scena had interpolations from a chorus of fishermen, suggesting the same concern for musical shape, as opposed to simple declamation. The score of *Il ballo delle ingrate* of the same year was published only in 1638, though the surviving libretto of the 1608 performance suggests that there were a number of changes in the published version. Whether all the instrumental sections were published is more doubtful, since as it stands the ballet is both short and somewhat lacking in proportion. Follino's description mentions the participation of all kinds of instruments, so it may well be that the string parts of the dances are a reduced arrangement catering for the tastes of a later period. The monodic opening section, a dialogue between Venus and Cupid, is written in a stricter recitative style than is usual in *L'Orfeo*, though the harmony is effective, and at one point there is a hint of a triple-time aria, looking forward to the style of the 1620s. The short duet which ends this dialogue is in Monteverdi's best vein, and the strophic-variation aria for Pluto surrounding the dances shows a melodiousness combined with a care for expressing the detail of the words worthy of his best madrigals. The concluding aria for the last remaining *ingrata* is the finest part of the work, a miniature masterpiece written in the same emotional spirit as the *Lamento d'Arianna*. The dances display the methods of rhythmic transformation common in pavan–galliard pairs, and their five-part texture emphasizes the three upper lines, which are allotted to violins. The production was probably quite elaborate, with machines or *carri* for Venus and Cupid and an *intermedio*-like representation of the jaws of Hades. The lack of virtuosity in the women's parts, as in the surviving scena from *L'Arianna*, almost certainly stems from the employment of the actress Virginia Andreini after the death of Caterina Martinelli, but if this caused practical difficulties at the time the exploitation of a limited vocal range and a simpler melodic style in the *ingrata*'s aria showed the way forward to a genuine dramatic manner in solo music.

7. LATER DRAMATIC WORKS. Monteverdi's next surviving theatre piece, *Tirsi e Clori* (1616), was also a ballet written for Mantua, but is on a smaller scale and lacks the *intermedi* ingredients of *Il ballo delle ingrate*. The musical forces show the trend towards the monochrome string ensemble and away from the variety of the Renaissance orchestra: Monteverdi asked for nine players of the viola da braccio family and eight singers, two of whom take the parts of Thyrsis and Chloris. The continuo team is equally modest, with a chitarrone and

harpsichord (or a harp for Chloris) to accompany the two protagonists and a spinet and two lutes to support the general ensemble. The work is in the form of a dialogue madrigal, a type popular by 1616, with flowing triple-time melody after the manner of the monodic aria, followed by the ballet, an extended madrigal for five voices (notwithstanding the eight suggested by Monteverdi) with more complicated rhythms than in the dance music of either *L'Orfeo* or *Il ballo delle ingrate*. Noticeably there are no allegorical elements in the brief story of pastoral courtship. That this is symptomatic of Monteverdi's thinking about the nature of music drama is revealed by a series of letters to Striggio concerning the music for *Le nozze di Tetide*, a *favola marittima*, which he started to compose later the same year. He thought at the outset that the libretto was to be set completely to music in the manner of *L'Arianna*. For this purpose, however, it seemed, because of the lack of human interest, very inadequate:

I see that the characters are winds, *amoretti*, *zeffiretti* and sirens, so that many sopranos will be needed; and also that the winds – west winds and north winds – have to sing. How, dear sir, since winds do not speak, shall I be able to imitate their speech? And how, by such means, shall I be able to move the passions? Ariadne moved the audience because she was a woman, and Orpheus did the same because he was a man and not a wind ... I find that this tale does not move me at all and is even difficult to understand; nor do I feel that it can naturally inspire me to a moving climax. Ariadne inspired in me a true lament, and Orpheus a true prayer, but I do not know what this will inspire in me.

This letter, one of the first contributions to an aesthetic of opera written by a composer who had experience of the genre, was in fact based on a misunderstanding, since the verse was intended for a set of *intermedi*; it is interesting that when this was explained to him Monteverdi did not challenge its suitability. He wrote madrigals for the nereids and solo music for Venus, the latter with fashionable echo effects, and he suggested dancing at certain points. Thus he was clearly differentiating by this time between operas, serious works that must move the affections, and less organic forms of entertainment. The correspondence about the abortive *Andromeda* of 1618–20 reveals nothing of aesthetic importance except that Monteverdi was still interested in madrigalian choruses and dances. The conception of the lost *Apollo* emerges even more vaguely from the letters, but it seems to have been some kind of dramatic cantata, the centrepiece of which was a lament, presumably monodic.

As a piece of music-theatre *Apollo* may thus have resembled Monteverdi's next such work to survive, *Combattimento di Tancredi e Clorinda* (1624), a setting of stanzas from Tasso's epic poem *Gerusalemme liberata*. This in itself denotes that it was not to be a conventional operatic work, since, whereas he usually insisted on all kinds of changes and additions to librettos to make them more effective for his purposes, he here set a text that afforded no opportunity for this kind of adaptation. The scene is that of a fight in single combat between a Crusader, Tancred, and the Muslim girl Clorinda, of whose sex he could not be aware since she was dressed in armour; Monteverdi used a narrator to sing the words not given to these two protagonists. The form of the cantata (for want of a better word) is therefore based on the dialogue madrigal. The central action, however, is largely created by the orchestra of strings, the writing for which demonstrates the potentialities of the *stile concitato*, with its division of long notes into short, measured repeated notes – not, as has

sometimes been stated, with the modern string tremolando. Though in outline the work is not all that different from *Tirsi e Clori*, the writing for both instruments and voices is completely different. The vocal parts are set as expressive arioso, at times highly ornamented, and lack the pure lyricism of the earlier piece. The absence of theatrical realism implied by the use of a narrator is more than made up for by the realistic effects of the orchestra, which imitates the trotting of horses in triple time, the clashing of swords by pizzicato and the shortness of breath in the dying Clorinda by sustained bowing changing suddenly from *forte* to *piano* and by both instruments and the voice as Clorinda actually dies. What could so easily have been simply a demonstration of an academic idea is in fact a vivid drama of human feeling.

It is evident from the important series of letters to Striggio in 1627 (see fig.3) about the lost opera *La finta pazza Licori* that human psychology was now Monteverdi's principal concern in dramatic music. This opera was planned as a comedy, which was certainly unusual at this time and suggests that Giulio Strozzi's drama had been written as a play rather than for musical setting. There is no mention of any allegorical figures, but the heroine, Licoris, intended for the singer Margherita Basile, was to simulate madness in order to make Amyntas desire to marry her. The complicated psychology of the heroine was one of the greatest attractions of this idea for Monteverdi, who instructs the singer to act 'from the single word rather than the sense of the phrase'. Realism was again to be sought: offstage music and noises, arias (one a lullaby) and the necessity for as much variety as possible are mentioned in the descriptions of how Strozzi was adapting the play to Monteverdi's needs. The fact that three virtuoso singers were available made them reorganize the plot to give each a more equal role than in the first conception, where the burden was very strongly on Licoris. While it is impossible to surmise exactly what form Monteverdi's music took, the correspondence indicates a radical departure from the earlier operas in aim and approach in spite of the fact that the royal occasion for which it was designed was not basically different from the one for which *L'Arianna* had been composed. The letters concerning the *intermedi* at Parma in 1628 show a more conventional attitude, indicating that Monteverdi still subscribed to the idea of a difference in seriousness between an opera and other theatre music.

The ballet for Ferdinand III published in the eighth book of madrigals is not strikingly original in plan. It consists of strophic variations for tenor, with instrumental ritornellos, followed by two choral madrigals using the *stile concitato*; the latter were originally separated by dances, but these were not printed. The ritornellos are scored for two violins and continuo, but the five-part texture of the choruses and the style of the tenor solo are both developed from *Tempro la cetra* and *Tirsi e Clori* of some 20 years earlier.

Little is known about the conception of the three operas of Monteverdi's final years or even about the conditions under which they were performed. One, *Le nozze d'Enea con Lavinia*, is lost, but the synopsis and scenario, which do survive, indicate that it was 'a tragedy with a happy ending'. There were dances and choruses, first in *intermedi* between the acts and later integrated into the drama. The authenticity of one of the two surviving works, *Il ritorno d'Ulisse in patria*, has

3. Final page of autograph letter (10 September 1627) from Monteverdi to the Mantuan court chancellor, Alessandro Striggio, giving his reasons for refusing to return to the service of the Gonzagas (Archivio di Stato, Mantua; trans. in Arnold and Fortune, p.73)

sometimes been challenged, since its only surviving score is in Vienna and is different in many details from the manuscript librettos presumably used in Venice. The style of the music is so like that of Monteverdi's other late works that there can be few doubts that the Vienna score is by him, but it may well have been altered by another hand. The opera was first performed in Venice early in 1640, given in Bologna later that year, and repeated in Venice the following Carnival. It is known that some of the singers at St Mark's were given leave of absence to go to Bologna, presumably to take part in the performances there; this may explain the preponderance of male roles of quite modest proportions, whereas in other Venetian operas of the 1640s both women and castratos were used more lavishly. The demands on the designer and machinist were little different from those in the early operas, and, with the frequent participation of gods, the libretto still shows elements from *intermedi*. But the Homeric basis of the story allows for much of the interest in human emotion on which the correspondence concerning *La finta pazza Licori* insisted, and Badoaro provided a great variety of characters, from the comic, represented by Iro, the parasite accompanying Penelope's suitors, to the intensely serious, Ariadne-like figure of Penelope herself. There is also a genuine attempt at dialogue between the participants, and a grand climax, allowing for the equivalent of Orpheus's 'Possente spirto' at the moment when Ulysses defeats the suitors through being the only one to have the strength to draw his bow. Musically, the score is remarkable for its lack of academicism compared with the style that might have been expected from Monteverdi's letters and eighth book of madrigals. The climactic scene uses the *stile concitato* most effectively.

Elsewhere he displayed complete mastery of the genres in which he had been working for over 30 years. Much of Penelope's music consists of expressive recitative. It is somewhat less dissonant than his earliest music in this manner, but it shows a notable command of phrase structure, sometimes involving the repetition of words, which, while never obscuring their meaning, gives the recitative a hitherto unrivalled sense of shape. The variety of closed forms is equally noteworthy. The duets are specially fine and never obstruct the movement of the drama. Both strophic variation and the ostinato bass are freely used in the closed forms, where the melodic writing varies from smoothly flowing triple-time arias to catchy ariettas. It is clear that the orchestral and choral music is incomplete in the Vienna manuscript, but five-part textures are again common, and the strings are occasionally used to accompany the voice. Monteverdi's intentions are sometimes obscure – for example, when only a single chord, meant to be repeated but with no other instructions, is given to accompany the departure of the Thracian boat escorting the sleeping Ulysses – but this very fact shows that the orchestra was exploited for such effects; and as was customary, ritornellos are used to shape the vocal music.

Monteverdi's final opera, *L'incoronazione di Poppea*, is on an even more ample scale and involves a still greater number of characters. The principal parts – Poppaea, Nero (written for a high castrato) and Octavia (taken by Anna Renzi, one of the most celebrated singers of the mid-17th century) – require first-class singers, and a number of minor roles demand considerable skill.

G. F. Busenello's libretto still contains allegorical elements, and the dénouement, whereby the sleeping Poppaea is protected from murder by Love, relies literally on a *deus ex machina*. In part because the story is an adaptation of Tacitus and no longer a matter of mythology, supernatural characters play a proportionally lesser role in the opera, which has a strongly human basis. The characters represent a cross-section of society ranging (apart from deities) from the emperor and his consort and their courtiers and associates to servants and common soldiers. In spite of this immense range the libretto is skilfully constructed, so the lack of continuity sometimes apparent in *Il ritorno d'Ulisse* is rarely found, and cause and effect follow each other cogently, only a few disparate scenes providing obvious relief from the progress of the drama.

Monteverdi set the libretto with considerable freedom, repeating and rearranging passages to heighten the dramatic effect, as in the confrontation between Nero and Seneca in the first act. He consistently underscored variety of emotion within a single character, and Nero is drawn in a way reminiscent of Monteverdi's instructions concerning Licoris, in that a single phrase can suddenly change his mood, giving a lively, realistic picture of a neurotic ruler. The music has greater variety than any other opera by Monteverdi, and the purely solo music is intrinsically more interesting than that of *Il ritorno d'Ulisse*. There are specially fine laments, written in the customary arioso, for the deposed empress, Octavia, and Poppaea's husband, Otho. Nero's music is still more remarkable; in it the detailed imagery of the verse is set with the utmost imagination, such devices as the *stile concitato* having lost their academic flavour and become an essential expression of mood. The duets are frequent, and in them Monteverdi displayed an astonishing capacity for expressing widely differing kinds of love-making, from the flirtatiousness of the valet and the maid (some of whose music, however, is of questionable authenticity) to the highly charged sexuality between Nero and Poppaea, seen at its best in the final ground, which may, however, be by Benedetto Ferrari (see Chiarelli, 1974).

A serious problem in assessing the opera is that both surviving musical sources are posthumous and were probably meant for performances outside Venice by travelling companies, such as that at Naples in 1651. Thus the original music has often been transposed and otherwise rewritten, and the parts adjusted to allow doubling of roles and to eliminate complicated machinery. A certain amount of the music is probably not by Monteverdi, and the instrumental ensemble, which may well in its original form have been similar to that of *Il ritorno d'Ulisse*, has been arranged for two violins and bass in one score, for four-part ensemble in the other.

Despite the uncertainties caused by these changes, it is generally possible to follow the workings of Monteverdi's dramatic imagination. The scene of the death of Seneca, a chromatic madrigal in a style whose origins go back to Monteverdi's Mantuan years, shows a tragic power rarely seen in 17th-century opera. From the point of view of construction the most impressive flair is shown in the way that closed forms never seem to be the object of the music but convey necessary elements of the drama; with few exceptions it is thus impossible to extract the arias and duets from the fabric of the opera. The realism of the world picture given by *L'incoronazione di Poppea* has a strange by-product in that Nero and Poppaea are anti-hero and anti-heroine, and virtue is defeated in their victory. The idea of the opera yet remains a typically 17th-century allegory of the triumph of love in which the fate of individual human beings is less important. For all that, it is difficult not to see Monteverdi's experience of princes and their courts in this work, his greatest masterpiece and arguably the finest opera of the century.

8. SACRED MUSIC. The multiplicity of styles in Monteverdi's sacred music owes much to the fact that although he spent the greater part of his working life in the service of the church he was not so employed during the vital years of his early maturity. His music therefore does not fit naturally into a continuing tradition, and it shows many signs of individuality, not only in details of style but also in his general approach to its peculiar problems. Just as there is no evidence to suggest that he was ever a choirboy at Cremona Cathedral, equally there is none to show that he was seriously concerned in the composition of church music in his pre-Mantuan years. The *Sacrae cantiunculae* (1582) consists not of liturgical pieces but of motets probably written to acquire contrapuntal technique. As such they reveal an efficiency surprising for a boy of 15, though both in the handling of words and in a lack of interesting sonorities they also show some inexperience. At Mantua, Monteverdi seems to have had no responsibility whatever for church music until his promotion to *maestro di cappella* in 1601; and for the rest of his career there his duties in this sphere were nominal, especially up to 1609, while Gastoldi was in charge of the music at the ducal church of S Barbara. It may have been because there was no church musician of any eminence in Mantua from that year that Monteverdi was

stimulated to the composition of the music included in the grand collection published in 1610, though its dedication to the pope indicates an outward-looking ambition rather than a desire to please his employer. The music, however, so strongly reflects the resources and attitudes common at Mantua that it is unique in the history of church music and belongs to neither of the established Roman and Venetian traditions so influential at this period.

The full title of this famous volume is *Sanctissimae virgini missa senis vocibus ad ecclesiarum choros ac Vespere pluribus decantandae – cum nonnullis sacris concentibus ad sacella sive principum cubicula accommodata*. It is clear from this that there are three elements in the collection: a mass; the vesper psalms and *Magnificat* settings appropriate to festivals of the Virgin Mary; and motets of a not strictly liturgical nature. It has sometimes been interpreted to mean that these three elements were intended to be kept separate in performance, but the motets are placed unusually in between the settings of the vesper psalms, thus encouraging the belief that they were considered part of the Vespers music and acted as antiphon substitutes in a well authenticated manner of the time. There still remains the problem of why Monteverdi provided two settings of the *Magnificat*, which are so similar in technique and material that they must be considered alternatives rather than complementary. It has been suggested that one was meant for First Vespers, the other for Second, but there is no evidence that the music was designed for the monastic observance that this implies rather than for the public ceremonial or princely devotions for which most of the music was conceived. Monteverdi's liturgical intentions are thus open to varying interpretations. His general intention, to show himself a capable composer in differing styles of church music and to make plain his belief in the *prima* and *seconda prattica*, is hardly in doubt. The mass is a monument of the *prima prattica*. Written on themes from Gombert's motet *In illo tempore* (published in 1554), its academic intent is clear from the printing of ten *fughe* or contrapuntal tags from the motet at the head of the mass in the partbooks. It thus differs considerably from the masses using motets as parody material common in the later decades of the 16th century. Not only is there a more thorough polyphonic working-out of these tags but there is much close canonic writing and few places where imitative counterpoint gives way to the sonorous homophony of the Roman composers. Austerity rules too in the treatment of the words, for the conventional painting of the text is almost completely lacking. The mass is therefore most unusual for its period, its main resemblances to other settings lying in the diatonic harmony, with its many academic progressions, and in the wide range between upper and lower parts, which results in great splendour of sound.

The vesper psalms, on the other hand, are in the modern style, though they are not entirely *seconda prattica* works, since formal design, not the words, was the primary consideration. The mixture of elements is unique. Much of the melodic material is derived from plainsong, which is sometimes used as cantus firmi in long notes, sometimes woven into the fabric of counterpoint through the use of strong rhythms and imitative phrases. In *Dixit Dominus* it is the basis of a strophic-variation form, and in the hymn for Vespers, *Ave maris stella*, it is given the accentuation of a strophic hemiola

song. Chordal chanting in the manner of *falsobordone* is freely used in several places. Alongside these seemingly backward-looking elements are traits derived from the most recent madrigal style, notably trios with decorated melody, 'walking' bass patterns given to the continuo instruments, and ritornellos (sometimes optional) for a five-part instrumental ensemble. The larger-scale works show a knowledge of the Venetian style, though the use of *cori spezzati* rarely resembles that of the Gabrielis since the use of plainsong material does not allow for closely argued dialogue. The psalm settings are, however, conceived sectionally, verse by verse, the sections ending with full cadences, and the diversity between them is emphasized by complete changes of sonority, a trio of upper voices, for example, being replaced by one of lower voices or some similar effect. This is the antithesis of 16th-century practice and is one of the earliest appearances of a method that became the norm in later Baroque music. Where counterpoint is still extensively employed, as in *Lauda, Jerusalem*, the close imitations and dense textures of the mass on *In illo tempore* are also found.

The motets in the collection are the most thorough-going exhibitions of the modern style and the *seconda prattica*. They were written with Mantuan virtuoso singers in mind, and few church works of the time equal them in their exploitation of ornamental melody, in which figuration developed in secular monody is freely used in ensemble. Harmonically they are akin to the arioso sections in the operas, dissonance arising from the conflict between the slower movement of the bass and the anticipations or delays in the melody, which itself uses such expressive devices as the descending 6th and augmented and diminished intervals to express the words. One motet is an echo piece, less in the manner of Venetian echo motets than of theatre music such as Peri's 'Dunque fra torbid'onde' in the Florentine *intermedi* of 1589. Instruments are prominent in two items. The opening versicle, *Domine ad adiuvandum*, is remarkable for being the toccata from *L'Orfeo* with added choral parts chanting the words rhythmically. The other, the *Sonata sopra 'Sancta Maria'*, is in effect a large-scale 'quilt' canzona, with a soprano repeating a plainsong prayer to the Virgin Mary 11 times. Though there were precedents for it, the virtuosity of the instrumental writing and the expansiveness of its form make this unique too. The *Magnificat* settings bring all the afore-mentioned devices into play. The smaller one is for six voices and organ and is thus one of the first concertato settings. It is composed in separate sections, each using a different combination of voices, but unity is achieved by the constant repetition of a plainsong cantus firmus. The ornamental melody suggests that it was intended for solo voices though it is possible that some verses were sung chorally. The larger setting is designed in the same way except that the inclusion of instruments makes possible even greater variety between the sections. Operatic influences are here very strong, one section being virtually an echo scene, another using cornett and violin duets in the manner of Orpheus's great aria in *L'Orfeo*. In one verse, treated in the manner of the *Sonata sopra 'Sancta Maria'*, the plainsong cantus firmus is accompanied by instruments playing lively rhythms.

Whether Monteverdi composed further church music in his years at Mantua is unknown, and dating his Venetian works is difficult since they appeared in two collections, both huge, one published under his supervision in 1640, the other issued posthumously in 1651. Some developments in style can be traced by means of various works by him that appeared in anthologies between 1615 and 1629, but they are mainly pieces for modest forces, and thus do not give a rounded picture. It seems certain that much of his church music for Venice is lost, for, since he was expected to compose fresh music for the important festivals each year, even the two ample collections can hardly represent 30 years' work. The surviving works suggest that he continued to develop the three major trends revealed in the 1610 volume, adapting them to the changing tastes of three decades. He largely abandoned the older Venetian style, using *cori spezzati*, in favour of various types of concertato music, in which the expansive manner of the late Renaissance was reduced to the more restricted but elegant style of the early Baroque period. He continued to make use of the *prima prattica*, in which he composed at least two masses and several psalms. The extreme scholarliness of the 1610 mass is, however, modified in the two later mass settings. Both are for four voices with organ bass and use the old *misura da breve* and white note values. Dissonance is restricted to prepared suspensions and passing notes that move by step, while the melody and verbal underlay follow the principles of Zarlino. The main difference between this style and that of the 16th century lies in its diatonicism, the increasing regularity of rhythm and the predictability of its imitative counterpoint, whose texture is rarely varied by homophony. There is little word-painting, though suspensions express the word 'passus' in one of the masses, and Monteverdi was obviously determined to remain strictly within the tenets of the *prima prattica* and to essay a pure musical idiom. The resulting music is thus somewhat lacking in emotional power, though it is of profound historical importance in the development of the *stile antico*, which was practised successfully in Venice by several composers even in the 18th century.

The works written in the concertato manner are mainly psalm settings for Vespers and were probably meant for ceremonial occasions at St Mark's. In keeping with the general trend of the time, they are for comparatively small instrumental forces; two violin parts are normal, with trombones to support the voices (though the parts are often optional), and occasionally a bassoon is given an independent part. The brilliance of the Gabrielian orchestra is thus substantially reduced to monochrome. The writing for voices also tends to be of a less obviously virtuoso nature, though it is often both effective and imaginative. The earliest of Monteverdi's published Venetian choral works are four motets (in *RISM* 1620³); they are in a style akin to that of the Cremona madrigals, with the concrete images painted in an almost Marenzian way, and the continuo is little more than a *basso seguente*. There are some similar works in the retrospective collections, but the bulk of the concertato music uses the continuo as an essential feature, and it often acts as an important structural device. Monteverdi did not repeat the experiment of the Vespers music in using plainsong cantus firmi as unifying agents, probably because the harmonic implications of modal material were difficult to reconcile with the increasing diatonicism of 17th-century music. Instead he sought formal designs either in rondo structures or in repeated bass figuration. There are a number of rondo motets, in which a solo group of two or three singers

usually alternates with a tutti repeating a refrain. Unlike earlier Venetian rondo motets, in which the refrains are settings of the word 'Alleluja', Monteverdi repeated words from the psalm, even though this destroyed their continuity; he thus shows his concern for musical design at the expense of the text. He did likewise in works where there is no rondo form but merely short repetitions of motifs and phrases. Ostinato basses allowed for textual continuity, and Monteverdi showed a mastery of the genre to an even greater extent than in his secular music, since his psalm settings are often much longer than the *Lamento della ninfa* and the 1632 *Zefiro torna*. His tour de force occurs in a setting of *Laetatus sum*, where a single-bar figure is repeated over 100 times while variety is achieved through a succession of duets for differing combinations of voices, violins, trombones and bassoon. The melodies in such works are often close to those in contemporary secular songs, and Monteverdi used his own popular canzonetta *Chiome d'oro* in a setting of *Beatus vir*, which mixes ostinato and rondo techniques. As a result he forged an attractive, modern style unusual in church music at this time.

Monteverdi's Venetian motets for a few voices are more closely related to those in the 1610 collection, though with necessary modifications to suit Venetian conditions. His first published solos and duets appeared in anthologies from 1615 onwards and show that, lacking the virtuosos of Mantua, he largely renounced decorative melody in favour of a pleasant tunefulness. Some of the motets of the 1620s especially owe much to the secular arias of the songbooks and achieve a lightness that makes them seem secular in spirit. Other pieces look back to the intensity of the 1610 motets, especially four Marian motets (published in *RISM* 1625²), which seem to derive from the version of the *Lamento d'Arianna* as a prayer to the Blessed Virgin. These works use virtuoso *fioriture*, dissonance and expressive melody to give extraordinarily passionate meaning to the words in the *seconda prattica* manner. There is also a small group of works which are constructed sectionally; with their passages of quasi-recitative and aria they look forward to the later Baroque solo cantata.

The fact that in much of Monteverdi's sacred music secular material and techniques are to be found is of great significance in the history of church music, since many 17th-century church composers were not experienced in opera or other modern genres. By his application of methods first explored in secular music he helped to prevent the ossification of style increasingly encouraged by the Roman school with their preference for the *stile antico*.

9. HISTORICAL POSITION. Monteverdi's reputation, both in his lifetime and subsequently, has been that of a revolutionary, responsible to a considerable degree for the drastic changes in musical style that took place around 1600. This picture, encouraged by the polemic with Artusi, was confirmed in essentials by the two leading historians of the 18th century, Martini and Burney, probably because Artusi was more accessible than scores of Monteverdi's madrigals (the original sources being partbooks); and it persisted during most of the 19th century. Increased knowledge of the background of the period has modified this point of view in recent years. Monteverdi can now be seen as a principal figure in a progressive movement that included a num-

ber of composers and theorists. His greatest gifts lay in finding how traditional means could be applied to novel ends. Thus he persisted with the ensemble madrigal when the logical step for a composer interested in the declamation of the words was to adopt monody after the Florentine manner. His early operas were full of devices developed in *intermedi* and ballets. His church music is, in the *prima prattica* works, very traditional; elsewhere it is a mixture of traditional and new techniques, as in the Vespers of 1610, where cantus firmus technique and operatic scena mingle to produce a unique effect. His one real invention was the *stile concitato*, which has no exact precedent, though with its vivid realism the practical result is reminiscent of the battle pieces of the 16th century. As a theorist he was unable, even after a lifetime's thought, to arrive at a complete system or aesthetic of composition. His originality here lay in his realization that there was not one method of approach, but two, to the problems involved and that it was possible to use traditional as well as new techniques in attaining the desired goal of moving the passions.

It was because of his moderate views that Monteverdi's influence was less than might have been assumed for so famous and long-lived a composer. Few Italian composers followed his madrigal style, since the younger ones in particular were absorbed in the writing of monodic works. In this sphere his invention of the lament was particularly influential, for the genre became fashionable at the hands of such composers as d'India, Saracini and, later, Cavalli. Neither did his operas give rise to direct imitations. The style of the early works remains unique, while that of the later works was taken up less by his Venetian successors than has often been imagined. The profound humanity based on a historical theme which is the essence of *L'incoronazione di Poppea* has no exact equivalent in the works of Cavalli, though comic personages do infiltrate the operas of the period around 1650. The *stile concitato* certainly inspired: in Italy it was used by Grandi and Merula, while in Germany, Schütz made it an integral part of his style. It was in northern countries too that the theoretical basis of the *stile concitato* took root in the attempt by Schütz's pupil Christoph Bernhard and others to categorize musical figuration to correspond with human emotions, a process that contributed to the emergence of the doctrine of the Affections. It was in the practical application of this expression of human emotions in music that Monteverdi rightly held himself to be a master; and his position in music history rests on the fact that he showed how this could be done.

### WORKS

Editions: *C. Monteverdi: Tutte le opere*, ed. G. F. Malipiero (Asolo, 1926–42, rev. 2/1954; with added vol.xvii [suppl.], 1966) [M]
    *C. Monteverdi: Opera Omnia*, ed. Fondazione Claudio Monteverdi, IMa, *Monumenta*, v (1970–)
    *C. Monteverdi: Composizioni vocali profane e sacre (inedite)*, ed. W. Osthoff (Milan, 1958) [O]

#### DRAMATIC

L'Orfeo, favola in musica (A. Striggio (ii)), Mantua, Feb 1607 (Venice, 1609); M xi, 1
L'Arianna, opera (O. Rinuccini), Mantua, 28 May 1608, music lost except for lament (see 'Secular vocal')
Il ballo delle ingrate, ballet (Rinuccini), Mantua, 1608, pubd in Madrigali guerrieri et amorosi, 1638; M viii, 314
Prologue to L'Idropica, comedy with music (G. B. Guarini), Mantua, 2 June 1608, music lost
Tirsi e Clori, ballet (Striggio), Mantua, 1616, pubd in Concerto: settimo libro, 1619; M vii, 191
Le nozze di Tetide, favola marittima, begun 1616 but never completed, lost

Andromeda, opera (E. Marigliani), begun 1618–20 but never completed, lost
Apollo, dramatic cantata, never completed, lost
Combattimento di Tancredi e Clorinda (Tasso), Venice, 1624, pubd in Madrigali guerrieri et amorosi, 1638; M viii, 132
La finta pazza Licori (G. Strozzi), intended for Mantua, 1627, but never perf., music lost
Gli amori di Diana e di Endimione (A. Pio), Parma, 1628, music lost
Mercurio e Marte, torneo (C. Achillini), Parma, 1628, music lost
Proserpina rapita, opera (Strozzi), Venice, 1630, music lost except for 1 trio (see 'Secular vocal': Come dolce hoggi)
Volgendo il ciel, ballet, Vienna, ?1636, pubd in Madrigali guerrieri et amorosi, 1638; M viii, 157
Il ritorno d'Ulisse in patria (G. Badoaro), Venice, 1640; M xii
Le nozze d'Enea con Lavinia, opera, Venice, 1641, music lost
La vittoria d'Amore, ballet, Piacenza, 1641, music lost
L'incoronazione di Poppea (G. F. Busenello), Venice, 1642; M xiii

Prologue to La Maddalena, sacra rappresentazione (G. B. Andreini), 1617 (see 'Sacred vocal': Su le penne de' venti)

#### SECULAR VOCAL

Canzonette, 3vv (Venice, 1584) [1584]
Il primo libro de madrigali, 5vv (Venice, 1587) [1587]
Il secondo libro de madrigali, 5vv (Venice, 1590) [1590]
Il terzo libro de madrigali, 5vv (Venice, 1592) [1592]
Il quarto libro de madrigali, 5vv (Venice, 1603) [1603]
Il quinto libro de madrigali, 5vv, bc (Venice, 1605) [1605]
Musica tolta da i madrigali di Claudio Monteverde e d'altri autori, e fatta spirituale da Aquilino Coppini, 5, 6vv (Milan, 1607[20]) [incl. 11 sacred contrafacta of madrigals by Monteverdi] [1607[20]]
Scherzi musicali di Claudio Monteverde, raccolti da Giulio Cesare Monteverde suo fratello, 3vv (Venice, 1607[21]) [1607[21]]
Il secondo libro della musica di Claudio Monteverde e d'altri autori, fatta spirituale da Aquilino Coppini, 5vv (Milan, 1608) [incl. 8 sacred contrafacta of madrigals by Monteverdi] [1608]
Il terzo libro della musica di Claudio Monteverde e d'altri autori, fatta spirituale da Aquilino Coppini, 5vv (Milan, 1609) [incl. 19 sacred contrafacta of madrigals by Monteverdi] [1609]
Il sesto libro de madrigali, 5vv, con uno dialogo, 7vv, bc (Venice, 1614) [1614]
Concerto: settimo libro de madrigali, con altri generi di canti, 1–4, 6vv, bc (Venice, 1619) [1619]
Scherzi musicali cioè arie, et madrigali in stil recitativo, con una ciaccona . . . raccolti da Bartholomeo Magni, 1, 2vv, bc (Venice, 1632) [1632]
Madrigali guerrieri et amorosi con alcuni opuscoli in genere rappresentativo, che saranno per brevi episodii frà i canti senza gesto: libro ottavo, 1–8vv, insts, bc (Venice, 1638) [1638]
Madrigali e canzonette . . . libro nono, 2, 3vv, bc (Venice, 1651) [1651]

Works in 1594[15], 1605[12], 1624[11], C. Milanuzzi: Quarto scherzo delle ariose vaghezze . . . con una cantata et altre arie del Signor Monteverde, e del Sig. Francesco suo figliolo, 1v (Venice, 1624 [lost], 2/1624), 1634[7]

A che tormi il ben mio, 5vv, 1587; M i, 8
A Dio, Florida bella (G. B. Marini [Marino]), 5vv, insts, 1614; M vi, 38
Ah, che non si conviene romper la fede?, 2vv, 1619; M vii, 62
Ah dolente partita (Guarini: Il pastor fido) (= O infelix recessus), 5vv, 1603; M iv, 1
Ahi, che si parti il mio bel sol adorno, 3vv, I-MOe; M xvii, 38
Ahi, com'a un vago sol (= Vives in corde), 5vv, 1605; M v, 62
Alcun non mi consigli, 3vv, 1651; M ix, 42
Alle danze, alle gioie, 3vv, 1651; M ix, 68
Al lume delle stelle (Tasso) (= O rex supreme), 4vv, 1619; M vii, 129
Altri canti d'amor, 6vv, 2 vn, 4 va, 1638; M viii, 2
Altri canti di Marte (Marini) (= Pascha concelebranda) (2p. Due belli occhi fur l'armi [ = Ergo gaude, laetare and Lauda, anima mea]), 6vv, 2 vn, 1638; M viii, 181
Amarilli onde m'assale (G. Chiabrera), 3vv, 1607[21]; M x, 31
Amor che deggio far?, canzonetta, 4vv, 2 vn, chit/hpd, 1619; M vii, 182
Amorosa pupilletta, 3vv, 1607[21]; M x, 44
Amor per tua mercè vatene a quella, 5vv, 1587; M i, 11
Amor, se giusto sei (= Amemus te), 5vv, 1605; M v, 81
Amor, s'il tuo ferire, 5vv, 1587; M i, 54
Anima del cor mio, 5vv (= Anima quam dilexi), 5vv, 1603; M iv, 88
Anima dolorosa (= Anima miseranda), 5vv, 1603; M iv, 84
Anima mia, perdona (Guarini: Il pastor fido) (= Domine Deus) (2p. Che se tu se'il cor mio [ = O gloriose martyr], 5vv, 1603; M iv, 26
A quest'olmo, a quest'ombre (Marini), 6vv, 2 vn, 2 rec/fl, 1619; M vii, 14
Ardo, avvampo, mi struggo ( = Alleluja, kommet, jauchzet and Frewde, kommet, lasset uns gehen), 8vv, 2 vn, 1638; M viii, 107
Ardo e scoprir, ahi lasso, io non ardisco, 2vv, 1638; M ix, 32
Ardo, sì, ma non t'amo (Guarini) (2p. Ardi o gela a tua voglia (Tasso), risposta; 3p. Arsi e alsi a mia voglia (Tasso), contrarisposta), 5vv,

1587; M i, 61

Armato il cor d'adamantina fede (= Heus, bone vir), 2vv, 1632; M ix, 27

Augellin, che la voce al canto spieghi, 3vv, 1619; M vii, 98

A un giro sol de' bell'occhi lucenti (Guarini) (= Cantemus), 5vv, 1603; M iv, 49

Baci soavi e cari (Guarini), 5vv, 1587; M i, 14

Batto qui pianse Ergasto (Marini), 5vv, hpd, 1614; M vi, 101

Bel pastor dal cui bel guardo (Rinuccini), 2vv, 1651; M ix, 1

Bevea Fillide mia (G. Casoni), 5vv, 1590; M ii, 15

Cantai un tempo, e se fu dolc'il canto (P. Bembo), 5vv, 1590; M ii, 102

Canzonette d'amore, 3vv, 1584; M x, 3

Che dar più vi poss'io? (= Qui regnas), 5vv, 1605; M v, 51

Ch'io ami la mia vita, 5vv, 1587; M i, 1

Chiome d'oro, bel thesoro, canzonetta, 2vv, 2 vn, chit/hpd, 1619; M vii, 176

Ch'io non t'ami, cor mio (Guarini), 5vv, 1592; M iii, 76

Ch'io t'ami e t'ami più de la mia vita (Guarini: Il pastor fido) (= Te sequar) (2p. Deh, bella e cara [= Sancta Maria]; 3p. Ma tu più che mai dura [= Spernit Deus]), 5vv, 1605; M v, 39

Chi vol haver felice e lieto il core, 'cantato a voce piena, alla francese' (Guarini), 5vv, 1638; M viii, 280

Chi vuol veder d'inverno un dolce aprile, 3vv, 1584; M x, 17

Chi vuol veder un bosco, 3vv, 1584; M x, 23

Clori amorosa (Chiabrera), 5vv, 1607²¹; M x, 54

Come dolce hoggi l'auretta spira (Strozzi, from Proserpina rapita), 3vv, 1651; M ix, 60

Come farò, cuor mio?, 3vv, 1584; M x, 14

Con che soavità, labbra odorate (Guarini), 1v, str, lutes, hpds, org, 1619; M vii, 137

Cor mio, mentre vi miro (Guarini) (= Jesu, dum te), 5vv, 1603; M iv, 7

Cor mio, non mori? (= Jesu, tu obis), 5vv, 1603; M iv, 11

Corse a la morte il povero Narciso, 3vv, 1584; M x, 15

Cruda Amarilli (Guarini: Il pastor fido) (= Felle amaro), 5vv, 1605; M v, 1

Crudel, perchè mi fuggi? (Tasso), 5vv, 1590; M ii, 83

Damigella tutta bella (Chiabrera), 3vv, 1607²¹; M x, 40

De la bellezza le dovute lodi, 3vv, 1607 (doubtful)

Dice la mia bellissima Licori (Guarini), 2vv, 1619; M vii, 58

Di far sempre gioire amor speranza, 3vv, 1651; M ix, 50

Dolcemente dormiva la mia Clori (Tasso), 5vv, 1590; M ii, 78

Dolci miei sospiri (Chiabrera), 5vv, 1607²¹; M x, 52

Dolcissimi legami di parole amorose (Tasso), 5vv, 1590; M ii, 19

Dolcissimo uscignolo, 'cantato a voce piena, alla francese' (Guarini), 5vv, 1638; M viii, 271

Donna, nel mio ritorno (Tasso), 5vv, 1590; M ii, 44

Donna, s'io miro voi, giaccio divengo, 5vv, 1587; M i, 58

Ecco di dolci raggi (2p. Io che armato sin hor [= Spera in Domino]), 1v, 1632; M x, 81

Eccomi pronta ai baci (Marini), 3vv, 1619; M vii, 111

Ecco mormorar l'onde (Tasso), 5vv, 1590; M ii, 68

Ecco Silvio (Guarini: Il pastor fido) (= Qui pependit) (2p. Ma se con la pietà [= Qui pietate]; 3p. Dorinda, ah dirò mia [= Maria, quid ploras]; 4p. Ecco piegando le ginocchie a terra [= Te, Jesu Christe]; 5p. Ferir quel petto, Silvio [= Pulchrae sunt]), 5vv, 1605; M v, 14

Ecco vicine, o bella tigre, 2vv, 1619; M vii, 71

E così a poc'a poco torno farfalla (Guarini), 6vv, 1605; M v, 96

Era l'anima mia già presso a l'ultim' hore (Guarini) (= Stabat virgo), 5vv, 1605; M v, 9

Eri già tutta mia, 1v, 1632; M x, 80

Et è pur dunque vero, 1v, insts, 1632; M x, 82

Filli cara e amata (A. Parma), 5vv, 1587; M i, 21

Fugge il verno dei dolori (Chiabrera), 3vv, 1607²¹; M x, 34

Fumia la pastorella (A. Allegretti), 5vv, 1587; M i, 27

Già mi credev'un sol esser in cielo, 3vv, 1584; M x, 18

Giovinetta ritrosetta, 5vv, 1607²¹; M x, 50

Gira il nemico insidioso, 3vv, 1638; M viii, 75

Giù li a quel petto giace, 3vv, 1584; M x, 20

Godi pur del bel sen felice, 3vv, 1584; M x, 19

Hor, care canzonette, 3vv, 1584; M x, 24

Hor ch'el ciel e la terra (Petrarch) (= O du mächtiger Herr) (2p. Così sol d'una chiara fonte [= Dein allein ist ja]), 6vv, 2 vn, 1638; M viii, 39

I bei legami (Chiabrera), 3vv, 1607²¹; M x, 29

Il mio martir tengo, 3vv, 1584; M x, 9

Incenerite spoglie (see Sestina)

Interrotte speranze (Guarini), 2vv, 1619; M vii, 94

Intorno a due vermiglie, 5vv, 1590; M ii, 29

Io ardo, si ma'l fuoco di tal sorte, 3vv, 1594¹⁵; M xvii, 1; O, 2

Io mi son giovinetta (= Rutilante in nocte), 5vv, 1603; M iv, 59

Io mi vivea com'aquila, 3vv, 1584; M x, 11

Io son fenice e voi sete la fiamma, 3vv, 1584; M x, 22

Io son pur vezzosetta pastorella (Guarini), 2vv, 1619; M vii, 41

La bocc'onde l'asprissime (E. Bentivoglio), 5vv, 1590; M ii, 75

La fiera vista, 3vv, 1584; M x, 4

La giovinetta pianta (= Florea serta), 5vv, 1592; M iii, 1

Lamento d'Arianna: Lasciatemi morire (Rinuccini), 5vv, 1614; M vi, 1

Lamento d'Arianna: Lasciatemi morire (Rinuccini), 1v (Venice, 1623); M xi, 161

Lamento della ninfa: Non havea Febo ancora (Rinuccini), 1–4vv, 1638: M viii, 286

Lamento d'Olimpia: Voglio morir: van'è'l conforto tuo, 1v, GB-Lbm; O, 10

La mia turca che d'amor, 1v, in C. Milanuzzi: Quarto scherzo delle ariose vaghezze (Venice, 2/1624); M ix, 117

La pastorella mia spietata (Sannazaro), 3vv, 1607²¹; M x, 41

La piaga c'ho nel core (= Plagas tuas), 5vv, 1603; M iv, 41

Lasciatemi morire (see Lamento d'Arianna)

La vaga pastorella sen va tra fiori, 5vv, 1587; M i, 50

La violetta (Chiabrera), 3vv, 1607²¹; M x, 48

Lidia, spina del mio core, 5vv, 1607²¹; M x, 56

Longe da te, cor mio (= Longe a te), 5vv, 1603; M iv, 92

Luci serene e chiare, 5vv, 1603; M iv, 35

Lumi miei, cari lumi (Guarini), 5vv, 1592; M iii, 99

Maledetto sia l'aspetto, 1v, 1632; M x, 76

Mentre io miravo fiso (Tasso), 5vv, 1590; M ii, 58

Mentre vaga Angioletta ogn'anima (Guarini), 2vv, 1638; M viii, 246

M'è più dolce il penar per Amarilli (Guarini: Il pastor fido) (= Animas eruit), 5vv, 1605; M v, 56

Misero Alceo, 5vv, insts, 1614; M vi, 91

Ninfa che scalza il piede, 1–3vv, 1638; M viii, 259

Non così tosto io miro (Chiabrera), 3vv, 1607²¹; M x, 38

Non è di gentil core (degl'Atti), 2vv, 1619; M vii, 8

Non giacinti o narcisi (Casoni), 5vv, 1590; M ii, 24

Non havea Febo (see Lamento della ninfa)

Non m'è grave'l morire, 5vv, 1590; M ii, 92

Non partir, ritrosetta, 3vv, 1638; M viii, 305

Non più guerra, pietate (Guarini), 5vv, 1603; M iv, 72

Non si levav'ancor (Tasso), 5vv, 1590; M ii, 1

Non sono in queste rive fiori (Tasso), 5vv, 1590; M ii, 35

Non vedrò mai le stelle, 2vv, 1619; M vii, 66

Non voglio amare per non penare, 3vv, 1651; M ix, 58

Occhi miei, se mirar, più non debb'io, 3vv, 1594¹⁵; M xvii, 2; O, 3

Occhi un tempo, mia vita, occhi di questo cor fido sostegno (Guarini), 5vv, 1592; M iii, 82

O come è gran martire (Guarini) (= O dies infelices), 5vv, 1592; M iii, 8

O come sei gentile, caro augellino (Guarini), 2vv, 1619; M vii, 41

O come vaghi, o come cari, 2vv, 1624¹¹; M x, 102

O dolce anima mia (Guarini), 5vv, 1592; M iii, 19

Ogni amante è guerrier, 2–3vv, 1638; M viii, 88

Ohimè ch'io cado, ohimè ch'inciampo, 1v, in C. Milanuzzi: Quarto scherzo delle ariose vaghezze (Venice, 2/1624); M ix, 111

Ohimè, dov'è il mio ben?, 'romanesca' (B. Tasso), 2vv, 1619; M vii, 152

Ohimè, il bel viso (Petrarch), 5vv, 1614; M vi, 70

Ohimè, se tanto amate (Guarini), 5vv, 1603; M iv, 54

O mio bene, o mia vita, 3vv, 1651; M ix, 95

O Mirtillo, Mirtill'anima mia (Guarini: Il pastor fido) (= O mi Fili), 5vv, 1605; M v, 5

O primavera, gioventù de l'anno (Guarini: Il pastor fido) (= Praecipitantur), 5vv, 1592; M iii, 62

O rosetta, che rosetta (Chiabrera), 3vv, 1607²¹; M x, 43

O rossignuol ch'in queste verdi fronde (Bembo), 5vv, 1592; M iii, 33

O sia tranquill'il mare, 2vv, 1638; M ix, 36

O viva fiamma, o miei sospiri ardenti, 2vv, 1619; M vii, 47

Parlo, miser'e taccio? (Guarini) (= Longe, mi Jesu), 3vv, 1619; M vii, 116

Perchè fuggi tra salci, ritrosetta? (Marini), 2vv, 1619; M vii, 76

Perchè, se m'odiavi, 1v, 1634⁷; M xvii, 24

Perchè se m'odiavi, 3vv, 1651; M ix, 79

Perchè t'en fuggi, O Fillide?, 3vv, 1638; M viii, 295

Perfidissimo volto (Guarini), 5vv, 1592; M iii, 68

Piagne e sospira (Tasso), 5vv, 1603; M iv, 96

Più lieto il guardo, 1v, 1634⁷; M xvii, 22

Poi che del mio dolore, 5vv, 1587; M i, 24

Presso un fiume tranquillo, dialogue (Marini), 7vv, insts, 1614; M vi, 113

Prima vedrò ch'in questi prati, 3vv, 1605¹²; M xvii, 5; O, 6

Qual si può dir maggiore, 3vv, 1584; M x, 2

Quando dentro al tuo seno, 3vv, 1651; M ix, 56

Quando l'alba in oriente (Chiabrera), 3vv, 1607²¹; M x, 36

Quando sperai del mio servir mercede, 3vv, 1584; M x, 13

Quante son stelle in ciel (G. B. da Cerreto), 3vv, 1594¹⁵; M xvii, 3; O, 4

Quel augellin che canta (= Qui laudes), 5vv, 1603; M iv, 66

Quell'ombra esser vorrei (Casoni), 5vv, 1590; M ii, 49

Quel sguardo sdegnosetto, 1v, 1632; M x, 77

Questa ordì il laccio (Strozzi), 5vv, 1587; M i, 46

Questi vaghi concenti, 9vv, 1605; M v, 104

Questo specchio ti dono, Rosa, 5vv, 1590; M ii, 87

Qui rise, O Tirsi (Marini), 5vv, insts, 1614; M vi, 77

Raggi, dov'è il mio bene?, 3vv, 1584; M x, 6

Rimanti in pace a la dolente e bella Fillida (L. Celiano), 5vv, 1592; M iii, 104

S'andasse amor a caccia (T. Tasso), 5vv, 1590; M ii, 53

Se i languidi miei sguardi, 'lettera amorosa', 1v, 1619; M vii, 160

S'el vostro cor, madonna (Guarini), 2vv, 1619; M vii, 90

Se nel partir da voi, vita mia, 5vv, 1587; M i, 36

Se non mi date aita, 3vv, 1594[15]; M xvii, 4

Se per estremo ardore morir potesse un core (Guarini), 5vv, 1592; M iii, 41

Se per havervi oimè, 5vv, 1587; M i, 5

Se pur destina e vole il cielo, 'partenza amorosa', 1v, 1619; M vii, 167

Se pur non mi consenti, 5vv, 1587; M i, 18

Sestina: Lagrime d'amante al sepolcro dell'amata [incipit: Incenerite spoglie] (S. Agnelli), 5vv, 1614; M vi, 46

Se tu mi lassi, perfida (Tasso), 5vv, 1590; M ii, 65

Se vittorie si belle, 2vv, 1638; M ix, 21

Sfogava con le stelle (Rinuccini) (= O stellae), 5vv, 1603; M iv, 15

Sì ch'io vorrei morire (= O Jesu, mea vita), 5vv, 1603; M iv, 78

Si come crescon alla terra i fiori, 3vv, 1584; M x, 21

Si dolce è'l tormento, 1v, in C. Milanuzzi: Quarto scherzo delle ariose vaghezze (Venice, 2/1624); M ix, 119

Si si ch'io v'amo, occhi vaghi, occhi belli, 3vv, 1651; M ix, 82

Soave libertate (Chiabrera), 2vv, 1619; M vii, 85

Son questi i crespi crini?, 3vv, 1584; M x, 10

Sovra tenere herbette, 5vv, 1592; M iii, 13

Stracciami pur il core (Guarini), 5vv, 1592; M iii, 26

Su su, su che'l giorno è fore, 3vv, 1584; M x, 12

Su su, su pastorelli vezzosi, 3vv, 1638; M viii, 310

Su su, su pastorelli vezzosi, 3vv, 1651; M ix, 89

Taci, Armelin, che taci, 3vv, 1624[11]; M ix, 106

T'amo, mia vita (Guarini) (= Gloria tua), 5vv, 1605; M v, 90

Tempro la cetra (Marini), 1v, str, 1619; M vii, 1

Ti spontò l'ali amor, la donna mia (F. Alberti), 5vv, 1590; M ii, 97

Tornate, o cari baci (Marini), 2vv, 1619; M vii, 81

Tra mille fiamme e tra mille cathene, 5vv, 1587; M i, 39

Troppo ben può questo tiranno amore (Guarini) (= Ure me), 5vv, 1605; M v, 71

Tu dormi? Ah crudo core (= O Jesu, lindere meinen Schmertzen), 4vv, 1619; M vii, 123

Tu ridi sempre mai, 3vv, 1584; M x, 16

Tutte le bocche belle in questo nero volto (Alberti), 5vv, 1590; M ii, 39

Una donna fra l'altre honesta e bella vidi (= Una es), 5vv, hpd, 1614; M vi, 29

Usciam, ninfe, homai fuor di questi boschi, 5vv, 1587; M i, 42

Vaga su spina ascosa (Chiabrera) (= Ave regina mundi and Jesum viri senesque), 3vv, 1619; M vii, 104

Vaghi rai di cigli ardenti (Chiabrera), 3vv, 1607[21]; M x, 46

Vago augelletto, che cantando vai (Petrarch) (= Resurrexit de sepulcro and Veni, veni, soror mea), 6–7vv, 2 vn, db, 1638; M viii, 222

Vattene pur, crudel, con quella pace (Tasso), 5vv, 1592; M iii, 48

Vita de l'alma mia, 3vv, 1584; M x, 4

Vivrò fra i miei tormenti (Tasso), 5vv, 1592; M iii, 87

Voglio di vita uscir, 1v, I-Nf; O, 18

Voi pur da me partite (Guarini) (= Tu vis a me), 5vv, 1603; M iv, 44

Volgea l'anima mia soavemente (Guarini) (= Ardebat igne), 5vv, 1603; M iv, 20

Vorrei baciarti, O Filli (Marini), 2vv, 1619; M vii, 52

Zefiro torna (Petrarch), 5vv, 1614; M vi, 22

Zefiro torna, 'ciacona' (Rinuccini), 2vv, 1632; M ix, 9

### SACRED VOCAL

Sacrae cantiunculae . . . liber primus, 3vv (Venice, 1582) [1582]

Madrigali spirituali, 4vv (Brescia, 1583) [1583]

Musica tolta da i madrigali di Claudio Monteverde e d'altri autori, fatta spirituale da Aquilino Coppini, 5, 6vv (Milan, 1607[20]) [incl. 11 contrafacta of madrigals by Monteverdi] [1607[20]]

Il secondo libro della musica di Claudio Monteverde e d'altri autori, fatta spirituale da Aquilino Coppini, 5vv (Milan, 1608) [incl. 8 contrafacta of madrigals by Monteverdi] [1608]

Il terzo libro della musica di Claudio Monteverdi e d'altri autori, fatta spirituale da Aquilino Coppini, 5vv (Milan, 1609) [incl. 19 contrafacta of madrigals by Monteverdi] [1609]

Sanctissimae virgini missa senis vocibus ad ecclesiarum choros ac Vespere pluribus decantandae – cum nonnullis sacris concentibus ad sacella sive principum cubicula accommodata, 1–3, 6–8, 10vv, insts, bc (Venice, 1610) [1610]

Selva morale e spirituale, 1–8vv, insts (Venice, 1641) [1641]

Messa, 4vv, et salmi, 1–8vv, concertati, e parte da cappella, et con le letanie della beata vergine, 6vv (Venice, 1650) [1650]

Works in 1615[13], 1617[3], 1620[2], 1620[3], 1622[2], P. P. Lappi: Concerti sacri . . . libro secondo (Venice, 1623), 1624[2], 1625[1], 1625[2], 1627[1], 1627[4], 1629[5], 1641[2], 1641[3], 1642[4], 1645[3], 1649[6], 1651[2]

#### (Latin)

Missa de cappella, 6vv, 1610 (on Gombert's In illo tempore); M xiv, 57

Messa da cappella, 4vv, org (with alternative settings of Crucifixus, 4vv, 4 trbn/va da braccio; Et resurrexit, 2vv, 2 vn; Et iterum venturus est, 3vv), 1640; M xv, 59

Messa da cappella, 4vv, org, 1650; M xvi, 1

Ab aeterno ordinata sum, 1v, 1640; M xv, 189

Adoramus te, Christe, 6vv, bc, 1620[3]; M xvi, 439

Amemus te (= Amor, se giusto sei), 5vv, 1609

Angelus ad pastores ait, 3vv, 1582; M xiv, 36

Animas eruit (= M'è più dolce il penar), 5vv, 1608

Anima miseranda (= Anima dolorosa), 5vv, 1609

Anima quam dilexi (= Anima del cor mio), 5vv, 1609

Ardebat igne (= Volgea l'anima mea), 5vv, 1609

Ave Maria, gratia plena, 3vv, 1582; M xiv, 15

Ave regina mundi (= Vaga su spina ascosa), 3vv, in P. P. Lappi: Concerti sacri . . . libro secondo (Venice, 1623)

Beatus vir, 6vv, 2 vn, 3 va da brazzo/trbn, 1640; M xv, 368

Beatus vir, 5vv, 1640; M xv, 418

Beatus vir, 7vv, 2 vn, 1650; M xvi, 167

Cantate Domino, 2vv, 1615[13]; M xv, 409

Cantate Domino, 6vv, bc, 1620[3]; M xvi, 422

Cantemus (= A un giro sol), 5vv, 1609

Christe, adoramus te, 5vv, bc, 1620[3]; M xvi, 428

Confitebor tibi, Domine, 4vv, 1627[4]; O, 45

Confitebor tibi, Domine, 3vv, chorus 5vv, 1640; M xv, 297

Confitebor tibi, Domine, 3vv, 2 vn, 1640; M xv, 338

Confitebor tibi, Domine, 5vv or 1v and 4 str, 1640; M xv, 352

Confitebor tibi, Domine, 1v, 2 vn, 1650; M xvi, 129

Confitebor tibi, Domine, 2vv, 2vn, 1650; M xvi, 144

Credidi propter quod locutus sum, 8vv, 1640; M xv, 544

Currite populi, T, 1625[2]; M xvi, 491

Deus tuorum militum, 1v, 2 vn, 1640 (= Sanctorum meritis (ii) and Iste confessor); M xv, 614

Deus tuorum militum, 3vv, 2 vn, 1640; M xv, 636

Dixit Dominus (i), 8vv, 2 vn, 4 va/trbn, 1640; M xv, 195

Dixit Dominus (ii), 8vv, 2 vn, 4 va/trbn, 1640; M xv, 246

Dixit Dominus (iii), 8vv, 1650; M xvi, 54

Dixit Dominus (iv), 8vv, 1650; M xvi, 94

Domine Deus (= Anima mia, perdona), 5vv, 1609

Domine, ne in furore, 6vv, bc, 1620[3]; M xvi, 432

Domine Pater et Deus vitae meae, 3vv, 1582; M xiv, 17

Ecce sacrum paratum, 1v, 1625[2]; M xvi, 497

Ego dormio et cor meum vigilat, 2vv, 1625[1]; M xvi, 481

Ego flos campi, 1v, 1624[2]; M xvi, 464

Ego sum pastor bonus, 3vv, 1582; M xiv, 6

En gratulemur hodie, 1v, 2 vn, 1651[2]; M xvi, 517

Ergo gaude, laetare (= Due belli occhi, 2p. of Altri canti di Marte), 6vv, 1641[3]

Exulta, filia Sion, 1v, 1629[5]; M xvii, 8; O, 32

Exultent caeli, 5vv, 1641[3]; M xvii, 15; O, 39

Felle amaro (= Cruda Amarilli), 5vv, 1607[20]

Florea serta (= La giovinetta pianta), 5vv, 1608

Fugge, anima mea, mundum, 2vv, vn, 1620[3]; M xvi, 444

Gloria in excelsis Deo, 7vv, 2 vn, 4 va da braccio/trbn, 1640; M xv, 117

Gloria in excelsis Deo, 8 vv, I-Nf; O, 65

Gloria tua (= T'amo, mia vita), 5vv, 1607[20]

Haec dicit Deus (= Voi ch'ascoltate in rime sparse), 5vv, 1642[4]

Heus, bone vir (= Armato il cor), 2vv, 1642[4]

Hodie Christus natus est, 3vv, 1582; M xiv, 26

Iam moriar, mi Fili, 'Pianto della Madonna sopra il Lamento d'Arianna', 1v, 1640; M xv, 757

In tua patientia, 3vv, 1582; M xiv, 34

Iste confessor (= Deus tuorum militum and Sanctorum meritis (ii)), 1v, 2 vn, 1640; M xv, 618

Iste confessor (= Ut queant laxis), 2vv, 2 vn, 1640; M xv, 622

Jesu, dum te (= Cor mio, mentre vi miro), 5vv, 1609

Jesum viri senesque (= Vaga su spina ascosa), 3vv, 1641[2]

Jesu, tu obis (= Cor mio, non mori?), 5vv, 1609

Jubilet tota civitas, 1v, 1640; M xv, 748

Justi tulerunt spolia impiorum, 3vv, 1582; M xiv, 50

Laetaniae della beata vergine, 6vv, 1650; M xvi, 382

Laetatus sum, 6vv, 2 vn, bn, 2 trbn, 1650; M xvi, 231

Laetatus sum, 5vv, 1650; M xvi, 276

Lapidabant Stephanum, 3vv, 1582; M xiv, 1

Lauda, anima mea (= Due belli occhi, 2p. of Altri canti di Marte), 6vv, 1641[3]

Lauda, Jerusalem, 3vv, 1650; M xvi, 344

Lauda, Jerusalem, 5vv, 1650; M xvi, 358

Lauda, Sion, salvatorem, 3vv, 1582; M xiv, 42

Laudate Dominum, 5vv, chorus 4vv, 2 vn, 4 va/trbn, 1640; M xv, 481

Laudate Dominum, 8vv, 2 vn, 1640; M xv, 503

Laudate Dominum, 8vv, 1640; M xv, 521

Laudate Dominum in sanctis eius, 1v, 1640; M xv, 753

Laudate Dominum, B, 1650; M xvi, 227

Laudate Dominum, B, 1651[2]; M xvi, 519

Laudate Dominum, 6vv, org, D-Kl

Laudate pueri, 5vv, 2 vn, 1640; M xv, 438

Laudate pueri, 5vv, 1640; M xv, 460

Laudate pueri, Dominum, 5vv, 1650; M xvi, 211

Lauda, anima mea (= Due belli occhi, 2p. of Altri canti di Marte), 6vv, 1641[3]

Longe a te (= Longe da te, cor mio), 5vv, 1609

Longe, mi Jesu (= Parlo, miser'o taccio?), 3vv, 1649[6]
Magnificat, 8vv, 2 vn, 4 va/trbn, 1640; M xv, 639
Magnificat, 4vv, 1640; M xiv, 703
Maria, quid ploras? (= Dorinda, ah dirò mia, 3p. of Ecco Silvio), 5vv, 1607[20]
Memento [Domine, David] et omnis mansuetudinis, 8vv, 1640; M xv, 567
Nisi Dominus, 3vv, 2 vn, 1650; M xvi, 299
Nisi Dominus, 6vv, 1650; M xvi, 318
O beatae viae, O felices gressus, 2vv, 1620[2]; M xvi, 454
O bone Jesu, illumina oculos meos, 3vv, 1582; M xiv, 44
O bone Jesu, o piissime Jesu, 2vv, 1622[2]; M xvi, 506
O crux benedicta, 3vv, 1582; M xiv, 25
O dies infelices (= O come è gran martire), 5vv, 1608
O Domine Jesu Christe, 3vv, 1582; M xvi, 29
O gloriose martyr (= Che se tu se'il cor mio, 2p. of Anima mia, perdona), 5vv, 1609
O infelix recessus (= Ah dolente partita), 5vv, 1608
O Jesu, mea vita (= Sì ch'io vorrei morire), 5vv, 1609
O magnum pietatis opus, 3vv, 1582, M xiv, 22
O mi Fili (= O Mirtillo), 5vv, 1608
O quam pulchra es, 1v, 1625[2]; M xvi, 486
O rex supreme (= Al lume delle stelle), 4vv, 1649[6]
O stellae (= Sfogava con le stelle), 5vv, 1609
Pascha concelebranda (= Altri canti di Marte), 6vv, 1641[3]
Pater, venit hora, 3vv, 1582; M xiv, 33
Plagas tuas (= La piaga c'ho nel core), 5vv, 1609
Plorat amare (= Piagne e sospira), 5vv, 1609
Praecipitantur, Jesu Christe (= O primavera), 5vv, 1608
Pulchrae sunt (= Ferir quel petto, 5p. of Ecco Silvio), 5vv, 1607[20]
Quam pulchra es, 3vv, 1582; M xiv, 13
Qui laudes (= Quel augellin che canta), 5vv, 1609
Quia vidisti me, Thoma, credidisti, 3vv, 1582; M xiv, 40
Qui pependit (= Ecco Silvio), 5vv, 1607[20]
Qui pietate (= Ma se con la pietà, 2p. of Ecco Silvio), 5vv, 1609
Qui regnas (= Che dar più vi poss'io?), 5vv, 1608
Qui vult venire post me, 3vv, 1582; M xiv, 48
Resurrexit de sepulcro (= Vago augelletto), 6–7vv, 1649[6]
Rutilante in nocte (= Io mi son giovinetta), 5vv, 1609
Salve, crux pretiosa, 3vv, 1582; M xiv, 38
Salve, O regina, 1v, 1624[2]; M xvi, 475
Salve regina, 1v, 1625[2]; M xvi, 502
Salve regina, 2vv, 2 vn, 1640; M xv, 724
Salve regina, 2vv, 1640; M xv, 736
Salve regina, 3vv, 1640; M xv, 741
Sancta Maria (= Deh, bella e cara, 2p. of Ch'io t'ami e t'ami più), 5vv, 1607[20]
Sancta Maria, succurre miseris, 2vv, 1627[1]; M xvi, 511
Sanctorum meritis inclita gaudia (i), 1v, 2 vn, 1640; M xv, 606
Sanctorum meritis inclita gaudia (ii) (= Deus tuorum militum and Iste confessor), 1v, 2 vn, 1640; M xv, 610
Spera in Domino (= Io che armato sin hor), 1v, 1642[4]
Spernit Deus (= Ma tu più che mai dura, 3p. of Ch'io t'ami e t'ami più), 5vv, 1607[20]
Stabat virgo (= Era l'anima mia), 5vv, 1607[20]
Surgens Jesus, Dominus noster, 3vv, 1582; M xiv, 46
Surge propera, amica mea, 3vv, 1582; M xiv, 8
Te, Jesu Christe (= Ecco piegando, 4p. of Ecco Silvio), 5vv, 1607[20]
Te sequar (= Ch'io t'ami), 5vv, 1608
Tu es pastor ovium, 3vv, 1582; M xiv, 19
Tu vis a me (= Voi pur da me partite), 5vv, 1609
Ubi duo vel tres congregati fuerint, 3vv, 1582; M xiv, 11
Una es (= Una donna fra l'altre), 5vv, 1609
Ure me (= Troppo ben può questo tiranno amore), 5vv, 1607[20]
Ut queant laxis (= Iste confessor), 2vv, 1640; M xv, 629
Veni in hortum meum, 3vv, 1582; M xiv, 3
Venite siccientes ad aquas Domini, 2vv, 1624[2]; M xvi, 467
Venite, videte martyrem, 1v, 1645[3]; M xvii, 25
Veni, veni, soror mea (= Vago augelletto), 6–7vv, 1649[6]
Vespro della Beata Vergine, 'composto sopra canti fermi', 6vv, 6 insts, 1610:
    Domine ad adiuvandum, 6vv, 3 trbn, 2 cornetts, 6 str; M xiv, 123
    Dixit Dominus, 6vv, 6 insts; M xiv, 133
    Nigra sum, 1v; M xiv, 150
    Laudate pueri, 8vv, org; M xiv, 153
    Pulchra es, amica mea, 2vv; M xiv, 170
    Laetatus sum, 6vv; M xiv, 174
    Duo Seraphim clamabant, 3vv; M xiv, 190
    Nisi Dominus, 10vv; M xiv, 198
    Audi coelum, 1v, chorus 6vv; M xiv, 227
    Lauda, Jerusalem, 7vv; M xiv, 237
    Sonata sopra 'Sancta Maria', 1v, 2 cornetts, 3 trbn, 2 vn, vc; M xiv, 250
    Ave maris stella, 2vv, chorus 8vv (2 choirs), 5 insts; M xiv, 274
    Magnificat, 7vv, 2 fl, 2 rec, 3 cornetts, 2 trbn, 2 vn, vc; M xiv, 285
    Magnificat, 6vv, org; M, xiv, 327
Vives in corde (= Ahi, com'a un vago sol), 5vv, 1607[20]

*(Italian)*

Afflitto e scalz'ove la sacra sponda, 4vv, 1583
Aventurosa notte, 4vv, 1583
Chi vol che m'innamori, 3vv, 3 str, 1640; M xv, 54
Dal sacro petto esce veloce dardo, 4vv, 1583
Dei miei giovenil anni, 4vv, 1583
D'empi martiri, 4vv, 1583
È questa vita un lampo, 5vv, 1640; M xv, 35
Laura del ciel sempre feconda, 4vv, 1583
L'empio vestia di porpora, 4vv, 1583
Le rose, gli amaranti e gigli, 4vv, 1583
L'human discorso, 4vv, 1583
Mentre la stell'appar, 4vv, 1583
O ciechi il tanto affaticar, 5vv, 2 vn, 1640; M xv, 1
Sacrosanta di Dio verace imago, 4vv, 1583
Spuntava il dì, 3vv, 1640; M xv, 42
Su le penne de' venti (prol to La Maddalena), 1v, 5 insts, 1617[3]; M xi, 170
Voi ch'ascoltate in rime sparse (Petrarch) (= Haec dicit Deus), 5vv, 2 vn, 1640; M xv, 15

*(German)*

Alleluja, kommet, jauchzet (= Ardo, avvampo), 8vv, 1649[6]
Dein allein ist ja (= Così sol d'una chiara fonte, 2p. of Hor ch'el ciel e la terra), 6vv, 1649[6]
Frewde, kommet lasset uns gehen (= Ardo, avvampo), 8vv, 1649[6]
O du mächtiger Herr (= Hor ch'el ciel e la terra), 6vv, 1649[6]
O Jesu, lindere meinen Schmertzen (= Tu dormi?), 4vv, 1649[6]

## BIBLIOGRAPHY

### SOURCE MATERIAL

G. Sommi Picenardi: 'D'alcuni documenti concernenti Claudio Monteverde', *Archivio storico lombardo*, 3rd ser., iv (1895)
G. F. Malipiero: *Claudio Monteverdi* (Milan, 1929)
Anon.: 'Preziose scoperte di autografi di Claudio Monteverdi', *La bibliofilia*, xxxviii (1937)
R. Lunelli: 'Iconografia monteverdiana', *RMI*, xlvii (1943), 38
C. Gallico: 'Newly Discovered Documents concerning Monteverdi', *MQ*, xlviii (1962), 68
A. Rosenthal: 'A Hitherto Unpublished Letter of Claudio Monteverdi', *Essays Presented to Egon Wellesz* (Oxford, 1966), 103
F. Lesure: 'Un nouveau portrait de Monteverdi', *RdM*, liii (1967), 60
G. de Logu: 'An Unknown Portrait of Monteverdi by Domenico Feti', *The Burlington Magazine*, cix (1967), 706
Monteverdi's letters: a selection in Eng. trans. with commentary, in D. Arnold and N. Fortune, eds.: *The Monteverdi Companion* (London, 1968), 19–87
W. Siegmund-Schultze: 'Beiträge zu einem neuen Monteverdi-Bild', *Wissenschaftliche Beiträge der Universität Halle*, ser. G, viii/1 (1968), 11
*Monteverdi: lettere, dediche e prefazioni*, ed. D. de' Paoli (Rome, 1973)
*The Letters of Claudio Monteverdi*, ed. and trans. D. Stevens (London, 1980)

### BIOGRAPHY AND CRITICAL STUDIES

G. M. Artusi: *L'Artusi, ovvero Delle imperfettioni della moderna musica*, i (Venice, 1600); ii (Venice, 1603)
——: *Discorso secondo musicale di Antonio Braccino da Todi* (Venice, 1608, repr. 1924)
F. Caffi: *Storia della musica sacra nella già cappella ducale di San Marco in Venezia dal 1318 al 1797* (Venice, 1854–5, repr. 1931)
P. Canal: *Della musica in Mantova* (Venice, 1881)
S. Davari: *Notizie biografiche del distinto maestro di musica Claudio Monteverdi* (Mantua, 1884)
E. Vogel: 'Claudio Monteverdi', *VMw*, iii (1887), 315–450
A. Bertolotti: *Musici alla corte del Gonzaga in Mantova dal secolo XV al XVIII* (Milan, 1890/R1969)
H. Goldschmidt: *Studien zur Geschichte der italienischen Oper* (Leipzig, 1901–4/R1967)
——: Monteverdis Ritorno d'Ulisse, *SIMG*, iv (1902–3), 671
——: 'Claudio Monteverdis Oper: Il ritorno d'Ulisse in patria', *SIMG*, ix (1907–8), 570
G. Cesari: 'Die Entwicklung der Monteverdischen Kammermusik', *IMusSCR*, iii *Vienna 1909*, 153
H. Leichtentritt: 'Claudio Monteverdi als Madrigalkomponist', *SIMG*, xi (1909–10), 255–91
R. Schwartz: 'Zu den Texten der ersten fünf Bücher der Madrigale Monteverdis', *Festschrift Hermann Kretzschmar* (Leipzig, 1918), 147
L. Schneider: *Un précurseur de la musique italienne aux XVIe et XVIIe siècles: Claudio Monteverdi: l'homme et son temps* (Paris, 1921)
R. Haas: 'Zur Neuausgabe von Claudio Monteverdis "Il ritorno d'Ulisse in patria" ', *SMw*, ix (1922), 3–42
A. Tessier: 'Les deux styles de Monteverde', *ReM*, iii/8 (1922), 223–54
H. Prunières: *La vie et l'oeuvre de C. Monteverdi* (Paris, 1926, 2/1931; Eng. trans., 1926/R1972)
——: 'Monteverdi's Venetian Operas', *MQ*, x (1924), 178
C. van den Borren: ' "Il ritorno d'Ulisse in patria" de Claudio

Monteverdi', *Revue de l'Université de Bruxelles*, iii (1925)

J. A. Westrup: 'Monteverde's "Il ritorno d'Ulisse in patria" ', *MMR*, lviii (1928), 106

A. Tessier: 'Monteverdi e la filosofia dell'arte', *RaM*, ii (1929), 459

K. F. Müller: *Die Technik der Ausdrucksdarstellung in Monteverdis monodischen Frühwerken* (Berlin, 1931)

H. F. Redlich: *Claudio Monteverdi: ein formgeschichtlicher Versuch* (Berlin, 1932)

J. A. Westrup: 'The Originality of Monteverde', *PMA*, lx (1933–4), 1

W. Kreidler: *Heinrich Schütz und der Stile Concitato von Claudio Monteverdi* (Stuttgart, 1934)

G. Benvenuti: 'Il manoscritto veneziano della "Incoronazione di Poppea" ', *RMI*, xli (1937), 176

H. F. Redlich: 'Notationsprobleme in Cl. Monteverdis "Incoronazione di Poppea" ', *AcM*, x (1938), 129

J. A. Westrup: 'Monteverdi and the Orchestra', *ML*, xxi (1940), 230

——: 'Monteverdi's "Lamento d'Arianna" ', *MR*, i (1940), 144

P. Collaer: 'L'orchestra di Claudio Monteverdi', *Musica*, ii (Florence, 1943), 86

B. Lupo: 'Sacre monodie monteverdiane', *Musica*, ii (Florence, 1943), 51–85

F. Torrefranca: 'Il lamento di Erminia di Claudio Monteverdi', *Inedito*, ii (1944), 31; suppl., 1

O. Tiby: *Claudio Monteverdi* (Turin, 1944)

D. de' Paoli: *Claudio Monteverdi* (Milan, 1945)

L. Ronga: 'Tasso e Monteverdi', *Poesia*, i (1945)

H. F. Redlich: 'Monteverdi's Religious Music', *ML*, xxvii (1946), 208

A. Einstein: *The Italian Madrigal* (Princeton, 1949/*R*1971)

H. F. Redlich: *Claudio Monteverdi: Leben und Werk* (Olten, 1949; Eng. trans., rev., 1952)

J. A. Westrup: 'Monteverdi and the Madrigal', *The Score*, i (1949), 33

L. Schrade: *Monteverdi, Creator of Modern Music* (London, 1950/*R*1964)

W. Apel: 'Anent a Ritornello in Monteverdi's Orfeo', *MD*, v (1951), 213

M. le Roux: *Claudio Monteverdi* (Paris, 1951)

C. Sartori: *Monteverdi* (Brescia, 1953)

A. A. Abert: *Claudio Monteverdi und das musikalische Drama* (Lippstadt, 1954); review by L. Ronga, *RMI*, lvii (1955), 140

D. Arnold: 'Notes on Two Movements of the Monteverdi "Vespers" ', *MMR*, lxxxiv (1954), 59

W. Osthoff: 'Die venezianische und neapolitanische Fassung von Monteverdis "Incoronazione di Poppea" ', *AcM*, xxvi (1954), 88

H. F. Redlich: 'Claudio Monteverdi: Some Problems of Textual Interpretation', *MQ*, xli (1955), 66

W. Osthoff: 'Zu den Quellen von Monteverdis Ritorno d'Ulisse in Patria', *SMw*, xxiii (1956), 67

D. Arnold: ' "Seconda pratica": a Background to Monteverdi's Madrigals', *ML*, xxxviii (1957), 341

——: 'Monteverdi's Church Music: Some Venetian Traits', *MMR*, lxxxviii (1958), 83

W. Osthoff: 'Neue Beobachtungen zu Quellen und Geschichte von Monteverdis "Incoronazione di Poppea" ', *Mf*, xi (1958), 129

——: 'Zur Bologneser Aufführung von Monteverdis "Ritorno d'Ulisse" im Jahre 1640', *Anzeiger der phil.-hist. Klasse der Österreichischen Akademie der Wissenschaften*, xcv (1958), 155

D. Stevens: 'Ornamentation in Monteverdi's Shorter Dramatic Works', *IMSCR*, vii *Cologne 1958*, 284

J. A. Westrup: 'Two First Performances: Monteverdi's "Orfeo" and Mozart's "Clemenza di Tito" ', *ML*, xxxix (1958), 327

F. B. Zimmerman: 'Purcell and Monteverdi', *MT*, xcix (1958), 368

G. Pannain: 'Studi monteverdiani', *RaM*, xxviii (1958), 7, 97, 187, 281; xix (1959), 42, 95, 234, 310; xxx (1960), 24, 230, 312; xxxi (1961), 14; *Quaderni della RaM*, iii (1965), 13

D. D. Boyden: 'Monteverdi's *violini piccoli alla francese* and *viole da brazzo*', *AnnM*, vi (1958–63), 387

L. Passuth: *A mantuai herceg muzsikusa, Claudio Monteverdi korának regényes története* (Budapest, 1959; Ger. trans., 1959 as *Monteverdi: der Roman eines grossen Musikers*)

W. Osthoff: *Das dramatische Spätwerk Claudio Monteverdis* (Tutzing, 1960)

D. Arnold: 'The Monteverdian Succession at St Mark's', *ML*, xlii (1961), 205

W. Osthoff: 'Monteverdis Combattimento in deutscher Sprache und Heinrich Schütz', *Festschrift Helmuth Osthoff* (Tutzing, 1961), 195

D. Stevens: 'Where are the Vespers of Yesteryear?', *MQ*, xlvii (1961), 315

F. Ghisi: 'L'orchestra in Monteverdi', *Karl Gustav Fellerer zum 60. Geburtstag* (Cologne, 1962), 187

D. Arnold: ' "L'incoronazione di Poppea" and its Orchestral Requirements', *MT*, civ (1963), 176

——: *Monteverdi* (London, 1963)

——: 'The Monteverdi Vespers – a Postscript', *MT*, civ (1963), 24

S. Reiner: 'Preparations in Parma – 1618, 1627–28', *MR*, xxv (1964), 273

R. Tellart: *Claudio Monteverdi: l'homme et son oeuvre* (Paris, 1964)

G. Biella: 'La Messa, il Vespro e i sacri concenti di Claudio Monteverdi nella stampa Amadino del 1610', *Musica sacra*, 2nd ser., ix (Milan, 1964)

D. Arnold: ' "Il ritorno d'Ulisse" and the chamber duet', *MT*, cvi (1965), 183

G. Biella: 'I "Vespri dei Santi" di Claudio Monteverdi', *Musica sacra*, 2nd ser., xi (Milan, 1966), 144

A. Damerini: 'Il senso religioso nelle musiche sacre di Claudio Monteverdi', *CHM*, iv (1966), 47

*RIM*, ii/2 (1967) [special Monteverdi no.]

C. Gallico: 'Monteverdi e i dazi di Viadana', *RIM*, i (1966), 242

D. Arnold: 'Monteverdi and the Art of War', *MT*, cviii (1967), 412

——: *Monteverdi Madrigals* (London, 1967)

——: 'Monteverdi the Instrumentalist', *Recorder and Music Magazine*, ii (1967), 130

G. Barblan and others: *Claudio Monteverdi nel quarto centenario della nascita* (Turin, 1967)

S. Bonta: 'Liturgical Problems in Monteverdi's Marian Vespers', *JAMS*, xx (1967), 87

N. Fortune: 'Duet and Trio in Monteverdi', *MT*, cviii (1967), 417

C. Gallico: 'La "lettera amorosa" di Monteverdi e lo stile rappresentativo', *NRMI*, i (1967), 287

E. Santoro: *La famiglia e la formazione di Claudio Monteverdi: note biografiche con documenti inediti* (Cremona, 1967)

D. Stevens: '*Madrigali guerrieri, et amorosi*: a Reappraisal for the Quatercentenary', *MQ*, liii (1967), 161; also pubd in D. Arnold and N. Fortune, eds.: *The Monteverdi Companion* (London, 1968)

——: 'Monteverdi's Venetian Church Music', *MT*, cviii (1967), 414

D. Arnold and N. Fortune, eds.: *The Monteverdi Companion* (London, 1968)

N. Pirrotta: 'Early Opera and Aria', *New Looks at Italian Opera: Essays in Honor of Donald J. Grout* (Ithaca, 1968), 39–107

——: 'Scelte poetiche di Monteverdi', *NRMI*, ii (1968), 10–42, 226

*Congresso internazionale sul tema Claudio Monteverdi e il suo tempo: Venezia, Mantova e Cremona 1968*

N. Anfuso and A. Gianuario: '*Lamento d'Arianna*': *Studio e interpretazione sulla edizione a stampa del Gardano, Venezia 1623* (Florence, 1969)

A. Gianuario: 'Proemio all' "Oratione di Monteverdi" ', *RIM*, iv (1969), 32

N. Pirrotta: 'Early Venetian Libretti at Los Angeles', *Essays in Musicology: in Honor of Dragan Plamenac* (Pittsburgh, 1969), 233

D. Arnold: 'Monteverdi's Singers', *MT*, cxi (1970), 982

N. Anfuso and A. Gianuario: *Preparazione alla interpretazione della Poïesis Monteverdiana* (Florence, 1971)

T. Antonicek: 'Claudio Monteverdi und Österreich', *ÖMz*, xxvi (1971), 266

W. Frobenius: 'Zur Notation eines Ritornells in Monteverdis "L'Orfeo" ', *AMw*, xxviii (1971), 201

K. R. Mays: *Harmonic Style in the Madrigals of Claudio Monteverdi* (diss., Indiana U., 1971)

D. Arnold: 'A Background Note on Monteverdi's Hymn Settings', *Scritti in onore di Luigi Ronga* (Milan and Naples, 1973), 33

D. Stevens: 'Monteverdi's Necklace', *MQ*, lix (1973), 370

A. Chiarelli: '*L'incoronazione di Poppea* o *Il Nerone*: problemi di filologia testuale', *RIM*, ix (1974), 117–51

S. Reiner: 'La vag'Angioletta (and others), Part I', *AnMc*, no.14 (1974), 26–88

C. Gallico: ' "contra Claudium Montiuiridum" ', *RIM*, x (1975), 346

H. Hell: 'Zu Rhythmus und Notierung des "Vi ricorda" in Claudio Monteverdis *Orfeo*', *AnMc*, no.15 (1975), 87–157

J. G. Kurtzman: 'Some Historical Perspectives on the Monteverdi Vespers', *AnMc*, no.15 (1975), 29–86

D. Stevens: 'Monteverdi, Petratti, and the Duke of Bracciano', *MQ*, lxiv (1978), 275

——: *Monteverdi: Sacred, Secular and Occasional Music* (Rutherford, 1978)

D. de' Paoli: *Monteverdi* (Milan, 1979)

J. G. Kurtzman: *Essays on the Monteverdi Mass and Vespers of 1610* (Houston, 1979)

DENIS ARNOLD (text, bibliography),
ELSIE M. ARNOLD (work-list)

**Monteverdi, Francesco.** Italian singer and composer, elder son of Claudio Monteverdi; *see* MONTEVERDI, CLAUDIO, §3.

**Monteverdi, Giulio Cesare** (*b* Cremona, baptized 31 Jan 1573; *d* Salò, Lake Garda, probably in 1630 or 1631). Italian composer, organist and writer on music, younger brother of Claudio Monteverdi. He became organist of Mantua Cathedral on 1 April 1600 but left to return to his native town only five months later. In August 1602 he was in the service of the Duke of Mantua, his salary two years later being only 7 scudi a month. He wrote the music for the fourth *intermedio* (to words by Chiabrera) in the performance of Guarini's play *L'Idropica* given on 2 June 1608 during the wedding celebrations at the Mantuan court, and an opera by him, *Il rapimento di Proserpina* (libretto by Ercole Marigliani), was given at Casale Monferrato in 1611; all this music is lost. In 1612 he was dismissed, along with his brother and other artists, from the Gonzaga family's service. He soon became organist of the principal church at Castelleone, in the province of Cremona, where he seems to have remained until, in 1620, he was appointed *maestro di cappella* of Salò Cathedral. He probably died of the plague of 1630–31, since his successor was appointed in 1631 and nothing further is heard of him. The small amount of his music to survive shows to some extent the influence of his brother. His one collection is *Affetti musici, ne quali si contengono motetti a 1–4 et 6 voci, per concertarli nel basso per l'organo* (Venice, 1620). Its 25 motets are competent in the manner of the concertato for few voices; they lack secular influences but are pleasantly melodious. There is a madrigal for three voices and continuo (in *RISM* 1605¹²), and his two pieces in his brother's three-part *Scherzi musicali* (1607²¹), each with a three-part ritornello, are very similar in style to the rest of the volume (edns. in *C. Monteverdi: Tutte le opere*, ed. G. F. Malipiero, x, Asolo, 1929, 58ff). He is more important for the fact that he edited that volume and in doing so included as a *Dichiaratione* a detailed explanation (facs., ibid, 69ff; Eng. trans. in O. Strunk: *Source Readings in Music History*, New York, 1950, pp.405ff) of Claudio's ideas as expressed in the preface to his fifth book of madrigals written in response to Artusi's attacks on him.

BIBLIOGRAPHY
P. Guerrini: 'La cappella musicale del duomo di Salò', *RMI*, xxxix (1922), 108
P. M. Tagmann: *Archivalische Studien zur Musikpflege am Dom von Mantua (1500–1627)* (Berne, 1967), 43, 45, 66, 80

For further bibliography *see* MONTEVERDI, CLAUDIO.
DENIS ARNOLD

**Monteverdi Choir.** London chamber choir founded in 1964; *see* LONDON, §VI, 3(ii).

**Montevideo.** Capital of Uruguay. Sacred music was first heard at S Francisco, which was founded in 1724 with a rudimentary choir; its first organ was inaugurated in 1772. The church's first musicians were the organists Tiburcio Ortega (*c*1780), Bruno Barrales (1786) and Benito de San Francisco (1800); the most important *maestros de capilla* were Blas Perera (*c*1803), Hermenegildo Ortega (*c*1810), José María de Arzac (until 1830), Juan José de Sostoa (*c*1800) and Manuel Úbeda (1802).

The foundation stone of Montevideo Cathedral was laid in 1790 and the building was consecrated on 21 October 1804 by the Bishop of Buenos Aires, Benito Lué y Riega. It had a choir and later an organ, both initially rather elementary, but improved after 1830. It employed some good organists, including Sostoa (*c*1750–1813) and Arzac (1832–6), and three important *maestros de capilla* who were also accomplished composers – the Spaniard Antonio Saenz (from 1829), the Italian José Giuffra (who lived in Montevideo from 1850) and the Spaniard Carmelo Calvo (from 1871).

Sacred music heard in Montevideo until the mid-18th century consisted of popular religious songs of Spanish origin, accompanied by the harp, cittern and other instruments. In the second half of the century the same works were heard, but the settings were more elaborate, often for three or four voices and sometimes with organ accompaniment. A third period of religious music after 1830 was directly influenced by opera, and partly by Italian sacred music.

The archives of S Francisco contain primitive liturgical songs and polyphonic works; there are 194 complete works from the colonial period to 1890, of which the most important historically is Manuel Úbeda's Mass for All Souls Day (1802), the first known composition written in Uruguay. There are also some religious works of the colonial period in the musicology section of the National History Museum.

Theatre music was derived initially from the Spanish theatre and was heard in the Casa de Comedias from 1793; the repertory consisted of *tonadillas escenicas* (musical comedies), *melólogos* (operettas) and zarzuelas, and their greatest popularity lasted until about 1825, by which time more than 300 operettas had been performed. The composers and some of the most famous works were Pedro Aranaz (*El chusco y la maja* and *El chasco del mesón*), Pablo Esteve (*El granadero, Los esclavos del mundo, La jardinerita del gusto, La cortesana pastora, El amante tímido,* etc), Fernando Ferandiere (*Los españoles viajantes*), Manuel García (*El majo y la maja*) and Blás Laserna (*El novio sin novia, La vida del petimetre, El tribunal de las quejas, Los majos celosos, El marido sagaz,* etc).

From 1820 a taste for Italian opera developed which led in 1856 to the opening of the Teatro Solís, one of the largest in South America (2500 seats). The major works by Rossini, Bellini, Donizetti, Pacini, Mercadante, Paisiello, Pavesi, Paer and Ricci were performed, as were all of Verdi's; 70 operas were given between 1830 and 1859. The companies were all foreign, mostly Italian, and gave performances annually between May and August. They included the Tanni brothers (1820–40), Ida Edelvira (1851–3), Piacentini (1849–54), Rossi Guerra-Luisia-Oliveri (1850), Biscacianti (*c*1854), Vera Lorini (1855–7), Tamberlick (1857), Bishop and Lelmi (1858), Lagrange-Mirate (1859), Carlotta Patti (1870), Adelina Patti (1888), Roberto Stagno (1888), Darclée (from 1890), Regina Paccini (from 1890) and Eva Tetrazzini (1894).

Of later theatres San Felipe (1879), the Politeama (*c*1890) and the 500-seat Cibils (1893) no longer exist. The Stella d'Italia (400 seats) has been much altered since its opening in 1900, by which time there were 15 theatres. The Urquiza (3000 seats) opened in 1905 with Sarah Bernhardt in Sardou's *La sorcière*; it was bought in 1930 by the national broadcasting service (SODRE) as a studio-auditorium and continued to function until it burnt down in September 1971. There are also several much less important theatres, including the Zabala, Artigas, 18 de Julio and the Albeniz.

Early concert life grew out of the drawing-room music of the colonial salons. The small groups (duos, trios, quartets) which performed in salons became larger, forming on the one hand quartets, quintets, etc, and on the other small orchestras. These ensembles eventually performed in public theatres and thus became the first vehicles of symphonic performance. They were often supported by music societies, and generally met weekly or fortnightly. They were usually made up of local performers and European musicians who had settled in Montevideo, and occasionally visiting foreign soloists joined their performances. The orchestra of the Beethoven Society (1897–1902), under the Spanish conductor Manuel Pérez-Badía, introduced the Classical symphonic repertory to Uruguay; the National Orchestra (1908–14) under the Uruguayan composer and violinist Luis Sambucetti was important because it performed not only contemporary European works (particularly Debussy, Franck, Ravel, Rimsky-Korsakov), but also new works by Uruguayan composers. The Uruguayan Orchestral Society (1929–31), conducted by José Segú, Benone Calcavecchia and Vicente Pablo, played the standard symphonic repertory.

OSSODRE (SODRE Symphony Orchestra) was founded on 20 June 1931, and remains the most important symphony orchestra in the country. Its first concert was conducted by Vicente Pablo, and its subsequent conductors have been Uruguayan and foreign. The Municipal Symphony Orchestra, the next in importance, was founded by Carlos Estrada in July 1959 and conducted by him until his death in 1970, when Hugo López was appointed his successor. The Montevideo Chamber Orchestra was founded in 1936, also by Carlos Estrada. Other lesser orchestras include that of the Anglo-Uruguayan Institute, Audem, Sambucetti, Euterpe, Anfión and the Young Musicians.

The main concert halls are that of La Lira Conservatory (600 seats), used in 1878–1950; that of the Verdi Institute (800 seats, 1890), which after alterations is still in use as the Verdi Hall; the Victoria Hall (600 seats, opened c1920), now the Victoria Theatre; and the Vaz Ferreira Auditorium in the National Library (opened 1972).

Public musical education began in the late 19th century; between 1873 and 1904 six conservatories were founded, each with its own choir and orchestra. La Lira Conservatory (1873) performed chiefly chamber music until 1900 and later concentrated on symphonic and choral music; it also has its own quartet. The Verdi Institute (1890), which also has its own quartet, orchestra and choir, performed chamber works and, after 1900, symphonic works. Montevideo also has the Franz Liszt Musical Academy, the Falleri Music School, the Montevideo Musical Conservatory and the National Conservatory of Music, which is part of the University of the Republic (founded 1849). The Institute of Musicology (founded 1946) is part of the Faculty of Humanities; the professor of musicology is appointed by the Faculty of Humanities, and the chair of composition is controlled by the National Conservatory of Music.

The City of Montevideo International Piano Competition, founded in 1968, is an important biennial event, and there are occasional festivals of Latin American music.

SODRE, the official broadcasting service, has five transmitters and a television channel, all of which broadcast music and cultural programmes.

BIBLIOGRAPHY

L. Ayestarán: *La música en el Uruguay*, i (Montevideo, 1953)

S. Salgado: *Breve historia de la música culta en el Uruguay* (Montevideo, 1971)

SUSANA SALGADO

**Montfort, Corneille de.** See BLOCKLAND, CORNELIUS.

**Montfort, Hugo von.** See HUGO VON MONTFORT.

**Montgomerie, Hugh.** See EGLINTON, HUGH MONTGOMERIE.

**Montgomery, Kenneth** (*b* Belfast, 28 Oct 1943). British conductor. He studied at the RCM, London, with Boult, and in Siena with Celibidache. In 1963 he joined the Glyndebourne staff as assistant chorus master while studying with John Pritchard, and in 1965–6 he worked with Schmidt-Isserstedt at Hamburg, returning to Glyndebourne in 1967 when he conducted *L'elisir d'amore*. He was a staff conductor with Sadler's Wells Opera (1967–70) where he conducted a wide repertory while continuing his association with Glyndebourne, at the festival and on tour. In 1970 he became assistant conductor of the Bournemouth SO and Sinfonietta, and was director of the Sinfonietta (1973–5). In the meantime he had conducted *Il re pastore* (1971) and *Oberon* (1972) at Wexford and begun his association with the Netherlands Opera, conducting *L'Ormindo* (1971), *Ariadne auf Naxos* (1972) and *Capriccio* (1975). At Glyndebourne he conducted *Le nozze di Figaro* and *La Calisto* in 1974, *The Rake's Progress* (1975), *Falstaff* and *Così fan tutte* (1976). In 1975 Montgomery made his Covent Garden début with *Le nozze di Figaro*, and was appointed musical director of Glyndebourne Touring Opera, with whom he conducted *Der Freischütz* in 1976. That year he became principal conductor of the Netherlands Radio Orchestra and resigned his Glyndebourne post.

ALAN BLYTH

**Monti.** Italian family of singers and at least one composer, prominent in the 18th century in the development of Neapolitan *opera buffa*.

(1) **Anna Maria** [Marianna] **Monti** (*b* Rome, 1704; *d* ?Naples, after 1727). Singer. She made her début at the Teatro dei Fiorentini, Naples, at the age of 13, singing the second comedienne's part in the Piscopo-De Falco dialect opera *Lo mbruoglio d'ammore* (1717) in the first regular full season of the new genre of comic opera. She sang regularly at the Fiorentini until 1727, specializing in comic servant roles. She should not be confused with her Neapolitan cousin of the next generation, (4) Marianna Monti.

(2) **Grazia Monti** (*b* ?Rome; *fl* Naples, 1728). Singer, sister of (1) Anna Maria Monti. She appeared at the Teatro Nuovo in Naples at least once, in G. de Majo's *chelleta pe' museca*, *La Milorda* (1728), but is not otherwise known.

(3) **Laura Monti** (*b* ?Rome, after 1704; *d* Naples, 1760). Singer, younger sister of (1) Anna Maria Monti. Between 1726 and 1732 she was a member of comic opera companies at the Teatro Nuovo, and like her sisters sang second and third comic parts. In 1733 the royal theatre S Bartolomeo engaged her as replacement for Celeste Resse to sing opposite the comic singer Gioacchino Corrado in intermezzos performed in the theatre's serious operas. She held this position until 1735, when Carlo III replaced intermezzos with ballets to improve the theatre's declining artistic tone. Among Laura's roles was Serpina in the première of Pergolesi's *La serva padrona* in 1733; Hasse and Leo also wrote parts for her. In summer 1738 she took part in some of the productions celebrating Carlo III's marriage to

Maria Amalie of Saxony: a *burletta* performed in the summer residence at Aversa, and, on 10 July at the newly opened theatre S Carlo, Federico and Auletta's expanded intermezzo *La locandiera* – the first and for many years the only comic opera produced in the royal theatre. The Monti–Corrado team so entertained the queen that she requested them to sing for her all their old intermezzo parts at the Teatrino di Corte. In 1743 she sang at the Teatro Nuovo; in the same year she applied unsuccessfully for admission to the S Carlo cast. After appearances in 1745–6 at the Fiorentini she seems to have retired with her husband, the court official Girolamo Martinez.

(4) **Marianna Monti** (*b* Naples, 1730; *d* Naples, 1814). Soprano, cousin of the above three sisters. She made her début on the Naples comic stage in Carnival 1746 in the Trinchera–Conforto opera *La finta vedova* at the Teatro dei Fiorentini. From then until 1759 she appeared regularly there and at the Teatro Nuovo, singing, like her cousins, the comic female servant parts. For concerts and theatre work she was reputed to earn 450 to 500 ducats a year, with which, being unmarried, she helped support numerous relations. Her contract for the suspended original production of *Il Socrate immaginario* in 1775 stipulated a salary of 150 ducats, only 20 less than Paisiello's fee for the music. She enjoyed the patronage of the Marchese di Gerace, in whose house she often appeared for concerts, 'richly dressed'. Taking offence at the couple, the Uditore dell'Esercito (one of the city's theatrical censors) had them arrested suddenly in early August 1760; the singer was confined in the Conservatorio di S Maria del Buon Principio ossia di S Antoniello, and the nobleman in the Castelnuovo. This action seems to have been ill-judged, for the marchese's wife immediately petitioned the king for her husband's release, and depositions appeared promptly from the parishes of Marianna Monti's residence, testifying to her 'honest, philanthropic life, without any scandal' and to her regular attendance at church. The marchese was set free on condition that he pay a monthly maintenance charge of seven ducats for Marianna in the convent, but she was to remain confined for a further six months. By October talk had sufficiently subsided for her to be sent home 'on physician's advice', but she remained under house arrest. In the following month she successfully petitioned to leave her home in order to go to church – and also to fulfil her contractual obligations to sing at the nearby Fiorentini theatre during the autumn season. This was her first season of star billing, a rank she held until her retirement.

For almost 20 years she was perhaps Naples's most popular *prima buffa*. The best composers of the period created roles for her: Cocchi, Latilla, Logroscino, Jommelli, Traetta, Piccinni, Sacchini, Guglielmi, Paisiello and Cimarosa. Her style almost certainly influenced the development of Neapolitan *opera buffa*. She helped to popularize in the south the modern comic opera dramaturgy that Goldoni had developed for Venice, with its greater variety of vocal textures and aria forms, and its longer and more complex finales. This dramaturgy was introduced in Naples in the early 1760s particularly by the librettist Antonio Palomba; in Croce's opinion Marianna Monti was mainly responsible for Palomba's notable success. Her public career ended with the Palomba–Curci *farsa*, *Il millantator*, during Carnival 1780 at the newly opened Teatro del Fondo. Thereafter she declined into a poverty only alleviated two years before her death by a royal pension.

(5) **Gaetano Monti** (*b* Naples, c1750; *d* ?Naples, ?1816). Organist and composer, younger brother of (4) Marianna Monti. Early biographers' reports that he was born either around 1740 or 1760 at Fusignano, and that he was the brother of the poet and librettist Vincenzo Monti (1754–1828), are unfounded. He is not known to have studied at any of the Naples conservatories, but probably received early training at home among his family.

According to Florimo, Gaetano first appeared in public in 1758 at the age of eight, singing a skirt part in a revival of Piccinni's *Il curioso del suo proprio danno* at the Teatro Nuovo along with his sister Marianna who had the lead. This short part, that of Stellante, was probably written specially for him, since the character did not appear in the original production of 1756 and was in excess of the seven characters customary for *opere buffe* of this period. In 1776 he was admitted to the musical staff of the Philippine Tesoro di S Gennaro as *organista straordinario*, a position he appears to have held until at least 1788. After writing one serious opera for Modena in 1775, he confined himself to productions for the comic stage, works which usually contained a part for his sister until her retirement in 1780. According to Villarosa he also composed a quantity of church music (none of which is known to survive), and he had the reputation of 'un buon Maestro di musica'; in 1776 the impresarios of the S Carlo listed him among the 20 best composers then living in Naples. His two most popular operas, *Le donne vendicate* and *Lo studente*, were performed outside Naples as well as revived there; Gerber remarked on the popularity of his music in Germany.

## WORKS

*(comic operas; music lost unless otherwise indicated)*

L'Adriano in Siria (opera seria, Metastasio), Modena, Corte, 31 Jan 1775
Il cicisbeo discacciato, Naples, Nuovo, spr. 1777
La fuga (G. B. Lorenzi), Naples, Nuovo, sum. 1777; score, *I-Nc*
Il geloso sincerato (Lorenzi), Naples, Fondo, aut. 1779
Le donne vendicate (G. Palomba), Naples, Nuovo, 17 Oct 1781; also known as Il gigante; score, *I-Nc*
La contadina accorta (intermezzo a 5), Rome, Capranica, 4 Jan 1781; score, ?*D-Dlb*
Lo sposalizio per dispetto (G. Bertati), Venice, S Moisè, 26 Dec 1781
Il Molaforbice (G. Palomba), Naples, Nuovo, 26 Dec 1781
La viaggiatrice di bell'umore (intermezzo a 5), Rome, Capranica, carn. 1782
Lo studente (S. Zini), Naples, Nuovo, carn./spr. 1783
La donna fedele (Zini), Naples, Fondo, ?1 Sept 1784

Arias in Tritto's La Scuffiara, Naples, 1784; several numbers in revival of Gazzaniga's La donna soldato, Naples, S Ferdinando, 1793; music in I tre gobbi (intermezzo), *I-Nc*

6 concerti a 6, *I-MC*; aria, *GB-Lbm*

## BIBLIOGRAPHY

*FétisB*; *GerberNL*
P. Napoli-Signorelli: *Vicende della coltura nelle due Sicilie* (Naples, 1784–6), v, 564ff
C. A. de Rosa [Marchese di Villarosa]: *Memorie dei compositori di musica del Regno di Napoli* (Naples, 1840), 119
F. Florimo: *La scuola musicale di Napoli e i suoi conservatorii* (Naples, 1880–83/R1969), ii, 196; iv
M. Scherillo: *L'opera buffa napoletana durante il settecento: storia letteraria* (Naples, 1883, 2/1916/R), 115, 346f, 365ff, 403ff, 449f
B. Croce: *I teatri di Napoli: secolo XV–XVIII* (Naples, 1891/R1968), 250ff, 287f, 371, 372ff, 469, 637
U. Prota-Giurleo: 'Monti', *RicordiE*
M. F. Robinson: *Naples and Neapolitan Opera* (Oxford, 1972), 186f, 209ff

JAMES L. JACKMAN

**Monti, Giacomo** (*fl* Bologna, 1639–89). Italian music publisher, father of Pier Maria Monti. He began his publishing activities in Bologna in 1632, establishing a printing press near the church of S Matteo delle Pescherie. Two years later he entered into partnership with Carlo Zenero, and the press was moved to the street of S Mamolo in 1638. Its first musical publication was Corbetta's *Scherzi armonici: suonate sopra la chitarra spagnola* (1639), followed in the same year by Piccinini's *Il secondo libro di intavolature di liuto*. Shortly thereafter the partnership was dissolved, and Monti continued the business alone, publishing mostly historical and sacred works. In 1662 he resumed his musical activities, having moved to a shop under the vault of the Pollaroli, and until 1689 his musical production was intense, consisting chiefly of works by Bolognese composers. He seems to have worked completely independently at first. During this period his typographical mark was a figure of S Petronio, the patron saint of Bologna.

In about 1668 the Bolognese bookseller Marino Silvani associated himself with Monti, at first using his presses for several of the anthologies he himself edited (*Sacri concerti*, 1668; *Nuova raccolta di motetti sacri*, 1670; *Canzonette per camera a voce sola*, 1670; *Scelta di suonate a 2 violini e bc. per organo*, 1680), as well as for music by Filippini (op.10), G. B. Bassani (opp.1 and 5), Albergati (op.2), Domenico Gabrielli (op.1) and Corelli (reprint of op.1), all within the period 1683–4. Apparently Silvani and Monti then made an agreement that gave Silvani the exclusive rights to sell Monti's publications. From 1685 all the publications of Giacomo Monti carried the indication 'sold by M. Silvani at the sign of the violin', and the typographical mark was nearly always a violin with the motto 'UTREleves MIserum FAtum SOLitosque LAbores'. The secular production of the firm during this period was somewhat limited but included madrigals by G. B. Bassani, Mazzaferrata, G. B. Bianchi and G. M. Bononcini and canzonettas and chamber cantatas by G. M. Bononcini, Cazzati, Cherici, Legrenzi, Cossoni, Mazzaferrata and Penna. For sacred and instrumental music, however, production was far more extensive, preferred authors being G. P. Colonna, Cossoni, Filippini, G. B. Vitali, G. Bononcini, G. B. Degli Antonii, G. B. Bassani, Mazzaferrata, Cazzati, Albergati, Corelli, Berardi and Penna. Between 1681 and 1685 the firm printed an index (undated) of its published works (*Indice dell'opere di musica sin'hora stampate da Giacomo Monti in Bologna*). In 1689 the business passed to Pier Maria Monti.

BIBLIOGRAPHY

F. Vatielli: 'Editori musicali dei secoli XVII e XVIII', *Arte e vita musicale a Bologna* (Bologna, 1927/*R*1969), 239
A. Sorbelli: *Storia della stampa a Bologna* (Bologna, 1929)
L. Gottardi: *La stampa musicale in Bologna dagli inizi fino al 1700* (diss., U. of Bologna, 1951)
C. Sartori: *Dizionario degli editori musicali italiani* (Florence, 1958)
ANNE SCHNOEBELEN

**Monti, Pier Maria** (*fl* Bologna, 1689–1709). Italian music publisher, son of Giacomo Monti. He succeeded his father in 1689, taking over a well-established printing house that had been active in Bolognese music publishing since 1639. Like his father's, his publications were sold by Marino Silvani, and later also by Lelio della Volpe. The composers whose works were published by the Monti firm during these 20 years (mostly between 1690 and 1695) included G. Bononcini, Domenico Gabrielli, Corelli, G. P. Colonna, Elia Vannini, Jacchini, G. B. Bassani and Francesco Passarini. Monti's last musical edition seems to have been a reprint of Paradossi's *Il modo di suonare il sistro* (1702). After his death his heirs continued the non-musical part of the firm's publishing activities, becoming the official printers for the Holy Office; the music publishing was taken over by the Silvani firm. In general the typography of the Monti press (both father and son) lacks care and elegance and has a commercial character.

For bibliography *see* MONTI, GIACOMO.

ANNE SCHNOEBELEN

**Monti, Vittorio** (*b* Naples, 6 Jan 1868; *d* Naples, 20 June 1922). Italian violinist and composer. He was a pupil of Pinto (violin) and Serrao (composition) at the Naples Conservatory and of Sivori in Paris, where he settled in 1886. He was a violinist in the Lamoureux Orchestra and from 1900 directed a music-hall orchestra. Later he devoted himself to teaching the violin and the mandolin (for which he wrote a tutor) and to composition. He composed a ballet, *Il giardino incantato* (Naples, 1891), several short operettas and other stage works, notably *Noël de Pierrot* (Paris, 1900), and many other light vocal and instrumental pieces, of which a violin *Csárdás* achieved widespread popularity.

ANDREW LAMB

**Monticelli, Angelo Maria** (*b* Milan, 1710–15; *d* Dresden, 1764). Italian castrato soprano. After his stage début in Rome about 1730 Monticelli appeared in Venice, Milan and Florence. He was the first man in the opera company at the King's Theatre in London from 1741 to 1744 when, according to Horace Walpole, he was 'infinitely admired'. He sang there again in 1746, in a season which included two works by Gluck. He returned to the Continent and sang in various opera houses, although his voice was apparently declining. In the mid-1750s he settled at Dresden where he worked under Hasse. Burney praised his acting, his clear sweet voice and his good taste.

OLIVE BALDWIN, THELMA WILSON

**Montichiaro, Zanetto di.** *See* ZANETTO DI MONTICHIARO.

**Montirandé** (Fr.). A 16th- and 17th-century variety of BRANLE in duple metre with dotted rhythms. It was mentioned by Arbeau (as the 'branle de mostierandel'), Mersenne ('branle de montirandé') and François de Lauze, who defined it simply as the fifth branle of a series (*Apologie de la danse*, 1623; ed. J. Wildeblood, 1952). Examples can be found in Jean d'Estrée's *Tiers livre de danseries* (1559), Anthoine Francisque's *Le trésor d'Orphée* (1600) and Michael Praetorius's *Terpsichore* (1612). A manuscript in Uppsala contains a number of *montirandés* for ensemble.

BIBLIOGRAPHY

*BrownI*
J. J. S. Mráček: *Seventeenth-century Instrumental Dances in Uppsala, Univ. Libr. I. Mhs 409* (diss., Indiana U., 1965)

**Montisarduus, Hieronymus.** *See* MONTESARDO, GIROLAMO.

**Montpellier Codex** (*F-MO* H196). *See* SOURCES, MS, §V, 2.

**Montre** (Fr.). An ORGAN STOP.

**Montreal.** Largest city in Canada. It has long been a leader in the country's musical life, challenged only by Toronto. It is a bilingual city (roughly three quarters French- and one quarter English-speaking), and music is one of the few cultural activities that unites and receives support from both language groups.

1. History. 2. Institutions.

1. HISTORY. Founded by the French as a missionary outpost in 1642, the early colony was too preoccupied with such basics as shelter, food and defence to pay much attention to cultural development. Music consisted of French folksongs and, in the religious services, some plainchant and a few motets. It was discovered that the Indians of the region responded readily to liturgical music, and the latter became a vital tool in their conversion to Catholicism: native children were taught canticles and simple Gregorian chant, with words in the appropriate Indian language. A number of musical instruments were brought by the colonists, and particularly by those who were sent to govern them. There are 17th-century references to flutes, trumpets, drums, fiddles, lutes and guitars, which were played in connection with wedding celebrations, government functions and military ceremonies.

Quebec City, founded 34 years earlier than Montreal, was the seat of French government, and secular music developed more rapidly there than in the purely religious settlement of Montreal; however, the commercial and military importance of Montreal – the highest navigable point on the St Lawrence River at that time – soon came to be recognized and exploited, and the town began to lose its exclusively religious character. By the end of the 17th century an imported French organ had been installed in the parish church; the first recorded organist is J.-B. Poitiers du Buisson (1645–1727), who took up the post at the age of 60. Although the existence of secular instrumental music in 17th- and early 18th-century Montreal is confirmed by the records of an occasional ball organized by a government official or a member of the seigneurial class, such activity was discouraged by the Gentlemen of St Sulpice, the seigneurs of the Montreal settlement. Music remained either a folk tradition, barely tolerated by the church, or an instrument of the divine service. The music of the native tribes was not regarded as worthy of notice. A few Indian tunes were written down as curiosities in the 17th century, but only when they showed some resemblance to European music.

After the conquest of Canada by the British (1759), the bands of British regiments stationed in the larger towns formed the nucleus of a new and somewhat more active musical life. Army commissions were purchased by the wealthy, and commanding officers vied with each other in the quality of their bands; the musicians, many of them German, seem to have been both competent and versatile. In Montreal they gave regular weekly concerts of about two hours on the old Champs de Mars, and the bands also provided the musicians for the frequent balls held during the winter.

Montreal acquired a French musician of some wit and skill during the American Revolution: Joseph Quesnel (1749–1809), a sea-captain from St Malo captured by a British frigate in 1799 while running supplies and ammunition from France to the USA. After his release he eventually settled in the Montreal area, managing the general store of Boucherville, an adjacent village, and writing songs, chamber operas, and quantities of essays and poetry. One of his operas, *Colas et Colinette, ou Le bailli dupé* (1788), was performed in Montreal in 1790; it is a pleasant if rather conventional work, owing more to Grétry than to Mozart. Quesnel arrived in Canada as a mature musician, and Montreal had as little influence on his work as he had on the citizens of his adopted country. His assessment of the cultural life of the town was not high; in one of his poems, *Epitre à M Généreux Labadie*, he wrote: 'At table they sing you an old Bacchic song; in church there were two or three old motets, accompanied by organs missing their bellows'.

In 1848 the first Philharmonic Society was organized in Montreal by an English organist, R. J. Fowler, for the presentation of orchestral and choral works. Fowler's musical resources must have been severely limited at the time, and the career of the organization was ended abruptly by the great cholera epidemic of 1852. Sporadic attempts were made to organize concerts on a regular basis, but the majority were short-lived. The first group to survive for any length of time was the Montreal Mendelssohn Choir, founded in 1864 and conducted by Joseph Gould (1833–1913), who continued to direct the group of some 100 voices in several concerts each year until the choir's dissolution in 1894. The extensive collection of musical material acquired by the organization was left to the faculty of music at McGill University.

A few French choral groups enjoyed brief success during the same period: La Société Musicale des Montagnards Canadiens, Les Orphéonistes de Montréal (both founded by François Benoit) and the Société Ste-Cécile, founded by Adélard J. Boucher. The latter also launched a music publishing business and acted as an impresario for visiting artists.

The development of Boston and New York was much more rapid than that of the French and British settlements in Canada, and by the mid-19th century the musical celebrities of Europe already found it profitable to tour the USA, with brief sallies into the larger Canadian towns across the frontier. In this way Montreal heard such musicians as Patti, Christine Nilsson, Gottschalk, Joseffy, Bülow, Rubinstein, Wieniawski, Vieuxtemps and Ole Bull. In 1850 a touring orchestra from Berlin, known as the Germanians, gave nine performances in Montreal's Theatre Royal with great success.

The revival of the Philharmonic Society of Montreal in 1877 was an event of great consequence in the development of musical taste in the city. In its 22 years of activity it presented over 120 large orchestral and choral works, many of them for the first time in Canada. Although choral groups were flourishing at this period the formation of an adequate orchestra presented problems; musicians were imported from Boston, Quebec City and Ottawa to supplement the local band for the society's concerts. The first director of the Philharmonic concerts was P. R. McLagan, succeeded in 1879 by Joseph Gould and Fred E. Lucy-Barnes. In 1880 the direction of the concerts was taken over by Guillaume Couture, who continued to lead the performances until 1899, when the organization suspended its activities. During that period the Philharmonic Society presented such important works as Handel's *Judas Maccabaeus* and *Acis and Galatea*; Mendelssohn's *Elijah* and *St Paul*; Mozart's *Requiem* and that of Cherubini; Schumann's *Das Paradies und die Peri*; Haydn's *The Creation* and *The Seasons*; Beethoven's Ninth Symphony and *Christus am Ölberge*; a concert version of Wagner's *Der fliegende Holländer*; and the first Canadian performance of Saint-Saëns's *Samson et Dalila*.

Guillaume Couture, who sustained the Philharmonic Society and accounted for much of its success, was the first outstanding Montreal-born musician. In 1873 he was sent by a generous patron to Paris to complete his studies. He returned to Canada permanently in 1878, and after the failure of the Philharmonic Society in 1899 confined himself to teaching and to his post as organist of the Cathedral of St Jacques. Several of his pupils contributed significantly to Montreal's musical development. Another musician of importance in Montreal during the last quarter of the 19th century was the Belgian violin virtuoso Frantz Jehin-Prume, teacher of Ysaÿe and successor to Bériot as violinist to the Belgian king. He toured with the Rubinsteins, Jenny Lind, Esipova and others, and during one of his American visits married the Canadian soprano Rosita del Vecchio. Settling in Montreal in the 1860s, he organized and conducted a number of orchestral and chamber music concerts, exercising considerable influence on the quality of music in the city, both through the imaginative choice of programmes and his professional level of performance. He was also a close friend and supporter of Calixa Lavallée, who composed Canada's national anthem and was one of the country's most gifted and productive musicians.

2. INSTITUTIONS. Towards the end of the 19th century a number of attempts were made in Montreal to form a permanent orchestra, the most important being that of Joseph Goulet, a Belgian violinist who went to Montreal in 1890. He organized the remnants of a short-lived cooperative orchestra founded by Guillaume Couture, and from 1897 was able to sustain a series of four or five concerts annually for more than ten years, under the name of the Montreal SO.

Following the development of the film soundtrack in the late 1920s many of the pit musicians, who supplied background music and accompaniments for cinemas and vaudeville houses, found themselves unemployed. Their situation was aggravated in 1929 by the financial crisis and subsequent depression. A group of these musicians approached Douglas Clarke, dean of the faculty of music at McGill University, with a view to forming an orchestra with Clarke at its head. The orchestra offered 25 programmes in its first season (1930–31), but this was reduced to 20, then 18, in succeeding seasons. Concerts took place at His Majesty's Theatre on Sunday afternoons, and the programmes compared favourably with those of other American orchestras.

Clarke, a pupil of Vaughan Williams and Holst, was a well-schooled and perceptive musician. He refused payment for his services throughout the 11-year existence of the orchestra and contributed generously to its collection of scores and parts. He led the musicians through the first Montreal performances of many works now regarded as part of the standard repertory, and he invited leading musicians to take part in the concerts either as guest conductors or as soloists, among them

Enescu, Kubelík, Bauer, Zimbalist, Holst and Grainger. In 1934 the board of directors of the Montreal Orchestra split in a dispute with Clarke over the choice of programmes, and the dissatisfied faction, largely French-speaking and led by Athanase David, set up a new series of concerts under the name of Les Concerts Symphoniques. Performances were given in the auditorium of the Plateau School; there were a dozen concerts that year, and most of the musicians were those employed by the Montreal Orchestra. Whereas before 1930 there had been no permanent orchestra, by 1935 the community was called upon to support two.

Lacking overall musical direction, the programmes of Les Concerts Symphoniques were uneven; the conducting, assigned largely to local musicians of modest talents, was even more so. One of the founders of the new concert series was Wilfrid Pelletier, a Montreal conductor on the staff of the Metropolitan Opera in New York. His commitments in New York prevented him from playing a very active role in the direction of the Concerts Symphoniques in the early years, but his association with the organization later became closer, and the quality of performance improved.

An important offshoot of Les Concerts Symphoniques was an annual summer festival, first held in 1936, in which Wilfrid Pelletier played a more creative role. These summer concerts began with large choral works, but by 1945 the project had expanded to include opera, ballet, orchestral concerts and theatre in both French and English. Between 1941 and 1944 Beecham led a number of the choral performances. The Montreal Festivals enjoyed their greatest popularity during the 1950s, although a notable event was the Contemporary Music Week in July 1961, which attracted leading composers from most Western countries.

Clarke's Montreal Orchestra was dissolved in 1941, and the Concerts Symphoniques continued alone; in the 1940s the Belgian Désiré Defauw was engaged as artistic director. The rift between the two language groups gradually closed. Programmes became bilingual, and in 1954 the organization was renamed Orchestre Symphonique de Montréal – Montreal SO, a name that has been retained. Permanent musical directors succeeding Defauw have been Klemperer (1950–53), Markevich (1956–60), Mehta (1961–7), F.-P. Decker (1968–75), Frühbeck de Burgos (1975–6) and Charles Dutoit (1978–). In 1976 the orchestra were engaged for 46 weeks, with two main subscription series, four large choral concerts, a series of popular concerts in a large sports arena and an educational series for young people, with commentary in English and French, under the direction of Mario Duschenes.

The first attempt to establish a permanent opera company in Montreal was made in 1910. Generously underwritten by F. D. Meighen, the company was headed by Albert Clerk-Jeannotte, a singing teacher at the McGill Conservatorium. Organized as a repertory company, it mounted 13 operas in its first three-month season, and included a tour of Toronto, Rochester, Quebec City and Ottawa. The personnel numbered as many as 100 instrumentalists and singers, including 23 principals. Most of the singers were guests (e.g. Leo Slezak), but there were several Canadians, some of whom have distinguished themselves abroad (e.g. La Palme Issaurel and Mme Edvina). The theatres of the time were not large enough to make Meighen's scheme workable; the company was kept afloat for four years, then disbanded just before World War I. For many years Montreal was dependent on occasional visits by the Metropolitan Opera of New York and by smaller touring companies.

In 1936 Les Variétés Lyriques was founded by Lionel Daunais and Charles Goulet. With a repertory made up largely of popular operettas by Friml, Lehár, Lecocq, Messager and others, they won a large public (17,000 subscribers annually), particularly among the French-speaking community. During the next 19 years at the Monument National, the company offered over 1000 performances of 83 works, of which 13 were from the serious opera repertory. With the development of national television networks in the 1950s their audience dwindled, and the company closed at the end of the 1955 season.

Meanwhile, in 1942 the Opera Guild of Montreal was founded with Pauline Donalda as artistic director. The aims of the company were much more modest and realistic than Meighen's. Beginning with two productions annually, each of which was given two performances, its programme was cut back in 1950 to one opera a year. Local artists were strongly supported, and although most of the operas were chosen from the popular repertory, more adventurous items were included, such as *The Golden Cockerel* (1944), *The Love of Three Oranges* (1952), *Louise* (1953), *Boris Godunov* (1954), *Falstaff* (1958) and *Macbeth* (1959). The musical director of the company for 19 of its 28 years was the Russian conductor Emil Cooper, who had directed the première of *The Golden Cockerel* in Moscow in 1909. The guild closed in 1969.

From 1964 Montreal's opera programme was augmented by productions organized by the Montreal SO in collaboration with the directors of the Place des Arts. The quality of performance was high, and opera became a regular feature of the orchestra's season, supported by additional subsidies from both the Canada Council and the Minister of Cultural Affairs of the Province of Quebec. In 1971, wishing to consolidate its opera investments, the Quebec government formed l'Opéra du Québec, which absorbed the opera programme of the Montreal SO as well as a small company in Quebec City, the Théâtre Lyrique de la Nouvelle France. Excellent productions of such works as *Otello*, *Salome*, Puccini's *Il trittico* and *Tristan und Isolde* were offered, along with standard repertory, first in the Place des Arts, then in Quebec's Grand Théâtre. However, the arrangement was awkward: Quebec performances were required to use the Quebec orchestra and chorus, which involved additional expensive rehearsal time. In some instances the production never left Montreal because the cost of remounting it in Quebec was prohibitive. After four seasons the Quebec Minister of Cultural Affairs suspended the operation, which already had an accumulated deficit of more than a million dollars.

The Little Symphony, an ensemble patterned on the late 18th-century orchestra, flourished between 1942 and 1951, offering a mixture of classical and modern works. Conductors were engaged on a permanent basis, and they included Bernard Naylor, George Schick, Fritz Mahler and Carl Bamberger. The role of the Little Symphony was taken over by the McGill Chamber Orchestra, which continues to offer a popular series of eight concerts each season under its founder and permanent conductor, Alexander Brott. Basically a string orchestra (it began in 1939 as a quartet), the McGill Chamber Orchestra varies in size from 12 to 25 musicians; its concerts are given in the Théâtre Maisonneuve.

The Ladies' Morning Musical Club, founded in 1882, is one of the oldest musical organizations on the continent. Despite the name, the annual 13 recitals and chamber concerts take place in the afternoon and are not confined to ladies. The club has a record of unusual success in finding gifted performers, from Ysaÿe to Ferrier, before their reputations had carried them beyond its financial capabilities. Similar in its objectives is the Pro Musica Society, founded by Constant Gendreau in 1948, which offers eight concerts annually, also at the Théâtre Maisonneuve.

A wide spectrum of the new music is offered by the Société de Musique Contemporaine du Québec, founded in 1965. The musical director is the well-known Canadian composer Serge Garant, who has trained a basic ensemble of 12 musicians to meet the exigencies of this specialized repertory. Six concerts a year, international in character, are given in the Pollack Hall of McGill University.

Montreal's Place des Arts (completed in 1967) consists of three modern concert halls: the Salle Wilfrid Pelletier (capacity 3000; see illustration), the Théâtre Maisonneuve (capacity 1200) and the Théâtre Port Royal (capacity 823). All three are used both for plays and for music, although the Salle Wilfrid Pelletier is used mainly by the Montreal SO. Although the completion of the theatre complex relieved some of the pressure for adequate accommodation for the arts, there is still an urgent need for a medium-sized hall suitable for chamber music. The Salle Claude Champagne (capacity 1600) is a fine hall built by the Ecole Vincent d'Indy, with an organ by Casavant; however, its location on the slope of Mount Royal is daunting in winter. Pollack Hall (capacity 600) was opened in the Strathcona Music Building of McGill University in 1975, but, designed to meet the needs of the music faculty, its availability to other music organizations is strictly limited; it is regularly used, however, by the Société de Musique Contemporaine du Québec.

During the 18th century and most of the 19th, music education in Montreal consisted of little more than basic solfège and classroom singing; only a few private teachers offered more advanced training. From 1876, however, a number of attempts were made to create a specialized music school, but most of them were short-lived (including the Conservatoire de Musique de Montreal, which relied for its support on a public lottery). With the creation of the Dominion College of Music in 1894 music education had a more solid basis; for about 50 years it organized graded examinations, issuing degrees and diplomas in association with Bishop's College (now Bishop's University). In 1904 the McGill Conservatorium was founded through a gift of Lord Strathcona and Mount Royal, chancellor of McGill University. In 1921 the university formed a faculty of music, associated with the conservatorium, with H. C. Perrin as dean. The department and conservatorium (now the preparatory school) continue to thrive, having had a particularly active period of growth during the decade 1965–75.

In 1905 Alphonse Lavallée Smith founded the Conservatoire National de la Musique, which offered courses leading to music degrees in association with the Université de Montréal, and which continued to play an important role through the 1930s. In 1933 the nuns

*Interior of the Salle Wilfrid Pelletier in the Place des Arts, Montreal*

of Les Saints Noms de Jésus et Marie founded the Ecole Vincent d'Indy, which soon won a fine reputation for musical instruction, both practical and theoretical. The school later became associated with the University of Sherbrooke, and offers degree courses. The Conservatoire de Musique et d'Art Dramatique was created by the government of Quebec Province in 1943; it is a scholarship school, supported completely by government funds, and has branches in other principal cities of the province. It offers certificates and prizes along the lines of the Paris Conservatoire. In 1950 the university founded its own faculty of music offering French-speaking courses in interpretation, composition, musicology and music education.

ERIC McLEAN

**Montreux.** Swiss town. Until the last quarter of the 19th century there was nothing in its musical life to distinguish it from other Swiss centres of comparable size. Its celebrated climate attracted increasing numbers of foreigners and this led in 1881 to the foundation of the Kursaal Orchestra, which gave about 30 concerts annually until 1914, when it was disbanded because of the war; such conductors as Oskar Jüttner and Ernest Ansermet chose novel and eclectic programmes. From 1911 to 1914 Ansermet gave the first Swiss performances of many French and Russian works, including Stravinsky's Symphony in E♭ (2 April 1914).

Between the two wars Montreux suffered a depression and was musically less active, apart from its folk

festivals, e.g. the Fête des Narcisses. Interest revived in 1946, when the Septembre Musical was started; this later became known as the Montreux Music Festival and now ranks as one of the most important in western Europe. Most of the great orchestras of Europe, the USA and Japan have performed there under the most famous conductors. Programmes also include chamber music concerts and recitals, and in recent years the traditional repertory has been extended by concerts of contemporary and avant-garde music. The town of Vevey enlarges the festival's scope by organizing performances of oratorios, church music and organ music. Permanent collaboration was gradually established between the festival and conductors living in Montreux (Paul Kletzki, Carl Schuricht).

The pleasant climate and beauty of the surroundings have always attracted musicians; Tchaikovsky worked on his Fourth Symphony there in 1877 and his Violin Concerto in the following year. Chausson composed his *Poème* for violin and orchestra there in 1896, and Stravinsky completed *The Rite of Spring* and *Le rossignol* there in 1913 and 1914. Other musicians of distinction including Furtwängler, Hindemith and Duparc lived for some years in or near Montreux.

BIBLIOGRAPHY

E. Ansermet and I. Stravinsky: 'Unveröffentliche Briefe', *Neue Zürcher Zeitung*, no.317 (1970)
J. Burdet: *La musique dans le canton de Vaud au XIXème siècle* (Lausanne, 1970)

PIERRE MEYLAN

**Montsalvatge, Xavier** (*b* Gerona, 11 March 1912). Spanish composer and critic. He studied at the Barcelona Conservatory with Millet, Morera, Costa and Pahissa (1923–36). In 1934 he received the most important conservatory award, the Rebell Prize, for his Impromptus for piano, and two years later he was awarded the Pedrell Prize for the *Suite burlesca*. By temperament he tends towards the plastic and theatrical, and he is particularly conscious of rhythm; so an early interest in the ballet was natural. In 1936–7 he worked on the ballet *El ángel de la guarda*, which remains unpublished, and subsequently he developed a close association with the Goubé–Alexander company. This connection led to the composition of some 20 ballets, of which the most outstanding are *La muerte enamorada* (1943), *Manfred* (1945) and *La Venus de Elna* (1946). It was at this time, too, that he began work as a critic; he became music critic of the weekly *Destino* of Barcelona in 1942, and in 1962 he began to write for the *Vanguardia española*. He has taught in Barcelona at the San Jorge Academy (since 1962) the Destino Seminary (since 1969) and the Conservatory (since 1970).

Montsalvatge felt it necessary to depart from certain Germanic traditions in Catalan music, and he came nearer to the diverting style of Les Six, besides incorporating the expressive and structural innovations of Stravinsky. At the same time he wanted to acquire Catalan qualities distinct from those implicit in his use of folk music. These concerns bore fruit in his 'West Indian' works, which he created, to use his own words, 'in West Indian musical style, which was itself originally Spanish, exported overseas and then reimported into our country, and which finds a place at the periphery of our traditions as a new, vague and evocative manifestation of musical lyricism'. He has also remarked that, for him, 'the sardana has the same traditional spirit and the same profound resonance as a habanera'. Typical of his West Indian manner are the Divertimento (1941), the *Cuarteto indiano* (1952) and above all the *Canciones negras* (1945–9). Rather as an appendage to these there appeared a number of works relating to the world of children (as attractive to Montsalvatge as it was to Lorca); these include the magic opera *El gato con botas*, staged at the Barcelona Liceo in 1948, and the *Canciones para niños* (1953) on poems of Lorca, to which was added a narration with orchestral accompaniment, *Viaje a la luna*, first performed at Barcelona in 1966. In other pieces of this period Montsalvatge expressed something of the romantic sentiment of earlier Catalan musicians, while using the popular traditions of the country; among such compositions are the *Poema concertante* for violin and orchestra (1951) and the *Concierto breve* for piano and orchestra (1953).

In the ensuing years Montsalvatge's thinking and methods underwent a decisive change. He saw no need to adhere rigidly to new ideas if they invalidated what had gone before; and he affirmed that it was as necessary to alter the hierarchy of tonality as to reinterpret tonality. Placed as he was between the nationalist generation and the vanguard, he was perhaps obliged to adopt an eclectic posture, which has enabled him to write scores of individuality, maturity and high quality. A new and apparently definitive style was established in the *Cinco invocaciones al Crucificado* (1969) and pursued in *Laberinto*, *Homenaje a Manolo Hugué*, the Cello Sonata and the overture *Reflexus*; yet Montsalvatge's sense of the function of a work and his belief in music as a vehicle for expressive communication have led him to take a distinctive point of departure for each composition. Thus in the opera *Una voce in off* (1962), to an Italian text, his closeness to Puccini resembles that of Menotti, while the Cantata on poems of Maragall (1958) alludes to previous generations of Spanish composers, in spirit if not in style. But, whatever the technique, the music is structurally firm, imaginatively orchestrated and motivated by an inner core of conviction.

WORKS
*(selective list)*

Operas: El gato con botas, 1948; Una voce in off (1, Montsalvatge), 1962; Babel-1948 (4, Montsalvatge), 1968
Ballets: La muerte enamorada, 1943; Manfred, 1945; La Venus de Elna, 1946; Perlimplinada, 1956, collab. Mompou
Orch: Poema concertante, vn, orch, 1951; Concierto breve, pf, orch, 1953; Caleidoscopio, 1955; Partita, 1958; Danzas concertantes, 1962; Desintegración morfológica de la Chacona de Bach, 1963; Laberinto, 1971; Reflexus, ov., 1974; Conc. capriccio, harp, orch, 1976; Conc. per un virtuoso, hpd, orch, 1977
Vocal: Canciones negras, 1v, pf, 1945, orchd 1949; Egloga del Tajo, chorus, orch, 1945; Canciones para niños (Lorca), 1953; Cantata (Maragall), 1958; Paisatge del Montseny, 1v, small orch, 1961; 5 invocaciones al Crucificado, S, ens, 1969; Homenaje a Manolo Hugué, S, orch, 1972; Sum vermis, S, 2 pf, 2 perc, 1974
Inst: Variaciones sobre la españoleta de G. Farnaby, vn, pf, 1946; Cuarteto indiano, str qt, 1952; Sketch, vn, pf, 1953; Self-paráfrasis, cl, pf, 1953; Sonata concertante, vc, pf, 1972; Spanish Sketch, vn, pf, 1972; Serenata a Lydia, fl, pf/chamber orch, 1972–3; Aureola, org, 1973
Other works: choral pieces; music for pf, org, gui; arrs.; incidental music, film scores

Principal publishers: Salabert, Southern, Unión Musical Española

BIBLIOGRAPHY
M. Valls: *X. Montsalvatge* (Barcelona, 1969)
E. Franco: *Xavier Montsalvatge* (Madrid, 1975)
ENRIQUE FRANCO

**Montserrat.** Benedictine monastery near Barcelona. It has been a very important centre of pilgrimages and devotion to the Virgin Mary from the 11th century. Music has played an important role in these activities especially since the foundation of the Escolanía in the 12th century. The *Llibre Vermell*, a 14th-century manuscript in the monastery archives, records details of the musical life at Mary's shrine. Two abbots, A. P. Ferrer (13th century) and Garcías de Cisneros (16th century), regulated in their *constitutiones* and *regula puerorum* the life of the *escolans* (boy singers) and their participation in the religious services. The Escolanía was at its zenith from the beginning of the 17th century until its destruction by Napoleon's army (1811); it could be classified as a music school where boy singers were trained. Joan March (1582–1658), who succeeded Victoria as organist of the convent of Descalzas Reales in Madrid, was the first to give the Escolanía its characteristic traits. The pupils of Joan Cererols, who taught there, were much admired throughout Spain and some of his works were published in Mestres de l'Escolanía de Montserrat. Miguel López was a choirboy and later a choirmaster at the Escolanía. His works, mostly in a manuscript entitled *Miscellanea musicae* (in *E-Boc*), are indicative of his creative mind and of the performing resources of the Escolanía, which had both singers and an orchestra. His treatise, *Exagoga ad musicem*, is lost. The Escolanía had many of its best teachers during the 18th century: Josep Martí (1719–63), Benet Julià

(1727–87), Anselm Viola (1738–98) and Narciso Casanovas. Outstanding students included Soler and Sor. Many of the works of these composers are unpublished; some, however, have been recorded. Following the destruction of the monastery and the Escolanía in 1811 and the subsequent musical decline, musical life was eventually restored in 1852 by Jacint Boada. Manuel Guzmán (1846–1909) consolidated it, and his disciples, Anselm Ferrer, Angel Rodamilans and David Pujol had contributed to its success by 1953 when Ireneu Segarra became director. Efforts have been made since then to continue to publish the works of the masters of the Escolanía and to provide the new liturgy with suitable music; international meetings of composers have been held to carry out these objectives.

BIBLIOGRAPHY

P. Burgos: *Libro de la història y milagros de nuestra Señora de Montserrate* (Barcelona, 1550, 2/1605)
J. M. Marvà: *Memorial o tratado en favor de los niños escolanes y seminario de nuestra Señora de Montserrat* (Toulouse, 1650)
B. Saldoni: *Reseña histórica de la Escolanía de Montserrat* (Madrid, 1856)
A. Albareda: *Història de Montserrat* (Montserrat, 1931, 5/1972)
A. Ramón Arrufat: *Llibre d'or de l'Escolanía de Montserrat* (Barcelona, 1936)
H. Anglés: 'El "Llibre Vermell" de Montserrat y los cantos y la danza sacra de los peregrinos durante el siglo XIV', *AnM*, x (1955), 45
A. Caralt: *L'Escolanía de Montserrat* (Montserrat, 1955)

IRENEU SEGARRA

**Montserrat, Andrés de.** *See* MONSERRATE, ANDRÉS DE.

**Monza, Carlo** (*b* Milan, *c*1735; *d* Milan, 19 Dec 1801). Italian composer. He studied with G. A. Fioroni and probably also with G. B. Sammartini, with whom he was closely associated. When Sammartini was promoted to *maestro di cappella* of the ducal court in Milan (8 November 1768) Monza succeeded him as organist, and on Sammartini's death (15 January 1775) as *maestro*. By this time he held similar posts at three Milanese churches (S Maria Segreta, S Giovanni in Conca and the Chiesa della Rosa), and had established himself as an important church and theatre composer. He was elected a member of the Accademia dei Pugni (Alessandro Verri's letter of 10 December 1768), and the Accademia Filarmonica, Bologna (2 May 1771, test piece in *I-Bc*). On 28 December 1787 he was appointed *maestro* of Milan Cathedral, having twice failed to obtain this post (1773, 1778); he abandoned his successful opera career and became a remarkably active composer of sacred music. A long illness led the cathedral chapter in 1793 to seek a replacement for Monza, and in 1795 Zingarelli was officially named his successor, although the post was eventually filled in September 1801 by Quaglia. In 1796 the French occupation of Milan forced the dissolution of the ducal chapel, which, under Monza, had performed regularly at the ducal church of S Gottardo and for special feasts at other Milanese churches. After the Austrians recaptured Milan in April 1799, Monza signed a petition to reopen S Gottardo, but this failed with the return of the French in June 1800.

Monza was among the best of late 18th-century Italian church composers. Although his music for S Gottardo is lost, 228 works for Milan Cathedral are extant in its archive, and demonstrate that he could equal Fioroni's archaic contrapuntal style or, in his brilliant solo motets, the theatrical style of his own operas. Burney wrote favourably of Monza's sacred music that he heard in Milan and Florence in 1770 and

called him, along with Melchiorre Chiesa, the best composer of theatre music in Milan. In the same year Alessandro Verri reported that Monza's opera *Germanico in Germania* was well received in Rome. Several collections of his instrumental music were published in London in the 1780s; a group of six attractive string quartets with programmatic titles is in the Paris Conservatoire library.

WORKS

OPERAS

*(serious, in 3 acts, unless otherwise indicated)*

Olimpiade (Metastasio), Milan, Regio Ducal, May 1758; *P-La* [2 copies]
Sesostri re d'Egitto (Zeno and Pariati), Milan, Regio Ducal, 26 Dec 1759; *I-Nc*, *P-La* [2 copies], *GB-Lam* [13 arias]
Achille in Sciro (Metastasio), Milan, Regio Ducal, 4 Feb 1764; *I-Nc*, *P-La* [2 copies]
Temistocle (Metastasio), Milan, Regio Ducal, 1 Jan 1766; *I-Nc*, *P-La* [2 copies]
Oreste (M. Verazzi), Turin, Regio, carn. 1766; *P-La*
Demetrio (Metastasio), Rome, Dame, 3 Jan 1769; *F-Pc*, *I-Bc*, *Rdp*, *P-La*
Adriano in Siria (Metastasio), Naples, S Carlo, 4 Nov 1769; *I-Nc*, *D-RH* [1 aria]
Germanico in Germania (N. Coluzzi), Rome, Dame, 7 Jan 1770
La lavandara astuta (comic, P. Chiari, after Galuppi: Il marchese villano), Milan, Regio Ducal, 2 July 1770, pasticcio; arias *A-Wn*
Nitteti (Metastasio), Milan, Regio Ducal, 22 Jan 1771; *P-La* [for Venetian revival, 1777]
Aristo e Temira (2, Count Salvioli), Bologna, Comunale, May 1771
Berenice, Turin, Regio, ?1771; *I-Bc*
Antigono (Metastasio), Rome, Argentina, carn. 1772
Il [finto] cavalier parigino (comic, 2), Milan, Regio Ducal, 3 Sept 1774 [? 1st perf. Rome, 1770]; *I-Rdp*, ?*H-Bn*
Alessandro nelle Indie (Metastasio), Bologna, Comunale, Jan 1775; arias *I-MAc* [dated ?1770]
Cleopatra (C. Olivieri), Turin, Regio, 26 Dec 1775
Caio Mario (G. Roccaforte), Venice, S Benedetto, Ascension Fair 1777
Attilio Regolo (Metastasio), composed for Munich, 1777, not perf.; *D-Mbs*
Ifigenia in Tauride (B. Pasqualigo), Milan, La Scala, Jan 1784; *F-Pc*, *P-La* [2 copies]
Enea in Cartagine (2, G. M. D'Orengo), Alessandria, Città, Oct Fair 1784 [? 1st perf. Turin, 1770]
Erifile (G. De Gamerra), Turin, Regio, 26 Dec 1785; *P-La*, *I-Gi(l)* [1 aria]
Miscellaneous arias: *A-Wgm*; *B-Br*; *D-Dlb*, ?*Bds*, ?*K*, *RH*, *W*; *F-Pc*; *GB-Lbm*, *T*; *I-Fc*, *Gi(l)*, *Mc*, *MAc*, *MOe*, *Nc*, *PAc*, *Rc*, *Tn*, *Vnm*

OTHER VOCAL

Cantatas: Non temer, bell'idol, S, orch, *D-Bds*; Pria di sorger dall'onda, S, bc, *I-Gi(l)*; Tirsi e Licori, S, S, 2 ob, 2 hn, str, *MAc*
Sacred: 13 masses, 20 Gloria, 2 Credo, 8 Credo–Sanctus–Benedictus, Sanctus–Benedictus, 4 ints, 2 graduals, 18 offertories, 13 antiphons, 37 hymns, 2 post-hymns, 36 psalms, 17 Ecce nunc, 11 Magnificat, 11 Magnificat–Pater noster, 11 Pater noster, Post Magnificat, 19 solo motets, 21 motets, 2vv, 5 motets, 3–8vv, Litany, 3 Lucernario, all *I-Md*, many autograph; 10 Gloria, 8 Credo, Antiphon, 3 psalms, all *F-Pc*; 2 hymns, *I-NOVd*; solo motet, *Vnm*; Pange lingua, in Musica sacra (Milan, n.d.)
Examination pieces, *I-Bc*

INSTRUMENTAL

Orch: 2 ovs., D, *I-Gi(l)*; 4 ovs., 3 in D, 1 in B♭, *Mc*; 4 syms., D, *Mc*; other syms., *CH-Zz*, *D-DS*, *I-MAc*
Chamber: 6 Str Trios, op.1 (London, *c*1781); 6 Str Qts, op.2 (London, *c*1782); 6 Sonatas, hpd, vn acc., op.3 (London, *c*1786–8); str trios: 1, ?*D-Bds*, 7, *Mbs*, 2, *F-Pc*, 6, *I-Gi(l)*, 1, *Vqs*; 7 notturne, str trio, *I-Gi(l)*; str qts: 6, *F-Pc*, 1, *D-RH*; Sonata, fl, 2 vn, 2 hn, b, C, *I-Gi(l)*; 2 sonatas, saltero, b, C, G, *Gi(l)*; Sonata, hpd, vn acc., *F-Pc*
Kbd: hpd sonatas: ?*D-Bds*, G, *I-Gi(l)*, A, *Mc*, B♭, *Mc*, *F-Pc*, G, A, *GB-Lbm*; org sonatas: G, *I-Mc*, B♭, *Mc*, *Gi(l)*; Pastoral, org, ?*D-Bds*; 6 Variations, hpd, *I-MOe*

BIBLIOGRAPHY

*EitnerQ*
Correspondence with G. B. Martini, *I-Bc*, *Bsf*
C. Burney: *The Present State of Music in France and Italy* (London, 1771, 2/1773); ed. P. Scholes as *Dr. Burney's Musical Tours* (London, 1959)
*La galleria delle stelle: almanacco per l'anno 1775* (Milan, 1775)
G. B. Martini: *Serie cronologica de' principi dell'Accademia de' Filarmonici di Bologna* (Bologna, 1776), 39
J.-B. de La Borde: *Essai sur la musique ancienne et moderne*, iii (Paris, 1780/R1972), 206

*Gazzetta di Milano*, xxxv (20 Dec 1780)
L. Torri: 'Una lettera inedita del Padre G. B. Martini', *RMI*, ii (1895), 262
E. Greppi and A. Giulini, eds.: *Carteggio di Pietro e di Alessandro Verri*, ii (Milan, 1910), 95; iii (1910), 156; xi (1940), 215
G. G. Bernardi: *La musica nella Reale accademia virgiliana di Mantova* (Mantua, 1923), 171f
D. Bartha and L. Somfai: *Haydn als Opernkapellmeister* (Budapest, 1960), 39, 240, 377
C. Sartori: 'G. B. Sammartini e la sua corte', *Musica d'oggi*, new ser., iii (1960), 106
——: 'Sammartini post-mortem', *Hans Albrecht in memoriam* (Kassel, 1962), 155
G. Barblan: 'La musica in Milano nell'età moderna', *Storia di Milano*, xvi (Milan, 1962), 645, 652, 656f, 659
F. Mompellio: 'La cappella del Duomo dal 1714 ai primi decenni del '900', *Storia di Milano*, xvi (Milan, 1962), 558ff
U. Prota-Giurleo and L. Paduano: 'Monza, Carlo', *MGG*
W. A. Bauer and O. E. Deutsch, eds.: *Mozart Briefe und Aufzeichnungen*, i (Kassel, 1962), 321f; ii (1962), 113, 299; v (1971), 236, 428, 498
M. Viale Ferrero: *La scenografia del '700 e i fratelli Galliari* (Turin, 1963), 255, 259, 265f
                                          SVEN HANSELL

**Monza, Carlo Antonio** (*b* ?Milan, late 17th century; *d* Vercelli, 1736). Italian composer. He is identified as Milanese in some printed librettos (Ancona, 1717, 1722); Fétis, however, wrote that Brescia was his birthplace (and misspelt his name 'Manzo'). He was a priest, but available information suggests that he turned only late to the composition of oratorios. Up to 1724 he composed operas and even managed a theatre, the Teatro della Munizione in Messina. After launching an operatic career in Venice he spent 15 years in southern Italy serving, at least briefly, the governor of Lecce (Puglia), according to a serenade of 1 October 1709 celebrating the birthday of Charles III, King of Naples (later Charles VI of Austria). Scores of four operas in the Royal Academy of Music, London, are probably by Monza but the places and dates of their performances are still unknown. A fifth opera for which no printed libretto has been found is *Tamerlano*; despite Vianello's claim that it was written by the Carlo Monza of the later 18th century (who, as far as is known, is unrelated to Carlo Antonio Monza), it is not elsewhere listed among the works of that later, better-known composer.

In 1735, a year before his death, Monza became *maestro di cappella* and canon at one of the two cathedrals in Vercelli (in Piedmont, not Sardinia as Eitner believed). An oratorio he directed there in 1736 was a revival of his *La fedeltà costante*, composed for Ancona in 1725. The S Filippo Neri priests in Rome and Bologna performed other of his oratorios, so it is likely that further research will disclose that churches of the order elsewhere also used his music. On some scores (*GB-Lam*) he is named 'Carlino Monza'.

### WORKS
(*lost unless otherwise stated*)

OPERAS

Paride ed Ida, Venice, S Angelo, 1706, collab. A. B. Coletti
Alessandro in Susa (G. Frigimelica Roberti), Venice, S Giovanni Grisostomo, 1708
Sidonio (P. Pariati), Naples, Fiorentini, 13 Jan 1714
La principessa fedele, Messina, della Munizione, 1716, ? collab. M. A. Gasparini, 16 arias, *GB-Lam*
La Circe in Italia, Rome, della Pace, carn. 1717
Carlo in Allemagna, *c*1719, *Lam*
La Floridea regina di Cipro, Ancona, Fenice, carn. 1723
Cambise, Messina, della Munizione, 1724
Il più fedel tra i vassalli (F. Silvani), 19 arias, *Lam*
Scipione nelle Spagne (Zeno), *Lam*
Tigrane, 16 arias, *Lam*
Tamerlano, Milan, ?before 1758

SACRED VOCAL

Per la solenne translazione de' Sacri Corpi de SS Martiri Valentino ed Ilario protettori della città di Viterbo (oratorio), Viterbo, 1724
S Filippo Neri (oratorio), Rome, Nuova, 1725
La fedeltà costante di S Giovanni Nepomuceno (oratorio), Ancona, 1725
Martirio del glorioso vescovo S Giagio (oratorio), Bologna, Galliera, 1728

Other uncatalogued sacred music, *I-VCd*

### BIBLIOGRAPHY
*EitnerQ*; *FétisB*
C. A. Vianello: *Teatri, spettacoli, musiche a Milano nei secoli scorsi* (Milan, 1941), 276
U. Manferrari: *Dizionario universale delle opere melodrammatiche*, ii (Florence, 1955), 352
                                          SVEN HANSELL

**Monza, Maria** (*fl* 1729–41). Italian soprano. She was the daughter of Bartolomeo Monza, a barber who in 1737–8 was the last director of the Hamburg Opera. She sang in three operas at Venice between 1729 and 1731 and two at Prague in 1734–5. At Hamburg she appeared in a number of concerts, singing 'the most beautiful arias of the best Italian masters' on 5 April 1736, and doubtless at the opera. On 23 April 1738 she put on a 'serenade' at the Drillhaus. Handel engaged her in 1740 for his last London opera season, but she arrived too late to sing in *Imeneo* (22 November) and made her début at Lincoln's Inn Fields on 10 January 1741 as Nerea in *Deidamia*. She sang (probably in Italian) in revivals of *L'Allegro*, the bilingual *Acis and Galatea* (Filli) and *Saul* (Merab) in the early months of 1741 and had a benefit concert at Hickford's Room on 28 April. According to Mrs Pendarves 'her voice is between Cuzzoni's and Strada's – strong, but not harsh, her person *miserably bad*, being very low, and *excessively* crooked'. Burney dismissed her by implication as 'below criticism', but that is certainly unjust. Handel, who had finished *Deidamia* before her arrival and written the part of Nerea for a singer of limited capacity, recomposed it for Monza, making heavy demands on technique and flexibility and extending the compass to two octaves (*b* to *b''*).

                                          WINTON DEAN

**Monzani, Tebaldo** [Theobald] (*b* Duchy of Modena, 1762; *d* London, 14 June 1839). Italian flautist, instrument maker and publisher. He apparently played both the flute and the oboe, but gave up the latter after moving to England, where he became well known as a solo and orchestral flautist. In 1787 he established premises in London where from various addresses he published his own compositions (mainly for flute) and other works. From 1789 he sometimes employed the piano maker and music publisher JAMES BALL to print and sell his publications. In 1800 Monzani entered a partnership with GIAMBATTISTA CIMADOR as Monzani & Cimador, from about 1803 occupying a building known as the Opera Music Warehouse. From 1805 Monzani continued alone as Monzani & Co. until about 1807, when he established a partnership with Henry Hill and the firm became Monzani & Hill; about 1815 it obtained royal patronage as 'music seller to the Prince Regent'. The partnership was dissolved in 1829 and Henry Hill and his sons continued the business until 1845, when the firm was sold by auction.

Monzani and his successors issued much sheet music, especially Italian vocal pieces, but their publications also included the piano works of Mozart and Beethoven. Monzani made many flutes and clarinets and had a high reputation as a craftsman. He also wrote a tutor,

*Instructions for the German Flute* (1801, 3/?1820). His son Willoughby became a flautist and was described by W. N. James (1826) as 'perhaps the most promising performer in England'.

BIBLIOGRAPHY
W. N. James: *A Word or two on the Flute* (Edinburgh, 1826)
R. S. Rockstro: *A Treatise on the Construction, the History and the Practice of the Flute* (London, 1890, 2/1928/R1967)
C. Humphries and W. C. Smith: *Music Publishing in the British Isles* (London, 1954, 2/1970)
O. Neighbour and A. Tyson: *English Music Publishers' Plate Numbers in the First Half of the Nineteenth Century* (London, 1965), 11
P. Bate: *The Flute* (London, 1969)
WILLIAM C. SMITH/PETER WARD JONES

**Monzino, Francesco di.** *See* FRANCESCO CANOVA DA MILANO.

**Mood.** English vernacular for Latin *modus*: the relationship between long and breve in the late medieval system of mensuration. *See* NOTATION, §III, 3.

**Moode, Henry.** *See* MUDD family.

**Moody [Manners], Fanny** (*b* Redruth, Cornwall, 23 Nov 1866; *d* Dundrum, Co. Dublin, 21 July 1945). English soprano. She studied with Charlotte Sainton-Dolby, making her début in April 1885 in a memorial concert for her teacher at the Prince's Hall, London. Her stage début was as Arline in *The Bohemian Girl* at Liverpool in February 1887 with the Carl Rosa Company, of which she remained the leading soprano until 1898. Then, with the bass Charles Manners, whom she married in 1890, she founded the Moody-Manners Opera Company (1898–1916). In 1892 she sang Tatyana in the first English performance of *Eugene Onegin* at the Olympic Theatre, London. She created Rosalba, in Pizzi's opera of that name, and Militza in McAlpin's *The Cross and the Crescent*, in the Covent Garden seasons that she organized with Manners (1902–3). Her repertory also included Elsa, Gounod's Marguerite and Juliet, Leonora (*Il trovatore*) and Santuzza. Her pleasant light soprano voice and charming stage personality were widely admired.

BIBLIOGRAPHY
P. Graves: 'The Moody-Manners' Partnership', *Opera*, ix (1958), 558
HAROLD ROSENTHAL

**Moody-Manners Company.** English opera company. It was established in 1897, after a successful opera tour in South Africa, by the Irish bass Charles Manners and his wife, the soprano Fanny Moody, to produce grand opera in English. At first they toured the provinces; by 1902 there were two Moody-Manners companies on the road. The principal company, with 175 members, gave seasons that year and in 1903 at Covent Garden, at Drury Lane in 1904 and later at other London theatres. With the Carl Rosa Company, it was the principal training ground for British artists in the years before World War I.

Manners encouraged British composers to write for his company, offering prizes for operas. The resulting works included McAlpin's *The Cross and the Crescent*, produced at Covent Garden in 1903, and Nicholas Gatty's *Greysteel*, produced at Sheffield in 1906. In Sheffield Manners sponsored special opera festivals in 1904 and 1906, the profits of which helped to found Sheffield University. A successful season in Glasgow in 1906 led to the creation of the Glasgow Grand Opera Society which, in the interwar years, put on a number of enterprising seasons under Erik Chisholm. The company's music library is now in the Mitchell Library, Glasgow. By 1910 Manners faced financial difficulties and had to disband one of his two companies; his dream of founding a national English opera company centred in London was not realized. After Manners reduced his activities, Joseph O'Mara, a member of the Moody-Manners Company, formed his own group for provincial touring and occasional seasons in the London suburbs. The Moody-Manners Company gave its last performance in May 1916.

HAROLD ROSENTHAL

**Moog, Robert A(rthur)** (*b* Flushing, NY, 23 May 1934). American inventor of the 'Moog synthesizers' and other instruments. He took degrees in physics from Queens College, New York, and electrical engineering from Columbia University, and the PhD in engineering physics from Cornell University in 1965. He founded the R. A. Moog Co. in Trumansburg, New York, in 1954 for the manufacture of theremins. In 1965 the company started making electronic music synthesizers, which became its principal concern. The firm merged with MuSonics in 1971 to form Moog Music Inc. and moved to Williamsville, New York. In 1973 it became a subsidiary of Norlin Industries.

Moog's first synthesizers were designed in collaboration with the composer Herbert A. Deutsch. The composer Walter Carlos has collaborated in the design of the equipment since 1964. Other composers who have worked with Moog include Vladimir Ussachevsky, Lejaren Hiller, Gustav Ciamaga, John Cage, David Tudor, Gordon Mumma, Richard Teitelbaum, Emmanuel Ghent, John Charles Eaton, Jon Weiss, Chris Swanson and David Borden.

With the success of Walter Carlos's 'Switched-on Bach' recording (released commercially in February 1969), which uses a Moog synthesizer, and the worldwide distribution of Moog equipment, Moog's name, perhaps more than any other, became widely identified with the commercial electronic synthesizer. Moog Music Inc. manufactures both modular synthesizers and components, in which voltage control is the basic operating technique, and non-modular performance instruments such as the Mini-Moog and Sonic VI. Robert Moog is active in musical research and in the development of new instruments, with a particular interest in evolving more sophisticated control devices and more complex ways of applying control signals to add aural interest to sounds. *See also* THEREMIN and SYNTHESIZER.

HUBERT S. HOWE JR

**Moondaye, John.** *See* MUNDY, JOHN.

**Moondaye, William.** *See* MUNDY, WILLIAM.

**Moonie, W(illiam) B(eatton)** (*b* Stobo, Peeblesshire, 29 May 1883; *d* Edinburgh, 8 Dec 1961). Scottish composer, son of James A. Moonie, a well-known Edinburgh musician. He studied under Niecks at Edinburgh University (MusB 1902). The Bucher Scholarship took him in 1905 to Frankfurt, and he returned to Edinburgh three years later to take up a teaching appointment. On his father's death in 1923, he took over Mr Moonie's Choir. In 1937 the Glasgow Grand Opera Society produced *The Weird of Colbar*, which was broadcast in 1939 in an abridged version. Edinburgh University awarded him an honorary MusD.

### WORKS
*(selective list)*

Operas: The Weird of Colbar (G. M. Reith), perf. 1937; Lucy Ashton (Moonie), completed 1961
Orch: 2 syms.; 1745, concert ov.; Burns, suite, small orch; Cromer, suite; Pan, 4 dances; 4 Highland Airs; Land of Heather, suite; Prelude and Fugue, str; Scottish Lyric Pieces, op.34; The Highland Division, grand march; Meditation, pf, str; Riders of the Sidhe; Springtide on Tweed
Choral: Caledonia, ode; Glenara, ballad; Glide Gentle Streams (Herrick); The Ship, choral epilogue (E. Albert); Song of Roland (Scott-Moncrieff); Woodland Scene; Dumbarton's Drums, arr.; Edward! Edward!, arr.
Inst: Pf Trio; Perthshire Echoes, suite, pf; Scottish dance arrs., pf
Songs

MAURICE LINDSAY/R

**Moor, de.** *See* MOORS family.

**Moór, Emanuel** (*b* Kecskemét, 19 Feb 1863; *d* Chardonne, 20 Oct 1931). Hungarian composer, pianist and inventor. At an early age he began to study the organ, first locally, then in Prague. Subsequently he studied in Vienna and Budapest; then followed a period of musical activity in Szeged, where he taught, conducted light opera and considered becoming an architect. In 1885–7 he toured in Europe and America (where he was director of the Concerts Artistiques) as accompanist (to Lilli Lehmann and others), pianist and conductor. In 1888 he married, and went to England; then he settled in Switzerland. There Henri Marteau asked him to write a Violin Concerto for him; further commissions followed from Casals, Ysaÿe and Flesch. His feverish activity as a composer was interrupted by World War I; after his second marriage (1923), to the pianist Winifred Christie, he was mainly occupied with his invention, the EMANUEL MOÓR PIANOFORTE, as well as with other projects to do with the design of musical instruments.

### WORKS
*(selective list)*

Operas: La Pompadour (2, L. von Ferro, A. Moór, after Musset), Cologne, 22 Feb 1902; Andreas Hofer (4), Cologne, 9 Nov 1902; Hochzeitsglocken (1), Kassel, 2 Aug 1908; Der Goldschmied von Paris (3, T. Rehbaum); Hertha (3, D. Hollins), inc.
Orch: Serenade, str, 1881; 3 pf concs., 1886, 1888, 1906; 8 syms., 1893, 1895, 1895, 1898, 1901, 1906, 1906, 1908–10; Conc. Ov., 1893; 4 vn concs., 1905–7; 2 vc concs., 1905–6; Improvisation on an Orig. Theme, 1906; Triple Conc., vn, vc, pf, 1907; Rhapsody, vn, orch, 1907; 2 Rhapsodies, vc, orch, 1907, 1911; Pensées symphoniques, 1908; 5 Concertstück: pf, orch, ?1908; vn, vc, orch, 1909; pf, orch, 1909; vn, orch; va, orch; Chant funèbre, 1909; 5 Impressions, 1910; Chant héroïque, 1911; Harp Conc., 1913; Va Conc.
Vocal: La jeune tarantine, Mez, orch; Mass, solo vv, chorus, orch; Stabat mater, A, female vv, orch/org, 1911; Requiem, 4 solo vv, chorus, orch, 1916; songs
Chamber, incl. 2 pf qnts, 2 str qts, 2 pf trios, suites, 12 vn sonatas, 7 vc sonatas, 3 pf sonatas, works for harp

### BIBLIOGRAPHY
E. Blom: 'Emanuel Moór Pianoforte', *Grove 5*
J. S. Weissmann: 'Moór, Emanuel', *Grove 5* [with fuller work-list]
M. Pirani: *Emanuel Moór* (London, 1959)

JOHN S. WEISSMANN/R

**Moor, Karel** (*b* Belgrade, 26 Dec 1873; *d* Prague, 30 March 1945). Czech composer, conductor and writer on music. He studied at the Prague Organ School (1895), took the state examination in singing at Vienna (1896) and went to Castelli in Trieste for further lessons

(1900). Until 1923, when he settled permanently in Prague, he held a succession of brief conducting or teaching appointments throughout Czechoslovakia and Yugoslavia; he was conductor of the Czech PO (1902), a theatre conductor in Brno (1908), a schoolteacher in Stip (1916) and a choirmaster and bandmaster in Sinj and Sarajevo (1918–23). In Prague he held several jobs as a choirmaster or bandmaster. His music is late-Romantic, and his pan-Slavonic feelings are evident in the use of Russian, Serbian and Slovak themes.

### WORKS
*(selective list)*

Operas: Hjördis (4, F. Khol, after Ibsen), 1899, rev. 1901, Prague, 1905; Vij (1, Khol, after Gogol), 1901, Prague, 1903, rev. 1910; Poslední akord [The last chord] (I. L. Pohl), 1929, Prague, 1930; Pan amanuensis na venku [Mr amanuensis in the country] (Putování za novelou [In search of a novella]) (3, E. Pauk, after F. J. Rubeš), Prague, 1930; W. A. Mozart (3, F. Francl, S. Mann), Prague, 1934
Operettas: Pan profesor v pekle [Mr professor in hell] (3, A. Rajská-Smolíková, after K. Vaurien [E. Pauk]), 1906–7, Brno, 1908, rev. 1922; Výlet pana Broučka do měsíce [Mr Brouček's excursion to the moon] (3, V. Merhaut, Moor, after S. Čech), 1908–10, Jaroměř, 1910; Jeho krásná neznámá [His beautiful unknown woman] (3, K. Tobis, J. Kohout), Prague, 1926; Vzhůru do pekel [Up to hell] (operetta-revue, J. L. Novák), Prague, 1929; Svatební valčík [Bridal waltz] (3, Pohl), Prague, 1931; Noční Prahou [By night through Prague] (3, A. Přerovský-Caletka), Prague, 1933
Ballets: Golem, ballet pantomime (2, V. Pirnikov), 1928, Plzeň, 1929; Pan (3, Pirnikov), 1928, Plzeň, 1929
Orch: Polonia, sym. poem, 1897; Polské tance, 1897; Česká suita, 1926; 4 other sym. poems, suites, ovs.
Melodramas (P. Bezruč), cantata, many songs, choruses, inst pieces

Principal publishers: Dilia, Divadelní Zastup, Eberle, Lidové Umění, Švejda, Thalia, Universum

### WRITINGS
*Karl Martens* (Prague, 1906)
*Vzpomínky* [Reminiscences] (Plzeň, 1917)
*V dlani osudu* [In the hands of fate] (Nový Bydžov, 1947)
Articles in *Narodni obzor*

### BIBLIOGRAPHY
O. Sv.: 'Karel Moor', *Ohlas od Nežárky*, 1/20 (1920), 2
'Kapelník a hudební skladatel Karel Moor' [Kapellmeister and composer Moor], *Hudební zpravodaj*, ii/1 (1933), 3
M. Šimáček: 'Karel Moor šedesátníkem' [Moor's 60th birthday], *Československé divadlo*, xvi (1933), 292
H. D.: 'Jubilea', *Tempo*, xiii (1933–4), 237
J. Balda: 'Český muzikant Karel Moor', *Divadlo*, xxix (1943), 106

MÍLAN KUNA

**Moor, William.** *See* MORE, WILLIAM.

**Moorat, Joseph (Samuel Edward)** [Ward, Joseph S.] (*b* Bath, 26 Oct 1864; *d* Farnborough, Hants., 10 Aug 1938). English composer. He came of old Roman Catholic families, English on his mother's side and Armenian on his father's. Educated at Downside, he was a self-taught composer and an instinctive melodist. Since his father opposed a musical career he published his early works under the pseudonym 'Joseph S. Ward'. Later he collaborated with Laurence Housman on several musical plays, writing continuous, integrated music that was admired at home and abroad: it pleased Elgar, and critics praised it above Housman's literary contribution.

### WORKS
*(selective list)*

Musical plays: Bethlehem (L. Housman), 1902; Japonel: a Summer Day's Dream (Housman), 1903; Prunella, or Love in a Dutch Garden (Housman, Granville Barker), 1904; The Chinese Lantern (Housman), 1908; The Snow Queen (after Andersen), 1910; Nazareth (Housman), 1919; As You Like It (Shakespeare), 1920
Other works: c250 songs (Herrick, A. E. Housman, L. Housman, Moore, Shakespeare, Shelley, Swinburne, K. Tynan etc), 4 hymns

GRAHAM HATTON

**Moore, Douglas S(tuart)** (*b* Cutchogue, NY, 10 Aug 1893; *d* Greenport, NY, 25 July 1969). American composer, teacher and writer. His ancestors were among the first to settle in the north fork of Long Island in 1640, and it was there that Moore spent most of his free time. His operas are generally concerned with rural or pioneer life; his numerous songs and instrumental pieces often draw on folk genres. Moore's music studies began conventionally in Brooklyn; his first composition, characteristically a song (though without words), was probably written when he was 13. At Hotchkiss School, collaboration with his classmate Archibald MacLeish quickened his desire to become a composer, and at Yale (BA 1915, BM 1917) he continued to write college and popular songs, such as *Goodnight Harvard* and *Naomi, my Restaurant Queen*, while pursuing serious studies primarily with Parker. Moore then served in the navy, writing further popular songs, several of which were later included in the *Songs my Mother never Taught me*. In later years Moore sometimes regretted that he had not emulated the career of another Yale graduate, Cole Porter, but the commitment to serious music prevailed.

Leaving the navy in 1919 he remained in Paris to study the organ with Tournemire and composition with d'Indy and Boulanger. The harmonic and tonal influence of d'Indy is present in Moore's later work, but the relationship with Boulanger was less rewarding. In 1921 Moore accepted a position with the Cleveland Museum, where he initiated a concert series and played the organ; in Cleveland he also studied with Bloch and acted at the Playhouse. After another year of study in Paris on a Pulitzer Travelling Scholarship he was appointed in 1926 to teach at Barnard College, Columbia University, where he remained until his retirement in 1962. In his positions as executive officer from 1940 and MacDowell Professor from 1943 he reinvigorated the music department, and his administrative abilities, together with his bright urbane manner and catholic taste, made him an effective leader of many American composers' organizations, several of which he helped to found. Moore was president of both the National Institute and the American Academy of Arts and Letters, and he received honorary degrees from the following universities: Adelphi, Cincinnati, Columbia, Rochester and Yale. Other awards made to him included the Pulitzer Prize (1951) and a Guggenheim Fellowship.

Moore's most distinctive music is to be found in his vocal works, particularly the operas; *The Devil and Daniel Webster* and *The Ballad of Baby Doe* became staple items in the modern American repertory. His dramatic sense is evident in his choice of subject, keen timing and musical characterization, accurate colloquial prosody and dominating vocal line. In the later operas the instrumental accompaniments are more discriminate, effective and individual. Although Moore's purely instrumental work is unpretentious, it is far from trivial.

### WORKS
#### OPERAS
White Wings (chamber opera, P. Barry), 1935
The Headless Horseman (S. V. Benet), 1936
The Devil and Daniel Webster (Benet), 1938, New York, 18 May 1939
The Emperor's New Clothes (R. Abrashkin), 1948, New York, 19 Feb 1949, rev. 1956
Giants in the Earth (A. Sundgaard, after Rolvaag), 1950, 28 March 1951, rev. 1963
The Ballad of Baby Doe (folk opera, J. Latouche), 1956, Central City, Col., 7 July 1956
Gallantry ('soap opera', Sundgaard), 1957, New York, 15 March 1958

Wings of the Dove (E. Ayer), 1961, New York, 12 Oct 1961
The Greenfield Christmas Tree (Sundgaard), 1962, Baltimore, 8 Dec 1962
Carrie Nation (W. N. Jayme), 1966, Lawrence, Kansas, 28 April 1966

#### ORCHESTRAL
4 Museum Pieces, 1923; The Pageant of P. T. Barnum, 1924; Moby Dick, 1929; Comedy Ov. on an American Theme, 1932; Village Music, 1941; In memoriam, 1943; Sym., A, 1945; Farm Journal, 1947; Cotillion, 1952; 3 works for band

#### CHAMBER AND INSTRUMENTAL
Vn Sonata, 1929; Str Qt, 1933; Wind Qnt, 1942; Down East Suite, vn, pf, 1944; Cl Qnt, 1946 (1962); Pf Trio, 1953
c18 keyboard works incl. Passacaglia, org, 1939

#### VOCAL
Choral works incl. Simon Legree (V. Lindsay), 4 male vv (1938); Perhaps to Dream (Benet), 3 female vv (1938); Prayer for the United Nations (Benet); S/Bar, chorus, pf/orch (1943); Dedication (MacLeish), 6vv (1943)
Songs incl. Come Away, Death (Shakespeare), 1925; Sigh No More, Ladies (Shakespeare), 1927; 3 Sonnets of John Donne (1942); Adam Was my Grandfather (Benet), 1942; Not This Alone (P. Underwood), 1943; Under the Greenwood Tree (Shakespeare), 1944; Old Song (Roethke), 1947; Dear Dark Head (S. Ferguson), 1958

#### MISCELLANEOUS
Incidental music incl. Jesse James (J. M. Brown), Much Ado about Nothing (Shakespeare), Twelfth Night (Shakespeare), Oh, Tennessee (Moore), The Road to Rome (R. Sherwood)
Music for documentary films: Power in the Land (1940), Youth Gets a Break (1940), Bip Goes to Town (1941)

MSS in *US-Wc*; some smaller works, sketches, correspondence, *NYcu*
Principal publishers: Carl Fischer, G. Schirmer, Galaxy, Boosey & Hawkes

### WRITINGS
*Listening to Music* (New York, 1932, enlarged 2/1937)
*From Madrigal to Modern Music: a Guide to Musical Styles* (New York, 1942)

### BIBLIOGRAPHY
J. Edmunds and G. Boelzner: *Some Twentieth Century American Composers* (New York, 1959–60) [incl. bibliography]
H. Weitzel: *A Melodic Analysis of Selected Vocal Solos in the Operas of Douglas Moore* (diss., New York U., 1971)
D. J. Reagan: *Douglas Moore and his Orchestral Works* (diss., Catholic U. of America, 1972)

JACK BEESON

**Moore, Gerald** (*b* Watford, 30 July 1899). English pianist. His first piano lessons were from Wallis Bandey at Watford School of Music. In 1913 his family emigrated to Canada, where he studied further with Michael Hambourg and made his first recital appearances as soloist and accompanist. Returning to England in 1919, Moore had lessons with Mark Hambourg, son of his professor in Canada, undertook recital tours as an accompanist, and in 1921 began a long career with HMV as a recording artist. Sir Landon Ronald advised him to specialize in piano accompaniment, advice that Moore found congenial. In 1925 he began working as accompanist to John Coates, from whom he claims to have learnt his art and craft, and with whom he made his first important London appearances in 1926. From that time until his retirement from the platform in 1967, Moore accompanied virtually every eminent solo singer and instrumentalist in recitals, abroad as well as in Britain, and raised the art of accompanying at the piano from servility to the highest prestige. Moore's strength lay not only in the vastness of his repertory, nor even in the beauty of his legato playing, his subtle command of pedalling, and his mastery of tone colour, but more especially in his chameleonic empathy with every musical partner – whether Casals, Shalyapin or a young débutant recitalist – and his readiness to turn every partnership to musical advantage of a refreshing and inspiriting nature.

Moore was a magnificent interpreter of the duo-sonata repertory even though he never formed a regular partnership for such work. In later years he abandoned solo instrumental recitals to concentrate on his favourite repertory of the song. His lieder performances with Fischer-Dieskau and Schwarzkopf, especially in Schubert, Wolf and Richard Strauss, were paragons for their generation and vastly expanded the known recital repertory. A large number of them were recorded, including all Wolf's mature songs, over 500 by Schubert, and almost all Strauss's. Moore was equally expert and illuminating in Spanish *canciones* (notably with Los Angeles), and French *mélodies* with Maggie Teyte. His partnerships, in earlier years, with Gerhardt, Elisabeth Schumann, McCormack and Hotter were equally celebrated, so cunningly did Moore modulate his range of keyboard colour to match the voice of his partner. He began a subsidiary career as a lecture-recitalist when, during World War II, Myra Hess invited him to lecture on the art of accompaniment at her lunchtime National Gallery concerts. This lecture, repeated throughout Britain, assumed literary form as *The Unashamed Accompanist*, and caused further stir when Moore began to give annual lecture tours of the USA in 1954. He gave master classes on the interpretation of song as far afield as Salzburg, Barcelona, Stockholm, Helsinki, Tokyo, New York and Chicago. After his retirement he continued to make gramophone records and in 1971 was artistic director of an immensely successful summer song festival at London's South Bank arts centre.

The Grand Prix du Disque, usually given to outstanding soloists, was awarded four times to Moore as accompanist. He won the Cobbett Gold Medal in 1951, was made a CBE in 1954 and Hon. RAM in 1962, the year in which he was president of the Incorporated Society of Musicians. He received the honorary degrees of DLitt from Sussex University in 1968 and MusD from Cambridge University in 1973, when he was also awarded the Hugo Wolf Medal of Vienna. In addition to his books Moore has published folksong arrangements and piano transcriptions of favourite songs.

WRITINGS

*The Unashamed Accompanist* (London, 1943, rev. 2/1957)
'The Accompanist', *A Career in Music*, ed. R. Elkin (London and Bournemouth, 1950), 95
*Singer and Accompanist* (London, 1953)
*Am I too Loud? Memoirs of an Accompanist* (London, 1962)
*The Schubert Song Cycles* (London, 1975)
*Farewell Recital* (London, 1978)

BIBLIOGRAPHY

F. F. Clough and G. J. Cuming: 'Gerald Moore: Sketch for a Discography', *Audio & Record Review*, iv (1964), 81
WILLIAM S. MANN

**Moore, Grace** (*b* Jellicoe, Tenn., 5 Dec 1901; *d* nr. Copenhagen, 26 Jan 1947). American soprano. She studied singing with Marafioti in New York, and then appeared in revue and operetta. She sailed for Europe in 1926, and worked with Richard Berthélemy at Antibes, making her Opéra-Comique début in 1928. That year she also made her Metropolitan Opera début as Mimì, remaining there until the 1931–2 season, singing such roles as Lauretta, Tosca, Manon, Fiora (*L'amore dei tre re*) and Louise, and returning in 1934–5 and 1937–9. She appeared at Covent Garden in 1935 as Mimì, and continued to give concerts internationally until her death in an aeroplane accident. She made several films, the most important of which was *One Night of Love* (1934). Hers was a glamorous personality, earning the American accolade of 'star of stage, screen and radio';

and a sensuous, substantial voice, though it lacked technical finish.

BIBLIOGRAPHY

O. Thompson: *The American Singer* (New York, 1937), 384ff
G. Moore: *You're Only Human Once* (Garden City, NY, 1944/R1977)
A. Faria-Artsay: 'Grace Moore', *Hobbies*, lxvii (1963), 31
R. Celletti: 'Moore, Grace', *Le grandi voci* (Rome, 1964) [with opera discography by S. Smolian]
MAX DE SCHAUENSEE

**Moore, Thomas (i).** English 17th-century printer. He worked in London and was the first to introduce the 'new tied' note into musical typography, wherein the tails of quavers and semiquavers are joined instead of being printed separately. This device, together with the new rounded head, is used in the second book of *Comes amoris* (1688), the first book (1687) having the old lozenge-shape notes. In later years Moore was associated with J. Heptinstall, another London printer. In 1700 William Pearson made great improvements in the tied note, and Fougt, at a much later date, effected still greater improvements.

FRANK KIDSON/R

**Moore, Thomas (ii)** (*b* Dublin, 28 May 1779; *d* Sloperton Cottage, nr. Devizes, 26 Feb 1852). Irish poet and musician. A 'show child', as he described himself in his *Memoirs*, he gave recitations and took part in private theatricals; he published some verses by the age of 11, and at 14 contributed to the *Anthologia hibernica*. As a boy, he learnt French and Italian, and studied music independently and with his sister's teacher. In 1793 Trinity College, Dublin, was opened to Catholics, and Moore went there in 1794; while a student, he made his translation of the odes of Anacreon. Though a friend of Robert Emmet and other revolutionaries, he was not involved in any conspiracy; and in 1799 he went to London and entered Middle Temple as a law student. He made himself a popular figure socially with his verses and his singing; he also wrote the libretto for Michael Kelly's opera *The Gipsey Prince* (1801), and in 1802–3 wrote the words and often the music of many songs which won instant popularity. In 1803 he took up the post of registrar in the admiralty court of Bermuda, but soon relinquished it to a deputy and returned by way of Canada, where he composed his *Canadian Boat Song*. *Epistle Odes and Other Poems* appeared in 1806, and the scathing review in the *Edinburgh Review* by Francis (later Lord) Jeffrey led to a duel, interrupted by the police; Jeffrey's pistol was found to be unloaded, and the two men then became warm friends.

When in 1807 the publisher William Power, impressed by the success of George Thomson's collections, proposed a selection of Irish songs, Moore provided words and tunes, with accompaniments by Sir John Stevenson. The *Irish Melodies* began serial publication in 1808, eventually (after a dispute between Power and his brother James over rights) reaching ten numbers and a supplement by 1834. For the purpose, Moore raided the collections made by Edward Bunting (who was much upset), making only minor musical alterations but freely using originally light or comic melodies for new serious words. It was this collection above all which clinched Moore's already enormous popularity. In March 1811 he married Elizabeth (Bessie) Dyke, an Irish actress, and in the same year wrote the text and (with C. E. Horn) music for an unsuccessful comic opera, *M.P. or The Blue Stocking* and published a *Melologue upon National Music*. By now rich and famous, he could command an advance of £3000 for *Lalla Rookh*: the first edition sold out in a fortnight, and it was reprinted six times in as many months. In 1816 he published the first number of *Sacred Songs*, with music selected and composed by himself and Stevenson, and in 1818 there followed the first of *A Selection of Popular National Airs*. In the same year he learnt of his Bermudan deputy's embezzlement, and became liable for the loss of £6000. Refusing help, he retreated to Paris, also visiting Italy, before returning to England in 1822; by the writings of his exile years he was able to settle a reduced debt of £740. He also published lives of Sheridan (1825), Byron (1830) and Fitzgerald (1831). In his latter years, despite the happiness of his marriage and the support of friends who included Byron, Canning, Peel and Russell (who arranged a pension of £3000 for him), he was ill and depressed: all his five children were dead by 1846, and in these last years his mind began to fail.

Byron, who was devoted to him, wrote that, 'Moore has a peculiarity of talent, or rather talents, – poetry, music, voice, all his own; and an expression in each, which never was, nor will be, possessed by another' (Journal, 22 November 1813); and Sydney Smith called him, 'a gentleman of small stature, but full of genius, and a steady friend of all that is honourable and just' (*Edinburgh Review*, 1824). In his day, Moore won a vast following for his verses, songs and stories, partly through his personal charm as a reciter and singer; but an age which delighted in national lore and the revelation of folk melody was ready to find potency even in Moore's feeblest verses (Coleridge was a rare dissenter). Abroad, the enthusiasm for Scott and Burns and all things Scottish was easily extended to include Moore as their counterpart, with his apparent embodiment of the Irish soul in verse and song; and though the work includes covert references to Irish patriotism, the orientalism of *Lalla Rookh* played expertly on Romantic sensibilities that were still enraptured by the *1001 Nights* (whose pattern of a narrative framework for interpolated stories, here in verse, Moore copied). Berlioz, who first read Moore's work in translations by Gounet and others, found it full of 'splendid images' (*Mémoires*), and set and often quoted it.

Though not a methodical collector of Irish folk music, nor markedly skilful as an adapter or arranger, Moore did much by his personal qualities to kindle interest in these little-known tunes. As a poet, he appealed to a wide range of taste with the *Irish Melodies*, and the story-poems of *Lalla Rookh* long attracted composers for their simple and exotic subjects and their opportunities for colourful music.

### WORKS SET TO MUSIC
*(musical settings follow each work or portion of work)*

*The Gipsey Prince*, opera lib: M. Kelly, 1801
*M.P. or The Blue Stocking*, opera lib: C. E. Horn and Moore, 1811
*Lalla Rookh*, story with 4 interpolated poems (London, 1817): G. Bantock (sym. poem, 1902); F. Clay (choral work, 1877); Félicien David (opera, 1859); C. E. Horn (opera, 1818); J. Jongen (sym. poem, 1904); A. Rubinstein (opera: Feramors, 1863); A. M. Smith (ov., c1865); Spontini (tableaux vivants, 1821; opera: Núrmahal, 1822)
   'The Veiled Prophet of Khorassan': C. V. Stanford (opera, 1881)
   'Paradise and the Peri': J. F. Barnett (choral work, 1870); W. S. Bennett (fantasy-ov., 1862); I. I. Kryzhanovsky (cantata); Schumann (choral work, 1841–3); V. A. Zolotarev (choral work, 1900)
   'The Fire-worshippers': Bantock (choral work, 1892)
   'The Light of the Haram': A. G. Thomas (opera, 1879)

Songs to Moore poems by Berlioz, Cornelius, Duparc, Hindemith, J. Ireland, A. Jensen, A. Mackenzie, Mendelssohn, H. Parry, S. I. Taneyev, F. Walker, P. Warlock, Weber, etc

### EDITIONS AND COLLECTIONS
The melodies were collected and in some cases altered by Moore; the name of the composer of the accompaniment follows each setting.
*A Selection of Irish Melodies* (Irish trad.): J. Stevenson, nos.8–10 rev. H. Bishop (London, 1808–34, enlarged 4/1859 with accs. by M. Balfe, 8/1893); Glover (Dublin, 1860); rev. and ed. G. A. Macfarren (London, 1859–61)
*Sacred Songs* (Irish trad.): Stevenson (London, 1816)
*A Selection of Popular National Airs* (Irish trad.): Stevenson, nos.2–6 rev. Bishop (London and Dublin, 1818–28) [incl. Moore's *Melologue upon National Music*, orig. pubd 1811]

### BIBLIOGRAPHY
J. Russell, ed.: *Memoirs, Journals and Correspondence of Thomas Moore* (London, 1853–6)
J. Power: *Notes from the Letters of Thomas Moore to his Music-publisher* (New York, 1854)
R. Prothero, ed.: *The Works of Lord Byron: Letters and Journals* (London, 1898–1901)
S. Gwynn: *Thomas Moore* (London, 1905)
P. H. Muir: 'Thomas Moore's *Irish Melodies* 1808–1834', *The Colophon*, xv (1933), Oct
W. F. Trench: *Tom Moore* (Dublin, 1934)
S. MacCall: *Thomas Moore* (Dublin, 1936)

JOHN WARRACK

**Moorehead** [Moorhead], **John** (*b* Ireland, *c*1760; *d* nr. Deal, March 1804). Irish violinist and composer. He received his first musical instruction in Ireland, but went to England when young and was for several years engaged in the orchestras of various country theatres. He was one of the violins at the Worcester Festival of 1794, and in 1795 was in London as principal viola at Sadler's Wells Theatre. In 1798 he was engaged in the orchestra at Covent Garden and soon after employed to compose songs and overtures for that theatre.

In 1802 he became insane and, after a series of assaults and property destruction, was confined successively in Tothill Fields Prison and Northampton House, Clerkenwell. On his liberation he entered the navy as a common sailor, and was quickly promoted to bandmaster, but a short time afterwards he hanged himself in a fit of insanity.

His brother, Alexander Moorehead, was also a violinist of merit and led the orchestra at Sadler's Wells Theatre; he also became insane, and died in an asylum at Liverpool in 1803.

### WORKS
*(all published and first performed in London, unless otherwise stated)*

THEATRICAL
*(all publications are vocal or pf scores; MS libs in US-SM)*
CG – *Covent Garden Theatre*    SW – *Sadler's Wells Theatre*
The Philosopher's Stone [? = The Philosopher, or The Turns of Fortune (comedy)], SW, 1795
Birds of a Feather, or Buz and Mum (comic piece, ?Moorehead), SW, 25 July 1796; 2 songs (1796); collab. Attwood
The Naval Pillar, or Britannia Triumphant (interlude, T. J. Dibdin), CG, 7 Oct 1799 (1799), lib pubd; incl. music of Calcott, Linley
The Volcano, or Rival Harlequins (pantomime, T. J. Dibdin, C. Farley), CG, 23 Dec 1799, ov. (c1800), lib pubd
Boadicea, or The British Amazon (serious pantomime, C. Dibdin), SW, 14 April 1800
Old Fools, or Love's Stratagem (burletta, C. Dibdin), SW, 14 April 1800
Il Bondocani, or The Caliph Robber (comic opera, T. J. Dibdin), CG, 15 Nov 1800 (1801), lib pubd; collab. Attwood
Harlequin's Tour, or The Dominion of Fancy (pantomime, T. J. Dibdin), CG, 22 Dec 1800 (c1800), lib pubd; collab. Attwood
Perouse, or The Desolate Island (pantomime, J. Fawcett), CG, 28 Feb 1801, ov. pubd (1801), lib pubd; collab. Davy
Harlequin Benedick, or Mother Shipton's Ghost (pantomime, C. Dibdin), SW, 29 June 1801, lib pubd
The Cabinet (comic opera, T. J. Dibdin), CG, 9 Feb 1802 (1802), lib pubd; collab. Reeve, Davy, Corri, Braham
Speed the Plough, or The Return of Peace (musical play, C. Dibdin), SW, 1 May 1802

Family Quarrels (comic opera, T. J. Dibdin), CG, 18 Dec 1802 (c1802), lib pubd; collab. Braham, Reeve

Harlequin's Habeas, or The Hall of Spectres (pantomime, T. J. Dibdin), CG, 27 Dec 1802, ov. pubd (1802), lib pubd; collab. Braham, Davy

OTHER WORKS

Duo concertante no.1, 2 vn (1799)

Several singly pubd songs

Tunes in contemporary collections, incl. Busby's Monthly Musical Record (1800), Hime's Pocket Book, rec/vn (Dublin, c1800)

BIBLIOGRAPHY

T. J. Dibdin: *Reminiscences*, i (London, 1827), 317ff

L. M. Middleton: 'Moorehead, John', *DNB*

C. Dibdin: *Professional & Literary Memoirs*, ed. G. Speaight (London, 1956), 42f

W. H. HUSK/FRANK KIDSON/R

**Moorish music.** *See* MAURITANIA.

**Moors** [Mors, Morss, de Moer, de Moor]. South Netherlands family of organists, organ builders and instrument makers. The Lier branch of the family included Mark (i) (*d* Lier, 1525), who built a 'manucordium' in 1508 for the future Emperor Charles V; Hendrik, who built a small organ for Charles in 1517; Mark (ii) (*d* after 1535), who was a member of Charles's chapel; and several organists of the church of St Gommaar: Bernhard (i), Bernhard (ii) (*d* 1558; son of Mark (i)), and Bernhard (iii) (*d* 1597; possibly the son of Bernhard (ii)).

The Antwerp line was founded by Anton (i) (*d* Antwerp, 1539), who was organist of the abbey of St Michiel in the city, as well as a maker of organs and other instruments. He built small organs for the royal chapels in Brussels (1514) and The Hague (1515), and a clavichord for Eleonore of Habsburg, Charles V's sister, in 1516; in 1529 he was working for Margaret of Austria. Of the sons of Anton (i), the organ builder Cornelis (*b* Antwerp, c1500; *d* Antwerp, 1557) remained in his home town, but the organ builder Anton (ii) (*b* Antwerp, c1500; *d* before August 1562) and the organists Jakob (*b* Antwerp, c1515; *d* ?Berlin, between 1585 and 1602) and Hieronymus (*b* Antwerp, 1521; *d* Schwerin, 16 Dec 1598) went to northern Germany. Cornelis built organs for St Michiel, Ghent (before 1542), St Walburga, Oudenaarde (1542–3), St Katharina, Mechlin (before 1543) and elsewhere. Hieronymus was court organist to Duke Albrecht of Mecklenburg by 1538, and also organist of Schwerin Cathedral from 1552. Hieronymus's son Anton (iii) (*b* Schwerin, c1555; *d* Rostock, 1619) was organist of St Jakobi, Rostock from 1573 to 1613, as well as a court musician at Güstrow from time to time. Jakob entered the service of the court at Mecklenburg about 1548, became court organist to Elector August of Saxony in Dresden (1554), and moved to Berlin in 1557 to be organist at the court of Elector Joachim II Hector of Brandenburg. Jakob's son Joachim (*b* ?Berlin, c1560; *d* after 1605) was court organist, first in Dresden, 1579–81, and subsequently in Berlin. Anton (ii)'s major work was a large new organ for Onze Lieve Vrouw in Dendermonde. He worked also for Duke Albrecht of Mecklenburg, from 1555 to 1557, in Schwerin Cathedral (major repairs and enlargement) and Güstrow Cathedral in 1558, and for Elector Joachim II Hector in Berlin from 1559 to 1560. The specification of the 'Mary Organ' in Berlin suggests that it is also the work of Anton (ii) . On the evidence of the Schwerin contract of 1555, Anton (ii) was among those leading Brabantine

organ builders who had improved on the indigenous type of instrument by grafting on to it the 'new and strange voices' brought to the Low Countries by the Rhenish masters Hans Suys (*see* SUISSE) and PETER BREISIGER.

BIBLIOGRAPHY

A. Werckmeister: *Organum Gruningense redivivum* (Quedlinburg and Aschersleben, 1705, 2/1932)

O. Kade: 'Die Organistenfamilie Mors im 16. Jahrhundert', *MMg*, xxix (1897), 43

W. Haacke: *Die Entwicklungsgeschichte des Orgelbaus im Lande Mecklenburg-Schwerin* (Wolfenbüttel and Berlin, 1935)

H. H. Steves: 'Der Orgelbauer Joachim Wagner', *AMf*, iv (1939), 321; v (1940) 17, 230

J.-A. Stellfeld: 'Bronnen tot de geschiedenis der Antwerpse clavecymbelen orgelbouwers in de XVIe en XVIIe eeuwen', *Vlaams Jb voor muziekgeschiedenis*, iv (1942), 1–110

B. de Keyser:'Figuren uit vlaanderens orgelhistorie', *De schalmei*, iii (1948), 78

M. A. Vente: *Die brabanter Orgel* (Amsterdam, 1958, 2/1963)

——: 'Mors', *MGG*

HANS KLOTZ

**Moos, Paul** (*b* Bad Buchau, nr. Ulm, 22 March 1863; *d* Raeren, nr. Aachen, 27 Feb 1952). German writer on music and aesthetics. Following early commercial training he studied at the universities of Tübingen and Munich and at the Akademie der Tonkunst, Munich (with, among others, Rheinberger and Thuille). After sojourns in Italy and in Berlin, where he was much influenced by Eduard von Hartmann, he settled at Ulm in 1899 as a freelance writer on music. In 1929 he received an honorary doctorate from the University of Erlangen and in 1932 retired to Göppingen. His importance lies in his work on the history of music aesthetics and his determined championship of it as a discipline. He allied himself not with the psychological and empirical view of aesthetics, but with the concrete idealism perfected, in his view, by Hartmann, and first applied to music by the Danish scientist Hans Christian Oersted (1777–1851). Moos defined aesthetics as the intellectual penetration of the symbolic content of a work of art as represented in ideas perceived through the senses; he maintained that an understanding of aesthetics was to be achieved more easily through a philosophical approach than by historical or artistic studies, since 'the intellectual–metaphysical dimension exists only in the consciousness and therefore eludes the empirical grasp'. Though he greatly admired Hartmann's philosophy, he did not accept it uncritically, as is shown by his corrections to Hartmann's conception of the emotions and affections in music, as well as in his amplification of Hartmann's one-sided remarks about vocal music. It is work such as this that highlights Moos's particular significance: through the powerful innate musicianship that he brought to bear on his abilities as a thinker, music occupies a central position in his work as an aesthetician.

WRITINGS

*Moderne Musikästhetik in Deutschland: historisch-kritische Übersicht* (Berlin and Leipzig, 1902; rev. and enlarged, 1922 as *Die Philosophie der Musik von Kant bis Eduard von Hartmann*)

*Richard Wagner als Ästhetiker* (Berlin and Leipzig, 1906)

'E. T. A. Hoffmann als Musikästhetiker', *Die Musik*, vi (1906–7), 67

'Bernard Shaw und sein Wagner-brevier', *Die Musik*, vii (1907–8), 49

'Psychologische Musikästhetik', *ZIMG*, ix (1907–8), 100

'Volkelt's Einfühlungslehre', *Riemann-Festschrift* (Leipzig, 1909), 40

'Die Ästhetik des Rhythmus bei Theodor Lipps', *IMusSCR*, iii Vienna 1909, 345

'Volkelts ästhetische Normen', *Festschrift . . . Rochus Freiherrn von Liliencron* (Leipzig, 1910/R1970), 138

*Die deutsche Ästhetik der Gegenwart: mit besonderer Berücksichtigung der Musikästhetik*, i: *Die psychologische Ästhetik* (Berlin and Leipzig, 1920); ii: *Die deutsche Ästhetik der Gegenwart: Versuch*

*einer kritischen Darstellung* (Berlin, 1931)
'Beziehungen der jüngsten Musikwissenschaft zur Ästhetik', *Kongressbericht: Leipzig 1925*, 405, 414
'Gehören Gluck, Händel und Bach zur barocken Kunst ihrer Zeit', *GfMKB, Lüneburg 1950*, 195
'Bemerkungen zum Thema "Sinn und Wesen in der Musik"', *Mf*, iv (1951), 205
*Die Lehre vom Erhabenen in der deutschen Ästhetik* (MS, see Mies)

BIBLIOGRAPHY
A. Drews: 'Die Philosophie der Musik', *Die Musik*, xv (1922–3), 356
J. H. Wetzel: 'Köpfe im Profil, xiii: Paul Moos', *Die Musik*, xviii (1925–6), 485
H. Engel: 'Paul Moos zum Gedächtnis', *Mf*, v (1952), 361
P. Mies: 'Paul Moos zum Gedächtnis: aus seinen Briefen', *Musicae scientiae collectanea: Festschrift Karl Gustav Fellerer* (Cologne, 1973), 386

based on *MGG* (xvi, 1288–9) by permission of Bärenreiter
WOLFGANG SCHMIDT-BRUNNER

**Moosburg Gradual** (*D-Mu* 2° 156). *See* SOURCES, MS, §II, 8.

**Mooser, (Jean Pierre Joseph) Aloys** (*b* Fribourg, baptized 27 June 1770; *d* Fribourg, 19 Dec 1839). Swiss organ builder and piano maker. He was the son of the organ builder Joseph Anton Moser (1731–92), of Niederhelfenschwil, St Gall, who had settled in Fribourg in the 1760s. He studied with his father, who himself had been schooled in the south German organ-building tradition under Johann Michael Bihler of Konstanz, and was thus not a pupil of Silbermann as is sometimes erroneously recorded. Working in Fribourg, he became the best-known Swiss organ builder of the first half of the 19th century. His organs reflect a south German and early Romantic style. The source of his reputation is the large organ in St Nicolas's Cathedral in Fribourg (1824–34), whose Vox humana, with Swell mechanism, aroused special enthusiasm. Its fame, in fact, rests not only on its quality as an instrument, but above all on a pastoral fantasia, the 'Gewitter', by the cathedral organist Jacques Vogt (1810–69), which has remained on cathedral recital programmes.

Mooser was also well known as a piano maker; the Parisian piano maker Erard attempted to interest him in a collaboration. He had sons who were organ and piano makers, including Joseph, Alexander and Moritz, but their reputations waned after their father's death.

BIBLIOGRAPHY
R. A. Mooser: 'Aloys Mooser, facteur d'orgues à Fribourg', *Nouvelles étrennes fribourgeoises*, lxviii (1935), 119
FRIEDRICH JAKOB

**Mooser, R(obert) Aloys** (*b* Geneva, 20 Sept 1876; *d* Geneva, 24 Aug 1969). Swiss musicologist and music critic. His mother was Russian and his father, Jean-Louis (who worked for a time in St Petersburg), was a son of the organ and piano maker Joseph Mooser (1794–1876). He studied the organ with O. Barblan and theory in Geneva, and then (1896) composition with Balakirev and orchestration with Rimsky-Korsakov in St Petersburg, concurrently working there as organist at the French Protestant church (1896–1909), music critic of the French periodical *Journal de St-Pétersbourg* and a member of the directorate of the Imperial Theatre (1899–1904). Subsequently he was music critic of the Geneva periodical *La Suisse* (1909–62) and director of Auditions du Jeudi, the Geneva concert series of modern music (1915–21). The independent periodical *Dissonances* which he directed, edited and published (1923–46) was particularly concerned with modern,

Swiss and Russian works and strenuously opposed German and Italian fascism during the war. Geneva University awarded him an honorary doctorate in 1956.

Mooser (with Willi Schuh) was the leading music critic in Switzerland, and in the French-speaking area his fame was comparable to Ansermet's; his criticism shows an independence of all schools and doctrines. He enthusiastically supported Honegger, Frank Martin and Malipiero, and though he never appreciated Schoenberg (whom he compared with Meyerbeer), he nevertheless recognized the importance of such figures as Webern, Apostel, Berg, Lutosławski and Nono. His restrained opposition to Messiaen, Boulez, Stockhausen and serial music of the 1960s showed him (in his 80s) to be open to all contemporary developments and prepared to make a thorough study of music otherwise alien to him. His highly informative studies of Russian music history have become standard works in the subject, and his study of the Genevan composer and violinist Gaspard Fritz gives a multi-faceted account of Genevan musical life from 1750 to 1850.

WRITINGS
*Contribution à l'histoire de la musique russe: l'opéra comique français en Russie au XVIIIᵉ siècle* (Geneva, 1932, 2/1954)
'Aloys Mooser, facteur d'orgues à Fribourg', *Nouvelles étrennes fribourgeoises*, lxviii (1935), 119
'Un musicien espagnol en Russie: contribution à la biographie de V. Martin y Soler et à la bibliographie de ses oeuvres', *RMI*, xl (1936), 432
'Violonistes-compositeurs italiens en Russie au XVIIIe siècle', *RMI*, xlii–lii (1938–50)
*Opéras, intermezzos, ballets, cantates, oratorios joués en Russie durant le XVIIIᵉ siècle* (Geneva, 1945, 3/1964)
*Regards sur la musique contemporaine, 1921–1946* (Lausanne, 1946)
*Annales de la musique et des musiciens en Russie au XVIIIᵉ siècle* (Geneva, 1948–51)
*Panorama de la musique contemporaine, 1947–1953* (Geneva, 1953)
*Aspects de la musique contemporaine, 1953–1957* (Geneva, 1957)
*Visage de la musique contemporaine, 1957–1961* (Paris, 1962)
'Grétry sur les scènes russes du XVIIIe siècle', *Liber amicorum Charles van den Borren* (Antwerp, 1964), 114
'L'apparition des oeuvres de Mozart en Russie', *MJb 1967*, 226
*Deux violonistes genevois: Gaspard Fritz (1716–1783), Christian Haensel (1766–1850)* (Geneva, 1968)
'Un musicista veneziano in Russia: Calterizo Cavos', *NRMI*, iii (1969), 13

BIBLIOGRAPHY
*SML*
*Schweizer Musikbuch*, ii: *Musikerlexikon* (Zurich, 1939), 144
C. Tappolet: 'La musique à Genève au XIXe et au XXe siècle', *L'histoire de Genève de 1798 à 1931* (Geneva, 1956) 638
M. Mila: 'R.-Aloys Mooser (1876–1969)', *NRMI*, iii (1969), 902
A. Jacquier: 'Hommage à Aloys Mooser (1876–1969)', *SMz*, cx (1970), 160
C. Tappolet: *La vie musicale à Genève au dix-neuvième siècle (1814–1918)* (Geneva, 1972), 136
JÜRG STENZL

**Moraes Pedroso, Manuel de.** *See* PEDROSO, MANUEL DE MORAES.

**Morago, Estêvão Lopes** (*b* Vallecas [now in Madrid], *c*1575; *d* probably at Orgens, nr. Viseu, after 1630). Portuguese composer of Spanish birth. He studied from 1592 to 1596 with Filipe de Magalhães at the Colégio dos Moços do Coro maintained by Évora Cathedral and received his bachelor's degree on 3 March 1596. On 15 August 1599 he was appointed *mestre de capela* of the cathedral at Viseu, Portugal, probably on the recommendation of the new bishop, who had been a canon of Évora Cathedral. He became a priest and a licentiate before 27 September 1605, when the bishop instituted him in a benefice of the church of S Pedro de Cota, to which a half-pay canonry at the cathedral was added on 5 January 1608. After a quarter-century as *mestre de capela* he wished to see through the press a substantial amount of his church music, and on 14 January 1626 the Viseu chapter gave him a month's leave to negotiate personally with the royal printer at Lisbon. Unable to secure a favourable contract, he returned to Viseu to supervise the copying of one of the two surviving manuscript collections of his music, the title-page of which is dated 15 August 1628. Immediately afterwards he seems to have left for a short visit to Spain. He then continued as *mestre de capela* until April 1630. Later that year, in a gift copy of Magalhães's *Officium defunctorum*, he signed himself a friar minor, possibly as a result of his retiring to the Franciscan house at Orgens, two miles from Viseu.

The two surviving manuscript miscellanies of Morago's liturgical music (both in *P-Va*) are the above-mentioned collection dated 1628, which is a Vesperal of 111 folios containing three psalms, 18 hymns and four odd-verse *Magnificat* settings, and a 149-folio *Livro da Coresma* (Coleção 771), which is, however, misnamed, because the 81 compositions in it include in addition to Lenten music various works for Sundays in Advent, Christmas, Purification and the Office of the Dead. 35 motets (28 for four voices, five for five, one for six and one for double choir), eight four-part Christmas responsories, three psalms (two for four voices and one for double choir), 18 four-part hymns and four *Magnificat* settings (three for four voices and one for six) are edited in PM, ser.A, iv (1961). The sustained popularity of 12 of Morago's hymns, the texts changed to agree with Urban VIII's revision, can be demonstrated by their having been copied into 18th-century partbooks (of which only the tenor book is now extant, at Viseu). The second of his invitatories for Christmas matins, *Christus natus est nobis*, survives at Viseu with an added continuo part. But like his teacher and his Portuguese contemporaries Brito, Cardoso and Lobo, he always remained too much the Peninsular conservative to write for continuo, to forgo imitation and the equality of the voices or to venture far into chromaticism. For dramatic effect, however, he did place adjacent to each other chords as disparate as those of G minor and E major and Bb and A major. To add to the harmonic tension he frequently changed accidentals in successive imitative entries (occasionally he wrote an inverted final entry). Many chordal sequences are found in his more expressive motets, as also are chains of suspensions and passing and changing notes. Occasionally he violated the spirit of Renaissance music by mixing the extremes of fast and slow motion in the same motet, and six of his eight Christmas responsories are in fast triple metre. His shorter motets are frequently monothematic. He sometimes confirmed his endings with long pedals. Despite the triple canon closing his *Magnificat* on the 8th tone he could not begin to match the contrapuntal pyrotechnics of his Spanish contemporaries Vivanco and Aguilera de Heredia; nor was he fastidious about avoiding forbidden consecutives.

BIBLIOGRAPHY

M. Joaquim: 'Um inédito musical', *Brotéria*, xxx (1940), 497
——: *Em louvor do grande polifonista Estêvão Lopes Morago* (Oporto, 1948)
ROBERT STEVENSON

**Moral, Pablo del** (*fl* 1765–1805). Spanish violinist and composer. In 1777 he was violinist at the royal chapel of St Cayetan in Madrid; by then he had also been standing in for more than eight years for violinists attached to the theatrical companies of Madrid. In 1778,

after public competition, he was officially named 'violinist of the Madrid theatres', and about the same time began to compose *tonadillas*. In 1790, again after public competition, he was appointed 'composer to the theatres of Madrid', with the responsibility of composing 40 *tonadillas* each year 'as well as everything else needed in the way of music'. In March 1792 he was obliged to abandon the post for reasons of health, but by April 1797 he was able to resume. In 1804 a new post of theatre composer was created, identical with Moral's, and awarded to the Italian G. M. Francesconi, a mediocre but conceited composer, much given to intrigue; Moral, affronted, resigned on 17 April 1805 and disappeared from public life.

In Moral's time the *tonadilla escénica* lost its directness and simplicity, often becoming a miniature comic opera with Italianate music. Subirá published one of his *tonadillas*, *La ópera casera* (1799), in which there is some virtuoso vocal writing entirely operatic in character. About 150 of his *tonadillas* survive, as well as an opera *La dama inconstante*, several *sainetes* and other theatre music (*E-Mm*); he also composed sacred music, of which two masses, two Compline settings, a *Salve regina* and a litany are known (*MO*).

BIBLIOGRAPHY

*LaborD*
J. Subirá: *La tonadilla escénica* (Madrid, 1928–30)
——: *La tonadilla escénica: sus obras y sus autores* (Barcelona, 1933)
JOSÉ LÓPEZ-CALO

**Morales, Cristóbal de** (*b* Seville, *c*1500; *d* ?Marchena, between 4 Sept and 7 Oct 1553). Spanish composer, widely recognized as the first major composer from the Iberian peninsula and the most important figure in early 16th-century Spanish sacred music.

1. Life. 2. Posthumous reputation. 3. Works.

1. LIFE. The addition of the Latinized 'hyspalensis' after his name in contemporary documents signifies that he was born in Seville. Long after he had left his native city and won fame elsewhere, he remembered his Sevillian origin with what now seems a certain fierce pride. In Rome, for instance, where in 1544 he published 16 masses in sumptuous twin folio volumes, he signed himself 'Christophorus Morales Hyspalensis', not only in the Latin dedications but also at the beginning of each mass.

Morales's pride in being known as a Sevillian seems not misplaced, for he was the beneficiary of an exceptionally rich musical heritage. Two 15th-century theoretical treatises, one by Fernand Esteban and the other anonymous (1480), show that musical studies at Seville were equal to those at Salamanca during that period. The first two printed Spanish music books (1492 and 1494) appeared at Seville – the chief city of the world, according to the printer's boast on the title-page of the former. Of the three principal composers in Spain during Morales's earliest years, Anchieta, Francisco de Peñalosa and Pedro de Escobar, two held official positions at Seville Cathedral: Peñalosa, the Spanish composer whose technique most closely resembles that of Morales, was a canon; and Escobar became *maestro de capilla* in 1507. Though not so widely known as Peñalosa, whom Leo X called to Rome to serve in the papal choir, Escobar was known in his own century as far away as Guatemala. Morales thus had no need to look beyond Seville for musical instruction. He may also have profited from the instruction of Escobar's successor as *maestro de capilla*, Pedro Fernández de Castilleja, who was appointed on 13 August 1514 and remained in the post for 35 years.

Morales's education extended beyond music. His lengthy Latin dedications (*Missarum liber primus* and *Missarum liber secundus*, 1544) show him a master of Ciceronian prose, suggesting that he must have had a thorough classical training. In the first of these dedications he in fact claimed that from a very early age (*ab ineunte aetate*) he had wholeheartedly addressed himself to the liberal arts (Trivium and Quadrivium); he had worked sedulously in them so that no-one engaged in his own art might despise his preparation in the others.

His first professional appointment outside Seville was as *maestro de capilla* of Avila, the oldest Gothic cathedral in Spain. He assumed the post on 8 August 1526 with an annual salary of 100 ducats (37,500 maravedís). Two years later he transferred to Plasencia with a much higher salary (60,000 maravedís) and a half prebend that obliged him to attend chapter meetings until 7 May 1529. On 4 February 1530 the Plasencia chapter granted him a month's leave to attend his sister's wedding in Seville and 40 gold ducats to defray the costs of his sister's dowry; he overstayed his leave and his salary was temporarily suspended on 31 March. By 9 December 1531 he had resigned, whereupon the post was offered to Diego Bruxelas at only 50,000 maravedís. Morales probably went next to Naples, but his first documented appointment in Italy was as a singer in the papal choir at Rome (1 September 1535).

The papal choir had included Spanish singers a full century before Morales; the Spanish popes, Calixtus III and Alexander VI, had particularly favoured them. Julius II (1512) tried to end the dominant position of the French and Spanish in the choir, but his successor, Clement VII, continued to rely heavily on them. Morales therefore found himself but one of several Spaniards when he joined the choir, and before he left a decade later two more had been added. The Sistine diaries show that a strong clannish spirit prevailed among the Spaniards, and it is likely that they were Morales's closest personal associates. He acknowledged in his *Missarum liber secundus* that he owed his appointment to the personal interest of Paul III. During the ten years he was in the choir, Paul III (who became pope in 1534) enlarged it from 24 to 33, raised the pay of its members and imposed new regulations. Because of his exceptional liberality to singers, later historians of the papal choir looked back on his tenure as a golden age. Morales profited greatly from the pope's musical interests.

Although Morales was described on joining the choir as 'clericus hispalensis d[iocesis]', he was probably not a presbyter but a deacon at most. In order to share in all the monetary gifts and feasts from which the choir benefited beyond the regular salary, he paid ten ducats into the chest on the day of his formal admission, to be divided among the choir's older members. His own regular salary was fixed at eight ducats a month. He was also given a servant and, when he travelled in the pope's retinue to Nice, Loreto or Bologna, a horse. His actual earnings always greatly exceeded his official salary. On Charles V's entry into Rome in April 1536, for instance, he had an opportunity to sing for the emperor and to share with the other choir members a handsome gift. One reason for the rapid diffusion of his own music throughout Europe was the opportunity to perform it

frequently before the greatest rulers.

Morales's earliest dated composition for an official event is the six-part motet *Jubilate Deo omnis terra*, written for the peace celebration at Nice in June 1538. The pope, though unable to bring Charles V and François I face to face at Nice, at least prevailed upon them to sign a ten years' peace treaty: Morales's motet was sung in celebration of that happy event. It has two long movements throughout which one voice repeats the word 'gaudeamus' to a Gregorian ostinato figure while the other five discourse on the merits of the pope, the emperor and the king. The work survived its occasion, remaining popular in Spain and elsewhere even after Morales's death. Valderrábano (1547) and Fuenllana (1554) made intabulations of it for one and two vihuelas respectively, and it was published in vocal partbooks in Lyons (1542) and Venice (1549).

Among Morales's other occasional compositions is the six-part motet *Gaude et laetare ferrariensis civitas*, sung at Ferrara Cathedral on Sunday, 9 March 1539, to celebrate the elevation of Ippolito II d'Este to a cardinalate. Ippolito had been named at the consistory of 20 December 1538, and had used the intervening time to prepare for the public announcement, made at Ferrara with pomp and splendour enhanced by poems, congratulatory addresses and musical compliments. Morales again used an ostinato construction: one voice sings the Gregorian chant associated with the words 'Magnificabo nomen tuum in aeternum' while the other five praise the cardinal and the city of Ferrara. This and other occasional compositions of Morales are by no means inferior in quality to his other works.

As a daily record of the choir's activities was kept, it is still possible to reconstruct Morales's activities during nearly the entire period of his membership. The choir occasionally performed in the Sistine Chapel but more often in the Pauline Chapel or in churches outside the Vatican. It consisted entirely of men; the treble parts were sung by falsettists. Morales himself was once thought to have been a falsettist (like many other Spaniards in the choir during his century), but evidence from the Sistine diaries seems to show that he was a baritone. His masses of 1544, written specially for the choir, give some idea of the skills of its singers.

Morales's first printed works appeared in 1539: two four-part motets published by Moderne at Lyons as part of the anthology *Motteti del fiore* (*RISM* 1539[11]). In that year his madrigal *Ditimi o si o no* was published at the instance of Arcadelt, who was then *maestro* of the Cappella Giulia and who a year later joined Morales in the papal choir. Morales published no other secular music, nor music with Italian text. In 1540 three of his masses were printed by Scotto at Venice. After such small beginnings a steady stream of his works flowed for the next 20 years from music presses at Lyons, Wittenberg, Nuremberg, Augsburg, Antwerp, Milan, Rome and above all Venice.

Morales's next important journey was in September 1539, when he accompanied the pope on a month's trip to Loreto. On 4 April 1540, having served his first five-year term in the choir (after which, according to the choir constitution, he was entitled to ten months' paid leave in his own country), he left for Spain. He was in Rome again on 25 May 1541 but was not singing regularly again until the autumn. His second five years in Rome are notable for the wide publication his works achieved, but his health seems to have declined during that period. In 1536 he was absent for nine days from the choir because of illness, in 1537 for 14, in 1543 for 35 and in 1544 for 90.

Morales's last extensive journey as papal chorister took place in spring 1543. On 4 March the pope left Rome, reaching Bologna two weeks later and until 1

CHRISTOPHORI
MORALIS HYSPA
LENSIS MISSARVM
·LIBER SECVNDVS·

*Title-page of Morales's 'Missarum liber secundus' (1544) showing the composer presenting the volume to Pope Paul III*

July the papal retinue moved through northern Italy. On 16 May Morales obtained special leave for a short excursion to Genoa, where Emperor Charles V was expected. The exact nature of Morales's private business cannot be determined, but he may have spent his time exploring possibilities for a change of service from the pope to the emperor. The pope met the emperor at Busseto for four days from 21 June. As at Nice, the meeting was a spectacular event: Titian painted the pope and emperor, and the noblemen of Spain and Italy attended performances by the papal and imperial choirs. Soon thereafter the papal choir members were rewarded with three months' vacation. In spite of this and other opportunities for recuperation, Morales was ill during the winters of 1543–4 and 1544–5, losing respectively 36 and 42 consecutive days.

Several other members of the choir, such as Festa and Arcadelt, were prolific composers, and Morales also had opportunities for contact with those in Paul III's employ who were eminent in the other arts. Nevertheless, when the time came in 1545 for his second ten months' leave with pay, he resigned from the choir. His dedications in both 1544 books of masses show him to have been

searching actively for more lucrative employment. In the first he promised Cosimo de' Medici, the Grand Duke of Tuscany, to dedicate all future works to him if he would take him under his protection. That Duke Cosimo did not rise to the offer is evident from the second dedication, in which Morales boldly asked the pope to confer an ecclesiastical dignity on him. The pope, however, delayed doing so, giving lucrative benefices to three others in the choir, Arcadelt, Danckerts and Ivo Barry, none of whom had distinguished himself as a composer of sacred music; Arcadelt was, moreover, Morales's junior in the choir by some five years. Even the small benefice in Cuenca diocese conferred on Morales some time before April 1545 slipped out of his hands in that month.

Morales left Rome on 1 May 1545. He may have returned to Seville: Guerrero wrote (*Viage de Hierusalem*, 1590) that he studied with Morales in Seville when he was 18 (in 1545). On 31 August, having passed the prescribed tests, Morales became *maestro de capilla* of the Spanish primatial cathedral at Toledo. The Toledo governing body set his annual salary at 43,500 maravedís – a sum much larger than that paid to the previous *maestro* – because of his reputation gained from the publication in Rome of his two books of masses; but it was little more than he had earned at Avila. According to an agreement with the Toledo authorities he was obliged to board and lodge the choirboys out of the sum paid to him. The following year, 1546, was one of high prices and food shortages there. In March and again in October Morales was forced to borrow. To make matters worse, he fell gravely ill, and on 9 August 1547 he renounced his position as *maestro de capilla* and the associated prebend. His reason was clear: he had come to Toledo to make money and instead had run into debt. Further, it was a position to which he was musically unsuited. He had built his reputation with *a cappella* works, but at Toledo organs were in constant use in the 16th century during most of the liturgical year. Two organists were paid during Morales's tenure, one of them the blind Francisco Sacedo. Morales could undoubtedly have adapted his style to Spanish practice as Victoria later did under similar circumstances. However, only one of the various Morales masses copied into the Toledo choirbooks can reasonably be regarded as a product of his time there, a *Missa cortilla* ('short mass').

On leaving Toledo Morales returned to Andalusia. In *El arte tripharia* (1549) Juan Bermudo described him as *maestro de capilla* to the Duke of Arcos at Marchena, a post he held from 1548 to 1551. On 20 October 1550 Morales wrote a commendatory letter for inclusion in the second edition of Bermudo's *Declaración de instrumentos*. He praised Bermudo's method of instruction because it progressed from the easy to the difficult, the known to the unknown; he also approved of Bermudo's combination of brevity and thoroughness, his fluent and easy style and his insistence that theory and practice go hand in hand. Morales's remarks on educational method are particularly interesting, for among his opponents at Toledo was the schoolmaster. Whether he was himself as progressive as were the methods he admired in Bermudo cannot be ascertained, but he did have at least two pupils after his return from Italy whose success would commend even the most obscure of teachers – Francisco Guerrero and Juan Navarro.

On 27 November 1551 Morales was appointed *maestro de capilla* of Málaga Cathedral. There, during the last two years of his life, he was even unhappier than he had been at Toledo. A week after his appointment the cathedral chapter had to order the singers to obey him. Shortly before Christmas he moved into a house provided by the chapter; presumably he was responsible, as he had been at Toledo, for boarding and educating the choirboys. Frequent lapses in discipline provoked reprimands and the imposition of fines by the cathedral chapter. Thus in August, when the post of *maestro de capilla* at Toledo unexpectedly fell vacant, Morales wrote asking to be considered. A determined minority (including the schoolmaster) pronounced against inviting him back. Although the governing body could have allowed his immediate return without further formality, the members instead voted that he must stand trial in open competition just as he had done eight years before when first appointed. The four other competitors were persons of no consequence and Morales was one of the most eminent composers in Europe. (Just at this time Rabelais wrote of a fanciful garden in which he imagined he heard 'Morales. . .& autres joyeulx musiciens. . .mignonnement chantans'.) Morales, however, accordingly submitted his application on 4 September 1553. But he was not to compete: by the beginning of October he was dead.

2. POSTHUMOUS REPUTATION. Morales's reputation continued to grow during the 30 years after his death through the steady spread of his compositions through France, Germany, Italy, Spain and the Low Countries. His fame travelled as far as Mexico, where his music was chosen for performance in 1559 at the commemorative services for Charles V; Cervantes de Salazar (*Túmulo imperial*, 1560) praised the choice of Morales's music for the occasion. The earliest printed polyphony copied for use in the New World was one of Morales's books of masses of 1544. His works appeared in at least 65 prints before 1600. Because of his international popularity his bibliography is extremely complicated, more nearly comparable with Lassus's than with Victoria's or Guerrero's. The gathering of references to his music from theoretical sources is a no less complex task. A list of those theorists who within 100 years of his death cited his works as technical models includes Bermudo and Montanos in Spain, Zacconi, Artusi, Baccusi, De Grandis, Bonini and Cerone in Italy, and António Fernândez, Álvarez Frouvo and Nunes da Silva in Portugal.

An early 18th-century view was stated by Andrea Adami da Bolsena (1711), who listed Morales as the most important composer in the papal chapel between Josquin and Palestrina; Adami particularly praised the masses because of their polish, their learned contrivance and their elevated style. He called Morales's *Lamentabatur Jacob* the most precious work in the Sistine Chapel archives, referring to it as 'a marvel of art'. Fornari (*Narratione istorica*, 1749), discussing Palestrina's text-setting in the *Missa Papae Marcelli*, praised Morales as the composer who first showed how to set words intelligibly in a contrapuntal fabric. Late 19th-century historians saw Morales through Wagnerian eyes, but at least in that century many of his works were published in modern score. Eslava and Pedrell did him disservice by attributing to him Victoria's highly expressive motet *O vos omnes*, which

they called Morales's most typical work (Pedrell discovered his error when he came to edit the complete works of Victoria).

Bermudo, himself a Spaniard, called Morales 'the light of Spain in music', but at the same time listed 'the excellent Morales' together with the 'profound Gombert' as foreign. In his *Declaración de instrumentos*, 1555, he said that he regarded 'our Morales as a foreign composer because, although his music possesses the charm and pleasing sound of Spanish music, yet at the same time it does not lack the profundity, the technical skill and the artifice of foreign music'.

3. WORKS. Almost all Morales's works are liturgical. Rubio (1969) published an extensive analysis of his musical style, comparing his procedures bar by bar with those of his Spanish forebears and contemporaries and such Franco-Flemish masters as Josquin, Gombert, Clemens non Papa, Arcadelt and Willaert. He sought to prove that Morales avoided anticipations, did not allow a voice to rise a 4th from the leading-note in a final cadence, and in two-part writing avoided upper auxiliary suspensions beginning as dissonances. Rubio noted that these and other rules were broken in five Lamentations ascribed to Morales in the two 1564 Venetian prints (Rampazetto and Gardane); and he found all five ascribed not to Morales but to his fellow member of the papal choir, Costanzo Festa (in *I-Rvat* C.G.XII–3, ff.18–37). Copied in 1543 while both were in Rome, this manuscript also contains three Lamentations correctly attributed to Morales; the authentic works transgress none of his self-imposed rules.

These 'rules' usually echo procedures already current in the works of Morales's Netherlands contemporaries, as well as in those of Francisco de Peñalosa, Alonso de Alva, Pedro de Escobar and Francisco de la Torre, all active at Seville in Morales's youth. The synthesis and the spirit were of course his own. Distinguishing characteristics of his style include: (*a*) a typically Peninsular fondness for what can be called functional harmony; (*b*) cross-rhythms in which one or more voices sing melodic figures whose natural rhythms run counter to the written metre; (*c*) occasional use of conflicting rhythms, for example three against four; (*d*) frequent use of melodic sequence and melodic repetition, but not of harmonic sequence or repetition; (*e*) no ascending crotchet leaps in melismatic passages; (*f*) motivic use of short melodic phrases; (*g*) frequent recourse, especially in early works, to the incomplete cambiata, which lacks the stepwise turn upwards on the fourth note later deemed indispensable; (*h*) leaps from dissonances that cannot be justified even as incomplete cambiatas; (*i*) harmonic cross-relations, guaranteed by explicit accidentals, of the type favoured by Tudor composers; (*j*) a systematic use of consecutives, excluded from Palestrina's style; (*k*) an impartial use of all the modes, including the Phrygian and its plagal; and (*l*) occasional harmonic daring, such as the use of a diminished triad in root position on a relatively strong beat. Bermudo called particular attention to this last trait of Morales's style which now, given the uncertainty regarding the use of accidentals in 16th-century music, might be subject to 'correction' if it were not for Bermudo's authority and citation of example. Other 16th-century theorists, also aware of Morales's individuality (for example Artusi in *L'arte del contrappunto*, 1586, and Zacconi in *Prattica di musica*, 1596), even cited Morales as an authority for procedures that could not be justified from the works of Palestrina.

With the exception of the two motets *Jubilate Deo* and *Gaude et laetare ferrariensis civitas* (each commissioned to celebrate a specific event), all Morales's motets (more than 100) are essentially sacred. He drew his text from responsories, antiphons, psalms, hymns, various biblical passages and other sacred sources. He often used associated Gregorian chant incipits as a melodic point of departure (e.g. *Puer natus est*) or as an ostinato figure (e.g. the five-voice *Tu es Petrus*), but he seldom borrowed entire melodies. The texture of the motets is characterized by free imitation with exceptional use of homophonic sections to stress important sections or words, a procedure typical of polyphonic composers of his epoch. He also showed a preference for the use of an ostinato as a formal device in his motets (e.g. the five-voice *Tu es Petrus, Exaltata est sancta Dei genetrix, Emendemus in melius* etc), as well as a variety of external formal structures, including the repetition of entire sections.

The two sets of *Magnificat* settings were perhaps the best known of Morales's works; 16 editions appeared between 1542 and 1619. They are permeated with Gregorian cantus firmi and, unlike those by Gombert or Clemens, each voice typically enters with the same melody and then continues in free counterpoint. His settings of the Lamentations are characterized by a sober homophonic style, with only brief interruptions of imitative counterpoint and largely conjunct melodic movement, a restrained treatment that had characterized Lamentations settings back to Dufay. The two masses for the dead and the *Officium defunctorum* are the most extreme examples of Morales's sobriety of style.

He had thorough command of the musical techniques practised on the Continent during the first half of the 16th century; his style is best compared to Josquin, Gombert and Clemens rather than to his Spanish contemporaries, even though he was not without certain Peninsular characteristics. He composed in all the important sacred forms and his masses use the cantus firmus, parody, paraphrase and ostinato techniques; his use of such techniques is simpler and more direct than that of his Netherlands contemporaries, and his music shows a special care for clarity and concision of form.

Rubio saw Morales as a precursor of Palestrina; he cited Palestrina's familiarity with Morales's music and detailed the characteristics of Morales's style and technique that can be said to have influenced Palestrina. But Morales, like Josquin, was as deeply concerned with expressing the meaning of the text as he was with clarity, and freely abandoned his self-imposed rules to that end; it is there that his real genius lay.

For illustration from a Morales *Magnificat, see* GARDANE.

## WORKS

Principal sources only; instrumental intabulations are listed only when the vocal model is not extant; for full list of intabulations see *BrownI*.

Edition: *C. de Morales: Opera omnia*, ed. H. Anglès, MME, xi, xiii, xv, xvii, xx, xxi, xxiv, xxxiv (1952–) [A]

### MASSES

Missarum liber primus (Rome, 1544) [1544a]
Missarum liber secundus (Rome, 1544) [1544b]
Others in *E-GRcr, Mmc, Tc, TZ, Vp; I-Ma, Rvat;* Guatemala Cathedral
Missa 'Aspice Domine', 4vv, 1544a; A xi, 35 (on Gombert's motet; different Ag II in *E-Mmc*)
Missa 'Ave Maria', 4vv, 1542³, 1544b; A xv, 32
Missa 'Ave maris stella', 5vv, 1544a; A xi, 104 (canonic)
Missa 'Benedicta es caelorum regina', 4vv, 1544b; A xv, 1 (on Mouton's motet, with quotations from Josquin)
Missa 'Caça', 4vv, *Mmc* (with different Ag), *TZ, Vp;* A xxiv, 1 (quotes from ensalada by M. Flecha (i))

Missa cortilla, 4vv, *Mmc, Tc,* Guatemala Cathedral (lacks Ag II); A xxiv, 18
Missa de beata virgine, 4vv, 1540⁴, 1544a; A xi, 1
Missa de beata virgine, 5vv, 1540³, 1544b; A xv, 66
Missa 'Desilde al cavallero', 4vv, *I-Ma;* A xxiv, 58 (on popular Sp. song)
Missa 'Fa re ut fa sol la' [= Missa cortilla]
Missa 'Gaude Barbara', 4vv, 1544b; A xxi, 34
Missa 'L'homme armé', 4vv, 1544b; A xxi, 67
Missa 'L'homme armé', 5vv, 1540³, 1544a; A xi, 193
Missa 'Mille regretz', 6vv, 1544a, *Rvat* (with different San, Ag I, III); A xi, 238; xxiv, 123 (on Josquin's chanson)
Missa pro defunctis, 4vv, *E-Vp;* ed. in Musica liturgica, ii/1 (Cincinnati, 1960)
Missa pro defunctis, 5vv, 1544b; A xv, 114
Missa 'Quaeramus cum pastoribus', 5vv, 1543¹, 1544a; A xi, 148 (on Mouton's motet)
Missa 'Quem dicunt homines', 5vv, 1544b; A xxi, 89 (on Richafort's motet)
Missa 'Si bona suscepimus', 6vv, 1544a; A xi, 274 (on Verdelot's motet)
Missa 'Tristezas me matan', 5vv, *I-Rvat;* A xxiv, 83 (on popular Sp. song)
Missa 'Tu es vas electionis', 4vv, 1544b; A xxi, 1 (tenor mass on versicle from M. de Eguía, Liber processionarius, Alcalá, 1526)
Missa 'Ut re mi fa sol la', 4vv, *E-GRcr, Mmc, TZ* (with add. Osanna), Guatemala Cathedral; A xxiv, 36
Missa 'Vulnerasti cor meum', 4vv, 1542³, 1544a; A xv, 70 (on ?Févin's motet)

### MAGNIFICAT, LAMENTATIONS

Magnificat, 4vv (Venice, 1542⁹)
Magnificat . . . liber primus (Venice, 1545) [1545a]

*(verses set polyphonically are given in square brackets)*

Magnificat primi toni, 4–6vv, 1542⁹, *E-Tc* (different Anima mea and Quia respexit), *P-Cug* (different Suscepit Israel); A xvii, 1 [odd]
Magnificat primi toni, 4–6vv, 1542⁹; A xvii, 8 [even]
Magnificat secundi toni, 4–6vv, 1542⁹; A xvii, 17 [odd]
Magnificat secundi toni, 4–6vv, 1542⁹, *I-Rvat* C.G. (Suscepit Israel with opt. added parts by Soriano and Palestrina); A xvii, 25 [even]
Magnificat tertii toni, 4–6vv, 1545a; A xvii, 34 [odd]
Magnificat tertii toni, 4–6vv, 1545a, *Rvat* C.G. (Esurientes, Sicut locutus est, Fecit potentiam with opt. parts by Palestrina); A xvii, 41 [even]
Magnificat quarti toni, 4–6vv, 1542⁹; A xvii, 50 [odd]
Magnificat quarti toni, 4–6vv, 1542⁹, *Rvat* C.G. (Sicut erat with opt. parts by Palestrina); A xvii, 57 [even]
Magnificat quinti toni, 4–6vv, 1545a; A xvii, 65 [odd]
Magnificat quinti toni, 4–6vv, 1545a; A xvii, 75 [even]
Magnificat sexti toni, 4–6vv, 1542⁹; A xvii, 84 [odd]
Magnificat sexti toni, 4–6vv, 1542⁹, *Rvat* C.G. (Esurientes with opt. part by Palestrina); A xvii, 91 [even]
Magnificat septimi toni, 4–6vv, 1542⁹; A xvii, 100 [odd]
Magnificat septimi toni, 4–6vv, 1542⁹; A xvii, 109 [even]
Magnificat octavi toni, 4–6vv, 1545a; A xvii, 119 [odd]
Magnificat octavi toni, 4–6vv, 1545a; A xvii, 126 [even]

Lamentationi, 4–6vv (Venice, 1564) (4 by Morales; 5 others attrib. Morales are by C. Festa); ed. in Watkins
Lamentations, 5vv, Puebla Cathedral, Mexico (with prologue: Et factum est post capitem)

### MOTETS ETC

Accepit Jesus panes, 4vv, *E-E, Vp;* A xx, 10
Ad tante nativitatis, 4vv, *Tc;* A xxxiv, 19
Agnus redimit ovis, 4vv, *Tc* 21
Andreas Christi famulus, 5vv, 1556⁶; A xiii, 157
Andreas Christi famulus, 8vv, 1564¹; A xxxiv, 102
Antequam comedan suspiro, 4vv, 1541⁴; A xiii, 42
Apostole Christi Jacobe, 4vv, *V;* A xxxiv, 64
Asperges me, Domine, 4vv, in C. de Morales: Missarum liber primus (Lyons, 1545); A xxxiv, 10
At ille dixerunt (see Cum natus esset Jesus)
Ave Domine Jesu Christe, 4vv, 1543⁵; A xx, 22
Ave Maria, gratia pleni, 5vv, *Sc, I-Rvat;* A xiii, 75 (fuga in subdiapason)
Ave regina caelorum, 5vv, *E-Vp;* A xiii, 132 (fuga in subdiapason)
Beati omnes, 6vv, 1553⁶; A xx, 153
Candida virginitas, 4vv, 1543⁵; A xx, 70
Christus resurgens, 5vv, *A-Wn;* A xx, 107
Circumdederunt me, 5vv, *E-Tc;* A xxxiv, 88
Clamabat autem mulier Chananea, 5vv, *Tc;* A xiii, 96 (also attrib. Rore)
Clementissime Christi confessor, 4vv, 1543⁵; A xx, 94
Conceptio tua genetrix virgo, 6vv, *Vp*
Cum natus esset Jesus (2p. At ille dixerunt; 3p. Et ecce stella), 1541³; A xiii, 79 (2p. pubd separately 1549¹⁴)
Descendit angelus, 4vv, 1552³⁵; A xxxiv, 127 (intabulation)
Dixit Dominus, 4vv, *Mmc* 13230
Domine Deus, Agnus Dei, 3vv, 1549¹⁴; A xxxiv, 1

Ecce virgo concipiet, 4vv, *Sc*; A xiii, 8
Egredientem de templo, 4vv, *Tc* 21
Emendemus in melius, 5vv, *E*; ed. in HAM, i (1946), 138; A xxxiv, 73
Exaltata est sancta Dei genetrix, 6vv, *I-Rvat*; A xiii, 174
Gaude et laetare ferrariensis civitas, 6vv, 1549³; A xiii, 192
Gloriosus confessor Domini, 5vv, *E-Tc*; A xx, 139
Hi sunt olivae duae, 4vv, *Tc* 25
Hoc est praeceptum meum, 5vv, *Vp*
Hodie si vocem eius, 4vv, Puebla Cathedral, Mexico (part of the Officium defunctorum)
Inclina, Domine, aurem tuam (2p. In die tribulationis; 3p. Confitebor tibi), 4vv, 1541⁵; A xiii, 48 (2p. pubd separately 1549¹³)
In die tribulationis (see Inclina, Domine, aurem tuam)
In illo tempore assumpsit Jesus, 4vv, *E-GRcr, Tc*; A xxxiv, 39
In illo tempore cum turba plurima, 4vv, *GRcr, Tc*; A xxxiv, 27
In illo tempore dixit Jesus modicum, 4vv, 1543⁵; A xx, 40
In illo tempore stabant autem, 4vv, 1543⁵; A xx, 76
Inter natos mulierum, 4vv, 1543⁵; A xiii, 69
Inter vestibulum et altare, 4vv, *Mmc, I-Rvat*; A xiii, 24
Israel es tu, Rex Davidis, 4vv, *E-Tc* 22
Jam non dicam vos servos, 4vv, 1539¹¹; A xx, 50
Jubilate Deo omnis terra, 6vv, 1542⁵; A xiii, 184
Lamentabatur Jacob, 5vv, 1543³; A xiii, 102
Manus tuae Domine, 5vv, *Ac, E*; A xxxiv, 130
Miserere nostri Deus, 4vv, 1543⁵; A xx, 55
Missus est Gabriel, 4vv, 1542³
Nobis datus, nobis natus, 4vv, *Tc*
Noctis recolitur, 4vv, *Sc* (inc.), *Tc*
O crux, ave, spes unica, 4vv, *E*; A xx, 103
Officium defunctorum, 4vv, *Ac, GRcr*; ed. F. Pedrell, Hispaniae schola musica sacra, i (Barcelona, 1894)
O Jesu bone, 4vv, 1545²; A xx, 14
O magnum mysterium, 4vv, *Mmc, Vp*; A xx, 7
O sacrum convivium, 5vv, *A-Wn, E-Mmc, Tc, Vp, I-Rvat*; A xiii, 115
Pastores, dicite, quidnam, 4vv, 1546⁹; A xiii, 12
Pater noster, 5vv, *Rvat*; A xx, 117
Peccantem me quoditie, 4vv, *E-Vp*; A xxxiv, 30
Per tuam crucem, 4vv, *Tc, Vp*; A xiii, 36
Puer natus est nobis, 3vv, 1543⁶; A xx, 1
Puer qui natus est, 5vv, 1541³
Quanti mercenarii, 6vv, 1558⁴; A xiii, 166
Quod Eva tristis, ?4vv, *Sc* (inc.)
Quoniam Deus magnus, 4vv, Puebla Cathedral, Mexico (part of Officium defunctorum)
Quoniam ipsius est mare, 4vv, Puebla Cathedral, Mexico (part of Officium defunctorum)
Regina caeli, laetare, 4vv, *E-Tc, Vp*; A xiii, 66
Regina caeli, laetare, 5vv, *Tc* 21
Regina caeli, laetare (i), 6vv, *Vp*; A xx, 135
Regina caeli, laetare (ii), 6vv, *Vp*; A xxxiv, 95
Sacerdos et pontifex, 4vv, *Vp*; A xxxiv, 66
Sacris solemnis Joseph vir, 4vv, Venegas de Henestrosa, Libro de cifra (Alcalá, 1557); ed. in MME, ii (1944), 136 (intabulation)
Salve nos, stella maris, 5vv, *Tc*; A xx, 101 (canon in diapason)
Salve regina, 4vv, *Boc, Mmc, Vp*; A xxxiv, 56
Salve regina, 5vv, *Sc, Tc, I-Rvat*; A xiii, 137
Sancta et immaculata virginitas, 4vv, 1541⁴; A xiii, 17
Sancta Maria, succurre miseris, 4vv, 1543⁵; A xx, 82
Sancte Antoni pater monachorum, 4vv, 1541⁴; A xx, 86
Signum crucis, 4vv, 1543⁵; A xx, 36
Simile est regnum caelorum, 4vv, *E-GRcr, Tc*; A xxxiv, 21
Solemnis urgebat, 4vv, *Tc* 25 (canon in diatessaron)
Spem in alium nunquam habui, 4vv, 1541³; A xxxiv, 79
Sub tuum presidium configimus, 4vv, 1539¹¹; A xx, 63
Tu es Petrus, 3vv, 1543⁶; A xx, 4
Tu es Petrus, 5vv, 1541³; A xiii, 144
Tu lumen splendor, 4vv, *GU, Tc* 18
Vae Babylon, 4vv, 1546⁸; A xxxiv, 33
Veni Domine, 4vv, 1554³²  (intabulation)
Veni Domine, et noli tardare, 6vv, 1549³; A xx, 146
Verbum iniquum et dolosum, 5vv, 1554³²; A xiii, 122 (intabulation)
Victimae paschali laudes, 4vv, 1546⁹
Vidi aquam egredientem, 4vv, *Tc* 21 (dated 1549)
Virgo Maria, 5vv, 1554³²; A xxxiv, 117 (intabulation)

SECULAR

Caronte, 5vv, 1584¹⁵ (intabulation)
De Antequera sale el Moro, 4vv, 1554³²; ed. in GBM, 114 (intabulation)
Ditimi o si o no, 4vv, 1539²⁴
Juicio fuerte sera dado y muy, *E-Tc* 21 (dated 1549)
Si vos uviera mirado, 3vv, *Bc*, 1556³⁰ (anon.); ed. J. Bal y Gay, *Cancionero de Upsala* (Mexico City, 1944)

DOUBTFUL AND MISATTRIBUTED WORKS

Ad Dominum cum tribularer, 4vv, 1543⁵
Adest dies, 4vv, 1543⁵

Andreas Christi Sancte Andrea, ora pro nobis, 5vv, 1547²⁵ (intabulation)
Cantate Domino, 4vv, 1543⁵
Cum inducerunt puerum Jesum, 4vv, 1543⁵
Ecce amica mea, 4vv, 1543⁵
Haec est vera, 4vv, 1546⁹
Inclina, Domine, aurem tuam, 3–4vv, *P-Cug* (attrib. Morales), 1543⁵, 1546⁹ (both anon.); A xxxiv, 45
Immutemur habitu, 4vv, 1546⁹, 1556⁹ (both attrib. Morales), *E-Tc, I-Rvat* (both attrib. Escobedo); A xiii, 28
Ingrediente Domino, 4vv, 1543⁵
In illo tempore . . . nolite, 4vv, 1543⁵
In tua patientia, 4vv, 1543⁵
Job tonso capite, 5vv, 1549⁷; A xx, 126 (probably by Clemens non Papa)
Martinus Abrahe, 4vv, 1543⁵
O beatum pontificem, 4vv, 1543⁵
O vos omnes (attrib. Morales in H. Eslava, Lira sacro-hispana, 1st ser., B (Madrid, 1869) and F. Pedrell, Hispaniae schola musica sacra, i (Barcelona, 1894); actually by Victoria)
Omni mal de amor procede, 4vv (attrib. Morales in 1552⁴⁷; actually by Trombincino)
O quam veneranda, 4vv, 1543⁵
Paulus apostolus, 4vv, 1543⁵
Quando lieta sperai, 5vv (attrib. Morales in 1584¹⁵; actually by Rore)
Qui consibilitur me, 5vv, *F-Pn*; A xxxiv, 68
Vigilate et orate, 4vv, *E-E*; A xxxiv, 43

BIBLIOGRAPHY

R. Mitjana y Gordón: *Estudios sobre algunos músicos españoles del siglo XVI* (Madrid, 1918)
——: 'Nuevas noticias referentes a la vida y las obras de Cristóbal de Morales', *Música sacro-hispana*, xii/2 (1919), 15
J. B. Trend: 'Cristóbal Morales', *ML*, vi (1925), 19
——: 'Catalogue of the Music in the Biblioteca Medinaceli', *Revue hispanique*, lxxi (1927), 485–524
H. Anglès: 'Les musiciens flamands en Espagne et leur influence sur la polyphonie espagnole', *IMSCR, v Utrecht 1952*, 47
R. Stevenson: 'Music Research in Spanish Libraries', *Notes*, x (1952–3), 49
*AnM*, viii (1953) [8 articles on Morales, pp. 3–176]
R. Stevenson: 'Cristóbal de Morales: a Fourth-centenary Biography', *JAMS*, vi (1953), 3–42
G. Watkins: *Three Books of Polyphonic Lamentations, 1549–1564* (diss., U. of Rochester, NY, 1953)
H. Anglès: 'Cristóbal de Morales y Francisco Guerrero', *AnM*, ix (1954), 56
G. Reese: *Music in the Renaissance* (New York, 1954, rev. 2/1959)
R. Stevenson: 'Anuario musical, vol.viii', *ML*, xxxvi (1955), 287
R. Stevenson: *Spanish Cathedral Music in the Golden Age* (Berkeley and Los Angeles, 1961)
P. Colino: 'Desde Roma: El P. Samuel Rubio defiende su tesis doctoral', *Tesoro sacro musical*, 1 (1967), 60
H. Anglès: 'Latin Church Music on the Continent: Spain and Portugal', *NOHM*, iv (1968), 381
——: 'Problemas que presenta la nueva edición de las obras de Morales y de Victoria', *Renaissance-muziek 1400–1600: donum natalicium René Bernard Lenaerts* (Louvain, 1969), 21
V. Pérez-Jorge: 'Rubio, P. Samuel, OSA: Cristóbal de Morales', *Tesoro sacro musical*, lii (1969), 7
S. Rubio: *Cristóbal de Morales: estudio critico de su polifonía* (El Escorial, 1969)
——: 'Las dos ediciones de las *Lamentaciones*, de Morales, del año 1564, son una farsa editorial', *Tesoro sacro musical*, lii (1969), 25
R. Stevenson: *Renaissance and Baroque Musical Sources in the Americas* (Washington, DC, 1970)
S. G. Cusick: *Valerio Dorico: Music Printer in Sixteenth-century Rome* (diss., U. of North Carolina, 1975)
J. J. Rey: 'Enríquez de Valderrábano: siete obras de Cristóbal de Morales para una y dos vihuelas', *Tesoro sacro musical*, lix/1 (1976), 3

ROBERT STEVENSON

**Morales, Melesio** (*b* Mexico City, 4 Dec 1838; *d* Mexico City, 12 May 1908). Mexican composer. He studied with Agustín Caballero, Felipe Larios (1817–75), Antonio Valle (?1825–76) and Cenobio Paniagua. At the age of 12 he passed off a composition of his own as a 'mazurka by Thalberg'; when the deception was discovered he began to be taken seriously as a composer. At 18 he sketched his first opera, *Romeo e Giulietta* (on Romani's libretto). After revising the orchestration three times he succeeded in getting it performed by the resident Italian company on 27 January 1863. One of the singers, Roncari, advised him to leave Mexico and make a name in Europe. He was unable to leave, however, until the spring of 1866, and in the meantime his second opera, *Ildegonda*, was produced (27 December 1865) after Maximilian had personally intervened to guarantee the costs of production.

Morales spent three years in Europe and shortly before his return saw *Ildegonda* produced at the Teatro Pagliano in Florence (December 1868), where it was received with great acclaim. As predicted his reputation in Mexico was tremendously enhanced by his European success, and he returned a conquering hero. At the Mexico City Conservatory he organized his own department of composition, 'founded on Neapolitan principles', and numbered among his pupils Gustavo E. Campa, Ricardo Castro and Julián Carrillo. Of his later operas two were produced at the Gran Teatro Nacional, Mexico City, *Gino Corsini* (14–15 July 1877) and *Cleopatra* (14–21 November 1891). His last opera, the one-act *Anita*, dealing with the 1867 siege of Puebla, shows *verismo* influence. All his librettos were written in Italian. Morales was the first to conduct Beethoven's symphonies in Mexico. His own orchestral fantasy *La locomotiva*, performed for the opening of the Mexico–Puebla railway (16 November 1869), was an early attempt at an orchestral interpretation of the sound of a locomotive. Almost 100 of his works were published, many of them in Italy, including excerpts from *Ildegonda*.

BIBLIOGRAPHY
O. Mayer-Serra: *Música y músicos de Latinoamérica*, ii (México City, 1947), 660ff
E. de Olavarría y Ferrari: *Reseña histórica del teatro en México* (Mexico City, 1961), i, 670ff, 699; ii, 973f, 1363f
R. Stevenson: *Music in Mexico* (New York, 1952, 2/1971), 197ff
ROBERT STEVENSON

**Morales, Olallo (Juan Magnus)** (*b* Almeria, 15 Oct 1874; *d* Tällberg, 29 April 1957). Swedish composer, conductor and critic, of Spanish birth. He moved to Sweden at the age of seven and, after schooling in Göteborg, he studied the piano and composition at the Stockholm Conservatory (1891–9) and in Berlin (1899–1901). He was music critic of the *Göteborgs handels- och sjöfartstidning* (1901–5), the *Dagens nyheter* (1909–11) and the *Svenska dagbladet* (1911–18), and conductor of the Göteborg SO (1905–9). From 1917 to 1939 he taught conducting and other subjects at the Stockholm Conservatory, where in 1921 he was made professor. He was secretary to the Academy of Music (1918–40) and undertook numerous public commissions. As a conductor he appeared in Scandinavia, Germany and Switzerland. His colourful music combines a Spanish impressionism with Nordic romanticism.

WORKS
(*selective list*)
Orch: Försommar [Early summer], ov., 1898; Sym., g, 1901; Abu Casems tofflor [Abu Casem's slippers], ov., 1926; Vn Conc., d, 1943; Camachos bröllop [Camacho's wedding], ballet and suite, 1944; Pastoraluvertyr (Sommarmusik), 1948
Pf: Sonata, D♭, 1902; Nostalgia, 1920, orchd; Balada andaluza, 1946
Other works: choral music, songs, chamber pieces

Principal publishers: Elkan & Schildknecht, Foetisch, Nordiska musikförlaget, Ries & Erler, Simrock

WRITINGS
with T. Norlind: *Kungliga musikaliska akademien 1771–1921* (Stockholm, 1921)
*Kungliga musikaliska akademien 1921–31* (Stockholm, 1932)
*Kungliga musikaliska akademien 1931–41* (Stockholm, 1942)
*Handbok i dirigering* (Stockholm, 1946)

BIBLIOGRAPHY
W. Seymer: 'Olallo Morales', *Svenska män och kvinnor*, v (Stockholm, 1949), 335
G. Percy: 'Morales, Olallo', *Sohlmans musiklexikon* (Stockholm, 1948–52, rev. 2/1975–9)
ROLF HAGLUND

**Morales, Pedro García** (*b* Huelva, 1879; *d* Huelva, 9 Dec 1938). Spanish violinist, composer and musicologist. He studied music, philosophy and arts at Seville University, and the piano, violin, viola, harmony and composition at the Royal College of Music, London. Remaining in England for most of his life, he helped to make Spanish music known there through his appearances as a solo violinist and conductor. He was also a poet, writer and musicologist, providing all of the Spanish entries for *A Dictionary of Modern Music and Musicians* (London, 1924). Of his compositions, *Boceto andaluz* for violin and orchestra (1911) and *Bagatela* for violin and piano (1912) were first performed by Kreisler. He also wrote songs to texts by his friend Jimenez and other Spanish, British and Italian poets.

CARLOS GÓMEZ AMAT

**Morality play.** See MEDIEVAL DRAMA.

**Moralt** [Muralter, von Muralt]. German family of musicians, represented by 18 members in the Munich Hofkapelle between 1787 and 1920, and best known for the celebrated Moralt String Quartet of the 19th century.

(1) **Adam Moralt** (*b* c1741; *d* Munich, 2 Nov 1811). He was orchestral manager at Mannheim, and went with the electoral court when it moved to Munich in 1778. No fewer than seven of his sons joined the Munich Hofkapelle. Through his wife Maria Anna Kramer the family was related to the London musical family Cramer.

(2) **Johann Wilhelm Moralt** (*b* Mannheim, 1774; *d* after 1842). Viola player, son of (1) Adam Moralt. He must have gone to London at an early age; he played a prominent part in English musical life, and until 1842 was principal violist in the Philharmonic Concerts.

(3) **Joseph Moralt** (*b* Schwetzingen, 5 Aug 1775; *d* Munich, 13 Nov 1855). Violinist, son of (1) Adam Moralt. He was a supernumerary member of the Hofkapelle from 1787, soon became an official court musician and was made leader in 1800. With his brothers (4) Johann Baptist Moralt, Philipp (1780–1830) and Georg (1781–1818), whose place was taken at his death by Jakob (1780–1820), he formed a string quartet which from 1800 often gave concerts, even abroad, in Switzerland, France and elsewhere – the first quartet known to have toured. Joseph was one of the founders of the Munich Musical Academy, and in its concerts made his mark as a 'fiery and discreet' conductor (Spohr). He also conducted the Italian Opera and from 1827, when he was appointed director of instrumental music at court, the German Opera.

(4) **Johann Baptist Moralt** (*b* Mannheim, 10 March 1777; *d* Munich, 7 Oct 1825). Violinist and composer, son of (1) Adam Moralt. He was a violin pupil of Johann Baptist Geiger and Carl Cannabich. He served the Munich Hofkapelle from 1792 and had been promoted to 'court musician' by 1798. He studied composition under Joseph Grätz and produced a large num-

ber of instrumental works, some of which became known outside Munich. In collaboration with colleagues in the court orchestra he also published a collection of violin duets for beginners. His instrumental music belongs to the Mannheim–Munich tradition. Various contributions by J. B. Moralt to the contemporary attempts at reforming church music also received more than merely local recognition.

WORKS

Inst: Concertante, 2 vn (Mainz, n.d.); Sym., E♭ (Bonn, n.d.); Sym., G (Leipzig, n.d.); 2 fl qts (Munich, n.d.); Leçons méthodiques, vn (Mainz, n.d.); Concertante, fl, ob, *D-Mbs*

Vocal: Deutsches Traueramt, 4vv, org (Munich, n.d.); choral pieces in K. A. von Mastiaux: Vollständige Sammlung der besten alten und neuen Melodien (Leipzig and Munich, 1812–19); Deutsche Messe, *Mbs*

**(5) Clementine Moralt** (*b* Munich, 9 Oct 1797; *d* Munich, 7 July 1845). Contralto, daughter of (1) Adam Moralt. She was appointed a court singer in 1818 and from 1820 to 1843 was a contralto at the Munich Opera. In 1823 she married the highly esteemed bass Giulio Pellegrini (1806–58).

**(6) Peter Moralt** (*b* Munich, 23 Sept 1814; *d* after 1866). Violinist, grandson of (1) Adam Moralt. From 1828 he was a violinist in the Hofkapelle, was appointed a court musician in 1835 and from 1853 to 1865 acted as a conducting member of the court orchestra. From 1830 to 1840 he led a second Moralt Quartet, with his brother August (1811–86) and his cousins (7) Wilhelm Moralt and Anton (1812–83) as partners. After 1840 lengthy concert tours as a soloist took him to north Germany, London, St Petersburg and elsewhere. He retired in 1866.

**(7) Wilhelm Moralt** (*b* Munich, 3 July 1815; *d* Munich, 25 Dec 1874). Violinist, grandson of (1) Adam Moralt. He was second violin in the younger Moralt Quartet, and gained popularity through his compositions and arrangements for the zither, which were published mostly by Aibl (Munich).

A later member of the family, a great-grandson of the Jakob Moralt who played in the first Moralt Quartet, was the conductor RUDOLF MORALT.

BIBLIOGRAPHY

F. J. Lipowsky: *Baierisches Musik-Lexikon* (Munich, 1811/*R*1971)

'Nekrolog [J. B. Moralt]', *AMZ*, xxviii (1826), col.42 [cf also many other references to the family in this journal]

H. Bihrle: *Die musikalische Akademie in München* (Munich, 1911)

M. Zenger: *Geschichte der Münchener Oper* (Munich, 1923)

A. Aschl: *Die Moralt* (Rosenheim, 1960)

FOLKER GÖTHEL

**Moralt, Rudolf** (*b* Munich, 26 Feb 1902; *d* Vienna, 16 Dec 1958). German conductor, nephew of Richard Strauss. He studied under Courvoisier and Schmid-Lindner at Munich University and Academy, and was engaged as répétiteur at the Munich Staatsoper under Walter and Knappertsbusch (1919–23). He was conductor at the Kaiserslautern Städtische Oper, from 1923 to 1938, and musical director at the German Theatre, Brno, from 1932 to 1934. After a brief return to Kaiserslautern he was appointed to Brunswick in 1934 and to Graz in 1937. That year he also made his début in Vienna, where he was chief conductor at the Staatsoper from 1940 until his death. A reliable, unaffected and deeply understanding conductor, he was responsible for a high standard of repertory performances at Vienna for almost 20 years, and was deeply disappointed that none of the eight new productions in the rebuilt Staatsoper's first season in 1955 was as-

signed to him. Overshadowed by the more famous conductors of his time, his stylistic competence and excellent baton technique nevertheless achieved many notable performances, especially of works by Mozart, Wagner, Pfitzner and Richard Strauss. He appeared at the 1952 Salzburg Festival and as guest conductor in many other European cities and in South America. His records include Mozart's *Don Giovanni*, Strauss's *Salome*, the first recording of Lehár's *Giuditta*, and a version of Beethoven's Mass in C that was much admired in the 1950s.

GERHARD BRUNNER

**Moran, Robert (Leonard)** (*b* Denver, 8 Jan 1937). American composer. He studied composition with Apostel in Vienna (1957–8) and with Milhaud and Berio at Mills College (1961–3). From 1964 to 1972 he taught composition in San Francisco, where he directed the West Coast New Music Ensemble from 1968. He has also toured as a pianist and lecturer throughout the USA and Europe. In his music he seeks the involvement of the performer through indefinite notation and mixed-media situations. He is best known for works requiring a great number of people and a great variety of means, pieces such as *Hallelujah*, which used most of the 75,000 population and resources of Bethlehem, Pennsylvania: bands, rock groups, choirs, carillons, motor cars, house lights and broadcasting stations.

WORKS

(*selective list*)

4 Visions, fl, str qt, harp, 1963; Interiors, ens/orch/perc ens, 1964; Bombardments no.2, 5 perc, 1964; L'après-midi du Dracoula, any insts, 1966; For Organ, org (1–3 players), 1967; Titus no.1, amp motor car, performers, tape, 1967; Jewel-encrusted Butterfly Wing Explosions, mixed media, orch, 1967–8; Bank of America Chandelier, 4 perc, 1968; 39 Minutes for 39 Autos, mixed media, 1968; Let's Build a Nut House, chamber opera, 1, 1969; Silver and the Circle of Messages, chamber orch, 1970; Hallelujah, mixed media, 1971; Divertissement no.3 (street opera), 1971; Evening Psalm of Dr Dracula, prepared pf, tape, 1973

Principal publishers: Hansen, Peer, Peters, Schott, Universal

BIBLIOGRAPHY

R. Moran: 'Hallelujah', *Numus West* (1972), Feb, 28

'Conversation with Robert Moran', *Numus West* (1973), March, 30

DON WALKER

**Morari, Antonio** (*b* Bergamo; *d* Munich, early 1597). Italian violinist and composer resident in Germany. He is known to have worked at the Bavarian court at least from 1562, and from 1568 he is regularly listed in the court accounts. His brothers Giovanni Battista and Annibale were also employed there as string players. Several factors indicate the high regard in which he was held at court: a salary sometimes higher than that of the Kapellmeister, Lassus; gifts of money; a large discretionary allowance; extra allowances for a servant and a horse; and many long visits to Italy (doubtless on behalf of the duke). Still more significant were his promotion to the positions of chamber musician and chief instrumentalist and the fact that he was the first Bavarian musician to be designated 'Konzertmeister'; it is to be assumed that in this capacity he directed the instrumentalists, as Lassus did the singers. He retired on full pay in 1583 because of ill-health. He published *Il primo libro de madrigali a quattro voci* (Venice, 1587); there is also one five-part madrigal by him in *RISM* 1575[11] and another in 1585[17] and two of his motets, one for five voices, the other for six, in 1583[2].

BIBLIOGRAPHY

A. Sandberger: *Beiträge zur Geschichte der bayerischen Hofkapelle unter Orlando di Lasso*, iii (Leipzig, 1895)

W. Boetticher: *Orlando di Lasso und seine Zeit* (Kassel, 1958), 522ff, 534, 621, 715, 829
——: *Aus Orlando di Lassos Wirkungskreis* (Kassel, 1963), 125
H. Leuchtmann: *Orlando di Lasso*, i: *sein Leben* (Wiesbaden, 1976), 108, 114, 192
HORST LEUCHTMANN

**Morata, Ginés de** (*fl* 16th century). Spanish composer resident in Portugal. Of his life it is known only that he was choirmaster to the Dukes of Braganza in Portugal at some time during the 16th century. He is known by four four-part motets (three in *P-VV*, the other in *E-Mmc*) and 12 canciones and villancicos, six for three voices and six for four (all in *Mmc* and in *Cancionero musical de la Casa de Medinaceli*, ed. M. Querol Gavaldá, MME, viii–ix, 1949–50). His compositions may be few in number, but they are of high quality, especially the canciones and villancicos, and they place him among the leading Spanish composers of the 16th century.

BIBLIOGRAPHY
M. Joaquim: 'A propósito dos livros de polifonía existentes no Paço Ducal de Vila Viçosa', *AnM*, ii (1947), 69
——: *Vinte livros de música polifónica do Paço Ducal de Vila Viçosa* (Lisbon, 1953)
JOSÉ LÓPEZ-CALO

**Morata, Juan José Joachín** (*b* Geldo, 1769; *d* Valencia, 4 Feb 1840). Spanish composer. He served as a chorister in Segorbe Cathedral; by the time he was 15 he had written music for the church, and he became *maestro de capilla* there in 1786. From 1793 to 1815 he was *maestro de capilla* at Játiva, but returned to his old post in Segorbe in 1815 and remained until 1829, when he became master at the College of Corpus Christi in Valencia. Among his works are nine masses (including a Requiem), nine Lamentations, motets, psalms and 79 villancicos for various festive occasions (mostly in *E-SEG*). Two 19th-century copies of a *Magnificat* and *Beatus vir*, both in five parts, by 'Morata' (*CU*) may also be his works.

ELEANOR RUSSELL

**Moratelli, Sebastiano** (*b* Vicenza, 1640; *d* Heidelberg, 1706). Italian composer and instrumentalist. He went to Vienna before 1660 and entered the emperor's service as a chamber musician. He was also music master to the Dowager Empress Eleonore and her daughter Maria Anna Josepha. When the archduchess married the future Elector Palatine Johann Wilhelm he went at the dowager empress's request to the Palatine court at Düsseldorf. He remained a member of the court from 1679 until his death. Correspondence between the elector and the Emperor Leopold I reveals that he was supplying the court with dramatic music for Carnival by 1681. In November 1685 he accompanied the elector and his wife to Vienna, and he went there again in 1689. He was appointed Kapellmeister not later than 1687. In November 1685 he was described as court chaplain and in 1688 as honorary chaplain to the electress; he was appointed spiritual counsellor to the elector before 1695. Because of ill-health he was increasingly assisted from 1696 by his younger colleague and eventual successor, J. H. von Wilderer. In October 1705 the elector sent him to Heidelberg to recover his health, but he died there. Extant documents (in *D-Mbs*, *DÜha* and *KA*) indicate that as a musician he was highly esteemed by his contemporaries. Rapparini stated that he composed several operas and serenades and praised him above all for the naturalness and expressive power of his recitatives. Not a note of his music survives. On the basis of extant librettos, all by Rapparini, the following operas can certainly be ascribed to him: *Erminia ne' boschi* (December, 1687), *Erminia al campo* (Carnival, 1688), *Didone* (1688), *I giochi olimpici, ovvero Che fingendo si prova un vero affetto* (1694) and *Il fabbro pittor* (1695). He may also have written the festival opera *La gemma Ceraunia* (N. Minato) performed at Heidelberg in 1687.

BIBLIOGRAPHY
*EitnerQ*
G. M. Rapparini: *Le portrait du vrai mérite dans la personne serenissime de Monseigneur l'Electeur Palatin* (MS, *D-DÜl*, 1709); ed. H. Kühn-Steinhausen (Düsseldorf, 1958)
F. Walter: *Geschichte des Theaters und der Musik am kurpfälzischen Hofe* (Leipzig, 1898/R1968)
A. Einstein: 'Italienische Musiker am Hofe der Neuburger Wittelsbacher, 1614–1716: neue Beiträge zur Geschichte der Musik am Neuburg-Düsseldorfer Hof im 17. Jahrhundert', *SIMG*, ix (1907–8), 336–424
F. Lau: *Geschichte der Stadt Düsseldorf* (Düsseldorf, 1921)
G. Croll: 'Musikgeschichtliches aus Rapparinis Johann-Wilhelm-Manuskript (1709)', *Mf*, xi (1958), 257
G. Steffen: *Johann Hugo von Wilderer (1670–1724), Kapellmeister am kurpfälzischen Hofe zu Düsseldorf und Mannheim* (Cologne, 1960)
GERHARD CROLL, SIBYLLE DAHMS

**Moravec, Ivan** (*b* Prague, 9 Nov 1930). Czech pianist. He studied in Prague with Grünfeld, then with Štěpánova-Kurzová (1952–3), and later, at Michelangeli's invitation, at his master classes in Arezzo (1957 and 1958). He made his début on Prague Radio in 1946, his London début in 1959, his first American recording in 1962, and his New York début with Szell and the Cleveland Orchestra in 1964. From his first European tour he won praise for his rhythmic precision, clarity of articulation, sonorous tone and cantabile playing. His sense of style and of a work's structure is supported by unusual musicality and power of expression. His repertory comprises mainly Chopin, Debussy, Ravel, Beethoven and Brahms's concertos. He has returned to the USA regularly for concerts and recordings and has also played in Canada and Japan. In 1967 he began to teach at the Prague Academy (AMU) and he has given master classes in Europe and the USA.

BIBLIOGRAPHY
*ČSHS*
J. Kozák: *Československí koncertní umělci a komorní soubory* [Czechoslovak concert artists and chamber ensembles] (Prague, 1964), 63ff
A. Chekouras: 'The Master Class Concept', *Clavier*, ix/2 (1970), 15
ALENA NĚMCOVÁ

**Moravia.** Region of central Europe, now part of CZECHOSLOVAKIA.

**Moravia, Jerome of.** *See* JEROME OF MORAVIA.

**Moravian Quartet (i).** Czech string quartet. It was active in Brno from 1923 to 1959, and was formed by František Kudláček (*b* Milevsko, 11 May 1894; *d* Brno, 26 Aug 1972) who remained its first violin throughout. The other members who were constant from the mid-1920s were Josef Jedlička (*b* Kroměříž, 2 Jan 1904), violin, Josef Trkan (*b* Brno, 30 Dec 1897; *d* Brno, 18 April 1941), viola, and the cellist Josef Křenek (*b* Vienna, 20 May 1898; *d* Prague, 9 Nov 1976). An important ensemble in Moravia, they played many contemporary works as well as the standard repertory, and gave the posthumous première of Janáček's String Quartet no.2 'Intimate Letters' at Brno in 1928, performing it according to the composer's instructions given during rehearsals before his death. The quartet also toured in Germany, Italy and Austria.

BIBLIOGRAPHY
J. Vratislavský: *Moravské kvarteto* (Prague, 1961)
ALENA NĚMCOVÁ

**Moravian Quartet (ii).** Czech string quartet. It was formed in 1964 by players from the Brno State PO. The members since 1965 have been Rudolf Šťastný (*b* Zábřeh na Moravě, 31 Dec 1933) and Ludvík Borýsek (*b* Dolní Němčí, 21 Feb 1944), violins, Jiří Beneš (*b* Komárno, 24 Sept 1928), viola, and Jiří Havlík (*b* Horka nad Moravou, 6 Dec 1936), cello. After winning the 1965 Quartetto Italiano Competition they toured widely in Europe and made their British début in 1969. They are chiefly known for their accomplished performances of new works, many of which are written specially for them by young composers. They are an independent ensemble of the Brno State PO and have made many records.

BIBLIOGRAPHY
J. Bártová: 'Provedli na padesát novinek' [They have performed over 50 new works], *HRo*, xxv (1972), 403
ALENA NĚMCOVÁ

**Moravians, American.** A religious sect that established communities during the mid-18th century in Pennsylvania and North Carolina and produced a highly developed musical culture for over 100 years.

1. History. 2. Musical structure and sources.

1. HISTORY. The origins of the Moravian Church in America (or Unitas Fratrum) can be traced back more than five centuries to the Bohemian Brethren, followers of the Czech martyr Jan Hus. The Unitas Fratrum was organized in Bohemia in 1457 and for almost two centuries led a precarious existence in Bohemia, Moravia and Poland. Never a large denomination, and without official recognition or support, the brethren nevertheless contributed much to Bohemian culture and education. The Thirty Years War destroyed much of their work and drove them into hiding, and the Peace of Westphalia (1648) left their lands under the control of the Roman Catholic Church, which continued the persecution begun more than three decades earlier.

In 1722 some remnants of the Bohemian Brethren took refuge on the estate of Count Nikolaus Ludwig von Zinzendorf in Saxony. They built the town of Herrnhut and over the next several years revitalized and renewed their church. Many of the customs and services unique to the Moravian Church date from these years: the love feast (*Liebesmahl*), the song hour (*Singstunde*), the choir system and the book of *Daily Texts*. The role and influence of Zinzendorf in the renewed Moravian Church was central to its development.

Within ten years of its renewal at Herrnhut, the Moravian Church began sending missionaries to various lands to preach to the 'heathen'. The first group of Moravians to reach North America arrived in 1735 at Savannah, Georgia. Because of an imminent war with Spain over disputed territory and the Moravians' conscientious objection to bearing arms, they abandoned the Georgia settlement in 1740 and in 1741 established the town of Bethlehem in east-central Pennsylvania. From here other communities were founded: Nazareth

(1748) and Lititz, Pennsylvania (1756), and Salem, North Carolina (1766, now Winston-Salem); smaller communities and 'preaching stations' were also established (Graceham, Maryland; Hope, New Jersey; Dover, Ohio), but music reached its highest development in the church communities.

From its renewal in 1722 the Moravian Church placed strong emphasis on music, both congregational and concerted. Music played a part in all its services and was almost continuous in the love feast and song hour. The Moravians who colonized Pennsylvania and North Carolina carried on this musical tradition as much as they were able in the wilderness. At first their music consisted largely of hymns accompanied by a few instruments such as horns, trumpets, flutes and violins. As the communities became more settled, organs were built for the churches, and orchestras (collegia musica) were organized among the men of the congregation. These not only accompanied the concerted anthems sung by the choir but often met several times during the week to rehearse and perform orchestral and chamber music imported from Europe.

This intense musical activity required a large amount of music, most of which was provided by composers within the Moravian Church itself. German Moravian composers such as Christian Gregor (1723–1801), Johann Christian Geisler (1729–1815), Johann Ludwig Freydt (1748–1807) and others wrote hundreds of anthems with orchestral accompaniment. Appropriate choruses by non-Moravian composers were also widely used. Many of the American Moravian communities had members who wrote hymns, songs, anthems and liturgical music for the specific needs of the congregations.

The first Moravians in America known to have composed music were Johann Christoph Pyrlaeus (1713–85) and Christian Friedrich Oerter (1716–93), who wrote liturgical music as early as 1747. Pyrlaeus was also the leader of a collegium musicum organized in Bethlehem in 1744. The first composer to write concerted anthems in America was Jeremiah Dencke (1725–95), who arrived in Bethlehem in 1761. Dencke's earliest surviving anthem, dated 1766, is a doxology for a provincial synod held in Bethlehem that year. In 1765 he wrote two groups of songs for love feasts, on 29 August and 7 September (his earliest surviving compositions), and in 1767 and 1768 he wrote special music for Christmas love feasts.

The arrival in 1770 of JOHANN FRIEDRICH PETER (1746–1813) and his brother Simon Peter (1743–1819) began a period of musical excellence in American Moravian communities that lasted well into the 19th century. J. F. Peter, who worked in all the major American Moravian communities, was the most important Moravian musician and composer of his time in America, and his anthems are among the best in the Moravian repertory. His brother, who was more important as a minister and teacher than as a composer, went to Salem in 1782 and spent the rest of his life there. He wrote only four known works, but each displays a remarkable talent.

Following the Peter brothers to America were Georg Gottfried Müller (1762–1821), a talented violinist who arrived in 1784, and JOHANNES HERBST (1735–1812), an excellent organist who came in 1786. Müller was a minister and congregational leader at Lititz and at Beersheba, Ohio. He is known to have composed nine anthems; the eight that survive are of high quality.

Herbst's more than 100 anthems were widely used in Moravian communities during the late 18th and early 19th centuries.

In 1795 David Moritz Michael (1751–1827) went to America for 20 years' service. He worked mostly in Nazareth and Bethlehem, and was a versatile musician: he could play many instruments and was a capable orchestra leader; he directed the first American performance of Haydn's *The Creation* at Bethlehem in 1811. His compositions include over a dozen anthems, 16 suites (*Parthien*) for woodwind sextet, and a monumental setting of Psalm ciii for soloists, chorus and orchestra.

Johann Christian Bechler (1784–1857) arrived in America in 1806 to teach at the newly founded theological seminary at Nazareth. From 1829 he was the pastor of the Salem congregation and after his consecration as a bishop (1835) went to Sarepta, Russia. An enthusiastic lover of music, Bechler composed hymns, anthems, liturgies and a few pieces for wind instruments.

In addition to these European musicians there was also a group of composers born and trained in America who began contributing to American Moravian music during the 1790s. Jacob Van Vleck (1751–1831) and Johann Christian Till (1762–1844) were the earliest; both wrote anthems, hymns and liturgies. Peter Wolle (1792–1871), a student of Michael and Bechler, edited the first Moravian tune book published in America, *Hymn Tunes Used in the Church of the United Brethren* (Boston, 1836); he wrote about 16 anthems and sacred songs, several of which were published (an unusual occurrence for Moravian music of that time).

About 1840 the musical life in American Moravian communities began to decline because of changes in musical taste, the opening of previously closed communities to secularizing influences (the communities of Bethlehem, Nazareth, Lititz and Salem were owned by the Moravian Church, and residence there had been restricted to its members), and perhaps a decreasing need for new music, as much useful music was easily available. The love feasts, song hours and other services had become more recreative than creative. Two composers active during this time deserve mention, however: Francis Florentine Hagen (1815–1907) and Edward W. Leinbach (1823–1901), both born in Salem. Leinbach stayed there, serving as organist, violinst and general town musician. He is known primarily for his remarkable setting of the *Hosanna*, but also wrote hymn tunes. Hagen entered the ministry and served in Pennsylvania, North Carolina, New York and Iowa. He wrote about a dozen anthems, some of which are harmonically daring, and a delightful overture for orchestra.

The music of the 18th- and 19th-century American Moravians was not widely known beyond the limits of their towns. Although such men as Benjamin Franklin and the Marquis of Chastellux (quoted in Rau, 1927) and the Rev. John C. Ogden wrote enthusiastically of the musical life in Bethlehem, this music had little or no direct influence on the main stream of contemporary American sacred music.

2. MUSICAL STRUCTURE AND SOURCES. The musical life of the American Moravian communities revolved around the musical needs of the church. The choir system divided the congregation administratively by age, sex and marital status: there were separate choirs of young boys, young girls, older boys, older girls, single men, single women, married people, widows and widowers; each choir had a member designated as its spiritual leader; there were often special residences for each choir, particularly the older unmarried men and women, and each had its own devotionals and festivals. The principal musical service was the love feast, a simple, non-sacramental meal shared by the congregation. The love feast had a particular theme, expressed in a continuous succession of anthems, hymns, sacred duets and solo songs compiled for the occasion. They were held frequently on church and choir festival days, for various celebrations (e.g. of welcome or farewell) and for personal anniversaries of important or beloved members of the congregation. The song hour, a less formal musical service consisting entirely of hymns, was organized around a single thought or subject; the music was sung by the congregation with organ accompaniment. Song hours were held several evenings a week to learn new music and share in the joy of singing.

The principal musical form was the anthem or 'coro', scored for mixed chorus (usually SSAB) and a small instrumental ensemble (usually strings and organ, occasionally with wind instruments). Some composers, principally Herbst and Bechler, also wrote solo songs (or 'ariettas') with keyboard accompaniment. The anthem was used mostly in the love feast; its text was compiled from biblical sources and the Moravian hymnal, and until about 1850 was usually in German. Hymns were sung at all the Sunday services: the German preaching service, the English preaching service, the individual choirs' devotionals etc. The hymns were selected from the *Gesangbuch, zum Gebrauch der evangelischen Brüdergemeinen* (Barby, 1778), sung to chorale melodies (many dating from the Bohemian Brethren) collected in the *Choral-Buch enthaltend alle zu dem Gesangbuch der Evangelischen Brüder-Gemeinen von Jahre 1778 gehörige Melodien* (Leipzig, 1784).

The American Moravian musical manuscripts are held in the Archives of the Moravian Church at Bethlehem, and the Moravian Music Foundation at Winston-Salem; both are under the administration of the Moravian Music Foundation. The congregational music collections of Bethlehem, Nazareth and Lititz, and Dover, Ohio, as well as the Bethlehem and Lititz collegia musica collections, are virtually intact in the Bethlehem archives. The Salem congregation, Salem collegium musicum and Bethania congregation collections are in the Winston-Salem archive. The Moravian archives consist of approximately 10,000 manuscripts including some 7000 individual works; about two-thirds of these were written by composers connected with the Moravian Church, and about 30% of the total are by American Moravian composers.

For a Moravian musical score *see* UNITED STATES OF AMERICA, fig.2.

BIBLIOGRAPHY
(* – reprinted by the Moravian Music Foundation)
J. Ogden: *An Excursion into Bethlehem and Nazareth in Pennsylvania in the year 1799* (Philadelphia, 1800)
J. Henry: 'Music at Bethlehem and Nazareth', *Sketches of Moravian Life and Character* (Philadelphia, 1859)
R. A. Grider: *Historical Notes on Music in Bethlehem, Pa. from 1741 to 1871* (Philadelphia, 1873, *1957)
[A. G. Rau]: 'The Moravian Contribution to Pennsylvania Music', *Church Music and Musical Life in Pennsylvania in the Eighteenth Century*, ii (Philadelphia, 1927)
T. M. Finney: 'The Collegium Musicum at Lititz, Pennsylvania, during the Eighteenth Century', *PAMS 1937*, 45

A. G. Rau and H. T. David: *A Catalog of Music by American Moravians, 1742–1842* (Bethlehem, Penn., 1938/*R*1970)

H. T. David: 'Musical Life in the Pennsylvania Settlements of the Unitas Fratrum', *Transactions of the Moravian Historical Society*, xiii (1942, *1956), 19

D. M. McCorkle: 'The Moravian Contribution to American Music', *Notes*, xiii (1955–6, *1956), 597

——: 'The Collegium Musicum Salem: its Music, Musicians and Importance', *North Carolina Historical Review*, xxxiii (1956, *1956), 483

——: *Moravian Music in Salem* (diss., Indiana U., 1958)

W. H. Armstrong: *Organs for America* (Philadelphia, 1967)

H. H. Hall: *The Moravian Wind Ensemble: a Distinctive Chapter in America's Music* (diss., George Peabody College for Teachers, Nashville, Tenn., 1967)

J. T. and K. G. Hamilton: *History of the Moravian Church* (Bethlehem, Penn., 1967)

M. P. Gombosi: *Catalog of the Johannes Herbst Collection* (Chapel Hill, 1970)

E. V. Nolte: 'Sacred Music in the Early American Moravian Communities', *Church Music* (St Louis, 1971, *1971), no.2, p.16

K. Kroeger: 'Moravian Music in 19th Century American Tunebooks', *Moravian Music Foundation Bulletin*, xviii/1 (1973), 1

——: 'Moravian Music in America: a Survey', *Unitas fratrum* (Utrecht, 1975), 387

F. A. Cumnock: *Catalogue of the Music of the Salem Congregation* (in preparation)

KARL KROEGER

**Morawetz, Oskar** (*b* Světlá nad Sázavou, 17 Jan 1917). Canadian composer and pianist of Czech origin. He studied the piano in Prague with Karel Hoffmeister and in 1937 was offered a conducting post by Szell at the Prague opera. However, with the advent of Nazism Morawetz realized that his future as a conductor and concert pianist was doomed unless he were to flee his homeland. Having lived for brief periods in Vienna and Paris, where he managed to continue his piano studies with Julius Isserlis and Lazare Lévy, he decided in 1940 to settle in Toronto, where by this time his immediate family had already taken up residence. Continuing his musical education at the University of Toronto with Leo Smith and Alberto Guerrero, he received the BMus in 1944 with his String Quartet no.1 and the DMus in 1953 with his Symphony no.1. In 1958 he was appointed professor of theory and composition at the university.

As a composer Morawetz is completely self-taught, and it is his belief that every composition has to come from a deeply felt experience. His works first achieved prominence after he had twice won a nation-wide competition sponsored by the Composers, Authors and Publishers Association of Canada, with his First Quartet (1944) and his *Sonata tragica* for piano (1945). Other honours of international importance followed. In 1962 Zubin Mehta awarded him first prize for his Piano Concerto no.1 in a competition sponsored by the Montreal SO, and, besides conducting the first performance of this work in 1963, Mehta introduced Morawetz's Sinfonietta for wind instruments and percussion (1965). In 1971 Morawetz received an award from the Segal Foundation of Montreal for his *From the Diary of Anne Frank*, described as 'the most important contribution to Jewish music in Canada'. He has also received the Canada Council's Senior Arts Fellowship twice (1961 and 1974).

Some of Morawetz's earlier orchestral works, such as the *Carnival Overture* (1946), the *Divertimento* for strings (1948, revised 1954) and the *Overture to a Fairy Tale* (1956), have become popular for their colourful orchestration and rhythmic vitality, capturing a cheerful mood of Slavonic flavour. But most of his works are serious, often tragic in nature, and these are partly influenced by the events of World War II. This applies for instance to his finest and most frequently performed quartet, the Second (1952–5), where the mysterious atmosphere opening the second movement came to his mind after seeing war scenes on film. In the dynamic climax of this movement, the clustered trills combined with the main themes are reminiscent of menacing military drums.

Outstanding among the numerous piano works are the Scherzo (1947), which has effectively achieved the status of a minor classic for Canadian pianists, the Fantasy, Elegy and Toccata (1958), the First Concerto (1962) and the Suite (1968). The textures of Morawetz's piano writing vary with each movement, so that, for instance, the Fantasy is basically in a free sonata form, the Elegy mixes impressionist pedal chords with diatonic counterpoint, and the Toccata is a study in *moto perpetuo*, where the final section reaches a dynamic power of orchestral proportions.

In wanting to write music which is immediately accessible to the mind as well as the emotions, Morawetz often reflects the meaning and mood of any text he sets. This pattern is already evident in the early songs such as *Mother, I cannot mind my wheel*, which uses a rather Schubertian spinning-wheel motif throughout, while *The Juggler* (Four Songs, 1966) is depicted by means of rhythm in perpetual motion. A number of Morawetz's songs have been orchestrated, perhaps preparing the way for his most expressive work and one which is particularly characteristic of his later manner, *From the Diary of Anne Frank* (1970). Present in this piece are the most salient features of his style, which is associated with the highly charged late Romantic styles of Mahler and Berg. In this respect Morawetz holds a unique position among Canadian composers, since intentionally he does not align himself with the contemporary avant garde.

Morawetz's block chords are not used solely for impressionist colour effect, but rather as part of the contrapuntal thinking; the structure and orchestration of these blocks serve to subdivide extended musical lines. Organic unity is achieved by the cyclic recurrence of themes or the contrapuntal combination of them for dramatic climax, as in the orchestral interlude in *Anne Frank* after her exclamation: 'Lies is for me a symbol of the suffering of all the Jews'. Morawetz set here the rather telling and dramatically ironic segment in which Anne feels deep guilt at her inability to help her friend Lies. The musical style is expressionistic, with the vocal line declaimed partly in recitative and partly in melody. This prayer-like section employs muted brass and bells, and solemn chord changes contribute to the suspension of time. In *Reflections after a Tragedy* (1969) some of the same mannerisms recur to recall the horror of the war: a plaintive melody in the woodwinds, a 'frightened' dialogue between two trumpets accompanied by a snare drum and accented tremolos in the strings, muted violins and brass, march-like rhythms and a prayer articulated by dirge bells.

If there is one strong informing element in Morawetz's imagination it may be his desire to come to grips with the past as well as to redeem it. This would account for his neo-Romantic style and also his preoccupation with contemporary tragedies.

## WORKS
### (selective list)

#### ORCHESTRAL

Carnival Ov., 1946; Divertimento, str, 1948, rev. 1954; Fantasy, 1952; Sym. Scherzo, 1952; Dirge, 1951–3; Sym. no.1, 1951–3; Ov. to a Fairy Tale, 1956; Sym. no.2, 1959; Capriccio, 1960; Pf Conc. no.1, 1962; Sinfonietta, str, 1963, rev. 1968; Passacaglia on a Bach Chorale, 1964; Sinfonietta, wind insts, perc, 1965; 2 Preludes, vn, chamber orch, 1965, rev. 1972; Conc., brass qnt, orch, 1968; Memorial to Martin Luther King, vc, wind insts, perc, 1968, rev. 1974; Reflections after a Tragedy, 1969; Psalm, str, 1971; Sym. Intermezzo, 1971

Improvisation, vc, orch, 1973; Fantasy, vn, orch, 1974; Harp Conc., 1975

#### VOCAL

With orch: Keep us Free, chorus, orch, 1951; From the Diary of Anne Frank, S, orch, 1970; A Child's Garden of Verses, A/Mez, orch, 1971; orchd songs

Unacc. choral: Two Contrasting Moods (A. Lampman), 1966; Crucifixion (spiritual), 1968; Who has allowed us to suffer? (A. Frank), 1970, rev. 1972; The Song my Paddle Sings (P. Johnson), 1975

Songs: The Fly (Blake), 1947; The Chimney-sweeper (Blake), 1947; Mad Song (Blake), 1947; Piping down the valleys wild (A. Wilkinson), 1947; Elegy 'I am so tired' (Wilkinson), 1947, orchd 1947; Cradle Song (Blake), 1949; I love the jocund dance (Blake), 1949, orchd 1949; Land of Dreams (Blake), 1949, orchd 1949; To the Ottawa River (Lampman), 1949; When we two parted (Byron), 1949; Grenadier (Housman), 1950, orchd 1950; Mother, I cannot mind my wheel (Landor), 1955; My true love hath my heart (Sidney), 1955; Sonnets from the Portuguese (E. B. Browning), 1955; Father William (Carroll), 1957, arr. S, B, chamber orch, 1973; 4 Songs (B. Carman), 1966

#### CHAMBER AND INSTRUMENTAL

Chamber: Str Qt no.1, F, 1944; Duo, vn, pf, 1947; Str Qt no.2, a, 1952–5; Sonata no.1, vn, pf, 1956; Str Qt no.3, F, 1959; Trio, fl, ob, hpd/pf, 1960; 2 Fantasies, vc, pf, 1962, rev. 1970; 2 Preludes, vn, pf, 1965, rev. 1972; Suite, fl, pf, 1972

Pf: Sonata tragica, 1945; Scherzo, 1947; Fantasy, d, 1948; Tarantelle, 1949; Ballade, 1950; Fantasy on a Hebrew Theme, 1951; Scherzino, 1953; Fantasy, Elegy and Toccata, 1958; 10 Preludes, 1966; Suite, 1968

Principal publishers: MCA, Gordon V. Thompson

### BIBLIOGRAPHY

K. MacMillan and J. Beckwith, eds.: *Contemporary Canadian Composers* (Toronto, 1975)

DORITH R. COOPER

**Morawski-Dąbrowa, Eugeniusz** (*b* Warsaw, 2 Nov 1876; *d* Warsaw, 23 Oct 1948). Polish composer and teacher. In 1904 he completed his studies at the Warsaw Music Institute as a pupil of Noskowski; he also studied painting. Exiled by the Russian authorities in 1908, he settled in Paris and continued his education with Gédalge (counterpoint) and Chevillard (orchestration), while studying painting further at the Académie Julien and later at the Académie Colorossi with Bourdelle. He returned to Poland in 1930 as director of the Poznań Conservatory. After several months he moved to Warsaw and, in 1932, succeeded Szymanowski as director and professor of composition at the conservatory. He held that position until 1939. His music, distinguished by colourful instrumentation and rich harmony, descends from the late Romantics and from Debussy.

## WORKS
### (selective list)

Stage: Aspazja (opera, after A. Świętochowski), n.d.; Lilla Weneda (opera, after J. Słowacki), n.d.; Salammbô (opera, after Flaubert), n.d.; Krak i smok [Krak and the dragon], ballet, 1930; Świtezianka [The mermaid of Świteź], ballet, perf. 1931; Miłość [Love], ballet, perf. 1932

Orch: 6 syms., b, e, g, 'Prometheus', 'Fleurs du mal', 'Vae victis'; 2 pf concs.; Vn Conc.; Finale, f, pf, orch; Don Quixote, sym. poem, perf. 1912; Ulalume, sym. poem, perf. 1925; Nevermore, sym. poem, perf. 1938; Miłość [Love], sym. poem, n.d.

Inst: 7 str qts, 2 vn sonatas, 8 pf sonatas

TERESA CHYLIŃSKA

**Morceau** (Fr.). PIECE.

**More [Moor], William** (*b* ?Reading, *c*1490; *d* ?London, ?25 March 1565). English composer and harper. According to Flood (who cited no authority), More became blind at an early age. He was a harper to Henry VIII probably by 1511, and performed in the New Year court celebrations in 1512. Shrewsbury Corporation, which entertained More in 1520, described him as 'the principal harper of England'. More remained a Roman Catholic through the religious troubles of the 1530s and for the rest of his life. On 20 November 1539 he was a prisoner in the Tower of London for his part in the affairs of the Abbot of Reading, who had been executed five days before: apparently More had carried letters between the abbots of Reading, Glastonbury and Colchester. The use of a minstrel for secret communications was by no means new, but More's position and blindness must have helped to raise him above suspicion. The king forgave his harper's possible treason, for More was apparently released in time for the New Year festivities of 1540, and his payments as royal harper continued unchanged.

In the 1540s More was well known both as a harper and as a composer. Thomas Whythorne copied 'divers songs and sonnets that were made by . . . Mr Moor, the excellent harper' and listed him among the 'Masters of Music'. In the king's household, too, More was given the style of 'Master' – always a sign of high standing. He remained the royal harper under Edward VI and Mary, and in the first year of her reign, on 3 June 1559, Elizabeth I granted him wages for life of 12d. per day.

More's only surviving music is in the British Museum. A four-part textless piece, *Levavi oculos*, is in Add.30480–4, and an 18th-century copy is in Add.31226. A single part of *Ad Dominum contribularem* (originally for five voices) is in Harl.7578.

### BIBLIOGRAPHY

F. A. Gasquet: *Henry VIII and the English Monasteries* (London, 1888, 7/1920)

H. C. de Lafontaine: *The King's Musick* (London, 1909)

E. Stokes: 'Lists of the King's Musicians, from the Audit Office Declared Accounts', *MA*, i (1909/R1973), 56

W. H. G. Flood: 'New Light on Late Tudor Composers: VII William More', *MT*, lxvi (1925), 328

G. Hayes: *King's Music* (Oxford, 1937)

J. M. Osborn, ed.: *The Autobiography of Thomas Whythorne* (Oxford, 1961)

P. Marr: *Reading Abbey: an Introduction to Music at the Abbey* (Reading, 1971)

RICHARD RASTALL

**Moreau, Henri** (*b* Liège, baptized 16 July 1728; *d* Liège, 3 Nov 1803). Belgian church musician, teacher, composer and theorist. First trained in Liège, he was sent for study to the Collège Liégeois in Rome in 1752, and recalled to Liège in 1758 as *maître de chant* at the collegiate church of St Paul where he served most of his life. After a long career as a composer and teacher of repute (Grétry studied with him from 1758 to 1761), he was made a corresponding member of the Institute of France in 1798. His surviving music (all at the Royal Conservatory in Liège, Fonds Terry) includes several sacred works for voices and orchestra (a *Te Deum*, *Jam de coelo*, *Alme chorae festinate* and three *Tantum ergo*) and a cantata on a Walloon text; a lost set of trio sonatas was published in Liège (*c*1777). Moreau also wrote two treatises: *L'harmonie mise en pratique* (Liège, 1783), a pedagogical work for composition students based on the theories of Rameau and Tartini, and an unpublished *Nouveaux principes d'harmonie, selon le système d'Antoine Ximenez* [Eximeno], *précédés d'observations sur la théorie de Rameau* (MS, c1800, Fonds Terry), which reflected a concern for balancing rules with a natural aesthetic of composition.

BIBLIOGRAPHY
P. Bergmans: 'Moreau, Henri', *BNB*
A. Auda: *La musique et les musiciens de l'ancien pays de Liège* (Brussels, 1930), 176f
J. Quitin: *Les maîtres de chant et la maîtrise de la collégiale Saint-Denis, à Liège, au temps de Grétry* (Brussels, 1964), chap.5
ALBERT COHEN

**Moreau, Jacobus Franciscus** [Jacob François] (*b* ?Flanders, *c*1684; *d* Rotterdam, 9 Oct 1751). Netherlands organ builder. His parents probably moved to The Hague after his birth. On 7 September 1724, as 'Organ builder Jacob François Moreau of The Hague', he married Isabella Philippa de la Haye (daughter of the organ builder Louis de la Haye the elder of Ghent, who had settled in Antwerp). Later Moreau moved to Rotterdam. He is known to have worked in Brielle (1722); Rotterdam (Oosterkerk and Grote Kerk, 1722–6); Steenbergen (1729); Gouda (Grote Kerk St Jan, 1732–6, three manuals, 52 stops; still extant); Goes (Grote Kerk, 1738); again Rotterdam (Oude Kerk, 1744; and in Baarland and Oosterhout (both extant).

Moreau's specifications followed the style developed by north German masters who had settled in the north Netherlands. His style of voicing however was individual: G. J. Vogler compared Müller's organ in Haarlem and Moreau's instrument in Gouda with two women, one 'belle, superbe, fière', the other (which he preferred) 'douce, aimable, traitable'. The simple frontage of the Gouda instrument follows the style of Walloon organ cases. Moreau's work was continued by his son Johannes Jacobus (*d* c1762) and his nephew Louis de la Haye the younger.

BIBLIOGRAPHY
J. Hess: *Beschrijving van het groot en uitmuntend orgel in de St. Jans kerk te Gouda* (Gouda, 1764)
——: *Dispositien der merkwaardigste Kerk-orgelen, welken in de zeven Vereenigde Provincien als mede in Duytsland en elders aangetroffen worden* (Gouda, 1774)
N. A. Knock: *Dispositien der merkwaardigste Kerk-orgelen welken in de Provincie Friesland, Groningen en Elders aangetroffen worden* (Groningen, 1788/*R*1959)
J. Hess: *Dispositien van kerk-orgelen, welke in Nederland worden aangetroffen, vervolg* (Amsterdam, 1907)
A. Bouman: *Orgels in Nederland* (Amsterdam, 1943, rev., enlarged 3/1964 as *Nederland . . . orgelland*)
F. Peeters and M. A. Vente: *De orgelkunst in de Nederlanden van de 15e tot de 18e eeuw* (Antwerp, 1971; Eng. trans., 1971)
HANS KLOTZ

**Moreau, Jean-Baptiste** (*b* Angers, 1656; *d* Paris, 24 Aug 1733). French composer and teacher. He was trained at Angers Cathedral and early in his career served as *maître de musique* at the cathedrals of Langres (at least in 1681 and until February 1682) and then Dijon. He is then heard of in Paris in January 1687, when a *Te Deum* by him (now lost) was sung at St Cosme in thanksgiving for Louis XIV's recovery from illness; his divertissement *Les bergers de Marly* was performed at court later that year.

Moreau came under royal notice just as Louis was organizing work at the school for young noblewomen founded in 1682 by Mme de Maintenon and established at St Cyr in 1686. The king invited him to provide music for the school – at which, along with Nivers and

later also with Clérambault, he served as *musicien ordinaire* – and it is in this connection that he achieved his most lasting fame, particularly in collaboration with Racine. Moreau set Duché de Vancy's *Jonathas* in 1688 and Racine's *Esther* the following year; the performance of the latter was attended by the king, who is said to have been extremely pleased with it. He was indeed Racine's favourite composer, and in addition to *Esther*, they produced *Athalie* for St Cyr in 1691 (it was revived in 1701). Moreau also composed for St Cyr settings of Racine's *Cantiques spirituels* (published in 1695 as *Cantiques chantez devant le Roy*) as well as an *Idylle sur la naissance de notre Seigneur* and at least four dramatic works to texts by other authors.

Performances at St Cyr were not open to the public, and Moreau found it harder to achieve public success. In addition to the *Te Deum* of 1687 he wrote a *grand motet, In exitu Israel*, and a Requiem, and in 1697 produced in Paris his choruses from *Esther* under the title *Concert spirituel, ou Le peuple juif délivré par Esther*. He also composed occasional divertissements, one, *Le feu de joye*, for the Dauphin, and another, *Zaïre* (to a text by Alexandre Laînez), for performance at Fontainebleau. Laînez, known for his libertine verse at a time when the king had become strictly religious, persuaded Moreau to write music of a popular nature for *Zaïre*: the composer won considerable public success by doing so but forfeited the esteem of the king. In 1694 he was appointed superintendent of music in Languedoc, a post that was tantamount to exile; but he soon sold this benefice and returned to Paris, where he taught singing at the Jesuit convent of St Sulpice.

Moreau played a not unimportant role in establishing the motet (particularly the *petit motet*) in France. But he is more important for his contributions to *Esther* and *Athalie*, which consist of a series of short, contrasting recitatives and choruses, notable for their elegant simplicity and careful word-setting. His *Cantiques* are much shorter, but the individual movements, for solo voices and unison female chorus, are longer. His achievements as a composer still await more detailed assessment.

Moreau was considered in his own day an exceptionally fine teacher of both composition and singing; his composition students included Montéclair, Clérambault and Dandrieu. Singers whom he taught included his daughter Marie-Claude and Louise Couperin. His manual *L'art mélodique* is lost, but is known to have demanded rhythmic and melodic finesse.

WORKS

Editions: 'Musique des choeurs d'Esther et d'Athalie et des cantiques spirituels', ed. P. Mesnard, *Grand écrivains de la France* (Paris, 1873), suppl. [M]
　　*The Solo Song, 1580–1730*, ed. C. MacClintock (New York, 1973) [S]

Choeurs de la tragédie d'Esther (Paris, 1689)
La musique d'Athalie (Paris, ?1691)
Cantiques chantez devant le roy (Paris, 1695): A la louange de la charité; Plaintes d'un chrétien, M; Sur les vaines occupations, S, M; Sur le bonheur des justes et sur le malheur des réprouvés, M

Idylle sur la paix, Idylle sur la naissance de notre Seigneur, *F-V*
Intermedia: Jonathas (Duché de Vancy), 1688, lost; Judith (Abbé Boyer), lost; Jephté (Abbé Boyer), 1692, *Pn, V*; Absalon (Duché de Vancy), 1702, lost; Débora (Duché de Vancy), 1706, lost
3 divertissements: Les bergers de Marly, 1687; Le feu de joye; Zaïre: all lost
Requiem, lost; Te Deum, 1687, lost, announced in Le Mercure, Feb 1687; In exitu Israel, lost, announced in Le Mercure, June 1691

BIBLIOGRAPHY
J. Tiersot: 'Les choeurs d'Esther de Moreau', *RHCM*, ii (1903)

M. Garros: 'Mme de Maintenon et la musique', *Rapports et communications de la Société française de musicologie* (1943), 8
L. Boulay: 'Les cantiques spirituels de Racine mis en musique au XVIIe siècle', *XVIIe siècle*, xxxiv (1957), 79

EDITH BORROFF

**Moreau, Simon** (*fl* 1553–58). Composer. He is known only for seven motets and one chanson published in collections by Phalèse, Susato and Waelrant between 1553 and 1558.

WORKS

Comeditis carnes, 5vv, 1555[8]
Deus misereatur nostri, 5vv, 1557[3]
Ecce ego mitto vos, 5vv, 1553[13]
Expurgate vetus fermentum, 6vv, 1554[5]
Praeparate corda vestra, 5vv, 1553[15]
Sancta et immaculata, 5vv, 1553[12]
Tu es Petrus, 5vv, 1553[11]

Ung jour advint, 4vv, 1556[19]

F. J. DE HEN

**Morecock, Robert** (*b* c1510; *d* 15 June 1582). English church musician and composer. He was clerk of the choir and master of the choristers at the London parish churches of St Mary Woolnoth (1542–5) and St Michael, Cornhill (1547–9). By 1551 he had become a Gentleman of the Chapel Royal, and he retained this position until his death. He is a more plausible candidate than THOMAS MERICOCKE for identification with the 'mr. moorecocke' whose three-part setting of *Gloria, laus et honor*, the hymn sung in the Sarum rite during the procession before Mass on Palm Sunday, is in *GB-Lbm* R.M.24.d.2.

ROGER BOWERS

**Moreira, António Leal** (*b* Abrantes, 1758; *d* Lisbon, 21 Nov 1819). Portuguese composer. On 30 June 1766 he entered the Lisbon Seminário Patriarcal, where he studied with João de Sousa Carvalho. In 1775 Carvalho made him his teaching assistant. On 19 May 1777 his *Missa do Espirito Santo* was sung at the acclamation of Maria I, and on 8 August of that year he was inducted into the Lisbon Brotherhood of S Cecilia. He was organist of the Seminário Patriarcal and after 1 February 1787 *mestre de capela* of the royal chapel, for which he composed most of his numerous sacred works.

As a stage composer Moreira had a career second only to that of his brother-in-law Marcos Portugal. In 1782 his serenata *Bireno ed Olimpia* and in 1783 his *opera seria Siface e Sofonisba*, both with librettos by the court poet Gaetano Martinelli, were performed at the Queluz theatre to celebrate royal family events. The serenata *Ascanio in Alba*, to the same Giuseppe Parini libretto used by Mozart, followed in 1785, and the same year the opera *L'imenei di Delfo* was staged for a double royal wedding at the Ajuda palace. This was followed by a staged oratorio, *Ester* (1786), and three more *opere serie*. In 1790 he became music director of the fashionable theatre in the Rua dos Condes, then the Lisbon home of Italian opera. In 1793 Luisa Todi came from Madrid to sing in his serenata *Il natale augusto*, performed in the palace of Anselmo José da Cruz Sobral to celebrate a royal birth of 29 April.

On 30 June 1793 Moreira conducted at the opening of the S Carlos opera house, continuing as music director until Marcos Portugal's return to Lisbon in 1800. After Antonio Teixeira he was the first to compose stage works with Portuguese texts; he wrote for S Carlos, in addition to three Italian operas, the serenata *Os voluntarios do Tejo* (1793) and two operas with librettos by

the Brazilian mulatto Domingos Caldas Barbosa, *A sàloia namoranda ou O remedio é casar* (1793) and *A vingança da cigana* (1794). This latter, which is still performed, features a 'black' character who sings in a minstrel style (a style which Moreira had used two years earlier in his *modinha Moda de Zambumba*) and another character who imitates the musical styles then typical of Naples, Paris, London, Madrid and Lisbon. His only opera to be performed outside Portugal was his last, the *opera buffa Il disertore francese*, first performed at the Carignano in Turin during Carnival 1800 and repeated on 9 July at La Scala.

Although heavily influenced by Paisiello and Cimarosa, Moreira's stage and sacred works are among the most solidly constructed, technically competent and inspired Portuguese masterpieces. Of his many pupils, at least two, Antonio José Soares and José Marques, rose to eminence in the early 19th century.

WORKS

STAGE

Bireno ed Olimpia (serenata, G. Martinelli), Queluz, 1782; Siface e Sofonsba (opera seria, Martinelli), Queluz, 5 July 1783, *P-La*; Ascanio in Alba (serenata, G. Parini), Queluz, 1785, *La*; L'imenei di Delfo (drama lirico alegórico), Ajuda, 12 April 1785, *La*; Ester (oratorio), Ajuda, 19 March 1786, *La*; Artemisia, regina di Caria (opera seria), Ajuda, 1787, *La*; Gli eroi spartani (opera seria), Ajuda, 21 Aug 1788, *La*; Gli affetti del genio lusitano (drama lirico alegórico), Ajuda, 1789, *La*; Il natale augusto (serenata, Martinelli), Ajuda, 21 April 1793
Raollo (opera seria) Lisbon, S Carlos, 1793; Os voluntarios do Tejo (serenata), S Carlos, 1793; A sàloia namorada ou O remedio é casar (farce, D. Caldas Barbosa), S Carlos, 1793; A vingança da cigana (drama joco-serio, Caldas Barbosa), S Carlos, 1794; L'eroina lusitana (opera seria, Martinelli), S Carlos, 21 March 1795; La serva riconoscente (opera buffa), S Carlos, 1798; Il disertore francese (opera buffa), Turin, Carignano, carn. 1800

OTHER WORKS

Sacred: 5 villancicos, 1779, *P-EVp*; 4 masses, 2 Magnificat, 11 sets of responsories, psalms, matins, others, *La*; others, *Lf, Ln, Lc*
Other: Moda de Zambumba, 3vv, pf acc., in *Jornal de modinhas*, xxxii (1792); Sinfonia, F, 1803, *La*; 3 sinfonias, *Ln*

BIBLIOGRAPHY

*DBP*, ii, 105ff, 454ff
M. A. Machado Santos: *Biblioteca da Ajuda: catálogo de música manuscrita*, iii (Lisbon, 1960), 83ff
C. Gatti: *Il teatro alla Scala, nella storia e nell'arte, 1778–1963*, ii (Milan, 1964), 18

ROBERT STEVENSON

**Moreira Sá e Costa, Leonilde.** Portuguese pianist, wife of Luis Costa; *see* COSTA (i), (18) Luis.

**Morel.** A number of musicians of this name were active in England, France and the Netherlands in the 16th century.There is no evidence that they were related to each other or to the French composer Clement Morel.

A composer called Morel (*fl* ? c1543–70), probably of Netherlands origin, may have been in England in the service of Henry Fitzalan, Earl of Arundel. One of his chansons, *Bon jour bon an*, appears in an Arundel manuscript (*GB-Lbm* Roy.App.49–54), and another manuscript (*Lbm* Roy.8.G.VII) contains a puzzle canon, *Honi soit quil maly pense*, with an inscription: 'Morel viro praeclarissimo domino comiti de Arundell'. In the British Library copy of Susato's *L'unziesme livre contenant 29 chansons* (*RISM* 1549[29]), the chanson *Content ou non il fault* is ascribed to Clement Morel in the three lower parts but is anonymous in the superius partbook. A 16th-century scribe has added 'Morel ex familia excellen comtis d'arundell' to the superius and has erased the first name from the other partbooks. A similar emendation appears in the chanson *Vivions, vivons joyeusement* in the British Library copy of Phalèse's *Premier livre des chansons* (*RISM* 1554²²) which formerly belonged to Arundel. This not only suggests that Morel was employed there, but also raises the possibility that some chansons in continental publications are misattributed to Clement Morel.

Jenin Morel, a Netherlander, was a singer in Charles V's chapel from 1518 to 1521. Jean Morel was listed as a 'basse-contre' in the chapel of Philip II of Spain in 1561, described as 'newly arrived from Flanders'. His name reappears in the Spanish court records of 1566 and 1572. Nicholas (or Nicolas) Morel (*b* Rouen, ? *c*1550) was *maître des enfants de choeur* at Rouen Cathedral. In 1584 at the Puy de Musique at Evreux he received a silver lyre for his chanson *Je porte en mon bouquet*; two years later he was awarded a silver lute for his *D'ou vient belle*. Both these works are now lost.

BIBLIOGRAPHY

*FétisB*

E. vander Straeten: *La musique aux Pays-Bas avant le XIXe siècle* (Brussels, 1867–88/*R*1969), i, 246; vii, 295, 302; viii, 41ff, 49, 52, 81, 98

JANE A. BERNSTEIN

**Morel, Clement** [Clemens] (*fl* Nevers, 1534–52). French composer. In 1552 he was *maître des enfants* in Nevers and declined an invitation to the Sainte-Chapelle, Bourges. His first chanson appeared anonymously in an anthology printed by Attaingnant in 1534 but was ascribed to him in another of Attaingnant's anthologies two years later. 13 more chansons by him were included in Attaingnant's second series (1536–49); the rest were printed by Du Chemin, Susato, and Phalèse. Most of his settings are courtly poems with decasyllabic lines by François I and his generation (e.g. Marot, Fontaine), set for four voices in the style of Sermisy, Sandrin and the contemporary Parisian school; he respected the prosody and generally preferred homophony enlivened with a few imitative entries. His motets (published at Lyons, Paris, Antwerp and Nuremberg) are more consciously polyphonic.

WORKS

4 motets, 4vv, 1539¹¹, 1551¹, 1553⁵ (1 also attrib. S. Moreau)
18 chansons, 4vv, 1534¹³, 1536⁴, 1536⁵, 1540¹¹, 1543⁸, 1546¹⁴, 1549²⁰, 1549²¹, 1549²⁹, 1552⁴, 1554²², 1557¹¹; 1 ed. in PÄMw, xxiii (1899/*R*)

BIBLIOGRAPHY

F. Lesure: 'Some Minor Composers of the 16th Century', *Aspects of Medieval and Renaissance Music: a Birthday Offering to Gustave Reese* (New York, 1966), 543

FRANK DOBBINS

**Morel, François (d'Assise)** (*b* Montreal, 14 March 1926). Canadian composer. He studied with Champagne at the Montreal Conservatory (1944–53). Unlike many of his contemporaries who continued their training in Paris, he remained in Montreal, though his contacts with Varèse in New York in 1958 were decisive. Also in that year he helped to found the association Musique de Notre Temps, which aimed to promote contemporary music, and from that time he has worked for the CBC as a composer of incidental music, popular songs, etc. His concert works are almost all instrumental; a few of his essays in electronic music were withdrawn because their fixity prevented them from evolving with society, and a similar concern has led him to recast some works. His output may be divided into three phases: the first culminated with *L'étoile noire* for orchestra (1962), which was also a departure point for a slow progress, until 1968, towards

a more individual style characterized by a search for restraint through more deliberate organization; *Départs* and *Radiance* marked the beginning of a period of greater maturity.

Several works of the first period show the effect of ideas that Morel received during his studies. He followed Champagne's advice in only gradually liberating himself from chosen models: the orchestral *Esquisse* (1946–7), for example, was stimulated by Debussy's *Images*; the *Quatre chants japonais* (1949) are reminiscent of Ravel; and the rhythmic experiments of the String Quartet no.1 (1952) were influenced by Bartók and Stravinsky. In *Antiphonie* for orchestra (1953) he used a plainsong *Salve regina* to give continuity to the music, treating it in an austere modal style that owes something to Messiaen. But the use of spatial movement in handling an immobile theme shows that Morel's ideas were already moving in a direction that was to be encouraged by his meetings with Varèse. The impact of this encounter was demonstrated most obviously in *Boréal* for orchestra (1959) and *Nuvattuq* for flute (1967); it also led to the composition of *L'étoile noire*.

The second period of Morel's development is defined by his use of 12-note serial principles and by a predilection for Varèsian ensembles of wind and/or percussion. *L'étoile noire* derives its 12-note series from Beethoven's op.135; the Second Quartet (1962–3) is constructed on a mirror series based on the B–A–C–H motif; the Sinfonia for jazz band (1963) also uses a mirror series; *Nuvattuq* (1967) is built on two series, one a permutation of the other; and the series of *Prismes-anamorphoses* is made up entirely of tones and semitones. This last work is notable for its alternation of strict sections with freer passages, often non-serial. The subsequent third period saw a continued subordination of serial organization to the need for motivic refinement. With *Radiance* (1970–72) he returned to the full orchestra after a gap of ten years; the work derives a serial rhythmic structure from the intervals of the pitch set.

WORKS

(*selective list*)

Orch: Esquisse, small orch, 1946–7; Antiphonie, 1953; Rituel de l'espace, 1958–9; Boréal, 1959; L'étoile noire, 1961–2; Trajectoire, small orch, 1967; Radiance, 1970–72; Jeux, 1976

Ens: Str Qt no.1, 1952; Cassation, 7 wind, 1954; Litanies, wind, harp, pf, cel, perc, 1955–6, rev. 1970; Sym. pour cuivres, brass, perc, 1956; Spirale, wind, harp, cel, perc, 1956; Rythmologue, 8/6 perc, 1957, rev. 1970; Le mythe de la roche percée, wind, perc, 1960–61; Qnt, 2 tpt, hn, trbn, tuba, 1962; Requiem for Winds, wind, harp, cel, perc, 1962–3; Str Qt no.2, 1962–3; Sinfonia, jazz band, 1963; Etude en forme de toccate, 2 perc, 1965; Neumes d'espace et reliefs, wind, harp, cel, perc, 1967; Prismes-anamorphoses, wind, harp, cel, pf, perc, 1967; Départs, 12 str, harp, gui, 2 perc, 1968–9; Iikkii, 18 insts, 1971

Solo inst: Ronde enfantine, pf, 1949; 2 études de sonorité, pf, 1952–4; Prière, org, 1954; Nuvattuq, fl, 1967; Alleluia, org, 1964–8; Me duele Espana, gui, 1975

Songs for S, pf: 4 chants japonais, 1949; Les rivages perdus (W. Lemoyne), 1954

Principal publishers: Berandol, Canadian Music Centre, Jaymar, Ricordi

BIBLIOGRAPHY

F. Morel: 'Edgard Varèse ou la conscience du son et de l'espace', *Liberté 59*, i/5 (1959), 287

B. Lagacé: 'François Morel, musicien canadien', *Liberté 60*, ii/1 (1960), 66

*Trente-quatre biographies de compositeurs canadiens/Thirty-four Biographies of Canadian Composers* (Montreal, 1964) [Radio Canada publication]

F. Morel: 'Faire sonner la musique'; 'Quintette pour cuivres', *Musiques du Kébèk*, ed. R. Duguay (Montreal, 1971)

LYSE RICHER-LORTIE

**Morel, Jacques** (*fl c*1700–40). French viol player and composer. He was a pupil of Marin Marais, to whom he dedicated his *1er livre de pièces de violle*. In these four suites for seven-string bass viol he adopted Marais' signs for bowing and ornamentation, though his suites are generally simpler than those of Marais. They are printed in score, 'pour la commodité de ceux qui voudront les jouër sur le clavecin'. He also published a setting in French of the *Te Deum* (Paris, 1706), dedicated to the Duke of Aumont, and a volume of solo cantatas entitled *Les Thuilleries* (Paris, 1717). It is uncertain whether he was related to 'Le Sieur Morel, former organist at Soissons', whose book of pieces for the five-string pardessus de viole was announced in the *Mercure de France* (December, 1749). In 1730 his privilege to publish 'des pièces de viole et autres pièces de musique' was renewed and his *1er livre* was probably reprinted at that time (see Clérambault's copy, *F-Pn* Rés.856, in which several alterations were made, including the removal of the date in the privilege).

Three other musicians of the name Morel have been confused with Jacques. Antoine Morel, a *basse-taille* singer, was at the royal chapel in 1669 and later at the Opéra, where he created two Lully roles (Arcas in *Thésée*, 1675; Indien Chantant in *Le triomphe de l'amour*, 1681). Another Morel (first name unknown, called 'de la Ferronerie') was active in Paris from about 1696 to about 1739; several of his chansons appeared in the *Mercure de France*, 1727–39, and other vocal pieces were issued in Ballard's *Recueils* or survive in manuscript (*F-Pn*, *GB-Lbm*). A harpsichord maker called Morel lived in the rue Quincampoix in Paris in the 1770s.

BIBLIOGRAPHY

*WaltherML*

J. A. Vertrees: *The Bass Viol in French Baroque Chamber Music* (diss., Cornell U., 1978)

MARY CYR

**Morel, Jean** (*b* Abbeville, 10 Jan 1903; *d* New York, 14 April 1975). French conductor and teacher. In Paris he studied the piano with Isidore Philipp, theory with Noël Gallon, music history with Maurice Emmanuel, composition with Gabriel Pierné, and the lyric repertory with Reynaldo Hahn. From 1921 to 1936 he taught at the American Conservatory in Fontainebleau. During this period he also conducted a variety of French orchestras, but both the educational side of his work and the American link were to bear the more evident fruit. From 1940 to 1943, having moved to the USA, he taught at Brooklyn College, but it was in his dual capacity, 1949–71, as a teacher at the Juilliard School of Music, New York, and as conductor of the Juilliard Orchestra that he wielded his strongest influence on a generation of American students. He conducted opera in Rio de Janeiro and Mexico and at New York City Center, and also, from 1956, at the Metropolitan Opera.

BERNARD JACOBSON

**Morel, Octave.** *See* MAILLARD, JEAN (ii).

**Morelia.** City in Mexico. It was founded in 1541 by Viceroy Mendoza as Valladolid and was renamed Morelia in 1828. In 1580 the Cathedral of Michoacán was moved to Valladolid from Pátzcuaro, where it had been from 1540. Pátzcuaro was the largest centre of instrument making (recorders, shawms, trumpets and bells) in 16th-century Mexico, and at a Corpus Christi procession in 1556 the earliest extant *zarabanda* was sung there. The first virtuoso Indian organists mentioned by name in a colonial Mexican imprint were a father and son who were cathedral organists at Pátzcuaro in 1567 and at Valladolid after 1602 respectively. Morelia Cathedral, dedicated in 1705, was built between 1660 and 1744, and the leading colonial *maestro de capilla* was José Gavino Leal, active from 1732 to 1768. The Colegio de Santa Rosa de Santa María founded for poor girls in 1738 was active as a music school from 1756 to about 1857 when it was suppressed by anticlericalists; it has an archive containing not only works by Gavino Leal but also by Gregorio Remacha (dated 1738–60), Manuel de Zendexas (1758, 1763), Cayetano de Perea (1771), Francisco Javier Ortiz de Alcalá (1754, 1768, 1776) and other local musicians. Overtures by Rodil and Sarrier indicate a high level of instrumental performance at the college around 1780. Elízaga, a child prodigy born in 1786 at Valladolid and trained there from 1795 to 1799 by the eminent cathedral organist José María Carrasco, was later patronized by the Emperor Iturbide and his wife, both of whom were natives of the town.

The Teatro de Ocampo, constructed in 1828–9, was rebuilt in 1869–70 and inaugurated with a brilliant vocal and instrumental concert on 15 September 1870. Leading 19th-century Morelia musicians included the organist Ramón Martínez Avilés, the composer of sacred music Benito Ortiz, the internationally acclaimed writer of popular music Miguel Lerdo de Tejada (1869–1944) and the military band director Encarnación Payén. Miguel Bernal Jiménez, the most widely known Morelia composer, organist and scholar of the 20th century, studied with Ignacio Mier Arriaga in the Escuela Popular de Bellas Artes de la Universidad Michoacana (founded *c*1920). In 1957 Alfonso Vega Núñez became director of the school; he was also cathedral organist and arranged international organ festivals for many years. Other important 20th-century figures are Bonifacio Rojas, director of both the Conservatorio de las Rosas (refounded in 1939) and the Escuela de Música Sagrada, and Rubén Valencia Cortés, the leading avant-garde composer. From 1939 to 1956 a valuable sacred music quarterly, *Schola cantorum*, was published at Morelia. The Niños Cantores de Morelia was a boys' choir that toured extensively in the USA and Europe in the 1950s.

BIBLIOGRAPHY

D. Basalenque: *Historia de la provincia de San Nicolas de Tolentino de Michoacan* (Mexico City, 1673), f.21*v*

*Magestuosa real pyra* (Mexico City, 1727)

*Breve noticia de las solemnes exequias de la Reina Nuestra Señora Doña Maria Isabel Francisca de Braganza y Borbón* (Mexico City, 1820), 21

J. de la Torre: *Bosquejo histórico y estadistico de la ciudad de Morelia* (Mexico City, 1883), 196

M. Bernal Jiménez: *El archivo musical del Colegio de Santa Rosa de Santa Maria de Valladolid: siglo XVIII: Morelia colonial* (Mexico City, 1939)

J. Trinidad Sánchez Frías: 'La música vernácula', *IV centenario Morelia monografía 1541–1941* (Morelia, 1941), 119

J. Romero Flores: *Historia de la ciudad de Morelia* (Mexico City, 1952), 247f

J. M. Marín: 'La obra del Maestro Miguel Bernal Jiménez', *Boletin mensual de la Universidad Michoacana*, no.3 (1956), 5

M. Talavera: *Miguel Lerdo de Tejada: su vida pintoresca y anecdótica* (Mexico City, 1958)

ROBERT STEVENSON

**Morell, Thomas** (*b* Eton, 18 March 1703; *d* Turnham Green, London, 19 Feb 1784). English author, scholar and librettist. He was educated at Eton and King's College, Cambridge, and entered the church, becoming a Doctor of Divinity in 1743. He was a Fellow of King's and from 1737 held the college living of Buckland in Hertfordshire, but lived chiefly at Turnham Green. His interests were scholarly and worldly rather than pastoral, though he was in demand as a preacher; he delivered the Three Choirs Festival sermon in Worcester Cathedral in 1746. He edited and translated a number of Greek plays, revised Greek and Latin dictionaries, turned Chaucer's *Canterbury Tales* into contemporary verse, and published *Poems on Divine Subjects*, an incomplete epic (*Hope*), sermons and miscellaneous journalism. He became a Fellow of the Royal Society and assistant secretary of the Society of Antiquaries in 1768, and chaplain to the Portsmouth garrison in 1775. Some of his MSS are in the British Library.

In 1746 Handel approached Morell for an oratorio text on the recommendation of the Prince of Wales. This resulted in Morell's supplying the librettos of *Judas Maccabaeus*, *Alexander Balus*, *Joshua* (conjecturally), *Theodora*, *Jephtha* and *The Triumph of Time and Truth* (dubbed on music previously composed to Italian words). He probably adapted *The Choice of Hercules* from a poem by Robert Lowth, but has been wrongly credited with the *Occasional Oratorio* and *Solomon*. After Handel's death he and the younger J. C. Smith concocted two pasticcio oratorios, *Nabal* (1764) and *Gideon* (1769), from the composer's works. Late in life Morell wrote a valuable account of his collaboration with Handel, containing some characteristic anecdotes and illustrating the facility with which he composed and improvised. Morell was a lover of music and played the organ, but his literary talents were slight. He spiced his insipid and limply constructed texts with quotations from Milton, Shakespeare, Dryden, Pope, Addison and others, without a corresponding enrichment of their content. Morell was of a convivial and improvident disposition, often in debt, and a friend of Hogarth and Garrick as well as Handel (who left him a legacy of £200). Hogarth's painting of him (1762) 'in the character of a cynic philosopher', seated by an organ, was engraved by James Basire.

BIBLIOGRAPHY
W. Dean: *Handel's Dramatic Oratorios and Masques* (London, 1959)
WINTON DEAN

**Morellati, Paolo** (*b* Vicenza, 1740; *d* Vicenza, 16 Feb 1807). Italian keyboard instrument maker and composer. He studied in Bologna with Martini from April 1762 to November 1763; his counterpoint exercises and 44 of his letters to Martini are extant (in *I-Bc*). In October 1763 he was admitted to the Accademia Filarmonica. From 1768 until his death he was organist at Vicenza Cathedral.

Morellati was known primarily as a maker of harpsichords and pianos; only a few of his compositions (those from the period of his study with Martini) seem to be extant (in *I-Bc*). Morellati constructed a piano with a new kind of hammer mechanism (an escapement action) and described it in a letter published in the *Giornale enciclopedico* (vii, July 1775) and the *Antologia di Roma* (xli, 1780, p.324). Sacchi wrote that in 1775 Morellati gave an excellent harpsichord he had made to Farinelli, who in turn presented it to the Duke of Parma. There are unconfirmed reports that Morellati

collaborated with the Erards as well as with English and German piano makers, and that he declined the offer of a position in London.

He was the father of Pietro Morellati, who succeeded him as organist at Vicenza Cathedral in 1807, and Stefano Morellati (1772–1794), a double bass player, who studied with Dragonetti and succeeded him in the Eretenio theatre orchestra at Vicenza.

BIBLIOGRAPHY
*SchmidlD*
G. Sacchi: *Vita del Cavaliere Don Carlo Broschi* (Venice, 1784)
L. Torri: 'Paolo Morellati', *Il pianoforte*, i (1920), May, 5
G. Mantese: *Storia musicale vicentina* (Vicenza, 1956), 101ff, 120, 147
HOWARD BROFSKY

**Morelli, Cesare** (*fl* late 1660s–1686). Italian singer, lutenist and composer of Flemish origin. He was taught music in Rome. After visiting England he spent four years in the service of a Portuguese nobleman in Lisbon where he was discovered in 1673 by Thomas Hill, a merchant friend of Samuel Pepys. On Hill's recommendation, Pepys took him into his service, and Morelli eventually arrived in London in April 1675. Pepys was highly impressed with his abilities, commenting that 'he is a thorough-bred scholar, and may be the greatest master of music of any we have'. His Catholicism, however, proved a great burden to Pepys during the persecution of Catholics in London in 1678, and consequently Morelli was forced to spend most of his time in the country. He nevertheless was able to teach Pepys to play the guitar, and he kept him supplied with songs until, in 1682, he returned to Flanders. Four years later he unsuccessfully asked Pepys to try to get him a place in James II's Catholic chapel, after which he is not heard of again. The songs that he wrote out for Pepys, which survive in four volumes (*GB-Cmc* Pepys 2591 and 2802–4), are for bass (to suit Pepys's voice) with simple tablature accompaniment. They include some by Morelli himself, among them a recitative setting of 'To be, or not to be', as well as arrangements of operatic arias by Carissimi, Cesti, G. B. Draghi, Lully, Reggio and Stradella. His other known works are a lute piece (in *J-Tn* n-4/42) and a duet which is included in a folio of Italian arias in the Royal Music Library (*GB-Lbm* RM 23.f.4).

BIBLIOGRAPHY
F. Bridge: *Samuel Pepys, Lover of Musique* (London, 1903)
A. Bryant: *Samuel Pepys: the Years of Peril* (London, 1948)
ROGER SHORT

**Morena [Meyer], Berta** (*b* Mannheim, 27 Jan 1878; *d* Rottach-Egern, Tegernsee, 7 Oct 1952). German soprano. She studied in Munich with Sophie Röhr-Brajnin and Aglaja von Orgeni, and made her début at the Munich Hofoper as Agathe (*Der Freischütz*). She remained with the company until her farewell in 1927, being especially admired in Wagner roles. She sang at the Metropolitan Opera (début March 1908 as Sieglinde) until 1911 and in the 1924–5 season, as Elisabeth, Beethoven's Leonore, Brünnhilde and Santuzza. When she appeared at Covent Garden in 1914, as Isolde, Sieglinde and Kundry, she was praised more as an actress (she was a woman of great beauty and distinctive stage presence) than as a singer; but she remained a Munich favourite until her retirement, after which she taught.

BIBLIOGRAPHY
A. Vogl: *Berta Morena und ihre Kunst* (Munich, 1919)
HAROLD ROSENTHAL

**Morendo** (It.: 'dying'; gerund of *morire*). A word used in musical scores as an instruction to die away gradually, characteristically found at the end of a section, as for instance at the end of the slow movement in Beethoven's String Quartet op.74. It is particularly common in Verdi's work. *Smorzando* has a similar meaning but is less strongly confined to the ends of sections; *diluendo* and CALANDO also appear. Koch (*Musikalisches Lexikon*, 1802) gave an entry under 'Moriente' (the present participle of *morire*).

For bibliography *see* TEMPO AND EXPRESSION MARKS.

DAVID FALLOWS

**Moreno (Andrade), Segundo Luis** (*b* Cotacachi, Ecuador, 3 Aug 1882; *d* Quito, Ecuador, 18 Nov 1972). Ecuadorian musicologist, composer and educationist. His early educational and musical experiences were confined to Cotacachi until he entered the National Conservatory of Music in Quito in October 1906. There his principal teacher, Dominico Brescia, persuaded him to begin collecting and studying the indigenous music of his own country. From 1915 until 1937 Moreno was a band director in the Ecuadorian army, a post which caused him to be stationed in various parts of Ecuador thus giving him the opportunity of learning the musical traditions of the Indians in many provinces.

Moreno was director of the conservatories in Cuenca (1937–40) and in Guayaquil (1940–45). The musical examples and descriptions of ceremonies which appear in Moreno's musicological writings are particularly important since they often constitute the only surviving records of these indigenous practices.

WRITINGS

'Música en el Ecuador', *El Ecuador en cien años de independencia*, ed. J. Gonzalo Orellana (Quito, 1930), 187–276
*La Campaña de Esmeraldas de 1913–1916 encabezada por el Coronel Graduado Don Carlos Concha Torres* (Cuenca, 1939)
'La música criolla en el Ecuador', *América: revista de la Asociación de escritores y artistas americanos*, iii/3 (1939), 60
*Música y danzas autoctonas del Ecuador* (Quito, 1949)
*La música de los Incas* (Quito, 1957)
*Cotacachi y su Comarca* (Quito, 1966)
'El equinoccio de setiembre en Cotacachi (la Fiesta de Santa Ana)', *Revista del folklore ecuatoriano*, ii (1966), 189
*Historia de la música en el Ecuador*, i (Quito, 1972)

BIBLIOGRAPHY

O. Meyer-Serra: *Música y músicos de Latinoamérica*, ii (Mexico City, 1947), 66
A. Morlás Gutiérrez: *Florilegio del pasillo ecuatoriano* (Quito, 1961), 208ff
C. Sigmund: *Segundo Luis Moreno: his Contributions to Ecuadorian Musicology* (diss., U. of Minnesota, 1971)

CHARLES SIGMUND

**Moreno Gans, José** (*b* Algemesi, Valencia, 3 March 1897). Spanish composer. He studied harmony and composition with del Campo at the Madrid Conservatory and then, under a grant from the Conde de Cartagena Foundation, continued his studies in Paris, Vienna and Berlin. In 1928 he won the National Music Prize for *Pinceladas goyescas*, a brilliantly orchestrated work in which he attempted to depict impressions of different streets painted by Goya. He won the prize for a second time in 1933 with the Violin Sonata in F minor. Among his other works are the *Sinfonía de estampas*, a Symphony in A major for small orchestra, a Piano Concerto, a String Quartet in D major and a Piano Sonata in C major.

ANTONIO RUIZ-PIPÓ

**Moreno Polo** [Moreno y Polo, Moreno], **Juan** (*fl* 1754–76). Spanish organist and composer. He was a priest and organist at Tortosa Cathedral. A manuscript of organ and harpsichord pieces (sonatas, fugues, hymn verses etc) signed by him and dated from 1754 to 1776, formerly in the possession of Pedrell, is now in the Biblioteca Central, Barcelona. Additional *pasos* and sonatas are at Montserrat and a large group of sacred vocal pieces is also at the Biblioteca Central, Barcelona, though these bear only the name Moreno. Pedrell held his works in high regard, considering him a pioneer in the high Classical style of Haydn and Mozart. Three of his organ pieces were published in *El organista litúrgico español* (Barcelona, 1905), nine organ and vocal pieces in *Salterio sacro-hispano* (Madrid, 1905–8), two keyboard pieces in the second volume of *Antología de organistas clásicos españoles* (Madrid, 1908, 2/1968), and two organ pieces in J. Muset's *Early Spanish Organ Music* (New York, 1948). They reveal many of the traits of his Spanish contemporaries – a mixture of *stile antico* (with dense imitation and liturgical cantus firmi) and the newer textures and figures of the Rococo. A certain harmonic boldness is present, but also the usual Spanish weakness (in the longer pieces) of over-repetition of a single motif. The vocal works are more conservative than those for keyboard, with polychoral effects that often suggest the early Baroque.

His brother, José Moreno Polo (*b* Hoz, nr. Saragossa; *d* Madrid, buried 23 Sept 1774), according to Latassa first served as organist at the Pilar in Saragossa and Albarracin Cathedral, where he was ordained priest, and then entered the royal chapel in Madrid (2 June 1757) in the new position of fourth organist, becoming third organist in 1768 after Nebra's death. Although Latassa credited José with more than 100 sonatas and other keyboard works, none has been found bearing his Christian name, and Pedrell believed all existing Moreno compositions to have been the work of Juan.

BIBLIOGRAPHY

F. de Latassa y Ortín: *Biblioteca nueva de los escritores aragoneses que florecieron desde el año de 1753 hasta el de 1795*, v (Pamplona, 1801), 222
F. Pedrell: 'Notas biográfico-bibliográficas', *Antología de organistas clásicos españoles*, ii (Madrid, 1908, 2/1968)
J. Subirá: 'Necrologías musicales madrileñas (años 1611–1808)', *AnM*, xiii (1958), 217

ALMONTE HOWELL

**Moreno Torroba, Federico** (*b* Madrid, 3 March 1891). Spanish composer, conductor and critic. He began music studies with his father, José Moreno Ballesteros, an organist and teacher at the Madrid Conservatory; later he was a composition pupil of del Campo. His earliest compositions were orchestral pieces, notably *Cuadros castellanos* (*c*1920). He then followed his predecessors in trying to create a true Spanish opera, producing *La virgen del Mayo* (1926) and *Maria la tempránica* (1930). However, he had most success with his light and subtle zarzuelas, pieces wide in their appeal but retaining a purity of style. Moreno Torroba achieved similar prominence through his guitar works, promoted by Segovia and others; his writing for the guitar shows the influence of central Spanish folk music.

WORKS

(*selective list*)

Zarzuelas: La mesonera de Tordesillas, 1925; La pastorella, 1925; La marchenera, 1929; Baturra de Temple, 1929; Luisa Fernanda, 1932;

Xuanón, 1933; La caravana de Ambrosio, 1934; La chulapona, 1934; Paloma Moreno, 1936; Monte Carmelo, 1936; Sor Navarra, 1936; Oro de Ley, 1938; Cascabeles, 1940; Maravilla, 1941; Polonesa, 1941; La caramba, 1942; La ilustra moza, 1943; Baile de Trajes, 1944; La canción del organillo, 1945; Orgullo de Jalisco, 1947; La niña del Polisón, 1948; El diablo en Sierra Morena, 1952; La boda del Señor Bringas, 1953; Hola Ciqui, 1953; Maria Manuela, 1953; La mujer de Aquella Noche, n.d.; Una noche en Aravaca, n.d.; Azabache, n.d.; Lolita Dolores, n.d.

Gui: Nocturno, 1926; Suite castellana, 1926; Burgalesa, 1928; Preludio, 1928; Serenata burgalesca, 1928; Pièces caractéristiques, 1931; Madroños, 1954; Guitarra española, 1960; Suite miniatura, 1960; Sonatina, 1965

Gui, orch: Concierto de Castilla, 1960; Homenaje a la seguidilla, 1961; Concierto en flamenco, 1962; Dialogo, a, n.d.

Principal publishers: Ricordi (Buenos Aires), Shott (Mainz), Unión Musical Española

### WRITINGS
*Discursos leidos ante la Academia de bellas artes de San Fernando en la recepción publica del Señor Don Federico Moreno-Torroba el dia 21 de febrero de 1935* (Madrid, 1935)

CHARLES RICHARD

**Morera, Enrique** [Enric] (*b* Barcelona, 22 May 1865; *d* Barcelona, 12 March 1942). Spanish composer. The family moved to Argentina in 1867, and the young Morera studied the violin, trumpet and organ in Córdoba. In 1883 he returned to Barcelona, where he became a pupil of Albeniz (piano), Vidiella (piano), Pedrell (harmony) and Chioffi (violin), and where he played in the Liceo Orchestra. He returned in 1886 to Argentina, but two years later he moved to Brussels and lived there for five years; he studied with Gilson and Fièvez and appeared at a public recital with Ysaÿe. In 1893 he went back to Barcelona, where he gained a reputation as a temperamental and craftsmanlike composer, principally through the orchestral pieces *Dansa dels gnoms* and *Introducció a l'Atlàntida*. He founded the Catalunya Nova choral society (1895), which he conducted for 14 years, and the Teatre Liric Català (1901). After a period in Madrid he returned again to Barcelona in 1905; this time he enjoyed a warmer reception—indeed, his stage works were greeted with acclaim. He made a further visit to Argentina (1909–11), where the president invited him to form a conservatory, and then settled in Barcelona as deputy director of the municipal music school. His compositions were strongly influenced by folk music, and he was one of the most popular of the Catalan nationalist composers.

### WORKS
(*selective list*)
Operas: La fada, 1, 1897; La devoción de la cruz, 3, 1904; Emporium, 3, 1906; Bruniselda, 3, 1908; Titaína, 3, 1908; La feréstega domada, 3, 1910; El mestre, 3, 1921; Don Joan de Serrallonga, 3, 1921; La nit d'amor, 1; Tassarba, 1

Zarzuelas: La canción del náufrago, 1904; El tío Juan, collab. R. Chapí; La vuelta de Pierrot

Orch: Danza dels gnoms, 1893; Introducció a l'Atlántida, sym. poem, 1893; Vc Conc., 1917; Poema de la nit i del dia,, 1919

Chamber music, pf pieces, incidental music, lyric scenes, many songs, many choral pieces, many sardanas

Principal publisher: Unión Musical Española

### BIBLIOGRAPHY
I. Iglesias: *Enric Morera* (Barcelona, 1921)
E. Morera: *Moments viscuts* (Barcelona, 1936)
J. Pena: *Enric Morera* (Barcelona, 1937)

ANTONIO RUIZ-PIPÓ

**Morera, Francisco** (*b* Villa de San Mateo, Castellón, 4 April 1731; *d* Valencia, 19 Oct 1793). Spanish composer. In 1741 he became a chorister at Valencia Cathedral, where he remained until on 15 June 1753 he was made acting organist at the Colegio del Patriarca in the same city; his appointment was made permanent on 7 June 1755, by which time he had composed 'many works, which on being sung were warmly applauded'. In 1757 he competed for the post of choirmaster at the cathedral, which was awarded to Pascual Fuentes. Later that year he went as organist to Castellón, and in April 1758 he was appointed choirmaster at Cuenca Cathedral. Finally, on 18 July 1768, on the strength of his reputation and without the usual competition, he was appointed to the same post at Valencia Cathedral, where he remained until his retirement in July 1793, three months before his death. His music includes many masses, a requiem, psalms and other Latin works as well as 217 Spanish villancicos (mostly in *E-VAc* and *CU*; also *MO*, *VAcp*).

### BIBLIOGRAPHY
*LaborD*
J. Ruiz de Lihory: *La música en Valencia: diccionario biográfico y crítico* (Valencia, 1903)
V. Ripollés: *El villancico i la cantata del segle XVIII a València* (Barcelona, 1935) [incl. villancico *Un niño que es el movil*, 1786, 8vv]
J. Piedra: 'Organistas valencianos de los siglos XVII y XVIII', *AnM*, xvii (1962), 141–78
R. Navarro Gonzalo: *Los maestros de capilla de la catedral de Cuenca* (Cuenca, 1974)

JOSÉ LÓPEZ-CALO

**Moresca** [morisca]. (1) A dance of exotic character which occurred widely in Europe during the Renaissance. Generally there was a Moorish element in the costumes or action; the dance often took the form of a stylized battle between Moors and Christians, reminiscent of the medieval wars in Spain. Certain recurring features of the *moresca*, however, are apparently of more ancient origin. Blackening of the face, bells attached to costumes, the presence of a fool (sometimes a man disguised as a woman) and the sword-play element itself have been traced back by Sachs and others to primitive fertility rites. The English morris dance – a variety of the *moresca* encountered as early as the 14th century – displays many of these features.

In the latter part of the 15th century *moresche* were danced in carnival processions and (especially in Italy) in *intermedi* between the acts of courtly dramatic entertainments. Although the dance is mentioned frequently in such connections, no detailed choreographic descriptions from this period survive. Some indication of the character of the *moresca* can be obtained from contemporary sculptures and paintings; for instance, a set of 16 statuettes carved by Erasmus Grasser in 1480 for the town hall at Munich clearly convey the grotesque, whirling movement of the dance. In the courtly sphere the *moresca* seems to have been performed mostly by professional dancers, to the accompaniment of pipes and tabors.

Musical sources for the *moresca* are not plentiful. There are a few 16th-century German examples, of which the earliest is Weck's *Tancz der schwarcz Knab* in J. Kotter's keyboard tablature (*c*1513; printed in Merian). Arbeau in *Orchésographie* (1588) recounted having seen in his youth 'la dance des Morisques' performed as a solo dance by a young man with the usual blackened face, and bells attached to his legs. Arbeau described the *moresca* as in 'mesure binaire', and he gave for it the tune shown in ex.1. Another version of this tune appears in Susato's third book of dance-tunes (Antwerp, 1551) under the title 'La Morisque basse danse'. A *moresca* tune in different rhythm was given by Mersenne in *Harmonie universelle* (1636–7; see ex.2).

*Moresca: engraving by Israel van Meckenem, second half of the 15th century; see also* DANCE, *fig.7*

Other tunes occur in English sources, e.g. 'The Kinges Morisck', which appears in *Parthenia Inviolata* (no.1) and the Fitzwilliam Virginal Book (no.247); the metrical change in this piece is typical.

Ex.1 Arbeau: Air de la Morisque, *Orchésographie*, f.94*v*

Ex.2 Mersenne: La Moresque, *Harmonie universelle* (Livre second des chants, p.171)

In the 17th century the term 'moresca' was also applied to ballet or pantomimic dance in opera, for example, the *moresca* at the end of Monteverdi's *Orfeo* (1607).

(2) A type of VILLANELLA, whose text parodied the dialect spoken by Africans living in parts of Venice and Naples. Examples are found in collections issued by Barré (1555) and Scotto (1560); Lassus included six *moresche* in his *Libro de villanelle, moresche ed altre canzoni* (Paris, 1581), three for four voices and three for six. The musical style of the vocal *moresca* was lively and uncomplicated, characterized by rhythmic freedom, much chordal writing and repetition, and occasional passages in parallel 5ths.

BIBLIOGRAPHY

C. Sharp and H. C. MacIlwaine: *The Morris Book* (London, 1907–13, rev. 2/1912–24)

W. Merian: *Der Tanz in den deutschen Tabulaturbüchern* (Leipzig, 1927/*R*1968), 52

O. Gombosi: 'The Cultural and Folkloristic Background of the Folia', *PAMS 1939*, 88

P. Nettl: 'Die Moresca', *AMw*, xiv (1957), 165

H. Engel: 'Moresca', *MGG*

For further bibliography *see* DANCE.

ALAN BROWN

**Moreschi, Alessandro** (*b* Montecompatri, nr. Rome, 11 Nov 1858; *d* Rome, 21 April 1922). Italian soprano, generally reckoned to have been the last castrato. *See* CASTRATO.

**Moretus, Jean** (*b* ?Antwerp, 1543; *d* Antwerp, 1610). Flemish printer who managed the Antwerp publishing business established by CHRISTOPHER PLANTIN.

**Morgan, Justin** (*b* West Springfield, Mass., 1747; *d* Randolph, Vermont, 2 March 1798). American composer; *see* PSALMODY (ii), §II.

**Morgan, Thomas** (*fl* 1691–9). Organist and composer, probably Irish. It seems very likely that the 'Mr Morgan' to whom a number of late 17th-century songs and instrumental pieces are attributed was the Thomas Morgan appointed organist of Christ Church Cathedral, Dublin, in 1691, who left almost immediately for England 'to endeavour to attain the perfection of an Organist'. *Mercurius musicus* (1699) contains a song stated to be 'the last he made in Ireland'. His *Collection of new Songs . . . and a Sonata for two Flutes* (1697) contains pieces from Motteux's *Europe's Revels* (1697) and Powell's *Imposture Defeated* (1697), on the whole of rather inferior quality. John Eccles's *Theatre Musick* (1698) contains instrumental music by Morgan, as do several MSS in *GB-Lbm* (e.g. Harl.4899, and Add.30839, 35043, etc). *Come, come, ye inhabitants of heaven*, described as 'A Mad Song . . . being the last he made', was published separately in 1699.

IAN SPINK

**Morganfield, McKinley.** *See* MUDDY WATERS.

**Morhange, Valentin.** *See* ALKAN, VALENTIN.

**Morhard** [Mohrhardt, Mohrhart], **Peter** (*d* Lüneburg, 1685). German composer and organist. He is first heard of in 1662, when he became organist of the Michaeliskirche, Lüneburg; he held the post until his death and was succeeded in it by his eldest son, Friedrich Christoph. His nine surviving chorale arrangements, which were recorded about 1660 in the tablature in which they have survived, show typical stylistic features of the generation of north German organists between the pupils of Sweelinck and Buxtehude, though in the quality of their contrapuntal writing they fall short of works by, for instance, Weckmann or Tunder. They show the influence of Scheidemann, but it does not follow that he must have been his pupil. The types of chorale arrangement that Morhard took over from Scheidemann were almost exclusively the modern ones, for example the organ chorale with decorated cantus firmus and above all the chorale fantasia typified by its virtuosity, refined sonority and plentiful use of echo effects.

WORKS

Org arrs.: Kyrie; Allein zu dir, Herr Jesu Christ; Alle Welt, was lebt [kreucht] und webet; Aus tiefer Not schrei ich zu dir; Gelobet seist du, Jesu Christ; Herr Gott, dich loben wir; Meine Seele erhebt den Herren; Wacht auf, ihr Christen alle; Was fürchtst du, Feind Herodes, sehr: *D-Lr*; some ed. in CEKM, xxiii (1973)

11 vocal works, formerly in *Lm* according to Seiffert, now lost
1 cantata, formerly in library of St Jacobi, Stettin, according to Freytag, now lost
1 sonata, 2 vn, 2 va, bn, bc; lost, cited in Walther

BIBLIOGRAPHY
*WaltherML*
M. Seiffert: 'Die Chorbibliothek der St. Michaelisschule in Lüneburg zu S. Bachs Zeit', *SIMG*, ix (1907–8), 610
F. Dietrich: *Geschichte des deutschen Orgelchorals im 17. Jahrhundert* (Kassel, 1932), 59f
W. Freytag: *Musikgeschichte der Stadt Stettin im 18. Jahrhundert* (Greifswald, 1936), 141
W. Apel: *Geschichte der Orgel- und Klaviermusik bis 1700* (Kassel, 1967; Eng. trans., rev. 1972)

WERNER BREIG

**Mori.** English family of musicians.

**(1) Nicolas Mori** (*b* London, 24 Jan 1796 or 1797; *d* London, 14 June 1839). Violinist and music publisher. The son of an Italian wig-maker in the New Road, London, he performed as a child prodigy, playing a concerto to his teacher, Barthélemon, at the age of eight. After six years' study with Viotti he was a soloist at the second Philharmonic Society concert in 1814; from 1816 he was for many years one of the leaders of that orchestra, playing at 92 concerts of the society. He led the King's Theatre orchestra under Costa until 1839 and played in many London concerts and provincial festivals. The *Quarterly Musical Magazine* admired his bold, free and commanding bow-arm, his firm, full and impressive tone and the force, precision and facility of his playing; the *Harmonicon* called him in 1824 'one of the finest violin-players in Europe'.

Mori composed a number of works for the violin. In 1819 he married Elizabeth Lavenu, widow of the publisher Lewis LAVENU; from about 1828 until his death the firm operated as Mori & Lavenu.

**(2) Frank** [Francis] **Mori** (*b* London, 21 March 1820; *d* Chaumont, France, 2 Aug 1873). Composer and conductor, son of (1) Nicolas Mori. A well-known London musician, he directed the short-lived London Orchestra in 1854, an early attempt to establish a permanent orchestra in the capital. He composed a cantata *Fridolin* (Worcester Festival, 1851), an operetta *The River Sprite* (Covent Garden, 9 February 1865, vocal score published) on a libretto of George Linley, and many ballads. Ballads were also published at about the same time by 'Frank Mori the younger'.

**(3) Nicholas Mori** (*b* London, 14 Jan 1822; *d* ?c1890). Composer, son of (1) Nicolas Mori. He studied with his father and C. Lucas and later in Paris. He wrote music to W. S. Gilbert's fairy comedy *The Wicked World* (1873) and published several fantasias for violin and piano on operatic and popular melodies.

BIBLIOGRAPHY
*Quarterly Musical Magazine*, iii (1821), 323
E. W. Duffin: *Particulars of the Illness and Death of the late Mr. Mori the Violinist* (London, 1839)
E. Heron-Allen: 'Mori, Nicolas', *DNB*
C. Humphries and W. C. Smith: *Music Publishing in the British Isles* (London, 1954, 2/1970)

KEITH HORNER

**Moriani, Napoleone** (*b* Florence, 10 March 1808; *d* Florence, 4 March 1878). Italian tenor. Of professional middle-class background, he studied law until convinced that his vocal gifts assured him of a stage career. His opera début was at Pavia in 1833 in Pacini's *Gli arabi nelle Gallie*. His period of great fame began in 1838, but his career was cut short by an early deterioration of his voice, highly marked by 1845. From 1840 to 1844 he frequently sang in Vienna and Germany as well as in Italy; in 1841 he was made a *Kammersänger* to the Austrian emperor. In summer 1844 and 1845 he sang in London, where he pleased the public but not the press, and in winter 1844–5 and 1845–6 at Madrid, where he was awarded the Order of Isabella; he also appeared at Lisbon and Barcelona. After singing in Italy for two years, he had his last important engagements at the Théâtre-Italien, Paris (where he had made his début in October 1845), in 1849–50 and at Madrid in autumn 1850. He retired the next year.

Moriani combined sweetness of tone with great dramatic intensity. With his gaunt, cadaverous good looks he excelled in death scenes and was known as 'il tenore della bella morte'. Impressed by his performance in revivals of Donizetti's *Lucia di Lammermoor* and *Pia de' Tolomei*, composers wrote for him parts portraying the hero in a prolonged death agony, as in Vaccai's *La sposa di Messina* (Venice, 1839) and Federico Ricci's *Luigi Rolla* (Florence, 1841), which concerns a sick genius. Other important premières in which he took part included Mercadante's *Le due illustri rivali* (Venice, 1838), Donizetti's *Maria di Rudenz* (Venice, 1838) and *Linda di Chamounix* (Vienna, 1842). For a revival of *Attila* at La Scala in 1847 Verdi wrote for him a romanza to be inserted into the last act. He provides an interesting footnote to Verdian history: he was almost certainly the father of Giuseppina Strepponi's two illegitimate children.

BIBLIOGRAPHY
A. Ghislanzoni: 'Il re dei tenori', *Gazzetta musicale di Milano*, xxxiii (1878), 115
L. Neretti: 'Dalle carte di un celebre tenore', *Musica d'oggi*, xvii (1935), 7
R. Celletti: 'Moriani, Napoleone', *ES*
F. Walker: *The Man Verdi* (London, 1962)

JULIAN BUDDEN

**Mori da Viadana, Jacobi.** See MORO, GIACOMO.

**Morigi, Angelo** (*b* Rimini, 1725; *d* Parma, 22 Jan 1801). Italian violinist and composer. He was a pupil of Tartini for the violin and of Vallotti for theory. In 1750 he appeared in London, and his first compositions were published there. He entered the service of the Duke of Parma in about 1758 (according to the dedication of his sonatas op.4), became first violinist on 1 April 1766, and was appointed director of music on 6 September 1773. He was well regarded both as a violinist and as a teacher of composition, his most successful pupil being Bonifazio Asioli who posthumously published Morigi's counterpoint treatise. Morigi's compositions resemble Tartini's, tending in melody and texture towards the early *galant* style. A letter to Padre Martini in 1772 reflects his dissatisfaction with the new, more brilliant style, and perhaps explains why all of his published works appeared early in his career.

WORKS
6 Sonatas, 2 vn, bc (London, *c*1751)
[6] Sonate, vn, b, op.2 (London, *c*1753)
6 Concertos in 7 Parts, vn, str, op.3 (London, *c*1756; 2/Amsterdam, 1759)
6 sonate, vn, b, op.4 (Parma, 1759; 2/as op.1, Paris, n.d.)
3 sonatas, vn, b, *B-Bc*, *US-BE*; duet, ob, bn, *I-Gi(l)*

WRITINGS
*Elementi e regole di contrappunto* (MS, *I-PAc*)

*Trattato di contrapunto fugato* (Milan, *c*1815, 2/*c*1820; Ger. trans., 1816)

BIBLIOGRAPHY

L. Torchi: 'La musica instrumentale in Italia nei secoli XVI, XVII e XVIII', *RMI*, vi (1899), 722; pubd separately (Turin, 1901/*R*1969)
A. Moser: *Geschichte des Violinspiels* (Berlin, 1923, rev. and enlarged 2/1966–7)
N. Pelicelli: 'Musicisti in Parma nel secolo XVIII', *NA*, xi (1934), 267

CHAPPELL WHITE

**Mörike, Eduard (Friedrich)** (*b* Ludwigsburg, 8 Sept 1804; *d* Stuttgart, 4 June 1875). German writer, clergyman and teacher. He studied at the monastery school in Urach and theology at the university of Tübingen, where he met Maria Meyer, the 'Peregrina' of his poems and the model for Elisabeth in his novella *Maler Nolten* (1832). He was ordained in 1826 but retired from the Church in 1843. In 1851 he married and settled in Stuttgart as a teacher of literature at the Katharinenstift.

Mörike had special affinities with music: personally, professionally and above all creatively. These affinities are manifest in his poetry, which though first published in 1838 elicited only a sporadic (and hardly commensurate) response until Hugo Wolf's 57 settings of the 1880s. This half-century hiatus suggests that Mörike's highly charged and highly coloured language had to await a complex and chromatic musical equivalent for its significant embodiment.

Its inherent musicality had simple and strong foundations; in folksong, in hymn metres, and in the general German tradition. At least one poem (*Zum neuen Jahr*) was written to an existing tune; another (*Chor jüdischer Mädchen*) was part of an unfinished opera; a third (*Ach, nur einmal*) is prefaced by a melody quoted from Mozart – about whom Mörike wrote the justly famed novella, *Mozart auf der Reise nach Prag* (1855), which is as notable for its intuitive critical insight as for its beauty of form and phrase. Mörike's social circle included the amateur pianist Wilhelm Hartlaub and composer Friedrich Kauffmann (and his son Emil, later a friend of Wolf's); these relationships occasioned several poems on music as well as the earliest settings of the lyrics, by the Kauffmanns. Their plain diatonic style was also common to Silcher (one song) and later Hugo Distler (48 partsongs). Schumann (five songs, four partsongs), Franz (nine songs) and Brahms (two songs, one duet) found more complex equivalents, but the deepest musical strata of Mörike remained for the most part unmatched.

These elements can be classified as relating to melody, rhythm and motif. In the first case, poetic echo-refrains (as in *Agnes*) or puns (*Elfenlied*) or deliberate vowel patterns and cadences require an analogous turn of musical phrase. Next, Mörike's familiarity with classical verse forms and metres made him a master of the significant stress and placement of key words. More subtly, he used relevant rhythms to unify a poem (e.g. the cantering beats of *Der Gärtner*, or the insistent feet that begin *Fussreise*). Finally his favourite unifying images are often themselves either directly musical (e.g. the wind-blown harp notes that symbolize lament in *An eine Aeolsharfe*) or are readily translatable into sonorous terms (e.g. the breezes that signify love in *Lied vom Winde*, *Begegnung* etc).

These latter devices of relevant unifying rhythm and motif are the precise poetic counterpart of the fully evolved lied form itself, which may in part explain the often-remarked Mörike–Wolf affinity. Othmar Schoeck's 47 settings also repay study from this standpoint.

BIBLIOGRAPHY

H. Maync: *Eduard Mörike: sein Leben und Dichten* (Stuttgart and Berlin, 1902, 2/1913)
J. H. Kneisel: *Mörike and Music* (New York, 1949)
S. S. Prawer: *Mörike und seine Leser: Versuch einer Wirkungsgeschichte* (Stuttgart, 1960)
W. Rehm: 'Mörike, Eduard', *MGG* [with list of writings and fuller bibliography]
E. Sams: 'Homage to Eduard Mörike', *MT*, cxvi (1975), 532 [with list of settings]

ERIC SAMS

**Morin, Charles.** See CRABBÉ, ARMAND.

**Morin, Jean-Baptiste** (*b* Orleans, 1677; *d* Paris, 1754). French composer. He received his early training as a chorister at St Aignan in Orleans and throughout his career he served the royal family of Orleans – as *maître de chapelle* to the Abbesse de Chelles (a daughter of Philippe III, Duke of Orleans and Regent) and as *ordinaire de la musique* in the duke's household in Paris. Like other musicians working for Philippe III, he was greatly influenced by his employer's love of Italian music, and it was no mere coincidence that the earliest works in the repertory of the 18th-century French cantata – a form deeply indebted to Italian models – came from a circle of musicians (Morin, Bernier, Stuck, Campra) in the service of the Duke of Orleans.

Morin's cantatas represent his most important contribution to French music. Uniting French and Italian styles, they broke new ground in French vocal chamber music and set a fashion which few composers could resist. His first volume of such works appeared in 1706 (although Morin stated that these cantatas had been circulating in manuscript for some years), and so popular were they that a second edition was issued three years later. His second and third volumes of *cantates françaises* appeared in 1707 and 1712. The preface to Morin's first volume explains the composer's aim:

I have done all that I can to retain the sweetness of our French style of melody, but with greater variety in the accompaniments and employing those rhythms and modulations characteristic of the Italian cantata. For convenience of performance I have included in this volume only one cantata that needs an instrumental ensemble. Thus with only a solo voice, harpsichord and bass viol one can easily perform most of this chamber music. I have also added one duo cantata.

Morin's 18 published cantatas all reflect in some way a union of French and Italian styles (although some individual movements closely resemble the conventional French *air*), and while they do not take pride of place in the cantata repertory their influence was nevertheless decisive.

Morin himself, however, regarded his divertissement *La chasse du cerf* (1708) more highly than all his other works. Not only did it receive royal approval, but its popularity was sustained long after his cantatas had been superseded by those from other composers. It is easy to see why this divertissement (to words by Séré de Rieux) caught the public fancy: not only are the elaborate 18th-century conventions and intricate manoeuvres of the royal sport of hunting faithfully followed in the work's structure, but the music itself captures the scene very vividly. Ideally the work requires hunting horns and trumpets (undoubtedly borrowed from the royal *écurie* when it was performed at court), but Morin realistically reduced the published score to a trio texture (violins, oboes and continuo), marking those places where brass could be used. Despite its novelty *La chasse du cerf* owes much to the experience Morin gained in his first two books of cantatas; upon these pioneering works also rests his reputation in the history of early 18th-century French music.

### WORKS
*(all printed works published in Paris)*

#### CANTATAS
Bk 1 (1706): Euterpe; L'impatience; Circé; L'Amour devoilé; Enone; Les amants mécontents

Bk 2 (1707): L'absence; L'aurore; La rose; L'incertitude; Bachus; Junon et Pallas

Bk 3 (1712): Le sommeil d'Amour; L'absence; La jeune Flore; La nauffrage d'Ulisse; Don Quixote; Psiché et ses soeurs

Esther (mentioned in *Mercure de France*, 1724, lost); Philomèle, *F-Pn* (doubtful authorship); Airs in Ballard's *Recueil* (1707)

#### DIVERTISSEMENTS, ETC
La chasse du cerf(1709); La chasse du coeur, parody (1752); L'Himen et l'Amour (1714); Le triomphe de l'Amour et de l'Himen, parody (1747); Fanfares in Les dons des enfans de Latone (1734)

2 books of motets (1704, 1709); Ad mensam and Venite, exsultemus; Te Deum, lost

### BIBLIOGRAPHY
C. Brainne, J. Debarbouiller and C. F. Lapierre: *Les hommes illustres de l'Orléanais*, i (Orleans, 1852)

D. E. Tunley: *The Eighteenth-century French Cantata* (London, 1974)

DAVID TUNLEY

**Morini (Siracusano), Erica** (*b* Vienna, 5 Jan 1904). American violinist of Austrian birth. The daughter of professional musicians, she was taught by her father until the age of seven, when she became one of the first female violin pupils at the Vienna Conservatory, studying with Otakar Ševčík. Her successful Viennese début in 1916 led to an invitation from Nikisch to perform with the Leipzig Gewandhaus Orchestra and the Berlin PO. In the 1920–21 season she travelled to the USA, where she made her concerto début at the Metropolitan Opera under Bodansky and gave four much-praised recitals at Carnegie Hall and elsewhere. Her large sympathetic tone and reliable technique were especially notable. On her return to Europe after three years she was admired as one of the finest string players of a particularly brilliant generation. She left Austria during the Anschluss and settled in New York where her abilities were further developed. Her playing has always been characterized by a generous emotional response to the music, but at her best she also displayed a degree of interpretative adaptability to an extremely wide repertory.

RICHARD BERNAS

**Morino, Egidius de.** *See* EGIDIUS DE MURINO.

**Morisca.** *See* MORESCA.

**Morison, Elsie (Jean)** (*b* Ballarat, Victoria, 15 Aug 1924). Australian soprano. After winning the Melba Scholarship in 1943, she studied with Clive Carey at the Melbourne Conservatory and in 1946, still with Carey, at the RCM, London. She made her English début at the Albert Hall, in *Acis and Galatea* in 1948, and that autumn joined Sadler's Wells Opera, appearing regularly there until 1954. She played Anne Trulove in the first British staging of *The Rake's Progress* (Edinburgh Festival, 1953). After her Covent Garden début (21 December 1953) as Mimì, she sang regularly with that company until 1962. In such roles as Susanna, Pamina, Marzelline, Micaela, Antonia (*Les contes d'Hoffmann*), Mařenka, and Blanche in the first British production (in English) of Poulenc's *Dialogues des Carmélites* (1958), she was admired for the touching sincerity of her acting and the lyrical warmth of her voice. In 1955 she created the title role of Arwel Hughes's *Menna* for the Welsh National Opera. She sang frequently in oratorio and was a distinguished Handelian. She married the conductor Rafael Kubelík in 1963.

HAROLD ROSENTHAL

**Moritz,** Landgrave of Hessen-Kassel (*b* Kassel, 25 May 1572; *d* Eschwege, 15 March 1632). German patron and composer. He succeeded his father as Landgrave of Hessen-Kassel in 1592 and ruled until 1627, when, under the pressures of the Thirty Years War, he abdicated in favour of his son and retired to Eschwege. He encouraged an exceptionally flourishing musical life at his court and himself studied music from 1586 onwards with his Kapellmeister, Georg Otto. He also encouraged drama, and the Ottoneum, completed in 1605 and named after Otto, was the earliest court theatre in Germany. His patronage not only of music and the theatre but of other branches of art and learning earned him the title 'Moritz der Gelehrte' (Moritz the Learned), and the Landgraf-Moritz-Stiftung, an important musicological institution founded in Kassel in 1955, is named after him. He was the first to encourage the talents of Schütz, who was a choirboy in his Kapelle. He financed his first visit to Italy, in 1609, and appointed him court organist on his return in 1613. Reluctantly, but with a good grace, he allowed him to move to the electoral court at Dresden in 1615, and he presented him with a medallion and other gifts; in 1619 he unsuccessfully tried to persuade him to return as Kapellmeister after Otto's death. The forces in Moritz's Kapelle were modest but were augmented for occasions such as the christening of his son in 1600, when 36 instrumentalists were among the performers. His library (in *D-Kl*) contained concerted works of the time by Giovanni Gabrieli, Schütz and other composers, which suggests that up-to-date music was performed at the court, and Hans Leo Hassler, John Dowland, Christoph Demantius and Alessandro Orologio were among the prominent composers who worked at or visited his court, dedicated works to him or corresponded with him.

Moritz's own music is conservative. His output, especially of sacred music, was large, but much of it is lost. The sacred works include both solo settings and four-part harmonizations of hymns and psalms, as well as a number of psalms, motets and *Magnificat* settings written either in the *stile antico* or in the Venetian polychoral manner, all without continuo except the 12-voice setting of Psalm cl. The secular music includes groups of Italian madrigals and villanellas and a number of pavans, galliards and intradas for a generally unspecified ensemble; of the four pieces for which instruments are indicated two are for broken consort and two are for homogeneous groups, of cornetts and trombones respectively. Moritz also completed and prepared for the press a number of works by Valentin Geuck, who was employed at his court and died young in 1596.

### WORKS

#### VOCAL
24 melodies, 1v, in S. Schadaeus: Christlich Gesangbuch von allerhandt geistlichen Psalmen und Liedern (Geissmar, 1601, 2/1612 with harmonizations); 13 ed. in Winterfeld; 14 ed. in K. Ameln and C.

Mahrenholz: *Handbuch der deutschen evangelischen Kirchenmusik*, ii–iii (Göttingen, 1942)
30 motets, 3–5vv, 1603³, 1603⁴, 1604⁵: 4 ed. in Blume
31 songs, 1–4vv, in Psalmen Davids, nach frantzösischer melodey (Kassel, 1607)
Hosianna, 8vv, 1618¹
Magnificat, 3vv, inc.; Magnificat, 4vv; 2 Magnificat in 12th mode, 1600; 2 psalms, 12vv, 1 with bc: *D-Kl*
24 villanellas, 4vv; madrigals, songs, other vocal works: *Kl*; 4 fugues, 5 madrigals, ed. in EDM, 2nd ser., *Kurhessen*, i/2 (1938)

INSTRUMENTAL

1 pavan, lute, 1610²³; ed. in Schott's Series of Early Lute Music, i (London, 1958)
Pavans, galliards, intradas, various insts., *Kl*; some ed. in EDM, 2nd ser., *Kurhessen*, i/1 (1936)

For complete list including lost works see *MGG*

BIBLIOGRAPHY

C. von Winterfeld: *Der evangelische Kirchengesang*, ii (Leipzig, 1845/R1966)
E. Zulauf: *Beiträge zur Geschichte der landgräflich-hessischen Hofkapelle zu Cassel bis auf die Zeit Moritz' des Gelehrten* (Kassel, 1902)
F. Blume: Introduction to *Geistliche Musik am Hofe des Landgrafen Moritz von Hessen* (Kassel, 1931); repr. in *Zeitschrift des Vereins für Hessische Geschichte und Landeskunde*, lxviii (1957), 131
H. Birtner: 'Heinrich Schütz und Landgraf Moritz von Hessen', *Hessenland*, xlvi (1935), 100
H. Grössel: *Georgius Otto: ein Motettenkomponist des 16. Jahrhunderts* (Kassel, 1935)
W. Dane: 'Briefwechsel zwischen dem landgräflich-hessischen und dem kurfürstlich-sächsischen Hof um Heinrich Schütz (1614–1619)', *ZMw*, xvii (1935–6), 343
C. Engelbrecht: *Die Kasseler Hofkapelle im 17. Jahrhundert* (Kassel, 1958)
——: 'Musik und Theater in Kassel von den Anfängen bis zum Tode des Landgrafen Friedrich II.', *Theater in Kassel* (Kassel, 1959)
E. Gutbier: 'Valentin Geuck und Landgraf Moritz von Hessen, die Verfasser einer Musiklehre', *Hessisches Jb für Landesgeschichte*, x (1960)
W. Blankenburg: 'Landgraf Moritz von Hessen-Kassel', *Musik und Kirche*, xlii (1972), 131

*See also* KASSEL *and* SCHÜTZ, HEINRICH.

HORACE FISHBACK

**Morlacchi, Francesco (Giuseppe Baldassare)** (*b* Perugia, 14 June 1784; *d* Innsbruck, 28 Oct 1841). Italian composer and conductor. A pupil of his uncle, the cathedral organist L. Mazzetti, and of Luigi Caruso, director of the music school in the monastery of the Padri dell'Oratorio in Perugia, he began to compose sacred music at an early age, including a mass and an oratorio, *Gli angeli esultanti al sepolcro* (1803). From 1803 to 1804 he studied in Loreto with Nicola Zingarelli, whose teaching proved not to his liking, and in 1805 he continued his studies with Padre Mattei at the Liceo Filarmonico in Bologna. There, in the same year, he received his diploma for the cantata *Il tempio della gloria*, written in honour of the coronation of Napoleon as King of Italy and first performed at the Teatro Maggiore. Morlacchi was also elected a member of the Accademia Filarmonica. During this time he wrote other choral works, including a *Te Deum* and a *Pater noster* which were performed on a number of occasions, a *Cantata in lode della musica* and the *Canto dell' Ugolino* on a text by Dante.

Morlacchi made his début as an opera composer in 1807 with *Il poeta in campagna* in Florence and *Il ritratto* in Verona. *Il Corradino*, an *opera seria* first performed in Parma in 1808, marked the beginning of his extraordinarily successful career as a composer for the stage, though he continued to write sacred works (notable is a *Miserere a 16*, written for Bologna, 1807). His renown had spread quickly, and leading opera houses, in Milan and Rome, commissioned operas from him; *La principessa per ripiego* (1809) and *Le Danaidi*

(1810), both first performed in Rome, enjoyed great success throughout Italy.

Morlacchi also scored a considerable triumph with the lyric cantata *Saffo*, written for the celebrated contralto Maria Marcolini and first performed at La Scala. Through this singer, who had sent reports of Morlacchi to the Saxon minister Count Camillo Marcolini, a relative of hers, he was brought to the notice of the Dresden court; in September 1810, he was summoned to the Italian Opera in Dresden on Marcolini's recommendation as assistant to the Kapellmeister Joseph Schuster. In 1811 he was appointed Kapellmeister for life. Between 1817 and 1826 Carl Maria von Weber also worked in the city as Kapellmeister of the German Opera, whose development Morlacchi understandably strove to restrain. His best years were between 1810 and 1816, when he did a great deal for the administration and artistic furtherance of the royal chapel at Dresden; the musicians greatly valued his exceptional, dynamic talent as a conductor, his brilliant musicianship and his versatility on a variety of instruments: the violin, piano, clarinet, flute, bassoon, horn and cello. His organizing ability and diplomatic skill, his capacity for discovering virtuoso voices, and his authoritative musicianship must also be recognized. These have been widely underestimated; nevertheless, his indisputable human failings – vanity, self-aggrandizement, love of intrigue and chauvinism – which constantly showed themselves in the rivalry with Weber, undoubtedly caused difficulties in his administration. In fact it was the rivalry of their factions, not personal differences between Morlacchi and Weber, that caused both men, especially Morlacchi, to behave unreasonably; later, their relations improved.

As Kapellmeister of the Italian Opera, supported by the influential Italian party at court and enjoying the special protection of the all-powerful minister, Count von Einsiedel, Morlacchi staged a representative selection of Italian operas in Dresden. His performances did not consist only of the successful operas of his day, but included among oratorios Bach's *St Matthew Passion* (1833), performed in aid of a pension fund he had set up in 1829 for widows and orphans of members of the chapel, and Handel's *Messiah* (1834), in the Palm Sunday concerts given by the royal chapel. He was highly praised and esteemed as a composer of opera and sacred music at the court of Dresden, where he scored conspicuous successes with his operas *Il nuovo barbiere di Siviglia* (1816), *La simplicetta di Pirna* (1817), *La gioventù di Enrico V* (1823), *Il Colombo* (1828) and *Il rinnegato* (1832). With these he instilled into his brilliant, effective if superficial style slightly more depth under the influence of German music, without achieving a quality which could have won a significant place in music history for his long-forgotten, wide-ranging compositions. Of Morlacchi's *Il nuovo barbiere di Siviglia*, written immediately after Rossini's *Il barbiere di Siviglia*, Weber remarked: 'The fellow has little musical knowledge, but he has talent, a flow of ideas and especially a fund of good comic stuff in him'. The technical handling of vocal parts in comic scenes especially, with their bravura coloraturas, ornamented cadenzas and expressive cantilenas, is one of the most successful features of Morlacchi's stage compositions which, with their piquant rhythms and dynamic climaxes, approach Donizetti and Rossini in style. His later works show an increasingly colourful instrumentation, and follow Weber's example in making frequent use of the clarinet, horn and cello. Superficial treatment and threadbare harmony are characteristic of the sacred works; significantly, in the requiem for King Friedrich August I of Saxony (1827), the operatic, dramatic sections are the best.

During his years in Dresden, Morlacchi also composed numerous operas and sacred works for his homeland. After the performance of his *Oratorio della Passione* in Perugia in 1816 he was awarded the Order of the Golden Spur and was granted the title Conte Palatino e Lateranense by Pope Pius VII. He died en route from Dresden to Pisa, where he was hoping to regain his health after two years of suffering from consumption. After the official closing of the Italian Opera in Dresden (31 March 1832) it was the downfall of Spontini in Berlin (April 1841), and the deaths of Morlacchi and his colleague Joseph Rastrelli (November 1842), together with the rise of Wagner as Kapellmeister of the Dresden Opera (1843–9), that marked the end of the supremacy of Italian opera in German theatres.

## WORKS

### OPERAS

Il poeta in campagna ossia Il poeta spiantato (farce, 1), Florence, Teatro della Pergola, Feb 1807
Il ritratto ossia La forza dell'astrazione (opera giocosa, 1, L. Romanelli), Verona, Teatro Filarmonico, April 1807
Il Corradino (opera seria, 2, A. S. Sografi), Parma, Teatro Ducale, 25 Feb 1808
Enone e Paride (opera seria, 2), Livorno, Teatro degli Avvalorati, aut. 1808
Oreste (opera seria, 2, L. Bottoni), Parma, Teatro Ducale, 26 Dec 1808
Rinaldo d'Asti (opera giocosa, 2, J. Ferretti), Parma, 1808
Il tutore deluso (G. Rosseau), Parma, Teatro S Caterina, spr. 1809, doubtful
Il Simoncino (farce, 1), Rome, Teatro Valle, June 1809
La principessa per ripiego (opera giocosa, 2, Ferretti), Rome, Teatro Valle, aut. 1809
Le avventure di una giornata (opera buffa, 2, Romanelli), Milan, La Scala, 26 Sept 1809
Le Danaidi (opera seria, 2, S. Scatizzi, after Metastasio: Ipermestra), Rome, Teatro Argentina, 11 Feb 1810
Raoul di Créqui (opera giocosa, 2, G. Artusi), Dresden, Hoftheater, April 1811
La capricciosa pentita (opera giocosa, 2, Romanelli), Pavia, Nuovo Teatro dei Quattro Signori, 1812
Il nuovo barbiere di Siviglia (opera giocosa, 4, G. Petrosellini and C. Sterbini), Dresden, Hoftheater, May 1816
La simplicetta di Pirna (opera buffa, 2), Pillnitz bei Dresden, Königliches Theater, Aug 1817
Laodicea (opera seria, 2, G. B. Bordese), Naples, Teatro S Carlo, 13 Jan 1818
Gianni di Parigi (opera seria, 2, F. Romani), Milan, La Scala, 29 May 1818
Donna Aurora ossia Il romanzo all'improvviso (opera buffa, 2, Romani), Dresden, Hoftheater, 1819
Tebaldo e Isolina (2, G. Rossi), Dresden, Hoftheater, 1820
La gioventù di Enrico V (2, Romani), Dresden, Hoftheater, 4 Oct 1823
Ilda d'Avenello (opera seria, 2, Rossi), Venice, Teatro la Fenice, carn. 1824
I saraceni in Sicilia ossia Eufemia da Messina (grand opera, Romani), Venice, Teatro la Fenice, carn. 1828; Dresden, Hoftheater, March 1832 as Il rinnegato
Il Colombo (2, Romani), Genoa, Teatro Carlo Felice, 28 June 1828
Don Desiderio ovvero Il disperato per eccesso di buon cuore (opera buffa, 2, B. Morelli), Dresden, Hoftheater, aut. 1829
Francesca da Rimini (Romani), 1836, inc.

### OTHER WORKS

Oratorios: Gli angeli esultanti al sepolcro, 1803; Oratorio della Passione (Metastasio), 1811; Isacco (Metastasio), 1817; La morte d'Abele (Metastasio), 1821
Other vocal: 13 masses, requiem, offertories, settings of Salve regina and Magnificat, vespers, cantatas, solo songs
Inst: La tempesta, sinfonia; str qt; short pieces for pf and org

## BIBLIOGRAPHY

'Verzeichnis sämtlicher Compositionen des Kapellmeisters Ritter Morlacchi bis 1822', *AMZ*, v (1823), 174
G. B. Rossi-Scotti: *Della vita e delle opere del cavaliere Francesco Morlacchi* (Perugia, 1860)
M. M. von Weber: *Carl Maria von Weber*, ii (Leipzig, 1864)
U. Manferrari: *Dizionario universale delle opere melodrammatiche*, ii (Florence, 1945)
H. Schnoor: *Dresden: vierhundert Jahre deutscher Musikkultur* (Dresden, 1948)
W. Fischer, ed.: *In memoriam Francisci Morlacchi* (Innsbruck, 1952)
H. Schnoor: *Weber: Gestalt und Schöpfung* (Dresden, 1953)
G. Ricci des Ferres-Cancani: *Francesco Morlacchi, un maestro italiano alla corte di Sassonia (1784–1841)* (Florence, 1956)
I. Sampson: 'Morlacchi, Francesco', *ES*
W. Becker: *Die deutsche Oper in Dresden unter der Leitung von Carl Maria von Weber, 1817–1826* (Berlin, 1962)
J. Warrack: *Carl Maria von Weber* (London, 1968)

DIETER HÄRTWIG

**Morlaye, Guillaume** (*b* ?Paris, *c*1510; *d* after 1558). French lutenist, editor and composer. He lived in Paris and was active as a 'marchant et joueur d'instruments' from 6 August 1541 when he took on an apprentice and agreed to teach him the viol and the lute. He maintained a variety of commercial interests; in 1548 he was involved in slave-trading and between 1549 and 1553 he dealt in engravings. On 13 February 1552 he obtained from Henri II a ten-year privilege to print, or have printed, music by his teacher, Alberto da Ripa, and tablatures for guitar, spinet and other instruments. On 19 April Michel Fezandat made an agreement with him to bear the whole cost of printing in return for half the proposed 1200 copies; Morlaye had simply to provide corrected proofs. The collaboration proved fruitful and during the next six years Fezandat printed under Morlaye's privilege three guitar (or cittern) books and four lutebooks, and the partbooks of two collections of four-voice psalms. Morlaye's voice, lute and Christian charity were praised in poems by Jacques Grévin published in 1560, probably after Morlaye's death. Apart from the collection for soprano and lute arranged from psalm harmonizations by Certon, Morlaye's intabulations are varied; they usually include a few opening *fantaisies* (short chordal pieces in rambling style), transcriptions of secular and sacred chansons (mostly of four-voice pieces by Parisian composers of the preceding decade, e.g. Sandrin, Janequin, Mithou), a few frottolas, *villanesche*, madrigals and motets; the largest group consists of dances, mainly galliards, pavanes, branles and allemandes, and includes some sets of variations on grounds such as the 'Hornepype d'Angleterre' and 'Conte Clare'.

## WORKS

*(published in Paris)*

### INTABULATIONS

*(lute)*

Premier livre de tabulature de leut, contenant plusieurs chansons, fantasies, pavanes et gaillardes, composées par maistre Guillaume Morlaye joueur de leut, et autres bons autheurs (1552[34])
Premier livre de psalmes mis en musique par maistre Pierre Certon . . . reduitz en tabulature de leut par maistre Guillaume Morlaye, 1v, lute (1554); ed. R. de Morcourt, Les luthistes (Paris, 1957)
Second livre de tabulature de leut, contenant plusieurs chansons, fantaisies, motetz, pavanes et gaillardes: composées par maistre Guillaume Morlaye (1558[18])
Troisiesme livre de tabulature de leut . . . par maistre Guillaume Morlaye (1558[19])

*(guitar)*

Le premier livre de chansons, gaillardes, pavanes, branles, almandes, fantaisies, reductz en tabulature de guiterne par maistre Guillaume Morlaye (1552[32])
Quatriesme livre contenant plusieurs fantasies, chansons, gaillardes, paduanes, branles, reduictes en tabulature de guyterne, et au jeu de la cistre, par maistre Guillaume Morlaye, et autres bons autheurs (1552[33]) (incl. 27 works by Morlaye)
Le second livre de chansons, gaillardes, paduanes, branles, almandes,

fantasies, reduictz en tabulature de guiterne, par maistre Guillaume Morlaye joueur de leut (1553[34])

### EDITIONS

Premier livre de tabulature de leut, contenant plusieurs chansons et fantasies, composées par feu messire Albert de Rippe de Mantoue (1552[36])

Second livre de tabulature de leut, contenant plusieurs chansons, motetz et fantasies, composées par feu messire Albert de Rippe (1554[34])

Troisieme livre de tabulature de leut . . . par feu messire Albert de Rippe (1554[35])

Quatriesme livre de tabulature de leut . . . par feu messire Albert de Rippe (1554[36])

Cinquiesme livre de tabulature de leut . . . par feu messire Albert de Rippe (1555[36])

Sixiesme livre de tabulature de leut, contenant plusieurs chansons, fantasies, motetz, pavanes, et gaillardes composées par feu messire Albert de Rippe (1558)

Premier livre de psalmes et cantiques en vulgaire françoys (1552[3])
Second livre de psalmes et cantiques en vulgaire françoys (1553[18])

### BIBLIOGRAPHY

J.-G. Prod'homme: 'Guillaume Morlaye, éditeur d'Albert de Ripe', *RdM*, ix (1925), 157

F. Lesure: Introduction to *Psaumes de Pierre Certon réduits pour chant et luth*, ed. R. de Morcourt, Les luthistes (Paris, 1957)

D. Heartz: 'Parisian Music Publishing under Henri II', *MQ*, xlvi (1960), 448

FRANK DOBBINS

**Morley, Thomas** (*b* Norwich, 1557 or 1558; *d* London, early Oct 1602). English composer, editor, theorist and organist. He was the most influential figure, as writer and editor as well as composer, in the Elizabethan vogue for the Italian madrigal, which reached its peak during the eight years in which his works first appeared in print (1593–1601). Although a taste for madrigalian music can be discerned in England for a much longer period, it was Morley who appears to have been chiefly responsible for grafting the Italian shoot on to the native stock and initiating the curiously brief but brilliant flowering of the madrigal that constitutes one of the most colourful episodes in the history of English music.

1. LIFE. A note, 'Thomas Morley aetatis suae 19 an° Domini 1576', appended by John Sadler to one part of his copy of *Domine, non est exaltatum cor meum* (*GB-Ob* Mus.Sch.E.1–5), is the sole record of Morley's date of birth. His origins have recently been uncovered by Watkins Shaw. It appears that his father was a Norwich brewer named Francis Morley, who may also have been a verger at the cathedral between 1562 and 1566. It is reasonable to suppose that Thomas was a chorister there, but the first surviving record connecting him with the cathedral is a patent of reversion from the dean and chapter dated 16 September 1574, promising him the position of master of the choristers (including the duties of organist) when it was vacated by its current occupant, Edmund Inglott. The post was at various times before and after promised to others, including the author Thomas Tusser and Inglott's son, William. But when Inglott died early in 1583 it was indeed Morley who succeeded him.

Morley's early life, however, cannot all have been spent in East Anglia. When he came to publish *A Plaine and Easie Introduction to Practicall Musicke* in 1597 he dedicated it to Byrd, whom he addressed as his master. We cannot know when or for how long Morley studied under Byrd: Shaw suggested from about 1572 to 1574, between the time his voice broke and the reversionary grant mentioned above, and he cited a special payment made to 'domino Morley' in 1575–6 as evidence that he was resident in Norwich at that time, perhaps as a lay clerk at the cathedral. However long or short that period

of study, it nevertheless formed his initial habits of musical thought. These are most clearly evident in his Latin motets and Anglican church music and in the relatively small amount of his surviving instrumental music, but they also affect his response to the Italian idiom in a number of interesting ways.

In May 1587 Morley's house and chambers at Norwich were leased to one Thomas Brown, and the last payment to him as cathedral organist was made in July of that year. The next certain records of him are that he graduated BMus at Oxford in July 1588 and that a son, Thomas, was buried on 14 February 1589 at St Giles, Cripplegate, London. The parish register describes Morley as 'organist'. The fact that he was so at St Paul's is made clear by a reference in the printed text of the Elvetham entertainment (1591), during which the queen 'gave a newe name unto one of their Pavans, made long since by master Thomas Morley, then organist of Paules church'.

It must have been before his promotion to St Paul's that Morley began to digest more fully, and perhaps to imitate, the Italian manner he so energetically promoted during the following decade. He may have been encouraged by the presence at Thorpe-by-Norwich of a musically educated squire, Edward Paston, who owned a considerable collection of books and music. Many of his manuscript partbooks survive, several of them devoted exclusively to Italian madrigals. The connection between the two men is not entirely fanciful, for in a letter dated 3 August 1587 to the 4th Earl of Rutland, a kinsman by marriage, Paston recommended as someone to teach his daughters the virginal the unnamed bearer who, he wrote, 'was placed at Norwich Organest, And by my perswacion, he hath left his rome to come to your L.'. The date, just after Morley's last Norwich payment, and the wording suggest very strongly that the person in question ('such as in my Judgement your L. shall hardlie get the like') was no ordinary parish church organist but Morley himself, who may have spent up to a year with the family before going to St Paul's.

Another reason for Morley's friendship with Paston and, as Shaw pointed out, for his desire to leave the puritanically inclined establishment at Norwich may have been his Roman Catholic leanings. These come to light in a correspondence between the notorious Charles Paget, a Catholic intriguer and double agent, and Thomas Phellippes, secretary to Sir Francis Walsingham. In a letter from the Low Countries dated 3 October 1591 Paget indicated not only that Morley (like Alfonso Ferrabosco (i)) was employed as a spy for the government but also that there was some reason for Catholics to trust him as a genuine believer, 'reconciled' (i.e. reconverted) to the Roman church. The passage reads as follows:

Ther is one Morley that playeth on the organes in poules that was with me in my house. He seemed here to be a good Catholicke and was reconsiled, but notwith-standing suspecting his behaviour I entercepted letters that Mr. Nowell [possibly Dean of St Paul's or Henry Nowell the courtier whose elegy concludes the *Canzonets* of 1597] wrote to him Wherby I discovered enoughe to have hanged him. Neverthelss he shewing with teares great repentaunce, and asking on his knees forgiveness, I was content to let him goe. I here since his comming thether he hath played the promoter and apprehendeth Catholickes.

Phellippes's draft reply confirms Morley's activity: 'It is true that Morley the singing man employeth himself in that kind of service . . . and hath browht diverse into danger'.

Morley was sworn in as a Gentleman of the Chapel

Royal on 24 July 1592. Coming hard on the heels of the above events, the appointment can possibly be interpreted as a reward for political services as well as an acknowledgment of musical excellence. In November of the same year the Cheque Book records his promotion from Epistler to Gospeller.

In 1593 appeared the first of the 11 publications on which Morley's subsequent reputation rests. During this last and most productive period of his life and at least from 1596, he lived in the parish of St Helen's, Bishopsgate. The dedication of the *Canzonets* of 1595 to Lady Periam suggests that Morley may have married again at this time. The contents were 'destinated by my Wife (even beefore they were borne) unto your Ladiships service . . . not being able as heertofore still to serve you'. She is named as Suzan in the parish registers recording the birth of a daughter, Frauncys (19 August 1596), who was buried on 9 February 1599, a son, Christopher (26 June 1599), and a daughter, Anne (28 July 1600). In the first of these entries Morley is described as a 'Musitian', in the others as 'gent.', a status he would seem to have attained by the valuation of his property at £5 in the Rolls of Assessments for Subsidies dated 1598 and 1600, a sum indicating a fair standard of middle-class prosperity. Shakespeare, living in the same parish, was similarly assessed in the 1598 document. The possibility of a connection between the two men has been the subject of much speculation. All that is known for certain is that Morley set a Shakespeare lyric, 'It was a lover and his lass', which was published in *The First Booke of Ayres* (1600). There is no evidence one way or the other that the setting was used in a production of *As You Like It*. And in spite of many ingenious attempts to wed the lyric from *Twelfth Night* to the tune in the *First Booke of Consort Lessons* (1599), 'O mistress mine, where are you roaming?' refuses to fit the popular song which, as Tomkins's list (in *F-Pc* Rés.1122) conveniently explains, is entitled 'O mistress mine, I must'.

In later years Morley was much involved in printing and publishing. The monopoly over music printing that Byrd had held expired in 1596. In a letter of 23 July 1598 to Sir Robert Cecil, Morley petitioned that the new monopoly, for the receipt of which he was prepared to offer half the proceeds to Christopher Heybourne, Ferdinando's brother, should cover 'all, every and any music'. It seems that he had his eye not on such peripheral matters as ruled paper ('it will be little worth') or even partbooks ('the bounteous reward of your Honour to me [for the dedication of the *Balletts* of 1595] was more worth to me than any book or books whatsoever') but on the lucrative business in books of metrical psalms. He was granted the patent on 28 September 1598 and accordingly arranged that the first publications issued under his control should include a metrical psalter with music by Richard Alison (and with an extract from the patent figuring prominently among the preliminaries) and a pocket psalter issued by Barley, differing little from that of Thomas East (1592) save for a few new settings, among them four by Morley himself. The Stationers' Company, with which the patent was registered on 6 October 1598, itself held a patent for the psalter, assigned to John Day, and there ensued a battle between the composer and the printer in which even the Bishop of London failed to arbitrate. But the House of Commons took up the whole issue and ruled in 1600 that no further monopoly on music would be granted

after the expiry of Morley's patent. Some information about the operation of the patent emerges from the lawsuit over the printing of Dowland's *Second Booke of Songs* (1600) by Thomas East, to whom on 19 May 1600 Morley assigned rights under the patent for a period of three years. Eastland, the publisher, paid Morley and Heybourne 40s. before printing began; and afterwards he had to find another £9 10s., almost as much as the total cost of East's labour.

On 7 October 1602 George Woodson was sworn in as a Gentleman of the Chapel Royal 'in Thomas Morley's room'. Some writers have suggested that Morley resigned from the chapel at this time on account of the increasing ill-health to which he refers in the *Plaine and Easie Introduction* (1597) and again in the preface to the *First Booke of Ayres* (1600). The appearance of his name on the title-page of Dowland's *Third and Laste Booke of Songs* (1603) and the republication of the 1593 *Canzonets* in 1606 with 'some Songs added by the Author' have been taken to support the conclusion that he died at some later date before 1608, when Weelkes included in his *Ayres* a 'Remembrance of my friend M. Thomas Morley', *Death hath deprived me of my dearest friend*. Yet there is no indication of anyone else's having left the Chapel Royal in such a manner, posts there being held (often long past a time when the occupant could be expected to serve usefully) for life; and the references in 1603 and 1606 are misleading, the first being the result of the three-year contract with East, the second copied from the title-page of the 1602 edition. The question is most likely resolved by the discovery in the Act Book of the London Archdeaconry Court (*GB-Lgc* 9050/3, f.165r) of letters of administration dated 11 October 1602 to 'Suzunne Morley'. The parish named is that of St Andrew's, Holborn, rather than St Helen's, Bishopsgate, and there are many other Thomas Morleys in the city records of the time; but the widow's first name and the proximity of the date to that of the Chapel Royal reference seem more than mere coincidences, and it is reasonable to assume in the absence of further evidence that the musician died early in October 1602.

2. WORKS. Morley's musical activities were both more extensive and more varied than those of most English composers of the period. As a composer he evidently tried to emulate his master, Byrd, in the variety of forms and styles he cultivated. His earliest known works are, not surprisingly, two motets, *Domine, Dominus noster* and an ambitious full-scale psalm setting, *Domine, non exaltatum cor meum*; they date from 1576 and clearly reflect the influence of the recently published *Cantiones sacrae* of Byrd – indeed, Morley literally transcribed the last five breves of Byrd's *Libera me, Domine, et pone me* for the conclusion of *Domine, Dominus noster*. Another five-part motet, *Gaude Maria virgo*, is a reworking of a piece by Peter Philips, as Lionel Pike has shown. The four motets in the *Plaine and Easie Introduction* show Morley in more complete control of his material, and the two six-part pieces in Thomas Myriell's manuscript anthology *Tristitiae remedium* (1616) – particularly *Laboravi*, which Weelkes in turn imitated – are very impressive indeed.

If the Latin music is serious and weighty, the English sacred music is barely recognizable as the work of the master of the light madrigal and canzonet. Nowhere is the contrast more striking than in *Nolo mortem pec-*

catoris, a macaronic carol cast in the severe Edwardian anthem mould of Tallis and Tye. Indeed, its style is sufficiently archaic for a shadow of doubt to linger around Myriell's ascription of the piece to Morley. By contrast, the funeral sentences, though ostensibly in the same style, are worlds removed in terms of melodic and harmonic fluency; a late-Elizabethan graciousness shines through their restraint. The five-part full service ('The Three Minnoms') is modelled on Byrd's Third Service; and much of the verse music is similarly Byrdian in manner, particularly Out of the deep. Morley's largest service is unusual in comprising some full movements (Venite, Kyrie and Creed), a Te Deum and Benedictus with some solo passages, and a Magnificat and Nunc dimittis in an ornate verse style to some extent free of Byrd's influence but still, in contrast to the comparable service by the more ambitious and less skilful Edmund Hooper, Morley's contemporary, a model of the traditional Anglican values of simplicity and clarity.

The keyboard compositions are again reminiscent of Byrd, but here the pupil falls far short of the master. There is a charming alman and a good set of variations on Go from my window, but the Quadro Pavan (a mere two statements of the bass with decorated repetitions) is typical in not sustaining a promising opening; and the popularity of the Pavan in F (set by Farnaby and also included in Rosseter's Lessons for Consort as Southerne's Pavan) is inexplicable in view of its clumsy phrasing and lifeless divisions. The pavan that appears in Robert Dowland's Varietie of Lute Lessons (1610) was set for keyboard by 'Mr Heybourne', the brother, Ferdinando, of the courtier with whom Morley shared the profits of the printing monopoly, and for consort by Peter Philips: perhaps it was the pavan from the missing pavan and galliard for lute in the First Booke of Ayres (1600), but Heybourne and Philips each pairs it with a different galliard. Morley's contribution to instrumental ensemble music consists primarily of the important First Booke of Consort Lessons, containing pieces arranged for the specifically English consort of treble and bass viols, flute, lute, cittern and pandora. Unlike Rosseter, Morley omits to acknowledge the original composers, and only one of the pieces, an arrangement of See, see, myne owne sweet jewell entitled Joyne hands, can definitely be attributed to him. The pieces without words in the Canzonets of 1595, though each entitled 'fantasie', are identical to the texted pieces in style and are not specifically designated as instrumental; they were no doubt primarily intended for use as solmization songs. A fantasy entitled Tow Trebels appears in its source (GB-Lbm 37402–6) immediately after an anonymous piece in the same style that may also have been written by Morley; both may derive from vocal models.

If none of this 'English' music had survived, Morley's reputation would remain undiminished by virtue of his madrigalian works. Yet his achievement in connection with the Italian style does not depend upon his ability simply as a composer but also as an editor, translator, arranger, propagandist and entrepreneur, roles which are all reflected in his publications. As editor and translator he produced two anthologies of Italian music of the lighter sort in 1597 and 1598, and in 1595 he published in simultaneous English and Italian editions a book of canzonets and one of balletts that are largely 'arrangements' of popular Italian pieces by Felice Anerio

(Canzonette a 4 voci, 1586) and Gastoldi (Balletti, 1591) respectively. The Consort Lessons of 1599, as mentioned above, is another exercise in the art of arranging, this time of English popular music, much of it associated with the theatre and the dance floor. The Plaine and Easie Introduction of 1597 is, among other things, a colourful piece of propaganda for Italian music, and a measure of its success in this regard is the degree to which posterity has adopted the notion of a brilliant Elizabethan musical achievement arising mainly from the adoption by English composers of Italian styles, a view that has only recently come fully into question. Finally, there are what may be called Morley's entirely original works, though again some of their contents are heavily indebted to models, and the derivation of other pieces will no doubt be discovered. The Canzonets to Three Voyces (1593) and Madrigalls to Foure Voyces (1594) are the most successful in terms of the complementary balance between Morley's individuality as an artist and his remarkable synthesis of Italian style and English training. The pieces in Canzonets to Five and Six Voices (1597), which are often expansive to the point of losing the focus and conciseness of the earlier works, make a gesture in the direction of yet another contemporary musical fashion by including a lute accompaniment to the majority of pieces. It is no surprise, therefore, to find Morley turning to the lute air for his last effort, and even though he confesses himself 'no professor thereof, but like a blind man groping for my way' in the preface to The First Booke of Ayres (1600), one or two of the songs, including the Shakespeare setting, are among the most delightful in the repertory.

It seems almost as though Morley sought by sheer effort to transform the musical world bequeathed to him by Byrd, and before his comparatively early death he had to a large extent achieved his aims, by stimulating an enormous musical fashion that he himself, always with an eye to business, was already in process of deserting for new and potentially more profitable ventures. It is fitting, however, that his list of publications concludes with The Triumphes of Oriana (1601), a collection of madrigals by 23 musical compatriots that Morley most probably conjured into being some time in the late 1590s as an entertainment to honour his queen and to enhance his (and the madrigal's) cause. It is perhaps significant that, of his two contributions to the collection, Arise, awake was a rearrangement of Adiew, adiew, you kind and cruel from the Canzonets of 1597, and Hard by a cristall fountaine a rewriting of Croce's Ove tra l'herbe e i fiori, which had come from Il trionfo di Dori – the collection on which The Triumphes was modelled – by way of Yonge's second Musica transalpina (1597). And yet here as elsewhere the accusation of plagiarism must be resisted, for the 16th century saw nothing wrong in imitation and borrowing but considered them, on the contrary, normal artistic practices. In this case, as Kerman aptly remarked (1962, p.209), 'Morley's composition, using identical material, has life and breadth, and is actually more true to the madrigal ideal which with Croce was already stale'; for Morley, like Handel and other great borrowers, constantly took full and confident possession of what he borrowed and added considerable musical interest to the loan.

Morley, then, was the true begetter of the English madrigal and the greatest influence on its subsequent development. Yet, as has been pointed out, he was not a 'madrigalist' in the strictest sense of the word, for although in the *Plaine and Easie Introduction* he showed himself fully conversant with all the Italian forms and with the aesthetic considerations behind them, in his own work he favoured the light canzonet style and rarely ventured beyond the less serious kind of madrigal. Within these limits he paradoxically tended to elaborate and develop his material, often for purely musical reasons, in a manner that his Italian contemporaries might not have understood but that his master Byrd would at least have appreciated. This can be seen by comparing his arrangements with their models: *Sing wee and chaunt it*, for instance, enlivens Gastoldi's penny-plain *A lieta vita* by numerous small touches of the most musical kind; but when Morley goes further, as in *What saith my daintie darling?*, based on the same composer's *Piacer, gioia*, the simple delicacy of the original tends to be lost in the welter of counterpoint and harmonic detail. The comparative stodginess of the 1597 *Canzonets* ultimately results from this very tendency to carry each contrapuntal idea a little too far and in the process to diffuse (and therefore defuse) what is ideally a pithy, epigrammatic style.

Morley's lack of interest in dramatic effects, chromatic harmony and even in word-painting of more than an elementary and perfunctory kind places him in sharp contrast to Weelkes and even to the Byrd of the 1589 and 1591 *Cantiones sacrae*. *Deep lamenting* is perhaps his most extremely expressive piece. The refined understatement and subtle treatment of verse that marks the work of Wilbye is also beyond him. The only genre in which he could sustain musical invention successfully over a large stretch is the narrative madrigal (e.g. the marvellous *Hoe, who comes here?*), which seems to have been an original conception. Yet to label him a 'conservative' is, as usual in the case of so talented a composer, to miss the point. It is not even a question of his falling back on an undemanding idiom, but, like Byrd, of his making a positive choice about the way of setting poetry to music that, given the nature of the verse, satisfied the primary criterion of appropriateness or decorum (and incidentally may have won him Byrd's permission to publish). And still today it is the restraint and balance of his settings that guarantee them serious critical consideration while their exuberance and exquisite grace win them affection. Where else in the whole body of English madrigals is there a piece that better exemplifies these virtues than the deservedly well-known *Aprill is in my mistris face*? Morley's strength as a composer, then, lies largely in his sense of style rooted in a surely self-imposed restraint (that Weelkes, for instance, rarely exercised), and it is perhaps not surprising that his energy, which despite illness must have been immense, spilled out in so many other directions. Yet though he had a considerable effect on his successors and there were several reprints of his sets in the early 17th century, nothing is more poignantly expressive of the short life of the movement he initiated and the values he represented than the pointed avoidance of his work by the Jacobean anthologists. It is to the gloomy motets that Myriell paradoxically turned for 'tristitiae remedium', rather than to the gay, graceful and more polished works of the printed sets.

One work that has kept Morley's name constantly before the musical public is *A Plaine and Easie Introduction to Practicall Musicke*, perhaps the most famous musical treatise in the English language. The research it entailed must have been immense; and the lengthy passages on obsolescent matters show that Morley was not entirely willing to spare the reader the pains and labour he himself bemoans in the preface. (The absence of any detailed account of the modes is an intriguing exception, as several writers have pointed out.) In many cases his discoveries led him to take up the cudgels against traditional English practices, and in matters of notation, for instance, he appears to have had an effect in changing the practice of East's printing house. The book is indeed based largely on the authority, and sometimes the very examples, of authors who are mostly but not always acknowledged (see Harman's edition for the details). Yet Morley's method of presenting his material is original and well-considered and his literary style delightful. The book is also, as its title-page boasts, eminently practical – from its division of the material into three sections, with the thornier problems relegated to appendices, to its examples brilliantly constructed to show the pitfalls into which the student of counterpoint habitually falls. Byrd's teaching, as Morley acknowledged, must be reflected on many of its pages, however little the master can have shared his pupil's enthusiasm for all manifestations of Italian musical art. Above all, the book is lively and passionate in manner, written from a refreshingly sceptical point of view that finds expression, for instance, when the pupil Philomathes is confronted with a particularly obscure and difficult table taken from Gaffurius's *De proportionibus musicis*: 'As for musick, the principal thing we seek in it, is to delight the eare, which cannot so perfectly be done in these hard proportions, as otherwise'.

For relevant illustrations *see* EDUCATION IN MUSIC, fig.6, MADRIGAL, fig.8, and PITCH NOTATION.

### WORKS

Editions: *T. Morley: A Plaine and Easie Introduction to Practicall Musicke*, ed. R. A. Harman (London, 1952, 2/1963) [H]
   *T. Morley: Canzonets to 2 Voices (1595), Canzonets to 3 Voices (1593)*, ed. E. H. Fellowes, rev. T. Dart, EMS, i (2/1956) (texted items only from 1595 edn.) [EMS i]
   *T. Morley: Collected Motets*, ed. H. K. Andrews and T. Dart (London, 1959) [M]
   *T. Morley: The First Booke of Consort Lessons*, ed. S. Beck (New York, 1959) [B]
   *T. Morley: Keyboard Works*, ed. T. Dart in English Keyboard Music, xii–xiii (London, 1959) [D]
   *The Triumphes of Oriana*, ed. E. H. Fellowes, rev. T. Dart, EM, xxxii (1962) [EM]
   *T. Morley: Madrigals to 4 Voices (1594)*, ed. E. H. Fellowes, rev. T. Dart, EMS, ii (2/1963) [EMS ii]
   *T. Morley: Ballets to 5 Voices (1600)*, ed. E. H. Fellowes, rev. T. Dart in EMS, iv (2/1966) [EMS iv]
   *T. Morley: The First Booke of Ayres*, ed. E. H. Fellowes, rev. T. Dart, EL, xvi (3/1966) [EL]
   *T. Morley: Canzonets to 5 and 6 Voices (1597)*, ed. E. H. Fellowes, rev. T. Dart, EMS, iii (2/1966) [EMS iii]

(*all printed works published in London*)

#### SERVICES

First Service [The Verse Service] (Ven, TeD, Bs, Ky, Cr, Mag, Nunc), verse [Ven, Ky, Cr, full], 5vv, 1641[5], *GB-Cpc, Cu, DRc, GL, Lbm, Lcm, Llp, Ob, Och, Ojc, T, US-NYp* [at least 3 different Kyries extant]; Ven, TeD, Bs, Ky, Cr, ed. E. H. Fellowes (London, 1931, rev. 1963); Mag, Nunc, ed. F. Burgess and R. Shore (London, 1913), ed. B. Rainbow (London, 1955)
Second Service ['The Three Minnoms or Pricksemibref'] (Mag, Nunc), full, 5vv, 1641[5], *GB-Cpc, Cu, DRc, Llp, Och, Ojc, Y*; ed. R. Greening and H. K. Andrews (London, 1957)
Short Service (Mag, Nunc), full, 4vv, *Cu, Lbm, Llp, Ob, Ojc, WB*; ed. C. F. Simkins (London, 1956)
Burial Service (see I am the resurrection)
Preces, Responses and Ps cxix.145–76 (145. I call with my whole heart; 153. O consider mine adversity; 161. Princes have persecuted me; 169. Let my complaint), full [vv. 169–76 verse], 5vv, *Lcm, T* (inc.); Preces and Responses ed. I. Atkins and E. H. Fellowes (London, 1933), ed. H. W. Shaw (London, 1966)

Behold, the Lord cometh out (doubtful), *PB*
How long wilt thou forget me (Ps xiii), verse, 5vv, in J. Clifford: The
Divine Services and Anthems (1663, enlarged 2/1664), *Ckc*, *Cpc*,
*DRc*, *Lbm*, *Lcm*, *Llp*, *Ojc*, *T*, *Y*, *US-NYp*
I am the resurrection [Burial Service] (2p. I know that my Redeemer
liveth; 3p. We brought nothing into this world; 4p. Man that is born
of a woman; 5p. In the midst of life; 6p. I heard a voice from heaven),
full, 4vv, *GB-Lbm*, *Ob*, *T*; ed. C. F. Simkins (London, 1961)
I call with my whole heart (see Preces, Responses and Psalm)
I heard a voice from heaven (6p. of I am the resurrection)
I know that my Redeemer liveth (2p. of I am the resurrection)
In the midst of life (5p. of I am the resurrection)
Let my complaint (see Preces, Responses and Psalm)
Man that is born of a woman (4p. of I am the resurrection)
Nolo mortem peccatoris . . . Father I am thine only Son, full, 4vv, *Lbm*;
ed. S. T. Warner, rev. J. Morehen (London, 2/1967)
O consider mine adversity (see Preces, Responses and Psalm)
O God our Lord (doubtful), *LF* (inc.), *PB*
O Jesu meek, verse, 5vv, in J. Clifford: The Divine Services and
Anthems (1663, enlarged 2/1664), *Ckc*, *Lcm*, *T*
Out of the deep (i) [Eng. version of De profundis], full, 6vv, *DRc*, *Lbm*,
*Ob*, *Y*
Out of the deep (ii), verse, 5vv, 1641⁵, *Ckc*, *Cu*, *DRc*, *GL*, *Lbm*, *Lcm*,
*Llp*, *Ob*, *Och*, *Ojc*, *T*, *WB*, *Y*, *US-NYp*; ed. in TCM, lxxi (1933)
Princes have persecuted me (see Preces, Responses and Psalm)
Teach me thy way, O Lord, full, 5vv, *GB-Cu*
Thou knowest, Lord, full, 4vv, in W. Boyce: *Cathedral Music* (1760–
78), *Lbm*; ed. C. F. Simkins (London, 1961)
We brought nothing into this world (3p. of I am the resurrection)

O God, my God (Ps xxii), 1599⁹
Our ears have heard our fathers tell (Ps xliv), 1599⁹
Put me not to rebuke, O Lord (Ps xxxviii), 1621¹¹ (same tune as O God,
my God)
The Lord is our defence (Ps xlvi), 1621¹¹
The Lord's Prayer, 1599⁹
The man is blest (Ps i), 1621¹¹ (same tune as The Lord is our defence)
There is no God (Ps xiv), 1599⁹, 1621¹¹

Agnus Dei, 4vv; H 317
De profundis clamavi, 6vv
Dentes tui sicut greges (2p. of O amica mea)
Domine, Dominus noster, 5vv, 1576
Domine fac mecum, 4vv; H 314
Domine, non est exaltatum cor meum, 5vv, 1576
Eheu sustulerunt Dominum, 4vv
Gaude Maria virgo (2p. Virgo prudentissima), 5vv
Heu mihi, Domine, 5vv (inc.)
In manus tuas, 5vv (inc.)
Laboravi in gemitu meo, 5vv
Nolo mortem peccatoris (see 'Anthems')
O amica me (2p. Dentes tui sicut greges), 5vv
Virgo prudentissima (2p. of Gaude Maria virgo)

Canzonets, or Little Short Songs to Three Voyces (1593, enlarged
3/1602 as Canzonets . . . with Some Songs added by the Author; Ger.
trans. 1624/R1957) [1593]
Madrigalls to Foure Voyces: the First Booke (1594, enlarged 2/1600 as
Madrigalls . . . with Some Songs added by the Author) [1594]
The First Booke of Balletts to Five Voyces (1595, 3/1600) [1595a]
Il primo libro delle ballette, 5vv (1595, It. edn. of 1595a) [1595b]
The First Booke of Canzonets to Two Voyces (1595/R1954) [It. edn.
was produced, now lost] [1595c]
Canzonets or Little Short Aers to Five and Sixe Voices (1597) [1597a]
Canzonets . . . to Foure Voyces: Celected out of the Best and Approved
Italian Authors (1597) [1597b]
Madrigales: The Triumphes of Oriana to 5. and 6. Voices (1601¹⁶)
[1601¹⁶]
Madrigals in *A Plaine and Easie Introduction to Practicall Musicke*
(1597/R1971) [1597c]

About the may-pole new (= Al suon d'una sampogna), 5vv, 1595a (? on
Trofeo); EMS iv, 39
Adiew, adiew, you kind and cruel, 5vv, 1597a [reworked as Arise,
awake]; EMS iii, 12
Aprill is in my mistris face, 4vv, 1594; EMS ii, 1
Arise, awake, you silly shepherds sleeping, 5vv, 1601¹⁶ [reworking of
Adiew, adiew, you kind and cruel]; EM, 136
Arise, get up, my deere, 3vv, 1593; EMS i, 101
Ay me, the fatall arrow, 5vv, 1597a, EMS iii, 47
Beesides a fountaine, 4vv, 1594; EMS ii, 62
Blow, shepherds, blow, 3vv, 1593; EMS i, 39

Cease, myne eyes, 3vv, 1593; EMS i, 78
Clorinda false, adieu, 4vv, 1594; EMS ii, 4
Come, lovers, follow me, 4vv, 1594; EMS ii, 45
Cruell, wilt thou persever?, 5vv, 1597a; EMS iii, 55
Cruel, you pul away to soone, 3vv, 1593; EMS i, 9
Daintie fine sweet nimphe (= Vezzosette ninfe), 5vv, 1595a (on
Gastoldi, 1591); EMS iv, 1
Damon and Phyllis squared, 5vv, 1597a; EMS iii, 63
Deep lamenting, grief bewraying, 3vv, 1593; EMS i, 44
Doe you not know?, 3vv, 1593; EMS i, 84
Dye now, my heart, 4vv, 1594; EMS ii, 92
False love did me inveagle, 5vv, 1597a; EMS iii, 5
Farewell, disdainfull, 3vv, 1593; EMS i, 51
Flora, wilt thou torment mee?, 2vv, 1595c (on F. Anerio's Flora, morir
debb'io, 1586); EMS i, 20
Fly love, that art so sprightly, 5vv, 1597a; EMS iii, 1
Fyer, fyer (= A la strada), 5vv, 1595a (on Marenzio, 1585); EMS iv, 53
Fyre and lightning from heaven, 2vv, 1595c (on F. Anerio's Caggia
fuoco dal cielo, 1586); EMS i, 19
God morrow, faye ladies of the may, 3vv, 1593; EMS i, 27
Goe yee, my canzonets, 2vv, 1595c (on F. Anerio's Gitene canzonette,
1586); EMS i, 1
Good love, then flie thou toe her, 6vv, 1597a; EMS iii, 98
Hard by a cristall fountaine, 6vv, 1601¹⁶ (on Croce's Ove tra l'herbe,
1592); EM, 238
Harke; Alleluia cheerely, 6vv, 1597a; EMS iii, 114
Hark, jolly shepheards, 4vv, 1594; EMS ii, 78
Help, I fall, ladie, 4vv, 1594; EMS ii, 20
Hoe, who comes here?, 4vv, 1594; EMS ii, 84
Hould out, my hart, 3vv, 1593; EMS i, 21
I follow, loe, the footing, 5vv, 1597a; EMS iii, 78
I goe before, my darling, 2vv, 1595c; EMS i, 8
I love, alas, I love thee (= Innamorato sono), 5vv, 1595a; EMS iv, 68
In dewe of roses, 4vv, 1594; EMS ii, 29
In every place, 4vv, 1594; EMS ii, 34
In nets of goulden wyers, 2vv, 1595c (on Felis's Di vaghe fila d'oro,
1585); EMS i, 22
I saw my lovely Phillis (= Madonna mia gentile), 5vv, 1595a; EMS iv,
26
I should for griefe and anguish, 2vv, 1595c (on F. Anerio's Io morirei
d'affano, 1586); EMS i, 26
I will no more come to thee, 4vv, 1594; EMS ii, 56
Joy doth so arise, 3vv, 1593; EMS i, 4
Ladies, you see time flieth, 6vv, 1597a; EMS iii, 108
Ladie, those cherris plentie (= Al primo vostro sguardo), 5vv, 1595a (?
on Marenzio, 1584); EMS iv, 63
Ladie, those eyes, 3vv, 1593; EMS i, 16
Lady, if I through grief, 3vv, 1593; EMS i, 72
Lady, why grieve you still mee?, 4vv, 1594; EMS ii, 24
Lady, you thinke you spite me, 5vv, 1597a; EMS iii, 68
Leave, alas, this tormenting (= Non mi date tormento), 5vv, 1595a (? on
Ferretti, 1569); EMS iv, 76
Leave now mine eyes lamenting, 2vv, 1595c; EMS i, 17
Loe heere another love, 2vv, 1595c (on Vecchi's Ecco novello Amor,
1585); EMS i, 14
Lo, she flyes (= Fugirò tant'Amore), 5vv, 1595a (? on Marenzio, 1584);
EMS iv, 71
Love learnes by laughing, 3vv, 1593 [3/1602 only]; EMS i, 107
Love's folke in greene araying, 5vv, 1597a; EMS iii, 18
Love tooke his bowe and arrow, 5vv, 1597a; EMS iii, 24
Lo, where with floury head, 5vv, 1597a; EMS iii, 29
Miraculous love's wounding, 2vv, 1595c (on F. Anerio's Miracolo
d'amore, 1586); EMS i, 11
My bonny lasse shee smyleth (= Questa dolce sirena), 5vv, 1595a (on
Gastoldi, 1591); EMS iv, 23
My hart, why hast thou taken? (= Perche tormi il cor mio), 4vv, 1597b,
1597c (? on Croce, 1588); ed. in Murphy; EMS ii, 117
My lovely wanton jewell (= La bella ninfa mia), 5vv, 1595a; EMS iv, 45
My nymph, the deere, 5vv, 1597a; EMS iii, 50
No, no, Nigella (= Possa morir chi t'ama), 5vv, 1595a (on Gastoldi,
1591); EMS iv, 19
No, no, thou doest but flout mee, 4vv, 1594; EMS ii, 51
Now is the gentle season (2p. The fields abroad), 4vv, 1594; EMS ii, 38
Now is the month of maying (= Se ben mi c'ha bon tempo), 5vv, 1595a
(on Vecchi, 1590) [arr. P. Rosseter for mixed consort in Lessons for
Consort (London, 1609)]; EMS iv, 8
Now must I dye, alas, recureless, 3vv, 1593; EMS i, 66
O flye not, O take some pittie, 3vv, 1593; EMS i, 56
O griefe, even on the bud, 5vv, 1597a; EMS iii, 33
On a faire morning, 4vv, 1594 [2/1600 only]; EMS ii, 109
O sleep, fond fancy, 3vv, 1597c; EMS i, 115
O sweet, alas, what say you? (2p. of Sport wee, my lovely treasure)
O thou that art so cruel, 2vv, 1595c (on F. Anerio's O tu che mi dai
pene, 1586); EMS i, 24
Our bonny bootes could toote it, 5vv, 1597a; EMS iii, 41
Phillis, I faine wold die now (= Filli morir vorei) [Dialogue of 7 voc.],

7vv, 1595a (? on Croce, 1592); EMS iv, 85
Round about a wood, 4vv, 1594 [2/1600 only]; EMS ii, 104
Sayd I that Amarillis, 5vv, 1597a; EMS iii, 59
Say, deere, will you not have me?, 3vv, 1593; EMS i, 97
Say, gentle nymphes, 4vv, 1594; EMS ii, 99
See, see, myne owne sweet jewell, 3vv, 1593 [= Joyne hands in Consort Lessons, 1599]; EMS i, 1
Shoot, false love, I care not (= Viver lieto voglio), 5vv, 1595a (on Gastoldi, 1591); EMS iv, 4
Since my teares and lamenting, 4vv, 1594 (on Lassus's Poi che'l mio largo pianto, 1583¹⁵); EMS ii, 17
Singing alone satte my sweet Amarillis (= Amore l'altro giorno), 5vv, 1595a; EMS iv, 13
Sing wee and chaunt it (= A lieta vita), 5vv, 1595a (on Gastoldi, 1591); EMS iv, 11
Sov'raign of my delight, 5vv, 1597a; EMS iii, 36
Sport wee, my lovely treasure (2p. O sweet, alas, what say you?), 4vv, 1594; EMS ii, 68
Spring tyme mantleth every bough, 3vv, 1593 [3/1602 only]; EMS i, 113
Stay, hart, runne not so fast, 6vv, 1597a; EMS iii, 89
Still it frieth (= Ard'ogn'hora il cor), 4vv, 1597b, 1597c; ed. in Murphy; EMS ii, 121
Sweet nimphe, come to thy lover, 2vv, 1595c (on F. Anerio's Su questi fior t'aspetto, 1586); EMS i, 6
The fields abroad (2p. of Now is the gentle season)
Thirsis, let pittie move thee, 3vv, 1593; EMS i, 61
This love is but a wanton fit, 3vv, 1593 [3/1602 only]; EMS i, 109
Those dainty daffadillies (= Le rose frond'e fiori), 5vv, 1595a (on Marenzio, 1584); EMS, iv, 60
Though Philomela lost hir love, 3vv, 1593 [2/1602 only]; EMS i, 111
Thus saith my Galatea (= Al piacer alla gioia), 5vv, 1595a (on Gastoldi, 1591); EMS iv, 36
What ayles my darling?, 3vv, 1593; EMS i, 92
What saith my daintie darling? (= Piacer, gioia), 5vv, 1595a (on Gastoldi, 1591); EMS iv, 32
When, loe, by breake of morning, 2vv, 1595c (on F. Anerio's Quando la vaga Flori, 1586); EMS i, 3
Where art thou, wanton?, 3vv, 1593; EMS i, 87
Whether awaie so fast?, 3vv, 1593; EMS i, 32
Why sit I heere complaining?, 4vv, 1594; EMS ii, 10
Why weepes, alas, my lady? (= Non dubitar), 5vv, 1595a (? on Ferretti, 1569); EMS iv, 81
You blacke bright starres, 5vv, 1597a; EMS iii, 72
You that wont to my pipes' sound (= Ninfe belle), 5vv, 1595a (on Gastoldi's Vaghe ninfe, 1591); EMS iv, 50

Some sacred contrafacta from 1593 and 1594, *GB-Och* 739–43

*(Italian)*

A la strada (= Fyer, fyer), 5vv, 1595b
A lieta vita (= Sing wee and chaunt it), 5vv, 1595b
Al piacer alla gioia (= Thus saith my Galatea), 5vv, 1595b
Al primo vostro sguardo (= Ladie, those cherris plentie), 5vv, 1595b
Al suon d'una sampogna (= About the may-pole new), 5vv, 1595b
Amore l'altro giorno (= Singing alone satte my sweet Amarillis), 5vv, 1595b
Ard'ogn'hora il cor (= Still it frieth), 4vv, 1597c
Filli morir vorei (= Phillis, I faine wold die now), 7vv, 1595b
Fugirò tant'Amore (= Lo, shee flyes), 5vv, 1595b
Innamorato sono (= I love, alas, I love thee), 5vv, 1595b
La bella ninfa mia (= My lovely wanton jewell), 5vv, 1595b
Le rose frond'e fiori (= Those dainty daffadillies), 5vv, 1595b
Madonna mia gentile (= I saw my lovely Phillis), 5vv, 1595b
Ninfe belle (= You that wont to my pipes' sound), 5vv, 1595b
Non dubitar (= Why weepes, alas, my lady?), 5vv, 1595b
Non mi date tormento (= Leave, alas, this tormenting), 5vv, 1595b
Piacer, gioia (= What saith my daintie darling?), 5vv, 1595b
Perche tormi il cor mio (= My hart, why hast thou taken?), 4vv, 1597c
Possa morir chi t'ama (= No, no, Nigella), 5vv, 1595b
Questa dolce sirena (= My bonny lasse shee smyleth), 5vv, 1595b
Se ben mi c'ha bon tempo (= Now is the month of maying), 5vv, 1595b
Vezzosette ninfe (= Daintie fine sweet nimphe), 5vv, 1595b
Viver lieto voglio (= Shoot, false love, I care not), 5vv, 1595b

Mi sfidate guerrera, 5vv, *Lbm* (textless after incipit)

### SOLO SONGS

The First Booke of Ayres or Little Short Songs to Sing and Play to the Lute with the Base Viole (1600/*R*1970), EL: Absence, hear thou my protestation; A painted tale; Can I forget what reason's force; Come, sorrow, come; Faire in a morne; I saw my ladye weeping; It was a lover and his lasse; Love winged my hopes; Misteresse mine, well may you fare; Shee straight hir light greene silken cotes (2p. of Thirsis and Milla); Thirsis and Milla (2p. Shee straight hir light greene silken cotes); What if my mistresse now; Who is it that this darke night; With my love my life was nestled

*(listed in index but missing from extant copy)*
Fantasticke love (2p. Poore soule); Much have I loved; Poore soule (2p. of Fantasticke love); Sleepe slumbring eyes (song with this title, *Och* incl in facs. 1970 and *EL*); What lack ye, Sir?; White as lillies; Will ye buy a fine dogge? (song with this title, *Och* incl. in facs. 1970 and *EL*)

### KEYBOARD

Pavan and galliard, F [arr. P. Rosseter for mixed consort as Southernes Pavan in Lessons for Consort (London, 1609); arr. G. Farnaby, kbd]; D i, 2
Quadro Pavan; D i, 8
Passymeasures Pavan; D i, 14
Pavan and galliard, a [pavan arr. F. Cutting, lute, *Cu*]; D i, 16
Galliard, G; D i, 21
Alman, C; D ii, 7
Nancy, variations; D ii, 8
Fantasia, d; D ii, 12
Go from my window, variations; D ii, 17
Pavan and galliard, d, 'set by Mr. Heyborne' (*see* OTHER INSTRUMENTAL); D ii, 2

### OTHER INSTRUMENTAL

9 'fantasie': Il doloroso; La Girondala; La rondinella; Il grillo; Il lamento; La caccia; La sampogna; La Sirena; La Torello [Tortorella in tenor part index, and in 1619 edn.]: a 2, The First Booke of Canzonets to Two Voyces (1593, 2/1619); ed. D. H. Boalch (Oxford, 1950)
6 sol-faing songs, a 2, in *A Plaine and Easie Introduction* (1597); H, 89
Aria, a 3, in *A Plaine and Easie Introduction* (1597); H, 98
Pavane and galliard, lute, lost (list in index of The First Booke of Ayres, 1600)
Pavan, lute, 1610²³ [arr. F. Richardson alias Mr. Heyborne, for kbd, see D i, 2; arr. P. Philips for consort a 5, *Lbm*]
La fantasia (? 2p. Tow Trebels), a 5, *Lbm* (fantasia anon., attrib. Morley in Edwards)
Sacred End Pavin, lute, *NL-Lt*, Thysius; Reading, Berkshire County Record Office, Trumbull; R. Spencer's private collection, Woodford Green, Essex, Braye lutebook; attrib. Morley in P. Rosseter: Lessons for Consort (London, 1609), anon. in other sources

### ARRANGEMENTS
*(conjectural attributions in parentheses)*

The First Booke of Consort Lessons, made by Divers Exquisite Authors, for 6 Instruments to Play Together, the Treble Lute, the Pandora, the Cittern, the Base-Violl, the Flute and Treble Violl (1599, corrected and enlarged 2/1611; both inc.); B: The Quadro Pavin (R. Alison); The Galliard to the Quadro Pavin (Alison); De la Tromba pavin (Alison); Captaine Pipers pavin (J. Dowland); Galliard to Captayne Pipers pavin (Dowland); Galliard, Can shee excuse (Dowland); Lacrime pavin (Dowland); Phillips pavin (P. Philips); Galliard to Phillips pavin (Philips); The Frogge galliard (Dowland); Alison's knell (Alison); Goe from my window (Alison); In Nomine pavin (? N. Strogers)

My Lord of Oxenfords Maske; Mounsiers Almaine; Michel's galliard; La Volto; Balowe; O mistresse mine; Sola soleta (G. Conversi, Canzoni, 1572); Joyne hands (Morley, reworking of See, see myne owne sweet jewell, 1593); La coranta; The Lord Sowches Maske (? G. Farnaby); The Batchelars Delight (Alison) (1611 edn.); Responce pavin (Alison) (1611 edn. only)

### EDITIONS

Canzonets or Little Short Songs to Foure Voyces: celected out of the Best and Approved Italian Authors (1597); ed. in Murphy
Madrigals to Five Voyces: celected out of the Best Approved Italian Authors (1598); ed. in Murphy
Madrigales: the Triumphes of Oriana to 5 and 6 voices (1601¹⁶) [in 2/1601 Kirbye's piece appears with text With angel's face and brightness]; ed. W. Hawes (London, 1814); EM

### WRITINGS

*A Plaine and Easie Introduction to Practicall Musicke* (1597/*R*1971); facs. ed. E. H. Fellowes (London, 1937); H

### BIBLIOGRAPHY

O. Bekker: *Die englischen Madrigalisten William Byrd, Thomas Morley und John Dowland* (Leipzig, 1901)
E. H. Fellowes: *English Madrigal Verse* (Oxford, 1920, 3/1967 rev. F. W. Sternfeld and D. Greer)
——: *The English Madrigal Composers* (Oxford, 1921, 2/1948)
——: *The English Madrigal* (Oxford, 1925/*R*1952)
P. Warlock [pseud. of P. Heseltine]: *The English Ayre* (Oxford, 1926)
M. Dowling: 'The Printing of John Dowland's *Second Booke of Songs or Ayres*', *The Library*, 4th ser., xii (1932), 365
J. Pulver: 'The English Theorists: xiii – Thomas Morley', *MT*, lxxvi (1935), 411
B. Pattison: 'Notes on Early Music Printing', *The Library*, 4th ser., xix (1939), 389

H. E. Bush: 'The Recognition of Chordal Formation by Early Music Theorists', *MQ*, xxxii (1946), 227

R. T. Dart: 'Morley's Consort Lessons of 1599', *PRMA*, lxxiv (1947–8), 1

A. Obertello: *Madrigali italiani in Inghilterra* (Milan, 1949)

J. R. King: *An Aesthetic and Musical Analysis of the Madrigals of Thomas Morley, with Special Reference between Text and Music and Some Comparison with the Madrigals of John Wilby, John Bennet, and the 'Triumphs of Oriana'* (diss., U. of Toronto, 1950)

R. Stevenson: 'Thomas Morley's "Plaine and Easie" Introduction to the Modes', *MD*, vi (1952), 177

J. Kerman: 'Morley and the "Triumphs of Oriana" ', *ML*, xxxiv (1953), 185

D. Arnold: 'Croce and the English Madrigal', *ML*, xxxv (1954), 309

J. E. Uhler: 'Thomas Morley's Madrigals for Four Voices', *ML*, xxxvi (1955), 313

D. Arnold: 'Gastoldi and the English Ballett', *MMR*, lxxxvi (1956), 44

D. Brown: 'Thomas Morley and the Catholics: Some Speculations', *MMR*, lxxxix (1959), 53

T. Dart: 'Morley and the Catholics: Some Further Speculations', *MMR*, lxxxix (1959), 89

R. C. Strong: 'Queen Elizabeth I as Oriana', *Studies in the Renaissance*, vi (1959), 251

F. B. Zimmerman: 'Italian and English Traits in the Music of Thomas Morley', *AnM*, xiv (1959), 29

D. Brown: 'The Style and Chronology of Thomas Morley's Motets', *ML*, xli (1960), 216

E. Doughtie: 'Robert Southwell and Morley's *First Booke of Ayres*', *LSJ*, iv (1962), 226

J. Kerman: *The Elizabethan Madrigal: a Comparative Study* (New York, 1962)

R. Spencer: 'Two Missing Lute Parts for Morley's Consort Lessons', *LSJ*, iv (1962), 31

T. Dart: 'A Suppressed Dedication for Morley's Four-part Madrigals of 1594', *Transactions of the Cambridge Bibliographical Society*, iii (1963), 401

C. A. Murphy: *Thomas Morley Editions of Italian Canzonets and Madrigals* (Tallahassee, Florida, 1964)

W. Shaw: 'Thomas Morley of Norwich', *MT*, cvi (1965), 669

D. Greer: 'The Lute Songs of Thomas Morley', *LSJ*, viii (1966), 25

P. J. Seng: *The Vocal Songs in the Plays of Shakespeare* (Cambridge, Mass., 1967) [incl. complete bibliography of Morley–Shakespeare literature]

R. Illing: 'Barley's Pocket Edition of Est's Metrical Psalter', *ML*, xlix (1968), 219

L. Pike: ' "Gaude Maria Virgo": Morley or Philips?' *ML*, l (1969), 127

J. Buttrey: 'Music for Elizabeth I', *Records and Recording*, xiii/7 (1970), 15

L. M. Ruff: 'The Social Significance of the 17th century English Music Treatises', *The Consort*, xxvi (1970), 412

R. J. McGrady: 'Thomas Morley's *First Booke of Ayres*', *MR*, xxxiii (1972), 171

W. Edwards: *The Sources of Elizabethan Consort Music* (diss., U. of Cambridge, 1974)

C. A. Monson: *Voice and Viols in England, 1600–1650: the Sources and the Music* (diss., U. of California, Berkeley, 1974)

M. Chibbett: 'Dedications in Morley's Printed Music', *RMARC*, xiii (1977), 84

PHILIP BRETT

**Morley, William** (*d* London, 29 Oct 1721). English composer. He collaborated with John Isham in composing *A Collection of New Songs* (London, *c*1710). On 17 July 1713, described as 'pleb.', he took the Oxford degree of BMus along with Isham. Both appear to have been subordinate colleagues of William Croft, who took his doctorate a week earlier. Along with three others, Morley was admitted a Gentleman of the Chapel Royal on 8 August 1715, on the enlargement of the establishment by George I, and his death (not 1731 as formerly cited) is noted in the Chapel Royal Cheque Book. Morley is remembered because of the faint interest attaching to his putative authorship of an early instance of the Anglican double chant. Boyce's *Cathedral Music* (1760–73; ii, 306) includes a double chant in D minor without a composer's name which Joseph Warren in his edition of Boyce (1849; iii, 471) attributed to William Morley without naming his authority and with an inaccurate biographical note (ibid, 31). The source of the chant given by Boyce has not been discovered; it ap-

peared in *Cathedral Chants* (ed. A. Bennett and W. Marshall, London, 1829) as 'said to be' by Thomas Morley but 'more probably' by William Morley.

WATKINS SHAW

**Morley College.** London college of adult education; *see* LONDON, §VII, 4.

**Morley-Pegge, Reginald (Frederick)** (*b* London, 17 Jan 1890; *d* Cobham, Surrey, 1 June 1972). English horn player and scholar. His aptitude for brass instruments revealed itself during his schooldays, and at 21 he entered the Paris Conservatoire, taking the conducting class and studying under Brémond, who had revived the teaching of valve-horn there in 1896. Though trained on the French valved instrument, to which he remained faithful until quite late in life, Morley-Pegge became an acknowledged master of hand-horn technique, which he regarded as indispensable. During a long career he played in the following orchestras: Symphonique de Paris, Colonne, Concerts Paulet, Paris Radio, Reid; International Ballet and Ballet des Champs Elysées. In his Paris days Morley-Pegge recatalogued and photographed the wind instruments of the Conservatoire collection. He was a founder-member of the Galpin Society. As a musician the style and integrity of Morley-Pegge's performance were much admired, and his profound knowledge of the literature and history of his instrument commanded world-wide respect.

WRITINGS

'The Evolution of the Large Bore Brass Mouthpiece Instrument', *Musical Progress and Mail* (1940), March–June

'Horn', 'Serpent', 'Valve', 'Ophicleide', 'Hibernicon', 'Regent's Bugle', *Grove 5*

'The Regent's Bugle', *GSJ*, ix (1956), 91

'The "Anaconda" ', *GSJ*, xii (1959), 53

*The French Horn* (London, 1960, rev. 2/1973)

PHILIP BATE

**Mornable** [de Mornable], **Antoine** [Anthoine] (*b* ?*c*1515; *fl* 1530–53). French composer, active in Paris. After serving as a chorister at the Sainte-Chapelle until his voice broke, he was educated at the expense of the canons there between December 1530 and December 1532. His first works were printed by Attaingnant in 1534; the same publisher issued a volume of 25 motets and a book of 17 psalms (paraphrased by Marot) in 1546. Both volumes refer to the composer as 'de Mornable', but this form is not found in subsequent anthologies. The title-page of the motets designates him 'most learned musician', but the book of psalms specifies that he was *maître de chapelle* and valet to Count Guy XVII of Laval, a Protestant sympathizer.

Mornable also wrote 43 chansons which were published in collections, mostly by Attaingnant, between 1538 and 1553. The majority are courtly pieces in the style of Claudin de Sermisy and show Mornable's penchant for setting *épigrammes*. An increasing preference for homophony, already illustrated in the psalms of 1546, can be seen in the two *airs* of 1553, *Je ne me confesseray point* and *Je ne sçay que c'est qu'il me fault*, both of which contrast sections in duple and triple metre with great charm.

WORKS

Motetorum musicalium, liber primus, 5, 6, 8vv (Paris, 1546)
Livre second contenant XVII pseaulmes de David, 4vv (Paris, 1546)
Magnificat [primi toni], 4vv, 1534[7]
3 motets, 3–6vv, in 1534[9], 1539[10]
43 chansons, most 4vv, in 1538[11], 1538[14], 1538[15], 1540[14], 1542[13],

$1542^{14-15}$, $1543^{11-12}$, $1544^{7-8}$, $1545^7$, $1545^8$, $1546^7$, $1546^{12}$, $1547^{11}$, $1549^{19}$, $1549^{20}$, $1549^{22}$, $1553^{20}$

For full titles of pieces printed by Attaingnant, see D. Heartz: *Pierre Attaingnant: Royal Printer of Music* (Berkeley and Los Angeles, 1969)

BIBLIOGRAPHY

M. Brenet: *Les musiciens de la Sainte-Chapelle du Palais* (Paris, 1910)
P. Pidoux: 'Les Psaumes d'Antoine de Mornable, Guillame Morlaye et Pierre Certon', *AnnM*, v (1957), 179

FRANK DOBBINS

**Mörner, Carl-Gabriel Stellan** (*b* Ystad, 10 July 1915; *d* Stockholm, 18 Jan 1977). Swedish writer on music. He studied at Uppsala University, 1937–42, under Svensson (theory) and Moberg (musicology). After working as a librarian in Stockholm (1940–53), he took the doctorate at Uppsala with a dissertation on Wikmanson and Silverstolpe. He was head of the gramophone archive of Swedish Radio, 1953–67. His publications include books on Mozart (1944, rev. 2/1965) and Haydn (1945) and on cataloguing and classification (1962), as well as many articles in periodicals (including *STMf*, *Bibliothekbladet* and *Haydn-Studien*) and music criticism for *Svenska dagbladet*. He edited volumes of symphonies and polyphonic songs respectively for the Haydn and Mozart complete editions.

**Mornington, Garret Wesley,** 1st Earl of (*b* Dublin, 19 July 1735; *d* Kensington, 22 May 1781). Irish composer. His father, Richard Colley (Cowley) (*c*1690–1758), came from an established family of Anglo-Irish landowners, and changed his surname to Wesley on being made heir of Dangan Castle by a distant cousin, Garret Wesley. He named his son after his benefactor. (The surname was not changed to Wellesley until after the death of the 1st Earl.) The father was created Baron Mornington in 1746, and on his death on 31 January 1758 the son inherited the barony. He was created Earl of Mornington and Viscount Wellesley on 2 October 1760: it is said that he owed this honour to his musical talent, which had gained him the favour of George III. His second son was the great Duke of Wellington, who was a talented violinist in his youth, but deliberately broke his fiddle when he thought it might distract him from his career. There is no evidence to connect this family with that of John Wesley.

Mornington's father 'played well (for a gentleman) on the violin', and the boy showed a precocity which attracted the notice of Daines Barrington, who later compared him with Mozart, Samuel Wesley and Crotch. In 1748 Mrs Delany wrote:

My godson, Master Wesley, is a most extraordinary boy; ... he is a very good scholar, and whatever study he undertakes he masters it most surprisingly. He began with the fiddle last year, he now plays everything at sight; he understands fortification, building of ships, and has more knowledge than I ever met with in one so young.

He also demonstrated early ability in playing the organ and the harpsichord, and in composition. He entered Trinity College, Dublin, in 1751, graduating BA in 1754 and MA in 1757. In the latter year he founded an amateur musical society in Dublin called the Academy of Music which became well known for its charitable concerts. He was also elected to the Irish House of Commons as member for Trim, but left the following year to take his father's place in the House of Lords. In 1764 he was made MusD and elected the first professor of music in the University of Dublin, a post he retained until 1774. The latter part of his life was spent mostly in London.

As a composer Mornington is known chiefly for his glees, most of which were first published posthumously in collections. The Catch Club of London awarded him prizes in 1776, 1777 and 1779, the last for *Here in cool grot*, which became his most popular piece. His glees are among the most smoothly melodious of their period: two of the best are *Come, fairest nymph* and *When for the world's repose my Chloe sleeps*. Mornington also wrote three madrigals, which show at least a superficial connection with the Elizabethan madrigal. All his part-songs show a due sensitivity to word-setting, though their phrase structure is influenced by that of instrumental music.

Among the unpublished music is a cantata, *Caractacus*. The statement that he wrote cathedral music for St Patrick's, Dublin, and that it is preserved there, is found in earlier editions of *Grove* and other reference books, but seems to be a myth (see *PMA*, xxvi, 1900, p.113). His double chant is the only composition still in regular use, but in a debased form; the original version (in *PMA*, xxvi, p.92) is in its cool serenity among the best of Anglican chants.

WORKS

19 glees, 10 catches, 3 madrigals, 1 ode; the glees and madrigals were published collectively, ed. H. R. Bishop (London, 1846)
Caractacus, cantata, *EIRE-Dtc*; Venite, *Dtc*; chants
March as performed at the installation of ... the Duke of Bedford, pf (Dublin, *c*1770)

BIBLIOGRAPHY

D. Barrington: *Miscellanies* (London, 1781), 317ff
G. E. C[okayne]: *The Complete Peerage* (London, 1887–98, rev. 1936), ix, 235, 236
J. S. Bumpus: 'Irish Church Composers and the Irish Cathedrals, I', *PMA*, xxvi (1899–1900), 90
E. Longford: *Wellington: the Years of the Sword* (London, 1969)

NICHOLAS TEMPERLEY

**Moro** [da Viadana], **Giacomo** [Mori da Viadana, Jacobi] (*b* Viadana, nr. Mantua; *fl* 1581–1610). Italian composer. He may have been a Servite monk. According to title-pages he worked in Viadana in 1581, in Bologna in 1599 and in Fivizzano, near Carrara, in 1604. His two earliest volumes were secular (canzonets and madrigals respectively), and he then produced two collections for liturgical rites, Vespers and the Office of the Dead. But he is better known for the collections of *Concerti ecclesiastici* that appeared after the turn of the 17th century, in which he followed close upon the heels of Viadana (a colleague from the same town) in experimenting with the new concertato style for a small number of voices with indispensable basso continuo. His 1604 collection is a particularly practical compendium including a *Magnificat*, Compline music, a mass on Giovanni Gabrieli's *Lieto godea* and, a Litany of the Santa Casa, Loreto, and some motets, all for double choir, as well as newer-style pieces for one to four voices and organ (these include a *Magnificat* too, for two voices); there are also two four-part canzonas for instruments.

WORKS

*(all pubd in Venice except anthologies)*

Canzonette alla napoletana primo libro, 3vv, con un dialogo e 2 canzonette, 4vv (1581)
Gli encomi musicali, 4, 5vv (1585)
Psalmi ad vespertinas omnium solemnitatum horas, beataeque virginis canticum, 5vv (1595)
Officium et missa defunctorum, 8vv (1599)
Concerti ecclesiastici ... si contengono mottetti, Magnificat, e falsibordoni, 1–8vv, alcuni ... vv/insts, 1 Compieta, 8vv, con le sue antiphone della beate virgine, messa, 8vv, litanie che si cantano nella Santa Casa di Loreto, 8vv, canzoni, a 4, insts, bc, op.8 (1604; rev. 2/1613, 1–4vv, bc (org))
Libro terzo de' concerti ecclesiastici ... contengono motetti e Magnificat, 1–4vv, con alcune canzonette alla francesa, 3, 4vv, bc, op.10 (1607)

1. Bendīr (frame drum) player, Ouzad

2. Ghaiṭa (shawm) player, Marrakesh

3. Gnawa group, Marrakesh, playing qarqabat (iron clappers) and gunbri (skin-bellied lute)

Quarto libro de' concerti ecclesiastici, 1–4vv, bc (org) (1610)
Sacrarum cantionum mentioned in *EitnerQ*
19 motets in 1616[2], 1621[2], 1622[2], 1623[2], 1627[1], 1627[2], 1638[5]; 1 motet, 8vv, *D-Bds*
1 madrigal in 1588[14]

JEROME ROCHE

**Moro, Il.** *See* RATTI, BARTOLOMEO.

**Morocco.** North African kingdom. The music of Morocco can best be understood as the co-existence, sometimes the fusion, of Sudanic, west African and Egyptian-Asiatic musical styles. A linguistic parallel is found in the two quite different – but distantly related – languages of the country, Arabic and Berber. In general Berber music and language flourish in the countryside, while Arabic language and Arab-style music are found in the cities. Just as there is an underlying relationship between the Berber and Semitic language systems, so there is an ancient likeness between the musics of these groups, since Egypt has acted as a cultural matrix. The instruments now played by Moroccan Berbers closely resemble those of ancient Egypt: the *gunbri* (skin-bellied lute; see fig.3) seems very similar to the ancient Egyptian lute, and the *bendīr* (frame drum; fig.1) is an archetypal Mediterranean drum.

Morocco, Egypt and west Africa form the three points of a cultural triangle: various groups have passed freely across the trade routes that connect these three points, bringing not only their goods but also their cultural traditions. Thus, the instruments of ancient Egypt were brought directly into west Africa; goods and ideas flowed easily from the Guinea coast through Timbuktu (now Tombouctou, in Mali) to Fez and back. Under Islam Egyptian influence on Moroccan music remains strong; popular singers and players from Egypt have large and devoted followings in Morocco. The European continent has also played a role in Moroccan music, particularly in its art music which is believed to be derived from that of Muslim Spain.

One of the most striking aspects of Moroccan music is the prevalence of outdoor ceremonial music played upon instruments reminiscent of the *musique haute* category of western Europe in the Middle Ages and Renaissance. On Friday nights members of various Muslim brotherhoods process with musical accompaniment to the tombs of their saints. Typical instruments are the *ghaiṭa* (shawm; fig.2) and the *bendīr* and *ṭabl* (cylindrical drum). The same instruments and groups function in other outdoor activities, such as snake-charming, which, although now used to induce tourists to part with coins, has a strongly ritualistic aspect. The music performed by these shawm and drum players fits into the great chain of musics, stretching from India to the Atlantic, that depend for their organization on a combination of rhythmic and melodic modes. Although improvised elaboration and heterophony are an important part of the music, its basic structure is of a scale pattern interacting with a rhythmic mode.

Another group of outdoor musicians, the Gnawa, seems to have cultural affinities with west Africa. Its antecedents are said to come from the Guinea coast (hence the name); its patron saint is Bilāl, who was Mohammed's Ethiopian slave, the first person to perform the call to prayer (Arabic: *a dhān*). Its instruments are the *ganga* (side drum) and the *qarqabat* (iron clappers 30 cm long; fig.3). This group performs in the streets for coins but is also adept at healing the sick.

The music of the Moroccan Berbers of the Middle Atlas, the High Atlas and the pre-Saharan regions in the south frequently entails the mass participation of the members of a tribe; for example, the *aḥwash* dance, as performed at the oasis of Tafraoute in the south, is done by women in the afternoon and by men in the evening, although in other places men and women perform it together (see fig.4). The performers stand shoulder to shoulder, sometimes moving in a line, sometimes forming a circle. The singing is antiphonal, two equal groups responding to one another, after beginning with a solo by the group leader. The music is frequently in a pentatonic mode; there is much hand-clapping; the drumming (on frame drums) becomes polyrhythmic as the music develops. Several aspects of Moroccan Berber performance are related to west African style.

Professional musician-dancers from Tafraoute travel as itinerant troupes throughout the country. These groups often perform at Marrakesh, where, clad in white robes, they dance, sing and play on the *gunbri* and the one-string skin-bellied fiddle (fig.5). As in the oasis, their singing is antiphonal and strophic.

In Morocco, as in all the countries of the Maghrib, there is the type of art music called *mūsīqī andalusī* ('Andalusian music'), which was formerly played in wealthier households (like chamber music in Europe), and now flourishes with official encouragement on the national radio and in conservatories, where amateurs often study it. It was originally the court music of Muslim Andalusia, and was carried from there to north Africa by the many intellectuals, artisans and musicians who fled after the fall of the kingdom of Granada in 1492. Andalusian music is like the western European category of *musique basse*, being played on the quiet in-

*4. Frame drums accompanying the aḥwash dance for the Fête du Trône at Imlil in the High Atlas*

H. G. Farmer: *Oriental Studies: Mainly Musical* (London, 1953)
A. de Larrea Palacín: *Canciones juglarescas de Ifni* (Madrid, 1956–7)
A. Essayd: 'La musique berbère au Maroc', *La musique dans la vie*, ed. T. Nikiprowetsky, i (Paris, 1967), 241
T. Grame: 'Music in the Jmā al-Fna of Marrakesh, Morocco', *MQ*, lvi (1970), 74

THEODORE GRAME

5. *Soussi rabāb (one-string fiddle) player, Marrakesh*

struments: *'ud* (Arab lute), *rabāb* (fiddle), *kamānja* (fiddle; now often used to mean the western European violin), *ṭār* (tambourine) and the *darabukka* (single-headed pottery drum). In modern performances the cello and the piano are often used as well. Certain *nawbāt* (suites) are traditionally assigned to specific hours of the day (a practice reminiscent of north Indian music). The performance of a *nawba* commences with a solo improvised prelude that is analogous to the *ālāp* of Indian music and the *taqsīm* of the eastern Arab-Turkish tradition, and in some ways to the prelude of the European dance suite. Like the dance suite, the *nawba* proceeds through a group of movements which vary in 'metre' (in this context, rhythmic mode), mood and tempo, but which use the same 'key' (here, melodic mode). Certain popularized forms of this music can now be found in night clubs and restaurants, and are sometimes used to accompany dancers.

*See also* ARAB MUSIC; BERBER MUSIC; NORTH AFRICA.

BIBLIOGRAPHY
G. L. Africano: *A Geographical Historie of Africa* (London, 1600/R1969)
A. Paris: 'Haouach à Telouet', *Hespéris*, i (1921), 209
J. Rouanet: 'La musique arabe', *EMDC*, I/v (1922), 2676–2812
R. Brunel: *Essai sur la confrérie religieuse des 'Aïssâoûa au Maroc* (Paris, 1926)
E. A. Westermarck: *Ritual and Belief in Morocco* (London, 1926)
R. d'Erlanger: *La musique arabe* (Paris, 1930–59)
H. G. Farmer: *An Old Moorish Lute Tutor* (Glasgow, 1933)
E. M. von Hornbostel and E. Lachmann: 'Asiatische Parallelen zur Berber Musik', *Zeitschrift für vergleichende Musikwissenschaft*, i (1933), 25
P. Thornton: *The Voice of Atlas* (London, 1936)
A. Chottin: *Tableau de la musique marocaine* (Paris, 1939)
H. G. Farmer: 'Early References to Music in the Western Sūdān', *Journal of the Royal Asiatic Society* (1939), 569
*La Nawbah dans le maghreb arabe* (Tunis, n.d.)
P. García Barriuso: *La música hispano-musulmana en Marruecos* (Larache, 1941)

**Moroi, Makoto** (*b* Tokyo, 17 Dec 1930). Japanese composer, son of Saburō Moroi. In 1952 he graduated from the Tokyo Geijutsu Daigaku (National University of Fine Arts and Music), where he had been a pupil of Ikenouchi; he also studied Gregorian chant privately with Paul Anouilh, and Renaissance and Baroque music with Eta Harich-Schneider. His career started brilliantly in 1953 when two of his works won international prizes: the Partita for flute (1952), a rhapsodic, 12-note piece full of virtuoso writing and rhythmic and dynamic complexities, won an ISCM prize; and the Composition no.1, Moroi's first orchestral work, received a prize at the Belgian Queen Elisabeth Competition, as well as the first prize in the Japanese radio music competition and the government-sponsored Art Festival prize. He was awarded a second ISCM prize, for the piano composition *Alpha and beta*, in 1955. In May of that year he went to Europe, where he worked in the Cologne electronic music studio. He returned to Tokyo after eight months and began work at the studio of Japanese radio: in autumn 1956 he completed there his first piece in the new medium, Seven Variations, composed with the assistance of Mayuzumi. The two composers were principal promoters of the summer festivals of new music, given under the aegis of the Institute for Twentieth-century Music from 1957 to 1963. In 1958 Moroi won yet another ISCM prize for *Kihaku na tenkai* (or *Développements raréfiants*), a 12-note suite for soprano, singing in Sprechgesang or recitative style, and chamber orchestra. His other awards include an Otaka Prize (1963) for the *Kyōsō-kumikyoku* (or Suite concertante) for violin and orchestra, and an Italia Prize (1965) for the music drama *Gyosha Paeton* ('Phaeton the charioteer'). In 1964 he met Chikuho Sakai, a *shakuhachi* player, and began to take a serious interest in the instrument; he wrote the virtuoso Five Pieces (1964) for Sakai and, gradually, extended his interests to other Japanese instruments. In 1968 he was appointed professor of composition at the Osaka Geijutsu Daigaku. He made several trips abroad in 1970–71 and was guest composer at the Brahmshaus, Baden-Baden, in 1971.

Moroi is one of the leading composers who have actively introduced Japanese audiences to various contemporary techniques, including 12-note methods, further ramifications of serialism, and aleatory music. He is also keenly concerned with contrasting sonorities and instrumental capabilities, as is shown particularly well in his chamber works, such as the *Itsutsu no epigram* (or *Cinq épigrammes*) for seven instruments (1962), a suite of short Webernian pieces with much use of tremolo and repeated notes. Moroi's music is, however, quite unlike Webern's in its tendency to the lyrical and rhapsodic, which is still more striking in his larger compositions, among them the Symphony (1968) for a Wagnerian orchestra. This work is in two movements, of which the first includes a passage for strings in 52 parts and two brilliant percussion cadenzas; the coda to the second movement uses a tape of a pre-recorded performance. Virtuoso writing and rhapsodic form, principal features of the Symphony, are also characteristic of Moroi's pieces for traditional Japanese instruments.

## WORKS
*(selective list)*

INSTRUMENTAL

Orch: Composition no.1, 1953, no.2, 1958, no.3, 1958, no.4, 1960; Schönberg shō [Ode to Schoenberg], 1961; Kyōsō-kumikyoku (Suite concertante), vn, orch, 1963; Toccata, Sarabande and Tarantella, pf, 2 str orchs, 1964; Kain no gen'ei [Vision of Cain], sym. sketch for ballet, 1966; Pf Conc. no.1, 1966; Sym., 1968; 3 Movts, shakuhachi, str, perc, 1970; Pf Conc. no.2, 1971–; Kyōsō kōkyōkyoku – gūtai, Jap. insts, orch, 1973; Kōkan, Jap. perc, pf, orch

Chamber: Chamber Music no.1, 1950, no.2, 1950, no.3, 1951, no.4, 1954; Itsutsu no epigram (5 épigrammes), fl, cl, vib, cel, harp, vn, vc, 1962; Taiwa godai [5 conversations], 2 shakuhachi, 1966; Godan henyō no shirabe [5 metamorphic strata], shakuhachi, shamisen, koto, jūshichigen, 1967; Contradiction, koto, shakuhachi, 1972; Contradiction no.2, shakuhachi, koto, shamisen, jūshichigen, 1972; Hanafuda denki, Jap. insts, 1976

Solo inst: Sonata da camera, pf, 1950–51; Partita, fl, 1952; Alpha and beta, pf, 1954; 5 Pieces, shakuhachi, 1964; Iroha tatoebanashi hachidai [8 parables], pf, 1967; Les farces, vn, 1970; Sinfonia for S.M., sanjūgen, 1972; Phantasie und Fuge, org, 1978

VOCAL AND TAPE

Dramatic: Pitagoras no hoshi [Stars of Pythagoras] (music drama), 1v, insts, tape, 1959; Akai mayu [Red cocoon] (music drama), chorus, orch, tape, 1960; Nagai nagai michi ni sotte (Die lange, lange Strasse lange) (music drama), chorus, orch, tape, 1961; Yamauba [Mountain witch] (opera-ballet), solo vv, orch, tape, 1962; Gyosha Paeton [Phaeton the charioteer] (music drama), solo vv, chorus, orch, tape, 1965

Choral: Chamber Cantata no.1, 1959, no.2, 1959; Waga Izumo [Izumo, my home], S, Bar, chorus, orch, tape, 1970; Hanafuda denki [A romance of playing cards], chorus, koto, jūshichigen, 1972

Solo vocal: Kihaku na tenkai (Développements raréfiants), S, chamber orch, 1957; Aru shu no bagateru (Une espèce de bagatelle), S, pf, 1957

Tape: 7 Variations, 1956, collab. Mayuzumi; Henshin [Transfiguration], 1958; Variété, 1962; Shō sanke [Small confession], 1968, rev. 1969

Principal publisher: Ongaku-no-Tomo Sha

BIBLIOGRAPHY
K. Akiyama: 'Moroi Makoto', *Record geijutsu* (1972), Nov, 359
MASAKATA KANAZAWA

**Moroi, Saburō** (*b* Tokyo, 7 Aug 1903; *d* Tokyo, 24 March 1977). Japanese composer. He graduated from Tokyo University in 1928, presenting a dissertation on musical forms. At this time he headed the Suruya group, which gave seven concerts of new music between 1927 and 1931. From 1932 to 1934 he was in Berlin, studying composition with Schrattenholz and orchestration with Gmeindl at the Staatliche Hochschule für Musik. While there he composed the Piano Concerto in C and the First Symphony, both of which were performed in Berlin for broadcasting; they were played again in Tokyo soon after his return, establishing him as the principal advocate in Japan of the German school. The years between 1936 and 1944 proved to be his most fruitful period, during which he wrote, among many other works, two symphonies and three concertos (some of these were heard in Germany as well as Japan); after the war he produced only a few works. He has served as jury member of the Japanese music competition (1935), inspector of music and adult education for the Ministry of Education (1946–64), director of the Tokyo Metropolitan SO (1965–6) and director of the Senzoku Gakuen Academy of Music, Tokyo (from 1967).

Moroi is a direct descendant from the German academic tradition. His music is always tonal and displays a mastery of polyphonic writing, thematic treatment and orchestration. He is particularly concerned with questions of form, and most of his works are in the standard 'absolute' forms. One of the leading teachers of European music in Japan, he has had a number of distinguished private pupils, among them Dan, Irino, Shibata and Toda.

## WORKS
*(selective list)*

Orch: Pf Conc., C, 1933; 5 syms., 1934, 1938, 1944, 1951, 1970; Vc Conc., d, 1936; Bn Conc., 1937; Vn Conc., 1939; Kōkyōteki nigakushō (Symphonischer Zweisatz), 1942; Sinfonietta, B, 1943; Allegro, pf, orch, 1947; Pf Conc. no.2, 1977

Choral: Taiyō no otozure [A visit of the sun], fantasy oratorio, Bar, female vv, orch, 1968

Chamber: Sonata, vc, pf, 1930; Str Qt, 1933; Pf Qt, 1935; Sonata, va, pf, 1935; Trio, va da gamba, vc, hpd, 1936; Sonata, fl, pf, 1937; Str Sextet, 1939; Str Trio, 1940

Songs: Kaze [Wind], Hikari [Light], Konoha [Leaves], 1v, pf, 1926; Ichō [Ginko tree], 1v, pf, 1927; Rinjū [The deathbed], Asa no uta [Morning song], 1v, vc, 1928; Shōnen [A boy], 1v, pf, 1931; Imo yo [My sister], Haru to akanbo [Spring and baby], 1v, pf, 1935

Pf: 2 sonatas, 1933, 1940; Suite, 1942; Preludio ed allegro giocoso, 1971

Principal publisher: Ongaku-no-Tomo Sha

WRITINGS
*Ongaku keishiki no genri* [The principles of musical forms] (diss., U. of Tokyo, 1928; Tokyo, 1932, as *Ongaku keishiki ron*)
*Ongaku kyōiku ron* [Music education] (Tokyo, 1947)
*Kinō-wasei hō* [Functional harmony] (Tokyo, 1948)
*Bētōven gengaku shijūsō-kyoku* [Analysis of Beethoven's string quartets] (Tokyo, 1949)
*Junsui tai i hō* [Strict counterpoint] (Tokyo, 1949)
*Ongaku jiten* [Music dictionary] (Tokyo, 1949)
*Romanha ongaku no chōryū* [Current of Romantic music] (Tokyo, 1950)
*Ongaku to shikō* [Music and thinking] (Tokyo, 1953)
*Bētōven piano sonata* (Tokyo, 1958)
*Gakushiki no kenkyū* [Historical research on musical forms], i–v (Tokyo, 1957–67)

MASAKATA KANAZAWA

**Moross, Jerome** (*b* Brooklyn, NY, 1 Aug 1913). American composer. He held a Juilliard Fellowship (1931–2) and graduated from New York University in 1932. During the 1930s he supported himself by writing music and playing the piano for the theatre. He spent the years 1940–48 in Hollywood, arranging and orchestrating scores by Copland (*Our Town*), Adolph Deutsch (*Action in the North Atlantic*), Frederick Hollander (*Conflict*), Franz Waxman (*God is my Co-pilot*) and Hugo Friedhofer (*Best Years of our Lives*). Moross's first original film score was for *Close-up* (1948), and thereafter he divided his time between work for the cinema and music for the theatre and concert hall. His First Symphony was conducted by Beecham in Seattle in 1942.

Moross has been concerned to evolve hybrid theatre forms out of elements relating to both popular art genres. His music combines the ambience of simple rural America with the urban sophistication of jazz to produce a tense steely grandeur and an extreme lyricism. Triadic harmony contrasts with highly dissonant elements, rhythms are strong, rugged and assertive (e.g. in *The Last Judgement*). The aggressive, spotlit scoring uses instruments at the upper extremes of their ranges – as when a D trumpet crowns the climax of the First Symphony's fugal finale – and the counterpoint is clean and sharp. Moross has often borrowed from rags, blues and stomps (e.g. in *Frankie and Johnny*), but a more gentle lyrical quality asserts itself in such scores as *The Eccentricities of Davy Crockett*. He is important as a composer for films: his *The Big Country* score is among the finest written for westerns and his music for *The War Lord* was an important part of Hollywood's single attempt to create a genuine medieval atmosphere.

## WORKS
STAGE

Ballet Ballads (four ballet operas, 1, J. Latouche): Susanna and the Elders, 1940–41; Willie the Weeper, 1945; The Eccentricities of

Davy Crockett, 1945; Riding Hood Revisited, 1946
The Golden Apple (opera, 2, J. Latouche), 1949–50
Gentlemen, Be Seated! (opera, E. Eager), 1955–6

ORCHESTRAL

Paeans, 1931; Those Everlasting Blues (A. Kreymborg), v, small orch, 1932; Biguine, 1934; Frankie and Johnny, ballet suite, 1937–8; A Tall Story, 1938
Symphony no.1, 1941–2; Variations on a Waltz, 1946–66
Music for the Flicks, film suite, 1952–65; The Last Judgement, ballet suite, 1953; The Big Country, film suite, 1958

CHAMBER

Recitative and Aria, vn, pf, 1944
Sonatinas for Divers Instruments: no.1, cl choir, 1966; no.2, db, pf, 1966; no.3, ww qnt, 1970; no.4, brass qnt, 1969

FILM MUSIC
(selective list)

When I Grow Up, 1950; The Sharkfighters, 1952; Captive City, 1952; Hans Christian Andersen (including ballet, The Little Mermaid, based on themes by Liszt), 1952; The Seven Wonders of the World (part score), 1955; The Proud Rebel, 1957; The Big Country, 1958; The Jayhawkers, 1959; The Adventures of Huckleberry Finn, 1959
The Mountain Road, 1960; Five Finger Exercise, 1961; The Cardinal, 1963; The War Lord, 1965; Rachel, Rachel, 1967; The Valley of Gwangi, 1968; Hail, Hero, 1969
Music for TV series: Wagon Train, Lancer

PEGGY GLANVILLE-HICKS/CHRISTOPHER PALMER

**Morpain** (*fl* mid-16th century). French composer of six four-voice chansons published in collections by Attaingnant (1539[17], 1540[17], 1545[8], 1547[8]), listed in D. Heartz: *Pierre Attaingnant, Royal Printer of Music* (Berkeley and Los Angeles, 1969).

**Morris, Gareth (Charles Walter)** (*b* Clevedon, 13 May 1920). English flautist. After private tuition with Robert Murchie from the age of 12, he completed his training at the RAM, making his début as a soloist at the Wigmore Hall, London, in 1939. He appeared frequently with such well-known chamber orchestras as the London Chamber Orchestra and the Boyd Neel Orchestra, and this led to a distinguished career as a soloist and member of ensembles such as the Dennis Brain and London Wind Quintets. In 1945 he began to teach the flute at the RAM and from 1948 to 1972 was principal flautist in the Philharmonia (later New Philharmonia) Orchestra, as well as lecturing and writing extensively. He gave the first performances in England of Poulenc's Flute Sonata (with the composer), and the concertos for flute by Gordon Jacob and for flute and horn by Rawsthorne, both dedicated to him. A player of great style and individuality, Morris has throughout his career remained faithful to the wooden flute with thinned head on which his technique was formed; as a pupil of Murchie he may be regarded as a descendant of the great English school of flute playing.

PHILIP BATE

**Morris, Harold** (*b* San Antonio, Texas, 17 March 1890; *d* New York, 6 May 1964). American composer and pianist. He studied at the University of Texas (BA) and the Cincinnati Conservatory (MM 1922, honorary MusD 1939), his teachers including Kelley, Rothwell, Scalero and Godowsky. For a time he toured the USA and Canada as a solo pianist. He taught at the Juilliard School (1922–39) and Teachers College, Columbia University (1935–46), and was guest professor at several universities, including Rice Institute, where he gave the lectures published as *Contemporary American Music* (Houston, 1934). In addition, he was active in associations promoting modern music, serving on the ISCM directorate. His music won many awards and

was often performed in the 1940s. The style shows neo-romantic traits: much of the music is programmatic or impressionistic, and the influence of Skryabin can be detected in the harmonic and tonal thinking. Some of the thematic material, as well as the use of Afro-American rhythms, draws on both black and white Southern folk music. Morris's form, though skilful, sometimes appears contrived.

WORKS
(selective list)

Orch: Poem, after Tagore: Gitanjali, 1915; Dum-a-lum, variations on a Negro spiritual, chamber orch, 1925; Sym. no.1, after Browning: Prospice, 1925; Pf Conc. on Two Negro Themes, 1927; Suite, chamber orch, 1927; Vn Conc., 1938; Passacaglia and Fugue, 1939; American Epic, 1942; Heroic Ov., 1943; Sym. no.2 'Victory', 1943; Sym. no.3 'Amaranth', 1946
Chamber: 2 pf trios, 1917, 1933; Sonata, vn, pf, 1919; 2 str qts, 1928, 1937; 2 pf qnts, 1929, 1937; Suite, pf, str, 1943
Pf: 4 Sonatas, many pieces

BARBARA HAMPTON

**Morris, R(eginald) O(wen)** (*b* York, 3 March 1886; *d* London, 14 Dec 1948). English musical scholar, teacher and composer. He was educated at Harrow and at New College, Oxford, and studied music at the Royal College of Music in London, where he became a member of the teaching staff. In 1926 he was appointed head of the department of theory at the Curtis Institute in Philadelphia but left after two years; he returned to England and continued teaching at the RCM until his death.

His first book, *Contrapuntal Technique in the 16th Century*, has had a lasting influence on teaching in England and elsewhere. It broke new ground by drawing a clear distinction between the various national schools of composition; and by insisting, with trenchant wit, that the study of counterpoint should be based on the works of the composers who wrote it, rather than on arbitrary rules invented by later theorists. The textbooks that followed came from long teaching experience, and were skilfully designed to satisfy the needs of the average student.

Young composers taught by him at the RCM benefited immeasurably from his clarity of mind and rigorous intellect; yet they were allowed to develop in their different ways, for though he spotted the weak link in any chain of musical thought instantly, he never imposed either his own solution or his own personality.

As a composer Morris was, undeservedly, less recognized. His music was not experimental and was therefore unfashionable; yet it reflected the man, and its cool, fastidious clarity, spiced with the diatonic clashes of the English polyphonists, provided just the vehicle he required. The *Canzoni ricertati* for strings show how powerfully he was influenced by his study of polyphonic methods, while the choral setting of Herrick's *Corinna's Maying* and the folksong arrangements are delightful evidence of his lighter vein. One of his most striking works is the Suite for solo cello and orchestra, written in the Lydian mode and originally called *Partita lidica*; in it he seems to have allowed himself a greater freedom of expression than usual.

It is hard to say whether his abandonment of composition at about 50 was because of lack of public response, or simply because he had nothing to say. Certainly he never spoke of his own works and, as Edmund Rubbra wrote, 'even to mention them was latterly the gravest of social indelicacies'. Few people knew that for many years he was a regular contributor of crossword puzzles to *The Times*.

## WORKS

*(all printed works published in London)*

### VOCAL

4 Elizabethan Songs, 1v, pf, 1921: Follow your saint (Campion), There is a lady, Maids are simple (Campion), It fell on a summer's day (Campion), *GB-Onc*

6 English Folk-Songs, 6vv (1929): Seventeen come Sunday, Brisk young sailor (I), Brisk young sailor (II), The lawyer, Tarry Trowsers, The cuckoo

Hunting song (W. Scott), 4 male vv (1930); There is a garden (Campion), 4 male vv (1930)

5 English Folk-Songs, 5vv (London, 1931): Blow away the morning dew, Cold blows the wind, High Germany, The turtle dove, The mare and the foal

Since thou, O fondest (Bridges), 4vv (1932); Corinna's Maying (Herrick), chorus, orch (1933)

### INSTRUMENTAL

Qt in miniature, *Onc*, *Lcm*; Fantasy, str qt (1922)

Toccata and Double Fugue; Symphony, D; Sinfonia, C; Concertino, F; Suite, B♭: all *Lcm*, some also *Onc*

Concerto, g, vn, orch (1930); Concerto Piccolo, a, 2 vn, str orch (1930)

Concertino da camera, a, qnt (version of movts 1, 2, 4 of Concerto Piccolo), *Onc*

Suite in F, vc, orch (1931)

[6] Canzoni ricertati, str orch/qt (1931)

### WRITINGS

'A Memoir of George Butterworth', *George Butterworth 1885–1916* (London and York, 1918)

'Hubert Parry', *ML*, i (1920), 94

'Maurice Ravel', *ML*, ii (1921), 274

*Contrapuntal Technique in the 16th Century* (Oxford, 1922)

*Foundations of Practical Harmony and Counterpoint* (London, 1925)

with H. Ferguson: *Preparatory Exercises in Score-reading* (London, 1931)

*Figured Harmony at the Keyboard* (London, 1931)

'An Introduction to Music', *An Outline of Modern Knowledge*, ed. W. Rose (London, 1931), 1003–54

*The Structure of Music* (London, 1935)

*Introduction to Counterpoint* (London, 1944)

*Oxford Harmony*, i (London, 1946/R1974)

### BIBLIOGRAPHY

W. H. Mellers: 'The Music of R. O. Morris', *MO*, lxiv (1940–41), 437

G. Finzi: Obituary, *RCM Magazine*, xlv (1949), 54

E. Rubbra: 'R. O. Morris: an Appreciation', *ML*, xxx (1949), 107

M. Roberts: 'R. O. Morris 1886–1948: a Tribute', *Music in Education*, xiii (1949–50), 50

H. C. COLLES/HOWARD FERGUSON

**Morris dance.** English folkdance; *see* ENGLAND, §II, 6(i).

**Morrison, (Stuart) Angus** (*b* Maidenhead, 28 May 1902). English pianist. He studied the piano with Harold Samuel and composition with Dunhill and Vaughan Williams at the RCM, London, and joined the teaching staff there in 1926. He made his début at the Wigmore Hall in 1923 and later formed a trio with Jean Pougnet and Anthony Pini. A sensitive, reticent pianist, he had a highly developed ear for subtleties of nuance and phrasing. His repertory included Classical and Romantic works, but he often gave prominence to the music of Debussy, Ravel and other French composers of their time. He wrote vividly on Reynaldo Hahn (*Recorded Sound*, 1966, no.21, p.11) whom he met when he was ten, and who fostered his love of French art. He also supplied valuable source material on his friends Lambert and Walton for R. Shead's *Constant Lambert* (London, 1973) and H. Ottaway's 'Walton's First and its Composition', *MT*, cxiv (1973), 998. He was made a CBE in 1979.

FRANK DAWES

**Morrow, (Norman) Michael (MacNamara)** (*b* London, 2 Oct 1929). Director and co-founder of the ensemble Musica Reservata; *see* MUSICA RESERVATA (ii).

**Morrow, Walter** (*b* Liverpool, 15 June 1850; *d* Wimbledon, 21 Dec 1937). English trumpeter. He studied with the younger Thomas Harper at the RAM and began to play the cornet and slide trumpet at London concerts in about 1873. When Harper retired in 1885 Morrow was generally regarded as the foremost English trumpeter, playing first trumpet at the Philharmonic concerts, the Handel festivals and elsewhere. Towards 1910 he began to give up concert work. He was a professor at the RCM from 1894 to 1920, and also at the Guildhall School of Music. He was an accomplished pianist.

Morrow's knowledge of the trumpet's history made him share with Harper a distaste for the prevailing habit of playing orchestral trumpet parts on the cornet; but unlike Harper, Morrow was not content to use the slide trumpet where feasible and otherwise the cornet. He insistently advocated the use of the valve trumpet in F, then hardly known in England, on the grounds that it alone had the proper length of tubing to reproduce the classical trumpet tone. Among London players he set a fashion for it which lasted roughly from 1898 to 1905, by which time the modern B♭ trumpet had arrived in England. Morrow was opposed from the beginning to the B♭ trumpet, which has merely the tube length of a cornet. He revived the F trumpet at the RCM from about 1910, persuading Stanford to insist that students orchestrate for this instrument, but because of pressure from his colleague John Solomon and his best pupil Ernest Hall (the leading British player of the following years), he began to teach and use the B♭ trumpet, at least occasionally, from about 1912. Morrow also had made a two-valve trumpet in A that he introduced at the Leeds Festival of 1886 (*see* BACH TRUMPET). His F trumpet and slide trumpet are now in the Horniman Museum, London. He made a translation (London, *c*1907) of Julius Kosleck's F trumpet method.

ANTHONY C. BAINES/EDWARD H. TARR

**Mors [Morss].** *See* MOORS family.

**Morselli, Adriano** (*b* Venice; *d* 1691 or 1692). Italian librettist. He wrote at least 18 opera librettos which were performed and printed in Venice between 1679 and 1693. The composers who set them included G. F. Tosi, C. F. Pollarolo, G. M. Martini, Domenico Gabrielli, Domenico Freschi, Antonio Giannettini, M. A. Ziani and G. B. Bassani. After writing a few heroi-comic texts Morselli was for five years house author of the demanding Teatro Grimani di S Giovanni Grisostomo. For this theatre he wrote librettos in a predominantly elevated style, wholly (or almost wholly) serious in character and enhanced by ballets, the use of stage machinery and occasional choruses. Like the work of GIROLAMO FRIGIMELICA ROBERTI (who succeeded him at S Giovanni Grisostomo), his last two texts have deliberate reference to French classical tragedy. Contemporaries considered both writers to be 'learned' librettists.

### BIBLIOGRAPHY

R. S. Freeman: *Opera without Drama: Currents of Change in Italian Opera, 1675–1725, and the Roles Played therein by Zeno, Caldara, and Others* (diss., Princeton U., 1967)

K. Leich: *Girolamo Frigimelica Robertis Libretti (1694–1708): ein Beitrag insbesondere zur Geschichte des Opernlibrettos in Venedig* (Munich, 1972)

KARL LEICH

**Morsolino, Antonio** (*fl* 1588–94). Italian composer. In 1588 he was commissioned by Count Marc'Antonio Martinengo of Villachiara to collect and edit an anthology of madrigals by 18 Italian composers all set to the same text, which had been written by Martinengo himself. The result, *L'amorosa Ero*, was published in Brescia (*RISM* 1588[17]; ed. H. B. Lincoln, Albany, NY, 1968), and includes one setting by Morsolino. He also contributed eight pieces to *Il primo libro delle canzonette a tre voci* (*RISM* 1594[15]). Uomobono Morsolino, organist of Cremona Cathedral, 1591–1611, who wrote four canzonettas for the same publication, was probably a relative.

BIBLIOGRAPHY
A. Anzellotti: 'Una gara musicale nel secolo XVI', *NA*, xi (1934), 225
HARRY B. LINCOLN

**Mortari, Virgilio** (*b* Passirana di Lainate, Milan, 6 Dec 1902). Italian composer. He studied with Bossi at the Milan Conservatory, then with Pizzetti, and took a diploma at the Parma Conservatory in 1928. After beginning his career as a pianist, he turned his attention to composition and teaching: he was on the staff of the Venice Conservatory (1933–40) and served as professor of composition at the Rome Conservatory (1940–73). In addition he was superintendent of La Fenice, Venice (1955–9), and vice-president of the Accademia di S Cecilia, Rome. His music was influenced at first by Pizzetti, but he later adopted a principally neo-classical style, with frequent humorous touches and a tendency to use popular tunes. Together with Casella he wrote *La tecnica dell'orchestra moderna* (Milan, 2/1950).

WORKS
(*selective list*)

Operas: Secchi e Sberlecchi (A. Beltramelli), Udine, 1927; La scuola delle mogli (C. V. Ludovici, after Molière), 1930, rev., Milan, 1959; La figlia del diavolo (C. Pavolini), Milan, 1954; Il contratto (G. Marotta, B. Randone), Rome, 1964
Other stage works: L'allegra piazzetta, ballet, Rome, 1945; Resurrezione e vita (sacro teatro, O. Costa) [after old Venetian music], Venice, 1954; Alfabeto e sorpresa, divertimento scenico, 3 solo vv, 2 pf, Venice, 1959
Vocal orch: Stabat mater, 1947; Requiem, 1959
Orch: Rapsodia, 1930; Fantasia, pf, orch, 1933; Piccola serenata, vn, orch, 1947; Minuetto, notturno e marcia, 1949; Arioso e toccata 'La strage degli innocenti', 1957; Eleonora d'Arborea, 1968
Other works: choral pieces, songs, chamber and pf works
Edns.: works by Cimarosa, Galuppi, Monteverdi, Mozart, Pergolesi, Purcell, A. Scarlatti, Vivaldi

BIBLIOGRAPHY
R. Mariani: 'Musicisti del nostro tempo: Virgilio Mortari', *RaM*, x (1937), 255
M. Mila: 'La scuola delle mogli', *Cronache musicali 1955–59* (Turin, 1959)
ALBERTO PIRONTI

**Mortaro, Antonio** (*fl* 1587–1610). Italian composer. He became a Franciscan friar at Brescia in 1595, and by 1598 had taken the post of organist at the Franciscan monastery in Milan. He was organist at Novara Cathedral in 1602, but returned to Brescia after 1606. He was one of the more important transitional church composers whose works span the pre-continuo and the continuo epochs, and his output also includes a large number of canzonets and some madrigals, and instrumental works, some in keyboard or lute tablature. The majority of his sacred music is for double or triple choir in the Venetian manner of the Gabrielis, although there are conventional polyphonic motets in the 1602 volume and five-part psalms with continuo in that of 1608 (in a more forward-looking style). The three-part motets of 1598, though less impressive, are historically more noteworthy in being mostly scored for two equal voices and a bass in a style that is as close to concertato as one can get without basso continuo – and this four years before anyone actually published motets with continuo. Other collections of trio motets followed in 1603 and 1610, the latter having continuo, and all Mortaro's contributions to Donfrid's *Promptuarii*, vol.ii (1623[2]) are for this medium (those in Reininger's anthology, 1626[2], however, are all for SATB). The trio medium is apparent in Mortaro's four volumes of *Fiammelle amorose*, canzonets with a pleasing rhythmic gaiety, although here the upper voices are usually not equal. Whatever medium he chose, his works were popular and widely disseminated in anthologies over a 40-year period.

WORKS
SACRED

Missae, motecta, cantica BVM, 8, 12vv, liber 2 (Venice, 1595)
Partitio sacrarum cantionum, 3vv (Milan, 1598)
Psalmi ad vesperas, triaque cantica BVM, 8vv (Venice, 1599)
Messa, salmi, motetti, et Magnificat, 3 choirs (Milan, 1599)
Sacrarum cantionum, 5–8vv, liber 1 (Milan, 1602)
Sacrae cantiones, 3vv (Venice, 1603)
Missarum, sacrarum cantionum, 9vv, liber 3 (Venice, 1606)
Il primo libro delli salmi, 5vv, bc, op.13 (Venice, 1608)
Il secondo libro delle messe, salmi, Magnificat, canzoni da suonare e falsi bordoni, a 13 (Milan, 1610)
Sacrae cantiones, 3vv, bc (Venice, 1610)
1 motet in 1600[2]; 1, 1613[1]; 3, 1616[2]; 2, 1622[2]; 5, 1626[2]; 2, 1626[4]; 2, 1627[1]; 2, 1627[2]; 3 psalms, 1587[1]; 1 Magnificat, 1600[1]; 2 tricinia, 1605[1]

SECULAR

Fiammelle amorose, 3vv, libro 1 (Venice, 2/1594)
Il secondo libro delle fiammelle amorose, 3vv (Venice, 1590)
Il terzo libro delle fiammelle amorose, 3vv (Venice, 1592)
Il quarto libro delle fiammelle amorose, 3vv (Venice, 1596)
Il primo libro de canzoni da sonare a 4 (Venice, 1600)
2 canzonets, 1599[14]; 5 canzonas, 1599[19]; 3, 1607[29]; 1, 1609[33]; 1 madrigal, 1624[16]
Various works in MS, *A-Wn*, *D-Bds*, *D-Mbs*, *GB-Lcm*, *PL-WRu*

BIBLIOGRAPHY
C. Krebs: 'Girolamo Dirutas Transilvano', *VMw*, viii (1892), 307
L. Torchi: 'La musica istrumentale in Italia', *RMI*, iv (1897), 607
P. Guerrini: 'Per la storia della musica in Brescia', *NA*, xi (1934), 11
G. Reese: *Music in the Renaissance* (London, 1954, rev. 2/1959), 545
J. L. A. Roche: *North Italian Liturgical Music in the Early 17th Century* (diss., U. of Cambridge, 1968)
JEROME ROCHE

**Mortellari, Michele** (*b* Palermo, *c*1750; *d* London, 27 March 1807). Italian composer and teacher. He was a pupil of Piccinni in Naples, and between 1770 and 1785 about 20 operas by him were performed, mostly in Venice, but also in Rome, Florence and several of the main towns in northern Italy. In 1785 he settled in London, composing and teaching singing; Mrs Billington is said to have studied with him during her first Covent Garden season in 1786. Among his stage works produced in London were the pasticcio *Didone* (1786) and the operas *Armida* (1786) and *Venus and Adonis*, first performed at the Hanover Square Rooms on 8 May 1787. Probably identical with the 'Mr Mortellari' who played the trumpet at the Pantheon Theatre during the season of 1790–91, he was described by the *Gentleman's Magazine* as 'a gentleman of much celebrity in the musical world'. He travelled to Italy and Russia in the late 1790s, but remained based in England. Apart from his operas he also wrote church music, cantatas and other vocal works; the ballet *La fille sauvage* (1805) may also have been by him.

A Michele (C. M.) Mortellari, generally assumed to have been the elder Michele Mortellari's son, played the harpsichord at the King's Theatre from about 1804 to 1806, and was a composer of ballet music and songs.

Another member of the family, Antonio (A. B.) Mortellari, was possibly a brother of the younger Michele, but more likely a cousin who went to England as a protégé of the successful elder Michele. Also a composer of songs, he had two daughters who became well-known singers ('The Misses Mortellari'), one of whom, Marietta Augusta, sang at the King's Theatre, under her married name, as Signora Woolrych.

MOLLIE SANDS/R

**Mortelmans, Lodewijk** (*b* Antwerp, 5 Feb 1868; *d* Antwerp, 24 June 1952). Belgian conductor and composer. He studied with Jan Blockx and Peter Benoit at the Antwerp School of Music, and in 1893 he took the Belgian Prix de Rome. Appointed professor of counterpoint and fugue at the Antwerp Conservatory in 1902, he directed that institution from 1924 until 1933. He was the first director and conductor of the Nouveaux Concerts d'Anvers, founded in 1914. Mortelmans's teaching attracted many gifted pupils, among them de Jong and Peeters. An enthusiast for the Flemish movement, he was president of the Society of Flemish Composers and made many settings of Gezelle, the leading Flemish poet of the 19th century. His works include symphonic poems and other orchestral works, instrumental pieces, songs and choral music, and the opera *De kinderen der zee*.

His son Ivo (Oscar) Mortelmans (*b* Antwerp, 19 May 1901) was known as a composer, especially of choral and dramatic works, conductor and writer on music.

BIBLIOGRAPHY

*AMe*

L. van Riel: 'Lodewijk Mortelmans', *ML*, ii (1921), 107

W. Weyler: *Vlaamse tondichters*, i (Brussels, 1937), 11f

J. L. Broeckx: *Lodewijk Mortelmans* (Antwerp, 1945)

HERBERT ANTCLIFFE/CORNEEL MERTENS

**Mortensen, Finn (Einar)** (*b* Oslo, 6 Jan 1922). Norwegian composer. He studied harmony with Eken and counterpoint with Egge in Oslo, and composition with Bentzon in Copenhagen (1956); both Egge and Bentzon have greatly influenced his music. From 1948 to 1966 he taught music theory at the Norwegian Correspondence School, where he had been a pupil in 1940, and he was then director of the Norwegian state concerts (1967–8). He taught composition at the Oslo Conservatory (1970–73) and was appointed professor of composition at the Oslo Musikkhøgskolen in 1973. Other important posts he has held are the chairmanship of Ny Musikk (1961–4, 1966–7), the presidency of the Society of Norwegian Composers (from 1972) and the vice-presidency of TONO, the Norwegian performing rights society.

Mortensen's opp.3–6 form a distinctive group of early works, neo-classical, polyphonic and clearly diatonic; the Symphony op.5 is indebted to Egge, Lie and Bruckner. However, from the early 1940s he had been experimenting with Schoenbergian 12-note techniques without using them compositionally. Work on the Symphony convinced him of the limitations of tonality and brought his work to a standstill. The deadlock was relieved by his studies with Bentzon, and Mortensen was also encouraged by the reception accorded the Wind Quintet at the 1956 ISCM Festival. During the next few years he wrote a number of 12-note instrumental pieces, chief among them the piano works op.7 and op.13 (the latter performed at the 1960 ISCM Festival).

His use of serialism became more systematic after 1960, a development evident in the orchestral *Evolution* op.23, in which a series of chords is hurled with increasing intensity against a sustained high violin note. This eruptive expressive power is still more strongly felt in the Piano Concerto. In the Sonata for two pianos op.26 Mortensen introduced aleatoricism, and after 1971 he concentrated on a new form of serial technique in which melody, for a long time of lesser importance, returns to a principal role.

WORKS

Orch.: Sym., op.5, 1953; Pezzo orchestrale, op.12, 1957; Evolution, op.23, 1961; Tone Colours, op.24, 1962; Pf Conc., op.25, 1963; Phantasy, op.27, pf, orch, 1965–6; Per orchestra, op.30, 1967; Hedda, op.42, 1973

Chamber: Str Trio, op.3, 1950; Wind Qnt, op.4, 1951; Sonata, op.6, fl, 1953; Sonatina, op.9, cl, 1957; Sonatina, op.10, balalaika, pf, 1957; 5 Studies, op.11, fl, 1957; Sonatina, op.14, va, 1959; Sonatina, op.15, ob, pf, 1959; Fantasy, op.16, bn, 1959; Sonata, op.17, vn, pf, 1959; Sonatina, op.18, va, pf, 1959; Pf Qt, op.19, 1960; 3 Pieces, op.21, vn, pf, 1961–3; 12-tone Music, op.22 no.3, amateur wind, 1961–4; Music, op.22 no.5, amateur str, 1971; Chamber Music, op.31, cl, bn, tpt, trbn, perc, vn, db, 1968; Constellations, op.34, accordion, gui, perc, 1971; New Serialism I, op.35, fl, cl, 1971; Suite, op.36, wind qnt, 1972; Serenade, op.37, vc, pf, 1972; New Serialism II, op.38, fl, cl, bn, 1972; 3 Pieces, op.39, accordion, 1973; New Serialism III, op.40, str trio, 1973; Construction, op.41, hn, 1973

Vocal: Duo, op.8, S, vn, 1956; Tre ved stranden [Three on the shore], op.20 (P. Brekke), female chorus 4vv, 1961; Greners tyngde [The weight of branches], op.33 (Brekke), S, pf, 1971

Pf: Sonatina no.1, op.1, 1943, rev. 1948; Sonatina no.2, op.2, 1949, rev. 1952; Sonata, op.7, 1956; Fantasy and Fugue, op.13, 1958; 12 Short 12-tone Pieces, op.22 nos.1–2, for children, 1961–4; Nocturne, op.22 no.4, 1968; Sonata, op.26, 2 pf, 1964; Pf Piece, op.28, 1966; Drawing, op.29, 1966; Impressions, op.32, 2 pf, 1971; Sonata, op.43, 2 pf, 1973–4

Principal publisher: Norsk Musikforlag

BIBLIOGRAPHY

S. Lind: 'Finn Mortensen', *Nutida musik*, vii/5 (1963–4), 16

A. Nordheim: 'Finn Mortensens nye verk: en klaverkonsert', *Dansk musiktidsskrift*, xxxviii/8 (1963), 303

RANDI MARGRETE SELVIK

**Mortensen, Otto (Jacob Hübertz)** (*b* Copenhagen, 18 Aug 1907). Danish composer, pianist and teacher. In 1925 he entered the Copenhagen Conservatory, where he studied with Jeppesen (theory), Rung-Keller (organ) and Christiansen (piano). He left the conservatory in 1929 after taking the final examination as organist and pianist, and he made his début as a concert pianist in Copenhagen the following year. During the 1930s he studied in Berlin (1930) and Paris (1939, under Milhaud and Desormière); in 1956 he took a master's degree at the University of Copenhagen. He was opera répétiteur at the Royal Theatre in Copenhagen (1937–56) and has appeared as a guest conductor for Danish Radio and the Tivoli; from 1942 to 1966 he taught at the Copenhagen Conservatory and from 1966 to 1974 was lecturer in music at the University of Århus.

Mortensen's fairly sparse output centres on vocal music. Among his instrumental works, the Wind Quintet is notable for its balanced form on a traditional basis. His vocal music is also bound by tradition, but his rare talent for an independent, lyrical continuation of Nielsen's romance tradition has earned him a reputation as the most convincing and convinced song composer of his generation, at a time in Danish music when the romance tradition has been seen more as a burdensome inheritance to be avoided than a challenge to be taken up. Mortensen became involved in popular musical work in the years after 1930; he has written finely constructed choral arrangements of his own songs and Danish folktunes, as well as educational works.

## WORKS
*(selective list)*

Orch: Koncertstykke, fl, vc, pf, orch, 1935; Kirgisisk suite, 1935; Ov., g, 1943; Pf Conc., 1945; Sym., 1957

Choral: Farvel, frost, og velkommen, foraar (Herrick), chorus, fl, str, 1932; Verdenshjørnerne (T. Larsen), chorus, str, pf, perc, 1933, rev. 1936; cantatas, songs, etc

Chamber: Str Qt no.1, 1937; Quatuor concertant, fl, pf trio, 1944; Wind Qnt, 1944; Sonata, ob, pf, 1953; Str Qt no.2, 1955

Songs with orch: 3 sange (T. Lange), A, orch, 1933; Jeg har en sortnende hede (S. Hallar), lv, str, 1940

Songs with pf: 10 danske sange (1940); 2 sange (1942); 10 sange af nordiske digtere (1944); 4 Songs (L. Hughes, J. W. Johnson, R. Frost, W. J. Turner) (1945); 3 Songs (Nash, Belloc, Masefield) (1947); 3 sange (Andersen) (1950); 7 sange (1951); others, school songbooks

Incidental music: Nederlaget (N. Grieg), 1937; Caesar og Cleopatra (Shaw), 1946; Fluerne (Sartre), 1946

Educational: Klaverskole, 1933, collab. O. Jacobsen; rec works, canons

Principal publisher: Hansen
MSS in *DK-Kk*

## WRITINGS

*Harmonisk analyse efter grundbas-metoden* (Copenhagen, 1954)

'The Polish Dance in Denmark', *Chopin Congress: Warszawa 1960*, 572

'Über Typologisierung der Couranten und Sarabanden Buxtehudes', *DAM*, vi (1972)

NIELS MARTIN JENSEN

**Morthenson, Jan W(ilhelm)** (*b* Örnsköldsvik, 7 April 1940). Swedish composer and theorist. He studied composition with Mangs, Lidholm and Metzger, electronic music with Koenig and aesthetics at Uppsala University; in 1963 he attended the Darmstadt summer courses. In his book *Nonfigurative Musik* (1966) he argued that developments in composition have rendered music of directed movement impossible, since the breakdown of tonal harmony has been followed by similar processes of neutralization in instrumentation, presentation and form. His works take note of the far-reaching consequences of this point of view. After the *Wechselspiel* series (1960–61), which he later criticized as idealistic and formalistic, he made several studies of timbre over various chords (*Coloratura* series, 1962–4) and essays in octave harmony (*Antiphonia I–III*, 1963–70), striving in both groups for the most static form. A note of social-cultural criticism appeared most evidently in his work after 1968, for example in *Decadenza II*, 'a funeral march for the decline of instrumental music and musical life over 100 years' which brings together musical characteristics from Bruckner onwards. In the same way he concentrated on church music in *Decadenza I*, funeral music in *Farewell*, string music in *Senza*, the demagogy and mass effect of orchestral music in *Colossus*, and music's demand for physical achievement in *Labor*. He has also worked with visual images in a series of film and videotape pieces, moving from simple changing shades of colour in *Interferences I* through lines, volumes and light intensities in *Lux sonora* to the environmental composition *Camera humana*. In the *Sensory Project* series he has explored aural and visual stimuli at the limits of perception, believing that artists of the future may have to work below the threshold of consciousness. On the other hand, his mixed-media piece *Citydrama* used the whole city of Bonn for four days in 1973.

## WORKS
*(selective list)*

Mixed-media: Colossus, harp, pf, perc, orch, tape, slides, film, 1970; Decadenza II, orch, tape, slides, film, 1970; Citydrama, 1973

Orch: Coloratura II–IV, 1962–4; Antiphonia I–III, 1963–70; Senza, str, 1970; Life, T, chamber ens, orch, 1971; 5 Pieces, 1974

Vocal: Chains-Mirrors, S, tape, 1963; Alla marcia, chorus, orch, 1973

Chamber: Wechselspiel I, vc, 1960; Wechselspiel II, fl, tape, 1961;

Wechselspiel III, pf, perc, 1961; Interjections, perc, 1961, realized Caskel; Courante I–III, pf, perc, 1964, realized Welin; Down, fl, 1972; Labor, ens, 1972; Video I, 8 str, 1972; Soli, wind qnt, 1974; Unisono, bn, hpd/harp, 1975

Org: Some of these, 1961, realized Welin; Pour Madame Bovary, 1962; Encores, 1964; Eternes, 1965; Decadenza I, 1968; Farewell, 1970

Tape: Förspel – Epsilon – Eridani – Efterspel, 1967; Neutron Star, 1967; Spoon River, 1967; Ionosphères I, 1969; Zero, 1969; Ultra, 1970

Videotape: Supersonics, 1970; Interferences I, 1970; Lux sonora, 1970; Sensory Project I–III, 1970–72; Camera humana, 1972

Principal publisher: Nordiska Musikförlaget

## WRITINGS

'Arbetsbok', *Nutida musik*, vi/8 (1962–3), 4

'Det absolut musikaliska', *Nutida musik*, vi/8 (1962–3), 22

'Chains-Mirrors', *Nutida musik*, vii/2 (1963–4), 35

'Nonfigurativ musik', *Nutida musik*, vii/7 (1963–4), 16

with J. Bark: 'Två spår', *Rondo* (1964), no.1, p.6

'Det sköna och det svåra', *Paletten* (1965), no.2, p.58

'Slapstick och datakval: om sextiotalets musik', *Medicinska föreningens tidskrift* (1965), 246

'Experiment i tomhet', *Nutida musik*, ix/3 (1965–6), 20

*Nonfigurative Musik* (Stockholm, 1966) [in Ger. trans.]

'Concert – go home', *Nutida musik*, xi/3–4 (1967–8), 38

'Epsilon Eridani', *Nutida musik*, xi/3–4 (1967–8), 39

'Move against the Beat', *Nutida musik*, xi/3–4 (1967–8), 40

'Nonfigurative Musik', *International Music Educator* (1969), no.2, p.14 [in Ger., Eng. and Fr. trans.]

'Om Ionosphères och Zero', *Nutida musik*, xiii/3 (1969–70), 30

'Den svenske tonsättarens situation', *Nutida musik*, xiv/2 (1970–71), 33

'1970', *Nutida musik*, xiv/3 (1970–71), 12

'Den elektroniska musikens ideologi', *Nutida musik*, xv/2 (1971–2), 25

'Metamusik', *Nutida musik*, xv/2 (1971–2), 42

'Europa efter Cage', *Nutida musik*, xvi/2 (1972–3), 51

'Den beställde komponisten', *Nutida musik*, xvii/4 (1973–4), 5

'Labor', *Nutida musik*, xvii/3 (1973–4), 36

'Musik i ljud och bild', *Nutida musik*, xvii/2 (1973–4), 20

'Den musikaliska kvalitetens ideologi', *Tonfallet*, vii (1974), no.9, p.6; no.10, p.4

'Den strukturella musikens situation', *Artes* (1975), no.1, p.45

## BIBLIOGRAPHY

K. Linder: 'Sex unga tonsättare', *Nutida musik*, vi/8 (1962–3), 13

L. G. Bodin and B. E. Johnson: 'Semikolon; akustiska betraktelsebilder: en intervju med Jan W. Morthenson', *Ord och bild* (1965), 473

O. Nordwall: 'Musikestetisk absolutism', *Musikkultur* (1967), no.2, p.24

M. Gräter: 'Elektronik als Kompositionselement und Gestaltungsmittel im Fernsehen', *NZM*, cxxxiii (1972), 77 [on *Supersonics* and *Lux sonora*]

G. Bergendal: 'Jan W. Morthenson – på marsch', *Nutida musik*, xvii/4 (1973–4), 11

ROLF HAGLUND

**Mortier, Pierre** (*d* Amsterdam, 18 Feb 1711). Amsterdam printer; he copied some of the publications of ESTIENNE ROGER.

**Morton, 'Jelly Roll'** [Ferdinand Joseph] (*b* ?Gulfport, Mississippi, 20 Sept 1885; *d* Los Angeles, 10 July 1941). Black American jazz composer and pianist. He grew up in New Orleans, where there was an identification with European culture, but there is little evidence that this was a significant influence on him or that his formal musical training was exceptional. He worked there as a pianist, taking as his model the jazz pianist–composer Tony Jackson. From about 1904 he became itinerant, at first returning periodically to New Orleans. He often engaged in such illicit activities as pool playing and procuring, but his interest in music predominated. By 1911 the jazz pianist James P. Johnson had heard him play his *Jelly Roll Blues* in New York and considered his style advanced for its time; two years later the piece was published in Chicago. In 1913 Morton was in St Louis and from 1917 to 1922 he lived in Los Angeles, where he enjoyed great success. In 1923, using Chicago as his base, he made his first recordings, of which two early sextet performances, *Big Fat Ham* and *Muddy Water Blues*, and a series of piano solos revealed a mature post-ragtime style of composition and improvisation. By 1926–7 Morton was recording with his Red Hot Peppers, well-rehearsed ensembles of seven or eight players (and sometimes quartets and trios); their recordings included superb versions of his early piano pieces *Grandpa's Spells*, *The Pearls* and *Wolverine Blues* and introduced such excellent and previously unrecorded pieces as the three-part *Dead Man Blues* and the highly praised and intricately structured *Black Bottom Stomp*. In 1928 Morton moved to New York and there recorded more works. With such pieces as *Tank Town Bump* (1929) and *Harmony Blues* (1930) he gradually turned to larger ensembles and more elaborately harmonized ensemble writing, but also to greater use of solo improvisation, as in *Blue Blood Blues* (1930). These later records influenced certain bands in the south-west, particularly Benny Moten's.

Although pieces like *Shoe Shiner's Drag*, *Wolverine Blues*, *Milenburg Joys* (on which Morton collaborated) and particularly *King Porter Stomp* continued to be played and to be influential throughout the 1930s, Morton's performances came increasingly to be regarded as old-fashioned, and his career declined. In 1938 he was in Washington, DC, and through the efforts of the folklorist Alan Lomax recorded for the Library of Congress an extensive series of performances (issued in 1948 and 1957) in which he was a charming raconteur, an autobiographer of little modesty, a jazz historian, the genre's first theorist and a leading pianist–composer. This eventually led to further recordings and a renewed career.

Morton was the first significant jazz composer. Although he did not begin recording until the mid-1920s his work may be said to synthesize the features of New Orleans jazz (and perhaps Afro-American music in general) before Louis Armstrong's great innovations had begun to have an effect. His points of departure were Missouri or 'classic' ragtime and the developing idiom of instrumental blues. His piano pieces bear at least a formal resemblance to ragtime compositions; but his music exceeded ragtime's limits by its more complex, tango-derived syncopation, polyphonic bass lines and formal cohesion (brought about by thematic relationships and subtly linked tonalities) and, most important, by his use of written and improvised variation. He developed a jazz ensemble style in which simple homophony, solo choruses and 'breaks', and improvised polyphony take turns; the best examples are his fine recordings of 1926–7. His concern for the compositional aspect of jazz was unusual in the New Orleans style and places him alongside Ellington and Monk as one of the most important composer–pianists in jazz history. (*See* JAZZ, fig.5.)

### WORKS
*(selective list; dates are of first recording)*

Edition: *The Collected Piano Music of Ferdinand 'Jelly Roll' Morton*, ed. J. Dapogny (Washington, DC, 1977)

Pf: London Blues, 1923; New Orleans Blues, 1923; Wolverine Blues, 1923; King Porter Stomp, 1923; The Pearls, 1923; Kansas City Stomps, 1923; Perfect Rag, 1923; Stratford Hunch, 1923; Grandpa's Spells, 1923; Frog-i-Moore (Froggy Moore) Rag, 1924; Mamanita, 1924; Jelly Roll Blues, 1924; Shreveport Stomp, 1924; The Crave, 1939; Creepy Feeling, 1939; Mister Joe, 1939; Sweet Substitute (song), 1939

Ensemble: Big Fat [Foot] Ham, 1923; Muddy Water Blues, 1923; Black Bottom Stomp, 1926; Dead Man Blues, 1926; Grandpa's Spells, 1926; Jungle Blues, 1927; The Pearls, 1927; Wolverine Blues, 1927; Kansas City Stomps, 1928; Shoe Shiner's Drag

(London Blues), 1928; Tank Town Bump, 1929; New Orleans Bump, 1929; Harmony Blues, 1930; Blue Blood Blues, 1930

Principal publishers: Carew (Tempo Music), Melrose

### BIBLIOGRAPHY
A. Lomax: *Mister Jelly Roll* (New York, 1950, 2/1973)
W. Russell: 'Morton and *Frog-i-more Rag*', *The Art of Jazz*, ed. M. Williams (New York, 1959), 33
R. Hadlock: 'Morton's Library of Congress Albums', *Jazz*, i (1959), 133
M. Williams: 'Jelly Roll Morton', *Jazz*, ed. N. Hentoff (New York, 1959), 59
K. Hulsizer: 'Morton in Washington', *This is Jazz*, ed. K. Williamson (London, 1960), 202
D. Locke: 'Jelly Roll Morton: the Library of Congress Recordings', *Jazz Journal*, xiii (1960), Jan, 15
G. Waterman: 'Jelly Roll Morton', *Jazz Panorama*, ed. M. Williams (New York, 1962), 31
M. Williams: *Jelly Roll Morton* (London, 1962)
——: *Jazz Masters of New Orleans* (New York, 1967), 38ff
G. Schuller: *Early Jazz* (New York, 1968), 134–74
M. Williams: *The Jazz Tradition* (New York, 1970), 16–46
MARTIN WILLIAMS

**Morton** [Mourton, Moriton], **Robert** (*b* *c*1430; *d* 1476 or later). English composer. All the surviving documents bearing on his life concern his years as *clerc* and *chappellain* in the chapel choir of the Burgundian court from 1457 to 1476, the final decade of the long reign of Philip the Good and the first eight years of the brief and tumultuous reign of his son Charles the Bold. The document of late 1457 appointing Morton and authorizing payment for clothes describes him as 'chappellain angloix' and is the only evidence that he was English; the wording of the document seems to imply that he was already resident in Brussels at the time. Because of a lacuna in the documents for the following years, the first surviving payment to him as a member of the chapel is from October 1460: here, and in all subsequent documents, he is styled 'Messire' – a title which, in these particular documents, means that he is a priest. Thus it remains difficult to explain why Morton remained in the humble position of *clerc* for 15 years when most were promoted to *chappellain* after about three years. Morton's promotion occurred some time between 20 June 1471 and 20 July 1472: again, a lacuna in the surviving documents makes a more precise date unattainable.

Morton was seconded to the household of Charles, Count of Charolais, the future Duke Charles the Bold, from 1 June 1464 to 12 March 1465 and again for three months some time between 1 October 1465 and 31 September 1466. He was given leave of absence from 20 July to 13 August 1470. In 1475 his appearances in the daily chapel accounts are more irregular, and he was paid only a quarter of his full wage for that year. On 1 February 1476 his position as a chaplain was taken by Pierre Basin, apparently in immediate fulfilment of an expectative granted a year earlier (see Pirro, p.118). The lack of any reference to 'feu Messire Morton' – which would be normal in such documents – makes it unlikely that Morton died then; and there is some evidence that he was still alive in 1478, being paid his earlier wages in retrospect after the chaos of Charles the Bold's campaigns. (A reference in *FétisB* to a document attesting his presence at the chapel in 1478 seems to go back to an earlier misreading of that document by Pinchart, corrected by implication in Pinchart, 1881; see Fallows, 1978, pp.275ff: unfortunately the document itself cannot now be traced.)

Further oblique clues to his life survive. His rondeau *Le souvenir* recalls the arms of Claude Bouton (*b* ?1488),

'Souvenir tue', and might indicate some connection with the Bouton family, at least one of whom was prominent at the Burgundian court during Morton's time there. The rondeau *Il sera pour vous/L'homme armé* refers jokingly to Simon le Breton (*see* SIMON, §1) whose retirement from the court chapel in May 1464 may have provided the occasion for the song (see Fallows, 1978, pp.204ff). The poem *Mon bien, m'amour, ma joye et mon desir*, printed in *Le jardin de plaisance* (Paris, 1501) and normally considered the correct poem for the music *Mon bien ma joyeux*, has the acrostic MARIE M[O]RELET, though no person of this name has been identified. And the anonymous rondeau *La plus grant chiere* (ed. in Marix, 1937, p.86; text in Marix, 1939, p.207) describes vividly how Morton and Hayne van Ghizeghem astonished everybody with their singing and playing at Cambrai.

Only secular works survive; and all are ascribed simply 'Morton' or, in the case of *I-Fn* 176, 'Mortom' (perhaps 'Mortoni'). None of his songs appears in any English source. Moreover English style is difficult to find in them: *Mon bien ma joyeux* has the close imitations on an F major triad that are characteristic of John Plummer; and *Pues serviçio* has several times been described as English in style though further information shows it to be almost certainly Spanish in origin. The true stylistic context for all eight reasonably secure works of his is in the music of the Burgundian court. *Cousine* and *Que pourroit plus faire* have the kind of metrical irregularity found in, for instance, the anonymous *La plus grant chiere*; *N'aray je jamais* and *Le souvenir* have the fluid melodic style that is apparent also in the early works of Hayne van Ghizeghem and Busnois; *Mon bien ma joyeux* seems to be a reworking of the musical material in the anonymous bergerette *Greveuse m'est vostre acointance* (*US-Wc* M2.1 L25), following a tradition of reworking common among the court composers of the time; moreover, the revision of *Il sera pour vous/L'homme armé*, adding a voice and perhaps turning it into an instrumental piece, shows clear influence from the *Missa 'L'homme armé'* of Busnois – if the original version is from 1464, this version would probably date from the early 1470s when Busnois' star was rising.

Given that context, certain individual stylistic traits can be noted. All his secure pieces have an extreme melodic economy; they avoid the simple 'filling' patterns that a composer such as Hayne would often give to the contratenor between musico-poetic lines in the discantus and tenor; but the contratenor often uses wide leaps more frequently than in the works of his contemporaries; and a preference for the contratenor to use leaps of a 5th tends to anchor the tonalities.

The four songs listed here as doubtful are all ascribed to Morton in a single manuscript, *I-PEc* 431. Three of them have conflicting ascriptions elsewhere, of which two seem decidedly more convincing (those for *Vien avante* and *Pues serviçio*); the fourth, *Elend du hast*, fits stylistically very closely with the German songs of the time. Certainly all four stand apart from the relatively coherent stylistic profile of the eight more secure works, and they are unlikely to have anything to do with the Burgundian court. While a firm conclusion on these ascriptions cannot yet be hoped for, the pieces are best considered doubtful.

Morton's personal fame was not widespread. Only

*N'aray je jamais* is ascribed to him in more than one source. Yet there is ample testimony to his achievement. He was mentioned by Hothby (see *JAMS*, viii, 1955, p.95) and Tinctoris (*CS*, iv, 200). And his most successful pieces were exceptionally widely distributed. *Le souvenir* has 14 musical sources (including three intabulations) and was used as the basis for two works by Tinctoris and one by Arnolfo Giliardi. *N'aray je jamais* has 15 musical sources and was used for a motet and three mass cycles (among them Josquin's *Missa 'Di dadi'*). These two songs represent a peak in the music of the Burgundian court only to be equalled by Hayne van Ghizeghem in his *De tous biens plaine* and *Allez regrets*; and they are Morton's true claim to recognition.

### WORKS
*(all for 3vv and probably rondeaux)*

Editions: *Der Kopenhagener Chansonnier*, ed. K. Jeppesen (Copenhagen and Leipzig, 1927, rev. 2/1965) [J]
        *Les musiciens de la cour de Bourgogne au XVe siècle (1420–1467)*, ed. J. Marix (Paris, 1937) [M]
        *The Mellon Chansonnier*, ed. L. L. Perkins and H. Garey (New Haven and London, 1979) [P]
        *R. Morton: The Collected Works*, ed. A. W. Atlas (New York, in preparation)

*(for full source information see Atlas edn.)*

Cousine trop vous abusés; ed. in Plemenac, p.172
Il sera pour vous conbatu/L'homme armé, P 125 (combinative chanson, anon. in unique source; rev. version, 4vv, in *I-Rc* 2856, ascribed 'Borton', M 96)
Le souvenir de vous me tue, J 37 (also intabulated as Salve radix Josophanie; added 4th voice in *PEc* 431)
Mon bien ma joyeux (text incipit evidently corrupt, and perhaps for poem Mon bien, m'amour, ma joye et mon desir in *Le jardin de plaisance*), M 98
N'aray je jamais mieulx que j'ay, J 4 (added 4th voice in three sources, P 95)
Paracheve ton entreprise, P 145 (= La perontina, M 97)
Plus j'ay le monde (= Madonna bella)
Que pourroit plus faire une dame (= Numine Ihesu celice)

#### DOUBTFUL WORKS
*(forms uncertain)*

C'est temps perdu, M 95 (ascribed 'Caron' in *I-Rc* 2856)
Elend du hast umbfangen mich, M 240 (= Lent et scolorito and Vive ma dame par amours)
Pues serviçio vos desplaze, M 93 (ascribed 'Enrrique' in *E-Mp* 1335, ed. in MME, v (1947), 34; text by Pere Torroella)
Vien avante morte dolente, M 94 (ascribed 'Basin' in *I-Rc* 2856)

### BIBLIOGRAPHY
*FétisB*
A. Pinchart: *Archives des arts, sciences et lettres*, iii (Ghent, 1881)
J. Marix: *Histoire de la musique et des musiciens de la cour de Bourgogne sous le règne de Philippe le Bon (1420–1467)* (Strasbourg, 1939/R1972)
A. Pirro: *Histoire de la musique de la fin du XIVe siècle à la fin du XVIe* (Paris, 1940)
D. Plemenac: 'The "Second" Chansonnier of the Biblioteca Riccardiana (Codex 2356)', *AnnM*, ii (1954), 105–87
B. Trowell: *Music under the Later Plantagenets* (diss., U. of Cambridge, 1959)
P. Gülke: 'Morton, Robert', *MGG*
H. M. Brown: *Music in the French Secular Theater, 1400–1550* (Cambridge, Mass., 1963)
D. Fallows: 'English Song Repertories of the Mid-fifteenth Century', *PRMA*, ciii (1976–7), 61
——: *Robert Morton's Songs: a Study of Styles in the Mid-fifteenth Century* (diss., U. of California, Berkeley, 1978)
                                                DAVID FALLOWS

**Morungen, Heinrich von.** *See* HEINRICH VON MORUNGEN.

**Mosca, Giuseppe** (*b* Naples, 1772; *d* Messina, 14 Sept 1839). Italian composer. He studied composition and counterpoint with Fenaroli at the Conservatory of S Maria di Loreto in Naples; in 1791 his first opera, *Silvia e Nardone*, was performed at the Tordinona in

Rome. For 12 years he worked as a composer for various Italian theatres, presenting his operas in Rome, Naples, Venice and elsewhere, usually with much success. In 1803 he went to Paris as *maestro al cembalo* at the Théâtre-Italien; he composed additional music when required, but wrote no operas (the two operas that Florimo attributed to him in this period were by his brother). When Spontini assumed the directorship of the theatre (1810), Mosca returned to Italy.

After the success of Rossini's *La pietra del paragone* (1812), Mosca accused Rossini of having plagiarized his *I pretendenti delusi* (1811), particularly the device of the crescendo, circulating copies of his music as proof. The charge was repeated by critics until Radiciotti discovered that the crescendo had been used (by Simone Mayr in *Lodoiska*, 1796) before Mosca's first use of it in *Il folletto* (1797). Certainly Mosca's musical style shows a remarkable similarity to Rossini's in many respects – melodic turns, orchestral melodies under vocal patter, multipartite ensemble structures – but it would be difficult to decide from a study of the music who influenced whom.

In 1817 Mosca went to Palermo as musical director of the Teatro Carolino, but he gave up the post after the Revolution of 1820. A return to Milan revived his career; after several years of touring, however, he settled in Messina as director of another theatre, succeeding Platone (1827). He wrote no more operas. Fétis described him as a musician without genius, but gifted with stupendous facility.

### WORKS

42 operas, incl. Silvia e Nardone, Rome, 1791; Il folletto (C. Battimelli), Naples, 1797, *I-Nc*; Chi si contenta gode (Le nozze in fieva) (B. Sivoli), Rome, 1798, *Mr*; Ifigenia in Aulide (Zeno), Rome, 1799; Il sedicente filosofo (G. Foppa), Milan, 1801, *F-Pc*, *I-Fc*; Ginevra di Scozia, ossia Ariodante (G. Rossi), Turin, 1802; I pretendenti delusi (L. Prividali), Milan, 1811, *Bc*, *Fc*, *Mr*, *Nc*; I Tre mariti (La moglie di tre mariti) (G. Rossi), Venice, 1812; *GB-Lbm*, *I-Nc*; Il finto Stanislao re di Polonia (Rossi), Venice, 1812; Gli amori e l'arme (G. Palomba), Naples, 1812, *Nc*; Le bestie in uomini (A. Anelli), Milan, 1812; La gazzetta (Avviso al pubblico; Il matrimonio per concorso) (Rossi), ? Venice, 1812; La diligenza a Joigni, ossia Il collaterale (Palomba), Naples, 1813, autograph *Nc*; La gioventù di Enrico V (F. Romani), Palermo, 1817, *Fc*; Attila, ossia Il trionfo del re dei Franchi (S. Sografi), Palermo, 1818, *Mc*; L'abate de l'epée (L. Riccuti), Naples, 1826, *Nc*

### BIBLIOGRAPHY

*EitnerQ*; *FétisB*
'Verzeichniss sämmtlicher Compositionen des Hrn. Joseph Mosca bis zum Frühjahr 1821 inclusive', *AMZ*, xxiii (1821), col.477
F. Florimo: *La scuola musicale di Napoli e i suoi conservatorii*, ii (Naples, 1882/*R*1969), 450ff
G. Radiciotti: *Gioacchino Rossini*, iii (Tivoli, 1927), 97
O. Tiby: *Il Real Teatro Carolino* (Palermo, 1957)
MARVIN TARTAK

**Mosca, Luigi** (*b* Naples, 1775; *d* Naples, 13 or 30 Nov 1824). Italian composer. Although most early sources say that he was a student at the Turchini conservatory, most also state that, like his brother Giuseppe, he was a pupil of Fenaroli, who taught at the Loreto. He was for many years *maestro al cembalo* at the S Carlo opera house. Through the intervention of his friend and protector Paisiello he also became, at some time after 1802, *vice-maestro* of the royal chamber and chapel; he kept this post under the Bourbon Restoration. By the first decade of the century he was considered one of the best singing teachers in Naples, and when Zingarelli became director of the Naples Conservatory in 1813 Mosca was made *primo maestro di canto*. He was a member of the Naples Accademia di Belle Arti.

Mosca's first opera, *L'impresario burlato*, was suc-

cessfully performed at the Teatro Nuovo in 1797. Though he travelled through Italy staging his operas, all were originally written for Naples except *L'italiana in Algeri* (Milan, 1808; reset by Rossini in 1813). In 1816 he directed the music for Paisiello's funeral, conducting the latter's requiem. He also composed much sacred music himself.

Luigi Mosca's musical style seems more interesting than Giuseppe's. Prota-Giurleo and Paduano noted his aptitude for setting specific dramatic situations, his ability to build a scene, his richer harmonies etc. Whatever their musical differences, neither brother's music outlasted him, and their works are dim reflections of their greatest Italian contemporary, Rossini.

### WORKS

Operas: 16 operas, incl. L'impresario burlato (F. Signoretti), Naples, 1797, *B-Bc*, *I-Fc*, *Nc*; Gli sposi in cimento (S. Zini), Naples, 1800, *Nc*; L'impostore (A. Tottola), Naples, 1802, *Nc*; La vendetta feminina, Naples, 1803; L'italiana in Algeri (A. Anelli), Milan, 1808, autograph *Mr*; La sposa a sorte (G. Palomba), Naples, 1810, *Nc*; Il salto di Leucade (G. Schmidt), Naples, 1812, *Nc*
Other works: Gioas, oratorio, Palermo, 1806; sacred works, *I-Mc*, *Nc*

### BIBLIOGRAPHY

*EitnerQ*
C. A. de Rosa [Marchese di Villarosa]: *Memorie dei compositori di musica del regno di Napoli* (Naples, 1840)
F. Florimo: *La scuola musicale di Napoli e i suoi conservatorii*, iii (Naples, 1883/*R*1969), 82ff
U. Prota-Giurleo and L. Paduano: 'Mosca', *MGG*
MARVIN TARTAK

**Moscaglia, Giovanni Battista** (*b* ?Rome; *fl* 1559–1590). Italian composer and poet. He served as 'cantore, sopranus' in the Cappella Giulia from 21 March 1559 to 31 August 1560. Although he seems to have remained in Rome after 1560, as shown by several title-pages, there is no evidence of his holding any salaried appointment. In Rome he was associated with such composers as G. M. Nanino, Macque, Stabile, Zoilo, Giovannelli and Marenzio, all of whom set his texts to music on at least one occasion. Moscaglia asked each of these men, among others, to compose a setting for one of his poems to be included in his second book of madrigals for four voices, saying in his dedication that since he was 'unable to set them all to music myself for lack of time, I gave part of them to these excellent musicians of Rome'. Although his dedication was signed on 10 September 1582 the book was not published until 1585. Marenzio apparently tired of waiting for the appearance of his madrigal and published it in his own volume of madrigals for four voices. Two of Moscaglia's dedications indicate that he also knew some important patrons of northern Italy. His third book of madrigals for five voices is dedicated to Count Mario Bevilacqua of Verona, leader of the Accademia Filarmonica. In 1587 Moscaglia visited Ferrara, where he was cordially received; on 30 June he dedicated his fourth book of madrigals to Don Alfonso d'Este, uncle of Duke Alfonso II, in gratitude for his favour. A book of *napolitane* for three voices, published in 1585, contains a dedication written by Moscaglia's wife, Lucretia Guidotti, following a common tradition in the late 16th century that composers affected lack of interest in 'minor' forms such as the canzonetta and villanella.

Moscaglia was popular with anthologists in his day; eight of his madrigals appeared in various collections and were reprinted as late as 1630. His *Due rose fresche* from the second book of madrigals for four voices is transcribed for lute in Joachim van den Hove's *Delitiae musicae* (1612). His last extant published work was one piece for four voices included in a collection of 1590.

### WORKS

Il secondo libro de madrigali, 5vv (Venice, 1579)
Il terzo libro de madrigali, 5vv (Venice, 1585)
Il secondo libro de madrigali con alcuni di diversi eccellenti musici di Roma, 4vv (Venice, 1585); 1 piece transcr. lute, 1612[18]
Il primo libro delle napolitane, 3vv (Venice, 1585)
Il quarto libro de suoi madrigali, 5vv (Venice, 1587)
Several madrigals, 1582[4], 1583[10], 1585[19], 1586[9], 1587[6], 1590[15]

### BIBLIOGRAPHY

A. Einstein: *The Italian Madrigal* (Princeton, 1949/*R*1971)

STEVEN LEDBETTER

**Moscheles, Ignaz** (*b* Prague, 23 May 1794; *d* Leipzig, 10 March 1870). German pianist, conductor and composer of Czech birth. His piano lessons began early, and from 1804 to 1808 he was taught by B. D. Weber, director of the Prague Conservatory, who insisted on an exclusive study of Bach, Mozart and Clementi. But already Moscheles had discovered the 'Pathétique' Sonata, and was keen to explore every new Beethoven piano work. In 1808 he moved to Vienna, where he could come closer personally and musically to Beethoven, while studying counterpoint with Albrechtsberger and composition with Salieri. By 1814, when the publisher Artaria commissioned him to prepare a piano reduction of Beethoven's *Fidelio*, he was one of Vienna's most popular pianists, and his career as a virtuoso had begun. The brilliant display piece *La marche d'Alexandre* op.32 (1815) met with tremendous success at his recitals and became a favourite with other aspiring pianists (later including Schumann). Between 1815 and 1825 his travels as a recitalist took him throughout Germany, often to Paris and London, and also back to Prague. He was first heard in London at a Philharmonic concert on 11 June 1821, and was hailed as an equal and friend by Clementi and J. B. Cramer. It was in 1824

*Ignaz Moscheles: lithograph (1846) by Charles Baugniet*

that Moscheles met the 15-year-old Mendelssohn in Berlin and gave him some finishing lessons on the piano.

In March 1825 Moscheles married Charlotte Embden (1805–89) from Hamburg, and they settled in London, where he taught the piano at the Royal Academy of Music and built up a circle of talented pupils, including Litolff and Thalberg. He also became a conductor to the Philharmonic Society (co-director from 1832 to 1841); he conducted the first London performance of Beethoven's *Missa solemnis* in 1832 and very successful performances of the Ninth Symphony in 1837 and 1838. His edition and translation of Schindler was published as *The Life of Beethoven* (London, 1841). He often played in society, and produced many lightweight piano works in a fashionable idiom for publishers' commissions. At the same time he established a series of 'classical chamber concerts' or 'historical soirées', in which he contributed to the newly awakened interest in earlier music by playing Scarlatti and Bach on the harpsichord. The Moscheles family was often host to Mendelssohn in London: the two composers played Mendelssohn's Two Piano Concerto in E in 1829, and the Mozart Two Piano Concerto in 1832, and Moscheles went to Leipzig to appear with Mendelssohn in his first Gewandhaus concerts in 1835. He also met Chopin and with him played his own *Grande sonate* op.47 to the French royal family in Paris in 1839.

Moscheles finally left London in 1846 to become principal professor of piano at the Leipzig Conservatory, recently founded by Mendelssohn, remaining there for the rest of his life. Mendelssohn's death in 1847 was a profound blow, and he resolved to maintain the high standard of teaching for which his former pupil would have wished. He taught his unique piano method to many pupils, whom he treated with an almost paternal interest, often inviting them to continue instruction at his home, and finding them suitable professional openings.

Moscheles brought a crisp and incisive touch to his own piano playing, and he phrased with clarity and precision. He admired the pianistic innovations of Chopin and Liszt, but was not convinced of their aesthetic validity: though he commissioned Chopin's *Trois nouvelles études* for his piano method, he found the showy and effeminate side of Chopin's virtuosity distasteful. His own piano improvisations were marked by brilliance and variety; some of their atmosphere is probably captured in small pieces like the *Präludien* op.73 or the grander sets of variations on well-known melodies. Moscheles had a great respect for earlier music (he was active both as an editor and as an interpreter of Handel, Haydn, Mozart and Clementi, as well as Weber). The programme of his first 'historical soirée' (February 1837) included two Beethoven sonatas (op. 31 no.2 and op.81*a*), a Weber sonata, three preludes and fugues from the '48' and some Scarlatti and Handel pieces played on a 1771 harpsichord, some of his own newest studies, and vocal items by Purcell, Mozart and Mendelssohn. Hanslick assessed Moscheles as one of the last great representatives of the classical school and also the beginner of a new epoch.

The vast majority of Moscheles's compositional output is piano music, of which only the sonatas are of consequence; the many fantasias, rondos and variations are ephemeral music intended for salons or for the newly expanding amateur market. Schumann considered Moscheles one of the best sonata composers of his generation: certainly the one-movement *Sonate mélancolique* op.49 and the two duet sonatas are imaginatively written, the former with noble restraint. His later *Hommage à Händel* op.92 for two pianos is a tasteful parody, showing his interest in Baroque music. His piano method is best represented in his sets of studies, which are still used: Schumann saw these as bridging the gap between the age of Clementi and that of Chopin and being indebted to Bach's *Clavierübung*.

Many of Moscheles's sonatas were written in the Beethovenian environment of Vienna; with the development of his travelling career, he turned more to display pieces and piano concertos, the latter forming the bulk of his small orchestral output. Of these the best, no.3 op.60 in G minor, is still known today: it is masculine in spirit, taking its inspiration from Beethoven, and has delicate touches of orchestration (though Moscheles complained that he found writing for the orchestra difficult). Later in life he turned to song-writing, in addition to producing the better-known sets of studies (opp.70 and 95). His output also includes chamber works such as the Sextet op.35 and the Septet op.88, both of which include piano and are texturally akin to miniature piano concertos.

In all his more serious works Moscheles was capable of skilfully wrought musical structures, in which a classical balance of thematic ideas is tempered with an early Romantic dynamism. Pathos in general, or chromaticism in particular, are never overplayed, and his music is never sentimental. That this restraint and discernment was as characteristic of the man as of his music can be seen from his wife's biography of him, a fascinating if not always reliable account of his times, which records his dealings with and feelings about many great musicians of the early 19th century.

## WORKS

For complete list see C. Moscheles (1872); many works were published in Leipzig or Vienna, undated, within a few years of composition, but a few appeared first in Berlin or Paris.

### ORCHESTRAL
Sym. no.1, C, op.81, 1829
Ov. 'Jeanne d'Arc', after Schiller, op.91, 1835
Pf concs.: no.1, F, op.45, 1819; no.2, E♭, op.56, 1825; no.3, g, op.60, 1820; no.4, E, op.64, 1823; no.5, C, op.87, 1826; no.6 'Fantastique', B♭, op.90, 1833; no.7 'Pathétique', c, op.93, 1835–6; no.8 'Pastorale', D, op.96, 1838
8 other works with solo inst: La marche d'Alexandre, pf, op.32, 1815; Französisches Rondo, pf, vn, op.48, 1819; Fantaisie ... et variations sur Au clair de la lune, pf, op.50, 1821; Souvenirs d'Irlande, pf, op.69, 1826; Anklänge aus Schottland, pf, op.75, 1826; Fantaisie sur des airs des bardes écossais, pf, op.80, 1828; Souvenirs de Danemarc, pf, op.83, 1830; Duo concertant, variations on march from Weber's Preciosa, 2 pf, op.87b, 1833 [collab. Mendelssohn]

### PIANO
*(for 2 hands unless otherwise stated)*
Sonatas and sonatinas: Sonatine, G, op.4, before 1815; Sonate, D, op.22, before 1815; Sonate caractéristique, B♭, op.27, 1814; Grosse Sonate, E, op.41, 1816; Grande sonate, E♭, 4 hands, op.47, 1816; Sonate mélancolique, f♯, op.49, 1814; Grande sonate symphonique no.2, b, 4 hands, op.112, 1845
Pedagogical works: [24] Studien, op.70, 1825–6; 50 Präludien, op.73, 1827; [12] Charakteristische Studien, op.95, 1836; Méthode des méthodes [collab. Fétis], 2 studies pubd as op.98, 1840/*R*1973; [59] Tägliche Studien über die harmonisierten Skalen, 4 hands, op.107, 1842; 2 other sets of studies
Other works: Variations sur un thème de Händel, op.29, 1814; Allegri di bravura, op.51, 1821; Hommage à Händel, 2 pf, op.92, 1822–33; Hommage à Weber, 4 hands, op.102, 1842; c100 other works, incl. 9 for pf duet

### OTHER WORKS
Chamber: Sextet, E♭, vn, fl, 2 hn, vc, pf, op.35, 1815; Fl Sonata, A, op.44, 1819; Sonata, G, fl/vn, pf, op.79, 1828; Pf Trio, c, op.84,

1830; Septet, D, vn, va, cl/vn, hn/va, vc, db, pf, op.88, 1832; Vc Sonata, E, op.121, 1850; 13 other works
Songs: 3 erotische Lieder (E. Ludwig), op.16, ? before 1815; 6 Lieder (L. Uhland, others), op.97, ?c1840; Freie Kunst (Uhland), B/A, op.116, ?c1845; 6 Lieder (Rückert, E. Geibel, Uhland, L. Hölty, F. von Schlecta), op.117, ?c1845; 6 Gesänge, op.119, ?c1845; Frühlingslied, S/T, op.125, ?c1850; 6 Lieder, op.131, ? after 1850; 4 Duette, S, A, op.132, ? after 1850
Numerous edns. and arrs., incl. works by Beethoven (Choral Fantasia, Christus am Oelberg, Egmont Ov., Fidelio, syms., pf concs., pf trios, vn sonatas, vc sonatas, pf sonatas and variations), Clementi (pf sonatas), Handel (L'allegro, il pensieroso ed il moderato, kbd suites), Haydn (pf sonatas), Weber (pf works)

### BIBLIOGRAPHY
E. Hanslick: *Geschichte des Concertwesens in Wien* (Vienna, 1869–70/*R*1971)
C. Moscheles, ed.: *Aus Moscheles' Leben* (Leipzig, 1872; Eng. trans., 1873) [incl. list of works]
*Thematisches Verzeichniss im Druck erschienener Compositionen von Ignaz Moscheles* (Leipzig, 1885/*R*1966)
F. Moscheles, ed.: *Briefe von F. Mendelssohn-Bartholdy an Ignaz und Charlotte Moscheles* (Leipzig, 1888; Eng. trans., 1888/*R*1970)
F. Moscheles: *Fragments of an Autobiography* (London and New York, 1899)
M. Kreisig, ed.: *Robert Schumann: gesammelte Schriften* (Leipzig, 5/1914)
H. Engel: *Die Entwicklung des deutschen Klavierkonzertes von Mozart bis Liszt* (Leipzig, 1927/*R*1971)
P. Egert: *Die Klavier-Sonate im Zeitalter der Romantik* (Berlin, 1934)
I. Heussner: *Ignaz Moscheles in seinen Klavier-Sonaten, Kammermusikwerken, und -Konzerten* (diss., U. of Marburg, 1963)
W. S. Newman: *The Sonata since Beethoven* (Chapel Hill, 1969, rev. 2/1972)
J. Roche: 'Ignaz Moscheles: 1794–1870', *MT*, cxi (1970), 264
JEROME ROCHE

**Moscow** (Russ. Moskva). Capital city of the USSR and the RSFSR since 1918. It is the most important centre of Soviet musical culture. The city was founded in the 12th century and despite Tartar invasions expanded to become the national capital in the 16th century. In 1703 Peter the Great moved the capital to St Petersburg (now Leningrad), and Moscow declined; it was burnt after the Napoleonic invasion (1812), but prospered later in the 19th century. After the Revolution it again became the capital.

1. Before 1600. 2. 1600–1703. 3. 1703–1918. 4. Since 1918.

1. BEFORE 1600. The earliest written evidence of musical life in Moscow dates from the end of the 15th century, and relates to the activities of the two Moscow choirs of that period, the *gosudarevï pevchiye d'yaki* (ruler's singing clerks) and the *patriarshiye pevchiye diaki i podd'yaki* (patriarchal singing clerks and sub-clerks). The former was established by Ivan III after 1472 and took part in all solemn acts of worship and in various court ceremonies. The singers were considered to be in the service of the court, and enjoyed the privileges of courtiers; the choir was firmly established in a superior position to the patriarchal choir, both in performance and in the solution of all problems connected with singing. The patriarchal choir grew out of an earlier metropolitan choir and was of secondary importance. These Moscow choirs became the centre of professional musical culture: music education was concentrated there, chant books were copied out, and their performing style served as a model for other ensembles. Professional training and a thorough knowledge of chant (not only the melodies but also the nature of their performance) was required of the singers belonging to the two choirs. The repository of chant book manuscripts of the singing clerks was the first Russian music library. A census of the city carried out shortly after Ivan IV's Reign of Terror (1547–84) had ended marks

the first appearance of professional singers in Moscow: they had no connection with the church and did not take holy orders, and they constituted the tsar's choir in the service of the state. Such civilians made up the choirs of the patriarch and of several high church dignitaries who followed his example. Famous singers and *ustavshchiki* (precentors), such as Ivan Nos and Fyodor Khristianin, both of whom had many pupils, were already active at the court of Ivan IV in the 16th century.

2. 1600–1703. With the consolidation of Moscow's importance as the musical centre of Russia in the 17th century, the work of correcting the chant books, improving the ancient *kryukovaya* (hook) system of notation and unifying the forms of the ecclesiastical chant was carried out. Special commissions of experts on ecclesiastical chant (the so-called *didaskalï*) were set up; two of these (1665 and 1668) were engaged in establishing model versions of the chants, and were headed by Alexander Mezenets, music scholar and monk of the Savvino-Storozhevsky Monastery and later a proof corrector at the Moscow printing press. Ivan Shaydur, a Moscow clerk and music theorist, improved the hook notation. At about this time the new polyphonic style known as *partesnoye peniye* (part-singing), originally taken over from the Ukraine, became widespread in Moscow. Nikolay Diletsky, the most important theorist of part-singing, worked in Moscow from 1670 to 1680. The Moscow school of polyphonic singing (Vasily Titov and others) took shape during the 17th and 18th centuries.

The music of that time was not, however, confined to church music. The singing of folksongs and the playing of instruments were widespread in Moscow. The art of the *skomorokhi* (itinerant artists) was especially popular, despite the prohibitions of the church; they were musicians, singers and acrobats who gave improvised performances, often satirizing the clergy, in the squares and streets. The songs and dances of the *skomorokhi* were accompanied by the *gudok* (rebec), *gusli* (zither), *rozhok* (wooden trumpet), *sopel'* (oboe) and *volïnka* (bagpipe). The *skomorokhi* were known as the 'funny people' or the 'cheerful ones'. Secular elements also penetrated the work of the tsar's singers, helped by their independence from the church authorities and by the fact that the tsar's choir (with 170–80 members in the second half of the 17th century) seldom performed at its full strength: the rites of the Orthodox Church did not require so many singers. The singing clerks were sent in small groups to many different secular festivities, court celebrations, welcomes and dinners and as a sign of the tsar's special favour they were allowed to sing in private houses. They were also the first to perform secular cantatas, works composed for the victory of Russian armies at Azov and performed in the streets of Moscow at a specially erected triumphal arch, and the first Russian composers to write for voice and for different instruments, including the organ. The secular orientation of the tsar's choir is also revealed in such details as the clerks' dress: the patriarchal singing clerks were supposed to wear a garment similar to a deacon's cassock of dark cloth, whereas the clothes of the tsar's singers sparkled with bright colours and were made of various materials (crimson breeches, several layers of caftan lined with hare and squirrel fur and made of the English cloth so highly valued at that time – scarlet, cherry or green, trimmed with beaver or blue

fox fur, with silver or gilt buttons). Each clerk owned a horse with silver-mounted harness, and thus it is understandable that their appearance in the tsar's train in the streets of Moscow should so grip the imagination of foreign travellers.

With the development of the city's musical culture secular music became more widespread. The penetration of new forms of western European art furthered this diffusion: there are early records of an Italian organist visiting Moscow, and in 1586 Queen Elizabeth I of England had sent a small Positive organ and virginals to the Tsaritsa Irina Fyodorovna. As early as the first quarter of the 17th century there were violinists (former *skomorokhi*) in the service of the court. Instrumental music was heard increasingly frequently in the palaces of the educated boyars, several of whom (including A. S. Matveyev and V. V. Golitsïn) maintained domestic instrumental ensembles comprising viols, violins, woodwind and brass.

In early 17th-century Moscow there were many instrumentalists among whom the trumpeters enjoyed special respect, although contemporary archives shed no light on the term 'trumpeter', and it is impossible to determine exactly what instrument was played. A particularly large number of trumpeters appeared in 1660, suggesting an increasing public interest in music. Their performing skill was prized and they were sufficiently highly paid for almost every trumpeter to purchase his own courtyard. In 1660 special teachers, *mastera trubnovo ucheniya* (masters of trumpet teaching), like S. Burakov, appeared among the trumpeters. During this period the first state school for wind players, the S'ezhey Dvor Trubnovo Ucheniya (Assembly Court of Trumpet Teaching), was opened. The number of musicians constantly increased, as did the flow of foreign instrumentalists to Moscow. Sometimes they were specially invited by the tsar's court to explain developments in Western music, and also to accompany dramatic productions.

The picture of Moscow's musical life was changing. Gradually players of *rozhok*, *gusli* and other folk instruments disappeared and organ playing became widespread and was a favourite pastime at court and in the boyars' homes. An organ stood in the Granovitaya Palata (Faceted Palace), where solemn state ceremonies took place; as early as the mid-16th century the organ had been used widely, not only at court and in the houses of the aristocracy but also in folk music. In one of the resolutions of the Stoglavïy Sobor (Assembly of 100) indignation was expressed that not a single folk celebration, fair or wedding went by without organ music (in this case a portative organ was mentioned). It is characteristic that in Russia the organ was used exclusively for secular purposes. In the 1650s there was a workshop for keyboard instruments under the jurisdiction of the Moscow Grand Palace, producing organs and harpsichords. The greatest Moscow organist and organ builder of the time was S. Gutovsky, who worked in the Oruzheynaya Palata (Armoury Palace) from 1654 to 1665. In collaboration with his pupils he built a large number of organs for the Faceted Palace and the houses of eminent boyars. Gutovsky was also the founder of music printing in Russia, for which he constructed a press in 1677.

During the 17th century stage drama also began to develop in Moscow. Religious plays, especially the *Peshchnoye deystvo* ('Play of the furnace') enacted in churches shortly before Christmas, were an important element of the church's culture. Despite their conventional content these plays were genuine theatrical presentations with costumes, elaborate scenery and even some mechanical contrivances; the production of the *Play of the Furnace* required extensive preliminary preparation, and each year this task was assigned to a new producer chosen from among the most experienced singing clerks. In 1672 the first court theatre was built; music – the chorus, instrumental ensemble and, in particular, the organ – played an important part in its performances. The organ was used to accompany all productions, and incidental music was played on it during the intervals. Precise details of the organ repertory of this period are not known, but there is evidence to suggest that it included works by Sweelinck, Scheidt and several Polish composers.

A public theatre existed in Moscow from 1702 to 1706; the building erected specially for it in Red Square was named the Komediynaya Khoromina (Palace of Comedy). In 1731 a group of Italian singers and musicians in the service of the Polish king went on tour to Moscow and mounted Ristori's *Calandro*, the first opera staged in Russia. In 1742 Hasse's *La clemenza di Tito* was sumptuously produced for the coronation of the Empress Elisabeth, in a specially built theatre seating 1000. In 1759 Locatelli's opera company first introduced comic opera to the Moscow public. Moscow's educational institutions played a significant part in the development of drama at this time: the study of music was compulsory, and student productions of the so-called 'school dramas' were put on twice a year by the pupils of the Moscow Slavonic–Greek–Latin Academy. They also played instruments and accompanied the singing of *kantï* at public debates and examinations.

The development of Russian military music in the mid-17th century played an important part in the general growth of musical culture in Moscow. The training of Russian wind players began at that time; regular orchestras consisting of nine 'oboists' (the general term for military musicians) and 16 company drummers were introduced into infantry regiments (apart from the guards) at the beginning of the 18th century as part of Peter the Great's plan to establish a regular national army. Garrison schools were set up in which the children of serving soldiers could learn to sing and play instruments. Military musicians took part in official state ceremonies and in the specially festive folk processions usually arranged after military victories. Also linked with these state celebrations was the development of a distinctive musical–poetic genre, the 'panegyric' or *privetstvenniy kant* (welcome song), one of the typical features of Russian artistic culture of the first quarter of the 18th century.

3. 1703–1918. With the reforms of Peter the Great secular music came to have a much more prominent place in Russian life. The founding of St Petersburg, to which the court moved, also had an effect on the musical culture of Moscow, which changed radically during the 18th century. At the beginning of the century Russian music was represented by its rich heritage of folksong, by ecclesiastical chants and by the simplest domestic genres; by the end of the century Russian opera was taking shape, symphonic and chamber music were being written by Russian composers, and early examples of the Russian song were beginning to appear. The musical needs of Russian society were growing, its tastes were changing and the circle of educated music lovers was expanding. In spite of the fact that St Petersburg drew great artistic forces to the court, Moscow formed its own professional musical circles. Of particular importance were the serf musicians, who performed as soloists and in the many large serf orchestras.

New educational institutions began to play a significant part in Moscow's musical life in the second half of the 18th century: the university, the Blagorodniy Pansion (Boarding School for the Nobility) attached to it, and the Vospitatel'niy Dom (Foundling Hospital), where the teaching of music was established on a serious basis and where stage works, including operas, were produced. The university theatre, which later merged with Locatelli's Italian opera company, was founded under the auspices of the university in 1757. The official opening of the new theatre in the Operniy Dom (Opera House) was in 1759. A new musical genre, Russian comic opera, evolved in the 1770s in Moscow; and in 1779 *Mel'nik-koldun, obmanshchik i svat* ('The miller-magician, cheat and matchmaker'), with a libretto by Ablesimov and music by Sokolovsky, was produced in the theatre on the Znamenka. Shortly before this Johann Kerzelli, a member of a family of Czech musicians who made a great contribution to Moscow's musical life in the last quarter of the 18th century and the beginning of the 19th, wrote a comic opera *Derevenskiy vorozhey* ('The village sorceress'). Members of the Kerzelli family were active in various spheres, as composers, conductors, teachers and organizers of concerts and schools of music. Johann Kerzelli opened a music college with a special department for 'the highborn nobility, the bourgeoisie and serfs' in 1772, and in 1783 M. F. Kerzelli opened a music school intended primarily for the training of serf musicians. I. F. Kerzelli was a composer and conductor who worked as musical director of the Petrovsky Theatre (built in 1780) from 1801; in 1802 Mozart's Requiem was given its first performance in Russia under his direction. His activities laid the foundations for the intensive development of concert life in the first half of the 19th century. The conductors and composers Mathias Stabinger and A. and F. Sartori were also concert organizers.

The imperial theatre was established in Moscow in 1806; this initially brought together a drama and an opera company that numbered among its members many gifted actors, singers, dancers and musicians from the best serf theatres in Moscow, those of the Sheremet'yevs, the Yusupovs, the Stolïpins and the Apraksins. Plays, operas and ballets were staged at the theatre in its early days, but later a separation took place: from 1824 the drama company began to perform in the newly opened Malïy Theatre, and in 1825 the Bol'shoy Theatre, where operas and ballets were given, opened on the site of the Petrovsky Theatre. The Bol'shoy burnt down in 1853 and was rebuilt in 1856. Verstovsky, composer of the popular opera *Askol'dova mogila* ('Askol'd's tomb', 1834), held various posts in the Moscow directorate of the imperial theatres between 1825 and 1860, and contributed much to raising the standards of Moscow opera. Concert life, too, was developing. The performance in 1811 of Degtyaryov's patriotic oratorio *Minin i Pozharsky ili Osvobozhdeniye Moskvï* ('Minin and Pozharsky, or The liberation of Moscow') was a great event.

*1. The Bol'shoy Theatre: early 19th-century engraving*

Public concerts were given daily, or even twice daily, principally during Lent, when the state theatres were closed; they were given by foreign virtuosos, Moscow musicians, soloists from the Russian and Italian opera companies, and also for charity by aristocratic amateurs. From the 1820s concerts were arranged by the theatre directorate (including works by Beethoven performed under the direction of Friedrich Scholz and N. E. Kubishta); and concerts were also given in the Blagorodnoye Sobraniye (Assembly of the Nobility; now the Dom Soyuzov, House of Unions) and the Nemetskoye Sobraniye (German Assembly). Important Russian performers began to appear at this time: the pianist and composer Daniil Kashin, the pianist Alexoy Zhilin, and other musicians who had settled in Moscow, like Johann Hässler, John Field, Josef Genishta, Kubishta, Villuan (teacher of Anton Rubinstein) and Dubuque. At the same time there were performances by visiting celebrities such as Lipiński, Vieuxtemps and Berlioz. A key figure of the 1840s and 1850s was the conductor Ivan Johannes, musical director of the Bol'shoy Theatre from 1841, who conducted the first Moscow production of Glinka's *A Life for the Tsar* in 1842; he also directed Sunday concerts at the theatre and conducted the student orchestra of Moscow University from 1850. He gave the first Moscow performances of *Jota aragonesa* and *Kamarinskaya*, and he championed the symphonic works of Mozart and Beethoven. Other popular performers of the period included the singers Elizaveta Sandunova and Alexander Bantïshev, the violinists Gavrila Rachinsky and Nikolay Afanas'yev, and the guitarists Semyon Aksyonov and Mikhail Vïsotsky, the last two being outstanding representatives of the Moscow guitar school founded by Andrey Sikhra. The guitar was widely used as a concert instrument; the gypsy choruses and their singers

(women soloists with guitar accompaniment) who appeared at the beginning of the 19th century gave added colour to Moscow's musical life and became exceptionally popular. The gypsy choirs directed by Il'ya Sokolov and I. V. Vasil'yev enjoyed particular fame between 1820 and 1860, and the singing of Sokolov's gypsy chorus was much admired by Liszt, who went on tour to Moscow in 1842; their repertory consisted of Russian folksongs and songs on subjects drawn from everyday life. Under the influence of the distinctive style of the gypsies the popular genre known as the gypsy song appeared in Russian vocal music, strongly influencing the songs of the Moscow composers Alexander Gurilyov and Alexander Varlamov.

Until the mid-19th century Moscow's musical life was to a great extent centred on a great number of domestic milieux. In the 1820s the artistic tone was set by the circles of Wielhorski and Volkonskaya, and later by those of Botkin, Bakunin and Stankevich. The social upsurge of the 1850s and 1860s, which had an effect on the democratic trend of Russian culture with its enlightening tendencies, laid the basis for a new fruitful stage in the growth of musical Moscow. A number of artistic societies arose, the most important being the Artistichesky Kruzhok (Artistic Circle); this existed from 1865 to 1883, and included among its members Ostrovsky, Nikolay Rubinstein and the actor P. M. Sadovsky. It also played a large part in arousing interest in Russian folksong; it arranged performances of new literary and musical works and organized lectures and stage productions, thus raising the standards of Moscow's social and artistic life. The founding in 1859, on the initiative of Nikolay Rubinstein, of the Moscow branch of the Russkoye Muzïkal'noye Obshchestvo (Russian Musical Society) brought a radical change in the style of concert life and in the organization of musical education.

It is above all with the name of Rubinstein that the most productive stage in the growth of social musical life in Moscow is linked: he was the first director (from 1860) of the symphony concerts of the Moscow branch of the Russian Musical Society and the first director of the Moscow Conservatory. The symphony concerts of the Russian Musical Society took place in the halls of the Assembly of the Nobility and in the Manezh (where public concerts were given). The repertory consisted basically of important symphonic and choral works. After Rubinstein's death Max Ermandsdörfer (1882–4) and Vasily Safonov (1889–1905) conducted the Russian Musical Society's concerts. Concerts were also given by the Moscow Philharmonic Society (founded 1883; directed by Pyotr Shostakovsky until 1895), the Russian Choral Society (from 1878) and the Moscow Synodal Choir.

In 1860 the Russian Musical Society formed its music classes, on the basis of which the Moscow Conservatory was opened in 1866, with such eminent musicians as Tchaikovsky, Rubinstein, Laub, Kashkin and Larosh on its teaching staff. Tchaikovsky's career at the conservatory was of outstanding significance; his music instigated a compositional trend that can conditionally be called the 'Moscow School' (Taneyev, Arensky, Rakhmaninov and others). The educational society Kruzhok Russkoy Muzïki (Russian Music Circle, 1896–1912) played a large part in championing Russian music, as did Savva Mamontov's Moskovskaya Chastnaya Russkaya Opera (Moscow Private Russian Opera). Mamontov brought together in this theatre the leading figures in Russian art, including singers (Vladimir Lossky, Pyotr Olenin, Anton Sekar-Rozhansky, Shalyapin, Nadezhda Zabela-Vrubel', Vera Petrova-Zvantseva, Nadezhda Salina and Elena Tsvetkova), composers (Vasilenko, Ippolitov-Ivanov, Kalinnikov, Rakhmaninov and Rimsky-Korsakov) and artists. Besides Russian works the company performed Western classics, always adhering to its principles of realism in art. Under various names the theatre was in existence from 1885 to 1904; its artistic traditions were kept alive by Sergey Zimin, whose private opera company was founded in 1904 and continued to perform until 1924. From 1907 until 1913 the singer Mariya Deysha-Sionitzkaya organized concerts of new Russian and Western music; and from 1909 the critic Derzhanovsky and the conductor Saradzhev arranged a series of concerts called Evenings of Contemporary Music.

During the early 1900s there was also considerable expansion in the Bol'shoy Theatre's activities; its opera repertory was augmented by several artistically outstanding productions; and many operas by Rimsky-Korsakov, Arensky, Koreshchenko and Rakhmaninov had their premières there. At the same time Alexander Gorsky joined the ballet company as ballet master and developed the traditions of Russian ballet, drawing it closer to dramatic art; the dancer V. D. Tikhomirov also played an important role as ballet master, training a whole generation of dancers. Among the conductors at the Bol'shoy were Rakhmaninov (1904–6) and Václav Suk (from 1906), and its singers included Shalyapin, Sabinov and Nezhdanova. The greatest foreign conductors, pianists, violinists and cellists appeared regularly on the Moscow concert platform during these years (Nikisch, Mengelberg, Hofmann, Busoni, Godowsky,

Kreisler, Ysaÿe, Jan Kubelík, Casals) as well as many famous singers.

Influenced by the ever-increasing demand for musical education, private schools with high teaching standards opened, notably the music schools of the Gnesins and of V. Y. Zograf-Plaksina, and the music courses of E. N. Vizler and others. Music-teaching establishments also existed under the auspices of a music educational institution, the Betkhovenskaya Studiya (Beethoven Studio, founded in 1911 by the pianist David Shor), which arranged historical concerts, lecture-recitals and musical evenings. Such a thriving musical life created ideal conditions for music publishing. Small firms gave way to the large music-publishing houses of Gutheil (1859), Jurgenson (1861) and the Russkoye Muzïkal'noye Izdatel'stvo (known in the West as Editions Russes de Musique, founded by Koussevitzky in 1909, which purchased the Gutheil firm in 1914).

With the revolutionary events of 1905 Moscow saw the publication of new journals dealing with social problems: *Muzïkal'nïy truzhennik* ('Musical labourer', 1906–10), *Muzïka i zhizn'* ('Music and life', 1908–12) and *Orkestr* (1910–12); the influential journal *Muzïka* (1910–16) championed contemporary music. At the same time important new concert organizations were established: the Moskovskaya Simfonicheskaya Kapella (Moscow Symphonic Chapel, 1901–17) of Vyacheslav Bulïchev, the Istoricheskiye Kontsertï (Historic Concerts, 1907–17) of Sergey Vasilenko and the Kontsertï Kusevitskovo (Concerts of Koussevitzky, 1908). There was also an increase in music education: by arranging lecture-recitals leading figures in the art world made music more accessible to the general public. In 1906 the first Narodnaya Konservatoriya (People's Conservatory) in Russia was opened in Moscow; it was part of the established Obshchestvo Narodnïkh Universitetov (Society of People's Universities).

During these years the collecting of and research into folksongs flourished. Of particular importance were the activities of the Muzïkal'no–Etnograficheskaya Komissiya (Music–Ethnography Commission), formed in 1901 and attached to the ethnography department of the Obshchestvo Lyubiteley Estestvoznaniya, Antropologii i Etnografii (Society of Lovers of Natural Science, Anthropology and Ethnography) under the auspices of Moscow University. The ethnography department had been engaged in research into folk music since the time of the staging of the ethnographical exhibition in Moscow in 1867, and it published the journal *Etnograficheskoye obozreniye* ('Ethnographical review') from 1889. Several important Moscow musicians, composers and folklorists (Taneyev, Yuly Mel'gunov, Dmitry Arakchiyev, Evgeniya Linyova and others) took part in the work of the Music–Ethnography Commission, which conducted folklore expeditions, arranged scientific lectures, published writings and organized ethnographical concerts. The concerts known as Krest'yanskiye Kontsertï (peasant concerts) of the famous folklore collector and performer Mitrofan Pyatnitsky were of great significance and featured the well-known folksinger Irina Kolobayeva ('Arinushka'). The Russian folk choir organized by Pyatnitsky was the basis for the Russkiy Narodnïy Khor (Russian Folk Choir), which now bears his name. At that time, too, the Prechistenskiye Besplatnïye Kursï dlya Vroslïkh Rabochikh i Rabotnits (Prechistensky free courses for adult men and women workers) were being given; such outstanding artists as Igumnov and Sobinov took part in the concerts relating to the courses. The widening of musical audiences was typical of Moscow's social life in the period immediately preceding the October Revolution.

4. SINCE 1918. The changes wrought by the Revolution laid the foundations for the new Soviet era in the musical life of Moscow. A new mass concert audience emerged. In her reminiscences of old Moscow, the writer Marietta Shaginian told of the narrowness of the musical circles in pre-Revolutionary Moscow: 'all knew one another, knew one another's tastes and circumstances, and knew what one another's opinions would be, and somehow nobody in this circle came up with any new or surprising thoughts' (*Noviy mir*, 1943, no.4, p.110). Lenin's signing of the Decree of the Soviet of People's Commissars of 12 June 1918 about the nationalization of the Petrograd and Moscow Conservatories laid the foundation for 'state musical construction'. It chiefly affected the performance of music; concerts, lectures and stage productions drew vast audiences, and the musicians of Moscow took part passionately in the promotion of musical culture. 'We must perform the Russian classics, now that we can better acquaint the workers with the Russian classics', Lenin said to N. B. Podgoretskaya, an artist at the Bol'shoy Theatre (*SovM*, 1947, no.6, p.49). During those years chamber music, both instrumental and vocal, was of particular importance in the promotion of classical music largely because of the mobility of chamber ensembles and their ability to perform away from the concert platform. String quartets were established in Moscow: in 1918 Lev Tseytlin organized a quartet named after Lenin, and in 1919 David Kreyn led a quartet, later the Stradivarius Quartet; others were a quartet founded at the Moscow Conservatory in 1923 (from 1931 known as the Beethoven Quartet), the Moscow Conservatory Students' Quartet (1925, the Komitas Quartet from 1932), the Glier Quartet (1927) and the Bol'shoy Theatre Quartet (1931). They performed not only in established concert halls but also in factories, mills and industrial works, acquainting the Moscow public with the repertory and stimulating an interest in chamber music.

New institutions developed simultaneously to supervise the city's musical life: the Muzïkal'nïy Otdel Narodnovo Komissariata Prosveshcheniya (MUZO Narkompros; Music Department of the Commissariat for Public Education) with its concert section, the Khudozhestvenno-prosvetitel'nïy Otdel Voyennovo Komissariata (Art Education Department of the Military Commissariat), the Muzïkal'nïy Otdel Proletkul'ta (Music Department of Proletkul't), which played a significant role in mass music educational work during this period (among its leading figures were Alexander Kastal'sky, B. B. Krasin and Nadezhda Bryusova). In 1918 the Khudozhestvenno-prosvetitel'nïy Otdel Moskovskovo Soveta Rabochikh i Krest'yanskikh Deputatov (Art Education Department of the Moscow Council of Worker and Peasant Deputies) established a theatre and music section, which, on the whole, was engaged in arranging concerts for worker audiences in different areas of Moscow, and in directing local arts institutions; it sanctioned the opening and closing of Moscow arts establishments, saw to the registering of concerts and to the booking of

concert venues, and subsidized music theatres (with the exception of the Bol'shoy Theatre). Many Moscow musicians organized music studios in factories and mills. One of the first stages of acquainting the workers with art was the organization of music circles in factory clubs. In the early years of the Revolution a new type of musical propaganda campaign and educational work, the so-called 'concert meetings', became widespread; these took place in theatres and concert halls and generally drew large audiences. Lenin, Kalinin, Lunacharsky or Sverdlov delivered speeches on topical political questions, followed by the concert section and a lecture: papers alternated with musical programmes by the finest artists in Moscow. In the 1920s concerts for workers, given in the Grand Hall of the Moscow Conservatory by the Korporatsiya Artistov-solistov Bol'shovo Teatra (Corporation of Solo Artists of the Bol'shoy Theatre) under its music director Nikolay Golovanov, enjoyed enormous popularity, as did the chamber concerts given by the Stradivarius Quartet in the so-called 'Betkhovenskiy Zal' (Beethoven Hall, formerly the tsar's foyer of the Bol'shoy Theatre).

Recalling the elated artistic atmosphere of those years, Szigeti (one of the first foreign musicians to appear in Moscow in the 1920s) wrote in his memoirs: 'I cannot forget the sight of those innumerable crowds, moving about, becoming excited, talking and applauding in the intervals between the numbers' (*SovM*, 1958, no.12, p.80). New experimental groups were organized, the work of the old music theatres (faced with the problem of large-scale cultural promotion and education) was revised, and the work of music educational institutions was reorganized. On the initiative of Stanislavsky, the Opernaya Studiya Bol'shovo Teatra (Bol'shoy Theatre Opera Studio) was opened in 1918; in 1926 it was reorganized as the Opernïy Teatr-Studiya Stanislavskovo (Stanislavsky Opera Theatre Studio), and on the basis of this the Opernïy Teatr imeni Stanislavskovo (Stanislavsky Opera Theatre) was founded in 1928. In 1919 Vladimir Nemirovich-Danchenko founded his Muzïkal'naya Studiya Moskovskovo Khudozhestvennovo Teatra (Moscow Arts Theatre Music Studio), reorganized in 1926 as the Muzïkal'nïy Teatr imeni Nemirovicha-Danchenko (Nemirovich-Danchenko Music Theatre). In their work both theatres put forward the innovatory ideas of their musical directors, exerting great influence on Moscow's dramatic culture. In 1941 the theatres were combined in the Muzïkal'nïy Teatr imeni K. S. Stanislavskovo i V. I. Nemirovicha-Danchenko (Stanislavsky–Nemirovich-Danchenko Music Theatre), the most important music theatre after the Bol'shoy.

One of the leading figures in Moscow's concert life was the conductor Alexander Khessin, director and principal conductor of the concert department of MUZO Narkompros from 1920. The first state concert organizations were established in Moscow: the Gosudarstvennaya Filarmoniya (State Philharmonic, from 1920), the Rossiyskaya Filarmoniya (Rosfil; Russian Philharmonic, 1925–8), Sovetskaya Filarmoniya (Sovfil; Soviet Philharmonic, 1928–31) and the Moskovskaya Filarmoniya (Moscow Philharmonic, from 1931). They were granted the right to invite foreign artists, and despite the difficult external conditions musical life flourished; Shalyapin, Nezhdanova, Igumnov, Gol'denveyzer and many other Russian musicians took part in concerts. Mozart's

Requiem, Beethoven's *Missa solemnis* and masterpieces of Russian classical music were heard, and foreign musicians began to make tours to Moscow: the conductor Oscar Fried first appeared in 1921, and was followed by Ansermet, Walter, Abendroth and Klemperer, the violinists Szigeti and Huberman, the pianists Petri and Zecchi and many others.

In Moscow during the 1920s new ideas about orchestral playing and about different forms of group performance were formed. In this respect the most important events were the organization in 1922, on the initiative of Tseytlin, of the Pervïy Simfonicheskiy Ansambl' bez Dirizhora (Persimfans; First Conductorless Symphony Ensemble), and in 1928 of the Ansambl' Krasnoarmeyskoy Pesni (Red Army Song Ensemble). Persimfans was a first-class symphony orchestra, based on the full artistic and material equality of its members; its membership comprised the finest artists of the Bol'shoy Theatre orchestra, and professors and talented students of the orchestral faculty at the Moscow Conservatory. The conductorless orchestra aimed to revise the methods of symphonic performance, relying on the creative initiative of each of its members, and applying to a symphonic group the rehearsal methods used in chamber music. Persimfans was striking for its group concentration, its virtuoso playing and brightness of sound, its expressiveness and its artistic interpretation. The early flourishing of concert life in new post-Revolutionary Moscow is closely connected with Persimfans, which exerted great influence on the formation of the leading Moscow schools of instrumental performance, and helped to raise the standards of orchestral playing in the USSR. Following the example of Persimfans, conductorless órchestras were organized in Leningrad, Kiev, Voronezh and other towns, and also in several towns in other countries (Leipzig, New York). The importance of Persimfans's ten years of activity (1922–32) was enormous, and its weekly subscription concerts (given in the Grand Hall of the Moscow Conservatory) had sensational success; concerts were also given in factories and mills. The programmes included works from Bach and Beethoven to Wagner, Richard Strauss, Prokofiev, Stravinsky and Hindemith.

The Red Army Song Ensemble, founded by Alexander Alexandrov, originally comprised 12 members, and developed into a first-class performing group – the Krasnoznamennïy Ansambl' Pesni i Plyaski Sovetskoy Armii imeni A. V. Alexandrova (Alexandrov Order of the Red Banner Soviet Army Song and Dance Ensemble) – combining a men's choir, a dance group and a mixed orchestra. During the 1920s and 1930s creative associations involving various groups of composers and musicians were founded in Moscow: the Assotsiatsiya Sovremennoy Muzïki (Association for Contemporary Music), Rossiyskaya Assotsiatsiya Proletarskikh Muzïkantov (Russian Association of Proletarian Musicians), Ob'yedineniye Revolyutsionnïkh Kompozitorov i Muzïkal'nïkh Deyateley (Association of Revolutionary Composers and Musicians) and Proizvodstvennïy Kollektiv Studentov-kompozitorov Moskovskoy Konservatorii (Production Group of Student Composers of the Moscow Conservatory). Music journals were published, including *K novïm beregam* ('Towards new shores', 1923), *Muzïkal'naya nov'* ('New ground in music', 1923–4), *Sovremennaya muzïka* ('Contemporary music', 1924–9), *Muzïkal'noye obrazovaniye* ('Musical education', 1925–30) and *Muzïka i*

*revolyutsiya* ('Music and revolution', 1926–9). Research centres were created, such as the Gosudarstvennïy Institut Muzïkal'noy Nauki (State Institute for Music Research, 1921) and the music section of the Gosudarstvennaya Akademiya Khudozhestvennïkh Nauk (State Academy of Artistic Sciences). Nikolay Garbuzov, Mikhail Ivanov-Boretsky and Konstantin Kuznetsov played a great role in the organization of research work. In 1927 Lev Oborin, a pupil at the Moscow Conservatory, became the first Soviet prizewinner at an international music competition (the Chopin Piano Competition in Warsaw). A number of new performing groups were organized: the Bol'shoy Simfonicheskiy Orkestr Vsesoyuznovo Radio (Grand Symphony Orchestra of All-Union Radio, 1931), the Gosudarstvennïy Simfonicheskiy Orkestr Soyuza SSR (USSR State SO, 1936) and the Gosudarstvennïy Russkiy Narodnïy Orkestr (State Russian Folk Orchestra), reorganized from the Radio Folk Instrument Orchestra and named after Nikolay Osipov in 1946; the Russkiy Narodnïy Khor imeni M. E. Pyatnitskovo (Pyatnitsky Russian Folk Choir) became a professional group of the Moscow Philharmonic.

During the 1930s the importance of Moscow as a centre of the development of multi-national art in the USSR increased. The Vsesoyuznaya Olimpiada Teatrov i Iskusstv (All-Union Olympiad of Theatres and the Arts), offering a wide survey of the music of the Soviet peoples, took place in 1930, when the Armenian opera *Almast* by A. S. Spendiarov was given its première. The Dekadï Natsional'novo Iskusstva (Festivals of National Art) were systematically staged in Moscow from 1936 to 1960. A large number of artists, composers, folk musicians, artists from opera and drama theatres, choirs and instrumental and choreographic groups took part, and to coincide with each festival an exhibition of the painting and sculpture of the particular republic was mounted. All the festivals ended with a grand concert of national works, classical music and dancing. The Festivals of National Art, of which 30 took place in Moscow, contributed to the exchange of artistic experience, and helped to introduce the finest works of national art into the stage and concert repertories.

The Ansambl' Sovetskoy Operï Vserossiyskovo Teatral'novo Obshchestva (Soviet Opera Ensemble of the All-Union Theatrical Society), organized in Moscow in 1934, played a great role in the promotion of opera in concert performance. It acted as a sort of laboratory for Soviet opera, midway between the composer and the opera theatre, and approved new works, many of which were then staged in opera theatres in different towns of the USSR. Over 75 operas were performed by the ensemble, many of them for the first time in the USSR, including Shaporin's *The Decembrists* (1937), Prokofiev's *War and Peace* (1944) and *Semyon Kotko* (1957), Molchanov's *Dawn* (1954) and Shebalin's *The Taming of the Shrew* (1958). The most important centre of musical drama in Moscow was the Bol'shoy Theatre, the principal conductors of which were Suk (1906–33), Samosud (1936–43), Pazovsky (1943–8), Golovanov (1948–53) and Melik-Pashayev (1953–62); Fayer was ballet conductor (1923–62). Among the company's singers were Nezhdanova, Derzhinskaya, Obukhova, Stepanova, Barsova, Sobinov, Migay, Grigory and Alexander Pirogov, Reyzen and Kozlovsky.

Composition was invigorated and musical performance stimulated by the founding in Moscow of the

Soyuz Kompozitorov (Composers' Union) in 1932 and of the Orgkomitet Soyuza Kompozitorov SSSR (Organizing Committee of the USSR Composers' Union) in 1939, and also by the establishment of the Composers' Union theory and research journal *Sovetskaya muzïka* in 1933, and by the systematic staging of the Vsesoyuznïye Konkursï Muzïkantov-ispolniteley (All-Union Performers' Competitions), the first of which was held in 1933. Many distinguished Soviet composers, conductors and performers worked in Moscow and were pupils at the Moscow Conservatory, which at this time developed into a vast teaching complex, including the conservatory itself, the Tsentral'naya Muzïkal'naya Shkola-desyatiletka (Central Secondary Music School), a music school and children's primary school and an Opernaya Studiya (Opera Studio), opened in 1933; it also had 'national' departments (Kazakh, Kirgiz, Bashkir etc), preparing music specialists for the union and autonomous republics.

The events of World War II determined a new direction and content for Moscow's musical life. Although many musical groups and institutions were evacuated the intensity of their work was not diminished. Moscow musicians formed numerous front-line brigades and ensembles, and carried out a large amount of work in the artistic service of military units. Moscow composers wrote a great number of patriotic songs; of these, Alexander Alexandrov's *Svyashchennaya voyna* ('The holy war'), which the troops sang on their way to the front, became the musical emblem of World War II. The Gosudarstvennïy Russkiy Khor Soyuza SSR (USSR State Russian Choir) was organized in Moscow in 1942, the Institut Istorii Iskusstv Akademii Nauk SSSR (Institute for the History of the Arts of the USSR Academy of Sciences) in 1943 (among its founders was the academician Boris Asaf'yev), and the Muzïkal'no-pedagogicheskiy Institut imeni Gnesinïkh (Gnesin Music Teachers' Training College) in 1944.

After the war the intensity of Moscow's musical life continued to increase steadily. New performing groups were organized: the Kvartet Moskovskoy Filarmonii (Moscow Philharmonic Quartet, 1946, renamed the Borodin Quartet in 1955); the Moskovskiy Kamernïy Orkestr (Moscow Chamber Orchestra, 1956), directed by Rudolf Barshay; the Ansambl' Skripachey Bol'shovo Teatra (Bol'shoy Theatre Violin Ensemble, 1956), directed by Yu. M. Reyentovich; the Kvartet Aspirantov Moskovskoy Konservatorii (Quartet of Postgraduates of the Moscow Conservatory, 1957, renamed the Prokofiev Quartet in 1962); the Kvartet imeni Glinki (Glinka Quartet, 1968, formerly the USSR Composers' Union Quartet); and the Kamernïy Orkestr Studentov Moskovskoy Konservatorii (Moscow Conservatory Students' Chamber Orchestra, 1961), which was directed by Mikhail Terian and awarded the first prize at the Karajan International Competition for Young Orchestras in West Berlin in 1972. An important event for music-theatre in Moscow was the founding of the Detskiy Muzïkal'nïy Teatr (Children's Music Theatre, 1965), and the Kamernïy Opernïy Teatr (Chamber Opera Theatre, 1970), directed by Boris Pokrovsky. The 1-y Vsesoyuznïy S'yezd Sovetskikh Kompozitorov (First All-Union Congress of Soviet Composers), held in Moscow in 1948, endorsed the regulations and chose the board of the USSR Composers' Union, and played an enormous role in the improvement of the training of young composers. Among the many talented composers and musicologists active in the city Shostakovich, who lived and worked in Moscow from 1943, played a considerable part in the education and development of composers; Sviridov also lived and worked in Moscow from 1955. From 1945 performers' competitions were resumed: in 1958 the Mezhdunarodnïy Konkurs imeni P. I. Chaykovskovo (International Tchaikovsky Competition), which takes

*2. The opening ceremony of the first International Tchaikovsky Competition (1958) in the Grand Hall of the Moscow Conservatory*

place every four years, was inaugurated, as were the annual music festivals Moskovskiye Zvyozdï (Moscow Stars) and Russkaya Zima (Russian Winter). After the war many foreign opera companies appeared in Moscow, including those of La Scala, Covent Garden, the Berlin Komische Oper, the Vienna Staatsoper and the Royal Swedish Opera, as have the symphony orchestras of Prague, Bucharest, New York, Boston, Philadelphia, Cleveland and Paris, in addition to many solo artists. International music congresses, seminars, conferences and creative meetings of composers, musicologists and musicians have taken place in the city.

BIBLIOGRAPHY

*Bol'shoy Moskovskiy teatr i obozreniye sobïtiy predshestvovavshikh osnovaniyu pravil'novo russkovo teatra* [The Moscow Bol'shoy Theatre and a survey of the events leading to the founding of a true Russian theatre] (Moscow, 1857)

S. Kniglikov: *Obzor deyatel'nosti muzïkal'no-dramaticheskovo uchilishaba Moskovskovo filarmonicheskovo obshchestva za vremya s 1878 do 1888 god* [An account of the activity of the music drama school of the Moscow Philharmonic Society, 1878–88] (Moscow, 1888)

N. D. Kashkin: *Pervoye 25-letiyu Moskovskoy konservatorii: istoricheskiy ocherk* [The first 25 years of the Moscow Conservatory: a historical study] (Moscow, 1891)

N. Dmitriyev [pseud. of N. D. Kashkin]: *Opernaya stsena Moskovskovo imperatorskovo teatra* [The opera stage of the Moscow Imperial Theatre] (Moscow, 1897)

N. Manïkin-Nevstruyev, ed.: *Imperatorskoye Russkoye muzïkal'noye obshchestvo, Moskovskoye otdeleniye: simfonicheskiye sobraniya 1–500* [The Imperial Russian Musical Society, Moscow Section: symphonic meetings 1–500] (Moscow, 1899) [statistical index]

——: *Kratkiy istoricheskiy ocherk imperatorskovo Russkovo muzïkal'novo obshchestva 1860–1900* [A short historical study of the Imperial Russian Musical Society 1860–1900] (Moscow, 1900)

I. Lipayev: *Moskovskoye filarmonicheskoye obshchestvo: istoricheskaya spravka* [The Moscow Philharmonic Society: historical information], *RMG* (1903), no.44, col.47

*Kruzhok lyubiteley russkoy muzïki, x: 1896–1906: sbornik programm* [The Russian Music Lovers' Circle: 1896–1906: a collection of programmes] (Moscow, 1906)

Yu. Engel': 'Narodnaya konservatoriya' [The national conservatory], *Muzïkal'nïy truzhennik* (1908), no.20, p.10

N. Kashkin: *Moskovskoye otdeleniye Russkovo muzïkal'novo obshchestva: ocherk deyatel'nosti za pyatidesyatiletiye 1860–1910* [The Moscow section of the Russian Musical Society: a study of its 50 years' activity, 1860–1910] (Moscow, 1910)

*Russkoye khorovoye obshchestvo v Moskve* [The Russian Choral Society in Moscow], xxv (Moscow, 1910)

V. Metallov: *Sinodal'noye uchilishche tserkovnovo peniya v evo proshlom i nastoyashchem* [The Synodal School of Church Singing, past and present] (Moscow, 1911)

P. A. Rossiyev: 'Artisticheskiy kruzhok v Moskve' [The artistic circle in Moscow], *Istoricheskiy vestnik* (1912), no.6, pp.878–920; no.7, p.111–41

*Otchot obshchestva 'Muzïkal'no-teoreticheskaya biblioteka v Moskve' za pervïye chetïre goda eyo deyatel'nosti 1909–1912* [An account of the music theory library in Moscow society in its first four years, 1909–1912] (Moscow, 1913)

V. Yakovlev: 'Moskovskaya opernaya stsena v sorokovïkh godakh' [The Moscow opera stage in the 1940s], *Vremennik russkovo teatral'novo obshchestva* (Moscow, 1924), 91–141

M. V. Ivanov-Boretsky: *Pyat' let nauchnoy rabotï Gosudarstvennovo instituta muzïkal'noy nauki (GIMNa) 1921–1926* [Five years of research work at the State Institute for Music Research] (Moscow, 1926)

O. Chayanova: *Teatr Maddoksa v Moskve 1776–1825* [Maddox's theatre in Moscow, 1776–1825] (Moscow, 1927)

A. Khokhlovkina, V. Yakovlev and S. M. Popov: 'Muzïkal'naya Moskva i Betkhoven' [Musical Moscow and Beethoven], *Kniga o Betkhovena: k 100-letiyu so dnya smerti kompozitora, 1827–1927*, ed. K. A. Kuznetsov (Moscow, 1927), 111–157

A. Tsukker: *Pyat' let Persimfansa* [Five years of Persimfans] (Moscow, 1927)

*Gosudarstvennaya Opernaya Studiya-teatr imeni narodnovo artista Respubliki K. S. Stanislavskovo* [The Stanislavsky State Opera Studio-Theatre] (Moscow, 1928)

*Pyat' desyat let teatral'noy shkolï 1878–1928* [50 years of the theatre school, 1878–1928] (Moscow, 1929) [on the Moscow Philharmonic Society Music and Drama School, the State Institute of Music Drama etc]

N. Findeyzen: *Ocherki po istorii muzïki v Rossii* [Studies in the history of music in Russia], ii (Moscow, 1929)

*Sorok let Moskovskovo gosudarstvennovo tekhnikuma imeni Gnesinïkh 1895–1935: sbornik* [40 years of the Moscow State Gnesin Technical School 1895–1935: a collection] (Moscow, 1935)

P. A. Markov: *Vl. I. Nemirovich-Danchenko i muzïkal'nïy teatr evo imeni* [Nemirovich-Danchenko and the music theatre named after him] (Moscow, 1936)

I. Martïnov: *Narodïy khor* [The folk choir] (Moscow, 1944, 2/1947, enlarged 3/1950 as *Gosudarstvennïy russkiy narodnïy khor imeni Pyatniskovo* [The State Russian Pyatnitsky Folk Choir], 4/1953)

*Pyat'desyat let Gosudarstvennovo muzïkal'novo uchilishche imeni Gnesinïkh 1895–1945: sbornik* [50 years of the Gnesin State Music School 1895–1945: a collection] (Moscow, 1945)

N. Bryusova: 'Massovaya muzïkal'no-prosvetitel'naya rabota v pervïye godï posle Oktyabrya' [Mass music education in the early years after October], *SovM* (1947), no.6, p.49

K. Kuznetsov: 'Iz muzïkal'novo proshlovo Moskvï' [From the musical past of Moscow], *SovM* (1947), no.5, p.35

*Teatr* (1951), no.5 [special issue for 175th anniversary of the Bol'shoy Theatre]

L. V. Polyakova: *Molodyozh' opernoy stsenï Bol'shovo teatra* [The young members of the Bol'shoy Theatre] (Moscow, 1952)

A. Shaverdian: *Bol'shoy teatr Soyuza SSR* [The USSR Bol'shoy Theatre] (Moscow, 1952)

*Istoriya Moskvï* [The history of Moscow] (Moscow, 1952–9)

V. A. Natanson: *Iz proshlovo Moskovskovo universiteta* [From the past of Moscow University] (Moscow, 1955)

S. Migay: 'Kontsertï dlya naroda: vospominaniya o muzïke v godï stanovleniya Sovetskoy vlasti' [Concerts for the people: reminiscences about music in the years of Soviet power], *SovM* (1957), no.11

I. Yampol'sky: *Gosudarstvennïy kvartet imeni Bol'shovo teatra Soyuza SSR 1931–1956* [The State Bol'shoy Theatre Quartet 1931–56] (Moscow, 1957)

*Bol'shoy teatr: opera: balet* (Moscow, 1958)

A. Shteynberg: 'Kerzinskiy ukrzhok lyubiteley russkoy muzïki' [The Kerzin Russian Music Lovers' Circle], *Voprosï muzïkoznaniya*, iii, ed. Yu. V. Keldïsh (Moscow, 1960), 598

E. Grosheva: *Bol'shoy teatr v evo proshlom i nastoyashchem* [The Bol'shoy Theatre, past and present] (Moscow, 1962)

L. Royzman: 'Iz istorii organnovo iskusstva v Rossii vo vtoroy polovine XVIII stoletiya' [From the history of the art of the organ in Russia in the second half of the 18th century], *Voprosï muzïkal'no-ispolnitel'skovo iskusstva*, iii, ed. A. A. Nikolayev (Moscow, 1962), 306, 311, 327, 330

I. Yampol'sky: *Zasluzhennïy kollektiv Respubliki Gosudarstvennïy kvartet imeni Betkhovena* [Honoured collective of the Republic State Beethoven Quartet] (Moscow, 1963)

A. Shilov: *Krasnoznamennïy ansambl' Sovetskoy Armii* [The Order of the Red Banner Soviet Army Ensemble] (Moscow, 1964)

N. Moleva: 'Teatr na Krasnoy ploshchadi: publikatsiya arkhivnïkh materialov' [The theatre on Red Square: publication of archive material], *SovM* (1966), no.6

*Moskovskaya konservatoriya 1866–1966* [The Moscow Conservatory 1866–1966] (Moscow, 1966)

*Vospominaniya o Moskovskoy konservatorii* [Reminiscences of the Moscow Conservatory] (Moscow, 1966)

A. Medvedev: *Ansambl' skripachey GABTa* [The GABTa violin ensemble] (Moscow, 1966)

N. Moleva: 'Muzïka i zrelishcha v Rossii v XVII stoletii' [Music and entertainments in Russia in the 17th century], *Voprosï istorii* (1971), no.11, p.143

S. Stepanova: *Muzïkal'naya zhizn' Moskvï v pervïye godï posle Oktyabrya* [Musical life in Moscow in the early years after October] (Moscow, 1972)

L. Ginzburg and Ya. Platek, eds.: *Moskovskaya filarmoniya* [The Moscow Philharmonic] (Moscow, 1973)

I. M. YAMPOL'SKY

**Mosel, Giovanni Felice** (*b* Florence, 1754; *d* after 1812). Italian violinist and composer. He studied the violin with his father (who had been a pupil of Tartini) and during his childhood appeared at concerts in Florence, where he completed his studies under Pietro Nardini. He was a player in the grand ducal orchestra and, on his teacher's death in 1793, succeeded him as conductor, a post he held for several years. In 1812 he was leader of the Pergola theatre orchestra.

WORKS

12 duets, 2 vn: op.1 (Florence and Paris, 1783), op.3 (Venice, 1791); 6 str qts (Paris, 1785); Serenata, fl, 2 va, vc (Venice, n.d.)

Syms.; trios, 2 vn, vc; sonatas, vn, b: all unpubd, mentioned by Fétis

BIBLIOGRAPHY
C. Gervasoni: *Nuova teoria di musica* (Parma, 1812), 195
O. Racster: *Chats on Violins* (London, 1905)
R. Gandolfi: 'La cappella musicale della corte di Toscana (1539–1859)', *RMI*, xvi (1909), 506

SERGIO MARTINOTTI

**Mosel, Ignaz Franz von** (*b* Vienna, 1 April 1772; *d* Vienna, 8 April 1844). Austrian writer on music, conductor and composer. He conducted the first musical festivals of the Gesellschaft der Musikfreunde in the imperial riding-school in Vienna (1812–16). He was ennobled and made a *Hofrat*. From 1820 to 1829 he was vice-director of the two court theatres, and from 1829 till his death principal *custos* of the Imperial Library. Mosel was one of the three chief mourners at Beethoven's funeral. Although his own compositions were forgotten even in his lifetime, and his arrangements and editions are useless by today's standards, his work at the theatres and in the Imperial Library enabled him to write authoritatively about contemporary musical figures and ideas.

WORKS
3 stage, all MSS in *A-Wn*: Die Feuerprobe (Singspiel, J. Sonnleithner), 1811; Salem (lyric tragedy, I. F. Castelli), 1813; Cyrus und Astyages (heroic opera, M. von Collin), 1818; incidental music for numerous plays, mostly *Wn*
Masses, psalms, cantatas, songs, instrumental works, some pubd, others mostly *Wgm* and *Wn*
Arrs., all pubd Vienna, c1801–32: J. Haydn: Die Schöpfung, L. Cherubini: Medea, Les deux journées, W. A. Mozart: Così fan tutte, Don Giovanni [all for str qt]; additional instrumentation for G. F. Handel: Samson, Israel in Egypt, Jephtha

WRITINGS
*Versuch einer Ästhetik des musikalischen Tonsatzes* (Vienna, 1813, 2/1910)
*Über das Leben und die Werke des Anton Salieri* (Vienna, 1827)
*Geschichte der k. k. Hofbibliothek in Wien* (Vienna, 1835)
*Über die Original-Partitur des Requiems von W. A. Mozart* (Vienna, 1839)
Articles in various periodicals, incl. 'Die Tonkunst in Wien während der letzten 5 Dezennien', *Stuttgart's Jb der deutschen Tonkunst 1842*

BIBLIOGRAPHY
*FétisB*
A. Schmidt: 'I. F. Edler von Mosel', *Denksteine* (Vienna, 1848)
R. Batka: 'Moseliana', *Musikbuch aus Österreich*, vii–ix (Vienna, 1911–12)

C. F. POHL/BRUCE CARR

**Möseler, Karl Heinrich.** German music publisher, owner of the firm of KALLMEYER from 1947 to 1951.

**Moseley, Carlos (Du Pré)** (*b* Laurens, South Carolina, 21 Sept 1914). American orchestra manager and administrator. After graduating from Duke University (1935) he did postgraduate work at the University of Michigan and the Philadelphia Conservatory. He subsequently studied the piano under Harold Morris and Olga Samaroff and appeared in recitals and as a soloist, winning the MacDowell Young Artists Competition in 1939. During and after the war he held various government positions, and then became director of the school of music and professor of music (piano) at the University of Oklahoma at Norman (1950–55). He was director of press and public relations (1955–9), associate managing director (1959–61) and managing director (1961–70) of the New York PO and in 1970 was appointed president of the New York Philharmonic Symphony Society. This was the first time a major American symphony orchestra had appointed a professional, salaried president.

Moseley has made a lasting impression on the history of the New York PO. Besides working as an administrator he has helped to shape its artistic policies, in the later years of Leonard Bernstein's tenure as conductor and especially from 1969 in the years under Pierre Boulez. Certain innovations – notably the successful summer 'Rug Concert' series begun in 1974 – are almost wholly due to Moseley; his working relationship with Boulez has been a model of how artistic and administrative activities can unite to achieve a result that is both artistically fruitful and appropriate to the needs of the time.

PATRICK J. SMITH

**Moser.** German family of musicians.

**(1) Andreas Moser** (*b* Semlin an der Donau, 29 Nov 1859; *d* Berlin, 7 Oct 1925). Violinist, teacher, writer on music and editor. He first studied engineering and architecture, then turned to music in 1878, becoming a violin pupil of Joachim in Berlin. He was briefly employed as orchestral leader in Mannheim in 1883, but because of an arm ailment he gave up a performing career and became a teacher. From 1884 to 1888 he was a private teacher in Berlin, and from 1888 to 1925 he taught at the Hochschule für Musik there. He was made a professor in 1900, and in 1925 he received an honorary degree from the University of Berlin.

Moser is known chiefly for his writings on the violin, its music and its performers. His biography of Joachim (written for Joachim's jubilee in 1899 and expanded to two volumes after his death) and his edition of Joachim's correspondence are standard reference works. He also edited the Brahms–Joachim correspondence for the Deutsche Brahms Gesellschaft and wrote teaching methods for the violin, and articles on violin playing and violin music; he prepared editions of many standard repertory works for string instruments, including the parts to the complete quartets of Beethoven and Mozart and the 30 'famous' Haydn quartets. His three-volume violin tutor (1905), written in collaboration with Joachim, was widely used in its time.

WRITINGS
*Joseph Joachim* (Berlin, 1898, rev., enlarged 4/1908; Eng. trans., 1900)
with J. Joachim: *Violinschule*, i–iii (Berlin, 1905, rev. 2/1959 by M. Jacobsen)
ed.: *J. Brahms: Briefwechsel*, v–vi (Berlin, 1908) [correspondence with Joachim]
ed., with Johannes Joachim: *Briefe von und an Joseph Joachim*, i–iii (Berlin, 1911)
*Methodik des Violinspiels*, i–ii (Leipzig, 1920)
*Geschichte des Violinspiels* (Berlin, 1923, rev., enlarged 2/1966–7)
*Technik des Violinspiels*, i–ii (Leipzig, 1925)

BIBLIOGRAPHY
H. J. Moser: 'Andreas Moser', *Berliner MusikJb*, ed. A. Ebel (Berlin and Leipzig, 1926), 106

**(2) Hans Joachim Moser** (*b* Berlin, 25 May 1889; *d* Berlin, 14 Aug 1967). Musicologist, son of (1) Andreas Moser. From 1907 he studied musicology, German philology and history at the universities of Berlin (with Kretzschmar and Wolf), Marburg (with Schiedermair) and Leipzig (with Riemann and Schering), and in 1910 took the doctorate with a dissertation on musical societies in Germany during the Middle Ages. Concurrently he studied composition (with H. von Eyken, R. Kahn and G. Jenner) and singing (with O. Noë and F. Schmidt), later giving recitals as a bass-baritone. After army service in World War I he completed his *Habilitation* at Halle in 1919 with a study of the history of string playing in the Middle Ages, and became successively a *Privatdozent* (1919) and reader (1922) at the

University of Halle, reader at the University of Heidelberg (1925–7) and honorary professor at the University of Berlin (1927–34). He was also director of the National Academy of Church and School Music (1927–33), where he reformed the curriculum for music teaching in higher education and raised the standards for important posts in church music as well as furthering music-making among the young and in the home. With the advent of the Nazi regime he had to give up his public offices, and he was retired in 1934; however he was still able to work as a writer and from 1940 to 1945 he was in charge of the Reichsstelle für Musik-Bearbeitungen. He took up teaching again in 1947 as a professor at the University of Jena and at the Weimar Musikhochschule; in 1950 he returned to Berlin, and was director of the city's conservatory until 1960.

Moser had an extraordinarily creative personality. He was a scholar of enormous knowledge and memory and engaged in unusually versatile research with amazing energy. As well as his specifically musical talents, he had a particular flair for correlating history and art history in music history; he wrote comprehensive and distinguished works on music history and several biographical studies. Both his musicological and pedagogical books are marked by originality of design, treatment and style. These qualities mark his *Geschichte der deutschen Musik* (written when he was 30), a notable national music-cultural history with an unusual arrangement of material, precise characterization of individuals and an acute selection of detail. Further significant achievements such as monographs on Paul Hofhaimer (1929) and Heinrich Schütz (1936) followed this early principal work; his important works on Lutheran church music and the polyphonic Gospel settings (1931) prepared the way for a revival of interest in these subjects. His research also produced substantial discoveries relating to music history: the tablatures of Lübbenau and Vienna, the madrigals of Knüpffer and G. M. Cesari and the accompanied partsong with basso continuo. His intensive effort and alert academic curiosity are evident in his numerous writings (over 1500 publications), which cover a wide variety of subjects including music sociology, the geography of civilization, music teaching, music aesthetics, acoustics and the history of individual genres of forms. His music encyclopedia (1932–5) was an outstanding achievement and had an extensive readership even among laymen. Moser also arranged Handel and Weber operas, worked as a translator and wrote novels, short stories and a comedy; among his compositions are many songs and the children's opera *Der Reisekamerad* (1931).

## WRITINGS

*Die Musikergenossenschaften im deutschen Mittelalter* (diss., U. of Rostock, 1910)
with O. Noë: *Technik der deutschen Gesangskunst* (Berlin, 1911)
'Die Entstehung des Dur-Gedankens: ein kulturgeschichtliches Problem', *SIMG*, xv (1913–14), 270
'Zur Frage der Ausführung der Ornamente bei Sebastian Bach', *BJb*, xiii (1916), 159
*Das Streichinstrumentenspiel im Mittelalter* (Habilitationsschrift, U. of Halle, 1919); pubd in A. Moser: *Geschichte des Violinspiels* (Berlin, 1923, rev., enlarged 2/1966–7), 1–34
'Zur Rhythmik der altdeutschen Volksweisen', *ZMw*, i (1918–19), 225
*Geschichte der deutschen Musik* (Stuttgart and Berlin, 1920–24, enlarged 2/1968)
'Atonale Geschichtsklitterung', *AMz*, l (1923), 623
*Musikalisches Wörterbuch* (Leipzig and Berlin, 1923)
'Über die Eigentümlichkeit der deutschen Musik begabung', *JbMP 1924*, 35
'Kleine Beiträge zu Beethovens Liedern und Bühnenwerken', *NBJb*, ii (1925), 43

'Die musikalische Jugendbewegung', *Schulmusikalische Zeitdokumente: Vorträge der VII. Reichsschulmusikwoche in München* (Leipzig, 1929), 52
*Paul Hofhaimer: ein Lied- und Orgelmeister des deutschen Humanismus* (Stuttgart and Berlin, 1929, enlarged 2/1966)
*Die Ballade* (Berlin, 1930)
*Die Epochen der Musikgeschichte im Überblick* (Stuttgart and Berlin, 1930)
*Die mehrstimmige Vertonung des Evangeliums* (Leipzig, 1931; vol.i R1968)
*Musiklexikon* (Berlin, 1932–5, 4/1955; suppl. 1963)
'Zum Bau von Bachs Johannespassion', *BJb*, xxix (1932), 155
*Corydon: das ist Geschichte des mehrstimmigen Generalbass-Liedes und des Quodlibets im deutschen Barock* (Brunswick, 1933)
'Musik für Gesang', *Das Atlantisbuch der Musik*, ed. F. Hamel and M. Hürlimann (Berlin and Zurich, 1934), 651–87
*Die Melodien der Luther-Lieder* (Leipzig and Hamburg, 1935)
*Johann Sebastian Bach* (Berlin, 1935)
'Musikalische Kulturgeographie', *Die Musik*, xxviii (1935–6), 43
*Tönende Volksaltertümer* (Berlin, 1935)
*Heinrich Schütz: sein Leben und Werk* (Kassel, 1936, rev. 2/1954; Eng. trans., 1959)
*Lehrbuch der Musikgeschichte* (Berlin, 1936, 13/1959)
'Daniel Speer', *AcM*, ix (1937), 99
*Das deutsche Lied seit Mozart* (Berlin and Zurich, 1937, rev. 2/1968)
*Die Musikfibel* (Leipzig, 1937)
'Zur Aufführungspraxis bei Heinrich Schütz', *SMz*, lxxvii (1937), 29
'Georg Friedrich Händel zwischen deutscher und englischer Welt', *Deutsch-Englische Hefte* (1938), no.p.165
*Kleine deutsche Musikgeschichte* (Stuttgart, 1938, 3/1949)
'Frauen schreiben Musik', *Der Silberspiegel*, v (1939), 1230, 1248
'Pfitzners Liedschaffen', *AMz*, lxvi (1939), 297
*Allegemeine Musiklehre* (Berlin, 1940)
*Christoph Willibald Gluck* (Stuttgart, 1940)
*Kleines Heinrich-Schütz-Buch* (Kassel, 1940; Eng. trans., 1967)
*Carl Maria von Weber* (Leipzig, 1941)
'Der Humor in der Musik', *Neues Musikblatt*, xx (1941), 1
*Georg Friedrich Händel* (Kassel, 1941)
'Die Opernbühne Friedrichs des Grossen', *200 Jahre Preussischer Staatsoper* (Berlin, 1942), 12
*Goethe und die Musik* (Leipzig, 1949)
'Kompositionsunterricht als Stillehre', *Musikblätter* (Berlin, 1950), no.6, p.121
*Lebensvolle Musikerziehung* (Vienna, 1952)
*Musikgeschichte in hundert Lebensbildern* (Stuttgart, 1952)
'Bach als Zwölftöner?', *Das Musikleben*, vi (1953), 86
'Diabolus in musica', *Musikerziehung*, vi (1953), 131
*Die evangelische Kirchenmusik in Deutschland* (Berlin, 1953)
'Max Regers Orchesterwerke', *Max Reger: Festschrift* (Leipzig, 1953), 21
*Musikästhetik* (Berlin, 1953)
'Das deutsche Volkslied in der Kunstmusik', *Hausmusik*, xviii (1954), 38
'Der Wechsel nationaler und universaler Epochen in der Musikgeschichte des Abendlandes', *Universitas* (1954), 39
*Die Musikleistung der deutschen Stämme* (Vienna, 1954)
*Die Tonsprachen des Abendlandes* (Berlin and Darmstadt, 1954)
'Über den Sinn der Musikforschung', *Festgabe für Hans Joachim Moser* (Kassel, 1954), 158
*Harmonielehre*, i (Berlin 1954–5)
*Blinde Musiker aus sieben Jahrhunderten* (Hamburg, 1956)
*Dietrich Buxtehude* (Berlin, 1957)
*Musik in Zeit und Raum* (Berlin, 1960) [collected essays]
*Bachs Werke: ein Führer für Musikfreunde* (Kassel, 1964)
'Luther als Musiker', *Speculum artis musicae: Festgabe für Heinrich Husmann* (Munich, 1970), 229

## EDITIONS

with O. Albrecht and H. Lucke: *Luthers Lieder*, Werke, xxxv (Weimar, 1923)
*Minnesang und Volkslied* (Leipzig, 1925)
*C. M. von Weber: Musikalische Werke* (Augsburg and Leipzig, 1926–33)
*Die weltlichen Liedsätze des Adam von Fulda*, 'Leben und Lieder des Adam von Fulda', *Jb der Staatlichen Akademie für Kirchen und Schulmusik*, i (Leipzig, 1927–8), appx
with F. Piersig: *Carmina*, NM, liii (1929)
with E. Bernoulli: *Das Liederbuch des Arnt von Aich* (Kassel, 1930)
*Frühmeister deutscher Orgelkunst*, Staatliche Akademie für Kirchen-und Schulmusik, i (Leipzig, 1930)
*J. P. Krieger: 24 Lieder und Arien*, NM, clxxiv–clxxv (1930)
*J. V. Rathgeber: Ohrenvergnügendes und gemüthergötzendes Tafelconfect*, EDM, 1st ser., xix (1942)
*J. Herold: Historia des Leidens und Sterbens unser Herrn und Heilands*, MAM, iv (1955)
*Das deutsche Sololied und die Ballade*, Mw, xiv (1957; Eng. trans., 1958)

G. Rhau, ed.: *Vesperarum precum officia*, Musikdrucke aus den Jahren 1538 bis 1545 in praktischer Neuausgabe, iv (Kassel, 1960)
A. *Hammerschmidt: Weltliche Oden*, EDM, 1st ser., xliii (1962)
H. *Schütz: Italienische Madrigale*, Neue Ausgabe sämtlicher Werke, xxii (Kassel, 1962)
*Geistliche Konzerte um 1700*, EDM, 1st ser., xlv–xlvi (1970)

BIBLIOGRAPHY

A. Moser: 'Hans Joachim Moser', *Berliner Musik Jb*, ed. A. Ebel (Berlin and Leipzig, 1926), 106
L. M. Walzel: 'Hans Joachim Moser', *Musikerziehung*, v (1952), 217
*Festgabe für Hans Joachim Moser* (Kassel, 1954) [incl. complete list of publications compiled by Heinz Wegener]
W. Vetter: 'Gedanken zur musikalischen Biographie', *Mf*, xii (1959), 141
Obituary: G. Hausswald, *Musica*, xxi (1967), 250; A. A. Abert, *AcM*, xl (1968), 91; O. Söhngen, *Mf*, xxi (1968), 154

**(3) Edda (Elisabeth) Moser** (*b* Berlin, 27 Oct 1941). Austrian soprano of German birth, daughter of (2) Hans Joachim Moser. She studied at the Berlin Conservatory with Hermann Weissenborn and Gerty König. Her début was at the Städtische Oper in 1962, in the small role of Kate Pinkerton, after which she sang for a year in the Würzburg Opera chorus; engagements followed at Hagen and Bielefeld. She has appeared regularly at Vienna, Salzburg (from 1970) and Hamburg; since her Metropolitan Opera début in 1968 as Wellgunde (*Das Rheingold*) her roles there have included Donna Anna, the Queen of Night and Liù. Equally at home in contemporary music, she has sung and recorded Henze's *Cantata della fiaba estrema*, *Being Beauteous* and *Das Floss der Medusa* under the composer, the last at its première in Vienna (1970); her repertory also includes works by Fortner, Zimmermann, Nono and Stravinsky. Moser's voice is a powerful dramatic coloratura soprano, used with remarkable accuracy and musicianship.

R. J. PASCALL (1), ANTON WÜRZ (2),
HAROLD ROSENTHAL (3)

**Möser, Karl** (*b* Berlin, 24 Jan 1774; *d* Berlin, 27 Jan 1851). German composer and violinist. He was a pupil of his father, Böttcher and Haack, and played in Friedrich Wilhelm II's private quartet. He then undertook concert tours, visiting London and meeting Rode and Viotti, contact with whom caused him to revise his playing method. He returned to Berlin in 1797, then went to St Petersburg (1807–11), going back to Berlin as Konzertmeister of the reorganized Hofkapelle. He began regular chamber music evenings with his quartet in 1813, which by 1816 developed into symphony concerts. In 1825 he became director and by his retirement in 1842 was titular Kapellmeister. He is less important for his compositions, mostly songs and pieces for violin and orchestra, than for his position in Berlin's musical history (he conducted several local Beethoven premières, notably Symphony no.9, 1826) and for his beneficent influence on violin playing and teaching there.

**Moser, Rudolf** (*b* Niederuzwil, 7 Jan 1892; *d* Silvaplana, 20 Aug 1960). Swiss composer. He studied first at Basle, including musicology under Nef, then at Leipzig (1912–14), under Reger, Sitt and Klengel. Further studies in Basle and Geneva followed, under Huber, Suter, Lauber and Nef. He became choirmaster at Basle Cathedral and teacher in composition at the conservatory there; he also played the viola in a string quartet. Moser occupies a special place among Swiss composers through his efforts to combine a modern and individual expression with a use of the church modes in his many-sided output, which includes *Die Fischerin* (1935,

Singspiel after Goethe) and other dramatic works, much choral music, songs, many concertos and miscellaneous orchestral works, chamber and keyboard music.

BIBLIOGRAPHY

H. Ehinger: 'Moser, Rudolf', *MGG* [with work-list]
H. Buchli: *Rudolf Moser* (Zurich, 1964)

HANS EHINGER/R

**Mosewius, Johann Theodor** (*b* Königsberg, 25 Sept 1788; *d* Schaffhausen, 15 Sept 1858). German conductor. After studying law, he turned to music and became musical director of the Königsberg theatre (1814). In 1816 he moved to Breslau, where he founded a quartet society, a Singakademie and a *Liedertafel*, also becoming successively teacher at the university (1827), head of the Akademisches Institut für Kirchenmusik (1831), director of music at the university (1832) and founder of the Musikalischer Cirkel for the practice of secular music (1834). At the institute he introduced Italian works as well as music by Mendelssohn, Loewe, Spohr, Marx and others. One of the earliest 19th-century champions of Bach, both as performer and as scholar, he became known in England through two pamphlets first published in the *Allgemeine musikalische Zeitung*, *J. S. Bach in seinen Kirchenkantaten und Choralgesängen* (1845) and *J. S. Bachs Matthäus-Passion* (1852), whose copious music examples helped draw attention to Bach's music in England.

BIBLIOGRAPHY

C. Hoffmann: *Die Tonkünstler Schlesiens* (Breslau, 1830)
A. Kempe: *Erinnerungen an Ernst Theodor Mosewius* (Breslau, 1859)
*Verzeichnis von Musikalien aus dem Nachlass des verstorbenen Herrn Dr. J. Th. Mosewius* (Breslau, n.d.)

GEORGE GROVE/JOHN WARRACK

**Moskova, Joseph Napoléon Ney**, Prince de la (*b* Paris, 8 May 1803; *d* St Germain-en-Laye, 25 July 1857). French statesman, scholar and composer. As a boy he showed great aptitude for music and composed a mass, performed at Lucca, where he lived after his father's death. In 1831 he became a member of the Chambre des Pairs, and in Paris he contributed articles to several publications, especially the *Revue des deux mondes* and the *Constitutionnel*, which excited considerable interest. With Adolphe Adam he founded the Société des Concerts de Musique Religieuse et Classique, and published much of the Renaissance, Baroque and Classical vocal music performed by the society in the 11-volume *Recueil des morceaux de musique ancienne*. He was intimate with the singer Delsarte and with the composer Niedermeyer, whom he helped to found the Ecole de Musique Religieuse. In 1831 Choron's pupils performed one of his masses, which was highly praised by Fétis. Although naturally inclined to the madrigal style and sacred music, the prince also wrote two one-act operas, *Le Cent-Suisse* (1840) and *Yvonne* (1855).

GUSTAVE CHOUQUET/R

**Moskva** (Russ.). MOSCOW.

**Mos longus, mediocris, lascivus.** Three levels of tempo, reflecting stylistic categories of music, formulated by PETRUS LE VISER during the 1290s.

**Mosolov, Alexandr Vasil'yevich** (*b* Kiev, 29 July 1900; *d* Moscow, 11 July 1973). Russian composer. He received some music lessons from his mother, the singer N. A. Mosolova, and studied at a Moscow high school until 1917. From 1918 to 1920 he took part in the civil war in Kotovsky's brigade. He began to compose in 1921 and studied privately with Glier in 1922; he then attended the Moscow Conservatory (1922–5) as a pupil of Glier (harmony and counterpoint), Myaskovsky (composition) and Prokofiev and Igumnov (piano). In the 1920s he joined the Association for Contemporary Music (ASM) and his works were heard in western Europe. Mosolov lived in Moscow until 1937, working as a concert pianist and playing his own pieces. Early in his career he composed intensively (from 1924 to 1926 he produced about 30 works); the music of this period was marked by drama, a nocturnal urban quality (for example, in the piano sonatas and the symphonic poem *Sumerki*), parody (in the *Chetïre gazetnïkh ob'yavleniya*) and Musorgskyan intensity (in the *Tri detskikh stsenki*). Mosolov also contributed to the modern 'barbarism' movement, somewhat influenced by Honegger and Satie – a strain notably expressed in *Zavod* ('The foundry'), which attracted attention through its use of a metal sheet to create the sound of clashing iron and steel. He turned to socialist themes in the late 1920s in the operas *Geroy* ('The hero') and *Plotina* ('The dam').

Many of these early works (among them a symphony and two sonatas, opp.21a and 22) were lost when a case of MSS was stolen. In the period 1927–31 Mosolov's work was severely criticized by the Russian Association of Proletarian Musicians. The result was a long interruption of his work and a change in style: his music became melodically and harmonically simpler and he abandoned urban subject matter. From 1939 to his death he lived in Moscow, but made many expeditions to the Turkmen and Kirghiz republics investigating folk music; this interest gave rise to the three orchestral songs of op.33 and the Piano Concerto no.2 on Kirghiz themes. In the 1950s he collected peasant songs in the Kuban and Stavropol regions, and in the 1960s in northern Russia. During this period he wrote extensively in large-scale genres, employing elements of folk melody, harmony and polyphony. In his last years his compositional activity was linked with the Northern Folk Choir.

### WORKS
(*selective list*)

ORCHESTRAL
Sumerki [Twilight], op.9, sym. poem, ?1925; Zavod [The foundry], op.19, orch episode from ballet Stal, 1926–8; Stal, op.19a, ballet suite, perf. 1927; Pf Conc. no.1, op.14, 1927; Sym., op.20, ?1928–9, lost; Pf Conc. no.2, 1932; Harp Conc., 1939; Vc Conc., 1945; Torzhestvennaya oda [Ceremonial ode] (1947); Sym. no.1 'Kubanskaya', 1950; Sym. no.3 (Simfonia-pesnya [Sym.-song]), B, 1950; Kubanskaya syuita, folk insts (1954); Sym. no.2, C, 1959; Elegicheskaya poema, vc, orch, 1961; Sym. no.5, a, 1965; Sym. no.6, inc.

VOCAL
Operas: Geroy [The hero], op.28, 1, 1927; Plotina [The dam] (5, Y. L. Zadïkhin), ?1929–31; Signal (O. Litovsky), 1941, lost; Maskarad (after Lermontov) (1944)
Choral: ?, op.8 (Mayakovsky), lost; Sfinx (Wilde), T, chorus, orch, ?1925, lost; Goroda-geroy [Town hero] (oratorio, Zharov) (1945); Rodina [Native land] (cantata, A. Prokofiev) (1949); Pesni krasnodarskovo kraya [Songs of the Krasnodar region] (1959); Slava Moskve [Hail Moscow], oratorio, chorus, orch, 1967; Narodnaya oratoriya [People's oratorio], 1970; many other choruses and folksong arrs.
Solo vocal (with pf unless otherwise stated): 4 Poems (Pushkin, Goethe, Khodasevich), 1924; 4 pesni, op.7, lost; 10 stikhotvorenii [10 poems], op.10 (Blok), 1v, pf/ens; 3 vokaliza, op.13, perf. 1926, ?lost; 10 chetverostishiï [10 quatrains], op.16, Mez, pf, perf. 1929, ?lost; 3 detskikh stsenki [3 children's scenes], op.18, S/T, pf, perf. 1926; 4 gazetnïkh ob'yavleniya [4 newspaper announcements], op.21, 1926; Sonata, op.22 (textless), lost; Skorpion, op.25 (S. V. Shervinsky), lost; 3 Songs, op.33 (N. Samolevska), 1v, orch (1933); Schastliviy put [Happy path] (Zharov) (1941); Chekh i sokol [The Czech and the falcon] (A. Maykov) (1941); 3 elegii (D. Davïdov) (1946); Slava

velikomu oktyabryu [Hail great October] (Zharov), Bar, orch (1947); 3 romansa (Pushkin) (1949); Kabardinskie romansï, 1955

CHAMBER AND INSTRUMENTAL
Elegiya, op.2, vc, pf, lost; Legenda, op.5, vc, pf, 1924; 3 liricheskie p'yesï, va, pf, perf. 1925–6, lost; Ballada, op.17, cl, vc, pf, perf. 1926, ?lost; Sonata, op.21a, va, lost; Str Qt no.1, a, op.24, 1926; 4 kadentsii i koda, op.26, str qt, lost; Tantseval'naya syuita, op.27, pf trio, perf. 1929, ?lost; Sonatina, vc, pf, 1946; 4 p'yesï, bn, pf (1946); Tantseval'naya syuita, harp (1947); Str Qt no.2 'na patrioticheskie temï 1812', 1963
Pf: 5 sonatas: c, op.3, 1924; 'Iz starïkh tetradey' [From old notebooks], b, op.4, 1923–4; op.6, ?lost; op.11, 1925; d, op.12, 1925; 2 noktyurna, op.15, 1926; 3 p'yesï, 2 tantsa, op.23 (1928, 1930); Turkmenskie nochi (1929)

Principal publishers: Muzgiz, Universal

BIBLIOGRAPHY
V. Belyaev: 'A. V. Mosolov', *Sovremennaya muzïka* (1926), no.13–14, p.81
'Levïy flang sovremennoy muzïki' [The left flank of contemporary music], *Muzïka i revolyutsiya* (1927), no.1, p.3
M. Ivanov-Boretsky: 'Simfonicheskiy kontsert ASM v oznamenovanie deyatel'nosti oktyabrya' [The ASM symphony concert in commemoration of the events of October], *Muzïkal'noye obrazovaniye* (1928), no.1, p.72
V. Belyaev: 'Fortepiannïy kontsert Mosolova', *Sovremennaya muzïka* (1928), no.30, p.142

INNA BARSOVA

**Mosonyi, Mihály** [Brand, Michael] (*b* Boldogasszonyfalva, Hungary [now Frauenkirchen, Austria], 4 Sept 1815; *d* Pest, 31 Oct 1870). Hungarian composer, teacher and writer on music. Like Liszt, he was born in the border region between Hungary and Austria at the meeting-point of several cultures. His name was originally Michael Brand, the same as his father and grandfather, and his first language was German. He was the fourth of 11 children in a family of furriers. According to a fragmentary autobiography music was pursued by the peasants in his birthplace, and there he had the opportunity to learn the usual wind instruments in his youth in the peasant manner. Boldogasszonyfalva was a famous place of pilgrimage, and in its church, built by Prince Pál Esterházy, Mosonyi had the opportunity to practise the organ and, between the ages of 10 and 12, to deputize for the cantor. In 1829 he left home to work as a church officer in Magyaróvár, where he taught himself music by copying Hummel's manual of exercises for the piano. About 1832 he arrived in Pozsony (now Bratislava) as a student. At that time Pozsony was the seat of the royal family and the capital of Hungary, and its cultural life was dominated by the nearby imperial city of Vienna. Mosonyi became acquainted with the great works and resolved to devote himself to music. He earned a living by teaching reading and writing, copying music, and working as a newspaper distributor and typesetter for a printing firm. In Pozsony he studied the piano and music theory with Károly Turányi, who later became Kapellmeister in Aachen. Turányi and another patron, Count Károly Keglevich, obtained for Mosonyi a position as a piano teacher at the residence of Count Péter Pejachevich in the Slavonian village of Rétfalu. There he spent seven years (1835–42), becoming an accomplished pianist and, with the help of Reicha's theoretical works, a composer. The compositions he finished in Rétfalu – the Grand Duo for piano, the first four of his seven string quartets and an overture – reveal a diligent pupil of the Classical style.

In 1842 Mosonyi moved to Pest, where he worked until his death. He never held a public, municipal or ecclesiastical position, nor was he in the service of a theatre, teaching institute or aristocratic household. He was one of the first independent musicians in Hungary to earn a living by teaching the piano and composition. His most famous pupils were Kornél Ábrányi (the elder), who later edited the weekly music journal *Zenészeti lapok*, Gyula and Sándor Erkel (the sons of Ferenc), and the future director of the Budapest Academy of Music, Ödön Mihalovich. He was encouraged to compose by the stimulating intellectual atmosphere in Pest in the decade before the Hungarian War of Independence (1848–9): the Hungarian Theatre (later the National Theatre) had been opened in 1837, followed three years later by the conservatory of

*Mihály Mosonyi*

the Music Society of Pest-Buda (later the National Conservatory); in 1844 Ferenc Erkel had written Hungary's national anthem, and in 1840 and 1844 Erkel's first two operas, *Bátori Mária* and *Hunyadi László*, were performed. In April 1843 Mosonyi's Overture was given its first performance under the direction of Louis Schindelmeisser; the following March his First Symphony received its première, and a month later his first mass was heard in Pest. The success of these works led to Mosonyi's being appointed assistant archivist of the Pest-Buda Music Society on 27 September 1844. Both this symphony and the Sextet of 1844 reflect the influence of Beethoven, while the Piano Concerto, also completed in 1844, represents a step towards Romanticism. In this work Mosonyi succeeded in constructing a large one-movement form with the recognizable contours of the traditional three movements, and thus anticipated a development in cyclical composition that has been widely credited to Liszt.

On 3 October 1846 Mosonyi married Paulina Weber, sister of the famous portrait painter Henrik Weber. In the same year he began writing his Second Symphony, which was not performed until ten years later. Mosonyi took part in the War of Independence as a member of the National Guard, his musical contribution to the cause being an arrangement of the *Marseillaise* for baritone solo, mixed choir and orchestra. In 1849 he wrote a mass (his third) in memory of his benefactor and godfather Peter Piller. The early death of his wife (13 July 1851) brought on an emotional crisis, making it impossible for him to compose

for two years. The elegiac autumnal lyricism of the German songs (1853–4), which were published by Breitkopf & Härtel, reflect his grief and show him a fully-fledged Romantic.

The critics at the première of Mosonyi's First Symphony had been justified in singling out the influence of Beethoven and the composer's distance from any aspirations to write in a national style. In the finale of his Second Symphony (first performed on 30 March 1856), however, he first made use of Hungarian idioms; his personal acquaintance with Liszt in the same year was decisive in his development. Liszt, who contributed to the festivities at the consecration of the Basilica in Esztergom (Gran) with his *Missa solemnis*, then asked Mosonyi to set the Propers of the Mass, the Offertory and the Gradual. (Mosonyi's pieces, unperformed in Esztergom because the *regens chori* Sayler had also made settings of the Offertory and Gradual, were first performed in Pest on 24 August 1856 under the direction of Liszt.) Mosonyi, who took part in the performance of Liszt's mass as a double bass player, did not recognize the true importance of Liszt as a composer or of his musical reforms until he had attended the rehearsals. From 1856 the two men were on close terms, as friends and colleagues. In honour of Mosonyi, Liszt had the main motif in the Agnus Dei of his mass appear in a solo for the double bass. In 1860 Mosonyi transcribed Liszt's *Missa solemnis* for piano four hands, to the composer's great satisfaction. Liszt invited Mosonyi to Weimar for the first performance of his *Faust-Symphonie* in September 1857, and looked through Mosonyi's German romantic opera *Kaiser Max auf der Martinswand*, finished in 1857, in the hope of presenting it there.

But these hopes were not fulfilled. Liszt pointed out dramatic errors which he asked Mosonyi to correct. He worked again on the opera until 1858, then abandoned it in favour of other works. Liszt's criticism and notices in the Hungarian press encouraged him to turn his attention to raising the status of Hungarian art music. In 1857, on the occasion of the first visit to Hungary by the Empress (later Queen) Elisabeth, Mosonyi composed a piano piece in the Hungarian style, *Pusztai élet* ('Puzsta life'). A whole year of compositional activity followed its favourable reception, and from about 1859 he wrote a series of new works in the national style. To give an outward gesture of his stylistic transformation, he took the Hungarian name of Mosonyi in 1859, after his place of birth (the county of Moson).

In creating a national style of art music Mosonyi could proceed from the already existing melody and rhythm of the *verbunkos* and *csárdás* and of Hungarian popular art song. His greatest task was to shape larger forms and a consistent musical language from the elements of the compact, small forms of dance and song. At first he followed Romantic models, composing mood and character-pieces after the example of Schumann's *Kinderszenen* (*Magyar gyermekvilág*, 1859), and studies after Chopin and Liszt (*Tanulmányok zongorára*, 1860). Mosonyi later used parts of these works for piano in his cantatas and operas. His *Hódolat Kazinczy Ferenc szellemének* ('Homage to Kazinczy'), originally for piano but later orchestrated, is a stylized Hungarian rhapsody, while *Gyász hangok Széchenyi István halálára* ('Funeral music for Széchenyi', also originally written for piano) is a symphonic poem built on a

'Hungarian ostinato'. *Hódolat* is the first work in the symphonic literature to use the cimbalom, which had previously been used only in gypsy bands. Mosonyi's Hungarian ostinato on the notes G–B♭–C♯–F♯ was later used by Liszt in his Hungarian historical portraits. The beginning of the struggle for national independence in 1859–60 contributed to the popularity of Mosonyi's first Hungarian work. The nationwide festivities celebrating the centenary of the birth of the poet and language revivalist Ferenc Kazinczy – which developed into a celebration of the free national spirit – inspired Mosonyi's Kazinczy cantata *A tisztulás ünnepe az Ungnál* ('Festival of purification at the River Ung', 1859). The text of his cantata, based on the conquests of the Hungarians in the 9th century, gave the composer occasion to put himself forward as a reformer of the Hungarian musical language and a representative of what he called a 'spiritual conquest'. The appearance of the first weekly music journal in Hungary, *Zenészeti lapok* (1860), gave Mosonyi the opportunity to voice his aesthetic principles. His basic programme was 'to create, alongside the German, Italian, and French musical currents in music, a fourth world-famous style, the Hungarian'. In his articles Mosonyi fought for the cultivation and unity of Hungarian provincial composers, and also for Hungarian performances of the music of Liszt and Wagner, as well as for general musical education of the public. The last-named objective made him a forerunner of Kodály. Wagner, who became acquainted with some of Mosonyi's compositions on the occasion of his first trip to Hungary in 1863, praised the synthesis of the national and popular elements with the international in a piece from the *Tanulmányok zongorára*.

In 1861 and 1862 Mosonyi composed the Hungarian operas *Szép Ilonka* ('Pretty Helen') and *Álmos*. In the first he sought to build a grandiose form exclusively out of elements from Hungarian popular art song. In the second, whose theme was once more the early conquests of the Hungarians, he sought to synthesize certain expressive possibilities in Hungarian *verbunkos* music with those in Wagner's music dramas. *Szép Ilonka* met with no great success (Liszt composed a Fantasia on motifs from it in 1867); *Álmos* was never performed in the composer's lifetime.

In 1865 Mosonyi went to Munich to attend the first performance of *Tristan und Isolde*. In the same year he played the double bass in the first performance in Pest of Liszt's *Legende der heiligen Elisabeth*. In his last years Mosonyi composed noteworthy Hungarian art songs and ballads, and a series of choral works and cantatas of less importance. In 1870, a few months before his death, he was appointed to the programme selection committee of the Pest National Theatre and made a member of the committee to prepare the Hungarian Beethoven centenary festival. He died with many ambitious hopes for a Hungarian national music.

### WORKS

#### OPERAS

Kaiser Max auf der Martinswand (3, E. Pasqué), 1856–7, unperf.
Szép Ilonka [Pretty Helen] (5, rev. 4, M. Fekete, after M. Vörösmarty), Pest, National Theatre, 19 Dec 1861, vocal score (Pest, 1862)
Álmos (3, E. Szigligeti), 1862, Budapest, Royal Hungarian Opera, 6 Dec 1934

#### VOCAL

Sacred choral: 5 masses, 1840–66; Jubilate Deo, 1843; Gradual, 1843; Lauda Sion, 1855; Offertory and Gradual, for Liszt's Missa solemnis, 1856; Gebet des Herrn; Halotti ének [Funeral song], 1865; Ave verum, Tui sunt, Ave Maria, all late 1860s; Libera me, 1870, ed. (Budapest, 1871)
Cantatas: A tisztulás ünnepe az Ungnál 886-ik esztendöben [Festival

of purification at the River Ung in 886] (F. Kazinczy), 1859; Dalra magyar! [Sing, Hungarian!] (E. Abrányi), 1869; Cantate a zenekedvelök dalcsarnokának megnyitási ünnepére [Cantata for the inauguration of the concert hall of the Pest Amateur Music Society] (J. Komócsy), 1870
Other secular choral: Chor zur Feyer des Tondichters Herrn Fr. Erkel, 1844; A dalárda [The choral society] (I. Szepessy), 1857; Üdvözlet [Greeting], 1857; Völkerfrühling, 1857; Fel fel a vérzö kebelröl [Up from the bleeding bosom], 1863; Tavaszi dal [Spring song] (L. F. Takáts), 1863; Keserü pohár [Cup of bitterness] (Vörösmarty), 1863; Bordal [Drinking-song] (J. Arany), 1864; A nagyszombati dalárda jelvénye [Motto of the Nagyszombat Choral Society], 1864; Kemény-induló [Kemény march] (K. Tóth), 1865; A pacsirta [The lark], 1865; Ébresztö [Reveille], 1865; Szellemvilág [World of the spirits], 1865; Dalárok karéneke [A song to sing], 1866; Szentelt hantok [Consecrated graves] (Komócsy), 1868–9; Gróf Batthiány Lajos emlékének [In memory of Count Batthiány], 1870
Songs: An Juma, c1850; Aus einsamer Zelle (Menner), c1850; Wunsch im Frühlinge, c1850; Wiegenlied (Stütze), 1850; Du schönes Fischermädchen (Heine), 1853; Ob ich dich liebe? (Ronninger), c1853; 6 Lieder (N. Lenau, R. Burns, E. Geibel), op.5 (Leipzig, 1853); Schilflieder (Lenau), op.6 (Leipzig, 1854); A szerelem, a szerelem [Love, love] (S. Petöfi) (Pest, 1860); Letészem a lantot [I lay aside my lyre] (Arany) (Pest, 1863); Hat népdal [6 folksongs] (Tóth) (Pest, 1863); Gara Mária (Tóth) (Pest, 1864); Mátyás anyja [Mátyás's mother] (Arany) (Pest, 1864); Szentelt hantok [Consecrated graves] (Komócsy) (Pest, 1869); Boldogság emléke [Souvenir of happiness] (Komócsy) (Pest, 1870)

#### INSTRUMENTAL

Orch: Ov., b, 1841–2; 2 syms., D, 1843–4, a, 1846–56; Pf Conc., e, 1844, ed. (Budapest, 1966); A honvédek (Honvéds), fantasia, 1860; Gyász hangok Széchenyi István halálára [Funeral music for Széchenyi], 1860; Hódolat Kazinczy Ferenc szellemének [Homage to Kazinczy], 1860; Ünnepi zene [Festival music], 1860
Chamber: 7 str qts, D, g, a, f, c, b, before 1844; Ballade, vn, pf, 1841; Sextet, 2 vn, 2 va, 2 vc, 1844; Grand Nocturne, pf trio, 1845; Pf Trio (Vienna, 1851); Romance, vn, pf/str, 1861
Pf (2 hands unless otherwise stated): Grand Duo, 4 hands, 1837–8; 3 Klavierstücke, op.2 (Pest, 1855); 2 Perlen, op.3 (Pest, 1856); Pusztai élet [Puzsta life] (Pest, 1857); Magyar gyermekvilág [Hungarian children's world], i–iii (Pest, 1859); Hódolat Kazinczy Ferenc szellemének (Pest, 1859), arr. orch; Tanulmányok zongorára, a magyar zene elödásának képzésére [Studies for development in the performance of Hungarian music], i–iv (Pest, 1860); Magyar zeneköltemény [Hungarian musical poem] (Pest, 1860); Gyász hangok Széchenyi István halálára (Pest, 1860), arr. orch; Ünnepi zene, 4 hands (Pest, 1864), arr. orch; Variations on a theme of S. Elemy (Pest, 1863); Az égö szerelem hármas szine [Three colours of burning love], 4 hands (Pest, 1864); Bandérium induló [Band march] (Pest, 1867)
Numerous arrs., incl. Beethoven: Syms. 1–9, pf 4 hands (Pest, 1866); Liszt; Missa solemnis (Graner Messe), pf 4 hands (Pest, 1865); Rákóczi March, pf (Pest, 1863); Rouget de Lisle: Marseillaise, Bar, vv, orch, 1848; Schubert: Erlkönig, orch, 1853

#### BIBLIOGRAPHY

K. Ábrányi: *Mosony Mihály élet és jellemrajza* [Mosonyi, his biography and character] (Pest, 1872)
B. Fabó: 'Mosonyi Mihályról', *Zeneközlöny*, xiii (1915), 1
B. Bartók: 'Two Unpublished Liszt Letters to Mosonyi', *MQ*, vii (1921), 520
K. Isoz: 'Liszt Ferenc három kiadatlan levele Mosonyi Mihályhoz' [3 unpublished letters of Liszt to Mosonyi], *Magyar könyvszemle*, xxxiii (1926), 309
J. Káldor: *Michael Mosonyi* (Dresden, 1936)
I. Sonkoly: 'Mosonyi Mihály ismeretlen kéziratai' [Unkown Mosonyi manuscripts], *Zenei szemle*, v (1948), 264
B. Szabolcsi: *A XIX. század magyar romantikus zenéje* [Hungarian Romantic music of the 19th century] (Budapest, 1951)
F. Bónis: *Mosonyi Mihály* (Budapest, 1960)
——: 'Die ungarischen Opern Mihály Mosonyis', *SM*, ii (1962), 139–87
B. Szabolcsi: *A Concise History of Hungarian Music* (London, 2/1965; Hung. orig., 1947)
F. Bónis, ed.: *Magyar zenetörténeti tanulmányok Mosonyi Mihály és Bartók Béla emlékére* [Studies on the history of Hungarian music, in memory of Mosonyi and Bartók] (Budapest, 1973) [incl. biographical articles by F. Bónis, C. Landon, M. Gollowitzer, I. Lakatos and A. Valkó]
                                                      FERENC BÓNIS

**Moss** [Mosse], **John** (*fl* London, 1662–84). English composer, bass viol player and teacher. The first known reference to Moss is in the minutes of the Westminster Corporation of Music (*GB-Lbm* Harl.1911). In 1662 he repeatedly failed to answer a summons to appear before the corporation and was fined £3 for contempt. In 1669 he was apprehended for teaching music without a licence but must have mended his ways, for in July 1679 he was made an assistant to the corporation. In the meantime he had been teaching music at Christ's Hospital, at any rate in 1674 and 1675. On the recommendation of Lord Chief Justice North he became a member of the King's Private Musick in 1678, filling the vacancy caused by the death of John Jenkins. His name disappears from the royal music records after 1684.

According to John Playford, performance on the bass viol 'lyra way' had been 'much improved by the excellent Inventions and Skill' of Moss and others. Moss contributed suites (though this term is not used) in each of the four standard tunings to *Musick's Recreation*. *Lessons for the Base-Viol*, printed in tablature to be played 'lyra way' with the support of a thoroughbass instrument, comprises 26 suites intended as teaching pieces and arranged, as in many didactic works of the period, so as to take the pupil through 'all [the] Keys usually play'd on in the Scale'. The preface to the *Lessons*, addressed 'to his Present and Quondam Scholars', stresses that the music is not too difficult and observes that 'the commonest Instruments in use, as the *Violin*, and *Gittar* have far more difficult Stops than any that I have here made use of'. Nearly all of Moss's suites, including that for harpsichord in *Melothesia*, consist of four movements: Almain, Corant, Saraband and Jig-almain (a type of jig in slow quadruple time).

### WORKS

Jigg, hpd, in Musick's Hand-maide (London, 1663[7])
Prelude, 4 suites, in Musicks Recreation on the Viol, lyra way (London, 3/1669[9])
26 suites, in Lessons for the Base-Viol in the Common Tunings (London, 1671)
Suite in F, hpd, in Melothesia, ed. M. Locke (London, 1673[9])
Songs and catch in Select Ayres and Dialogues (London, 1669), The Musical Companion, ii (London, 1672[5]), New Ayres and Dialogues, ed. J. Banister and T. Low (London, 1678[4]), Choice Ayres and Songs, ii (London, 1679[7]); and song: Love's a blind passion (London, c1700)
Bass viol pieces in *GB-Lcm* II.F.10 and *Ob* Mus.Sch.F.572

### BIBLIOGRAPHY

*CSPD* (1678), 141
H. C. de Lafontaine: *The King's Musick* (London, 1909/R1973)
J. Pulver: *A Biographical Dictionary of Old English Music* (London, 1927)
S. Jeans: 'The Easter Psalms of Christ's Hospital', *PRMA*, lxxxviii (1961–2), 53

MICHAEL TILMOUTH

**Mossi, Giovanni** (*b* Rome, late 17th century; *d* ?Rome, mid-18th century). Italian composer and violinist. He was an outstanding pupil of Corelli. He seems to have travelled little, for his fame as a performer remained local, though his compositions, published at Amsterdam between 1716 and 1733, circulated widely. He was undoubtedly close to the Ottoboni family (whose patronage Corelli had enjoyed), and the dedication of his op.4 (c1720) would indicate that he was in the service of Princess Vittoria Altieri-Pallavicini.

Mossi's six published sets of instrumental music comprise 26 concertos and 36 sonatas. Confusion over opus numbering has arisen from the existence of a few examples of op.4 and op.6 incorrectly designated op.2 and op.3 respectively. Mossi's stylistic debt to Corelli is evident, though there is a tendency to first-violin prominence in his concertos once the writing ceases to be imitative or fugal. As in other neo-Corellian contemporaries (e.g. Dall'Abaco, G. M. Alberti), much of the ornamentation required in slow movements is written out by the composer. Although Mossi's surviving works

are exclusively for strings, a lively concern with sonority is found in one concerto, op.4 no.12, where four obbligato violin parts are complemented by the same number of ripieno parts. Reports of Mossi's music are without exception favourable, though no detailed study of it has yet appeared in print.

### WORKS
*(all printed sets published in Amsterdam)*

op.
1 [12] Sonate, vn, vle/hpd (1716)
2 VIII concerti, a 3 e a 5 (c1720)
3 VI concerti a 6 (c1720)
4 [12] concerti a 6 e 10 (c1726)
5 12 sonate o sinfonie, vn, vc (1727)
6 [12] Sonate da camera, vn, vc/hpd (1733)
Works by Mossi in VI concerts à 5 et 6 instruments par messieurs Mossi, Valentini et Vivaldi (Amsterdam, 1716), Six Solos or Sonatas for a Violin (London, c1750), A Third Collection for the Violin of the Newest English Airs and Minuets (Dublin, c1726)
Concerto a 2 violini concertati, *D-Dlb*

### BIBLIOGRAPHY

L. Torchi: 'La musica istrumentale in Italia', *RMI*, vi (1899), 284
——: *La musica istrumentale in Italia* (Turin, 1901)
K. Brückner: *Giovanni Mossi, seine Umwelt und seine Sonaten* (diss., U. of Munich, 1920)
A. Moser: *Geschichte des Violinspiels* (Berlin, 1923, rev., enlarged 2/1966–7)

MICHAEL TALBOT

**Mosso** (It.: 'agitated'; past participle of *muovere*, to move). A word that appears by itself as a tempo designation but is more often found in such contexts as *più mosso* (faster) and *meno mosso* (slower). *Allegro assai mosso* was normally the fastest tempo mark for Verdi.

*See also* TEMPO AND EXPRESSION MARKS.

DAVID FALLOWS

**Mostart [Mostaert], David** (*b* Amsterdam, c1560; *d* Amsterdam, 1615). Dutch schoolmaster, public official and amateur musician. He was first of all a school teacher, then public notary in Amsterdam. He revised the Datheen Psalter, the official psalter of the Dutch Reformed Church, by providing all the verses of a psalm with the melody. His work appeared as *De Psalmen Davids van P. Dathenus geheel op muzyk-noten* (Amsterdam, 1598); this edition seems to be lost, but the second edition (Amsterdam, 1614) is extant. He also wrote a short rhyming treatise on music, *Korte onderwysinghe van de musyk-konste* (Amsterdam, 1598), which is lost too; it was possibly part of the 1598 edition of the psalter. In it he proposed a solmization system for all seven notes in the octave.

### BIBLIOGRAPHY

J. C. Boers: 'David Mostart', *Bouwsteenen: JVNM*, i (1869–72), 25
J. I. Doedes: 'David Mostart', *Bouwsteenen: JVNM*, ii (1872–4), 111
D. F. Scheurleer: 'Het muziekleven van Amsterdam', *Amsterdam in de zeventiende eeuw*, iii (The Hague, 1904), 44, 80

RUDI A. RASCH

**Mosto, Francesco** (*b* Udine, probably before 1550; *d* after 1590). Italian instrumentalist, brother of Giovanni Battista Mosto. A son of the head of Udine's *piffari*, he was a cornett player and trombonist, together with his three brothers, at the Munich court in 1568; unlike them he did not return home after his father's death but remained in Bavaria until 1579. During that time he accompanied Lassus to Italy on searches for singers for the court. In 1581 he became one of the salaried players at St Mark's, Venice (he was appointed because he was a particularly fine player). It is not known how long he stayed there, but from 1587 to 1590 he was one of the trumpeters at the court at Graz, where he also seems to have carried on a flourishing trade selling instruments to other courts.

BIBLIOGRAPHY
H. Federhofer: *Musikpflege und Musiker am Grazer Habsburgerhof der Erzherzöge Karl und Ferdinand von Innerösterreich (1564–1619)* (Mainz, 1967)

DENIS ARNOLD

**Mosto, Giovanni Battista** (*b* Udine, probably before 1550; *d* Karlsburg [now Alba Iulia], June 1596). Italian instrumentalist and composer, brother of Francesco Mosto. He was a son of the head of the *piffari* at Udine and studied with Claudio Merulo. He was employed by the Bavarian court at Munich in 1568 as a cornettist and trombonist; he left the following year with his brothers Nicolò and Bernardo. In 1570, following his father's death, he was made one of the *piffari* of Udine, sharing his father's stipend with Nicolò. He was given a rise in pay in 1573 for assuming additional duties in the cathedral, but by the end of that year he had left Udine, probably to return to Munich, where he was employed in the later 1570s. In November 1580 he became *maestro di cappella* at Padua Cathedral. Though he was an energetic director he was for some reason not re-elected to his post in 1589 and went into the service of Prince Sigismond Báthory of Transylvania. He remained with him until 1595, when he returned to Padua to be once again appointed *maestro di cappella* at the cathedral. In the following year he returned to Transylvania to collect his family and possessions but died shortly after leaving for Italy.

Mosto was a competent composer of madrigals, contributing to many of the major anthologies of the later 16th century as well as publishing four volumes of his own music; his contribution to *De floridi virtuosi d'Italia, il primo libro de madrigali* (2/1586) was reprinted by Thomas Morley in his *Madrigals to 5 Voyces: Celected out of the Best Approved Italian Authors* (London, 1598). In style he belonged to the Venetian school and approached Andrea Gabrieli in his manipulation of short, pleasant, singable phrases and in his bright diatonic harmony.

WORKS
Il primo libro de madrigali, 5vv (Venice, 1578)
Il secondo libro de madrigali, 5vv (Venice, 1584)
Il terzo libro de madrigali, 5vv (Venice, 1588)
Il primo libro de madrigali, 6vv (Venice, 1595)
Madrigals in 1577[7], 1579[2], 1582[5], 1583[14], 1584[4], 1585[10], 1586[1], 1586[8], 1586[11], 1587[7], 1590[15], 1591[10], 1593[3], 1594[6], 1598[2], 1598[15], 1605[9]

BIBLIOGRAPHY
G. Vale: 'La cappella musicale del duomo di Udine', *NA*, vii (1930), 118
E. Haraszti: 'S. Báthory, Prince de Transylvanie et la musique italienne', *RdM*, xii (1931), 190
R. Casimiri: 'Musica e musicisti nella cattedrale di Padova nei sec. XIV, XV, XVI', *NA*, xviii (1941), 113
A. Garbelotto: 'Codici musicali della Biblioteca capitolare di Padova', *RMI*, liv (1952), 306
W. Boetticher: *Orlando di Lasso und seine Zeit* (Kassel and Basle, 1958)
E. Zottoviceanu: 'Nouvelles données sur Giovanni Battista Mosto et ses relations avec la Transylvanie', *Musica antiqua Europae orientalis IV: Bydgoszcz 1975*, 369
H. Leuchtmann: *Orlando di Lasso, i: Sein Leben* (Wiesbaden, 1976), 155, 158

DENIS ARNOLD

**Mostras, Konstantin (Georgiyevich)** (*b* Ardzhenka, 16 April 1886; *d* Moscow, 6 Sept 1965). Russian violinist, teacher and composer. He studied the violin with Boris Sibor at the Moscow Philharmonic School of Music and Drama until 1914, and taught there himself (1914–22). During this period he performed in quartets and other ensembles. From 1922 he taught the violin at the Moscow Conservatory where he became head of the violin department and where in 1931 he introduced his own course on violin technique. From 1922 to 1932 he was also one of the organizers and directors of Persimfans, the first conductorless symphony orchestra. But his chief importance was in the teaching activities that played a significant role in the development of a Soviet violin school. Among his pupils were Ivan Galamian (who later won fame as a teacher in New York), Mikhail Terian and Marine Yashvili. He wrote and edited numerous instructional works and transcriptions for the violin, including *Pedagogicheskiy repertuar dlya skripki i fortep'yano* ('A pedagogic repertory for violin and piano'; nine collections of pieces in collaboration with I. M. Yampol'sky, 1939–40), and in collaboration with David Oistrakh an edition of Tchaikovsky's Violin Concerto with a commentary on technique (Moscow, 1947). His compositions include studies for violin solo, and his writings on violin technique are of great value. He was made Doctor of Arts (1941), and Honoured Art Worker of the RSFSR (1937).

WRITINGS
*Intonatsiya na skripke* [Intonation on the violin] (Moscow and Leningrad, 1947, 2/1963)
*Ritmicheskaya distsiplina skripacha* [The rhythmical discipline of the violinist] (Moscow, 1951)
*Dinamika v skripichnom iskusstve* [The dynamics of the art of violin playing] (Moscow, 1956)
*Sistema domashnikh zanyatiy skripacha* [A system of home studies for the violinist] (Moscow, 1956)
*Metodicheskiy kommentariy k 24 kaprisam dlya skripki solo N. Paganini* [A technical commentary on Paganini's 24 Caprices for violin solo] (Moscow, 1959)

I. M. YAMPOL'SKY

**Moszkowski, Moritz** (*b* Breslau, 23 Aug 1854; *d* Paris, 4 March 1925). German pianist and composer of Polish descent. He studied first at Dresden, then in Berlin with Wüerst and Kullak. He settled in Berlin and taught the piano at Kullak's academy for many years, although he also toured extensively as a pianist. He appeared in London at the Philharmonic concerts in 1886, and was frequently heard in England later, both as pianist and conductor; as a composer he had much success with several light works. He retired to Paris in 1897 and was elected a member of the Berlin Academy in 1899.

Moszkowski's most popular works were the two books of piano duets, *Spanische Tänze* op.12, also arranged for solo piano as the demand for them grew; these are marked by a superficial picturesqueness which, if not genuinely Spanish, is at least sufficiently exotic. Later he tried to reproduce the music of other countries in the orchestral suite *Aus aller Herren Ländern* op.23, but he was still regarded chiefly as an interpreter of Spain. It was perhaps for this reason that he tried his hand at an opera on a Hispanic-Moorish subject, *Boabdil, der letzte Maurenkönig*, modelled on Meyerbeerian grand opera. It was produced in Berlin on 21 April 1892, but, though given in Prague and New York (in English) the following year, it was not widely successful and soon disappeared from the stage. Its ballet music, however, similar in style to the earlier *Spanische Tänze*, long remained in concert programmes. A three-act ballet, *Laurin*, followed in 1896. Well written and highly effective, Moszkowski's lighter music had a legitimate place in its time; the more serious large-scale works, although competently turned out, had little originality or vitality. His brother Alexander (1851–1934) was a writer on music.

WORKS
Stage: Boabdil, der letzte Maurenkönig (opera, 3, C. Wittkowsky), Berlin, 21 April 1892; Laurin (ballet), 1896; Don Juan und Faust (incidental music, Grabbe)

Orch: Serenata, op.15; Jeanne d'Arc, sym. poem, op.19; Aus aller Herren Ländern, suite, op.23; Vn Conc., C, op.30; 2 orch suites, opp.39, 47; Pf Conc., E, op.59; Phantastischer Zug

Chamber: 3 Pieces, vc, pf, op.29; Scherzo, vn, pf; 2 Concertstücke, vn, pf

For pf: Spanische Tänze, op.12; 3 Concert Studies, op.24; Barcarolle, op.27; Miniatures, op.28; Suite, op.50

BIBLIOGRAPHY
A. C. Kalischer: 'Moszkowski als Opernkomponist', *Nord und Süd*, lxii (1892), 26
R. Sietz: 'Moritz Moszkowski', *MGG*
                                    J. A. FULLER MAITLAND/R

**Moszumańska-Nazar, Krystyna** (*b* Lwów, 5 Sept 1924). Polish composer. She studied composition with Wiechowicz and the piano with Hoffman at the Kraków Conservatory, where she returned as lecturer. Her best works deploy advanced techniques in music of clear form and rhythm. The *Musica per archi* won a gold medal in Buenos Aires, and *Hexaèdre* received an honourable mention in the International Competition of Women Composers at Mannheim in 1961.

WORKS
(*selective list*)

Orch: Pf Concertino, 1954; Allegro symphonique, 1957; Hexaèdre, 1960; Musica per archi, 1962; Exodus, orch, tape, 1964; Variazioni concertanti, fl, chamber orch, 1966; Pour orchestre, 1969

Other: Interpretations, fl, perc, tape, 1967; 3 Concert Studies, perc, 1970; 9 Bagatelles, pf, 1972; Bel canto, S, cel, perc, 1972; Str Qt, 1973–4; From End to End, 2 perc, 1976

Principal publisher: Polskie Wydawnictwo Muzyczne

BIBLIOGRAPHY
H. Schiller: '"Muzyka na smyczki" Krystyny Moszumańskiej-Nazarowej', *Ruch muzyczny* (1963), no.22, p.13
                                MIECZYSŁAWA HANUSZEWSKA

**Mota, José Viana da.** *See* VIANNA DA MOTTA, JOSÉ.

**Motellus** (Lat.). MOTET; *see also* MOTETUS.

**Moten, Bennie** [Benjamin] (*b* Kansas City, Missouri, 13 Nov 1894; *d* Kansas City, 1935). Black American jazz pianist and band-leader. He studied the piano with two of Scott Joplin's pupils and began working professionally in 1918 as leader of a ragtime trio. By 1922 his group had expanded to six members, and in the next year they issued their first recordings, playing mostly blues with a heavy, 'stomping' beat. Within ten years Moten's ensemble included among its members such outstanding performers as Walter and 'Hot Lips' Page, Eddie Durham, Ben Webster, Buster Smith, Count Basie and the blues singer Jimmy Rushing, and had largely established the 'Southwestern' or 'Kansas City' style of orchestral jazz. This style – based on a four-beat bar, flexible rhythm section, frequent blues devices and advanced arrangements (by Durham, Basie and Eddie Barefield) with orchestral riffs – is well represented in a series of ten performances from the group's final recording session in 1932, the finest of these being *Moten's Swing*, *Toby*, *Prince of Wales* and *Lafayette*. On Moten's death his group was led jointly for a short while by Basie and Moten's brother 'Buster' (Ira) Moten, and from 1936 its personnel and style went on, through the Count Basie Orchestra, to become an important force in 'swing' big band music, and a formative influence on bop and modern jazz.

BIBLIOGRAPHY
F. Driggs: 'Kansas City and the South West', *Jazz*, ed. N. Hentoff (New York, 1959), 189–231
G. Schuller: *Early Jazz* (New York, 1968), 283ff
A. McCarthy: *Big Band Jazz* (London, 1974), 33ff
                                        GUNTHER SCHULLER

**Motet.** One of the most important forms of polyphonic music from about 1220 to 1750. No single set of char-

acteristics serves to define it generally, except in particular historical or regional contexts. It originated as a liturgical trope but soon developed into the pre-eminent form of secular art music during the late Middle Ages. The medieval motet was a polyphonic composition in which the fundamental voice (tenor) was usually arranged in a pattern of reiterated rhythmic configurations, while the upper voice or voices (up to three), nearly always with different Latin or French texts, generally moved at a faster rate. In the first half of the 15th century the motet's liturgical ties were restored, and it continued to evolve by adapting a number of forms and styles borrowed in part from the chanson, tenor mass and, later, the madrigal. In the 16th century the motet achieved its classical synthesis in the context of the Franco-Netherlands style of Josquin and his successors. Important vernacular sub-species developed later, particularly in England (*see* ANTHEM, §I) and Germany, but the motet has since been defined as a sacred polyphonic composition with Latin text, which may or may not have *colla voce* or independent instrumental accompaniment.

I. Medieval. II. Renaissance. III. Baroque. IV. After 1750.

### *I. Medieval*

1. Ars Antiqua. 2. England. 3. Ars Nova.

1. ARS ANTIQUA. The history of the medieval motet is rooted in the organa of Léonin's *Magnus liber*, specifically, in their discant sections, in their modernizations by Pérotin, and in the clausulas, which originated as detached discant sections and thereafter developed into a distinct genre of self-contained and independently shaped pieces of music based on Gregorian melismas (*see* DISCANT and CLAUSULA). Consistent with the traditions of *prosa* and prosula, as well as the general medieval concept of the consanguinity of music and poetry, the motet came into being with the application of a poetic text to the duplum of the clausula. (Figs.1–2, p.622, show the clausula *Johanne* and the motet derived from it by addition of the text 'Clamans in deserto' to the upper voice.) By and large, clausulas seem to have been predestined to be wedded to appropriate verses; the resulting pieces were called 'motelli' (from Fr. *mot*: 'word'), a term that soon gave way to 'moteti'. A possible reason why it was necessary at first to trope pre-existing clausulas in order to compose motets involves a notational problem: the graphic fixation of durational values originated in melismatic discant, and the conception of rhythm in polyphony was configurational (ligatures). For several decades the 13th century possessed no system of individual notational symbols with which to express rhythms in music *cum littera*, such as the upper voices of motets. Under these circumstances it seems difficult to imagine the composition or the rehearsal of a motet without the aid of a melismatic model. The marginal indications of the beginnings of motetus texts for the clausulas in the St Victor manuscript (*F-Pn* lat.15139) may be cited in this connection. Moreover, the only time Johannes de Garlandia cited both words and music of a certain motetus part, he wrote the example in ligature notation *sine littera*. Evidently the clausulas were a pivotal phenomenon; their use as substitutes for old-fashioned passages in pre-existing organa points to the past, but their adaptation as motets explains their continued cultivation. A good many are not known as motets and were probably not equipped with a text. Yet, on the whole, clausulas with patterned

Ex.1

[No - - - - strum est im-ple-tum gau-di-um per a - zi-mum sit a - ni-mum pa-scha___ le - tum,

No - - - - strum est im-ple-tum gau-di-um per a - zi-mum sit a - ni-mum pa-scha le - tum,

No - - - - strum

le - to le - tum est de - le - tum ex - u - lat ex - i - li-um post tri - du - um    ces-sat va - cu-um tu-um mors

le - to le - tum est de - le - tum ex - u - lat ex - i - li-um post tri - du - um    ces-sat va - cu-um tu-um mors

de - cre - tum,    am - ple-xa - tur par - vu-lum dat o - scu-lum dat a - nu-lum pa-ter et vi - tu-lum,

de - cre - tum,    am - ple-xa - tur par - vu-lum dat o - scu-lum dat a - nu-lum pa-ter et vi - tu-lum,

o   quam dul - ce fer - cu-lum in a - ra cru-cis tor - ri-dum,    a___ quo flu - it sa - pi-dum

o   quam dul - ce fer - cu-lum in a - ra cru-cis tor - ri-dum,    a   quo flu - it sa - pi-dum___

cru - or po - cu - lum    no - - - strum.]

cru - or po - cu - lum    no - - - strum.

tenors doubtless came to be viewed as potential motets. The earliest of these 'troped discant passages' and 'troped clausulas' derived the manner of applying poetry to the upper voice or voices from the troped organa. With the added trope-like text for the upper voices, the passage shown in ex.1, separated from the Pérotinian organum triplum *Alleluia, Pascha nostrum*, is a motet; without it, it would be a clausula.

The musical phraseology of most clausulas and Notre Dame motets, while carefully planned, exhibits no regularity. The structure of ex.1, made up of phrases of four, eight and 12 beats, could be summarized as follows: *upper voices* (8 + 12L) + 2(12 + 8L) + 3(4L), *tenor* 9(4 + 4L), if L stands for a long or its equivalents. Since the versification has to accord with the musical

phrases of the pre-conceived clausula (or discant section), it cannot be regular. Irregularity of verse structure thus became a hallmark of the 13th-century motet, as the primary measuring tool was the pre-conceived music with its varied phrase layout.

On the other hand, the poetry also affected the music. A decisive result of the adaptation of text to clausulas concerns the weight and articulation of the notes. A comparison of any motet with the ligature notation of the melismatic original shows how the propulsive flow of the melismatic phrases is profoundly affected by the declamatory individualization of each note. The words often convert the iambic (upbeat–downbeat) implications of the binary ligatures into truly trochaic rhythms (strong beat–weak beat).

Finally, ex.1 demonstrates another Pérotinian innovation. The Gregorian melisma is repeated (see I and II in ex.1), causing a rhythmic redistribution of its pitch content in the second statement. The purpose of this device is obviously a more expansively shaped superstructure. Tenor repetition, often involving more than two statements as well as rhythmic redistributions, soon developed into a favourite compositional procedure. Another device that began to appear is the application of two different tenor patterns to two successive statements of one plainchant melisma.

In ex.1 the duplum and triplum have parallel phrasing and can therefore deliver the added text like two voices of a polyphonic conductus. Such motets (for three voices) are therefore commonly referred to as conductus motets in modern commentaries. However, a good number of clausulas began to free the duplum phrases from their dependence on the tenor; some of them overlap the tenor patterns. For composers of the time the potential complexity of phrase structure in clausulas for more than two voices was an adventurous challenge. But the device of staggered phrases also wreaks havoc with the procedure of turning three-voice clausulas into conductus motets. Since any attempt at such a conversion would necessarily entail more or less extensive adjustments in the music, it is understandable that only very few such pieces were made into conductus motets.

In the case of many a conductus motet appearing in more than one source, the various versions of the tenor and duplum agree, since they are generally based on a two-part clausula, while those of the subsequently added triplum usually vary. This feature shows up the fundamental cleavage between conductus and motet. In the former, the text governs the tenor and all superimposed voices, binding the parts together. A polyphonic conductus is a setting of poetry, in which the chief function of music is rather comparable to manuscript illumina-

tion; the upper voices decorate the tune, which jointly with them decorates the text. The motet lacks the unifying bond of one text; it is not poetry set to music. Both textually and musically tenor and duplum are two distinct entities. From the beginning of its existence the motet aimed for individualization of its voices, and the conductus motet therefore remained a transitional phenomenon. To make a motet out of a three-part clausula with overlapping phrases in duplum and triplum was at first simply inconceivable, and the triplum was therefore dropped. Apart from the conductus motets, almost all the motets in the earliest sources (*I-Fl* Plut.29.1, *D-W* Helmstedt 1099 (Heinemann catalogue 1206) [W2], *Mbs* Mus.ms.4775, *E-Mn* 20486; *see* SOURCES, MS, §III–VI) are for tenor and duplum only, as are most clausulas. The motet at first had to abandon composition for three or four parts as it came to grips with the problems posed by the genre.

The triplum received definition as soon as it was animated by a text of its own with independent rhyme scheme and versification. The 'double motet', that is, the motet with two different texts for duplum and triplum, is a rigorously logical concept of marvellous daring. (Not until the operatic ensemble of Mozart's time did polytextuality again appear as a compositional principle.) Of the 69 motets in *I-Fl* 29.1, the earliest major source to transmit such compositions, only three are double motets. It is all the more astonishing that one of these (875), in combining three voices whose differentiation extends not only to the texts, but also to the music, already fully realizes the potential of the genre, which might be described as the joining of diverse entities (ex.2). The poem of the duplum praises the deeds of the dedicated clerics, while the triplum castigates the 'hypocritical pseudo-bishops, vile slayers of the church'. The tenor, which originated as a two-part clausula, proceeds in longs and double longs, the duplum in longs and

Ex.2

breves, and the newly added triplum almost exclusively in breves. Moreover, the voices, like those of most other medieval double motets, are differentiated in their phrase structure: almost all the phrases of the duplum are four or six beats long, while the phrase structure of the lively triplum is more varied; its first half is ordered as follows: 2(4L) + 5L + 2(4L) + 1L + 2(2L) + 6L + 4L + 3L + 6L + 5(5L). It is possible to view this arrangement as consisting of three sections (22, 23 and 25 beats), with the phrases proceeding mainly in fours, sixes and fives respectively.

It is the epoch-making achievement of Pérotin and his generation to have added to the traditional numerical order of music, as embodied in the consonant intervals, the numerically founded arrangement of durational values, as embodied in rhythm and the coordination of phrases. A well-made 13th-century motet, then, is a concise tonal, temporal and poetic form, whose superstructure, erected on the staked-out notes of the cantus firmus, is designed proportionally to unfold, demonstrate and articulate the fundamental numerical theme given by the tenor. The motet is a polyphony of tones, of texts and of interrelated numbers governing rhythms and phrase structure. Such structures are not accompanied songs or duets that 'express' their texts. The role of poetry in a medieval motet is best defined by analogy with the stained-glass windows in a Gothic church. The poetic images in the upper voices relate to the music in the same way as do the historiated windows to the structure of which they are components. The music does not accompany, elucidate or intensify; rather, the poetry illuminates and coordinately reflects the structure of the music.

The three most important developments affecting the motet in the first two decades of the 13th century were the loosening of tenor rhythms, the formulation of the system of rhythmic modes and the introduction of the vernacular. The earliest tenor patterns containing breves seem like diminutions of their predecessors (ex.3). But

Ex.3
(a)

soon composers took to writing clausulas and motets with lively and increasingly varied tenor patterns, including the new rhythms codified in the system of rhythmic modes. While these rhythmic innovations might still be ascribed to Pérotin, the introduction of the vernacular into motet polyphony was a step he evidently did not cultivate. Just as the polyphonic *musica mensurata* had for the first time furnished a reliable musical yardstick with which to measure Latin poetry, the musical setting of French poems was now also drawn into its orbit. (Figs.3–4, pp.622–3, show the motet of fig.2 with substitution of the vernacular text 'Ne sai que ie die' in the upper voice.) The intrusion of French poetry into cantus firmus polyphony must have occurred very soon after the development of the modal system.

The appearance of the French language and of the rhythms of the 2nd mode seem to have been corollary

phenomena, for the 'iambic' mode is more commonly associated with French than with Latin texts. French motets rapidly became more prominent than those with Latin poetry, and few of the French texts maintained a trope-like relationship with the cantus firmus. The dwindling topical connection with the chant is specially well demonstrated by the occasional practice of combining a French triplum (contrafactum or original) with a Latin motetus, thereby adding another element to the individualization of the upper voices. But even a good many poems in the Latin motets either retain only a topical connection with the text of the cantus firmus, while giving up the assonances characteristic of troped organa and troped clausulas, or else depart altogether from the tenor's words and their connotations. Other motets, Latin as well as French, continued to cultivate assonance with the tenor label, but rather than reflecting liturgical necessity the device now betokened poetic ingenuity and delight in punning (e.g. *Maniere esgarder/ Manere*).

Latin motets predominantly concern the Virgin Mary. Less common topics that crop up more and more rarely deal with liturgical occasions in the Temporale or Sanctorale or with moral exhortation. Most French motet poems deal with love – courtly, urban or pastoral. A few other texts reflect the convivial life in the city (i.e. Paris); the rest are either Marian or hortatory. The earliest motets, such as *Nostrum* (ex.1), were still closely related to the genre of troped organa and may have been used within their appropriate organa, but there is no question that, on gaining musical independence, clausula and motet (Latin as well as French) soon shed their umbilical connection with church and liturgy. Liturgical ordering of motets, still observed in the first of the two motet fascicles in *I-Fl* 29.1 and in *D-Mbs* Mus.ms.4775, is

Ex.4
(a) *F-MO* H 196, no.192

(b) *F-MO* H 196, no.219

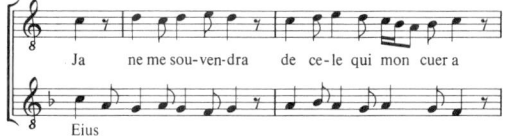

given up in the second motet fascicle of *I-Fl* 29.1 and is replaced by alphabetical arrangement in *D-W* Helmstedt 1099 (Heinemann catalogue 1206) [W2]. Evidently, motets became mostly pieces of clerical and aristocratic chamber music, whose patterned Gregorian tenors are likely to have been performed instrumentally.

The enormous vogue for French motets for two voices – often, like many French double motets, incorporating refrains from song literature – seems to have been in full swing by about 1230 and continued for most of the century. They bespeak the far-reaching secularization of the genre. Their tenors do not favour the traditional slow, steady patterns, but tend to approximate the rhythmic quality of the motetus. No other type of motet shows a comparable decline in the old-fashioned tenors without breves; in fact, it seems as though for much of the century the motet frequently was on the point of transforming itself into another genre, the polyphonic song (exx.4a–b).

Since a motet could be viewed as a song accompanied by a tenor (often exhibiting patterns of a liveliness commensurate with the motetus), it was only one step further to treat the motetus as an unaccompanied song. There are numerous cases of motets appearing in certain sources without tenors or with tenors notated in so corrupt and useless a manner as to indicate complete lack of comprehension and sympathy on the part of the scribe. Presumably the motetus parts in these sources were then performed freely, like trouvère songs. These developments often caused a corrosion of the integrity of the cantus firmus in the process of composition; changes in structure and pitch content in deference to the upper voice are by no means uncommon. Particularly striking are motetus parts that quote chanson refrains (including the *motets entés*, in which new text and music are added or 'grafted' between parts of one refrain) and motets with upper voices shaped like rondeaux; necessarily the tenors are often unpatterned or irregularly shaped, and in the cases of rondeau motets they are bent to fit the form of the motetus with its reiterations and recurrences of phrases. (The main sources of such motets are *F-Pn* fr.12615, fr.884 and fr.845.)

The type of motet that occasioned the break with the tradition and repertory of Notre Dame was the French double motet, which became increasingly prominent during the second half of the century (main sources: *F-Pn* n.a.fr.13521, *MO* H196, *D-BAs* Lit.115). (Fig.5 below shows a French double motet which derives from that of figs.3–4 by addition of a triplum with the text 'Quant vient en mai'.) A marginal development that was destined to remain largely unsuccessful was the attempt to revive four-part writing by combining three separately texted voices over a tenor. In most of these 'triple motets' the quadruplum was added to a pre-existing double motet, generally with dubious contrapuntal success and often, as in the case of many double motets, without any regard for topical correlation of the poems. It is in the French double motets, however, that the next phases in the evolution of the species occurred. The very rhythm that had engendered the modal system proved to be its undoing, since it was the long in the 2nd mode that had a marked tendency towards subdivision. Moreover, 6th-mode tripla, some of which halved several of the breves not only melismatically but even syllabically, became quite common. The increasing subdivision of the breve and the consequent lengthening

Ex.5

(a) *F-Pn* lat. 11266, no. 6

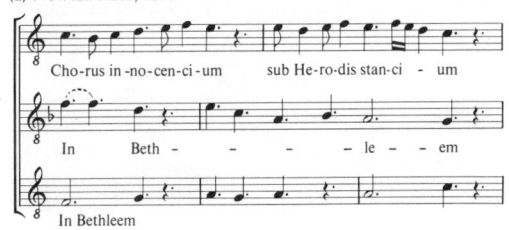

Cho-rus in -no-cen-ci-um sub He-ro-dis stan-ci - um

In Beth – – – le – – em

In Bethleem

(b) *D-Mbs* Clm. 14523, f. 154*r*

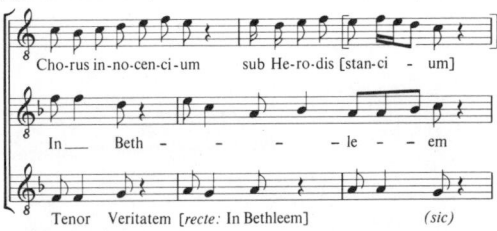

Cho-rus in-no-cen-ci-um sub He-ro-dis [stan-ci – um]

In___ Beth – – – le – – em

Tenor Veritatem [*recte:* In Bethleem] (*sic*)

Ex.6 *D-BAs* lit. 115, no. 36

Po – vre se-cours ai en-co-re re – co-vré

Gau-de cho-rus___ om – ni – um fi –

Angelus

a ma da-me que i'a-voi-e ser – vi a sa vo – lon-té

- de – li – – um ro – sa___ fra – grans___

of long and breve caused some motets originally composed in relatively slow modes (e.g. 3rd and 5th; ex.5a) to be converted to faster rhythms (e.g. 6th and 2nd; ex.5b). But in effect the frequent association of a 2nd-mode motetus, with more than half its longs dissolved into ornaments, and a 6th-mode triplum reduced modality to little more than a residual code that hardly reflected the musical actuality (ex.6). In fact, this deceleration of long and breve helped to condition musical hearing to such an extent as to affect the performance of organa, since both Franco of Cologne and Anonymous IV recommended that in organal passages the tenor adjust itself to dissonances by resting or subtly detouring to a more consonant note.

The dissolution of the modal system, which was a result of the proliferation of shorter note values and of the increasing, at times nearly prose-like, prolixity of the French texts of the tripla, produced the notational reforms codified by Franco of Cologne. The notational individualization of rhythmic values further undermined modal rhythm. The mingling of rhythms appropriate to the 'inconsistent' 1st and 2nd modes, which formerly occurred only in some cases of refrain citation, now

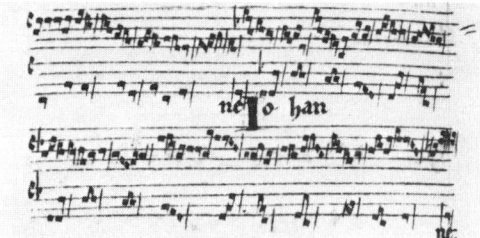

1. *I-Fl Plut. 29.1, f.164v: clausula 'Johanne' (from 'Alleluia, Inter natos'; Flotzinger no.Cl.2148)*

2. *I-Fl Plut. 29.1, f.409v: two-voice motet 'Clamans in deserto/Johanne'*

3. *D-W Helmstedt 1099 (Heinemann catalogue 1206) [W2], f.219av: French contrafactum, 'Ne sai que ie die/Johanne', of fig.2*

became possible. In view of the ternary organization of rhythm, however, motets with duple rhythm (i.e. binary subdivision of the long) were still exceedingly rare.

In the Franconian motet style – a generic stylistic term, since Franco's authorship is not established for any specific composition – the natural, more or less foursquare and dance-like swing of the modal phrases gave way to a more complicated phrase structure, whose relatively complex rhythms are defined by the underlying inescapable regularity of the neutral beats of the breves. A modal phrase in a Notre Dame composition is generally a rhythmically homogeneous, indivisible whole, but a phrase in a Franconian motet contains a chain of any number of perfections, the number being determined by the composer. A new way of measuring time by mechanical units impinged on organic time as experienced. Significantly, the appearance of this new style coincided with the invention of the mechanical clock, which from the later 13th century gradually displaced the older clock types (operating with water or sand) and the sundial.

It was at this time (the second half of the 13th century) that Notre Dame ceased to be both model and leader in music. With the advent of the new notational system, clausulas were no longer necessary and ceased to be written. Chants other than the traditional Gregorian melismas began to appear as motet tenors. Fewer and fewer concordances or contrafacta of Notre Dame compositions are found. The enormous inter-

national dissemination of Notre Dame motets (Spain, England, Italy, Germany) and their endless adaptations (new texts, new tripla etc) not only betokens their popularity in educated circles but also reveals them as a kind of ready-made proving ground for the study and practice of motet techniques. Towards the end of the 13th century this communal aspect of art music gave way to a situation where individual compositions were no longer subject to remodelling. The disappearance of notational ambiguity made each composition a finished product.

One of the trends that developed in the late 13th century was the so-called Petronian motet style, motets by or exhibiting the characteristic compositional technique of Petrus de Cruce (sources: *F-MO* H196 and *I-Tr* Vari 42). A second major type shares with the Petronian motet its cultivation of French poetry and, insofar as it is already prominently represented among the motets for two voices, its tendency towards accompanied-song texture. In contrast to the Petronian style, however, the tenor of this type is lively, at times to the point where its patterns are no longer modal but approximate the rhythm of the upper voices. Some cantus firmi are so closely adapted to the design of the motetus as to include semibreves or hocket passages (e.g. *F-MO* H196, no.294). Furthermore, the dissolution of the modal system enabled composers to introduce secular cantus firmi (refrain songs, dance-tunes, street cries), invariably retaining their original rhythms and shapes.

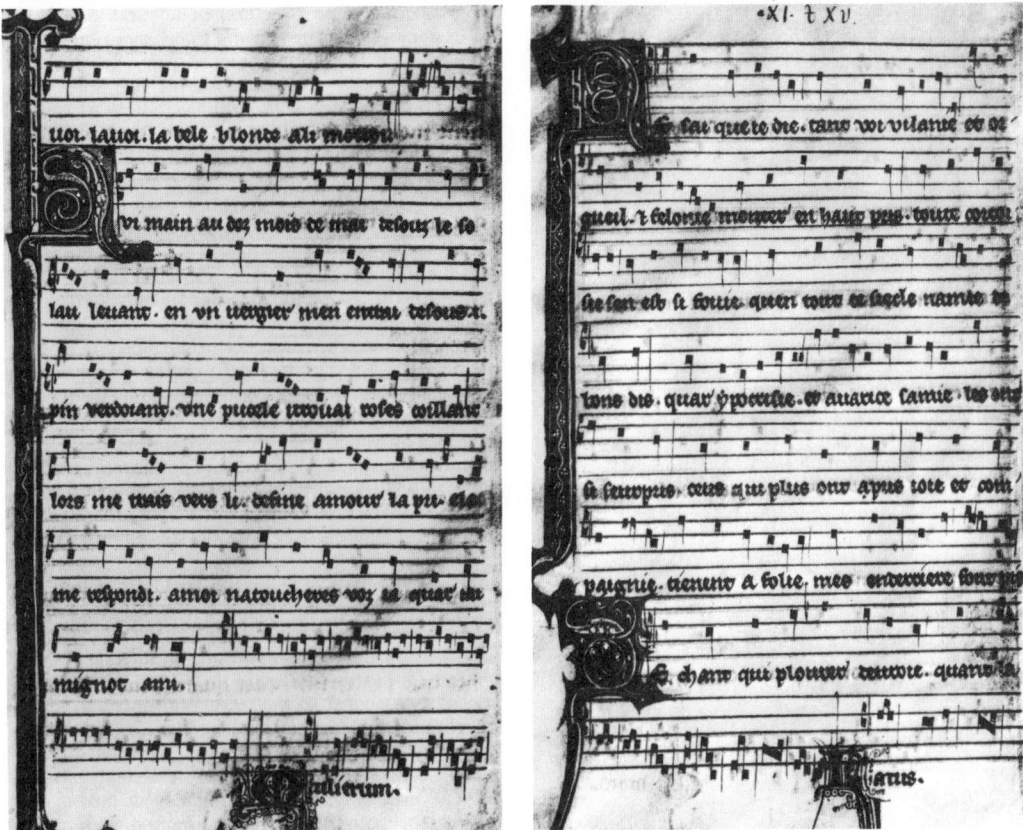

4. *F-MO H196, ff.234v* (*final staff, left*)*–235r: fig.3* (*with tenor erroneously designated 'Mulierum'*) *in a more advanced notation*

An additional sub-species was the Latin double motet, which seems to have led an existence mainly apart from the prominent Parisian tradition. As a more or less distinct type it evidently branched off early in the 13th century from the Pérotinian conductus motet; its manuscript distribution (mainly *D-BAs* Lit.115, *DS* 3471 and *E-BUlh*) indicates that it was cultivated particularly in areas peripheral to central France. Generally, motets of this type exhibit a continuing affinity with the conductus. Their texts retain a traditional trope relationship to the cantus firmus and are therefore topically affiliated to each other. In fact, several examples betray an attitude that bypasses the clausula and recalls the troped organum, since they elaborate Gregorian melodies which usually do not belong to the specialized clausula repertory. A further frequent characteristic is perspicuity of form, often delineated by partial isomelic or, more rarely, isorhythmic correspondences and, in a number of cases, by melismatic caudas. The simpler compositions exhibit uncomplicated phrase designs, with the upper voices either declaiming their related texts homorhythmically or mutually alternating syllabic and melismatic passages. But many apparently peripheral works exhibit a fine concern for elegant phrase structure, often supported by unusual cantus firmi that were evidently selected for their conciseness or their patently repetitive design. For example, *F-MO* H196, no.49 imaginatively articulates its overall length of 60 longs as follows: *triplum* 5(8L) + 4L + 2(8L),

*motetus* 6(7L) + 2(9L), *tenor* 10(2 + 4L).

In the consonant flow of its voices, regulated by good melodic design and proper counterpoint, and in the measured disposition of its elements and structural members, the 13th-century motet is an aural manifestation of numerical 'musical' proportions. Just as architecture was regarded in the Middle Ages as a visual demonstration of musical proportions, music (i.e. measured discant) was by the end of the 13th century described (by Johannes de Grocheo) in architectural terms: 'The tenor, however, is that part upon which all others are founded, just as the parts of a house or building are erected upon its fundament. It is their yardstick and gives them quantity'. Visual evidence of this view of the motet may be seen in the way its voice parts were written in manuscripts after the mid-13th century: triplum either on the left half of a page or on the verso of a folio; duplum on the right half of a page or on the recto facing the triplum; tenor under both voices on the bottom of the page, with the appropriate Gregorian word or words placed like a label below its initial notes. In the earliest manuscripts, the voices are notated successively, often continuing from the recto of a folio to its verso. Thus, motets at first could not be performed from the book. Evidently the advances of the Franconian era account for the new arrangement, since the rhythmically unambiguous Franconian notation of music *cum littera* (chiefly the motet) made sight-reading possible. The growth of this skill, for which some evidence begins

5. *D-BAs Lit.115, f.44v: double motet 'Quant vient en mai/Ne sai que ie die/Johanne' (but with tenor, of which only the opening is shown, erroneously designated 'Amoris') in Aristotelian notation (left-hand column staves 5–9, and right-hand column)*

to crop up in the early 14th century, may therefore be said to be due to the development of the motet in the preceding decades. (Figs.1–5 show the development of a two-voice clausula into a two-voice Latin motet, a two-voice French motet in earlier and later notational forms, and a French double motet.)

2. ENGLAND. Cantus firmus motets were quite rare in England, but works that look and act like motets and were apparently referred to as such were composed in great numbers. They differ from their continental counterparts in that the upper voices – nearly always two – are based on a *pes*, which in many cases supports voice exchange. In contrast to the tradition launched by the continental clausula motet, which is texted music, an English *pes* motet generally makes the impression of a musical setting of poetry.

Instead of the double-versicle structure necessary for *pedes* supporting voice exchange, the *pes* in many motets consists of only one melodic element, stated more than twice and thus producing a melodic ostinato or ground, over which the upper voices unfold without voice exchange. Sometimes such a *pes* was a well-known tune, such as a snatch of a popular song, a refrain or a dance phrase (ex.7). Many such *pes* motets exhibit

sophisticated phrase structures of admirable elegance, for example *Te domine laudat/Te dominum clamat (GB-Ob 20, no.71; for facsimile see* WORCESTER POLYPHONY), whose *pes* consists of five statements, the last incomplete: *triplum* [2(8L) + 2(10 + 8L) + 8L] + [10L + 2(10 + 8L) + 14L] + 10L + 8L, *duplum* [(2 + 8L) + 2(10 + 8L) + 14L] + [2(8L) + 2(10 + 8L) + 8L] + 8L + 10L, *pes* 4[5(6L)] + 3(6L). Each upper voice therefore consists of one double phrase (14L) and 14 phrases (the ten-beat phrases are actually eight-beat phrases extended by short melismas), which accommodate the eight couplets of their respective poems.

The English partiality to homogeneous and tonally unified compositions seems to have prevented the technique of the continental motet from spreading in 13th-century England. In France the matter of tonal unity was relatively unimportant, as is attested by the practice of writing clausulas and motets; many of the chant melismas on which they are based are not tonal units. Even many of the freely-composed continental pieces of the 13th and 14th centuries lack an unequivocal tonal centre. Moreover, in contrast to the *pes* motet with its relatively homogeneous texture and sonority, the continental motet characteristically forges unity out of antinomic components. The French tradition of imposing repetitive rhythmic ostinato patterns on cantus firmi and keeping the upper voices strictly syllabic is evident in relatively few English compositions of the time.

After 1300 the expansion of the two-voice framework beyond one octave resulted in more four-part writing (two or three texted upper parts and two or one untexted lower voices). It also caused the decline of voice exchange, with the individual voice-exchange passages growing ever lengthier. Among the few motets with voice exchange of the early 14th century there are, in addition to some freely-composed pieces, two compositions which, in contrast to the voice-exchange motets of the 13th century, are both based on a liturgical cantus firmus (*prosa*) throughout (*GB-Onc* 362, no.17; *F-MO* H196, no.323). The result of the association of voice exchange in the upper voices with a plainsong cantus firmus is that the quality of regular harmonic alternation, of a varied ostinato, so characteristic of the 13th-century compositions, is absent from these later works. There are also three motets (*GB-Ob* Hatton 81, no.4; *Ob* Mus.E.7, no.7; *Onc* 362, no.7) in which voice exchange is applied to the cantus firmus by dividing it into phrases, which, mutually alternating with free counterpoint, are repetitively divided among the two lower voices of these four-part compositions so that one has phrases in the order *XAYBZC*, while the other has *AXBYCZ* (*A, B, C* are phrases of the cantus firmus and *X, Y, Z* are free counterpoint). But in all cantus firmus motets voice exchange gives the impression of a traditional device that has become extrinsic.

In many 14th-century motets without cantus firmi the design was evidently dictated by the top voice or voices, so the cantus firmus is treated with an unusual lack of orderly regularity with respect to rhythm and phrasing. A case in which the irregular shape of the cantus firmus is the result of the neatly laid-out phrase design of the upper voices is the motet *Januam/Jacintus/Jacet*

Ex.7 Pes of *GB-Ob* 20 no.10

*granum* (*Onc* 362, no.2). It is noteworthy that this piece, which treats the cantus firmus as an element of secondary structural importance, presents the first known case of a *solus* tenor (here labelled 'tenor per se'), which is a conflation of the pitches of the two bottom voices into one optional substitute part.

Many cantus firmus motets written in the early 14th century are constructed in a fashion that has come to be called isoperiodic. In these the phrases are usually of the same length but are laid out so as to produce overlaps between voices. While in 13th-century English polyphony isoperiodicity was relatively rare and harmony and tonality fused the three or four lines of a composition, these latter factors were now either given up or made secondary in structural importance to the regular interlacing of phrases. Thus, three of the four voices of *Petrum cephas/Petrus pastor* (*Ob* Mus.E.7, no.2) are arranged as follows (pointed brackets indicate rests that are not part of a phrase): triplum 12(9L), duplum <7L> + 10(9L) + 11L, tenor <7L> + (4 + <3L>) + 10(6 + <3L>) + 4L. (The *quartus cantus* is free.) The nine-bar phrases are eight-bar units lengthened by initial arses. While the beginning of each duplum phrase coincides with the last note of each triplum phrase, the beginning of the latter coincides with the last note of each tenor unit; furthermore, the end of each duplum phrase and the beginning of each tenor unit coincide. Isoperiodic designs involving even all four voices in the production of a repetitive pattern of overlapping phrases are not uncommon.

In several motets (almost complete) the middle voice moves only in slow note values in a manner usually associated with motet tenors (in two cases the voice has been identified as a Gregorian cantus firmus); whenever it rests the outer voices form parallel 6ths. Each of these pieces was to some extent conceived as a duet around the cantus firmus. In *Zelo tui langueo/Reor nescia* (*Lbm* Sloane 1210, no.13) the unlabelled middle voice, consisting of four statements of melody, has phrases of three longs and one long rest. The surrounding two voices are made up of four-bar phrases (six breves per bar), arranged so as to produce a regular catenary arrangement of rests. Each phrase consists of two parts, with the consequent linked to its antecedent by filler material that has the quality of an arsis taking the place of a rest (ex.8). Since the top voice enters one bar before and the

Ex.8

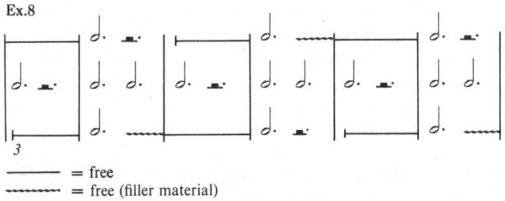

3

――――― = free

┄┄┄┄┄ = free (filler material)

bottom voice one bar after the tenor's entrance in bar 2, the periods concluding the piece are five and three bars long respectively. The diagram in ex.8 clearly shows that isorhythm began as a clarification of the cadential points of phrase structures. The other four motets of this type represent further steps in the evolution; in each case the phrases of the two outer voices maintain a repetitive rhythmic similarity, which is more or less isorhythmic.

Ostinatos and varied ostinatos that are freely invented

or perhaps borrowed from popular sources provided bases for another type of motet written during the first half of the 14th century, the successor to the ostinato *pes* motet of the 13th century. All such motets exploit the principle of sectional variation in so consistent a manner as to suggest their designation as 'variation motets' (e.g. *Cgc* 543/512, nos.1 and 5). Several other compositions also exploit the principle of sectional acceleration. For instance, the fragmentary motet with the duplum *O regina glorie* (*Ob* 20, no.36), an astonishingly sophisticated specimen probably dating from the late 13th century, consists of two sections, whose respective phrase ingredients relate as 4:3. The tenor's irregular rhythms in the second section (color II) prove that the proportionality of the composition is governed by the upper voices. The most impressive piece of this type, one of the last representatives of voice-exchange technique, has an extraordinarily expansive (354-bar) and complex design. In each of the five sections of this fragmentary motet, *De sancta Katerina* (*Rota versatilis* in *Lbm* Add.40011B, ff.4*v*, 5*v*, 6*v*, 7*v*; *Lbm* 24198, no.1; *Ob* 652, no.1), the two freely-composed lower voices (instrumental) are stated twice, with the upper voices engaging in voice exchange from one half to the other. Thus, the five stanzas of the poem, each a quatrain of specific verse structure, are sung twice. The sections are carefully constructed as a particular embodiment of the fundamental numerical proportions 12:8:4:9:6. The notational and general palaeographic evidence indicates that the work cannot have been composed any later than the second decade of the 14th century.

The extant sources seem to indicate that no indigenous motet techniques continued in England beyond the middle of the 14th century and that those relatively few motets written thereafter were largely influenced by continental techniques. Nevertheless, knowledge of English medieval polyphony is far too fragmentary to permit definite conclusions.

3. ARS NOVA. The reduction of the several motet types flourishing in France at the turn of the 13th century to one definitive type capable of accommodating endless variety is the new 'maniere des motets' (*Les règles de la second rhétorique*) invented by Philippe de Vitry. The most prominent practitioner of the strophic motet was apparently Machaut, though Gace de la Buigne wrote (*Roman des deduis*, *c*1370): 'Phelippe de Vitry ot nom, Qui mieulx fist motets que nulz hom'. The major features distinguishing Machaut's motets from Vitry's are his preference for French texts (except in his late motets); his use of secular tenors in three compositions; the strophic isorhythmic structure (*see* ISORHYTHM) in all the others, and the relatively larger number of his motets in which color and talea overlap (ex.9) (both devices were still rarely employed by Vitry); and his preference for structures based on fewer but longer tenor taleae.

The motet differed from the polyphonic chanson not only in conception and structure but also in style. The two upper voices had largely given up the sharp differentiation they possessed in the Petronian motet. The possibility of combining two unrelated poems in the upper voices ceased to exist, since the selection of the tenor was no longer determined by arbitrary considerations of contrapuntal convenience but was governed by the need for its text to correspond like a motto to the poetic conceit of the upper voices. This procedure was

Ex.9 Machaut tenors
(a) Motet no.9

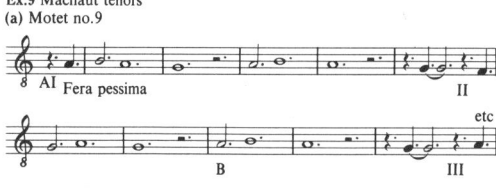

AI   Fera pessima                                    II

                                        etc

          B                            III

(b) Motet no.14

AI   Quia amore langueo

                                        etc

     B              II                 C

Letters:   Colores
Numerals: Taleae

first reported by Egidius de Murino (*CS*, iii, 124*a*). The practice, which originated around the turn of the century, might be called reverse textual troping, since the relevance of the texts is motivated not liturgically but poetically. The primacy of the poetic impulse (but not of the poetic composition) is a feature the motet shares with the accompanied song. The triplum poems are always longer than those of the motetus and therefore, in contrast to most motetus poems, are strophic in structure; but the rhythmic character of both voices, which have lost all modal constraints, is often nearly the same. As a result, the declamation, whose concern with prosody is anything but vital, is rapid in the triplum, but slower and, in contrast to 13th-century tradition, fairly melismatic in the motetus, though short melismas also occur in most tripla. The poetic and musical structures are frequently not isomorphic, but composers evidently sympathized less and less with the seemingly haphazard attitude implied by Egidius de Murino's statement that 'it is sometimes necessary to spread many notes over few words [and sometimes many words] over few beats'. (It indicates, however, that the musical structure continued to be primary in the 14th century.) Although a number of motets composed in the first half of the 14th century still reveal the composer's rather cavalier attitude in fitting the poetry to the music, several others show great care in the structural coordination of music and poetry. The melodic design of the upper voices clearly shows that each phrase is a separate component which requires no linking to its predecessor by such means as motivic relationships, sequences or contrast. Since the composition is not the product of free melodic invention, a motet sounds stiffer and more formal than a chanson, not only because of its massive fundament – now often consisting of tenor and contratenor, a voice of similar range and facture – but because the melodic design of the upper voice is more restricted; even rhythmically it is more conservative. Rooted in the pitches of the cantus firmus, motetus and triplum are pre-eminently concerned with the harmonious unfolding of numerical gestalts.

The presence of a cantus firmus, which had always caused the motet tenor to be regarded as the 'dignior pars' (Anonymous VII), in no case automatically implies liturgical function. The original trope-like nature of the motet was a fleeting phenomenon, whose inevitability was eliminated when clausula and motet were recog-

nized as entities divorced from the chant that furnished the tenor notes. Undoubtedly a remark by Guillaume Durand (*d* 1334) that properly 'the impious and irregular music of motets and similar compositions should not be performed in church' indicates not his desire for the elimination of the motet as a species, but for its relegation to its appropriate sphere. Certainly motets with suitable texts must have been performed in church; but the primary raison d'être of the motet was surely more than ever to function as the most sublime product of *ars musica*, which addressed itself to the 'learned and those who prize artistic subtlety' (Grocheo). Though originating as clerical chamber music, it was produced in the 14th century by and for 'accomplished musicians and lay connoisseurs' (Jacques de Liège). Its prestige, at least since the mid-13th century, is attested by the many 13th-century musical manuscripts devoted more or less exclusively to it; 14th-century musical sources, most of which mix the genres, as a rule place the motets at the beginning.

The apprehension of 14th-century motets may at first seem a forbidding task, since they are of much broader dimensions than those of the Ars Antiqua. But far from being arcane intellectual constructs that resist aural perception, 14th-century isorhythmic motets are strophic variations, and the listener's sense of recurrence, though differently activated, is hardly less keen than in such early 17th-century strophic variations as the prologue or Orpheus's Act 3 aria in Monteverdi's *Orfeo*. Perception of the proportioned relationships within a motet is not essentially more problematic than perception of the proportioned relationships of the structural members in Gothic architecture. Isorhythmic passages are recurring rhythmic ornaments that emphasize structure.

Panisorhythm, a schematic procedure not practised by Vitry and still rare in Machaut's motets and those contained in the Ivrea manuscript (*I–IV*), increased in importance around the middle of the century. The development towards panisorhythm goes hand in hand with a tendency to forgo the traditional structure of the upper voices that divides the talea into proportioned component phrases. Increasingly, motets appear in which one or both of the upper voices are not subdivided at all (e.g. Machaut, Schrade edn. no.21, and several Ivrea motets). Such motets are panisorhythmic or nearly so. The formal changes experienced by the motet in the second half of the century resulted from the monumentalism that began to affect it. The level of articulation had passed from the component phrases of the taleae to the monolithic taleae themselves; usually both the structure of the poetry and its declamation are closely moulded to the strophic design of the music. Isorhythm in the upper voices no longer functioned as carefully spaced, ornamental emphasis of the articulation of phrase structure but had become of central importance, and with the elimination of the structural subdivisions of the taleae the elements of form became vast. In the panisorhythmic motets of the late 14th century the phrase was no longer a formal component.

Numerical significance was restored to the motet on a larger plane than before through the extended use of diminution, a device that had been optional since Vitry's day. Both diminution and other changes in mensuration were applied to motet tenors (and contratenors) of the late 14th century for the sake of numerically proportioned sectional design. One of the earliest specimens of the 'mensuration motet' is *Ida capillorum matris/Portio nature/Ante thronum* (*F-CH* 564, no.102), whose concordance in the Ivrea manuscript makes it the most progressive motet in that source; it may have been composed in the late 1360s. Its eight taleae are divided into four pairs, each of which apportions a different mensuration to the two lower voices. Necessarily, the isorhythmic shaping of the upper voices applies only to the two halves of each pair, so the piece actually constitutes a double strophic variation form; the upper voices form strophic subdivisions of the strophic sections established by the lower voices. The lengths of these four sections yield the proportion 6:4:3:2. Each section is based on one color of the tenor (and contratenor); the overlapping of color and talea structure that occurs in about a quarter of Machaut's motets is given up for the sake of clearer definition of the expanding form. Another striking example is *Sub Arturo/Fons citharizantium/[In omnem terram]* (*F-CH* 564, no.111), whose motetus text states that the tenor 'is repeated twice, each time reduced by the hemiola proportion' (i.e. 9:6:4). In most compositions of this type the structure of the poetry, with its growing tendency towards arcane references and recondite imagery, is carefully integrated with the musical design.

Many large-scale mensuration motets of increasing complexity can be found in the English and French sources of the late 14th century and early 15th. Its ultimate degree was achieved by French composers of the early 15th century (e.g. Billart, Brassart, Grenon). For instance, the rhythm of the four tenor sections of Grenon's *Ave virtus/Prophetarum/Infelix* is governed successively by *modus maior*, *modus minor*, *tempus* and *prolatio* (*see* NOTATION, §III, 3). The arrangement of the subordinate 'prolacions' yields for the length of the four colores the proportion 8:6:2:1. But since each of the last two sections contains two colores (and two taleae), the four sections together represent the Pythagorean proportions 4:3:2:1.

Since in all such motets the main emphasis is no longer on strophic isorhythm but on variety of sectional mensuration, a logical conclusion of this development is the appearance of mensuration motets without isorhythm. Three compositions by Dufay are outstanding representatives of this final structural type of the medieval motet, which is related to the Burgundian cantus firmus mass. The sections of nos.11, 12 and 13 (in CMM, i) of his 'isorhythmic' motets present the following proportions respectively: 6:4:2:3, 12:4:2:3, 6:3:4:2:6:3; isorhythmic repetition no longer subdivides the sections.

As in the early 20th-century symphony, the huge proportions to which the isorhythmic motet by English, Burgundian and Franco-Flemish composers of the early 15th century had grown indicated its imminent demise; already in the later 14th century music manuscripts generally gave increasing prominence to polyphonic chansons. Both in size and in sound the motet tended to become unwieldy. Its enormous structural members were based on large areas of unvarying sonority established by the long durational values of the tenor (and contratenor). The motets of the Chantilly repertory particularly are bedecked with richly ornamental upper parts of manneristic rhythmic intricacy.

Moreover, the motet assimilated two features that had been essentially foreign to it since its birth – isomelism

and imitation. The latter had been known to motet composers of the Ars Antiqua, who often correlated identical text phrases occurring successively in the two upper voices by associating them with the same pitches (e.g. *F-MO* H196, nos.95, 308). But this is not so much a matter of imitation as of musico-textual identity, reflecting the same melos principle that made a triplum into a distinct entity, once it had been separated from the duplum by its own text. True imitation was so uncommon as to be negligible. In the 14th century, too, imitation in the upper voices is of no significance. Generally it occurs only in the introitus with which Vitry and other composers prefaced some of their motets; in such introductions the tenor rests or is freely composed. The reason for the absence of imitation from the body of the motet is surely less the contrapuntal difficulties presented by the cantus prius factus than the fact that devices of melodic integration are essentially foreign to structures based, ever since the appearance of the clausula, on the disposition of temporal units (rhythm and phrases).

These circumstances also explain the relative rarity of isomelism in the motets of Vitry's and Machaut's time. Since there were certainly more contrapuntal opportunities for strophic isomelic correspondences than 14th-century motet composers cared to exploit, isomelism, like imitation, must be recognized as essentially extrinsic to the medieval motet.

The increasing importance of both devices around 1400 is symptomatic of a profound shift from the shaping of a composition by means of numerical coordination of heterogeneous, hierarchically ordered durational components, in which melodic considerations are of no structural importance, to the creation of a musically and textually homogeneous contrapuntal fabric from one congenial set of melodic cells. The many significant changes in style and technique occurring in motets composed at this time have been demonstrated as preeminently due to Italian influences, absorbed and transformed by such northern composers resident in Italy as Ciconia and Dufay. Before the early 15th century, motet production in medieval Italy had been negligible; the extant pieces number fewer than half a dozen and demonstrate a fundamental distrust of the species. Even more than the 13th-century English composers the Italians shied away from the cantus firmus and evidently tended to mould their motets into non-isorhythmic secular forms, like madrigals. All of Ciconia's dozen motets have tenors with bass-like support quality, rather than Gregorian cantus firmi. All but two are tonally unified, and their melodic style has a flexibility relating them to the other sphere of polyphony (song) that was not structurally governed by the tenor. Their clear sectional articulation is produced by various means, such as isomelic endings of taleae, structurally placed melismas and cadential arrest of motion preceded by climactic acceleration. Furthermore, the composers active in northern Italy evidently were the first to transfer the technique of imitation from monotextual duets, where it was at home, to the motet. Since monotextual motets were now written more frequently and the poems of a polytextual composition were usually of the same length and had similar versification and related subject matter, the two upper voices, which had already occupied the same range in many 14th-century French motets, were now assimilated by melodic cross-references, by similar rhythmic facture and by declamation.

All these progressive features can be found in a number of Dufay's 14 isorhythmic and mensuration motets. In these works, composed 100 years after Vitry and some 200 years after Pérotin, Dufay achieved a last magnificent synthesis of the traditions of numerically constructed cantus firmus polyphony with the new forces that hastened its decline. Like the motets by Dunstable and his English contemporaries, composed as elaborations of the liturgy and legitimized by pertinent cantus firmi, most motets by French composers of the early 15th century are sacred *pièces de circonstance*, hallowed by relevant liturgical fundaments that the Middle Ages knew as divinely inspired, sacrosanct and eternally valid.

### II. Renaissance

1. Dufay and his contemporaries. 2. Later 15th century. 3. Josquin. 4. Josquin's contemporaries and successors: (i) France (ii) Netherlands (iii) Italy. 5. Peripheral traditions: (i) Spain (ii) Germanic territories (iii) England. 6. Second half of the 16th century.

1. DUFAY AND HIS CONTEMPORARIES. The first half of the 15th century was a period of transition and transformation in the history of the motet. By the 1420s isorhythmic and mensural structures – cultivated during the 14th century to the virtual exclusion of all others – had reached a degree of complexity that was to be less and less in harmony with developing stylistic tendencies. However, because isorhythm had come to be linked with compositions written to celebrate festal and ceremonial occasions, the strength of that tradition maintained its use in the motet until the mid-15th century. This is demonstrated by late examples such as Dufay's *Nuper rosarum*, intended for the dedication of Brunelleschi's cathedral in Florence in 1436, or Brassart's *O rex Fridrice/In tuo adventu*, written on the death of his imperial patron in 1440. Only after the principles of isorhythmic composition began to be freely adapted for cyclic settings of the mass Ordinary shortly before the middle of the century was their rigorous application to the motet relinquished completely.

The abandonment of strict isorhythm was accompanied by a shift in the primary function of the motet. Composers in the first half of the 15th century began to return to the liturgical and devotional contexts in which the genre had originated, thus diminishing the relative significance of its role as a festal piece or a vehicle for social comment. The impetus for this development may have come from England; to judge from isorhythmic English works like Dunstable's *Veni Sancte Spiritus*, the original liturgical associations of the motet seem never to have been forgotten there. However, favoured texts were no longer linked topically to responsorial chants but were rather related primarily to the cult of the Virgin. They were both liturgical and devotional, in prose and in verse, and none was more frequently set than the Marian antiphons. In England these were generally composed with the traditional plainchant as an inner or – more rarely – an upper or migrating voice, usually in a discant style consonant almost throughout and not far removed from the improvised counterpoint of faburden that was to have such an impact on developments on the Continent. The motets of Leonel Power and his immediate English contemporaries include a substantial number of this type.

Composers on the Continent, lacking a compositional tradition for texts of this kind, experimented with a variety of established structural principles and contrapuntal techniques. The diversity of the solutions tried in the first half of the 15th century is well illustrated by a substantial repertory of motets included in the major sources of the period. English and Franco-Flemish composers are best represented, but the manuscripts are primarily from Savoy and northern Italy (*I-Bc* Q15; *Bu* 2216; *OA* A1 D19; *GB-Ob* Can.Misc.213; the earlier layers of the Trent MSS). Simple homophonic compositions, of which the anonymous *Verbum caro factum est* is fairly typical (ex.10), clearly show the influence of improvised discant and the consonant sonorities associated with it. The rhythmic simultaneities of the three voices are only lightly veiled by the melodic ornamentation of the highest part, and all could easily bear the text. Even when no liturgical melody is present, nor direct evidence of borrowed contrapuntal techniques such as fauxbourdon, compositions of this kind may still have been modelled on the English pieces with which they are frequently found in the sources; they are very similar in conception to Dunstable's *Quam pulchra es* and a number of Power's early works with no known cantus firmus.

The treble-dominated style of soloistic secular song was also adopted for Latin words. Binchois' *Domitor Hectoris* (ed. in *MD*, ii, 1948, p.66) and Feragut's *Francorum nobilitati* (*Polyphonia sacra*, ed. C. van den Borren, 1932, no.40) are relatively early works of a non-liturgical nature written essentially in that manner. When a liturgical text was similarly handled, the plainchant to which it was sung was frequently retained in the polyphony. It was most often placed at the top of the contrapuntal structure as the text-bearing line, with its contours reshaped in accordance with the melodic ideal of the chanson (but still recognizable to the informed listener).

This solution – in contrast to the cantus firmus treatment usually practised by the English – was in keeping with contemporary French style, and it led to the establishment of the devotional song motet for three voices as a distinct type. Such works were typically based on non-liturgical texts although some drew on the liturgy as well. Most are addressed to the Virgin, but some honour popular saints instead. As befits their modest sonorities, their scope was usually restricted, conceivably because of the quasi-private use for which they were intended. Inevitably the treble-dominated style came to be tempered considerably in the 16th century by a totally vocal conception and the increasing prevalence of systematic imitation, but a three-voice texture and a modest, songlike setting continued for several generations to be used for well-loved Marian and hagiographic texts. Evidence of a lasting affection for motets of this type is provided by 16th-century collections devoted wholly to works for three voices such as *Trium vocum cantiones centum* (Nuremberg, 1541), *Motetta trium vocum ab pluribus authoribus composita* (Venice, 1543), *Elettione de motetti a tre voci libro primo* (Venice, 1549) and *Libro secondo de li motetti a tre voci* (Venice, 1549).

Alongside a generally experimental trend, continental composers tended in the first half of the 15th century to revert to certain aspects of the 14th-century motet tradition, either borrowing them consciously and directly or deriving them second-hand from song forms. They juxtaposed vocal and instrumental pairs of voices, for example, linking them by range as well as by mode of performance, and pointed up the differences between the

Ex.10 Anon.: *Verbum caro factum est, I-Bu 2216*

Ver-bum ca-ro fac-tum est de vir-gi-

-ne__ Ma-ri - - a    In hoc an-ni

1)
cir - cu-lo    vi-ta da-tur se - cu-

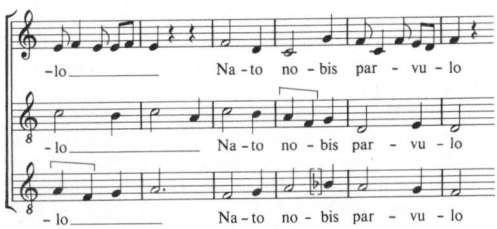

-lo_____    Na-to no-bis par-vu-lo

1) *f'* in the MS

two groups by contrasts in rhythmic activity and melodic interest.

The innovatory combination of different compositional traditions is reflected in works such as Arnold de Lantins' four-part *Tota pulchra es* (*Polyphonia sacra*, no.41). There, at the start, the upper pair of voices is clearly distinguished from the lower pair by more animated rhythms and a more conjunct melodic style, even though the tenor is also texted in the manuscript. However, as the counterpoint unfolds the tenor declaims a number of phrases homophonically with the higher voices, and the obviously instrumental contratenor assumes the same rate of motion.

Dufay adopted for three-part song motets a treble-dominated texture derived from the chanson, even before he had abandoned isorhythmic structures. Sometimes he combined a melodically predominant cantus with such motet-related features as a text-bearing pair of upper voices and polytextuality. Sometimes he

introduced passages of chordal homophony suggestive of improvised discant. He turned consistently to the style of solo song, with little modification, for his settings of the antiphons for the *Magnificat* and for two presumably early versions of the processional antiphons for Compline: *Ave regina celorum* and *Alma Redemptoris mater* (*Opera omnia*, v, ed. H. Besseler and G. de Van, CMM, i/5, 1966, nos.48, 50). In each the chant provides the melodic substance of the cantus part. However, Dufay's polyphonic antiphons also include a nearly equal-voiced three-part treatment of *Alma Redemptoris mater* (*Opera omnia*, v, no.47) with the chant in the tenor and text in all voices. A stylistically similar elaboration of *Ave regina celorum* (*Opera omnia*, v, no.49) is syllabic, declamatory and fully texted but shows no trace of a borrowed plainsong.

During the second half of the 15th century, with the clarification and consequent reduction of stylistic possibilities, experimentation began to give way little by little to a redefinition of the motet as a genre. New compositional traditions were thus established, many of which were adhered to until the rise of monody brought about a stylistic transformation of the motet. Already with the liturgical repertory of Dufay and, to a lesser degree, his immediate contemporaries, one can see the beginnings of characteristic procedures for hymn and *Magnificat* settings that were to be observed for more than a century. In both, successive verses of the text alternate between plainsong and polyphony, and the chant melody also usually figures prominently in the part-writing. As a rule the borrowed line is carried by the cantus, where it contributes to a modest impression of treble-domination in the customary texture of three parts (*see* HYMN, §III, 2, and MAGNIFICAT, §2).

A decisive impetus for the development of the motet in this period came indirectly from the traditional cantus firmus structures of the 14th century, through their transformation in the polyphonic mass cycles of the 1440s and 1450s. There the mathematical severity of isorhythmic and mensural patterns was either substantially tempered, if only by their extension over a large cyclic form, or virtually dissolved. At the same time the medieval hierarchy of voices had begun to break down, despite the adherence to the tenor cantus firmus as a structural armature for the composition, in deference to an increasingly vocal conception of part-writing and a concomitant trend towards melodic and rhythmic equalization of the parts. In addition, the sonorous possibilities were enriched by an ever more regular use of the *contratenor bassus* – not infrequently an optional part in the 14th-century motet even when present. The four voices of such a polyphonic texture were also spread more evenly over the ranges now considered standard for the human voice.

Thus the tenor cantus firmus was newly transformed and reintegrated into motet composition, and in the process a compositional tradition was forged that was to prove particularly tenacious. This development is exemplified by Dufay's *Ave regina celorum*, written just a decade before his death in 1474. It was perhaps not the first work of its kind – other composers may have taken the crucial step before Dufay – but it reveals clearly its relationship both to the cantus firmus masses of Dufay's maturity and to the earlier isorhythmic motet structures from which they were derived. The extended introductory duos (where the plainsong functions as a melodic element in the continental manner), the use of the antiphon melody as a tenor cantus firmus set off at its entry by prolonged note values, the addition of a low contratenor, the division of the piece into two sections under contrasting mensurations, and the bitextuality created by the troping of Dufay's personal supplications in every part except the tenor – all these features reflect compositional procedures characteristic of the 14th-century isorhythmic motet (see ex.11). At the same time the work owes to the cyclic masses of the immediately preceding decades the vocal character of its part-writing and the supple handling of its borrowed chant; the tenor becomes increasingly indistinguishable from the

Ex.11 Dufay: *Ave regina celorum*

surrounding voices, both rhythmically and melodically, as it proceeds from its initial entry to the concluding cadence of each section. That Dufay drew consciously for this motet on the compositional procedures that he had developed in his cantus firmus masses is suggested by the extensive three-voice passage common to it and to the second Agnus Dei of the cyclic mass based on the same liturgical chant.

2. LATER 15TH CENTURY. With the next generation of composers, the motet built on a tenor cantus firmus became once again an important stylistic type. Of the eight motets that can be attributed to Johannes Regis, Dufay's 'clerc' (and possibly his pupil), all but one are of this kind. Regis increased the potential sonority of his works by weaving four additional voices around the tenor, but he usually engaged all five parts simultaneously only at the culmination of a section. More often he intensively exploited the possibilities for contrasts in range, timbre and density by alternating duos, trios and the full ensemble. The texts he set were almost exclusively festal or occasional in intent, and he selected his cantus firmus in each case from a liturgical chant providing both a suggestive symbolic association with the words declaimed by the other voices and – since the borrowed melodies retained their traditional texts – an appropriate commentary upon them. The resulting bitextuality revived the 'reverse textual troping' of the early 14th century.

It is probably because of this symbolic and associative significance that cantus firmi, borrowed or contrived, continued to be used for festal and ceremonial motets throughout the 16th century. In time the device itself acquired the venerability of tradition, contributing thereby to the desired effect. Moreover, later composers tended to give it even greater prominence by reverting to the extended note values of an earlier period. They also greatly increased its weight on occasion, by presenting it in strict imitation in two or more voices and by sustaining it with the full sonorities of five, six or even more parts.

Despite the apparent homogeneity of Regis's known motets, his immediate contemporaries continued to experiment with the compositional solutions that had been evolved for the genre. Like Dufay, Ockeghem turned to cantus firmus techniques in setting the Marian antiphons. However, with the exception of the two large works for five voices, *Celeste beneficium* and *Gaude Maria, virgo*, both cast in essentially the same structural mould as Dufay's *Ave regina*, his treatment of borrowed material is characteristically unconventional. In one version of the *Salve regina* the chant is carried mainly by the superius, and its function is clearly more melodic than structural even though it migrates occasionally to both altus and tenor. The liturgical melody is similarly handled in his *Alma Redemptoris mater*, but with a triplum-like voice laid over it in an unusually high register, whereas in a second *Salve regina* the chant is consigned solely to the *bassus*.

At the same time Ockeghem continued to experiment with further solutions for compositions of this sort, providing settings of both liturgical and devotional texts without reference to a chant melody. The angelic salutation of the Annunciation, *Ave Maria, gratia plena*, though used as an antiphon in several contexts, he treated melismatically in a freely-composed contrapuntal style for four voices of equal rhythmic activity and melodic interest. For the prayer to the Virgin *Intemerata Dei mater*, which has no place in the liturgy, he produced an imposing work for five voices. Dividing it into three sections with different mensurations, he contrasted full sonorities with duos and trios in different registers, and juxtaposed the independent, contrapuntal part-writing and melismatic text-setting of the initial and final sections with the syllabic, declamatory style of the intervening passages.

Busnois also relied upon the cantus firmus principle for compositions based on liturgical chants, but, like Ockeghem, he used it somewhat freely. In a setting of the Easter sequence *Victimae paschali laudes*, he embellished the chant elaborately and placed it in the altus. For one version of the Marian antiphon *Regina coeli* he gave the traditional melody to the *bassus*, while for another (ed. A. Smijers, *Van Ockeghem tot Sweelinck*, i, 16) he doubled it canonically at the 5th between the lower two voices. Two other motets, *Anthoni usque limina* (ed. C. L. W. Boer, *Het Anthonius Motet van Anthonius Busnois*, 1940) and *In hydraulis* (DTÖ, xiv–xv, Jg.vii, 105), have a distinctly personal stamp: he apparently wrote the texts himself and constructed the cantus firmi according to rigidly schematic designs. The only analogous composition by Ockeghem is the enigmatic *Ut heremita solus* (GMB, no.52), for which the tenor has to be extrapolated from an elaborate combination of notational and verbal canons; the resulting puzzle presumably sorely taxed the imagination even of those familiar with such devices, since Petrucci deemed it necessary to publish a resolution together with the instructions. The Ockeghem work is exceptional in this respect, for while complex canonic manipulation of the tenor cantus firmus was fairly common in masses of the period, it was not often used in the motet.

With another unusual work, the motet-chanson written for the death of Binchois in 1460, Ockeghem may have been responsible for establishing a new compositional genre. The use of the vernacular for the primary text has usually caused such works to be considered with chansons, but serious compositions can also be regarded as a sub-species of the motet, since they derive from it their most salient traits: the simultaneous setting of two different texts and the adoption of a pre-existing melody as the tenor cantus firmus. Dufay's *Je ne puis plus/Unde veniet* was evidently earlier than Ockeghem's motet-chanson, since it was included in *GB-Ob* Can.Misc.213, but its intention seems humorous and its tradition more distinctly secular than the epitaphs by Ockeghem and composers of the following generation. Although they display a superficial structural resemblance to bitextual chansons where both the borrowed tenor and its text stem from a popular repertory of French song, epitaphs on the passing of a personage of note, such as those included in the collection prepared for Margaret of Austria (*B-Br* 228), are more serious in intent and, as a result, in style. The thoroughly motet-like facture of *Nymphes des bois*, Josquin's *déploration* on the death of Ockeghem, is a case in point. When it is compared with the popular character of the combinatorial chansons added to the final layer of the Dijon chansonnier, for example, the distinctions are clearly illustrated.

The structural and stylistic affinities between the motet and the tenor mass, due to their common origins and to cross-currents of influence in the second half of the 15th century, are also illuminated by the develop-

ment of the *motetti missales*. Their beginnings appear to be attributable to northern composers working at the Sforza court in Milan. Both Compère and Weerbeke wrote, probably in the 1470s, motet cycles to be performed during the celebration of the Mass, and were shortly followed by Gaffurius and other, unidentified composers. The individual pieces were intended to be sung in place of certain mass chants – introit, Gloria, Credo, offertory, Sanctus, Agnus Dei, and *Deo gratias* – and at the Elevation. The texts were taken from the liturgy itself (antiphons, hymns and responsories) and from devotional sources (*prosae*, rhymed prayers, rhymed offices etc) and were sometimes composite, consisting of a series of appropriate related statements drawn from a variety of sources.

There are several traits by which the *motetti missales* reveal their relationship to the cyclic mass: a common final, identical or at least similar clefs, a recurring sequence of alternating mensurations, and like structures or shared musical material. In addition, the texts of a given cycle (except the Elevation motet, which always refers to the Eucharist) all share a common theme, usually concerned with either the cult of the Virgin or feasts of the Lord. As a result they impart to the cycle a Proper character in the same sense that a tenor cantus firmus can provide a Proper reference for a setting of the mass Ordinary.

Textual centonizations were used not only for the *motetti missales* but, more importantly, as a basis for motet composition generally for several decades before and after the turn of the 15th century. Unlike settings of chants, such as the Marian antiphons, that have a traditional liturgical function, motets of this type raise questions as to their intended purpose. A partial answer is suggested by the motet cycles. Although their cultivation seems to have been a localized and transitory practice, it provides an interesting indication of the liturgical use to which individual motets may have been put, even within the context of the mass.

It is also possible to see in these compositions, particularly those of Weerbeke, the gradual crystallization of the musical style that was to characterize the motet throughout the 16th century, beginning with the mature works of Josquin. Weerbeke's setting of *Ave regina* (*in loco* Agnus Dei) for the cycle *Ave mundi domina* (ed. in Archivium musices metropolitanum mediolanense, xi, 1963, p.28) makes systematic use of paired imitation; two-voice textures in a variety of combinations alternate with the full complement of four, and the contrapuntal character of the initial section is juxtaposed with the chordal declamation of the solemn *O salutaris hostia* that was sung during the Elevation (see ex.12).

The word-generated figures that begin the imitative phrases, the clear cadential articulation that ends them and the syllabic, homorhythmic style of the closing section are generally regarded as reflecting Italian tastes and influence. However, this style, with each note carrying a corona as here, appears in the works of northern composers as early as Johannes de Lymburgia and the young Dufay. A type of homophonic declamation deriving from the natural rhythm of the Latin is also found, for example in the *secunda pars* of the late five-voice *Intemerata Dei mater* (ed. A. Smijers, *Van Ockeghem tot Sweelinck*, i, 3) by Ockeghem, who apparently never visited Italy. Since the supposed Italian models have yet to be identified, definitive conclusions are difficult to draw.

Ex.12 Gaspar van Weerbeke: *Ave regina caelorum*

canonic structure expands the customary fabric of four voices to six. Josquin also contrived his own cantus firmi, as in the five-voice *Illibata Dei virgo* (*Werken*, ix, no.27), where the tenor consists solely of the hexachord syllables *la*, *mi*, *la*, conceivably a reference to the virgin, *Ma-ri-a*. In his motets Josquin even quoted secular melodies, such as *D'ung aultre amer* and *De tous biens playne* –albeit without their texts – clearly for the same sort of associative significance that they carried when adopted as cantus firmi for mass cycles (e.g. *Werken*, ix, no.26 and xxiv, no.40).

As syntactic imitation became increasingly important, Josquin applied the technique to the handling of pre-existing as well as original melodic material. The voices were then assimilated to each other both melodically and rhythmically, and the cantus firmus permeated the entire contrapuntal fabric, as in his four-voice *Virgo prudentissima* (*Werken*, ix, no.25) and *Mittit ad virginem* (*Werken*, ii, no.3). This development was virtually inevitable for Josquin, who consistently retained with any liturgical text the melody traditionally associated with it. Thus in his four-voice *Ave Maria, gratia plena* (*Werken*, i, no.1) he derived the melodic material for the opening biblical salutation from the related chant, providing a fourfold statement of it as a series of regular points of imitation. The rest of the text is composed of five regular strophes of four lines each, which he set as successive units, articulated not only cadentially but also by means of contrasts in part-writing. The result is a compendium of the contrapuntal techniques in use in motet composition by the turn of the century: successive points of imitation, homophonic declamation, free contrapuntal writing, contrasting textures and timbres resulting from the alternation of duos and trios in different registers with the full choir, and rhythmic variety achieved by a proportional shift from the prevailing binary metre to a ternary one (see ex.13).

This arsenal of compositional procedures undoubtedly facilitated the innovations with which Josquin is generally credited. However important his contributions to the codification of style for traditional categories of the genre – the polyphonic settings of antiphons, sequences and devotional Marian texts – they were significantly complemented, if not completely matched, by those of his immediate contemporaries such as Alexander Agricola, Compère, Isaac and Obrecht. His most important motets historically are perhaps those based on texts for which no similar conventions existed, the lyrical and subjective poetry of the Old Testament and in particular that of the psalms. He appears to have been one of the first to draw on them for a substantial number of works. In these the venerable techniques of cantus firmus and canon gave way to an increasing reliance on syntactic imitation as a basic compositional procedure. At the same time the melodic figures with which successive phrases begin are more closely tied to the natural rhythms and inflections of the Latin words. Homophonic declamation continued to function as an articulating device and as an element of stylistic variety, but its rhetorical possibilities, which had always been important, received even greater stress; the dramatic change in texture produced by its introduction served at once to draw the listener's attention to a new phrase of text and to make it clearly audible.

Presumably in response to a burgeoning interest among humanist men of letters in the relationship be-

3. JOSQUIN. The key figure in the development of the motet in the late 15th century and early 16th was undoubtedly Josquin. All the compositional solutions that had become traditional for the genre found a place in his works. There is a reference to the melodic use of liturgical chant in his simultaneous setting of the two Marian antiphons *Alma Redemptoris mater* and *Ave regina celorum* (*Werken*, vii, no.21). Moreover, from his literal quotation of the opening of Ockeghem's elaboration of the first of those chants one can assume a conscious allusion to the usage of the previous generation. The use of a tenor cantus firmus, selected for its symbolic significance, is exemplified in his six-voice setting of the Gospel text *In illo tempore stetit Jesus* (*Werken*, xxxviii, no.55), where the antiphon for Vespers on Easter Sunday, *Et ecce terrae motus*, is laid out in long note values, particularly extended at its initial appearance, and carries its original text.

Canonic doubling of the tenor was also used by Josquin to give greater prominence and weight to the borrowed chant, as in *Benedicta es, celorum regina* (*Werken*, xxxv, no.46) or, yet more rigidly, in *Veni Sancte Spiritus* (*Werken*, xxxvi, no.49). In both, the

Ex.13

tween a musical text-setting and its affective impact upon the listener, Josquin also began to explore more fully in motets of this type a dimension only occasionally entered by earlier masters such as Busnois and Ockeghem: the illustration and symbolization of verbal conceits by musical gestures. Examples of his attempts in this regard are numerous, but none is more striking than his setting of David's lament for the death of Absalom (see Osthoff, ii, p.382). The exceptionally low range of the work, and the flats that it carries, both in the signature and as accidentals, are undoubtedly intended to reflect the extreme grief expressed by the text. Similarly, alternate syllabic declamation and melismatic extension of musical phrases portray respectively the exclamations and weeping of the mourning king and culminate in a final descending pattern that depicts the words 'non vivam ultra sed descendam in infernum plorans'.

4. JOSQUIN'S CONTEMPORARIES AND SUCCESSORS. By the time of Josquin's death, early in the 1520s, the motet as a genre appears to have been largely defined, and the musical language associated with it until at least the end of the 16th century was fully formed in all its essentials. The tendency, clearly discernible in Josquin's mature works, towards an ever fuller submission of compositional procedures to the meaning and requirements of the text was to have highly significant ramifications, not only for the motet but also for secular music. However, it is evident from the delineation of regional and personal styles that seems to have begun at about the same time, that Josquin's attention to musical rhetoric was not shared to an equal degree by all his immediate and younger contemporaries.

(i) France. Antoine de Févin and Jean Mouton, with whom Josquin is reported to have been associated at the French court, made only occasional attempts at musical symbolism. Mouton in particular was evidently more concerned with the finely chiselled and balanced melodic lines that Glarean so admired and with clear, coherent formal structures. This can be seen in his settings of plainchant sequences, which he treated much more consistently than Josquin as a sort of variation chain based on paired repetitions of the pre-existing melody. He also followed the repetition schemes characteristic of the liturgical chant in his settings of invitatory antiphons and great responsories, categories of chant to which Josquin gave scant attention.

Mouton's choice of such texts was motivated partly at least by the formal possibilities inherent in them. This is strongly suggested by other compositions such as the ceremonial motet *Non nobis, Domine* (Cw, lxxvi), written to celebrate a French royal birth in 1510, on which similar repetition patterns are also imposed. The acclamation 'Ergo clamemus . . . vivat rex!' functions as a refrain; it is heard twice in each of the two *partes*, first at about the mid-point, in the binary rhythms characteristic of the composition, and again at the end, with a shift to ternary metre. Not only are the corresponding passages the same in the two *partes* but the binary and ternary passages are also closely related to each other through the use of common musical material. Thus they serve both to articulate formally the individual *pars* and to create a clear overall design.

This stylistic trend was in no way inimical to the style of Josquin's mature works. Indeed the basic compositional procedures were the same: syntactic imitation and homophonic declamation in alternation with reduced or changing numbers of voices as an added element of variety. But the emphasis was much more on rational ordering of the musical structure than on rhetorical gesture derived from verbal meaning. Of the composers of the next generation a considerable number – most of whom had connections of some sort with the French royal chapel – elected to follow Mouton in that respect and to cultivate what was becoming a traditional French style. Since some (such as Verdelot, Jacquet de Berchem, Lhéritier and Willaert) crossed the Alps to the south seeking lucrative positions, they also contributed to the dissemination of the style in Italy. In France, where it had originated, it was carried to its greatest degree of refinement – one bordering on facility – by Sermisy, Certon and, to a lesser degree, other composers associated with the musical institutions of the court and the capital.

(*ii*) *Netherlands*. In the regions of Franco-Flemish culture the distinctive stylistic proclivities of a number of Josquin's younger contemporaries also spawned a somewhat different tradition. Gombert, for example, followed French models in some important respects. Although reportedly a 'disciple' of Josquin, he generally restricted his use of liturgical melodies to the two contexts in which they had become traditional for Mouton and his emulators, the setting of Marian antiphons and tenor cantus firmus compositions. In the latter case the borrowed chant was usually given to a fifth or sixth voice and used with its original text for its symbolic or associative significance. Gombert also adopted for a number of his motets the repetition pattern and, like Mouton, the bipartite division of the responsory.

But at the same time Gombert showed the influence of the earlier Netherlands tradition, as represented in the works of Agricola, La Rue and Obrecht, in his preference for full contrapuntal textures. His reliance on homophony was generally rather slight. Although he turned from freer contrapuntal part-writing to a systematic use of syntactic imitation, he maintained thick sonorities by avoiding the bicinia characteristic of both Josquin and, to some degree, his French colleagues, and by adopting regular, closely-spaced entries for individual voices. His use of five or even six voices (instead of the normal four) in nearly two-thirds of his motets contributes to the same effect. A humanistic concern for verbal meaning and intelligibility had tempered the abstract, even arbitrary relationship between word and note often found in the writing of his immediate predecessors, but it is reflected in Gombert's compositions mainly in a more regular declamation of the text and a curtailment of cadential melismas. The Netherlands style, as Gombert helped to define and exemplify it, was confirmed and established by Crecquillon, his somewhat younger successor at the imperial court, and by Clemens non Papa, Crecquillon's immediate contemporary. Individual distinctions can be made, but the essential characteristics of style are common to all three.

(*iii*) *Italy*. From the early 15th century Italy became a veritable province of Franco-Netherlands musical culture. A steady stream of singers and composers came south across the Alps to staff the chapels established at the leading courts and churches of such important centres as Milan, Venice, Florence, Ferrara, Naples and Rome. Virtually every important figure of the late 15th century and early 16th was at some time in his career on Italian soil; Agricola, Isaac, Compère, Weerbeke, Obrecht and Josquin were only a few of them. The influence of the northerners was felt not only in their contributions to the motet repertory that came to be disseminated there but also in their teaching activities.

After the accession of Leo X to the papal throne in 1513, the decisive influence appears, however, to have been French. This may have been due largely to the decidedly francophile tastes of both Leo X and his successor but one, Clement VII (also a Medici), and to the considerable prestige of the papal chapel in which those predilections were mirrored. The motet publications of Antico and Petrucci give special status to the works of Févin and Mouton and show that composers in the orbit of the French royal chapel were in the ascendancy. The flow of compositions, and of musicians, was undoubtedly encouraged by the meeting between Leo X and François I at Bologna in 1515. The French presence in the duchy of Milan, following the victory at Marignano in that year, must also have contributed to the same trend. Events such as these reinforced the French orientation of the important musical establishment maintained by the dukes of Este in Ferrara and facilitated the circulation of music by masters of the French royal chapel that had begun through that channel about the turn of the century. As a result, not only the papal chapel but also a good deal of Italian musical life was dominated by the French style well into the second half of the 16th century. Even the few native composers known to have been active during this period emulated their northern neighbours. The most noteworthy is Costanzo Festa, who set the lament on the death of Queen Anne of Brittany, *Quis dabit oculis*, a text previously treated by Mouton, whose setting he clearly followed. Nevertheless, it was undoubtedly the Italians who first developed, from antiphonal elements in the polyphonic style of northern composers, the practice of writing motets for divided choirs (*cori spezzati*) that came to be a hallmark of ceremonial music at the basilica of St Mark's, Venice. Francesco Santa Croce, whose origins and career have both been traced to the Venetian states, set the compline psalms for divided choir, and these were included in a manuscript now in Verona (*I-VEaf* 218) that was probably copied in the late 1530s. The liturgical practice of singing alternate verses of the psalms from opposite sides of the choir presumably gave rise to polyphonic settings intended for similar performance. But the paired bicinia that figure so prominently in the motets of the Josquin generation, and the contrasting combinations of two and more voices that came into play even earlier, both lent themselves admirably to a spatial division between groups of singers that were treated antiphonally. When the vesper psalms composed in this manner by Willaert and Berchem were published in 1550 (*I salmi appertinenti ali vesperi per tutte le feste dell'anno ... parte spezzadi accomodati da cantare a uno et a duoi chori*) the polychoral style was provided with a prestigious example that was widely circulated and presumably regularly heard at St Mark's, which was ideally suited to an effective deployment of divided choirs. The stage was thus set not only for the dissemination of this style into every leading musical centre of western Europe but also for the extraordinary development of festal music in Venice by Andrea and Giovanni Gabrieli.

5. PERIPHERAL TRADITIONS.
(*i*) *Spain*. The cultivation of the motet seems to have come to Spain relatively late. Not until Aragon and Castile were united in 1474 under Ferdinand and Isabella is there evidence of an important musical establishment where motets would have been composed and sung regularly. In fact the beginnings of a significant Spanish tradition may date from the visits to Spain in 1502 and again in 1506 of Philip the Handsome and Joanna of Castile. They were attended

on both occasions by the distinguished chapel maintained by them in the best tradition of the ducal house of Burgundy. Among the composers then in Spain were Pierre de La Rue and Alexander Agricola as well as lesser men such as Orto, Braconnier and Divitis.

The leading composers at the Spanish court under Ferdinand and Isabella, Juan de Anchieta and Francisco de Peñalosa, wrote motets in a style not far removed from that of the Netherlanders they presumably emulated. Liturgical melodies were used both as tenor cantus firmi and as the melodic substance of the superius, as was traditional for Marian antiphons. The polyphonic complexity of the northern style seems not to 'ave been entirely compatible with Spanish tempera-r,ent, however, and Anchieta in particular was inclined to adapt to his motets the syllabic homophony of his secular pieces.

The Spanish presence in the Low Countries under the Habsburgs made possible a continuing Netherlands influence on Spanish composers through most of the 16th century. But equally important for Spanish composers of that period was their association with Franco-Flemish musicians at the papal court. Peñalosa was there in 1517, and Morales, a seminal figure for the Spanish tradition, spent a decade there from 1535. The musical style that was to have the most decided effect on Morales is revealed in his choice of motets as mass models; for example, there are two by Mouton and one each by Gombert, Richafort and Verdelot. His own motets show the systematic use of syntactic imitation characteristic of his generation, the adoption of a cantus firmus with its original text for symbolic reasons – both are exemplified in his celebrated five-voice *Emendemus in melius* (HAM, no.128) – and an affinity for the balanced symmetry of the respond form. A move towards fuller sonorities and a more homophonic texture – even when the compositional procedure is essentially contrapuntal in nature – is discernible; these traits became increasingly marked on the Continent after the middle of the century.

At the same time, the motet tradition continued to be cultivated vigorously in Spain even by those composers who never left their native country. This is amply demonstrated by Guerrero and a number of composers of secondary importance who continued to build on the same stylistic foundation.

(ii) *Germanic territories.* Just as Franco-Flemish musicians took the newly defined style of the Latin motet to Spain, so also did they take it to the regions of Germanic culture. One of the key figures was undoubtedly Isaac, who was associated with the imperial chapel of Maximilian I from 1496 for the rest of his life. His influence is most directly evident in the works of his pupil Senfl, who served with him in Maximilian's chapel and then in the 1540s moved to the ducal court of Bavaria in Munich. No less important for the development of the motet in Germanic territories was Josquin himself. Although he may never have been east of the Rhine, his works were much admired there (especially by Luther) and widely disseminated by publishers such as Forster, Hans Ott, and Berg & Neuber.

The development of the Latin motet was inhibited in some areas by the Reformation, which emphasized congregational participation and the use of the vernacular. But, as in France, the compositional procedures developed for setting Latin texts were also adopted to the vernacular. Just as Goudimel had set the French Psalter both in the familiar style for singers of limited skill and in a more polyphonic vein for the better-trained, Johann Walter (i) provided polyphony for the chorales in both styles, treating the traditional melodies as they were generally treated in the Tenorlied.

In the second half of the 16th century, however, polyphonic settings of Latin texts – many by Catholic composers – gradually regained ascendancy over music sung in the vernacular during Lutheran services. This was undoubtedly due in part to the activity of the Protestant printer Georg Rhau, who published a series of collections (1538–51) devoted to polyphonic settings of the Roman liturgy for both the Mass and Vespers. Particularly significant are the psalm motets (following Josquin's models) and settings of the Gospel readings, both because of their large number and the frequency with which they could have been used in the liturgy. Indeed, Berg & Neuber printed (1554–5) a five-volume repertory of Gospel motets for the main feasts of the entire liturgical year, and there is evidence that these were sung not only in conjunction with but also in lieu of the prescribed readings for the Mass well into the 17th century.

(iii) *England.* The history of the motet in England after the generation of Power and Dunstable shows a gap that can only partly be filled by the repertory of the Eton Choirbook. These works demonstrate that in the second half of the 15th century English composers had lost none of their fondness for plainsong settings of the Marian antiphons, particularly the *Salve regina*, or for devotional texts in honour of the Virgin. However, the settings they provided have a monumental character only occasionally adumbrated in the mass compositions of the Old Hall Manuscript. They are mainly for five or six voices and are divided into half a dozen or more separate sections. The juxtaposition of choirs with varying numbers of voices and different ranges, together with a melismatic, freely contrapuntal style, suggests that motets such as those written by Regis, Busnois and Ockeghem were taken as models. It may have been the latter's motet for 36 voices that prompted compositions such as Robert Carver's 19-voice *O bone Iesu* and Tallis's *Spem in alium* for 40 voices.

There is little if any syntactic imitation in the works of the earlier generation of composers, which included Banaster, Cornysh and Fayrfax. After the accession of Henry VIII in 1509, however, contacts with musicians on the Continent began to increase markedly; it was presumably from continental models that Taverner, for example, adopted a tenor cantus firmus treatment in even semibreves and breves for his settings of *Dum transisset*. Perhaps more significant for the developing English tradition was the gradual assimilation of a more syllabic approach to text setting and the concomitant organization of contrapuntal writing into points of imitation. An early example is (?Richard) Sampson's *Quam pulchra es* (*GB-Lbm* Royal II E.ii), which dates from about 1516. The discant style that was such a distinctive trait of English music in the first half of the 15th century continued, nonetheless, to be used effectively, as can be seen from Taverner's *Christe Iesu*.

Henry VIII's break with Rome in 1534 and his subsequent dissolution of the monasteries, with their musical institutions, imposed a restraint on the development of the Latin motet much more stringent than that caused by the Reformation in Germany. It may also help to account for the unusual emphasis on polyphonic psalm settings by somewhat later figures such as Tye and Robert White; presumably these were intended to replace plainsong, which was no longer in use. But as in other Protestant areas compositional skills associated with the motet were transferred to the setting of texts in the vernacular. Thus the anthem was born of the earlier genre.

6. SECOND HALF OF THE 16TH CENTURY. The 16th-century motet saw a final synthesis in the works of Palestrina and Lassus, each of whom represented a separate stylistic tradition. The more conservative was certainly Palestrina, which may be explained in part by the atmosphere engendered by the Counter-Reformation. However, it is also clear that his stylistic antecedents lie primarily with the French composers of the generation after Mouton. This is indicated first of all by his selection of motets as models for mass composition; these include four by Jacquet of Mantua, two by Lhéritier and one each by De Silva, Richafort, Moulu and Carpentras. Palestrina's choice of texts and their treatment lead to the same conclusions; in his settings of sequences and traditional Marian antiphons he retained the chant as an important melodic element in the polyphony, something he rarely did with other liturgical genres.

Palestrina showed his concern for formal order and clarity by mirroring the paired repetitions of the sequence in a variation chain, and by adhering to the liturgical design of the responsories that constitute roughly half of his motet repertory. Most of his motets are for five or six voices, but even in those works he was inclined to handle the parts in contrasting pairs, as he did systematically in his four-voice compositions. Everywhere the alternation between imitative polyphony and an occasional passage in homophony provides the basic substance of his part-writing. Only in a general preference for fuller textures and sonorities and in a handful of psalm compositions for divided choir can one detect the general direction of contemporary stylistic change.

Palestrina's compositional style also provided the matrix for the artistic culmination of the Spanish tradition as embodied in the motets of Victoria. Like Morales, Victoria spent a significant length of time in Rome, which was all the more critical for him in that it began when he was only 17 and lasted more than 20 years. Although his total repertory is much smaller than Palestrina's, he set many of the same texts and handled them in much the same way. But his motets are distinguished by a more generally homophonic texture and by a livelier interest in harmonic colour, which he pursued by means of signed accidentals usually suggested by the meaning of the words.

An overriding concern for a vivid musical depiction of the text is primarily responsible for the essential stylistic differences between Palestrina and Lassus. In contrast to Palestrina's carefully balanced lines and smooth rhythms, those of Lassus respond to certain textual conceits with wide leaps and relatively sharp rhythmic contrasts. Whereas Palestrina made only occasional, discreet use of pictorial devices, Lassus drew on a wide repertory of rhetorical gestures borrowed from the contemporary madrigal. His reliance on the musical vocabulary of Italian secular music is undoubtedly a result of his service as a young man at the court of Ferdinando Gonzaga, as opposed to the ecclesiastical context within which Palestrina spent his entire life. In addition, Lassus cultivated a declamatory chordal style in which the harmonic rhythm is surprisingly static for the period, and the vertical sonorities are thus strongly perceived. Even imitative passages are so treated that the impression of homophony is only moderately disturbed.

From the ducal court of Bavaria in Munich, where Lassus served from 1556 until his death, his motet style was disseminated through areas of Germanic culture by a number of talented pupils, including Reiner, Lechner, Eccard, Aichinger and – indirectly through Giovanni Gabrieli – H. L. Hassler. Essentially the same manner of motet composition flourished also at the imperial court of Vienna, where Vaet served as the Kapellmeister from 1564 to 1567, followed by Monte from 1569 to 1603. Jacob Handl also represents this tradition: even though he is not known to have had any direct connection with Lassus, his skilful and expressive use of rhetorical gestures points to Lassus's influence.

It may have been Monte who took to England the dramatic chordal style characteristic of Lassus. He visited there in 1554–5, becoming acquainted with Thomas Byrd, whose son, William, achieved the final synthesis of the Latin motet in the British Isles. There are some typically conservative traits in Byrd's output of motets, such as the eight-voice crab canon in his *Diliges Dominum* (*Works*, i, 232). But he revealed his interest in Monte's style in his eight-voice *Quomodo cantabimus* of 1583 (*Works*, ix, 99), an answer to the latter's setting (also for eight voices) of the initial verses of the same psalm, *Super flumina Babylonis*. Perhaps in response partly to Monte's example and partly to the growing interest in the Italian madrigal in England from the 1580s, Byrd also made considerable use of pictorial devices in some of his motets; his *Vigilate* (*Works*, ii, 120) is a well-known example.

Early in the 16th century it had been Italian composers who first developed the polychoral style. Similarly, at the end of the century it was once again an Italian, Giovanni Gabrieli, who perceived in the performance traditions of *cori spezzati* the seeds of a new manner. From the relatively rapid interchange of short homophonic phrases between choirs of voices, or voices and instruments, was born the concertato principle. It can be heard in, for instance, Gabrieli's *In ecclesiis* (HAM, no.157; see §III, 2(i) below), a work that clearly presages the transformation of the motet in the 17th century.

### III. Baroque

1. General. 2. Italy. 3. Germany. 4. France.

1. GENERAL. After 1600 the motet lost its traditional position as a central musical genre. With the assimilation and integration of *seconda prattica* elements, it abandoned some of its classical characteristics; but at the same time it became during the 17th century an important point of departure for a range of new forms of sacred vocal composition, such as the cantata, and in this development its earlier, leading role was at least

partly restored.

The motet's development into a peripheral genre is demonstrated in a growing terminological imprecision, whereby in the 17th and 18th centuries the term 'motet' came to denote any kind of vocal music with liturgical affiliations. Indeed, the functional definition of the motet as a piece belonging to the liturgy remained the decisive factor, regardless of its musical nature. Texts were mainly biblical, drawn from psalms, lessons, antiphons, canticles and so on, but they also included free poetry with liturgical *de tempore* designations (e.g. Marian sequences for the Catholic Church, or chorales for the Protestant). Catholic motets were invariably in Latin, but, after the Reformation, Protestant motets were predominantly in the vernacular.

Independently of its historical development as a genre, the term 'motet' was itself introduced in the mid-17th century as a stylistic concept, and, as in the systematizations of Marco Scacchi, Athanasius Kircher and others, the 'stylus motecticus' became a subdivision of the 'stylus ecclesiasticus'. It was thus categorized as a style of composition, derived from the traditional polyphonic language of the 16th-century *ars perfecta*. 'Stylus motecticus' represents a retrospective musical language, especially that of Palestrina and his tradition, and was applied to other genres, such as the mass. The term 'motet' thus signified both a genre and a style. Motet and motet style, though originally congruent, were not necessarily in any way identical after 1600.

In the 17th and 18th centuries motets were often summarily described as 'concerted', and the term 'motetto concertato' appears with some frequency after the middle of the 17th century. Praetorius (*Syntagma musicum*, iii, 1618, p.6) stated that the names 'concerti, motetti, concentus etc' were analogous and interchangeable. The concerto principle appeared in various ways as a universal element of the *seconda prattica* in motet composition, even in the retrospective *stile antico* motet; yet the term 'concerted motet' obscured distinctions between the different types of post-1600 motet. The common structural element was the technique of stringing together passages of contrasting themes and motifs to match the individual lines of text. This fragmented, varied construction was expressly referred to in Walther's definition (1732) of motet style.

The history of motet composition after 1600 divides into two independent lines of development, which were manifested nationally, regionally and denominationally in several different ways: the choral motet proper continued the 16th-century tradition in various directions; and the vocal concerto, which arose from the motet of the *cori spezzati* type, assimilated the principles of monody and gradually integrated instrumental elements.

The essential structure of the older motet style was retained in the true choral motet, especially in the Palestrinian motet predominant in the Catholic south (Italy, Austria and south Germany) and exclusively used in the Iberian peninsula, where Counter-Reformation orthodoxy prevailed. This *stile antico* was particularly preserved and promoted in the mass, as laid down by papal decree (Urban VIII, 1623) and as practised in the Sistine Chapel, which provided a decisive lead until the 19th century. The tradition of following Palestrina's style necessarily resulted in apathy and conformity in the mass as well as the motet, which came to be characterized by studious craftsmanship, with

schematic sequences of motif and monotonous harmony. On the other hand there was a trend towards contrapuntal techniques, such as canons and inversions, a trend reflected in the theoretical treatises of the time (Fux, Martini, Paolucci). In the late 17th century there was a tendency towards a functionally harmonic conception of counterpoint, with an increasingly periodic style of vocal melody and even da capo form (Caldara, Lotti). The *a cappella* ideal appeared by the 17th century in so modified a form that instrumental doubling – often with cornetts and trombones, to create an archaic effect – with continuo accompaniment in *basso seguente* style was normal.

Implicit in the sacred vocal concerto, on the other hand, is a complex range of combinations of voices and instruments which, in conjunction with episodic structure, resulted by the late 17th century in the splitting-up of the motet into isolated units. The concerted motet thus began to comprise a number of separate movements, incorporating elements such as aria and recitative formerly considered foreign to the form. This was the origin of the Italian orchestral motet (e.g. Scarlatti, Durante, Leo and Pergolesi) and of the *grand motet* in France (e.g. Charpentier, Lully, Lalande, Campra and Rameau). The development of the English verse anthem and of the cantata in its various forms also derives from this new motet style.

## 2. ITALY.

(i) *Up to 1650.* The era of the Baroque concertato motet begins with the publication in 1602 of Viadana's *Cento concerti ecclesiastici*, for one to four voices with, for the first time, organ continuo. The idea was prompted not so much by any hankering after change as by the increasingly inadequate performance of unaccompanied church music: the solo motets in particular were conceived in the most conservative style. What the collection achieved was to prove the feasibility of a small-scale medium, using a handful of modest voices, and to break the dominance of the *a cappella* approach in sacred music. At the same time the use of the organ continuo opened up new possibilities with the conventional four- to six-part texture. Contrasts of texture and sonority could be exploited, and counterpoint became harmonically based, since it was heard against a background of simple chord progressions. The Venetian printers produced a flood of publications of small-scale, practical church music for the provincial cities of northern Italy, by composers who were often quite talented; most of it consisted of motets to be sung at Mass or at the Offices on principal feasts and saints' days. In the context of the new style the word 'concerto' was frequently used as a synonym for motet. The motets in Monteverdi's Vespers collection of 1610 do not fit so easily into this picture: they are virtuoso pieces conceived in an experimental style for court singers.

In the hands of composers like Alessandro Grandi (i) and Ignazio Donati, the smaller types of concertato motet quickly reached a high artistic level in the decade 1610–20. Grandi in particular was an assured master of melody. This gift was combined with a grasp of polyphonic techniques in his duet motets for equal voices and continuo, the best of which are those with intense, prayerful texts or with words from the Song of Songs, which drew from him powerful, impassioned music. Donati excelled in works for four or five voices with organ, where he could play off different combinations of singers and build up telling climaxes by means of a 'textural crescendo'. In this very popular type of piece the text would be divided into sections, each with a characteristic motif that could be developed contrapuntally; sometimes, however, a refrain form with solos and duets offset by a repeated tutti was used, or a motet might be in the form of a dialogue in which one or more voices would represent different scriptural characters (see DIALOGUE, §4).

The refrain form was specially appropriate to the massive, elaborate Venetian motets that Giovanni Gabrieli wrote during his last years, often involving the principle of *cori spezzati*. In these the word 'Alleluia' was frequently set to a dance-like triple-time passage, which through its recurrence could bind a large work together. Gabrieli also pioneered the 'mixed concertato' style in the large motet, assigning particular sections to solo voices, instruments and a full choir and orchestra called 'cappella': *In ecclesiis* (HAM, no.157) is a deservedly famous work of this type in which all these innovatory techniques are handled with mastery. After Gabrieli this grandiose approach tended to be restricted to psalm and mass composition; motets were in general small-scale works for everyday church use or even 'spiritual recreation'.

To this end Venice in the 1620s created a vogue for small motets for one or two voices with obbligato violins and continuo, the sacred parallel of the early secular cantata. Grandi proved a pioneer here: he introduced delightful, idiomatically written sinfonias for the violins which acted as refrains, and tried out variation and strophic-bass techniques borrowed from secular music. Sometimes the violins not only provided a refrain but joined in dialogue with the voice. This medium and the simpler monodic solo motet (without violins) were the types that most clearly pointed the way for the Baroque motet. The monodic type, too, became established only in the 1620s: a fine anthology is the Venetian *Ghirlanda sacra* (1625), which contains four of Monteverdi's few contributions to the genre. Compared with the sacred duet, therefore, the solo motet had taken root slowly: the oft-repeated claim that the Florentine monodists had an immediate, important effect on sacred music can be discounted. Nevertheless, the type did call for more virtuosity in the way of vocal ornamentation, an indispensable part of the art of monody.

In Rome the conservative atmosphere militated to some extent against the introduction of the various progressive ideas from the north. Older composers perpetuated the ideal of Palestrinian polyphony in the *stile antico*, but some younger ones (Agazzari, Landi and G. F. Anerio) preferred concertato writing in an unadventurous Viadana-like idiom. Solo motets, for example those by Kapsberger, could all too easily be dogged by mere ornamental note-spinning at the expense of real melody. It was only with the development of oratorio that Roman church music achieved a new lease of life in the 1640s, as can be seen from the anthologies of motets published later in that decade. Refrain forms with instrumental sinfonias, a bel canto style of melodic writing and a wider range of keys are all found here; and in Carissimi, Rome had at last found a really talented composer who could infuse spiritual fervour into motets as well as into oratorios. Other notable composers of motets in the first half of

the 17th century were G. B. Crivelli, Merula, Giovanni Priuli, Rigatti, Rovetta and Orazio Tarditi.

(*ii*) *After 1650.* By 1650 liturgical composition was declining, and with the competition of opera and instrumental music the number of motet publications was decreasing. Opera became an attractive source of income to composers who held church posts, and motets tended to be produced only in places with opera houses and by composers (Cavalli, Legrenzi, P. A. Ziani) who were as well known for their operas as for their sacred music. The mellifluous vocal writing in some of Legrenzi's motets is obviously derived from opera, although in others he used dialogue effects between two characters which are not necessarily operatic but hark back to the dialogue motets of the early 17th century. Instrumental music was becoming an increasingly important part of the church service, with the development of the violin family, and sonatas and concertos were displacing occasional motets at Mass. Motets themselves often involved a pair of violins as well as voices. The concertato motet for four to six voices and organ had petered out by 1650, leaving the chamber-like combinations of solo, duet and trio, with or without violins, as the preferred textures for the Italian motet. With a smaller demand for occasional motets to be sung at Mass, the texts set most commonly were the four Marian antiphons for Vespers and Compline.

Important composers of motets in the mid-Baroque period include the prolific Cazzati, best known for his instrumental music written for S Petronio, Bologna: he was one of the few north Italians to write motets in both the archaic *stile antico* and the up-to-date manner. A later Bolognese was G. P. Colonna, some of whose motets include violins (to be expected, in view of the excellence of the Bologna church orchestra). Other notable composers in north Italian cities were Bassani at Ferrara and Petrobelli at Padua, both of whom included instrumental parts in their motets, and Brevi at Milan, who published solo motets of the monodic type. It is interesting that all this published music was modest in its requirements; large-scale motets were not disseminated through publication, but this is not to say that they were not composed. Intended for special celebrations in individual places, such as that of a church's patron saint, their usefulness was local and they survive only in manuscript form.

The co-existence of old and new ways continued to be a marked feature in Rome: publications of old-style pieces by such men as Francesco Foggia or Benevoli were distinguished by Latin title-pages. Their music was largely in a retrospective *a cappella* style, while at the same time, between 1650 and 1680, Graziani published many volumes of solo motets. The tension between the two styles resulted in a gradual modification of the pure Palestrina idiom under the influence of Baroque approaches to phrase structure and tonality. The Marian antiphons of the Bernabei family are either in a very pallid version of the old style, lacking rhythmic verve and modal colouring (Giuseppe Antonio's *Regina caeli*), or more dramatic in feeling (his father Ercole's *Salve regina*), taking Victoria rather than Palestrina as a starting-point. In some of the motets of Lotti, a prominent Venetian opera and oratorio composer, the updating of the old style is complete: *In omni tribulatione*, though unaccompanied, has a chromatic theme and a rich harmonic language. Even if the linear treatment of dissonance conformed to 16th-century conventions, chords such as the diminished 7th were introduced for expressive purposes. Lotti also wrote more modern motets such as *Columbae innocentes* for soprano, two violins and organ.

In the hands of Neapolitan opera composers such as Alessandro Scarlatti, Francesco Durante and Leo, the orchestral motet – in effect a more lavishly scored version of the solo motet with violins – came nearest to the current operatic forms of the day. Scarlatti's *Audi filia*, a festive motet for St Cecilia's Day, has oboes as well as strings in the orchestra and consists largely of elaborate solo sections with a chorus entering only at the end; as in the operatic aria, vocal and instrumental material was closely integrated within a taut ritornello structure. Other motets by Scarlatti make use of distinct recitative and da capo aria schemes, again imported from opera. In general the emphasis is on musical organization and display rather than fervent declamation of the text in the manner of earlier Baroque Italians.

3. GERMANY.

(i) *The generation of Schütz.* The Catholic regions of Germany showed a clear dependence on Italy in nearly every aspect of sacred music, and the most original development after 1600 in the choral motet was in Lutheran Germany. In contrast to the Calvinist regions of Switzerland and the Netherlands, where psalm settings were the only polyphonic genre (exemplified by Sweelinck's psalm motets), and even England, where the anthem had in effect replaced the motet, by the second half of the 16th century the Lutheran areas had a broadly based motet tradition capable of further development. Three main types had evolved: the motet in free, lightly imitative style ('Liedmotette') with occasional cantus firmus elements (used by Eccard, Hassler and Lechner); the chorale motet in a markedly contrapuntal cantus firmus style (*see* CHORALE SETTINGS, §I); and the text-motet ('Spruchmotette'), presenting settings of key verses mainly from the Gospels, the Psalter or the Song of Songs. This last type in particular soon gained increasingly in importance since there was a great liturgical demand for music illustrating pithy biblical texts (or 'Kernsprüche', which became a popular title for such collections. This soon led to the publication of sets of Gospel texts covering the church year (for example by Melchior Vulpius, Andreas Raselius, Christoph Demantius and Melchior Franck), and this was echoed in the 18th century by the seasonal cantatas which also chiefly derived their texts from the Gospels. The expressive style of Lassus and his followers (such as Jacob Handl) exerted a greater influence in northern and central Germany than the textually less committed manner of the Palestrina school. This repertory was handed down in printed collections (especially Bodenschatz's *Florilegium portense*, 1618) and performed well into the 18th century, and the musical–rhetorical principles of the Latin motet (as codified in the numerous treatises on *musica poetica*) was transferred directly to the German text-motet. An important stylistic advance was the inclusion of madrigal elements in early 17th-century music, as shown particularly in motets called 'sacred madrigals', for example J. H. Schein's *Israelis Brünlein* (1623) and Schütz's *Cantiones sacrae* (1625), but also apparent as early as 1606 in Lechner's *Deutsche*

*Sprüche von Leben und Tod* (MS). One remarkably informative collection, including the most varied kinds of motet-style treatment of a text, is *Angst der Hellen und Friede der Seelen*, published by Burkhard Grossmann in 1623 and consisting of commissioned settings of Psalm cxvi by the most esteemed motet composers of the time: Franck, Nicolaus Erich, Michael Praetorius, Schütz, Schein and Demantius among others. This remarkable volume demonstrates the flexible application of various techniques, ranging from chordal homophony and *falsobordone* to regular points of imitation and more refined contrapuntal intricacies; at the same time it represents a selection of the most characteristic approaches, from the plain concerto manner of Praetorius to the highly individual musical language of the young Schütz. The climax of powerful and vivid musical illustration of text combined with elaborate counterpoint came in Schütz's later works, especially his *Geistliche Chor-Music* (1648), *Zwölff geistliche Gesänge* (1657) and *Deutsches Magnificat* (1671). The *Geistliche Chor-Music* represents the programmatic counterpart to his *Symphoniae sacrae* (see below) in that it is based exclusively on the 'stylus. . .without Bassum Continuum' (to quote Schütz's foreword) and incorporates as 'necessary Requisita . . .Dispositiones modorum; Fugae simplices, mixtae, inversae; Contrapunctum duplex; Differentia Styli in arte Musica diversi; Modulatio vocum; Connexio subjectorum, etc'. In the *Geistliche Chor-Music* Schütz forged a motet style that renounces the overemphasis on madrigalisms (which still prevailed in the *Cantiones sacrae*) and aims at a perfect balance between contrapuntal organization and the musical interpretation of the text. His appreciation and treatment of German in terms of a natural prosody is both exemplary and unprecedented. The *Deutsches Magnificat*, one of his very last works, forms the logical conclusion of his late motet style in that it abandons the emphatic accentuation of single words or phrases by rhetorical or other expressive devices in favour of a more detached, harmonically orientated style.

Although the true choral motet figures prominently in Schütz's output, it is outnumbered and dominated by the vocal concerto, which had developed around 1600 as a new branch of the motet in Italy. Giovanni Gabrieli's *Sacrae symphoniae* (1597) and Viadana's *Cento concerti ecclesiastici* (1602) served as starting-points and models for German composers of the vocal concerto. The sacred vocal concerto (*geistliches Konzert*, *Psalmkonzert* etc) is based on the same repertory of liturgical texts as the traditional motet and follows the same formal (i.e. sectional) organization. The Venetian type of polychoral motet, in which contrasting choirs functioned as heterogeneous elements, with instruments taking a supplementary or complementary role, reached a climax in Germany at the beginning of the 17th century in Praetorius's *Musae Sioniae* (1605–7), Schütz's *Psalmen Davids* (1619) and Samuel Scheidt's many motets for two or more choirs. Because of the great expenditure involved, performance of these monumental works was necessarily restricted to centres with large musical establishments and to special occasions. During the Thirty Years War (1618–48) the use of several choirs became exceptional and then disappeared entirely; it enjoyed only a modest revival in the motets for double choir written in central Germany around 1700 (members of the Bach family composed several such works).

This situation demanded the swift development and dissemination of the concertato solo motet, which was far less demanding and more practical to perform. Originally these *geistliche Konzerte* were written for solo voices and continuo (e.g. Schein's *Opella nova*, 1618–26, or Schütz's *Kleine geistliche Concerte*, 1636–9), representing in effect a reduced form of the polychoral motet. Obbligato instruments were soon added, and a fully independent instrumental ensemble resulted. This development is most clearly seen in the three parts of Schütz's *Symphoniae sacrae* (1629, 1647, 1650), in which various kinds of concerto for both large and small forces were published, and Scheidt's *Concertus sacri* (1622). Implicit in the sacred concerto is a complex range of possible combinations of vocal and instrumental parts in conjunction with the sectional structure of the motet. In the second half of the 17th century this resulted in its being split up into separate units, which in turn led to its developing into independent sections or movements using elements foreign to the motet such as aria, chorale and finally recitative. The cantata derives from this development of the concerted motet. In line with this tradition, J. S. Bach referred both to his early cantata on a purely biblical text, *Gott ist mein König*, bwv71 (1708), and to his late parody of Pergolesi's *Stabat mater* as 'motetto'.

*(ii) The generation of Bach.* No particular Schütz tradition was established in central Germany in the late 17th century. Hammerschmidt, Christoph Bernhard and J. R. Ahle appear in a limited way as followers of Schütz in their motets but could not command his breadth or depth. Within the repertory of concerted liturgical *de tempore* music the small- and large-scale types of *geistliches Konzert* gradually merged into, and were finally absorbed by, the emerging cantata (*see* CANTATA, §II). But composition of the choral motet proper continued within the framework of the flourishing Kantorei tradition, especially in Thuringia and Saxony. As the cantata came to the fore the motet was increasingly confined to weddings, funerals and similar special services. Stylistically there was a clear movement towards homophonic textures, above all in the chordally based works for double chorus from the circle round the Bach family. There was a marked preference for a combination of biblical quotation and chorale, also a characteristic of J. S. Bach's work. In the motets of the older Bachs, Georg Böhm, P. H. Erlebach, Sebastian Knüpfer, Johann Schelle and their contemporaries, modern structural elements such as ritornello form and fugal technique appeared. The fact that the ideal of a single musical structure with contrasting, thematically unified sections or parts conflicted with the traditional motet form (whose irregular, sectionalized structure depended entirely on the phrases of the text) clearly hastened the gradual decline of the motet genre.

J. S. Bach's motets represent the culminating point of the genre in the 18th century, though they amount to an insignificant proportion of his total output (six works: four for double chorus, one each for four- and five-part chorus). They fall entirely within the tradition of the central German motet, which is especially clear in *Fürchte dich nicht*, where there is a chordal opening section with alternating choirs and a fugue with cantus firmus (a simultaneous combination of two different texts and compositional elements; it is modelled on a work by Johann Christoph Bach). Peculiarities of Bach's motet composition include an ingenious stratification of the text for reciprocal interpretations (for instance in *Der Geist hilft*, where the first chorus sings 'denn wir wissen nicht, was wir beten sollen' and the second 'der Geist hilft'); contrast of texture; large-scale formal organization (as in *Jesu meine Freude*, in 11 symmetrical corresponding parts); the 'instrumentalizing' of vocal parts by virtuoso declamation in figurative instrumental style; and the application of contemporary Italian instrumental concerto form (slow–fast–slow – e.g. in *Singet dem Herrn*, which is divided into three such sections). Above all, his works are marked by their close affinity between musical expression and textual meaning. In the motets, unlike the choral cantatas (which are more unified in motif and on a larger scale), textual relevance of the musical material corresponds more openly to the smaller scale of the sectional principle. Nevertheless, the musical underlining of single words or groups of words is clearly integrated in a coherent and unified thematic–motivic context. The interpretation of the meaning and expressive qualities of larger text units rather than single words relates to the ideals of the doctrine of the Affections; it is here that the chief conceptual difference between the motet of Schütz's generation and that of Bach's principally lies.

All Bach's motets belong to his first years in Leipzig (1723–31), and this accounts for the singular stylistic position occupied by *O Jesu Christ, meins Lebens Licht* bwv118, called 'motet' in Bach's autograph scores, in which the presence of obbligato instruments, not typical of the chorale motet proper, forms a bridge to the chorale concerto and chorale cantata – another example of the interrelation of genres. This is further demonstrated in the fact that motet-like principles predominate in the chorale cantatas (and in others, for example no.106).

Like Bach's, Telemann's small number of motets (some of them of the strict *stile antico* type) are peripheral works: when the rise of 18th-century rationalism led to the decline of liturgical musical traditions, Protestant motet writing died away. But apart from Bach's successors (Harrer, Doles, Homilius, Kirnberger and J. A. Hiller) some notable compositions appeared, distinguished by their contrapuntal purity and cantabile quality. These stylistic trends were no doubt concessions to prevailing taste, but at the same time they show the influence of a new retrospective orientation (Harrer studied Palestrina; Kirnberger edited works by Hassler): this represents one of the earliest instances of the musical historicism that characterized the 19th- and 20th-century motet.

4. FRANCE.

*(i) The early 17th century.* A conservative style rooted in Franco-Netherlands polyphony dominated the French motet in the early 17th century. French composers were reluctant to introduce elements from the *stile concertato* and slow to adopt the continuo in religious music. For Mersenne, the 'impressive harmony and rich counterpoint' of Du Caurroy's motets was such that 'all the composers of France take him for their master'. The motets of Du Caurroy's *Preces ecclesiasticae* (1609) and those of Jean de Bournonville, André Péchon and Charles d'Ambleville exemplified this late Renaissance style, which was not seriously challenged in

the first quarter of the century.

By the 1630s the most original motet composer was Guillaume Bouzignac, whose music was not widely disseminated. He wrote probably about 100 motets. He absorbed Italian and Catalan influences and created a dialogue motet of great dramatic intensity, for example by juxtaposing solo voice and tutti and by using speech rhythms and textual repetition.

Jean Veillot, Thomas Gobert and Nicolas Formé were concerned in the evolution of the double-chorus concertato motet. Veillot was one of the first to compose independent *symphonies* and to use instruments to double the chorus (*O filii et filiae* and *Sacris solemniis*, for example); all three used the *grand* and *petit choeurs* that became the hallmark of the later Versailles motet. As early as 1646, Gobert noted that the '*grand choeur*, in five parts, is always sung by many voices. The *petit choeur* is composed only of solo voices' (letter of 17 October to Constantijn Huygens). Few double-chorus motets by Formé and Veillot and none by Gobert survive, largely because little original sacred music of the early 17th century was published; for the same reason the double-chorus motets of Gonet, Solon and Penne, the motets of Cambert and Eustache Picot and the late motets of Moulinié are lost or exist only in fragmentary form.

In the preface to his *Meslanges de sujets chrétiens* of 1658, Etienne Moulinié commented on 'certain passages . . . which are rather bold and which may pass for licence in the opinion of those who prefer the austerity of the old style to the *agréments* of the new'. He was presumably referring to those passages for solo voices (*récits*) and chorus that borrow the short phrases, the dance rhythms and even certain roulades from contemporary *airs de cour*. Also new in France in the late 1640s was the use of the continuo in religious music, as in Moulinié's *Meslanges* and in Constantijn Huygens's *Pathodia sacra et profana* (1647). In 1652 Ballard brought out Henry Du Mont's *Cantica sacra*, with continuo parts printed separately for the first time in France.

(*ii*) *The mid-17th century.* Du Mont, a Walloon, who arrived in France in 1638, assumed a position in French religious music 'somewhat comparable to that of Haydn in the symphony and the string quartet' (Garros, p.1598). He introduced to France the *petit motet* of one, two or three voices and continuo in collections issued between 1652 and 1671. Here motets with Italianate chains of suspensions, light polyphony, 'affective' melodic and harmonic intervals, echo effects, dialogue techniques and word-painting co-exist with motets exhibiting such French characteristics as more syllabic rendering of the text, use of melodies of restricted range and shorter phrases, basic diatonicism and rhythmic organization corresponding to popular French dances. Du Mont's 20 *grands motets* open the history of the Versailles motet. Composed over his 20 years as *sous-maître* in the royal chapel, they were printed (post-humously in 1686) 'by express order of His Majesty', like the 24 *grands motets* of Pierre Robert (1684) and the 11 of Lully (1684). These formed an impressive repertory for the king's chapel at the time of his move to Versailles. Louis XIV preferred Low Mass. Perrin wrote: 'there are ordinarily three [motets], one *grand*, one *petit* for the Elévation and a *Domine salvum fac regem*' (a motet setting of Psalm xix.10 that served as a salutation to the king and closed both Low and High Mass) (*Cantica pro capella regis*, 1665).

Structurally the Versailles *grand motet* of this period is an extension of earlier models by Formé and Veillot. It is typically a psalm setting in which the versicles are musically arranged as a series of episodes, incomplete in themselves, for solo voice, ensemble and chorus. The five-part chorus is divided into a *grand* and a *petit choeur*, and the five-part orchestra provides independent *symphonies*, marks important structural divisions, generally doubles the chorus and contributes solo obbligato parts for some of the *récits*. The *grands motets* of the above composers differ only in details. All are very long (Lully's *Te Deum*, for example, has over 1200 bars), all have weighty homophonic choruses with unceasing speech rhythms, often of hypnotic power, and all use melodic formulae and scoring practices found in contemporary stage music and *airs de cour* (for instance, the bass 'double continuo' *air*). In effect, the *grand motet* from this period to the Revolution is a secularized 'concert spirituel' without liturgical function.

(*iii*) *The late 17th century.* The two composers who best represent the motet in quality and quantity at the turn of the century are Charpentier and Lalande. Charpentier composed *grands motets* for the dauphin's chapel (after 1679), for the Jesuit church of St Louis (1684–98) and for the Sainte-Chapelle (1698–1704); he wrote *petits motets* for his patroness, Mlle de Guise (about 1673–88), and for various convents. He obviously regarded his oratorios as motets, since he used that title for many of them. Lalande wrote only *grands motets*, to be heard by the few attending the king's Mass at the royal chapel and, from 1725, by the crowds at the Concert Spirituel (where one of his motets was usually featured in each programme).

Although profiting from his exposure to music by Carissimi, Francesco Beretta and other Roman composers when he was in Italy, Charpentier's only departure from the French motet tradition seems to be his predilection for four-part rather than five-part textures. His harmonic language is richer than that of his predecessors. He used augmented chords and dissonances, such as the mediant 9-7-♯5 chord, with telling effect. In general, his harmonic vocabulary is conservative; his melodic style derives from the French *air de cour* and from the organic use of such ornaments as *ports de voix* and *coulés*; French dance is an important source for his rhythmic organization; and though more contrapuntally orientated than Lully's, his textures remain basically homophonic. His *petits motets* are the most important examples of the genre before François Couperin. Many are *élévations* or Marian antiphons; 30 are *leçons de ténèbres*. He preferred countertenor, tenor and bass or three women's voices for his numerous *petits motets* in trio texture.

Lalande's *grands motets* (about 70 in all) represent the highpoint of the Versailles motet. In many of his later motets (or second versions of earlier ones) he expanded the solo and ensemble episodes into autonomous sections, which were often preceded by *ritournelles*; in this respect the *grand motet* came to resemble the German church cantata at the time of Bach. Dubbed a 'Latin Lully' by his pupil Collin de Blamont, Lalande 'humanized' the *grand motet* without compromising its kingly role: that is, he was particularly sensitive to the meaning of the Latin psalm texts and interpreted the words through expressive harmonies and appropriate melodic figures. He converted the stiff, formal solo *récits* of (for example) Lully and Robert into graceful, even *galant airs*, often providing them with a delicate counterpoint through obbligato instruments, for instance using the typical pre-Rameau opera scoring of soprano and flute accompanied by a violin. Lalande made use of massive blocks of sound in the grandiose five-part, homophonic choruses, but also composed fugal choruses of great breadth in which polyphonic tension is strongly maintained, as in the 'Requiem aeternam' in *De profundis*. He used the orchestra more imaginatively than his predecessors, and at times (following the tentative lead of Du Mont) allowed it a degree of independence, freeing it from merely doubling the vocal lines: see, for example, the second version of the chorus 'Vitam petiit' from *Domine, in virtute tua*. These traits, considered 'ingenious disparities' in their day ('Avertissement' to *Motets de Feu M. Delalande*, 1729), were no doubt responsible for the great popularity of his motets as concert pieces throughout the 18th century.

During the last two decades of the 17th century many *petits motets* were composed for convents. Those by Nivers and Clérambault for St-Cyr are typical: they are scored for two or three voices, and their simple diatonic melodies are laden with French vocal *agréments*. Brossard composed three volumes of *petits motets* (printed in 1695, 1698 and 1703) for the choir schools at Strasbourg and Meaux; though harmonically conservative, they include original touches, and they have detachable 'Alleluia' or 'Amen' finales should they 'appear to be a little long' ('Avertissement' from *Elévations et motets*, 1695).

*(iv) The 18th century.* The Lalande *grand motet* served as both inspiration and obstacle to change for later 18th-century composers. From Campra and Bernier to Mathieu and Giroust, the *sous-maîtres* of the royal chapel were reluctant to alter the basic form of the Versailles motet. Within this tradition, some of the 45 motets by Gervais, the three surviving by Colasse, the six of Minoret, the 11 by Bernier, the *Te Deum* by Collin de Blamont and most of the 26 *grands motets* by Henry Madin ('one of the best motet composers of this century', according to Titon du Tillet) deserve attention. On the other hand, the patina of Italianisms brings little life to most of the motets by Lallouette, Courbois, Pétouille, Guignard, Gomay and Gaveau, which remain exercises in the 'old style'.

In Campra's *grands motets* for the royal chapel, composed between 1723 and 1741, there are solemn homophonic choruses, well-planned double fugues and effective ostinato basses as well as virtuoso 'arias', often accompanied with brilliant instrumental obbligatos. Campra and Rameau made a descriptive agent of the motet orchestra in the manner of the large choral–orchestral complexes of their *tragédies lyriques*. In Campra's *Lauda Jerusalem* and Rameau's *Deus noster refugium*, for example, the violins constantly penetrate the chorus in rapid, concerto-like passages to create exciting 'storm' scenes. Further operatic inroads are found in the opening countertenor *récit* of Rameau's masterpiece, *In convertendo*, which resembles an elegiac monologue from *Hippolyte et Aricie* or *Castor et Pollux* and introduces the fluctuating metres of French recitative. Boismortier and Blanchard further expanded

the role of the orchestra in the *grand motet*, especially with respect to woodwind and brass instruments. Da capo *airs* and elaborate *symphonies* assured these works a place in the repertory of the Concert Spirituel along with the 12 *grands motets* by Mondonville.

The important *grand motet* composers from the early and middle years of the 18th century continued to dominate the music heard at the royal chapel up to the Revolution. This is verified by a Ballard publication (*Livre de motets pour la chapelle du roy*) of the years 1787–92. The 1792 volume gives a list of titles and texts of motets, presumably those performed at the royal chapel between January and June that year: it includes 14 by Lalande, 13 by Campra, four by Bernier, five by Gervais, 25 by Madin and a few by Devins, Gilles, Michel and Vignot.

The *grands motets* of most Parisian and provincial composers follow the uniform style emanating from Versailles. Henry Desmarets composed 16 *grands motets* between 1704 and 1708 for the Duke of Lorraine's chapel in Lunéville. Four of his psalm settings in the Bibliothèque Nationale are long even by the standards of the genre, averaging more than 100 pages each; they include passages of polyphonic concentration rare in French music of the time (for example 'Laboravi in gemitu meo' from *Domine, ne in furore*). Gilles composed 12 *grands motets*, some of which remained in the repertory of the Concert Spirituel up to the end of the 18th century. Although they are more intimate in style, and although their solo *récits* and some of their homophonic choruses reflect the asymmetrical phrase groupings of Provencal melody, these works conform in large measure to the Versailles motet.

Less governed by tradition than the *grand motet*, the *petit motet* absorbed more and more elements from both French and Italian opera and cantata around 1700. The numerous motets of Daniel Danielis, with their frequent modulations, vocalises and text repetitions, persuaded Le Cerf de la Viéville that the composer was indeed Italian. In the 'Avertissement' to the first book of Lochon's motets (1701), the printer Ballard claimed that Lochon 'by his genius has found the secret of uniting Italian design and expression with French delicacy and gentleness'. Campra made a similar claim, apropos his cantatas, seven years later; all four books of his *petits motets* were printed before the cantatas and may be thought of as preliminary studies in the *goûts-réunis*. His third book (1703) includes a motet (*Quis ego, Domine*) 'à la manière italienne'; in his fourth, the many da capo *airs*, sequential vocal melismas, triadic melodies and mechanical rhythmic pulsations clearly reveal a debt to the Italian sonata and concerto.

The *petits motets* in two books (1704, 1709) by Morin and the 12 *Motets à I, II et III voix* by Foliot also combine French and Italian features and, like those of Brossard, may be abridged, 'in order not to prolong the Divine Office' ('Avertissement' to Foliot's collection). The *petits motets* of François Couperin are on a more elevated musical plane, and there is little parroting of Italian devices. For Couperin *goûts-réunis* consisted of a natural synthesis of French melodic shapes and dance rhythms with Italian vocalises, abrupt changes of tonality and discreet chromaticism. In his three collections of psalm verses (1703, 1704, 1705), Couperin wisely set only the verses best suited to his particularly lyrical, intimate musical style. His masterpieces are surely the three *Leçons de tenébres* composed between 1713 and 1717 for the convent at Longchamp: nowhere else, except possibly in some of his keyboard pieces, did Couperin make more effective use of French vocal *agréments* as an organic and expressive part of the musical line. Like many cantatas and *cantatilles*, some *petits motets* were fashioned for performances by well-known opera singers at the Concert Spirituel and other concerts. Mouret's *petits motets* (published posthumously in 1742) were ideal for this environment (*O sacrum convivium* includes a vocal cadenza); the composer was director of the Concert Spirituel from 1728 to 1734.

Dufourcq (p.109) suggested that the performance of motets at the Concert Spirituel 'might have killed religious music' in France. The French motet had never had a liturgical function, so it was never bound to stay in the sanctuary; but whether or not the lack of a specific function or the new spirit of rationality diminished religious music is immaterial to the fact that the latter half of the 18th century lacked motet composers of the calibre of Charpentier and Lalande.

*IV. After 1750.* It is impossible to trace any continuous line of development in the history of the motet after 1750. The form never regained the central position it had occupied in the music of the Middle Ages or the Renaissance; nor did it claim the attention of leading composers to the extent it had in the Baroque period. In addition the weight of ecclesiastical tradition kept church music so far removed from stylistic developments in secular music that very few important 19th-century composers were able to write motets in a style that was not to some extent assumed. For this reason the motets of Liszt, Brahms and Verdi, among others, rarely show them at their best or most characteristic. The main concern of the student of post-Baroque motets is to distinguish the form from other sacred pieces closely resembling it, to observe the influences (ecclesiastical as well as musical) that have determined its character and to isolate those composers and those works that have contributed most to the form.

1. Latin motets, 1750–1830. 2. The 19th-century Latin motet. 3. The German Protestant motet. 4. The 20th century.

1. LATIN MOTETS, 1750–1830. Salzburg and Vienna were the most important centres for the Latin motet during the late 18th century. J. E. Eberlin, composer of over 300 motets, was Kapellmeister at Salzburg from 1749 until his death in 1762, and in Vienna the orchestral motet of the Neapolitan school – represented at its fullest flowering by such prolific and successful motet composers as Hasse and Jommelli – had, even before 1750, been cultivated with notable success by Fux, Caldara and others. The motet figures hardly at all among the extant works of Joseph Haydn, but his younger brother Michael is important both for his own compositions in this form and for the influence that his church music as a whole exercised on Mozart. Like those of Michael Haydn, Mozart's motets are mostly brightly coloured, extrovert works, expressing a resplendent dogma rather than a strongly personal faith. Some use deliberately archaic, Baroque-style, Fuxian counterpoint; most use the harmonic and instrumental textures of the new symphony and call for four-part chorus (SATB) with an orchestra of symphonic proportions. Examples can be found which do not fit this description, but they were generally written for

performance outside Vienna and Salzburg. For example, the antiphon *Quaerite primum regnum Dei* K86/73v, written at Bologna in 1770 as part of the required examination for admission to the Accademia Filarmonica, calls only for organ accompaniment from a figured bass. The brilliant motet for solo soprano and orchestra, *Exsultate, jubilate* (K165), was written for the famous castrato Venanzio Rauzzini and performed by him in Milan in 1773. And the very last motet, *Ave verum corpus* (K618), written for the feast of Corpus Christi at Baden in 1791, is exceptional in its intimate, expressive homophony, discreetly accompanied by strings and continuo only. Beethoven's settings of the Roman liturgy are confined to the two great masses, but Schubert's interest in church music extended to the composition of several splendid motets, scored, like Mozart's, for chorus and orchestra and sometimes including parts for solo voices.

2. THE 19TH-CENTURY LATIN MOTET. From about 1830 onwards the influential Cecilian movement sought actively to replace the worldly, symphonic church music of the Viennese school with a 'purer' style, based on the *a cappella* masses and motets of the late Renaissance. In Germany the reforms of Caspar Ett, August Eduard Grell (a prolific composer of motets), Carl Proske and others resulted in the formation in 1869 of the Allgemeiner Deutscher Cäcilien-Verein, presided over by F. X. Witt. Closely bound up with this and similar movements in other countries (notably France) was a renewed interest in the music of Palestrina. Giuseppe Baini's critical biography appeared in 1828, and in 1863 there was initiated the collected edition of Palestrina's works under the editorship of F. X. Haberl, president of the Cäcilienverein from 1899. This had been preceded by a number of important publications of Renaissance music, including *Musica divina* (edited by Proske and J. Schrems, 1853–63) and *Trésor musical* (edited by R. J. van Maldeghem, 1865–93). In France, Alexandre Choron's Institution Royale de Musique Classique et Religieuse was founded in 1818 for the performance of Renaissance music and resuscitated in 1854 as the Ecole Niedermeyer. The study of Gregorian chant and 16th-century polyphony was of primary importance in its curriculum. The Société de Musique Vocale Religieuse et Classique (founded in 1843) and the Schola Cantorum (1896) likewise encouraged a conservative attitude towards church music.

The effects of these reforms – one of them the composition of a vast quantity of third-rate church music – were felt in all Catholic countries, but it was in France especially that the motet enjoyed an unbroken tradition. Gounod's main contributions to the form are contained in the *Motets solennels* of 1864 and the three volumes of *Chants sacrés* (1879), but he also wrote several psalms, hymns and graduals. Franck's *Trois motets* (*O salutaris*, *Ave Maria* and *Tantum ergo*) of 1858 are for solo soprano and baritone, chorus and organ, and he wrote about a dozen similar pieces that could properly be classed as motets. Berlioz's *Tantum ergo* and *Veni, creator* and the 20 motets of Saint-Saëns are also noteworthy. Chausson published three sets of motets (opp.6, 12 and 16) between 1883 and 1891, and Fauré's religious compositions include a number of motets that reflect the traditions of the Ecole Niedermeyer, where he studied for about ten years.

The ideals of the Cecilian movement also found expression in Liszt's church compositions, most of which contrast sharply with the flamboyant virtuoso piano works by which he is best known. Many of the shorter ones require only chorus and organ; they include an *Ave verum corpus*, a setting of *O salutaris hostia*, dedicated to Haberl, and two settings of *Tantum ergo*, dedicated to Witt. Bruckner also lent at least nominal support to the Cecilian movement, although his own church music was founded on a sincere and direct faith and a reverence for the whole musical tradition that supported it. He revived the style of the Viennese school in his large orchestral masses and *Te Deum* and reached back towards the Venetians of the 16th and 17th centuries in some of his motets. Their archaism leads even to the occasional use of modal harmony (e.g. the Aeolian *Asperges me*, the Phrygian *Pange lingua* and the Lydian *Os justi*), though Bruckner's language in these works is not pastiche. He wrote about 40 motets in all, the majority being either unaccompanied or with only organ in support. They represent a peak in the Catholic motet of the late 19th century attained by no other composer except Verdi, some of whose late motets (*Quattro pezzi sacri*) have much in common with the devout spirit of Bruckner's.

3. THE GERMAN PROTESTANT MOTET. Pursuing a development largely independent of Catholic traditions, the motet of the German Protestant Church was almost as backward-looking in style. Schütz and Bach were to the Lutheran composer what Palestrina and Lassus were to the Catholic. The Protestant motet, with a vernacular text often selected from the Bible, was usually distinguished from the cantata (as it had been by Bach) by its more contrapuntal style and its lack of independent accompaniment. Chorale melodies were often used as a kind of cantus firmus (as in Bach's *Jesu meine Freude*), and many motets were composed for double chorus (like Bach's *Singet dem Herrn* and some motets by Schütz). The modest achievements of the second half of the 18th century are seen in the motets of Bach's sons Carl Philipp Emanuel and Johann Christoph Friedrich and more particularly in those of his pupils G. A. Homilius (most of whose 60 or more motets date from after 1755) and J. F. Doles (whose motets include 15 for double chorus). Other composers include J. H. Rolle, who wrote more than 60 motets, and J. A. Hiller, whose funeral motet *Alles Fleisch ist wie Gras* was particularly admired.

It was not until well into the 19th century that the Protestant motet again attracted the greatest composers, and even then it rarely inspired their finest works. Mendelssohn wrote both Latin and German motets, but more important are the seven German motets, mostly to biblical texts, by Brahms (opp.29, 74 and 110) and his three *Fest- und Gedenksprüche* op.109, also to biblical words. These were published in the same year (1890) as the three motets op.110 and, like the first and last of that set, are scored for eight-part chorus, divided into two equal parts. The two earlier sets are deliberately archaic in their use of late Baroque chorale harmony, chorale-prelude technique and Bachian counterpoint, and the effect is sometimes rather impersonal. The retrospective elements in the two later sets (e.g. the scoring for double chorus, their indebtedness to the German lied tradition, and the occasional modal harmonies) are more successfully absorbed into the composer's personal style. Composed near the end of the 19th century, they

occupy a position in the history of the German motet analogous to that of Verdi's late examples in the much longer history of the Latin motet.

4. THE 20TH CENTURY. The motet has been accorded a place of even less importance in the 20th century than in the 19th, at least by major composers. The *Motu proprio* of Pope Pius X (1903), as well as extolling Gregorian chant and the style of Palestrina as 'the supreme model of all sacred music', specifically laid down that

the antiphons of the Vespers must be as a rule rendered with the Gregorian melody proper to each. Should they, however, in some special case be sung in figured music, they must never have either the form of a concert melody or the fullness of a motet or a cantata.

The *Motu proprio* was directed mainly against the 'theatrical style, which was in the greatest vogue, especially in Italy, during the last century'. The motets of G. F. Ghedini and Ettore Desderi in Italy and those of Florent Schmitt, d'Indy, Poulenc and Messiaen in France show in varying degrees the effects of Pius X's reforms. Among recent composers of Latin motets in Germany are J. N. David, Hermann Schroeder and Joseph Ahrens. The German Protestant motet is best represented by Reger, Arnold Mendelssohn, Heinrich Kaminski, Ernst Pepping and Hugo Distler.

In England the Renaissance conception of the motet as a short *a cappella* composition to a Latin text persisted into the 20th century; very few works, therefore, complement the orchestral motets of the Viennese school or the German Protestant motets of the 19th century. During the 18th and 19th centuries the Latin church music of Tallis and Byrd (like that of Palestrina and Lassus) had not only been cherished by antiquarians but also sung regularly (in translation) in Anglican churches and cathedrals and often reprinted. The Motett Society met regularly in London between 1841 and 1857 to rehearse works by early composers, and they published as 'anthems' with English words motets by Tallis, Byrd, Gibbons, Palestrina, Lassus and Victoria.

In the 20th century, Latin motets began to be sung to their original words in Anglican services, but as far as original church music is concerned the motet has naturally taken second place to the anthem. Stanford's three Latin motets op.38 (1905) – *Justorum animae*, *Coelos ascendit* and *Beati quorum via* – have established themselves in the repertory of most English cathedrals, and Edmund Rubbra (a Roman Catholic) has successfully recaptured the flavour of Tudor (and earlier) styles in several of his motet compositions. Bernard Naylor's nine motets of 1951-2 (to English texts), arranged as a cycle for the nine major feast days of the church year, are a landmark in the development of the motet in England.

BIBLIOGRAPHY
GENERAL

H. Leichtentritt: *Geschichte der Motette* (Leipzig, 1908/R1967)

H. Besseler: *Die Musik des Mittelalters und der Renaissance*, HMw (1931)

F. Blume: *Die evangelische Kirchenmusik*, HMw, x (1931, rev. 2/1965 as *Geschichte der evangelischen Kirchenmusik*; Eng. trans., enlarged, 1974 as *Protestant Church Music: a History*)

H. J. Moser: *Die mehrstimmige Vertonung des Evangeliums*, i (Leipzig, 1931/R1968)

O. Ursprung: *Die katholische Kirchenmusik*, HMw, ix (1931/R)

M. F. Bukofzer: *Studies in Medieval and Renaissance Music* (New York, 1950)

R. Dammann: 'Geschichte der Begriffsbestimmung Motette', *AMw*, xvi (1959), 337–77

A. Hughes and G. Abraham, eds.: *Ars Nova and the Renaissance, 1300–1540*, NOHM, iii (1960)

L. Finscher: 'Motette', *MGG*

E. Apfel: *Beiträge zu einer Geschichte der Satztechnik von der frühen Motette bis Bach* (Munich, 1964)

E. Nievergelt: 'Die Motette', *Der evangelische Kirchenchor*, lxxii (1967), 83

H. Hüschen, ed.: *Die Motette*, Mw, xlvii (1974; Eng. trans., 1976)

### MIDDLE AGES

E. Ludwig: 'Die mehrstimmige Musik des 14. Jahrhunderts', *SIMG*, iv (1902–3), 16–70

——: 'Die 50 Beispiele Coussemakers aus der Handschrift von Montpellier', *SIMG*, v (1903–4), 177–224

P. Aubry: *Cent motets du XIIIe siècle* (Paris, 1908)

F. Ludwig: *Repertorium organorum recentioris et motetorum vetustissimi stili* (Halle, 1910); vols.i/B, ii repr. in SMM, vii–viii (1961–2); vols.i/A, ii ed. L. Dittmer, Musicological Studies, vii (Brooklyn, 1964), xvii (Brooklyn, 1972)

——: 'Die Quellen der Motetten ältesten Stils', *AMw*, v (1923), 185–222, 273–315; repr. in SMM, vii (1961)

——: 'Die geistliche, nichtliturgische und weltliche einstimmige und die mehrstimmige Musik des Mittelalters', *Handbuch der Musikgeschichte*, ed. G. Adler (Frankfurt, 1924, rev. and enlarged 2/1930/ R1961), 157–295

H. Besseler: 'Studien zur Musik des Mittelalters', *AMw*, vii (1925), 167–252; viii (1926), 137–258

F. Gennrich: 'Trouvèrelieder und Motettenrepertoire', *ZMw*, ix (1926–7), 8–39, 65–85

H. Anglès, ed.: *El códex musical de Las Huelgas* (Barcelona, 1931/R1977)

J. Handschin: 'Zur Geschichte von Notre Dame', *AcM*, iv (1932), 5, 49, 104

C. van den Borren, ed.: *Polyphonia sacra: a Continental Miscellany of the Fifteenth Century* (Burnham, Bucks., 1932)

Y. Rokseth: *Polyphonies du XIIIe siècle* (Paris, 1935–9)

E. Dannemann: *Die spätgotische Musiktradition* (Strasbourg, 1936)

H. Husmann: 'Die Motetten der Madrider Handschrift und deren geschichtliche Stellung', *AMf*, ii (1937), 173

G. Kuhlmann: *Die zweistimmigen französischen Motetten des Kodex Montpellier* (Würzburg, 1938)

G. D. Sasse: *Die Mehrstimmigkeit der Ars Antiqua in Theorie und Praxis* (Leipzig, 1940)

H. Nathan: 'The Function of Text in French 13th-century Motets', *MQ*, xxviii (1942), 445

H. Tischler: *The Motet in 13th-century France* (diss., Yale U., 1942)

——: 'English Traits in the Early 13th-century Motet', *MQ*, xxx (1944), 458

Y. Rokseth: 'La polyphonie parisienne du treizième siècle', *Les cahiers techniques de l'art*, i/2 (1947), 33

J. Handschin: 'The Summer Canon and its Background', *MD*, iii (1949), 55–94; v (1951), 65–113

R. H. Hoppin: 'Rhythm as a Structural Device in the Motet around 1400', *JAMS*, iii (1950), 157

A. Auda: *Les 'motets Wallons'* (Brussels, 1953)

W. Apel: 'Remarks about the Isorhythmic Motet', *L'Ars Nova: Wégimont II 1955*, 139

L. Schrade: 'Unknown Motets in a Recovered Thirteenth-century Manuscript', *Speculum*, xxx (1955), 404

M. F. Bukofzer: 'The Unidentified Tenors in the MS La Clayette', *AnnM*, iv (1956), 255

R. H. Hoppin: 'Some Remarks a propos of *Pic*', *RBM*, x (1956), 105

G. Reichert: 'Das Verhältnis zwischen musikalischer und textlicher Struktur in den Motetten Machauts', *AMw*, xiii (1956), 197

H. Tischler: 'The Evolution of the Harmonic Style in the Notre-Dame Motet', *AcM*, xxviii (1956), 87

S. E. Brown jr: 'New Evidence of Isomelic Design in Dufay's Isorhythmic Motets', *JAMS*, x (1957), 7

F. Gennrich: *Bibliographie der ältesten französischen und lateinischen Motetten* (Darmstadt, 1957)

R. H. Hoppin: 'A Fifteenth-century "Christmas Oratorio" ', *Essays on Music in Honor of Archibald Thompson Davison* (Cambridge, Mass., 1957), 41

——: 'The Cypriot-French Repertory', *MD*, xi (1957), 79–125

U. Günther: 'The 14th-century Motet and its Development', *MD*, xii (1958), 27–58

F. Ll. Harrison: *Music in Medieval Britain* (London, 1958, 2/1963)

E. Apfel: *Studien zur Satztechnik der mittelalterlichen englischen Musik* (Heidelberg, 1959)

H. Tischler: 'The Evolution of Form in the Earliest Motets', *AcM*, xxxi (1959), 86

E. Apfel: 'Über einige Zusammenhänge zwischen Text und Musik im Mittelalter, besonders in England', *AcM*, xxxiii (1961), 47

G. Birkner: 'Motetus und Motette', *AMw*, xviii (1961), 183

U. Günther: 'Das Wort-Ton-Problem bei Motetten des späten 14. Jahrhunderts', *Festschrift Heinrich Besseler* (Leipzig, 1961), 163

R. H. Hoppin, ed.: *The Cypriot-French Repertory*, CMM, xxi/2 (1961)

G. Reichert: 'Wechselbeziehungen zwischen musikalischer und textlicher Struktur in der Motette des 13. Jahrhunderts', *In Memoriam Jacques Handschin* (Strasbourg, 1962), 151

E. H. Sanders: 'Peripheral Polyphony of the 13th Century', *JAMS*, xvii (1964), 261

U. Günther, ed.: *The Motets of the Manuscripts Chantilly, Musée Condé, 564 (olim 1047) and Modena, Biblioteca estense, D.M.5, 24 (olim lat.568) (14th c.)*, CMM, xxxix (1965)

F. Matthiassen: *The Style of the Early Motet* (Copenhagen, 1966) [review in *Notes*, xxiv (1967–8), 33]

P. Petrobelli: 'Due motetti francesi in una sconosciuta fonte Udinese', *CHM*, iv (1966), 201

S. Davis: 'The Solus Tenor in the 14th and 15th Centuries', *AcM*, xxxix (1967), 44

F. Ll. Harrison: '*Ars nova* in England: a New Source', *MD*, xxi (1967), 67

H. Husmann: 'Ein Faszikel Notre-Dame-Kompositionen', *AMw*, xxiv (1967), 1

E. H. Sanders: 'Die Rolle der englischen Mehrstimmigkeit des Mittelalters in der Entwicklung von Cantus-firmus-Satz und Tonalitätsstruktur', *AMw*, xxiv (1967), 24–53

H. Tischler: 'Another English Motet of the 13th Century', *JAMS*, xx (1967), 274 [see also G. A. Anderson: 'Addendum', *JAMS*, xxi (1968), 381]

——: 'Some Rhythmic Features in Early 13th-century Motets', *RBM*, xxi (1967), 107

G. A. Anderson: 'Notre Dame, Bilingual Motets: a Study in the History of Music c1215–1245', *MMA*, iii (1968), 50

S. Davis: 'The Solus Tenor: an Addendum', *AcM*, xl (1968), 176

F. Ll. Harrison, ed.: *Motets of French Provenance*, PMFC, v (1968)

G. A. Anderson: 'A Small Collection of Notre Dame Motets', *JAMS*, xxii (1969), 157–96

——: 'Newly Identified Clausula-motets in the Las Huelgas Manuscript', *MQ*, lv (1969), 228

——: 'Newly Identified Tenor Chants in the Notre Dame Repertory', *ML*, l (1969), 158

——: 'Clausulae or Transcribed-motets in the Florence Manuscript?', *AcM*, xlii (1970), 109

R. Hammerstein: 'Über das gleichzeitige Erklingen mehrerer Texte', *AMw*, xxvii (1970), 257–86

K. Hofmann: 'Zur Entstehungs- und Frühgeschichte des Terminus Motette', *AcM*, xlii (1970), 138

J. Stenzl: 'Eine unbekannte Sanctus-motette vom Ende des 13. Jahrhunderts', *AcM*, xlii (1970), 128

G. A. Anderson: 'Notre-Dame Latin Double Motets', *MD*, xxv (1971), 35

K. Hofmann: *Untersuchungen zur Kompositionstechnik der Motette im 13. Jahrhundert* (Neuhausen, 1972)

G. A. Anderson: 'Motets of the Thirteenth-century Manuscript La Clayette', *MD*, xxvii (1973), 11; xxviii (1974), 5–37

E. H. Sanders: 'The Medieval Motet', *Gattungen der Musik in Einzeldarstellungen: Gedenkschrift für Leo Schrade*, i (Berne and Munich, 1973), 497–573

C. W. Warren: 'Brunelleschi's Dome and Dufay's Motet', *MQ*, lix (1973), 92

G. A. Anderson: 'A Unique Notre-Dame Motet Tenor Relationship', *ML*, lv (1974), 398

——: Introduction to *Motets of the Manuscript La Clayette*, CMM, lxviii (1975)

For further bibliography *see* ORGANUM AND DISCANT: BIBLIOGRAPHY

### RENAISSANCE

T. Kroyer: *Ludwig Senfl und sein Motettenstil* (Munich, 1902)

A. Orel: 'Einige Grundformen der Motettkomposition im 15. Jahrhundert', *SMw*, vii (1920), 48–101

K. Dèzes: 'Der Mensuralcodex des Benediktiner-Klosters Sancti Emmerami zu Regensburg', *ZMw*, x (1927–8), 65–105

K. P. Bernet Kempers: *Jacobus Clemens non Papa und seine Motetten* (Augsburg, 1928)

E. Loge: *Eine Messen- und Motettenhandschrift des Kantors Matthias Krüger aus der Musikbibliothek Albrechts von Preussen* (Kassel, 1931)

H. Eppstein: *Nicolas Gombert als Motettenkomponist* (Würzburg, 1935)

E. Lowinsky: 'Zur Frage der Deklamationsrhythmik in der a-capella-Musik des 16. Jahrhunderts', *AcM*, vii (1935), 62

J. Schmidt-Görg: 'Zu einigen Motetten des 16. Jahrhunderts', *ZMw*, xvii (1935), 47

H. Anglès: 'Un manuscrit inconnu avec polyphonie du XVe siècle conservé à la cathédrale de Ségovie (Espagne)', *AcM*, viii (1936), 6

E. Lowinsky: 'Das Antwerpener Motettenbuch Orlando di Lassos und seine Beziehungen zum Motettenschaffen der niederländischen Zeitgenossen', *TVNM*, xv/1 (1936), 1–43

W. Stephan: *Die Burgundisch-niederländische Motett zur Zeit Ockeghems* (Kassel, 1937/R1973)

L. Balmer: *Orlando di Lasso Motetten: eine stilgeschichtliche Studie* (Berne and Leipzig, 1938)

O. Strunk: 'Some Motet Types of the 16th Century', *PAMS 1939*, 155

M. van Crevel: 'Secret Chromatic Art in the Netherlands Motet?', *TVNM*, xvi/4 (1946), 253–304

C. van den Borren: 'Quelques reflexions à propos du style imitatif syntaxique', *RBM*, i (1946–7), 14

G. de Van: 'A Recently Discovered Source of Early 15th Century Polyphonic Music', *MD*, ii (1948), 5–74

E. E. Lowinsky: 'A Newly Discovered 16th Century Motet Manuscript', *JAMS*, iii (1950), 173–232

H. Besseler: 'The Manuscript Bologna, Biblioteca Universitaria 2216', *MD*, ix (1952), 39

G. d'Alessi: 'Precursors of Adriano Willaert in the Practice of Coro Spezzato', *JAMS*, v (1952), 187

R. Dammann: 'Spätformen der isorhythmischen Motette im 16. Jahrhundert', *AMw*, x (1953), 16

P. Mohr: *Die Handschrift B 211–215 der Proske-Bibliothek zu Regensburg* (Kassel, 1955)

G. Reaney: 'The Manuscript Oxford, Bodleian Library, Canonici Miscellany 213', *MD*, ix (1955), 73–104

A. Seay: 'An "Ave maris stella" by Johannes Stochem', *RBM*, xi (1957), 93

H. Kellman: 'The Origins of the Chigi Codex', *JAMS*, xi (1958), 6

H. Glahn: 'Et fransk musikhåndskrift fra begyndelsen af det 16. århundrede', *Fund og forskning*, v–vi (1958–9), 90

W. Gerstenberg: 'Zur Motette im 16. Jahrhundert', *Festschrift Alfred Orel* (Vienna and Wiesbaden, 1960), 73

D. Launay: 'A propos de quelques motets polyphoniques en l'honneur de Saint Martin: contribution à l'histoire du motet aux XVIe et XVIIe siècles', *RdM* xlvii (1961), 67

J. A. Mattfeld: 'Some Relationships between Texts and Cantus Firmi in the Liturgical Motets of Josquin des Pres', *JAMS*, xiv (1961), 159

L. Finscher: 'Zur Cantus-Firmus-Behandlung in der Psalm-Motette der Josquinzeit', *Hans Albrecht in Memoriam* (Kassel, 1962), 55

J. Kerman: 'The Elizabethan Motet: a Study of Texts for Music', *Studies in the Renaissance*, ix (1962), 273–308

H. Osthoff: *Josquin Desprez* (Tutzing, 1962–5)

E. H. Sparks: *Cantus Firmus in Mass and Motet, 1420–1520* (Berkeley, 1963)

S. W. Kenney: *Walter Frye and the 'Contenance Angloise'* (New Haven, 1964)

W. Kirsch: 'Zum Verhältnis von Motettenstil und liturgisch-musikalischer Praxis im 16. Jahrhundert', *GfMKB, Leipzig 1966*, 196

E. E. Lowinsky: *The Medici Codex of 1518* (Chicago, 1968)

T. L. Noblitt: 'The Ambrosian Motetti Missales Repertory', *MD*, xxii (1968), 77

R. Strohm: 'Ein unbekanntes Chorbuch des 15. Jahrhunderts', *Mf*, xx (1968), 40

A. Dunning: *Die Staatsmotette, 1480–1555* (Utrecht, 1969)

L. L. Perkins: *Opera Omnia Johannis Lhéritier*, CMM, xlviii (1969)

R. J. Snow: 'The Mass-motet Cycle: a Mid-fifteenth-century Experiment', *Essays in Musicology in Honor of Dragan Plamenac* (Pittsburgh, 1969/R1977), 301

H. L. Marshall: *The Four-voice Motets of Thomas Crecquillon* (Brooklyn, 1970)

W. Denhard: *Die deutsche Psalmmotette in der Reformationszeit* (Wiesbaden, 1971)

H. C. Slim: *A Gift of Madrigals and Motets* (Chicago, 1972)

L. Finscher: 'Zum Verhältnis von Text und Musik in der Motette der Josquinzeit', *Renaissance-Studien: Helmuth Osthoff zum 80. Geburtstage* (Tutzing, 1977)

W. Kirsch: 'Zur Funktion der tripeltaktigen Abschnitte in der Motetten des Josquin-Zeitalters', *Renaissance-Studien: Helmuth Osthoff zum 80. Geburtstage* (Tutzing, 1977)

E. Nowiacki: 'The Latin Psalm Motet, 1500–1535', *Renaissance-Studien: Helmuth Osthoff zum 80. Geburtstage* (Tutzing, 1977)

AFTER 1600

M. Brenet: *La musique sacrée sous Louis XIV* (Paris, 1899)

——: *Les concerts en France sous l'ancien régime* (Paris, 1900/R1969), 169

——: 'La musique dans les églises de Paris, de 1716 à 1738 d'après les almanachs du temps', *Tribune de Saint-Gervais* (Paris, 1903), 71

——: 'Notes sur l'introduction des instruments dans les églises de France', *Riemann-Festschrift* (Leipzig, 1909), 277

M. Seiffert, ed.: *Thüringische Motetten aus der ersten Hälfte des 18. Jahrhunderts*, DDT, xlix–1 (1915/R) [incl. important preface]

F. Blume: *Das monodische Prinzip in der protestantischen Kirchenmusik* (Leipzig, 1925/R1975)

K. G. Fellerer: *Der Palestrinastil und seine Bedeutung in der vokalen Kirchenmusik des 18. Jahrhunderts* (Augsburg, 1929/R1972)

A. A. Abert: *Die stilistische Voraussetzungen der 'Cantiones Sacrae' von H. Schütz* (Wolfenbüttel, 1935)

A. Adrio: *Die Anfänge des geistlichen Konzerts* (Berlin, 1935)

M. Schneider, ed.: *Altbachisches Archiv*, EDM, 1st ser., i–ii (1935) [incl. important preface]

A. E. Schröder: *De meerstemmige muziek op de Lamentaties van Jeremia van de 15. tot de 18. eeuw* (diss., U. of Louvain, 1948)

J. E. Richards: *The 'Grand Motet' of the Late Baroque in France as Exemplified by Michel-Richard de Lalande and a Selected Group of his Contemporaries* (diss., U. of Southern California, 1950)

W. Ehmann: 'Aufführungspraxis von Bachs Motetten', *Musik und Kirche*, xxi (1951), 49

N. Dufourcq: 'La musique religieuse française de 1660 à 1789', *ReM* (1953–4), no.222, p.89

A. Verchaly: 'La musique religieuse française de Titelouze à 1660', *ReM*, (1953–4), no.222, p.77

C. Barber: *The Liturgical Music of Marc-Antoine Charpentier* (diss., Harvard U., 1955)

J. Heinrich: *Stilistische Untersuchungen zur 'Geistlichen Chormusik' von Heinrich Schütz* (diss., U. of Göttingen, 1956)

W. Morgan: *The Choral Motet (1650–1750)* (diss., U. of South Carolina, 1956)

R. G. Pauly: 'The Motets of Michael Haydn and of Mozart', *JAMS*, ix (1956), 67

A. Forchert: *Das Spätwerk des Michael Prätorius* (Berlin, 1957)

D. Launay: 'Les motets à double choeur en France, dans la première moitié du XVIIe siècle', *RdM*, xl (1957), 173

J. E. Richards: 'Structural Principles in the Grands Motets of Michel-Richard Delalande (1657–1726)', *JAMS*, xi (1958), 119

D. Arnold: 'The Significance of "Cori Spezzati"', *ML*, xl (1959), 4

M. Garros: 'La musique religieuse en France de 1600 à 1750', *Histoire de la musique*, ed. Roland-Manuel, i (Paris, 1960), 1591

D. Launay: 'A propos de quelques motets polyphoniques en l'honneur de Saint-Martin: contribution à l'histoire du motet aux XVIe et XVIIe siècles', *RdM*, xlvii (1961), 67

U. Siegele: 'Bemerkungen zu Bachs Motetten', *BJb*, xlix (1962), 33

W. Braun: 'Samuel Scheidts Bearbeitungen alter Motetten', *AMw*, xix–xx (1962–3), 56

D. Launay, ed.: *Anthologie du motet latin polyphonique en France (1609–1661)*, PSFM, 1st ser., xvii (1963)

R. Bullivant: 'Zum Problem der Begleitung der Bachschen Motetten', *BJb*, lii (1966), 59

F. Krummacher: 'Motetten und Kantaten der Bachzeit in Udestedt/Thüringen', *Mf*, xix (1966), 402

W. P. Cole: *The Motets of Jean-Baptiste Lully* (diss., U. of Michigan, 1967)

H. T. McElrath: *A Study of the Motets of Ignatio Donati (1575–1638)* (diss., U. of Rochester, 1967)

J. L. A. Roche: *North Italian Liturgical Music in the Early 17th Century* (diss., U. of Cambridge, 1968)

M. L. White: *The Motets of Luigi Cherubini* (diss., U. of Michigan, 1968)

H. Ambrose: *The Anglican Anthems and Roman Catholic Motets of Samuel Wesley (1766–1837)* (diss., Boston U., 1969)

P. A. Brandvik: *Selected Motets of Alessandro Scarlatti* (diss., U. of Illinois, 1969)

A. C. Howie: *The Sacred Music of Anton Bruckner* (diss., U. of Manchester, 1969)

S. H. Hansell: 'Sacred Music at the 'Incurabili' in Venice at the Time of J. A. Hasse (1720–80)', *JAMS*, xxiii (1970), 282

P. Oboussier: 'Couperin Motets at Tenbury', *PRMA*, xcviii (1971–2), 17

K. Fischer: *Die Psalmkompositionen in Rom am Ende des 16. und zu Beginn des 17. Jahrhunderts (ca. 1570–1630)* (diss., U. of Cologne, 1972)

J. R. Anthony: *French Baroque Music from Beaujoyeulx to Rameau* (London, 1973, rev. 2/1978)

G. Beechey: 'Hindemith's Motets', *MT*, cxiv (1973), 1276

F. Krummacher: 'Textauslegung und Satzstruktur in J. S. Bachs Motetten', *BJb*, lx (1974), 5–43

A. Lewis and N. Fortune, eds.: *Opera and Church Music, 1630–1750*, NOHM, v (1975)

P. Oboussier: 'Lalande's Grands Motets', *MT*, cxvii (1976), 483

G. Ebensberger: *The Motets of Francis Poulenc* (diss., U. of Texas, in preparation)

F. F. Mueller: *Austrian Sacred Choral Music between Schubert and Bruckner* (diss., U. of Illinois, in preparation)

ERNEST H. SANDERS (II), LEEMAN L. PERKINS (II), CHRISTOPH WOLFF (III, 1, 3), JEROME ROCHE (III, 2), JAMES R. ANTHONY (III, 4), MALCOLM BOYD (IV)

**Motet-chanson.** A term used to describe a category of works found in musical sources of the late 15th and early 16th centuries. Normally appearing in secular chansonniers, they have the scope of a chanson but a sacred Latin text. A famous and characteristic example is Walter Frye's *Ave regina celorum*. A chansonnier will often begin and end with a prayer in this way.

DAVID FALLOWS

**Motetus.** Medieval term (13th, 14th and early 15th centuries) for the voice immediately above the tenor in motets; it was also used to designate the entire composition, whether it consisted of two or more voices.

Notre Dame motets developed from some of the discant sections of Notre Dame organa and many of the clausulas. When French poetry began to be applied to their upper voice(s), the voice part above the tenor ceased to be called 'duplum'. All pre-Franconian writers (Johannes de Garlandia, Anonymous VII, Lambertus, Anonymous Sowa's, Amerus, Anonymous IV) used the term *motellus*, a Latin diminutive of the French word *mot*, which in the 12th century often denoted a stanza or strophe of French poetry. Probably the invention of short French poems tailored to fit duplum parts of melismatic discant polyphony, as well as the frequent insertion of chanson refrains, caused the change in terminology that eventually gave the genre its name.

In the earliest stages of the motet (e.g. *I-Fl* 29.1), when only Latin texts appear, the compositions were sometimes called 'tropi' or 'prose', and Garlandia and Anonymous IV used both *discantus* and *motellus* to designate the voice above the tenor in motets. The term *motellus* was soon evidently applied to all such polyphonic compositions, whether the texts were French or Latin. The form *motetus*, which appeared first in Franco's authoritative treatise and thenceforth replaced the earlier term, may well have been coined in analogy to *hoquetus*.

*See also* MOTET, §I.

BIBLIOGRAPHY
R. Dammann: 'Geschichte der Begriffsbestimmung Motette', *AMw*, xvi (1959), 337–77
G. Birkner: 'Motetus und Motette', *AMw*, xviii (1961), 183
R. A. Rasch: *Johannes de Garlandia*, Musicological Studies, xx (Brooklyn, 1969), 280f
K. Hofmann: 'Zur Entstehungs- und Frühgeschichte des Terminus Motette', *AcM*, xlii (1970), 138
ERNEST H. SANDERS

**Motif** [motive]. A short musical idea, be it melodic, harmonic or rhythmic, or all three. A motif may be of any size, though it is most commonly regarded as the shortest subdivision of a theme or phrase that still maintains its identity as an idea. It is most often thought of in melodic terms, and it is this aspect of motif that is connoted by the term 'figure'. Thus, for example, in the opening theme of Beethoven's Sonata in E op.109 a case could be argued for either half a bar or one bar constituting a motif, though the latter interpretation would probably be favoured by most listeners, since the two pairs of notes together form an identifiable contour; the two-note members might then be called 'cells' (see ex.1).

The rhythmic motif may be defined by analogy with the melodic type: a short, characteristic sequence of accented and unaccented, or short and long articulations, sometimes including rests. Rhythmic motifs may be bound up with a class of melodic ideas (probably the most famous being that in Beethoven's Fifth Symphony), or they may exist as rhythmic ideas in themselves, with little or no melodic interest, for instance the

Nibelungs' motif from *Das Rheingold*, scene iii (ex.2). A repeated harmonic pattern is seldom perceived independently of rhythmic and melodic contours and may hardly therefore be designated 'motif'; however, the harmonic element may contribute potently to a composite motif, as often in the LEITMOTIF of 19th-century opera.

In Riemann's theory of rhythm, motif can take on a purely metric connotation. The principle of *Vierhebigkeit*, or four-bar regularity in phrase structure, enables one to divide the phrase into two 'half-phrases', and to divide each of these into two motifs, each a bar long (Ger. *Taktmotiv*). The principle of this kind of subdivision is discussed further in RHYTHM.

Taken in its totality – a combination of melodic, rhythmic and harmonic elements – the motif is the building-block of polyphonic structures, the first and most important of which is THEME. Theme and motif have usually been contrasted, theme being viewed as a self-contained idea, as opposed to the elemental, incomplete nature of the motif. In fact the relationship between motif and theme is analogous to that between theme and an entire movement or composition: in each case the smaller unit is incomplete, yet it has a special identity with important consequences for the shape and structure of the larger.

WILLIAM DRABKIN

**Motive.** *See* MOTIF.

**Moto** (It.: 'movement', 'motion'). A word found within the tempo designation *con moto* (with movement) but particularly common as a qualification of another tempo mark: *allegro con moto* was often used by Haydn and Beethoven. MOTO PERPETUO (perpetual motion) is found more often as a description or title of a piece comprising an uninterrupted succession of quick notes than as an instruction of any kind. *Moto* is also applied in Italian writings to contrapuntal contexts: *moto contrario* is 'contrary motion'; *moto obliquo* is 'oblique motion'; and *moto retto* is 'similar motion'.

*See also* TEMPO AND EXPRESSION MARKS.

DAVID FALLOWS

**Moto perpetuo** (It.: 'perpetual motion'; Lat. *perpetuum mobile*). A title sometimes given to pieces in which rapid figuration is persistently maintained. Familiar examples are the finale from Weber's First Piano Sonata, Mendelssohn's op.119 and Paganini's *Allegro de concert* op.11 for violin and orchestra. There are many others for which the exhibition of a performer's digital agility seems the sole justification.

The quality of perpetual (not necessarily rapid) movement has, however, always been a resource capable of yielding valuable results. The continuous forward momentum of many Baroque movements is due to the relentless persistence of a *Gehende-bass* ('walking bass'). Continuous movement is implied in the character of dances like the tarantella, and may justifiably be employed to achieve brilliance in forms like the Toccata (e.g. Schumann's op.7) or in the finale of a larger work (e.g. Haydn's String Quartet op.64 no.5). It is used in Chopin's B♭ minor Piano Sonata op.35 to achieve a close of feverish brilliance; Chopin often used effects of perpetual motion in his studies. In song accompaniments, far from being a purely mechanical device, it may appropriately reflect the mood of the verse. The desperation in Schubert's *Erstarrung* (*Winterreise*, no.4) is achieved partly through such means; the momentary cessations of movement in his settings of *Erlkönig* and *Gretchen am Spinnrade*, and in the finales

Ex.1

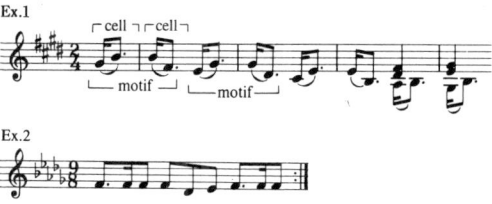

Ex.2

of Beethoven's piano sonatas op.26, op.31 no.3 and op.54, sensitively articulate the design of movements all of which rely heavily on the device of *moto perpetuo*. Johann Strauss the younger wrote his well-known *Perpetuum mobile* op.257 as a 'musikalischer Scherz' ('musical joke').    MICHAEL TILMOUTH

**Motown.** A term for the regional variant of Afro-American recorded popular music (e.g. rhythm and blues, soul music, rock music) from Detroit, Michigan, beginning in the early 1960s. The term 'Motown' is apparently a contraction of 'Motortown', referring to the city's principal industry of manufacturing cars. The 'Motown sound' contrasts with that of other regional centres of black popular music (e.g. Chicago, Memphis and New York) in its greater reliance on the conventions of mainstream Anglo-American urban popular music (such as sophisticated arrangements, with large studio orchestras usually including strings) and a muting of the vigorous Afro-American music sound ideals and performing practices. The result is a product sufficiently refined for large-scale acceptance by whites. The chief creator of the 'Motown sound' was Berry Gordy jr, a record producer who formed a highly successful recording and publishing business, the Motown Corporation (the first large American music firm owned and controlled by blacks).

BIBLIOGRAPHY
D. Morse: *Motown and the Arrival of Black Music* (London, 1971)
ROBERT WITMER

**Motsev, Alexander** (*b* Lom, 16 Oct 1900; *d* between Lom and Sofia, 24 Dec 1964). Bulgarian music folklorist. He studied music theory with Dobri Khristov and music history, education and aesthetics with Stoyan Brashovanov at the State Academy of Music in Sofia, where he graduated in 1925. From 1925 to 1938 he taught music at the gymnasium in Lom; he also produced a dozen operettas and operas (including Gluck's *Orfeo* and Flotow's *Martha*) with an amateur company and formed an amateur choir which gave concerts in Romania and Yugoslavia. In 1938 he moved to Sofia, where he taught as a school music teacher, and from 1942 until 1945 he studied musicology with Erich Schenk in Vienna. On his return he taught in the same Sofia Gymnasium and, for a short time, music history and solfège at the Sofia Music School. Until 1956 he worked as adviser for the Central House of Folk Art in Sofia. He died in a car accident.

WRITINGS
*Ritam i takt v balgarskata narodna muzika* [Rhythm and metre in Bulgarian folk music] (Sofia, 1949)
*Rabota nad ispalnenieto i agogikata na pesenta* [Work on the performance and accentuation of song] (Sofia, 1953)
*Balgarskata narodna muzika* [Bulgarian folk music] (Sofia, 1954)
'Taktovete s hemiolno udalzheni vremena v zapisite na balgarskite folkloristi' [Types of bars with hemiola lengthening in the notation of Bulgarian folklorists], *IIM*, ii–iii (1956), 319–50
*Kharakterni ritmi v tvorchestvoto na balgarskite kompozitori* [Characteristic rhythms in the works of Bulgarian composers] (Sofia, 1957)
*Ornamenti v balgarskata narodna muzika* [Ornaments in Bulgarian folk music] (Sofia, 1961)
'Struktura i formi na balgarskite narodni pesni' [Structures and forms in Bulgarian folk songs], *IIM*, xv (1970), 5–95
Numerous articles on folk music and education
LADA BRASHOVANOVA

**Motta, José Vianna da.** *See* VIANNA DA MOTTA, JOSÉ.

**Motte, Diether de la** (*b* Bonn, 30 March 1928). German composer and teacher. He studied composition with Maler, the piano with Hansen and choral conducting with Thomas at the Nordwestdeutsche Musikakademie, Detmold, and attended classes given by Leibowitz, Krenek, Fortner and Messiaen at the Darmstadt summer courses. In 1950 he was appointed lecturer at the Evangelische Landeskirchenmusikschule in Düsseldorf, where from 1955 he was also active as a music critic. He was then a reader for the publishing house of Schott (1959–62) before his appointment as lecturer (1962) and then professor of composition and theory (1964) at the Hamburg Musikhochschule. In 1972 he was elected vice-president of the Freie Akademie der Künste, Hamburg. Never attached to a group or school, he has been decisively influenced by 'singing' music – the gamelan and Gregorian chant, Schubert and Berg. Numerous 'visible music' compositions led him to a new conception of opera in *So oder so*, in which pantomime has an important part. He is married to Helga de la Motte-Haber.

WORKS
*(selective list)*
Conc. for Orch., 1963; Sym., 1964; Wie eine Rose (Jimenez), chorus, 1964; Pf Conc., 1965; Septet, cl, bn, tpt, trbn, perc, vn, db, 1965; 3 Gesänge (Gryphius), Bar, org, 1966; Die Niemandsrose (Celan), Bar, 7 insts, 1966; Sym. Ov., 1966; Fl Conc., 1967; Es wartet alles auf Dich (Ps civ), chorus, 5 insts, org, 1968; Der Aufsichtsrat (opera, R. Schneider), Hanover, 1970; Orgelstück mit Fenstern, org, 1970; Haus-Konzert, Tafel-Musik, Klang-Wege, orch, 1971; So oder so (opera, de la Motte), 1972–4; Conc. avventuroso, small orch, 1974; Echokonzert, vc, orch, 1976; Hörtheater (5 pieces), 1976
Chamber and pf music, tape compositions, 'visible music'

Principal publisher: Bärenreiter

WRITINGS
*Hans Werner Henze: Der Prinz von Homburg* (Mainz, 1960)
'Elegie für junge Liebende', *Melos*, xxviii (1961), 152
'Kontrapunkt', *Terminologie der neuen Musik*, Veröffentlichungen des Instituts für neue Musik und Musikerziehung Darmstadt, v (Darmstadt, 1965)
'Reform der Formenlehre?', *Probleme des musiktheoretischen Unterrichts*, Veröffentlichungen des Instituts für neue Musik und Musikerziehung Darmstadt, vii (Darmstadt, 1967)
'Die Sprache der neuen Musik', *Musica*, xxi (1967), 49
'Ich bin gespannt, wie es weitergeht', *Musik und Verlag: Karl Vötterle zum 65. Geburtstag* (Kassel, 1968)
*Musikalische Analyse* (Kassel, 1968, 2/1973)
ed.: H. Grabner: *Allgemeine Musiklehre* (Kassel, 10/1970)
'Konzerte im Wandel(n)', *Musica*, xxv (1971), 121
*Harmonielehre* (Kassel and Munich, 1976)

BIBLIOGRAPHY
K. Grebe: 'Musik für ein singendes Orchester: Diether de la Motte – ein Porträt', *Musica*, xxi (1967), 155
MONIKA LICHTENFELD

**Motte-Haber, Helga de la** (*b* Ludwigshafen, 2 Oct 1938). German musicologist. From 1957 she studied psychology at Vienna University with H. Rohracher, at Hamburg University with P. R. Hofstätter, and at Mainz University with A. Wellek, obtaining a final diploma in psychology at Mainz in 1961. She then studied musicology with G. von Dadelsen and H. P. Reinecke at Hamburg University, where she took the doctorate in 1967 with a dissertation on experimental psychological investigations into the classification of musical rhythms. She worked freelance at the Staatliche Institut für Musikforschung in Berlin (1965–72), and in 1971 completed her *Habilitation* in systematic musicology at the Technical University of Berlin. In 1972 she became a research fellow and professor at the Pädagogische Hochschule in Cologne. She specializes in experimental psychology with reference to music.

WRITINGS
*Ein Beitrag zur Klassifikation musikalischer Rhythmen experimental-psychologische Untersuchungen* (diss., U. of Hamburg, 1967, Cologne, 1968)
'Musikalische Begabung und ihre Messbarkeit', *Forschung in der*

*Musikerziehung*, ii (1969), 69

'Über musikalische Urteilsbildung', *Forschung in der Musikerziehung*, i (1969), 11

'Über die Gegenstände und Methoden der Musikpsychologie', *IRMAS*, i (1970), 83

'Die Schwierigkeit, Trivialität in der Musik zu bestimmen', *Studien zur Philosophie und Literatur des 19. Jahrhunderts*, vi (1972), 171

'Die Anwendung der Bedingungsvariation bei musikpsychologischen Untersuchungen ein Methodenexperiment', *Jb des Staatlichen Instituts für Musikforschung Preussischer Kulturbesitz* (1972), 154

'Das singende und klingende Plakat: Werbung durch Musik', *Sprache im technischen Zeitalter*, xlii (1972), 143

*Musikpsychologie: eine Einführung* (Cologne, 1972)

'Der Einfluss psychologischer Variablen auf das ästhetische Urteil', *Jb des Staatlichen Instituts für Musikforschung Preussischer Kulturbesitz* (1973), 163

'Musik und Informationstheorie', *NZM*, Jg.135 (1974), 78

HANS HEINRICH EGGEBRECHT

**Motteux, Peter Anthony** [Pierre Antoine] (*b* Rouen, 25 Feb 1663; *d* London, 18 Feb 1718). English man of letters of French birth. As a Huguenot he was forced to leave France after the revocation of the Edict of Nantes in 1685. He settled in London, becoming naturalized in 1686. In 1692 he initiated the *Gentleman's Journal*, a monthly magazine – the first of its kind – which attempted to cater for a wide range of tastes and included comments on music as well as a music supplement. Difficulties in production forced him to abandon it at the end of 1694. He turned to translation and playwriting. He completed Thomas Urquhart's translation of Rabelais (1693–4) and produced the best-known translation of *Don Quixote* (1701). His dramatic works include a number of masques and musical interludes: *The Taking of Namur* (1695), *The Loves of Mars and Venus* (performed with Edward Ravenscroft's *The Anatomist*, 1696), *Europe's Revels for the Peace* (1697) and *Acis and Galatea* (performed originally with *The Mad Lover*, *c*1700) – all set mainly by John Eccles (with assistance from Gottfried Finger in *The Loves of Mars and Venus*) – *Britain's Happiness* (1704), set by both Richard Leveridge and John Weldon, and *The Mountebank* (performed in his own *Farewell Folly*, 1707), set by Leveridge. In 1698 he turned John Fletcher's *The Island Princess* into a semi-opera which was set by Daniel Purcell, Jeremiah Clarke and Leveridge and enjoyed considerable success. His occasional and other verses were set at the time by Eccles and J. W. Franck, among others.

Motteux was also involved in the first productions of all-sung opera in England. He is generally regarded as having been responsible for the translation and adaptation for Thomas Clayton of the libretto of *Arsinoe*, produced on 16 January 1705, and he certainly provided the English texts for Giuseppe Fedeli's *The Temple of Love* (1706), the pasticcio *Thomyris* (1707) and the opera *Love's Triumph* (1708). Once Italian operas came to be performed in their original language, however, Motteux ceased to write for the theatre.

BIBLIOGRAPHY

R. N. Cunningham: *Peter Anthony Motteux, 1663–1718: a Biographical and Critical Study* (Oxford, 1933)

M. Tilmouth: 'A Calendar of References to Music in Newspapers Published in London and the Provinces (1660–1719)', *RMARC*, i (1961/*R*1968), 13, 35

MARGARET LAURIE

**Mottl, Felix (Josef)** (*b* Unter-St Veit, Vienna, 24 Aug 1856; *d* Munich, 2 July 1911). Austrian conductor, composer and editor. He was admitted as a boy soprano to the Löwenburg Seminary in Vienna, and then studied at the Vienna Conservatory, where he was in Bruckner's theory class. Soon he was appointed co-répétiteur at the opera house and conductor of the Academic Wagner Society, Vienna. In 1876, with Hans Richter's help, he was enlisted at Bayreuth to prepare for the first Wagner Festival, and he became one of the most active members of the so-called 'Nibelungen-Kanzlei'. Liszt facilitated the performances of his three-act opera *Agnes Bernauer* at Weimar (1880). From 1881 Mottl was conductor at the court opera and the Philharmonic Society of Karlsruhe, where he made operatic standards virtually second to none in Germany: all Wagner's works were given, as well as Berlioz's *Béatrice et Bénédict* (1888) and *Les troyens* (the first stage performance of all five acts, in German) on 6 and 7 December 1890. He also secured recognition for Cornelius's *Der Barbier von Bagdad*, which had been neglected since 1858, by re-orchestrating it and performing it in 1884.

In 1886 Mottl conducted for the first time at Bayreuth, when he was jointly in charge of *Tristan und Isolde* and *Parsifal*. He remained a regular guest conductor there, and his reputation from this time was inseparable from his Wagner performances. On 17 April 1894 he gave a Wagner concert in the Queen's Hall, London, the first of many concerts in England. The *Musical Times* reported, 'His "readings" were marked by singular clearness, delicacy and energy, great rhythmic freedom, and exceptionally strong contrasts of all kinds. Not a detail, not a point was lost'. He conducted Wagner's *Ring* cycle at Covent Garden in 1898 and repeated it in 1890, also conducting *Fidelio*, *Tannhäuser* and *Lohengrin*.

During a visit to New York in 1903 Mottl prepared the first American performances of *Parsifal* at the Metropolitan Opera House; he declined to conduct them, because of protests by the Wagner family that the copyright had not yet expired, and Alfred Heitz conducted instead. Mottl did, however, conduct other works. Alma Mahler noted that 'he made the mistake of not taking the American public seriously' and that his initial performances proved a disappointment.

Mottl left Karlsruhe in 1903 to take charge of the Munich opera house and direct the Akademie der Tonkunst. Again he brought distinction to the institutions in which he worked. He arranged and performed Bellini's *Norma* and Donizetti's *L'elisir d'amore*, and published a newly orchestrated version of Gluck's *Alceste* (Bonn, 1911). He collapsed while conducting *Tristan und Isolde* and died a few days later; he was survived by his widow, the soprano Zdenka Fassbender.

Besides editing the vocal scores of Wagner's operas Mottl made orchestral arrangements of songs by Mozart, Schubert, Wagner and Loewe, and of Chabrier's *Bourrée fantasque*; he also arranged ballet suites from music by Gluck (1896 and *c*1901), Rameau (1899), Grétry (*c*1901) and Lully (*c*1902). His compositions include a string quartet (1904), many songs, the one-act opera *Fürst and Sänger* and the one-act dance-play *Pan im Busch* (1881).

For a photograph of Mottl *see* RICHTER, HANS.

BIBLIOGRAPHY

E. Istel: Obituary, *Die Musik*, xl (1910–11), 118

W. Krienitz: Obituary, *Wagner-Jb*, iv (1912), 202

A. Einstein: *Neues Musik-Lexikon* (Berlin, 1925)

W. Krienitz: 'F. Mottls Tagebuch Aufzeichnungen 1873–76', *Neue Wagner-Forschungen* (Karlsruhe, 1943), no.1, pp.167–239

A. Mahler: *Gustav Mahler: Memories and Letters* (London, 1946, enlarged 3/1973), 129

P. A. Scholes: *The Mirror of Music* (London, 1947), 388
R. Delage, ed.: 'Correspondance inédite entre Emmanuel Chabrier et
Félix Mottl', *RdM*, xlix (1963), 61–107

DAVID CHARLTON

**Mottl-Fassbender, Zdenka.** *See* FASSBENDER, ZDENKA.

**Motto.** A term used for a brief phrase or motif that
recurs at various points in a work. It may be applied to
masses of the 15th and 16th centuries unified by the
appearance of the same brief phrase at the beginning of
each movement, as in such parody masses as Morales's
*Missa 'Mille regretz'* (*see* HEAD-MOTIF). In the 17th and
18th centuries, it is commonly applied to a figure at the
beginning of an aria (*see* DEVISENARIE) where the
'motto' is stated by the voice and followed by the opening
ritornello, as in 'Lo farò, dirò spietato' in Act 1 of
Handel's *Rodelinda* (1725). In music of the 19th century, it may apply to a phrase that dominates a composition or recurs within it, generally appearing at the
opening and at decisive moments in the course of the
movement or the work: examples are Beethoven's
'Lebewohl' Piano Sonata op.81*a*, Berlioz' *Symphonie
fantastique* (where the *idée fixe* may be called a motto)
and Tchaikovsky's Symphonies nos.4 and 5.

**Motz, Georg** (*b* Augsburg, 24 Dec 1653; *d* Tilsit [now
Sovetsk], 25 Sept 1733). German composer, musician
and writer on music. According to an autobiographical
statement printed in Mattheson, he began his musical
training at Augsburg under the guidance of Georg
Schmezer. At the age of 16 he went to Worms to
complete his schooling. A journey to Vienna and the
neighbouring spa of Baden brought him to the notice of
Prince Johann Seyfried of Eggenberg, who employed
him as a musician at his residence near Graz. During
this period he also spent some time at Ljubljana when
his employer held court there in the winter. In 1679 he
received permission to make a four-month journey to
Venice, Padua, Ferrara, Bologna, Florence, Siena and
Rome. On returning to Eggenberg in August he fell
seriously ill and after recovering decided in 1680 that
for health reasons he must leave Styria. He moved to the
court of his former employer's brother, Duke Johann
Christian, at Krumau (now Český Krumlóv), Bohemia,
where he became court organist. Because of his
Protestant faith, however, he became badly estranged
from religious circles there, and he left within a year. He
then travelled north, stopping at Hamburg, Lübeck,
Danzig and Königsberg, until finally he went to Tilsit,
where on 8 May 1682 he was appointed Kantor of the
Provincial School. He remained at Tilsit until his death.

Motz received Mattheson's warmest praise as 'one of
the best Kantors in Germany, who may with honour be
called a *musicus eruditus*'. None of his music survives,
and he is known now exclusively as an effective and
outspoken writer opposing critics of church music. His
treatise *Die vertheidigte Kirchen-Music* convincingly
challenges the denunciation of the use of music in the
Protestant church made by CHRISTIAN GERBER in his
book *Unerkandte Sünden der Welt*. Although Gerber
used scripture and the words of Luther to prove that
practices in the sphere of church music at the time were
sacrilegious, Motz was able to destroy his criticisms
point by point by showing that both the Bible and
Luther strongly supported music in the church. He
quoted also from a large number of theorists of the 16th,

17th and 18th centuries, including Bartolus, Lorber,
Lippius, Listenius, Praetorius and Printz, to support his
arguments. Writing with perception and humour, he
clearly made Gerber look ignorant of the very sources
he quoted and showed up his pseudo-moralizing about the
sins of church music as foolish. His treatise and its
continuation of 1708 are significant documents of the
early 18th century for the musico-sociological conflicts
arising within the German Protestant church as the
impact of secular musical styles became ever more central to concepts of sacred music.

WRITINGS
*Die vertheidigte Kirchen-Music oder klar und deutlicher Beweis welcher
gestalten Herr M. Christian Gerber ... in seinem Buch, welches er
Unerkandte Sünden der Welt nennet ... da er von dem Missbrauch
der Kirchen-Music geschrieben zu Verwerfung der musicalischen
Harmonie und Bestraffung der Kirchen-Music zu weit gegangen* (n.p.,
1703)
*Abgenötigte Fortsetzung der vertheidigten Kirchen-Music* (n.p., 1708)
*Grosse unbegreifliche Weisheit Gottes, in dem Gnadengeschencke der
geistlichen Sing- und Klingkunst*, lost, MS once owned by Mattheson
BIBLIOGRAPHY
J. Mattheson: *Grundlage einer Ehren-Pforte* (Hamburg, 1740); ed. M.
Schneider (Berlin, 1910/*R*1969)

GEORGE J. BUELOW

**Moucqué, Antoine.** *See* MOUQUÉ, ANTOINE.

**Moud, Henry.** *See* MUDD family.

**Moulaert, Pierre** (*b* St Gilles, Brussels, 24 Sept 1907; *d*
Uccle, Brussels, 13 Nov 1967). Belgian critic and composer. Son of Raymond Moulaert, he studied the violin
and theory at the Brussels Conservatory, and worked as
a violinist at the Théâtre Royal de la Monnaie. His most
important post as a critic was with the daily *Dernière
heure*; at the Brussels Conservatory he was successively
professor of solfège (from 1937) and harmony (from
1964). Coming to composition through practical work
for the theatre and cinema, he remained, in his few
concert works, close to convention, although he
produced original effects of timbre in such works as the
Concertino for flute, oboe and strings (1954), and there
are bold rhythmic ideas in, for example, *Séquences*
(1964) for orchestra. His use of counterpoint was
thorough and strict, but also clear and elegant (e.g. the
String Quartet, 1956). Moulaert's music is published by
CeBeDeM, which holds his MSS.

HENRI VANHULST

**Moulaert, Raymond (Auguste Marie)** (*b* Brussels, 4 Feb
1875; *d* Ixelles, Brussels, 18 Jan 1962). Belgian composer, pianist and teacher. He studied the piano and
theory at the Brussels Conservatory, but was self-taught
in composition. Returning to teach at the conservatory,
he remained there for 43 years, most notably as professor of counterpoint (1927–40); he was also professor of
harmony and counterpoint at the Chapelle Musicale
Reine Elisabeth. He was elected a member of the
Belgian Royal Academy in 1955, and in 1958 he
received the Prix Quinquennial of the Belgian government. As a composer, he excelled in songwriting, and
his best work in the genre (the five cycles of *Poèmes de
la vieille France*) recalls Fauré. He wrote for the
orchestra in a Bartókian manner, often using variation
techniques within strict forms, as in the *Symphonie de
fugues*. He edited Lully's *Alceste* (Paris, 1932) for
Prunières' complete edition.

## WORKS
*(selective list)*

Orch: Fanfares, 1930; Symphonie de valses, 1936; Tpt Concertino, 1937; Pf Conc., 1938; Rhapsodie écossaise, pf, orch, 1940; Symphonie de fugues, 1942–4; Etudes symphoniques, 1943

Choral: Poèmes de la vieille France (1917–20); La lanterne magique (Carême), 1947; Mass, 1949; Petites légendes, 2 vols., 1950

Inst: Andante, fugue et final, ob, ob d'amore, eng hn, heckelphone, 1907; Divertimento, str trio, 1936; Suite, 3 trbn, 1939; Sonata, vc, pf, 1942; Concert, wind qnt, harp, 1950; kbd pieces

Songs: 20 mélodies et poèmes (1914–17); Poèmes de la vieille France (1917–43); Zes oud-nederlandse gedichten, 1925; 2 poèmes en vieille langue anglaise, 1929; Rime dell'Italia antica, 1930; Chansons du châtelain de Coucy, 1945; orch songs

Principal publishers: Brogneaux, CeBeDeM, Chester, Salabert

### BIBLIOGRAPHY
*Catalogue des oeuvres de compositeurs belges: Raymond Moulaert* (Brussels, 1954) [CeBeDeM publication]

R. Wangermée: *La musique belge contemporaine* (Brussels, 1959), 124f

'Raymond Moulaert', *Annuaire du Conservatoire royal de Bruxelles*, lxxxv (1962), 39

P. Tinel: 'Notice sur Raymond Moulaert', *Annuaire de l'Académie royale de Belgique*, cxxix (1963)

*Music in Belgium* (Brussels, 1964) [CeBeDeM publication]
HENRI VANHULST

**Moule-Evans, David** (*b* Ashford, Kent, 21 Nov 1905). English composer. He gained an open scholarship in 1924 to the RCM, where he studied under Sargent and Howells. He won the Mendelssohn Scholarship in 1929 and obtained a DMus at Oxford in the following year. His Concerto for String Orchestra won a Carnegie Publication Award in 1928, and his Symphony in G (1944) won first prize in the Australian Jubilee Competition in 1952. He has written a number of substantial orchestral pieces, of which the overture *Spirit of London* (1942), the *Vienna Rhapsody* (1943) and the orchestral poem *September Dusk* (1945) are perhaps the most notable and popular. *The Haunted Place* (1944), for string orchestra, was also well received. Among his chamber works the Violin Sonata in F♯ minor (1956) and the Piano Sonata (1966) are outstanding, and they represent a move away from the straightforward traditional style that had served his more popular orchestral works. He has also written songs, partsongs and music for many documentary films. In 1945 he joined the teaching staff of the RCM as professor of composition and theory. Serious illness in 1968 brought his composing career to an end, although he continued to teach. His principal publishers are Joseph Williams and Stainer & Bell.

MICHAEL HURD

**Moulinié** [Moulinier, Moulinière, Molinié], **Etienne** (*b* Languedoc, *c*1600; *d* Languedoc, after 1669). French composer. As a child he sang in the choir of Narbonne Cathedral. In 1624 he came to Paris, where his older brother Antoine (*d* Paris, 8 Aug 1655) was a singer in the king's chamber. Antoine recognized Etienne's talent and used his influence as a valet and officer in the royal service to assist his career. In 1628 Etienne became director of music to Gaston of Orleans, the king's younger brother, and remained in this post until Gaston's death on 2 February 1660; Gaston was very fond of music and particularly of *ballets de cour*. Moulinié wrote both sacred and secular music, for one or more voices unaccompanied or accompanied by either lute or continuo, and also composed music for ballets and dance pieces for other occasions. From 1634 to 1649 he served as music master to Gaston's daughter, Mlle de Montpensier, for whose *Ballet des quatres*

*monarchies chrétiennes* (1635) he composed the solo *airs*. After Gaston's death he received a small payment from his estate, but it was necessary for him at a relatively advanced age to seek new employment. In 1661 he became director of music to the estates of Languedoc and remained so until his death.

Moulinié's many *airs de cour* are typical of the genre in that they are simple, strophic and basically syllabic, but they are unusual in being freer rhythmically. The appearance in print of many *airs* within a single year in three versions – for four voices, solo voice with lute, and unaccompanied solo voice – attests to their popularity. In one instance, *Enfin la beauté*, the lute adds a ritornello that is absent in the purely vocal versions, and in another, *D'où sort cette grande clarité*, the vocal part in the version with lute is transposed. Moulinié's skill as a composer is evident in *Quoy faut-il donc vous dire adieu*, where the initial phrase is developed to a degree rare in 17th-century *airs de cour*. The *airs* were so admired that they were used for sacred songs with new texts in *Despouille d'Egypte* (Paris, 1629) and *La philomele seraphique* (Tournai, 1632). Heinrich Albert included *Est-ce l'ordonnance des cieux* in his *Arien*, vii (Königsberg, 1648) with a new German text, *So ist es denn des Himmels Will*, by Andreas Adersbach. Perhaps some of the unusual qualities of Moulinié's *airs* come from his awareness of non-French vocal music, particularly that of Spain and Italy. Spanish song and dance were popular in Paris, but only Moulinié among French composers actually published *airs* in Italian and Spanish. The Spanish songs do not display any features of the *tonada humana*, but one of them, *Repican las campanillas*, was copied and adapted by Dutch composers many times and even appeared in greatly revised German versions. The Italian influence on Moulinié eventually proved stronger: all his later compositions, most of which are sacred, include a figured bass, and the polyphonic choral works include some antiphony.

### WORKS

Edition: *Airs de cour pour voix et luth (1603–1643)*, ed. A. Verchaly (Paris, 1961) [contains 7 of Moulinié's airs]

Airs avec la tablature de luth, 5 vols. (Paris, 1624–35)

Airs de cour à 4 et 5 parties, 5 vols. (Paris, 1625–39)

Missa pro defunctis, 5vv (1636); ed. D. Launay (Paris, 1952)

Meslanges de sujets chrestiens, cantiques, litanies et motets, 2–5vv, bc (Paris, 1658)

Airs à 4 parties, bc (Paris, 1668)

Motets offerts à la province de Languedoc (1668), lost

21 airs, 1624[10] (from Airs avec la tablature, i, ii); 10 airs, 6 Sp. songs, 1626[11] (some from Airs avec la tablature, ii); 5 airs, 1 in 1628[10], 1 in Chansons pour dancer et pour boire, iv (Paris, 1630), 1 in 1631[4], 2 in 1633[3]

10 airs, F-Pn Rés.Vm[7] 510, Rés.Vma 571

10 sacred contrafacta, 5 in 1629[7], 4 in 1632[3], 1 in H. Albert, Arien, vii (Königsberg, 1648)

Texts of works for which the music is lost survive in P. Perrin: *Les oeuvres de poésie* (Paris, 1661)

### BIBLIOGRAPHY
M. M. McGowan: *L'art du ballet de cour en France, 1581–1643* (Paris, 1963)

D. Launay: 'La "Paraphrase des psaumes" de Godeau et ses musiciens', *RdM*, l (1964), 30–75

L. E. S. J. de Laborde: *Musiciens de Paris, 1535–1792*, ed. Y. de Brossard (Paris, 1965)

M. Jurgens: *Documents du minutier central concernant l'histoire de la musique (1600–1650)* (Paris, 1967)

J. H. Baron: 'Dutch Influences on the German Secular Solo-continuo Lied in the Mid-seventeenth Century', *AcM*, xliii (1971), 43
JOHN H. BARON

**Moulton Piper, Dorothy.** *See* MAYER, DOROTHY.

Moulu [Moullu, Molu], Pierre (*b c*1480–90; *d c*1550). French or Flemish composer. The texts of two of his compositions offer circumstantial evidence that he was employed at the French royal chapel for a time during the first quarter of the 16th century. *Fiere attropos mauldicte et inhumaine*, a rondeau using as cantus firmus an antiphon for Good Friday (*Anxiatus est in me spiritus meus*), laments the death of France's sovereign lady, doubtless Anne of Britanny (*d* 1514); the composition resembles Josquin's *déploration* for Ockeghem in many ways and may have been modelled on it. Moulu's motet *Mater floreat florescat* pays tribute to the most celebrated musicians of France, arranged roughly in chronological order. The first part praises Dufay, Regis, Baziron, Agricola, Obrecht, Compère, Eloy, Hayne van Ghizeghem and La Rue, and ends, 'may the incomparable Josquin win the prize'. The second half names younger composers, all active during the first half of the 16th century and many of them known to have sung in the French royal chapel: Longueval, Lourdault, Prioris, the brothers Févin, Hilaire, Divitis, Brumel, Isaac, Nynot (Ninot le Petit), Mathurin Forestier, Bruhier and Mouton. The composition may have been written and first performed for the triumphal entry into Paris on 12 May 1517 of the newly crowned wife of François I, Queen Claude. That Moulu should have been the musical spokesman for the French court on these occasions suggests his close association with the chapel there, but no archival documents confirm this hypothesis.

Pierre de Ronsard in the dedication to *Livre des meslanges* (Paris, 1560) mentioned Moulu as a student of Josquin Desprez. Whether Ronsard's remark is intended to be taken literally or not, Moulu's music does in fact show the influence of Josquin in many ways. While in his motets Moulu still made use of older scaffolding techniques like cantus firmus either simply or in canon, he often paraphrased borrowed material and frequently constructed his compositions quite freely as a chain of points of imitation. His fairly syllabic style reveals his concern for good text declamation, which is not, however, invariably observed. His best-known mass, the *Missa 'Alma Redemptoris mater'*, paraphrasing the Marian antiphon, reveals a curious constructivist tendency in Moulu's personality: it is composed so that it can be performed either as it stands or by omitting all of the rests longer than a minim. Two of his other masses also paraphrase chants as well as incorporating some references to polyphonic motets. (Crawford argued that the motets were composed later and allude to the masses.) Moulu's *Missa 'Missus est Gabriel'* parodies Josquin's motet. Likewise most of his chansons are based on borrowed material, chiefly popular urban melodies, which Moulu treated with considerable contrapuntal sophistication in a manner typical of French composers of the first quarter of the 16th century.

WORKS

Edition: *Treize livres de motets parus chez Pierre Attaingnant en 1534 et 1535*, ed. A. Smijers and A. T. Merritt (Monaco and Paris, 1934–64) [SM]

MASSES

Missa 'Alma Redemptoris mater', 4vv, *RISM* 1522
Missa 'Missus est Gabriel angelus', 4vv, *F-CA* 4 (on Josquin's motet)
Missa 'Mittit ad virginem', 4vv, *P-C* M.M.2
Missa 'Stephane gloriose', 4vv, 1540[1]

MOTETS

Adest nobis dies laetitiae, 4vv, *I-MOd* IX; Alleluia, Regem ascendentem, 4vv, *USSR-KAu* 1740, lost; Domine Dominus noster, 4vv, *D-Kl* 4, 24; Fiere attropos, 5vv, ed. in MRM, iii–v (1968); Inducta est

caro mea, 4vv, *Rp* B2111–15; In hoc ego sperabo, 3vv, 1542[18]; In pace, 5vv, SM x
Mater floreat, 4vv, ed. in MRM, iii–v (1968); Ne projicias, 6vv, SM x; Oculi omnium, 3vv, 1565[2]; O dulcis amica Dei, 5vv, *I-Bc* Q19; Oremus pro conctis, 4vv, *Bc* R141, vol.iii; Quam dilecta, 3vv, 1565[2]; Regina caeli, 4vv, 1535[4]
Salve Barbara martyr, 7vv, *Pc* A17; Salve regina Barbara, 4vv, *Bc* Q19; Sancta Maria, Dei mater, 4vv, *Bc* R141, vol.iv; Saule, Saule, 5vv, SM viii; Sicut malus, 3vv, ed. Y. Rokseth, *Treize motets et un prelude . . . parus chez Pierre Attaingnant* (Paris, 1930); Tu licet [= 'Crucifixus' from Missa 'Alma Redemptoris mater'], 2vv, 1549[16]; Virgo carens criminibus, 4vv, *D-Rp* B220–22; Vivo ego, 3vv, 1565[3]; Vulnerasti cor meum, 5vv, ed. in MRM, iii–v (1968)

CHANSONS

Au bois, au bois, madame, 4vv, ed. H. M. Brown: *Theatrical Chansons of the Fifteenth and Early Sixteenth Centuries* (Cambridge, Mass., 1963); En despit des faux mesdisans, 6vv, 1572[2]; Et d'où venes vous, 3vv, ed. in *Theatrical Chansons* (Cambridge, Mass., 1963); Hellas, hellas madame, 4vv, 1528[9]; J'ay mis mon cueur, 7vv, 1572[2]; La rousée de moys de may, 6vv, 1572[2]; N'aymés jamais ces gens, 3vv, 1536[1]; Voicy le may, 4vv, 1530[5]

J'ay . . ., 3vv, *I-Bc* Q19 (text missing)
Canon, a 3, L. Zacconi: *Prattica di musica*, i (Venice, 1592/*R*1967), chap.56

WORKS WITH CONFLICTING ATTRIBUTIONS

In illo tempore, accesserunt ad Jesum, 4vv, attrib. Mouton in 1537[1], attrib Moulu in *I-Bc* Q19
Quam pulchra es, 4vv, attrib. Josquin in 1537[1]; attrib. Mouton in 1519[2], attrib. Moulu in *Bc* Q19

BIBLIOGRAPHY

Y. Rokseth: 'Un motet de Moulu et ses diverses transcriptions pour orgue', *Kongressbericht: Basel 1924*, 286
J. G. Chapman: *The Works of Pierre Moulu: a Stylistic Analysis* (diss., New York U., 1964)
D. Crawford: 'Reflections on Some Masses from the Press of Moderne', *MQ*, lviii (1972), 82

HOWARD MAYER BROWN

**Mounsey, Ann (Sheppard)** (*b* London, 17 April 1811; *d* London, 24 June 1891). English organist, teacher and composer. She studied under Logier, and was alluded to by Spohr in his account of his visit to Logier's academy in 1820. She held several positions as organist in London churches and in 1834 she became an associate of the Philharmonic Society. In 1843 she gave the first of six series of Classical Concerts, at Crosby Hall, London, for one of which Mendelssohn composed *Hear my Prayer* for voice and organ, first performed on 8 January 1845. On 28 April 1853 she married W. Bartholomew and in the same year composed the oratorio *The Nativity*, which was performed on 17 January 1855, under the direction of John Hullah at St Martin's Hall. Mounsey was well known in London as a teacher; she published more than 100 songs, 40 partsongs and a large number of works for piano and for organ.

Her sister Elizabeth Mounsey (*b* London, 8 Oct 1819; *d* London, 3 Oct 1905) was an organist and composer; she was organist of St Peter, Cornhill, from 1834 (when she was 14) to 1882. She also played the guitar, and composed for the organ, the piano and that instrument.

BIBLIOGRAPHY

E. Polko: *Reminiscences of Felix Mendelssohn-Bartholdy* (London, 1869), 220
L. Spohr: *Autobiography*, ii (London, 1878), 99f

GEORGE GROVE/R

**Mountain dulcimer.** *See* APPALACHIAN DULCIMER.

**Mount Athos.** *See* ATHOS, MOUNT.

**Mount-Edgcumbe, Richard,** 2nd Earl of (*b* Plymouth, 13 Sept 1764; *d* Richmond, Surrey, 26 Sept 1839). English opera enthusiast and amateur composer. An only child,

Richard Edgcumbe married in 1789, by which time he was already Tory MP for Fowey. On his father's death in 1795 he was elevated to the peerage and became Lord Lieutenant of Cornwall. Frequent visits to London and some to Italy were made mainly for the purpose of going to operas. When he himself composed an Italian opera to words by Metastasio, Brigitta Banti generously agreed to sing in it at her benefit performance; *Zenobia* (King's Theatre, 22 May 1800) was announced as 'composed by an English Gentleman'. 'Having granted the use of this opera to Banti only, I withdrew it immediately, and would not permit it to be again represented for the manager, who requested to have it.' This explanation of apparent failure comes from *Musical Reminiscences, containing an Account of the Italian Opera in England from 1773* (1824). The book, which is Lord Mount-Edgcumbe's chief claim to fame, is vividly and garrulously readable, and surprisingly free from anti-English bias. The fourth edition (1834) includes an account of the music festival that year in Westminster Abbey. None of Lord Mount-Edgcumbe's music has been published. When he was a child, his portrait was painted by Reynolds.

ROGER FISKE

**Mouqué** [Moucqué, Mocke, Mocqué], **Antoine** (*b* Ostend, 1 Aug 1659; *d* Ostend, 23 Aug 1723). Flemish composer, organist and singer. He began as a choirboy at the principal church of Ostend, SS Peter and Paul, and in 1677 became a salaried singer there. He had meanwhile completed his studies in the humanities with the Oratorian fathers at Ostend. On 9 August 1680 at Louvain he became a novice in their order, but he soon left to go to Bruges as a vicar and substitute organist at St Donaas. In 1689 he was again mentioned as a salaried musician at SS Peter and Paul, Ostend, and on 27 April 1691 was appointed *phonascus* there. He remained in this post until his sudden death, though there was in theory a break in his service from 16 July 1706 to 6 August 1709. On 20 September 1692 he was ordained a priest at Bruges. In 1711 he was asked to go to Antwerp to try out the new carillon for Ostend and in 1722 to go to Bruges to test the new clock for the market tower. No music by him has survived, though he appears to have been a prolific composer. The Ostend town accounts show that between 1690 and 1719 he was paid nine times for church compositions, including three masses and a collection of carols, which he dedicated to the magistrate. Works by him are also listed in four 18th-century inventories of music belonging to the principal churches of Oudenaarde (1734 and 1752), Ostend (1747) and Ghent (1754). These include an 'Opus Soloon', a Passion with Lamentations, an antiphon with *Magnificat*, a *Salve regina* and a *Regina coeli*. In 1706 Etienne Roger of Amsterdam advertised a printed collection of motets by him for one to five voices and instruments. His name also appears with those of Corelli, G. B. Vitali and others in a privilege dated 1695 awarded to the Bruges printer François van Heurck. Swert called him 'a famous musician very well versed in every sort of instrumental music'.

BIBLIOGRAPHY

A. Félibien: *Conférences de l'Académie royale de peinture et de sculpture* (Amsterdam, 1706), appx: 'Catalogue de livres de musique qui se vendent à Amsterdam chez Estienne Roger mais qui ne sont point de son impression'

P. de Swert: *Chronicon congregationis Oratorii Domini Jesus per provinciam archi-episcopatus mechliniensis diffusae, 1626–1729*

(Lille, 1740), 132

E. vander Straeten: *La musique aux Pays-Bas avant le XIX<sup>e</sup> siècle*, i (Brussels, 1867/R1969), 212, 217, 226; v (Brussels, 1880/R1969), 220, 236

D. van de Casteele: 'Une expertise de la tour des Halles, à Bruges, le 31 décembre 1722', *Annales de la Société d'émulation de Bruges*, xxi (iii/4) (1869), 321

D. van de Casteele and E. vander Straeten: *Maîtres de chant et organistes de Saint-Donatien et de Saint-Sauveur à Bruges* (Bruges, 1870), 40, 47

[C. van Iseghem]: 'Antoine Mouqué: sa vie, ses oeuvres', *La feuille d'Ostende* (5, 8 and 12 April 1894)

P. Bergmans: 'Mouqué, Antoine', *BNB*

R. Vannes: *Dictionnaire des musiciens (compositeurs)* (Brussels, 1947), 289

GODELIEVE SPIESSENS

**Mouret, Jean-Joseph** (*b* Avignon, 11 April 1682; *d* Charenton, 22 Dec 1738). French composer. He was the son of an Avignon silk merchant, Jean-Bertrand Mouret, and his wife, Madeleine Menotte. Durey de Noinville related that the father, an amateur violinist, saw to it that Mouret 'perfected himself in the art of music'; it is reasonable to assume that he was trained at the choir school of Avignon's Notre Dame des Doms where the young Rameau was appointed temporary organist in January 1702.

By 1707 Mouret was in Paris, where his excellent singing voice and personal charm enabled him to move with ease in 'the best company'. He was appointed *maître de musique* for the Marshall of Noailles. In 1708 or 1709 he was named *Surintendant de la musique* at the court of Sceaux where he composed much of the music for the Duchess of Maine's 'Grandes Nuits' (1714–15). From 1714 to 1718 he directed the orchestra at the Paris Opéra. By 1716 he was composing divertissements for Dancourt's comedies at the French Theatre. That year the New Italian Theatre reopened, thanks to the regent, and in 1717 Mouret began 20 years of employment there as composer-director. At this time and until 1734, Mouret, his wife (Marie Prompt) and daughter lived 'beside the Café de la Régence' on the Place du Palais Royal. In 1718 he obtained a royal privilege (renewed the year he died) to publish his own music. On 2 February 1720 he became an *ordinaire du Roy* as a singer of the king's chamber. Many of his motets, cantatas and *cantatilles* were composed for performance at the Concert Spirituel which he headed as artistic director from 1728 to 1734. If frequent mention in the influential *Mercure de France* is to be taken as measure, Mouret was the most popular composer of the Regency (1715–24).

It is thus surprising to realize that his popularity was ephemeral, and to find that he was quickly stripped of income and prestige. The difficulties of his last years were partly actuated by the interminable financial and legal problems attendant on his directorship of the Concert Spirituel. When in December 1734 the Académie Royale de Musique took over the administration of the Concert Spirituel, Mouret lost his position to Jean-Féry Rebel. After the death of the Duke of Maine two years later, Mouret was no longer retained at Sceaux, and in 1737 he lost his post at the Italian Theatre. In four years he was left essentially without employment and dependent on the kindness of such friends as the Prince of Carignan who gave him a pension of 1000 livres. The first signs of his insanity were noted in 1737, and on 14 April 1738 he was sent to the Fathers of Charity at Charenton, where he died eight months later.

Mouret shared in the innovating spirit that characterized the best in French stage music between Lully and Rameau. His *Le mariage de Ragonde* (1714) is a true lyric comedy composed more than 30 years before Rameau's *Platée*. In his *opéra-ballet*, *Les fêtes ou Le triomphe de Thalie*, the humiliating defeat of Melpomene (muse of tragedy) by Thalia (muse of comedy) in the prologue, which the librettist La Font boldly set on the stage of the Paris Opéra, resulted in a *succès de scandale*. Pressure obliged the authors to remove the heretical 'Triomphe de Thalie' from the title and to add a new entrée ('La critique des fêtes de Thalie') in which La Font 'assigned all the merit of its success to the music and dance' (preface). Although not (as Loewenberg claimed in *Annals of Opera*) the work in which the 'comic element was first introduced into the sphere of French opera' (see, for example, Campra's *Les fêtes vénitiennes* of 1710), *Les fêtes de Thalie* deals with flesh and blood characters, soubrettes and coquettish widows, who were costumed 'à la française'. 'La Provençale', a new entrée added in 1722, even makes use of Provençal dialect and popular instruments from the Midi.

Mouret's melodic gifts earned him the posthumous title of 'musicien des grâces'. They may be seen to better advantage in the music of *Les fêtes de Thalie*, *Les amours de Ragonde* and the divertissements of the Italian Theatre than in his more pretentious (and less successful) *tragédies lyriques* and *ballets-héroïques*. There is simplicity and naturalness in the former music that avoids triteness through asymmetrical phrase groupings and rhythmic contrasts. There is also keen observation of the entire spectrum of French stage music resulting in a highly developed sense of musical gesture; in *Le procès des théâtres* (1718), for example, Mouret characterizes musically the quarrelsome protagonists in the battle for supremacy in the theatrical world.

Mouret's motets, cantatas and *cantatilles*, designed for specific vocalists and solo instrumentalists at the Concert Spirituel, have a superficial elegance and brilliance exemplified in the extended vocalises of the Alleluia finales to many of the motets (*O sacrum* even has a soprano cadenza). Only in the *Cantemus Domino* and in the poignant 'Ora pro nobis' of the *Regina coeli* does the music illuminate the text.

The *Suites de symphonies* by Mouret and similar works by Jacques Aubert and Etienne Mangeant moved the small ensemble in France closer to an orchestral concept through their use of specific instrumentation. Dating from 1729, Mouret's *Suites* gave unusual attention to combinations of timbres. The first suite is scored for trumpet in D, first and second violins, oboes, bassoon, bass and timpani; the second suite, a 'joyeuse musique de table' (Viollier), contains nine binary dances; the instrumentation, clearly indicated, exploits colour contrasts between horns and strings.

## WORKS

*(all printed works published in Paris unless otherwise stated)*

### STAGE

*(all first performances in Paris unless otherwise stated)*

Les fêtes ou Le triomphe de Thalie (opéra-ballet, La Font), Opéra, 14 Aug 1714; prol, 3 entrées: La fille, La veuve, La femme (1714; 2/1720 as Les fêtes de Thalie); new entrées: La critique des fêtes de Thalie, added 9 Oct 1714 (1714); La veuve coquette, added 12 March 1715 (1720); La Provençale, added 17 Sept 1722 (1722); full score, 1745, *F-Pn*; full score (as Le triomphe de Thalie), *Po*

Le mariage de Ragonde et de Colin ou La veillée de village (comédie lyrique, Nericault–Destouches), Sceaux, Dec 1714; 3 acts: La soirée de village, Les lutins, La noce et le charivari (lib, 1714; music, 1738); revised as Les amours de Ragonde ou La soirée de village, Opéra, 30 Jan 1742

Ariane (tragédie lyrique, P.-C. Roy, Lagrange), Opéra, 6 April 1717; prol, 5 acts (1717)

Pirithous (tragédie lyrique, La Serre), Opéra, 26 Jan 1723; prol, 5 acts (1723)

Les amours des dieux (ballet-héroïque, L. Fuzelier), Opéra, 14 Sept 1727; prol, 4 entrées: Neptune et Amymone, Jupiter et Niobe, Apollon et Coronis, Ariane et Bacchus (1727)

Le prince de Noisy, Théâtre Français, 1730; divertissement for a comedy by d'Aigueberre (c1730)

Le triomphe de sens (ballet-héroïque, Roy), Opéra, 5 June 1732; prol, 5 entrées: L'odorat; Le toucher; La vue; L'ouie, added 8 July; Le goût, added 14 Aug (1732)

Les grâces (ballet-héroïque, Roy), Opéra, 5 May 1735; prol, 3 entrées: La grâce ingénue, La grâce mélancolique, La grâce enjouée

Le temple de Gnide ou Le prix de la beauté (Bellis, Roy), Opéra, 7 Nov 1741; divertissement, 1 act (1741)

Recueil des divertissements du Nouveau Théâtre Italien, augmenté de toutes les symphonies, accompagnements, airs de violons et de flûtes, de hautbois, de musettes, airs italiens et de plusieurs divertissements qui n'ont jamais paru (c1737); incl. divertissements by Mouret for 452 plays

Divertissements for 9 comédies françaises, part in *F-Pcf*

### VOCAL

Motets, 1–2vv, insts (1742): Usquequo Domine, Regina coeli, Quemadmodum, Nunc dimittis, Cantate Domino, O sacrum, Benedictus, Laudate nomen Domini, Cantemus Domino, Venite exultemus Domino

Cantates françoises, 1v, insts, livre premier (c1718): Andromède et Persée, ed. R. Blanchard (Paris, 1973); L'absence; La naissance du bal

L'heureux hazard, cantate, B, insts, *Pc*

Cantatilles françoises (1718–38): Eglé; Hymne à l'Amour; Echo; Leda; L'Amour vainqueur; Thétis; Le raccomodement; Epitalame; L'Amour et l'Hymen

L'été, cantatille, *Pn*

Amour, tout l'univers soumis à ton empire, cantatille, *Pc*

[19] Airs sérieux et à boire, 1–2vv, acc. (1719)

Second recueil d'[19]airs sérieux et à boire, 1–2vv, acc. (1719)

IIIme livre d'[20]airs sérieux et à boire, et de plusieurs parodies bachiques, 1–2vv, acc. (1727)

3 airs, S, B, bc, *F-A* 1171

Airs, cantatas, cantatilles and sacred contrafacta in over 50 18th-century anthologies, incl. Recueil des divertissements pour le Nouveau Théâtre Italien (Paris, 1713–37); Meslanges de musique latine, françoise et italienne (1725, 1729), 1 air, ed. in Le pupitre, vi (Paris, 1968); Nouveau recueil de chansons choisies (The Hague, 1723–43); Nouveau Théâtre de la Foire (1758); Nouvelles poésies morales (1737); Nouvelles poésies spirituelles et morales (1730–37); Recueil complet de vaudevilles et airs (1755); Ballard's Recueil d'airs sérieux et à boire (1711–18); Recueil de chansons nouvelles et vaudevilles (1737); Le Théâtre de la Foire ou L'Opéra Comique (1721–34); Le Théâtre de M. Favart ou Recueil des comédies, parodies et opéras comiques (1763–72); for others see *RISM*

### INSTRUMENTAL

Concert de chambre à deux et trois parties, vns, recs, obs, suivi d'une suite d'airs à danser ... premier livre (1718)

Fanfares, tpts, timbales, vns, obs, avec une suitte de simphonies mêlées de cors de chasse (c1729); ed. R. Viollier (Paris, c1937) and M. Sanvoisin (Paris, 1970)

Concert de chambre à deux et trois parties ... second livre (1738)

6 sonatas, 2 rec, 1729, *F-A*; ed. R. Viollier (Wilhelmshaven, 1975)

### BIBLIOGRAPHY

Durey de Noinville: *Histoire du théâtre de l'Académie royale de musique* (Paris, 1757/R1972)

A. Pougin: 'Mouret', *Revue et Gazette musicale de Paris*, xxvi (1859), 412; xxvii (1860), 18,127

L. de La Laurencie: 'La musique française de Lulli à Gluck', *EMDC*, I/iii (1921), 1385

P.-M. Masson: 'Le ballet héroïque', *ReM*, ix (1928), 132

R. Viollier: 'Un compositeur d'opéra sous la régence: Jean-Joseph Mouret', *Mitteilungen der Schweiz*, i (1934), 68

——: 'Un opéra-ballet au xviiie siècle', *RdM*, xvi (1935), 78

——: 'Les symphonies de Jean-Joseph Mouret', *RdM*, xvii (1936), 182

——: 'Les divertissements de Jean-Joseph Mouret pour la "Comédie Italienne" à Paris', *RdM*, xviii (1939), 65

——: 'La musique à la cour de la Duchesse du Maine', *ReM*, xx (1939), no.193, p.96; xxi (1939), no.194, p.133

C. le Gras: 'Jean-Joseph Mouret, "le musicien des grâces" ', *Mémoires de l'Académie de Vaucluse*, 3rd ser., iii (Avignon, 1939), 115

R. Viollier: *Jean-Joseph Mouret, le musicien des grâces* (Paris, 1950/R1976)

M. Barthélemy: 'Les divertissements de Jean-Joseph Mouret pour les comédies de Dancourt', *RBM*, vii (1953), 47

R. Viollier: 'Mouret, Jean-Joseph', *ES*

J. Robert: 'Comédiens, musiciens et opéras à Avignon', *Revue de la Société d'histoire du théâtre*, xvii (1965), 275

J. R. Anthony: *French Baroque Music from Beaujoyeulx to Rameau* (London, 1973, rev. 2/1978)

D. Tunley: *The Eighteenth-century French Cantata* (London, 1974)

JAMES R. ANTHONY

**Mourky** [mourqui]. *See* MURKY.

**Mourtois, Jean.** *See* COURTOIS, JEAN.

**Mourton, Robert.** *See* MORTON, ROBERT.

**Mousikon.** *See* AKOLOUTHIAI.

**Moussorgsky, Modest Petrovich.** *See* MUSORGSKY, MODEST PETROVICH.

**Mouth organ** (Ger. *Mundharmonika*). A free-reed wind instrument; *see* HARMONICA (i). From this, in studies of oriental music, a Western taxonomic term for the numerous and varied mouth-blown instruments of south-east Asia and the Far East (Chinese *sheng* etc) in which free reeds of brass or bamboo are employed. For illustrations, *see* HARMONICA (i) and REED INSTRUMENTS; for references to illustrations of non-Western mouth organs, *see* Appendix A.

**Mouthpiece** (Fr. *embouchure* [of clarinets and saxophones, *bec*]; Ger. *Mundstück*). That part of a wind instrument which is placed in or against a player's mouth, and which, together with the lips or a cane REED, forms the tone generator.

In brass instruments (including obsolete side-hole types) it is roughly bell-shaped but is much modified by external ornament. Internally it has three important elements: the cup (Fr. *bassin*); the throat (Fr. *grain*) (or orifice at the base of the cup); and the backbore (Fr. *queue*) (or expansion) which leads to the main tubing. All three have much influence on the characteristic tone and behaviour of the instrument. The cup varies from shallow hemispherical to deeply conical. The throat may be relatively large, small, sharp-edged, rounded off, or,

in such as the horn, virtually non-existent. (This applies also to the backbore.) The rim applied to the lips varies according to individual convenience.

In clarinets and the like the mouthpiece is roughly conical externally for some $\frac{2}{3}$ of its length, after which it is obliquely chamfered off to a chisel-shaped tip (*see* CLARINET, fig.2). Opposite the chamfer is a flat table tangential to the surface, and against this the flat reed is placed. The table is slightly curved towards the tip and this 'lay' allows the reed to vibrate under the influence of the breath and control of the lips. In the upper part of the table is a rectangular or keystone-shaped slot through to the interior. The internal 'tone chamber' may be a simple extension of the main bore of the instrument or it may be enlarged in various ways which have much influence on its internal tuning and general behaviour. Such mouthpieces are today made of wood and various synthetics, others of metal and (more rarely) glass.

PHILIP BATE

**Mouton, Charles** (*b* 1626; *d* after 1699). French lutenist and composer. He probably spent part of his youth at the court of Savoy in Turin. He seems to have learnt the lute from Denis Gaultier. He settled in Paris in 1678. In 1691 he was mentioned as a lute teacher: among his pupils were Milleran, Le Sage de Richée and the daughter of the engraver Edelinck, who showed his thanks by engraving his portrait after the painting in the Louvre by Francis de Troyes. He was one of the last of the 17th-century school of French lutenists and is known to have composed only lute music.

WORKS

Pieces de luth sur differents modes (Paris, 1698 or 1699, 2/1710); 2 bks, each containing 4 suites; edns. of 7 pieces in Lindgren

2 other bks, mentioned by E. Roger and *WaltherML*, lost

Pieces in *A-SF*; ?*CS-Pu* (Lobkowitz); *F-Pn* (especially Rés.823), *B*; *D-Bds*, *As*

BIBLIOGRAPHY

A. Lindgren: 'Ein Lautenbuch von Mouton', *MMg*, xxiii (1891), 46

M. Brenet: 'Notes sur l'histoire du luth en France', *RMI*, vi (1899), 1

L. de La Laurencie: *Les luthistes* (Paris, 1928)

M. Rollin: 'La suite pour luth dans l'oeuvre de Charles Mouton', *ReM*, no.226 (1955), 76

JOËL DUGOT

**Mouton, Jean** (*b* Holluigue [now Haut-Wignes], nr. Samer, 1459 or earlier; *d* St Quentin, 30 Oct 1522). French composer, one of the most important writers of motets of the early 16th century.

1. LIFE. His epitaph, now lost but originally in the collegiate church of St Quentin where he was buried, gave his full name as 'Maistre Jehan de Holluigue, dit Mouton'. Contemporary documents describing him as 'Sameracensis' confirm that his native village, Holluigue, is in fact the Haut-Wignes near Samer. He was appointed a singer and teacher of religious subjects (*écolâtre-chantre*) in the collegiate church of Notre Dame in Nesle (département of Somme, arrondissement of Péronne) in 1477. In 1483 he was made *maître de chapelle* in Nesle. By this time he was a priest and thus at least 25 years old. How long he stayed in Nesle is not clear. Perhaps he obtained his master's degree, possibly in Paris, after leaving Nesle and before going to Amiens Cathedral, where he was in charge of training the choirboys in 1500. A document from that year lists him as *maître des enfans* and one of the organizers of a performance of a mystery play.

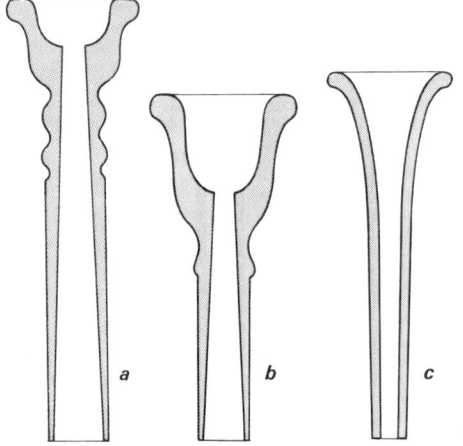

*Mouthpieces of (a) a trumpet, (b) a trombone, (c) a horn*

In September 1501 he took charge of music in the collegiate church of St André in Grenoble. Part of his duties included teaching choirboys plainchant and polyphony. He did not stay there long; by the middle of 1502 he had left without the permission of the chapter. Possibly he had joined the chapel of Queen Anne of Brittany by then. She and her husband, Louis XII, visited Grenoble in June 1502 and they may have taken Mouton with them when they departed. Records from her chapel do not survive, but other evidence proves that Mouton entered her service during the first decade of the 16th century. In 1509 the queen interceded personally on Mouton's behalf to obtain for him a position as canon at St André in Grenoble, a post he held *in absentia* and which enabled him to draw income from a benefice conferred on him in 1510.

Mouton remained attached to the French court for the rest of his life, serving first Anne and then François I. He seems to have been the official court composer during much of this time, commissioned to write music to celebrate important events both public and private. Thus the text of his motet *Christe redemptor, O rex omnipotens*, with its closing salutation, 'fit regi felicitas, reginae fecunditas', suggests that it was intended for a royal wedding, perhaps that of Anne and Louis XII in 1499, even before Mouton was engaged at the court. *Caeleste beneficium*, a motet that may not be by Mouton, praises St Anne and incorporates a prayer for an heir; it may have been performed at the *Mystery of the Five Annes*, given in the queen's honour on the occasion of her second coronation in Paris on 18 November 1503. At least one of Mouton's motets for St John the Baptist (*Inter natos mulierum* and *Regem confessorum*) may have been ordered by Anne to commemorate the saint in 1506, after she had been cured of an illness, ostensibly by application of one of his relics. Mouton's motet *Non nobis Domine* celebrated the birth in 1510 of Renée, second daughter of Anne and Louis XII. His moving *Quis dabit oculis* laments the queen's death in 1514.

Mouton doubtless composed *Christus vincit* in honour of Leo X's election as pope in 1513. Lowinsky argued persuasively that *Missus est angelus Gabriel* was written for the entry of Louis XII's new wife, Mary Tudor, into Paris on 6 November 1514. Less than a year after his remarriage Louis XII died. The records show that Mouton took part in his funeral service, but no special music composed by him for the event has yet been identified.

Mouton's motet *Domine salvum fac regem*, on the other hand, is likely to have been composed for the coronation in 1515 of François I in Rheims Cathedral. During his first year as king, François won a notable victory at the Battle of Marignano, an event celebrated in Mouton's *Exalta Regina Galliae*. Several months later, in December 1515, François and Leo met in Bologna to discuss peace. The meeting was enlivened by many musical performances by both the papal and the royal chapels. The pope was very favourably impressed by the musicians in the king's service, and he rewarded some of them; he named Mouton, for example, an apostolic notary. A number of 16th-century sources stress that Mouton was one of Leo's favourite composers, a judgment that may date from their meeting in Bologna. Glarean, for example, who studied in Paris between 1517 and 1522 and knew the composer, stated that Leo was fond of Mouton's masses. Glarean also wrote that he spoke with the composer through an interpreter, a

curious fact since, as a priest and a composer of sacred music, Mouton should have known Latin fluently.

According to Lowinsky (but see L. Perkins's review, *MQ*, lv (1969), 255), Mouton may have been the editor-in-chief of the Medici Codex, an elegantly illuminated manuscript prepared in 1518 as a wedding gift for Lorenzo de' Medici, Duke of Urbino, and his young bride, Madeleine de la Tour d'Auvergne. Mouton's official position at court during this time is shown by a letter written that same year by the Duke of Ferrara's representative at the French court, excusing himself for his inability to send the duke any new compositions by Mouton, since the composer had shortly before returned to Paris from Amboise in order to compose new music in honour of the birth of the Dauphin. (The music has apparently not survived.)

Although no proof exists it seems virtually certain that Mouton accompanied François to his meeting with Henry VIII of England at the Field of the Cloth of Gold in 1520. Various commentators reporting on the event noted that the performances by the two rival chapel choirs were as elaborate then as they had been five years before in Bologna.

In Mouton's last years he was granted a benefice at St Quentin. Although no church records survive from those years, Mouton may have been elected a canon on the death of Compère in 1518. Mouton was buried in St Quentin. His epitaph described him as 'en son vivant chantre du roy, chanoine de Thérouanne et de cette église'. His connection with Thérouanne is otherwise recorded only in the document appointing him apostolic notary, where he is referred to as 'clericus Morinensis dioc.' (i.e. a cleric from the diocese of Thérouanne).

Quite apart from his stature as a composer and his position as one of the leading musicians at the French court, Mouton deserves a place in history as the teacher of Adrian Willaert, himself one of the greatest teachers of the 16th century, and hence a direct link in the tradition of Franco-Netherlands composers who most influenced the direction of Italian music during the high Renaissance.

2. WORKS. More than 100 motets, about 15 masses and more than 20 chansons by Mouton survive. Over 50 of these were published during his lifetime. Petrucci devoted an entire volume to his masses (1515) and the Parisian firm of Le Roy & Ballard brought out a posthumous collection of his motets (1555). The remainder are preserved in numerous manuscript and printed anthologies scattered throughout many European libraries.

Pierre de Ronsard, in the dedication to *Livre des meslanges* (Paris, 1560), cited Mouton as a pupil of Josquin Desprez, and Teofilo Folengo in some verses from his *Opus... macaronicorum* (1521) prophesied that Mouton was a composer whose music would be mistaken for Josquin's. Nevertheless it seems unlikely that Mouton actually studied with the older composer, although they may have known each other at the French court. Both Kast and Lowinsky pointed out that various other early 16th-century composers imitated Josquin's mannerisms more closely than Mouton did. Even though both composers employed many of the same techniques – paired imitation, canonic cantus firmi and so on – Mouton displayed a personality totally unlike that of Josquin. Although his music at times produces brilliant effects, by and large Mouton wrote placid, smoothly flowing polyphony, with great technical finish and superb contrapuntal command, but without the flashes of fire of the older and greater master. As Lowinsky has pointed out: 'The evenness of his temperament, the steadiness of his character, the solidity of his craftsmanship equipped him for a position of highest official importance'. That judgment corresponds well with the opinion of Glarean, who praised Mouton for his smoothly flowing melody ('facili fluentem filo cantum') and for his industry and application ('studio ac industria').

The smooth flow of Mouton's melody stems in large part from the stately regular pace at which much of his music moves. Short notes are used mostly to break up this slow, regular motion rather than to offer genuine rhythmic contrast. The melodic contours themselves tend to be rather short-spanned; Mouton's penchant for clear, sharply profiled motifs perhaps reflects the rational and precise spirit of his specifically French rather than Flemish heritage. Mouton was often indifferent to good text declamation: his music is filled with incorrect accentuations and other infelicities in the way he combines words and notes, a trait indicating that he was more interested in purely musical design than in expression. On the other hand, he sometimes took care to match the text carefully to his melodic lines, particularly in his political motets where the words are particularly important. In both the motet for François' coronation, *Domine salvum fac regem*, and that celebrating the Battle of Marignano, *Exalta Regina Galliae*, for example, the words can be clearly understood and the textual and musical accents usually coincide. Mouton was fond of full sonorities; all voices are consistently brought in soon after the initial point of imitation (although the entrance of a cantus firmus is often long delayed) and he normally kept all voices active most of the time. In spite of this, the texture is usually clear and transparent, owing partly to his care in keeping the various voice ranges separate.

On the other hand, the uniformity of his music should not be exaggerated, for it does reflect a diversity of approaches, as Kast has emphasized in his edition of five of the composer's motets (Cw, lxxvi). Kast may well be premature in his attempt to distinguish four distinct style periods in Mouton's work since few of the motets can be precisely dated and stylistic criteria are unreliable in the absence of a complete edition, but he presented a convincing outline of the composer's development from a young man, fascinated by purely musical design and constructive elements, to a mature artist, mixing judiciously homophony or near-homophony with imitative sections and adopting a more humanistic attitude towards the texts he set. Dammann emphasized the change of style that took place about the turn of the century, in motets like *Sancti Dei omnes*, *O Maria, virgo pia* and *O quam fulgens*, when Mouton's music became more chordally orientated, perhaps as a result of his confrontation with Italian music, and particularly *laude*.

Along with secular motets, composed for political or other official events, Mouton set some texts appropriate for specific liturgical occasions, including sequences (*Ave Maria . . . virgo serena*, and *Benedicta es caelorum regina*), responsories (*Antequam comedam* and *Christus resurgens*) and antiphons (*Beata Dei genitrix*); some verses honouring various saints and presumably meant to be sung at services commemorating their subjects (*Amicus Dei Nicolaus* for St Nicholas, and *Christum regem regum* for St Andrew); and some biblical texts of a sort that had seldom been set polyphonically before the late 15th century, like psalms (*De profundis*, surviving only in a lute arrangement, and *Usquequo Domine*), and evangelia, that is, settings of the epistle or gospel of the Mass (those motets beginning *In diebus illis* or *In illo tempore*). In addition there are a number of Marian texts, several hymns (*O Maria piissima* and *O Maria, virgo pia*) and various sacred verses not yet identified as belonging to a specific liturgical or para-liturgical occasion. Many of these are pieced together from several liturgical or biblical sources.

Mouton's dazzling contrapuntal skill is shown in those compositions in which all of the voices are canonic, *Nesciens mater virgo virum*, for example, a quadruple canon partly based on a plainchant. Frequently he constructed his motets around a central canon, either derived from a Gregorian cantus prius factus (*Salva nos, Domine* and *Per lignum salvi facti sumus*), or based on apparently free material (*Peccata mea, Domine*). Those motets that do not make use of some scaffolding technique sometimes paraphrase a chant (as in *Noli flere, Maria* and *Regem confessorum Dominum*), but usually quite freely; the composer assimilated the chant so well into his own melodic style that the original is sometimes difficult to disentangle. In those motets which seem to be based entirely on free material, Mouton sometimes repeated sections in a formally significant way, either by ending each of the two *partes* with the same music (Dammann claimed that *Non nobis Domine* (1510) is the earliest datable responsory motet in *aBcB* form) or by introducing a phrase which returns in the manner of a ritornello, or at the very least by reworking previous motivic material in a later section using a free variation technique. Also some motets (for example, the brief, *lauda*-like *In omni tribulatione*) are entirely free of borrowed material, scaffolding techniques or repetition schemes; they depend for their effect on successive points of imitation, on melodic coherence or simply on the regular and steady rhythmic flow and the interplay between harmony and counterpoint.

Mouton's masses span the transition from cantus firmus technique to the new procedures of paraphrase and parody. Most of them seem to date from the mature years, particularly the decade between 1505 and 1515. Mouton took his cantus firmi either from chant (*Alma Redemptoris mater*) or used one voice from a polyphonic composition (for example, the tenor of Févin's motet *Benedictus Dominus Deus*). More often than not the cantus firmus is not sharply differentiated rhythmically from the other voices, but rather smoothly incorporated into the texture. Some of the masses paraphrase monophonic material, and several, including that based on Richafort's motet *Quem dicunt homines*, are fully-fledged parody masses, among the earliest to use that compositional process. Perhaps parody technique was first extensively applied to cyclic masses in the circles associated with the French court in the early years of the 16th century. Indeed, Mouton may have composed his *Missa 'Quem dicunt homines'* in competition with Divitis and both masses may have been intended for performance at the meeting between François I and Leo X in Bologna in 1515.

Like his motets, Mouton's chansons display a variety of styles. Some are canonic, like *En venant de Lyon* and the lament on the death of Févin, *Qui ne regrettoit*.

Some are three-part popular arrangements, apparently paraphrasing now lost popular monophonic tunes. Some, like *Jamais jamais* in the *Odhecaton*, and *Resjouissez vous bourgeoises*, are wittily imitative pieces, influenced in their strongly metrical melodic style by popular tunes. Some of those for five and six voices resemble motets in their contrapuntal complexity. And at least one chanson, *De tous regretz*, is not unlike a later Parisian chanson in the manner of Claudin de Sermisy.

### WORKS
*(only principal sources listed)*

Editions: *J. Mouton: Opera omnia*, ed. A. C. Minor, CMM, xliii/1– (1967–) [M]

*Treize livres de motets parus chez Pierre Attaingnant en 1534 et 1535*, ed. A. Smijers and A. T. Merritt (Monaco and Paris, 1934–64) [SM]

*Van Ockeghem tot Sweelinck*, ed. A. Smijers (Amsterdam, 1939–56) [S]

*The Medici Codex of 1518*, ed. E. E. Lowinsky, MRM, iii–v (1968) [L]

#### MASSES AND MASS SECTIONS

Missarum . . . liber primus, 4vv (Fossombrone, 1515)

Missa 'Alleluya', 4vv, M i, 1; Missa 'Alma Redemptoris mater', 4vv, M i, 37; Missa 'Argentum et aurum non est mihi', 4vv, M vii; Missa 'Benedictus Dominus Deus', 4vv, M i, 72 (on A. de Févin's motet); Missa d'Allemagne [= Missa 'Regina mearum']; Missa 'Dictes moy toutes vos pensées', 4vv, M ii, 1 (on Compère's chanson); Missa 'Ecce quam bonum', 4vv, M ii, 51; Missa 'Faulte d'argent', 4vv, M ii, 89; Missa 'L'homme armé', 4vv, M v (also attrib. Forestier); Missa 'L'oserai je dire', 4vv, M iii, 1

Missa 'Quem dicunt homines', 4vv, M iii, 40 (on Richafort's motet); Missa 'Regina mearum', 4vv, M iii, 65; Missa sans cadence, 4vv, M iii, 102; Missa 'Tu es Petrus', M iv, 1; Missa 'Tua est potentia', 4vv, M iv, 42; Missa 'Verbum bonum', 4vv, M iv, 79 (on Therache's motet); Missa, *I-CMac*

Credo, 4vv

#### MAGNIFICAT SETTINGS

Magnificat primi toni, 4vv, *D-Ju* Cod.20, ff.7v–13r
Magnificat primi toni, 4vv, *Ju* Cod.20, ff.13v–19r
Magnificat quarti toni, 4vv, *NL-L* Cod.E
Magnificat quarti toni, 4vv, S vi, 1
Magnificat quinti toni, 4vv, *L* Cod.B
Magnificat sexti toni, 4vv, S vi, 81
Magnificat octavi toni, 4vv, *I-Bc* Q19
Fecit potentiam [quinti toni], 2vv, 1543[19]
Magnificat, 4vv, even verses only, and Magnificat, 4vv, beginning 'Anima mea' in *E-Tc*, choirbook without siglum; the first is probably concordant with one of the others above.

#### MOTETS

Selecti aliquot moduli, liber primus, 4–8vv (Paris, 1555) [1555[a]]

Alleluia confitemini Domino, 4vv, 1545[2]; Alleluia noli flere Maria, 4vv, 1547[6] (attrib. Gascongne in 1545[2]); Amicus Dei Nicolaus, 4vv, 1519[1]; Angelus ad pastores ait, 4vv, 1554[10]; Antequam comedam suspiro, 5vv, SM xi, 146; Ave fuit prima salus, 4vv, Cw, lxxvi (1959), 25; Ave Maria gemma virginum, 8vv, SM iii, 173; Ave Maria gratia Dei plena per saeculum, 4vv, *GB-Cmc* Pepys 1760; Ave Maria gratia plena, 3vv, 1541[2]; Ave Maria gratia plena, 4vv, *I-Bc* Q19; Ave Maria . . . virgo serena, 5vv, *Bc* Q19; Ave sanctissima Maria, 4vv, Cw, lxxvi (1959), 14; 50; Ave virginum gemma Katharina, 4vv, *Fn* Magl.XIX 58 (II.I.232); Ave virgo caeli porta, 4vv, 1520[4]

Beata Dei genitrix, 4vv, 1514[1]; Benedicam Dominum, 6vv, Cw, lxxvi (1959), 9; Benedicite, Agimus tibi, 4vv, *GB-Cmc* Pepys 1760; Benedicta es caelorum regina, 4vv, MME, xv (1954), 185; Benedictus Domine Deus Israel, 4vv, 1555[a]; Bona vita, bona reflectio, 4vv, *I-Fn* Magl.XIX 58 (II.I.232); Caeleste beneficium introivit, 4vv, 1514[1] (attrib. A. de Févin in *GB-Cmc* Pepys 1760); Candida Phoebus moneas, 4vv, *F-CA* 124; Christe redemptor, O rex omnipotens, 4vv, 1521[5]; Christum regem regem adoremus, 4vv, SM iv, 78; Christus vincit, Christus regnat, 4vv, 1521[4]; Confitemini Domino quoniam bonus, 4vv, SM xi, 47; Confitemini Domino quoniam bonus, 6vv, *I-Rvat* C.S.38; Congregatae sunt gentes, 4vv, 1519[1]; Corde et animo Christo canamus, 4vv, L iv, 137

Da pacem Domine, 6vv, 1555[a]; De beata virgine [= Salve mater Salvatoris]; De profundis, 4vv, 1558[20] (lute intabulation); Domine Deus exercituum, 4vv, *GB-Lcm* 2037; Domine Dominus noster, 4vv, 1538[6]; Domine salvum fac regem, 4vv, L iv, 142; Dulces exuviae, dum fata, 4vv, 1559[2]; Ecce Maria genuit nobis salvatorem, 4vv, 1514[1]; Ego sum qui sum, 4vv, *I-Bc* Q27; Egregie Christi martyr Christophore, 4vv, *A-Wn* 15941 (attrib. A. de Févin in 1514[1]); Elisabeth Zachariae magnum, 4vv, 1559[2] (attrib. La Fage in 1519[1]);

Exalta regina Galliae, 4vv, L iv, 132, Cw, lxxvi (1959), 32; Exsultet conjubilando Deo, 8vv, 1555[a]

Factum est silentium in caelo, 4vv, 1519[1]; Felix namque es, 4vv, 1521[3]; Filiae Jerusalem, 4vv, *D-B* Mus.14800; Gaude Barbara beata, 4vv, 1514[1]; Gaude virgo Catherina, 4vv, SM vii, 162, S 209 (attrib. Gombert in 1539[4]); Gratia plena ipsa, 4vv, *A-Wn* 15941; Homo quidam fecit cenam, 4vv, SM i, 196; Illuminare Hierusalem, 4vv, 1519[1]; Impetum inimicorum, 4vv, 1528[2]; In diebus illis dum complerentur dies, 4vv, *I-Bc* Q19; In diebus illis filius Diocletiani, 4vv, *VEcap* DCCLX; In exitu Israel [= Nos qui vivimus]; In illo tempore accesserunt, 4vv, 1537[1] (attrib. Moulu in *Bc* Q19); In illo tempore Maria Magdalene, 4vv, 1521[5]; In illo tempore postquem consummati sunt, 4vv, 1554[10]; In omni tribulatione, 4vv, L iv, 201 (also attrib. Moulu); Inter natos mulierum, *Bc* Q20

Jocundare Jerusalem, 4vv, 1521[5]; Lauda Christum, 3vv, 1541[2]; Laudate Deum in sanctis, 4vv, 1514[1]; Lectio Actuum Apostolorum [= In diebus illis dum complerentur]; Libera animam meam, 4vv, 1545[7]; Maria virgo semper laetare, 4vv, 1519[1], SM i, 82 (Gascongne); Miseremini mei saltem vos, 4vv, SM i, 176 (attrib. Richafort in 1519[3]); Miserere mei Deus, 4vv, 1538[6]; Missus est angelus Gabriel, 5vv, L iv, 360 (Mouton), *Josquin Desprez: Motetten*, Werken, i/3, fasc.6 (1924), 82 (Josquin); Moriens lux amantissima, 5vv, *Bc* Q19

Nesciens mater virgo virum, 8vv, SM iii, 43, L iv, 207; Nobis sancti spiritus, 4vv, *GB-Lcm* 2037; Noe noe noe psallite, 4vv, SM ii, 86; Noe noe noe, puer nobis nascitur, 4vv, *Lbm* Add.19583; Noli flere, Maria, 4vv, *A-Wn* 18825; Nolite confidere, 2vv, 1545[6]; Non nobis Domine, 4vv, Cw, lxxvi (1959), 1 (attrib. Gascongne in 1535[3]); Nos qui vivimus . . . in exitu, 4vv, 1514[1]; O amica mea [= Quam pulchra es]; O beate Sebastiane [= Sancte Sebastiane]; O Christe redemptor [= Christe redemptor]; O Domine Jesu Christe, 4vv, G. Rhau: Musikdrucke, iii (Kassel, 1955), 147; O Maria piissima stella maris, 6vv, 1555[a]; O Maria virgo pia, 4vv, 1505[2]; O pulcherrima mulierum, 4vv, *E-Bc* 941; O quam fulges in aetheris, 4vv, 1505[2]; O salutaris hostia, 4vv, 1521[6]

Peccantem me quotidie, 5vv, SM iii, 98; Peccata mea, Domine, 5vv, L iv, 241; Per lignum salvi facti sumus, 5vv, L iv, 246; Puer natus est nobis, 4vv, G. Rhau: Musikdrucke, iii (Kassel, 1955), 15; Puer natus est nobis, 4vv, *I-Bc* Q19; Quaeramus cum pastoribus, 4vv, S 201; Quam pulchra es, amica mea, 4vv, 1519[2] (attrib. Josquin in 1537[1], attrib. Moulu in *Bc* Q19); Quam pulchra es, et quam decora, 4vv, *F-CA* 124; Quis dabit oculis nostris, 4vv, Monumenta polyphoniae italicae, ii (Rome, 1936), 113; Regem confessorum Dominum, 4vv, *I-Fn* Magl.XIX 58 (II.1.232); Reges terrae congregati sunt, 4vv, SM i, 16; Regina caeli laetare, 4vv, *Rvat* C.S.42; Rex pacificus hodie natus est, 4vv, 1554[10]

Salva nos, Domine, 6vv, L iv, 227, CMM iii/4 (1952), 65 (Willaert), G. Rhau: Musikdrucke, iii (Kassel, 1955), 149 (La Rue); Salvator mundi, salva nos, 4vv, SM xiii, 137; Salve mater Salvatoris, 4vv, S 207; Sancte Sebastiane, ora pro nobis, 4vv, 1521[5]; Sancti Dei omnes, 4vv, Cw, lxxvi (1959), 15 (Mouton), *Josquin Desprez: Motetten*, Werken, v/20, fasc.46 (1957), 27 (Josquin); Si oblitus fuero tui, 4vv, *F-CA* 124; Spiritus Domini, 4vv, 1540[7]; Surge Petre et induete, 4vv, *USSR-KAu* 1740; Surgens Jesus a mortuis, 4vv, 1545[2]; Suscipe Domine munera, 4vv, *I-VEcap* DCCLX; Tota pulchra es, 4vv, 1521[6]; Tua est potentia, 5vv, L iv, 250; Usquequo Domine oblivisceris me, 4vv, *I-Bc* Q20; Veni ad liberandum nos Domine, 4vv, *MOd* IX; Verbum bonum et suave, 8vv, 1564[1]; Verbum caro factum est, 6vv, formerly Breslau City Library mus.VI

#### CHANSONS

Adieu mes amours, 4vv, ed. E. Bernoulli: *Aus Liederbüchern der Humanistenzeit* (Leipzig, 1910), 63; Ce que mon cueur pense, 5vv, 1572[2]; De tous regretz, 4vv, Cw, lxi (1958), 24; Dieu gard de mal, 3vv, *GB-Cmc* Pepys 1760; Du bon du cueur, 5vv, 1572[2]; En venant de Lyon, 4vv, ed. D. Heartz, *JAMS*, xiv (1961), 16; Jamais jamais, 4vv, ed. H. Hewitt: *O. Petrucci: Harmonice musices Odhecaton A* (Cambridge, Mass., 1942), 296; Jamais n'aymeray masson, 3vv, 1520[6]; Je le lairay, 4vv, ed. H. M. Brown: *Theatrical Chansons of the Fifteenth and Early Sixteenth Centuries* (Cambridge, Mass., 1963), 109; Je ne puis, 4vv, *F-Pn* nouv.acq.fr.4599

La la la l'oysillon, 4vv, ed. H. M. Brown: *Theatrical Chansons* (Cambridge, Mass., 1963), 135; La roussée du mois de may, 5vv, 1545[14]; Le berger et la bergère, 5vv, 1572[2]; Le grant desir d'aymer, 3vv, 1520[6]; Le vilain jaloux, 4vv, *I-Bc* Q19; Payne trabel, 1547[25] (arr. two vihuelas); Prens ton con grosse garsse, 3vv, 1536[1]; Qui ne regrettoit, 4vv, ed. D. Plamenac, *RBM*, vi (1952), 19; Resjouissez vous bourgeoises, 4vv, ed. in Haar, 155; Veleci velela ma mère, 4vv, *Fc* Basevi 2442; Vray dieu d'amours, 5vv, 1572[2]; Vray dieu qu'amoureux ont de peine, 6vv, 1572[2]

#### DOUBTFUL WORKS

Missa 'Da pacem', 4vv, attrib. Mouton in *USSR-KAu* 1740, lost; *Josquin Desprez: Missen*, Werken, iv/19, fasc.34 (Amsterdam, 1953) (Josquin)

Missa 'Sancta Trinitas', 4vv, M iv (also attrib. A. de Févin)

Magnificat quarti toni, 4vv, attrib. Mouton in *E-MO* 769, attrib. Willaert in *NL-L* Cod.E

Te Deum, 4vv, attrib. Mouton in *USSR-KAu* 1740, lost; attrib. Silva in *I-Bc* Q20; attrib. Josquin in *D-ROu* Mus.Saec.XVI-49; anon. in 1537[1], *D-Rp* A.R.940/41, A.R.1018, C.120, *Dlb* 1/D/6, *As* 31
Christus resurgens ex mortuis, 5vv, attrib. Mouton in *A-Wn* 18825; attrib. Richafort in 1554[10]
Gloriosi principes terrae, 5vv, S viii, 93 (Mouton), L iv, 380 (Erasmus Lapicida)

BIBLIOGRAPHY
C. Gomart: 'Notes historiques sur la maîtrise de Saint-Quentin et sur les célébrités musicales de cette ville', *Bulletin de la Société académique de Saint-Quentin* (1850), 43
M. Brenet: 'Jean Mouton', *Tribune de Saint-Gervais*, v (1899), 323
J. Delporte: 'L'école polyphonique franco-flamande: Jean Mouton', *Revue liturgique et musicale*, xvi/3 (1932), 72; xvii/4 (1933), 109; xviii/6 (1934), 96; xix/2 (1935), 33
——: 'Nouveaux documents sur Jean Mouton', *Musique et liturgie*, xxi (1937), 7
L. Royer: 'Les musiciens et la musique à l'ancienne collégiale Saint-André de Grenoble du XVe au XVIIIe siècle', *Bibliothèque d'humanisme et renaissance*, iv (1937), 237–73
B.-A. Wallner: 'La messe *Quaeramus cum pastoribus* de Cristobal Morales et son modèle, le motet de Jean Mouton', *Musica sacra*, xlv (1938), 172
F. Lesure: 'Un document sur la jeunesse de Jean Mouton', *RBM*, v (1951), 177
A. C. Minor: *The Masses of Jean Mouton* (diss., U. of Michigan, 1951)
R. Dammann: *Studien zu den Motetten von Jean Mouton* (diss., U. of Freiburg, 1952)
D. Plamenac: 'Deux pièces de la renaissance tirées de fonds florentins', *RBM*, vi (1952), 12
R. Dammann: 'Spätformen der isorhythmischen Motetten im 16. Jahrhundert', *AMw*, x (1953), 16
J. M. Shine: *The Motets of Jean Mouton* (diss., New York U., 1953)
P. Kast: *Studien zu den Messen des Jean Mouton* (diss., U. of Frankfurt am Main, 1955)
——: 'Zu Biographie und Werk Jean Moutons', *Kongressbericht: Wien Mozartjahr 1956*, 300
——: 'Remarques sur la musique et les musiciens de la chapelle de François 1er au camp du drap d'or', *Fêtes et cérémonies au temps de Charles Quint [Fêtes de la Renaissance II]:CNRS Bruxelles, Anvers, Gand, Liège 1957*, 135
L. Lockwood: 'A View of the Early Sixteenth-century Parody Mass', *Queens College Twenty-fifth Anniversary Festschrift* (New York, 1964), 53
E. E. Lowinsky, ed.: *The Medici Codex of 1518*, MRM, iii–v (1968)
A. Dunning: *Die Staatsmotette 1480–1555* (Utrecht, 1970)
L. Lockwood: 'Jean Mouton and Jean Michel: New Evidence on French Music and Musicians in Italy, 1505–1520', *JAMS*, xxxii (1979), 191–246

HOWARD MAYER BROWN

**Movement** (Fr. *mouvement*; Ger. *Satz*; It. *movimento*). Term applied to any portion of a work sufficiently complete in itself to be regarded as an entity; normally such portions are most obviously distinguishable by differences of tempo or 'movement'. Thus one refers to the 'first' or 'last' movement, or to a 'fast' or 'slow' movement, suite, of a sonata, symphony, suite, concerto etc.

MICHAEL TILMOUTH

**Movie music.** *See* FILM MUSIC.

**Movius, Caspar** (*b* ?Lenzen, Brandenburg; *fl* 1633–59). German composer and schoolmaster. He is described on the title-pages of some of his works as 'Leontinus Marchicus', which probably denotes that he was born at Lenzen. In 1634 he was a student of theology at Rostock, where all his known publications appeared. In 1636 he was deputy rector of the school at Stralsund. He belonged to, and enjoyed a high reputation among, the active group of north German composers who were primarily engaged in producing music – particularly psalm settings and chorale arrangements – for the Lutheran church. His first two publications are devoted to small-scale pieces with continuo, which, however, really belong to the tradition of bicinia and tricinia, since the continuo part is texted and may therefore be sung if desired. *Triumphus musicus* is a collection of ten

German pieces based on chorale texts and melodies, the majority for double choir; they thus belong with the many chorale compositions produced in north Germany at this time by Scheidemann, Weckmann, Tunder and others. Movius did not generally exploit colourful virtuoso effects to the same extent as many of his contemporaries, but the final piece in the collection, marked 'Concert', is an exception, for its two upper parts contain florid and dramatic writing, while the other four act as a contrasting tutti. The double-choir pieces, with their high and low voice groupings, show the influence of Venetian polychoral music.

WORKS
*(all printed works published in Rostock)*
Hymnodia sacra, 2vv, bc (1634, 2/1639); 1 piece from 2/1639 pubd separately 1633
Psalmodia sacra nova, das ist, Geistliche Concerten newes Werck, 3vv, bc (1636)
Triumphus musicus spiritualis, 6, 8vv, bc (1640)
Odae ecclesiasticae, 1–4vv, bc (1659), lost
Several pieces in J. M. Dilherr: *Seelenmusik* (Nuremberg, 1654)
10 sacred vocal works, incl. 8 from Triumphus musicus, *D-Bds*, *Lr*, *PL-WRu*, *USSR-KA*

BIBLIOGRAPHY
M. H. Schacht: *Musicus danicus, eller Danske sangmester* (MS, *DK-Kk*, completed 1 Jan 1687; ed. G. Skjerne, Copenhagen, 1928)
G. Schünemann: 'Matthaeus Hertel's theoretische Schriften', *AMw*, iv (1922), 348, 350
W. Müller: 'Stralsunds liturgisch-musikalische Reformationsarbeit von der Einführung der evangelischen Lehre (1525) bis zum Ende des 30-jährigen Krieges (1648)', *Baltische Studien*, new ser., xxx/1 (1928)

A. LINDSEY KIRWAN

**Moxica** (*fl* c1475). Spanish composer. Only two pieces by him are known, the canciones *Dama mi gran querer* and *No queriendo sois querido* (both included in the Cancionero Musical de Palacio, *E-Mp*; ed. MME, v, 1947, nos.8, 22). The first is a setting of a poem by Pedro Gonzalez de Mendoza who in 1473 was cardinal and from 1485 to 1495 Archbishop of Toledo. Perhaps, as Stevenson suggested, Moxica was attached to Mendoza's household. The piece is in the style of the earlier generation of Spanish 15th-century composers. The melodic range is restricted, phrases end with long melismas and the contra leaps an octave to the 5th of the final chord. *No queriendo sois querido* is more rhythmically animated. The C minor of the initial refrain sets off the B♭ and E♭ major chords used for the more optimistic text of the stanza.

BIBLIOGRAPHY
F. Asenjo Barbieri, ed.: *Cancionero musical de los siglos XV y XVI* (Madrid, 1890), 59
R. Stevenson: *Spanish Music in the Age of Columbus* (The Hague, 1960), 242
G. Haberkamp: *Die weltliche Vokalmusik in Spanien* (Tutzing, 1968), 172f

ISABEL POPE

**Moyle** [née **Brown**], **Alice (Marshall)** (*b* Bloemfontein, 25 Dec 1908). Australian ethnomusicologist. She graduated as a bachelor of music at Melbourne University (1930) and later took the BA (1954) and MA (1957) at Sydney University. She gained the doctorate in 1975 with a dissertation on north Australian music, a taxonomic approach to the study of aboriginal song performances. During the course of her ethnomusicological research she has been a teaching fellow in the music department of Sydney University (1960–63), a research officer at the Australian Institute of Aboriginal Studies (1964–5) and a research fellow of the music department of Monash University (1965–73); she became a research fellow at the Australian Institute of Aboriginal Studies in 1973 and a research officer in

1974. Her work embraces field collection, documentation, analysis, cataloguing (for computerized retrieval) and the transfer to disc and film of performances of Australian aboriginal music.

WRITINGS

*Know your Orchestra* (Melbourne, 1948) [written as A. Brown]

'Sir Baldwin Spencer's Recordings of Australian Aboriginal Singing', *Memoirs of the National Museum of Victoria*, xxiv (1959), 7

'Bara and Mamariga Songs on Groote Eylandt', *Musicology*, i (Sydney, 1964), 15 [special issue of *Canon*, xvii]

'A Handlist of Field Collections of Recorded Music in Australia and Torres Strait', *Occasional Papers in Aboriginal Studies*, vi (1966), 1–227; pubd separately (Canberra, 1966)

'Songs from the Northern Territory', IAS-M-001/5 [disc notes]

'Tasmanian Music, an Impasse?', *Records of the Queen Victoria Museum, Launceston* (1968), no.26, p.1

'Aboriginal Music on Cape York', *Musicology*, iii (Sydney, 1968–9), 8

'Source Materials: Aboriginal Music of Australia and New Guinea', *EM*, xv (1971), 81

WERNER GALLUSSER

**Moyne, Jean-Baptiste.** *See* LEMOYNE, JEAN-BAPTISTE.

**Moyse, Marcel (Joseph)** (*b* St Amour, Jura, 17 May 1889). French flautist. He studied the flute at the Paris Conservatoire under Paul Taffanel, Adolphe Hennebains and Philippe Gaubert, and chamber music with Lucien Capet, winning a *premier prix* in 1906. He became solo flautist with the Pasdeloup Orchestra, Paris, in 1918 and with the Société des Concerts du Conservatoire. From 1913 to 1938 he was solo flautist at the Opéra-Comique and from 1922 to 1933 with the Concerts Straram. He was professor of the flute at the Paris Conservatoire (1932–49) and a member of the Conseil Supérieur de la Radio-Diffusion Française (1936–9). Moyse was soloist under such conductors as Walter, Toscanini, Mengelberg, Klemperer and Strauss. He made many recordings, including several for teaching purposes issued on his own label, and in 1928 he won a *grand prix du disque* for his recording of Mozart's D major Flute Concerto. Ibert's Flute Concerto was written for him, and he gave the first performance in 1933. He has written many pedagogical works for the flute. In 1934 he was made a member of the Légion d'honneur and later a commandant. In 1933 he formed the Moyse Trio with his son Louis Moyse (*b* Scheveningen, 1912) and daughter-in-law Blanche Honegger Moyse (*b* Geneva, 1909), pianist and violinist respectively. The trio won a *grand prix du disque* in 1935 for a recording of Bach and toured Europe, South America and the USA up to 1950. In 1931 its members were among the founders of the Marlboro School and the Marlboro Festival in Vermont.

**Moyzes, Alexander** (*b* Kláštor pod Znievom, northwest Slovakia, 4 Sept 1906). Slovak composer and teacher, son of Mikuláš Moyzes. He entered the Prague Conservatory in 1925 to study composition, conducting and the organ, and he graduated from Novák's master class in 1930. He was appointed to teach theory and composition at the Bratislava Academy of Music and Drama in 1929; in 1941 he was made professor at the Bratislava Conservatory and chief music adviser to Bratislava radio. At the inception of the Bratislava College of Musical Arts Moyzes was appointed professor of composition, and he was rector of the institution from 1965 to 1971. Most of the Slovak composers of the mid-20th century were his pupils, and he chaired the Slovak Composers' Union (1969–70). Awards made to him include the Bratislava Civic Prize (1937) and the

State Prize (1956); he was created Artist of Merit in 1961 and National Artist in 1966.

Moyzes's first creative period (1929–33) constituted an important and radical movement to modernize Slovak music; his Symphony no.1 (1929) symbolizes the beginning of new Slovak music in the inter-war years. Somewhat influenced by the European avant garde, he also drew on the characteristic features of Slovak folk music. The cantata *Demontáž* ('The dismantling', 1930) shows an attitude of social criticism. In a second phase (1934–50) Moyzes developed the national element in his music through the use of historic and patriotic subject matter, in addition to continuing to employ peasant materials, particularly in his many folk choruses. His third period, which began in 1951, exhibits a tendency to synthesize the innovatory aspects of his first manner with ethnic characteristics.

WORKS
*(selective list)*

Orch: Sym. no.1, 1929; Ov., op.10, 1929; Na horách spievajú [They sing in the mountains], op.15, 1933; Sym. no.2, op.16, 1932–41; Jánošíkovi chlapoi [Jánošik's boys], op.21, ov., 1934–43; Nikola Šuhaj, op.22, ov., 1934; Dolu Váhom [Down the Váh], op.26, 1935–45; Sym. no.3, 1942; Sym. no.4, op.38, 1947; Tance z Pohronia [Dances from Hron], op.43, 1950; Sym. no.7, 1955; Tance z Gemera, op.51, 1950; Vn Conc., op.53, 1958; Sonatina giocosa, op.58, str, 1962; Fl Conc., op.61, 1967; Sym. no.8, 1968; Partita, op.67, 1970; Sym. no.9, op.69, 1971; Musica istropolitana, str, 1974; Jánošik, 1976

Vocal: Farby na palete [Colours on a palette], song cycle, 1928; 12 Folksongs, op.9, 1v, pf, 1929; Demontáž [The dismantling], op.12, cantata, 1930; Znejú piesne na chotári [Songs resound in the country], op.40, S, T, chorus, orch, 1948; V jeseni [In autumn], op.56, Mez, orch, 1960; Ranná rosa [Early dew], op.59, Mez, orch, 1963; Udatný kráľ [The deposed king], opera, 1966; choruses

Chamber: Vest-pocket suita, vn, pf, 1928; Str Qt, a, op.8, 1929–42; Jazzova sonata, 2 pf, 1932; Wind Qnt, op.17, 1933; Fox etuda, pf, 1935; Str Qt no.2, 1969; Sonatina, fl, gui, 1975

Incidental music for the theatre, cinema and radio

Principal publishers: Opus, Panton, Slovenský hudobný fond, Supraphon, Universal

BIBLIOGRAPHY

L. Burlas: *Alexander Moyzes* (Bratislava, 1956)

I. Hrušovský: *Slovenská hudba* (Bratislava, 1964), 163

LADISLAV BURLAS

**Moyzes, Mikuláš** (*b* Zvolenská Slatina, central Slovakia, 6 Dec 1872; *d* Prešov, 2 April 1944). Slovak composer and teacher. He received his musical education at a teachers' institute and as an external student at the Budapest Academy of Music. After working as a music teacher and organist in various towns in his native region, which was then part of Hungary, he settled in Prešov in 1908 as a teacher. He began to draw on folk elements before 1918 and established himself as a pioneer of Slovak national music; after 1918 he wrote chamber and orchestral works in the main.

WORKS
*(selective list)*

Masses: Missa solemnis, C, 1906; Mass, d, 1929

Melodramas: Siroty [Orphans], 1921; Lesná panna [Maid of the woods], 1922; Čertova rieka [The devil's river], 1940

Orch: 2 suites, 1931, 1932; Malá vrchovská symfónia [Little highland sym.], 1937; Naše Slovensko [Our Slovakia], festival ov., 1938

Chamber: 4 str qts: D, 1926, a, 1929, f♯, 1932, G, 1943; Wind Sextet, A♭, 1934

Org: 3 Fugues, 1911; Rozpomienka [Recollection], 1911; Elegy, 1911; Intermezzo, 1911; Capriccio, 1926; Scherzoso, 1929; Toccata and Fugue, 1940

Folksong arrs., choruses, songs, teaching works

Principal publishers: Bratia Mandlovci, Molnár Eugen, Röder, Rozsnyai Károly, Slovenské hudobné vydavateľstvo, Závodský Jozef

MSS in *CS-BRnm*

BIBLIOGRAPHY

Z. Bokesová: *Sedemdesiatročný Mikuláš Moyzes* [Moyzes at 70] (Bratislava, 1942)

J. Kresánek: 'Mikuláš Moyzes-myslitel' ' [Moyzes, thinker], *Slovenské pohl'ady*, lviii (1942), 557

Z. Bokesová: 'Mikuláš Moyzes: klasik slovenskej hudby' [Moyzes, a classic of Slovak music], *Hudobnovedné štúdie* (Bratislava, 1955)

I. Hrušovský: *Slovenská hudba* [Slovak music] (Bratislava, 1964), 97

LADISLAV BURLAS

**Mozahili.** One of the three voices of Georgian ecclesiastical polyphony; *see* GEORGIAN RITE, MUSIC OF THE.

**Mozambique** [Moçambique]. African state.

1. History and ethnography. 2. Music areas. 3. Instruments and instrumental music. 4. Vocal music.

1. HISTORY AND ETHNOGRAPHY. After about four centuries of Arab influence and settlement on coastal islands such as Moçambique and Ibo, the first Portuguese, Pero da Covilhã, reached Moçambique Island and Sofala in 1489. Rapid settlement followed and within a century most of the coastline had been colonized. In 1752 the General Government of Mozambique was created. The main areas of development were Moçambique Island, the lower Zambezi and Manica highlands, and the coastal area from Inhambane southwards. Except for the Tete area in the Zambezi valley, however, Portuguese rule was finally established in the interior only in the early 20th century (the final campaign was in 1912). Lourenço Marques (now

*1. Map of Mozambique showing the distribution of the principal peoples*

Maputo) became the capital in 1897. Mozambique became independent in June 1975.

The Zambezi valley divides the primarily matrilineal peoples of the north from the patrilineal peoples of the south; it also marks the approximate southern limit of Swahili or Arab influence, which was manifested in trade and the introduction of slavery and Islam. The north is inhabited by the Swahili, whose territory extends along the coast into Tanzania; the Makonde, who are also divided between Tanzania and Mozambique, and who are noted for their rich sculptural tradition, their masked dances, and other cultural features more typical of central than east African peoples (*see* TANZANIA, §6); the Makua group, the largest; and the Maravi group (which includes the Cewa, Mang'anja, Ngoni and Yao) (see map, fig.1).

The Zambezi valley and delta have been an access route for at least three groups of invaders: the Indonesians, who also settled in other large African river valleys, and are presumed to have come in about 500; the Portuguese, who established military posts and engaged in extensive trade and agriculture from the 16th century; and the Nguni invaders who, originally escaping from warfare in Natal at the beginning of the 19th century, marauded throughout central Mozambique until the end of the century, finally settling among the Maravi people. The heterogeneous population of this area includes the Chikunda, the Nyungwe (including the Sena-Tonga and the Tavara), the Sena and the Cuabo. Many of the Shona peoples (who include the Manyika, Barwe, Utee and Ndau sub-groups) consider themselves closely linked with the culture of the Shona of Zimbabwe (Rhodesia), and were adherents of the Monomotapa empire in the 16th and 17th centuries.

The Thonga group, consisting of Tswa, Tsonga, Ronga and Shangana, predominate in the south. In the 19th century the Shangana were conscripted into the armies of the Nguni, who controlled southern and parts of central Mozambique, Zimbabwe and Malawi throughout the century.

The Chopi are a small isolated group (*c*250,000) related culturally to the Shona of Zimbabwe, and famous for their xylophone orchestras. Their land is fertile, and abundant crops allow them much leisure for music-making. Since 1975 patronage of xylophone orchestras has passed from chiefs to political officials and there has been a move towards the establishment of Chopi orchestras as a 'national' music.

2. MUSIC AREAS. The music of Mozambique may be considered in relation to three main areas. In northern Mozambique the music is generally hexa- or heptatonic: there are many kinds of drums and drumming styles but only simple xylophones and lamellaphones. Some singing in parallel 3rds occurs among the Makua, Makonde and Ndonde; otherwise singing is monophonic or with movement in parallel 4ths and 5ths. Various elements indicate Arab influence: ornamented monophonic singing, timbre and intonation, the use of drone, the characteristic lowering of the voice by a whole tone at the end of a long held note, and the use of one-string spike fiddles and *daira* (tambourines). Much of the population is Muslim, particularly along the coast. The central area (as also the Chopi and Tswa further south) has many complex types of xylophone and lamellaphone and many string and wind instruments; drums are less

common. The music is generally heptatonic and poly-phonic, mostly using 4ths and 5ths in oblique rather than parallel part movement. In the south, among the Thonga and Ndau (and also the Ngoni further north), musical bows, lamellaphones and guitars are common. The use of drums is relatively limited. Melodies are penta- and hexatonic, vocal harmonies consisting mostly of 4ths and 5ths in parallel movement.

## 3. INSTRUMENTS AND INSTRUMENTAL MUSIC.

(*i*) *Idiophones*. These are among the most important in-struments and include the xylophone and lamellaphone, many varieties of rattle (made of gourd, tin, basket, reed-raft, fruit shell, seed-pod, moth cocoon, palm leaf etc), and percussion beams, clappers, iron sheets, pipes etc. Slit-drums and bells, characteristic of central and west African music, are not used in Mozambique.

There are four distinct xylophone traditions. The best known is that of the Chopi xylophone orchestras (Port. *marimbeiros de Zavala*; fig.2*a* overleaf) associated with the dance known as *mgodo*, the 'classical' music of the Chopi. The *mgodo* performers are male xylophone play-ers, rattle players and dancers, who also sing. There are between five and 30 xylophones (*mbila*, plural *timbila*), usually about 12, carefully constructed in five sizes and tuned to cover a range of four octaves (Table 1). The four higher-pitched instruments are played seated; the four-note *chinzumana* is played standing, and provides a deep rhythmic drone. The slats are made of highly re-sonant sneezewood (*Ptaeroxylon obliquum*) and require tempering by fire before they will ring. Each slat has its own resonator, made from the shell of a wild orange tuned in sympathy with it. A single central member forms the frame, with holes for the attachment of the resonators. As with many African xylophones a buzzing membrane is attached over a small hole in the side of each resonator. A peculiarity of the Chopi instrument is the use of a small cylindrical piece of gourd, one of whose ends is fixed to the resonator surrounding the membrane to make the tone rounder. In all, about 15 different natural products are used.

The tuning system is equi-heptatonic (i.e. with seven intervals to the octave, each about 170 cents). This has been used as evidence by Jones and others to associate the xylophones of Africa with those of Indonesia. The absolute pitch of the tonic, which is variously called *dikokoma dawumbila* ('the note which gives the quality of the *mbila*'), *chilanzane* ('the first note of the highest instrument') or *hombe* ('the great note'), does not vary from village to village by more than about 100 cents. Many Chopi musicians have a sense of absolute pitch. Hugh Tracey (1948) described in detail the physical arrangement of the orchestra and dancers, the structure of the movements (usually 10 or 11) and the high degree of control exercised by the leaders of the orchestra and dance group through rehearsal and by aural and visual cuing. The musical texture is complex and dense owing to the variety of ways in which each of the many players may present his tune. The two hands of the xylophonist move in rhythmic counterpoint, which experienced players vary continuously throughout a performance. Rhythmic patterns of two against three and three against four are always present. Some types of tunes appear to be harmonically based; the preferred intervals are 4ths, 5ths and octaves, as in most southern African music, although 3rds, 6ths and to a lesser extent 7ths and 9ths

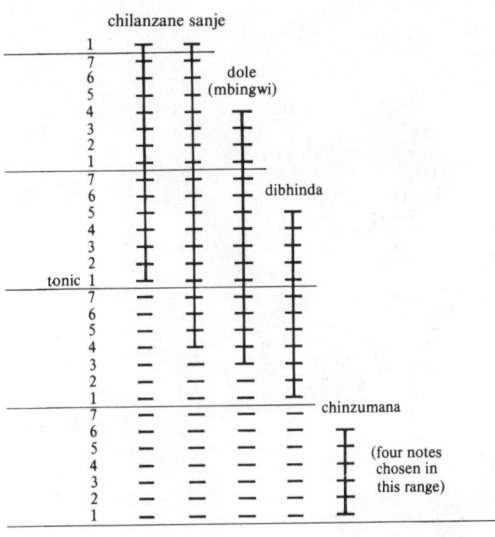

TABLE 1: Relative compass of the five xylophones of the Chopi orchestra

occur; chord movement is rarely parallel. In other pieces the music is dependent on the words, and some-times moves in parallel 4ths and 5ths. In many tunes there is a harmonic alternation between chords based on the tonic and chords based on the note immediately above. The tunes are based on cyclic patterns which vary from four rattle beats to 32 (frequently 8, 12, 16, 20, 24 or 26 beats). The *mgodo* serves as recreation and as a means of social control at the village level; at the national level it is a source of pride and provides a sense of identity both for the Chopi and for Mozambique.

The Tswa people are immediate neighbours of the Chopi. Their *muhambi* xylophone resembles that of the Chopi (i.e. an equi-heptatonic fixed-key instrument with individual gourd resonators) but has lighter keys and beaters, giving a different tone quality. It is played by adults, mostly in groups of three, accompanied by dan-cers, singers and three drums, in a suite of three or four contrasting movements, which often include elements of drama or mime. The style is related to that of the Chopi but is freer in form, and includes more improvisation and use of parallel octave part movement. This simpler type of performance may well be the original from which the Chopi developed their complex orchestral style. Xylophones made by the Tswa are bought and played by neighbouring peoples, the Shangana and the Ndau-Shanga, who adapt their own musical styles to it.

The third xylophone tradition is that of the Mang'anja, Podzo, Cuabo, Yao, Sena, Barwe and Ndau peoples in the lower Zambezi area. Their heptatonic instruments include the free-key type (with rough slats or logs laid across two long bundles of grass; fig.2*b*) and the trough-resonated type (with all the keys sharing a common resonator box), as well as those with individual gourd resonators (fig.2*c*). While they are generally played singly, there is always more than one player to an in-strument. The players sit either together on one side or on opposite sides, and beat the keys in the centre with

(b)

2. Xylophones: (a) mbila orchestra of the Chopi people, Zandamela; note the double-bass xylophones at the back, and rattle players in front; (b) valimba with keys resting on bundles of grass, Sena people, Rotanda; (c) valimba with individual gourd resonators, Sena people, Macossa

(a)

(c)

soft-tipped sticks. The compass varies from about ten notes in the simpler types to four octaves in the gourd-resonated types. The parts interlock rhythmically; some of the music is related to that of the lamellaphone traditions and has a strong harmonic framework. The xylophone is usually called *valimba*, and less commonly *varimba*, *ulimba*, *madudu*, *bachi*, *mambira*, *marimba* or *ngambi*. It is normally played for young people's dances at night, accompanied by singing, rattles and sometimes a drum.

The fourth xylophone tradition is that of the Makua and Makonde peoples. Their hexatonic free-key log xylophones (with six to eight keys resting on two banana trunks, or on a pair of logs padded with grass) are always played by two players sitting opposite each other. In contrast to the lower Zambezi xylophone tradition, the keys are struck not at the centre but at the ends, with plain wooden sticks. As in other African log xylophone traditions (in Uganda, Zaïre, Cameroon etc) the playing technique requires the interlocking of the two parts at high speed. The Makua call this instrument *mangwilo*, the Makonde *dimbila*.

There are three main lamellaphone performing traditions, found in the north, the Zambezi basin and in the south. In the north, among the Makonde and Makua, the lamellaphone is known as *shitata*, *chityatya* etc, and is a small instrument with calabash resonator and seven or eight keys (similar to the *malimba* of southern Tanzania), played solo with the thumbs and one forefinger. The Zambezi basin tradition is the richest of the three and extends into most of Zimbabwe and parts of Zambia, Malawi and Transvaal. There are at least nine types of lamellaphone, mostly calabash-resonated with slightly wedge-shaped bodies and from 8 to over 30 keys: the tuning of these instruments is heptatonic (with a tendency to equal spacing) and harmony is important, the style being based on chord sequences of 4ths and 5ths. Up to five men play together, producing complex polyphony. The nine main types are *kalimba* (Nsenga, Ngoni, Cewa, Nyungwe and Chikunda peoples); *ndimba* (Nsenga); *karimba* (Nyungwe, Chikunda, Sena-Tonga and Tavara); *njari* (Nyungwe, Sena-Tonga, Manyika and Utee); *njari huru* (Chikunda); *hera* or *matepe* Tonga, Nyungwe, Sena); *mbira huru* (Manyika); and *nyonganyonga* (Barwe, Gorongozi and Sena). *Mbira*, *marimba* and *nsansi* are broad generic names also used in this area. Some of the instruments in this family (the *njari*, *hera* and *mbira huru*) are played in ancestral spirit ceremonies; the others are usually played for entertainment. The southern instrument, called *mbira dza vaNdau* by the Ndau and *timbila* by the Tsonga, is related to the above group, and is widely played in Mozambique south of Beira (fig.3). It has hexatonic tuning with widely differing intervals, and three manuals of keys. It is played by young men for entertainment and courting, and also by a class of older minstrels known as *varombe* who entertain professionally, sometimes achieving a wide reputation. Several Mozambique radio stations broadcast traditional music; players such as António Gande (an Ndau musician from Chingune Island) and Lázaro Vinho (a blind Nyungwe *njari* player from Tete) were well known as broadcasters in the early 1970s (for further discussion of lamellaphones in Mozambique see LAMELLAPHONE, §§2, 3).

*(ii) Membranophones*. Drums are played by all the peoples of Mozambique, but the number of types and the

3. *Mbira dza vaNdau (lamellaphone) of the Ndau people, with bottle-top buzzers and calabash resonator*

frequency with which they are played decrease towards the southern end of the country. Most drums are single-headed with pegged skins and cylindrical or conical bodies, open at the lower end. They are tuned by heating, or sometimes by using tuning-paste. Double-headed drums were formerly rare, but are now more common throughout the country, particularly in towns, because they can easily be constructed from metal cans with the two opposite heads laced together. The friction drum is played by the Swazi to accompany dancing and by the Makonde during puberty ceremonies. Tambourine-type frame drums called *daira* are played near the island of Moçambique and in other areas influenced by Islam in the north, and also in the south by the Thonga during their spirit-possession ceremonies. Closed bowl-shaped drums are used by the Chopi, Ndau and Sena-Tonga for the same purpose.

Throughout the country drums are played together in ensemble, usually a minimum of three (see fig.4). The highest-pitched drum usually marks the time, the lowest is the leader. There are several musical styles in which drums are prominent. The *likhuba* (of the Mang'anja and Sena peoples) is a drum-chime consisting of up to ten drums tuned to a pentatonic scale; the leader plays five

4. *Sena drummers from Mutarara district accompanying the likhuba dance in Bulawayo, Zimbabwe*

or six of these with his hands, accompanied by three or four other drummers, rattles, singing and solo exhibition dancing. The Ndau *muchongoyo* ensemble consists of three double-headed drums beaten by one or two players with sticks, and (with singing and hand-clapping) provides a virtuoso polyrhythmic accompaniment to a unison-dance team performing acrobatic and humorous movements. The Nyungwe *kangoma kabodzi* is a more modern dance form, accompanied by virtuoso drumming on one tall, cylindrical drum. The most characteristic of a remarkable variety of Makonde drums are the slender *neya* drum and the small closed *singanga* drum, whose foot is extended into a narrow spike one metre in length. Ten or more *singanga* may be used simultaneously as part of a drum ensemble.

(*iii*) *Aerophones*. Horn, bone and wood whistles, and end- and side-blown bamboo flutes, are played in some parts of Mozambique, mostly by herdsmen for private enjoyment. The Chopi, Tsonga and Ndau of the south play globular flutes or ocarinas of gourd or clay. Ensembles of single-note stopped flutes, common in other parts of southern Africa, are found only among the Chopi, where boys perform the *chimveka* circle-dance in the fields at night, playing in hocket fashion. The magnificent *nyanga* (panpipes) dance of the Nyungwe is a circle-dance performed by 20 to 30 men, each with two-, three- or four-note panpipes making in all a heptatonic compass of three and a half octaves (fig.5). The men dance irregularly phrased steps as they play, interspersing sung notes with blown notes, and each interlocking his part with that of the others so that there is a continuous sound of both blown and sung notes, to which the voices of women singers are added. (*See* STOPPED FLUTE ENSEMBLE.)

Antelope horns, particularly of the kudu and sable,

with a lateral mouth-hole near the tip, are blown as signal or ceremonial instruments in many districts. Kazoos called *malipenga* are used in ensembles with drums by the Cewa near Lake Malawi. The instruments are made in various sizes from the straight or curved neck of a gourd, closed at the smaller end with a nasalizing membrane, and with a lateral mouth-hole for singing into near the same end. *Malipenga* dances are said to have originated in military drill music in Tanzania and Malawi during the early 20th century.

(*iv*) *Chordophones*. Many types of MUSICAL BOW are still played in the south. They include the popular braced *chitende* with a gourd resonator, used widely by men for topical and humorous songs, the *kadimbwa* (of the Nyungwe and Sena-Tonga), resonated with the mouth, and the *chizambi* (of the Tsonga, Chopi and Ndau), which is sounded by rubbing the notched body of the bow with a small rattle stick. In the northern half of Mozambique two string instruments are popular. The board zither, known variously as *bangwe*, *pango*, *bango* etc, is played mainly by the Cewa and Yao peoples near Malawi and Lake Malawi, but is also found among the Makua and Makonde. Its single wire or fibre string is stretched seven times from end to end through holes near each end. The player usually strums all the strings with the right index finger, while damping those notes that are not required with the left fingers. The far end of the instrument is sometimes put in a calabash or metal tin for resonance. Among the Mang'anja and Sena of the central Zambezi the instrument has nine to 12 strings which the player plucks (fig.6). The other northern instrument is the long-necked, one-string spike fiddle (Swahili *rabeka*, Lomwe *takare*, Meto *chikwesa*, Cewa *mugole*, Mang'anja *siribo*). It is played by wandering troubadours, some of them blind or crippled, who sing

*5. Part of a nyanga (panpipes) ensemble of the Nyungwe people at Nsava, near Tete*

ballads, epic poems or humorous and satirical songs to its accompaniment. The body of the fiddle is like a small drum and is made of calabash, wood or coconut shell covered with an antelope or lizard skin. The use of a tuning-loop which passes around the neck and the wire or sisal string is distinctive.

4. VOCAL MUSIC. Whereas instruments are nearly always played by men, most singing is by groups of women, who provide an essential accompaniment to many dances and communal performances. The tone of their voices is typically shrill and piercing, designed, like many instrumental timbres, to cut through a welter of polyphonic sound. Yodelling by both men and women is important in central Mozambique (for example in men's lamellaphone songs and women's polyphonic pounding-songs) and also to a lesser extent among the Makua in the north. On Moçambique and Ibo islands in the north large, well-rehearsed choirs of women, beautifully and uniformly dressed in bright costumes and with faces whitened, sing dramatic and romantic songs to the accompaniment of several *daira* and hand-clapping. Thonga men in the south form vocal dance groups called *makwaya* (from 'choir') which sing topical and satirical songs in a vigorous style which was first developed in the mining compounds of South Africa.

In addition to the two traditional harmonic styles using either 4ths and 5ths or 3rds (see §2) there is a third style which uses the triadic harmonies of Euro-American popular and church music. Apart from being used in towns and mission centres this style has had considerably less influence in Mozambique than in most other African countries. Popular music has been influenced by Portuguese music and by the urban musics of neighbouring African states. The guitar, introduced in the 16th or 17th century, is popular in the south. The musical influence of other settler groups such as Indians and Chinese has been minimal. The slow rate of urbanization and development in the country has meant that many traditional cultures have been left relatively undisturbed. This, coupled with Portuguese tolerance of folk arts, has favoured one of the strongest and most varied musical cultures in Africa. Numerous recordings of the traditional music of Mozambique are held at and published by the International Library of African Music, Rhodes University, Grahamstown, South Africa.

BIBLIOGRAPHY

H. A. Junod: *Les chants et les contes des Ba-Ronga, de la baie de Delagoa* (Lausanne, 1897)
G. M. Theal: *Records of South-eastern Africa* (Cape Town, 1899–1903) [with reports from J. dos Santos (1586) and A. Fernandes (1560, 1562)]
H. P. Junod: 'The *Mbila* or Native Piano of the Tshopi Tribe', *Bantu Studies*, iii (1927–9), 275
P. R. Kirby: 'Chopi Instruments and Music', *The Musical Instruments of the Native Races of South Africa* (Oxford, 1934/R1953), 57
H. T. Tracey: 'Três dias com os Ba-Chope', *Moçambique*, xxiv (1940), 23
——: 'Música, poesia e bailados Chopes', *Moçambique*, xxx (1942), 69–112
——: 'Marimbas, os xilofones dos Changanes', *Moçambique*, xxxi (1942), 49
B. Marques: *Musica negra: estudos de folclore Tonga* (Lisbon, 1943)
H. T. Tracey: 'The Poetry of the Bachopi Ballet', *Nada*, xxi (1944), 6
——: *Chopi Musicians: their Music, Poetry and Instruments* (London, 1948/R1970)
N. dos Santos jr: 'A chitata: contribuição para o estudo dos instru-

6. *Bangwe (board zither) played by the blind Sena musician Francisco Singirira, at Mutarara*

mentos musicais dos indígenas de Moçambique', *Garcia de Orta*, vi/2 (1958), 347, 527
——: 'O pango ou panco', *Garcia de Orta*, vi/3 (1958)
G. Kubik: 'Letters to the Editor', *African Music*, iii/1 (1962), 113
——: 'Discovery of a Trough Xylophone in Northern Mozambique', *African Music*, iii/2 (1963), 11
F. P. Marjay: *Mozambique* (Lisbon, 1963)
A. M. Jones: *Africa and Indonesia: the Evidence of the Xylophone and Other Musical and Cultural Factors* (Leiden, 1964/R1971)
G. Kubik: 'Recording and Studying Music in Northern Moçambique', *African Music*, iii/3 (1964), 77
——: 'Transcription of Mangwilo Xylophone Music from Film Strips', *African Music*, iii/4 (1965), 35
M. Dias: 'Os instrumentos musicais de Moçambique', *Geographica*, ii/6 (1966), 2
M. and J. Dias: *Os Macondes de Moçambique*, iii (Lisbon, 1970)
T. F. Johnston: 'Xizambi Friction-bow Music of the Shangana-Tsonga', *African Music*, iv/4 (1970), 81
A. Tracey: 'The Matepe Mbira Music of Rhodesia', *African Music*, iv/4 (1970), 37
T. F. Johnston: 'Shangana-Tsonga Drum and Bow Rhythms', *African Music*, v/1 (1971), 59
——: *The Music of the Shangana-Tsonga* (diss., U. of Witwatersrand, 1971)
A. Tracey: 'The Nyanga Panpipe Dance', *African Music*, v/1 (1971), 73
J. A. R. Wembah-Rashid: ' "Isinyago and Midimu", Masked Dancers of Tanzania and Mozambique', *African Arts*, iv/2 (1971), 38
T. F. Johnston: 'Possession Music of the Shangana-Tsonga', *African Music*, v/2 (1972), 10
G. Kubik: 'Transcription of African Music from Silent Film: Theory and Methods', *African Music*, v/2 (1972), 28
A. Tracey: 'The Original African Mbira?', *African Music*, v/2 (1972), 85
T. F. Johnston: 'Mohambi Xylophone Music of the Shangana-Tsonga', *African Music*, v/3 (1973–4), 86
C. Wittig: 'Chopi Orchestral Xylophone Music: the Mgodo of Mbanguzi', Kaleidophone KS 2202 [disc notes]
ANDREW TRACEY

**Mozarabic rite, music of the.** One of the principal branches of Christian liturgical chant in the west during the Middle Ages. It was sung in the Iberian peninsula, but its interest and importance reach beyond that to touch other repertories of chant such as the Gregorian, Ambrosian and Gallican.

1. History. 2 Sources and notation. 3. Musical forms in the Office. 4. Musical forms in the Mass.

1. HISTORY. The repertory of Mozarabic chant belongs to the rite observed by Spanish Christians until its suppression in favour of the Roman rite in 1085. The

term 'Mozarabic' refers to Christians living under Muslim domination. It is generally applied to the rite because its principal surviving documents date from the period after the Muslim invasion of the Iberian peninsula in 711. The term, however, is not strictly appropriate in some respects, for the formation of the rite clearly antedates the Muslim invasion. And many of the surviving MSS, though copied in the Mozarabic period, were copied in lands already reconquered from the Muslims by Christian rulers. Alternatives such as 'Visigothic' and 'Hispanic' are, however, equally inappropriate in some respects.

The earliest evidence for the existence of a rite essentially like that preserved in later MSS is found in the writings of ISIDORE OF SEVILLE (d 636). His *Etymologiae* and *De ecclesiasticis officiis* contain descriptions of the mass which closely parallel the later liturgical and musical documents themselves. Furthermore, the process of unification within the Iberian peninsula and parts of southern France was evidently already well advanced by 633, for in that year the fourth council of Toledo met under Isidore's leadership to decree the observance of 'one order of prayer and singing in all Spain and Gaul'. Only about 70 years later was the oldest surviving liturgical document for this rite copied. This is the *Orationale* of Verona, which, although it does not contain musical notation, does contain prayers and text incipits for antiphons and responsories. Comparison of this MS with the musical MSS of the 10th and 11th centuries makes it clear that the musical repertory too must have been set largely before 711.

The Mozarabic rite began to give way to the Roman rite as the reconquest of the peninsula gradually proceeded. The Roman rite entered Catalonia as early as the 8th century, but it was not until 1071 that it was adopted in Aragon. In 1076, it was adopted in parts of Castile and León, though surviving MSS from these territories make it clear that the Mozarabic rite had been observed here in the years immediately following the reconquest.

Toledo, the seat of the Spanish Church, was not recaptured from the Muslims until 1085. Hence, it was not until that year that the Roman rite could be imposed on the Spanish Church as a whole through the appointment of a French archbishop. Although Pope Alexander II had approved the Mozarabic service books as recently as 1065, Pope Gregory VII made their suppression official. Only a few parishes in Toledo itself were allowed to continue in the observance of their ancient rite. Whether the rite continued to be observed in territory held by the Muslims as late as 1492 is not known.

In the late 15th century, Cardinal Jiménez de Cisneros embarked on a project to restore the rite. He published a missal in 1500 and a breviary in 1502. These were based on MSS some of which are still preserved in Toledo. They transmit a form of the rite which was not, however, found in the majority of the MSS preserved there, or in any of the MSS from northern Spain. Scholars disagree over which form of the rite is the more ancient. New musical MSS were also copied at this time, though their melodies, copied in rhythmic notation, are evidently different from those of the older, non-diastematic sources.

The restoration of the rite received added impetus from Cardinal Lorenzana in the late 18th and early 19th centuries with the publication of new books and with increased support for the Mozarabic chapel in Toledo Cathedral. Except for relatively brief periods, this chapel has functioned continuously since that time, and services are still held daily. A few churches elsewhere in Spain have received permission to celebrate the Mozarabic Mass, but none does so on a regular basis.

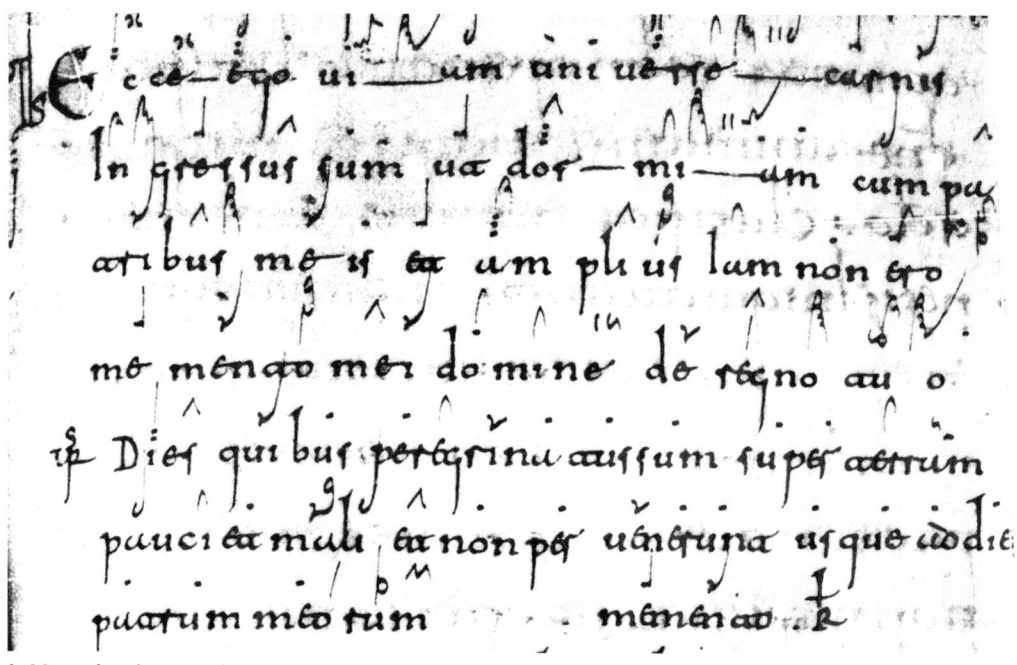

1. *Mozarabic chant, northern notation (S Domingo de Silos, Archivo del Monasterio 4 (Liber ordinum), f.85)*

2. SOURCES AND NOTATION. There are more than 20 surviving MSS and as many more fragments containing musical notation for Mozarabic chant. With only five exceptions, all of these sources employ non-diastematic notation. The exceptions are four MSS copied during and after Cisneros's restoration of the rite around 1500 and one 11th-century MS which contains about 20 melodies in Aquitanian neumes. Hence, the melodies will forever remain indecipherable, unless new sources are discovered which employ a more advanced notation. It is unlikely, however, that such sources ever existed, for the rite was suppressed and the copying of MSS virtually ceased at just the period in which diastematic notation came into general use. Even scribes in Toledo, where the rite was observed after 1085, seem not to have bothered to recopy their melodies in a notation like that of the French MSS which had been brought by the new archbishop in that year.

On notational grounds, the MSS (excluding those copied during and after Cisneros's restoration) may be divided into two broad classes: those employing northern notation and those employing Toledan notation. These labels should not be taken to represent the actual geographical state of affairs in the 11th century and before. It is not certain, for example, that all of the Toledan MSS were actually copied in Toledo, and we have no idea at all of what notations might have been used in the southern half of the peninsula.

The northern notation is found primarily in MSS copied in the provinces of León (e.g. the antiphoner *E-La* 8) and Castile (e.g. *GB-Lbm* Add.30851, from S Domingo de Silos). It bears some resemblance to neumatic notations found elsewhere in Europe and is characterized by a predominance of upright neumes employing vertical strokes (see fig.1 and ex.1).

By contrast, vertical strokes are almost totally lacking in Toledan notation, the neumes being generally inclined to the right. There are, furthermore, two types of Toledan notation. The first is found in MSS which embody the liturgical tradition of the north (referred to in the literature as tradition A). This notation includes a large number of delicate, rounded strokes (see fig.2). The second type of Toledan notation is found only in MSS embodying a different liturgical tradition (tradition B), and is much coarser and more angular in appearance (see fig.3).

The chronology of the sources, and thus the relative antiquity of the notations which they contain, is not yet fully established, especially with respect to Toledan sources. The latter have been thought to include MSS copied as early as the 9th century. The MSS in question may, however, actually date from the 12th century and in some cases from as late as the 13th and 14th centuries (Mundó). The idea that non-diastematic notation continued in use into the 14th century must, of course, raise serious questions, but it is important to note that the earlier dating of these MSS is not firmly based.

Dates for a number of the northern MSS were provided by their copyists. All of these fall within the 11th century. Others, such as the antiphoners of León and S Millán de la Cogolla (*E-Ma* Aemil.30), have been assigned by scholars to the 10th century, though further study may show that some of these, too, should be placed in the 11th century.

The organization of the MSS into types and the arrangement of material within each of the types (for which see the writings of Pinell) are peculiar to the

Ex. 1

Mozarabic rite. For example, material which, in service books for the Roman rite, would be divided between the antiphoner (containing chants for the Office) and the gradual (containing chants for the Mass) is present in a single book in the Mozarabic rite. The León antiphoner is such a book, and is thus from the Roman point of view not strictly an antiphoner at all. Within this volume all of the music for both the secular Office and the Mass appears in a single series which mixes the feasts of the Lord and the feasts of the saints in the order in which they would normally occur during the liturgical year. This series is followed by Offices and Masses for the Common of Saints, ordinary Sundays, and various special occasions such as marriages and deaths. Other sources, such as the antiphoner of S Millán de la Cogolla, add to this same arrangement all of the Proper prayers for both Mass and Office.

3. MUSICAL FORMS IN THE OFFICE. The musical forms encountered in Mozarabic chant present a number of analogies with those of the Roman rite. For example, a comparable distinction exists between antiphonal and responsorial singing. And the Mozarabic chant may be seen to make use of three styles: syllabic, neumatic and melismatic, much as in Gregorian chant. In the following descriptions of the principal musical items in both the Mozarabic Office and Mass, some of these analogies will be discussed further. The items from the Mass are presented here in the appropriate liturgical order.

2. Mozarabic chant, Toledan notation, tradition A (E-Tc 35.4, f.44)

(i) *Antiphons.* These number approximately 3000 in the surviving MSS and are generally moderate in length, employing a simple syllabic or moderately neumatic style. Descriptions of the singing of antiphons found in the writings of Isidore of Seville and in the second prologue to the antiphoner of León make it clear that the alternation of two choirs was used, much as it is in Gregorian chant. Mozarabic MSS show, furthermore, that the verse or verses following the antiphons were sung to simple recitation formulae much like the Gregorian psalm tones. Unfortunately, however, there is very rarely musical notation for an entire verse. Instead, most antiphons are simply provided with the incipit of a single verse, usually without any notation at all. This was presumably done because the formulae were simple and so well known that there was no need to write them down, at least not for every antiphon.

The exact number of antiphonal psalm tones used in Mozarabic chant has not so far been ascertained because of the fragmentary nature of the evidence. Certainly one cannot show that there were eight tones corresponding to eight modes, as in Gregorian chant. Nevertheless,

there are at least two tones which recur often enough to suggest that the application of the psalm tones depended on some scheme for classifying melodies, a scheme analogous to the modal system of Gregorian chant. Evidently these psalm tones could be modified slightly in order to adapt them to individual antiphons, though these modifications are not so numerous or extensive as the Gregorian *differentiae.*

The structure of the two most common tones is simple, consisting of an intonation of two or four elements, apparently applied without regard for text accent, a recitation tone, perhaps modified by an occasional elevation, and a final cadence consisting in one case of two elements and in the other of four elements applied mechanically to the final syllables of the verse. Whether these psalm tones were divided into two parts by a medial cadence is not clear.

The verse incipits provided for the antiphons are frequently not drawn from the beginning of a psalm, nor do the MSS always concord well in the choice of verse for a given antiphon. It is thus often doubtful, in the secular Office at least, whether an entire psalm was to

3. Mozarabic chant, Toledan notation, tradition B (E-Mn 10.110, f.XXXVIIv)

accompany each antiphon, though the descriptions of antiphonal singing mentioned above always refer to the singing of 'verses' between the two choirs. Only in the monastic Office does it seem clear that entire psalms were sung with antiphons and that there was some provision for singing the entire psalter on a regular basis. For this purpose, however, psalters provided with antiphons were used in conjunction with other books containing other types of music such as the responsories. There seems to have been no single book which contained all of the music for the monastic Office.

At Matins, pairs of antiphons are each combined with an *Alleluiaticus* (the term for alleluiatic antiphons; see below) and a responsory to form *missae*, the number of which varies with the solemnity of the feast. Normally, the notation of the four pieces within any single *missa* does not suggest that they share common musical material. But a few *missae*, which definitely postdate the oldest core of the repertory, do display a musical unity brought about by shared material, sometimes extending to the responsory as well as the antiphons and *Alleluiaticus*.

Another regular feature of Matins is a group of three antiphons, one drawn from each of the three *Psalmi canonici* (Psalms iii, l and lvi in the numbering of the Vulgate) and each presumably accompanied by the singing of the appropriate psalm. Although they do not follow one another immediately in the service, the three pieces are generally cut from the same melodic stock.

(ii) *Alleluiatici*. These are simply alleluiatic antiphons, and they share the psalm tones and musical style of the antiphons just described. The rubrics in the sources, however, clearly distinguish these pieces from the remaining antiphons, and they occur only at specific points in the liturgy: as the third item in the *missae* at Matins and as the second antiphon at Vespers. Even during parts of Lent, when the word 'alleluia' is eliminated from the liturgy, pieces drawn from the alleluiatic psalms and bearing the rubric for the *Alleluiatici* continue to appear in the appropriate places at Matins and Vespers.

(iii) *Responsories*. Approximately 500 responsories survive, and they bear a strong resemblance to the Great Responsories of the Gregorian chant. They occur at Matins as the last item of each *missa* (see above) and at certain of the lesser hours. Their style is generally neumatic, as illustrated in ex.1 by one of the few melodies which have survived in both Mozarabic and decipherable Aquitanian neumes.

Most responsories are provided with a single verse which is written out complete with musical notation, and the MSS embody four clearly distinguishable traditions for the psalm tones to which these verses are sung. The northern sources transmit two of these traditions, one in sources from the region of León and the other in sources from the Rioja (the Ebro River valley above and below the city of Logroño) and neighbouring Castile. The melodies of these two traditions clearly correspond to one another, and since neither seems clearly to have been derived from the other, they must have descended from a common archetype dating from before the 10th century and the earliest surviving northern sources.

Studies of early Spanish monasticism suggest that, following their reconquest in the 8th century, parts of Castile were colonized by monks from Galicia, and that it was from Castile that the Rioja was colonized. The organization of monastic life in all three of these regions

clearly sets them apart from León. Hence, it is not surprising that the musical MSS from Castile and the Rioja should present a tradition different from that of the Leonese MSS. And even though we have no musical sources from Galicia before the colonization of Castile, we may conclude that the differences between the two northern traditions reach back as far as the 8th century.

Of the two northern traditions, the Leonese is the more elaborate and systematic. Seven different tones occur more than once in the sources from León, but two of these appear much more frequently than the others (227 and 150 times, respectively, in a total of almost 500 pieces in the antiphoner of León). This suggests immediately that, here again, there was some scheme for the classification of melodies which formed the basis for the assignment of a particular psalm tone to each responsory. But it seems not to have been a scheme as elaborate as the system of eight modes found in the Gregorian chant.

The application of the more common psalm tones to the responsory verses follows extremely closely certain principles, especially in the Leonese sources. As in the Gregorian Great Responsories, the melodies are generally bipartite, certain formulae (notably the final cadences) remaining fixed while others are adjusted to the structure of the text in question. These adjustments are carried out through the addition of single notes and through the contraction or division of more complex neumes. Even the adjustable formulae, however, are modified within narrow limits, and here the accentuation of the text clearly provides the guiding principle. In fact the treatment of accentuation in these melodies, unlike that in their Gregorian counterparts, is so careful that it provides clear evidence for some of the kinds of changes which were taking place in Latin on the Iberian peninsula just at the time when the vernacular began to emerge. The grammatical construction of the texts also exercises a clear influence on the melodies, for clauses and phrases in the text are punctuated through the introduction of secondary mediants and intonations. The verse in ex.1 presents one of the tones from the Rioja tradition.

The Toledan sources also transmit two traditions for the responsorial psalm tones, and these differ markedly from one another as well as from the two northern traditions. The two Toledan musical traditions correspond to the two liturgical and notational traditions found in these MSS. In the sources which agree liturgically with the northern MSS, there are again two tones which account for the great majority of examples. But neither of these tones corresponds clearly to any of the northern tones, even allowing for the considerable differences between the two notational systems. The melodies of the responsories themselves are clearly the same in these Toledan MSS and in the northern MSS, but responsories assigned to a single tone in one tradition are divided among several tones in the other. In general, these Toledan tones are much less elaborate and systematic than those of either northern tradition.

The Toledan sources which embody liturgical tradition B present four distinct responsorial psalm tones, and of these, one accounts for more than half of the total. It is treated with much the greatest consistency, but none of the four is applied to its texts as systematically as are the northern tones, and none significantly resembles tones in any other tradition.

An understanding of this last Toledan tradition must await a better knowledge of the liturgical tradition with which it is associated. But if we compare the remaining three traditions for the responsorial psalm tones, several conclusions emerge. The responsories themselves are the same in these three traditions, allowing for minor variants and notational differences. Consequently the disparity between the psalm tones of the two northern traditions on the one hand and the Toledan tradition on the other suggests that the psalm tones were transmitted orally long after the responsories themselves had been written down. By the time the psalm tones were written down, individual melodies and the criteria for applying them had evidently undergone considerable change in different parts of the peninsula, and they must have been written down only after the Toledan and northern notations had become quite distinct.

The existence of two quite distinct notational systems transmitting a single repertory of responsories can perhaps be attributed to the Muslim domination of large parts of the peninsula. Musical notation of the type found in the MSS of western chant generally can only have been in its very first stages, if that, at the time of the Muslim invasion in 711. The Toledan and northern notations must therefore have become distinct only after the Muslims were in control of much of Spain. Northern notation probably developed on the Christian side of the frontier. Toledan notation probably developed among Christians living in territories on the Muslim side of the frontier and is thus Mozarabic properly so called. And until it moved to the south of Toledo, opening the way for the suppression of the rite altogether, it was this frontier, marked with fire and blood, that kept the two notational and musical traditions separate.

These conclusions about regional differences in the Mozarabic chant and its notations have been based almost exclusively on a study of the responsories for the Office and their psalm tones. But many of them could doubtless be confirmed by systematic studies of other types of chant.

(iv) *Matutinaria*. Occurring only at Matins, these pieces are evidently antiphons which are set apart from the others because their texts treat the appropriate themes for the early morning hours. They are normally provided with a notationless incipit for one verse.

(v) *Benedictiones*. Not to be confused with the *Benedictiones* of the Mass, these are antiphons sung to the accompaniment of *Daniel* iii.52, 'Benedictus es Domine Deus', and the verses following. The sources occasionally provide the normal rubric for antiphons along with the rubric *BNS* which always accompanies these pieces. Since the verse to follow was invariable, the sources do not always provide an incipit for it.

(vi) *Soni*. These often melismatic melodies occur at both Matins and Vespers. Their style and formal design, which resemble those of the *Sacrificia* of the Mass (see below), make it clear that they are soloistic chants at least in part. Their refrain form suggests that they might be responsorial chants, but they are not mentioned in the prologues to the antiphoner of León as numbering among those pieces which were sung in the manner of responsories. The numbering of their verses also suggests that they belong to a separate category, for the first verse following the initial refrain always bears the rubric *II* instead of the *VR* of clearly responsorial chants. These melodies occasionally include long melismas (often on the word 'Alleluia') which embody the double

versicle structure of the *sequentiae* found in other chant repertories. With only the rarest exceptions in peripheral sources, these melismas were apparently not provided with *prosae*.

(vii) *Laudes*. Pieces bearing this title occur at Matins, at some of the lesser hours, and at the Mass. The singing of Alleluia is a prominent feature of all of them except during Lent, when this word is suppressed throughout the liturgy.

(viii) *Psallendi*. These pieces occur at Matins and Vespers, generally without a verse following, though they were to be followed always by the Doxology. What melodies, if any, were to be used for this latter is not known, nor can it be said with certainty how the piece as a whole was performed and by whom. The closest analogy outside of the Mozarabic chant is provided by the *Psallendae* of the Ambrosian chant, though there are no concordances between the two groups.

(ix) *Vespertini*. The prologues to the antiphoner of León identify these as having been sung in the manner of responsories. Neumatic in style, they occur as the first item at Vespers and bear some resemblance to the Ambrosian *Lucernaria*, their texts dealing with the traditional subjects of light, evening, night and the like. Although the term 'Vespertinus' goes back at least as far as the Council of Merida in 666, the term 'Lucernarium', describing what is certainly the same item in the liturgy, may be found in the *Regula monachorum* of Isidore of Seville and in the canons of the first council of Toledo, which met between 397 and 400. Some Toledan MSS employ the rubric *Lm*, which should perhaps be interpreted as standing for *Lucernarium*, given the Spanish tradition for this term.

There are not sufficient Vespertini to provide a different piece for each feast. Hence, many of them are repeated during the course of the year. Within this limited repertory (fewer than 70 examples in the antiphoner of León) there is a considerable variety of forms. For example, although the Vespertini are grouped among the responsorial pieces, about a quarter of them (notably those assigned to the ferias of Lent) lack verses. Almost another quarter include two or more verses, one of these pieces including as many as nine.

How the pieces without verses were performed is not clear. The pieces with verses were almost certainly performed by soloists and a choir, as were other responsorial pieces. The verses were evidently performed by the soloists alone in most cases, for each verse is generally followed in the MSS by an indication to repeat the final portion of the refrain. This method of responsorial singing corresponds with the description by Amalar of responsorial singing among the Franks. Only when the music of the refrain and the verse is the same (or when the two at least end with the same material) is the repetition of part of the refrain omitted. In such cases, the choir presumably joined the soloists in singing the final portion of the verse.

The number of verses included in any one piece seems to be an index of the solemnity of the feast to which it is assigned. The composition of the texts with multiple verses, furthermore, makes it clear that these pieces are not remnants of a practice in which all Vespertini consisted of entire psalms, for some of them intermingle psalmodic and non-psalmodic verses.

The Vespertini illustrate most clearly the use of centonate composition in the Mozarabic chant (*see* CENTONIZATION). Some of them employ common melodic formulae in such a way as to eliminate any possibility that one melody served as the model for the remainder. Among the Vespertini without verses, however, there is one melody which was simply provided with different texts for different days in Lent.

(x) *Preces*. Occurring in both the Office and the Mass, the Preces, in their most highly developed form, present us with rhythmic poetry composed in relatively short strophes separated by a brief refrain. Musically, this refrain may be entirely separate from the strophe or it may be the final phrase in what is essentially a single musical statement comprising both a strophe and a refrain. The melodies range between a simple syllabic and a moderately neumatic style.

The tradition of the Preces reaches back at least into the 7th century and offers one of the principal points of contact between the Mozarabic and Gallican rites. It is generally thought that the texts shared by the two rites are Spanish in origin. Only two of these texts, however, can be shown to have employed the same melodies in France and Spain, and their distribution in Spanish sources suggests that they may have originated in France. Among Spanish MSS, those associated with Toledo, and particularly those embodying liturgical tradition B, are richest in Preces.

(xi) *Hymns*. Mozarabic MSS present texts for numerous hymns, many of which are common to other rites. But only a very few examples include musical notation. Hymns are assigned to Matins, Vespers and a number of the lesser hours.

4. MUSICAL FORMS IN THE MASS.

(i) *Praelegenda*. These correspond in function to the Gregorian introits and, like them, are examples of antiphonal psalmody. In fact, some melodies in the Mozarabic rite serve both as Praelegenda for the Mass and as antiphons or *Alleluiatici* for the Office. In general, the MSS do not provide complete verses for the Praelegenda. But enough verses are provided with notation to reveal that they employed the same psalm tones as those found among the antiphons for the Office.

(ii) *Gloria in excelsis Deo*. Although this text and melodies for it rarely appear in the MSS, the antiphoner of León contains several versions among the pieces for ordinary Sundays.

(iii) *Trisagion*. The threefold singing of *Agios* to melodies which are at times quite melismatic is provided for in the MSS on only a few occasions. The texts sometimes present only the transliterated Greek, sometimes both the Greek and a Latin translation sung to the same melody; and in one case the Latin alone is given. The only rubric employed for these pieces is *GRC*, which is also used in the Office for antiphons with texts in transliterated Greek.

(iv) *Benedictiones*. All texts for the Benedictiones of the Mass are drawn from the Canticle of the Three Children in the book of *Daniel*. Because their melodies are neumatic and even moderately melismatic, all verses in each piece are written out with notation. Within each piece, all verses employ much the same melodic material, and each is followed by the repetition of a refrain, a feature built into the scriptural text itself.

(v) *Psalmi*. Although scholars have generally employed the term 'Psallenda' (singular 'Psallendum'), the sources suggest that 'Psalmi' (singular 'Psalmo') ought to be preferred. In the antiphoner of León, these pieces are referred to as *Psalmi pulpitales*. They correspond to the Gregorian graduals in a number of respects.

Like the Vespertini, they are numbered among the responsorial pieces by the author of the second prologue to the antiphoner of León. They are generally neumatic or melismatic in style, most consisting of a refrain and a single verse. As with the Vespertini, part of the refrain is repeated after the verse unless the refrain and verse share the same melody. Only five out of more than 120 surviving examples have non-psalmodic texts.

Only nine examples include more than a single verse, and these nine are assigned to the Sundays in Lent, with the exception of the first, and to Tuesday, Wednesday, Thursday and Friday of Holy Week. The number of verses gradually increases as the weeks pass, and the Psalmo for Good Friday in the antiphoner of León includes a total of 15 verses. This artificial arrangement alone suggests that these pieces are not remnants of an earlier practice in which all of the Psalmi consisted of whole psalms. The structure of the texts adds some support to this notion, for the verses are not always presented in the order in which they occur in the psalm itself. Thus, at the very least, a considerable amount of rearranging was done in the course of abbreviating them. If the Psalmi (and perhaps analogous pieces in other rites) originally consisted of whole psalms, it seems likely that nothing of the original melodies has been preserved for us.

(vi) *Clamores*. Only about 20 feasts are provided with Clamores, and these pieces, though always identified by the appropriate rubrics, clearly form part of a continuous piece with the Psalmi. A Clamor normally consists of two parts separated by the acclamation *Deo gratias*, the melody for which is invariable. Following the second part of the Clamor, it is the refrain from the preceding Psalmo that is repeated. If the concept of mode is applicable to these melodies at all, each Clamor must be in the same mode as its associated Psalmo. And since parts of the Clamor melody are always the same, it would appear that all Clamores and all of their associated Psalmi must be in the same mode. The 20 or so feasts to which these pieces are assigned are among the most ancient and important of the liturgical year. Hence, it appears that the oldest core of the Psalmo repertory is constructed from a single mode, even though the notation for these pieces does not suggest significant melodic similarities among them. It is not possible to say, however, how many other Psalmi might be in this same mode or how many other modes might be represented in the repertory of Psalmi as a whole.

The Clamores also bear on the question of whether the Psalmi might originally have included more than one verse as a general rule. The text for a Clamor is almost always taken from the psalm which provides the text for its Psalmo, and such an addition would have been pointless if the Psalmo already consisted of the entire psalm. Hence, if the Clamores and Psalmi are of equal antiquity, as is generally agreed, the Psalmi for which we have Clamores must not have consisted originally of entire psalms.

(vii) *Threni*. The 11 pieces bearing this name substitute for the Psalmi on certain days in Lent. Their texts are drawn from the books of *Job*, *Jeremiah* and the *Lamentations of Jeremiah*, and in the antiphoner of León all 11 pieces begin with the same refrain followed by three or four verses. Furthermore, all of the pieces, and all verses within each piece, make use of the same melismatic melody. As with the Psalmi in which refrain and verse share the same melody, the refrain of the Threni is not repeated after each of the verses. Hence, it is not entirely clear that they should be regarded as responsorial pieces. Their closest analogue in Gregorian chant is the tract, though this substitutes not for the gradual in Lent but for the Alleluia.

(*viii*) *Laudes*. The Laudes of the Mozarabic Mass correspond clearly to the alleluias of the Roman Mass. Outside Lent these pieces begin with the singing of the word 'alleluia' to a lengthy melisma. This is followed by a verse (though the usual rubric for verses does not appear here) which is neumatic in style, and this in turn is followed by a repetition, sometimes modified or expanded upon, of the initial alleluia melisma. Since the Laudes are grouped among the pieces sung in the manner of responsories, it seems likely that they were performed in much the same manner as the Gregorian alleluias, though the MSS do not indicate the specific roles of the soloists and choir. Like the Gregorian alleluias, too, the Laudes for the Mass may be grouped into a number of melodic families.

The Mozarabic Mass includes an item with the title 'Laudes' in Lent too. But since the word 'alleluia' itself is suppressed during this season, the Laudes of Lent have quite a different form from their non-Lenten counterparts. In most respects, they resemble the Psalmi and the Vespertini, for they are neumatic in style and consist of a refrain followed by one or two verses. And unless refrain and verse share the same melody, the final portion of the refrain is repeated after each verse.

(*ix*) *Sacrificia*. These correspond in function to the Gregorian offertories and are often quite long and highly melismatic. Each consists of a refrain followed by one or more verses (usually not from the Psalter), though the first verse following the refrain always bears the roman numeral *II*. In this and other respects, they resemble the Soni of the Office, and in fact, an occasional piece serves in both categories. In this connection, it should be remembered that in the Gallican rite the piece which corresponds to the Gregorian offertory and the Mozarabic Sacrificium is called the Sono.

The final portion of the refrain is repeated after each of the verses, and in this respect the Sacrificia resemble the Psalmi and other responsorial pieces. But the second prologue to the antiphoner of León does not include them in this category. Hence, because of other peculiarities such as the scheme for numbering their verses, they are best placed in a separate category along with the Soni.

(*x*) *Ad Pacem*. The few melodies sung during Mass at the giving of the kiss of peace bear only the rubric 'ad pacem'. They are, however, antiphons which share the psalm tones found with the antiphons of the Office.

(*xi*) *Ad Sanctus*. Chants bearing this rubric are provided for only a few important feasts. The texts, of which there are several different examples, are related to, but not the same as, the Sanctus of the Roman Mass. The rubric 'ad sanctus' is occasionally applied also to the Latin version of the Trisagion, which normally precedes the Benedictiones of the Mozarabic Mass.

(*xii*) *Ad confractionem panis*. Sung at the breaking of the bread, this piece most often bears the rubric *RS* for responsory. Unlike the responsories for the Office, however, it is rarely provided with a verse, even though a few melodies serve in both Office and Mass. The characteristic formulae for the verses of the Office responsories are never presented with the pieces for the Mass.

(*xiii*) *Ad Accedentes*. These melodies correspond in function to the communion antiphons of the Roman rite. They are similar to the Office antiphons in style and in the treatment of their verses, sharing with them the same psalm tones.

## BIBLIOGRAPHY

### EDITIONS

C. Blume: *Die mozarabischen Hymnen des alt-spanischen Ritus*, Analecta hymnica, xxvii (Leipzig, 1897)

M. Férotin: *Le liber ordinum en usage dans l'église wisigothique et mozarabe d'Espagne du V au XI siècle*, Monumenta ecclesiae liturgica, v (Paris, 1904)

J. P. Gilson: *The Mozarabic Psalter*, Henry Bradshaw Society, xxx (London, 1905)

M. Férotin: *Le liber mozarabicus sacramentorum et les manuscrits mozarabes*, Monumenta ecclesiae liturgica, vi (Paris, 1912)

J. Vives: *Oracional visigótico*, Monumenta hispaniae sacra, Serie litúrgica, i (Barcelona, 1946)

*Antifonario visigótico mozárabe de la Catedral de León*, Monumenta hispaniae sacra, Serie litúrgica, v/2, Facsímiles musicales, i (Madrid and Barcelona, 1953)

L. Brou and J. Vives: *Antifonario visigótico mozárabe de la Catedral de León*, Monumenta hispaniae sacra, Serie litúrgica, v/1 (Barcelona and Madrid, 1959)

I. Fernández de la Cuesta: 'El "Breviarium gothicum" de Silos', *Hispania sacra*, xvii (1964), 393–494

### CATALOGUES, ETC

W. M. Whitehill and J. Pérez de Urbel: 'Los manuscritos de Santo Domingo de Silos', *Boletín de la Real academia de la historia*, xcv (1929), 521–601

W. M. Whitehill: 'A Catalogue of Mozarabic Liturgical Manuscripts Containing the Psalter and Liber Canticorum', *Jb für Liturgiewissenschaft*, xiv (1934), 95

A. Millares Carlo: *Manuscritos visigóticos: notas bibliográficas*, Monumenta hispaniae sacra, Subsidia, i (Barcelona and Madrid, 1963); first published in *Hispania sacra*, xiv (1961), 337–464

K. Gamber: *Codices liturgici latini antiquiores* (Freiburg, 1963)

J. M. Mora Ontalba: 'Bibliografía general, ediciones de textos, trabajos y repertorios', *Estudios sobre la liturgia mozárabe*, ed. J. F. Rivera Recio (Toledo, 1965), 165

J. M. Pinell: 'Los textos de la antigua liturgia hispánica: fuentes para su estudio', ibid, 109–64

D. M. Randel: *An Index to the Chant of the Mozarabic Rite* (Princeton, 1973)

### SECONDARY LITERATURE

J. F. Riaño: *Critical and Bibliographical Notes on Early Spanish Music* (London, 1887/R1971)

W. Meyer: *Die Preces der mozarabischen Liturgie*, Abhandlungen der königlichen Gesellschaft der Wissenschaften zu Göttingen, Philologisch-historische Klasse, new ser., xv/3 (Berlin, 1914)

W. C. Bishop: *The Mozarabic and Ambrosian Rites: Four Essays in Comparative Liturgiology*, ed. C. L. Feltoe (London, 1924)

J. Pérez de Urbel: 'Origen de los himnos mozárabes', *Bulletin hispanique*, xxviii (1926), 5, 113, 209, 305

G. Prado: *Manual de liturgia hispano-visigótica o mozárabe* (Madrid, 1927)

——: *Historia del rito mozárabe y toledano* (Santo Domingo de Silos, 1928)

——: 'Mozarabic Melodies', *Speculum*, iii (1928), 218

P. Wagner: 'Der mozarabische Kirchengesang und seine Überlieferung', *Spanische Forschungen der Görresgesellschaft*, 1st ser., i (1928), 102–41

F. Cabrol: 'Mozarabe (Messe)', *Dictionnaire de théologie catholique*, x (Paris, 1929)

C. Rojo and G. Prado: *El canto mozárabe* (Madrid, 1929)

P. Wagner: 'Untersuchungen zu den Gesangstexten und zur responsorialen Psalmodie der altspanischen Liturgie', *Spanische Forschungen der Görresgesellschaft*, 1st ser., ii (1930), 67–113

H. Anglés: *El codex musical de Las Huelgas*, i (Barcelona, 1931)

W. S. Porter: 'Early Spanish Monasticism', *Laudate*, x–xii (1932–4), excerpted and trans. as 'Monasticismo español primitivo', *Hispania sacra*, vi (1953), 3–36

——: 'Studies in the Mozarabic Office I: the Verona Orationale and the Leon Antiphoner', *Journal of Theological Studies*, xxxv (1934), 266

H. Anglès: *La música a Catalunya fins al segle XIII* (Barcelona, 1935)

F. Cabrol: 'Mozarabe (La liturgie)', *Dictionnaire d'archéologie chrétienne et de liturgie*, xii/1 (Paris, 1935)

A. Millares Carlo: *Los códices visigóticos de la catedral toledana: cuestiones cronológicas y de procedencia* (Madrid, 1935)

G. M. Suñol: *Introducció a la paleografia Gregoriana* (Barcelona, 1925; Fr. trans., 1935)

H. Anglès: 'La música medieval en Toledo hasta el siglo XI', *Spanische Forschungen der Görresgesellschaft*, 1st ser., vii (1938), 1–68

L. Brou: 'Un passage de Tertullien conservé dans un répons pour la fête de S. Jean-Baptiste', *Ephemerides liturgicae*, lii (1938), 237

——: 'Le répons "Ecce quomodo moritur" dans les traditions romaine et espagnole', *Revue bénédictine*, li (1939), 144

H. Anglès: 'Hispanic Musical Culture from the 6th to the 14th Century', *MQ*, xxvi (1940), 494–528

——: *La música española desde la edad media hasta nuestros días* (Barcelona, 1941)

J. Enciso: 'El breviario mozárabe de la Biblioteca nacional', *Estudios bíblicos*, ii/2 (1943), 189

G. Prado: *Valoración y plan de reforma del rito mozárabe* (Madrid, 1943)

R. E. Messenger: 'Mozarabic Hymns in Relation to Contemporary Culture in Spain', *Traditio*, iv (1946), 149

L. Brou: 'Etudes sur la liturgie mozarabe: le trisagion de la Messe d'après les sources manuscrites', *Ephemerides liturgicae*, lxi (1947), 309

——: 'Le Psallendum de la Messe et les chants connexes', *Ephemerides liturgicae*, lxi (1947), 13–54

P. David: *Etudes historiques sur la Galice et le Portugal du VI au XII siècle* (Lisbon and Paris, 1947)

C. J. Bishko: 'Salvus of Albelda and Frontier Monasticism in Tenth-century Navarre', *Speculum*, xiii (1948), 559–90

L. Brou: 'Les "Benedictiones" ou cantique des trois enfants dans l'ancienne Messe espagnole', *Hispania sacra*, i (1948), 21

——: 'Les chants en langue grecque dans les liturgies latines', *Sacris erudiri*, i (1948), 165; iv (1952), 226

——: 'Bulletin de liturgie mozarabe, 1936–48', *Hispania sacra*, ii (1949), 459

——: 'Liturgie "mozarabe" ou liturgie "hispanique"?', *Ephemerides liturgicae*, lxiii (1949), 66

M. Huglo: 'Mélodie hispanique pour une ancienne hymne à la Croix', *Revue grégorienne*, xxviii (1949), 191

L. Brou: 'L'antiphonaire wisigothique et l'antiphonaire grégorien du VIII siècle', *AnM*, v (1950), 3

J. Moll Roqueta: 'Nuevos hallazgos de manuscritos mozárabes con neumas musicales', *AnM*, v (1950), 11

J. Pérez de Urbel: 'La reconquista de la Rioja y su colonización espiritual en el siglo X', *Estudios dedicados a Menéndez Pidal* (Madrid, 1950), i, 495–534

C. J. Bishko: 'Gallegan pactual monasticism in the repopulation of Castile', *Estudios dedicados a Menéndez Pidal* (Madrid, 1951), ii, 513–53

L. Brou: 'L'Alleluia dans la liturgie mozarabe', *AnM*, vi (1951), 3–90

——: 'Séquences et tropes dans la liturgie mozarabe', *Hispania sacra*, iv (1951), 27

——: 'Un antiphonaire mozarabe de Silos d'après les fragments du British Museum', *Hispania sacra*, v (1952), 341

——: 'Fragments d'un antiphonaire mozarabe du monastère de San Juan de la Peña', *Hispania sacra*, v (1952), 35–65

——: 'Notes de paléographie musicale mozarabe', *AnM*, vii (1952), 51

S. Corbin: *Essai sur la musique religieuse portugaise au moyen âge (1100–1385)* (Paris, 1952)

M. Huglo: 'Source hagiopolite d'une antienne hispanique pour le Dimanche des Rameaux', *Hispania sacra*, x (1952), 367

M. L. Povés: 'Los fragmentos de códices visigóticos de la Catedral de Santo Domingo de la Calzada', *Revista de archivos, bibliotecas y museos*, lviii (1952), 517

H. Allinger: *The Mozarabic Hymnal and Chant with Special Emphasis on the Hymns of Prudentius* (diss., Union Theological Seminary, New York, 1953)

H. Anglès: 'Mozarabic Chant', *NOHM*, ii (1954), 81

L. Brou: 'Le joyau des antiphonaires latins', *Archivos leoneses*, viii (1954), 7–114

M. C. Díaz y Díaz: 'Los prólogos del antiphonale visigothicum de la Catedral de León (León, Arch. Cat. 8)', *Archivos leoneses*, viii (1954), 226–57

J. Moll Roqueta: 'El canto mozárabe', *Arbor*, xxviii (1954), 380

J. Pérez de Urbel: 'Antifonario de León: el escritor y la época', *Archivos leoneses*, viii (1954), 115

J. M. Pinell: 'Las "missae", grupos de cantos y oraciones en el oficio de la antigua liturgia hispana', *Archivos leoneses*, viii (1954), 145–85

J. Vives: 'Fuentes hagiográficas del antifonario de León', *Archivos leoneses*, viii (1954), 288

L. Brou: 'Notes de paléographie musicale mozarabe', *AnM*, x (1955), 23

M. Huglo: 'Les "preces" des graduels aquitains empruntées à la liturgie hispanique', *Hispania sacra*, viii (1955), 361

J. Vives: 'En torno a la datación del antifonario legionense', *Hispania sacra*, viii (1955), 117

J. Pinell: 'El "matutinarium" en la liturgia hispana', *Hispania sacra*, ix (1956), 61

——: 'Vestigis del lucernari a occident', *Liturgica*, i (1956), Cardinali I. Schuster in memoriam, *Scripta et documenta*, vii (Montserrat, 1956), 91–149

A. A. King: *Liturgies of the Primatial Sees* (London, 1957)

J. M. Pinell: 'El oficio hispano-visigótico', *Hispania sacra*, x (1957), 385–427

L. Brou: 'Etudes sur le missel et le bréviaire "mozarabes" imprimés', *Hispania sacra*, xi (1958), 349–98

A. Franquesa: 'El codice emilianense 60 y sus piezas litúrgicas', *Hispania sacra*, xii (1959), 423

M. Rabanal Alvarez: 'Sobre algunas piezas griegas (transcritas) del antifonario visigótico-mozárabe de la Catedral de León', *Archivos leoneses*, xiii (1959), 67

L. Brou: 'Deux mauvaises lectures de chanoine Ortiz dans l'édition du bréviaire mozarabe de Ximenez: lauda, capitula', *Miscelánea en homenaje a Monseñor Higinio Anglés* (Barcelona, 1958–61), i, 173

H. Husmann: 'Alleluia, Sequenz und Prosa im altspanischen Choral', ibid, i, 407

E. Werner: 'Eine neuentdeckte mozarabische Handschrift mit Neumen', ibid, ii, 977

B. Thorsberg: *Etudes sur l'hymnologie mozarabe* (Stockholm, 1962)

J. López-Calo: 'Responsorium', §IV, *MGG*

J. M. Martín Patino: 'El breviarium mozárabe de Ortíz: su valor documental para la historia del oficio catedralicio hispánico', *Miscelánea Comillas*, xl (1963), 205–97

M. S. Gros: 'Les fragments parisiens de l'antiphonaire de Silos', *Revue bénédictine*, lxxiv (1964), 324

L. Brou: 'Ediciones de textos, investigaciones y estudios de los últimos treinta años', *Estudios sobre la liturgia mozárabe*, ed. J. F. Rivera Recio (Toledo, 1965), 2–31 [includes supplement by J. M. Pinell]

M. C. Díaz y Díaz: 'El latín de la liturgia hispánica', ibid, 55–87

E. Jammers: *Tafeln zur Neumenschrift* (Tutzing, 1965)

R. E. Messenger: 'The Mozarabic Hymnal', *The Hymn*, xvi (1965), 49

A. M. Mundó: 'La datación de los códices litúrgicos visigóticos toledanos', *Hispania sacra*, xviii (1965), 1

G. Prado: 'Estado actual de los estudios sobre la música mozárabe', *Estudios sobre la liturgia mozárabe*, ed. J. F. Rivera Recio (Toledo, 1965), 89

J. Bernal: 'Primeros vestigios del lucernario en España', *Liturgica*, iii (1966), *Scripta et documenta*, xvii, 21

M. S. Gros: 'El ordo romano-hispánico de Narbona para la consagración de iglesias', *Hispania sacra*, xix (1966), 321–401

J. Janini: 'Los fragmentos visigóticos de San Zoilo de Carrión', *Liturgica*, iii (1966), *Scripta et documenta*, xvii, 73

J. M. Pinell: 'Las horas vigiliares del oficio monacal hispánico', ibid, 197–340

R. F. Lechner: 'Mozarabic Rite', *New Catholic Encyclopedia*, x (New York, 1967)

I. Wortman: 'Mozarabic Rite, Chants of', ibid

C. W. Brockett jr: *Antiphons, Responsories and other Chants of the Mozarabic Rite* (Brooklyn, 1968)

D. M. Randel: *The Responsorial Psalm Tones for the Mozarabic Office* (Princeton, 1969)

——: 'Responsorial Psalmody in the Mozarabic Rite', *Etudes grégoriennes*, x (1969), 87–116

H. Anglès: 'Spanisch-mozarabische Liturgie', *Geschichte der katholischen Kirchenmusik*, ed. K. G. Fellerer, i (Kassel, 1972), 208

I. Fernández de la Cuesta and C. del Alamo: 'Fragmento de un salterio visigótico con notación musical', *Revista de Musicologia*, ii (1979), 9

DON M. RANDEL

**Mozart.** South German–Austrian family of musicians.

**(1) (Johann Georg) Leopold Mozart** (*b* Augsburg, 14 Nov 1719; *d* Salzburg, 28 May 1787). Composer, violinist and theorist.

1. LIFE. He was the son of an Augsburg bookbinder, Johann Georg Mozart (1679–1736), and attended the Augsburg Gymnasium (1727–35) and the Lyceum adjoining the Jesuit school of St Salvator there (1735–6). After his father's death he was directed towards a clerical career by his teachers and patrons, and in 1737 moved to Salzburg where on 26 November he enrolled at the Benedictine University. There he studied philosophy and jurisprudence, taking the bachelor of philosophy degree in the next year with public commendation; in September 1739, however, he was expelled for poor attendance at the college. He thereupon became a valet and musician to the Salzburg canon and president of the consistory Johann Baptist, Count of Thurn-Valsassina and Taxis, to whom he dedicated his six trio sonatas 'per chiesa e da camera' op.1 (1740),

which he himself engraved in copper. Shortly thereafter he appeared as a composer of German Passion cantatas and Latin school-dramas, and as a result he obtained a post in 1743 as fourth violinist in the court orchestra of the prince-archbishop. In addition he was made violin teacher to the choirboys of the cathedral oratory in the next year; later, in 1777, he also became a keyboard instructor there. It has been suggested that the court Kapellmeister at the time, Johann Ernst Eberlin (like Mozart a Swabian), was Mozart's teacher in composition; but this supposition, while attractive, lacks documentary support. In 1757 Mozart was appointed composer to the court and chamber; the next year he advanced to the post of second violinist in the court orchestra, and in 1763 to deputy Kapellmeister.

By this time Mozart had married Anna Maria Pertl, the wedding having taken place on 21 November 1747; of their seven children only two, (2) Maria Anna (*b* 1751) and (3) Wolfgang Amadeus (*b* 1756), survived to adulthood. In the same year as Wolfgang's birth Leopold published his *Versuch einer gründlichen Violinschule*, an epoch-making work of German music theory which made its 37-year-old author well-known, indeed famous, in European musical circles. In the preceding autumn, of 1755, Lorenz Mizler had petitioned for Mozart's membership in his Societät der Musicalischen Wissenschaften in Leipzig; the petition failed, however, for reasons unknown. Even the theorist F. W. Marpurg actively sought Mozart's collaboration; the anonymous 'Nachricht von dem gegenwärtigen Zustande der Musik . . . zu Salzburg' in the third volume of his *Historisch-kritische Beyträge* (1757) is generally held to be Mozart's, and Marpurg himself devoted a very flattering passage of his *Kritische Briefe* (i, 1759) to Mozart.

Around 1760 Mozart was at the height of his creativity. Shortly afterwards, however, as his daughter 'Nannerl' later reported, he 'gave up both violin instruction and composition in order to direct that time not claimed in service to the prince to the education of his two children'. Indeed, he seems to have composed rarely after 1762, and not at all from 1771, the year of his last work with a substantiated date of composition (the Symphony in D, no.25). Works by Mozart appeared in Breitkopf's catalogues for the last time in 1775. There is no 'late period' in Leopold Mozart's oeuvre.

The 'miracle which God let be born in Salzburg' changed Leopold's life; the recognition of this miracle must have struck the sober, critical, thoroughly 'reasonable' man with all the force of a divine revelation. It is particularly telling that he felt his responsibility to be not merely a father's and teacher's, but a missionary's as well: the 'miracle' required not just the most painstaking care and instruction, but was to be proclaimed to an unbelieving world ('I owe this act to Almighty God, otherwise I should be the most thankless creature', he wrote in a letter of 30 July 1768; 'And if it is ever to be my duty to convince the world of this miracle, it is so now, when people are ridiculing whatever is called miracle and denying all miracles. Therefore they must be convinced'). The numerous artistic and educational journeys which Leopold accordingly undertook – some with his entire family and others with Wolfgang alone – were financially dangerous and taxed to the extreme the patience of his overlord, the prince-archbishop; further, they must certainly have contributed to Wolfgang's weak health and premature physical collapse. Yet

Wolfgang's universal artistic development would have been unimaginable without these journeys.

This second period in Leopold Mozart's life can thus be understood only in its relation to Wolfgang's. It is as though Leopold gave up his own life to become a peripheral figure, albeit the most important one, in the biography of his son. His collaboration in Wolfgang's early works (up to about 1765–6) was probably quite considerable, though he seldom drew direct attention to it (an exception was the *Gallimathias musicum* K32). He played a more noticeable role as proofreader, editor and sometimes copyist; until the early 1770s scarcely a single autograph of Wolfgang's is without additions or alterations in his father's hand. Even later on, the notices of authorship and date are frequently by Leopold, who apparently preserved his son's manuscripts with painstaking orderliness. It was also Leopold who in 1768 drew up a manuscript catalogue of the most important works to that date. Thus the elder Mozart fulfilled a universal function as teacher, educator and private secretary to his son, and when necessary also served as valet, impresario, propagandist and travel organizer. Despite his own many rebuffs and setbacks at court, he was not beyond attempting to mediate in the ever worsening relations between his son and Prince-Archbishop Colloredo. The personal tragedy of his later life – the increasing alienation of his son, the misalliance (as he saw it) with Constanze Weber – was made the more severe as he saw the failure of his ambitions: Wolfgang was unable to reach a worldly position appropriate, in Leopold's opinion, to his genius. In spring 1785, while visiting Vienna, Leopold experienced his son's triumphs, noticed (not without mistrust) his apparent affluence, and heard with pride and satisfaction Haydn's famous words in praise of Wolfgang. He did not witness the financial catastrophe; he died, alone in spirit, in Salzburg. He was buried in the cemetery of St Sebastian. On the same day his long-standing friend Dominicus Hagenauer, Abbot of St Peter's in Salzburg, noted in his diary:

Leopold Mozart, who died today, was a man of much wit and wisdom, and would have been capable of good services to the state beyond those of music . . . He was born in Augsburg, spent most of his days in court service here, and yet had the misfortune always to be persecuted and was by far less beloved here than in other great places of Europe. He reached an age of 68 years.

Mozart's personality could not be more accurately summarized. Highly educated and with wide-ranging interests, an admirer of Gottsched as well as of Gellert (with whom he maintained a correspondence), a friend of Wieland, he was for almost a full half-century the only intellectual in the Salzburg court chapel. J. I. Bieling, T. F. Lipowsky, F. S. Rainprechter, Heinrich Marchand and the latter's sister Margarete Danzi, in addition to his own children, were among his pupils. A portrait of him (possibly by Lorenzoni, *c*1765; fig.1) and a drawing (probably by Count Firmian, *c*1762) survive (*A-Sm*); an engraving by J. A. Friedrich after M. G. Eichler appears as the frontispiece of his *Violinschule*. He is also depicted on the Carmontelle and Della Croce family paintings (see figs.3 and 9 below).

2. WORKS. Leopold Mozart's compositions are difficult to evaluate as long as it remains unclear to what extent his surviving works are representative of his entire oeuvre; further, any attempt to put his works into chronological order faces virtually insurmountable difficulties. The wide-ranging quality of his output seems

*1. Leopold Mozart: portrait (c1765) attributed to Pietro Antonio Lorenzoni in the Mozart Museum, Salzburg*

appear. In addition he has brought forth many concertos, in particular for the transverse flute, oboe, bassoon, Waldhorn, trumpet etc; countless trios and divertimentos for various instruments; 12 oratorios and a number of theatrical items, even pantomimes, and especially certain occasional pieces such as martial music . . . Turkish music, music with 'steel keyboard' and lastly a musical sleigh ride; not to speak of marches, so-called 'Nachtstücke' and many hundreds of minuets, opera dances and similar items.

The 'Nannerl Notebook', which Leopold began in 1759, served the young Wolfgang as well from 1760, and preserves some of his earliest compositions from the years 1761–3, most of them in Leopold's hand (though later some were entered by Wolfgang himself). As regards keyboard technique the book leads from the simplest of minuets to more demanding pieces by Agrell, Tischer and Wagenseil, and even to the level of a concerto (an unpublished fragment in G at the end of the book). Most of the anonymous pieces are probably Leopold's (the minuet and trio no.17, for example, are piano arrangements of his *Hochzeitsminuette* nos.9–10); the aria with variations in A, commonly attributed to Leopold or to Wagenseil (as no.96 in Scholz-Michelitsch's catalogue), is probably an early version of C. P. E. Bach's variations W118 no.2, circulated in manuscript. The so-called 'Notebook for Wolfgang' of 1762 is (contrary to Hermann Abert's view) an anonymous volume, most likely of central German provenance, with a forged dedication from Leopold to Wolfgang dating from the late 19th century.

The *Violinschule* of 1756 is of outstanding importance, a didactic work, which can stand alongside the corresponding essays by Quantz (on the flute, 1752) and C. P. E. Bach (on the keyboard, 1753). As regards its teaching of technique, Mozart in essence transmitted the Italian method, drawing particularly on Tartini; the general historical chapters bespeak his thorough knowledge of music theory as early as Glarean and Gaffurius. The violin method is also a valuable source for studying contemporary performing practice, musical taste and outlook. It should not be regarded as universally applicable to the music of W. A. Mozart and his contemporaries. Other projected literary works, including a biographical sketch of Wolfgang as a child prodigy (planned for a later edition of the violin method) and an edition of the travel letters, were never realized.

only in part explicable by its chronology; the particular occasion for each piece and the demands of the patron concerned played at least equally important roles. That he was capable of significant work as a composer is perhaps best shown in his great Sacrament Litany in D (1762) and the three piano sonatas that were published in his lifetime. His numerous, well-wrought symphonies mainly sought a light, conventional tone; outbursts of genius such as appear in the Symphony in F (no.5, c1760; unfortunately not published) are rare. It speaks for itself that a number of Leopold's compositions were until the 1960s or 1970s held to be Wolfgang's work (e.g. K115/166d and 116/90a). The much discussed 'popular' bias affects only one part of his work, and while certainly the most obviously attractive part it is not necessarily one of special importance. The frank naturalism that Mozart sought in performing his programmatic works is noticeable: in addition to bagpipes and hurdy-gurdy, the 'Bauernhochzeit' ('Peasant Wedding') Divertimento calls for a dulcimer and *ad libitum* whoops, whistles and pistol shots; the Sinfonia 'da caccia' demands, besides a bugle and a hunting-horn, boxes of ammunition and, if possible, dog yelps and various human cries of the chase. Curiously, Mozart seems to have composed nothing at all for his own instrument, the violin. The cursory list of works printed in Marpurg's *Historisch-kritische Beyträge* (iii, 1757) shows the uncertain basis at present for judging Mozart as a composer, and how little is actually known about this aspect of his activity:

Of Mr Mozard's compositions, which have become well-known in manuscript, one should mainly point out the many contrapuntal and other church items; further a great number of symphonies, some only à 4 but others with all the customary instruments; likewise more than 30 large serenades in which solos for various instruments

## WORKS

(*for detailed lists see Seiffert, 1908, Theiss, 1942, and Carlson, 1976*)
Editions: *L. Mozart: Ausgewählte Werke*, ed. M. Seiffert, DTB, xvii, Jg. ix/2 (Leipzig, 1908/*R*) [S]
    *W. A. Mozarts Werke*, ed. L. von Köchel and others (Leipzig, 1877–83, suppls. 1877–1910/*R* with changes) [W]

s – no. in Seiffert (1908)
т – no. in Theiss (1942)
к – no. in Köchel (6/1964)

### VOCAL

Sacred cantatas (oratorios), school dramas: Christus begraben (I. A. Weiser), Salzburg, 1741, rev. 1755, only libs extant; Antiquitas personata, Salzburg, 1742, pr. scenario extant; Christus verurteilt (Weiser), Salzburg, 1743, only lib extant; Der Mensch ein Gottesmörder (Weiser), early 1740s, parts *I-BZf* (see Tagliavini, 1963; Münster, 'Augsburger Gymnasialjahre', 1965); Geistliches Schäfergedicht [Der gute Hirte] (J. A. Schachtner), Salzburg, after 1754, only lib extant; Oratorium pro Quadragesima, MS copy formerly in collection of J. Liebeskind; other passion cantatas, lost, containing the extant arias: Du wahrer Mensch und Gott, s4.18, ed. in S; Weicht, zweifelnde Klagen, s4.19; So straft Herodes die Verräter, s4.20, ed. in S

Masses: Missa solemnis, C, s4.1, also falsely attrib. J. E. Eberlin; Missa solemnis, C, s4.2, before 1764; Missa [brevis], A [see Seiffert, p.xlix], parts *A-Sd*; Missa brevis, F [к116/90a and ккА18–19], frag., ed. in W xxiv, no.33, see Plath, *MJb 1971–2*; Missa brevis, C, к115/166d, partly identical with s4.2, frag., autograph *D-OF*, ed. in W xxiv, no.28, see Pfannhauser (1971–2); Sanctus–Agnus, C, s4.11, lost; Missa 1ma Ssmae Trinitatis, C, s4.4, score *A-Sca*, spurious; Gloria–Credo–Sanctus, A, s4.5, spurious, by J. E. Eberlin; Missa solemnis, C, s4.3, ĸAC1.20, ?by C. Vogel; Missa pastoritia, C, spurious, by B. Grueber, see Plath (1974)

Litanies: Litaniae de venerabili, C, s4.6, ed. in S; Litaniae Lauretanae de BVM, Eb, s4.7; Litaniae de BVM, Eb, s4.8; Litaniae Lauretanae, F, s4.9; Litaniae Lauretanae, G, s4.10; Litaniae de venerabili sacramento, E, see Seiffert, p.xlix, 1762, autograph *Sd*, see Senn, 1971–2, ed. in *W. A. Mozart: Neue Ausgabe sämtlicher Werke*, X:28/3–5/i (1973); Litanei, D, formerly *LA*

Other church music: Dixit Dominus, Magnificat, C, parts *D-Asa*; Miserere, F, s4.12, lost; Tantum ergo, s4.16; Veni Sancte Spiritus, C, s4.17; Offertorium de tempore et sub exposito venerabili (Convententur sedentes), s4.13, ĸAC3.09, ed. in W iii/23; Offertorium de Ssmo Sacramento (Parasti mensam), s4.14, ed. in S; Ad sacram Communionem (Confitemini Domino), s4.15; Aria (Rorate coeli), Bb, parts *YU-Zha*; Cantata pro Communione (Pulcherrimus mortalium), A, parts *D-Asa*; Aria de BVM (Helle Sonn' der düstren Sterne), D, parts *Asa*; Offertorium (Jubilate Domino), C, parts *Asa*; Cantata ad Communionem (Surgite), C, parts *D-TIT*; Offertorium Ss Trinitate (Omnes hodie), D, parts *Asa*, *TIT*; Aria [de Passione] (Traure, o verwaiste Seele), F, parts *A-Sn*; Aria pro Adventu (Christen, auf), Eb, parts *Sn*; Aria pro Adventu (Nur im Paradeyss), D, parts *Sn*; Offertorium, C, parts *SEI*; Sequenza (Veni Sancte Spiritus), autograph *GÖ* (doubtful)

Secular lieder: Bey dem Abschiede (Du dauerst mich) (J. C. Günther) and Die Rangordnung (Den Schönen, die mit holden Blicken), autograph, Hummel collection, Florence; Der Mensch seufzt stets in Kreuz und Weh, 1 Jan 1761, autograph *H-Bn*; Die grossmütige Gelassenheit (Ich hab' es längst gesagt) (Günther), ĸ149/125*d*, autograph *A-LIm*, ed. in W vii/1; Die Zufriedenheit im niedrigen Stande (Ich trachte nicht nach solchen Dingen) (F. R. L. von Canitz), ĸ151/125*f*, autograph *LIm*, ed. in W vii/1; Geheime Liebe (Was ich in Gedanken küsse) (Günther), ĸ150/125*e*, autograph *H-Bn*, ed. in W vii/1; 15 Lieder (Gellert), ĸAC8.32–46, possibly by L. Mozart, see Plath (1971–2); cadenzas for J. C. Bach arias, ĸ293*e*, see Plath (1971–2)

### SYMPHONIES

C: no.1, s3.1, TH.I, parts *D-B*; no.2, s3.2, TD.1, parts *HR*; no.3, s lost work no.1, TH.III.1, ĸAC11.01, 1st vn part *Mbs*

D [1–13]: no.1 'De gustibus non est disputandum', s3.3, TD.2, parts *HR*; no.2 'De gustibus non est disputandum', s3.4, TD.3, parts *HR*; no.3 'Non è bello quello che è bello mà quello che piace', s3.5, TD.4, parts *HR*; no.4, s3.6, TD.5, parts *HR*; no.5, s3.7, TD.6, parts *HR*, ed. in S; no.6, s3.8, TD.7, parts *HR*; no.7, s3.9, TD.8, parts *HR*; no.8, s3.10, TD.9, parts *HR*; no.9, s3.11, TD.10, parts *HR*; no.10, s3.12, TD.11, parts *HR*; no.11, s3.13, TD.11, parts *HR*; no.12, s3.14, TD.13, parts *HR*; no.13 'Non è bello quello che è bello mà quello che piace', s3.15, TD.14, parts *HR*

D [14–25]: no.14, s3.16, ĸ81/73*l*, probably by W. A. Mozart, see Seiffert pp.xxxviiiff and Köchel (6/1964); no.15, s3.17, TG.II, frag. parts *HR*, *A-Sca*, also attrib. B. Galuppi; no.16, TG.I, frag. parts *D-HR*; no.17, s lost work no.2, TD.16, parts *HR*; no.18, s lost work no.3, TH.III.2, parts *Asa*; no.19, s lost work no.4, TH.III.3, lost; no.20, parts *A-Ik*; no.21, parts *Ik*; no.22, parts *D-Asa*; no.23 'Jagd Parthia', formerly *A-LA*, lost; no.24, inc. parts *D-Asa*; no.25, TD.15, formerly *DO*, modern MS copy extant

Eb: no.1, formerly *A-LA*, lost

F: no.1, s3.18, TD.17, parts *D-HR*; no.2, s3.19, TD.18, parts *HR*; no.3, s3.20, TD.19, parts *Mbs*, *Asa*; no.4, s lost work no.5, TH.III.4, parts *HR*; no.5, c1760, parts *Tl*; no.6, parts *Asa*

G [1–9]: no.1, s3.21, TD.20, parts *HR*; no.2 'Sinfonia burlesca', s3.22, TD.21, parts *D-Asa*, ed. in S and in Diletto musicale, no.83 (Vienna, 1970); no.3 'Sinfonia pastorella', s3.23, TD.22, ĸAC11.13, parts *D-Asa*, *HR*, MS copies in score *A-Wgm*, *D-B*; no.4, s3.24, TD.23, parts *HR*; no.5, s3.25, TD.24, parts *HR*; no.6, s3.26, TD.25, parts *HR*; no.7, s3.27, TD.26, parts *HR*; no.8, s3.28, TD.27, ĸAC11.09, attrib. L. Mozart in Breitkopf catalogue suppl.X (1775), 3, but cf Köchel (6/1964); no.9 'Sinfonia da caccia', s3.29, TD.28, parts *HR*, *A-Wgm*, ed. in S and in Concertino, no.100 (Mainz, 1967), Eulenburg, no.580 (London, 1968) and in Diletto musicale, no.311 (Vienna, 1970)

G [10–20]: no.10, s lost work no.6, TH.III.5, lost; no.11, s lost work no.7, TH.III.6, lost; no.12, s lost work no.8, TH.III.7, lost; no.13, s lost work no.9, TH.III.8, lost; no.14, parts *D-Asa*; no.15, formerly *A-LA*, lost; no.16, parts *D-Asa*, ed. in NM, no.217 (1965), attrib. W. A. Mozart by Abert (1964, also *MJb 1964*); no.17, parts *A-Gd*, ed. in Diletto musicale, no.293 (Vienna, 1970); no.18, parts *Gd*, ed. in Eulenburg, no.539 (London, 1956); nos.19–20, formerly *LA*, lost

A: no.1, s3.30, TH.II, parts *D-Asa*; no.2, inc. parts *Mbs*

Bb: no.1, s lost work no.10, TH.III.9, parts *Asa*; no.2, s lost work no.11, TH.III.10, formerly *A-LA*, lost; no.3, s lost work no.12, TH.III.11, lost; no.4, formerly *LA*, lost; no.5, 1753, parts *Gd*, ed. in Diletto musicale, no.294 (Vienna, 1970); no.6, ĸAC11.02, formerly *LA*, W viii/i, see Köchel (6/1964); no.7, formerly *D-ZL*, lost; no.8,

s1.12, TA.III.1, arr. kbd in Raccolta delle megliore sinfonie, iii (Leipzig, 1761)

2 syms., discovered by Riemann, see *RiemannL 11*, 1218: 1 lost, 1 = Sym., D, no.17; 3 pastoral syms., lost, see letters of 15, 18 and 29 Dec 1755 to J. J. Lotter; Post Sym., lost, see note in MS of Sym., G, no.9, *A-Wgm*

A. A. Abert further attrib. W. A. Mozart's Symphony ĸ45*a* to Leopold; see Abert (1964, also *MJb 1964*)

### DIVERTIMENTOS, PARTHIAS, SERENADES

C: no.1 'Partia', parts *CH-Zz*, listed as sinfonia in *A-LA* and *D-ZL* thematic catalogues; no.2 'Parthia', formerly *A-LA*, lost; no.3 'Parthia', formerly *LA*, lost

D: no.1 'Divertimento militare cioè Sinfonia', s3.31, TE.I, parts *D-HR*, ed. in S; no.2 'Partita', s3.32, TE.III, score *GB-Lbm*, see Breitkopf catalogue V (1765), 13; no.3 'Die Bauernhochzeit, Divertimento', s3.33, TE.II, 1755, score and parts *D-B*, ed. in S and in Diletto musicale, no.259 (Vienna, 1972); no.4 'Parhia', formerly *A-LA*, lost; no.5 'Partita', mentioned in Breitkopf catalogue V (1765), 13; no.6 'Divertimento', s lost work no.13, TH.III.12, lost; no.7 'Serenata', parts *SEI*, movts iv and v identical with Tpt Conc. s3.34/TF.I, trio of movt iii identical with Vn Sonata ĸ6

F: no.1 'Die musikalische Schlittenfahrt, Divertimento', s1.11, TA.III.3 and E.V, 1755, parts *D-Mbs* [different work of same title by Wassmuth in *D-B* (attrib. L. Mozart and Wassmuth), rev. in *ZI* (attrib. W. A. Mozart, numerous later edns. as work of L. Mozart), cf Valentin, 1942–3]

G: no.1 'Cassatio', TE.VI, arr. L. Mozart from anon. 'Berchtesgadener Musik', see Münster (1969), ed. in Diletto musicale, no.300 (Vienna, 1974)

2 serenades, lost, mentioned in letter of 10 April 1755 to J. J. Lotter; 'Chinese' and 'Turkish' music, lost

### OTHER ORCHESTRAL

Concs.: Tpt Conc., D, s3.34, TF.I, Aug 1762, autograph *D-Mbs*, ed. in S, in Organum, 3rd ser., xxix (Leipzig, 1930), in Concertino, no.98 (Mainz, 1967), cf Serenata, D, no.7; Conc., 2 hn, Eb, s3.35, TF.II, 3 Aug 1752, parts *HR* (partly autograph); Ob Conc., F, mentioned in Breitkopf catalogue III (1763), 29, lost; Pf Conc., G, ĸAC15.02, only autograph sketches extant; 5 fl concs., lost, mentioned in letter of 24 Nov 1755 to J. J. Lotter (with incipits); 2 concs., 2 hn, D, mentioned in *D-SI* thematic catalogue, doubtful

Dances: 12 menuetti fatti per le nozze del Signore Francesco Spangler, s3.36, TE.IV, parts *A-Sca*, minuets nos.9 and 10 = minuet and trio no.17 in Nannerl Notebook; Minuet, ĸ64, possibly by L. Mozart, see Plath (1971–2)

### CHAMBER, KEYBOARD

Chamber, 3 insts, some with kbd: Sonate 6 per chiesa e da camera, 2 vn, b, s2.Trios 7–12, TC.II, parts (Salzburg, 1740), no.2 ed. in S, no.4 ed. in Hausmusik, no.177 (Vienna, 1955); 6 divertimentos, 2 vn, vc, s2.Trios 1–6, TC.I, parts *D-Mbs*, nos.1, 2, 4 ed. in S, 3 ed. in Organum, 3rd ser., xxx (Leipzig, 1930), no.1 ed. in Concertino, no.99 (Mainz, 1959); 3 trios, hpd obbl, vn, vc, s2.Trios 13–15, TC.III, parts *D-MMm*, formerly cycle of 6 works, nos.1, 3 and 6 lost, no.5 ed. in S; Divertimento, 2 vn, vc, parts *HR*; Divertimento, vn, vc, vle, parts *HR*; Parthia di Rane, vn, vc, b, formerly *A-LA*, lost; Divertimento, fl, vn, b, formerly *D-SI*, lost

Vn duos: 16 in 1st edn. of violin method (1756), ed. in Thesaurus musicus, vi (Budapest, 1959, 2/1965); 12 in Fr. edn. of violin method (1770), with Caprice, vn solo, s2. Solos, Duos, TB.I.II, nos.3 and 7 from sonatas nos.4 and 2 of G. P. Telemann: 18 canons mélodieux ou 6 sonates en duo (Paris, 1738), remainder probably by V. Roeser, duos ed. in Hortus musicus, no.78 (Kassel, 1951, 2/1963)

Kbd: 3 Sonaten, s1.1–3, TA.I.1.3, in Haffner's Oeuvres mêlées, iv (1759), vi (1760), ix (1762–3), ed. in S; 7 pieces in Der Morgen und der Abend ... oder 12 Musikstücke, kbd, ed. L. Mozart (Salzburg, 1759), nos.1, 6, 8, 11, 12 by J. E. Eberlin, remainder by L. Mozart, nos.8 and 10 ed. in S; Tempo di menuetto, 1 Jan 1761, autograph *H-Bn*; most of anon. pieces of the Nannerl-Notenbuch [minuet no.17 and trio identical with Hochzeitsminuette s3.36/TE.IV nos.9–10, aria and variations in A by ?C. P. E. Bach (see Plath, *MJb 1971–2*, 337)]

### THEORETICAL WORKS

*Versuch einer gründlichen Violinschule* (Augsburg, 1756/R1976, repr. 1922, 2/1769–70, enlarged 3/1787/R1956, 4/1800; Dutch trans., 1766/R1965; Fr. trans., 1770; numerous other unauthorized reprintings and edns; Eng. trans., 1939 [?1948], 2/1951) [see also vn duos above]

'Nachricht von dem gegenwärtigen Zustande der Music Sr. Hochfürstl. Gnaden des Erzbischoffs zu Salzburg im Jahre 1757', in F. W. Marpurg: *Historisch-kritische Beyträge zur Aufnahme der Musik*, iii (Berlin, 1757/R1970), 183

Various letters, notebooks etc, ed. in *Mozart: Briefe und Aufzeichnungen*, ed. W. Bauer, O. E. Deutsch and J. Eibl (Kassel, 1962–75); see also bibliography

Pedagogical: Nannerl-Notenbuch, 1759, *A-Sm*, part ed. E. Valentin

(Munich, 1956, 2/1969) [see also kbd works]; 'Notenbuch, seinem Sohne Wolfgang Amadeus . . . geschenkt', 1762, spurious; see Plath, *MJb 1971–2*, 337

## BIBLIOGRAPHY

### LIFE

J. E. Engl: 'Leopold Mozarts (des Vaters) Grabstätte', *Jahresbericht der Internationalen Stiftung Mozarteum*, xvii (1897), 24; xviii (1898), 27 [repr. in *Studien über W. A. Mozart*, v (1898), 3]

F. Wagner: 'Ein neues Bild Leopold Mozarts', *Mozart-Jb*, iii (1929), 303

O. E. Deutsch: 'Vater Mozarts Ende', *National-Zeitung Basel: Sonderausgabe* (30 May 1937), no.241

F. Posch: 'Leopold Mozart als Mensch, Vater und Erzieher der Aufklärung', *Neues Mozart-Jb*, i (1941), 49

H. F. Deininger, ed.: *Augsburger Mozartbuch*, Zeitschrift des Historischen Vereins für Schwaben, lv–lvi (1942–3) [incl. A. Sandberger: 'Festrede gehalten anlässlich der Eröffnung des Augsburger Mozarthauses', 31; E. F. Schmid: 'Mozart und das geistliche Augsburg', 40]

E. F. Schmid: *Ein schwäbisches Mozartbuch* (Lorch and Stuttgart, 1948)

——: 'Leopold Mozart', *Lebensbilder aus dem Bayerischen Schwaben*, iii (Munich, 1954), 346

——: 'Leopold Mozart: Vater und Mentor', *ÖMz*, xi (1956), 27

——: 'Neues zu Leopold Mozarts Bildungsgang', *Acta Mozartiana*, iii/1 (1956), 21

*Neues Augsburger Mozartbuch*, Zeitschrift des Historischen Vereins für Schwaben, lxii–lxiii (1962) [incl. O. E. Deutsch: 'Ein Rezept für den sterbenden Vater Mozart', 329; A. Layer: 'Leopold und Wolfgang Mozarts schwäbischer Bekannten- und Freundeskreis in Salzburg', 293; 'Beziehungen von Leopold und Wolfgang Amadeus Mozart zu Musikern des Augsburger Domstiftes', 245; 'Mozart und der fürstbischöflich Augsburgische Hof', 263; E. F. Schmid: 'Neues zu Leopold Mozarts Bildungsgang', 200; W. Senn: 'Zur Erbteilung nach Leopold Mozart', 383; E. Valentin: ' "Was der Schüler beobachten muss . . .": zu Leopold Mozarts Lehrtätigkeit', 324]

*De familie Mozart in Nederland* (The Hague, 1965) [exhibition catalogue]

J. Kay: *Mein Sohn Wolfgang Amadeus: Glück und Tragik des Vaters Leopold Mozart* (Vienna, 1965)

W. Lievense: *De familie Mozart in Nederland: een reisverslag* (Hilversum, 1965)

R. Münster: '. . . beyn Herzoge Clemens . . .: ein Beitrag zum Thema Mozart in München', *MJb 1965–6*, 133

——: 'Neues zu Leopold Mozarts Augsburger Gymnasialjahren', *Acta Mozartiana*, xii (1965), 57

L. Wegele: 'Augsburg und die Mozart', *Musik in der Reichsstadt Augsburg*, ed. L. Wegele (Augsburg, 1965), 149

R. Münster: 'München und Wasserburg am Inn als Stationen der Mozartreisen von 1762 und 1763', *Acta Mozartiana*, xv (1968), 32

L. E. Staehelin: *Die Reise der Familie Mozart durch die Schweiz* (Berne, 1968)

A. Layer: 'Leopold Mozart im Urteil seiner Zeitgenossen', *Schwäbische Blätter für Heimatpflege und Volksbildung*, xx (1969)

L. Wegele, ed.: *Leopold Mozart, 1719–1787: Bild einer Persönlichkeit* (Augsburg, 1969)

A. Layer: *Eine Jugend in Augsburg – Leopold Mozart 1719–1787* (Augsburg, 1976)

M. H. Schmid: *Mozart und die Salzburger Tradition* (Tutzing, 1976)

### WORKS

M. Friedlaender: 'Leopold Mozarts Klaviersonaten', *Die Musik*, iv/1 (1904), 38

W. Renz: 'Leopold Mozart als Komponist', *Die Musik*, iv/4 (1905), 351

M. Seiffert: 'Vorwort', *Ausgewählte Werke von Leopold Mozart*, DTB, xvii, Jg.ix/2 (1908/R) [with list of works; see review by J. Liebeskind, *ZIMG*, xi (1909–10), 361]

G. Schünemann: 'Leopold Mozart als Komponist', *AMz*, xxvi (1909), 1039

E. L. Theiss: *Die Instrumentalwerke Leopold Mozarts nebst einer Biographie* (diss., U. of Giessen, 1942; extracts in *Neues Augsburger Mozartbuch*, Zeitschrift des Historischen Vereins für Schwaben, lxii–lxiii (1962), 397–468) [with list of works]

E. Valentin: 'Musikalische Schlittenfahrt, ein Wolfgang Amadeus Mozart zugesprochenes Gegenstück zu Leopold Mozarts Werk', in H. F. Deininger, ed.: *Augsburger Mozartbuch*, Zeitschrift des Historischen Vereins für Schwaben, lv–lvi (1942–3), 440

E. F. Schmid: 'Leopold Mozart und die Kindersinfonie', *MJb 1951*, 69

E. Simon: *Mechanische Musikinstrumente früherer Zeiten und ihre Musik* (Wiesbaden, 1960) [incl. 4 pieces from Der Morgen und der Abend]

W. Plath: 'Beiträge zu Mozart-Autographie, I: die Handschrift Leopold Mozarts', *MJb 1960–61*, 82–118

L. F. Tagliavini: 'Un oratorio sconosciuto di Leopold Mozart', *Festschrift Otto Erich Deutsch* (Kassel, 1963), 187

A. A. Abert: 'Methoden der Mozartforschung', *MJb 1964*, 22 [on

Wolfgang's and Leopold's Lambach symphonies]

——: 'Stilistischer Befund und Quellenlage: zu Mozarts Lambacher Sinfonie K V Anh.221 = 45a', *Festschrift Hans Engel* (Kassel, 1964), 43

R. Münster: 'Wer ist der Komponist der "Kindersinfonie"?', *Acta Mozartiana*, xvi (1969), 76

M. H. Schmid: *Die Musikaliensammlung der Erzabtei St. Peter in Salzburg. Katalog I: Leopold und Wolfgang Amadeus Mozart, Joseph und Michael Haydn* (Salzburg, 1970)

K. Pfannhauser: 'Epilegomena Mozartiana', *MJb 1971–2*, esp. 299–304

W. Plath: 'Zur Echtheitsfrage bei Mozart: 2. Leopold Mozart', *MJb 1971–2*, 20

W. Senn: 'Das wiedergefundene Autograph der Sakramentslitanei in D von Leopold Mozart', *MJb 1971–2*, 197

W. Plath: 'Leopold Mozarts Pastoralmesse: unecht?', *Acta Mozartiana*, xxi (1974)

A. Weinmann: 'Neue Ergebnisse der RISM-Quellenforschung', *ÖMz*, xxix (1974), 440 [on Serenade in D, no.7]

D. Carlson: *The Sacred Vocal Works of Leopold Mozart* (diss., U. of Michigan, 1976) [with list of works]

### VIOLIN METHOD

K. Gerhartz: 'Die Violinschule von Leopold Mozart (1756)', *Mozart-Jb*, iii (1929), 243–302

K. von Fischer: 'Eine Neubearbeitung von L. Mozarts Violinschule aus dem Jahre 1804: ein Stilvergleich', *Mf*, ii (1949), 187

W. Egk: 'Anmerkungen zur Violinschule von Leopold Mozart', *Gestalt und Gedanke*, iv (1957), 28

W. Lidke: 'Übereinstimmung und Gegensatz der Violinschulen von Leopold Mozart und Louis Spohr', *Festschrift Louis Spohr* (Weimar, 1959), 67

E. Melkus: 'Über die Ausführung der Stricharten in Mozarts Werken', *MJb 1967*, 244

D. Themelis: 'Violintechnik in Österreich und Italien um die Mitte des 18. Jahrhunderts', *Der junge Haydn*, ed. V. Schwarz (Graz, 1972)

### CORRESPONDENCE, NOTEBOOKS

R. Genée: 'Mozarts musikalische Erziehung und ein bisher unbekannt gebliebenes Notenbuch von Leopold Mozart', *Mitteilungen für die Mozart-Gemeinde in Berlin*, iii (1908), 71

H. Abert: 'Leopold Mozarts Notenbuch von 1762', *Gluck-Jb*, iii (1917), 51–87

A. Schurig: *Leopold Mozarts Reiseaufzeichnungen 1763–1771* (Dresden, 1920) [facs. edn.]

H. Wiedenmann: 'Briefe von Leopold Mozart', *Zeitschrift des Historischen Vereins für Schwaben und Neuburg*, xlix (1933), 132 [letters to J. J. Lotter]

O. E. Deutsch and B. Paumgartner: *Leopold Mozarts Briefe an seine Tochter* (Salzburg and Leipzig, 1936)

L. Weinhold: 'Ein ungedruckter Brief Leopold Mozarts', *Neues Mozart-Jb*, ii (1942), 231

H. Klein: 'Ein unbekanntes Gesuch Leopold Mozarts von 1759', *Neues Mozart-Jb*, iii (1943), 95

E. Schenk: 'Ein unbekannter Brief Leopold Mozarts', *Sitzungsberichte der Österreichischen Akademie der Wissenschaften, phil.-hist. Klasse*, ccxxv/1 (Vienna, 1947)

E. H. Müller von Asow: 'Leopold Mozarts Münchener Reise 1786', *Musikerziehung*, viii (1954–5), 236

A. Kozár: *Wolfgang Amadeus Mozart (1756–1791) im Spiegel der Briefe seines Vaters Leopold Mozart: ein Beitrag zur Kulturgeschichte des 18. Jahrhunderts* (diss., U. of Graz, 1955)

A. Ostoja: *Mozart e l'Italia* (Bologna, 1955)

E. H. Müller von Asow: 'Zu Leopold Mozarts Wiener Reise 1785', *Musikerziehung*, ix (1955–6), 113

O. E. Deutsch: 'Drei neue Briefe von Leopold Mozart', *SMz*, xcvi (1956), 44

——: 'Leopold Mozart über seinen jungen Sohn', *Neue Zürcher Zeitung* (22 Jan 1956)

——: 'Noch ein Brief von Leopold Mozart', *SMz*, xcvi (1956), 291

H. Klein: 'Unbekannte Mozartiana von 1766/67', *MJb 1957*, 168

O. E. Deutsch: 'Ein neuer Brief Leopold Mozarts an seine Tochter', *Wissenschaft und Praxis: eine Festschrift . . . Bernhard Paumgartner* (Zurich, 1958), 57

D.-R. de Lerma: 'Händel-Spuren im Notenbuch Leopold Mozarts', *Acta Mozartiana*, v/1 (1958), 15

——: 'The Nannerl Notebook', *MR*, xix (1958), 1

H. Klein: 'Drei unbekannte Tagebuchnotizen über Leopold Mozart', *Neues Augsburger Mozartbuch*, Zeitschrift des Historischen Vereins für Schwaben, lxii–lxiii (1962), 137

W. Plath: 'Leopold Mozarts Notenbuch für Wolfgang (1762) – eine Fälschung?', *MJb 1971–2*, 337

For further bibliography see under (3) Wolfgang Amadeus Mozart, esp. biographies by Abert, Einstein, Schenk, Schurig and genealogical studies.

**(2) Maria Anna (Walburga Ignatia) Mozart** ['Nannerl'] (*b* Salzburg, 30 or 31 July 1751; *d* Salzburg, 29 Oct 1829). Pianist, daughter of (1) Leopold Mozart. She received her first music lessons from her father in 1758 and showed an early talent scarcely inferior to her brother's. Her first musical tour with her parents and brother took her in January 1762 to Munich, her second in September 1762 to Vienna, her third (which lasted until 1766) in June 1763 across western Europe, including London and Paris, where Baron Friedrich Melchior Grimm judged that she played the piano brilliantly and performed the greatest and most difficult pieces with an astonishing precision. In September 1767 Nannerl travelled again to Vienna with her father and brother, but without the expected success.

From 1769 onwards Nannerl was permitted to show her artistic gifts only at home. While her brother triumphed as a composer and virtuoso abroad, she remained with her mother in Salzburg. Nannerl tried her own hand as a composer, with results that met her brother's approval, but none of her compositions survives. In 1775 she and her father went to Munich for the première of *La finta giardiniera*, and again in 1781 for that of *Idomeneo*. On 23 August 1784 she married Johann Baptist von Berchtold zu Sonnenburg (*b* 22 Oct 1736; *d* 26 Feb 1801), a councillor and magistrate at St Gilgen. They had three children, Leopold Alois Pantaleon (1785–1840), Jeanette (1789–1805) and Maria Babette (1790–91). In early 1792 Nannerl wrote down some facts and recollections about her late brother for his biography by Schlichtegroll, in response to questions sent to her; her material (now in *A-Sm*), also used by Nissen, represents an important source for Mozart's early years in particular. Her diaries and letters, too, are central documents for the study of the Mozart family. Her brother, who wrote several works for her, including miscellaneous minuets and the Divertimento K251, was closely bound to her, at least until the time of their marriages.

After her husband's death in 1801 she returned to Salzburg with her children, and led a simple and peaceful life. She was active as a piano teacher; many pupils from bourgeois circles were keen to study with the great Mozart's sister. She was blind from 1825, and when Vincent and Mary Novello visited her in 1829 they found her 'blind, languid, exhausted, feeble and nearly speechless'; Mary Novello also remarked on her poverty and loneliness. In accordance with her will she was buried in the churchyard of St Peter's Abbey, Salzburg. Besides the childhood portrait ascribed to P. A. Lorenzoni (fig.2), she is depicted in the Carmontelle and (particularly well) in the Della Croce Mozart family portraits (figs.3 and 9 below).

BIBLIOGRAPHY

W. Hummel: *Nannerl: Wolfgang Amadeus Mozarts Schwester* (Vienna, 1952)
N. Medici di Marignano and R. Hughes: *A Mozart Pilgrimage: Being the Travel Diaries of Vincent and Mary Novello in the Year 1829* (London, 1955/*R*1975)
W. Hummel: 'Tagebuchblätter von Nannerl und Wolfgang Mozart', *MJb 1957*, 207
D.-R. de Lerma: 'The Nannerl Notebook', *MR*, xix (1958), 1
W. Hummel, ed.: *Nannerl Mozarts Tagebuchblätter mit Eintragungen ihres Bruders Wolfgang Amadeus* (Stuttgart, 1958) [see also K. Pfannhauser, *Mitteilungen der Internationalen Stiftung Mozarteum*, viii/1–2 (1959), 11]
W. Hummel: 'Nannerl Mozarts Tagebuchblätter: neue Funde – neue Fragen', *Mitteilungen der Internationalen Stiftung Mozarteum*, vii/3–4 (1958), 7

**(3) (Johann Chrysostom) Wolfgang Amadeus Mozart** (*b* Salzburg, 27 Jan 1756; *d* Vienna, 5 Dec 1791). Austrian composer, son of (1) Leopold Mozart. Along with Haydn, his senior by 24 years, and Beethoven, his junior by 15, he is one of the composers who brought the Viennese Classical style to its height. He was a child prodigy, and the experience of traversing musical Europe in that capacity during his most impressionable years not only left indelible marks on his character but was also far-reaching in its effects as regards the kind of composer he was to become. His style essentially represents a synthesis of many different elements, each taken for a while into his idiom, then in part rejected, in part absorbed. His mature music, distinguished by its melodic beauty, its formal perfection and its richness of harmony and texture, is deeply coloured by Italian opera though rooted in Austrian and south German traditions. Unlike Haydn and Beethoven, he excelled in every medium current in his time (especially in chamber music for strings, in the piano concerto and in opera): he thus may be regarded as the most universal composer in the history of Western music.

1. Ancestry and early childhood. 2. Paris and London, 1763–6. 3. Vienna and Italy, 1766–71. 4. Italian journeys, 1771–3. 5. Early instrumental works. 6. Early sacred music. 7. Early dramatic music. 8. 1773–4: the Vienna visit and its musical aftermath. 9. 1775–7: Salzburg. 10. 1777–80: Mannheim, Paris, Salzburg. 11. Music of 1777–80. 12. 1780–81: Munich. 13. Early Viennese years, 1781–4. 14. 1782–4: vocal works. 15. 1781–4: chamber and instrumental music. 16. 1781–4: orchestral music. 17. Vienna and Prague, 1785–8. 18. 1785–8: chamber and instrumental music: (i) Works without piano (ii) Works with piano. 19. 1785–8: orchestral music: (i) Piano concertos (ii) Symphonies. 20. Key associations. 21. Last years, 1789–91. 22. The Da Ponte operas. 23. Late instrumental works. 24. Late vocal music. 25. Appearance, iconography. 26. Posthumous reputation; Mozart studies.

*2. Maria Anna ('Nannerl') Mozart: portrait (1763) attributed to Pietro Antonio Lorenzoni in the Mozart Museum, Salzburg*

1. ANCESTRY AND EARLY CHILDHOOD. Wolfgang Amadeus Mozart, as he is universally known, was baptized in Salzburg Cathedral on the day after his birth as Joannes Chrysostomus Wolfgangus Theophilus. The first two names come from St John Chrysostom, whose feast falls on 27 January; the last was the name of his godfather, Joannes Theophilus Pergmayr (Mozart sometimes preferred the Latin form, Amadeus, more often Amadè, Amadé or the Italian Amadeo, and occasionally the German Gottlieb). He was the seventh and last child born to (1) Leopold Mozart and his wife Anna Maria, née Pertl (*b* St Gilgen, 25 Dec 1720; *d* Paris, 3 July 1778); only he and (2) Maria Anna (generally called 'Nannerl') survived infancy. He was born in a house in the Getreidegasse, now a Mozart museum.

The paternal ancestry of the family has been traced back with some degree of certainty to Ändris Motzhart, who lived in the Augsburg area in 1486; the name is first recorded, for a Heinrich Motzhart in Fischach, in 1331, and appears in other villages south-west of Augsburg, notably Heimberg, from the 14th century. The surname was spelt in a variety of forms, including Mozarth, Mozhard and Mozer. Several early members of the family were master masons (i.e. architects), builders, craftsmen and sculptors; two, in the late 16th and early 17th centuries, were artists. Mozart's great-grandfather David (*c*1620–1685) was a master mason, his grandfather Johann Georg (1679–1736) a master bookbinder in Augsburg. Others of his paternal ancestors were from Baden-Baden and Ober Puschthain. His mother's family came mainly from the Salzburg region (her father held administrative appointments at Hüllenstein, near St Gilgen), but one branch may be traced to Krems-Stein and Vienna. They mostly followed lower middle-class occupations; some were gardeners.

Mozart showed his musical gifts at an extremely early age. In his sister's music book, his father noted that he had learnt some of the pieces when he was four. His earliest known compositions, an Andante and Allegro K1*a* and *b*, were written, Leopold noted, early in 1761, when he was five. They are very brief, and modelled on the little pieces, many of them north German in origin, that his sister had been given to play (and which he also learnt; the 'Wolfgang Notenbuch' is a forgery). As they survive only in his father's handwriting, it is impossible to determine how far they are Mozart's own work.

Mozart's first known public appearance was at Salzburg University in September 1761, when he took part in a theatrical performance with music by Eberlin. Like other parents of his time, Leopold Mozart saw nothing improper in exhibiting, or in exploiting, his son's God-given genius for music. He took Wolfgang and Nannerl to Munich, for about three weeks from 12 January 1762, where they played the harpsichord before the Elector of Bavaria. No documentation survives for that journey. Later ones are better served – Leopold was a prolific correspondent and also kept travel diaries. The next started on 18 September 1762, when the entire family set off for Vienna; they paused at Passau and Linz for the children to perform before local noblemen or to give concerts. Except for a spell in December at Pressburg (Bratislava), at the invitation of a group of Hungarian patrons, they remained in Vienna until the end of the year, playing at the homes of various noblemen and appearing twice before Maria Theresia and her consort at Schönbrunn. The empress sent them a set of court clothes, which they wore for the well-

*3. Leopold Mozart and his children: watercolour (probably 1763–4) by Louis Carrogis de Carmontelle in the British Museum, London*

known paintings later done in Salzburg, probably by P. A. Lorenzoni. Leopold's reports of the children's triumphs, in letters to his friend and landlord Lorenz Hagenauer, are corroborated by the diary entries of Count Zinzendorf (see Deutsch, 1962): Mozart 'plays marvellously, he is a child of spirit, lively, charming'.

The family returned to Salzburg on 5 January 1763. In February Mozart played the violin and harpsichord in a concert at the Salzburg court. A report in an Augsburg newspaper in May tells of the kinds of performance: he could play in an adult manner, improvise in various styles, accompany at sight, play with a cloth covering the keyboard, add a bass to a given theme, and name any note that was sounded. There are numerous anecdotes about his precocity, most of them coming from accounts of him prepared after his death by his sister and a family friend, J. A. Schachtner (a poet, Salzburg court trumpeter, violinist and cellist). One story tells of his remembering, correctly, that Schachtner's violin was tuned an eighth of a tone lower than his own; another, of his taking a second violin part at sight and playing it perfectly, although he had had no violin lessons. Those events were in 1763. He was only four or five when, according to Schachtner, he tried to compose a concerto, which looked 'a smudge of notes' but Leopold found 'correctly and properly' composed. Schachtner further wrote of his docile and tender disposition: he was afraid of the trumpet, demonstratively affectionate with friends, high-spirited, eager to learn anything but preoccupied with music. He was also proud and ambitious, and willing to play only before people who took music seriously.

2. PARIS AND LONDON, 1763–6. It was natural that Leopold Mozart should want to take his son to Paris and London, the largest and most prosperous musical centres in Europe. The family set out on this ambitious trip in their own carriage, with a servant, on 9 June 1763: their intention was to visit every significant musical centre on the route, particularly those with courts where the children might be heard and generous gifts bestowed. Mozart usually played the local church organ at towns where they made overnight stops. They also did a great deal of sightseeing.

Their first important stop was Munich, where Mozart played at court. Next they went to Augsburg, Leopold's birthplace; here there was no court and they gave three public concerts. They travelled on to Ludwigsburg, the Duke of Württemberg's summer residence (the duke was away, but they met Jommelli, his Kapellmeister, and the violinist Nardini); then to Schwetzingen, the summer palace near Mannheim of the Elector Palatine Carl Theodor, who heard the children on 18 July. They passed on to Mainz; the elector there was ill, so they gave a public concert instead of playing at court. In August they were in Frankfurt, performing four or five times. They played again in Mainz, then in Koblenz, and in Aachen before Princess Anna Amalia of Prussia (who piqued Leopold by compensating them only with kisses). They now passed into the Austrian Netherlands, to Brussels, where they spent six weeks, having waited five of them for permission to play before the governor, Prince Charles of Lorraine.

They reached Paris on 18 November, and remained there for five months except for two weeks at Versailles, where on 1 January 1764 they played before Louis XV. No doubt they gave other private performances; they also met several musicians active in Paris, notably the Germans Schobert and Eckard, as well as Baron Grimm, a leading figure in literary circles. There Mozart published two pairs of sonatas for keyboard and violin – his first music to appear in print – with dedications to a royal princess and to a lady-in-waiting. They gave two public concerts and then, in April, left for London.

The family spent 15 months in England. They appeared at court, where George III gave Mozart some difficult tests at the keyboard soon after their arrival and twice more in the succeeding months; the children were heard at four concerts, one of them in Ranelagh Pleasure Gardens, and Leopold invited music lovers to visit them in private and put Mozart's 'Talents to a more particular Proof'. Mozart was extensively tested by the philosopher Daines Barrington, who in 1769 furnished a report on him to the Royal Society; it mentions among other things his improvisations at the harpsichord, including songs of love and of rage in an operatic style. Among the composers the family met in London was J. C. Bach, who was particularly friendly; this was the beginning of a lifelong influence. They improvised together on the harpsichord, but there is no evidence that Bach, as is sometimes said, gave Mozart lessons. While the Mozarts were in London, Leopold was ill, and they moved to the suburban calm of Chelsea; it was probably there that Mozart composed his first symphonies, some of which were given at their next con-

certs. Here and elsewhere the advertisements lopped a year off his age.

After this profitable period in London, the family travelled to Dover (pausing at Canterbury to attend a race meeting and stay with Horace Mann; a planned concert there was evidently cancelled) and embarked for Calais on 1 August 1765. They were obliged to wait a month at Lille, as Mozart was ill, before going on through Ghent and Antwerp, where he played on the local organs, to The Hague, arriving on 10 September. There they gave two public concerts and played before the Princess of Nassau-Weilburg, to whom Mozart dedicated a set of six keyboard and violin sonatas published in The Hague. Some keyboard variations on Dutch songs and a *Gallimathias musicum* (a potpourri) also come from the months in the Netherlands. In The Hague first Nannerl and then Wolfgang succumbed to 'intestinal typhoid'. They moved on in January 1766, and gave concerts in Amsterdam, Utrecht and Antwerp before returning through Brussels to Paris, where they remained for two months. Baron Grimm again heard the children and commented on Mozart's 'prodigious progress' since the preceding visit. He mentioned his symphonies, which had been well received in Paris, and referred to his encounters with experienced musicians, in which the boy had undergone the most difficult tests that could be devised and had left his interlocutors baffled. Mozart (as Daines Barrington also said) sang weakly but with great expression, and was 'une des plus aimables créatures qu'on puisse voir, mettant à tout ce qu'il dit et ce qu'il fait de l'esprit et de l'âme avec la grâce et la gentillesse de son âge'. The final stage of the homeward journey took several more months. They paused to play in Dijon, Lyons, Lausanne and Zurich; then they went into Germany and spent 11 days at Donaueschingen, with four-hour musical sessions with the Prince of Fürstenberg on nine of the evenings. They passed on through Dillingen and Augsburg to Munich, where they appeared at court (Mozart had to improvise on a theme supplied by the elector) and where Mozart was again briefly ill. They arrived back in Salzburg on 29 or 30 November, bearing a large number of gold rings, watches and snuffboxes.

3. VIENNA AND ITALY, 1766–71. Mozart spent the next nine months in Salzburg; during this period he wrote some fugues, but there is no evidence that he had any formal musical tuition. Nor, probably, did he – at any time – undergo formal schooling. He learnt Latin when young, and soon had a command of Italian (later also some French and English); the report that he enjoyed arithmetic is borne out by various numerical games and jottings on his manuscripts. A remark by Schachtner implies, probably correctly, that all his tuition came from Leopold.

During these months he arranged some concertos, from sonatas mainly by composers he had met in Paris, and wrote three vocal works – a Latin comedy *Apollo et Hyacinthus* for the university, the first act of a joint work, the oratorio *Die Schuldigkeit des ersten Gebots* (Michael Haydn and Adlgasser wrote Acts 2 and 3), and a piece of Passion music. It was probably this last that, according to Daines Barrington, Mozart composed in isolation in a locked room so that the Archbishop of Salzburg could satisfy himself that the claimed compositions were in fact the child's own work; traditionally the piece concerned has been thought to be *Die*

*4. A page from Mozart's 'Die Schuldigkeit des ersten Gebots' K35 (opening of no.4), composed early 1767 (Royal Library, Windsor Castle)*

*Schuldigkeit*, but the state of the autograph, with Leopold's emendations, rules it out.

In September 1767 the family set out for Vienna; their 15 months there are documented by Leopold's letters to Hagenauer. The visit was presumably timed to coincide with the festivities planned for the marriage of an archduchess, who however died during a smallpox epidemic before the wedding date. The combination of court mourning and the risk to their health induced Leopold to take his family out of Vienna after six weeks, on 26 October, to Brünn (Brno) and then to Olmütz (Olomouc). There Mozart and then Nannerl had mild attacks of smallpox. In December they returned to Brünn, giving a concert there, and arrived on 10 January 1768 in Vienna, where they were soon heard at court. By the beginning of February Leopold had conceived a plan for Mozart to compose an opera for production there; the emperor gave his consent and Gluck offered guarded encouragement. It was to be an *opera buffa*, called *La finta semplice*. The plan was unsuccessful. Leopold's letters, and his indignant petition in September to the emperor, tell a sordid story of intrigues. Mozart may however have had some small compensation for the suppression of *La finta semplice* if, as is generally supposed, his one-act Singspiel *Bastien und Bastienne* was given privately, about October, at the home of Dr Franz Anton Mesmer, the inventor of 'magnetism therapy'. Moreover, on 7 December, he directed a performance before the imperial court of a substantial, festal mass setting (K139/47a), along with other works (notably a trumpet concerto, now lost), at the dedication ceremony of the Waisenhauskirche. About the end of the year they set out for Salzburg, probably pausing at the Lambach monastery, presenting to the library scores of symphonies by both Leopold

and Wolfgang. This may have been in return for hospitality; they often stayed at monasteries rather than inns during their travels.

The Mozarts arrived back in Salzburg on 5 January 1769 and remained there nearly a year. During that time *La finta semplice* was performed at the theatre in the archbishop's palace, probably on or about 1 May, and Mozart wrote a new mass setting (K66) for performance, in October, at the first Mass celebrated by his friend Cajetan Hagenauer (Father Dominicus). To this period also belong some other, shorter sacred works, several sets of minuets for dancing, and three substantial orchestral serenades or cassations, of which two were probably 'Finalmusiken' for the ceremonies traditionally held by the faculties of Salzburg University at the end of the academic year. On 27 October Mozart was appointed, on an honorary basis, Konzertmeister to the Salzburg court.

Leopold had long planned to take his son to Italy, and was anxious to do so while Wolfgang was young enough for his talents to arouse wonder. He was doubtless also keen to visit the land that was the main source of stylistic novelty at the time, particularly in opera. They set out on 13 December, this time without Mozart's mother or sister. Their letters home are the principal source of information on their journey and activities.

The journey followed the now usual pattern: they paused at any town where a concert could be given, or where an influential nobleman might wish to hear Mozart play. They travelled to Innsbruck, giving a concert privately there, then to Rovereto, where Mozart played privately and on the organ at S Marco. In Verona he played at S Tommaso and at the Accademia Filarmonica, where he was given improvisation and sight-reading tests, and produced an impromptu written

5. *Wolfgang Amadeus Mozart: portrait (early 1770) probably by Saverio dalla Rosa, formerly attributed to Felice Cignaroli (private collection); the music he is playing is presumed to be by Mozart himself (this is its only source) and is entered in the Köchel catalogue (3/1937) as* K72a

piece. He also had a portrait painted, probably by Saverio dalla Rosa (fig.5); the piece of music shown on the harpsichord is taken to be a work by him, otherwise unknown (K72a). They next paused at Mantua, where the surviving programme of his concert, in the monthly series given by the Accademia Filarmonica, shows that he was put through tests of a particularly stringent kind. They passed on to Cremona, hearing there an opera by Hasse, to Milan, where they arrived on 23 January 1770. Here their chief patron was Count Firmian, the Austrian minister plenipotentiary, at whose house Mozart played several times as well as giving a public concert. Milan was an important cultural centre. They met G. B. Sammartini, the senior composer there, and Piccinni, and initiated arrangements for Mozart to write the first opera for the Carnival season in December; it seems that he was required to prove his ability to fulfil such a commission by submitting some arias (K88/73c, 77/73e).

They left Milan on 14 March; stopping the next night at an inn in Lodi, Mozart completed his first string quartet. They travelled through Parma, where they met the soprano Lucrezia Aguiari, reaching Bologna on 24 March; there they spent five days, giving a concert at Count Pallavicini's house, twice visiting the esteemed theorist and composer Padre Martini, with whom Mozart wrote some fugues, and meeting the famous castrato Farinelli. At Florence, where he played twice,

privately, he met the castrato Manzuoli, an old acquaintance from London, and the English composer Thomas Linley, a boy of his own age, with whom he quickly made friends.

Mozart and his father then passed on to Rome, where they arrived on 10 April, in time for Holy Week, and stayed for a month. They gave several performances in private houses, and did much sightseeing. In the Sistine Chapel they heard the *Miserere* for double choir of Gregorio Allegri (1582–1652), traditionally, Leopold wrote, considered the exclusive preserve of the choir there; Mozart wrote it out from memory on a single hearing. He composed at least two symphonies in Rome. On 14 May they reached Naples, where they stayed until 25 June: they gave several concerts, did more sightseeing (including Pompeii and Vesuvius) and probably made two visits to the opera, one of them for Jommelli's *Armida*, which Mozart thought 'beautiful, but much too broken up and old-fashioned for the theatre'. Then they returned to Rome, where the papal Order of the Golden Spur was conferred on Mozart, and he had an audience with the pope; Gluck and Dittersdorf had also received the order, but Mozart's was in a higher rank, that of knight.

They left Rome on 10 July and travelled, through Loreto, Spoleto and Rimini, to Bologna. The summer was spent nearby at Count Pallavicini's house, where Mozart composed some sacred works and canons (and possibly symphonies) and received the libretto and cast list of his opera for Milan. Before they left Bologna he underwent and passed tests for admittance to membership of the ancient and esteemed Accademia Filarmonica; the surviving manuscripts of his test piece (an antiphon on a cantus firmus, K86/73*v*), with annotations by Martini, and his clean copy of a reworking, suggest that he had help. A similar honour from the Verona Accademia Filarmonica followed in 1771.

The Mozarts reached Milan on 18 October 1770. Work could now start in earnest on the composition of the opera, *Mitridate, rè di Ponto*. The libretto, by Vittorio Amadeo Cigna-Santi after Racine, had been set by Quirino Gasparini for Turin in 1767. Leopold discussed in his letters various intrigues among the singers, including the possibility of their substituting certain of Gasparini's settings for Mozart's; one of Gasparini's may in fact have been sung in the performance. He also reported the singers' enthusiastic approval of the music, but did not mention that – as the autograph material shows – Mozart rewrote several arias, presumably because the first versions failed to please. There were three recitative rehearsals, two preliminary orchestral rehearsals and two full ones in the theatre, and a dress rehearsal. The première, at the Regio Ducal Teatro, was on 26 December 1770; including the ballets (by other composers), it lasted six hours. Leopold had not been confident that the opera would be a success, but it was, and there were 22 performances of which Mozart, in the traditional way, directed the first three from the harpsichord.

The Mozarts left Milan on 14 January 1771 for Turin, then had four days back in Milan before going on to Venice, where they spent a happy month from 11 February with friends of the Hagenauers and gave a concert; they then moved on to Padua and Verona, pausing briefly to play in each, then back to Salzburg, where they arrived on 28 March. During these 15 months Mozart had increasingly added postscripts, usually addressed to his sister, to his father's letters home, supplementing Leopold's sharp, hard-headed, detailed reports with some high-spirited, boyish observation or an affectionate greeting, and occasionally some absurd obscenity. Later his notes often contained cryptic, amorous messages to girls in Salzburg.

4. ITALIAN JOURNEYS, 1771–3. Before they left Italy the Mozarts laid plans for return journeys. A contract had been agreed for a further Milan opera at the end of 1772, and apparently an oratorio had been commissioned for Padua (though seemingly it was never performed); an opera for Venice was mooted, but Mozart would have had to be there when he was already committed to Milan, and the negotiations came to nothing.

The second Italian visit was in fact in 1771, not 1772. At Verona in March 1771 Leopold had received a letter commissioning a serenata or *festa teatrale* from Wolfgang for performance in Milan the following October on the marriage of the Archduke Ferdinand (his letter home expresses delight at news of the commission, but the idea must have been contemplated earlier: Burney, who saw the Mozarts in Bologna in the summer, referred in his diaries on 30 August 1770 to Mozart's projected opera for this wedding).

So Mozart had barely five months at home in 1771; during that time he wrote the Paduan oratorio, *La*

*Betulia liberata*, some sacred works and probably some symphonies. He and his father arrived in Milan on 21 August. About a week later he was given the libretto, by Giuseppe Parini, for the serenata, *Ascanio in Alba*. Leopold remarked on the friendship and respect with which Mozart was treated by everyone, including Hasse (who was composing an opera for the festivities) and the singers. By 23 September the score was complete; there were separate ballet and choral rehearsals, and four general rehearsals, before the performance on 17 October. According to Leopold it was 'an extraordinary success . . . I am sad to say that Wolfgang's serenata has completely overshadowed Hasse's opera'. There were at least two, possibly four, further performances. The Mozarts remained until 5 December in Milan, where Wolfgang wrote a divertimento and at least one symphony, and they gave a concert. It seems that Mozart applied for employment in Archduke Ferdinand's service; a letter to the archduke from his mother, the Empress Maria Theresia, advised him against burdening himself with such useless people, and that the Mozarts' habit of going 'about the world like beggars' would degrade his service. Others, it seems, felt similarly. By 15 December the Mozarts were back in Salzburg.

The next ten months were spent at home. Just after their return the prince-archbishop, Sigismund, Count Schrattenbach, died: he had been a tolerant employer, ready to allow Leopold prolonged (if sometimes unpaid) spells of leave. His successor, Hieronymus, Count Colloredo, was enthroned on 14 March 1772. For the celebrations Mozart composed a serenata, *Il sogno di Scipione*, possibly performed in May. These were prolific months: Mozart composed eight symphonies, four divertimentos and some substantial sacred works. On 9 July he was formally taken into the employment of the court, with a salary as Konzertmeister of 150 florins; he had held the post in an honorary capacity for nearly three years.

The third and last Italian journey began on 24 October 1772. Probably Mozart had been sent the libretto and cast list for the new Milan opera, *Lucio Silla*, during the summer, and had already set the recitatives; at any rate, it was the composition of a string quartet that occupied him on the journey. On his arrival in Milan he had to adjust the recitatives to accommodate changes made by the poet, Giovanni de Gamerra. He then wrote the choruses, and composed the arias for the singers in turn, having first heard each of them sing so that, in the accepted way, he could suit the music to their voices. There was a recitative rehearsal, then three rehearsals with orchestra and a dress rehearsal, interspersed with lengthy musical parties in the evenings given by Count Firmian. The première, on 26 December, which began three hours late and lasted six, was a mixed success, mainly because of a patchy cast, but the opera ran for 26 performances. In January Mozart wrote a solo motet, *Exsultate, jubilate*, for the primo uomo in the opera, Venanzio Rauzzini, who was himself a composer; some string quartets also belong to these months in Milan. The Mozarts remained there until the beginning of March: Leopold, anxious to find his son a post outside Salzburg, had applied to the Grand Duke of Tuscany and feigned illness to postpone the return journey while awaiting a reply. If one came, it was unfavourable.

They arrived back in Salzburg on 13 March. The next four months were spent at home, where Wolfgang composed four symphonies, a mass and probably some shorter sacred works and two divertimentos.

5. EARLY INSTRUMENTAL WORKS. The question of how much of the early music attributed to Mozart he himself actually composed can never be fully answered. That many of these pieces survive only in his father's hand, or in composite autograph, often with heavily corrected texts, does not necessarily argue conclusively against Mozart's authorship; and stylistic arguments are even more hazardous. Doubtless Leopold sometimes wrote down Wolfgang's improvisations, made fair copies, partial or complete, of Wolfgang's unclear originals, and inserted corrections of his own. Doubtless, too, he made suggestions that found their way into Wolfgang's own copies. Particular suspicion, however, is bound to attach to those items where the surviving manuscripts are largely in Leopold's hand, including the earliest keyboard pieces and parts of the Paris keyboard and violin sonatas, K6–9, especially K8. (For a full and penetrating discussion, see Plath, 1960–61.)

Mozart's earliest claimed compositions were short keyboard pieces, probably dating from his sixth year. Although most of them survive only in Leopold's hand, these simple works are likely to be at least partly Mozart's own; and Leopold left enough of naive charm and harmonic solecism for plausibility. They imitate the manner of the keyboard miniatures in the notebooks Leopold drew up for his children's use. In the sonatas for keyboard and violin published in Paris in 1764 – works in the most popular and commercially salable form of the day – the models were the sonatas of Schobert and the other Germans in Paris. The music is somewhat mechanical in its textures (with much Alberti bass) and its melodic matter, with heavy reliance on sequential patterns; much here seems to represent an inventive boy's exploration of harmonic and textural possibilities.

The London sonatas, for keyboard and violin with optional cello (K10–15), show the same influences and preoccupations. But the London symphonies, or such of them as survive, represent a large step forward. Less so the very first (K16), which uses cliché with a mildly appealing simplicity and enthusiasm, than K19 in D, which shows in the first movement a remarkable grasp of the principles of J. C. Bach's symphonic style, for example the dramatic contrast of a *forte* motto opening with a *piano* continuation and the hint of a cantabile second subject, and possesses an Andante of Italianate melodic grace. Both symphonies have vigorous finales in 3/8 time, of a kind favoured by J. C. Bach and many Italian and English symphonists. As a parody of a well-formed style, this is an astonishing piece of work for a boy of nine, and its technical accomplishment is equally impressive. The same line of development is pursued in the B♭ Symphony K22 composed in The Hague, with its sharply outlined form and the maturer command of texture shown in the small-scale imitative writing. The accompanied sonatas written a few weeks later in The Hague (K26–31) sometimes show a neater handling of form than the earlier ones.

The next group of instrumental works comprises four keyboard 'concertos', prepared, presumably, for concert tours: they consist of sonata movements, mostly by German composers active in Paris (including Raupach, Honauer and Schobert), to which Mozart added orchestral tuttis and accompaniments, making other minor

changes here and there. More important are the symphonies composed during or around the Vienna visit of 1767–8, where the influence of the Viennese symphonic style is seen. It is notable in the full, energetic orchestral style of K43, and in its inclusion of a minuet; slightly less so in K45, a spirited D major work with strong *opera buffa* overtones (it was in fact used as the overture to *La finta semplice*); and strikingly evident in K48, which has a first movement showing strong momentum, busy textures, a substantial development section and a well-defined recapitulation. This is Mozart's earliest symphony first movement to include a clearly marked restatement of the primary material; previous ones follow the extended binary form preferred by J. C. Bach and many Italians. The Andantes are mostly binary movements of a simple melodic cast; that of K43 draws on a duet from *Apollo et Hyacinthus*. There are typically sturdy Viennese minuets, and finales which retain gigue-like rhythm but are more fully worked out and formally neater and better defined. Stylistic arguments indicate that the 'New Lambach' symphony, rather than the 'Old Lambach' K45a, may be Mozart's.

Three serenades probably date from the following summer, K100/62a, 63, and 99/63a. Following the Austrian serenade tradition, represented at Salzburg by Michael Haydn, each has six or more movements and an associated introductory (and perhaps valedictory) march; there is a bustling, rather loosely textured opening allegro, two or even three cheerful minuets, and a rollicking finale. The most refined invention is reserved for the slow movements, of which one generally has a concertante part (in K63 for violin, 100/62a for oboe and horn) and the other is of a straightforward melodic character; K100/62a, in eight movements, also has concertante parts in a fast movement and the trio of one of its minuets, a pattern that later became standard.

The next orchestral works date from the first Italian journey. Probably Mozart wrote five symphonies in Italy. The four in D, K81/73l, 97/73m, 95/73n and 84/73q (the authenticity of K81 and 84 has been questioned, though not convincingly), may be the ones referred to in Mozart's letter of 4 August 1770: 'habe ich schon 4 itallienische Sinfonien componirt'. They are alike in their light textures, their lively, mechanical string figuration and their slender thematic material. Their first movements mostly have little or no development but a full recapitulation. Also from the Italian journey is K74 in G, similar in pattern to the D major works, whose linked first two movements suggest that it may originally have been intended as an opera overture, presumably to *Mitridate*. The manner of these symphonies shows Mozart influenced by the music he encountered in Italy, and keen to please Italian audiences, or both. There may also have been an element of emulation and competition, a pattern that was to continue.

Further symphonies followed between and during the two briefer Italian journeys. The more extreme aspects of Italian style have disappeared in K73, 75 and 110/75b, but the formal pattern remains. Of the three symphonies from late 1771, K96/111b is much concerned with orchestral brilliance and in particular the kind of imperious effect associated with the use of trumpets and drums in a C major work, and K112 is notable mainly for its first movement, a well-formed example of the *buffo* manner. K114 in A, composed back in Salzburg, embodies new elements. There is a chamber-music fineness of style, and a particular care over proportion and harmonic logic. While in most symphonies the outer movements require oboes and horns, and occasionally flutes instead of oboes in the slow movements, here there are flutes in all but the Andante; doubtless the choice of the higher instruments was dictated by textural considerations contingent on the use of high-pitched horns, needed in A major, but Mozart characteristically let the softer-toned wind section colour the actual invention.

Seven further symphonies belong to 1772. The first two (K124 and 128) show no special advance, except possibly in incorporating something close to development procedures in a predominantly *buffo* context, and in the growing textural interest of their slow movements; the next, K129, reverts surprisingly to the manner of J. C. Bach. All three throw greater weight on the finale than hitherto, and K130 goes further, with the most substantial finale Mozart had yet composed – in full sonata-allegro form, with a brief development but an extended second group. This symphony is exceptional, too, for the three-bar phrases in its Andantino and for its orchestration, with flutes preferred to oboes and (no doubt because extra players were briefly available) four horns. K132, Mozart's first symphony in E♭ since K16, and again requiring four horns, is more assured; its opening motto phrase, treated with the *forte–piano* polarity favoured by J. C. Bach, is one of a kind Mozart often used in this key (cf K364/320d, 375, 449, 482). The style is predominantly *buffo*, and the 'development' a neatly proportioned transition. For the slow movement, a 3/8 Andante, Mozart later provided a replacement, a 2/4 Andantino, shorter but texturally less plain. There is a minuet embodying a good deal of small-scale imitative treatment, a harmonically quizzical trio, and a *gavotte en rondeau* finale, more boisterously Viennese than French. The stylistic synthesis that this symphony represents is maintained in K133, whose D major brilliance places it firmly in the line of the Italianate symphonies. But it is texturally richer and better developed; and the implied 'Mannheim crescendo' of the opening is counterpoised by another Mannheim usage, the dramatic reappearance of the opening material, not previously recapitulated, in the coda. The influence of Haydn has been remarked (Wyzewa and St Foix, 1912–46), and of M. G. Monn (Fischer, Neue Mozart-Ausgabe preface). This group ends with another work in A (K134), like K114 using flutes and horns and in a more chamber-musical style. Its first movement is among Mozart's most closely argued, and its opening phrase is much heard in the exposition tuttis and in the development; the primary theme recurs at the end of the exposition, a usage associated with Haydn, lending logic to the absence of a full recapitulation. The expressive melodic tag that begins the Andante is one that Mozart specially favoured (cf 'Porgi amor', *Le nozze di Figaro*).

The symphonies of this group (which may be augmented by two: Mozart added finales, K120/111a and 161/141a, to make concert works out of two-movement overtures) were probably composed mainly for use in Salzburg, perhaps in connection with Mozart's post as Konzertmeister. Various other orchestral works were written for specific occasions. The three keyboard concertos K107 arranged, probably in 1772 (not 1765, as was long stated), from J. C. Bach sonatas may have been intended for performance on tour, when just two

violins and a bass instrument could be called upon; Leopold copied out the sonatas, Mozart added the ritornellos and accompaniments (see fig.6). A 'Concerto ò sia Divertimento' K113 was written in Milan, his first use of clarinets; he revised it early in 1773, with oboes, english horns and bassoons, enabling the clarinets to be omitted.

The term 'divertimento' implies performance by a small ensemble, one to a part; 'serenade' implies orchestral performance. Four works of 1772 are known as 'divertimento', but for K131 the title is unauthentic and the work has characteristics in common with the cassations or serenades of 1769 and 1773–4. It has seven movements, and is scored for strings with only single oboe, flute and bassoon but (like the contemporary symphonies) four horns; there is some concertante flute writing and much ingenious, witty solo use of the horn ensemble, especially in the minuets and their trios. The work has the relaxed gait and loose structure typical of the Salzburg serenades, with an Adagio, clearly intended for solo strings, in the customary sensuous vein. The occasion for its composition is unknown, but the time of year means that its use on Colloredo's name day or for university Finalmusik cannot be excluded. For the three works for strings K136–8/125a–c, sometimes misleadingly known as 'Salzburg symphonies', the title 'divertimento' is again not Mozart's own, but that these compact and assured three-movement pieces are solo rather than orchestral music is made clear beyond doubt by style; they are in effect lightweight string quartets. The similarity between the openings of the first and last movements of K136 has often been noted and is perhaps the most obvious among the numerous resemblances to be found between themes in different movements of a single work in Mozart's music of all periods, whether intentional, unconscious or fortuitous (for discussions of Mozart and cyclic form, see Engel, 1962–3, and Marx, 1971).

Apart from the single quartet (K80/73f) of 1770, to whose three movements he later added a rondeau in gavotte rhythm, Mozart's first true string quartets belong to the period of the third Italian journey. Each is in three movements, and the models are Italian, especially the quartets of G. B. Sammartini. The first, K155/134a, is in the manner of the 'divertimentos' K136–8; but in most of the remainder a genuine quartet style is apparent. The development section of K156/134b, with imitations against a dominant pedal figure, is both true quartet writing and true development, an unsurprising coincidence; and there are some carefully worked four-part textures in the slow movements, for example the E minor Adagio of the same quartet. Both this and K158 end with substantial minuets, in the favoured Italian style – on which Mozart had remarked in letters of 24 March and 29 September 1770. These six quartets follow, exceptionally, a cyclic key scheme, D–G–C–F–B♭–E♭, and four have minor-key middle movements, among them a fiery and extended G minor Allegro in K159.

6. EARLY SACRED MUSIC. The first vocal work in the Köchel catalogue is the 'madrigal' *God is our refuge* K20, presented at Leopold's wish to the British Museum as an example of his son's work; most of the handwriting is Leopold's. Sacred music occupied Mozart a good deal in the ensuing years. More than a dozen short liturgical or para-liturgical pieces were written up to

6. *Part of the autograph MS of Mozart's Piano Concerto in D* K107 *no.1 (3rd movement) after J. C. Bach (D-B Mus.ms.autogr.Mozart 107); both Leopold's and Wolfgang's handwriting may be seen*

1773, as well as four masses and two litany settings. Stylistically, the models were clear; it is not surprising that, of the works by other composers that Mozart copied out, most of those formerly accepted as his own are sacred music. They include items by Eberlin, Michael Haydn, his own father, the younger Reutter, Padre Martini and Quirino Gasparini. Such were the composers he sought to emulate; the tradition was essentially Italian, imported to Austria, and its most famous representative was Hasse.

Mozart's first mass was the ceremonial K139/47a. Though nominally in C minor, it is mainly in the major; minor-key introductions lend solemnity to three movements. It has the usual mixture of solo items and choruses, which are mostly homophonic (the choir in block chordal writing against busy string textures) apart from the extended fugues that traditionally concluded the Gloria and Credo sections. Particularly original are the sombre textures of the 'Qui tollis', in F minor, the introduction (with trumpets and drums) to the 'Crucifixus' and the opening of the Agnus Dei on a trio of trombones. Probably from much the same time comes a *Missa brevis* (K49/47d), a brisk setting of the kind preferred for everyday liturgical use; it has only one, brief fugue, and its most interesting feature is the 'Et incarnatus' chorus with a light, ethereal texture and a chromatic treatment of 'passus et sepultus est'. Another *Missa brevis* (K65/61a) is equally perfunctory, apart from a chromatic duet setting of the Benedictus. A companion to K139, and more assured, especially in its

'rauschende Violinen' ('rushing violins') in the Austrian tradition, is the 'Dominicus' mass K66: the figuration of the G minor 'Qui tollis' is on the same pattern as that in the Agnus Dei of the Requiem (K626), and there are striking contrasts of texture and pace in the C minor 'Crucifixus'.

Mozart's first liturgical work, the offertory *Scande coeli limina* K34, consists of a graceful aria and a chorus of almost banal simplicity; but the pieces that followed, like the contemporaneous masses, show how quickly he grasped the techniques of choral writing, using plain block harmony, and applied the standard forms to church music. The *Regina coeli* K108/74d and *Litaniae lauretanae* K109/74e of 1771 include confident homophonic choral writing and ensembles or arias in the supplicatory style suggested by the texts; the longer *Litaniae de venerabili altaris sacramento* K125 of a year later shows more individuality of invention and a powerful command of writing for choir and orchestra, as well as considerable grasp of dramatic effect, with strong chordal writing against rushing violins, in such movements as the 'Verbum caro factum' and the 'Tremendum'. This work also contains tender arias, a lengthy choral fugue (of which Mozart made a shorter version) and, in the opening Kyrie, an elaborate ritornello structure with three levels – orchestra, chorus and soloists. His sacred music of 1770 includes some *a cappella* items, cantus firmus workings and canons, written in Italy and probably intended as contrapuntal studies for Padre Martini: these are his only technical exercises to survive, although possibly the *Te Deum* K141/66*b*, closely modelled on one by Michael Haydn, should be regarded in the same light. Mozart's best-known sacred piece of the early years is the Rauzzini motet *Exsultate, jubilate* K165/158*a*, a miniature vocal concerto in three movements, full of felicitous invention and culminating in a brilliant 'Alleluia'. Three of Mozart's 'church sonatas', for three-part strings with organ continuo and intended for performance between the Epistle and Gospel of the Mass, date from the period up to 1773; these early examples are brief, sonata-form miniatures, but Mozart later allowed the form to be extended, in proportion to the mass settings with which the pieces were associated, and in his last church sonatas the orchestral forces are larger and the organ part blossoms into first an obbligato accompaniment and ultimately a solo role.

7. EARLY DRAMATIC MUSIC. It is clear from Daines Barrington's story of his tests in 1764–5 that Mozart was by then already familiar with dramatic composition; he was able to improvise a plausible 'Song of Love' and 'Song of Anger', and to precede each with a proper 'five or six lines of a jargon recitative'. The Metastasio setting *Va, dal furor portata* K21/19*c*, if elementary in its invention, shows a knowledge of the standard mode of treatment for such a text, as do the Metastasio settings of the following months, of which *Per pietà* K78/73*b*, probably written in 1766, represents an attempt at the typical E♭ *aria di affetto* manner. Several of these also show a grasp of the style of obbligato (or accompanied) recitative.

His first more extended essay in dramatic music was the act he contributed to *Die Schuldigkeit des ersten Gebots* K35, a 'sacred Singspiel' in which a Christian Spirit and a Worldly Spirit compete. That Mozart, at the age of 11, could write music to reflect the sense of the text is not surprising; the tradition was an established one, and the emotion is generalized (with dance rhythms and bravura for the Worldly Spirit and soberer music for the other participants). Five of the arias are in full da capo form, with middle sections usually in contrasting tempo and metre; one, referring to the last trump ('Posaunenschall'), has an alto trombone obbligato and a rich accompaniment with divided violas. The invention is generally more elaborate here than in the school-drama *Apollo et Hyacinthus*, where the rhythms of the Latin verse often induced Mozart to compose in a somewhat facile triple metre. Here too there are several full da capo arias. Musically the duets are of particular interest, one being the graceful piece that found its way into the Symphony in F K43, the other a striking dialogue for the angry Melia and the innocent Apollo, where changes in texture and key already support the sense of the drama. Both these works belong in a tradition firmly established in Salzburg; Mozart must have been familiar with examples by such composers as Eberlin and Adlgasser.

For Mozart's next stage work, *La finta semplice* K51/46*a*, a new range of techniques needed to be acquired. This was a full-length *opera buffa* demanding from him first of all a command of the Italian language, then a grasp of the more rapid and fragmented mode of setting that a *buffo* context required, an ability to delineate an emotion quickly, a knowledge of the range of effective orchestral cliché that supplied much of the accompaniment, and a control of the extended, multi-section finale of the Goldoni–Galuppi tradition favoured in Vienna. The mastery of these techniques, in which he was admittedly helped by Coltellini's efficient but unsubtle libretto (after Goldoni), shows an amazing gift – even if partly one of deft imitation of his models – for a boy of 12 whose contacts with *opera buffa* must have been few. The actual invention is often on a fairly routine level, but there are several numbers of considerable interest, among them an echo aria (with an oboe providing the echo, and two english horns in the accompaniment), a drinking-song, an exquisitely scored aria in E for Rosina (the 'feigned simpleton' of the title) with divided violas and prominent bassoons, and a duel duet. The arias are generally shorter than those of the preceding works, and full da capo form appears only once; one aria comes from *Die Schuldigkeit*, now shortened, and another uses an idea from *Apollo*. *Bastien und Bastienne* K50/46*b*, composed just after *La finta semplice* though possibly begun earlier, is altogether simpler and more direct in style, both because of its topic, rural love, and because it belongs to the Singspiel tradition rather than the more sophisticated one of *opera buffa*.

With this selection of styles already mastered, Mozart ventured into the most important musical-theatrical form of his day, *opera seria*, with *Mitridate, rè di Ponto* K87/74*a*. The rejected drafts, totalling 11, suggest the extent to which he had to meet the singers' requirements. It has been remarked (by Tagliavini, 1968) that in several details of form and treatment Mozart modelled his setting on Quirino Gasparini's. The music of *Mitridate* is expansive, but there are no full da capo arias; eight are in shortened da capo form (often with middle sections in contrasting metre and tempo), four are in alternating slow and fast tempos, while six follow a sonata-like pattern and two a binary one. The most striking aria is a G minor Allegro agitato for the prima donna, with violin tremolandos, chromaticisms and a fragmented melodic line to represent the sense of the text.

*La Betulia liberata*, composed in summer 1771, is Mozart's first setting of an extended Metastasio text. The libretto is concerned more with the moral quality of the tale than with its drama: the story of Judith and Holophernes is related wholly from within the besieged Bethulia. That ensures a setting somewhat formal and abstract in tone: even the dramatic central event of the work, Judith's killing of Holophernes, is related in a subdued obbligato recitative. The overture, in D minor (all Mozart's others of the period are in D major), is dark-toned and forceful, with thematic links between the outer movements, and perhaps with a Gluckian flavour; more markedly Gluckian is the C minor chorus for the Israelites at prayer, led by Ozias, which recalls the elegiac opening chorus of *Orfeo*. But *Betulia liberata* is no reform work, and stands firmly in the Metastasian tradition, with extended arias, often including bravura writing, and sometimes partial da capos.

Mozart's next two dramatic works were of the serenata or *festa teatrale* type, *Ascanio in Alba* K111 and *Il sogno di Scipione* K126. The style of the former, written to be performed alongside Hasse's *Ruggiero*, has been compared with Hasse's (Engel, 1960–61). It is a leisurely work, with pastoral choruses and ballets interspersed with the arias, among which those for Ascanio, sung by the alto castrato Manzuoli, are especially sympathetic. *Il sogno di Scipione*, composed for Salzburg rather than Italy, has a Metastasio text dating back to

1735. Like *Die Schuldigkeit*, it is a 'morality' – Scipio is wooed by Constancy and Fortune. The music is less tellingly characterized than that of the earlier work; the arias, mostly in shortened da capo form, are lengthy (averaging 185 bars, the highest figure for any Mozart work) and contain much bravura writing. It ends with an outburst in obbligato recitative from the rejected Fortune, followed by a *licenza* aria, of which two settings survive.

The final and most significant work of this group is an *opera seria*, *Lucio Silla*, written at the end of 1772. It suffers from a verbose, sententious and ill-motivated libretto; but a more individual, less convention-bound expression of emotion may be found in this score than in any hitherto. This is true particularly of the music for the role of Junia, whose opening aria alternates between an intense Adagio and a fiery Allegro, and whose choral scene at her father's tomb again recalls Gluck. Her other music includes a conventional bravura aria and an aria of agitation. That role was written for Anna de Amicis; Rauzzini's primo uomo role is more conventionally brilliant although it includes an elaborate Adagio aria in Act 2 and a pathetic farewell minuet. The role of Celia, too, has a certain individuality, partly for its unusual light coloratura (doubtless designed for the singer's particular qualities). Sulla's, written for a novice, and reduced by Mozart's omission of two arias, is in the vein customary for an *opera seria* tyrant. The terzetto where, against the smooth lines and the sweet 3rds and 6ths of the lovers, Sulla expresses his anger is an early example of simultaneous differentiated characterization; and the obbligato recitatives are notably more powerful in expression than in any preceding work by Mozart.

**8. 1773–4: THE VIENNA VISIT AND ITS MUSICAL AFTER-MATH.** Mozart and his father, having returned from Italy in March 1773, stayed in Salzburg until early summer. About this time the family moved from their apartment in the Getreidegasse to a large one in the Hannibalplatz (now Makartplatz). The move reflects the family's prosperity; although Leopold's salary had sometimes been withheld during his absences, the gifts they received had no doubt compensated. The family was, it seems, keenly conscious of its status in Salzburg society; their friends were professional people rather than fellow musicians, and they took care to be on good terms with the local nobility. They were not, however, content. Leopold's standing in the local musical establishment was less high than he wished, and he saw poor prospects there for his son.

It was probably to seek an opening for him at the imperial court that, after a busy four-month spell – which saw the composition of four symphonies, three serenades or divertimentos and a mass – Leopold took his son to Vienna. They arrived about 17 July and spent some ten weeks there; among the people they met were Dr Mesmer, the ballet-master J. G. Noverre, and the court Kapellmeister Giuseppe Bonno. Mozart played a violin concerto at a nearby monastery, and his Mass K66 was directed by Leopold at the Jesuit church. They had an audience with the Empress Maria Theresia, but if (as cryptic remarks in Leopold's letters imply) the intention was to secure a post, they were unsuccessful.

In other ways, however, the visit to Vienna was not unproductive, for it seems to have stimulated an intensification in Mozart's style. This has commonly been ascribed to his presumed contact with Joseph Haydn's latest music, in particular his string quartets (opp.9 and 17 and the recently published op.20); and doubtless Mozart also encountered other new Viennese music that interested him. While in Vienna he composed a set of six quartets K168–73, in a style markedly more Viennese than that of the Milanese set. Textures are more fully worked, with much imitative writing, not only in the development sections but integral to some of the thematic material on its first statement (even in one minuet, in K172, and in the Andante of K171). The carefree Italianate manner appears in some movements, like the first of K169 and 172 and some of the finales; but in others – like the variations (much in Haydn's manner) opening K170, or the Allegro of K171 with its recurring Adagio introduction and curiously varied pace, or above all the intense, chromatic Allegro of the D minor Quartet K173 – an altogether more intellectual approach to quartet composition is in evidence. So is it, still more, in the fugal finales of K168 and 173: not, like many quartet finales of the time, sonata movements with fugal sections but entire fugues, like those of Haydn's op.20 nos.2, 5 and 6. These were Mozart's first fugues outside church music, and are likely to have been provoked by Haydn's example. Their counterpoint is not Bachian, but in the traditional Austrian manner of Fux, and not without a certain selfconsciousness. Resemblances to works by several composers have been remarked, ranging from Handel (the F minor Andante theme in K168, no less indebted however to Haydn's op.20 no.5) to Gluck and to Gassmann. For the string quintet K174, Mozart's first, started early in 1773 and completed with some revisions at the end of the year, Michael Haydn provided the model with some quintets also from 1773. This is more polished and relaxed than the quartets, and the ensemble with two violas is treated in a variety of ways, notably in dialogues between first violin and first viola, with the richer sonorities used to good advantage. A comparison between the first version of the finale and the final one, where Mozart added a new theme at the beginning and turned his original opening idea into a subsidiary one, is instructive.

In Vienna Mozart completed a serenade (K185/167a) with a violin concerto section, probably for Salzburg University Finalmusik; it also has connections with the Andretter family, for whom he had written, most likely just before leaving for Vienna, a good-humoured divertimento (K205/167A). On his return he wrote several symphonies and his first original piano concerto. This last, K175, recalls in its manner the J. C. Bach parodies of two years before, but is larger in scale and surprisingly well developed in its finale, which starts with a contrapuntal gesture that recurs in various ways. Mozart later revived the work, equipping it in about 1782 with a new finale, the Rondo K382 (actually a theme and variations), which is out of style with the remainder of the concerto and on a level of charming triviality.

The symphonies, of which four were written shortly before the Viennese journey, a group immediately after, and a further group in 1774 – the dates are not entirely certain – are more important: it could be said that two of these, the earliest Mozart works to have an inalienable place in the concert repertory, mark his emergence from a preternaturally gifted youth into a great composer. The first four (K184/161a, 199/161b, 162, 181/162b) are reversions to the Italian type, with much brisk and mechanical figuration, simple textures, and three-movement form: in K184 and 181 the movements follow without a break, along the pattern of the Italian overture. K184 is the strongest of these, with a C minor Andante whose main theme is built on imitative writing; its dramatic style, marked in the driving unison passages and the sharp dynamic contrasts, was acknowledged by its adoption in the 1780s as overture to Gebler's *Thamos, König in Ägypten*, for which Mozart wrote incidental music.

K182/173dA, composed a few days after Mozart's return from Vienna, moves little beyond the preceding group. But K183/173dB, the 'little G minor', his first minor-key symphony besides the overture to *La Betulia liberata*, is music of a different temper. The urgent tone of the repeated syncopated notes at the start represents something new, and so do the dramatic falling diminished 7th and the repeated thrusting phrases that follow. The increased force of the musical thinking is seen in the strong sense of harmonic direction, the taking up of melodic figuration by the bass instruments, and the echo sections, which are no longer merely decorative but add intensity. Although the E♭ Andante is soft-textured music, with bassoons constantly echoing the violins, it is often chromatic, and the tone of the work is maintained, especially in the fiery finale. This tone is not unique among works of the period; there was a wave of minor-key symphonies – including G minor ones by Haydn (no.39), Vanhal and J. C. Bach (op.6 no.6) in the same manner as K183 (particularly J. C. Bach's, where there is even figuration close to Mozart's) – which have been cited as musically analogous to the 'Sturm und Drang' movement in German literature.

Some biographers have suggested a personal 'romantic crisis' behind this symphony, but no known biographical circumstance supports that idea; such a work must, however, signify something in terms of spiritual development, even if, as is possible, it was written in emulation of similar works by other composers. No less of a landmark is the Symphony in A K201/186a, of April 1774 – also personal in tone, perhaps indeed more individual in its combination of an intimate, chamber music style with a still fiery and impulsive manner. The gentle appoggiatura phrase and dipping octave of the opening is dramatized and intensified by its *forte* repetition with the bass instruments in imitation. The Andante, calling for muted strings, is no different in its melodic style from several earlier ones, though it is more eloquent; here again elaborated repetition intensifies the music. The finale has an unusually long development section, urgent in tone, with much use of string tremolando and imitation between basses and first violins.

In May 1774 Mozart composed a further symphony, K202/186b, a D major work of a less developed and fairly light, divertimento-like character. The Symphony in C K200/189k probably dates from November 1774 (or possibly 1773; the year is illegible on the autograph). It is far from the ceremonial manner associated with C major and the use of trumpets and drums in his earlier symphonies; the style is lighter, more *buffo*, the textures finer, the thematic ideas in the spirited outer movements neatly argued (and, like those of K202, seemingly related to one another).

Several other works of interest date from 1774. There are two concertos, the Concertone K190/186E for two violins and orchestra, with solo parts for oboe and cello, and the Bassoon Concerto K191/186e. The

Concertone ('large concerto') is a leisurely, amiable work in the sinfonia concertante style of J. C. Bach, with much dialogue and sequence: it has a minuet-rondo finale, a type J. C. Bach favoured. So has the Bassoon Concerto, whose particular interest lies in Mozart's brilliant assumption of a style to exploit the instrument's special qualities – its contrasts of register, its staccato, its latent eloquence. The occasions for which these works were composed, in spring 1774, remain unknown. In the summer Mozart wrote a serenade K203/189b, containing a violin concerto, probably for university Finalmusik or possibly for celebrations on Archbishop Colloredo's name day (it has been called the 'Colloredo Serenade').

The Colloredo connection is more firmly established with the sacred works of this period. Colloredo was a reformist churchman with, for his day, an austere view on music for worship. In a well-known letter of 1776 Mozart wrote to Padre Martini: 'a mass, with the whole Kyrie, the Gloria, the Credo, the Epistle sonata, the Offertory or Motet, the Sanctus and the Agnus, must last no more than three-quarters of an hour'. The masses of 1774, K192/186f and 194/186h, are of this type, unlike his only other since Colloredo's accession, the *Missa in honorem sanctissimae Trinitatis* K167, whose unusual setting with four trumpets (two high and two low) and chorus without soloists makes clear that it was meant for a special occasion. That work totals 863 bars; K192 and 194 have respectively 290 and 457. This style, more condensed than in the earlier *missae breves*, demanded a minimum of word repetition (some texts are even treated in continuous dialogue), simple choral declamation, and sparing musical treatment of verbal meaning, as well as unbroken Gloria and Credo settings without extended final fugues, though sometimes an imitative point is briefly worked out. As exercises in concision and ingenuity, they are impressive. The most interesting movement is the Credo of K192, held together by a motivic treatment of the word 'Credo' to the traditional tag, based on the 'Lucis creator' plainchant, which Mozart used contrapuntally many times, most famously in the finale of his last symphony. Here it is sometimes treated contrapuntally, sometimes merely harmonized; the phrase gives rise to fugatos at 'Crucifixus' and 'Et vitam venturi', but its recurrences mostly serve as an affirmation of 'Credo'. The device is not, however, original; there existed a well-established Austrian tradition of 'Credo masses', to which composers like Donberger, Francesco Conti and Holzbauer had contributed, and with which Mozart must have been familiar (see Reichert, 1955). He had opportunity for sacred composition in a more expansive manner with the Lorettine litany setting K195/186d, whose scale suggests it may have been written for Salzburg Cathedral; it is a relatively elaborate, polished essay in the traditional Salzburg manner, like the previous setting (K109/74e), with choruses in a free homophonic style and much expressive melody and bravura writing for the soloists. Settings of the *Dixit* and *Magnificat* of the same period (K193/186g) contain some vigorous counterpoint.

9. 1775–7: SALZBURG. During summer 1774 Mozart received a commission to write an *opera buffa* for the Carnival season in Munich. He started work about September, and left Salzburg with his father on 6 December, probably with the score near-complete; his

7. *Mozart wearing the insignia of the Golden Spur: anonymous portrait (1777) in the Civico Museo Bibliografico Musicale, Bologna*

sister joined them later. The première of the opera, *La finta giardiniera*, was to have been on 29 December but was postponed to Friday 13 January (Mozart told his mother not to be worried by the unpropitious date). According to Mozart's report to his mother the opera was much applauded and there were two repeat performances. The work was later (1780) given by Johann Heinrich Böhm's travelling company, who performed it in German as a Singspiel, with spoken dialogue; as the autograph score of Act 1 is lost, and no original printed libretto is known, this version was preferred until the discovery of a source with the Italian original and its publication in the Neue Mozart-Ausgabe (1978).

*La finta giardiniera*, written just before Mozart's 19th birthday, was his first *opera buffa* for six and a half years. The libretto, generally thought to have been prepared by Coltellini after Calzabigi, had been set by Anfossi for Rome in 1774; Mozart may have known Anfossi's setting. It is a tale of disguises and mistaken identities. Although several of the arias are in the simple, direct manner called for by the straightforward humour of the plot, others, including two agitated ones in minor keys and several in amorous or pathetic mood, hint with their richer harmony and texture at Mozart's growing resources for the musical depiction of character and situation. There are two mad scenes, and two ensemble finales, that of Act 1 notable for its crisp and ingenious vaudeville-like treatment of the comic

situation at the beginning, that of Act 2 for its poetic opening (where the characters are lost in a wood); but the structure of these extended scenes is not entirely sure, and in any case is hampered by the libretto.

While the Mozarts were in Munich they took part in local musical life; Leopold conducted liturgical music by Wolfgang in performances at court and they played at academies. They also went to masked balls. Mozart wrote an offertory *Misericordias Domini* K222/205a, in an elaborate, learned style, borrowing an Eberlin theme for the purpose; he later sent the work to Martini for approval. He was doubtless anxious to impress the court, for the idea of an appointment in Munich was never far from his mind or his father's. He took part in a keyboard contest with the virtuoso Ignaz van Beecke, also a former child prodigy: according to C. F. D. Schubart Mozart played weightily and sight-read perfectly but Beecke surpassed him in every other respect.

Mozart's earliest surviving piano sonatas date from about this time: K279–83/189d–h were seemingly written as a group, K284/205b a little later. They are not works of great individuality; their general style is most of all akin to that of J. C. Bach's sonatas, as in the graceful first movement of K283, although certain movements, like the second of K280, look to Haydn. The final sonata, written for Baron Thaddäus von Dürnitz (an amateur bassoonist for whom he probably wrote the duet sonata K292/186c), is longer and more brilliant; its pseudo-orchestral first movement anticipates the sonatas of 1777–8, and it is unusual in having a polonaise-rondeau central movement and a variation finale. The set may have been composed with a view to publication, but only the last sonata was printed in Mozart's lifetime. Approaches to publishers at this period met with no success.

Mozart returned to Salzburg on 7 March, and there began a period that apparently he found depressing. Opportunities in the Salzburg musical establishment were limited, and the archbishop was ungenerous over leave; feeling his talent stifled in provincial Salzburg, Mozart pined for the larger musical world where since childhood he had won so much applause. Leopold, ambitious for his son and almost pathologically suspicious and discontented – Hasse, in 1771, had commented sharply on this – no doubt fed his frustration. Convinced, probably correctly, that the archbishop looked on them unfavourably, the Mozarts felt insecure in his domain.

The period in Salzburg began, however, with a commission for a work to be performed on the visit of Archduke Maximilian Franz, on 23 April: a setting of Metastasio's *Il rè pastore*. Contemporary writers called it a 'Serenada' or 'Cantate', which implies that it was given in concert or semi-staged form. In the Metastasian tradition, the drama, and thus the musical clothing of it too, are highly stylized; the aria texts deal with the claims of love and of duty, and the deft libretto contrives opportunities for pathetic farewells and occasional passionate expression. That the musical setting is somewhat static is inevitable, but the arias show a grace and polish in keeping with the text and a nice appreciation of scale – prolonged arias like those in the earlier Italian works are rare. The incipient characterization of *La finta giardiniera*, however, was scarcely followed up in *Il rè pastore*; the text offered no real scope for it.

Mozart's other principal compositions of 1775 were instrumental: they comprise another serenade (K204/213a), almost certainly written as university Finalmusik, and five violin concertos. These represent – excluding the violin concertos built into serenades – his total output of concertos for the instrument, or at least of undoubtedly authentic ones. (Two more are ascribed to him, K268/C14.04 in E♭ and K271a/271i in D, which may include music of Mozart's in adulterated form: their sources are dubious and their style uncharacteristic. The 'Adelaïde Concerto', allegedly from 1766, is a forgery, probably written in the early 1930s.) The five fully genuine works span from April to December 1775 and show a steady gain in mastery of the form. In the first two, K207 and 211, the balance between virtuoso violin writing and thematic treatment is not quite assured; the solo passage-work does not relate entirely convincingly with the general musical fabric, particularly in K211, whose rather halting and formal first movement recalls late Baroque or early Rococo concertos like some of Tartini's and those of his successor Nardini, whom Mozart had met at Stuttgart and probably Florence. K216 in G, beginning with a theme from an aria ritornello in *Il rè pastore*, is altogether more confident in style and makes in its Adagio a new, telling use of expressive violin cantilena. So does K218; these two concertos also have in common finales in a variety of tempos and metres, at different levels of sophistication, including courtly dances alongside folk themes (among them, in K216, a musette-like melody whose origins account for Mozart's calling this the 'Strasbourger-Concert'; see Bartha, 1956). Suggestions that K218 was modelled on a Boccherini concerto are mistaken; the alleged source is another modern forgery. The diversity of material in the final work of the group, K219 in A, reflects Mozart's newly acquired control with its happy and graceful themes, its counter-subjects and its dialogues; the poetic Adagio episode introducing the soloist in the first movement and the 'Turkish' episode set into the minuet finale are specially notable. The occasions that called forth these concertos are unknown, but probably they were mostly composed for Mozart himself or for a friend called Kolb at Salzburg; later they were played by Antonio Brunetti, the Salzburg Konzertmeister from 1776, for whom Mozart supplied a new movement (K261) to replace the 'studied' Adagio of K219, and a Rondo K269/261a, probably to replace the one in K207.

In 1776 Mozart wrote a number of piano (or harpsichord) concertos, and his treatment of that form underwent an analogous development. The occasion for the composition of the first, K238 in B♭, is not known; the second, K246 in C, was written for the Countess Lützow, a member of a prominent Salzburg family. K238 is an amiable work, essentially in a *galant* manner, with fluent passage-work taking its place neatly in the structure; it marks no departure. In the K246 opening movement the soloist, for the first time, has a distinctive, lyrical secondary theme not heard in the preceding ritornello, a clear hint of the coming expansion of the form's scale and range although the actual invention is fairly conventional. The finale follows the minuet-rondo design favoured in several earlier concertos, as does that of the three-piano concerto K242, composed about the same time for the Lodrons, another leading Salzburg family – an ingeniously contrived work that also exists in a two-piano version. By the beginning of 1777, stimulated by the visit of a French keyboard virtuoso, Mlle Jeunehomme, Mozart was ready to write a concerto on a far larger scale. K271 in E♭, quite apart from the inherent attractiveness, vitality and grace of its ideas, is one of Mozart's most subtle and highly organized works of any period in matters like its thematic relationships, its handling of phrase length and cadence to increase tension and strengthen its resolution, and, most strikingly, in its richly developed relationship between soloist and orchestra. It begins, arrestingly and unconventionally, with the piano answering in the second bar the orchestra's fanfare-like opening phrase; and though this dialogue has no effect on the movement's basic formal outlines it establishes an unusually flexible treatment of soloist and orchestra and gives rise to a large variety of possibilities, adventurously and wittily explored – not least the later exchange in dialogue roles, at the recapitulation, and the piano's unorthodox final intervention in the ritornello following the cadenza. There is a sombre C minor Andantino, notable for its exploitation of the violins' dark lowest register, its chromatic melody and affective harmony, and its elaborately embellished solo line. The finale is an extended rondo whose brilliant passage-work assumes a symphonic character, and whose thrust is tellingly relieved by an interpolated minuet, of which each strain is repeated with florid decoration. K271, written in the month of Mozart's 21st birthday, represents a new maturity, technical and emotional.

A stream of lighter instrumental works had flowed

from Mozart's pen during the time between *Il rè pastore* and summer 1776. They include divertimentos for a wind band of pairs of oboes, bassoons and horns, cheerful outdoor music on a smallish scale, with brief sonata movements, variations and a polonaise and a contredanse as well as minuets; there are six in this group, though there may be doubts about the authenticity of the last, K289/271*g*. On a less unpretentious level are various occasional works, divertimentos and serenades, including two substantial, six-movement works (K247 and 287/271*H*) composed for the name days of Countess Lodron: each has two minuets and two slow movements (one an Adagio in the traditional amorous serenade style), with fast movements often including material of an almost rumbustiously popular character. At least two actual folk melodies appear in K287. These works are for two violins, viola, double bass (rather than cello) and two horns: they are solo, not orchestral, music. So is the septet divertimento K251, for the same combination plus oboe, traditionally supposed to have been composed for Nannerl Mozart, probably on her name day. There are two echo serenades, the charming K239 'Serenata notturna', consisting of a march-like first movement, a minuet and a rondo (with rustic episodes), where a group of two violins, viola and

double bass is set against full strings and timpani; and the Notturno K286/269*a*, where the dialogue among four orchestras of strings and horns is ingenious and humorous, depending on echo effects. The single substantial orchestral work of the period is the noble Serenade K250/248*b*, composed for the marriage of Elisabeth Haffner, daughter of a prominent Salzburg citizen. This is a nine-movement work, with three minuets and an interpolated violin concerto, whose lithe, sparkling rondo is a tour de force both of composition and execution. The scale and character of the music, particularly its *maestoso* opening, make clear Mozart's view of the grandeur of the occasion; this is the weightiest and most symphonic of Mozart's occasional works to date, without prejudicing the D major trumpet-and-drum brilliance typical of the medium. A flute concerto by Mozart is said to have been performed in July 1777, but no such work is known; an oboe concerto may also belong to this period.

Mozart's other sphere of activity in these years was church music, required of him in connection with his court duties. He had composed one short mass, K220/196*b*, about the time of *La finta giardiniera* (it follows the tradition of cyclic use of material, the music for the Kyrie recurring at 'Dona nobis pacem'); four

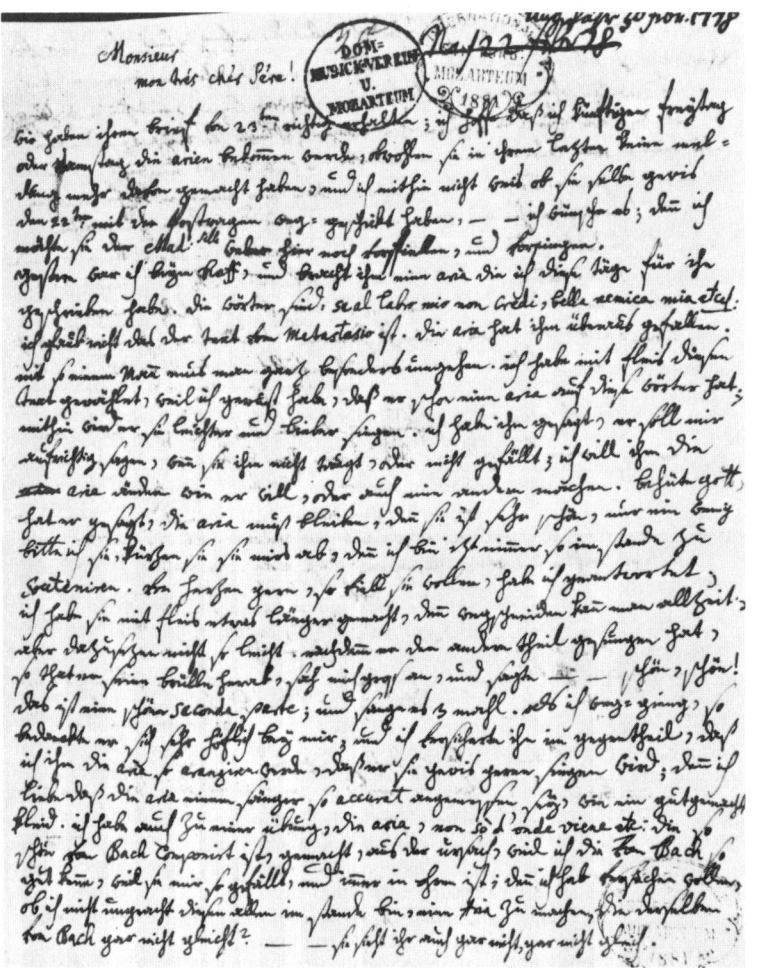

8. *Autograph letter from Mozart to his father (dated '30' February 1778), written from Mannheim; it refers to the aria 'Se al labbro' K295 that he composed for Anton Raaff (Mozart Museum, Salzburg)*

more, all in C major to accommodate the trumpets favoured in Salzburg, followed in 1776 and one in 1777. None requires violas, which evidently were not used, or were used merely to double the bass line, at Salzburg. The longest and most elaborate is the first, K262/246a, probably composed for Salzburg Cathedral at Easter 1776; it has, besides the customary concluding fugues to the Gloria and Credo, contrapuntal writing even at the Kyrie and the 'Et incarnatus', and extended orchestral ritornellos. The Benedictus, usually a solo movement followed by a separate Osanna or a repeat of the preceding one, is here set with solo phrases to the 'Benedictus' words and choral refrains to the 'Osanna', in a single movement. Points of interest in the next three, K257, 258 and 259, all of them of the *missa brevis* type, are in K257 the use of a repeated Credo motto, though not contrapuntally as in K192, and the appearance of the four-note 'Credo' phrase used in K192 in its Sanctus; in K258 the interesting solo–chorus treatment of the Benedictus and the curiously solemn florid writing of the last movement; and in K259 the use of the organ as a solo instrument in the Benedictus. This group of compact, direct pieces, firmly in the Austrian tradition of church music and indeed of the region's natural and gracefully decorative Rococo art as a whole, is rounded off by K275/272b, a work on a modest scale and of a simpler and more intimate character – in B♭, it lacks the usual trumpets. There are several epistle sonatas of this period, no doubt originally associated with particular masses: attractive pieces in an airily tuneful style, emphasizing the lack of any sharp distinction in Mozart's attitude to sacred and secular. Mozart's most important church work in this period, however, is the *Litaniae de venerabili altaris sacramento* K243. It embraces several styles unselfconsciously and without incongruity: simple homophonic choruses, dramatic ones, fugues, a plainchant setting, and expressive arias with florid embellishment.

10. 1777–80: MANNHEIM, PARIS, SALZBURG. The Mozarts' discontent with their situation in Salzburg came to a head during 1777. In August Mozart wrote a carefully worded petition – there is almost an undertone of insolence to it – asking the archbishop for his release from employment. In his faintly sarcastic note of reply the archbishop released both father and son; but Leopold could not afford to go and was evidently reinstated. So on this next journey Mozart was accompanied by his mother. The numerous and long letters exchanged between father and son during his 16 months' absence (this was the first time they had been away from one another) cast a sharp light on their relationship, particularly if read with some scepticism as to Mozart's frankness and indeed his truthfulness.

Mozart and his mother set out, in their own chaise, on 23 September. At Munich, where they spent 17 days, Mozart offered his services to the elector, and met with a polite refusal: 'there is no vacancy here'. At Augsburg they remained a fortnight: Mozart visited the piano maker J. A. Stein, amazed the monks at the Heiligkreuz canonry with his fugal improvisations, attended an academy with the town patricians (where he was discomfited at being teased over the Order of the Golden Spur that he wore) and gave a concert including several of his recent works. He spent some time with his relatives and struck up a vivacious friendship with his cousin Maria Anna Thekla (his 'Bäsle', affectionate

diminutive of *Base*, 'cousin'): in the ensuing months he wrote her several letters, full of the obscene childish humour, characteristic of Salzburg, that also runs through his letters home; there is no reason to imagine that their friendship was in any way sexual, as has been suggested. Mozart and his mother left Augsburg on 26 October and, after pausing at Hohenaltheim in the hope of playing to the Prince of Oettingen-Wallerstein, reached Mannheim on 30 October.

Mannheim was an important musical centre, with a fine orchestra and a court devoted to music under the lavish patronage of the Elector Carl Theodor. Mozart remained there until the middle of March. His letters give a graphic picture of musical life and the musical people there. He quickly became friendly with Cannabich, the Konzertmeister, and with others, including the Kapellmeister, Holzbauer (whose opera *Günther von Schwarzburg* and a mass impressed him), and particularly the flautist J. B. Wendling. He soon met the elector, talked to him about his children's musical tuition, and dropped hints about his interest in remaining at Mannheim; but it was another month before the elector made clear that there was no post for him. Mozart was acutely disappointed. It was now a bad time of year for travelling. So he found work, as well as diversion, in Mannheim: he did some teaching, wrote flute quartets and concertos for a Dutchman ('de Jean': possibly Dejong), and remained for three more months, taking part in much music-making. During that time he fell in love with Aloysia Weber, a soprano, aged 16, daughter of a copyist, and travelled with her and her father to Kirchheimboland to perform to the Princess of Nassau-Weilburg. He postponed moving on to Paris, and put to Leopold the notion of taking her to Italy to become a prima donna. This naive proposal infuriated Leopold: he had been pouring forth advice since Mozart had left home – on routes, potential patrons, letters of introduction, ways of ingratiating himself with influential people, money matters and countless other topics – and was now distracted by his son's ill-conceived schemes, his dilatoriness, his irresponsibility over money and his apparent family disloyalty. The contrast between Mozart's gossipy, high-spirited, often frivolous letters and his father's increasingly anxious and irritable ones is revealing. Finally, on 11–12 February 1778, Leopold ordered his son onwards: '*Off with you to Paris!* and that soon, find your place among great people – aut Caesar aut nihil'. Further, Mozart's mother was to accompany him to Paris; Mozart had hardly shown himself fit to travel alone.

The Mozarts left Mannheim on 14 March and arrived in Paris nine days later. Mozart followed up various connections, through German acquaintances, Baron Grimm and the Palatine ambassador, and found work. He composed additional music, mainly choruses, for a performance at the Concert Spirituel of a *Miserere* by Holzbauer and, according to his letters home, a sinfonia concertante K Anh.9/297B for flute, oboe, bassoon and horn, for his Mannheim friends; that, however, if it ever was composed, was suppressed by the Concert Spirituel director, Joseph Legros, and like the *Miserere* movements is lost. (A work in E♭ for oboe, clarinet, bassoon and horn, K Anh.9/C14.01, discovered much later in an early 19th-century copy, has been reckoned to be a version of that work; but its credentials are dubious, and any music by Mozart that it may contain can be only in a corrupt form.) Mozart was not happy in

Paris; his letters make clear that he heartily despised French music and French taste, that he was unwilling to be duly deferential to possible patrons, and that like his father he always suspected malicious intrigue. He undertook a little teaching (his letter to Leopold of 14 May tells fascinatingly of his methods with an untalented composition pupil) and accepted some private commissions; he also hoped to write an opera. A post as organist at Versailles was offered to him, he told his father, but he intended to decline it. Two new works had hearings in June: a group of ballet pieces, for Noverre, given with a Piccinni opera, and a symphony composed for the Concert Spirituel, performed on 18 June and several times repeated. The symphony was warmly received, and after its success, Mozart wrote, 'I went off to the Palais Royal, where I had a large ice, and said the rosary as I had vowed to'.

By that date Mozart's mother was ill with a fever. They tried the usual family remedies, then called in Grimm's doctor; but nothing could be done, and on 3 July she died. Mozart's communication of the news to his father shows a new maturity and sensitivity. He wrote to say that she was critically ill, and by the same post wrote to the Abbé Bullinger, a close friend in Salzburg, telling him what had happened. Leopold was thus prepared when Bullinger broke the news to him. Mozart now went to stay with Grimm, who soon wrote frankly and pessimistically to Leopold about his son's prospects in Paris, pointing out that his visit had unfortunately coincided with the Gluck–Piccinni controversy, and that he would have done better in Paris with half the talent and double the shrewdness. Meanwhile Mozart had another symphony given at the Concert Spirituel, on 8 September (he claimed in a letter that it was a new work, but that seems to be untrue), renewed his old acquaintance with J. C. Bach, over from London to hear the Paris singers before composing an opera, and wrote a scena for Bach's friend the castrato Tenducci (now lost). His friendship with Grimm (an ardent Piccinniste; Mozart was anxious to keep clear of the controversy) deteriorated. Mozart owed him money, and reacted in a manner typical of one who feels an irksome obligation.

On 27 August Leopold wrote to Mozart, enjoining on him the need to work towards earning a living in Paris. Four days later he wrote again: Mozart must come back to Salzburg, where a better post was open to him; he would still be a Konzertmeister, but now court organist, with accompanying duties, rather than violinist. The archbishop had offered a salary increase and generous leave. So Mozart, who had hoped to escape from the provincial atmosphere of Salzburg and to secure a full Kapellmeistership – although, as Leopold pointed out, he was too young for that – set out for home. He left on 26 September; Grimm arranged the journey and put him on a slow coach through Nancy to Strasbourg, where he gave three unprofitable concerts. Then he went to Mannheim, where he remained a month, although, as Carl Theodor had become Elector of Bavaria and moved to Munich, the orchestra was largely disbanded. There he heard a melodrama (a theatrical work consisting of declamation with music) by Georg Benda, and resolved to write one himself; the work, *Semiramis*, was listed in the Gotha *Theater-Kalender* from 1779 but, even if written, was never performed and is now lost. He also started writing a concerto for piano and violin. Leopold, incensed at his son's having gone to Mannheim,

where there were no opportunities, summoned him home. Mozart reached Munich on 25 December. There he remained – again to the irritation of Leopold, who was afraid that his dawdling might jeopardize the Salzburg appointment – until 11 January: he presented dedication copies of a set of sonatas, newly arrived from the engraver in Paris, to the Electress Elisabeth Auguste, and stayed with the Webers. His reception from Aloysia, now singing in the court opera, was apparently cool; 'I really cannot write – my heart is too full of tears', he wrote to Leopold. And it seems that his inquiries about a post or an opera commission there proved fruitless. He arrived home, anxious about the welcome he would receive, in mid-January.

Mozart had been away 16 months. He had received no worthwhile offer of a post or even a major commission; he had fallen deeply in love and been disappointed; his mother had died; his actions had worsened the family finances and strained the family affections – though there is no doubt that the eagerness to see one another again, repeatedly expressed in the father–son correspondence, was genuine and indeed heartfelt. His letters of these months hint at several important aspects of his personality. He had always been told by Leopold to be natural and friendly with noblemen but aloof, 'like an Englishman', with other musicians; deeply implanted in him was a mistrust of his own professional colleagues (perhaps exaggerated in his letters, to satisfy his father), and that consorted uneasily with his natural youthful openness and liveliness. His comments on musical matters often show a certain arrogance; he knew the extent of his own skills, could see the weaknesses of other men's, and (as his music repeatedly bears out) was keen to outshine any potential rival. He had a strong and sincere, quite conventional, religious feeling, with a hint of selfconscious moral rectitude, in no way contradicted by his smutty humour.

Immediately on his return Mozart formally petitioned the archbishop for his new appointment as court organist, which was granted with a salary of 450 gulden (the same as his predecessor Adlgasser's). His duties included playing in the cathedral, at court and in the chapel, composing as required, and instructing the choirboys. The years 1779–80 were uneventful for him. He wrote several sacred works, and symphonies, presumably for use in court ceremonial; also from this period came some concertos and, each summer, a divertimento or serenade. His interest in dramatic music remained strong, and when Johann Heinrich Böhm's troupe visited Salzburg in mid-1779 and winter 1779–80 Mozart's music to Gebler's *Thamos, König in Ägypten*, may have been used. He began work on a Singspiel, now known as *Zaide*, intended either for this troupe or for Emanuel Schikaneder's, in Salzburg for winter 1780–81, or with thoughts of production in the new German opera house in Vienna.

11. MUSIC OF 1777–80. Like the journeys of his youth, the 1777–8 one to Mannheim and Paris had its influence on his music. The first and most obvious echo of the Mannheim style came in the Piano Sonata K309/284*b*, written for Cannabich's young daughter Rosa (its Andante was designed, Mozart said, to portray her): Mozart's sister wrote that 'anyone could see it was composed in Mannheim', and Leopold that 'it has something of the mannered Mannheim style about it, but so little that your own good style is not spoilt'. They were

9. *The Mozart family; portrait (c1780) by Johann Nepomuk della Croce in the Mozart Museum, Salzburg; Mozart's mother (d 1778) is depicted in her portrait of c1775 (probably by Lorenzoni or Franz Joseph Degle)*

doubtless referring to such characteristics as the sharp dynamic contrasts in the first two movements and the aura of 'sensibility', even expressive affectation, that pervades the Andante. A similar atmosphere is evident in the Andante of the next sonata, K311/284c, though the lines are less elaborate, and the work as a whole is of a more brilliant and expansive cast. These two were published in Paris by Mozart's friend Mme Heina (her husband had been Mozart's only companion at his mother's funeral), along with his first minor-key sonata, K310/300d in A minor, probably also composed there. He may have written the A minor work for his performances in the Parisian salons; it follows up the tradition of fiery keyboard writing that Schobert and others had pursued in Paris, though Mozart's textures are less orchestral than theirs, the sense of agitation more consistent and deeper.

The six sonatas for piano and violin printed in Paris and dedicated to the electress were begun in Mannheim early in 1778, and they bear the impress of the local style. That however is not the sole influence; when passing through Munich Mozart had commented favourably on a set of sonatas by Joseph Schuster, then popular there, and had thought of writing a similar set. Schuster's (ed. in NM, nos.229, 232–3) are texturally slender but ingenious, and their use of the 'accompanying' violin is enterprising for the date. Mozart employed several of his devices, and in particular derived from Schuster the structure of the first movement of K303/293c where, in effect, the Adagio introduction

represents the first subject and recurs at the recapitulation. The emotional world of these sonatas is however closer to that of Mannheim than that of Schuster's light, crisp pieces, and each sonata touches on a different aspect of Mannheim expressiveness. At one extreme is K304/300c, Mozart's only work in E minor, with its spare textures and hesitant, wistful manner representing a world of delicate sensibility – its concluding minuet in particular, a rondo on an elegant, pathetic melody of a French cast with a gentle second episode in E major providing harmonic balm. At the other is K306/300l in D, the only three-movement sonata of the published set, a showy and energetic piece with a hint of orchestral style in some of the keyboard writing and a finale in two contrasting tempos and metres. Those two were probably the last to be written. The individuality of expression in these sonatas, and the inventiveness yet essential simplicity of the piano–violin textures, is also evident in such movements as the graceful finale of K302/293d in E♭. One further sonata was written in Mannheim, a three-movement work in C (K296) in a light, almost playful style, composed for Mozart's pupil Therese Serrarius, daughter of his landlord there.

Other products of the Mannheim months are Mozart's flute works, written slowly and unwillingly for a patron; the commission was never finished, the fee never fully paid. The second of the two concertos (K313–4/285c–d) is probably an arrangement of an oboe concerto, possibly the one referred to in a letter as having been written for the Salzburg oboist Ferlendis, and thus rather earlier. Both are essentially in the manner of the violin concertos of 1775, with no perceptible Mannheim influence; an additional Andante (K315/285e) may have been intended as a simpler slow movement for K313 rather than as part of a third concerto. Mozart wrote that he had composed three flute quartets for 'De Jean', but only two (K285 and 285a) can be assigned to this period. Of his other two, K298 is much later (1786–7), and K Anh.171/285b, if fully authentic, probably belongs to the early Viennese years. Mozart told his father that he disliked the flute; but the writing is too professional and idiomatic to betray anything of the kind. He wrote again for flute in Paris, a double concerto with harp (his only work for that instrument) for the Count (not Duke) of Guines and his daughter, composed with care and evident affection as well as a sharp sense of a style apt for aristocratic French patrons: the Andantino, with divided violas, has a sensuous warmth, and the finale is a courtly gavotte.

The most significant Paris work is the symphony written for the Concert Spirituel and, following Leopold's counsel, carefully tailored to local taste. It begins with the obligatory *premier coup d'archet*, made the more sharply effective by the *piano* phrase that follows; marked dynamic contrasts, vivacious rhythms, powerful unison and octave passages, brilliant tuttis, and exposed writing (equally for the string and wind sections) characterize the first movement, a specially inventive piece, obviously designed to dazzle the Parisians' ears and exploit their large orchestra. That such was Mozart's purpose is left in no doubt by his letter of 3 July 1778, in which he referred to the unusual *piano* opening of the finale and the effect it had. The familiar 6/8 Andante, the weight of evidence suggests, was composed later as a replacement for the original, simpler 3/4 movement. The other surviving Paris work is the ballet *Les petits riens*, which contains some sharply characterized dances of an aptly elegant kind, though it is not easy to be certain which of the smaller pieces are Mozart's new movements and which the 'wretched old French airs' that he said were included.

The Mannheim and Paris experiences left their mark on the music composed on his return home; he was doubtless pleased to display his command of international styles in provincial Salzburg. That command is especially clear in the orchestral music. Soon after his return he wrote two symphonies, of which the first, no.32 (in the traditional numbering) in G K318 is in Italian overture form – possibly it was intended for a theatrical performance, but there is no firm evidence. It consists of an Allegro into which, at the end of the development section, an Andante, is inserted; then the Allegro resumes, with its second subject, and finally the first subject returns. This 'reversed recapitulation', favoured by certain Mannheim composers, ought not be regarded as progressive or innovatory; rather it represents an older, binary pattern, in which the first subject was not recapitulated at all, now supplemented by the rhetorical device of having the opening music crown the movement by serving as coda. Mozart did this in the first movements of two sonatas (K306 and 311) and in the Andante of his next symphony, K319 in B♭. While K318 bears, in its brilliant and prolonged tuttis and its dramatic style, signs of Mozart's recent experiences, K319 is a much more chamber-musical work, in the Salzburg tradition. Interestingly, the 'development' sections in its original three movements –

the minuet was added later – each begin with fresh material (with thematic links between them, incidentally): this too, often reckoned as bold or forward-looking, is again a reversion to an earlier procedure.

These works were followed by Mozart's last Salzburg serenade, K320 (see fig.10), probably composed as university Finalmusik. Its concertante insertion is a pair of movements with solo woodwind instruments, mainly flute and oboe, but sometimes a six-part ensemble; the whole work has an opulence of orchestration beyond that of the preceding serenade, K250. Its first movement in particular, though in Mozart's typically extrovert D major manner, has tuttis of exceptional variety and ingenuity, using (as does Symphony no.32) Mannheim-style crescendos, and the finale incorporates hints of contrapuntal development, while the D minor Andantino touches on emotions of a sombre kind not normal to serenades. The use of a posthorn in the second trio of the second minuet gives the work its nickname. This group of works ends with the vigorous and spacious Symphony no.34 in C K338, composed a year later, in August 1780, by when the stylistic novelties were more fully assimilated: the tone is assured and individual. Here the first-movement 'development' makes no reference to exposition material, and there is both a normal recapitulation and a last-minute reappearance of the first subject. There are three movements; the minuet K409/383f may have been intended for it but scarcely accords with it in style.

Mozart composed a further four substantial instrumental works in this period: a piano and violin sonata (K378/317d); his last Salzburg divertimento, K334/320b, for strings and horns, possibly intended for the Mozarts' friends the aristocratic Robinig family, and notable for its exquisitely graceful first minuet; and two double concertos. That for two pianos K365/316a is a work of vivacity and charm, with much ingenious dialogue; it is not known to have been commissioned and was probably intended for Mozart and his sister. That for violin and viola, the Sinfonia concertante K364/320d, is a major work, comparable in its significance to the Piano Concerto K271, also in E♭. The sinfonia concertante was a favoured form in Mannheim and Paris, with their orchestras of virtuosos; Carl Stamitz composed several for violin and viola. Mozart possibly wrote one for wind, and began one for piano and violin, of which he wrote 120 bars, and one for string trio, of which he wrote 134. He may have stopped work because there was no likelihood of a commission or performance; but the possibility should not be overlooked that the intractable formal problems posed by the instrumental layout gave him pause. In K364 they are less acute, for it is a double concerto rather than an ensemble one, and the instruments can interchange material freely; they mostly play separately, in dialogue – the viola often taking over phrases heard on the violin, presenting them in a different light and turning them in different directions – and come together only at the ends of sections. The orchestral writing is markedly Mannheim-influenced, and enhanced by the rich texture of divided violas, needed to reflect the violin–viola symmetry. An impassioned, elegiac tone, characteristic of Mozart's C minor slow movements, marks the Andante, its dialogues full of unexpected melodic twists leading to highly chromatic harmonies.

The vocal works of this period are comparatively few. Mozart wrote four arias on the Mannheim and Paris journey. For Aloysia Weber he set first a Metastasio text, *Non sò d'onde viene*, K294: 'because I know [J. C.] Bach's setting so well, and like it so much . . . I wished to see whether I could not write an aria totally unlike his'. It is indeed like J. C. Bach in style, but not like his setting; it is an eloquent *aria d'affetto*, written lovingly for Aloysia's voice. An ornamented version, prepared for her instruction, is extant. *Io non chiedo* K316/300b, presented to her in Munich, tests her coloratura. He also composed an aria for Dorothea Wendling, and one for the elderly tenor Raaff, a good friend to him at Mannheim, beautifully suited to his old-fashioned portamento style and allowing him generous opportunities for breath. Back in Salzburg, Mozart wrote four substantial sacred works. First among them is the Coronation Mass K317, traditionally believed to have been composed for the ceremonial crowning of an image of the virgin in a church near Salzburg. Written in March 1779, it has claims to be counted Mozart's finest Salzburg mass. It is in *missa brevis* style, but less condensed than his earlier examples and considerably tauter in structure, with more use of recurring material (in particular, the 'Dona' matching the Kyrie). The symphonic drive of the Credo is broken off for an Adagio 'Et incarnatus', touching on distant keys and with delicate violin arabesques; and the Agnus is a soprano solo whose resemblance to 'Dove sono' in *Le nozze di Figaro* has often been remarked.

In the next (and last) of the Salzburg masses, K337, the Agnus, with solo oboe, bassoon and organ, resembles the Countess's other aria in *Figaro*; this, also a short mass, is otherwise of limited interest, apart only from the exceptional treatment of the Benedictus as a severe *a cappella* fugue. Mozart's only two complete settings of the vesper psalms were composed in 1779–80, probably for use in Salzburg Cathedral. Each is a sequence of six movements, not (like a mass or litany setting) a unity; only the keys of the outer movements correspond. Most movements have a basis of homophonic choral writing with solo episodes, but in each work the pattern is changed for the 'Laudate pueri', at first strictly fugal or canonic, and generally contrapuntal throughout, and also for the succeeding 'Laudate Dominum', a soprano aria – in K321 with organ obbligato, and in K339 a simple long, floating melody whose beguiling beauty attracted many 19th-century arrangers.

The technique of writing vivid dramatic music to support declaimed speech – picked up from Benda, and to have been applied in *Semiramis* – was used in *Zaide*, as the unfinished, untitled Singspiel to a text arranged by J. A. Schachtner is known. Its opening scene in particular is striking, with chromatic harmonies and highly expressive figuration supporting the enslaved hero's words of despair; and it culminates in a minuet aria of exquisite grace in the manner of J. C. Bach. *Zaide* was left incomplete presumably because performance prospects had faded; but it has several strong and elaborately worked items, notably a fiery G minor aria for the heroine Zaide and two ensembles, the second of them a quartet in which the characters' differentiated expressions of love, anxiety and vengeance are treated in the same way as in the later *Idomeneo* quartet. But the opera's topic and characterization generally make it more readily seen as a step towards *Die Entführung*. The other dramatic music of this time consists of three

10. *First page of the autograph MS of Mozart's 'Posthorn' Serenade* K320, *composed 1779 (D-Bds)*

choruses, two of them probably reworkings of ones composed in 1773, three entr'actes and a melodrama for Gebler's play *Thamos, König in Ägypten*, his only incidental theatre music (Mozart was a keen follower of theatre, non-musical as well as musical). The serious, intense tone of the instrumental pieces – most likely composed in 1776–7, though the whole achieved its final form probably in 1779 – and the exalted nature of the ritual music in the new final chorus testify to Mozart's involvement in the drama, which like *Die Zauberflöte* deals with the triumph of good over evil. When *Thamos* fell out of the repertory Mozart's music was used in K. M. Plümicke's play *Lanassa*.

12. 1780–81: MUNICH. During summer 1780 Mozart received the commission he had long hoped for to compose an opera for Munich; probably Raaff had helped him secure it. The Salzburg cleric Gianbattista Varesco was engaged to prepare a libretto based on Danchet's *Idomenée*, set by Campra (Paris, 1712). The plot concerns King Idomeneus of Crete, who promises Neptune that if spared from a shipwreck he will sacrifice the first person he sees, and is met on landing by his son Idamantes. Mozart began to set the text in Salzburg: he already knew several of the singers, from Mannheim, and could draft some of the arias in advance. On 5 November he left for Munich to complete the task, working with the singers, the intendant (Count Seeau), the designer (Lorenzo Quaglio) and the ballet-master (Le Grand, in effect the producer too). His letters to Leopold, who was in close touch with Varesco, provide a fascinating picture of the genesis of the work and in particular of the ways in which it was modified during rehearsal. The matters that chiefly occupied Mozart's mind – apart from assuring his father about the singers' enthusiasm – were, first, the need for cuts, because the text was overlong; second, the need to make the action more natural; and third, the need to accommodate the requirements (and the weaknesses) of the singers. As rehearsals, act by act, continued during December, more cuts were made. Even after the libretto was sent to the printer at the beginning of January Mozart continued to trim the score and eventually it was decided to have a second libretto printed to show the final text (although in the event still more adjustments were made, as the performing score makes clear). Because of the opera's excessive length at the rehearsals, Mozart omitted at this late stage not only much recitative of both kinds but also sections of the ceremonial choral scenes and three arias in the last act. The planning, and composition, of the opera had in fact been seriously miscalculated: the libretto was far too long, particularly for the elaborate, expansive setting Mozart envisaged and the ruthless cutting necessitated by the realization of this at so late a stage was bound to affect the work's proportions. The opera was performed, after postponements, on 29 January 1781. Leopold was now in Munich, so Mozart sent no report; but clearly it was a considerable success.

In *Idomeneo* Mozart depicted serious, heroic emotion with a richness unparalleled elsewhere in his works. He certainly set great store by the opera himself. Although nominally an *opera seria*, it departs substantially from tradition: with its French source, it has a more natural attitude to emotion, a more complex structure, and a greater emphasis on the participation of the chorus, while its scoring – for the virtuoso Mannheim orchestra,

now at Munich – is exceptionally full and elaborate. Gluck's influence, notable in Mozart's setting of the oracle scene with trombones (cf *Alceste* – though the idea, in any case obvious in view of the association of trombones with ritual, was put forward by Leopold), is often remarked. The influence of Piccinni's French operas – Mozart had heard *Roland* in Paris – is also strong; so perhaps is that of Holzbauer's *Günther von Schwarzburg*. Mozart had no interest in eliminating either bravura singing, which he used to a dramatic rather than an exhibitionist end (as above all in Idomeneus's 'Fuor del mar'), or, unlike Gluck in his 'reform operas', in eliminating simple recitative – though he often elided recitative of either kind with the lyrical music so as to make the texture more continuous.

A remarkable feature is the opera's abundance of orchestral recitative, much of it vigorous and dramatic, and often extremely colourful and expressive in its harmony, sharply reflecting the sense of the words. Some of it involves the use of motif: it is clear that Mozart employed certain patterns of phrase throughout the opera with consistent reference to individual characters and their predominant emotions, like Ilia's grief and Electra's jealousy (see Heartz, 1974; also *MJb 1973–4*, 82ff). There are also fairly well defined relationships between particular keys and the dramatic contexts in which they appear, affecting the recitative as well as the arias; similar patterns may be found in the later operas. An unorthodox key treatment – a false recapitulation in C minor in a D minor aria – is clearly intended to suggest that Electra is disorientated or even unhinged. The traditional device of analogy between natural events and represented emotion is used with particular force in the same aria, Electra's in Act 1, where the storm at sea is paralleled by her turbulence; and Idomeneus's 'Fuor del mar', a traditional simile aria, gains special force because it is the raging sea itself that is responsible for the raging emotion within him. If the music for Idamantes is less inspiring, that may be because Mozart found the singer, an inexperienced castrato, inadequate; but the richness and warmth of the music for Ilia, notably her E♭ *aria d'affetto* with prominent wind parts, speak unmistakably of Dorothea Wendling's capacities as well as Mozart's sympathy for the character. In the opera's orchestration many new and brilliant details are to be found, like the evocative flute, oboe and violin passages in 'Fuor del mar' (as in bars 9–10) or the solemn effect of the big choral scenes: sustained wind against inexorable string triplets and muted trumpet fanfares in 'O voto tremendo', or pizzicato violin arpeggios against wailing flute and oboe phrases in Idomeneus's prayer. Of the individual numbers, however, the most powerful is the Act 3 quartet in which Idamantes resolves to seek death, a tour de force in which intensely chromatic music embraces truthfully four characters' diverse emotions.

*Idomeneo* had three performances in Munich. Later in 1781 Mozart considered revising it 'more in the French manner', with a bass Idomeneus (as he had initially expected to have for the première) and a tenor Idamantes, but his hopes came to nothing. He did however give a performance, probably a concert one, at the Auersperg palace in Vienna in 1786, for which he arranged the castrato part of Idamantes for a tenor, writing an extended new aria with violin obbligato and a new duet, and making other modifications and cuts.

While he was in Munich Mozart composed a number

of short vocal works, his Oboe Quartet, and possibly the Serenade K361/370a (or part of it) and three piano sonatas. These, K330/300h, 331/300i and 332/300k, long ascribed to his months in Paris but now known to belong to this period in Munich or Mozart's early years in Vienna, are among his most popular keyboard works, especially K332 in F (which in its 1784 published form has a richly embellished slow movement recapitulation, presumably Mozart's own second thoughts) and K331 in A, famous for its first movement, a 6/8 pastoral theme with variations, and its 'Rondo alla turca' finale, a brilliant response to the current fashion for janissary music.

Mozart, his father and his sister remained in Munich until early March. They then spent a few days in Augsburg, no doubt visiting their relatives. On 12 March Mozart, back in Munich, was summoned to Vienna, where the Archbishop of Salzburg and his retinue were resident during celebrations of the accession of Emperor Joseph II.

13. EARLY VIENNESE YEARS, 1781–4. Mozart arrived in Vienna on 16 March and was required to stay with the archbishop's entourage. At table he was placed below the valets but above the cooks; fresh from his triumphs in Munich, where noblemen had talked with him on equal terms, he was insulted and resentful. He equally resented the archbishop's refusal to let him earn money by playing at concerts. His letters home over the next three months reflect not only his increasing irritation – many sections are written in the cipher Mozart and his father used for material they did not want the Salzburg censors to understand – but also a growing enthusiasm for the possibility of earning his own living in Vienna. On the evening of an entertainment given by the archbishop, for which he supplied a rondo for the violinist Brunetti, a song for the castrato Ceccarelli and a sonata for himself (K373, 374 and 379/373a), he could, had the archbishop released him, have played before the emperor and earned the equivalent of half his annual Salzburg salary. On 9 May matters came to a head, and at a stormy interview with the archbishop, who according to Mozart poured out abuse unworthy of his station and his calling, Mozart asked for his discharge. At first he was refused, but at an interview with the chief steward Count Arco on 9 June he was finally and decisively released from Salzburg service, 'with a kick on my arse ... by order of our worthy Prince Archbishop', he wrote. Leopold's letters of these months do not survive, but their content is easily inferred from Mozart's replies. Clearly he was apprehensive for his own situation and anxious about his son's future. Mozart replied with strong – almost too strong – protestations about his honour, about how ill he had been used, and about the rosy prospects of a career in Vienna; he also answered various reproaches about supposed improper behaviour and failures in his religious observations, and his answers ring true.

By this time Mozart had moved from the quarters occupied by Colloredo's retinue to the house of his former Mannheim friends the Webers. In 1780 Aloysia had married a court actor, Joseph Lange, and now Mozart's name came to be linked with that of the third of the four daughters, Constanze. In a letter to Leopold, Mozart dismissed such rumours as 'entirely groundless': he had never thought less of getting married, which would be a misfortune to him, and anyway he did not love the girl. But to scotch the gossip he moved elsewhere in September. He was making a modest living by teaching, one of his three or four pupils (see Hamann, 1962–3) being Josepha von Auernhammer, for whom he wrote his two-piano sonata and to whom he dedicated a set of accompanied sonatas, published by Artaria in November; she was very ugly – Mozart was repelled by her amorous feelings towards him – but musically talented and a true friend. Probably she later saw some of his publications through the press. At the end of July Mozart had been given a libretto for a Singspiel, Die Verführung (later Entführung) aus dem Serail, on which he unhurriedly worked; it was soon clear that there was no prospect of an early production. Other compositions included a wind serenade for a group of 'poor beggars who ... play quite well together' to perform to a lady on her name day; he wrote it 'quite carefully' as an influential court official was to hear it. The 'poor beggars' surprised Mozart by playing it to him on his own name day two weeks later. During these months he took part in concerts in various noblemen's houses. In December he played at court in a private, informal competition with Clementi; they improvised, separately and together, and played sonatas. In a letter to his father Mozart called Clementi a 'mere technician'; Clementi later spoke of him more generously. Although Mozart was evidently regarded as the winner, his hopes for a court appointment were no nearer to fulfilment.

During the autumn and winter of 1781–2 the relationship between Mozart and Constanze Weber grew deeper. Mozart did not refer to her in his numerous letters home between his urgent denials of 25 July and his firm statement on 15 December of his love for her. On that date he wrote to Leopold of his virtuous life as regards relationships with women, his need for a domestic existence (which he said would represent an economy) and his conviction that Constanze was a paragon despite the unpleasantness of her family. Events gave Mozart little choice: doubtless through his future mother-in-law's scheming, he was placed in a position where, because of his alleged intimacy with Constanze, he was required to agree to marry her or to compensate her. The letters containing Leopold's reactions were later destroyed by Constanze.

Mozart's main energies during the early part of 1782 were concentrated on the completion of Die Entführung aus dem Serail. He may have given his first Viennese concert (or 'academy') in March; he certainly took part in one in the Augarten in May. During this time he played regularly in Sunday concerts at the home of Baron Gottfried van Swieten. Act 1 of Die Entführung had been finished the previous August, when Mozart had hoped for a production in the autumn; the remainder was written by May, and rehearsals began at the beginning of June. The première, on 16 July, was evidently a success – Mozart's letter home describing it does not survive, but he referred to the 'good reception' after the second performance three days later. According to Niemetschek's biography of Mozart (1798), the emperor remarked that the opera had 'very many notes', to which Mozart replied 'Exactly the necessary number, your majesty'. Gluck, the doyen of composers in Vienna, with whom Mozart had lately become friendly, requested an extra performance. The opera remained in the repertory for several years and was soon given in various German cities. Other works of these months include, besides the accompanied sonatas for publication, the Haffner Symphony (written as a serenade for the ennoblement of Sigmund Haffner in Salzburg), a further wind serenade, a group of piano concertos intended for publication, and the first of a set of string quartets.

A few days after the première of *Die Entführung* the difficult situation in the Weber family came to a head and Mozart decided to go forward with marriage arrangements. He wrote to his father on 31 July 1782 asking his consent (also expressing pain at Leopold's cool reaction to the opera's success); on 2 August the couple took communion together, on 3 August the contract was signed, on 4 August they were married at St Stephen's Cathedral. On 5 August Leopold's grudging consent arrived. Constanze was 20, Mozart 26. Their marriage seems to have been very happy. Constanze was loyal and affectionate, if sometimes a shade thoughtless. Mozart occasionally reproached her, for not writing to him, or for frivolous behaviour; she may not have shared his long-practised disdainful attitudes. According to Mozart's description of her to Leopold, she had no wit, but plenty of common sense and the kindest heart in the world. None of Constanze's letters to Mozart survives; her few to his relatives testify to her poor literacy and her almost embarrassing eagerness to please. His to her testify to a relationship of warmth and intimacy, and often sound a note of almost paternal solicitude for her health and well-being. There is little reason to imagine that she was solely, or even primarily, to blame for their chronic money troubles, which began only weeks after their marriage when they had to borrow from the friend, Baroness Waldstätten, who had provided their bridal supper. It has often been suggested that Constanze was extravagant, and indeed Mozart felt bound to deny it, to Leopold, even before their marriage. The truth probably lies somewhere near Nannerl's statement, in 1792, that Mozart was incapable of managing his own financial affairs and that Constanze was unable to help him. In this context it is interesting to note that Leopold, in a letter to Baroness Waldstätten shortly after the wedding, set down his own thoughts on his son: the familiar complaint that Wolfgang was apt to procrastinate is enlarged upon, and his tendency to be easygoing or indolent on the one hand is contrasted with his impatience and impetuousness on the other.

Mozart was anxious to take his wife to Salzburg, to meet his father and sister. To Leopold's irritation, the visit was several times postponed: because of the weather, because of Mozart's pupils, because of his concert commitments (including an important academy of his own before the emperor on 23 March), and because Constanze was pregnant. Their first child, Raimund Leopold, was born on 17 June 1783, while Mozart was working on his D minor String Quartet. Then again he delayed, ostensibly because he was afraid that in Salzburg he could be arrested by the archbishop. He and Constanze set out in July (leaving behind their child, who died on 19 August) and spent about three months in Salzburg. Clearly Mozart had had anxieties about the success of the visit, and particularly about his father's reactions to Constanze; and one may infer from the later correspondence that these months were not wholly happy. Mozart's two violin–viola duets probably date from this period, allegedly written for Michael Haydn, behindhand with a commission; and the Kyrie and Gloria of the mass he had resolved to write in

thanks for his marriage had their first hearing, possibly with Constanze singing, at St Peter's Abbey on 26 October (the work, K427/417a, was never completed). He also conferred with Varesco about a libretto for a new comic opera. On the return journey he paused at Linz, where he composed a symphony – no.36 in C K425 – 'at breakneck speed' for a concert, as he did not have one with him. Probably the Piano Sonata K333/315c dates from this time.

Back in Vienna, Mozart resumed his teaching, which provided his basic income, and entered on what were the busiest, the most successful and probably the happiest months of his life (despite an illness, possibly a kidney infection, in August). In a letter home he listed his engagements over five weeks, covering the Lenten concert season, including 19 concerts during the month of March, mostly at the houses of Count Johann Esterházy and the Russian ambassador, Prince Golitsïn, but including concerts of his own, both private and at the theatre. In February he had started keeping a list of his new works, *Verzeichnüss aller meiner Werke* (see fig. 11), recording the incipit and the date of each; many of the entries however were made well after the actual time of composition, and several dates must be wrong. The first works noted are the great piano concertos from K449 onwards, most of them composed for the concerts in which he was engaged; other early entries are for the Quintet for piano and wind, which Mozart counted 'the best work I have composed', and the Sonata for piano and violin K454, written for the violinist Regina Strinasacchi – this is the work he is said to have performed from a blank or fragmentary copy, and it is clear from the autograph that the violin part was written first and the piano one added later. This sonata, with two others for solo piano (K284, 333), was published by Torricella, and three (K330–32) were issued by Artaria; other publishers made available in manuscript the group of piano concertos written in 1782–3, K413–5/387a, 385p, 387b, which Artaria printed in 1785, and a wind-band arrangement (not by Mozart) of *Die Entführung*. A wind serenade of Mozart's was given at a concert by Anton Stadler, the clarinettist; this may have been the Serenade for 13 instruments K361/370a, probably begun in Munich in 1781 and completed in Mozart's early months in Vienna. In the first days of 1785 Mozart completed the last two of the six quartets published by Artaria later in the year with a dedication to Haydn. His second child, (5) Carl Thomas Mozart, was born in September 1784.

14. 1782–4: VOCAL WORKS. Mozart's correspondence with Leopold about *Idomeneo* gives a picture of the mechanics of planning an opera for the stage. That about *Die Entführung* is revealing in other ways. Mozart's letter of 26 September 1781 refers not only to some restructuring of the libretto (to expand Osmin's part, and to move an ensemble to a more effective position) but also to specific expressive devices: the key relationships, which he said needed some degree of remoteness to express Osmin's immoderate rage, and the orchestration, where the violins in octaves expressed Belmonte's throbbing heart, and muted violins with flute the 'whispering and sighing'. He further referred to the 'sacrifice' of one of the arias for Constanze (that his fiancée and his heroine shared a name was coincidental), 'Ach ich liebte', to the singer's 'flexible throat', and mentioned that

*11. The first page of Mozart's 'Verzeichnüss aller meiner Werke', begun in February 1784 (GB-Lbm Loan 42/1)*

he had included the lively janissary chorus and the drinking-duet to please the Viennese taste. In another letter, evidently responding to Leopold's criticism of the literary quality of J. G. Stephanie's libretto, he pointed out that it 'could hardly be better written for music', adding: 'in an opera the poetry must be altogether the obedient daughter of the music ... when music reigns supreme and one listens to it, all else is forgotten'.

Music indeed reigns supreme in *Die Entführung*; in fact the force and the scale of the music, and certain aspects of its structure (like the integration of the overture and the opening aria), carry the work beyond the accepted limits of the Viennese Singspiel tradition to which it belongs. The colourful 'Turkish' music (exotically scored, with piccolo and an enlarged percussion section) and the comic scenes with the Pasha's grotesque steward, Osmin, belong squarely in that tradition, as do the vaudeville finale and the songs for the servant Pedrillo – one is a 'Moorish' ballad with pizzicato accompaniment, the other the parody 'Frisch zum Kampfe', where the grandiose, military D major setting with trumpets and drums is contradicted by music to represent his quaking with fear. On a different plane are, above all, the deeply felt arias for Constanze in Act 2: first a chromatic lament, using material from *Zaide*, given a particularly pessimistic slant by its ending in the home key, G minor, with material earlier heard in B♭ major; and the expansive 'Martern aller Arten', 293 bars long with an undramatically lengthy opening ritornello of 60 bars, with four obbligato instruments, where although there may seem to be further concessions to Cavalieri's throat the bravura is not without dramatic function. Other noteworthy features are Belmonte's ardent arias and the quartet finale to the second act, resembling the chain finales of *opera buffa* but, unlike them, not propelling the action.

It is characteristic of the Singspiel that the crucial elopement scene is not set to music but conducted in spoken dialogue.

The German opera company for which *Die Entführung* was composed lasted only briefly. Mozart, though an enthusiast for opera in German, now sought Italian librettos. He started work on two comic operas during 1783, one, *L'oca del Cairo*, with Varesco, and the other, *Lo sposo deluso*, with Lorenzo da Ponte; but he soon abandoned them, doubtless because he came to realize how feeble were the librettos. He composed a number of separate arias during this period, including a group for insertion in Anfossi's *Il curioso indiscreto* for singers (among them Aloysia Lange) unsuited by the existing ones. Also for his sister-in-law was *Mia speranza adorata* K416, in the increasingly popular rondò form, with a slow section followed by a fast one (sometimes twice over, *ABAB*), which Mozart later often employed in his operas. From 1783 or rather later come a group of vocal chamber pieces, notturnos for two sopranos and bass with clarinets or basset-horns, lighthearted yet with an operatic vein of expression, apt to their Metastasio texts: these were written for a circle of friends connected with Gottfried von Jacquin, whom Mozart apparently permitted to pass the pieces off as his own.

Mozart had little call to compose sacred music during this period. A beautiful and richly scored Kyrie K341/368a, in D minor (in contradistinction to the C major of most of the Salzburg church music), dates from just after *Idomeneo*; the next sacred work is the C minor Mass K427/417a, partly written by January 1783, and left incomplete. Written not to commission but in fulfilment of a vow, it was to have been a large-scale 'cantata mass', unlike any other of Mozart's, and is reckoned to have been designed for Constanze to sing. The special stylistic features of the C minor Mass require that it be viewed in the wider context of Mozart's activities and compositions of the period. In 1782 he had come into contact with Baron Gottfried van Swieten, at whose house he regularly played. Van Swieten, while ambassador in Berlin, had developed a taste for late Baroque music, then little heard in Vienna except in antiquarian musical circles. Mozart's interest was caught, and he sent home for fugues by the Bachs (C. P. E. and W. F. as well as J. S.) and Handel. Various of his works of these months reflect his response to the challenge of a new technique. He copied several Bach fugues and attached new preludes to some of them, in a solemn but personal vein, showing no awareness of stylistic incongruity; about the same time he wrote a suite, sometimes unauthentically called 'in the style of Handel', and several fugues for keyboard. Almost all these pieces were left unfinished. Some were composed at the behest of Constanze, who liked fugues. His persistent failure to complete them suggests not only that Mozart lost interest once he had met the form's basic challenges but also that he regarded fugue as essentially irrelevant to his real manner of musical expression. Some scholars (notably Einstein, 1945) have ascribed a deep significance to Mozart's encounter with Bach and with fugue in particular; but although some absorption of contrapuntal techniques cannot be excluded, their influence on Mozart's central musical development is easily overrated.

The contrapuntal treatment in certain instrumental works of this period, for example the String Quartet in G K387, can be traced to other influences; and the fugues in the C minor Mass do not significantly depart from the traditional Austrian ecclesiastical model. The work is however marked by a certain archaic flavour, new in Mozart's music, that seems likely to derive from his experiences at van Swieten's. It is noticeable not only in the statuesque, grave choruses (some in eight parts, or five, as well as the customary four), among which the massive and relentless 'Qui tollis' on an ostinato bass of the Baroque descending tetrachord pattern is the most powerful, but also in several of the solo items, like the 'Domine Deus' duet or the 'Quoniam' trio, which have some almost Handelian counterpoint, figuration and bare continuo texture. Others of the solos are in the usual Austrian church style, with expressive melody and florid decoration, like the 'Laudamus te' and particularly the 'Et incarnatus', with wind obbligatos. The work has often been criticized for inconsistency of style. The Kyrie and Gloria were completed, and for the Sanctus and Benedictus Mozart's intentions for completion are easily deduced; but only part of the Credo was written, and none of the Agnus Dei. Einstein called the work a noble torso. In 1785 Mozart re-used the complete numbers, to a libretto specially provided (perhaps by Da Ponte), along with two new arias, to form a cantata *Davidde penitente* K469 for performance at the Vienna Tonkünstler-Sozietät.

15. 1781–4: CHAMBER AND INSTRUMENTAL MUSIC. Mozart's first Viennese publication was a set of six piano and violin sonatas. It included K296, composed at Mannheim but not published in the earlier set; K378/317*d*, written either in Salzburg or early in 1781 before his arrival in Vienna; and K379/373*a*, composed just after his arrival for Colloredo's entertainments. These sonatas are broader in conception than the earlier ones. The first-movement development sections normally begin with fresh material; an exception is the particularly brilliant K377/374*e* in F where the first subject is thoroughly worked out and the development section elided with the recapitulation. That sonata ends with an extended minuet-rondo, in the *amoroso* style of J. C. Bach, following a variation movement. K379 in G ends with variations, and begins with a short but intense Adagio leading directly into a G minor Allegro of exceptional vigour; perhaps the unorthodox form and the temper of the music reflect Mozart's way of asserting himself at the archbishop's soirée. K376/374*d*, again in F, almost reverts to the playful mood of the Serrarius sonata K296, apart from its Andante, characterized by veiled accompanying textures as well as its unusual form. The final sonata, K380/374*f* in E♭, is the grandest in manner with its rhetorical contrasts between full chords and rapid passage-work and its strong sense of harmonic direction. A reviewer of the publication in Cramer's *Magazin der Musik* (4 April 1783) commented not only on the richness of the ideas and the signs of Mozart's genius but particularly on the ingenuity with which the violin accompaniment is combined with the keyboard so that the instruments 'are always kept in equal prominence'. They remain piano sonatas with accompaniment, and contain entire pages where the violin part could be omitted without damaging the music's continuity; but increasingly the violin part, instead of merely filling in harmonically, supporting, or adding interest to the texture, carries essential material, melodic or even contrapuntal, or engages in dialogue. Mozart's sonatas, both the 1778 set and these, have conspicuously more textural variety and fullness than most others of the time.

Mozart began work on a small further group of accompanied sonatas for Constanze, probably late in 1782; but they suffered the fate of most of the music intended for her and were left unfinished. They are miniature in scale and slender in content; one was evidently to have included a fugue. There exist completions by Maximilian Stadler. The K454 sonata for Strinasacchi is however in the mainstream of Mozart's development. The violin part, understandably, has even greater prominence, and the work is virtually a duo with the instruments on equal terms. It is interesting to note that again the first movement development begins with new material (more precisely, a figure from the exposition's cadence chords); the succeeding sonata, K481, of 1785, notable particularly for the far-reaching enharmonic modulations of its Adagio, has parallel treatment at the corresponding point. K454 is however of unprecedented richness in the variety of its melodic material, its phrase structure and its harmonic pace as well as its texture.

But the central chamber works of this period are the six string quartets dedicated to Haydn. Mozart's personal acquaintance with Haydn probably dated from 1781. Where or how they met, and the degree of intimacy of their friendship, is uncertain, but it is known that they were at quartet parties together more than once. The English composer Stephen Storace gave such a party in 1784, reported in Michael Kelly's *Reminiscences* (1826), where the players were Haydn, Dittersdorf, Mozart and Vanhal. Another took place on Leopold's visit to his son in 1785, when Haydn said to him: 'Before God, and as an honest man, I tell you that your son is the greatest composer known to me in person or by name. He has taste, and, what is more, the greatest knowledge of composition'. Mozart chose to dedicate his first mature quartets not to a noble patron for the favour of gifts in return, but to the acknowledged master of the string quartet. In his warm, florid Italian dedication, he referred to Haydn as his 'most dear friend' and to the elder composer's expressed satisfaction with the works (see fig.12).

12. Title-page of the six string quartets, K387, 421/ 417b, 428/421b, 458, 464 and 465 (Vienna: Artaria, 1785)

Mozart also referred to his quartets as 'the fruits of long and laborious endeavour', a claim that is borne out by the state of the autographs and the existence of numerous rejected sketches. That he sought to emulate Haydn's op.33, published in 1781, can scarcely be doubted. Like Haydn's, these works are characterized by textures conceived not merely in four-part harmony but as four-part discourse, with the actual musical ideas ineluctably linked to a freshly integrated treatment of the medium. The debt to Haydn lies rather in this general approach to quartet style than in the specific resemblances that have been pointed out (like the kinship of the minuets of the Eb quartets, op.33 no.2 and K428/421b), though such resemblances are sufficiently marked to leave no doubt about Mozart's knowledge of the Haydn works or his interest, conscious or no, in vying with them.

The Mozart works form a collection more heterogeneous than any set of Haydn's. They do however have several features in common, some of them new to Mozart's music. One is the use of counterpoint for intensification: in for example the first movements of the

D minor, K421/417b, the most sombre and dramatic work in the set, and of K464 in A, where each of the principal themes is soon subjected to imitative treatment. The Andante of K428 follows a similar procedure, supported by an increasing level of chromaticism; the upward-resolving appoggiaturas have prompted comparisons with *Tristan und Isolde*. This quartet as a whole is remarkable for its chromatic writing; also notable is the multiplicity of motif in its first movement. The most famous use of dissonance is, of course, in the C major K465 whose slow introduction (Mozart's only one in a string quartet) became an analytical *cause célèbre* (see Vertrees, 1974). K458 (the 'Hunt', after its 6/8 opening), the most relaxed of the six, inaugurates the second half of the set, which Leopold understandably regarded as lighter in style than the first, and is the only one with a development section quoting no exposition material; but its coda, with contrapuntal discussion of the opening theme, draws the movement together. Its Adagio, also lacking development, has some textural detail of exceptional richness. The minuet (placed before rather than after the slow movement), notable for the unorthodox phrase structure of its eight-bar opening strain, is much briefer than the others, several of which are in effect miniature sonata-form designs; their trios are often in the minor mode, with invention of a more sophisticated cast. Two quartets have variation movements, K421 (finale, on a theme akin to that of the variation finale of Haydn's op.33 no.5 but also to a variation in the K377 sonata) and K464 (slow movement). Each follows to some degree the 'quatuor concertant' scheme whereby the instruments take turns at carrying the main interest, but this potentially banal notion is transfigured by Mozart's textural inventiveness into a pattern of increasing complexity and, again, intensification. Two of the finales are of particular interest. That of K464 is virtually a monothematic movement, built from the pair of tags heard in the first four bars. That of K387 begins with a fugal exposition, and incorporates another (on a theme contrapuntally compatible with the first) in its second subject; it is not however a fugal movement like those in Haydn's op.20 or Mozart's K173, but a sonata-type form (a rounded binary, for it lacks a first-group recapitulation) with fugal material. To cite this as a sign of Bachian influence is to disregard the fact that a steady stream of sonata-type movements with fugal sections had been composed during Mozart's time, including many by composers whose work he knew, like Michael Haydn, F. X. Richter and Wagenseil.

Other chamber works of this period include two duets for violin and viola, written with an ingenuity that goes some way towards concealing the textural thinness of the medium, and various arrangements of Bach fugues, with and without preludes (the exact number is in doubt); there is also the ingeniously composed horn quintet, set with two violas so that the solo instrument is not too readily covered, and the happy oboe quartet written in Munich at the time of *Idomeneo*. More important than these is the Quintet for piano and wind K452, a difficult medium because of the limited capacities of the wind instruments (oboe, clarinet, bassoon, horn) to blend or to sustain a prolonged line, and the risk of their sound beginning to cloy. Mozart designed his melodic material accordingly, casting it in short phrases which create and resolve tensions at a rapid rate. The result is a work of exceptional mastery and inventiveness, melodically, rhythmically and in its use of instrumental sonority.

Wind music proper falls into a separate category, being designed rather for open-air band performance than as chamber music. Mozart's three substantial wind serenades date from around this time; they are his last works for wind ensemble, apart from some small masonic pieces and the lightweight divertimentos K Anh.229/439b, which are contemporary with the similarly scored Jacquin notturnos (and which survive in some state of disorder; see Flothuis, 1973–4). The earliest of them is probably K375, originally for pairs of clarinets, bassoons and horns but more familiar in its later form, with additional oboes making up the standard 'Harmonie' ensemble. It opens with the martial rhythm Mozart often used in works in Eb, and is on the expansive, leisurely scale apt to serenade music; there are five movements, with two minuets. Its companion piece K388/384a, Mozart's first true C minor work, is presumably the 'Nacht musique' that, according to a letter, he was required to write in great haste. The fact that Mozart later arranged it for string quintet (K406/516b) is in itself a commentary on its character. A work of driving energy and consistent intensity, with its chromatic writing, its strikingly unorthodox phrase structure, its pulsating inner parts and its vigorous sforzandos, it lifts the wind serenade medium to a level perhaps out of accord with its social purpose; the learned canons of the minuet and especially its trio (4 in 2, al rovescio), indebted more to Haydn (cf Symphonies 44, 47) than to the Baroque, demand a more attentive listener than do the serenades of Mozart's youth, as indeed do the instrumental ingenuities of the concluding variations. For enterprise in the handling of instrumental colour, however, the Serenade for 13 instruments, or 'Gran Partita', K361/370a, stands supreme: this is a seven-movement work, for the eight-part Harmonie ensemble supplemented by two basset-horns, two horns and double bass. By using thematic material of a dialogue character, or involving contrasts between the tutti and smaller groups, Mozart allowed the maximum scope for varied instrumental combinations; and the inclusion of a variation movement, and of two trios to each of the minuets, provided yet more opportunities for kaleidoscopic writing. The expressive variety and instrumental range of these works stand without parallel in wind music.

Despite Mozart's activities as pianist and piano teacher, this period produced little solo piano music. Except in so far as they provide a commentary on his preoccupations at the time, the abortive fugues, the prelude and fugue K394/383a and the pseudo-Baroque dance suite K399/385i are unimportant. The fantasias of the same period (these works are all, plausibly, supposed to belong to 1782), which include the one in D minor K397/385g, argue that his interest in the Bach family extended to Carl Philipp Emanuel, whom he is reputed to have admired but whose influence on him is otherwise small; Mozart's sympathy for the north German style must have been limited. The fantasias were all left unfinished. To some extent they may represent written-out versions of his concert improvisations. So too do the variations, of which one important set (K455) and one whose entire authenticity has been much argued (K460/454a) belong to this period. K455 typifies, as much as any single work can, Mozart's variation technique: it comprises a series of variations of progressive brilliance interspersed with others of textural ingenuity,

including one in the tonic minor, has an Adagio as the penultimate variation and finally an extended one in a changed metre. The only sonata of these years is K457 in C minor, which was published in 1785 along with the Fantasia K475; the pairing implies that continuous performance was intended, with the formal orderliness of the sonata resolving the tensions of the impassioned and irregular fantasy, notable for its remote modulations and its unpredictable structure and textures. The sonata is itself the most forceful – it has been called Beethovenian, and certainly it influenced Beethoven – that Mozart composed, taut in form and characterized by the driving, triadic themes of its fast movements, which enfold an Adagio notable for the increasingly elaborate embellishments of the main theme.

Finally mention should be made of Mozart's two strongly contrasted two-piano works, the brilliant, good-humoured Sonata in D K448/375a and the Fugue in C minor K426. The latter, based on a theme of Baroque ancestry, is elaborately worked, using inversions and many varieties of stretto, and derives a certain harshness from the prevalence of chromatic appoggiaturas. Neither the counterpoint nor the treatment, with a homophonic final climax, could be called Bachian. In 1788 Mozart arranged the fugue for strings, prefixing it with an Adagio (K546). These are Mozart's only two-piano works, apart from some fragments and the incomplete Larghetto and Allegro in Eb (Kdeest; see Croll, 1964).

16. 1781–4: ORCHESTRAL MUSIC. The series of piano concertos that Mozart composed in Vienna are probably his greatest achievement in instrumental music. They represent a corpus of music of exceptional quality and originality, far beyond the concertos of his predecessors or his contemporaries in their scale, their thematic richness and their subtle, highly developed relationship between soloist and orchestra.

The origins of the structural patterns of Mozart's piano concerto opening movements lie in the ritornello form of the aria or concerto first movement of the late Baroque, expanded in the light of the sonata principle. Closely analogous structures may be found in the arias of his early operas. This was a form that varied considerably according to the character of the material, except in its basic scheme of tonalities, which essentially conformed to the sonata pattern used in virtually all Mozart's and his contemporaries' music. The commonest schemes in his concerto first movements of this period usually follow some such lines as these: an opening ritornello in the tonic, comprising a primary theme and (after a tutti) a secondary one, with a cadential group; then, in effect, a sonata-form exposition for soloist and orchestra, beginning with the former primary theme (sometimes with prefatory solo material), including the former secondary theme and often a new solo one, both in the dominant, and cadential material; a central ritornello; a widely modulating development or 'free fantasia', with sequential writing and solo bravura and little thematic working; a recapitulation, including material from both the opening ritornello and the exposition, now in the tonic; and a cadenza and closing ritornello. Mozart's thematic fertility and his particular method of devising flexible links, between themes, bravura passages and ritornello material, ensured a high level of interest within each concerto as well as great variety within the series as a whole.

Mozart wrote three piano concertos in 1782–3 and

six in 1784; a further eight were to follow. He described the 1782–3 set to his father (28 December 1782):

These concertos are a happy medium between what is too easy and too difficult; they are very brilliant, pleasing to the ear, and natural, without being vapid. There are passages here and there from which connoisseurs alone can derive satisfaction; but these passages are written in such a way that the less learned cannot fail to be pleased, though without knowing why.

K413/387a is the slightest and most conservative of these three: its finale reverts to the minuet-rondo type favoured by J. C. Bach and used by Mozart as far back as 1774. K415/387b is in the pompous, formal manner of many of Mozart's C major symphonies, with brisk, military rhythms and brilliant passage-work; Mozart's sketches show that he planned a C minor Adagio, then settled for a graceful Andante in F (he used the C minor material for a pair of slow episodes in the 6/8 finale). The most distinctive of these three works is K414/385p, with its exceptionally delicate orchestral layout, its easy succession of melodies, and its unassuming bravura writing. The main theme of the Andante quotes, not necessarily intentionally, an overture by J. C. Bach (to *La calamità dei cuori*, 1763, published 1770); the music's elegiac character has led to its being interpreted as an act of homage to J. C. Bach, who had lately died. Mozart wrote two finales, the Rondo K386 being presumably a rejected first attempt; that both are 2/4 Allegrettos, light and gentle in character, suggests that he had a clear view of the kind of movement he wanted to write before finding the right material.

These concertos, Mozart said, were written for performance with an orchestra including oboes and horns – in fact K413 additionally calls for bassoons, 415 for bassoons, trumpets and drums – or even 'a quattro', presumably meaning just four string instruments, which made them apt for domestic use. The next, K449 in E♭, composed for Mozart's pupil Barbara Ployer, can also be played with strings alone. Although it thus lacks the variety of colour that marks the greatest of the series, it may be counted as the first of the mature concertos. Its opening movement, like that of K414, abounds in melodic ideas, but here they are more diverse in character, and the form is enlarged so as to comprehend a wider range of material. There is an unusually taut development section, built on a phrase from the cadential group. This movement has something close to the textbook 'double exposition', otherwise unknown in the mature works, by virtue of its modulation to the dominant in the opening ritornello. The finale is Mozart's most brilliant, elaborate and ingenious to date. Outwardly a sonata-rondo, of a specially complex kind, it incorporates procedures closely akin to those of monothematic movements, sonata or ritornello, and at the same time its opening theme is subjected to constant melodic variation – to the extent that a coda turning to 6/8 metre, a procedure normal in variation movements, seems a natural outcome. Its contrapuntal inclinations have also been much remarked.

Mozart composed the next two works, K450 in B♭ and 451 in D, to play at concerts. 'They are both concertos to make you sweat', he wrote to Leopold (26 May 1784). K450 represents a distinct advance in its newly elaborate writing for wind instruments and in its reconciliation of a more selfconscious virtuoso style with, again, a wide range of thematic material; in K451, in the tradition of brilliant D major music (the orchestra includes trumpets and drums), the style is again virtuoso, and there is a new, spacious symphonic character, but the music is more homogeneous and lacks the thematic variety and interest of the other concertos of this period. The next two were composed for Barbara Ployer (K453 in G) and the blind virtuoso pianist Maria Theresia von Paradis (K456 in B♭), though Mozart undoubtedly played them himself; both, particularly K453, are technically less demanding than the two preceding. The use of wind instruments is even more elaborate; much of the principal thematic material is entrusted to them, and this strikingly affects the nature and phrase structure of that material, especially in the dialogue themes of the first movement of K456. The two opening movements follow virtually identical groundplans, and share too a new method of weaving piano bravura writing into interesting, often motivically constructed orchestral textures, so that it becomes less of an end in itself, more of a continuation of the musical development. The Andante of K453 is characterized by its distant, often dramatic modulations and its rich woodwind writing; the finale is a set of variations (mainly double ones), on a theme close to one Mozart noted in his commonplace book as sung by his pet starling. The K456 slow movement, in G minor, is (like that of K450) a set of variations, whose expressive force is barely lessened by their being somewhat schematic for a work otherwise so fluid; possibly they also seem foursquare, but the strains are in fact of eight and 13 bars. The finale (again like that of K450) is of the 'hunting' type. With K459 in F, the last of the 1784 concertos, the finale (560 bars long) bears more weight; it is in a variety of sonata-rondo form, enriched by fugato episodes and much semi-contrapuntal use of orchestral material against piano bravura. This follows a pastoral Andantino and a martial first movement, thematically less varied than its predecessors but no less tautly developed, exploiting the march-like rhythm that Mozart had also used to begin K451, 453 and 456.

Mozart's only other concerto of the early 1780s is K417, for horn. Of the next for horn, K447, the Romance probably dates from 1784 but the outer movements are seemingly later (1786–7). These works, and K495 of 1786, are altogether smaller in scale than the piano concertos, and do not have a comparable subtlety, though basically they follow the same formal outlines. Composed for Joseph Leutgeb, an old Salzburg friend who was now a Viennese cheesemonger, they exhibit, not least in their multi-coloured autograph annotations, Mozart's humour. They also, characteristically, show Mozart turning the natural horn's limitations to profitable ends, even to the point where the different timbre of stopped notes may be musically advantageous. Each concerto possesses, predictably, a spirited 'hunting' finale. K417 and 495 have much in common; K447 is the most adventurous, with unusual scoring – clarinets and bassoons replace the oboes and horns – and a slow movement in A♭ rather than B♭, meaning that the available natural notes fall differently in the scale and so give rise to a new range of melodic possibilities. K412/386b, long dated 1782, has been established (by Tyson) as from 1791; it comprises a compact, neatly turned first movement and a 'hunting' rondo, incomplete in the autograph (the sole true source: the score sometimes dated 1787 is probably a 1792 completion).

Mozart had no regular call to compose symphonies in these years as he did concertos. Between 1781 and 1788 his few symphonies were written as occasional pieces; no.35 was originally a serenade, composed for the Haffner family in Salzburg at the time of the *Entführung* première, and written in the brilliant and effective serenade key, D major, which Leopold (according to Mozart's letter of 27 July 1782) favoured. It originally had five movements, with two minuets. The autograph makes clear that the flutes and clarinets in the outer movements – this is Mozart's only symphony with eight woodwind – were added later. The music is essentially in the serenade manner, with dashing outer movements, a warm-toned Andante and a formal, foursquare minuet; but the substance of the first is strengthened by the way its main motif is woven into the texture, and the finale is a brilliant *moto perpetuo*, recalling that of the Paris Symphony. That a serenade could take its place as a symphony is in itself a commentary on the course Mozart's music was taking. Symphony no.36, hastily composed at Linz, does not pursue that course much further: in spite of its slow introduction, a new feature for a Mozart symphony, it is primarily an extrovert work, clear and spacious in its form, with sturdy, emphatic tuttis. Viennese influence, specifically Haydn's, has been noted in the use of an introduction, the siciliana-style slow movement (though the F minor episode in its development was surely suggested by one in the Michael Haydn symphony to which Mozart at the same time composed an introduction) and the ländler-type trio; the wit in the finale, with its successive instrumental sallies, seems wholly personal.

17. VIENNA AND PRAGUE, 1785–8. At the end of 1784, on 11 December, Mozart had become a freemason at the lodge 'Zur Wohlthätigkeit'. The master there was Baron von Gemmingen, whom he had met in 1778 and whose *Semiramis* he had planned to set; the master at another lodge Mozart attended, 'Zur wahren Eintracht', of which Haydn was briefly a member in 1785, was the well-known scientist Ignaz von Born. Mozart's lodge was later amalgamated into 'Zur gekrönten Hoffnung'. He wrote some music for masonic ceremonial and for other use at lodge meetings. The society was essentially one of liberal intellectuals, concerned less with political ideals than with the philosophical ones of the Enlightenment, including Nature, Reason and the brotherhood of Man. Although there was tension between Austrian freemasonry and the Catholic church, the organization was in no sense anti-religious; membership was perfectly compatible with Mozart's faith, and there is no reason to think that he abandoned his religion even if his formal observances became less regular.

Mozart's surviving correspondence for 1785, and indeed the ensuing years, is sparse. A few letters from Leopold, visiting his son in Vienna for ten weeks early in the year, to Nannerl (now Frau Berchtold zu Sonnenburg) give a graphic account of Mozart's activities: they comment on his lavish apartment, the bustle of his daily life and the character of his latest music. Leopold attended several of his concerts; during the Lenten season Mozart gave six at the Mehlgrube and one at the Burgtheater, and took part in various others. He also gave three later in the year, during Advent. This period represents the peak of his reputation as composer and pianist. *Die Entführung* was carrying his name to many German cities. His teaching activities continued: one of his pupils was the English composer Thomas Attwood, whose surviving exercises illuminate Mozart's careful, systematic teaching methods, and perhaps carry hints as to how Mozart himself had been taught (see Heartz, 1973–4). A good deal of his music was published, in

print or in manuscript copies. At the end of the year the *Wiener Zeitung*, in a concert review, referred to Mozart's 'merited fame' and said that he was 'universally valued'. In spite of all this he was in financial straits; a plea for a loan, probably not the first, went to his friend the composer and publisher F. A. Hoffmeister in November. Compositions of 1785 include three piano concertos, a replacement Andante for a violin concerto, a piano quartet, several songs and various masonic works – a cantata, a funeral piece, songs and choruses, and (for brother masons but probably not for ritual use) some movements for clarinets and basset-horns. There were also arias for use in other composers' operas.

Opera remained central to Mozart's ambitions. His short Singspiel *Der Schauspieldirektor* K486 was completed early in 1786 for performance in the Orangery in Schönbrunn Palace, along with a work by the court composer Salieri; both were commissioned for a visit by the Governor-General of the Austrian Netherlands. In March a private performance of the revised version of *Idomeneo* (see §12 above) was given. But his main project was the collaboration with Da Ponte on *Le nozze di Figaro*. The topic was no doubt carefully chosen. Beaumarchais' play had been given in Paris in April 1784, and a German version had been printed in Vienna when, at the beginning of 1785, performances by Schikaneder's theatre company had been banned; further, the play was a sequel to *Le barbier de Séville*, of which Paisiello's operatic version had been a great success. Although both Da Ponte and Michael Kelly, the Irish tenor who first sang the roles of Basilio and Curzio, left garrulous memoirs, neither was specially informative about the opera's genesis. Letters from Leopold to Nannerl make it clear that composition had started by October or November 1785, and that there was a good deal of intrigue (allegedly by Salieri and Righini) against the opera. It finally came to the stage at the Burgtheater on 1 May 1786, and was well received; many items were applauded and encored at the first three performances, inducing the emperor to restrict encores at later ones to the arias. In Vienna the opera was given nine times in 1786, then revived for 26 performances in 1789–90; it was quickly taken up by travelling companies and widely performed in other German cities, usually in German.

The months in which *Figaro* had been composed were otherwise uneventful. The only important works besides the opera had been three piano concertos, one written in December 1785 and two in March 1786, the customary time of year for them because of the traditional Lenten concert season. That this year he gave only a single concert in Lent (there may have been others in Advent) must be a commentary on the fickle taste of the Viennese public. The fee of 450 gulden for *Figaro* – Da Ponte received 200 – did not lessen his financial anxieties. During the summer he was able to sell various recent works to the Prince of Fürstenberg, but his hopes of a retainer fee were not realized. In the autumn he conceived a plan for going to England, accompanying or following his friends Stephen and Nancy Storace, Kelly and Attwood, but that foundered when Leopold advised against it and declined to look after Mozart's children. A third child, Johann Thomas Leopold, was born on 18 October and died on 15 November.

Towards the end of the year, however, Mozart accepted an invitation to Prague, where *Figaro* had been a great success. He spent some four weeks there, from 11 January 1787; it is clear from a letter he wrote to Jacquin that he relished his popularity in the city. He saw one performance of *Figaro* and directed another, and gave a concert including a new symphony (K504) written for the occasion. He also went to a Paisiello opera but chatted through it. The Prague impresario Bondini commissioned him to write an opera for production the following autumn; on his return to Vienna he asked for another libretto from Da Ponte, who though engaged on texts for Salieri and Martín y Soler started work on *Don Giovanni*.

In April 1787 Mozart heard that his father was seriously ill, and wrote a letter of consolation, including a famous passage expressing his view, based on masonic teachings, of death: 'As death . . . is the true goal of our existence, I have formed during the last few years such close relations with this best and truest friend of mankind that his image is no longer terrifying to me but rather very soothing and consoling'. Leopold died at the end of May. Mozart renounced his share of the estate to Nannerl for 1000 gulden; he asked for his manuscripts to be sent to him, but some were given to the Heiligkreuz monastery at Augsburg and others evidently went astray.

Mozart is not known to have made any public appearance in Vienna during some eight months of 1787. In April he moved from his apartment behind the cathedral to what was presumably a more modest one; about that time he was briefly ill. Teaching activities continued: in the spring, he may have given lessons to Beethoven, then on his first, very brief visit to Vienna; he also taught Hummel who, not yet ten, probably lived with the Mozart family.

His compositions since the time of *Figaro* seem to have been planned primarily with a view to publication, which represented a source of ready cash. There were several chamber works, including a piano quartet, three piano trios and a string quartet in 1786 and two string quintets and a piano and violin sonata in 1787; most of them soon went into print, as did several songs. The reason for the composition of the K503 piano concerto is uncertain: it may have been intended for a projected series of Advent concerts, or possibly for performance in Prague. Nor is it known what occasions called forth the *Musikalischer Spass* or the *Kleine Nachtmusik*.

Those two works immediately preceded *Don Giovanni*. Mozart left for Prague on 1 October 1787, with much of the score written. The première had been planned for 14 October, but because of inadequate preparation *Figaro* was given instead and *Don Giovanni* was postponed until 29 October. According to Constanze's later recollection the overture, the last part of the opera to be written, was completed two days (not, as is often said, one) before. The Prague public received the work warmly; a newspaper report stated that Mozart was greeted with threefold cheers. He directed three or four performances before returning to Vienna in mid-November. He spent much time in Prague with the Dušek (Duschek) family in their villa outside the

13. *A page from the autograph MS of Mozart's 'Le nozze di Figaro'* K492, *1786 (Act 2 finale, beginning of the last scene) (D-Bds)*

city; the difficult aria *Bella mia fiamma* K528 was composed for Josefa, an old Salzburg friend.

Mozart arrived back in Vienna in mid-November and was soon offered the post of court *Kammermusicus*, at a salary of 800 gulden (Gluck, who had just died, had been paid 2000). He was apparently required to do little more than write dance music for court balls. Though not a court Kapellmeister, and not a Kapellmeister at all except in a very loose sense, he could at least sign himself as a court musician in the imperial and royal service. Clearly he welcomed this appointment, both for the dependable income associated with it and for its advancement of his standing in Viennese musical life. He had been hoping for something of the kind for five years; there is no reason to suppose that he specially valued independence from patrons. The extra income scarcely seems to have eased his situation. He moved to a new apartment, where a daughter (Theresia) was born on 27 December; she died on 29 June 1788, just after another move, to a smaller apartment in a suburb. By then the pitiful sequence of letters to Michael Puchberg, a merchant, freemason and musician, had begun. Four were written in June and July, pleading urgently for loans: one refers to Mozart's hopes of quick repayment when he received money for a planned concert series (which probably never took place); another to the poor response to his solicitation for subscriptions to the publication of his new string quintets, and to embarrassing debts to a former landlord; and a third to dealings with a pawnbroker. In one, requesting a large long-term loan, he wrote of 'black thoughts' that he could banish only 'with great effort', mentioning however that since the recent move he had been able to work more productively.

The works on which he was engaged were the three last symphonies, completed, according to his catalogue, on 26 June, 25 July and 10 August. The earlier part of 1788 had indeed been relatively unfruitful: there were various dances, a little piano music, songs and arias, a piano concerto (written in February, though no concert in Lent is documented) and three new items for the Viennese première of *Don Giovanni* on 7 May. The opera cannot have been unsuccessful, for it had 14 further performances, but there is evidence that the story of its having a mixed reception, with some of the audience regarding the work as prolonged, contrived and over-elaborate, is not unfounded. Similar criticisms were levelled at *Figaro* and *Die Entführung*. Later in 1788 Mozart composed more dance music, a piano trio, a string trio which he gave to Puchberg, and vocal canons; he also arranged *Acis and Galatea*, the first of several Handel works (to include *Messiah* in March 1789) for concerts under Baron van Swieten's auspices.

18. 1785–8: CHAMBER AND INSTRUMENTAL MUSIC.
(*i*) *Works without piano*. After the disciplined style of the six 'Haydn' quartets of 1782–5, Mozart's string chamber music of the following years is more relaxed and more expansive, and often more concerned with sensuous beauty of harmony or texture. The only quartet of these years is K499, known as the 'Hoffmeister' after its original publisher. Its first movement, Allegretto rather than the usual Allegro, is characterized by the all-pervading falling phrase of its opening theme, by its varied though less conscientiously egalitarian quartet writing, with the viola in particular colouring the texture, and by its chromaticisms and its

remote modulations. The minuet again is coloured by a high viola part, the Adagio by smooth, euphonious writing, with many parallel 3rds and 6ths – these intervals are prominent melodically throughout the quartet. The finale's rapid triplets, chromatically inflected, show high spirits tempered by hints of wryness in a way that was to become increasingly characteristic.

Mozart's two string quintets of spring 1787 represent a peak in his chamber music. He seems to have found the five-part texture easier to handle than four-part. The new possibilities of symmetry clearly attracted him: violin set against cello, with three-part harmony in the middle (K515, opening; K516, introduction to finale); a pair of violins against a pair of violas, above the cello (K515, first movement, bars 94ff); violin against viola with string trio accompaniment (K515, second movement; K516, third movement, bars 30f); and a high trio against a low one (K516, opening). Many other, more elaborate, quickly shifting patterns also appear; and there is a general harmonic and textural richness, without any thickness or heaviness, since the total tessitura is enlarged compared with the quartets. The C major K515 (perceptively discussed by Rosen, 1971, pp.264ff) is Mozart's longest four-movement chamber work, generously proportioned in every particular, with spacious, harmonically slow-moving themes and broad structural spans. The first movement is remarkable for its remote modulations and its complex rhythmic structure, in which the opening five-bar phrases, later tautened by overlapping into orthodox fours, represent one of many subtleties; it is balanced by a finale of 539 bars, more conventional in phrase structure but with a huge sonata-rondo framework embracing a great deal of contrapuntal development. Again it is touched by that ambivalent emotional quality of many of Mozart's overtly high-spirited finales of this period. The Andante is largely an elaborate dialogue for violin and viola, the minuet a highly individual movement using ten-bar phrases and intense chromaticisms (diminished 7ths with clashing appoggiaturas).

The complementary quality implied by the composition alongside a minor-key work of a major-key one in the same genre – Mozart's usual procedure in his maturity – is seen in other aspects of the C major and G minor quintets. The first movement of K516 is faster-moving harmonically and sharper in its melodic contours, with a more directly emotive thematic content in its aspiring phrases and falling chromaticisms, and a more closely imitative style. This emotive manner is maintained in the accented off-beat chords of the minuet, and in the softening of the trio's turn to the major, the more so because it takes the cadential phrase of the minuet as its starting-point. After an Adagio with all the instruments muted, enriched by much real five-part harmony, distant modulation and textures of a rare feathery beauty, a dark slow introduction precedes the finale proper, a G major Allegro in 6/8 which has been criticized as an abnegation of the consistent emotional world of the remainder of the work; again, however, there is a hint of ambiguity. The existence of a discarded G minor opening leaves no doubt that Mozart weighed different possibilities.

Only two other string works belong to this period. One is the C minor Adagio K546, a stern piece influenced by French-overture rhythms, which Mozart prefixed to a string arrangement of the two-piano fugue in C minor K426. The other is the 'divertimento' for string trio, K563 – so titled, no doubt, mainly because of its six-movement plan, with two minuets and a set of variations. Folklike melodies have been noted in the fourth and sixth movements. Though in no sense in the manner of the earlier divertimentos, it has by virtue of its light textures and concertante writing a generally less concentrated style than the quartets or quintets. Mozart's only string trio, it shows great resource in its handling of the limited medium in a lengthy work. The nocturne or *Kleine Nachtmusik*, for string quartet and double bass, shows in its direct, appealing invention the aristocratic ease and mastery that Mozart could now bring to entertainment music; its antithesis is the *Musikalischer Spass*, whose harmonic and rhythmic gaffes serve to parody the work of incompetent composers. Another kind of musical joke, a *quatuor d'airs dialogués*, is the flute quartet K298, with ideas from a song by F. A. Hoffmeister, a French traditional melody, and an aria from Paisiello's *Le gare generose* – this last fixing its date as not before autumn 1786. A dozen miniature duos for horns, a genre usually intended for open-air music-making, date from this period; they make the most of a medium severely circumscribed by the natural horn's limitations.

(ii) *Works with piano.* The first products of Mozart's new interest in the popular forms of keyboard chamber music from 1785 were two piano quartets, K478 in G minor and K493 in E♭, another of the characteristic major–minor pairs. While the piano trios are still to some extent accompanied sonatas, in the quartets the string ensemble is balanced against and contrasted with the piano, which has a role of a virtuosity akin to that in Mozart's concertos of the time. There is a major-key finale to K478, but its first movement has much of the intense, sombre character associated with G minor. The E♭ quartet is more lyrical and expansive, with extended second-group themes; written during the opening run of *Figaro*, it is a particularly happy work.

If the material of the trios is often more conventional, that is understandable in this extended piano-sonata form. The first and last of the group, K496 and K564, each in G, and each possessing a variation movement, particularly bear the imprint of the accompanied sonata style, though K496 has an Andante with elaborate yet economical four-part counterpoint, not unlike string quartet textures. K502 in B♭, though not stylistically very different, is more original and more concentrated in invention, with the second-group theme derived from the first, and continuously developed in a manner Mozart may have learnt from Haydn; that a new theme provides an interlude at the beginning of the development is however entirely characteristic, particularly in a movement with a thematically economical exposition. From mid-1788, the period of the last three symphonies, come three piano trios, one in G already referred to, and works in E (K542) and C (K548). This last, like K564, is polished but somewhat routine in its material and its procedures. K542, Mozart's only work in E, is richly poetic in its first movement, where the pellucid textures and graceful, chromatically inflected lines introduce hints of melancholy. Understandably, the trio with the truest three-instrument style is K498, for clarinet, viola and piano, probably composed for music-making with the Jacquin family; its veiled colour, its spare textures and

its concentrated use of material place it among the most unified in feeling of Mozart's works. Lastly among these keyboard chamber works, the K526 piano and violin sonata should be mentioned, Mozart's last full-scale work in the medium and the most integrated in its piano and violin writing: the first movement has a new level of elaboration in virtuoso interchange between the violin and the piano right hand, and the very brilliant finale shows an array of textures in which the priority between piano passage-work and lyrical accompaniment (often flowering into melody) varies fascinatingly.

To this period belong a number of important keyboard works, including two substantial duet sonatas, K497 and 521, which carry the form beyond its usual domestic context. K497 proclaims its seriousness with an Adagio introduction and maintains it in its extended scale and the unusual frequency of contrapuntal writing as opposed to the customary dialogues and homophonic accompaniments. Mozart's most persistently contrapuntal piano writing appears in K533, the sonata he put together by adding two movements to the Rondo K494 – which he expanded, supplementing it with a cadenza to give it weight more nearly to balance the new movements. The first is exceptionally spare in texture and economical in material, and contrapuntal thinking pervades all its sections; it also derives a strong sense of direction from its purposeful sequences and its free use of discord. The Andante looks to C. P. E. Bach in its affective appoggiaturas, but the intense chromaticism, remote modulations and release in florid melody are characteristically Mozartian. This remarkable movement also affords an outstanding example of the 'principle of increasing animation' in Mozart's music (Lowinsky, 1956), by which phrase lengths increase at the end of a period, stresses are shifted (often with overlapping phrases) and rhythms quickened; it was by such methods, and his use or subtle avoidance of symmetrical phraseology, that Mozart so successfully controlled the structure not merely of periods but also of sections and entire movements, perhaps even whole works. This control over pace, harmonic and rhythmic, is an important factor in Mozart's 'perfection of form'.

Some smaller piano works of these years typify particular tendencies. The Rondo K485 – a rondo only in title – is based on a melodic tag which Mozart used many times at different periods, and which also appears in J. C. Bach's music (op.11 no.6) in just the form used here; if this piece leans towards the urbane grace and brilliance of J. C. Bach, the A minor Rondo K511 is more akin to C. P. E. with its appoggiatura-laden, introspective tone. Other piano works of the period include a still more chromatic Adagio K540, a remarkably emotional work, characterized by suspensions and diminished 7ths, in a key (B minor) Mozart otherwise scarcely used. This highly personal piece was composed in the difficult spring of 1788. A little later, at the time of the last symphonies, came the popular sonata 'for beginners' K545. Its first movement includes Mozart's only true example – there is a remote parallel in the finale of the K387 quartet – of a recapitulation beginning in the subdominant; it is not, however, merely a transposed version of the exposition, for in order to fix the home key more firmly the transition moves on to the dominant before settling in the tonic. Even in conventionally planned sonata movements Mozart was inclined to adjust the recapitulation transition in order to consolidate the tonic.

19. 1785–8: ORCHESTRAL MUSIC.

(i) *Piano concertos*. The piano concertos of 1785, the pair in D minor K466 and C major K467, abandon certain aspects of the plan that had served for those of 1784. Each concerto of that group opened with a well-defined theme that the soloist could take up on (or immediately after) his initial entry. These two begin with material that does not lend itself to solo performance, and a new kind of integration between soloist and orchestra is implicit. So is a different kind of solo entry. K466 has a significant new theme for the soloist, which is apt only for a piano entry after a tutti and is used and developed in just that context in the development section. The movement's basic outline remains unaffected; during the statement of the opening primary material in the exposition proper its restless syncopations are glossed by urgent semiquaver figuration. In K467 the entry has a mild flourish of virtuosity before a trill which serves to accompany the orchestral motto theme, a theme whose symphonic character and contrapuntal potentialities find a clear analogy in the forceful and strongly directed piano bravura. Although its development section barely alludes to material stated earlier, this is Mozart's most densely argued concerto movement and among his broadest in structure. The novelty and increasingly symphonic nature of these first movements is paralleled by the departures in the other movements, less in the K466 Romance (in simple rondo form, with the traditional stormy second episode) than in the extraordinary Andante of K467, with its reliance on a new richness of cantilena, harmony and texture, or the K466 finale, constructed on a scale and with a density of argument comparable with the first movement's – it is in a variety of sonata-rondo form, with material exclusive to the soloist, and a substantial development section. The 'daemonic' character of K466 made it Mozart's most popular concerto in the 19th century. Beethoven wrote a characteristic pair of cadenzas for it.

The concertos written at the time of *Le nozze di Figaro* do not consistently pursue the new symphonic approach. All require clarinets, not previously used in piano concertos; the wind colouring, a feature of the concertos since K450, almost dominates K482 in Eb through its influence on the shape of the thematic material. This is a leisurely, expansive work, allowing the ear to relish the sensuous piano and wind sonorities, with an Andante in variation form (the wind dominate two of the variations) and a traditional 'hunting' finale that incorporates as an episode, like K271 in the same key, a slow minuet with a variation. The emphasis in K482 on bravura writing may be contrasted with the much more gentle nature of the passage-work in K488 in A; lacking its predecessor's trumpets and drums, this concerto draws on another, softer range of tone colours, of a piece with its graceful themes. Its first entry reverts to the usual pattern, but a departure is represented by the presentation of the new second-subject matter after, rather than before, the central ritornello, thus placing it analogously with the fresh development themes that Mozart often introduced; the analogy is pursued in that the entire development is based on this theme – which however is later recapitulated in the orthodox position. The Adagio, Mozart's only F# minor movement, is famous for its poetry and its pathos, derived from its gently falling phrases, siciliana rhythm, 'Neapolitan' harmony and expressive woodwind writing.

Those two concertos and the C minor K491, all composed during the writing of *Figaro*, make up a mutually complementary group, like the pairs already discussed; but the C minor is more profitably considered alongside the other 1786 concerto, the C major K503, for in these two the symphonic approach of K466 and 467 is pursued alongside the treatment of colour and character of K482 and 488. They are not however alike. K491, where the orchestra, uniquely, requires both oboes and clarinets, has many thematic ideas (though no true second-subject one in the first tutti): this material, some of it motivic, lends itself to development to an extent new in the concertos, and in the recapitulation it is drawn together, with the ideas re-ordered, elaborated and orchestrally enriched. In K503 the first-movement material is almost neutral in character, comprising broken-chord patterns, figures of three repeated notes (masonic significance has been ascribed to them) and scales; and its themes are relatively formal – bland, foursquare and minimally expressive. This concerto is thus in the line of descent from K415 and 451, but now the proportions are grander and the organization more taut, particularly through the capacity of the material to serve for contrapuntal working and rigorous, continuous development. The other movements show parallel features. In the C minor the second, like a Romance, is a rondo with faster-moving episodes where material stated by the wind band is elaborated by piano and strings. The finale is a set of variations, mainly double ones, the repeat of each strain in effect a new variation (as in K450, 453 and 456), allowing for greater elaboration and variety of orchestral colour without increasing the time-scale; two major-key sections (Ab, bar 97; C, bar 165) have the relaxing effect of episodes although they are thinly disguised variations.

There were no concertos in 1787. The solitary one of 1788, K537 in D, is to some extent in the manner of K503, with similar neutral material, but less amenable to strongly organized development and more inclined towards decorative passage-work; it is hard, especially in the Romance-type second movement, not to sense some falling off in inventive vigour. The solo part left hand is not complete in the autograph; Mozart, expecting to play the concerto himself, had no reason to fill in detail. Similar considerations naturally apply to ornamentation: many concertos have conspicuous lacunae in this respect, for example K488 and 491 (second movements) and K482 (finale, including the repeats of the interpolated minuet).

(ii) *Symphonies*. In his mature years Mozart wrote no symphonies for use in Vienna at least until his last three of 1788; he did however perform there some earlier ones, including sections of serenades and the revised version of the Haffner K385 (1782). That work and the symphony for Linz were the only ones he composed after he had settled in Vienna until late 1786, when he wrote the Prague Symphony K504, presumably for use in that city. It is in three movements, with no minuet – more probably because he had reason to think that the Prague audiences were accustomed to three-movement symphonies than for any aesthetic reason. While preserving much of the traditional D major brilliance, in style it is close to the K503 concerto: it depends more on the arrangement and development of motifs than on thematic material. The first movement, after a slow introduction, has a structure of great originality and integrity, borrowing perhaps from Haydn's so-called monothematic type: its initial second-group idea starts as a chromatically inflected variant of the first, with a contrapuntal and sequential continuation, but a distinct lyrical theme ensues. Further, the tutti material of the groups is similarly related. The development includes contrapuntal workings of various of these motifs, and elides with the recapitulation, which in turn fuses – using the ambiguity of the inflected variant – the two groups in an extraordinarily subtle way. It has been pointed out (Larsen, 1956) that this unconventional form is best understood in relation to ritornello structure, which in view of Mozart's recent preoccupation with the piano concerto is not entirely surprising. The Andante, though lyrical in temper, remains motivic in style: all its ideas are based on the changing and developing repetition of essentially brief figures. So in a more relaxed way is the finale.

The great triptych that stands at the end of Mozart's symphonic output is obscure in its origins. It is not clear why he should have written symphonies just then: if for a series of concerts (a letter to Puchberg suggests he had one in mind), concertos might have been more understandable. These works are mutually complementary, a pair that grew into three: the pairing of G minor with E♭ and C had recent precedents, in the piano quartets and the string quintets respectively. The E♭ symphony is scored with clarinets rather than the usual oboes. The G minor is without trumpets or drums; Mozart later rearranged the wind layout, incorporating parts for clarinets and modifying those for the oboes.

The treatment of form is plainer and more conventional in all three first movements than in that of the Prague Symphony. No.39 is especially clearcut: after a sombre slow introduction based on dotted rhythms, the material is consistently lyrical and the development so traditional as to start with a subdominant statement of a second-group theme. The basic material in no.40 is less homogeneous. Its impassioned opening, with its original and beautiful throbbing accompaniment on divided violas, is set against a secondary theme in dialogue, but the falling-note figure from the opening (cf K478) persists at various levels and lends an undercurrent of agitation. Here the development section, quickly contradicting the conventional tonal expectation, begins with the first-group material in F♯ minor and includes contrapuntal argument around it; there is more during the recapitulation. The passion and urgency generally ascribed to this symphony have not been universally acknowledged; Schumann spoke of grace and charm, and others have detected only *opera buffa* character (see Westrup, 1955). No.41 is more formal and consciously grand, with *forte–piano* contrasts at the opening, tuttis with military rhythms, new superimposed counterpoints and expansive second-group material. For all that, *opera buffa* is not far distant: the gestures of the first bars could be those of the Count's knocking at the door answered by the Countess's pleas (in *Figaro*), and a cadential theme (bar 101) is identical with one in an aria, 'Un bacio di mano' K541, composed for an Anfossi opera.

The slow movements are marked by a new tone in Mozart's music: their tutti sections, often in minor keys, with high violin writing, chromatic wind and low-lying harmony for the middle string instruments, have an almost anguished emotional force (no.39, bars 30ff;

no.41, bars 23ff). The Andante of no.39 makes much use of its two opening phrases; in sonata form without a development section, it has a recapitulation that is effectively a developmental elaboration of the exposition. The Andante of no.40 is more conventional in pattern, with a short development touching at its end heights of chromatic pathos (bars 69ff). Its basic two-note figure may be seen as linked with that of the first movement. Much the most complex in melodic structure, orchestration and chromatic harmony is the Andante of no.41, and here too, although there is a development section, new elaborations are introduced in the recapitulation; as in no.39, a *piano* statement of the opening material begins the coda.

14. *Wolfgang Amadeus Mozart: silverpoint drawing (1789) by Doris Stock; the original was destroyed in World War II*

The tendency to assign more weight to the finale of a multi-movement work can be seen in Mozart's symphonies since K130, and to some extent in his piano concertos (e.g. K466); Haydn was moving in the same direction. That of no.39 is relatively straightforward, a monothematic sonata-form movement, its secondary theme a varied version of the primary enhanced by a poetic, distantly modulating passage, with a vigorous development involving imitative writing. No.40 has a famously fiery finale, thematically rather foursquare (as indeed is the first movement); its remarkable development section begins with a tonally disorientating flourish, then embarks on a four-part contrapuntal working-out of the material, ending in the remote key of C♯ minor, where the music pauses before being wrenched back to the tonic for a regular recapitulation. The finale of no.41 is even more famed, for its 'fugue'. It does not possess a fugue, as such; rather, this is a sonata-form movement including fugal material. In this it is in the same tradition as the K387 quartet (see §15 above) and, more particularly, as symphonies by various Austrian composers, including Michael Haydn, which Mozart may be assumed to have known – though in scope and execution it far surpasses any models. To discover J. S. Bach's influence is to sentimentalize and to ascribe to Mozart 20th-century historical attitudes; if any more distantly past influence should be noted it might rather be that of Fux and his school, the more so as the four-note tag that serves as fugue subject has its ancestry in a plainchant, 'Lucis creator', extensively set by those composers. The movement sets out conventionally, then at the transition includes a fugal exposition on the opening subject; and its main second-group theme is workable in various degrees of close imitation. Much of the tutti and accompanying material, mostly scale figures, also proves to be amenable to contrapuntal treatment. Some of the possibilities are further explored in the development section, but it is not until the coda (at bars 371ff) that the whole is drawn together in an apotheosis of invertible five-part counterpoint without parallel in the symphonic literature.

20. KEY ASSOCIATIONS. These last four symphonies are in keys, D, E♭, G minor and C, with specially strong associations in Mozart's music. Much has been written about Mozart's comparative consistency in the use of keys for particular types of work. This should be seen in a wider context of key traditions and associations, and instrumental characteristics. C. F. D. Schubart (*Ideen zu einer Ästhetik der Tonkunst*, 1806; written in the 1780s) distinguished between the 'tinted' and neutral keys, referring to the keys with sharps in their signatures as 'wild and strong', those with flats as 'sweet and melancholy', and the neutral ones as 'innocent and simple'.

D major was orchestrally the most brilliant key, specially effective for string instruments, and preferred by Mozart for almost all his Salzburg serenades as well as his Italian symphonies and overtures and such concertos of a calculated brilliance as K451 and K537. D and C were the keys in which trumpets and drums were habitually used, and the extra depth of C seems to have led to Mozart's preferring it for works of a more ceremonious character, including several early symphonies, three mature piano concertos (K415, 467, 503) and Symphonies nos.34 and 41. E♭ was the traditional key of the operatic *aria d'affetto* and the warm emotion associated with it, reflected in such works as the Sinfonia concertante K364/320d and Symphony no.39; the use of the clarinet, regarded as a specially expressive instrument, was more common in this key. F and G were considered more neutral, and Mozart used them relatively infrequently in his mature music; F has certain pastoral associations, and the light quality of G, partly a result of high-pitched horns – still more marked in A and sometimes in B♭ – gave it associations with rural jollification, as in the choruses of *Le nozze di Figaro* and *Don Giovanni*. For his operatic love duets Mozart habitually used A major, with its associations of soft, warm texture; and in his operas D minor is almost invariably linked with ideas of vengeance. Minor keys however are relatively rare in any music of this period, and are never without special emotional significance of a dark or passionate kind; in his Viennese years Mozart wrote only two substantial instrumental works in D minor (K421/417b and 466) and three each in G minor (K478, 516 and 550) and C minor (K388/384a, 457

with 475, and 491). In his maturity he composed only single works in E major (K542), A minor (K310/300d) and E minor (K304/300c), a few movements in A♭ and no more than isolated ones in B minor (K540) or F♯ minor (K488); his only F minor works (K594 and 608) are for mechanical organ. Equal temperaments were not fully in use even for keyboard instruments in Mozart's time – this was a factor in the 'tinting' of the keys – and the unacceptability of certain intervals to his sensitive ear may have affected his choice.

Though his internal tonal contrasts, in development sections, range wide, Mozart was unadventurous compared with Haydn in his choice of keys for slow movements: in major-key works, he generally used the subdominant, less often the dominant and rarely the relative minor; in minor-key ones, commonly the relative major or the submediant. Mozart essentially used tonality to secure a broad unity, not for rhetorical effect; the very broadest of his tonally unifying schemes are found in his operas.

21. LAST YEARS, 1789–91. Early in 1789 Mozart accepted an invitation from Prince Karl Lichnowsky to accompany him on a journey to Berlin. They left on 8 April, pausing first at Prague (where Mozart visited friends and discussed with the impresario Guardasoni possibilities of a new opera commission) and then at Dresden. During six days there he played chamber music privately (including the K563 trio) and was unexpectedly asked to perform at court, where he played the K537 concerto; he heard a mass by J. G. Naumann, which he dismissed as 'very mediocre', and listened to the playing of J. W. Hässler, who had 'merely memorized old Sebastian Bach's harmony and modulations and could not play a fugue properly'. They moved next to Leipzig, where Mozart is said to have improvised at the Thomaskirche organ in the presence of J. F. Doles, the Kantor and a former Bach pupil. They reached Potsdam about 25 April, but Mozart returned to Leipzig (8–17 May) to give a concert (including the K456 piano concerto) which was well received though financially unrewarding. Little is known about his time in Potsdam and Berlin; probably he heard *Die Entführung* at the opera house, and he went to a concert at which Hummel played. He also appeared at court, on 26 May, and may have been invited to compose quartets for King Friedrich Wilhelm II, who was a cellist, and sonatas for the princess – he later told Puchberg that he was composing quartets and sonatas for the Prussian court, but made no reference to a commission (his letter, moreover, was partly motivated by a concern to reassure Puchberg about repayment of a proposed loan). He almost certainly started work on the quartets on the return journey; for K575 and part of K589 he used manuscript paper originating from a mill between Dresden and Prague (see Tyson, 1975, and fig.16). He arrived home on 4 June 1789; in his eight weeks away he had sent some 11 letters to his wife, full of news about his activities, eagerly affectionate and indeed sometimes very intimate in content, and showing concern not only about her health but also about the propriety of her conduct in his absence.

The letters to Puchberg this summer read pitifully. Both Mozart and his wife had spells of illness: he was unable, he said, to work, and he could secure only one subscriber, van Swieten, for a proposed concert series at his home (he had moved back to central Vienna at the beginning of the year); and Constanze had to go to Baden, a spa about 25 km from Vienna, for a cure. She was again pregnant; a daughter, Anna, was born in November and died the same day. While Constanze was in Baden, Mozart wrote two replacement arias for a new production of *Figaro* on 29 August; Adriana Ferraresi del Bene, who sang Susanna, was evidently not suited by the existing music. Cavalieri sang the Countess. The most important compositions of the summer were a piano sonata, and the clarinet quintet for Anton Stadler, first heard at a Tonkünstler-Sozietät concert in December. At the end of the year Mozart's main energies were expended on *Così fan tutte*, the third of his operas with Da Ponte. The others had been successes; they were travelling through the German lands and beyond and were generally well received, although many listeners found *Don Giovanni* bold, extravagant and complex. *Così fan tutte* had rehearsals on 31 December at Mozart's home and 21 January 1790 at the theatre; Puchberg and Haydn probably attended both. The première was on 26 January; there were four further performances, then a break because of the death of Joseph II in February, and five more in the summer.

Yet again, the fee for the opera seems to have had little effect on Mozart's financial situation. There were eight letters to Puchberg in the first half of 1790, requesting still larger loans and offering still less convincing promises of repayment. His poverty was not, however, desperate in the sense that he and his family

15. *Handbill for the concert Mozart gave in Frankfurt* (15 October 1790) *during the festivities on the coronation of Leopold II; the programme included the piano concertos* K537 *and* 459

starved or went unshod; basic necessities, like food, clothing, a carriage and servants, were cheap enough to be available to anyone in his social class. Constanze was able to take a cure at Baden, where Mozart spent some time in June. He still had his court salary and two pupils (he was anxious for more) as well as some income from publications; concert plans are often referred to in his correspondence, but whether they materialized is uncertain. He completed the third of the 'Prussian' quartets in June, and according to a letter to Puchberg had to sell the set for 'a trifle' to obtain cash quickly; they were not published until just after his death, and they bore no dedication to Friedrich Wilhelm II. In July he made two more Handel arrangements for van Swieten.

With the accession of the new emperor, Leopold II, Mozart hoped for preferment at court. None was forthcoming; but to take advantage of the coronation festivities, in which he had no official role, he went in September to Frankfurt, taking Franz de Paula Hofer, husband of his sister-in-law, and a servant. They arrived on 28 September. His concert, on 15 October (see fig.15), was apparently a success musically, although the orchestra was small (only five or six violins, according to an eye-witness, insufficient for works like the K459 and K537 piano concertos and the new 'grosse Symphonie' he gave); but it was poorly attended and financially a failure. Mozart's letters to Constanze are full of affectionate assurances about his anxiety to be home and optimistic suggestions about how they would overcome their money worries. On his return journey he gave a concert at Mainz, heard *Figaro* at Mannheim, and played before the King of Naples at Munich. He reached home about 10 November, joining Constanze at the new apartment in central Vienna to which she had just moved.

In December 1790 Mozart saw Haydn leave for London; he himself had just declined an invitation from an opera promoter there but had been promised another, like Haydn's, from J. P. Salomon. His compositions during the winter months include a string quintet (another followed in April), a piano concerto, two pieces for mechanical organ and numerous dances for court balls. He played a concerto at a concert organized by the clarinettist Josef Bähr in March; and an aria and a symphony, perhaps one of the last three, were given at the Tonkünstler-Sozietät concerts in April. During that month Mozart petitioned the city council for the reversion to the important and remunerative post of Kapellmeister at St Stephen's Cathedral, where the incumbent Leopold Hofmann was aged and ill; he was appointed assistant and deputy, without pay. Hofmann lived until 1793.

During the early summer Constanze, once more pregnant, was away at Baden; Mozart often visited her there, and became friendly with the choirmaster, Anton Stoll, for whom he composed the motet *Ave verum corpus*. Their sixth child, (6) Franz Xaver Wolfgang Mozart, was born in July. Mozart's frequent letters to Constanze suggest a happier frame of mind, with their affectionate concern and cheerful banter, the latter directed at F. X. Süssmayr, his pupil and a close friend in these months. It seems that financial matters were less pressing, and perhaps his spirits reflected the happy collaboration on which he was engaged with his old acquaintance the actor-manager Emanuel Schikaneder, whose company gave plays and Singspiels in a suburban theatre. This collaboration was on *Die Zauberflöte*, which occupied him during part of the summer. Early biographers suggested that in his wife's absence Mozart indulged in various kinds of excess during 1791, in company with Schikaneder, but there is no evidence of that, nor of any kind of loose living on Mozart's part at any time. Nothing more licentious than a fondness for billiards is reliably documented.

While he was at work on *Die Zauberflöte* he received another commission, when a stranger asked him to compose a requiem under conditions of secrecy. This commission came from Count Walsegg-Stuppach, who wanted to pass off as his own composition a requiem for his wife. Then, probably about the middle of July, Mozart was asked by the Prague impresario Guardasoni to write the opera for the festivities in September at Leopold II's coronation as King of Bohemia. This was to be *La clemenza di Tito*, a setting of Metastasio's 1734 text; the Dresden court poet Caterino Mazzolà was then in Vienna and it would seem probable that Guardasoni and Mozart arranged for him to cut and reshape the libretto to meet modern requirements. (Other possibilities have been put forward about the opera's origins, linking it with plans mooted by Guardasoni and Mozart in 1789, and attempting to explain how an aria apparently from the opera might have been performed in Prague as early as April 1791: see Volek, 1959; Lühning, 1974; and Tyson, 1975.)

Mozart set out for Prague on about 25 August, with his wife and Süssmayr. His earliest biographer, Niemetschek, said that he started work on the opera in the coach, and composed it in 18 days, but there are good reasons for believing that he had already written most of the ensembles and two of the arias for Titus (he knew the singer, the Ottavio in *Don Giovanni*), and had drafted more (see Tyson, 1975). The simple recitatives were supplied, it seems, by Süssmayr (see Giegling, 1967). Mozart had a spell of illness in Prague, but went to a performance of *Don Giovanni* on 2 September, finished work on *Tito* on 5 September, and conducted the première the next night. It apparently had only a mixed reception (the empress called it 'una porcheria tedesca'), but like most of Mozart's operas it soon rose in public esteem, and the final performance on 30 September was much applauded.

On that same night *Die Zauberflöte* had its first performance at the Theater auf der Wieden (or Freihaustheater) in Vienna, with Schikaneder as Papageno, the composer Benedikt Schack as Tamino and Mozart's sister-in-law Josepha Hofer as the Queen of Night. Again, initial reactions were cautious, but by 7 October Mozart could write to Constanze, at Baden, that several numbers had been encored and that the opera was steadily becoming more esteemed. Mozart took his mother-in-law to one performance, and to another his son Carl as well as Salieri and the soprano Cavalieri – Salieri greeted every item with 'bravo' or 'bello', Mozart noted. At another performance Mozart delighted the audience by playing the glockenspiel in the wings, deliberately mistiming it in relation to Schikaneder's actions. About this time he completed a clarinet concerto for Stadler; and in November he composed a masonic cantata, directing a performance on 18 November at his lodge.

That cantata was his last completed work. The illness he had suffered in Prague, which may have been linked with his spells of poor health the previous year, apparently never quite left him. Later accounts of his last

weeks tell of his working feverishly, on his return from Prague, at the Requiem, with premonitions of his own end; these seem hard to reconcile with the high spirits evident in his letters from much of October. At the end of November he was confined to bed, and attended by two leading Viennese doctors, Closset and Sallaba. He was nursed by Constanze and her youngest sister, Sophie. His condition seemed to improve on 3 December, and the next day a few friends (Schack, Hofer and the bass Gerl) gathered to sing over with him parts of the unfinished Requiem. That evening, according to the moving account of his death written by Sophie Haibel in 1825, his condition worsened; Closset, summoned from the theatre, applied cold compresses; and just before 1 a.m., on 5 December, Mozart died. The cause of his death was registered as 'hitziges Friesel Fieber' (severe miliary fever) and later diagnosed as 'rheumatische Entzündungsfieber' (rheumatic inflammatory fever) by a medical authority on evidence from Closset and Sallaba. That seems perfectly consistent with the symptoms and Mozart's medical history, more so than the various rival diagnoses, such as uraemia; there is no evidence to support the anyway improbable notion that he was poisoned, by Salieri or anyone else (for a full discussion see Bär, 1966, 2/1972). He was quietly buried in a mass grave, in accordance with contemporary Viennese custom, at St Marx churchyard outside the city, on 7 (not 6) December. If, as later reports say, no mourners attended, that is consistent with Viennese burial customs at the time; but Jahn (1856) wrote that Salieri, Süssmayr, van Swieten and two other musicians were present. The tale of a storm and snow is false: the day was calm and mild.

The obituary notices were unanimous in acknowledging Mozart's greatness. Various concerts and requiems were given in his memory, including some for Constanze's benefit. The estate was considerable, though its financial valuation was small (for details, including the books and music in Mozart's library, see Deutsch, *Mozart: die Dokumente seines Lebens*, 1961, Anh.II). Constanze applied for and was granted a court pension, which amounted to one third of Mozart's salary; Puchberg did not press for the money due to him, about 1000 gulden, but later asked for it and was repaid. In the ensuing years Constanze sold many of Mozart's manuscripts, a large proportion in 1799–1800 to the publisher J. A. André.

22. THE DA PONTE OPERAS. It is clear from Mozart's correspondence that serious opera and German opera were his dominating interests. When, however, the demand for opera at the Viennese court theatre was primarily for *opera buffa*, he fell in with it, once he could find a librettist to supply him with adequate texts. Da Ponte, as his memoirs indicate, took care to suit his librettos to the composers for whom they were intended. His three for Mozart, *Le nozze di Figaro* (1786), *Don Giovanni* (1787) and *Così fan tutte* (1790), exhibit an exceptional complexity of character and motivation; their plots contain many traditional and conventional elements, but treated in such a way as to allow a new seriousness.

The most straightforwardly comic is probably *Le nozze di Figaro*. Many political elements in Beaumarchais' original, including most of the direct expressions of social resentment, were pruned by Da Ponte; but the social tensions remain, to be expressed in, for example, Figaro's 'Se vuol ballare' in Act 1, the Act 2 finale, and the Count's music early in Act 3. The nature of the individual arias also reflects the social standing of the various characters: this may be exemplified by a comparison between the two D major vengeance arias, the blustery, parodistic 'La vendetta' for Bartolo and the Count's 'Vedrò, mentr'io sospiro', with its overtones of power and menace, or between the breadth and smoothness of the Countess's phraseology as opposed to Susanna's. Arias showing extensions of the emotional range of *opera buffa* include the two in which the Countess mourns the loss of her husband's love, Cherubino's two evocations of adolescent passion (particularly 'Non so più') and Figaro's cynical tirade against woman's infidelity.

Some of the ensembles carry more complex kinds of expression, like the ironic humour of 'Via resti servita'; and one, the Letter Duet, is a musical-dramatic tour de force, the music representing the dictation of a letter, with phrases realistically repeated and a condensed recapitulation serving for the reading-back of the text. In general however the ensembles, following *opera buffa* tradition, carry the action forward. This applies particularly to the finales. The first of the four acts in fact ends with an aria rather than an ensemble, the brilliant 'Non più andrai', a favourite ever since Mozart's time; and the third ends with a dance scene, which uses, as the only concession to Spanish local colour, a traditional fandango melody, close to that in Gluck's ballet *Don Juan*. (The opera clearly prefigures the new two-act structure used in *Don Giovanni* and *Così fan tutte*; the traditional three-act plan is altogether abandoned.) The other two finales are long, multi-section ensembles, with changes in tempo, metre, tonality and orchestration resolving existing tensions and creating new ones, always closely keyed to the action. Several such sections, especially in Act 2, are in effect substantial, symphonically developed movements (for example the B♭ Allegro, bar 167). In the Act 4 finale, particularly, passing modulation is used strikingly to mark out incident, and the mock pleas of love from Figaro to the 'Countess' – Susanna in disguise – are paralleled by the parodying character of the music. Each extended finale is strengthened by its unity of key, so that the pull of tonality draws them together: that of Act 2 begins and ends in E♭, that of Act 4 in D, the basic key of the opera (an increasingly common procedure in contemporary *opera buffa*). It is the symphonic force of the music, and its high degree of orchestral elaboration, that lends life to the characters, depth to the situations and seriousness to their resolution, and places the opera apart from the generality of Italian *opere buffe* of the period, however closely it may resemble those of such composers as Sarti, Anfossi, Paisiello, Cimarosa or Martín y Soler in its manner and its material.

Recent research on *Figaro* has thrown important new light on Mozart's method of composition. Analysis of papers and inks in the available part of the autograph implies that he did not compose the opera from beginning to end within six weeks as Da Ponte sent him the libretto (Da Ponte's tale – anyway belied by biographical evidence), but according to the character of the items: first the playful-undramatic ones, then the comic-dramatic, third the action scenes and last the lyrical arias (Köhler, 1967). The arrangement of numbers in the autograph of Act 3, available only since 1980, seems to preclude the revised order suggested in 1965 (Moberly

and Raeburn) and since then widely accepted.

While *Don Giovanni*, like *Figaro*, is based on the tensions of class and sex, its plot, which dates back at least to the time of Tirso de Molina (1571–1641), is less obvious material for an *opera buffa* (strictly, it is a *dramma giocoso* in the tradition deriving from Goldoni): partly because of the serious and supernatural issues involved, and partly because the story was simply too short. Da Ponte drew on what was in effect a one-act libretto by Bertati, set by Gazzaniga for Venice early in 1787, and filled it out with extra episodes; it accordingly lacks the integrity of the *Figaro* plot, with its close network of functional relationships. But the force and the 'daemonic' character of the music have exercised a special fascination for audiences and for connoisseurs, giving rise to a vast literature, critical, interpretative and purely fanciful, by among others E. T. A. Hoffmann, Kierkegaard, Mörike, Baudelaire, Gounod and Jouve.

A difference in approach between *Don Giovanni* and *Figaro* is evident in the long and tonally unified scene that opens the opera: the overture, in D minor and major; a comic aria in F major for Leporello; an ensemble in B♭ as Anna pursues Giovanni from her chamber; a modulating scene as Giovanni fights and kills the Commendatore; a brief simple recitative, then an orchestral one for Anna and Ottavio, leading to their duet, back in D minor. Much of the opera's basic material is thus exposed in what is virtually an unbroken musical span. The more conventionally *buffo* material that ensues takes the normal form of alternating simple recitative and lyrical numbers – among the latter are Leporello's Catalogue Aria (in an unusual fast–slow pattern) and two movements establishing Elvira's grotesque, tragi-comic situation (the first with overdramatic leaps and pauses, the second in an old-fashioned, pseudo-Handelian style) – before the quartet 'Non ti fidar', in which the serious and comic sides converge, and which leads with only a very brief, non-modulating recitative to Anna's recognition of Giovanni and her call for vengeance: again the serious side of the opera is sustained by virtually continuous music.

The material that follows – including two scenes for Zerlina and Masetto, the Act 1 finale, the mock seduction of Elvira, Leporello's escape, and various arias – is, essentially, interposed, with some of its ideas borrowed from Bertati's text; its links with the outer parts of the opera are fragile. It also contains Giovanni's own three arias, all to some extent conventional in type (the serenade with mandolin may be compared with 'In Mohrenland' from *Die Entführung*), as well as music providing social characterization comparable with that of *Figaro*, in Zerlina's simple tuneful songs and, more particularly, in the extraordinary ball scene of the Act 1 finale: here different groups dance simultaneously to the aristocratic minuet, the middle-class contredanse and the peasant German dance, played by three stage orchestras. This finale is another long, composite movement in a closed tonal scheme, though the resolution of one section by the next is less striking than in the parallel (Act 2) finale in *Figaro*, reflecting the more episodic nature of the plot.

The plot's main thread resumes in the cemetery scene and (after Anna's final aria, in the two-tempo rondò form normally reserved for the prima donna) the supper scene, an extended finale. Its first part includes passages, played by a stage band, from popular operas by Martín y Soler, Sarti and Mozart himself (*Figaro*), as table-music; in its central part, as the statue of the Commendatore consigns Giovanni to hell, the original tonic of D minor is at last established, with the music heard at the beginning of the overture. The climax is heightened by the use of trombones to suggest solemnity and the supernatural, the hieratic dotted rhythms, the extreme chromaticism, and the changing harmonic movement, growing increasingly irregular until it lurches wildly as Giovanni is overcome by the flames. But this is an *opera buffa*, and throughout the scene, cowering under the supper table, is Leporello, proffering advice and the common man's wry or facetious observations, just as he had while Giovanni killed the Commendatore and during the mock seduction (to genuinely tender music) of Elvira: comedy subsists alongside serious drama, and both are reflected in the music. And at the end of the opera, the remaining characters draw the moral and plan their future in a cheerful sextet, in G and finally D major.

For the Vienna performances of 1788 Mozart made various revisions: there was a replacement aria for Ottavio, a dramatically feeble duet scene for Zerlina and Leporello, and a scena for Elvira; it has been suggested, though probably mistakenly, that the final sextet was omitted. Both Ottavio's arias, and the new scene for Elvira, are commonly given in present-day performances although their inclusion scarcely strengthens the dramatic structure or the characterization.

*Così fan tutte*, composed just over two years after *Don Giovanni*, and also having sources in Tirso de Molina, is widely reckoned to be the most carefully and symmetrically constructed, and the most consistent in style, of the three Da Ponte operas. It has also been the one most severely criticized for moral shortcomings. The subject of the comedy, feminine fickleness, was found shocking even quite shortly after the opera's composition, and is made the more so by the convention (standing equally in *Figaro* and *Don Giovanni*) that the action should span no more than 24 hours. The opera is however susceptible of more positive interpretations, for example as a commentary on the strength and uncontrollability of amorous feelings and on the value of a mature recognition of them.

The plan of the opera and the make-up of the cast lend themselves to symmetrical treatment, with three men (a pair of officers and their friend) and three women (two sisters and their servant), each having an aria in each act, and with a treatment of the ensemble movements calculated so that the four principals are kept in their pairs (officers, sisters) and given relatively little personal identity until well on in Act 2 – by which point the sisters are emotionally affected by the 'Albanians', their disguised lovers. Thus their arias in Act 1, Dorabella's 'Smanie implacabili' and Fiordiligi's 'Come scoglio', while basically serious music, embody an element of parody: the emotions voiced, and the musical style in which they are couched, are as disproportionate to the situation as are the self-dramatizing protestations of a romantic girl. The music, in fact, truthfully represents the situation's different levels. There is a similar duality to the two quintets in Act 1, the over-emotional 'Sento, o Dio' and 'Di scrivermi ogni giorno', a touching farewell against Alfonso's chuckles. Further, the music often parodies particular styles and works.

While in Act 1 the emotions expressed are those conventionally considered proper to the situations, in Act 2 they become more personal in tone. The arias' messages are no longer simply the predictable ones; and the two sisters and the two officers are differentiated from one another in a way that lends logic to the original couplings. In particular the dilemma of the sterner sister, Fiordiligi, is strongly conveyed in the heroic music of her rondò aria 'Per pietà'; the pain of her capitulation, represented by a piercingly chromatic oboe phrase in her duet with Ferrando, is contrasted with the ease with which Dorabella, whose Act 2 aria is playful, joins in a sensuous duet with Guglielmo. And the quicksilver emotions of Ferrando, represented in the phraseology and particularly the key scheme of his aria 'Tradito, schernito' (C minor–E♭–C minor–C major: an uncommon pattern for Mozart), are set against the cynicism of Guglielmo, expressed partly in his aria but more so in the canonic quartet in the wedding scene, where Mozart characteristically made a virtue of necessity by assigning different music, and words to match, to the baritone, who could not join in the canon at a pitch apt to sopranos and a tenor. This solemn canon, for the wedding toast, is one section of the second-act finale, which later introduces allusively quotations from music heard earlier in the opera – the march at the officers' departure, two numbers familiar from the scenes where the officers were disguised, and one mystifying passage (bar 496) which can only be a quotation of material Mozart decided to omit.

The canonic music, like that in the final sextet of *Don Giovanni*, draws on a tradition now familiar chiefly through Rossini's finales (*Il barbiere di Siviglia*, Act 1) and Beethoven ('Mir ist so wunderbar', *Fidelio*); Mozart must have known the examples in Martín y Soler's *Una cosa rara* and Storace's *Gli equivoci*. Precedents may be found for several other features of Mozart's Da Ponte operas, including in several cases clear reminiscences, in music by Sarti, Gazzaniga, Piccinni, Paisiello and others (some are cited by Dent, 1913; Abert, 1919; Einstein, 1945; etc). Sometimes, as in the 6/8 G major peasants' music in *Don Giovanni*, this was partly a matter of common coin. But the subtlety of characterization, the richness of orchestral development, the tonal and symphonic control of long expanses of music, the vitality of the recitative (simple as well as obbligato) and the range of serious emotion combine to place these three works on a different plane from other *opere buffe* of their time.

23. LATE INSTRUMENTAL WORKS. *Così fan tutte* has certain characteristics – irony, restraint, serene detachment, symmetry – distinct from the other Da Ponte operas, and these have been seen as elements of a specific Mozartian 'Spätstil'. Some commentators have dated this style back to the time of the last three symphonies (summer 1788), others to that of *Don Giovanni* (autumn 1787) or a few months before – to the period of the two great string quintets and, significantly, the letter to Leopold about death. How this late style may relate to the circumstances of Mozart's life, like his lack of professional progress, his financial troubles, his marriage, his father's death, and in particular his embracing of freemasonry, is of course open to speculation. It may seem that these changes represented a slow process, starting after (or even during) the period of his most lyrical music – early 1784 to summer 1786 – and continuing, with several important landmarks, including the K503 concerto and the Prague Symphony as well as

16. *Autograph MS from Mozart's String Quartet in D* K575, *1789, end of the first movement* (GB-Lbm Add.37765, f.4v)

the works just cited, so that by 1789 he had arrived at a style noticeably more austere and refined, more motivic and contrapuntal, more economical in the use of material, and harmonically and texturally less rich. His late music is melodically less abundant and less expansive; there are fewer new themes in development sections or in exposition codas, and second-group themes are more often derived from primary ones by some form of extension or contrapuntal treatment. Contact with Haydn's mature music may have stimulated this last development, but in general Mozart was now past the stage when he would omnivorously draw to himself all that he found worthwhile in other men's music. By the middle 1780s the process of synthesis that governed his earlier development had effectually finished, and the changes of this late period were of a more internal kind, with few parallels in other composers' music; arguably they may be regarded as analogous to the neo-classicism that was affecting the arts generally.

It has been suggested that at this time Mozart was finding composition increasingly difficult, and the multiplicity of extant sketches from his last years, mostly discarded beginnings, has been cited in support. Whether the existence of such sketches is evidential may be questioned since later material could anyway be expected to survive in larger quantities. Their existence also reflects the greater complexity of his later music. A certain amount of sketch material, mostly drafts of beginnings, from a few bars to entire expositions, but also detailed workings-out of brief passages, survives from most periods of Mozart's adult life; it testifies that composition was not as effortless to him as some

romantic biographers thought, and that his works were not always visualized entire in his mind before being consigned to paper.

He seems to have found the string quartet a specially difficult medium. For the three 'Prussian' quartets, K575, 589 and 590, there were several false starts, as in the quartets dedicated to Haydn, and work on them was strung out over many months (Mozart did not, however, as was long imagined, call on earlier material; see Tyson, 1975). He must have realized that the new, elaborately wrought four-part style he had previously used would not serve for the kind of concertante quartets he wanted to offer the cellist king of Prussia. To write quartets in which the cello was consistently prominent would have violated Mozart's ideas of stylistic integrity; except in the slow movements, where there was more scope, and the trio of K575, he arrived at a style in which each instrument was for symmetry's sake assigned melodic matter. For the last two movements of K589 and the last three of K590 the idea of the cello's prominence seems virtually to have been abandoned; perhaps the Prussian hopes had faded. Here the quartet style is closer to that of the Haydn set, particularly in the finale of K590; the finale of K575 is also more contrapuntal, and more closely organized, than any other movement in that work.

These quartets are polished music; but if they were the only examples of Mozart's 'late style' it would be hard to avoid regarding it as involving something of a falling off in inventiveness and ingenuity. While the two late quintets, K593 and 614, bear a similar relation to K515–16 as the 'Prussian' quartets to the Haydn ones, they make a more positive impression. Each first-movement Allegro (K593 has a Larghetto introduction, recurring in the coda) begins with a passage imitating horns, and that of K614, in 6/8 rhythm, retains something of a wind serenade atmosphere; K593 has a first movement in a style more spare in texture than the preceding quintets but polyphonically richer, particularly in the recapitulation where the exposition material is extended and elaborated. The Andante of K614 recalls the Romance style, with the recurrences increasingly complex in texture and the episodes representing development of the main theme; the K593 Adagio is altogether more intense with its chromaticisms, its dialogues between violin and cello across throbbing middle textures, and its great range of elaborations throughout every phase of the movement of the descending tetrachord figure heard at the start. The contrast of intensity persists. K614 has a ländler trio and a monothematic finale on a Haydn-like theme, including fugato treatment, while K593 has a sophisticated canonic minuet and a graceful dialogue-style trio, and a 6/8 finale whose main theme begins with a descending chromatic scale (the zigzag pattern long accepted was a publisher's emendation after Mozart's death) – it is contrapuntally developed, in light, open textures with a curiously cool, even astringent flavour.

The only other chamber works of the last years are of a more relaxed sort: a little Adagio and Rondo for musical glasses (or armonica), flute, oboe, viola and cello, of May 1791, whose sensitive blend of a true chamber style and the concertante writing needed if the medium is to be effective far surpasses the earlier works for a wind instrument with strings. The necessary mixtures of dialogue and accompaniment, of homogeneous and heterogeneous textures, called forth a special quality and style of invention, as in the Piano and Wind Quintet K452.

Keyboard music of this period includes two sonatas, the relatively slight B♭ K570 and, written just after the Berlin journey and presumably intended for the Prussian princess, K576 in D. It is not exactly a 'leichte Klaviersonate' such as, Mozart wrote, seemed appropriate to her, for though light in texture it is often contrapuntal: in both outer movements the main secondary material is contrapuntally derived from the primary, and in the first there is much contrapuntal working in the development and the recapitulation. Among other keyboard works are a gigue K574 composed in Leipzig, and fancifully supposed to be a homage to Bach, and the unfinished G minor Allegro K312/590d; these last two may have been intended for further Prussian sonatas. Also from this period are the two fantasias K594 and 608, composed for mechanical organ, an instrument whose high-pitched pipes Mozart found objectionable; they are commonly played as piano duets or organ solos. It is interesting to see how Mozart, with no established design to follow, set about composing such pieces: one is made up of a sonata-allegro in F major, with much busy, quartet-like contrapuntal texture, framed by a chromatic F minor Adagio; the other is a fugue in F minor, introduced by material of a rhetorical kind (which recurs at climactic points), interrupted by an A♭ Andante, and resuming with increased pace and contrapuntal complexity. They show Mozart finding new and imaginative responses even to a challenge he did not relish.

The last two orchestral works were concertos, in B♭ K595 for piano and in A K622 for clarinet. K595 broadly follows the formal pattern of the 1784 concertos, but has an unusual abundance of ritornello material. Other special features include a marked tendency for the music to oscillate between major and minor, and a link between ritornello figuration and piano passage-work; also notable is the development section, beginning with a series of strange, disorientating modulations, followed by material closely based on the exposition, worked contrapuntally and with little piano virtuosity. After a long ternary Larghetto, with a main melody of extreme simplicity and beauty in Romance style, the finale is in the traditional 6/8 'hunting' rhythm, less ebullient and more rarefied than Mozart's other examples. His last instrumental work, the Clarinet Concerto for Anton Stadler, was originally to have been a basset-horn concerto in G, and the first movement was sketched in that form before he decided in favour of Stadler's 'basset clarinet' (a clarinet with a downwards extension of a major 3rd, probably also intended in K581). The work survives only in an adaptation by its original publisher, and not until the 1960s were attempts made to restore it and perform it on an extended instrument. The discovery that it was composed for basset clarinet explains several puzzling features in the text, and the extra compass makes the exploitation of the clarinet's contrasting registers even more striking than in its familiar form. The gentle-toned orchestra, with flutes, bassoons and horns but not oboes, doubtless reflects a preference for tone-colours to offset the clarinet as well as the factors touched on earlier (see §5 above) regarding the orchestration of music in A major; and it helps impart to this graceful and lovingly written work a shading that it is tempting to regard as autumnal.

Mozart's large output of dance music ought not to be passed over. He composed, for dancing, about 120 minuets, more than 50 German dances or ländler and some 40 contredanses; nearly all the German dances and about one third of each of the other types postdate his court appointment. Some were composed each winter from 1787–8 to 1790–91. Most are 16 or 32 bars long, for strings (without viola) and varied wind. One is struck by the craftsmanship and the artistic invention he brought even to these humble pieces, and in particular by his capacity for overcoming the rhythmic monotony of 16-bar phrases, by the ingenious variety of colour, and above all by the melodic felicity that enabled him to offer piquant little surprises to those of the dancers who cared to listen.

24. LATE VOCAL WORKS. In his last months Mozart wrote major works in three genres with which he had scarcely been occupied for almost a decade: Singspiel, *opera seria* and sacred music. The two theatrical forms, in particular, had undergone considerable change since the time of *Die Entführung* (1782) and *Idomeneo* (1781).

The first of the three to be composed was *Die Zauberflöte*, which was well under way by 11 June 1791, as a reference in a letter to Constanze makes clear, and probably complete in July but for three vocal items, the overture and the march. It has many sources. Schikaneder apparently drew its basic plot from Liebeskind's 'Lulu oder Die Zauberflöte', published in Wieland's collection of fairy tales, *Dschinnistan* (1786–

9); this was a source for other operas given at the Freihaustheater and the rival Leopoldstädter-Theater, including several that Mozart knew, like Müller's *Kaspar der Fagottist* and Schack's *Der Stein der Weisen*, and which themselves may have provided ideas for Schikaneder and Mozart. Another source for the magical elements was Philipp Hafner's play *Megära* (1763). Many of the ritual elements are derived from Jean Terrasson's novel *Sethos* (1731), which has an ancient Egyptian setting, from contemporary freemasonry and possibly from other theatrical works of the time. The whole belongs firmly in the established traditions of Viennese popular theatre. Claims have been made on behalf of C. L. Giesecke, a poet and a member of the company, as author of the libretto, in the light of his own reported assertions about 30 years later; but they lack plausible support, and the arguments in favour of Schikaneder's authorship seem incontrovertible. The possibility that Giesecke, who put together Wranitzky's *Oberon* text, may have suggested ideas or helped over details cannot be ruled out.

Another hotly disputed point regarding *Die Zauberflöte* concerns a possible reshaping of the plot while composition was in progress. The opera begins as if a traditional tale of a heroic prince (Tamino) rescuing a beautiful princess (Pamina) at the bidding of her mother (the Queen of Night) from her wicked abductor (Sarastro) – like the basic plan of 'Lulu'. It soon transpires, however, that the abductor is beneficent and that it is the princess's mother who is wicked. One is tempted to think that this shift can only represent a change in plan by Schikaneder and Mozart; but the moral ambiguities that demand explanation if it does not – Sarastro's employment of the evil Monostatos, for example, or the Queen and her Ladies' gifts of the benevolently magical flute and bells to Tamino and Papageno, or Pamina's fear of Sarastro – are not out of line with Viennese popular theatrical traditions, nor with symbolic interpretations of the work.

*Die Zauberflöte* is distinguished from the bulk of contemporary Singspiels not merely by the quality of its music but also by the serious meanings that underlie what on the surface may seem childish pantomime or low comedy. In style it is diverse. The overture, in the 'masonic' key of E♭ (with three flats), embodies fugal writing, and it also at once implies masonic symbolism: the introduction sounds three chords, two of them twice, and thus signifies the number 3 (or possibly the masonic feminine number 5); it recurs with a less ambiguous three times three chords, and also appears in that form in the ritual scenes of Act 2. Papageno's strophic comic songs are in the same cheerful manner as those of other contemporary Singspiels, and close too to some of Mozart's own lieder of the preceding years. The songs for the serious characters, while rarely using the extended forms of Italian opera, are more Italianate, like

*17. Sketches for 'La clemenza di Tito' K621 (nos.10, 15 and 1), 1791 (S-Uu Vokalmusik Handskrift 133, f.8v); these are working sketches, showing Mozart's working-out of detailed passages, as opposed to the 'melodic sketches' (of which more survive) in which he drafted the line of continuity of a section or movement, or his many 'false starts'*

Tamino's lyrical Portrait Aria, or the high coloratura ones that portray the Queen of Night with such fierce brilliance. Pamina's 'Ach ich fühl's' falls in between; its simple, intimate manner could not belong to a Countess or an Elvira in a like situation, and indeed reflects her more universal, idealized character as well as the different social ambience for which this opera was intended. The music for the Three Ladies is distinguished from that for the Three Boys in style and texture, the former intense and calling for vibrant tone, the latter cool and pellucid, representing at its height the element of serenity remarked earlier as characteristic of Mozart's late style.

The ritual music, including the songs for Sarastro, the choruses, certain ensembles and the cantus firmus 'chorale prelude' setting for the music of the Men in Armour, falls into yet another category. Stylistic parallels can be found, not surprisingly, in Mozart's masonic music, which includes four cantatas, among them one composed at the time of *Die Zauberflöte* and one just after, and which mostly contain songs and choral music in the solemn, exalted tone heard here; they share too the same masonic symbols in key, rhythm, instrumentation and other particulars. Most of the music in the two extended finales is of this kind.

Much has been written about freemasonry in *Die Zauberflöte* (see particularly Nettl, 1957; Chailley, 1968; and Thomson, 1977). It has been suggested that the characters stood for people involved in the recent history of freemasonry – the Queen of Night for Maria Theresia, its oppressor, Tamino for Joseph II, Sarastro for the scientist Ignaz von Born or the Italian masonic martyr Cagliostro. Such particularizations are unlikely to have been in the authors' minds, and may seem to narrow the work, for the characters here, unlike those of the Da Ponte operas, are generalized and symbolic: for example Papageno and Papagena as children of nature, Tamino and Pamina as ideal beings seeking full realization and, especially, ideal union. In this *Die Zauberflöte* may be thought to pursue the theme of self-knowledge predicated in *Così fan tutte*. More broadly, it has been persuasively argued (Koenigsberger, 1975) that the opera is susceptible to interpretation in the light of the philosophical, cosmological and epistemological background of 18th-century freemasonry as an allegory about 'the quest of the human soul for both inner harmony and enlightenment', with the main characters 'joint participants in one being, one psyche, or one soul'. Such interpretations help explain how what may superficially seem a mixture of the sublime (musically) and the ridiculous (textually) melds into an opera not only theatrically effective but also of a philosophical or religious quality. Goethe tried to write a sequel to it; Bernard Shaw called it 'the music of my own church'.

Until the 1960s, Mozart scholars were inclined to dismiss *La clemenza di Tito* as an opera written hurriedly and with distaste. That it was written hurriedly, even if not as hurriedly as has been supposed, is probably true; but there is no reason to imagine that Mozart had reservations about composing it. Serious opera had always attracted him; and many composers were setting Metastasio's classical librettos modified to meet contemporary taste through the addition of ensembles and choruses. Mozart noted *Tito* in his catalogue as 'ridotto a vera opera' by Mazzolà, who removed 18 arias and added four, and supplied two duets, three trios and finale ensembles.

The opera was composed in a style more austere than that of the Da Ponte operas or *Die Zauberflöte*. This traditionally has been attributed to Mozart's alleged haste; but on other occasions he composed quickly and elaborately, and there is no reason to think that the opera would have been substantially different had he had longer. Its style is appropriate to its topic. The indebtedness of the original Metastasio libretto to French classical models has been pointed out (Moberly, 1974), and in its reduced form it may be seen as conforming to the neo-classical ideals then rapidly gaining ground in Germany. Mozart responded with restrained orchestral writing, smooth, broad vocal lines, and relatively brief numbers.

It is clear that the aria lengths were carefully planned. In Act 2 both the prima donna (Vitellia) and primo uomo (Sextus) have full-length rondò arias, Vitellia's being the movement, 'Non più di fiori', that may have been composed earlier. An interesting feature is the appearance of related material in the two sections; there is evidence that this was an afterthought. This aria has an obbligato part for basset-horn, and Sextus's Act 1 aria, 'Parto', has one for clarinet; these were composed for Stadler. Both Sextus's arias involve progressive increases in tempo, no doubt intended to represent the screwing up of his courage. The arias for the secondary characters, even Titus, are much shorter. The trios embody some degree of simultaneous representation of different emotions, as in the *opere buffe*. The Act 1 finale however moves in a sense opposite from that of the traditional, accelerating *opera buffa* ensemble of confusion: it starts Allegro and ends Andante, with the principals on the stage bewailing the betrayal of Titus while the groans of the populace are heard in the distance. *La clemenza di Tito*, compared with the preceding operas, is no less refined in craftsmanship, and it shows Mozart responding with music of restraint, nobility and warmth to a new kind of stimulus.

Mozart's last work was the Requiem. Besides the little funeral motet *Ave verum corpus*, of June 1791, it was his first sacred work since the abandoned C minor Mass (1783). It was, as we have seen, left unfinished. On his death Constanze, or someone acting for her, gave the score first to Joseph Eybler to complete, but he did little more than add orchestral parts in certain skeletal passages. Eventually Süssmayr undertook responsibility for its completion. He afterwards claimed that the Sanctus, Benedictus and Agnus Dei were wholly his own work. He adapted Mozart's music of the opening two movements for the 'Lux aeterna' and 'Cum sanctis tuis', and orchestrated all the movements from the 'Dies irae' to the 'Hostias', for most of which Mozart had left a figured bass and in several movements at least a top line to indicate the continuity (his customary mode of drafting a score). To what extent Süssmayr's claims were true must remain uncertain. The evidence is untrustworthy: it was in his interest to say that much of the work was his own, and in Constanze's to say that her husband had virtually completed it. She said that she passed sketch material to Süssmayr, who was close to Mozart in those last weeks and may have known the composer's detailed intentions; but one is bound to wonder why Constanze did not turn to him immediately. On the evidence embodied in the extant material – Mozart's manuscript with Eybler's additions, Süssmayr's copy, and a few inconclusive sketches – Mozart's contributions to the remaining movements

*18. Wolfgang Amadeus Mozart: unfinished portrait (probably 1789) by Joseph Lange in the Mozart Museum, Salzburg*

must remain a matter for conjecture. Süssmayr's completion has however been criticized, as clumsy and untrue to Mozart, by Richard Strauss, Bruno Walter and many others; several other completions have been essayed, notably by Benjamin Britten (1970) and Franz Beyer (published 1971).

The Requiem is less diverse in style than the C minor Mass. Its tone, in the form in which it survives (for Mozart might have orchestrated later movements differently), is determined by the sombre basset-horns and bassoons that comprise the woodwind section; there are also trumpets and timpani, and the traditional trombones of liturgical music, as well as strings and continuo. The increasingly contrapuntal style of Mozart's later years, too, and the plainer melodic writing, conduce to a greater consistency. Several of the solo movements, notably the 'Recordare', involve contrapuntal treatment, and even some of the dramatic choruses, for example the 'Confutatis' and the 'Rex tremendae majestatis', embody canonic writing. The most dramatic, the 'Dies irae', remains largely homophonic. Mozart followed established Austrian traditions in several choral numbers. The opening 'Requiem aeternam' and the 'Quam

olim Abrahae' fugue are influenced by Michael Haydn's Requiem of 1771 (which also used plainchant at 'Te decet hymnus'), and the influence of Gassmann and others in the Austrian, Fuxian tradition has been noted. The fugue subject of the Kyrie, embodying a characteristic falling diminished 7th, has been cited as an example of the influence of Bach or Handel but this is a traditional phrase with obvious contrapuntal potentialities, used in various forms by many composers including Haydn and Mozart himself (K426). Here it is treated in a straightforward double fugue; the 'Quam olim Abrahae', with its chromatic subject, its awkward rhythms and its ostinato string accompaniments, is less conventional. To what extent Mozart's ideas may have been used in the movements claimed by Süssmayr cannot be deduced on stylistic grounds; commentators have often reckoned however that the perfunctory 'Osanna' settings are unlikely to be Mozart's (though his too are usually brief), that the Benedictus seems too characteristic to be wholly Süssmayr's, and that the sombre D minor music that begins the Agnus Dei could well incorporate Mozartian material. Whether Mozart intended the music of the opening movements to be used for the last ones it is impossible to say, but there is precedent in his earlier works (for example the Mass K317); and it at least ensures that the Requiem ends in fully authentic tones.

25. APPEARANCE, ICONOGRAPHY. There are surprisingly few descriptions of Mozart's appearance. Several observers commented on his small stature; as a child he was short, and in about 1785 an anonymous English traveller (quoted by King, 1973–4) set his height at 'not more than about five feet and four inches'. All agreed, too, on his slight build, and several noted his habitual pallor and his fine fair hair. His sister reported that, though handsome as a child, he suffered some disfigurement from smallpox and became sallow after visiting Italy. The English traveller and Hummel noted a melancholy expression, but Hummel, Kelly and others remarked on his bright eyes and animated countenance when aroused – 'as impossible to describe it, as it would be to paint sunbeams' (Kelly).

Most of the authentic portraits, engravings and the like are reproduced in Deutsch's *Mozart und seine Welt in zeitgenössischen Bildern* (1961). Of them, the earliest of any importance is the Verona portrait of 1770, probably by Saverio dalla Rosa (fig.5). The Della Croce family portrait of about 1780 (fig.9) was noted by Nannerl as giving a particularly good likeness; the one of Mozart as Knight of the Golden Spur (fig.7) gives a similar, rather severe appearance. A softer, more pensive expression is shown on the famous unfinished portrait by Joseph Lange, husband of Mozart's sister-in-law Aloysia, probably from 1789 (fig.18); also from his late years comes, besides various medallions, silhouettes and engravings, the sensitive silverpoint drawing by Doris Stock, done in Dresden in 1789 (fig.14).

26. POSTHUMOUS REPUTATION; MOZART STUDIES. To judge by the more than conventionally laudatory tone of the obituaries and other tributes, Mozart's reputation stood high in Vienna and throughout the German lands at the time of his death. Although his music was widely criticized as audacious, too highly flavoured, and too complex for the ordinary listener to follow, it was widely understood that he was an artist far out of the ordinary, on a par with the other great Viennese composer of the time, Haydn. His operas, led by *Die Zauberflöte* and *Don Giovanni*, and at first *La clemenza di Tito*, were widely performed (though often in corrupt versions) and published many times over in the last years of the 18th century and the first of the 19th. His main mature works, of which only a small proportion were printed in his lifetime, began to appear in print. In 1798 Spehr of Brunswick and Breitkopf & Härtel of Leipzig embarked on collected editions, the former of his keyboard works, the latter more comprehensive; several other sets with similar aims were inaugurated in the following decades. The André firm in Offenbach, who negotiated with Constanze over Mozart's manuscript material, also published many of his works, some in critical editions.

Early biographies include the obituary of Schlichtegroll (1793), which uses Nannerl's and J. A. Schachtner's recollections, and Niemetschek's important life (1798). Comparisons of Mozart and Haydn were published by I. F. Arnold (1810) and Stendhal (1814). In 1828 the substantial biography by Georg Nikolaus Nissen, Constanze's second husband, was pub-

lished; in the next year Constanze and Nannerl met Vincent and Mary Novello, in Salzburg on a Mozart pilgrimage, and talked to them about Mozart (see Medici and Hughes, 1955).

In the mid-19th century interest in Mozart grew along with the general growth of interest in music of the past; most writers on his music, viewing it in the context of Beethoven and the early Romantics, and Bach, tended to dwell on its purity, beauty and sweetness. Nissen's biography was the main source for others of the 1840s, like those of Oulibicheff (Ulïbïshev) and Holmes. The first substantial scholarly biography, embodying fresh research, appeared in the centenary year, 1856 – Otto Jahn's *W. A. Mozart*. Six years later came Ludwig von Köchel's chronological thematic catalogue of Mozart's works, which, ahead of its time in scholarly method, gave the fullest possible source information; and Köchel was influential in the publication of the Breitkopf & Härtel collected edition, which began in 1877 and was largely finished in six years.

In the early decades of the 20th century Mozart scholarship made particular progress, with the beginning in 1912 of Wyzewa and Saint-Foix's highly schematic analytical and stylistic study of his works, the appearance in 1913 and 1914 of Dent's study of the operas and Schiedermair's critical edition of the letters, and the publication in 1919–21 of Hermann Abert's substantial revision of Jahn's biography. The first series of Mozart yearbooks began in the 1920s, lasting only three issues, like the second series in 1941–3, but including research more solid than the *Mitteilungen* of the leading Mozart societies, those in Berlin, Salzburg and Vienna. Mozart studies in England in the 1930s were stimulated by the scholarly and collecting activities of C. B. Oldman and later A. H. King, by the coming to England of Paul Hirsch and his Mozart collection, and by the appearance in 1938 of Emily Anderson's translation of the letters, the most complete edition then to be had. In 1937 Einstein published the third edition of the Köchel catalogue, following up Paul Graf von Waldersee's revision of 1905 with a more radical one involving much renumbering for his new chronology, which was based as much on stylistic argument as on source studies; there was a reprint with a supplement in 1947. Einstein's deeply perceptive if over-romantic book on the composer appeared in 1945.

The range of Mozart's works familiar to the musical public had not been large in the 19th century; in the 20th it greatly increased, with performances of more of the piano concertos and symphonies in particular, and the revival of *Idomeneo* and *Così fan tutte*, which entered the repertory only from the 1950s; by the 1970s, with the more general acceptance of *opera seria* conventions, a reconsideration of the dramatic viability of *La clemenza di Tito* was under way, and the earlier operas too had occasional revivals. Mozart's operas have occupied a specially prominent role at the Salzburg Festival and at the small opera house at Glyndebourne, Sussex (founded in 1934). The influence of the gramophone in the dissemination of his music, with the appearance, in the 1960s and 1970s of complete recordings of many entire categories of his works, has been profound.

All these developments were much encouraged by the bicentenary celebrations of 1956, which themselves came early in a new wave of Mozart scholarship. A third yearbook series had been instituted in 1950, by the

Internationale Stiftung Mozarteum in Salzburg, and the early 1950s also saw the foundation of a new series of *Mitteilungen* from the Mozarteum and of *Acta Mozartiana*. Still more crucial was the institution in 1955 of the Neue Mozart-Ausgabe, published by Bärenreiter, a new critical edition of all Mozart's works, with full prefaces and (eventually) critical commentaries. Its work was however hampered by the removal in World War II and the unavailability until 1980 of most of the largest single collection of Mozart autographs, that of the Prussian State Library, Berlin.

The most important individual Mozart scholar in the mid-20th century was O. E. Deutsch, who prepared, in association with the Neue Mozart-Ausgabe, a documentary biography (1961, supplement in 1978), a pictorial study of Mozart's life (1961) and, with W. A. Bauer and J. H. Eibl, a complete, critical edition of the family correspondence, richly annotated. The huge growth in Mozart studies is shown in Schneider and Algatzy's valuable *Mozart-Handbuch* of 1962, which contains a bibliography of nearly 4000 items, and by Angermüller and Schneider's even larger bibliography in

the *Mozart-Jahrbuch 1975* (supplement in 1978). In 1964 the sixth edition of the Köchel catalogue appeared, with adjustments to the chronology, generally based on more exact palaeographic methods than Einstein's, with further revisions to the numbering system and a more rationally organized series of appendices dealing with unauthentic or doubtful works and arrangements. The work of the Neue Mozart-Ausgabe, in association with the 'Mozart towns' Augsburg, Salzburg and Vienna, has provoked a new wave of textual and source scholarship, typified by the searching, detailed autograph studies of Wolfgang Plath, which along with Alan Tyson's paper studies have involved a re-examination of the dating of certain works and have raised questions of authenticity. Mozart's methods of composition, which have fascinated commentators since the time of Niemetschek and Rochlitz – paticularly the semi-myth of his conceiving works entire in his head before committing anything to paper – have been the subject of recent research; scholars have also particularly given attention to Mozart's methods of articulating the drama in his operas and to the underlying structures of his compositions.

## WORKS

Editions: *W. A. Mozarts Werke*, ed. L. von Köchel and others (Leipzig, 1877–83, suppls. 1877–1910/*R* with changes) [MW]

    *W. A. Mozart: Neue Ausgabe sämtlicher Werke*, ed. E. F. Schmid, W. Plath and W. Rehm, Internationale Stiftung Mozarteum Salzburg (Kassel, 1955–) [NMA; nos. shown, e.g. Series (IV): Werkgruppe (3)/Abteilung (2)/Band (i), page (273) – IV:3/2/i, 273; Abteilung and Band nos. not always applicable]

Catalogue: *Chronologisch-thematisches Verzeichnis sämtlicher Tonwerke Wolfgang Amade Mozarts*, ed. L. von Köchel (Leipzig, 1862; 2/1905 ed. P. Graf von Waldersee; 3/1937 ed. A. Einstein, with suppl. 1947; 6/1964 ed. F. Giegling, A. Weinmann and G. Sievers)

| | |
|---|---|
| K  – no. in Köchel, 1862; for items not in 1862 edn., no. from 2/1905 or 3/1937 given | A  – Anhang [appx]; applicable only to edns. of Köchel before 6/1964 |
| K⁶ – no. in Köchel, 6/1964; nos. preceded by A, B or C in appendices | BH – no. in Breitkopf edn |
| | (D) – date from MS of work (not always clear) |
| sk – associated sketch, draft or frag. material | (L) – date from Mozart's letters |
| | (C) – date from Mozart: Verzeichnüss aller meiner Werke (1784–91) |

Editions published in Mozart's lifetime are noted in the Remarks column, excluding arrangements, and, generally, pf reductions; references to movements are shown in small roman, e.g. K320/iii.

Items are arranged in each category by order of K⁶ numbers.

| K | K⁶ | Title | Key | Scoring | Composition | MW | NMA | Remarks |
|---|---|---|---|---|---|---|---|---|
| | | | | MASSES, MASS MOVEMENTS, REQUIEM | | | | |
| 33 | 33 | Kyrie | F | SATB, str | Paris, 12 June 1766 (D) | III/i, 2 | | |
| 139 | 47a | Missa solemnis | c | S, A, T, B, SATB, 2 ob, 4 tpt, 3 trbn, timp, str, org | ?Vienna, aut. 1768 | I/i, 117 | I:1/1/i, 37 | 'Waisenhausmesse'; perf. orphanage in Rennweg, Vienna, 7 Dec 1768 |
| 49 | 47d | Missa brevis | G | S, A, T, B, SATB, [3 trbn,] str, org | Vienna, Oct–Nov 1768 (D) | I/i, 1 | I:1/1/i, 3 | frag. alternative settings of Gloria and Credo, KA20a/626b,25 |
| 65 | 61a | Missa brevis | d | S, A, T, B, SATB, str, org | Salzburg, 14 Jan 1769 (D) | I/i, 33 | I:1/1/i, 159 | perf. Salzburg, collegiate church, 5 Feb 1769 |
| 66 | 66 | Missa | C | S, A, T, B, SATB, 2 ob, 2 hn, 2 [+2] tpt, [3 trbn,] timp, str | Salzburg, Oct 1769 (D) | I/i, 49 | I:1/1/i, 185 | 'Dominicus' Mass; perf. Salzburg, St Peter, 15 Oct 1769, for Cajetan Hagenauer; extra wind pts. by Mozart and Leopold |
| 140 | C 1.12 | Missa brevis | G | S, A, T, B, SATB, 2 vn, b | ?Salzburg, 1773 | — | I:1/1/i, 285 | doubtful; incl. in K³ as 235d; MS pts. have autograph corrections |
| 167 | 167 | Missa | C | SATB, 2 ob, 4 tpt, [3 trbn,] timp, 2 vn, b, org | Salzburg, June 1773 (D) | I/i, 179 | I:1/1/ii, 3 | 'In honorem Ssmae Trinitatis' |
| 192 | 186f | Missa brevis | F | S, A, T, B, SATB (2 tpt), [3 trbn,] 2 vn, b, org | Salzburg, 24 June 1774 (D) | I/i, 239 | I:1/1/ii, 75 | tpts added later by Mozart (tpt 2 = K626b,20) |
| 194 | 186h | Missa brevis | D | S, A, T, B, SATB, [3 trbn,] 2 vn, b, org | Salzburg, 8 Aug 1774 (D) | I/i, 265 | I:1/1/ii, 121 | sk K91/186i, MW, XXIV, no.32 |
| 220 | 196b | Missa brevis | G | S, A, T, B, SATB, 2 tpt [3 trbn,] timp, 2 vn, b, org | 1775–6 | I/i, 291 | I:1/1/ii, 163 | 'Spatzenmesse' |
| 262 | 246a | Missa [longa] | C | S, A, T, B, SATB, 2 ob, 2 hn, 2 tpt, [3 trbn, timp,] 2 vn, b, org | Salzburg, 1775 | I/ii, 119 | I:1/1/ii, 197 | |

| K | K⁶ | Title | Key | Scoring | Composition | MW | NMA | Remarks |
|---|---|---|---|---|---|---|---|---|
| 257 | 257 | Missa | C | S, A, T, B, SATB, 2 ob, 2 tpt, [3 trbn,] timp, 2 vn, b, org | Salzburg, Nov 1776 (D) | I/ii, 1 | I:1/1/iii | 'Credo' |
| 258 | 258 | Missa brevis | C | S, A, T, B, SATB, 2 tpt, timp, 2 vn, b, org | Salzburg, Dec 1776 (D) | I/ii, 55 | I:1/1/iii | 'Spaur' |
| 259 | 259 | Missa brevis | C | S, A, T, B, SATB, 2 tpt, timp, 2 vn, b, org | Salzburg, Dec 1776 (D) | I/ii, 89 | I:1/1/iii | 'Organ solo' |
| 275 | 272b | Missa brevis | Bb | S, A, T, B, SATB, 2 vn, b, org | Salzburg, late 1777 | I/ii, 183 | I:1/1/iv | perf. Salzburg, St Peter, 21 Dec 1777 |
| 317 | 317 | Missa | C | S, A, T, B, SATB, 2 ob, 2 hn, 2 tpt, 3 trbn, timp, 2 vn, org | Salzburg, 23 March 1779 (D) | I/ii, 207 | I:1/1/iv | 'Coronation' |
| 337 | 337 | Missa solemnis | C | S, A, T, B, SATB, 2 ob, 2 bn, 2 tpt, [3 trbn,] timp, 2 vn, b, org | Salzburg, March 1780 (D) | I/ii, 255 | I:1/1/iv | frag. of different Credo in MW, XXIV, no.135 |
| 341 | 368a | Kyrie | d | SATB, 2 fl, 2 ob, 2 cl, 2 bn, 4 hn, 2 tpt, timp, str, org | ?Munich, 1780–81 | III/i, 31 | | |
| 427 | 417a | Missa | c | 2 S, T, B, SSAATTBB, fl, 2 ob, 2 bn, 2 hn, 2 tpt, 3 trbn, timp, str, org | Vienna, cJuly 1782–May 1783 | XXIV, no.29 | I:1/1/v | Credo inc., Agnus Dei not composed; Kyrie, Gloria perf. Salzburg, St Peter, 25 Oct 1783; see Davidde penitente K469 |
| 626 | 626 | Requiem | d | S, A, T, B, SATB, 2 basset hn, 2 bn, 2 tpt, 3 trbn, timp, str, org | Vienna, late 1791 | XXIV, no.1 | I:1/2/i–ii | inc.; completed by F. X. Süssmayr |

Kyrie frags.: C (49 bars), KA18/166f; D (12 bars), KA19/166g; G (34 bars), KA16/196a, ?1788–9; C (9 bars), KA13/258a, ?1788–9; Eb (34 bars), K322/296a, ?early 1778, MW, III/i, 11; KA12/296b, lost; C (37 bars), K323, ?1788–9, MW, III/i, 22; D (11 bars), KA14/422a, ?1783, Gloria frag.: C (26 bars), KA20/323a, ?1788–9. Sanctus/Benedictus frag.: Eb (18 bars), K296c. Osanna frag.: C (21 bars), K223/166e, ?1772.

Doubtful and spurious masses (selective list): d, K90 (Kyrie), ?copy of another composer's work, MQ, xxvii (1951), 1; C, K115/166d, MW, XXIV, no.28, inc., ?by Leopold; F, K116/90a, MW, XXIV, no.33 with 417B (Quoniam), by Leopold (see Plath, MJb 1971–2, 21); C, KA185/C1.01, Novello no.17; Eb, KA235f/C1.02, by B. Schack, in Periodical Collection of Sacred Music, no.4 (May 1831), 'additions by Mozart'; Eb KA186/C1.03, Novello nos.13, 16; G, KA232/C1.04, Novello no.12 ('Twelfth Mass'); Bb, KA233/C1.06, Novello no.7; G, K140/C1.12, see above; G ('Missa solemnis pastorita'), Kdeest/C1.18 (Munich, 1946); d ('Requiem brevis'), KA237/C1.90, Novello no.18; Kyrie, C, K340/C3.06; Kyrie, C, K221/A1, MW, XXIV, no.34, by Eberlin

| | | | | | LITANIES, VESPERS, VESPER PSALMS | | | |
|---|---|---|---|---|---|---|---|---|
| 109 | 74e | Litaniae Lauretanae BVM | Bb | S, A, T, B, SATB, [3 trbn,] 2 vn, b, org | Salzburg, May 1771 (D) | II, 1 | I:2/i, 3 | |
| 125 | 125 | Litaniae de venerabili altaris sacramento | Bb | S, A, T, B, SATB, 2 ob/fl, 2 hn, 2 tpt, [3 trbn,] str, org | Salzburg, March 1772 (D) | II, 13 | I:2/i, 23 | |
| 195 | 186d | Litaniae Lauretanae BVM | D | S, A, T, B, SATB, 2 ob, 2 hn, [3 trbn,] str, org | Salzburg, May 1774 (D) | II, 63 | I:2/i, 135 | |
| 193 | 186g | Dixit Dominus, Magnificat | C | S, T, SATB, 2 tpt, 3 trbn, 2 vn, b, org | Salzburg, July 1774 (D) | II, 169 | I:2/ii, 1 | |
| 243 | 243 | Litaniae de venerabili altaris sacramento | Eb | S, A, T, B, SATB, 2 ob/fl, 2 bn, 2 hn, 3 trbn, str, org | Salzburg, March 1776 (D) | II, 109 | I:2/i, 251 | |
| 321 | 321 | Vesperae de Dominica | C | S, A, T, B, SATB, [bn,] 2 tpt, [3 trbn,] timp, 2 vn, b, org | Salzburg, 1779. | II, 193 | I:2/ii, 33 | |
| 339 | 339 | Vesperae solennes de confessore | C | S, A, T, B, SATB, [bn,] 2 tpt, [3 trbn,] timp, 2 vn, b, org | Salzburg, 1780 (D) | II, 237 | I:2/ii, 101 | |

Frag.: Magnificat, C, K321a, NMA, I:2/ii, 18 (7 bars)

| | | | | | SHORT SACRED WORKS | | | |
|---|---|---|---|---|---|---|---|---|
| 20 | 20 | God is our refuge | g | SATB | London, July 1765 | III/i, 47 | III:9, 2 | motet; autograph (partly in Leopold's hand) given to GB-Lbm, July 1765 |
| 33c | 33c | Stabat mater | | SATB | Paris and Salzburg, 1766 | — | — | lost; in LC |
| 34 | 34 | Scande coeli limina | C | S, SATB, 2 tpt, timp, 2 vn, b, org | Kloster Seeon, Bavaria, early 1767 | III/ii, 1 | I:3, 3 | offertory |
| 47 | 47 | Veni Sancte Spiritus | C | S, A, T, B, SATB, 2 ob, 2 hn, 2 tpt, timp | Vienna, aut. 1768 | III/i, 48 | I:3, 12 | |

| K | K⁶ | Title | Key | Scoring | Composition | MW | NMA | Remarks |
|---|----|-------|-----|---------|-------------|----|----|---------|
| 117 | 66a | Benedictus sit Deus | C | S, SATB, 2 fl, 2 hn, 2 tpt, timp, str, org | Vienna, Oct–Nov 1768 | III/ii, 21 | I:3, 25 | offertory; ? = 47b, perf. at Waisenhauskirche, Vienna, 7 Dec 1768 |
| 141 | 66b | Te Deum | C | SATB, 4 tpt, [timp,] 2 vn, b, org | Salzburg, end 1769 | III/i, 133 | I:3, 43 | |
| 143 | 73a | Ergo interest | G | S, str, org | Salzburg, late 1773 | III/ii, 37 | I:3, 62 | motet |
| 85 | 73s | Miserere | a | ATB, b | Bologna, July–Aug 1770 | III/i, 58 | I:3, 69 | last 3 verses ?incorrectly attrib. J. André in one MS |
| 44 | 73u | Cibavit eos | a | SATB, org | 1770 | XXIV, no.31 | | antiphon, doubtful; see Federhofer, MJb 1960–61, 43 |
| 86 | 73v | Quaerite primum | d | SATB | Bologna, 9 Oct 1770 | III/i, 62 | I:3, 73 | antiphon; exercise for Accademia Filarmonica, Bologna |
| 108 | 74d | Regina coeli | C | S, SATB, 2 ob/fl, 2 hn, 2 tpt, timp, str, org | Salzburg, May 1771 | III/i, 63 | I:3, 74 | |
| 72 | 74f | Inter natos mulierum | G | SATB, 2 vn, b, org | Salzburg, May–June 1771 | III/ii, 9 | I:3, 9 | offertory; for feast of St John the Baptist, 24 June |
| 127 | 127 | Regina coeli | B♭ | S, SATB, 2 ob/fl, 2 hn, str, org | Salzburg, May 1772 | III/i, 87 | I:3, 120 | |
| 165 | 158a | Exsultate, jubilate | F | S, 2 ob, 2 hn, str, org | Milan, Jan 1773 | III/ii, 43 | I:3, 157 | motet, for Rauzzini; perf. Milan, 17 Jan 1773 |
| 197 | C3.05 | Tantum ergo | D | SATB, 2 tr, str, org | ?Salzburg, 1774 | III/i, 149 | I:3, 276 | doubtful; see Münster, Acta Mozartiana, x (1963), 54 |
| 198 | C3.08 | Sub tuum praesidium | F | S, T, str, org | ?Salzburg, 1774 | III/ii, 73 | I:3, 177 | offertory, doubtful, incl. in K³ as 158b; ?adaptation of secular work |
| 222 | 205a | Misericordias Domini | d | SATB, 2 vn, [va,] b, org | Munich, early 1775 | III/ii, 77 | I:3, 182 | offertory |
| 260 | 248a | Venite populi | D | SSAATTBB, 2 vn ad lib, b, org | Salzburg, mid-1776 | III/ii, 91 | I:3, 199 | |
| 277 | 272a | Alma Dei creatoris | F | S, A, T, SATB, 2 vn, b, org | Salzburg, 1777 | III/ii, 111 | I:3, 223 | offertory |
| 273 | 273 | Sancta Maria, mater Dei | F | SATB, str, org | Salzburg, 9 Sept 1777 (D) | III/ii, 103 | I:3, 234 | gradual, for feast of BVM, 12 Sept |
| A1 | 297a | Miserere (8 movts) | | SATB, orch | Paris, March–April 1778 | — | — | for work by Holzbauer; lost; see letter, 5 April 1778 |
| 146 | 317b | Kommet her, ihr frechen Sünder | B♭ | S, str, org | Salzburg, ?March–April 1779 | VI/i, 81 | I:4/iv, 33 | aria |
| 276 | 321b | Regina coeli | C | S, A, T, B, SATB, 2 ob, 2 tpt, timp, 2 vn, b, org | Salzburg, ?1779 | III/i, 118 | I:3, 243 | |
| 343 | 336c | O Gottes Lamm; Als aus Aegypten | F; C | S, b | Prague, or Vienna, ?early 1787 | III/i, 154 | III:8, 30 | Ger. sacred songs |
| 618 | 618 | Ave verum corpus | D | SATB, str, org | Baden, 17 June 1791 (D) | III/ii, 123 | I:3, 261 | motet |

Frag.: In te Domine speravi, C, ᴋA23/166h (34 bars), 1774
Doubtful or spurious works (selective list):
    copied by Mozart: Lacrimosa, c, ᴋA21/A2, MW, XXIV, no.30, by Eberlin; Justum deduxit (hymn), ᴋ326/A4, MW, III/ii, 117, by Eberlin; Adoramus te (hymn), ᴋ327/A10, MW, III/ii, 121, by Q. Gasparini; De profundis (psalm), ᴋ93/A22, MW, III/ii, 18, by G. von Reutter (ii); Memento Domine David (psalm), by Reutter
    others: Salve regina, ᴋ92/C3.01; Salus infirmorum (hymn), ᴋ324/C3.02; Sancta Maria (hymn), ᴋ325/C3.03; Tantum ergo, B♭, ᴋ142/C3.04, MW, iii/1, 144, and NMA, I:3, 270 (?by J. Zach; see Münster, Acta Mozariana, x (1963), 54; xii (1965), 9); Convertentur sedentes (offertory), ᴋ177 and 342/C3.09, MW, III/ii, 59, by Leopold; Venti, fulgura, procellae (motet), ᴋdeest (see de Nys, Acta Mozartiana, xviii (1971), 7, and MJb 1971–2, 37)

CHURCH SONATAS

| K | K⁶ | Key | Scoring | Composition | MW | NMA |
|---|----|-----|---------|-------------|----|----|
| 67 | 41h | E♭ | 2 vn, b, org | Salzburg, 1772 | XXIII, 1 | VI:16, 2 |
| 68 | 41i | B♭ | 2 vn, b, org | Salzburg, 1772 | XXIII, 3 | VI:16, 4 |
| 69 | 41k | D | 2 vn, b, org | Salzburg, 1772 | XXIII, 5 | VI:16, 6 |
| 144 | 124a | D | 2 vn, b, org | Salzburg, 1774 | XXIII, 7 | VI:16, 8 |
| 145 | 124b | F | 2 vn, b, org | Salzburg, 1774 | XXIII, 9 | VI:16, 11 |
| 212 | 212 | B♭ | 2 vn, b, org | Salzburg, July 1775 (D) | XXIII, 11 | VI:16, 13 |
| 241 | 241 | G | 2 vn, b, org | Salzburg, Jan 1776 (D) | | VI:16, 16 |
| 224 | 241a | F | 2 vn, b, org | Salzburg, early 1780 | XXIII, 14 | VI:16, 18 |
| 225 | 241b | A | 2 vn, b, org | Salzburg, early 1780 | XXIII, 18 | VI:16, 22 |
| 244 | 244 | F | 2 vn, b, org [solo] | Salzburg, April 1776 (D) | XXIII, 21 | VI:16, 25 |
| 245 | 245 | D | 2 vn, b, org [solo] | Salzburg, April 1776 (D) | XXIII, 24 | VI:16, 28 |
| 263 | 263 | C | 2 tpt, 2 vn, b, org [solo] | Salzburg, Dec 1776 | — | VI:16, 32 |
| 274 | 271d | G | 2 vn, b, org | Salzburg, 1777 (D) | XXIII, 27 | VI:16, 36 |
| 278 | 271e | C | 2 ob, 2 tpt, timp, 2 vn, b, org | Salzburg, March–April 1777 | XXIII, 30 | VI:16, 39 |
| 329 | 317a | C | 2 ob, 2 hn, 2 tpt, timp, 2 vn, b, org [solo] | Salzburg, ?March 1779 | XXIII, 41 | VI:16, 49 |
| 328 | 317c | C | 2 vn, b, org [solo] | Salzburg, ?early 1779 | XXIII, 36 | VI:16, 60 |
| 336 | 336d | C | 2 vn, b, org [solo] | Salzburg, March 1780 | XXIII, 51 | VI:16, 65 |

Frag.: D, ᴋA65a/124A

ORATORIOS, SACRED DRAMAS, CANTATAS

| K | K⁶ | Title (description, libretto) | Scoring | Composition | MW | NMA | Remarks |
|---|---|---|---|---|---|---|---|
| 35 | 35 | Die Schuldigkeit des ersten Gebots (pt i of sacred drama, 3, I. A. Weiser) | 3 S, 2 T, 2 ob/fl, 2 bn, 2 hn, trbn, str | Salzburg, early 1767 | V/i | I:4/i | perf. Salzburg, 12 March 1767; pt ii by J. M. Haydn, pt iii by A. C. Adlgasser |
| 42 | 35a | Grabmusik (cantata) | S, B, SATB, [2 ob,] 2 hn, str | Salzburg, 1767 | IV/1, 1 | I:4/iv, 1 | ?perf. Salzburg Cathedral, 7 April 1767; final recit and chorus added c1773 |
| 118 | 74c | La Betulia liberata (oratorio, 2, Metastasio) | 4 S, T, B, SATB, 2 ob/fl, 2 bn, 4 hn, 2 tpt, str | Italy and Salzburg, March–July 1771 | IV/2, 1 | I:4/ii | commissioned in Padua, apparently not perf. |
| 429 | 468a | Dir, Seele des Weltalls (cantata, L. L. Haschka) | T, TTB, fl, 2 ob, cl, 2 hn, bn, str | Vienna, 1785 | XXIV, no.36a–b | I:4/iv, 96 | inc.; partly completed M. Stadler |
| 469 | 469 | Davidde penitente (oratorio, 2, ?Da Ponte) | 2 S, T, SATB, 2 fl, 2 ob, 2 cl, 2 bn, 2 hn, 3 trbn, timp, str | Vienna, March 1785 | IV/2, 1 | | music from Mass K427/417a except for 2 arias, 6 and 11 March 1785 (C); perf. Burgtheater, 13 March |
| 471 | 471 | Die Maurerfreude (cantata, F. Petran) | T, TTB, 2 ob, cl, 2 hn, str | Vienna, 20 April 1785 (C) | IV/1, 24 | I:4/iv, 35 | perf. Lodge 'Zur gekrönten Hoffnung', 24 April 1785 (Vienna, 1785) |
| 619 | 619 | Die ihr des unermesslichen Weltalls Schöpfer ehrt (cantata, F. H. Ziegenhagen) | S, pf | Vienna, July 1791 (C) | VII/1, 82 | I:4/iv, 59 | |
| 623 | 623 | Laut verkünde unsre Freude (cantata, E. Schikaneder) | 2 T, B, fl, 2 ob, 2 hn, str | Vienna, 15 Nov 1791 (C) | IV/1, 40 | I:4/iv, 65 | perf. Lodge 'Zur neugekrönten Hoffnung', 18 Nov 1791 |
| 623 | 623a | Lasst uns mit geschlungnen Händen | S, ? | Vienna, ?Nov 1791 | | | frag. of 32 bars, appended to 1st edn. of K623, pubd 1792; ?spurious |

OPERAS, MUSICAL PLAYS, DRAMATIC CANTATAS

| K | K⁶ | Title (description, libretto) | Scoring | First perf. | MW | NMA | Remarks |
|---|---|---|---|---|---|---|---|
| 38 | 38 | Apollo et Hyacinthus (Lat. intermezzo, 3, ?P. F. Widl) | 2 S, 2 A, T, B, 2 ob, 2 hn, str | Salzburg University, 13 May 1767 | V/ii | II:5/i | perf. with Widl's Lat. play, Clementia Croesi |
| 51 | 46a | La finta semplice (opera buffa, 3, M. Coltellini after Goldoni) | 3 S, 2 T, 2 B, 2 fl/eng hn, 2 ob, 2 bn, 2 hn, str | Salzburg, Archbishop's palace, 1 May 1769 | V/iv | II:5/ii | composed Vienna, mid-1768 |
| 50 | 46b | Bastien und Bastienne (Singspiel, 1, F. W. Weiskern and J. A. Schachtner after J. J. Rousseau: Le devin du village) | S, T, B, 2 ob/fl, 2 hn, str | Vienna, F. A. Mesmer's house, ?Sept–Oct 1768 | V/iii | II:5/iii | |
| 87 | 74a | Mitridate, rè di Ponto (opera seria, 3, V. A. Cigna-Santi after G. Parini and Racine) | 4 S, A, 2 T, 2 fl, 2 ob, 2 bn, 4 hn, str | Milan, Regio Ducal Teatro, 26 Dec 1770 | V/v | II:5/iv | |
| 111 | 111 | Ascanio in Alba (festa teatrale, 2, Parini) | 4 S, T, SATB, 2 fl, 2 ob/eng hn/ serpentini, 2 bn, 2 hn, 2 tpt/hn, timp, str | Milan, Regio Ducal Teatro, 17 Oct 1771 | V/vi | II:5/v | for wedding of Archduke Ferdinand of Austria and Maria Ricciarda Berenice of Modena |
| 126 | 126 | Il sogno di Scipione (serenata, 1, Metastasio) | 2 S, 3 T, 2 fl, 2 ob, 2 bn, 2 hn, 2 tpt, timp, str | Salzburg, Archbishop's palace, cMay 1772 | V/vii | II:5/vi | ? for installation of Colloredo as Prince-Archbishop of Salzburg |
| 135 | 135 | Lucio Silla (opera seria, 3, G. de Gamerra) | 4 S, 2 T, SATB, 2 ob/fl, 2 bn, 2 hn, 2 tpt, timp, str | Milan, Regio Ducal Teatro, 26 Dec 1772 | V/viii | II:5/vii | |
| 196 | 196 | La finta giardiniera (opera buffa, 3, ?Calzabigi rev. Coltellini) | 4 S, 2 T, B, 2 fl, 2 ob, 2 bn, 2 hn, 2 tpt/hn, timp, str | Munich, Assembly Rooms, 13 Jan 1775 | V/ix | II:5/viii | perf. as Singspiel, Die verstellte Gärtnerin, Augsburg, 1 May 1780 |
| 208 | 208 | Il rè pastore (dramma per musica, 2, after Metastasio) | 3 S, 2 T, 2 fl, 2 ob/eng hn, 2 bn, 2 hn, 2 tpt/hn, str | Salzburg, Archbishop's palace, 23 April 1775 | V/x | II:5/ix | |
| A11 | 315e | Semiramis (duodrama, O. von Gemmingen) | | ?Mannheim, Nov 1778 | — | — | lost; ?never started |
| 345 | 336a | Thamos, König in Ägypten (play with music, 5, T. P. Gebler) | B, SATB, 2 fl, 2 ob, 2 bn, 2 hn, 2 tpt, 3 trbn, timp, str | Salzburg, ?1776–9 | V/xii | II:6/i | ? 2 choruses composed Vienna, 1773; final version ?1776–9 |
| 344 | 336b | Zaide (Singspiel, 2, Schachtner, after F. J. Sebastiani: Das Serail) | S, 2/3 T, 2 B, 2 fl, 2 ob, 2 bn, 2 hn, 2 tpt, timp, str | Salzburg, 1779–80 | V/xi | II:5/x | inc.; lacks ov. and final chorus |

| K | K⁶ | Title (description, libretto) | Scoring | First perf. | MW | NMA | Remarks |
|---|---|---|---|---|---|---|---|
| 366 | 366 | Idomeneo, rè di Creta (opera seria, 3, G. Varesco after A. Danchet: Idomenée) | 3 S, 3 T, B, SATB, 2 fl, 2 ob, 2 cl, 2 bn, 2 hn, 2 tpt, timp, str | (i) Munich, Hoftheater, 29 Jan 1781 (ii) Vienna, Auersperg Palace, March 1786 | V/xiii | II:5/xi | with ballet, K367 perf. with K489, 490, both composed by 10 March 1786 (C) |
| 384 | 384 | Die Entführung aus dem Serail (Singspiel, 3, J. G. Stephanie jr after C. F. Bretzner: Belmonte und Constanze) | 2 S, 2 T, B, SATB, 2 fl/pic, 2 ob, 2 cl/basset hn, 2 bn, 2 hn, 2 tpt, timp, str | Vienna, Burgtheater, 16 July 1782 | V/xv | II:5/xii | vocal score (Vienna, 1785); for addl march see Croll, Mitteilungen der Internationalen Stiftung Mozarteum, xxviii/1–2 (1980), 2 |
| 422 | 422 | L'oca del Cairo (opera buffa, 3, Varesco) | 3 S, 2 T, 2 B, [chorus,] 2 ob, 2 bn, 2 hn, str | — | XXIV, no.37 | II:5/xiii | Salzburg and Vienna, late 1783, inc.; 1 trio complete, 6 nos. sketched; see Holschneider, Mf, xv (1962), 231 |
| 430 | 424a | Lo sposo deluso (opera buffa, 2, ?Da Ponte) | 2 S, 2 T, 2 fl, 2 ob, 2 bn, 2 hn, 2 tpt, timp, str | — | XXIV, no.38 | II:5/xiv | ?begun 1783; only ov., trio and qt completed, 2 other nos. sketched |
| 486 | 486 | Der Schauspieldirektor (Singspiel, 1, Stephanie jr) | 2 S, T, B, 2 fl, 2 ob, 2 cl, 2 bn, 2 hn, 2 tpt, timp, str | Schönbrunn Palace, Orangery, 7 Feb 1786 | V/xvi | II:5/xv | completed Vienna, 3 Feb 1786 (C), see Kunze, MJb 1962–3, 156 |
| 492 | 492 | Le nozze di Figaro (opera buffa, 4, Da Ponte after Beaumarchais) | 5 S, 1/2 T, 3/4 B, SATB, 2 fl, 2 ob, 2 cl, 2 bn, 2 hn, 2 tpt, timp, str | (i) Vienna, Burgtheater, 1 May 1786 (ii) Vienna, Burgtheater, 29 Aug 1789 | V/xvii | II:5/xvi | completed Vienna, 29 April 1786 (D); excerpts, vocal score (Berlin, 1790) with arias K577, 579 |
| 527 | 527 | Il dissoluto punito, ossia Il Don Giovanni (opera buffa, 2, Da Ponte) | 3 S, T, 4 B, SATB, 2 fl, 2 ob, 2 cl, 2 bn, 2 hn, 2 tpt, 3 trbn, timp, mand, str | (i) Prague, National Theatre, 29 Oct 1787 (ii) Vienna, Burgtheater, 7 May 1788 | V/xviii | II:5/xvii (concert version of ov., IV: 11/x, 23 | Prague, 28 Oct 1787 (C); excerpts, vocal score (Speyer, 1788) and (Vienna, 1790–91) with addns K540a, b, c |
| 588 | 588 | Così fan tutte, ossia La scuola degli amanti (opera buffa, 2, Da Ponte) | 3 S, T, 2 B, SATB, 2 fl, 2 ob, 2 cl, 2 bn, 2 hn, 2 tpt, timp, str | Vienna, Burgtheater, 26 Jan 1790 | V/xix | II:5/xviii | Jan 1790 (C); excerpts, vocal score (Vienna, 1790) |
| 620 | 620 | Die Zauberflöte (Singspiel, 2, E. Schikaneder) | 7 S, 2 A, 4 T, 5 B, SATB, 2 fl/pic, 2 ob, 2 cl/basset hn, 2 bn, 2 hn, 2 tpt, 3 trbn, timp, glock, str | Vienna, Theater auf der Wieden, 30 Sept 1791 | V/xx | II:5/xix | vocal nos. begun July 1791 (C), ov. and march completed 28 Sept 1791 (C); excerpts, vocal score (Vienna, 1791–2) |
| 621 | 621 | La clemenza di Tito (opera seria, 2, C. Mazzolà after Metastasio) | 4 S, T, B, SATB, 2 fl, 2 ob, 2 cl/basset hn, 2 bn, 2 hn, 2 tpt, timp, str | Prague, National Theatre, 6 Sept 1791 | V/xxi | II:5/xx | for Prague coronation of Leopold II; completed 5 Sept 1791 (C); plain recits ?not by Mozart; see Giegling, MJb 1967, 121; Plath, MJb 1971–2, 34 |

BALLET MUSIC

| K | K⁶ | Title | Scoring | Composition | MW | NMA | Remarks |
|---|---|---|---|---|---|---|---|
| A207 | C27.06 | [?for Ascanio in Alba] | | ?Milan, late 1771 | — | | 9 nos. only extant, arr. pf; see Plath, MJb 1964, 111 |
| A109 | 135a | Le gelosie del serraglio [for Lucio Silla] | | ?Milan, late 1772 | — | | ?doubtful; autograph incipits for ballet of 32 nos., 6 from J. Starzer: Le cinque soltane; see Senn, Acta Mozartiana, xxxiii (1961), 169 |
| A10 | 299b | Les petits riens | 2 fl, 2 ob, 2 cl, 2 bn, 2 hn, 2 tpt, timp, str | Paris, May–June 1778 | XXIV, no.10a | II:6/ii, 13 | perf. 11 June 1778, Opéra, Paris, after Piccinni: Le finte gemelle; 20 movts, ov. and 13 (of 20) by Mozart |
| A103 | 299d | La chasse (rondo) | 2 fl, 2 ob, 2 bn, 2 hn | ?Salzburg, 1778 | | II:6/ii, 112 | 1 movt |
| 300 | 300 | [Gavotte] | 2 ob, 2 bn, 2 hn, str | ?Paris, early 1778 | | II:6/ii, 46 | ?discarded movt of Les petits riens |
| 367 | 367 | [Ballet for Idomeneo] | | | | | see 'Operas' |
| 446 | 416d | [Pantomime] | str | Vienna, Feb 1783 | XXIV, no.18 | II:6/ii, 120 | perf. Vienna, Hofburg, 3 March 1783; only 5 of at least 15 nos. extant |

Frag.: sketches K299c, for a ballet of 27 nos., ?Paris, early 1778

DUETS AND ENSEMBLES FOR SOLO VOICES AND ORCHESTRA

| K | K⁶ | First words (author) | Voices | Accompaniment | Composition | MW | NMA | Remarks |
|---|---|---|---|---|---|---|---|---|
| 389 | 384A | Welch ängstliches Beben (Bretzner) | T, T | fl, ob, bn, 2 hn, str | Vienna, April–May 1782 | XXIV, no.42 | | intended for Die Entführung aus dem Serail k384; inc. |
| 479 | 479 | Dite almeno in che mancai (G. Bertati) | S, T, B, B | 2 ob, 2 cl, 2 bn, 2 hn, str | Vienna, 5 Nov 1785 (C) | VI/ii, 70 | II:7/iii, 101 | for F. Bianchi: La villanella rapita, perf. Burgtheater, 28 Nov 1785 |
| 480 | 480 | Mandina amabile (Bertati) | S, T, B | 2 fl, 2 ob, 2 cl, 2 bn, 2 hn, str | Vienna, 21 Nov 1785 (C) | VI/ii, 87 | II:7/iii, 143 | as 479 (Paris, 1789–90) |
| 434 | 480b | Del gran regno delle amazzoni (G. Petrosellini: Il regno delle amazoni) | T, B, B | 2 ob, 2 bn, 2 tpt, str | ?Vienna, end 1785 | XXIV, no.44 | II:7/iv, 154 | 106 bars, inc., sketch |
| 489 | 489 | Spiegarti non poss'io | S, T | 2 ob, 2 bn, 2 hn, str | Vienna, 10 March 1786 (C) | V/xiii | II:5/xi, 376 | for Idomeneo k366 |
| 540b | 540b | Per queste due manine (Da Ponte) | S, B | 2 fl, 2 ob, 2 bn, 2 tpt, str | Vienna, 28 April 1788 (C) | V/xviii | II:5/xvii, 497 | addn to Don Giovanni k527 |
| 625 | 592a | Nun liebes Weibchen | S, B | | | | | see 'Arrangements' |
| 615 | 615 | Viviano felici (T. Grandi: Le gelosie villane) | S, A, T, B | | Vienna, 20 April 1791 (C) | — | — | lost; known only from Mozart's catalogue; for perf. of Sarti: Le gelosie villane |

VOCAL ENSEMBLES WITH PIANO OR ENSEMBLE

| K | K⁶ | First words (author) | Voices | Accompaniment | Composition | MW | NMA | Remarks |
|---|---|---|---|---|---|---|---|---|
| A24a | 43a | Ach, was müssen wir erfahren | S, S | pf | ?Vienna, Oct 1767 | — | III:9, 51 | |
| 436 | 436 | Ecco quel fiero istante (Metastasio: Canzonette) | S, S, B | 3 basset hn | ?Vienna, 1783–6 | VI/ii, 65 | III:9, 31 | notturno; ?partly by G. von Jacquin; see Plath, MJb 1971–2, 35 |
| 437 | 437 | Mi lagnerò tacendo (Metastasio: Siroe) | S, S, B | 2 cl, basset hn | ?Vienna, 1783–6 | VI/ii, 67 | III:9, 35 | as 436 |
| 438 | 438 | Se lontan ben mio (Metastasio: Strofe per musica) | S, S, B | 2 cl, basset hn | ?Vienna, 1783–6 | XXIV, no.46 | III:9, 29 | as 436 |
| 439 | 439 | Due pupille amabile | S, S, B | 3 basset hn | ?Vienna, 1783–6 | — | III:9, 26 | as 436 |
| 346 | 439a | Luci care, luci belle | S, S, B | 3 basset hn | ?Vienna, 1783–6 | — | III:9, 42 | as 436 |
| 441 | 441 | Liebes Mandel, wo is's Bandel (?Mozart) | S, T, B | str | Vienna, ?1783 | VII/1, 25 | III:9, 7 | |
| 532 | 532 | [Grazie agl'inganni tuoi] (Metastasio: La libertà di Nice) | S, T, B | fl, cl, 2 hn, 2 bn, b | ?Vienna, 1787 | VII/1, 73 | III:9, 62 | 26 bars without words based on M. Kelly's duet, 'Grazie agl'inganni tuoi' |
| 549 | 549 | Più non si trovano (Metastasio: L'Olimpiade) | S, S, B | 3 basset hn | Vienna, 16 July 1788 (C) | VI/ii, 185 | III:9, 44 | authenticity of acc. doubtful |
| A5 | 571a | Caro mio Druck und Schluck (Mozart) | S, T, T, B | ?pf | ?Vienna, 1789 | XXIV, no.50 | III:9, 64 | inc. |

Doubtful: Liebes Mädchen, S, S, B, k441c/C9.04, also ascribed to Haydn

ARIAS AND SCENES FOR VOICE AND ORCHESTRA

| K | K⁶ | First words (author) | Accompaniment | Composition | MW | NMA | Remarks |
|---|---|---|---|---|---|---|---|
| | | | | *for soprano* | | | |
| 23 | 23 | Conservati fedele (Metastasio: Artaserse) | str | The Hague, Oct 1765 | VI/i, 9; XXIV, no.54 | II:7/i, 13 | rev. Jan 1766; ? earlier version; ?(The Hague, 1766) |
| 70 | 61c | A Berenice . . . Sol nascente | 2 ob, 2 hn, str | Salzburg, ?Dec 1766 | VI/i, 23 | II:7/i, 47 | ?licenza for Sarti: Vologeso, Salzburg, 28 Feb 1767, or for perf. March 1769 |
| 78 | 73b | Per pietà, bell'idol mio (Metastasio: Artaserse) | 2 ob, 2 hn, str | c1766 | VI/i, 49 | II:7/i, 17 | |
| — | — | Cara se le mie pene | 2 hn, vn, va, b | Salzburg, c1769 | — | II:7/i, 59 | |
| A2 | 73A | Misero tu non sei (Metastasio: Demetrio) | | Milan, 26 Jan 1770 (L) | — | — | lost; known only from letter, 26 Jan 1770 |
| 88 | 73c | Fra cento affani (Metastasio: Artaserse) | 2 ob, 2 hn, 2 tpt, str | Milan, Feb–March 1770 | VI/i, 66 | II:7/i, 65 | |
| 79 | 73d | O temerario Arbace . . . Per quel paterno amplesso (Metastasio: Artaserse) | 2 ob, 2 bn, 2 hn, str | c1766 | VI/i, 54 | II:7/i, 23 | |
| 77 | 73e | Misero me . . . Misero pargoletto (Metastasio: Demofoonte) | 2 ob, 2 bn, 2 hn, str | Milan, March 1770 | VI/i, 33 | II:7/i, 83 | |

| K | K⁶ | First words (author) | Accompaniment | Composition | MW | NMA | Remarks |
|---|---|---|---|---|---|---|---|
| 82 | 73o | Se ardire, e speranza (Metastasio: Demofoonte) | 2 fl, 2 hn, str | Rome, 25 April 1770 (D) | XXIV, no.48a | II:7/i, 103 | |
| 83 | 73p | Se tutti i mali miei (Metastasio: Demofoonte) | 2 ob, 2 hn, str | Rome, April–May 1770 | VI/i, 60 | II:7/i, 115, 177 | 2 versions |
| 74b | 74b | Non curo l'affetto (Metastasio: Demofoonte) | 2 ob, 2 hn, str | Milan or Pavia, early 1771 | — | II:7/i, 125 | |
| 217 | 217 | Voi avete un cor fedele (after Goldoni: Le nozze di Dorina) | 2 ob, 2 hn, str | Salzburg, 26 Oct 1775 (D) | VI/i, 93 | II:7/i, 147 | ? for Galuppi: Le nozze di Dorina |
| 272 | 272 | Ah, lo previdi . . . Ah, t'invola agl'occhi miei (V. A. Cigna-Santi: Andromeda) | 2 ob, 2 hn, str | Salzburg, Aug 1777 (D) | VI/i, 119 | II:7/ii, 23 | |
| 294 | 294 | Alcandro lo confesso . . . Non sò d'onde viene (Metastasio: L'Olimpiade) | 2 fl, 2 cl, 2 bn, 2 hn, str | Mannheim, 24 Feb 1778 (D) | VI/i, 134 | II:7/ii, 41, 151 | 2 versions |
| 486a | 295a | Basta vincesti . . . Ah, non lasciarmi (Metastasio: Didone abbandonata) | 2 fl, 2 bn, 2 hn, str | Mannheim, 27 Feb 1778 (D) | XXIV, no.61 | II:7/ii, 77 | see Plath, *Festschrift Walter Senn* (Munich and Salzburg, 1975), 174 |
| 316 | 300b | Popoli di Tessaglia . . . Io non chiedo (Calzabigi: Alceste) | ob, bn, 2 hn, str | Paris, July 1778; Munich, 8 Jan 1779 (D) | VI/i, 164 | II:7/ii, 85 | |
| A3 | 315b | [Scena] | ob, 2 cl, 3 hn, pf, str | St Germain, Aug 1778 | — | — | lost; for Tenducci; see Oldman, *ML*, xlii (1961), 44 |
| A11a | 365a | Warum, o Liebe . . . Zittre, töricht Herz (?F. A. C. Werther) | | Munich, Nov 1780 | — | — | lost; sung in Gozzi: Le due notti affannose, trans. Werther (Salzburg, 1 Dec 1780) |
| 368 | 368 | Ma che vi fece . . . Sperai vicino (Metastasio: Demofoonte) | 2 fl, 2 bn, 2 hn, str | Salzburg, 1779–80 | VI/i, 183 | II:7/ii, 107 | |
| 369 | 369 | Misera! dove son . . . Ah! non son io (Metastasio: Ezio) | 2 fl, 2 hn, str | Munich, 8 March 1781 (D) | VI/i, 198 | II:7/ii, 125 | |
| 374 | 374 | A questo seno . . . Or che il cielo (G. de Gamerra: Sismano nel Mogol) | 2 ob, 2 hn, str | Vienna, April 1781 (L) | VI/i, 206 | II:7/ii, 135 | |
| 119 | 382h | Der Liebe himmlisches Gefühl | [2 ob, 2 hn, str] | ?Vienna, 1782 | XXIV, no.40 | II:7/ii, 203 | acc. extant only in kbd red. |
| 383 | 383 | Nehmt meinen Dank | fl, ob, bn, str | Vienna, 10 April 1782 (D) | VI/i, 217 | II:7/iii, 3 | |
| 416 | 416 | Mia speranza adorata . . . Ah, non sai qual pena (G. Sertor: Zemira) | 2 ob, 2 bn, 2 hn, str | Vienna, 8 Jan 1783 (D) | VI/ii, 2 | II:7/iii, 11 | |
| 178 | 417e | Ah, spiegarti, oh Dio | | ?Vienna, June 1783 | XXIV, no.41 | II:7/iii, 210 | acc. extant only in kbd red., ?version of к418 |
| 418 | 418 | Vorrei spiegarti, oh Dio | 2 ob, 2 bn, 2 hn, str | Vienna, 20 June 1783 (D) | VI/ii, 11 | II:7/iii, 25 | for Anfossi: Il curioso indiscreto, Burgtheater, 30 June 1783 |
| 419 | 419 | No, che non sei capace | 2 ob, 2 hn, 2 tpt, timp, str | Vienna, June 1783 (D) | VI/ii, 21 | II:7/iii, 37 | as к418 |
| 490 | 490 | Non più, tutti ascoltai . . . Non temer, amato bene | 2 cl, 2 bn, 2 hn, vn solo, str | Vienna, 10 March 1786 (C) | V/xiii | II:5/xi, 192 | for Idomeneo к366 |
| 505 | 505 | Ch'io mi scordi di te . . . Non temer, amato bene | 2 cl, 2 bn, 2 hn, pf, str | Vienna, 26 Dec 1786 (D) | VI/ii, 100 | II:7/iii, 175 | text from 1786 addn to Idomeneo к490 |
| 528 | 528 | Bella mia fiamma . . . Resta, o cara (D. M. Scarcone: Cerere placata) | fl, 2 ob, 2 bn, 2 hn, str | Prague, 3 Nov 1787 (DC) | VI/ii, 146 | II:7/iv, 37 | for Josefa Dušek |
| 538 | 538 | Ah se in ciel, benigna stella (Metastasio: L'eroe cinese) | 2 ob, 2 bn, 2 hn, str | Vienna, 4 March 1788 (DC) | VI/ii, 161 | II:7/iv, 57 | |
| 540c | 540c | In quali eccessi ... Mi tradi (Da Ponte) | fl, 2 cl, bn, 2 hn, str | Vienna, 30 April 1788 (DC) | V/xviii | II:5/xvii, 511 | addn to Don Giovanni к527 |
| 569 | 569 | Ohne Zwang, aus eignem Triebe | 2 ob, 2 bn, 2 hn, str | Vienna, Jan 1789 (C) | — | — | lost; Mozart's catalogue: 'Eine teutsche Aria' |
| 577 | 577 | Al desio di chi ch'adora (?Da Ponte) | 2 basset hn, 2 bn, 2 hn, str | Vienna, July 1789 (DC) | V/xvii | II:5/xvi, 602 | addn to Le nozze di Figaro к492 |
| 578 | 578 | Alma grande e nobil core (G. Palomba) | 2 ob, 2 bn, 2 hn, str | Vienna, Aug 1789 (DC) | VI/ii, 187 | II:7/iv, 91 | insertion in Cimarosa: I due baroni, Burgtheater, Sept 1789 |
| 579 | 579 | Un moto di gioia (?Da Ponte) | fl, ob, bn, 2 hn, str | Vienna, Aug 1789 | VII/1 | II:5/xvi, 597 | addn to Le nozze di Figaro к492 |
| 580 | 580 | Schon lacht der holde Frühling | 2 cl, 2 bn, 2 hn, str | Vienna, 17 Sept 1789 (DC) | XXIV, no.48 | II:7/iv, 168 | insertion for Ger. version of Paisiello: Il barbiere di Siviglia, not used; orch inc. |

| K | K⁶ | First words (author) | Accompaniment | Composition | MW | NMA | Remarks |
|---|---|---|---|---|---|---|---|
| 582 | 582 | Chi sa qual sia (?Da Ponte) | 2 cl, 2 bn, 2 hn, str | Vienna, Oct 1789 (DC) | VI/ii, 195 | II:7/iv, 105 | for Martin y Soler: Il burbero di buon cuore, Burgtheater, 9 Nov 1789 |
| 583 | 583 | Vado, ma dove? (?Da Ponte) | 2 cl, 2 bn, 2 hn, str | Vienna, Oct 1789 (DC) | VI/ii, 203 | II:7/iv, 115 | as 582 |

Frags.: Per quel paterno amplesso (Metastasio: Artaserse), κ73*D*, 3 bars only, *c*1766; In te spero (Metastasio: Demofoonte), κ440/383*h*, MW, XXIV, no.47, 81 bars, v and b only

| K | K⁶ | First words (author) | Accompaniment | Composition | MW | NMA | Remarks |
|---|---|---|---|---|---|---|---|
| | | | | *for alto* | | | |
| 255 | 255 | Ombra felice . . . Io ti lascio | 2 ob, 2 hn, str | Salzburg, Sept 1776 (D) | VI/i, 103 | II:7/ii, 3 | text from M. Mortellari: Arsace (Padua, 1775) |
| | | | | *for tenor* | | | |
| 21 | 19*c* | Va dal furor portata (Metastasio: Ezio) | 2 ob, 2 bn, 2 hn, str | London, 1765 | VI/i, 1 | II:7/i, 3, 163 | 2 versions, 1 ed. Leopold |
| 36 | 33*i* | Or che il dover . . . Tali e cotanti sono | 2 ob, 2 bn, 2 hn, 2 tpt, timp, str | Salzburg, Dec 1766 | VI/i, 13 | II:7/i, 33 | licenza perf. anniversary of Archbishop Sigismund's consecration, 21 Dec 1766 |
| 71 | 71 | Ah più tremar non voglio (Metastasio: Demofoonte) | 2 ob, 2 hn, str | Salzburg, late 1769–early 1770 | XXIV, no.39 | II:7/iv, 145 | only 48 bars extant |
| 209 | 209 | Si mostra la sorte | 2 fl, 2 hn, str | Salzburg, 19 May 1775 (D) | VI/i, 83 | II:7/i, 131 | |
| 210 | 210 | Con ossequio, con rispetto | 2 ob, 2 hn, str | Salzburg, May 1775 (D) | VI/i, 87 | II:7/i, 139 | |
| 256 | 256 | Clarice cara | 2 ob, 2 hn, str | Salzburg, Sept 1776 (D) | VI/i, 113 | II:7/ii, 15 | |
| 295 | 295 | Se al labbro mio non credi | 2 fl, 2 ob, 2 bn, 2 hn, str | Mannheim, 27 Feb 1778 (D) | VI/i, 148 | II:7/ii, 59, 167 | 2 versions; text from Hasse: Artaserse |
| 435 | 416*b* | Müsst'ich auch durch tausend Drachen | fl, ob, cl, 2 bn, 2 hn, 2 tpt, timp, str | ?Vienna, 1783 | XXIV, no.45 | II:7/iv, 162 | orch inc. |
| 420 | 420 | Per pietà non ricercate | 2 cl, 2 bn, 2 hn, str | Vienna, 21 June 1783 (D) | VI/ii, 31 | II:7/iii, 51 | for Anfossi: Il curioso indiscreto, not perf. |
| 431 | 425*b* | Misero! o sogno . . . Aura che intorni spiri | 2 fl, 2 bn, 2 hn, str | ?Vienna, Dec 1783 | VI/ii, 39 | II:7/iii, 81 | |
| 540*a* | 540*a* | Dalla sua pace (Da Ponte) | fl, 2 ob, 2 bn, 2 hn, str | Vienna, 24 April 1788 (DC) | V/xviii | II:5/xviii, 489 | addn to Don Giovanni κ527 |
| | | | | *for bass* | | | |
| 432 | 421*a* | Così dunque tradisci . . . Aspri rimorsi atroci (Metastasio: Temistocle) | 2 fl, 2 ob, 2 bn, 2 hn, str | ?Vienna, 1783 | VI/ii, 55 | II:7/iii, 67 | |
| 512 | 512 | Alcandro, lo confesso . . . Non sò d'onde viene (Metastasio: L'Olimpiade) | fl, 2 ob, 2 bn, 2 hn, str | Vienna, 19 March 1787 (D) | VI/ii, 120 | II:7/iv, 3 | |
| 513 | 513 | Mentre ti lascio (Angioli–Morbilli: La disfatta di Dario) | fl, 2 cl, 2 bn, 2 hn, str | Vienna, 23 March 1787 (DC) | VI/ii, 133 | II:7/iv, 19 | |
| 539 | 539 | Ich möchte wohl der Kaiser sein (J. W. L. Gleim) | pic, 2 ob, 2 bn, 2 hn, perc, str | Vienna, 5 March 1788 (DC) | VI/ii, 177 | II:7/iv, 79 | Ger. warsong for F. Baumann, Leopoldstädter-Theater, 7 March 1788 |
| 541 | 541 | Un bacio di mano (?Da Ponte) | fl, 2 ob, 2 bn, 2 hn, str | Vienna, May 1788 (C) | VI/ii, 180 | II:7/iv, 83 | for Anfossi: Le gelosie fortunate, Burgtheater, 2 June 1788 |
| 584 | 584 | Rivolgete a lui lo sguardo (Da Ponte) | 2 ob, 2 bn, 2 tpt, timp, str | Vienna, Dec 1789 (C) | VI/ii, 209 | | for Così fan tutte κ588; replaced by 'Non siate ritrosi' |
| 612 | 612 | Per questa bella mano | fl, 2 ob, 2 bn, 2 hn, db solo, str | Vienna, 8 March 1791 (DC) | VI/ii, 224 | II:7/iv, 123 | |
| A245 | 621*a* | Io ti lascio | str | ?Prague, Sept 1791 | | II:7/iv, 139 | ?only vn pts by Mozart, rest by Jacquin; see Kunze, *MJb 1967*, 205; Plath, *MJb 1971–2*, 35 |

Frags.: Un dente guasto, κ209*a*, 16 bars extant, sum. 1772; Männer suchen stets zu naschen, κ433/416*c*, ?1783, MW, XXIV, no.43, orch barely sketched

SONGS
(*pf acc. unless otherwise stated*)

| K | K⁶ | Title | First words | Key | Author | Composition | MW | NMA | Remarks |
|---|---|---|---|---|---|---|---|---|---|
| 53 | 47*e* | An die Freude | Freude, Königin der Weisen | F | J. P. Uz | Vienna, aut. 1768 | VII/1, 2 | III:8, 2 | (Vienna, *c*1768) |
| 147 | 125*g* | | Wie unglücklich bin ich nit | F | | Salzburg, ?1775–6 | VII/1, 4 | III:8, 4 | |

| K | K⁶ | Title | First words | Key | Author | Composition | MW | NMA | Remarks |
|---|-----|-------|-------------|-----|--------|-------------|-----|-----|---------|
| 148 | 125h | Lobegesang auf die feierliche Johannisloge | O heiliges Band der Freundschaft | D | L. F. Lenz | Salzburg, ?1775–6 | VII/1, 5 | III:8, 4 | |
| 307 | 284d | Ariette | Oiseaux, si tous les ans | C | A. Ferrand | Mannheim, wint. 1777–8 | VII/1, 12 | III:8, 6 | |
| 308 | 295b | Ariette | Dans un bois solitaire | A♭ | A. H. de la Motte | Mannheim, wint. 1777–8 | VII/1, 14 | III:8, 8 | |
| 343 | 336c | [2 Ger. church songs] | | | | | | | see 'Short sacred works' |
| 392 | 340a | | Verdankt sei es dem Glanz | F | J. T. Hermes | Vienna, 1781–2 | VII/1, 24 | III:8, 15 | |
| 391 | 340b | [An die Einsamkeit] | Sei du mein Trost | B♭ | Hermes | Vienna, 1781–2 | VII/1, 23 | III:8, 16 | |
| 390 | 340c | [An die Hoffnung] | Ich würd' auf meinem Pfad | d | Hermes | Vienna, 1781–2 | VII/1, 22 | III:8, 17 | |
| 349 | 367a | Die Zufriedenheit | Was frag ich viel | G | J. M. Miller | Munich, wint. 1780–81 | VII/1, 18 | III:8, 12 | 2 versions, one with mand acc. |
| 351 | 367b | | Komm, liebe Zither | C | | Munich, wint. 1780–81 | VII/1, 21 | III:8, 14 | mand acc. |
| A25 | 386d | [Gibraltar] | O Calpe! | D | J. N. C. M. Denis | Vienna, end 1782(L) | — | III:8, 72 | only pf pt. sketched |
| 178 | 417e | | Ah, spiegarti, o Dio | | | | | | see 'Arias and Scenes . . .' (soprano) |
| 468 | 468 | Lied zur Gesellenreise | Die ihr einem neuen Grade | B♭ | J. F. von Ratschky | Vienna, 26 March 1785 (C) | VII/1, 34 | III:8, 18 | acc.: org in autograph, pf in Mozart's catalogue |
| 472 | 472 | Der Zauberer | Ihr Mädchen, flieht Damöten ja! | g | C. F. Weisse | Vienna, 7 May 1785 (C) | VII/1, 36 | III:8, 20 | (Vienna, 1788) |
| 473 | 473 | Die Zufriedenheit | Wie sanft, wie ruhig | B♭ | Weisse | Vienna, 7 May 1785 (C) | VII/1, 38 | III:8, 22 | |
| 474 | 474 | Die betrogene Welt | Der reiche Tor | G | Weisse | Vienna, 7 May 1785 (C) | VII/1, 40 | III:8, 24 | (Vienna, 1788) |
| 476 | 476 | Das Veilchen | Ein Veilchen | G | J. W. von Goethe | Vienna, 8 June 1785 (C) | VII/1, 42 | III:8, 26 | (Vienna, 1789) |
| 483 | 483 | | Zerfliesset heut', geliebte Brüder | B♭ | A. V. von Schlittersberg | Vienna, end 1785 | VII/1, 44 | III:9, 20 | masonic song, with male chorus |
| 484 | 484 | | Ihr unsre neuen Leiter | G | Schlittersberg | Vienna, end 1785 | VII/1, 46 | III:9, 22 | masonic song, with male chorus |
| 506 | 506 | Lied der Freiheit | Wer unter eines Mädchens Hand | F | J. A. Blumauer | Vienna, ? end 1785 | VII/1, 48 | III:8, 28 | (Vienna, 1786) |
| 517 | 517 | Die Alte | Zu meiner Zeit | e | F. von Hagedom | Vienna, 18 May 1787 (C) | VII/1, 50 | III:8, 32 | (Vienna, 1788) |
| 518 | 518 | Die Verschweigung | Sobald Damötas Chloen sieht | F | Weisse | Vienna, 20 May 1787 (C) | VII/1, 52 | III:8, 34 | (Vienna, 1788) |
| 519 | 519 | Das Lied der Trennung | Die Engel Gottes weinen | f | K. E. K. Schmidt | Vienna, 23 May 1787 (C) | VII/1, 54 | III:8, 36 | (Vienna, 1789) |
| 520 | 520 | Als Luise die Briefe | Erzeugt von heisser Phantasie | C | G. von Baumberg | Vienna, 26 May 1787 (DC) | VII/1, 58 | III:8, 40 | |
| 523 | 523 | Abendempfindung | Abend ist's | F | ?J. H. Campe | Vienna, 24 June 1787 (C) | VII/1, 60 | III:8, 42 | (Vienna, 1789) |
| 524 | 524 | An Chloe | Wenn die Lieb' aus deinen blauen | E♭ | J. G. Jacobi | Vienna, 24 June 1787 (C) | VII/1, 64 | III:8, 46 | (Vienna, 1789) |
| 529 | 529 | Des kleinen Friedrichs Geburtstag | Es war einmal, ihr Leutchen | F | J. E. F. Schall | Prague, 6 Nov 1787 (C) | VII/1, 68 | III:8, 50 | (Vienna, 1788) |
| 530 | 530 | Das Traumbild | Wo bist du, Bild | E♭ | L. H. C. Hölty | Prague, 6 Nov 1787 | VII/1, 70 | III:8, 52 | |
| 531 | 531 | Die kleine Spinnerin | Was spinnst du | C | | Vienna, 11 Dec 1787 (C) | VII/1, 72 | III:8, 54 | (Vienna, 1787) |
| 552 | 552 | Beim Auszug in das Feld | Dem hohen Kaiser-Worte treu | A | | Vienna, 11 Aug 1788 (C) | — | III:8, 56 | (Vienna, 1788) |
| 596 | 596 | Sehnsucht nach dem Frühlinge | Komm, lieber Mai | F | C. A. Overbeck | Vienna, 14 Jan 1791 (C) | VII/1, 77 | III:8, 58 | (Vienna, 1791) |
| 597 | 597 | Im Frühlingsanfang | Erwacht zum neuen Leben | E♭ | C. C. Sturm | Vienna, 14 Jan 1791 (C) | VII/1, 78 | III:8, 59 | (Vienna, 1791) |
| 598 | 598 | Das Kinderspiel | Wir Kinder | A | Overbeck | Vienna, 14 Jan 1791 (C) | VII/1, 80 | III:8, 60 | (Vienna, 1791) |
| 619 | 619 | | Die ihr des unermesslichen Weltalls | | | | | | see 'Oratorios' |

Lost: Per la ricuperata salute di Ophelia (Da Ponte), KA11a/477a (set by Mozart, Salieri and 'Cornetti', mentioned in *Wienerblättchen*, 26 Sept 1785); Des Todes Werk and Vollbracht ist die Arbeit der Meister (G. Leon), Kdeest. 1786–90, see NMA, III:8, 78
Frags.: Ja! grüss dich Gott, K441a, 20 bars, ?Vienna, 1783; Einsam bin ich, KA26/475a, 8 bars, ?Vienna, 1785
Doubtful and spurious:

к52/46*c*: Daphne deine Rosenwangen, arr. by Leopold of Meiner Liebsten schöne Wangen (Bastien und Bastienne к51/46*b*) with new text, MW, VII/1, 1; NMA, II:5/iii, 90

к149/125*d*, Ich hab' es längst (Die grossmütige Gelassenheit), 1 by Leopold; MW, VII/1, 6; see Ballin, *Acta Mozartiana*, viii (1961), 18

к150/125*e*, Was ich in Gedanken küsse (Geheime Liebe), MW, VII/1, 7; as 149

к151/125*f*, Ich trachte nicht (Die Zufriedenheit), MW, VII/1, 8; as 149

к152/210*a*, Ridente la calma (canzonetta), adapted arr., ?by Mozart, of aria by Mysliveček, see MW, VII/1, 9; Flothuis, *MJb 1971–2*, 241

к350/C.8.48, Wiegenlied, by B. Flies, MW, VII/1, 20

### CANONS

| K | K* | Work and type | Key | Composition | MW | NMA | Remarks, alternative texts |
|---|---|---|---|---|---|---|---|
| 89*a*I | 73*i* | canon 4 in 1 | A | 1772 | — | III:10, 71 | |
| 89 | 73*k* | Kyrie, 5 in 1 | G | 1772 | III 1. 5 | III:10, 3 | |
| 89*a*II | 73*r* | 1 Incipe Menalios, 3 in 1 | F | 1772 | — | III:10, 73 | |
| | | 2 Cantate Domino, 8 in 1 | G | | | | |
| | | 3 Confitebor, 2 in 1 (+1) | C | | | | |
| | | 4 Thebana bella cantus, 6 in 2 | B♭ | | | | |
| ʌ109*d* | 73*x* | 14 canonic studies | | 1772 | | | |
| — | | canon 8 in 1 | a | ?Italy or Salzburg, 1770–71 | — | — | see Zaslaw, *MJb 1971–2*, 419 |
| 229 | 382*a* | canon 3 in 1 | c | ?Vienna, *c*1782 | VII/2, 2 | III:10, 80 | Sie ist dahin (Hölty) |
| 230 | 382*b* | canon 2 in 1 | c | ?Vienna, *c*1782 | VII/2, 4 | III:10, 83 | Selig, selig (Hölty) |
| 231 | 382*c* | Leck mich im Arsch (Mozart), 6 in 1 | B♭ | ?Vienna, *c*1782 | VII/2, 5 | III:10, 11 | Lasst froh uns sein (Breitkopf) |
| 233 | 382*d* | Leck mir den Arsch (Mozart), 3 in 1 | B♭ | ?Vienna, *c*1782 | VII/2, 11 | III:10, 17 | Nichts labt mich mehr (Härtel) |
| 234 | 382*e* | Bei der Hitz' im Sommer ess ich (Mozart), 3 in 1 | G | ?Vienna, *c*1782 | VII/2, 13 | III:10, 20 | Essen, trinken (Breitkopf) |
| 347 | 382*f* | canon 6 in 1 | D | ?Vienna, *c*1782 | VII/2, 15 | III:10, 84 | Wo der perlende Wein (Breitkopf): Lasst uns ziehn (Köchel) |
| 348 | 382*g* | V'amo di core teneramente, 12 in 3 | G | ?Vienna, *c*1782 | VII/2, 16 | III:10, 24 | |
| 507 | 507 | canon 3 in 1 | F | Vienna, after 3 June 1786 | VII/2, 18 | III:10, 86 | Heiterkeit und leichtes Blut (Härtel) |
| 508 | 508 | canon 3 in 1 | F | Vienna, after 3 June 1786 | VII/2, 18 | III:10, 88 | Auf das Wohl aller Freunde (Härtel) |
| — | 508*A* | canon 3 in 1 | C | Vienna, after 3 June 1786 | — | | |
| 508*a* | 508*a*, 1–2 | 2 canons 3 in 1 | F | Vienna, after 3 June 1786 | | III:10, 89 | |
| 508*a* | 508*a*, 3–8 | 6 canons 2 in 1 | F | Vienna, after 3 June 1786 | | III:10, 90 | |
| — | — | 8 canons 2 in 1 | F | Vienna, after 3 June 1786 | | III:10, 90 | |
| — | — | canon 4 in 1 | F | Vienna, ?sum. 1786 | — | III:10, 97 | |
| 232 | 509*a* | Lieber Freistädtler, lieber Gaulimauli (Mozart), 4 in 1 | G | Vienna, after 4 July 1787 | VII/2, 8; XXIV, no.52 | III:10, 27 | Wer nicht liebt Wein (Härtel) |
| 283 | 515*b* | canon 4 in 2 | F | Vienna, 24 April 1787 (D) | VII/2, 1 | III:10, 96 | Ach! zu kurz (Härtel) |
| 553 | 553 | Alleluia, 3 in 1 | C | Vienna, 2 Sept 1788 (C) | VII/2, 19 | III:10, 32 | |
| 554 | 554 | Ave Maria, 4 in 1 | F | Vienna, 2 Sept 1788 (C) | VII/2, 20 | III:10, 34 | |
| 555 | 555 | Lacrimoso son'io, 4 in 1 | a | Vienna, 2 Sept 1788 (C) | VII/2, 21 | III:10, 36 | text earlier set by Caldara; Ach zum Jammer (Breitkopf) |
| 556 | 556 | Grechtelt's enk (Mozart), 4 in 1 | G | Vienna, 2 Sept 1788 (C) | VII/2, 23 | III:10, 38 | Alles Fleisch (Breitkopf) |
| 557 | 557 | Nascoso è il mio sol, 4 in 1 | f | Vienna, 2 Sept 1788 (C) | VII/2, 25 | III:10, 40 | text earlier set by Caldara |
| 558 | 558 | Gehn wir im Prater (Mozart), 4 in 1 | B♭ | Vienna, 2 Sept 1788 (C) | VII/2, 27 | III:10, 43 | Alles ist eitel hier (Breitkopf) |
| 559 | 559 | Difficile lectu mihi mars (Mozart), 3 in 1 | F | Vienna, 2 Sept 1788 (C) | VII/2, 29 | III:10, 47 | Nimm, ist's gleich warm (Breitkopf) |
| 560*a* | 559*a* | O du eselhafter Peierl! (Mozart), 4 in 1 | F | Vienna, 2 Sept 1788 (C) | VII/2, 36 | III:10, 49, 55 | versions к560, MW, VII, 2, 31, in F or G with slightly different words; Gähnst du (Breitkopf) |
| 561 | 561 | Bona nox! bist a rechta Ox (Mozart), 4 in 1 | A | Vienna, 2 Sept 1788 (C) | VII/2, 37 | III:10, 62 | Gute Nacht (Breitkopf) |
| 562 | 562 | Caro bell'idol mio, 3 in 1 | A | Vienna, 2 Sept 1788 (C) | VII/2, 39 | III:10, 65 | text earlier set by Caldara; Ach süsses teures Leben (Breitkopf) |
| 562*a* | 562*a* | canon 4 in 1 | B♭ | ?Vienna | — | III:10, 98 | |
| ʌ191 | 562*c* | [? for 2 vn, va, b] 4 in 1 | C | ?Vienna | XXIV, no.51 | III:10, 68 | |

### SYMPHONIES, SYMPHONY MOVEMENTS

| K | K* | BH | Key | Movts | Scoring | Composition | MW | NMA | Remarks |
|---|---|---|---|---|---|---|---|---|---|
| 16 | 16 | 1 | E♭ | 3 | 2 ob, 2 hn, str | London, 1764–5 | VIII/i, 1 | IV:11/i | |
| ʌ220 | 16*a* | | a/?A | | | ?London, 1765 | — | — | lost; in Breitkopf catalogue |

| K | K⁶ | BH | Key | Movts | Scoring | Composition | MW | NMA | Remarks |
|---|---|---|---|---|---|---|---|---|---|
| 19 | 19 | 4 | D | 3 | 2 ob, 2 hn, str | London, 1765 | VIII/i, 37 | IV:11/i | |
| A223 | 19a | | F | | | ?London, 1765 | — | — | lost; in Breitkopf catalogue, frag. in Leopold's MS |
| A222 | 19b | | C | | | ?London, 1765 | — | — | lost; in Breitkopf catalogue |
| 22 | 22 | 5 | B♭ | 3 | 2 ob, 2 hn, str | The Hague, Dec 1765 | VIII/i, 47 | IV:11/i | |
| 76 | 42a | 43 | F | 4 | 2 ob, 2 hn, str | ?Vienna, 1767 | XXIV, no.3 | IV:11/i | |
| 43 | 43 | 6 | F | 4 | 2 ob/fl, 2 hn, str | Vienna, 1767 | VII/i, 56 | IV:11/i | |
| 45 | 45 | 7 | D | 4 | 2 ob, 2 hn, 2 tpt, timp, str | Vienna, 16 Jan 1767 (D) | VIII/i, 69 | IV:11/i | adapted as ov. to La finta semplice |
| A221 | 45a | | G | 3 | 2 ob, 2 hn, str | ?Vienna, 1768 | — | IV:11/i | 'Old Lambach'; pts. A-La, attrib. Mozart, ?incorrectly |
| — | — | | G | 3 | 2 ob, 2 hn, str | ?Vienna, 1768 | — | | 'New Lambach' (Kassel, 1965); pts. LA, attrib. Leopold; see Abert, MJb 1964, 24, and Festschrift Hans Engel (1964), 43 |
| A214 | 45b | | B♭ | 4 | 2 ob, 2 hn, str | ?Vienna, 1768 | — | IV:11/i | |
| 48 | 48 | 8 | D | 4 | 2 ob, 2 hn, 2 tpt, timp, str | Vienna, 13 Dec 1768 (D) | VIII/i, 81 | IV:11/i | |
| A215 | 66c | | D | | 2 ob, 2 bn, 2 hn, str | ?Salzburg, 1769 | — | — | lost; incipit in Breitkopf catalogue; ? perf. Mantua, 16 Jan 1770 |
| A217 | 66d | | B♭ | | 2 fl, 2 hn, str | ?Salzburg, 1769 | — | — | lost; see 66c |
| A218 | 66e | | B♭ | | 2 fl, 2 ob, 2 bn, 2 hn, str | ?Salzburg, 1769 | — | — | lost: see 66c |
| 73 | 73 | 9 | C | 4 | 2 ob/fl, 2 hn, 2 tpt, timp, str | Salzburg, early sum. 1772 | VIII/i, 97 | IV:11/i | |
| 81 | 73l | 44 | D | 3 | 2 ob, 2 hn, str | Rome, April 1770 | XXIV, no.4 | IV:11/i | also attrib. Leopold |
| 97 | 73m | 47 | D | 4 | 2 ob, 2 hn, 2 tpt, timp, str | Rome, April 1770 | XXIV, no.4 | IV:11/i | |
| 95 | 73n | 45 | D | 4 | 2 fl, 2 tpt, str | Rome, April 1770 | XXIV, no.5 | IV:11/ii | |
| 84 | 73q | 11 | D | 3 | 2 ob, 2 hn, str | Milan or Bologna, 1770 | VIII/i, 121 | IV:11/ii | also attrib. Leopold, Dittersdorf and others; see LaRue, MJb 1971–2, 48 |
| 74 | 74 | 10 | G | 3 | 2 ob, 2 hn, str | Milan, 1770 | VIII/i, 110 | IV:11/ii | |
| A216 | C11.03 | — | B♭ | 4 | 2 ob, 2 hn, str | Milan or Salzburg, 1770–71 | — | — | K³74g, doubtful; see Allroggen, AnMc, no. 18 (1978), 237 |
| 75 | 75 | 42 | F | 4 | 2 ob, 2 hn, str | Salzburg, 1771 | XXIV, no.2 | IV:11/ii | |
| 110 | 75b | 12 | G | 4 | 2 ob/fl, 2 bn, 2 hn, str | Salzburg, July 1771 (D) | VIII/i, 135 | IV:11/ii | |
| 120 | 111a | | D | 1 | 2 fl, 2 ob, 2 hn, 2 tpt, timp, str | Milan, Oct–Nov 1771 | XXIV, no.9 | IV:11/ii | finale, to form sym. with ov. Ascanio in Alba K111 |
| 96 | 111b | 46 | C | 4 | 2 ob, 2 hn, 2 tpt, timp, str | Milan, Oct–Nov 1771 | XXIV, no.6 | IV:11/ii | |
| 112 | 112 | 13 | F | 4 | 2 ob, 2 hn, str | Milan, 2 Nov 1771 (D) | VIII/i, 149 | IV:11/ii | |
| 114 | 114 | 14 | A | 4 | 2 fl/ob, 2 hn, str | Salzburg, 30 Dec 1771 (D) | VIII/i, 161 | IV:11/ii | |
| 124 | 124 | 15 | G | 4 | 2 ob, 2 hn, str | Salzburg, 21 Feb 1772 (D) | VIII/i, 175 | IV:11/ii | |
| 128 | 128 | 16 | C | 3 | 2 ob, 2 hn, str | Salzburg, May 1772 (D) | VIII/i, 187 | IV:11/iii, 1 | |
| 129 | 129 | 17 | G | 3 | 2 ob, 2 hn, str | Salzburg, May 1772 (D) | VIII/i, 199 | IV:11/iii, 15 | |
| 130 | 130 | 18 | F | 4 | 2 fl, 4 hn, str | Salzburg, May 1772 (D) | VIII/i, 215 | IV:11/iii, 31 | |
| 132 | 132 | 19 | E♭ | 4 | 2 ob, 4 hn, str | Salzburg, July 1772 (D) | VIII/i, 233 | IV:11/iii, 52 | alternative slow movts; see Plath, Mf, xxvii (1974), 93 |
| 133 | 133 | 20 | D | 4 | fl, 2 ob, 2 hn, 2 tpt, str | Salzburg, July 1772 (D) | VIII/i, 252 | IV:11/iii, 78 | |
| 134 | 134 | 21 | A | 4 | 2 fl, 2 hn, str | Salzburg, Aug 1772 (D) | VIII/i, 271 | IV:11/iii, 102 | |
| 161, 163 | 141a | 50 | D | 3 | 2 fl, 2 ob, 2 hn, 2 tpt, timp, str | Salzburg, 1773–4 | XXIV, no.10 [163 only] | IV:11/iii, 123 | movts K161 from ov. Il sogno di Scipione K126 with finale K163 |
| 184 | 161a | 26 | E♭ | 3 | 2 fl, 2 ob, 2 bn, 2 hn, 2 tpt, str | Salzburg, 30 March 1773 (D) | VIII/ii, 58 | IV:11/iv, 15 | |
| 199 | 161b | 27 | G | 3 | 2 fl, 2 hn, str | Salzburg, 10 [?16] April 1773 (D) | VIII/ii, 79 | IV:11/iv, 37 | |
| 162 | 162 | 22 | C | 3 | 2 ob, 2 hn, 2 tpt, str | Salzburg, 19 [?29] April 1773 (D) | VIII/ii, 1 | IV:11/iv, 1 | |
| 181 | 162b | 23 | D | 3 | 2 ob, 2 hn, 2 tpt, str | Salzburg, 19 May 1773 (D) | VIII/ii, 13 | IV:11/iv, 57 | |
| 182 | 173dA | 24 | B♭ | 3 | 2 ob/fl, 2 hn, str | Salzburg, 3 Oct 1773 (D) | VIII/ii, 39 | IV:11/iv, 75 | |
| 183 | 173dB | 25 | g | 4 | 2 ob, 2 bn, 4 hn, str | Salzburg, 5 Oct 1773 (D) | VIII/ii, 39 | IV:11/iv, 87 | |

| K | K* | BH | Key | Movts | Scoring | Composition | MW | NMA | Remarks |
|---|---|---|---|---|---|---|---|---|---|
| 201 | 186a | 29 | A | 4 | 2 ob, 2 hn, str | Salzburg, 6 April 1774 (D) | VIII/ii, 117 | IV:11/v, 1 | |
| 202 | 186b | 30 | D | 4 | 2 ob, 2 hn, 2 tpt, str | Salzburg, 5 May 1774 (D) | VIII/ii, 141 | IV:11/v, 26 | |
| 200 | 189k | 28 | C | 4 | 2 ob, 2 hn, 2 tpt, timp, str | Salzburg, 17 [?12] Nov 1774 [?1773] (D) | VIII/ii, 95 | IV:11/iv, 107 | |
| 121 | 207a | | D | 1 | 2 ob, 2 hn, str | Salzburg, end 1774–early 1775 | X, 42 | IV:11/v, 44 | finale, to form sym. with ov. La finta giardiniera K196 |
| | | | D | 4 | 2 ob, 2 bn, 2 hn, 2 tpt, str | | — | IV:11/vii, 1 | movts from Serenade K204/213a |
| 102 | 213c | | C | 1 | 2 ob/fl, 2 hn, 2 tpt, str | Salzburg, April and Aug 1775 | XXIV, no.8 | IV:11/v, 139 | finale, to form sym. with versions of ov. and 1st aria of Il rè pastore K208 |
| | | | D | 4 | 2 ob, 2 bn, 2 hn, 2 tpt, timp, str | | — | IV:11/vii, 31 | movts from Serenade K250/248b with new timp pt. |
| 297 | 300a | 31 | D | 3 | 2 fl, 2 ob, 2 cl, 2 bn, 2 hn, 2 tpt, timp, str | Paris, June 1778 | VIII/ii, 157 | IV:11/v, 57 | 'Paris'; 2 slow movts, original in 1st edn. (Paris, 1788) |
| A8 | 311A | | | | | | — | — | never written; see Zaslaw, MT, cxix (1978), 753 |
| 318 | 318 | 32 | G | 1 | 2 fl, 2 ob, 2 bn, 4 hn, 2 tpt, timp, str | Salzburg, 26 April 1779 (D) | VIII/ii, 197 | IV:11/vi, 3 | ov., ? for Zaide K344/366b |
| 319 | 319 | 33 | B♭ | 4 | 2 ob, 2 bn, 2 hn, str | Salzburg, 9 July 1779 (D) | VIII/ii, 213 | IV:11/vi, 23 | 3rd movt (minuet) later addn; (Vienna, 1785) as op.7 no.2 |
| | | | D | 3 | 2 ob, 2 bn, 2 hn, 2 tpt, str | | — | IV:11/viii, 89 | movts from Serenade K320 with added timp |
| 338 | 338 | 34 | C | 3 | 2 ob, 2 bn, 2 hn, 2 tpt, timp, str | Salzburg, 29 Aug 1780 (D) | VIII/ii, 239 | IV:11/vi, 59 | minuet (after 1st movt) cancelled in autograph; see K409/383f |
| 409 | 383f | | C | 1 | 2 fl, 2 ob, 2 bn, 2 hn, 2 tpt, timp, str | ?Vienna, May 1782 | X, 48 | IV:11/x, 3 | minuet, ? for K338 |
| 385 | 385 | 35 | D | 4 | 2 fl, 2 ob, 2 cl, 2 bn, 2 hn, 2 tpt, timp, str | Vienna, July 1782 (D) | VIII/iii, 1 | IV:11/vi, 113 | 'Haffner'; orig. intended as serenade, with March K408,2/385a and another minuet (lost); fls and cls later addns; (Vienna, 1785) as op.7 no.1 |
| 425 | 425 | 36 | C | 4 | 2 ob, 2 bn, 2 hn, 2 tpt, timp, str | Linz, Oct–Nov 1783 | VIII/iii, 37 | IV:11/viii, 3 | 'Linz' |
| 444 | 425a | 37 | G | | 2 ob, 2 hn, str | ?Linz, Nov 1783, or later | VIII/iii, 81 | | introduction for M. Haydn: Sym. P16 |
| 504 | 504 | 38 | D | 3 | 2 fl, 2 ob, 2 bn, 2 hn, 2 tpt, timp, str | Vienna, 6 Dec. 1786 (C) | VIII/iii, 97 | IV:11/viii, 63 | 'Prague' |
| 543 | 543 | 39 | E♭ | 4 | fl, 2 cl, 2 bn, 2 hn, 2 tpt, timp, str | Vienna, 26 June 1788 (C) | VIII/iii, 137 | IV:11/ix, 1 | |
| 550 | 550 | 40 | g | 4 | fl, 2 ob, (2 cl,) 2 bn, 2 hn, str | Vienna, 25 July 1788 (C) | VIII/iii, 181 | IV:11/ix, 63, 125 | 2 versions, 1st without cls |
| 551 | 551 | 41 | C | 4 | fl, 2 ob, 2 bn, 2 hn, 2 tpt, timp, str | Vienna, 10 Aug 1788 (C) | VIII/iii, 230 | IV:11/ix, 187 | 'Jupiter' |

Doubtful or spurious: K17/C11.02, B♭ [BH no.2] MW, VIII/i, 13; KA216/C11.03, B♭, MW, XXIV, no.63; K18/A51, E♭ [BH no.3], MW, VIII/i, 23 (by C. F. Abel); K98/C11.04, F, MW, XXIV, no.56; K291/A52, Fugue, D, by M. Haydn, MW, XXIV, no.11; K311a/C11.05, B♭, ?spurious, '2nd Paris symphony' Frags., sketches: KA100/383g, E♭, lost, pt. of 1st movt formerly extant; K383i, C, ? for sym. or ov.

CASSATIONS, SERENADES, DIVERTIMENTOS, MISCELLANEOUS WORKS

| K | K* | Title | Key, movts | Scoring | Composition | MW | NMA | Remarks |
|---|---|---|---|---|---|---|---|---|
| 32 | 32 | Gallimathias musicum | | hpd, 2 ob, 2 hn, 2 bn, str | The Hague, March 1766 | XXIV, no.12 | IV:12/i, 3 | |
| 41a | 41a | 6 divertimentos | | fl, hn, tpt, trbn, vn, va, vc | Salzburg, 1767 | — | — | lost; in LC |
| 100 | 62a | Cassation | D, 8 | 2 ob/fl, 2 hn, 2 tpt, str | Salzburg, 1769 | IX/i, 33 | IV:12/i, 67 | with march K62 |
| 63 | 63 | Cassation | G, 7 | 2 ob, 2 hn, str | Salzburg, 1769 | IX/i, 1 | IV:12/i, 25 | |
| — | — | Cassation | C | | ?Salzburg, 1769 | — | — | lost; see letter, 18 Aug 1771 |
| 99 | 63a | Cassation | B♭, 7 | 2 ob, 2 hn, str | Salzburg, 1769 | IX/i, 19 | IV:12/i, 45 | |
| 113 | 113 | Divertimento | E♭, 4 | 2 cl, 2 bn, 2 hn (or 2 ob, ?2 cl, 2 eng hn, 2 bn, 2 hn), str | Milan, Nov 1771 | IX/ii, 1 | IV:12/ii, 3 | 'Concerto o sia Divertimento'; rev. orch. early 1773 |
| 136–8 | 125a–c | 3 Divertimentos | | | | | | see 'Chamber Music: String Quartets' |

| K | K⁶ | Title | Key, movts | Scoring | Composition | MW | NMA | Remarks |
|---|---|---|---|---|---|---|---|---|
| 131 | 131 | Divertimento | D, 7 | fl, ob, bn, 4 hn, str | Salzburg, June 1772 | IX/ii, 15 | IV:12/ii, 29 | |
| 205 | 167A | Divertimento | D, 5 | 2 hn, bn, str (solo) | Salzburg, ?1773 | IX/ii, 73 | VII:18, 7 | with march K290/167AB |
| 185 | 167a | Serenade | D, 7 | 2 ob/fl, 2 hn, 2 tpt, vn solo, str | Vienna, July–Aug 1773 | IX/i, 61 | IV:12/ii, 76 | with march K189/167b |
| 203 | 189b | Serenade | D, 8 | 2 ob/fl, bn, 2 hn, 2 tpt, vn solo, str | Salzburg, Aug 1774 (D) | IX/i, 97 | IV:12/iii, 7 | with march K237/189c |
| 204 | 213a | Serenade | D, 7 | 2 ob/fl, bn, 2 hn, 2 tpt, vn solo, str | Salzburg, 5 Aug 1775 (D) | IX/i, 133 | IV:12/iii, 60 | with march K215/213b; see also 'Symphonies' |
| 239 | 239 | Serenata notturna | D, 3 | 2 vn, va, db (solo); str, timp | Salzburg, Jan 1776 (D) | IX/i, 177 | IV:12/iii, 114 | |
| 247 | 247 | Divertimento | F, 6 | 2 hn, str (solo) | Salzburg, June 1776 (D) | IX/ii, 98 | VII:18, 28 | with march K248; sk, K288/246c |
| 250 | 248b | Serenade | D, 9 | 2 ob/fl, 2 bn, 2 hn, 2 tpt, vn solo, str | Salzburg, June 1776 (D) | IX/i, 193 | IV:12/iv, 8 | 'Haffner'; with march K249; see also 'Symphonies' |
| 251 | 251 | Divertimento | D, 6 | ob, 2 hn, str (solo) | Salzburg, July 1776 (D) | IX/ii, 121 | VII:18, 67 | |
| 286 | 269a | Notturno | D, 4 | 4 groups, each 2 hn, str (solo) | Salzburg, Dec 1776–Jan 1777 | IX/i, 293 | IV:12/v | |
| 287 | 271H | Divertimento | B♭, 6 | 2 hn, str (solo) | Salzburg, June 1777 | IX/ii, 168 | VII:18, 103 | |
| 320 | 320 | Serenade | D, 7 | 2 fl/pic, 2 ob, 2 bn, 2 hn, posthorn, 2 tpt, timp, str | Salzburg, 3 Aug 1779 (D) | IX/i, 325 | IV:12/v | 'Posthorn'; with 2 marches, K335/320a; see also 'Symphonies', 'Concertos (wind insts)' |
| 334 | 320b | Divertimento | D, 6 | 2 hn, str (solo) | Salzburg, 1779–80 | IX/ii, 208 | VI:18, 158 | with march K445/320c |
| 477 | 479a | Maurerische Trauermusik | c | 2 ob, cl, 3 basset hn, dbn, 2 hn, str | Vienna, Nov 1785 | X, 53 | IV:11/x,11 | July 1785 (C) |
| 522 | 522 | Ein musikalischer Spass | F, 4 | 2 hn, str (solo) | Vienna, 14 June 1787 (C) | X, 58 | VII:18, 223 | sk, KA108/522a |
| 525 | 525 | Eine kleine Nachtmusik | G, 4 | 2 vn, va, vc, b (solo) | Vienna, 10 Aug 1787 (C) | XIII, 181 | IV:12/vi, 43 | orig. 5 movts, 2nd lost; sk KA69/525a |

Frag.: K246b/320B, 2 hn, str, end 1772–early 1773

WIND ENSEMBLE

| K | K⁶ | Title | Key | Scoring | Composition | MW | NMA | Remarks |
|---|---|---|---|---|---|---|---|---|
| 33a | 33a | Solos | | fl, [?bc] | Lausanne, Sept 1766 | — | — | lost; in LC |
| 33h | 33h | Piece | | hn [+?] | ?Salzburg, 1766 | — | — | lost; mentioned in Leopold's letter, 16 Feb 1778 |
| 41b | 41b | Pieces | | 2 tpt/2 hn/2 basset hn | Salzburg, 1767 | — | — | lost; in LC |
| 186 | 159b | Divertimento | B♭ | 2 ob, 2 cl, 2 eng hn, 2 hn, 2 bn | Milan, March 1773 | IX/ii, 57 | VII:17/i | |
| 166 | 159d | Divertimento | E♭ | 2 ob, 2 cl, 2 eng hn, 2 hn, 2 bn | Salzburg, 24 March 1773 (D) | IX/ii, 47 | VII:17/i | |
| 213 | 213 | Divertimento | F | 2 ob, 2 bn, 2 hn | Salzburg, July 1775 (D) | IX/ii, 83 | VII:17/i | |
| 240 | 240 | Divertimento | B♭ | 2 ob, 2 bn, 2 hn | Salzburg, Jan 1776 (D) | IX/ii, 89 | VII:17/i | |
| 252 | 240a | Divertimento | E♭ | 2 ob, 2 bn, 2 hn | Salzburg, early 1776 | IX/ii, 147 | VII:17/i | |
| ✓188 | 240b | Divertimento | C | 2 fl, 5 tpt, timp | Salzburg, mid-1773 | IX/ii, 69 | VII:17/i | |
| 253 | 253 | Divertimento | F | 2 ob, 2 bn, 2 hn | Salzburg, Aug 1776 (D) | IX/ii, 152 | VII:17/i | |
| 270 | 270 | Divertimento | B♭ | 2 ob, 2 bn, 2 hn | Salzburg, Jan 1777 (D) | IX/ii, 159 | VII:17/i | |
| 289 | 271g | Divertimento | E♭ | 2 ob, 2 bn, 2 hn | ?Salzburg, 1777 | IX/ii, 198 | VII:17/i | ?doubtful |
| 361 | 370a | Serenade | B♭ | 2 ob, 2 cl, 2 basset hn, 2 bn, 4 hn, db | Vienna, 1781 or 1781–4 | IX/i, 399 | VII:17/ii, 141 | |
| 375 | 375 | Serenade | E♭ | (2 ob,) 2 cl, 2 bn, 2 hn | Vienna, Oct 1781 | IX/i, 455 | VII:17/ii, 3, 41 | obs added in 2nd version, July 1782 |
| 388 | 384a | Serenade | c | 2 ob, 2 cl, 2 bn, 2 hn | Vienna, ?July 1782 or late 1783 | IX/i, 481 | VII:17/ii, 97 | arr. as str qnt, K406/516b |

| K | K⁶ | Title | Key | Scoring | Composition | MW | NMA | Remarks |
|---|----|-------|-----|---------|-------------|----|----|---------|
| ᴀ229 | 439b | 5 divertimentos | B♭ | 2 basset hn/cl, bn; 3 basset hn | Vienna, ?1783 or later | XXIV, no.62 | VIII:21, 67, 78, 89, 105, 114 (also 167) | see Whewell, *MT*, ciii (1962), 19; Flothuis, *MJb 1973–4*, 202 |
| 411 | 484a | Adagio | B♭ | 2 cl, 3 basset hn | ?Vienna, end 1785 | X, 80 | VII:17/ii, 223 | |
| 410 | 440d | Adagio | F | 2 basset hn, bn | ?Vienna, end 1785 | X, 79 | VIII:21, 120 | |
| 487 | 496a | 12 Duos | | 2 hn [?basset hn] | Vienna, 27 July 1785 (D) | XXIV, no.58 | VIII:21, 49 | |

Frags., sketches: Andante ᴋ384B, 2 ob, 2 cl, 2 bn, 2 hn; March ᴋ384b, 2 ob, 2 cl, 2 bn, 2 hn; Allegro ᴋ384c, 2 ob, 2 cl, 2 bn, 2 hn; Allegro assai, B♭, ᴋA95/484b, 2 cl, 3 basset hn; Adagio, F, ᴋA93/484c, cl, 3 basset hn; Allegro, F, ᴋ484e, basset hn, str inst; Adagio, C, ᴋA94/580a, ? cl, 3 basset hn (or eng hn, 2 hn/basset hn, bn)

Doubtful: 4 partitas, 2 ob, 2 cl, 2 bn, 2 hn, F, B♭, E♭, B♭, incl. movts from ᴋA17.04–5, arrs. of movts from ᴋ361/370a, movts in *CS-Pu*; 5 Pièces d'harmonie, 2 ob, 2 cl, 2 bn, 2 hn (Leipzig, 1802): B♭, after ᴋ361/370a; E♭, ᴋA226/C17.01; B♭, after ᴋ361/370a; B♭, ᴋA227/C17.02; E♭, ᴋA228/C17.03; Partita, E♭, 2 ob, 2 cl, 2 bn, 2 hn, ᴋAC13.07, inc., *CS-Pu*; see Leeson and Whitwell, *ML*, liii (1972), 377

Spurious: Divertimento, C, ᴋ187/C17.12, 2 fl, 5 tpt, timp, MW, IX/ii, 63, arr. by Leopold of dances by Starzer and Gluck; see also 'Arrangements', ᴋ626b, 28

MARCHES

| K | K⁶ | Key | Scoring | Composition | MW | NMA | Remarks |
|---|----|----|---------|-------------|----|----|---------|
| 41c | 41c | | 2 ob, bn, 2 hn, 2 vn, b | Salzburg, 1767 | — | — | lost; in LC |
| 62 | 62 | D | 2 ob, 2 hn, 2 tpt, str | Salzburg, 1769 | — | IV:12/i, 63 | quoted in letter, 4 Aug 1770; used in Mitridate, ᴋ87/74a ? for Cassation, ᴋ100/62a |
| 290 | 167AB | D | 2 hn, str | Salzburg, sum. 1772 | X, 19 | VII:18, 3 | with Divertimento, ᴋ205/167A |
| 189 | 167b | D | 2 fl, 2 hn, 2 tpt, 2 vn, b | Vienna, July–Aug 1773 | X, 1 | IV:12/ii, 70 | with Serenade, ᴋ185/167a |
| 237 | 189c | D | 2 ob, 2 bn, 2 hn, 2 tpt, 2 vn, b | Salzburg, Aug 1774 | X, 10 | IV:12/iii, 3 | with Serenade, ᴋ203/189b |
| 215 | 213b | D | 2 ob, 2 hn, 2 tpt, str | Salzburg, Aug 1775 | X, 7 | IV:12/iii, 55 | with Serenade, ᴋ204/213a |
| 214 | 214 | C | 2 ob, 2 hn, 2 tpt, str | Salzburg, 20 Aug 1775 (D) | X, 4 | IV:13/1/ii | |
| 248 | 248 | F | 2 hn, str | Salzburg, June 1776 (D) | X, 13 | VII:18, 23 | with Divertimento, ᴋ247 |
| 249 | 249 | D | 2 ob, 2 bn, 2 hn, 2 tpt, str | Salzburg, 20 July 1776 (D) | X, 16 | IV:12/iv, 3 | with Serenade, ᴋ250/248b |
| 335 | 320a | D | 2 ob/fl, 2 hn, 2 tpt, str | Salzburg, Aug 1779 | X, 22 | IV:13/1/ii | 2; with Serenade, ᴋ320 |
| 445 | 320c | D | 2 hn, str | Salzburg, sum. 1780 | X, 114 | VII:18, 155 | with Divertimento, ᴋ334/320b |
| 408/1 | 383e | D | 2 ob, 2 hn, 2 tpt, timp, str | Vienna, 1782 | X, 28 | IV:13/1/ii | |
| 408/3 | 383F | C | 2 fl, 2 bn, 2 hn, 2 tpt, timp, str | Vienna, 1782 | X, 36 | IV:13/1/ii | |
| 408/2 | 385a | D | 2 ob, 2 bn, 2 hn, 2 tpt, timp, str | Vienna, 1782 | X, 32 | IV:13/1/ii | |
| 544 | 544 | D | fl, hn, str | Vienna, June 1788 (C) | — | | lost |

All surviving marches listed above in NMA IV:13/1/ii

DANCE MUSIC

| K | K⁶ | No. | Keys | Scoring | Composition | MW | NMA | Remarks |
|---|----|-----|------|---------|-------------|----|----|---------|
| | | | | | *Minuets (* – without trio)* | | | |
| 41d | 41d | | various | | Salzburg, 1767 | | | lost; in LC |
| 65a | 61b | 7 | G, D, A, F, C, G, D | 2 vn, b | Salzburg, 26 Jan 1769 | XXIV, no.13 | IV:13/1/i, 1 | |
| 103 | 61d | 19 | C, G, D, F, C, A*, D, F, C, G, F, C, G, B♭, E♭, E*, A*, D, G* | 2 ob/fl, 2 hn/tpt, 2 vn, b | Salzburg, spr.–sum. 1772 | | IV:13/1/i, 11, 78, 80 | orig. 20; rearranged by Mozart as 19 |
| 104 | 61e | 6 | C, F, C, A*, G, G | pic, 2 ob, 2 hn/tpt, 2 vn, b | Salzburg, late 1770–early 1771 | | IV:13/1/i, 28 | nos.1, 2 arr. from M. Haydn ᴘ79, nos.1, 3; see Senn, *MJb 1964*, 71 |
| 61g | 61g | 2 | A*, C | 2 fl, str | Salzburg, early 1770 | | IV:13/1/i, 40, 92 | no.1 doubtful; no.2 known only in kbd transcr., trio also in ᴋ104/61e, 3 |
| 122 | 73t | 1 | E♭* | 2 ob, 2 hn, 2 vn, b | ?Bologna, Aug 1770 | XXIV, no.13a | IV:13/1/i, 10 | |
| 164 | 130a | 6 | D, D, D, G, G, G | fl, ob, 2 hn/tpt, 2 vn, b | Salzburg, June 1772 (D) | XXIV, no.57 | IV:13/1/i, 45 | |
| 176 | 176 | 16 | C, G, E♭*, B♭*, F, D, A, C, G, B♭*, F, D, G, C, F, D | 2 ob/fl, 2 hn/tpt, 2 vn, b | Salzburg, Dec 1773 (D) | | IV:13/1/i, 51 | |
| 363 | 363 | 3 | D*, B♭*, D* | 2 ob, 2 bn, 2 hn, 2 tpt, timp, 2 vn, b | ?Vienna, c1782–3 | XXIV, no.14 | IV:13/1/ii | |
| 409 | 383f | 1 | C | | | | | see 'Symphonies', ᴋ409/383f |
| 461 | 448a | 6 | C, E♭, G, B♭, F, D* | 2 ob/fl, 2 bn, 2 hn, 2 vn, b | Vienna, early 1784 | XI, 158 | IV:13/1/ii | no.6 inc. |
| 463 | 448c | 2 | F*, B♭* | 2 ob, bn, 2 hn, 2 vn, b | Vienna, early 1784 | XI, 169 | IV:13/1/ii | short minuets with contredanses |
| 568 | 568 | 12 | C, F, B♭, E♭, G, D, A, F, B♭, D, G, C | 2 fl/pic, 2 ob/cl, 2 bn, 2 hn, 2 tpt, timp, 2 vn, b | Vienna, 24 Dec 1788 (C) | XI, 1 | IV:13/1/ii | (Vienna, 1789) |

| K | K⁶ | No. | Keys | Scoring | Composition | MW | NMA | Remarks |
|---|---|---|---|---|---|---|---|---|
| 585 | 585 | 12 | D, F, B♭, E♭, G, C, A, F, B♭, E♭, G, D | 2 fl/pic, 2 ob/cl, 2 bn, 2 hn, 2 tpt, timp, 2 vn, b | Vienna, Dec 1789 (C) | XI, 19 | IV:13/1/ii | |
| 599 | 599 | 6 | C, G, E♭, B♭, F, D | 2 fl/pic, 2 ob/cl, 2 bn, 2 hn, 2 tpt, timp, 2 vn, b | Vienna, 23 Jan 1791 (C) | XI, 37 | IV:13/1/ii | |
| 601 | 601 | 4 | A, C, G, D | 2 fl/pic, hurdy-gurdy, 2 ob/cl, 2 bn, 2 hn, 2 tpt, timp, 2 vn, b | Vienna, 5 Feb 1791 (C) | XI, 46 | IV:13/1/ii | with German Dances κ602 |
| 604 | 604 | 2 | B♭, E♭ | 2 fl, 2 cl, 2 bn, 2 tpt, timp, 2 vn, b | Vienna, 12 Feb 1791 (C) | XI, 53 | IV:13/1/ii | with German Dances κ605 |

Doubtful or spurious (see Plath, *MJb 1971–2*, 33); 6 Minuets, D, D, D, G, G, G, κ105/61*f*, NMA IV:13/1/i, 34; 6 Minuets, C, A*, D*, B♭, G, C, κ61*h*, NMA, IV:13/1/i, 40; Minuet, D, κ64 (? by Leopold)

### German dances, ländler

| K | K⁶ | No. | Keys | Scoring | Composition | MW | NMA | Remarks |
|---|---|---|---|---|---|---|---|---|
| 509 | 509 | 6 | D, G, E♭, F, A, C | 2 fl/pic, 2 fl, 2 ob, 2 cl, 2 bn, 2 hn, 2 tpt, timp, 2 vn, b | Prague, 6 Feb 1787 (C) | XI, 56 | IV:13/1/ii | |
| 536 | 536 | 6 | C, G, B♭, D, F, F | pic, 2 fl, 2 ob/cl, 2 bn, 2 hn/tpt, timp, 2 vn, b | Vienna, 27 Jan 1788 (C) | XI, 72 | IV:13/1/ii | (Vienna, 1789) |
| 567 | 567 | 6 | B♭, E♭, G, D, A, C | pic, 2 fl, 2 ob/cl, 2 bn, 2 hn, 2 tpt, timp, 2 vn, b | Vienna, 6 Dec 1788 (C) | XI, 80 | IV:13/1/ii | (Vienna, 1789) |
| 571 | 571 | 6 | D, A, C, G, B♭, D | 2 fl/pic, 2 ob/cl, 2 bn, 2 hn/tpt, timp, perc, 2 vn, b | Vienna, 21 Feb 1789 (C) | XI, 92 | IV:13/1/ii | |
| 586 | 586 | 12 | C, G, B♭, F, A D, G, E♭, B♭, F, A, C | 2 fl/pic, 2 ob/cl, 2 bn, 2 hn, 2 tpt, timp, perc, 2 vn, b | Vienna, Dec 1789 (C) | XI, 106 | IV:13/1/ii | |
| 600 | 600 | 6 | C, F, B♭, E♭, G, D | pic, 2 fl, 2 ob/cl, 2 bn, 2 hn, 2 tpt, timp, 2 vn, b | Vienna, 29 Jan 1791 (C) | XI, 127 | IV:13/1/ii | |
| 602 | 602 | 4 | B♭, F, C, A | 2 fl/pic, 2 ob/cl, 2 bn, 2 hn/tpt, timp, hurdy-gurdy, 2 vn, b | Vienna, 5 Feb 1791 (C) | XI, 139 | IV:13/1/ii | with Minuets κ601 |
| 605 | 605 | 3 | D, G, C | 2 fl/pic, 2 ob, 2 bn, 2 hn/tpt, 2 post-horns, timp, 5 sleighbells, 2 vn, b | Vienna, 12 Feb 1791 (C) | XI, 145 | IV:13/1/ii | with Minuets κ604; no.3, Die Schlittenfahrt, ? composed separately |
| 606 | 606 | 6 | B♭ | 2 vn, b [wind pts. lost] | Vienna, 28 Feb 1791 (C) | XXIV, no.16 | IV:13/1/ii | 'Ländlerische'; with Contre-danse κ607/605a |
| 611 | 611 | 1 | C | 2 fl, 2 ob, 2 bn, 2 tpt, timp, hurdy-gurdy, 2 vn, b | Vienna, 6 March 1791 (C) | XI. 144 | IV:13/1/ii | 'Die Leyerer'; = κ602, no.3 |

### Contredanses

| K | K⁶ | No. | Keys | Scoring | Composition | MW | NMA | Remarks |
|---|---|---|---|---|---|---|---|---|
| 123 | 73g | 1 | B♭ | 2 ob, 2 hn, 2 vn, b | Rome, 13–14 April 1770 | XI, 152 | IV:13/1/i, 7 | |
| 101 | 250a | 4 | F, G, D, F | 2 ob/fl, bn, 2 hn, 2 vn, b | Salzburg, ?early 1776 | IX/1, 57 | IV:13/1/i, 67 | 'Serenade' |
| — | 269b | 12 | G, G, C, D | | Salzburg, ?early 1776 | | | nos.1, 2, 3, 12 extant in kbd red. only; others lost; nos.2, 12 = κ101/250a nos.2, 3 |
| 267 | 271c | 4 | G, E♭, A, D | 2 ob/fl, bn, 2 hn, 2 vn, b | Salzburg, early 1777 | XI, 154 | IV:13/1/i, 71 | |
| 462 | 448b | 6 | C, E♭, B♭, D, B♭, F | 2 ob, 2 hn, 2 vn, b | Vienna, Jan 1784 | XI, 165 | IV:13/1/ii | wind insts added later |
| 463 | 448c | 2 | F, B♭ | 2 ob, bn, 2 hn, 2 vn, b | Vienna, Jan 1784 | XI, 169 | IV:13/1/ii | each preceded by a minuet |
| 510 | C13.02 | 9 | D, D, D, B♭, D, D, F, B♭, C | 2 pic, 2 ob/fl, 2 cl, 2 hn, 2 tpt, timp, 2 vn, b | ?Prague, early 1787 | XI, 173 | IV:13/1/ii | probably not authentic |
| 534 | 534 | 1 | D | pic, 2 ob, 2 hn, side drum, 2 vn, b | Vienna, 14 Jan 1788 (C) | XXIV, no.27 | IV:13/1/ii | Das Donnerwetter; extant only in pf red. |
| 535 | 535 | 1 | C | pic, 2 cl, bn, tpt, side drum, 2 vn, b | Vienna, 23 Jan 1788 (C) | XI, 184 | IV:13/1/ii | La bataille [The Siege of Belgrade] |
| 535a | 535a | 3 | C, G, G | | Vienna, ?early 1788 | | | only pf version extant; sk κA107/535b |
| 565 | 565 | 2 | B♭, D | 2 ob, 2 hn, bn, 2 vn, b | Vienna, 30 Oct 1788 (C) | — | | lost |
| 587 | 587 | 1 | C | fl, ob, bn, tpt, 2 vn, b | Vienna, Dec 1789 (C) | XI, 188 | IV:13/1/ii | Der Sieg vom Helden Coburg |
| 106 | 588a | 3 | D, A, B♭ | 2 ob, 2 bn, 2 hn, 2 vn, b | Vienna, Jan 1790 | XXIV, no.15 | IV:13/1/ii | with ov. |

| K | K⁶ | No. | Keys | Scoring | Composition | MW | NMA | Remarks |
|---|---|---|---|---|---|---|---|---|
| 603 | 603 | 2 | D, B♭ | pic, 2 ob, 2 bn, 2 hn, 2 tpt, timp, 2 vn, b | Vienna, 5 Feb 1791 (C) | XI, 191 | IV:13/1/ii | |
| 607 | 605a | 1 | E♭ | fl, ob, bn, 2 hn, 2 vn, b | Vienna, 28 Feb 1791 (C) | XXIV, no.17 | IV:13/1/ii | Il trionfo delle dame; with German Dances K606 |
| 609 | 609 | 5 | C, E♭, D, C, G | fl, side drum, 2 vn, b | Vienna, 1791 | XI, 194 | IV:13/1/ii | |
| 610 | 610 | 1 | G | 2 fl, 2 hn, 2 vn, b | Vienna, 6 March 1791 (C) | XI, 200 | IV:13/1/ii | Les filles malicieuses |

CONCERTOS, CONCERTO MOVEMENTS

*piano*

| K | K⁶ | Title | BH | Key | Scoring | Composition | Cadenzas K624/626a | MW | NMA | Remarks |
|---|---|---|---|---|---|---|---|---|---|---|
| 37,39–41 107, 1–3 | 37, 39–41 107, 1–3 | | 1–4 | | | | | | | see 'Arrangements' see 'Arrangements' |
| 175 | 175 | Concerto | 5 | D | pf, 2 ob, 2 hn, 2 tpt, timp, str | Salzburg, Dec 1773 (D) | 1–4 | XVI/i, 131 | V:15/i, 3 | (Vienna, 1785), op.7; see K382 below |
| 238 | 238 | Concerto | 6 | B♭ | pf, 2 ob/fl, 2 hn, str | Salzburg, Jan 1776 (D) | 5–7 | XVI/i, 165 | V:15/i, 89 | |
| 242 | 242 | Concerto | 7 | F | 3 pf, 2 ob, 2 hn, str | Salzburg, Feb 1776 (D) | — | XVI/i, 197 | V:15/i, 155 | also version for 2 pf |
| 246 | 246 | Concerto | 8 | C | pf, 2 ob, 2 hn, str | Salzburg, April 1776 (D) | 8–14 | XVI/i, 289 | V:15/ii, 3 | |
| 271 | 271 | Concerto | 9 | E♭ | pf, 2 ob, 2 hn, str | Salzburg, Jan 1777 | 15–22 | XVI/ii, 1 | V:15/ii, 65 | |
| 365 | 316a | Concerto | 10 | E♭ | 2 pf, 2 ob, 2 bn, 2 hn, str | Salzburg, 1779 | 23–4 | XVI/ii, 53 | V:15/ii, 145 | |
| 382 | 382 | Rondo | | D | pf, fl, 2 ob, 2 hn, 2 tpt, timp, str | Vienna, March 1782 | 25–6 | XVI/iv, 359 | V:15/i, 67 | new finale for K175 (Vienna, 1785) |
| 414 | 385p | Concerto | 12 | A | pf, 2 ob, 2 hn, str | Vienna, 1782 | 27–36 | XVI/ii, 133 | V:15/iii, 3 | (Vienna, 1785) as op.4 no.1; sk K385o |
| 386 | 386 | Rondo | | A | pf, 2 ob, 2 hn, str | Vienna, 19 Oct 1782 (D) | — | | V:15/viii, 173 (inc.) | ? intended as finale for K414/385p |
| 413 | 387a | Concerto | 11 | F | pf, 2 ob, 2 bn, 2 hn, str | Vienna, 1782–3 | 37–8 | XVI/ii, 101 | V:15/iii, 67 | (Vienna, 1785) as op.4 no.2 |
| 415 | 387b | Concerto | 13 | C | pf, 2 ob, 2 bn, 2 tpt, timp, str | Vienna, 1782–3 | 39–41 | XVI/ii, 163 | V:15/iii, 127 | (Vienna, 1785) as op.4 no.3 |
| 449 | 449 | Concerto | 14 | E♭ | pf, 2 ob, 2 hn, str | Vienna, 9 Feb 1784 (DC) | 42 | XVI/ii, 205 | V:15/iv, 3 | |
| 450 | 450 | Concerto | 15 | B♭ | pf, fl, 2 ob, 2 bn, 2 hn, str | Vienna, 15 March 1784 (C) | 43–5 | XVI/ii, 241 | V:15/iv, 67 | |
| 451 | 451 | Concerto | 16 | D | pf, fl, 2 ob, 2 bn, 2 hn, 2 tpt, timp, 2 vn | Vienna, 22 March 1784 (C) | 46–7 | XVI/ii, 285 | V:15/iv, 137 | (Paris, c1785); ornamentation of ii, K624/626aII, M |
| 453 | 453 | Concerto | 17 | G | pf, fl, 2 ob, 2 bn, 2 hn, str | Vienna, 12 April 1784 (C) | 48–51 | XVI/iii, 22 | V:15/v, 3 | (Speyer, 1789) as op.9; sk KA65/452c |
| 456 | 456 | Concerto | 18 | B♭ | pf, fl, 2 ob, 2 bn, 2 hn, str | Vienna, 30 Sept 1784 (C) | 52–7 | XVI/iii, 55 | V:15/v, 71 | |
| 459 | 459 | Concerto | 19 | F | pf, fl, 2 ob, 2 bn, 2 hn, str | Vienna, 11 Dec 1784 (C) | 58–60 | XVI/iii, 119 | V:15/v, 151 | sk KA59/459a [466a in K³] |
| 466 | 466 | Concerto | 20 | d | pf, fl, 2 ob, 2 bn, 2 hn, 2 tpt, timp, str | Vienna, 10 Feb 1785 (C) | — | XVI/iii, 181 | V:15/vi, 3 | |
| 467 | 467 | Concerto | 21 | C | pf, fl, 2 ob, 2 bn, 2 hn, 2 tpt, timp, str | Vienna, 9 March 1785 (C) | — | XVI/iii, 237 | V:15/vi, 93 | sk KA60/502a |
| 482 | 482 | Concerto | 22 | E♭ | pf, fl, 2 cl, 2 bn, 2 hn, 2 tpt, timp, str | Vienna, 16 Dec 1785 (C) | — | XVI/iv, 1 | V:15/vi, 177 | |
| 488 | 488 | Concerto | 23 | A | pf, fl, 2 cl, 2 bn, 2 hn, str | Vienna, 2 March 1786 (C) | 61 | XVI/iv, 67 | V:15/vii, 3 | sk KA58/488a, A63/498b, A64/488c, 488d |
| 491 | 491 | Concerto | 24 | c | pf, fl, 2 ob, 2 cl, 2 bn, 2 hn, 2 tpt, timp, str | Vienna, 24 March 1786 (C) | — | XVI/iv, 121 | V:15/vii, 85 | sk KA62/491a |
| 503 | 503 | Concerto | 25 | C | pf, fl, 2 ob, 2 bn, 2 hn, 2 tpt, timp, str | Vienna, 4 Dec 1786 (C) | — | XVI/iv, 185 | V:15/vii, 256 | |
| 537 | 537 | Concerto | 26 | D | pf, fl, 2 ob, 2 bn, 2 hn, 2 tpt, timp, str | Vienna, 24 Feb 1788 (C) | — | XVI/iv, 253 | V:15/viii, 3 | 'Coronation'; sk KA57/537a, A61/537b |
| 595 | 595 | Concerto | 27 | B♭ | pf, fl, 2 ob, 2 bn, 2 hn, str | Vienna, ?1788–91, 5 Jan 1791 (C) | 62–4 | XVI/iv, 309 | V:15/viii, 93 | (Vienna, 1791) as op.17 |

Frag.: for vn, pf, in D, KA56/315f, MW, XXIV, no.21a; sk material noted above is in NMA, V:15/viii, 188ff *strings*

| K | K⁶ | Title | Key | Solo | Accompaniment | Composition | MW | NMA | Remarks |
|---|---|---|---|---|---|---|---|---|---|
| 190 | 186E | Concertone | C | 2 vn | solo ob, vc; 2 ob, 2 hn, 2 tpt, str | Salzburg, 31 May 1774 (D) | XII/i, 167 | V:14/ii, 3 | |
| 207 | 207 | Concerto | Bb | vn | 2 ob, 2 hn, str | Salzburg, 14 April 1775 (D) | XII/i, 1 | V:14/i | |
| 211 | 211 | Concerto | D | vn | 2 ob, 2 hn, str | Salzburg, 14 June 1775 (D) | XII/i, 27 | V:14/i | |
| 216 | 216 | Concerto | G | vn | 2 ob, 2 hn, str | Salzburg, 12 Sept 1775 (D) | XII/i, 49 | V:14/i | |
| 218 | 218 | Concerto | D | vn | 2 ob, 2 hn, str | Salzburg, Oct 1775 (D) | XII/i, 83 | V:14/i | |
| 219 | 219 | Concerto | A | vn | 2 ob, 2 hn, str | Salzburg, 20 Dec 1775 (D) | XII/i, 113 | V:14/i | |
| 261 | 261 | Adagio | E | vn | 2 fl, 2 hn, str | Salzburg, 1776 | XII/i, 145 | V:14/i | for K219 |
| 269 | 261a | Rondo | Bb | vn | 2 ob, 2 hn, str | Salzburg, 1776 | XII/i, 150 | V:14/i | ? for K207 |
| 364 | 320d | Sinfonia concertante | Eb | vn, va | 2 ob, 2 hn, str | Salzburg, 1779 | XII/i, 211 | V:14/ii, 57 | |
| 373 | 373 | Rondo | C | vn | 2 ob, 2 hn, str | Vienna, 2 April 1781 (D) | XII/i, 159 | V:14/i | fl arr. in D KA184 not authentic |
| 470 | 470 | Andante | A | vn | 2 ob, 2 hn, str | Vienna, 1 April 1785 (C) | — | — | lost; ? for concerto |

Doubtful and spurious violin concertos: in D, K271a/271i, ?incl. authentic material (see King, 1978, pp.31f, and Mahling, *MJb 1978–9*, 252); in Eb, K268/C14.04, MW, XXIV, ?incl. authentic material (see Oldman, *ML*, xii, 1931, p.174; King, 1978, pp.31ff); 'Adelaide Concerto', in D, KA294a/C14.05, by its 'editor', H. Casadesus (Mainz, 1930).
Lost and frag.: vc, F, K206a, lost; Sinfonia concertante, vn, va, vc, A, KA104/320e

*wind instruments*

| K | K⁶ | Title | Key | Solo | Accompaniment | Composition | MW | NMA | Remarks |
|---|---|---|---|---|---|---|---|---|---|
| 47c | 47c | Concerto | | tpt | | Vienna, Nov 1768 | — | — | lost; see Leopold's letter, 12 Nov 1768 |
| 191 | 186e | Concerto | Bb | bn | 2 ob, 2 hn, str | Salzburg, 4 June 1774 (D) | XII/ii, 1 | V:14/iii | |
| 271k | 271k | Concerto | | ob | | Salzburg, 1777 | | | mentioned in letter, 14 Feb 1778; ?lost, or K314/285d |
| 313 | 285c | Concerto | G | fl | 2 ob, 2 hn, str | Mannheim, early 1778 | XII/ii, 73 | V:14/iii | |
| 314 | 285d | Concerto | C/D | ob/fl | 2 ob, 2 hn, str | Mannheim, early 1778 | XII/ii, 104 | V:14/iii | ob version, ?K271k |
| 315 | 285e | Andante | C | fl | 2 ob, 2 hn, str | ?Salzburg, 1779–80 | XII/ii, 129 | V:14/iii | |
| A9 | 297B | Sinfonia concertante | | fl, ob, bn, hn | | ? Paris, April 1778 | | | lost (if written); see A9/C14.01 |
| A9 | C14.01 | Sinfonia concertante | Eb | ob, cl, bn, hn | 2 ob, 2 hn, str | | XXIV, no.7a | | doubtful; K³ 297b; ?later arr. of KA9/297B; see *MJb 1971–2*, 56; and Leeson and Levin, *MJb 1976–7*, 70 |
| 299 | 297c | Concerto | C | fl, harp | 2 ob, 2 hn, str | Paris, April 1778 | XII/ii, 21 | V:14/iii | |
| 320 | 320 | Sinfonia concertante | G | 2 fl, 2 ob, 2 bn | | | | | iii and iv of Serenade K320; see letter of 29 March 1783 |
| 371 | 371 | Rondo | Eb | hn | 2 ob, 2 hn, str | Vienna, 21 March 1781 (D) | XXIV, no.21 | V:14/v | inc. |
| 412 | 386b | Concerto | D | hn | 2 ob, 2 bn, str | Vienna, 1791 | XII/ii, 135 | V:14/v | ii inc.; version in *USSR-Lit* (K514) is ?1792 completion |
| 417 | 417 | Concerto | Eb | hn | 2 ob, 2 hn, str | Vienna, 27 May 1783 | XII/ii, 149 | V:14/v | |
| 447 | 447 | Concerto | Eb | hn | 2 cl, 2 bn, str | Vienna, ?1784–7 | XII/ii, 167 | V:14/v | |
| 495 | 495 | Concerto | Eb | hn | 2 ob, 2 hn, str | Vienna, 26 June 1786 (C) | XII/ii, 187 | V:14/v | |
| 622 | 622 | Concerto | A | cl | 2 fl, 2 bn, 2 hn, str | Vienna, Oct 1791 | XII/ii, 207 | V:14/iv | orig. solo part, with range to written c, lost |

Doubtful: bn, F, KA230/196d; bn, Bb, AC14.03, spurious; ?others for bn, lost
Frag. movts: ob, F, K293/416f, MW, XXIV, no.20; hn, Eb, K370b; hn, E, K494a; basset hn, G, K584b/621b (= i of K622)

CHAMBER
*Strings and wind*

| K | K⁶ | Title | Key | Scoring | Composition | MW | NMA | Remarks |
|---|---|---|---|---|---|---|---|---|
| 292 | 196c | Duo | Bb | bn, vc | Munich, early 1775 | X, 75 | VIII:21, 7 | |
| 285 | 285 | Quartet | D | fl, vn, va, vc | Mannheim, 25 Dec 1777 (D) | XIV, 307 | VIII:20/2, 3 | |
| 285a | 285a | Quartet | G | fl, vn, va, vc | Mannheim, Jan–Feb 1778 | | VIII:20/2, 25 | |
| A171 | 285b | Quartet | C | fl, vn, va, vc | ?Vienna, 1781–2 | | VIII:20/2, 33 | ii, arr., ?not by Mozart, from Serenade K361/370a; see Leavis, *ML*, xliii (1962), 48; (Speyer, 1788) as op.14 |

| K | K⁶ | Title | Key | Scoring | Composition | MW | NMA | Remarks |
|---|----|-------|-----|---------|-------------|-----|------|---------|
| 298 | 298 | Quartet | A | fl, vn, va, vc | Vienna, 1786–7 | XIV, 310 | VIII:20/2, 51 | |
| 370 | 368b | Quartet | F | ob, vn, va, vc | Munich, early 1781 | XIV, 327 | VIII:20/2, 65 | |
| 407 | 386c | Quintet | E♭ | hn, vn, 2 va, vc | Vienna, end 1782 | XIII, 41 | VIII:19/2, 1 | |
| 581 | 581 | Quintet | A | cl, 2 vn, va, vc | Vienna, 29 Sept 1789 (C) | XIII, 112 | VIII:19/2, 15 | sk ĸA88/581a |

Frags.: B♭, ĸA91/516c and E♭, ĸ516d, cl, 2 vn, va, vc; F, ĸA90/580b, cl, basset hn, vn, va, vc

*String quintets: 2 vn, 2 va, vc*

| K | K⁶ | Key | Composition | MW | NMA | Remarks |
|---|----|-----|-------------|-----|------|---------|
| 174 | 174 | B♭ | Salzburg, Dec 1773 | XIII, 1 | VIII:19/1, 3 | |
| 515 | 515 | C | Vienna, 19 April 1787 (C) | XIII, 54 | VIII:19/1, 27 | (Vienna, 1789); sk ĸA80/514a, A87/515a, A79/515c |
| 516 | 516 | g | Vienna, 16 May 1787 (C) | XIII, 85 | VIII:19/1, 63 | (Vienna, 1790); sk ĸA86/516a |
| 406 | 516b | c | Vienna, 1788 | XIII, 23 | VIII:19/1, 91 | arr. from Serenade ĸ388/384a |
| 593 | 593 | D | Vienna, Dec 1790 (C) | XIII, 132 | VIII:19/1, 113 | sk ĸA83/592b |
| 614 | 614 | E♭ | Vienna, 12 April 1791 (C) | XIII, 156 | VIII:19/1, 143 | sk ĸA81/613a, A82/613b |

Doubtful: 3 preludes, see 'Arrangements'; spurious: ĸ46, MW, XXIV, no.22; arr. of movts from Serenade ĸ361/370a

*String quartets*

| K | K⁶ | Title | Key | Composition | MW | NMA | Remarks |
|---|----|-------|-----|-------------|-----|------|---------|
| 80 | 73f | Quartet | G | Lodi, 15 March 1770 (D) | XIV, 1; XXIV, no.55 | VIII:20/1/i, 3 | iv added Vienna, late 1773, or Salzburg, early 1774 |
| 136 | 125a | Divertimento | D | Salzburg, early 1772 | XIV, 278 | IV:12/vi, 3 | |
| 137 | 125b | Divertimento | B♭ | Salzburg, early 1772 | XIV, 287 | IV:12/vi, 19 | |
| 138 | 125c | Divertimento | F | Salzburg, early 1772 | XIV, 294 | IV:12/vi, 30 | |
| 155 | 134a | [Quartet] | D | Bolzano, Verona, Oct–Nov 1772 | XIV, 8 | VIII:20/1/i, 17 | |
| 156 | 134b | Quartet | G | Milan, end 1772 | XIV, 15 | VIII:20/1/i, 31 | |
| 157 | 157 | Quartet | C | Milan, end 1772–early 1773 | XIV, 21 | VIII:20/1/i, 41 | |
| 158 | 158 | Quartet | F | Milan, end 1772–early 1773 | XIV, 29 | VIII:20/1/i, 57 | |
| 159 | 159 | Quartet | B♭ | Milan, early 1773 | XIV, 36 | VIII:20/1/i, 69 | |
| 160 | 159a | Quartet | E♭ | Milan, early 1773 | XIV, 45 | VIII:20/1/i, 85 | |
| 168 | 168 | Quartet | F | Vienna, Aug 1773 | XIV, 52 | VIII:20/1/i, 99 | |
| 169 | 169 | Quartet | A | Vienna, Aug 1773 (D) | XIV, 60 | VIII:20/1/i, 113 | |
| 170 | 170 | Quartet | C | Vienna, Aug 1773 (D) | XIV, 69 | VIII:20/1/i, 129 | |
| 171 | 171 | Quartet | E♭ | Vienna, Aug 1773 (D) | XIV, 77 | VIII:20/1/i, 145 | |
| 172 | 172 | Quartet | B♭ | Vienna, ?Sept 1773 | XIV, 86 | VIII:20/1/i, 159 | |
| 173 | 173 | Quartet | d | Vienna, [Sept] 1773 (D) | XIV, 96 | VIII:20/1/i, 175 | |
| 387 | 387 | Quartet | G | Vienna, 31 Dec 1782 (D) | XIV, 106 | VIII:20/1/ii, 3 | (Vienna, 1785) as op.10 no.1 |
| 421 | 417b | Quartet | d | Vienna, June 1783 | XIV, 124 | VIII:20/1/ii, 33 | (Vienna, 1785) as op.10 no.2 |
| 428 | 421b | Quartet | E♭ | Vienna, June–July 1783 | XIV, 137 | VIII:20/1/ii, 85 | (Vienna, 1785) as op.10 no.4 |
| 458 | 458 | Quartet | B♭ | Vienna, 9 Nov 1784 (C) | XIV, 152 | VIII:20/1/ii, 57 | 'Hunt' (Vienna, 1785) as op.10 no.3; sk ĸA68/589a |
| 464 | 464 | Quartet | A | Vienna, 10 Jan 1785 (C) | XIV, 168 | VIII:20/1/ii, 111 | (Vienna, 1785) as op.10 no.5; sk ĸA72/464a |
| 465 | 465 | Quartet | C | Vienna, 14 Jan 1785 (C) | XIV, 186 | VIII:20/1/ii, 145 | 'Dissonance' (Vienna, 1785) as op.10 no.6 |
| 499 | 499 | Quartet | D | Vienna, 19 Aug 1786 (C) | XIV, 206 | VIII:20/1/iii, 3 | 'Hoffmeister' (Vienna, 1786) |
| 546 | 546 | Adagio and Fugue | c | Vienna, 26 June 1788 (C) | XIV, 301 | IV:11/x, 47 | ?for str orch; fugue arr. from ĸ426 |
| 575 | 575 | Quartet | D | Vienna, June 1789 (C) | XIV, 226 | VIII:20/1/iii, 37 | 'Prussian' |
| 589 | 589 | Quartet | B♭ | Vienna, May 1790 (C) | XIV, 242 | VIII:20/1/iii, 65 | 'Prussian'; sk ĸA75/458a, 71/458b |
| 590 | 590 | Quartet | F | Vienna, June 1790 (C) | XIV, 258 | VIII:20/1/iii, 93 | 'Prussian'; sk ĸA73/589b |

Frags.: F, ĸ168a, early 1775; C, ĸA77/405a, c1790; ĸA76/417c, after 1786; e, ĸ417d, c1789; g, with ĸ453b, ?1783; g, ĸA47/587a, c1789; for sk dating see Tyson: *Mozart's Workshop*

Doubtful: 6 preludes, see 'Arrangements'; spurious: B♭, C, A, E♭, ĸA210–13/C20.01–04 (Mainz, 1932) by J. Schuster; see Finscher, *Mf*, xix (1966), 270

*String sonatas, duos, trios*

| K | K⁶ | Title | Key | Scoring | Composition | MW | NMA | Remarks |
|---|----|-------|-----|---------|-------------|-----|------|---------|
| 33b | 33b | Solos | | vc, b | Donaueschingen, Oct 1766 | — | — | lost; in LC |
| 41g | 41g | Nachtmusik | | 2 vn, b | ?Salzburg, 1767 | | | lost; see Nannerl's letter, 8 Feb 1800 |
| 46d | 46d | Sonata | C | vn, b | Vienna, 1 Sept 1768 (D) | — | VIII:21, 3 | |
| 46e | 46e | Sonata | F | vn, b | Vienna, 1 Sept 1768 (D) | — | VIII:21, 5 | |
| 266 | 271f | Trio | B♭ | 2 vn, b | Salzburg, early 1777 | XXIV, no.23 | VIII:21, 61 | |
| 404a | 404a | 4 preludes | | vn, va, vc | Vienna, 1782 | | | doubtful; for fugues by J. S. and W. F. Bach; see 'Arrangements' |
| 423 | 423 | Duo | G | vn, va | ?Salzburg, sum. 1783 | XV, 1 | VIII:21, 15 | |
| 424 | 424 | Duo | B♭ | vn, va | ?Salzburg, sum. 1783 | XV, 9 | VIII:21, 33 | |

| K | K⁶ | Title | Key | Scoring | Composition | MW | NMA | Remarks |
|---|---|---|---|---|---|---|---|---|
| 563 | 563 | Trio | E♭ | vn, va, vc | Vienna, 27 Sept 1788 (C) | XV, 19 | VIII:21, 121 | 'Ein Divertimento … di sei pezzi'; sk KA66/562e |

Frags.: G, KA66/562e, vn, va, vc; Fugue, G, K443/404b, completed by M. Stadler

### Keyboard and two or more instruments

| K | K⁶ | Title | Key | Scoring | Composition | MW | NMA | Remarks |
|---|---|---|---|---|---|---|---|---|
| 10–15 | 10–15 | 6 sonatas | | hpd, vn [vc] | | | | see 'Keyboard and violin' below |
| 254 | 254 | Divertimento | B♭ | pf, vn, vc | Salzburg, Aug 1776 (D) | XVII/2, 2 | VIII:22/2, 56 | (Paris, c1782) as op.3 |
| 442 | 442 | Trio | d | pf, vn, vc | Vienna, ?1783–90 | XVII/2, 20 | — | inc.; finished by M. Stadler; ? three separate movts, in d, G, D, associated fortuitously |
| 452 | 452 | Quintet | E♭ | pf, ob, cl, bn, hn | Vienna, 30 March 1784 (C) | XVII/1, 2; XXIV, no.59 | VIII:22/1, 107 | sk KA54/452a |
| 478 | 478 | Quartet | g | pf, vn, va, vc | Vienna, 16 Oct 1785 (D) | XVII/1, 32 | VIII:22/1, 1 | (Vienna, 1785–6) |
| 493 | 493 | Quartet | E♭ | pf, vn, va, vc | Vienna, 3 June 1786 (D) | XVII/1, 62 | VIII:22/1, 53 | (Vienna, 1787) as op.13; sk KA53/493a |
| 496 | 496 | Trio | G | pf, vn, vc | Vienna, 8 July 1786 (C) | XVII/2, 46 | VIII:22/2, 78 | (Vienna, 1786); sk KA52/495a |
| 498 | 498 | Trio | E♭ | pf, cl, va | Vienna, 5 Aug 1786 (C) | XVII/2, 68 | VIII:22/2, 104 | (Vienna, 1788) as op.14; sk KA51/501a |
| 502 | 502 | Trio | B♭ | pf, vn, vc | Vienna, 18 Nov 1786 (C) | XVII/2, 86 | VIII:22/2, 129 | (Vienna, 1788) as op.15 no.1 |
| 542 | 542 | Trio | E | pf, vn, vc | Vienna, 22 June 1788 (C) | XVII/2, 110 | VIII:22/2, 160 | (Vienna, 1788) as op.15 no.2 |
| 548 | 548 | Trio | C | pf, vn, vc | Vienna, 14 July 1788 (C) | XVII/2, 132 | VIII:22/2, 188 | (Vienna, 1788) as op.15 no.3 |
| 564 | 564 | Trio | G | pf, vn, vc | Vienna, 27 Oct 1788 (C) | XVII/2, 150 | VIII:22/2, 212 | (London, 1789) |
| 617 | 617 | Adagio and Rondo | c | armonica, fl, ob, va, vc | Vienna, 23 May 1791 (C) | X, 85 | VIII:22/1, 146 | sk KA92/616a |

### Keyboard and violin

| K | K⁶ | Title | Key | Composition | MW | NMA | Remarks |
|---|---|---|---|---|---|---|---|
| 6–7 | 6–7 | 2 sonatas | C, D | Salzburg, Paris, 1762–4 | XVIII/i, 2, 12 | VIII/23/i, 2, 12 | (Paris, 1764) as op.1 |
| 8–9 | 8–9 | 2 sonatas | B♭, G | Paris, 1763–4 | XVIII/i, 20, 26 | VIII:23/i, 20, 26 | (Paris, 1764) as op.2 |
| 10–15 | 10–15 | 6 sonatas | B♭, G, A, F, C, B♭ | London, 1764 | XVIII/i, 34, 42, 47, 54, 62, 72 | VIII:22/2, 2, 12, 18, 26, 36, 48 | (London, 1765) as op.3; vc ad lib |
| 26–31 | 26–31 | 6 sonatas | E♭, G, C, D, F, B♭ | The Hague, Feb 1766 | XVIII/i, 78, 84, 90, 96, 100, 106 | VII:23/i, 34, 40, 45, 50, 54, 59 | (The Hague and Amsterdam, 1766) as op.4 |
| 301 | 293a | Sonata | G | Mannheim, early 1778 | XVIII/ii, 18 | VIII:23/i, 66 | (Paris, 1778) as op.1 no.1 |
| 302 | 293b | Sonata | E♭ | Mannheim, early 1778 | XVIII/ii, 32 | VIII:23/i, 78 | (Paris, 1778) as op.1 no.2 |
| 303 | 293c | Sonata | C | Mannheim, early 1778 | XVIII/ii, 44 | VIII:23/i, 88 | (Paris, 1778) as op.1 no.3 |
| 305 | 293d | Sonata | A | Mannheim, early 1778 | XVIII/ii, 64 | VIII:23/i, 107 | (Paris, 1778) as op.1 no.5 |
| 296 | 296 | Sonata | C | Mannheim, 11 March 1778 (D) | XVIII/ii, 2 | VIII:23/i, 139 | (Vienna, 1781) as op.2 no.2 |
| 304 | 300c | Sonata | e | Paris, early sum. 1778 | XVIII/ii, 54 | VIII:23/i, 98 | (Paris, 1778) as op.1 no.4 |
| 306 | 300l | Sonata | D | Paris, sum. 1778 | XVIII/ii, 76 | VIII:23/i, 118 | (Paris, 1778) as op.1 no.6 |
| 378 | 317d | Sonata | B♭ | Salzburg, early 1779 or Vienna, 1781 | XVIII/ii, 140 | VIII:23/i, 154 | (Vienna, 1781) as op.2 no.4 |
| 372 | 372 | Sonata | B♭ | Vienna, 24 March 1781 | XVIII/ii, 98 | VIII:23/ii, 154 | Allegro only, inc.; completed by M. Stadler |
| 379 | 373a | Sonata | G | Vienna, April 1781 | XVIII/ii, 160 | VIII:23/ii, 3 | (Vienna, 1781) as op.2 no.5 |
| 359 | 374a | Variations | G | Vienna, June 1781 | XVIII/ii, 290 | VIII:23/ii, 136 | on La bergère Célimène, Fr. song, anon. (Vienna, 1786) |
| 360 | 374b | Variations | g | Vienna, June 1781 | XVIII/ii, 300 | VIII:23/ii, 144 | on Hélas, j'ai perdu mon amant, Fr. song, anon. (Vienna, 1786) |
| 376 | 374d | Sonata | F | Vienna, sum. 1781 | XVIII/ii, 108 | VIII:23/ii, 16 | (Vienna, 1781) as op.2 no.1 |
| 377 | 374e | Sonata | F | Vienna, sum. 1781 | XVIII/ii, 124 | VIII:23/ii, 32 | (Vienna, 1781) as op.2 no.3 |
| 380 | 374f | Sonata | E♭ | Vienna, sum. 1781 | XVIII/ii, 172 | VIII:23/ii, 48 | (Vienna, 1781) as op.2 no.6 |
| 403 | 385c | Sonata | C | Vienna, Aug–Sept 1782 | XVIII/ii, 198 | VIII:23/ii, 152 | inc.; completed by M. Stadler |
| 404 | 385d | Sonata | C | Vienna, ?1782 (? or c1788) | XVIII/ii, 208 | VIII:23/ii, 164 | Andante and Allegretto, inc. |
| 402 | 385e | Sonata | A | Vienna, Aug–Sept 1782 | XVIII/ii, 190 | VIII:23/ii, 173 | inc.; completed by M. Stadler; sk KA48/385E |
| 396 | 385f | Sonata movt | c | Vienna, Aug–Sept 1782 | — | VIII:23/ii, 181 | inc.; completed by M. Stadler; see Eppstein, Mf, xxi (1968), 205 |
| 454 | 454 | Sonata | B♭ | Vienna, 21 April 1784 (C) | XVIII/ii, 210 | VIII:23/ii, 64 | (Vienna, 1784) as op.7 no.3 |
| 481 | 481 | Sonata | E♭ | Vienna, 12 Dec 1785 (C) | XVIII/ii, 232 | VIII:23/ii, 82 | (Vienna, 1786) |
| 526 | 526 | Sonata | A | Vienna, 24 Aug 1787 (C) | XVIII/ii, 252 | VIII:23/ii, 100 | (Vienna, 1787); sk KA50/526a |
| 547 | 547 | Sonata | F | Vienna, 10 July 1788 (C) | XVIII/ii, 276 | VIII:23/ii, 122 | 'für Anfänger' |

Frags.: G, KA47/546a; B♭, KA46/374g [pf, vc]
Spurious: K55–60/C23.01–6, MW, XVIII, 114ff, see Neumann, MJb 1965–6, 152; Plath, MJb 1968–70, 368ff; K61, MW, XVIII, 172, by H. F. Raupach

KEYBOARD
*Sonatas*

| K | K⁶ | Key | Composition | MW | NMA | Remarks |
|---|---|---|---|---|---|---|
| | | | *(solo keyboard)* | | | |
| A199–202 | 33d–g | G, B♭, C, F | 1766 | — | — | lost; known from Breitkopf catalogue |
| 279–83 | 189d–h | C, F, B♭, E♭, G | Munich, early 1775 | XX, 1 | IX:25 | |
| 284 | 205b | D | Munich, Feb–March 1775 | XX, 46 | IX:25 | (Vienna, 1784) as op.7 no.2 |
| 309 | 284b | C | Mannheim, Oct–Nov 1777 | XX, 64 | IX:25 | (Paris, 1782) as op.4 no.1 |
| 311 | 284c | D | Mannheim, Nov 1777 | XX, 92 | IX:25 | (Paris, 1782) as op.4 no.2 |
| 310 | 300d | a | Paris, sum. 1778 | XX, 78 | IX:25 | (Paris, 1782) as op.4 no.3 |
| 330 | 300h | C | Munich or Vienna, 1781–3 | XX, 106 | IX:25 | (Vienna, 1784) as op.6 no.1 |
| 331 | 300i | A | Munich or Vienna, 1781–3 | XX, 118 | IX:25 | (Vienna, 1784) as op.6 no.2 |
| 332 | 300k | F | Munich or Vienna, 1781–3 | XX, 130 | IX:25 | (Vienna, 1784) as op.6 no.3 |
| 333 | 315c | B♭ | Linz and Vienna, 1783–4 | XX, 146 | IX:25 | (Vienna, 1784) as op.7 no.1 |
| 457 | 457 | c | Vienna, 14 Oct 1784 (C) | XX, 160 | IX:25 | pubd with Fantasia κ475 (Vienna, 1785) as op.11 |
| 533 | 533 | F | Vienna, 3 Jan 1786 (C) | XXII, 44 | IX:25 | incl. rev. of Rondo κ494; (Vienna, 1788) |
| 545 | 545 | C | Vienna, 26 June 1788 (C) | XX, 174 | IX:25 | 'für Anfänger' |
| A135 | 547a | F | ?Vienna, summer 1788 | — | — | doubtful; finale = transposed version of κ545, iii |
| 570 | 570 | B♭ | Vienna, Feb 1789 (C) | XX, 182 | IX:25 | first edn. (1796) with vn acc., probably spurious; sk κΑ31/569a |
| 576 | 576 | D | Vienna, July 1789 (C) | XX, 194 | IX:25 | |

Frags., sketches: F, κΑ29, 30, 37/590a–c, 1789–90

| K | K⁶ | Key | Composition | MW | NMA | Remarks |
|---|---|---|---|---|---|---|
| | | | *(keyboard duet)* | | | |
| 19d | 19d | C | London, May 1765 | — | IX:24/2, 2 | (Paris, 1788); see Tyson, *MR*, xxx (1969), 98 |
| 381 | 123a | D | Salzburg, mid-1772 | XIX, 32 | IX:24/2, 20 | (Vienna, 1783) as op.3 no.1 |
| 358 | 186c | B♭ | Salzburg, late 1773–early 1774 | XIX, 18 | IX:24/2, 36 | (Vienna, 1783) as op.3 no.2 |
| 497 | 497 | F | Vienna, 1 Aug 1786 (C) | XIX, 46 | IX:24/2, 54 | (Vienna, 1787) as op.12 |
| 521 | 521 | C | Vienna, 29 May 1787 (C) | XIX, 80 | IX:24/2, 106 | (Vienna, 1787) |
| | | | *(for 2 keyboards)* | | | |
| 448 | 375a | D | Vienna, Nov 1781 | XIX, 126 | IX:24/1, 2 | |

Frags.: ? Sonata, G [Allegro, κ357/497a (98 bars) and Andante, κ357/500a (158 bars)], MW, XIX, 2, 10 and NMA, IX:24/2, 142

*Variations*

| K | K⁶ | Theme | Key | Composition | MW | NMA | Remarks |
|---|---|---|---|---|---|---|---|
| | | | | *(solo keyboard)* | | | |
| A206 | 21a | ?orig. | C | ?London, 1765 | — | — | lost; in Breitkopf catalogue |
| 24 | 24 | Dutch song (Laat ons juichen) by C. E. Graaf | G | The Hague, Jan 1766 | XXI, 1 | IX:26, 3 | (The Hague, 1766) |
| 25 | 25 | Willem van Nassau (Dutch national song) | D | Amsterdam, Feb 1766 | XXI, 6 | IX:26, 9 | (The Hague, 1766) |
| 180 | 173c | Mio caro Adone from Salieri: La fiera di Venezia (Vienna, 1772) | G | Vienna, aut. 1773 | XXI, 22 | IX:26, 15 | (Paris, 1778) |
| 179 | 189a | Minuet [finale of Ob Conc. no.1, 1768] by J. C. Fischer | C | Salzburg, sum. 1774 | XXI, 12 | IX:26, 20 | (Paris, 1778) |
| 354 | 299a | Je suis Lindor (song in Beaumarchais: Le barbier de Séville, by A. L. Baudron) | E♭ | Paris, early 1778 | XXI, 58 | IX:26, 34 | (Paris, 1778) |
| 265 | 300e | Ah vous dirai-je, maman (Fr. song) | C | Vienna, 1781–2 | XXI, 36 | IX:26, 49 | (Vienna, 1785) |
| 353 | 300f | La belle françoise (Adieu donc, dame françoise, Fr. song) | E♭ | Vienna, 1781–2 | XXI, 50 | IX:26, 58 | (Vienna, 1786) |
| 264 | 315d | Lison dormait from N. Dezède: Julie (Paris, 1772) | C | Paris, late sum. 1778 | XXI, 26 | IX:26, 67 | shortened (Paris, 1786); (Vienna, 1786) |
| 352 | 374c | Dieu d'amour (March), chorus from Grétry: Les mariages samnites (Paris, 1776) | F | Vienna, June 1781 | XXI, 44 | IX:26, 82 | (Vienna, 1786) |
| 398 | 416e | Salve tu, Domine, chorus from Paisiello: I filosofi immaginarii (Vienna, 1781) | F | Vienna, March 1783 | XXI, 68 | IX:26, 90 | (Vienna, 1786) |
| 460 | 454a | Come un agnello from Sarti: Fra i due litiganti (Milan, 1782) | A | Vienna, ?June 1784 | XXI, 84 | IX:26, 154 | autograph has 2 variations; version with 8 variations doubtful: see *MJb 1958*, 18; *MJb 1959*, 127, 140; *MJb 1971–2*, 55; *MJb 1978–9*, 112; (Vienna, 1784) |
| 455 | 455 | Les hommes pieusement (Unser dummer Pöbel meint) from Gluck: La rencontre imprévue | G | Vienna, 25 Aug 1784 (C) | XXI, 74 | IX:26, 98 | (Vienna, 1785); earlier version 1783 |
| 500 | 500 | probably orig. | B♭ | Vienna, 12 Sept 1786 (C) | XXI, 94 | IX:26, 112 | |
| 54 | 547b | probably orig. | F | Vienna, July 1788 | | IX:26, 157 | 1st edn. (1795) has spurious 4th variation; re-used by Mozart, with vn κ547 |
| 573 | 573 | Minuet [from Vc Sonata op.4 no.6] by J. P. Duport | D | Potsdam, 29 April 1789 (C) | XXI, 100 | IX:26, 120 | (Berlin, 1791); see Hortschansky, *Mf*, xvi (1963), 265 |

| K | K⁶ | Theme | Key | Composition | MW | NMA | Remarks |
|---|---|---|---|---|---|---|---|
| 613 | 613 | Ein Weib ist das herrlichste Ding, by B. Schack or F. Gerl | F | Vienna, March 1791 | XXI, 108 | IX:26, 132 | theme from music to Schikaneder play Der dumme Gärtner, 1789 (Vienna, 1791) |

Frag.: E♭, ᴋ236/588b, theme by Gluck, ?intended for variations

| | | | | *(piano duet)* | | | |
|---|---|---|---|---|---|---|---|
| 501 | 501 | probably orig. | G | Vienna, 4 Nov 1786 (C) | XIX, 108 | IX:24/ii, 96 | |

### Miscellaneous

| K | K⁶ | Title | Key | Composition | MW | NMA | Remarks |
|---|---|---|---|---|---|---|---|
| | | | | *(solo keyboard)* | | | |
| — | 1a | Andante | C | Salzburg, early 1761 | — | | |
| — | 1b | Allegro | C | Salzburg, early 1761 | — | | |
| — | 1c | Allegro | F | Salzburg, 11 Dec 1761 | | | |
| — | 1d | Minuet | F | Salzburg, 16 Dec 1761 | | | |
| 1 | 1e | Minuet | G | Salzburg, Dec–Jan 1761–2 | XII, 2 | | |
| — | 1f | Minuet | C | Salzburg, Dec–Jan 1761–2 | | | |
| 2 | 2 | Minuet | F | Salzburg, Jan 1762 | XXII, 3 | | |
| 3 | 3 | Allegro | B♭ | Salzburg, 4 March 1762 | XXII, 38 | | |
| 4 | 4 | Minuet | F | Salzburg, 11 May 1762 | XXII, 3 | | |
| 5 | 5 | Minuet | F | Salzburg, 5 July 1762 | XXII, 4 | | |
| 9a | 5a | Allegro | C | sum. 1763 | — | | |
| 9b | 5b | Andante | B♭ | sum. 1763 | — | | |
| — | 33B | [without title] | F | Zurich, Oct 1766 | — | | |
| 41e | 41e | Fugue | | Salzburg, 1767 | — | — | lost; in LC |
| 72a | 72a | Allegro | G | ?Verona, Jan 1770 | — | | inc.; only source is S. dalla Rosa portrait |
| 94 | 73h | Minuet | D | Salzburg, 1769 | XXII, 5 | | |
| 284a | 284a | 4 preludes | | | | | identical with ᴋ395/300g |
| 284f | 284f | Rondo | | Mannheim, Nov 1777 | | | lost; mentioned in letter, 29 Nov 1777 |
| 395 | 300g | Capriccio | C | Munich, Oct 1777 | XXIV, no.24 | | |
| 315a | 315g | 8 minuets | | Salzburg, late 1773 | — | | |
| 400 | 372a | Allegro | B♭ | Vienna, 1781 | XXIV, no.26 | | inc.; completed by M. Stadler |
| 401 | 375e | Fugue | g | Vienna, early 1782 | XXII, 34 | | inc.; completed by M. Stadler; also duet version |
| 153 | 375f | Fugue | E♭ | ?Salzburg, 1783 | XXIV, no.25 | | inc.; completed by S. Sechter |
| 394 | 383a | Prelude and fugue | C | Vienna, early 1782 | XX, 20 | | |
| 396 | 385f | Fantasia | c | Vienna, early 1782 | XX, 214 | IX:25 | inc.; orig. with vn, see 'Chamber music' |
| 397 | 385g | Fantasia | d | Vienna, early 1782 or 1786–7 | XX, 220 | IX:25 | last 10 bars (not in 1st edn.) probably spurious; see Plath, *MJb 1971–2*, 31 |
| 399 | 385i | Suite | C | Vienna, early 1782 | XXII, 28 | | sarabande inc. |
| 154 | 385k | Fugue | g | Vienna, early 1782 | XXIV | | inc. |
| 453a | 453a | Funeral march | c | Vienna, 1784 | — | | |
| 475 | 475 | Fantasia | c | Vienna, 20 May 1785 (C) | XX, 224 | IX:25 | pubd with Sonata ᴋ457 (Vienna, 1785) as op.11 |
| 485 | 485 | Rondo | D | Vienna, 10 Jan 1786 (D) | XXII, 8 | IX:25 | (Vienna, c1786) |
| 494 | 494 | Rondo | F | Vienna, 10 June 1786 (D) | XXII, 14 | IX:25 | (London, 1788), (Speyer, 1788); rev. version in Sonata ᴋ533 |
| 511 | 511 | Rondo | a | Vienna, 11 March 1787 (CD) | XXII, 20 | IX:25 | (Vienna, 1787) |
| 540 | 540 | Adagio | b | Vienna, 19 March 1788 (C) | XXII, 56 | | ?(Vienna, 1788) |
| 574 | 574 | Gigue | G | Leipzig, 16 May 1789 (D) | XXII, 60 | | |
| 355 | 576b | Minuet | D | Vienna, ?1786–7 | XXII, 6 | | trio by M. Stadler; see King (1955, 3/1970), 222f; Badura-Skoda, *NZM*, Jg. 127 (1966), 468 |
| 236 | 588b | Andantino | E♭ | | XXII, 55 | | see 'Arrangements' |
| 312 | 590d | Allegro | g | Vienna, 1789–90 | XXII, 39 | | inc.; ? for a sonata; see Plath, *MJb 1971–2*, 30f; Tyson, *Mozart's Workshop* |

Frags.: Fugue, D, ᴋ73w, early 1773; Fugue, G, ᴋᴀ41/375g, 1777; Fugue, F, ᴋ375h; Fugue, F, ᴋᴀ33 and 40/383b; Fugue, c, ᴋᴀ39/383d; Adagio, d, ᴋᴀ34/385h, 1786–7; Fantasia, f, ᴋᴀ32/383C; Minuet, D, ᴋᴀ34/576a, 1786–7

| K | K⁶ | Title | Key | Composition | MW | NMA | Remarks |
|---|---|---|---|---|---|---|---|
| | | | | *(2 keyboards)* | | | |
| 426 | 426 | Fugue | c | Vienna, 29 Dec 1783 (D) | XIX, 118 | IX:24/1, 39 | (Vienna, 1788); arr., with new introduction, for str, K546 |
| — | — | Larghetto and Allegro | E♭ | ?Vienna, 1782–3 | — | IX:24/1, suppl. | inc.; completed by M. Stadler; see Croll, *MJb 1962–3*, 708; *MJb 1964*, 28 |

Frags.: Grave-Presto, B♭, ᴋᴀ42/375b (52 bars), MW, XXIV, 60 and NMA, IX:24/1, 46; movt, B♭, ᴋᴀ43/375c (15 bars), NMA, IX:24/1, 49; Fugue, G, ᴋᴀ45/375d (23 bars), NMA, IX:24/1, 50; Allegro, c, ᴋᴀ44/426a (22 bars), NMA, IX:24/1, 51

| K | K⁶ | Title | Instrument | Key | Composition | MW | NMA | Remarks |
|---|---|---|---|---|---|---|---|---|
| | | | *(for mechanical organ or armonica)* | | | | | |
| 594 | 594 | Adagio and Allegro | mechanical org | f | Vienna and elsewhere, Oct–Dec 1790 | XXIV, no.27a | IX:27 | |
| 608 | 608 | [Fantasia] | mechanical org | f | Vienna, 3 March 1791 (C) | X/100 | IX:27 | |
| 616 | 616 | Andante | mechanical org | F | Vienna, 4 May 1791 | X/109 | IX:27 | arr. pf (Venice, 1791) |
| 356 | 617a | Adagio | armonica | C | Vienna, 1791 | X/84 | IX:27 | |

Frags. for mechanical org.: Adagio, d, ᴋᴀ35/593a; Andante, F, ᴋ615a

MISCELLANEOUS

| K | K⁶ | Title | Key | Composition | MW | NMA | Remarks |
|---|---|---|---|---|---|---|---|
| ᴀ109b, 15a–ss | 15a–ss | London Sketchbook | | London, 1765 | — | | short pieces on 2 staves for kbd or sketches for orch |
| — | 32a | Capricci | | ?1764–6 | — | — | lost; see Constanze's letter to André, 2 March 1799; ?in LC |
| 41f | 41f | Fugue a 4 | | Salzburg, 1767 | — | — | lost; in LC |
| 393 | 385b | Solfeggios for voice | | Vienna, ?Aug 1782 | XXIV, no.49 | | |
| — | 385n | Fugue a 4 | A | Vienna, ?1782 | — | | frag. |
| 443 | 404b | Fugue a 3 | G | Vienna, ?1782 | — | | inc.; completed by M. Stadler |
| — | 453b | Exercise book for Barbara Ployer | | | — | | facs. in Lach, *Mozart als Theoretiker* (Vienna, 1918) |
| 485a | 506a | Attwood Studies | | Vienna, 1785–6 | — | X:30, 1 | |
| ᴀ294d | 516f | Musikalisches Würfelspiel | C | Vienna, 1787 | — | | |
| ᴀ78 | 620b | [contrapuntal study] | b | Vienna, ?Sept 1791 | | | chorale setting; ?sketch for Die Zauberflöte ᴋ620 |

ARRANGEMENTS ETC

| K | K⁶ | Orig. composer, work | Orig. scoring | Key | Mozart's scoring | Date of arr. | MW | NMA | Remarks |
|---|---|---|---|---|---|---|---|---|---|
| 37 | 37 | i H. F. Raupach, op.1 no.5 ii ? iii L. Honauer, op.2 no.3 | kbd | F | kbd, 2 ob, 2 hn, str | Salzburg, April 1767 | XVI/i, 1 | X:28/ii, 3 | |
| 39 | 39 | i Raupach, op.1 no.1 ii J. Schobert, op.17 no.2 iii Raupach, op.1 no.1 | kbd | B♭ | kbd, 2 ob, 2 hn, str | Salzburg, June 1767 | XVI/i, 35 | X:28/ii, 45 | |
| 40 | 40 | i Honauer, op.2 no.1 ii J. G. Eckard, op.1 no.4 iii C. P. E. Bach, w117 | kbd | D | kbd, 2 ob, 2 hn, str | Salzburg, July 1767 | XVI/i, 67 | X:28/ii, 84 | cadenza ᴋ624/626aII, C |
| 41 | 41 | i Honauer, op.1 no.1 ii Raupach, op.1 no.1 iii Honauer, op.1 no.1 | kbd | G | kbd, 2 ob, 2 hn, str | Salzburg, July 1767 | XVI/i, 99 | X:28/ii, 125 | |
| 107, 1 | 107, 1 | J. C. Bach, op.5 no.2 | kbd | D | kbd, 2 vn, b | 1772 | — | X:28/ii, 165 | cadenzas ᴋ624/626aII, A–B |
| 107, 2 | 107, 2 | J. C. Bach, op.5 no.3 | kbd | G | kbd, 2 vn, b | 1772 | — | X:28/ii, 187 | |
| 107, 3 | 107, 3 | J. C. Bach, op.5 no.4 | kbd | E♭ | kbd, 2 vn, b | 1772 | — | X:28/ii, 203 | |
| 284e | 284e | J. B. Wendling, conc. | fl, str | | ?addl. wind | Mannheim, Nov 1777 | — | — | lost; see letter, 21 Nov 1777 |

| K | K⁶ | Orig. composer, work | Orig. scoring | Key | Mozart's scoring | Date of arr. | MW | NMA | Remarks |
|---|---|---|---|---|---|---|---|---|---|
| 404a | 404a | 6 preludes and fugues | kbd | | vn, va, vc | Vienna, 1782 | — | | doubtful; see Kirkendale, JAMS, xvii (1964), 43 and Mf, xviii (1965), 195; Holschneider, Mf, xvii (1964), 51 |
| | | 1 p ?orig., f J. S. Bach BWV853 | | d | | | | | |
| | | 2 p ?orig., f BWV883 | | g | | | | | |
| | | 3 p ?orig., f BWV882 | | F | | | | | |
| | | 4 p BWV527/ii, f BWV1080 no.8 | | F | | | | | |
| | | 5 p, f BWV526/ii, iii | | E♭ | | | | | |
| | | 6 p ?orig., f W. F. Bach Fugue no.8 | | f | | | | | |
| 405 | 405 | J. S. Bach 5 fugues BWV871, 876, 878, 877, 874 | kbd | c, E♭, E, d, D | 2 vn, va, vc | Vienna, 1782 | — | | see Kirkendale, MJb 1962–3, 140 |
| — | — | J. S. Bach BWV891 | kbd | c | 2 vn, va, vc | ?Vienna, 1782 | — | | see Croll, ÖMz, xxi (1966), 508 |
| — | — | 6 preludes and fugues | kbd | | 2 vn, va, vc | ?Vienna, 1782 | — | | very doubtful; see Kirkendale, JAMS, xvii (1964), 43 |
| | | 1 p ?orig., f J. S. Bach BWV548 | | e | | | | | |
| | | 2 p ?orig., f BWV877 | | d | | | | | |
| | | 3 p ?orig., f BWV876 | | E♭ | | | | | |
| | | 4 p ?orig., f BWV891 | | b | | | | | |
| | | 5 p ?orig., f BWV874 | | D | | | | | |
| | | 6 p ?orig., f BWV878 | | E | | | | | |
| — | — | 3 preludes and fugues | kbd | | 2 vn, 2 va, vc | ?Vienna, 1782 | — | | very doubtful; see Kirkendale, JAMS, xvii (1964), 43 |
| | | 1 p ?orig., f J. S. Bach BWV849 | | d | | | | | |
| | | 2 p ?orig., f BWV867 | | a | | | | | |
| | | 3 p ?orig., f BWV546 | | c | | | | | |
| 470a | 470a | G. B. Viotti, Vn Conc. no.16 | | | addl tpt, timp | Vienna, April 1785 | — | | lost Andante K470 ? intended for this |
| A109g no.19 | 537d | C. P. E. Bach, Ich folge dir, from Auferstehung und Himmelfahrt Jesu (1787) | T, tpt, str | | addl fl, ob, tpt | Vienna, Feb 1788 | — | | |
| 566 | 566 | G. F. Handel, Acis and Galatea (1718) | S, T, T, T, B, rec, 2 ob, bn, 2 vn, va, bc | | addl 2 fl, 2 cl, bn, 2 hn | Vienna, Nov 1788 | — | X:28/1/i | |
| 572 | 572 | Handel, Messiah (1742) | S, A, T, B, SATB, 2 ob, 2 tpt, timp, str | | addl 2 fl, 2 cl, 2 bn, 2 hn, 3 trbn, rev. tpt parts | Vienna, March 1789 | — | X:28/1/ii | |
| 591 | 591 | Handel, Alexander's Feast (1736) | S, T, B, SATB, 2 rec, 2 ob, 3 bn, 2 hn, 2 tpt, timp, str | | addl 2 fl, 2 cl, rev. tpt parts | Vienna, July 1790 | — | X:28/1/iii | |
| 592 | 592 | Handel, Ode for St Cecilia's Day (1739) | S, T, SATB, fl, 2 ob, 2 tpt, timp, lute, str | | addl fl, 2 cl, 2 bn, 2 hn, rev. tpt parts | Vienna, July 1790 | — | X:28/1/iv | |
| 625 | 592a | ? B. Schack, Nun liebes Weibchen, duet, in Schikaneder's play Der Stein der Weisen | S, B, ?pf | | S, B, fl, 2 ob, 2 bn, 2 hn, str | Vienna, Aug 1790 | — | VI/2, 235 | ?orig. |
| 624 | 626aII, D–O | Cadenzas | kbd | | various | | | | D(A61a), F–G, H for J. S. Schroeter op.3 nos.1, 4, 6; K for I. von Beecke Conc. in D; N, O for unknown conc; L lost; E, I unauthentic |
| | 626b, 28 | C. W. Gluck, gavotte from Paride ed Elena (1769) | orch | | 2 fl, 5 tpt, timp | | | | ? Mozart's contribution to Divertimento K187 |
| — | — | L. Mozart: Litaniae de venerabili altaris sacramento (1762) | S, A, T, B, SATB, 2 hn, str | | various changes | | — | X:28/3–5/i | |

19 cadenzas K293e for J. C. Bach arias, 1772–3, some not authentic: see Plath, MJb 1960–61, 106, and MJb 1971–2, 20

## BIBLIOGRAPHY

CATALOGUES, BIBLIOGRAPHIES, LETTERS, DOCUMENTS

L. von Köchel: Chronologisch-thematisches Verzeichnis sämtlicher Tonwerke Wolfgang Amade Mozarts (Leipzig, 1862; 2/1905 ed. P. Graf von Waldersee; 3/1937 ed. A. Einstein, repr. 4/1958, 5/1963, with suppl. 3/1947; 6/1964 ed. F. Giegling, A. Weinmann and G. Sievers, repr. 7/1965) [reviews by A. H. King, Mf, xviii (1965), 307 and B. E. Wilson, Notes, xxi (1963–4), 531; corrections and suppls. by P. W. van Reijen, MJb 1971–2, 342–401]

C. von Wurzbach: *Mozart-Buch* (Vienna, 1869)

H. de Curzon: *Essai de bibliographie mozartienne: revue critique des ouvrages relatifs à W. A. Mozart et ses oeuvres* (Paris, 1906)

L. Schiedermair, ed.: *Die Briefe W. A. Mozarts und seiner Familie: erste kritische Gesamtausgabe* (Munich and Leipzig, 1914)

O. Keller: *W. A. Mozart: Bibliographie und Ikonographie* (Berlin, 1927)

E. Anderson, ed.: *Letters of Mozart and his Family* (London, 1938; rev. 2/1966 ed. A. H. King and M. Carolan)

O. E. Deutsch, ed.: *Wolfgang Amadeus Mozart: Verzeichnis aller meiner Werke: Faksimile der Handschrift mit dem Beiheft 'Mozarts Werkverzeichnis 1784–1791'* (Vienna, 1938; Eng. edn., 1956)

E. Müller von Asow, ed.: *Gesamtausgabe der Briefe und Aufzeichnungen der Familie Mozart* (Berlin, 1942)

——: *Wolfgang Amadeus Mozart: Verzeichnis aller meiner Werke und Leopold Mozart: Verzeichnis der Jugendwerke W. A. Mozarts* (Vienna, 1943, 2/1956)

O. E. Deutsch: *Mozart: die Dokumente seines Lebens, gesammelt und erläutert* (Kassel, 1961; Eng. trans., 1965, 2/1966; suppl. 1978)

W. A. Bauer, O. E. Deutsch and J. H. Eibl, eds.: *Mozart: Briefe und Aufzeichnungen* (Kassel, 1962–75) [complete edn.; for later discoveries see G. Croll, *MJb 1967*, 12, and R. Angermüller and S. Dahms-Schneider, *MJb 1968–70*, 211–41]

O. Schneider and A. Algatzy: *Mozart-Handbuch: Chronik, Werk, Bibliographie* (Vienna, 1962)

R. Angermüller and O. Schneider: 'Mozart-Bibliographie (bis 1970)', *MJb 1975*

——: *Mozart-Bibliographie 1971–1975 mit Nachträgen bis 1970* (Kassel, 1978)

O. Wessely: 'Ergänzerungen zur Mozart-Bibliographie', *SMw*, xxix (1978), 37–68

ICONOGRAPHY

O. Keller: *W. A. Mozart: Bibliographie und Ikonographie* (Berlin, 1927)

R. Tenschert: *Wolfgang Amadeus Mozart 1756–1791: sein Leben in Bildern* (Leipzig, 1935)

R. Bory: *La vie et l'oeuvre de Wolfgang-Amadeus Mozart par l'image* (Geneva, 1948) [also Eng. edn.]

G. Rech: *Wolfgang Amadeus Mozart: ein Lebensweg in Bildern* (Munich and Berlin, 1955)

O. E. Deutsch: 'Mozart's Portraits', *The Mozart Companion*, ed. H. C. R. Landon and D. Mitchell (London, 1956, 2/1965), 1

R. Petzoldt: *Wolfgang Amadeus Mozart: sein Leben in Bildern* (Leipzig, 1956, 2/1956)

E. Valentin: *Mozart: eine Bildbiographie* (Munich, 1959; Eng. trans., 1959)

O. E. Deutsch: *Mozart und seine Welt in zeitgenössischen Bildern* (Kassel, 1961) [in Ger. and Eng.]

A. Hutchings: *Mozart: the Man, the Musician* (London, 1976)

SPECIALIST PUBLICATIONS

*Mitteilungen für die Mozartgemeinde in Berlin* (1895–1925)

*Mozarteums-Mitteilungen* (1918–21)

*Mozart-Jb*, i–iii (1923–9)

*Bulletin de la Société d'Etudes Mozartiennes*, i (Paris, 1930–32)

*Tagung der Internationalen Stiftung Mozarteum: Salzburg 1931*

*Wiener Figaro*, Mitteilungen der Mozartgemeinde Wien (1931–)

*Neues Mozart-Jb*, i–iii (1941–3)

*MJb 1950–* [with annual bibliography up to 1975]

*Mitteilungen der Internationalen Stiftung Mozarteum* (1952–)

*Acta Mozartiana*, Mitteilungen der Deutschen Mozart-Gesellschaft (1954–)

Prefaces and Critical Commentaries to all vols. of *W. A. Mozart: Neue Ausgabe sämtlicher Werke* (Kassel, 1955–)

*Internationale Mozartkonferenz: Praha 1956*

*Kongressbericht: Wien Mozartjahr 1956*

*Les influences étrangères dans l'oeuvre de Mozart: CNRS Paris 1956*

'W. A. Mozart emlékére', *Zenetudományi tanulmányok*, v (1957)

'Mozart und Italien: Rom 1974', *AnMc*, no.18 (1978)

SKETCHES, FRAGMENTS, RESEARCH, AUTHENTICITY

L. Schiedermair: *W. A. Mozarts Handschrift in zeitlich geordneten Nachbildungen* (Bückeburg and Leipzig, 1919)

M. Blaschitz: *Die Salzburger Mozart-Fragmente* (diss., U. of Bonn, 1924; part pubd in *Jb der philosophischen Fakultät, Bonn 1924–5*)

C. B. Oldman: 'Mozart and Modern Research', *PRMA*, lviii (1931–2), 43

R. Engländer: 'Die Mozart-Skizzen der Universitätsbibliothek Uppsala: eine entstehungsgeschichtliche Studie', *STMf*, xxxvii (1955), 96; suppl. in *Mf*, ix (1956), 307

W. Plath: 'Das Skizzenblatt KV.467a', *MJb 1959*, 114

——: 'Beiträge zur Mozart-Autographie I: die Handschrift Leopold Mozarts', *MJb 1960–61*, 82–118

W. Senn: 'Mozarts Skizze der Ballettmusik zu Le gelosie del serraglio', *AcM*, xxxiii (1961), 169

A. A. Abert: 'Methoden der Mozartforschung', *MJb 1964*, 22 [on Lambach symphonies]

H. Engel: 'Probleme der Mozartforschung', *MJb 1964*, 38

E. Hess: 'Ein neu entdecktes Skizzenblatt Mozarts', *MJb 1964*, 185

W. Plath: 'Bemerkungen zu einem missdeuteten Skizzenblatt Mozarts', *Festschrift Walter Gerstenberg* (Wolfenbüttel, 1964)

——: 'Der Ballo des "Ascanio" und die Klavierstücke KV Anh. 207', *MJb 1964*, 111

——: 'Der gegenwärtige Stand der Mozart-Forschung', *IMSCR*, ix *Salzburg 1964*, 47, 88

G. Rech: 'Mozart: Results of Present-day Research on his Works', *Universitas*, vii (1965), 355

W. Plath: 'Überliefert die dubiose Klavierromanze in As, KV-Anh.205, das verschollene Quintett-Fragment KV-Anh.54 (452a)?', *MJb 1965–6*, 71

R. D. Levin: 'Das Konzert für Klavier und Violine D-Dur KV Anh. 56/315f und das Klarinettenquintett B-Dur, KV Anh. 91/516c: ein Ergänzungsversuch', *MJb 1968–70*, 304 [in Eng.]

K. Pfannhauser: 'Epilegomena Mozartiana', *MJb 1971–2*, 268–312

W. Plath: 'Leopold Mozarts Notenbuch für Wolfgang (1762): eine Fälschung?', *MJb 1971–2*, 337

W. Plath and others: 'Zur Echtheitsfrage bei Mozart', *MJb 1971–2*, 19–67 [incl. discussions]

N. Zaslaw: 'A Rediscovered Mozart Autograph at Cornell University', *MJb 1971–2*, 419

D. N. Leeson and D. Whitwell: 'Mozart's Thematic Catalogue', *MT*, cxiv (1973), 781

A. H. King: 'Some Aspects of Recent Mozart Research', *PRMA*, c (1973–4), 1

W. Senn: 'Beiträge zur Mozartforschung', *AcM*, xlviii (1976), 205

W. Plath: 'Beiträge zur Mozart-Autographie II: Schriftchronologie 1770–1780', *MJb 1976–7*, 131–73

A. Tyson: *Mozart's Workshop* (Berkeley and Los Angeles, in preparation)

MANUSCRIPTS, SOURCES, PUBLICATION

O. E. Deutsch and C. B. Oldman: 'Mozart-Drucke: eine bibliographische Ergänzung zu Köchels Werkverzeichnis', *ZMw*, xiv (1931–2), 135, 337

G. de Saint-Foix: *Les éditions françaises de Mozart (1765–1801)* (Paris, 1933)

H. G. Farmer and H. Smith: *New Mozartiana: the Mozart Relics in the Zavertal Collection at the University of Glasgow* (Glasgow, 1935/R1976)

A. H. King: 'A Census of Mozart Musical Autographs in England', *MQ*, xxxviii (1952), 566; repr. in King (1955)

O. E. Deutsch: 'Mozarts Nachlass: aus den Briefen Constanzes an den Verlag André', *MJb 1953*, 32

——: 'Mozarts Verleger', *MJb 1955*, 49

A. H. King: *Mozart in the British Museum* (London, 1956/R1975)

H. Moldenhauer: 'Übersicht der Musikmanuskripte W. A. Mozarts in den Vereinigten Staaten von Amerika (1956)', *MJb 1956*, 88

*Mozart en France* (Paris, 1956) [*F-Pn* exhibition catalogue]

L. Nowak: 'Die Wiener Mozart-Autographen', *ÖMz*, xi (1956), 180

A. Weinmann: *Wiener Musikverleger und Musikalienhändler von Mozarts Zeit bis gegen 1860* (Vienna, 1956)

M. and C. Raeburn: 'Mozart's Manuscripts in Florence', *ML*, xl (1959), 334

L. Finscher: 'Maximilian Stadler und Mozarts Nachlass', *MJb 1960–61*, 168

A. Holschneider: 'Neue Mozartiana in Italien', *Mf*, xv (1962), 227

W. Senn: 'Die Mozart-Überlieferung im Stift Heilig Kreuz zu Augsburg', *Neues Augsburger Mozartbuch* (Augsburg, 1962), 333–68

K.-H. Köhler: 'Die Erwerbung der Mozart-Autographe der Berliner Staatsbibliothek: ein Beitrag zur Geschichte des Nachlasses', *MJb 1962–3*, 55

'Mozart-Autographe: Verzeichnis der verschollenen Mozart-Autographe der ehemaligen Preussischen Staatsbibliothek Berlin', *MJb 1962–3*, 306 [see also Acta Mozartiana, xii (1965), 66]

W. Plath: 'Miscellanea Mozartiana I', *Festschrift Otto Erich Deutsch* (Kassel, 1963), 135

W. Rehm: 'Miscellanea Mozartiana II', *Festschrift Otto Erich Deutsch* (Kassel, 1963), 141

H. Federhofer: 'Mozartiana im Musikaliennachlass von Ferdinand Bischoff', *MJb 1965–6*, 15

G. Croll: 'Zu den Verzeichnissen von Mozarts nachgelassenen Fragmenten und Entwürfen', *ÖMz*, xxi (1966), 250

D. Kolbin: 'Autographe Mozarts und seiner Familie in der UdSSR', *MJb 1968–70*, 281

W. Plath: 'Mozartiana in Fulda und Frankfurt', *MJb 1968–70*, 333

M. H. Schmid: *Die Musiksammlung der Erzabtei, St. Peter in Salzburg: Katalog I. Teil: Leopold und Wolfgang Mozart, Joseph und Michael Haydn*, Schriftenreihe der Internationalen Stiftung Mozarteum, iii–iv (Salzburg, 1970)

BIOGRAPHIES, STUDIES OF LIFE AND WORKS

F. Schlichtegroll: 'Johannes Chrysostomus Wolfgang Gottlieb Mozart', *Nekrolog auf das Jahr 1791* (Gotha, 1793), ed. L. Landshoff (Munich, 1924); as *Mozarts Leben* (Graz, 1794/R1974) [see also Favier, 1976]

F. X. Niemetschek: *Leben des k.k. Kapellmeisters Wolfgang Gottlieb Mozart nach Originalquellen beschrieben* (Prague, 1798, enlarged

2/1808; Eng. trans., 1956) [see also Favier, 1976]

[I. F. Arnold]: *Mozarts Geist: seine kurze Biographie und ästhetische Darstellung* (Erfurt, 1803)

I. F. Arnold: *Galerie der berühmtesten Tonkünstler des 18. und 19. Jahrhunderts ... W. A. Mozart und Joseph Haydn: Versuch einer Parallele* (Erfurt, 1810, 2/1816)

Stendhal [M.-H. Beyle]: *Lettres ... sur le célèbre compositeur Haydn: suivies d'une vie de Mozart et considérations sur Métastase* (Paris, 1814, rev. 2/1817 as *Vies de Haydn, de Mozart et de Métastase*; Eng. trans., 1972)

P. Lichtenthal: *Cenni biografici intorno al celebre maestro Wolfgang Amadeo Mozart* (Milan, 1816)

G. N. Nissen: *Biographie W. A. Mozarts nach Originalbriefen* (Leipzig, 1828/R1964 and 1972)

A. D. Oulibicheff: *Nouvelle biographie de Mozart* (Moscow, 1843, 2/1890–92)

E. Holmes: *The Life of Mozart* (London, 1845, 2/1878, repr. 1932)

O. Jahn: *W. A. Mozart* (Leipzig, 1856, 2/1867; ed. H. Deiters, 3/1889–91, 4/1905–7; Eng. trans., 1882) [for later edns. see H. Abert, 1919–21]

L. Nohl: *Mozart* (Leipzig, 1863, enlarged 2/1877 as *Mozarts Leben*, rev. 3/1906)

G. Nottebohm: *Mozartiana* (Leipzig, 1880/R1972)

W. W. F[owler]: *Stray Notes on Mozart and his Music* (Edinburgh, 1910)

T. de Wyzewa and G. de Saint-Foix: *Wolfgang Amédée Mozart: sa vie musicale et son oeuvre* (Paris, 1912–46) [iii–v by Saint-Foix alone]

A. Schurig: *Wolfgang Amadeus Mozart: sein Leben und sein Werk* (Leipzig, 1913, 2/1923)

H. de Curzon: *Mozart* (Paris, 1914, 2/1927)

E. W. Engel: *Wolfgang Amade Mozart* (Vienna, 1914)

H. Abert: *W. A. Mozart: neu bearbeitete und erweiterte Ausgabe von Otto Jahns 'Mozart'* (Leipzig, 1919–21, 3/1955–66)

J. S. J. Kreitmeier: *W. A. Mozart: eine Charakterzeichnung des grossen Meisters nach literarischen Quellen* (Düsseldorf, 1919)

L. Schiedermair: *Mozart: sein Leben und seine Werke* (Munich, 1922, rev., enlarged 2/1948)

B. Paumgartner: *Mozart* (Berlin, 1927, enlarged 6/1967)

D. Hussey: *Wolfgang Amade Mozart* (London, 1928)

M. Davenport: *Mozart* (New York, 1932)

H. Ghéon: *Promenades avec Mozart* (Paris, 1932, 7/1948; Eng. trans., 1932 as *In Search of Mozart*)

R. Haas: *Wolfgang Amadeus Mozart* (Potsdam, 1933, 2/1950)

E. F. Schmid: *W. A. Mozart* (Lübeck, 1934, enlarged 3/1955)

E. Blom: *Mozart* (London, 1935, 3/1975)

A. Boschot: *Mozart* (Paris, 1935, 2/1949)

W. J. Turner: *Mozart: the Man and his Works* (London, 1938, 3/1966)

A. Einstein: *Mozart: his Character, his Work* (Eng. trans., New York, 1945; Ger. orig., 1947, 4/1960)

R. Tenschert: *Wolfgang Amadeus Mozart* (Salzburg, 1951; Eng. trans., 1952)

E. Schenk: *Wolfgang Amadeus Mozart: eine Biographie* (Vienna and Zurich, 1955, rev. 2/1975; Eng. trans., abridged, 1960 as *Mozart and his Times*)

F. Hadamowsky and L. Nowak: *Mozart: Werk und Zeit* (Vienna, 1956)

J. N. Burk: *Mozart and his Music* (New York, 1959)

J. and B. Massin: *Wolfgang Amadeus Mozart: biographie, histoire de l'oeuvre* (Paris, 1959, 2/1971)

C. Haldane: *Mozart* (London, 1960)

F. Blume: 'Mozart, Wolfgang Amadeus', *MGG* [iconography by W. Rehm, bibliography and work-list by F. Lippmann, list of edns. by R. Schaal]

S. Sadie: *Mozart* (London, 1966)

A. H. King: *Mozart: a Biography with a Survey of Books, Editions and Recordings* (London, 1970)

M. Levey: *The Life and Death of Mozart* (London, 1971)

G. Favier, ed.: *Vie de W. A. Mozart par Franz Xaver Niemetschek précédée du nécrologe de Schlichtegroll* (St Etienne, 1976) [in Ger. and Fr., with introduction and notes]

A. Hutchings: *Mozart: the Man, the Musician* (London, 1976)

W. Hildesheimer: *Mozart* (Frankfurt am Main, 1977; Eng. trans., 1979)

I. Keys: *Mozart: his Life in his Music* (London, 1980)

LIFE: PARTICULAR ASPECTS AND EPISODES

F. Rochlitz: 'Verbürgte Anekdoten aus Wolfgang Gottlieb Mozarts Leben: ein Beitrag zur richtigeren Kenntnis dieses Mannes, als Mensch und Künstler', *AMZ*, i (1798–9), 17, 49, 81, 113, 145, 177, 289, 480, 854; iii (1800–01), 450, 493, 590

L. da Ponte: *Memorie di Lorenzo da Ponte, da Ceneda: scritte da esso* (New York, 1823–7; Eng. trans., 1929/R1967)

E. Mörike: *Mozart auf der Reise nach Prag* (Stuttgart and Augsburg, 1856; Eng. trans., 1934, 1946) [novel]

C. F. Pohl: *Mozart and Haydn in London* (Vienna, 1867/R1970)

A. J. Hammerle: *Mozart und einige Zeitgenossen: neue Beiträge für Salzburgische Geschichte, Literatur und Musik* (Salzburg, 1877)

K. Prieger: *Urtheile bedeutender Dichter, Philosopher und Musiker über Mozart* (Wiesbaden, 1885–6)

R. Procházka: *Mozart in Prag* (Prague, 1899; rev. and enlarged by P. Nettl as *Mozart in Böhmen*, 1938)

E. K. Blümml: *Aus Mozarts Freundes- und Familienkreis* (Leipzig, 1923)

O. E. Deutsch: *Mozart und die Wiener Logen: zur Geschichte seiner Freimaurer-Kompositionen* (Vienna, 1932)

P. Nettl: *Mozart und die königliche Kunst: die freimaurerische Grundlage der Zauberflöte* (Berlin, 1932, enlarged 2/1956)

W. Kipp: *Mozart und das Elsass* (Colmar, 1941)

H. A. Thies: *Mozart und München: ein Gedenkbuch* (Munich, 1941)

E. F. Schmid: 'Mozart und das geistliche Augsburg, insonderheit das Chorherrenstift Heiligkreuz', *Augsburger Mozartbuch* (Augsburg, 1942–3), 40

E. J. Luin: 'Mozarts Aufenthalt in Rom', *Neues Mozart-Jb*, iii (1943), 45

E. Schenk: 'Neues zu Mozarts erster Italienreise: Mozart in Verona', *Neues Mozart-Jb*, iii (1943), 22

I. Hoesli: *W. A. Mozart: Briefstil eines Musikgenies* (Zurich, 1948)

A. B. Gottron: *Mozart und Mainz* (Baden-Baden and Mainz, 1951)

M. Fehr and L. Caflisch: *Der junge Mozart in Zürich: ein Beitrag zur Mozart-Biographie auf Grund bisher unbekannter Dokumente* (Zurich, 1952)

M. Kenyon: *Mozart in Salzburg* (London, 1952)

E. J. Luin: 'Mozart: Ritter vom Goldenen Sporn', *SMw*, xxii (1955), 30

N. Medici di Marignano and R. Hughes: *A Mozart Pilgrimage: Being the Travel Diaries of Vincent and Mary Novello in the Year 1829* (London, 1955/R1975)

A. Ostoja: *Mozart e l'Italia* (Bologna, 1955)

E. Schenk: 'Mozart in Mantua', *SMw*, xx (1955), 1

G. Barblan and A. della Corte: *Mozart in Italia* (Milan, 1956)

O. E. Deutsch: 'Phantasiestücke aus der Mozart-Biographie', *MJb 1956*, 46

L. E. Staehelin: 'Neues zu Mozarts Aufenthalten in Lyon, Genf und Bern', *SMz*, xcvi (1956), 46

O. E. Deutsch: 'Aus Schiedenhofens Tagebuch', *MJb 1957*, 15

P. Nettl: *Mozart and Masonry* (New York, 1957/R1970)

A. Greither: *Wolfgang Amadé Mozart: seine Leidensgeschichte aus Briefen und Dokumenten zusammengestellt* (Heidelberg, 1958)

W. Hummel: *Nannerl Mozarts Tagebuchblätter, mit Eintragungen ihres Bruders Wolfgang Amadeus* (Salzburg, 1958)

E. F. Schmid: 'Zur Entstehungszeit von Mozarts italienischen Sinfonien', *MJb 1958*, 71

E. Winternitz: 'Gangflow Trazom: an Essay on Mozart's Script, Pastimes, and Nonsense Letters', *JAMS*, xi (1958), 200

H. F. Deininger and J. Herz: 'Beiträge zur Genealogie der ältesten schwäbischen Vorfahren W. A. Mozarts', *Neues Augsburger Mozartbuch* (Augsburg, 1962), 1–76

O. E. Deutsch: 'Mozart in Zinzendorfs Tagebüchern', *SMz*, cii (1962), 211

H. W. Hamann: 'Mozarts Schülerkreis', *MJb 1962–3*, 115; suppl. by C. Bär, *Acta Mozartiana*, xi (1964), 58

O. E. Deutsch: 'Die Legende von Mozarts Vergiftung', *MJb 1964*, 7 [with discussion by C. Bär]

L. Wegele: 'Die Mozart: neue Forschungen zur Ahnengeschichte Wolfgang Amadeus Mozarts', *Acta Mozartiana*, xi (1964), 18; also in *Mitteilungen der Internationalen Stiftung Mozarteum*, xii/3–4 (1964), 1

W. Lievense: *De familie Mozart in Nederland: een reisverslag* (Hilversum, 1965)

C. Bär: *Mozart: Krankheit, Tod, Begräbnis*, Schriftenreihe der Internationalen Stiftung Mozarteum, i (Kassel, 1966, rev. 2/1972)

A. R. Mohr: *Das Frankfurter Mozart-Buch* (Frankfurt, 1968)

L. E. Staehelin: *Die Reise der Familie Mozart durch die Schweiz* (Berne, 1968)

A. Greither: *Die sieben grossen Opern Mozarts: mit ein Pathographie Mozarts* (Heidelberg, 2/1970) ['Pathographie' not in 1956 edn.]

H. Schuler: *Die Gesamtverwandtschaft Wolfgang Amadeus Mozarts* (Essen, c1972)

——: *Die Vorfahren Wolfgang Mozarts* (Essen, 1972)

J. H. Eibl: 'Die Mozarts und der Erzbischof', *ÖMz*, xxx (1975), 329

M. H. Schmid: *Mozart und die Salzburger Tradition* (Tutzing, 1976)

K. Thomson: 'Mozart and Freemasonry', *ML*, lvii (1976), 25

——: *The Masonic Thread in Mozart* (London, 1977)

C. Bär: 'Er war ... kein guter Wirth: eine Studie über Mozarts Verhältnis zum Geld', *Acta Mozartiana*, xxv (1978), 30

ESSAYS, COLLECTIVE WORKS

D. F. Tovey: *Essays in Musical Analysis* (London, 1935–44) [on κ297/300a, 338, 425, 543, 550, 551; 250/248b; 414/385p, 450, 453, 488, 491; 218, 219, 261, 313/285c, 314/285d, 315/285e, 299/297c, 622; 452; 497]

H. F. Deininger, ed.: *Augsburger Mozartbuch: Zeitschrift des historischen Vereins für Schwaben*, lv–lvi (Augsburg, 1942–3)

E. F. Schmid: *Ein schwäbisches Mozartbuch* (Stuttgart, 1948)

A. H. King: *Mozart in Retrospect: Studies in Criticism and Bibliography* (London, 1955, 3/1970/R1976)

A. Einstein: *Essays on Music* (New York, 1956) [incl. 8 on Mozart]

H. C. R. Landon and D. Mitchell, eds.: *The Mozart Companion*

(London, 1956, 2/1965)

P. Schaller and H. Kühner, eds.: *Mozart-Aspekte* (Olten and Freiburg, 1956) [symposium]

*Neues Augsburger Mozartbuch: Zeitschrift des historischen Vereins für Schwaben*, lxii–lxiii (Augsburg, 1962)

F. Blume: *Syntagma musicologicum: gesammelte Reden und Schriften* (Kassel, 1963) ['Haydn und Mozart', 571; 'Wolfgang Amadeus Mozart', 583; 'Wolfgang Amadeus Mozart: Geltung und Wirkung', 670; 'Mozarts Konzerte und ihre Überlieferung', 686; 'Requiem und kein Ende', 714]

P. H. Lang, ed.: *The Creative World of Mozart* (New York, 1963)

*Mozartgemeinde Wien 1913 bis 1963: Forschung und Interpretation* (Vienna, 1964)

E. Wellesz and F. Sternfeld, eds.: *The Age of Enlightenment 1745–1790*, NOHM, vii (1973)

*Festschrift Erich Valentin zum 70. Geburtstag* (Regensburg, 1976) [incl. 12 essays on Mozart]

WORKS: STYLE, INFLUENCES, PARTICULAR ASPECTS

A. Heuss: 'Das dämonische Element in Mozarts Werken', *ZIMG*, vii (1905–6), 175

G. Schünemann, ed.: *Mozart als achtjähriger Komponist: ein Notenbuch Wolfgangs* (Leipzig, 1909)

R. Lach: *W. A. Mozart als Theoretiker* (Vienna, 1918)

F. Torrefranca: 'Le origini dello stile Mozartiano', *RMI*, xxviii (1921), 263; xxxiii (1926), 321, 505; xxxiv (1927), 1, 169, 493; xxxvi (1929), 373

W. Lüthy: *Mozart und die Tonartencharakteristik* (Strasbourg, 1931/R1974)

C. Thieme: *Der Klangstil des Mozartorchesters* (Leipzig, 1936)

A. Einstein: 'Mozart's Choice of Keys', *MQ*, xxvii (1941), 415; repr. in Einstein (1945)

A. H. King: 'Mozart's Counterpoint: its Growth and Significance', *ML*, xxvi (1945), 12; repr. in King (1955)

J. Chantavoine: *Mozart dans Mozart* (Paris, 1948)

E. J. Dent: 'Mozart: Lecture on a Master Mind', *Proceedings of the British Academy*, xxxix (1953), 181

J. A. Westrup: 'Cherubino and the G minor Symphony', *Fanfare for Ernest Newman* (London, 1955), 181

D. Bartha: 'Mozart et le folklore musical de l'Europe centrale', *Les influences étrangères dans l'oeuvre de Mozart: CNRS Paris 1956*, 157

F. Blume: 'Mozart's Style and Influence', *The Mozart Companion*, ed. H. C. R. Landon and D. Mitchell (London, 1956, 2/1965), 10

I. M. Bruce: 'A Note on Mozart's Bar-rhythms', *MR*, xvii (1956), 35

H. T. David: 'Mozartean Modulations', *MQ*, xlii (1956), 193; repr. in Lang (1963)

H. Engel: 'Mozarts Instrumentation', *MJb 1956*, 51

E. E. Lowinsky: 'On Mozart's Rhythm', *MQ*, xlii (1956), 162; repr. in Lang (1963)

E. F. Schmid: 'Mozart and Haydn', *MQ*, xlii (1956), 145

B. Szabolcsi: 'Die "Exotismen" Mozarts', *Internazionale Mozart-konferenz: Praha 1956*, 181; Eng. trans., *ML*, xxxvii (1956), 323

E. Valentin: *Der früheste Mozart* (Munich, 1956) [in Ger. and Eng.]

——: *Leopold Mozart: Nannerls Notenbuch 1759* (Munich, 1956)

E. Hertzmann: 'Mozart's Creative Process', *MQ*, xliii (1957), 187; repr. in Lang (1963)

W. Siegmund-Schultze: *Mozarts Melodik und Stil* (Leipzig, 1957)

K. F. Müller: *Leopold Mozart: Werkverzeichnis für W. A. Mozart (1768): ein Beitrag zur Mozartforschung* (Salzburg, 1958)

H. Engel: 'Haydn, Mozart und die Klassik', *MJb 1959*, 46–79

G. Massenkeil: *Untersuchungen zum Problem der Symmetrie in der Instrumentalmusik W. A. Mozarts* (Wiesbaden, 1962)

H. Engel: 'Nochmals: thematische Satzverbindungen und Mozart', *MJb 1962–3*, 14

I. R. Eisley: 'Mozart and Counterpoint: Development and Synthesis', *MR*, xxiv (1963), 23

M. Chusid: 'The Significance of D minor in Mozart's Dramatic Music', *MJb 1965–6*, 87

S. Davis: 'Harmonic Rhythm in Mozart's Sonata Form', *MR*, xxvii (1966), 25

W. Kirkendale: *Fuge und Fugato in der Kammermusik des Rokoko und der Klassik* (Tutzing, 1966), 184–215; Eng. trans., enlarged (1979), 152–81

H. Beck: 'Harmonisch-melodische Modelle bei Mozart', *MJb 1967*, 90

I. Kecskeméti: 'Barockelemente in den langsamen Instrumentalsätzen Mozarts', *MJb 1967*, 182

M. S. Cole: 'The Rondo Finale: Evidence for the Mozart–Haydn-Exchange?', *MJb 1968–70*, 242

M. Flothuis: *Mozarts Bearbeitungen eigener und fremder Werke*, Schriftenreihe der Internationalen Stiftung Mozarteum, ii (Salzburg, 1969)

H. Federhofer: 'Mozart als Schüler und Lehrer in der Musiktheorie', *MJb 1971–2*, 89

K. J. Marx: *Zur Einheit der zyklischen Form bei Mozart* (Stuttgart, 1971)

C. Rosen: *The Classical Style: Haydn, Mozart, Beethoven* (London, 1971, 2/1973), 183–325

D. Heartz: 'Thomas Attwood's Lessons in Composition with Mozart', *PRMA*, c (1973–4), 175

'Tonartenplan und Motivstruktur (Leitmotivtechnik?) in Mozarts Musik', *MJb 1973–4*, 82–144 [discussions]

'Typus und Modell in Mozarts Kompositionsweise', *MJb 1973–4*, 145–78 [discussions]

U. Toeplitz: *Die Holzbläser in der Musik und ihr Verhältnis zur Tonartwahl* (Baden-Baden, 1978)

SACRED WORKS

W. Pole: *The Story of Mozart's Requiem* (London, 1879)

E. Lewicki: 'Über Mozarts grosse c-Moll-Messe und die Endgestaltung ihrer Ergänzung', *Mozart-Jb*, i (1923), 69

K. A. Rosenthal: 'The Salzburg Church Music of Mozart and his Predecessors', *MQ*, xviii (1932), 559

——: 'Mozart's Sacramental Litanies and their Forerunners', *MQ*, xxvii (1941), 433

K. G. Fellerer: *Mozarts Kirchenmusik* (Salzburg, 1955)

G. Reichert: 'Mozarts "Credo-Messen" und ihre Vorläufer', *MJb 1955*, 117

K. Geiringer: 'The Church Music', *The Mozart Companion*, ed. H. C. R. Landon and D. Mitchell (London, 1956, 2/1965), 361

H. Federhofer: 'Probleme der Echtheitsbestimmung der kleineren kirchenmusikalischen Werke W. A. Mozarts', *MJb 1958*, 97; suppl., *MJb 1960–61*, 43

A. Hess: 'Zur Ergänzung des Requiems von Mozart durch F. X. Süssmayr', *MJb 1959*, 99

K. Pfannhauser: 'Mozarts kirchenmusikalische Studien im Spiegel seiner Zeit und Nachwelt', *KJb*, xliii (1959), 155

F. Blume: 'Requiem but no Peace', *MQ*, xlvii (1961), 147; repr. in Lang (1963) and [Ger.] in Blume (1963)

I. Kecskeméti: 'Beiträge zur Geschichte von Mozarts Requiem', *SM*, i (1961), 147

K. Marguerre: 'Mozart und Süssmayer', *MJb 1962–3*, 172

O. E. Deutsch: 'Zur Geschichte von Mozarts Requiem', *ÖMz*, xix (1964), 49

L. Nowak: 'Das Requiem von W. A. Mozart', *ÖMz*, xx (1965), 395

R. Federhofer-Königs: 'Mozarts "Lauretanische Litaneien" KV 109 (74e) und 195 (186d)', *MJb 1967*, 111

A. Holschneider: 'C. Ph. E. Bachs Kantate "Auferstehung und Himmelfahrt Jesu" und Mozarts Aufführung des Jahres 1788', *MJb 1968–70*, 264

F. Beyer: 'Mozarts Komposition zum Requiem: zur Frage der Ergänzung', *Acta Mozartiana*, xviii (1971), 27

G. Duda: 'Neues aus der Mozartforschung', *Acta Mozartiana*, xviii (1971), 32 [on Requiem]

C. Rosenthal: 'Der Einfluss der Salzburger Kirchenmusik auf Mozarts kirchenmusikalische Kompositionen', *MJb 1971–2*, 173

L. Nowak: 'Wer hat die Instrumentalstimmen in der Kyrie-Fuge des Requiems von W. A. Mozart geschrieben? Ein vorläufiger Bericht', *MJb 1973–4*, 191

K. G. Fellerer: 'Liturgische Grundlagen der Kirchenmusik Mozarts', *Festschrift Walter Senn* (Munich and Salzburg, 1975), 64

'Sektion Kirchenmusik', *MJb 1978–9*, 14 [4 articles]

OPERA

A. D. Oulibicheff: *Mozarts Opern: kritische Erläuterungen* (Leipzig, 1848)

C. Gounod: *Le Don Juan de Mozart* (Paris, 1890; Eng. trans., 1895/R1970)

E. Komorzynski: *Emanuel Schikaneder: ein Beitrag zur Geschichte des deutschen Theaters* (Vienna, 1901, rev. 2/1951, 3/1955)

E. J. Dent: *Mozart's Operas: a Critical Study* (London, 1913, 2/1947)

E. Lert: *Mozart auf dem Theater* (Berlin, 1918)

A. Lorenz: 'Das Finale in Mozarts Meisteropern', *Musik*, xix (1926–7), 621

E. Blom: 'The Literary Ancestry of Figaro', *MQ*, xiii (1927), 528

R. Dumesnil: *Le Don Juan de Mozart* (Paris, 1927)

F. Brukner: *Die Zauberflöte: unbekannte Handschriften und seltene Drucke aus der Frühzeit der Oper* (Vienna, 1934)

P. Stefan: *Die Zauberflöte: Herkunft, Bedeutung, Geheimnis* (Vienna, 1937)

E. Komorzynski: 'Die Zauberflöte: Entstehung und Bedeutung des Kunstwerks', *Neues Mozart-Jb*, i (1941), 147

H. F. Redlich: 'L'oca del Cairo', *MR*, ii (1941), 122

P. J. Jouve: *Le Don Juan de Mozart* (Fribourg, 1942; Eng. trans., 1957)

L. Conrad: *Mozarts Dramaturgie der Oper* (Würzburg, 1943)

E. Wellesz: 'Don Giovanni and the dramma giocoso', *MR*, iv (1943), 121

C. Benn: *Mozart on the Stage* (London, 1946, 2/1947)

A. H. King: 'The Melodic Sources and Affinities of Die Zauberflöte', *MQ*, xxxvi (1950), 241; repr. in King (1955)

S. Levarie: *Mozart's 'Le nozze di Figaro': a Critical Analysis* (Chicago, 1952/R1977)

H. Engel: 'Die Finali der Mozartschen Opern', *MJb 1954*, 113

C. Raeburn: 'An Evening at Schönbrunn', *MR*, xvi (1955), 96

A. Greither: *Die sieben grossen Opern Mozarts: Versuche über das Verhältnis der Texte zur Musik* (Heidelberg, 1956, enlarged 2/1970)

L. F. Tagliavini: 'L'opéra italien du jeune Mozart', *Les influences étrangères dans l'oeuvre de Mozart: CNRS Paris 1956*, 125

C. Raeburn: 'Die textlichen Quellen des "Schauspieldirektor" ', *ÖMz*, xiii (1958), 4

J. A. Westrup: 'Two First Performances: Monteverdi's "Orfeo" and Mozart's "La clemenza di Tito" ', *ML*, xxxix (1958), 327

T. Volek: 'Über den Ursprung von Mozarts Oper "La clemenza di Tito" ', *MJb 1959*, 274

C. Bitter: *Wandlungen in den Inszenierungsformen des 'Don Giovanni' von 1787 bis 1928* (Regensburg, 1961)

B. Szabolcsi: 'Mozart et la comédie populaire', *SM*, i (1961), 65

S. Kunze: 'Mozarts Schauspieldirektor', *MJb 1962–3*, 156

F.-H. Neumann: 'Zur Vorgeschichte der Zaide', *MJb 1962–3*, 216–47

A. Livermore: 'The Origins of Don Juan', *ML*, xliv (1963), 257

B. Brophy: *Mozart the Dramatist: a New View of Mozart, his Operas and his Age* (London, 1964)

C. Floros: 'Das "Programm" in Mozarts Meisterouvertüren', *SMw*, xxvi (1964), 140–86

C. Raeburn: 'Die Entführungsszene aus "Die Entführung aus dem Serail', *MJb 1964*, 130

A. Rosenberg: *Die Zauberflöte: Geschichte und Deutung* (Munich, 1964)

A. Livermore: 'Così fan tutte: a Well-kept Secret', *ML*, xlvi (1965), 316

R. Moberly and C. Raeburn: 'Mozart's "Figaro": the Plan of Act III', *ML*, xlvi (1965), 143; repr. in *MJb 1965–6*, 161

R. Münster: 'Die verstellte Gärtnerin: neue Quellen zur authentischen Singspielfassung von W. A. Mozarts La finta giardiniera', *Mf*, xviii (1965), 138

P. Branscombe: ' "Die Zauberflöte": some Textual and Interpretative Problems', *PRMA*, xcii (1965–6), 45

M. Chusid: 'The Significance of D minor in Mozart's Dramatic Music', *MJb 1965–6*, 87

D. J. Keahey: 'Così fan tutte: Parody or Irony', *Paul A. Pisk: Essays in his Honor* (Austin, 1966), 116

A. A. Abert: 'Beiträge zur Motivik von Mozarts Spätopern', *MJb 1967*, 7

B. Brophy: 'The Young Mozart', *Opera 66*, ed. C. Osborne (London, 1967)

F. Giegling: 'Zu den Rezitativen von Mozarts Oper "Titus" ', *MJb 1967*, 121

G. Gruber: 'Das Autograph der "Zauberflöte" ', *MJb 1967*, 127–49; *MJb 1968–70*, 99–110

D. Heartz: 'The Genesis of Mozart's Idomeneo', *MJb 1967*, 150; repr. in *MQ*, lv (1969), 1

K.-H. Köhler: 'Mozarts Kompositionsweise: Beobachtungen am Figaro-Autograph', *MJb 1967*, 31

R. B. Moberly: *Three Mozart Operas: Figaro, Don Giovanni, The Magic Flute* (London, 1967)

A. A. Abert: ' "La finta giardiniera" und "Zaide" als Quellen für spätere Opern Mozarts', *Musik und Verlag: Karl Vötterle zum 65. Geburtstag* (Kassel, 1968), 113

J. Chailley: *'La flûte enchantée', opéra maçonnique: essai d'explication du livret et de la musique* (Paris, 1968; Eng. trans., 1972)

F. R. Noske: 'Musical Quotation as a Dramatic Device: the Fourth Act of Le nozze di Figaro', *MQ*, liv (1968), 185; repr. in Noske (1977)

L. F. Tagliavini: 'Quirino Gasparini and Mozart', *New Looks at Italian Opera: Essays in Honor of Donald J. Grout* (Ithaca, 1968), 151 [on *Mitridate*]

S. Döhring: 'Die Arienformen in Mozarts Opern', *MJb 1968–70*, 66

H. Federhofer: 'Die Harmonik als dramatischer Ausdrucksfaktor in Mozarts Meisteropern', *MJb 1968–70*, 77

F. Giegling: 'Metastasios Oper "La clemenza di Tito" in der Bearbeitung durch Mazzola', *MJb 1968–70*, 88

K.-H. Köhler: 'Figaro-Miscellen: einige dramaturgische Mitteilungen zur Quellensituation', *MJb 1968–70*, 119

C.-H. Mahling: 'Typus und Modell in Opern Mozarts', *MJb 1968–70*, 145

G. Rech: 'Bretzner contra Mozart', *MJb 1968–70*, 186

E. M. Batley: *A Preface to The Magic Flute* (London, 1969)

C. Henning: 'Thematic Metamorphoses in Don Giovanni', *MR*, xxx (1969), 22

F. Noske: 'Social Tensions in "Le nozze di Figaro" ', *ML*, l (1969), 45; repr. in Noske (1977)

A. A. Abert: *Die Opern Mozarts* (Wolfenbüttel, 1970); Eng. version in *NOHM*, vii (1973)

B. Brophy: ' "Figaro" and the Limitations of Music', *ML*, li (1970), 26

F. R. Noske: 'Don Giovanni: Musical Affinities and Dramatic Structure', *SM*, xii (1970), 167–203; repr. in *Theatre Research/ Recherches téâtrales*, xiii (1973), 60 and in Noske (1977)

A. Williamson: 'Who was Sarastro?', *Opera*, xxi (1970), 297; see also 695f

H. H. Eggebrecht: *Versuch über die Wiener Klassik: die Tanzszene in Mozarts 'Don Giovanni'* (Wiesbaden, 1972)

H. Keller: 'Mozart's Wrong Key Signature', *Tempo* (1972), no.98, p.21 [*Così fan tutte*]

S. Kunze: *Don Giovanni vor Mozart: die Tradition der Don Giovanni-Opern im italienischen Buffo-Theater des 18. Jahrhunderts* (Munich, 1972)

H. Goldschmidt: 'Die Cavatina des Figaro', *BMw*, xv (1973), 185

R. B. Moberly: 'Mozart and his Librettists', *ML*, liv (1973), 161

B. Williams: 'Passion and Cynicism: Remarks on "Così fan tutte" ', *MT*, cxiv (1973), 361

D. Heartz: 'Raaff's last Aria: a Mozartian Idyll in the Spirit of Hasse', *MQ*, lx (1974), 517 [from *Idomeneo*]

——: 'Tonality and Motif in Idomeneo', *MT*, cxv (1974), 2

H. Lühning: 'Zur Entstehungsgeschichte von Mozarts "Titus" ', *Mf*, xxvii (1974), 300: see also xxviii (1975), 77, 312; xxix (1976), 127

R. B. Moberly: 'The Influence of French Classical Drama on Mozart's "La clemenza di Tito" ', *ML*, lv (1974), 286

G. Gruber: 'Bedeutung und Spontaneität in Mozarts "Zauberflöte" ', *Festschrift Walter Senn* (Munich and Salzburg, 1975), 118

D. Koenigsberger: 'A New Metaphor for Mozart's *Magic Flute*', *European Studies Review*, v (1975), 229–75

H. L. Scheel: ' "Le mariage de Figaro" von Beaumarchais und das Libretto der "Nozze di Figaro" von Lorenzo da Ponte', *Mf*, xxviii (1975), 156

A. Tyson: ' "La clemenza di Tito" and its Chronology', *MT*, cxvi (1975), 221

H. Abert: *Mozart's 'Don Giovanni'* (London, 1976) [Eng. trans. from Abert, 1919–21]

C. Gianturco: *Le opere del giovane Mozart* (Pisa, 1976, enlarged 2/ 1978)

R. Angermüller: 'Wer war der Librettist von "La finta giardiniera"?', *MJb 1976–7*, 1

W. Mann: *The Operas of Mozart* (London, 1977)

F. Noske: *The Signifier and the Signified: Studies in the Operas of Mozart and Verdi* (The Hague, 1977)

R. Angermüller: 'Mozart and Metastasio', *Mitteilungen der Internationalen Stiftung Mozarteum*, xxvi/1–2 (1978), 12

D. Heartz: 'Mozart's Overture to Titus as Dramatic Argument', *MQ*, lxiv (1978), 29

——: 'Mozart, his Father and "Idomeneo" ', *MT*, cxix (1978), 228

C. Osborne: *The Complete Operas of Mozart* (London, 1978)

S. Vill, ed.: *Così fan tutte: Beiträge zur Wirkungsgeschichte von Mozarts Oper* (Bayreuth, 1978)

D. Heartz: 'Mozart and his Italian Contemporaries: La clemenza di Tito', *MJb 1978–9*, 275

——: 'The Great Quartet in Mozart's *Idomeneo*', *Music Forum*, v (in preparation)

MISCELLANEOUS VOCAL

M. J. E. Brown: 'Mozart's Songs for Voice and Piano', *MR*, xvii (1956), 19

A. Orel: 'Mozarts Beitrag zum deutschen Sprechtheater: die Musik zu Geblers "Thamos" ', *Acta Mozartiana*, iv (1957), 43, 74

H. Engel: 'Hasses Ruggiero und Mozarts Festspiel Ascanio', *MJb 1960–61*, 46

C. B. Oldman: 'Mozart's Scena for Tenducci', *ML*, xlii (1961), 44

S. Kunze: 'Die Vertonungen der Arie "Non sò d'onde viene" von J. Chr. Bach und von W. A. Mozart', *AnMc*, no.2 (1965), 85

A. Dunning: 'Mozarts Kanons', *MJb 1971–2*, 227

S. Dahms: 'Mozarts festa teatrale "Ascanio in Alba" ', *ÖMz*, xxxi (1976), 15

ORCHESTRAL

D. Schultz: *Mozarts Jugendsinfonien* (Leipzig, 1900)

S. Sechter: *Das Finale von W. A. Mozarts Jupiter-Symphonie*, ed. F. Eckstein (Vienna, 1923)

H. Schenker: 'Mozart: Sinfonie g-Moll', *Das Meisterwerk in der Musik*, ii (1926), 105

A. E. F. Dickinson: *A Study of Mozart's Last Three Symphonies* (London, 1927, 2/1940)

G. de Saint-Foix: *Les symphonies de Mozart* (Paris, 1932; Eng. trans., 1947)

N. Broder: 'The Wind-instruments in Mozart's Symphonies', *MQ*, xix (1933), 238

C. M. Girdlestone: *W. A. Mozart et ses concertos pour piano* (Paris, 1939, rev. 2/1953, 3/1978; Eng. trans., enlarged, 1948)

G. Dazeley: 'The Original Text of Mozart's Clarinet Concerto', *MR*, ix (1948), 166; see also J. Kratchovil, *Internationale Mozartkonferenz: Praha 1956*, 262, and E. Hess, *MJb 1967*, 18

A. Hutchings: *A Companion to Mozart's Piano Concertos* (London, 1948, 2/1950)

G. de Saint-Foix: 'La jeunesse de Mozart: 1771: les diverses orientations de la symphonie', *MJb 1950*, 14, 116

H. Engel: 'Über Mozarts Jugendsinfonien', *MJb 1951*, 22

G. Hausswald: *Mozarts Serenaden: ein Beitrag zur Stilkritik des 18. Jahrhunderts* (Leipzig, 1951, rev. 2/1975)

H. Engel: 'Der Tanz in Mozarts Kompositionen', *MJb 1952*, 29

J. N. David: *Die Jupiter-Sinfonie: eine Studie über die thematisch-melodischen Zusammenhänge* (Göttingen, 1953)

H. Beck: 'Zur Entstehungsgeschichte von Mozarts D-Dur Sinfonie, K.V.297: Probleme der Kompositionstechnik und Formentwicklung in Mozarts Instrumentalmusik', *MJb 1955*, 95

F. Blume: 'The Concertos, I: their Sources', *The Mozart Companion*, ed. H. C. R. Landon and D. Mitchell (London, 1956, 2/1965), 200

H. Keller: 'K503: the Unity of Contrasting Themes and Movements', *MR*, xvii (1956), 48, 120

H. C. R. Landon: 'The Concertos, II: their Musical Origin and Development', *The Mozart Companion*, ed. H. C. R. Landon and D. Mitchell (London, 1956, 2/1965), 234

J. P. Larsen: 'The Symphonies', *The Mozart Companion*, ed. H. C. R. Landon and D. Mitchell (London, 1956, 2/1965), 156

E. J. Simon: 'Sonata into Concerto: a Study of Mozart's First Seven Concertos', *AcM*, xxxi (1959), 41

C. Bär: 'Die "Musique vom Robinig" ', *Mitteilungen der Internationalen Stiftung Mozarteum*, ix/3–4 (1960), 6

——: 'Die Lodronschen Nachtmusiken', *Mitteilungen der Internationalen Stiftung Mozarteum*, x/1–2 (1961), 19

——: 'Zum "Nannerl-Septett" KV 251', *Acta Mozartiana*, ix (1962), 24

——: 'Die "Andretterin-Musik": Betrachtungen zu KV 205', *Acta Mozartiana*, x (1963), 30

A. A. Abert: 'Stilistischer Befund und Quellenlage: zu Mozarts Lambacher Sinfonie KV Anh. 221 = 45a', *Festschrift Hans Engel* (Kassel, 1964), 43

H. Tischler: *A Structural Analysis of Mozart's Piano Concertos* (New York, 1966)

I. Kecskeméti: 'Opernelemente in den Klavierkonzerten Mozarts', *MJb 1968–70*, 111

M. W. Cobin: 'Aspects of Stylistic Evolution in two Mozart Concertos: K.271 and K.482', *MR*, xxxi (1970), 1

J. Kerman, ed.: *Mozart: Piano Concerto in C Major, K.503* (New York, 1970) [score and essays]

D. Forman: *Mozart's Concerto Form: the First Movements of the Piano Concertos* (London, 1971)

W. Plath and others: 'Zur Echtheitsfrage bei Mozart', *MJb 1971–2*, 19–67 [with discussions of кAnh.9/Anh.C14.01 and к84/73q]

P. Benary: 'Metrum bei Mozart: zur metrischen Analyse seiner letzten drei Sinfonien', *SMz*, cxiv (1974), 201

S. Wollenberg: 'The Jupiter Theme: New Light on its Creation', *MT*, cxvi (1975), 781

L. Meyer: 'Grammatical Simplicity and Relational Richness: the Trio of Mozart's G minor Symphony', *Critical Inquiry*, ii (1976), 693–761

A. H. King: *Mozart String and Wind Concertos* (London, 1978)

C. Wolff: 'Zur Chronologie der Klavierkonzert-Kadenzen Mozarts', *MJb 1978–9*, 235

R. Strohm: 'Merkmale italienischer Versvertonung in Mozarts Klavierkonzerten', *AnMc*, no.18 (1978), 219

CHAMBER AND ENSEMBLE MUSIC

T. F. Dunhill: *Mozart's String Quartets* (London, 1927, 2/1948)

A. Einstein: 'Mozart's Ten Celebrated String Quartets', *MR*, iii (1942), 159

R. S. Tangemann: 'Mozart's Seventeen Epistle Sonatas', *MQ*, xxxii (1946), 588

W. Fischer: 'Mozarts Weg von der begleiteten Klaviersonate zur Kammermusik mit Klavier', *MJb 1956*, 16

J. Kratochvíl: 'Betrachtungen über die Urfassung des Konzerts für Klarinette und des Quintetts für Klarinette und Streicher von W. A. Mozart', *Internazionale Mozartkonferenz: Praha 1956*, 262

S. T. M. Newman: 'Mozart's G minor Quintet (KV.516) and its Relationship to the G minor Symphony (KV.550)', *MR*, xvii (1956), 287

A.-E. Cherbuliez: 'Bemerkungen zu den "Haydn"-Streichquartetten Mozarts und Haydns "Russischen" Streichquartetten', *MJb 1959*, 28

E. Hess: 'Die "Varianten" im Finale des Streichquintettes KV.593', *MJb 1960–61*, 68

K. Marguerre: 'Mozarts Klaviertrios', *MJb 1960–61*, 282

M. Whewell: 'Mozart's Bassethorn Trios', *MT*, ciii (1962), 19

A. Palm: 'Mozarts Streichquartett d-Moll, KV 421, in der Interpretation Momignys', *MJb 1962–3*, 256

W. Kirkendale: 'More Slow Introductions by Mozart to Fugues of J. S. Bach?', *JAMS*, xvii (1964), 43

L. Finscher: 'Mozarts Mailänder Streichquartette', *Mf*, xix (1966), 270

A. H. King: *Mozart Chamber Music* (London, 1968)

K. Marguerre: 'Die beiden Sonaten-Reihen für Klavier und Geige', *MJb 1968–70*, 327

G. Croll and K. Birsak: 'Anton Stadlers "Bassettklarinette" und das "Stadler-Quintett" KV581: Versuch einer Anwendung', *ÖMz*, xxiv (1969), 3

W. J. Mitchell: 'Giuseppe Sarti and Mozart's Quartet K.421', *CMc*, no.9 (1969), 147

W. S. Newman: 'The Duo Texture of Mozart's K.526: an Essay in Classic Instrumental Style', *Essays in Musicology in Honor of Dragan Plamenac* (Pittsburgh, 1969), 191

W. Hümmeke: *Versuch einer strukturwissenschaftlichen Darstellung der ersten und vierten Sätze der zehn letzten Streichquartette von W. A. Mozart* (Münster, 1970)

I. Hunkemöller: *W. A. Mozarts frühe Sonaten für Violine und Klavier* (Berne and Munich, 1970)

F. László: 'Untersuchungen zum Mozarts "zweiten" Opus 1, Nr.1', *MJb 1971–2*, 149

D. N. Leeson and D. Whitwell: 'Mozart's "Spurious" Wind Octets', *ML*, liii (1972), 377

R. Hellyer: 'Mozart's Harmoniemusik', *MR*, xxxiv (1973), 146

M. Flothuis: 'Die Bläserstücke KV 439b', *MJb 1973–4*, 202

J. A. Vertrees: 'Mozart's String Quartet K465: the History of a Controversy', *CMc*, no.17 (1974), 96

A. Tyson: 'New Light on Mozart's "Prussian" Quartets', *MT*, cxvi (1975), 126

D. N. Leeson and D. Whitwell: 'Concerning Mozart's Serenade in B♭ for Thirteen Instruments, K.361 (370a)', *MJb 1976–7*, 97–130

KEYBOARD

F. Lorenz: *W. A. Mozart als Klavierkomponist* (Breslau, 1866)

H. Schenker: 'Mozart: Sonate a-Moll', *Der Tonwille*, ii (1922), 7

——: 'Mozart: Sonate C-Dur', *Der Tonwille*, iv (1923), 19

N. Broder: 'Mozart and the "Clavier" ', *MQ*, xxvii (1941), 422; repr. in Lang (1963)

H. Ferguson: 'Mozart's Duets for One Pianoforte', *PRMA*, lxxiii (1946–7), 35

W. Mason: 'Melodic Unity in Mozart's Piano Sonata K332', *MR*, xxii (1961), 28

K. von Fischer: 'Mozarts Klaviervariationen: zur Editions- und Aufführungspraxis des späten 18. und frühen 19. Jahrhunderts', *Hans Albrecht in memoriam* (Kassel, 1962), 168

G. Croll: 'Zu Mozarts Larghetto und Allegro Es-Dur für 2 Klaviere', *MJb 1964*, 28

H. Neumann and C. Schachter: 'The Two Versions of Mozart's Rondo K494', *Music Forum*, i (1967), 1–34

R. Rosenberg: *Die Klaviersonaten Mozarts: Gestalt- und Stilanalyse* (Hofheim, Hesse, 1972)

W. Plath: 'Zur Datierung der Klaviersonaten KV 279–284', *Acta Mozartiana*, xxi (1974), 26

*Piano Quarterly*, no.95 (1976) [Mozart issue]

PERFORMING PRACTICE

R. Elveis: *Untersuchungen zu den Tempi in Mozarts Instrumentalmusik* (diss., U. of Berlin, 1952)

W. Fischer: 'Selbstzeugnisse Mozarts für die Aufführungsweise seiner Werke', *MJb 1955*, 7

H. Albrecht, ed.: *Die Bedeutung der Zeichen Keil, Strich und Punkt bei Mozart* (Kassel, 1957)

E. and P. Badura-Skoda: *Mozart-Interpretation* (Vienna and Stuttgart, 1957; Eng. trans., 1962 as *Interpreting Mozart on the Keyboard*)

P. Mies: 'Die Artikulationszeichen Strich und Punkt bei Wolfgang Amadeus Mozart', *Mf*, xi (1958), 428

A. B. Gottron: 'Wie spielte Mozart die Adagios seiner Klavierkonzerte', *Mf*, xiii (1960), 334

C. Bär: 'Zum Begriff des "Basso" in Mozarts Serenaden', *MJb 1960–61*, 133

W. Gerstenberg: 'Authentische Tempi für Mozarts "Don Giovanni" ', *MJb 1960–61*, 58

R. Münster: 'Authentische Tempi zu den sechs letzten Sinfonien W. A. Mozarts?', *MJb 1962–3*, 185

C. Bär: 'Zu einem Mozart'schen Andante-Tempo', *Acta Mozartiana*, x (1963), 78

Z. Śliwiński: 'Ein Beitrag zum Thema: Ausführung der Vorschläge in W. A. Mozarts Klavierwerken', *MJb 1965–6*, 179

C.-H. Mahling: 'Mozart und Orchesterpraxis seiner Zeit', *MJb 1967*, 229

S. Babitz: 'Some Errors in Mozart Performance', *MJb 1968–70*, 62

H. Engel: 'Interpretation und Aufführungspraxis', *MJb 1968–70*, 7 [with proceedings of colloquium of Zentralinstitut für Mozartforschung, 1968]

E. Melkus: 'Über die Ausführung der Stricharten in Mozarts Werken', *MJb 1968–70*, 244

——: 'Zur Auszierung der Da-capo-Arien in Mozarts Werken', *MJb 1968–70*, 159

T. Harmon: 'The Performance of Mozart's Church Sonatas', *ML*, xxxiv (1970), 51

N. Zaslaw: 'Mozart's Tempo Conventions', *IMSCR*, xi *Copenhagen 1972*, 720

M. Bilson: 'Some General Thoughts on Ornamentation in Mozart's Keyboard Works', *Piano Quarterly*, no.95 (1976), 26

**(4) (Maria) Constanze** [Constantia] **(Caecilia Josepha Johanna Aloisia) Mozart** [née Weber; later Nissen] (*b* Zell, Wiesental, 5 Jan 1762; *d* Salzburg, 6 March 1842). Soprano, wife of (3) Wolfgang Amadeus Mozart and later of his biographer Georg Nikolaus Nissen. She was the third of four daughters of the bass, prompter and copyist Fridolin Weber, and thereby related to the composer Carl Maria von Weber (*see* WEBER). Though not gifted with any great musical talent, she had a pleasing, well-trained voice and possessed some skill on the piano. She first met Mozart in 1777–8 in Mannheim; he did not direct his attentions to her then but to her elder sister Aloysia, who rejected him. Constanze moved with her family to Vienna in September 1779; from 2 May 1781 Mozart took lodgings with her mother, and on 4 August 1782

*19. Constanze Mozart, née Weber: portrait (probably 1782) by Joseph Lange in the Hunterian Art Gallery, Glasgow University*

married Constanze in St Stephen's. There were six children, of whom two, (5) Carl Thomas and (6) Franz Xaver Wolfgang, survived to maturity. During a visit to Salzburg, she sang one of the soprano parts in a performance at St Peter's Abbey of the Kyrie and Gloria of her husband's Mass in C minor K427/417*a* (26 October 1783). The coincidence of names has led to the unfounded suggestion that she was portrayed in *Die Entführung* in the character of Constanze.

After Mozart's death she was allowed a pension of one third of his salary. She attempted to improve her unsettled financial position by arranging concerts with his works in various cities, herself singing in several of them. She organized several performances of *La clemenza di Tito*. In 1797 she had a vocal score of *Idomeneo* arranged from Mozart's autograph and published by Breitkopf & Härtel, though without financial success, and in 1800 she sold his remaining manuscripts to the publisher André after first having them set in order by the Abbé Maximilian Stadler and Nissen, who in part managed her affairs. Nissen was a Danish diplomat; she probably first met him in 1797 when he lodged in rooms in her house. They were married on 26 June 1809 in Pressburg (Bratislava) Cathedral. There were no children of her second marriage. In 1810 the couple moved to Copenhagen and in 1821 to Salzburg, where Nissen collected materials for his biography. He died on 29 March 1826, however, before its publication, and left Constanze the responsibility of completing the work and seeing it through the press. The rest of her life was uneventful. Her character is an interesting study: after Mozart's death she seems to have lost all traces of the slovenliness and improvidence that reputedly helped

to wreck his affairs, and, as her diary and correspondence show, became a capable business woman and a devoted mother. Two portraits survive, one from 1782 by her brother-in-law Joseph Lange (Hunterian Art Gallery, Glasgow University; fig.19) and one from 1802 by Hans Hansen (*A-Sm*).

BIBLIOGRAPHY

A. Schurig, ed.: *Konstanze Mozart: Briefe–Aufzeichnungen–Dokumente 1782–1842* (Dresden, 1922)

J.-G. Prod'homme: 'The Wife of Mozart: Constanze Weber', *MQ*, xiii (1927), 384

H. G. Farmer and H. Smith: *New Mozartiana: the Mozart Relics in the Zavertal Collection at the University of Glasgow* (Glasgow, 1935/R1976)

R. Tenschert: 'Mozarts Kompositionen für Konstanze', *Mozart-Almanach auf das Jahr 1941*, 97

O. E. Deutsch: 'Mozarts Nachlass: aus den Briefen Constanzes an den Verlag André', *MJb 1953*, 32

N. Medici di Marignano and R. Hughes: *A Mozart Pilgrimage: Being the Travel Diaries of Vincent and Mary Novello in the Year 1829* (London, 1955/R1975)

R. Schaal: 'Zwei unveröffentlichte Dokumente von Constanze Nissen', *Acta Mozartiana*, xiii (1966), 89

J. H. Eibl: 'Aus den Briefen Constanze Mozarts an die Verleger Breitkopf & Härtel und Johann André', *Musik und Verlag: Karl Vötterle zum 65. Geburtstag* (Kassel, 1968), 238

R. Angermüller and S. Dahms-Schneider: 'Neue Brieffunde zu Mozart', *MJb 1968–70*, 211–41

O. Biba: 'Zu Konstanze Mozarts Pensionsbezug', *Mitteilungen der Internationalen Stiftung Mozarteum*, xx (1972), 20

For further bibliography see under (3) Wolfgang Amadeus Mozart, esp. biographies by Abert, Einstein, Schenk, Schurig

**(5) Carl Thomas Mozart** (*b* Vienna, 21 Sept 1784; *d* Milan, 2 Nov 1858). Second and elder surviving son of (3) Wolfgang Amadeus and (4) Constanze Mozart. Without finishing his schooling, for some of which he was under Franz Xaver Niemetschek in Prague, he went to Livorno in 1797 to begin his apprenticeship with a commercial firm. He planned to open a piano business in the following years, but the project failed for lack of funds. He moved to Milan in 1805 and studied music with Bonifazio Asioli, but gave up his music studies in spring 1810 and became an official in the service of the Viceroy of Naples in Milan. In that year his mother gave him his father's piano. His relationship with his step-father Georg Nikolaus Nissen was particularly happy. He several times visited Salzburg, notably for the unveiling of the Mozart monument in 1842 and at the centenary celebrations in 1856, and Vienna. Much of his correspondence was published in the Mozarteum *Mitteilungen* (1918–21, 1961).

For bibliography see under (6) Franz Xaver Wolfgang Mozart

**(6) Franz Xaver Wolfgang** ['Wolfgang Amadeus'] **Mozart** (*b* Vienna, 26 July 1791; *d* Carlsbad, 29 July 1844). Composer and pianist, the sixth child and younger surviving son of (3) Wolfgang Amadeus and (4) Constanze Mozart. He received his first piano instruction in 1796 from the Mozart biographer, Franx Xaver Niemetschek, in Prague, where he lived with the Dušek family. In Vienna he continued his studies under Sigismund Neukomm, Andreas Streicher, J. N. Hummel, Antonio Salieri, G. J. Vogler and Georg Albrechtsberger. His first compositions, which include the Piano Quartet op.1, appeared in 1802. On 30 March 1807 Salieri declared his pupil to possess 'a rare talent for music', and prophesied a career for him 'not inferior to that of his celebrated father'. On 22 October 1807 Franz Xaver went to Lemberg (now L'vov). In Podkamien he accepted a post as tutor in the home of Count Viktor Baworowski, a position he held until December 1810. In 1811 he became a music teacher in the home of the imperial chamberlain, Janiszewski, in Sarki (near Lemberg). He gave up that post in 1813 and lived as a freelance musician in Lemberg, where he supervised the training of Julie Baroni-Cavalcabó. From 1819 to 1821 he undertook an extended concert tour during which he played in Kiev, Warsaw, Copenhagen (where he saw his mother and stepfather, Georg Nikolaus Nissen), Hamburg, Berlin, Leipzig, Dresden (where he visited his cousin, Carl Maria von Weber), Prague, Vienna, Venice, Milan (where he visited his brother Carl), Zurich, Berne, Frankfurt am Main, Mannheim, Augsburg, Munich and Salzburg (where he visited his aunt, (2) Maria Anna). In 1822 he returned to teach in Lemberg; in 1826 he went to Salzburg to see his mother. In the same year he renewed his studies in counterpoint with Wagenseil's pupil, Johann Mederitsch or Gallus (1752–1835), who bequeathed him all his compositions. Also in that year he founded the Cäcilien-Chor in Lemberg, but in 1838 he left Lemberg and settled in Vienna. In 1841 he was made honorary Kapellmeister of the Dom-Musik-Verein and the Mozarteum in Salzburg, and in 1842 he stayed with his brother there during celebrations on the unveiling of the Mozart memorial; at the festival concert he played his father's D minor Piano Concerto K466. In December of the same year the Congregazione ed Accademica Santa Cecilia in Rome named him *maestro compositore onorario*. In his will Franz Xaver stipulated, among other things, that any of his father's autographs found in his papers, his father's portrait and piano, as well as his own library, should be given to the Dommusik-verein and the Mozarteum as a lasting memorial to his father. This Mozart-Nichlass passed partly to the Internationale Stiftung Mozarteum and partly to the consistorial archive in Salzburg.

The brilliant pianistic figuration prominent in Franz Xaver's music reveals the particular influence of his teacher Hummel. The more relaxed quality and richer sonority of his piano writing, as reflected especially in his Second Piano Concerto (1818), however, hint at the characteristic piano style of Chopin and Liszt.

## WORKS

For further details, see Hummel (1956), 314ff; all printed works published in Vienna, unless otherwise stated.

### VOCAL

With orch: Der erste Frühlingstag, cantata, 4 solo vv, chorus, op.28 (1827); Festchor, cantata, solo vv, chorus, op.30 (1842) [for unveiling of Mozart memorial in Salzburg]; Aria buffa, 1v, op.13, *A-Sm* (autograph dated 15 Jan 1808), *GB-Lbm* (autograph), for inc. facs. see Hummel, 322f [for insertion in W. A. Mozart: Der Schauspieldirektor]; Lied für die heilige Christnacht, 2 S, org, private collection, Vienna; Cantata for Haydn's birthday, 1805, lost

Choral without orch: Die Nacht (Uz), 3vv, composed 1826, pubd in *Wiener Zeitschrift*, li (1839); Frühlingsgruss (Die Frühlingsgöttin nahet), 3vv, pf (Dresden, n.d.); Von der Hoheit lichtem Glanz umflossen, 4 solo vv, 1828, autograph, *A-Sm*; Pour des morts, autograph, *Sm* [15 nos. incl. lieder]

Lieder with pf: Romanze (In der Väter Hallen ruht) (Stollberg), op.12 (1808) [for (4) Constanze]; Arietta (In questa tomba oscura) (1808); 8 deutsche Lieder (1810); 6 Lieder, op.21 (Hamburg, 1820); An Emma (Weit in nebelgraue Ferne) (Schiller), op.24 (Hamburg, 1820); 3 deutsche Lieder, op.27 (1820); Vaudevilles, autograph, *Sm* [16 sketches for Fr. songs]; Erinnerung (Byron), *Wst*; Ständchen, *Wgm* (inc.)

2 untitled duets, *Wgm*; for other works cited in auction catalogues see Hummel (1956), 319

### INSTRUMENTAL

Orch: 2 pf concs., C, op.14 (Leipzig, 1809), ed. R. Angermüller (Salzburg, 1972), Eb, op.25 (Leipzig, 1818); Konzertvariationen, pf, orch (Graz, 1820); Sinfonia, D, autograph, *A-Sm* (2 movts); 12 Minuets and Trios (1808)

Chamber: pf qt, op.1 (1802), ed. in Diletto musicale, no.180 (Vienna, 1966); Sei piccoli pezzi, fl, 2 hn, op.11 (1808); 2 vn sonatas, Bb, op.7 (1808), F, op.15 (Leipzig, 1813); Grande Sonate, E, vn/vc, pf, op.19 (Leipzig, 1820), ed. W. Boettcher for vc (Mainz, 1969); Rondo (Sonate), fl, pf, autograph, *Sm*, ed. R. Ermeler (Wilhelmshaven, 1962)

Pf: Sonata, op.10 (Offenbach, 1808); 12 Polonaises, op.17 (Leipzig, c1815), op.22 (Leipzig, 1820), op.26 (Padua, after 1820); 11 sets of variations: Minuet from Don Juan (1805); Russian theme (1809); theme, G, op.13 (1810); March from Coriolan, op.16 (Leipzig, 1813); Air russe variée, op.18 (Milan, 1820); Romance by Méhul, op.23 (Leipzig, 1820); Veränderungen über einen Walzer (1824); March from Aline (before 1828); Variations sur un thème favorit (n.d.); 2 other sets (n.d.); Rondo, F, 1802, autograph, *Sm*; Allegretto, 9 Aug 1841, facs. of autograph, *Sm*; Adagio, autograph, *Sm*; for details of other works in autograph, *Sm*, and in auction catalogues see Hummel (1956), 318–19

### BIBLIOGRAPHY

A. Fuchs: 'Biographische Skizze von Wolfgang Amadeus Mozart (dem Sohne)', *Allgemeine Wiener Musik-Zeitung*, iv/11 (1844)
——: 'Gedächtnisfeier am Sterbetag W. A. Mozarts des Sohnes', *Allgemeine Wiener Musik-Zeitung*, v/107 (1845)
——: 'W. A. Mozart's (des Sohnes) Vermächtnis an das Mozarteum in Salzburg', *Allgemeine Wiener Musik-Zeitung*, v/6 (1845)
A. Schmid: 'W. A. Mozart (Sohn)', *Denksteine* (Vienna, 1848), 75
J. Fischer: *Wolfgang Amadeus Mozart (Sohn): eine biographische Skizze, sowie zwei bisher unbekannte Briefe Mozart's (Vater)* (Carlsbad, c1888)
J. E. Engl: 'Die den Vater überlebenden Söhne Carl und Wolfgang und die übrigen Kinder W. A. Mozarts', *Jahresbericht der Internationalen Stiftung Mozarteum*, xiii (1893), 41; also in *Studien über W. A. Mozart*, ii (Salzburg, 1894), 4
O. E. Deutsch: 'Der Sohn: eine Studie über W. A. Mozart den Jüngeren mit neuen Mitteilungen', *Musica divina*, ii (1914), 362
E. K. Blümml: 'Mozarts Kinder: eine Matrikelstudie', *Mozarteums-Mitteilungen*, i/3 (1918–19), 1
K. Geiringer: 'W. A. Mozart the Younger', *MQ*, xxvii (1941), 456
A. E. Schroeder: 'De betekenis von Mozart's zoon Wolfgang Amadeus aan de hand van zijn reisdagboek (1819–1821)', *RBM*, iv (1950), 111
A. vander Linden: 'Lettres de W. A. Mozart junior', *RBM*, v (1951), 147–76
W. Hummel: 'W. A. Mozarts Söhne: Quellen und Schrifttum zur Darstellung ihrer Lebensbilder', *MJb 1954*, 65

——: *W. A. Mozarts Söhne* (Kassel and Basle, 1956)
C. Nemeth: 'Der "Fest-Chor" und ein unbekanntes Autograph von W. A. Mozart Sohn', *ÖMz*, xiii (1958), 302
W. Hummel: 'W. A. Mozart-Sohn im Banne der Romantik', *Mitteilungen der Internationalen Stiftung Mozarteum*, xi (1963), 18
K. M. Pisarowitz and W. Hummel: 'Frühe Briefe des Mozart-Sohnes Wolfgang Amadeus (1791–1844)', *Mitteilungen der Internationalen Stiftung Mozarteum*, xi (1963), 21
W. Hummel: 'Bücherschau: 10 Jahre W. A. Mozart Söhne', *Mitteilungen der Internationalen Stiftung Mozarteum*, xv (1967), 19
A. vander Linden: 'Le dernier fils de W. A. Mozart', *Bulletin de la Classe des Beaux-arts de l'Académie royale de Belgique*, l (1968), 46
R. Angermüller and S. Dahms-Schneider: 'Neue Brieffunde zu Mozart', *MJb 1968–70*, 211–41
D. Kolbin: 'Lwower Lithographie des Porträts von Franz Xaver Mozart', *Mitteilungen der Internationalen Stiftung Mozarteum*, xx/3–4 (1972), 1

For further bibliography see under (3) Wolfgang Amadeus Mozart
WOLFGANG PLATH (1)
RUDOLPH ANGERMÜLLER (2, 4 with C. B. OLDMAN, 5, 6)
STANLEY SADIE (3, work-list with ANTHONY HICKS)

**Mozarteum.** Conservatory in Salzburg founded in 1841 as the Dommusikverein und Mozarteum; *see* SALZBURG, §4.

**'Mozart' fifths** (Ger. *Mozartquinten*). Consecutive 5ths occurring when the German 6th chord resolves directly to the dominant (*see* CONSECUTIVE FIFTHS, CONSECUTIVE OCTAVES, ex.9).

**Mozart societies.** The most important organization named after Mozart and aiming to promote his music is the Salzburg Dommusikverein und Mozarteum – now the Internationale Stiftung Mozarteum – founded in 1841 by Franz von Hilleprandt to renew the city's musical activity after its cessation in the Napoleonic wars; it has developed as one of the central institutions of Salzburg's musical life, and with its offshoots, the Internationale Mozart-Gemeinde, Zentralinstitut für Mozartforschung and the Mozart-Museum (in the house where he was born), is one of the most important centres of Mozart scholarship (for its history, *see* SALZBURG). Since the first half of the 19th century numerous Mozart societies have been founded in other parts of Europe. The earliest was that formed in Prague in 1837 to commemorate the 50th anniversary of the première of *Don Giovanni*; it erected a Mozart monument and founded a Mozart museum, which was moved to the Villa Bertramka in 1927. A Mozart-Stiftung was founded in Frankfurt am Main in 1837 to help talented musicians learn composition. The Berlin Mozartgemeinde was founded in 1894 as a branch of the Internationale Mozart-Gemeinde and was active until the 1930s, publishing research material in its *Mitteilungen*; it was re-established after World War II by H. J. Moser. The Dresden Mozart-Verein was founded in 1897 to perform Mozart's works; it revived the Mass in C minor in 1901. The Vienna Mozartgemeinde was formed in 1941, and has sponsored such diverse activities as concerts, commemorations, awarding a Mozart medal, encouraging young performers and publishing the bulletin *Wiener Figaro*. In 1951 E. F. Schmid founded the Deutsche Mozart-Gesellschaft in Augsburg to coordinate the numerous local German societies; it has promoted annual Mozart festivals and published *Acta mozartiana* from 1953. Mozart societies have also been founded in the Netherlands (1902), Budapest (1926) and Zurich (1940).

based on *MGG* (ix, 839–42) by permission of Bärenreiter
WALTER HUMMEL

**Mozeen,** Mrs. *See* EDWARDS (ii).

**mp.** *Mezzopiano* (It.: 'moderately soft'); *see* MEZZO, MEZZA.

**Mraczek** [Mráček], **Joseph Gustav** (*b* Brno, 12 March 1878; *d* Dresden, 24 Dec 1944). Czech composer. He studied under his father, the cellist František Mráček (1842–98), at Brno and at Vienna Conservatory under Grädener, Hellmesberger and Löwe. He led the Brno theatre orchestra, 1897–1902, and taught the violin at the conservatory from 1898. In 1919 he moved to Dresden, teaching composition at the conservatory and, until 1924, conducting the Dresden PO. Among his orchestral music *Max und Moritz* (1912), a brilliantly orchestrated piece in the Strauss manner based on Wilhelm Busch's nursery stories, was especially popular.

WORKS
*(selective list)*
Dramatic: Der gläserne Pantoffel, opera, Brno, 1902; Der Traum (after Grillparzer), opera, Brno, 1909; Kismet, ballet, Munich, 1912; Aebelö (Nikisch), opera, Breslau, 1915; Ikdar (Glück), opera, Dresden, 1921; Madonna am Wiesenzaun oder Herrn Dürers Bild (Ostermann), opera, Hanover, 1927; Der Liebesrat, unperf; Der arme Tobias, radio/concert opera, 1936
Other: Rustans Traum, symphonic poem, 1911; Max und Moritz, symphonic burlesque, 1912; Orientalische Skizzen, chamber orch, 1918; Eva, symphonic poem, 1922; Variété, scenes for orch, 1928; also chamber, choral and pf music, songs

BIBLIOGRAPHY
E. H. Müller: *Joseph Gustav Mraczek* (Dresden, 1917)
ALFRED LOEWENBERG/R

**Mravina** [Mravinskaya], **Evgeniya Konstantinovna** (*b* St Petersburg, 16 Feb 1864; *d* Yalta, 25 Oct 1914). Russian soprano. She studied with Pryanishnikov who, as one of the foremost operatic baritones of the day (he was the first St Petersburg Onegin), was able to teach her much about the musical and dramatic interpretation of operatic roles; as a result Mravina became probably the first Russian female singer to regard opera as more than a concert in costume. From 1886 to 1897 she sang at the Mariinsky Theatre, including in her repertory the parts of Antonida in *A Life for the Tsar* and Lyudmila in Glinka's second opera, Tatyana in *Eugene Onegin*, and roles in operas by Gounod, Meyerbeer and Wagner. An outstandingly beautiful woman, she possessed a voice of exceptional purity and an ability for irreproachable enunciation; yet these natural attributes were at the service of an intelligent mind and were always used to appropriate dramatic and musical ends.

BIBLIOGRAPHY
E. Stark: *Peterburgskaya opera i eyo mastera 1890–1910* [The St Petersburg Opera and its masters 1890–1910] (Moscow, 1940)
E. Alexeyeva: 'Evgeniya Mravina', *SovM* (1964), no.4, p.92
A. Kollontay: 'Iz vospominaniy' [Reminiscences], *SovM* (1964), no.4, p.98
E. Mravina: 'Stranichka memuarov' [A page of memoirs], *SovM* (1964), no.4, p.99
A. Grigoreva: *E. K. Mravina* (Moscow, 1970)
M. MONTAGU-NATHAN/JENNIFER SPENCER

**Mravinsky, Evgeny (Alexandrovich)** (*b* St Petersburg, 4 June 1906). Soviet conductor. He studied at the Leningrad Conservatory, graduating from Vladimir Shcherbachov's composition class in 1930 and Alexander Gauk's conducting class in 1931. From 1932 to 1938 he was conductor of the Leningrad Academic Opera and Ballet Theatre (now the Kirov). In 1938 he won first prize in the All-Union Conductors' Competition in Moscow, and became chief conductor of the Leningrad PO; under his direction the orchestra has won international acclaim, touring in many countries (including Finland, Czechoslovakia, West Germany and Italy). He was made People's Artist of the USSR in 1954.

Mravinsky is an outstanding representative of the Soviet school of orchestral conductors: he combines acute perception with respect for the score, breadth of style with fine attention to detail; and he achieves subtle gradations of colour and an ideal balance between orchestral groups. In spite of meticulous preparation, his performances are marked by an atmosphere of spontaneous emotion, for behind his economy of gesture lies a resolute temperament. He has a broad repertory, founded on the works of Beethoven and Tchaikovsky, and is particularly noted for his interpretations of the music of Soviet composers: Prokofiev, Myaskovsky, Khachaturian, Kabalevsky, Shcherbachov, Shteynberg and Shostakovich, the premières of whose symphonies nos.5, 6, 8 (dedicated to him), 9 and 10 he conducted.

BIBLIOGRAPHY
V. Bogdanov-Berezovsky: *Sovetskiy dirizhor* [A Soviet conductor] (Leningrad, 1956)

I. M. YAMPOL'SKY

**Mṛdaṅgam.** Indian double-headed barrel drum; *see* BANGLADESH, §5, and INDIA, SUBCONTINENT OF, §§I, 3 (ii); II, 6(iii); VII, 4(ii).

**MS.** (1) *Mano sinistra* (It.: 'left hand'); *see* ABBREVIATIONS.

(2) Manuscript; *see* AUTOGRAPH; SOURCES, MS; SOURCES OF INSTRUMENTAL ENSEMBLE MUSIC TO 1630; SOURCES OF KEYBOARD MUSIC TO 1600; SOURCES OF LUTE MUSIC.

**Mshvelidze, Shalva Mikhaylovich** (*b* Tbilisi, 28 May 1904). Soviet composer, teacher and ethnomusicologist. His interest in music began in the Tbilisi Gymnasium choir. Later, after the family had moved to Surami in east Georgia, he took part in folk ensembles and, from 1920 to 1925, directed amateur student and army choirs, teaching and performing mostly folksongs. He entered the choir-training department of the Tbilisi Conservatory but, on the recommendation of Arakishvili, transferred to the composition class. There he studied with Bagrinovsky and also had lessons at the Leningrad Conservatory with Shcherbachov, Tyulin, Shteynberg and Ryazanov. He graduated from the Tbilisi Conservatory in 1930 and then undertook postgraduate studies with Shcherbachov. His ethnomusicological research, which has become an important part of his wide activities, began with expeditions in 1927. In 1929 he began teaching at the Tbilisi Conservatory, where he was made professor in 1942. He has held administrative posts at various times, notably as deputy director of the Tbilisi Opera and Ballet Theatre, head of the educational institutions department of the board for art affairs of the Georgian SSR Sovnarkom (Council of People's Commissars), and director and artistic director of the Georgian State Song and Dance Ensemble. He has also been chairman of the board of the Georgian Composers' Union (1941–51), a board member of the Composers' Union of the USSR and a deputy to the Supreme Soviet of the Georgian

SSR (1951–6). The honours he holds include the titles Honoured Art Worker of the Georgian SSR (1941) and People's Artist of the Georgian SSR (1958), the State Prize (1942, 1947), the Paliashvili Prize (1972), the Nehru State Prize of India (1973), the Order of Lenin, the Order of the Red Banner of Labour (twice) and the Order of Friendship of the Peoples of the USSR.

Mshvelidze has played an important part in the formation and development of 20th-century Georgian music. As in the work of his contemporaries, forms and modes of thought new to Georgian music originated and became established in his music, which shows the achievement of an organic fusion of national traditions and European music in general. In particular, Mshvelidze laid the foundations for Georgian epic symphonism, for which his symphonic poem *Zviadauri* (1940) was the first significant model. Here the ideas of Vasha Pshavela's poem *Stumar–maspindzeli* ('Guest and host') – a tragic collision of high humanist ideals with the stern traditions of mountain tribes – are laid bare. A close connection with the modal and cadential features of archaic Georgian folk music marks the work; its dramatic structure is founded on the transformation of contrasting themes, representing images in the poem, which are developed in a rhapsodic manner peculiar to the composer. His characteristic programmaticism is also present in the following works stimulated by the events of World War II: the First Symphony (1943), dedicated to the heroic defence of the Caucasus, and the Second (1944), sub-titled *Sikharulisa da gamardzvelis simfonia* ('Symphony of joy and victory'). The Third Symphony (1952) earned him a wide reputation; distinguished by a stylistic expansion, it illustrates the reclamation of the waste region at Samgori (near Tbilisi) by juxtaposing contrasted musical pictures of the desert's past and its subsequent bringing to life. Mshvelidze's studies in the 1950s of Indian music and its local variants led to the composition of the Indian Suite for orchestra (1955), which won him the Nehru Prize. His Fourth Symphony (1968) is dedicated to the 50th anniversary of the October Revolution.

As an opera composer, Mshvelidze has developed the tradition of the national classics. This is shown with particular force in *Ambavi Tarielisa* ('The legend of Tariel'), based on *Vepkhis tkaosani* ('The knight in the tigerskin') by the 12th-century Georgian poet Shota Rustaveli. The work is in the heroic-epic mould: strongly developed choral scenes occupy an important place in the dramatic structure, and the opera's measured narrative character lends it the quality of an oratorio. Mshvelidze produced a second epic piece in *Didostatis mardzhvena* ('The hand of a great master'), a monumental music drama treating the tragic fate of the architect Arsakidze and his beloved, the clash of powerful human passions against a broad panorama of 11th-century Georgia, and the history of the building of the Svetitskhoveli Temple, a classic of Georgian architecture. Here again the work depends to a great extent on the chorus, and it achieves an expressive combination of archaic folk strata and developed recitative and arioso.

WORKS
*(selective list)*

Operas: Ambavi Tarielisa [The legend of Tariel] (4, A. Pagava, after Rustaveli), Tbilisi, 1946, rev. 1966; Didostatis mardzhvena [The hand of a great master] (N. Dzidzishvili, after K. Gamsakhurdia), Tbilisi, 1961; Dzhariskatsis kvrivi [Widow of a soldier], 1967; Aluda Ketelauri, 1972
Oratorios: Kavkasioni, 1949; Vekam v predan'ye [The legend to survive the centuries], 1970

Orch: Zviadauri, sym. poem after Pshavela, 1940; 4 syms., 1943, 1944,
1952, 1968; Mindiya, sym. poem after Pshavela, 1950; Indian Suite,
1955; Polyphonic Suite, 1956; Na prostorakh Birmï [In the plains of
Burma], suite, 1958; Vepkhi da mokme [The tiger and the young
man], sym. poem after trad. poem, 1962
Other works: songs, choruses, folksong arrs., chamber pieces, pf and
org compositions, incidental music, film scores

Principal publishers: Muzfond Gruzii (Tbilisi), Muzgiz, Muzïka,
Sovetskiy Kompozitor (Moscow and Leningrad)

### WRITINGS

'Khalkhurobisa da realizmis gzit' [Along the path of folk style and
realism], Sabchota khelovneba (Tbilisi, 1958), no.6, p.10
Sakravtmtsodneoba [The study of instruments] (Tbilisi, 1965)
'Indoetis musikosebtan' [Among India's musicians], Sabchota khelov-
neba (1967), no.9, p.55
'Muzïka stranï chudes' [The music of the land of wonders], SovM
(1967), no.8, p.116
'Kartuli musikis didi moamage' [A great figure in Georgian art],
Sabchota khelovneba (1973), no.3, p.4

### BIBLIOGRAPHY

A. Ostretsov: 'Zviadauri Sh. Mshvelidze', SovM (1941), no.3, p.40
V. Donadze: Sh. Mshvelidze (Tbilisi, 1946)
M. Koval': 'K novïm tvorcheskim uspekham' [Towards new creative
successes], SovM (1950), no.1, p.4
V. Belïy and V. Vanslov: 'Novoye v gruzinskom simfonizme'
[Something new in Georgian symphonism], SovM (1954), no.9, p.9
A. Tsulukidze: 'Tret'ya simfoniya Sh. Mshvelidze' [Mshvelidze's Third
Symphony], SovM (1955), no.2, p.28
E. Dzidzadze: 'Kartuli sabchota opera' [A Georgian Soviet opera],
Sabchota khelovneba (1958), no.3, p.33
G. Toradze: Simfonicheskiye poemï Shalvi Mshvelidze Zviadauri i
Mindiya (Moscow, 1958)
M. Pichkhadze: 'Indiyskaya syuita Sh. Mshvelidze', SovM (1959), no.9,
p.35
G. Ordzhonikidze: 'Opera epos', SovM (1962), no.11, p.13
——: '60 let bol'shomu khudozhniku' [A great artist's 60th birthday],
SovM (1964), no.6, p.11
A. Shaverzashvili: Fugi Sh. Mshvelidze (Tbilisi, 1964)
A. Tsulukidze: Sh. Mshvelidze (Tbilisi, 1964)
A. Shaverzashvili: 'Simfoniuri orkestris teoriuli sapudzvlebi'
[Theoretical foundations of the symphony orchestra], Sabchota
khelovneba (1966), no.7, p.24
G. Toradze: 'Tret'ya simfoniya Sh. Mshvelidze', Sovetskaya simfoniya
za 50 let, ed. G. Tigranov (Leningrad, 1967), 211
A. Khachaturian: 'Sh. Mshvelidze: 70 let', SovM (1974), no.11, p.36
E. Machavariani: 'Beseda s Sh. Mshvelidze' [A chat with Mshvelidze],
SovM (1974), no.11, p.38

EVGENY MACHAVARIANI

**Mt'açmideli, George** (d 1065). Hymnographer of the
Georgian Church; see GEORGIAN RITE, MUSIC OF THE.

**Mubārak Shah.** See SHARḤ MAWLĀNĀ MUBĀRAK SHĀH
BAR ADIVĀR.

**Muck, Carl** (b Darmstadt, 22 Oct 1859; d Stuttgart, 3
March 1940). German conductor. The son of a gifted
amateur musician, he studied classical philology in
Heidelberg and Leipzig. In 1880, the year he obtained
his PhD, he made his début in the Leipzig Gewandhaus
with Scharwenka's Piano Concerto in B♭ minor. Without
ever completing any real course in conducting, he
devoted himself from that time onwards to conducting
operas. After engagements in Zurich, Salzburg, Brno
and Graz he was appointed principal Kapellmeister at
Angelo Neumann's Deutsches Landestheater in Prague
in 1886. Even at that early date he laid the foundations
of his reputation as a conductor of Wagner's works with
exemplary performances of the Ring. In 1892 he
became principal Kapellmeister of the Berlin Opera,
where he was appointed general music director in 1908.
From 1894 to 1911 he directed the Silesian music
festivals in Görlitz as guest conductor, Wagnerian performances at Covent Garden in London, and the
Parsifal performances in Bayreuth after 1901. In 1912
he took over the directorship of the Boston SO, and
from 1922 to 1933 he conducted the Hamburg PO.

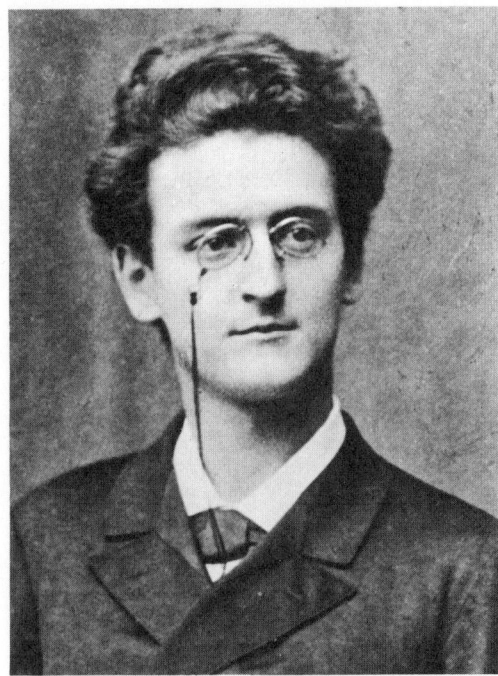

*Carl Muck*

An advocate of Classical and Romantic rather than
modern music, Muck had an unerring ear. He was an
unrelentingly strict orchestra trainer, and always intent
on absolute fidelity to the score. Contemporaries described his conducting as strikingly economical, and
praised his sense of form and the strict rhythm of his
interpretations. Muck, who conducted the Parsifal performances in Bayreuth for almost three decades (where,
according to the singer Frida Leider, he preferred
unusually slow tempos), was considered in his time to be
the greatest conductor of Wagner's works. However, he
also enjoyed unchallenged supremacy as an interpreter
of Bruckner's symphonies (which he gave without cuts).
Despite his lack of sympathy for most 20th-century
music, he supported some contemporary works, including Schoenberg's Five Orchestral Pieces op.16 and
Stravinsky's Pulcinella.

### BIBLIOGRAPHY

W. Zinne: 'Carl Muck', Die Musik, xvii (1924–5), 669
K. Stephenson: Hundert Jahre Philharmonische Gesellschaft in
Hamburg (Hamburg, 1928)
H. Schonberg: The Great Conductors (New York, 1967), 216ff
J. J. Badel: 'The Strange Case of Dr. Karl Muck, who was Tor-
pedoed by The Star-spangled Banner during World War I', High
Fidelity, xx/10 (1970), 55

HANS CHRISTOPH WORBS

**Mudarra, Alonso** (b Palencia diocese, Spain, c1510;
d Seville, 1 April 1580). Spanish vihuelist and composer.
He was brought up at Guadalajara in the households of
the third and fourth dukes of Infantado, Diego Hurtado
de Mendoza (1461–1531) and Iñigo López de Mendoza
(1493–1566). In 1529 the latter accompanied Charles
V on a visit to Spanish territories in Italy; it is likely that
Mudarra travelled with him. His elder brother
Francisco represented Seville Cathedral as procurator
at the papal court in Rome from about 1539 to 1555; he
also held a Seville canonry. With the aid of his brother's
powerful influence Alonso became a Seville Cathedral

canon on 18 October 1546. During the next 34 years he played an increasingly important role in cathedral affairs: in 1556 he took charge of the annual Corpus Christi festival arrangements, in 1560 he persuaded the chapter to hire two of the best shawm players in Spain, from 1566 to 1573 he headed the committee that arranged the purchase and installation of a new organ (built by the Flemish Mestre Jox), and on 20 March 1568 he was elected major-domo of the cathedral, in charge of all disbursements. After his death, his possessions were sold by auction and the money distributed to the Sevillian poor on 6 June 1582 according to the provisions of his will.

On 7 December 1546 Mudarra's *Tres libros de musica en cifras para vihuela* (dedicated to a royal councillor, Luis Zapata) was published in Seville. The volume contains over 70 compositions for six-course vihuela, four-course guitar and voice and vihuela. The instrumental pieces include 27 fantasias, eight tientos (one of which is ciphered for harp in a 14-line tablature), two pavans based on the folia and one on the *passamezzo antico*, a galliard, and sets of chain variations on the familiar *Conde claros* and *Guardame las vacas*. Mudarra also intabulated seven mass sections by Josquin and one by Fevin, and motets by Gombert and Willaert. Among the songs with vihuela accompaniment are pieces with Latin texts; he was the first in Spain to set texts by Horace, Ovid and Virgil; also included are settings of the Italians Petrarch and Sannazaro, and five villancicos and three *romances* in Spanish and Galician. His *Nisi Dominus* was the first *fabordón* psalm printed in Spain. The *Fantasia que contrahaze la harpa en la manera de Ludovico* (Ferdinand V's court harpist) uses extremely daring dissonances and is the first printed piece to use the descending Phrygian tetrachord which is now considered a hallmark of the Andalusian style. Like other Spanish vihuelists and composers, Mudarra used mensuration signs to indicate tempo: Ø for allegro, C for moderato and ¢ for lento (see Jacobs). Luis Venegas de Henestrosa reprinted for keyboard a number of Mudarra's compositions and intabulations; some of the tientos which Mudarra had published as preludes to the fantasias were placed by Henestrosa after their respective fantasias.

#### WORKS

Tres libros de musica en cifras para vihuela (Seville, 1546); ed. in MME, vii (1949); 20 pieces transc. for kbd in L. Venegas de Henestrosa: Libro de cifra nueva para tecla, harpa, y vihuela (Alcalá de Henares, 1557); ed. in MME, ii (1944)

#### BIBLIOGRAPHY

J. Ward: 'The Editorial Methods of Venegas de Henestrosa', *MD*, vi (1952), 108, 111
——: 'The Use of Borrowed Material in 16th-century Instrumental Music', *JAMS*, v (1952), 93
——: *The Vihuela de mano and its Music (1536–1576)* (diss., New York U., 1953), 375f; music suppl., 11f, 24, 42f
M. Schneider: 'Un villancico de Alonso de Mudarra procedente de la música popular granadina', *AnM*, x (1955), 79
R. Stevenson: *Spanish Cathedral Music of the Golden Age* (Berkeley and Los Angeles, 1961), 141f, 149, 154f, 158f, 160, 162, 226f, 231
C. Jacobs: *Tempo Notation in Renaissance Spain* (New York, 1964)
ROBERT STEVENSON

**Mudd** [Mudde, Mud]. English family of composers and organists active as church musicians in the 16th and 17th centuries. Many works are ascribed in manuscript sources merely to 'Mudd' or 'Mr Mudd' and may not be attributed definitely to any member of the family.

**(1) Henry** [Harry] **Mudde** [Moode, Moud, Mudge] (*d* London, ?c1588). In 1573 he was described as 'organ

player' of St Paul's Cathedral and in 1574 as one of the vicars-choral there. From 1575 until his death he held the office of parish clerk at St Dunstan-in-the-West, London, where he seems to have directed the music. A four-part In Nomine (in *GB-Ob*) is attributed to him.

**(2) John Mudd** (*b* London, 1555; buried Peterborough, 16 Dec 1631). Son of (1) Henry Mudde. He was educated at St Paul's School and matriculated at Gonville and Caius College, Cambridge, in 1573. After his graduation in 1576 he is not heard of until, on 7 July 1582, he was appointed Master of the Choristers at Southwell collegiate church. From Michaelmas 1583 until his retirement in June 1631 he was organist at Peterborough Cathedral. Two anthems can be attributed to him: *Plead thou my cause* and *Sing joyfully*. He should not be confused with the John Mudd who is recorded as a minor canon at St Paul's in 1636 and 1638 and who died in 1639.

**(3) Thomas Mudd** [Mudde] **(i)** (*b* London, c1560; *d* after 1619). Son of (1) Henry Mudde. He was educated at St Paul's School and matriculated at Gonville and Caius College, Cambridge, in 1577; at the request of the dean of St Paul's he was awarded an exhibition which he held from 1578 until 1587. He was apparently refused his degree at Caius, on religious grounds, and took the BA at Peterhouse (1581) and the MA at Pembroke College (1584); he was elected to a fellowship there and later a music lecture was established for his benefit. He was evidently a well-known musician in his day as Francis Meres listed him as one of England's 16 'excellent musitians' (*Palladis Tamia*, 1598). He left Cambridge to become rector of Cooling, Kent (from 1592), and vicar of Cobham, Kent (1603–19). It is often difficult to differentiate between the works of Thomas Mudd (i) and Thomas Mudd (ii) when they are simply signed or attributed to 'Thomas Mudd', but the following can be ascribed to Thomas (i): a five-part In Nomine, a five-part *In Nomine de profundis*, two anthems (*I will always give thanks* and *Lord, hear my voice*), two keyboard pieces and nine short viol pieces.

**(4) Thomas Mudd** **(ii)** (*b* ?Peterborough; *d* probably at Durham, buried 2 Aug 1667). Son of (2) John Mudd. In 1619 he was a chorister at Peterborough Cathedral; he succeeded his father as cathedral organist on 9 June 1631 but remained there only until 1632. His name next appears in the accounts of Exeter Cathedral (1660–61), though at that time he held no official position there. He then returned to Peterborough Cathedral where, in 1662, he was made a petty canon on condition that he took holy orders; he did not do so and by the end of the same year he was organist at Lincoln Cathedral but was soon dismissed for his unruly behaviour and drunkenness. On 5 March 1664 he was appointed organist at Exeter Cathedral, but he held this post for little more than a year. On 20 August 1666 he became Master of the Choristers at York Minster, but this appointment lasted only two weeks; the record of his burial at Durham refers to him as the organist of York Minster. The Service in D (in *GB-Ob*) may be attributed to him.

#### WORKS

*(many attributed to 'Mudd', or 'Mr Mudd' etc in the sources)*
Full Service (TeD, Jub, Ky, Cr, San), D, *GB-Ob* [by Thomas Mudd (ii)]
Full Service (TeD, Jub, Ky, Cr, San, Mag, Nunc), d, *EL*
Service ['Mr Mudd's First Service'] (TeD, Jub, Mag, Nunc), d, *PB*
Service ['Mr Mudd's Second Service'] (TeD, Jub, Mag, Nunc), *PB*
Te Deum, *Ob*, *T*, Susi Jeans's private collection, Dorking, Surrey
Magnificat, *WB*; New Magnificat in G sol re ut, *WB*
Bow down thine ear, verse, anthem, *EL* (inc.)
I will always give thanks, verse anthem, *Cjc* (wrongly attrib. John

Mudd; inc.), *Cp*, *DRc* (inc.), *EL*, *Lbm* (inc.), *LF* (inc.), *T* (inc.), *US-SM* (inc.); text pr. in J. Clifford, The Divine Services and Anthems (London, 1663) [by Thomas Mudd (i)]

I will sing the mercies of the Lord, verse anthem, text only in Anthems to be Sung . . . in the Cathedral Church of the Holy and Undivided Trinity in Dublin (Dublin, 1662)

Hear my crying, O God, anthem, *Cp* (attrib. 'Mudd' in index, attrib. 'Hutchinson of York' in some partbooks)

Laudate Dominum, 3vv, bc, *Ge*

Let thy merciful ears, full anthem, 4vv, *Cp* (inc.), *DRc*, *Lbm* (inc.), *Y* (attrib. Strogers; inc.); ed. in TCM, xxxv (n.d.), attrib. T. Weelkes

Lift up your heads, verse anthem, inc., *DRc*, *Lbm* (attrib. J. Hutchinson)

Lord [O Lord], hear my voice when I cry, verse anthem, music lost, *Lbm*, *Ob* [by Thomas Mudd (i)]

O clap your hands, verse anthem, *Cp* (inc.)

Of mortall men [Southwell Anthem], *Cp* (attrib. 'Mudd' in index, attrib. Hutchinson on some partbooks)

O God, thou art my God, verse anthem, inc., *DRc*, *Lbm*, *LF*

O God who hast prepared, full anthem, 4vv, *DRc*, *EL* (inc.), *Lbm*; ed. J. Morehen (Croydon, 1965)

Plead thou my cause, full anthem, *LF* (inc.) [by John Mudd]

Sing joyfully, anthem, 6vv, insts, *Lbm* (attrib. 'Mr Mudd of Peter'; inc.) [by John Mudd]

We beseech thee, O Lord, full anthem, *EL* (inc.)

In Nomine, a 4, *Ob* [by Henry Mudde]

In Nomine, a 5, *Lbm*; In Nomine de profundis, a 5, *T* (inc.); 9 pieces, 3 viols, bc, *Lbm*; A Lesson of Voluntarie, The Answer to ye Former Lesson, kbd, *F-Pn* [all by Thomas Mudd (i)]

### BIBLIOGRAPHY

Act of Court Books of the Mercers Company, London (MS)

J. Venn and S. C. Venn: *Admissions to Gonville and Caius College* (London, 1887)

A. Attwater: *A Short History of Pembroke College, Cambridge* (Cambridge, 1936, 2/1973)

J. Noble: 'Le répertoire instrumental anglais: 1550–1585', *La musique instrumentale de la Renaissance: CNRS Paris 1954*, 91

P. le Huray: *The English Anthem, 1603–1660* (diss., U. of Cambridge, 1959)

SUSI JEANS

**Muddy Waters** [Morganfield, McKinley] (*b* Rolling Fork, Mississippi, 4 April 1915). Black American blues singer and guitarist. He first learnt the harmonica and changed to the guitar when he was 17. In 1941–2 he was recorded in Mississippi for the Library of Congress; his *I be's Troubled* and *Country Blues* from these sessions show the influence of Son House, whom he knew personally, and the recordings of Robert Johnson. In 1943 he moved to Chicago, where in 1947 he began to record commercially under the name Muddy Waters. By this time he had taken up the electric guitar, which he played with a vibrant slide technique, singing with a louder and harder voice. From 1950 he recorded regularly with the harmonica player Little Walter, with whom he made the splendidly integrated *Louisiana Blues* (1950); they were soon joined by Muddy Waters's half-brother Otis Spann (pianist) and Jimmy Rogers (second guitarist) to form the nucleus of a long-lived blues band based in Chicago. By 1953 Muddy Waters was performing such dramatically phrased songs as *I'm your Hoochie Coochie Man* (1953) and *Manish Boy* (1955); these established him among the most important postwar blues singers, and set the model for later performances such as *Got my Mojo Working* (1956) and *Tiger in your Tank* (1960), which in their declamatory style and loud amplification express the militant spirit of the ghetto at that time. In the 1960s Muddy Waters toured extensively in the USA and Europe, but lost much of his black audience and frequently re-recorded his songs of the 1950s without meeting their standards. A serious car accident in 1970 obliged him to sing from a chair from then onwards.

### BIBLIOGRAPHY

P. Oliver: *Muddy Waters* (Bexhill, 1964)

P. Welding: 'Interview with Muddy Waters', *American Folk Music Occasional* (New York, 1970), no.2, p.2

PAUL OLIVER

**Mudge, Richard** (*b* Bideford, Devon, 1718; *d* ?Bedworth, Warwicks., April 1763). English cleric and composer. It is not possible to identify with complete certainty the 18th-century composer designated 'Mr Mudge'; he is most likely to have been Richard Mudge, son of the clergyman Zachariah Mudge (1694–1769), a friend of Dr Johnson and master of Bideford grammar school. Richard Mudge entered Pembroke College, Oxford, in 1735 and, after being ordained, became vicar at Great Packington near Birmingham; a 'Rev. Mr Mudge' of Birmingham subscribed to numerous music publications in the 1750s. In 1756 he became rector of Bedworth, Warwickshire, under the patronage of the Earl of Aylesford, whose family had musical connections most notably through Handel's friend and librettist Charles Jennens.

Aside from a *Medley Concerto, with French Horns* which appears in the catalogue of the Oxford Musical Society (*c*1770), the composer 'Mr Mudge' is known only through a set of *Six Concertos in seven parts . . . to which is added a 'Non nobis Domine' in eight parts* (London, 1749). They are written for two solo violins with string ripieno, but the first has an added solo trumpet and the last a solo part for organ or harpsichord. To this is added a short Adagio for five-part string orchestra (two violins, two violas and bass) at the climax of which three voices sing the canon 'Non nobis Domine', attributed to Byrd, around which the strings provide counterpoint. The concertos are noteworthy examples of the late Baroque concerto grosso style, and show Mudge to have been a composer of considerable skill and a flair for the unconventional. Gerald Finzi prepared modern editions of all the concertos, of which three were published (nos.1, 4 and 6).

### BIBLIOGRAPHY

J. H. Mee: *The Oldest Music Room in Europe* (London, 1911)

G. Finzi: Preface to *Richard Mudge: Concerto No.4* (London, 1954)

RICHARD GORER/CHARLES CUDWORTH

**Mudie, Thomas Molleson** (*b* Chelsea, London, 30 Nov 1809; *d* London, 24 July 1876). English composer of Scottish descent. He was one of the ten successful candidates for entry into the Royal Academy of Music in the severe first examination of 1823. He became a pupil of Crotch for composition, of Cipriani Potter for piano and of Willman for clarinet, and was regarded as one of the best pupils of his time. From 1832 to 1844 he was a professor of piano at the RAM; during this time many of his compositions were performed at the Society of British Musicians (founded 1834). From 1844 to 1863 he lived in Edinburgh as a private teacher. While there he published several piano pieces and songs, and wrote accompaniments to many songs in Wood's collection *Songs of Scotland*. In 1863 he returned to London. His earlier compositions show considerable technical mastery: the Symphony in B♭ is especially notable, and contains a minuet with two trios, all three finally played simultaneously as a coda. His music was formerly in the library of the RAM but most of it is now missing.

### WORKS

Syms., E♭, 1827, *GB-Lam*; C, 1830; B♭, 1831; F, 1835; D, 1837

Pf Qt, e♭, 1843; Pf Trio, D, 1843

48 pieces, pf solo; 6 pf duets; 19 pf fantasias on Scottish airs, etc

Deh, proteggi, chorus, orch, 1825, *Lam*

24 sacred songs; 3 sacred duets; 3 chamber anthems, 3vv; 42 secular songs; 2 secular duets

### BIBLIOGRAPHY

*The Harmonicon*, viii (1830/*R*1971), 217; ix (1831), 123

*Musical Magazine* (1835), 40, 109

*Musical World*, v (1837), 11; xviii (1843), 158, 183

MT, xvii (1876), 563
G. A. Macfarren: 'Mudie, Thomas Molleson', Grove 1
                    G. A. MACFARREN/NICHOLAS TEMPERLEY

**Muelas, Diego de las** (d Madrid, 1743). Spanish composer. After several years as *maestro de capilla* at Astorga he was appointed on 26 January 1719 to succeed Antonio Yanguas as *maestro de capilla* at Santiago de Compostela Cathedral. In 1723 he moved in the same capacity to Encarnación Convent in Madrid (under the jurisdiction of the Archbishop of Santiago), remaining there until his death. His villancicos with string accompaniment were sung as far away as Guatemala up to 1775; a double-choir villancico with harp surviving at Morelia shows that his reputation extended to Mexico. His motets for Sundays in Advent and Lent and for Holy Week continued to be sung at Santiago into the 19th century. Six motets for three to eight voices were published in *Lira sacro-hispana* (17th century, i/1, 101ff, ed. H. Eslava). A vast quantity of his music survives at Montserrat (see *LaborD*).

BIBLIOGRAPHY
S. Tafall: 'La capilla de música de la Catedral de Santiago: notas históricas', *Boletín de la Real academia gallega*, xxvi (1931), Aug, 107
J. López Calo: 'El archivo de música de la Catedral de Santiago de Compostela', *Compostellanum*, iii (1958), 314
R. Stevenson: *Renaissance and Baroque Musical Sources in the Americas* (Washington, 1970), 91, 190
                                                    ROBERT STEVENSON

**Muelen, Servais vander.** See MEULEN, SERVAES VANDER.

**Mueller von Asow** [Müller], **Erich H(ermann)** (b Dresden, 31 Aug 1892; d Berlin, 4 June 1964). German musicologist. He studied with Riemann and Schering at the University of Leipzig where he received a doctorate in 1915 with a dissertation on the Mingotti opera company (1732–56). After serving as the assistant director of the Neue Theater, Leipzig, he became the artistic director of the international festival for modern music in Dresden in 1917. In the following year he was appointed director of the Wernow Theater and from 1919 he was a music critic in Berlin and Dresden. In 1926 he joined the staff of the Dresden Pädagogium der Tonkunst, of which he soon became director (1927–33). On his 50th birthday he was created a Knight of the Order of the Crown, Romania.

In 1945 Mueller von Asow founded and became the first director of the Internationales Musiker-Brief-Archiv in Berlin. His research resulted in editions of the letters and other contemporary documents of Schütz, Bach, Mozart, Brahms and others, and although they are sometimes faulty, they make primary source material easily accessible. His chief contribution to musicology, however, is his thorough and extremely detailed thematic catalogue of Richard Strauss's works.

WRITINGS
*Die Mingottischen Opernunternehmungen, 1732–1756* (diss., U. of Leipzig, 1915; Dresden, 1917 as *Angelo und Pietro Mingotti: ein Beitrag zur Geschichte der Oper im XVIII. Jahrhundert*)
*Joseph Gustav Mraczek* (Dresden, 1917)
'Die Komponisten und die Werke', *Erstes modernes Musikfest zu Dresden . . . 1917*, 23–150
ed.: *Deutsches Musiker-Lexicon* (Dresden, 1929, 2/1954 with H. Mueller von Asow as *Kürschners Deutscher Musiker-Kalender*)
ed.: *Festschrift Johannes Biehle zum sechzigsten Geburtstage überreicht* (Leipzig, 1930) [incl. 'Die alte Orgel in der evangelischen Pfarrkirche zu Hermannstadt [Sibiu]', p.31]
*Die Musiksammlung der Bibliothek zu Kronstadt* (Kronstadt [Braşov], 1930)
*Dresdner Musikstätten* (Dresden, 1931)

ed.: *Heinrich Schütz: Gesammelte Briefe u. Schriften* (Regensburg, 1931, 2/1950)
ed.: *An die unsterbliche Geliebte: Liebesbriefe berühmter Musiker* (Dresden, 1934, 3/1962)
ed.: *The Letters and Writings of Georg Frideric Handel* (London, 1935; Ger. trans., 1949) [incl. Mainwaring's biography]
ed.: *Johann Sebastian Bach: Gesammelte Briefe und Schriften* (Regensburg, 1938, 2/1950)
*Egon Kornauth: ein Bild von Leben und Schaffen des mährischen Komponisten* (Vienna, 1941)
ed.: *Briefe Wolfgang Amadeus Mozarts* (Berlin, 1942) [facs. and edn. of the letters of W. A. Mozart and his family; 2/1949 as *Wolfgang Amadeus Mozart: Briefwechsel und Aufzeichnungen*]
ed.: *Johannes Brahms und Mathilde Wesendonck: ein Briefwechsel* (Vienna, 1943)
ed.: *Wolfgang Amadeus Mozart: Verzeichnis aller meiner Werke* (Vienna and Leipzig, 1943, 2/1956)
*Max Reger und seine Welt* (Berlin, 1944) [incl. 132 illustrations]
ed.: *Max Reger: Briefwechsel mit Herzog Georg II von Sachsen-Meiningen* (Weimar, 1949)
'Der Gesamtkatalog der Musiker-Briefe', *IAML, Lüneburg 1950*, 35
'Musikerepistolographie', *Kongressbericht: Wien Mozartjahr 1956*, 430
'Ein ungedruckter Brief Mahlers', *ÖMz*, xii (1957), 63
'Zu einer unbekannten Photographie Constanze Mozarts', *ÖMz*, xiii (1958), 93
*Richard Strauss: thematisches Verzeichnis* (Vienna and Wiesbaden, 1959–74) [continued by A. Ott and F. Trenner]
'Hermann Cohen: ein Lieblingsschüler Franz Liszts', *ÖMz*, xvi (1961), 443
'Richard Strauss und Giuseppe Verdi', *ÖMz*, xvi (1961), 348
'Ein ungedruckter Brief von Henri Vieuxtemps an W. A. Mozart Sohn', *SMw*, xxv (1962), 389
ed. with H. Mueller von Asow: *The Collected Correspondence and Papers of Christoph Willibald Gluck* (London, 1962)
BIBLIOGRAPHY
'Mueller von Asow, Erich Hermann', *Kürschners deutscher Musik-Kalender*, ed. H. and E. H. Mueller von Asow (Berlin, 2/1954) [incl. complete list of writings up to 1954]
                                                    M. E. C. BARTLET

**Mueren, Florentijn Jan Van der.** See VAN DER MUEREN, FLORENTIJN JAN.

**Muffat, Georg** (b Mégève, Savoy, baptized 1 June 1653; d Passau, 23 Feb 1704). German composer and organist of French birth, father of Gottlieb Muffat. He considered himself a German, although his ancestors were Scottish and his family had settled in Savoy in the early 17th century. He was a prominent composer of instrumental music who was particularly important for the part he played in introducing the French and Italian styles into Germany.

1. LIFE. Muffat went as a boy to Alsace, then to Paris to study with Lully and others from 1663 to 1669. He returned to Alsace to become a student, first at the Jesuit college at Sélestat in 1669, then in 1671 at a similar institution at Molsheim, where he was appointed organist to the exiled Strasbourg Cathedral chapter. By 1674 he was in Ingolstadt, Bavaria, and matriculated as a law student. He had left Alsace when war was imminent, and in the autobiographical foreword to his *Florilegium primum* he referred to his subsequent flight 'to Vienna in Austria, Prague and then finally to Salzburg and Passau'. At the Viennese court he found a patron in the Emperor Leopold I but received no official appointment. In 1677 he was in Prague and the following year took up a post at Salzburg as organist and chamber musician to Archbishop Max Gandolf, Count of Kuenberg. His employer granted him leave to visit Italy in the 1680s: he studied in Rome with Pasquini, heard Corelli's concerti grossi and composed works which were performed at Corelli's house, and later published in his own *Armonico tributo*. The visit ended in September 1682. After the archbishop's death in 1687 he continued to work under his successor but eventually left Salzburg, disappointed with the unfavourable atmosphere there.

Early in 1690 he was in Augsburg for the coronation of the Emperor Leopold's eldest son Joseph as Roman king and he made a personal presentation of his *Apparatus musico-organisticus* to Leopold, its dedicatee. From later that year until his death he was Kapellmeister at the court of Johann Philipp of Lamberg, Bishop of Passau, and tutor to the pages there.

2. WORKS. Muffat's only known work dating from before his Italian visit is a violin sonata, composed at Prague in 1677, which is also his only extant autograph. Almost all of his music has survived only in the original printed editions, whose multilingual forewords show that he regarded himself as a pioneer in bringing French and Italian styles directly from their sources to German-speaking countries. His special contribution lay in the detailed information about Lully's and Corelli's practices which he provided for German performers.

The *Armonico tributo*, like Corelli's op.6, belongs to the early development of the concerto grosso. Though defined as 'chamber sonatas suitable for few or many instruments', the five works in the collection are based on the concerto principle of alternating groups. They are notated for five-part strings throughout, using the letters 'T' and 'S' to denote tutti and solo passages (the latter always have the Corellian trio texture of two violins and bass). This compressed notation may have been necessitated by the prohibitive cost of producing a full edition at the time: later the music reappeared in concertos nos.2, 4, 5, 10, 11 and 12 of the *Ausserlesene Instrumental-Music*, newly arranged and with explicit concerto grosso scoring. Like Corelli's op.6 the *Armonico tributo* displays no fixed formal scheme. The number of movements varies between five, six and seven, with a mixture of *da chiesa* and *da camera* elements similar to that in Corelli's last four concertos. Whereas Corelli used only the four basic dances and two additional ones, the gavotte and minuet, Muffat added to these the borea (bourrée) and balletto, as well as an aria, passacaglia and rondeau. The style of his dances suggests French influence in its harmonic simplicity, flowing melody and clearly articulated phrases. The rondeau (in Sonata no.3) is based on the French form, while the passacaglia (in Sonata no.5) reflects Lully's practice of interspersing trio episodes among five-part passages and follows the French custom of repeating the theme in rondeau fashion throughout. Corelli's influence appears in the non-dance movements, where two types of slow movement recur: one in simple homophonic style with successions of chords, sometimes broken up by rests, the other in a more continuous contrapuntal style, with characteristic chains of suspensions. In faster movements such features as running basses, sequences on standard chord progressions, rapid tutti-solo contrasts, echo effects and lively contrapuntal writing are clearly derived from Corelli's concerto style.

When Muffat drew on these early works for the *Ausserlesene Instrumental-Music* he altered the number, order and length of movements, filled out the texture and assigned a continuo to both concertino and ripieno; in one case he distributed movements from a sonata among two concertos (nos.10 and 12). The original Corellian basis remains, however, not only in the sonata arrangements but also in the six newly composed concertos, which retain the characteristic trio grouping and the mixture of elements seen in the *Armonico tributo*. Muffat's foreword explains that this mixture makes the concertos unsuitable either for use purely in church or for dancing but that they are appropriate for performance at court and state ceremonies or entertainments and at musical gatherings. Their individual Latin titles refer to the various such occasions on which they were originally performed and have no programmatic significance. The foreword also makes some suggestions for performance, stressing that the scoring may be adapted to the resources available. Among specific instructions are references to bowing, to the precise attack of the first note and to the extremes of dynamics and tempo which characterize the Italian manner. In the foreword to the *Florilegium primum* Lully's style is equally aptly summed up as 'natural and flowing, rejecting all superfluous artifice, extravagant runs, frequent and awkward leaps . . .'. The foreword to the second volume describes in greater detail the method of performing ballets 'à la Françoise' and provides a substantial treatise on bowing and ornamentation, copiously illustrated.

The orchestral suites of the *Florilegia* are among the best of a group of works in this form written by German composers under Lully's influence: others are the *Composition de musique* by Kusser (1682) and the *Journal du printemps* by J. C. F. Fischer (1695). Kusser, who, like Muffat, studied with Lully, was apparently the first to add the French overture to the German orchestral suite: Muffat followed his example in his *Florilegia*. Almost all the opening movements have the customary first section with dotted rhythms, followed by a lively fugal section often in triple time. The other movements vary in number, arrangement and type from one suite to another. They cover a wide range of dances similar to Fischer's in the *Journal* and going beyond the limited forms of earlier works such as J. H. Schmelzer's *Balletti francesi* of the 1660s and 1670s. Most of the seven 'fascicles' (i.e. suites) of the first *Florilegium* comprise standard dances. The saraband, gavotte, minuet, bourrée and gigue are among the most frequent; other movements include the air, rondeau, chaconne and passacaille, and there are also specialities such as the echo and traquenard (used by Fischer too). The eight fascicles of the second *Florilegium* use more descriptive titles implying dramatic ballets, although the music itself is not overtly descriptive. The internal structure owes much to Lully. Whereas in Schmelzer's suites the sections of a binary movement are usually undeveloped and equal in length, Muffat followed Lully in enlarging the second section to as much as twice the length of the first, with further extension achieved by the use of the *petite reprise*. His first sections are generally longer than Schmelzer's and show Lully's influence in their tendency to create a composite structure from recurring elements, often $ABA^1B^1$. The five-part string texture of the *Florilegia*, like that of Kusser's *Composition*, is modelled on music for the '24 violons'. The individual parts are always shapely, and the general style is elegantly sophisticated in comparison with the robust manner of earlier German orchestral suites. Among stylistic details showing French influence are some characteristic triple-time rhythms with the accent on the second beat, and a liking for graceful feminine endings at cadences in triple time.

Muffat's versatile musicianship extended beyond orchestral composition into a variety of fields. His MS treatise on continuo practice, *Regulae concentuum partiturae*, is outstanding among similar German works of the 17th century for its large quantity of fully figured and realized examples. His contribution to solo organ music survives in the *Apparatus musico-organisticus*, a characteristically eclectic publication incorporating both Lullian and Corellian elements. The main part consists of 12 large-scale toccatas arranged in the order of the church tones. Their multisectional structure, extreme contrasts and variety of figuration within one piece are reminiscent of the toccatas of Frescobaldi, whom Muffat mentioned in his foreword as a forerunner. Another model could have been Pasquini, whose absorption of Italian chamber and continuo idioms into solo keyboard music is a progressive feature found also in the *Apparatus*. The transfer of orchestral and chamber idioms to the keyboard is significant in view of later Baroque trends. Among the six or so sections of one toccata, which are contrasted in time signature, tempo, texture and style, there may be sections of pure toccata writing with runs over or beneath chords, imitative sections in *sonata da chiesa* style, sometimes suggesting two violins over a continuo bass, extended fugues, often with gigue subjects like those favoured by Froberger and Italianate *durezze e ligature* sections. The French style appears in the tenth toccata, where a pompous opening Adagio is followed by a lively fugal Allegro, with a final Adagio related in style to the first, clearly forming a French overture. Stylistic details in these toccatas encompass Frescobaldian chromatic effects and Lombard rhythms, stock Corellian harmonic sequences, recitative-like melody and mechanical patterns of the kind found in Italian violin music. The Passacaglia shows an interesting combination of the French rondeau form and the Italian variation (freely treated). More than any other of his publications the *Apparatus* demonstrates the wide range of ideas that Muffat absorbed during his varied career.

*Beginning of the first toccata from Georg Muffat's 'Apparatus musico-organisticus' (1690)*

## WORKS

Armonico tributo: 5 sonatas, str, bc (Salzburg, 1682); ed. E. Schenk, DTÖ, lxxxix (1953); lute version of passacaglia from Sonata no.5, ed. A. Koczirz, DTÖ, 1, Jg.xxv/2 (1918/*R*)
Apparatus musico-organisticus: 12 toccatas, 1 ciaccona, 1 passacaglia, aria with variations: all org (Salzburg, 1690)
Suavioris harmoniae instrumentalis hyporchematicae florilegium primum: 7 orch suites, a 4/5, bc (Augsburg, 1695); ed. H. Rietsch, DTÖ, ii, Jg.i/2 (1894/*R*); foreword ed. and trans. O. Strunk, *Source Readings in Music History* (New York, 1950), 442ff
Florilegium secundum: 8 orch suites a 4/4, bc (Passau, 1698); ed. H. Rietsch, DTÖ, iv, Jg.ii/2 (1895/*R*)
Ausserlesene Instrumental-Music: 12 concerti grossi (Passau, 1701); ed. E. Luntz, DTÖ, xxiii, Jg.xi/2 (1904/*R*); lxxxix (1953)
Sonata, vn, bc, 1677, holograph, *CS-KRa*; Preludes, dances, kbd, *A-Wm*

### LOST WORKS

Marina Armena, opera, 5 Sept 1679, Salzburg, Akademie-Theater
Königin Mariamne, opera, Sept 1680, Salzburg, Akademie-Theater
Le fatali felicità di Plutone, *c*1688, Salzburg, Hoftheater; lib, inc., *Wn*

### DOUBTFUL WORKS

Missa 'In labore requies', 8vv, 12 insts, *Ee*
Keyboard pieces, *Wm* XIV 743

## WRITINGS

Regulae concentuum partiturae, *c*1699, *Wm*; ed. H. Federhofer, MSD, iv (1961)
Nothwendige Anmerkungen bey der Musik, lost

## BIBLIOGRAPHY

L. von Stollbrock: *Die Komponisten Georg und Gottlieb Muffat* (Rostock, 1888)
——: 'Georg Muffat und sein "Florilegium"', *MMg*, xxii (1890), 87
——: 'Georg Muffats musiktheoretische Abhandlung', *MMg*, xxiii (1891), 37
E. von Werra: 'Georg Muffat ... und Gottlieb Muffat...: bio-bibliographische Studien', *KJb*, viii (1893), 42
A. Schering: 'Georg Muffat: "Ausserlesene mit Ernst und Lust gemengte Instrumental-Musik", 1701', *ZIMG*, v (1903–4), 365
K. Nef: *Geschichte der Sinfonie und der Suite* (Leipzig, 1921)
A. Kutscher: *Vom Salzburger Barocktheater zu den Salzburger Festspielen* (Düsseldorf, 1939)
A. Liess: *Wiener Barockmusik* (Vienna, 1946), 44ff, 98f, 113
A. Goehlinger: 'Georges Muffat', *Caecilia*, lxii (1954), 177
——: 'Georg Muffat', *Zeitschrift für Kirchenmusik*, lxxiv (1954), 194
F. Raugel: 'Georg Muffat en Alsace', *RdM*, xxxvi (1954), 143
R. Walter: 'Georg Muffat und sein "Apparatus musico-organisticus"', *Musik und Altar*, xi (1959), 116
H. Federhofer: 'Biographische Beiträge zu Georg Muffat und Johann Joseph Fux', *Mf*, xiii (1960), 130
A. Layer: 'Georg Muffats Ausbildungsjahre bei den Jesuiten', *Mf*, xv (1962), 48 [see also H. Federhofer, ibid, 367]
K. Cooper and J. Zsako: 'Georg Muffat's Observations on the Lully Style of Performance', *MQ*, liii (1967), 220
F. W. Riedel: 'Der Einfluss der italienischen Klaviermusik des 17. Jahrhunderts auf die Entwicklung der Musik für Tasteninstrumente in Deutschland ...', *AnMc*, no.5 (1968), 18
W. Kolneder: *Georg Muffat zur Aufführungspraxis* (Strasbourg, 1970)
S. Harris: 'Lully, Corelli, Muffat and the Eighteenth-century String Body', *ML*, liv (1973), 197
K. Schütz: 'Die Toccaten des Apparatus musico-organisticus von Georg Muffat', *De ratione in musica: Festschrift Erich Schenk* (Kassel, 1975), 117

SUSAN WOLLENBERG

**Muffat, Gottlieb** [Theophil] (*b* Passau, baptized 25 April 1690; *d* Vienna, 9 Dec 1770). German composer and organist, son of Georg Muffat. He was the leading keyboard composer in Vienna in the early 18th century.

1. LIFE. Muffat led a more stable existence than his father, entering the musical establishment at the Viennese court early in his career and remaining there for over half a century. It may be assumed that as a child he was taught by his father. He probably did not leave Passau before 1704, the year of his father's death. The first report of his presence in Vienna dates from 1711, when he became *Hofscholar* under the supervision of Fux (some sources incorrectly give the date as 1706). The education of scholars at the imperial court included performance on the organ and other

instruments, continuo playing, singing and counterpoint. Muffat was appointed official court organist in 1717: he was required to play for services in the Hofkapelle and to provide continuo accompaniment for performances of operas. At this time he received a grant for a period of study abroad, but there is no record of the exact date or place of his visit. Subsequently he acquired additional duties at court, including the tuition of various children of the imperial family, among them the future Empress Maria Theresia. On the strength of his devoted service Fux recommended him for a rise in salary in 1723, the year in which he assisted at the famous ceremonial performance of Fux's opera *Costanza e fortezza* in Prague. Three years later, in the preface to his first publication, the *72 Versetl sammt 12 Toccaten*, he acknowledged his great debt to Fux ('without flattery the best master in the world'). In 1729 he was promoted to second organist. After the death of the Emperor Karl VI in 1740 and with the accession of Maria Theresia, the resources of the Hofkapelle were reorganized, bringing Muffat his final promotion to first organist in 1741. He seems to have written no more music after this. A projected sequel to his second publication, the *Componimenti musicali* (*c*1739), never materialized, and all later 18th-century sources of his works are copies of pieces in earlier MSS. He was pensioned off in 1763 (some sources have 1764).

2. WORKS. Unlike his versatile father, Muffat chose to restrict himself almost exclusively to one field, that of keyboard music. He came at the end of a long line of Baroque organists and keyboard composers working in Vienna and was the only contemporary of Bach there to make a substantial contribution to the keyboard repertory in both quantity and quality. Much of his music remained unpublished and is still not generally known: it covers a wider range of forms than the two published collections alone would suggest. Although he lived until 1770, he belongs musically to the late Baroque period rather than to the age of Haydn; his keyboard works never desert traditional Baroque structures (toccata, complete fugue, dance suite, ciaccona).

Muffat's conservatism is most evident in his fugues. His reputation as a contrapuntist rests primarily on the short liturgical fugues of the *72 Versetl*, whose survival was aided by the issue of new editions from *c*1800 and by the incorporation of extracts into fugal treatises (e.g. Marpurg's of 1753–4). However, the versets are overshadowed by the archaic grandeur of the unpublished ricercares. These form the largest single collection of such pieces composed in the early 18th century. They are unusual for their time in having no introductory toccatas or preludes: in this they resemble Bach's *Art of Fugue* and like that work are notated in open score, following earlier Baroque usage for strict contrapuntal keyboard pieces. Fux's pupils owned printed editions and personal MS copies of ricercares by 17th-century composers such as Frescobaldi, G. B. Fasolo, Froberger, Battiferri, Fabrizio Fontana and Poglietti. Muffat's own ricercares show that he was familiar with these models: their fluid continuity is quite different from the stiff, artificial rhythmic style of Fux's 'species' in the *Gradus* and is much closer to the true spirit of *stile antico* than to Fux's artefact. Among individual elements showing the influence of the older ricercare are the strong modal flavour, especially in Phrygian pieces such as no.4 (see ex.1); some angular chromatic subjects recalling the *Recercar cromaticho* in Frescobaldi's *Fiori*

Ex.1

*musicali*; and the use of sectional structures. The ricercares observe the traditional differentiation in character from the 19 canzonas appended to them in being stylistically related to the 16th-century vocal motet, while the canzonas are in a livelier, more idiomatically instrumental style. Several of the canzonas are sectional in form also, most notably no.11. This is a true variation canzona whose rhythmic transformation of a theme throughout successive sections (including a gigue-like version) follows a favourite 17th-century practice.

Muffat's versets, like his ricercares, belong to a well-established tradition. His chief predecessors in this field were Kerll (*Modulatio organica*, 1686), the anonymous author of the *Wegweiser* (1689) – an organ tutor containing versets for practice – Speth (*Ars magna*, 1693) and Murschhauser (*Octi-tonium*, 1696). These publications were all familiar to Viennese organists in the early 18th century. Muffat used the same kind of external structure as they did, arranging his pieces according to the order of the church tones, with a short introductory toccata and a regular number of versets in each tone. He followed their internal structure also in the miniature fugal form of his versets. Like Murschhauser he left the function of the versets open and avoided reference to chant, so they are not restricted to one part of the liturgy. The elimination of chant is one aspect of a general process of secularization culminating with Muffat: more than his predecessors, he used strongly secular, even rustic, subjects (often in dance rhythms). He also applied a wide range of ornamentation symbols and provided an explanatory table similar to the one in the *Componimenti*. Although French composers were using copious ornamentation and secular dance styles in liturgical organ music from at least the mid-17th century, Muffat was the first among Austro-German composers to absorb these trends fully into the traditional verset. Apart from the *72 Versetl* his liturgical organ music includes some mass movements and a series of 12 short preludes in various keys, all cadencing on a preparatory E major chord.

Muffat's chief contribution to the organ prelude (under various titles) is preserved in a Viennese MS notated in so-called Italian organ tablature with two staves respectively of six and eight lines, again in accordance with earlier Baroque notation for such works. Among the pieces are 24 large-scale toccatas in the order of the church tones, each followed by a capriccio in the same tone: Muffat seems to have invented this particular pairing. The system of church tones was apparently ingrained in his musical thinking, for he used it not only for the versets and toccatas but also for the first eight ricercares. His toccatas are of two main types: the first is a unified form like an extended *intonazione*, consisting of florid runs above or beneath chords, sometimes with imitation between the hands. The virtuoso element here is confined to the manuals: like most South German composers, Muffat made very little independent use of the pedals. A second type of toccata is modelled more on Georg Muffat's *Apparatus*, using a sectional design with contrasts in tempo, time signature and texture. The varied styles of individual sections encompass those of the French overture (no.11) and the Italian trio sonata (no.10), further indicating the influence of his father's toccatas. With the capriccios one title is applied to a wider range of works than in the case of the toccatas: improvisatory preludes, invention-like pieces in free contrapuntal style, more directly tuneful ones such as the expressive *Capriccio desperato* R165, some in the style of a dance, and others based on special devices (recalling Frescobaldi) such as no.12, R159, which exploits syncopation.

Some of the shorter improvisatory capriccios and toccatinas from the same MS reappear in other MSS as preludes to suites. A feature they share is the grandiose succession of arpeggiated chords at the opening: Muffat provided a prelude in similar style for Fux's Partita in A minor, and Fux's own 'harpeggio' and capriccio preludes are examples of this Viennese speciality. Muffat's suites invariably have some kind of introductory movement: his use of the French overture or prelude-and-fugue form suggests the influence of Fux and of Handel (1720 set of suites). There are MS copies in Muffat's hand of suites by both these composers: to Handel's he added ornamentation symbols, sometimes to pieces which were totally unornamented in the original. His own suites similarly use lavish ornamentation, clearly under French influence. In addition to Handel and Fux, Couperin is an important model for the form and style of his suites. Following both Couperin and Fux he kept vestiges of the traditional order of dances and added extras (usually towards the end) such as the menuet and rigaudon, two favourite dances with Fux, or character-pieces with Couperinesque titles such as *La plainte d'une ame abandonnée* or *La coquette*. He also used free pieces entitled 'Finale' to replace the gigue at the end of four of his suites: these are modern in style, with short, simple phrases and instant repetition of motifs. Some of his most attractive and up-to-date music is contained in the suites: while his ricercares belong to the traditional Italian side of Viennese keyboard music, his suites belong to the progressive French side.

Among features worthy of special mention are Muffat's frequent use of the French *petite reprise*; the advanced nature of his binary designs, with second halves often at least twice as long as the first and perhaps encompassing a final return to the original material in the tonic; his free treatment of key, allowing excursions into the relative minor or major or into the tonic minor for slow movements (saraband and air) and trios to minuets; and his successful combination of *galant* traits in melody, rhythm and texture, with a thorough mastery of counterpoint (as one would expect of a pupil of Fux). Although Muffat's keyboard music would seem to be more limited in scope than the total output of his father, there are signs of the same eclectic approach – for example in the fact that he was equally at home in the thoroughly old-fashioned form of the ricercare and in the forward-looking 2/4 or 3/8 *galant* suite finales.

The sources and survival of Muffat's works present some special problems and points of interest. The lack of extant autographs and the ambiguous methods of ascription in some of the extant MS copies create some insoluble problems of authenticity. It is also impossible to establish a precise chronology, as so few of these copies are dated: moreover, Muffat is not a composer whose work seems to reveal any clear chronological development on internal evidence alone. The circulation of some of his pieces in MS copies during the 18th century was quite widespread, a notable example being the Canzona no.7 R250. In the early 19th century it was ascribed to Frescobaldi (together with two of his

other canzonas, R251 and 254) in Clementi's *Selection of Practical Harmony*, and this false attribution gained general credence among subsequent editors of keyboard anthologies (e.g. AMI, iii). Some of the music of the *Componimenti* has also become known under the name of Handel, who incorporated direct borrowings from it into various works, including the Ode for St Cecilia's Day, as well as taking material from Muffat's unpublished music for one of his organ concertos.

WORKS

*(all for kbd unless otherwise stated)*

Editions: G. *Muffat*, ed. F. W. Riedel, Die Orgel, ii/8, 10, 13, 16, 17 (Lippstadt, 1957–61) [R]

G. *Muffat: Componimenti musicali*, ed. G. Adler, DTÖ, vii, Jg.iii/3 (1896/*R*) [A]

G. *Muffat: 72 Versetl und 12 Toccaten für Orgel und Klavier*, ed. G. Adler, DTÖ, lviii, Jg.xxix/2 (1922/*R*) [V]

J. J. Fux: *Werke für Tasteninstrumente*, ed. F. W. Riedel, Sämtliche Werke, vi/1 (Graz, 1964) [F]

*Riedel nos.*

| | |
|---|---|
| 1–84 | 72 Versetlsammt 12 Toccaten (besonders zum Kirchen-Dienst bey Choral-Aemtern und Vesperen dienlich) (Vienna, 1726), V; facs. in Monuments of Music and Music Literature in Facsimile, i/18 (New York, 1967) |
| 85–135 | Componimenti musicali per il cembalo, 6 suites, 1 ciaccona (Augsburg, *c*1739), A; facs. in Monuments of Music and Music Literature in Facsimile, i/8 (New York, 1967) |
| 136–211 | 24 toccatas with 24 capriccios; 12 capriccios; 3 toccatinas; 4 preludes; 9 capriccios, *A-Wm, Wn, D-B, H-Bn*; selections in R ii/8, 10, 13 |
| 212–62 | 32 ricercares, 19 canzonas, 1733 at latest, *A-GÖ, Wm, D-B, H-Bn, US-NYp*; 2 in R ii/8, 17 |
| 263–74 | 12 preludes, R ii/16 |
| 275–8 | 4 fugues, R ii/17 |
| 279 | Fugue on Easter alleluia, R ii/17 |
| 280–322 | 2 organ masses, *D-BEU* |
| 323–7 | Partita, *A-Wn*, holograph |
| 328–35 | Partita, *D-B*, holograph |
| 197, 336–41 | Partita, *A-Wm* |
| 342–8 | Partita, *D-B* |
| 349 | Prelude to Fux's partita, F appx 62 |
| 350 | Ciaccona, 1733 at latest, *A-Wn* |

DOUBTFUL WORKS

351–495; Anh. 1–11: Preludes, dances, etc, *Wm, Wn, D-BEU, Mbs, H-Bn*

OTHER WORKS

Sonata pastorale, 2 vn, bc, 1727 at latest, *A-Wn*
Salve regina, 2vv, 2 vn, va, vc, org, *Gd*
Full thematic catalogues in Riedel (MS, n.d.), and in Wollenberg (MS)

BIBLIOGRAPHY

L. von Köchel: *Die kaiserliche Hof-Musikkapelle in Wien von 1543 bis 1867* (Vienna, 1869)

L. von Stollbrock: *Die Komponisten Georg und Gottlieb Muffat* (Rostock, 1888)

E. von Werra: 'Georg Muffat ... und Gottlieb Muffat ...: bio-bibliographische Studien', *KJb*, viii (1893), 42

M. Seiffert: *Geschichte der Klavier-Musik* (Leipzig, 1899)

S. Taylor: *The Indebtedness of Handel to Works by Other Composers* (London, 1906)

P. Robinson: 'Muffat's "Componimenti"', *ZIMG*, ix (1907–8), 123 [see also W. Wolffheim, ibid., 188]

J. H. Knöll: *Die Klavier- und Orgelwerke Theophile Muffats* (diss., U. of Vienna, 1916)

A. Liess: *Wiener Barockmusik* (Vienna, 1946), 113ff

S. T. Morris: *Gottlieb Muffat's Clavier Suites* (diss., Boston U., 1959)

F. W. Riedel: *Quellenkundliche Beiträge zur Geschichte der Musik für Tasteninstrumente in der 2. Hälfte des 17. Jh. (vornehmlich in Deutschland)* (Kassel, 1959)

——: *Thematischer Katalog der von den Organisten der kaiserlichen Hofkapelle in Wien unter Ferdinand III bis Karl VI komponierte Musik für Tasteninstrumente* (MS, n.d., in author's possession)

——: *Das Musikarchiv im Minoritenkonvent zu Wien*, CaM, i (1963)

——: 'Der Einfluss der italienischen Klaviermusik des 17. Jahrhunderts auf die Entwicklung der Musik für Tasteninstrumente in Deutschland ...', *AnMc*, no.5 (1968), 18

S. Wollenberg: 'Handel and Gottlieb Muffat: a Newly Discovered Borrowing', *MT*, cxiii (1972), 448

——: *Thematic Catalogue of the Keyboard Works of Gottlieb Muffat* (MS in author's possession)

S. Dahms: 'Neues zur Chronologie der Opern von Biber und Muffat', *ÖMz*, xxix (1974), 362

S. Wollenberg: *Viennese Keyboard Music in the Reign of Karl VI*

(*1712–40*) (diss., U. of Oxford, 1975)
——: 'The Keyboard Suites of Gottlieb Muffat (1690–1770)', *PRMA*, cii (1975–6), 83
B. Baselt: 'Muffat and Handel: a Two-way Exchange', *MT*, cxx (1979), 904

SUSAN WOLLENBERG

**Muffler pedal.** *See* MODERATOR PEDAL.

**Mugnone, Leopoldo** (*b* Naples, 29 Sept 1858; *d* Capodichino, Naples, 22 Dec 1941). Italian conductor and composer. The son of the principal double bass in the Teatro S Carlo orchestra, he studied at the Naples Conservatory, composing and producing a comic opera when he was 12. While still in his teens he composed two operettas and *La rosella*, a romance which became a popular success, and made his conducting début in comic opera at the Naples Teatro La Fenice (not the Venice La Fenice as in some references). He became conductor at the Teatro Costanzi, Rome, and in 1888 won a contract giving him the musical direction of operas published by Sonzogno and their performances outside Italy. In this capacity he conducted the première of Mascagni's *Cavalleria rusticana* (Rome, 1890) and began to tour abroad, visiting Paris in 1889 and London in 1905–6, conducting the first Covent Garden production of Giordano's *Andrea Chénier* in 1905 and the British première of Giordano's *Fedora* there the next year. Meanwhile he did much to encourage French opera in Italy with productions of works by Bizet and Massenet, and in 1900 he conducted the première of *Tosca* at Rome. His friendly relations with Puccini were disrupted by a disagreement over the musical direction of *Madama Butterfly* at Rome in 1908, but Mugnone later introduced to Italy the only Puccini opera published by Sonzogno, *La rondine*, shortly after its Monte Carlo première in 1917. He also conducted the premières of Franchetti's *La figlia di Iorio* (La Scala, 1906) and Giordano's *Mese mariano* (Palermo, 1910), and took the latter on a South American tour during which he conducted *Götterdämmerung* and Charpentier's *Louise* in addition to Italian works.

Mugnone's interpretations of *Otello* and *Falstaff* were regarded by Boito as particularly notable, and he conducted *Nabucco* at La Scala in 1913 as part of the Verdi centenary celebrations; Beecham considered him the best Italian conductor of his time. Mugnone returned to Covent Garden in 1919, when he gave the British première of Mascagni's *Iris*, and again in 1925, when he was summoned to rescue some of the Italian performances that had suffered at other hands. He appeared frequently as a symphonic conductor at the Augusteo, Rome, and composed two mature operas in the *verismo* style. His extensive personal papers, which include correspondence with Verdi, Puccini, Mascagni, Leoncavallo, Massenet and Richard Strauss, were presented to the museum libraries at La Scala, the Rome Opera and the Naples Conservatory.

WORKS

Il dottor Bartolo Salsapariglia (opera), Naples, 1870–71; Don Bizzarro e le sue figlie (operetta, 1, E. Golisciani), Naples, Nuovo, 1875; Mamma Angot al serraglio di Costantinopoli (operetta, 3, Golisciani), Naples, Nuovo, 1875; Il Birichino (opera, 1, Golisciani), Venice, Malibran, 1892; Vita brettone (opera, 3, Golisciani), Naples, S Carlo, 1905

BIBLIOGRAPHY

'Leopoldo Mugnone', *Teatro illustrato*, x (1890), 66
T. Ruffo: *La mia parabola artistica* (Milan, 1937), 231ff
P. Panichelli: *Il 'Pretino' di Giacomo Puccini* (Pisa, 1940, 4/1962), 89ff
E. de Leva: 'Leopoldo Mugnone nel dolore e nell'arte', *Corriere di Napoli* (6 Aug 1941)

A. de Angelis: 'Aneddoti su Mugnone', *Voce d'Italia* (23 Nov 1941)
——: 'Leopoldo Mugnone era timido come Verdi', *Giornale d'Italia* (11 April 1958)

CLAUDIO CASINI

**Muḥammad ibn 'Abd al-Ḥamīd.** *See* AL-LĀDHIQĪT.

**Mühlen, Raimund von zur.** *See* ZUR MÜHLEN, RAIMUND VON.

**Mühlfeld, Richard (Bernhard Herrmann)** (*b* Salzungen, 28 Feb 1856; *d* Meiningen, 1 June 1907). German clarinettist. He was the youngest of four brothers, all of whom received their first musical training from their father; he played the violin and clarinet in the spa orchestra at Salzungen under his father's direction until he obtained a post in 1873 as violinist at the court of Saxe-Meiningen. In 1879 he was made principal clarinettist at Meiningen, an appointment he retained until his death. When von Bülow was court conductor, Mühlfeld took sectional rehearsals of the orchestra; his thoroughness in this was recognized as contributory to its reputation for attention to detail. Mühlfeld also conducted his own male-voice choir, and was made music director of the court theatre in 1890.

When Brahms visited Meiningen in March 1891, the court conductor Fritz Steinbach drew his attention to Mühlfeld's excellence as a clarinettist. Mühlfeld was asked to play privately to Brahms, who, although he had written nothing for a year, was immediately interested, and composed his Trio op.114 and Quintet op.115 during the following summer. Mühlfeld gave the first performances at Berlin on 12 December 1891 of the Trio with Brahms and Hausmann, and of the Quintet with the Joachim Quartet. In 1894 Brahms wrote his two Sonatas op.120 and gave the first performances of them with Mühlfeld at Vienna on 7 January 1895. Brahms derived so much pleasure from their many performances of the sonatas throughout Germany and Austria that he gave Mühlfeld all performing right fees during his lifetime, all fees from their joint performances, and the MSS of both sonatas after publication.

Mühlfeld gained an international reputation. He visited England many times, performing Brahms's works with the Joachim Quartet and Fanny Davies. Other composers who wrote for him were Gustav Jenner, Henri Marteau and Karl Reinecke. He was rewarded with several decorations by the Duke of Saxe-Meiningen and received the Royal Bavarian Gold Medal of Ludwig. He used Baermann system 18-keyed clarinets made by Ottensteiner of Munich. His interpretations were said to be dramatic and very moving.

BIBLIOGRAPHY

M. Kalbeck: *Johannes Brahms* (Vienna, 1904–14)
F. May: *The Life of Johannes Brahms* (London, 1905, 2/1948)
J. Brahms: *Briefwechsel* (Berlin, 1907–19)
C. Mühlfeld: *Die herzogliche Hofkapelle in Meiningen* (Meiningen, 1910)
A. Moser, ed.: *Briefe von und an Joseph Joachim* (Berlin, 1911–13; Eng. trans., 1913)
G. Toenes: 'Richard Muehlfeld', *The Clarinet*, xxiii (1956)
B. Portnoy: 'Brahms' Prima Donna', *Woodwind World*, iv (1963), 12
P. Weston: *Clarinet Virtuosi of the Past* (London, 1971)

PAMELA WESTON

**Mukwamya.** Alternative spelling of *maqwāmiyā*, an Ethiopian prayer stick used as a percussion instrument; *see* ETHIOPIAN RITE, MUSIC OF THE.

**Mul, Jan** (*b* Haarlem, 20 Sept 1911; *d* Overveen, nr. Haarlem, 30 Dec 1971). Dutch composer. After early lessons with Andriessen and several years at the Roman

Catholic School of Church Music, Utrecht, he studied composition with Dresden at the Amsterdam Conservatory. With two other Andriessen pupils, De Klerk and Strategier, he formed the 'Trium Puerorum', a church music group. Mul was music editor of the *Volkskrant* and constantly active in music administration; he was president of the Society of Dutch Composers, the Bureau for Music Copyright and the Federation of Professional Artists' Associations.

### WORKS
(*selective list*)

Dramatic: De varkenshoeder (opera, 1, after Andersen), 1952; 1 other 1-act opera, film scores

Sacred choral: 14 masses incl. Missa 'Causa nostrae laetitiae', Missa 'L'homme désarmé', Missa canonica; Stabat mater, 1934; Te Deum, 1936; many Proper psalm settings

Secular choral: Egmont onthalst (cantata, Hooft), 1938

Orch: Sinfonietta, 1957; Conc., pf 4 hands, 1962; Confetti musicali, 1965; Ik, Jan Mul, 1965; Divertimento, pf, orch, 1967

Chamber works; pf pieces incl. Sonata, 1940; songs

Principal publisher: Donemus

### BIBLIOGRAPHY
W. Paap: 'De varkenshoeder van Prenen en Mul', *Mens en melodie*, viii (1953), 175
H. Andriessen: 'Jan Mul', *Sonorum speculum* (1961), no.8, p.2
J. Mul: 'Sinfonietta', *Sonorum speculum* (1962), no.12, p.14
ROGIER STARREVELD

**Mulder, Ernest Willem** (*b* Amsterdam, 21 July 1898; *d* Amsterdam, 12 April 1959). Dutch composer and theoretician. He studied the piano under Schulz and composition under Zweers at the Amsterdam Conservatory, where he taught as professor of theory and composition for many years. The best known of his 30 or so works are the *Maria-motetten*, five pieces for soprano and various instrumental ensembles (1945), which won the Visser-Neerlandia Prize. He also composed a Requiem (1932), a *Stabat mater* (1948), four symphonies, chamber music, songs and the *Ars contrapunctica*, a series of studies for ensembles (1938–40).

### WRITINGS
*Harmonieleer* (Utrecht, 1947–52)
*Das Lied von der Erde* (Amsterdam, 1951)
*Polyphonie* (Utrecht, 1955)
ROGIER STARREVELD

**Muldowney, Dominic** (*b* Southampton, 19 July 1952). English composer. He studied composition at Southampton University with Harvey, in London with Birtwistle and at York University with Rands and Blake. From 1974 to 1976 he was composer-in-residence to the Southern Arts Association, and from 1976 resident composer to the National Theatre, London.

### WORKS
Stage: Klavier-Hammer, 1 or more pf, 1973; An Heavyweight Dirge, T, Bar, Mez, fl + sax/cl + sax, pf, perc, 2 vn, vc, 1971; Da capo al fine (ballet), tape, 1975; The Earl of Essex's Galliard (T. Ward), 3 actors, dancer, cl, bn, cornet, tbn, perc, vn, db, 1975–6

Orch: Driftwood to the Flow, 18 str, 1972; Music at Chartres, 16 insts, 1974; Perspectives, 1975; 3 Part Motet, 1976

Choral: Bitter Lemons (Durrell), S, S, A, A, SSAA, 1970; Cantata, S, T, 2 speakers, SATB, 2 vc, perc, 1975; 6 psalms, S, T, chorus, wind, opt. tape, 1979

Chamber: Str Qt, 1973; Lovemusic for Bathsheba Evergreen and Gabriel Oak, fl, ob, cl + sax, pf, b gui, 2 perc, va, vc, 1974; Solo/Ensemble, fl + pic, cl, pf, perc, va, vc, 1974; From Arcady (1) vn, 1976, (3) eng hn, va, vc, 1976, (4) 4 ob, 1977 (2) basset hn, tuba, 1978; Double Helix, 8 players, 1977; 5 melodies, 4 sax, 1978; Garland of chansons, 6 ob, 3 bn, 1978; 3 Hymns to Agape, ob, ob d'amore, eng hn, 1978; A First Show, perc, tape, 1978

Principal publishers: Novello, Universal

**Mulè, Giuseppe** (*b* Termini Imerese, nr. Palermo, 28 June 1885; *d* Rome, 10 Sept 1951). Italian composer. He studied at the Palermo Conservatory, where he was appointed director in 1922, leaving three years later to take a similar post at the Conservatorio di S Cecilia, which he held until 1943. His talent for organization was recognized by the fascist government; he was made national secretary of the Sindacato dei Musicisti, which he and Lualdi represented in parliament from 1929.

Mulè's music was at first influenced by the 'realist' school, and in particular by Mascagni; but he soon came under the spell of the folksong and landscape of Sicily. Returning to the sources of Sicilian folk music he discovered the spiritual world of Greek tragedy, and he wrote much music for performances in the open-air theatre at Syracuse. This was a field in which Mulè excelled. But in his operas, too, the dramatic emotion and atmosphere bear the stamp of a racial instinct, evident as much in legendary or mythical drama as in popular comedy. Moreover, Mulè's harmony, though it never freed itself wholly from derivative elements, is often distinctively rugged, exotic and tritone-obsessed. A first step in this direction is apparent in the immature *La baronessa di Carini*, e.g. in the oddly effective orchestral prelude, with its rasping bass tritones (though the piece resolves into pure Mascagni at the end). A far more extreme example of Mulè's individuality is the first half of his last opera, *La zolfara* – particularly the extraordinary 'whiplash' dance, which shows him as a kind of lesser Sicilian counterpart to Bartók. Yet even in this boldest of his operas he lacked the courage to defy conservative taste to the end: the dénouement is disappointingly tame and sentimental. Among the intervening operas, which represent intermediate stages in Mulè's evolution from *La baronessa* to *La zolfara*, the most celebrated was *Dafni*. Though not his most perfect work (it is uneven, and lacks the concision of the slightly mawkish but evocative *La monacella della fontana*), it contains some of his finest music, particularly in Act 1, which expresses in more complex terms the same archaic, atavistic spirit that pervades the best of the Syracuse scores.

### WORKS
(*selective list*)

Operas: La baronessa di Carini (F. P. Mulè), Palermo, 1912; Al lupo! (F. P. Mulè), Rome, 1919; La monacella della fontana (G. Adami), Trieste, 1923; Dafni (E. Romagnoli, after Theocritus), Rome, 1928; Liolà (A. Rossato, after Pirandello), Naples, 1935; Taormina (Adami), San Remo, 1938; La zolfara (Adami), Rome, 1939

Incidental music: intermezzos, choruses, dances (Aeschylus, Aristophanes, Euripides, Sophocles, Theocritus, a few Italian plays)

Oratorio: Il cieco di Gerico, 1910

Orch: Sicilia canora, 1924; La vendemmia, sym. poem, 1936; Tema con variazioni, vc, orch, 1940; other pieces

Chamber: Adagio, vc, pf, 1903; Str Qt; other works

Songs, film scores

Principal publisher: Ricordi

### BIBLIOGRAPHY
G. Nataletti: 'La *Dafni* di Giuseppe Mulè', *Italia musicale*, iv/4–5 (Genoa, 1931), 1
*Giuseppe Mulè*, Collana di autori contemporanei italiani (Milan, early 1930s) [Ricordi publication, with long extracts from press criticism]
M. Saint-Cyr: 'Giuseppe Mulè', *Rassegna dorica*, v (Rome, 1933–4), 3
A. Gasco: 'La prima rappresentazione di "Dafni" del maestro Mulè al Teatro Reale dell'opera (marzo 1928)', *Da Cimarosa a Strawinsky* (Rome, 1939), 475
J. C. G. Waterhouse: *The Emergence of Modern Italian Music (up to 1940)* (diss., U. of Oxford, 1968), 533ff
ALFREDO CASELLA/JOHN C. G. WATERHOUSE

**Mulet, Henri** (*b* Paris, 17 Oct 1878; *d* Draguignan, Provence, 20 Sept 1967). French composer and organist. As a boy he often played the harmonium for services at the Sacré Coeur, deputizing for his father, Gabriel Mulet, who was choirmaster there. He studied from 1890 at the Paris Conservatoire, where his teachers included Delsart for the cello (*premier prix* 1893),

Leroux and Pugno for harmony (*premier prix* 1896) and Guilmant and Widor for the organ (*second prix* 1897). At the same time he was a member of the Concerts du Chatelet and organist of St Pierre de Montrouge, and he later taught at the Ecole Niedermeyer (1899–1917) and the Schola Cantorum (1924–31). In 1922 the Schola published his attack on organ construction, *Les tendances néfastes et antireligieuses de l'orgue moderne*, which followed similar articles in the *Tribune de St Gervais*. Appointments as organist took him from St Pierre et Ste Marie des Batignolles (1910) and St Eustache et St Roch (1912) to his most important post, that of titular organist at St Philippe du Roule (1922–37). In 1937 he burnt most of his manuscripts, sold his piano and possessions, and moved to Draguignan. His abrupt departure was reportedly caused by despair at financially disastrous contracts exploited by foreign publishers. Isolated, disillusioned, disgusted with his contemporaries (who regarded him as an enigma, though respecting his musicianship), he continued to play at Draguignan Cathedral until 1958, when failing health and poverty forced a move to a convent, La Maison des Petites Soeurs des Pauvres. His output is almost unknown except for two organ works: the *Esquisses byzantines*, stimulated by architectural features of the Sacré Coeur, and the stirring *Carillon sortie*. Tournemire considered him a great artist, a mystic and a gifted improviser.

### WORKS

Org: Méditation religieuse, ?1896; Prière, ?1902; Esquisses byzantines, 10 pieces, ?1914–19; Carillon sortie; Offertoire funèbre; Petit offertoire; Sortie douce
Orch: Dans la vallée du tombeau, sym. poem; Fantaisie pastorale; Paysage d'hiver; Paysages crépusculaires; Suite sur des airs populaires; Scherzo marche; La toussaint, sym. poem
Harmonium: Angelus; Offertoire; Sortie
Pf: Danse persane; Petit lied
Ob: 2 noëls

Principal publishers: Leduc, Senart

### BIBLIOGRAPHY

'Henri Mulet Paris, 1878. 1967, Draguignan', *The Diapason* (1968), March

JENNIFER BATE

**Muling** [Mulinus], **Johannes.** *See* STOMIUS, JOHANNES.

**Muller.** *See* MALER.

**Müller.** German family of string players. Aegidius Christoph Müller (*b* Görsbach, 2 July 1765; *d* Brunswick, 14 Aug 1841), *Hofmusikus* to the Duke of Brunswick, had four sons who formed a string quartet. The eldest, Karl (Friedrich) Müller (*b* Brunswick, 11 Nov 1797; *d* Brunswick, 4 April 1873), was the leader of the quartet and, until 1830, Konzertmeister to the Duke of Brunswick. The second violinist, (Franz Ferdinand) Georg Müller (*b* Brunswick, 30 July 1808; *d* Brunswick, 22 May 1855), was until 1830 Kapellmeister to the same duke. The other members of the quartet were (Theodor Heinrich) Gustav Müller (*b* Brunswick, 3 Dec 1799; *d* Brunswick, 7 Sept 1855), the violist, and (August) Theodor Müller (*b* Brunswick, 27 Aug 1802; *d* Brunswick, 20 Oct 1875), the cellist. Besides playing in the quartet, Theodor Müller was a successful teacher in Brunswick for over 40 years, numbering among his pupils Bernhard Cossmann, Wilhelm Fitzenhagen, Robert Hausmann and his nephew Wilhelm Müller. As employees of the duke the brothers were forbidden to perform publicly and were compelled to rehearse in secret, coached by their father. They resigned in 1830 and made their public début in

Hamburg the following year. In 1832–3 they played in Berlin, acquiring a distinguished reputation; they then embarked on the first of many tours which took them to Germany, France, Denmark, the Netherlands and Russia. The works of Haydn, Mozart and Beethoven comprised their principal repertory. The quartet was dissolved on Gustav Müller's death in 1855.

Karl Müller's four sons formed a second quartet soon afterwards. They were Karl Müller-Berghaus (*b* Brunswick, 14 April 1829; *d* Stuttgart, 11 Nov 1907), the leader of the quartet and married to the singer Elvira Berghaus; Hugo Müller (*b* Brunswick, 21 Sept 1832; *d* Brunswick, 26 June 1886), the second violinist; Bernhard Müller (*b* Brunswick, 24 Feb 1825; *d* Rostock, 4 Sept 1895), the violist; and Wilhelm Müller (*b* Brunswick, 1 June 1834; *d* New York, Sept 1897), the cellist. As a quartet they were appointed to the ducal court at Meiningen but also toured extensively, visiting France, Denmark and Russia. In 1866 they went to Wiesbaden, but soon moved on to Rostock, settling there when Karl was made Kapellmeister (Auer replaced him on the quartet's tours). The quartet was disbanded in 1873 when Wilhelm replaced Jules de Swert as solo cellist of the royal chapel in Berlin and teacher at the Hochschule für Musik (he was also a member of the Joachim Quartet for ten years). Despite their distinguished ensemble playing, they were hampered by their unsuitable choice of repertory and never achieved the status of the earlier quartet.

Two other musicians named Müller, apparently unrelated to the above-named Müllers, were active in Germany as cellists. Hippolyte Müller (*b* Hildburghausen, 16 May 1834; *d* Munich, 23 Aug 1876) made his début at the age of 11, studied with Joseph Menter and was appointed to the royal chapel and conservatory in Munich in 1854. Valentin Müller (*b* Münster, 14 Feb 1830; *d* after 1868) also studied with Menter, then went to Brussels in 1848 to become a pupil of Servais. He was a deputy teacher at the conservatory and for a time a member of the Maurin Quartet. In 1868 he moved to Frankfurt am Main to join the Museums-Gesellschaft Quartet and to teach at the conservatory.

LYNDA LLOYD REES

**Müller** [Schmid], **Adolf** [Adolph] (*b* Tolna, Hungary, 7 Oct 1801; *d* Vienna, 29 July 1886). Austrian composer and Kapellmeister. Orphaned at an early age, he was brought up by an aunt and trained for the stage. He received his first musical instruction from Joseph Rieger, cathedral organist at Brünn (Brno), and is reported to have appeared in public as a pianist at the age of seven. After engagements as actor and singer at Prague, Lemberg (Lwów) and Brünn he moved to Vienna in 1823. He continued his musical studies under Joseph von Blumenthal and on 27 February 1823 his cantata *Österreichs Stern* was performed at the University of Vienna on the occasion of Francis I's birthday. A Singspiel, *Wer andern eine Grube gräbt, fällt selbst hinein*, was given in the Theater in der Josefstadt on 13 December 1825, and in December 1826 he became famous overnight with his score to *Die schwarze Frau*, Meisl's enormously popular parody of Boieldieu's *La dame blanche*. In this year he was engaged as singer at the Kärntnertor-Theater, where he rapidly advanced to the position of Kapellmeister and gave up his acting and singing activities. At Beethoven's funeral he sang second tenor in B. A. Weber's *Rasch tritt der Tod den Menschen an*, after a last rehearsal for

*Die erste Zusammenkunft*, his first Singspiel for the Court Opera, which had its première that night (29 March 1827). In 1828 Müller became Kapellmeister at the Theater an der Wien under Karl Carl, and until 1847 he was director of music at this theatre or at Carl's other theatre, that in the Leopoldstadt suburb. In 1847 he returned to the Theater an der Wien, under new management, and continued as music director until 1878; among his late scores are those for some of Ludwig Anzengruber's plays. Müller was married in 1827; of his three children the most famous was Adolf Müller jr (*b* Vienna, 15 Oct 1839; *d* Vienna, 14 Dec 1901), also a Kapellmeister and talented composer.

Müller's output was prodigious even by the prolific standards of his time. Throughout a long working life (his last [?] new score was performed in January 1878) he produced new Singspiels and *Posse* scores at an average of more than one a month, apart from his duties as arranger, conductor and director. Wurzbach in his incomplete list included about 580 theatre scores for the period up to 1868 including roughly 4500 individual musical numbers; Müller himself made several manuscript copies of many of his scores and arranged some of his most popular numbers for other instruments. Not surprisingly, the bulk of his output proved ephemeral, yet many of his 41 scores to Nestroy's plays are still performed in Vienna, and at his best his music has more than mere melodic charm to commend it. There are innumerable witty, effective *couplets*, and on occasion extended concerted numbers and large-scale quodlibets; the instrumentation is neat though usually unadventurous. He also composed a mass (performed in the court chapel in 1842) and other pieces of church music, some 400 songs and instrumental chamber music. His *Grosse Gesangschule in vier Abtheilungen* (published by Haslinger, Vienna, and in a French edition), and also an *Accordeon-Schule* (published by Diabelli, 1854) were popular in their time.

There are large numbers of Müller's autograph scores in the principal Viennese libraries, especially the Stadtbibliothek and Nationalbibliothek. Many songs from his popular theatre scores were brought out in series by Haslinger, Diabelli, Spina and others.

BIBLIOGRAPHY

C. von Wurzbach: 'Müller, Adolph', *Biographisches Lexikon des Kaiserthums Oesterreich*, xix (Vienna, 1868) [incl. almost complete list of works, 1825–68]

J. Nestroy: *Sämtliche Werke*, ed. F. Brukner and O. Rommel (Vienna, 1924–30)

F. Hadamowsky: *Das Theater in der Wiener Leopoldstadt* (Vienna, 1934)

A. Bauer: *Die Musik Adolph Müllers in den Theaterstücken Johann Nestroys* (diss., U. of Vienna, 1935)

——: *150 Jahre Theater an der Wien* (Zurich, Leipzig and Vienna, 1952)

——: *Opern und Operetten in Wien* (Graz and Cologne, 1955)

——: *Das Theater in der Josefstadt zu Wien* (Vienna and Munich, 1957)

PETER BRANSCOMBE

**Müller, August Eberhard** (*b* Northeim, 13 Dec 1767; *d* Weimar, 3 Dec 1817). German conductor, flautist, keyboard player and composer. He was first taught the keyboard and organ by his father, the organist Matthäus Müller, and later took lessons in harmony and composition with J. C. F. Bach in Bückeburg. In 1786 he began to study law at Göttingen, where he attracted attention as a flautist in the informal concerts at the home of the Officer of Justice, Püttner. He then made concert tours in northern Germany and lived for a time in Brunswick. In 1788 he married the pianist Elisabeth Catherina

Rabert in Magdeburg, and in the following year succeeded her father as organist at the Ulrichskirche there. From 1792 he conducted the Masonic concerts and the private concerts of the nobility. During the 1792–3 season he appeared in Berlin, where he made the acquaintance of several important people. On J. F. Reichardt's recommendation he became organist at the Nikolaikirche, Leipzig, in 1794 and also joined the Gewandhaus orchestra as first flautist. His wife played there regularly as a pianist in Mozart concertos. In 1800 he became assistant at the Thomaskirche to the aging Kantor J. A. Hiller, whom he succeeded in 1804. He continued the concerts begun by Hiller at the Thomasschule and the church, and in them he conducted several of Bach's cantatas, probably for the first time since the composer's death. In 1810 he left Leipzig to become musical director of the Weimar court orchestra and court opera, which entailed teaching duties at the Gymnasium and the teacher-training college; he was also responsible for the Stadtkirche music.

Müller was a capable organist and keyboard player as well as a proficient flautist. Goethe, who always had difficulties with the opera in Weimar, valued him as an energetic Kapellmeister. He had an excellent ear and tried to raise the standard of the performances. His Singspiel *Der Polterabend* was unsuccessful, but his flute concertos and various piano works were well received. His sacred works were also praised (*AMZ*, iv, 1801–2, col.233), but only a few survive. The starting-point for his compositions was Mozart, whose influence is predominant in the early works. The later piano capriccios, opp.29, 31, 34 and 41, and the Variations on Mozart's 'Ein Mädchen oder Weibchen' op.32, however, reveal virtuoso developments in piano technique approaching those of Liszt. Müller did much to propagate the works of Mozart and Haydn: in addition to performing their works he prepared piano arrangements for Breitkopf & Härtel and assisted that firm as an adviser and co-worker in the publication of their first complete editions. Beethoven wrote to Breitkopf (3 September 1806) that he held Müller in high esteem as an artist. Müller's pedagogic works had a great influence in his lifetime. Besides a guide to Mozart's keyboard concertos and tutors for the flute and keyboard, he published a *Klavier- und Fortepiano-Schule* (1804) as a revised, much enlarged sixth edition of Löhlein's *Clavierschule*; this was revised by Czerny as late as 1825.

WORKS
*(published in Leipzig unless otherwise stated)*

VOCAL

Der Polterabend (Singspiel, 1, A. Wolff), Weimar, 1813 or 1814; vocal score (*c*1820)

Cantatine zu Familienfesten, 4vv, chorus, insts (n.d., after 1817); sacred cantatas, Gerechte frohlocket dem Herrn, *D-B*, *Dlb*, Preis und Dank, *Dlb*, *GOa*, Siehe, ich verkündige euch, *B*; Te Deum, D, *Dlb*; Psalm cxii, *Dlb*; [12] deutschen Lieder, i (Hamburg, 1796), ii (n.d.); other lieder pubd separately

ORCHESTRAL

Fl concs.: op.6 (Berlin, *c*1794); op.7 (Berlin, *c*1794), lost; op.10 (Offenbach, *c*1795); op.16 (*c*1798); op.19 (1801); op.20 (*c*1801); op.22 (*c*1804); op.24 (*c*1806); op.27 (*c*1807), lost; op.30 (*c*1809); op.39 (*c*1817)

Polonoise, fl, orch, op.23 (*c*1805)

Grande fantaisie, fl, orch, op.40 (*c*1818)

Kbd concs.: op.1 (Berlin, *c*1792); op.21 (*c*1802)

KEYBOARD

Sonatas: 3, op.3 (Offenbach, 1792); 3, op.5 (Offenbach, 1793); 3, op.7 (*c*1795); 3, op.14 (?1801); 3, op.18 (?1802); 1, op.26 (*c*1806); 1, op.36 (1813)

Caprices: op.4 (Offenbach, 1793); 6, op.29 (*c*1808); 3, op.31 (*c*1809); 3, op.34 (*c*1812); 3, op.41 (*c*1818)

Variations: op.8 (1795); op.9 (Hamburg, 1796); op.12 (*c*1796); op.32

(c1810); op.35 (c1813); op.37 (1813); others
Other: Sammlung von Orgelstücken . . . 12 leichte und 6 schwere Sätze, org (1798); Walzer in 12 Durtönen, op.33 (1810)

OTHER INSTRUMENTAL

Fl duets: 3 grands duos concertants, op.11 (Hamburg, n.d.); 3, op.13 (c1797); 20 petits duos, op.19 (Paris, n.d.); 3 duos concertants, op.28 (1807)
Solo fl: Theme favorit de W. A. Mozart varié (1801); 6 variations (Hamburg, n.d.)
Grande sonate, pf, acc. vn, vc, op.17 (1800)
Grande sonate, pf, fl, op.38 (c1814)

PEDAGOGICAL

*Anweisung zum genauen Vortrage der Mozartschen Clavier-Concerte* (1796)
*Klavier- und Fortepiano-Schule* (Jena, 1804 [as 6th edn. of G. S. Löhlein: *Clavierschule*, 1765]; 8/1825, ed. C. Czerny)
*Kleines Elementarbuch für Klavierspieler* (c1807)
*Elementarbuch für Flötenspieler* (c1815)
*Cadenzen zu den 8 vorzüglichsten Clavier-Conzerten von W. A. Mozart* (c1818)
Several collections of practice pieces, fl, pf

BIBLIOGRAPHY

*EitnerQ*; *GerberNL*
Reviews, notices etc, *AMZ*, i–xix (1798–1817)
A. Dörffel: *Geschichte der Gewandhausconcerte zu Leipzig* (Leipzig, 1884)
W. Nagel: 'Zur Lebensgeschichte August Eberhard Müllers', *Die Musik*, ix/4 (1909–10), 84
W. Bode: *Die Tonkunst in Goethes Leben* (Berlin, 1912)
G. Haupt: *A. E. Müllers Leben und Klavierwerke* (diss., U. of Leipzig, 1926)
N. Broder: 'The First Guide to Mozart', *MQ*, xlii (1956), 223

GUNTER HEMPEL

**Müller, Christian** (*b* Andreasberg, Harz, Feb 1690; buried Amsterdam, 8 March 1763). German organ builder. He was active in Holland and West Frisia, and is best known for his large organ in the Grote Kerk (St Bavo) in Haarlem (1735–8; three manuals, 60 stops; restored 1959–61). He also built organs in Alkmaar, Amsterdam, Beverwijk, Leeuwarden and elsewhere. The materials and workmanship of Müller's organs are of high quality, but their scalings are relatively unimaginative (all the diapasons in Alkmaar, Beverwijk and Haarlem have exactly the same proportions). Müller's production was carried on by his pupil Johann Heinrich Hartmann Bätz (1709–70), from Frankenroda in Thuringia; Bätz's most important work is in Zierikzee (1770).

BIBLIOGRAPHY

H. L. Oussoren: 'De orgelbouwer Christiaan Müller en zijn werk', *Prospectus van het Haarlemmer orgelconcours in 1959*, 8
——: 'Het Christian Müller-orgel in de Grote of St. Bavokerk te Haarlem', *Nederlandse orgelpracht*, ed. J. F. Obermayr and others (Haarlem, 1961), 38–85

HANS KLOTZ

**Müller, Eduard** (*b* Basle, 12 Oct 1912). Swiss organist. He studied at the Basle Conservatory with Adolf Hamm and in Leipzig with Günther Ramin. In 1934 he was appointed organist and choirmaster of St Paul's church, Basle, and in 1939 teacher of organ, harpsichord and thoroughbass at the Schola Cantorum Basiliensis (where Gustav Leonhardt was among his pupils), as well as in 1945 at the conservatory. Müller gives numerous concerts in Switzerland and abroad, and has an unusually large repertory. His careful feeling for style is demonstrated in a large number of gramophone recordings which include the complete set of Handel's organ concertos. He is also engaged in editing the continuo parts for the Neue Bach-Ausgabe.

JÜRG STENZL

**Müller, Erich H(ermann).** *See* MUELLER VON ASOW, ERICH H.

**Müller** [Miller; Krasinsky, Graschinsky], **Ernest Louis** (*b* Warsaw, 26 Oct 1740; *d* Paris, 15 April 1811). Flautist and composer resident in France. He may have been born Krasinsky, though Choron maintained that this was a pseudonym and further distinguished him from a German composer of flute music by that name. He was living in Berlin in about 1760, and in 1768 he moved to France in the service of the wealthy amateur and flautist Chevalier de Salles, first at Dijon and later at Auxonnes. In 1776 he settled in Paris, but his career was greatly handicapped by a tendency to drink. Through the help of the violinist and ballet-master Pierre Gardel he was able to obtain ballet commissions for the Opéra; they brought him some considerable fame and were frequently revived well into the 1820s. He also composed flute duets and *duos concertans* for flute and violin which were apparently known throughout Europe, and Choron mentioned the extraordinary popularity in Germany of a volume of flute trios by him. His step-daughter Marie Elizabeth Miller (1770–1823) achieved fame as a dancer, and married Gardel in 1795.

WORKS

STAGE

*(all performed at Paris Opéra)*

Le déserteur (ballet pantomime, 3, M. Gardel), 21 Oct 1786; (rev. P. Gardel), 16 Jan 1788, *F-Po*
Télémaque dans l'île de Calypso (ballet héroïque, 3, P. Gardel), 23 Feb 1790, *Po*
Psyché (ballet pantomime, P. Gardel), 14 Dec 1790, *Po*

INSTRUMENTAL

Point d'orgue, vn, dans tous les tons (Paris, 1778)
6 duos concertans, fl, vn (Paris, 1781; 2/as op.1, London, n.d.), collab. L. Vogel
At least 30 duos, 2 fl, opp.4–5, 7–8, 26 (Paris, 1787 and later)
Trios, 3 fl, cited by Choron

BIBLIOGRAPHY

*FétisB*; *GerberNL* ('Krasinsky')
A. Choron and F. Fayolle: *Dictionnaire historique des musiciens* (Paris, 1810–11)
T. Lajarte: *Bibliothèque musicale du théâtre de l'Opéra* (Paris, 1878), esp. ii, 53

ROGER COTTE

**Müller, Fidel.** *See* MOLITOR, FIDEL.

**Müller, Franz.** *See* MÜLLER, SILVERIUS.

**Müller, Georg Gottfried** (*b* 1762; *d* 1821). American Moravian violinist and composer; *see* MORAVIANS, AMERICAN.

**Müller, Heinrich** (*b* Lübeck, 18 Oct 1631; *d* Rostock, 17 Sept 1675). German poet and theologian. His father had fled from Rostock to Lübeck when Mecklenburg was occupied by Wallenstein's armies. The family returned to Rostock in 1644, and Heinrich entered the university there at the age of 13. In 1647 he went to Greifswald to study theology, returning in 1650 to Rostock, where he received the master's degree. He then spent a year visiting various universities, including those at Danzig, Königsberg, Helmstedt, Wittenberg, Leipzig and Jena, after which, in 1651, he gave lectures on philosophy at the University of Rostock. At the age of 21 he became a doctor of theology of Helmstedt University. In 1653 he became archdeacon at the Marienkirche, Rostock. In 1659 he was appointed professor of theology, as well as pastor at St Marien. He was made city superintendent in 1671.

Theologically, Müller remained within the confines of Lutheran orthodoxy, but as a writer he leaned towards the mystical-erotic tradition, following Philipp Nicolai, in which godly love in the heart of the believer was seen as an intensification of the Lutheran doctrine of justification by faith. He was one of those late Baroque mystical poets who scorned the world and wrote ecstatic works in praise of Heaven (e.g. *Himmlischer Liebeskuss*, 1659) and Christ. Alongside the emphasis on Heaven an almost self-indulgent subjectivism is found in his song texts. His mystical spiritualism heralded the beginnings of Pietism and through his major song publication influenced the hymn writers Johann Franck, Paul Gerhardt, Johann Heermann and Johann Rist. This publication is *Geistliche Seelenmusik bestehend in zehn Betrachtungen und 400 auserlesenen geist- und kraftreichen sowohl alten als neuen Gesängen mit allerhand schönen, unter andern fünfzig ganz neuen Melodien gezieret* (Rostock, 1659, rev. 2/1668; the ten *Betrachtungen* (meditations) repr. as *Hymnologia sacra*, Nuremberg, 1728). It is a collection of both old and new songs. Among the latter are ten sacred poems under a separate title, *Himmlische Liebesflamme*, by Müller himself. The old songs consist of 112 from the 16th century: Müller was one of the first poets to remould 16th-century sacred songs, thereby contributing to the reform of the Protestant hymn. His collection includes 126 melodies with continuo, 50 of them by Nikolaus Hasse. The meditations are in prose and are concerned with the value and use of sacred songs.

BIBLIOGRAPHY
E. E. Koch: *Geschichte des Kirchenlieds und Kirchengesangs* (rev., enlarged Stuttgart, 3/1866–77/R1973), iv
J. Zahn: *Die Melodien der deutschen evangelischen Kirchenlieder*, vi (Gütersloh, 1893/R1963)
M. Schmidt: 'Müller, Heinrich', *Die Religion in Geschichte und Gegenwart*, iv (Tübingen, 1960)
JERROLD C. BAAB

**Müller, Iwan** (*b* Reval [now Tallinn], Estonia, 3 Dec 1786; *d* Bückeburg, 4 Feb 1854). German clarinettist and basset-horn player. He was also active as an inventor: in 1808 he produced an 18-key basset-horn, and in 1809 a prototype clarinet of the class now known as 'simple system'. The clarinet had 13 keys, seven of which were new, and gave much better intonation through more carefully placed holes. Müller was the first to use stuffed pads over counter-sunk tone-holes, and in 1817 invented the metal ligature. Early in his career he added three keys to the bassoon, which he played at that time, and later claimed the invention of the alto clarinet.

Müller was no less energetic as a performer; his 'carrière agitée', as Fétis called it, took him to all major European cities. Wherever he went he advertised his new clarinet, and his success as an artist inspired composers to write specifically for it. His style was brilliant and expressive, though impetuous and somewhat lacking in polish. From 1800 he was in St Petersburg, where he became an imperial chamber musician. He left in 1807 and travelled through Austria and Germany to Paris, where he spent considerable periods throughout his life, though without any fixed appointment. Müller lived in England from 1815 to 1820 and during 1829. In later years he made several extremely successful Italian tours and ended his days as court musician to the Prince of Schaumburg-Lippe. He dedicated his tutor of 1825 to George IV of England. His studies are still used today, but his numerous concert pieces are no longer popular.

BIBLIOGRAPHY
*FétisB*
W. Tenney: 'Ivan Mueller and his New Clarinet', *Woodwind Magazine*, iii (1951)
F. G. Rendall: *The Clarinet* (London, 1954, 3/1971)

O. Kroll: *Die Klarinette* (Kassel, 1965; Eng. trans., enlarged, 1968)
P. Weston: *Clarinet Virtuosi of the Past* (London, 1971)
PAMELA WESTON

**Müller, Johann** (*fl* 1656–82). German singer, instrumentalist and composer. Gerber's remarks about him distort those of Walther; Eitner (in his second and third 'Müller' entries) confused various composers. Müller studied composition with Peranda. From 1656 he was a member of the Dresden Hofkapelle. About 1666 he is recorded as an alto singer and as an instrumentalist there and in 1676 as being 'attached to' the Kapelle; he is named in a salary document of 1680, and in 1682 he is mentioned as music master to the choirboys and thus must still have been a member of the Kapelle. He may be identical with the schalmei player of the same name mentioned in 1692 (but definitely not with the court organist Hans Müller, who was engaged in 1615). Of the few works identified as his, two, the ten-part *O Jesu Christe, Gottes Sohn* and five-part *Dein Wort ist meines Fusses Leuchte*, are in the Bokemeyer Collection. The concertos mentioned in the Catalogus CAS (*D-Dlb* Mus.2118-E-503; see Steude) – *Fürwahr er trug unsere Krankheit*, for 18 voices, *Age homo numeremus*, for six voices, and *Cogita, o homo*, for seven voices – are lost, as too is his important contribution to the 17th-century *historia*, *Die Aufferstehung unsers Herrn und Heilands Jesu Christi* (1676). The two concertos marked 'Molitor' (= 'Müller') in the inventory of the Michaelisschule, Lüneburg – *Si Deus pro nobis*, for three voices and *Wie lieblich sind deine Wohnungen*, for ten or 15 voices – may also be by Johann Müller.

BIBLIOGRAPHY
*EitnerQ*; *GerberNL*; *WaltherML*
M. Fürstenau: *Zur Geschichte der Musik und des Theaters am Hofe zu Dresden* (Dresden, 1861–2/R1971)
M. Seiffert: 'Die Chorbibliothek der St. Michaelisschule in Lüneburg', *SIMG*, ix (1907–8), 593
W. Steude: 'Die *Markuspassion* in der Leipziger Passionen-Handschrift des Johann Zacharias Grundig', *DJbM*, xiv (1969), 96
H. Kümmerling: *Katalog der Sammlung Bokemeyer* (Kassel, 1970)
WOLFRAM STEUDE

**Müller, Johann Adam.** See MOLITOR, ALEXIUS.

**Müller, Johann Daniel** (*fl* Frankfurt am Main, mid-18th century). German musician. He was concert director in Frankfurt am Main around the middle of the 18th century, and he edited a hymnbook for the organ there in 1754 for the printing house of Stocks Erben, Schilling & Weber, under the title *Vollständiges Hessen-Hanauisches Choral-Buch, welches so wohl die Melodien der 150. Psalmen Davids, als anderer in beyden evangelischen Kirchen unseres Deutschlands bisher eingeführten alten und neuen Lieder in sich fasset ... auf gantz neue Art eingerichtet*. The preface states that the printers had originally planned only to issue a new edition of Johann Michael Müller's hymnbook, but because of the increased number of songs they decided in favour of the form presented. Instead of about 300 melodies, the later work contained almost 1000, arranged according to the strophic structure of the text. The settings are characteristic of the 17th century (with emphasized series of basic notes and consonant intervals between descant and bass): according to the preface, the bass lines are not set too chromatically because a hymn should be played quite naturally and without exaggerated affectation so that the melody can be clearly heard by the congregation. Zahn listed a number of melodies which were published for the first time in this hymnbook and which are probably Müller's own work. His identification with other musicians of the same name is questionable (see Blankenburg).

BIBLIOGRAPHY

*EitnerQ*

J. Adlung: *Anleitung zu der musikalischen Gelahrtheit* (Erfurt, 1758/*R*1953), 670; (2/1783)

C. F. Becker: *Die Choralsammlungen der verschiedenen christlichen Kirchen* (Leipzig, 1845), 190f

C. von Winterfeld: *Der evangelische Kirchengesang und sein Verhältniss zur Kunst des Tonsatzes*, iii (Leipzig, 1847/*R*1966), 536f

S. Kümmerle: *Encyklopädie der evangelischen Kirchenmusik*, ii (Gütersloh, 1890), 319f

J. Zahn: *Die Melodien der deutschen evangelischen Kirchenlieder*, vi (Gütersloh, 1893/*R*1963), 339f

M. Blindow: *Die Choralbegleitung des 18. Jahrhunderts in der evangelischen Kirche Deutschlands* (Regensburg, 1957)

W. Blankenburg: 'Müller, Johann Daniel', *MGG*

GÜNTER THOMAS

**Müller, Johann Michael** (*b* Schmalkalden, 21 Nov 1683; *d* Hanau, 14 Sept 1743). German composer. He was musical director and organist in Hanau from 1706: he was also appointed *Präzeptor* at the reformed Gymnasium in 1713 and became deputy headmaster in 1737. His hymnbook for the organ, published in Frankfurt, contains a poem of dedication by Telemann (Zahn mentioned a group of melodies which appeared here for the first time and which were probably composed by Müller himself). This went through two editions and was then replaced by the considerably more comprehensive hymnbook of Johann Daniel Müller.

WORKS

Neu-aufgesetztes, vollständiges und nach der neu- und reinesten Composition eingerichtetes Psalm- und Choral-Buch, in welchem nicht allein die 150 Psalmen Davids, sondern auch die gebräuchlichste Evangelisch-Lutherische Kirchen-Gesänge, nebst des Neanders Bundes-Liedern, so bisshero nach keinen bekandten Melodien gesungen worden, in fügliche Melodie gesetzt, pt.i (Frankfurt am Main, 1718), pt.ii (Frankfurt am Main, 1719)

Anhang zu dem Müllerischen Psalmen- und Choral-Buch (Frankfurt am Main, 1739)

12 sonatas, ob solo, 2 ob/vn, taille, bn, bc (Amsterdam, n.d.), lost, cited in Walther and Gerber

Variirte Chorale und Psalmen, pt.i (Frankfurt am Main, 1735), pt.ii [incl. preludes, fugues and 1 org conc.] (Frankfurt am Main, 1737): lost, cited in Adlung, Gerber and Göhler

BIBLIOGRAPHY

*EitnerQ*; *GerberL*; *GerberNL*; *WaltherML*

J. Adlung: *Anleitung zu der musikalischen Gelahrtheit* (Erfurt, 1758/*R*1953, 2/1783)

C. F. Becker: *Die Choralsammlungen der verschiedenen christlichen Kirchen* (Leipzig, 1845), 183ff

S. Kümmerle: *Encyklopädie der evangelischen Kirchenmusik*, ii (Gütersloh, 1890), 320f

J. Zahn: *Die Melodien der deutschen evangelischen Kirchenlieder*, vi (Gütersloh, 1893/*R*1963), 301f, 315, 326

A. Göhler: *Verzeichnis der in den Frankfurter und Leipziger Messkatalogen der Jahre 1564 bis 1759 angezeigten Musikalien* (Leipzig, 1902/*R*1965), iii, 16

GÜNTER THOMAS

**Müller, Johann Nicolaus** (*b* c1700; *d* after 1749). German organist and composer. According to his publications he was also a sworn legal notary (*Act[uarius] justit[iae] jur[atus]*) in Wurzbach, Lobenstein (Thuringia). His simple, rather naive keyboard suites *Des musicalischen Frauenzimmers musicalisches Divertissiment* (Nuremberg, from 1736) were popular in their day and included many types of dance in the French and Italian styles. Only the last set of six (not three) is extant (*D-Mbs*). Nor did his *Harmonische-Kirchen-Lust: bestehend aus XII. Arien XII. Praeludien und XII. kurzen leichten Fugen vor Orgel und Clavier* (Nuremberg) survive World War II, but the 12 fugues

that survive in manuscript (*D-B* 15708/10) are probably a contemporary copy. Like south German models, the writing is more fugato than fugal, without regular counter-subjects, strict part-writing or obbligato pedal. The best examples show a certain flair for keyboard writing in a somewhat vapid Italian style. The motet *Schaffe in mir Gott ein reines Herze* (27 May 1677; *D-B* 15708) is probably by the J. N. Müller named on the rolls of the Thomasschule, Leipzig, 1665–74.

BIBLIOGRAPHY

G. Frotscher: *Geschichte des Orgel-Spiels und der Orgel-Komposition* (Berlin, 1935–6, enlarged 3/1966)

HUGH J. MCLEAN

**Müller, Johann Patroklus.** *See* MÖLLER, JOHANN PATROKLUS.

**Müller, Maria** (*b* Litoměřice, 29 Jan 1898; *d* Bayreuth, 13 March 1958). Czech soprano. She studied in Vienna with the Danish tenor Erik Schmedes and made her début as Elsa at Linz in 1919. Engagements followed at the German Theatre in Prague and in Munich, and in 1925 she made her début as Sieglinde at the Metropolitan, New York. She remained there until the 1934–5 season, singing leading parts in a number of American premières, including the title role in Alfano's *Madonna imperia* (1928), Mariola in Pizzetti's *Fra Gherardo* (1929), Dorota in *Schwanda* (1931) and Amelia in *Simon Boccanegra* (1932). In Berlin, at the Städtische Oper under Bruno Walter, she was first heard as Euryanthe in 1926, and she later sang at the Staatsoper until 1943. After World War II she sang again at the Städtische Oper, but was not in good health and soon retired to live at Bayreuth, her spiritual home. There she had sung regularly from 1930 to 1944 (Senta, Eva, Elisabeth, Elsa and Sieglinde). At Salzburg she appeared in 1931 (Eurydice), 1933 (Reiza) and 1934 (Donna Elvira). Her Covent Garden début was as Eva in 1934 under Beecham, and she sang Sieglinde in the 1937 *Ring* cycles under Furtwängler. Her large repertory included the title roles in *Die aegyptische Helena*, *Jenůfa*, Iphigenia in Gluck's *Iphigénie en Tauride*, Djula in Gotovac's *Ero s onoga svijeta* ('Ero from the other world'), Pamina, Tosca and Marguerite.

Maria Müller possessed a warm, vibrant voice. She sang Elsa and Elisabeth with a rare purity of tone, and her Sieglinde, while not quite so womanly as Lotte Lehmann's, was a moving creation.

HAROLD ROSENTHAL

**Müller, Matthias.** Inventor of the UPRIGHT PIANOFORTE, also developed independently by JOHN ISAAC HAWKINS.

**Müller** [Miller, Millner, Müllner], **Silverius** [Franz] (*b* Oberhöflein, Lower Austria, 27 Feb 1745; *d* Vienna, 21 Aug 1812). Austrian composer and teacher. He entered the Piarist order on 3 October 1764 and took the name Silverius a Sancto Leopoldo instead of his baptismal name, Franz; he was ordained on 22 December 1770. He received his musical education at the Piarist Gymnasium at Horn. Between 1770 and 1783 he worked chiefly as *regens chori* and *instructor musicae* at three Piarist colleges, Maria Treu, Vienna, and those at Günzburg and Krems. Because of the reforms of the Emperor Joseph II there were fewer opportunities for such employment after 1783 and Müller subsequently worked for his order not as a musician but as a prefect and, from 1800, as professor of classical literature and philosophy at the Löwenburg Konvikt, Vienna. In 1796 he visited Naples for study purposes. His music won a certain admiration in his day; the most important is his chamber music, which deploys Classical forms in a lively manner. The Mass in D stands out among his church music, which follows the conventions of the time.

### WORKS

Str qts: 6 (Vienna, 1785); 6 (Vienna, 1795), announced but probably not pubd; 3 as op.3 (Vienna, 1803); 6 as op.2, *A-Wgm* (? copied from unknown pubn); 13, *I-Mc*; 6, *CS-J* (inc.)

Other inst: 6 str qnts, *A-Wgm*; 2 pf qts, *I-Mc*; 6 duos, vn, va, *A-Wgm*; 6 fl qts, lost (cited in Traeg's catalogue, 1799); Marsch beym Abzug der Franzosen, pf, 1806, *Wn*

Vocal: 6 neue Lieder beym Clavier oder bey der Harfe zu singen (Vienna, before 1799); 2 masses, C, *SEI*, D, *Wp*; motet, offertory, *CS-Bm*

### BIBLIOGRAPHY

O. Biba: *Der Piaristenorden in Österreich: seine Bedeutung für bildende Kunst, Musik und Theater im 17. und 18. Jahrhundert* (Eisenstadt, 1975), 131, 157f, 164ff, 179

For fuller bibliography see *MGG*

based on *MGG* (xvi, 1303–4) by permission of Bärenreiter

OTTO BIBA

**Müller, Therese.** *See* MALTEN, THERESE.

**Müller, Valentin.** *See* MOLITOR, VALENTIN.

**Müller, Wenzel** (*b* Tyrnau [now Trnava], 26 Sept 1767; *d* Baden, nr. Vienna, 3 Aug 1835). Austrian composer and Kapellmeister. Following his father's early death Müller and his mother moved from Altstadt (Stare Město) to Kornitz (Koričany) in the same area of south-east Moravia. Taught by the local schoolmaster, Müller could soon play all the instruments of the orchestra and began to compose. At the age of 12 he wrote a mass for the ordination of an older brother. He was sent to study at the Benedictine foundation of Raigern (Rajhrad), near Brno, where he concentrated on mastering wind instruments. Taught and encouraged by the choirmaster, Maurus Haberbauer, he also composed wind pieces and church music. When the prelate Ottmar went to Johannisberg (the seat of Count Schaffgotsch, Prince-Bishop of Breslau) he took Müller with him, and Dittersdorf became his teacher. In 1782 Müller joined Waizhofer's theatre company at Brno as third violinist and composed a successful Singspiel, *Das verfehlte Rendezvous, oder Die weiblichen Jäger*. Encouraged by the comic actor and singer Anton Baumann, and by the new theatre director Bergopzoomer, Müller made excellent progress. The story that Emperor Joseph II heard Müller, was impressed by him and determined to send him to Italy to study, must be discounted on grounds of chronology. Müller did however embark on a planned concert tour with the Willmann family in 1786 that was abandoned only when he was taken on as Kapellmeister by Marinelli at Vienna's Leopoldstädter-Theater ('The tenth of May I Wenzel Müller was formally engaged as Kapellmeister', he wrote in his diary – the first definitely authenticated date since his birth).

Müller's first Vienna appearance was on 30 May 1786, when he conducted the Leopoldstadt première of Gassmann's *Die Gräfin* (*La contessina*). From then until 1830, with the exception of an engagement in Prague, he served as Kapellmeister to the Leopoldstädter-Theater, for most of that time being in charge of the theatre's musical activities. Not yet 19 at the time of his appointment, he had the task of making the musical side of Marinelli's performances worthy of the actors' skills (these included his friend Baumann, and Johann 'Kasperl' Laroche). Under Müller the orchestra was

enlarged and improved, and the appointment of Ferdinand Kauer as second Kapellmeister, and later as head of the theatre's own music school, meant that the company was assured a steady supply of well-trained singers and musicians.

Müller's autograph diary contains a wealth of fascinating information about performances at the theatre, as well as its social and economic circumstances. For several years he listed the number of performances he had to conduct and the number of new scores he wrote; in 1794 he was exceptionally busy, conducting on no fewer than 225 evenings, though in this year he wrote a mere seven 'operas' (the title loosely used for Singspiels of some pretension) as opposed to 15 or 20 theatre scores in other years. His first major success as a composer was achieved with *Das Sonnenfest der Braminen* (9 September 1790; text by Hensler), given over 90 times in 15 years and published by at least three German houses. *Das Neusonntagskind*, the first of the Singspiels adapted by Joachim Perinet from originals by Philipp Hafner, was given on 10 October 1793 and heard over 160 times in the Leopoldstadt alone. The première was Müller's first benefit night, and as he said in his diary, 'I won my musical renown [*Credit*] with this opera; this opera is known in every land'. The 1790s were splendid years for this theatre – the abandonment of the National-Singspiel left the field wide open, and the enterprising Marinelli stepped in; as proof of the theatre's renown, there was a remarkable number of royal and imperial visitors. Müller's most popular scores of this period include [*Kaspar*] *Der Fagottist oder Die Zauberzither, Die Schwestern von Prag, Die zwölf schlafenden Jungfrauen, Das lustige Beilager* and *Die Teufelsmühle am Wienerberg* (163 performances in the Leopoldstadt before 1860).

The first few years of the 19th century contained no major successes for Müller, which may well account in part for his decision to accept an invitation from the director, Liebich, to become Kapellmeister at the German Opera in Prague, a post he held from March 1807 until May 1813; his daughter Therese (the distinguished operatic soprano Madame Grünbaum, born 24 August 1791) was engaged as singer at the same time. It is clear from contemporary reports that Müller was not equal to the demands of his Prague contract (even Weber, his successor, was exercised to improve standards); there is, however, a valuable report on Müller as a conductor from J. F. Reichardt, who heard him conduct *Das Neusonntagskind* at Prague November 1808:

The finale of the second act was performed entirely comically by all the cast, with Italian liveliness. Most of the waltzes and other folk melodies were, however, played and sung much more slowly and gracefully than almost anywhere else, whereby the whole took on a *gemütlich* quality, which obviously pleased all hearers and assuredly has something national about it.

Müller resumed his duties at the Leopoldstädter-Theater on 15 June 1813; he recovered much of his former fire and enthusiasm, owing at least in part to the successes of his daughter, son-in-law and, later, granddaughter Caroline (who made a successful début at the Court Opera in August 1829, aged 15). Müller's numerous popular Singspiels, parodies and *Posse* scores after his return from Prague include *Tankredi, Aline, oder Wien in einem andern Weltteil* (1822; based on Berton's opera), *Der verwunschene Prinz* (1818; based on Seyfried's arrangement of Grétry's *Zémire et Azor*) and his scores for Raimund's *Der Barometermacher auf der Zauberinsel* (1823), *Die gefesselte Phantasie* and

*Der Alpenkönig und der Menschenfeind* (both 1828). He continued to write scores until the year before his death, not without meeting charges of self-plagiarism.

Of all the regular composers of music for the Viennese *Volkstheater* Müller was the most popular and the best; some of his scores, especially for Raimund's works, are still regularly performed; and a number of his songs rapidly achieved lasting success in the guise of street songs and *Volkslieder* (*Wer niemals einen Rausch gehabt, Lieber kleiner Gott der Liebe, So leb denn wohl, du stilles Haus*). Although later in his career he was seldom as ambitious, a number of his early operas fully deserve that title: the finale to Act 1 of *Die unruhige Nachbarschaft* is so extensive that it was bound as a separate manuscript volume (now in the Bavarian State Library, Munich); the first finale to *Die Schwestern von Prag*, with its interrupted serenades, beatings and nightwatchman's call, is also a full-scale ensemble. Müller was at his best and most characteristic in simple, unpretentious songs and duets. The famous quintet from *Der Alpenkönig* is nothing more than a simply harmonized refrain with contrasting solos. His scoring is simple but almost always effective. He experimented eagerly and with success in operatic parody and in melodrama (*Der verwunschene Prinz* includes four melodramas, one of them comic). Müller's most obvious weakness lies in his general inability to develop his ideas or string them together to any cumulative effect. This fact alone would be sufficient to discount Bauernfeld's anecdote of Mozart's having tapped Müller on the shoulder after one of his concerted finales and said: 'Wenzel, I should like to have composed that myself'. Yet in solo song (easily the most important single category in contemporary Viennese theatre) Müller achieved an astonishing number of successes in all types, especially with tender, reflective numbers, but also with gay or satirical and occasionally (*Die Teufelsmühle*) with effectively sinister songs.

### WORKS
*(principal sources for MSS and early prints: A-Wgm, Wn, Wst, D-Bds)*

THEATRICAL

Selective list from c250 titles; all works cited were first performed at the Leopoldstädter-Theater, Vienna; many appeared contemporaneously in vocal scores or excerpts.

Das Sonnenfest der Braminen (heroic-comic Singspiel, 2, K. F. Hensler), 9 Sept 1790

[Kaspar] Der Fagottist, oder Die Zauberzither (Singspiel, 3, J. Perinet), 8 June 1791

Das Neusonntagskind (Singspiel, 2, Perinet, after Hafner), 10 Oct 1793

Die Schwestern von Prag (Singspiel, 2, Perinet, after Hafner), 11 March 1794

Der alte Überall und Nirgends (play, with songs, 5, Hensler), 10 June 1795

Das lustige Beilager (Singspiel, 2, Perinet, after Hafner), 14 Feb 1797

Die zwölf schlafenden Jungfrauen (play, with songs, 4, Hensler), 12 Oct 1797

Der Sturm, oder Die bezauberte Insel (heroic-comic opera, 2, Hensler, after Shakespeare), 8 Nov 1798

Die Teufelsmühle am Wienerberg (legend, with songs, 4, Hensler), 12 Nov 1799

Die Belagerung von Ypsilon (caricature, with songs, 2, Perinet, after Hafner), 4 May 1804

Die neue Alceste (caricature opera, 3, Perinet, after Pauersbach and Richter), 12 June 1806

Der Schlossgärtner und der Windmüller (comic opera, 1, B. J. Koller), 1 July 1813

Der Fiaker als Marquis (comic opera, 3, A. Bäuerle), 10 Feb 1816

Tankredi (comic parody, 2, Bäuerle), 25 April 1817

Doktor Fausts Mantel (Zauberspiel, 2, Bäuerle), 11 Dec 1817

Der verwunschene Prinz (parody, with songs, 2, Bäuerle), 3 March 1818

Die travestirte Zauberflöte (farce, with songs, 2, K. Meisl), 13 Aug 1818

Die Fee aus Frankreich, oder Liebesqualen eines Hagestolzen (fairy tale, with songs, 2, Meisl), 23 Nov 1821

Aline, oder Wien in einem andern Weltteil (Zauberoper, 3, Bäuerle), 9 Oct 1822

Der Barometermacher auf der Zauberinsel (Zauberposse, with songs and dances, 2, F. Raimund), 18 Dec 1823

Herr Josef und Frau Baberl (farce, with songs, 3, J. A. Gleich), 11 May 1826

Die gefesselte Phantasie (Zauberspiel, with songs, 2, Raimund), 8 Jan 1828

Der Alpenkönig und der Menschenfeind (Zauberspiel, 2, Raimund), 17 Oct 1828

Der Sieg des guten Humors, oder Die Lebenslampen (Zauberspiel, with songs, 3, J. Schickh), 17 Sept 1831

c225 other operas, Singspiels, plays with music, pantomimes, ballets, melodramas

Other works (?most lost), incl. church music, syms., chamber music and wind pieces, pf pieces

BIBLIOGRAPHY

W. Müller: *Kaiser.- königl. priviligirtes Theater in der Leopoldstadt in Wien* (MS, *A-Wst*) [diary of theatre events]

—: *Die von mir Wenzel Müller Kapellmeister . . . componirten Opern von 1786 bis 1828* (MS, *A-Wn*) [inc.]

J. F. Reichardt: *Vertraute Briefe geschrieben auf einer Reise nach Wien* (Amsterdam, 1810)

W. Blum: 'Wenzel Müller, der eigentliche Schöpfer echter Volks-Musik', *Allgemeine Theater-Zeitung*, xxviii/161–2 (Vienna, 1835)

W. A. Riehl: *Musikalische Charakterköpfe: ein kunstgeschichtliches Skizzenbuch* (Stuttgart, 1853–60)

C. von Wurzbach: *Biographisches Lexikon des Kaiserthums Oesterreich*, xix (Vienna, 1868), 407 [with list of stage works]

E. von Bauernfeld: *Aus Alt- und Neu-Wien* (Vienna, 1872)

O. Teuber: *Geschichte des Prager Theaters*, ii (Prague, 1885)

H. Riemann: *Opern-Handbuch* (Leipzig, 1887–93)

W. Krone: *Wenzel Müller: ein Beitrag zur Geschichte der komischen Oper* (diss., U. of Berlin; Berlin, 1906) [with list of stage works]

W. A. Bauer and H. Kraus, eds.: *Raimund-Liederbuch* (Vienna, 1924)

A. Orel, ed.: *F. Raimund: Die Gesänge der Märchendramen*, Sämtliche Werke, vi (Vienna, 1924)

L. Raab: *Wenzel Müller: ein Tonkünstler Altwiens* (Baden, 1928) [with list of stage works]

F. Hadamowsky: *Das Theater in der Wiener Leopoldstadt* (Vienna, 1934)

P. Branscombe: 'An Old Viennese Opera Parody and a New Nestroy Manuscript', *German Life & Letters*, xxviii (1975), 210

PETER BRANSCOMBE

**Müller, Wilhelm** (*b* Dessau, 7 Oct 1794; *d* Dessau, 30 Sept 1827). German poet. He studied classical philology in Berlin, and after fighting in the War of Liberation, he became part of the Berlin circle that included Brentano and Arnim; he also came to know Tieck and Carl Maria von Weber in Dresden. His 77 *Gedichte aus den hinterlassenen Papieren eines reisenden Waldhornisten* (1821 and 1824), which included *Die schöne Müllerin* and *Winterreise*, were dedicated to Weber, 'master of German song, as token of friendship and admiration'. After Italian travels he returned to Dessau in 1819.

To his contemporaries, Müller was known as a Byronic imitator of Greek lyrics who keenly supported the Greek war of independence; he was also strongly influenced by folk poetry, on which many of his lyrics are modelled. *Die schöne Müllerin* originally arose from a private entertainment influenced by Paisiello's *La molinara*. While he fell too often into the weaker conventions of folk poetry even when describing a rejection of love he had himself experienced, his best lyrics have an untainted charm and a gift for simple words and images that influenced Heine. Their appeal to Schubert, for his two great song cycles, lay in Müller's ability to provide suggestive imagery for music and to portray emotions in verse from which the feeling of country life and scenery was never far. Other composers who set his poetry include Brahms (*Vineta* from op.42, *Die Braut* from op.44) and Goetz (*Es liegt so abendstill*, op.11).

BIBLIOGRAPHY

P. S. Allen: 'Müller and the German Volkslied', *Journal of English and Germanic Philology*, ii (1898–9), 283–322; iii (1900–01), 35, 431; pubd separately (Chicago, 1901)

B. Hake: *Wilhelm Müller: sein Leben und Dichten* (diss., U. of Berlin, 1907); chap.4 'Die schöne Müllerin' pubd separately (Berlin, 1908)
K. Helm: 'Müller, Wilhelm', *MGG* [incl. list of settings]

JOHN WARRACK

**Müller-Blattau, Joseph** [Josef] **M(aria)** (*b* Colmar, Alsace, 21 May 1895; *d* Saarbrücken, 21 Oct 1976). German musicologist. He studied musicology with Friedrich Ludwig at the University of Strasbourg, composition and conducting with Hans Pfitzner and the organ with Ernst Münch at Strasbourg Conservatory. After World War I he continued his studies with Wilibald Gurlitt at the University of Freiburg, taking the doctorate in 1920 with a thesis on the history of the fugue. In 1922 he completed his *Habilitation* with a work on Schütz's pupil Christoph Bernhard at Königsberg University where he directed the musicology seminar. He was promoted to reader in 1928. He was subsequently on the staff of the universities of Frankfurt am Main (1935–7), Freiburg (1937–9) and Saarbrücken (1952–64); he was also director of the Staatliche Hochschule für Musik (1952–8). Besides his work on Bernhard, Müller-Blattau is chiefly known for his studies of German folksong and medieval monophonic music, of which he produced important editions; he also worked on the relationship between words and music there and in opera.

### WRITINGS
*Grundzüge einer Geschichte der Fuge* (diss., U. of Freiburg, 1920; Königsberg, 1923, rev. 3/1963)
*Das Elsass, ein Grenzland deutscher Musik* (Freiburg, 1922)
*Die Kompositionslehre Heinrich Schützens in der Fassung seines Schülers Christoph Bernhard* (Habilitationsschrift, U. of Königsberg, 1922; Leipzig, 1926, 2/1963)
*Geschichte der Musik in Ost- und Westpreussen von der Ordenszeit bis zur Gegenwart* (Königsberg, 1931, enlarged 2/1968)
*Hamann und Herder in ihren Beziehungen zur Musik* (Königsberg, 1931)
*Das deutsche Volkslied* (Berlin, 1932, 2/1958)
*Einführung in die Musikgeschichte* (Berlin, 1932, 2/1941)
*Georg Friedrich Händel* (Potsdam, 1933, 2/1959) [2nd edn. lacks the numerous illustrations of the 1st]
*Zur Erforschung des ostpreussischen Volksliedes* (Halle, 1934)
ed.: *Hohe Schule der Musik* (Potsdam, 1935) [incl. 'Der Lehre von den Elementen', i, pp.1–227, and 'Die Lehre vom Führen und Folgen in Chor und Orchester (Dirigierlehre)', ii, pp.257–516]
*Geschichte der deutschen Musik* (Berlin, 1938, 3/1942; Fr. trans., 1943)
*Hans Pfitzner* (Potsdam, 1940, rev. 2/1969)
*Gestaltung – Umgestaltung: Studien zur Geschichte der musikalischen Variation* (Stuttgart, 1950)
ed.: *Taschenlexicon der Fremd- und Fachwörter der Musik* (Berlin, 1951)
*Das Verhältnis von Wort und Ton in der Geschichte der Musik: Grundzüge und Probleme* (Stuttgart, 1952)
*Die Volksliedsammlung des jungen Goethe* (Kassel, 1955)
'Über das Opernlibretto: ein Zwiegespräch zwischen Dichter und Komponist', *NZM*, cxxii (1961), 4
*Von der Vielfalt der Musik: Musikgeschichte – Musikerziehung – Musikpflege* (Freiburg, 1966)
'Goethes Kantate zur Jubelfeier der Reformation (1817): ein Beitrag zur Religiosität des späten Goethe', *Festschrift für Walter Wiora* (Kassel and Basle, 1967), 405
*Goethe und die Meister der Musik* (Stuttgart, 1969)
'Goethes Weg zum Schaffen Johann Sebastian Bachs', *Speculum musicae artis: Festgabe für Heinrich Husmann* (Munich, 1970), 245
'Aus der Geschichte des elsässischen Volksliedes', *Musicae scientiae collectanea: Festschrift Karl Gustav Fellerer* (Cologne, 1973), 390
'Grösse und Glanz der Barockoper', *Festschrift für Ernst Hermann Meyer* (Leipzig, 1973), 223

### EDITIONS
with F. Ranke: *Das Rostocker Liederbuch* (Halle, 1927)
*Die zwei ältesten Königsberger Gesangbücher von 1527* (Kassel, 1933)
with A. Jeziorowski: *Masurische Volkslieder* (Berlin and Leipzig, 1934)
*Preussische Festlieder: zeitgenössische Kompositionen zu Dichtungen Simon Dachs*, EDM, 2nd ser., Ostpreussen und Danzig, i (1939)
with M. Lang: *Zwischen Minnesang und Volkslied: die Lieder der Berliner Handschrift Germ.Fol.922* (Berlin, 1941)
*Heeger-Wüst: Pfälzische Volkslieder* (Mainz, 1963)

with H. Moser: *Deutsche Lieder des Mittelalters von Walther von der Vogelweide bis zum Lochamer Liederbuch: Texte und Melodien* (Stuttgart, 1968)
*Die Fuge: von Georg Friedrich Händel bis zur Gegenwart*, Mw, xxxiii (1968; Eng. trans., 1968)

### BIBLIOGRAPHY
W. Salmen, ed.: *Festgabe für Joseph Müller-Blattau zum 65. Geburtstag* (Saarbrucken, 1960, 2/1962)
J. M. Müller-Blattau: *Von der Vielfalt der Musik: Musikgeschichte – Musikerziehung – Musikpflege* (Freiburg, 1966) [incl. list of writings]
C.-H. Mahling, ed.: *Zum 70. Geburtstag von Joseph Müller-Blattau* (Kassel, 1966)

M. E. C. BARTLET

**Müller-Hartmann, Robert** (*b* Hamburg, 11 Oct 1884; *d* Dorking, Surrey, 15 Dec 1950). German composer. He studied at the Stern Conservatory, Berlin, and was a lecturer at Hamburg University, 1922–33; he settled in London in 1937. As a composer he did not adhere to any of the modern schools. His orchestral works, some given their premières by Strauss, Muck and Busch, include a symphony (1926), several suites and variation sets; he also wrote many chamber works and songs. He published *Aufgaben zur Harmonielehren* (Leipzig, 1928) and translated into German *The Pilgrim's Progress* of Vaughan Williams, whom he much admired.

ALFRED LOEWENBERG/R

**Müller-Hermann, Johanna** (*b* Vienna, 15 Jan 1878; *d* Vienna, 19 April 1941). Austrian composer. She studied with Adler and Zemlinsky and later with J. B. Foerster, whom she succeeded at the Neues Wiener Konservatorium. Her works show the influence of Brahms and Reger in their adherence to traditional forms and tonality, though they also reflect Schoenberg's harmonic richness and Schreker's instrumentation. She wrote several large-scale choral works, notably the oratorio *In Memoriam* (Whitman), as well as orchestral and chamber music, piano pieces and songs.

KARL GEIRINGER/R

**Müller von Asow, Erich H(ermann).** See MUELLER VON ASOW, ERICH H.

**Müller von Kulm, Walter** (*b* Basle, 31 Aug 1899; *d* Arlesheim, 3 Oct 1967). Swiss composer. He studied in Aarau and at Basle and Zurich conservatories, also taking musicology, philosophy and psychology at Basle University. He was director of Basle Conservatory (1947–64) and founding editor of the *Schweizerische musikpädagogische Blätter* (1949). His theoretic and pedagogic studies were expressed in his *Grundriss der Harmonielehre* (Basle, 1948). His creative work is manifold: his vocal music particularly is permeated by spiritual and ethical strength and abundant in harmonic colour and rhythmic force. He wrote an opera *Der Erfinder* (Wälterlin, 1936–44), *Klaggesang* (Goethe, 1925–32) and oratorios *Vater unser* (1945) and *Petrus* (1960); among his orchestral compositions are a symphony (1928) and concerted works for violin, flute, saxophone and clarinet. He also wrote chamber and keyboard music.

KURT VON FISCHER/R

**Müller-Zürich** [Müller], **Paul** (*b* Zurich, 19 June 1898). Swiss composer. He added Zürich to his surname to avoid confusion with other Müllers. He was a pupil of Andreae and Jarnach at the Zurich Conservatory (1917–19) and then studied in Paris and Berlin. In 1927 he returned to the Zurich Conservatory as a lecturer in theory; he remained there, also teaching conducting and composition, until his retirement in 1969. In addition, he held a lectureship in music theory at Zurich University (1959–70). As director of the Elisabeth Schmid Choir (1931–9), the Lucerne Chamber Choir (1948–55) and other choruses he gave performances of old and new music; he has also directed the Unterstrass Male-Voice Choir of Zurich and the Zurich Academic Orchestra. His appearances as an orchestral conductor, notably in Zurich and Winterthur, have been principally in performances of his own works.

Müller-Zürich belongs to the large group of major Swiss composers (others were Beck and Burkhard) who, at first more or less firmly entrenched in Romanticism, adopted Baroque canonic and other contrapuntal techniques and the concertante principle, arriving eventually at a neo-Baroque style characterized by advanced but tonal harmony. In Müller's case it was above all an acquaintance with the music of the Renaissance Netherlanders, Monteverdi and Purcell that brought the change in direction, one that had been anticipated by Reger, who was another strong influence on him (see the early string quartets and the Violin Sonata op.5). Baroque forms such as toccatas and fugues occur frequently in his work, whose primarily diatonic and often modal character has not been obscured by an increasing chromaticism in later compositions, even in those which re-introduce late-Romantic harmonies. Other attributes of his style are strict formal integrity, a feeling for architecture and transparent part-writing which eschews contrapuntal virtuosity for clarity and audibility. His choral polyphony is eminently singable (reflecting his experience with choirs). All of these characteristics have made it possible for him to write popular music without making important concessions, whether for such genres as the *Festspiel* or for amateur choruses or orchestras. Among the honours he has received are the Music Prize of the City of Zurich (1953) and the Composer's Prize of the Schweizerischer Tonkünstlerverein (1958), of which he was vice-president (1955–60) and president (1960–63). He is a council member of the Pro Helvetia Foundation.

### WORKS
(*selective list*)
DRAMATIC AND VOCAL

Dramatic: Die Simulanten, op.7, play with music, 1922; Dr Faust, op.9, puppet-play score, 1922; Festspiel der Schweizerischen Landesausstellung 1939, op.30, 1939; Jedema, op.31, 1941; Der Herr beschirmt syne Kilchen, op.34, radio score, 1941; Feuer vom Rütli, op.35, Freilichtspiel, 1941; Festspiel, op.44, 1947

Choral: Te Deum, op.11, solo vv, chorus, orch, 1924; Chor der Toten, op.16, chorus, wind orch, db/org; Kleine Messe, op.17, vv, insts, 1931; 3 geistliche Chöre, op.18, female vv, str, hpd, 1931; Te Deum II, op.20, female vv, insts, 1933; Mein Vaterland, op.27, male vv, orch; Der Sonnengesang, op.29 (St Francis), solo vv, female vv, 6 insts, 1939; Dona pacem, chorus, orch, 1946; Friede auf Erden, op.42, A, male vv, org; Mein Land, op.47, solo vv, chorus, orch, 1950; Aus Knechtschaft zur Freiheit, op.48, solo vv, chorus, orch, 1950; Gesänge von Gott, op.49, male vv, orch; Von Werktag und Sonntag, op. 55, female vv, orch; Psalm cxlviii, op.67, chorus, orch, 1964; Psalm ciii, op.71, chorus, youth chorus, ob, bn, str qt, org, 1969; other pieces for unacc. chorus, youth chorus, etc

Solo vocal: 4 Duette, op.15, S, A, orch/pf, 1928; 2 Barockgesänge, op.33, S, cl, vn, pf, 1941; Psalm xci, op.39, female 1v, org, 1943; An die Toten, S, vn, vc, 1958; songs with pf

INSTRUMENTAL

Orch: Little Sym., D, op.3, 1920; Little Serenade, chamber orch, 1921; Hymnus, op.14, 1927; Conc., f, op.24, va, small orch, 1934; Conc., G, op.25, vn, small orch, 1935; Conc., op.28, org, str, 1938; Hochzeitstanz, 1939; Sym., C, op.40, str, 1944; Sym., D, op.43, 1947; Sym., E, op.53, str, fl, 1952; Vc Conc., op.55, 1954; Sinfonischer Prolog, op.57, 1955; Sinfonische Suite, E, op.59, 1956–7; Vn Conc. no.2, op.60, 1957; Conc., op.61, 2 vn, str, hpd, 1958;

Sinfonietta, op.66, 1964; Sonata, op.72, str, 1967–8

Chamber: Str Qnt, F, op.2, 1919; Str Qt no.1, E♭, op.4, 1921; Sonata no.1, B, op.5, vn, pf, 1922; Marienleben, op.8, 10 insts, 1928; Präludium, Arie und Fuge, op.21, ob, bn, hn, tpt, str qnt, 1933; Sonata no.2, op.32, vn, pf, 1941; Petite sonate, op.37, cl, pf, 1942; Fantasie und Fugue, E, op.45, vn, org, 1949; Str Trio, C, op.46, 1950; Little Suite, op.51, hn, va, harp, 1952; Sonata, op.52, vn, 1952; Elegie, vc, pf, 1955; Tema con variazioni, 3 rec/vn; Str Qt no.2, op.64, 1960; Canzone, op.64a, str qt, 1961; Trio, op.70, fl, cl, pf, 1965–6

Org: 3 toccatas, C, op.12, 1925, D, op.38, 1943, a, op.50, 1952; Präludium und Fuge, c, op.22, 1934; Canzone, e, 1936; Choraltoccata über 'Eine feste Burg', op.54, org, 2 tpt, 2 trbn, 1953; 4 Choralfantasien, opp.56, 58, org, 2 tpt, 2 trbn; Passacaglia, op.65; chorales and chorale intonations

Principal publishers: Ahn & Simrock, Hug, Schott (Mainz)

### BIBLIOGRAPHY
P. Müller-Zürich: *Das Büchlein vom Eidgenössischen Wettspiel* (Thalwil, 1940)
E. Hess: 'Zum 50. Geburtstag Paul Müllers', *SMz*, lxxxviii (1948), 201
W. Schuh: *Festschrift Tonkünstlerverein II* (Zurich, 1948)
R. Wittelsbach: 'Paul Müller', *SMz*, xciv (1954), 9
P. Mieg: 'Paul Müller', *40 Schweizer Komponisten der Gegenwart* (Amriswil, 1956)
E. de Stoutz: 'Paul Müller', *SMz*, xcviii (1958), 241
H. Funk: 'Paul Müllers choralgebundene Orgelmusik', *SMz*, ci (1961), 229
F. Jakob: *167. Neujahrsblatt der Allgemeine Musikgesellschaft Zürich* (Zurich, 1963)

FRITZ MUGGLER

**Mulligan, Gerry** [Gerald Joseph] (*b* New York, 4 June 1927). American jazz saxophonist and arranger. He grew up in Philadelphia, where he wrote for Johnny Warrington's radio band. In 1946 he worked with Gene Krupa both as an instrumentalist and as an arranger. He also provided scores for Elliot Lawrence and in 1948 began an association with the Claude Thornhill band which led to his involvement in Miles Davis's influential Capitol recordings. The formation in 1952 of his 'piano-less quartet' with the trumpeter Chet Baker brought Mulligan an international reputation; he has led numerous groups of varying instrumentation in the USA and elsewhere.

An important, versatile figure of the 'cool' jazz movement, Mulligan first achieved notice as an arranger, and his early *Disc Jockey Jump* for Krupa (1947), pitting a small group against the full ensemble, foreshadowed the resourcefulness of such later, more personal works as *Funhouse* (1951) and *Walkin' Shoes* (1952). As an improviser he was slower to develop, but then established himself as an outstanding baritone saxophonist, with a style that convincingly wed the harmonic and melodic characteristics of his own generation to a more traditional rhythmic discipline.

### BIBLIOGRAPHY
M. Harrison: 'An Ensemble Style for Jazz', *These Jazzmen of our Time*, ed. R. Horricks (London, 1959), 68
M. Harrison: 'Gerry Mulligan', *Jazz Review*, iii (1960), Aug, 23
M. James: *Ten Modern Jazzmen* (London, 1960), 93ff
W. Mellers: *Music in a New Found Land* (London, 1964), 357f
J. Goldberg: *Jazz Masters of the Fifties* (New York, 1965), 9ff
A. Tercinet: 'Mulligan Revisited', *Jazz Hot*, xxxviii (1972), June, 23

MICHAEL JAMES

**Mulliner, Thomas** (*fl* 1563). English anthologist and composer. His main importance is as the compiler of the Mulliner Book (*GB-Lbm*), an eclectic collection of keyboard music, original and arranged, sacred and secular, of the period *c*1530–75. It has been suggested that he was in some way associated with Redford (*d* 1547) at St Paul's in London, but nothing certain is known. Nevertheless, an early period in London appears likely in view of the repertory of the MS and Mulliner's friendship with John Heywood, who witnessed his ownership of the book. There is no evidence that Mulliner held any post at St Paul's; the 18th-century statement to that effect on the MS is so far unsupportable. The only contemporary record of his career is as 'modulator organum' in an entry of 3 March 1563 at Corpus Christi College, Oxford.

He presumably arranged the vocal pieces in the Mulliner Book himself; in addition his initials are attached to two compositions in it: a fragment of a part-song, *The higher that the cedar tree* and *The Queen of Scots Galliard* for cittern (both printed in Stevens, 1952).

BIBLIOGRAPHY
D. Stevens, ed.: *The Mulliner Book*, MB, i (London, 1951, 2/1954)
D. Stevens: *The Mulliner Book: a Commentary* (London, 1952)
JOHN CALDWELL

**Mulliner Book** (*GB-Lbm* Add. 30513). *See* SOURCES OF KEYBOARD MUSIC TO 1660, §2(vi).

**Mullings, Frank** (*b* Walsall, 10 May 1881; *d* Manchester, 19 May 1953). English tenor. He studied singing at the Birmingham School of Music (1905–9), gained experience in concert and oratorio, and in 1913 sang Tristan with notable success under Beecham in Birmingham. His first performance as Othello was in Manchester (1916), his Covent Garden début being in the English première of de Lara's *Naïl* (1919), with *Pagliacci* and *Parsifal* following later that year. As principal dramatic tenor in the British National Opera Company (1922–9), he also sang Apollo in the première of Boughton's *Alkestis* (Covent Garden, 1924) and had such roles as Siegfried, Tannhäuser and Radamès in his repertory. From 1930 to 1945 he sang mainly in concert, and taught at the Birmingham School of Music (1927–46). Recordings show a strong, heroic voice of distinctive timbre, sometimes uncomfortably produced but beautiful in the middle register. Tributes by Beecham, Newman, Cardus and others testify to his greatness as an operatic artist; many considered his Tristan, Othello and Canio the finest heard in England in living memory.

BIBLIOGRAPHY
J. Fryer and J. B. Richards: 'Frank Mullings', *Record Collector*, vii (1952), 5 [with discography]
J. B. STEANE

**Müllner, Silverius** [Franz]. *See* MÜLLER, SILVERIUS.

**Multiple stopping.** Whereas a single stopped string on any string instrument produces one note, fingers can be pressed down on two, three or four strings to produce double, triple or quadruple stops, that is, multiple stops. The technique of multiple stopping was well known among viol players, as can be seen in such treatises as Ganassi's *Regola rubertina* (1535), Christopher Simpson's *Division Viol* (1659) and Mersenne's *Harmonie universelle* (1636). Three- and four-note chords were, however, arpeggiated, the curvature of the early bow precluding the playing of three or four notes simultaneously except possibly in the case of the LIRONE, whose bridge was low and flat. Double-stop techniques were well developed.

The music of the violin family was very simple until virtuoso technique was demanded by Biagio Marini in his sonatas for violin, op.8 (1626–9). In the fourth sonata, 'per sonar con due corde', double stops occur in a complex contrapuntal section. The second sonata uses 'scordatura' for the first time in violin music; this technique was later developed by Biber (1644–1704), who added more difficult and even some impossible multiple stops, playable only by the employment of scordatura. Open strings are often used. The peak of artistic perfection in the use of multiple stops was reached by Bach in his suites for solo cello and in the sonatas and partitas for solo violin.

In general, the Germans and Bohemians of the late 17th and early 18th centuries were more fascinated by multiple stops than virtuosos of other countries, but the sonatas of J.-M. Leclair (1697–1764), who worked primarily in Paris, are full of octaves and 10ths as well as the more usual 3rds and 6ths. As for Italy, Corelli's sonatas op.5 employ multiple stops as a normal part of violin technique, and in the next generation Paganini achieved a brilliance in their performance probably unsurpassed to this day.

Many difficulties arise in the reading of multiple stops in 17th- and 18th-century violin literature: what is written by the composer is often musically neither possible nor even desirable to play; it is therefore to be assumed that what is written is not what the composer expected to hear. For example, parts often indicate sustained three- and four-note chords: it is left to the performer's discretion to interpret the notation according to the performing practice of the time, and to sustain what is feasible both technically and musically. In Baroque music the word 'arpeggio' appears frequently; in other cases the performer must arpeggiate even without instruction, as in the Chaconne of Bach's second Partita for solo violin. In most cases the strings are stopped as for simultaneously sounding multiple stops, although the notes sound contiguously. Geminiani, in *The Art of Playing on the Violin* (1751), gave 18 ways of arpeggiating a chord progression.

In around 1780 the Tourte bow revolutionized the technique of the violin family by allowing a larger and more sustained tone and the simultaneous sounding of three-note chords. The cello method of Louis Duport (1749–1819) set the technical norm for modern cello playing, specifically treating the subject of double stops which had been largely neglected in methods until then. In 1834 *L'art du violon* by Pierre Baillot standardized the practice of double-stop scales for the violin.

In the 20th century the methods of Auer, Flesch, Dotzauer and Piatti are standard texts for string players wishing to practise double stops. In the music of the present century difficult multiple stops are common. Bartók, for example, wrote for minor 9ths just as Paganini used octaves, and Schoenberg delighted in combinations of false and natural harmonics.

BIBLIOGRAPHY
F. Geminiani: *The Art of Playing on the Violin* (London, 1751/R1952 with introduction by D. Boyden)
T.-J. Tarade: *Traité du violon* (Paris, 1774/R1972)
P. Baillot: *L'art du violin* (Paris, 1834)
D. Boyden: *The History of Violin Playing from its Origins to 1761* (London, 1965)
——: 'Violinspiel', *MGG*
SONYA MONOSOFF

**Mumma, Gordon** (*b* Framingham, Mass., 30 March 1935). American composer, performer of electronic music and hornist. He studied at the School of Music (1952–3) and at the Institute of Science and Technology (1959–62) of the University of Michigan, and has held lectureships at Brandeis (1966–7), Buffalo (1968), the University of Illinois (1969–70), Berkeley (1971) and

Dartmouth College (1972). From 1957 to 1964 he collaborated with Ashley and with the visual artist Milton Cohen on mixed-media 'Space Theater' productions involving light projections, dance, sculpture and electronic sound improvisation. He was also a co-founder with Ashley of the Cooperative Studio for Electronic Music (1958–66) in Ann Arbor, where, with other composers, artists and architects, he established the ONCE Festival (1961–8), which he co-directed until 1966. In that year he joined Merce Cunningham's company as a composer and performer, and also co-founded the Sonic Arts Union in New York. Mumma's compositions often contain instructions for movement or gesture; many require various types of amplification and electronic modification through 'cybersonic circuits' which he has developed.

### WORKS
*(selective list)*

Densities, tape, 1959; Pf Suite, 1959; Vectors, tape, 1959; Mirrors, tape, 1960; Meanwhile, a Twopiece, perc, tape, 1961; A Quarter of Fourpiece, 4 insts, 1960–62; Epoxy (Sequence I), tape, 1962; Very Small Size Mograph 1962, any number of pfs and players, 1962; Medium Size Mograph 1962, pf (any number of players), 1962; Large Size Mograph 1962, pf, 1962; Medium Size Mograph 1963, pf, cybersonic circuits, 1963; Megaton for William Burroughs, live elec, 1963

Music for the Venezia Space Theater, tape, 1964; Very Small Size Mograph 1964, pf duet, 1964; Small Size Mograph 1964, pf duet, 1964; The Dresden Interleaf 13 February 1945, tape, 1965; Horn, hn, cybersonic circuits, 1965; Le Corbusier, orch, org, tape, cyber-sonic circuits, 1965; Second Horn, hn, cybersonic circuits, 1965; Mesa, cybersonic bandoneon, 1966; Diastasis, and in Beer, 2 cyber-sonic gui, 1967; Hornpipe, cybersonic hn, 1967

Swarmer, vn, concertina, saw, cybersonic circuits, 1968; Beam, vn, va, cybersonic modification, digital control circuitry, 1969; Conspiracy 8, digital computer (up to 8 players), collab. S. Smoliar, 1970; I Saw her Dance, crosscut saw, dancer, slides, tape, 1970; Telepos, dancers, elec, 1971; Ambivex, elec, 1972; Phenomenon Unarticulated, dancers, elec, 1972

### WRITINGS

'The ONCE Festival and how it Happened', *Arts in Society*, iv (1967), 381

'Technology in the Modern Arts: Music and Theatre', *Chelsea* (1967), nos.20–21, p.99

'Home Canning: Guerrilla Facility', *Electronic Music: a Listener's Guide*, E. Schwartz (London and New York, 1973), 244

'Live-Electronic Music', *The Development and Practice of Electronic Music*, ed. J. Appleton and R. Perera (Englewood Cliffs, NJ, 1975)

### BIBLIOGRAPHY

U. Kasements: 'Current Chronicle', *MQ*, 1 (1964), 515
H. W. Hitchcock: *Music in the United States: a Historical Introduction* (Englewood Cliffs, NJ, 1969), 249

GERALD WARFIELD

**Münch [Munch], Charles** (*b* Strasbourg, 26 Sept 1891; *d* Richmond, Virginia, 6 Nov 1968). French conductor and violinist. His father was a professor at the Strasbourg Conservatory, and he first studied the violin there and later with Flesch in Berlin. In 1912 he went to Paris to study with Lucien Capet, but as a resident of Alsace he was conscripted into the German army for war service, 1914–18. He became a professor of the violin first at the Strasbourg Conservatory (in 1919) and then at Leipzig, where he led the Gewandhaus Orchestra under Furtwängler, 1926–33. On his return to Paris in 1933 he financed his conducting début (which, he later said, he had been unable to afford sooner), and its success enabled him to concentrate on conducting. Based in Paris for the next 15 years, he played an increasingly important part in introducing new works into the programmes of the Lamoureux and Straram Orchestras, the Concerts Siohan and the newly founded Orchestre Symphonique de Paris. He played a similar role after taking over the direction of the Société

Philharmonique de Paris in 1935 and the Société des Concerts du Conservatoire in 1937, and became admired for performances in which a sensitive feeling for tone-colour was balanced by a strong architectural sense. During these years, when he was also a professor at the Ecole Normale de Musique, he gave the first performances of many works by such composers as Honegger, Roger-Ducasse, Ropartz, Roussel and Schmitt, and (in 1945) of Messiaen's *L'Ascension*.

Münch toured widely as a conductor in Europe, including concerts with the BBC SO in 1938, and in 1946 made his American début with the Boston SO and other orchestras. Two years later he succeeded Koussevitzky as chief conductor of the Boston orchestra and remained until 1962, resuming the policy initiated there by Monteux in the 1920s of making the Boston SO the chief agent for the introduction of new French music to the American public, as well as of new works by Barber, Foss, Piston, Schuman, Sessions and others. He was welcomed in Boston for the feeling of spontaneity he brought to his performances, and under his direction the Boston SO maintained a high standard of brilliance and discipline that reflected his own dynamic personality. He returned to France after leaving Boston, and in 1967 shared with Baudo the formation and direction of L'Orchestre de Paris, with which he was on an American concert tour when he died. He wrote *Je suis chef d'orchestre* (Paris, 1954; Eng. trans., 1955).

### BIBLIOGRAPHY

'There will be Joy', *Time* (19 Dec 1949), 26
G. Collard: 'Charles Münch', *Audio & Record Review*, ii/9 (1963), 16 [with discography by F. F. Clough and G. J. Cuming]

MARTIN COOPER

**Münch, Hans** (*b* Mühlhausen, 9 March 1893). Swiss conductor and composer, cousin of Charles Münch. His father was the conductor Eugen Münch (*d* 1897). He received some musical education from Albert Schweitzer before going to Basle in 1912. At the conservatory there his teachers were Hans Huber (composition), Adolf Hamm (organ) and Emil Braun (cello). He was a cellist in the Basle Orchestra (1914–26), taught the piano at the Basle Conservatory (1918–32) and conducted the Basle Bach Choir (1921–6). He succeeded Hermann Suter in 1925–6 as the conductor of the two oldest choirs in Basle, the Gesangverein and the male-voice Liedertafel. From 1935 to 1966 he had charge of the concerts of the Basle Allgemeine Musikgesellschaft in succession to Weingartner. In these programmes he showed a preference for Bruckner, Reger and Strauss, and for Berlioz, Ravel and Debussy. He was an extremely versatile conductor whose essential qualities found their finest expression in his interpretations of late Romantic orchestral music. He was director of the Basle Music School and the conservatory from 1935 to 1947, and in 1939 the university conferred on him an honorary doctorate.

### BIBLIOGRAPHY

*SML* [with work-list]
F. Morel: *Die Konzerte der AMG in Basel 1926–1951* (Basle, 1951), 23
*100 Jahre Basler Liedertafel* (Basle, 1952), 67
*50 Jahre Konservatorium Basel* (Basle, 1955), 31
H. Oesch: *Die Musik-Akademie der Stadt Basel* (Basle, 1967)
A. Müry: 'Dr. h.c. Hans Münch zum 80. Geburtstag', *SMz*, cxiii (1973), 86
T. Seebass: *Die Allegemeine Musikgesellschaft Basel 1876–1976* (Basle, 1976), 31

JÜRG STENZL

**Münchhausen, Adolph** [August], Baron von (*b* Brunswick, *c*1755; *d* Paris, 1811). German diplomat and musical dilettante. He was chamberlain to the Duke of Brunswick-Lüneburg, from 1788 was in the service of the Prince of Prussia, and from 1799 lived in Munich and Paris. He composed symphonies, chamber music and keyboard sonatas in a *galant* style similar to that of J. C. Bach, and his *Dix ariettes allemandes* contain folk material and show a talent for melodies. Gerber considered Münchhausen a good keyboard and glass harmonica player and a creditable composer, although elsewhere his works were criticized for their antiquated forms and ornamentation.

WORKS

Orch: 3 syms., op.1 (Berlin and Amsterdam, ?1791); 2 syms., op.5 (Berlin and Amsterdam, 1790); 2 concs., hpd/pf, op.7 (Paris, n.d.); 2 simphonies concertantes, opp.9–10 (Paris, n.d.); Symphonies périodique (Mainz, 1800)

Chamber: 3 sonatas, hpd/pf 4 hands, 2 as op.2 (Paris, 1793), 1 as op.3 (Paris, ?1793); 3 duos, vn, va, op.8 (Berlin and Amsterdam, 1797); Sonate, hpd/pf, va/fl, op.8 (Mainz, c1800); Grande sonate, pf, va, op.10 (Paris, n.d.), lost; Sonate, harp (Paris, n.d.)

Vocal: 10 ariettes allemandes, 1v, hpd/pf, op.4 (Berlin and Amsterdam, 1793)

BIBLIOGRAPHY

*GerberNL*
C. von Ledebur: *Tonkünstler-Lexicon Berlin's* (Berlin, 1861/*R*1965)
T.-M. Langner: 'Münchhausen, Adolph Baron von', *MGG*
HEINRICH SIEVERS

**Munchheimer, Adam.** *See* MINCHEJMER, ADAM.

**Münchinger, Karl** (*b* Stuttgart, 29 May 1915). German conductor. He studied at the Musikhochschule, Stuttgart, and at the Leipzig Conservatory (conducting under Abendroth). After working in Stuttgart as organist and choirmaster, he was first appointed conductor of the Hanover SO (1941–3). As soon as the war ended he founded the Stuttgart Chamber Orchestra, one of the most successful chamber orchestras of its time. Münchinger conducted its first concert at the Furtbachhaus, Stuttgart, on 18 September 1945, and remained its artistic director. His principal débuts have been on successive tours with the orchestra, including Paris, London and Madrid (1949), central and South America (1952), the USA (1954), the Far East (1955) and the USSR (1959), and their joint reputation has been enhanced by numerous widely praised gramophone records. These include three sets of Bach's Brandenburg Concertos (successively in mono, stereo and quadraphonic recording) and the major choral works of Bach.

Münchinger's repertory is based on Bach, but extends to Classical composers, and to a modest range of music for strings by Britten, Berkeley, Hindemith and others. He has appeared with success as a guest conductor with larger orchestras in Europe and the USA, and in 1966 he formed the Stuttgart Klassische Philharmonie (45 players) by supplementing the nucleus of the chamber orchestra to enable them to extend their repertory to larger works. Münchinger's conducting style lies between academic rigour and romantic expressiveness, characterized in performance by extreme clarity of texture, and elegance, spirit and richness of tone. He has received the German Federal Cross of Merit and the French Order for Art and Literature.

WOLFRAM SCHWINGER

**Munck, (Pierre Joseph) Ernest,** Chevalier de (*b* Brussels, 21 Dec 1840; *d* London, 19 Jan 1915). Belgian cellist. He learnt the cello from his father, François de Munck

(1815–54), and Servais at Brussels Conservatory (*premier prix* 1855). He toured in Britain in 1855 and settled there, teaching at the GSM; he was in Paris, 1868–70, playing in the Maurin Quartet and with his brother Camille, a violinist, and from 1871 was solo cellist in the Weimar Hofkapelle. He married the singer Carlotta Patti in 1879; they undertook tours and lived for a time in the USA. Back in London in 1893, he became a professor at the RAM. He wrote some cello music, including a *Concerto dramatique*, and edited classical works. He owned a Stradivari cello labelled 1710 but in fact from about 1730.

LYNDA LLOYD REES

**Munclinger, Milan** (*b* Košice, 3 July 1923). Czech flautist and conductor. He studied at the Prague Conservatory (1942–8) and the Academy of Musical Arts (1946–50) (conducting with Doležil, Dědeček and Talich, composition with K. Janeček and Krejčí), and at Prague University (musical sciences). During World War II he worked as an orchestral player in the Leipzig Gewandhaus Orchestra and at the opera in Breslau. He was the founder and from 1951 the artistic director of the ensemble Ars Rediviva with which he performs pre-Classical and Classical works. He is concerned with questions of the reproduction of historical music, which he edits for performance by the ensemble or for publication. He also appears as a solo flautist and conductor. As a player and realizer of 17th- and 18th-century music Munclinger strives to combine stylistic authenticity with a 20th-century approach. He participates in numerous gramophone recordings and is a frequent guest at European music festivals and concert halls.

ALENA NĚMCOVÁ

**Mundharmonika** (Ger.). HARMONICA; *see also* MOUTH ORGAN.

**Mundstück** (Ger.). MOUTHPIECE.

**Mundy** [Moondaye, Munday, Monday, Mondy, Mundies]**, John** (*b c*1555; *d* Windsor, 29 June 1630). English composer and organist, son of WILLIAM MUNDY. He received the BMus at Oxford on 9 July 1586 and the DMus on 2 July 1624, and according to Wood was held 'in high esteem for his great knowledge in the theoretical and practical part of music'. He succeeded either John Merbecke or Richard Farrant as organist at St George's Chapel, Windsor, where he worked for more than 40 years. There is no documentation to support the contention that he also became organist at Eton College in the late 1580s. He apparently continued to serve at Windsor until his death and is buried in the cloisters at St George's Chapel.

Mundy was a versatile and sometimes highly effective composer. His *Songs and Psalmes* (1594) for three to five voices, comprising both sacred and secular works, follows the pattern of Byrd's *Psalmes, Sonets and Songs* (1588). The secular songs use imagery sparingly, although some (e.g. *Of all the birds*, *Heigh ho!*, and *Penelope*) are at once madrigalian and yet for their time conservative and restrained in their treatment of the texts. The settings contain much imitative polyphony, frequent interchange of melodic and rhythmic motifs between the voices, contrasts of texture, and modal fluidity within a broad but conservative harmonic range. Most of the formal designs mirror the poetic structure of the texts. The psalms in the collection are mostly metrical settings from the Sternhold and Hopkins Psalter. Stylistically they closely resemble the secular pieces: there is some restrained word-painting, notably in *Blessed art thou* and *Lord to thee I make my moan*; they are modally flexible and the textures essentially polyphonic within a clear chordal framework. The prose psalms in the collection are perhaps less successful; they lack the forward thrust of most of the songs and metrical psalms and show Mundy's apparent difficulty in sustaining musical interest over broader spans.

Many extant manuscript works are ascribed simply to 'Mundy' (for discussion of this *see* MUNDY, WILLIAM. The five verse anthems that are attributed to John Mundy are harmonically conservative and somewhat lacking in flow and continuity. His setting of *Blessed art thou* for two tenor soloists, while not a parody, shares some common features with its predecessor in the *Songs and Psalmes*. Here, and in *O Lord our governor*, Mundy frequently used sequential repetition to increase dramatic tension, and in *O Lord our governor* applied a strophic variation principle in which the first three choruses act as refrains between the verses. *Sing joyfully*, for solo bass and four vigorous obbligato instrumental parts, contains much vivid word-painting. Among Mundy's Latin pieces is the lovely *In te Domine speravi*, with a seven-voice section generated by gymel, dividing the altos and basses. In his *Delamentacione Jeremie* he set the introductory announcement polyphonically and the sections headed by the Hebrew letters 'Daleth' and 'Lamed' to extended musical melismas. His *Dum transisset sabbatum*, a festal respond (*Mark* xvi.1.), quotes in the superius the third Sarum respond for Easter Matins, providing in the customary manner a full cadential close on 'aromata' to allow for the performance of the plainsong verse.

Mundy's keyboard pieces (in the Fitzwilliam Virginal Book) include a setting of *Robin*, clearly related to Farnaby's *Bonny sweet Robin*, but a 4th higher. Seven of the eight variations on *Goe from my window* are also attributed in the same book to Morley. Mundy's *Faire Wether* fantasia, one of the most unusual pieces in the collection, is a somewhat abrupt and naive though nevertheless effective succession of 'Faire Wether', 'Lightning' and 'Thunder', ending with 'A Cleare Day'. His pieces for instrumental ensemble include a six-part *Judica me Deus*, which may originally have been a setting of Psalm xlii, and five In Nomines, all with the customary plainsong fragment in long note values.

### WORKS

[12] Songs and [15] Psalmes, 3–5vv (London, 1594); ed. in EM, xxxv/2 (1924, rev. 2/1961 by T. Dart and P. Brett, incl. 1 more song)
1 madrigal, 5vv, 1601[16]

#### ANTHEMS
*(verse unless otherwise stated)*

Blessed art thou that fearest God, *GB-DRc, GL, Lbm, T, Y*
Give laud unto the Lord, full, 5vv, *Cp, DRc, Lbm, Y*
O give thanks unto the Lord, full, 5vv, *DRc, Lbm, Lcm, LF, Ob, Och, Ojc, T, Y, US-BE, SM, NYp*
O God, my strength and fortitude, *GB-DRc, Lbm, Y*
O Lord our Governor, in J. Clifford: The Divine Services and Anthems (London, 1663), *DRc, Lbm, Lcm, Och, T, Y, US-NYp* (attrib. E. Smith in some other sources)
Send aid, inc., *GB-DRc, Lbm, Y*
Sing joyfully unto God our strength, *Lbm*; ed. E. H. Fellowes (London, 1937)

#### LATIN SACRED

Aedes nostra sancta, 5vv, *GB-Och*; Delamentacione Jeremie, 5vv, *Och*; Dominus illuminatio mea, 3vv, *Lbm*; Dum transisset sabbatum, 6vv, *Och*; In te Domine speravi, 5–7vv, *Och*; Judica me Deus, 6vv, *Lbm* (textless); Kyrie 'in die pasche', 4vv, *Lbm*

#### INSTRUMENTAL

2 fantasias (1 entitled Faire Wether), Goe from my window, Munday's Joy, Robin: ed. J. A. Fuller Maitland and W. B. Squire, The Fitzwilliam Virginal Book (London, 1894–9/R1963)
5 In Nomines, a 5, 6, *GB-Lbm, Ob*

For works ascribed in sources to 'Mundy' and for bibliography *see* MUNDY, WILLIAM.

GILBERT L. BLOUNT

**Mundy** [Moondaye, Munday, Monday, Mondy, Mondie etc], **William** (*b* c1529; *d* ?London, probably before 12 Oct 1591). English composer, father of JOHN MUNDY. He was the son of Thomas Mundy, a sexton at St Mary-at-Hill, London, succeeded Thomas Giles as head chorister of Westminster Abbey in 1543, was at St Martin Vintry in 1547 and by 1548 was a parish clerk at St Mary-at-Hill. He became a vicar-choral of St Paul's Cathedral and was elected a Gentleman of the Chapel Royal on 21 February 1564. On 12 October 1591 Anthony Anderson was sworn Gentleman of the Chapel Royal in succession to Mundy, who had presumably died shortly before. He was highly regarded by his contemporaries, according to Robert Dow (in *GB-Och* 987), Thomas Whythorne, in his autobiography, John Baldwin (in *Lbm* R.M.24.D.2) and Morley, in his *Plaine and Easie Introduction* (1597).

It is difficult to assign with certainty to William or John Mundy compositions ascribed to 'Mundy'. At least four complete or fragmentary services are so ascribed and of the remainder only four can definitely be ascribed to William Mundy. The Evening Service 'in C fa ut', for instance, may well be by John Mundy, though in places it closely resembles William's *Sive vigilem*. Most of the surviving manuscripts, which date mainly from after 1625, offer little help in solving the problem. William Mundy's two settings of the Evening Service are quite contrapuntal; the service 'in medio chori' is an elaborate, highly florid setting for nine voices containing passages for high voices alone, perhaps imitating some of the earlier Spanish pieces for high *voces aequales*. The later services alternate more systematically between homophonic and polyphonic textures, and the five-part Evening Service 'to Mr Parsons' contains sections of madrigalian colour.

While not all of Mundy's full anthems are of equal merit, *O Lord, the maker* and *O Lord, I bow the knees* are of some interest; both were widely disseminated and they are among the earliest Elizabethan anthems of any substance. The former, for Compline, is in the common bipartite form with an optional repeat of the second section, while the latter is through-composed and is Mundy's largest-scale imitative anthem: it is possibly an adaptation of one of his Latin motets that is now lost. The verse anthem *Ah, helpless wretch* is particularly interesting as being one of the earliest verse anthems. It is scored for solo alto and five-part choir with organ and arises from an amalgam of the early metrical psalm, the consort song and the full anthem.

Mundy's large-scale votive antiphons are highly complex, fluid and ornate and are in the tradition of the Eton Choirbook pieces. They are similar in structure to the multipartite motets of such continental composers as Josquin, and although they contain marked textural contrasts, usually coinciding with the sectional divisions, their overall effect is of thick, heavy scoring, lacking any strong directional melodic or rhythmic impetus. Cadence points usually confirm only the progenitor mode: in *Vox Patris caelestis* the music centres on D consistently over a span of 261 bars; and in *Maria virgo sanctissima* there is only one deviation from internal cadences on F. Full-voice sections commonly open homophonically for purposes of impact, and then dissolve into non-imitative polyphony, at its most florid in the final 'amen' sections.

Sections of several works, including the impressive *Miserere mei Deus* for six voices, are found in a number of sources. Mundy's earliest and generally least effective Latin pieces appear in *GB-Lbm* 17802–5; the most interesting is the processional *In exitu Israel* for Easter Vespers, composed jointly by Sheppard, Byrd (possibly Thomas Byrd) and Mundy. The two four-part settings of the Mass *Upon the Square* are based on the Kyrie melodies for Lady Mass in the Sarum Rite, and, unlike other English mass settings of the time, set the five sections of the Ordinary almost in full, with a few slight textual modifications. Other manuscripts include several florid though incomplete *Magnificat* settings and two striking pieces, *Beatus et sanctus* and *Sive vigilem*.

### WORKS

Edition: *W. Mundy: Latin Antiphons and Psalms*, ed. F. Ll. Harrison, EECM, ii (1963) [H]

#### SERVICES

First Service, in d sol re, 4–6vv, *GB-Cp, DRc, GL, Lbm, Lcm, Och, Y*, 1641⁵
Short Service, 4vv, *Cp, Cpc, DRc, Llp* (different Cr), *Och, Ojc* (different Cr)
Evening Service 'to Mr Parsons', 5vv, *Cp, DRc, Y*
Evening Service 'in medio chori', 9vv, *Cp*

#### ANTHEMS
(*full unless otherwise stated*)

Ah, helpless wretch, verse, A, 5vv, org, *GB-DRc, GL, Lbm, Lcm* (attrib. Parsons), *Ob, Ojc, T*, 1641⁵; ed. P. le Huray (London, 1965)
Bow down thine eye, 4vv, inc., *Lcm* (adaptation of Adolescentulus)
Increase my joy (text only), in J. Clifford, The Divine Services and Anthems (London, 2/1664)
Lay not up your treasures, inc., *Cp* (anon., offertory to the First Service)
Let the sea make a noise, 6vv (textless), *Lbm*
My song shall be of mercy, inc., *Lbm*
O Lord, I bow the knees, 5vv, *GB-Cfm, Cpc* (attrib. Tallis), *DRc, EL, GL, Lbm, LF, Llp, Lsp, Ob, Och, Ojc, T, WRch, Y, US-BE, NYp*, 1641⁵
O Lord, the maker of all things, 4vv, *GB-DRc, EL, GL, Lbm, Lcm, Och, Ojc, T, WB, WRch, Y, US-BE, NYp*, 1641⁵; ed. P. le Huray (London, 1965)
O Lord, the world's saviour, 4vv, *GB-DRc, EL, GL, Lbm, Lcm, Och, Ojc, WRch, Y, US-BE*, 1641⁵
Prepare you, time weareth away, 4vv, *GB-Lbm*
Save me, O God, for thy name's sake (text only), *Lbm, Ob*
The secret sins (text only), verse, *Lbm, Ob*
This is my commandment, 4vv (also attrib. Tallis and Johnson), *GB-Cp, DRc, Lbm, Ob, US-NYp*

#### LATIN SACRED

Mass Upon the Square (2 settings), 4vv, *GB-Lbm*
Kyrie, 4–5vv, *Lbm*

Adhaesit pavimento, 5vv, H; Adolescentulus sum ego (2p. Tribulacio), 6vv, H; Alleluia, 4vv, *Lbm*; Alleluia, 4vv, *Lbm*; Beati immaculati, 5vv, H; Beatus auctor, 5vv, *Och*; Beatus et sanctus, 5vv, *Och*; Domine, non est exaltatum, 6vv, H; Domine, quis habitabit, 6vv, H; Eructavit cor meum, 6vv, H; Exurge, Christe, 4vv, *Lbm* (and as Tres partes in una, kbd transcr. ed. in MB, i, 1951); Gaude virgo mater, inc., *Ob*; In aeternum, 6vv, H; In exitu Israel, 4vv, *Lbm* (collab. Sheppard and ?Thomas Byrd); Magnificat, 4vv, *Lbm*; Magnificat, inc., *Lbm, Ob*; Magnificat, inc., *Ob*; Magnificat, *Och* (frag.); Maria virgo sanctissima, 6vv, H; Memor esto, 5vv, H; Miserere mei Deus, 6vv, inc., *Lbm, Lcm, Ob, T*, Spetchley Park, Worcester; Noli aemulari, 5vv, H; O admirabile, 5vv (textless); O mater mundi, 5vv (textless), *CH, Lbm*; Sive vigilem, 5vv, *Och*; Veni Creator Spiritus, 5vv, *Och*; Videte miraculum, 5vv, *Och*; Vox Patris caelestis, 6vv, H

#### INSTRUMENTAL

In Nomine, on D, a 5, *Ob*

#### WORKS BY EITHER JOHN OR WILLIAM MUNDY
(*all ascribed 'Mundy'*)

##### SERVICES

Evening Service, in C fa ut, 5vv, *GB-Cp, DRc*
First Evening Service, inc., *Lbm*

Fourth Evening Service, inc., *Lbm*
Second Service, in F fa ut, 4vv, *DRc, Lbm, Lcm, Ob*
Service in Four Parts for Men, *Cp, DRc, Lbm*
Service in Three Parts for Men, *Cp, DRc*
Te Deum (Eng. text) for Five Men's Voices, inc., *Lbm*
Whole Service for Two Basses, ?5vv, *DRc* (organbook only)
Te Deum, Benedictus for Trebles (Eng. text), 5vv, *US-NYp*

##### ANTHEMS
(*all full*)

A new commandment, 4vv, *US-NYp*
Behold it is Christ, 4vv, *GB-Lbm, US-NYp*
Blessed is God in all his gifts, 4vv, *GB-Cp*
God be merciful unto us, inc., *Lbm*
He that hath my commandments, 4vv, *DRc, Lbm, US-NYp*; ed. P. le Huray (London, 1965)
In God alone is all my trust, inc., *GB-Lbm*
Let us now laud, 4vv, *DRc, Lbm, US-NYp*; ed. P. le Huray (London, 1965)
Praise the Lord, O ye servants, 4vv, *GB-Lbm, US-NYp*
Rejoice in the Lord alway, 4vv, *GB-DRc, Lbm*
Teach me, O Lord, inc., *Lbm*

##### LATIN SACRED

Deus misereatur nostri, 6vv, *Lbm* (? by White); Dulcior melle, 3vv (textless), *Lbm*; Mi Deus eripe me, inc., *US-SM*

##### INSTRUMENTAL

In Nomine, on D, a 5, *GB-Lbm*; Sermone blando, a 5, *Lbm, Lcm, Ob, US-NYp, Ws*; A Solfinge Song, inc., *GB-Lbm*; untitled piece, a 5, *Lbm*

### BIBLIOGRAPHY

A. Wood: *Athenae oxonienses* (London, 1691–2); ed. and enlarged P. Bliss (London, 1813–15)
E. H. Fellowes: *The Music of St. George's Chapel* (London, 1927)
H. Baillie: 'Squares', *AcM*, xxxii (1960), 178
J. D. Bergsagel: 'An Introduction to Ludford', *MD*, xiv (1960), 105
H. Baillie: 'Some Biographical Notes on English Church Musicians Chiefly Working in London (1485–1569)', *RMARC*, ii (1962), 18–57
J. Kerman: *The Elizabethan Madrigal* (New York, 1962)
——: 'The Elizabethan Motet: a Study of Texts for Music', *Studies in the Renaissance*, ix (1962), 273–308
J. D. Bergsagel: 'The Date and Provenance of the Forrest–Heyther Collection of Early Tudor Masses', *ML*, xliv (1963), 240
P. le Huray: *Music and the Reformation in England, 1549–1660* (London, 1967)
R. W. Bray: 'British Museum Add. MSS 17802–5 (the Gyffard Partbooks): an Index and Commentary', *RMARC*, vii (1969), 31
A. Langford: *Music for the English Prayerbook from Tallis to Tomkins* (diss., U. of Reading, 1970)
W. A. Edwards: 'The Performance of Ensemble Music in Elizabethan England', *PRMA*, xcvii (1970–71), 113
R. W. Bray: 'The Part-books Oxford, Christ Church, Mss. 979–983: an Index and Commentary', *MD*, xxv (1971), 179
P. Doe: 'Another View of Music Ficta in Tudor Music', *PRMA*, xcviii (1971–2), 113
R. T. Daniel and P. le Huray: *The Sources of English Church Music*, EECM, suppl.i (1972)
G. L. Blount: *The Sacred Vocal Music of John Mundy* (diss., U. of California, Los Angeles, 1974)
R. G. Reeve: *The Life and Works of William Mundy* (diss., U. of London, in preparation)

GILBERT L. BLOUNT, ROBERT REEVE

**Munerat, Jean le.** *See* LE MUNERAT, JEAN.

**Munfurt, Hugo von.** *See* HUGO VON MONTFORT.

**Munich** (Ger. München). Capital of the state of Bavaria, Federal German Republic.

1. Before 1651. 2. 1651–1806. 3. 1806–1918. 4. Since 1918. 5. Musical education and musicology.

1. BEFORE 1651. Munich was the seat of the dukes of Upper Bavaria from 1255, and the capital of the whole duchy from 1550. Records of early musical activity in the city are sparse. Since the parish schools taught singing as well as Latin and German, it may be assumed that music was heard at services in the oldest church in Munich, St Peter's (first mentioned 1225), from an early date. The parish of Munich was divided in 1271 and the little Marienkapelle became the parish church of Our

Lady (Frauenkirche). Gregorian chant (in the so-called Germanic dialect) is reported as being sung in both churches and in the Franciscan friary on the Anger at about this period. In 1384 St Peter's acquired a new, larger organ and the new Frauenkirche (built 1468–88) had a splendid instrument installed in 1491, which was mentioned by Zarlino (*Supplementi musicali*, 1588).

Equally little is known of the music enjoyed by the citizens. It is safe to assume that domestic music-making was carried on, but there is no extant record of it. The city normally maintained four pipers and one drummer for all public and private occasions; they were sometimes augmented by the court trumpeters, just as the city pipers helped out at court on occasion. It was not unknown for a city piper to be in the court service at the same time. The head of the Bavarian musicians' guild, the *Spielgraf*, was always one of the court trumpeters from the 15th century onwards. The city musicians did not in any case form a guild until after the Thirty Years War. The art of Meistergesang did not flourish to any notable extent in Munich, although Hans Sachs studied there under the linen-weaver and Meistersinger Leonhard Nonnenpeckh.

The music of the court is the most fully documented: the trumpeters and drummers essential to the court's dignity are on record as permanent members of the household at an earlier date than the chapel musicians. Itinerant minstrels were well received. Music at the court of Munich began to flourish in the 15th century, when Conrad Paumann was the court organist. The first evidence of a chapel of priests and clerks comes from the time of Duke Albrecht IV (1440–1508); it included two Bavarian musicians who had formerly worked in London. Closer connections with the court of Burgundy were fostered by the engagement of Ludwig Senfl, previously a singer in, and director of, the court chapel of Emperor Maximilian I. The Kantorei of singers and instrumentalists which he built up was independent of clerical control; it provided secular entertainment as well as fulfilling religious duties and was capable of performing the large repertory of the age. After Senfl's death the standing of the chapel waned, but it revived with the advent of Lassus. The earliest record of his residence in Munich is 1557, and under him music in Bavaria rose to a high level of importance. He was officially appointed Hofkapellmeister in 1563 and vigorously set about reorganizing the Kantorei. From then on Munich was a musical centre of significance, with a chapel that could stand comparison with those of the emperor, the King of France and even the pope. The summit of its achievement under Lassus was the music for the wedding of Wilhelm, the duke's heir, and Renata of Lorraine in 1568. On this occasion the Kantorei was built up to larger numbers than ever before.

The court of Munich was European in its musical outlook. Lassus, by birth a Walloon and educated in Italy, composed in all the national styles of the age and directed an ensemble which originally had a strong Netherlands contingent but gradually recruited more and more Italians. Duke Albrecht V (1550–79) founded Munich's reputation as a home of the arts, not only by his generous endowment of music at court, but also by his collections, which form the nucleus of the present-day Bavarian state library, the state art collections and other institutions. Adam Berg opened his printing house in 1564 and founded Munich's reputation as a publishing centre, particularly with his music publications,

including numerous editions of Lassus's works. Munich had much to offer to the musicians it attracted from abroad: Andrea Gabrieli and his nephew Giovanni were among those who played under Lassus. For two years after 1568 Duke Albrecht and his son maintained a chapel each, the latter employing at his residence in Landshut some of the musicians originally engaged to augment the chapel for his wedding. This proving prohibitively expensive Wilhelm had to give up his chapel, and from then on the Munich Kantorei continually oscillated between reductions and increases in numbers until the accession of Duke Maximilian (1597), when the musical establishment was finally cut and the great efflorescence of Bavarian music ended. Lassus had succeeded Ludwig Daser as Kapellmeister; his own successors, up to the middle of the 17th century, were his deputy Fossa, his son and grandson, both Ferdinand, Giovanni Battista Crivelli and Giovanni Giacomo Porro.

The church music of 16th-century Munich did not flourish with the music at court. Polyphony with instrumental accompaniment was heard in the Frauenkirche in the mid-15th century, but it was rare before the end of the century, not least for financial reasons. On festive occasions the churches had to help each other out or call on the court musicians or the city pipers if they wanted to perform polyphonic music, and great events like the funeral of Albrecht V in 1579 were accompanied only by choral monody. The reform of church music, after the introduction of the Roman rite laid down by the Council of Trent, began at the court in 1581, with the parish churches following suit in the early 17th century, and eventually polyphony became the rule in all the churches, though it did not gain a footing in St Peter's until c1635.

Religious life took on new impetus with the arrival of the Jesuits, whom Albrecht V invited to Munich in 1559. Before the end of the year they had opened a grammar school and an educational institute for poor scholars; they recruited court musicians to teach music. The free tuition and the academic standards of the Jesuits immediately deprived the parish schools of pupils, fees and choirboys. The Jesuit church, St Michael's (consecrated 1597), became the centre of church music in Munich. The Jesuits' Latin plays, with casts of hundreds, also attracted attention away from the plays performed in the Rathaus by the city poet and his pupils, travelling players or craftsmen (*Esther* 1567, *Samson* 1568, *Cenodoxus* 1607). Lassus probably composed choruses for some of the Jesuit plays.

The Corpus Christi processions held since 1343 had become occasions of great splendour, for which the court made itself solely responsible, providing the costumes, paying most of the cost of the ostentatious decorations and employing the full strength of the court musicians, beside whom the four city pipers could not hope to shine. In this way the music of the townspeople and of the two parish churches was overshadowed by that of the court and the Jesuits, and was unable to develop independently. The Thirty Years War, which reduced the whole of Germany to cultural stagnation, also hindered the advent of Italian opera in Munich, so that the next stage in the musical history of the city did not begin until the second half of the 17th century.

2. 1651–1806.

(i) *Opera*. The opera house beside the Salvatorkirche was originally a granary, converted by the Elector

1. *The Bavarian court chapel under Orlande de Lassus: miniature by Hans Mielich from the Mielen Codex, 16th century* (*D-Mbs Mus.Ms.AII, f.186r*)

Maximilian I (1597–1651). Music at court benefited greatly from the enthusiasm of Henriette Adelheid of Savoy, the wife of the elector's son and heir, Ferdinand Maria. Concerts, musical theatre and ballet were performed, including Maccioni's dramatic cantata *L'arpa festante* (1653) and *La ninfa ritrosa* (perhaps by Zambonini, 1654). The magnificent productions mounted from 1656 onwards, under the direction of the Hofkapellmeister Kerll, put the Munich court opera on a level equal to any in Europe. Kerll's own operas and those of his successor Ercole Bernabei (Hofkapell-meister 1674–87) are lost, but some scores by Steffani (Kammermusikdirektor 1681–8) and Giuseppe Antonio Bernabei (Hofkapellmeister 1688–1732) have survived. Changes resulted from the appointment of Elector Maximilian II Emmanuel (1680–1725) as governor of the Netherlands and from the War of the Spanish Succession (1701–14): the electoral chamber musicians, under Pietro Torri and later E. F. dall'Abaco, followed the elector to Brussels and to exile in France; virtually the only music still performed at court in Munich, under Antonio Bernabei, was at religious services. During the

Austrian occupation opera was performed in German by travelling companies, augmented by such individual court musicians as Schuechbauer. Meanwhile at the elector's court in the Netherlands a taste for the French style in the manner of Lully, which had already gained ground in Munich, finally prevailed. Prominent composers of instrumental music of the early years of the century included, besides dall'Abaco, Brescianello, Pez and Mayr. On Maximilian's return in 1715 a number of French musicians also came to Munich, among them Jacques Loeillet who remained in the service of the court until 1732. Music and drama at court revived in the years up to 1725, with such sumptuous productions as the operas by Torri (Hofkapellmeister 1732–7) and Albinoni performed on the occasion of the marriage of the heir apparent, Karl Albrecht (1722), with magnificent sets by Giuseppe Galli-Bibiena. During the electorate of Karl Albrecht (1726–45, emperor from 1742), after a short break musical pursuits at the court continued, with a distinct return to the Italian style. They were interrupted once again by the unhappy outcome of the War of the Austrian Succession (1741–5) and the two-year exile of Karl Albrecht, but under Maximilian III Joseph (1745–77), a zealous patron of music, the court musicians were again brought up to full strength after a few years. The elector, himself a musician and a composer, preferred Neapolitan opera. Besides the composers who were in the elector's service, Porta (Hofkapellmeister 1737–55), Ferrandini, Francesco Peli, Aliprandi and Bernasconi (Hofkapellmeister 1755–84), music was commissioned from Sales, Antonio Tozzi, Traetta, Sacchini and others. Germans who wrote for the stage included J. A. Camerloher, F. C. T. Cröner, Joseph Michl, Naumann and the elector's sister, Maria Antonia Walpurgis of Saxony. The only Gluck work heard, apart from performances by travelling companies, was a much-adapted *Orfeo* given during Carnival 1773. On the other hand Mozart's *La finta giardiniera* (Salvatortheater, 1775) was commissioned for the programme of *opera buffa* initiated at his own risk by the Intendant of court music, Count Seeau. The Residenztheater (fig.2) in the electoral palace, also known as the Cuvilliéstheater, was opened in 1753; it was destroyed in World War II but rebuilt on the original pattern and reopened in 1958. The elector's cousin Duke Clemens of Bavaria (*d* 1770) also maintained his own ensemble of singers and instrumentalists at this period; he patronized the education of gifted musicians generously and had close ties with the Jesuits. Some of his musicians, Holzbogen, Kirmayr, Haindl and Vogl, belonged to a circle of Munich composers who were overshadowed by the Mannheim composers gathered by Carl Theodor (1778–99). Despite such honoured names as Cannabich and Toeschi, the Mannheim composers did not reach their former standing in Munich; they did not create anything equivalent to the Viennese Classical tradition, but with Winter, Danzi and Fränzl they prepared the ground for the Romanticism of Weber and Spohr. In 1787 Carl Theodor banned Italian opera, which had reached its peak with Mozart's *Idomeneo* (1781). Thereafter the repertory consisted predominantly of German translations of French and Italian operas, and of Singspiels by Schubaur, Gleissner, Destouches and Winter. Count Seeau, who encouraged German theatre, ended his 45 years in office in 1799, leaving his successor, Babo, to cope with the results of his indescribable misman-

agement. In the opening years of the new century music at the court laboured under stringent economies and the 'French requisition' of scores and parts. In succession to Johann Friedrich Eck, Carl Cannabich, a skilful orchestral trainer, became the last electoral director of music in 1800.

(*ii*) *Church music.* The principal institutions were the Jesuit college and church of St Michael and the associated Seminarium Gregorianum, which was famous for its music teaching. Court musicians were among the teachers, and the students swelled the ranks of the chorus in the court opera. The greater part of the music for the Lenten meditations, held annually until 1776, was by Bavarian composers. Franz Xaver Murschhauser was the most important of the choirmasters and composers of church and organ music at the collegiate church of Unsere Liebe Frau. Of his successors, Christoph Hirschberger (in office 1742–56) and Joseph Adam Obermiller (1757–69) should be mentioned for their church music and their sacred dramatic works. The music at the older Munich parish church of St Peter was reorganized from 1649 and a school of singing and instrumental playing was founded. The inventories of 1655 and 1662 testify to a comprehensive repertory, from Senfl to Kerll. Victorin and Pez were the best known musicians at St Peter's. Musical standards were high, particularly in the 18th century, at some of the religious houses in the city: those of the Augustines, Hieronymites and Franciscans, and the nunneries on the Anger and the Ridler Regelhaus among the female foundations. The court heard sacred music in its chapel and, on feast days, also in the Theatinerkirche, built in 1675. The scope of the repertory is indicated by a thematic catalogue compiled *c*1810–40, which lists the names of 89 composers. Sacred oratorios by Pampani, Bernasconi, Jommelli and Myslivecek were among those performed during Lent in the court theatre or in the chapel.

### 3. 1806–1918.

(*i*) *Opera.* During the first decades of the 19th century there were many new musical enterprises in the city, but at the same time the standard of public taste declined. The 1787 ban on Italian opera was lifted in 1805, and that genre dominated the repertory again from 1816. The dilapidated Salvatortheater was pulled down in 1802; the Hof- und Nationaltheater designed by Karl von Fischer, completed in 1818, was rebuilt in 1823 (see fig.3) after a fire (and again in 1963, having been destroyed in 1943). The most notable works to receive their first performances in the Residenztheater at this time were Weber's *Abu Hassan* (1811) and Meyerbeer's first opera *Jephthas Gelübde* (1812). Both composers remained in Munich for some time, Weber hoping in vain, like Mozart before him, for a conducting post. At the Theater am Isartor (opened 1812), under the musical direction of Peter von Lindpaintner, Singspiels and farces in the Viennese manner by Müller, Röth, Lindpaintner, Weigl and others were performed. It was closed by Ludwig I in 1825, in the interests of more lofty cultural aspirations. After Winter's death in 1825 the direction of the operas was undertaken by Ferdinand Fränzl (retired 1827) and Joseph Stuntz. Partly because of the inefficient division of responsibility between Stuntz and the Konzertmeister Moralt, standards steadily dropped until 1836 when, under the excellent Intendant Küstner, Franz Lachner took on the fundamental reorganization of the repertory and, as a first-rate orchestral trainer, restored the court ensemble to its former heights. His own opera *Catarina Cornaro* was a great success. He also directed new works by Spohr, Lortzing, Marschner, Gounod and Verdi, and in spite of a personal lack of sympathy for Wagner's work he conducted the first performances there of *Tannhäuser* and *Lohengrin*. In 1864 Wagner himself was invited to Munich by Ludwig II, but his plans for the reform of the Musikschule and the Wagner Festival Theatre designed by Semper did not materialize. Wagner's extravagant style of living, at the king's expense, and the offensive behaviour of his supporters led to his having to leave the city after 18 months. Ludwig remained, notwithstanding, the chief patron of the composer and of his work. The first performances of *Tristan und Isolde* (1865) and *Die Meistersinger* (1868), conducted by Hans von Bülow, were outstanding triumphs for Wagner. Against the composer's will the king ordered the first performances of *Das Rheingold* (1869) and *Die Walküre* (1870), conducted by Franz Wüllner. Lachner, virtually ousted from office when Bülow arrived, retired in 1868; but it was he who instigated the award of the Order of Maximilian to Brahms and Wagner in 1872. On Hermann Levi's appointment as Hofkapellmeister in 1872, Munich became one of the principal centres for the performance of Wagner's music dramas, a tradition that was carried on by such men as Zumpe, Mottl and Fischer. Richard Strauss and Kienzl also spent short periods as young men conducting the Munich opera and, like Levi, played a part in the Mozart renaissance. The Munich opera festival dates from 1875, when the Intendant Carl von Perfall organized a 'festival summer' with operas by Mozart, Wagner and others. The true, eventual founder was Ernst von Possart, under whom the Prinzregententheater was opened for festival performances in 1901. The last royal Generalmusikdirektor was Bruno Walter, from 1913 to 1922. The climax of his memorable term of office was the première of Pfitzner's *Palestrina* (1917). The Theater am Gärtnerplatz, opened in 1865, was devoted to operetta.

(*ii*) *Concerts*. In 1811 some of the court musicians formed the Musikalische Akademie, which still exists, and organized subscription concerts. The lack of a dominating personality as conductor and public preference for the entertaining and undemanding led to a marked decline in the number of these concerts in the 1820s, until they were abandoned altogether in 1832. By contrast the evenings of music and recitation organized by private societies giving themselves such names as 'Harmonie', 'Frohsinn' and 'Museum', at which famous virtuosos like Hummel and Moscheles could be heard, were always well attended. Secular choral singing was cultivated by male choral societies; at least 30 were

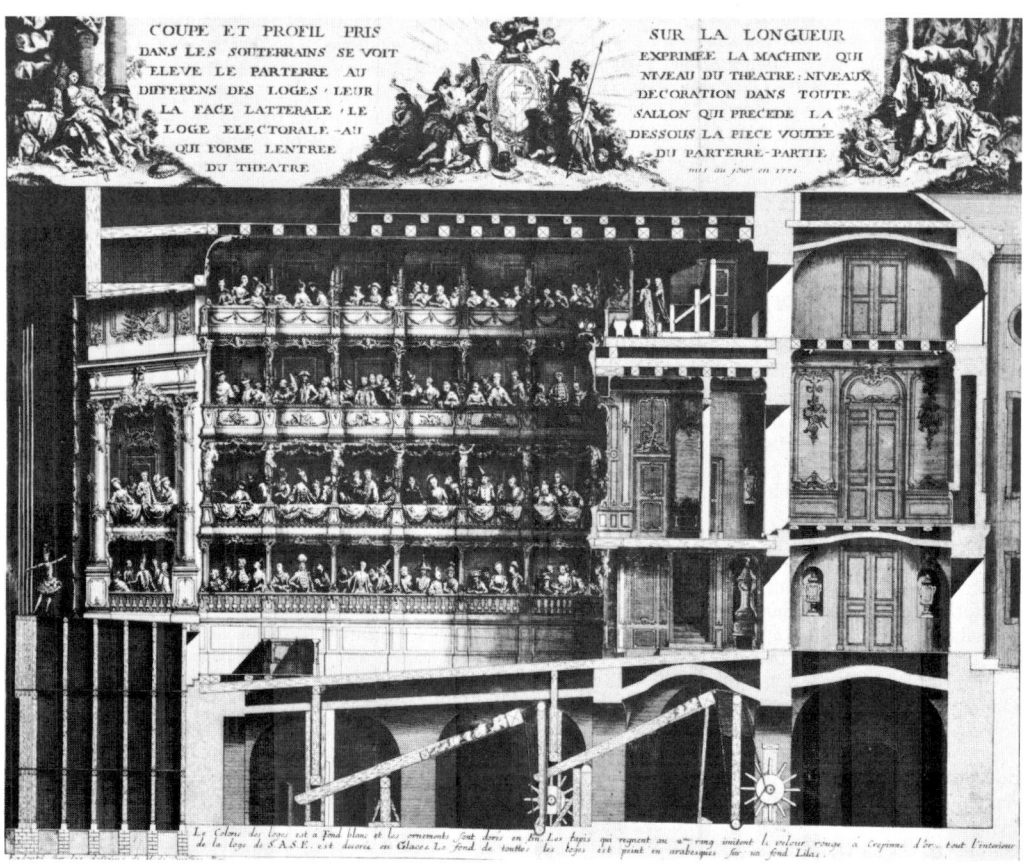

2. Cross-section of the Munich Residenztheater opened in 1753: engraving (1771) by Valerian Funck after François de Cuvilliés

*3. The Hof- und Nationaltheater, Munich: lithograph (1825) by G. Kraus*

founded by 1874, including the Liederkranz (1826), Bürgersängerzunft (1840), Liedertafel (1841) and Akademischer Gesangverein (1861). In addition to the Musikalische Akademie, revived by Lachner, the Oratorienverein, founded by Carl von Perfall in 1854 and conducted for many years by Rheinberger, the Lehrergesangverein (1878) and the Porges'scher Chorverein (1886) all organized large-scale choral concerts. Among the amateur orchestras the two outstanding were the Wilde Gung'l, founded 1864 and directed by Franz Strauss from 1875, and the Neuer Orchesterverein (1879). Concerts were given by the Musikalische Akademie in the Odeon, opened in 1828 (burnt down in 1944), and in 1893 the private Kaim orchestra inaugurated another series of symphony concerts which proved very popular and took place from 1895 in the Tonhalle (also destroyed in 1944). The conductors of this orchestra included Zumpe, Löwe and Weingartner. Towards the end of the 19th century the school of Munich composers led by Ludwig Thuille began to gain a reputation which spread beyond the city.

(*iii*) *Church music.* The secularization of the monasteries in 1803 was a setback for church music, but from 1816 Schmid and Ett at St Michael's set a shining example in their revival of classical vocal polyphony and the resumption of the south German tradition of sacred instrumental music, especially the work of Michael Haydn. In the Frauenkirche, raised to cathedral in 1823, the choirmaster Anton Schöfl and his son Johann Baptist were equally diligent in pursuing both traditions. The Cecilian reforms in the second half of the century had a far-reaching effect on the repertory. The royal Vokalkapelle performed in the newly built court church of Allerheiligen from 1837. It was conducted by Winter, Aiblinger and Stuntz before its reorganization in 1864, when it came under the baton of Franz

Wüllner, who was replaced in 1877 by Rheinberger, much esteemed as a composer of church music. At their popular soirées the royal choir also performed some secular works. Danzi and Winter were among the first to compose music for the Lutheran church established at the court in the early years of the century. From 1842 to 1854 the Lutheran St Matthew's boasted one of the leading organists of the day in Johann Herzog. A synagogue was opened in 1826 and in its early years commissioned compositions from Stuntz and Ett.

4. SINCE 1918. The representatives of the Munich school active in the early years of the century, such as Courvoisier, von Franckenstein and von Waltershausen, were succeeded by Haas, Kaminski and others of the present day such as Fritz Büchtger, Karl Höller, Harald Genzmer, Günther Bialas, Wilhelm Killmayer, Hans Ludwig Hirsch and Josef Anton Riedl, while Carl Orff and Karl Amadeus Hartmann achieved international standing. Under Knappertsbusch and Krauss the Munich opera built up a resounding reputation, specializing in the works of Richard Strauss, whose *Friedenstag* and *Capriccio* had their first performances in Munich (1938 and 1942). Until the Nationaltheater, destroyed in 1943, was reopened in 1963, the opera company played in the Prinzregententheater. Its principal conductors have included Ferdinand Leitner, Georg Solti, Ferenc Fricsay, Rudolf Kempe, Joseph Keilberth and, from 1971, Wolfgang Sawallisch. The Gärtnertheater is devoted mainly to comic opera, operetta and musicals; musical stage works can also be heard occasionally in such other theatres as the Schauspielhaus. The popular puppet theatre has a tradition dating from 1859 and performs works by Haydn, Mozart and Orff.

In 1924 the Kaim orchestra became the Munich PO and it is now financed by the city. Conductors have included Pfitzner, von Hausegger, Kabasta and Rosbaud, and Rudolf Kempe directed the orchestra, 1967–76. Orchestras founded since 1945 include the Bavarian RSO (conductors Eugen Jochum, Rafael Kubelik), the Radio Orchestra (Kurt Eichhorn), the private Kurt Graunke Orchestra (which runs its own subscription concerts) and the Munich Chamber Orchestra (Hans Stadlmair). The Philharmonic Choir (Rudolf Zöbeley) and the Bach Choir (Karl Richter) are the best-known choral societies; the Bach Orchestra is associated with the latter.

The Capella Antiqua (Konrad Ruhland) and the Capella Monacensis (Kurt Weinhöppel) specialize in the interpretation of medieval music, as did the Studio der Frühen Musik (Thomas Binkley; disbanded 1977). Christian Döbereiner and the Bach Society (whose conductors included Carl Orff) set new standards in the performance of Baroque music. The concerts and recordings of the Musica Bavarica chamber orchestra (Alois Kirchberger) specialize in the Bavarian musical tradition since the 17th century. There are also several chamber music societies in the city. The Association for Contemporary Music founded in 1929 was re-formed in 1945 as the Studio for New Music. In 1946 Karl Amadeus Hartmann founded the internationally famous Musica Viva concerts, which champion the contemporary cause with exemplary performances.

The cathedral choir became one of the leading German *a cappella* choirs under Ludwig Berberich. Under his successors Johannes Hafner and Max Eham it has concentrated on carrying out the changes in its role resulting from the liturgical reforms of the Second Vatican Council, which have restricted the old tradition of orchestral masses. Other Catholic churches where music is important are St Michael's, St Peter's, St Kajetan's and St Ludwig's. Lutheran church music is represented by the Bach Choir (Karl Richter), the motet choir of St Matthew (R. Zöbeley) and other bodies, which also, however, include the Catholic repertory.

5. MUSICAL EDUCATION AND MUSICOLOGY. The theory and practice of music are taught at the Städtische Singschule (founded 1830), the Richard-Strauss-Konservatorium (formed from the Trappsches Konservatorium in 1957), and the Staatliche Hochschule für Musik (previously the Königliche Musikschule, 1846–92, and the Akademie der Tonkunst, 1892–1946). The chair of musicology at the university has been held by Adolf Sandberger, Rudolf von Ficker, Thrasybulos Georgiades and (from 1973) Theodor Göllner; von Ficker and Georgiades were also chairmen of the Musikhistorische Kommission of the Bayerische Akademie der Wissenschaften, which is responsible for the complete Lassus edition. The Gesellschaft für Bayerische Musikgeschichte, founded in 1958, is devoted to research and publication (Denkmäler der Tonkunst in Bayern). The complete edition of Wagner's works is appearing under the auspices of the Bayerische Akademie der Schönen Künste. The musical collections of the Bayerische Staatsbibliothek and the Städtische Musikbibliothek contain abundant source material for research and performance. Other notable collections include the Theatermuseum, the large municipal collection of instruments in the Stadtmuseum and the instrument collections in the Deutsches Museum and the Nationalmuseum. Major exhibitions have been mounted (some with comprehensive catalogues) on Richard

Strauss (1964), Max Reger (1968), Hans Pfitzner (1969), Carl Orff (1970) and Werner Egk (1971).

### BIBLIOGRAPHY

#### GENERAL
E. Bücken: *München als Musikstadt* (Munich, 1923)
O. Ursprung: *Münchens musikalische Vergangenheit* (Munich, 1927)
A. Kaul: 'München', *MGG*
H. Schmid: 'Musik', *Handbuch der bayerischen Geschichte*, ed. M. Spindler (Munich, 1967)
R. Münster and H. Schmid, eds.: *Musik in Bayern*, i: *Bayerische Musikgeschichte* (Tutzing, 1972)

#### BEFORE 1651
B. Stubenvoll: *Geschichte des Königlichen Erziehungsinstitutes für Studirende in München* (Munich, 1874)
K. Trautmann: 'Italienische Schauspieler am bayerischen Hofe', *Jb für Münchener Geschichte*, i (Munich, 1887), 193–312
K. von Reinhardstöttner: 'Zur Geschichte des Jesuitendramas in München', *Jb für Münchener Geschichte*, iii (Bamberg, 1889), 53–176
K. Trautmann: 'Archivalische Beiträge zur Geschichte der Schulkomödie in München', *Mitteilungen der Gesellschaft für deutsche Erziehungs- und Schulgeschichte* (Berlin, 1891), 61
A. Sandberger: *Beiträge zur Geschichte der bayerischen Hofkapelle unter Orlando di Lasso* (Leipzig, 1894–5)
A. Schulz: *Die St.-Michaels-Hofkirche in München* (Munich, 1897)
L. Söhner: *Die Musik im Münchner Dom unserer lieben Frau in Vergangenheit und Gegenwart* (Munich, 1934)
W. Boetticher: *Orlando di Lasso und seine Zeit*, i: *Monographie* (Kassel and Basle, 1958)
——: *Aus Orlando di Lassos Wirkungskreis: neue archivalische Studien* (Kassel, 1963)
E. Straub: *Repraesentatio Majestatis oder churbayerische Freudenfeste: die höfischen Feste in der Münchner Residenz vom 16. bis zum Ende des 18. Jahrhunderts* (Munich, 1969)
H. Leuchtmann: 'Orlando di Lasso in München', *Oberbayerisches Archiv*, xcvii (Munich, 1973), 1
——: *Orlando di Lasso*, i: *Sein Leben* (Wiesbaden, 1976); ii: *Briefe* (Wiesbaden, 1977)

#### 1651–1806
L. Westenrieder: 'Von dem Zustand der Musik in München', *Jb der Menschengeschichte in Bayern*, i/2 (Munich, 1783), 366
F. J. Lipowsky: *Baierisches Musiklexikon* (Munich, 1811)
F. M. Rudhart: *Die italiänische Oper von 1654–1787*, Geschichte der Oper am Hofe zu München, i (Freising, 1865)
L. Schiedermair: 'Die Anfänge der Münchener Oper', *SIMG*, v (1903–4), 442
P. Legband: 'Münchener Bühne und Literatur im 18. Jahrhundert', *Oberbayerisches Archiv*, li (1904), 1–546
H. Uffinger: *Die Grundlagen des Münchener Konzertlebens* (diss., U. of Munich, 1941)
H. Bolongaro-Crevenna: *L'arpa festante: die Münchner Oper 1651–1825* (Munich, 1963)
R. Münster: *Die Musik am Hofe Max Emanuels, Kurfürst Max Emanuel: Bayern und Europa um 1700*, i (Munich, 1976) [exhibition catalogue]
Introductions to the DTB volumes of Kerll, Pez, Murschhauser, Steffani and dall'Abaco

#### 1806–1918
E. Rutz: *Der Münchener Liedertafel Stiftungs- und Sonnwendfeste in den Jahren 1842–1866* (Munich, 1867)
E. von Destouches: 'Geschichte der Sangespflege und der Sängervereine in der Stadt München', *Festzeitung zum II. deutschen Sängerbundesfest* (Munich, 1874), 5
F. Grandaur: *Chronik der Königlichen Hof- und Nationaltheaters in München* (Munich, 1878)
*Der Oratorien-Verein in München in den ersten 25 Jahren seines Bestehens (1854–1879)* (Munich, 1879)
O. J. Bierbaum: *Fünfundzwanzig Jahre Münchner Hoftheater-Geschichte* (Munich, 1892)
K. von Perfall: *Ein Beitrag zur Geschichte der königlichen Theater in München (1867–1892)* (Munich, 1894)
H. Bihrle: *Die Musikalische Akademie München 1811–1911* (Munich, 1911)
M. Zenger: *Geschichte der Münchener Oper*, ed. T. Kroyer (Munich, 1923)
*Festschrift zum 50jährigen Bestehen der Akademie der Tonkunst in München 1874–1924* (Munich, 1924)
P. Busse: *Geschichte des Gärtnerplatztheaters in München* (Munich, 1924)
J. Peslmüller and F. Weber: *Die Städtische Singschule München von 1830–1930* (Munich, 1930)
O. Mainer: '90 Jahre Münchner Bürgersängerzunft', *Münchner neueste Nachrichten* (1931), no.315

Werden und Wirken der Münchener Philharmoniker ... und des Konzertvereins München e.V. (Munich, 1934)

F. Ihlau: *Die Entwicklung der Musikberichterstattung in den 'Münchener neuesten Nachrichten' bis zum Jahr 1860* (diss., U. of Munich, 1935)

P. Beckers: *Die nachwagner'sche Oper bis zum Ausgang des 19. Jahrhunderts im Spiegel der Münchner Presse* (diss., U. of Munich, 1936)

W. Eichner: *Münchens Entwicklung als Musikstadt* (diss., U. of Munich, 1951)

E. J. Luin: 'Das künstlerische Erbe der Kurfürstin Adelaide in ihren Kindern, Enkeln und Urenkeln', *Festgabe für ... Kronprinz Rupprecht von Bayern* (Munich, 1953), 152

A. Aschl: *Die Moralt* (Rosenheim, 1960)

K. Hommel: *Die Separatvorstellungen von König Ludwig II. von Bayern* (Munich, 1963)

*Orchesterverein 'Wilde Gung'l' 1864–1964: Festschrift* (Munich, 1964)

H.-I. Irmen: *Gabriel Josef Rheinberger als Antipode des Cäcilianismus* (Regensburg, 1970)

SINCE 1918

*Lehrergesangverein München 1878–1938* (Munich, 1939)

A. Berrsche: *Trösterin Musica* (Munich, 1942, 3/1964)

H. Wagner: *Münchner Theaterchronik 1750–1950* (Munich, 1950–60) [with supplement to 1960]

*Magie der Oper: München 1947–51* (Ulm, 1952)

H. Friess: *300 Jahre Münchener Oper* (Munich, 1953)

W. Zentner: *Sechzig Jahre Münchner Philharmoniker 1893–1953* (Munich, 1953)

F. Lutz: *125 Jahre Städtische Singschule München 1830–1955* (Munich, 1955)

*Die Münchner Theater*, ed. Freunde des Nationaltheaters (Munich, 1957)

K. H. Ruppel: *Musica viva* (Munich, 1959)

*Festschrift zum 150jährigen Jubiläum 1811–1961: Musikalische Akademie – Bayerisches Staatsorchester* (Munich, 1961)

H. Friess and R. Goldschmidt: *Nationaltheater München: Festschrift der Bayerischen Staatsoper zur Eröffnung des wiederaufgebauten Hauses* (Munich, 1963)

W. Panofsky: *Musiker, Mimen und Merkwürdigkeiten im Hof- und Nationaltheater* (Munich, 1963)

P. Schallweg, ed.: *Festliche Oper: Geschichte und Wiederaufbau des Nationaltheaters in München* (Munich, 1964)

*100 Jahre Theater am Gärtnerplatz München* (Munich, 1965)

A. Ott, ed.: *Die Münchner Philharmoniker 1893–1968* (Munich, 1968)

G. Benker: *Reise durch das konzertante Bayern* (Munich, 1968)

E. Nick: *Münchner Musikberichte* (Tutzing, 1971)

K.-R. Danler: *Musik in München 1945–1972* (Munich, 1972)

LIBRARIES AND COLLECTIONS

J. J. Maier: *Die musikalischen Handschriften der Königlichen Hof- und Staatsbibliothek in München*, i: *Die Handschriften bis zum Ende des 17. Jahrhunderts* (Munich, 1879, rev., enlarged, in preparation).

K. A. Bierdimpfl: *Die Sammlung der Musikinstrumente des baierischen Nationalmuseums* (Munich, 1883)

B. A. Wallner: 'Die Gründung der Münchener Hofbibliothek durch Albrecht V. und Johann Jacob Fugger', *ZMw*, ii (1919–20), 294

R. Schaal: 'Die vor 1800 gedruckten Libretti des Theatermuseums München', *Mf*, xi (1958), 58

C. Gottwald: *Die Musikhandschriften der Universitätsbibliothek München* (Wiesbaden, 1968)

HORST LEUCHTMANN, ROBERT MÜNSTER

**Munkittrick, Howard.** *See* TALBOT, HOWARD.

**Münnich, Richard** (*b* Berlin, 7 June 1877; *d* Weimar, 4 July 1970). German musicologist and music educationist. He studied musicology with Bellermann, Friedlaender and Stumpf at Berlin University, where he took the doctorate in 1902 with a dissertation on Kuhnau; later he was a composition pupil of Grabert. He taught at the Riemann Conservatory, Stettin (from 1904), at several schools in Berlin (from 1908) and at the Klindworth-Scharwenka Conservatory (from 1910), while also serving as director of the Charlottenburg Chorverein (1908–14). In 1918 he founded (and until 1920 directed) an association of secondary school music teachers in Prussia. Concurrently he edited a journal of school music (1918–25) and was co-editor (1928–34) and editor (from 1934) of the *Zeitschrift für Schulmusik*. He taught at the Charlottenburg Akademie für Kirchen- und Schulmusik (1928–34) before becom-

ing professor and director of the school music department at the Weimar Hochschule für Musik (1935–49); he continued teaching there until 1964, also serving as principal (1944–5) and an honorary governor (1957–70). Münnich was an early campaigner for the reform of school music teaching and its establishment on a scientific basis; his 'Jale' method, a syllabic tonal and rhythmic system, combined the advantages of sol-fa with those of the 'Tonwort' system of Eitz and achieved considerable currency.

WRITINGS

*Johann Kuhnau: sein Leben und seine Werk* (diss., U. of Berlin, 1902; *SIMG*, iii (1901–2), 473–509)

'Von der Entwicklung der Riemannschen Harmonielehre und ihrem Verhältnis zu Oettingen und Stumpf', *Riemann-Festschrift* (Leipzig, 1909), 60

'Ein Brief Esaias Reussners', *Festschrift ... Rochus Freiherrn von Liliencron* (Leipzig, 1910/R1970), 173

'Konkordanz und Diskordanz', *ZIMG*, xii (1910–11), 46–90

*Zilchers Dehmel-Zyklus* (Charlottenburg, 1911)

'Zur Theorie des Leitklangs', *Festschrift Hermann Kretzschmar* (Leipzig, 1918/R1973), 101

'Musikstundenzahl in der höheren Schule', *Musikpädagogische Gegenwartsfragen*, ed. L. Kestenberg (Leipzig, 1928)

'Lessing und die Musik', *Zeitschrift für Schulmusik*, ii (1929)

ed. with H. Martens: *Beiträge zur Schulmusik* (Lahr, 1930–32)

*Jale: ein Beitrag zur Tonsilbenfrage* (Lahr, 1930, 2/1959)

*Die Suite* (Berlin, 1931, 2/1957 ed. H. W. Schmidt)

ed.: *Aus Robert Schumanns Briefen und Schriften* (Weimar, 1956)

ed.: *E. T. A. Hoffmann: musikalische Novellen und Schriften nebst Briefen und Tagebuchaufzeichnungen* (Weimar, 1961)

ed.: *D. Diderot: Rameaus Neffe* (Weimar, 1964)

BIBLIOGRAPHY

*Festschrift zum siebzigsten Geburtstag von Richard Münnich* (Weimar, 1947) [unpubd typescript with biography by H. Kirmsse]

*Festschrift Richard Münnich zum achtzigsten Geburtstage: Beiträge zur Musikästhetik, Musikgeschichte, Musikerziehung* (Leipzig, 1957) [incl. H. Grossmann: 'Verzeichnis der Schriften Richard Münnichs', 128; A. Krause: 'Richard Münnich: ein Leben für die Musikerziehung', 133]

G. Braun: *Die Schulmusikerziehung in Preussen* (Kassel and Basle, 1957)

W. Friedrich, ed.: *Münnich-Festschrift: Richard Münnich zum achtzigsten Geburtstage* (Berlin, 1957) [unpubd typescript]

80th birthday tributes: H. Fischer, *Musik im Unterricht*, xlviii (1957), 232; H. Grossmann, *Musik und Gesellschaft*, vii (1957), 352; A. Krauss, *Musik in der Schule*, viii (1957), 159

A. Krauss: 'Richard Münnich, dem Nestor der deutschen Schulmusikerziehung, zum 90. Geburtstag', *Musik in der Schule*, xviii (1967), 210

Obituary: H. Grossmann, *Musik in der Schule*, xxi (1970), 468; R. Günther, *Musik und Bildung*, iii (1971), 44

**Muñoz Molleda, José** (*b* La Línea de la Concepción, Cadiz, 16 Feb 1905). Spanish composer. He studied with Del Campo at the Madrid Conservatory, where in 1934 he won the Rome Prize. His compositions are in a neo-Romantic style, recalling Ravel in the Piano Concerto, and he has cultivated an Andalusian picturesqueness. He is a member of the San Fernando Academy.

WORKS

(*selective list*)

Dramatic: La niña de plata y oro (ballet), 1936–7; La rosa viva (ballet), 1954; film scores

Oratorio: La resurrección de Lázara, solo vv, chorus, orch, 1936–7

Orch: Postales madrileñas, 1931; Scherzo mácabro, sym. poem, 1932; De la torre alta, sym. poem, 1932; Pf Conc., 1935; Fantasía romántica, 1943; Introducción y fugado, 1945; Miniaturas medievales, 1952

Chamber: Str Qt, 1934; Divertimento, 6 insts, 1944; Qnt, 1950; Trio, fl, vc, pf, 1951; Str Qt, 1952

Songs

Principal publisher: Unión Musical Española

GUY BOURLIGUEUX

**Munrow, David (John)** (*b* Birmingham, 12 Aug 1942; *d* Chesham Bois, Bucks., 15 May 1976). English player of early wind instruments. After leaving school he spent

*The Early Music Consort of London: (from left to right) Christopher Hogwood (harp), David Munrow (flute), James Tyler (lute), Oliver Brookes (rebec) and James Bowman*

a year teaching in South America, then read English at Pembroke College, Cambridge (1961–4), where he was prominent in university musical life, founding a group to perform early music. He subsequently spent a year studying 17th-century music at Birmingham University. His year in South America had given him experience of folk music, which he heard and played on the descendants of earlier instruments, and was a valuable foundation for his later studies of the playing techniques of those earlier instruments; he built up an extensive collection of folk and early art instruments.

Munrow was soon in demand as a recorder player, and formed his own recorder consort. In 1967 he began part-time lecturing at Leicester University, and in 1969 started to teach the recorder at the RAM. He made many broadcasts, and his series 'Pied Piper' (1971–6) was very successful; its following was not limited to the younger listeners for whom it had been intended originally. In 1967 he formed the Early Music Consort of London, with James Bowman, Oliver Brookes (viols) and Christopher Hogwood (harpsichord), joined in 1969 by James Tyler (lute). The consort, which aimed to perform early music in a way at once authentic and attractive, was first heard in London in 1968 but had given its début in Louvain in 1967. Besides regular concerts it provided 'period' music arranged by Munrow for television and films, and gave the first performances of several works, including Peter Dickinson's *Translations* (1971) and Lutyens's *The Tears of Night* (1972). Peter Maxwell Davies scored for the group as a stage band in his opera *Taverner* (1972).

The consort gave polished and thrilling performances of medieval and Renaissance music. Its style was considered brash by some critics, but it brought to enthusiastic audiences a large, important repertory of music previously regarded primarily as the domain of scholars.

Munrow's exuberance guided and dominated the group's work and his industry and musicianship were responsible for many attractive and well-balanced performances and recordings. Had he not ended his life, he would surely have come to be reckoned, as to some degree he already was, one of the most influential musicians of his generation.

WRITINGS

*Instruments of the Middle Ages and Renaissance* (London, 1976) [with discs]

BIBLIOGRAPHY

D. Fallows: Obituary, *MT*, cxvii (1976), 596

H. M. Brown: '*Instruments of the Middle Ages and Renaissance*: in memoriam David Munrow', *Early Music*, iv (1976), 288 [review]

'Tributes to David Munrow', *Early Music*, iv (1976), 376

DAVID SCOTT

**Münster, Joseph Joachim Benedict** (*b* Gangkofen, nr. Salzburg, ?30 Jan 1694; *d* after 1751). German composer and theorist. He matriculated at Salzburg University in 1710, but in 1712 his father's death and his mother's immediate remarriage ended his studies. By 1715, the year he married, he was working as schoolmaster and choirmaster at the church of St Zeno in Bad Reichenhall. He later changed his profession from teaching to law, while retaining his post as choirmaster. As well as several volumes of church music, he produced a manual of sight-singing, *Musices instructio*, which was published in the 1730s and went into nine editions, and a plainsong manual, *Scala Jacob*, in 1743.

Münster was one of the first composers to publish simple church music for parish choirs in the style popularized by JOHANN VALENTIN RATHGEBER from 1721 onwards. The psalms in both collections are through-composed, and neither solo nor tutti parts present the performers with difficulties. However, despite the description of his style as 'comico-ecclesiastical' on the title page of his 1743 Vespers, the general effect of the music is dull. He had little talent either for musical organization – most of his psalm settings are rather shapeless – or for writing good tunes, especially in choral passages; even in the longer psalms of 1729 his tuttis consist largely of repeated-chord declamation. Münster is unusual among composers of church music at this time in giving a tempo marking for each psalm: almost all are very slow.

As a theorist, Münster was old-fashioned. The *Musices instructio*, intended, according to the preface, to enable young people to learn singing as easily as possible, is based on the hexachord system, and is redolent of an earlier century.

### WORKS
*(all pubd in Augsburg)*

op.
1   Sacrificium vespertinum (1729), vesper psalms
2   VIII lytaniae ... cum IX antiphonis (c1735)
3   Epithalamion mysticum (1740), 60 German arias
4   Helicon sacer (1743), 4 antiphons, 5 psalms for Vespers
?5  Solsequium (c1745), concertos
6   Fons signatus (1751), 7 litanies, 1 Te Deum

### WRITINGS
*Musices instructio ... Kürtzist doch wohl gründlicher Weg ... die Edle Sing-Kunst ... zu erlernen* (?1732 [*GerberNL*], 9/1781)
*Scala Jacob ascendendo et descendendo* (1743, 2/1756)

ELIZABETH ROCHE

**Münster, Robert** (*b* Düren, 3 March 1928). German music librarian. He studied musicology with von Ficker and Georg Reichert at Munich University (1949–56); at the same time he continued his private studies in music theory (with H. W. von Waltershausen) and piano (with W. von Hoeselin). He took his doctorate in Munich in 1956 with a dissertation on Toeschi's symphonies. From 1957 to 1959 he was assistant to E. F. Schmid on the editorial staff of the Neue Mozart-Ausgabe. In 1961 he completed the state examinations in higher librarianship and in 1969 was appointed director of the music collection in the Bavarian State Library in Munich. Münster's main interest has been the opening up of new music collections in Bavaria, as well as the music history of this region. He is the historical editor of the gramophone record series Musica Bavaria. Other research interests include Mozart, on whom he has written a number of articles; he has also edited music by Boccherini, Cannabich, Mysliveček and other 18th-century composers.

### WRITINGS
*Die Sinfonien Toeschis* (diss., U. of Munich, 1956)
'Fragmente zu einer Musikgeschichte der Benediktinerabtei Tegernsee', *Studien und Mitteilungen zur Geschichte des Benediktinerordens*, lxxix (1968), 66
'Die erste Symphonie d-Moll von Hermann Goetz', *Mf*, xxii (1969), 162
*Carl Orff: das Bühnenwerk* (Munich, 1970) [exhibition catalogue]
with R. Machold: *Thematischer Katalog der Musikhandschriften der ehemaligen Klosterkirchen Weyarn, Tegernsee und Benediktbeuern* (Munich, 1971)
ed., with H. Schmid: *Bayerische Musikgeschichte*, Musik in Bayern, i (Tutzing, 1972)
'Die handschriftlichen Nachlässe in der Musiksammlung der Bayerischen Staatsbibliothek', *Beiträge zur Musikdokumentation: Franz Grasberger zum 60. Geburtstag* (Tutzing, 1975), 259
'Mozart bearbeitet Cannabich', *Festschrift Walter Senn* (Munich and Salzburg, 1975), 142
'Mozarts Kirchenmusik in München im 18. und beginnenden 19. Jahrhundert', *Erich Valentin zum 70. Geburtstag* (Regensburg, 1976)

### BIBLIOGRAPHY
*Mitteilungsblatt der Gesellschaft für bayerische Musikgeschichte*, iii (1967), 33 [incl. list of writings to 1967]

HANS HEINRICH EGGEBRECHT

**Munter** (Ger.: 'merry', 'cheerful', 'brisk', 'vigorous'). Perhaps the nearest German equivalent of the Italian

ALLEGRO. Schumann used it twice in *Album für die Jugend* op.68: the 'Soldatenmarsch' is marked *munter und straff* with the translation *gaio e deciso*, and 'Fröhlicher Landmann' has *frisch und munter*, translated *animato e grazioso*. It is otherwise relatively rare.

*See also* TEMPO AND EXPRESSION MARKS.

**Munzinger, Karl** (*b* Balsthal, canton of Solothurn, 23 Sept 1842; *d* Berne, 16 Aug 1911). Swiss conductor and composer. He studied first in Basle (1859–60), then at the Leipzig Conservatory (1860–63) under Hauptmann, Reinecke, E. F. Richter and Moscheles. He later taught the piano and was organist at Wesserling in Alsace. In 1866 he was appointed director of the Solothurn Liedertafel and Cäcilienverein, whose standards he greatly improved. He succeeded A. Reichle as conductor of the concerts of the Musikgesellschaft in 1884 and through his activities he exercised a profound influence on the musical life of Berne. One characteristic of his conducting was the range of music he performed; he introduced to Berne works by Brahms, Wagner, Berlioz and Bach. Though his output as a composer is rather small, his cantatas and *a cappella* compositions were once very popular throughout Switzerland; one of his major works was the music for a pageant commemorating the 700th anniversary of the foundation of Berne. He also composed piano pieces, organ music, a piano quartet and a mass.

### BIBLIOGRAPHY
*SML*
E. Refardt: 'Munzinger, Karl', *Historisch-biographisches Musikerlexikon der Schweiz* (Leipzig and Zurich, 1928)

F. R. BOSONNET

**Muradeli, Vano Il'ich** (*b* Gori, Georgia, 6 April 1908; *d* Tomsk, 14 Aug 1970). Russian composer. He studied composition with Barchudarian and Bagrinovsky at the Tbilisi Conservatory, from which he graduated in 1931. Subsequently he was a composition pupil of Shekhter and Myaskovsky at the Moscow Conservatory. He was a praesidium member of the Composers' Union organization committee (1939–48), and in his last years he headed the Moscow branch of the union. During the war he led the central song ensemble of the Soviet Navy, and he is best-known for his choral and vocal pieces; the song *Bukhenval'dskiy nabat* ('The Buchenwald alarm') achieved international fame. His work shows a striving for monumentality, propagandist effectiveness and oratorical pathos. Among the awards he received was the title People's Artist of the USSR.

### WORKS
*(selective list)*

Dramatic: Velikaya druzhba [The great friendship] (opera), Moscow, 1947; Oktyabr' (opera), 1961; Moskva–Parizh–Moskva [Moscow–Paris–Moscow] (operetta), 1969; incidental music, film scores
Orch: Gruzinskaya simfonicheskaya plyaska [Georgian sym. dance], 1939; 2 syms., 1938, 1975; Prazdnichnaya uvertyura [Festive ov.], 1969
Choral: Put' pobedï [The way of victory], sym. poem, chorus, orch (1950); Naveki vmeste [Forever together], cantata, female v, chorus, orch, 1959; S nami Lenin [Lenin is with us], cantata, B, chorus, orch, 1960
More than 200 songs, incl. Boyevaya komsomol'skaya [The fighting Komsomol](V. Vinnikov); Komsomol'skaya dal'nevostochnaya [The Komsomol of the Far East] (A. Gatov); Zhdi menya [Wait for me] (K. Simonov); Pesnya o druz'yakh [Song about friends] (A. Oyslender); Gimn mezhdunarodnovo soyuza studentov [Hymn of the International Students' Union](L. Oshanin); Gimn Moskvï[Hymn of Moscow] (A. Kovalenkov); Pesnya bortsov za mir [Song of the warriors for peace] (V. Kharitonov); Rossiya, rodina moya [Russia, my homeland] (Kharitonov); Druzhba vsevo dorozhe [Friendship is dearest of all] (E. Iordkovsky); Edyom mï, druz'ya [We are on our

way, friends] (Iordkovsky); Val's mechtï i druzhbï [Waltz of dreams and friendship] (S. Bogomozav); Bukhenval'dskiy nabat [The Buchenwald alarm] (A. Sobolev); Tovarishch Zorge [Comrade Zorge] (B. Dvornov); Kremlyovskiye kurantï [The Kremlin chimes] (A. Zharov); Marsh kosmonavtov [March of the cosmonauts] (E. Dolmatovsky); Partiya – nash rulevoy [The Party is our helmsman] (S. Mikhalkov); Tomskiy val's [The Tomsk waltz] (V. Pukhnachev); Polya Rossii [The field of Russia] (A. Kovalenkov)

Principal publishers: Muzïka, Sovetskiy Kompozitor

BIBLIOGRAPHY
G. Polyanovsky: 'Pesni Vano Muradeli', *SovM* (1965), no.5, p.87
M. Byalik: 'V partiture i na stsene' [In score and on the stage], *SovM* (1965), no.3, p.49 [on various stagings of *Oktyabr'*]
T. Khrennikov: 'Pamyati druga' [In memory of a friend], *Sovetskaya kul'tura* (1970), no.98
A. Spadavekkia: 'Pamyati Vano Il'icha Muradeli', *SovM* (1970), no.11, p.46

GALINA GRIGOR'YEVA

**Muralter** [Muralt, von]. *See* MORALT family.

**Muratore, Lucien** (*b* Marseilles, 29 Aug 1876; *d* Paris, 16 July 1954). French tenor. He began his career as an actor, appearing occasionally with Sarah Bernhardt, then studied at the Paris Conservatoire before making his début at the Opéra-Comique in 1902, as the King in Hahn's *La carmélite*. In 1905 he moved to the Opéra, where he remained until 1912. During this period he created roles in three operas by Massenet, Theseus in *Ariane* (Opéra, 1906), the title role in *Bacchus* (Opéra, 1909) and Lentulus in *Roma* (Monte Carlo, 1912), as well as Prinzivalle in Février's once popular *Monna Vanna* (Opéra, 1909) and Ulysses in Fauré's *Pénélope* (Monte Carlo, 1913). He was also a notable interpreter of Faust, Des Grieux, Don José and Sigurd (Reyer). From 1913 to 1922 he sang in the USA, in Boston and Chicago. Although Muratore's voice was not intrinsically of great beauty he used it with an intensity of expression that is conveyed even on his early recordings, and with a skill and artistry that made him an outstanding singing actor. He retired during the 1930s and became a teacher; the tenor Kenneth Neate was among his pupils. In 1943 he settled in Paris and was manager of the Opéra-Comique. From 1913 to 1927 he was married to Lina Cavalieri.

BIBLIOGRAPHY
K. Neate: 'Lucien Muratore', *Opera*, v (1954), 674
R. Celletti: 'Muratore, Lucien', *Le grandi voci* (Rome, 1964) [with opera discography by J. P. Kenyon and R. Vegeto]

ALAN BLYTH

**Murdoch, William (David)** (*b* Bendigo, 10 Feb 1888; *d* Holmbury St Mary, Surrey, 9 Sept 1942). Australian pianist and writer. He studied music at Melbourne University, going to London in 1906 to the RCM with a Clerke scholarship. On leaving in 1910, he began a career as solo pianist, touring five continents. An exceptional sense of tonal values and responsibility made him an ideal member of chamber combinations. In recitals the Chamber Music Players, a quartet including (besides Murdoch) Albert Sammons, Lionel Tertis and Lauri Kennedy, were noted for their rare balance as well as for the soundness of their interpretations. In May 1919 Murdoch took part in the first performance of Elgar's Piano Quintet. Among his recordings are Elgar's Violin Sonata, with Sammons, and Ireland's Second Violin Sonata, with Catterall. He taught at the RAM from 1930 to 1936.

Murdoch composed a few songs and piano pieces and published transcriptions from the works of Bach, Handel and Vivaldi. He was the author of *Brahms* (London, 1933) and *Chopin: his Life* (London, 1934) and wrote articles on modern piano music.

FERRUCCIO BONAVIA/FRANK DAWES

**Mure, Sir William** (*b* Rowallan Castle, 1594; *d* Rowallan Castle, 1657). Scottish poet and amateur musician. He compiled two important MS music books. *GB-Eu* La.III.487 (*c*1616) is a small book containing simple pieces for the lute, several being arrangements of Scottish melodies. In it are two compositions by Mure, one on f.24, the other – 'For kissing, for clapping, for loving, for proving (set to the Lute by Mr Mure)' – on f.25. *Eu* La.III.488, copied at about the same period, contains cantus parts of vocal and instrumental works by leading composers of the time, none of whom are named. None of the vocal lines have words.

Transcriptions of two pieces from *Eu* La.III.487 (Volt, Currant) are in Lumsden: they are both (different) settings of the well-known tune 'La volta'. Another is in Elliott and Shire, as are six pieces from *Eu* La.III.488.

BIBLIOGRAPHY
T. Boyne: 'Mure, Sir William', *DNB*
D. Lumsden, ed.: *Anthology of English Lute Music* (London, 1953), nos.30, 31
K. Elliott and H. M. Shire, eds.: *Music of Scotland 1500–1700*, MB, xv (London, 1957, 2/1964), nos.41, 45, 47, 50, 54, 55, 85

DIANA POULTON

**Mureşianu, Iacob** (*b* Braşov, 11 July 1857; *d* Blaj, 6 June 1917). Romanian composer, teacher and conductor. He was the son of a journalist, folklorist and music lover, and received his first musical instruction from his family; at the age of six he appeared as a concert pianist in a literary festival of the Astra, the association for Romanian culture, science and literature. While he was attending the Polytechnic School in Vienna he also appeared as a pianist and composer in amateur circles in the city. Later he attended classes by Jadassohn, Weidenbach and Reinecke at the Leipzig Conservatory; his successes in Leipzig included a Mendelssohn prize (1883) and a concert appearance as accompanist to Joachim. On his return to Romania he settled in Blaj, one of the old centres of Romanian culture, where he became very active as a teacher and a school and church choirmaster, conducting the musical society and the school orchestras. He also founded a music review, *Musa română* ('Romanian muse'), which appeared, with interruptions, from 1888 to 1907.

In his criticism and in his letters Mureşianu set out his aesthetic of music, which he always held to be part of a general culture and not merely a decoration to life. At the same time he worked for a national style in professional music, founding his idiom more on the authentic folklore of different regions than on the gypsy fiddlers' music. His review also published many of his own compositions and those of his contemporaries. His ideas and their expression greatly contributed to the development of a national style in Romanian music. In his seven ballads and poems he drew on oratorio style, the most important of them, *Mânăstirea Argeşului* ('The monastery of Arges'), being performed both in the concert hall and on stage as an opera. His symphonic overture *Ştefan cel Mare* ('Stephen the Great') is one of the first Romanian pieces of programme music. As a forerunner of the school of Romanian piano music, he wrote miniatures in a Romantic style, a rhapsody and fantasies on folk themes and many dances collected in different regions of the country. His five vaudevilles and an operetta *Millo director*, all based on comedies by Vasile Alecsandri, were given by amateur theatre companies. His choruses and songs for schools, salons and musical societies were all composed according to the same ideals that motivated his 'professional' music.

## WORKS

Edition: *Opere alese de Iacob Mureşianu* [Selected works of Mureşianu], ed. N. Parocescu (Bucharest, 1958) [P]
Principal MS collections: *R-Ba*, Biblioteca Uniuni Compozitorilor din RSR, Bucharest

### STAGE
*(all texts after V. Alecsandri)*

Vaudevilles: Scara mîţei [Cat's cradle]; Rusaliile [Pentecost]; Florin şi Florica; Cinel-cinel [Riddle-me-ree!]; Nunta ţărănească [Peasants' wedding]
Millo director [Director Millo] (operetta, 1), 1910, orchd Iuliu Mureşianu

### CHORAL WITH ORCHESTRA
All texts by Alecsandri; works are for solo vv and chorus with orch/pf acc. unless otherwise stated

Mânăstirea Argeşului [The monastery of Arges], dramatic poem, 1884, rev. 1895
Erculeanul [Hercules], ballads, 1890, P
Năluca [The phantom], poem, 1893
Brumărelul [The frosty boy], ballad, with narrator, 1897, P
Brâncoveanu Constantin, dramatic poem, 1905
Şoimul şi floarea fegului [The falcon and the beech-flower], ballad, 1906
Muieruşca din Braşeu [The woman of Braşov], ballad

### OTHER VOCAL
*(published in Musa română, Blaj, 1888–1906, unless otherwise stated)*

[39] Cîntece corale [Choral songs], unison vv (Bucharest, n.d.)
De la poarta badii-n sus [From the uncle's gate above] (popular text), mixed chorus (1906)
For male vv: Lume, lume [World, world] (popular text) (1888); Cheruvic [Cherubic hymn] (1888); Responsorii (1888); Jelui-m-aş şi n-am cui [I shall lament, but I have nobody] (popular text), P; Cucuşor [Cuckoo] (popular text), P
Songs, for 1v, pf: Nu plînge [Do not cry] (I. Neniţescu) (1888); Flori de nufăr [Water-lilies] (V. Alecsandri) (1888); Dor de mare [Sea fever] (Neniţescu) (1888); Tu m-ai iubit [You loved me] (Neniţescu) (1888); Intoarcerea în ţară [Return to the homeland] (Alecsandri), P

### INSTRUMENTAL
*(printed works published in Musa română unless otherwise stated)*

Orch: Ştefan cel Mare [Stephen the Great], ov., 1882; Dorule, odorule [Dear, darling], dance; O noapte pe Tîmpa [A night on Timpa]; Elegie, str
La mormîntul unui amic [At the grave of a friend], vn, pf (1906)
For pf solo: Suvenir de Nasaud, op.24 (Bucharest, n.d.); Marşul lui Horia [Horia's march] (Braşov, n.d.); Cimpoiul [The bagpipe], capriccio (1888); Cunună de flori romăne [A garland of Romanian flowers] (1888); Capriccio, f (1888); Jocuri din Banat [Dances from Banat] (1906); Caprice-étude (1906); Capriccio, f♯ (1906); Impromptu (1906); Scherzo (1907)

## BIBLIOGRAPHY

R. Ghircoiaşiu: 'O sută de ani dela naşterea lui Iacob Mureşianu' [100 years after the birth of Mureşianu], *Steaua*, viii/6 (1957), 70
G. Merişescu: *Iacob Mureşianu: viaţa şi opera* [Mureşianu: life and works] (Bucharest, 1966)
Z. Vancea: *Creaţia muzicală românească, sec.XIX–XX*, i (Bucharest, 1968)
V. Cosma: 'Mureşianu, Iacob', *Muzicieni români: lexicon* (Bucharest, 1970) [with complete list of works]

ROMEO GHIRCOIAŞIU

**Muret [Muretus], Marc-Antoine de** (*b* Muret, Limoges, 12 June 1526; *d* Rome, 4 June 1585). French composer and jurisconsult. His humanist Latin poetry and classical erudition were greatly admired. After teaching at Auch (from 1544) and then Bordeaux (from 1547), he spent several years in Paris as regent of the College of Boncourt where he helped the young poets of the Pléiade and wrote a commentary explaining the mythological allusions of Ronsard's *Amours*. He also composed four-voice settings of an ode and sonnet by Ronsard, the latter being included in the musical appendix of the first edition of the *Amours*; a third chanson by

Muret was printed by Attaingnant's widow in 1553. All three pieces are in a simple homophonic style and might be described as competent rather than inspired. According to the late 16th-century bibliographer La Croix du Maine, Muret also wrote the texts of 19 *chansons spirituelles* set by Claude Goudimel and published by N. du Chemin in 1555. Having been accused of immorality, the poet fled to Italy, where he spent the rest of his life, living in Venice, Padua and Ferrara before settling in Rome and taking holy orders in 1576.

## WORKS

Ma petite colombelle toute belle (Ronsard), 1552[4-5], ed. in Thibault and Perceau
Las je me plains de mille (Ronsard), 1552[6], ed. in Tiersot
Venez sus donc, venez embrassez moy, 1553[20]

## BIBLIOGRAPHY

A. du Verdier and La Croix du Maine: *Les bibliothèques françaises*, iii (Paris, 1772), 345
C. Dejob: *M.-A. de Muret* (Paris, 1881)
J. Tiersot: *Ronsard et la musique de son temps* (Paris, 1901)
G. Thibault and L. Perceau: *Bibliographie des poésies de P. de Ronsard mises en musique au XVIe siècle* (Paris, 1941)
F. Lesure and G. Thibault: 'Bibliographie des éditions musicales publiées par N. du Chemin', *AnnM*, i (1953), 269–373

FRANK DOBBINS

**Muricy, (João Cândido de) Andrade** (*b* Curitiba, 4 Dec 1895). Brazilian music critic and writer. From 1911 he studied solfège and the piano with Marieta Beltrão and Hugo de Barros and harmony and counterpoint with the Swiss organist and conductor Leo Kessler; subsequently he studied in Rio de Janeiro with Luciano Gallet and Tomás Terán and took a law degree at the university (1918). He was appointed professor of music history and aesthetics at the Universidade do Distrito Federal (1935) and succeeded Oscar Guanabarino as music critic of the *Jornal do comércio* (1939) before occupying the chair of the history of music education and music aesthetics at the Conservatório Nacional de Canto Orfeônico directed by Villa-Lobos (1942). He has been director of the Teatro Municipal at Rio de Janeiro, president of the Brazilian Academy of Music and a member of the Federal Council of Culture. The Brazilian Academy of Letters awarded him the Machado de Assis Prize (1972) for his entire writings, of which half are music criticism.

## WRITINGS

'Música brasileira moderna', *Revista da Associação brasileira de música*, i/1 (1932), 2
'Mário de Andrade, musicólogo', *Revista brasileira de música*, i (1934), 128
'Meia hora com Itiberê da Cunha', *Festa*, i/5 (1934), 7
'Condor (1891): notas sôbre a estética dessa ópera', *Revista brasileira de música*, iii (1936), 300
'Panorama da música brasileira', *Revista brasileira de música*, iv (1937), 95
'Villa-Lobos', *Bulletin of the Pan American Union*, xxix (1945), 1
'A Academia brasileira de música', *Música sacra*, v/9 (1945), 165; vi/1 (1946), 13; vii/2 (1947), 24; vii/3 (1947), 13
*Caminhos de música* (Curitiba, 1946)
'Lorenzo Fernândez', *Música sacra*, viii/10 (1948), 181
*Villa-Lobos: uma interpretação* (Rio de Janeiro, 1961)

## BIBLIOGRAPHY

*Quem é quem nas artes e nas letras do Brasil* (Rio de Janeiro, 1966), 160

GERARD BÉHAGUE

**Muris, Johannes de.** *See* JEHAN DES MURS.

**Muristus** [Mūriṣṭus, Mīrisṭus, Mūrṭuš]. Inventor of organ-like instruments. His name appears only in medieval Arabic sources and he has been inconclusively identified with various Greek technical writers, notably with Ctesibius by Farmer. Two devices were attributed to him. One had 12 pipes, their valves operated in an unspecified fashion, and supplied with wind by the lung power of four men; the other was a primitive quasi-siren, with a hydraulic wind apparatus similar to that of the hydraulis, and therefore looked upon by some as its forerunner.

BIBLIOGRAPHY

H. G. Farmer: *The Organ of the Ancients: from Eastern Sources, Hebrew, Syriac and Arabic* (London, 1931), 16ff, 60ff, 127ff
J. Perrot: *L'orgue de ses origines hellénistiques à la fin du XIIIe siècle* (Paris, 1965; Eng. trans., adapted, 1971), 189ff

JAMES W. Mc KINNON

**Murky** [murky bass, mourqui, mourky, murki]. A style of keyboard writing (or a piece in that style) in which the bass consists of an extended pattern of alternating octaves; the term 'murky bass' has been applied to any accompaniment pattern of the type. This style of composition flourished in Germany from the 1730s in works directed towards the growing public of dilettantes and amateurs. The murky bass most often appears in writing which presents only one or two bass notes in each bar, thus generating rhythmic interest in what was essentially a slow harmonic rhythm. In the absence of the continuo, the broken-octave pattern could also fill out the texture and sonority without taxing the skill of an amateur performer.

Most accounts of the origin of the murky derive from F. W. Marpurg's anecdote in his *Kritische Briefe* of 1759: Seedo (*d* 1754), a composer of ballad operas and later a chamber musician in Berlin, was asked in 1720 to set some jocular poems to music, and his attempts to reflect these whimsical texts in music led to the mildly redundant bass pattern which he called 'murky'. The style quickly became popular, and the murky was known as a dance type in southern Germany later in the 18th century. Halski has suggested that the murky was a Polish folkdance, named after the village of its origin, Murka.

References to the murky by C. P. E. Bach and Adlung indicate that it was a widespread keyboard genre, if not one highly esteemed by trained musicians. One of the earliest collections was *XII Murki fürs Klavier* (*c*1727) by Balthasar Schmid of Nuremberg; Sperontes' four-volume song collection *Singende Muse an der Pleisse* (1736–45); DDT, xxxv–xxxvi, 1909/*R*) contains a number of murkys identified as such both by title and by the accompaniment pattern. The murky bass frequently appears also in German songs of the later 18th century and in collections of miniature dance pieces. Perhaps the most famous example occurs in the first movement of Beethoven's Piano Sonata op.13.

BIBLIOGRAPHY

G. A. Sorge: *Vorgemach der musicalischen Composition* (Lobenstein, 1747)
J. Adlung: *Anleitung zu der musikalischen Gelahrtheit* (Erfurt, 1758/*R*1953, 2/1783)
C. P. E. Bach: *Versuch über die wahre Art das Clavier zu spielen* (Berlin, 1759; Eng. trans., 1949)
F. W. Marpurg: *Kritische Briefe über die Tonkunst* (Berlin, 1759), no.36
——: *Clavierstücke mit einem practischen Unterricht für Anfänger und Geübtere*, ii (Berlin, 1762)
H. C. Koch: *Musikalisches Lexikon* (Frankfurt, 1802/*R*1964)
G. Schilling, ed.: *Encyclopädie der gesammten musikalischen Wissenschaften oder Universal-Lexikon der Tonkunst* (Stuttgart, 1835–42/*R*1973)
C. F. Weitzmann: *Geschichte des Klavier-Spiels und der Klavier-Literatur* (Leipzig, 1863; Eng. trans., 1894)
W. Tappert: 'Der Murky', *Die Tonhalle*, i (1868), 1
C. R. Halski: 'Murky: a Polish Musical Freak', *ML*, xxxix (1958), 35

DOUGLAS A. LEE

**Murray, Sonny** [James Arthur] (*b* Philadelphia, 21 Sept 1937). Black American jazz drummer. After attending the Schillinger School in Philadelphia he moved to New York (1957), where he continued his studies at the Manhattan School of Music and played with the trumpeter Henry 'Red' Allen. In the late 1950s he began to work with the pianist Cecil Taylor, and he toured Scandinavia with him in 1962. The following year he joined the New York Contemporary Five, and in 1964 Albert Ayler's band. He appeared with Ayler later that year in Denmark, Sweden and the Netherlands, remaining with him in 1965 after his return to the USA; he then worked and recorded with groups of his own in both the USA and Europe.

Generally held to be the outstanding drummer of 'free jazz', Murray extended Elvin Jones's aim to free the jazz drummer from his orthodox role as time keeper and to construct a unique style out of patterns previously regarded as subordinate to the main beat. The hitherto untapped potential of this method was revealed in his *D trad, that's what* with Taylor (1962), but it was in performances such as *Children* (1964) that his conception of stratified and constantly shifting percussive arrays matured. *Angel Son* (1969) represents a further advance in terms of tone-colour and dynamic interest.

BIBLIOGRAPHY

J. Cooke: 'New York Nouvelle Vague', *Jazz Monthly*, xi (1965), Aug, 14
——: 'Sonny Murray', *Jazz Monthly*, xiii (1967), Nov, 13
——: 'Sonny Murray in Paris', *Jazz Monthly*, xviii ((1973), Jan, 16

MICHAEL JAMES

**Murrill, Herbert (Henry John)** (*b* London, 11 May 1909; *d* London, 25 July 1952). English composer and administrator. He was educated at Aske's School, Hatcham, where he won the Musicians' Company Carnegie Scholarship to the GSM, but he relinquished it to study at the RAM (1925–8) under Bowen, Marchant and Alan Bush. As organ scholar at Worcester College, Oxford (1928–31), he made further studies under Harris, Walker and Allen. While he was still at the university his opera *Man in Cage* was produced for a run at the Grafton Theatre, London (1930). He worked as a school music master, organist and choirmaster until 1935, when he became musical director for the Group Theatre (Westminster Theatre, London). He joined the BBC in 1936, became music programme organizer in 1942, did war service in the intelligence corps (1942–6) and then returned to the BBC to become assistant head of music (1948) and finally head of music (1950). In addition, he was a professor of composition at the RAM from 1933 until his death. As a composer his affinities were Francophile and mildly middle-Stravinskian, both influences tempered by an English kind of neo-classicism. He wrote mainly in smaller forms, but his output includes a polished string quartet and two cello concertos, of which the second is a rhapsodic, one-movement work sub-titled 'El cant dels ocells', based on the Catalan folksong of that name and dedicated to Casals. Murrill was married to Vera Canning, the cellist.

WORKS

*(selective list)*

DRAMATIC

Opera: Man in Cage (G. Dunn), 1929; London, Grafton, 1930
Ballet: Picnic, 1927

Incidental music: The Dance of Death (Auden), The Dog Beneath the Skin (Auden, Isherwood), No more Peace (E. Toller), Fulgens and Lucrece (H. Medwall), Music at Night (Priestley), Richard III (Shakespeare)
Film scores: And so to Work, The Daily Round

VOCAL

Choral: Love not me for Comely Grace, unacc., 1932; Brother Petroc's Carol, unacc., 1940; 2 Songs from Shakespeare's 'Twelfth Night', unacc., 1941; In Youth is Pleasure, vv, pf, 1943; Magnificat and Nunc dimittis, SATB, org, 1945; The Souls of the Righteous, unacc., 1947
Songs: Self-portrait (Dunn), 1v, pf, 1928; 3 Carols, 1v, ob, 1928; 2 Songs (Herrick), 1v, pf, 1938

INSTRUMENTAL

Orch: 3 Hornpipes, 1932; Vc Conc. no.1, 1935; Set of Country Dances, str, 1945; Vc Conc. no.2 'El cant dels ocells', 1950
Chamber: Capriccio, vc, pf, 1932; Prelude, Cadenza and Fugue, cl, pf, 1932; 3 Pieces, vc, pf, 1938; Str Qt, 1939; 4 French Nursery Songs, vc/va, pf, 1941; Sonata, rec/fl, hpd/pf, 1950
Pf: Sonatina, 1930; 4 Studies, 1931; 2 Impromptus, 1933; Play for Pleasure, children's pieces, 1935; Suite française, hpd/pf, 1938; Toccatina, 1939; Canzona, 1939; Presto alla giga, 1939; Dance on Portuguese Folksongs, 1940; Caprice on Norfolk Folk Tunes, 1940
Edns. of trio sonatas by Arne and Boyce; arrs. of works by Walton and others, pf 4 hands/2 pf

Principal publishers: Hinrichsen, Oxford University Press

RONALD CRICHTON

**Murrin, Jacobus** (*fl* early 15th century). French composer. He was a priest at Aix-en-Provence in 1423. His only known work is a three-part Credo (in *F-APT*; ed. in CMM, xxix, 1962) which like its counterpart from the same manuscript – a three-part Gloria by Susay – is strictly chordal except in the Amen where minims are introduced.

BIBLIOGRAPHY

J. Handschin: 'Zur Geschichte von Notre Dame', *AcM*, iv (1932), 55
H. Stäblein-Harder: *Fourteenth-century Mass Music in France*, MSD, vii (1962), 64f, 95f

GILBERT REANEY

**Murschhauser, Franz Xaver** (*b* Zabern, Alsace, baptized 1 July 1663; *d* Munich, 6 Jan 1738). German composer and theorist. His career can be traced first to Munich, where he was a singer and instrumentalist at St Peter's School in 1676. There he received music lessons initially from Kantor Siegmund Auer and later, in 1683, from the composer and teacher Johann Caspar Kerll, with whom he studied until Kerll's death in 1693. In 1691 Murschhauser became music director at the parish church of Munich, the church of Our Lady, where he remained for the rest of his life.

His two published volumes of music exhibit south German characteristics of organ music written for use with the Catholic liturgy. Both the *Octi-tonium novum organicum* and the *Prototypon longo-breve organicum* include cyclic compositions of free toccata-like fantasies and fugues written to the psalm tones and based on plainsong melodies. The works are important for their variety and the distinction of the fugal writing (see Frotscher). Murschhauser's treatise, *Academia musico-poetica bipartita*, although planned for teaching students composition, is an ultra-conservative manual primarily derived from 17th-century concepts of sacred vocal music. Perhaps the most noteworthy aspect of its contents, in four major sections (1. Von der Music insgemein und insonderheit von denen Intervallis Musicis; 2. Von denen Consonantibus; 3. Von denen Dissonantibus; 4. Von denen Tonis Choralibus, und Figuratis), is the remoteness of Murschhauser's method from 18th-century sacred and secular music. The treatise was attacked with devastating satire by Mattheson in the opening volume of his *Critica musica*,

in the first section entitled 'Die melopoetische Licht-Scheere'. As a result, Murschhauser's intrinsically unimportant treatise retains significance as the catalyst for Mattheson's valuable testimony to the continuing conflict in the 18th century between 'old-fashioned' composers still pursuing the contrapuntal practice of late 16th-century sacred music and 'modern' composers largely influenced by the idiom of Italian opera.

WORKS

Octi-tonium novum organicum, octo tonis ecclesiasticis, ad Psalmos, & magnificat, org (Augsburg, 1696) [89 pieces]; DTB, xxx, Jg.xviii (1917)
Vespertinus latriae et hyperduliae cultus, vv, insts (Ulm, 1700) [10 ps and 1 Laudate]; as Psalmi vespertini (Augsburg, 1728)
Prototypon longo-breve organicum, org, pt.i (Nuremberg, 1703) [34 pieces], pt.ii (Nuremberg, 1707) [34 pieces]; DTB, xxx, Jg.xviii (1917)

Other kbd works in *A-Wn*, Berlin Singakademie, *D-He*

WRITINGS

*Fundamentalische kurz- und bequeme Handleitung sowohl zur Figural als Choral Music* (Munich, 1707)
*Academia musico-poetica bipartita, oder: hohe Schul der musicalischen Compositions*, pt.i (Augsburg, 1721) [pt.ii not pubd]

BIBLIOGRAPHY

*WaltherML*
J. Mattheson: *Critica musica* (Hamburg, 1722–5/*R*1964)
G. Frotscher: *Geschichte des Orgel-Spiels und der Orgel-Komposition*, (Berlin, 1935–6, enlarged 3/1966), 527ff

GEORGE J. BUELOW

**Murska, Ilma di.** See DI MURSKA, ILMA.

**Mŭrțus.** See MURISTUS.

**Musa** [West, Wesch], **Anthonius** (*b* Wiehe, *c*1490; *d* Merseburg, shortly before 22 June 1547). German composer. He was given the name Musa during his days in the Erfurt humanist circle around Helius Eobanus Hessus. He studied in Erfurt from 1506 and at Leipzig University in 1509, and obtained the master's degree in Erfurt in 1517. There he became a faithful supporter of Martin Luther and the Reformation. At that time he probably met Conrad Rein, who had moved to Erfurt from Nuremberg in 1515 and who may have taught him composition. Musa was a pastor in Erfurt from 1521 and was probably involved in producing the two *Erfurter echiridien* (1524), which are among the earliest hymnbooks of the Reformation. From 1524 to 1536 he was pastor and superintendent in Jena; he was appointed superintendent in Rochlitz in 1537 and finally, from 1544, he was a superintendent and member of the Merseburg consistory. In all these places he played a considerable part in furthering the cause of the Reformation. Melchior Graupitz composed a five-voice epitaph for him.

For a theologian who was not a professional composer Musa's surviving works are astonishingly numerous; and many other works are probably lost. His five-voice setting of Psalm i, in German, is particularly remarkable because the genre of the German psalm motet and the first settings of lengthy spiritual texts in the vernacular became established only after Stoltzer's setting of the German Psalter in 1524. Musa generally composed in a conservative style, but was forward-looking in his frequent use of the 6-5 chord at cadences ($II_7b$–V–I). It is not possible to make a final assessment of his works for most of them survive incomplete.

WORKS

3 mass sections, *D-Els*; 3 Latin motets, 4–5vv, *Els*; responsory, 4–5vv, *Z 73*
Gloria, 5vv, 9 Latin motets, 4–5vv, German psalm motet, 5vv, *H-BA 22–3* (all inc.)

BIBLIOGRAPHY

H. Albrecht: 'Zwei Quellen zur deutschen Musikgeschichte der Reformationszeit', *Mf*, i (1948), 242–85

R. Jauernig: 'Antonius Musa, ein unermüdlicher Erbauer lutherischer Kirchentums', *Des Herren Name steht uns bei*, ed. K. Brinkel and H. von Hintzenstern (Berlin, 1961), 118

F. Krautwurst: 'Musa, Anthonius', *MGG*

W. Dehnhard: *Die deutsche Psalmmotette in der Reformationszeit* (Wiesbaden, 1971)

FRANZ KRAUTWURST

**Musae** (Lat.). MUSES.

**Musaeus.** Legendary figure of Greek literature and religion. Musaeus is first mentioned *c*440 BC by a tragic poet (possibly Euripides, in *Rhesus* 945–7) as a citizen of Athens who had been trained by the MUSES and APOLLO. The latter reference can only be to the art of singing to the lyre. Aristophanes (*Frogs*, l.1038) named Musaeus among the most ancient poets and spoke of him as a healer and a source of oracles, while PLATO (*Republic*, ll.364e3–4) mentioned liturgical handbooks by 'Musaeus and Orpheus, offspring of Selene and the Muses', used in the rites of the mysteries. His role as musician had no importance for either author. In the 2nd century AD, however, Pausanias (1.xxv.7) noted the belief that Musaeus sang on the hill of the Muses at Athens, and stressed his close relations with the city.

These references touch upon the chief attributes of Musaeus: his place as a singer in the far-distant past, the strong local ties with Athens, his connection with the mysteries (those of Demeter at Eleusis) and the near-identification with Orpheus. Certain hymns in honour of the Eleusinian goddesses were attributed to him, and he has even been thought to be merely an eponymous representation of the mysteries. During the Hellenic period, Orphic writers and others actually claimed that Musaeus had invented the hexameter and that Homer later borrowed it, along with much poetry composed by Musaeus or Orpheus.

BIBLIOGRAPHY

O. Kern, ed.: *Orphicorum fragmenta* (Berlin, 1922)

H. Diehls, ed.: *Die Fragmente der Vorsokratiker* (Berlin, rev. 11/1964 by W. Kranz; Eng. trans., 1948)

For further bibliography see GREECE, §I.

WARREN ANDERSON

**Mūsā ibn-Maimūn** (*b* 1135; *d* 1204). Jewish music theorist; *see* JEWISH MUSIC, §I, 13(iii).

**Musard, Philippe** (*b* Tours, 1793; *d* Auteuil, 31 March 1859). French composer and conductor. He came from a poor background. He learned the horn and to some degree the violin, and played for low-class dances. He probably began composing early. Pougin (*FétisB*) stated that Musard paid an early visit to London, and the publication of a large number of his quadrilles there from 1817 seems to corroborate this. Musard's French successes began after 1830, when he conducted at masked balls at the Théâtre des Variétés and was then invited to direct a series of popular concerts and dances on the Champs-Elysées. *Concerts-Musard* became fashionable, and took place at the Salles Valentino and Vivienne. At the same time he conducted masked balls at the Salle Ventadour and the Opéra-Comique. In 1835 and 1836 Musard had his greatest success, conducting the balls at the Opéra, with a full-size orchestra, gimmicks with pistol shots and the new popularity of the galop fully exploited.

His reputation secure, Musard went to England and first appeared on 12 October 1840 as conductor of the Promenade concerts at the Drury Lane Theatre; the next season he appeared in a similar role at the Lyceum Theatre, until the end of 1841. He continued to be a popular conductor until 1845. In France he was considered the doyen of dance composers and popular conductors until 1852, but after he retired to Auteuil he was forgotten, and his death was little noticed by the musical press.

Musard's full scores (*F-Pn*) show that he chiefly used the full complement of woodwind and strings with horns, *cornets à pistons*, trombones and ophicleide. His various shorthand techniques may one day be of interest to the historian of popular music. Pougin suggested that Musard was the first dance composer to use trombones for the principal melody; it may be more accurate to say that a typical Musard melody line employed trombones, ophicleide, *cornets à pistons*, first violins and flutes, with the lower strings, woodwind and horns accompanying. For the Opéra balls Musard's band is supposed to have included 48 violins, 14 cornets and 12 trombones. According to some sources Musard used about 90 players in all his concerts.

Musard was necessarily a showman, but not as flamboyant as Jullien. A contemporary account of his manner in *Le ménestrel* was reprinted by Fétis. He wrote mostly waltzes and quadrilles, many based on operatic tunes but many also of his own invention. His evident versatility was shown in two more serious projects of the early 1830s: a set of three string quartets and the beginnings of a *Nouvelle méthode de composition musicale*, dedicated to Reicha (who seems to have taught him for some time, probably in the late 1820s).

BIBLIOGRAPHY

*FétisB*

A. Carse: *The Life of Jullien* (Cambridge, 1951), 4ff

GUSTAVE CHOUQUET/DAVID CHARLTON

**Muscadin.** A dance similar to the allemande presumably named after the wine called muscadin. Settings of the melody associated with it and variations upon it occur in the Fitzwilliam Virginal Book (edn. Leipzig, 1899/*R* New York, 1963) and other sources of English keyboard music. That by Giles Farnaby (MB, xxiv, no.38) is also found under the title *Kempes moris*, which suggests that the tune was danced to by William Kempe, the well-known Elizabethan dancer and comic actor who performed in England and on the Continent.

MICHAEL TILMOUTH

**Muscarini, Girolamo.** See MONTESARDO, GIROLAMO.

**Musculus, Balthasar** (*b* ?Neustadt an der Orla, Thuringia, ?*c*1540; *d* probably between 1595 and 1597). German music editor, composer and schoolmaster. He was most probably the 'Balthasar Meuslin a Neapoli ad Orlam' who matriculated at the University of Jena in the summer of 1557. He first worked in his native town, whence in 1575 he sent several songs (probably his lost print of that year) to the town councillors of Amberg and Nördlingen and in 1579 some partbooks to Naumburg an der Saale. Later, he was headmaster of the school at Ziegenrück, Thuringia, until 1595. Since his publication of 1597 was edited for him he was probably dead by then. The four-part songs that make up the *40 schöne geistliche Gesenglein*, which from 1597 always appeared alongside pieces by Jacob Meiland, Orazio Vecchi and other composers, are anonymous settings of German texts, partly in the expressive polyphonic style of the late Netherlands motet, partly in a simple homophonic song style that shows the influence of the Italian villanella and canzonetta. Since they exhibit such a variety of styles and are of such differing quality, it must be assumed that only a few were composed by Musculus himself; some indeed are known to be by Jacob Meiland, Georg Körber, Antonio Scandello and Gallus Dressler. The popularity of the collection and its widespread use in Protestant grammar schools is demonstrated by the large number of editions and by the frequency with which individual pieces were reprinted. Further work needs to be done on the sources; five editions have been established.

WORKS

35 kurze christliche Gesänglein, 4vv (Nuremberg, 1575), lost (according to Göhler); ? rev. as 40 teutsch geistliche Gesänglein, 4vv (Nuremberg, 1587), lost (according to Göhler); ? rev. as 40 schöne geistliche Gesenglein . . . jetzt aber von neuem ubersehn, corrigirt und mit etlichen Gesenglein gemehrt, 4vv (Nuremberg, 1597?); rev. as Ausserlesene . . . Gesänglein, von newem übersehen und gebessert, darbey auch etliche . . . Horatii Vecchi, Regnardi . . . und anderer auff . . . componirte Gesäng, 4–6vv (Nuremberg, 1622¹⁵); rev. as Sacra Cithara, das ist 80 schöne geistliche Gesäng . . . auctoribus Balthasare Musculo, Horatio Veccho, 4, 5vv (Nuremberg, 1625⁶) [incl. total contents of 1597 edn.]

2 hymns, 1610¹², 1637²
2 hymns in E. Widmann: Geistliche Psalmen, Hymni und andere Kirchengesänge (Rothenburg, 1639)
2 hymns, 2 motets in L. Erhard: Harmonisches Chor- und Figural Gesang-Buch (Frankfurt am Main, 1659)
3 hymns in C. Huber: Geistliche Seelen-Music (St Gall, 1682)

2 motets, 3 hymns, D-Bds, Z

BIBLIOGRAPHY

EitnerQ; GerberNL; WaltherML
J. Zahn: Die Melodien der deutschen evangelischen Kirchenlieder (Gütersloh, 1889–93/R1963)
E. Bohn: Fünfzig historische Concerte (Breslau, 1893), 95f
A. Göhler: Verzeichnis der in den Frankfurter und Leipziger Messkatalogen der Jahre 1564 bis 1759 angezeigten Musikalien (Leipzig, 1902/R1965)

FRANZ KRAUTWURST

**Musel, Corneille.** See NERVIUS, LEONARDUS.

**Muselar** (Dutch). A term used by C. Douwes (Grondig ondersoek van de toonen der musijk, Franeker, 1699) and revived by modern writers to designate Flemish virginals which, having their keyboards placed off-centre to the right, consequently have strings that are centrally plucked for most of the instrument's range. This gives the muselar a distinctive flute-like tone of great beauty, quite unlike that produced by any of the registers of a harpsichord or by a virginal of any other design, and since the late 1960s several makers have constructed replicas of the 17th-century originals.

BIBLIOGRAPHY

G. Leonhardt: 'In Praise of Flemish Virginals of the Seventeenth Century', Keyboard Instruments, ed. E. M. Ripin (Edinburgh, 1971), 43

EDWIN M. RIPIN

**Muses** (Gk. Mousai, Moisai; Lat. Musae, also Camenae, from cano). The Muses are of unknown origin. They have been explained as water-nymphs who frequented mountain springs or streams. None of the etymologies proposed for the singular Mousa has won general acceptance.

The poet HOMER called upon one or more of the Muses at certain crucial points in his writings. In the Odyssey (xxiv.60), 'Muses nine in all' mourn Achilles. This ambiguous phrase probably generated the later belief in nine as the canonical number, observed everywhere except at Delphi and Sicyon. Homer remained imprecise, even omitting the distinctive name from the opening line ('Sing, goddess . . .') of his Iliad. By way of genealogy, he offered only the phrase 'daughter of Zeus' (Odyssey i.10). His successor HESIOD, writing probably in the late 8th century BC, provided the Muses with a mother as well: she is Mnemosyne or 'Memory', obviously an allegorical figure (Theogony, ll.915–18). More significantly, he described vividly how they visited him on Helicon and endowed him with the knowledge and command of words to be a rhapsode (ll.22–34). For him, they numbered precisely nine and had individual names (ll.75–9). They had particular fields of activity attributed to them principally by late writers, though the distinctions between these fields are somewhat blurred: Clio [Klio] (history, shown in representational art with the kithara), Euterpe (lyric, shown with the double aulos), Thalia (comedy, light poetry, the idyll), Melpomene (tragedy, Aeolic poetry and songs of mourning), Terpsichore (choral lyric and dance, shown with the lyre), Erato (song and the dance, and erotic lyric, sometimes shown with the lyre), Polymnia or Polyhymnia (hymns, dance and mime, shown with the barbiton), Urania (astronomy) and their chief, Calliope or Calliopea (heroic poetry and playing on string instruments) – the true leader of the Muses being of course Apollo Mousagetēs. This system of associating specific literary forms, fields of study and musical instruments with individual Muses is not Hellenic. It first took on a recognizable degree of fixity in the literature and art of the later Roman Empire.

The Muses eventually came to be linked with all the arts and sciences that later antiquity recognized as liberal pursuits. Originally their proper province included no more than the sung or chanted word with musical accompaniment and, secondarily, the dance. This had changed by the time of Hesiod, whose didactic epic was recited. By his time, however, Homeric poetry had established the Muses as an embodiment, collective or individual, of the forces of knowledge and inspiration within the singer. The dancer in Homer is an entertainer; the bard presents, by contrast, an august figure. As a follower of the Muses, instructed and inspired by them, he possesses an almost sacerdotal function. The vatic tradition thus begun has survived as a prominent aspect of European literary and musical Romanticism.

With reference to language, the most striking gift of the Muses is the term mousikē. Once descriptive of all that was thought to come within their varied domain, it underwent a reductive process to provide at length our present-day concept. The Muses themselves remain quintessentially Hellenic, without true analogues in any other mythology, representations of the ideal of supreme bodily and intellectual grace.

BIBLIOGRAPHY

P. Boyancé: Le culte des Muses chez les philosophes grecs (Paris, 1937)
W. H. Otto: Die Musen und der göttliche Ursprung des Singens und Sagens (Düsseldorf, 1955, 2/1956)
E. Barmeyer: Die Musen (Munich, 1968)
For further bibliography see GREECE, §I.

WARREN ANDERSON

**Muset, Colin** (fl c1200–50). French trouvère poet and composer. Allusions in his works to people and places have led to the conclusion that he was probably active in the first half of the 13th century in and around Champagne and Lorraine. Not all the works with such references, however, have been definitely attributed to him. *Quant je voi le tens refroidier* is probably addressed to Gui de Joinville, seigneur of Sailly from 1206 to 1256; *Devers Chastelvilain* tells of two kings, probably Louis IX of France and Thibaut, King of Navarre from 1234, and praises the hospitality of the seigneur of Châteauvillain, probably Simon de Broyes (1199–1258): both songs are of doubtful authorship. On the other hand *Or voi le dous tens* is certainly Muset's work; it is addressed to a 'bone duchesse' – perhaps one of several duchesses of Lorraine from the first three-quarters of the century.

The definite works are of a considerable variety of types: a *lai* (*Sospris sui*), a *descort* (*Or voi le dous tens*), a *tenson* (*Biaus Colins Musés*) and a number of songs which refer to eating and drinking (e.g. *Sire cuens*). Most interesting historically are the references to instruments and the playing of instruments (by which means Muset revealed his profession as a jongleur): he mentioned 'la viele et l'archet' (in *Volés öir muse Muset*), the 'flajoet' (*En mai*), 'flaihutel' and 'tabor' (*Encontre le tens novel*); the 'muse' (*Volés öir muse*) may refer to the cornemuse (as well as being a pun on his own name).

Over half Muset's poems have survived without their melodies. A curious and very clear division exists: one group of songs is transmitted without music in one small group of sources, and a quite different repertory, with melodies, in another group. *Trop volentiers chanteroie* is the one exception in that it survives with melody in the first group. It is, therefore, difficult to determine the actual extent of Muset's work; the confusion of sources may be related to his presumed humble origin. The existing melodies are basically simple in style and form, with a great deal of repetition of smaller melodic elements, a limited compass and a prevalence of syllabic settings. This 'folksong' style is perhaps another indication of the composer's profession as a jongleur. In *Sire cuens* text and music together present a clear picture of the wandering popular musician.

WORKS

Edition: *Les chansons de Colin Muset*, ed. J. Bédier and J. Beck (Paris, 1912) [B]; 2/1938 without music [Bw]

(*nm – no music*)

Biaus Colins Musés, je me plaing d'une amour, R.1966, B 20 (tenson with Jacque d'Amiens; nm)
En ceste note dirai, R.74, B 19 (Muset names himself in the text)
Encontre le tens novel, R.582, B 16 (nm)
En mai, quant li rossignolet, R.967, B 7 (Muset names himself in the text)
Mout m'anüe d'iver que tant a duré, R.428, B 3 (nm)
Or veul chanter et solacier, R.1313, B 8 (nm)
Or voi le dous tens repairier, R.1302, B 14 (nm)
Sire cuens, j'ai vielé, R.476, B 22
Sospris sui d'une amourete, R.972, B 4 (nm)
Trop volentiers chanteroie, R.1693, B 12
Une nouvele amourete que j'ai, R.48, B 10 (nm)
Volés öir muse Muset, R.966, B 1

DOUBTFUL WORKS

Bel m'est li tans, R.284, Bw 18 (nm)
De la procession, R.1881 [contrafactum: Devers Chastelvilain], Bw 21
Devers Chastelvilain, R.123 [contrafactum: De la procession], B 25
Hideusement va li mons empirant, R.340, B 26
Il me convient renvoisier, R.1300, Bw 16
Je chantasse d'amoretes, R.989, Bw 17 (nm)
Quant je voi iver retourner, R.893, Bw 27
Quant je voi le tens refroidier, R.1298, Bw 13 (nm)
Quant li malos bruit, R.2079, Bw 15 (nm)

BIBLIOGRAPHY

P. Aubry: *Trouvères et troubadours* (Paris, 1909, 2/1910; Eng. trans., 1914), 113–16 [incl. edn. of *Sire cuens*]
A. Jeanroy and A. Langfors: *Chansons satyriques et bachiques* (Paris, 1921)
F. Gennrich: 'Muset, Colin', *MGG*

ROBERT FALCK

**Musette** (Fr.). (1) A small bagpipe, especially one of aristocratic design which achieved popularity in France in the 17th and early 18th centuries. Courtly ladies and gentlemen would perform in pastoral costume, and treatises were written describing the instrument, with instructions on how to play it and pieces in a special musette tablature. Two such treatises are: Borjon de

*Portrait (1737) by Hyacinthe Rigaud of Gaspard de Gueidan playing the musette, in the Musée Granet, Aix-en-Provence*

Scellery, *Traité de la musette* (Lyons, 1672) and Jacques Hotteterre, *Méthode pour la musette* (Paris, 1737). Many compositions were written for the musette in the 1720s and 1730s. J. B. Boismortier's works include numerous pieces for one and two musettes, for musette combined with other instruments, and a collection of songs accompanied by musette. Other pieces are in works by J.-B. Anet, Jacques Hotteterre (op.8), J. P. Rameau, Montéclair, and in Henry Expert's edited collection *Amusements des musiciens français du XVIIIᵉ siècle* (Paris, n.d.). For an account of the physical characteristics of this instrument *see* BAGPIPE, §5.

(2) The 'musette de Poitou' of the 17th century was a simple bagpipe, and like the *biniou* of Brittany was accompanied by an 'hautbois de Poitou' (a bagless chanter played by another man), or by a consort of such instruments including a bass. The consort was described and illustrated by Mersenne (in *Harmonicorum libri xii*, book 5, proposition 34) and is repeatedly mentioned in documents relating to musicians of the Grande Ecurie du Roi at Versailles, who included a group called Les

Musettes et Hautbois de Poitou; among its members were Jean Hotteterre (1) and later the flautist Michel de La Barre: see M. Benoit, *Musiques de cour* (Paris, 1971). The 'hautbois de Poitou' had a wooden reed-cap, shown in the frontispiece of C. E. Borjon's *Traité de la musette* (Lyons, 1672).

Many specimens of the 'hautbois de Poitou' in museum collections probably date from the 18th century, and it was following the same tradition that Paris woodwind makers began in the 1830s to produce the small oboe without reed-cap which has since been called 'musette'. It supplied rural colour to the urban *bal musette* and was further popularized at concerts like those of L. A. Jullien, who himself performed on it in England in imitation of the Scottish bagpipe. Pitched a 5th above the oboe and 31 to 36 cm in length, it is made in two joints and has seven finger-holes, a thumb-hole and two vents in the bell. The reed is shaped like that of an oboe, but is a little smaller. Later a simple keywork was added, and such models, usually made of blackwood, were still offered for sale in the 1930s for domestic amusement, along with similarly constructed flageolets. Another type with a wider bore, modelled on the Breton bombarde, was introduced about the middle of the 19th century by Frédéric Triébert: it was named in advertisements 'hautbois pastorale', and subsequently even fitted with a keywork of the Boehm system.

(3) A dance-like piece of pastoral character whose style is suggestive of the sound of the musette or bagpipe. The bass part generally has a drone (*bourdon*) on the tonic and the upper voice or voices consist of melodies in conjunct motion, sometimes but not always in quick note values. Any metre may be used and the tempo is moderate.

The dance which bears the name and was performed to the music has a languid, fragile character. It was danced in French ballet as early as Campra's *Les ages* (1718), and in his earlier opera-ballet *Les muses* (1703) the sound of the musette is imitated in a minuet of an entrée, *La pastorale*. Other appearances of pieces called musette were in Destouches' opera *Callirhoé* (1712) and Lalande and Destouches' *Les éléments* (1721). Handel included one in the overture to *Alcina* (1735) (and in his Concerto grosso op.6) and Mozart composed one for *Bastien und Bastienne* (1768) to announce the arrival of the Sorcerer.

Ex.1 Couperin: Muséte de taverni, XVe ordre (*Troisième livre*, 1722) Première partie

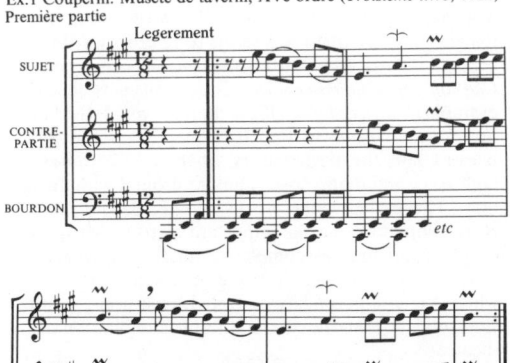

Musettes were also composed for keyboard, the execution of which, according to Türk (*Clavierschule*, 1789, p.401), should be 'schmeichelnd und geschleift' ('coaxing and slurred'). Perhaps the most elegant examples are the *Muséte de choisi* and *Muséte de taverni* for two harpsichords by François Couperin (*Pièces de clavecin*, XVe ordre, 1722). These were written to be performed one after the other and the imitative beginning of the *Muséte de taverni* (ex.1) recalls the rustic sound of two bagpipes. Bach called a movement of his Third English Suite 'Gavotte ou la musette' and in the 20th century the form has been used by Selim Palmgren in his *Country Dance* (*Musette*) (1922) and Schoenberg in the Suite for piano op.25 (1925).

(4) An ORGAN STOP.

BIBLIOGRAPHY

J. G. Sulzer: *Allgemeine Theorie der schönen Künste*, iii (Leipzig, 1793), 780

E. de Bricqueville: *Les musettes* (Paris, 1894)

C. Sachs: *Eine Weltgeschichte des Tanzes* (Berlin, 1933; Eng. trans., 1937/*R*1963)

F. B. Lindemann: *Pastoral Instruments in French Baroque Music: Musette and Vielle* (diss., Columbia U., 1978)

ANTHONY C. BAINES (1, 2), MEREDITH ELLIS LITTLE (3)

**Musgrave, Thea** (*b* Barnton, Midlothian, 27 May 1928). Scottish composer. She studied for three years at the University of Edinburgh and privately with Gál before going to Paris in 1950 to work with Boulanger. She remained with Boulanger until 1954, but meanwhile her music began to arouse interest in Scotland. In 1953 she fulfilled her first commission (from the Scottish Festival at Braemar) with the *Suite o' Bairnsangs*, and in the following year the BBC (Scotland) commissioned a major vocal work, the *Cantata for a Summer's Day*. During this period she also composed two medium-length stage works, the ballet *A Tale for Thieves* and the chamber opera *The Abbot of Drimock*.

These early scores are predominantly diatonic in style and show a predilection for ancient, dialect or in other ways picturesque texts. In the years following her return from Paris, however, Musgrave's style underwent a gradual change towards chromaticism and her forms became more abstract. From this period date her first important instrumental works: the Piano Sonata, the String Quartet, *Obliques* for orchestra and, a little later, *Colloquy* for violin and piano, and the Trio for flute, oboe and piano. By 1960, the year of the Trio, Musgrave was using a fairly orthodox serial technique (there is already a free but distinct serialism deployed in the *Triptych* for tenor and orchestra, a short setting of a text by Chaucer, which had its first performance at a Prom in 1960). In 1959 she had taken up an extramural lectureship for London University at Teddington. At this time her position was thoroughly representative of the *via media* of British music: a tempering of strict orthodoxy with an instinctive moderation which also disposed her against experiment with any more *outré* forms of the avant garde. The tone of her music was serious but not solemn, its personality somewhat retiring.

The 1960s brought a notable enlargement, at first slowly, later with extreme rapidity. The main catalyst for this change was the opera *The Decision*, to which Musgrave devoted most of her energies during 1964 and 1965. (It was staged by the New Opera Company at Sadler's Wells Theatre in 1967.) This was her biggest undertaking to date and, for all the prevailing sombreness appropriate to the subject of a mining accident and the conflicting moral dilemmas in which it places those involved, its music shows a marked enrichment of both expressive and technical means, as compared with the two main works which immediately preceded it: *The Phoenix and the Turtle*, a well-wrought but elusive (as well as allusive) setting of the Shakespeare poem, commissioned for the 1962 Proms; and the Sinfonia of 1963, a serial work of no great individuality. *The Decision* forced an extroversion which these earlier works had generally lacked, and the benefit is apparent in most of Musgrave's subsequent work. *Nocturnes and Arias* (1966) stands slightly apart in being based on actual material from the opera. The first technical departures came in the Second and Third Chamber Concertos, both also written in 1966. Here for the first time Musgrave wrote asynchronous music (i.e. music where each part is fully notated but need not be exactly coordinated with the others). In the Second Concerto there are also Ivesian borrowings from popular music. But, whereas in Ives such quotations often have an impressionistic function, Musgrave uses the tunes as *dramatis personae*, giving the music the character of a charade or harlequinade (there is some parallel with the role of *commedia dell'arte* characters in the Venetian classical theatre). In later works, many of them concertos, this dramatic function is taken over by solo instrumentalists performing simple gestures, such as standing up to play solo or climactic passages, moving physically around the orchestra or around the hall etc.

Since *The Decision* Musgrave has composed mainly to commission. In 1967 she wrote the Concerto for Orchestra for the Feeney Trust, and in the same year the Royal Philharmonic Society commissioned the Clarinet Concerto (this was not, however, performed until 1969). *Night Music*, the concerto-like *Memento vitae* and the Viola Concerto (first performed by her husband, Peter Mark) were all composed for the BBC. In 1969 Scottish Theatre Ballet produced the full-length ballet *Beauty and the Beast* at Sadler's Wells Theatre, London. There are also works for solo instrumental or chamber forces, including some (the Impromptu for flute and oboe, and the Music for Horn and Piano) which develop in an étude-like manner the concerto techniques already mentioned. *Soliloquy* for guitar and *From One to Another* for viola use the solo instrument in conjunction with a pre-recorded tape – a further extension of what Musgrave calls the 'dramatic-abstract' procedures of her works of the period. Finally, the chamber opera *The Voice of Ariadne*, commissioned by the Royal Opera House for performance at the 1974 Aldeburgh Festival by the English Opera Group, renders these procedures concrete, and may be seen as the natural culmination of the theatrical tendencies in Musgrave's concert works since *The Decision*. In *The Voice of Ariadne* the asynchronous techniques of the concertos are carried over with good effect into the vocal ensembles, where they become a natural extension of what has always been an essentially declamatory type of music.

Musgrave's output covers a wide range, from full-length stage works to simple *a cappella* choral motets, music for brass band and a set of teacher–pupil piano duets called *Excursions*. However, since 1966 her music has been predominantly instrumental, and if these works leave a stronger impression than their predecessors, it is above all because they are more brilliant and direct. The

*Thea Musgrave*

instrumental works of the late 1950s and early 1960s, while tending towards serial procedure, are technically conservative or, where more ambitious, inclined to mannerism (for instance, rising semiquaver figuration and augmented octave pedals recur repeatedly). In the later works serialism is subsumed in a confident, individual atonal style, drawing new rhythmic and structural energy from the bolder, less inhibited instrumental writing. Lutosławski's 'controlled aleatoricism' is used freely and with definite harmonic and textural purpose. In contrast, the solo lines regain something of Musgrave's early lyricism, recapturing spontaneity without loss of sinew. On these and other grounds, *Night Music*, the Horn Concerto and the Viola Concerto, in particular, must count among the most striking achievements in British music since 1960.

This is not to discount Musgrave's earlier works, which are seldom less than effective. The vocal works before *The Decision* are eclectic in style, but with a tendency to florid and rhapsodic word-setting which remains characteristic and seems to refer forward to the bravura instrumental writing of the concertos. The early *Cantata for a Summer's Day* is an unusually felicitous example of melodrama. Of the mature works, the ballad *Sir Patrick Spens* (written for Peter Pears and Julian Bream) and the declamatory *Song for Christmas* for high voice and piano cover familiar ground with distinction. The earlier stage works, up to *Beauty and the Beast*, impress rather as important steps in Musgrave's development than as completely fulfilled achievements. *The Voice of Ariadne*, coming after a series of works in which the composer has perfected a naturally gestural style, may be considered a first fertile exploitation of the theatre.

## WORKS
### STAGE

A Tale for Thieves, ballet, 1 (after Chaucer: The Pardoner's Tale), 1953

The Abbot of Drimock (chamber opera, 1, M. Lindsay), 1955; Park

Lane Opera Group, 1958; staged, London, Morley College, 1962
Marko the Miser (children's tale, Afanas'yev, trans. Samson), 1962; Farnham Festival of Schools' Music, 1963
The Decision (opera, 3, Lindsay), 1964–5; New Opera Company, cond. L. Lovett, Sadler's Wells, 30 Nov 1967
Beauty and the Beast, ballet, 2, C. Graham, 1968–9; Scottish Theatre Ballet, Sadler's Wells, 19 Nov 1969
The Voice of Ariadne (opera, 3, A. Elguera, after James: The Last of the Valerii), 1972–3; English Opera Group, Aldeburgh, Maltings, 11 June 1974
Orfeo (ballet), dancer, fl, tape, 1975
Mary, Queen of Scots (opera, 3, Musgrave); Edinburgh, King's, 6 Sept 1977
A Christmas Carol (opera, 2, Musgrave, after Dickens), 1978–9; Virginia Opera, Norfolk, Virginia, 7 Dec 1979

ORCHESTRAL

A Tale for Thieves, suite [from ballet], 1953; BBC Scottish SO, cond. I. Whyte, 1957
Divertimento, str, 1957; Eric Roberts String Orch, 1957
Obliques, 1958; BBC Scottish SO, cond. C. Davis, 8 Jan 1959
Scottish Dance Suite, 1959; BBC Scottish SO, cond. Lockhart, 17 Aug 1961
Theme and Interludes, amateur orch, 1960
Perspectives, ov., 1961; Scottish National Orch, cond. Gibson, Stirling, 21 May 1961
Sinfonia, 1963; BBC Northern SO, cond. Horenstein, Cheltenham, 3 July 1963
Festival Overture, 1965; Scottish National Orch, cond. Gibson, Glasgow, 18 Sept 1965
Variations, brass band, 1966
Nocturnes and Arias, 1966: Beromünster RO, cond. Del Mar, Zurich, 3 Nov 1968
Concerto for Orchestra, 1967; City of Birmingham SO, cond. Rignold, Festival Hall, 8 March 1968
Clarinet Concerto, 1967; de Peyer, BBC SO, cond. Davis, Festival Hall, 5 Feb 1969
Night Music, chamber orch, 1969; BBC Welsh Orch, cond. Carewe, Cardiff, 24 Oct 1969
Memento vitae, conc. in homage to Beethoven, 1970; BBC Scottish SO, cond. Loughran, 21 March 1970
Horn Concerto, 1971; Tuckwell, Scottish National Orch, cond. Musgrave, Glasgow, City Hall, 1 May 1971
Viola Concerto, 1973; P. Mark, Scottish National Orch, cond. Musgrave, Albert Hall, 13 Aug 1973
Orfeo II, fl, 15 str, 1975

VOCAL

2 Songs (Pound), Bar, pf, 1951; Suite o' Bairnsangs (Lindsay), 1v, pf, 1953; 4 Madrigals (Wyatt), chorus, 1953; Cantata for a Summer's Day (Hume, Lindsay), speaker, S, A, T, B, fl, cl, str qt, db, 1954; Song of the Burn (Lindsay), chorus, 1954; 5 Love Songs (medieval English), S, gui, 1955; 4 Portraits (Davies), Bar, cl, pf, 1956; A Song for Christmas (attrib. Dunbar), S/T, pf, 1958
Triptych (Chaucer), T, orch, 1959; D. Robertson, LSO, cond. M. Davies, Albert Hall, 14 Sept 1960
Make ye merry for him that is come (15th century), children's chorus, female chorus, org ad lib, 1961
Sir Patrick Spens (trad.), T, gui, 1961; Pears, Bream, Aldeburgh, June 1961
The Phoenix and the Turtle (Shakespeare), small chorus, orch, 1962; Ambrosian Singers, BBC Scottish SO, cond. Del Mar, Albert Hall, 20 Aug 1962
2 Christmas Carols in Traditional Style (N. Nicholson), SA, TB ad lib, str, 1963
The Five Ages of Man (Hesiod, trans. R. Lattimore), chorus, orch, 1963; Norwich Festival Choir and PO, Norfolk County Youth Brass Ens, cond. Mackerras, Norwich, 6 June 1964
John Cook, chorus, 1964
Memento creatoris (Donne), chorus, org ad lib, 1967; Purcell Singers, cond. I. Holst, Aldeburgh, 6 June 1967
Primavera, S, fl, 1971; D. Dorow, Zagreb, May 1971
Rorate coeli (Dunbar), unacc, 1974; rev. 1976

CHAMBER AND INSTRUMENTAL

Pf Sonata no.1, n.d., withdrawn; Pf Sonata no.2, 1956; Str Qt, 1958
Colloquy, vn, pf, 1960; Parikian, Crowson, Cheltenham, July 1960
Monologue, pf, 1960; Trio, fl, ob, pf, 1960; Serenade, fl, cl, harp, va, vc, 1961
Chamber Concerto no.1, ob, cl, bn, hn, tpt, trbn, str trio, 1962; Scottish National Orch, Glasgow, 26 April 1962
Excursions, pf duet, 1965; Sonata for Three, fl, vn, gui, 1966
Chamber Concerto no.2, pic + fl + a fl, cl + b cl, vn + va, vc, pf, 1966; Vesuvius Ens, Dartington, Aug 1966
Chamber Concerto no.3, cl, bn, hn, str qt, db, 1966; Melos Ens, Queen Elizabeth Hall, 16 Oct 1967
Impromptu no.1, fl, ob, 1967
Music for Horn and Piano, 1967; Tuckwell, Kitchin, Zagreb, May 1967

Soliloquy, gui, tape, 1969; Elegy, va, vc, 1970
From One to Another, va, tape, 1970; Mark, Los Angeles, Nov 1970
Impromptu no.2, fl, ob, cl, 1970; Cardiff Wind Ens, 16 Nov 1971
Space Play, wind qnt, str qt, 1974; London Sinfonietta, Queen Elizabeth Hall, 11 Oct 1974
Orfeo I, fl, tape, 1975

Principal publishers: Chester, Novello

WRITINGS

'The Decision', MT, cviii (1967), 988
'A New Viola Concerto', MT, cxiv (1973), 790
'Mary Queen of Scots', MT, cxviii (1977), 625

BIBLIOGRAPHY
S. Bradshaw: 'Thea Musgrave', MT, civ (1963), 866
M. Lindsay: 'The Disaster and The Decision', Opera, xviii (1967), 874
A. Payne: 'Thea Musgrave's Clarinet Concerto', Tempo (1969), no.88, p.50
N. Kay: 'Thea Musgrave', Music and Musicians, xviii/4 (1969), 34
S. Walsh: 'Musgrave's "The Voice of Ariadne"', MT, cxv (1974), 465
L. East: 'The Problem of Communication – Two Solutions: Thea Musgrave and Gordon Crosse', British Music Now, ed. L. Foreman (London, 1975), 19ff

STEPHEN WALSH

**Mushāqa, Mikhā'īl** [ibn Jurjīs al-Lubnānī] (b Rokhmaya, 1800; d Damascus, 1888). Arab music theorist and writer. He was the most important modern Arab writer on the theory of music. He spent his youth at Dair al-Qamar, but in 1819 was in Egypt and settled at Damascus in 1820. There he lived professionally as a physician but privately as a man of letters for the rest of his days, save for his years of study at the Qaṣr al-'Ain School of Medicine, Cairo (1845–6). Being deeply interested in the physical sciences, he began as early as 1830 to take an interest in the theory of music, and took lessons from the best masters, including the sheikh Muḥammad al-'Aṭṭār, 'a master of several sciences and much learning'. The sheikh had written a book on the theory of music which did not satisfy Mushāqa, with the result that he himself published his Risāla al-shihābiyya fīl-ṣinā'a al-mūsīqiyya ('Shihabian treatise on the art of music'), the name being due to the Emīr Muḥammad Fāris Shihāb. The precise date of its composition is not known, but the oldest manuscript is dated 1840. In this work Mushāqa was the first to codify and explain the modern quarter-tone system of the Arabs. It circulated mainly in manuscript until 1899, when Ronzevalle edited the text in the journal Al-Machriq, and as a separate issue of 1900; but it had already been translated into English by Eli Smith. In 1913, when other, more correct manuscripts became available, a new Arabic text was published, by Ronzevalle.

BIBLIOGRAPHY
E. Smith: 'A Treatise on Arab Music chiefly from a Work by Mikhâil Meshâkah, of Damascus', Journal of the American Oriental Society, i (1849), 171–218
H. von Helmholtz: Die Lehre von den Tonempfindungen als physiologische Grundlage für die Theorie der Musik (Brunswick, 1863; Eng. trans., 1875/R1954, 3/1895 as On the Sensations of Tone)
J. P. N. Land: 'Recherches sur l'histoire de la gamme arabe', 6ème congrès international des orientalistes: Leiden 1883, 75
M. Collangettes: 'Etude sur la musique arabe', Journal asiatique, 10th ser., iv (1904), 365–422
P. L. Ronzevalle: 'Un traité de musique arabe moderne', Mélanges de la faculté orientale, vi (Beirut, 1913), 1 [incl. Fr. trans.]
'Mushāka, Mīkha'il ibn Djirdjis al-Lubnānī', The Encyclopaedia of Islam, suppl. (Leiden and London, 1938)

H. G. FARMER/R

**Mushel', Georgy** (b Tambov, 29 July 1909). Soviet composer. He studied with Starikov (piano) at the Tambov Music Technical College (1926–30) and with Myaskovsky and Gnesin (composition) and Oborin (piano) at the Moscow Conservatory. His performance of his First Piano Concerto at the final examination (1936) won Prokofiev's approval, and in the same year he was invited to teach composition at the newly opened Tashkent Conservatory, where he was later made professor. Like other Russian composers living in Uzbekistan, he took an active part in creating the first Uzbek works in the major European genres. He worked closely with V. Uspensky in studying all aspects of Uzbek folk music, a collaboration which led to the composition of the music drama *Farkhad i Shirin* (1937), which, with Vasilenko and Ashrafi's *Buran*, played an important role in establishing the Uzbek musical theatre. Mushel' then wrote the first Uzbek symphony (1938), on themes from folklore, and the earliest chamber pieces to be composed in the republic (two violin suites). The 1940s and 1950s saw the composition of his finest orchestral work, the Third Symphony, and of a series of organ pieces, which have been taken up widely by Soviet and foreign performers. Since the early 1950s he has produced several ballets on exotic Eastern subjects. His style developed under the influence of various tendencies which determined the evolution of European music in the 1920s and 1930s: the innovations of Debussy, Ravel and Prokofiev, as well as specific Uzbek modes and rhythms, have had most effect on him. Pre-eminently an instrumental composer, he typically maintains in his music an associative link with visual phenomena; indeed, his scores are sometimes illustrated with his own pictures (he is a talented watercolourist). In 1944 he received the title Honoured Art Worker of the Uzbek SSR.

### WORKS
*(selective list)*

Opera: Farkhad i Shirin (music drama), 1937, collab. V. A. Uspensky; rev. as opera, Tashkent, Navoyi, 15 May 1957
Ballets: Balerina, 1951, Tashkent, 1952; Tsvetok schast'ya [Flower of happiness], 1958, Chelyabinsk, 1959; Kashmirskaya legenda, 1961, Tashkent, 1961; Samarkandskaya legenda, 1970, Samarkand, 1970
Orch: 6 pf concs., 1936, 1943 rev. 1958, 1943, 1950, 1951, 1962; 3 syms., 1938, 1941, 1943; Vn Conc., 1945, rev. 1962; Musical Opening Day, suite, 1965; ballet suites
Vocal: Kantata o Farkhadstoye, solo vv, chorus, orch, 1942; songs
Inst: Org Suite no.1, 1948; Poema, org, vc, 1949; Sonata, fl, pf, 1951; Sonata, vn, pf, 1952; Sonata, vc, pf, 1955; Rozovaya sonatina [Rose sonatina], pf, 1966; 6 Org Pieces (1971); 24 Preludes and Fugues, pf, 1975; other works

Principal publishers: Gosizdat UzSSR, Muzïka, Sovetskiy kompozitor

BIBLIOGRAPHY
Ya. Pekker: *Georgy Mushel'* (Moscow, 1966)

L. M. BUTIR

**Mushtaq.** Sassanid panpipes; *see* PERSIA, §3(ii).

**Musica Antiqua.** The original name of the Ensemble Musica Antiqua, founded in 1958 by RENÉ CLEMENCIC.

**Musica da camera** (It.). CHAMBER MUSIC.

**Musica enchiriadis.** One of the best-known medieval Latin writings on music – at least by reputation – for every general history of music devotes attention to it as the beginning of a theory of polyphonic music. This characterization distorts the work's significance in its own time, as will be seen below.

1. General. 2. Manuscript sources. 3. Authorship. 4. Dating. 5. Provenance. 6. Theory of the 'Musica enchiriadis' and 'Scolica enchiriadis'. 7. Influence of the 'Musica enchiriadis' and 'Scolica enchiriadis'.

1. GENERAL. *Musica enchiriadis* (*ME*) is generally thought to have been written about 900 in the north of the West Frankish empire. It was first printed by Gerbert in 1784 as one of a large group of works

attributed to Hucbald of St Amand. Although the attribution was not well founded, the considerable discussion it has provoked persists to this day. A number of other highly interesting Latin treatises of approximately the same date, also anonymous, are frequently found in physical juxtaposition to *ME* in the manuscripts, and share conceptual, stylistic and notational features with it. They are *Scolica enchiriadis* (*SE*; often misnamed 'Scholia enchiriadis'), *Commemoratio brevis de psalmis et tonis modulandis* (*CB*), the so-called *Alia musica* (*AM*), and a short essay on dividing the monochord beginning with the words 'Super unum concavum lignum' (*Super*).

The questions of the date, authorship, provenance and original form of the text of these works are rendered difficult by the absence of a reliable modern edition of *ME*. (One has been in preparation for some years by H. Schmid.) *AM* has been edited twice, although inadequately, by Mühlmann and Chailley, but a reliable text of *CB* has yet to appear. A discussion of *ME* on the basis of Gerbert's text is nonetheless feasible, since he used enough manuscripts of several families to produce a version sufficiently accurate for a coarse-grained exposition, though not for detailed philological or semantic study.

2. MANUSCRIPT SOURCES. There exist about 40 manuscript sources of *ME*, almost always associated with one or more of the other works mentioned above. This is an exceptionally large number for so early a work, and makes it by this measure alone one of the three or four most important – in the sense of popular – writings of the Middle Ages. By way of contrast, the probably contemporaneous work of Hucbald, *De harmonica institutione*, is found in only seven manuscripts. The great majority of *ME* manuscripts were copied before 1200; there seems to be no preponderance of sources from one region. The oldest of them – by the dates of copying – appear to be *F-VAL* 337 (formerly 359, and 325), and *D-BAs* HJ.IV.20 (var.I). There is no palaeographic evidence permitting a date more specific than the early 10th century.

The sources may be classed as follows by their contents: family A comprises the majority and is characterized by the pair *ME*, *SE*, often followed by *Super* and sometimes preceded by Boethius on music; family B offers the succession *ME–SE–CB* in nine manuscripts, followed in four instances by *Super* and, in whole or in part, *AM* (*CH-E* 79 seemingly has a different recension of *CB*); family C contains *ME* alone in a very different version beginning with chapter 9 of Gerbert's text and concluding with a unique text published by Coussemaker (*CS*, ii, 74–8). In each of four manuscripts of this family (three of the 11th century, one of the 15th) *ME* is preceded by Boethius on music; these are also the only sources with an attribution to Hucbald.

3. AUTHORSHIP. There is no explicit statement in the text of the author's name; conclusions have, therefore, been based first on inscriptions and title; second, on attributions by early commentators; and finally, on deductions from political or cultural history. The inscriptions may be readily arranged in four groups. The first group contains four manuscripts with the following at the head: 'Incipit Inchiriadon Uchubaldi Francigene' (or variants), and which begin with chapter 9 of the Gerbert text. None of the manuscripts antedates the 11th century. It was on the basis of this inscription

that the longstanding attribution to Hucbald was made. It is, of course, not impossible that someone named Hucbald – not necessarily the famous Hucbald from St Amand – rearranged the *ME* text, adding to it another brief section on organum.

A second group ascribes the work to a certain Abbot Odo, sometimes of Cluny (878–942), sometimes not. Most of these ascriptions are 16th century or later. That of *B-Br* 10114/6, reading 'Incipit Enchiridion Obdonis abbatis', seems to be authentically 11th century.

In the third and largest group, no author's name is given, unless indeed 'Enchiriadis' is taken as a personal name in the genitive case. There are many minor variants in such inscriptions, but the following is typical: 'Incipit liber Enchiriadis de musica' (*F-Pn* lat.7212 and 7211). In any event, the commonly accepted title 'Musica enchiriadis' has no particular claim to originality.

A fourth class of manuscripts attributes the work to Hogerus or Otgerus (of which the form Nogerus appears to be a misreading). One very early source is in this group, *F-VAL* 337, of the 10th century. Partly because of the paramount importance of this manuscript and partly because of Smits van Waesberghe's advocacy, there has been recent support for this author, whoever he might be. Smits van Waesberghe proposed to identify him as Otgerus, Count of Laon and Abbot of St Amand between 924 and about 952.

Early commentators made few attributions. Hermannus Contractus, writing at least a century after the writing of *ME*, did not give an author's name ('quidam enchiriadis musicae auctor'), and references by Guido of Arezzo and Wilhelm of Hirsau to an 'Enchiridion Oddonis' are now understood to refer to the dialogue attributed to Odo. A 14th-century citation by Marchetto da Padova reads 'Harmonia, ut Ubaldus refert, est diversarum vocum coadunatio', which is the incipit of the four manuscripts of the third family mentioned above, the only ones to which the name of Hucbald is attached. It seems likely, therefore, that Marchetto made his citation from a source of that family.

The most intriguing of medieval citations comes from the 11th-century bibliographer Sigebert of Gembloux (*fl* 1071–1112), who referred to a 'librum de musicis notis et symphoniarum modis', where it is possible to see and understand how the intervals of the concords differ from one another; this work he ascribed to 'Notgerus abbas'. A similar title was given to *ME* in *B-Br* 10078/95, an 11th-century manuscript from Gembloux itself, the author, however, being designated Otgerus. (Sigebert's words are not available in a philologically reliable edition.) This appears to lend strong support to Smits van Waesberghe's theory of authorship; yet Gembloux is geographically close to St Amand and this corroboration ought not to be considered wholly independent. In his next entry Sigebert referred to *SE* (under the title 'Dialogus de ratione musicae') as the work of a certain Enchiriades.

Various other ascriptions deduced from the political and cultural context in which it is assumed *ME* arose are possible, but all are based on indirect and unconvincing evidence.

4. DATING. These doubts concerning the authorship of *ME* are not otiose, as they have much to do with its dating. If Smits van Waesberghe is correct in his theory of authorship, *ME* and its dependent treatises must have been written as much as three generations later than some current estimates, and the chronology of Western music theory would need drastic modification. For example, from 1927 Handschin maintained that Scotus Erigena must have borrowed from *ME*, necessitating an early *terminus ante quem* of about 860. This thesis has recently been supported by Dronke, relying on another set of textual parallels. Such drastic disagreement aggravates a current tendency to resolve the problem rather crudely by taking an approximate mean date of about 900.

5. PROVENANCE. There are indications of an extraordinary interest in music theory during the 9th century in the monasteries of what is now northern France and Belgium; it is thus plausible that *ME*, at least, if not the other treatises of the group, originated there. The question has, however, always been prejudged because of the specious priority given to Hucbald of St Amand, and the provenance from St Amand of one of the oldest manuscripts. Confirmatory evidence for an origin in this area is not lacking; yet the assumed provenance of the extant sources does not suggest any particular place of origin.

6. THEORY OF THE 'MUSICA ENCHIRIADIS' AND 'SCOLICA ENCHIRIADIS'. The discussion here assumes that there are no important differences between the Gerbert text and the original. *ME* is best known for its instructions for parallel or mostly parallel organum (also called 'cantilena diaphonia') and its odd ideographic diastematic notation, called Daseian. Careful reading shows these to be secondary to the work's central concern, a theory of the tetrachord as an organizing principle for song in general, and for individual pitches. It is, therefore, a prescriptive theory of tonal order with didactic applications. (*See* NOTATION, fig. 11; SCORE, fig. 1.)

The tendency to treat the topics of parallel organum and the Daseian notation as primary is a projection of music historians' concern with causation and evolution on to the past; greatest significance is naturally attributed to things useful in establishing a chain of events between past and present. Moreover, the history of Western art music has been made to revolve around music notation and artistic polyphony. In fact, the organum of *ME* and *SE* is now seen to have little to do with polyphony in the sense of independent part-writing, and much to do with the reinforcement of melody, as a liturgically determined decoration, or part of a general process of troping, if not also a feeble reflection of early medieval secular or folk music. Another point, however, may be made: that the sensuous impact of organum validated the concept of the tetrachord and the arithmetical doctrine involved in defining it.

The notion of the tetrachord as such was hardly original, and we need seek no further for a proximate source than Boethius, styled in *ME* a 'doctor magnificus'. But that author provided no link between Hellenistic music theory and the liturgical music of Western Christianity; the importance of *ME* may be seen in having provided such a link, as Hucbald also did, in a way more sophisticated and respectful of Boethian authority, in *De harmonica institutione*. Both authors, however, related the church modes to their tonal systems by designating as the principal tetrachord that comprising the final notes (*d e f g*) of the modes.

The distinctive achievement of the author of *ME* was the abandonment of the old Greek distinction between conjunct and disjunct tetrachords. This nevertheless resulted in the manifest absurdity of augmented octaves, as well as chromatic notes outside the diatonic system of plainchant, points which such later writers as Hermannus Contractus quite properly rejected as discordant with the actual tonal system in use. But, as stated above, the tetrachord concept was not devised for descriptive purposes, but as a prescriptive approach to an already established tonal order (knowledge of which was assumed) integrated with a method of sight-singing, note-reading and transposition. Such an approach incidentally avoided the very real difficulties other writers had at approximately the same time in applying the Boethian octave species and modes to Christian liturgical music. It should be added that the tetrachord was not justified in any elaborate manner, but was stated as representing the natural order of notes proceeding from low to high. That the theory of *ME* was more than description or pedagogy may be seen in the constraints placed on the *vox organalis* (i.e. that added to a plainchant) added at the 5th below, producing oblique motion in otherwise strictly parallel settings. It is also clear that the author of *ME* was aware of the naturalness of the octave produced by ensembles of mixed voices, and it may be safely assumed that he was not attempting a reform. The famous augmented octaves may have arisen from a certain theorist's myopia, or excessive zeal to avoid the problems of octave species. *ME* also contains important remarks of an aesthetic or philosophic character (although the authenticity of chapter 19 in which some of the most significant are found may be questioned). These call insistently for a close coordination between text and melody, and also rhythm and tempo.

The first word of the title of *SE* is usually incorrectly cited in modern discussions as 'scholia', under the mistaken impression that it is a commentary on *ME*. It is, rather, a dialogue between master and pupil. The word actually seen in virtually all manuscripts, 'scolica', designates the scholastic use intended for *SE*. Particularly in the first and much of the second of *SE*'s three parts, the matter of *ME* was restated in a way particularly appropriate to the classroom. This does not apply to the rest, which deals extensively with Boethian, i.e. Pythagorean, proportional arithmetic, in a fashion perhaps intended to be more didactically practical than Boethius himself. This element particularly, not found in *ME*, creates the impression of independent authorship, as do certain uses of the Daseian signs and much emphasis on the pentachord and transposition in the parts having to do with singing. Nevertheless, it is not possible to deny the quite concrete affinity with *ME* established by a similar concern with the tetrachord, and by the use of Daseian notation.

7. INFLUENCE OF THE 'MUSICA ENCHIRIADIS' AND 'SCOLICA ENCHIRIADIS'. The subsequent history of these two works presents a number of problems which may be solved once the relationships between manuscripts and their relative chronology is better understood. For example, it is not certain whether *CB* and *AM* are to be considered additions to the original nucleus (*ME* and *SE*, with or without *Super*), or whether they were part of an original corpus which dropped away in the course of time. Similarly, the significant textual variants may stem from author's revisions or may be the work of later scribes or scholiasts. It is necessary also to consider the relationships to *ME* of various so-called 'organum

treatises' of the 10th and 11th centuries, such as that of Paris (*F-Pn* lat.7202) or Milan (*I-Ma* M 17 sup.).

Other medieval authors seem to owe little to *ME* or *SE* in terms of borrowed ideas or literal copying. The notations of the Oddonian *Dialogus* and Guido's works, as well as the 11th-century notions of hexachord and interval species, may possibly be regarded as reactions to *ME*'s non-cyclical (i.e. at the octave) tetrachords and the visually difficult Daseian signs. In any event, the invention of hexachords and a fully-fledged doctrine of the species of the 4th and 5th, related to the octave, must have rendered *ME* and *SE* obsolete, except in areas such as Germany in which the practice of parallel organum lingered.

BIBLIOGRAPHY

*CS*, ii, 74–8
*GS*, i, 152–212; Eng. trans. by L. Rosenstiel as *Music Handbook* (Colorado Springs, 1976)
R. Schlecht, trans.: 'Musica enchiriadis von Hucbald', *MMg*, vii (1875), 1, 93; viii (1876), 89
H. Müller: *Hucbalds echte und unechte Schriften über Musik* (Leipzig, 1884)
P. Spitta: 'Die Musica enchiriadis und ihre Zeitalter', *VMw*, v (1889), 443–82
H. Sowa: 'Textvarianten zur Musica enchiriadis', *ZMw*, xvii (1935), 194
O. Strunk, ed. and trans.: *Source Readings in Music History* (New York, 1950), 126–38 [part 2 of *SE* only]
J. Smits van Waesberghe: 'La place exceptionnelle de l'Ars musica', *Revue grégorienne*, xxxi (1952), 81
E. Waeltner: *Das Organum bis zur Mitte des 11. Jahrhunderts* (diss., U. of Heidelberg, 1955)
——: 'Der Bamberger Dialog über das Organum', *AMw*, xiv (1957), 175
L. B. Spiess: 'The Diatonic Chromaticism of the Enchiriadis Treatises', *JAMS*, xii (1959), 1
P. Dronke: 'The Beginnings of the Sequence', *Beiträge zur Geschichte der deutschen Sprache und Literatur*, lxxxvii (1965), 43
J. Smits van Waesberghe: *Musikerziehung*, Musikgeschichte in Bildern, iii/3 (Leipzig, 1969), 104f
R. L. Crocker: 'Hermann's Major Sixth', *JAMS*, xxv (1972), 19
                                                  LAWRENCE GUSHEE

**Musica ficta** (Lat.: 'false' or 'feigned music'). The term used loosely to describe accidentals added to sources of early music, by either the performer or the modern editor. More correctly it is used for notes that lie outside the predominantly diatonic theoretical gamut of medieval plainchant, whether written into the source or not. Although the term 'musica ficta' died out during the 16th century, the principle of adding accidentals in performance prevailed well into the following century.

1. Before *c*1500: (i) Introduction and early references (ii) Notation (iii) Theorists' rules (iv) Signatures (v) Tinctoris. 2. *c*1500 to *c*1600: (i) Notation (ii) Performing practice (iii) Contemporary theory and 'rules'. 3. After 1600.

1. BEFORE *c*1500.

(i) *Introduction and early references*. The terms 'musica ficta' and the synonymous 'musica falsa' (more common in the 13th century) were used by music theorists from the mid-13th century to denote chromatic notes alien to the hexachords that had formed the basis for musical instruction since they were first established by Guido of Arezzo in 1025–6. The hexachords built on *G*, *c* and *f* (and their upper octaves, *g*, *c'*, *f'*, *g'*) comprised the 'white' notes of the modern diatonic scale from *G* to *e''* with the addition of *b♭* and *b♭'*: these were defined as the hexachords of *musica vera* or *recta* (La Fage, Anonymous I) and the constituent pitches similarly as those of *musica vera* or *recta*. The internal arrangement in each hexachord was identical (tone–tone–semitone–tone–tone, identified by the syllables *ut–re–mi–fa–sol–la*), the main purpose of the system being to contain and demonstrate the position of the semitone. The singer moved up and down the overlapping hexachords as the music required, making transitions (known as mutations or *coniuncte*) on notes common to two hexachords, though never between the notes bounding the semitone step *mi–fa*. The application of *musica ficta* was considered part of the performer's art; this is why the terminology of singing teaching rather than that of speculative theory is used for most contemporary statements on the subject: some references also occur in vernacular writings of a non-technical nature. But as with so many other lost traditions of performance, the modern editor lacks sufficient evidence to enable him to make with confidence the decisions taken by medieval singers, especially when more than one solution may be possible in a given situation.

The system of solmization was originally designed for plainchant (which made little or no use of notes extraneous to the hexachords) and had to be extended to cope with the growing demands of polyphony. It was by transposing *recta* hexachords to alien pitches that semitone steps other than B–C, E–F, A–B♭ could take their place within the solmization system. The range of available *ficta* hexachords was increased and rationalized until, in the 1430s, Ugolino of Orvieto recognized a complete system of *ficta* hexachords whose sole purpose was to accommodate chromatic notes. Before it was adulterated by the extra demands of polyphony, the *recta* system as applied to plainchant was not incompatible with the modes, but the introduction of *ficta* notes led theorists from the 13th century onwards (e.g. Johannes de Grocheo) to repudiate the application of modes to polyphony; indeed, it was not until the late 15th and early 16th centuries (Tinctoris, Glarean) that serious attempts were made to assign polyphonic compositions to specific modes.

Even before Guido's hexachords were introduced, B♭ was recognized as part of the regular (*recta*) system of available notes. In addition, earlier theorists made allowance for chromatic alteration other than the alternative inflections of B, although the terms *musica ficta* or *falsa* were not used. The Enchiriadis treatises of about 900 give the earliest explicit and extensive theoretical account of chromatic alteration. The anonymous author of the *Scolica enchiriadis* defined *absonia* (elsewhere *dissonantia*) as the lowering or raising of a note from its normal pitch. The word *vitium* is used in this context and seems to imply no more than a disturbance of the normal scale, the force being very similar to that of the later *falsa* (the term *falsus sonus* in fact appears in this treatise; *GS*, i, 177). The *absonia* arises from faulty intonation (a 'vice' of the human voice to which instruments are less subject) or, more importantly, from the nature of the music, where it has the effect of transplanting or restoring the mode.

Using Daseian signs the author set up tetrachords (disjunctly, with a central semitone flanked by two tones) yielding the remarkable scale *G–A–B♭–c–d–e–f–g–a–b♮–c′–d′–e′–f♯′–g′–a′–b♭′–c♯″* (Spitta, Jacobsthal, Spiess). This is proposed in addition to the more normal scale, and is specially suited to organum at the 5th: the early use of such extreme chromatic notes seems to be connected with polyphony. For plainchant the author was more conservative but no less ingenious. He evolved a system of pentachords involving *recta* forms as well as the *absonia*. The pitches of *e♭* and *f♯* are introduced by changing the Daseian name on one note –

in effect a mutation. By extending the tetrachord system to cover the legitimate transpositions of the pentachords with *absonie*, Jacobsthal further advanced the possibility that the Enchiriadis treatises also allow for *c♯, g♯, d♯* and *A♭*.

Odo (10th century) also referred to the 'vice' of additional semitones outside the 'prefixed rule' (*GS*, i, 272) and cited chants in which *b♭, e♭, c♯* and *f♯* are required. The derivation of chromatic notes by modal transposition is clearly specified by some 11th-century theorists. Berno of Reichenau recognized transposition of modes up a 5th to make *f* and *f♯* available, or up a 4th to produce *e* and *e♭* in both cases transposing from *b*, for which both natural and flat forms are available (*GS*, ii, 75). Johannes Afflighemensis gave more detail but only accepted transpositions up a 5th and only for those modes (1–3) that would not thereby lose their identity (*GS*, ii, 248; ed. J. Smits van Waesberghe, p.101). He also provided for a process of 'emendation' in a few places where the notes can neither be sung at original pitch nor transposed. Odo allowed 'emendation' where necessary, that is, where the piece could not be sung in another mode. Such prescriptions already anticipate later warnings against using *ficta* when the situation could be corrected by other means. The usual reason given for melodic alterations to chant is the avoidance of the tritone. The development of a system of modal transpositions coincided with the rise of a clearer notation of fixed pitches which, however, had very little capacity as yet to cope with chromatic notes.

The first uses of the terms *falsa* or *ficta* are by the 13th-century theorists Johannes de Garlandia and Magister Lambertus. Johannes defined *musica falsa* as 'when we make a tone into a semitone and vice versa' (*CS*, i, 166), a definition later used by Philippe de Vitry (*CS*, iii, 26; see Reaney, Gilles and Maillard, p.22). Lambertus already showed dissatisfaction with the designation *falsa*, 'for it is necessary for achieving good consonance' (*CS*, i, 258); 'it is not so much false as unusual'. Jerome of Moravia equated it with the *synemmenon* (synonymous with *coniuncta*) and based his exposition not on hexachords but on tetrachords. Most other definitions of the 13th and 14th centuries repeat or only slightly vary these. Walter Odington wrote of 'movable solmization names' (*CS*, i, 216), Coussemaker's Anonymous II of 'false mutation, or *falsa musica*' (*CS*, i, 310). An anonymous treatise of 1375 (Crocker, 1967) rejects the terms *falsa* and *ficta*, preferring *coniuncta*, and defines the problem in terms of 'imaginary transposition' of hexachords.

Theorists were divided in opinion about the use of *ficta* in plainchant but those who declared themselves on the subject recognized the need for it in polyphony. Jacques de Liège asserted its importance in plainchant (*CS*, ii, 293ff); Jerome of Moravia, however, allowed it in polyphony but excluded it from plainchant (*CS*, i, 86). Johannes de Garlandia, in his treatise on plainchant and measured music, specified its use in polyphony ('organis'; *CS*, i, 166). Vitry also affirmed its role in polyphony as not false but true and necessary, because, he said, no motet or rondellus could be sung without it (*CS*, iii, 18; Reaney, Gilles and Maillard, p.23). The anonymous Paris theorist of the Berkeley Manuscript (who explicitly dealt with plainchant and specific categories of polyphony) exemplified the *coniuncta* from chant, contrary to 13th-century principles. The early 15th-century Anonymous XI (*CS*, iii, 429) said that *coniuncte* were necessary in both plainchant and polyphony.

(*ii*) *Notation*. The 13th-century theorists already mentioned also defined the signs for notating *musica ficta*. Johannes de Garlandia said each tone is divisible into two semitones, and these can be notated (*CS*, i, 166). Lambertus prescribed ♭ and ♮ for the points at which mutations are to be made (*CS*, i, 258). Theorists up to and including Prosdocimus and Ugolino (first half of the 15th century) admitted only these two signs, to distinguish the soft and hard forms of B. The single exception is Marchetto (*c*1318), who used an obliquely written ♯ to distinguish the enharmonic semitone step (e.g. F–F♯) from the smaller semitone (e.g. F♯–G) which corresponds to *mi–fa* in solmization. Although scribes used either ♯ or ♮ for the 'hard' B, the distinction does not seem to have been meaningful. Not until Hothby (*d* 1487) are three possible positions, ♭, ♮ and ♯, distinguished for each degree of the scale. Nowhere in the period up to 1450 is there any direct theoretical admission that ♭ lowers or that ♮ raises a note: ♮ simply denotes *mi* and ♭ *fa* (that is, they indicate where the semitone lies in relation to the accidental). *Mi–fa* is always a minor semitone, a minor semitone always *mi–fa*. Consequently, in rare cases (Ugolino's treatise and some practical examples), one or other sign may be used to bring the adjoining note to within a semitone of the signed note and not vice versa. In other words, ♭ placed on G may not affect the pitch of G but indicate that, since G is to be sung *fa*, *mi* should be a semitone below it on F♯. The presence of a ♭ on F would not in any case lower its pitch. Occasionally the letters 'F', 'C' and 'G' are used instead of the ♭ sign to indicate the 'soft' forms of those pitches.

Although a means of notation existed it was, for the reasons given above, neither complete nor watertight. There was no need to notate every occurrence of *mi* and *fa*, and in practice this meant that many notes that required chromatic inflection lack the sign – an accidental – that signals this inflection to the modern musician. In practice only a small proportion of the accidentals required in performance were actually notated, though the number indicated (and required) shows a steady increase during the period up to about 1400. The polyphonic and secular monophonic sources of the 13th century add F♯, C♯ and E♭ to make distinctions parallel to that between B♭ and B♮ found in plainchant sources. Theorists were reticent about omissions until the late 14th century, when the Paris treatise (now in *US-BE*) states that in practice one very rarely found the signs for *fa* and *mi* marked. Prosdocimus de Beldemandis, writing in his counterpoint treatise (*c*1410), addressed to composers rather than to singers, inveighed against the use of too much *musica ficta*. However, it is clear from his exposition and his examples that he envisaged many inflections, and it seems most likely that he was enjoining composers to leave the application of *musica ficta* to the singers, and perhaps also to avoid situations in which too much would be required. The 14th century saw a spectacular increase in marked accidentals until, around 1400, D♯, D♭, G♯, A♭ and G♭ are specifically notated and intended in certain sophisticated repertories such as those of the Chantilly and Old Hall Manuscripts. These were exceptional: some sources remained very sparing in their indications, and there is a general decline in the number indicated from about 1400 onwards.

The main reason for the incomplete provision of accidentals is, as explained above, that the signs were used to indicate solmization and only incidentally did they also indicate inflection. An important secondary reason is the medieval musician's reluctance to admit in theory or to notate in practice something that lay outside the regular, respectable system, although all theorists who discussed the matter acknowledged that it was necessary to good results. For both these reasons, the responsibility for providing the appropriate inflections rested with the performer and, today, rests with the modern editor, who acts on the medieval performer's behalf.

The cross-section of required accidentals that found its way on to the pages of medieval manuscripts includes pitches that fall within the system of *musica recta* as well as many that lie outside it. Additional accidentals required in performance similarly include both *recta* and *ficta* notes. It is therefore not possible to equate *musica ficta* simply with added accidentals. (In modern editions it is usual to distinguish editorial accidentals from those of the source by placing the former above the note, or in brackets, or in small type; with regard to the placing of editorial accidentals, see especially Anglès, 1954; Hewitt, 1942; Jeppesen, 1927; and Lowinsky, 1964 and 1967.)

The placing of accidentals in the sources is not without ambiguities. Some scribes placed the accidental near, above or below the affected note, without regard for the correct placing on the staff: this is particularly common in some late 14th- and early 15th-century Italian and south German sources. Other scribes placed the accidental well in advance of – or even after – the note to which it applied. In view of the close connection between the 'signs' of *musica ficta* and the practice of solmization, it may be that such pre-placing serves as a deliberate advance warning of mutation. Thus the progression *fa–mi* (between which no mutation can take place) is very often preceded, rather than divided, by the ♮ sign indicating *mi*. A consequence of this (solmization) function of an accidental sign is that it does not necessarily apply to more notes than the one to which it most directly refers. In some situations a larger context will be affected, but an accidental, written or not, may easily be overruled (for the sake of contrapuntal propriety) on subsequent appearances of the note.

(*iii*) *Theorists' rules*. This evidence of the musical sources, some at least of which were used by performers, is one of the twin foundations on which the performer's art of applying *musica ficta* can partly be reconstructed. For the performers will have applied certain principles which can partly be recovered from theorists, though oral tradition surely accounts for much that is now not known. The other foundation is the theoretical evidence. Since this is drawn largely from counterpoint treatises and takes the view of the composer rather than that of the performer, one of its main values is the light it casts on how the performers should adjust to each other: many of the theoretical rules are given in terms of harmonic progressions in two parts (appropriate to the compositional principle of superimposed duets then current) rather than for isolated melodic lines. It is also worth noting that some of the most important clues occur not in separate chapters devoted to *musica ficta* but in general discussions of counterpoint.

Since rules for *ficta* are necessarily related to changes

in musical style, it is particularly important not to project rules backwards to a period earlier than that in which they were formulated. Even in the writings of 13th-century theorists, both harmonic and melodic reasons for applying *musica ficta* are given. Johannes de Garlandia gave principally melodic rules, requiring 'leading notes' to be a semitone from their destination (*CS*, i, 115). Although the Enchiriadis treatises and other early writings forbid the melodic tritone, this prohibition no longer figures among 13th-century rules. Lambertus stated that the main purpose of *musica ficta* was to achieve perfect vertical consonances on 5ths, octaves and other perfect intervals (*CS*, i, 258): this clearly applies only to polyphony.

These principles are incorporated in the more fully developed expositions of the 14th century, of which that by Jehan des Murs is the fullest and clearest. His rules (*CS*, iii, 71–3) state that, for melodic progressions, lower returning notes (e.g. in the progression G–F–G) should be raised (G–F♯–G); and that leading notes approached by any other means (e.g. by leap) should be raised (e.g. D–F♯–G; this is also implied by the author of the *Quatuor principalia*, *CS*, iv, 250). His harmonic rules state that the sounding of *mi* against *fa* is forbidden in vertical perfect intervals (i.e. 5ths and octaves are to be perfect; this rule is ubiquitous in treatises); and that a perfect interval should be approached by the nearest imperfect interval – a major 3rd will expand to a 5th, a major 6th to an octave, a minor 3rd will contract to a unison, and so on; where one of the parts proceeds by step, this step will, in practice, be a semitone (see ex.1*a*; if both proceed by step, only one will be a semitone). Several theorists gave the important qualification to these rules that they should be effected where possible without resort to *musica ficta*: if the interval or progression can be corrected within the system of *musica recta*, this should be done (see Prosdocimus de Beldemandis, *c*1410, *CS*, iii, 196–9; Ugolino of Orvieto, *c*1435, *Declaratio*, ii, 45). Whereas Jehan des Murs' examples invariably sharpen a leading note in the upper part, using *musica ficta*, one progression may be corrected within the *recta* system by flattening the lower note instead of sharpening the upper, thus placing the semitone step in the lower part (ex.1*b*). A further consequence of the second harmonic rule, applicable to most music up to 1450, is the 'double leading note cadence' in which ex.2*a* results from the superimposition of the legitimate two-part progressions exx.2*b* and 2*c*. (The 'correctness' of this progression has nothing to do with perfecting the vertical 4th, which was not at this period considered a perfect interval for purposes of counterpoint, despite its acoustical status.)

Theorists of the 13th to 15th centuries said surprisingly little about the melodic interval of the tritone. Prosdocimus's music examples make it clear that the

leading note principle is to be observed even when the interval preceding the leading note step is forced thereby to be a tritone. An anonymous 15th-century theoretical fragment from Seville (Gallo, 1968) does state explicitly that melodic tritones should be avoided when they return within their own confines, that is, when they are not ancillary to a leading note. True chromatic progressions (e.g. F–F♯–G) are both allowed in theory (Marchetto, *GS*, iii, 82–3) and prescribed in manuscript sources.

In addition to giving rules in specific terms, theorists also expressed the reasons for using *ficta* in more metaphysical terms: for acquiring greater perfection, so that imperfect intervals may acquire some perfection by closer adhesion to perfect ones; for the 'colouring' of dissonances or imperfect intervals; and for the sake of sweeter harmony. From the earliest references in the 13th century onwards, the reasons are also classed as *causa necessitatis* ('by reason of necessity', which aligns with the perfection of vertical consonances) and *causa pulchritudinis* ('by reason of beauty', which corresponds to melodic reasons for chromatic alteration). (See also §2, iii below.)

(*iv*) *Signatures*. The phenomenon of 'key' signatures during this period is not illuminated by any of the theorists: at the same time it has proved to be one of the most provoking and controversial issues and has served as the starting-point for many of the most important recent discussions of early *ficta*. The signatures in question are always of flats, and the nub of the problem is that the number of flats indicated at the beginning of the staves very often differs between different voice-parts of the same piece, the lower part or parts having, usually, one flat more than the upper. From the top downwards, a three-part piece might have parts with signatures of –, –, B♭; –, B♭, B♭; B♭, B♭, B♭ and E♭; B♭, B♭ and E♭, B♭ and E♭. Apel claimed that these 'partial' signatures implied bitonality, the signatures having the modern significance of inflecting all notes written at that pitch level. Lowinsky on the other hand maintained that the basis of 'conflicting' signatures was mainly practical, the signature being omitted when no note of that pitch was required. Hoppin proposed, since the difference in signatures tends to represent pitch levels about a 5th apart, that modal transposition was involved. All these views assume that the signatures have a significance approximately equivalent to that of a modern key signature, affecting all notes at the written pitch of the accidental, perhaps also of its octave transpositions. The possibility remains, however, that they denote the transposition of hexachord systems, especially since hexachords rather than modes form the basis of medieval discussions of *ficta* in polyphony. If the hexachords on G, C and F are transposed one degree flatwards, in the case of a single flat in the signature the hexachords for that part will be on C, F and B♭, leaving two hexachords common to both a signatured and an unsignatured part, and thus a considerable range of *recta* notes, including B♭, which a simultaneous unsignatured part is perfectly free to use. Both parts are also free to add *ficta* where necesary, the naturalizing of B in a part with a flat signature being no more serious than the sharpening of F in an unsignatured part. Such transpositions of the entire hexachord system seem to have been counted as transposed *recta*, transposition of isolated hexachords as *ficta*. Where there is a signature, the *recta* priorities are established for the duration of the signature, and the singer is free

Ex.1
(a)                                    (b)

Ex.2
(a)        (b)        (c)

to use the normal hexachord relationships, applying rules and priorities within them. The distinction between applying chromatic alteration by means of transposition and by means of individual emendation does, after all, go back to the 11th-century theorists.

Many changes can be traced from the last quarter of the 15th century onwards. These are due to gradual changes in compositional technique and the approach to dissonance on the one hand, and on the other to attempts (coinciding with the effects of humanism on music theory) to change the theoretical basis of music, restoring the status of the modes (Tinctoris, Glarean) and superseding the old hexachord system by the octave (Ramos), together with fixed designations for ♭, ♮ and ♯ degrees (Hothby).

(v) *Tinctoris*. Important observations on accidentals are found in the writings of Tinctoris, though modern quotations of his remarks on this subject often fail to take account of the context in which he made them. In the 12 treatises that constitute his *summa* on the music of his time, written between about 1472 and about 1485, Tinctoris's highly systematic exposition of the concepts of gamut, hexachord system, mode and counterpoint are so ordered as to give only brief mention to those deviations occasioned by the needs of musical practice or by *ficta* elements outside the system. In his *Diffinitorium* (1472) Tinctoris gave a classic definition of *musica ficta* as being 'cantus praeter [not propter] regularem manus traditionem editus' ('a way of singing apart from the regular ordering of the [Guidonian] hand'); that the authentic reading is 'praeter' not 'propter' is explicitly clear from at least one authoritative manuscript source and was pointed out by Ambros (*Geschichte der Musik*, ii, 171).

The longest passage by Tinctoris on accidentals occurs in his treatise on the formation of the 'modes', or 'tones' as he called them, *Liber de natura et proprietate tonorum* (chap.8). He presented the modes as being the diverse linear products of the collocation of the several diatonic species of the perfect 4th and 5th. In this chapter, dealing with the 6th mode (the plagal form of the F mode), Tinctoris made clear that in practice the 5th and 6th modes use B♭ not B♮. He added some general comments on the use of the flat, both in linear and in two-part contrapuntal writing. First, the necessity for the flat is twofold – to create perfect consonances in polyphony and to avoid the linear or vertical tritone. Second, the 'signature flat' (or, as he put it, the flat at the beginning of the staff) affects the whole segment (whether of music or of staff is not clear) for which it is given, while the 'accidental' flat lasts as long as the hexachord segment (the *deductio*) before which it is placed. Third, the formation of these two modes with B♭, to avoid the tritone, is well known, so much so that the flat need not always be written down, and if it is, it may be considered an 'ass's mark' – not that all explicit accidentals may be so regarded, but specifically or primarily the flat needed for the 5th and 6th modes (the example illustrating this remark is monophonic). Fourth, linear tritones should also be avoided in other modes, but in polyphony they are sometimes unavoidable, because of inadmissible vertical intervals that may otherwise result, and in such cases the sign ♮ should be used; this passage significantly indicates that for Tinctoris, in two-part polyphony at least, when vertical tritone problems clash with linear tritones the former

should take precedence, and it also indicates a rational basis for the use of the natural sign, namely to prevent a *ficta* flat which the singer, following his own part, would normally adopt. Fifth, what is true of the tritone in regular modes is also true of irregular ones in *musica ficta* (i.e. the system of *musica recta* as transposed). Finally, the linear tritone is less difficult to sing when approached by step than by leap.

2. *c*1500 TO *c*1600. Throughout this period the concepts embodied in and entailed by the medieval term *musica ficta* continued to play a role in the interpretation of polyphonic music, and the term itself remained in use by theorists. So long as the traditional gamut and hexachord system stood as the basis of musical structure, the distinction between *musica recta* and *musica ficta* (Bent, 1972) must have influenced both composition and performance, and those accidentals that were *extra manum* (outside the Guidonian hand) were considered variable units within a basically diatonic system. Broad developments in musical practice during the period 1450–1600 rendered the interpretation of unspecified accidentals even more problematic than in the past. These developments include the gradual increase in the number of voices normally used for vocal polyphony, the multiplication of variant versions of works as a result of the invention of music printing, and the rise of experimental chromatic and enharmonic tone systems (such as that of Vicentino) along with the freer exploitation of chromatic degree-inflection by composers outside the ranks of theorists. The period as a whole evidently witnessed a gradual evolution from a prevailing view that the addition of unspecified accidentals by performers was, no doubt in varying degrees, a normal practice, to a prevailing view that such additions were no longer generally regarded as necessary and that composers, copyists and printers alike were becoming accustomed to the specification of many of the necessary accidentals. Although this latter view apparently took hold by degrees rather than at once, it became more widely held after 1600 than previously. Changes of musical style in the early Baroque period did cause another phase of fluidity in the use of accidentals (see §3), yet the much stronger effect of the inclination to notate accidentals coincided with changing developments in notation and performing practice after about 1600. Thus one can assert with confidence that from about 1450 to about 1600 such a development took place; but it is by no means clear how to derive from it specific standards of interpretation for accidentals in pieces from particular periods, regions, repertories or sources. Thus the basic problems of *musica ficta* remain as controversial throughout the 16th century, and a wide variety of views have been expressed on the subject by modern scholars.

Not only has no single formula been devised that seems readily applicable to all types of *musica ficta* problems, but it seems likely that an attitude of intelligent and well-informed relativism on the matter is historically more realistic than an apocalyptic vision of a universal solution for all cases. In broad terms the problem rests on two parallel inequalities: one lies in the divergence of readings in contemporary musical sources, the other in the relationship of the notation in these sources to the pertinent theoretical literature. The latter ought ideally to provide a set of procedures that would govern the treatment of accidentals, but the treatises are often abstract and elliptical in their discussion of the subject.

*(i) Notation.* In mensural notation from about 1450 to about 1540 flat signs were in normal and regular use, as accidentals and as signatures, and there is ordinarily no doubt about their meaning. Sharp signs, on the other hand, are extremely scarce in sources of vocal polyphony of the late 15th century and early 16th, whether manuscript or, after 1501, printed. The sharp is used only as an accidental in this entire period, with one or two very particular exceptions in which it appears as a signature (e.g. to express the relationship of a canon at the 5th above, in Willaert's *Musica nova* of 1559). From 1540 on, especially in Italian prints, the sharp sign becomes more frequent, but its placing is still free; it may appear below or before or, sometimes, even after the note affected. When it appears between and below two notes of the same apparent pitch there can be substantial doubt as to whether it refers to both notes (which should therefore have the same pitch) or whether it signals a chromatic inflection from the first note to the second. (For conflicting views on some relevant cases in printed sources of Italian madrigals see Kroyer, 1902, and Ficker, 1914.) The normal sign for the sharp in this period is ✕, but variants of this sign appear. The sign ♮, which had been the traditional sign for *b quadratum* in contradistinction to *b rotundum*, returned around 1540 as a distinctive symbol and attained its modern meaning; Einstein (*The Italian Madrigal*, i, 412) noted its use in a Vicentino madrigal collection of 1542.

It should be noted that in lute and other instrumental tablatures of the period accidentals are always specified in full, and some scholars (e.g. Apel) take these sources as being vitally important for the practices of the time. On the other hand, there is no reason to assume that the practices followed by instrumentalists were carried over into the vocal literature, where the tradition of solmization and *musica ficta* particularly applies. There is however much evidence of the increasingly explicit use of accidentals in vocal music itself (see Kroyer) and there can be no doubt that this is closely related to the move towards greater use of chromatic degree-inflection as a tonal device – the two are inseparably linked. Chromaticism is particularly visible in the madrigal from about mid-century, and was greatly developed later by Marenzio and Gesualdo. This type of degree-inflecting chromaticism is actually a tendency away from the medieval tradition of *musica ficta*, with its hexachord basis for the singing of unspecified accidentals. The two patterns co-existed during the 16th century.

Stemming from the concept of *musica ficta* and significantly extending it are works that explore chromatic notes by transposing hexachords to positions other than their traditional ones. Significant works in this tradition are Josquin's *Fortuna d'un gran tempo*, Willaert's puzzle duo (originally conceived as a quartet) *Quid non ebrietas* (Lowinsky, 1943 and 1956) and Greiter's *Passibus ambiguis* (Lowinsky, 1956–7). All of these use hexachord transposition through the circle of 5ths; this is also applied in those examples of motets of the mid-16th century with unspecified chromaticism discovered and described by Lowinsky (1946). The 'secret chromatic art' involved here is in each case a considerable extension of traditional *musica ficta*, in which an entire passage and not merely a single note or a cadence is open to a chromatic interpretation. While the thesis advanced by Lowinsky is still controversial, he brought strong evidence in its favour. Similarly originating in *musica ficta* is a type of chromaticism based on transposition using flat signatures.

Less indebted to the tradition of *musica ficta* than to the more 'progressive' and experimental wing of 16th-century theory are pieces based on chromatic and enharmonic experimentation in imitation of the ancient genera, as well as those originating in a fresh use of chordal chromaticism of a colouristic type. Combining in varying degrees all of these tendencies is an extraordinary chromatic chanson by Guillaume Costeley, *Seigneur Dieu* (see Levy, 1955), which is one of the most remarkable experiments of the century. It should be noted that wherever hexachord chromaticism is used the traditional notational function of the flat is the same (an instruction to sing 'fa') and thus implies the continuity of the solmization traditions, while in degree-inflected chromaticism an increasing departure from notational traditions is evident.

*(ii) Performing practice.* On this crucial aspect of the problem little can be said, but one must be wary of the facile assumption that singers of the period were universally cognisant of the 'right' approach to the problem and solved it uniformly. On the contrary, there is persuasive evidence that 16th-century musicians found it difficult to know how to apply those rules of *musica ficta* that were espoused by theorists of their own times. As early as 1524 Giovanni Spataro wrote to Pietro Aaron (in a passage later used verbatim by Aaron in the supplement to his *Toscanello in musica* of 1529, but without credit to Spataro; trans. from Lockwood, 1968):

thus the musician or composer is obliged to indicate his intention, in order that the singer may not chance to do something that was never intended by the composer . . . the singer is not to be expected, on first reading, to sing the proper notes in the places where this sign [♭] may occur, inasmuch as it may belong there, or may not belong there.

In the 1550s the Roman singer and writer Ghiselin Danckerts in an unpublished treatise illustrated the problem from the performer's point of view by means of an anecdote concerning a dispute between two singers of the church of S Lorenzo in Damaso, Rome, which must have occurred between 1538 and 1544 (Lockwood, 1965). The dispute was over the proper way to add accidentals to a composition by the papal singer Juan Escribano. According to Danckerts, he himself was eventually asked to judge the matter, and he explained his decision in substantial detail. Since concrete evidence of actual choices of accidentals made in performance is virtually non-existent, one can only surmise that practices must indeed have differed from place to place and time to time, and that it would probably be a severe historical misjudgment to assume any prevailing uniformity of practice. On the other hand, much can be learnt about the prevailing theoretical assumptions on which judgments and choices could have been made by knowledgeable singers.

*(iii) Contemporary theory and 'rules'.* In a thorough exposition of the rules of *musica ficta* that were propagated throughout this period, Lowinsky (1964) summed up the prevailing rules under the headings of *causa necessitatis* ('by reason of necessity') and *causa pulchritudinis* ('by reason of beauty'). The former heading includes: first, the rule prohibiting the simultaneous

sounding of *mi* against *fa*, that is, diminished octaves and 5ths between two simultaneously sounding voices; second, the rule known from a schoolboy jingle as 'una nota super la, semper est canendum fa' ('a note above *la* is always sung *fa*'), to prevent a linear tritone when a line ascends above the syllable *la* (Pietro Aaron in his *Lucidarium*, 1545, showed this was by no means a universally applicable doctrine); and third, the prohibition of false relations.

Under the heading *causa pulchritudinis* Lowinsky included: first, the rule governing the *subsemitonium modi*, that is, the raising of the leading note at cadential formulae; second, the rule of propinquity, that is, approaching a perfect consonance in two voices by the nearest imperfect consonance; and third, the rule of ending on a complete triad (according to Lowinsky this was known only in the 16th century).

These rules undoubtedly constituted a set of guidelines, inherited from earlier periods (e.g. see §1, iii, above), which 16th-century musicians could recognize as being broadly applicable; Aaron specifically referred to 'ordinary and special rules devised by musicians', and Danckerts referred to reasons for the insertion of accidentals which are directly equivalent to the first three rules cited above. Among the many problems still unsolved is that of how to apply the rules when one contradicts the other or when more than one is applicable. This was illustrated in the period itself by Aaron, in the supplement to his *Toscanello in musica*, where he quoted a passage from the bass part of the third Agnus Dei of Josquin's *Missa 'L'homme armé' super voces musicales* (see ex.3). As Aaron explained, the tritone *f–b* cannot be changed to *f–b♭* since that in turn would cause a diminished 5th *b♭–e*: 'thus the singer will be obliged to sing the harsh tritone for the sake of that interval [a 5th] or rather that syllable which occurs in the position of *hypate meson*, called *E la mi*; because in order to accommodate the interval in the most convenient way, he is forced to break the rule'.

Ex.3

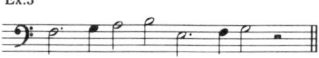

Similar problems inevitably arise in the music of the period. Yet it would be erroneous to assume, as some have done, that because *musica ficta* cannot be applied with absolute consistency and rigour, it ought not to be applied at all in vocal music. There is ample testimony by reliable writers showing that despite the problems inherent in the tradition, it continued to have meaning throughout the 16th century. It has been suggested (Lockwood, 1968) that one useful approach may consist in analysing individual pieces with regard to the definition of classes of linear, harmonic and contrapuntal movement that may require unspecified accidentals, together with exhaustive study of the relevant sources for each work. In this way one may study the problem as consisting of the relationship between those accidentals that are specified and those that are required by the known rules. Since for each of these categories both positive and negative possibilities exist, there will be four potential categories for each situation. By examining these in relation to one another and to the composition as a whole, more and less plausible solutions may emerge.

3. AFTER 1600. Accidentals in the Baroque period, like many other features of notation and performance, went through a long and intermittent transition from the greater fluidity of earlier periods towards the greater fixity of later periods. In early Baroque music accidentals were still a responsibility shared by the composer and the performer and open to a choice of solutions; hence modern editors and performers are concerned primarily with deciding which accidentals are most satisfactory within the original boundaries of the style. By 1700, much of the responsibility for deciding on accidentals and inflections had passed to the composer or printer, but even in late Baroque music the performer will sometimes still have to add accidentals.

Several principles seem to apply to much Baroque music, probably throughout the period, though with numerous exceptions. Most derive directly from earlier practice. Perhaps the most important general point is that accidentals in Baroque music still serve to inflect a note, giving it a new relative position compared with what in its context it would otherwise have had. This is different from the modern absolute effect of a notated accidental. Thus Christopher Simpson wrote in his *Principles of Practical Musick* (1665): 'That ♭ takes away a *Semitone* from the Sound of the Note before which it is set, to make it more *grave* or *flat*: This ♯ doth add a semitone to the Note to make it more *acute* or sharp'. Hence written C♭ after C♯ may (by inflecting the note a semitone down) mean a modern C♮; and written B♯ after B♭ may mean a modern B♮. This principle was still expressed, with reservations, by Francesco Geminiani (*The Art of Playing on the Violin*, London, 1751, p.3):

A Sharp (♯) raises the Note to which it is prefixed, a Semitone higher . . . A Flat (♭) on the contrary renders the Note to which it is prefixed, a Semitone lower . . . This Rule concerning the Flats and Sharps is not absolutely exact; but it is the easiest and best Rule that can be given to a Learner. This Mark (♮) takes away the Force of both the Sharp and the Flat and restores the Note before which it is placed to its natural Quality.

The natural sign was rare (and strictly applicable only to B) through much of the Baroque period, but came into common though far from exclusive use (applicable to any note) in later Baroque music.

By Baroque convention, a flat or a sharp 'serves only for that particular Note before which it is placed' (Christopher Simpson). Although this was always the theoretical understanding, in practice inconsistencies are numerous, and more or less regular exceptions were to some extent recognized. Notes immediately repeated, or with only one or two other notes intervening, usually (though not invariably) retain the force of an accidental applied to the first of them. This tendency is somewhat weakened if there is a change of harmony and greatly weakened if there is an intervening rest, or the start of a new phrase (see ex.4); still more so if more than one of these circumstances coincide (e.g. if both a rest and the start of a new phrase interrupt the series of repeated notes).

It was only in the Classical period that the convention of an accidental ceasing to apply after a bar-line received explicit recognition. D. G. Türk (*Clavierschule*, 1789, p.46) wrote that accidentals 'are valid only through one bar; yet one must not wish to observe this rule too strictly, for such a modifying sign often remains valid through several bars, or indeed so long, until it is cancelled by a ♮'. Ex.4 shows an example of this effect in Monteverdi's *Orfeo*; the upper voice has the precaution-

Ex.4 Monteverdi: *Orfeo*, Act 2

ary cancellation of the sharp at the start of the new phrase. The same effect should be understood in the lower voice.

An extension of this understanding of the duration of an accidental, which is clearly derived from earlier practice, is still found widely in early Baroque music, but less so thereafter: while a part remains within the compass of the same hexachord (i.e. without the need for mental mutation into a different hexachord for solmization), there is a strong tendency for the force of an accidental to persist. On any theoretical basis, this should have applied only to flats, but by analogy (or by transposition), it actually applied to sharps as well. In performance, this possibility should on no account be overlooked (at least in all music of the 17th centuury).

Whereas the force of a modern accidental can only extend forwards, that of a Baroque accidental could, and frequently did, also extend backwards – a principle of great importance in early Baroque music. This is not merely a matter of the admittedly careless placing in printed music, and still more in manuscripts, of the actual signs for accidentals (so much so that it sometimes seems that anywhere within reas-onable distance around the note meant to be affected, and where there might happen to be room on the paper); but it is also a matter of definite convention, the exis-tence of which was brilliantly noticed, though not fol-lowed up, by Jeppesen (1923). An accidental of which the force extends backwards (as well as forwards) may be called 'retrospective'. The plainest cases are those in which a dissonant suspension on a dominant 5-4 resolves ornamentally on to the leading note in a domin-ant 5-3. Here it was still extremely common in early Baroque music, and not uncommon later, to place the necessary sharp on the main note of resolution but not on the preceding ornamental note or notes (where it is nevertheless ordinarily required; see ex.5). Retrospec-

Ex.5

tive accidentals can occur in the figuring of continuo basses as well as in the written-out parts of a composi-tion.

The use of retrospective accidentals in sources of 17th-century music evidently goes far beyond anything that the appearance of the original printed volumes and manuscripts implies (the trouble being precisely that retrospective accidentals look no different from normal ones). There are, of course, many passages that on first thoughts might well appear to need retrospective ac-cidentals, but that prove on careful consideration not to need and sometimes not to tolerate such a solution. But passages where a retrospective accidental provides the most musicianly solution seem to be extremely numer-ous before and during the early Baroque period, and to a lesser but not inconsiderable extent thereafter.

Many interpretations of accidentals may be suggested by both the melody and the harmony. Baroque melody has some tendency to ascend with sharps and naturals and descend with naturals and flats; to flatten the peak note of a phrase when that note immediately falls again; to sharpen the trough note of a phrase when that note immediately rises again (thus serving as a leading note); to sharpen the 6th of the scale when the 7th is sharpened (to serve as leading note); and generally (though not invariably) to avoid augmented 2nds. Baroque harmony has some tendency to change with a new phrase; to end a minor passage in the major (Picardy 3rd); and to insist on regular (sharp or sharpened) cadential leading notes in dominant to tonic progressions or interrupted cadences. But melodic considerations may prevail over harmonic ones to produce, for example, a diminished- or augmented-octave clash (ex.6).

Ex.6 Coprario: Fantasia *Chi pue mirarvi*

There are ways in which the notation can be actively misleading as to the presence of certain accidentals. Whereas figured basses may use the usual methods of notating accidentals, they carry some particular patterns of error, such as ♭ wrongly written for 6 or 6 for ♭.

Tablature does not notate accidentals separately, but simply shows the fingerings that will produce them so that no ambiguity should arise; but, of course, mis-takes can occur. When tablature doubles staff notation, one helps to check the other, but it cannot be assumed (in cases of discrepancy) that the tablature is necessarily right. When tablature stands alone, it may be somewhat more reliable than staff notation, but it is by no means sacrosanct, for tablature not infrequently shows a wrong fingering.

Precautionary accidentals occur often, but very inconsistently, in places where Baroque conventions require them in order to prevent excessive ambiguity. Nevertheless, ambiguities abound for the modern musician as, presumably, they did for the Baroque musician. In practice it is much more important to work out for each passage a suitable scheme of accidentals, reasonably consistent within itself but not rigorously so, than it is to seek an unattainable certainty. It would have been somewhat contrary to the spirit of Baroque music, and especially of early Baroque music, for the composer to assume or for the performer to attempt any such consistent and predictable pattern.

## BIBLIOGRAPHY

M. Gerbert, ed.: *Scriptores ecclesiastici de musica sacra* (St Blasien, 1784/*R*1963, 2/1905, 3/1931)

C.-E.-H. de Coussemaker: *Histoire de l'harmonie au moyen-âge* (Paris, 1852), 295–349

——: *Scriptorum de musica medii aevi nova series* (Paris, 1864–76/*R*1963)

A. de La Fage: *Essais de diphtérographie musicale* (Paris, 1864)

G. von Tücher: 'Zur Musikpraxis und Theorie des 16. Jahrhunderts, v: Accidentien und Musica Ficta', *AMZ*, viii (1873)

R. Schlecht: 'Über den Gebrauch des Diesis im 13. u. 15. Jahrhundert', *MMg*, ix (1877), 79, 99

R. Hirschfeld: 'Notizien zur mittelalterlichen Musikgeschichte (Instrumentalmusik und Musica Ficta)', *MMg*, xvii (1885), 61

P. Spitta: 'Die Musica Enchiriadis und ihre Zeitalter', *VMw*, v (1889), 443–82

G. Jacobsthal: *Die chromatische Alteration im liturgischen Gesang der abendländischen Kirche* (Berlin, 1897/*R*1970)

W. Schmidt: *Die Calliopea legale des Johannes Hothby* (Leipzig, 1897)

H. Riemann: *Geschichte der Musiktheorie im IX.–XIX. Jahrhundert* (Leipzig, 1898, 2/1921; Eng. trans., 1962/*R*1974)

T. Kroyer: *Die Anfänge der Chromatik im italienischen Madrigal des XVI. Jahrhunderts* (Leipzig, 1902/*R*1968)

J. Wolf: *Geschichte der Mensuralnotation* (Leipzig, 1904/*R*1965), i, 109ff

A. Einstein: 'Claudio Merulos Ausgabe der Madrigale des Verdelot', *SIMG*, viii (1906–7), 220–54, 516

H. Riemann: 'Verloren gegangene Selbstverständlichkeiten in der Musik des 15.–16. Jahrhunderts', *Musikalisches Magazin*, xvii (Langensalza, 1907)

E. Wilfort: 'Glareans Erwiderung', *ZIMG*, x (1908–9), 337

*IMusSCR*, iii *Vienna 1909* [articles by Bernoulli, Chilesotti, Kroyer, Schwartz, Wolf]

R. von Ficker: 'Beiträge zur Chromatik des 14. bis 16. Jahrhunderts', *SMw*, ii (1914), 5

K. Dèzes: *Prinzipielle Fragen auf dem Gebiet der fingierten Musik* (diss., Humboldt U., Berlin, 1922)

K. Jeppesen: *Palestrinastil med soerligt henblik paa dissonansbehandlingen* (Copenhagen, 1923; Eng. trans., 1927, 2/1946)

E. Frerichs: 'Die Accidentien in Orgeltabulaturen', *ZMw*, vii (1924–5), 99

K. Jeppesen: *Der Kopenhagener Chansonnier* (Copenhagen, 1927)

W. Apel: *Accidentien und Tonalität in den Musikdenkmälern des 15. und 16. Jahrhunderts* (Strasbourg, 1937/*R*1972)

——: 'Accidentals and the Modes in 15th- and 16th-century Sources', *BAMS*, ii (1937), 289

——: 'The Partial Signatures in the Sources up to 1450', *AcM*, x (1938), 1

J. Levitan: 'Adrian Willaert's Famous Duo *Quidnam ebreatis*', *TVNM*, xv/3 (1938), 166f; xv/4 (1939), 193–233

W. Apel: 'A Postscript to "The Partial Signatures in the Sources up to 1450"', *AcM*, xi (1939), 40

C. Fox: 'Accidentals in Vihuela Tablatures', *BAMS*, iv (1940), 22

W. Apel: *The Notation of Polyphonic Music, 900–1600* (Cambridge, Mass., 1942, rev. 5/1961), 104ff, 120

H. Hewitt: *Harmonice Musices Odhecaton A* (Cambridge, Mass., 1942), 16

L. Hibberd: '*Musica ficta* and Instrumental Music, c1250–c1350', *MQ*, xxviii (1942), 216

E. E. Lowinsky: 'The Goddess Fortuna in Music, with a Special Study of Josquin's *Fortuna d'un gran tempo*', *MQ*, xxix (1943), 45–77

W. Apel: 'Musica ficta', *Harvard Dictionary of Music* (Cambridge, Mass., 1944, rev. 2/1969)

E. E. Lowinsky: 'The Function of Conflicting Signatures in Early Polyphonic Music', *MQ*, xxxi (1945), 227–60

M. van Crevel: 'Secret Chromatic Art in the Netherlands Motet?', *TVNM*, xvi/4 (1946), 253–304

E. E. Lowinsky: *Secret Chromatic Art in the Netherlands Motet* (New York, 1946/*R*1967)

L. Schrade: 'A Secret Chromatic Art', *JRBM*, i (1946), 159

M. Johnson: 'A Study of Conflicting Key-signatures in Francesco Landini's Music', *Hamline Studies in Musicology*, ii (1947), 27

J. Smits van Waesberghe, ed.: *Johannes Afflighemensis (Cotto): De musica cum tonario*, CSM, i (1950)

R. Hoppin: 'Partial Signatures and Musica Ficta in Some Early Fifteenth Century Sources', *JAMS*, vi (1953), 197

H. Anglès, ed.: *C. de Morales: Opera omnia*, MME, xv (1954); xx (1959)

E. E. Lowinsky: 'Conflicting Views on Conflicting Signatures', *JAMS*, vii (1954), 181

S. Clercx: 'Les accidents sous-entendus et la transcription en notation moderne', *L'Ars Nova: Wégimont II 1955*, 167

K. Levy: 'Costeley's Chromatic Chanson', *AnnM*, iii (1955), 3–263

G. Reaney: 'Musica Ficta in the Works of Guillaume de Machaut', *L'Ars Nova: Wégimont II 1955*, 196

R. Hoppin: 'Conflicting Signatures Reviewed', *JAMS*, ix (1956), 97

E. E. Lowinsky: 'Adrian Willaert's Chromatic Duo Re-examined', *TVNM*, xviii/1 (1956), 1–36

——: 'Matthaeus Greiter's *Fortuna*: an Experiment in Chromaticism and in Musical Iconography', *MQ*, xlii (1956), 500; xliii (1957), 68

L. Spiess: 'The Diatonic "Chromaticism" of the *Enchiriadis* Treatises', *JAMS*, xii (1959), 1

A. Seay, ed.: *Ugolino of Orvieto: Declaratio musicae disciplinae*, CSM, vii (1959–62)

N. Pirrotta: 'Laurentius de Florentia', *MGG*

E. E. Lowinsky: *Tonality and Atonality in Sixteenth-century Music* (Berkeley, 1961, rev. 2/1962)

G. Haydon: 'The Case of the Troublesome Accidental', *Natalicia musicologica Knud Jeppesen* (Copenhagen, 1962), 125

N. Pirrotta, ed.: *The Music of Fourteenth-century Italy*, CMM, viii/3 (1962)

C. Dahlhaus: 'Zu Costeleys chromatischer Chanson', *Mf*, xvi (1963), 253

E. E. Lowinsky: Introduction to *Musica nova*, ed. C. Slim, MRM, i (1964), pp.xiii–xxi

G. Massera: 'Musica inspettica e accordatura strumentale', *Quadrivium*, vi (1964), 85

G. Reaney, A. Gilles and J. Maillard, eds.: *Philippe de Vitry: Ars nova*, CSM, viii (1964)

L. Lockwood: 'A Dispute on Accidentals in Sixteenth-century Rome', *AnMc*, no.2 (1965), 24

H. Kaufmann: 'A "Diatonic" and a "Chromatic" Madrigal by Giulio Fiesco', *Aspects of Medieval and Renaissance Music: a Birthday Offering to Gustave Reese* (New York, 1966), 474

A. Seay: 'The 15th Century Coniuncta: a Preliminary Study', *Aspects of Medieval and Renaissance Music: a Birthday Offering to Gustave Reese* (New York, 1966), 723

R. Crocker: 'A New Source for Medieval Music Theory', *AcM*, xxxix (1967), 161

E. E. Lowinsky: Introduction to *O. Petrucci: Canti B*, ed. H. Hewitt, MRM, ii (1967), pp.ix–xiv

A. Seay, ed.: *Concerning Music – De musica; Johannes de Grocheo* (Colorado Springs, 1967)

C. Dahlhaus: 'Zur Akzidentiensetzung in den Motetten Josquins des Prez', *Musik und Verlag: Karl Vötterle zum 65. Geburtstag* (Kassel, 1968), 206

F. A. Gallo: 'Alcune fonte poco note di musica teorica e pratica', *L'ars nova italiana del trecento: convegni di studi 1961–1967* (Certaldo, 1968), 49

C. Jacobs: 'Spanish Renaissance Discussion of Musica Ficta', *Proceedings of the American Philosophical Society*, cxii (1968), 277

E. Kottick: 'Flats, Modality and Musica Ficta in some Early Renaissance Chansons', *JMT*, xii (1968), 264

L. Lockwood: 'A Sample Problem of *Musica Ficta*: Willaert's *Pater noster*', *Studies in Music History: Essays for Oliver Strunk* (Princeton, 1968), 161

E. E. Lowinsky: 'Echoes of Adrian Willaert's Chromatic "Duo" in Sixteenth- and Seventeenth-century Compositions', *Studies in Music History: Essays for Oliver Strunk* (Princeton, 1968), 183–238

C. Dahlhaus: 'Tonsystem und Kontrapunkt um 1500', *Jb des Staatlichen Instituts für Musikforschung* (1969), 7

A. Hughes: 'Ugolino: the Monochord and Musica Ficta', *MD*, xxiii (1969), 21

K. P. Bernet Kempers: 'Accidentals', *Renaissance-muziek 1400–1600: donum natalicium René Bernard Lenaerts* (Louvain, 1969), 51

G. Reaney: 'Accidentals in Early Fifteenth-century Music', *Renaissance-muziek 1400–1600: donum natalicium René Bernard Lenaerts* (Louvain, 1969), 223

D. Crawford: 'Performance and the Laborde Chansonnier: Authenticity of Multiplicities: Musica ficta', *College Music Symposium*, x (1970), 107

R. Bray: 'The Interpretation of Musica Ficta in English Music, c1490–c1580', *PRMA*, xcvii (1970–71), 29

G. G. Allaire: *The Theory of Hexachords, Solmization and the Modal System*, MSD, xxiv (1972)

P. Doe: 'Another View of Musica Ficta in Tudor Music', *PRMA*, xcviii (1971–2), 113

M. Bent: 'Musica Recta and Musica Ficta', *MD*, xxvi (1972), 72

A. Hughes: *Manuscript Accidentals: Ficta in Focus, 1350–1450*, MSD, xxvii (1972)

H. Tischler: ' "Musica Ficta" in the Thirteenth Century', *ML*, liv (1973), 38; also pubd in *IMSCR*, xi *Copenhagen 1972*, 695

D. Harrán: 'New Evidence for Musica Ficta: the Cautionary Sign', *JAMS*, xxix (1976), 77

R. Bray: 'Sixteenth-century *Musica Ficta*: the Importance of the Scribe', *Journal of the Plainsong and Mediaeval Music Society*, i (1978), 57

MARGARET BENT (1 i–iv), LEWIS LOCKWOOD (1 (v), 2), ROBERT DONINGTON (3), STANLEY BOORMAN (bibliography)

**Musica figurata** (Lat.). Figural music; *see* FIGURAL, FIGURATE, FIGURED.

**Musical.** See MUSICAL COMEDY.

**Musical Antiquarian Society.** An organization founded in London for the 'publication of scarce and valuable works by early English composers'. Its first publications appeared from the firm of William Chappell in 1840. In a year it gathered nearly 1000 subscribing members who received the publications at cost price. By its dissolution in 1847 the society had issued 19 large folio scores, including Byrd's five-part Mass and the first book of *Cantiones sacrae*, Wilbye's *First Set of English Madrigals*, masques and madrigals by Gibbons, Purcell's *Dido and Aeneas*, *King Arthur*, *Bonduca* and the Ode for St Cecilia's Day, works by Morley, Weelkes, Dowland and East, and several anthologies of Elizabethan and Jacobean vocal music.

**Musical Art Society.** New York choir active from 1894 to 1920; *see* NEW YORK, §7.

**Musical Association.** *See* ROYAL MUSICAL ASSOCIATION.

**Musical bottles.** *See* BOUTEILLOPHONE.

**Musical bow** (Fr. *arc musical, arc sonore*; Ger. *Musikbogen*; It. *arco sonore*; Sp. *arco musical*). A bow-shaped string instrument consisting solely of a flexible stave, curved by the tension of a string (or strings) stretched between its ends, any associated resonator being either unattached, or detachable without destroying the sound-producing apparatus (see figs.1 and 2). Sachs and Hornbostel classified both the musical bow and the 'stick zither' (which has a rigid stave) as types of bar zither (*see* INSTRUMENTS, CLASSIFICATION OF). *See also* the entry 'Musical bow' in Appendix A.

1. History. 2. Structure. 3. Resonators. 4. Technique.

1. HISTORY. The musical bow, in various forms, is widely distributed in Africa, America, Oceania, parts of Asia and formerly to a small extent in Europe (East Prussia, the Netherlands, Italy, Latvia and Lithuania). It is frequently played recreationally as a solo instrument or (with a resonator) for song accompaniment, and in some areas is important in magic or religion. In the cave Les Trois Frères in south-western France a rock painting from *c*15,000 BC shows musical use of a bow in a religious ceremony (according to the Abbé Breuil; *see* EUROPE, PREHISTORIC, fig.2).

Whether the archer's bow or the musical bow came first has long provoked conjecture and contention. Apollo was both an archer and the god of music; Homer and Euripides refer to the musical note emitted by the archer's bowstring and the delight it gave to the ear. Legend in north India names the simple *pinâka* musical bow as the prototype of all string instruments and ascribes its invention to the god Śiva. In Japan legend traces the origin of the *koto* (fretted long zither) to the god Ameno Kamato who placed six archers' longbows

close together with their strings uppermost. A southern African Bushman rock painting reported by G. W. Stow depicts similar use of seven shooting bows (see frontispiece in Kirby).

The notion that all string instruments evolved from the musical bow was dismissed by Balfour in the late 19th century, but he firmly believed that the musical bow had evolved from the shooting bow. Montandon, however, asserted that the weapon evolved from the musical bow, after the musical bow had changed from an original idiochord form (in which the string is a partially detached strip from the same piece of cane as the stave, lifted on bridges) to heterochord form (with a tied-on string). Hornbostel (p.135) objected that the shooting bow was already known in the earliest cultures. He favoured Sachs's claim that weapon and instrument originated independently but had later become similar in shape.

According to Sachs the earliest musical bow had a separate resonator (the stick being pressed against a vessel placed on the ground) and this had developed via an intermediate form (the ground zither) from the percussion beam (a pole suspended in two nooses and struck with two sticks). Sachs (1940, p.56) held that 'those forms of bow which we have good reason to believe are the oldest have nothing to do with a hunters' bow' (being generally too long for shooting, and some of them idiochord, with bridges) and were not associated with hunters' beliefs and ceremonies: in many cases only women play them, and they may serve variously to induce meditation, invoke the spirits or accompany initiation.

Some peoples who play musical bows hunt without bows and arrows (as was true of the Zulu in former times), while others (such as the Dan of the Ivory Coast) use a different form of bow for their hunting. The Dan ascribe their musical bow to a genie who used to play it to warn animals of approaching hunters; absent-mindedly he once left it on an ant heap, and a hunter appropriated it. On the other hand, there is clear evidence that Bushmen of southern Africa have long played tunes on their hunting bows, and continue this practice in modern times. In this instance at least, elaborate origin theories have seemed superfluous to some scholars: Kirby in his extensive Bushman studies chose to adopt Balfour's practical view that 'the idea of adapting the shooting bow to musical purposes ... might well arise in more than one centre, since it involves little more than the appreciation of the musical qualities in the twang of the bow-string, a thing which is almost forced upon the attention of the archer' (Balfour, p.86).

Musical bows are usually played singly, but a few instances of multiple use are known. The pluriarc (which is really a bow lute) resembles a series of bows with a common resonator. The terms 'ground bow' or 'earth bow' are misnomers (*see* GROUND HARP). The arched harp of Sumeria (depicted on a vase from *c*3000 BC) has some bow-like features and is regarded by Sachs (1940, p.80) as a descendant of the musical bow. Similar arched harps (also called bow harps) survive in many parts of Africa north of the equator (*see* HARPS, AFRICAN).

2. STRUCTURE. The stave varies from about 50 cm to 3 metres in length with different varieties. It may be of round, semicircular or flat section, and often tapers towards the ends. The dividing line between musical bows

*1. Mouth-resonated musical bow of the Fula people, Wala region, Senegal*

and stick zithers (with a rigid stave) is often uncertain, especially with idiochord varieties. Bow staves are usually made from a single length of wood or cane, but a few types have two or three sections (Xhosa *umrubhe*; Sotho *setolotolo*). 'Scraped bows' (Ger. *Schrapbogen*), found in India, central and southern Africa and South America, have serrations along one side of the stave (the instrument being sounded by scraping across these with a stick or rattle-stick). With other types of bow, the string may be set in vibration by plucking it with finger-tip or plectrum, by tapping it with a small stick or grass stalk, by stroking it with a friction stick (in Colombia, South Africa, Loango and Marquesas) or with a sub-sidiary bow (in Patagonia), which, among the Araucano and Chaco in South America, is interlinked with the main bow.

The Aeolian bow, sounded by the force of wind or breath, is exemplified by the tiny 'whizzing bow' swung round like a bullroarer (and thus qualifying as a 'free aerophone') which is found sporadically in west Africa (Liberia), China, Indonesia and eastern Brazil. It is also used, attached to large kites, in Indonesia and eastern Asia (Java: *sundari*; Laos: *tamoo*). Bows sounded with the breath are confined to the South African GORA and its derivatives and the Javanese *bajang kĕrek*.

Both idiochord and heterochord musical bows may have one or more strings. The string of the heterochord bow may be made from rattan, vegetable fibre, sinew, twisted animal hairs or wire. It may either vibrate as a whole, or be divided into unequal segments (usually two) by a bridge (*see* MVET) or by a 'brace' (also called 'tuning noose' or 'tension noose') – a loop, passing round both stave and string, which keeps the string pulled inwards, towards the stave. Some braced bows, such as the *egoboli* of Uganda, have an additional smaller noose near each end for making finer adjustments of the string tension. In rare cases a single bowstring may be laced more than once across the curved frame of the stave, as

in the *adungu* of the Acoli in Uganda. The breath-sounded *gora* is exceptional in that a piece of quill connects the string with the stave at one end.

3. RESONATORS. As far as supplementary resonance is concerned, bows may be subdivided into two broad categories: those without and those with an attached resonator. The first of these may be further divided between bows played entirely without a resonator and others played with a separate resonator. The first of these two types is rare, the north Indian *pināka* being a reported example (Balfour, p.54). Whizzing bows perhaps qualify but are usually considered aerophones. Bows with a separate resonator include the mouth bow, in which the player's mouth cavity supplies resonance: this type is widespread in Africa, South America and Oceania. The stave may be held against either the player's teeth or his slightly parted lips, or the string may vibrate freely between the lips (fig.1). Some types in India, Africa, America and Borneo have an independent resonator (calabash, bowl, pot, skin bag or basket).

Bows with an attached resonator usually have an open-ended gourd attached in some way to the stave on the opposite side to the string; these, known as gourd bows, are common in equatorial and southern Africa and among Afro-Americans in South America. The bow is usually held vertically, with the opening in the gourd facing the player's body (fig.2). The Indian *tuila* and instruments like the *nenjenje* of the Medje in central Africa have similar features but, having rigid flat bars, are really stick zithers. In southern Africa two typical mono-heterochord gourd bows are the Zulu *ugubhu* (unbraced, with resonator near the bottom of the stave) and *umakhweyana* (braced, with the resonator near the centre, attached to the brace; *see* NGUNI MUSIC, §3 and fig.3). The opening in the gourd resonators of the Zulu instruments is mostly between 5 and 7 cm in diameter, but in those of most other ethnic groups the hole is larger, or a hemispherical half gourd may be used. In some areas supplementary rattles, bells or jingles are attached to the stave, or used with the beater, and the *kalumbu* of the Valley Tonga (Zambia) may

Ex.1 Music for *umqunge* (mouth bow), Mpondo, Xhosa, South Africa, sounded by stroking the string with a friction stick (Rycroft, 1966)

o unstopped

● stopped with left thumb

have a mirliton attached to the gourd. In the case of another smaller variety of mono-heterochord gourd bow found in east, central and west Africa, the half-gourd resonator is placed over the player's mouth (e.g. the *ekitulenge* of the Konjo in Uganda). A U-shaped gourd bow with five to seven strings (known as the forked harp and sometimes nicknamed the belly-harp) is used in the savannah region of west Africa; the *seperewa* of Ashanti is a typical example.

4. TECHNIQUE. The fundamental pitch of a musical bow is often varied by the performer. In bows with a bridge or brace the two unequal segments of the string yield different pitches. Additional pitches may be produced on braced and unbraced bows by stopping the string at one or more points with a finger, thimble, small stick or (in Brazil) the edge of a coin; harmonics are also often played. On some varieties with an unattached resonator harmonics are produced by touching the string at a nodal point with a finger or with the chin. With many other types the resonance frequency of the resonator is continually altered while playing to amplify one or other of the higher harmonics. The fundamental then serves only as a drone (or provides a simple ground bass if its pitch is varied) while selectively resonated upper partials are used for the melody. With mouth bows the volume of the player's mouth cavity is varied, as in the case of the jew's harp (see ex.1). The effective compass is usually from about *f'* to *e'''*. Which harmonic partials fall within this range depends on the tuning of the fundamental: partials 4 to 13 (from a fundamental pitch *G*) have been noted for the Venda *tshigwana*.

Pitch on mono-heterochord gourd bows is varied by finger-stopping (as with the unbraced Zulu *ugubhu*), and also, in the case of braced bows like the *umakhweyana*, through striking alternate segments of the string. The 3rd, 4th and 5th partials above each fundamental may be selectively amplified through covering the opening of the gourd to a varying extent, thereby altering its resonance frequency, as in ex.2. This is achieved by moving it closer to, or further from, the chest while playing (*see* NGUNI MUSIC, §3). The musical purpose of such movements was misunderstood by earlier investigators, including Kirby (p.198) and Sachs (1940, p.57). A few instances have been reported of players expanding and

2. *Braced musical bow (umuduli) with gourd resonator, Rwanda*

contracting their stomach muscles instead of moving the instrument. A !Kung Bushman was observed by England doing this with a tin can (in lieu of a gourd) held against his shooting bow to serve as an unattached resonator; it seems likely, however, that he was imitating the gourd-bow technique of some neighbouring peoples. Gourd bows are generally used for self-accompaniment while singing and, certainly among the Nguni, the instrumental ostinato serves as a substitute chorus part, against which the performer takes the antiphonal role of the leading singer.

The largest collection of recordings of African musical bows is housed at the International Library of African Music, Rhodes University, Grahamstown, South Africa.

Ex.2 Zulu *ugubhu* (unbraced gourd bow), sounded by striking the string with a piece of thatching grass (Rycroft, 1976)

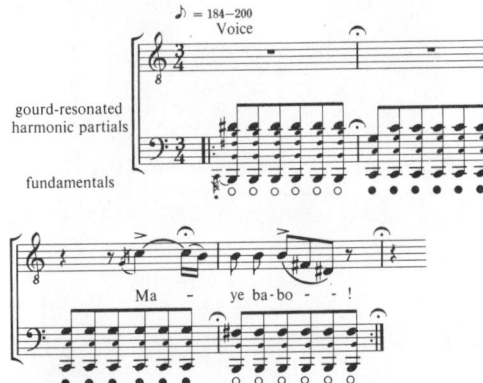

gourd-resonated harmonic partials

fundamentals

Ma - ye ba-bo - - !

o unstopped
● stopped between left thumb-nail and forefinger

BIBLIOGRAPHY
G. Fritsch: *Die Eingeborenen Süd-Afrikas* (Breslau, 1872), 20, 132f, 190f, 225, 327f, 427, 439f
O. T. Mason: 'Geographical Distribution of the Musical Bow', *American Anthropologist*, x (1897), 377
H. ten Kate: 'Geographical Distribution of the Musical Bow', *American Anthropologist*, xi (1898), 93
H. Balfour: *The Natural History of the Musical Bow* (Oxford, 1899)
B. Ankermann: 'Die afrikanischen Musikinstrumente', *Ethnologisches Notizblatt*, iii/1 (1901), 1–134
L. Frobenius: 'Die Saiteninstrumente der Naturvölker', *Prometheus*, xii (1901), 625, 648
G. Montandon: 'La généalogie des instruments de musique et les cycles de civilisation', *Archives suisses d'anthropologie générale*, iii (1919), 1–71
C. Sachs: *Geist und Werden der Musikinstrumente* (Berlin, 1929)
E. M. von Hornbostel: 'The Ethnology of African Sound-instruments', *Africa*, vi (1933), 129, 277–311
P. R. Kirby: *The Musical Instruments of the Native Races of South Africa* (London, 1934, 2/1965)
K. G. Izikowitz: *Musical and other Sound Instruments of the South American Indians* (Göteborg, 1935)
T. Norlind, ed.: *Systematik der Saiteninstrumente* (Stockholm, 1936)
C. Sachs: *The History of Musical Instruments* (New York, 1940)

G.-J. Duchemin: 'Autour d'un arc musical du Saloum oriental', *Première conférence internationale des africanistes de l'ouest: Dakar 1945*, 248

J. Kunst: *The Music of Java* (The Hague, 1949, enlarged 3/1973), 232f

F. Ortiz: *Los instrumentos de la música afrocubana* (Havana, 1952–5)

K. P. Wachsmann: 'The Sound Instruments', in M. Trowell and K. P. Wachsmann: *Tribal Crafts in Uganda* (London, 1953), 311–415

D. K. Rycroft: 'Tribal Style and Free Expression', *African Music*, i/1 (1954), 16

H.-H. Wängler: 'Über südwestafrikanische Bogenlieder', *Afrika und Übersee*, xxxix (1954–5), 49; xl (1955–6), 163

C. M. Camp and B. Nettl: 'The Musical Bow in Southern Africa', *Anthropos*, l (1955), 65

H. Fischer: *Schallgeräte in Ozeanien* (Strasbourg, 1958)

J. S. Laurenty: *Les cordophones du Congo Belge et du Ruanda-Urundi* (Tervuren, 1960)

S. Marcuse: 'Musical Bow', *Musical Instruments: a Comprehensive Dictionary* (New York, 1964)

G. List: 'The Musical Bow at Palenque', *JIFMC*, xviii (1966), 36

D. K. Rycroft: 'Friction Chordophones in South Eastern Africa', *GSJ*, xix (1966), 84

N. M. England: 'Bushman Counterpoint', *JIFMC*, xix (1967), 58

G. Kubik: *Mehrstimmigkeit und Tonsysteme in Zentral- und Ostafrika* (Vienna, 1968), 50ff, pl.2

D. Taylor: 'The Music of Some Indian Tribes in Colombia', *Recorded Sound*, xxix–xxx (1968), suppl.

D. K. Rycroft: *Zulu, Swazi and Xhosa Instrumental and Vocal Music* (Tervuren, 1969) [with disc]

G. Kubik: *Musica tradicional e aculturada dos !Kung' de Angola* (Lisbon, 1970), 30ff

T. Johnston: 'Xizambi Friction-bow Music of the Shangana-Tsonga', *African Music*, iv/4 (1970), 81

H. Zemp: *Musique Dan* (Paris, 1971)

H. Tracey: *Catalogue: the Sound of Africa Series* (Roodepoort, 1973)

M. Davidson: 'Some Patterns of Rhythm and Harmony in Kalumbu Music', *African Music*, v/3 (1973–4), 70

D. K. Rycroft: 'The Zulu Bow-songs of Princess Magogo', *African Music*, v/4 (1976), 41

DAVID K. RYCROFT

**Musical box.** A MECHANICAL INSTRUMENT, invented at the close of the 18th century. Originally the musical box consisted of several metal teeth, arranged in radial fashion and sounded by a disc furnished with fine steel pins. At the beginning of the 19th century the disc was replaced by a steel comb with a number of teeth of different lengths and pitches. These teeth were sounded by pins fixed to a steel cylinder, and the cylinder was revolved either manually, by a small crank handle, or by a spring mechanism. Even movement was maintained by a fan connected with the cylinder by means of a gearing.

The first musical boxes, at that time called *carillons à musique* and provided with 15 to 25 teeth arranged in a scale, were made by the Swiss watchmakers at the end of the 18th century. In 1815 Jérémie Recordon and Samuel Junod established factory production of musical boxes in Switzerland. Since that time the entire manufacture of these musical instruments has been concentrated in Switzerland, where famous firms were founded in St Croix (D. Lecoultre, J. Recordon, S. Junod) and especially in Geneva (Aubert, Capt, Curting, David, Durand & Meyer, Golay, Granger, Liodet, Piguit, Rochat Frères, Nicole Frères, etc). Musical boxes with a fine and clear tone were also manufactured after 1813 by F. Řebiček in Bohemia, who won first prizes at the world exhibitions in London and Paris, surpassing such outstanding world manufacturers as A. Olbrich in Vienna, Lecoultre, Gublet, the Jaccard brothers from St Croix, and Doës in Geneva. Around 1835 musical boxes were made as toys, without a spring mechanism, but with a crank handle for manual operation. Over several years they spread all over the world. They had metal boxes, were small, round, brightly painted and played only one short melody. Larger types of musical boxes made in Geneva were called *cartels* and supplied

finer music for more demanding and discriminating listeners.

Musical boxes were characterized by a rather monotonous sound, and to remedy this some manufacturers tried to introduce various effects. These were tremolo (repetition of the main note), or the addition of small drums, bells, free reeds, etc. The music was varied further by the use of two or more combs in the instrument. Such musical boxes were made under various names (Fortepiano, Picolo, Aeolian Harp, Quatuor, Sublime Harmony, Flutina) by the Swiss firms Nicole, Paillard, Baker-Troll and others.

In 1862 A. Paillard in St Croix invented means of exchanging the cylinders, which were placed on a revolving shaft. This invention was perfected in 1879 by H. Metert in Geneva. Another important innovation was the standardization of cylinders, which made it possible to use the same cylinder in other musical boxes. The cylinder revolved six times around the axis in a spiral fashion, thus allowing a longer playing-time. In an attempt to dispense with the winding-up of the musical box, two or even more springs were used. Nicole made musical boxes with as many as four springs, so that his instruments played without interruption or winding-up for up to three hours.

Despite all the improvements and innovations (more than 400 patents were taken out) the basic weak point of musical boxes – their limited capacity to play musical compositions – was not removed. Few instruments with interchangeable discs were manufactured, and these were very expensive. The problem was solved by P. Lochmann by the introduction of an interchangeable metal disc in place of the cylinder. His instrument was called the POLYPHON; it was mass-manufactured from 1886 and the last was made as late as in the 1920s. German makers were most important in this field, especially in Leipzig; their instruments were variously called Fortuna, Comet, Kalliope, Celesta, etc.

The manufacture of musical boxes has survived to a limited degree in Switzerland, and today there is a certain revival of interest in these instruments all over the world. Among those who have contributed to the resumption of their manufacture are P. Rochat in

*Orchestral cylinder musical box by Paillard Vaucher Fils, Swiss, c1888 (private collection)*

Geneva and H. Thorens in St Croix; recently Japan has begun to manufacture musical boxes.

BIBLIOGRAPHY

M. M. Curtis: *Story of Snuff and Snuffboxes* (New York, 1935)
R. and M. Norton: *A History of Gold Snuff Boxes* (London, 1938)
J. E. T. Clark: *Musical Boxes, a History and an Appreciation* (Birmingham, 1948, 2/1952)
R. Mosoriak: *The Curious History of Music Boxes* (Chicago, 1953)
A. Buchner: *Hudebni automaty* (Prague, 1959; Eng. trans., 1959)
D. Tallis: *Musical Boxes* (London, 1971)
A. Ord-Hume: *Musical Box* (London, 1980)
——: *Restoring Musical Boxes* (London, 1980)

ALEXANDR BUCHNER

**Musical clock.** A clock combined with a MECHANICAL INSTRUMENT which played music at regular time intervals (every quarter of an hour, half-hour, or hour) or at will. In the Middle Ages astronomical clocks were equipped with carillons (the earliest account from 1352 mentions a carillon in Strasbourg), and in the 16th and 17th centuries there was a great upsurge in the construction of carillons in Flanders and Holland, whence they spread into a number of other countries, especially France and Germany. When spring mechanisms were invented, small carillons were built in portable clocks. These clocks were extremely expensive, but later on cheaper wooden musical clocks with glass carillons were made in the Black Forest region. In these musical clocks eight to sixteen glass bells played short folksongs by means of a cylinder. As early as the 16th century watches were equipped with miniature carillons, and from the 18th century these watches were combined with miniature musical instruments based on the comb mechanism. In the first half of the 19th century the metal bells of the carillon were replaced either by chromatically tuned metal rods, arranged in the manner of the xylophone, or (more frequently) with comb mechanisms, as in the MUSICAL BOX.

In the 18th century the manufacture of musical clocks was concentrated in London. There these instruments were made by outstanding clockmakers, including Barbot, William Carpenter, James Cox, R. Fleetwood, Fox & Sons, Fromanteel & Clark, Henderson, George Higginson, Thomas Larrymore, Marriott, Eardley Norton, Robert Philip, Robert Sellers, Tomlin, and Williamson; musical clocks built by all these clockmakers are now in the largest collection of musical clocks, in the Imperial Palace Museum in Peking. In the 1760s Frederick the Great invited watchmakers from Switzerland to establish the manufacture of musical clocks in Berlin. Among well-known Berlin manufacturers are Konrad Ehrbar, Christian Möllinger, Johann Elfroth and the court watchmaker Pohlmann; the cylinders were pinned by the musician Kummer. While the London manufacturers for the most part made musical clocks with carillons, the Berlin makers concentrated upon flute-playing clocks. Later, the manufacture of musical clocks spread to Paris, Dresden and Prague, but mainly to Vienna, where clocks were made by J. A. Hoyer and J. Janisch. Large flute-playing clocks, in fact orchestrions (*see* ORCHESTRION) combined with clocks, were made by the Maelzel brothers in Vienna.

Flute-playing clocks played arrangements of music (overtures, arias, parts of flute concertos and sonatas, marches and dance music), but also compositions written exclusively for them. Gerber mentioned in his encyclopedia a flute-playing clock constructed by Primitivus Němec, Prince Esterházy's librarian, whose cylinder

played music written by Mozart and Haydn for this instrument. 32 compositions by Haydn for flute-playing clock were published by Nagel in Hanover in 1931 and by Bärenreiter in Kassel in 1954. There are also 28 compositions by C. P. E. Bach, three compositions by Mozart and three by Beethoven.

As well as flute-playing clocks, harp-playing clocks were made, equipped with a stringed automatophon. In Cöthen Castle there was a harp-playing clock made by Johannes Zacharias Fischer from Halle; it was destroyed during World War II. On the cylinders of that instrument were compositions by J. S. Bach (which were published by A. Klughardt in 1897). At the beginning of the 19th century musical boxes almost completely replaced flute-playing and harp-playing clocks.

BIBLIOGRAPHY

G. Kinsky: 'Beethoven und die Flötenuhr', *Beethoven-Almanach*, ed. G. Bosse (Regensburg, 1927)
E. F. Schmid: 'Joseph Haydn und die Flötenuhr', *ZMw*, xiv (1931–2), 193
S. Harcourt-Smith: *A Catalogue of Various Clocks* (Peiping, 1933)
A. Chapuis: *Le Grand Frédéric et ses horlogers* (Lausanne, 1938)
A. Orel: 'Andante für eine Walze: sekundäre Quellen zu Mozarts KV. 616', *Acta Mozartiana*, iii/4 (1956), 3
A. Buchner: *Hudebni automaty* (Prague, 1959; Eng. trans., 1959)

ALEXANDR BUCHNER

**Musical comedy** [musical play, musical]. The chief form of popular musical theatre in the English-speaking world during the 20th century. Musical comedy, which developed from comic opera and burlesque in London during the 1890s, consists of a loose plot combining comic and romantic interest and a musical score of catchy songs, ensembles and dances. It reached its most durable musical form in the 1920s and 1930s in the works of Jerome Kern, George Gershwin, Richard Rodgers and other American songwriters. The term 'musical play' indicates a work with a more substantial plot and musical score, as in Leonard Bernstein's *West Side Story*. The term 'musical' has become current since World War II to cover the two forms, but 'musical comedy' is still conveniently used for the whole genre from the 1890s to the present day. There is no precise or internationally consistent distinction between musical comedy and OPERETTA, but the latter term usually indicates an older-style work with a romantic, Ruritanian story and a score using 19th-century European musical styles.

Further discussion of the styles used in musical comedy will be found in POPULAR MUSIC, §§I and II.

1. Nature and development. 2. Britain up to World War I. 3. Britain since World War I. 4. The USA up to World War II. 5. The USA since World War II.

1. NATURE AND DEVELOPMENT. The prime purpose of the musical comedy or musical play has always been to entertain audiences who look for lighthearted relief rather than for intellectual stimulation. Accordingly, what has usually been of greatest importance is a quota of good tunes to catch the audience's imagination, to be hummed on the way home, and to be recognized when played outside the theatre by dance orchestras, military bands, salon ensembles or on the radio.

The structure of the early British musical comedies was essentially that of comic opera, with a typical two-act score consisting of about 20 numbers including opening choruses for each act, an extended first-act finale, assorted songs and duets (often with a chorus refrain or danced repeat), concerted pieces and even snatches of recitative. Musical comedy gradually moved away from the comic opera pattern (as did continental operetta) as less care was given to the structure and development of a score and more to making individual numbers memorable. Initially this meant that catchy numbers submitted by other composers were interpolated into a score, often at the suggestion of star performers. By the very nature of the operation, it was these special 'additional numbers' that made the greatest impression on the public, and in due course the role of the specialist songwriter increased, soon equalling that of more traditionally trained musicians.

With the rise of a new generation of songwriters (particularly in the USA) during and after World War I, the extended finales, elaborate ensembles and detailed part-writing were dropped altogether, and during the 1920s hit numbers began to be driven home even more firmly than before by being reprised later in the show. The influence of American musical comedy after World War I also brought a significant change in song styles. Vocal writing had always been simple and frequently limited to a range of an octave, in deference to performers chosen more for their ability to put over a number than for their singing skill, and so it remained. But where Edwardian musical comedy composers relied on fluent melody with regular rhythms, often in waltz or march time, postwar American songwriters used syncopation and such dance rhythms as the one-step and foxtrot. In addition there was an important change in the style of lyrics: in early British musical comedies they were purely escapist, as in Lionel Monckton's 'Soldiers in the Park' (from *The Runaway Girl*, 1898); in American musical comedy of the 1920s and 1930s the subjects were more down-to-earth. At first the songs were just rhythmic tunes fitted with words, but songwriters gradually paid greater attention to a closer integration of verbal and musical phrases. In Jerome Kern's 'Who?' from *Sunny* (1925) the key word is regularly held for two whole bars, and in the songs of Rodgers and Hart the wit was more incisive, the verbal and musical patterns more original and varied. 'Blue Room' from *The Girl Friend* (1926) shows a sensitive interplay of words and music, with the repeated pivotal $c'$ helping to establish a rhyme on the last syllable but one of the line.

The change from composer to songwriter brought with it some technical problems. Whereas an Edwardian composer like Sidney Jones had been a skilled musician technically equal to constructing a full score, the specialist songwriters were often relatively untrained. Even if they had the ability to harmonize and orchestrate, the demand for new numbers for a constant stream of new shows was such that they did not have the time. They commonly submitted their scores to trained musicians for harmonic correction, and the orchestration was left to specialists, usually theatre conductors.

The dependence of songwriters on the assistance of specialists to harmonize, 'correct' and score their tunes was not necessarily new, or unique to musical comedy. Sullivan frequently left it to his conductor to compile overtures from themes in his comic operas. Gaston Serpette is known to have orchestrated some French operettas by other composers in the late 19th century, and Schoenberg performed similar services in Vienna in the early 20th century. Musical comedy differed from operetta precedents in the extent to which it became acceptable, even respectable, for composers to use this assistance. After World War I, songwriters no longer needed or acquired the technical skills of their comic opera predecessors. In England Noël Coward's creations were taken down and harmonized by his regular amanuensis Elsie April; in the USA Irving Berlin could play the piano only in the key of F♯, and used a special attachment to change key. By the 1930s the use of orchestrators was standard: before World War II they were often uncredited, but in postwar American musicals orchestrators like Robert Russell Bennett were named. So widely accepted did the use of such professionals become that even a classically trained musician like Leonard Bernstein used the assistance of Sid Ramin and Irwin Kostal for the orchestration of *West Side Story* (1957).

A conventional theatre orchestra of about 30 players accompanied early British musical comedy, while for the American-style works staged between the wars various ad hoc combinations were used. The pit orchestra for Gershwin's *Girl Crazy* (performed in New York, 1930) included the distinguished jazz musicians Benny Goodman, Glenn Miller, Red Nichols, Gene Krupa, Jack Teagarden and Jimmy Dorsey; in London in the 1930s the pit orchestra was often a regular dance band such as that of Debroy Somers or Carroll Gibbons, who provided their own orchestrations. After World War II big 'production numbers' were generally scored for the sound of an American show band, while in the more serious musical plays, where the aim was to make the music integral to the development of the plot, the techniques of film music, with a conventional range of orchestral instruments and effects, were used to depict mood, period or locale.

Since the earliest years of the genre there have been two principal traditions for musical comedy: the song-and-dance musical, derived largely from vaudeville and revue, linked the musical and choreographic numbers with a rather flimsy and contrived plot, often romantic; the 'musical play' sought a closer integration between the plot (which might have serious overtones) and the musical and spectacular elements of the show.

2. BRITAIN UP TO WORLD WAR I. The immediate ancestors of musical comedy on both sides of the Atlantic are the comic operas, burlesques and extravaganzas of the second half of the 19th century. The term 'musical comedy' was used in a general sense to describe certain British and American works in the 1870s and 1880s (see §4), but the credit for establishing musical comedy as a genre belongs to the London theatre manager George Edwardes. In October 1892, at the Prince of Wales Theatre, Edwardes produced a 'musical farce' *In Town*, composed by F. Osmond Carr, with a loose and vaguely topical plot, plentiful song-and-dance numbers, and featuring popular performers of the comic opera stage and a galaxy of female beauty. A year later at the same theatre Edwardes staged *A Gaiety Girl* with music by Sidney Jones, and for the first time a work was described simply as 'musical comedy'. A contemporary press report stressed the weakness of the plot but went on to describe *A Gaiety Girl* as 'one of the most curious examples of dramatic architecture that we have for some time seen. It is sometimes sentimental drama, sometimes comedy, sometimes almost light opera, and sometimes downright "variety show"; but it is always light, bright and enjoyable'. The formula was evidently popular with the public, and Edwardes began to adapt it for his other theatres.

At Edwardes's Gaiety Theatre the retirement of his burlesque stars brought about the demise of that pun-laden form; but in introducing the 'musical farce' *The Shop Girl* in November 1894 Edwardes took care to maintain continuity by stressing its 'variety show' aspect. With its sumptuous contemporary dresses, youthful cast, romantic plot and catchy tunes, *The Shop Girl* established the formula for the Gaiety musical comedy. Its score was by the Belgian Ivan Caryll, with additional numbers provided by Lionel Monckton; between 1894 and 1909 the pair collaborated on ten more musical comedies for the Gaiety, almost all of which ran for over a year. The emphasis on the chorus of 'Gaiety Girls' and on leading ladies such as Ellaline Terriss and later Gertie Millar was reflected in the many 'girl' titles such as *The Circus Girl* (1896) and *The Runaway Girl* (1898).

Meanwhile, at Daly's Theatre, Edwardes was developing a variant formula with a more consistent romantic plot, with comic relief restricted to secondary characters, and with a more substantial musical score, which was closer to traditional English light or comic opera. *An Artist's Model* (1895), with music by Sidney Jones, was followed by the same composer's *The Geisha* (1896), the latter running for two years. First announced as a 'comedy opera' (a common alternative to 'comic opera'), *The Geisha* finally bore the designation 'musical play', a description which continued to be used for works with a more consistent plot. At a time when French operettas and the comic operas of Gilbert and Sullivan had, like burlesque, lost much of their appeal, musical comedies at the Gaiety and musical plays at Daly's became the fashionable forms of popular musical theatre in London.

Edwardes's success soon encouraged other managers to copy his formula. Particularly successful works from other managements included *Florodora* (1899) with music by Leslie Stuart and *A Chinese Honeymoon* (1901) with music by Howard Talbot. Musical comedy spread round Britain and reached the Commonwealth and the USA. As early as 1894 an Edwardes company took *A Gaiety Girl* to New York and it was followed by a steady flow of later works. On the Continent many British musical comedies were staged in operetta theatres; around the turn of the century, for example, *The Runaway Girl* was at the Theater an der Wien and *Florodora* at the Bouffes Parisiens. The success of Jones's *The Geisha* surpassed even that of an earlier Japanese subject, *The Mikado*, and on German stages exceeded that of any current native work.

The style of Edwardian musical comedy represented a mixture of the lighter elements of the Savoy Operas of Gilbert and Sullivan with the topical comic songs of the music hall. At Daly's in particular the former constituent was more prominent, especially in the works of Sidney Jones, whose technical accomplishments enable him to bear comparison with Sullivan. Elsewhere the scores were often collaborations, with a theatre conductor such as Caryll or Talbot writing the choruses and concerted numbers and a songwriter such as Monckton or Rubens contributing the catchy solo songs for individual performers. In this way arose collaborations such as those between Caryll and Monckton, Talbot and Rubens, Jones and Rubens, and Monckton and Talbot, their scores often given a uniform finish by a professional orchestrator. It is worth noting that, whereas Caryll and Jones in particular provide a link with the earlier comic opera days, Monckton, Rubens and Stuart may be seen more as forerunners of theatre song stylists like Kern (who learnt his trade in London during this period), Gershwin, Porter and Coward.

The actual content of any musical comedy score was flexible, with new numbers frequently introduced to suit individual performers. These were often completely extraneous songs, many of them American vaudeville numbers. The musical standards of performers cannot always have been very high, for vocal compass was rarely very wide and part-writing was rudimentary. Generally there was no attempt at musical characterization nor any evocation of geographical setting; the latter ranged widely (Japan, China, Ceylon, Germany, the Netherlands, Denmark, the Balkans) but the musical style always remained distinctively English.

Edwardian musical comedy reached its zenith with *Miss Hook of Holland* by Paul A. Rubens (1907), *Our Miss Gibbs* by Caryll and Monckton (1909), *The Arcadians* by Monckton and Talbot (1909) and *The Quaker Girl* by Monckton (1910). Thereafter its appeal declined in favour of Viennese operetta and ragtime-inspired revue. Only in the special conditions of wartime did Edwardian-style musical comedy enjoy its last big successes with Rubens's *To-night's the Night* (1915) and particularly *The Maid of the Mountains* (1916) with a score by Harold Fraser-Simson and additional numbers by James W. Tate. The latter achieved a run of 1352 performances, a record for a musical play exceeded only by the 2238 performances of *Chu Chin Chow* (1916), a 'musical tale of the east' with music by Frederic Norton.

3. BRITAIN SINCE WORLD WAR I. Although ragtime and jazz were to have more impact on revue than on musical comedy, American composers and styles increasingly influenced the British musical stage. *To-night's the Night* had included two numbers by Jerome Kern, and the reversal of British and American dominance was symbolized by the importation of several works with scores by Ivan Caryll, by then settled in America. The romantic Ruritanian musical play was disappearing in favour of American song-and-dance musicals with their added emphasis on chorus dancing. But, for the present, London remained the musical comedy capital; Vincent Youmans's *No, No, Nanette* was successful in London before it was produced in New York, and many Americans wrote works specially for London, including Kern's *The Cabaret Girl* (1922), Gershwin's *Primrose* (1924), Rodgers and Hart's *Evergreen* (1930) and Cole Porter's *Nymph Errant* (1933).

Among British composers Noël Coward was exceptional in capturing some of the sophistication of American songwriting, although he often relied more on European influences, as in *Bitter Sweet* (1929) and *Operette* (1938). One of the most prolific British theatre composers between the wars was Vivian Ellis, who produced many light musical comedies for London, including *Mr Cinders* (with Richard Myers, 1929), *Jill Darling* (1934) and *Under Your Hat* (1938). In similar vein were several shows composed jointly by Jack Waller (1885–1957) and Joseph Tunbridge (1886–1961), including *For the Love of Mike* (1930), *Yes, Madam?* (1934) and *Please Teacher!* (1935). Another successful British composer of songs in the light, syncopated style of the time was Noël Gay, whose biggest musical comedy success was *Me and My Girl* (1937)

*1. Scene from Ivor Novello's musical comedy 'Glamorous Night' (1935) at the Theatre Royal, Drury Lane*

which included 'The Lambeth Walk' and ran for 1646 performances. Other musical plays followed the romantic Ruritanian style of continental operetta, for example *Balalaïka* (1936) with music by George Posford and Bernard Grun (1901–72), and above all such works of Ivor Novello as *Glamorous Night* (1935; see fig.1), *Careless Rapture* (1936) and *The Dancing Years* (1939).

British musicals continued to serve as a link between continental and American styles during World War II, among them *Old Chelsea* (1943), with music by two central European musicians, Richard Tauber and Grun, and *The Lisbon Story* (1943), a musical play by Harry Parr Davies which broke fresh ground with its up-to-date spy story and the death of the leading lady. In the decade after the war Vivian Ellis collaborated with A. P. Herbert on *Bless the Bride* (1947), successfully evoking the light opera style of half a century earlier, and Novello returned to Ruritanian subjects in *King's Rhapsody* (1949). Somewhat more modern were Davies's *Blue for a Boy* (1950), Coward's *Ace of Clubs* (1950) and Posford's *Zip Goes a Million* (1951). By 1950, however, American productions were increasingly taking over the London musical theatre; even the native success *Love from Judy* (1952) was composed by an American, Hugh Martin (*b* 1914). Yet the two most successful London musicals during the 1950s, both running for over 2000 performances, were low-budget productions which provided a sharp antidote to

American brashness. *The Boy Friend* (1953), with music by Sandy Wilson, was a nostalgic look at the 1920s musicals of Gershwin, Rodgers, Youmans and Coward, while *Salad Days* (1954), with music by Julian Slade (which beat the London long-running record of *Chu Chin Chow*), combined a simple old-fashioned story with equally simple tunes and a two-piano accompaniment.

The spirit of the times was more accurately captured by *Fings ain't wot they used t'be* (1959) with music by Lionel Bart; and this was followed by other successful works from the same composer, of which *Oliver!* (after Dickens, 1960) set another new long-running record for London with 2618 performances. Other successes of the 1960s included *Stop the World – I want to get off* (1961) by Leslie Bricusse (*b* 1931) and Anthony Newley (*b* 1931), *Pickwick* (after Dickens, 1963) with music by Cyril Ornadel, *Half a Sixpence* (after Wells, 1963) with music by David Heneker (*b* 1906), *Robert and Elizabeth* (based on the lives of Robert Browning and Elizabeth Barrett, 1964) with music by Ron Grainer (*b* 1922), *Charlie Girl* (1965) with music by John Taylor and Heneker, and *The Canterbury Tales* (after Chaucer, 1968) with music by Richard Hill and John Hawkins. As in New York, long runs, source material of proven appeal, hit songs for the media and star names became increasingly important, though the dominance by American works and performers meant that British writers and singers could no longer achieve fame or fortune within the confines of London. Few British musicals since World War I have gained extensive international popularity, and British writers have seldom captured the incisiveness of American songwriting. Many of the most successful British works in that time have not even reached New York, and of those that have, few have achieved long runs. Exceptions include *Oliver!*, *Stop the World – I want to get off* and *Half a Sixpence*, all well received in New York. Particularly noteworthy was the international success of the rock musical *Jesus Christ, Superstar* (1971), with lyrics by Tim Rice and music by Andrew Lloyd Webber (*b* 1948). The fact that it received its stage première in New York, however, demonstrated the current low standing of London musical theatre.

4. THE USA UP TO WORLD WAR II. The early history of American musical comedy was dominated by European works and styles. Besides the successful productions of British musical comedies by visiting British companies, many Edwardian shows were adapted for performance by American casts. There were also a number of European composers active in New York, among them Kerker, Luders, Victor Herbert, Ludwig Englander, Rudolf Friml and Sigmund Romberg. Friml's romantic musical plays *Rose-Marie* (with Herbert Stothart, 1924) and *The Vagabond King* (1925), and Romberg's *The Student Prince in Heidelberg* (1924), *The Desert Song* (1926) and *The New Moon* (1928) were among the most successful works of the American musical stage in the 1920s. However, with ragtime having already sown the seeds of a new style of popular music, these works came to be classed with European operetta and British musical comedy as representative of an old-fashioned culture alien to the spirit of a developing nation.

The works of George M. Cohan were the immediate forerunners of an essentially American musical comedy style. His earliest shows were little more than extensions of vaudeville routines, but *Little Johnny Jones* (1904) had all the main elements of American musical comedy. By contrast with the romanticized subjects, idealized characters and more extended writing of European and British works, this was a simple show with American characters and a story line linking dances and songs such as 'Give my regards to Broadway'. Cohan's popularity began to fade around 1914, and the native successes of the following years showed that no individual style of musical comedy had yet been firmly established. *Going Up* (1917) was a successful work by the ragtime composer Louis A. Hirsch (1887–1924), while *Irene* (1919), with a score by Harry Tierney, was still highly dependent on European escapism and musical style. However, it was also during these years that the acknowledged founding father of American musical comedy, Jerome Kern, was attracting attention with his first complete musical comedy scores.

Kern received his early training in London as a songwriter for British musical comedies. In the USA he provided extra numbers to be inserted into adaptations of European shows, such as 'How'd you like to spoon with me?' for Caryll's *The Earl and the Girl* (1905) and 'They didn't believe me' for Jones and Rubens's *The Girl from Utah* (1914). Then, with Guy Bolton and P. G. Wodehouse, Kern created a series of intimate shows at the 300-seat Princess Theatre using a small orchestra and chorus and functionally simple sets and costumes; the first show, *Nobody Home* (1915), an adaptation of Rubens's book for his British musical comedy *Mr. Popple* (*of Ippleton*) (1905), was a moderate success. Two ensuing productions, *Very Good, Eddie* (1916) and *Oh Boy!* (1917), were outstanding situation comedies with catchy songs that not only possessed witty lyrics and rhymes but also contributed to the action. Kern's subsequent works, including *Sally* (1920) and *Sunny* (1925), both written as vehicles for the singer Marilyn Miller, were more conventional in staging, but they contained songs such as 'Look for the silver lining' and 'Who?', which further established an American style of musical comedy songwriting.

By the mid-1920s other teams of writers were establishing themselves. Prominent among the composers was George Gershwin, who, after composing for several spectacular revues, wrote the score of *Lady, be Good!* (1924) with his brother Ira Gershwin as lyricist. Besides the title song and 'Fascinating rhythm', it featured the singing and dancing of Fred and Adele Astaire, who helped to make tap-dancing a popular feature of musical comedies of the 1920s. The Gershwins continued with *Tip Toes* (1925), *Oh Kay!* (1926) and *Funny Face* (1927); their *Girl Crazy* (1930) introduced two new stars in Ethel Merman, who sang 'I got rhythm', and Ginger Rogers with 'Embraceable you'. Another composer who made a significant (though brief) contribution was Vincent Youmans, whose *No, No, Nanette* (1924) and *Hit the Deck* (1927) contained songs such as 'Tea for two' which for many people epitomize the spirit of the decade. Other teams who turned to musical comedy from the world of revue included that of the lyricists B. G. DeSylva and Lew Brown and the composer Ray Henderson, whose *Good News!* (1927) featured the song 'The best things in life are free'. The following year the New York theatre was introduced to the highly sophisticated and often risqué songs of the lyricist and composer Cole Porter, whose *Paris* (1928) contained the song 'Let's do it'.

Despite successful individual songs and routines, these shows were often little more than vehicles for individual stars with contrived boy-meets-girl situations and happy endings, songs that for the most part were just catchy tunes with lyrics tagged on, and occasional spectacular 'production numbers'. A more creative approach characterized the works of the composer Richard Rodgers and the lyricist Lorenz Hart: such shows as *The Girl Friend* (1926) produced songs with a more inventive matching of lilting tunes and adult wit and sentiment (together with ingenious rhyme schemes), and other shows experimented with musical comedy conventions and subject matter. *Dearest Enemy* (1925) was concerned with American history and *Peggy-Ann* (1926) with dream psychology. In 1927 New York first saw *Show Boat*, with book and lyrics by Oscar Hammerstein II and music by Kern, a work that firmly pointed the way to the Broadway musical play of the 1940s. By contrast with the usual procedure of building a show around songs and performers, *Show Boat* boasted a cohesive story into which were integrated songs that contributed to the action by creating mood, revealing character or advancing the plot.

In *The Cat and the Fiddle* (1931) and *Music in the Air* (1932) Kern made further breaks with conventional precedents; like *Show Boat*, the former revolved around a 'show within a show', a procedure whereby the internal show, integral to the story, provided an excuse for

*2. Scene at the Ascot races from the film version (1961) of 'My Fair Lady', with lyrics by Alan Jay Lerner and music by Frederick Loewe*

*3. Scene from the first London production (1958) of 'West Side Story', with lyrics by Stephen Sondheim and music by Leonard Bernstein*

introducing a big set number. Thereafter Kern concentrated on films in Hollywood. Cole Porter continued the song-and-dance tradition of the 1920s musical with *Gay Divorce* (1932), in which Fred Astaire sang 'Night and day', and followed it with *Anything Goes* (1934) and others, while the Gershwins wrote works of increasing seriousness. Their *Strike Up the Band* (1930) was a satirical look at war and big business, and *Of Thee I Sing* (1931) ridiculed the American presidential system and became the first musical play to win a Pulitzer Prize for drama. In their final Broadway collaboration, *Porgy and Bess* (1935), the Gershwins raised musical comedy to the level of opera.

Other important American songwriters wrote musical comedies in the 1930s, including Irving Berlin, whose *Face the Music* (1932) was a lighthearted musical comedy set against a background of police and political corruption during the Depression, and Arthur Schwartz, who with his regular lyricist Howard Dietz (*b* 1896) wrote *Revenge with Music* (1934), an adaptation of Pedro de Alarcón's *El sombrero de tres picos*. Harold Arlen was the composer of *Hooray for What?* (1938), a warning about the dangers of the armament race presented within the conventional musical comedy framework, and Vernon Duke composed the commercially unsuccessful but artistically highly-regarded Negro folk musical *Cabin in the Sky* (1940).

Another composer with origins in European serious music was Kurt Weill, who began his American career with *Johnny Johnson* (1936), a bitter yet amusing anti-war piece. His *Knickerbocker Holiday* (1938) had a historical subject that drew analogies with Fascist oppression and a score that included Weill's most celebrated American number, 'September Song', while the subject of *Lady in the Dark* (1941) was psychoanalysis. Weill's works did a good deal to further the idea of the American musical play, with set numbers played down in the interests of integration of plot and music. At a time when the use of professional harmonizers, arrangers and orchestrators was standard practice, Weill was exceptional in completing his own scores.

Perhaps the most significant works of the late 1930s, however, in terms of both their song content and their development of the musical comedy formula, came from Rodgers and Hart. In *On your Toes* (1936) the subject was ballet, and the score featured a quasi-jazz ballet sequence 'Slaughter on Tenth Avenue' as well as such hit numbers as 'There's a small hotel'. *I'd Rather be Right* (1937) was another political satire, featuring George M. Cohan as a US president with a striking resemblance to Franklin D. Roosevelt, while *The Boys from Syracuse* (1938) was based on Shakespeare's *The Comedy of Errors*. *Pal Joey* (1940) featured a cast of thoroughly disreputable characters and a story of blackmail, illicit love affairs and various types of skulduggery.

5. THE USA SINCE WORLD WAR II. After his partnership with Hart ended in 1943, Rodgers collaborated with Oscar Hammerstein II. Their first work inaugurated a new era for the American musical. *Oklahoma!* (1943) was based on a proven play (Lynn Riggs's *Green Grow the Lilacs*), it had credible characters and dialogue, and its plot was unusually well constructed. Such musical comedy conventions as the opening chorus were set aside in the interests of the play's development, the melodies were written to fit the lyrics

rather than the reverse, and the songs and dances were of genuine musical substance. *Oklahoma!* began the American musical's period of greatest national and international acclaim, helped by gramophone records and film versions. It established a vogue for the more logically constructed musical play, with increasing importance attached not only to composers and lyricists but also to book authors, directors, choreographers and orchestrators. Directors such as George Abbott, Joshua Logan and Jerome Robbins (also a choreographer), writers such as Comden and Green, Herbert and Dorothy Fields, Howard Lindsay and Russell Crouse, Abe Burrows, and Moss Hart, choreographers such as Agnes De Mille, George Balanchin, Robert Alton and Patricia Birch and orchestrators such as Robert Russell Bennett, became essential contributors to American musical theatre.

Rodgers and Hammerstein continued to write a series of musicals of exceptional popularity, including *Carousel* (1945), with a somewhat unsavoury hero who (departing further from the conventions of musical comedy) was murdered, *Allegro* (1947), with an ancient-Greek-style chorus, *South Pacific* (1949), *The King and I* (1951), *Flower Drum Song* (1958) and *The Sound of Music* (1959). They were also responsible as producers for *Annie Get your Gun* (1946), a Wild West musical with music and lyrics by Irving Berlin including an unusually large number of hit songs. Berlin also wrote *Call me Madam* (1950), and Cole Porter, after some years in eclipse, achieved his greatest success with *Kiss me Kate* (1948), based on Shakespeare's *The Taming of the Shrew*, which developed the idea of the play within a play, the lyrics appropriating some of Shakespeare's lines.

Whereas the loose plots of the pre-World War II shows had almost automatically been set in America, the search for varied and interesting plots for the postwar musicals produced a more international element. *The King and I* was set in 19th-century Siam, Cole Porter's *Can-can* (1953) in Paris during the 1890s and *The Sound of Music* in Austria in 1938. *Fanny* (1954) with music by Harold Rome was set in modern Marseilles, while two fantasy musicals – both produced in 1947 – offered interesting comparisons. *Finian's Rainbow*, with a score by Burton Lane, featured Irishmen in a Southern American state, and *Brigadoon*, with lyrics by Alan Jay Lerner and music by Frederick Loewe, had American tourists in Scotland. After *Paint your Wagon* (1951), Lerner and Loewe created the extremely popular *My Fair Lady* (1956), from Shaw's *Pygmalion*. Whereas Duke and Weill consciously assimilated American life and musical styles during the 1930s, this most successful musical of the 1950s had a European setting and a score by a composer of European origin which was consciously European in style.

Perhaps the most significant works to develop the musical play in the 1950s were those by Leonard Bernstein and Frank Loesser. Bernstein's *On the Town* (1944) was followed by *Wonderful Town* (1953), *Candide* (after Voltaire, 1956) and *West Side Story* (1957, lyrics by Stephen Sondheim), a transformation of Shakespeare's *Romeo and Juliet* into a story of gang warfare in the West Side of New York. It represented a highpoint in the musical play's fusion of elements of American life with an originality of staging and mastery of varying musical forms. Loesser's *Guys and Dolls*

(1950) was another work with a well-integrated story and songs and dances in varying styles, while *The Most Happy Fella* (1956), of which he was sole author, had an extended score of almost operatic proportions. Loesser's *How to Succeed in Business without Really Trying* (1961), set in a large office, was another musical to win a Pulitzer Prize.

Two other works on characteristically American subjects were *The Pajama Game* (1954), about trade unionism, and *Damn Yankees* (1955), about a baseball championship, both from the successful but short-lived partnership of two composer-lyricists, Richard Adler and Jerry Ross (1926–55). Meanwhile the song-and-dance musical comedy tradition was kept alive most notably through several star-vehicle works with scores by Jule Styne. They included many successful show songs in the postwar American style: *High Button Shoes* (1947) with Phil Silvers was followed by *Gentlemen Prefer Blondes* (1949) which featured Carol Channing and the song 'Diamonds are a girl's best friend'; *Bells are Ringing* (1956) had Judy Holliday and 'The party's over'; in *Gypsy* (1959) it was Ethel Merman and 'Let me entertain you'; and *Funny Girl* (1964) gave fame to Barbra Streisand. Another show that owed a good deal to a big production number ('76 Trombones') was *The Music Man* (1956) with music by Meredith Willson (*b* 1902).

The new generation of composers during the 1960s worked in a changed financial system for the musical. In earlier days musical shows had made their profits largely from provincial tours, but the reduced opportunities for touring and increased costs of production made a long Broadway run ever more important. Although the musical theatre continued to prosper, the opportunity for composers to make a name with a string of successes had disappeared with the necessity for fewer new works and longer runs, the greater degree of collaboration involved in production of an integrated work and the longer gestation period required. Among composers of individual successes in the 1960s were Charles Strouse (*b* 1928), whose *Bye Bye Birdie* (1960) was a spoof of the rock and roll idol; Jerry Herman (*b* 1932), whose *Hello Dolly!* (1964) and *Mame* (1966) were both song-and-dance musical comedies adapted from successful plays and dependent on star leading ladies and successful title songs; and Cy Coleman (*b* 1929) whose *Sweet Charity* (1966) featured the big production number 'If my friends could see me now'. Two composer-lyricists, Bob Merrill (*b* 1921; *Carnival,* 1961) and Stephen Sondheim (*A Funny Thing Happened on the Way to the Forum,* 1962), were also associated with successes as lyricists to other composers.

Works with non-American subjects included the extremely popular *Fiddler on the Roof* (1964), based on a series of Yiddish short stories about Jews in Russia by Sholom Aleichem; Jerry Bock (*b* 1928) incorporated elements of Yiddish folksong into his score. *Man of La Mancha* (1965), with a score by Mitch Leigh (*b* 1928), was based on Cervantes's *Don Quixote,* and *Cabaret* (1966), set in Berlin between the wars, had a score by John Kander (*b* 1927) that successfully evoked setting and period. *The Fantasticks* (1960), with a score by Harvey Schmidt (*b* 1929), was produced on a modest budget in the Greenwich Village section of New York (far from the commercial theatre centre), and provides a model of the 'off-Broadway' musical; it had been performed over 7000 times by 1977. Another notable off-Broadway production was the rock musical *Hair* (1967), which began at Joseph Papp's innovatory Public Theatre; its score by Galt MacDermot (*b* 1928) incorporated electronic sounds.

In the early 1970s few new works appeared to counter the claims that the American musical was an anachronistic form. Some of the successful Broadway shows were revivals (Tierney's *Irene,* Kern's *Very Good, Eddie* and Youmans's *No, No, Nanette*), reworkings of earlier shows (Bernstein's *Candide*) or nostalgic pastiches such as *Over Here!* (1973) starring the Andrews Sisters. Among the most promising new works was Sondheim's play with music *A Little Night Music* (1973), which had long runs in New York and London; the serious nature of its play is matched in the music with reflective ballads, clever patter-songs, contrapuntal vocal ensembles and even a double quintet. A more recent success was *A Chorus Line* (1975), a vigorous exposé of Broadway back-stage, with music by Marvin Hamlisch.

Since the war there has been a period of maturity and diversification in the American musical; furthermore, the more substantial plots, the growing international acceptance of American popular music in general, and the increased use of non-American subjects have made the American musical more readily acceptable abroad. Of musical comedies written between the wars, *No, No, Nanette* was exceptional in being staged in translation in the operetta theatres of Europe (and elsewhere), but since World War II such shows as *Porgy and Bess, Kiss me Kate, The Pajama Game, My Fair Lady, West Side Story, Hello Dolly!, Fiddler on the Roof, Man of La Mancha* and *Hair* have been received enthusiastically around the world – notably in Walter Felsenstein's Komische Oper in East Berlin.

BIBLIOGRAPHY

D. Forbes-Winslow: *Daly's: the Biography of a Theatre* (London, 1944)

J. W. McSpadden: *Operas and Musical Comedies* (New York, 1946, rev. 2/1951)

E. Short: *Fifty Years of Vaudeville* (London, 1946)

B. Atkinson: *Broadway Scrapbook* (New York, 1947)

W. J. Macqueen-Pope: *Gaiety: Theatre of Enchantment* (London, 1949)

C. M. Smith: *Musical Comedy in America* (New York, 1950)

A. E. Wilson: *Edwardian Theatre* (London, 1951)

J. Burton: *The Blue Book of Broadway Musicals* (New York, 1952, 2/1969)

J. Mattfeld: *Variety Music Cavalcade: Musical-historical Review* (New York, 1952, rev. 3/1971)

P. G. Wodehouse and G. Bolton: *Bring on the Girls!* (New York, 1953)

W. J. Macqueen-Pope: *Nights of Gladness* (London, 1956)

D. Ewen: *Complete Book of the American Musical Theater* (New York, 1958, rev. 3/1976 as *New Complete Book of the American Musical Theater*)

B. A. L. Rust: *London Musical Shows on Records, 1894–1954* (London, 1958, rev. 2/1977)

D. C. Blum: *A Pictorial History of the American Theatre, 1860–1960* (Philadelphia, 1960)

S. Green: *The World of Musical Comedy* (New York, 1960, rev. 2/1974)

L. Moore, M. Sands and B. Sobel: 'Musical Comedy', *ES*

D. Ewen: *The Story of America's Musical Theater* (Philadelphia, 1961, rev. 2/1968)

R. Lewine and A. Simon: *Encyclopedia of Theatre Music* (New York, 1961)

A. Churchill: *The Great White Way* (New York, 1962)

G. Hughes: *Composers of Operetta* (London, 1962)

M. Lubbock and D. Ewen: *The Complete Book of Light Opera* (London, 1962)

H. H. Taubman: *The Making of the American Theatre* (New York, 1965, rev. 2/1967)

L. Engel: *The American Musical Theatre: a Consideration* (New York, 1967)

D. Ewen: *Composers for the American Musical Theatre* (New York, 1968)

A. Laufe: *Broadway's Great Musicals* (New York, 1969)

R. Mander and J. Mitchenson: *Musical Comedy: a Story in Pictures* (London, 1969)

B. Atkinson: *Broadway* (New York, 1970)

T. Vallance: *The American Musical* (New York, 1970)

S. Green: *Ring Bells! Sing Songs! Broadway Musicals from the 1930s* (New York, 1971)

L. Engel: *Words with Music* (New York, 1972)

A. Wilder: *American Popular Song: the Great Innovators, 1900–1950* (New York, 1972)

R. Lewine and A. Simon: *Songs of the American Theater* (New York, 1973)

M. Wilk: *They're Playing our Song: from Jerome Kern to Stephen Sondheim* (New York, 1973)

S. Green: *Encyclopaedia of the Musical* (New York, 1976)

E. Mordden: *Better Foot Forward: the History of American Musical Theater* (New York, 1976)

A. Jackson: *The Book of Musicals from Show Boat to A Chorus Line* (London, 1977, rev. 2/1979)

G. M. Bordman: *The American Musical Theatre: a Chronicle* (New York, 1978)

W. T. Stanley: *Broadway in the West End: an Index of Reviews of American Theatre in London, 1950–1975* (Westport, Conn., 1978)

ANDREW LAMB

**Musical Fund Society.** Charitable organization founded in Philadelphia in 1820, probably the oldest music society in the USA; *see* PHILADELPHIA, §7.

**Musical glasses** [armonica; harmonica; glass harmonica]. Bell-type instruments made of glass or other brittle material that if rubbed in a certain fashion will respond like the strings of a bowed instrument, though with less capacity for nuance. They may also be struck, with moderate force, for quasi-plucking and melodic tremolo effects as on a xylophone, a method that prevails in Asia.

While it is not always possible to distinguish various types of bell or gong-chime among descriptions of ancient instruments, musical glasses in the West were evidently derived from Asian antecedents, particularly in Persia from the 11th century onwards. The earliest known European allusion to musical glasses occurs in Gaffurius's *Theorica musicae* (Milan, 1492), which contains a woodcut showing the musical use of vessels in a 'Pythagorean experiment' (see fig.1). An inventory made in 1596 of the Ambras collection (now in the Kunsthistorisches Museum, Vienna) describes 'Ain Instrument von Glaswerck', three and a third octaves in compass (see Primisser, 1819). These and similar phenomena, such as 'making a cheerful wine-music', described by Harsdörffer, may well have grown up independently of oriental influences, which seem however to have been fairly strong. Diderot referred to the use of musical glasses in ancient Persia; such musical practices had doubtless become known to western Europe through reports of early travellers.

It was apparently during the early 18th century that the glasses came into serious musical use, having been previously regarded in Europe as only a quasi-scientific toy or novel amusement for social gatherings. The sound was produced by striking the sides of the glasses with a stick, which was sometimes muffled. In England the more refined technique of stroking the rims with the fingertips seems to have been first used in 1744 by an Irishman, Richard Pockrich, whose glasses were graded by size and tuned by the addition of water where required to raise their natural pitch. In a concert at the Haymarket Theatre, London (23 April 1746; reported in the *General Advertiser*), Gluck played a concerto on 26 glasses; he gave another in Copenhagen in 1749. In London, newspaper announcements testify to the growing popularity of musical glasses in the 1750s. One

*1. Musical glasses used in a 'Pythagorean experiment': woodcut from Gaffurius, 'Theorica musicae' (1492)*

particularly notable performer was Ann Ford, who married Philip Thicknesse, Gainsborough's friend and biographer. She published the first known method for the instrument in 1761 (unique copy now in *US-CA*) and gave explicit instructions for the use of the moistened pads of the fingers – with precise application of varying degrees of pressure – on the sides and rims of the glasses. Meanwhile, in spring 1761 Benjamin Franklin, then on a visit to England, heard Edmund Delaval, a fellow of Pembroke Hall, Cambridge, play on the glasses. Franklin was so impressed with the instrument that he decided to improve it. He took the bowls of the glasses and fitted them concentrically (the largest on the left) on a horizontal rod, which was actuated by a crank attached to a pedal (see fig.2). Careful gradation of size ensured a more consistently accurate scale than was possible with water tuning, while the close proximity of the rims (which would be well moistened before use) enabled the player to produce chords and runs with far greater ease than had been possible when each glass stood separate on its base. In a letter (see Sparks) to an Italian scientist named Beccaria, Franklin proposed to call his instrument the 'armonica', as a compliment to the musical Italian language. (The intrusive 'h', of German origin, has no original authority, and only serves to confuse this instrument with the modern harmonica proper, i.e. the mouth organ.) Sonneck has shown that the date of Franklin's invention, also popularly known as the 'glassy-chord', cannot be later than autumn 1761. The name of the earliest known maker of the armonica is given in

*2. Benjamin Franklin playing the musical glasses: portrait by Alan Foster (b 1892) (private collection)*

*3. Bruno Hoffmann playing the musical glasses, 1971*

Jackson's *Oxford Journal* (29 May 1762) as Charles James of Purpool Lane, near Gray's Inn, London, who stated that he manufactured expressly for Franklin from the beginning. In a slightly later development of the armonica, the rims of the glasses (at least for half the length of the spindle) were moistened automatically by means of a shallow trough of water through which they could pass as the spindle revolved. It is not known to whom the credit for this innovation belongs.

Franklin's invention achieved a certain popularity in America, but exercised far more influence in Europe, where it seems to have been introduced by Marianne Davies, a virtuoso who is thought to have received her own armonica from Franklin. She began to tour Europe in 1768, moving in the highest society. In 1773 she became known to the Mozart family, and caused Leopold Mozart to express an interest in owning an armonica himself. She also met Anton Mesmer, the originator of 'magnetism', who developed an enduring devotion to the instrument and used it to induce a receptive state in his hypnotic subjects. As on the glasses (i.e. the instrument in its original form), some of the finest armonica players were women, for instance Marianne Kirchgessner, the remarkable blind performer who became famous throughout Europe between 1790 and her death in 1808; Mozart composed his exquisite Quintet K617 for armonica, flute, oboe, viola and cello for her in 1791.

There is ample testimony that the practice of eliciting sounds from the revolving bowls of the glasses was apt to have a deranging effect on the nerves of the player. Sachs attributed this to 'the irritating permanence of extremely high partials and the continuous contact of the sensitive fingers with the vibrating bowls'. In some German towns the armonica was banned by the police.

Various improvements were attempted, aiming to eliminate the fingers as the means of contact: several types of keyboard were devised, by Hessel at St Petersburg (1782), by H. Klein at Pressburg, by Röllig and by D. J. Nicolai at Görlitz (all 1784), and by Francis Hopkinson in America in 1787; P. J. Frick, a virtuoso armonica player, had introduced pads as early as 1769; and in 1779 Mazzucchi applied a form of violin bow to the instrument. But direct hand contact could not be rivalled for natural tone quality, whatever the gain might otherwise be in facility and speed of execution.

The heyday of the armonica in Europe lasted until about 1830. Its distinctive tone of vibrant, piercing sweetness caught the imagination of various French and German Romantic writers; Goethe, for instance, wrote that in the sustained chords of this music he could detect 'Die Herzblut der Welt'. Even while the àrmonica was at the height of its popularity, the earlier form never quite lost its appeal; Ann Ford, for instance, was still playing the musical glasses in 1790. After the armonica had become a museum piece, the glasses lingered, at least in Britain, throughout the 19th century, and were often heard in music halls and sometimes at evangelical meetings. In the 20th century they have been revived by the German virtuoso Bruno Hoffmann (see fig.3), whose playing of the Mozart quintet has been recorded.

### BIBLIOGRAPHY

G. P. Harsdörffer: *Deliciae physico-mathematicae* (Nuremberg, 1677), 147

A. Ford: *Instructions for the Playing of the Musical Glasses* (London, 1761)

D. Diderot, ed.: 'Verres, musique des', *Encyclopédie*, xvii (Paris, 1765)

K. L. Röllig: *Ueber die Harmonika* (Berlin, 1787)

J. C. Muller: *Anleitung zum Selbstunterricht an der Harmonika* (Leipzig, 1788)

F. C. Bartl: *Nachrichten von der Harmonika* (Prague, 1796)
G. von Graubenfeld: *Aestetische Gedänken über Bartl's Tasten-harmonika* (Vienna, 1798)
F. Rochlitz: 'Ueber die vermeintliche Schädlichkeit des Har-monikaspiels', *AMZ*, i (1798), 97
A. Primisser: *Die Kaiserlich-Königliche Ambraser-Sammlung* (Vienna, 1819), 219
J. Sparks, ed.: *The Works of Benjamin Franklin*, vi (Boston, 1840), 245
C. F. Pohl: *Zur Geschichte der Glasharmonika* (Vienna, 1862; Eng. trans., 1862)
D. J. O'Donoghue: *An Irish Musical Genius: Richard Pockrich, the Inventor of the Musical Glasses* (Dublin, 1899)
O. G. T. Sonneck: 'Benjamin Franklin's Musical Side', *Suum cuique* (New York, 1916)
W. Lüthge: 'Die Glasharmonika, das Instrument der Wertherzeit', *Der Bär* (1925), 98
C. Sachs: *History of Musical Instruments* (New York, 1940), 404
A. H. King: 'The Musical Glasses and Glass Harmonica', *PRMA*, lxxii (1945–6), 97
B. Hoffmann: 'Glasharmonika und Glasharfe', *Musica*, iv (1950), 327
——: 'Glasharmonika', *MGG* [incl. list of music for the armonica]
A. H. King: 'Some Notes on the Armonica', *MMR*, lxxxvi (1956), 61
B. Matthews: 'The Davies Sisters, J. C. Bach and the Glass Har-monica', *ML*, lvi (1975), 150

ALEC HYATT KING

**Musical Institute.** New York choral society founded in 1844, merged in 1849 with the Sacred Music Society to form the New York Harmonic Society; *see* NEW YORK, §7.

**Musical Institute of London.** A society founded on 22 November 1851 'for the cultivation of the art and science of music ... for the holding of conversazioni, for the reading of papers upon musical subjects, and the performance of music in illustration'. Its membership ultimately comprised 180 Fellows, including a good representation of the most outstanding scholars, editors, executants, collectors and publishers of the time, 42 associates, and an honorary Fellow (Spohr). The first president was John Hullah, and the first vice-presidents were Sterndale Bennett, Charles Lucas and Ouseley. The institute maintained premises at 34 Sackville Street, Piccadilly, with a reading room and a fine library; the plan for a museum of musical instruments did not materialize. Although the institute was dissolved in summer 1853, and the promised volume of transactions was probably never printed, its work – however limited in achievement – anticipated that of the Musical Association by over 20 years. (Indeed, the early membership of the latter included some of the same names.) The institute may therefore be regarded as the earliest organization of its kind devoted to the scholarly study of music. (*See also* ROYAL MUSICAL ASSOCIATION.)

BIBLIOGRAPHY
A. H. King: 'The Musical Institute of London and its Successors', *MT*, cxvii (1976), 221

ALEC HYATT KING

**Musical play.** *See* MUSICAL COMEDY.

**Musical saw.** *See* SAW, MUSICAL.

**Musical Society of London.** Society active between 1858 and 1867 as a splinter group of the New Philharmonic Society; *see* LONDON, §VI, 4(ii).

**Musica poetica** (Lat.). Composition in close relationship with the sound, structure and meaning of a text; *see* FIGURES, DOCTRINE OF MUSICAL.

**Musica reservata (i).** Musical term found with various definitions and implications in sources from 1552 to 1625.

1. Original uses of the term. 2. Modern interpretations.

1. ORIGINAL USES OF THE TERM. Ever since the term 'musica reservata' was discovered at the end of the 19th century, its interpretation has been of major concern to musicologists. It is generally assumed to refer to a central aspect of the style or performance of music in the second half of the 16th century. Since the term appears relatively rarely, and explanations are sometimes obscure or altogether contradictory, great care is needed when looking for a clear-cut definition. The sources that mention the term are as follows:

| | |
|---|---|
| 1552 | A. P. Coclico: *Compendium musices* and *Consolationes piae* |
| 1555 | Two letters from Dr Seld to Duke Albrecht V of Bavaria |
| | N. Vicentino: *L'antica musica ridotta alla moderna prattica* |
| 1559 | J. Taisnier: *Astrologiae iudiciariae isagogica* |
| c1560 | Samuel Quickelberg's comments on Lassus's penitential psalms |
| c1559–71 | Treatise from the Synod of Besançon |
| 1582 | E. Hoffmann: *Doctrina de tonis* |
| 1610 | A. Brunelli: *Regole et dichiarationi de alcuni contrappunti doppii* |
| 1611 | R. Ballestra: *Sacrae symphoniae* |
| 1619 | Reference to Biagio Marini at the Neuburg court |
| 1625 | J. Thuringus: *Opusculum bipartitum*, a copy of Hoffmann |

Those sources that do more than mention the term, and include details that could help to achieve an understand-ing of it, suggest that four aspects of music may be involved: musical expression of the meaning of the text; rhythm; chromaticism or the use of chromatic notes; performing practice.

The best-known description of *musica reservata* is that given by Samuel Quickelberg, a humanist of Netherlands extraction living at the ducal court in Munich. He made the following comment (printed in Crevel, p.300) on Lassus's penitential psalms (com-posed c1560):

Thus the illustrious prince commissioned his most excellent musician, Orlandus Lassus, more distinguished and polished than any our century has produced, to compose these psalms, mostly for five voices. Lassus expressed these psalms so appropriately in accommodating, according to necessity, thoughts and words with lamenting and plaintive tones, in expressing the force of the individual affections, and in placing the object almost alive before the eyes, that one is at a loss to say whether the sweetness of the affections enhanced the lamenting tones more greatly, or whether the lamenting tones brought greater ornament to the sweetness of the affections. This genre of music they call *musica reser-vata*. In it, whether in other songs [*carminibus*], which are virtually innumerable, or in these, Orlandus has wonderfully demonstrated to posterity the outstanding quality of his genius.

Here *musica reservata* is presented as the expression of the affect and meaning of the words. However, the frequency and intensity of these features appear to be no greater in Lassus's penitential psalms than in the rest of his works. The value of Quickelberg's definition of *musica reservata* is reduced for two reasons: first, such musical word-painting and portrayal of affect were precisely the central characteristics of most music writ-ten around 1560; second, he omitted any mention of the specific compositional techniques used in this period. Moreover, it has been pointed out that Quickelberg's description has much in common with musical ideals which for some time had been widely held among humanists.

A short anonymous treatise in the acts of the Synod

of Besançon from 1559 to 1571 (see Bäumker) seems to imply that *musica reservata* was concerned with rhythm; part of the text suggests that a characteristic was the practice of 'fuggir la cadenza'. The pupil is given the following rule:

One should tend to make voices progressing in diverse and (as far as possible) contrary motion unite at last in perfect consonances and return to a certain mode. However, in a continuous rhythm you will avoid the cadence [*clausulam*] so that there might result what is called *musica reservata*.

*Musica reservata* was used in two sources to mean the use of the *genus chromaticum*. It first occurs in this sense in a treatise by Jean Taisnier, astrologer and mathematician. He had travelled widely, and was also active as a musician at the court of Charles V and other places. In his treatise, *Astrologiae iudiciariae isagogica* (Cologne, 1559), he listed alongside other classifications of music a category of music both 'ancient and modern – called new or "reservata" by some who have held that the application of one or the other *diesis* or *diaschisma* in a secular song or motet turns the diatonic genre into the chromatic'. The second source is Eucharius Hoffmann's *Doctrina de tonis* (Greifswald, 1582) which was copied word for word by Joachim Thuringus in his *Opusculum bipartitum* (Berlin, 1625). The relevant passage runs as follows: 'Today, however, it [the chromatic genre] is being restored to singing by certain people and by them this is called *musica reservata*, since it is almost entirely reserved for certain musical instruments and has not been accepted or practised in singing'. Although the source of Hoffmann's description of the chromatic genre was clearly Nicola Vicentino's *L'antica musica ridotta alla moderna prattica* (Rome, 1555/R1959), Hoffmann stands alone in his distinctly questionable etymological explanation of the word *reservata*. There has been much controversy about the correct interpretation of a phrase in this passage from Vicentino's *L'antica musica*:

... they understand that (as the ancient authors prove) the chromatic and enharmonic music was fittingly reserved [*reservata*] for another purpose than [was] the diatonic, for the latter was sung, for the benefit of ordinary ears, at public festivals in places for the community: the former was used for the benefit of trained ears at private entertainments of lords and princes, in praising great personages and heroes.

Some scholars (Jeppesen and Lowinsky) have suggested translations of the critical section in the following manner: 'the chromatic and enharmonic *musica reservata* deservedly had a different application from that of the diatonic'. However, well-founded grammatical objections have been raised to this translation by Schrade, Palisca and others.

Two statements in documents have been brought forward as evidence for the view that *musica reservata* means performance by soloists. In 1611 Reimundo Ballestra's *Sacrae symphoniae* appeared in Venice; in a document (see Federhofer, 1952) the pieces are described as *Musicalische Symphonien und Harmonien, ausser etlicher reservata*. As well as works written in the concertato style (*Symphonien*) and others in the *a cappella* and the polychoral style (*Harmonien*), there are some in which sections for soloists with organ continuo alternate with passages for the full ensemble. It is these last works which some musicologists identify as the 'etlicher reservata' group. The second piece of possible evidence for this interpretation is the title 'musico riservato', which was given in about 1619 to Biagio Marini, a violin player who was active at the Neuburg court. A

document (see Clark, 1957) runs as follows: 'Marino .... will be "musico riservato" and with his violin should not be in the midst of the concerti grandi where he cannot be heard well'. From this it would appear that Marini as a 'musico riservato' was a soloist, not one of the ripieno players. However, the words 'musico riservato' may mean no more than a special musician, that is, one who is 'reserved' for special purposes, and in any case it is unlikely that it has any connection with *musica reservata*.

On the other occasions when the words *musica reservata* appear in contemporary documents the texts explain no more than do those discussed above, either about the technical character of compositions or about their performance. According to some of these sources *musica reservata* was in the 1550s both a new and a controversial kind of music, clearly distinguishable from other contemporary repertories. A Dr Seld, an imperial vice-chancellor resident in Brussels, was commissioned to find musicians in the Netherlands for the chapel of Duke Albrecht V of Bavaria, his former sovereign. In a letter of 22 September 1555 (Crevel, p.295) Seld recommended to him Philippe de Monte, describing him as 'incontrovertibly the best composer in the whole land, especially in the new manner and "musica reservata"'. Even though the terms 'new manner' and 'musica reservata' can not necessarily be equated, Seld's remark on the replacement of Cornelius Canis by Nicolas Payen as imperial Kapellmeister seems to indicate the relative novelty of the fashion: '... and so "musica reservata" will become still more the fashion than heretofore'. Seld's statement 'that he [Canis] could not well reconcile himself to it' provides sufficient grounds for thinking that *musica reservata* was not greeted with universal approval. Novelty and controversy are also apparent in Taisnier's comments: in the passage quoted above, the terms *musica moderna*, *musica nova* and *musica reservata* are all used to mean the same thing. Taisnier's objection to this new music becomes clear in the course of his declarations. He sharply attacked the way the 'moderns' contravened the rules of traditional modality, their disregard for the intricacies of mensural theory, their use of certain figures (semiminim runs, canons and repetitions) to express the sense of the text and their new notational techniques. What Taisnier missed in the way of complex mensural practice in modern compositions and what he complained about in part-writing were precisely what Coclico praised in his *Compendium musices* of 1552 as the new musical ideals: the rejection of mensural subtleties and the rise of a text-setting style that laid greater emphasis on the content of the text. There are, however, difficulties about Coclico's declaration in the *Compendium musices* that he wrote his treatise 'in order to call to light again [*in lucem revocare*] this music which they ordinarily refer to as *reservata*'. This passage suggests a revival of an ancient musical practice which had fallen into disuse, but such an interpretation is highly suspect in view of the humanists' fondness for images of revival and restoration. The words *musica reservata* also appear on the title-page of Coclico's *Consolationes piae*, a collection of motets dating from 1552 (ed. in EDM, 1st ser., xlii, 1958). The pieces reveal in fact a tendency to extreme word-painting, and some of the motets, with their extensive use of accidentals, have links with the similar chromatic experiments in some of Josquin's work. Coclico claimed to have been taught by Josquin and to be handing on his compositional practice and thinking.

Seld also mentioned *musica reservata* in connection with a singer in a letter of 28 April 1555 (Crevel, p.294). He reported that a singer named Fux had an audition, after which Seld invited him 'and others of our group to my home. As we sang all sorts of "reservata" and music unknown to him, I consider that he is secure enough in all of them so that he, as all the others say, can compare favourably with any alto of the Imperial Chapel'.

An explanation of the word *riservato* to mean a complicated manner of composition seems to be suggested by a passage from Antonio Brunelli's *Regole et dichiarationi de alcuni contrappunti doppii* (Florence, 1610), in which he referred to 'regole piu riservate e recondite'. Although additional confirmation of this interpretation of *reservata* can be inferred if one includes among Ballestra's 'etlicher reservata' the elaborate, two-text homage motets in his *Sacrae symphoniae* (Federhofer, 1952, 1957) it is quite possible that, by associating *riservato* with *recondito*, Brunelli is using the word in a different, more general, sense. Whether it is possible to equate 'osservata', which occasionally occurs, with *reservata* remains questionable (see Sandberger, Crevel, Meier, *MGG* and Reese). It is perhaps misleading to mention here the words 'reservato ordine' found in Vincenzo Ruffo's *Opera nuova di musica intitolata armonia celeste* (Venice, 1556); they may mean no more than 'restrained orderliness' (see Osthoff, Einstein, Palisca).

2. MODERN INTERPRETATIONS. As they have gradually become known in musicological circles, these sources have given rise to various contradictory interpretations. Many musicologists, accepting Quickelberg's definition, have been of the opinion that *musica reservata* is music with heightened expressiveness, presenting the text to the listener with a greater intensity, although they have been unable to agree on any specific devices that might have been cultivated to this end (Sandberger). In this connection, the relationship between *musica reservata* and rhetorical figures has been examined in various ways (Brandes, Unger, Meier, Leuchtmann). Others understand *musica reservata* as music that is restrained in its expression (Bernet Kempers), as music that is characterized by its restraint in the use of figuration (Ursprung) or as a musical style with improvised ornamentation (Huber). It is also occasionally linked with what is known as mannerism in music (Palisca, Hucke). The most recent research (Meier, *MGG*, Federhofer, *RiemannL 12*) stresses sociological aspects which have already been considered occasionally by Lowinsky and others. These authors agree that *musica reservata* was reserved for a particular section of the public, whose members regarded themselves as connoisseurs. Lowinsky holds this view because of his interpretation of the passage from Vicentino discussed above, Federhofer (1952, 1957) does so on the grounds of the description of works in *reservata* style in Ballestra's publication, while Meier (*MGG*) stresses the musical education of that particular class.

Thus *musica reservata* does not appear to be characterized by a single musical technique, but rather by many factors, namely by 'the use of unusual means, by striking modulations, lavish use of chromaticism, enharmonic changes, *musica ficta*, affected artistic counter-

point or mannerist and eccentric traits' (Federhofer, *RiemannL 12*), or else by 'special refinements in its musical structure, such as the intensive portrayal of the imagery and affect of words, the use of chromaticism or else just complex contrapuntal structures' (Meier, *MGG*). This interpretation of the term *musica reservata* has the advantage that contemporary statements that may appear contradictory can be related to a single (if somewhat unspecific) concept of a relatively exaggerated means of expression. The question whether *musica reservata* is 'a term whose significance has been overestimated' (Federhofer, *RiemannL 12*) is one that can be answered satisfactorily only when a definitive interpretation of the term is reached. Recent research accepts that this is a problem which is still open-ended and which will perhaps never be finally resolved.

BIBLIOGRAPHY

*RiemannL 12*
A. P. Coclico: *Compendium musices* (Nuremberg, 1552/*R*1954)
W. Bäumker: 'Über den Kontrapunkt: eine kurze Anweisung aus dem XVI. Jahrhundert', *MMg*, x (1878), 63
A. Sandberger: *Beiträge zur Geschichte der bayerischen Hofkapelle unter Orlando di Lasso*, i, iii (Leipzig, 1894–5/*R*)
K. Huber: *Ivo de Vento* (Lindenberg in Allgäu, 1918)
K. P. Bernet Kempers: *Jacobus Clemens non Papa und seine Motetten* (Augsburg, 1928), 77
H. J. Moser: *Die mehrstimmige Vertonung des Evangeliums* (Leipzig, 1931/*R*1968)
O. Ursprung: *Die katholische Kirchenmusik* (Potsdam, 1931–3)
H. Brandes: *Studien zur musikalischen Figurenlehre im 16. Jahrhundert* (Berlin, 1935)
T. Kroyer: 'Von der Musica reservata des 16. Jahrhunderts', *Festschrift Heinrich Wölfflin* (Dresden, 1935), 127
L. Balmer: *Orlando di Lassos Motetten: eine stilgeschichtliche Studie* (Berne, 1938)
H. Osthoff: *Die Niederländer und das deutsche Lied (1400–1640)* (Berlin, 1938)
M. van Crevel: *Adrianus Petit Coclico* (The Hague, 1940)
H. Unger: *Die Beziehungen zwischen Musik und Rhetorik im 16. bis 18. Jahrhundert* (Würzburg, 1941)
H. Leichtentritt: 'Musica riservata', *BAMS* (1942), no.6, p.18 [abstract]
E. Lowinsky: *Secret Chromatic Art in the Netherlands Motet* (New York, 1946/*R*1967)
L. Schrade: Review of E. Lowinsky: *Secret Chromatic Art*, *JRBM*, i (1946), 165
A. Einstein: *The Italian Madrigal* (Princeton, 1949/*R*1971)
H. Federhofer: 'Eine neue Quelle der musica reservata', *AcM*, xxiv (1952), 32
E. R. Sholund: *The Compendium musices by Adrianus Petit Coclico* (diss., Harvard U., 1952)
G. Reese: *Music in the Renaissance* (New York, 1954, rev. 2/1959), 511ff
W. Boetticher: 'Neue Lasso-Funde', *Mf*, viii (1955), 385
K. Jeppesen: Review of G. Reese: *Music in the Renaissance* (New York, 1954), *MQ*, xli (1955), 390
B. Meier: 'Eine weitere Quelle der musica reservata', *Mf*, viii (1955), 83
——: 'The Musica Reservata of Adrianus Petit Coclico and its Relationship to Josquin', *MD*, x (1956), 67–105
W. Clark: 'A Contribution to Sources of Musica Reservata', *RBM*, xi (1957), 27
H. Federhofer: 'Monodie und Musica reservata', *DJbM*, ii (1957), 30
W. Boetticher: *Orlando di Lasso und seine Zeit* (Kassel and Basle, 1958)
B. Meier: 'Reservata-Probleme, ein Bericht', *AcM*, xxx (1958), 77
H. Leuchtmann: *Die musikalischen Wortausdeutungen in den Motetten des Magnum opus musicum von Orlando di Lasso* (Strasbourg and Baden-Baden, 1959)
C. V. Palisca: 'A Clarification of "Musica Reservata" in Jean Taisnier's "Astrologiae", 1559', *AcM*, xxxi (1959), 133
H. Hucke: 'Das Problem des Manierismus in der Musik', *Literaturwissenschaftliche Jahrbücher der Görres-Gesellschaft*, new ser., ii (Berlin, 1961)
B. Meier: 'Musica reservata', *MGG*
H. Federhofer: *Musikpflege und Musiker am Grazer Habsburgerhof der Erzherzöge Karl und Ferdinand von Innerösterreich (1564–1619)* (Mainz, 1967)

ALBERT DUNNING

**Musica Reservata (ii).** British early music ensemble. It was founded in the mid-1950s by the writer and broadcaster Michael Morrow, the conductor and harpsichordist John Beckett, the recorder player John Sothcott and the countertenor Grayston Burgess, and is directed by Morrow. It was called Musica Reservata because of Morrow's opinion that it was most unlikely that any performance of early music, however carefully researched, could be a true reproduction of the original sounds. His own preference was for a harsh-toned and stark approach, modelled to some extent on eastern European folksingers and embodied most strikingly in the singing of Jantina Noorman. Musica Reservata gave its first public concert at Fenton House, London, in 1960, but its greatest influence was perhaps not felt until 1967 on the occasion of its first South Bank concert: this was at a time when performers of early music were beginning to draw large audiences but favoured a more gentle and romantic sound, and the impact of Musica Reservata in the following years led to a widespread preference for a more direct and aggressive manner of performance. This resulted largely from Morrow's extreme approach – at least in the early stages – and over the next ten years Musica Reservata remained at the centre of substantial controversy while continuing its innovatory approach to historical authenticity. The group has made many records, among which particular mention should be made of two containing French and Italian dance music of the 16th century; they reflect Morrow's own intensive research into that repertory and the nature of its transmission.

DAVID FALLOWS

**Music Association of Ireland.** An organization founded in 1948 to promote the performing arts in Ireland through lectures and concerts, and to encourage composers and performers. It has arranged several festivals, including the Bach Bi-centenary Commemoration (1950) and the Handel Festival (1959), and organizes the Dublin Festival of 20th Century Music (from 1969). From 1957 it arranged début recitals for young Irish performers and from 1954 sponsored concert tours throughout the country. The association has formed several affiliated organizations: chamber music groups, the Composers' Group, the Irish Youth Orchestra and a programme of school concerts. The journal *Counterpoint* is published monthly.

**Musica Viva Australia.** Australian organization. Based in Sydney, with representatives in Melbourne, Adelaide, Brisbane, Hobart and Perth, it specializes in promoting chamber music tours by Australian performers at home and abroad, and tours by artists from overseas. It was first formed as Sydney Musica Viva by a group of musicians including Richard Goldner, who organized the first concert in December 1945 at the Sydney Conservatorium; a small nucleus of players was formed who, during the next five years, established Musica Viva's aim of presenting superior performances of chamber music. The members were Richard Goldner, Robert Pikler, Edward Cockman, Kathleen Tuohy, Maureen Jones and, later, Lois Simpson, Theo Salzman and William Krasnik. Regina Ridge was appointed manager in 1950 and did much to develop the organization during the 25 years she worked for it. By the 1970s regular subscribers to concert series in Sydney, Melbourne, Canberra, Adelaide and Brisbane numbered 8250. The Australia Council has provided funds for tours to be extended to more distant parts of the country, and (from 1969) to Europe, North America, south-east Asia and the Pacific. Australian music, including many works directly commissioned by Musica Viva, is an important feature of all tours. Australian tours are organized for leading ensembles from Europe, and special educational tours for young listeners.

ANN CARR-BOYD

**Music Corporation of America.** See MCA MUSIC.

**Music Critics Association** (MCA). An association of music critics in the USA and Canada who review for newspapers, magazines and broadcast media. An outgrowth of discussions between critics and conductors during an American Symphony Orchestra League symposium in 1952, the MCA was inaugurated by a three-year series of workshops funded by the Rockefeller Foundation and sponsored by the New York Music Critics Circle, the New York Philharmonic and the Symphony League. Since its incorporation in 1957 it has sponsored annual courses for younger professionals and senior critics in an effort to promote high standards of music criticism, encourage educational opportunities and increase general interest in music. The MCA Musicultura programme sends a critic to study each autumn at the Eduard van Beinum Foundation at Breukelen in the Netherlands. Its quarterly newsletter is published at the association's headquarters in Rockville, Maryland. Past presidents Miles Kastendieck and Irving Lowens as well as Paul Henry Lang and Virgil Thomson have been elected to life membership. The president from 1975 was Elliott W. Galkin.

RITA H. MEAD

**Music dealers and antiquarians.** The study of the retail distribution of music, both in and out of print, has been virtually untouched by the music historian. Few of the major studies on important music publishers have mentioned the methods used to distribute the publications to the public. This article will attempt to gather the little information published so far.

1. Music dealers and collectors to 1800. 2. Auction and trade catalogues to 1800. 3. Music dealers and antiquarians after 1800.

1. MUSIC DEALERS AND COLLECTORS TO 1800. From the beginning, music dealers were inseparably linked with the music publishers. The MS scriptorium and the early printing house each served as the distributor for the goods that it produced. By the early 16th century an international web united the book trade of Europe, so that many of the publisher-dealers in the major centres strove to have an international selection subject to the vagaries of politics and the difficulties of transport. Moreover, in order to sell the average impression of 1000 copies, it was necessary for the 16th-century printer to arrange for the export of his publications. The international book fairs held first at Lyons and Frankfurt and later at Leipzig provided opportunities for this. The fair catalogues, the earliest trade bibliographies, were doubtless as useful to dealers then as such catalogues are today. In addition many must have issued their own lists in an effort to distribute their publications. Unfortunately none survives earlier than the two catalogues of GIACOMO VINCENTI and GARDANE issued in Venice in 1591.

If the printer and the publisher were but rarely separable in the first century of printing, the publisher and the dealer never were. The 17th century maintained this tradition. The one important development was an ever-increasing stock of other publishers' issues available for sale at any publisher-dealer's shop. Foreign imprints on sale often reflected political alliances; for instance, the great book fairs of Leipzig and Frankfurt did not have as much influence on the music available in the London shop of JOHN WALSH (i) as the strong English trade ties with Amsterdam. Another method used for financing publication was to sell shares in the enterprise; it also served as an aid for the distribution of books to dealers, although usually on a more local level. Several publisher-dealers would subscribe and on publication receive a proportional number of copies. Music was also sold on subscription to private individuals. Usually this method of distribution also served as a means of financing the publication. The benefit to the subscriber lay in the lower price he paid. This marketing method was fairly common in England in the early 1700s and in Germany in the latter part of the 18th century.

Generally speaking, until the end of the 17th century dealers had only new publications for sale. Little antiquarian interest was expressed by music collectors. One should not, however, discount the role collectors played in influencing the direction of publishing and selling. Surely such avaricious acquisitors as FERNANDO COLÓN, JOHN IV of Portugal, Johann Heinrich Herwart and later SAMUEL PEPYS could not have amassed such rich collections without the assistance of music dealers. But they usually collected contemporary music. A few retrospective bibliographies were issued. *La libraria* (1550) by ANTONFRANCESCO DONI and Andrew Maunsell's *Seconde Parte of the Catalogue of English Printed Books* (1595) both contain lists of music publications. In 1592 Georg WILLER published a list of the music publications of the preceding 28 years. GEORG DRAUDIUS issued two similar catalogues in 1611 and 1625 in which, unfortunately, all of the titles have been translated into Latin, thus causing considerable confusion to successive generations of bibliographers. In 1653 John Playford (i) (*see* PLAYFORD) published *A Catalogue of All the Musik-bookes that have been Printed in England*, a list which contains most of the major publications of the first half of the century.

Evidence of interest in antiquarian music, that is, out-of-print or generally unavailable items, can be observed among collectors of the 18th century. Charles Burney, the intrepid traveller and music historian, often commented in the diary of his journey on the problems of seeking out the rare and unusual publication. Here too Burney admitted to a book collector's vice: 'I went into la rue St Jacques (a long street filled with book-sellers) not so much to purchase books as to collect catalogues to examine at my leisure'. He also remarked on the lack of specialized music dealers in towns that had no music publishers, a confirmation of the link between these two trades. But specialists in music were certainly not the only suppliers with whom Burney dealt for he found 'old authors on the subject of music . . . and as to the new, I met with many that I was unable to find elsewhere', in the shops of the general booksellers of Venice.

Burney also found in Italy another collector who shared his interest in the historical: Padre GIOVANNI BATTISTA MARTINI. Documents in Martini's library reveal many of the problems and practices of the collector in the 18th century. His friends were always on the lookout for items that might interest him, even those who lived in other countries, such as the German music historian and collector MARTIN GERBERT von Hornau. On one occasion Martini exchanged copies of his own publications for a collection of some now invaluable Petrucci prints.

2. AUCTION AND TRADE CATALOGUES TO 1800. Begun in its modern form in Holland in the late 16th century, the book auction had spread to France, England and northern Germany by the end of the 17th century. It is one of the earliest indications of a developing historical awareness of books. Auction sales devoted exclusively to musical items have always been very rare, but those that have occurred have often been important. One of the earliest was an anonymous sale held at Dewing's Coffee-House, London, on 17 December 1691. The catalogue (*GB-Lbm*) contains a listing of an astonishing anonymously assembled collection of music, much of it Italian and mostly dating from the early decades of the 17th century.

Auction sales were not popular with all dealers. Henry Playford had already abandoned this method by the time of the Dewing sale, for he remarked on the title-page of his 1690 catalogue that this collection was:

formerly designed to have been sold by way of Auction but the Reason of its being put off was, That several Gentlemen, Lovers of Musick living remote from London, having a desire for some of this Collection and could not be there, they are here set down in Order, with the Rates, being lower than could be afforded otherwise.

Playford's reasons are rather curious; many of his contemporaries dealt with the problem of out-of-town clients by providing bidding agents in the manner still employed in the sales room today. Furthermore, increased prices could only benefit the seller. Playford did not entirely divorce himself from the auction room. An advertisement for one of his new publications appeared at the end of the Dewing sale catalogue and his name was often among those dealers from whom copies of catalogues were available before an auction sale.

Burney's compatriot, collector and rival historian John Hawkins preserved several other catalogues; for example, in the *General History* he reproduced the contents of the catalogue for the Thomas Britton sale (6–8 December 1714) (the original catalogue was presumably destroyed in the fire in Hawkins's library in 1785). Britton was considered an extraordinary man by his contemporaries. According to Hawkins, he was a friend of John Bagford, the 17th-century amasser of an important collection of materials on the history of printing (now in *GB-Lbm*). Together they agreed to try to salvage any old MSS that they found. Furthermore, Britton's large music collection reflects very clearly the programmes of chamber music performed at the musical concerts that he sponsored.

The regular music trade also developed. In general it remained in the domain of the publisher-dealer, but he expanded his shop and improved his catalogues to assist the prospective buyer in making his selection. The justly famous Breitkopf catalogues underscore the vastness of some publisher-dealers' undertakings. The attention that Breitkopf paid to publication details and the large stock of scores available in MS copies indicate his intention to reach a larger clientèle than just the musically-inclined population of Leipzig. A foreign audience may also help to explain his introduction of thematic incipits into these lists.

Breitkopf was not alone in issuing catalogues. Most by other dealers are not thematic and many reflect an appeal to a local clientèle. The recently discovered Leuckart catalogues are excellent examples. They contain a repertory consisting mainly of printed chamber music published in northern and central Europe, in contrast to the Breitkopf lists, which often include imprints from more distant English and Parisian publishers.

The non-thematic catalogues, whether French, English or German, often closely resemble the Leipzig book fair catalogues of the time. The musical contents of these later Leipzig trade lists have not been adequately investigated, nor has the role of these fairs in the dissemination of music been studied. Clearly they are the direct forerunners of the important Whistling–Hofmeister series of trade publications which have served so well as an aid in the identification of 19th-century music publications.

In mid-18th-century London several firms of booksellers dealt largely in out-of-print materials. These dealers, Osborne, Payne, Wagstaff and Evans, issued numerous long catalogues notable mostly for the quantity of material amassed and for the uniformity and low level of the prices. Doubtless these sales enriched the music collections of Johann Pepusch, William Boyce and many others. The lack of specialized catalogues and the evenness of the prices indicates that no true antiquarian market yet existed.

3. MUSIC DEALERS AND ANTIQUARIANS AFTER 1800. Although the early music historians did have some effect on the public's interest in the music of the past, it was not until the Romantic revival that this movement received any real impetus. Then the developing interest led to the founding of music faculties, the production of bibliographies and the growth of historical research. The rise of a true music antiquarian business parallels the rise of the scientific study of music. It is hardly surprising that the period that witnessed the publication of the works of Forkel, Coussemaker, Eitner and Fétis should have required such specialized dealers. As the Romantic movement found its first roots in Germany, so too did the first specific music antiquarian lists come from there.

In the mid-19th century the character of auction and bookdealers' catalogues underwent a transformation. The descriptions of items to be sold became more historical, and much more attention was paid to detail. A number of German antiquarian dealers began to issue catalogues of music. Some of these were published in conjunction with the dispersal of specific collections. The catalogue of the music collection of A. Westrow compiled by the Berlin bookseller R. Friedländer & Sohn in 1853 is but one example. Other dealers were issuing catalogues of composite collections: for instance, L. E. Lanz of Weilberg issued a catalogue in 1854 entitled *Verzeichnis einer Sammlung antiquarischer Musikwerke.*

One of the most active firms was the house of List & Franke in Leipzig. Within a year of its founding in 1862 it offered for sale no fewer than five important German collections of music. The descriptive notes are often in French rather than German, highlighting the international attention paid to such sales. The use of French was not unique to these German catalogues; indeed, many of the 18th-century English catalogues had French or Latin prefaces. The same period witnessed the establishment of one of the most influential of all music antiquarians, LEO LIEPMANNSSOHN. His firm,

founded first in Paris in 1866, reopened in Berlin in 1873 and under his successor, Otto Haas, ultimately moved to London.

In the early 19th century American music dealers opened their shops with a stock consisting mainly of musical instruments and domestically published popular sheet music. As in Europe most music dealers were also publishers and some instead of relying on postal orders bravely opened retail outlets in several cities. The Board of Music Trade of the USA, founded in 1855, was an organization dedicated to protecting the interests of dealers and teachers. The board issued a catalogue of publications (1869), intended as a tool for the teacher and the amateur as well as the dealer. In the board's opinion European music publications were expensive in contrast to the American. It is indicative of the high cost and consequent lack of interest in European art music that it was excluded from the original American music copyright law of 1831.

Most American music antiquarian firms were founded after World War II when the rapid growth of music departments made university libraries a ready market for out-of-print materials. But the demand for some titles soon exhausted the supply and today a dealer who formerly sold exclusively antiquarian material will also stock reprints and current imprints; some have also entered the reprint field themselves. As in Europe not all dealers having rare music materials restrict their trade exclusively to music.

The music trade continues to flourish. Both publishing house outlets (some selling works issued by many publishers beside their own imprints) and unaffiliated music shops co-exist. European imprints to be sold in the USA are often assigned to one publisher or dealer who functions as the distributor; frequently confusion is caused by a rapid turnover in assignees. 'Popular' music is still generally sold in different shops from 'art' music.

BIBLIOGRAPHY

*BurneyH*; *HawkinsH*

A. Göhler: *Verzeichnis der in den Frankfurter und Leipziger Messkatalogen der Jahre 1564 bis 1759 angezeigten Musikalien* (Leipzig, 1902/R1965)

A. Rosenthal: 'The Music Antiquarian', *FAM*, ii (1953), 80

R. Schaal: 'Musikverlag und Musikalienhandel', *MGG*

Å. Davidsson: *Bibliographie zur Geschichte des Musikdrucks* (Uppsala, 1965)

B. S. Brook: 'Preface', *The Breitkopf Thematic Catalogue, 1762–1787* (New York, 1966)

J. LaRue: 'Ten Rediscovered Sale-catalogues: Leuckart's Supplements, Breslau 1787–1792', *Musik und Verlag: Karl Vötterle zum 65. Geburtstag* (Kassel, 1968), 424

D. Epstein: 'Preface', *Complete Catalogue of Sheet Music and Musical Works published by the Board of Music Trade of the United States of America, 1870* (New York, 1973) [facs. edn.]

LENORE CORAL

**Music drama.** By the description 'A Musical Drama' Handel's *Hercules* (1745) was distinguished from, on the one hand, an opera and, on the other, 'An Oratorio, or Sacred Drama'. In 19th-century and current usage, the meanings attached to the term 'music drama' derive from the ideas formulated in Wagner's *Oper und Drama*; it is applied to his operas and to others in which the musical, verbal and scenic elements cohere to serve one dramatic end. In a letter of 1869, Verdi distinguished between a mere opera of the old sort and the *dramma musicale* that he believed his *La forza del destino* to be. English usage often hyphenates the words, music-drama, to stress the *Gesamtkunstwerk* conception that was Wagner's – and, for that matter, Verdi's –

intention. Current theatrical practice tends to destroy this unity and to perform music dramas with the original music and words but freshly invented scenic elements.

In the 17th century, *dramma musicale* was one of the terms used to describe a play written for musical setting, for example G. A. Cicognini's texts for Cavalli's *Giasone* and Cesti's *Orontea* (both 1649) and Francesco Sbarra's for Cavalli's *Alessandro vincitor di se stesso* (1650). In this sense it means much the same as *dramma per musica*, *opera musicale*, *favola dramatica musicale* and other such terms.

*See also* DRAMMA PER MUSICA and OPERA.

ANDREW PORTER

**Music Educators National Conference.** An organization of music teachers in the USA with members engaged in teaching at all educational levels. Founded in 1907 as a group of music supervisors, it adopted its present name in 1940 and became affiliated with the National Education Association in 1956. The federation of MENC consists of state associations divided regionally, one auxiliary (the Music Industry Council) and six national organizations representing band and choral directors, string, wind and percussion instructors, and band and orchestra associations. Its programme includes conferences, commissions and projects to further music education. It sponsors the Contemporary Music Project and the Historical Research Center, publishes a wide range of books, pamphlets, films and other material about music education and produces the *Journal of Research in Music Education* and its official monthly magazine, the *Music Educators Journal*.

RITA H. MEAD

**Musicescu, Gavriil** (*b* Ismail, 1 April 1847; *d* Iaşi, 20 Dec 1903). Romanian composer, teacher and choirmaster. He began his musical instruction at the Theological Seminary of Huşi, and in the first years of the new Iaşi Conservatory he attended its viola, singing and theory classes. Having made his mark as choirmaster in Ismail, he received a bursary to study in St Petersburg at the conservatory and at the Imperial Chapel as a pupil of Huncke and Bachmetyev. On returning home he became professor and later director of the Iaşi Conservatory and conductor of the Metropolitan Choir, where he had sung as a student. He developed a new repertory of European religious and secular pieces and of his own music, and by travelling through the Romanian provinces he developed a tradition of choral culture. This was a difficult struggle, as he had to contend with critics who opposed the performance of folk music in public concerts. Other academic critics objected to his modal harmony, inspired as it was by folksong; and the church authorities criticized his palaeography of the old psalms and monodies and their harmonization. Musicescu may be regarded as a founder of the Romanian choral school, and an early practitioner of modal harmony. His compositions make use of the variety of folksong – lyrical melodies, ballads, patriotic songs and romances – for chorus or solo voices. He also wrote two liturgies, some works for choir and cherubic hymns, which, as major choral forms, aroused new interest in music in Romania.

WORKS

Edition: *Opere alese de Gavriil Musicescu* [Selected works of Musicescu], ed. G. Breazul (Bucharest, 1958) [B]

SACRED CHORAL

Liturgical hymns: Imnele dumnezeescei liturghii, op.1 (Bucharest, 1869); Imnurile dumnezeescei liturghii, op.3 (Bucharest, 1870); Imnele Sfintei Liturghii, chorus, pf (Leipzig, 1900)

Psalms: Rînduiala vecerniei de sîmbătă seara [Saturday evening vespers], 1883 (Leipzig, c1883); Anastasimatariu (Leipzig, 1884–9); Rînduiala Sfintei Liturghii [Service of the Holy Liturgy] (Leipzig, 1885); 17 Axioane intrebuinţate în serviciul Bisericii Ortodoxe [17 axions for the Orthodox service] (Leipzig, 1897); Catavasiile serbătorilor de peste an prelucrate [The Katabasiōas of the feasts of the year] (Leipzig, 1899)

Înnoeşte-te noule Ierusalime [Renew thyself, Jerusalem], 1887 (Leipzig, 1900), B; 4 sacred concertos, 2 in B; 3 cherubic hymns, 2 in B; other works in B

SECULAR VOCAL

12 melodii naţionale, arr. chorus, pf, op.31, 1889 (Leipzig, 1889); 25 Cînturi [25 songs], unison vv, 1898 (Leipzig, 1898)

For 1v, pf: Rîndunica [The swallow], B; O, dacă n-ai nimic a-mi spune [Oh, if you have nothing to say to me], B; Hora de la Plevna [Plevna's round dance] (V. Alecsandri), op.17 (Vienna, n.d.), B; În grădină [In the garden] (I. Neniţescu), with vn, op.26, 1884, in *Arta* (1884), no.2

INSTRUMENTAL

7 melodii, arr. pf, 1884, B; songs and romances, vn, pf

WRITINGS

*Curs practic de muzică vocală* (Leipzig, 1877)

'Cîteva curinte despre muzică' [Some words on music], *Lyra română* (1880), nos.5–8

'5000 lei noi' [5000 new lei], *Arta* (1884), no.11

'Naţionalism sau cîntecele populare' [Nationalism and popular song], *Arta* (1885), no.7

*O întîmpinare la raportul Comisiunii Sfintul Sinod* [Discussion of the report of the Commission of the Holy Synod] (Iaşi, 1900)

'Cîntările bisericeşti şi muzică poporană' [Church songs and popular music], *Conferinţă sosţinută la Societate universitară din Iaşi* (1901) [in B]

BIBLIOGRAPHY

A. Atanasiu: *Gavriil Musicescu* (Iaşi, 1904)

S. Stoicescu: *Lui Gavriil Musicescu: omagiu* [Homage to Musicescu] (Bucharest, 1934)

G. Breazul: *Gavriil Musicescu* (Bucharest, 1962)

Z. Vancea: *Creaţia muzicala româneasca, sec.XIX–XX* (Bucharest, 1968)

V. Cosma: 'Musicescu, Gavriil', *Muzicieni români: lexicon* (Bucharest, 1970)

ROMEO GHIRCOIAŞIU

**Music Group of London.** English chamber ensemble. It was founded formally in 1966 and grew out of the cello and piano duo of Eileen Croxford and David Parkhouse, and of the Boise Trio, which consisted of those two and the violinist Hugh Bean and which had already been giving concerts for ten years. Other members have included Jack Brymer and Keith Puddy, clarinets; Alan Civil, horn; Roger Birnstingl, bassoon; Frances Mason, Roger Garland, Perry Hart and Andrew Watkinson, violins; Christopher Wellington, viola; and Keith Marjoram, double bass. Between 1976 and 1978 Frances Mason and Ralph Holmes served successively as leader.

The ensemble, which is the resident chamber music group at the RCM, London, has toured throughout Europe and in the USA, Canada, the Middle and Far East, and Australia. Its regular membership, which is sometimes augmented for larger works, allows it an unusually flexible repertory, reflected in the group's many gramophone recordings; these include the standard trios and sonatas by Beethoven, Mendelssohn and others, and a number of 20th-century British pieces for different ensembles. The group's performances have been praised as much for their range of style as for technical polish.

BERNARD JACOBSON

**Music hall.** A type of entertainment place which flourished in Britain during the late 19th century and early 20th, where drinking might be enjoyed together with musical acts and in particular popular songs. By exten-

*1. Weston's Music Hall, Holborn, c1860: unsigned lithograph*

sion the term is applied to the form of entertainment itself, and 'music hall' was the main source of popular song of its time. Similar forms of entertainment flourished in other countries, for example in the USA as 'vaudeville'. The term 'music hall' entered the French language to describe such night spots as the Moulin Rouge and Casino de Paris which flourished from the end of the 19th century as successors to the *cafés-chantants* and *cafés-concerts* (*see* CABARET).

1. Rise and decline of British music hall. 2. The music of the halls.

1. RISE AND DECLINE OF BRITISH MUSIC HALL. Convivial drinking and music-making have long been associated, and the ancestry of music hall may be found in the catch clubs which flourished widely in England from the mid-17th century and particularly during the late 18th. During the 1830s and 1840s, London taverns with a music licence (such as the Mogul, Drury Lane) offered the working classes an evening of communal singing while they drank; in more Bohemian, all-male song and supper rooms (such as the Coal Hole, Strand, or Evans's late Joy's, Covent Garden) supper could be enjoyed to the accompaniment of singing which ranged as the evening progressed from popular ballads to coarse songs. The proprietor acted as host and chairman, and the clientèle joined in the entertainment. In the expanding suburbs there were also taverns offering entertainment for the local working class, such as the Eagle or Grecian Rooms in the City Road immortalized in the song *Pop goes the Weasel*:

> Up and down the City Road,
> In and out the Eagle,
> That's the way the money goes. . . .

With the taverns there grew up character singers who travelled from one to another giving their acts several times in an evening, and the public taste for the entertainment they provided steadily developed. The term 'music hall' seems to have been first used in 1848 when the Surrey Music Hall opened in Westminster Bridge Road; and the following year Charles Morton (1819–1904), later dubbed 'father of the halls', took over the Canterbury Arms in Lambeth and built a hall large enough for 700 people with a platform at one end. In 1851 the Mogul Saloon itself was refurbished as the Middlesex Music Hall, and other halls opened, such as Wilton's in Whitechapel, Collins's in Islington and Weston's in Holborn (see fig.1). In 1856 Morton further enlarged the Canterbury, and in 1861 he opened perhaps the most celebrated of music halls, the Oxford, in Oxford Street.

The entertainment at these halls contained a wide variety of musical items, including ballads and other popular songs, 'nigger minstrel' acts, selections from popular operas and also comic turns and monologues (dramatic performances were forbidden under the terms of the licence). The audience sat at tables in the body of the hall, where they were served with drinks, and the chairman presided at his own table below or to one side of the platform. The audience participated by joining in the choruses of the songs and in verbal interplay with the chairman, himself often a retired performer. Entertainment increasingly gained precedence over convivial drinking, and it is significant that the Alhambra in Leicester Square was converted in 1860 to have a proscenium arch. In 1878 the London County Council sought to exercise control over the music halls by requiring a proscenium arch and a fire curtain dividing the stage from the body of the hall and by confining liquor to bars at the back of the hall. Some famous haunts were unable to meet the requirements and were closed, for example Wilton's (though the building survives) and the Winchester (formerly the Surrey).

The music-hall business continued to expand as syndicates built large 'variety' theatres throughout the country. In London several theatres were converted to music hall and others were built for the purpose. The intimate nature of the old halls was disappearing and the chairman was often replaced by an indicator board identifying each act by a number. Performers required stronger projection of their voices, and better material, but remained able to travel up and down the country giving their acts.

The turn of the century represents the 'golden age' of music hall as a source of popular song. By World War I it was on the decline. The respectability bestowed by the first Royal Command Performance at the Palace Theatre in 1912 and the bestowing of knighthoods for services to music hall were fundamental incongruities; but neither these nor the final banning of drinks from the back of the auditorium in 1914 were more than incidental factors. Music hall in its expanded form had run its course as a popular type of entertainment in the face of such new attractions as the cinema, revue and (later) radio. Variety theatres were converted to other uses or demolished. The successors to the original music halls are found in working-men's clubs and night-club cabaret; and relics of the style of entertainment appear in Christmas pantomimes with their chorus singing, 'principal boys' and 'pantomime dames'.

2. THE MUSIC OF THE HALLS. In the later variety shows, the forms of entertainment included such non-musical acts as conjurors or acrobats. But the basic entertainment remained musical, as it had been in the older genuine music halls. The opening programme of the Oxford included among its artists Santley and Mme Parepa, and it was at the Canterbury Hall that excerpts from Gounod's *Faust* were first heard in England. Later the Alhambra and the Empire were famous for their ballets; they helped to revive a taste for the genre, then out of favour. At the Hippodrome in 1911 and 1912 Leoncavallo and Mascagni conducted their most famous operas, and Leoncavallo wrote his *Zingari* for that theatre, as did Leo Fall *The Eternal Waltz* and Imre Kálmán *The Blue House*.

Popular songs, however, were the most typical product of the music halls. Dispersed throughout the country not only by the variety theatres themselves but also as sheet music, they mostly dealt with topical or everyday subjects. Neither verses nor music sought artistic merit; an appealing verbal phrase allied to a catchy musical one was quite enough, in the hands of a good artist, to make a successful music-hall song. The performer mattered as much as the song, and both were more important to devotees than the identity of the author of words or music. The music was at times obviously derivative, the words banal, the humour unsubtle. It did not matter, for example, that when Wilkie Bard sang 'I want to sing in op'ra' the tune quoted was not operatic but Arditi's *Il bacio*. The singers, though each having his individuality, often fell into such categories as the Cockney or coster singer, the blackened-faced 'coon', or the male impersonator.

The early music-hall stars, up to about 1880, were mostly male. Without the benefit of gramophone records and the ubiquity that the variety theatres were to give music-hall artists their names remain little known: W. G. Ross, Sam Cowell (1820–64), Harry Clifton (1824–72), Sam Collins (1827–65), Arthur Lloyd (1839–1904), Vance (1838–88), George Leybourne (1842–84), Harry Rickards (1842–1911), Harry Liston (1843–1929) and G. H. Macdermott (1845–1933). A few of their songs have remained familiar, for example Clifton's *Polly Perkins of Paddington Green*, Leybourne's *Champagne Charlie* and *The Flying Trapeze* and Macdermott's *We don't want to fight, but by Jingo if we do* (which added the word 'jingoism' to the English language). When the music hall entered its 'variety' phase women gained more prominence, and Nelly Power (1853–87) first sang *The boy I love is up in the gallery*, later taken over by the greatest of all music-hall singers, Marie Lloyd (1870–1922). Dan Leno (1860–1904; see fig.2), who was also a celebrated pantomime dame, Little Tich (1868–1928; he gave the word 'tich' to the language) and George Robey (1869–1954) were stars of music hall who were primarily comedians, but the following, among the most celebrated of music-hall singers, may be cited along with the songs they sang: Charles Coborn (1852–1945: *Two lovely black eyes*; *The man who broke the bank at Monte Carlo*), Eugene Stratton (1861–1918: *Little Dolly Daydream*; *The Lily of Laguna*), Albert Chevalier (1861–1923: *My old Dutch*; *Wot cher!* or *Knocked 'em in the Old Kent Road*), Gus Elen (1863–1940: *It's a great big shame*), Vesta Tilley (1864–1952: *Jolly good luck to the girl who loves a soldier*), Harry Champion (1866–1942: *Any old iron*; *Boiled beef and carrots*),

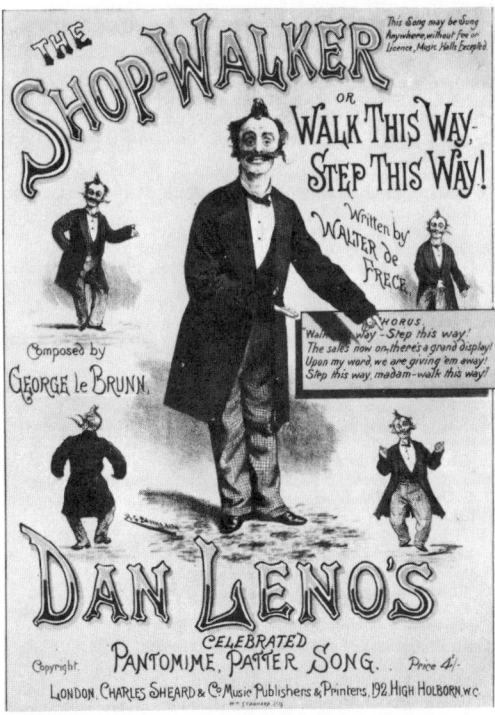

2. Cover of the song 'The Shop-walker' by George Le Brunn, as sung by Dan Leno

Harry Lauder (1870–1950: *I love a lassie*; *Roamin' in the gloamin'*; *Keep right on to the end of the road*), Vesta Victoria (1874–1951: *Daddy wouldn't buy me a bow-wow*; *Waiting at the church*), Florrie Forde (1874–1941: *Down at the old Bull and Bush*; *She's a lassie from Lancashire*), Hetty King (1883–1972: *All the nice girls love a sailor*), Will Fyffe (1885–1947: *I belong to Glasgow*) and Ella Shields (1879–1952: *Burlington Bertie from Bow*, itself a parody of another song, *Burlington Bertie*).

By comparison with the singers, the writers of the songs are rarely fêted, although some singers, such as Albert Chevalier and Harry Lauder, wrote their own material. However, certain composers may be singled out from the mass for the quality or in some cases the quantity of their contributions: Alfred Lee (*Champagne Charlie*; *The Flying Trapeze*), George Le Brunn (*Oh, Mister Porter*; *It's a great big shame*), Leslie Stuart (*Soldiers of the Queen*; *The Lily of Laguna*; *Little Dolly Daydream*), Fred Gilbert (*The man who broke the bank at Monte Carlo*; *At Trinity Church*), Felix McGlennon (*Comrades*; *Sons of the Sea*), Fred W. Leigh (*Put on your tat-ta little girlie*; many in collaboration with others), Charles Collins (*Any old iron*; *Boiled beef and carrots*), C. W. Murphy (*Has anybody here seen Kelly?*; *Hold your hand out, naughty boy*), Harry von Tilzer (*Down at the old Bull and Bush*; *Riding on top of the car*), Herman E. Darewski (*I used to sigh for the silvery moon*; *In the twi-twi-twilight*) and James W. Tate (*A broken doll*; *I was a good little girl*).

BIBLIOGRAPHY
GENERAL

C. D. Stuart and A. J. Park: *The Variety Stage* (London, 1895)
G. F. Scotson-Clark and G. Gamble: *The 'Halls'* (London, 1899)
H. C. Newton: *Idols of the Halls* (London, 1928)
A. Haddon: *The Story of the Music Hall* (London, 1935)
M. W. Disher: *Winkles and Champagne* (London, 1938)
D. Gilbert: *American Vaudeville: its Life and Times* (New York, 1940)
S. T. Felstead: *Stars who made the Halls* (London, 1946)
H. Scott: *The Early Doors* (London, 1946)
W. Macqueen-Pope: *The Melodies Linger on* (London, 1951)
C. Pulling: *They were Singing* (London, 1952)
J. Feschotte: *Histoire du Music-hall* (Paris, 1965)
R. Mander and J. Mitchenson: *British Music Hall* (London, 1965, 2/1974)
C. MacInnes: *Sweet Saturday Night* (London, 1967, 2/1969)
D. Howard: *London Theatres and Music Halls, 1850–1950* (London, 1970)
G. J. Mellor: *The Northern Music Hall* (London, 1970)
P. Davison: *Songs of the British Music Hall* (New York, 1971)
P. Gammond: *Your own, your very own* (London, 1971) [with detailed bibliography]
P. Honri: *Working the Halls* (Farnborough, 1973)
D. F. Cheshire: *Music Hall in Britain* (Newton Abbot, 1974)
R. Busby: *British Music Hall* (London, 1976)

BIOGRAPHICAL

J. Nash: *Stories and Anecdotes* (London, n.d.)
——: *The Merriest Man Alive* (London, n.d.)
A. Chevalier and B. Daly: *Albert Chevalier: a Record by himself* (London, 1896)
A. Chevalier: *Before I forget* (London, 1901)
D. Leno: *Hys Booke: a Volume of Frivolities* (London, 1901)
T. E. Dunville: *The Autobiography of an Eccentric Comedian* (London, n.d.)
W. H. Morton and H. C. Newton: *Sixty Years' Stage Service* (London, 1905)
J. H. Wood: *Dan Leno* (London, 1905)
G. Robey: *My Life up to Now* (London, 1908)
H. Relph ['Little Tich']: *A Book of Travels (and Wanderings)* (London, 1911)
G. H. Chirgwin: *Life and Reminiscences* (London, 1912)
H. Lauder: *At Home and on Tour* (London, 1912)
——: *A Minstrel in France* (London, 1918)
R. G. Knowles: *A Modern Columbus* (London, 1918)
H. Lauder: *Roamin' in the Gloamin'* (London, 1927)
A. Roberts: *Fifty Years of Spoof* (London, 1927)
H. Randall: *Harry Randall, Old Time Comedian* (London, n.d.)

C. Coborn: *The Man who Broke the Bank* (London, n.d.)
G. Robey: *Looking back on Life* (London, 1933)
M. W. Disher, ed.: *The Cowells in America* (London, 1934)
Lady de Frece [V. Tilley]: *Recollections of Vesta Tilley* (London, 1934)
N. Jacob: *Our Marie* (London, 1936)
W. Macqueen-Pope: *Marie Lloyd, Queen of the Music-halls* (London, n.d.)
A. E. Wilson: *Prime Minister of Mirth* (London, 1956)
P. Cotes: *George Robey* (London, 1972)
D. Farson: *Marie Lloyd and the Music Hall* (London, 1972)

ANDREW LAMB

**Musici, I.** Italian chamber ensemble. It was formed in March 1952 by 12 students at the Accademia di S Cecilia, Rome, and consists of six violins, two violas, two cellos, double bass and harpsichord, playing without a conductor. Toscanini described the ensemble as 'Twelve capable, twelve very capable lads of eighteen, a perfect chamber orchestra. I applauded them'. Concert tours in Europe, and later to the USA, Canada, central and South America, South Africa, Australia and Japan soon made I Musici known outside Italy, and numerous recordings, which have won many prizes and awards, gained the group an even wider audience. Although their reputation was originally founded on music by Italian Baroque composers like Albinoni, Bononcini, Corelli, Locatelli, Scarlatti, Torelli and, in particular, Vivaldi, I Musici also play works by Bach, Handel and Mozart, as well as music by 20th-century composers, including Barber, Bartók, Britten, Hindemith, Martin and Respighi. Until 1968 the leader of the ensemble was the violinist Felix Ayo, who also frequently appeared as soloist. The group was then led by Salvatore Accardo and Pina Carmirelli, and in the mid-1970s the players included Anna Maria Cotogni, Arnaldo Apoltoli, Walter Galozzi, Luciano Vicari and Italo Colandrea (violins), Carmen Franco and Paolo Centurione (violas), Francesco Strano and Mario Centurione (cellos), Lucio Buccarella (double bass) and Maria Teresa Garatti (harpsichord and piano). Despite changes of personnel, I Musici's style has remained remarkably constant, with emphasis on brilliance, firmness of attack and a high level of discipline.

ELIZABETH FORBES

**Musicians' Benevolent Fund.** An English institution founded by Victor Beigel in 1921 as the Gervase Elwes Memorial Fund. Elgar was president until his death. It was originally intended to assist young musicians, but soon after its foundation it was renamed the Musicians' Benevolent Fund and became a registered charity, aiming to provide financial relief for musicians in need. It maintains a convalescent home and residential homes for the elderly. An annual concert in aid of the fund is given in London on St Cecilia's Day.

**Musicians' International Mutual Aid Fund.** Fund created in 1974 by the INTERNATIONAL MUSIC COUNCIL.

**Musicians' Union.** British trade union. It was formed in 1921 by the amalgamation of the National Orchestral Union of Professional Musicians (founded 1891 and mainly London-based) and the Amalgamated Musicians' Union (founded 1893 in Manchester and Birmingham and later active throughout the provinces). The union's main aim is the improvement of the social and economic status of musicians, and with over 36,000 members in the mid-1970s it is the second largest musicians' organization in the world (after the American Federation of Musicians). It operates through negotiated agreements with such bodies as broadcasting organizations, opera houses, the British Phonographic Industry, the Association of British Orchestras and the Film Production Association. Its policy is to achieve the highest degree of organization in all areas of the musical profession, defined as 'those engaged in performing, teaching or writing music'. Instrumentalists constitute the greater part of its membership, singers usually being members of the British Actors' Equity Association, with which the union developed close links in the 1970s. It participates in several other organizations in order to achieve its objectives, such as the Trades Union Congress, the Federation of Theatre Unions and the Federation of Broadcasting Unions. It was a founder-member of the National Music Council, and its experience in all areas of British musical life has made it an advisory body to organizations concerned with the musical profession, broadcasting etc.

BIBLIOGRAPHY
H. G. Farmer: 'Musicians' Union', Grove 5

**Music Library Association.** An association founded in 1931 to promote the establishment, growth and use of music libraries in the USA. It encourages the collection of music and music literature, furthers studies in music bibliography and works for increased efficiency in library service and administration. It has developed a standard code for descriptive cataloguing of printed music and recordings and has initiated specialized education for music librarians. The official MLA journal *Notes* (begun in 1943) contains reviews of books, music and records; other publications include *A Checklist of Thematic Catalogues*, *Manual of Music Librarianship*, and a series of valuable indexes to composers' works.

RITA H. MEAD

**Musico** (It.: 'musician'). The medieval distinction between a self-trained amateur musician and a professionally trained 'musicus' was carried over into the original usage of the Italian word 'musico'. In this sense it is found as late as 1781 in G. B. Martini's *Storia della musica*, but in the common parlance of the 17th and 18th centuries its meaning changed a good deal. First it was applied to any professional musician, especially one associated with secular music; then to a musician associated with the opera; to an operatic singer; to an operatic singer of mediocre talent; and finally to a castrato usually with derogatory implications. Pier Francesco Tosi, who was himself a castrato, referred to singers in his *Opinioni de' cantori antichi, e moderni* (1723) by such respectful terms as 'cantore', 'soprano', 'maestro', and even 'professore'; when he used 'musico', which he did rarely, he implied a mediocre singer.

OWEN JANDER

**Music of the spheres.** A Pythagorean doctrine postulating harmonious relationships among the planets governed by their proportionate speeds of revolution and by their fixed distance from the earth. Belief in a universe ordered by the same numerical proportions that produce musical harmonies is hinted at in surviving fragments of pre-Socratic Greek philosophers such as Anaximander and Parmenides. The Greeks attributed ideas about a harmonious universe to the 'Chaldeans' or Babylonians, from whom Jewish beliefs about an orderly cosmos hymning the praises of its Creator (expressed in the *Psalms*, the visions of Isaiah and Ezekiel,

and the Talmudic treatise *Yoma*) may also have been derived (for further details *see* MESOPOTAMIA, §10). The relationships of Indian and Chinese cosmologies to those of the ancient Near East have not been determined.

Pythagoras and his followers developed a series of analogies between musical consonances – derived from proportionate lengths of a stretched string – and natural phenomena. In Plato's *Timaeus* the creation of the World-Soul, a model for the physical universe, is accomplished through the use of Pythagorean proportions; duple and triple geometric series are filled in with arithmetic and harmonic means, as a result of which one can see 'the whole heaven to be a scale and a number' (Aristotle, *Metaphysics*). The musical scale thus produced is that of Pythagorean tuning, and the World-Soul is created through the use of a kind of celestial monochord.

As described in the *Timaeus* the cosmic scale is not actual music but the foundation for the Greek science of harmonics. In the myth of Er (*Republic*, p.617b, ll.4–7) Plato described the universe as a set of concentric rings (planets) on the surface of each of which a Siren sits singing; together they form a harmonious sound, after Plato's time interpreted literally as the music of the spheres – audible to but unnoticed by mortals who hear it from birth (*see* PLATO, §2).

The influence of these two Platonic myths was great and long-lasting despite Aristotle's rejection of a sonorous universe in favour of his own silent, frictionless spheres (*De caelo* ii, 9; *see* ARISTOTLE, §2). In neo-Platonic commentaries, particularly those on Cicero's *Somnium Scipionis* (itself derived from the myth of Er), the planetary harmony of the Sirens was conflated with the Timaeus scale. Aristides Quintilianus extended cosmic harmony to include the sublunary elements (fire, air, water and earth), the seasons, the tides, the growth of plants, and – as a microcosmic mirror of the universe – man's growth and behaviour. Ptolemy in his *Harmonics* distinguished between cosmic and psychic harmony; these categories became, in the Latin of Boethius, *musica mundana* and *humana*, to which was added the music played and sung by men (*musica instrumentalis*). The place of music in the medieval Quadrivium is a result of the central importance of neo-Pythagorean thought in late antiquity.

Jewish belief in angelic habitation of the universe, coloured by Gnostic angelology and given canonic standing in the 6th-century Dionysian hierarchies of angels (*see* JEWISH MUSIC, §I, 13), led to a belief in *musica celestis*, the angelic music seen in countless medieval and Renaissance paintings and combined with *musica mundana* in the blazing vision of light and sound of Dante's *Paradiso*.

Pythagorean ideas about cosmic harmony continued to be elaborated by neo-Platonists from Carolingian times until the end of the Renaissance. These ideas strongly influenced astronomers and astrologers, physicians, architects, humanist scholars and poets. There were occasional musical representations of planetary harmony; an example is the tableau *L'armonia delle sfere* designed for the Florentine *intermedi* of 1589 (*see* PLATO, §9–10).

Perhaps the last creative statement of the idea of the music of the spheres was made by Kepler (*Harmonices mundi*, 1619); but cosmic imagery of Pythagorean cast has persisted in the work of later philosophers (Leibniz,

Schopenhauer), astronomers (J. E. Bode) and polymaths (Mersenne, Kircher). There are 20th-century writers such as Hans Kayser who might be called neo-Pythagoreans, and 20th-century musicians such as Hindemith for whom the music of the spheres has remained a vital if metaphorical concept (*see* PLATO, §11).

BIBLIOGRAPHY

A. Boeckh: 'Über die Bildung der Weltseele im Timaeos des Platon', *Gesammelte kleine Schriften*, iii (Leipzig, 1866), 109–80
A. von Thimus: *Die harmonikale Symbolik des Altertums* (Cologne, 1868)
C. von Jan: 'Die Harmonie der Sphären', *Philologus*, lii (1893), 13
E. Frank: *Plato und die sogenannten Pythagoreer* (Halle, 1923)
J. Handschin: 'Ein mittelalterlicher Beitrag zur Lehre von der Sphärenharmonie', *ZMw*, ix (1926–7), 193
F. Cornford: *Plato's Cosmology* (New York, 1937)
L. Spitzer: 'Classical and Christian Ideas of World Harmony', *Traditio*, ii (1944), 409–64; iii (1945), 307–64
J. Handschin: 'The Timaeus Scale', *MD*, iv (1950), 3–42
J. Hutton: 'Some English Poems in Praise of Music', *English Miscellany*, ii, ed. M. Praz (Rome, 1951), 1–63
R. Brumbaugh: *Plato's Mathematical Imagination* (Bloomington, Ind., 1954)
J. Haar: *Musica mundana: Variations on a Pythagorean Theme* (diss., Harvard U., 1961)
R. Hammerstein: *Die Musik der Engel: Untersuchungen zur Musikanschauung des Mittelalters* (Berne and Munich, 1962)
D. Walker: 'Kepler's Celestial Music', *Journal of the Warburg and Courtauld Institutes*, xxx (1967), 228
K. Meyer-Baer: *Music of the Spheres and the Dance of Death* (Princeton, 1970)
J. Haar: 'Pythagorean Harmony of the Universe', *Dictionary of the History of Ideas* (New York, 1973), iv, 38f

JAMES HAAR

**Musicology** (Fr. *musicologie*; Ger. *Musikwissenschaft*, *Musikforschung*; It. *musicologia*).

I. Nature of musicology. II. Disciplines of musicology. III. National traditions of musicology.

### I. Nature of musicology

1. Definitions. 2. Musicology as scholarly method. 3. Musicology as an area of knowledge. 4. Historical and systematic musicology.

1. DEFINITIONS. The term 'musicology' has been defined in many different ways, almost all of them reflecting one of two fundamentally different viewpoints: they are formulated in terms of either the methods of musicologists or the subject matter of the study. The two might be thought mutually complementary, one defining the discipline, the other the phenomena to be investigated. However, they represent a difference of philosophical standpoint, one seeing it as an activity in which people engage, the other as an area of knowledge that exists regardless of that activity.

The approach through method places emphasis on musicology as a form of scholarship characterized by the procedures of research, drawing attention to their precision and rigour. A simple definition in these terms would be: 'the scholarly study of music'. Many musicologists would in fact prefer to describe their work as 'musical scholarship' (the latter word laying emphasis on the attainment of learning by the individual scholar) rather than use a term whose meanings have become clouded and confused through careless usage.

The approach through the subject matter, on the other hand, in specifying the area often draws attention to that which musicology has disregarded or undervalued. Thus a committee of the AMS in 1955 defined it as 'a field of knowledge having as its object the investigation of the art of music as a physical, psychological, aesthetic, and cultural phenomenon' (*JAMS*, viii, 153). The last of these four attributes in particular gives the definition

considerable breadth, although music, and music as an 'art', remains firmly at the centre of the investigation.

Yet a third view, which neither of these definitions fully implies, has claimed the attention of musicologists in recent years. This is the belief that the advanced study of music should be centred not on music but on Man, the musician, acting within a social and cultural environment. This shift from music to Man, from product (which tends to imply fixity, 'composition') to producer or participant, carries with it a shift of method. The traditional apparatus of historical inquiry is not designed to cope with the new elements that come into play as music merges into a continuum of activities such as ritual, dance and language, all governed by social forces: various contributing disciplines are now involved, among them anthropology, ethnology, linguistics, economics and sociology, which place the study within the discipline of the social sciences. This type of inquiry, which is associated with ethnomusicology, is particularly appropriate where little or no historical information is available and no body of music theory exists. Causality must be traced not through events in time but through social forces which are present. For this reason ethnomusicological inquiry has been directed towards non-European music. Where, as with China and India, historical information and a body of music theory do exist, it has been possible to engage also in such traditionally historical studies as those of notation, theoretical interpretation, archives and performing practice. Ethnomusicologists feel that their discipline does not need to be justified as a branch of musicology; rather they would identify it with the main trunk. Harrison (1963) has expressed it in the following terms: 'It is the function of all musicology to be in fact ethnomusicology; that is, to take its range of research to include material that is termed "sociological" ' (*see also* ETHNOMUSICOLOGY).

2. MUSICOLOGY AS SCHOLARLY METHOD. To describe musicology as a 'method' is to imply that it proceeds according to logical principles; to call that method 'scholarly' is to imply that its processes are applied on a well-informed basis and operated on the soundest available criteria. In the broadest sense it implies that musicology is 'scientific'. 'Science' in current vocabulary is an extremely elastic term: there is no word in the English language that conveys the breadth of meaning suggested by the German 'Wissenschaft'. Both it and the Latin term 'scientia' basically mean 'knowledge', but 'Wissenschaft' can be applied with equal relevance to the body of knowledge encompassing natural and cultural phenomena.

Until the second half of the 19th century the study of music was regarded not as an independent discipline but as that part of general knowledge which gave theoretical handling to specifically musical questions. It was Chrysander who in 1863 contended that musicology should be treated as a science in its own right, on a level equal to that of other scientific disciplines. The quantitative methods of natural science had of course been brought to bear on music as a physical phenomenon by the ancient Greeks: the Pythagoreans studied number as the prime condition of musical sound, and numerical relationships as the underlying laws of harmony in music, in man and in the spheres. This study continued throughout the Middle Ages as part of *ars musica*, itself part of the Quadrivium along with arithmetic, geometry and astronomy. Much later, in the 18th century, during the years spanned by the careers of Joseph Sauveur (1653–1716), Leonhard Euler (1707–83) and Ernst Chladni (1756–1827), attention was given to studies in acoustics and the physics of sound. These three men, significantly, were scientists by training: Sauveur and Euler mathematicians, and Chladni a physicist. Similarly in the 19th century many musical scholars were influenced by Hermann von Helmholtz (1821–94), an anatomist and physiologist, and Friedrich Carl Stumpf (1848–1936), both of whom worked on the psychology of hearing and sought to give tangible explanations to many aesthetic matters that had been considered intangible. Their work played an important part in a general trend towards determinism – a belief that all musical phenomena and experiences have attributable causes.

It was during this latter period that the term 'Musikwissenschaft' came into use. It appeared as early as 1827, in the title of a work by the German education-ist Johann Bernhard Logier, and became established in the early 1860s; its acceptance was reflected in the title of the journal *Vierteljahrsschrift für Musikwissenschaft* founded in 1885, and that of the term 'Musikforschung' in the name of the Gesellschaft für Musikforschung instituted by Commer and Eitner in 1868. The phrase 'musikalische Wissenschaft' had been in use since the 18th century, and 'Tonwissenschaft' since the second half of the 18th century. 'Musikologie' was used for a subdivision in 1885 roughly equivalent to 'ethno-musicology' (see §4 below).

However, scholars in the historical and critical fields of musicology have been more attracted by the spirit than by the techniques of the natural sciences. When a musicologist speaks of scientific method, he usually has in mind the methods of the so-called cultural sciences: history, sociology, anthropology and philosophy. These disciplines share a common respect for the use of critical standards in the treatment of evidence, for the employment of objective criteria in the evaluation of the sources, and for the responsibility of the scholar to bring his findings to a community of informed specialists.

Such principles of investigation, now taken for granted, have not always been observed. They are, in fact, of fairly recent origin, born in Western thought as part of that intellectual current known as the Enlightenment, the period in European history when most of the patterns of modern humanistic scholarship began to take shape. Cultural historians may differ as to the precise time span, but most will agree in placing the beginnings of the Enlightenment towards the end of the 17th century when the philosophical innovations of Descartes had made their impact on European thought, and when the methods of empiricism had replaced an uncritical reliance on the authority of the Church or myth. This was the time when the Benedictine scholars of the Congregation of St Maur in Paris, led by Jean Mabillon (1632–1707) and Bernard de Montfaucon (1655–1741), established the principles of Latin and Greek palaeography and diplomatic. It was an age of rationalism and scepticism, personified most vividly in the figure of Voltaire and in the work of the *philosophes* which culminated in the great French *Encyclopédie*. From this period dates the establishment of some of the major learned societies and academies of science and letters, notably those in Great Britain and France, the Royal Society (1662, but dating informally back to

1645), the Académie Francaise (1635) and the Académie des Inscriptions (1663).

Musicology, insofar as it reflects the cultural aims of 17th- and 18th-century society, is circumscribed by strict spatial and temporal boundaries. It would be incorrect to speak of musicology in the context of ancient, medieval, or Renaissance ideas. The term is not a label that can be affixed to any form of musical learning regardless of time or place. On the contrary, it can be understood only as a manifestation of west European thought during the past 250 years or more. Man's musical experience has, undeniably, been accompanied in every age and society by a body of esoteric knowledge. Musicology, however, is a phenomenon of the modern world, and was until recently more or less confined to the Western and European dimensions of that world. Its geographical confines have been responsible for the shape the discipline has taken in the 20th century, and also accounts for some of the criticism to which it has been subjected in recent years.

3. MUSICOLOGY AS AN AREA OF KNOWLEDGE. The effort to determine the scope of musicology as a special province or aggregate of fields has prompted much discussion. The issues have revolved around classification: how are the various areas of study to be distributed, or ordered along a scale of significance? What one age regards as important may be given a lesser position by the next. Attempts to define the scope of musical scholarship lead almost inevitably towards an arrangement in which certain areas are taken to represent the core while others occupy auxiliary positions. Since the early 19th century historical studies have occupied the centre ground, but each age brings its own scale of values to bear on the general pattern, and this leads to a constantly changing disposition of emphasis. For example, a typical 18th-century framework designed to contain the whole of musical learning was fashioned by Nicolas Etienne Framery in 1770. Framery's 'Tableau de la musique et de ses branches' (see illustration) is a hierarchical scheme encompassing the entire discipline of music, which is subdivided at first level into three branches: acoustic, practical and historical. Acoustics is then subdivided three times, and represents the quantitative sciences and metaphysics; musical history is similarly subdivided to include the study of music and of musicians, native and foreign, of the past and present. Musical practice is broken down into two parallel divisions, 'Composition' and 'Execution', which in turn yield further subdivisions, sacred and secular, vocal and instrumental, native and foreign, and then institutions and musical genres. A place is also provided within musical practice for certain major interdisciplinary areas: music and poetry, music and dance, music and theatrical setting, music and elocution, the construction of instruments, music theory and instruction. Framery's design is a thoroughly rationalistic one, comprehensive, symmetrical and essentially static.

A few years later the Göttingen music historian Johann Nikolaus Forkel (1749–1818) brought out his map of musical knowledge in a pamphlet entitled *Über die Theorie der Musik, insofern sie Liebhabern und Kennern notwendig und nützlich ist* (1777). The scheme was revised and presented in an expanded form in his *Allgemeine Geschichte der Musik* (i, 1788). Forkel offered a fivefold approach to musical knowledge embracing the physics of sound, the mathematics of sound, musical grammar, musical rhetoric and music criticism. If history is not represented here it is because Forkel took it for granted. Implicit in his scheme is a concept of growth or progressive change in which the unfolding of Man's musical powers is paralleled by his attainment of mastery in the arts of language. Forkel's historical bias is best displayed in the organization of his *Allgemeine Litteratur der Musik* (1792), a bibliography of writings on music from antiquity to Forkel's own time. This work is divided into two main sections, one devoted to the literature of music history, the other to the literature of theory and practice. The fundamental distinction made here between historical and non-historical writings foreshadows a dichotomy that has marked the discipline from Forkel's day to the present, the distinction between historical and systematic musicology.

4. HISTORICAL AND SYSTEMATIC MUSICOLOGY. It was Guido Adler who, in a paper printed in the first issue of the *Vierteljahrsschrift für Musikwissenschaft* (1885) – 'Umfang, Methode und Ziel der Musikwissenschaft' – codified the division between the historical and the systematic realms of music study and tabulated their substance and method. The main outline, as repeated with slight modifications in Adler's *Methode der Musikgeschichte* (1919, p.7), was as follows:

MUSICOLOGY

I. The historical field (the history of music arranged by epochs, peoples, empires, countries, provinces, towns, schools, individual artists):

A. Musical palaeography (semiography) (notations).
B. Basic historical categories (groupings of musical forms).
C. Laws: (1) as embodied in the compositions of each epoch; (2) as conceived and taught by the theorists; (3) as they appear in the practice of the arts.
D. Musical instruments.

II. The systematic field (tabulation of the chief laws applicable to the various branches of music):

A. Investigation and justification of these laws in: (1) harmony (tonal); (2) rhythm (temporal); (3) melody (correlation of tonal and temporal).
B. Aesthetics and psychology of music: comparison and evaluation in relation to the perceived subjects, with a complex of questions related to the foregoing.
C. Music education: the teaching of (1) music in general; (2) harmony; (3) counterpoint; (4) composition; (5) orchestration; (6) vocal and instrumental performance.
D. Musicology (investigation and comparative study in ethnography and folklore).

The 'Musicology' of II.D is the subdivision 'Musikologie' rather than 'Musikwissenschaft', which circumscribes the entire field.

In his tabulation Adler listed the auxiliary sciences of musicology. These are, for the historical field: general history, palaeography, chronology, diplomatic (i.e. the form of manuscript documents), bibliography (i.e. the form of printed books), library and archive science, literary history and languages; liturgical history; history of mime and dance; biography, statistics of associations, institutions and performances; and, for the systematic field: acoustics and mathematics, physiology (aural sensations), psychology (aural perception, judgment, feeling), logic (musical thought), grammar, metrics and

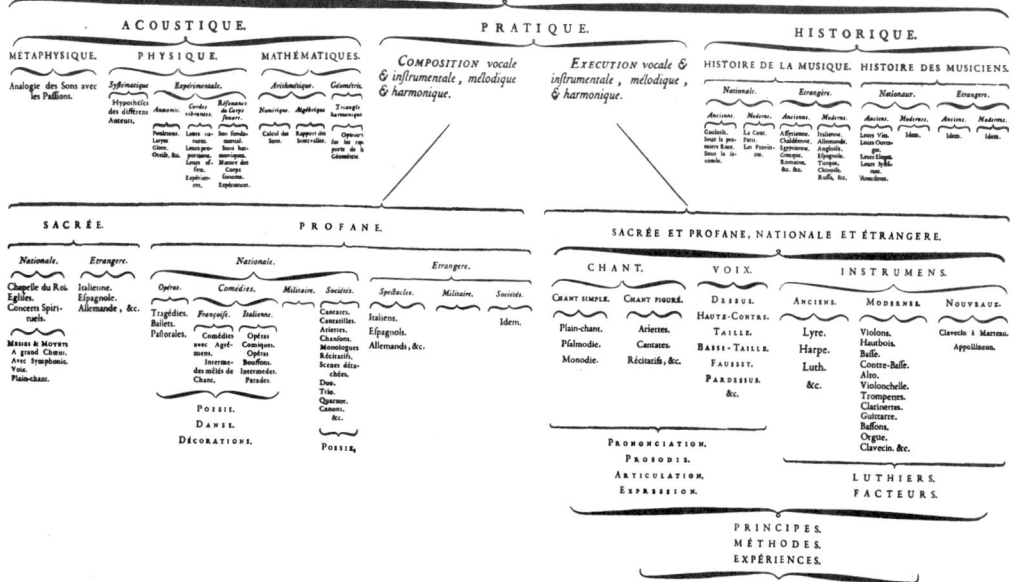

*'Tableau de la musique et de ses branches' by Nicolas Etienne Framery, from 'Journal de musique historique, théorique et pratique' (January 1770)*

poetics, education, aesthetics etc. More recent methodologists, notably Hans-Heinz Dräger (1955), have refined and modified Adler's scheme, adding for example recording techniques, without changing its essential polarity. Dräger, however, introduced into his scheme the categories of music sociology and interdisciplinary subjects, though leaving the main weight heavily on the two original categories. In spite of the apparent equilibrium of the two sections of Adler's outline, history carries the greater weight, as it did in Adler's career as a musicologist.

Systematic musicology is usually defined in negative terms, as a configuration of disciplines that have little in common except for the fact that they are non-historical in nature. This concept has undergone a striking reversal in recent years. Far from being a kind of 'dumping ground' for matters of secondary interest to historians, the systematic approach has come to be regarded as leading to fundamental research into the nature and properties of music, not only as an art but as a sociological, acoustical, physiological and psychological phenomenon. Moreover, all of Adler's historical subject areas are capable of study from a non-historical viewpoint, and such study has been attempted in some of them – for example in the semiological approach to musical notations and in typological classifications of musical forms. Systematic musicology, in the eyes of such scholars as Walter Wiora, is not a mere extension of the musicologist's views but a complete reorientation of his outlook towards the discipline. It calls for the reopening of some of the basic questions that have occupied men's minds from antiquity, and still call for resolution in modern terms: What is music? What function does it perform in society? What is the role of value in the musical experience? Of tradition? Perhaps what emerges from this is that there are two fundamentally different approaches to all musical material – one which seeks to trace its development in the course of time (sometimes called the 'diachronic' view), and one which examines it as a phenomenon among comparable phenomena, seeking to place it within a classification scheme irrespective of the passage of time (the 'synchronic' view). Neither can be sustained exclusive of the other, but each has its value, and the two aspects exist in a constant tension. Ultimately the synchronic view is the more empirical (i.e. it deals with things as they are) and the diachronic view the more interpretative (since the past itself exists as a collection of images 'frozen' in time, between which the historian constructs lines of cause and effect).

### II. Disciplines of musicology

1. Historical method. 2. Theoretical and analytical method. 3. Textual criticism. 4. Archival research. 5. Lexicography and terminology. 6. Organology and iconography. 7. Performing practice. 8. Aesthetics and criticism. 9. Dance and dance history.

1. HISTORICAL METHOD. The study of history requires a theory of history, a framework of ideas or set of assumptions of which the historian may or may not be aware, but which guide his work (see HISTORIOGRAPHY). As the art historian E. H. Gombrich (1969) has observed:

Without such an idea history could never be written at all. The infinite array of documents and monuments which the past has bequeathed to us cannot be grasped without some principle of relevance, some theory which brings order into the atomic facts as a magnet creates configurations out of inert iron filings.

Historical thinking in the 18th century was inextricably tied to an idea of progress. The history of music in Burney's terms was marked by a continuing advance towards perfection that, in his view, reached its zenith in the music of his own day. Burney's contemporaries, Hawkins and Forkel, gave substantial support to this view though with some modifications. In the 19th century the naive belief in the perfectibility of Man and his arts was replaced by more sophisticated concepts of historical continuity derived from the theory of evolution and the metaphysics of Hegelian idealism. Historical phenomena came to be explained in terms of biological metaphors. Art forms and the cultures that sustained them were treated as living organisms subject to birth, growth, decline and dissolution. Linear progress was replaced by cyclic progression, or by a periodic fluctuation between phases such as the alternating Dionysian and Apollonian principles described by Curt Sachs in *The Commonwealth of Art* (1946).

In adopting these dynamic but deterministic explanations of historical change, music took its cue from art history. The art historians, having gained academic authority at least a generation in advance of their colleagues in music, were in a position to share their concepts of periodization, continuity and style. Many of the terms used by music historians to subdivide the flow of time (Renaissance, Mannerism, Baroque, Classicism) were lifted from architecture and the other visual arts. Particularly influential in this respect was the work of Heinrich Wölfflin (1864–1945), the successor to Jacob Burckhardt at Basle. For Wölfflin art history was 'a history without names', that is, it discounted biographical facts and concerned itself chiefly with forms and styles determined by the innate artistic vision of the creator and the beholder. The prime object for the historian is the individual work of art approached through those qualities it shares with other manifestations of the culture. Viewed in this light, art history and musicology as well are to be regarded as branches of cultural history. The cultural-historical emphasis was in part a protest against positivism, a reaction against some of the more rigid theories of historical progression mentioned above. The aim of the cultural historian is to apprehend the cohesive elements within a given culture. He seeks to become so thoroughly immersed in 'the spirit of the age' (the Zeitgeist) that he can identify its imprint in every expression of the culture – in costume and decoration, in institutions, ideas and art forms. Through an imaginative re-creation of a past society, the cultural historian seeks to draw parallels and establish relationships that cut across the traditional subject boundaries. The prototype for this kind of historical writing on music was furnished by August Wilhelm Ambros, a man whose wide cultural experience embraced not only the tonal but the visual arts as well. Ambros's approach was made more explicit in the style-orientated methodology of the Viennese musicologist Guido Adler (1855–1941). It was given a broad conceptual foundation by the philosopher Wilhelm Dilthey (1823–1911). In his concept of *Geistesgeschichte*, Dilthey expounded a methodology for the humane sciences as distinct from the mechanistic ones.

Although the approach through cultural history has lost favour with some scholars in recent years, it still has its champions among modern musicologists. One of its leading advocates was Wilibald Gurlitt (1889–1963) of the University of Freiburg. In Gurlitt's view 'every stylistic epoch has its own beauty, its own meaning, and occupies its own position on the scale of artistic values' (1948). The pursuit of the unique concentration of values expressed by a cultural epoch presents a challenge to the imagination and understanding. In the hands of a sensitive and cultivated scholar the writing of cultural history has the quality of a creative art. But the method has traps for the unwary. It can lead to historicism, to historical and aesthetic relativism, to the belief that the only significant thing that can be observed about a historical event or work of art is its particularity. Furthermore, it encourages a superficial desire to seek and to impose relationships where they may not be present. It maintains the position that the function of the musicologist and the critic is to penetrate to the cultural meaning of an art object and transfer that meaning verbally to the mind of the hearer or observer. This stress on the interpretative function of the scholar gave rise to the doctrine of hermeneutics as articulated by Hermann Kretzschmar (1848–1924) and his successor at Berlin, Arnold Schering (1877–1941), in the early years of the 20th century. In Schering's hands the search for analogous symbols and meanings in music and literature was carried to extremes in which certain works by Beethoven were supplied with programmes derived from the plays of Shakespeare and Schiller. (*See also* HERMENEUTICS and ANALYSIS, §III.)

Fundamental to the music historian is the concept of style, for the historical phenomena with which he is concerned are not biographical facts or events. These are only the 'factual' framework within which he views his object of attention: the musical substance of works of art. Style is for him a classificatory concept: a style is a set of features, and compositions in that style are compositions that have those features in common. Styles are not fixed and mutually exclusive; they are arbitrary ways of seeing data; they may overlap, and some may wholly contain others. But a stylistic category, once it has been set up, can function as a norm against which data are assessed. It can be used as a test: for example, in order to ascertain whether an anonymous composition might reasonably be ascribed to a given composer, or at least to the orbit of a certain group of composers whose style is well determined; or to see whether a work whose composer is known contains features of another style, and thus to posit a line of influence from that style to the composer or vice versa. It is from a corpus of judgments of this sort that broader stylistic categories can be established: the style of the Renaissance, French 18th-century style, operatic style and so on – styles defined by time, by place and by function. Bukofzer (1957) said that 'the description of the origin and development of styles, their interrelations, their transfer from one medium to another, is the central task of musicology'. Yet ultimately style is only a convenience: this part of the task of musicology is the charting of the evolution of music itself (*see also* STYLE).

## 2. THEORETICAL AND ANALYTICAL METHOD.

Theory and analysis differ in essence from historical inquiry. History is concerned with the arrangement of events in time, and searches for chains of cause and effect which bind those events. It tends also to stress the conscious aspects of social life: the record of demonstrable past events, the reasons in men's minds, the circumstances and conditions of life. Theory and analysis, on the other hand, examine phenomena rather than events; they are concerned with how things work rather than why they arise; they deal not with arrangement in time, or causality, but with relationships; they delve into the unconscious since they seek to discover the structural laws underlying complex phenomena (the laws of form and of style, for example, in music) and the processes by which they operate (the process of harmony, or the compositional process).

Theory is by far the oldest branch of the study of music, and arguably the broadest in scope. It has its roots in the writings of the ancient Greeks and a powerful tradition extending through the Middle Ages and Renaissance to modern times. Moreover other cultural traditions, notably those of the Arab countries, Iran, India, China and Japan, have bodies of theory which go back at least 1000 years and cover similar subjects in a way that is not matched by parallel lines of historical inquiry. Analysis is a much more recent concept, though its methods can be seen at work in the Middle Ages and were clearly formed by the 17th century.

As to the scope of music theory, it embraces the examination of the fundamental materials of music (the acoustics of pitch systems, tunings, scales, tonality, interval ratios, consonance and dissonance, pulse, measure and duration), the structuring of such materials into melody, counterpoint, harmony, rhythm and form, the expression of these structures in written form and their realization through instrumental and vocal techniques. It covers these from the points of view of the philosopher, the composer, the notator, the performer, the teacher and (more recently) the listener.

The Greek theoretical tradition dealt with three broad issues: the materials of scales, modes and melodic motion (Aristoxenus, 4th century BC); musical intervals as part of a cosmological system of ratios (the Pythagoreans and Ptolemy, 2nd century); and the effects of music on people and its uses in education (Aristides Quintilianus, 3rd century). The principal transmitters of Greek theory to the early Middle Ages were Boethius (*c*480–*c*524), Cassiodorus (*c*485–*c*580) and Isidore of Seville (*c*559–636). In certain respects medieval theorists after them upheld the issues of Greek theory: inheriting from Boethius a classification of music into *mundana* (cosmic), *humana* (of the human mind) and *instrumentalis* (practical) they continued the speculative discussion of music as part of the cosmos, though with less strength than the theorists of the Renaissance for whom it was once again a live issue; they also continued to evolve the theory of scales and modes in a powerful and central line of discussion which extended unabated into the Renaissance (Tinctoris, Aaron, Zarlino, Glarean and others); they were much occupied with intervallic ratio, consonance and dissonance. The great difference between these medieval writers and the Greek theorists is that they can be seen to have been battling with problems of a practical nature: modal theory was concerned with executant problems such as how to make the transition from antiphon to psalm verse smoothly, and intervallic theory with how to generate polyphony in live performance without running into tonal impasses (especially *Musica enchiriadis* and the 12th-century *Ad organum faciendum* treatises, but also the faburden and discant treatises of the 14th and 15th centuries). Melodic and intervallic theory were also concerned with tonal orientation through the gamut, solmization, the eminently practical and spontaneous device of the Guidonian hand, and *musica ficta*. (*See also* MODE, §§II–III; MUSICA FICTA; ORGANUM, §§2–4; SOLMIZATION, §I.)

Moreover, medieval rhythmic theory tends to be presented in modern textbooks as part of the development of notation. It is much more a process of reducing to some graspable framework the concepts of time, time measurement and organization – concepts still overwhelmingly problematic to modern philosophers. That framework had to serve performers in an aural tradition just as much as composers and literate performers. Hence rhythmic notation was only a symptom and surface manifestation of rhythmic conceptions that were evolving and changing from at least as early as the 8th century. First, by reference to the 'feet' of classical poetic theory, rhythmic formulae (based on alternation of long and short time units) were probably used one after another in a chain which 'filled up' available time. Then the notion of internally reorganizing these formulae evolved. It was only at this stage, the turn of the 12th century, that a notational system and accompanying theory developed: the rhythmic modal system, with formula chains represented by ligature chains. Significantly, although modal theory was not expressed in notational terms until the 13th century (with Johannes de Garlandia and Anonymous IV), discussion of the 'feet' of poetics can be found in Boethius, and their direct application to musical metre was stated as early as 1025–6 by Guido of Arezzo.

The enormous step from modal rhythm to the mensural system of the later Middle Ages typifies the process of theoretical formulation. It involved a total reconceptualization of how music occupies the dimension of time. In place of formulae being 'packed' end to end into a vacant time space, that time space itself was 'charted' by a metrical grid system not unlike the grid of longitude and latitude which charts the earth's surface. Of course, the earth's surface is two-dimensional whereas time is one-dimensional; but a more important difference is that medieval theorists (particularly Franco of Cologne, Jehan des Murs, Philippe de Vitry and Marchetto da Padova) provided a system of several grids based on differing subdivisions of note values at several levels: the mood, time and prolation that constituted mensuration. (*See also* NOTATION, §III, 2–4, and RHYTHM, §II, 5–7.)

It was in the early 17th century, with the doctrines of rhetorical device and of the Affections, associated with the *seconda prattica*, that the concept of the form of a piece of music, and hence the technique of formal analysis, had its origin. It appeared with the writings of Joachim Burmeister (in particular *Musica poetica*, 1606), and carried with it a terminology for describing types of texture, vocal grouping, repetition, sequence and antiphony – a terminology derived from the techniques of rhetorical discourse. The most elaborate analyses of musical devices and their associated emotions were given by Johann Mattheson (1739; *see* RHETORIC AND MUSIC). This approach to analysis through definable affects has been revived in the 20th century in Kretzschmar's 'hermeneutics' and Schering's 'musical symbolism'.

The Baroque period also produced a host of practical tutors for performers: manuals of the vocal embellishment of polyphonic lines in compositions, such as those by Girolamo Dalla Casa and Bovicelli (1584, 1594), methods of playing instrumental divisions, such as that by Christopher Simpson (1659), and above all manuals

on improvisation at the keyboard over a figured bass by such writers as Agazzari (1607), Locke (1673) and Saint-Lambert (1680) and the theory of thoroughbass method by Penna (1672), Heinichen (1728) and others.

The acknowledgment, most radically by Rousseau (1683) and Masson (1699), that from among the eight modes theoretically available only two were used in practice, prepared for another momentous reformulation. This was Rameau's new conception of harmony (1722). It rested on the principle of what is now called 'pitch class' – the identity of a note with all its octave replicates. This entailed the principle of inversion, whereby a triad might appear with any one of three bass notes, and the concept of fundamental bass – a bass made up of the roots of all the chords in a progression, which underlies (without being fully sounded) and functions as the generator of that progression. Rameau's theory spread through the work of Marpurg, Kirnberger, Fétis, Day and countless other theorists of the late 18th and the 19th centuries, was further refined in the work of Hugo Riemann and still powerfully influences modern harmonic thinking (including for example the theories of Hindemith and even the analytical formulations of Allen Forte).

Two developments of the 18th and 19th centuries profoundly affected musical thought. The first was the growth of a scientifically based acoustics, founded by Joseph Sauveur (1701), who himself influenced Rameau, and continued by Hermann von Helmholtz (1863) and Carl Stumpf (1883–90). The second was the creation of formal models for the construction of compositions. Such models can be found in the late Renaissance and the Baroque period, and even traced back to the Middle Ages, but did not talk, as did 19th-century theory, in terms of specific musical identities. It was only with Koch (1793), Reicha (1832) and A. B. Marx (1837–47) that the composer could find formal models set out, like templates, ready to be filled with musical content. Originally part of the tradition of *Kompositionslehre* but subsequently, with Leichtentritt, to become in its own right the branch *Formenlehre*, this approach still provides the basis for the identification of such movement forms as sonata form, song form, variation form and so on. It was thus that a technique designed for the composer became a technique for the listener and analyst.

In the early 20th century Heinrich Schenker's questioning of the validity of chord labelling (i.e. the giving of an individual tonal identity to every chord in a passage of music) led to his radical idea that chords could be embellishments of underlying chords in just the way that notes can be embellishments of underlying notes. From this developed his concept of structural levels, each more 'fundamental' and less embellished that the last, and of 'reduction' from surface structure to fundamental structure (*Ursatz*) by passage through these levels (*Schichten*). Schenker underpinned his entire scheme with the primacy of the major triad; to him every valid tonal composition was an activation of the major triad, a realization of its full potential, a 'composing out' of it. Schenker's theories have wide influence in modern German and Austrian theory, and have profoundly affected American theory and analysis, but have penetrated only slightly to many other countries.

Not unrelated to Schenker's work, and broader in base though ultimately less influential, has been the analytical work of Lorenz on Wagner's later operas. Lorenz's work had two main aspects. Like Schenker he sought large-scale tonal movement by tracing extended tonal areas and charting them together. He had, however, a more general notion of tonal unity and worked without a preconceived fundamental pattern. On the other hand he defined temporal units of structure, using elements of received *Formenlehre* with the addition of his own arch form (*Bogenform*), and then traced these upwards to ever higher levels of structure in a hierarchical scheme which owes something to Schenker's theory of structural levels. Through what might be called macrotonality and macrorhythm Lorenz tried to uncover the 'large-scale architectonics' of music.

Rudolph Réti sought unity not in tonal movement but in thematic material. For him the fundamental structuring process in music from the 18th century onwards was transformation. His method of analysis is that of reduction applied to the contrasting thematic materials of a work so as to disclose an underlying intervallic motif. That motif is often found to be constantly present, saturating the texture. However, Réti went further. His analyses seek to show that composition proceeds by thematic evolution, by transformation towards a goal of intensification followed by thematic resolution. It accounts for music as a linear phenomenon, unified by the constant presence of the motif from which the transformation proceeds, not as a hierarchical phenomenon or as a structure built of formal units. The method of the British analyst Hans Keller similarly seeks the unity that underlies contrasting themes. His 'functional analysis' seeks 'the unifying *functions* of the living organism which is a musical work of art'. It eschews verbal description. In 1956 Keller evolved a method of analytical demonstration which dispensed with the written and spoken word altogether. This relied exclusively on sounded musical examples showing the 'basic ideas' from which themes are derived. Keller presented a series of such analytical demonstrations through the medium of radio.

In 1923 Knud Jeppesen published his study of Palestrina's style and the dissonance. It was the first truly scientific examination of a style, and was seen by the author as a first step towards a study of 'the laws of musical evolution' based on comparison of variant styles. Jeppesen, significantly, stated at the outset that 'music is, in its way, a language'. His study of melody, harmony and dissonance is distributional; that is, it locates all occurrences of a particular element (the downward leap from an accented crotchet, for example), and examines the context within which each falls in order to discover the syntactical laws by which that element is governed. This is essentially the method by which the linguist works when examining syntactic laws in a language, and it is the method adopted by those analysts who in recent years have explored musical semiology, particularly Ruwet, Nattiez and Lidov. Semiology sees music as a network of relations between elements, all governed by laws of structure. It compares all elements with all other elements in the structure, determining which may co-exist with which, and which are inimical to each other. It does this for different levels of structure (usually starting with the smallest elements and ending with the definition of the largest structural units), with the aim of a complete and rigorous statement of structure as the final product. Semiology strives above all for objectivity and achieves it through

the elimination of all preconceived notions about the music. Some American analysts have used linguistic models, for example Forte in his 'parsing' of structures by Webern, and Kassler in his testing of Schenker's theories; so too have Scandinavian scholars such as Lindblom and Sundberg, in their work on melody (1970). The objectivity of these methods invites the use of the computer, whose logic ensures rigorous adherence to the criteria that have been laid down, and which can handle complex data in large quantities. For the latter reason the computer lends itself well to the systematic examination of an entire stylistic field, as in the Princeton project on the style of Josquin's music.

Another external model that has been applied to music is that of information theory. Using the methods of this theory, Kraehenbuhl and Coons have sought to account for some of the expressive characteristics of musical sequences ('Information as a Measure of Experience in Music', *Journal of Aesthetics and Art Criticism*, xvii (1958–9), 510). They address themselves to the experience the listener undergoes when hearing a work, and consider the listener's mind as a system which at each point predicts what is to come on the basis of what has already been heard. As the work proceeds, the network of probabilities becomes more and more complex. At any one point, by information theory, total confirmation of a prediction yields 'no information' (a condition termed 'redundancy'); partial confirmation yields partial information, total non-confirmation yields maximum information ('entropy'). Put in another way, that which lives up to expectations is least random, that which constantly surprises is most random in structure. This theory can be used in analysis to test the degree of coherence of a work, to locate the high and low points of intensity and the gradations between these points. It can be used in composition to procure a desired formal shaping.

The most important body of compositional theory in the 20th century is undoubtedly that of serialism. Schoenberg's work on 12-note method, and that of Leibowitz, Rufer, Rochberg and others, was continued by the writings of Milton Babbitt, who has used group theory to predict certain general properties of 12-note compositions. Boulez has extended the discussion of set organization to the parameters of duration, tempo, dynamic, timbre, the control of texture and of the physical placing of sound sources, and to the coordination of these parameters (*see* SERIALISM and TWELVE-NOTE COMPOSITION).

For the analysis of atonal music which is not serially ordered Allen Forte has formulated the concept of pitch-class sets (unordered sets of pitches irrespective of octave register), relations of identity and similarity between such sets, and interrelated groups of sets, known as set complexes. This provides a coherent method for determining pitch structure particularly useful in music based on configurations of notes other than the major and minor scales and on chords not formed by the superposition of 3rds.

*See also* ANALYSIS and THEORY, THEORISTS.

3. TEXTUAL CRITICISM. Textual criticism embraces several central sciences: palaeography (the decipherment of handwritings), diplomatic and bibliography (the study of the formal make-up of manuscripts and printed books respectively), editorship and collation (the identification of errors in the text of a document and the

reconciliation of variant readings). Ancillary to these are such sciences as the studies of printing techniques and processes, of paper manufacture, of binding, of illumination and of book illustration. All these bodies of knowledge contribute directly to the establishment of a critical text. The first five have venerable scholarly traditions extending back into the early 19th century; the rest have developed in the 20th century, with such works as Charles Briquet's *Les filigranes* (Geneva, 1907), Allan Stevenson's *The Problem of the Missale speciale* (London, 1967) and Charlton Hinman's *The Printing and Proof-reading of the First Folio of Shakespeare* (Oxford, 1963) as landmarks.

In the context of music, the decipherment of notational systems (ekphonetic, neumatic, mensural, tablature etc; *see* NOTATION, §I) forms an important part of musical palaeography – though the decipherment of verbal text matter remains a vital skill which is given far too little attention by musicologists. The special demands of music on printing – multiple impression, the production of specialist characters of highly complex kinds, engraving etc – all require study as processes; they carry their own peculiarities and tendencies to particular errors which must be known before the text can be fully elucidated (*see* PRINTING AND PUBLISHING OF MUSIC). The procedures of music writing, of the production and copying of the musical source, are again activities not yet fully appreciated in their own terms; to understand the 'psychology' of the producer of a text is half the battle in understanding the text itself (*see* SOURCES, MS, §I).

In the study of music printing the groundwork was laid by scholars like Anton Schmid in his survey of the output of the Petrucci press (1845), by Robert Eitner, and by Emil Vogel in his *Bibliothek der gedruckten weltlichen Vocalmusik Italiens* (1892). Vogel's work has been carried on by Claudio Sartori in his *Bibliografia della musica strumentale italiana stampata in Italia fino al 1700* (1952–68) and by Howard Mayer Brown in his *Instrumental Music Printed Before 1600* (1965). Basic studies of early French music printers and publishers have been made by François Lesure and Geneviève Thibault, of the early English by Charles Humphries and William C. Smith, and of the early Viennese by Alexander Weinmann. A model of descriptive bibliography covering the activities of the earliest French music publisher, Pierre Attaingnant, is in Daniel Heartz's *Pierre Attaingnant, Royal Printer of Music* (1970). The same kind of critical scrutiny directed towards manuscripts draws on the techniques and resources of palaeography.

In manuscript studies much attention has been given in recent years to the 18th century. Studies involving paper-making, the distribution of watermarks and handwriting have brought about important revisions in the chronology of the works of J. S. Bach, Mozart and his father, and Haydn. Moreover, a new understanding of the creative processes of composers – notably of Beethoven and Wagner – has been growing as a result of close examination of preparatory materials such as sketchbooks, drafts and preliminary scores.

The principles of editing are another supporting science of musicology. They embrace not only the surface questions such as how to distinguish editorial emendation and interpretation from original reading and how to lay out suppressed readings in a critical commentary along with a description of sources (although these are matters on which no conformity has been reached among scholars), but also the much more fundamental issues of how far editors should go in correcting and interpreting a text; and whether the variants of a particular text are separate entities or lead back hierarchically to an original exemplar, and thus whether the readings given in an edition of a work with many variant sources should seek to establish by reconstruction a hypothetical archetype, or simply present the best surviving text intact, or set out the variants or alternatives in several textual traditions (*see* EDITING).

In music, the concepts of 'Urtext' and of critical edition are in principle distinct. Urtext attempts to present the contents of an original source free of all editorial additions (slurs, bowing marks, extra dynamics etc): it is pure, yet is to some extent a translation into modern notation. Further to the same end of the spectrum is the so-called diplomatic transcription – a hand facsimile of the original notation still much used in German dissertations but properly replaced by the photographic facsimile. The critical edition, at the other end of the spectrum, is a presentation of the text after it has been subjected to critical scrutiny and a certain construction placed on it.

Many scholars at the beginning of the 20th century (e.g. Aubry and Beck) were trained as philologists before turning to musical scholarship. They brought a particular awareness of the problems of textual transmission, above all to the thorny field of medieval monophony. The series Paléographie Musicale (1889–) published by the monks of Solesmes exemplifies this dual approach to textual criticism which combines facsimiles of original sources with editions in more modern notation, later to be attempted systematically by Beck in his Corpus Cantilenarum Medii Aevi (1927–38) for all surviving troubadour and trouvère song (never completed). The Solesmes monks have always been among the most critical and scientific textual scholars and their recent text-analytical work in *Le graduel romain* (Solesmes, 1957–) is highly sophisticated.

Textual criticism was itself a product of the search for authenticity which began in the 19th century and has preoccupied 20th-century historical thought. In music this was manifested particularly in the production of critical editions of the works of leading composers. Following the foundation of the Bach Gesellschaft in 1850, European scholars started a series of Gesamtausgaben, definitive editions of the complete works of Beethoven, Mozart, Lassus, Palestrina, Schubert, Schumann, Schütz and Victoria, among others. Few of these sets reached the state of completeness envisaged by their editors, but they marked significant steps in the development of editorial techniques and in the bibliographical control of sources. Parallel to the Gesamtausgaben were the Denkmäler sets devoted to the publication of 'monuments' of national music. Among the earlier projects of this nature were Franz Commer's Collectio Operum Musicorum Batavorum (1844–58), a pioneer edition of early Flemish music, and Robert Julien van Maldeghem's *Trésor musical* (1865–93). These established a continuing pattern of critical editions of historically significant music originating in Germany, Austria, France, Italy, Belgium, the Netherlands, England etc (*see* EDITIONS, HISTORICAL).

An important adjunct to text-critical study is the compilation of inventories and cataloguing of primary source materials. The towering figure in this was

Robert Eitner (1832–1905) who published numerous music catalogues and inventories in *Monatshefte für Musikgeschichte* (1869–1904) and who brought the results of his vast knowledge of European archives into evidence in his ten-volume *Biographisch-bibliographisches Quellen-Lexikon der Musiker und Musikgelehrten der christlichen Zeitrechnung bis zur Mitte des 19. Jahrhunderts* (1900–04). The ideals that Eitner initiated in this great work have served musical scholarship for more than 60 years and are still alive in the form of an 'International Inventory of Musical Sources' (RISM) published under the auspices of the International Musicological Society and the International Association of Music Libraries. The catalogues of the works of individual composers – those by Köchel for Mozart, Schmieder for J. S. Bach, Hoboken for Haydn, Zimmerman for Purcell, Rufer for Schoenberg, for example – often give information on the textual transmission of each individual work, enabling the user to locate all primary material and know its status. The first part of Ludwig's *Repertorium* (1910) was a model of another type of source catalogue: the *catalogue raisonné* of the materials of a repertory laid out according to stylistic dictates and explained as an evolutionary picture (*see* THEMATIC CATALOGUE).

4. ARCHIVAL RESEARCH. Archives are the residue of documents issued in the process of some sort of administration – whether it be of central government or a private business, a ducal household or a parish church. They are of interest to the historian for study of the institution to which the archives refer, or for study of people or objects or events concerned with that institution. Their essential feature is that they are generated automatically in the process of administration, and this makes them in principle different from almost all other sources of history. Unlike a chronicle, a diary or a newspaper report, they are not a conscious historical record involving selection of fact according to some criterion. They record everyday detail as faithfully as the unusual and the recorder is in the strict sense not a participant in the events recorded. It is these factors that historians in the mid-19th century recognized. As the centralization of archives into principal depositories got under way during the early part of the century and the science of archive keeping began to develop, historians turned to them as objective truth. 'Ultimate history' (Acton, 1896) seemed only a generation or two away. National series of archive transcripts were begun: Monumenta Germaniae Historica (1826–), Collection de Documents Inédits sur l'Histoire de France (1850–), the British Rolls Series and Calendars (1856–) and others. Only slowly was it realized that the proper use of archives could be made only after painstaking study of how the administration itself worked, and that even then error and fabrication could be uncovered.

In musicology there has been a little activity in producing transcripts, either of entire series of documents concerning musical administration (such as Edward Rimbault's *The Old Cheque-book, or Book of Remembrance of the Chapel Royal*, London, 1872), or of selected musical items from more general documents (such as those in Casimiri's periodical *Note d'archivio*, 1924–42, relating to the Sistine Chapel in Rome, and Lafontaine's *The King's Musick*, 1909, relating to the English Chapel Royal). There has been an upsurge of archival research in the patient combing of archives in Italy by American and English scholars for evidence of musical activities and institutions in the late medieval and Renaissance city states (*see* ARCHIVES AND MUSIC).

5. LEXICOGRAPHY AND TERMINOLOGY. The lexicography of music is a form of applied scholarship the object of which is to condense, organize (normally in alphabetical order) and clarify the terms musicians use to communicate their ideas about and their experience of their art; it is commonly extended to include biographical material on individual musicians. This interest has given rise to a long tradition of dictionary making beginning with Brossard and extending through Walther, Rousseau, Grassineau and Koch to such distinguished modern representatives of the genre as Apel's *Harvard Dictionary of Music* (2/1969) and the subject volume of the *Riemann Musik-Lexikon* ('Sachteil', 12/1967). (*See* DICTIONARIES AND ENCYCLOPEDIAS OF MUSIC.)

Musical dictionaries reflect the use of terms in all kinds of primary sources, musical, theoretical and documentary. At the same time, they themselves become historical phenomena furnishing primary evidence of the musical mentality of past eras. It is obvious that terms change their meanings in time, that they coalesce in groups or undergo mutations. The phenomenon of 'term-families' and their behaviour was of particular interest to Wilibald Gurlitt who projected a *Handwörterbuch der musikalischen Terminologie* that would trace the lineage of the vocabulary of music in a manner similar to that used in the *Oxford English Dictionary*. Such a handbook would provide a historical analysis of musical terms according to their inherent relationships and family groupings. His scheme is now in the process of being realized by H. H. Eggebrecht: the first issue of a handbook under Gurlitt's title came out in 1972. The historical analysis of terms has its obvious use as a means to gaining an understanding of the development of concepts, but there is another aspect of the relationship between word and music that confronts the musicologist with a perpetual dilemma – the need to apply verbal symbols to an art that conveys its meanings through the medium of sound. One can talk or write about music, but the experience of music itself can be known only through its own 'language', the language of sound. The effort to resolve the disparity between verbal and tonal discourse has been a lifelong preoccupation for Charles Seeger. He has seen little chance of bringing these two realms of meaning into complete coincidence. It is the fate of the musicologist to suffer what Seeger called the 'linguocentric predicament'.

6. ORGANOLOGY AND ICONOGRAPHY. The study of musical instruments (organology) has attracted scholars since at least the 17th century. Michael Praetorius included in his *Syntagma musicum* (ii, 1618) an important section on instruments, with detailed illustrations drawn to scale. Similar discussions are found in the encyclopedic works of Mersenne (1636) and Kircher (1650). Insofar as the modern study of historical performing practices involves authentic reconstruction and restoration of instruments of former centuries, it has benefited from the observations of such early scholars.

The term 'organology' was introduced in 1941 by Nicholas Bessaraboff. Bessaraboff felt that if a good musicologist ought to play an instrument whose music was of particular interest to him, then a good organologist, concerned with its acoustical design and mechanics, ought to be able to build a specimen. This form of what might be called 'applied organology' has flourished since World War II and has made notable advances beyond the achievements of such early 20th-century pioneers as Dolmetsch, Galpin and the promulgators of the German *Orgelbewegung* of the 1920s.

Since the late 18th century an interest in ancient and exotic instruments has served an ethnomusicological purpose by providing a common method of approach to the music of diverse remote cultures. Guillaume André Villoteau (1759–1839) made the first scientific study of Egyptian music largely on the basis of depictions of instruments in ancient tombs and temples. The study of organology came into its own after the 19th-century development of instrument museums in Western centres: Berlin, Brussels, Cologne, Copenhagen, The Hague, Leipzig, Nuremberg, New York, Prague etc. Once these collections had become established, scholars confronted new and fruitful challenges of description and classification. Curt Sachs's *Real-Lexikon der Musikinstrumente* (1913), the first effort to systematize knowledge of musical instruments on a worldwide basis, and the classificatory system devised jointly by Sachs and Erich von Hornbostel were based on Victor Mahillon's extensive instrument collection in the Brussels Conservatory. The study of musical instruments *per se* became an important resource for comparative musicology (e.g. Hornbostel's adducing of panpipe tunings as evidence of a cultural connection between Brazil and Polynesia), but ethnomusicologists have tended to favour subordinating a 'purely' organological approach to a more comprehensive penetration of the individual musical contexts or styles involved.

Iconography, the study of visual materials related to music, shares the subject matter of organology insofar as it is concerned with the representation of instruments in works of art, but the musical information to be gained from prints, paintings, sculpture and other visually apprehended artefacts covers a wide territory, embracing performing practice, music sociology, the arts of the musical theatre and the portraiture of musicians. It provides information about such specific matters as the size of a concert room, the way of holding a bow, the construction of an instrument, the size and grouping of a choir, operatic costume and stage design. It often supplies the sole surviving evidence on a question of organology or performing practice; for historical questions in ethnomusicology it is frequently the only available type of evidence.

The realization of the vast potential of visual materials in affording information not available through any other medium began in the first two decades of the 20th century in the work of Buhle, Galpin, Scheurleer and others. Kinsky's *Geschichte der Musik in Bildern* (1929) was the first significant publication in the field. But Kinsky's modest effort, designed for musical amateurs, was greatly expanded in the subsequent *Musikgeschichte in Bildern* (1961–), a multi-volume work founded by Heinrich Besseler and Max Schneider. With the growth of research has come an awareness of the many reasons for distrusting iconographical evidence: lack of skill on the part of the artist, copying of other traditions or styles, imaginative invention or the basing of imagery on theatrical scenery or action, or symbolic purpose. Consequently iconography has become more analytical and interpretative in nature. Distinguished scholars of instrumental iconography,

pictorial biography and the iconography of music in cultural life include Howard Mayer Brown, Alexandr Buchner, Reinhold Hammerstein, Edward Lowinsky and Emanuel Winternitz.

As the scope of iconography has become apparent, the need for bibliographical control at international level was realized. The 'International Repertory of Musical Iconography' (RIdIM) was established in 1971 to catalogue all source materials (*see* ICONOGRAPHY OF MUSIC).

7. PERFORMING PRACTICE. Performing practice is the study of the way music was performed in past times. Indeed, the discipline can hardly be said to have existed (save to an unimportant extent in a few 16th- and 17th-century treatises that deal with the music of the ancient Greeks and Romans) until after the various revivals of earlier music began in the 19th century, for example Mendelssohn's performances of music by J. S. Bach and the publication of historical editions of old music and of critical editions of the works of Bach, Handel and others. The existence of monumental and critical editions naturally led to more frequent performances of 'historical' music, although most performers in the 19th century and surprisingly many in the 20th have assumed that older music must be 'improved' by performing it, for instance, on modern instruments with their greater volume and brilliance and generally better mechanical efficiency. A number of musicians, on the other hand, realized that since the actual sound of music is important to the understanding of it, performances of older works might reveal unexpected meanings if they were played in a manner as close as possible to that heard by the original audiences. Obsolete instrumental techniques and conventions of performance (improvising embellishments, realizing keyboard parts from figured and unfigured basses, adding implied accidentals, inventing appropriate scoring where none is indicated and so on) have had to be relearnt. An important landmark in the history of the revival of older musical practices was the publication in 1915 of Arnold Dolmetsch's book on the interpretation of music in the 17th and 18th centuries, and a number of other studies appeared about the same time or in the following few decades: Beyschlag on ornamentation (1908), F. T. Arnold on figured bass (1931) and Robert Haas on performing practice in general (1931). Much of this early work centred on the problems of performing music by J. S. Bach and his contemporaries.

Since World War II scholars have developed and refined many of the conclusions about the way music was performed in the 17th and 18th centuries, and they have begun to investigate similar problems in earlier and later repertories. Robert Donington, Thurston Dart, Frederick Neumann, Sol Babitz, Michael Collins and Putnam Aldrich have been important among postwar scholars in advancing ideas about performing Baroque music; their ideas have not always been accepted by the musical world or even by the scholarly community. Instrument makers and performers, as well as professional scholars, have had an important influence, and books like that on harpsichord making by the American builder Frank Hubbard have had an influence as wide as or wider than that of his instruments.

Scholarly work on the performance of music since 1750 has been scant (but there is an important study by Paul and Eva Badura-Skoda on performing conventions in Mozart's keyboard music) and so instrument makers and instrumentalists have led the way in teaching how late 18th- and early 19th-century music was performed in its own time. The revival of medieval and Renaissance music, on the other hand, has involved the active collaboration of makers, players and scholars. To a greater extent even than the study of later music, research into the performance of music before 1500 involves the evaluation of archival notices, literary works and works of art with musical subject matter, as well as the analysis of theoretical treatises and the evidence of the musical sources themselves. For these earlier repertories, moreover, the traditional tasks of editors – to add *musica ficta* and the texts in vocal compositions in a way that makes them easier to sing – overlap with those of scholars and performers concerned to understand the conventions of performance in earlier times. (*See also* PERFORMING PRACTICE.)

8. AESTHETICS AND CRITICISM. Aesthetic questions are present in almost all types of musicological writing. They arise when music historians discuss the role of music in a social milieu or the impact of personal environment on individual musical development, or liken music to other arts, or define the terms of a specific style; they are raised by acousticians who seek their bases in physical properties; they are invoked by analysts as foundations for theories and methods of operating, and underlie their attitudes towards musical material, the process of hearing and the function of performance; they appear constantly in the writings of music critics wherever the criteria for judgment of craftsmanship, imagination in composition, and technical skill and interpretative insight in performance come into play; they penetrate the works of iconographers and experts in performing practice, just as they do the deliberations of performers, when leaping the gap – imaginative, despite its historical conditioning – between evidence and statement or performance. They are thus expressed in many different styles of writing: scientific, scholarly, literary, philosophical. They also occur outside the literature of musicology, in systematic philosophical writings from Pythagoras to Leonard Meyer, and in general histories of art and culture.

Musical aesthetics seeks to answer the questions 'What does music mean?', 'What is the place of music in human life, and in the system of reality?', 'What is excellence in music?'. Answers have been provided by some of the world's greatest philosophers: Plato and Aristotle, St Augustine, Thomas Aquinas, Kepler, Leibniz, Descartes, Rousseau, Kant, Hegel, Schopenhauer, Nietzsche and Marx. Scholars in acoustics and psychology, such as Stumpf, Helmholtz and Seashore, have made a large contribution. So have general aestheticians like Adorno, Croce, Langer and Zuckerkandl.

Specialist writing in musical aesthetics extends back to the Middle Ages, above all in the speculative tradition which was inherited from classical Greek philosophy, and which extended through the Renaissance to the early Baroque period. It was with the theory of emotive meaning in music, the so-called doctrine of the Affections, that aesthetics took on a sharply different character. Scheibe and Mattheson were the most important figures in the development of this theory. In the 19th century Hanslick's theory of music as 'sounding form in motion' founded a line of aesthetic thought

which rejected emotional and programmatic interpretations of music, a formalism that has been followed by Combarieu, Stravinsky, Langer and others. Kurth's theory of music as a stream of tension, and as expression of the will (in the Schopenhauerian sense) belongs to the same line of thought. Kretzschmar, on the other hand, took the view that music had meaning and emotional state, and that these could be directly deduced. There is now an important body of Marxist aesthetic theory in music, particularly in the work of Lissa and Supičić. Many composers have contributed brilliantly to the theory of aesthetics, among them Wagner and Busoni, Henry Cowell, Hindemith, Schoenberg, Sessions, Schaeffer and Stockhausen. (*See* AESTHETICS OF MUSIC.)

9. DANCE AND DANCE HISTORY. Dance history offers valuable information for the musicologist as it does for the historian of theatre and the anthropologist. It provides specific data on questions of tempo, phrasing, rhythm and style in performance. In particular, it can supply margins of tempo and patterns of articulation and accentuation for the performer. It can also offer additional evidence concerning many aspects of Renaissance and Baroque improvisatory practices. For the authentic re-creation of early musical theatre – *intermedi*, masques, ballets and operas – it furnishes not only the essential choreographic components but also a wide range of evidence as to stage production and physical movement. It makes possible the presentation of functional dance music in its full context and heightens stylistic awareness in the performer of non-functional, stylized dance music such as the English virginal repertory, the keyboard suites of J. S. Bach and the minuet movements of Haydn and Mozart.

The writing of dance history goes back at least to the 17th century. Authors as early as Praetorius, Mersenne, Mattheson and Cahusac showed a historical sense in their discussion of dance. The initial impetus to modern dance history was given by the publication of important 15th-century dance manuals at the beginning of the 20th century: Closson published the Brussels basse danse manuscript in 1912, Mazzi two Italian manuscripts in 1914 and 1915, and Scholderer the manual of Michel de Toulouse in 1936.

The groundwork of modern scholarly investigation was laid by the generation of Aeppli, Bukofzer, Gombosi, Kinkeldey, Prunières, and above all Sachs, with his *Weltgeschichte des Tanzes* (1932). A shift towards the practical execution of historical dances, their steps and features of style came in the 1950s with the writings and activities of Mabel Dolmetsch, Melusine Wood and Karl Heinz Tauber. A more recent generation of researchers, most of them university-trained, has since brought recognition to the field of dance history as a scholarly discipline: Ingrid Brainard, Meredith Ellis Little, Wendy Hilton, Julia Sutton and Shirley Wynne. Parallel with this has come the study and publication of musical sources by Frederick Crane, Daniel Heartz, Lawrence Moe, Eileen Southern and John M. Ward. The broader social and political context of dance has been explored by Marie-Françoise Christout, Jean-Michel Guilcher, Jean Jacquot, François Lesure and Margaret McGowan. Several systems have been evolved for notating dance, of which Labanotation, devised by Rudolf von Laban, is the most widely used. (*See also* DANCE.)

*III. National traditions of musicology.* Just as there are recognizable national styles in musical composition, so too are there patterns in scholarship that owe their character to the presence of national traditions, ideas and institutions peculiar to a given country or language group. The objectives of scholarship are international, but it is instructive to follow the various native strands and note how they fuse into the total pattern. The present discussion nevertheless can only make passing reference to the principal events and individuals within the major countries.

1. France. 2. Italy. 3. Great Britain and the Commonwealth countries. 4. Germany and Austria. 5. Other west European countries. 6. The Soviet Union. 7. Eastern Europe. 8. The United States of America.

1. FRANCE. If modern musicology is a product of the Enlightenment, then France is the logical place to begin a discussion of national schools. French learning was emulated throughout Europe as the source and centre of rationalism. The rationalistic spirit revealed itself first of all in the work of the lexicographers, in the dictionaries of Sébastien de Brossard and Jean-Jacques Rousseau, culminating in the great *Encyclopédie* of Diderot and D'Alembert, and beyond that in the musical volumes of the *Encyclopédie méthodique* (1791–1818) edited by Framery, Ginguené and Momigny. French learning was also disseminated in the writings of a group of aestheticians (the Abbé Dubos, Crusaz, Batteux and Chabanon) all preoccupied in some degree with the classic concept of art as 'imitation of nature'. Much of their argument was channelled into the prevailing controversy over the merits of French as against Italian opera.

France had less to offer in writings on music history. After the efforts of Pierre Bonnet-Bourdelot early in the century there was only one work of any significance – J.-B. de La Borde's four-volume *Essai sur la musique ancienne et moderne* (1780), a provocative but uneven work important chiefly for the attention it draws to the early French chanson. In 1756, however, a Benedictine monk, Philippe-Joseph Caffiaux, had produced a systematic history of music from pre-history to contemporary times in seven volumes, but it was never published (MS in *F-Pn*). Finally, the theoretical works of Rameau were fundamental to French musical learning in the 18th century; they provided a focal point for the discussion of a host of crucial problems confronting composers and scholars alike.

After the disruptive events of the French Revolution a new generation of music scholars came to the fore. Prominent among them was Alexandre Choron (1771–1834), a man of broad knowledge and high didactic aims who was director of the Opéra in 1816 and for a brief period was involved in efforts to establish the Paris Conservatoire as the 'Ecole Royale de Chant et de Déclamation'. His lifelong objective was to revitalize the training of musicians in France and to raise the level of musical understanding of the public in general. He was well versed in the German and classical writings on music, but Italy remained for him the prime source of musical excellence, as demonstrated in his best-known work, *Principes de composition des écoles d'Italie* (1808, in three volumes; 2/1816, in six). As a teacher, writer and administrator, Choron exerted a profound influence on his contemporaries.

A more direct precursor of modern historical methods was François-Louis Perne (1772–1832), whose research centred on the music of the Middle Ages and antiquity. He was among the first to transcribe the music of Machaut and the Chastelain de Couci, and he made a rather misguided effort to restore the musical notation of ancient Greece to modern practice. A model of erudition of another kind was presented by Guillaume André Villoteau (1759–1839), who was chosen to accompany Napoleon's army to Egypt as a member of a scientific commission to study the culture of that country. His monographs treating of Egyptian music, musical instruments and iconography are pioneer works of ethnomusicology.

The central position in French musicology in the first half of the 19th century was occupied by François-Joseph Fétis (1784–1871), whose range of musical activity was extraordinarily comprehensive, embracing history, theory, music education, composition and the sociology of music. Prodigious in energy and prolific in output, Fétis dominated the music scholarship of his generation, overshadowing the work of all his colleagues. He is best known today for his *Biographie universelle des musiciens*, published in eight volumes between 1833 and 1844. The journal *Revue musicale*, which he founded in 1827, served as a medium for the expression of his views as a critic and historian until it merged with Schlesinger's *Revue et gazette musicale* in 1835. In 1833 Fétis left Paris to become director of the Brussels Conservatory. His series of historical concerts with commentary, given in Paris between 1832 and 1835, awakened public interest in the music of the past. With Raphael Kiesewetter he was one of the first to stress the importance of the Netherlands school in the history of early European music. In a competition set by the Dutch government for the best essay on the subject 'The Contribution of the Netherlanders to the History of Music in the 14th, 15th and 16th Centuries', Fétis's text was rated a close second and was published along with Kiesewetter's prizewinning work.

In the shadow of Fétis's vigorous personality, a distinguished group of French music scholars was active in the first half of the 19th century, including Adrien de La Fage (1805–62), a pupil of Choron and friend of Baini (Palestrina's biographer) in Rome. La Fage's interests ranged from plainchant and the music of the Near East to music bibliography and source studies in general. He collaborated with Choron on the latter's *Nouveau manuel complet de musique vocale et instrumentale* (1838–9) and wrote his own *Histoire générale de la musique et de la danse* (1844) emphasizing ancient and oriental practices. His best-known book was published posthumously under the title *Essais de dipthérographie musicale* (1864), a collection of notes and commentary related to early printed and manuscript sources, many of them deriving from Baini's library. Several of these French scholars were archivists or librarians associated with one or more of the Parisian collections undergoing rapid expansion at that time. One such was Auguste Bottée de Toulmon (1797–1850), a lawyer by training who served as librarian of the Conservatoire from 1831 to 1848; he produced a number of important monographs, on the medieval chanson, medieval musical instruments, and the life of Guido of Arezzo.

An interest shared by many of these early 19th-century French musicologists was the improvement of church music performance through the reconstruction of organs and restoration of the authentic corpus of the chant. A leader in this movement was Joseph Louis d'Ortigue (1802–66), best known for his *Dictionnaire liturgique, historique et théorique de plain-chant et de musique d'église* (1854, in collaboration with Théodore Nisard). Others concerned with chant reform include La Fage, Jean-Louis-Félix Danjou (1812–66), who with Stéphan Morelot (1820–99) edited the *Revue de la musique religieuse, populaire, et classique* from 1845 to 1849, Alexandre Vincent (1797–1868) and Félix Clément (1822–88). In its critical approach to chant sources the work of these men foreshadowed that of the monks of Solesmes later in the century. Another important figure, Aristide Farrenc, compiled jointly with his wife, the pianist and composer Jeanne-Louise Farrenc, a 23-volume set of early keyboard music, Le Trésor des Pianistes (1861–72). A selection of early vocal music was edited by Le Prince de la Moskowa (son of Marshal Ney) in his 11-volume *Recueil des morceaux de musique ancienne* (1843). Charles Bordes (1863–1909) was responsible for an *Anthologie des maîtres religieux du XVe au XVIIe siècle* and Henry Expert (1863–1952) produced several well-edited sets of Renaissance French music. Of great significance still is the work of Edmond de Coussemaker (1805–76), a Franco-Belgian lawyer who came to medieval studies through reading Fétis's *Revue musicale*. Best known among his editions is *Scriptorum de musica medii aevi* (1864–76), an anthology of medieval writings on music modelled on a similar collection produced by Martin Gerbert nearly 100 years earlier (see §4 below), the *Scriptores ecclesiastici de musica sacra* (1784).

All of these scholars, with the exception of Fétis, were amateurs in the best sense; they were largely self-taught in music, and pursued careers as doctors, lawyers and public officials. The French were slow in giving institutional support to research in music: it was not until 1872 that a chair in music history was added to the staff of the Conservatoire. By the second half of the 19th century, however, French musicology began to take on a professional character: a new generation of scholars had emerged, some, notably the medievalist Pierre Aubry (1874–1910) and Jules Ecorcheville (1872–1915), harshly critical of Fétis's dogmatism and frequent inaccuracies. A major effort to establish France as the centre of musical learning was made by Albert Lavignac (1846–1916) and Lionel de La Laurencie (1861–1933) who joined forces to edit the great *Encyclopédie de la musique et dictionnaire du Conservatoire* (1920–31). La Laurencie himself produced the definitive study *L'école française de violon de Lully à Viotti* (1922–4). Romain Rolland (1866–1944) was one of the many contributors to the *Encyclopédie*. Marie Bobillier (1858–1918), who published under the name Michel Brenet, was a prolific writer on early French music. Henry Prunières (1886–1942) founded a new *Revue musicale* in 1920.

The first French doctoral dissertation on a musical subject was completed by Jules Combarieu in 1894: *Les rapports de la musique et de la poésie*. This was followed a year later by Romain Rolland's study *L'origine du théâtre lyrique moderne*. It was Rolland who occupied the first chair in music history at the Sorbonne, beginning in 1904. He was succeeded by André Pirro (1869–1943), one of the giants of modern French musicology. In addition to his basic research in the music of the late Baroque (J. S. Bach, Schütz and Buxtehude) and the 15th century, Pirro claimed a long line of distinguished pupils including Yvonne Rokseth, Jeanne Marix,

Geneviève Thibault, Jacques Chailley, Armand Machabey, Elisabeth Lebeau, Nanie Bridgman, Vladimir Fédorov, Paul Henry Lang and Dragan Plamenac.

The Société Française de Musicologie was founded in 1917 with Lionel de La Laurencie as its first president and has published the *Revue de musicologie* since 1922. For a short time after World War I France served as the home of the International Musicological Society, promoting its activities and publishing its journal, the *Bulletin de la société 'Union musicologique'* (1921–6). In the years since World War II, French musicology has undergone significant developments. One important factor in its growth has been the consolidation under one administration of the three major music libraries in Paris, the Bibliothèque de l'Opéra, the Bibliothèque du Conservatoire and the music division of the Bibliothèque Nationale. Some of the most productive scholars in France have been associated with this newly founded institution: François Lesure, Nanie Bridgman and Vladimir Fédorov. In 1953 Jacques Chailley became professor of music history at the Sorbonne and director of the Musicological Institute at the University of Paris. Among the senior scholars of this period were Marc Pincherle, a specialist in the violin music of the late Baroque and Classical periods, and Geneviève Thibault (Countess of Chambure) who encouraged and influenced scholarship throughout the world, particularly in the fields of the 16th-century chanson, organology and iconography.

The humanities division of the Centre National de la Recherche Scientifique has since the early 1950s brought small international groups of musical specialists together for intensive discussion of chosen problems. Some of these 'colloques', many under the direction of Jean Jacquot, have explored the interrelationship of poetry and music, and theatre and music, while others have centred on instrumental music, acoustics, style, the Renaissance and Baroque, and the 18th and 20th centuries. Their proceedings have been published within the general series Le Choeur des Muses, which also includes editions.

The search for a fully deployed 'science' of music is still a strong intellectual current in France. The early acoustical work of Pierre Schaeffer in his experimental studio, which started in 1942 and later came under the auspices of the ORTF, led eventually to his formulation of a 'morphology and typology' of all musical objects in his *Traité des objets musicaux* (1966). The same spirit fired the theoretical formulations of Pierre Boulez, notably in his essay 'Technique musicale' in *Penser la musique aujourd'hui* (1964), and also the rigorous analytical apparatus of Nicolas Ruwet and Jean-Jacques Nattiez in their musical semiotics (*see* SEMIOLOGY). It is most fully expressed in the scheme to establish an Institut de Recherche et de Coordination Acoustique/Musique (IRCAM), headed by Boulez and housed on the central Parisian site known as the 'Petit-Beaubourg' within a vast complex of buildings constituting a centre for contemporary art. This institute is to have four divisions: the Section Instruments et Voix, investigating natural sounds under the direction of Vinko Globokar; the Studios de Musique Electronique et Electro-Acoustique under Luciano Berio; the Département des Ordinateurs, investigating sound synthesis under Jean-Claude Risset in collaboration with Iannis Xenakis; and the 'unite mobile' under Diego Masson. It represents an international and interdisciplinary enterprise of an ambitiousness that is wholly French.

2. ITALY. Before the 20th century the state of musicology in Italy presented a strange contrast between the richness of the country's archives and the failure of its scholars to make the best use of them. Italian scholarship of the 19th and early 20th centuries produced little to compare with Einstein's study of the Italian madrigal, Haberl's collected edition of Palestrina's music, or the pioneer work on several important Italian composers undertaken by foreign scholars. The reasons for this may be sought in the national temperament, in the failure of universities to stimulate interest in historical studies, in the lack of funds available for research, in the haphazard organization of certain libraries (a situation not entirely remedied today), and perhaps also in the sheer quantity of material available. One result of all this was that scholars worked, often in isolation, on whatever came nearest to hand, and it is only quite recently that a broader sphere of interest and a more sophisticated methodology have raised the status of Italian musicology to international levels.

Italy's contribution to music theory in the 18th and 19th centuries should not be overlooked, however. Burney met numerous learned musicians, collectors, theorists and historians during his Italian tour (1770), and even before this F. A. Calegari, his pupil Vallotti, and Tartini at Padua were looking for a theoretical basis for music founded on mathematical principles. Vallotti's ideas were systematically expounded in treatises by L. A. Sabbatini published in Venice about the end of the century. Sabbatini had been a pupil at Bologna of Padre Martini, a central figure in the Italian musical Enlightenment, whose reputation as a historian and theorist was unsurpassed. His three-volume *Storia della musica* (1757–81), though incomplete, badly proportioned and marred by archaic methodology, was of wide influence; and his two-volume *Saggio fondamentale pratico di contrappunto* (1774–5) was an admired textbook on the contrapuntal practice of the old and new styles. Martini's interest in the past as a lesson for the present was very similar to ours, and his voluminous correspondence and library (now in *I-Bc*) represent in the first place a source of information about musical activity in the broadest sense. His methods were modelled on those of Muratori, the founder of modern Italian historiography, in nearby Modena.

Petrobelli (*AcM*, xliii, 1971) has identified three main lines of activity in 19th-century Italian musicology. The first, which he referred to as the 'true' Italian tradition, concerned primarily with sacred music, can be traced at least as far back as Pitoni (1657–1743). Though conservative and even archaic in his own music, he must be regarded as a forerunner in historical musicology. His *Notizie dei maestri di cappella*, containing copious information on some 1500 musicians active in Rome and elsewhere between 1000 and about 1700, was never published, but Baini drew on it for his study of Palestrina (1828) and for his projected *Storia della cappella pontificia*. The former is a key document in the history of music biography and a starting-point for the 19th-century cult of Palestrina and the *a cappella* style. It was soon followed by a seven-volume edition of Palestrina's works edited by Pietro Alfieri. Following in the tradition of Baini, the Abbé Santini assembled at

Rome a remarkable collection of manuscripts and transcriptions which ultimately found its way into the cathedral library at Münster (now in *D-MÜs*).

A second area of activity in the 19th century is represented by the extremely valuable (if not invariably accurate) documentary work of 'local' music historians, such as Francesco Caffi's on the music at St Mark's, Venice, and Gaetano Gaspari's on that of S Petronio, Bologna. Perhaps the most important of these local historians was Francesco Florimo, whose well-known account of the Neapolitan conservatories appeared in four volumes (1880–83). This interest in local music history, often motivated by a scholar's pride in the place where he was born or brought up, has been continued in the 20th century (usually on a more scientific basis), for example by Francesco Vatielli at Bologna, Raffaele Casimiri at Rome, Ulisse Prota-Giurleo at Naples, Mario Fabbri at Florence, and Roberto Pagano in Sicily.

Petrobelli's third category comprises 19th-century writers with a more comprehensive outlook. The interests of Abramo Basevi (1818–85) extended to contemporary German music as well as older Italian music, as did those of Alberto Mazzucato at the Milan Conservatory. Mazzucato's ideas on music history were systematically presented in the writings of his pupil Amintore Galli. An attempt to cover early Italian music comprehensively was made by Luigi Torchi in his *L'Arte Musicale in Italia*, projected in 34 volumes, of which only seven reached publication. At about the same time Oscar Chilesotti brought out a nine-volume set of early French and Italian music, mostly for lute and guitar, under the title Biblioteca di Rarità Musicali.

An influential figure in the early part of the 20th century was Fausto Torrefranca, whose writings were motivated by nationalism (*Le origini italiane del romanticismo musicale*, 1930) and by the 'neo-idealistic' philosophy and historiographic methods of Benedetto Croce (*La vita musicale dello spirito*, 1910). Following in the same trend was Andrea Della Corte, co-author with Guido Pannain of the first large-scale Italian history of music (1936). Gaetano Cesari was the first Italian scholar to profit from a thorough musicological training, which he received in Munich from Sandberger and Kroyer. In 1931 he founded the historical series Istituzioni e Monumenti dell'Arte Musicale Italiana, on which Giacomo Benvenuti, another Sandberger pupil, also worked. Benvenuti inaugurated another important series, I Classici Musicali Italiani, in 1941. The Istituto Italiano per la Storia della Musica, founded in 1938, published Casimiri's edition of Palestrina and works by other Renaissance and Baroque composers. More recently Italian musicology has earned international recognition through the work of such scholars as Nino Pirrotta and Pierluigi Petrobelli.

A central figure in musical activity and organization during the 20th century was Guido Maria Gatti, author of several books, editor with Andrea Della Corte of what was long the standard Italian musical dictionary, general editor of the dictionary and encyclopedia *La musica*, and music editor of two other encyclopedias. In 1920 he founded the periodical *Il pianoforte*, which in 1928 became the *Rassegna musicale*; publication ceased in 1962, but a series of *Quaderni* followed. The most authoritative Italian music periodical from 1894 until it ceased publication in 1955 was the *Rivista musicale italiana*, published by the Bocca brothers of Turin; others include Ricordi's *Gazzetta musicale di Milano* (1842–1966, with several changes of title), and *Note d'archivio*, a mine of documentary information on early Italian music and musicians which Raffaele Casimiri edited from 1924 until his death in 1943.

In an effort to place Italian musicology on a sounder footing the Associazione dei Musicologi Italiani was founded at Ferrara in 1908 by Guido Gasperini. An important result was the publication between 1909 and 1941 of a series of catalogues of Italian libraries and archives. The project remained unfinished and the results were uneven, but many of the catalogues were of outstanding quality, notably those of the Biblioteca Estense in Modena and the Biblioteca del Conservatorio di Musica in Naples. The association's activities ceased after Gasperini's death in 1942, but a new organization, the Società Italiana di Musicologia, was founded in 1964 with its own journal, the *Rivista italiana di musicologia*; and in 1967 Italian Radio supported the foundation of the *Nuova rivista musicale italiana*. Since 1966 . the Ufficio Ricerca Fondi Musicali Italiani, directed by Claudio Sartori, has been engaged in the finding and cataloguing of musical material.

Italian universities were slow to recognize the importance of musicological studies. Musicology in Italy thus owes much to a group of research institutes supported, in part, by public funds. The Istituto di Studi Verdiani at Parma, the Accademia Tartiniana at Padua and the Fondazione Rossini at Pesaro are all engaged in scholarly research into those composers whose names they bear, and the Cini Foundation at Venice has assembled an important collection, in photographic reproduction, of Venetian musical sources, as well as organizing conferences on Venetian opera. Courses and conferences are also arranged each year at Certaldo, Boccaccio's birthplace, for the study of 14th- and 15th-century music, and at Siena by the Accademia Chigiana, whose valuable bulletin, *Chigiana*, is published by Olschki of Florence. The same publishers issue important series of monographs (Historiae Musicae Cultores) and editions (e.g. Archivium Musices Metropolitanum Mediolanense). Another important research journal, *Analecta musicologica*, is published by the German–Italian Institute at Rome.

3. GREAT BRITAIN AND THE COMMONWEALTH COUNTRIES. Musicology in Britain has grown out of certain particularly strong and long-lived traditions: the collecting and study of musical instruments, the science of acoustics, the performing of early music (with the allied practices of textual criticism and editing) and to some extent also the collecting and editing of folksong. The development of music history as a scholarly discipline came, in a sense, rather later, although it has roots extending back to the 17th century. Its pre-Victorian manifestations were very much part of the amateur tradition of music study that has always been an element of British musicology. In those earlier times, all music other than contemporary music was termed 'ancient music' and thought of as the domain of the 'antiquary'.

Roger North (1653–1734) stands at the beginning of the English Enlightenment and was a man in whom the spirit of the Enlightenment was clearly visible. Furthermore, he represents an abiding tradition in British musical scholarship in placing emphasis on music not as a subject for speculation but as a living art to be enjoyed

and understood in performance. North, a member of a distinguished family, was trained for a career in law but retired in 1688 to devote himself to music and gardening. He regarded himself as an amateur musician. He cultivated music in its widest dimensions, was fascinated by the ideas that move men to create it, and filled notebooks with observations related to theory and musical composition, history, aesthetics and performing practice. These views were consolidated in a series of treatises of which *The Musicall Grammarian* and *Memoires of Musick* were the most important. He continually redrafted and revised his writings but never brought them to publication. North, though not a profound music historian or speculative theorist, had vision and a lively curiosity, and was free from pedantry.

A more traditionally orientated musician was J. C. Pepusch (1667–1752). His fame rests chiefly on his association with John Gay as musical arranger of *The Beggar's Opera* (1728), but his contemporaries knew him as a student of ancient music and theory. The crowning achievements of English music historiography in the 18th century were the general histories of Charles Burney and John Hawkins. Hawkins's *General History of the Science and Practice of Music* appeared complete in five volumes in 1776. The first volume of Burney's *General History of Music from the Earliest Ages to the Present* was issued in the same year, but the author did not finish his work until 1789. The magnitude of these accomplishments is astonishing considering that Hawkins and Burney worked independently and without significant antecedents.

The two main preoccupations of 19th-century music historians were church music and the Elizabethan 'Golden Age' of English music. The critical study of church music arose at about the time that the monks of Solesmes were beginning their work in France on plainchant; it was associated in part with the Oxford Movement for liturgical reform, and later with the so-called English Renaissance at the end of the century. Two scholars represent the study of church music at the turn of the century: Walter Howard Frere (1863–1938), Bishop of Truro, and Edmund H. Fellowes (1870–1951), a minor canon of St George's Chapel, Windsor. Frere was concerned with the study of medieval plainchant, but he also did much to establish the forms of liturgy in late medieval England, particularly the Use of Sarum, and produced editions of the main Sarum liturgical books. His work was continued by Anselm Hughes (1889–1974). Fellowes produced his standard history of *English Cathedral Music from Edward VI to Edward VII* (1942) and biographies of Byrd (1923, superseded by a second in 1936) and Gibbons (1925), as well as studies of the English madrigal and its composers and many editions of 16th- and 17th-century sacred and secular music (see below).

The first important 20th-century history of music in English was *The Oxford History of Music* (1901–5), written from very different standpoints by H. E. Wooldridge, Hubert Parry, J. A. Fuller Maitland, Henry Hadow, Edward Dannreuther and H. C. Colles, with an introductory volume by Percy Buck. Parry in particular, in his volume on the 17th century, took a Darwinian evolutionary approach to music history which he had already applied in *The Art of Music* (1893, enlarged as *The Evolution of the Art of Music*, International Scientific Series, lxxx, 1896), and which has characterized much English historical writing since. The successor to *OHM*, *The New Oxford History of Music*, was under the direction of Egon Wellesz and Jack Westrup – two great Oxford historians, the latter one of the most influential minds in English music historiography – and Gerald Abraham, noted particularly for his work on Russian and east European music. Another scholar of profound influence, in England and internationally, was Edward J. Dent (1876–1957), professor at Cambridge, whose main field of research was Italian Baroque opera, and who did much to bring little-known music of the past and present to a wider audience.

British historical writing prides itself on its strong critical tradition, cultivating descriptive and evaluative prose. An interest in musical aesthetics goes back to the 18th century, with a group of writers concerned chiefly with the relationship between music and poetry. Its principal member was Charles Avison, a composer–critic whose *Essay on Musical Expression* appeared in 1752. A few years later John Brown published his *Dissertation on the Union and Power, the Progressions, Separations, and Corruptions of Poetry and Music* (1763), which was followed by Daniel Webb's *Observations on the Correspondence between Poetry and Music* (1769) and James Beattie's *Essays on Poetry and Music* (1776).

Occasional reviews of music and musical performances began to appear during the second half of the 18th century in monthly journals such as the *Gentleman's Magazine* and *European Magazine*, but it was not until the early 19th century, with such publications as *The Harmonicon* (1823–33) and the *Musical World* (1836–91) that independent music journalism was firmly established. The *Musical Times*, which has been in continuous publication since 1844, combines unusually wide coverage of musical events with well-informed criticism and articles of general and scholarly interest. The *Musical Antiquary* (1909–13) was short-lived but set a new standard in the presentation of musical scholarship, while both the title and the contents of *Music & Letters* (founded 1920) are representative of the best traditions in English musicology. Since 1940 the broad approach of *Music & Letters* has been complemented by the more closely analytical emphasis of another quarterly journal, *Music Review*. Newspaper music journalism has always been of a high standard, elegant and well informed. Among the most famous critics in the late 19th and early 20th centuries were George Bernard Shaw, Ernest Newman and Neville Cardus, and these have been followed by Martin Cooper, William Mann, Jeremy Noble, Andrew Porter, Stanley Sadie and others in the principal newspapers and weekly and monthly magazines. Critical and historical traditions come together in the work of writers such as the Handel scholar Winton Dean, the medievalist John Stevens and the writer on German and Russian Romantic music John Warrack.

The tradition of collecting musical instruments is a very old one, and Britain houses several fine collections which furnish primary material for research. These include the Russell Collection of keyboard instruments in Edinburgh, the Bate Collection of wind instruments in Oxford, the Colt Collection of keyboard instruments in Kent, and the collections at the Ashmolean, Oxford, and the Victoria and Albert Museum, the Horniman Museum and the Royal College of Music, London.

Francis Galpin (1858–1945), working at the same time as Hornbostel and Sachs, was one of the first to write in a scholarly way about instruments in his *Old English Instruments of Music* (1910). He investigated not only European instruments but also those of the Near East, and his private collection numbered more than 500 instruments. The Galpin Society, founded in 1946, publishes an annual journal which is indispensable to anyone interested in early instruments, with articles by such scholars as Philip Bate, Anthony Baines and Peter Williams (who also edits the important *Organ Year Book*, founded 1970). The quarterly *Early Music*, which started publication in 1973, devotes many of its pages to articles on instruments.

The twin traditions of performing and editing early music go back to the 18th century. Pepusch was one of the founders of the Academy of Ancient Music in the 1720s, the first of a series of associations devoted to the performance of early music. Others were the Apollo Society (1731), the Madrigal Society (1741) and the Noblemen's and Gentlemen's Catch Club (1761). The repertory of these singing societies was drawn from English and Italian partsongs of an earlier period together with contemporary catches and glees.

The members of the Dolmetsch family were the most influential figures in the early 20th century in bringing about performances of Renaissance and Baroque music on authentic instruments such as lutes, viols, recorders and crumhorns. Arnold Dolmetsch (1858–1940) pioneered the accurate restoration of old instruments and the making of reproductions; he also researched and edited early instrumental music, and instituted festivals of early music. The Viola da Gamba Society (founded 1956) and the Lute Society (1948) continue to encourage authentic performance, and produce their own journals as forums for the discussion of performing practice, instruments and sources. This activity resulted in the setting up from the 1950s onwards of many instrument makers who based their designs on original instruments, as well as of a number of professional groups whose players were thoroughly versed in early performing practice and whose singers were trained in vocal production and ornamentation appropriate to specific musical styles.

The performance of 17th- and 18th-century opera, particularly the operas of Monteverdi, Purcell and Handel under Westrup at Oxford University from the 1920s onwards and under Anthony Lewis at Birmingham University in the 1940s to 1960s, was an important venture. Lewis, on the staff of the BBC from 1935 and in charge of music on the Third Programme in the mid-1940s, brought such music to a still wider public. The spirit of all these operatic ventures derived from the work and teaching of Dent, who saw performance as the ultimate goal of scholarship.

The histories by Burney and Hawkins were remarkable for their extensive examples of early music, and the English were among the first to edit early music on a large scale. A collection, *Cathedral Music*, was projected by John Alcock and Maurice Greene and completed by William Boyce between 1760 and 1778. The edition, representing a continuous tradition from Tye and Tallis to Purcell and Croft, was further revised and expanded in 1790 by Samuel Arnold. It was Arnold who made the first collected edition of the works of a major composer, namely Handel. The set was issued in 180 instalments between 1787 and 1797 and, for its time, was a creditable undertaking, but unfortunately Arnold, for all his enthusiasm, was not equipped to fulfil his promise that the work would be 'correct, uniform, and complete'. The many collections of catches and glees that appeared at intervals thoughout the century displayed great antiquarian interest. One of the most conspicuous examples of this kind was Thomas Warren's *Collection of . . . Catches, Canons, and Glees* (c1775–), which contained 652 pieces, many of them transcribed from 16th-century sources. Another edition devoted to the music of the past was William Crotch's *Specimens of Various Styles of Music* (1807–8), one of the first historical anthologies of music designed for teaching purposes. Crotch's selection is unusual in the amount of folk or national music that it contains, of both Eastern and Western origin. John Stafford Smith published a similar anthology in 1812 under the title *Musica Antiqua: a Selection of Music of this and other Countries from the Commencement of the 12th to the Beginning of the 18th Century.*

The British Musical Antiquarian Society published music of the Elizabethan and Jacobean periods, and also of Purcell, between 1840 and 1847 (three decades before Eitner began his *Publikationen*). The Purcell Society, founded in 1876, embarked on its edition of Purcell's music in 1878, in collaboration with the publishing firm of Novello; it was eventually completed with volume xxxiii in 1965. In 1898 John Stainer published his collection of medieval music, *Dufay and his Contemporaries*. The earliest English counterparts of the great German and Austrian Denkmäler editions, which began in 1892, were the publications of the Plainsong and Mediaeval Music Society (founded 1888) which date from 1891 onwards: Edmund Fellowes's 36-volume English Madrigal School (1913–24) and 32-volume English School of Lutenist Song-writers (1920–32), and the jointly edited Tudor Church Music (1922–9). Fellowes also produced a collected edition of the works of Byrd (1937–50). Thurston Dart later revised much of Fellowes's work, as well as engaging in several important projects of his own. His editorial methods, which combined exact scholarship with sympathetic awareness of the needs of performers, were widely imitated. He was associated with the most important series of scholarly editions to appear since World War II, Musica Britannica, launched in 1951 by the Royal Musical Association, with Anthony Lewis as general editor and Stainer & Bell as publishers.

As early as 1851 a learned society had been founded in London 'for the cultivation of the art and science of music'. This was the Musical Institute of London, presided over by John Hullah. It was dissolved two years later, but in 1874 the Musical Association (since 1944 the Royal Musical Association) was founded by John Stainer and William Pole 'for the investigation and discussion of subjects connected with the art and science of music'. The 'science' referred to was acoustics, a study strongly cultivated in Britain from the mid-19th century to the mid-20th by such scholars as Pole himself (a civil engineer by profession), Alexander Ellis, James Jeans and Alexander Wood; its major practical manifestation was the scientifically designed Royal Festival Hall, built in 1951. Since its formation the RMA has extended its activities, and its published *Proceedings*, together with a *Research Chronicle*, now constitute a major contribution to English musicology.

From its earliest times British musicology has placed great emphasis on research into folksong and popular music. The tradition extends from Bishop Percy's *Reliques* (1765) and Edward Jones's *Musical and Poetical Relicks of the Welsh Bards* (1784) to the 20th century. Joseph Ritson (1752–1803) introduced critical methods in place of the casual amateurism of Percy, and the Anglican clergyman John Broadwood was one of the first to collect (in 1843) songs directly from the lips of living singers. His methods were followed by his niece, Lucy Broadwood, and by another clergyman, Sabine Baring-Gould. Two of the leading 19th-century students of British popular song were Edward F. Rimbault (1816–76) and William Chappell (1809–88). Rimbault was a versatile if not very precise scholar who played an active part in the formation of both the Musical Antiquarian and the Percy Societies. William Chappell is best remembered for his *Popular Music of the Olden Time* (1845–9), a work of enduring value. Towards the end of the century Frank Kidson, Cecil Sharp and Ralph Vaughan Williams were collecting and editing folksongs – still part of a living tradition. Kidson was a founder-member of the Folk Song Society in 1898; Sharp and Vaughan Williams later became members. In 1932 the society joined with the English Folk Dance Society (founded 1911) to form the English Folk Dance and Song Society. More recent studies in English folk music have owed much to the research and activities of Maud Karpeles, A. L. Lloyd and Frank Howes, editor of the *Folk Song Journal* and its successor the *Journal of the English Folk Dance and Song Society* from 1927 to 1945.

Many younger British scholars have adopted a more anthropological approach to the study of Britain's folk music, and much research has been undertaken into the folk music of non-European countries, notably by Hugh Tracey, A. M. Jones and John Blacking on African music, Laurence Picken on Chinese music and Turkish folk instruments, and an important group of scholars at the School of Oriental and African Studies, London University.

In 1740 the young James Grassineau, encouraged by Pepusch, published *A Musical Dictionary*. This turned out to be something more than the mere translation of Brossard's *Dictionaire* that had been planned, and was in fact the first substantial work of its kind in the English language. Busby's *Complete Dictionary* (1786), Burney's articles for Rees's *New Cyclopaedia* (1802–20), Busby's *Musical Biography* (1814) and Sainsbury's *Dictionary of Musicians* (1824) are among the more important lexicographical works between Grassineau's and the first edition of Grove's *Dictionary of Music and Musicians*. This was completed in 1890 and, in its subsequent revisions, has remained the most comprehensive and authoritative English-language work of its kind. Percy Scholes's *Oxford Companion to Music* (1938) showed a more idiosyncratic approach to lexicography, but contained much information not readily accessible elsewhere, and Eric Blom's *Everyman's Dictionary of Music* (1946) was more useful and reliable than its small size might suggest. Both these works subsequently appeared in several new editions.

The role of the universities in the advancement of British musicology was not a prominent one before World War II, although the influence of isolated scholars such as Donald Tovey at Edinburgh and Dent at Cambridge was profound on those students who came into contact with them. Oxford and Cambridge have continued to play a leading role, partly because of their rich archival resources, but also because of the example and teaching reforms of Jack Westrup at Oxford and Thurston Dart and his predecessors at Cambridge. Dart was also for a time professor at King's College, London University, and his influence was felt by a whole generation of British scholars. Many other British universities now have important music faculties, several of which encourage research at postgraduate level.

The development of musicological studies in the English-speaking countries of the Commonwealth is relatively recent. Only in the case of New Zealand have the traditional ties with Great Britain remained strong, through the interchange of scholars. Peter Platt, an English scholar trained at Oxford, taught at Otago (1957–75); John Steele, a New Zealander, studied early English keyboard music at Cambridge and returned to teach at Otago; and several New Zealand scholars have settled in Britain. In Australia, American models have tended to prevail, for example in the graduate school established at Adelaide under Andrew D. McCredie and in the links between conservatory and music department there and at other centres. English scholars have, however, held important posts, notably David Galliver and Donald Peart; Peart and Frank Callaway have been particularly active in music education studies. Other active scholars are Gordon Anderson, Peter Dennison and David Tunley. Two university departments, at Perth and Adelaide, are concerned in the publication of valuable musicological yearbooks. Canadian musicology has naturally been orientated towards the USA rather than Great Britain (or France), and there are several significant graduate schools, notably at Toronto University, on the American pattern; music education is a favoured field of study. Notable scholars include Helmut Kallmann, Maria Rika Maniates, Hugh McLean and H. Colin Slim.

4. GERMANY AND AUSTRIA. During the course of the 18th century the centre of gravity in music moved from south to north European countries. The same was true of music scholarship. Two names, from among many, may be mentioned as representative of that trend. One was Martin Gerbert (1720–93), abbot of St Blasien, who first submitted the music of the Middle Ages to critical scholarship. His history of sacred music, *De cantu et musica sacra* (1767), was used heavily by Burney and Forkel, as was his anthology of medieval treatises, *Scriptores ecclesiastici de musica sacra* (1784). The other was Ernst Ludwig Gerber (1746–1819) who began by revising and expanding the biographical entries in Walther's *Lexicon* (1732) and concluded by producing a biographical reference work on a scale unprecedented for his time: *Historisch-biographisches Lexikon der Tonkünstler* (1790–92), followed by a four-volume *Neues historisch-biographisches Lexikon der Tonkünstler* (1812–14).

Germany led the rest of Europe in establishing the academic discipline of modern music scholarship. The German university system provided the institutional framework within which the new field could evolve; as a result, German musicology of the 19th century established a record of productivity unrivalled by any other nation. Critical editions, definitive biographies, bibliographies and catalogues were issued in a profusion that was not disrupted by two world wars. At the same time the emerging discipline enjoyed an enviable relationship

with the press. The great publishing houses of Breitkopf & Härtel and C. F. Peters in Leipzig, and Schott in Mainz, were generous in their support of scholarly activity, not only in the publication of editions and research monographs but through the issuing of periodicals to spread the results of research. The *Allgemeine musikalische Zeitung*, founded in 1798 in Leipzig by Friedrich Rochlitz, was the prime example of such a journal. It served as a model for *Cäcilia*, published by Schott in Mainz and edited successively by Gottfried Weber and Siegfried Dehn from 1824 to 1848, and also for the *Berliner allgemeine musikalische Zeitung*, edited by A. B. Marx from 1824 to 1830. Another important journal of criticism was Robert Schumann's *Neue Zeitschrift für Musik*, which began its long run in 1834 and still continues. By the end of the 19th century German musicology had reached a high level of professionalism clearly reflected in such journals as the *Vierteljahrsschrift für Musikwissenschaft* edited jointly by Chrysander, Spitta and Adler from 1885 to 1894, the *Jahrbuch der Musikbibliothek Peters*, 1894–1940, founded by Emil Vogel, and Robert Eitner's *Monatshefte für Musikgeschichte*, 1869–1905.

Johann Nikolaus Forkel (1749–1818) stands at the head of the new breed of academic musician that came into being in the early 19th century. He spent the greater part of his career at the Georg-August University at Göttingen, which he first attended in 1769 as a student of jurisprudence, and afterwards served as organist of the university church and as music director in 1779; he was awarded an honorary doctorate in 1787. Among Forkel's many important publications was the first musicologically orientated bibliography of music books (*Allgemeine Litteratur der Musik*, 1792), a history of music (*Allgemeine Geschichte der Musik*, 1788–1801), and the first attempt at a biography of J. S. Bach (*Über J. S. Bachs Leben, Kunst und Kunstwerke*, 1802). Göttingen in the late 18th century was a centre of lively intellectual activity. The university was founded in 1734 by the Elector of Hanover, who was also George II of England; it was noteworthy for its Anglo-German studies and for a school of 'universal historians' that developed there under the leadership of such men as Johann Christoph Gatterer, J. C. Schölzer and Johann von Müller. They advocated a view of history that extended far beyond the traditional emphasis on political and military affairs, and provided a framework for Forkel's studies in the history of music.

Forkel was not an isolated example. In 1779, the year in which he was appointed university music director at Göttingen, Daniel Gottlob Türk (1750–1813) was granted a similar post at Halle, where he lectured in music history, theory and aesthetics. From that time onwards a widening circle of German universities and research institutes brought music into their curricula with men such as Franz Joseph Fröhlich at Würzburg, Christian Friedrich Michaelis at Leipzig, Ferdinand Gassner at Giessen, Adolf Bernhard Marx at Berlin, and Carl Breidenstein at Bonn. Breidenstein was the first musician to occupy a professorial chair in music (1826), but it was not until 1870 that the Viennese music critic Eduard Hanslick became the first to bear the title *Professor ordinarius* in music history and aesthetics at the University of Vienna. The first German professorship of equal rank was held by Gustav Jacobsthal at the University of Strasbourg in 1897. Between 1904 and 1960 no fewer than 21 German universities inaugurated full professorships at the level of *ordinarius*, and their first occupants make an impressive list of scholars:

1904 Berlin: Hermann Kretzschmar
1909 Munich: Adolf Sandberger
1915 Bonn: Ludwig Schiedermair
1918 Halle: Hermann Abert
1920 Breslau: Max Schneider
1920 Göttingen: Friedrich Ludwig
1920 Leipzig: Hermann Abert
1921 Heidelberg: Theodor Kroyer
1928 Kiel: Fritz Stein
1929 Freiburg: Wilibald Gurlitt
1932 Cologne: Theodor Kroyer
1935 Frankfurt am Main: Joseph Müller-Blattau
1944 Königsberg: Hans Engel
1946 Mainz: Franz Arnold Schmitz
1946 Marburg: Hans Engel
1946 Münster: Werner Korte
1947 Jena: Hans Joachim Moser
1952 Tübingen: Walter Gerstenberg
1956 Hamburg: Heinrich Husmann
1958 Saarbrücken: Joseph Müller-Blattau
1960 Würzburg: Georg Reichert

The German university system provided academic ranks for a host of other distinguished scholars who contributed to the growing literature of their field. An outstanding example was Hugo Riemann (1849–1919), the dominant figure in German musicology in the opening years of the 20th century. In the range and authority of his writing and teaching, Riemann invites comparison with Fétis (see §1 above). Both men had a universal appetite for knowledge. In a letter to Hans Huber in 1898, inquiring about a possible position at the University at Basle, Riemann modestly described his special province as 'music theory from A to Z, music history, including aesthetics and acoustics, keyboard instruction and performing practice'. Apart from his numerous monographs and manuals, Riemann made a number of important editions of early music (for example, volumes of music by the Mannheim school in Denkmäler der deutscher Tonkunst), and some 50 volumes of early chamber music under the title Collegium Musicum. His *Musik Lexikon*, first published in 1882, maintains his enormous influence in its 12th edition (1959–75).

Parallel to the Viennese school of Classical composers there was a 'Viennese school of musical scholarship' in the 19th century that exerted considerable influence on the development of musicology in the German-speaking countries. The central figure was Raphael Georg Kiesewetter (1773–1850), a civil servant in the office of the Austrian War Ministry (it was he who was successful against Fétis in the competition for the prize essay on the music of the Netherlanders). His interest in early secular vocal music led to a comprehensive treatment of the subject extending from the early Middle Ages to the birth of the monodic style (*Schicksale und Beschaffenheit des weltlichen Gesanges*, 1841). He also conducted investigations into Arabian music, tuning and temperament, and the musical instruments of the Middle Ages. He was the author of an outline history of music, the first of its kind, based on cultural epochs identified with the careers of the great creative musicians of the past (*Geschichte der europäisch-abendländischen Musik*, 1834). A younger colleague of Kiesewetter in the ministry office was Franz Sales Kandler (1792–1831) who took the advantage afforded by his diplomatic status to travel extensively in Italy observing and transcribing early music, the results of which he sent back to Vienna for Kiesewetter. Kandler established a close relationship with the Roman

historian and biographer of Palestrina, Giuseppe Baini, and in fact prepared a condensed German translation of Baini's work. A member of the same circle of music-loving public officials was Aloys Fuchs (1799–1853), an avid collector of musical autographs to whom we owe the preservation of a great many of the autograph scores of Viennese composers.

Anton Schmid (1784–1847), head of the music division of the Austrian National Library, was a specialist in the history of music printing. He produced an important monograph *Ottaviano dei Petrucci da Fossombrone . . . und seine Nachfolger im 16. Jahrhunderte* (1845), and contributed a series of bibliographical papers to the periodical *Cäcilia* based on the library's holdings in early printed music. He is also remembered as the author of the first critical biography of Gluck (1845).

The leading music historian of the late 19th century was a product of the Viennese group, although he was born near Prague. He was August Wilhelm Ambros (1816–76), a nephew of Raphael Kiesewetter and a man of broad cultural experience. His *Geschichte der Musik* appeared in four volumes between 1862 and 1878. Ambros's death interrupted the work before it had progressed much beyond 1600, but his observations on early polyphony, based on original research, set the standard for all subsequent research in this area.

Hanslick's successor as professor of music at the University of Vienna was Guido Adler (1855–1941), whose long career spanned the most productive period in Austro-German musicology. With Chrysander and Spitta he was co-editor of the *Vierteljahrsschrift für Musikwissenschaft*; he was also the founder and general editor of the Denkmäler der Tonkunst in Österreich (1894–). Adler's work was always historical in approach, but he saw that to write a comprehensive history of music was beyond the powers of any 20th-century scholar to accomplish alone. He collaborated with some of the most distinguished specialists of his generation to produce a *Handbuch der Musikgeschichte* (1924, 2/1930) that served as a basic text for students of historical musicology for the first half of the century.

The tasks German musicology set for itself in the 19th century were far-ranging and the results were often brilliant, establishing the boundaries and the substance of the discipline until at least the end of World War II. Faced with a flood of newly discovered source materials, many of the major names of this period contributed monumental catalogues, bibliographies, and thematic indexes. Among the most influential of these were Robert Eitner's ten-volume *Biographisch-bibliographisches Quellen-Lexikon* (1900–04) and Eitner and Haberl's *Bibliographie der Musik-Sammelwerke des XVI. und XVII. Jahrhunderts* (1877), Friedrich Ludwig's *Repertorium organorum recentioris et motetorum vetustissimi stili*, i/1 (1910; later completed by Gennrich), Emil Vogel's *Bibliothek der gedruckten weltlichen Vocalmusik Italiens* (1892), and Johannes Zahn's six-volume *Die Melodien der deutschen evangelischen Kirchenlieder* (1889–93).

A high standard was established for thematic indexing by the classic achievements of Nottebohm for Beethoven's works (1868; fully revised by Halm and Kinsky, 1955) and Ludwig von Köchel for Mozart's (1862, 3/1937 ed. Einstein, 6/1964). Among the new directions taken by German scholarship in the later

19th century was the Gesamtausgabe, the complete edition of the works of a major composer. This was frequently a joint enterprise involving the cooperation of several editors. From the founding of the Bach Gesellschaft in 1851, and its pioneer effort to publish all Bach's works, the pattern was set for a series of critical editions for such composers as Handel (1858), Palestrina (1862), Mozart (1876), Schubert (1883), Beethoven (1884) and Lassus (1894). Parallel to these series of editions was the appearance of studies of the life and works of individual composers, using increasingly refined musicological methodology. Philipp Spitta's remarkable two-volume study of J. S. Bach (1873–80) became a model for such studies.

During the first third of the 20th century German musicology advanced rapidly along these lines, and the profusion of scholarly publications that appeared placed German scholars in the front rank of musicology. From a long list of notable musicologists may be singled out Heinrich Besseler for his studies of medieval and Renaissance music; Hans Joachim Moser, especially for his studies of German church music; Johannes Wolf for his works on musical notation; Peter Wagner for his study of Gregorian chant and history of the mass (1914); Arnold Schering for his history of the oratorio (1911), history of the music of Leipzig (1927, 1941), study of performing practice in early music (1931) and aesthetic study of symbolism in music (1941). Schering also contributed a new kind of musicological tool, the anthology of old music *Geschichte der Musik in Beispielen* (1931), and Georg Kinsky compiled his anthology of pictorial material relating to music history *Geschichte der Musik in Bildern* (1929). Ernst Bücken, expanding Adler's original concept of a collaborative history written by specialists, edited and himself contributed to the monumental ten-volume *Handbuch der Musikwissenschaft* (1927–31). Its volumes were by some of the most distinguished German musicologists of these generations: Robert Lachmann, Curt Sachs, Heinrich Besseler, Robert Haas, Hans Mersmann, Otto Ursprung and Friedrich Blume.

In the same period Erich von Hornbostel and Curt Sachs carried out the basic work of classification and historical investigation of musical instruments; the significant results were published in Sachs's *Real-Lexikon der Musikinstrumente* (1913) and *Handbuch der Musikinstrumentenkunde* (1920). As each new generation of university students completed doctoral courses in musicology, and as German publishers expanded their support of musicological research of all kinds, it seemed certain that Germany would always dominate musicology on the international level. Indeed, it was through German initiative – by Oskar Fleischer and Max Seiffert – that the Internationale Musikgesellschaft was founded in 1899. It was disbanded in 1914, but during the Beethoven centenary celebrations in Vienna in 1927 a new organization, the Internationale Gesellschaft für Musikwissenschaft, was founded, with Guido Adler as honorary president and Peter Wagner as president.

However, as with all aspects of German and Austrian culture and life, the politics of National Socialism led to destruction and to the end of German domination in musicology. The subsequent collapse of the nation during World War II was one reason for the deterioration of musicological scholarship. A second reason, however, grew out of the darkest aspects of the Nazi era – the enforced emigration for racial reasons of many of Germany's and Austria's foremost musicologists, including Willi Apel, Manfred Bukofzer, Hans David, Alfred Einstein, Karl Geiringer, Otto Gombosi, Paul Nettl, Curt Sachs, Leo Schrade and Emanuel Winternitz, to name but a few who fled from Europe. Not only were German universities severely crippled by this removal of so many scholars, but the country as a whole was cut off from the extraordinary growth of the discipline in other parts of the world, especially the USA, where most of Germany's displaced musicologists had settled.

Since 1945 the traditions of scholarship formerly characterizing German musicology have slowly been restored, although many of the postwar achievements belong, at least for West Germany, to broader cooperative efforts within an international framework; in East Germany the chief emphasis has lain on the study of music in relation to different kinds of social system. The concerns of scholars before the 1930s with such projects as complete editions continue. Many of the old complete editions have been discontinued and new ones have begun to replace them, for example for Schütz, Bach, Handel and Mozart. Among the factors re-establishing Germany and Austria as centres of musicological accomplishment has been the continuing generous support of publishing houses. Not only have those firms with distinguished heritages, like Breitkopf & Härtel, Schott and Universal, remained active in musicology, but new firms such as Bärenreiter and Henle have become prominent. The appearance of good, scholarly editions has moved hand in hand with the study of performing practice, manifested in practical terms by such groups as the Capella Antiqua of Munich and the Concentus Musicus of Vienna.

Although established before World War II (in 1924), Bärenreiter under the leadership of its founder Karl Vötterle must be considered the single most important publisher of musicological work in the postwar decades. Among an extraordinary series of new complete editions, catalogues, facsimile editions and smaller publications, its greatest single enterprise has been *Die Musik in Geschichte und Gegenwart*; the first fascicle appeared in 1949, the last 30 years later. Prepared under the distinguished editor and scholar Friedrich Blume, this vast research encyclopedia (14 volumes and two of supplements) perhaps symbolizes better than any other work the position of German musicology in the second half of the 20th century. Edited with profound knowledge and care for detail, *MGG* has long been reckoned the most important single source of musicological knowledge for almost every facet of Western music history. It is, nevertheless, an international effort, with a large proportion of articles by scholars from the world at large. While the work's emphasis is profoundly German, *MGG* was the first international musicological effort of any size to be brought to completion.

As before the collapse of Germany during World War II, musicology again has a prominent role in most German universities. While several senior figures long remained influential (Bruno Stäblein, Walter Wiora), many important teaching posts are held by a middle generation of scholars (including Carl Dahlhaus, Hellmut Federhofer and Ludwig Finscher), whose range of interests is wide and whose names become increasingly significant through their own work and their participation in international meetings and research projects. While the German monopoly in musicology has clearly been broken for ever, it is also clear that German musicological scholarship has regained a central position in the international community of scholars.

5. OTHER WEST EUROPEAN COUNTRIES. The smaller countries of western Europe have naturally leant heavily on their larger neighbours in the development of musicological studies, and in particular many of them have leant on Germany. Their own traditions have been relatively late in developing and have not always been distinctive – depending, to some extent, on the musical past of the country concerned. A typical case is that of Switzerland, at the junction of three larger cultures. Scholars in that country have worked extensively on the history of Swiss music (notably the Protestant psalm), and have been avid in the production of dictionaries and periodicals; but apart from a continuing interest in medieval and Renaissance studies it would be hard to discover any national pattern in the work of such distinguished scholars of different generations as Peter Wagner, Jacques Handschin, Kurt von Fischer (a profoundly influential figure internationally) and Martin Staehelin. The activities of the Schola Cantorum Basiliensis, with which August Wenzinger and Wulf Arlt have worked, show an interest in the practical application of musicological knowledge.

Studies of performing practice, and of instruments, have characterized musicology in the Low Countries, typified by the instrument collecting of D. F. Scheurleer (1855–1927) and more recently by the conservation work of J. H. van der Meer, the performances of Gustav Leonhardt, the publications of Frits Knuf, and the historical instrument designs of Flentrop. Historical musicology (and the Dutch society for its study, the Vereniging voor Nederlandse Muziekgeschiedenis, founded in 1868 – the oldest in the world) is represented in the Netherlands by Albert Smijers, the first reader in the subject at a Dutch university (Utrecht, 1928), editor of the Josquin edition and student of other Franco-Flemish music, as well as the teacher of a generation of Dutch scholars including Eduard Reeser; also by scholars as diverse in their interests as Joseph Smits van Waesberghe, a chant scholar, and Frits Noske, whose work on song and opera covers the 17th to 19th centuries and whose interest in socio-musicology represents a significant new trend. The convergence of historical, sociological and ethnomusicological traditions (inherited primarily through Jaap Kunst, organologist and scholar of Indonesian music) typifies Dutch musicology in the 1970s. In Belgium, Robert Julien van Maldeghem (1810–93) produced an edition of early Flemish music in 29 volumes, defective as to editorial procedure but a valuable source for later scholars; and Edmond vander Straeten issued an eight-volume work documenting the activities of early Flemish musicians throughout Europe during the period of their greatest influence, *La musique aux Pays-Bas avant le XIXe siècle* (1867–88). Musicological studies were introduced at universities in 1931, partly through Ernest Closson's initiative; a specially influential figure was Charles van den Borren, who at Brussels and Liège taught Suzanne Clercx-Lejeune, Albert vander Linden and Robert Wangermée; his son-in-law was Safford Cape, with whom he founded the Pro Musica Antiqua

ensemble. A tradition of ecclesiastical musical studies is represented by Jozef Robijns and René Bernard Lenaerts.

Similar traditions have influenced Spanish musicology, with such scholar–priests as Higini Anglès, José María Llorens Cisteró and José López-Calo prominent in the uncovering of their country's heritage of ecclesiastical music. But important work was early accomplished by M. H. Eslava y Elizondo (1807–78) in his ten-volume Lira Sacro-Hispana and F. A. Barbieri (1823–94) in his edition of the 15th- and 16th-century Cancionero Musical de Palacio. The true father of modern Spanish musicology, however, was Felipe Pedrell (1841–1922), a composer, teacher, writer and music editor. He is best known for his editions of sacred music by early Spanish composers, Hispania Schola Musica Sacra (1894–8), and keyboard music by Cabezón, and especially for the complete edition of the works of Victoria; another important student of the national musical past, besides Anglès, was José Subirá Puig, a prolific writer particularly on Spanish dramatic music.

Scandinavian scholars, though much occupied with their national musical past, have tended to look to the German-speaking countries, particularly Switzerland, for their training. Tobias Norlind (1879–1947), the senior Swedish figure, studied at Leipzig and Munich; his pupil Carl-Allan Moberg (1896–1978), considered the founder of Swedish musicology, studied in Vienna and Fribourg; and Moberg's successor, Ingmar Bengtsson, studied in Basle. Moberg's research embraced early Swedish music and Swedish folksong, and Bengtsson worked on J. H. Roman and other Swedish composers before turning to socio-musicological studies. Also influential in Sweden was the influx of refugee scholars from Germany in the 1930s. In Denmark musicology has been longer established: Angul Hamerik (1848–1931) was awarded the earliest doctorate in music (1892) and obtained the first lectureship in musicology at Copenhagen (1896); he was a teacher of Erik Abrahamsen (in 1926 the first Danish professor of musicology) and the great Palestrina scholar Knud Jeppesen (the first professor at Århus, 1946). Jens Peter Larsen's work on the Classical era, and the involvement of several Danish scholars in Byzantine studies, have helped give the country's musicology a special character as well as an international standing. In Norway the first musicological chair was established in 1956 at Oslo, for Olav Gurvin (1893–1974), who had studied in Heidelberg and Berlin; he and Ole Sandvik (1875–1976) had given the first regular university lectures in music in 1937–9. Folk music studies form the bulk of these men's work; the investigation of the national musical past, including the Protestant church music tradition, has always occupied an important place in Scandinavia. The founder of Finnish musicology was Ilmari Krohn (1867–1960), who studied at Leipzig and Weimar, and founded the Finnish Musicological Society in 1916; his chief work was on theory, church music and Finnish folk music. The research of Erik Tawaststjerna on Sibelius and his contemporaries is among the most notable recent Finnish musical scholarship.

6. THE SOVIET UNION. Scholarly investigation of Russian music history began in the 18th century, especially after the rule of Peter the Great (1689–1725),

when sustained contacts with west European countries were established. The first significant publications were by foreigners in Russia, for example Leonhard Euler's *Tentamen novae theoriae musicae* (1739) and a lecture by Georg-Wolfgang Krafft (1701–54) on consonance (delivered in Latin in 1742 and published in Russian in 1744). Both were well-known mathematicians. Jacob von Stählin (1709–85) was the first to publish information about music in Russia, 'Nachrichten von der Musik in Russland' in Haigold's *Beylagen zum neuveränderten Russland*, ii (Riga and Leipzig, 1770). The first music periodical established in Russia was published by a German: Johann Daniel Gerstenberg's *Magasin musical de St. Pétersbourg* (1794). Towards the end of the 18th century the Russians began investigating their musical legacy by collecting folksongs (Trutovsky) and studying the rich domain of church music. The first to assemble data on Russian chant was Evfimy Bolkhovitinov (1767–1837), better known as Metropolitan Evgeny of Kiev, whose 1797 lecture on the subject was published two years later.

Some early 19th-century Russian writers preferred to study European music. Count Grigory Orlov (1777–1826), for example, published his *Essai sur l'histoire de la musique en Italie* (1832), and Alexander Ulïbïshev (1794–1858) and Wilhelm von Lenz (1808–83) their writings on Mozart and Beethoven.

Prince Vladimir Odoyevsky (1804–69), though basically an amateur, played an important role in the study of Russian music and may be viewed as one of the founders of musicology in Russia. Despite some earlier work, it was in the 1860s that the scholarly investigation of Russian chant history began, with the research of Dmitry Razumovsky (1818–89), Stepan Smolensky (1848–1909), Ivan Voznesensky (1838–1910) and especially Vasily Metallov (1862–1926) and Anatoly Preobrazhensky (1870–1929).

Apart from an article by Alexey Veselovsky in *Russkii vestnik* (1866), the first significant attempt at a history of Russian music in the Russian language was Vladimir Mikhnevich's *Istoricheskiye etyudï russkoy zhizni: ocherk istorii muzïki v Rossii v kulturno-obshchestvennom otnoshenii* ('Historical studies of Russian life: essay on the history of music in Russia in relationship to culture and society'; St Petersburg, 1879). In the next four decades, which led to the establishment of the Soviet Union, a number of writers specialized in aspects of Russian music history. Probably the most significant were Vsevolod Cheshikhin (1865–1934), a historian of Russian opera, and Nikolay Findeyzen (1868–1928), founder and editor of the important periodical *Russkaya muzïkal'naya gazeta* (1893–1918) and of the annual *Muzïkal'naya starina* ('Musical past'; 1903–11). Findeyzen's lifework, *Ocherki po istorii muzïki v Rossii s drevneyshikh vremyon do kontsa XVIII v.* ('Essays on the history of music in Russia from the earliest times to the end of the 18th century'; 1928–9), is still the most comprehensive survey of Russian music. The high level of analytical and historical musicology attained in the pre-revolutionary period is also exemplified in articles by a variety of writers on the 19th century and on contemporary music in the periodical *Muzïkal'nïy sovremennik* ('The musical contemporary'; 1915–17), edited by Andrey Rimsky-Korsakov (1878–1940), biographer of his father and a first-rate scholar.

There were significant developments between the wars. Perhaps most far-reaching and internationally recognized was the publication of original scores of Musorgsky's works under the editorship of Pavel Lamm, starting in 1928. This gave a strong impetus to systematic, critical study of sources. Even more significant were attempts to re-examine the basic postulates of music as an art, its components and its impact on the listener. These problems were studied from a theoretical point of view with a strong tendency to formulation in Marxist terms and, from the 1930s, in accordance with the officially promulgated concepts of socialist realism. Among the leaders of these studies were Boris Asaf'yev (who also wrote under the pseudonym Igor Glebov), a scholar of great erudition who formulated the concept of *intonatsiya* dealing with the creation of audio-imagery by association with familiar melodic patterns, and Boleslav Yavorsky, the creator of a concept of harmonic rhythm in his theory of 'auditory gravitation'. Important in the historical field since the mid-1930s has been Tamara Livanova, whose works, especially her classic book *Ocherki i materialï po istorii russkoy muzïkal'noy kulturï* ('Essays and documents on the history of Russian musical culture'; 1938), are among the most scholarly in Russian musicology, as are also Boris Yarustovsky's on dramaturgy. A number of scholars have tried to write comprehensive histories of world music, notably Roman Gruber.

Most of the younger scholars active since 1945 have specialized in aspects of Russian music and of other ethnic groups in the USSR, and the number of publications has greatly increased. Periodicals and yearbooks appear in growing numbers. Music bibliography has not only kept up with current publications but also given retrospective coverage (for example in Livanova's *Muzïkal'naya bibliografiya russkoy periodicheskoy pechati XIX v.*). Lexicography has also developed: Boris Shteynpress and Izrail' Yampol'sky are prominent in this area. Yury Keldïsh, author of a history of Russian music and an account of music in 18th-century Russia, was chief editor of a collective history of music of the peoples of the USSR (*Istoriya muzïki narodov SSSR*); he is also the editor of the largest Russian music encyclopedia, *Muzïkal'naya entsiklopediya*, and chief editor of the first Russian equivalent of the Denkmäler series under the title Pamyatniki Russkoy Muzïki. There are many biographical studies of Russian composers and their works; Semyon Ginzburg compiled an anthology of Russian art music up to Glinka (*Istoriya russkoy muzïki v notnïkh obraztsakh*), and studies of Russian chant have been resumed. A notable theorist is Lev Mazel', while Vladimir Protopopov is active in Western and Russian polyphony. Abram Gozenpud works on Russian opera; scholars of folk traditions include Isaly Zemtsovsky and Robert At'ayan (Armenian music).

7. EASTERN EUROPE. As with the Soviet Union, musicology has in the past been preoccupied with particular fields: with the history of church music and opera, with local music history, and increasingly with folk music. Marxist ideology has in recent years fostered the systematic and social study of music, and it is in this part of the world that the SOCIOLOGY OF MUSIC has become an independent discipline with rigorous standards.

The first important musicological publication on Polish music was the biographical dictionary *Les musiciens polonais et slaves anciens et modernes* (1857) by the pianist and amateur scholar Wojciech Sowiński (1805–80). In the same year Józef Sikorski (1813–96) founded a significant periodical, *Ruch muzyczny*, but it lasted only five years. An anthology of the rich legacy of church music, Monumenta Musices Sacrae in Polonia (1885–96), was initiated by Józef Surzyński (1851–1919). Much of the work of the 19th-century scholars dealt with Chopin, including that of Maurycy Karasowski, also the author of the first history of opera in Poland (*Rys historyczny opery polskiej*, 1859). The first full-scale history of Polish music seems to have been that by Aleksander Poliński, *Dzieje muzyki polskiej* (1907). No fewer than eight Poles obtained doctorates in musicology at German universities in the first decade of the 20th century. In 1911 the first chair in musicology was established in Poland, in Kraków. By World War I a group of scholars was already producing significant and lasting work. Among the next generation of scholars were Hieronim Feicht, Józef Chomiński and Zofia Lissa, a leading thinker in musical aesthetics and historiography and one of the most influential musicologists in eastern Europe. The two main centres of publication for music scholarship are Warsaw and Kraków, to which must be added Bydgoszcz, where triennial conferences have been held since 1966 under the title Musica Antiqua Europae Orientalis for scholars of eastern European music. The youngest generation includes Stefan Jarociński, Bogusław Schäffer, Zygmunt M. Szweykowski and Mirosław Perz.

Romania had a forerunner of musicology in the humanist Dimitrie Cantemir (1673–1723), who wrote a description of Romanian music (1716), studied Turkish music and devised a notational system for recording it. Before the 20th century there were individual attempts at collecting church music, notably by Anton Pann (1797–1854); Eusebius Mandyczewski (1857–1929), the great scholar and editor active in Vienna, was of Romanian origin. Modern scholarship began only after World War I with the ethnomusicological studies of Constantin Brăiloiu and the musicological work of George Breazul and Ioan D. Petrescu (1884–1970), who studied church music and its relationship to Byzantine music. The younger generation of scholars includes Viorel Cosma; his generation has worked particularly on the history of Romanian music, with special emphasis on the music of Enescu.

In Bulgaria, except for some studies in folk music, scholarly activities did not really begin until the work of Ivan Kamburov and Stojan Brashovanov, author of the first history of Bulgarian music (1946). Since 1945 there has been a much greater emphasis on scholarly work, supported by the Institute of Musicology founded in 1948 as part of the Bulgarian Academy of Sciences. An important writer on Bulgarian music is Venelin Krastev, author of several monographs; he was responsible for the first comprehensive encyclopedia of Bulgarian music.

The first systematic gathering of data about Czech musicians seems to be the *Allgemeines historisches Künstler-Lexikon* (1815) of Bohumír Dlabač. The beginnings of a more systematic study of the Czech and Slovak musical past appear in the works of Otakar Hostinský (1847–1910), who trained a generation of scholars, among them Dobroslav Orel, Otakar Zich and most notably Vladimir Helfert (1886–1945), a fine scholar particularly active after the creation of an independent Czechoslovakia in 1918. Otakar Šourek (1883–1956) devoted himself to the study of Dvořák. The three most important centres of musicological studies are Prague, Brno and Bratislava. In Prague scholarly activities are directed by Bohumír Štědroň, joint editor of the dictionary *Československý hudební slovník* (1963–5). The important centre in Brno was long directed by Jan Racek, who has not only written a comprehensive history of Czech music up to the beginning of the 19th century and been principal editor of the series Musica Antiqua Bohemica, but has specialized particularly in Italian monody. The Bratislava group was formed around Orel. The finest anthology of Czech music before Smetana was prepared by Jaroslav Pohanka (1924–64). Historical studies are well supported by a profusion of periodicals and publications of high quality.

Hungarian musical scholarship before 1918 was closely tied to that of Austria. Liszt's writings about gypsy music aroused much interest in traditional folk music, on which Kodály and Bártok later contributed studies. The first Hungarian music periodical, *Zenészeti lapok* ('Musical leaflets'), was founded in 1860 by Kornél Ábrányi, and Emil Haraszti (1885–1958) did much to make Hungarian music known in other countries. Modern musicological studies came into their own after 1918, especially in the work of Bence Szabolcsi, pre-eminent as a student of the distant past as well as of more recent developments in Hungarian music; Otto Gombosi, a medievalist of unusually broad erudition; and Dénes Bartha, well known for his work on Haydn as well as on Hungarian music. The Haydn studies of László Somfai (*b* 1934) are in the forefront of present research on the composer.

In Yugoslavia the 19th-century beginnings of music historiography can be traced to those areas belonging to the Austrian Empire before 1918. Perhaps the most significant figure was the ethnomusicologist Franjo Kuhač (1834–1911), who fancifully claimed Croatian origin for Haydn, Tartini and Liszt. In Slovenia Peter Radics published *Frau Musica in Krain* (1877), which marks the beginning of interest in the Slovenian musical past; the first true scholar, however, was Josef Mantuani (1860–1933), long active in Vienna. Dragan Plamenac (*b* 1895) is a scholar of international reputation whose interests have centred on the music of the 14th to 16th centuries; his contributions to scholarship include an edition of Ockeghem's works. The greatest progress in musicology since 1945 has been achieved in Slovenia; at the University of Ljubljana the first and so far the only chair of musicology was founded in 1962. It is occupied by Dragotin Cvetko, the most erudite and best-informed modern scholar in Yugoslavia. In Croatia the teacher and author Josip Andreis has trained a whole generation of fine scholars; and Ivo Supičić has created an important centre for the sociology and aesthetics of music in Zagreb. In Serbia the beginnings of music historiography were made by the composer–scholars Miloje Milojević (1884–1946) and Kosta Manojlović (1890–1949). Several studies on the history of Serbian music have been produced by Stana Đurić-Klajn (*b* 1908), editor of a number of journals. Musicological studies are mainly centred on research institutes in Belgrade (founded in 1948), Zagreb (1967) and Ljubljana.

8. THE UNITED STATES OF AMERICA. Musicology was

slow to respond to Ralph Waldo Emerson's call for distinctive American contributions to humanistic disciplines in an address 'The American Scholar' (1837), for the field was at that time scarcely in existence in a formal sense in Europe. It began in the USA in the later 19th century with distinctive though necessarily isolated achievements by scholars who lacked the institutional bases that were later created by the development of the field as an intellectual enterprise. To its earliest phase belong such efforts as J. S. Dwight's *Journal of Music* (1852–81), which included material on music history, and the work of Lowell Mason, who combined the roles of music teacher, editor and collector of rare music. Intellectually more distinguished though geographically more isolated was the achievement of A. W. Thayer (1812–97), the great pioneer of serious Beethoven biography, who spent all his later life as United States consul at Trieste.

The first important American-based scholar, in the true sense, was Oscar George Theodore Sonneck (1873–1928), who was born in the USA, trained in Germany, and for 15 years was chief of the Music Division of the Library of Congress (1902–17). Sonneck was not only instrumental in building the great music collection of the Library of Congress; he was also the author of essays and studies on a variety of musicohistorical subjects and the compiler of a bibliography of early American music and of a richly annotated *Catalogue of Opera Librettos Printed before 1800* (1914). He was also the founder-editor of the *Musical Quarterly* (published by G. Schirmer) which began publication in 1915 and remains the most widely circulated American periodical containing serious writing on music.

Between the wars American musicology began to establish its roots in American institutions of higher learning, and formed the professional ties that would make possible its growth as a scholarly discipline. As early as 1915 the *Musical Quarterly* had issued a programme for the field in an article by Waldo Selden Pratt entitled 'On Behalf of Musicology'. Although the term 'musicology' at first rang strangely in American ears, the field by the early 1930s was fast acquiring in academic circles the status accorded to any other branch of humanistic scholarship. A seminal figure in the establishment of musicology in the American university was Otto Kinkeldey (1878–1966). Like Sonneck, Kinkeldey was trained in Germany, where he was not only awarded the PhD but was also in 1910 named Royal Prussian Professor of Musicology at the University of Breslau. On returning to the USA in 1914 he became head of the Music Division of the New York Public Library, and in 1930 professor of musicology at Cornell University, the first such chair to be established in an American university. Kinkeldey was the first president of the American Musicological Society.

On 3 June 1934, in a private house at 25 Washington Square North, New York, nine people founded the American Musicological Society. In the mid-1970s the society, whose *Journal* has been issued regularly since 1950, had a national membership of more than 3000, and it has long been accepted as the central professional association for music scholarship in America. In addition to the annual meeting of the entire society, its 15 constituent regional chapters hold their own regular meetings throughout each year, at which scholarly papers are given. In 1961 the society was host to the

eighth congress of the International Musicological Society in New York, and in 1977 to the twelfth congress at Berkeley, California. Although members of the AMS are active in every field of study, the main line of American musicology has so far been undeniably directed towards the Western historical tradition. In 1954 the Society for Ethnomusicology was founded; this serves as a focus for the active field of ethnomusicology and issues its own journal, *Ethnomusicology*. Like the AMS in 1934, the Society for Ethnomusicology was accepted in 1955 by the American Council of Learned Societies as a constituent member. Yet despite this formal separation there are many signs of mutual awareness of the common interests that can unite traditional musicological disciplines and their ethnomusicological counterparts. For example, the important set of essays entitled *Musicology* (1963), published in the series Humanistic Scholarship in America, was written by two scholars who were then principally distinguished for their work in music history, Frank Ll. Harrison (from Great Britain) and Claude V. Palisca, and by the ethnomusicologist Mantle Hood. More recently Harrison has devoted himself to full-time teaching and research in the field of ethnomusicology.

Since the first American PhD in musicology was awarded at Cornell University in 1932 (to J. Murray Barbour), the field has spread widely among universities. Music in any form was relatively late in entering American university curricula as a separate subject, but it has undergone enormous growth in the past 75 years. Today few universities or colleges in the USA can fail to offer, in addition to practical vocal and instrumental music-making, at least elementary courses devoted to music theory and to music history in one or more of its phases. Many offer much more, including courses in theory, analysis and related fields, and a full range of courses in the history and literature of music, often supplemented by courses in one area or more of non-Western music.

The large number of PhDs awarded in musicology since 1945 is indicative of a growing population of American-trained scholars, but also indicates the creation of university positions on a larger scale than before, although conditions of economic retrenchment have recently reduced the earlier trend. In part, the significant role of American musicology in every field of study now being pursued in the discipline is attributable to its substantial number of practitioners, to the location of its research bases in universities, and to the research support available to American scholars through such private organizations as the Guggenheim Foundation, the American Council of Learned Societies and the federally supported National Endowment for the Humanities. Even more, it is attributable to the contributions of a score of eminent scholars who, in the generation after Kinkeldey, actually created the field in its more modern forms in the USA. Among these seminal teacher-scholars were three of the founder-members of the AMS: Gustave Reese, Charles Seeger and Oliver Strunk. The first and last of these trained generations of scholars at, respectively, New York University and Princeton University. To their names must be added those of Paul Henry Lang, Glen Haydon, Donald J. Grout, Charles Warren Fox and Arthur Mendel.

During the Nazi period, the collapse of scholarly and all other civilized values in Germany brought to the

USA a large number of significant figures in musical scholarship, including Willi Apel, Manfred Bukofzer, Hans David, Alfred Einstein, Karl Geiringer, Otto Gombosi, Paul Nettl, Erich Hertzmann, Edward Lowinsky, Curt Sachs, Leo Schrade and Emanuel Winternitz. All these men taught at major institutions and had vital roles in the training of younger American scholars now active; all of them, furthermore, published their work in English and brought European backgrounds and modes of approach to the fields in which they specialized. With the recovery of Europe after World War II, the increasing internationalization of the discipline was felt in many ways: in the resumption of European travel and research by American scholars, in their contacts with foreign scholars and some scholarly enterprises, and in the presence of other major foreign scholars in American teaching posts; among the latter was Nino Pirrotta, who taught at Princeton, Columbia and then for many years at Harvard before returning to his native Italy. Such teachers as these laid the foundations for a postwar generation of American scholars, among them Barry S. Brook, Howard Mayer Brown, James Haar, Daniel Heartz, Joseph Kerman, Jan LaRue, Lewis Lockwood and Claude V. Palisca.

Musicology in the USA has reached a stage at which it may be described as a solidly established field of scholarship embracing a vast spectrum of interests. At distant ends of the arc these interests may be said to coalesce in the work of large groups of scholars sharing common approaches: at one end is a group concerned with Western historical musicology in all its forms, fields and sub-disciplines (ranging from archival work to performing practice, which manifested itself in, for example, the pioneer work of the New York Pro Musica and the authentic instrument designs of such men as Hubbard and Dowd); and at the other end, a growing number in the field of ethnomusicology, seen not simply as the study of music in social and cultural context but as distinctly involved in ethnological and anthropological approaches. In addition to these more or less clearly definable segments of the active scholarly population, there is growing evidence of the opening of the discipline to new or formerly less emphasized dimensions of the field, among them such areas as speculative and descriptive theory and analysis (notably Milton Babbitt and Allen Forte), contemporary music, historiography, folk and popular music, and – too long neglected by American music historians – the music history of the American continent (to which such scholars as Gilbert Chase, Robert Stevenson and H. Wiley Hitchcock have contributed substantially). Already in use are new technological means for research, preeminently the computer, which will have an important impact not only on methods of research but also on dissemination of its findings, and on the very choice and definition of subjects to be investigated. Hazardous as it may be to speculate on the future, it appears that pluralistic definitions of the field are the only realistic ones, and that the spectrum is likely to widen still more.

Perhaps the greatest challenge facing American musicology, now that its place among the academic disciplines is a settled matter, is to make its impact felt outside its own domains – on the world of performance, in conservatories, in concert life, and even in the commercialized music industries. At present American musicology has barely breached the long-established barriers that divide the forces of serious intellectual life

from the vast media that produce and disseminate music (especially as published and recorded). One result is the continued isolation of scholarship from practical musical life, the proliferation of much traditional misinformation, and the perpetuation of long-established and deeply entrenched attitudes about music, largely inherited from the 19th century. Yet it may not be too optimistic to speculate whether, if the universities are indeed advance guards of the forms of knowledge that will eventually be assimilated by the public at large, the eventual importance of disciplined knowledge of and about music may be more strongly felt in American society in the future than it has been in the past.

## BIBLIOGRAPHY

F. Chrysander: Preface to *Jb für musikalische Wissenschaft* (Leipzig, 1863)
G. Adler: 'Umfang, Methode und Ziel der Musikwissenschaft', *VMw*, i (1885), 5
——: 'Musik und Musikwissenschaft', *JbMP 1898*, 27
H. Kretzschmar: 'Kurze Betrachtungen über den Zweck, die Entwicklung und die neuesten Zukunftsaufgaben der Musikhistorie', *JbMP 1907*, 83
H. Riemann: *Grundriss der Musikwissenschaft* (Leipzig, 1908)
G. Adler: *Der Stil in der Musik*, i: *Prinzipien und Arten des musikalischen Stils* (Leipzig, 1911)
W. S. Pratt: 'On Behalf of Musicology', *MQ*, i (1915), 1
J. Wolf: 'Musikwissenschaft und musikwissenschaftlicher Unterricht', *Festschrift Hermann Kretzschmar* (Leipzig, 1918/R1973), 175
G. Adler: *Methode der Musikgeschichte* (Leipzig, 1919)
H. Kretzschmar: *Einführung in die Musikgeschichte* (Leipzig, 1920)
E. Bücken: 'Grundfragen der Musikgeschichte als Geisteswissenschaft', *JbMP 1927*, 19
T. Haapanen: 'Gegenwärtiger Stand der Musikwissenschaft in Finnland seit 1923', *AcM*, i (1928–9), 46, 53
D. Iselin: 'Die Musikwissenschaft an den schweizerischen Universitäten', *AcM*, i (1928–9), 27, 39
C.-A. Moberg: 'Musik und Musikwissenschaft an den schwedischen Universitäten', *AcM*, i (1928–9), 54; ii (1930), 10
E. J. Dent: 'The Scientific Study of Music in England', *AcM*, ii (1930), 83
A. Pirro: 'L'enseignement de la musique aux universités françaises', *AcM*, ii (1930), 26, 45
H. Zenck and H. Schultz: 'Die Musikforschung in Leipzig und ihre Neuorganisierung', *AcM*, ii (1930), 56
E. J. Dent: 'Music and Music Research', *AcM*, iii (1931), 5
K. Herbst: 'Musikpsychologie und Musikwissenschaft: eine grundsätzliche Betrachtung über E. Kurths *Musikpsychologie*', *AcM*, iii (1931), 64
E. Haraszti: 'Fétis fondateur de la musicologie comparée', *AcM*, iv (1932), 97
O. Strunk: *The State and Resources of Musicology in the United States* (Washington, 1932)
H. Osthoff: 'Die Anfänge der Musikgeschichtsschreibung in Deutschland', *AcM*, v (1933), 97
H. Edelhoff: *Johann Nikolaus Forkel: ein Beitrag zur Geschichte der Musikwissenschaft* (Göttingen, 1935)
O. Kinkeldey: 'Changing Relations within the Field of Musicology', *PAMS 1936*, 42
G. Pietzsch: 'Zur Pflege der Musik an den deutschen Universitäten', *AMf*, i (1936), 257, 424; iii (1938), 302; vi (1941), 23
E. J. Dent: 'The Historical Approach to Music', *MQ*, xxiii (1937), 1
W. D. Allen: *Philosophies of Music History* (New York, 1939)
W. Gurlitt: 'Der gegenwärtige Stand der deutschen Musikwissenschaft', *Deutsche Vierteljahrsschrift für Literaturwissenschaft und Geistesgeschichte*, xvii (1939), 1–82
C. Seeger: 'Systematic and Historical Orientations in Musicology', *AcM*, xi (1939), 121
G. Haydon: *Introduction to Musicology* (New York, 1941/R1959)
J. Wolf: 'Musik und Musikwissenschaft', *Von deutscher Tonkunst: Festschrift zu Peter Raabes 70. Geburtstag* (Leipzig, 1942), 38
P. H. Lang: 'Musical Scholarship at the Crossroads', *MQ*, xxxi (1945), 371
S. Clercx-Lejeune: 'Définition de la musicologie et sa position à l'égard des autres disciplines qui lui sont connexes', *RBM*, i (1946), 113
C. Sachs: *The Commonwealth of Art* (New York, 1946)
O. Kinkeldey: 'Musical Scholarship and the University', *JRBM*, i (1946–7), 10
Y. Rokseth: 'Musical Scholarship in France during the War', *JRBM*, i (1946–7), 81
G. Haydon: 'Musicology in the United States: a Survey of Recent Trends', *MTNA Proceedings*, xli (1947), 321
P. H. Lang: 'On Musicology', *MQ*, xxxiii (1947), 557

L. Schiedermair: *Einführung in das Studium der Musikgeschichte* (Bonn, 1947)

W. Franck: 'Musicology and its Founder, Johann Nicolaus Forkel (1749–1818)', *MQ*, xxxv (1949), 588

J. Handschin: 'Musicologie et musique', *IMSCR, iv Basle 1949*, 9; also in *Revue internationale de musique*, new ser. (1950–51), no.9, p.220

H. Hickmann: 'Über den Stand der musikwissenschaftlichen Forschung in Ägypten', *IMSCR, iv Basle 1949*, 150

R. Wangermée: 'La musique ancienne contre la musique d'aujourd'hui', *Polyphonie*, iii (1949), 12

C. Seeger: 'Music and Musicology in the New World', *HMYB*, vi (1949–50), 36

H. Engel: 'Die Entwicklung der Musikwissenschaft, 1900–1950', *NZM*, Jg.111 (1950), 16

J. Kunst: *Ethno-musicology: a Study of its Nature, its Problems, Methods and Representative Personalities* (The Hague, 1950, rev. 3/1959)

E. Reeser: 'Musikwissenschaft in Holland', *AcM*, xxxii (1950), 160

L. Ronga: 'Musicologia e filologia musicale', *RaM*, xx (1950), 1

C. Seeger: 'Systematic Musicology: Viewpoints, Orientations and Methods', *JAMS*, ii (1951), 240

R. Wangermée: *François-Joseph Fétis, musicologue et compositeur* (Brussels, 1951)

Yu. Kremlyov: 'Über einige Fragen der sowjetischen Musikwissenschaft', *Musik und Gesellschaft*, ii (1952), 184

F. Blume: 'Musikforschung und Musikleben', *GfMKB, Bamberg 1953*, 7

K. G. Fellerer: *Einführung in die Musikwissenschaft* (Münchberg, 1953)

A. H. King: 'Musikwissenschaft in England: Ursprung und Quellen', *Musik der Zeit* (1953), no.4, p.57

F. Lesure: 'Musicologie et sociologie', *ReM* (1953), no.221, p.4

H. J. Moser: 'Über den Sinn der Musikforschung', *Festgabe für Hans Joachim Moser* (Kassel, 1954), 158

B. Nettl: *Theory and Method in Ethnomusicology* (New York, 1954)

H.-H. Dräger: 'Musikwissenschaft', *Universitas litterarum: Handbuch der Wissenschaftskunde*, ed. W. Schuder (Berlin, 1955), 635

M. Bukofzer: 'Musicology: the Anatomy of a Temporal Art', *Frontiers of Knowledge in the Study of Man*, ed. L. White (New York, 1956), 166

F. Bose: 'Südamerikanische Musikforschung', *AcM*, xxix (1957), 43

M. Bukofzer: *The Place of Musicology in American Institutions of Higher Learning* (New York, 1957/R1977)

J. Handschin: 'Der Arbeitsbereich der Musikwissenschaft'; 'Belange der Wissenschaft'; 'Gedanken über moderne Musikwissenschaft'; 'Humanistische Besinnung'; 'Über das Studium der Musikwissenschaft'; 'Vom Sinn der Musikwissenschaft', repr. in *Gedenkschrift Jacques Handschin* (Berne, 1957), 23; 60; 51; 376; 38; 29

H. Heckmann: 'Musikwissenschaftliche Unternehmungen in Deutschland seit 1945', *AcM*, xxix (1957), 75

A. Mendel, C. Sachs and C. C. Pratt: *Some Aspects of Musicology* (New York, 1957/R1977 in single vol. with Bukofzer, 1957) [incl. A. Mendel: 'The Services of Musicology to the Practical Musician'; C. Sachs: 'The Lore of non-Western Music', 19–48; C. C. Pratt: 'Musicology and Related Disciplines', 51–88]

O. Wessely: 'Die österreichische Musikforschung nach dem zweiten Weltkrieg', *AcM*, xxix (1957), 111

C. N. Brăiloiu: 'Musicologie et ethnomusicologie aujourd'hui', *IMSCR, vii Cologne 1958*, 17

J. Chailley, ed.: *Précis de musicologie* (Paris, 1958)

S. Clercx-Lejeune: 'La musicologie en Belgique depuis 1945', *AcM*, xxx (1958), 199; xxxi (1959), 130

E. Gerson-Kiwi: 'Musicology in Israel', *AcM*, xxx (1958), 17

H. Husmann: *Einführung in die Musikwissenschaft* (Heidelberg, 1958)

F. Lesure: 'La musicologie française depuis 1945', *AcM*, xxx (1958), 3

H. Rosenberg: 'Musikwissenschaftliche Bestrebungen in Dänemark, Norwegen, und Schweden in den letzten ca. 15 Jahren', *AcM*, xxx (1958), 118

H. P. Schanzlin: 'Musikwissenschaft in der Schweiz (1938–1958)', *AcM*, xxx (1958), 214

R. Allorto and C. Sartori: 'La musicologia italiana dal 1945 a oggi', *AcM*, xxxi (1959), 9

F. Blume: 'Was ist Musik?: ein Vortrag', *Musikalische Zeitfragen*, v (1959); repr. in *Syntagma musicologicum*, i (Kassel, 1963), 872

J. L. Broeckx: *Methode van de muziekgeschiedenis* (Antwerp, 1959)

D. Cvetko: 'Les formes et les résultats des efforts musicologiques yougoslaves', *AcM*, xxxi (1959), 50

D. Devoto: 'Panorama de la musicología latino-americana', *AcM*, xxxi (1959), 91

L. Hibberd: 'Musicology Reconsidered', *AcM*, xxxi (1959), 25

N.-E. Ringbom: 'Die Musikforschung in Finnland seit 1940', *AcM*, xxxi (1959), 17

D. Carpitella: 'Rassegna bibliografica degli studi di etnomusicologia in Italia dal 1945 a oggi', *AcM*, xxxii (1960), 109

L. S. Janković: 'La situation actuelle de l'ethnomusicologie en Yougoslavie', *AcM*, xxxii (1960), 94

M. S. Kastner: 'Veinte años de musicología en Portugal (1940–1960)', *AcM*, xxxii (1960), 1

R. Katzarova-Koukoudova: 'L'ethnomusicologie en Bulgarie de 1945 à nos jours', *AcM*, xxxii (1960), 77

G. Knepler: 'Reaktionäre Tendenzen in der westdeutschen Musikwissenschaft', *BMw*, ii/2 (1960), 3

C. Seeger: 'Toward a Unitary Field Theory for Musicology', *Selected Reports*, iii (1960), 172–210

E. Weber: 'L'enseignement de la musicologie en France', *Annales de l'université de Paris*, xxx (1960), 398

S. Goldthwaite: 'The Growth and Influence of Musicology in the United States', *AcM*, xxxiii (1961), 72

A. Mendel: 'Evidence and Explanation', *IMSCR, viii New York 1961*, ii, 3

W. Wiora: 'Musikgeschichte und Urgeschichte', *STMf*, xliii (1961), 375; repr. in *Historische und systematische Musikwissenschaft* (Tutzing, 1972), 88

——: 'Musikwissenschaft und Universalgeschichte', *AcM*, xxxiii (1961), 84

W. Wiora and H. Albrecht: 'Musikwissenschaft', *MGG*

W. Graf: 'Neue Möglichkeiten, neue Aufgaben der vergleichenden Musikwissenschaft', *SMw*, xxv (1962), 231

A. Machabey: *La musicologie* (Paris, 1962)

'Die Natur der Musik als Problem der Wissenschaft', *Musikalische Zeitfragen*, x (1963) [incl. articles by W. Wiora, C. Dahlhaus, H.-H. Dräger, H.-P. Reinecke, F. Winckel, P. Collaer, H. Pfrogner, G. Albersheim, L. Finscher, G. N. Reichert, H. Eckardt]

K. G. Fellerer: 'Musik und Musikwissenschaft', *A Ettore Desderi nel suo 70. compleanno* (Bologna, 1963), 61

E. Haraszti: 'La musicologie, science de l'avenir', *Histoire de la musique*, ii, ed. Roland-Manuel (Paris, 1963), 1549

F. Ll. Harrison, M. Hood and C. V. Palisca: *Musicology* (Englewood Cliffs, NJ, 1963) [incl. F. Harrison: 'American Musicology and the European Tradition', 3–85; M. Hood: 'Music, the Unknown', 217–326; C. V. Palisca: 'The Scope of American Musicology', 89–213]

E. C. Krohn: 'The Development of Modern Musicology', *Historical Musicology*, ed. L. B. Spiess (New York, 1963), 153

F. Y. Nomura: 'Musicology in Japan since 1945', *AcM*, xxxv (1963), 45

L. B. Spiess, ed.: *Historical Musicology* (New York, 1963)

A. Wellek: *Musikpsychologie und Musikästhetik: Grundriss der systematischen Musikwissenschaft* (Frankfurt am Main, 1963)

V. Duckles: *Music Reference and Research Materials: an Annotated Bibliography* (New York, 1964, 3/1974)

A. Hughes: 'Ninety Years of English Musicology', *Liber amicorum Charles van den Borren* (Antwerp, 1964), 93

A. P. Merriam: *The Anthropology of Music* (Evanston, Ill., 1964)

*CMc* (1965–), no.1–

S. Erdely: *Methods and Principles of Hungarian Ethnomusicology* (Bloomington, Ind., and The Hague, 1965)

F. Hoerburger and W. Suppan: 'Die Lage der Volksmusikforschung in den deutschsprachigen Ländern: ein Bericht über die Jahre 1945 bis 1964', *AcM*, xxxvii (1965), 1

J. Kerman: 'A Profile for American Musicology', *JAMS*, xviii (1965), 61

E. A. Lippman: 'What Musicology Should Be?', *CMc* (1965), no.1, p.55

E. Lowinsky: 'The Character and Purpose of American Musicology: a Reply to Joseph Kerman', *JAMS*, xviii (1965), 222

W. Suppan: *Volkslied: seine Sammlung und Erforschung* (Stuttgart, 1965)

C. Dahlhaus: 'Historismus und Tradition', *Zum 70. Geburtstag von Joseph Müller-Blattau* (Kassel, 1966), 46

M. Donà: 'La musicologia in Italia', *CHM*, iv (1966), 94

K. G. Fellerer: 'Zur musikalischen Akustik im 18. Jahrhundert', *Zum 70. Geburtstag von Joseph Müller-Blattau* (Kassel, 1966), 80

W. Gurlitt: 'Hugo Riemann und die Musikgeschichte'; 'François-Joseph Fétis und seine Rolle in der Geschichte der Musikwissenschaft', *Musikgeschichte und Gegenwart*, ed. H. H. Eggebrecht, ii (Wiesbaden, 1966), 103; 123

H. Hüschen: 'Universität und Musik', *MGG*

F. W. Riedel: 'Zur Geschichte der musikalischen Quellenüberlieferung und Quellenkunde', *AcM*, xxxviii (1966), 3

W. Szmolyan: 'Die Musikwissenschaft an Österreichs Universitäten', *ÖMz*, xxi (1966), 55

G. Abraham: 'Musical Scholarship in the 20th Century', *SMA*, i (1967), 1

F. Blume: 'Das musikalische Kunstwerk in der Geschichte', *Festschrift Bruno Stäblein* (Kassel, 1967), 9; repr. in *Syntagma musicologicum*, ii (Kassel, 1973), 47

——: 'Historische Musikforschung in der Gegenwart', *IMSCR, x Ljubljana 1967*, 13; repr. in *Syntagma musicologicum*, ii (Kassel, 1973), 34; Eng. trans., *SMA*, ii (1968), 1

H. A. Brockhaus: 'Zur Problematik der Musikhistoriographie', *Hundert Jahre Reclams Universal-Bibliothek* (Leipzig, 1967), 306–46

A. Chodkowski: 'Les études musicologiques en Pologne', *Musique en Pologne*, ii (1967), 17

S. Claro: 'Hacia una definición del concepto de musicología: contribución a la musicología hispano-americana', *Revista musical chilena* (1967), no.101, p.8

E. Doflein: 'Historismus und Historisierung in der Musik', *Festschrift für Walter Wiora* (Kassel, 1967), 48

V. Ernst: 'Über die Einheit von historischer und systematischer Musikwissenschaft', *BMw*, ix (1967), 91

M. M. Gallagher: 'The State of Musicology in American Universities', *Student Musicologists at Minnesota* (1967), 1–51

F. Grasberger: 'Musik und Forschung: ein historischer Rückblick', *ÖMz*, xvii (1967), 641

H. Heckmann, ed.: *Elektronische Datenverarbeitung in der Musikwissenschaft* (Regensburg, 1967)

M. Kolinski: 'Recent Trends in Ethnomusicology', *EM*, xi (1967), 1

W. F. Kümmel: 'Die Anfänge der Musikgeschichte an den deutschsprachigen Universitäten', *Mf*, xx (1967), 262

——: *Geschichte und Musikgeschichte: die Musik der Neuzeit in Geschichtsschreibung und Geschichtsauffassung des deutschen Kulturbereichs* (Kassel, 1967)

L. Schrade: 'Eine Einführung in die Musikgeschichtsschreibung älterer Zeit', *De scientia musicae studia atquae orationes*, ed. E. Lichtenhahn (Berne and Stuttgart, 1967), 17

A. N. Sohor: '50 Jahre sowjetische Musik im Spiegel der sowjetischrussischen Musikwissenschaft', *BMw*, ix (1967), 181

L. Treitler: 'On Historical Criticism', *MQ*, liii (1967), 188

R. T. Watanabe: *Introduction to Music Research* (Englewood Cliffs, NJ, 1967)

H. C. Wolff: 'Grenzen der Musikwissenschaft', *Festschrift für Walter Wiora* (Kassel, 1967), 661

H. A. Brockhaus: 'Musikwissenschaft als Leitungswissenschaft', *Musik und Gesellschaft*, xviii (1968), 747

Y. Chartier: 'La musicologie à l'université – méthodes et expériences', *Revue de l'Université d'Ottawa*, xxxviii (1968), 405

M. Griffel: 'Musicological Method in American Graduate Schools', *CMc* (1968), no.6, pp.7–50

D. J. Grout: 'Current Historiography and Music History', *Studies in Music History: Essays for Oliver Strunk* (Princeton, 1968), 23

D. Harrán: 'Musical Research in Israel: its History, Resources and Institutions', *CMc* (1968), no.7, p.120

R. Heinz: *Geschichtsbegriff und Wissenschaftscharakter der Musikwissenschaft in der zweiten Hälfte des 19. Jahrhunderts* (Regensburg, 1968)

H. Kier: *Raphael Georg Kiesewetter (1773–1850): Wegbereiter des musikalischen Historismus* (Regensburg, 1968)

W. Konen: 'Zur Verteidigung der historischen Musikwissenschaft', *Kunst und Literatur*, xvi (1968), 199

A. Liess: 'Zur Problematik der Musikgeschichte als Wissenschaft und Unterrichtsfach', *Musikerziehung*, xxii (1968), 6, 55

G. Rouget: 'L'ethnomusicologie', *Encyclopédie de la Pléiade, ethnologie générale*, i (1968), 1339–90

Yu. Semtsovsky: 'Heute und Morgen der Musikfolklore-Forschung', *Kunst und Literatur*, xvi (1968), 640

F. Blume: 'Musicology in German Universities', *CMc* (1969), no.9, p.52; repr. in *Syntagma musicologicum*, ii (Kassel, 1973), 14

H. Engel: 'Musikwissenschaft und ihr Studium', *Aspekte*, ii (1969), 32

H. Federhofer: 'Gegenwartsprobleme der Musikforschung', *Musikerziehung*, xxii (1969), 147

A. Geering: 'Musikwissenschaft in der Schweiz', *ÖMz*, xxiv (1969), 177

E. H. Gombrich: *In Search of Cultural History* (Oxford, 1969)

A. Liess: 'Aktuelle Probleme der Musikgeschichtsschreibung', *NZM*, Jg.130 (1969), 139

G. S. McPeek: 'Musicology in the United States: a Survey of Recent Trends', *Studies in Musicology: Essays ... in Memory of Glen Haydon* (Chapel Hill, 1969), 260

A. P. Merriam: 'Ethnomusicology Revisited', *EM*, xiii (1969), 213

E. H. Meyer: 'Über die wechselseitige Beziehung musikwissenschaftlicher und kompositorischer Tätigkeit', *BMw*, xi (1969), 235

E. Schenk: 'Musikwissenschaft an der Universität Wien', *Sborník prací filosofické fakulty brněnské university*, H4 (1969), 7

F. Schneider: 'Die Musikwissenschaft in der DDR', *BMw*, xi (1969), 163

H. Tischler: 'And What is Musicology?', *MR*, xxx (1969), 253

L. Treitler: 'The Present as History', *PNM*, viii/1 (1969), 1–58

E. Weber: 'La musicologie dans les universités françaises', *Revue historique* (1969), no.490, p.373

A. Wellek: 'Gegenwartsprobleme systematische Musikwissenschaft', *AcM*, xli (1969), 213

W. Wiora, ed.: *Die Ausbreitung des Historismus über die Musik* (Regensburg, 1969)

H. C. Wolff: 'Die Geschichte der Musikwissenschaft an den Universitäten Leipzig und Berlin', *Sborník prací filosofické fakulty brněnské university*, H4 (1969), 97

B. Brook, ed.: *Musicology and the Computer: Musicology 1966–2000: a Practical Program* (New York, 1970) [incl. 'Computer Applications to Music and Musicology: Bibliography', 229–70, and papers by L. Dittmer, J. LaRue, E. Lippman, L. Lockwood, C. V. Palisca, F. Zimmerman, A. Mendel]

V. Duckles: 'Patterns in the Historiography of 19th Century Music', *AcM*, xlii (1970), 75

H. H. Eggebrecht, ed.: 'Reflexionen über Musikwissenschaft heute', *GfMKB, Bonn 1970*, 615–97; see also *Musikwissenschaft heute* [pre-publication of statements made at *IMSCR*, xi *Copenhagen 1972*]

A. Liess: *Protuberanzen*, i: *Zur Theorie der Musikgeschichte* (Vienna, 1970)

H. B. Lincoln, ed.: *The Computer and Music* (Ithaca, NY, 1970)

H. B. Lincoln: 'The Current State of Music Research and the Computer', *Computers and the Humanities*, v (1970), 29

J. Maillard: 'The Many Faces of Medieval Musicology', *SMA*, iv (1970), 1

B. S. Brook and L. B. Plantinga, eds.: 'Patterns in the Historiography of 19th-century Music', *AcM*, xliii (1971), 248–82 [from symposium with statements by W. Austin, B. S. Brook, V. Duckles, V. Fédorov, G. Knepler, F. Lesure, L. Lockwood, R. M. Longyear, F. Noske, P. Petrobelli, L. B. Plantinga, A. Ringer, B. Schwarz, M. Velimirović, R. Wangermée]

C. Dahlhaus, ed.: *Einführung in die systematische Musikwissenschaft* (Cologne, 1971, 2/1975)

M. Hood: *The Ethnomusicologist* (New York, 1971)

A. D. McCredie: 'Systematic Musicology – some 20th-century Patterns and Perspectives', *SMA*, v (1971), 1–35

B. S. Brook, E. O. D. Downes and S. Van Solkema, eds.: *Perspectives in Musicology* (New York, 1972) [15 papers on perspectives and lacunae in musicological research, listed below]

M. Babbitt: 'Contemporary Music Composition and Music Theory as Contemporary Intellectual History', ibid, 151–84

F. Blume: 'Musical Scholarship Today', ibid, 15

G. Chase: 'American Musicology and the Social Sciences', ibid, 202

L. H. Corrêa de Azevedo: 'The Present State and Potential of Music Research in Latin America', ibid, 249

V. Duckles: 'Musicology at the Mirror: a Prospectus for the History of Musical Scholarship', ibid, 32

F. Ll. Harrison: 'Music and Cult: the Functions of Music in Social and Religious Systems', ibid, 307

M. Hood: 'The Consensus Makers of Asian Music', ibid, 290

G. Knepler: 'Music Historiography in Eastern Europe', ibid, 227

H. C. R. Landon: 'Two Research Lacunae in Music of the Classic Period', ibid, 136

P. H. Lang: 'Musicology and Related Disciplines', ibid, 185

F. Lesure: 'Archival Research: Necessity and Opportunity', ibid, 56

E. E. Lowinsky: '*Secret Chromatic Art* Re-examined', ibid, 91–135

J. H. K. Nketia: 'The Present State and Potential of Music Research in Africa', ibid, 270

G. Reese: 'Perspectives and Lacunae in Musicological Research', ibid, 1

E. Winternitz: 'The Iconology of Music: Potentials and Pitfalls', ibid, 80

K. von Fischer: 'The Interpretation of Musical Sources', *FAM*, xix (1972), 148

A. Lönn: 'Trends and Tendencies in Recent Swedish Musicology', *AcM*, xliv (1972), 11

D. Schjelderup-Ebbe: 'Neuere norwegische musikwissenschaftliche Arbeiten', *AcM*, xliv (1972), 25

T. Schousboe: 'Dänische musikwissenschaftliche Publikationen seit 1958', *AcM*, xliv (1972), 1

W. Wiora: *Historische und systematische Musikwissenschaft* (Tutzing, 1972)

G. Chase: 'The Musicologist as Historian: a Matter of Distinction', *Notes*, xxix (1972–3), 10

F. Blume: 'Musik und Musikwissenschaft', *Syntagma musicologicum*, ii (Kassel, 1973), 1

O. Elschek: 'Gegenwartsprobleme der musikwissenschaftlichen Systematik', *AcM*, xlv (1973), 1

K. P. Etzkorn, ed.: *Music and Society: the Later Writings of Paul Honigsheim* (New York, 1973)

B. Jarustovsky: 'Soviet Musicology', *AcM*, xlvi (1974), 50

D. Harrán: *Musicologia: tehumin u-megamot* [Musicology: areas and purposes] (Jerusalem, 1975)

'Musikvetenskap: synpunkter på en översikt', *STMf*, lvii (1975), 7–56 [contributions by J. Bärmark, I. Bengtsson, O. Edwards, P. Gronow, S. Hansell, K. Johannesson, F. Krummacher, P. Lindblom, A. Lönn, F. Mathiassen, T. Stenström, J. Sundberg, M. Tegen]

M. Querol Gavaldá: 'Die Musikwissenschaft in Spanien', *ÖMz*, xxx (1975), 208

'Memorandum über die Lage der Musikwissenschaft in der Bundesrepublik Deutschland', *Mf*, xxix (1976), 249

J. Bek, J. Fukač and I. Poledňák: 'Česka hudební věda 1945–1975' [Czech musicology 1945–75], *HV*, xiii (1976), 3 [with Ger. summary]

L'. Chalupka: 'Slovenská musikológia v rokoch 1945–1975', *HV*, xiii (1976), 99

W. S. Newman: 'Musicology in the United States in 1975', *AcM*, xlviii (1976), 284

——: 'Musicology in the United States in 1976', *AcM*, xlix (1977), 269

T. Straková: 'Die tschechische Musikwissenschaft in den Jahren 1945–1975', *AcM*, xlix (1977), 103 [see also V. Karbusicky, p.280]

R. Stevenson: 'American Musical Scholarship: Parker to Thayer', *19th Century Music*, i (1977–8), 190

D. Cvetko: 'Der gegenwärtige Stand der jugoslawischen Musikwissenschaft', *AcM*, li (1979), 151

P. Petrobelli: 'Musicologia: ma quale?', *RIM*, xiv (1979), 184

D. Fallows, A. Whittall and J. Blacking: 'Musicology in Great Britain since 1945', *AcM*, lii (1980), 38–68

VINCENT DUCKLES
(with HOWARD MAYER BROWN, GEORGE J. BUELOW, MARK LINDLEY, LEWIS LOCKWOOD, MILOŠ VELIMIROVIĆ and IAN D. BENT)

**Music printing and publishing.** *See* PRINTING AND PUBLISHING OF MUSIC.

**Music Publishing Co.** English firm of music publishers founded and directed by GEORGE HENRY DAVIDSON.

**Music Teachers National Association.** An American organization founded in 1876 by Theodore Presser, a musician and publisher, to aid teachers, raise standards of music education and gain recognition for the profession. Its members have included teachers, performers, composers and conductors. In 1883 it helped to establish an international pitch and promoted an international copyright law; in 1967 it approved a national certification plan for qualified teachers. To attract young people into the profession the association holds auditions at local schools and at the state and national levels. Its official publication is the *American Music Teacher*.

RITA H. MEAD

**Music theatre** (Ger. *Musiktheater*). A catch-phrase that became common in the 1960s, particularly among composers, producers and critics who had artistic or social objections to the cost of traditional grand opera and the conservatism of grand opera companies and their audiences. It was, and is, loosely used in three senses: (1) to designate musical works for small or moderate forces that involve a dramatic element in their presentation. Such works have included small-scale operas (e.g. Goehr's *Naboth's Vineyard*, composed for the London Music Theatre Ensemble); song cycles with instrumental accompaniment that are 'staged' and enacted on a concert platform (e.g. Davies's *Eight Songs for a Mad King*); and pieces by Ligeti (*Aventures* and *Nouvelles aventures*), Cardew (school operas), and Kagel (numerous works, some, indeed, with no recognizably 'musical' component; Kagel formed a group for their performance) that resist any precise definition. Stravinsky's *The Soldier's Tale* and *Reynard*, Weill's *Mahagonny-Songspiel* and Hindemith's *Wir bauen eine Stadt*, for children, – and, for that matter, Monteverdi's *Tancredi e Clorinda* – are earlier examples. (2) To describe either an opera in which the theatrical element is deemed powerful enough to compensate for an indifferent or insubstantial score (e.g. 'Penderecki's *The Devils of Loudun* may not be very good music but is excellent music theatre'), or any uncommonly dramatic opera. (3) To describe a manner of opera performance in which the acting and staging are thought to be so vivid as to compensate for mediocre, or complement admirable, singing and playing. In this sense Walter Felsenstein's carefully acted productions of the traditional operatic repertory are called 'music theatre'. In the latter two senses 'music theatre' is little more than a handy term of approval used, in the age-old struggle for supremacy that underlies the history of opera and has prompted so many 'reforms', to champion the claims of 'drama' against those of 'music'.

BIBLIOGRAPHY

W. Felsenstein and S. Melchinger: *Musiktheater* (Bremen, c1961)

W. Felsenstein, G. Friedrich and J. Herz: *Musiktheater: Beiträge zur Methodik und zu Inszenierungs-Konzeptionen* (Leipzig, 1970)

*Yale/Theatre*, iv/3 (1973) [special 'Music and Theatre' issue]

P. P. Fuchs, ed. and trans.: *The Music Theater of Walter Felsenstein: Collected Writings* (New York, 1975)

ANDREW PORTER

**Music therapy.** The use of music to cure, alleviate or stimulate. It is familiar from the Greek myths and the Old Testament, and has been increasingly used in the treatment of mental and physical handicaps and emotional disturbance, but there is as yet little theoretical work to explain its effectiveness. Music can affect function at a basic level of sensory response, as is indicated by cases of patients suffering from brain injury who, after months of deep coma, regain consciousness after continuous exposure for a day or two to a radio music programme (Taylor, 1971) and by cases of musicogenic epilepsy, such as that of a man who invariably lost consciousness at the sound of bells (Poskanzer, Brown and Miller, 1962). But, apart from such cases of brain pathology, it is difficult to distinguish the effects of music as purely physiological in terms of sensory function rather than entirely emotional. How, for instance, should one interpret observed changes in listeners' respiration rates caused by changes in musical tempo: as a move towards rhythmic synchrony akin to marching in step, or as increased emotional arousal? Studies using the galvanic skin response, which measures the reduction in electrical resistance of the skin indicative of changed emotional states, have shown that when listening to music children are more responsive than adults, manic depressives more than schizophrenics (Weidenfeller and Zimny, 1962) and women more than men (Sears, 1958). A direct correlation between the galvanic skin response and the importance of music in the life of the subject has been found (but see Sears, 1958).

Of the elements of music – pitch, intensity, melody, harmony and rhythm – it is rhythm that is acknowledged to be the vital therapeutic factor by virtue of its power to focus energy and to bring structure into the perception of temporal order. Music is unique among therapies in that this structuring of the 'specious present' (i.e. the present as it flows into the past; Clay, 1882) can stimulate the passive or withdrawn patient into a more alert response, both cognitive and social, to his immediate environment. In the case of emotional illness it can serve to make the patient more accessible; for physical disabilities it can be used to organize the sequence of small goals in acquiring muscular skill and control; and for mental retardation it can assist in the acquisition of elementary concepts. In the musical treatment of all three groups of disorders the progress towards 'doing' behaviour involves also that towards 'communicating' behaviour, and both mentally retarded and autistic children frequently respond to music where all else has failed. Music is an expressive vehicle for relief of emotional tension; it bypasses the speech difficulties of the disabled and the 'dangers' of verbal language for emotionally ill patients.

Therapy is chosen according to each patient's particular needs and can include singing, dancing, clapping and percussion games, playing musical instruments and listening, either individually or in groups. For child and adult mental retardates music therapy takes place in schools or hospitals; in either setting it engenders the same complement of cognitive and social redevelopment. The repetitive songs or clapping games seem by their simple predictability to give the retardate experience of security, order and achievement. Often hyperactive retarded children (who generally have a short span of attention and are better disposed to things than to people) begin both to socialize and to control their powers of attention through these musical group games. With cerebral-palsied or brain-damaged children it is important to suit the music to the type of handicap; for example, 'sedative' music is relaxing to athetoids, whereas 'stimulating' music assists coordination in spastics (Schneider, 1957).

Music therapy has been used to improve motor coordination in cerebral palsy and in muscular dystrophy cases. It is also used to teach breath and diction control where there is severe speech impairment, and is effectively used as a background in speech-therapy sessions to increase participation (Ditson, 1961). Research indicates that music evokes in the brain-damaged child a basic level of stimulation which makes learning possible, perhaps because its continuity of sound and variety of pattern have a particular effect on the non-specific arousal pattern in the brain. That background music causes in these patients a reduction of tension as well as constant stimulation may show it to be beneficial in a manner similar to that of 'background music' to the work-performance of normally healthy people.

The exclusion of sensory input by the individual is manifest in the extremes of mental illness (e.g. in catatonic schizophrenia) where, though totally inaccessible, the patient is nevertheless overaroused and vigilant and can handle only a lower than normal environmental stimulation. The most impressive effects of music therapy are shown in the treatment of childhood autism, where such exclusion of environmental stimulation is characteristic. Autistic children are often intelligent and extremely musical (Sherwin, 1953; Anastasi and Levee, 1960). Nordoff and Robbins (1965) gave a detailed account of a type of music therapy that proves particularly effective in establishing an initial responsiveness in autistic children. The therapist improvises piano music to accompany whatever erratic or obsessively regular beating of drums the child produces, and then gradually introduces rhythms that induce the child to follow and words that evoke a personal response and sense of identity. Therapy thus repairs autistic distortions of ego-development by the child's moving from fear to trust in a relationship sustained by musical rather than verbal colloquy.

Though the most spectacular results have been achieved with autism, music therapy has been used for all types of emotional illness and for many other physical ones. It seems, however, unlikely at present that any unitary theory of music therapy could account for the wide variety of physical, mental and psychological syndromes and deficiencies for which it seems to be effective. One can only speculate that, as well as increasing social accessibility and response, it may be conducive to the optimal level of non-specific arousal necessary to well-being. An important factor in the various stresses that engender illness, particularly mental illness, is that though the eyes can be closed the ears cannot; thus control of auditory stress is through the manipulation of attention, such habits becoming in time involuntary. By marshalling and re-educating faulty attentional processes, and doing so by invoking the expressive use of gesture without involving the possible emotional dangers of verbal language, music therapy tends towards establishing a more natural physical and psychological balance.

BIBLIOGRAPHY

R. Browne: *Medicina musica* (London, 1729)
R. Brocklesby: *Reflections on Antient and Modern Musick with the Application to the Cure of Diseases* (London, 1749)
J.-L. Roger: *Tentamen de vi soni et musices in corpus humanum* (Avignon, 1758; Fr. trans., 1803)
H. Chomet: *Effets et influence de la musique sur la santé et sur la maladie* (Paris, 1874; Eng. trans., 1875)
E. R. Clay: *The Alternative: A Study in Psychology* (London, 1882), 167
A. F. Savill: *Music, Health and Character* (London, 1923)
S. Licht: *Music in Medicine* (Boston, 1946)
D. Soibelman: *Therapeutic and Industrial Uses of Music* (New York, 1948)
S. D. Mitchell: 'Music and Psychological Medicine', *PRMA*, lxxvii (1950–51), 27
A. C. Sherwin: 'Reactions to Music of Autistic (Schizophrenic) Children', *American Journal of Psychiatry*, cix (1953), 823
B. Fields: 'Music as Adjunct in Treatment of Brain-damaged Patients', *American Journal of Physical Medicine*, xxxiii (1954), 273
E. H. Schneider: 'Relationships between Musical Experiences and Certain Aspects of Cerebral Palsied Children's Performance on Selected Tasks', *Music Therapy 1956*, ed. E. T. Gaston (Lawrence, Kansas, 1957)
W. W. Sears: 'The Effects of Music on Muscle Tonus', *Music Therapy 1957*, ed. E. T. Gaston (Lawrence, Kansas, 1958), 199
A. Anastasi and R. F. Levee: 'Intellectual Defect and Musical Talent: a Case Report', *American Journal of Mental Deficiency*, lxiv (1960), 695
R. Ditson: 'A Study of the Effects of Moderate Background Music on the Behavior of Cerebral Palsied Children', *Bulletin of the National Association of Music Therapy*, x (1961), 6
D. C. Poskanzer, A. E. Brown and H. Miller: 'Musicogenic Epilepsy caused only by a Discrete Frequency Band of Church Bells', *Brain*, lxxxv (1962), 77
E. W. Weidenfeller and G. H. Zimny: 'Effects of Music upon GSR of Depressives and Schizophrenics', *Journal of Abnormal and Social Psychology*, lxiv (1962), 307
J. and M. A. Guilhot and J. Jost: *Musique, psychologie et psychothérapie* (Paris, 1964)
*Music Therapy, Tension and Relaxation: A Symposium* (London, 1964)
*Journal of Music Therapy* (1964–) [USA]
P. Nordoff and C. Robbins: *Music Therapy for Handicapped Children* (New York, 1965)
J. Alvin: *Music for the Handicapped Child* (London, 1965, rev. 2/1976)
——: *Music Therapy* (London, 1966, rev. 2/1975)
J. P. B. Dobbs: *The Slow Learner and Music* (London, 1966)
*British Journal of Music Therapy* (1969–)
J. D. Taylor: 'Radio I: an Unexpected Response', *The Lancet* (1971), no.7729, p.881
M. Priestley: *Music Therapy in Action* (London, 1976)

NATASHA SPENDER

**Musikalisches Magazin.** Austrian firm of music publishers. It was founded by the composer Leopold Kozeluch, whose first works written in Vienna were published by Artaria and by Torricella; the desire for more profit led him to publish his works himself. On 14 April 1784 the *Wiener Zeitung* carried his first advance announcement of his two piano concertos op.12, which appeared on 1 September; on 12 November 1785 it advertised the opening of his music and art shop, the beginning of his publishing business.

Because of Kozeluch's activities as a composer, especially from 1792 when he became court composer, he was obliged to engage his brother Anton (*b* 9 Dec 1752, baptized Antonín Tomáš; *d* Vienna, 4 July 1805), who had come to Vienna in 1788, as business manager; it was at this time that the firm began to trade under the name Musikalisches Magazin, later changed to Kozeluchsche Musikhandlung. Anton did not apply to the Vienna city council for the licence left by his brother until 29 May 1802. The firm's activity however ceased completely in 1803 and the licence left to Anton Kozeluch's widow passed to Ludwig Maisch. Compared with Artaria the Musikalisches Magazin was insignificant, and lacked a definite policy. Nevertheless the publishing programme included Haydn's 'Tost' quartets, a piano reduction of Mozart's *Die Zauberflöte* and reprints of several of his works, and 13 pieces by Ignaz Pleyel. Kozeluch's own compositions make up the bulk of the output. Other composers published included Kauer, J. G. Lickl, Lipavský, Wenzel Müller, Paradis, Pasterwitz, Rieder, Vanhal, Anton Wranitzky and their lesser contemporaries.

BIBLIOGRAPHY

A. Weinmann: *Verzeichnis der Verlagswerke des Musikalischen Magazins* (Vienna, 1950)
M. Poštolka: *Leopold Koželuch; život a dílo* (Prague, 1964)
A. Weinmann: 'Supplement zum Verlagverzeichnis des Musikalischen Magazins in Wien', *Beiträge zur Geschichte des Alt-Wiener Musikverlages*, 2nd ser., xiv (1970)
——: *Verzeichnis der Musikalien des Verlages Maisch-Sprenger-Mathias Artaria* (Vienna, 1970)

ALEXANDER WEINMANN

**Musikbogen** (Ger.). MUSICAL BOW.

**Musikforschung** (Ger.). MUSICOLOGY.

**Musikgeschichtsschreibung** (Ger.). HISTORIOGRAPHY.

**Musikkorps** (Ger.). MILITARY BAND.

**Musikwissenschaft** (Ger.). MUSICOLOGY.

**Musin.** *See* FURLANETTO, BONAVENTURA.

**Musique concrète.** *See* ELECTRONIC MUSIC.

**Musique de chambre** (Fr.). CHAMBER MUSIC.

**Musique de la Chambre.** One of the divisions of the French court musical establishment; *see* PARIS, §§II, 1; V, 1.

**Musique de la Chapelle.** One of the divisions of the French court musical establishment, known as Musique de la Chapelle Royale in the 17th and 18th centuries; *see* PARIS, §§II, 1; V, 1.

**Musique de l'Ecurie.** One of the divisions of the French court musical establishment, known as Musique de la Grande Ecurie in the 17th and 18th centuries; *see* PARIS, §§II, 1; V, 1.

**Musique mesurée, musique mesurée à l'antique.** Late 16th-century French settings of VERS MESURÉS, poetry that applies the quantitative principles of classical Greek and Latin to French.

**Musique Vivante.** French ensemble founded in 1966 by DIEGO MASSON.

**Musorgsky** [Moussorgsky], **Modest Petrovich** (*b* Karevo, Pskov district, 21 March 1839; *d* St Petersburg, 28 March 1881). Russian composer. His life was extremely unstable, and at the time of his death some of his most important compositions were left unfinished. His greatest achievements were as a composer of operas and solo songs. He was an unorthodox harmonist and he discovered a way of writing for the voice that was both lyrical and true to the inflections of speech. He was the most strikingly individual Russian composer of the later 19th century.

1. Life. 2. Posthumous completion of works. 3. Style and aesthetic.

1. LIFE. Musorgsky was the youngest son of a well-to-do landowner, but had peasant blood, his paternal grandmother having been a serf. According to a not altogether reliable autobiographical sketch written in 1881, under his nurse's influence he became familiar with Russian folk tales, and it was mainly this contact with the spirit of the life of the people which impelled him to improvise music before he had learnt even the most elementary rules of piano playing. His mother gave him his first lessons, and he made such progress that at the age of seven he could play short pieces by Liszt. When he was nine he performed a Field concerto before a large audience in his parents' house, and in August 1849 he began to have piano lessons with Anton Herke, a pupil of Henselt. His general education was continued first at a preparatory school, then with a tutor, and in 1852 he entered the Cadet School of the Guards in St Petersburg, where, according to his elder brother, he was particularly interested in history and German philosophy. During his first year at the Cadet School he composed a *Porte-enseigne polka*, dedicated to his schoolfellows, which was published at his father's expense. He was in the school choir, and the religious instructor, Father Krupsky, encouraged him to study the church music of Bortnyansky and other Russian composers of the early 19th century. The piano lessons with Herke ended in 1854. Musorgsky had learnt nothing of harmony or composition; nevertheless in 1856 he tried to write an opera based on Victor Hugo's *Han d'Islande*. The same year he left the Cadet School and entered the Preobrazhensky Regiment of Guards. Borodin, who met him at this period, described him as an elegant piano-playing dilettante.

In 1857 Musorgsky made the acquaintance of Dargomïzhsky, already an established composer, and César Cui, like himself a young military officer who dabbled in composition; through them, in turn, he met Balakirev and Stasov. Before long he induced Balakirev, his senior by only three years, to give him lessons in musical form, based mainly on Beethoven's symphonies (which they played in four-hand arrangements) but also on compositions by Schubert, Schumann, Glinka and others. From this period date a song, *Gde tï, zvezdochka* ('Where art thou, little star?'), and a *Souvenir d'enfance* for piano; in 1858 he wrote more songs, piano sonatas in E♭ major and F♯ minor, and the introduction to an opera based on Ozerov's play *Edip v Afinakh* ('Oedipus in Athens'), a project abandoned in 1860. During the summer of 1858 he passed through a nervous or spiritual crisis and on 17 July he resigned his commission; work with Balakirev was resumed later in the year and in November he composed two scherzos for piano, one in C♯ minor, the other in B♭ (he orchestrated the latter with Balakirev's assistance). A visit to Moscow in the summer of 1859 fired his patriotic imagination and provided him with one of the deepest experiences of his youth. He wrote to Balakirev, 'You know I have been a cosmopolitan, but now I have undergone a sort of rebirth: I have been brought near to everything Russian'. But this mood was not reflected in his next compositions, a mildly Schumannesque *Impromptu passionné* for piano, suggested by two characters in Herzen's novel

*Who is to Blame?*, and a projected cantata, *Marsh Shamilya* ('Shamil's march') for tenor and bass, chorus and orchestra. On 23 January 1860 his Scherzo in B♭ was conducted by Anton Rubinstein at a concert in St Petersburg of the newly founded Russian Music Society.

The year 1860 was marked by another nervous crisis. Musorgsky wrote, 'During the greater part of this time, from May to August, my brain was weak and in a state of violent irritability'. But in the autumn he announced his recovery and his intention to put all his 'musical sins' in order and begin a new period of his creative life. He may already have toyed with the idea of an opera based on Gogol's story *Vecher nakanune Ivana Kupala* ('St John's eve'), and he now seems to have thought of using material originally intended for this in a setting of the witches' sabbath scene on the Bare Mountain from a play *Ved'ma* ('The witch') by an army comrade, Baron Georgy Mengden. Shortly afterwards, in the winter of 1860–61, he produced an Allegro in C for four hands, a duet transcription in C minor of his C♯ minor Scherzo, the beginnings of two movements of a Symphony in D and an 'essay in instrumentation', *Alla marcia notturna*. That his nervous irritability was not entirely calmed appears from his petulant complaints that Balakirev was 'keeping him in leading-strings' and from his rejection of an opportunity to have the temple scene from his *Oedipus* performed by the Russian Music Society. (The scene was, however, given a concert performance in the Mariinsky Theatre, St Petersburg, on 18 April 1861, under K. N. Lyadov.)

The emancipation of the serfs in March 1861 involved Musorgsky in family difficulties. He was obliged to spend a great part of the next two years in the country, assisting his only surviving brother in the management of the family estate of Karevo. The D major Symphony came to nothing, and both Stasov and Balakirev regretfully agreed that 'Musorgsky is almost an idiot'. Yet he had already written the characteristic *Intermezzo in modo classico* (inspired by a country scene) in its original form for piano solo (winter 1860–61), and in the summer of 1863 he composed two songs, a setting of 'An die Türen will ich schleichen' from *Wilhelm Meister* and a translation of Byron's *Song of Saul before the Battle*, all of which announce the imminence of artistic maturity. *Tsar' Saul* ('King Saul') may have been written under the influence of Serov's opera *Judith*, which Musorgsky had recently heard; under the combined impact of *Judith* and the reading of Flaubert's *Salammbô* he began in the autumn of 1863 to write the libretto of an opera on *Salammbô*, interweaving his own verses with borrowings from Heine and Russian poets, and taking his stage directions wholesale from Flaubert. The music of *Salammbô*, on which he worked intermittently until the summer of 1866, includes a certain amount of self-borrowing from *Oedipus*, but some of it, in turn, was later transferred with little alteration to *Boris Godunov*.

Financial straits now obliged Musorgsky to enter the civil service. On 13 December 1863 he was posted to the chief engineering department of the Ministry of Communications, with the rank of collegiate secretary, and on 1 February 1864 he was appointed assistant head clerk of the barracks section of the department. This period of service lasted less than four years; on 13 December 1866 he was promoted to the rank of titular councillor, but on 10 May 1867 he was dismissed from the Ministry. Even before entering the service and beginning *Salammbô* Musorgsky had settled again in St Petersburg (autumn 1863) in conditions that, under the influence of Chernïshevsky's recently published novel *Chto delat'?* ('What is to be done?'), had suddenly become popular among the younger Russian intellectuals: he joined a commune with five other young men, living in the same flat and ardently cultivating and exchanging advanced ideas on art, religion, philosophy and politics. One member of the commune, V. A. Loginov, provided him with the theme of his *Duma* ('Rêverie') for piano. *Salammbô* was one of the books read by the commune and, according to Stasov, it was during the years of communal life that Musorgsky absorbed those views (put forward above all in the writings of Chernïshevsky and Dobrolyubov) on 'artistic truth' and the necessity of subordinating art to life, which he spent his remaining years in working out. The earliest evidence of the new tendency was the first version of the song *Kalistratushka*. Further essays in the same direction were the two piano pieces *Iz vospominaniy detstva* ('From memories of childhood'), written in April 1865 after his mother's death. That last event was the probable cause of Musorgsky's first serious bout of dipsomania, which ended in an attack of delirium tremens necessitating his removal from the commune to his brother's flat in the autumn of 1865.

Work on *Salammbô* seems to have been abandoned in the summer of 1866, although *Porazheniye Sennakheriba* ('The destruction of Sennacherib') for chorus and orchestra (January 1867; performed in St Petersburg, under Balakirev, two months later) belongs to the same circle of ideas. But between 14 September and 9 October 1866 Musorgsky had written three songs: *Svetik Savishna* ('Darling Savishna'), *Akh tï, p'yanaya teterya!* ('You drunken sot!') and *Seminarist* ('The seminarist'), which unmistakably mark the beginning of the full stream of musical naturalism and ironic, realistic comedy in song; the flow of songs in this vein continued throughout 1867. In that year two of them, *Darling Savishna* and *Hopak*, together with *Otchevo, skazhi* ('Tell me why') of nine years earlier, were published by Johansen: these were the first of Musorgsky's works to appear in print since the *Porte-enseigne polka*. Freed from government service and living in the country at his brother's house at Minkino during the summer of 1867, Musorgsky occupied himself with orchestral composition and the piano transcription of movements from Beethoven's quartets; the orchestral works were a piece based on the early *Witch* music, *Ivanova noch' na Lïsoy gore* ('St John's Night on the Bare Mountain'), an orchestral version of the *Intermezzo in modo classico*, with an additional trio, and an unfinished symphonic poem *Podibrad Cheshskiy* ('Poděbrad of Bohemia'), inspired by the Pan-Slav Congress held earlier in the summer.

Returning to St Petersburg in the autumn, Musorgsky, like the other members of the Balakirev–Stasov circle (who had just been ironically dubbed the 'Moguchaya Kuchka', or 'Mighty Handful') became especially interested in Dargomïzhsky, then engaged on his most extreme experiment in operatic naturalism, *Kamennïy gost'* ('The stone guest'). Musorgsky found his own tendencies strongly reinforced, and on 23 June 1868 embarked on his own most daring essay, a setting of Gogol's prose comedy *Zhenit'ba* ('The marriage'); the first act was completed by 20 July, but the work was carried no farther. The completed act was privately per-

*1. Modest Petrovich Musorgsky: portrait (1881) by I. E. Repin in the State Tretyakov Art Gallery, Moscow*

formed at Cui's on 6 October, the composer himself singing the part of the hero; but even Dargomïzhsky and his other friends felt that experimentalism had been carried too far. Stasov alone was roused to closer interest in Musorgsky's work and from that time onwards became his adviser and champion. Musorgsky was by this time interested in a fresh project, in which he was able to blend realism with his older strain of romantic lyricism, an opera on the subject of *Boris Godunov*, to his own libretto based partly on Pushkin's play. The first scene was completed in vocal score on 12 November. On 2 January 1869 Musorgsky re-entered the government service as assistant head clerk in the third section of the forestry department of the Ministry of State Property. He was able to live with old friends, the brother and sister A. P. and N. P. Opochinin, and in these settled conditions the original version of *Boris*, in seven scenes, was completed in vocal score by the end of July 1869 and in full score on 27 December. A fortnight before the completion of the full score Musorgsky was promoted to the rank of collegiate assessor.

In July 1870 Musorgsky began negotiations for a production of *Boris* and embarked on the composition of a new opera, *Bobïl'*, the music of one completed scene of which was later transferred to *Khovanshchina*. In the autumn he wrote four naturalistic studies of child life. These songs to his own words were published, together with one earlier piece in the same vein, as a cycle, *Detskaya* ('The nursery'); two more were added in the second edition. But Musorgsky was soon obliged to return to *Boris*. On 22 February 1871 the opera

committee of the Mariinsky Theatre rejected his score and, very easily offended though he was, he began with unusual meekness to recast his work, introducing the present third act and the final scene of riot and anarchy, eliminating the scene before St Basil's Cathedral and making other drastic changes. This second version, consisting of a prologue and four acts, was completed in full score on 5 July 1872. During the latter part of the work (autumn 1871 onwards) Musorgsky shared an apartment with another composer of the Balakirev group, Rimsky-Korsakov, then engaged on his opera *The Maid of Pskov*, and in the spring of 1872 both composers interrupted their operas to collaborate with two others of their circle (Borodin and Cui) in a projected opera-ballet, *Mlada*, which was never completed. For part of his contribution to *Mlada* Musorgsky again drew on his old *Oedipus* music and his *St John's Night on the Bare Mountain*; *Mlada* in turn yielded material for later compositions. From that period the Balakirev circle tended to disintegrate.

On 17 February 1872 the finale of the first act of *Boris* was performed at a concert of the Russian Music Society in St Petersburg, under Nápravník, and on 15 April Balakirev conducted the polonaise at a concert of the Free School of Music. But in the autumn the opera committee of the Imperial Theatres rejected the second version, as it had the first. Nevertheless, on the initiative of some of the singers and in defiance of the committee, three scenes from *Boris* were performed as part of a benefit performance for the stage manager of the Mariinsky Theatre on 17 February 1873, and met with

*2. Scene showing the death of Boris in the first production of 'Boris Godunov' at the Mariinsky Theatre, Leningrad in 1874: engraving*

great success. A month or two later the publisher Bessel announced that he had acquired the rights in the opera and opened subscriptions for the vocal score. This was issued in January 1874 (it represents a modification of the second version), and on 8 February 1874 *Boris Godunov* was produced at the Mariinsky Theatre, St Petersburg, for the benefit of the singer Yuliya Platonova. It was repeated a week later, and eight more performances were given in the course of the season.

Since June–July 1872 Musorgsky had on Stasov's suggestion been collecting historical and musical material for another historical opera, *Khovanshchina*, dealing with the political disturbances under the regency which preceded Peter the Great's full accession to the throne. Instead of writing a complete libretto, or at least preparing a scenario, he appears to have confused himself by too much study of historical sources and then to have written fragments of libretto with too little reference to a definite plan. From this period date most of Musorgsky's dicta on the function of art, the value of technique and so on, all expressed in letters to his confidant Stasov. In the summer of 1873 he formed a close friendship with a family connection, Count A. A. Golenishchev-Kutuzov, a poet of some ability, and agreed to share a flat with him. At the same period he began the music of *Khovanshchina*, on which he continued to work intermittently until August 1880, although most of it was written in 1873 and 1875–6. He was no longer capable of sustained effort; under the influence of heavy drinking his character had begun to deteriorate seriously, and he confessed to 'fits of dementia'. Stasov failed to induce him to visit Liszt, who had expressed admiration of *The Nursery*, and his friend's temporary absence in western Europe removed a restraining influence. Nevertheless Musorgsky earned official promotion to the grade of court councillor (13 December 1873) and was made senior head clerk of his department (17 March 1875).

Even the successful production of *Boris* had an unfortunate effect on the composer personally: it inflated his self-esteem and, owing to several unlucky circumstances, wounded it at the same time. Little was done to *Khovanshchina* in 1874, although the familiar 'introduction' dates from September of that year. From June to November Musorgsky composed the song cycle *Bez solntsa* ('Sunless') to poems by Golenishchev-Kutuzov; in June he also wrote the cycle of piano pieces *Kartinki s vïstavki* ('Pictures at an exhibition'), suggested by a memorial exhibition of the architectural drawings, stage designs and watercolours of his friend Victor Hartmann, who had died the year before. A more serious deflection from *Khovanshchina* was the idea of a comic opera based on Gogol's short story *Sorochinskaya yarmarka* ('Sorochintsy fair'), which occurred to him that summer, though he temporarily abandoned the project early in 1875. During the first half of 1875 he wrote the first three numbers of a new song cycle to Golenishchev-Kutuzov's words, *Pesni i plyaski smerti* ('Songs and dances of death'). When the poet, who married a few months later, went off to the country, Musorgsky was given a home by a retired naval officer, P. A. Naumov. At the same time he had drifted away from his earlier musical friends, Cui and Rimsky-Korsakov, partly because of their pursuit of different musical ideals, partly because of their very different ways of life.

During the spring of 1876 Musorgsky and Lyudmila Shestakova, Glinka's sister, were much concerned in organizing the jubilee celebrations of the bass singer Osip Petrov, the first Varlaam in *Boris*. This event seems to have turned his thoughts back to *Sorochintsy Fair*, which he had conceived from the outset with Petrov in mind, and during the latter part of 1876 he worked at both the Gogol opera and *Khovanshchina*. The next year he thrust *Khovanshchina* aside entirely in favour of *Sorochintsy Fair*, but after Petrov's death (14 March 1878) he cooled towards that in turn. At this period he was experimenting with a type of compromise between lyrical melody and subtly accurate, naturalistic declamation, 'the incorporation of recitative in melody.... I should like to call it "intelligently justified" melody'. The results are apparent in some passages of the two operas and, more immediately, in a group of songs to poems by Alexey Tolstoy composed between 17 March and 2 April 1877. On 14 July the same year he completed a short choral piece, *Iisus Navin* ('Jesus Navin'), based on two numbers from *Salammbô*. During the earlier part of 1878 Musorgsky appears to have led a more respectable life. Balakirev, just beginning to show himself again in the musical world after six years of retirement, was 'pleasantly surprised' on meeting him. On 4 June Musorgsky was promoted to collegiate councillor. Later in the summer there was a serious relapse but, thanks to the efforts of Stasov and Balakirev, he was transferred from the forestry department to a temporary post in the Revision Commission of Government Control, whose director, the folksong enthusiast T. I Filippov, proved exceedingly lenient.

The following year Filippov was even so complaisant as to allow Musorgsky leave for a three-months concert tour in the Ukraine, Crimea and towns along the Don and the Volga. An old acquaintance, the contralto Darya Leonova, invited him to make this provincial tour as her accompanist, and between 11 August and 29 October they gave concerts at Poltava, Elizavetgrad, Nikolayev, Kherson, Odessa, Sevastopol, Yalta, Rostovna-Donu, Novocherkassk, Voronezh, Tambov and Tver (see Keldïsh and Yakovlev, 1932, for full programmes). Besides accompanying Leonova, who naturally included some of his songs in her programmes, Musorgsky appeared as soloist in transcriptions of excerpts from his operas, including the Coronation Scene from *Boris*, the March of the Preobrazhensky Guards from *Khovanshchina* and the *Bare Mountain* music (now described as 'a musical picture from a new comic opera, *Sorochintsy Fair*'). At the later concerts he also played a 'grand musical picture', *Burya na Chernom more* ('Storm on the Black Sea'), which was never written down. Two slighter travel impressions for piano, *Na yuzhnom beregu Krïma* ('On the southern shore of the Crimea'), were published the following year.

On 13 January 1880 Musorgsky was at last obliged to leave the government service, but Filippov and other friends guaranteed him a monthly pension of 100 rubles on condition that he finish *Khovanshchina*. Unfortunately, shortly afterwards another group of well-wishers offered him a sum of 80 rubles on condition that he finish *Sorochintsy Fair* within a year. (They also pressed him to make piano arrangements of excerpts from it for the publisher Bernard, and the popular *Hopak* first appeared in this form.) In consequence both operas remained unfinished. During this last year of his life Musorgsky made further appearances as Leonova's accompanist. She also took him with her to her summer villa at Oranienbaum and employed him as accompanist, theory teacher and factotum in the music school which she instituted in St Petersburg; he composed a number of folksong arrangements and vocalises for the pupils there. Besides working at his two operas he contemplated writing an orchestral suite on oriental themes and composed (January or February 1880) a trio *alla turca* for a processional march on a Russian folksong, originally part of the *Mlada* music. This 'new' march, intended to accompany one of a series of *tableaux vivants* of the reign of Alexander II, was performed under the title *Vzyatiye Karsa* ('The capture of Kars') by Nápravník at a concert of the Russian Music Society in St Petersburg on 30 October.

On 15 February 1881 Musorgsky made his last public appearance, when Rimsky-Korsakov conducted *The Destruction of Sennacherib* at a concert of the Free School of Music, and he acknowledged the applause. Eight days later he went to Leonova (according to her own account) 'in a state of great nervous excitement', saying 'that there was nothing left for him but to go and beg in the streets'. That evening he had a fit of alcoholic epilepsy. He spent the night at Leonova's house and the next day (24 February) had three more fits. On 26 February he was removed by his friends to the Nikolayevsky Military Hospital. There was a temporary improvement (14–17 March) during which Repin painted his famous portrait, but on 28 March he died. He was buried in the Nevsky Cemetery two days later.

2. POSTHUMOUS COMPLETION OF WORKS. Comparatively few of Musorgsky's works were published during his lifetime, and the editing of the posthumous publications was mainly – at first solely – carried out by Rimsky-Korsakov; these were issued by Bessel. In Rimsky-Korsakov's opinion Musorgsky, though 'so talented, original, full of so much that was new and vital', revealed in his manuscripts technical clumsiness, 'absurd, disconnected harmony, ugly part-writing, sometimes strikingly illogical modulation, sometimes a depressing lack of it, unsuccessful scoring of the orchestral things.... Publication without some setting in order by a skilled hand would have had no sense, except a biographical–historical one'. If an 'archaeologically exact edition' was called for after 50 years, one could always be produced; 'what was needed at the moment was an edition for performance, for practical artistic aims, for familiarization with his enormous talent, not for the study of his personality and artistic transgressions'.

Accordingly every composition that passed through Rimsky-Korsakov's hands was to a greater or lesser degree 'corrected' by him. In the case of the *Bare Mountain* music he entirely rejected the completed orchestral version of 1867 (which was not published until 1968) and composed what was virtually a new orchestral piece on Musorgsky's various materials, most nearly approximating to the version with chorus that Musorgsky had prepared for *Sorochintsy Fair*. The most important, and most necessary, of Rimsky-Korsakov's immediate tasks was the completion and orchestration of *Khovanshchina*, produced by an amateur group in St Petersburg on 21 February 1886; the vocal score of the Rimsky-Korsakov version was published by Bessel in 1883. Passages omitted by Rimsky-Korsakov were orchestrated by Ravel and Stravinsky and inserted for the first Paris production (5 June 1913); Stravinsky composed the final chorus afresh from Musorgsky's themes, and this was published by Bessel in 1913. These insertions in the Rimsky-Korsakov version were balanced by drastic cuts. Rimsky-Korsakov later turned his attention to the compositions published in Musorgsky's lifetime and produced editions which for a number of years supplanted the authentic texts. When in 1898 Belyayev reissued the seven songs originally published by Johansen 30 years earlier, they were anonymously edited by Rimsky-Korsakov. He also edited for Bessel in 1908 new editions of the songs originally published by that firm, making few changes but producing a 'free paraphrase' of the first number of *The Nursery*.

All these re-editions are of minor importance compared with Rimsky-Korsakov's versions of *Boris Godunov*. As early as 1888 he rescored the polonaise, in 1891–2 the Coronation Scene; in 1896 he produced a completely new version of the opera with drastic cuts, wholesale rewriting and complete rescoring of the surviving text, insertion of a certain amount of new music composed by himself and transposition of the order of the last two scenes. This version was produced privately in the Great Hall of the St Petersburg Conservatory on 10 December 1896, by the Mamontov Opera Company with Shalyapin (Moscow, 19 December 1898; St Petersburg, 19 March 1899), and by the Imperial Theatres, again with Shalyapin (Moscow, 26 April 1901; St Petersburg, 22 November 1904). The vocal score was published by Bessel. During 1906–8 Rimsky-Korsakov prepared a fresh version, also published in vocal score by Bessel, in which he restored the cuts but not the original text and left in his own additions. For the Paris production of *Boris* (19 May 1908), the first in western Europe, he composed two new passages for the Coronation Scene.

Rimsky-Korsakov left the fragmentary *Salammbô* untouched, but a year or two before his death he decided on the publication of the single act of *The Marriage*; the vocal score, edited by him with the relatively few changes mentioned in the preface to the score, was published by Bessel in 1908. He also began the orchestration, but completed only a few pages; the single act was subsequently orchestrated by the Soviet conductor Alexander Gauk (and supposedly by Ravel, but the matter is controversial). In 1931 Ippolitov-Ivanov composed and orchestrated the three remaining acts of Gogol's comedy. Rimsky-Korsakov made no attempt to edit *Sorochintsy Fair* (apart from the *Bare Mountain* music inserted in it); on his suggestion the completion of the libretto was entrusted to Golenishchev-Kutuzov, that of the music to A. K. Lyadov. Little was done, but in 1886 Bessel published Khivrya's song and Parasya's *dumka* with piano, and the *hopak* for piano solo (all three in practically pure texts), and during the period 1904–14 a series of further numbers: (*a*) the *parobok*'s *dumka*, edited and orchestrated by Lyadov, with a vocal score (1904); (*b*) Lyadov's orchestration of the *hopak* with a 'piano arrangement', essentially identical with the 1886 edition (1904); (*c*) Lyadov's rewritten version of the introduction, in full score and piano arrangements; (*d*) Introduction and Fair Scene, edited by V. G. Karatïgin in vocal score (1912); (*e*) the scene between Cherevik and the *kum*, edited by Karatïgin in vocal score (1912); (*f*) the comic scene from Act 2, edited by Karatïgin in vocal score (1912); (*g*) Parasya's *dumka*, orchestrated by V. A. Senilov (1912); and (*h*) Khivrya's song, orchestrated by Lyadov, with vocal score essentially identical with the 1886 edition (1914). Karatïgin's edition and completion of the finale of Act 2 was engraved but never published. Of the Lyadov–Karatïgin numbers (*c*), (*d*) (Fair Scene only) and (*f*) were first performed as illustrations to a lecture on *Sorochintsy Fair* by Karatïgin, given privately at Count Osten-Drizen's in St Petersburg, with piano and without chorus, on 29 March 1911; they were repeated in public and with costumes and scenery, with the addition of the finale of Act 2, in the Comedia Theatre, St Petersburg, on 30 December of the same year. On 21 October 1913, a pastiche of all the available numbers in the Lyadov and Karatïgin editions, with Rimsky-Korsakov's version of the *Bare Mountain*, was produced at the Moscow Free Theatre, the lacunae in the action being filled with spoken dialogue by K. A. Mardzhanov; the numbers edited by Karatïgin were orchestrated by Yu. S. Sakhnovsky, who also composed a few additional passages. This production caused legal action by Bessel on a point of copyright, and Sakhnovsky's score was suppressed. In 1915 César Cui prepared a complete

musical version, using all the available numbers and in some cases Lyadov's orchestration, and composing additional music, partly on Musorgsky's themes, as required; the vocal score of Cui's version was published by Bessel in 1916, and on 26 October 1917 it was produced at the Theatre of Musical Drama, Petrograd. Another complete version was prepared by N. N. Tcherepnin in Paris after the Russian Revolution. This was based on the existing editions by Lyadov, Karatïgin and Cui, but Cui's additions were not used; Tcherepnin filled the lacunae with music borrowed from *Salammbô*, songs and other works by Musorgsky. Tcherepnin's version, the one usually performed outside Russia, was produced at Monte Carlo on 17 March 1923 and published in vocal score by Bessel in 1924.

One other garbled text must be mentioned: that of the collection of songs from the years 1857–66 entitled by Musorgsky *Yunïye godï* ('Years of youth'). It was acquired by Charles Malherbe, archivist of the Paris Opéra, in 1909. The collection consists partly of songs hitherto unknown, partly of variants of published songs. Four of the former were published as a supplement to the *Bulletin français de la S.I.M.* (1909) and, in an edition by Karatïgin, by Bessel's firm in 1911. In 1923 Bessel issued in Paris the whole collection except for the last number (a duet arrangement of Gordigiani's *Ogni sabato*), four songs being reprinted from Karatïgin's edition, 12 inaccurately copied from the Paris autograph and one (*Kalistrat*) reprinted from the Rimsky-Korsakov edition of the variant not in the Paris collection.

From about 1908 onwards growing dissatisfaction with the Rimsky-Korsakov versions of Musorgsky's music, particularly that of *Boris*, was felt both in Russia and in western Europe, and a vigorous campaign for the publication and performance of the true texts was carried on by Russian and Western critics, led in England and France by M. D. Calvocoressi. In 1928 the Russian State Music Publishing Corporation at last embarked on a 'complete collected edition' of Musorgsky's music in accordance with the composer's manuscripts, embodying all textual variants and provided with elaborate critical apparatus. This edition, of which Pavel Lamm was editor-in-chief, was interrupted in 1939 by the outbreak of war. At the same time *Khovanshchina* was completed by Lamm and Asaf'yev and orchestrated by Asaf'yev in a version faithfully embodying all the material left by Musorgsky; *Sorochintsy Fair* was completed in the same spirit in 1930 by Vissarion Shebalin. Musorgsky's 1869 version of *Boris* was produced in Leningrad on 16 February 1928 and in London (at Sadler's Wells) on 30 September 1935. Lamm's edition of the full score of *Boris*, a conflation of sources, was superseded in 1975 by David Lloyd-Jones's, which restores Musorgsky's own full score as the basic text while printing other sources separately.

3. STYLE AND AESTHETIC. During the last year of his life Musorgsky wrote an autobiographical sketch, inaccurate in many respects but concluding with a statement of his artistic position that could hardly be bettered:

Musorgsky cannot be classed with any existing group of musicians, either by the character of his compositions or by his musical views. The formula of his artistic *profession de foi* may be explained by his view of the function of art: art is a means of communicating with people, not an aim in itself. This guiding principle has defined the whole of his creative activity. Proceeding from the conviction that human speech is strictly controlled by musical laws (Virchow, Gervinus), he considers the function of art to be the reproduction in musical sounds not merely of feelings, but first and foremost of human speech. Acknowledging that in the realm of art only artist–reformers such as Palestrina, Bach, Gluck, Beethoven, Berlioz and Liszt have created the laws of art, he considers these laws as not immutable but liable to change and progress, like everything else in man's inner world.

But if Musorgsky could not class himself with any existing group of musicians, he could very easily have placed himself beside other artists, the great Russian novelists of his day and such painters as Kramskoy, Surikov, Gey and Repin. He shared with these (particularly with the painters): a disdain for formal beauty and technical polish and every other manifestation of 'art for art's sake'; the desire to relate his art as closely as possible to life, especially to that of the Russian masses; to nourish his art on events and in turn to employ it as a medium for communicating human experience; and a somewhat selfconscious and aggressive Russianness and an intense sympathy with the Russian peasant, newly freed from serfdom. The philosophical basis of their outlook was stated most satisfactorily by Chernïshevsky in his dissertation *Esteticheskiye otnosheniya iskusstva k deystvitel'nosti* ('The aesthetic relationship of art and reality', St Petersburg, 1855) and his own criticism of it in the journal *Sovremennik*.

Musorgsky's earlier, lyrical and romantic compositions, written before he had arrived at this viewpoint, reveal the influences of Glinka, Balakirev and (in the case of *Salammbô*) Serov, of Schumann and (a little later) Liszt and Meyerbeer. The harmonic language of these works is limited and conventional, their workmanship amateurish; the instrumental pieces reveal the structural weaknesses that mark even his mature essays in instrumental music: squareness, primitiveness, lack of organic cohesion. Yet more personal traits soon begin to show themselves. The main theme of the *Intermezzo in modo classico* (1861) is doubly characteristic in that its origin was pantomimic (it was suggested by the sight of peasants plunging heavily through deep snowdrifts on a sunny winter day) and that, although the composer himself described it as 'in modo classico' and 'à la Bach', its separate motifs show an affinity with Russian folk melody. In the song *Kalistratushka* (1864), of which the first version is called 'study in folk style', the voice part, already fully typical of Musorgsky's mature type of free, asymmetrical lyrical melody, is very close to folk melody, while the cadential dissolution of the harmony into bare octaves (e.g. at the end of the first vocal phrase) is also typical of the Russian folk polyphony recorded by Melgunov, Kastal'sky and others; an actual folktune appears in the piano part in the *tranquillo* section.

This predominantly lyrical strain in Musorgsky's style was never completely submerged at any period; but, side by side with the lyrical songs of 1866–8, *Evreyskaya pesnya* ('Hebrew song'), *Po nad Donom sad tsvetet* ('The garden by the Don'), *Detskaya pesenka* ('Child's song') and others, sharply opposed tendencies appear. Instead of lyrical melody the voice parts of such songs as *Darling Savishna*, *The Seminarist* and *You Drunken Sot!* (all 1866) are attempts at 'quasi-phonographic' representation of human speech, not of speech in general but the peculiar speech of sharply realized individuals: a village idiot babbling out his amorous plea to the village beauty, a theological student allowing erotic thoughts to creep into his memorizing of Latin nouns of the third declension, a woman scolding a drunken husband. Some degree of stylization is inevitable in the

3. *Page from the autograph MS of the vocal score of Musorgsky's opera 'Boris Godunov' (2nd version, 1871–2, rev. 1873) showing the original ending of Act 1 scene ii (USSR-Mcm)*

musical representation of speech, but Musorgsky aimed at the minimum possible; when, from time to time, he abandoned represented speech, he naturally lapsed into his lyrical folksong-like idiom or, as in *The Seminarist*, deliberately imitated the music of the Orthodox Church. At the same time the piano parts are contrived to underline the characterization of the vocal line with pantomimically inspired motifs and unorthodox and empirical, but often strikingly evocative, harmony. In his songs of this type Musorgsky showed not so much a subjective sympathy for his characters as an ability to put himself in their place: *Svetik Savishna*, *Ozornik* ('The ragamuffin'), *Sirotka* ('The orphan') and *The Nursery*. Even a comic character, as in *The Seminarist*, is rendered with only slight exaggeration, as a good actor might play the part. But a little later, perhaps under the influence of Dargomïzhsky's songs, this ironic-comic element became exaggerated into less objective and thus less effective satire, as in *Kozyol* ('The he-goat'), *Klassik* ('The classicist') and *Rayok* ('The peepshow'), the last two being lampoons of the composer's musical enemies. These tendencies – 'recorded' speech with the minimum of stylization, pantomimic instrumental motifs and empirical, expressionistic harmony, satirical comedy – are manifested in their most extreme forms and without lyrical relief in *The Marriage*.

In *Boris Godunov* these two tendencies, the lyrical and the naturalistic, exist side by side in nearly perfect equilibrium. In *Khovanshchina* and the later songs they tend to be fused rather than opposed, and the lyrical element tends to gain the upper hand. In the *Sunless* cycle a new element of subjective pessimism makes its appearance, though in no work of Musorgsky is his empirical harmony more subtly effective. The *Pictures at an Exhibition*, dating from the same year as *Sunless* (1874), reveal the characteristic juxtaposition of lyrical and pantomimic (and comic) elements. After 1874 a gradual falling-off in quality is perceptible in all Musorgsky's work, though even the fragments of *Sorochintsy Fair* show him still striving to learn from folk music and the intonations of folk speech (in both cases, those of the Ukraine), still mingling pure lyricism with satirical comedy.

*Boris Godunov* and *Khovanshchina* are, like all the Russian historical operas of that period, offshoots of Meyerbeerian grand opera, however much they may differ from the prototypes in musical language, in musical and dramatic technique and in aesthetic point of view. Musorgsky's originality as a dramatic composer is most easily gauged by reference to that standard. In place of well-made theatrical plots there are cross-sections of the life of a whole people; instead of conventionalized characters in *Boris* (though hardly in *Khovanshchina*), sharply realized individuals. The personal tragedy of Boris is heightened, not weakened, by being set against a wholly living background not only of the court circle (his children, the treacherous boyar Shuysky) but of the Russian people generally, represented by individuals such as the various monks, the police officers, the idiot, the innkeeper, even the anonymous members of the crowd; as a result Boris himself comes to stand for the entire suffering nation. In *Khovanshchina* the same thing is attempted much less successfully; neither the elder Khovansky nor Dosifey is presented in the round, as Boris is; the forces opposed to them are shown only in the person of the lay figure Shaklovity, while the forces opposed to Boris are per-

sonified in the very human Pretender. Even 'the people' in *Khovanshchina* have less vital representatives. The score of *Khovanshchina* contains some of Musorgsky's best lyrical writing (for example, the introduction and Golitsïn's departure into exile), one of his finest strokes of musical irony (the snatch of folksong sung by Shaklovity over the elder Khovansky's dead body) and some typical pantomimic effects (such as the scribe's 'writing' figure); but it lacks the dramatic incisiveness of the earlier work. Few operas contain so little dead matter as *Boris*, particularly in its original version of 1869; apart from the grandeur and depth of the treatment as a whole, episodic as that whole is, the score is full of singularly effective subtleties of every kind. Musorgsky did not use leitmotifs as Wagner did, but in the more limited way common in the third quarter of the 19th century; however, he used the device in a quite peculiar manner, to make points that could hardly be made by other means. A single theme serves in *Boris* both for the real, murdered Tsarevich and for the Pretender, the false Dmitry, and so reflects the superstitious doubt and confusion in Boris's mind; in *Khovanshchina* the theme of Marfa's conjuration scene is later linked in turn with the fates of the elder Khovansky, Golitsïn and Andrey Khovansky – all Tsar Peter's enemies are doomed. Of the innumerable very different subtleties of harmony and orchestration in *Boris* it must suffice to mention the simple, solemn trombone chords in the second scene of the Prologue, just before Boris's call to 'pay a solemn tribute to the tombs of Russia's rulers', the grating harmonies of the high string tremolo of the hallucination scene, the bare open 5ths on the second syllable of the word 'Siberia' in the map scene, the harmonic setting of the treacherous Shuysky's account to the Duma of the tsar's hallucinations. Musorgsky's orchestration is seldom beautiful for its own sake; his harmony would often be nonsensical as absolute music; but he used both with infallible instinct as instruments of dramatic expression. As a musical translator of words and all that can be expressed in words, of psychological states and even physical movements he is unsurpassed; as an absolute musician he was hopelessly limited, with remarkably little ability to construct pure music or even a purely musical texture.

### WORKS

Edition: *M. P. Musorgsky: Polnoye sobraniye sochineniy* [Complete collection of works], ed. P. Lamm, with B. V. Asaf'yev (Moscow, 1928–34/R1969, 1939 [addl vol.viii]) [L]

STAGE

Han d'Islande (opera, after Hugo), projected 1856

Edip v Afinakh [Oedipus in Athens] (opera, after Ozerov), projected 1858–60

Salammbô (opera, after Flaubert), 1863–6, inc.

Zhenit'ba [The marriage] (comic opera, Gogol), 1868, Act 1 only, St Petersburg, Suvorin Theatre School, 1 April 1909, L iv/2

Boris Godunov (opera, Musorgsky, after Pushkin and Karamazin): 1st version, 7 scenes, 1868–9, Leningrad, 16 Feb 1928; 2nd version, prol and 4 acts, 1871–2, rev. 1873, vocal score (1874), St Petersburg, Mariinsky Theatre, 8 Feb 1874; ed. D. Lloyd-Jones (London, 1975)

Bobïl' [The landless peasant] (opera, after Spielhagen: Hans und Grete), projected 1870

Mlada (opera-ballet, V. A. Krilov), collab. Rimsky-Korsakov, Borodin, Cui, projected 1872, L iv/3, vii/1

Khovanshchina (opera, Musorgsky), 1872–80, completed and orchd Rimsky-Korsakov, St Petersburg, 21 Feb 1886, L iv/3, vii/2

Sorochinskaya yarmarka [Sorochintsy fair] (comic opera, after Gogol), 1874–80, completed and orchd Lyadov, V. G. Karatïgin and others, Moscow, Free Theatre, 21 Oct 1913 and St Petersburg, Comedia Theatre, 30 Dec 1913, L iii

Pugachovshchina (opera, after Pushkin), projected 1877

CHORAL

Marsh Shamilya [Shamil's march], T, B, chorus, orch, 1859
Porazheniye Sennakheriba [The destruction of Sennacherib], 1866–7 (1871), rev. 1874
Iisus Navin [Jesus Navin], A, B, chorus, pf, 1874–7
3 vocalises, 3 female vv, 1880
5 Russian folksongs, arr. 4 male vv, 1880: Skazhi, devitsa milaya; Tï vzoydi, solntse krasnoye; U vorot, vorot batyshkinïkh; Uzh tï, volya, moya volya, with 2 solo T; no.5, inc.

ORCHESTRAL

Scherzo, B♭, 1858, orig. for pf, L vii/4
Alla marcia notturna, 1861
Symphony, D, projected 1861–2
Ivanova noch' na Lïsoy gore [St John's Night on the Bare Mountain], 1867
Intermezzo symphonique in modo classico, b, 1867, orig. for pf, with new trio, L vii/5
Podibrad Cheshskiy [Poděbrad of Bohemia], sym. poem, projected 1867
Vzyatiye Karsa [The capture of Kars], march, 1880

PIANO

(in L viii unless otherwise stated)

Porte-enseigne polka, 1852 (1852); Souvenir d'enfance, 1857; 2 sonatas, E♭, f♯, 1858, no.1 inc., both lost; Scherzo, c♯, 1858; Scherzo, B♭, 1858, orchd; Impromptu passionné, 1859; Ein Kinderscherz, 1859, rev. 1860 (1873); Preludio in modo classico, 1860, lost; Intermezzo in modo classico, 1860–61 (1873), orchd 1867, rearr. pf, 1867; Menuet monstre, 1861, lost
Iz vospominaniy detstva [From memories of childhood], 1865: 1 Nyanya i ya [Nurse and I], 2 Pervoye nakazaniye: Nyanya zapirayet menya v temnuyu komnatu [First punishment: Nurse shuts me in a dark room]; Duma [Rêverie], on a theme of V. A. Loginov, 1865; La capricieuse, on a theme of L. Heyden, 1865; Shveya [The seamstress], scherzino, 1871 (1872)
Kartinki s vïstavki [Pictures at an exhibition], suite, 1874, L viii/2;
Burya na Chernom more [Storm on the Black Sea], 1879, lost; Na yuzhnom beregu Krïma [On the southern shore of the Crimea], 1880 (1880); Méditation, albumleaf, 1880 (1880); Une larme, 1880; Au village (Quasi fantasia), ?1880; arr. of Fair Scene and Hopak from Sorochintsy Fair
For pf 4 hands: Allegro and scherzo for a sonata, C, 1860 [scherzo based on Scherzo, c♯, pf solo]; 4-hand arrs., L vii/1, 3, 4

SONGS

(for 1v, pf, and in L v unless otherwise stated)

Gde tï, zvezdochka? [Where art thou, little star?] (N. Grekov), 1857, rev. with orch, 1858
Meines Herzens Sehnsucht, 1858
Otchevo, skazhi [Tell me why], 1858 (1867)
Vesyolïy chas [Hour of jollity] (A. Kol'tsov), 1858, 2nd version 1859
List'ya shumeli unïlo [Sadly rustled the leaves] (after Pleshcheyev), 1859
Chto vam slova lyubvi? [What are words of love to you?] (A. Ammosov), 1860
Mnogo est' u menya teremov i sadov [I have many palaces and gardens] (Kol'tsov), 1863
Pesn' startsa: Stanu skromno u poroga [Old man's song] (Goethe, trans.), 1863
Tsar' Saul [King Saul] (Byron, trans. P. Kozlov), 1863, 2nd version 1863 (1870–71)
No esli bï s toboyu ya vstretit'sya mogla [But if I could meet thee again] (V. Kurochkin), 1863
Duyut vetrï, vetrï buynïye [The wild winds blow] (Kol'tsov), 1864
Kalistratushka (Nekrasov), 1864, 2nd version as Kalistrat, 1864
Noch' [Night] (after Pushkin), 1864, orchd 1868, 2nd version 1864 (1870–71), L vii/3
Molitva [Prayer] (Lermontov), 1865
Otverzhennaya: opit rechitativa [The outcast: essay in recitative] (I. Holz-Miller), 1865
Kolïbel'naya pesnya [Lullaby] (Ostrovsky, from Voyevoda), 1865, 2nd version as Spi, uspi krest'yanskiy sïn [Sleep, sleep, peasant son], 1865
Malyutka: Akh, zachem tvoy glazki poroyu? [Dear one, why are thine eyes sometimes so cold?] (Pleshcheyev), 1866
Ich wollt' meine Schmerzen ergössen (Heine), 1866
Iz slyoz moikh [From my tears] (Heine, trans. M. Mikhaylov), 1866
Svetik Savishna [Darling Savishna] (Musorgsky), 1866 (1867)
Akh tï, p'yanaya teterya! [You drunken sot!] (Musorgsky), 1866
Seminarist [The seminarist] (Musorgsky), 1866
Hopak (Shevchenko, trans. Mey), 1866 (1867), rev. with orch, 1868, L vii/6
Pesn' Yaremï 'Na Dnepre' [Yarema's song 'On the Dnieper'] (Shevchenko, trans. Mey), 1866, lost, 2nd version 1879
Evreyskaya pesnya [Hebrew song] (Mey), 1867 (1868)
Strekotun'ya beloboka [The magpie] (Pushkin), 1867 (1870–77)
Po gribï [Gathering mushrooms] (Mey), 1867 (1868)
Pirushka [The feast] (Kol'tsov), 1867 (1868)

Ozornik [The ragamuffin] (Musorgsky), 1867 (1870–71)
Kozyol: svetskaya skazochka [The he-goat: a worldly story] (Musorgsky), 1867 (1868)
Klassik [The classicist] (Musorgsky), 1867 (1870)
Po nad Donom sad tsvetet [The garden by the Don] (Kol'tsov), 1867
Sirotka [The orphan] (Musorgsky), 1868 (1870–71)
Kolïbel'naya Eryomushki [Eremushka's lullaby] (Nekrasov), 1868 (1870–71)
Detskaya pesenka [Child's song] (Mey), 1868 (1870–71)
Detskaya [The nursery] (Musorgsky) (1870): 1 S nyaney [With nurse], 1868; 2 V uglu [In the corner], 1870; 3 Zhuk [The cockchafer], 1870; 4 S kukloy [With the doll], 1870; 5 Na son gryadushchiy [Going to sleep], 1870; 6 Poyekhal na palochke [On the hobby-horse], 1872; 7 Kot Matros [The cat Sailor], 1872 [6 and 7 in 2/1873]
Rayok [The peepshow] (Musorgsky), 1870 (1870–71)
Vechernyaya pesenka [Evening song] (?Pleshcheyev), 1871
Bez solntsa [Sunless] (Golenishchev-Kutuzov), 1874 (1874): 1 V chetïryokh stenakh [Between four walls]; 2 Menya tï v tolpe ne uznala [Thou didst not know me in the crowd]; 3 Okonchen prazdnïy, shumnïy den' [The idle, noisy day is ended]; 4 Skuchay [Boredom]; 5 Elegiya [Elegy]; 6 Nad rekoy [On the river]
Zabïtïy [Forgotten] (Golenishchev-Kutuzov), 1874
Nadgrabnoye pis'mo [Epitaph] (Musorgsky), 1874, inc.
Krapivnaya gora [The nettle mountain] (Musorgsky), 1874, inc.
Pesni i plyaski smerti [Songs and dances of death] (Golenishchev-Kutuzov): 1 Kolïbel'naya [Lullaby], 1875; 2 Serenada [Serenade], 1875; 3 Trepak, 1875; 4 Polkovodets [The field-marshal], 1877
Neponyatnaya [The sphinx] (Musorgsky), 1875
Ne bozhniim gromom udarilo [Not like thunder, trouble struck] (A. K. Tolstoy), 1877
Gornimi tikho letela dusha nebesami [Softly the spirit flew up to heaven] (Tolstoy), 1877
Spes' [Pride] (Tolstoy), 1877
Oy, chest' li to molodtsu len pryasti? [Is spinning man's work?] (Tolstoy), 1877
Rassevayetsya, rasstupayetsya [It scatters and breaks] (Tolstoy), 1877
Videniye [The vision] (Golenishchev-Kutuzov), 1877
Strannik [The wanderer] (Rückert, trans. Pleshcheyev), 1878
Pesnya Mefistofelya o blokhe [Mephistopheles' song of the flea] (Goethe, trans. A. Strugovshchikov), 1879

BIBLIOGRAPHY

V. V. Stasov: 'Modest Petrovich·Musorgsky: biografichesky ocherk', [Biographical essay], Vestnik Evropï (1881), no.5, pp.285–316; no.6, pp.506–45
P. d'Alheim: Moussorgski (Paris, 1896)
M. D. Calvocoressi: Moussorgsky (Paris, 1908, rev. 2/1911; Eng. trans., 1919)
M. Olenina d'Alheim: Le legs de Moussorgski (Paris, 1908)
MS (1917), Jan–Feb [special issue, incl. Musorgsky's autobiographical note]
V. Karatïgin: Musorgskiy (Petrograd, 1922)
J. Handschin: Mussorgski: Versuch einer Einführung (Zurich, 1924)
R. Godet: En marge de Boris Godunof (Paris and London, 1926)
V. Belyayev: 'Boris Godounov' in its Genuine Version (London, 1928)
I. Glebov [B. V. Asaf'yev]: K vosstanovleniyu Borisa Godunova Musorgskovo [On the restoration of Musorgsky's Boris Godunov] (Moscow, 1928)
S. Lopashev and others: Musorgskiy i evo 'Khovanshchina': sbornik statey [Musorgsky and his Khovanshchina: a collection of essays] (Moscow, 1928)
I. Glebov: 'Die ästhetischen Anschauungen Mussorgskijs', Die Musik, xxi (1929), 561
V. Belyayev and others: Boris Godunov: stat'i i issledovaniya [Boris Godunov: essays and papers] (Moscow, 1930)
V. Fédorov: 'Sur un manuscrit de Moussorgskii: les différentes éditions de ses lieder', RdM, xiii (1932), 10
Yu. Keldïsh and V. Yakovlev, eds.: M. P. Musorgskiy k pyatid'esyatoletiyu so dnya smerti: stat'i i materialï [On the 50th anniversary of Musorgsky's death: essays and material] (Moscow, 1932)
A. N. Rimsky-Korsakov, ed.: M. P. Musorgskiy: pis'ma i dokumentï [Letters and documents] (Moscow and Leningrad, 1932)
Yu. Keldïsh: Romansovaya lirika Musorgskovo [Musorgsky's lyrical songs] (Moscow, 1933)
V. Fédorov: Moussorgsky (Paris, 1935)
A. A. Golenishchev-Kutuzov: 'Vospominaniya o M. P. Musorgskom' [Memories of Musorgsky], Muzikal'noe nasledstvo, ed. M. V. Ivanov-Boretsky, i (Moscow, 1935)
K. Nilsson: Die Rimskij-Korsakoffsche Bearbeitung des 'Boris Godunoff' von Mussorgskij als Objekt der vergleichenden Musikwissenschaft (Münster, 1937)
G. Abraham: 'The Fair of Sorochintsy and Cherepnin's Completion of it', On Russian Music (London, 1939), 216
A. Frankenstein: 'Victor Hartmann and Modeste Musorgsky', MQ, xxv (1939), 268
Yu. Keldïsh, ed.: M. P. Musorgskiy: pis'ma k A. A. Golenishchevu-

*Kutuzovu* (Moscow and Leningrad, 1939)

*SovM* (1939), April [special issue, incl. Musorgsky's autobiographical note]

N. Tumanina: *M. P. Musorgskiy: zhizn i tvorchestvo* [Life and works] (Moscow and Leningrad, 1939)

M. D. Calvocoressi: *Mussorgsky* (London, 1946, rev. 2/1974)

J. Leyda and S. Bertensson, eds.: *The Musorgsky Reader: a Life of M. P. Musorgsky in Letters and Documents* (New York, 1947/R1970)

A. S. Ogolevets, ed.: *V. Stasov: izbrannïye stat'i o M. P. Musorgskom* [Selected articles on Musorgsky] (Moscow, 1952)

T. N. Livanova and others, eds.: *B. V. Asaf'yev: Izbrannïy trudï* [Collected works], iii (Moscow, 1954)

M. D. Calvocoressi: *Modest Mussorgsky: his Life and Works* (London, 1956/R1967)

V. A. Vasina-Grossman: 'Vokal'noe tvorchestvo Musorgskovo', *Russkiy klassicheskiy romans XIX veka* (Moscow, 1956)

A. Orlova: *Trudï i dni M. P. Musorgskovo: letopis' zhizni i tvorchestva* [Works and days of Musorgsky: a chronicle of his life and work] (Moscow, 1963)

A. Ogolevets: *Vokal'naya dramaturgiya Musorgskovo* (Moscow, 1966)

G. Abraham: *Slavonic and Romantic Music* (London, 1968) [incl. 'Mussorgsky's *Boris* and Pushkin's', p.178; 'The Mediterranean Element in *Boris Godunov*', p.188]

V. I. Serov: *Modest Musorgsky* (New York, 1968)

A. A. Orlova and M. S. Pekelis, eds.: *M. P. Musorgskiy: literaturnoye naslediye* (Moscow, 1971)

D. Lloyd-Jones: *Boris Godunov: Critical Commentary* (London, 1975)

S. I. Shlifshteyn: *Musorgskiy: khudozhnik, vremya, sud'ba* [Musorgsky: artist, time, fate] (Moscow, 1975)

R. W. Oldani: 'Boris Godunov and the Censor', *19th Century Music*, ii (1978–9), 245

E. R. Reilly: *A Guide to Mussorgsky: a Scorography* (New York, 1980) [rev., enlarged edn. of essays on *Boris Godunov* etc pubd in *Musical Newsletter*]

GERALD ABRAHAM

**Mussele, Corneille.** *See* NERVIUS, LEONARDUS.

**Musset, (Louis-Charles-)Alfred de** (*b* Paris, 11 Dec 1810; *d* Paris, 2 May 1857). French poet. Although he had no deep understanding of music, despite his early study of the piano and later activities as a music critic, Musset was sensitive to its emotional effect, as is shown by his *Stances à la Malibran*. One of his early works, *La quittance du diable*, resembles an *opéra comique* in style, and music plays an important decorative or evocative role in many of his *Comédies et proverbes*, as well as in his lyric poems. Musset identified music with melody, preferably Italian, such as he heard sung by the great artists of the Théâtre Italien, in particular Rubini, Mario, Pasta and Malibran; and in his criticism written for the *Revue des deux mondes* from 1833 onwards he was actively hostile to what he considered 'learned' music. By this he meant Berlioz and Meyerbeer, whose claims he rejected for those of his particular favourite Rossini. Denying Diderot's claim that operatic melody is exaggerated declamation, he insisted on identifying bel canto with 'la pensée pure'.

Apart from the overtly musical *Chansons à boire*, his works are interspersed with lyrics which by their form, language and character invite a musical setting (famous examples are *Beau chevalier, qui partez pour la guerre, A St Blaise, à la Zuecca, J'ai perdu ma force et ma vie*). Romantic disillusion and ennui, the *mal de siècle*, finds elegant and charming expression in his work and attracted many musicians of the generation following his own. The elegiac aspect of music, perfectly summed up in his *Stances à la Malibran*, was his chief concern, and he expressed it in a much quoted couplet: 'les plus désespérés sont les chants les plus beaux, et j'en connais aucuns qui sont de purs sanglots'. This might be applied to much of Bellini's and some of Chopin's music, and Musset met both composers in the Princess Belgioioso's salon during the 1830s. The only other function of music in Musset's work is to provide an element of the picturesque, whether in its exotic form (the guitars of Spain and Italy) or in the more homely popular vein of *Mimi Pinson est une blonde*. No importance should be attached to the line in his *Les marrons du feu* – 'C'est la musique, moi, qui m'a fait croire en Dieu'. Music was for Musset a sentimental adornment rather than a spring of faith.

BIBLIOGRAPHY

G. Rouchez: 'Le sentiment musical chez les écrivains de 1830, Alfred de Musset', *Courrier musical* (15 July 1904), 424

F. Noske: *La mélodie française de Berlioz à Duparc* (Amsterdam and Paris, 1954), 65ff

T. Marix-Spire: *Les romantiques et la musique* (Paris, 1955), 302ff

L. Maurice-Amour: 'Musset, la musique et les musiciens', *Revue des sciences humaines* (1958), Jan, 31

MARTIN COOPER

**Mussio, Emanuele.** *See* MUZIO, EMANUELE.

**Mustafà, Domenico** (*b* Sterpara, nr. Perugia, 14 April 1829; *d* Montefalco, nr. Perugia, 18 March 1912). Italian soprano castrato and composer. He entered the choir of the Sistine Chapel in 1848 and later became its director, holding the post until his retirement in 1895. Emma Calvé, who took singing lessons from him in 1891, described certain notes in his voice as 'strange, sexless, superhuman, uncanny', while Wagner considered casting him as Klingsor in *Parsifal*. His compositions include settings of *O salutaris hostia*, *Tu es Petrus*, *Miserere* and *Dies irae*, many other sacred works and some songs.

BIBLIOGRAPHY

A. De Angelis: *Domenico Mustafà e la Cappella Sistina* (Bologna, 1926)

E. Calvé: *Sous tous les ciels j'ai chanté* (Paris, 1940)

A. Heriot: *The Castrati in Opera* (London, 1956)

ELIZABETH FORBES

**Mustel, Victor** (*b* Le Havre, 13 June 1815; *d* Paris, 26 Jan 1890). French manufacturer of harmoniums. His several inventions resulted in the instrument known as the Mustel organ. Orphaned at the age of 12, he was apprenticed to a shipbuilder and in 1838 set up in business for himself in that trade in Sanvic. Endowed from youth with a peculiarly constructive genius, he first attempted to make musical instruments by devoting himself to the improvement of an accordion which he had bought at Le Havre. Elated with his success, he disposed of his workshop in May 1844 and set out for Paris with his wife and two children. For the next nine years he worked in several different workshops, but never obtained high wages. In 1853 he determined to start in business for himself as a harmonium maker, and in 1855 he exhibited his harmonium with 'Double Expression' and a new stop (Harpe éolienne), for which he gained a medal of the first class. For the first year after this Mustel (now assisted by his two sons) did fairly well, but business rapidly declined, and he would perhaps have been obliged to give up but for the sale of a little land which he had inherited from his father. Even in 1866 his receipts did little more than cover costs, but from that date the firm of Victor Mustel & ses Fils gained a reputation as noteworthy in England as in France. The present name of the firm is Mustel & Cie.

The inventions due to the Mustels are the 'double expression' (patented in 1854), whereby the natural preponderance of the bass notes over those of the treble is, with complete power of increase and decrease in either half, brought under direct control of the player by means of knee pedals (*genouillères*) that control the energy and pressure of the wind; the 'Forte expressif', a divided swell governed by pneumatic action; and the 'Harpe éolienne', a tremolo register of two ranks of vibrators, 2′ pitch, which offer a gently beating variation to the unison by being slightly higher and lower than the normal pitch of the instrument, the impression of which remains unimpaired. Later Mustel inventions were the Typophone and Métaphone. The first of these is a keyboard percussion instrument made of tuning-forks in resonance boxes of the proper acoustic capacity. The principle is very similar to that of the celesta. The Métaphone (patented 1878) was devised by Mustel's son Charles to soften the strident tones of the harmonium. This softening effect is produced by a sliding shutter of leather to each compartment and governed by draw-stops, as with other modifications of tone and power.                                       A. J. HIPKINS/R

**Muta** (It.: 'change'). A performing instruction: 'Muta in La' would mean change to an instrument in A, or change the tuning-crook of a wind instrument to put it in A.

**Mutation.** In solmization, changing from one hexachord to another. *See* SOLMIZATION, §I, 3.

**Mutation stop.** In modern organ usage, mutations are those single-rank stops, usually of wide or fairly wide-scaled pipes with a high lead content, pitched at the 5th, 3rd, 7th, 9th, etc, of an upper octave; hence their other names: 'overtone stops', *Aliquotstimmen*, etc. Common examples are the Nasard, Larigot and Tierce; sometimes the stop has two ranks (e.g. Terzian), in which case it really belongs to the mixtures; sometimes the stop is scaled, voiced and constructed of a metal suitable for a Principal rank (e.g. Twelfth), in which case it is not a Flute mutation. Historically, the picture is not simple. *Mutationen* could mean any stops, a synonym for *Stimmen* (J. B. Samber, 1707); in late medieval contracts, *mutaciones* denoted much the same as *jeux* or *jochs*, i.e. registrations or, simply, different sounds (Minorites' church, Barcelona, 1480); in classical French usage, mutation stops include any rank (such as 2′ flutes or even solo reeds) which are of wide scale or drawn outside the *plein jeu* chorus (Paris, 1647). The term does not refer to the 'changing' of the fundamental tone to an overtone, as often stated in English sources, but to the varieties of tone or *mutaciones* such stops afford.                                      PETER WILLIAMS

**Mutazione** (It.). In the Italian poetic forms of the 14th-century BALLATA and 16th-century BARZELLETTA, a pair of lines having identical scansion and end rhymes, usually forming part of the stanza. *See* FROTTOLA, §2.

**Mute** (Fr. *sourdine*; Ger. *Dämpfer*; It. *sordino*). A mechanical device used on musical instruments to muffle the tone (i.e. to alter the timbre; the volume is usually somewhat decreased in the process).

In instruments of the violin family the typical mute takes the form of a three-pronged clamp (sometimes two- or five-pronged), made of such materials as metal (particularly steel and aluminium), ivory, bakelite or wood (especially ebony and boxwood) (see fig.1). Attached to the bridge, the mute absorbs some of the vibrations and makes the sound relatively veiled and a bit nasal; the degree of muting and the difference of tone-colour

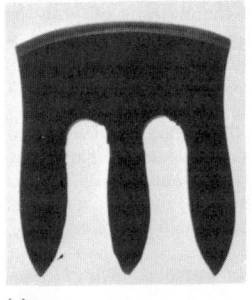

*1. Mutes for instruments of the violin family: (a) a conventional three-pronged mute; (b) a Roth (or Roth-Sihon) mute*

depend on the material used for the mute, its mass and the firmness with which it is attached to the bridge. Originally a separate accessory, the mute is sometimes installed on the instrument between bridge and tailpiece, to be pushed up against the bridge for muting as needed. 'Practice' mutes are exceptionally heavy, and are used to decrease the volume to a fraction of the normal sound for convenience when practising (they are not used in concert performance). A 'wolf mute' is sometimes used to correct the WOLF effect at the major 6th or 7th above the open G string of the cello.

The mute has been used on bowed string instruments since at least the 17th century, and was described by Mersenne in 1636. Mutes are specified in all five string parts in several passages in Act 2 (scenes iii and iv) of Lully's *Armide* (1686), among them the famous air 'Plus j'observe' (scene iii). Similarly Purcell specified mutes for the violins in the air 'See, even night herself is here' from *The Fairy Queen* (1692).

*2. Horn mutes: (a) all-purpose mutes made of fibreboard and wood, with cork strips which prevent the conical portion actually closing the bell and raising the pitch (the interior shape is a hollow cylinder, the lower half of which serves as a resonance chamber); (b) mute made of brass and cork, producing a brassier tone than (a) and raising the pitch by a semitone (the interior shape follows the outline of the exterior)*

Two debated points about the meaning of 'with the mute' may be settled here. First, in works that consist of several movements the instruction *con sordino* ('with mute') applies only to the movement concerned. Thus, in Mozart's String Quintet in G minor (K516), the term *con sordino* over all parts at the beginning of the third movement applies only to that movement. Second, the claim that *con sordino* is synonymous with 'soft' is disproved by the specified variety of dynamic markings in the movement just mentioned, including *piano*, *forte*, *crescendo*, and *sforzando*.

The typical mute for brass instruments is a cone-shaped air chamber inserted in the bell, and is usually made of cardboard, fibre, wood, or aluminium. Fig.2 shows typical orchestral mutes. A much greater variety of mutes of different shapes and tone-colours is used in popular music (e.g. the 'wa-wa' dance-band mute).

All brass instruments may be muted. The first was undoubtedly the trumpet, for which Mersenne illustrated a mute in 1636 (see fig.3). This early mute, unlike most modern ones, changed the pitch, raising it a whole tone – a transposition that had to be allowed for by the player. The mute tends to subdue the tone of the brass, giving it a certain mystery in soft passages (e.g. in Debussy's *Nuages*). A muted brass instrument is also capable of a metallic and nasal effect; and in loud passages the tone is very penetrating. The muted trumpet played *fortissimo* produces one of the most piercing sounds in the orchestra (e.g. in Stravinsky's *Petrushka*). A special metallic, brassy effect (*cuivré*) is sometimes called for (usually marked *sf*), particularly on the horn: the player mutes the instrument by hand-stopping and, by means of lip tension and hard blowing, produces a *sforzando* that is piercing, pungent and brassy. As indicated, this effect often concludes with a sudden softness. When muting the horn by hand-stopping, the tube is closed completely by inserting the hand into the bell. The pitch is raised by a semitone, a factor that must be taken into account in playing. Hand-stopping is generally indicated by a cross (+) for 'stopped' (*bouché*) and cancelled by *o* for 'open' (*ouvert*). There is some difference in tone-colour between the mute sound resulting from hand-stopping and that from a mechanical mute. Mutes are used on trombones and tubas to reduce volume and to change the tone-colour.

Among woodwind instruments, the flute is virtually never muted. In the 18th century the oboe was occasionally muted by inserting cottonwool, paper or pear-shaped pieces of hardwood into the bell. Some 18th-century specimens of the wooden oboe mute have survived; this type of mute imparts a curious veiled quality throughout the range, most evident in the notes which issue through the lower holes. Muting is now generally accomplished by stuffing a handkerchief into the bell. The same method is used by French players to mute the bassoon for very soft notes in the deepest register. German bassoonists prefer a mute that consists of a brass cylinder wound round with some soft material. A species of clarinet mute must have existed in the 18th century, although nothing precise is known about it. In 1785 the records of a firm of instrument makers named Tuerlinckx, in Mechlin, listed an order for '23 clarinets with A-joints and *sourdine*' sold to a military band (see *Bulletin du Cercle archéologique, littéraire & artistique de Malines*, xxiv, 1914, p.176). Berlioz muted the clarinet by wrapping the bell in a bag of cloth or leather, an example which evidently had no

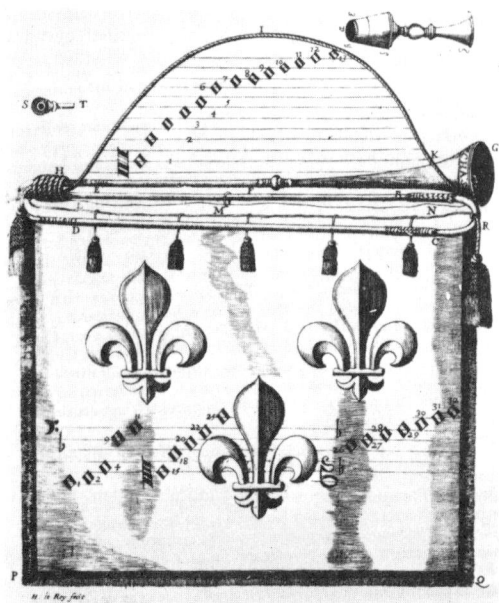

*3. Trumpet and mute (top right): engraving from Mersenne's 'Harmonie universelle' (1636–7)*

imitators, although later (*c*1930) a somewhat similar cardboard megaphone enjoyed a short vogue among dance musicians.

Kettledrums are muted by placing a cloth or handkerchief on the drumhead, opposite the striking point (the Italian instruction for this is *coperti*, 'covered').

On the harp, a species of muted tone may be produced by a method of plucking that stops the string as soon as the note is produced (*sons étouffés*). This sound resembles a short, dry, string pizzicato, quite different from the usual warm, vibrant tone of the harp as normally plucked (*laissez vibrer*).

A mute effect is also possible on the harpsichord and piano. On the former, a device called a 'harp' stop (sometimes called 'buff') presses felts or leathers against a whole set of strings, thereby muting the tone and shortening its period of resonance, the resulting sound being almost like pizzicato. The piano has both dampers and mutes. The damper, which is made of felt, is used not to dampen (i.e. to lessen or muffle) the sound but to extinguish it. When the damper pedal is depressed, all the dampers are raised from the strings, allowing them to ring freely, also inducing sympathetic vibrations from other strings. If the damper pedal is not used, the strings are automatically dampened and cease to sound the moment the finger releases the key. The 'soft' pedal is the modern version of a mute on the piano. It reduces the volume of sound by shifting the whole row of hammers a short distance to the right (Ger. *Verschiebung*, 'shifting') so that (in the modern grand piano) they hit only two of the three strings for each note (or, in the lower register, one of two). In Beethoven's time, the row of hammers could be moved to strike either one string (called *una corda*) or two strings (*due corde*) of the normal three. In his Hammerklavier Sonata op.106 (third movement), Beethoven called for *una corda*, then 'gradually two, then three strings', an effect no longer possible on the modern piano.

Some early pianos had true mute stops – strips of leather, cloth or other material interposed between hammers and strings to mute and change the timbre. In 1783 Broadwood of London patented (under the name 'sourdin') a mute stop in which a long strip of leather was applied against the strings by the action of a pedal. Several of Beethoven's pianos (e.g. his Erard of 1803) were equipped with mute stops. Some modern upright pianos still use a strip of felt to achieve this muting effect.

The term 'sordino', however, has caused some confusion, as it is also the normal term for a damper. The direction *senza sordini* evidently requires the damper pedal to be depressed to raise the dampers. The first edition of Beethoven's Piano Sonata op.27 no.2 gives the direction, 'One should play this whole piece very delicately and *senza sordino*'; and above the bass staff, 'always pianissimo and *senza sordino*'. Interpreted literally, this seems to mean that the damper pedal should be kept down continuously from the beginning to the end of the movement. The result is a confusion of blurred harmony, less so perhaps in the weak-toned Viennese pianos of Beethoven's time than on modern instruments. No really satisfactory explanation of this direction has yet been offered, despite the suggestion that Beethoven's *senza sordino* meant 'without a mute stop' (see D. Arnold and N. Fortune, eds.: *The Beethoven Companion*, London, 1971, p.50ff).

BIBLIOGRAPHY
C. Forsyth: *Orchestration* (London, 1914, 2/1935, repr. 1948)
W. Piston: *Orchestration* (New York, 1955)
A. Baines: *Woodwind Instruments and their History* (London, 1957, 3/1967)
R. Russell: *The Harpsichord and Clavichord* (London, 1959, rev. 2/1973)
D. D. Boyden: *The History of Violin Playing from its Origins to 1761* (London, 1965)
W. S. Newman: 'Beethoven's Pianos versus his Piano Ideals', *JAMS*, xxiii (1970), 484

DAVID D. BOYDEN

**Müthel, Johann Gottfried** (*b* Mölln, Lauenburg, 17 Jan 1728; *d* Bienenhof, nr. Riga, 14 July 1788). German composer. He received his earliest musical instruction from his father Christian Caspar Müthel (organist from 1717 at St Nicolai's, Mölln), and later from Paul Kuntzen at Lübeck. In 1747 he was appointed chamber musician and organist at the court of Mecklenburg-Schwerin under Duke Christian Ludwig II. Among his functions there was teaching music to the Crown Prince Ludwig and Princess Anna Amalie. In 1750 he was granted a year's leave of absence. He first visited Bach at Leipzig and was kindly received by the family; after Bach's death he visited J. A. Hasse at Dresden, C. P. E. Bach at Potsdam and Telemann in Hamburg. In 1753, at his brother's instigation, he took over the Russian Privy Councillor O. H. von Vietinghoff's small musical establishment at Riga; two years later he was offered in addition the post of organist at the principal church at Riga. He soon felt so much at home in the generous and liberal middle-class society of Riga that he refused all offers of posts elsewhere.

Müthel, who remained a bachelor, was looked upon as an oddity at Riga. Extremely introverted as both man and artist, he began experimenting from about 1750 in self-expression, striving to depict his inner life in music; he has therefore been called one of the most self-willed musical representatives of the early 'Sturm und Drang'. Always desiring originality in his works, he confessed that he composed slowly, and only when he felt in the

right mood; at such times he rested as little as possible. Until recently his known output seemed relatively small, but the discovery in the Pretlack music library (see Jaenecke, 1973) of a probable ten further works represents an important addition. His keyboard music is undoubtedly the most important part of his oeuvre. Burney considered his clavier sonatas to be among the most significant works of the period and praised in particular the considerable technical demands they imposed (which permit assumptions about Müthel's own pianistic ability), and the virtuoso and often wilful passage-work. In his middle movements Müthel strove exaggeratedly for expression, in this respect far exceeding his model, C. P. E. Bach. Their bizarre and occasionally mannered style is most obviously felt in the brittle melodic lines and jagged rhythms, often broken up into tiny units. Similar stylistic features characterize his concertos. His keyboard variations are among the boldest and most original compositions of the kind between Bach and Beethoven. In the few surviving organ works Bach's influence is unmistakable but not oppressive.

WORKS
Concs.: 2 for hpd (Riga and Mitau, 1767); 6 for hpd, *D-Bds*; 2 for hpd, *B*; 1 for 2 bn, str, *Bds* [6 hpd concs. ed. in Denkmäler norddeutscher Musik, iii–iv (Munich, 1975)]
Kbd: 3 sonates et 2 ariosi avec 12 variations, hpd (Nuremberg, 1756), ed. in Mitteldeutsches Musikarchiv, 1st ser., vi–vii (Leipzig and Wiesbaden, 1955); Duetto, 2 kbd (Nuremberg, 1771), ed. in NM, clxxvi (1954); 5 sonatas, hpd, *Bds*, 3 doubtful, 2 ed. in Organum, 5th ser., xxix (1961), xxxiii (1964); 8 sonatas, *B*, doubtful attrib.; technical exercises [incl. fantasy ed. in Mw, xliii (1971)], 3 chorales, prelude, fugue frag., org, *Bds*; other hpd pieces, *Bds*, some doubtful
Other: Auserlesene Oden und Lieder (Hamburg, 1759); Trinklied, 4vv, *Bds*; Sonata, fl, bc, *Bds*; Canon, *Dlb*

BIBLIOGRAPHY
C. Burney: *The Present State of Music in Germany, the Netherlands and United Provinces*, ii (London, 1773, 2/1775; Ger. trans., 1773/R1959 [incl. letter from Müthel]; ed. P. Scholes as *Dr. Burney's Musical Tours* (London, 1959)
R. Sietz: 'Die Orgelkompositionen des Schülerkreises um J. S. Bach', *BJb*, xxxii (1935), 64
L. Hoffmann-Erbrecht: *Deutsche und italienische Klaviermusik zur Bachzeit* (Leipzig and Wiesbaden, 1954)
——: 'Sturm und Drang in der deutschen Klaviermusik von 1753–1763', *Mf*, x (1957), 466
W. Reich: 'J. S. Bach und J. G. Müthel: zwei unbekannte Kanons', *Mf*, xiii (1960), 449
W. Salmen: 'J. G. Müthel, der letzte Schüler Bachs', *Festschrift Heinrich Besseler* (Leipzig, 1961), 251
E. Kemmler: 'Zur Biographie J. G. Müthels', *Musik des Ostens*, ii (1963), 226
E. Stam: 'Die von Wolfgang Reich veröffentlichten unbekannten Kanons J. S. Bachs und J. G. Müthels', *Mf*, xxi (1968), 317
L. Hoffmann-Erbrecht: 'Klavierkonzert und Affektgestaltung: Bemerkungen zu einigen d-Moll-Klavierkonzerten des 18. Jahrhunderts', *DJbM*, xvi (1971), 86
J. Jaenecke: *Die Musikbibliothek des Ludwig Freiherrn von Pretlack (1716–1781)* (Wiesbaden, 1973)

LOTHAR HOFFMANN-ERBRECHT

**Muti [Mutio], Giovanni Vincenzo Macedonio di.** *See* MACEDONIO DI MUTIO, GIOVANNI VINCENZO.

**Muti, Riccardo** (*b* Naples, 28 July 1941). Italian conductor. He took childhood piano lessons, graduated from the Naples Conservatory as a piano student of Vincenze Vitale, and began to read philosophy at Naples University. His chance replacement of a fellow student as conductor of a conservatory concert, however, led him to continue musical studies at the Milan Conservatory for five years as a pupil of Bruno Bettinelli for composition and Antonino Votto for conducting. He won the 1967 Guido Cantelli International Conductors' Competition and made his début the next year with the Italian RSO (RAI). His success led within a few years to engagements with leading orchestras in Europe and the USA. He was appointed principal conductor of the Florence Maggio Musicale in 1969, and in 1972 made his American début with the Philadelphia and other orchestras and his British début with the New Philharmonia, of which he became principal conductor in succession to Klemperer with effect from the 1973 Edinburgh Festival. In 1975 he was additionally appointed principal guest conductor of the Philadelphia Orchestra; that year he shared with Böhm the Vienna PO's tour of Japan. At the same time he has been equally active in opera, making his début in 1970 in Naples and Rome, appearing regularly at the Salzburg Festival from 1971 and frequently at Vienna, Paris and elsewhere. At Florence in 1972 he conducted the first uncut performance of Rossini's *Guillaume Tell*, and he has renewed public interest in other operas such as Spontini's *Agnes von Hohenstaufen*, *L'africaine*, and *Attila* and *I masnadieri*. His first gramophone recordings, of *Aida* and *Un ballo in maschera*, were specially praised for their dramatic immediacy and musical cogency, and in symphonic music his performances are admired for his blend of vitality and musical purpose with expressive warmth and sonority. Gifted with deep musical intuition and an efficient technique, he conducts much 20th-century music by, among others, Britten, Dallapiccola, Hindemith, Ligeti, Petrassi and Shostakovich, whose Symphony no.13 he introduced to the Italian concert repertory in 1970.

BIBLIOGRAPHY

F. Granville Barker: 'Riccardo Muti', *Records and Recording*, xviii/7 (1975), 12

LEONARDO PINZAUTI

**Mutis, Bartolomeo,** Count of Cesana (*b* ? *c*1575–80; *d* Vienna, Nov 1623). Italian singer and composer. He was a member of the family of the counts of Cesana, whose estates lay to the south-west of Belluno in the Veneto. He was appointed chaplain and tenor singer at the court of Archduke Ferdinand at Graz on 1 April 1604. He accompanied Ferdinand's sister, the Archduchess Constantia, on her journey to Poland in 1605 to marry King Sigismund III and in 1611 went to Vienna with the archduke to attend the wedding of the Emperor Matthias. When Ferdinand became emperor in 1619 Mutis moved to Vienna with the other Graz court musicians and remained there as court chaplain until his death. While in Graz he may have acted as almoner to one of Ferdinand's younger brothers, the Archduke Maximilian Ernst, to whom he dedicated his *Musiche a una doi e tre voci* (Venice, 1613; edn. in DTÖ, cxxv, 1973). This volume, which shows the influence of Italian monodists like Caccini, establishes him as the earliest exponent of secular monody in an Austrian court chapel. As well as three solo madrigals it includes six pieces, either madrigalian or aria-like, for two voices and five for three; the volume also contains a richly ornamented madrigal by the Graz court musician Francesco degli Atti (*b* Todi, *c*1574; *d* Vienna, early May 1631). There are also two two-part motets with continuo by Mutis in G. B. Bonometti, ed.: *Parnassus musicus Ferdinandaeus* (Venice, 1615).

BIBLIOGRAPHY

H. Federhofer: 'Graz Court Musicians and their Contributions to the *Parnassus musicus Ferdinandaeus* (1615)', *MD*, ix (1955), 225

——: *Musikpflege und Musiker am Grazer Habsburgerhof der Erzherzöge Karl und Ferdinand von Innerösterreich (1564–1619)* (Mainz, 1967)

HELLMUT FEDERHOFER

# Illustration Acknowledgments

We are grateful to those listed below for permission to reproduce copyright illustrative material, and those contributors who supplied or helped us obtain it. Every effort has been made to contact copyright holders; we apologize to anyone who may have been omitted. Brian and Constance Dear prepared the maps and technical diagrams, and Oxford Illustrators the typographic diagrams (except where otherwise stated). Photographs acknowledged to the following sources are Crown copyright: Her Majesty the Queen, the Victoria and Albert Museum (including the Theatre Museum), the Science Museum and the National Monuments Record. The following forms of acknowledgment are used where the copyright of an illustration is held by a contributor:

photo John Smith – John Smith is contributor and photographer
John Smith – John Smith is contributor and copyright holder
photo John Smith, London – John Smith is a contributor (not of the article concerned) and photographer
John Smith, London – John Smith is a contributor (not of the article concerned) and copyright holder.

Where illustrations are taken from books out of copyright, the full title and place and date of publication are given, unless in the caption.

**Meares** British Library, London
**Mechanical instrument** *1–3, 7, 9* after A. Buchner; *4, 6, 8* Alexandr Buchner; *5* Sotheby's Belgravia, London; *10* British Piano Museum Charitable Trust, London / photo Times Newspapers Ltd
**Medici** Soprintendenza alle Gallerie, Florence
**Medieval** Bibliothèque Nationale, Paris
**Medieval drama** *1* Archivio Capitolare, Modena; *2* Stiftsbibliothek, St Gall; *3, 4, 8* British Library, London; *5* photo Archives du Loiret, Orleans; *6* Giraudon, Paris; *7* Folger Shakespeare Library, Washington, DC
**Méhul, Etienne-Nicolas** *1* Photographie Bulloz, Paris; *2* Garland Publishing Inc., New York and London: from facs. of printed orchestral score (1978)
**Meistergesang** *1* Stadtarchiv, Memmingen; *2* Stadtbibliothek, Nuremberg / photo Armin Schmidt
**Melanesia** *1–4* Ministry of Information, Suva; *5, 8* Musée de l'Homme, Paris / photo L. Hughan (*5*), J. Guiart (*8*); *6* photo Kirk Huffman, Cambridge; *7* after D. A. Rawcliffe; *9, 11* Summer Institute of Linguistics, Papua New Guinea: from V. Chenoweth, ed., *Musical Instruments of Papua New Guinea* (1976) / photo G. Cloud; *10* Museum für Völkerkunde und Schweizerisches Museum für Völkskunde, Basle / photo René Gardi; *12* VEB Deutscher Verlag für Musik, Leipzig: from P. Collaer, *Musikethnologie*, 1: *Ozeanien*, Musikgeschichte in Bildern, i (1965); *13* photo Axel Poignant, London; *14–17* photo Hugo Zemp
**Melba, Nellie** Stuart-Liff Collection, Tunbridge Wells
**Melbourne** Picturepoint Ltd, London
**Melchior, Lauritz** Harold Rosenthal, London / photo Carlo Edwards
**Melodrama** Nationale Forschungs- und Gedenkstätten der klassischen deutschen Literatur, Weimar
**Melograph** *3* Magnes Press, Jerusalem: from D. Cohen and R. Katz, 'Remarks Concerning the Use of the Melograph in Ethnomusicological Studies', *Yuval*, i (1968)
**Melophone** Museum of Fine Arts, Boston
**Mendelssohn, Felix** *3* Archiv für Kunst und Geschichte, Berlin; *4* Mansell Collection, London; *5* Staatsbibliothek Preussischer Kulturbesitz, Berlin; *6* Richard Macnutt, Tunbridge Wells; *8* Music Division, Library of Congress, Washington, DC
**Mengelberg** Phonogram Ltd, London
**Menotti, Gian Carlo** Camera Press Ltd, London / photo Horst Tappe
**Menuhin** photo Clive Barda, London
**Merbecke, John** British Library, London
**Mercadante, Saverio** *1* Opera Rara Collection, London; *2* British Library, London
**Merighi, Antonia Margherita** Fondazione Giorgio Cini, Istituto di Storia dell'arte, Venice

**Mersenne, Marin** Bibliothèque Nationale, Paris
**Mesopotamia** *1, 3b, 5–7* Wilhelm Stauder (*1*, from W. Stauder, *Die Harfen und Leiern der Sumerer*, Frankfurt, 1957); *2, 3a* Trustees of the British Museum, London; *4* photo Maurice Chuzeville, Malakoff, France
**Messiaen, Olivier** *1, 2* Editions Alphonse Leduc, Paris
**Metronome** Gesellschaft der Musikfreunde, Vienna
**Mexico** *1a–c* VEB Deutscher Verlag für Musik, Leipzig: from S. Martí, *Musik des Altertums*, 7: *Alt-Amerika*, Musikgeschichte in Bildern, ii (1970); *1d* Popperfoto, London; *2, 3, 7* photo E. Thomas Stanford; *4* British Library, London; *5, 6* Musée de l'Homme, Paris / (*5a, 6*) photo L. Diguet
**Meyerbeer, Giacomo** *1, 3* Staatliches Institut für Musikforschung Preussischer Kulturbesitz, (*1*, Musikinstrumenten-Museum), Berlin; *2* Richard Macnutt, Tunbridge Wells; *4* SPADEM, Archives Photographiques, Paris / photo Nadar; *5* Mary Evans Picture Library, London
**Michelangeli, Arturo Benedetti** Deutsche Grammophon, London / photo Siegfried Lauterwasser
**Micronesia** *1* Raymond F. Kennedy; *2* from H. Tischner, *Kulturen des Südsee: Einführung in die Völkerkunde Ozeaniens* (Hamburg, 1958); *3* Barbara Smith; *4* Margaret Higgins, San Diego, California / photo Spencer L. Higgins, National Geographic Society, Washington, DC; *5* photo Barbara Smith
**Milan** *1–4* Civica Raccolta Stampe Achille Bertarelli, Milan; *5* Archiv für Kunst und Geschichte, Berlin
**Milanov, Zinka** Harold Rosenthal / photo Sedge Le Blang
**Milhaud, Darius** H. Roger-Viollet, Paris / photo Lipnitzki
**Military band** *1, 2* Royal Military School of Music, Kneller Hall, Twickenham; *3* BBC Hulton Picture Library, London
**Mingus, Charles** Photography 33, London
**Minnesang** *1, 2* Universitätsbibliothek, Heidelberg; *3* Staatsbibliothek Preussischer Kulturbesitz, Berlin
**Minstrel** *1* Bodleian Library, Oxford; *2* Bibliothèque Nationale, Paris
**Minstrelsy, American** Harvard Theatre Collection, Cambridge, Massachusetts
**Minuet** *1, 2* Eastman School of Music, University of Rochester, New York; *3* British Library, London
**Moderne, Jacques** *1, 2* British Library, London
**Moiseiwitsch, Benno** Harry L. Anderson, San Diego, California
**Mondonville, Jean-Joseph Cassanéa de** Musée Antoine Lécuyer, Saint-Quentin, France
**Mongol music** Věra Jislová, Prague: from L. Jisl, *Mongolei, Kunst und Tradition* (1960)
**Moniuszko, Stanisław** Eastfoto, New York
**Monochord** *2* University Library, Cambridge

879

**Monsigny, Pierre-Alexandre** *1* Richard Macnutt, Tunbridge Wells; *2* Bibliothèque Nationale, Paris

**Montagnana, Domenico** W. E. Hill & Sons, Great Missenden / photo Desmond Hill

**Monte, Philippe de** Bibliothèque Royale Albert Ier, Brussels

**Monteux, Pierre** Phonogram Ltd, London

**Monteverdi, Claudio** *1* Tiroler Landesmuseum Ferdinandeum, Innsbruck; *2* Music Division, Library of Congress, Washington, DC; *3* Archivio di Stato, Mantua

**Montreal** Office of the Agent General for Quebec, London

**Morales, Cristóbal de** Biblioteca Apostolica Vaticana, Rome

**Moresca** Bärenreiter-Verlag, Kassel

**Morocco** *1–3, 5* photo Jean Jenkins, London; *4* photo Hamish M. Brown, Kinghorn, Fife

**Moscheles, Ignaz** Royal College of Music, London

**Moscow** *1, 2* Society for Cultural Relations with the USSR, London

**Motet** *1, 2* Biblioteca Medicea Laurenziana, Florence; *3* Herzog August Bibliothek, Wolfenbüttel; *4* Bibliothèque Interuniversitaire, Section Médecine, Montpellier; *5* Staatsbibliothek, Bamberg

**Mozambique** *2–6* International Library of African Music, Grahamstown / photo Hugh Tracey (*2a*), Andrew Tracey (*2b–6*)

**Mozarabic rite, music of the** *1* Archivo del Monasterio, Santo Domingo de Silos; *2* Archivo y Biblioteca Capitulares, Toledo; *3* Biblioteca Nacional, Madrid

**Mozart** *1, 2, 5, 8, 9, 18* Internationale Stiftung Mozarteum, Salzburg; *4* HM the Queen; *6* Staatsbibliothek Preussischer Kulturbesitz, Musikabteilung, Berlin; *7* Civico Museo Bibliografico Musicale, Bologna; *10, 13* Deutsche Staatsbibliothek, Berlin; *11, 12, 16* British Library, London; *14* Musikbibliothek der Stadt Leipzig; *17* Universitetsbiblioteket, Uppsala; *18* Hunterian Art Gallery, University of Glasgow

**Muck, Carl** Boston Symphony Orchestra

**Muffat, Georg** British Library, London

**Munich** *1* Bayerische Staatsbibliothek, Munich; *2, 3* Theatermuseum, Munich

**Munrow, David** photo BBC, London

**Musette** SPADEM, Archives Photographiques, Paris / photo Caisse Nationale des Monuments Historiques et des Sites

**Musgrave, Thea** Report, London / photo Patrick Eagar

**Musical bow** *1* photo Gilbert Rouget, Paris; *2* photo Jos Gansemans, Tervuren

**Musical box** Sotheby's Belgravia, London

**Musical comedy** *1, 3* Mander and Mitchenson, London; *2* CBS Inc., New York / photo British Film Institute, London

**Musical glasses** *1* British Library, London; *2, 3* Bruno Hoffmann, Stuttgart / (*3*) photo Alan Clifton

**Music hall** *1, 2* Mander and Mitchenson, London

**Musicology** Bibliothèque Nationale, Paris

**Musorgsky, Modest Petrovich** *1* Novosti Press Agency, London; *2* Theatre Museum, Leningrad; *3* M. I. Glinka State Central Museum for Musical Culture, Moscow

**Mute** *1a, 2* David Boyden; *1b* photo Mick Baines, London